D1094543

THE
Word Finder

Compiled and edited by J. I. RODALE

With the collaboration of KINGSBURY M. BADGER, M. A.

THEODORE G. EHRSAM, M. A.   MABEL E. MULOCK, B. S.

EDWARD J. FLUCK, Ph. D.

Rodale Books, Inc.
EMMAUS, PENNSYLVANIA

Copyright 1947 by Rodale Press, Inc.

All rights reserved

Printed in U.S.A.

		24	26	28	30	29	27	25		hardcover
2	4	6	8	10	9	7	5	3		hardcover deluxe

PREFACE

What is the WORD FINDER? Is it a new kind of thesaurus? The answer is emphatically "no"! In a thesaurus one looks for substitutes for the word he has in mind. If he wishes to say "large," reference to a thesaurus will supply him with a better word such as "spacious." The WORD FINDER, on the other hand, does not merely yield a substitute word but produces an augmentative word, one to embellish and add to the idea. Thus, in the WORD FINDER by referring to the adjective *large* the user is taught to describe "how large?" by a selected list of words such as *incalculably, incredibly, preposterously, overwhelmingly, prodigiously, inordinately,* etc.

The WORD FINDER has been created to improve a writer's style by adding to the bare, essential words of a sentence. A thesaurus does not do that. It merely assists the user to change such a sentence as "This business had a loss" to some such variant as "This trade suffered a reversal." The WORD FINDER, however, teaches one that "business *droops, expires, falters, founders, simmers* and *succumbs,*" simply by referring to the noun *business*. And if none of these adjuvant words is precisely what the writer has in mind to describe a languishing trade, the WORD FINDER will tell him, also under the heading *business,* to see *occupation, trade, concern, enterprise, industry, work, commerce,* etc.

Nouns, verbs, and adjectives are listed, alphabetically arranged, and in connection with each such word a list of "augmentatives" is given, that is, words that can be used to condition such a noun, verb, or adjective. In the case of *hill,* for example, the WORD FINDER will furnish either adjectives, such as *gleaming, emerald, moon-swept, verdured, radiant, shadowed, naked, pastoral, defiant,* or verbs, as *hills dot, encroach, flank, greet, interpose,* etc. In the case of the verb *hinder* we are told that a thing can hinder us *unendurably, insurmountably, irritatingly, irksomely* or *burdensomely,* as well as that we should also consult the synonym entries, *retard* and *obstruct*.

It is a simple type of book to use, and immediate results follow in the form of vigorous and deft variety, essential to the creation of a literary style. By studying any particular word in the WORD FINDER along with its coupling expressions and synonyms, the user is enabled to develop a concept and build a thought in such a way that intricate sentences can be evolved from the study of that word. He will find that whatever particular idea he has in mind will rise to fluent proportions under the leavening influence of the WORD FINDER's associated words, that his vocabulary has been increased and his powers of self-expression immeasurably improved.

For example, the sentence, "His cheerful character charmed me very much," contains the adjective *cheerful*, the noun *character*, the verb *charmed*, and the adverbs *very* and *much*. Though it is grammatically correct and genial in thought, it is sadly lacking in specific statement and colorful diction. What exactly are the elements in a *character* that *charm*? And what are the suggestive ingredients of being *cheerful*?

On pages 182-183 of our WORD FINDER the noun *character* has grouped with it a selected list of adjectives that explain and describe it. After studying the columns of epithets descriptive of our word while bearing in mind that this is a *character* that *charms*, we reap a rich harvest of modifiers. Depending on the nature of the characteristics that charm us, we can depict our character as *fabulous, munificent, steadfast, liberal, intense, frivolous, gallant, chivalrous, artistic, elusive, exotic, gentle, jovial, airy, gay, sympathetic, magnanimous, many-sided, jaunty, bizarre, racy* and *whimsical*, to cite only a few of the appropriate words that will expand our idea. Thus, if we admire the fay, will-o'-the-wisp facets of a certain personality, we may say, "His elusive character charmed me very much," and we have started on our quest for the specific and the well-delineated. We have, of course, substituted *elusive* for *cheerful*, but *cheerful* and *charmed* are faintly synonymic anyhow, and our purpose is to show what a plenitude of ideas related to our original sentence may be found in the WORD FINDER, rather than merely to adorn the flimsiness of that original sentence.

Since the original modifier of *character* was *cheerful*, what can we learn about ways of modifying that adjective in our book? Words which describe adjectives, verbs, or other adverbs are known as adverbs. On page 189 we find a choice list of such adverbs in association with the word *cheerful*. If we wish to express what we feel about this charmingly elusive character, we can readily avail ourselves of the most pertinent of these modifiers for *cheerful* and transfer it to *elusive*. Thus, we should choose from some such qualifying words as *habitually, blithely, casually, oddly,* or *perplexingly*, if, let us say, we were charmed by the casually elusive character of a Britisher.

The verb of our original thought was *charmed*, and it was described by the barren, inexpressive adverbial phrase *very much*. On page 185 we find the noun *charm* with its cluster of associated adjectives, among which we note our selection for character, namely *elusive;* this confirms our concept that an elusive character can be charming. On page 186, however, appears the verb *charm*, marked (v) as are all the verbs in this book. Browsing among its adverbs and choosing a few of the most applicable, we find that we can say with import that an elusive character charms *subtly, mysteriously, hauntingly, inexplicably, piquantly,* or *irresistibly.*

VI

As we reflect over all the words associated with *character*, *cheerful*, and *charm*, which three alone we have studied, we find that from that glittering galaxy of modifiers we can create innumerable combinations relevant to our original thought, but more sumptuously expressed; for an instance, "His piquant charm was of a perplexingly elusive character, haunting, subtle; yet its very intensity was irresistible." From the delicate contours of a silhouette our character has been projected full-featured.

Only words that are evocative, that stimulate and unfurl the wings of the imagination, are of real assistance to the aspiring writer. These are the words that avoid the flat surface of the cliché, that give dimensional depth to the picture we are creating. We believe such words to be found in hitherto unprecedented numbers in this book. They are the ones which, starting from a single unit in combination with another word, will, as they round a phrase, multiply and burgeon into a complete thought, while at the same time often yielding an unlooked-for but brighter image.

The editors sincerely trust that all students of this book will succeed in sending *winged words* on far-flung odysseys to Fame.

EDWARD J. FLUCK, PH. D.

VII

PREFACE

To The Original Adjective-Finder

Adjectives have been excellently defined as "the words of our language that make everything clearer, plainer, more beautiful or more dreadful." Oral or written expression without any adjectives at all would be meager, monotonous, utterly drab and colorless. The word *adjective* comes from the Latin *adjectivus,* meaning "that is added." The only part of English speech to which an adjective may be added is of course a noun. (That is why, in this volume, nouns have been listed alphabetically, with fitting adjectives appended to each noun).

Adjectives are as life blood to the language. William Freeman, in his book *Plain English,* says, "One can't embark upon any type of narrative, from embittered conversation to the conventional post-card, without turning to the adjective for help." For this reason adjectives may be described as the paints with which one brightens and vivifies the scenes and events behind the printed words, and lends fascinating hues to what might otherwise be prosaic and deadly dry.

No matter what writers turn their attention to, they must draw upon the adjective. Of course in certain types of narrative there is less need of the descriptive paint-brush than in others. An interesting study of the actual use of adjectives in various fields of writing has recently been made by Dr. David P. Boder, head of the department of psychology at Lewis Institute. His study—which he has termed the A. V. Q. (Adjective-Verb Quotient)—is a measure of the ratio of adjectives to verbs employed by writers. For example, an A. V. Q. of 20 means that a writer uses 20 adjectives for every 100 verbs he employs. (For a discussion of the verb, see the introduction to THE VERB-FINDER). Dr. Boder has found that of the four principal fields of writing, drama has the fewest adjectives, with an average A. V. Q. of 11. Laws are next, with an A. V. Q. of 20. Fiction has an A. V. Q. of 35; scientific writing, 75. Business letters, according to Dr. Boder's findings, show a relative paucity of adjectives, with only 19 to every 100 verbs. Private letters by inexperienced writers have on an average but 22 adjectives to a hundred verbs. Advertisements, on the other hand, are lavish of adjectives, with an A. V. Q. of 78. Theses written by candidates for the Ph. D. degree are loaded with even more adjectives than are advertisements—88 to 100 verbs! Poetry has what is perhaps a golden mean for proportion of adjectives to verbs—an A. V. Q. of 36. Dr. Boder's studies in this field make it clear that writers use more adjectives than speakers do. The reason for this is not far to seek; writers closeted with their thoughts have unlimited time in which to select appropriate adjectives while those who express themselves orally and extemporaneously do not.

Adjectives suffer, as any part of speech is bound to, if not properly employed. And adjectives, perhaps more than any other part of our language, are subject to wide-spread misuse. The adjective, of all the parts of English speech, is the most recklessly overworked. Both inexperienced and half-educated writers use far too many, and use them far too loosely. The amateur tends to use the first adjective that enters his mind, though that adjective may be shoddy and threadbare from excessive use, or though it may not express exactly what he wishes to say. Wesseen, in his *Dictionary of English Grammar*, calls this *adjectivitis* (a coined word meaning the habit of using many adjectives, especially big ones.)

Poor writers and beginners obscure their meaning by weighting their sentences with too many adjectives. Dr. Boder found in the course of his researches that the fewer the adjectives, the easier any writing is to read. With experience and practice the writer learns to substitute for makeshift, trite adjectives others which express his meaning exactly and vividly. Daniel Webster, as a young man, was bombastic in his speeches, but it did not take him long to discover that the power of a sentence lies chiefly in its meaning, and that forceful writing is that which is most direct. Upon making this discovery Webster became "a great eraser of adjectives," and used only the plainest in his addresses. Yet he won immortality for his eloquence. "You will find," he said, "in my speeches to juries, no hard words, no Latin phrases, no *fieri facias;* and that is the secret of my style, if I have any."

Because the adjective is of all parts of speech the most frequently abused and misused, it has come to be regarded with a suspicious eye by many a worker in words. The late columnist, Arthur Brisbane, termed the adjective the enemy of the noun. Many years before Brisbane's time Voltaire meant exactly the same thing when he said that adjectives are frequently the greatest enemies of the substantives.

"An adjective is, indeed, an addition," wrote William Matthews, in his book, *Words; Their Use and Abuse.* "But, he concludes, "an addition may be an incumbrance, as even a dog finds out when a kettle is tied to his tail. Generally the weakness of a composition is just in proportion to the frequency with which this abused class of words is introduced."

Ernest Weekley, a well-known authority on words, expressed irritation because of the wide-spread tendency to overwork the adjective. For example, some years ago, after an attempt had been made upon the life of Mussolini, the President of the Irish Free State congratulated the Italian dictator upon his "providential escape" from an "odious attack," and sent his "earnest wishes" for a "speedy recovery" from the "infamous attempt" which had caused "utmost indignation."

This sort of thing—with reason—goads Mr. Weekley to exasperation, and in an essay on the adjective he has been led to condemn it as being perhaps our least essential part of speech. But neither Mr. Weekley nor any other worker in words worth his salt scorns the adjective in actual practice. For example, Mr. Weekley, in his book *Cruelty to Words*, speaks of "linguistic absurdities perpetrated by contemporary authors," and "a small leavening of peptonized uplift and dilettante pornography." Here are adjectives a-plenty, and employed by an authority who has declared the adjective the least important part of our language! And though Arthur Brisbane termed the adjective the enemy of the noun, a study of Brisbane's writings reveals that the columnist used approximately 42 adjectives to every 100 verbs he employed.

The adjective has come to have a somewhat unsavory reputation, then, not because there is anything inherently bad about it, but because it is the one part of speech first seized upon and worked to death by novices and inferior writers.

When properly used, however, the adjective is an indispensable tool in the hands of all who would communicate with their fellow men by means of words. Employed with discrimination and restraint it becomes a source of tremendous power. Selection of the exact adjective to convey their meaning has done as much as anything to lend beauty and strength to the writings of men whose names have long since become household words wherever English is spoken. Thomas De Quincy, for example, famed for his style, was a master of the adjective. A single sentence from the pen of the man who wrote *The Confessions of an English Opium Eater* serves to show this:

"His diction blazed up into a sudden explosion of prophetic grandeur."

Had De Quincy used an adjective in connection with the word "diction," this fine sentence would have been spoiled.

Just as an adjective thoughtlessly or carelessly placed can wreck an otherwise excellent sentence, so a fitting adjective inserted at just the proper place can build magic into a sentence. The William

x

Saroyan play, *Love's Old Sweet Song*, offers an interesting example. Walter Huston, in the role of the leading male character, approaches an ornamental stone lion and in expressing disgust with the situation in which he finds himself, gestures toward the figure, referring to it not as "That lion!" but rather, as "That Abyssinian lion!" The adjective Abyssinian, as the author intended, brings a roar of laughter from the audience.

The danger in using adjectives lies in employing overworked and "tired" adjectives, or adjectives unsuited to the noun with which they are joined. That is the *raison d'etre* for the present volume. In the following pages a host of adjectives, each group appended to the noun modified, offers the user of this book a wide choice in the words so vital to memorable writing.

Very simple adjectives have been avoided except where their use in connection with certain nouns appears to be somewhat unusual. This point is worth a second glance—for quite simple adjectives have frequently aided authors in the moments of their greatest genius. Ernest Hemingway, in describing one of his characters, writes:

"His face was small and white and he had tight lips."

How simple are these adjectives: "small," "white," tight!" And yet they enable one to see that character immediately—and not only to see him, but to be on guard against him.

Indeed, Hemingway is famed for the simplicity of his style. At the other extreme there are writers who do not hesitate to use three words where one would suffice. Rufus Choate, the famous American states-man and orator, was such a man. So prodigal he was of adjectives that it was said that he "drove a substantive-and-six" whenever he spoke. When Chief-Justice Shaw, before whom Choate frequently pleaded, heard that a new edition of *Worcester's Dictionary* was off the press and that it contained 2,500 new words, he cried out, "For heaven's sake, don't let Choate get hold of it!"

Perhaps Choate frightened those who knew him with his verbiage, but he was so skilled in the use of words that he succeeded in spite of an overloaded style. A person of less experience or skill is almost certain to fall disastrously into the octopus arms of elaborate language. And curiously enough, it frequently happens that the amateur writer seeks to express himself in a more or less highly ornamented manner, usually with sad results.

The student, and even the practiced writer, cannot be advised too strongly against the use of long, unusual words. The urge to show off to the reader must be kept down. Not only will the worker in words —if he would possess a clear, vigorous style—guard against employing too many adjectives, but he will avoid the pitfalls and detours and handicaps that are likely to be encountered through the use of excessively elaborate adjectives. The simple adjective is almost always preferable to the unusual adjective.

Of course an adjective not met every day may be employed with profit if it expresses the author's thought better than any other word could, but in general the student—in using the present volume—will find it to his advantage to select such simple and yet vivid adjective-noun combinations as "casual visitor," "speechless agony," "misty diplomacy," "liquid gurgle," "giddy intoxication," and "silvery laughter."

Remember that adjectives—like visitors—become a nuisance only when there are too many of them. The adjective is never the enemy of of the noun until the adjective—like a drowning swimmer—drags down and strangles the noun.

J. I. RODALE.

PREFACE

To The Original Verb-Finder

THE POWER OF VERBS

There is an old saying that "fine words butter no parsnips." But of course they do, and always will—whenever the words have been fine enough. Words act. Think of the information, the insight, the entertainment that words provide through books, plays, radio programs, and sound motion pictures. Words are practical, practical even in the narrowest American sense; that is, they bring in money, support life. Let us be clearer by being more definite.

From the days when Anglo-Saxon and medieval minstrels earned their board by entertainment in mead-hall and castle, to modern times, word-craftsmen have moved and delighted their audiences by telling stories or by expressing thoughts, emotions, and aspirations at once personal and common to all people. In modern times such authors as Kipling, Shaw, Wells, Barrie, Masefield, and Bennett, to mention only a few, have achieved literary eminence by the power of fine words. They, like many other writers, not only have woven bright tapestries in poetry or prose, but also have buttered many a delicious parsnip. Robert Frost found the pen more powerful than the plow—even if he did have to go to England to make sure of it. Edgar Lee Masters wrote himself clear of the stifling influence of the small mid-western town. Edwin Arlington Robinson kept the wolf from his door for years by retelling for the modern world some of the most enchanting of the old romances, as well as by painting satirical portraits of New England townspeople. Arnold Bennett, through a tremendous amount of diligent work—he loved to gloat over the number of words he turned out every day—succeeded in becoming both a first-rate literary "merchant," as he liked to call himself, and one of the best novelists of his time. He lived zestfully by the power of words, and even realized his great desire to own a yacht.

Many other persons, perhaps no more gifted than we, have also succeeded. Although they have not profited greatly in a financial way, or become famous by their ability to write well, they have, nevertheless, shared with the eminent one satisfaction—that of expressing themselves adequately, of communicating their emotions, their thoughts, their opinions, attitudes, and ideals. By the power of well-wrought language they have achieved self-expression and have succeeded in rising from the buried life of a solitary organism to the rich life of communion with their fellows. Such satisfaction, such success is within the reach of all of us.

"But show us the road," people say. "What is the secret? Which way?" There is no one way, of course, for writing is a many-sided, complex art. Nor is there any formula for us to follow, for art is creative and imaginative, by no means a matter of slavish imitation or of scientific procedure. We need not despair, however,—not so long as we have the will to write. A close examination of what good writers produce, cannot fail to reveal to us something about how those works were produced, to give us some hints toward improvement. Arnold Bennett, whose improvement in style was due in large measure to his careful study of other writers, realized that the best novelists were word-conscious, that they sought constantly for strength, for clarity, precision. Incidentally, a good craftsman in writing must always be more than grammatically correct, and he will do well to keep ever in mind those three cardinal principles: strength, clarity, and precision. Bennett, by comparing and examining passages of equal length in the works of a great many novelists, discovered that the better artists—and the better merchants—chose lively adjectives and lively verbs. He discovered, furthermore, that adjectives, unless used charily, overornament; that nouns, unless cut down to a minimum, tend to overweight; but that verbs, if well chosen and skillfully handled, invigorate one's style.

We can see this for ourselves. Every day writers strive vainly to ornament and enrich their expression before they have learned to animate and strengthen it. The result of their striving is too often mere prettiness with no vigor beneath it, writing that is all sweetness and flourishes, a meal of all pastry, a beauty with no grain in it. This is a common fallacy among amateur writers, and even professional writers. They fail to see that ornamental adjectives often blur and obscure their meanings and that too many nouns, especially learned nouns—scientific, psychological, technical terms—bog it down. Expression demands life, not merely the trappings of life; vigor, not merely glitter. The sword must be keen that it may cut and thrust as well as glitter in the sun.

The true knight fought valiantly in battle; he did not spend most of his time strutting about with his plume, spear-pennant, and lady's scarf rippling in the breeze. The modern athlete, if he would excel on the field of competition, must display strength, agility, and sportsmanship, not merely a good sun-tan, bulging muscles, and his college or club colors. It is not enough that cathedrals be magnificently adorned with tapering spires and beautiful storied windows; they must be firmly braced and buttressed. Likewise, our written or oral expression must be keen-edged, powerful and agile, and well buttressed at the walls. Without a large number of carefully selected verbs, these essentials are impossible; moreover, selection, which is one of the cardinal principles of all art, is far more important than numbers.

Now, after so many generalizations, it is high time we substantiated what we have said about verbs by referring to particular passages in the writing of particular authors, for surely one good illustration is worth at least sixty generalizations.

Perhaps the most obvious use for verbs is to express physical action. In order to illustrate not a mere piling-up but a skillful selection of verbs, let us examine an action-scene from one of John Masefield's poems, *Dauber*. The poet transports his reader immediately to the deck of a clipper. The ship's painter, the "Dauber," and Si, the apprentice, stood by the rail while the swift ship *"tore"* on, *"straining"* her sheets and *"whitening"* her trackway.

> Her **clacking** tackle **tugged** at pins and cleats,
> Her great sails **bellied** stiff, her great masts **leaned:**
> They watched how the seas **struck,** and **burst,** and **greened.** *

On she sailed toward Cape Horn through snow and hail, her spars straining as she was tossed on the toppling billows. Just before she reached the cape, polar snow came *"tumbling"* and *"wavering"* down, *"furring* the ropes with white, *casing* the mast." At the cape all hands were called on deck to combat the storm, and the Dauber was sent aloft to furl one of the sails. As he lay out on the yardarm, *"gripping"* hard and *"clutching"* at the jack, he was sickened by the vast space that yawned just below his feet, where birds were *"mewing"* and *"wheeling."* He felt the wind *"hurl"* the ship on her side, and

> .darkness **speared**
> At her with wind; she **staggered,** she **careened,**
> Then down she lay. The Dauber felt her go;
> He saw the yard **tilt** downwards. Then the snow
> **Whirled** all about—dense multitudinous, cold—*

It was a terrific storm, one that *"whiffled* out men's tears" and put to a severe test their courage and endurance.

---

* Quoted by special permission of the publishers, The Macmillan Company, from *Poems* by John Masefield, 1935. (The boldface and italics are the editor's.)

While we are considering action and the sea, we recall those vigorous lines in Shakespeare's *HENRY V* in which the poet describes the effect of the blast of war on man, ending up with a fine picture of the sea drenching the rocks on the coast.

> Then lend the eye a terrible aspect;
> Let it **pry** through the portage of the head,
> Like the brass cannon; let the brow **o'erwhelm** it,
> As fearfully as doth a **galled** rock
> **O'erhang** and **jutty** his **confounded** base,
> **Swilled** with the wild and wasteful ocean.

Here the imagery of the sea and the coast is employed by the poet, not as the setting of a narrative poem, but to describe the appearance of man when the horrible spirit of war distorts his features. We recall, also, those famous lines from *MACBETH*. Macbeth is hounded by guilt and every noise *"appals"* him. He finds that all Neptune's ocean cannot wash the blood from his hands but that

> "............this my hand will rather
> The multitudinous seas **incarnadine**."

Thousands of such powerful lines could be culled from Shakespeare's works. A rereading of some of the famous passages reveals his chary use of lively adjectives, his strong contempt for mere prettiness, for what he called "silken terms" and "taffeta phrases," and his consummate mastery in the use of verbs. Reread, for example, Hamlet's advice to his players, or his soliloquies; Gloucester's speech in the opening scene of *Richard III;* Jacques' description of the seven ages of man, in *As You Like It;* the description of Cleopatra in her barge; Portia's mercy speech; Falstaff's witty lines, especially in *Henry IV* (Part I); or the splendid songs and sonnets. Cull a few phrases such as these:

> **Absent** thee from felicity awhile
> **Godlike** reason **to fust** in us unus'd
> Lilies that **fester**
> **Struts** and **frets** his hour
> Thoughts **people** this little world
> I am **unking'd** by Bolingbroke
> Let the **galled** jade **wince**, our withers are **unwrung.**
> **Screw** your courage to the sticking place
> The cliff that **beetles** o'er his base
> **Paragon** description
> **Beggars** description
> Native resolution **sicklied** o'er with the pale cast of thought
> Daffodils that come before the swallow **dares**

Shakespeare's use of the verb *dares* is an excellent example of the selection of a verb that is neither long nor rare but singularly apt. How better could he have distinguished the daffodil from other flowers or suggested the venturesome nature of the swallow than in these lines?

> " . . . . daffodils
> That comes before the swallow **dares**, and take
> The winds of March with beauty . . . ."

Another excellent example of fine selection is to be found in Ophelia's beautiful lament for Hamlet, in which she says,

> "Now see that noble and most sovereign reason,
> Like sweet bells **jangled**, out of tune and harsh."

"Sweet bells jangled." What a perfect phrase to suggest the contrast between noble reason and madness! On one side of the word *bells* we have the adjective *sweet,* and on the other side the verbal adjective, or participle, *jangled.*

So we might continue to quote from Shakespeare and other poets, from Shelly and Byron, Wordsworth and Coleridge, Tennyson and Browning, Keats, and many others. We recall the sound effects in the skating scene in Wordsworth's *Prelude* and in the scene toward the end of Tennyson's *Morte d'Arthur* in which Sir Bedevere carries Excalibur down to the edge of the mere. We remember, also, the remarkable description of storm-clouds in *The Testament of Beauty,* by Robert Bridges. Mention of Keats calls to mind many lines, especially those in his ode *To Autumn* in which he says of the bees, "Summer has *o'erbrimmed* their clammy cells." But since we must stop quoting somewhere, why not with this exceptionally fine example from Keats? Now let us turn to a consideration of the power of verbs in prose. It really makes little difference here whether we speak of poetry or prose, except that poetry is usually more concise and, consequently, more suitable for illustration. Certainly the need and selection of verbs is much the same.

In pure nature description one might not expect to find much action, certainly not so much as in an action-scene such as that quoted from *Dauber* or in any similar action-scene in prose. One might expect to find far fewer verbs than adjectives. Good description of nature, however, is never flat, static, motionless, but always alive. In his story, "The Lagoon," Conrad heightens an effect of stillness and immobility by emphasizing what action there is. Although the lagoon was *"bewitched into an immobility perfect and final",* the paddlers found themselves in a world not entirely devoid of motion. "The *churned-up* water *frothed* alongside with a *confused* murmur," the cry of a bird, "discordant and feeble, *skipped* over the smooth water," the voices of the paddlers *"reverberated* between the walls of vegetation," and "darkness *oozed* out from between the trees." In Mary Webb's novel, *Gone To Earth,* we find description that is surpassingly beautiful. Notice how much life she expresses in these two sentences, both of which describe Undern, a farm in Shropshire, England:

Even in May, when the lilacs **frothed** into purple, **paved** the lawn with shadows, **steeped** the air with scent; when soft leaves **lipped** each other consolingly; when blackbirds sang, **fell** in their effortless way from the green height to the green depth, and sang again—still, something that **haunted** the place set the heart **fluttering**.

In winter the yews and firs were like **waving** funeral plumes and **mantled**, headless goddesses; then the giant beeches would **lash** themselves to frenzy, and, **stooping**, would **scourge** the ice on Undern Pool and the **cracked** walls of the house, like beings **drunken** with the passion of cruelty. *

Here we have description that is alive, alive with suggestive and vigorous words, many of which are verbs.

Poets, novelists, historians; military leaders and peace-makers; statesmen, diplomats, lawyers; journalists, advertisers, and business men—all are men of action, wielders of words, wielders of verbs. Powerful words spurred Napoleon's men to push on over the Alps and down onto the fertile plains of Italy, just as, later, powerful words spurred the Italian army in its conquest of Ethiopia. No little eloquence was required to pass the Great Reform Bill of 1832 in England, or to free negro slaves in America. Salesmen cannot sell, business men cannot transact, diplomats cannot negotiate, lawyers can neither prosecute nor defend without forceful, convincing language. Without words our personalities become feeble and defunct; with words they spring into life. To express ourselves is to live—and where there's a will there's a word.

GUIDE TO THE USE OF VERBS

1. The Contents and Arrangement of the Thesaurus

Every workman requires the special tools, materials, and technique of his particular trade, and it is the function of the VERB-FINDER to provide the word-craftsman with these requisites. We must first go to the lumberyard and mill to see what materials and machinery we have with which to construct the furniture of our thoughts. In addition we must learn the technique of building.

The Arrangement of the Verbs

The Thesaurus consists of verbs, or action-words, listed alphabetically under nouns. These nouns are the subjects of our sentences, and they, together with the verbs listed below them, form the nuclei or cores of the sentences. Immediately below each noun a number of verbs are listed alphabetically with dashes following them, and under this list other verbs are arranged with dashes preceding them. The

* Quoted by special permission of the publishers, E. P. Dutton and Company, Inc., from *Gone To Earth*, by Mary Webb. (The boldface is the editor's.)

dashes are used to avoid needless repetition of the nouns. Notice that the verbs in the first list act upon the nouns, and that those in the second list carry out the action of the noun; that is, in the first list the noun is the receiver of the action, usually the object of the verb, and in the second list the doer of the action, or the subject of the verb. For example, under the noun *fire* you will find these two lists and these two relationships between noun and verb.

Fire

feed — (*Fire* is the object and receiver of action)
— crackles (*Fire* is the subject and doer)

Verb Forms

Obviously, not all forms of the verbs can be included in the lists, any more than all sizes and shapes of boards can be piled in the lumberyard. The carpenter must select suitable boards of approximately the right size and then shape them to his needs. Consequently, in the first list under each noun, that in which the verb precedes the dash, you will find the infinitive form of the verb (with the *to* omitted), which is exactly the same form as that of the first person singular of the present indicative. In the second list under each noun, that in which the dash follows the verb, you will find the third person singular or plural form of the present indicative, to agree with the noun preceding. For example:

Fish

prepare — (*Prepare* means *to prepare* or *I prepare*)
— squirms (*Squirms* means *It squirms*)

Brick

build with —s (*Build* means *to build* or *I build*)
—s crumble (*Crumble* means *They crumble*)

No verbals are listed. However, verbals and their value in writing will be discussed in another section of the "Guide."

2. How to Build Sentences

In the Thesaurus you will find thousands of sentences and suggestions for sentences right at hand. Given any thought or feeling that you want to express, all you have to do is to find the one best word to express the action that you want. The sentence is a unit of thought or predication containing a subject and predicate. Given a subject, you can easily find here the other element, the word to set it into motion, to make it alive—the verb.

Let us assume that you hear a bell ringing, and that you wish to communicate to us the sound that you hear and exactly how that sound affects you. It is not enough to say, "I hear a bell ringing." That communicates little, for there are all sorts of bells and all sorts of ringing sounds. *Bell* is your subject, however, and *rings* your action, at least tentatively. Now run your finger down the second column of verbs under *bell* and find a better verb. Perhaps you will choose *chimes, clangs, reverberates, sings,* or *tinkles.* It makes considerable difference. Or suppose you want to describe the way a bird moves through the sky. It is not enough to say "The bird moves," or even "The bird flies." Look down the list under *bird* until you come to a verb that will make the bird *dart, hover, float, wheel,* or what you will. This is the way to find your verb, whether you want a verb that will sell a shirt or one of the latest novels, or a verb that will make a poem magical. The same method enables you to find a verb that acts upon a noun used as its object. To express the idea of disposing of an argument, for example, run your finger down the first column under *argument* until you come to a verb, say *refute.* You now have your sentence: "I will refute the argument."

Cross References

If the procedure described above fails to provide you with the verb you are after, you can search elsewhere. At the foot of the verb lists you will usually find a number of guide words or cross references. "See" leads us, through these words, to other lists of verbs. We refer to these other lists in the following ways: from the generic to the specific word, from the specific to the generic, from synonym to synonym, and from the word listed to a word related but not synonymous. Let us explain.

(a) *Generic To Specific*

Suppose you have been trying to find a verb to express the sound (song or other sound) that a bird makes. Suppose that *bird,* although it has many such words listed, does not have the right one. Turn, then, to a specific kind of bird, such as *lark, nightingale,* or *grouse.* You will find that different and more specific verbs are listed under these headings to describe the characteristic sounds and actions of these very different birds. A few examples of this generic to specific reference are:

poetry—See *sonnet*
profession—See *teaching, law*
gem—See *diamond, ruby*

(b) *Specific To Generic*

This is, of course the exact opposite. Some examples are:

> diamond—See *gem*
> painting—See *art*
> bee—See *insect*
> musician—See *artist*
> law—See *profession*

It is well, if possible, to choose the word you want in the first place; that is, not to be talking vaguely about birds if you mean robins or about art if you mean painting. Nevertheless, you will often find it necessary and profitable to refer from the generic to the specific and from the specific to the generic word.

(c) *Synonym To Synonym*

Often you will find synonyms among your guide words. You will do well to use them. For example, after looking in vain for a verb to go with *courage*, you can easily and quickly turn to *bravery, fortitude,* or *valor.* Incidentally, in addition to finding the verb you are after, you may decide that *fortitude,* not *courage,* is the noun that you want.

(d) *The Related Word*

If you refer from *hand* to *claw,* which is not exactly a synonym, you will find good verbs for a claw-like hand. Likewise, if you refer from *anvil* to *bell* or from *art* to *artist* you will find verbs related to your subject. Sometimes you might well refer to a word whose meaning is directly opposite, to an antonym. Many verbs, for example, are used interchangeably with such pairs of words as the following:

Summer and *Winter, comparison* and *contrast, poetry* and *prose.*

3. How to Build Better Sentences

The best way to explain how to build better sentences is to build a few. Below you will find a series of sentences which, although grammatically correct, can stand considerable improvement:

> The red embers sent a strong and ruddy glow from the chimney. Dom Nicholas, the Picardy monk, stood before it. He pulled up his skirts and bared his fat legs to the comfortable warmth. His large shadow appeared in the middle of the room. The firelight shone on either side of his broad person, and in a little pool on either side of his feet, which were spread out. His face had the beery appearance of the continual drinker's, and it was bruised. It was covered with a network of veins, which were purple in ordinary circumstances, but were now violet. He had his back to the fire, but he was cold on the other side.

This is badly written. Why? In the first place, the style is monotonous and choppy because every sentence begins with the subject followed immediately by the verb; secondly, most of the verbs are weak or commonplace; and thirdly, there are too many verbs. If we substitute *diffused* for "*sent*", *straddled* for "*stood*", *picked* for "*pulled*", *escaped* for "*shone*", and *cut the room in half* for "*appeared in the middle of the room*," we will sharpen the picture by the use of stronger verbs. If we recast the second sentence by combining it with the third and by beginning it with a prepositional phrase, instead of with the usual subject-verb combination, we will create a much more compact sentence and relieve the paragraph of some of its monotony. We might write it this way:

> Before this straddled Dom Nicholas, the Picardy monk, with his skirts picked up and his fat legs bared to the comfortable warmth.

Thus, in combining the two sentences, we have used two participles instead of the two verbs, *picked* and *bared*. Participles often help us to condense and vary our sentences; moreover they add life to a sentence when used in place of commonplace adjectives. For example, if we place *arched* before "*chimney*" in the first sentence, *dilated* in place of "*large*" in the fourth, and *outspread* before "*feet*" in the fifth, we will greatly enhance the power of the description. Notice the unnecessary clause in the fifth sentence—"which were spread out". By rewriting the sentence with the participle *outspread* before "*feet*," we eliminate a whole clause, and thus condense the writing without losing any of the meaning. We see now that sentences can be improved in several ways: by substituting strong, precise, colorful, accurate verbs for weak, indefinite, colorless, and inaccurate verbs; by recasting sentences so as to vary, condense, and strengthen their structure by either adding verbals or converting verbs into verbals. Following these principles, we have transformed a crude paragraph into a remarkably fine paragraph. Here it is exactly as R. L. Stevenson wrote it in his story, "A Lodging for the Night:"

> A great pile of **living** embers **diffused** a strong and ruddy glow from the **arched** chimney. Before this **straddled** Dom Nicholas, the Picardy monk, with his skirts **picked** up and his fat legs **bared** to the comfortable warmth. His **dilated** shadow **cut** the room in half; and the firelight only **escaped** on either side of his broad person, and in a little pool between his **outspread** feet. His face had the beery, **bruised** appearance of the continual drinker's; it was covered with a network of **congested** veins, purple in ordinary circumstances, but now pale violet, for even with his back to the fire the cold **pinched** him on the other side. His cowl had half fallen back, and made a strange excrescence on either side of his bull neck. So he **straddled, grumbling,** and **cut** the room in half with the shadow of his portly frame. *

---

* Quoted by special permission of the publishers, Charles Scribner's Sons, from *New Arabian Nights*, by R. L. Stevenson. The editor wrote the first version for the purpose of showing how poor writing can be transformed into good writing. (The boldface is the editor's.)

What a striking portrait this is! Notice the use of the sharp verb *pinched* in place of *was* and of the participles *congested* and *grumbling*.

Since the paragraph above contains no infinitives—it is difficult to find any one selection that will illustrate everything—something remains to be said about the use of this type of verbal. The following words, uttered by Napoleon before his army in Milan, serve as a fine illustration of the effective use of infinitives:

> **To re-establish** the Capitol, **to set up** there the statues of the heroes, **to awaken** the Roman people which for centuries have been paralyzed by servitude—that is the fruit of your victories, that will amaze posterity.

What eloquent words—no matter what our feelings about war and peace—from this man of action! Take out the infinitives and you emasculate the sentence. How comparatively feeble it is when we rewrite it like this:

> The re-establishment of the Capitol, the erection of the statues of the heroes, the awakening of the Roman people which for centuries have been paralyzed by servitude—that is the fruit of your victories, that will amaze posterity.

Observe how heavy and academic this last version is. If you look at these two sentences, one above the other as they stand, you cannot fail to see the power of the infinitive.

4. Diction

A few words should be said about good and bad usage in verbs, for often we find ourselves uncertain as to whether or not a word has been generally accepted as good English. How can we be sure? The VERB-FINDER should help us here. To avoid unnecessary verbiage and confusion, the editors have arranged the verbs in the Thesaurus as simply as possible. You will find only three classifications: slang, colloquialism, and general usage.

Slang

Slang expressions, although sometimes extremely forceful, are often limited in use to a small locality or to a small number of people, to the college campus, to the Southwest, or to baseball, for example. Consequently, outside of its own little sphere it may mean nothing. Moreover slang is often too indefinite, too vague in meaning, to be of much value. For these reasons, when you see a verb listed with quotation marks around it, take care to avoid it in formal writing and to use it informally only where it will be understood. If, however, you feel that the word is sufficiently definite and more vigorous than any other you can think of, use it—but always with quotation marks to indicate that you know exactly what sort of word you are using. Although the word may some day be accepted as respectable, at present it must be regarded as questionable.

Colloquialisms

These words, if a bit more respectable than slang, are to be avoided in formal writing, because they are usually peculiar to one section of the country. However, authors often, and rightly, use colloquialisms in dialogue, for which the spoken word rather than the written or literary word is more appropriate.

Good Usage

We are correct when we say that usage determines what is right or wrong in language. Certainly usage is the power behind the dictionary. But we must qualify our statement, for not every word in common usage is the best word or even a good word. The standard for good usage is the standard set by the language customs of the better writers and speakers. In general, the most intelligent, the best educated, the most highly cultured, the most expressive people attain to the most effective and most beautiful expression. On the other hand, in general, persons of lesser intelligence, education, and culture use poorer language; they tend toward the mediocre and the trite, and even fall into barbarisms, improprieties, clumsiness, and confusion. We might make a table like this:

Good Usage (Formal)

Choice Diction (the best)
Good Diction (superior)
Fair Diction (tending toward the mediocre and trite)

Good and Bad Usage (Informal)

Slang
Colloquialisms

Bad Usage (Inexcusable)

Archaisms
Vulgarisms or Barbarisms
Improprieties or Malapropisms
Affection and Pedantry

If we keep in mind some such distinctions in diction we can be liberal and flexible without being uncertain and inconsistent. The VERB-FINDER concerns itself with the first two categories only. The greater part of the Thesaurus is devoted to the first, but the second, because of the good in it, cannot be ignored.

5. The Verb-Finder As a Source of Information

In addition to performing its chief function, that of aiding us in expressing ourselves, The VERB-FINDER also furnishes encyclopedic information. By consulting the verb lists we can obtain valuable information about many subjects and can even construct fairly good dictionary definitions. Certainly a good way to characterize or define a person or thing is to state what that person or thing does, what its actions are. How, for example, can we define a snob, except by stating how a snob acts? What is a snob? The VERB-FINDER tells us that the snob *apes, affects, pretends, cringes, worships, swaggers, overbears,* etc. Do not such verbs characterize this sort of person through his actions? Here is the definition of *snob* given in Funk and Wagnall's unabridged *DICTIONARY*:

> A person who vulgarly **affects** gentility, or **pretends** to a superiority he does not possess; one who **apes** and **cringes** to his superiors and is **overbearing** to those upon whom he looks as beneath him; one who regards wealth or position rather than character. *

In the same way we could find out a great deal about the habits of birds or termites or horses; about the nature and function of literature or sculpture or biology; about the characteristics of salesmen, artists, fools, clowns, sages, philosophers, lovers, or thieves.

KINGSBURY M. BADGER

---

*The boldface, which does not appear in the dictionary, is the editor's.

A

ABANDON

adjectives

delightful; gleeful; unconscious; passionate; drunken; increasing; intoxicated; idolatrous; hilarious; airy; fanatical; reckless; artistic; dissolute; emotional; melodramatic; universal; insane; humorous; bird-like; wild; childish; desolate; mystic; sensual; cruel; wanton; natural; boyish; typical; joyful; delirious; carefree; ecstatic.

ABANDON (*v*)

adverbs

shamelessly; ingloriously; regretfully; dramatically; definitely; recklessly; simultaneously; reluctantly; prudently; despairingly; eventually; inhumanly; cravenly; wantonly; childishly; temporarily; pusillanimously; faint-heartedly; pitiably; haplessly; remorsefully; ruefully; sullenly; woefully; wretchedly; contritely; dejectedly; dolefully; mournfully; dispiritedly; mirthlessly; tragically.

(See repudiate, forsake, waive, surrender.)

ABANDONED (*a*)

adverbs

delightfully; gleefully; hilariously; airily; recklessly; emotionally; insanely; crazily; ridiculously; wantonly; childishly; boyishly; ludicrously; lamentably; pitiably; unblushingly; provokingly; totally; shamefully; widely; maliciously; regretfully.

ABANDONMENT

adjectives

courageous; inhuman; introspective; hasty; moral; spontaneous; shameless; inglorious; melodramatic; notorious; cowardly; reluctant; prudent; despairing; criminal; crazy; odd.

ABASE (*v*)

adverbs

disgracefully; degradingly; humiliatingly; shamefully; mortifyingly; ruinously; brutally; belittlingly; calumniously; traducingly; mortifyingly; dishonorably; slanderously.

(See humiliate, degrade, disgrace.)

ABASEMENT

adjectives

servile; mortifying; humiliating; cruel; wilful; total; ultimate.

ABBE

adjectives

infidel; pleasure-loving; gay; witty; dissolute; dull; aristocratic.

ABBREVIATION

adjectives

offensive; delicate; apt; cryptic; unintelligible; suggestive; recognizable; remote; felicitous.

ABDICATE (*v*)

adverbs

altruistically; willingly; voluntarily; dramatically; ignominiously; unaccountably; cravenly; enforcedly; pusillanimously; submissively; shrewdly; pliantly; tractably; passively.

(See abandon, forsake, surrender, repudiate.)

ABDICATION

adjectives

dramatic; ignominious; unaccountable; altruistic; precipitate; unprecedented; reckless; voluntary; enforced.

ABDOMEN

adjectives

ample; protruding; protuberant; pendulous; flaccid; lean; monstrous; sagging.

verbs

develop—; distend—; enlarge—; exercise—; flatten—; knead—; massage—; relax—; rest on—; subject—; support—; thrust forward—; —is bounded by; —is composed of; —is lined; —juts out; —sags.

(See stomach, intestines, paunch, belly.)

ABDOMINAL

misc.

—surgery; —distress; mobilize the—contents.

ABERRATION

adjectives

vulgar; isolated; philosophic; abhorrent; dangerous; spiritual; noteworthy; marked; human; apparent; mental.

ABHOR (*v*)

adverbs

passionately; unqualifiedly; deeply; uncontrollably; vindictively; undyingly; vigorous-

1

ly; smoulderingly; malignantly; diabolically; vengefully; inimically; satanically;
malevolently; misanthropically; disdainfully.

(See detest, scorn.)

ABHORRENCE
adjectives
unqualified; modern; cold; hard-headed;
justified; passionate; rational; uncontrollable; utmost; inexpressive; well-organized;
sullen; deadly; respectful; furious; fierce;
stealthy; holy; professed; burlesqued.

ABHORRENT
adverbs
excruciatingly; loathsomely; impossibly;
utterly; completely; horribly; terribly; a-
bominably; odiously; repulsively; detestably; hatefully; shockingly; unspeakably.

ABIDE (*v*)
adverbs
faithfully; religiously; staunchly; temporarily; permanently; trustworthily; stoutly;
steadfastly; diligently; persistently; unabat-
ingly; deathlessly; enduringly; unfalteringly; firmly; constantly; assiduously.

ABILITY
adjectives
unexcelled; superior; transcendent; surpassing; brilliant; eminent; distinguished; commanding; promising; superb; never-failing;
proved; rare; unique; marked; conspicuous;
discernible; pronounced; obvious; manifest;
undeniable; surprising; amazing; astounding; extraordinary; remarkable; phenomenal; superhuman; inherent; innate; intrinsic;
natural; vast; immense; limited; mediocre;
middle; cold-blooded; uncanny; eerie; latent; administrative; artistic; executive;
forensic; histrionic; linguistic; organizing;
oratorical; recuperative; selective; story-
telling; mature; mystifying; embryonic; intuitive; sensitive; supposed; sheer; versatile; productive; respectable; slender; professional; superlative; dramatic; acquired;
individual; strategic; recognized; peculiar;
wonted; potential; striking; crafty; constructive; singular; conscienceless; overrated; intellectual; humble; undoubted; uncommon; critical; technical; variant; creative; doubtful; adroit; vocalistic; practical;
enhanced; discontented; melodic; universal;
conscious; humble.

verbs
analyze—; ascertain—; attribute—; bow to
—; bluster about—; confer—; demonstrate

—; destroy—; determine—; develop—; diminish—; display—; distrust—; donate—;
endow with—; enhance—; estimate—;
evince—; exhibit—; increase—; invest with
—; lack—; make use of—; manifest—;
mistreat—; outstrip—; outweigh—; pool—;
possess—; presume—; prove—; register—;
test—; vitiate—; weigh—; —develops; —
enables; —enhances; —falls short; —redeems; —undergoes.

(See talent, capability, capacity, faculty, power, skill.)

ABJECT
adverbs
inconceivably; hopelessly; mournfully; pitiably; incurably; basely; incredibly; piteously; horribly; tragically; unbelievably; singularly; miserably; comically; ridiculously;
ostensibly; ostentatiously; glumly; dismally;
disconsolately; moodily; heavily; ludicrously.

ABLE
adverbs
tremendously; extremely; wonderfully; adequately; marvelously; uncommonly; extraordinarily; astonishingly; brilliantly; superbly; surprisingly; amazingly; remarkably; particularly; consciously.

ABLUTION
adjectives
sacred; ordinary; daily; outward; unwonted; ritualistic.

ABNEGATION
adjectives
manly; unselfish; absolute; subtle; apostolic;
heroic; inspired; unsparing.

ABNORMAL
adverbs
grotesquely; distressingly; painfully; pitiably; noticeably; hideously; undoubtedly;
positively; emotionally; markedly; patently;
harmlessly; mildly; slightly; entirely; admittedly; grievously; repulsively; shockingly.

ABNORMALITY
adjectives
distressing; emotional; allied; fancied; imperceptible; marked; noticeable; hideous;
incredible; patent.

ABODE
adjectives
lonely; peaceful; august; blissful; ancient;
eternal; Elysian; sheltered; inaccessible;

dolorous; lasting; obscure; desolate; ancestral; claustral; comfortless; indispensable; serene; fit; fixed; permanent; primitive; sequestered; sybaritic; transient; immortal; ramshackle; dreadful; disconcerting; abandoned; secure; blest; troglodytic; unostentatious; luxurious; phantasmal; damp; dreary; perilous; abhorred; melancholy; mean; soft; eremitic; dread.

verbs
choose—; disdain—; make—with; retire to —; seek—; take up—; welcome to—.

ABOLISH (*v*)
adverbs
ultimately; effectually; virtually; universally; legally; permanently; entirely; dictatorially; tyrannically; destructively; obliteratingly; deleteriously.
(See annul, repeal.)

ABOLITION
adjectives
projected; forcible; universal; virtual; effectual; ultimate; immediate; instantaneous; gradual.

ABOMINABLE
adverbs
incredibly; intolerably; unbelievably; hatefully; utterly; completely; maliciously; oppressively; brutally; flagrantly; detestably; perniciously; viciously; deplorably; diabolically; execrably; noxiously; lamentably; hatefully; villainously; woefully; odiously; abhorrently; repulsively; invidiously; despicably.

ABOMINATION
adjectives
heathenish; hideous; dark; whitewashed; nondescript; loathsome; indescribable; foul; monstrous; gross.

verbs
behold—; cast away—; commit—; delight in—; work—; multiply—; overspread—; perpetrate—; provoke to—; turn away from —.

(See squalor, wickedness, aversion.)

ABORTION
adjectives
cruel; criminal; sterility-inducing; inadvisable; mutilating; illegal; wanton.

verbs
advise an—; anticipate—; avert—; balk at —; bring about—; cause—; contribute to—;

expose to—; frustrate—; have—; **impose** an—; indicate—; induce—; indulge in—; instruct about—; justify—; lead to—; legalize—; perform—; permit—; precede—; prevent—; procure—; produce—; prove—; provoke into—; resort to—; stop—; submit to—; terminate in—; tolerate—; treat—; undergo—; weaken by—; yield to—; — arises from; —occurs; —results.
(See miscarriage, failure, operation.)

ABOUND (*v*)
adverbs
plentifully; luxuriantly; astonishingly; endlessly; naturally; primevally; multitudinously; munificently; swarmingly; throngingly; monstrously; boundlessly; excessively; generously.
(See swarm.)

ABRUPT
adverbs
unpardonably, rudely; roughly; instinctively; unconsciously; unfortunately; startlingly; whimsically; intentionally; astonishingly; amusingly; offensively; ridiculously; inexcusably; unforgivably; unexpectedly; unreasonably; momentarily; habitually; unintentionally.

ABRUPTNESS
adjectives
embarrassed; off-hand; startling; uncompromising; whimsical; wolfish; characteristic; brusque; brisk; easy.

ABSCESS
adjectives
hidden; internal; monstrous; fatal; pestilent; cankerous; gnawing; tentacle-like.

verbs
confine—; develop into—; drain—; dress—; evacuate—; exude from—; give rise to—; incise—; inflame—; irritate—; lance—; poultice—; swab out—; —arises; —attains size; —becomes embedded; —bulges; — bursts; —destroys; —develops; —discharges; —forms; —grows; —infiltrates; —inflames; —occurs; —opens; —re-forms; —ruptures; —spreads; —swells.
(See sore, ulcer, tumor, boil.)

ABSCOND (*v*)
adverbs
villainously; faithlessly; vilely; treacherously; unexpectedly; basely; knavishly; mysteriously; monstrously; nefariously; odiously; lawlessly; mendaciously.
(See flee.)

adjectives

utter; cautious; restful; prolonged; total; unaccounted; trying; oppressive; frequent; momentary; undutiful; perilous; considerable; striking; enforced; protracted; continued; pleasing; unauthorized; comparative; apparent; voluntary; everlasting; occasional; intermittent (pl).

verbs

attend—; bear—; berate—; bewail—; deplore—; dote on—; endure—; lament—; mourn—; presuppose—; regret—; support by—; take advantage of—; wail—; grant—; yield to—; —diminishes; —draws; —grows; —increases; —kills; —lessens; —quickens.

ABSENT

(in mind or in person)

adverbs

conspicuously; unfortunately; unaccountably; frequently; irritatingly; apparently; voluntarily; inexcusably; noticeably; purposely; inexplainably; mysteriously; carelessly; usually; provokingly.

ABSOLUTION

adjectives

general; priestly; just; rapturous; timely; insincere; virtual; conscientious; serene; blissful.

ABSOLVE (v)

adverbs

religiously; entirely; wholly; thoroughly; certainly; partly; freely; leniently; placably; sympathetically; forbearingly; compassionately; palliatively.

(See free, pardon, release.)

ABSORB (v)

adverbs

incessantly; wholly; passively; profoundly; partially; racially; nationally; intelligently; intellectually; physically; studiously; hurtfully; mentally; accretively; electively; vocationally; bibulously; crapulently; canniballistically; edaciously; intemperately; ghoulishly.

(See monopolize, engross.)

ABSORBED

adverbs

ridiculously; tragically; utterly; profoundly; shamelessly; mentally; wholly; deeply; completely; rapturously; ecstatically; tensely; eagerly; anxiously; gloomily; ludicrously; foolishly; fatuously; amazingly.

ABSORBENT

adverbs

extraordinarily; scarcely; completely; gradually; quickly; remarkably; marvelously; notably; wonderfully; exceptionally; genuinely; astonishingly; unusually; unfailingly; singularly; particularly; unbelievably; highly.

ABSORPTION

adjectives

bookish; omnivorous; profound; tragic; unflattering; shame-faced; poetic; gradual; mental; tense; detached; droll; indecent; stolid; passive; demoniac; vigorous.

ABSTAIN (v)

adverbs

cautiously; perniciously; carefully; systematically; firmly; voluntarily; austerely; religiously; totally; wilfully; narrowly; wholesomely; cautiously; prudently; discreetly; circumspectly; scrupulously; squeamishly; judiciously; economically; frugally; parsimoniously; sparingly; penuriously; chastely.

(See refrain, withhold.)

ABSTEMIOUS

adverbs

ascetically; piously; wholly; strictly; austerely; rigorously; proudly; awkwardly; fanatically; ridiculously; absurdly; carefully; abominably; cautiously; correctly; habitually; warily; ostentatiously; inconspicuously; glaringly; conspicuously; reluctantly; unctuously; smugly; grimly.

ABSTEMIOUSNESS

adjectives

ascetic; austere; stern; rigorous; calculated; proud.

ABSTINENCE

adjectives

bigoted; excessive; prolonged; total; rash; systematic; forced; holy; marked; firm; strict; self-enforced; austere; cautious; pernicious; absolute; recurrent; partial; half-hearted; protracted; extreme; habitual.

ABSTRACT

adverbs

academically; infinitely; immeasurably; uncomfortably; abstrusely; indefinitely; illusively; remotely; undeniably; obscurely; completely; terribly; entirely; sheerly; thoroughly; immaterially; undefinably; immutably; vaguely; fantastically; chimerically;

4

extravagantly; eternally; evanescently; transcendentally; unverifiably; preternaturally; spiritually; mystically; conceptually; palpably; patently; speculatively; intuitively; ideologically; empirically; occultly; visionarily; doctrinally; hypothetically.

ABSTRACTION
adjectives
mysterious; intense; subtle; hazy; sublime; unquiet; meaningless; thoughtful; dreamy; noble; mythical; shadowy; gloomy; statistical; far-off; eerie; stony; melancholy; moody; tight-lipped; deep; dull; pernicious; wistful; lengthy; grandiose; grave; wonted.

ABSTRUSE
adverbs
disagreeably; unfortunately; vexatiously; remotely; obscurely; profoundly; extremely; unreasonably; unnecessarily; needlessly; foolishly; absurdly; foggily; senselessly; stupidly; inexpediently; enigmatically; annoyingly; heavily; injudiciously; incomprehensibly; highly; unwisely; preposterously; confusingly; bewilderingly; perplexingly; indiscreetly.

ABSURD
adverbs
palpably; perniciously; nakedly; impudently; ludicrously; manifestly; fantastically; quaintly; grotesquely; patently; tragically; comically; perversely; detestably; pathetically; ignominiously; ridiculously; monstrously; grossly; unreasonably.

ABSURDITY
adjectives
palpable; pernicious; unfathomable; essential; naked; impudent; ornithological; ludicrous; moral; manifest; fantastic; quaint; reigning; infantine; grotesque; patent; tragic; perverse; colossal; detestable; inadequate; pathetic; ignominious; cumulative (pl); assorted (pl); ridiculous; monstrous; wholesome; gross; intrinsic; raucous; unreasonable.

verbs
atone for—; behold—; condone—; excuse—; expose—; father—; grieve over—; perpetrate—; smile at—; —destroys; —falls away; —impairs; —saps; —undermines.
(See folly, foolishness, nonsense.)

ABUNDANCE
adjectives
copious; uninterrupted; lavish; unbelievable; natural; flowing; laudable; culinary; theoretical; coveted; peculiar; careless; needless; wasteful; economic; sheer.

verbs
bless with—; conserve—; diminish—; endow with—; groan under—; inherit—; lavish—on; partake of—; pile up—; pour —; sate with—; satiate with—; squander—; surround by—; tap—; weaken by—; — flows; —lies; —melts away.
(See plenty.)

ABUNDANT
adverbs
overwhelmingly; marvelously; happily; fortunately; lavishly; naturally; profusely; uncommonly; unusually; remarkably; ravishingly; staggeringly; surprisingly; unbelievably; incredibly; voluptuously; wonderfully; particularly; amazingly; astonishingly; extraordinarily; fabulously; immeasurably; incalculably; indisputably; inexpressibly; alarmingly.

ABUSE
adjectives
political; unintelligible; intemperate; personal; treasonable; alarming; existing; scurrilous; sore; glaring; triumphant; abundant; filthy; scandalous; pernicious; tyrannical; alleged; disastrous; noisy; humorous; false; indiscriminate; stupid; mighty; virulent; intolerable; horrible; obscene; vicious; violent; flagrant; inhuman; profane; foul; notorious; barefaced; arrogant; shameful.

verbs
brook—; check—; condone—; correct—; cry out at—; curb—; direct—against; drive to —; eliminate—; exchange—; heap—; incur —; pour—; prevent—; reckon up—; remedy —; shovel—on; spare—; spy into—; stumble on—; subject to—; thunder—; tolerate —; wipe out—; —blackens; —damns; — prevails; —s are rife; —s reckon up.
(See perversion, invective.)

ABUSE (v)
adverbs
profanely; notoriously; foully; arrogantly; barefacedly; grossly; scandalously; shamefully; intemperately; treasonably; indiscriminately; alarmingly; scurrilously; perniciously; tyrannically; stupidly; virulently; mightily; obscenely; viciously; violently; inhumanly; flagrantly; heinously; malevolently; malignantly; noxiously; tempestuously; truculently; atrociously; hellishly; roughly.
(See misuse, injure, violate.)

5

ABUSIVE

adverbs

inexcusably; tragically; absurdly; painfully; scathingly; blisteringly; scandalously; alarmingly; ferociously; noisily; intolerably; pugnaciously; truculently; inhumanly; foully; diabolically; inconceivably; incredibly; obscenely; cruelly; scurrilously; unpardonably; unforgivably; unreasonably; immoderately; virulently; rashly; criminally; preposterously; unbelievably; recklessly; terribly; humiliatingly; profanely; disgracefully; shamefully; insanely; crazily; appallingly; maliciously; lamentably; violently; destructively; rancorously; blasphemously; spitefully; wickedly; revoltingly; illegally; direly; deliriously; horribly.

ABYSS

adjectives

immovable; nethermost; awful; blossoming; unfathomed; threatening; watery; dolorous; howling; moral; infernal; financial; yawning; void; profound; desolate; murky; bottomless; sunless; horrible; widening; black; unavoidable; breath-taking; gaping; immeasurable; hellish; hideous; Stygian.

ACADEMIC

adverbs

incurably; consistently; abstrusely; formally; formidably; illusively; evasively; impracticably; idealistically; impractically; remotely; uselessly; patently; frankly; uncomfortably; completely; dangerously; intrinsically; vaguely; fantastically; unfortunately; dreamily; unserviceably; worthlessly.

ACCEDE (*v*)

adverbs

heartily; speedily; willingly; unconditionally; amicably; rationally; gladly; genially; grudgingly; boorishly; tacitly; affably; benevolently; courteously; complaisantly; civilly; chivalrously; deferentially.

(See agree, concur, comply.)

ACCELERATE (*v*)

adverbs

tremendously; expectedly; abruptly; naturally; foolhardily; thoughtlessly; mechanically; intemperately; instantaneously; promptly; hurriedly; startlingly.

(See hasten, quicken.)

ACCELERATION

adjectives

whirling; considerable; impressive; impetu-

ous; swift; easy; breath-taking; faulty; smooth; effortless.

ACCENT

adjectives

joyous; respectful; tender; well-bred; practiced; unctuous; affected; ornamental; mincing; vicious; blighting; coarse; peremptory; deliberate; icy; imperative; mocking; taunting; hurried; quivering; thick; clipped; mutilated; lingering; guttural; musical; silvery; mellow; pedantic; bell-like; clarion; insinuating; pleasant; droning; persuasive; melancholy; pitying; agonized; oratorical; professional; plebeian; objectionable; awed; faltering; half-impertinent; dispassionate; searching; trembling; gracious; musing; hushed; sober; measured; warning; meek; bluff; terrible; charming; feeble; soothing; compassionate; audible; smart; distinct; hollow; uncouth; haughty; ringing; honeyed; emphatic; nautical; swaggering; furious; mingled; tearful; crystal; pained; ecclesiastical; hesitant; wistful; authentic; melodious; sonorous; Teutonic; flippant; perceptible; provincial; circumflex; hesitating.

verbs

affect—; betray—; brook—; miss—; muffle —; reiterate in —s; —breaks; —echoes; —weakens.

(See stress, emphasis.)

ACCENT (*v*)

adverbs

nicely; pedantically; unctuously; joyously; tenderly; affectedly; mincingly; coarsely; deliberately; mockingly; tauntingly; quiveringly; lingeringly; musically; mellowly; insinuatingly; persuasively; falteringly; dispassionately; charmingly; soothingly; uncouthly; haughtily; emphatically; hesitantly; wistfully; melodiously; sonorously; flippantly; haltingly.

(See stress.)

ACCEPT (*v*)

adverbs

graciously; frankly; unreservedly; grudgingly; lifelessly; courteously; readily; cheerfully; fatalistically; passively; cautiously; phlegmatically; elatedly; enthusiastically; universally; bravely; casually; consciously; eagerly; generally; peacefully; credulously; thankfully; reluctantly; gratefully; reasonably; willingly; unhesitatingly; implicitly; philosophically; good-naturedly; slavishly; glibly; skeptically; impulsively, stoically; magnanimously; complacently.

(See approve.)

6

ACCEPTABLE

adverbs

unquestionably; charmingly; wholly; delightfully; genuinely; joyously; happily; providentially; luckily; gratifyingly; tragically; comically; vastly; duly; profoundly; admittedly; puzzlingly; infinitely; incalculably; immeasurably; particularly; personally; absolutely; frankly; socially; politically; officially; conventionally; widely; universally; locally.

ACCEPTANCE

adjectives

happy; warm; joyous; incoherent; complacent; wholesale; unanimous; fearless; impulsive; stoical; resigned; public; frank; modified; glib; skeptical; slavish; loathsome; unquestioning; ready; belated; simulated; good-natured; pacific; philosophic; reluctant; social; implicit; relieved; gracious; grudging; fatalistic; passive; phlegmatic; appreciatory; wide; delayed; patient; ironical; cheerful; general; unreserved; universal; credulous; grave; grandiloquent.

verbs

authorize—; coax—; confirm—; elicit—; find—; guarantee—; meet with—; presuppose—; —displays; —precludes.
  (See agreement, assent.)

ACCESS

adjectives

impregnable; casual; unrestricted; momentary; exclusive; strange; convenient; direct; expeditious; easy.

verbs

bar—; deny—to; desire—to; disdain—; give—; grant—; seek—; procure—; shut off—; stop up—; survey—; throng—.
  (See approach, admittance.)

ACCESSIBLE

adverbs

conveniently; easily; instantly; directly; serviceably; handily; immediately; instantaneously; casually; imperceptibly; inconspicuously; unobtrusively.

ACCESSORY

adjectives

agreeable; scenic; fashionable; cultured; gracious; impressive; colorful; distinctive; exquisite; decorative; tawdry; indispensable; unwilling; criminal.

ACCIDENT

adjectives

unlucky; capricious; untoward; melancholy; singular; unfortunate; comical; happy; felicitous; merest; incalculable; inescapable; preventable; frightful; pure; deplorable; subversive; divine; haphazard; perverse; monstrous; trivial; sheer; malignant; regrettable; vexing; inexplicable; minor; heart-breaking; curious; ghastly; providential; incredible; stupid; dreadful; fatal; predictable.

verbs

answer for—; barring—; breed —s; curb —s; excuse—; fake—; incapacitate by—; subject to—; trace to—; —befalls; —forces; —happens; —occurs; —oppresses; —places.
  (See event, mishap.)

ACCIDENTAL

adverbs

scarcely, obviously, presumably, luckily; purposely; wholly; comically; inexplicably; curiously; mysteriously; certainly; undoubtedly; admittedly; undeniably; ludicrously; purportedly; evidently; supposedly; awkwardly; tragically; plainly; rarely.

ACCLAIM

adjectives

critical; tumultuous; public; boisterous; deafening; wide-spread; enthusiastic; spontaneous; immeasurable; resounding; joyous; jubilant; riotous; grandiloquent; noisy; righteous; deserved; universal.

ACCLAIM (v)

adverbs

riotously; grandiloquently; enthusiastically; noisily; tumultuously; boisterously; deafeningly; spontaneously; resoundingly; jubilantly; joyously; obstreperously; thunderously; persistently; turbulently; vociferously; sepulchrally; blatantly; clamorously; flamboyantly.
  (See applaud, approve, cheer.)

ACCOMMODATE (v)

adverbs

effectually; appreciatively; easily; nobly; amiably; freely; generously; beneficently; benignly; graciously; impartially; magnanimously; altruistically; benignantly; legally; legitimately.
  (See favor, oblige.)

ACCOMMODATING

adverbs

ingratiatingly; amiably; delightfully; ob-

7

sequiously; ostentatiously; pompously; profusely; helpfully; fawningly; cordially; pretentiously; courteously; habitually; unusually; ominously; grudgingly; willingly; significantly; heartily; civilly; servilely; loftily; exceedingly; gravely; graciously; charmingly; freely; gruffly; politely; bluntly; splendidly; magnificently; surprisingly.

ACCOMMODATIONS
adjectives
luxurious; superior; splendid; modern; complete; princely; excellent; cheery; spacious; genial; straitened; pacific; dismal; comfortable; overnight; transient; capacious; commodious; sorry; mean; ordinary; slender; wretched.

ACCOMPANIMENT
adjectives
regrettable; picturesque; harmonic; supernatural; deprecatory; violent; aesthetic; invariable; undulating; confused; fearful; running; pleasurable; inharmonious; unsuitable; inevitable; throbbing; spirited; vague; faint; discordant; splendid; sinister; satiric; verdant; fiendish; bewitching; fitting; orchestral; indispensable; competent; riotous; listless; unhappy; staccato.

ACCOMPANY (v)
adverbs
listlessly; inevitably; invariably; delightedly; unhappily; fearfully; confusedly; harmoniously; unsuitably; spiritually; intelligently; discordantly; bewitchingly; competently; skillfully; dexterously; gaily; gladly; blissfully; rejoicingly; mirthfully; rapturously; dutifully.
(See escort, follow, attend.)

ACCOMPLICE
adjectives
menial; principal; provocative; vigilant; criminal; unwitting; dastardly; secret; willing; assiduous; inept; perfidious.

ACCOMPLISH (v)
adverbs
effectively; boastfully; deliberately; adequately; culturally; indefatigably; ultimately; substantially; peacefully; divinely; signally; impressively; skillfully; meritoriously; energetically; invincibly; irresistibly.
(See achieve, perform, execute.)

ACCOMPLISHED
adverbs
brilliantly; wonderfully; unusually; marvell-

ously; cleverly; incredibly; undoubtedly; distinctly; expertly; thoroughly; consummately; remarkably; politely; elegantly.

ACCOMPLISHMENT
adjectives
germinant; cultural; mental; limited; fatiguing; glittering; ultimate; substantial; brilliant; peaceful; divine; signal; human; impressive; creative; infinite (pl); successful; superb; scrupulous; notable; worthy; effete; versatile; effective; deliberate; boastful.

verbs
appraise —s; awe by—; credit with—; dwarf—; echo with—; enrich with—; gird oneself for—; hail—; lack—; marvel at—; praise—; strive for—; sum up —s; want (lack)—; —pales; —taunts.
(See achievement, action, deed feat.)

ACCORD
adjectives
complete; mutual; enthusiastic; technical; sweet; voluntary; sensual; solid; simple; superficial; perfect; generous; hearty; tumultuous; universal; widespread; peaceful; temporary; lasting; harmonious.

ACCORD (v)
adverbs
generously; universally; genially; voluntarily; willingly; grudgingly; superficially; beneficently; gladly; intelligently; benevolently; reasonably; magnanimously; graciously; impartially; altruistically; benignly.
(See agree, conform.)

ACCOST (v)
adverbs
cordially; genially; jovially; graciously; familiarly; rudely; roughly; heartily; acrimoniously; bitterly; bluffly; drunkenly; blithely; gleefully; mirthfully; vivaciously; exultantly; ecstatically; conceitedly; cheerily.
(See greet, address.)

ACCOUNT
adjectives
elaborate; detailed; full; minute; lengthy; analytical; concise; brief; condensed; picturesque; magnificent; beautiful; hackneyed; inspired; felicitous; scanty; fragmentary; sketchy; rambling; inadequate; exact; accurate; veracious; precise; factual; personal; intimate; unaffected; sincere; straightforward; biased; impartial; prejudiced; sober; childish; intelligible; cap-

able; continuous; straight-running; chimerical; absurd; amusing; humorous; whimsical; facetious; thrilling; breath-taking; hair-raising; blood-curdling; lurid; ambiguous; conflicting; contradictory; amazing; disquieting; alarming; ribald; sordid; sprawling; incoherent; statistical; romantic; syllogistic; proselytizing; ironical; informative; lusty; rigorous; indignant; delirious; articulate; uninhibited; charming; fascinating; delightful; absorbing; striking; graphic; vivid; animated; leisurely; belated; garrulous; circumstantial; exhaustive; specific; inferential; synthetic; punctilious; glowing; exaggerated; superficial; singular; unrhetorical; contemporary; profuse; inspired; gloomy; harrowing; technical; wiredrawn; conjectural; malicious; farcical; biographical; voluble; prosaic; racy; awful.

verbs
balance—; boost—; fabricate—; juggle —s; revel in —s; render—; settle—; tally up—; treble the—; attach to your—; call to—, give—of; open—; place to—; take—of; take into—; enliven—; favor with—; furnish—; launch upon—; peruse—; ramble through—; deny—; sum up—; supplement —; thrill to—; —amuses; —bores; —depicts; —differs; —entertains; —maneuvers; —wearies.
(See reckoning, bill, notice, history, report, record, narrative.)

ACCOUNTABLE
adverbs
personally; legally; entirely; wholly; scarcely; officially; morally; partially; solely; admittedly; seriously; terribly; unofficially; really.

ACCRETION
adjectives
scholastic; formalistic; enormous; elaborate; slow-forming; cumulative; natural; hidden; gradual.

ACCUMULATE (v)
adverbs
uselessly; painstakingly; laboriously; toilsomely; eccentrically; penuriously; cautiously; judiciously; prudently; close-fistedly; frugally; parsimoniously; economically; conservatively.
(See collect, gather.)

ACCUMULATION
adjectives
periodic; slow; colossal; perpetual; laborious; appalling; dangerous; insistent; use-

less; unsmiling; prodigious; ponderous; contorted; massive.

ACCUMULATIVE
adverbs
laboriously; ingeniously; peculiarly; unaccountably; painstakingly; instinctively; irresponsibly; habitually; dangerously; suspiciously; unsmilingly; laughingly; openly; furtively; surreptitiously; cleverly; cunningly; frankly; delightfully; deliriously; whimsically; garrulously; sincerely; unaffectedly; leisurely.

ACCURACY
adjectives
absolute; dependable; historical; businesslike; substantial; precise; unrivaled; scrupulous; tolerable; measurable; predictable; muscular; unfailing; blunt; remarkable; strict; deadly; guaranteed; mechanical; clock-like; excellent; uncanny; timed; impeccable; apparent; unctuous; machine-like; relentless; meticulous; unerring; horrible; photographic; sensitive; nautical; perfect; infinite; rhythmic; diabolical; humdrum; monotonous.

verbs
ascertain—; concede—; depend upon—; reveal—; scout—; test—; vouch for—; —fosters; —sustains
(See precision.)

ACCURATE
adverbs
absolutely; dependably; awfully; terrifyingly; scrupulously; tolerably; unfailingly; remarkably; strictly; uncannily; meticulously; monotonously; veritably; disturbingly; nakedly; essentially; unimpeachably; rigidly; mathematically; scientifically; carefully; particularly; astonishingly; insatiably; avidly; impartially; ostentatiously; punctiliously.

ACCUSATION
adjectives
frivolous; unfounded; monstrous; plaintive; vulgar; horrible; tearful; vague; rash; unanswerable; recurrent; merciless; mock; human; public; groundless; menial; eloquent; positive; keen; railing; sarcastic; indignant; constant; trumped up; nonsensical; sharp; determined; wild; unjust; false; cruel; revolting; wholesale (pl); grave; scurrilous; slanderous; violent; sensational; hasty; playful; vitriolic; villainous.

verbs
balk at—; bring—; clear—; contradict—;

9

counteract—; defend against—; deny—; disprove—; face—; headline—; heap —s; hurl—; level—at; parry—; refute—; resist —; roar —s; secure against—; set—; splutter—; uncover—; weigh—; withstand—.
(See charge, complaint.)

ACCUSE (v)
adverbs
publicly; consistently; unjustly; deliberately; scurrilously; falsely; sternly; vainly; frivolously; monstrously; plaintively; vulgarly; tearfully; vaguely; rashly; mercilessly; groundlessly; eloquently; indignantly; sarcastically; triumphantly; determinedly; wildly; cruelly; revoltingly; libellously; slanderously; sensationally; ruinously.
(See blame, charge.)

ACHE
adjectives
strange; dull; continual; yearning; maddening, hungry; trifling; brief; cold; numbing; throbbing; muscular; angry; bodily; intolerable; murderous; unbearable; agonizing; intermittent (pl).

verbs
aggravate—; allay—; alleviate—; assuage —; charm—; distress with—; fill with —s; harry by —s; hide—; increase—; mitigate —; mollify—; soothe—; subdue—; tantalize by—; torture by—; —abates; —contracts; —develops; —diminishes.
(See pain, agony, anguish, misery.)

ACHE (v)
adverbs
intolerably; dully; maddeningly; agonizingly; throbbingly; bitterly; sorely; mentally; dismally; tormentingly; torturingly; sharply; interminably; incessantly; monotonously; ceaselessly; periodically.
(See pain, suffer.)

ACHIEVE (v)
adverbs
unbelievably; secretly; laboriously; lastingly; consistently; tirelessly; honorably; gloriously; spiritually; conspicuously; momentously; splendidly; monumentally; superhumanly; signally; creatively; magnificently; spectacularly; breath-takingly; impressively; memorably; heroically; illustriously; valorously; fabulously; significantly.
(See accomplish, gain, acquire.)

ACHIEVEMENT
adjectives
solid; practical; lasting; remarkable; sci-entific; human; technological; metaphysical; civic; routine; happy; courageous; difficult; universal; authentic; fantastic; consistent; tireless; honorable; laureate; glorious; noble; conspicuous; spiritual; major; momentous; monumental; superhuman; signal; sublime; phenomenal; noteworthy; worthwhile; meritorious; creditable; praiseworthy; creative; constructive; colossal; vast; stupendous; magnificent; artistic; picturesque; rare; unparalleled; unique; spectacular; culminating; breath-taking; stirring; supreme; crowning; Homeric; impressive; memorable; heroic; valorous; illustrious; unfading; poetic; precocious; fabulous; laborious; subtle; immortal; significant; epoch-making; irreproachable.

verbs
belittle—; conceive—; denote—; disparage —; enhance—; facilitate—; hedge about—; laud—; meditate on—; mock at—; plan—; praise—; proclaim—; question—; reaffirm —; rejoice in—; strive toward—; —contributes to; —distinguishes; —goes unrecognized; —mocks.
(See accomplishment, action, deed, feat.)

ACID
adjectives
pungent; aromatic; biting; insidious; corrosive; baneful; mineral; powerful; fatal; astringent; violent; fuming.

verbs
immerse in—; isolate—; neutralize—; treat with—; —bites; —burns; —cauterizes; —corrodes; —dissolves; —eats; —etches; —evaporates; —meets; —penetrates; —scars; —sears; —seeps off.
(See chemical.)

ACID (a)
adverbs
bitterly; maliciously; viciously; purposely; unnecessarily; uncontrollably; hatefully; insidiously; sharply; cynically; spitefully; resentfully; venomously; intentionally; designedly; cunningly; insinuatingly; sarcastically; incisively; shrewdly; antagonistically; needlessly; unwisely.

ACKNOWLEDGE (v)
adverbs
gratefully; appreciatively; tacitly; thankfully; obsequiously; grudgingly; pusillanimously; handsomely; tardily; instinctively; cheerfully; profusely; indulgently; exuberantly; restrainedly; warmly; characteristically; graciously; jocosely; belatedly; glum-

10

ly; obstreperously; **boisterously**; taciturnly; **incoherently**.

(See admit, confess.)

ACKNOWLEDGMENT

adjectives
profuse; indulgent; exuberant; restrained; polite; conventional; frank; warm; characteristic; humiliating; enthusiastic; grateful; public; gracious; jocose; courteous; grim; belated; thankful; obsequious; tacit; grudging; handsome; **tardy**; appreciative.

ACQUAINT (v)

adverbs
intimately; minutely; partially; familiarly; imperfectly; mutely; affectionately; eagerly; reluctantly; entirely; affably; amiably; charitably; amicably; loyally; politely; piously; complacently.

(See tell.)

ACQUAINTANCE

adjectives
vast; mutual; desirable; intimate; eventful; favorable; brilliant; charitable; prosperous; common; conventional; casual; stray; select; congenial; slight; valued; ingenious; inaccurate; preliminary; fair; imperfect; superficial; extensive; critical; tolerable; nodding; astounding; injudicious; chance; passing; temporary; broad; well-born; garrulous; good-humored; varied (pl); amiable; numerous (pl); bowing; renewed; promiscuous; protracted; professional; informal; cursory; first-hand; incomplete.

verbs
bless with—; boast—; crave—; dim—; estrange—; exploit—; greet—; hold—; lend—; pursue—; put away—; renew—; resume—; strangle—; strike up—; urge—; —creeps; —is estranged; —widens.

(See intimacy, friendship, association, friend.)

ACQUAINTED

adverbs
intimately; slightly; favorably; unhappily; fortunately; unluckily; auspiciously; personally; directly; indirectly; well; happily; familiarly; casually; superficially; thoroughly; closely; generally; absolutely; naturally; remotely; barely; insufficiently; hardly; scarcely.

ACQUIESCE (v)

adverbs
grudgingly; silently; reluctantly; feelingly;
pleasantly; cheerfully; tepidly; carelessly; stolidly; sullenly; dignifiedly; cravenly; phlegmatically; grumblingly; tacitly; amiably; passively; candidly; complacently; fatalistically.

(See agree, assent, submit.)

ACQUIESCENCE

adjectives
stolid; tepid; agreeable; sullen; silent; dignified; polite; craven; unanimous; wise; courageous; phlegmatic; grumbling; delighted; tacit; stupid; amiable; passive; desperate; compulsory; candid; reluctant; fatalistic; cheerful; complacent; grudging; grim.

verbs
arrive at—; attain—; draw into—; signify —; soften into—; urge—; wheedle into—.

(See submission, agreement, compliance.)

ACQUIESCENT

adverbs
courteously; willingly; reluctantly; gruffly; grudgingly; graciously; cheerfully; necessarily; unwillingly; happily; pliantly; blithely; devotedly; wholly; glumly; half-heartedly; stolidly; timidly; stupidly; blindly; politely; passively; wisely; tacitly; complaisantly; sullenly; amiably; cunningly; shrewdly; casually; apparently; restrainedly; indifferently.

ACQUIRE (v)

adverbs
righteously; readily; patiently; instinctively; innocently; painfully; unjustly; gloriously; sensibly; ultimately; brutally; systematically; dictatorially; vigorously; ruthlessly; villainously; cruelly; treacherously; barbarously; legally; scientifically.

(See learn, master, attain.)

ACQUIREMENT

adjectives
scientific; glorious; systematic; consequent; linguistic; unrighteous; instinctive; innocent; painful.

ACQUISITION

adjectives
painful; noteworthy; desirable; permanent; eternal; arduous; exciting; superior; territorial; profitless; erudite; patient; mental; valuable; perfunctory; forcible; peaceful; cherished; long-sought.

ACQUISITIVE

adverbs
inordinately; insanely; avidly; eagerly; in-

curably; indiscriminately; universally; peculiarly; incorrigibly; distressingly; gloriously; happily; instinctively; painfully; embarrassingly; systematically; irreclaimably; hopelessly; promiscuously; vexatiously; shamelessly; perpetually; laboriously; insistently; appallingly.

ACQUIT (v)
adverbs
unhesitatingly; legally; unexpectedly; unanimously; generously; triumphantly; entirely; constitutionally; legitimately; tolerantly; graciously; licitly; condescendingly; acquiescently; deferentially.
(See absolve, justify, pardon.)

ACQUITTAL
adjectives
prompt; triumphant; unexpected; honorable; disquieting; undeserved; trumped-up.

verbs
advance toward—; argue for—; ballot for —; beg for—; concede—; decide on—; demand—; deny—; deserve—; direct—; earn —; effect an—; entreat for—; expect—; gain—; hope for—; justify—; merit—; move for—; order—; plead for—; produce —; provoke—; refuse—; request—; secure —; seek—; solicit—; vote on—; win—; —carries; —exonerates; —follows.
(See pardon.)

ACREAGE
adjectives
valuable; vast; fruitful; expansive.

ACRES
adjectives
wooded; impoverished; scant; unworked; well-fenced; paternal; suburban; airy; broad; rolling; broken; untilled; scrubby; verdant; denuded; cultivated; dead; ill-acquired.

ACRIMONIOUS
adverbs
pithily; dryly; sharply; tartly; pungently; wilfully; remorselessly; mercilessly; deliberately; ominously; obnoxiously; malignantly; destructively; roughly; bitterly; pertly; insolently; churlishly; crustily; snarlingly; bitingly; banefully; rancorously; quietly; unsparingly; chronically; unrelentingly; viciously; unnecessarily; hatefully; insidiously; venomously; cunningly; needlessly.

ACROBAT
verbs
—amuses; —arches his back; —awes; —

balances; —clowns; —contorts; —dances; —dazzles; —displays; —dives; —executes; —flexes; —flies; —flips; —folds; —frolics; —gyrates; —hangs; —hurtles; —leaps; —manipulates; —postures; —pyramids; —rebounds; —recovers; —relaxes; —revolves; —rolls; —soars; —somersaults; —spins; —swings; —thrills; —throws himself; —tumbles; —twirls; —twists; —vaults; —waddles; —whirls; applaud—; gape at—; gasp at—; marvel at—.

ACT
adjectives
virtuous; generous; gracious; unspeakable; self-confident; aggressive; dastardly; ruthless; loathsome; detestable; horrific; barbarous; ignominious; brutal; wilful; rash; servile; cowardly; militant; hostile; mutinous; lawless; illicit; churlish; unknown; condescending; reprehensible; compromising; unfortunate; suspicious; ungallant; unwise; impulsive; thoughtless; childish; gauche; dauntless; hardy; hazardous; official; ritualistic; conspicuous; overt; inopportune; voluntary; unremembered; well-planned; expressive; benevolent; needless; oppressive; conscientious; exasperating; arbitrary; sublime; amusing; incongruous; valid; symptomatic; disadvantageous; adumbrative; heroic; authenticated; meritorious; unfeeling; decisive; instinctive; valiant; beneficent; disinterested; crowning; innumerable (pl); offensive; daring; energetic; lugubrious; touching; specific; governmental; noble; salutary; impolitic; disdainful; violent; dishonorable; ferocious; generous; cogitative; unpopular; infamous; creative; atrocious; dreaded; mischievous; imposing; inexpiable; illogical; egotistic; compulsive; overbold; unwarrantable; disgraceful; unauthorized; superfluous; defensible; treasonable; climactic; derisive; craven; irrevocable; impudent.

verbs
achieve—; applaud—; behold—; betray—; bring to pass—; catch in the—; commend—; commit—; condemn—; derive from—; dispense with—; incite—; inspire—; perform —; provoke—; pursue—; smile upon—; take in—; urge in—; view—; visualize—; —abides; —blurs; —commences; —denotes; —overtakes; —unfolds; embody—in; frustrate—; galvanize into—; goad into—; govern—.

ACT
(*statute*)
abolish—; abrogate—; annul—; broaden—; design—; disallow—; invalidate—; invoke

—; make void—; outlaw—; proclaim—; put an end to—; repeal—; resurrect—; set aside—; supersede—; suspend—; term—; violate—.

(See bill.)

ACT (v)

adverbs
ignominiously; shamefully; disgracefully; irrationally; impulsively; impetuously; vengefully; abnormally; irregularly; generously; cautiously; coldly; officially; officiously; erratically; superfluously; adversely; involuntarily; admirably; imprudently; ostensibly; mercifully; independently; recklessly; detrimentally; impecuniously; deliberately; frivolously; graciously; viciously; self-confidently; aggressively; unspeakably; ruthlessly; detestably; brutally; wilfully; servilely; mutinously; churlishly; compromisingly; condescendingly; gallantly; impulsively; dauntlessly; disinterestedly; offensively; disdainfully; atrociously; illogically; treasonably,

(See behave, feign.)

ACTING

adjectives
immobile; technical; robust; allegorical; iridescent; extravagant; resolute; creditable; unnatural; effective; apt; adequate; inspired; imitative; wooden; facile; listless; pantomimic; sluggish; unconvincing.

ACTION

adjectives
intelligent; noble; efficient; authoritative; authenticated; sober; riotous; furious; hair-raising; intense; virile; vigorous; muscular; courageous; aggressive; direct; resolute; determined; independent; bold; gallant; heroic; positive; affirmative; decisive; vitalizing; tumultuous; perfidious; impetuous; lively; right; stimulating; frenzied; fervent; glorious; justifiable; regrettable; passionate; unrelated (pl); pointless; spectacular; futile; indiscreet; thoughtless; ill-advised; impulsive; commonplace; immoral; uncontrolled; desperate; contemptible; rash; unhesitating; ruthless; unsocial; negative; destructive; infernal; unconventional; drastic; menial; shameful; distressing; implacable; hysterical; mob; maternal; unprecedented; vivid; pending; coordinated; definite; prompt; preliminary; simultaneous; concerted; collective; selective; absurd; dramatic; restrained; involuntary; organized; unified; isolated; strenuous; mechanical; casual; singular; unguarded; unpremeditated; instinctive; punitive; ad-

mirable; favorable; laudable; unselfish; virtuous; righteous; conscientious; irritant; unscrupulous; individual; cordial; arbitrary; precipitate; abrasive; ill-considered; disinterested; excited; physiological; spirited; sweeping; chivalric; soothing; unopposed; insolent; pantomimic; rebellious; radical; postponed; vicious; incessant; automatic; emotional; enlightened; summary; ceaseless; engrossing; self-contained; lightning; distinguished; feverish; morbid; convulsive; vehement; uncertain; purgative; igneous; reflex; public-spirited; unobstrusive; meritorious; functional; dynamic; clannish; crude; awkward; insane; poisonous; reciprocal; inspired; adventurous; unheralded; unobserved; habitual; significant; deleterious; epic; atrocious; persistent; effectual; perturbative; accelerating; deplorable; trifling; magical; vacillating; prohibited; unholy; unforeseen; spontaneous; sporadic; headlong; logical.

verbs
accelerate—; account for—; advise—; affirm—; atone for—; authenticate—; authorize—; bare—; behold—; burst into—; call into—; chafe for—; classify—; clog—; concentrate—; condemn—; construe—; contemplate—; contrive—; control—; counterfeit—; crystallize—; embark on—; emulate—; enhance—; enter upon—; expedite—; dignify—; diminish—; disguise—; dwarf—; embody—in; frustrate—; galvanize into—; goad into—; govern—; hail—; hamper—; hasten—; hinder—; identify with—; imitate—; impede—; increase—; induce—; influence—; initiate—; intensify—; interpret—; introduce—; justify—; kindle into—; maintain—; motivate—; nullify—; paralyze—; perform—; pledge to—; postpone—; prescribe—; prod into—; produce—; put into—; quicken—; repeat—; repudiate—; restrain—; retard—; revel in—; reverse—; ripen into—; rue—; shame into—; snap into—; spring into—; spur to—; stimulate—; stint—; sum up—; support—; swing into—; threaten—; throw light on—; time—; underprop—; utilize—; weigh—; yield to—; —belittles; —betrays; —blasts; —centers; —confers; —contrives against; —conveys; —divorces from; —predominates; —proceeds from; —rends; —tires; —yields.

(See motion, gesture, act, operation.)

ACTIVE

adverbs
tremendously; keenly; perpetually; enormously; nervously; appallingly; seldom; ter-

13

ribly; amicably; despicably; charitably; helpfully; vitally; dramatically; ostentatiously; shamelessly; absurdly; villainously; ridiculously; admirably; efficiently; pompously; socially; ludicrously; perpetually; politically; singularly; habitually; uncommonly; infernally; vexatiously; suspiciously; subversively; constructively; excitedly; impudently; presumptuously; ardently; rebelliously; obtrusively; insanely; significantly; gravely; persistently.; disturbingly; noisily; amazingly; annoyingly; tirelessly; normally; surreptitiously; restlessly; furtively; openly; boldly; incessantly.

ACTIVITY
adjectives
intellectual; bustling; political; characteristic; extra-curricular; charitable; unavailing; elemental; intense; supporting; spasmodic; mischievous; feverish; exaggerated; volitional; sustained; pedagogical; commercial; unrivaled; spontaneous; volcanic; essential; potent; gastric; peculiar; mental; disquieting; productive; suspicious; erotic; cultural; infantile; unfettered; creative; mercantile; hampered; cataclysmic; magnetic; hive-like; fruitful; beneficent; unparalleled; throbbing; fiendish; functional; social; subversive; publicized; philanthropic; outstanding; recreational; buoyant; prodigious; ceaseless; energetic; incessant; tireless; editorial; violent; unedifying; frivolous; manifold; literary; accustomed; stunning; physiologic; purposeless; destructive; influential; malignant; cooperative; inspirational; painful; irresponsible; aesthetic; earthly; kaleidoscopic; zealous; wholesome; morbid; constructive; normal; disciplined; fascinating; dexterous; nefarious; frantic; surreptitious; clandestine; deficient; tortuous; expanding; multiple; conglomerate (pl); diversified; teeming; widespread; innumerable (pl); multifarious; incredible; nervous; passionate; eager; restless; strident; humming; hilarious; fertile; instigated; prosaic; bizarre; vicarious; villainous.

verbs
accompany—; administer—; boil with—; camouflage—; center—; chart—; condemn —; confine—; constitute—; contemplate—; control—; cramp—; cripple—; curb—; dedicate—; deliberate on—; diffuse—; direct —; display—; edge out—; embrace—; engage in—; examine—; focus—; frustrate—; guide—; hamper by—; hum with—; immerse in—; induce—; inhibit—; initiate—; interrupt—; involve—; kindle—; leap into

—; limit—; link—; maintain—; motivate —; nag into—; overshadow—; participate in—; pursue—; regulate—; restrict—; resume—; rouse—; seethe with—; spring into —; spur—; supervise—; undertake—; witness—; —abates; —defeats; —ebbs and flows; —excites; —flares into; —reigns; —stimulates.
(See action.)

ACTOR
adjectives
daring; conspicuous; tragic; eminent; gesticulating; diligent; impulsive; distinguished; celebrated; obscure; godlike; prominent; inimitable; popular; expert; unschooled; recalcitrant; "ham"; strolling; itinerant; persuasive; consummate; competent; forthright; character; skilled.

verbs
applaud—; greet—; key up—; prompt—; —acquits; —administers; —affects; —apes; —blunders through; —burlesques; —conforms to; —appears; —evokes; —executes; —forces; —gesticulates; —impersonates; —interprets; —mimics; —narrates; —parrots; —performs; —personifies; —radiates; —recites; —spouts; —suggests; —wails.
(See player, performer.)

ACTRESS
adjectives
gifted; distinguished; competent; charming; brilliant; subtle; exotic; fascinating; indomitable; obscure; hardened; stately; naturalistic; mediocre; energetic; spirited.

ACUMEN
adjectives
critical; philosophical; rare; financial; intellectual; penetrative; business; distinguished; acute.

ACUTE
adverbs
unwontedly; keenly; actually; remarkably; apparently; astonishingly; unexpectedly; surpassingly; shrewdly; cleverly; uncommonly; fairly; profoundly; thoughtfully; politically; sharply; discriminatingly; naturally; subtly; restlessly; prophetically; reassuringly; penetratingly; craftily.

ACUTENESS
adjectives
consummate; vicious; tense; native; unwonted; proverbial; incredible; godlike; rare; apparent.

14

ADAGE

adjectives
favorite; familiar; classic; oft-quoted; apt; well-phrased; clumsy; appropriate.

verbs
accept—; call to mind—; conceive—; disprove—; grasp—; interpret—; lean against —; paraphrase—; reiterate—; verify—; — expresses.
(See proverb, maxim, saying.)

ADAMANT

adverbs
wilfully; indomitably; bitterly; unyieldingly; obdurately; pitilessly; unrelentingly; unrepentantly; inexorably; stubbornly; obstinately; mulishly; doggedly; perversely; fanatically; pig-headedly; contumaciously; bigotedly.

ADAPT (v)

adverbs
admirably; skilfully; eminently; artistically; mentally; physically; intellectually; professionally; ingeniously; mechanically; adroitly; dexterously; aesthetically; craftily; competently; consummately; deftly; matchlessly; cleverly; efficaciously; factitiously; gracefully; scientifically; diplomatically; inventively; ingeniously; peerlessly; incomparably.
(See adjust, conform.)

ADAPTABILITY

adjectives
ready; wide-awake; facile; quick.
(See adaptation.)

ADAPTABLE

adverbs
complaisantly; hardly; readily; intelligently; graciously; easily; ingeniously; comfortably; moderately; scarcely; willingly; quickly; dexterously; cleverly; wisely; diplomatically; sagaciously; sympathetically; mercifully; affably; courteously; civilly; companionably; amiably; discreetly; judiciously; wisely.

ADAPTATION

adjectives
judicious; exquisite; conscious; functional; deliberate; scenic; terrestrial; approximate; stereotyped; passive; studious; agile; unfulfilled; inexpensive; ingenious; errant.

ADD (v)

adverbs
fondly; facetiously; significantly; intelligent-

ly; wearily; dreamily; sorrowfully; passionately; thoughtfully; mildly; parenthetically; frowningly; hopefully; bluntly; decisively; soothingly; carelessly; regretfully; stridently; hurriedly; unobtrusively; contemptuously; tremulously; doubtfully; self-reproachfully; wistfully; breathlessly; impressively; haughtily; needlessly; falteringly; graciously; tentatively; briskly; generously; coolly; cryptically; slyly; speedily; accurately; erratically; mentally; alternately; materially; freely; jerkily; vertically; diagonally; horizontally.
(See annex, join.)

ADDICT

adjectives
passionate; miserable; confirmed; incurable; depraved; pitiful.

ADDICTED

adverbs
miserably; unfortunately; hopelessly; tragically; incurably; ridiculously; pitifully; irreparably; comically; fatally; incorrigibly; lamentably; unhappily; absurdly; unluckily; distressingly; pathetically; laughably; unreasonably; strangely; curiously.

ADDICTION

adjectives
pedantic; stubborn; tiresome; conspicuous; learned; hopeless; desultory; violent; favorite.

ADDITION

adjectives
incongruous; anachronistic; desirable; simultaneous; pleasing; necessary; costly; significant; worthy; astonishing; dubious; immediate; unprofitable; meager; valuable; substantial; imaginative; gratuitous; indispensable; distinctive; popular.

ADDLED

adverbs
hopelessly; comically; strangely; disastrously; slightly; completely; sweetly; horribly; delightfully; indescribably; visibly; manifestly; uproariously; foggily; vociferously; dazedly; rosily; brokenly; incurably; pathetically; palpably.

ADDRESS

adjectives
impromptu; flattering; impending; emphatic; passionate; pithy; temperate; grave; inaugural; intuitive; masterly; graphic; soldier-like; moving; fervid; insinuating; il-

luminating; commemorative; laudatory; radical; carefully-worded; sensational; postprandial; lengthy; stirring; inspiring; rousing; keynote; eloquent; amatory; ardent; affectionate; lucid; preliminary; charming; naive; stumbling; halting; extempore; incoherent.

ADDRESS
verbs   (*speech*)
alter—; charge—with; compose—; concoct—; condense—; curtail—; expand—; grind out—; organize—; pour forth—; reel off—; thunder—.
(See speech, oration, sermon, lecture, discourse.)

ADDRESS (*v*)
adverbs
informally; cordially; intimately; affectionately; indiscriminately; pretentiously; exclusively; mournfully; passionately; extemporaneously; temperately; fervidly; insinuatingly; stirringly; inspiringly; rousingly; eloquently; ardently; lucidly; intelligently; pugnaciously; pointedly.
(See lecture, discourse.)

ADEPT
adverbs
expertly; scarcely; palpably; undoubtedly; cleverly; ingeniously; incredibly; marvellously; clearly; remarkably; smartly; unimaginably; surprisingly; dangerously; alarmingly; exceptionally; subtly; fearfully; comparatively; confidently.

ADEQUATE
adverbs
completely; excellently; pleasantly; delightfully; remarkably; providentially; sufficiently; scarcely; essentially; suitably; wholly; admirably; quite; satisfactorily; wonderfully; gratifyingly; fortunately; luckily.

ADHERE (*v*)
adverbs
rigidly; tenaciously; doggedly; staunchly; passionately; strictly; perversely; pertinaciously; scrupulously; unflinchingly; undeviatingly; formally; steadfastly; stubbornly; obstinately; blindly; unalterably; intractably; militantly; contentiously; cantankerously; incorrigibly; immovably; impassively; insistently; bigotedly; sullenly; waywardly, strenuously; religiously; moderately.
(See stick, cling.)

ADHERENCE
adjectives
lingering; firm; strict; scrupulous; unflinch-

ing; passionate; undiscriminating; rigid; undeviating; formal; steadfast; stubborn; obstinate; exact; staunch; apparent; blind; unalterable; inborn; tenacious; dogged; pertinacious; devout; perverse; rash; vigorous; unwise; smug; unswerving; ardent.

ADHERENT
adjectives
staunch; unquestioning; zealous; pious; numbered (pl); faithful; deluded; superstitious; loyal; devout; close; spirited.

ADIEU
adjectives
courtly; final; graceful; gentle; mute; sublime; fearful; silent; grave; painful; brash; condescending; disdainful; despairing; wistful.

ADIPOSE
adverbs
incredibly; irremediably; unfortunately; disagreeably; incurably; unacceptably; distressingly; absurdly; ridiculously; needlessly; ludicrously; damagingly; lamentably; sadly; dangerously; heavily; admittedly; unreasonably.

ADJECTIVE
adjectives
qualifying; explosive; unfactual; decorative; severe; impressive-sounding; apt; augmenting; glowing; sonorous; obsolete; laudatory; rapturous; nauseous; overworked; uncomplimentary; unfavorable; commendatory; descriptive; flattering; inept; obvious; appropriate; exact; distinctive; moving; brilliant; breezy; racy; lurid; lush; picturesque; suggestive; well-chosen; precise.

verbs
accompany by—; adorn with—; allot—; arrange—; attach—; avoid—; bandy—; choose—; classify—; compare—; depend on —; derive—; eliminate—; eschew—; exhaust—; group —s; indulge in —s; juggle —s; lavish —s on; overwork—; pile up —s; reject—; strike out—; stuff with —s; supply with —s; swamp with —s; transpose —s; —answers; —colors; —conveys; —defines; —denotes; —describes; —disappears; —explains; —expresses; —forms; —implies; —interprets; —limits; —modifies; —occurs; —s pad; —points out; —presents; —qualifies; —springs from; —supplies.
(See word.)

ADJUNCT

adjectives

impressive; non-essential; inevitable; external; unusual; absurd; impedimental; artificial.

ADJUST (v)

adverbs

delicately; improperly; satisfactorily; accurately; eventually; fortunately; happily; languidly; harmoniously; nervously; peaceably; enduringly; elaborately; amply; subtly; magnanimously; equitably; mathematically; minutely; precisely; punctiliously; specifically; exactly.

(See settle, fit.)

ADJUSTABLE

adverbs

amicably; easily; instantly; comfortably; necessarily; wisely; conveniently; fortunately; luckily; amazingly; extraordinarily; cunningly; cleverly; naturally; serviceably; handily; peaceably, sensibly.

ADJUSTMENT

adjectives

necessary; temporary; ultimate; long-awaited; peaceful; visual; constant; artistic; enduring; honorable; felicitous; elaborate; studied; rightful; immediate; patriotic; corresponding; ample; scientific; preliminary; harmonious; sensible; subtle; economic; discreet; enforced; poetical; complex; delicate; heart-rending; mental; compensating; calm; prompt; partial; compromised; amicable.

verbs

adopt—; advocate—; challenge—; effect—; honor—; postpone—; recommend—; reject —; stimulate—; submit to—; —obviates; —pleases; —prevents; —satisfies; —settles.

(See regulation, arrangement, settlement.)

ADMINISTER (v)

adverbs

efficiently; steadily; faithfully; methodically; internally; cautiously; economically; corruptly; benignly; wholesomely; incompetently; satisfactorily; formally; ecclesiastically; conventionally; customarily; domestically; wontedly; ethically; vigorously.

(See manage, regulate, settle.)

ADMINISTRATION

adjectives

successful; businesslike; memorable; subservient; corrupt; economical; incapable; filial; benign; stormy; incumbent; spiritual; contemporary; centralized; unified; communal; careful; incoming; civil; eventful; efficient; wholesome; bureaucratic; incompetent; judicial; provincial; internal; stern; progressive; partisan.

verbs

backbite—; consolidate—; dominate—; entrust with—; facilitate—; flout—; hamper —; repudiate—; set up—; —comes into power; —contemplates; —defends; —draws to a close; —justifies; —plows under; —refutes; —relegates to; —vindicates; —wields.

(See government.)

ADMINISTRATIVE

adverbs

capably; stormily; benignly; thoroughly; nonchalantly; conscientiously; patriarchally; paternally; ably; cleverly; sternly; severely; strictly; judiciously; wisely; tolerantly; wholesomely; busily; fussily; majestically; pompously; simply; arrogantly; officiously; laxly; loosely; democratically; dogmatically; tyrannically; sagely; affably; fairly; honestly; incorruptibly.

ADMIRABLE

adverbs

genuinely; virtuously; correctly; laudably; truly; really; unexpectedly; consciously.

ADMIRAL

adjectives

mustachioed; famed; stern; plucky; renowned; redoubtable; capable; undaunted.

ADMIRATION

adjectives

heartfelt; affectionate; ecstatic; whole-hearted; rapturous; unbounded; cordial; genuine; undying; profound; unstinted; grateful; modest; effusive; wistful; unfeigned; passionate; intense; open; frank; enthusiastic; reluctant; waning; grudging; fictitious; perverse; patriotic; youthful; girlish; wondering; amazed; hushed; puzzled; unabashed; sneaking; ardent; mirthful; self-contained; inexpressible; repressed; blind; mute; envious; reiterated; deluded; mutual; unmitigated; critical; loquacious; unrestrained; clamorous; passing; complacent; prolonged; smiling; unwilling; universal; ineffable; impersonal; respectful; astonished; reverent; calculating; noisy; untutored; outspoken; undisguised; unlimited; sympathetic; reciprocal; excessive; maudlin; rapt;

half-envious; magnanimous; indulgent; pitying; healthy; speechless; momentary; enhanced.

verbs
arouse—; challenge—; command—; draw—; elicit—; evoke—; excite—; express—; fill with—; inspire—; lose in—; mirror—; modify—; obtain—; profess—; reap—; reserve—; retain—; season—; strike with—; suppress—; temper—; utter—; win—; — abates; —beams; —buzzes; —cools; — haunts; —moves; —seizes; —wanes; — waxes.
(See amazement, wonder, astonishment, love, respect.)

ADMIRE (v)

adverbs
universally; prodigiously; immensely; gushingly; passionately; cordially; legitimately; tremendously; ardently; ecstatically; wholeheartedly; rapturously; effusively; profoundly; wistfully; intensely; mutely; unrestrainedly; loquaciously; complacently; clamorously; ineffably; reverently; outspokenly; frankly; undisguisedly; unboundedly; magnanimously; 'indulgently; unceasingly; fervently; legitimately; perfunctorily.
(See approve, appreciate.)

ADMIRER

adjectives
idolatrous; credulous; soft; ardent; fervent; enthusiastic; irresponsible; discriminating; solemn; passionate; devoted; staunch; countless (pl); sole; persistent; injudicious; quondam; appreciative; reluctant; blind; over-enthusiastic; fond; rival; well-bred; zealous; hearty.

verbs
abuse—; discourage—; displease—; humor —; indulge—; —acclaims; —adores; — amuses; —applauds; —deifies; —eulogizes; —fawns; —flatters; —glorifies; —gratifies; —idolizes; —lauds; —pays tribute; — pleases; —puffs; —renounces; —reveres; —s throng; —toasts; —worships.
(See favorite, follower, lover.)

ADMISSION

adjectives
grudging; heartfelt; inexorable; damaging; fatal; flattering; virtual; certain; tacit; frank; candid; liberal; naive; irreparable; plain-faced; blunt; obvious; rueful; reluctant; unguarded; brash; arrogant; gracious; ineluctable; quaint; final.

effusively; duly; solemnly; tearfully; parentally; cautiously; gently; paternally; prophetically; frantically; urgently; maternally; stingingly; harshly; bitterly; brutally; sternly; sensibly; ceremoniously; formally; puritanically; scrupulously; rigorously; stringently.
(See reprove, warn.)

ADMONITION

adjectives
soft-voiced; tearful; intensified; plain-spoken; parental; judicious; condescending; moral; cautious; stimulating; gentle; poetical; solemn; prophetic; grave; parting; frantic; urgent; forcible; affectionate; respectful; classical; discouraging; paternal; stinging; whispered; effusive; suave; bold; brazen; prosaic; tedious; beautiful.

verbs
cluck —s; elude—; heed—; merit—; —demoralizes; —distorts; —distracts; —repels; —scorches; —softens.
(See caution, warning, advice.)

ADOLESCENCE

adjectives
uneventful; painful; self-conscious; callow; awkward; gawky; supersensitive; vain; joyous; feverish; shy; coy; brash; brusque; carefree.
verbs
apply for—; authorize—; begrudge—; demand—; insure—; refuse—; win—.
(See entrance.)

ADMIT

adverbs
remorsefully; brashly; candidly; universally; reluctantly; arrogantly; ruefully; grudgingly; privately; semi-officially; willingly; graciously; equably; laughingly; knowingly; tacitly; humbly; formally; dubiously; unreservedly; savagely; unfeelingly; naively; bluntly; unguardedly.
(See acknowledge, confess, concede, grant.)

ADMITTANCE

verbs
buy—; crave—; deny—; desire—; gain—; grant—; request—; seek—.
(See entrance, admission.)

ADMONISH (v)

adverbs

ADOLESCENT

adverbs

delightfully; glowingly; dully; painfully; awkwardly; gawkily; sensitively; feverishly; shyly; joyously; obviously; incurably; alluringly; exuberantly; inexpressibly; unbelievably; markedly; radiantly; vividly; excitably.

ADOPT (v)

adverbs

gratefully; dogmatically; advantageously; ostensibly; unanimously; prudently; voluntarily; solemnly; vigorously; obstreperously; judiciously; arbitrarily; ultimately; frankly; deceitfully; apparently; formally; ceremoniously; prudishly; skilfully; tactfully; strategically.

(See espouse, support, maintain.)

ADOPTION

adjectives

solemn; vigorous; obstreperous; timely; judicious; grateful; dogmatic; ostensible; prudent; voluntary; ready.

ADORABLE

adverbs

mysteriously; utterly; altogether; delightfully; confoundedly; bewilderingly; amazingly; wondrously; unexpectedly; unimaginably; miraculously; graciously; coolly; warmly; radiantly; glowingly; joyously; unbelievably; consciously; contentedly.

ADORATION

adjectives

ecstatic; idolatrous; inarticulate; solemn; shy; passionate; young; breathless; unswerving; servile; filial; fervent; boyish; maternal; doglike; restrained; impassioned; cold; soft; silent; rapturous; mad; hushed; quiet; poetic; unlimited; deprecatory.

verbs

bestow—; fall in—; rear in—; repel—; yield to—; —buoys; —captivates; —enslaves.

(See worship, love, prayer, reverence.)

ADORE (v)

adverbs

blindly; angelically; ecstatically; inarticulately; solemnly; shyly; passionately; breathlessly; servilely; filially; fervently; restrainedly; boyishly; worshipfully; impulsively; wantonly; vehemently; warmly; carnally; ruttishly; meretriciously; faithfully; intensely; excessively; fondly; soulfully.

(See worship, reverence.)

ADORN (v)

adverbs

lavishly; sumptuously; elaborately; expensively; attractively; richly; architecturally; ceremonially; lustrously; artistically; triumphally; splendidly; decoratively.

(See decorate, ornament, embellish, gild.)

ADORNMENT

adjectives

lavish; extraneous; expensive; sculptural; architectural; curious; feminine; personal; lustrous; rich; sumptuous; elaborate; garish; gaudy; tasteful.

ADROIT

adverbs

marvellously; cleverly; incredibly; admirably; artfully; remarkably; dangerously; palpably; suspiciously; neatly; matchlessly; craftily; masterfully; wonderfully; uncommonly; consummately; innately; constitutionally; instinctively; inherently.

ADROITNESS

adjectives

masterly; neat; witty; technical; skilled; swift; matchless; wily; manual.

ADULATE (v)

adverbs

extravagantly; prodigally; servilely; vociferously; amorously; abjectly; indiscriminately; fulsomely; humbly; shrewdly; deceitfully.

(See praise, flatter.)

ADULATION

adjectives

tribal; hysterical; prodigal; vociferous; amorous; servile; abject; unnatural; fulsome; indiscriminate.

verbs

bask in—; deluge with—; enjoy—; expose to—; feast upon—; indulge in—; relish—; sicken by—; yield to—; —fatigues.

(See flattery, extravagance, praise, compliment.)

ADULATORY

adverbs

abjectly; fawningly; coquettishly; flatteringly; servilely; tribally; hysterically; politically; sycophantically; unctuously; officiously; ostentatiously; subtly; speciously; openly; disagreeably; disgustingly; blatantly; offensively; fulsomely; lavishly.

ADULT (a)

adverbs

surprisingly; completely; fully; obviously; fairly; precociously; prematurely; undeniably; wisely; mysteriously; emotionally; intellectually; uncommonly; buxomly; indescribably; consciously; appallingly; terribly; suddenly; unquestionably.

ADULTERY

verbs

commit—; condone—; forgive—; indulge in —; justify—; revel in—; take in—.
(See unfaithfulness.)

ADVANCE

adjectives

striking; logical; unflinching; subsequent; economic; orderly; general; sharp; courageous; intellectual; triumphant; successive; perpetual; incessant; definite; studious; haughty; unprecedented; spectacular; prodigious; dizzy; substantial; marked; distinct; material; noteworthy; trifling; modest; tenacious; reconnoitering; arduous; implacable; cautious; glacial; faltering; pugnacious; jaunty; ominous; bold; persistent; menacing; notable.

verbs

characterize—; check—; constitute—; discourage—; facilitate—; fear—; hinder—; mark—; pioneer in —s; reject —s; smile at —; —culminates; —terminates.
(See progress.)

ADVANCE (v)

adverbs

aggressively; cautiously; boldly; jauntily; ominously; menacingly; reluctantly; tremblingly; pugnaciously; progressively; ungracefully; simultaneously; hesitantly; secretly; persistently; hopelessly; inexorably; eagerly; notably; triumphantly; timidly; fearfully; compactly; materially; impulsively; awkwardly; unflinchingly; unprecedentedly; spectacularly; substantially; markedly.
(See progress, promote, enhance.)

ADVANCEMENT

adjectives

revolutionary; material; technical; significant; professional; cultural; economic; scientific; industrial; corresponding; spiritual; signal; long-sought; respective (pl).

verbs

contribute to—; deserve—; desire—; hope

for—; note—; promote—; strike a blow to —; strive for—.
(See promotion, progress.)

ADVANCES

adjectives

tender; lover-like; friendly; surreptitious; tactless; unwelcome; old-fashioned; formal; vigorous; amoristic; bold; boorish; bestial; intimate; circumspect.

ADVANTAGE

adjectives

irretrievable; vile; inevitable; inescapable; obvious; patent; remote; trifling; marked; private; educational; pecuniary; fallacious; immediate; inestimable; enduring; appreciable; unfair; hidden; incidental; underestimated; permanent; contingent; manifold; accidental; worldly; material; human; revolutionary; worth while; practical; unique; physical; substantial; undue; reciprocal; temporary; compensating; theoretical; reasonable; invaluable; surreptitious; matchless; graceless; definite; decisive; adventitious; base; hard-earned; initial; momentary; actual; cultural; exclusive; strategic; shameless; frail; selfish; perishable; unparalleled; mutual; overwhelming; hygienic; unsurpassed; decided; tangible; numerical; signal; partisan; insurmountable; incalculable; ineluctable; irresistible.

verbs

buy with—; cite—; confer—; contemplate —; derive—; discern—; embody—; enjoy —; forbear—; forego—; gain—; hold—; hold forth on the —s of; jeopardize—; lack —; let pass—; offset—; pay back with—; press—; press home—; reap—; sacrifice—; seize upon—; set—against; shear off—; stress—; surrender—; turn to—; use—; vouchsafe—; —accrues; —achieves; —is connected with; —feeds; —slips.
(See profit, victory, benefit.)

ADVANTAGEOUS

adverbs

politically; obviously; essentially; undoubtedly; suspiciously; practically; financially; eventually; immensely; socially; highly; materially; personally.

ADVENT

adjectives

illustrious; early; imposing; spectacular; exciting; miraculous; pretended; anticipated; long-awaited.

20

ADVENTURE

adjectives

lunatic; divers (pl); romantic; pioneering; nocturnal; foolish; intriguing; blithe; maritime; amusing; gustatory; prodigious; dramatic; weird; preposterous; boisterous; fascinating; glorious; royal; gallant; flagrant; healthful; spiritual; pleasurable; remarkable; scientific; desperate; petty; vicarious; glamorous; ludicrous; aesthetic; perilous; disgusting; intellectual; wearisome; terrifying; profitless; formidable; calamitous; extraordinary; countless (pl); notorious; stupendous; sensational; fruitful; curious; rambling; peaceful; gay; audacious; epic; colorful; picturesque; sparkling; piquant; joyous; sentimental; diverting; exuberant; chivalrous; colossal; uproarious; unprecedented; hazardous; astounding; extravagant; sordid; banal; indecorous; untoward; foolhardly; promiscuous; trying; unbelievable; singular; fantastic; fearful; incredible; curious; stimulating; stirring; hectic; mad, daring; breath-taking; strenuous; pathetic; amorous; mental; fearsome; quixotic; unique; exotic; stark; erotic; piscatory; disconcerting; picaresque; alcoholic; engrossing; comic; tragic; void; equivocal; agile.

verbs

achieve—; crown with—; dare—; dishonor —; dread—; embark on—; encounter—; expose to—; go in quest of—; hanker after —; hazard—; imperil—; mingle among —s; plunge into—; recount—; ride forth to—; risk—; search for—; seek—; set out upon —; thirst for—; thrill with—; urge to—; weave—; yearn for—; —awakens; —befalls; —diverts; —edges; —enlivens; — grips; —lurks; —sweeps over one; —thrills. (See quest.)

ADVENTURE (*v*)

adverbs

amorously; haphazardly; romantically; nocturnally; intriguingly; blithely; prodigiously; dramatically; preposterously; boisterously; gloriously; gallantly; vicariously; glamorously; perilously; breath-takingly; strenuously; fearsomely; quixotically; exotically; erotically.

(See dare, venture, happen.)

ADVENTURER

adjectives

venal; intrepid; astute; adroit; unscrupulous; reckless; ambitious; rapacious; martial; noisy; impudent: colossal; hardy; dauntless; despondent; amorous; born; charming; calculating; worthless; thieving; hard-bitten; lusty; penniless; unprincipled; sordid.

ADVENTUROUS

adverbs

madly; boldly; avidly; bravely; timidly; rashly; innately; daringly; carefully; crazily; recklessly; gloriously; notoriously; audaciously; romantically; dramatically; vicariously; courageously; foolishly; terribly; eagerly; inherently; joyously; colossally; foolhardily; singularly; breath-takingly; tragically; youthfully; fantastically; madly; boyishly; disconcertingly; incredibly; alarmingly; discreetly; constitutionally; extravagantly; hazardously.

ADVERSARY

adjectives

shallow; maimed; underrated; vanquished; doughty; imaginary; stubborn; stony; formidable; proud; courteous; intangible; hostile; vigorous; resolute; worthy; generous; stout; reluctant; well-matched; stalwart; sinister; deadly; harassed; venomous.

verbs

abash—; avenge one's—; battle with—; challenge—; combat—; conquer—; embrace —; fight against—; frustrate—; harass—; heckle—; mock at—; oppose—; overcome—; overpower—; overrule—; overthrow—; overwhelm—; provoke—; quell—; resist—; shake—; stir up—; summon—; take vengeance on—; terrify—; triumph over—; weed out —s; wrestle with—; —conquers; —defeats; —delivers; —fights; —gives battle; —rages; —strives; —struggles.

(See antagonist, enemy, opponent, foe.)

ADVERSE

adverbs

bitterly; fundamentally; persistently; openly; outspokenly; frankly; traditionally; formidably; irreconcilably; strangely; unaccountably; unfortunately; unhappily; powerfully; unmistakably; unmitigatedly; immoderately; unflaggingly.

ADVERSITY

verbs

acquaint with—; afflict with—; assay one's —ies; bruise with—; cast down by—; cross with—; deliver from—; distress by—; embrace—; endure—; redeem out of—; rejoice in—; smite with—; stand against—;

struggle against—; suffer—; withstand—; wound with—; —crosses; —tests; —threatens; —thwarts; —tries.

(See misfortune, disaster, trouble, affliction, calamity.)

ADVERTISE (v)

adverbs

consistently; effectively; dramatically; blatantly; extensively; intelligently; widely; truthfully; nationally; spectacularly; legally; enormously; limitedly.

(See announce, declare, publish, proclaim.)

ADVERTISEMENT

adjectives

circus; powerful; posthumous; gaudy; effective; urgent; fantastic; modest; glowing; spectacular; fraudulent; deceptive; blatant; shrill; prefatory; alluring; truthful; current; consistent; astute; dubious; adequate; seductive; dignified; exaggerated; misleading; objectionable; competitive; skilful; plaguy; unsharpened; productive.

verbs

accent—; alter—; analyze—; approve—; beautify—; believe—; belittle—; change—; complete—; creep into —s; criticize—; decorate—; discard—; follow through—; form—; heed—; identify—; illustrate—; insert—; issue—; launch—; lay out—; lengthen—; limit—; order—; overestimate —; overlook—; point up—; prepare—; purge—; react to—; recognize—; regulate —; respond to—; run—; scan—; solicit—; spoil—; survey—; turn to —s; underestimate—; weaken—; write—; —admonishes; —announces; —concentrates; —extols; — informs; —infuriates; —misleads; —represents; —warns.

(See announcement, notice, publication.)

ADVERTISING

verbs

abuse—; apply—; believe—; benefit by—; blame—; broaden—; buy—; campaign for —; charge for—; circularize—; clarify—; concentrate—; condemn—; continue—; contract for—; credit—; delineate—; display —; dissect—; disseminate—; eliminate—; emphasize—; employ—; exaggerate—; expend for—; experiment with—; exploit—; flash—; guide—; hail—; immunize to—; insist on—; intensify—; inveigh against—; issue—; judge—; learn—; mail—; minimize—; mislead by—; necessitate—; oppose—; overdo—; pay for—; parallel—;

peruse—; post—; pound away with—; prepare—; praise—; prolong—; promote with —; rate—; require—; resist—; revolutionize—; schedule—; segregate—; sell—; solicit—; specialize in—; spurn—; supplement —; survey—; teach—; time—; uphold—; undertake—; utilize—; value—; wage—; warn by—; welcome—; withhold—; —accomplishes; —advances; —appeals; —attracts; —builds; —colors; —embraces; — familiarizes; —features; —fosters; —increases; —influences; —informs; —infringes upon; —inspires; —invites attention; —markets; —merits; —ministers to; —offends; —organizes; —pays; —persuades; —popularizes; —profits; —promotes; —publicizes; —rewards; —sells; —speeds up; —standardizes; —stimulates; —stirs up; —succeeds; —suggests; —trade-marks; —transcends; —transforms; —urges.

(See announcement, notice, advertisement.)

ADVICE

adjectives

interested; sage; facetious; determinative; wholesome; admirable; rash; hasty; parental; urgent; salutary; serious; dissimilar; competent; authentic; unadulterated; old-fashioned; practical; shrewd; hard-headed; requisite; customary; proffered; medical; appropriate; moderate; supplemental; unprejudiced; concentrated; superfluous; brusque; disconcerting; unselfish; matrimonial; pregnant; brutal; subtle; impartial; conservative; canny; intelligent; expert; explicit; pertinent; dreary; resented; overweening; recurrent; interjected; cautionary; voluntary; unheeded.

verbs

adopt—; bombard with—; burst with—; consider—; consult—; counsel—; deliberate over—; disregard—; drum—into; adopt—; follow—; grind out—; hark to—; heap—; heed—; honor—; ignore—; impart—; judge —; lack—; modify—; ooze—; plan—; ponder—; profit by—; reckon—; regard—; relish—; seek—; shun—; solicit—; subscribe to—; supplant—; swallow up—; volunteer—; weigh—; —aids; —hinders; — leaks out.

(See counsel, instruction, information.)

ADVISABLE

adverbs

undoubtedly; scarcely; financially; discreetly; practically; profoundly; morally; urgently; politically; usually; selfishly; solidly; undeniably; particularly; honestly.

ADVISE (v)
adverbs
earnestly; briefly; urgently; unhesitatingly; fatally; needlessly; rightly; strenuously; coolly; sagely; rashly; shrewdly; moderately; wisely; incompetently; brusquely; disinterestedly; unselfishly; impartially; brutally; solemnly; subtly; explicitly; pertinently; drearily; overweeningly; intelligently; cleverly; cautiously.

(See admonish, counsel, inform.)

ADVISER
adjectives
competent; confidential; ill-humored; technical; conservative; sympathetic; prudent; facetious; spiritual; sagacious; influential; unscrupulous; resourceful; invaluable; altruistic; experienced.

ADVOCATE
adjectives
conspicuous; disinterested; benevolent; keen; stalwart; ardent; earnest; pioneer; militant; unselfish; persistent; distinguished; zealous; uncompromising; prominent; enthusiastic; sincere; warm; strenuous; erudite; adroit; exclusive; ingenious; notorious; active; argumentative; fearless; courageous; competent; aggressive; ironic; staunch; resourceful; idealistic; eloquent; loyal; tactful; obstinate; timorous; vigilant; virile; impassioned; able.

ADVOCATE (v)
adverbs
emphatically; disinterestedly; ostensibly; passionately; absurdly; warmly; fanatically; ardently; characteristically; openly; stalwartly; earnestly; militantly; unselfishly; persistently; zealously; uncompromisingly; eruditely; adroitly; ingeniously; notoriously; fearlessly; competently; idealistically; eloquently; obstinately; timorously; truculently.

(See defend, support.)

AERONAUT
adjectives
adventurous; ardent; intrepid; daring; seasoned; war-worn; accomplished; barnstorming; globe-circling; dashing.

AEROPLANE
verbs
ballast—; bank—; capture—; charter—; christen—; equalize—; experiment with—; explore with—; fabricate—; design—; ground—; herd in—; horse down—; hover in—; kick—into a spin; kite—; land—; lift —; modify—; navigate—; nose in—; overload—; "pancake"—; pilot—; propel—; revolutionize—; salvage—; shelter—; spiral —; stabilize—; stall—; sustain—; tilt—; underpower—; —alights; —attacks; —banks; —bombs; —cartwheels; —circles; —s compete for; —s convoy; —dashes; —dives; —drones; —flattens out; —folds up; —gleams; —glides away; —gyrates; —hovers; —loops; —manoeuvers; —pierces the sky; —pivots; —propels; —rains gas; —rises; —roars; —rolls; —scoots; —sheds its wings; —skids in; —skims the turf; —slips into the sky; —soars; —swirls; —swoops; —takes off; —taxies out; —throbs; —trundles on the field; —tumbles down; —twirls; —twists; —wings its way; —wings over; —winnows its way; —zooms; —floats down.

(See balloon, plane.)

AFFABILITY
adjectives
gracious; smiling; kindly; offensive; sardonic; rare; dry; dull; heartfelt; cordial; generous; insincere; pleasing; unwonted.

AFFABLE
adverbs
unaffectedly; courteously; comfortably; enthusiastically; pleasantly; placidly; unfailingly; graciously; smilingly; considerately; sincerely; genuinely; cordially; usually; singularly; quietly; remarkably; ostentatiously.

AFFAIR
adjectives
Gargantuan; spiritual; delicate; practical; multifarious; tumultuous; domestic; conventional; financial; droll; disagreeable; pressing; internal; personal; celebrated; complicated; instructive; public; petty; weighty; vast; grave; ecclesiastical; monotonous; corporate; clandestine; passing; quiet; prim; sublunary; uninteresting; intimate; detestable; charitable; masculine; elaborate; dramatic; vigorous; rustic; unsettled; momentous; foolish; flimsy; insignificant; wearisome; troublous; warlike; multitudinous (pl); provocative; secret; temporal; risky; supernatural; deplorable; fatal; community; wretched; barbarous; rollicking; primitive; hasty; reputable; gay; charming; harmless; enchanting; colorful; profitable; resplendent; spectacular; pretentious; colossal; rueful; painful; freakish; sordid; unsavory; tragic; diabolic; disreputable; ab-

surd; distasteful; scandalous; iniquitous; sanguinary; ferocious; blundering; dismal; apathetic; frail-looking; terrestial; academic; amorous; intricate; drawn-out; complex; droll; flippant; bewildering; laborious; different.

verbs
absorb in —s; administer —s; be conversant with—; carry on—s; change—s; characterize—; commit—to; con —s; scan—; conclude—; conduct—; connect—; control —; deal with —s; debate —s; detach from —s; dispute —s; embroil with —s; emerge from—; entangle in —s; expatiate —s; extricate from —s; grapple with —s; grasp —s; guarantee—; guide —s; hinder—; indulge in —s; intrude in —s; jumble up —s; manage —s; meddle in —s; muddle —s; operate —s; order —s; parallel—; persevere in—; pertain to—; picture—; place at the head of —s; pry into —s; shirk —s; snow under with —s; supervene in —s; support—; transact —s; travel from one—to another; undertake—; veil—; weather—; wind up —s; —drags; —intrigues; —prospers; —recurs; —rests; —ripens.
(See business, matter.)

AFFECT (*v*)
adverbs
gravely; materially; profoundly; visibly; powerfully; indirectly; strongly; detrimentally; vexatiously; adversely; vitally; poignantly; deeply; fundamentally; frequently; primarily; invariably; seriously; painfully; considerably; appreciably; enormously; variously; pleasantly; sensibly; injuriously; intimately; definitely; undoubtedly; differently; unconsciously; peculiarly.
(See touch, melt, incline.)

AFFECTED
adverbs
conceitedly; foppishly; pretentiously; sentimentally; stiltedly; mincingly; simperingly; stagily; abominably; absurdly; ridiculously; ludicrously; disgustingly; pathetically.

AFFECTION
adjectives
true-hearted; dramatic; warm; enthusiastic; filial; reciprocal; hysterical; nervous; natural; tepid; responsive; divine; purest; maternal; tender; intense; spasmodic; inordinate; domestic; dutiful; crushed; subtle; heartwarming; admiring; paternal; overflowing; sympathetic; ludicrous; disappointed; unreciprocated; mutual; demonstrative;

indiscriminating; mature; pious; wifely; unrequited; pastoral; temperate; inflammatory; untried; brotherly; peremptory; tempestuous; rabid; conjugal; well-grounded; doglike; overbrimming; sweet-toned; grateful; impulsive; healthful; involuntary; rational; perishable; playful; forced; respectful; ancient; concrete; trustful; overstrained; passionate; connubial; hollow; vulgar; vile; pretended; boundless; irrepressible; delirious; lasting; tacit; disinterested; sound; profound; nobler; generous; unreasoning; gleeful; coarse; tolerant; doubtful; confessed; foolish; blighted; wavering; long-suffering; stifled; sincere; beautiful; intimate; thoughtful; extreme; sheer; naive; frank; chaste; physical; unbounded; proud; tenacious; priceless; violent; immortal; sworn; zealous; sublime; sweet; sentimental; critical; undying; revived; ephemeral; embedded; calm; chilled; obvious; airy; childish; fastidious; quaint; aristocratic; stiff; awkward; disagreeable; languid; teasing; absurd; spruce; showy; deliberate; injudicious; comical; patent.

verbs
advert to—; alienate—; analyze—; arouse —; attach—to; awaken—; bear—; betoken —; bind by—; bless with—; blind by—; breed—; capture—; chain with—; coerce—; compel—; contain—; crave—; deflect—; demand—; denote—; desire—; detect—; disclose—; display—; earn—; eat up—; elicit —; enforce—; engage—; exempt from—; express—for; feed upon—; force—; gain—; impair—; impress by—; influence—; inspire with—; join in—; kindle—; lend—; manifest—; meet the demands of—; motivate by —; object to—; oppose—; overrule by—; pledge—; pour forth—; preserve—; pretend to—; produce—; promote—; regain—; regard with—; remove—; restrain—; reveal—; scatter—; sense—; shun—; speak—; starve for—; steal—; swear—; temper—; tender—; thwart—; transfer—; transplant —; uproot—; wean from—; weigh—; wrestle with—; —alternates; —bursts out; —ceases; —gets out of bounds; —grows; —links together; —prevails; —spreads; —springs from; —strays; —sways; —thickens; —turns; —warms; —wavers.
(See attachment, love, feeling, emotion.)

AFFECTIONATE
adverbs
enthusiastically; deeply; extremely; dutifully; heart-warmingly; tempestuously; gratifyingly; warmly; sincerely; temperately; im-

pulsively; playfully; naturally; paternally; respectfully; innately; essentially; confessedly; beautifully; sweetly; frankly; devotedly; apparently; incongruously; professedly; hypocritically; openly; sentimentally; truly; pretentiously; inherently; intensely; ludicrously; moderately; passionately; consistently; ostentatiously; maternally; spasmodically; obviously; steadily; tacitly; foolishly; intimately; proudly; furtively.

AFFILIATION
adjectives
growing; cosmopolitan; party; cultural; intimate; tender; undesirable.

verbs
arrange—; ascertain—; benefit by—; block —; deny—; destroy—; determine—; establish—; impute—with; maintain—; preclude —; recognize—; sponsor—; suspend—; wangle—; —aims at; —complicates; —engenders.
(See association, connection, relationship.)

AFFINITY
adjectives
peculiar; commercial; elective; natural; uncanny; temperamental; secret.

AFFIRM (*v*)
adverbs
plausibly; solemnly; plainly; distinctly; facetiously; venomously; categorically; definitely; significantly; constantly; vigorously; smilingly; glaringly; nonchalantly; gravely; splendidly; boldly; brazenly; swiftly; readily.
(See assert, state.)

AFFIRMATION
adjectives
smiling; glaring; nonchalant; grave; splendid; bold; brazen; ready; swift.

AFFLICT (*v*)
adverbs
distressingly; suddenly; desperately; irremediably; bitterly; poignantly; sharply; undeservedly; recurringly; harshly; fatally; brutally; temporarily.
(See persecute, scourge, harass, trouble.)

AFFLICTED
adverbs
distressingly; direly; tragically; unnecessarily; unfortunately; sadly; miserably; incurably; painfully; agonizingly; wretchedly; grievously.

AFFLICTION
adjectives
respiratory; corporal; irremediable; desperate; bitter; poignant; mute; sharp; undeserved; recurring; rending; harsh; fatal; brutal; palsied; temporary.

verbs
ameliorate—; amend—; bear—; bind in—; break with—; carry—; comfort—; conceal —; deliver—; diagnose—; endure—; grant refuge from—; purify by—; shake off—; visit in—; —bites; —follows; —grows; — persists; —prevents; —refines; —softens; —threatens.
(See trouble, tribulation, distress, grief, misfortune.)

AFFLUENCE
verbs
attain—; bask in—; enjoy—; glitter in—; manifest—; raise to—; reduce from—; revive—; wallow in—.
(See wealth, riches, abundance, plenty.)

AFFLUENT
adverbs
gorgeously; enormously; comfortably; fortunately; pleasantly; agreeably; serenely; snugly; enviably; complacently; sufficiently; smugly; graciously.

AFFORD (*v*)
adverbs
undoubtedly; scarcely; indiscriminately; abundantly; inadvertently.
(See furnish, yield, produce.)

AFFRAY
adjectives
murderous; nocturnal; head-punching; fierce; bloody; violent.

AFFRONT
adjectives
rude; personal; sacrilegious; deliberate; unmerited; unintentional; intolerable; vile; unnecessary; brutal; boorish; ill-mannered; brazen.

AFFRONT (*v*)
adverbs
impudently; brazenly; rudely; personally; sacrilegiously; deliberately; unmeritedly; unintentionally; intolerably; vilely; unnecessarily; brutally; boorishly; ill-manneredly.
(See insult, aggravate.)

AFFRONTED

adverbs

easily; definitely; slightly; quickly; increasingly; unreasonably; foolishly; senselessly; absurdly; unjustly; unfairly; deeply.

AFRAID

adverbs

superstitiously; timidly; childishly; queerly; curiously; dreadfully; horribly; perpetually; oddly; strangely; starkly; mysteriously; faint-heartedly; cautiously; timorously; extraordinarily; unquestionably; secretly; terribly; mortally; foolishly; frightfully; constantly; cravenly; temperamentally; distressingly; unwontedly; unusually; incredibly; shudderingly; surprisingly; unutterably; incomprehensibly; obviously; genuinely; suspiciously; idiotically; nervously.

AFTERMATH

adjectives

disastrous; psychological; barren; confused; melancholy; unfortunate; sordid; troublesome; hectic; sorry.

AFTERNOON

adjectives

inspiring; brilliant; dismal; gloomy; ghastly; cheerless; dull; restless; raw; fragrant; serene; wintry; rain-washed; humid; sunless; breezeless; tropical; drowsy; clement; drear; golden; rosy; rain-soaked; darkling; declining; showery; sweltering; formal; glamorous; sultry; miserable; fervid.

verbs

beguile—; devote—; fritter away—; nap away—; pass—; shadow—; tarry till—; while away—; —advances; —pales; —pauses; —pushes forward; —spends itself; —takes wing; —unrolls; —vanishes; —wanes; —wears on.

(See evening.)

AGE

adjectives

pastoral; comfortable; endless; bygone; primitive; seasoned; abominable; imponderable; distant; crabbed; prehistoric; graygrown; infidel; enlightened; feeble; unnumbered (pl); glorious; relative (pl); countless (pl); paleozoic; prolific; venerable; immemorial; aesthetical; barbarous; Pliocene; dim-lit; embittered; susceptible; infinite; green; polished; deathless; heroic; jostling; remote; pre-chromo; realistic; frostless; advancing; ripe; patriarchal; responsive; besotted; waning; historic; prudish; hoary; blissful; geologic; energetic; fabulous; middle; streamlined; advanced; receptive; decrepit; retirement; earnest; unregarded; tender; dingy; glamorous; roistering; marriageable; approaching; homely; renowned; rosy; honored; critical; heartless; prescribed; masquerading; electric; discreet; weak; dull; contented; mature; rotting; ambitious; exorbitant; muddled; revolutionary; live; unresting; premature; credulous; pre-scientific; weary; degenerate; fabled; classical; sententious; hectic; dateless; material; iron-bound; licentious; ruthless; flourishing; indeterminate; haggish; adolescent; sedate; debutante; disillusioned; discretionary; vast; eligible; unhonored; mellowed; inventive; withered; golden; machine; raucous; tabloid; pagan; graceless; robust; sordid; decayed; ripened; unorthodox; practical; vanished; leisurely; stalwart; toddling; primeval; hoary; talking; shallow; successive (pl); sentimental; dangerous; undiscriminating; independent; buried; innumerable (pl).

verbs

advance in—; attain—; clothe—in glory; come of—; decay with—; defy—; denote—; dim with—; enfeeble with—; ensnare with —; exempt from—; honor old—; incapacitate with—; increase with—; judge—; knock at the door of—; limit—; renew—; reveal—; scoff at old—; serve—; stoop with —; succumb to old—; —accounts for; —adorns; —s average; —cracks; —decays; —deposits; —diminishes; —dispels; —enfeebles; —honors; —impairs; —measures; —mellows; —prevails; —privileges; —retards; —shrivels; —steals on; —strikes; —wears; —withers; —wrinkles; —yellows; attribute to—; belong to—; classify —s; corrupt—; denounce—; designate—; divide into—; epitomize—; excel—; fade into —s; gild—; glorify—; mark—; mechanize—; outlive—; pervade—; proclaim—; represent —; symbolize—; terminate—; usher in—; —s behold; —recognizes.

(See maturity, era, epoch, generation.)

AGED

adverbs

prematurely; terribly; tragically; pathetically; patriarchally; dingily; ridiculously; mournfully; uncommonly; desolately; contentedly; rosily; datelessly; lamentably; comfortably; crabbedly; hoarily; feebly; incredibly; wondrously; mellowly; honorably.

adjectives

effective; volcanic; ordained; secret; external; conservative; all-sufficient; subtle; sole; appropriate; divine; supernatural; regulative; luciferal; technical; bureaucratic; bargaining; ubiquitous; organized; conducive; charitable; law-enforcing; mitigating; curative; myriad (pl).

verbs

administer—; assume—; consolidate—; develop—; create—; employ—; exclude from —; license—; obtain—; operate—; register with—; require—; squeeze (colloq.)—; terminate—; weld —s into a unit; —acts for; —advocates; —authorizes; —charges; —commissions; —functions; —handles; —offers; —places; —promotes; —recommends; —stimulates; —surrenders functions.

adjectives

dominant; consular; imaginative; enterprising; remedial; unscrupulous; catalytic; cleansing; stimulating; diplomatic; publicity; purchasing; fiscal; coloring; trustworthy; energetic; physical; involuntary; recruiting; confidential; vigilant; corrosive; superfluous; purifying; accredited; cajoling; advance; rapacious.

verbs

appoint—; authorize—; commission—; delegate to—; deliberate—; discredit—; employ —; endow—; evade—; exert—; direct—; frustrate—; hearten—; rely upon—; remunerate—; request—; vest in—; yield to—; —accounts for; —acts for; —agitates; —assists; —bickers; —conducts; —contrives; —deliberates; —distributes; —enforces; —exerts; —implies; —negotiates; —operates; —profits; —represents; —slumbers; —solicits; —stipulates; —transacts; —vanishes.
(See representative, operator, factor.)

AGGRAVATE (v)
adverbs
arrogantly; brutally; continually; obviously; detrimentally; unceasingly; painfully.
(See intensify, irritate, provoke.)

AGGREGATION
adjectives
enormous; notable; glamorous; indefinable; congenial; simple; continuous.

adjectives

wanton; wilful; jealous; conscienceless; fiery; brisk; ruthless; merciless; destructive; ill-timed.

verbs

anger by—; anticipate—; avenge—; bear—; bulwark against—; check—; crush with—; denounce—; dread—; encounter—; oppose —; protest against—; provoke—; renounce —; resent—; resist—; save from—; submit to—; surrender to—; wear out by—; —flourishes; —saps; —staggers; —undermines.
(See assault, attack, intrusion, invasion.)

AGGRESSIVE
adverbs
boldly; offensively; truculently; bluntly; presumptuously; impertinently; unbecomingly; unwarrantedly; daringly; courageously; fearlessly; calmly; steadily; persistently; incurably, gallantly; pluckily; heroically; confidently; doggedly; criminally; savagely; indomitably.

AGGRESSIVENESS
adjectives
male; crocodilian; dynamic; sullen; forced; predatory; war-like; unthinking; brutal.

AGGRESSOR
verbs
agitate against—; badger—; blockade—; curse—; defend against—; denounce—; disconcert—; disorganize—; mobilize against —; punish—; repel—; —assails; —assaults; —depresses; —encroaches; —invades; —provokes; —seizes; —sets upon; —sweeps; —attacks.
(See intruder, trespasser.)

AGGRIEVE (v)
adverbs
mortally; painfully; brutally; bitterly; deeply; heartlessly.

AGHAST
adverbs
utterly; wanly; amazingly; amazedly; astoundingly; wonderingly; blankly; staringly; breathlessly; wordlessly; indescribably; stupidly; tremulously; fearfully.

AGILE
adverbs
nimbly; gracefully; unusually; swiftly; briskly; actively; alertly; surprisingly;

youthfully; slenderly; clumsily; unexpectedly; quickly; dangerously; mentally; physically; smartly; light-footedly; spryly; fleetly;
trippingly; lightly

AGILITY

adjectives
graceful; grotesque; sailor-like; astonishing;
spidery; acrobatic; unsurpassed; feline;
tigerish; apish; rare; unusual.

AGITATE (v)

adverbs
convulsively; considerably; indescribably;
fiercely; greatly; gently; violently; internally; nervously; feverishly; vigorously; incessantly; recurrently; destructively; visibly;
intellectually; markedly.
(See disturb.)

AGITATION

adjectives
revolutionary; indescribable; gentle; violent;
profane; internal; nervous; legitimate;
gloomy; feverish; throbbing; vigorous; indignant; preliminary; incessant; convulsive;
recurrent; destructive; inner; student; bewildered; smothered; visible; intellectual;
marked; wearying; unflinching; wholesale;
righteous; wide-spread.

verbs
accustom to—; admire—; allay—; cease
—; discuss—; flutter in—; infect with—;
introduce—; keep in—; kindle—; menace
by—; express—; produce—; provoke—; resume—; stir—; set up—; understand—;
witness—; —arises; —arouses; —disorganizes; —disturbs; —excites; —ignites; —
impassions; —moves; —perturbs; —stirs;
—terrifies; —unsettles.
(See emotion, commotion, disturbance.)

AGITATOR

adjectives
veteran; headstrong; unscrupulous; earnest;
didactic; deft; extreme; sincere; dangerous; willing; adept.

AGONY

adjectives
profound; envenomed; tearless; inglorious;
mute; unattended; vulgar; unconquerable;
mortal; delirious; fiery; nervous; crowning;
supreme; keen; blank; dying; childless;
nameless; final; convulsive; hot; thudding;
acute; multitudinous (pl); cowardly; utter;
rending; loathsome; internal; remittent;
prolonged; heartfelt; mental; frightful; exquisite; stern; superstitious; unspeakable;
piercing; secret; prophetic; scathing; ill-
fated; amorous; helpless; concentrated;
cold; excruciating; human; unendurable;
spiritual; indescribable; invisible; throbbing; last; speechless; intensified; impotent;
bitter; blinding; benumbing; timeless; relentless.

verbs
alleviate—; convulsed in—; distort with—;
efface—; endure—; face—; impose—; prolong—; relish—; shriek in—; stir with—;
strive in—; struggle in—; wrench in—;
writhe in—; —abates; —clutches; —confuses; —despairs; —distresses; —shoots.
(See distress, pain, anguish, torture.)

AGREE (v)

adverbs
pleasantly; universally; tacitly; gravely;
solemnly; heartily; voluntarily; magnanimously; cheerfully; listlessly; cordially;
completely; meekly; mutually; fervently;
blandly; wholly; accordingly; passively;
unanimously; comfortably; reluctantly; privately; definitely; amicably; pacifically;
tentatively; sensibly; politely; reassuringly;
fatuously; verbally; voluntarily; vehemently; emphatically; unhappily; authoritatively; benignly.
(See accord, acquiesce, comply, grant.)

AGREEABLE

adverbs
consistently; obviously; openly; frankly;
sweetly; essentially; warmly; gratifyingly;
extremely; unaffectedly; courteously; comfortably; pleasantly; placidly; gravely; unfailingly; generously; graciously; smilingly;
considerately; sincerely; cordially; quietly;
remarkably; ostentatiously; charmingly; singularly; genuinely; happily.

AGREEMENT

adjectives
substantial; stringent; mutual; diplomatic;
tacit; loose; amicable; pacific; unanimous;
working; preliminary; undisclosed; tentative; moratory; provisional; corrupt; sensible; effective; water-tight; polite; blissful;
conscientious; hearty; reassuring; noncommittal; fatuous; despotic; verbal; voluntary;
vehement; emphatic; unhappy; compromising; iron-clad; binding; enforced; authoritative.

verbs
accept—; assent to—; avow—; breach of—;

28

bring to—; cement—; come to—; conform with—; consent to—; consolidate—; construct—; consummate—; declare—; default —; deny—; disregard—; dissent from—; enter into—; execute—; express—; formulate—; fulfill—; illustrate—; imply—; "junk"—; negotiate—; perfect—; prescribe —; reach—; repudiate—; sanction—; scrap —; set forth in—; shape into—; subject to—; tie down with—; violate—; —cements; —consolidates; —expires; —manifests; —reveals; —stands.

(See contract, compact, bargain.)

AGRICULTURAL

adverbs
seriously; playfully; spasmodically; seasonably; showily; enthusiastically; presumptuously; ridiculously; professionally; amateurishly; preachily.

AGRICULTURE

adjectives
scientific; crude; experimental; diversified; mechanical; variegated.

verbs
administrate—; appropriate—; classify—; commercialize—; conduct research in—; control—; cooperate in—; crystallize—; depress —; devastate—; develop—; doom—; educate—; employ in—; encourage—; exploit —; extend—; extend credit to—; feed—; foster—; grant to—; improve—; industrialize—; inflate—; instruct in—; insure—; isolate—; manage—; mechanize—; modernize—; nationalize—; organize—; pertain to —; promote—; protect—; regulate—; replenish—; reshape—; restrict to—; revolutionize—; subsidize—; subsist on—; supervise—; survey—; systematize—; teach—; —benefits from; —domesticates; —economizes; —experiments; —flourishes; —markets; —prospers; —rises; —succumbs to; —suffers; —unfolds; —yields.

(See industry.)

AID

adjectives
material; mutual; quickening; self-denying; welcome; preternatural; vigorous; positive; substantial; prompt; efficient; generous; invaluable; all-important; sovereign; practical; inconspicuous; artificial; fictitious; dubious; healthful; supernatural; gloomy; adventitious; reluctant; priceless; functional; loyal; extraneous; potential; enlightened; specific; vital; essential; sustaining; necessary.

verbs
abolish—; afford—; apply for—; apportion —; assist with—; assure—; avail of—; award—; call upon—; condone—; contribute—; deserve—; dispatch—; distribute—; enlist—; extend—; grant—; howl for—; interpose—; invoke—; lack—; lend—; limit —; march to—; offer—; pledge—; proffer —; prompt—; render—; require—; seek—; speed up—; subsidize—; support with—; swear—; trust in—; volunteer—; withhold —; —arrives; —disappears; —preserves; —redeems; —saves.

(See help, assistance, relief, cooperation, succor, subsidy.)

AID (v)

adverbs
gladly; secretly; modestly; materially; unquestionably; unobtrusively; treacherously; substantially; self-denyingly; vigorously; positively; promptly; efficiently; generously; invaluably; practically; inconspicuously; dubiously; gloomily; reluctantly; loyally; potentially; specifically; essentially; necessarily.

(See help, assist, foster.)

AILMENT

adjectives
neurotic; minor; correctible; physical; incurable; hereditary; emotional; imaginary; pernicious; childish; dreaded; mysterious; vague; mythical; chronic; feminine; nervous; obscure; grave.

verbs
complain of—; cure—; diagnose—; disregard—; ignore—; neglect—; relieve—; rout—; —indisposes; —springs from.

(See malady, illness, sickness, disease.)

AIM

adjectives
instructive; principal; lofty; undeviating; murderous; intelligible; unerring; ultimate; personal; heroic; apparent; conscious; poetic; unselfish; generous; fictitious; ulterior; illusory; deadly; deliberate; laudable; ambitious; elevated; unattainable; logical; altruistic; devotional; basic; sole; cherished; confessed; wild; sordid; infallible; sinister; paltry; futile; frustrated; irrelevant; altered; modest; fundamental; kindred; radical; novel; immediate; primal; vain; impracticable; double; sober; impossible.

verbs
applaud—; attain—; baffle—; cast out—; define—; design—; disguise—; dissipate—;

embrace—; encourage—; endorse—; fulfill—; picture—; promote—; propose—; realize—; restrict—; sanction—; set forth—; sum up—; wander from—; —conflicts; —elevates; —succeeds; —tends; affect—; avoid—; calculate—; direct—; estimate—; guide—; hinder—; lead—; level—; mark—; miss—; point—; take—; train—; —errs.

(See object, end, aspiration, purpose, direction.)

AIM (v)

adverbs
uselessly; deliberately; primarily; instructively; immediately; principally; loftily; undeviatingly; murderously; unerringly; apparently; heroically; consciously; poetically; unselfishly; generously; fictitiously; laudably; ambitiously; elevatedly; unattainably; logically; altruistically; basically; solely; confessedly; futilely; frustratedly; irrelevantly; modestly; fundamentally; radically; vainly; soberly; impossibly.

(See aspire, desire.)

AIMLESS

adverbs
lamentably; invariably; unfortunately; carelessly; happily; blithely; deplorably; unluckily; unhappily; moodily; gloomily; deliberately.

AIR

adjectives (*atmosphere*)
crisp; healthful; bracing; balmy; salt; mountain; vitalizing; tingling; invigorating; pungent; exhilarating; sparkling; scented; lofty; comfortable; luminous; polluted; vapory; unbreathed; troublous; sultry; jocund; frosty; ambient; stifling; glittering; precipitant; pernicious; darkened; shadowed; vital; dusky; misty; hushed; viewless; frigid; salubrious; tepid; muffled; wholesome; vibrant; vacant; raw; impalpable; thin; strangling; nocturnal; atmospheric; rarefied; enervating; delicious; genial; cleft; unjaded; foggy; fermenting; heavy; nipping; chilled; vivifying; interlunar; brisk; emerald; buoyant; singing; deoxidized; dewy; trackless; stinking; fetid; starry; caressant; scorching; tranquil; spiced; sharp; soothing; health-giving; circulating; conditioned; compressed; illimitable; translucent; moon-struck; wanton; sulphurous; pellucid; miasmic; penetrating; oppressive; desolate; pale; filtered; humidified; twilight; windless; tempest-charged; electric; upper; sanctified; cloudless; greedy; wholesome; dreamy; mineral; limpid;

startled; sun-sweetened; purgatorial; inclement; pestilential; highland; laughing; murky; soul-sustaining; heaven-high; infected; mellow; free; summering; mouldy; impregnated; vitiated; toxic; acrid; moontide; dust-scented; crystalline; smoke-saturated; balsam-laden; forest-scented; rainswept; clammy; roseate; lifeless; aromatic; ruffled; buxom; clinging; glimmering; pleasant; tropic; perfumed; empyreal; luscious; blue; stagnant; spreading; eddying; transparent; yielding.

verbs
admit—; ascend into—; bask in—; beat—; blacken—; bore through—; build in—; change—; charge—; choke—with dust; compose—; compress—; condition—; consume—; cool—; dance in—; darken—; dart through—; deprive of—; detect in—; diffuse—; disappear into thin—; dissipate into—; distribute—; drink—; embalm—with; embrace—; exhale—; exhaust—; expel—; expose to—; fan—; float through—; flush—; hallow—; heave into—; hurtle through—; impregnate—; infect—; inflame—; inhale—; inject—; liquidize—; load—; lope into—; melt into thin—; mix with—; mount into—; navigate—; penetrate—; perfume—; permeate—; pervade—; pierce—; purge—; purify—; pursue in—; putrefy—; ravish—; remove from—; rend—; ride—; ripple—; rise into—; rule—; sail in—; saturate—; scent—; seep into—; shelter from—; smite—; sniff—; split—; stir—; subject to—; support in—; surge into—; suspend in—; sweep—; taint—; tinge—; vanish into—; vitiate—; warm—; —blows; —circles; —circulates; —consists of; —conveys; —diffuses; —expands; —fans; —lulls; —murmurs; —palpitates; —reeks; —resounds; —reverberates; —rings; —ripples; —rushes by; —scintillates; —seeps in; —sighs; —singes; —stirs; —surges in; —surrounds; —swirls; —thickens; —throbs; —trembles; —whispers; —whistles.

(See atmosphere, wind, breeze, ether.)

AIR

adjectives (*attitude*)
racy; ironical; professional; coquettish; hesitating; surly; monastic; elegant; proud; condescending; saucy; insouciant; youthful; carefree; confident; joyous; buoyant; hospitable; grotesque; perky; deliberate; abstracted; mystic; druid-like; prehistoric; unctuous; becoming; serious; protecting; perplexed; ardent; businesslike; inquiring; passionate; prosperous; dolorous; pathetic;

discomfited; prophetic; judicial; desperate; peculiar; proprietary; confidential; indefinable; plaintive; dejected; distant; self-confident; rustic; cold; patient; fantastical; lackadaisical; pouting; well-bred; encouraging; calm; sweet; polished; devilish; dashing; unaffected; imposing; disappointed; striking; distinguished; excited; tragic; undaunted; artless; pompous; shamed; furtive; playful; genteel; wheedling; pensive; citified; injured; sedate; wanton; roguish; insulted; contrite; womanly; virginal; frivolous; feline; jaunty; meditative; bewitching; sinister; forbidding; portentous; sagacious; riotous; appreciative; courteous; unapologetic; candid; youthful; pitiless; voluptuous; simple; languid; reserved; threatening; imperious; intellectual; reminiscent; glib; deprecating; intolerant; patronizing; passionless; composed; comic; engaging; celestial; virtuous; elegant; exquisite; masterful; aggressive; knowing; shrewd; appraising, sophisticated; elaborate; obedient; tranquil; staid; quizzical; enigmatic; lofty; supercilious; possessive; matter-of-fact; nonchalant; detached; insolent; ominous; dissipated; moody; irrational; belligerent; calculating; obstinate; irritating; scandalized; dogged; harassed; martyred; injured; distraught; shrinking; crestfallen; disconcerted; motherly; suave; exotic; masculine; incorrigible; colloquial; cherubic; critical; indulgent; salubrious; appreciative; deferential; disarming; sly; accommodating; grandiose; spiritual; majestic.

verbs
acquaint with—; address with—; adopt—; affect—; ape—; assume—; bear—of; communicate—; describe—; draw up with—; feign—; give —s to; invest with—; manifest—; treat with—; unfold—; —excites; —pleases.

(See manner, mien, appearance, demeanor, expression.)

AIR
adjectives   *(tune)*
wizard; stirring; martial; light; melancholy; flippant; patriotic; lilting; mournful; plaintive; persistent; haunting; nostalgic; memorable; heartfelt; militant.

verbs
accompany—; arrange—; chorus—; compose—; harmonize—; hum—; play—; recognize—; sing—; spoil—; synchronize—; whistle—; —charms; —cheers; —enchants;

—expresses; —gladdens; —moves; —stirs. (See melody, tune.)

AIRPLANE
adjectives
multi-engined; droning; adventitious; obsolete; commercial; fleet; metal; transcontinental.

AIRY
adverbs
gracefully; exquisitely; boyishly; youthfully; lightly; cheerfully; inexpressibly; racily; blithely; gaily; elegantly; saucily; proudly; carelessly; joyously; confidently; buoyantly; mystically; prophetically; proprietarily; fantastically; devilishly; dashingly; imposingly; artlessly; playfully; wantonly; roguishly; jauntily; bewitchingly; engagingly; elegantly; superciliously; nonchalantly; suavely; smoothly; indulgently; disarmingly; slyly; fashionably; stagily; conceitedly; refreshingly; racially.

AISLE
adjectives
shadowy; cathedral; winding; grassy; gloomy; long-drawn; teeming; pillared; silent; narrow; raucous; leafy; forest; cloistered; slender; gorgeous; moldering.

verbs
amble down—; arch—; block—; bound down—; build—; divide into—; drift down —; extend—; flank—; form—; indicate—; labor up—; negotiate—; obstruct—; open —; pace—; separate by —s; speed down —; tear up—; traverse—; trip down—; walk down—; widen—; —bisects; —divides; —extends; —leads; —runs; —swallows one up.
(See passage.)

ALACRITY
adjectives
marvelous; gladsome; incredible; peculiar; sparkling; unequalled; comical; momentary; light-footed; nimble; feigned; eager; warlike; rhythmic; enthusiastic; headlong; keen; noteworthy; nervous.

ALARM
adjectives
serious; groundless; vague; superstitious; unnecessary; high; nocturnal; perpetual; tremulous; faint; profound; spectral; manifest; shrill; evident; grave; imminent; scandalized; unfounded; painful; imbecile; grim; mute; abrupt; midnight; uneasy; sounding; friendly; grisly; deadly; incessant.

31

verbs

answer—; bewilder by—; blow—; broadcast—; burden with—; check—; chime—; cry—; discourage undue—; excite—; exclaim in—; give rise to—; incite—; occasion—; peal—; produce—; recoil in—; respond to—; shake with—; shudder in—; signal—; sound—; strike—; suppress—; take—; transmit—; —awakens; —clangs; —demoralizes; —dismays; —disturbs; —notifies; —signifies; —spreads; —startles; —steals over one; —subsides; —summons; —surprises; —vanishes; —warns.

(See terror, fright, consternation, apprehension, panic, dismay, fear, dread, warning, signal.)

ALARM (v)

adverbs

sincerely; fearfully; seriously; astoundingly; exceedingly; groundlessly; unnecessarily; vaguely; superstitiously; perpetually; faintly; profoundly; manifestly; gravely; painfully; abruptly; incessantly.

(See terrify, frighten, scare.)

ALCOHOL

verbs

abstain from—; apply—; banish—; bloat with—; clean with—; concentrate—; condemn—; consume—; contain—; crave—; denature—; detect—; dilute—; dissolve in —; distill—; dose with—; ferment into—; formulate—; heat with—; indulge in—; injure with—; manufacture—; methylate—; power with—; prod with—; purvey—; redistill—; reduce to—; reek with—; reinforce by—; resist—; respond to—; restrict —; saturate with—; solace with—; stain with—; steep in—; stimulate with—; taint with—; utilize—; vaporize—; —accelerates; —contracts; —deadens; —depresses; —derives from; —dulls; —expands; —flames; —inebriates; —influences; —intoxicates; —menaces; —occurs in; —penetrates; —plays a role; —poisons; —preserves; —ravages; —retards; —soothes; —stimulates.

(See wine, liquor, whiskey, ale, etc.)

ALE

adjectives

nut-brown; home-brewed; spicy; unlimited; earth-cooled; bubbling; foam-flecked; gurgling; spirited; heaven-sent; sparkling; cheery; tempting; joyous.

verbs

appreciate—; brew—; consume—; deal in —; drink—; ferment into—; fill with—; flavor—; gulp down—; guzzle—; hop up —; imbibe—; medicate—; pour—; process —; revel in—; set up to a drink of—; swill—; warm with—; —inebriates; —intoxicates; —matures; —pacifies; —ripens; —sours; —stupefies.

(See beer, liquor.)

ALERT

adverbs

guardedly; extremely; wisely; resolutely; diabolically; eternally; zealously; embarrassingly; cautiously; suspiciously; terribly; comically; capably; amazingly; inordinately; passably; incessantly; mentally; nervously; uncommonly; keenly; coolly; warily; sharply; suavely; briskly; swiftly; signally.

ALERTNESS

adjectives

practical; mental; nervous; paradoxical; keen; fierce; flea-like; scientific; cool; quick; wary; sharp; sly; suave; brisk; swift; signal; undervalued.

ALIBI

adjectives

dubious; unquestioned; plausible; unbreakable; incontestable; air-tight; fantastic; faked; unprovable; admirable.

verbs

allege—; build—; concoct—; dispense with —; establish—; fabricate—; furnish—; introduce—; manufacture—; offer—; perjure —; pose—; prove—; regard—; resort to—; scrutinize—; set up—; snarl—; substantiate —; support—; tender—; verify—; —acquits; —bewilders; —confounds; —disconcerts; —proves.

(See plea, excuse.)

ALIEN

adjectives

unwashed; pseudo-intellectual; criminal; invading; objectionable; well-meaning; spying; unpatriotic; harmless.

verbs

admit—; appoint—; bilk—; comfort—; confuse—; defend—; define—; defraud—; delude—; dominate—; dupe—; exclude—; expel—; exploit—; hinder—; hoodwink—; incite—; legislate against—; naturalize—; outwit—; prejudice against—; restrict—; smuggle—; subsidize—; succor—; tolerate —; —agitates; —consumes; —demolishes; —domiciles; —immigrates; —rends; —resides; —sojourns in; —thwarts.

(See stranger, foreigner.)

adverbs
intrusively; irrelevantly; outlandishly; undeniably; ostentatiously; palpably; essentially; obviously; disagreeably; inimicably; inconceivably; unconcernedly; disinterestedly; relatively; discordantly; impertinently; fantastically; exotically; discordantly; incidentally; multifariously; remotely; strangely; unconformably; extraneously; exceptionally; inadmissably; objectionably; harmlessly; unpatriotically; unquestionably.

ALIENATE (v)
adverbs
irretrievably; completely; irreconcilably; temporarily; permanently; successfully; finally; spitefully.

(See transfer, separate.)

ALIENATION
adjectives
mental; complete; temporary; irreconcilable; permanent.

ALIMONY
verbs
appoint—; approve of—; award—; consent to—; decrease—; entitle to—; fall behind in—; imprison for—; lapse—; reward with—; seek—; settle—on; sue for—; win —; —supports.

(See allowance.)

ALIVE
adverbs
gaily; blithely; barely; resolutely; completely; eagerly; energetically; fortunately; happily; surprisingly; beamingly; briskly; industriously; alertly; animatedly; bustlingly; actively; diligently; friskily; restlessly; strenuously; gloriously; joyously; delightedly; rapturously.

ALLEGATION
adjectives
oft-repeated; prevailing; pointless; irrelevant; unsubstantiated; unsupported; insistent.

verbs
affirm—; blurt out—; declare—; deny—; disprove—; dispute—; disregard—; excuse —; hurl—; justify—; moderate—; overthrow—; persevere in—; plead—; propound —; protest—; prove—; refute—; reprove —; state—; voice—; —condemns; —effects; —supports; —validates; —warrants.

(See assertion, declaration, plea, statement.)

ALLEGE (v)
adverbs
emphatically; repeatedly; pointlessly; irrelevantly; insistently; heatedly.

(See state, maintain.)

ALLEGIANCE
adjectives
ill-defined; supreme; unflinching; unfaltering; passionate; vague; firm; absolute; self-sacrificing; divided; faithful; half-hearted; enthusiastic; constrained.

verbs
abandon—; affirm—; begrudge—; bid for —; cease—to; confer—; declare—; desert —; disavow—; dissolve—; exact—; follow with—; free from—to; gain—; imply—; pledge—; profess—; render—; renounce—; repudiate—; seek—; supplant—; swear—; throw off—; violate—; vow—; withdraw—; —binds; —comforts; —continues; —ties.

(See loyalty, devotion, fidelity, obedience.)

ALLEGORICAL
adverbs
abstrusely; openly; frankly; cleverly; disguisedly; ostensibly; ironically; typically; far-fetchedly; obtusely; complexly; incomprehensibly; palpably; evidently; thinly.

ALLEGORY
adjectives
horrid; tremendous; apt; philosophical; pompous; hidden; inappropriate; far-fetched.

ALLEVIATE (v)
adverbs
cheerily; markedly; tremendously; remarkably; slightly; apparently.

(See relieve, lighten, reduce, lessen.)

ALLEY
adjectives
blind; medieval; inclosing; labyrinthian; squalid; grimy; malodorous; slimy; unpromising; filthy; twisting; green; rat-infested.

verbs
approach—; border—; cower in—; lurk in —; saunter through—; skulk in—; slink through—; strike into—; —crawls with; —reeks; —resembles; —slumbers; —teems with; —turns; —twists; —winds.

(See street, passage, path, walk, way.)

ALLIANCE

adjectives

suspicious; entangling; defensive; amazing; long-desired; dubious; firm; treacherous; political; unholy; unspeakable; tribal; intimate; loose; epoch-making; bizarre; dissolved; prosperous; unhappy; matrimonial; iniquitous; extraneous; staunch; fitting; corrupt; unsurpassed; nuptial; accursed; formidable.

verbs

achieve—; acquire—; adhere to—; alter—; combine in—; conclude—; connect with—; contract—; contribute to—; defend—; deny —; disapprove of—; dissolve—; enhance —; entangle in —s; form—; found—; knit —; maintain—; preserve—; revise—; revoke—; sanction—; seek—; solidify—; stipulate—; terminate—; unite in—; —augments; —concludes; —crumbles; —discriminates against; —empowers; —enables; — enriches; —entangles; —fortifies; —insures; —knits; —maintains; —preserves; —promises; —reanimates; —reinforces; —rejuvenates; —revives; —solidifies; —stiffens; — stipulates; —sustains.

(See league, union, federation, coalition, relationship.)

ALLIGATOR

verbs

conserve —s; corner—; despatch—; exterminate —s; harpoon—; preserve—; prey upon—; prod—; spy on—; stock with —s; stuff—; —s abound; —attacks; —attains a length; —basks; —bellows; —burrows; — charges; —crawls; —crunches; —crushes; —deposits eggs; —devours; —draws his prey; —emits odors; —flips his tail; — floats; —frequents; —glides; —grunts; — hatches; —hibernates; —inhabits; —lashes; —lies in wait; —makes off with; —matures; —measures; —nips; —retreats; —roars; — slips into the water; —snaps; —splashes; —submerges; —suns; —surges; —swarms; —swings its tail; —tends its young; — thrashes about; —twists; —writhes.

(See reptile, crocodile.)

ALLOT (v)

adverbs

fairly; equitably; unjustly; unfairly; satisfactorily; magnanimously; impartially.

(See. apportion, distribute, divide.)

ALLOW (v)

adverbs

ultimately; generously; grudgingly; graciously; subsequently; tacitly; reluctantly; liberally; handsomely; munificently; reasonably; lavishly; regularly; intermittently; impartially.

(See permit, consent, tolerate.)

ALLOWABLE

adverbs

expressly; always; scarcely; socially; officially; legally; obviously; evidently; patently; unconditionally; reportedly; apparently; unquestionably; indubitably; undoubtedly; manifestly; definitely; explicitly; palpably.

ALLOWANCE

adjectives

liberal; generous; handsome; munificent; reasonable; meager; due; tolerable; lavish; modest; regular; intermittent; niggardly; kingly; stated.

verbs

admit—; allot—; apportion—; award—; concede—; continue—; deduct from—; draw from—; exhaust—; husband—; laud—; limit—; oppose—; pledge—; restrict—; sanction—; spurn—; tolerate—; —astounds; —shrinks; —staggers.

(See salary, wages, amount.)

ALLUDE (v)

adverbs

publicly; poetically; indelicately; pointedly; superciliously; jocosely; sarcastically; distinctly; crudely; obscurely; perplexingly; scripturally; casually; playfully; metaphorically; slyly; sneeringly; disdainfully; contemptuously; monotonously; personally; irreverently; subtly; timidly; blasphemously; insultingly; condescendingly; scurrilously; jocularly; abstrusely; respectfully.

(See hint, intimate, refer.)

ALLUREMENT

adjectives

economic; taunting; entrancing; delightful; exquisite; siren; agreeable; overpowering; female.

ALLURING

adverbs

mysteriously; utterly; delightfully; disturbingly; designedly; intentionally; confoundedly; diabolically; bewilderingly; amazingly; unquestionably; wondrously; unexpectedly; surprisingly; coolly; radiantly; joyously; quietly; consciously; unconsciously; tauntingly; tormentingly; overwhelmingly; provokingly.

ALLUSION

adjectives

happy; distinct; obscure; incidental; scholarly; crude; contemporary; sarcastic; pointed; topical; perplexing; scriptural; casual; facile; parting; playful; metaphorical; delicate; sly; biverbal; sneering; disdainful; contemptuous; literary; monotonous; personal; indecent; stray; well-timed; irreverent; laudatory; hidden; subtle; mythological; rambling; timid; blasphemous; insulting; condescending; scurrilous; jocular; abstruse; respectful.

verbs

accept—; discern—; endure—; explain—; insert—; sport with—; weave in —s; —s abound; —s clutter; —s crowd; —encumbers; —enriches; —implies; —suggests; —weighs down.

(See reference, hint, suggestion.)

ALLY

adjectives

ancient; formidable; constant; treacherous; invaluable; powerful; brilliant; faithful; indispensable; perfidious; distrustful; illustrious; staunch; natural; sturdy; vigorous; sympathetic; unmanageable; lifelong.

verbs

abuse—; alienate—; combine with—; consult—; defend—; forsake—; outrage—; seek—; take for—; unite with—; welcome —; —collapses; —concurs; —s connive; — contributes; —cools down; —forfeits.

(See colleague, friend, partner.)

ALLY (*v*)

adverbs

closely; inseparably; exclusively; treacherously; invaluably; faithfully; indispensably; perfidiously; staunchly; naturally; sturdily; sympathetically; vigorously.

(See join, associate.)

ALMS

verbs

allot—; bestow—; contribute—; dole out—; donate—; entreat for—; merit—; ministrate —; pilfer—; provide—; relieve with—; scatter—; scorn—; solicit—; support by—.

(See charity, dole, gift.)

ALOOF

adverbs

coldly; proudly; shyly; timidly; arrogantly; superciliously; intellectually; naturally; dreamily; discourteously; deliberately; resolutely; unsociably; impenetrably; ponderously; inscrutably; mysteriously; maddeningly; becomingly; gruffly; gravely; augustly; imposingly; absurdly; magnificently.

ALOOFNESS

adjectives

natural; sweet; drowsy; dignified; dreamy; dainty; unbending; icy; mystic; abstract; courteous; silent; defensive; impenetrable; absent-minded; Olympian; detached; despairing; pardonable; ponderous; inscrutable; effective; becoming.

verbs

attain—; enshroud in—; maintain—; preserve—; withdraw from—; wrap in—; — dehumanizes; —indicates; —induces; —inhibits; —leads to; —results in; —starves.

(See reserve.)

ALTAR

adjectives

garlandless; dreaded; cold; smokeless; nuptial; honored; glowing; conjugal; auspicious; idolatrous; brazen; impious; favored; lofty; sacrificial; venerable.

verbs

accept on—; adorn—; attend—; bow before —; burn at—; cast down—; consecrate—; dedicate at—; desecrate—; disparage—; elevate—; encrust—; enshrine on—; erect —; hang on—; inscribe on—; lure to—; offer on—; perform at—; raise—; rear—; repose on—; sacrifice at—; stagger to—; swear by—; vow at—; worship before—; —fumes with incense; —graces; —rises; —stands.

(See platform, bier.)

ALTER (*v*)

adverbs

placidly; ridiculously; radically; appreciably; considerably; materially; profoundly; conspicuously; extremely; subsequently; invariably; frankly; significantly; sensibly; quantitatively; mysteriously; extensively; basically; subtly; markedly; seriously; intangibly; indefinably.

(See vary, change, transform.)

ALTERABLE

adverbs

frankly; conveniently; easily; extensively; fortunately; unfortunately; always; happily.

ALTERATION

adjectives

frank; significant; sensible; trifling; quantitative; mysterious; basic; suggested; extensive; observable; subtle; marked; serious; intangible; indefinable.

verbs
detect—; dispute—; effect—; employ—; indicate—; modify—; ponder—; substitute —; yawn at—; —charms; —displeases; —effects; —enchants; —invalidates; —occurs; —offends; —pleases; —satisfies; —is wrought.
(See modification, change, variation.)

ALTERCATION
adjectives
monstrous; lurid; bitter; gesticulatory; high-pitched; wordy; domestic; deadly; unprovoked; violent; acrimonious.

ALTERNATION
adjectives
mad; periodical; endless; rapid; unconscious; intermittent; infinite.

ALTERNATIVE
adjectives
painful; pleasant; admirable; desperate; intolerable; unthinkable; dire; impossible; practicable; subtle; ghastly; grim; vague; contradictory; undesirable; inescapable; serious.

verbs
arrive at—; bewilder with—; conceive—; confront with—; countenance—; endorse—; explore—; extend—; mystify by—; propose —; reject—; request—; suggest—; —circumscribes; —curbs; —lies open; —limits; —puzzles; —remains.
(See option, preference.)

ALTITUDE
adjectives
bleak; dizzy; infinite; considerable; starlit; moderate; healthful; breezy; breath-taking; excessive; unbelievable; unattainable.

verbs
ascertain—; compute—; elevate—; exceed —; fix—; forfeit—; gain—; gauge—; heighten—; level off at—; maintain—; register—; rise to—; scale—; soar to—; —dazzles; —increases.

ALTRUISM
adjectives
genuine; noble; philanthropic; lofty; feeble; non-existent.

ALTRUISTIC
adverbs
sincerely; fanatically; pompously; vaingloriously; publicly; ostentatiously; extremely; instinctively; characteristically; truly; genuinely; amazingly; essentially; quixotically.

ALUMNUS
adjectives
distinguished; valuable; brother; successful; staunch; dependable; rabid; generous.

verbs
appeal to—; browbeat—; organize—; —associates; —i build; —celebrates; —i constitute; —i convene; —endows; —fosters; —i gather; —i nourish; —pledges; —relives; —i reunite; —revisits; —i stand behind.
(See graduate.)

AMALGAMATION
adjectives
compulsory; racial; ethnic; subtle; industrial; necessary; advantageous; vital.

AMATEUR
adjectives
persistent; enterprising; enthusiastic; complacent; inexperienced; deplorable; superficial; distinguished; literary; gifted.

verbs
bar—; brand as—; close to —s; define—; deride—; distinguish—; encourage—; exempt—; govern—; handicap—; outdistance —; purge —s; repudiate—; restrict —s; rule —s; safeguard—; sanction—; vindicate —; —aspires to; —attains; —barters; —competes; —cultivates; —devotes; —engages in; —participates; —preserves his status; —stresses.
(See novice.)

AMATEURISH
adverbs
hopelessly; youthfully; admittedly; eagerly; fancifully; fantastically; ambitiously; avidly; fervidly; enthusiastically; comically; pathetically; inexpertly; deplorably; unexpectedly.

AMAZE (v)
adverbs
perfectly; absolutely; ludicrously; indignantly; honestly; utterly; unboundedly; mutually; bewilderedly; unutterably; speechlessly; blankly; raptly; helplessly; ineffably; dumbfoundedly; haughtily; unconcealedly; senselessly; horribly.
(See astonish, surprise, astound.)

AMAZEMENT

adjectives

sheer; indignant; fond; honest; stupid; starry-eyed; stupefied; utter; mute; unbounded; rising; mutual; bewildered; half-incredulous; mocking; unutterable; speechless; critical; dawning; blank; rapt; wide-eyed; shocked; helpless; dumbfounded; ineffable; freezing; justifiable; startled; horrified; petrified; haughty; agonized; unconcealed; hurt; smothering; open-mouthed; uneasy; senseless.

verbs

augment—; confound with—; evince—; eye with—; feign—; overwhelm with—; paralyze with—; peer with—; petrify with—; smite with—; stupefy with—; —bewilders; —divulges; —manifests itself; —reveals; —seizes; —stuns.

(See astonishment, confusion, surprise, admiration, awe, bewilderment, perplexity, wonder.)

AMBASSADOR

verbs

accredit—; assign—; authorize—; charge —with; commission—; confer with—; delegate—; dismiss—; dispatch—; empower—; entrust—with; exchange —s; exclude—; exempt—; immunize—; induct—; install—; invest—with; maintain—; nominate—; ordain—; oust—; raise to the rank of—; recall—; retract—; suspend—; turn out—; unfrock—; —abrogates; —arbitrates; — arms with; —carries on; —conveys; — develops; —entreats; —has access to; — intercedes; —mediates; —ministers; —negotiates; —represents; —repudiates; — transmits.

(See agent, minister, official.)

AMBER

adjectives

limpid; pale; rich; clear; electrified; honey-colored; translucent; opaque.

AMBIGUITY

adjectives

unfortunate; verbal; apparent; subtle; disturbing; deliberate; undesirable.

verbs

admit—; brush away—; burden by—; clear away—; cling to—; develop—; disentangle —; dissolve—; distinguish—; express—; obscure with—; oppress with—; reduce—;

remove—; —clouds; —deludes; —occurs; —puzzles; —vanishes.

(See uncertainty, obscurity.)

AMBIGUOUS

adverbs

unfortunately; disturbingly; deliberately; undesirably; evasively; obscurely; distressingly; offensively; suspiciously; undeniably; quibblingly; equivocally; perplexingly; obscurely; mysteriously; vexatiously; seriously; irritatingly; vaguely; disagreeably; insidiously; stupidly; unwisely; objectionably; unacceptably; cunningly.

AMBITION

adjectives

forceful; unbounded; misplaced; personal; warring (pl); criminal; abstracted; reasonable; social; ancestral; uninstructed; worthy; unquenchable; industrial; average; grandiose; sole; thick-sighted; racial; lofty; cherished; lifelong; thwarted; worldly; vaulting; vain; conflicting (pl); daring; unprincipled; insane; intense; unbridled; noisy; darling; foiled; primary; disquieting; peculiar; fierce; humble; honorable; wandering; moderate; sensible; imperial; kingly; persistent; mad; tremendous; sublime; soaring; disappointed; desultory; insatiable; absurd; unreined; corrupt; beastly; misdirected; undying; healthy; satisfied; blind; august; youthful; vulgar; inordinate; life-ruling; troublous; sinister; irreconcilable; political; odious; crushed; tacit; impassioned; private; unscrupulous; persevering; senile; exalted; praiseworthy; modern; resolute; aggressive; consuming; gnawing; spurring; boastful; indiscreet; petty; visionary; conceited; dictatorial; egotistical; dynastic; abjured; hypertrophied; latent; innate; undeviating; tempered; boundless; distempered; focalized.

verbs

achieve—; attain—; badger—; balk—; betoken—; breed—; characterize—; cherish —; chill—; choke with—; commend—; control—; credit—; cultivate—; derive—; devour with—; direct—; display—; dose with —; drop—; dwarf—; endow with—; enslave—; entertain—; exaggerate—; extinguish—; feed with—; fire with—; fling away—; frustrate—; fulfill—; further—; gratify—; hamper—; honor—; humor—; infect with—; inflame with—; inspire—; master—; nurse—; overleap—; placate—; realize—; reawaken—; rein—; relinquish —; restrain—; satisfy—; scoff at—; scotch —; stifle—; stimulate—; subordinate—; temper—; thwart—; whet—; —burns; —s conflict; —emboldens; —lures; —overleaps itself; —pushes; —soars; —suffers; —vaults.

(See aspiration, desire, eagerness.)

AMBITIOUS

adverbs

socially; extremely; unspeakably; inordinately; profoundly; mercilessly; unscrupulously; politically; ruthlessly; odiously; laudably; properly; dangerously; admirably; industriously.

AMBLE (*v*)

adverbs

joyously; industriously; gently; languorously; lazily; impudently; lackadaisically.

(See walk.)

AMBUSH

verbs

assault from—; attack from—; capture by —; conceal in—; draw into—; elude—; employ—; encounter—; hide in—; lay—; lie in—; lurk in—; perish in—; post in—; set up—; station in—; suspect—; tempt into—; walk into—; waylay in—; —arises; —succeeds; —surprises.

(See trap.)

AMEN

adjectives

hearty; hasty; solemn; sincere; throaty; husky; heavenly.

AMENABLE

adverbs

pleasantly; personally; entirely; wholly; scarcely; seriously; terribly; directly; agreeably; accommodatingly; willingly; satisfactorily; sufficiently; fortunately; happily.

AMENDMENT

adjectives

belated; rash; drastic; pending; beneficent; continual.

verbs

abandon—; abrogate—; adopt—; allow—; alter—; complete—; concur with—; deliberate—; disagree with—; discuss—; dismiss —; initiate—; insert—; oppose—; propose —; ratify—; reject—; repeal—; resolve—; subject to—; substitute—; veto—; violate —; —adjusts; —alters; —betters; —compensates; —corrects; —deprives; —expiates; —gives birth to; —modifies; —overthrows; —provides; —reforms; —remedies; —removes; —restricts; —stands.

(See change, improvement, correction.)

AMENITY

adjectives

ancient; social; hard-won; nonsensical; accepted; expected.

AMERICAN

adjectives

dashing; chauvinist; adventurous; eminent; loud; red-blooded; level-headed; intellectual; sensitive; liberal; stout-hearted; rapid-fire; virile; swift-moving; industrial-minded.

adverbs

loyally; thoroughly; completely; independently; dauntlessly; proudly; consciously; resolutely; ostentatiously; ridiculously; adventurously; bravely; essentially; obviously; distinctively; characteristically; insistently; consistently; persistently; dashingly; steadily; coolly; charmingly; informally; violently; volubly; restrainedly; serenely; confidently; unmistakably; undeniably; loudly; quietly; palpably; evidently; level-headedly; stoutly; invincibly.

AMERICANISM

verbs

adhere to—; ally with—; appeal to—; assault—; assert—; assimilate—; awaken—; cherish—; cite—; cultivate—; defend—; develop—; deviate from—; embrace—; endow with—; establish—; explore—; express —; federate—; hearten by—; inculcate—; ingrain—; insure—; interfere with—; laud —; menace—; molest—; motivate by—; pledge to—; proclaim—; promote—; resist—; retain—; retreat to—; ripen—; safeguard—; surround by—; sympathize with—; tamper with—; threaten—; unite in—; uphold—; verse in—; vest in—; —converges with; —embraces; —flounders; —flourishes; —forges through; —fosters; —languishes; —progresses; —promotes; —signifies; —survives.

(See patriotism.)

AMIABILITY

adjectives

impassioned; delightful; sincere; disconcerting; utmost; gushing; easy-going; placid; unwonted; native; condescending; rarefied.

AMIABLE

adverbs

charmingly; unfailingly; always; sincerely; unaffectedly; calmly; serenely; happily; cheerily; naturally; bewitchingly; softly; gently; enchantingly; unwontedly; unusually; habitually; incomparably; modestly;

winningly; ineffably; genuinely; becomingly; refreshingly; wonderfully; sweetly; graciously; frankly.

AMITY

adjectives
godlike; cordial; ghastly; mutual; rough; genial; generous; feigned; jealous.

verbs
abide in—; bind in—; cultivate—; despise —; disrupt—; found upon—; knit in—; link in—; promote—; radiate—; restore—; swear—; unite in—; —conduces; —fosters; —insures.

(See friendship, harmony, good-will, peace.)

AMMUNITION

verbs
assign—; cap—; cast—; consume—; contract for—; discharge—; exhaust—; furnish—; fuse—; guard—; handle—; ignite —; insert—; jacket—; project—; protect ; ration out—; replenish—; safeguard—; secrete—; stack—; store—; transport—; —detonates; —embraces; —saves; —shatters; —undergoes improvement.

(See explosives, shells.)

AMOROUS

adverbs
ardently; erotically; tenderly; lovingly; excessively; ostentatiously; fervidly; adoringly; idolatrously; infatuatedly; passionately; rapturously; yearningly; coquettishly; excitedly; flirtatiously; sweetly; philanderingly; seductively; enchantingly; winningly; wooingly; devotedly.

AMOUNT

adjectives
sufficient; excessive; stipulated; immense; cumulative; dangerous; exhausting; vast; exorbitant; fabulous; incredible; gigantic; indecent; unreasonable; prodigious; unprecedented; fantastic; appalling; colossal; ruinous; incalculable; goodly; sizable; average; traditional; stated; strategic; proportionate; lucrative; harmonious; comfortable; infinite; negligible; inexhaustible; inadequate; moderate; insignificant; undue; maximum; requisite; definite; appreciable; trifling; minimum; perceptible; preponderant; staggering; unheard-of.

verbs
aggregate—; anticipate—; calculate—; compute—; diminish—; discount—; estimate—; expend—; forecast—; gauge—; indicate—;

magnify—; register—; sum up—; total—; view—; withdraw—; —dwindles; —exceeds; —recedes; —reverts; —rises.

(See quantity, total, sum.)

AMOUNT (v)

adverbs
collectively; sufficiently; excessively; immensely; cumulatively; dangerously; exhaustingly; vastly; exorbitantly; fabulously; incredibly; gigantically; indecently; unreasonably; prodigiously; unprecedently; fantastically; appallingly; colossally; ruinously; incalculably; sizably; proportionately; lucratively; harmoniously; infinitely; comfortably; inexhaustibly; moderately; insignificantly; definitely; appreciably; perceptibly; staggeringly.

(See reach, extend.)

AMOUR

adjectives
scandalous; classic; innocent; juvenile; delicate; passionate; fanciful; restless; discreet.

AMPHITHEATER

adjectives
Gargantuan; vast; immense; natural; wooded; colossal; sylvan; shaded; massive; florid; shadowy; splendid.

AMPLE

adverbs
generously; extensively; abundantly; liberally; amazingly; overwhelmingly; gratifyingly; astonishingly; capably; enormously; hugely; voluminously; immeasurably; immensely; magnificently; stupendously; splendidly; wastefully; boundlessly; illimitably; immoderately; incredibly; surprisingly; excessively; preposterously.

AMUSE (v)

adverbs
unconsciously; constantly; superficially; inwardly; genuinely; mightily; whole-heartedly; powerfully; secretly; libidinously; vociferously; considerably; indescribably; falteringly; undisguisedly; obviously; grimly; jovially; highly; impersonally; unspeakably; obscurely; good-humoredly; tolerantly; contemptuously; harmlessly; idly; endlessly; intimately; deliriously; detachedly; cynically; maliciously; puerilely; discreetly; ironically; benevolently; magnificently; haughtily; vaguely; wistfully; unconcealedly; emptily; sophisticatedly; insipidly; sheepishly; meretriciously; irritatingly; wholesomely; child-

ishly; intriguingly; fashionably; sparklingly; barbarously.

(See entertain, divert, please.)

AMUSED

adverbs

highly; slightly; definitely; postively; mildly; uproariously; unusually; tremendously; ingeniously; cleverly; constantly; greatly; gaily; indescribably; unspeakably; secretly; tolerably; heartily; idly; grimly; suitably; vaguely; foolishly; oddly; properly; fashionably; conventionally.

AMUSEMENT

adjectives

impersonal; unspeakable; obscure; good-humored; tolerant; worldly; contemptuous; harmless; favorite; abundant; hearty; secret; elegant; solitary; idle; puzzled; after-dark; racy; traditional; endless; intimate; delirious; detached; cynical; malicious; puerile; costly; discreet; innocent; sarcastic; healthy; ironic; benevolent; magnificent; mocking; mild; considerable; grim; undisguised; haughty; round-eyed; vague; wistful; unconcealed; empty; suppressed; sophisticated; scornful; wry; ribald; sly; reminiscent; facile; sheepish; heightened; meretricious; insipid; irritating; wholesome; childish; passing; intriguing; idle; fashionable; time-killing; sparkling; barbarous; evident.

verbs

absorb in—; afford—; attend with—; betray —; contrive—; crave—; cultivate—; dedicate to—; devise—; excite—; fall into—; indulge in—; revel in—; seek—; tickle with—; vary—; —affords; —attracts; —beguiles; —detains; —distracts; —diverts; —engages; —entertains; —grows out of; —invigorates; —relaxes.

(See diversion, entertainment, pastime, sport, pleasure.)

ANACHRONISM

adjectives

ineffective; moral; unconscious; flagrant; painful; bold; impossible.

ANAESTHETIC

verbs

absorb—; administer—; apply—; breathe—; confine—; discover—; dope with—; doze under—; drug with—; employ—; experiment with—; inhale—; inject—; introduce —; localize—; numb with—; relieve with —; sniff—; spray—; undergo—; —allays; —alleviates; —benefits; —benumbs; —comforts; —deadens; —depresses; —dulls; —freezes; —induces; —paralyzes; —relieves; —renders insensible; —restricts.

(See ether, chloroform.)

ANALOGOUS

adverbs

relatively; proportionally; approximately; closely; exactly; nearly; ridiculously; truly; interestingly; strikingly; internationally; remarkably.

ANALOGY

adjectives

striking; ironic; obvious; classic; intellectual; palpable; mysterious; astonishing; exaggerated; secret.

ANALYSIS

adjectives

scientific; flawless; exact; brilliant; learned; careful; thorough; logical; painstaking; vivid; keen-sighted; cautious; sound; cogent; revealing; trenchant; penetrating; rigorous; profound; probing; searching; minute; critical; intensive; microscopic; tortuous; shallow; abstruse; absorbing; unsparing; arbitrary; inadequate; illuminating; erroneous; obscure; involved; ruthless; merciless; complex; devastating; scathing; complete; frank; straightforward; philosophic; metaphysical; auditory; primary; legal; chemical; financial; exhaustive; elaborate; compact; comprehensive; thoroughgoing; grueling; final; interrelated; deliberate; cold; accurate; subtle; pedagogic; lucid; fine-spun; perspicacious; detailed; provocative; dispassionate; uncompromising; acute; ingenious; rational; intensive; tragic; patient; forceful; skilful.

verbs

answer with—; apply—; carry out—; clarify—; defy—; descend to—; display—; elude—; employ—; examine—; exhibit—; explain by—; introduce—; involve—; proceed by—; study—; submit to—; suggest—; summarize—; tabulate—; withstand—; yield to—; —assays; —breaks up; —concludes; —correlates; —cultivates; —decomposes; —defines; —determines; —differentiates; —discovers; —identifies; —precedes; —produces; —reduces; —resolves into; —restricts; —results in; —reveals; —separates; —solves; —teaches; —traces; —uncovers; —unearths.

(See investigation, examination.)

ANALYTIC

adverbs

brilliantly; learnedly; carefully; painstakingly; skilfully; cautiously; trenchantly; rigorously; profoundly; searchingly; minutely; critically; intensively; abstrusely; ruthlessly; mercilessly; scathingly; philosophically; primarily; exhaustively; tiresomely; coldly; offensively; accurately; impersonally; patiently; uncompromisingly.

ANALYZE (v)

adverbs

fully; scarcely; scientifically; adequately; exhaustively; flawlessly; exactly; brilliantly; learnedly; carefully; thoroughly; logically; painstakingly; vividly; skilfully; cautiously; soundly; cogently; penetratingly; rigorously; profoundly; probingly; searchingly; minutely; critically; intensively; microscopically; tortuously; shallowly; abstrusely; unsparingly; inadequately; involvedly; ruthlessly; mercilessly; devastatingly; scathingly; dispassionately; frankly; straightforwardly; philosophically; metaphysically; legally; chemically; financially; exhaustively; elaborately; comprehensively; finally; accurately; subtly; pedagogically; lucidly; perspicaciously; provocatively; dispassionately; uncompromisingly; ingeniously; rationally; patiently; forcefully.

(See discriminate, resolve.)

ANARCHIST

adjectives

moral; intellectual; communistic; theoretical; unthinking; rabid.

verbs

accuse—; apprehend—; combat—; condemn—; denounce—; disperse —s; execute—; expel—; take measures against—; —advocates; —blasts; —conceives; —denies; —disregards; —endeavours; —escapes; —executes; —maintains; —masses; —orates; —plunders; —promotes disorder; —rises; —rules; —scorns; —shatters; —struggles; —theorizes; —violates.

(See communist, terrorist.)

ANARCHISTIC

adverbs

ungovernably; dangerously; alarmingly; naively; youthfully; heedlessly; hatefully; enthusiastically; lamentably; deplorably; openly; actively; defiantly; insurgently; seditiously; restively; insubordinately; mutinously; rebelliously; violently; tumultuously; incorrigibly; persistently; obstinately; treasonably.

ANARCHY

adjectives

multitudinous; malignant; emulous; lawless; social; dormant; practical; moral.

verbs

abandon—; bear—; cast into—; conceive—; confuse—; control—; cope with—; crash into—; curse—; degrade by—; drift towards —; exclude—; expel—; fall under—; overthrow—; proclaim—; realize—; revive—; subject to—; suppress—; —abolishes; —advocates; —agitates; —appeals; —conflicts with; —confuses; —connotes; —degrades; —denounces; —destroys; —disorders; —dominates; —emancipates; —frees; —hurls back; —overlaps; —overthrows; —rages; —relates to; —repudiates; —resorts to; —strikes; —threatens; —violates.

(See revolution, confusion, chaos.)

ANATHEMA

adjectives

dire; violent; involuntary; incoherent.

ANATOMY

verbs

advance—; approach—; consult—; develop —; dissect—; practice—; protect—; rely on—; reveal—; segregate—; shrink—; shrivel—; sketch—; wither—; —admits; —analyzes; —applies to; —considers; —deals with; —defines; —denotes; —details; —detects; —develops; —dissects; —investigates; —produces; —rejects; —signifies; —specializes; —teaches; —traces; —treats of.

(See science.)

ANCESTOR

adjectives

rude; far-away; august; pious; dim; divine; symbolical; barbaric; martial; devout; renowned; remote; illustrious; cave-dwelling; heroic; primitive; forgotten; venerable; respected; roistering; adventurous; astute; seafaring; contemporary; solitary-minded; immortal; tainted; prehistoric; talented; frugal; lineal; immigrant; blue-blooded; aristocratic; benighted.

verbs

address—; anger—; bury with—; descend from—; hark back to—; honor—; idealize —; idolize—; inherit from—; invoke—; propitiate—; renounce—; revere—; sleep with—s; swear by—; trace—; venerate—; worship—; —bequeaths; —blesses; —counsels; —fades; —foreruns; —influences; —precedes; —vouchsafes.

(See father.)

41

adjectives

dubious; pre-human; illustrious; revolutionary; mixed; remote; rustic; insignificant; select; healthy; hard-working; shabby; spiritual; far-renowned.

ANCHOR

verbs

back—; cast—; cat—; come to—; drag—; drop—; fasten—; fish—; forge—; foul—; free from—; grapple with—; ground—; haul up—; heave up—; hoist—; hook—; let fall—; let go—; lie at—; lift—; load—; loose—; moor—to; raise—; rest—; ride at —; shackle—; shoe—; stow—; sweep for —; throw out—; tow—; weigh—; —bites bottom; —branches; —comes home; —drags; —entangles; —fixes itself to; —fouls; — holds; —moors; —resists; —rusts; —secures; —settles; —sinks; —slides down; —stabilizes; —strikes; —takes hold.

ANECDOTAL

adverbs

interestingly; racily; risquily; graphically; sentimentally; boisterously; insipidly; fruitily; drolly; ineptly; dismally; sparklingly; ponderously; edifyingly; endlessly; childishly; pertinently; entertainingly; startlingly; shockingly; amusingly; surprisingly.

ANECDOTE

adjectives

traditional; minute; chatty; amusing; sentimental; familiar; insipid; startling; authentic; childhood; trite; pertinent; fruity; long-buried; small-town; pointed; ponderous; sparkling; endless; harmless; edifying; illustrative; droll; badly-told; touching; gossipy; trifling; dismal; antique; inept; apt; satirical.

verbs

apply—to; avoid —s; collect —s; compile —s; dispel by means of —s; edit —s; elaborate—; enrich with —s; launch into—; manufacture—; narrate—; refer to—; reject—; relate—; retail —s; spice with —s; swell —s; venture—; weaken—; —betrays; —deals with; —entertains; —interests; — treats of.

(See story, narrative, incident.)

ANGEL

adjectives

ministering; painted; household; hovering; expectant; tutelary; accursed; avenging; light-invested; grave; rapturous; cheering; ancient; compassionate; invisible; bewitch-

ing; fallen; sensuous; rude; naughty; lugubrious; attendant; sorrowing; accusing; luminous; wrathful; flame-robed; benign; pearl-colored.

verbs

cast out—; conduct—; defy—; degrade—; deify—; etherealize—; exalt—; personify —; pray to—; summon—; transform into—; worship—; —appears; —ascends; —attends; —bears; —blesses; —descends; — exemplifies; —flutters; —guards; —hovers above; —ministers to; —proclaims; —represents; —salutes; —serves; —tends; — watches; —weeps.

(See God, cherub.)

ANGER

adjectives

murderous; sullen; slow; revengeful; momentary; disheartened; fatal; clamorous; fierce; hot; uneasy; headlong; savage; proud; righteous; wholesome; controlled; loyal; strident; terrified; tolerant; inordinate; unjust; unreasoning; merciless; dull; cold; stern; carnal; blistering; ferocious; injurious; mute; violent; implacable; assumed; well-feigned; sham; dumb; speechless; suppressed; smouldering; futile; white; pale; impotent; subdued; kindling; seething; blazing; scorching; consuming; flaring; whirlwind; devouring; passionate; incipient; latent; oblivious; quivering; cooling; frenzied; jealous; parental; blackbrowed; senseless; restrained; impetuous; uncharitable; genuine; uncontrollable; boisterous; arrogant; icy; savage; contemptuous; insane; confused; concentrated; puzzled; craven.

verbs

analyze—; blind with—; bristle with—; burn with—; cast—upon; cherish—; coddle —; control—; defer—; detour—; disarm—; exhibit—; expostulate in—; flash—; flush with—; incite—; kindle—; manifest—; pacify—; pale in—; project—; provoke—; rage in—; rebuke in—; repent—; revive—; scream in—; slay in—; sting with—; strike in—; swallow—; swell with—; unleash—; upbraid in—; vent—; vex with—; visit— upon; voice—; —abates; —blazes; —boils; —burns; —bursts out; —congeals; —consumes; —dies; —distresses; —exasperates; —falls; —flames; —flares up; —floods; —grieves; —inflames; —melts; —over-excites; —rages; —rises; —ruffles; —simmers; —startles; —subsides; —throbs; —wanes; —waxes.

(See fury, rage, wrath, exasperation, ire,

animosity, resentment, vexation, pique, frenzy.)

ANGER (v)

adverbs
violently; murderously; sullenly; slowly; revengefully; momentarily; fatally; clamorously; fiercely; hotly; savagely; inordinately; righteously; unjustly; unreasoningly; mercilessly; ferociously; injuriously; violently; implacably; speechlessly; futilely; impotently; passionately; frenziedly; jealously; senselessly; genuinely.

(See irritate, displease, offend, provoke.)

ANGLE

adjectives
salient; rakish; technical; astonishing; intricate; remote; projecting; peculiar; social; unfortunate; legal; odd; divergent (pl); elevated; oblique; obtuse; acute; precise; humanitarian.

verbs
bisect—; derive—; draw—; figure—; form —; increase—; inscribe—; maintain—; measure—; proceed from—; produce—; reckon—; trisect—; —adjoins; —corresponds.

ANGLER

adjectives
enthusiastic; insatiable; beginning; ardent; jubilant; expert; practiced; bungling; awkward; skilled; proficient; able.

ANGRY

adverbs
senselessly; sullenly; intolerably; hotly; obviously; righteously; foolishly; ridiculously; dangerously; icily; genuinely; uncontrollably; passionately; violently; sternly; implacably; unjustly; inordinately; insanely; naturally; ludicrously; unnaturally; curiously; strangely.

ANGUISH

adjectives
nameless; unspeakable; excessive; bodily; nauseating; dumb; mental; excruciating; keen; maddening; intolerable; sheer; startled; mortal; hopeless; indescribable; frightful; unbearable; bitter; profound; acute; tearless; soul-piercing; occult; strangling; perpetual; fierce; insufferable; universal; maternal; jealous; subdued; transient; dull; stifling; short-lived; audible; intimate; unuttered; grim; heart-rending; despairing; spiritual; killing; sickening; dark; abrupt;

amazed; insupportable; passionate; sensational.

verbs
burst with—; choke with—; consume with—; cry out in—; endure—; escape—; heal—; hearken to—; heed—; lessen—; overwhelm with—; soothe—; strike with—; suffer—; tremble with—; vent—; wring the mind with—; waste one's soul in—; writhe in—; —oppresses; —rends; —splits; —tears; — wrings.

(See distress, pain, anxiety, agony, misery, torture.)

ANGULAR

adverbs
forbiddingly; unattractively; raw-bonedly; repulsively; stiffly; absurdly; awkwardly; gawkily; pathetically; ludicrously; ridiculously; youthfully; painfully; pitifully; wretchedly; distressingly; crookedly.

ANGULARITY

adjectives
solid; raw-boned; stiff; absurd; awkward.

ANIMAL

adjectives
bold; pugnacious; ferocious; uncongenial; stiff-legged; indigenous; alpine; envenomed; elusive; heroic; familiar; social; patient; malignant; sensual; sentient; domesticated; performing; herbivorous; meek; rational; predatory; carnivorous; outlandish; articulate; restive; balky; well-groomed; ignoble; prowling; hunted; elusive; preternatural; reasoning; hoofed; pampered; white-sterned; emaciated; ruminant; noble; vigorous; throwing; marine; native; diabolical; graminivorous; frugivorous; armorial; agile; grotesque; docile; burly; aquatic; water-loving; amphibious; savage; invertebrate; porcine; devoted; thin-skinned; intelligent; responsive; affectionate; tractable; sagacious; helpless; magnificent; sleek; stunning; reclining; trapped; tethered; wounded; careening; stricken; harassed; fretting; snorting; panic-stricken; squealing; recalcitrant; maddened; infuriated; snarling; blood-thirsty; enraged; depraved; gregarious; prowling; omnivorous; albino; lower; furry; unshod; gaunt; cat-like; thick-skinned; sure-footed; nervous; stray; castrated; cautious; fabulous; marsupial; mangy; pachydermatous; oviparous; refractory.

verbs
breed—s; cage—; classify —s; clutch—;

conserve —s; corral —s; cross —s; decoy —; derive from—; discover—; distinguish —; domesticate—; dominate—; educate—; encounter—; ensnare—; exhaust—; exhibit —; experiment with—; exploit—; exterminate—; feed—; fondle—; groom—; harness —; improve—; infuriate—; inspect—; ·mate —; pat—; protect—; raise—; reproduce—; revert to—; search for—; stalk—; suffocate —; track—; train—; wheel—; —charges; —s cluster; —curls up; —feeds; —forages; —gestates; —gnaws; —hibernates; —hunts; —migrates; —s multiply; —occurs in; — perishes; —rages; —ranges; —reproduces; —roars; —scurries; —senses; —sniffs; — succumbs; —suckles.

(See beast, creature, brute.)

(See also specific animals, such as bear, cat, lion, etc.)

ANIMATE (v)

adverbs

impiously; fascinatingly; gladly; garrulously; characteristically; vividly; dazzingly; delightfully; picturesquely; mechanically; preternaturally.

(See stimulate, rouse.)

ANIMATED

adverbs

delightfully; eagerly; garrulously; excitedly; nervously; happily; rapturously; ecstatically; unusually; hilariously; gleefully; merrily; lightly; joyously; cheerfully; blithely; sparklingly; pleasingly; playfully; racily; energetically; vigorously; restlessly; resolutely; determinedly.

ANIMATION

adjectives

fascinating; glad; suspended; perspiring; garrulous; contagious; social; characteristic; vivid; dazzling; delightful; playful; transient; picturesque; returning; intense; mechanical; preternatural.

verbs

attain—; behold—; bestow—upon; buoy up with—; breathe out—; burst into—; counterfeit—; enliven with—; evince—; feign—; fire with—; impart—; incite to—; inject—; inspire with—; instil—; manifest—; provoke to—; recite with—; restore—; revive —; sparkle with—; suspend—; vitalize with —; woo with—; —enlivens; —fatigues; —flags; —flares up; —jades; —wearies.

(See vivacity, life, gayety.)

ANIMOSITY

adjectives

intensified; personal; sullen; jealous; ec-

clesiastical; rancorous; deep-seated; vindictive; savage; deadly; implacable; partisan; smouldering; relentless; emotional; bitter.

verbs

arouse—toward; bear—; break out into—; effect—; excite—; feed—; feel—; incite— ; incur—; inherit—; manifest—; nurse—; regret—; revive—; stir up—; tend toward —; unveil—; —alienates; —breaks up; — damages; —disrupts; —exists between; — hinders; —wavers.

(See rancor, hatred, enmity.)

ANKLE

adjectives

delicate; generous; fragile; beefy; bony; wrenched; swollen; immaculate; slender; aristocratic; well-turned.

ANNALS

adjectives

dramatic; fabulous; mythic; factual; voluminous; priceless; ancestral; contemporary; tragic; fragmentary; historic; literary; bloodstained; ancient; gossipy; racy.

ANNEX (v)

adverbs

formally; swiftly; utterly; forcefully; readily; craftily; partially.

(See take.)

ANNIHILATE (v)

adverbs

utterly; surely; swiftly; mercifully; unprecedentedly; craftily.

(See destroy.)

ANNIHILATION

adjectives

utter; sure; swift; terrible; bloody; merciful; beastly; unprecedented; crafty.

ANNIVERSARY

verbs

anticipate—; applaud—; commemorate—: dramatize—; fete—; institute—; observe—; disregard—; stamp—; —follows; —is marked by; —recurs.

(See observance, celebration, day, event.)

ANNOUNCE (v)

adverbs

flatly; vociferously; oracularly; mercifully; sententiously; paternally; clamorously; explicitly; pompously; publicly; simultaneously; reluctantly; solemnly; arrogantly; virtuously; ostentatiously; formally; blandly;

abruptly; jokingly; officially; unreservedly; significantly; jubilantly; gleefully; authoritatively; blithely; flatteringly; finally; mournfully; dramatically; haltingly; brazenly; prematurely; tersely; gayly; briskly.
(See proclaim, advertise, publish.)

ANNOUNCEMENT

adjectives
lurid; flattering; calamitous; conciliatory; final; implicit; successive (pl); encouraging; initial; mournful; drastic; dramatic; droning; halting; formal; brazen; devastating; pending; dire; premature; exclusive; vain-glorious; formidable; post-prandial; terse.

verbs
broadcast—; cheer—; confirm—; declare—; deliver—; dispatch—; disseminate—; misconstrue—; notify by—; reiterate—; rise at—; substantiate—; —astounds; —bursts upon; —gives notice; —proclaims; —publicizes; —overtakes; —takes by surprise.
(See proclamation, advertisement, notice.)

ANNOY (v)

adverbs
blusteringly; obviously; sorely; intensely; greatly; positively; unduly; temporarily; mildly; savagely; markedly; jealously; frivolously; unavoidably; excessively.
(See trouble, aggravate.)

ANNOYANCE

adjectives
petty; unconcealed; prolonged; unique; undue; shocked; temporary; intense; mild; savage; internal; mock; marked; aristocratic; impotent; sharp; repressed; obvious; inhospitable; nervous; dangerous; jealous; frivolous; unavoidable; private.

verbs
avoid—; condemn—; dislike—; flush with —; frown with—; generate—; molest with —; occasion—; plague with—; rumble in —; temper—; tolerate—; vent—; —disgusts; —injures; —persists; —returns; —troubles; —vexes.
(See vexation, irritation.)

ANNOYING

adverbs
mischievously; accidentally; disastrously; devilishly; diabolically; intentionally; outrageously; painfully; teasingly; persistently; unintentionally; purposely; defiantly; revengefully; abominably; exceptionally;

characteristically; wretchedly; tormentingly; maliciously; unbecomingly; increasingly; senselessly; unspeakably; deliberately.

ANNUL (v)

adverbs
virtually; wisely; quickly; unthinkingly; promptly; shrewdly.
(See abolish, reverse.)

ANOINT (v)

adverbs
sacrificially; religiously; perfunctorily; daily; occasionally.
(See smear.)

ANOMALY

adjectives
monstrous; dreadful; curious; noble; racial; peculiar.

ANONYMITY

adjectives
scrupulous; illegitimate; heartless; carefully-preserved; politic; necessary; defensive; desperate; cowardly; enforced.

verbs
bury in—; clothe in—; disguise in—; ensconce in—; hide in—; lend—; maintain —; mystify with—; preserve—; prowl in—; remain in—; resort to—; retire from—, skulk in—; slink in—; steal into—; surround with—; veil in—; write in—; —cloaks; —conceals; —impresses; —masks.
(See secrecy.)

ANONYMOUS

adverbs
mysteriously; naturally; obviously; necessarily; securely; safely; forever; scrupulously; legitimately; politically; defensively; timidly; bashfully; shyly; unaccountably; evasively; hopelessly; irretrievably; astonishingly; vaguely; perplexingly; undecipherably; unfathomably; enigmatically.

ANSWER

adjectives
definite; clinching; efficient; contemptuous; indignant; accurate; concrete; requisite; affirmative; negative; disconsolate; evasive; categorical; magnanimous; flippant; consenting; authoritative; verbal; comprehensive; bewildered; favorable; impatient; economical; unconsidered; worthy; doleful; enigmatical; discouraging; meaningless; deft; admissible; explicit; perfect; memorable; quavering; stubborn; sufficient; ready; boorish; cryptic; measured; boun-

tiful; definitive; vague; vehement; imperious; impertinent; oral; candid; argumentative; haughty; laconic; convincing; soul-sufficing; admirable; casual; amazing; proud; skilful; scorching; rash; incoherent; intelligible; insulting; fit; apt; indulgent; practical; animated; reassuring; respectful; impressive; comforting; satisfactory; courteous; illuminating; logical; conclusive; cool; pertinent; surly; equivocal; irritable; insolent; scathing; lame; harsh; dilatory; unorthodox; uninteresting; relevant; prodigal; disquieting; sardonic; pungent; sharp; exultant; dramatic; breathless; crushing; partial; tentative; cautious; inevitable; instantaneous; simultaneous; ultimate; rueful; unconscious; impromptu; time-honored; prescribed; mechanical; mollified; confident; significant; broken; impetuous; impulsive; fateful; matter-of-fact; irrefutable; agnostic; mild.

verbs

address—; appeal for—; approve—; bark —; bind to—; confine—; constitute—; defend—; deliver—; draw—from; echo—; entreat—; evade—; evolve—; exhort—; express—; extort—; fire back—; fling back —; frame—; fumble—; glean—; hang on —; hit ,upon—; justify—; marvel at—; merit—; mock—; muffle—; owe—; petition—; protest—; reject—; respond with—; signal—; snap—; stir to—; supply—; sustain—; sweeten—; tabulate —s; tear—from; volunteer—; word—; wrench—from; —accuses; —arises; —charges; —claims; —clamors; —contradicts; —implies; —informs; —invalidates; —pleases; —pledges; —rebuts; —reveals; —satisfies; —solves; —states.

(See reply, retort, response, defense.)

ANSWER (v)

adverbs

gruffly; candidly; haughtily; uncomfortably; energetically; evasively; bluntly; darkly; breathlessly; sulkily; affectionately; sagely; casually; volubly; listlessly; persistently; yawningly; carelessly; pointedly; enigmatically; stubbornly; proudly; definitely; tartly; hysterically; reluctantly; sadly; falteringly; unconcernedly; gravely; doggedly; directly; sententiously; completely; triumphantly; hoarsely; brusquely; laughingly; stolidly; cautiously; curtly; impatiently; nervously; desultorily; affirmatively; visibly; faithfully; bitterly; obstinately; thoughtfully; impetuously; effectually; guardedly; evasively; bravely; readily; distinctly; candidly; respectfully; emphati-

cally; squeamishly; ponderingly; surlily; coherently; challengingly; cynically; bashfully; knowingly; passionately; petulantly; hotly; non-committally; rancorously; instantly; simply; affirmatively; monosyllabically; laconically; directly; excitedly; evasively; indignantly; civilly; mechanically; fantastically; meekly; scoffingly; confusedly; definitely; pathetically; pertinaciously; wistfully; accurately; soothingly; tremulously; peevishly; disconsolately; evasively; categorically; verbally; comprehensively; bewilderedly; economically; worthily; dolefully; enigmatically; deftly; explicitly; perfectly; quaveringly; cryptically; measuredly; vehemently; imperiously; scorchingly; rashly; fitly; aptly; indulgently; animatedly; uninterestingly; relevantly; prodigally; disquietingly; sardonically; partially; tentatively; ruefully; matter-of-factly; mildly.

(See reply, respond, concede.)

ANSWERABLE

adverbs

personally; awfully; painfully; seriously; undoubtedly; terribly; officially; directly.

ANT

adjectives

antenna-manipulating; assiduous; destructive; exemplified; ever-questing; eternally-constructing; encroaching; frugal; formic-producing; garnering; gregarious; greedy; hoarding; harvesting; industrious; persistent; swarming; scurrying; sugar-seeking; store-collecting; troublesome; unpopular; wise.

verbs

burden—; combat —s; consider—; cultivate —s; disturb —s; examine—; exhibit —s; exterminate —s; fall victim to —s; infest with —s; go to —s; observe —s; purge of —s; spray —s; study—; teem with —s; —s abound; —accomplishes; —achieves; —accumulates; —s adapt themselves; —s amass; —ascends; —attacks; —bites; —bores into; —s build; —bustles; —s capture; —s collect; —s colonize; —s consolidate; —s construct; —s contend for; —s converge upon; —crawls; —s crowd; —defends; —s denude the area; —s deposit eggs; —descends; —despoils; —destroys; —s devastate; —devours; —digs; —dissects; —dominates; —dwells; —s eddy from; —emerges; —endures; —s enslave; —entombs; —excavates; —explores; —exudes; —s find their way; —s flit about; —s fly; —forages; —gathers; —gorges; —guards; —harvests; —hastens; —hatches; —heaps; —hibernates; —s hol-

low out; —hustles; —imprisons; —s insinuate themselves; —s invade; —labors; —lays up food; —mates; —s migrate; —s nest; —s nurse their young; —occupies; —s organize; —performs; —s pillage; —s preserve; —s pour in; —races; —s raid; —s ravage; —reconnoiters; —regurgitates; —roams; —roves; —rushes; —scouts; —scurries; —secretes; —seizes; —s share; —shears; —s socialize; —stings; —stores; —stows; —s stream up; —struggles; —s surge out; —survives; —s swarm; —s throng; —transports; —trudges; —utilizes; —vanishes; —wars.
(See insect, termite.)

ANTAGONISM

adjectives
political; bitter; surly; heartfelt; overwhelming; violent; subtle; mutual; professional; recurring; stiffening; fundamental; religious; bristling; deep-seated; social; sectional; persistent; racial; pronounced; ingrained; unrelenting, outspoken; vindictive; implacable; lofty; subdued; traditional; compromising; monosyllabic.

verbs
accentuate—; adjust—; balance—; conquer —; create—; develop—; express—; heighten —; increase—; mark—; oppose—; rack by —; risk—; rouse—; soften -; stimulate—; struggle with—; topple—; weaken—; —thwarts; —weakens.
(See opposition, hostility, resistance.)

ANTAGONIST

adjectives
legitimate; formidable; potential; appointed; contemptible; implacable; dreaded; defeated; crafty; redoubtable; irreconcilable; fallen; wary; agile; relentless; acrid.

verbs
admonish—; belittle—; best—; daunt—; defeat—; fence with—; overcome—; overpower—; overwhelm—; —argues; —assails; —battles; —collapses; —contends; —contests; —counteracts; —disputes; —languishes; —opposes; —relaxes; —slumps; —springs up.
(See opponent, rival, assailant, foe, adversary.)

ANTAGONISTIC

adverbs
violently; bitterly; subtly; fundamentally; persistently; racially; socially; politically; openly; outspokenly; vindictively; traditionally; formidably; unreasonably; irreconcil-

ably; relentlessly; utterly; strangely; inexplicably; essentially; palpably; undeniably; basically; alarmingly; unaccountably.

ANTAGONIZE (v)

adverbs
derisively; politically; bitterly; overwhelmingly; violently; professionally; recurringly; fundamentally; religiously; socially; sectionally; persistently; racially; outspokenly; vindictively; implacably.
(See oppose, hinder.)

ANTECEDENT

adjectives
mental; worthy; historic; dwarfish; undeniable; necessary; grammatical.

ANTHEM

adjectives
pealing; eternal; blessed; doleful; joyous; heavenly; resounding.

ANTIC

adjectives
unconscious; infantile; puerile; capricious; ridiculous; glib; sterile; gay; exuberant; mad; absurd; droll; small-boy; mechanical; erratic; drunken; boisterous.

ANTICIPATE (v)

adverbs
curiously; fondly; reasonably; pessimistically; confidently; mentally; ecstatically; gleefully; joyously; originally; pleasurably; eagerly; passionately; blissfully; gloatingly; hungrily; ardently; impatiently; avidly; tremblingly; greedily; reasonably.
(See expect, apprehend.)

ANTICIPATION

adjectives
unhesitating; sensitive; charming; bright; daring; joyful; mysterious; pleasurable; eager; greedy; sanguine; exhilarating; passionate; picturesque; lascivious; tingling; heightened; lively; thrilling; blissful; undefined; morose; gloating; hungry; ferocious; keen; alert; ardent; impatient; avid; trembling; crushing; panic-stricken; reasonable; quivering.

verbs
beam with—; delight in—; look forward with—; pardon—; resist—of; restrain—; revel in—; rob—; toil in—of; tremble in—; —cheers; —enhances; —excites; —gladdens; —incites; —stimulates.
(See expectation, hope.)

ANTICIPATORY

adverbs

joyously; mysteriously; pleasurably; excitedly; hysterically; passionately; thrillingly; hungrily; unreasonably; avidly; impatiently; ardently; keenly; hopefully; eagerly; charmingly; joyfully; mischievously; hastily; incontinently; fervently; anxiously; greedily; impetuously; crazily; madly; feverishly; nervously.

ANTIDOTE

adjectives

specific; effective; cursed; pungent; stupefying; vile.

ANTIPATHY

adjectives

blind; cordial; mortal; unaccountable; mutual; invincible; deep-rooted; natural; rational; bigoted; tacit; peculiar.

verbs

admit—; be born of—; date—; display—; dispose toward—; dwell in—; excite—; hold—; imply—; introduce—; mark—; remove—; rouse—; saturate with—; turn from—; —blazes; —burns; —manifests; —melts; —originates from; —prejudices; —puzzles; —restricts; —takes root.

(See aversion, enmity, dislike.)

ANTIQUARY

adjectives

ardent; musical; distinguished; honorary; eminent; passionate; shallow; classical; hoary; curious.

ANTIQUE

adjectives

charming; spurious; rare; valuable; precious; genuine; colorless; fraudulent.

adverbs

genuinely; expensively; unquestionably; authentically; truly; actually; veritably; really; pricelessly; richly; decoratively; garishly; gorgeously; gaudily; ornamentally; deceptively; fraudulently; cheaply; showily; smartly; trickily; foolishly; flimsily; absurdly; beautifully; unbelievably; spuriously.

ANTIQUITY

adjectives

unknown; remote; honorable; pagan; venerable; traceable; hoar; classical; quaint; dead; historical; respectable; solemn; remote; fabulous; feudal; fascinating; observable.

ANTISEPTIC

adjectives

powerful; intestinal; efficient.

verbs

act as—; advise—; apply—; bathe in—; compare—; develop—; dilute—; discard—; dust with—; embalm in—; employ—; expose to—; glaze with—; immerse in—; impregnate with—; inject—; introduce—; operate with—; paint with—; soak in—; sterilize with—; surround with—; swab with—; wash with—; wrap in—; —acts; —aids; —aims at; —arrests; —burns; —cleans; —combats; —counteracts; —destroys; —exercises; —fulfils; —functions; —influences; —inhibits; —insures; —irritates; —kills; —preserves; —prevents; —protects; —purifies; —reaches; —relieves; —removes; —renders; —replaces; —restrains; —restricts; —retards; —rids of; —serves; —sterilizes; —thwarts.

adverbs

genuinely; effectively; valuably; infallibly; powerfully; extremely; heroically; mildly; perfectly; soothingly; correctively; specifically; simply; safely; beneficially; beneficently; advantageously; commendably; highly; essentially.

ANTITHESIS

adjectives

vile; complacent; inharmonious; striking; complete; false.

ANTLERS

adjectives

budding; branching; cresting; clashing; defiant; deciduous; graceful; gouging; fathom-wide; interlocking; lordly; massive; menacing; pronged; palm-tree (moose); periodically-shed; regal; sail-like (moose); self-entrapping; tined; velvety; vigorously-beating; wicked.

verbs

adorn with—; bear—; brandish—; carry—; decorate with—; form—; gore with—; impale on—; lock—; mount—; ornament with —; renew—; shed—; snag—; solidify—; spear—; spike—; sprout—; stunt—; toss—; weaken—; —branch out; —develop; —fork; —menace; —pierce; —protrude; —rend; —stab; —threaten.

(See horn.)

ANVIL

adjectives

clanging; crude; fiery; harsh; hammer-worn; historic; mighty; massive; steely; spark-emitting; shaping; transforming; traditional; invincible; proving; resistant; unvarying; unyielding; Vulcan-symbolizing.

verbs

balance on—; beat on—; bend on—; clink on—; crack on—; fashion on—; flatten on—; forge on—; hammer on—; harden on—; jangle on—; shape on—; strike—; twist on—; —clashes; —resounds; —rings; —sustains.

(See bell.)

ANXIETY

adjectives

touching; breathless; irrepressible; excessive; torturing; slight; supreme; utmost; undue; considerable; deep; vague; absorbing; unsatisfied; paternal; indescribable; fretting; gnawing; indeterminate; haggard; unceasing; infinite; unavoidable; financial; perceptible; predominant; tender; insufferable; connubial; excited; feverish; brooding; trembling; pious; deep-seated; maternal; agonizing; bated; flushed; mortal; worldly; cruel; morbid; devastating; betrayed; hysterical; nerve-racking; frantic; breath-taking; mental; domestic; motherly; painful; intense; unjust; sleepless; poignant; sick; grueling; heart-broken; keen; acute; soul-searing; gratuitous; relieved; drab; unwarranted; common; unspoken; hidden; repressed; troublesome; throbbing; annoying; sudden; subconscious; discernible; undeceived; human; suppressed; wearisome; impatient.

verbs

accompany with—; betray—; burden with —; create—; disturb by—; evince—; free from—; gaze with—; harass with—; increase—; manifest—; overshadow with—; reveal—; seize by—; shake with—; strain with—; trouble with—; wear to shreds with—; —agitates; —clouds; —constricts; —depresses; —disturbs; —etches; —prevails; —seizes; —vexes.

(See solicitude, apprehension, worry, fear, care, misgiving.)

ANXIOUS

adverbs

over; unnaturally; painfully; laughably; ridiculously; pathetically; lamentably; curiously; eagerly; abnormally; naturally; touchingly; supremely; unduly; deeply; indescribably; perceptibly; tenderly; suspiciously; excitedly; frantically; frenziedly; inexplicably; nervously; timidly; terribly; keenly; pitiably; miserably.

APARTMENT

adjectives

luxurious; sumptuous; modern; bachelor; tawdry; gorgeous; immaculate; dignified; old-fashioned; impressive; swanky; spacious; cooped-up; dusty; dingy; squalid; isolated; unpersonalized; ground-floor; terraced; doll-size; private; commodious; magnificent; dirty; immense; whitewashed; dimly-lighted; home-like; shabby; imposing; distinctive; charming; elegant; well-ordered; ill-furnished; communal.

verbs

assign to—s; billet in —s; divide into —s; ensconce in—; fit out—; occupy—; wreck —.

(See room, house.)

APATHETIC

adverbs

stupidly; dully; strangely; abnormally; alarmingly; weakly; heavily; stolidly; vacantly; ridiculously; unnaturally; singularly; oddly; curiously; unaccountably; irritatingly; shockingly; callously; coldly; carelessly; hopelessly; unpardonably.

APATHY

adjectives

selfish; weary; dream-like; despairing; stagnant; incredible; dull; immovable; resigned; settled; curious; growing; strange; enveloping; political; unaffected; accustomed; complete.

verbs

denote—; disturb—; encounter—; engender —; escape—; free from—; forsake—; master—; overcome—; produce—; result in—; rouse from—; signify—; sink into—; suffer —; suppress—; tolerate—; —chills; —paralyzes; —prevails; —signifies.

(See indifference, lethargy.)

APE

adjectives

grotesque; lumbering; chattering; soot-colored; restless; anthropoid; man-like; monstrous.

verbs

descend from—; —chatters; —clambers; —claws; —crouches; —dances; —drops to earth; —gallops off; —imitates; —leaps;

—lodges in; —lumbers; —mimics; —plucks; —resembles; —screams; —springs; —sways; —swings; —yelps.

(See monkey, animal.)

APE (v)

adverbs

comically; sedulously; grotesquely; lumberingly; chatteringly; restlessly; monstrously; shamelessly; ludicrously.

(See imitate, mimic.)

APERTURE

adjectives

narrow; barred; grated; half-moon; yawning; ungarnished; ragged; circular; limiting.

APHORISM

adjectives

favorite; pregnant; cynical; resounding; sparkling; hackneyed; abominable; pithy; selfish.

APOLOGETIC

adverbs

awkwardly; humbly; sincerely; nervously; slavishly; hastily; instantly; preposterously; disgustingly; unnecessarily; skillfully; sufficiently; reluctantly; profoundly; deeply; tearfully; pathetically; incoherently; sheepishly; half-heartedly; confusedly; honestly; openly; generously; embarrassingly; miserably; eagerly.

APOLOGY

adjectives

practical; humble; voluble; metrical; nervous; groveling; abject; handsome; awkward; universal; hasty; muttered; cynical; preposterous; skillful; suitable; sufficient; sincere; rapturous; profound; exaggerated; strongly-worded; pathetic; pitiful; tearful; murmured; mumbled; incoherent; obscure; sheepish; mute; half-hearted; amazed; mental; public; automatic.

verbs

acknowledge—; attack—; attempt—; convey—; elicit—; express—; favor with—; imply—; indulge in—ies; plead for—; refuse—; shame into—; stammer—; tender—; trouble with—; wave aside—; —alters; —atones; —excuses; —vindicates.

(See defense, confession, excuse, plea, alibi.)

APOLOGY (v)

adverbs

meekly; pitifully; gruffly; profusely; humbly; volubly; nervously; abjectly; grovelingly; awkwardly; cynically; exaggeratedly; suitably; skillfully; pathetically; tearfully; incoherently; sheepishly; half-heartedly; automatically.

(See justify, defend, vindicate.)

APOSTLE

adjectives

current; intrepid; inspired; non-ecclesiastical; ordained; recalcitrant; self-appointed; subsequently-commissioned; specifically-chosen; treacherous; virtuous; world-denouncing.

verbs

alienate —s; bar —s; call —s; commission —s; delegate—; elect—; gain —s; gather —s; hail—s; initiate—; lead—s; martyr —s; ordain —s; persecute —s; quote—; regulate —s; select —s; send forth —s; —accompanies; —administers; —advocates; —executes; —leads; —performs miracles; —preaches; —proclaims; —records; —scatters.

(See witness.)

APPALLING

adverbs

grievously; sorely; bitterly; painfully; distressingly; excruciatingly; hauntingly; gruesomely; horridly; piercingly; tormentingly; torturingly; deplorably; disastrously; dreadfully; execrably; fearfully; frightfully; insufferably; insupportably; intolerably; odiously; oppressively; pathetically; ruefully; shockingly; woefully; touchingly; unbearably; terrifically.

APPARATUS

adjectives

dust-collecting; elaborate; abundant; scientific; perceptive; sentient; makeshift; curative; simple; intricate; complicated; ghastly; imperfect; digestive; inefficient; ingenious; culinary; new; ponderous; expensive; thinking; hefting; spectroscopic; murderous; solemn.

verbs

adapt—; adjust—; apply—; demonstrate—; design—; employ—; equip with—; evolve —; experiment with—; gear—; guard—; invent—; manipulate—; modernize—; provide—; put—in motion; set up—; simpli-

(See device, machine, tool.)

fy—; tinker with—; toy with—; —facilitates; —functions.

APPAREL

adjectives

glorious; superfluous; trim; homely; fashionable; smart; coarse; becoming; gorgeous; exquisite; ceremonious; luxurious; decorous; flamboyant; plain.

verbs

adorn in—; array in—; attire in—; behold —; change—; clothe in—; deck in—; don —; embroider—; equip with—; fashion—; fit—; furnish—; ornament—; outfit with—; prepare—; provide with—; rig with—; snatch at—; —beautifies; —conceals; —enhances; —proclaims.

(See clothing, dress, raiment.)

APPARENT

adverbs

plainly; conspicuously; downright; undeniably; clearly; definitely; flagrantly; glaringly; notoriously; openly; constantly; easily; strikingly; reasonably; shamefully; outrageously; dangerously; plaguedly; perilously.

APPARITION

adjectives

false; glorious; formidable; celestial; enchanting; distinguished; impatient; frightful; phenomenal; monstrous; intruding; startling; soulless; personal; exquisite; grisly; blushing; unpleasant; bloody; fantastic; overwhelming; ill-omened; black; ghostly; miraculous; horrid; singular; continuous.

verbs

authenticate—; believe in —s; disprove—; divine—; exhibit—; generate—; imagine—; occasion—; perceive—; produce—; shroud —; summon—; —s abound; —appears; —comes forth; —groans; —haunts; —lures; —suspends; —vanishes; —warns.

(See specter, ghost, phantom, illusion.)

APPEAL

adjectives

effective; universal; pathetic; emphatic; overt; contagious; impassioned; dramatic; modern; sorrowful; mute; unwitting; infinite; frail; sudden; potential; lamentable; eternal; frantic; mournful; diversified; rude; artless; inharmonious; constant; visible; urgent; boisterous; manifest; felicitous; irresistible; self-respecting; gastronomic; singular; persistent; troubled; popular; manly; matchless; unconscious; skillful; powerful; agonizing; unanswerable; eloquent; psychological; despairing; qualified; humanitarian; tragic; genuine; lasting; sad; unspoken; pitiable; speechless; crushing; fiery; piteous; tender; shrill; plaintive; hypnotic; sensuous; unavailing; habitual; emotional; enticing; alluring; joyous; visual; wonderful; deafening; logical; lovable; warm; convincing; devout; childish; rare; luxurious; stirring; lusty; courageous; challenging; feminine; public; delicate; artistic; magic; poetic; world-wide; human; timid; hurt; solemn; abject; weak; vague; adventurous; whimsical; strange; sensational; animated; electrifying; magnetic; tremendous; spectacular; imploring; wistful; timely; poignant; demagogical; superficial; panic-stricken; vain; inflammatory; dumb; admirable; olfactory; savory; mysterious; abnormal; sporadic; prophetic; distinct; comprehensive; gripping; unique; strong; intense; spontaneous; overbearing; sympathetic; strident; truculent; blatant; unvoiced.

verbs

abandon—; address—; admit—; afford—; bolster—; broadcast—; claim—; decline—; deny—, desist in—; discourage—; disregard—; enact—; exercise—; file—; give notice of—; grant—; institute—; invoke—; involve—; justify—; lose—; merit—; modify—; nullify—; present—; prevent—; privilege to—; prosecute—; provide—; provide security for—; question—; refuse—; regulate—; rely on—; render—; renew—; resist—; respond to—; review—; rule—; schedule—; stir by—; subject to—; submit to—; succumb to—; support—; voice—; whine—; yield to—; —engrosses; —fails; —reverses.

(See entreaty, petition, application, request, prayer.)

APPEAL (v)

adverbs

strangely; frantically; directly; strongly; confidently; constantly; irresistibly; forcibly; specially; powerfully; perpetually; effectively; dramatically; sorrowfully; mutely; strongly; mournfully; artlessly; rudely; urgently; boisterously; eloquently; tragically; piteously; tenderly; emotionally; shrilly; deafeningly; logically; stirringly; warmly; lustily; courageously; publicly; abjectly; wistfully; stridently; truculently; blatantly; outspokenly; mysteriously; grippingly; uniquely; sympathetically.

(See entreat, invoke.)

APPEAR (v)

adverbs

conspicuously; malignantly; impressively; presently; portentously; perpetually; tardily; distinctly; substantially; simultaneously;

miraculously; hesitatingly; posthumously; anonymously; manifestly; commandingly; mysteriously; astoundingly; exotically; flamboyantly; phlegmatically; demurely; ethereally; slovenly; ferociously; unhealthily; obtrusively; majestically; spectrally; inscrutably.

(See emerge, seem, look, resemble.)

APPEARANCE

adjectives

august; pompous; distinguished; stately; austere; noble; commanding; charming; cordial; worthy; antiquated; venerable; comfortable; immaculate; sleek; well-fed; quaint; luscious; artistic; dainty; lovely; comely; gorgeous; untidy; uncouth; angular; ungainly; forlorn; shabby; genteel; plaintive; somber; mysterious; weird; eerie; astounding; arresting; striking; singular; sprightly; grotesque; rakish; massive; robust; rugged; emaciated; deceitful; cadaverous; unearthly; desolate; quarrelsome; offending; miserable; sullen; disgusting; ungraceful; incongruous; gross; flamboyant; resentful; jaded; phlegmatic; grim; physical; youthful; nautical; grave-like; nun-like; orderly; unkempt; park-like; rabbit-like; clerk-like; mournful; exotic; ethereal; leonine; tolerable; ludicrous; poverty-stricken; fragile; casual; contrite; slovenly; dismaying; unfortunate; disjointed; sunken; bedraggled; animated; faint; diaphanous; picturesque; slothful; worm-eaten; contradictory; stern; benevolent; wretched; vulgar; dilapidated; external; promising; visual; ducal; inviting; ideal; squalid; sedate; outward; greasy; attractive; distinctive; ursine; demure; decorative; satanic; fearful; vacant; independent; portentous; beneficent; dignified; mottled; studious; stupid; timid; opalescent; ferocious; prepossessing; sickly; festive; reconciliatory; tawdry; impoverished; voluntary; scattered; deserted; prosperous; famished; thumbworn; unhealthy; reverential; respectable; swing-like; school-teacherish; unobstrusive; weedy; natty; frank; antediluvian; genuine; brave; flattering; material; palatial; battered; dressy; individual; variegated; watered; majestic; spectral.

verbs

come into—; detect—; disclaim—; discredit —; disfigure—; display—; involve—; greet —; judge by—; observe—; parade—; perceive by —s; present an—; preserve —s; put in—; ruffle—; transfigure—; transform —; —arrests; —belies; —repels.

(See aspect.)

APPEASE (*v*)

adverbs

inadequately; lightly; painstakingly; fully; completely.

(See pacify, calm, reconcile, propitiate.)

APPELLATION

adjectives

equivocal; false; incongruous; inappropriate; ill-mannered; heathenish; phantom; elegant; jocose; permanent; trite; hated; affectionate.

APPENDIX
(*anatomy*)

verbs

drain—; excise—; freeze—; incise—; inflame—; locate—; perforate—; remove—; —adheres; —bursts; —infects; —poisons; —ravages; —suppurates; —swells.

APPENDIX
(*book*)

adjectives

derogatory; contributory; complementary; concomitant; accessory; essential; explanatory; prolonged; solemn; supernumerary; superfluous; statistical.

verbs

advise by—; affix—; consult—; insert—; refer to—; relate in—; review in—; —concurs; —contributes; —directs; —guides; —introduces.

(See addition.)

APPERTAIN (*v*)

adverbs

unquestionably; undoubtedly; certainly; solely; exclusively.

APPETITE

adjectives

unmanageable; eager; inordinate; ravenous; cavernous; voracious; squeamish; keen; jaded; gluttonous; rude; depraved; abnormal; unappeased; phenomenal; prodigious; robust; natural; sharpened; vicious; eccentric; enormous; monstrous; gross; gigantic; sensitive; coarse; languid; sponge-like; pampered; devouring; herbivorous; rude; husky; boundless; leaden; capricious; perverted; obscene; unashamed; sleepy; sensual; catholic; brutish; perennial; inactive; lusty; insatiate; animal; satisfied; fleshy; overpowering; irrational; beastly; hearty; unreasonable; diseased; postponed; demoniac; surfeited.

verbs

acquire—; allay—; animate—; appeal to—; appease—; bury—; cloy—; comply with—;

curb—; delight—; deprave—; depress—; digest with—; express—; gorge—; govern—; gratify—; humor—; impair—; indulge—; obey—; pamper—; pervert—; preserve—; quench—; quicken—; raise—; reduce—; regulate—; relish—; revive—; sate—; satiate—; satisfy—; sharpen—; sicken—; staunch—; stimulate—; stir—; suffice—; suit—; yield to—; whet—; woo—; —anticipates; —diminishes; —drives; —dwindles; —gnaws; —grows; —increases; —languishes; —lessens; —returns; —sleeps.

(See desire, hunger, passion.)

APPLAUD (v)

adverbs

riotously; vociferously; warmly; valiantly; equally; tumultuously; spontaneously; hungrily; thunderously; deafeningly; lavishly; enthusiastically; uproariously; vigorously; wildly; irrepressibly; furiously; vehemently; clamorously; frantically; sycophantically.

(See cheer, laud, praise, admire.)

APPLAUSE

adjectives

spontaneous; thunderous; general; deafening; lavish; boisterous; kindly; willing; tumultuous; enthusiastic; whirlwind; uproarious; widespread; rapturous; intelligent; well-directed; vigorous; wild; hearty; irrepressible; furious; delirious; unqualified; vehement; rolling; sporadic; murmuring; rippling; prolonged; forced; warm; courteous; commendatory; heavy-handed; derisive; unbounded; mocking; frantic; vociferous; wondrous; controlled; inordinate; generous; singular; sycophantic; grateful; sarcastic; hollow; malicious; serious; clamorous; ecstatic; scattered.

verbs

acclaim by—; anticipate—; appreciate—; bask in—; chant—; clap—; commend—; demonstrate—; drink up—; echo—; envy—; express—; gain—; huzza—; laugh out—; long for—; love—; manifest—; merit—; murmur—; pronounce—; raise—; reap—; relish—; rock with—; shake with—; snap—; thunder—; trick into—; voice—; win—; —ascends; —breaks out; —bursts out; —crackles; —delights; —encourages; —gratifies; —interrupts; —lessens; —reverberates; —rings from.

(See cheers.)

APPLE

adjectives

smooth; polished; firm; cool; full-juiced; red-cheeked.

verbs

blight—; blow down—; bob for —s; bore into—; bruise—; bud —s; chip—; chop—; core—; crate —s; crop —s; crunch—; cultivate—; devour—; dice—; ferment —s; freeze—; gather —s; graft —s; harvest —s; hoard —s; market —s; munch —; palm—; pare—; plant —s; pluck —; preserve —s; press —s; propagate —s; quarter —; redden —s; scrape—; seed—; spray —s; store —s; taste—; vend —s; —s canker; —s ferment; —matures; —rots; —tempts; —s thrive.

(See fruit.)

APPLIANCE

adjectives

approved; base; complicated; suitable; adroit; crude; ingenious; rude; primitive.

APPLICANT

adjectives

gentle; clamorous; qualified; hopeful; admissible; profitable.

verbs

eliminate—; expose—; mortify—; place—; repulse—; —declares; —petitions; —qualifies.

(See candidate.)

APPLICATION

adjectives

diligent; intelligent; conscientious; rigid; assiduous; sedulous; steadfast; utmost; rigorous; concrete; fascinating; platonic; practical; universal; adroit; progressive; broad; specific; thorough; dynamic; degrading; perfunctory; strenuous; steadfast; presumptuous; unflinching; educated; continuing; pertinent; quantitative; undue; formalistic; correct; professional; ceaseless; industrial; systematic; repeated; inviting; ingenious; influential; superior; fruitful; admirable; economic; dexterous; unfriendly; timely.

verbs

attach—; consider—; cure with —s; demand —; detail—; justify—; petition for—; postpone—; present—; reconsider—; reject—; require—; solicit—; —eases; —kills; —modifies; —pends; request—.

(See use, request.)

APPLY (v)

adverbs

assiduously; indiscriminately; skilfully; ten-

derly; faithfully; diligently; ingeniously; luxuriously; extensively; incorrectly; dexterously; arbitrarily; consciously; comprehensively; advantageously; artificially; rigorously; directly; usefully; necessarily; promiscuously; adroitly; perfunctorily; professionally; ceaselessly; systematically; admirably; literally; liberally; scientifically; practically; universally.
(See use, utilize, practice, adapt.)

APPOINT (v)
adverbs
providentially; celestially; tentatively; publicly; clandestinely; arbitrarily; voluntarily.
(See establish, ordain, assign, allot.)

APPOINTMENT
adjectives
tentative; lifetime; public; onerous; clandestine; absolute; arbitrary; formal; voluntary.

verbs
assign—; benefit by—; cancel—; confirm—; decline—; decree—; designate—; direct—; dispose of—; engineer—; establish—; fix—; grant—; miss—; order—; perform—; ratify—; shuffle—; stipulate—; thrill by—; wangle—; —confers; —pays; —stands; —vests in one.
(See meeting.)

APPOINTMENTS
adjectives
luxurious; elegant; sumptuous; modernistic; dignified.

APPORTION (v)
adverbs
equitably; equally; fairly; justly; wisely; thoughtfully.
(See allot, distribute, grant, share.)

APPRAISAL
adjectives
silent; objective; luminous; shrewd; searching; rational; cool; desperate; intelligent; nimble; careful; adequate; critical; acute; technical; enlightening; scientific; convincing; prolonged; independent.

APPRAISE (v)
adverbs
critically; covertly; judiciously; conceitedly; knowingly; silently; objectively; shrewdly; rationally; coolly; intelligently; adequately; scientifically; independently.
(See judge, estimate.)

APPRECIATE (v)
adverbs
highly; adequately; justly; deeply; properly; particularly; readily; fully; correctly; sympathetically; mutually; genuinely; heartily; whole-heartedly; passionately; aesthetically; belatedly; artistically; profoundly.
(See esteem, prize.)

APPRECIATION
adjectives
intense; genial; detached; sympathetic; respectful; delicate; impersonal; laughing; bashful; mutual; poetic; innocent; definite; full; critical; hearty; high; true; genuine; discreet; wide; sensitive; wholehearted; clearer; deep; heightened; passionate; stunted; aesthetic; anticipated; patriotic; brilliant; cordial; amazed; generous; affectionate; splendid; reluctant; belated; keen; warmhearted; unsolicited; complete; proper; sensuous; fine; vivid; total; marked; flashing; humorous; expressed; emotional; rarefied; scant; supreme; increased; childish; sincere; oppressive; growing; loyal; hard-driven; rare; radiant; tentative; direct; intellectual; spiritual; alleged; artistic; enthusiastic; profound; youthful.

verbs
differ in—; drink in with—; evoke—; increase—; perceive with—; promote—of; recognize with—; stamp—; —grows; —increases; —rises.
(See esteem.)

APPRECIATIVE
adverbs
genially; sympathetically; laughingly; wholly; definitely; heartily; truly; genuinely; wholeheartedly; deeply; highly; passionately; discriminatingly; cordially; amazingly; pathetically; splendidly; keenly; warmly; completely; properly; childishly; sincerely; increasingly; oppressively; radiantly; delightfully; enthusiastically; gratifyingly; profoundly.

APPREHEND (v)
adverbs
readily; imperfectly; clearly; distinctly; nervously; tremblingly; fearfully; vaguely; acutely; undisguisedly; gnawingly.
(See dread, fear.)

APPREHENSION
adjectives
slumbering; uneasy; maternal; troublesome; nervous; wistful; sickening; sensitive; clammy; hazy; ghostly; trembling; frenzied;

lingering; quivering; fearful; shivering; fickle; rational; feigned; lively; vague; acute; undisguised; suppressed; gnawing; constant; religious; dismal; gloomy; ill-defined; cruel; despondent; remorseful; uncomfortable; foreboding; alarming; abject; distinct; unrelieved; sad; breathless; anguished; piteous; idle; grave; continuous; professed; indignant; daily; delighted; dread; warm; groundless; serious; vain; ever-present; nameless; instant; goading; painful; affected; supreme; right; puerile; terrible; mortal; cowardly; tempered; utmost; murky; miraculous.

verbs
allay—; arouse—; rise above—; becloud —; clear—; crystallize—; deny—; dull—; express—; free of—; ingrain—; look about with—; obtain—; profess—; rejoice in—; remove—; rest on—; sense with—; shake with—; strengthen—; torment by—; warrant—; wear out with—; —assails; — flames; —possesses; —seizes.
(See fear, dread, anxiety, distrust.)

APPREHENSIVE
adverbs
uneasily; nervously; fearfully; vaguely; acutely; constantly; occasionally; dismally; gloomily; cruelly; uncomfortably; alarmingly; distinctly; piteously; idly; gravely; professedly; groundlessly; seriously; namelessly; painfully; supremely; childishly; superstitiously; curiously; strangely; inexplicably; suddenly.

APPRENTICE
adjectives
idle; bright; haughty; hand-picked; drunken; able; practiced; clumsy.

verbs
abuse—; bind—; burden—; chastise—; contact—; dismiss—; employ—; engage—; enroll—; fledge—; instruct—; regulate—; remove—; retain—; school—; serve as—; teach—; —binds himself to; —gathers; — learns; —masters; —practices; —serves; —trains.
(See beginner, novice, student.)

APPRENTICESHIP
adjectives
weary; devious; tedious; long; arduous; strict; sordid; faithful.

APPROACH
adjectives
hackneyed; single; sociological; novel; or-

ganic; traditional; inevitable; oblique; tentative; obvious; impressive; immediate; logical; flanked; insidious; common-sense; majestic; tactful; critical; methodological; natural; simple; wary; galloping; fair; hushed; original; insinuating; wistful; cautious; illuminating; subtle; indirect; shamefaced; stealthy; boisterous; chic; affable; experimental; tolerable; warm; mutual; soft; ample; casual; rapid; cunning; active; timid; gradual; intimate; sympathetic; distant; tumultuous; extraordinary; speedy; hostile; irresolute; ironical.

verbs
bar—; betoken—; construct—; cover—; discover—; discuss—; disguise—; divert—; examine—; foresee—; herald—; hinder—; linger over—; obstruct—; reconstruct—; repel—; restore—; sense—; shun—; watch —; —bodes; --leads.
(See access, way, entrance.)

APPROACH (*v*)
adverbs
penitently; hilariously; noiselessly; devoutly; remotely; diffidently; cautiously; perilously; sinuously; stealthily; unwarily; dexterously; delicately; humbly; reluctantly; leisurely; suppliantly; obsequiously; blushingly; circumspectly; obliquely; irresolutely; casually; confidentially.
(See advance.)

APPROBATION
adjectives
individual; startled; enthusiastic; unmeasured; modest; full; audible; virtuous; general.

verbs
bestow—; concur in—; declare—; enjoy—; entertain—; express—; mark with—; meet with—; merit—; quote with—; receive—; revoke—; seal in—; voice—.
(See commendation, encouragement, admiration, approval, praise.)

APPROPRIATE (*v*)
adverbs
selfishly; unceremoniously; thievishly; eagerly; doubtfully; reverently; solely; wastefully; adequately; fraudulently; extravagantly; lavishly.
(See take, assume.)

APPROPRIATION
adjectives
wasteful; blind; adequate; permanent; con-

tinuing; ruthless; fraudulent; extravagant; lavish; excessive; passive; meager.

verbs
assign—; authorize—; bar—; bequeath—; carry on with—; default—; designate—; diminish—; draw—; economize on—; employ—; enact—; exceed—; expend—; finance—; grant—; legislate—; necessitate—; pass—; pinch—; reserve—; restrict—; set apart—; shave—; specify—; transfer—; triple—; —aids; —allows; —enables; —provides; pay—.
(See fund, tax.)

APPROVAL
adjectives
affectionate; highest; delighted; private; priceless; overwhelming; unqualified; monotonous; marked; reiterated; vigorous; patent; warm; unanimous; sage; genuine; condescending; frank; complete; roaring; tacit; maternal; hapless; loud; excited; free; world-wide; unrestrained; languid; partial; social; hearty; widespread; abject; masculine; enthusiastic; grudging; expressed; perfect; denominational; popular; surprised; intense; voiceless; unconscious; distant; reluctant.

verbs
authorize—; bask in—; beam—; clamor—; consent to—; imply—; insure—; intimate —; meet with—; nod—; roar—; sanction—; secure—; stamp with—; trick into—; win —; —encourages; —greets; —heartens.
(See approbation, sanction, commendation, indorsement, ratification.)

APPROVE (v)
adverbs
heartily; warmly; thankfully; strongly; unanimously; instinctively; deliberately; indifferently; condescendingly; cordially; unconditionally; thoughtlessly; entirely; unqualifiedly; rapturously; delightedly; privately; vigorously; sagely; completely; condescendingly; tacitly; partially; enthusiastically; grudgingly; reluctantly; overwhelmingly.
(See commend, sanction, favor.)

APPROXIMATION
adjectives
progressive; well-bred; thematic; urbane; close; clear; definite.

APRON
adjectives
gingham; ridiculous; filthy; frilled; generous; snowy; tiny; flowered; humble; vol-uminous; diminutive; coarse; greasy; billowy; prophylactic; womanish.

APT
adverbs
adroitly; cleverly; specially; dexterously; felicitously; expertly; intelligently; practically; technically; ably; artistically; capably; cunningly; deftly; handily; ingeniously; proficiently; scientifically; shrewdly; remarkably; unusually.

APTITUDE
adjectives
natural; intellectual; remarkable; judicial; military; special; mechanical; oratorical; hidden; artistic; singular; curious; high; unusual; characteristic; musical; surprising; versatile.

AQUEDUCT
adjectives
subterraneous; ancient; spacious.

ARAB
adjectives
tall; graceful; grave; dressed; big; powerful; harmless; wiry; black-browed; courteous; fine-looking; excited; chivalrous; imperturbable; amorous.

ARABESQUE
adjectives
elfin; exquisite.

ARBITER
adjectives
unprejudiced; just; trembling; implacable.

ARBITRARY
adverbs
overwhelmingly; extraordinarily; despotically; domineeringly; intolerably; paternally; patriarchally; dictatorially; imperiously; presumptuously; harshly; strictly; severely; tyrannically; oppressively; cruelly; haughtily; obdurately; positively; relentlessly; sternly; neatly; unreasonably; excessively; unbelievably; offensively; dangerously; alarmingly.

ARBITRATION
adjectives
compulsory; bloody; impartial; friendly.

verbs
abide by—; accept—; adopt—; advocate—; ascertain by—; compel—; conduct—; control by—; decide by—; discuss—; employ—;

obtain—; put to—; renounce—; respect—; seek—; submit to—; —adjusts; —adverts; —avoids; —awards; —conciliates; —considers; —determines; —judges; —negotiates; —referees; —results in; —settles; —succeeds.
(See decision.)

ARBOR

adjectives
rustic; flowering; sequestered; private; moving; gigantic; latticed; conical; bowery; sultry.

ARC

adjectives
deadly; skyward; graceful; fiery; luminous; friedelite; speed-blurred; controlling; unthinkable; zooming; ethereal; splendid; deficient; recurrent; flaming.

ARCADE

adjectives
blind; massive; sheltered; garish.

ARCH

adjectives
dignified; old; majestic; steel-trussed; artistic; echoing; horizontal; darkened; graceful; vast; livid; rustic; crumbling; leafy; peaked; magnificent; triumphal; subtle; elliptical; boundless; crystal; culminant; groined; successive; massive; shadowy; proscenium; titanic; accursed; rainbow; emerald; dazzling; topsy-turvy; inverted; cragged; shallow; stupendous; squashed; overworked; collapsed; glistening; flowery; melancholy; starry; tendriled; brazen; rising; interlacing; dim; somber; fretted.

verbs
adorn—; assemble—; cap—; construct—; crown—; develop—; employ—; erect—; form—; point—; span—; vault—; —carries; —commemorates; —curves; —gives way; —graces; —spans; —spreads; —strides over; —supports.
(See curve.)

ARCH (v)

adverbs
servilely; solidly; deeply; majestically; artistically; gracefully; magnificently; triumphally; massively.

ARCHAEOLOGIST

adjectives
distinguished; spectacular; venerable.

ARCHAEOLOGY

verbs
delve into—; derive from—; owe to—; study —; —absorbs; —accomplishes; —attempts; —attracts; —authenticates; —brings to light; —catalogues; —classifies; —collects; —compares; —concerns; —concludes; —conserves; —deals with; —deciphers; —decodes; —designates; —digs; —discovers; —disputes; —excavates; —fills in; —influences; —investigates; —marks; —misleads; —portrays; —preserves; —progresses; —recognizes; —reconstructs; —records; —rejects; —relates; —restores; —reveals; —scratches; —searches; —seeks; —sheds light upon; —surveys; —traces; —uncovers; —unravels.
(See science.)

ARCHAIC

adverbs
hopelessly; entirely; poetically; obviously; admittedly; veritably; venerably; traditionally; respectably; genteelly.

ARCHITECT

adjectives
philandering; eminent; self-constituted; consultant; ingenious; known; cunning; celebrated; fledgling; uninterested; creative; imaginative; successful; general; practical; exuberant; contemporary; admirable; lavish; discreet; romantic; symmetry-loving.

ARCHITECTURAL

adverbs
elaborately; chastely; unmistakably; charmingly; poetically; impressively; elegantly; tastefully; traditionally; nobly; ornately; rustically; historically; ecclesiastically; intricately; fantastically.

ARCHITECTURE

adjectives
primitive; diverse; ornate; semi-classic; elaborate; gilded; garbled; symphonic; charming; curious; rustic; organic; naval; noble; plastic; surrounding; historic; repellent; stodgy; colonial; editorial; ecclesiastical; florid; massive; distinctive; domestic; fantastic; traditional; impressive; intricate; tasteful; incrusted; elegant; incomparable; internal; diverse; rambling; poetic.

verbs
acquaint with—; adorn—; apply—; appreciate—; apprentice to—; build—; characterize—; conceive—; consider—; construct—; create—; crystallize—; decorate—; design

57

—; desolate—; destroy—; develop—; dress —; embellish—; embody in—; emphasize —; encourage—; enrich—; exhibit—; imitate—; immortalize—; practise—; preserve —; produce—; proportion—; raise—; regard—; regulate—; restore—; resuscitate —; revivify—; —adorns; —arises; —arranges; —consists; —designs; —details; —enables; —evolves from; —flourishes; —implies; —includes; —involves; —ornaments; —requires; —solves; —tends toward; —trains; —transfigures.

(See building, art.)

ARCHIVES
adjectives
historical; secret; incriminating; inexhaustible; enriched; treasured; indestructible; national; enduring.

verbs
burn—; conserve in—; deposit in—; preserve in—; record in—; register in—; rummage through—; store in—; superintend—; unlock—; —document; —include; —preserve; —record; —relate.

(See records, documents.)

ARCHWAY
adjectives
grated; sunken; ancient; ponderous; shining.

ARCTIC
adverbs
frigidly; frostily; rigorously; horribly; shiveringly; bleakly; coldly; freezingly; glacially; inclemently; piercingly; pinchingly; nippingly; rawly; intolerably; killingly; stiffly; frozenly; unbelievably; unbearably.

ARDENT
adverbs
youthfully; brightly; indiscreetly; amazingly; warmly; tenderly; generously; instinctively; impetuously; furiously; poetically; passionately; mutually; hastily; impulsively; irrepressibly; ingenuously; irresistibly; fervently; fervidly; anxiously; avidly; fondly; affectionately; devotedly; hungrily; yearningly; ambitiously; breathlessly; eagerly; insatiably; wistfully; sincerely; rapturously; ecstatically; racily; glowingly; feverishly; earnestly; emotionally; acutely; deeply.

ARDOR
adjectives
clean; bright; open-hearted; indiscreet; fiery; youthful; beauteous; amazing; cooled; revolutionary; tender; generous; characteristic; instinctive; inexplicable; impetuous; furious; sacrificial; covert; renewed; dampened; fastidious; poetic; passionate; mutual; tedious; professional; new-born; obsessing; war-like; wandering; hasty; impulsive; ready; redoubled; irrepressible; intrepid; exaggerating; emulous; heroic; ingenious; martial; patriotic; lyrical; military; submissive; irresistible; fervent.

verbs
burn with—; confine—; dampen—; effulge with—; electrify with—; extinguish—; fire with—; flame with—; heat with—; intensify—; pursue with—; radiate—; spend—; —abates; —swells; —wanes; —warms; —waxes.

(See eagerness, zeal, fervor, enthusiasm, warmth.)

ARDUOUS
adverbs
relatively; tremendously; overwhelmingly; formidably; unbelievably; supremely; gravely; seriously; administratively; physically; obviously; naturally; peculiarly; necessarily; unpleasantly; conspicuously; alarmingly; dishearteningly; incredibly; intricately; embarrassingly; perplexingly; complexly; desperately; perversely; occasionally.

AREA
adjectives
immense; unexplored; swampy; suburban; consolidated; misty; outlying; considerable; combined; vast; interior; populated; arid; scenic; circumscribed; stagnant; marshy; interstitial; limited; treeless; straggling; gale-swept; huge; enormous; bewildering; prolific; petty; devastated; inconspicuous; decreasing; unobstructed; forest; hazardous; widening; cultivable; superficial; diminished; liberal; super-productive; pestilential; varying; cleared; enveloping; trading; unpeopled; restricted; restoration; stone; faunal.

verbs
apply to—; approach—; bound—; cover—; cultivate—; define—; denude—; determine —; distinguish—; encircle—; enclose—; erect on—; excavate—; fence in—; give access to—; infest—; level—; limit—; measure—; reclaim—; remove from—; scatter over—; vacate—.

(See space, tract, portion, ground, yard.)

ARENA
adjectives
fit; conspicuous; commercial; frenzied; bloody; foggy; diplomatic.

verbs
combat in—; conflict in—; contend in—; display in—; emerge from—; enclose in—; flood—; jam—; perform in—; plunge into —; strew—; surround—; throng—.
(See space, field.)

ARGUE (*v*)
adverbs
persuasively; placatingly; elusively; understandingly; thoughtfully; drawlingly; fallaciously; rationalistically; preposterously; sensibly; captiously; lamely; fairly; roughly; impressively; profoundly; affirmatively; excitedly; hypercritically; vainly; irrationally; indefatigably; wisely; logically; adversely; scientifically; sophistically; deviously; contentiously; cantankerously; discursively; priggishly; clumsily; pettishly; hypothetically; ingeniously; crushingly; exhaustively; lucidly; formidably; tellingly; irrefutably; fruitlessly; acrimoniously; equivocally; irritatingly; stubbornly; superfluously; abusively; circuitously.

(See plead, remonstrate, discuss, dispute.)

ARGUMENT
adjectives
ingenious; powerful; affirmative; reasonable; sound; winning; crowning; notable; crushing; logical; acceptable; exhaustive; irresistible; conclusive; weighty; strong; favorable; effective; broad; doughty; truthful; unanswerable; cogent; forceful; basic; substantial; formidable; lucid; imaginative; eager; precious; matchless; intensive; illuminating; flawless; clear-cut; telling; close-knit; irrefutable; practical; heated; forensic; sonorous; eloquent; vehement; revolutionary; bitter; fiery; sharp; impassioned; ferocious; stale; fallacious; insidious; spurious; old; painful; futile; nervous; confused; specious; needless; feeble; conflicting; fruitless; influential; nation-wide; mild; half-playful; solemn; mathematical; typical; endless; extended; editorial; interminable; constant; protracted; final; prolific; deliberate; persistent; lengthy; wordless; delightful; good-selling; long-standing; widespread; impetuous; inevitable; rapid; brilliant; well-rounded; acrimonious; theistic; undeniable; utilitarian; scientific; moral; inconsiderable; violent; lofty; bloody; dispassionate; solid; grave; vulgar; absent; craven; staple; personal; positive; labored; rational; earnest; commonplace; hair-splitting; ampler; penetrating; embodied; outspoken; equivocal; irritating; convincing; coarse; adverse; timid; stub-

born; wearisome; wretched; judicious; superfluous; honest; enticing; slender; abusive; keen; potent; concise; odd; maternal; clear; close.

verbs
admit—; advance—; anticipate—; arm with —; arrange—; attack—; base—; bolster—; bolt—; bring forth—; burnish—; clinch—; color—; combat—; construct—; counter with —; debate—; deduce—; demolish—; derive —from; destroy—; dispense with—; dispute —; dread—; drive home—; employ—; engage in—; enumerate—; explain—; fashion —; force—; found on—; ground upon—; indulge in—; invalidate—; kindle—; maintain—; marshal —s; meet—; open—; oppose—; permit of—; premise—; proffer—; propose—; prove—; provoke—; pursue—; push—; qualify—; question—; rebut—; reduce to—; refute—; reiterate—; remove—; resume—; scorn—; settle—; sift—; steel with—; stir—; substantiate—; support —; weigh—; —appeals; —confounds; —depends on; —drones on; —fades away; —implies; —impresses; —infers; —involves; —rages; —rests on; —s simmer down; —s wax hot.
(See reason, proof, debate, discussion, dispute, controversy.)

ARGUMENTATIVE
adverbs
sagaciously; readily; disagreeably; hotly; sagely; offensively; cleverly; adroitly; ingeniously; reasonably; irresistibly; obstinately; pesteringly; abusively; stubbornly; convincingly; mulishly; irritatingly; dispassionately; earnestly; violently; acrimoniously; brilliantly; impetuously; interminably; endlessly; playfully; solemnly; fruitlessly; mildly; feebly; needlessly; nervously; insidiously; unnecessarily; ferociously; bitterly; significantly; foolishly; intelligently; astutely; shrewdly; vigilantly.

ARID
adverbs
dessicatingly; terribly; rainlessly; horribly; intolerably; unbearably; unproductively; wildly; fruitlessly; treelessly; dustily; insufferably; hopelessly; desperately; bitterly; malignly; pestiferously; agonizingly; heartbreakingly; destructively; murderously; joylessly; desolately; insupportably; dolorously.

ARISE (*v*)
adverbs
involuntarily; energetically; automatically;

spontaneously; pretentiously; incessantly; majestically; strenuously; readily; imperceptibly; irresistibly; hastily.

(See rise, ascend, mount, proceed.)

ARISTOCRACY

adjectives

odious; genuine; true; privileged; effete; heaven-descended; remarkable; gilded; canine; feudal; landed; moribund; pampered; devout; old; dominant; hereditary; high; admitted; recognized; idle; proud; democratic; industrial; sword-girt; phantasmal; martial.

verbs

attain—; break down—; choose from—; compose—; denote—; distinguish—; imperil —; oppose—; overthrow—; pervert—; privilege—; rank among—; strengthen—; vest in—; weaken—; —abuses; —administrates; —conforms; —degenerates; —develops from; —enlists; —fosters; —governs; —lolls; —predominates; —rules; —wields.

(See nobility, peerage, class, government.)

ARISTOCRAT

adjectives

bloated; proud; ante bellum; wealthy; exiled; hot-tempered; born; disgraced; snobbish; cosmopolitan; country; liberal; embryo; impoverished; stripling; emigrant; soft-voiced.

ARISTOCRATIC

adverbs

proudly; genuinely; truly; admittedly; tenaciously; inherently; innately; fantastically; snobbishly; nobly; actually; elegantly; unaffectedly; avowedly; unquestionably; palpably; essentially; stubbornly; ostentatiously; conspicuously; eminently; grandly; imposingly; magnificently.

ARK

adjectives

doveless; guarded; grounded.

ARM

adjectives

beautiful; tapering; superb; perfect; sculptured; marble-smooth; shaped; spiritual; graceful; delicate; slim; daisy-white; slender; golden; tender; soft; fragile; brawny; muscular; steel; iron; terrifying; strong; powerful; stout; tremendous; muscle-corded; firm; capable; sinewy; enormous; massive; mighty; bony; puny; thin; snaky; frail; lean; plump; thick; rounded; chubby; flab-

by; awkward; clumsy; grisly; profaning; threatening; offending; degraded; shattered; wounded; wasted; molded; numb; aching; bruised; limp; drowsy; languid; listless; waving; gesticulating; beckoning; outstretched; clutching; outflung; extended; proffered; hanging; rigid; outspread; wide-open (pl); reaching; classical; uplifted; imploring; dangling; upraised; crossed (pl); wan; throbbing; swaying; swinging; linked; shaking; silken; jeweled; uniformed; khaki-clad; veiled; soapy; bare; powdered; hirsute; overlong; fearful; willing; sheltering; protecting; pacifying; combined (pl); engulfing; encircling; supporting; wandering; longing; waiting; accusing; thankful; reluctant; yearning; affectionate; reassuring; flailing; nerveless; tremulous; developed; incredible; ineffective; enthusiastic; detaining; wriggling; reinforcing; impulsive; derisive; forging; bewildered; rapturous; whirlwind; alabaster; movable; crooked; potent; swirling; remorseless; glittering; generous; unsuspected; mutual; temporal; swordless; disposing; gigantic; resplendent; large; fetching; elephantine; revengeful; pendent; lithe; barren; seraphic; twining; motherly; impatient; fearsome; restful; despised; unwieldy; braving; stiffened; sausage-like; unloaded; gilded; speckled; gnarled; angular; hungry; aching; dingy; cautious; protesting; victorious; desolate; almighty; grotesque; ponderous; rebellious; shaggy; puissant; steadying; poetic; enticing; conjugal; wrathful; sustaining; furbished; oft-bended; pleached; dimpled; grounded; sinuous; shining; dazzling; figured; artificial; feeble; gross; snowy; loving; withered; impeccable; mailed; restful; troublesome; gorgeous; fondling; out-reaching; restraining; springy; naked; lascivious; locked (pl); municipal; amputated; freckled; unreasoning; chapel-like; dusky; official; embracing; unhallowed; burnished; alien; faith-clad; waxen; needful; hairy-fibred; sturdy; akimbo (pl); strangling; glowing; lily; secular; bandaged; steel-strong; dissonant; puffy; boneless; broken; stalwart; whirring; blazoned (pl); branching (pl).

verbs

amputate—; attach—to; bare—; bind—; cast —s around; clasp in —s; cradle in —s; cross —s; dangle on—; develop—; drive—through; embrace in —s; encircle in —s; encumber —s; enfold in —s; entwine in —s; extend —s; extricate —s; flap —s; fling—around; fold —s; gather in —s; hail

60

with open —s; hang on —s; leap into —s; lend—; lock —s; impair the use of —s; open —s; paralyze —s; proffer—; pluck from —s; recline on—; rotate —s; sling —s; stretch out —s; strip from —s; support in —s; tear from —s; uncover —s; wave —s; wind in —s; wound—; wrap in—; wreathe in —s; —bleeds; —s cling around; —s dandle; —hangs; —projects.
(See limb, wrist.)

ARM (v)
adverbs
imperfectly; impenetrably; superbly; powerfully; mightily; threateningly; incredibly; ineffectively; puissantly; sturdily; stalwartly.

ARMADA
adjectives
air; huge; mighty; ponderous; impressive; death-dealing.

ARMAMENT
adjectives
unchecked; formidable; excessive; national; increased; vaunted; enormous; splendid; considerable.

verbs
appropriate for—; discard—; equip with—; limit—; outlaw—; produce—; rebuild—; reduce—; rehabilitate—; replace—; scale down—; strip of—; —s collapse; —s exceed.
(See force, guns.)

ARM-CHAIR
adjectives
palatial; chintz-covered; cushioned; shabby; restful; spacious; luxurious.

ARMISTICE
adjectives
unspoken; assumed; undeclared; disregarded.

ARMOR
adjectives
adamantine; customary; shining; sun-bright; noticeable; virginal; magic; mortal; radiant; incongruous; elaborate; tough; chain; safest; steel-plated; jointless; impenetrable; protective; defensive; invisible; golden; horny; inviolate; spiritual; battered; granite; celestial.

verbs
buckle on—; burden with—; burnish—; clad in—; clothe in—; collect—; cover with

—; defend in—; design—; discard—; employ—; enclose in—; furnish—; harness in —; pad—; pierce—; plate with—; scar—; scour—; sheathe in—; stain—; strip off—; swagger in—; —clashes; —gives way; —hampers; —jingles; —protects; —resists; —shields.
(See steel.)

ARMS
adjectives   (*weapons*)
purposeful; puny; ruthless; skilfully-handled; unfriendly.

verbs
abate—; abolish—; bear—; burnish—; call to—; chastise with—; defend with—; display—; draw—; engage with—; excel in—; exploit with—; fire—; force with—; furnish —; groove—; invent—; lack—; lay down —; leap to—; march in—; notch—; order —; present—; rally to—; rattle—; repel with—; resist with—; rise in—; shoulder —; smuggle—; surrender—; take by force of—; take up—; throw away—; train in—; wield—; win with—; —clash; —run out.
(See weapons.)

ARMY
adjectives
bristling; cleverly-concealed; cold-staring; death-dealing; destruction-spilling; flashing; sullen; grim-looking; grisly; havoc-playing; malignant; murderous; make-shift; exalted; exultant; invincible; indefatigable; gallant; superb; glorious; determined; splendid; formidable; magnificent; picked; distressed; retreating; doomed; ragged; unpaid; disgruntled; decimated; demoralized; domestic; defeated; pathetic; tarnished; recalcitrant; standing; motor-camping; contending; organized; modern; vast; surging; invading; beleaguering; besieging; heterogeneous; overwhelming; furtive; ravishing; enraged; respective; heathen; cooperating; dwindling; fraternal; opposing; immense; precious; powerful; half-famished; dispersed; concentrated; rude; innumerable (pl); incompetent; victorious; scattered; solid; flying; compact; well-commanded; self-reliant; enthusiastic; principal; desolating; provisional; starry; wrangling; succoring; allied; obstinate; barefoot; omnipotent; shattered; phantom; insurgent; faithful; melancholy; deplorable; routed.

verbs
call out—; clothe—; command—; conscript into—; consolidate—; dash at—; defy—; demobilize—; disband—; discharge—; discipline—; dishearten—; dismiss—; disperse

—; double—; drill—; encompass—; engage—; enlist in—; equip—; evacuate—; furlough—; harry—; hire—; impress into—; improvise—; increase—; join—; mechanize —; mobilize—; motorize—; muster—; organize—; pledge—; provide—; provision —; raise—; recruit—; regiment—; route —; serve in—; supply—; support—; transport—; turn—to flight; —assembles; —blockades; —charges; —converges on; —crusades; —encamps; —intercepts; —mutinies; —pillages; —plunders; —retires; —retreats; —rumbles; —rushes in; —storms; —strikes; —swarms; —wages war.

(See troops, soldiers, forces.)

AROMA
adjectives
fruity; exquisite; peculiar; offensive; fragrant; spicy; pungent; delicious; pleasant; remote; earthly; preprandial; tempting; lingering; sickly; intoxicating; faint; ineffable; questionable; delicate; luscious; quick; penetrating.

verbs
breathe in—; dissipate—; exhale—; imitate —; send forth—; —escapes; —floats; —pervades.

(See perfume, fragrance, odor.)

AROMATIC
adverbs
pleasantly; spicily; fragrantly; redolently; sweetly; pungently; arrestingly; refreshingly; pleasingly; definitely; strongly; delicately; exquisitely; enchantingly; charmingly; drowsily; faintly; overpoweringly; delectably; softly; intoxicatingly; lingeringly; richly; attractively; exotically.

AROUSE (v)
adverbs
thoroughly; seditiously; instantaneously; antagonistically; suddenly.
(See excite, rouse, animate, stimulate.)

ARRAIGNMENT
adjectives
harsh; eloquent; appalling; incredible.

ARRANGE (v)
adverbs
dramatically; delicately; becomingly; temptingly; alphabetically; elaborately; admirably; systematically; beautifully; sensibly; exquisitely; harmoniously; ideally; felicitously; obviously; cleverly; efficiently; hideously; crudely; clumsily; finally; previously; complexly; artistically; mechanically; methodically; ostensibly; confidentially; painfully.

(See classify, dispose, devise, contrive.)

ARRANGEMENT
adjectives
balanced; careful; impeccable; admirable; ideal; pleasant; impromptu; serene; formal; elaborate; desirable; skilful; felicitous; fair; obvious; regular; clever; cordial; efficient; divine; empty; attractive; devious; inequitable; hideous; crude; clumsy; final, judgmatical; fiscal; temporary; previous; spacious; preconcerted; incompatible; defensive; complex; dinette; cunning; provident; inconsistent; due; pleasure-principle; special; dilapidated; artistic; compensatory; mechanical; disconcerting; free-wheeling; line; practical; rectilinear; methodical; curious; graceful; established; fairest; simple; credit; harmonious; picturesque; traditional; fitting; domestic; ostensible; existing; unnatural; systematic; complicated; unsatisfactory; municipal; judicious; ingenious; charming; reciprocal; habitual; old-fashioned; dexterous; cumbrous; confidential; countermanded; painful; spacious.

verbs
adapt—; adjust—; adopt—; cancel—; criticize—; declare—; design—; desire—; determine—; devise—; dispute—; elaborate—; enter into—; furnish—; improvise—; insure—; negotiate—; order—; prepare—; prevent—; reach—; register—; repudiate—; standardize—; style—; welcome—; —conforms to; —disposes of; —prevails.
(See contract, understanding.)

ARRAY
adjectives
formidable; imposing; glorious; impressive; prodigious; rich; colorful; fascinating; enticing; neat; disordered; unsightly; stubborn; bristling; bridal; superb; abounding; motley; glittering; formal; endless; giddy; heterogeneous; bewildering; astonishing; comprehensive; superficial; hostile; confused; gorgeous; meek; gallant; militant; vivid; festival; flimsy; tranquil; immense; bright; terrible; meteor-eclipsing; incomparable; undisciplined; loose; vast; inexhaustible; noble; scattered; threatening; ragged; magnificent; grand; feudal; symmetrical; complete; awful; martial; chaste; white; stern; cold; battle; goodly; wild; flowering.

verbs
attire in—; break—; challenge—; deck in
—; display—; draw up—; gaze at—; impose—; loose—; order—; outfit in—; rank
in—; renew—; review—; stand· in—; —
impresses; —stretches.
(See display, exhibition.)

ARRAY (v)
adverbs
tastefully; gloriously; handsomely; formidably; impressively; richly; colorfully; fascinatingly; enticingly; superbly; formally;
bewilderingly; superficially; vividly; gorgeously; incomparably; nobly.
(See arrange, marshal.)

ARREST
adjectives
arbitrary; capricious; frequent; summary;
indiscriminate; wrongful; friendly; dreamy;
injudicious; inspired; resisted; abrupt.

verbs
authorize—; charge with—; compel—; declare—; decree—; defend against—; delay
—; demand—; dispense with—; effect—;
enforce—; execute—; facilitate—; force to
—; immunize against—; interfere with—;
obtain—; order—; justify—; place under—;
procure—of; release from—; resist—; restrain from—; result in—; secure—of; stop
—; subject to—; warrant—; —deters; —s
outnumber; —prevents.
(See imprisonment.)

ARREST (v)
adverbs
arbitrarily; unjustly; capriciously; summarily; indiscriminately; wrongfully; abruptly;
injudiciously.
(See apprehend, stop, check, restrain.)

ARRIVAL
adjectives
mysterious; initial; late; speedy; unheralded; modest; merry; unconventional; noisy;
bustling; timely; impending; abstract; successful; adventitious; seasonable; welcome;
opportune; brilliant; unexpected; imminent;
dread; anticipated.

ARRIVE (v)
adverbs
jubilantly; ultimately; punctually; incessantly; tardily; mysteriously; unconventionally; bustlingly; adventitiously; seasonably;
opportunely; abruptly; expeditiously; slumberously.
(See come.)

adjectives
haughty; hard; cool; wounded; odd; splendid; stupid; vulgar; small; aesthetic; hot;
unresponsive; tactless; desperate; despotic;
supercilious; misstyled; unamiable; masculine; intellectual; tempered; monstrous; cynical; intolerable; meddlesome; ruffling;
crested; burgher; blustering; brash;
brusque; brisk; bristling; unbridled.

verbs
abandon—; disdain—; endure—; feed—;
humble—; loathe—; purge the soul of—;
satirize—; —causes; —indicates; —offends;
—repels; —vexes.
(See assumption, assurance.)

ARROGANT
adverbs
intolerably; justifiably; noticeably; smugly;
insolently; proudly; coolly; offensively; condescendingly; irritatingly; purposely; rudely; unpardonably; incurably; ridiculously;
laughably; splendidly; oddly; stupidly;
brashly; deplorably; uncivilly.

ARROW
adjectives
poisoned; fiery; answering; strong-shot;
vengeful; ultimate; barbed; ineffectual;
envenomed; burning; rankling; twanging;
buried; eagle-plumed; crafty; featherless;
swift; blunt; deadly; death-dealing.

verbs
aim—; barb—; bear—; discharge—; draw
—; drop—; feather—; fire—; imbed—;
lash—; let fly—; loose—; mark with—;
notch—; pierce with—; pinch—; place—;
point—; poison—; pour —s; release—; secure—; send—; shape—; shoot—; slay with
—; smite with—; string—; throw off—;
tip—; wound with—; —carries; —describes
an arc; —glances off; —goes to the mark;
—leaves; —passes; —penetrates; —pierces;
—quivers; —reaches; —rides; —slips; —
speeds; —wings.
(See dart, shaft.)

ART
adjectives
elaborate; consummate; undying; pleasurable; delicate; gentle; analogous; remarkable; serious; subtle; new; wonderful; ingenious; experienced; sophisticated; noblest;
superb; ripe; gracious; obliging; unsurpassable; fine; tedious; glowing; profound; proficient; great; simple; sincere; glorious;
pure; epic; meticulous; surpassing; graphic;

snubbed; aristocratic; modernistic; plastic; decorative; landscape; ancient; rustic; epistolary; contemporary; poetic; constructive; modern; applied; dramatic; elegant; antiquated; pyrotechnic; seeming; inscrutable; suave; finished; vanishing; fine; mystical; living; enviable; esoteric; replaced; cultured; lost; symbolic; fancy; hidden; servile; musical; colorless; blandishing (pl); kindred; perfidious; vital; culinary; fascinating; healing; peaceful; unpremeditated; specious; inventive; cunning; brain-spattering; baneful; fickle; windpipe-slitting; flawless; matchless; structural; virile; indigenous; superhuman; dreadful; tonsorial; imitative; classicizing; black; inharmonious; recreational; canonic; piscatorial; sunny; fertilizing; sublime; instrumental; regal; enrapturing; rational; idealistic; acquired; substantial; representative; lenient; vagrant; agile; equestrian; fearful; grotesque; public; deathless; prosperous; evasive; memorial; coarse; spiritual; abominable; inventive; exalted; mechanical; mortuary; histrionic; indifferent; vicious; living; coactive; quaint; empirical; irregular; incomprehensible; demoniacal; jealous; new-invented; loftier; orthodox; commercial; medical; ceramic; unhallowed; athletic; subservient; florid; classic; exquisite; practical; perishable; spontaneous; immature; elevated; patented; etched; menial; poor; low; voluptuous; illustrative; unlawful; rare; piquant; conspicuous.

verbs

animate—; apply—; appreciate—; attain—; awaken—; become—; breed—; caricaturize —; characterize—; choke—; compose—; comprehend—; conceive—; contrive by—; counterfeit—; cultivate—; dabble in—; deem —; devise—; devote to—; discriminate in —; display—; educate in—; elaborate—; embellish—; encourage—; etch—; evolve—; exaggerate—; execute—; exercise—; facilitate—; further—; glorify—; illustrate—; imitate—; inaugurate—; influence—; interpret—; limit—; master—; murder—; originate—; ply—; practise—; preserve—; produce—; purge—; pursue—; refine—; school in—; stifle—; supplement—; sustain —; systematize—; take refuge in—; trace—; verse in—; wed to—; —achieves; —assists; —attains; —builds; —conceals; —depicts; —derives from; —dies away; —disguises; —embodies; —enlightens; —evolves from; —excites; —expresses; —feigns; —flourishes; —functions; —imitates; —lags; —languishes; —ornaments; —portrays; —re-

flects; —remains; —reproduces; —reveals. (See literature, science.)

ARTERY

adjectives
pulsating; hardened; tiny; petty; spiritual; emotional.

verbs
block—; circulate in —s; drain—; expel from—; flow through—; incise—; involve —; ligate—; live in—; lodge in—; nourish —; obstruct—; pump through—; rupture—; sever—; terminate—; —s anastomose; —s ascend; —s branch; —s carry; —s contract; —s deteriorate; —s distribute; —s divide; —s empty; —s function; —s harden; —s join; —s spurt; —s supply; —s thicken; —s throb; —s unite.

ARTFUL

adverbs
instinctively; characteristically; slyly; craftily; subtly; insidiously; stealthily; smoothly; shrewdly; fiendishly; maliciously; astoundingly; astutely; cunningly; insinuatingly; trickily; habitually; adroitly; manifestly; openly; undeniably; knowingly; suavely; ingratiatingly; speciously; expertly; dangerously.

ARTICLE

adjectives (writing)
respective; undesirable; perfunctory; subsequent; able; valuable; detailed; forceful; inflammatory; unrelated; editorial; antiquarian; foregoing; explanatory; abusive; preliminary; hysterical; noteworthy; famous; fascinating; occasional; thought-provoking; enlightening; hypocritical; exasperating; comprehensive; arresting; lurid; delightful; frivolous; authentic; unusual; informative; striking; disturbing; sane; well-reasoned; sensible; condensed; inspired; vituperative; amusing; recent; fiery; stodgy; leading; stimulating; provocative; well-considered; critical; descriptive; proposed.

verbs
abolish—; administrate—; alter—; amend —; approve—; break—; combine —s; compose—; design—; dismiss—; dispute—; ease out—; emit—; enact—; entreat—; excerpt —; fashion—; form—; found upon—; invoke—; peruse—; point out—; prefix—; promote—; promulgate—; provide—; ratify—; reject—; revise—; rewrite—; sanction—; submit—; summarize—; swerve from—; transgress—; —asserts; —author-

izes; —binds; —compels; —concerns; —denotes; —effects; —exposes; —expostulates; —governs; —guarantees; —impeaches; —indicts; —libels; —regulates; —slanders; —specifies; —stipulates; —treats of.

(See detail, item, clause, editorial, essay.)

ARTICLE
adjectives (an object)
proprietary; admirable; charming; befrilled; practical; previous; metallic; objectionable; bloated; inferior; humblest; aggressive; cardinal; minutest; tempting; conspicuous; distinctive; cumbersome; superior; conceivable; forbidden; ancient; bulky; expensive; flimsy; showy; adulterated; intimate; plated; useful; novel; remarkable; superfluous; indispensable; harsher; inanimate; patented; preceding; fulminated; fugitive; non-durable; particular; obnoxious; important; suitable; necessary; principal; existing; resplendent; forbidden; unmistakable; toilet; serviceable; staple; unsightly; ornamental.

ARTICULATE (a)
adverbs
clearly; particularly; distinctly; emphatically; finely; especially; wonderfully; powerfully; unmistakably; cruelly; meticulously; precisely; exactly; easily.

ARTICULATE (v)
adverbs
precisely; faintly; meticulously; whisperingly; breathlessly; clearly.
(See speak.)

ARTICULATION
adjectives
supple; well-remembered; appreciative; meticulous.

ARTIFICE
adjectives
amazing; shallow; harmless; debasing; delicate; petty; plotted; ingenious; fictional; honest; dazzling; wicked.

ARTIFICER
adjectives
deft; cunning; fierce; sly; suave.

ARTIFICIAL
adverbs
subtly; stiffly; crudely; inelegantly; crassly; grotesquely; gracelessly; ponderously; highly; pretentiously; flashily; floridly; laugh-ably; ridiculously; awkwardly; offensively; outlandishly; affectedly; coquettishly; simperingly; mincingly; stagily; smoothly; slyly; cleverly; adroitly; ingeniously.

ARTILLERY
adjectives
active; coastal; defiance-roaring; doom-sounding; death-propelling; deafening; concerted; effective; earth-shaking; enormously-heavy; funeral-voiced; fierce-stabbing; incessant; liberal; offensive; reverberating; silenced; threatening; tumultuous; well-placed.

verbs
assign—; blast with—; capture—; command —; concentrate—; detail—; discharge—; disperse—; elevate—; employ—; encamp—; fear—; forge—; fortify—; improve—; introduce—; mechanize—; mount—; project —; reenforce with—; shelter from—; transport—; —attacks; —batters; —bears; —bombards; —breaks down; —concentrates on; —counters; —demolishes; —deploys; —destroys; —deteriorates; —devastates; —discharges; —fires; —forms; —handles; —harasses; —inflicts; —launches; —manoeuvers; —marches; —masses; —moves up; —occupies; —pounds; —projects; —pushes forward; —ranges; —reassembles; —repulses; —shells; —smashes; —supports; —thunders; —withdraws.
(See cannon, arms.)

ARTISAN
adjectives
tramping; skilled; capable; indolent; impatient; swarthy; humble; subordinate; simple; adroit.

ARTIST
adjectives
capable; excellent; first-rate; gifted; accomplished; competent; versatile; consummate; instinctive; true; creative; unerring; purposive; brilliant; conscientious; authentic; supreme; exquisite; cosmopolitan; keen-eyed; indefatigable; illustrious; great; cynical; world-famous; noted; distinguished; dissipated; weedy; sophisticated; temperamental; dissolute; adverse; melancholy; despairing; sought-after; pandering; un-business-like; impecunious; struggling; harassed; ragged; persecuted; misunderstood; detestable; sensitive; human; local; jealous; collaborating; fastidious; contemporary; eminent; eccentric; egotistic; excitable; fashionable; talented; outraged; accomplished; vulgar; scenic; native; mature; skilled;

65

well-known; inimitable; musical; liberal; unique; successful; sincere; decorative; technical; modern; renowned; interpretative.

verbs
confound—; encourage—; endow—; extol—; imitate—; inspire—; mark—; patronize—; remunerate—; revere—; —accomplishes; —apprehends; —attempts; —conceives; —contributes; —conveys; —creates; —cultivates; —designs; —displays; —elevates; —embodies; —employs; —endeavors; —entertains; —eschews; —executes; —expresses; —forges; —imbibes; —imitates; —opposes; —paints; —patterns; —portrays; —practises; —presents; —pursues; —renders; —reproduces; —reveals; —scorns; —sketches; —struggles with; —typifies; —unearths; —unfolds; —verses himself in.
(See sculptor, painter, musician, writer, poet, creator.)

ARTISTIC
adverbs
superbly; magnificently; delicately; actually; genuinely; indubitably; consummately; vividly; lustily; carefully; deftly; exultantly; studiedly; naturally; colorfully; richly; chastely; virginally; traditionally; radically; nostalgically; instinctively; inherently; innately; learnedly; creatively; unerringly; brilliantly; spontaneously; conscientiously; authentically; exquisitely; keenly; notably; temperamentally; sensitively; fastidiously; eminently; fashionably; inimitably; elegantly; gorgeously; magnificently; splendidly; radiantly; sublimely; bonnily; curiously; dazzlingly; passably; prettily; quaintly; showily; ingeniously; intrinsically; imitatively; academically; readily; correctly; easily; neatly; unaffectedly; crudely; ponderously; adroitly; cleverly; dexterously; intelligently; proficiently; skilfully; deftly; expertly; handily; critically; discriminatingly.

ARTISTRY
adjectives
superb; genuine; consummate; lusty; vivid; infinite; careful; deft; exalted; transcending; sheer; traditional; studied; fanatical.

ARTLESS
adverbs
unaffectedly; delightfully; refreshingly; sincerely; naively; touchingly; wondrously; manifestly; charmingly; ravishingly; exquisitely; deliciously; surprisingly; unbeliev-

ably; graciously; ingenuously; alluringly; adorably; innocently.

ASCEND (*v*)
adverbs
magically; majestically; simultaneously; directly; unwaveringly; lazily; leisurely; personally.
(See mount.)

ASCENDANCY
adjectives
inherent; moral; intellectual; growing; fatal; odious; papal; commercial; personal; complete.

ASCENDANT
adverbs
significantly; prominently; interestingly; materially; substantially; emphatically; chiefly; firmly; cardinally; markedly; primarily; remarkably; signally; vitally; influentially; preponderantly; prevalently; dominantly; authoritatively; absolutely; supremely; blessedly; happily; luckily; unfortunately; adversely; unluckily.

ASCENT
adjectives
marked; breakneck; preliminary; formidable; continual; toilsome; gentle; gradual; measureless; feasible; elevated; winding; tortuous; sheer; interminable; perilous.
verbs
accomplish—; attempt—; fear—; grade—; overcome—; schedule—; top—; —fatigues; —slopes; —tires; —wearies.
(See climb.)

ASCERTAIN (*v*)
adverbs
accurately; distinctly; dimly; instantaneously; vaguely; unhesitatingly.
(See discover.)

ASCETIC
adverbs
austerely; exceptionally; completely; incomprehensibly; obviously; excessively; terribly; remarkably; innately; naturally; puritanically; rigidly; rigorously; strictly; severely; harshly; arbitrarily; despotically; tyrannically; prudishly; haughtily.

ASCRIBE (*v*)
adverbs
unanimously; vaguely; openly; modestly; unsparingly; deliberately; unhesitatingly; villainously; frankly.
(See attribute, assign, impute.)

ASHEN

adverbs

pallidly; neutrally; coldly; colorlessly; dingily; dully; faintly; muddily; wanly; pearly.

ASHES

adjectives

quenchless; fallen; gossamer-like; glowing; whitening; lifeless; dreamless; smouldering; sparkless; venerated; charred; damped; cold; livid; vile; volcanic; blackened; dead; humble; feeble.

verbs

collect—; exhaust into—; flick—; gather—; grovel in—; heap—; mix with—; powder —; pulverize—; reduce to—; scorch to—; sift—; sprinkle with—; strew with—; throw out—; —char; —flame; —glow; —pirouette down; —remain; —rest; —settle; —smoulder.

(See cinders, remains, residue.)

ASK (*v*)

adverbs

courteously; equably; genially; discreetly; vaguely; pointedly; cannily; unctuously; spitefully; specifically; evasively; incredulously; querulously; swiftly; bluntly; huskily; contemptuously; relentlessly; persuasively; listlessly; compassionately; placidly; critically; guardedly; grouchily; shrewdly; brusquely; involuntarily; guilelessly; insistently; delicately; piteously; beseechingly; impressively; audaciously; plaintively; ironically; deadly; tremulously; naively; belligerently; provisionally; quizzically; socratically; apprehensively.

(See inquire, question, beg.)

ASPECT

adjectives

interesting; practical; picturesque; attractive; encouraging; smiling; humorous; prepossessing; pleasing; romantic; charming; benevolent; calm; noteworthy; absurd; sinister; ominous; accusing; contradictory (pl); dismal; diabolical; grim; forbidding; jaded; ludicrous; sensual; cynical; unnatural; maddening; gloomy; ridiculous; woebegone; volatile; evanescent; odd; grisly; irrational; controversial; shocking; ethical; ceremonial; physical; legal; psychic; religious; psychological; moral; genetic; scientific; obvious; broad; eternal; suggestive; original; fresh; superficial; ingratiating; beneficent; harsh; astonished; intimate; emotional; national; economic; conventional; unique; grave; for-

mal; ferocious; haggard; drawn; staring; piteous; forsaken; melancholy; wan; miserable; pallid; repulsive; formidable; enticing; cheery; weather-beaten; propitious; feminine; appealing; many-sided; festival; material; transitional; cadaverous; ironic; appalling; dark; interrelated (pl); insinuating; benignant; spiritual; unreal; artificial; unlovely; gloomy; tragic; mournful; neglected; mysterious; reverend; stern; belligerent; bleak; legal; aesthetic; incoherent; deserted; rustic; malign; utilitarian; forlorn; sanguine; primitive; alarming; supernatural; stunned; impressive; imposing; inspiring; weird; rigorous; chilling; intangible; classic; foreign; multiform; cultivated; settled.

verbs

accentuate—; adorn—; afford—; assume—; bear—; behold—; bend—; cloud—; color—; contemplate—; contrast—; dominate—; dramatize—; dwell on ; extol—; gaze at —; intensify—; meet—; muzzle—; regard —; stress—; take on—; turn—; view—; wear—; —speaks.

(See appearance, view, scene, expression, mien, look.)

ASPERSIONS

adjectives

obsolete; hasty; casual; thinly-veiled; bitter; subtle.

verbs

bespatter with—; cast—; let fall—; resort to—; vindicate from—; —besprinkle; —damage; —enrage; —infuriate; —soil; —stain.

(See slander, scandal, calumny.)

ASPIRANT

adjectives

baffled; literary; defeated; penitent; conscientious; judicial.

ASPIRATIONS

adjectives

generous; lofty; noble; national; boundless; passionate; vague; artistic; intellectual; glowing; elegant; pure; awakened; dictatorial; spiritual; unlimited; greedy; earnest; forgotten; exalted; exquisite; long-cherished; fond; sacred; speculative; political; moral; musical; social; scrupulous; secretive; rebuffed; undirected; ladylike; thwarted; professional; humdrum; poetic; determined; enthusiastic.

verbs

cherish—; deride—; dignify—; embody—;

fan with—; further—; give force to—; long with—; nurse—; realize—; restrain—; sigh with—; swamp—; thwart—; —is bounded by; —lifts him; —ripens; —soars.
(See ambition, desire, aim.)

ASPIRE (v)
adverbs
invariably; loftily; nobly; boundlessly; generously; passionately; artistically; intellectually; spiritually; earnestly; socially; professionally; poetically; determinedly; enthusiastically.
(See desire.)

ASS
adjectives
preposterous; incompetent; slow-gaited; conceited; affected; insignificant; arrant; pretentious; patient; gibbering; portentous; egregious; pompous.

verbs
act as—; brand—; breed —es; burden—; call—; corral —es; domesticate —es; employ —; harness—; overtake—; plow with —es; procure—; saddle—; shelter—; stall—; yoke —; —balks; —bears; —brays; —flees; —plods; —roams; —sniffs the wind; —strays; —subsists on.
(See animal.)

ASSAIL (v)
adverbs
abusively; fearlessly; unjustly; vituperatively; untruthfully; vaguely; furiously; keenly; constantly; perpetually; unrelentingly; doughtily; blood-thirstily; rudely; vociferously; audaciously; formidably; boldly.
(See attack.)

ASSAILANT
adjectives
fierce; quick; skillful; deadly; doughty; unrelenting; potent; unwary; blood-thirsty; rude; violent; savage; vociferous; audacious; powerful; bold; formidable; deceased.

ASSASSIN
adjectives
foiled; fiendish; jealous; vile; doomed; cool; professional; cowardly; terrorizing; wolfish; mercenary; well-meaning.

verbs
evade—; execute—; hire—; martyrize—; reward—; subdue—; —attacks; —conspires; —knifes; —lurks; —murders; —slays; —stabs; —terrorizes.
(See murderer.)

ASSASSINATE (v)
adverbs
treacherously; fiendishly; vilely; coolly; tragically.
(See kill.)

ASSASSINATION
adjectives
cold-blooded; murderous; foul; villainous; predatory.

verbs
accomplish—; aim at—; applaud—; attempt —; avert—; execute—; finish—; foment—; loathe—; pay for—; plot—; revenge—; witness—; —kindles.
(See murder, killing.)

ASSAULT
adjectives
intermittent; rude; meditated; critical; damnable; aggravated; gallant; fresh; feeble; furious; formidable; anonymous; salutary; murderous; vigorous; mock; contemplated; desperate; boisterous; drunken; base; vain; magnificent; counter; general; unprovoked; concentrated; criminal; inexplicable; destructive; terrific; simultaneous; felonious; courageous; vicious; serious; determined; savage; wicked; shrewd; frenzied; devastating; thorough-going.

verbs
aggravate—; bear—; carry by—; commit —; constitute—; counter—; defy—; fortify against—; gain by—; incur—; inflict—; intend—; make—upon; overthrow—; parallel—; project—; punish—; renew—; repeat —; repulse—; resist—; rush to—; scorn—; threaten with—; win by—; withstand—; —destroys; —produces; —weakens.
(See attack, charge, invasion, onslaught.)

ASSAULT (v)
adverbs
outrageously; violently; rudely; critically; damnably; gallantly; feebly; murderously; furiously; formidably; vigorously; desperately; boisterously; drunkenly; basely; vainly; magnificently; unprovokedly; criminally; inexplicably; destructively; simultaneously; feloniousiy; frenziedly; devastatingly.
(See attack, assail.)

ASSEMBLAGE
adjectives
vast; matchless; international; dazzling; brilliant; striking; immense; gracious; ad-

miring; hapless; motley; confused; popular; learned; glittering; melancholy; ludicrous; riotous; dreary; solemn; pitiful; plutocratic; chattering; variegated; august; hushed; listless; inattentive; public.

ASSEMBLE (v)
adverbs
elaborately; festively; tumultuously; confusedly; glitteringly; riotously; drearily; solemnly; pitifully; chatteringly; listlessly; publicly; inattentively.
(See congregate, gather, meet.)

ASSEMBLY
adjectives
fair; stormy; provincial; propitious; august; primary; legislative; glorious; numerous; gay; venerable; representative; illustrious; staid; significant; deliberative; electrified; distinguished; religious; truculent; uncongenial; periodical (pl); artless; orderly; polite.

verbs
address—; appoint to—; call—; compose—; convoke—; dismiss—; gather—; haunt—; lead—; organize—; pervade—; petition—; remodel—; salute—; set—against; unite in —; —abolishes; —adjourns; —annuls; —collects; —communes; —condemns; —congregates; —convenes; —decides; —decrees; —deliberates; —enforces; —excludes; —frames; —invests; —limits; —resolves; —suppresses.
(See meeting, congregation, council, conference.)

ASSENT
adjectives
unqualified; wordless; unanimous; preoccupied; spiritless; reluctant; deep-throated; provisional; silent; rational; requisite; cordial; vague; mournful; universal; callous; intellectual; placid; ready; brief; rapturous; smiling; rough; demure; enthusiastic; perfunctory; deliberate.

verbs
approve—; confess—; declare—; engage—; gain—; gesture—; imply—; mutter—; necessitate—; nod—; obtain—; promise—; purchase—; read—; require—; stir to—; vote—; vow—; win—; withdraw—; withhold—; yield—; —emanates; —signifies.
(See agreement, acquiescence, consent.)

ASSENT (v)
adverbs
grudgingly; appreciatively; graciously; solemnly; benevolently; ironically; indifferently; wordlessly; unanimously; unqualifiedly; spiritlessly; reluctantly; silently; cordially; vaguely; mournfully; callously; demurely; placidly; briefly; rapturously; enthusiastically; perfunctorily; deliberately.
(See concur, acquiesce, yield.)

ASSERT (v)
adverbs
positively; incredibly; blasphemously; unanimously; courageously; peremptorily; persistently; strenuously; dogmatically; emphatically; erroneously; eloquently; lustily; judicially; ignorantly; aggressively; boastfully; truculently; blandly; stalwartly; irresponsibly; autocratically; despotically; arbitrarily; fallaciously; contradictorily; presumptuously; vaingloriously; groundlessly; unequivocally; gratuitously.
(See affirm, state, say, declare.)

ASSERTION
adjectives
ignorant; lofty; vigorous; hare-brained; aggressive; emphatic; blundering; boastful; truculent; reiterated; extravagant; prior; impudent; audacious; wild; bland; complete; incredible; dogmatic; complimentary; intense; loud; incensed; controversial; irresponsible; sweeping; absolute; stalwart; astounding; autocratic; despotic; arbitrary; brutal; blustering; erroneous; pharisaical; fallacious; monstrous; disputable; contradictory; vainglorious; random; groundless; florid; deliberate; colorful; presumptuous; unequivocal; gratuitous.

verbs
affirm—; aver—; conclude—; contest—; contradict—; controvert—; credit—; declare —; defend—; flinch under—; justify—; maintain—; protest—; prove—; qualify—; refute—; sponsor—; support—; —contradicts; —elicits from; —liberates; —persuades; —sets free; —vindicates.
(See statement, declaration.)

ASSERTIVE
adverbs
loftily; aggressively; emphatically; boastfully; truculently; extravagantly; impudently; insolently; audaciously; arrogantly; blandly; confidently; dogmatically; irresponsibly; sweepingly; astoundingly; autocratically; despotically; imperiously; brutally; monstrously; vaingloriously; floridly; presumptuously; preposterously; unequivocally; heedlessly; rashly; brusquely; blatantly.

ASSESS (v)

adverbs

equitably; unjustly; annually; repeatedly.
 (See rate.)

ASSET

adjectives

dubious; distinct; domestic; inestimable; stupendous; valuable; perdurable; tangible; priceless; frozen; unassailable; paramount; strategic; scenic; compelling.

verbs

assess—s; bear—; capitalize on—; claim—; collect—s; dissolve—; distribute—s; earn —s; falsify—; fix—; freeze—; include—; inflate—s; inherit—; liquidate—; market—; note—; omit—; possess—; reduce—; represent—; salvage—; take over—; trade—; undervalue—; water—; work—; —s appear; —s increase; —s shrink; convert into —s; deduct from—; defer—.
 (See property, resources, effects, possessions.)

ASSEVERATE (v)

adverbs

repeatedly; hotly; continually; sincerely; persistently; whole-heartedly; coldly; pleasantly.
 (See declare.)

ASSIDUITY

adjectives

attentive; persevering; unremitting; discriminating; devastating; relentless; parental; bee-like; well-meaning.

ASSIDUOUS

adverbs

conscientiously; painfully; perseveringly; dependably; unremittingly; energetically; industriously; reliably; faithfully; amazingly; unusually; remarkably; loyally; uncomplainingly; unwaveringly; invariably; uniformly; persistently; constantly.

ASSIGN (v)

adverbs

subsequently; precisely; rigorously; pedagogically; frequently; unthinkingly.
 (See allot, apportion, appoint.)

ASSIGNMENT

adjectives

elaborate; roving; precise; glamorous; charming; pedagogical; rigorous; impossible; difficult.

verbs

accept—; administer—; advance—; allot—; alter—; appoint to—; apportion—; authorize—; block—; botch—; bungle—; create —; designate—; determine—; dispose of—; earn—; exempt from—; free from—; fulfill—; interest in—; merit—; muff—; nominate for—; pass—; point out—; reject—; relieve of—; set to—; share—; specify—; transfer—; wangle—; —consists of; —denotes; —pays.

ASSIMILATE (v)

adverbs

actively; readily; unhesitatingly; spiritually; painfully; whole-heartedly; easily.
 (See absorb.)

ASSIMILATION

adjectives

ready; spiritual; difficult.

ASSIST (v)

adverbs

industriously; chivalrously; materially; cordially; officiously; vigorously; effectively; financially; invaluably; charitably; generously; medically; professionally; scientifically; voluntarily; temporarily; mechanically; indispensably; skillfully; mutually; vicariously.
 (See help, aid.)

ASSISTANCE

adjectives

masculine; armed; pecuniary; financial; material; invaluable; ineffectual; extraneous; charitable; generous; medical; scientific; voluntary; professional; temporary; mechanical; outside; indispensable; skilled; additional; tactful; mutual.

verbs

accept—; afford—; contribute—; crave—; disdain—; entreat—; furnish—; further with—; lend—; limit—; present—; procure—; rely upon—; render—; requisition —; solicit—; swear—; win by—; —enables; —encourages.
 (See aid, relief, cooperation, help, support.)

ASSISTANT

adjectives

capable; patient; faithful; self-sacrificing; esteemed; untrained; temporary; fledgling; green-eyed; detached; ambidexterous; qualified; voluble; clinical; able; scholarly.

verbs
advance—; appoint—; choose—; dispatch
—; —accompanies; —aids; —cooperates;
—endeavours; —practices; —stands by.
  (See partner.)

ASSOCIATE
adjectives
habitual; blithe; old-time; ill-looking; dignified; daring; vulgar; confidential; barbarian; cherished; hardened; crafty; literary; business; questionable; unsavory;
droll; gallant; close; intimate.

verbs
applaud —s; exile —s; idolize —s; prevail
upon —s; —s accompany; —s ally with;
—s belong; —s cooperate; —s share; —s
unite.
  (See companion, colleague, partner.)

ASSOCIATE (v)
adverbs
inalienably; intimately; indissolubly, inseparably; profoundly; fraternally; indelibly;
habitually; vulgarly; daringly; confidentially; craftily; questionably; drolly; closely.
  (See connect.)

ASSOCIATION
adjectives
intimate; gloomy; ancestral; disparate;
incidental; promiscuous; philanthropic;
mournful; obscure; historical; tenuous;
scandalous; polite; charitable; congenial;
unpleasant; childish; cherished; tender;
undefinable; endearing; memorable; haphazard; obligatory; natural; exclusive;
ghastly; imperious; voluntary; indissoluble;
subtle; casual; facile; aesthetic; unanalyzed; curious; struggling; unsavory; venerable; daily; picturesque; legendary; democratic; classic.

verbs
admit to—; affiliate with—; awaken—;
combine in—; conceive—; confederate into
—; conjure up —s; connect with— ; deal
with—; disband—; disorganize—; disrupt
—; distinguish—; endow—; establish—;
exclude from—; expel from—; father—;
found—; frequent—; immortalize—; incorporate—; laud—; league into—; manage—; nurse—; oppose—; organize—; outlaw—; quarter at—; revive—; support—;
terminate—; unite in—; vouch for—; —
aims at; —classifies; —s combine; —confers upon; —flourishes; —fosters; —rivals;
—sets forth; —springs up.
  (See alliance, fellowship, affiliation, connection.)

ASSORTMENT
adjectives
imposing; varied; appealing; hideous; heterogeneous; distinguished; tangled; remarkable; excellent; amazing; complete; exceptional; motley; disintegrated; outstanding; vast; crude; comprehensive; diversified; odd; generous; extensive; incongruous; confused; conglomerated; concentrated;
balanced; weird.

ASSUME (v)
adverbs
presumptuously; gradually; voluntarily; dogmatically; hypothetically; commonly; vigorously; unconsciously; unlawfully; tacitly;
boastfully; superciliously; playfully; theatrically; irritatingly; erroneously; gratuitously; whimsically; groundlessly; complacently; fallaciously; blandly; smugly; ungraciously; baselessly; traditionally; fundamentally; falsely; imperturbably; candidly;
placidly; fatuously; humorously; viciously;
unpardonably; arrogantly; innocently.
  (See undertake, presume, accept, usurp.)

ASSUMPTION
adjectives
tacit; boastful; supercilious; theatrical;
sweeping; charitable; playful; irritating;
erroneous; verbal; gratuitous; transparent;
whimsical; preposterous; groundless; natural; complacent; calm; wearied; unparal-
lelled; fallacious; unwarranted; commonplace; absurd; precarious; mute; hereditary; bland; smug; ungracious; critical;
baseless; plausible; traditional; fundamental; reckless; false; imperturbable; candid;
gross; placid; random; shallow; unconcealed; fatuous; humorous; vicious; unproved; undue; gentlemanly; unpardonable;
arrogant; innocent.

verbs
accept—; adopt—; anticipate—; contest—;
grant—; guide by—; lay bare—; limit—;
pardon—; predicate upon—; proceed upon
—; steer clear of—; sustain—; take up—;
throw out—; verify—; warrant—; weigh
—; —holds; —implies; —leads.
  (See supposition.)

ASSURANCE
adjectives
gracious; positive; easy; lavish; pleasant;
solemn; full; happy; sincere; serene; unqualified; mute; respectful; modest; delicate; advance; dispassionate; tender; sufficient; renewed; calm; comforting; blissful; counterfeit; diplomatic; vain; insolent;

convincing; serious; limitless; reciprocal; mutual; characteristic; uncomfortable; ineffable; lukewarm; well-founded; disbelieved; inner; loquacious; inspiriting; exquisite; disheartening; definite; false; absolute; emphatic; melodious; tranquil; dampening; ponderous; smiling; gentle; cool; diminishing; considerable; significant; bland; waning; professional; swaggering; ineradicable; unwavering; infallible; magnificent; smug; defiant; blunt; insensitive; brassy.

verbs
breed—; confirm—; convey—; establish—; flash—; guarantee—; handle with—; inspire—; pledge—; procure—; promise—; renew—; rest in—; secure—; smile—.
(See confidence, conviction, trust.)

ASSURE (v)
adverbs
virtually; solemnly; diligently; indolently; secretly; vaguely; reasonably; positively; lavishly; serenely; unqualifiedly; mutely; respectfully; modestly; tenderly; diplomatically; insolently; convincingly; reciprocally; mutually; characteristically; absolutely; emphatically; tranquilly; blandly; professionally; swaggeringly; unwaveringly; infallibly; defiantly; bluntly.

ASTONISH (v)
adverbs
sublimely; rousingly; amazingly; silently; profoundly; inconceivably; utterly; unboundedly; inexpressibly; blankly; palpably; unmistakably; intensely; unaffectedly; ludicrously; dramatically.
(See amaze, astound, stagger.)

ASTONISHMENT
adjectives
respectful; amused; tempestuous; unrestrained; affronted; silent; rapturous; whimsical; fat; pure; feigned; involuntary; mute; profound; initial; inconceivable; liveliest; unspeakable; utter; unbounded; swift; indignant; delighted; ever-increasing; inexpressible; horrified; dull; dawning; contemptuous; blank; palpable; sardonic; unmistakable; puzzled; intense; fond; breathless; wordless; annoyed; unaffected; acute; uncomfortable; curious; faint; open-mouthed; petrified; bitter; wide-eyed; stupefied; ludicrous; dramatic; sheer; hurt; shocked; bored; bald.

verbs
benumb with—; blink with—; confuse—; elicit—; excite—; express—; feign—; gasp

with—; move to—; numb with—; paralyze with—; pretend—; quell—; restrain—; seize with—; stagger with—; stupefy—; supersede—.
(See amazement, surprise, wonder.)

ASTOUND (v)
adverbs
utterly; amazingly; thoroughly; completely; tremendously; dramatically; inexpressibly.
(See astonish, amaze, stagger.)

ASTUTE
adverbs
cleverly; keenly; sagaciously; sagely; wisely; craftily; cunningly; invariably; habitually; unfailingly; adroitly; customarily; discerningly; artfully; manifestly; undeniably; intelligently; shrewdly; deftly; ingeniously; insidiously; judiciously; learnedly.

ASTUTENESS
adjectives
habitual; strategical; devious; native; editorial; customary.

ASYLUM
verbs
abolish—; afford—; attend—; cast into—; claim—; commit to—; deliver up to—; devote to—; escape from—; establish—; flee from—; force into—; found—; guarantee—; grant—; harbor in—; huddle in—; incarcerate in—; invade—; limit—to; maintain—; maltreat in—; preside over—; provide—; refuse—to; remove from—; reside in—; restrict to—; retreat to—; sanctify—; seek—; support in—; torture in—; violate —; —accumulates; —cares for; —deals with; —protects; —shelters.
(See retreat, sanctuary, refuge, institution.)

ATHEISM
adjectives
uncompromising; overt; aggressive; militant; downright; courageous; swaggering.

verbs
cast off—; charge with—; clothe in—; countenance—; despise—; disprove—; destroy—; disapprove—; eradicate—; exhibit —; fall into—; incline toward—; inculcate—; justify—; mourn—; overthrow—; practice—; prate about—; pretend to—; proclaim—; recognize—; reject—; replace —; substitute—; support—; thunder—; unloose—; voice—; —acknowledges; —appears; —captivates; —conceives; —denies;

72

—disbelieves; —exists; —flounders; —grips; —grows; —lacks; —organizes; —philosophizes; —protests; —quiets down; —startles.
(See skepticism, disbelief.)

ATHEIST

adjectives
passionate; impious; positive; extreme; practical.

verbs
convert—; convince—; —arises; —confuses; —defames; —denies; —disbelieves; —discourses; —disregards.
(See skeptic, heretic.)

ATHEISTIC

adverbs
bigotedly; horribly; irreverently; impiously; perversely; fanatically; avowedly; sacrilegiously; profanely; heart-breakingly; grievously; tormentingly; obstinately; stubbornly; unhappily; irrationally; unreasonably; profoundly; irrevocably; immovably; obdurately; openly; essentially.

ATHLETE

adjectives
tall; wiry; well-built; fleet-legged; husky; energetic; lithe; young; scintillant; distinguished; professional; promising; splendid; all-around; barrel-chested.

verbs
address —s; applaud—; coach—; coddle—; condition—; debar—; develop—; commercialize—; exhaust—; experience—; fete—; fit—; govern—; honor—; inspire—; key up —; league —s; match—; oppose—; privilege—; proselyte—; provide for—; solicit—; stimulate—; strain—; subsidize—; time—; —accomplishes; —combats; —competes; —contends; —contests; —endures; —excels; —exhibits; —leaps; —overhauls; —strives; —surpasses; —trains; —vaults; —vies; —wrestles.
(See contestant, player.)

ATHLETIC

adverbs
splendidly; stoutly; noisily; sturdily; healthily; devotedly; robustly; heartily; vigorously; wholesomely; healthfully; magnificently; whole-heartedly; stockily; brawnily; ardently; assiduously; zealously; energetically; gravely; seriously.

ATHLETICS

verbs
bar—; bar from—; coach—; compete in—;

create—; develop—; dip into—; dispel—; draft into—; embrace—; encourage—; engage in—; enter into—; establish—; excel in—; favor—; further—; go in for—; improve—; interest in—; pertain to—; practise—; promote—; referee—; score—; skill in—; subordinate—; succeed in—; support —; teach—; train for—; undertake—; utilize—; witness—; —builds; —develops; —occupies; —stirs; —thrills.
(See game, exercise.)

ATMOSPHERE

adjectives
radiant; genial; congenial; rosy; general; ideal; blessed; refreshing; exhilarating; free; invigorating; gentle; homelike; calm; pure; enervating; charming; genteel; mirthful; enchanting; quiet; restful; exquisite; bracing; serene; cordial; genuine; healthful; happy; buoyant; delightful; queenly; hospitable; wholesome; agreeable; jolly; rare; admirable; weird; uncanny; indescribable; electric; amazing; 'spooky; exciting; creepy; gloomy; stratified; brutal; criminal; dingy; severe; restricted; unhappy; air-cooled; sinister; dire; hostile; uneasy; chilling; insidious; polluted; murky; smoky; terrible; fetid; soggy; sour; nauseous; poisonous; dim; small-town; rural; frozen; human; political; learned; adventurous; poetic; slumbrous; fairylike; cosmopolitan; humid; sultry; close; windless; stuffy; living; changed; sheltered; realistic; distinctive; intangible; unfathomable; essential; inimical; apprehensive; thunderous; balmy; swift-moving; colorful; unreal; cool; ethereal; misty; special; enveloping; natural; intoxicating; characteristic; refined; clean; correct; luxurious; pleasant; distinguished; cheerful; ambient; suffocating; limpid; burning; steaming; faint; foul; rayless; grim; tense; vapory; bell-clear; venomous; contagious; quivering; artistic; musical; charged; consistent; intimate; straitened; infective; spiritual; hot; scintillating; transparent; stagnant; ruffling; lucid; rosy; uninteresting; agitated; nervous; romantic; artificial; unearthly; fierce; factitious; sleepy; metropolitan; easy; controlled; surcharged; depressing; lost; medieval; continental; stilted; decorous; respectable; social; intellectual; dewy; drear; summer; frightening; intimate; choked; rich; subtle; unindividual; exciting; clarified; dense; ladylike; dismal; troublous; emotional; roseate; oil-reeking; picturesque; somber; country; sentimental; hallowed; poetic; humid; damp; burdensome; scientific; dust-

less; quivering; reactionary; provincial; pellucid; unconventional; thrilling; livable; indoor; germ-laden; putrid; festive; impersonal; disloyal; elastic; sun-warm; crystal; lifeless; mutual; beamless; evening; tranquil; emerald; precious; furnace-heated; authentic; oppressive; concentrated; uncongenial; wet; commonplace; rarefied; burning; impassive; remote; ever-stormless.

ATMOSPHERE
verbs (air)
absorb in—; adulterate—; analyze—; combine with—; compose—; constitute—; contaminate—; cool—; befoul—; cleanse—; erupt into—; escape into—; gain access to —; illuminate—; inhale—; invade—; filter —; float in—; mix in—; occupy—; pervade —; pump from—; rarify—; refresh—; release into—; smother in—of; surcharge—; —reeks.
(See air.)

ATMOSPHERE
(element or
verbs influence)
achieve—; break—; breathe—; capture—; charge—; create—; dispel—; dissipate—; distill—; drink in—; electrify—; enhance—; evoke—; indicate—; inform—; leaven—; load—; shatter—; surround—; —hinders; —inspires; —lends; —lures; —mingles; —promotes; —vivifies.
(See influence, environment.)

ATOM
adjectives
primordial; golden; pungent; intrusive; paltry; jarring; meditative; quenchless; homogeneous; gaseous; tormented; intelligent; throbbing; phosphorescent.

ATONE (v)
adverbs
fully; peacefully; heroically; bitterly; finally; vicariously; solemnly; sorrowfully; humbly.
(See pay.)

ATONEMENT
adjectives
heroic; final; least; bitter; vicarious; solemn; innocent.

verbs
emphasize—; make—; modify—; offer—; preach—; punish—; purify by—; refuse—; reject—; repent in—; reward—; sacrifice in—; set at—; —amends; —appeases; —

dawns; —expiates; —reconciles; —redeems; —repairs; —restores; —satisfies; —saves; —vindicates.
(See reparation, satisfaction.)

ATROCIOUS
adverbs
scandalously; outrageously; glaringly; notoriously; horribly; monstrously; inhumanly; harshly; ruthlessly; wickedly; abominably; savagely; barbarously; pitiably; remarkably; incredibly; unbelievably; inexpressibly; inconceivably.

ATROCITY
adjectives
Victorian; lugubrious; unbelievable; monstrous; unprovoked; barbaric; utter; cold-blooded; out-of-the-way.

verbs
attend with—; avenge—; commit—; defend from—; deserve—; expiate—; hide—; inflict—upon; revenge—; subject to—; —horrifies; —shocks; —stupefies.
(See outrage, crime, cruelty, wickedness, blunder.)

ATTACH (v)
adverbs
passionately; unfeignedly; exclusively; violently; devoutly; gratefully; justly; indissolubly; sentimentally; ardently; unashamedly; romantically; hopelessly; insanely; incestuously; uniformly; tenderly; fervidly; emotionally; recklessly; conjugally; avowedly; cynically; excessively; momentarily.
(See annex, fasten.)

ATTACHMENT
adjectives
sentimental; passionate; warped; ardent; violent; deep; affectionate; unashamed; romantic; hopeless; boundless; invisible; insane; warm; incestuous; altruistic; disinterested; uniform; prior; tender; honest; steady; unrequited; fervid; special; emotional; underlying; reckless; filial; conjugal; marked; lasting; growing; lukewarm; serious; avowed; cynical; excessive; momentary.

verbs
absorb by—; affect—; apprehend—; authorize—; cement—; command—; connect—; decree—of; deepen—; deprecate—; devote to—; divide—; enforce—; execute—; fasten —; further—; grant—; process—; recover by—; regulate—; secure—; seize in—; sympathize with—; tack on—; warrant—;

—binds; —perishes; —persists; —survives; —withstands.

(See affection, devotion.)

ATTACK

adjectives

smashing; savage; murderous; fiery; bold; homicidal; ripping; bulldog; tearing; deadly; devastating; ruthless; angry; fierce; brutal; reckless; terrific; treacherous; scathing; hurricane; severe; damaging; formidable; desperate; prolonged; diplomatic; merciless; literary; hand-to-hand; journalistic; verbal; demagogic; vehement; unrestrained; incessant; determined; inexorable; rapid; zestful; impetuous; correct; serious; unexpected; direct; surprise; resounding; logical; vague; mysterious; provocative; sudden; well-organized; sustained; widespread; subtle; persisting; counter; organized; vigorous; withering; open; pulmonary; precipitate; simultaneous; scientific; bitter; damaging; crushing; unprovoked; whirlwind; strategic; oblique; furious; hysterical; peculiar; systematic; secular; outside; ordered; infantry; desultory; threatened; blasphemous; lawless; decisive; barbarous; noisy; seditious; premature; subsequent; convulsive; contemplated; nocturnal; burglarous; unjust; insidious; unfortunate; indiscriminate; ill-natured; abrupt; outrageous; immediate; tumultuous; abortive; violent; ignoble; frontal; satirical; tireless; sagacious; spasmodic; censurable; epileptoid; premeditated; venomous.

verbs

anticipate—; avert—; block—; blunt—; carry—; change—; characterize—; conceive —; concentrate—; consolidate—; counter—; cure of—; defy—; desist from—; direct—; dislodge—; divert—; double—; foresee—; forestall—; guard against—; head off—; immunize against—; induce—; initiate—; intensify—; launch—; mass for—; mount to—; plan—; precipitate—; predispose to —; prepare for—; presage—; pretend—; proceed with—; proclaim—; recover from —; re-enforce—; repel—; repudiate—; repulse—; satirize—; shift—; soften—; subdue—; succeed in—; succumb to—; suppress —; survive—; sustain—; terminate—; throw off—; time—; unite in—; unleash—; usher in—; wind up—; —abates; —arises; — coincides; —defames; —excites; —impends; —injures; —occurs; —overthrows; —recurs; —seizes; —subsides; —succeeds; —sways; —swerves; —swings.

(See invasion, siege, attempt.)

ATTACK (v)

adverbs

ardently; simultaneously; bitterly; scurrilously; fiendishly; virulently; libelously; savagely; anonymously; ridiculously; characteristically; sorely; energetically; vehemently; criminally; unscrupulously; smashingly; murderously; devastatingly; ruthlessly; scathingly; treacherously; verbally; incessantly; determinedly; inexorably; impetuously; venomously; scientifically; unprovokedly; obliquely; blasphemously; decisively; barbarously; prematurely; insidiously; satirically.

(See assail, invade, combat.)

ATTAIN (v)

adverbs

ultimately; cheaply; effectually; artistically; modestly; legally; intellectually; profitably; educationally; singularly; ultimately; scientifically; technically; astronomically; linguistically; incomparably; rarely.

(See achieve, gain, acquire.)

ATTAINMENTS

adjectives

remarkable; artistic; desirable; modest; legal; mental; distinguished; unusual; intellectual; profitable; scholarly; educational; singular; ultimate; ornamental; eminent; scientific; technical; astronomical; linguistic; incomparable; rare.

ATTEMPT

adjectives

sincere; valiant; memorable; sympathetic; serious; honest; admirable; successful; elaborate; ingenious; ambitious; eloquent; careful; kindly; enlightened; reasonable; well-meaning; ill-directed; slow-witted; weak; faltering; feeble; sorry; slightest; bashful; ineffectual; unavailing; half-hearted; laughable; grotesque; hopeless; vain; unfortunate; clumsy; futile; stupid; foolish; fruitless; farcical; mock; foolhardy; despairing; inept; pitiful; nugatory; maladroit; murderous; outrageous; mad; disastrous; dreary; infamous; superhuman; bold; daring; heroic; spectacular; systematic; repeated; definite; organized; long-heralded; vituperative; obvious; belated; freest; picturesque; covert; blind; passionate; abortive; miscarried; unappreciated; curious; numerous; pretentious; early; labored; major; hurried; unsteady; involuntary; extreme; rash; remarkable; creditable; impious; patriotic; rude; youthful; vigorous; embarrassed; misguided; cramplike; isolated; memorable; inconsiderate; arduous; coquettish; ignoble; forcible; deliberate; laudable; forlorn; torturing; charitable; unconstitutional; wicked; complicated; brutal; discouraging; direct; previous; mimic; exorbitant; murderous; strange; unorganized; perpetual; chimerical; excellent; traitorous; premature; uncouth; half-satirical; despicable; inauspicious; villainous; experimental; bare.

verbs
acclaim—; afford—; applaud—; commence—; commit—; complete—; constitute—; defeat—; deter from—; discern—; essay—; evade—; fail in—; fall short in—; foil—; glorify—; honor—; indict for—; interpret—; justify—; oppose—; overcome—; put forth—; recognize—; repel—; repudiate—; restrain—; suffer from—; stimulate—; thwart—; undertake—; warrant—; —blinds; —confounds; —triumphs; —wearies; interrupt—.

(See trial, endeavor, effort, attack.)

ATTEMPT (v)
adverbs
desperately; amateurishly; repeatedly; strenuously; previously; feebly; inadvertently; valiantly; memorably; sincerely; ingeniously; eloquently; reasonably; enlightenedly; falteringly; ineffectually; unavailingly; half-heartedly; grotesquely; futilely; fruitlessly; farcically; ineptly; maladroitly; murderously; outrageously; odiously; hazardously; disastrously; infamously; superhumanly; heroically; spectacularly; daringly; systematically; vituperatively; obviously; picturesquely; covertly; abortively; pretentiously; laboriously; unsteadily; involuntarily; creditably; impiously; patriotically; misguidedly; memorably; arduously; coquettishly; ignobly; forcibly; laudably; forlornly; charitably; unconstitutionally; brutally; exorbitantly; prematurely; uncouthly; half-satirically; despicably; inauspiciously; villainously.

(See endeavor, strive, undertake.)

ATTEND (v)
adverbs
diligently; faithfully; habitually; punctually; consistently; patiently; strictly; frequently; numerously; successively; expertly; rarely; invariably; assiduously; casually; nightly; compulsorily; unavailingly; properly; medically; overflowingly; scantily; profes-

sionally; defectively; suitably; stolidly; unceremoniously; devotedly; cheerfully; intermittently.

(See guard, heed, listen.)

ATTENDANCE
adjectives
assiduous; casual; interminable; nightly; compulsory; constant; unavailing; unrelaxing; agitated; proper; medical; overflowing; increased; scanty; professional; slovenly; defective; suitable; stolid; unceremonious; regular; unasked; devoted; cheerful; surpassed; intermittent.

verbs
advise—; await—; charge for—; command—; compel—; continue—; dance—; delay—; engage—; exact—; expect—; gather in—; increase—; minister in—; order—; resume—; wait in—; win—; —dwindles; —falls off; —grows; —increases; —manifests.

(See audience, congregation.)

ATTENDANT
adjectives
faithful; trained; black-robed; courteous; general; unobtrusive; gaudy; official; mercenary; nervous; chattering; spectacled; skilled; constant; flustered; experienced; obsequious; diligent; brave; dissolute; whispering; excited; inspiring; inseparable; obliging; fez-covered.

ATTENTION
adjectives
gentle; popular; eager; favorable; considerate; respectful; flattering; courteous; charming; gracious; delicate; faithful; thoughtful; keen; interested; undisguised; open-mouthed; undivided; rapt; riveted; absorbed; precise; painstaking; critical; persistent; assiduous; meticulous; scrutinizing; scrupulous; particular; strict; studious; unremitting; unceasing; wide-eyed; skilled; intellectual; pusillanimous; unwavering; obsequious; irritating; odious; casual; unappreciated; scant; trifling; idle; surface; slight; wandering; excessive; concentrated; individual; general; underground; wide; alert; spurious; prompt; special; country-wide; final; increased; considerable; cursory; rival; calm; acute; anxious; unobtrusive; tactful; sharp; serious; deliberate; emphatic; sufficient; abstracted; frowning; ample; enwrapped; unreasoning; ungrudging; momentary; minute; precious; nocturnal; faintest; strained; vague; uninterrupt-

ed; polite; unwonted; willing; careful; admirable; well-meant; irksome; solitary; bland; impersonal; edifying; ill-omened; best; tense; languid; profound; watchful; painful; summary; supreme; deepest; unfatigued; hesitating; manual; undue; reluctant; early; marked; feigned; unwelcome; parental; benumbed; whole-souled; funny; startled; minimum; indifferent; exclusive; breathless; sour; statistical; forced; vital; rational; unflagging; close; listless; animated; universal; insensible; fawning; unmeasured; conscientious; uncaressing; vigilant; affectionate; mournful; cheap; fascinated; earnest; cataleptic; wifely; public.

verbs

absorb—; acquire—of; arouse—; arrest—; bestow—upon; bring to—; call—to; capture —; center—; chide into—; claim—; clamor for—; come to—; command—; compel—; compete for—; concentrate—; confine—; crave—; demand—; desire—; devote—; dictate—; direct—; dispose—; distract—; distribute—; divert—; draw—; enforce—; engage—; engross—; enlist—; escape—; exact—from; excite—; exercise—; exhaust —; exhibit—; fasten—; favor with—; fix —; flash—; focus—; gain—; garner—; hold in—; increase—; influence—; lavish —upon; lend—; load with—; locate—; maintain—; mark with—; merit—; monopolize—; object to—; observe with—; occupy —; pay—; provoke—; reap—; recall—; reduce—; register—; reject—; relax—; require—; resume—; rivet—; secure—; stand at—; stimulate to—; straighten up in—; strike—; strive for—; subject to—; summon—; sustain—; train—upon; turn—toward; warrant—; win—; yield—; —embarrasses; —flags; —lies in; —wanders; —wanes; attract—.

(See gaze.)

ATTENTIVE

adverbs

absorbingly; steadily; intently; alertly; critically; analytically; closely; remarkably; astoundingly; suspiciously; guardedly; mildly; noticeably; intelligently; breathlessly; eagerly; engrossingly; raptly; carefully; considerately; thoughtfully; scrupulously; deferentially; respectfully; obsequiously; decorously; immensely; favorably; courteously; charmingly; graciously; assiduously; unwaveringly; flatteringly; idly; excessively; generally; finally; calmly; anxiously; unobtrusively; tactfully; sharply; politely; earnestly.

ATTEST (v)

adverbs

explicitly; unequivocally; duly; sincerely; authoritatively; freely.

(See confirm, indorse, corroborate.)

ATTIC

adjectives

stuffy; dusty; cobwebby; unused.

verbs

betake oneself to—; climb to—; confine to—; construct—; decorate—; design—; designate to—; enclose—; insulate—; lock in—; lodge in—; modernize—; relegate to—; renovate —; rumble around—; rummage in—; scour —; seclude in—; store in—; utilize—; ventilate—; —contains; —covers; —extends; —holds.

(See garret, room, cellar.)

ATTIRE

adjectives

bedizened; elaborate; motley; disreputable; informal; injudicious; fit; scandalous; crumpled; male; hunting; gala; quaint; drab; fairest; elegant; gay; evening; holiday; unaccustomed; scanty; showy; absurd; feminine; careful; splendid; mourning; unceremonious; picturesque; ornamented; exquisite; tawdry; ostentatious; festal; negligent; substantial; wild; coarse; abbreviated; gaudy.

verbs

acquire—; adorn in—; array in—; checker —; costume in—; deck in—; decorate in—; don—; dress in—; equip with—; flash—; gear in—; outfit in—; pin on—; shroud in—.

(See dress, clothing, apparel, costume.)

ATTIRE (v)

adverbs

somberly; impeccably; fantastically; faultlessly; modishly; scrupulously; superbly; disreputably; informally; fittingly; scandalously; quaintly; drably; elegantly; scantily; unceremoniously; picturesquely; exquisitely; ostentatiously; negligently; coarsely; gaudily.

(See dress.)

ATTITUDE

adjectives

firm; oblivious; listless; denunciatory; truculent; philanthropic; apathetic; scrupulous; unsisterly; composed; studied; absolutory; pathetic; impassive; civilized; rebellious; disconsolate; misanthropic; sensible; figurative; contemptuous; hostile; lukewarm; egotistical; endless; assiduous; subtle; depressive; mental; indolent; contemplative; motionless; orientated; threatening; ridiculous; forlorn; political; basic; insidious; exulting; swaying; slouching; stoical; bellicose; favorable; submissive; positive; procrastinating; fearless; lofty; charming; gallant; gorgeous; piquant; reverent; exalted; resolute; cool; unbending; courageous; affirmative; adamantine; uncompromising; optimistic; light-hearted; complacent; cordial; self-sufficient; devil-may-care; overindulgent; carefree; depressed; serious; morose; sound; healthy; sane; natural; quiet; firm; eager; dignified; obliging; respectful; sympathetic; jubilant; conciliatory; enlightened; cultivated; timid; tolerant; cautious; generous; perfunctory; arrogant; supercilious; self-centered; disdainful; unsympathetic; condescending; patronizing; censorious; lordly; imperious; deprecatory; antagonistic; pugnacious; alien; militant; menacing; detestable; vengeful; devastating; preposterous; catastrophic; treasonable; unfriendly; transient; impolite; resentful; flippant; drooped; unfortunate; irreconcilable; condemnatory; suspicious; callous; pessimistic; dejected; ironical; overconfident; balanced; objective; unconventional; sudden; mature; fluid; familiar; injured; pragmatic; necessary; passive; watchful; worshipful; free; set; easy; quiescent; menial; annoying; defensive; condoning; sentimental; typical; talkative; realistic; various; restrained; destructive; ignorant; moral; ostrich; nonchalant; depreciatory; historical; nervous; benevolent; mutual; constrained; praiseworthy; infantile; graceful; belligerent; consistent; peculiar; suppliant; non-aggressive; defiant; untrammeled; presumptuous; judicial; helpless; negligent; characteristic; unsatisfactory; unpleasant; heroic; charming; strutting; comical; righteous; despondent; wholesome; unjust; hard-boiled; anachronistic; unlike (pl); crouching; fashionable; abnormal; chivalrous; discreet; penitential; peering; hypocritical; business-like; suggestive; forensic; fundamental; rigid; habitual; bipolar; ungraceful; tender; nonsensical; erect; resigned; traditional; warlike; emotional; mute; romantic.

verbs

abandon—; acquire—; adopt—; advocate —; analyze—; assume—; behave in—; breed—; choose—; color—; condemn—; define—; denote—; deplore—; discount—; distort—; dominate—; dramatize—; embrace —; emphasize—; encourage—; exalt—; examine—; exhibit—; explain—; expound—; express—; fall into—; gesture—; give rise to—; hold—; illuminate—; implant—; imply—; inculcate—; indicate—; ingrain—; interpret—; justify—; maintain—; manage —; manifest—; modify—; move to—; obsess with—; overcome—; persist in—; pervert—; portray—; posture—; preserve—; project—; reflect—; regard—; relax—; repose in—of; resent—; revere—; reverse—; sense—; stand in—; study—; —antagonizes; —applies; —implies; —menaces; —prejudices; —prevails; —reveals; —robs; —survives; —warns.

(See position, idea.)

ATTORNEY

adjectives

shyster; sneaking; incompetent; eminent; scurrilous; fashionable; prosecuting; well-tried; wealthy; astonished; illiterate; uneducated; brilliant.

verbs

appoint—; bar—; betray—; bind—; commission—; confer with—; confide in—; consult—; criticize—; delegate—; disbar—; discipline—; dispatch—; employ—; endorse —; engage—; ordain—; procure—; refer to—; reimburse—; retain—; train —s; — acknowledges; —acts; —administers; — advocates; —argues; —assails; —attacks; —bickers; —contracts for; —counsels; — cross-examines; —defames; —defends; — discusses; —examines; —exerts; —exposes; —formulates; —influences; —intercedes; —manages; —objects; —orates; —performs; —pleads; —practices; —prepares; —promotes; —prosecutes; —quibbles; —represents; —solicits; —sues for; —tries; —s wrangle.

(See lawyer.)

ATTRACT (v)

adverbs

instinctively; adroitly; romantically; magnetically; commandingly; irresistibly; profoundly; inescapably.

(See draw, engage, induce.)

ATTRACTION

adjectives

supreme; irresistible; queer; sweet; rare; natural; voluptuous; defective; dreadful; morbid; tragic; uncomfortable; fierce; insidious; unrivaled; loudly-heralded; dazzling; outstanding; overwhelming; principal; unusual; foremost; notable; cosmopolitan; physical; manifold; tidal; sexual; pastoral;

scenic; sartorial; historic; instant; growing; current; fleeting; scant; mutual; indefinable; obvious; chief; personal; myriad (pl); time-mellowed; casual; added; unspoken; spiritual; powerful; material; instinctive; clouded; poetical; limitless (pl); specific; resultant; acute; gratuitous; magnetic; electrostatic; hideous; fatal; permanent; feature; secret; coquettish; specious; mysterious; reciprocal; innumerable (pl); intellectual; accelerative; divine; enormous; sylvan; intrinsic; varying; imperious; conjugal; subtle.

verbs
admit—; augment—; cause—; center—; confess to—; exert—; force—; form—; illustrate—; yield to—; —adheres; —allures; —develops; —diminishes; —draws; —enhances; —fades; —lures; —recedes; —unsettles.
(See charm, fascination.)

ATTRACTIVE
adverbs
radiantly; irresistibly; rarely; sweetly; dazzlingly; overwhelmingly; indefinably; divinely; mysteriously; unutterably; powerfully; singularly; charmingly; alluringly; uncommonly; engagingly; undeniably; beautifully; bewitchingly; enchantingly; delightfully; exquisitely; interestingly; daintily; smartly; jauntily; bewilderingly; exotically; tormentingly.

ATTRACTIVENESS
adjectives
varied; bright; inevitable; annoying; physical; unusual; singular.

ATTRIBUTE
adjectives
supernatural; desirable; priceless; fundamental; fantastic; fearful; feminine; senseless; wonderful; detestable; recognizable; splendid; striking; peacock; literary; time-honored; chief; mistaken; characteristic; essential; accessory; homely; moral; intellectual; unalterable; judicial; human; highest; universal; gracious; noble; specific; conventional; sacred; productive; lofty; infinite; known; hereditary; striking; armorial; vacillating; diverse; sovereign; modified.

verbs
ascribe—to; credit with—; determine—; discover—; distinguish—; dramatize—; endow with—; enlarge—; estimate—; eulogize—; honor—; invest with—; limit—; manifest—;

mark—; possess—; recognize—; ridicule—; shed all —s; value—; —enhances.
(See characteristic, symbol, quality, property.)

ATTRIBUTE (*v*)
adverbs
invariably; solely; entirely; modestly; skilfully; chiefly; basely; falsely; absurdly; innocently; supernaturally; fantastically; senselessly; graciously; nobly; specifically; conventionally.
(See impute, ascribe.)

AUDACIOUS
adverbs
disconcertingly; dauntlessly; rashly; indiscreetly; injudiciously; hot-headedly; foolishly; impudently; incredibly; recklessly; serenely; amazingly; overbearingly; shamelessly; tragically; singularly; strangely; innately; crazily; notoriously; dramatically; terribly; inherently; colossally; foolhardily; breath-takingly; fantastically; alarmingly; offensively; constitutionally; temperamentally.

AUDACITY
adjectives
incredible; utmost; reckless; characteristic; rapid; serene; gay; gorgeous; winning; amazing; sheer; insolent; cynical; cool; unfailing; unparalleled; vigorous; indelicate; heroic; harmless; human; inward; personal; dissolute; splendid; unnecessary; supreme; brilliant; operative; adventurous; unheard-of; aggressive; masculine; magnificent.

verbs
admire—; assume—; cool—; counterfeit—; depart from—; encourage—; exhibit—; relapse from—; reprimand—; shame by—; tame—; thrill at—; venture forth with—; —affronts; —engenders; —perturbs; —shocks; disregard—.
(See recklessness.)

AUDIENCE
adjectives
intelligent; sympathetic; understanding; appreciative; meager; sophisticated; attentive; interested; discerning; approving; imposing; vociferous; distinguished; admiring; enchanted; happy; democratic; meticulous; hilarious; enthusiastic; frenzied; vast; crowded; wide; undetermined; large; huge; fair; capacity; slender; tense; hushed; expectant; whispering; breathless; startled; astonished; mystified; chilled; bewildered; hard-boiled; wayward; cynical; hostile;

critical; ribald; unprecedented; unseen; reading; special; famished; invited; dull; applauding; nightly; respectable; imaginary; apathetic; suspicious; technical; motley; martial; impromptu; select; laughing; legislative; eager; delighted; dead-struck; enormous; gloomy; indiscriminate; polished; tragic; absorbed; satisfied; circular; pitying; listless; reasonable; added; dreary; prospective; elect; stupid; unresponsive; advertent; haughty.

verbs
accustom to—; admit—; appeal to—; assemble—; break up—; command—; convulse—; crave—; delight—; dismiss—; draw—; enslave—; enthuse (colloq.)—; exhort—; grant—; harangue—; hypnotize —; inflame—; lend—; lure—; overwhelm —; panic—; scan—; seek—; survey—; sway —; vouchsafe—; win—; —acclaims; —applauds; —cheers; —claps; —demands; — detects; —gapes; —gasps; —groans; — hisses; —howls; —laughs; —listens; — melts away; —packs; —pays; —responds; —roars; —rustles; —sobs; —stamps; — swells; —thrills; —throngs; —weeps.
(See hearing, interview, conference, gathering.)

AUDITOR
adjectives
skilled; bated; confounded; enchanted.

AUDITORIUM
adjectives
tight-packed; seething; huge; crowded; firetrap.

verbs
assemble in—; fill—; hire—; jam—; occupy —; receive in—; reverberate through—; throng—; —accommodates; —echoes; —holds; —resounds; —rings with; —seats.
(See building, hall, arena.)

AUGMENT (v)
adverbs
currently; incredibly; scarcely; tremendously; indefinitely; continually.
(See swell, increase.)

AUGURY
adjectives
favorable; evil; happy; reassuring; fearful; grim; heathen; sinister.

AUNT
adjectives
thin; sallow; unflagging; gaunt; sophisti-

cated; worldly; ancient; strait-laced; maiden; pious.

AURA
adjectives
healthful; vague; flashing; evil; invidious; shimmering; tangible; smoky.

AUSPICES
adjectives
authoritative; pleasant; responsible; cordial; favorable; present; flattering; charitable.

AUSPICIOUS
adverbs
highly; opportunely; properly; suitably; happily; fairly; favorably; fortunately; luckily; providentially; remarkably; unusually; duly; consistently; gratifyingly; pleasantly; agreeably; fittingly; delightfully.

AUSTERE
adverbs
gravely; starkly; sombrely; monastically; harshly; puritanically; severely; rigorously; rigidly; uncompromisingly; inflexibly; unsparingly; arbitrarily; tyrannically; sternly; oddly; unfashionably; haughtily; soberly; odiously; unmitigatedly; unbendingly; unrelentingly.

AUSTERITY
adjectives
tempering; neat; wholesome; geometric; beautiful; dark; unrelieved; dignified; seeming; monastic; prayerful; natural; gentle; harsh; unyielding; famous; mild; hoar.

AUTHENTIC
adverbs
undeniably; unquestionably; admittedly; avowedly; unchallengedly; assuredly; professedly; palpably; obviously; evidently; apparently; absolutely; positively; categorically; genuinely; incontestably; indisputably; manifestly; unmistakably.

AUTHENTICITY
adjectives
doubtful; absolute; stylistic; altered; unmistakable; unquestioned; unforgettable.

verbs
accept—; command—; confirm—; dispute—; doubt—; entitle to—; insure—; profess—; prove—; question—; satisfy with—; stamp with—; testify to—; value—; verify—; —holds up; —stands.
(See accuracy.)

adjectives

veteran; competent; wild; versatile; accomplished; important; successful; prolific; eminent; favorite; distinguished; famous; modern; esteemed; engaging; amiable; vivacious; charming; noble; ardent; cheerful; well-meaning; inspiring; sane; disputatious; capricious; irresponsible; untrained; whimsical; perplexed; budding; unknown; putative; sentimental; dogmatic; forgotten; judicious; elusive; nascent; anonymous; irate; gregarious; antique; disillusioned; gifted; recent; alleged; striving; fearless; venerable; aspiring; delightful; remote; contemporary; cunning; neglected; profound; classical; agitated; anxious; vain; juvenile; comic; bigoted; superstitious.

verbs

acclaim—; acquaint with—; animate—; appreciate—; challenge—; criticize—; dishonor—; disturb—; employ—; engage—; enthuse (colloq.)—; exhaust—; frustrate—; honor—; inspire—; laud—; persecute—; plague—; rouse—; slander—; —bewitches; —casts about; —characterizes; —colors; —compels; —compiles; —composes; —creates; —cultivates; —dabbles; —declares; —dedicates; —describes; —devotes; —divines; —dreams; —edits; —exploits; —foreshadows; —gloats; —improvises; —indicates; —instigates; —labors; —languishes; —libels; —moralizes; —motivates; —objects; —originates; —philosophizes; —pirates; —plagiarizes; —produces; —pursues; —retires; —shapes; —soliloquizes; —translates; —voices; discuss—.

(See writer, poet.)

AUTHORITATIVE

adverbs

impressively; eminently; unquestionably; undisputedly; distinctly; reliably; responsibly; dependably; infallibly; highly; supremely; competently; expertly; peerlessly; imposingly; abundantly; respectably; quietly; learnedly; famously; deftly; academically; locally; legally; mildly; magisterially; uncompromisingly; pompously; imperially; condescendingly; truculently; brutally; studiously; specifically; directly; dogmatically; smoothly; suavely; conventionally; solemnly; delicately; finally; venerably; despotically; officially; divinely; habitually; undeniably; proudly; gently; unmistakably; cruelly; ostentatiously.

adjectives

leading; unimpeachable; acknowledged; accredited; recognized; renowned; eminent; unquestioned; well-known; undisputed; distinguished; reliable; responsible; dependable; prominent; infallible; high; foremost; supreme; unchallenged; competent; peerless; imposing; abundant; famous; respectable; quiet; learned; interesting; superior; deft; academic; civil; shocked; local; apostolic; outstanding; parental; legal; mild; arrogated; deputed; magisterial; uncompromising; constituted; imperial; sacred; express; crushing; appointed; condescending; revered; truculent; unique; adequate; humiliating; studious; practical; outraged; shadowy; specific; direct; limited; established; dogmatic; smooth; legitimate; apocryphal; mystic; coordinate; unbounded; sundry; conventional; solemn; centralized; concurrent; sufficient; executive; actual; delicate; minor; harassing; censorial; musical; administrative; standard; venerable; serious; delegated; ecclesiastical; parliamentary; despotic; base; brief; oracular; paramount; spiritual; dissolving; firm; provincial; far-distant; disciplinary; excellent; conferred; all-persuasive; scientific; territorial; governmental; antenatal; coercive; private; discretionary; ministerial; coequal; worn-out; military; provisional; ascertained; mellow; habitual; inspired; sovereign; central; weighty; grammatical; consular; divine; unassailable; sanctified.

verbs

abuse—; accept—; act with—; appeal to—; appoint to—; arm with—; aspire to—; assert—; attain—; boast—; carry—; challenge—; claim—; clothe with—; command—; confer—upon; confirm—; consult—; declare—; decree—; defy—; delegate—; derive—; desire—; discredit—; enforce—; entrust—; establish—; esteem—; execute—; exercise—; extend—; fetter—; flout—; grant—; heighten—; ignore—; inspire—; invest with—; lend—; limit—; mark with—; obey—; possess—; preserve—; pronounce—; question—; quote—; rebel against—; regard with—; register—; reject—; relinquish—; rely upon—; respect—; restrain—; revere—; revolt against—; ridicule—; speak with—; squelch—; submit to—; support—; uphold—; usurp—; weaken—; weigh—; wield—; wink at—; wrest—; yield to—; —s arrest; —s intervene; —s jockey; —melts away; —s speculate.

(See right, jurisdiction, influence, power.)

AUTHORIZE (v)

adverbs

specifically; confidentially; responsibly; infallibly; respectably; locally; magisterially; expressly; practically; specifically; directly; limitedly; legitimately; ecclesiastically; despotically; basely; governmentally; divinely; unassailably; grammatically.

(See confirm, justify.)

AUTOBIOGRAPHICAL

adverbs

honestly; inadvertently; factually; probably; possibly; embarrassingly; amusingly; lightheartedly; blithely; gaily; solemnly; revealingly; lustily; radiantly; indecently; decorously; selectively; happily; lustily; gustily; gloriously; delightfully; unexpectedly; helpfully; analytically; critically; literally.

AUTOBIOGRAPHY

adjectives

factual; honest; intimate; embarrassing; lusty; amusing; accurate; unbelievable.

AUTOCRACY

adjectives

malignant; church; incompetent; pernicious; monstrous.

AUTOCRAT

adjectives

rival; irresponsible; absolute; vigorous; beneficent; ruthless; ancient.

AUTOCRATIC

adverbs

imperiously; tyrannically; unyieldingly; inflexibly; hatefully; meanly; arbitrarily; insolently; arrogantly; overbearingly; openly; brazenly; audaciously; jauntily; teasingly; regally; offensively; obnoxiously; deplorably; intolerably; lamentably; unfortunately.

AUTOGRAPH

adjectives

interesting; stateliest; boldest; facsimile.

AUTOMATIC (n)

adjectives   (gun)

wicked; mean-looking; flashing; blue-nosed; compact; sputtering; deadly.

AUTOMATIC (a)

adverbs

entirely; conveniently; amazingly; optionally; originally; luckily; ingeniously; cleverly; smoothly.

AUTOMOBILE

adjectives

ancient; dusty; long; swerving; lean; unidentified; obsolete; two-seated; rusty; rattlesome; undependable; sleek; streamlined.

verbs

climb into—; construct—; crank—; demolish—; design—; develop—; enclose—; engage—; equip—; improve—; insure—; license—; pilot—; pour out of—; power—; salvage—; —careens; —chugs; —climbs; —crawls; —creaks; —cruises; —descends; —flashes by; —flits by; —hauls; —hurtles; —joggles; —jolts; —lumbers; —moans; —noses; —pants; —pokes; —quivers; —roars; —skids; —slips by; —snarls; —snorts; —spins; —squeaks; —s swarm; —swoops; —transports; —travels; —trundles; —whines; —whirs; —whizzes; —zooms.

(See wagon, train.)

AUTOPSY

adjectives

unfavorable; warmly controverted; ghastly; inevitable; long-drawn-out; purely experimental; gruesome; ensuing; consequent; co-incidental.

verbs

carry on—; complete—; conclude by—; consent to—; consider—; consult—; diagnose by—; dispense with—; evidence by—; examine by—; hold—; inspect—; observe—; order—; perform—; permit—; record—; refuse—; report on—; request—; require —; seek—; subject to—; testify to—; urge —; witness—; —confirms; —determines; —discloses; —discovers; —reveals; —verifies.

(See examination.)

AUTUMN

adjectives

first; radiant; rank; meek; eventful; distributed; colorful; ambient; bounteous; dreary; everlasting; sere; paradisaical; chill.

verbs

enter—; hail—; welcome—; —advances; —basks; —beams; —burnishes; —bursts; —clamors; —colors; —decays; —decks; —declines; —descends; —embellishes; —extends from; —fades; —flames; —flushes; —follows; —garners; —gleams; —harvests; —haunts; —heralds; —lavishes; —matures; —meditates; —merges; —mocks; —paints; —pierces; —pours; —precedes; —presses near; —reaps; —resigns; —ripens; —rushes

in; —rustles; —scatters; —shackles; —spreads; —sweeps in; —thwarts; —upbraids; —violates; —warns; —wreathes; —yields.
(See fall.)

AUXILIARY

adjectives
warlike; unexpected; disaffected; thundering.

AUXILIARY (v)

adverbs
patronizingly; officially; officiously; legally; cooperatively; helpfully.

AVAIL (v)

adverbs
freely; promptly; continually; unobtrusively; scarcely; covertly; openly; slyly; villainously; brutally.
(See use.)

AVAILABLE

adverbs
easily; instantly; immediately; presumably; always; undoubtedly; obviously; evidently; apparently; unquestionably; scarcely; seldom.

AVALANCHE

adjectives
hoofed; blinding; deep; startling; rocky; appalling; impending; sun-awakened; stupendous.

verbs
beat—; endure—; evade—; loose—; perish in—; precipitate—; protect against—; roll down in—; —crashes; —denudes; —descends; —destroys; —endangers; —gathers force; —masses; —occurs; —overwhelms; —plunges; —pours by; —roars; —rushes by; —suffocates; —swallows; —sweeps past; —washes along.

AVARICE

adjectives
besetting; anxious; sullen; pecuniary; insatiable; gripping; cruel; greedy.

verbs
decry—; deplore—; detest—; display—; evince—; gather with—; grovel in—; hoard in—; staunch—; take up with—; —acquires; —eats; —shrieks.
(See greed.)

AVARICIOUS

adverbs
incurably; avidly; insanely; peculiarly; incorrigibly; distressingly; painfully; embarrassingly; irreclaimably; hopelessly; shamelessly; appallingly; terribly; horribly; churlishly; sordidly; rapaciously.

AVENGE (v)

adverbs
horribly; sufficiently; fiercely; self-appointedly; blood-thirstily; cruelly; finally; primarily; satisfactorily.
(See punish, revenge, vindicate, retaliate.)

AVENGER

adjectives
fierce; blood-stained; unblamed; ordained; avowed; self-appointed.

AVENUE

adjectives
fine; moonlit; glittering; ignominious; trim; tidy; intersecting; cobble-stoned; open; fashionable; principal; diagonal; spacious; densely-shaded; leafy; dwarfish; continuous; noble; tree-lined; gorgeous; melancholy.

verbs
amble down—; approach—; border—; circle—; enter—; gain access to—; light—; litter—; locate on—; mark—; promenade —; shade—; shadow—; stroll down—; venture up—; —crosses; —extends; —leads to; —parallels.
(See road, thoroughfare, way, approach, street.)

AVERAGE

adjectives
well-gauged; inversely-proportioned; adjusted; stalwart; standardized; skeptical; unvarying; prevailing; weighted; weighty; timely.

verbs
adjust—; arrive at—; ascertain—; better —; compare—; compile—; derive—; determine—; diminish—; distribute over—; divide—; estimate—; evolve—; hit—; lower —; model on—; obtain—; propose—; reckon —; record—; refer—; reveal—; strike—; suggest—; yield—; —amounts to; —compares; —falls; —ranges; —rises; —varies; —yields.
(See amount.)

AVERSE

adverbs

persistently; unreasonably; ineradicably; unnaturally; innately; openly; avowedly; unrelentingly; tenaciously; immovably; inflexibly; headily; arbitrarily; mulishly; stubbornly; obstinately.

AVERSION

adjectives

persistent; marked; ineradicable; strong; unnatural; staunch; unconquerable; inherent; thorough; instinctive; deep-rooted; instantaneous; utter; hereditary; loathing; inexpressible; proportionate; decided; favorite; extreme; separate; marked; mutual; cold; feminine; undisguised; developed; unreasonable; deadly.

verbs

augment—; cement—; fix—; intimate—; produce—; purge of—; recollect with—; rid of—; side-track—; strengthen—; voice—; —estranges.

(See antipathy, dislike, hatred.)

AVERT (v)

adverbs

cleverly; happily; coldly; swiftly; thoughtfully; dexterously; skilfully; painstakingly; scarcely.

(See prevent.)

AVIATOR

adjectives

daring; illustrious; famous; amateur; imaginative; intrepid; fearless; skilled.

verbs

exhaust—; inform—; license—; overtake—; strain—; test—; —accomplishes; —achieves; —ascends; —attempts; —circles; —controls; —descends; —dips; —endures; —lands; —loops; —manipulates; —navigates; —operates; —perceives; —pilots; —somersaults; —speeds; —takes off; —transports; —views; —zooms.

(See flier, airplane.)

AVID

adverbs

childishly; unnaturally; fatally; obviously; extraordinarily; excessively; anxiously; ardently; breathlessly; hungrily; fantastically; impetuously; zealously; madly; curiously; fervently; queerly; insatiably; sedulously.

AVOCATION

adjectives

ecstatic; pleasant.

AVOID (v)

adverbs

zealously; openly; studiously; industriously; contemptuously; scrupulously; cautiously; purposely; persistently; honorably; sedulously; decorously; involuntarily; totally; vigilantly; absolutely.

(See parry, evade, shun, elude.)

AVOIDANCE

adjectives

total; vigilant; lazy; absolute.

AVOW (v)

adverbs

brutally; simply; enthusiastically; bluntly; plainly; ardently; ostentatiously; boldly; energetically; unequivocally; manfully; gratefully; daringly; commonly; sincerely; savagely; secretly.

(See acknowledge, admit, profess.)

AVOWAL

adjectives

brutal; simple; enthusiastic; blunt; plain; ardent.

AWAIT (v)

adverbs

tensely; anxiously; silently; impatiently; apprehensively; informally; excitedly; tremblingly; breathlessly; courageously.

(See look, wait.)

AWAKE (v)

adverbs

rudely; shudderingly; accidentally; muscularly; singularly; breathlessly; consequently; hauntingly; blissfully; manifestly; spiritually; mechanically.

(See wake.)

AWAKENING

adjectives

rude; first; startled; innocent; new; blissful; moral; consequent; modest; manifest; stormy; spiritual.

AWARD

adjectives

long-coveted; grudging; merited; carefully-computed; just; princely; bounteous; inconsequent.

verbs

adjudicate—; applaud—; arbitrate—; assign—; capture—; consider—; decide—; deliberate—; dispute—; earn—; embody—; examine—; furnish—; grant—; institute—;

judge—; merit—; please with—; praise—; pronounce—; provide—; submit—; win—.
(See decision, verdict, judgment.)

AWARE

adverbs

sensitively; painfully; acutely; vividly; sharply; keenly; curiously; psychically; subconsciously; sorely; uncomfortably; wretchedly; pleasingly; happily; rapturously; fully; intensely; suddenly; poignantly; astutely; wholly; neurotically; powerfully; perfectly; desperately; dimly; scarcely; barely; breathlessly.

AWARENESS

adjectives

neurotic; powerful; increased; sensitized.

AWE

adjectives

superstitious; deep; deferential; mysterious; simulated; joyous; strange; cringing; profound; candid; ineffable; vague; devout; tender; respectful; salutary; reverential; meaningful; undefined; fearful; slavish; unwilling; sacred; restraining; inspiring; trembling; adoring; mystic; silent; religious; hideous; inexpressible; supernatural; pious; rapt; ecstatic; dumb.

verbs

approach with—; awake—; bask in—; bind in—; breed—; command—; conduce—; create—; deepen—; develop—of; entertain —of; excite—; eye with—; fill with—; flock round in—; hold in—of; inspire with —; keep in—of; learn with—; mingle with —; oppress with—; overcome with—; remove—; shake with—; stand in—of; strike with—; —afflicts; —arises; —breeds; —overcomes; —shakes; —smites; —stirs; —strikes.
(See amazement, fear, reverence.)

AWKWARD

adverbs

clumsily; ungracefully; bashfully; shyly; gawkily; self-consciously; painfully; embarrassingly; ludicrously; laughably; ridiculously; intentionally; adorably; unconsci-

ously; charmingly; affectedly; momentarily; remarkably; flutteringly; clownishly; amusingly; pathetically; lamentably; unfortunately; helplessly; hopelessly.

AWKWARDNESS

adjectives

adorable; fumbling; mirth-provoking; pleased; unconscious; involuntary; slight; obvious; charming; blundering; affected; bristling; momentary.

verbs

begin in—; bungle with—; disperse—; encounter—; laugh at—; rebuke—; scorn—; —adheres; —embarrasses; —inconveniences.
(See clumsiness.)

AWNING

adjectives

luxuriant; striped; woven; rotting; shady; gaudy; ordinary; ready-made; gaily-colored.

AXE

adjectives

keen; lusty; glittering; gallant; rude; sounding; devastating; biting; consecrated.

verbs

apply—; chop with—; clasp—; cleave with —; condemn to—; cool—; execute with—; fashion—; fell with—; forge—; grind—; hack with—; heave—; helve—; hew with —; lay on—; resist—; scar—; shaft—; shape—; sharpen—; slay with—; stroke—; swing—; temper—; turn—; wedge—; whip —; wield—; yield to—; —chips; —cleaves; —decapitates; —falls; —gleams; —glitters; —hacks; —hews; —resounds; —rings; —rusts.
(See hatchet.)

AXIOM

adjectives

simple; religious; moral; accepted; fundamental; irrefutable; educing; settled; divine; intricate; established.

AZURE

adjectives

kindling; greenish; vivid; intense; clear; glowing; cold; cloudless; ambient; smiling; dazzling; beauteous; palpitating.

B

BABBLE

adjectives

charming; ceaseless; drunken; foolish; incoherent; literary; senseless; perpetual;
meaningless; idle; excited; irrelevant;
soothing; childish; idiotic; pleasant; prattling; confused.

BABBLE (v)

adverbs

drunkenly; grievously; ecstatically; idiotically; weirdly; ingeniously; charmingly; ceaselessly; incoherently; perpetually; meaninglessly; irrelevantly; confusedly.

(See murmur, prattle.)

BABE

adjectives

innocent; unmothered; speechless; maiden;
starving; wailing; nursing; testy; naked;
unborn.

BABOON

adjectives

malevolent; bouncing; dog-faced; patriarchal; chattering; grotesque; gaping;
smirking.

BABY

adjectives

healthy; fat; angelic; grown-up; pallid;
sickly-looking; unweaned; peaceful; bewitching; sturdy; squalling; new-born; lonesome; pitiful; wriggling; cunning; squeaking; babbling; sticky; petulant; strong-
lunged; appealing; featureless; blithesome;
staring; mewling; rosy-cheeked; tousled;
clamorous; stubborn; disobedient; delicate;
inopportune; undisciplined.

verbs

comfort—; cradle—; croon to—; fondle—;
indulge—; lull—; mother—; quiet—; rear
—; suckle—; swaddle—; tend—; train—;
treat as—; wean—; —babbles; —coos; —
creeps; —crows; —drools; —moans; —
pukes; —plains; —teethes; —toddles; —
weeps; —whimpers.

(See infant.)

BABYISH

adverbs

entrancingly; ridiculously; disgustingly; utterly; beamingly; angelically; sturdily;
cunningly; appealingly; rosily; delicately;
helplessly; clingingly; shyly; absurdly; a-
dorably; completely; artlessly; boisterously;
irresistibly; lovably; warmly; lustily; magically; mysteriously; excitedly.

BACHELOR

adjectives

virtuous; level-headed; arrant; vagrant;
typical; sexagenary; impeccable; desolate;
austere; dashing; predestined; crusty; cynical; solitary; elusive; confirmed; lonely;
gruff; perennial; wary; indignant; perpetual.

BACK

adjectives

expressive; prosperous; narrow; wiry; slender; straight; innocent-looking; broad; benevolent; roomy; rigid; brawny; powerful;
aching; inexorable; lovely; lithe; obtrusive;
bent; naked; cringing; arched; agile; discreet; wrenched; deliberate; lacerated;
burly; indiscriminate; stiffening; hairy; ram-
rod; contemptuous; incurious.

verbs

arch—; bear on—;, bow—; buckle on—;
clamor at—; huddle on—; hump—; mount
—; pluck from—; prick—; recline on—;
ride—; set upon—; strip—; sway—; up-
heave—; —arches; —creaks.

BACK (v)

adverbs

stealthily; consistently; obtrusively; cringingly; agilely; discreetly; deliberately; contemptuously.

(See support, indorse.)

BACKGROUND

adjectives

psychological; Puritan; political; historical;
rich; Quakerish; botanical; proletarian;
intellectual; educational; cultural; moral;
monotheistic; inherited; pictorial; blurred;
neutral; changeless; realistic; scenic; unwonted; stereotyped; garish; dense; serrated; meager; complex; star-flecked; shimmering; kaleidoscopic; broad; effective;
financial; conspicuous; attractive; authentic;
religious; fitting; immaterial; plain; harmonious; rocky; precipitous; theatrical; social; domestic; appropriate; technical; fascinating; vivid; lush; convincing; serene;
striking; unforgettable; imaginative; glamorous; enchanting; admirable; impressive;
shabby; sinister; cluttered; bizarre; weird-
est.

verbs

blend into—; broaden—; enhance—; fade

into—; form—; maintain—; melt into—; paint—; screen—; set into—; weave—; —blends; —brightens; —contrasts; —enhances; —looms; —sets off.

(See setting.)

BACON

adjectives

crisp; tender; tasty; mouldy; crackling; rank; sizzling; tempting.

BACTERIA

adjectives

antagonistic; classified; disease-producing; friendly; gram-positive; harmful; infectious; invading; injurious; lethal; minute; multitudinous; overwhelming; poisonous; secondary; succulent; swarming.

verbs

absorb—; activate—; annihilate—; attack —; class—; combat—; cultivate—; culture —; destroy—; discover—; disperse—; distribute—through; dose with—; examine—; filter—; group—; identify—; immunize against—; inhale—; inoculate with—; investigate—; isolate—; observe—; produce—; propagate—; protect against—; raise—; resist—; separate—; study—; treat —; —behave; —cause; —course through; —disturb; —enter; —form; —increase; —infect; —invade; —irritate; —multiply; —poison; —reproduce; —secrete; —split; —spoil; —survive; —swarm; —dwell.

(See organism, germs.)

BAD

adverbs

flagrantly; destructively; infinitely; harmfully; dangerously; mischievously; violently; vilely; irretrievably; inconceivably; poisonously; abominably; accursedly; perniciously; viciously; basely; deplorably; detestably; diabolically; disastrously; dreadfully; exceptionably; grievously; hatefully; malignantly; obnoxiously; venomously; virulently; manifestly; scandalously; irremediably; irrevocably; immeasurably.

BADGE

adjectives

corrupt; distinctive; decorative; decorous; distinguished; emblematic; glittering; heraldic; identifying; imperial; pompous; pretentious; tarnished; tawdry.

verbs

bear—; blazon with—; flash—; flaunt—; merit—; ornament—; wear—; work—; —betokens; —distinguishes; —heralds; —honors; —indicates; —marks; —signifies.

(See device, emblem.)

BADGER

adjectives

belligerent; biting; aggressive; defensive; fierce; hibernating; ungainly; moody.

verbs

bait—; snare—; trap— ; —s abound; —burrows; —charges; —claws; —digs; —dives in; —dwells; —excavates; —flattens out; —growls; —haunts; —hisses; —leaps; —lumbers; —mines; —plunges; —purrs; —retreats; —robs; —rushes; —senses; —seizes; —snarls; —sniffs; —squats.

(See animal.)

BADINAGE

adjectives

lazy; giddy; banal; good-natured; teasing; gay; cheap; frivolous; merciless; untimely.

BAFFLE (v)

adverbs

hopelessly; completely; genuinely; scarcely; continually; shrewdly; slyly; plainly.

(See thwart, frustrate.)

BAFFLING

adverbs

mysteriously; irritatingly; bewilderingly; unaccountably; disturbingly; genuinely; strangely; surprisingly; astonishingly; indescribably; fearfully; disappointingly; utterly; insuperably; dishearteningly; incommodiously; discouragingly; depressingly; terribly; vexatiously; seriously; alarmingly; perfectly; absolutely; incomprehensibly; inconceivably.

BAG

adjectives

sealed; sanitary; shiny; travel-worn; soggy; cloth-covered; bottomless; diminutive; bulky; pendulous.

verbs

bind in—; dip into—; purloin—; rifle—; seal—; secure in—; snatch—; stow—; trap in—; —bulges; —dangles; —emits; —hangs; —sags; —slides; —slips.

(See wallet, satchel.)

BAGGAGE

adjectives

unnecessary; hand, superfluous; mental; multitudinous; clumsy; ponderous; weighty.

verbs

abandon—; attend with—; convey—; dispatch—; encumber with—; lighten—; retrieve—; splotch—; stow—; transport—; tuck—away; —encumbers; —weighs.

(See satchel.)

BAGPIPE

adjectives

awesome; blood-chilling; dominant; droning; ear-splitting; eerie; fiercely-screaming; lamenting; long-winded; screeching; triumphant; victory-sounding; vengeful.

verbs

adjust—; blow upon—; compress—; elbow —; embrace—; esteem—; finger—; inflate —; introduce—; muffle—; press—; puff up —; regulate—; —bawls; —bellows; — chants; —cries; —drones; —emits; —expands; —groans; —harmonizes; —heaves; —labors; —mourns; —pipes; —proclaims; —rouses; —shrills; —sighs; —stirs; — swells; —wails; —whistles.

BAIL

adjectives

appointed; certified; forfeited; generous; responsible; specified; superficial; trifling; enforced; heavy; necessary; substantial.

verbs

admit to—; allow—; apply for—; assure—; bind with—; collect—; default—; demand —; deny—; designate—; dispense with—; enter—; exempt from—; fix—; forfeit—; furnish—; give—; grant—; gauge—; guarantee—; hold to—; insure by—; justify—; liberate on—; pledge—; post—; procure—; provide—; put up—; raise—; receive—; refund—; release on—; require—; risk—; satisfy with—; set—; set free on—; surrender—; —obligates; —releases.

(See security.)

BAIT

adjectives

tempting; dainty; false; seductive; coveted; treacherous; pernicious; alluring.

verbs

devour—; expose—; feed—; hold out—; proffer—; swallow—; —allures; —ensnares; —entices; —lures; —tempts; —traps.

(See lure, inducement, temptation.)

BALANCE

adjectives

unexpended; fabulous; unnatural; proper; delicate; subtle; artistic; comfortable; unpaid; neutral; sentimental; smooth; floating; adverse; peculiar; precarious; normal; miraculous; economic; trifling; workable; unfavorable; scrupulous; logical; physiological; trembling; accurate.

verbs

achieve—; adjust—; arrange—; attain—; augment—; bear—; bequeath—; control—; deflect—; determine—; disturb—; equalize —; even—; exhaust—; hang in—; hold—; lay in—; maintain—; measure—; reach—; readjust—; recover—; restore—; strike—; supply—; suspend on—; sway—; test—; tip —; totter in—; turn—; upset—; weigh in —; —turns.

(See scales, equilibrium.)

BALANCE (*v*)

adverbs

precariously; equally; ultimately; harmoniously; unskillfully; exactly; accurately; systematically; uncomfortably; cautiously; dexterously; eventually.

(See poise.)

BALCONY

adjectives

exquisite; overhanging; latticed; moon-drenched; screened; high-perched; vine-clad; narrow; grilled; delicate; frail.

verbs

crowd—; gain—; occupy—; overlook—; peer from—; rail—; salute from—; view from—; —encompasses; —overhangs; — projects; —swarms.

(See gallery.)

BALD

adverbs

shinily; fatly; rosily; hopelessly; nakedly; ruddily; ghastly; ridiculously; laughably; gracelessly; grossly; haggardly; hideously; unashamedly; odiously; shockingly; smilingly.

BALEFUL

adverbs

perniciously; terribly; venomously; malignantly; undeniably; villainously; exceptionally; sadly; grievously; deplorably; lamentably; woefully; shockingly; cruelly; detestably; infernally; irremediably; atrociously; malevolently; incorrigibly; brutally; unpardonably; incredibly; shamefully; iniquitously.

BALK (*v*)

adverbs

continually; cruelly; particularly; recalcitrantly; exasperatingly; pettishly; provokingly; irritatingly.

(See thwart, frustrate, baffle, disappoint.)

BALKY

adverbs

astonishingly; surprisingly; naturally; incorrigibly; wonderfully; unexpectedly; tormentingly; vexatiously; embarrassingly; stubbornly; obstinately; temperamentally; characteristically; abnormally; habitually; usually; uncompromisingly; invariably; consistently; inherently; innately; blithely; unreasonably; provokingly; unaccountably.

BALL
adjectives (dance)
inauguration; carnival; rustic; impromptu; magnificent; birthday; anniversary; annual; masquerade.

BALL
adjectives (object)
gilded; glowing; gleaming; bouncing; glittering; devil-guided; luminous; swift; gelatinous; fungous.

BALL
adjectives (sport)
back firing; catapulting, foul; fair; ricocheting; trenchant; tangential; sodden; speeding; bombastic; refractory.

verbs
bat—; bobble—; bunt—; chuck—; club—; control—; cover—; drive—; feed —s; fling —; foul—; fumble—; grip—; heave—; hurl —; inflate—; juggle—; lob—; loft—; muff —; pass—; pole—; pop—; project—; pursue—; release—; round into—; smash—; snare—; spear—; strike—; top—; toss—; trap—; waggle at the golf—; whip—; zip —; —bounds; —curves; —hops; —zooms.

BALLAD
adjectives
woeful; doleful; ribald; odious; patriotic; vigorous; dramatic; celebrated; tawdry; rude; merry; scurrilous; tender; lewd; blasphemous; interminable; vulgar; sentimental; brisk; ringing; homely; dolorous; obscene; raucous.

verbs
accompany—; carol—; characterize—; classify—; compose—; measure—; narrate—; print—; revive—; traduce—; translate—; wail—; —celebrates; —deals with; —exploits; —narrates; —relates; —survives; —swells.
(See poem, song.)

BALLET
adjectives
gaudy; glittering; dainty; sumptuous; exquisite; fairylike.

BALLOON
adjectives
gigantic; invisible; floating; lifeless; air-filled; gaseous.

verbs
anchor—; attach to—; ballast—; blow—; burst—; check—; command—; dispatch—; cut away—; deflate—; elevate—; experiment with —s; fire—; guide—; improve—; inflate—; liberate—; lift—; lighten—; man —; navigate—; power—; propel—; steady —; suspend—; swell—; —ascends; —circles; —collapses; —descends; —drifts; — expands; —explodes; —floats; —journeys; —kites; —rises; —sallies; —soars; —spins; —tosses; —wallows.
(See bladder, aeroplane.)

BALLOT
adjectives
approved; adopted; computed; disputed; fatal; political; polled, open; reformed; secret.

verbs
accede by—; acknowledge by—; agree by—; arrange—; assent by—; broadcast—; cast —; circulate —s; choose by—; deposit—; draw up—; employ—; hinge on—; inspect —; introduce—; record—; reform—; reject —; satisfy with—; stuff —s; tabulate —s; tally —s; tamper with —s; —acquits; —affirms; —ascertains; —condemns; —decides; —elects; —eliminates; —installs; —proclaims.
(See vote, ticket.)

BALLROOM
adjectives
huge; improvised; dimly-lit; crowded; decorated.

BALM
adjectives
soothing; fragrant; golden; philosophic; blissful; healing; temperate; assuaging; precious; unguentary; icy.

verbs
anoint with—; exude—; soothe with—; steep in—; yield—; wash off—; —assuages; —charms; —eases; —heals; —mitigates; — soothes; —trickles.
(See ointment, salve.)

BALMY
adverbs
soothingly; refreshingly; softly; comfortingly; curatively; quietly; coolly; gently; mild-

ly; blandly; healingly; gratifyingly; satisfactorily; remarkably; tenderly; mercifully; pleasantly; especially.

BALUSTRADE
adjectives
granite; terrace; sandstone; marble; graceful; wrought-iron; exquisite; carved; shining; quaint; twisting; serpentine; monstrous.

BAMBOO
adjectives
delicate-leaved; pliant; plaited; feathery.

BAN
adjectives
authoritative; blasphemous; cruel; common; harsh; inhibitory; legal; maledictory; proclamatory; senseless; tyrannical; unjust.

verbs
announce—on; command—on; contradict—; curse—; decree—; end—; enforce—; exempt from—; impose—; lift—; proclaim—; publish—; reaffirm—; remove—; renew—; send—; —deprives; —forbids; —offends; —outlaws; —prohibits.

(See notice, taboo, edict, proclamation, excommunication.)

BANAL
adverbs
monotonously; tritely; tiresomely; boringly; disagreeably; drearily; unceasingly; invariably; triflingly; vapidly; inanely; insipidly; intolerably; trivially; unbearably; exhaustingly; wearily; tediously; frivolously; senselessly; vacuously; insufferably; habitually; prosily; uninterestingly.

BANALITY
adjectives
routine; easy; preliminary; gross; unpleasant; boring; dreary; repetitious.

BANANA
adjectives
tempting; sun-hungry; lush; ripened.

BAND
adjectives (company)
aimless; diminished; detached; ferocious; foraging; gladsome; hunted; hapless; march-worn; pillaging; rapine; rollicking; straggling; vandalistic; victorious.

verbs
arm—; associate with—; attach to—; banish from—; bind in a holy—; captain—; collect—; compose—; disperse—; divide into —s; enlist in—; muster—; scatter—; summon—; unite in—; wander in—; —attacks; —invades; —pillages; —plunders; —pursues; —roves; —shrinks.

(See company, group, gang, troop.)

BAND
adjectives (fetter, tie)
ring-stacked; quivered; artful; swaddling; unrelieved; restraining; flexible; iridescent; metallic.

verbs
break asunder the—s; cancel—s; chain in —s; dissolve—; link in —s; release from —s; rend —s; strengthen —s; twist —s; untie —s; untwine —s; weaken—; —s bind; —s encircle; —s fetter; —s shackle.

(See tie, cord, bond, fetter, belt, bandage, chain.)

BAND
adjectives (group)
infuriated; angelic; cycling; alabaster; ruthless; scarlet; riotous; massed; melancholy; marauding; adverse; servile; devoted; encircling; colic; baleful; eager; doomed; notorious; peaceful; full; unbroken; bloody; amiable; swirling; murderous; numberless; resplendent; scattered; reckless; chosen; shadowy; formidable; violent; apathetic; restless; defiant; eternal; itinerant; enthralling; wandering; guerilla; fantastic; sullen; glittering; expectant; valiant; considerable; predatory; snail-like; gallant; mirth-breathing; heroic; enormous; mute; ghastly; scanty; boisterous; prying; mirthful; devoted; adventurous; ambitious; imperious; fairy; social; scattering; brazen; nondescript; partisan; thin; doughty; fierce; worn; insignificant; rival; small; well-armed; thundering; wild; howling; heretical; shabby; unkempt; conspicuous; feeble; mighty; unconquerable; inexhaustible; laborious; invading; brave.

BAND
adjectives (instrumental)
tuneful; stirring; gorgeously-arrayed; regimental; swing; jazz; competent.

verbs
assemble—; compose—; conduct—; engage —; group—; maintain—; organize—; pitch —; strike up—; supervise—; —arouses; —blares; —blasts on; —encourages; —harmonizes; —honors; —marches; —parades;

—performs; —renders; —serenades; —
toots; —troops.
(See orchestra.)

BANDAGE

adjectives
crimsoned; filthy; swathing; emergency;
bloodstained; saving.

verbs
apply—; attach—; border with—; change
—; discard—; fasten—; loose—; replace—;
sew—; sterilize—; stitch—; stripe with —s;
swathe in —s; tighten—.
(See band.)

BANDIT

adjectives
famous; amiable; cold-blooded; ferocious;
ruthless; wily; out-and-out; dark-visaged;
bold; outrageous; notorious; reckless; tantalizing; enraged; burly; restless; lawless.

verbs
defend—; execute—; grant sanctuary to—;
hire—; hunt—; imprison—; infest with —s;
organize—; outlaw—; seclude—; slay—; —
harries; —marauds; —s pillage; —s plunder; —s terrorize.
(See robber, burglar.)

BANDY (*v*)

adverbs
mercilessly; repeatedly; continuously; freely; haphazardly; thoughtlessly.
(See toss.)

BANG

adjectives
loud; emphatic; thudding; resounding; ear-
splitting.

BANG (*v*)

adverbs
fitfully; resoundingly; loudly; emphatically; terrifically; crashingly; tremendously;
explosively; thunderously; furiously.
(See thump, resound.)

BANISH (*v*)

adverbs
utterly; effectually; everlastingly; perpetually; dishonorably; eternally; inescapably;
deservedly; ultimately; reluctantly; cruelly.
(See dismiss, expel.)

BANISHMENT

adjectives
timely; everlasting; perpetual; honorable;
deadly; eternal; inescapable; deserved.

verbs
compel—; consent to—; decree—; doom to
—; order—; repeal—; reside in—; return
from—; suffer—.
(See exile, expulsion.)

BANJO

adjectives
melodious; melancholy; tuneless; twanging;
plunking; soul-fathoming; heart-voicing;
unstrung; voodoo-charming.

verbs
compose for—; employ—; excel at—; finger
—; fret—; harmonize with—; introduce—;
peg—; perform on—; pick—; pluck—; strike
—; string—; strum—; twitch—; —expresses; —lulls; —registers; —serenades; —
sings; —twangs; —vibrates.
(See instrument, music.)

BANK (finance)

adjectives
shiftless; leading; unthrifty; local; financial; depleted; impoverished; badly-man-
aged; safe; insured.

verbs
borrow from—; charter—; conduct—; consult—; deal with—; deposit in—; draw
upon—; equip—; loot—; patronize—; plunder—; run on—; wreck—; —acquires; —
advances; —advises; —amasses; —appropriates; —authorizes; —branches; —cashes;
—charges; —collapses; —consolidates; —
discounts; —dominates; —drafts; —expands; —finances; —flourishes; —guards;
—handles; —incorporates; —insures; —invests; —issues; —loans; —manages; —
mortgages; —negotiates; —operates; —profits; —rates; —regulates; —sanctions; —
serves; —transacts.
(See banker, firm, company, corporation.)

BANK (land)

adjectives
naked; oozy; perpendicular; shagged; grassy; wooded; precipitous; steep; slippery;
tottering; glorious; flowering; rocky; river;
mud; sloping; mossy; willow; sheltering;
forested; shelving; placid; tossing; pine-
clad; green-wooded; rugged; dirt; overhanging; miry; gentle; weedy; curving;
rain-gullied; clay; eroding; tree-lined;
heavily-wooded; glistening; caving; mosquito-infested; rabbit-riddled; willow-tufted;
low-lying; unlimited; enormous; smothering; noisy; frequented; fringed; deep; impassable; unmolested; storm-shaken; weary;
embroidered; permanent; high; bramble-

covered; primrose; cnalk; starred; settled; craggy; stifled; ash; wasted; picturesque; marshy; swampy; rugged; herbless; upland; tawny; bounding; beauteous; verdant; calm; rounding; porcelain; encompassing; lonesome; craggy; fraudulent; puddled; never-withering; glittering; blossom-laden.

verbs
bask on—; bound by —s; couch on—; fortify —s; overflow —s; scramble up—; shadow—; support—; swell over—; teeter on —; —encircles; —s rise.
(See ridge, pile.)

BANKER
adjectives
conservative; prosperous; resourceful; foremost; international; sophisticated; tall; dignified; mustached; gray-haired; trusted; rich; mean; bearded; cautious; private; leading; upstate; honest; hard-headed; prominent; defaulting; metropolitan; sagacious; astute; expert; established; benevolent; shortsighted; unscrupulous.

verbs
denounce—; envy—; protect—; —absconds; —collects; —contracts; —credits; —deals; —defaults; —embezzles; —executes; —investigates; —proffers; —provides; —refunds; —reimburses; —remits; —safeguards; —secures; —swindles; —traffics in.

BANKRUPT
adverbs
frequently; unfortunately; unhappily; profitably; conveniently; adroitly; inevitably; morally; irretrievably; unaccountably; mysteriously; surprisingly; seriously; temporarily; expediently; smartly; ingeniously; pitiably; dishearteningly; grievously; ruinously; touchingly; hopelessly; heartbreakingly.

BANKRUPTCY
adjectives
inevitable; economic; honest; moral; voluntary; irretrievable.

verbs
adjudge—; administer by—; administrate in —; annul—; arrange for—; arise from—; assent to—; authorize—; avoid—; commit to—; contract—; declare—; decree—; defer —; delay—; discharge from—; drift into—; effect—; embarrass into—; enter—; evade —; examine for—; face—; force into—; head for—; incur—; investigate—; involve

—; liquidate in—; petition for—; record—; reduce to—; relieve by—; save from—; seize in—; settle—; surrender to—; terminate in—; threaten with—; verge on—; — deprives; —divests; —solves; —threatens.
(See failure.)

BANNER
adjectives
bloodless; darkling; tattered; starry; spangled; elastic; prosperous; flaunting; murky; insurgent; bright-colored; gaudy; mimic; emblematical; superb; barbarous; gorgeous; unfurled; horse-tail; hostile; flapping; gay; flamboyant; victorious; appropriate; clustered; sinister; bloodstained; triumphant; rippling; holy; silken; star-faced; faded; historic; impalpable; crimsoned; ragged.

verbs
adopt—; bear—; flaunt—; flout—; gather round—; hail—; hang out—; hoist—; lift —; rally round—; serve—; spread—; stretch out—; unfurl—; unroll—; wave—; —dances; —droops; —flies; —flutters; —inspires; —rises into the air; —streams; —symbolizes; —undulates.
(See flag, standard, ensign.)

BANQUET
adjectives
unpretentious; sumptuous; diplomatic; delicious; fantastical; open-air; luxurious; artistic; unending; exotic; artificial; voluptuous; good-will; Lucullan; elaborate; stately; philanthropic.

BANTER
adjectives
familiar; good-natured; brilliant; delicate; contemptuous; gay; slow; facetious; witty.

verbs
assail with—; chide with—; engage in—; exchange—; indulge in—; pass for—; ridicule with—; turn to—; —entertains; —floats about.
(See ridicule, derision, mockery, repartee.)

BANTER (v)
adverbs
vivaciously; familiarly; brilliantly; delicately; contemptuously; gaily; facetiously; wittily; good-naturedly; slyly; cleverly; satirically.
(See jest, chaff.)

BAR
adjectives
unfeeling; resonant; colossal; extemporized;

92

statutory; invidious; anticipatory; inexorable; sullen; dissolving; alternating (pl); corporeal; multitudinous (pl); legal; oaken; drink-laden.

BAR
adjectives   (law)
lofty; magisterial; inviolable; relentless; arraigning; ruling; invincible.

verbs
accuse at—; address—; admit to—; appear before—; arraign before—; beseech—; bring to—; cajole—; call to—; defend at —; disagree with—; elect to—; expel from —; influence—; pass—; plead before—; reproach—; resign from—; solicit—; station at—; summon to—; —administers; —advises; —criticizes; —directs; —disciplines; — encourages; —establishes; —exercises; — governs; —grants; —orders; —privileges; —rules.
(See tribunal, law.)

BAR
adjectives   (obstruction)
basic; formidable; frowning; impassable; protective; forbidding; impenetrable; unscalable.

verbs
beat —s; cut —s; escape —s; fence in with —s; strengthen —s; —creates a barrier; — excludes; —hinders; —impedes; —obstructs; —prevents; —prohibits; —restrains.
(See barrier, obstruction, obstacle.)

BAR (v)
adverbs
strongly; unfeelingly; invidiously; inexorably; sullenly; corporeally; legally; determinedly; harshly; ultimately; utterly; unkindly; treacherously.
(See exclude, hinder, obstruct, restrain.)

BARBARIAN
adjectives
ferocious; sanguinary; tumultuous; idolatrous; lusty; obstinate; suspicious; bestial.

verbs
civilize—; conquer—; crush—; culture—; dominate —s; overcome—; quell—; repress —; subdue—; vanquish—; —imitates; —s overthrow; —pillages; —plunders; —subjugates; —sacks.
(See brute, savage, monster.)

BARBARISM
adjectives
medieval; colloquial; unenlightened; dark; heathen; unavoidable.

verbs
brand—; crash into—; degrade to—; descend to—; enslave by—; fall to—; rise from—; stave off—; succeed—.
(See brutality, anarchy.)

BARBARITY
adjectives
execrable; shocking; vulgar; calculated; legal; deliberate; indecent.

BARBAROUS
adverbs
fiercely; savagely; shockingly; deliberately; outlandishly; rudely; inhumanly; brutally; indecently; unforgivably; inherently; instinctively; heathenishly; triumphantly; vauntingly; mercilessly; fiendishly; oddly; uncouthly; bizarrely; grotesquely; cruelly; blatantly; flagrantly; incredibly.

BARD
adjectives
love-stricken; saturnine; high-dreaming; didactic; epic; merry; subtle; pied; mercenary; gifted.

BARE
adverbs
starkly; nakedly; pitiably; shamelessly; distressingly; skimpily; scantily; stingily; pathetically; austerely; painfully; grievously; unfortunately; wretchedly; miserably; cheerlessly; horribly; surprisingly; desolately; dismally; hopelessly; deplorably; utterly; unnecessarily.

BARGAIN
adjectives
mammoth; amazing; selfish; outstanding; remarkable; vaunted; sensational; sharp; fair; sordid; impious.

verbs
agree upon—; bind to—; buy a—; close a —; consider—; contract for—; discuss—; drive a—; enter into—; fulfill—; gobble up —; jump at—; maintain—; propose—; refuse—; release from—; rue—; seal—; search for —s; seize—; settle—; stipulate in—; strike—; strive for—.
(See transaction, contract.)

BARGAIN (v)
adverbs
collectively; indigently; amazingly; selfish

ly; remarkably; sensationally; sharply; fairly; sordidly; impiously; cleverly; shrewdly; stupidly; astutely.

(See agree, contract, stipulate.)

BARGE

adjectives
imperial; ungainly; gorgeous; state; abandoned; sluggish; dingy; gaily-painted; clumsy.

verbs
adorn—; anchor—; board—; christen—; command—; control—; convoy—; cushion —; decorate—; design—; dock—; equip—; escort—; fit out—; land—; lash—; launch —; license—; moor—; navigate—; pilot—; power—; propel—; rig—; shift—; stow—; straddle—; tow—; —coasts; —conveys; — discharges; —drifts; —journeys; —plies; —sails; —slips past; —trades; —transports; —tugs.

(See boat.)

BARK
(boat)

adjectives
venturous; perfidious; passing; stranded; swift-winged; lofty; fragile; floating; deep-drawing; foundering; proud; flying; frail; enchanted; storm-tossed.

BARK
(dog's)

adjectives
snappish; harsh; fiendish; welcoming; irritated; short; sharp; wild; eager; thundering; swaggering; acute; agonized; imperative; gay; high-pitched; teasing; expressive; ferocious; frenzied; staccato; frantic; furious; deafening; ecstatic; jubilant; ringing; desolate; muffled; defiant; confident; playful.

BARK
(tree)

adjectives
sapless; gnarled; rugged; indigenous; silvery; bruised; corrugated; peeling.

BARK (v)

adverbs
imperiously; lustily; inopportunely; explosively; joyously; injuriously; snappishly; harshly; fiendishly; welcomingly; irritatedly; sharply; wildly; eagerly; agonizedly; imperatively; teasingly; expressively; ferociously; frenziedly; frantically; deafeningly; jubilantly; desolately; defiantly; confidently; playfully.

(See shout.)

BARN

adjectives
substantial; commodious; solitary; comfortable; cool; tumble-down; ruinous; dilapidated; rickety; rambling; ramshackle; abandoned; neglected; decaying; well-filled; bulging.

verbs
construct—; equip—; erect—; fire—; forage in—; frame—; gather into—; house in—; install in—; remodel—; stable in—; stake out—; store in—; —collapses; —harbors; —shelters.

(See building.)

BAROMETER

adjectives
alternating; disconcerting; steadily-rising; unvarying; vacillating; threatening; faltering.

verbs
adjust—; affect—; compensate—; correct—; depend on—; devise—; employ—; equip with—; experiment with—; expose—; govern—; influence—; learn from—; read—; record—; rely on—; seal—; sheathe—; steady—; test—; throw off—; vouch for—; —assists; —climbs; —demonstrates; —determines; —falls; —fluctuates; —forecasts; —graduates; —indicates; —measures; — oscillates; —predicts; —records; —registers; —represents; —rises; —shows; —sinks; — soars; —threatens; —warns.

(See meter, thermometer.)

BARON

adjectives
medieval; villainous; cattle; feudal; despotic; coal; monocled; proud; impetuous; monstrous.

BARRACKS

adjectives
bleak; disciplinary; grim; cheerless; orderly; solid.

verbs
advance toward—; allot to—; arouse—; arrange for—; assault—; assign to—; censor —; command—; concentrate in—; confine to—; construct—; convert into—; dispatch to—; encamp in—; equip—; extend to—; file into—; fire on—; fortify—; guard—; invade—; protect—; quarter in—; repair to—; report to—; restrict to—; retire to—; sanitize—; station in—; superintend—; survey—; threaten—; —accommodate; —collapse; —house; —lodge; —resound; — spring up.

(See quarters, shelter, building.)

BARRAGE

adjectives
gigantic; advertising; incessant; verbal; rolling; murderous; leaden; shrapnel; deadly; fatal; vicious; violent.

verbs
advance under—; approach—; beat down —; concentrate—; create—; curtain with—; defend against—; defy—; denounce—; disperse—; establish—; extend—; invade—; lay down—; penetrate—; prolong—; reduce —; resist—; restrict—; retreat from—; strengthen—; sweep through—; —cuts off; —holds up; —obstructs; —parries; —protects; —surprises; —threatens.

BARREL

adjectives
dilapidated; hoopless; cobwebbed; moss-grown; sagging; scarred; slimy; stout; warped.

verbs
bung—; measure—; pipe—; pump from—; roll—; store in—; stove in—; tap—; valve —; —bulges; —reeks; —resounds; —thuds; —thunders; —tumbles.

BARREN

adverbs
monotonously; treelessly; desolately; endlessly; infinitely; alarmingly; frightfully; indescribably; immeasurably; comfortlessly; formidably; blankly; inhospitably; illimitably; boundlessly; terrifyingly; perilously.

BARRICADE

adjectives
verdant; feeble; defensive; disputed; stone; bristling; human; effective.

verbs
advance toward—; approach—; assault—; capture—; defend—; denounce—; entrench behind—; erect—; extend—; invade—; pile up—; strengthen—; support—; survey—; sweep through—; threaten—; withdraw—; —annoys; —bars; —blocks; —collapses; —confines; —cuts off; —defends; —fortifies; —parries; —prevents; —protects; —resists; —restricts; —withholds.
(See barrier, obstruction.)

BARRIER

adjectives
golden; external; sufficient; insuperable; material; formidable; subjective; effective;
feeble; obstinate; intervening; screening; conventional; fancied; invisible; insurmountable; stair-like; impassable; airy; serried; moss-draped; dismal; ancient; irregular; surf-beaten; absolute; stout; invincible; powerful; unconquerable; mighty; impenetrable; awesome; lofty; serious; eternal; natural; legal; psychological; economic; cultural; vast; lowered; inadequate; stubborn; artificial; puerile; indefinable; pitiless; traditional; countless (pl); imagined.

verbs
beat—; build—; burst—; confine by—; create—; cross—; erect—; flatten against—; follow—; form—; hurdle—; hurl against—; jump—; rail in with —s; smash—; step over —; strengthen—; surmount—; tear down—; vault—; —bounds; —hinders; —isolates; —limits; —looms; —obstructs; —prevents; —supports; —thwarts.
(See obstruction, barricade.)

BARRISTER

adjectives
conscientious; ambitious; overworked; struggling; smug; briefless; infant; sneering; brilliant; competent.

BASE

adjectives
substantial; solidified; tottering; commodious; crumbling; flattering; immutable; firm; circular.

verbs
advance to—; attach to—; break from—; build on—; challenge—; communicate with —; construct—; create—; decorate—; dump at—; enlarge—; establish—; gather at—; hollow—; issue from—; mould—; protect—; puncture—; rest on—; separate from—; set on—; situate at—; spread on—; store at—; —projects.
(See foundation, basis, bottom.)

BASE (*a*)

adverbs
intolerably; meanly; ignobly; obscurely; contemptibly; abjectly; unbecomingly; undisguisedly; shamefully; glaringly; flagrantly; unmistakably; palpably; nakedly; brazenly; shamelessly; flauntingly; sorrily; brutishly; rudely; fawningly; obsequiously; cringingly; sneakily; subtly.

BASE (*v*)

adverbs
primarily; wholly; unsoundly; substantially; totteringly; firmly; immutably.
(See depend.)

BASEBALL

verbs

blacken—; condemn—; destroy—; rebuke—; sponsor—; spread—; welcome—; —animates; —breeds; —engenders; —enlivens.

(See game.)

BASEMENT

adjectives

sunless; dark; stone; historical; excavated; dungeon-like; dank; damp; airless; musty; rat-infested.

verbs

climb from—; consist of—; drain—; excavate—; floor—; flood—; form—; relegate to—; rummage in—; well from—.

(See cellar.)

BASENESS

adjectives

inherent; forced; unconfinable; adroit; despicable; apparent; undisguised.

BASHFUL

adverbs

awkwardly; uneasily; boyishly; self-consciously; embarrassingly; uncomfortably; painfully; engagingly; charmingly; peculiarly; strangely; unwontedly; becomingly; naturally; modestly; timidly; fearfully; clumsily; foolishly; distressingly; ridiculously; pitiably; touchingly; adorably; comically; absurdly.

BASHFULNESS

adjectives

uneasy; maiden; engaging; virgin; childish; boyish; graceful; captivating; peculiar; shamefaced.

verbs

feign—; mask in—; shrink in—; —disturbs; —inhibits; —melts; —overcomes; —unfits.

(See modesty, shyness, diffidence.)

BASIC

adverbs

scientifically; fundamentally; essentially; indispensably; admittedly; emphatically; prescriptively; usually; ordinarily; officially; obviously; palpably; conspicuously; explicitly; positively; definitely; unavoidably.

BASIN

adjectives

remarkable; treeless; shallow; vast; starlit; drainage; rock-bottomed; tidal; empty; volcanic; gigantic; pitlike; lacustrine; rustic; beautiful; incrusted; weedy; marshy; na-

tural; fan-shaped; broad; spacious; sumptuous.

BASIS

adjectives

psychological; moral; social; military; commission; logical; scientific; voluntary; geographical; tangible; potential; essential; sustaining; concrete; apperceptive; experimental; daily; hypothetical; structural; universal; simplified; sound; economic; well-established; sensible; rationalized; secure; efficient; profitable; firm; prosperous; indispensable; healthy; solid; equitable; liberal; substantial; broad; possible; false; unsatisfactory; narrow; slippery; temporary; vast; meager; factual; ample; permanent; tenuous; inevitable; reliable; pecuniary; corporative; practical; immovable; flimsy; philosophical; physical; monarchical; creditable; feudal; mechanical; theoretical; dubious; imperishable; fantastic; enduring; lowest.

verbs

build upon—; establish a—; explain on—; form—; found on—; meet on—of; obtain—; place on—; rest on—; rise from—of; shake —; support on—; win a higher—; —consists.

(See foundation, base.)

BASK (v)

adverbs

obviously; torpidly; cozily; lazily; drowsily; blissfully; comfortably; sleepily; pleasantly; restfully.

(See luxuriate.)

BASKET

adjectives

enormous; rustic; severe; round; shallow; inexhaustible; wicker; huge; garlanded; split-oak; cup-shaped; upturned; filigree.

verbs

charge—; coil—; convey in—; cram in—; design—; fashion—; lattice into—; load—; measure in—; net—; provision—; stuff—; twine—; weave—.

(See case, chest, box.)

BASKING

adverbs

luxuriously; comfortably; buoyantly; joyously; prosperously; happily; warmly; radiantly.

BASS

adverbs

thunderingly; resonantly; deeply; breezily; boomingly; awfully; mightily; magnificently; toweringly; enormously; stupendously.

BASS
(fish)

adjectives

game; scrappy; small-mouthed; stern; skittish.

BASS
(voice)

adjectives

thunderous; resonant; bawling; masculine; profound; growling; deep; unruly; swelling; mellow; breezy.

BASTION

adjectives

sparkling; absurd; massive; futile; sloping; tower-like; coral.

BAT
(baseball)

adjectives

firm-resounding; decisive; sturdy; uncompromising; stout; spindly; threatening; relentless.

verbs

balance—; choose—; fling—; fondle—; grip —; oil—; paw—; release—; sandpaper—; scrape—; select—; shave—; shorten—; shoulder—; split—; swish—; tape—; weight —; wield—; —cracks; —flies; —slips; — splits.

(See club.)

BAT
(mammal)

adjectives

insectivorous; gloomy; grisly; monstrous.

verbs

attract—; disturb—; ensnare—; entice—; loose—; pursue—; strike—; trap—; —s a- bound; —clings; —flits; —hibernates; — lurks; —preys upon; —shuns; —sucks; — swoops; —terrorizes; —wheels; —whirls; —whirs; —wings.

(See animal, bird, insect.)

BATH

adjectives

chemical; imperceptible; ice; cold; Diocletian; perfumed; steaming; reducing; discomforting; relaxing; refreshing; portable; warm; soapy; splashing; freezing; medicated; involuntary; tepid; open-air; sun; modern; finely-appointed; immaculate; world-famous; well-equipped; radio-active; mud; matutinal.

verbs

administer—; arrange—; cure by —s; drain —; enter—; immerse in—; lather in—; loll in—; medicate—; perspire in—; rub in—; scald in—; sponge in—; steam in—; treat in

—; vaporize—; —enervates; —exhilarates; —refreshes; —relaxes.

(See water.)

BATHE (v)

adverbs

actually; chemically; steamingly; discomfortingly; comfortingly; refreshingly; soapily; splashingly; freezingly; involuntarily; tepidly; immaculately; daily; matutinally; thoroughly.

(See wash.)

BATHER

adjectives

ecstatic; adventurous; timid; floundering; inept; expert.

BATHING

adjectives

unexcelled; luxurious; indiscriminate; clear; clean; surf; safe; ocean.

BATON

adjectives

authoritative; commanding; directing; gilt; guiding; silencing; silver-tipped; suspended.

verbs

carry—; conduct with—; cudgel with—; dash—; direct with—; flourish—; lead—; mark with—; point—; signal with—; strike —; swing—; tap—; wave—; wield—; — guides.

(See wand, sceptre.)

BATTALION

adjectives

repulsed; puny; assaulting; steel-clad; potential; defending; staunch; sturdy; stalwart.

BATTER

adjectives

alert; deftly-moving; eagle-eyed; able-armed; wary; splendid; famous.

verbs

fan—; strike out—; —bats; —bunts; — crashes; —doubles; —drives; —flies; — fouls; —hits; —loops; —pops; —singles; —steals; —triples; —walks.

BATTERY

adjectives

sensitive; galvanic; pointed; discharged; weakened.

BATTLE

adjectives

bitter; hard-fought; furious; terrific; fierce;

raging; frantic; desperate; hot; bloody; savage; gory; gallant; sanguinary; thrilling; glorious; mighty; valiant; decisive; ceaseless; brief; impending; arduous; incessant; strenuous; historic; bloodless; inglorious; exhausting; hopeless; undercover; stiff; ironic; silent; pitched; fateful; phantom; life-long; offensive; parliamentary; dramatic; unrighteous; perpetual; discouraging; hereditary; nameless; memorable; earthly; childish; verbal; crashing; hand-to-hand; immediate; never-ending; weird; raging; naval; puny; intellectual; disastrous; losing.

verbs
arouse a—; clash in—; climax—; conflict in—; contend in—; create—; distinguish in —; doom to—; encounter in—; engage in—; finance—; gain in—; gird for—; give—; honor in—; join—; light the fuse of—; manoeuver—; offer—; overcome in—; pit in—; pitch—; precipitate—; premeditate—; provoke—; pursue—; slay in—; stay—; strive in—; subsist in—; sway—; triumph in—; wage—; —depends on; —ensues; —flashes; —presses; —rages; —rings; —swirls.
(See conflict, encounter, combat, fight, contest.)

BATTLE (v)
adverbs
fiercely; doggedly; invincibly; manfully; heroically; furiously; terrifically; desperately; gallantly; thrillingly; gloriously; valiantly; decisively; ceaselessly; briefly; arduously; incessantly; strenuously; hopelessly; exhaustingly; silently; fatefully; perpetually; childishly; verbally; intellectually; disastrously.
(See fight, encounter, combat.)

BATTLEFIELD
adjectives
immense; immortal; stupendous; rolling; ill-fated; scarred; silent; bloody; bone-strewn; glorious; memorial.

verbs
abandon on—; advance on—; assault on—; campaign on—; clash on—; concede on—; concentrate on—; encounter on—; enmesh on—; exhaust on—; fell on—; mass on—; occupy—; overthrow on—; perish on—; redden—; relinquish—; replace on—; slay on —; suffer on—; surprise on—; surrender on —; test on—; —lies; —reaps a harvest; —reeks; —stretches.
(See field, plain.)

BATTLELINE
adjectives
wavering; bent; far-flung; crushed; crumbling; tottering.

BATTLEMENTS
adjectives
frowning; massive; time-scarred; dim; castellated; crackling; imperial; haunted; escarped; cloud-capped; shining; narrow; gilded; tottered.

BAUBLE
adjectives
ingenious; gilt; worthless; imperial; silken; gorgeous; gleaming; heavy.

BAWD
adjectives
wicked; powdered; notorious; infamous; lewd; libidinous.

BAWL (v)
adverbs
hoarsely; plaintively; pitifully; intermittently; fitfully; loudly; wailingly.
(See cry.)

BAY
adjectives
land-locked; craggy; shallow; native; tranquil; yawning; eddying; noble; silvery; curving; regal; extensive; deep; protective; roaring; billowy; treacherous; glassy; squally; distant; sheltered; whispering; shimmering; murky; shark-infested; broadening; magnificent; protected; misted.

verbs
anchor in—; break on—; dredge—; drop into—; embark at—; enter—; put into—; recede into—; ride—; surround—; —eddies; —extends; —lashes the beach; —narrows; —widens.
(See ocean, river, gulf, harbor.)

BAYONET
adjectives
gleaming; pointless; glistening; fixed; bared; flashing; pitiless; ruthless; slanting; slashing; gory; grisly; merciless; murderous.

verbs
arm with—; attach—; charge with —s; clasp —; clutch—; connect—; defend with—; drive home—; equip with—; fix—; impale on—; insert—; jab with—; juggle—; raise —; repulse with—; rush with—; sheathe—; shield from—; spar with—; stab with—;

struggle with—; thrust—; vanquish with—; wield—; withdraw—; —catches; —flashes; —gores; —gouges; —pierces; —sticks.
(See dagger, weapon.)

BAZAAR

adjectives
straggling; languorous; Oriental; romantic; gay; grubby; modern; noisy.

BEACH

adjectives
artificial; accessible; secluded; clean; sloping; crescent; sandy; curving; private; sun-warmed; beautiful; commodious; gay; bright; fascinating; golden; rocky; pebbly; silvery; brilliant; sun-swept; gleaming; silent; desolate; shelving; surf-smoothed; windless; mosquito-infested; ancient; calcareous; foamy; private.

verbs
batter—; break on—; dawdle along—; drift on—; lash against—; pound—; ripple on—; roam—; run aground on—; settle on—; sprawl on—; stagger onto—; strand on—; strew—; throw up on—; —extends; —gleams; —stretches.
(See shore.)

BEACON

adjectives
eternal; indubitable; towering; revolving; long-distance; visual; dangerous; spiritual; gleaming; rebel; warning.

verbs
operate—; provide—; set—; —aids; —blazons; —circles; —directs; —guides; —identifies; —illuminates; —indicates; —leads; —lights; —marks; —notifies; —rotates; —shines; —signals; —swings; —warns.
(See fire, light, signal.)

BEADS

adjectives
wired; shining; iridescent; pale; gleaming; coiled; garish; many-colored; greasy; wooden; pea-sized; unstrung; cheap.

verbs
barter with—; color—; count—; crush—; dye—; facet—; fashion—; grind—; mould —; mount—; ornament with—; perforate —; pray with—; shape—; space—; string —; suspend—; trade—; trim with—; —glisten; —sparkle.
(See diamond, ornament, drop, jewel.)

BEAK

adjectives
curled; relentless; ravening; golden; brazen; Wellingtonian; lifelike; twisted; hooked; powerful; crooked; tuneless.

BEAM

adjectives (light)
quivering; hazy; dulled; transient; sunny; noonday; blessed; invisible; silvery; chaste; stray; steady; unwinking; eternal; creeping; intermittent; half-extinguished; bright; pallid; guiding; fervid; virgin; naked; feeble; divergent; crimson; intellectual; belated; transverse; kindly; slanting; piercing; horizontal; penetrating; weird; leaf-entangled; genial; blinding; sunny; burning; effulgent; gracious; glancing; refracted.

verbs
clothe in —s; emit—; enwreathe with —s; flash—; fling—; focus—; follow—; furnish —; gild with —s; isolate—; outshine—; play—upon; radiate—; shade—; shed—; shoot—; spot—; throw—; —blazes; —blinds; —brightens; —creeps up; —dazzles; —directs; —emanates from; —glitters; —guides; —penetrates; —pierces; —reflects; —scorches; —shines; —shoots forth; —slants; —sweeps.
(See ray, gleam.)

BEAM

adjectives (wood)
sagging; massive; uncovered; metal-weighted; rough; hand-hewn; exposed; blackened; tarred.

verbs
arch—; center—; cross —s; fell—; lay—; saw—; set—; split—; suspend from—; warp —; —connects; —extends; —projects; —strengthens; —supports.
(See timber.)

BEAM (v)

adverbs
affably; vaguely; benevolently; radiantly; hazily; transiently; sunnily; unwinkingly; chastely; steadily; eternally; intermittently; pallidly; fervidly; nakedly; intellectually; feebly; belatedly; slantingly; horizontally; penetratingly; weirdly; genially; blindingly; effulgently; graciously.
(See gleam, shine, glitter, glisten.)

BEAMING

adverbs
radiantly; joyously; fairly; delicately; beautifully; becomingly; bonnily; curiously; unconsciously; gorgeously; prettily; rosily;

smilingly; laughingly; ridiculously; foolishly; ruddily; sparklingly; mischievously; openly; innocently; girlishly; shyly; modestly; frankly; happily; brightly.

BEAR

adjectives

ponderous; huge; crafty; burly; brindled; fearless; monstrous; murderous; menacing; untamed; vicious; playful.

verbs

ambush—; bait—; cage—; chain—; confine—; exterminate —s; fatten—; harass—; madden—; roast—; skin—; stalk—; tame —; tether—; trap—; —attacks; —burrows; —charges; —claws; —climbs; —clowns; —dances; —flourishes; —forages; —gambols; —growls; —grunts; —hibernates; — hugs; —lumbers; —lurks; —migrates; — multiplies; —paws; —pounces on; —preys on; —ravages; —roars; —sheds; —shuffles; —whelps.

(See animal.)

BEAR (v)

adverbs

patiently; manfully; oppressively; prematurely; extremely; stiffly; valiantly; coldly; stoically; recklessly; philosophically; heavily; hurriedly.

(See endure, stand, tolerate.)

BEARD

adjectives

sheaved; vigorous; spreading; bushy; tawny; curly; peaked; dripping; comic; incipient; wiry; rippling; full; tangled; mangy; grizzled; downy; matted; filthy; forked; crisp; trim; close-cropped; well-clipped; Oriental; venerable; unshorn; hoary; foolish; overgrown; silken; military; telescopic; verdant; patriarchal; Mephistophelian.

verbs

acquire—; adorn with—; attain—; clip—; comb—; curl—; dignify with—; disguise by—; distinguish by—; drag by—; part—; paw—; pluck off—; pull—; run down—; scratch—; seize by—; shave—; singe—; smooth—; stroke—; style—; take by—; trim —; twitch—; waggle—; weep in—; — bristles; —blooms; —covers; —glistens.

(See hair, whiskers.)

BEARD (v)

adverbs

boldly; fearlessly; manfully; foolhardily; playfully; exasperatingly; foolishly; valiantly.

(See defy, oppose, encounter.)

BEARING (manner)

adjectives

modest; timid; manly; noble; courteous; polished; dignified; tranquil; unpretentious; unostentatious; imperial; austere; regal; lofty; haughty; patrician; godlike; majestic; jaunty; lively; gay; contemptuous; disdainful; martial; soldierly; military; clerkly; grave; staid; courteous; queenly; gallant; graceful; intimate; alarming; humble; courageous; worthy; unbridled; steadfast; chivalrous; heroic; imperious; rollicking; straightforward; immitigable.

BEARING (meaning)

adjectives

intimate; immediate; favorable; happy; vital; frank; tragic; popular; external; direct; mutual.

BEAST

adjectives

skulking; brutish; ingenious; ravenous; wily; unfriendly; elusive; slippery; wild; driveling; boisterous; unruly; unsavory; massive; infuriated; ill-trained; bloody; savage; grisly; predatory; formidable; monstrous; maddened; outlandish; venomous; grotesque; fabulous; cross-grained; beauteous; malicious; cowardly; sanguine; sulky; unkempt; jaded; voracious; undisciplined; squealing; nocturnal; four-footed; noble; lordly; cruel; murderous; ferocious; relentless; marauding; prowling; hostile; enraged; screaming; snarling; cornered; charging; frantic; restless; stamping; crouching; sagacious; cunning; well-bred; gaunt; hairy; stolid; plodding; shaggy; rugged; graceless; diminutive; foolish; prehistoric; sleek.

verbs

cage—; chase—; constrain—; depict—; flay —; hunt—; mount—; pen up—; shelter—; skin—; slash—; slaughter—; spare—; subdue—; track—; transform into—; —bays; —cries; —forages; —growls; —grunts; — prowls; —roams; —subsists; —yelps.

(See brute, monster, animal.)

BEAT

adjectives

receding; impatient; **dynamic**; incessant; steady; rhythmic.

BEAT (v)

adverbs

unmercifully; continuously; impatiently; in-

cessantly; rhythmically; languidly; mercilessly; boisterously; joyously; youthfully; manifestly; pleasantly; proportionately; regularly; audibly; unpitifully; unreasonably; horribly; uncontrollably; thoroughly; strenuously; burningly; merrily; lazily; lightly.
(See hammer, smite, strike, chasten.)

BEATIFIC
adverbs
ethereally; mysteriously; divinely; happily; ecstatically; gloriously; rapturously; mystically; devoutly; fervently.

BEATING
adjectives
merciless; tumultuous; fierce; unjust.

verbs
administer—; chastise with—; deserve—; endure—; flatten out with—; punish—; suffer—; throb from—; —intimidates
(See drubbing, defeat, blows.)

BEATING
adjectives (sound)
loud; insistent; barbaric; tumultuous; staccato.

BEATITUDE
adjectives
infinite; limitless; insouciant.

BEAU
adjectives
ardent; fascinating; devoted; distant; cool.

BEAUTIFUL
adverbs
gloriously; ethereally; dazzlingly; elusively; unearthly; fatally; fleetingly; intangibly; mysteriously; magnificently; fabulously; charmingly; radiantly; exquisitely; matchlessly; fiercely; surprisingly; exotically; sullenly; poignantly; bloomingly; naturally; simply; lustrously; languidly; compellingly; opulently; richly; wondrously; duskily; cruelly; stormily; vitally; singularly; vividly; gracefully; flawlessly; harmoniously; calmly; graciously; serenely; sweetly; childishly; unforgettably; innocently; imposingly; surpassingly; disdainfully; daintily; proudly; wildly; ineffably; triumphantly; ravishingly; weirdly; unconsciously; sternly; devastatingly; darkly; resplendently; robustly; infinitely; pensively; faultlessly; divinely; quietly; vivaciously; glamorously; glit-

teringly; glowingly; alluringly; unspeakably; adorably; startlingly; chastely; regally; terribly.

BEAUTY
adjectives
glorious; guarded; sable; animal; dazzling; uncultivated; moral; unearthly; distinctive; luscious; inexhaustible; famous; mortal; fleeting; iridescent; passionate; sensuous; gleaming; talented; mysterious; perpetual; mystic; homely; all-pervading; picturesque; infantile; notable; fabulous; radiant; exquisite; unmatched; haughty; reigning; stately; insistent; fierce; surprising; changeful; indescribable; celestial; sullen; naked; blooming; antique; poignant; morose; abstracted; delicate; poetic; unparalleled; mocking; unrivaled; natural; lustrous; wistful; ideal; rare; polished; perennial; languid; indefinable; compelling; opulent; rugged; matronly; rich; wondrous; original; verdant; dusky; cruel; peculiar; marvelous; stormy; despoiled; masculine; singular; indestructible; substantiated; transfigured; intellectual; graceful; harmonious; bedizened; unforgettable; luxurious; surpassing; sacred; evanescent; pictorial; breathless; crystal; excelling; considerable; spiritual; peerless; creative; dainty; speckled; wild; triumphant; weird; celebrated; impersonal; vaunted; plastic; blemished; stern; angelic; dismal; dark; earthly; comprehensible; robust; ripe; melodic; supernal; pensive; tragic; divine; intrinsic; vivacious; glittering; mellow; soul-awakening; tanned; alluring; exclusive; haunting; chaste; bridal; somber; unadorned; fadeless; geometric; impassioned; terrible; regal; majestic; voluptuous; sculptured; artistic; traditional; unexampled; rustic; enhanced; startling; unspeakable; glowing; patrician; pristine; tonic; glamorous; superlative; ornate; quiet; nymph-like; faultless; gnarled; debased; garnished; infinite; midnight; filmy; feathery; refined; gossamer; sheer; resplendent; impalpable; devastating; ravishing; beguiling; unique; lavish; ineffable; intoxicating; commanding; proud; lofty; disdainful; scornful; awesome; imposing; inherent; innocent; restful; unconscious; unspoiled; child-like; lyrical; ethereal; exotic; eerie; serene; calm; colorful; riotous; flawless; nonpareil; vivid; vital; lucid; transcendant; deathless; Grecian; statuesque; rural; odorous; pastoral; colonial; scenic; buxom; pagan; Botticellian; lush; creamy; elusive; fatal; still; sepulchral; guileless; proverbial; unattainable; unveiled; shroud-

ed; stage; intoxicating; sylvan; intangible; consummate.

verbs
achieve—; approve of—; array in—; a-waken—; bathe in—; bless with—; build—; capture—; commend—; deface—; depict—; desire—; desolate the—; drink up—; ena-mour of—; enhance—; envy—; excel in—; favor with—; gladden by—; glorify—; han-ker for—; heighten—; hunger for—; hyp-notize by—; impair—; lust for—; main-tain—; mar—; outrage—; perfect—; praise —; preserve—; recapture—; rejoice in—; restore—; seek—; smother—; soften—; stain—; surrender—; tinge with—; trample —; unfold—; unmask—; veil—; vouchsafe —; worship—; —abounds; —attracts; —captivates; —charms; —decays; —departs; —enchants; —endures; —enraptures; —en-trances; —excites; —fades; —fascinates; —glows; —shines; —stabs; —withers.
(See perfection, charm, loveliness, grace, harmony.)

BECKON (*v*)
adverbs
significantly; enticingly; captivatingly; smil-ingly; quaintly; repeatedly; imperceptibly.
(See wave.)

BED
adjectives
soft; snowy; luxurious; comfortable; lovely; quaint; chilly; four-poster; carved; musty; damp; ghoulish; spotless; wretched; pen-dent; curtained; sagging; painful; rocky; wholesome; cursed; barren; lustful; wormy; pensive; restless; regal; naked; sickly; fruitful; odorous; peaceful; creaking; make-shift; lumpy; hallowed; pebbly; nuptial; feverish; dying; sandy; virgin; sleepless; inviting; aching; pious; tumbled; weary; woeful; spectral; turfy; unhallowed; incest-uous.

verbs
canopy—; cast upon—; clamber into—; con-fine to—; convey to—; couch in—; deck—; decorate—; defile—; enclose—; flop into—; fold—; glide into—; hang from—; heave from—; hurl out of—; kneel beside—; lay out in—; loll on—; lounge on—; mattress—; pillow in—; prop in—; recline in—; repose in—; retire to—; roll in—; rouse from—; sink into—; slumber in—; spring from—; squirm in—; stagger from—; stow in—; strike—; toss in—; toss into—; tuck in—; usurp—; warm—.
(See cot, couch, mattress.)

BED (*v*)
adverbs
softly; luxuriously; quaintly; comfortably; mustily; damply; nightly.
(See rest.)

BEDECK (*v*)
adverbs
gaily; gorgeously; fabulously; lavishly; grandly; attractively; picturesquely; glori-ously.
(See ornament.)

BEDLAM
adjectives
clamorous; dreadful; foul; frantic; mind-sundering; raging; unsubdued.

verbs
lead into—; subject to—; —abates; —breaks out; —confuses; —deranges; —roars.
(See confusion, noise.)

BEDROOM
adjectives
gaudy; banal; voluptuous; charming; airy; dismal; silent; gloomy; ill-ventilated; dreary; diminutive.

verbs
air—; dash into—; deny—; emerge from —; furnish—; repair to—; retire to—; —contains.
(See room, apartment.)

BEE
adjectives
swarming (pl); laden; anxious; straggling; sucking; noontide; murmuring; stingless; maudlin; industrious; voluptuous; blunt-faced; sexless; restless; marauding; buzz-ing; bustling; busy.

verbs
handle—; keep —s; —alights on; —breeds; —bristles; —chases; —collects; —colonizes; —darts; —deposits; —dozes; —flits; —for-ages; —gathers; —gorges; —hibernates; —hums; —impregnates; —s issue; —labors; —mumbles; —murmurs; —nests; —ovi-posits; —perforates; —plies; —pollinates; —regurgitates; —secretes; —sips; —stings; —stores; —s swarm; —swoops down; —s throng; —tunnels; —wings its way.
(See insect.)

BEECH
adjectives
russet; stalwart; giant; leafy; serpent-root-ed.

adjectives
authentic; stout; frothy; pale; foamy; powerful; drowsy.

verbs
abstain from—; addict to—; annihilate—; age—; bottle—; brew—; concoct—; consume—; de-alcoholize—; down—; extract —; gulp—; guzzle—; hop up—; lap up—; manufacture—; market—; process—; quaff —; sample—; sip—; steep in—; stock—; stow away—; strengthen—; swill—; tap —; weaken—; —bubbles; —ferments; —flows; —foams; —froths; —glistens; —intoxicates; —quenches; —thickens; —winks.
(See ale, liquor.)

BEETLE

adjectives
noisome; infuriated; drowsy; iridescent; carnivorous; obscurely-colored; glistening.

verbs
armor—; attack —s; control —s; crush—; exterminate —s; infest with —s; plague with —s; sheathe—; spray—; —bites; —captures; —chews; —destroys; —devastates; —feigns; —forages; —gnaws; —menaces; —s ravage; —scurries along; —tears out; —tumbles along.
(See insect.)

BEFALL (v)

adverbs
occasionally; preposterously; happily; unaccountably; auspiciously; inadvertently; inexplicably.
(See happen.)

BEG (v)

adverbs
solicitously; ingratiatingly; deprecatingly; appealingly; importunately; urgently; embarrassedly; impudently; clamorously; reproachfully; whiningly; fawningly; grimacingly; piteously; pestiferously; professionally; earnestly.
(See beseech, implore, ask.)

BEGGAR

adjectives
sturdy; amiable; jolly; disciplined; filthy; whining; gloomy; worthless; disgraced; greedy; blind; wandering; monkish; implacable; stalwart; unclean; bareheaded; crippled; loathsome; fawning; grimacing; piteous; penniless; tattered; pestiferous; hideous; impudent; professional; formidable.

verbs
contribute to—; corrupt—; die a—; ease—; feast—; foster—; lodge—; reduce to—; relieve—; repel—; revive—; sink to—; spurn —; —s band together; —complains; —desires; —entreats; —implores; —intrudes; —loafs; —petitions; —pleads; —roams; —shirks; —starves; —struggles; —tramps along.

BEGIN (v)

adverbs
jerkily; resentfully; methodically; mechanically; earnestly; hesitatingly; ostensibly; clumsily; euphemistically; sarcastically; argumentatively; oracularly; surreptitiously; savagely; wistfully; eventually; contemporaneously; ecstatically; romantically; insidiously; auspiciously; appealingly; rapturously.
(See commence, originate.)

BEGINNER

adjectives
awkward; anxious; fearful; mere; over-confident; zealous; untried.

verbs
bestow on—; condition—; describe to—; educate—; encourage—; foster—; induce—; pit against—; reveal to—; school—; sponsor—; stimulate—; suggest to—; train—; trouble—; —acquires; —advances; —applies; —contacts; —copes with; —crams; —demands; —embarks on; —emerges; —errs; —experiences; —learns; —plunges into; —questions.
(See novice, apprentice, amateur.)

BEGINNING

adjectives
remote; slow; tentative; crude; auspicious; recorded; amateurish; nebulous; unworkable; humble; long-deferred; promising; simple; tragic; ambitious; mandatory; microscopic; substantial; inconspicuous; modest; casual; sweet; indestructible; unpropitious; unlimited; significant.

verbs
celebrate—; commemorate—; declare—; honor—; initiate—; mark—; proceed from —; read from—; trace—; —introduces; —leads off.
(See origin.)

BEGRUDGE (v)

adverbs
habitually; selfishly; unfeelingly; implac-

ably; cruelly; odiously; remorselessly;
frowningly.

(See deny.)

BEHAVE (v)

adverbs

unchastely; abhorrently; alluringly; treacherously; erratically; abominably; indifferently; unsociably; diabolically; errantly; debonairly; gawkily; ridiculously; prudently;
uncouthly; proverbially; boisterously; obtusely; ludicrously; conclusively; theatrically; drably; courteously; jocularly; artlessly;
imposingly; lasciviously; austerely; capric-
ously; speciously; decorously; callously; irreverently; obstreperously; generously; admirably.

(See act, bear.)

BEHAVIOR

adjectives

artless; imposing; offensive; lascivious; distant; picturesque; humorous; demonstrative;
objective; portentous; genetic; outward;
baffling; tormenting; prudential; austere;
blunt; infantile; rude; stupid; loutish; unfilial; capricious; unparalleled; highhanded; emotional; ungracious; specious; courteous; ingenious; mild; odd; cruel; frantic;
despicable; unbecoming; cowardly; disgusting; deferential; creditable; wanton; displeasing; suitable; individualistic; disheartening; noble; unique; odious; decorous; erratic; shameful; senseless; outrageous;
shocking; riotous; mysterious; instinctive;
decent; manly; intelligent; exceptional; reasonable; circumspect; polite; unmaidenly;
childish; detestable; inhuman; callous; irreverent; egocentric; annoying; insulting;
abominable; eccentric; obstreperous.

verbs

condone—; dignify—; interpret—; simulate
—; soften—; —implies; —improves; —infuriates; —pleases.

(See demeanor, conduct, manner, action.)

BEHEAD (v)

adverbs

publicly; cruelly; wantonly; outrageously;
heartlessly; shockingly; abominably; detestably.

(See execute.)

BEHOLD (v)

adverbs

gladsomely; earnestly; unblinkingly; respectfully; rapturously; tremblingly; blankly.

(See contemplate, gaze, look, observe.)

adjectives

sovereign; invisible; sinful; ungrateful;
stormy; neurotic; faulty; inner; loathed;
human; transformed; wayward; puny; delusive; reasonable; rare; radiant; rational;
uninhibited; amiable; jovial; lively; lovely;
sentimental; reasoning; semidivine; supernatural; mythological; legendary; unearthly; exalted; supreme; superior; forceful;
intrepid; corporeal; unfortunate; self-conscious; unsheltered; despicable; ominous;
intellectual; mysterious; rebellious; subtle;
wild; immortal; created; wondrous; incomprehensible; countless; deluded; satanic-look-
ing; helpless; finite; enchanted; malevolent;
celestial; terrestrial; infernal; articulate;
moral; responsible; spiritual; conscious;
unnatural; tame; passionless; progressive;
humble; supernal; incarcerated; physical;
transcendent.

verbs

corrupt—; eat into—; insinuate into—; oppose—; reject—; subjugate human —s; —s
differ.

(See individual.)

BELABOR (v)

adverbs

soundly; cruelly; wantonly; heartlessly;
persistently; grossly; unfeelingly; murderously.

(See beat.)

BELCH

adjectives

nauseating; embarrassed; resounding.

BELIEF

adjectives

comforting; sincere; inspiring; venerable;
sustaining; profound; cherished; traditional; calm; dispassionate; widespread; ingenuous; indestructible; unshakable; unswerving; staunch; rock-bound; deep-rooted; unwavering; overpowering; long-established; settled; personal; persistent; thoroughgoing; time-honored; inescapable; unquestioning; poetic; fantastic; weird; romantic; quaint; crazy; fanatical; blind;
senile; heretical; fatuous; illogical; widely-
varying; theosophical; medieval; atheistic;
religious; general; common; dogmatic; tottering; badly-shaken; pathetic; childlike;
implicit; tacit; supernatural; pragmatical;
ancient; serious; exacting; slow; rising;

important; indisputable; eager; unavoidable; prevailing; ineradicable; immemorial; confident; gross; unconscious; contrary; reasonable; theoretic; generous; universal; unassailable; vast; pious; ethical; fundamental; credulous; intellectual; old-fashioned; traditional; discreet; doctrinal; lingering; instinctive; cherished; unflattering; strange; irrational; adorable; spiritualistic; erroneous; grotesque; uncomprehending; popular; stubborn; independent; rote-learned; fatalistic; indomitable; unfounded; growing; stout; superstitious; honest; unstable; rooted; purposive; current; obstinate; divine; peremptory; vague; hoary; dangerous; prevalent; desirable; uncompromising; systematized; battered; consequent; conflicting (pl).

verbs

abandon—; allay—; alter—; annihilate—; apprehend—; arise from—; asphyxiate—; banish—; battle for—; bolster—; blot out—; break down—; cast out—; cherish—; cling to—, comfort in—; confide—; confirm—; conquer—; consider—; contradict—; convict on—; create—; credit—; delude into—; derive—; designate—; destroy—; dispel—; dissipate—; doubt—; draw—; drop—; embody—; embrace—; encourage—; endorse —; entertain—; establish—; evolve—; excite—; expel—; explain—; explode—; expound—; express—; favor—; fetter—; fix —; found upon—; free from—; imply—; incline to—; include—; indoctrinate—; influence—; inherit—; inspire—; justify—; labor under—; lend weight to—; manifest —; master—; nourish—; obliterate—; originate—; outgrow—; perpetuate—; persist in—; persuade in—; present—; profess—; realize—; reject—; relapse into—; relinquish—; repose—in; represent—; repudiate —; rest upon—; retain—; reverse—; rid of —; ripen into—; scotch—; share—; strengthen—; stress—; subdue—; submerge—; support—; surmise—; subscribe to—; trust in —; value—; vindicate—; voice—; waive—; wallow in—; warrant—; witness—; wound —; —s conflict; —decays; —dies; —disappears; —emerges from; —expires; —functions; —intrudes; —melts; —obsesses; — rests on; —springs from; —tempts; —totters; —vanishes; —wanders; —wanes; — waxes low.

(See faith, conviction, persuasion, assurance, doctrine, dogma, creed, opinion, view.)

BELIEVE (v)
adverbs
erroneously; candidly; passionately; frankly; ingenuously; assertively; infallibly; conscientiously; currently; popularly; deliberately; ardently; mournfully; instinctively; dispassionately; unshakably; unswervingly; staunchly; unwaveringly; persistently; unquestioningly; fatuously; illogically; religiously; dogmatically; pathetically; implicitly; tacitly; indisputably; immemorially; reasonably; fundamentally; irrationally; uncomprehendingly; obstinately; unfoundedly; fatalistically; superstitiously; uncompromisingly.

(See suppose.)

BELIEVER
adjectives
devout; ardent; passionate; true; firm; conscientious; tremendous; frantic; lifelong; unquestioning; consummate; fervent; enthusiastic; rapt.

BELITTLE (v)
adverbs
scoffingly; maliciously; subtly; justifiably; surreptitiously; obstreperously; venomously; insidiously; invidiously.

(See reduce.)

BELITTLEMENT
adjectives
malicious; subtle; justifiable.

BELL
adjectives
peaceful; enchanted; clinking; muffled; tinkling; gentian; chiming; mellow; shimmering; deep; oracular; old; cracked; twilight; clear-toned; insistent; tremulous; sullen; ponderous; clanging; gold-rimmed; discordant; warning; ringing; rankling; sleigh; jingling; pealing; rich-toned; musical; resonant; glittering; dazzling; brass; bronze; doleful; melancholy; drowsy; monotonous; jangling; feeble; faint; rusty; antique; little; clapping; sobbing; vesper; shrilling; sonorous; salvage; sweet; cracked; midnight; mournful; heavy-hanging; tolling.

verbs

adorn—; answer—; bear away—; bless—; cast—; clap—; coat—; consecrate—; crack —; fashion—; flare—; found—; gain—; hallow—; invert—; jangle—; lose—; mould —; muffle—; rattle—; recast—; rivet—; shake —s; shape—; silence—; strike—; swing—; trill—; tune—; —alarms; —assembles; —booms; —calls; —carols; — chimes; —clangs; —clashes; —ding-dongs; —heaves; —honors the dead; —invites; — knells; —marks the hour; —notifies; —

peals; —punctuates; —records; —reverberates; —rolls; —screams; —shrieks; —signals; —sings; —speaks; —strikes; —summons; —taunts; —tinkles; —tolls; —ushers
in; —vibrates.
  (See instrument, anvil.)

BELLE

adjectives
merciless; waltzing; ballet; faded; traditional; brilliant; raging.

BELLICOSE
adverbs
habitually; constitutionally; inherently; naturally; hopelessly; aggressively; truculently; atrociously; barbarously; brutally; cruelly; fiercely; hatefully; hard-heartedly; maliciously; obdurately; rancourously; resentfully; spitefully; uncharitably; venomously;
relentlessly; ruthlessly; outrageously; churlishly; invidiously; fiendishly.

BELLIGERENT
adverbs
naturally; habitually; inherently; incorrigibly; lamentably; incurably; racially; inveterately; intrinsically; fanatically; customarily; admittedly; contentiously; wrangl-
ingly; quarrelsomely; malevolently; cruelly;
cold-heartedly; irreconcilably; disturbingly;
riotously; aggressively; irretrievably; hopelessly.

BELLOW
adjectives
inflated; mysterious; bleating; righteous;
forty-acre; overpowering; epochal; hearty;
ludicrous; untuneful; cataclysmal; angry;
summoning; resonant; stupendous; ear-shat-
tering; huge; tempestuous; inhuman; fantastic; wonder-provoking; throaty; hoarse;
terrified; subterranean; hollow.

BELLOW (*v*)
adverbs
tumultuously; gloomily; piercingly; pleased-
ly; lustily; bleatingly; heartily; ludicrously;
untunefully; resonantly; inhumanly; throatily; subterraneanly; hollowly; barbarously.
  (See roar.)

BELLY
adjectives
remorseless; wrinkled; vile.

verbs
band—; belt—; constrict—; fill—; grovel
on—; inflate—; stuff—; swell—; thrust into

—; —aches; —bulges out; —contains; —
hungers; —protrudes; —swells; —vibrates.
  (See abdomen, paunch.)

BELONG (*v*)
adverbs
remotely; infinitely; notoriously; legally;
tacitly; anonymously; permanently; patriotically; temporarily; indefinitely; perpetually.

BELONGINGS
adjectives
countless; diminished; age-hoarded; scanty;
scattered; pathetic; vestigial.

verbs
carry—; cherish—; endow with—; increase
—; injure—; possess—; retrieve—; value
—.
  (See possessions, property.)

BELT
adjectives
tarnished; studded; endless; embroidered;
green-fringed; unbuckled; impenetrable; surrounding; inimitable; controversial; safety;
gentian; fertile; swaying; sequoia; flashing.

verbs
adorn with—; apply—; bind with—; carve
—; design—; emboss—; flap—; hang at—;
inlay—; join —s; load—; loose—; notch—;
pattern—; secure with—; strap—; tense—;
tighten—; tool—; unclasp—; —borders; —
confines; —conveys; —encircles; —girdles;
—restrains; —stretches; —supports; —surrounds.
  (See band.)

BEMOAN (*v*)
adverbs
miserably; piteously; sobbingly; gently;
chronically; unspokenly; tremulously; wailingly; wretchedly.
  (See lament, bewail, deplore.)

BENCH
adjectives   (furniture)
slab; roughly-carved; pew-like; crude; sun-
dried; high; dry; disfigured; secluded;
notched; Sheraton; offending; judicial;
rustic; sympathizing; elevated.

verbs
adorn—; decorate—; design—; display—;
indicate—; model—; occupy—; provide—;
reserve—; squat on—; tilt—; utilize—; work
at—; —affords; —serves; —supports; —
topples.
  (See seat, table, furniture, chair.)

BENCH

adjectives (legal)
dignified; exalted; honorable; judicial; learned; triumvirate; upper.

verbs
appoint to—; bring before—; elect to—; esteem—; occupy—; preside at—; resign from—; retire from—; return to—; serve at—; vacate—; —accepts; —affects; —approves; —ascertains; —charges; —conducts; —deems; —derives; —exemplifies; —fines; —fixes; —fulfills; —imposes; —judges; —pronounces; —sentences.

(See court.)

BEND

adjectives
distant; graceful; alternate; convex; keen; sharp; magisterial; sudden; tender; tolerant.

BEND (v)

adverbs
feebly; impulsively; confidentially; inextricably; mournfully; solicitously; alternately; magisterially; tenderly; tolerantly.

(See turn, curve.)

BENEDICTION

adjectives
low; gentle; healing; apologetic; silver; short; pontifical; perpetual; celestial.

verbs
accompany with—; apply—; attend—; bestow—upon; bless at—; implore—; kneel for—; perform—; pray at—; pronounce—; receive—; seek—; serve at—; shower —s upon; speak—; visit—upon; wreathe in—; —closes; —encourages; —inspires; —opens.

(See prayer, blessing.)

BENEFACTION

adjectives
unknown; gracious; admirable; notorious.

verbs
appeal for—; appreciate—; begrudge—; bestow—upon; cloak—; confer—; contribute —; demand—; expose—; imply—; influence —; judge—; launch—; menace—; offer—; owe to—; publicize—; reduce—; secure—; surprise by—; thwart—; volunteer—; withhold—; —elates; —redeems; —satisfies; —succors.

(See charity.)

BENEFACTOR

adjectives
anonymous; modest; silent; elderly; leading; munificent; life-long; potent.

verbs
appeal to—; betray—; burden—; depend on —; devote to—; distinguish—; employ—; flourish under—; inherit from—; —aids; —bequeaths; —cares for; —comforts; —counsels; —demands; —endows; —establishes; —finances; —fosters; —inquires; —institutes; —lavishes; —patronizes; —profits; —relieves; —retains; —satisfies; —shapes; —succors; —tempts; —volunteers.

BENEFICENCE

adjectives
magical; embodied; leading; heedless; iridescent.

BENEFICENT

adverbs
altruistically; amiably; benignly; charitably; considerately; generously; generally; good-naturedly; kindly; mercifully; sympathetically; tenderly; unselfishly; warmly; bountifully; graciously; indulgently; maternally; paternally; modestly; gently; anonymously; magnificently; simply; unassumingly.

BENEFICIAL

adverbs
permanently; desirably; cumulatively; particularly; reciprocally; mutually; enormously; surprisingly; extraordinarily; satisfactorily; gratifyingly; appreciably; economically; politically; internationally; ultimately; eventually; immensely; essentially; peculiarly; tolerably; generally; universally; absolutely; socially; financially.

BENEFIT

adjectives
permanent; community; important; practical; substantial; lasting; visible; far-reaching; anonymous; persuasive; sweet; merited; accrued; transforming; material; fixed; particular; cumulative; reciprocal; unsurpassed; mutual; enormous; inestimable; overwhelming; extraordinary; incalculable; remarkable; international; economic; educational; tolerable; especial; peculiar; corresponding; patriotic; public; conferred; positive; admitted; innumerable (pl); secluded; essential; immense; desirable; full; doubtful; immediate; surprising; unintended; ultimate; hazardous.

verbs
abolish—; acquire—; attend with—; bequeath —s; bestow—upon; claim—; con-

cede—; confer—upon; defend—; demand—; deprive of—; derive—; disable—; embrace —; enumerate —s; finance—; grant—of; load with —s; mark—; merit—; nullify—; proffer—; reap—; render—; reveal—; secure—; share—; stress—; yield —s; —s accrue; —occurs; —s proceed from.

(See profit, advantage, service, favor.)

BENEFIT (v)
adverbs
questionably; directly; substantially; visibly; anonymously; materially; particularly; cumulatively; reciprocally; unsurpassedly; mutually; inestimably; incalculably; internationally; economically; educationally; peculiarly; correspondingly; admittedly; essentially; unintentionally; ultimately.

(See help, avail.)

BENEVOLENCE
adjectives
unexpected; winged; remarkable; defective; private; expansive; factitious; tolerant; vague; world-wide; significant; muscle-loosening; red-blooded; social; despotic; easy; universal; dominant; sympathetic; amused; innate.

verbs
assist through—; assure one of—; contribute—; depend upon—; disguise—; dispense with—; encourage—; endow with—; exercise—; exploit—; expose—; flourish under —; manifest—; practice—; promote—; reform by—; rejoice in—; rouse—; support with—; surprise by—; withhold—; —aids; —consoles; —delights; —relieves; —shines.

(See bounty, charity, generosity.)

BENIGNANT
adverbs
graciously; invariably; consistently; tenderly; notably; amiably; big-heartedly; mildly; simply; warmly; tolerantly; gently; courteously; smoothly; generously; complacently; genially; thoughtfully; considerately.

BENIGNITY
adjectives
politic; hopeful; inexpressible; suave; soothing; gentle.

BENT
adjectives
artistic; philosophical; natural; immediate; practical.

BEQUEATH (v)
adverbs
mutely; subsequently; generously; acceptably; munificently; extravagantly; liberally; miraculously; unsparingly.

(See transmit.)

BEQUEST
adjectives
subsequent; munificent; acceptable; final; generous; scanty.

BERATE (v)
adverbs
morosely; abusively; furiously; heatedly; indignantly; vociferously; venomously; drunkenly; privately; desperately; deplorably; monstrously.

(See upbraid, reprimand, censure.)

BEREAVEMENT
adjectives
irreparable; personal; domestic; mitigated; intolerable; unforgettable.

BERRIES
adjectives
fresh-picked; luscious; delicious; bunched; packaged; frozen; helpless; scarlet.

verbs
consume—; crate—; crush—; cultivate—; devour—; enjoy—; feast on—; hull—; market—; pluck—; preserve—; relish—; wreathe with—; yield—; —crackle; —flourish; —redden; —ripen; —suspend from; —thrive.

(See fruit, vegetable, flower.)

BESEECH (v)
adverbs
unfeignedly; weepingly; vainly; piteously; charmingly; graciously; guilelessly; exquisitely; sentimentally; fanatically; piously; humbly.

(See beg, entreat, implore.)

BESIEGE (v)
adverbs
ineffectually; resolutely; foolhardily; miraculously; overwhelmingly; vigorously; ragingly; persistently; intermittently; intensively; desultorily.

(See surround, attack.)

BESIEGER
adjectives
arrogant; merciless; infuriated; intrepid; importunate; relentless; tireless; unreasoning; wrathful.

verbs

arm —s; take —s by surprise; taunt —s;
—s advance; —s assail; —s assault; —s
beleaguer; —s blockade; —s capture; —s
hem in.

(See fighter, soldier, troops.)

BESTIAL

adverbs

coarsely; horribly; brutally; fiercely; grossly; indecently; ribaldly; shamelessly; unbelievably; abusively; obscenely; evilly;
brutishly; violently; abominably.

BESTOW (v)

adverbs

gratuitously; felicitously; improperly; equally; facetiously; unwittingly; philanthropically; munificently; grudgingly.

(See grant.)

BET

adjectives

fatal; reckless; shrewd; timely; underhand
ed; unfair; unfortunate.

verbs

arouse—; balance—; cancel—; cover—; encourage—; forfeit—; hedge—; instigate—;
insure—; lay—; stake—; support—; —
stands; —surprises.

(See wager, stake.)

BETRAY (v)

adverbs

grossly; deliberately; hideously; vilely; viciously; virtually; infrequently; treacherously; incautiously; bluntly; subtly; heartlessly; venomously; emotionally; mentally.

(See reveal, disclose.)

BETRAYAL

adjectives

gross; deliberate; grave; hideous; vile; vicious.

verbs

avenge—; charge—; commit—; fume at—;
lead into—; —divulges; —exposes; —violates.

(See treason, treachery, exposure.)

BETRAYER

adjectives

accidental; circumspect; disloyal; shameless;
subtle; treacherous; unwitting.

verbs

accuse—; confront—; denounce—; dishonor
—; execute—; vindicate—; —deserts; —
discloses; —flees.

BETROTH (v)

adverbs

gladsomely; diplomatically; religiously; contemptuously; sordidly; inappropriately; beatifically.

(See give.)

BETROTHAL

adjectives

enforced; happy; opposed; favored; proclaimed; prolonged; signalized; unduly influenced.

verbs

compact—; compound—; consecrate—; consummate—; contract—; dissolve—; fulfill—;
honor—; promote—; ritualize—; sanction—;
solemnize—; violate—; —affiances; —binds;
—couples; —engages; —promises.

(See engagement.)

BETTERMENT

adjectives

permanent; material; economic; moral;
human; spiritual; lasting; civic.

BEVERAGE

adjectives

intoxicating; wholesome; fermented; distilled; seductive; beguiling; customary; exhilarating; soothing; mild; constant; limpid;
refreshing; invigorating; fragrant; thirst-
quenching.

verbs

brew—; carbonate—; consume—; devise—;
dispense—; dissolve into—; draw off—;
formulate—; infuse—; ladle—; medicate—;
quaff—; sip—; tap—; treat—with; weaken
—; —cools; —effervesces; —ferments; —
foams; —induces; —intoxicates; —percolates; —relieves; —satisfies; —warms.

(See drink, liquor, wine, beer, coffee, etc.)

BEWAIL (v)

adverbs

sepulchrally; mournfully; heartbrokenly;
blatantly; vigorously; hoarsely; stentoriously; stormily; fearfully; inarticulately;
raucously.

(See bemoan.)

BEWILDER (v)

adverbs

confusingly; completely; perplexingly; inscrutably; spiritually; pitifully; naively;
tragically; childishly.

(See confuse, perplex, mystify.)

BEWILDERED

adverbs

strangely; suddenly; hopelessly; helplessly; mysteriously; alarmingly; gravely; seriously; tragically; disastrously; completely; horribly; terribly; indescribably; obviously; manifestly; dazedly; brokenly; pathetically; laughably; ridiculously; foolishly; undeniably; significantly; painfully; confusedly; embarrassingly; ludicrously; bashfully; modestly; piteously; awkwardly; confoundedly; disturbingly; timidly; vaguely; dangerously; overwhelmingly; unluckily; miserably; wretchedly; indefensibly; ineptly.

BEWILDERMENT

adjectives

blank; growing; vague; dazed; helpless; elated; stunned; weary; hurt; spiritual; disgusted; pitiful; naive; added; incredulous; cross; seeming; sheer; complete; deep; suspicious; dazzling; tragic; childish.

verbs

extricate from—; hide—; lose in—; meet with—; stray in—; tangle in—; wander in —; —confuses; —grows; —perplexes.
(See confusion.)

BEWITCHING

adverbs

dangerously; enchantingly; charmingly; radiantly; indescribably; indefinably; marvelously; startlingly; fatally; ineffably; inexplicably; utterly; delightfully; designedly; diabolically; surprisingly; quietly; consciously; tauntingly; overwhelmingly; provokingly; tormentingly; youthfully; irresistibly; unconsciously.

BIAS

adjectives

distorting; grossest; racial; political; natural; beneficial; theoretic; considerable; economic; favorable; moral; elemental; personal.

verbs

deliver from—; free from—; —clouds; — crops up; —distorts; —inclines one toward; —influences; —leans; —misleads; —prejudices; —rejects; —slopes; —swerves; — warps.
(See prejudice.)

BIBLE

adjectives

consoling; dignified; family-recording; mutilated; treasured; time-honored; oft-perused; woe-comforting.

verbs

adopt—; advance—; blaspheme—; commend—; conflict with—; dethrone—; embellish—; embrace—; esteem—; execute—; inscribe in—; interpret—; misconceive—; mutilate—; preserve—; reject—; spread—; undermine—; —aims at; —appeals; —authorizes; —condemns; —decrees; —endures; —impresses; —inspires; —presents; —reveals; —sets forth; —stirs; —teaches; — unites; —veils.
(See book, scriptures.)

BIBLIOGRAPHY

adjectives

extensive; sketchy; elaborate; speculative; heavy; selective; analytical; complete; annotated; comprehensive; critical.

BICKER (*v*)

adverbs

constantly; cantankerously; perpetually; unappetizingly; pettishly; undiplomatically; uncharitably; blatantly; repulsively; incompatibly.
(See dispute.)

BICKERING

adjectives

unseemly; perpetual; unappetizing; petty; diplomatic; international.

adverbs

eternally; spitefully; ill-naturedly; nervously; feverishly; incessantly; tempestuously; fussily; intolerably; quarrelsomely; forever; habitually; ill-temperedly; unnecessarily; shrewishly; continually.

BID

adjectives

subtle; foolhardy; feathery; maddest; miraculous; casual; curt; collusive; contemptuous.

verbs

advance—; dispose of —s; double—; govern—; ignore—; pass—; rattle off —s; redouble—; reject—; retract—; run up—; shout—; submit—; withdraw—; —astounds; —s compete; —s pour in; —suffices.
(See proposal, offer.)

BID (*v*)

adverbs

mockingly; artfully; graciously; regretfully; shrewdly; imperiously; subtly; foolhardily; madly; casually; curtly; contemptuously.
(See offer, order, direct, ask.)

adverbs
graciously; astonishingly; miraculously; devotedly; pliantly; amiably; indifferently; apparently; cunningly; shrewdly; grudgingly; necessarily; glumly; stolidly; stupidly; passively; complacently; wisely; politely; suavely; cheerfully; blindly; blithely; unthinkingly; foolishly.

BIDE (v)

adverbs
patiently; habitually; naively; perpetually; ephemerally; transiently; independently; pensively.
(See inhabit, abide, endure.)

BIER

adjectives
watery; beckoning; hasty; hallowed; senseless; wretched; blazing.

verbs
array before—; deck—; decorate—; deposit on—; expose on—; file before—; kneel before—; mourn at—; repose on—; surround —; venerate—; weep at—; worship at—.
(See coffin, frame, grave, altar.)

BIGAMY

adjectives
defiling; forbidden; law-evading; ostracised; perfidious; shameful; titled; wretched.

verbs
charge with—; commit—; condone—; define—; imprison for—; live in—; loathe—; outlaw—; practice—.
(See crime.)

BIGOT

adjectives
fierce; intelligent; splendid; self-satisfied; pernicious; vicious; unsparing.

BIGOTED

adverbs
intolerably; fanatically; narrow-mindedly; obdurately; obstinately; incurably; persistently; hopelessly; offensively; arbitrarily; doggedly; incorrigibly; mulishly; inflexibly; perversely; pig-headedly; stubbornly; intractably; perniciously; wilfully; narrowly; dogmatically; arrogantly; imperiously.

BIGOTRY

adjectives
puritanical; sordid; religious; inveterate; unthinking; patent.

adjectives
abounding; acrid; complex; reactivated; yellow-green.

verbs
expel—; secrete—; store—; —collects; —converts; —flows; —reacts; —trickles.
(See fluid.)

BILL (invoice)

adjectives
preposterous; inevitable; exorbitant; unexpected; modest; staggering; delusive; long-unpaid.

BILL (law)

adjectives
substitute; pending; mandatory; feasible; amended; revised; comprehensive; militia; drafted; pork-barrel.

BILL (legislation)

adjectives
adopted; accepted; amended; contested; discussed; defeated; dismissed; parliamentary; petitionary; true; revised.

verbs
act on—; advocate—; challenge—; confer on—; confront with—; contest—; deliberate—; draft—; draw—; denounce—; enact —; frame—; hurry—through; incorporate in —; kill—; modify—; originate—; railroad —; reject—; retain—; slap through—; smother—; sponsor—; veto—; urge—; —entails; —looms; —provides; —sets forth; —stipulates.
(See law, legislation.)

BILL (money)

adjectives
limp; dejected; worn; crumpled; charitable; elusive; proud; defaced; carefully-fondled; ragged; crisp; faded; crinkled.

BILL (statement of account)

adjectives
adjusted; dunning; final; lavish; harassing; paltry; peccant; padded; uncollected; overwhelming.

verbs
deduct—; deliver—; discount—; draw up—; enter—; file—; foot—; forward—; pad—; render—; scale—; tuck—away; —itemizes; —overcharges; —s pour in; —s rain in.

adjectives

blatant; blazing; huge; glaring; inappropriate; inartistic.

verbs

censor—; crusade against —s; employ —s; greet with —s; plaster on—; post on—; rebel against —s; —blares; —campaigns; —coaxes; —s dot the highways; —informs; —s line; —s mar; —pictures; —promotes.
(See advertisement.)

BILLOW

verbs

bear on—; beset by—; cleave—; produce—; steer through—; swell into —s; swim through—; —beats; —breaks; —crests; —dances; —endangers; —foams; —overwhelms; —rages; —rears up; —roars; —rolls; —silvers; —surges; —sweeps on; —swells; —tosses up; —tumbles.
(See wave, breaker.)

BILLOW (*v*)

adverbs

softly; tumblingly; restlessly; dashingly; furiously; advancingly; foamingly; wrathfully; seethingly; multitudinously; glitteringly; darkly; crestedly.
(See pound.)

BILLOWS

adjectives

inky; heaving; crested; vibrant; slanting; wild-roaring; rocking; undulating; glittering; high; multitudinous; dark; solemn; breaking; proud; unreposing; tawny; ruffian; surging; unblended; foaming; unawakened; rolling; tempestuous; seething; wrathful; dancing; curling; building; ridgy; wafting; advancing; dashing; obedient; sleepless; furious; resistless; cruel; immense; endless; tumbling; glimmering; restless.

BIND (*v*)

adverbs

indubitably; beautifully; closely; exquisitely; intimately; firmly; conveniently; infinitely; eternally; irrevocably; inextricably.
(See fasten, tie, restrict, restrain.)

BINDING

adjectives

neat; original; practical; imperishable; ornate; exquisite; excellent; worn; mildewed; embossed; leather; drab; linen; luxurious.

BINDING (*a*)

adverbs

legally; morally; onerously; embarrassing-

ly; awkwardly; laboriously; perplexingly; formidably; desperately; dreadfully; outrageously; distressingly; vexatiously; uncomfortably; appallingly; alarmingly; unquestionably; definitely; positively; absolutely; securely; cruelly; truly; inescapably; conclusively; oppressively.

BIOGRAPHER

adjectives

distinguished; veracious; worthy; eulogistic; skilled; faithful; enthusiastic; pedestrian; debunking; ecclesiastical; iconoclastic.

BIOGRAPHICAL

adverbs

palpably; unmistakably; blatantly; evidently; undisguisedly; apparently; openly; flagrantly; accurately; historically; clearly; nakedly; pleasantly; slightly; pseudo-; cruelly; completely; purportedly; intentionally; carelessly.

BIOGRAPHY

adjectives

full-fledged; fascinating; literary; splendid; noble; notable; dignified; readable; compelling; painstaking; vital; rhapsodic; exuberant; fictionalized; authoritative; official; comprehensive; iconoclastic; miniature; definitive; pretentious; sensational; previous; informal; inclusive; reliable; remarkable; famous; picturesque; best-selling; meritorious; colorless; satisfactory; magnified; racy; critical; dull; drab; musty; hero-worshipping.

verbs

acquaint with—; attempt—; cultivate—; illuminate—; interpret—; launch—; live—; record in—; —accounts; —appeals; —attributes; —catalogues; —chronicles; —"debunks"; —defames; —delights; —details; —distorts; —enchants; —eulogizes; —exaggerates; —extols; —fires; —informs; —lauds; —narrates; —pictures; —portrays; —reveals; —sketches; —treats of; —twists; —unfolds.
(See life.)

BIRCHES

adjectives

superb; slim; silver; delicate; colored; snow-hung.

BIRD

adjectives

carrion; landward; flitting; red-breasted; homeward; chattering; fluttering; honeysucking; soaring; stuffed; widowed; songless; stripe-winged; glowing; ruffled;

choleric; captive; nesting; melodious; succulent; rapacious; flippant; full-throated; chirping; unclean; ominous; insolent; feathered; sober; morbid-looking; migratory; aquatic; timorous; joyful; frightened; grand-limbed; restless; gold-flecked; bewildered; caged; nest-deserted; reckless; human-hearted; singing; fledgling; unhappy; babbling; solemn; cruel; furtive; night; huge; deserted; callow; blind; bright-winged; predatory; cheerful; brooding; herald; unscared; dapple-breasted; silly; ragged; riotous; noxious; pigmy; tropical; sable; striking; raucous: contented; brilliant; ravenous; monstrous; bewildered; imprisoned; mateless; rare; unusual; strange; valuable; roosting; circling; wingless; timid; tenderest; startled.

verbs
breed —s; cage—; capture—; cripple—; dislodge—; encage—; exterminate—; fall prey to —s; flush—; kill off of peg ; scatter —s; stuff —s; teem with —s; —s anthem; —ascends; —babbles; —breeds; —broods; —builds; —calls; —carols; —chants; —cheeps; —cheers up; —chirps; —chitters; —s chorus; —s clamor; —s congregate; —croons; —s copulate; —crouches; —cuddles; —darts; —descends; —disgorges; —disports; —drifts; —dwells; —s enliven; —feeds; —fledges; —flits; —floats; —s flock; —flutters; —frequents; —gorges; —gossips; —gushes; —hatches; —haunts; —hovers; —inhabits; —lays; —lights upon; —mates; —migrates; —molts; —mounts; —nests; —s orient themselves; —s pair; —pecks; —perches; —pierces sky; —pipes; —pirouettes; —plaints; —plumes himself; —plunges; —pours out his song; —preens; —preys upon; —probes; —prunes; —s quarrel; —s race; —ranges; —rears; —s roost; —s ruffle their plumage; —s scatter; —s scold; —screams; —scuds; —scurries; —serenades; —shoots; —shuns; —sips; —skips; —soars; —sputters; —s stridulate; —s swarm; —sweeps; —swoops down; —taxies; —traces a circle in the air; —trills; —s troop; —twitters; —unfolds; —vanishes; —wanders; —warbles; —wheels; —whirls about; —whistles; —wings his way; —zooms.
(See animal, fowl.)

BIRTH
adjectives
checkered; illustrious; multiple (pl); doubtful; restless; mystic; abhorred; prodigious; timeless; visible; high; noble; royal; immortal; declining; exotic; heavenly; un-natural; approaching; violent; promiscuous; mortal; majestic; wondrous; adulterated; hallowed; painful; miraculous; princely; portentous; abortive; vernal; unexceptional; worthy; monstrous; ill-starred; fated; celebrated; virgin.

verbs
announce—; assist at—; attend at—; celebrate—; extol—; foretell—; govern—; herald—; honor—; manifest at—; preside over—; record—; register—; rejoice at—; restrict —s; travail in—; —s decline; —occurs.
(See beginning, origin, renaissance.)

BIRTHDAY
adjectives
happy; sad; romantic; memorable; unsung.

verbs
commemorate—; document—; endow on—; fete on—, honor on—; memorialize—; observe—; register—; trace—; —approaches.
(See anniversary.)

BIRTHPLACE
adjectives
forsaken; humble; remembered; sterile.

BIRTHRIGHT
adjectives
unattainable; unbound; bitter; unwhipped; unburned; unchained; separated; precious; inalienable; undeniable.

verbs
claim—; forfeit—; honor—; pawn—; retain—; rob of—; salute—; sell—; sway to —; —entitles; —privileges.
(See privilege, inheritance.)

BISCUITS
adjectives
delicious; crumbly; crisp; brown; golden-topped; delicate.

BISHOP
adjectives
affable; resident; pompous; dignified; massive; dutiful; esoteric; eccentric.

BISON
adjectives
attacked; watered; labored; tamed; horned; roaming; vagrant; herded; captured; slaughtered; conquered; hunted; skinned; galloping; thundered; inhabited; restricted; protected.

verbs
corral—; exterminate—; herd—; shelter—;
yoke—; —abound; —bellows; —charges;
—grazes; —pastures; —ranges; —roams;
—roars; —sheds; —stampedes; —vanishes.
(See ox, buffalo, animal.)

BIT

adjectives
needful; tempting; savory; checked; insignificant; fluffy; bright; picturesque; unrelated; choice; fragmentary; imaginary; premature; fantastic; mute; tuneless; disquieting; impossible; brilliant; incredible; dainty;
demoralized; charred; flimsy.

BIT

adjectives   (mouthpiece of bridle)
double; chain; cruel; champed; curbing; excruciating; maddening; torturous; vexing.

verbs
accustom to—; adjust—; attach to—; callous
to—; champ at—; choke on—; control with
—; cough out—; fight against—; jerk at—;
respond to—; ride—; run away from—; saw
at—; shy at—; slaver—; spit out—; stop
with—; swallow—; take—between teeth;
veer from—; yank at—; —chafes; —clamps
tongue; —curbs; —restrains; —slackens; —
subdues; —tames; —tortures.

BITE

adjectives
crisp; short; crunching; vicious; murderous;
prodigious; good-sized; furious; agonizing;
hurried; hasty.

verbs
down—; gulp—; inflict—; —cuts; —heals;
—pierces; —wounds.

BITE (v)

adverbs
savagely; impetuously; unmercifully; unexpectedly; annoyingly; passionately; viciously; daintily; crunchingly; murderously; agonizingly; hurriedly; hastily.
(See nibble, chew.)

BITING (a)

adverbs
sarcastically; bitterly; viciously; venomously; insidiously; hatefully; mercilessly; deliberately; churlishly; unsparingly; crustily;
insolently; obnoxiously; captiously; censoriously; caustically; acrimoniously; perversely; contumaciously; snappishly; peevishly;
uncivilly; ungraciously; abusively.

BITTER

adverbs
maliciously; shrewdly; enviously; viciously;
purposely; unnecessarily; uncontrollably;
insidiously; invidiously; sharply; cynically;
sarcastically; spitefully; jealously; intentionally; cunningly; ironically; insinuatingly; incisively; cruelly; brutally; unwisely;
atrociously; malevolently; tauntingly; caustically; diabolically.

BITTERNESS

adjectives
thwarted; rancorous; profound; political;
unserviceable; chill; quiet; corrosive; smiling; intense; loathsome; speculative; secret;
pent-up; sarcastic; extreme; sectional; unsparing; contradictory; personal; sardonic;
unrelenting; acrid; partisan; increased; concealed; concentrated; unspoken; undying;
chronic.

verbs
be devoid of—; brush aside—; erase—;
evoke—; fan—; intensify—; persecute with
—; taste—; temper—; —creeps into; —develops; —flames; —gnaws; —heats; —
vexes.
(See malice, rancor.)

BIVOUAC

adjectives
picturesque; solemn; miserable.

BLACK (n)

adjectives
solemn; rusty; pitchy; stark; shining; blistered; exploited; wicked; natural; dense;
lustrous; inky; midnight; conservative; rich;
dense; impenetrable; oppressive; sable;
ominous; heavy; palpable; murky; humid;
thick.

BLACK (a)

adverbs
rustily; dingily; deeply; lugubriously; formidably; gloomily; duskily; murkily; pitch-
ily; sombrely; richly; pallidly; dunly; faintly; dully; coldly; unearthly; sepulchrally;
mournfully; glossily; glassily; smoothly;
astonishingly; incredibly; unspeakably.

BLACKBIRD

adjectives
combative; chuckling; glinting; saucy; scolding; sooty; squabbling; planing; winging;
windy; timid.

verbs
—chatters; —chants; —claws; —flaps; —

114

flutes; —hovers; —migrates; —nests; —plasters; —preys on; —raids; —ravages; —sails off; —warbles.
 (See bird.)

BLACKGUARD
adjectives
dissipated; turbulent; foreign; drunken; brutal.

BLACKNESS
adjectives
inky; impenetrable; oppressive; pitchy; soft; sable; ominous; murky; cold; drizzling; unsociable; palpable; heavy; humid; piercing; peculiar; dripping; appalling; corrugated; musty; absolute; quivering; menacing; comforting; Cimmerian; Stygian.

verbs
engulf in—; grope through—; lose in—; peer into—; steer through—; —envelops.
 (See darkness.)

BLACKSMITH
adjectives
rural; gnarled; sinewy; mighty; brawny.

BLADDER
verbs
control—; dilate—; distend—; empty—; govern—; inflame—; regulate—; swell—; —bursts.

BLADE
adjectives   (grass)
trembling; springing; wind-rippled; dewy.

BLADE
adjectives   (man)
blushing; foppish; gay; desperate; roistering; brilliant; flashy; overdressed; jolly; generous.

BLADE
adjectives   (sword)
flashing; glittering; whirling; bright; heavy; broad; double-edged; sharp; dull; penetrating; rapier; projecting; fiery; lean; delicate; blameful; bloody; dripping; burnished; avenging; dry; scanty; polished; troublesome; flexible; unwithering; tremulous; freshly-springing; fratricidal; bayleaf-shaped; deadly; reddened; shining; scythe-shaped; trenchant; trusty; unsheathed; well-tempered; worthy.

verbs
carve with—; draw—; drive in—; flash—; forge—; grasp—; heave—; lash with—; redden—; send—home; sheathe—; temper —; withdraw—; —glances off; —lacerates; —pricks.
 (See knife.)

BLAMABLE
adverbs
partially; lamentably; unhappily; deplorably; unquestionably; entirely; seriously; directly; indirectly; morally; sinfully; deservedly; completely; personally; atrociously; criminally; enormously; outrageously; censurably; exceptionally; reprehensibly; unbelievably.

BLAME
adjectives
high-repented; worthy; moral; sinful; specific; small; ill-placed; complete; deserved; directed; heavenly.

verbs
absolve of—; account for—; accuse of—; allocate—; attach—to; avoid—; bear—; censure in—; charge with—; conceal—; deflect—; deserve—; devise—; expose to—; free from—; impute—to; incur—; lay—to; merit—; reproach with—; share—; stamp with—; trace—; vindicate one of—.
 (See censure, reproach, condemnation.)

BLAME (*v*)
adverbs
unjustly; morally; sinfully; specifically; completely; deservedly; prejudicially; unthinkingly; narrow-mindedly; puritanically.
 (See censure, reproach.)

BLAMELESS
adverbs
clearly; innocently; exceptionally; altogether; wholly; consciously; truly; undoubtedly; impeccably; virtually; artlessly; virtuously; happily; essentially; palpably; patently; indisputably; incontestably; indubitably; positively; absolutely; spotlessly; unquestionably.

BLAND
adverbs
inscrutably; gently; politely; mysteriously; amiably; civilly; complacently; courteously; genteelly; good-temperedly; obsequiously; suavely; urbanely; suspiciously; sweetly; affably; cordially; graciously; ingratiatingly; habitually; unfailingly; surprisingly; essentially.

BLANDISHMENT

adjectives
spider-like; sordid; paternal; artless; suave; sneering; oily.

BLANDNESS

adjectives
inscrutable; confidential; amazing; acquired; pretended.

BLANKET

adjectives
dripping; lovely; soaked; gaudy; bright-colored; impenetrable; shaggy; government; smelly; ragged; invisible; undulating; stretched; osier; sulphur; tasseled; warming; comfortable.

verbs
air—; clothe in—; divest of —s; double —s; envelop in —s; fold in—; immerse in—; pattern—; shelter with—; snuggle in—; tuck—in; weave—; wrap in—; —comforts; —consoles; —protects; —shields; —shrouds; —smothers.
(See robe.)

BLANKNESS

adjectives
oblivious; utter; lurid; strange; complete; devastating; overwhelming; inescapable; dire.

BLARE (v)

adverbs
steadfastly; vigorously; furiously; shrilly; howlingly; fearfully; cuttingly; startlingly; penetratingly; brassily; warningly; echoingly.
(See bellow.)

BLASPHEME (v)

adverbs
scandalously; fearfully; soul-searingly; abominably; raucously; mutteringly; luridly; crudely; shockingly; ominously.
(See swear.)

BLASPHEMOUS

adverbs
scurrilously; luridly; startlingly; horribly; unspeakably; soul-searingly; abominably; hideously; shrilly; raucously; noisily; inarticulately; mutteringly; unutterably; impiously; irreverently; brazenly; openly; wilfully; profanely; perversely; sacrilegiously; fanatically; scoffingly; desecratingly; irreligiously; cynically; intolerably; unbearably; terrifyingly; unregenerately; godlessly; unforgivably; diabolically; ruthlessly;
implacably; criminally; indefensibly; inexcusably; unpardonably; flagrantly; iniquitously; scandalously; wickedly; offensively; accursedly; indecorously; infamously; nefariously; obdurately; unconscionably; villainously.

BLASPHEMY

adjectives
loud; lurid; startling; horrible; unspeakable; soul-searing; abominable; willful; hideous; shrill; vast; raucous; intricate; illimitable; half-inarticulate.

BLAST

adjectives
overwhelming; vigorous; short; fierce; furious; golden; hoarse; challenging; unbroken; scorching; stentorian; summoning; shrill; chilling; stinging; icy; polar; startling; passing; careening; suffocating; howling; putrid; eddying; tremulous; stirring; modulated; bitter; spasmodic; heated; bleak; fearful; wintry; pitiless; furnace-like; roaring; infernal; scornful; woeful; cutting; unruly; nightly; parching; wailing; foul; stormy; raging.

verbs
blow—; loose—; prepare for—; set off—; shiver in—; shrink from—; spit out—; time —; unloose—; —bites; —bolts; —decapitates; —displaces; —envelops; —frees; —forces; —raves; —rends; —resounds; —rises; —roars; —rocks; —shakes; —shatters; —shocks; —startles; —unearths; —uproots; —vibrates; —withers.
(See explosion, discharge.)

BLAST (v)

adverbs
terrifically; overwhelmingly; vigorously; suffocatingly; thunderously; stunningly; tremendously; dynamically.
(See smite, destroy, frustrate.)

BLATANT

adverbs
clamorously; vociferously; cheeringly; uproariously; screamingly; stentoriously; offensively; unnecessarily; asininely; blunderingly; brainlessly; arrogantly; extravagantly; foolishly; heavily; ineptly; obtusely; senselessly; weakly; awkwardly; boorishly; lustily; indecorously; loudly; ribaldly; obstreperously; tawdrily; coarsely; cheaply; vulgarly; oddly; unwontedly; hoydenishly; monstrously; clownishly; outlandishly.

adjectives
ghastly; solstitial; supersolar; hospitable; fruitful; crimson; mellowed; meridian; fierce; brilliant; torrid; departed; passionate; leaping; flaring; cheery; unclouded; quenchless; final; distant; wondrous; continuous; garish; radiant; far-beaming; careless; sullen; comforting; noontide; bright; splendid; golden; hungry; glowing.

verbs
burst into—; confine—to; diffuse—; extinguish—; feed—; smother—; —beams; —flares up; —illumines; —ravages; —roars; —scorches; —sears; —springs up.
(See flame, fire, light.)

BLAZE (v)

adverbs
magnificently; spectacularly; terrifically; intensely; defiantly; crimsonly; torridly; passionately; flaringly; garishly; radiantly; sullenly; glowingly.
(See flame.)

BLAZONED

adjectives   (also emblazoned)
gloriously; goldenly; ceremoniously; glitteringly; grandly; magnificently; pretentiously; colourfully; punctiliously; properly; ritualistically; ceremonially; spectacularly; splendidly; fancifully; fantastically; ostentatiously; flamingly; garishly; gaudily; gaily; majestically; sumptuously; theatrically; noteworthily; deservedly; lustrously; distinctively; honorably; famously; sublimely; immortally; memorably; exaltedly; surpassingly; deathlessly; imperishably; prominently; proudly; imposingly.

BLAZONRY

adjectives
rich; barred; glorious; blood-red; historic; age-old; aristocratic; meaningful.

BLEAT (v)

adverbs
frantically.

BLEATING

adjectives
incessant; piteous; high-pitched; squeaky; helpless; ineffectual.

BLEED (v)

adverbs
internally; sorely; profusely; copiously; continually; excessively; fatally; terrifyingly; unexpectedly; intermittently.
(See exude.)

adjectives
continuous; excessive; fatal; forced; arrested.

verbs
arrest—; benefit from—; check—; coagulate—; combat—; control—; dread—; eliminate—; encourage—; impair by—; induce —; plug—; recover from—; reduce—; result in—; retard—; staunch—; suffer from —; tourniquet—; treat—; witness—; —ceases; —confines; —endangers; —enervates; —impoverishes; —increases; —irrigates; —saps; —shocks; —weakens.
(See hemorrhage.)

BLEMISH

adjectives
superficial; facial; physical; unsightly.

verbs
detect—; discern—; eradicate—; result in —; —blots; —disfigures; —flaws; —impairs; —marks; —mars; —scars; —slurs; —stains.
(See defect, fault, imperfection, flaw.)

BLEND (v)

adverbs
softly; intimately; pleasantly; indistinguishably; cunningly; curiously; skillfully; delicately; inextricably; mildly; expertly; exquisitely; amazingly; incredibly; magically; miraculously; mysteriously.
(See merge, combine, mix, assimilate.)

BLENDING

adjectives
extraordinary; delightful; special; uncopiable; mild; expert; discreet; mellow; master; subtle; delicate; rare; happy; strange; colossal; exquisite.

BLESS (v)

adverbs
sanctimoniously; benignly; spiritually; devoutly; reverently; graciously; silently; eternally; providentially.

BLESSED

adverbs
blissfully; happily; infinitely; richly; unquestionably; gratefully; ecstatically; gloriously; eternally; divinely; magically; mystically; endlessly; tenderly; devoutly; profoundly; fervently; sincerely; devotedly; reverently; immeasurably; warmly; thankfully.

BLESSING

adjectives

unexampled; greatest; inestimable; countless (pl); infinite; fervent; plural (pl); apostolic; unmitigated; needful; earthly; mutual (pl); manifold (pl); priestly; substantial; redeeming; unfelt; silent; certain; rich; supernatural; heavenly; abundant; guttural; over-cordial; unimpaired; unclouded; sundry (pl); unequivocal; endless; providential; choicest; valueless; lasting; lifelong; eternal.

verbs

abound with —s; bestow—upon; cherish—; consecrate with—; crown with —s; inherit —; invoke—; pour —s upon; pronounce—; prove—; realize—; render—; wish—upon; —s attend; —consoles; —descends upon; —s flow from; —hallows; —redeems; —thrills.
(See benediction, favor.)

BLIGHT

adjectives

devastating; mouldy; cruel; venomous; visible; premature; swarming.

BLIND

adverbs

falsely; defiantly; wilfully; mercifully; besottedly; heart-rendingly; wretchedly; pitiably; totally.
(See obscure.)

BLINDNESS

adjectives

obstinate; approaching; helpless; innocent; ultimate; mortal; burning; perspicacious; willful; social; pedantic.

BLINDS

adjectives

copper; painted; window; genteel; dilapidated; secret; shut; much-used.

BLINK (*v*)

adverbs

solemnly; approvingly; sleepily; drowsily; somnolently; shrewdly; sagaciously; dazedly; incessantly; intermittently.
(See wink, disregard, overlook.)

BLISS

adjectives

truest; rapturous; idiotic; unutterable; hysterical; mortal; conjugal; winged; ecstatic; endless; unforgettable; perennial; purest; youthful; dissolving; ambiguous; matchless; unclouded; virgin; visioned; perfect; connubial; extreme; dreamy; unearthly; ineffable; immortal; highest; domestic; private; perpetual; tranquil; coming; sensual; dead; inward; candid; nameless; eternal; transporting; audacious; mantling; faded; departed; foreshadowed; capricious; passive; paralyzed; everlasting; human; heavenly; imaginary; enormous.

verbs

abide in—; anticipate—; attain—; augment —; dampen—; deluge—; diffuse—; dwell in —; experience—; merit—; reign in—; renounce—; sever from—; share in—; violate —; wither—.
(See rapture, happiness, ecstasy.)

BLISSFUL

adverbs

delightfully; supremely; rapturously; gladly; happily; ravishingly; beatifically; joyously; transportedly; charmingly; joyfully; luxuriously; thrillingly; exquisitely; deliciously; incredibly; fascinatingly; blessedly; truly; idiotically; unforgettably; conjugally; amorously; enormously; eternally; dreamily; ineffably; perfectly; matchlessly; endlessly; youthfully; innocently; ecstatically.

BLISTER

adjectives

benign; dark; burning; malignant; tiny; suppurating; prurient; purulent; unsightly; watery.

verbs

absorb—; acquire—; apply to—; cover with —s; drain—; heal—; infect—; inflame to —; open—; paint—; plague with —s; puff into—; raise—; remove—; rub into—; suffer from—; swell into—; treat—; —annoys; —appears; —burns; —bursts; —inconveniences; —irritates; —pains; —drains.
(See ulcer, sore, boil.)

BLITHE

adverbs

infectiously; charmingly; cheerfully; gaily; healthily; contagiously; habitually; airily; exuberantly; heedlessly; carelessly; nimbly; affectionately; bewitchingly; teasingly; bewilderingly; childishly; girlishly; youthfully; wholeheartedly; enticingly; irresistibly; exhilaratingly; animatedly; gleefully; hilariously; friskily; bonnily; exultingly; happily; jauntily; jovially; joyously; jubilantly; joyfully; laughingly; merrily; mirthfully; playfully; rollickingly; spiritedly; vivaciously; trickily; winsomely.

adjectives

biting; dense; muffled; roaring; driving; raging; terrible; insect; blinding; numbing; howling; merciless; swirling.

verbs

dread—; forecast—; forewarn of—; perish in—; precede—; predict—; shelter from—; —blasts; —blinds; —freezes; —rages; —rattles; —redoubles its force; —rises; —shrieks; —suffocates; —tears; —wheels; —whines; —whirls.

(See wind, disaster, storm.)

BLOCK

adjectives

riveted; clanking; creaking; dedicated; bloody; lifeless; vertical; city.

BLOCKADE

adjectives

never-ending; actual; patulttle; economic; dilatory; menacing; complete; vertical; partial; inescapable; innumerable (pl).

verbs

break—; comply with—; cut off by—; denounce—; detail—; effect—; enforce—; engage in—; foil—; force—; impose—; insure—; maintain—; notify of—; patrol in —; penetrate—; proclaim—; raise—; relieve—; resort to—; retaliate for—; run—; slip out of—; smuggle through—; storm—; subject to—; succumb to—; surrender to—; sustain—; terminate—; undertake—; —binds; —checks; —compels surrender; confiscates; —denies; —detains; —distresses; —endangers; —interrupts; —isolates; —obtructs; —prohibits; —shuts off; —starves.

(See embargo.)

BLOCKHEAD

adjectives

babbling; inconceivable; prattling; idling; complete; accomplished; practiced; genial; harmless; silly; fond.

BLONDE

adjectives

blithe; fine; sandy; honey-colored; flamboyant; debonair; strident; incurable; brilliant; robust; vivacious; appealing; feather-headed; ravishing; pretty; irresponsible; peroxide; raucous; platinum; stringy; petite; insolent; attractive; natural; bleached; wistful.

adverbs

alluringly; rapturously; heavenly; divinely; seductively; naturally; artificially; goldenly; sandily; ruddily; tawnily; flamboyantly; stridently; brilliantly; vivaciously; bleachedly; attractively; provocatively; stringily; irresponsibly; prettily; ravishingly; featherheadedly; appealingly; irresistibly; enchantingly; refreshingly; winsomely; fascinatingly; daintily; felicitously; pleasantly; satisfyingly; tormentingly; disturbingly; grievously; inordinately; bewitchingly.

BLOOD

adjectives

distinguished; vigorous; fighting; chivalrous; tainted; foul; fraternal; stale; rank; polluted; dangerous; feverish; tingling; pounding; pulsing; oozing; flowing; mingled; foreign; human; hot; caked; dried; frozen; chilled; sluggish; innocent; spattered; quick; living; turbulent; bereaved; sacred; hostile; young; drowsy; precious; patriot; malapert; rushing; ebbing; jellied; trading; frolicsome; atoning; molten; violent; daring; kindred; nutrient; swift; basic; true; gummy; martyred; heretic; faultless; systolic; wicked; generous; pale; coursing; royal; aspiring; frothy; haughtiest; sanguine; congealed; arrested; excellent; noble; rare; sweet; comfortable; nomadic; corrupt.

verbs

aerate—; baptize in—; bathe in—; besmear with—; blend —s; chill—; cleanse—; congeal—; contaminate—; convey—; cool—; curdle—; defile with—; dilute—; dip in—; draw—; drip—; dye with—; effuse—; enrich—; expel—; fertilize—; flush with—; forfeit—; foul—; freeze—; go down in—; impoverish—; infect—; infiltrate—; infuse —; inhabit—; inoculate—; inure to—; invigorate—; issue from—; let—; oxygenate —; paint with—; poison—; pollute—; purge —; purify—; redden with—; seal with—; secrete—; shed—; soak in—; spill—; splash with—; spout—; stain with—; staunch—; steep in—; stimulate—; stir—; suck—; suffuse with—; swill—; taint—; taste—; thirst for—; transfuse—; wallow in—; win with —; write in—; yield—; —accumulates; —boils; —clots; —coagulates; —courses; —creeps through; —dribbles out; —flows; —gushes; —issues forth; —jets out; —leaps; —oozes; —palpitates; —pours from; —pulsates; —reabsorbs; —rises; —runs; —rushes through; —shoots forth; —spurts; —

stagnates; —streams; —surges; —tinkles;
—throbs; —wells up.

BLOOD PRESSURE
adjectives
alarming; apoplectic; choleric; devastating;
mounting; tremendous.

verbs
lower— —; normalize— —; relieve high—
—; — —descends; — —drops; — —endangers; — —rises; — —startles; — —threatens.
(See barometer.)

BLOODSHED
adjectives
wanton; continued; unspeakable; needless;
callous; ruthless.

verbs
attend with—; conquer without—; denounce
—; die in—; ease—; end in—; free from—;
instigate—; involve—; precipitate—; provoke—; result in—; revel in—; steep in—;
suffer—; terminate in—; win through—.
(See massacre, slaughter.)

BLOODTHIRSTINESS
adjectives
bestial; reckless; ghoulish; vampire; leech-
like; insatiable.

BLOODTHIRSTY
adverbs
insⁿtiably; recklessly; criminally; bestially;
cruelly; abominably; inhumanly; atrociously; brutally; infamously; iniquitously;
knavishly; profligately; scandalously; viciously; incorrigibly; lawlessly; nefariously;
sinfully; wickedly; horribly; unspeakably;
amazingly; systematically; inherently; savagely; ferociously; diabolically; feloniously;
fiendishly; flagitiously; foully; vilely; villainously.

BLOOD VESSEL
adjectives
bulging; bursting; flexible; heated; attenuated; overworked; straining; fragile.

verbs
block— —; burst— —; circulate through—
—; clog— —; contract— —; course through
— —; dilate— —; distend— —; disturb—
—; engorge— —; flex— —; harden — —s;
infect— —; line— —s; lodge in— —; narrow— —; puncture— —; retract— —;
rupture— —; sever— —; staunch— —;
tear— —; thin— —; twist— —; conveys
— —; — —pulsates; — —shrivels up; —
—s spring from; — —throbs; — —yields.
(See artery, vein.)

BLOOM
adjectives
gorgeous; glossy; girlish; delicate; lusty;
fragrant; glorious; lingering; artificial;
short-lived; semi-tropic; abundant; natural;
sweet; faded; bell-like; wonted; youthful;
overflowing; renovated; hopeful; welded;
roseated; manifold; definite; luxuriant; virgin; citrus; petaled; vivid; vernal; prolific; radiant; amethystine; braided; sensational; plenteous; bunchy; precious; exotic;
hidden; perfumed; wholesome; primeval;
straying; ethereal.

verbs
blast—; blight—; break into—; exalt—; nip
—; smother—; take—off; —colors; —culminates in; —exudes; —floresces; —flourishes; —flushes; —glows; —pales; —promises; —sparkles; —springs from; —tints.
(See blossom, vigor, flower.)

BLOOM (v)
adverbs
unchangingly; abundantly; magnificently;
lustily; gorgeously; glossily; youthfully;
overflowingly; luxuriantly; prolifically;
vernally; exotically; wholesomely; primevally; ethereally.
(See blossom.)

BLOSSOM
adjectives
gorgeous; exquisite; cheerful; bright; fabulous; pure; almond; varicolored; lace-like;
fragrant; golden; bursting; myriad; pendulous; showy; petaled; wholesome; marsh;
bloodlike; colorful; holy; peach; tender;
blazing; curious; living; blighted; pomegranate; sunlit; gaudy; meek; conical; embowering; faded; minute; brimstone; evanescent; odorous; latent; beauteous; topmost; phantom; vernal; winking; barren;
mimic; loveliest; storm-beaten; flaming;
proud.

verbs
bear—; burst into—; clip—; cover with —s;
nip—; press—; produce—; put forth —s;
scatter —s; shed —s; shower down —s;
trim—; yield—; —buds; —dances; —fades;
—flowers; —flutters down; —grows; —
opens; —promises; —unfolds; —withers.
(See bloom, flower.)

BLOSSOM (v)
adverbs
magnificently; simultaneously; luxuriantly;
fabulously; gorgeously; pendulously; colorfully; curiously; gaudily; conically; eva-

nescently; odorously; vernally; winkingly;
flamingly.
(See bloom, flower, prosper, thrive.)

BLOT
adjectives
unsightly; tarnished; shadowy; foul; indelible; wrinkled; messy; adulterate.

BLOT (v)
adverbs
remorselessly; indelibly; blackly; permanently; finally; eventually; carelessly; frequently.
(See spot, efface, obliterate.)

BLOTCH
adjectives
sickly; shadowy; ugly; pale; bloody.

BLOTCHY
adverbs
painfully; disagreeably; incurably; unpleas
antly; dingily; obnoxiously; disgustingly;
repulsively; distressingly; unbecomingly;
hopelessly; embarrassingly; disconcertingly;
mortifyingly; alarmingly; fearfully; strangely; oddly.

BLOUSE
adjectives
gaudy; flowered; sheer; soft; warm; padded; diaphanous.

BLOW
adjectives
powerful; hammer-like; heavy; severe;
fatal; irresistible; lethal; nasty; cruel;
treacherous; descending; resounding; per-
cussive; menaced; serious; decisive; frightful; painful; crushing; aggressive; perennial; threatened; echoless; irreparable;
doughty; well-directed; staggering; breathless; final; sharpest; faithless; severe;
swashing; annihilating; solid; hollow;
drunken; amorous; vicious; impending;
dull; dexterous; tetchy; ineradicable; heartless; sacrilegious; accusative; death-wind;
implacable; ineffective.

verbs
administer—; aim—; break—; breast—;
deal—; encounter—; evade—; exchange —s;
execute—; experience—; fall to —s; interchange —s; parry—; rain —s upon; reel
under—; strike—; stun with—; survive—;
thrust—; trade —s; —descends upon; —
resounds; —shatters; —smashes; —stretches
one out.
(See stroke.)

BLOW (v)
adverbs
adversely; ceaselessly; placidly; gustily;
violently; shrewdly; languorously; keenly;
incessantly; spasmodically; irresistibly; resoundingly; lethally; aggressively; annihil-
atingly; viciously; implacably.
(See howl, sigh, swirl.)

BLOWZY
adverbs
ruddily; healthily; sturdily; rosily; attractively; coarsely; blatantly; noticeably; carelessly; showily; floridly; sunnily; pleasantly; roughly; captivatingly; interestingly;
wholesomely.

BLUDGEON
adjectives
crude; effective; honest; critical; rough;
swift; devastating.

BLUE
adjectives
heavenly; silent; mermaid; exquisite; canonical; dim; celestial; iceberg; indigo;
bright; cadmium; intense; sky; glamorous;
turquoise; sapphire; brilliant; ordinary;
deep; chalcedony; larkspur; limpid; cobalt;
delicate; crystal; anemic; illimitable; somber; opalescent; glossy; boundless; uniform;
unbroken; dusty; remotest; wood-smoke;
cornflower; purest; periwinkle; light; luminous; royal; aquamarine; aerial; tropic;
pallid; sulphurous; frost.

BLUE
adverbs
ineffably; deeply; divinely; heavenly; unspeakably; indescribably; pleasantly; coldly; steely; affectionately; exquisitely; dimly; brightly; intensely; brilliantly; limpidly;
delicately; sombrely; boundlessly; dustily;
uniformly; remotely; purely; lightly; luminously; royally; frostily.

BLUEBIRD
adjectives
ever-welcome; flitting; glorious; luck-bear-
ing; joyful; memory-haunting; merry-
whistling.

verbs
—cheers; —pipes; —speeds; —warbles;
—whispers.
(See bird.)

BLUFF   (cliff)
adjectives
barren; wind-swept; somber; bare; grass-

grown; bold; low; hazy; fine; sand; scarped; rock-reared.

BLUFF
adjectives (lie)
unadulterated; superb; magnificent; brazen; bold; preposterous.

BLUFF
adjectives (speech or manner)
deceptive; frightening; hearty; imposing; offhanded; pretentious; surly; cruel.

verbs
attempt—; bet against—; boast—; call—; carry out—; get away with—; maintain—; —blinds; —deceives; —deters; —excuses; —frightens; —hoodwinks; —induces; —influences; —serves.
(See lie.)

BLUFF
adverbs
churlishly; rudely; captiously; discourteously; disrespectfully; ill-manneredly; impudently; uncivilly; mischievously; moodily; morosely; perversely; insultingly; impertinently; bitterly; bluntly; boorishly; coolly; grimly; harshly; peevishly; pertly; ruggedly; naturally; characteristically; unpardonably; inexcusably; unpleasantly; playfully; teasingly; tormentingly; nonsensically; disagreeably; unnecessarily; sarcastically; ironically; sourly; unceremoniously; tartly; sullenly; vulgarly; unintentionally; deliberately; indefensibly.

BLUFF (v)
adverbs
unnecessarily; superbly; brazenly; preposterously; boldly; magnificently; characteristically; inevitably; grossly; incredibly; unpardonably; faithlessly.
(See frighten, intimidate.)

BLUFFING
adjectives
brilliant; multifarious; inevitable; characteristic; unexpected.

BLUNDER
adjectives
unhappy; colossal; fateful; irretrievable; astounding; disastrous; egregious; political; awful; brave; absurd; idiotic; tactical; ill-judged; sad; marketing; glorious; gross; serious; irreparable; extravagant; incredible; recent; sorry; idiomatic; curious; unpardonable.

verbs
aggravate—; atone for—; commit—; denounce—; fall into—; redeem —s; repair —s; —confounds; —confuses; —disturbs; —troubles.
(See error, mistake.)

BLUNDER (v)
adverbs
grossly; ludicrously; chimerically; ineptly; awkwardly; colossally; fatefully; irretrievably; disastrously; egregiously; politically; idiotically; irreparably; incredibly; idiomatically; grammatically; unpardonably.
(See bungle.)

BLUNDERER
adjectives
inept; impudent; awkward; supposed; chagrined; finished.

BLUNDERING
adjectives
hopeless; bureaucratic; forward; silly; understandable; impudent.

BLUNT
adverbs
stupidly; boorishly; ignorantly; unintentionally; deliberately; sullenly; unceremoniously; ironically; unnecessarily; disagreeably; unpardonably; inexcusably; insolently; unpleasantly; characteristically; ruggedly; honestly; pertly; peevishly; sternly; severely; harshly; doggedly; rudely; captiously; discourteously; uncivilly; ungraciously; moodily; morosely; perversely; bitterly; coolly; clumsily; ineptly; exasperatingly.

BLUNTNESS
adjectives
occasional; astringent; exasperating; characteristic; righteous; permissible; ugly; accentuated; clumsy; bludgeoning; inept.

BLUR
adjectives
confused; dim; pale; ineffectual; misted; pensive; wavering; shapeless; golden; retreating; vague.

BLUSH
adjectives
soft; crimson; deep; modest; rare; palest; contagious; piteous; guilty; delicate; scarlet; hot; burning; suffusing; lovely; rising; bright; charming; gracious; guileless; west-

ern; innocent; telltale; pure; vivid; quick; eloquent; mellow; sudden; unseen; fleeting; short; boyish; puzzled; witching; unborrowed; exquisite.

verbs
color with—es; flash—; hide—; redden with —es; result in—; suffuse with—; —beautifies; —embarrasses; —glows; —heats; — inflames; —warms.
(See flush.)

BLUSH (v)
adverbs
furiously; miserably; coyly; elatedly; synthetically; disdainfully; ingenuously; modestly; delicately; eloquently; exquisitely; witchingly; easily.
(See flush, redden.)

BLUSTER (v)
adverbs
furiously; thunderously; fearsomely; tremendously; terrifically; ceaselessly; monotonously; wrathfully; heatedly; vigorously; vainly.
(See storm, rage, fume.)

BOAR
adjectives
urchin; snouted; angry; chafing; blunt; bloody; hideous; monstrous.

BOARD (commission)
adjectives
nonpartisan; expert; efficient; glowing; political; mirthful; superior; ancient.

BOARD (official body)
adjectives
assembled; directing; executive; governing; advisory; high; honorable; local.

verbs
abolish—; admit to—; bring before—; control—; create—; elect to—; enlarge—; entrust to—; establish—; organize—; provide —; refer to—; set up—; staff—; —administers; —adopts; —advises; —authorizes; —agrees; —arbitrates; —condemns; —convenes; —develops; —disposes of; —effects; —elects; —enacts; —enforces; —exercises; —investigates; —modifies; —operates; — outlines; —performs; —promotes; —provides; —reforms; —regulates; —relieves; —reports; —stimulates; —supports; — votes.
(See commission, committee.)

BOARD (wood)
adjectives
resplendent; stray; reeking; creaking; uncarpeted; shot-scarred; glistening; cypress; trophy-laden; decaying; rough-hewn; original; grub; sparing; wine-filled; ugly; sturdy; flimsy; scanty; groaning; festive; plenteous.

verbs
adjust—; burnish—; case with —s; cast upon —s; cover with —s; encase in —s; enclose in —s; finish off—; fit—; frame with —; hew—; measure—; patter over —s; plane—; preserve—; reinforce —s; sand—; scurry over —s; warp—; —bars; —creaks; —extends; —groans; —rots; —splinters; — splits; —warps.
(See table, stage.)

BOAST
adjectives
absurd; playful; empty; foolish; truthful; proudest; ordinary; unique; unadulterated; vapid; peerless; ignoble; honest; sentimental; fanatic; airy; childish; frantic; prattling; noisy; vain.

BOAST (v)
adverbs
justly; blatantly; unmitigatedly; exuberantly; arrogantly; intoxicatedly; hollowly; overweeningly; whimsically; vainly; egotistically; vapidly; ignobly; fanatically; prattlingly.
(See brag, vaunt.)

BOASTFUL
adverbs
extravagantly; absurdly; playfully; foolishly; proudly; vapidly; airily; childishly; boyishly; noisily; blatantly; egotistically; fantastically; grotesquely; palpably; manifestly; essentially; ludicrously; ridiculously; laughably; offensively; unpleasantly; egregiously; ignobly; ineffectually; inanely; senselessly; idiotically; preposterously; dexterously; adroitly; cleverly; indiscreetly; imprudently; feebly; flimsily; wishfully; stupendously; magnificently; splendidly; vaingloriously; blindly; blissfully.

BOASTING
adjectives
egotistical; vain; cursed; extravagant; blustering; bold; blatant.

verbs
glory in—; indulge in—; make good—; occasion—; speak in—; utter—; —extols; —

menaces; —occasions; —terrifies; —threatens.

(See display.)

BOAT

adjectives

crude; wooden; staunch; frail; uptilted; racing; comfortable; sunken; excursion; distant; tiny; fishing; plying; crowded; plunging; fragile; light; portable; lazy; vile; cheap; whirling; driving; moored; outward-bound; crewless; colossal; iron; vanished; half-beached; clumsy; swift; weather-beaten; well-manned; unanchored; pavilioned; worn-out; illuminated.

verbs

alight from—; anchor—; bail—; becalm—; capsize—; caulk—; detail—; fire up—; fit out—; heave to—; moor—; paddle—; pole —; propel—; punt—; push off—; reserve—; swamp—; —churns; —cleaves the water; —dances; —flops; —flounders; —founders; —glides; —grounds; —nuzzles; —outsails; —pitches; —plies; —ploughs; —sneaks; —swings; —touches at.

(See vessel, ship, canoe, launch, schooner, barge, tugboat.)

BOATMEN

adjectives

wrangling; grizzled; inexperienced; skillful.

BOB

adjectives

ravishing; tawny; smooth; smart; shoulder-length.

BOBOLINK

adjectives

joy-swelling; migratory; coy; rice-seeking; reed-swinging; throaty; questing.

verbs

—boasts; —broods; —chirps; —laughs; —prattles; —rattles.

(See bird.)

BOBWHITE

adjectives

covert; dun-colored; misleading; nature-sheltered; shy; sly; wary.

verbs

—bursts out; —calls; —darts; —displays; —feathers; —feigns; —fights; —flushes; —huddles; —preens; —prevs on; —puffs out; —sails; —struts; —swells; —trots; —twitters; —whirrs; —whistles; —wings.

(See quail, partridge, bird.)

BODEMENT

adjectives

tremendous; horrid; accurate; uncanny; precise.

BODICE

adjectives

slim; fitted; jeweled.

BODY

adjectives (group)

aggregate; august; responsible; disinterested; official; governing; obscure; civil; picturesque; upstanding; formidable; deliberative; eminent; hasty-witted; public; legislative; virtuous; specialized; illustrious; ecclesiastical; unsympathetic; artistocratic; insensate; permanent; obstructive; impartial; intermediary; heterogeneous; pigmy; arbitrating; expansive; elastic; appropriating; unfathomable; long-established; anxious; consulting; sensible; seeming; well-regulated; confirming; alterable; irresistible; distinct; reckless; contemptible; inanimate; numerous.

BODY

adjectives (substance)

clumsy; angular; boyish; deformed; dangling; hurtling; jerking; squatting; quivering; slouched; struggling; trembling; wan; palpitating; human; paralyzed; mummified; hairy; wrinkled; ruddy; compact; drenched; sodden; bleeding; jarred; relaxed; collapsed; huddled; slumped; sagging; defiant; swaggering; dainty; small-boned; shapely; graceful; delicate; striking; quick; wiry; supple; lithe; sturdy; swift; strong; heavy-muscled; hard; rugged; sinewy; young; vigorous; healthy; sound; vibrant; sensuous; amorous; yielding; passionate; stocky; weightless; stunted; shrunken; emaciated; meager; bronzed; slim; stiffened; taut; lethargic; slack; immovable; prone; lifeless; couchant; motionless; prostrate; huge; overgrown; vast; obese; mountainous; lanky; unclean; ragged; neglected; unshaven; detestable; overworked; meek; fear-driven; weary; worn; exhausted; charred; sick; strangled; ailing; poverty-weakened; disfigured; bruised; torn; jerking; swooning; soulless; negroid; paralyzed; covered; blanketed; relaxed; frozen; dense; unworthy; well-defended; minute; fever-stricken; anemic; religious; misshapen; pierced; organic; transparent; sovereign; inanimate; subterranean; visible; recumbent; influential; spontaneous; rotund; drowned; tattooed; inert; interlaced; unicellular; statuesque; squirming; convivial; flaccid; defunct; astral; adjacent; contradictory; segregated; idle; capable; cheerful; fluid; qualified; bigoted; unsound; chaste; branching; decent; convulsing; cigar-shaped; erect; twitching; Spagnuoled; decomposed; uncoffined; jovial; exhausted; plump; filiform; weazened; undivided; rubicund.

verbs
adapt—; anoint—; array—; attune—; bare —; batter—; bow—; bury—; cast out—; chill—; cleanse—; cling to—; commit—; consecrate—; consume—; contract—; deck —in; defile—; deplete—; discern—; dismember—; dispose of—; drag—; dwarf—; ease—; edify—; emaciate—; embrace—; endanger—; exhilarate—; expose—; exult in—; fetter—; floor—; gloat over—; govern—; incline—; inflict upon—; inter—; introduce into—; invest—; invigorate—; mangle—; pelt—; pommel—; preserve ⏐ reconstruct—; relieve—; reproduce—; rid —of; saturate—; splatter—; sponge—; stiffen—; sustain—; tenant—; torture—; transmit through—; triumph over—; twist—; vitalize—; waste—; wrap—in; —decomposes; —disintegrates; —festers; —flops; —gleams; —glides; —putrefies; —quivers; —rebels; —reigns; —responds; —slumps; —sprawls; —twitches; —vibrates; —wriggles; —writhes.
(See form, frame, carcass, corpse.)

BOG
adjectives
filthy; logical; sinking; swanky; sphagnous; treacherous; dangerous.

BOG (v)
adverbs
hopelessly; filthily; logically; treacherously; dangerously; fatally; irresistibly; obscurely; unprecedentedly; miserably.
(See fail.)

BOGGY
adverbs
muddily; plashily; squashily; quaggily; swampily; softly; unpleasantly; unhealthfully; unfortunately; pestiferously; undesirably; irrecoverably; irremediably; hopelessly; unluckily; deplorably; disturbingly; plaguedly; impracticably.

BOIL
adjectives   (tumor)
erupting; festering; hideous; throbbing; rest-robbing; purplish.

verbs
absorb—; cut—; dissect—; extirpate—; incise—; lance—; paint—; puncture—; — buds; —comes to a head; —disappeared; —forms.
(See abscess.)

BOISTEROUS
adverbs
broadly; intolerably; noisily; clamorously; uproariously; vociferously; turbulently; obstreperously; blatantly; fussily; breezily; convivially; festively; jovially; genially; happily; joyously; joyfully; wildly; madly; crazily; drunkenly; merrily; coarsely; crudely; pugnaciously; discordantly; angrily; excusably; childishly; rudely; Rotarily; uncontrollably; foolishly; fatuously; socially; perpetually; heedlessly; carelessly; thoughtlessly; deliberately; unpardonably; inexcusably; understandably; naturally; affectionately; fraternally.

BOISTEROUSNESS
adjectives
boyish; loud; unrestrained; broad; raucous.

BOLD
adverbs
offensively; audaciously; impudently; rashly; wantonly; indiscreetly; injudiciously; hotheadedly; foolishly; recklessly; presumptuously; amazingly; shamelessly; tragically; singularly; ridiculously; inexplicably; dramatically; inherently; fantastically; alarmingly; temperamentally; dangerously; courageously; adventurously.

BOLDNESS
adjectives
unprecedented; characteristic; decent; self-respecting; uncanny; prodigious; sublime; astonishing; pious; persistent; singular; ill-timed; ridiculous; easy; frank; habitual; felicitous; generous; extreme; foolish.

BOLE
adjectives
twisted; opalescent; resinous; hoary; bossy.

BOLT
adjectives
tremendous; heavy; flimsy; sulphurous; sharp; avenging; death-dealing; heaven-sent.

verbs
adjust—; apply—; clamp on—; connect—; discharge—; drive—; employ—; extract—; fasten—; forge—; heat—; hurl—; manipu-

BOMBAST

late—; rivet—; screw—; secure with—; shackle in —s; shoot—; sink—; snap—; strip—; stud—; thread—; tighten—; turn —; undo—; —bars; —expands; —fastens; —locks; —pins; —prevents; —rivets; —safeguards; —seals; —secures; —shrinks; —unties; —withstands.

(See bar.)

BOLT (v)

adverbs
hungrily; avidly; ferociously; grossly; hoggishly; brutishly; barbarously; unrestrainedly; sottishly; permanently.

(See gulp.)

BOMB

adjectives
unsuccessful; exploding; gas; incendiary; volcanic; time.

verbs
bombard with—; clock—; detonate—; direct—; discharge—; drop--; eject—; encase—; examine—; fill—; fire—; fling—; fuse—; hurl—; ignite—; project—; rain —s; release—; set—; shower with —s; time —; toss—; —batters; —bursts; —dynamites; —explodes; —s fly; —hammers; —hums; —plows through; —ruins; —scatters; —shatters; —ticks; —uproots.

(See projectile, shell.)

BOMB (v)

adverbs
cold-bloodedly; unsuccessfully; inhumanly; volcanically; ruthlessly; fiendishly; callously; devilishly; soullessly.

(See attack.)

BOMBARDMENT

adjectives
preliminary; serious; desultory; persistent; intermittent; intensive; aerial; constant; threatened.

verbs
assail with—; command—; concentrate—; conduct—; counter—; defend against—; direct—; flee from—; fortify against—; inflict—; plan—; prepare for—; resort to—; shatter with—; shelter from—; shudder under—; slacken—; unleash—; ward off—; —assails; —attacks; —batters; —damages; —demolishes; —demoralizes; —destroys; —disables; —disheartens; —dispirits; —injures; —reduces; —routs; —rumbles; —scatters; —thunders; —uproots.

(See attack, assault.)

BOMBASTIC

adjectives
oratorical; studied; stilted; rhetorical; empty; loud; pedantic; ranting.

adverbs
magnificently; absurdly; playfully; foolishly; proudly; inanely; vapidly; airily; noisily; childishly; blatantly; fantastically; joyously; ludicrously; ridiculously; laughably; offensively; unpleasantly; ineffectually; senselessly; idiotically; clownishly; preposterously; stupendously; splendidly; blissfully; intolerably; rudely; fatuously; deliberately; crudely; merrily; crazily; convivially; vociferously; uproariously.

BOND

adjectives (certificate or debenture)
corporation; government; interest-bearing; matured; municipal; negotiable; transferable; utility.

verbs
advise on —s; borrow on —s; cash —s; float —s; inherit —s; investigate —s; issue —s; liquidate—; market —s; number —s; print —s; recommend —s; register —s; repudiate —s; sell —s; serialize —s; transfer —s; —accumulates interest; —matures; —promises.

BOND

adjectives (investment)
dubious; crinkly; unimpeachable; funding; highly-secured; gilt-edged.

BOND

adjectives (tie)
textual; unbreakable; inescapable; economic; financial; confidential; cruel; weak; tacit; everlasting; powerful; tenacious; imperishable; invisible; sympathetic; secret; strong; invariable; delusive; indissoluble; indestructible; intellectual; countless (pl); subtle; artistic; single; merry; harmonious; conventional; natural; oppressive; fraternal; eternal; marriage; enduring; close.

verbs
burst —s; contract—; dissolve—; enter—; liberate from—; link with —s; loose —s; maintain—; pledge—; seal—; shatter—; snap —s asunder; tighten—; —cements; —confines; —connects; —constrains; —endures; —enslaves; —fetters; —imprisons; —manacles; —obligates; —restrains; —shackles.

(See band, tie, fetter, obligation, promise.)

BOND (v)

adverbs

indissolubly; unbreakably; inescapably; financially; tenaciously; imperishably; invisibly; conventionally; eternally; oppressively.

BONDAGE

adjectives

infantine; solemn; sweet; petted; deep; hereditary; deadly; commercial; intermittent; mysterious; improvised; voluntary; brittle; tolerable; wholesome; hard; magic; roseate; economical.

verbs

abolish—; bring into—; deliver from—; enforce—; enslave in—; escape from—; free from—; hold in—; impose—; pledge into —; reduce to—; return to—; rid of—; sell into—; serve out—; subject to—; tie in—; —degrades; —warps.

(See slavery, servitude, captivity, subjugation.)

BONE

adjectives

joint; marrow; gaunt; jutting; crumbling; bleached; ravaged-looking; dry; mighty; dismal; poor; tired; aching; trivial; massive; storm-chilled; unsightly; toothsome; aged; blanching; unrememberable; dissevered; aligned; queer-shaped; earthly; chivalric; delicate; distorted; empty; honored; sturdy; white-sown; sound; mastoid; unburied; grilled; uncoffined; shining; petrified; carious; honest; moldering; livid; weary; piteous; cowardly; frontal; pliable; marsupial; steely; brittle; immense; pulsant; femoral; prominent; canonized; spiced; high; saucer-like.

verbs

adhere to—; adjust —s; affect—; assemble —s; bend—; bleach —s; breed in —s; bruise —; cement—; crack—; crush—; cut to—; deform—; dislocate—; distort—; dry—; excavate —s; expose—; fertilize with —s; fracture—; freeze to—; gnaw—; graft—; grind —s; harden —s; heal—; infect—; inflame—; injure—; inter —s; knit—; lengthen—; operate on—; pick—; pierce—; plate —; protect—; rattle —s; realign—; reveal —; scatter —s; set—; shake—; soften—; splinter—; treat—; twist—; unite—; waste —s; wire—; wrap up —s; x-ray—; —s ache; —s creak; —s form; —s frame; — hinges; —s join; —s mature; —s remain; — rots.

BONFIRE

adjectives

solitary; glowing; tremendous; rejoicing.

BONNET

adjectives

dark; coquettish; delicate; starched; battered; flattened; sun; gigantic; hearse-plumed; amazing; poke; durable; dangling; orange-tawny.

BONNY

adverbs

blithely; airily; beautifully; buxomly; rosily; prettily; wholesomely; cheerfully; buoyantly; merrily; jestingly; gaily; lightly; winsomely; joyously; ecstatically; rapturously; simply; dearly; adorably; charmingly; enchantingly; bewitchingly; lovably; irresistibly; tormentingly; teasingly.

BONY

adverbs

awkwardly; fantastically; grotesquely; amusingly; pathetically; complacently; unbelievably; distressingly; angularly; terribly; horridly; oddly; touchingly; grievously; unthinkably; ludicrously; ridiculously; deplorably; lamentably; strangely; queerly; singularly; drolly.

BOOK

adjectives

vade-mecum; reference; glorified; guide; handy; narrow; thin; black; unacademic; unpretentious; amazing; disturbing; terrifying; strange; vital; dynamic; pregnant; monogrammed; original; incisive; passionate; ancient; worn; musty; dusty; littered; moldy; coverless; written; translated; polished; elegant; cynical; illustrated; inferior; painful; heartbreaking; obscure; condemned; ungraceful; dull; tedious; rejected; inadequate; incomplete; fuliginous; obscene; degrading; suggestive; immoral; dreadful; spectacular; shocking; devastating; ill-natured; cursed; blasphemous; seditious; banned; deliberate; quarrelsome; posthumous; sacred; unsigned; anonymous; educative; formidable; scientific; talking; racial; devotional; serious; realistic; truest; provocative; important; notable; warlike; venerable; sophisticated; wise; mature; delicate; learned; informative; readable; clever; agreeable; comprehensive; detailed; popular; best-selling; famous; hilarious; painful; funny; amusing; stimulating; quaint; priceless; rare; difficult; massive; well-made; clear; rich; authentic; factual; authoritative; absorbing; astonishing; accursed; bewitching; clarifying; diverting; enthralling; exhilarating; extraordinary; first; feminine; forthright; glamorous; glorious; heroic; human; hair-raising; irresistible; intimate; magnificent; practical; perfect; remarkable; readable; stirring; superb; scholarly; strangest; sensitive; timely; splendid; unique; vital; witty; grand; ephemeral; melancholy; useful; thought-provoking; valuable; exercise; scrambling; profitable; memorandum; stormy; edifying; musty; indecent; salable; lewd; elementary; illiterate; lucid; enjoyable; commonplace; censored.

verbs
adapt—; admire—; base on—; belittle—; clutch—; con—; cram—; dedicate—; depreciate—; disparage—; distort—; dive into —; edit—; elaborate—; enshrine—; fling —; illustrate—; label—; launch—; mutilate —; permeate—; peruse—; plot—; plunge through—; pour over—; preface—; propagate—; recommend—; resort to—; review —; revise—; ridicule—; satirize—; scan—; search—; slander—; succumb to—; summarize—; thumb—; tilt—; vend—; —abounds in; —breathes; —charms; —defiles; — details; —depresses; —disturbs; —documents; —embodies; —enchants; —enthralls; —inspires; —meanders; —oppresses; —ranks; —shocks; —sparkles; —surges; —transports.
(See volume, novel, fiction, story, biography.)

BOOKCASE
adjectives
bamboo; elegant; built-in; expensive.

BOOKISH
adverbs
hopelessly; learnedly; ostentatiously; arrogantly; proudly; unfortunately; quaintly; amusingly; complacently; colossally; tediously; monotonously; inordinately; obviously; studiously; ardently; unintelligently; vacuously; inanely; showily; blindly; pedantically; superficially; shrewdly; proverbially; profoundly; eruditely; consciously; academically; omnisciently.

BOOKKEEPER
adjectives
provincial; timid; expensive; overworked; lazy; ambitious.

BOOKLET
adjectives
descriptive; illustrated; attractive; authoritative; fascinating; explanatory; valuable;

informative; dainty; interesting; constructive; pictorial.

BOOM
adjectives (activity or prosperity)
amazing; exciting; fortune-rolling; gigantic; rapidly-subsiding; tidal-wave; overnight.

verbs
accelerate—; advance into—; buoy up by—; burst into—; daze by—; delay—; denote—; follow by—; foretell—; launch—; prepare for—; provoke—; revel in—; revive—; stimulate—; work up—; —advances; —bounds; —cheers; —collapses; —crashes; —encourages; —exhilarates; —fades; —follows; —induces; —prospers; —retards; —roars; —sets in; —swells.
(See prosperity, development.)

BOOM
adjectives (business)
postwar; periodic; unprecedented; glorious; fantastic.

BOOM
adjectives (noise)
dwindling; penetrating; deep; disturbing; muffled; incalculable; subdued.

BOOM (*v*)
adverbs
hollowly; deafeningly; penetratingly; disturbingly; muffledly; subduedly; sonorously; dully; monotonously; musically; thuddingly; resoundingly; intermittently.
(See roar.)

BOOMING
adjectives
hollow; sonorous; dull; perpetual; deep-toned; monotonous; musical.

BOON
adjectives
inestimable; priceless; immortal; unspeakable; delusive; blissful; greater; floral; choicest; smaller.

verbs
accord—; beseech—; bestow—; command —; confer—upon; court—; deny—; entreat —; favor with—; grant—; petition—; pray for—; request—; yield—.
(See blessing, advantage, favor, gift.)

BOOR
adjectives
sottish; churlish; ill-bred; insensible; ignor-

ant; thick-necked; rustic; lascivious; horny-handed; drunken.

BOORISH
adverbs
awkwardly; fantastically; inordinately; offensively; contemptibly; amusingly; unconsciously; unwittingly; artlessly; deliberately; morbidly; prodigiously; colossally; tediously; detestably; bluntly; insufferably; intolerably; unbearably; rudely; abominably; crudely; intentionally; carelessly; shockingly; stupidly; innately; churlishly; ignorantly; drunkenly; impudently; uncivilly; moodily; perversely; insultingly; bitterly; harshly; ruggedly; inexcusably; disagreeably; sourly; unceremoniously; sullenly; indefensibly; outrageously.

BOOTH
adjectives
gaudy; little; secluded; vine-covered; mushroom-topped; rustic; impermanent; miserable; demonstration.

verbs
assemble in—; conduct—; conduct to—; construct—; cover—; erect—; exhibit in—; huddle in—; lead to—; lodge in—; provide —; refresh at—; shelter in—.
(See shelter, stand.)

BOOTS
adjectives
squeaking; shining; swaggering; varnished; spurred; heavy; patched; elaborate; flat-soled; faultless; creaking; lustrous; lacquered; immaculate; fancy; neat; soft; studded; tight; high-heeled; close-fitting; dilapidated; clumsy; shapeless; patent-leather; elastic-sided; cavalier; flappy; muddy.

BOOTY
adjectives
hidden; magnificent; honeyed.

BORDER
adjectives
remote; rickety; dusky; inscribed; gaudy; beauteous; eternal; secluded; variegated; terraced; populous.

verbs
adjust—; broaden—; define—; enlarge—; establish—; extend—; fortify—; illustrate —; mark—; mass at—; menace—; pass through—; patrol—; post at—; ravage—; safeguard—; skirt—; touch—; widen—; —bounds; —limits; —margins; —outlines.
(See edge, limit, boundary, frontier.)

BORE
adjectives
deadly; highest; dreadful; everlasting; colossal; ignorant; ceaseless; veritable; incomparable; intimate; fearful; unmitigated; amiable; horrid; practiced.

BORE (v)
adverbs
faintly; heartily; dreadfully; everlastingly; colossally; ceaselessly; incomparably; unmitigatedly; horridly; agonizingly.
(See annoy, tire, trouble, vex.)

BOREDOM
adjectives
exasperated; intolerable; sinister; petulant; languid; passionless; unbearable; barren; solitary; sheer; genteel; gentlemanly; profound; drowsy; well-bred.

verbs
bear—; chase away—; consign to—, drug into—; endure—; experience—; free from —; pierce—; relieve—; sink into—; succumb to—; threaten with—; —annoys; —gnaws.
(See ennui, annoyance.)

BORESOME
adverbs
intolerably; profoundly; tiresomely; tediously; monotonously; irksomely; uniformly; terribly; inordinately; feebly; exhaustively; dully; mortally; prosily; disgustingly; unbearably; wearily; flatly; stupidly.

BORN (v)
adverbs
royally; posthumously; lowly; painlessly; humbly; legitimately; nobly.

BORROW (v)
adverbs
infrequently; constantly; boldly; shamelessly; persistently; frequently; habitually; cheerfully.
(See obtain, acquire.)

BORROWER
adjectives
solvent; would-be; shameless; infinite; unfortunate.

BOSOM
adjectives
ample; abundant; massive; extensive; capacious; expanded; capital; lovely; warm; flat; weak; aching; bare; maternal; austere; quickened; heaving; corseted; covert; jaded; melancholy; contented; placid; chill-

ed; plenteous; peaceful; brinish; immortal; faithless; complete; genial; tranquil; transparent; virginal; brassy; nectared; sad; blushing; sunburnt; sluggish; inconstant; soft-pleated; undefiled; quivering; virile; bloodless; hard; nursing; murmuring; glassy; palpitating; rock-ribbed; shieldless; agonized; fragrant; chaste; simple; writhing.

verbs
agitate—; assail—; bare—; beat—; chamber in—; cherish in—; clasp to—; cleanse—; embrace—; incense—; live in—; lurk in—; nestle in—; nurse in—; pacify—; pain—; perturb—; plant in—; pluck from—; shelter in—; soothe—; stir—; tear from—; vent—; warm—; wrestle in—; —burns; —heaves; —swells.
   (See breast.)

BOSS
adjectives   (colloq.)
political; nervous; high-strung; dominant; invisible; corrupt; arrogant; powerful; level-headed; department; egomaniac; brazen; bilingual; militant; argumentative.

verbs
anger—; esteem—; promote to—; —dictates; —discharges; —employs; —fires; —lashes; —leads; —manages; —masters; —orders.
   (See manager, employer, politician.)

BOSS (v)
adverbs
dreadfully; politically; nervously; dominantly; arrogantly; brazenly; argumentatively; dictatorially; highhandedly; imperiously; swaggeringly.
   (See direct, dominate.)

BOSSY
adverbs
disagreeably; ludicrously; infinitely; amusingly; officiously; ridiculously; despotically; tyrannically; pompously; characteristically; inherently; arrogantly; superciliously; loftily; clownishly; insistently; persistently; sharply; curtly; efficiently; offensively; detestably; shockingly; naturally; unreasonably; foolishly; excessively.

BOTHERSOME
adverbs
unduly; disagreeably; intolerably; annoyingly; vexatiously; incessantly; persistently; incorrigibly; incurably; offensively; detestably; shockingly; unreasonably; foolishly; noisily; pestiferously; tediously; stupidly; mortally; inordinately; terribly; disgustingly; cantankerously; unmanageably; insufferably; unendurably.

BOTTLE
adjectives
beautiful; shining; labeled; exquisite; spherical; grotesque; unique; ancient; flamboyant; reliable; venerable-looking; narrow-mouthed; half-empty; crown; coveted; unisonant (pl); unfinished.

verbs
brandish—; case —s; charge—; clink—; cluster —s; convey in—; cork—; drain—; drink—; invert—; manipulate—; pour into —; prepare—; produce—; proffer—; quaff from—; smash—; store in—; strain—; transfer to—; transport in—; —carries; —s clink; —contains; —crashes.
   (See glass.)

BOTTLE (v)
adverbs
effectively; exquisitely; reliably; permanently; temporarily; securely; skilfully; perpetually.

BOTTOM
adjectives
noble; shallow; luxuriant; sandy; sieve; fertile; blind; leaky; rugged.

verbs
anchor to—; drag—; dredge—; flounder on —; gauge to—; list at—; lower to—; plunge to—; probe to—; recede to—; rest on—; sink to—; transfix to—.
   (See base, foundation.)

BOUDOIR
adjectives
scented; perfumed; luxurious; frivolous; beautiful; alluring; enticing; sumptuous; beckoning.

BOUGH
adjectives
pendent; blossoming; projecting; breathless; fruited; pampered; untrimmed; feathery; colored; drooping; stony; topmost; shelving; unpeeled; majestic; prodigal; thick; snow-laden; fluttering; withered; naked; raven; arching; interlaced (pl); long; snow-hung; unwaving; sinewy; barren; fragrant; untrustworthy; clustering (pl); fresh; disenchanted; gnarled; splintered; hanging; billowy (pl); willing; treacherous; reluctant; nodding; denuded; springy;

mossy; stirring; ragged; beechen; innumerable (pl); dripping.

BOULDER
adjectives
fern-covered; huge; scattered; mighty; sun-warmed; tremendous; mossy; sheltering; flat-topped; great; loosened; granite, steel; ancient; glacial.

BOULEVARD
adjectives
spacious; crowded; engirdling; wintry; gay; bright; lighted; festive.

BOUND (v)
adverbs
joyously; gallantly; gracefully; exquisitely; superbly; lithely; sportively; animatedly; freely.
(See leap, spring, dance, frisk.)

BOUNDARY
adjectives
fairy; historical; established; frontier; opposite; outer; definite; geographical; intangible; material; titular; ill-defined; political; utmost.

verbs
break—; dispute—; disregard—; encroach upon—; enlarge—; extend—; fortify—; hang on—; hover over—; indicate—; limit —; line—; mark—; perceive—; reside on —; station at—; transcend —ies; widen—.
(See border, limit, barrier, edge, line.)

BOUNDS
adjectives
abolished; vaulting; narrow; visible; stone-troubled; mad; vulgar; utmost; firm; elastic; graceful; earthly

verbs
appoint—; break—; confine to—; extend—; hurdle—; infringe on—; leap—; narrow—; overleap all—; prescribe—; set—; transcend —; widen—.
(See boundary.)

BOUNTY
adjectives
beneficent; endless; essential; extravagant; munificent; questionable; reckless.

verbs
bestow—; collect—; deserve—; distribute —; earn—; merit—; pay—; proclaim—; reward with—; scorn—; share—; spread—;

taste—; value—; —encourages; —excels.
(See gift, favor, fee.)

BOUQUET
adjectives
lavish; huge; enormous; absurd; farewell; conventional; nightly; enchanting; exquisite; intriguing; distinctive; superb; animated; sumptuous; tasteful.

verbs
adorn with—; affix—; arrange—; bunch—; clasp—; clip—; cut—; display—; garnish with—; gather—; inhale—; lavish —s upon; pay tribute with—; sniff—; surrounded by —s; tie up—; toss—; wrap—; —cheers; —compliments; —conveys; —enhances.
(See flowers.)

BOURGEOIS
adverbs
obscurely; barbarously; humbly; boorishly; churlishly; roughly; savagely; snobbishly; flauntingly; obviously; manifestly; basely; evidently; indubitably; unquestionably; ignobly; meanly; sorrily; confessedly; admittedly.

BOURGEOISIE
adjectives (pl)
dispossessed; unconverted; all-pervading; prosperous; ambitious; wealthy; enfranchised; bloated; mercantile.

verbs
address—; besiege by—; class among—; clout (colloq.)—; control—; depend on—; despise—; distinguish—; enslave—; exclude —; familiarize with—; inveigh against—; mingle with—; rank among—; restrain—; tread on—; —arise; —cheer; —congregate; —decay; —gather; —resent; —revolt; —storm; —support; —surround; —triumph.
(See proletariat.)

BOUT
adjectives
match; stiff; humiliating; distressing; winding; dressing; wassail; exciting; boring.

verbs
cancel—; engage in—; indulge in—; stage —; take part in—; time—; witness—; —attracts; —draws; —thrills.
(See contest, conflict, battle.).

BOVINE
adverbs
stolidly; dully; ineptly; absolutely; stupidly; apathetically; calmly; serenely; indifferent-

ly; complaisantly; agreeably; blockishly; doltishly; heavily; idly; obtusely; simply; vacantly; witlessly; prosaically; ridiculously; reposefully; mildly; tranquilly; placidly; tamely; unconcernedly.

BOW
adjectives
noiseless; courteous; flourishing; profound; sweeping; chilly; polite; continuous; Oriental; ceremonious; unbent; mechanical; masculine; formal; conventional; hospitable; drowsy; serious; ironical; garish; humid; humble; grateful; obsequious; sycophantic; inimitable; magnificent; barbaric; sawing; whanging; romantic; historical; burlesque; mischievous; silent; amiable; exaggerated; sardonic; society; manly; valedictory; smashing; frigid; stiff; scarlet; prodigious; liberal; majestic; ethereal; transparent; unctuous.

BOW
adjectives (archery)
ashen; carefully-adjusted; curiously-fashioned; crude; pliant; servile; trusty; twanging.

verbs
arm with—; bend—; curve—; draw—; employ—; fashion—; form—; joint—; level—; release—; ripple from—; set—; shape—; shoot with—; spring—; string—; tense—; twang—; unleash—; —projects; —quivers; —retracts; —wavers.
(See arrow.)

BOW (v)
adverbs
discriminately; involuntarily; prematurely; languidly; ornately; gallantly; ironically; instinctively; profoundly; gravely; unctuously; passively; distantly; obsequiously; cringingly; formally; mockingly; deferentially; debonairly; submissively; desolately; haughtily; profoundly; dejectedly; Orientally; sweepingly; ceremoniously; drowsily; mechanically; sycophantically; sardonically; majestically.
(See incline, nod, yield, stoop.)

BOWELS
adjectives
lazy; lithe; firm-muscled; engorged; surfeited; stubborn.

verbs
clean out—; clear—; constipate—; dilate—; distend—; ease—; empty—; evacuate—; in-

fect—; inflame—; inject into—; insert in—; introduce into—; irritate—; line—; move—; open—; perforate—; purge—; regulate—; relax—; stimulate—; —move; —respond.
(See intestines.)

BOWER
adjectives
complete; myrtle; noontide; bloomless; wavy; heavenly; inmost; comfortless; leafy; over-arching; consecrated; moonlit; sylvan; pleached; native; roseate; apricot-silk; secluded; ravaged; amaranth; pleasant; lyric; noisome; blissful; fragrant; glimmering; newly-woven; close; enchanted; virgin; sequestered.

verbs
canopy with —s; cover—; dwell amid —s; entertain in—; entice into—; hide in—; idealize—; inhabit—; plant with—; shade—; steal into—; —droops; —shades; —thickens.
(See recess, cottage.)

BOWL
adjectives
unmingled; capacious; leathern; meager; ambrosial; flowing; enormous; sealed; pewter; lovely; cloisonne; shallow; flowered; fat; priceless; low; translucid; smooth; shining; adorned; brimming; nut-brown; coarse; coppery; hospitable; friendly.

BOX
adjectives
capacious; dreadful; cumbersome; spacious; stuffed; cozy; convenient; jolly; satin; alabaster; screened; unfurnished; pasteboard; triangular; poetical; wooden; gaudy; proscenium; uncompromising; sunken; hectagonal; oblong; tin; oversize.

verbs
collect in—; encase in—; hide in—; lock—; occupy—; partition—; restore to—; save in —; seal—; search—; shelter in—; —clatters; —contains; —yawns.
(See case, chest, basket.)

BOX (v)
adverbs
firmly; securely; clumsily; cumbersomely; conveniently; hectagonally; tastefully; sumptuously.
(See tie, enclose.)

BOX (v)
adverbs (prize fight)
invincibly; vigorously; violently; dexterously; nimbly; uncompromisingly; superbly.
(See slap.)

adjectives

stalwart; remarkable; inexperienced; un-equipped; boastful; unruly; dissolute; pre-cocious; clean-cut; nestling; disobedient; thoughtless; reckless; flint-hearted; peevish; starved; shelterless; amorous; military; ir-recoverable; stocky; round-faced; apple-cheeked; rollicking; red-haired; conscripted; sundry; dull; jolly; good-natured; laughing; active; fun-loving; handsome; radiant; live-ly; loving; good-looking; sturdy; absurd; lanky; chubby; honest; mischievous; lubber-ly; aggrieved; vociferous; barefoot; cool; silent; frantic; disappointed; irresponsible; incorrigible; devoted; taciturn; moody; thoroughbred; errant; waggish; flattering; well-grown; pestiferous; ungrateful; beau-tiful; fair; musing; ragged; cocksure; grin-ning; pernicious; lawless; criminal; medal-led; sheepish; bold; sanguine; quick; for-ward; capable; penitent; ruddy; sleeping; rare; rude; sympathetic; leprous; unbridled; unthinking; wayward; budding; white-headed; thin-faced; black-aproned; black-eyed; scornful; lascivious; patient; tender; serviceable; scrubbed; aristocratic; peevish; rascally; vigorous; enamored; swarthy; bril-liant; wild; weedy; daring; tiresome; non-sensical; turbaned; sordid; dreamy; wan-ton; winning; sassy; sportive; insolent; headstrong; ardent; healthy; robust; sedul-ous; aggressive; chivalrous; paltry; insipid; feeble-minded; stolid; clever; pugnacious; problem; gloomy; lonely; fragile; timid; impetuous; boisterous; fiery; heavy-hearted.

BOYCOTT

adjectives

fair; hampering; hostile; personal; private; protective; retaliatory; rigid; unwarranted; universal.

verbs

adopt—; approve—; assail—; coerce by—; counter—; discard—; formulate—; incur—; inflict—; instigate—; institute—; justify—; lift—; organize—; patronize—; prepare for —; proclaim—; punish with—; secure against—; shelter from—; stand firm on—; support—; sweep through—; threaten with —; urge—; warrant—; yield to—; —de-moralizes; —deprives; —incites; —injures; —outrages; —persecutes; —prevents; —pro-tects; —reduces; —starves.

(See embargo.)

BOYISH

adverbs

delightfully; remarkably; sturdily; stoutly;

adventurously; daringly; good-naturedly; impetuously; grinningly; happily; joyously; coaxingly; energetically; vigorously; re-freshingly; inextinguishably; vividly; irre-sistibly; robustly; ungovernably; hilarious-ly; facetiously; blithely; cheerfully; buoy-antly; merrily; triumphantly.

BOYLIKE

adverbs

refreshingly; charmingly; irresistibly; utter-ly; inexpressably; ineffably.

BRACE

adjectives

arching; auxiliary; extended; movable; strengthening; sustaining.

verbs

buckle on—; discard—; loosen—; regulate —; strap on—; —clasps; —connects; — holds; —pinches; —presses; —secures; — supports; —suspends; —tightens.

(See support, belt.)

BRACELET

adjectives

flaming; jingling; massive; jeweled; glitter-ing; diamond; flashing; glancing.

BRAG (v)

adverbs

immodestly; alcoholically; heartily; swag-geringly; idly; shamelessly; unrestrainedly; bullyingly; insolently; immoderately.

(See boast, vaunt.)

BRAGGADOCIO

adjectives

swaggering; hearty; idle; alcoholic.

BRAGGART

adjectives

strutting; cowardly; insolent; debonair; bullying; unscarred.

BRAID

adjectives   (stripe, ornament)

beaded; encrusting; curiously-patterned; glittering; intricately-woven; silken; em-broidered; tarnished.

verbs

adorn with—; attach—; deck in—; decorate with—; display—; embroider in—; entwine in—; envelop in—; exhibit—; flaunt—; in-terweave —s; knit in—; untwine—; wind

—; —binds; —denotes; —honors; —represents; —slips.

(See ornament.)

BRAID (v)

adverbs

skillfully; dexterously; nimbly; radiantly; verdantly; lustrously; heavily; intricately; curiously.

BRAIDS

adjectives

stubby; heavy; lustrous; jetty; shining; long; twisted; verdant; treble; radiant; glossy.

verbs

confine in—; do up in—; knot—; loose—; plait into—; snip—; tangle—; trim—; twist into—; uncoil—; —fly; —stream from.

(See hair.)

BRAIN

adjectives

editorial; reeling; sobering; inquisitive; clamoring; budding; shrinking; plotting; soothed; human; fevered; maddened; fabulous; boiled; whirling; busy; fertile; comprehensive; excited; dissolving; overseeing; keenest; overheated; immature; distempered; fruitful; logical; teeming; troubled; benumbed; sunburnt; tortured; tired; half-awakened; haunted; seething; rapt; bastard; dying; fatigued; maudlin; loyal; dull; cunning; drunken; scheming; throbbing; bewildered; heavily-taxed; misshapen; feverish; visioning; pure; devious; requisite; burning; addled; callow; young; confused; uncertain; grosser; amiable; brute; disordered; ruthless; maggoty; whisky-addled; flighty; emotive; calculating; celestial; erring; infernal; artless; shrewd; stifled; forging; cool; overtasked; wandering; vacant; sagacious; collective.

verbs

addle—; ballast—; bewilder—; clog—; confuse—; connect with—; craze—; cudgel—; dart through—; dash out—; emanate from —; endow with —s; force—; lash —s; nourish—; overtax—; perplex—; pound through—; prey upon—; rack—; rowel—; sear—; tax—; twist—; weigh upon—; —burns; —conceives; —devises; —fails; —functions; —invents; —lumbers; —races; —weaves; —whirls.

(See mind, intellect.)

BRAINLESS

adverbs

utterly; manifestly; feebly; heavily; blithely; cheerfully; obtusely; fatuously; blatantly; vacuously; incoherently obviously; evidently; oddly; crazily; unfortunately; lamentably; deplorably; admittedly; oafishly; loutishly.

BRAINY

adverbs

acutely; exceptionally; cleverly; astutely; profoundly; solidly; unusually; perspicaciously; reasonably.

BRAKE (n)

adjectives

dusky; shrieking; grinding; tricky; rasping; serviceable; shrill; inadequate; hissing.

verbs

adjust —s; apply—; clamp on—; contact—; depend on—; depress—; devise—; draw—; employ—; exercise—; fit with—; free—; jam on—; operate—; pedal—; press on—; regulate—; release—; tighten—; utilize—; —acts; —arrests; —checks; —controls; —fails; —grips; —locks; —reduces; —safeguards; —screams; —shrieks; —squeals.

BRAMBLES

adjectives

straggling; thorny; neglected.

BRANCH (division)

adjectives

collateral; subordinate; subsequent; specialized; rudimentary; purifying; despised; architectural; itinerant; local.

verbs

combine —es; consist of —es; corrupt—; diverge into —es; establish—; flourish in all —es; foster—; invest in—; manage—; propose—; separate into —es; spread out into —es; subdivide into —es; subordinate —es; —affiliates with; —booms; —flourishes; —represents; —springs up; —transacts.

(See department, division.)

BRANCH (tree)

adjectives

waxen; soft; wide; spreading; prominent; overhanging; gigantic; interlaced (pl.); rushing; grown; curving; circumstantial; fragrant; blazing; arching; swaying; murmuring; springy; moss-set; peaceful; long; pendulous; feathery; gnarled; picturesque; independent; coordinate; simpler; towering;

tasseled; gigantic; umbrageous; intruding; flowery; greenwood; nodding; flexible; loaded; heavy; somber; lopped; crackling; beauteous; stirring; thick-leaved; legitimate; plumy; luxurious; virgin; low-bent; delicate; shapely; shattered; phantom; profound; hoary; beauteous; obstructing; isolated; fatal; erect; verdant; flattened; crossing; covered; superfluous; naked; strong; thick; overambitious; luscious; knotted.

verbs
bow—; clip—; crash through—; gnarl—; graft—; hew—; lop off—; perch on—; rock —; trim—; —arches; —s cluster; —decays; —dips; —droops; —drops off; —flowers; —hangs low; —springs out; —supports; —tosses; —withers.
(See twig, limb.)

BRAND

adjectives
competitive; impious; petty; ensanguined; advertised; popular; faithful; largest-selling; reliable; searing; offensive; gloomy; smoldering; casual; blurred; wasted; glimmering; obscure; crooked; standard.

BRAND (v)

adverbs
epigrammatically; impiously; pettishly; popularly; offensively; casually; stigmatically; shamefully.
(See mark.)

BRANDISH (v)

adverbs
ferociously; victoriously; eloquently; proudly; heroically; gloriously; heatedly; furiously; exuberantly.
(See wave.)

BRANDY

adjectives
powerful; vile; cheap; canteen; aromatic; mulled; life-restoring.

verbs
age—; bottle—; distill—; entertain with—; flavor—; imbibe—; import—; mix with—; regale on—; sip—; tax—; —burns; —flavors; —intoxicates.
(See liquor, whiskey.)

BRASH

adverbs
impulsively; thoughtlessly; indiscreetly; touchily; testily; waspily; peevishly; fretfully; irascibly; rashly; foolhardily; incau-

tiously; carelessly; giddily; wildly; hotheadedly; precipitately; daringly; heedlessly; headily; jauntily.

BRASS

adjectives
unenduring; lusterless; winking; carved; glittering; burnished; time-stained; gorgeous; barbaric; tarnished.

BRASSY

adverbs
arrogantly; audaciously; flippantly; insolently; haughtily; impertinently; impudently; petulantly; saucily; shamelessly; terribly; dictatorily; presumptuously; bumptiously; superciliously; swaggeringly; intolerably; offensively; vexatiously; provokingly; unpleasantly.

BRAT

adjectives
furtive; howling; brawling; ill-mannered; ugly; puny; dirty; unwanted; cheeky; sweet; angelic; unruly; ungrateful; unteachable.

BRAVADO

adjectives
unmanly; soaring; humorous; polished; sheer; pure; pitiable; shallow; ferocious; speechless.

BRAVE (n)

adjectives
vanquished; murderous; sensible; aged; venerated; tremulous; reckless; selected; gifted; itinerant.

BRAVE (a)

adverbs
physically; indomitably; nobly; conspicuously; inherently; unflinchingly; heroically; magnificently; uncommonly; eminently; gallantly; resolutely; steadily; essentially; confidently; pluckily; valorously; valiantly; remarkably; unbelievably; sublimely; quietly; patiently; exceedingly.

BRAVE (v)

adverbs
defiantly; fearlessly; tremulously; recklessly; stalwartly; unselfishly; nobly; passionately; haughtily; staunchly; patriotically.
(See defy, dare.)

BRAVERY

adjectives
personal; shining; physical; insolent; sex-

ual; drunken; indomitable; reckless; flawless; noble; audacious; conspicuous; stupid; witless; inherent; unflinching; heroic; magnificent; outrageous; glittering; uncommon; fearful; unsurpassed.

verbs
act in—; add to—; admire—; display—; exhibit—; marvel at—; put on—; saturate with—; swagger in—; —amazes; —includes; —lies.
(See courage, heroism.)

BRAWL

adjectives
disreputable; drunken; street; friendly; desperate; private; coarsest.

verbs
approach—; batter in—; brook—; cause—; engage in—; force—; incite—; squabble in —; —clamors; —conflicts; —noises; —upsets.
(See quarrel, wrangle, row.)

BRAWNY

adverbs
extremely; indomitably; mightily; overpoweringly; stoutly; sturdily; vigorously; unbelievably; clumsily; awkwardly; admirably; amazingly; exceedingly; incredibly; undeniably; sufficiently.

BRAY (v)

adverbs
hideously; hoarsely; intermittently; solemnly; agonizingly; terrifyingly; idiotically; repeatedly; huskily.
(See howl.)

BRAZEN

adverbs
monstrously; shamelessly; daringly; boldly; presumptuously; unbecomingly; unsuitably; jauntily; airily; arrogantly; impudently; irreverently; disagreeably; ridiculously; offensively; detestably; hatefully; obnoxiously; excessively; foolishly; nauseatingly; indecently; insolently; incredibly; unwarrantably; atrociously; odiously.

BREACH

adjectives
formidable; continual; unpardonable; social; incurable; deplorable; irreconcilable; perceptible; dreadful; momentary; temporary; general; absolute; religious; flagrant; unhealed; monstrous; meditated.

verbs
excuse—; produce—; repair—; smooth over

—; suffer—; widen—; —damages; —disrupts; —fractures; —infracts; —infringes upon; —injures; —outlaws; —ruptures; — separates; —violates; —widens.
(See gap, violation, infringement, infraction.)

BREAD

adjectives
warm; stiff; frozen; daily; gnawed; moldy; sacred; rising; substantial; living; rain-soaked; wheaten; insipid; elfin; unleavened; bitter; blessed; broken; sliced.

verbs
apportion—; beg—; blacken—; break—with; brown—; consume—; cram with—; crave—; crumb—; deprive of—; devour—; dispense —; display—; divide—; earn—; knead—; munch—; nibble—; offer—; partake of—; prepare—; process—; provide—; ration—; restrict to—; sell for—; shape—; sustain with—; tax—; vend—; win—; —nourishes; —satiates; —stales; —strengthens.
(See food.)

BREADTH

adjectives
enormous; bare; unmoved; lyrical; viewless; diverse; endless; scant; epical; rippling; glassy; immoderate; spacious; ample; impassable.

BREAK

adjectives
appreciable; notable; numerous (pl.); unhappy; fatal; final; distinct; sharp; complete; agreeable; unhindered.

BREAK (v)

adverbs
eventually; unwarily; theoretically; treacherously; subsequently; deliberately; violently; unreasonably; forcibly; gratuitously; grimly; incoherently; intentionally; threateningly; advisedly; perilously; hilariously; fatally; distinctly; completely.
(See smash, shatter, burst, demolish.)

BREAKDOWN

adjectives
nervous; moral; universal; disastrous; incipient; mental; practical.

BREAKER

adjectives
foaming; ponderous; rising; swelling; ceaseless; never-silent; immense; wicked; enormous; tumbling; reasonless.

land among —s; warn of —s; —booms; —
verbs
crashes; —crushes; —dashes; —destroys;
—flies in; —foams; —lashes; —murmurs;
—passes over; —pounds; —rolls in; —subdues; —swells; —tumbles.
(See wave, billow.)

BREAKFAST
adjectives
sophisticated; substantial; hurried; magnificent; wedding; cheerful; gobbled; belated;
hearty; impromptu; leisurely; gloomy; abstemious; hospitable; pleasant; supplementary; wholesome.

verbs
adjourn to—; announce—; attack—; beckon
to—; bolt—; entertain at—; fast until—;
furnish with—; gobble—; gulp—; miss—;
partake of—; prepare—; provide—; relish
—; rush—; serve—; snatch—; take—; —
appeases; —replenishes; satiates.
(See meal, dinner, supper, food.)

BREAST
adjectives
defenceless; heaving; secret; cavernous;
beautiful; gloomy; dauntless; billowy;
brooding; snowy; throbbing; dolorous; tortured; rounded; large; tight; swollen; repentant; vast; soothing; barren; sanguine;
suckling; happy; glossy; greasy; watery;
inspired; boiling; bloody; obedient; elongated; half-tamed; calm; martyr; maternal;
well-developed; laboring; hideous; hollow-
swelling; feathered; torpid; shuddering;
fragrant; woolly; sunken; ample; misshap-
en; tumultuous; grief-filled; responsive;
troubled; palpitating; spotted; peaceable;
haughty; silent; careworn; panting; unconscious; pious; guileless; gentle; patriotic;
bare; careless; distended; vice-polluted;
faultless; oppressed; tawny; speckled; stimulated; supporting; snow-cold; tender; infinite; spangled; uplifted; wanton; sagging;
scourged; protruding; mailed; unwary; rugged; stormy; emaciated; full; dulled; immeasurable; harmless; devoted.

verbs
adorn—; bare—; beat—; boil in—; clasp
to—; cling to—; crush to—; distend—; disturb—; dry up—; ease—; exhaust—; expand
—; fold on—; harbor in—; inflame—with;
inflate—; infuse—with; inhabit—; lock in
—; lodge in—; nurse at—; penetrate—;
pillow on—; plant in—; rend—; smite—;
soothe—; strain to—; thunder in—; torment
—; trouble—; warm—; —burns with; —

flutters; —heaves; —secretes; —throbs.
(See bosom, chest, heart.)

BREASTWORK
adjectives
serpentine; substantial; gingerbread; military.

BREATH
adjectives
fiery; venomous; struggling; aimless; bated;
extinguished; unsavory; delighted; sweet-
scented; fragrant; idle; ryhthmic; vulgar;
warbling; unwholesome; morning; fearful;
quivering; foul; blessed; uneasy; snowy;
expiring; lightest; infant; untroubled;
stifled; stertorous; fetid; dumb; transitory;
quick; furtive; tender; ambient; delicate;
meager; surprised; hard; wicked; fluttering; damp; sobbing; quivering; dulcet;
common; harmonious; maiden; tremulous;
full; relieving; divine; clean; soft; rose-
laden; wine-laden; smoking; fugitive; bad;
cosmic; scorching; delicate; invisible; duteous; fleeting; deadly; rude; consuming;
sour; painful; blasting; feverous; spiritual;
tempestuous; undying; vital; icy; frightened; clear; cool; warm; natural; gasping;
miserable; transient; poisonous; cankering;
frosted; panting; rattling; ebbing; infantile;
golden; applausive; difficult; sugary; free;
audible; suspended; transparent; sharp;
worthless; royal; wanting; stinking; fatal;
passionate; hot; balsam; contagious; tobacco; scandalous; blighting; sulphurous; meditative; unanimous; offensive; prophet;
scant; pestilential; holy; failing; vile.

verbs
animate by—; bate—; catch—; discharge—;
draw—; exhale—; exhaust—; frost—; gasp
for—; inhale—; labor for—; lose—; murmur—; pen up—; poison—; puff out—; recover—; regain—; release—; revive—;
sigh—; smother—; stifles—; struggle for—;
suck in—; waste—; —emanates; —reeks.
(See air, respiration, breathing.)

BREATHE (*v*)
adverbs
stertorously; irregularly; assiduously; audibly; rhythmically; expiringly; uneasily;
untroubledly; transitorily; flutteringly; sobbingly; gaspingly; failingly.
(See inhale, pant, gasp.)

BREATHING
adjectives
cumbered; heavy; light; soft; shallow;
audible; regular; labored; peaceful; fervent;

placid; ryhthmical; tender; noisy; fluttered; holy; distressful; steady; abundant; hoarse; hurried; quickened; convulsive; alcoholic; long; quiet.

verbs
arrest—; choke—; correct—; ease—; hamper—; impede—; induce—; interfere with —; labor—; lessen—; obstruct—; restore —; smother—; stimulate—; train—.
(See respiration, breath.)

BREATHLESSNESS
adjectives
induced; parenthetical; distressing.

BREECHES
adjectives
tight; leather; drab; torn; baggy; muddy; tweed; nankeen.

BREED
adjectives
ancient; sporting; selective; unsocial; truer; elastic; pure-blooded; reckless; fabulous; recognized; superior; coarser; irritable; voracious.

verbs
adhere to—; ally—; characterize—; combine—; cross—; defile—; degenerate—; despise—; develop—; display—; distinguish —; domesticate—; examine—; exhaust—; exhibit—; exterminate—; generate—; improve—; mingle—; mix—; originate—; perpetuate—; preserve—; procreate—; propagate—; recognize—; strain—; —competes for; —overruns.
(See race.)

BREED (*v*)
adverbs
prodigiously; intelligently; luxuriantly; delicately; fabulously; superiorly; selectively.
(See multiply, rear, train.)

BREEDING
adjectives
artificial; exquisite; noble; gentle; courteous; virtuous; soft; tender; essential.

BREEDING
adjectives (animals)
straight-line; selective; fertile; aristocratic.

BREEZE
adjectives
sobbing; varying; desultory; increasing; favorable; roving; blessed; subtle; night;

summer; scented; playful; rising; steadying; native; faint; wayward; rude; slumbering; imperceptible; cooling; voluptuous; sportive; tonic; telltale; dying; sea; balmy; spicy; healthful; blistering; murmuring; chilling; southerly; fresh; blowing; sweeping; unsatisfied; zephyr; sluggish; nimble; ruffling; searching; western; fitful; sacred; wafting; whispering; treacherous; lightest; caressing; languorous; noiseless; lingering; river; lusty; passing; savage; crooning; tantalizing; penetrating; stray; pungent; stinging; vagrant; mild; raw; westerly; hovering; wanton; genial; odorous; vernal; polar; perfumed; salt-laden; lazy; casual; smoky; increasing; swift; uncontrollable; propitious; peaceful; refreshing; ocean; constant; soft; billowing; woodland; stirring; invigorating; tender; sweet; dependable; tantalizing; bracing.

verbs
bask in—; catch—; float in—; head into—; nod in—; rock with—; rustle in—; scent—; tremble in—; wave in—; —billows; —brushes; —caresses; —dies; —fans; —flutters; —freshens; —kisses; —lulls; —pauses; —ruffles; —rumples; —rustles; —scuds by; —sighs; —steals through; —stirs; —sweeps down; —tousles; —wafts; —wanders; —whistles.
(See wind, current.)

BREEZY
adverbs
delightfully; joyously; buoyantly; jovially; irresponsibly; gaily; vivaciously; brightly; wholesomely; heartily; irresistibly; flippantly; merrily; happily; gleefully; laughingly; rapturously; cheerfully; foolishly; childishly; youthfully; pleasantly; charmingly; exquisitely; daintily; agreeably; habitually.

BRETHREN
adjectives
dreamy; venerable; erring; cloudy; luckier; weak; civilized; wicked; twin-souled; speculative; fortunate; renegade; amiable; literary.

BREVITY
adjectives
laconic; pregnant; voluble; algebraic; tabloid; reassuring cynical; businesslike; curt; characteristic; voluminous; fallacious; laudable.

BRIBE
adjectives
base; timely; unworthy; innocent; custom-

ary; efficient; costly; enormous; extravagant; unclenched; septennial.

verbs

administer—; buy with—; condemn—; consent to—; consider—; exact—; extort—; forfeit—; offer—; pay—; pocket—; procure—; refuse—; surrender to—; tender—; yield to —; —abuses; —corrupts; —entraps; —induces; —influences; —offends; —perverts; —purchases; —purloins; —tempts.

(See inducement, graft.)

BRIBERY

adjectives

barefaced; corrupt; covert; daring; flagrant; offensive; open; surreptitious; vile.

verbs

accuse of—; achieve by—; acquit of—; arrest for—; charge with—; conceal—; convict of—; detect—; frustrate—; gain by—; obtain by—; practise—; punish—; purchase by—, remove for—; solicit—; yield to—; —flourishes; —motivates; —procures; —scandalizes; —sways; —tends to.

(See robbery, plunder.)

BRICK

adjectives

mellow; tawny; warm-toned; Georgian; adobe; harsh; sliding; smoke-blackened; enameled; soft; hard; front.

verbs

bake —s; base on —s; build with —s; cart —s; chisel—; construct of—; cut into—; dry —s; face with —s; fireproof —s; front with —s; harden into —s; heave —s; hem in with —s; inlay with —s; inscribe —s; knead into —s; lay —s; measure —s; pave with —s; prepare —s; pyramid —s; reinforce with —s; shape into —s; strain —s; toss —s; trowel —s; wall in with —s; —s collapse; —s crumble; —endures; mold into —.

(See stone.)

BRIDE

adjectives

peerless; prospective; insatiate; passionless; fastidious; virgin; beloved; blooming; perjured; pretty; bonny; first-made; affianced; gallant; truant; contraband; blushing; vivacious; country.

verbs

act as—; announce—; array—; assemble round—; attend—; bestow upon—; capture —; choose—; confuse—; congratulate—; costume—; dress—; drink to—; endow—;

fete—; give away—; greet—; indulge—; kiss—; pledge—; proclaim—; purloin—; serenade—; shower—; toast—; welcome—; win—; yearn for—; —blushes; —pales; —trembles.

(See queen, sweetheart.)

BRIDEGROOM

adjectives

destined; embarrassed; fickle; sturdy; youthful; happy; busy; shy; recreant; bold; brisk.

BRIDGE

adjectives

substantial; indigenous; antiquated; well-constructed; picturesque; rude; covered; mighty; famous; sturdy; swinging; massive; arched; iron; railroad; rustic; medieval; hideous; battered; spiritual; wooden; commodious; fortified; trembling; wide; narrow; rambling; portable; draw; proud; trussed.

verbs

arch—; block—; chain—; construct—; cross —; design—; destroy—; draw—; engineer —; flow under—; fortify—; gird—; imperil —; load—; lower—; overhaul—; patrol—; pattern—; plan—; strain—; suspend from —; sweep away—; —arches; —collapses; —connects; —conveys; —links; —spans; —supports; —surmounts; —totters; —unites.

(See span, support, structure.)

BRIDGE (v)

adverbs

successfully; picturesquely; massively; medievally; spiritually; proudly; tremblingly; diplomatically.

(See connect, link.)

BRIEF

adjectives

apostolic; honest; argumentative.

BRIEF (a)

adverbs

ridiculously; delightfully; agreeably; pitifully; disappointingly; tragically; mercifully; humanely; unreasonably; dramatically; smartly; inexcusably; characteristically; remarkably; satisfactorily; surprisingly; pleasantly; compactly; laconically; conveniently; curtly; commendably; strikingly; sensibly; wisely; prudently; tersely.

BRIEF CASE

adjectives

bulging; dog-eared; important-looking; mysterious; over-stuffed; resplendent; secret-charged; shabby; shiny; streamlined.

verbs
clasp— —; cram into— —; dig into— —; extract from— —; fasten— —; pack in— —; strap— —; stuff— —; whip open— —; — —bulges.
(See bag, satchel.)

BRIGADE
adjectives
advancing; combined; battle-toughened; favored; heroic; invincible; thundering.

verbs
command—; compose—; divide—; drill—; enlist in—; enroll—; form—; inspect—; instruct—; make up—; organize—; train—; transfer to—; transport—; —charges; —forages; —hunts; —marches.
(See gathering, regiment, troops, army.)

BRIGAND
adjectives
ferocious; ruthless; fugitive; veritable.

BRIGHT
adverbs
indescribably; dazzlingly; miraculously; ingeniously; amazingly; splendidly; magnificently; unbelievably; unusually; wonderfully; marvellously; artificially; scintillatingly; starrily; intolerably; painfully; bewilderingly; blindingly; unwontedly; suspiciously; crystally; luminously; radiantly; splendidly; unbearably; intensely; gaudily.

BRIGHTEN (v)
adverbs
intensely; momentarily; perceptibly; vividly; dazzlingly; artificially; bewilderingly; superficially; blindingly; unnaturally; intellectually; matchlessly.
(See cheer, illuminate.)

BRIGHTNESS
adjectives
tranquil; dazzling; artificial; scintillant; starry; shifting; shining; superficial; painful; intolerable; transcendent; bewildering; enlivening; unfathomed; expansive; glowing; gradual; sharp; windy; steely; rising; cold; blinding; unmoving; burning; unwonted; fiery; suspicious; poisonous; crystal.

BRILLIANCE
adjectives
youthful; mental; stylistic; dazzling; scintillating; roseate; intellectual; utmost; epigrammatic; feverish; crystal; signal; magnificent; polished; matchless; daring; spontaneous; eye-aching; uncanny; solemn; inevitable; lustrous.

verbs
boast—; hide—; impress with—; intensify —; polish into—; radiate—; shade—; shine in—; sing of—; sparkle with—; strike with —; —amazes; —dazzles; —overpowers; —pervades.
(See splendor.)

BRILLIANCY
adjectives
unnatural; dreamlike; exquisite; sufficient; solar; heightened; blinding; imposing; strange; ivory-like; technical; irregular; sparkling; superhuman.

BRILLIANT
adverbs
scintillatingly; miraculously; cleverly; ingeniously; notably; amazingly; signally; socially; intellectually; dazzlingly; smartly; inexpressibly; indescribably; surprisingly; splendidly; undoubtedly; incredibly; unusually; wonderfully; ostentatiously.

BRIM
adjectives
sparkling; medium-sized; huge; picot; glancing; rolling.

BRINE
adjectives
restless; bitter; mid-sea; rushing; audacious; fragrant; rolling; hoary; fateful; eye-offending; first-made; desolate; level; glassy; hissing.

BRING (v)
adverbs
lightly; finally; rarely; slyly; festinately; constantly; painfully; accordingly; vividly; inevitably; continuously; obviously; ultimately; simultaneously; vaguely.
(See carry, conduct, convey.)

BRINK
adjectives
plashy; dim; breezy; chilling; eternal; shadowy; rushy; precipitous; utmost; abrupt; sandy; giddy.

BRINY

adverbs

bitterly; brackishly; acridly; hotly; pungently; toughly; saltily; spicily; sharply; unsavorily; strongly; disagreeably; unpleasantly; horribly; aromatically; perceptibly; pleasingly; subtly; odoriferously; sufficiently; magnificently; properly.

BRISK

adverbs

tremendously; apallingly; helpfully; efficiently; singularly; habitually; excitedly; noisily; restlessly; nimbly; gracefully; energetically; cheerfully; actively; alertly; vivaciously; surprisingly; youthfully; capably; unexpectedly; quickly; dangerously; smartly; spryly; fleetly; trippingly; lightly; busily.

BRISKNESS

adjectives

keen; flavored; characteristic.

BRISTLE (v)

adverbs

defiantly; horridly; furiously; pugnaciously; militantly; bellicosely; belligerently; vindictively.

(See argue.)

BRITISH

adverbs

incurably; stolidly; loyally; sensibly; respectably; obstinately; stubbornly; proudly; unconditionally; obviously; manifestly; essentially; securely; permanently; urbanely; imperturbably; serenely; soundly; stoutly; devotedly; ardently; staunchly; punctiliously; incorruptibly; correctly; virtuously; shrewdly.

BRITISHER

adjectives

sound; solid; sensible; usual; well-fed; obstinate; muddling.

BRITTLE

adverbs

unfortunately; regrettably; exceedingly; smartly; delicately; crisply; lamentably; deplorably; deceptively; unexpectedly; surprisingly; slightly; highly; overly; extremely; evidently; unprofitably; unserviceably; inconveniently; impracticably.

BROAD

adverbs

splendidly; magnificently; illimitably; extensively; spaciously; liberally; boundlessly; infinitely; immensely; admirably; amply; adequately; grandly; majestically; expansively; inexpressibly; capaciously; roomily; extremely; enormously; endlessly; epically; immoderately; unbelievably.

BROADCAST

adjectives

commercial; unsponsored; regional; nationwide.

BROADCAST (v)

adverbs

grandiloquently; commercially; regionally; universally; temporarily; professionally; annually; popularly.

(See speak.)

BROADCLOTH

adjectives

bullet; lava; popular; shantung.

BROADEN (v)

adverbs

marvelously; appreciably; tremendously; noticeably; immeasurably; imperceptibly; abruptly; gradually.

(See enlarge, expand.)

BROADSIDE

adjectives

genuine; fearful; death-dealing; thundering; tremendous; crashing.

BROCADE

adjectives

jeweled; ancient; gorgeous; stiff; correct; bright; exquisite; historic.

BROCHURE

adjectives

innocent; artistic; modern; intimate; expensive; slender; rare.

BROGUE

adjectives

adorable; quaint; little; soft; clouted; brisk; Irish.

BROIL

adjectives

murderous; internal; prolonged; fierce.

BROKER

adjectives

disreputable; dummy; staid; loose-living; middle-aged.

BRONZE

adjectives

precious; valuable; burnished; enduring; immortal; inimitable; monumental; lined.

BRONZE (a)

adverbs

richly; tawnily; deeply; elaborately; strangely; incongruously; sumptuously; splendidly; magnificently; shimmeringly; ruddily; beautifully; superbly.

BROOD

adjectives

callow; straggling; lowering; hideous; unmanageable; erring; enormous; hapless; late-begotten; human; successive; spurious; shameful; dusky; hateful; writhing; silver; bastard; erratic; gorgeous; infernal; venomous; boreal; heavenly; noisy; viperous.

verbs

bring forth—; cherish—; cultivate—; exhibit—; gather—; give birth to—; hatch—; hover over—; incubate—; mother—; nest —; nourish—; nurse—; nurture—; orphan —; rear—; select—; tend—; tolerate—; warm—; —clucks; —follows; —originates from.

(See offspring, race, flock.)

BROOD (v)

adverbs

solitarily; somberly; vacantly; enviously; mournfully; reverently; haplessly; humanly; bitterly; maternally; superstitiously; fruitlessly; drearily; despondently.

(See ponder, meditate.)

BROODING

adjectives

subsequent; bitter; melancholy; constant; maternal; superstitious; concentrated; fruitless; dreary; despondent.

BROOK

adjectives

sluggish; delectable; south-sloping; unreposing; rapid; boisterous; wandering; brawling; glassy; careless; shallow; hidden; sedgy; rain-full; thirst-inviting; defiled; rippling; weedy; gushing; tumbling; mazy; copious; unsunned; struggling; babbling; gurgling; glittering; limpid; unseen; patient; peaceful; passionless; rushing; shrunken; inland; reedy; swift-running; crisped; hurrying; rushy; pellucid; happy; murmuring; narrow; silver; bisecting; cool; meandering; sweet; perennial; dancing; transparent; rocky; mountain; sparkling; companionable; pebbly; winding; wild; clear; woodland.

verbs

bog in—; bound—; bridge—; cast into—; frequent—; haunt—; pass over—; splash in—; swell—; wade in—; —babbles; —bubbles; —bursts forth; —chatters; —dances; —flows on; —frolics; —groans; —gurgles; —gushes; —murmurs; —races along; —rambles; —ranges; —sings; —swells; —whirls.

(See stream.)

BROOM

adjectives

careless; coarse; ever-questing; immaculate; industrious; lopsided; restless; rude.

verbs

apply—; brandish—; employ—; fill—; peddle —s; tie into—; trim—; twist—; wield —; —brushes; —collects; —delves; —gathers; —raises; —removes; —renews; —routs; —unearths.

(See brush.)

BROTH

adjectives

comforting; stomach-fortifying; satisfying; substantial; tasteless; watery.

verbs

ladle—; sip—; spoon—; strain—; test—; —nourishes; —simmers; —steams; —warms.

(See soup.)

BROTHER

adjectives

kind; indulgent; gentle; arbitrary; fiendish; cruel; illustrious; amorous; truant; healthful; affectionate; poor; unworthy; unemotional; new; distinguished; sworn; loftier; recreant; admirable; manly; ecclesiastical; true; foster; lost; ungrateful; renowned; awe-stricken; heroic; neglected; harrowed; malleable; rebellious; dismal; elder; serious; devoted; erring; unseemly; eligible; aristocratic; obvious; undeniable; slow-witted; indubitable; heavy-going; paretic; blood; model; imperial; puissant.

BROTHERHOOD

adjectives

bristly; critical; human; great; blood; subtle; meritable; idealized; diplomatic; close; cordial; indissoluble; spontaneous; sworn.

verbs

address—; ally with—; associate with—; band into—; cherish—; create—; devote to —; establish—; fraternize with—; fuse in —; head—; join—; league in—; obey—;

142

organize—; protect—; persecute—; **regale**
—; resign from—; rupture—; salute—; support—; sustain—; tie to—; unite—; —acts;
—aids; —arrays against; —convenes; —
declines; —equalizes; —flourishes; —instructs.

(See society, fellowship.)

BROTHERLY

adverbs
extremely; heart-warmingly; hardly; affectionately; cordially; intimately; sincerely; sympathetically; amicably; heartily;
benevolently; benignly; charitably; considerately; lovingly; unselfishly; tenderly; accommodatingly; good-naturedly; graciously;
warm-heartedly; adoringly; devotedly; fondly; adorably; charmingly; admirably; helpfully; companiably; congenially; surprisingly; unexpectedly.

BROUGHAM

adjectives
cozy; little; well-appointed; shiny.

BROW

adjectives
handsome; delicate; beautiful; illumined;
bland; amiable; fair; classical; lofty; manly; noble; social; lily; triumphant; low;
white; clouded; black; heavy; straight;
dark; blonde; rosy; sunburned; freckled;
bushy; shaggy; roughened; grizzled; thick;
puckered; ruffled; knotted; furrowed;
wrinkled; corrugated; contracted; drawn;
sad; troubled; overcast; mournful; brooding; swarthy; interrogative; scowling;
frowning; stormy; startled; puzzled; plucked; painted; fine; pencilled; arched; whimsical; thin; peaked; curved; meeting (pl.);
beetling; well-carved; prominent; level;
lifted; placid; tranquil; damp; perspiring;
fevered; heaving; crotchety; ironical; pimpled; elderly; austere; intelligent; glistening; deplorable; massive; haughty; dusky;
livid; thoughtful; withered; innocent; craggy; calm; angry; weather-beaten; clammy;
thorn-pierced; healthful; callow; serene;
high; cold; shadowy; intellectual; gloomy;
heated; royal; guilt-steeled; scarred; infant; sacred; surly; purpled; upturned;
snowy; unaltered; crownless; throbbing;
pensive; broiling; olive-tinctured; thunderblasted; burning; imperious; sun-kissed;
barbarian; hopeless; relaxed; rugged; imperial; bewitching; pale; amiable; unsullied;
bent; immense; blue-veined; threatening;
unkind; pain-knotted; laurel-laden; impenetrable; deep-pent; channeled; ingenuous;

contemptuous; stately; conquest-branded;
inky; triumphant; wreathed; pedantic; pitying; kindred; profulgent; wizard; animated;
stunned; mild; milky; crescent; haggard;
earnest; broad; gracious; bared; hooded;
bloodless; aching; youthful; dreamy; overhanging; polished; pallid; worn; drooping;
godlike; candid; transparent; bald; anxious;
smarting; bent; pretty; unsullied; mummied; unwritten; warlike; ensanguined;
resigned; sober; compressed; regent; dauntless; overwhelming; spiritual; hazel; burthened; projecting; mobile; airy; averted;
peaceful; bronzed; careworn.

verbs
arch—; contract—; crown—; elevate—;
flush—; furrow—; gild—; harden—; kiss
—; knit—; lift—; mop—; plait—; pluck
—s; pucker—; purse—; quirk—; shadow
—; singe—; smite—; smooth—; uplift—;
wrinkle—; —s bridge; —darkens; —menaces; —s struggle together; —throbs.

(See forehead, eyebrow, countenance.)

BROWBEATEN

adverbs
submissively; shamefully; meekly; disgracefully; humiliatingly; disconsolately; humbly;
abjectly; frightfully; horribly; terribly;
fearfully; unhappily; incredibly; astoundingly; alarmingly; coweringly; tremulously; dreadfully; nervously; portentously; unforgivably; evidently; visibly; indefensibly.

BROWN

adjectives
lustrous; vehement; russet; unsightly; golden; country; dainty; mellow; shining; turf;
ruddy; crisp; curious; grayish; glossy; twilight; yellowish; chestnut; pinkish; autumnal; gleaming; sedate.

BROWN (a)

adverbs
ruddily; lustrously; deeply; richly; gloriously; curiously; crisply; lightly; tawnily;
sumptuously; splendidly; superbly; shimmeringly; magnificently.

BROWSE (v)

adverbs
phlegmatically; contentedly; intellectually;
placidly; happily; abstractedly; absently.

(See nibble, feed, graze.)

BRUISE

adjectives
livid; marring; hurting; vast; innocent;
cruel.

verbs
apply to—; bandage—; heal—; incur—; inflict —s; produce—; receive—; salve—; soothe—; treat—; —dents; —disables; —discolors; —disfigures; —hurts; —infects; —injures; —lacerates; —mangles; —mars; —swells; —weakens.
(See injury, contusion.)

BRUISE (v)
adverbs
ineradicably; severely; agonizingly; disfiguringly; horribly; temporarily; villainously; mercilessly.
(See injure, hurt.)

BRUNETTE
adjectives
small; vivacious; indeterminable.

BRUNETTE (a)
adverbs
wondrously; gloriously; adorably; strikingly; petitely; vivaciously; piquantly; irresistibly; charmingly; saucily; startlingly; captivatingly; fascinatingly; distinctly; radiantly; glowingly; darkly; provocatively; astonishingly; starrily; artificially; naturally; skilfully; enchantingly; bewitchingly.

BRUSH
adjectives
deft; burnishing; illuminating; frugal; obliterating; purging; scavenging; sweeping.

verbs
apply—; attach—; cleanse with—; dust with —; employ—; paint with—; scrub with—; shape—; shine with—; smooth over with—; spread with—; stroke—; sweep with—; wipe with—; —refreshes; —renews; —revives.
(See broom.)

BRUSH (artist)
adjectives
potent; profound; lavish; fragrant; skillful.

BRUSH (plant)
adjectives
leafy; stunted; ragged; meager; aboriginal; sage; alert; tangled; fringing; rabbit; icy; dangerous; flaming; scrawny; crackling.

BRUSH (v)
adverbs
aimlessly; haughtily; hastily; tenderly; effectively; vivaciously; skillfully; interminably; monotonously.
(See wipe.)

BRUSQUE
adverbs
dashingly; fussily; hurriedly; impetuously; hastily; precipitately; urgently; expeditiously; fitfully; boisterously; furiously; outrageously; roughly; uproariously; violently; excitedly; stormily; extravagantly; ostentatiously; hysterically; uncontrollably; irrepressibly; turbulently; wildly; rampageously.

BRUTAL
adverbs
abominably; terribly; unspeakably; villainously; systematically; needlessly; inherently; harshly; sharply; savagely; coarsely; ferociously; nefariously; detestably; indecently; obtrusively; ostentatiously; foully; insolently; caustically; venomously; perversely; incorrigibly; inhumanly; cruelly; atrociously; obdurately; truculently; maliciously; intentionally; treacherously; outrageously; ruthlessly; stonily; barbarously; virulently; diabolically; invidiously; blatantly; flagrantly; openly; resolutely.

BRUTALITY
adjectives
quaint; sacrificed; horrible; primitive; suave; frantic; unspeakable; blind; amazing; unintelligent; villainous; continued; systematic; noisy; downright; needless; inherent; harsh; sharp; ugly; savage; coarse; ferocious; sheer.

verbs
appall by—; breed—; expose—of; imbue with—; inculcate—; indulge in—; refrain from—; subject to—; teach—; treat with—; —cuts; —degrades.
(See cruelty.)

BRUTE
adjectives
shy; perverse; treacherous; conscious; unfeeling; perfect; nasty; polite; ferocious; tawny; horrid; goaded; barbarous; hardy; lustful; grazing; repulsive; drunken; noxious; greedy; innocent; bristling; savage; ponderous; cowardly; self-confessed; surly; dangerous; ruffian; untamed; lowest; husky; sulky; selfish; canny; accursed; exhausted; avenging; cold-blooded; menacing; maddened; bulky; foul; bestial; blundering; evil; designing; ugly; meanest; villainous; merciless; gross; dissipated; burly; callous.

verbs
bring out—; charm—; ensnare—; hypnotize —; polish—; quell—; silence—; slay—;

tame—; worship—; —bolts; —charges; —rends; —survives; —thunders.
(See animal, beast.)

BUBBLE

adjectives
headed; ascending; crystalline; iridescent; innumerable (pl.); lazy; broken; pricked; intoxicating; soothing; pretty; sparkling; flimsy; flattened; beaded; wandering; empty.

verbs
agitate into —s; blow —s; cover with —s; delude with —s; emit —s; produce —s; send forth —s; —amuses; —dances; —dissipates; —drifts; —escapes; —explodes; —fascinates; —floats; —rises; —scintillates; —springs from; —swells.
(See balloon.)

BUBBLE (v)

adverbs
gayly; effervescently; hissingly; foamingly; exhilaratingly; joyously; sputteringly.
(See flow, whirl.)

BUCK (v)

adverbs
spiritedly; suddenly; abruptly; belligerently; spitefully; venomously; wildly.
(See prepare, plan.)

BUD

adjectives
springing; kindling; swaying; bloomless; sluggish; tender; dejected; bursting; fadeless; unexpanded; flower-enfolding; sweetest; masked; dripping; wayside; sulking; terminal; leaf-enfolded; axillary.

verbs
blast—; blight—; clip—; form—; frost—; graft—; kill—; nip—; sprout —s; —s appear; —breaks into bloom; —bursts forth; —s cluster; —s crowd together; —decorates; —develops; —expands; —flowers; —glistens; —matures; —multiplies; —produces; —projects; —promises; —prospers; —reveals; —sprouts; —swells; —unfolds.
(See flower, plant, bulb.)

BUDGET

adjectives
biennial; admirable; bearskin; balanced; moderate; scanty; heart-shaking; ordinary; family; tentative; extraordinary.

verbs
balance—; institute—; jeopardize—; promulgate—; prune—; reduce—; shape—; slash—; stagger under —s; swell—; tax—.
(See estimate, plan.)

BUDGET (v)

adverbs
impecuniously; meticulously; biennially; admirably; annually; tentatively; shrewdly; dexterously; wisely; conservatively.

BUFF

adjectives
rich; golden; glowing.

BUFFALO

adjectives
aggressive; belligerent; bellowing; charging; furious; grunting; humping; powerful; possessive; primitive; prairie-lording; stampeding; roaming.

verbs
domesticate—; exterminate—; farm with—; herd—; overrun with—; plough with —s; protect—; pursue—; stampede—; tame—; teem with—; water—; yoke—; —gores; —grazes; —grunts; —lumbers; —ranges; —roams; —wallows in mud.
(See bison, ox, animal.)

BUFFETINGS

adjectives
reminiscent; repeated; merciless; unkind; intermittent.

BUFFOON

adjectives
enormous; gluttonous; ordinary; stammering; pantomime.

BUFFOONERY

adjectives
exhibitionist; engaging; wanton; mad.

BUG

adjectives
annoying; encroaching; gregarious; insidious; invincible; inoffensive; obnoxious; over-companionable; persevering; patrolling; pestiferous; shelter-seeking; shrilly-serenading; undaunted; diminutive; droning; hovering; jeweled; predatory; piping; snug; vagrant; villainous; vigorous; wiggling.

verbs
destroy—; dissect—; exterminate —s; observe—; spray—; swat—; —s blight; —s bore; —s breed; —s lurk; —stings; —sucks.
(See insect.)

BUGLE

adjectives

blaring; bold; dominant; duty-calling; invocative; piercing; silence-shattering; rousing; sonorous; lamenting; peace-lulling.

verbs

assemble at—; awaken by—; march to—; overblow—; rally to—; respond to—; retire to—; scale—; sound—; —alarms; —arouses; —blares; —blasts; —calls; —declares; —echoes; —orders; —signals; —summons; —trumpets; —wails; —wakens; —warns.

(See instrument, horn, trumpet.)

BUILD

adjectives

elephantine; slender; sinewy; enduring; curious; heroic; gigantic; warlike; sturdy; ascetic; proportional.

BUILD (v)

ostensibly; impregnably; simultaneously; airily; irrevocably; variously; intelligently; synthetically; stoutly; expressly; sturdily; magnificently; substantially; enduringly; proportionally; secularly; incomparably; ecclesiastically; shabbily.

(See erect, construct, raise.)

BUILDER

adjectives

timid; prominent; independent; empire; sturdy; hard-working; ambitious; wonderful; body; pioneer; home; prospective; vigorous; devastating.

verbs

—alters; —bids; —commissions; —constructs; —contracts for; —designs; —determines; —develops; —directs; —draws; —employs; —erects; —establishes; —estimates; —excavates; —fireproofs; —guarantees; —initials; —leases; —operates; —profits; —remodels; —renovates; —specifies; —submits; —undertakes.

(See carpenter.)

BUILDING

adjectives

imposing; magnificent; attractive; palatial; rich; adorned; handsome; spacious; wonderful; beautiful; pretentious; fine; substantial; comfortable; monster; mammoth; giant; towering; commercial; Gargantuan; ancient; antiquated; century-old; grim; obsolescent; vestigial; solid; massive; great; stone; immense; gawky; ramshackle; barnlike; flimsy; rickety; rambling; straggling; squatting; cluttered; dirty-looking; sour; dingy; grimy; false-fronted; smoke-stained; bleak; gloomy; wretched; ugly; forlorn; sinister; peculiar; somber; severe; white-walled; red-roofed; multicolored; gaunt; red-bricked; weathered; ivy-grown; long; flat; low; clustered; silent; gilt-domed; unique; sun-flooded; commodious; consistorial; barrack-like; pagan; secular; combustible; oppressive; aggressive; impertinent; tame; uninteresting; proposed; dismal; conventual; tumble-down; unpretentious; heterogeneous; detached; ill-looking; conservative; irregular; opulent; profane; speculative; old-fashioned; well-constructed; extensive; monumental; decayed; moss-covered; useful; ghostlike; worthy; notable; beggarly; ruinous; eccentric; contemporaneous; flanking; arsenal-like; murky; unoccupied; sleepy; deserted; shabby; admonitory; elegant; dilapidated; ecclesiastical; capacious; incomparable; proud; drab.

verbs

clutter up—; demolish—; design—; dominate—; enlarge—; erect —s; evacuate—; extend—; inhabit—; lodge in—; modernize —; raze—; renovate—; restore—; revolutionize—; segregate into—; separate—; throng through—; —looms; —pierces; —straddles; —towers.

(See edifice, structure, house, barn.)

BULB (light)

adjectives

feeble; electric; flickering; unveiled; rarefied; myriad (pl.); inanimate.

BULB (plant)

adjectives

spring; early-flowering.

verbs

bury—; cultivate—; insert—; market—; raise—; sow—; uproot—; —blossoms; —buds; —bursts; —develops; —dilates; —flowers; —nourishes; —radiates; —sends off roots; —stores; —takes root; —tides over.

(See flower, plant, bud.)

BULGE

adjectives

inquisitive; disconcerting; noticeable; awkward.

BULGE (v)

adverbs

roundly; awkwardly; disconcertingly; noticeably; inquisitively; prominently; pro-

trudingly; enormously; horribly; abnormally; grotesquely.
(See swell, protrude.)

BULK

adjectives

grotesque; enormous; huge; tremendous; great; black; haughty; proper; mastodonic; insufficient; surging; tawny; cumbrous; low; broad; shadowy; imposing; shaggy; massive; shattered; considerable; vast; languid; full; voluptuous; overgrown; ugly; wavering; helpless; insufficient; ponderous; credent; colossal; crude; patched; bluff; terrifying; faceless; non-irritating; Amazonian; flying; clean-limbed; portly; physical; crushing; overwhelming; threatening.

BULK (v)

adverbs

enormously; heavily; cumbrously; overwhelmingly; threateningly; ponderously; terrifyingly; portentously.

BULKY

adverbs

enormously; awkwardly; immensely; massively; mightily; monstrously; crudely; inelegantly; lumpishly; stupendously; grotesquely; queerly; strangely; imposingly; overwhelmingly; ponderously; suspiciously; clumsily; unnecessarily; laughably; ridiculously; deceptively; ludicrously; grossly; delusively.

BULL

adjectives

incorrigible; snorting; mad; infuriated; rumbling; fretful; savage; raging; veritable.

verbs

bait—; brand—; breed—; bring—to bay; castrate—; chafe—; combat—; enrage—; exhibit—; infuriate—; jab—; market—; mistreat—; outnumber —s; plague—; rope —; slaughter—; slay—; torment—; torture —; —bellows; —butts; —charges; —collapses; —emerges; —gores; —grazes; —leaps; —paws; —perspires; —rages; —retires; —rushes; —snorts; —vaults; —wearies; raise—.
(See animal, cattle.)

BULLDOG

adjectives

hideous; squirming; pedigreed; ferocious.

BULLET

adjectives

moaning; well-directed; paper; answering; shrieking; ricocheted; caroming; whistling; spattering; soft-nose; flattened; harmless; powder; telltale; whining; whizzing; fiery; screaming; thudding; dum-dum; explosive.

verbs

cap—; design—; hail —s; jacket—; mold —s; project—; riddle with —s; shower —s; squirt —s; stream —s; —attains a speed; —s buzz by; —careens; —glances off; —grazes; —s hammer; —s patter; —penetrates —pierces; —ricochets; —s spatter; —speeds toward; —swerves; —wavers; —whines; —whistles by; —s wing past.
(See shot, projectile.)

BULLETIN

adjectives

confidential; monotonous; public.

BULLY

adjectives

beastly; blustering; loutish; strutting; prostrate.

BULLY (v)

adverbs

mildly; blusteringly; loutishly; struttingly; overbearingly; diplomatically; pertly; flatly; endlessly; securely; firmly.
(See intimidate.)

BULWARK

adjectives

sturdy; mighty; everlasting; broken; seaward; riddled; splintered; heaven-sustaining; granite; eternal; flimsy; invulnerable.

BUMP

adjectives

dull; heavy; inadvertent.

BUMPKIN

adjectives

small-town; awkward; city; country; overgrown.

BUMPTIOUS

adverbs

aggressively; offensively; disagreeably; absurdly; impertinently; ridiculously; egotistically; presumptuously; pretentiously; vainly; boastfully; ostentatiously; priggishly; unblushingly; brazenly, ludicrously; laughably; quaintly; comically; stupidly; boyishly; fantastically; immensely; complacently; foolishly; senselessly; extravagantly.

BUN

adjectives

delectable; indigestible; round; flat; plump.

BUNCH

adjectives

scattered; beautiful; horrible.

BUNDLE

adjectives

withered; compact; parti-colored; ribboned; exceptional; fine; emaciated; darkish; unwieldy; swaddled; inert; flat; sodden; queer-shaped; precious; muddy; helpless; numerous (pl.); cached; wrinkled; endless; malevolent.

verbs

bind in—; collect in—; contain in—; disorder—; encumber with —s; fasten in—; gather—; group in —s; load down with —s; shift —s; untie—.

(See parcel, package.)

BUNDLE (v)

adverbs

unceremoniously; compactly; inertly; flatly; endlessly; securely; firmly; unceremoniously.

(See bind, tie, roll.)

BUNGALOW

adjectives

rose-clad; richly-furnished; swanky; luxurious; screened; rustic; rambling; dark; unpretentious; beloved; picturesque.

BUNGLE (v)

adverbs

tragically; atrociously; characteristically; repeatedly; ineptly; generally; idiotically; diplomatically; strategically.

BUNGLING

adjectives

general; inept; patient; characteristic; repeated.

BUNGLING (a)

adverbs

awkwardly; clumsily; boorishly; loutishly; shyly; bashfully; ineptly; inexpertly; unskilfully; self-consciously; incompetently; vexatiously; hopelessly; diffidently; timidly; pitifully; helplessly; pathetically; plaintively; outlandishly; pitiably; miserably; sorrily; sadly; grievously.

BUOY

adjectives

dancing; heaving; ringing; rocking; warning.

BUOYANCY

adjectives

reckless; supreme; glad; youthful; virile; unutterable; natural; positive.

BUOYANT

adverbs

positively; joyously; affectedly; naturally; supremely; happily; suddenly; excitedly; unexpectedly; blithely; gleefully; rapturously; lightly; airily; gaily; hilariously; jovially; warmly; delightfully; delightedly; briskly; cheerily; jauntily; jubilantly; lightheartedly; disarmingly; merrily; playfully; irrepressibly; laughingly; smilingly; engagingly; irresistibly; confidently; enthusiastically; fervently; hopefully.

BURDEN

adjectives

grievous; financial; intolerable; painful; unwomanly; deadly; increasing; mutual; fragrant; double; various (pl); accumulated; racking; enticing; unnecessary; venerable; drowsy; precious; fatal; sinister; clattering; unescapable; never-lifted; serious; economic; appropriate; perpetual; fiery; passive; insufferable; monstrous; secret; baneful; oppressive; onerous; corresponding; expensive; equivalent; sweet; heavy; clerical; sheer; melancholy; aggravating; grim; common; unequal; unjust; dangerous; inevitable; cold; prodigious; ever-growing; staggering; crushing; unendurable; unbearable; cumbersome; over-heavy; dreadful; terrific; gruesome; undue; unusual; strange; pitiful; manifold (pl).

verbs

absorb—; ameliorate—; assume—; bear—; bend under—; chafe at—; deliver of—; ease—; groan under—; hamper with—; impose—; labor under—; lay on—; lighten —; load with—; overwhelm with—; shift —; shoulder—; stagger under—; suffer under—; support—; sustain—; unload—; —bows one down; —crushes.

(See load, cargo, weight, oppression, encumbrance.)

BURDENSOME

adverbs

grievously; financially; socially; intolerably; painfully; increasingly; unnecessarily; inescapably; seriously; economically; insuffer-

148

ably; monstrously; really; oppressively; aggravatingly; vexatiously; irritatingly; unequally; unjustly; dangerously; prodigiously; unendurably; dreadfully; terrifically; unduly; unusually; strangely; pitifully; calamitously; disastrously; unfortunately; tragically; gravely; cumbrously; embarrassingly.

BUREAU
adjectives
topographical; time-blackened; well-organized; devoted; legal; complete; self-supporting.

BUREAUCRACY
adjectives
smug; Teutonic; decadent; hardhearted; centralized.

BUREAUCRATIC
adverbs
complexly; unfortunately; portentously; ominously; dangerously; smugly; comfortably; democratically; autocratically; dictatorially; dominantly; imperiously; administratively; absolutely; arbitrarily; undeniably; hopelessly; irresistibly; terribly; unluckily; fairly; justly; unjustly; surprisingly; increasingly; overwhelmingly.

BURGLAR
adjectives
apprehensive; cautious; cunning; conscientious; felonious; stealthy; unscrupulous; chagrined; amateur; bungling; professional.

verbs
absolve—; accuse—; acquit—; apprehend —; condemn—; convict—; denounce—; detect—; imprison—; investigate —s; jail —s; protect against—; shield—; slay—; vindicate—; wound—; —alarms; —arouses; —invades; —plunders; —sacks; —terrorizes.
(See robber, highwayman, bandit.)

BURIAL
adjectives
obscure; golden; forgotten; Christian; interesting; hasty; premature; decent; respectable; proper; reverent; dismal; pagan.

verbs
assist at—; attend—; authorize—; commend to—; conceal by—; consecrate at—; console at—; draw out—; embalm for—; entitle to—; eulogize at—; notify of—; preach at —; preside over—; solemnize—; superintend—; uncover—; —disposes of.
(See death, funeral.)

BURLESQUE
adjectives
credible; polite; modified; exuberant; profane; farcical; vulgar; risque.

BURLESQUE (a)
adverbs
broadly; racily; absurdly; comically; cleverly; ludicrously; bombastically; caustically; sarcastically; ironically; satirically; extravagantly; cuttingly; adroitly; drolly; farcically; politely; profanely; coarsely; laughably; monstrously; ridiculously; refreshingly; delightfully; oddly; bizarrely; preposterously; unpardonably; whimsically; quizzically; uproariously; clownishly; chaffingly; scurrilously; derisively; scoffingly; exquisitely; deftly; expertly.

BURLESQUER
adjectives
hilarious; sheer; apt; clever; practiced.

BURN (v)
adverbs
destructively; smolderingly; luridly; noisily; mortally; inwardly; radiantly; shockingly; ruddily; intensely; steadfastly; dimly; sullenly; fitfully; ardently; distressfully; miraculously; inadvertently; glowingly.
(See scorch, consume.)

BURNING
adjectives
senseless; everlasting; endless.

BURRO
adjectives
dusty; dirty; shaggy; lop-eared; lazy; baldfaced; bobbing; munching.

BURST
adjectives
instant; passionate; indignant; convulsive; periodical; dreadful; sudden; fresh; unexplained; fiery; ungovernable; resplendent; scented; spontaneous.

BURST (v)
adverbs
turbulently; spontaneously; impetuously; appallingly; scornfully; involuntarily; hoarsely; ceaselessly; indignantly; periodically; ungovernably; resplendently.
(See break.)

BURTHEN
adjectives
breathless; delicate; sad; weighty; sorry.

adverbs

quietly; reverentially; worshipfully; solemnly; splendidly; impecuniously; shabbily; awesomely; spectacularly.

(See hide, conceal.)

BUS

adjectives

shrieking; steady; dependable; rumbling; lantern-hung; lumbering; gaudy; sight-seeing.

verbs

board—; enter—; jam—; route—; station —; —conducts; —crawls along; —disgorges passengers; —flounders; —jolts; —rolls along; —rumbles; —snorts; —traverses.

(See automobile.)

BUSH

adjectives

tough; elder; laurel; sickly; interminable; towering; rose; fiery; projecting; elderberry; pathless; silent; clustering; naked; sheltering; berried; whortleberry; embracing; sparse; spiny; flourishing; jessamine; spreading; secret; scrubby; gnarled; stiff; stunted; woody; flowering; scraggly; unkempt; mesquite; indigo; patient; blooming; broad; pyramidical; gorse; vase-shaped; irregular; curious; round-topped; twiggy; shriveled; stumpy; sodden.

verbs

conceal in—; cultivate—; dwell in—; grow over with—es; hide in—; lie in—; lose in—; nest in—; nestle in—; prune—; pry in—; shroud in—; skirt—; spring from—; take to —; tangle in—; wind in and out among—es; —blooms; —blossoms; —branches; —flourishes; —protects; —screens; —spreads; —tangles; —yields.

(See shrub, thicket.)

BUSINESS

adjectives

queer; fateful; ugly; hypothecary; mercantile; intelligent; stirring; fascinating; centralized; stiff; ungentle; bloody; snug; unpleasant; keyhole; curious; suspended; profitable; complicated; awkward; terrible; remunerative; weary; rationalized; wretched; unreasonable; sordid; ethical; vengeful; phenomenal; tidy; bustling; superfluous; reputable; flourishing; dangerous; serious; reliable; shameful; discouraging; dubious; late-afternoon; ecclesiastical; villainous; dreadful; dreary; executive; temporal; poor; single; roaring; delightful; toilsome;

prosperous; urgent; abstract; illegal; deplorable; unsound; definite; rascally; foul; weighty; stern; solemn; unavoidable; congenial; tedious; momentous; rural; legitimate; extensive; fiery; scratchy; urgent; civil; thriving; swift; blistering; risky; petty; competitive; extended; ordinary; solvent; brisk; lifelong; arduous; tangled; sorry; scurvy; delectable; unscrupulous; dirty; fast-growing; perfunctory; uncrowded; paramount; timely; weighty; subnormal; domestic; miserable; chancy; piratical; prodigious; nefarious; litigated; experimental; well-managed; urgent; hazardous; irrational; creative; exclusive; detailed; ruined; illustrious; muddled; tranquil; reckless; speculative; banking; primary; astounding; fecund; roundabout; essential; menaced; dull; drab; trivial; slack; stupid; pure; unmitigated; heartbreaking; backbreaking; brusque; honest; successful; sound; interesting; lucrative; blessed; rushing; gigantic; immense; tremendous; colossal; modern; increasing; dismal; shady; distasteful; degrading; unsavory; despicable; dark; knavish; damnable; cruel; fearful; ugly; tedious; distressing; nervy; nasty; sad; tiresome; unconstructive; stable; droll; ticklish; queer; silly; increasingly-profitable; substantial; amazing; ever-increasing; secure; ready-made; dependable; troublesome.

verbs

absorb—; accommodate—; adjust—; administer—; badger—; blast—; bolster—; charge with—; confess to—; corrupt—; debate—; democratize—; depress—; derive—; disorganize—; dispose of—; disrupt—; dominate —; drum up—; embark into—; employ in —; endanger—; envelop in—; establish—; evolve—; expedite—; exploit—; foster—; increase—; interfere with—; liquidate—; make inroads into—; meddle in—; mess up —; nurse—; plunge into—; quit—; regulate —; restrict—; resurrect—; revivify—; shift —; slow down—; speed up—; stabilize—; stimulate—; suspend—; swallow up—; symbolize—; tie up—; transact—; undertake—; underwrite—; wrap up in—; —booms; —bounds up; —branches out; —climbs; —droops; —expands; —expires; —falters; —flourishes; —flows; —founders; —lags; —looms; —nets; —simmers; —succumbs.

(See occupation, trade, matter, affair, interest, concern, enterprise, duty, industry, work, commerce.)

BUSINESSLIKE

adverbs

insistently; consistently; briskly; cheerfully;

alertly; keenly; intelligently; curiously; terribly; unreasonably; delightfully; urgently; definitely; positively; absolutely; thriftily; competently; competitively; thoroughly; ordinarily; ardently; scrupulously; astoundingly; essentially; dully; brusquely; honestly; successfully; soundly; immensely; tremendously; tediously; drolly; comically; amazingly; dependably; actively; assiduously; devotedly; eagerly; energetically; industriously; officiously; vigilantly; notably; smartly; zealously; shrewdly; courteously; methodically; craftily; astutely; cleverly; uniformly; capably; ingeniously; felicitously.

BUSINESSMAN
adjectives
average; hard-boiled; shrewd; prudent; substantial.

BUST
adjectives
laurel crowned, glowing; imperial; negligible; animated; portrait-like; protuberant; resurrected; placid; sculptured.

BUSTLE
adjectives
empty; heroic; sudden; feverish; indescribable; silent; hospitable; intervening; noisy.

BUSTLE (v)
adverbs
valorously; heroically; feverishly; indescribably; hospitably; noisily; officiously; clamorously; indignantly.
(See stir.)

BUSTLING
adverbs
restlessly; fitfully; eagerly; zealously; inefficiently; noisily; happily; affectionately; fondly; vexatiously; everlastingly; ceaselessly; cheerily; moodily; hastily; ardently; actively; energetically; industriously; assiduously; diligently; earnestly; enthusiastically; nervously; excitedly; impetuously.

BUSY (v)
adverbs
hurriedly; interferingly; noisily; officiously; irritatingly; animatedly; industriously; ambitiously; casually; perfunctorily.

BUSY (a)
adverbs
agreeably; delightfully; ceaselessly; charmingly; briskly; cheerfully; intelligently; constantly; curiously; unreasonably; competently; ordinarily; astoundingly; tremendously; comically; amazingly; actively; eagerly; zealously; energetically; smartly; ostentatiously; craftily; cleverly; capably; boyishly; noisily; happily.

BUSYBODY
adjectives
gifted; interfering; old; free lance; gaping; nosy.

BUTCHER
adjectives
benevolent; inexorable; unfeeling; latent; mortal; skilled.

BUTCHER (v)
adverbs
indiscriminately; dexterously; inexorably; unfeelingly; mortally; professionally; methodically; heartlessly; cruelly; wantonly; atrociously
(See slaughter, kill.)

BUTCHERY
adjectives
horrible; atrocious; deadly; murderous; wartime.

BUTLER
adjectives
impassive; peremptory; perfect; shrinking; hovering; worried; excellent; solemn; diminutive; competent; grizzled.

BUTTER
adjectives
rancid; molten; honeyed.

verbs
adulterate—; cart—; churn into—; color—; crock—; daub with—; deal in—; draw—; exude—; flavor—; grease—; lay on—; market—; melt—; mould—; pot—; ration out—; ripen—; separate—; solidify—; spread—; stir in—; test—; thicken—; work—.

BUTTER (v)
adverbs
sufficiently; goldenly; lavishly; liberally; scantily; meagerly; penuriously; politically.

BUTTERFLY
adjectives
painted; giddy; ingenious; chromatic-winged; bright; honey-sipping; social; gilded; quivering; sipping; marrying; blossom-like; slim; jet; loppy-winged; admired; gaudy; lazy; dainty; fluttering; poising.

verbs

attract—; distinguish—; frame—; hurt—; identify—; preserve—; pursue—; —beautifies; —ies cluster; —flits about; —flutters; —ies gather; —ies hibernate; —lays eggs; —migrates; —mimics; —pollinates; —spins; —sports; —twinkles.
(See moth.)

BUTTON

adjectives

saucer; shining; blue-jerkined; glittering; showy; blazing; fantastic.

verbs

adorn with —s; attach—; card —s; decorate with —s; drill —s; fondle—; grind —s; mold —s; ornament with —s; perforate —s; polish—; press out —s; sew on—; sort —s; stamp out —s; stud with —s; undo—; —affixes; —decorates; —fastens; —signifies.
(See knob, ornament.)

BUXOM

adverbs

agreeably; cheerfully; delightfully; attractively; genially; gaily; hilariously; noisily; lightly; merrily; joyously; charmingly; entrancingly; seductively; captivatingly; fascinatingly; humorously; vivaciously; bonnily; cheerily; gleefully; heartily; jauntily; jovially; jubilantly; playfully; sportively.

BUY

adjectives

exceptional; special; extraordinary.

BUY (v)

adverbs

secretly; eagerly; dearly; methodically; recklessly; exceptionally; extraordinarily.
(See purchase.)

BUYER

adjectives

reluctant; unintelligent; reckless; unwilling; avid; adept; ultimate; discriminating; prospective; timorous.

verbs

cater to—; coax—; coddle—; commission—; employ—; forewarn—; petition—; —bargains; —dickers; —obtains; —s pour in; —purchases.
(See customer.)

BUYING

adjectives

hand-to-mouth; cash; unintelligent; abnormal; collective; curtailed.

BUZZ

adjectives

humming; roaring; somnolent; baleful.

BUZZ (v)

adverbs

violently; roaringly; somnolently; balefully; monotonously; grindingly; painfully; repeatedly; intermittently; raucously; irritatingly.
(See hum, murmur.)

BUZZARD

adjectives

eternal: circling; watchful; carrion-feeding; waiting; patient.

verbs

—dips; —flaps his wings; —hovers; —soars.
(See bird, fowl.)

BUZZING

adjectives

loud; melancholy; repeated; intermittent; raucous.

BY-PRODUCT

adjectives

dubious; usual; unforeseen.

BYSTANDERS

adjectives

casual; innocent; mere; fascinated; inoffensive-looking; pathetic; sympathetic; superstitious.

verbs

collide with—; entertain—; regale—; strike —; —boo; —cheer; —gather; —hoot; —recognize; —threaten; —witness.
(See spectator, crowd.)

BYWAY

adjectives

deserted; dark; bowered; romantic.

C

CAB

adjectives
dilapidated; high; ridiculous; dejected; creaking; hansom; ramshackle.

CABIN

adjectives
malodorous; ruined; dreary-looking; little; sweet; deserted; primitive; ugly; tumble-down; abandoned; friendly; roomy; win-dowless; stuffy; spacious; airy; adobe; rus-tic; frontier; willow; dilapidated; dismal; second-class; unventilated; sanitary; lonely; embowered; remote; populous; tourist.

verbs
allot—; approach—; confine to—; coop in—; crawl into—; dwell in—; huddle in—; in-habit—; lodge in—; occupy—; situate—; thatch—; —flames; —shelters.
(See hut, house, compartment, cottage.)

CABINET

adjectives
quaint; treasure; lacquered; sound-proof; bedstead; canopied; moist; drunken; medi-cine; reliable; antiquated.

CABINET

adjectives   (governmental)
austere; absolute; didactic; dictatorial; dis-organized; resolute; united; unsympathetic; vacillating; weak-kneed.

verbs
address—; appoint to—; call—; consult—; convoke—; corrupt—; dismiss—; dissolve—; elect to—; represent in—; summon—; —ad-ministers; —advises; —confers; —consists; —convenes.
(See committee, council, ministry.)

CABLE

adjectives
heavy; electric; steel-wire; enormous; light; underground; overhead.

verbs
insulate—; lay—; reclaim—; reenforce—; sheathe—; snap—; solder—; stretch—; —communicates; —connects; —rusts; —trans-mits.
(See rope, line, chain, conduit, pipe.)

CACKLE

adjectives
sickly; vacant; occasional; sociable; foolish; prodigious.

CACKLE (v)

adverbs
obstreperously; sociably; harshly; prodigi-ously; raucously; stridently; disagreeably; triumphantly; proudly; jubilantly; exuber-antly.
(See laugh, chatter, babble.)

CACTUS

adjectives
spiny; mammoth; massive; hardy; scraggly; fantastic; prickly; succulent; large.

CAD

adjectives
sensual; slimy; rotten; brutal; discreet; elderly; ineffable.

CADAVEROUS

adverbs
horribly; forbiddingly; frightfully; spectral-ly; foully; grimly; gruesomely; hideously; haggardly; monstrously; odiously; shocking-ly; stiffly; uncannily; fearfully; alarming-ly; incredibly; dreadfully.

CADENCE

adjectives
self-possessed; monotonous; odd; singsong; calm; deep; mimic; best-measured; tinkling; merry; queer; wild; sardonic; nasal; minor; rollicking; weird; hideous; entreating; slightest; slurred; strange; rhythmic; musi-cal; affectionate; lingering; effective; gentle; elegant; exotic; passionate; varied; soul-like; plagal; pathetic; pleading; enchanting; sorrowful.

CAFE

adjectives
innumerable (pl); continental; eccentric; gaudy; dingy; sumptuous; garish; gay; air-conditioned; pleasant; obscure; modest; smart; modern.

CAFFEINE

adjectives
unfriendly; stimulating.

CAGE

adjectives

subterranean; quarantined; awful; gilded; bamboo; wire; delicate; adjourning; wicker; pretty.

verbs

bar—; beat—; burst—; chain—; confine in —; convey in—; coop in—; escape from—; fetter in—; flit from—; hoist—; house in—; imprison in—; muffle in—; release from—; seal—; thrive in—; transport in—; wire in —.

(See prison.)

CAKE

adjectives

huge; fluffy; stale; abominable; peatlike; fresh; big; luscious; ancestral; oaten; incalculable; sacrificial; decomposed; fatal; successful; election; rich; moist; tender; smooth; white; pound; futile.

verbs

celebrate with—; crust—; decorate—; feast on—; flavor—; frost—; ice—; knead—; mix—; moisten—; mold—; munch on—; ply with—; regale with—; relish—; shape —; share—; spice—; squash—; sweeten—; yearn for—; —appeals; —appeases; —attracts; —crumbles; —falls; —rises; —stales.

(See bread.)

CALAMITY

adjectives

sudden; near; appalling; frightful; dire; staggering; tremendous; universal; public; painful; evident; undeserved; national; family; inevitable; crowning; impending; ominous; dreadful; absurd; mysterious; natural; inexhaustible; grotesque; unspeakable; ultimate; extraordinary; surrounding; bitter; colossal; temporal; undisguised.

verbs

afflict with—; avert—; avoid—; bear—; beset with—ies; drive to—; free from—; inflict with—; investigate—; involve—; laugh at—; mourn—; overcome—; restore from—; rush to—; save from—; survive—; —arises; —confounds; —damages; —descends; —distresses; —foreshadows; —injures; —menaces; —recurs; —smites; — threatens; —troubles.

(See misfortune, disaster, adversity.)

CALCULABLE

adverbs

easily; accurately; obviously; analytically; rationally; fairly; exhaustively; arithmetically; scientifically; precisely; exactly; laboriously; imposingly; impressively.

CALCULATE (*v*)

adverbs

mentally; abstractly; arithmetically; shrewdly; convincingly; precisely; astronomically; mathematically; slavishly; systematically; perpetually; strikingly; nicely; artfully.

(See compute, reckon.)

CALCULATION

adjectives

abstruse; optimistic; hasty; mental; abstract; pragmatic; intricate; colorless; chill; arithmetical; trained; shrewd; barren; imposing; convincing; rough; mental; unsettling; hard; stupendous; easy; moderate; absurd; deliberate; prudent; precise; laborious; memorable; astronomical; elaborate; vain; mathematical; calm; monotonous; craniometrical; cool; systematic; slavish; perpetual; reasonable.

verbs

adjust—; adopt—; arrange—; average—; check—; cite—; compute—; denounce—; err in—; estimate—; facilitate—; frame—; perform—; prove—; reckon—; speed—; tabulate—; think out—; upset—; —deceives; — determines; —fits; —indicates; —results in.

(See computation, reckoning.)

CALDRON

adjectives

seething; spiteful; great; live; bubbling; ancestral; hellish; boiling; monstrous; magic.

verbs

agitate—; cook in—; cool—; fry in—; steep in—; —boils; —bubbles; —overflows; — pours out; —seethes; —simmers; —steams.

(See kettle, pot.)

CALENDAR

adjectives

proposed; universal; unscriptural; modern; present; scientific.

verbs

appear on—; count on—; designate on—; introduce—; judge by—; keep—of; pencil —; readjust—; reckon by—; regulate—; revise—; scratch out of—; —computes; —denotes; —determines; —s differ; —groups; —indicates; —measures; —serves; —signifies.

(See list, schedule.)

CALF

adjectives

capering; soft-eyed.

verbs
beget—; corral—s; fatten—; fetter—; groom—; infect—; lasso—; offer—; pasture—; pet—; rend—; sacrifice—; slaughter—; stable—; —bawls; —browses; —grazes; —kicks; —shies; —suckles; —whines.
(See animal.)

CALF
adjectives   (leg)
well-turned; unwearying; aching; pretty.

CALIBER
adjectives
high; stern; rare; meager; spectacular; mental; various.

CALL
adjectives
urgent; impatient; hurried; frantic; startled; strenuous; amazing; mystic; persistent; insistent; ceaseless; gallant; thrilling; voiceless; feeble; muffled; strong; canny; joyous; ringing; strident; clarion; screeching; staccato; calm; melodious; loud; musical; excited; effectual; pitiful; petulant; stirring; incoming; home-coming; solemn; doleful; providential; skyward; languid; vigorous; cheering; quavering; inconsiderate; bugle; emphatic; clamorous; person-to-person; night; echoing; high-pitched; immediate; impassioned; immortal.

verbs
evade—; ignore—; register—; respond to —; rise at—; trumpet—; whistle—; yield to—; —beckons; —bursts forth; —deludes; —drifts; —gladdens; —saddens.
(See shout, cry, summons, invitation.)

CALL
adjectives   (visit)
deathless; enormous; unending; ceremonious; emergency; neighborly; unexpected; convenient; innumerable (pl); close; honorable; hasty; protracted; reliable; bewildering; personal.

CALL (v)
adverbs
insistently; urgently; frantically; persistently; feebly; ringingly; stridently; screechingly; melodiously; musically; pitifully; petulantly; dolefully; languidly; passionately; vigorously; quaveringly; clamorously; emphatically; echoingly; irresistibly; officially; severely; alternately; bluntly; facetiously; despairingly; technically; irreverently;

extemporaneously; plaintively; mysteriously; familiarly; delicately; subsequently; indifferently; timorously; imperiously; cordially; tauntingly; cautiously; virtually; proverbially; unconscionably; sportively; graciously; lustily.
(See summon, bid, invite.)

CALLER
adjectives
white-haired; talkative; bedraggled; irate; bashful; unexpected; disappointed.

CALLING
adjectives
suitable; honorable; money-making; effectual; incessant; primordial; gainful; lawful.

verbs
answer—; awake to—; bend to—; consider —; continue in—; exalt—; exercise—; feel —; follow—; give up to—; heed—; profess to—; succeed in—; surrender to—; —bids; —invites; —invokes; —summons.
(See vocation, occupation, trade, profession.)

CALLOUS (a)
adverbs
coldly; unfeelingly; stolidly; senselessly; obtusely; apathetically; strangely; abnormally; weakly; heavily; vacantly; singularly; oddly; curiously; unaccountably; irritatingly; vexatiously; coolly; unpardonably; inexcusably.

CALLOUSNESS
adjectives
extreme; bitter; cruel; harsh; icy; incurred; repellent; brutal; self-imposed; criminal.

verbs
breed—; develop—; display—; expose to—; immunize to—; relapse into—; —blinds; —forms; —grows; —prevents; —ridicules.
(See callous, cruelty.)

CALLOW
adverbs
crudely; intolerably; uncompanionably; insufferably; rawly; youthfully; unintelligently; rudimentally; coarsely; thoughtlessly; heedlessly; vacuously; fatuously; surprisingly; awkwardly.

CALLUS (n)

adjectives

burning; carefully-tended; horny; leathery; reducible; stubborn; thickening; toil-worn; cushiony; cracked; shell-like.

verbs

apply to—; cut—; expose—; form—; pad—; peel—; press on—; rub into—; salve—; scrape—; slice—; soften—; soothe—; treat —es; wear —es; —aches; —burns; —hardens; —indurates; —irritates; —pains; —thickens.

(See callousness.)

CALM

adjectives

imperturbable; equable; deathly; reproachful; ominous; unutterable; desolate; sullen; philosophic; mental; studied; sensual; false; somber; solemn; classic; customary; comparative; jaded; forced; alert; secretive; unnatural; dovelike; delightful; unbroken; untroubled; restful; flawless; concentrated; hallowed; inmost; underlying; Sabbath; delicious; sweet; bitter; disciplined; stately; unalterable; shimmering; breathless; expressionless; succeeding; prosaic; windless; splendid; night; rigid; eternal; perfect; disquieting; outward; threatening; mysterious; legislative; passionless; remote; lucid; constant; serene; professional; melancholy; colossal; awful; inward; solid; habitual; unapologetic; sad; sacred; stolid; maddening; level; shuddering; kindred; dead; planetary; everlasting; propitious; apparent; judicial.

verbs

agitate—; break—; bring—; disturb—; end —; maintain—; preserve—; retain—; shatter—; suspend—; —bewitches; —delays; — detains; —enchants; —endures; —irritates; —rests; —settles on; —soothes.

(See tranquillity, stillness, serenity.)

CALM (a)

adverbs

pleasantly; delightfully; comfortingly; comfortably; habitually; sweetly; imperturbably; serenely; equitably; ominously; unutterably; philosophically; unnaturally; restfully; inwardly; unalterably; splendidly; mysteriously; perfectly; maddeningly; apparently; suddenly; strangely; pathetically; judicially; indulgently; coolly; placidly; gravely; passively; patiently; quietly; soberly; tranquilly; deliberately; silently; amicably; gently; smoothly; mildly; nonchalantly.

CALM (v)

adverbs

ominously; philosophically; falsely; soberly; soberly; mentally; comparatively; unnaturally; expressionlessly; prosaically; outwardly; mysteriously; passionlessly; professionally; serenely; propitiously; judicially; apparently.

(See lull, appease, hush.)

CALMNESS

adjectives

perfect; deathlike; icy; irritating; tense; sleepy; sudden; terrible; deliberate; strange; stony; peculiar; solitary; intrepid; honest; dreadful; collected; pathetic; fierce; unwonted; unmerciful; dreamy; judicial; proud; displeasing; settled; cold; imperturbable.

CALORIES

adjectives

accumulated; actinic; beneficial; burdening; life-sustaining; stored-up.

verbs

burden with—; calculate—; contain—; define—; determine—; express in—; govern —; increase—; lessen—; measure—; obtain —; regulate—; require—; supply—; vary—; —suffice.

(See unit.)

CALUMNIATORY

adverbs

criminally; scandalously; grossly; wilfully; flagitiously; dangerously; substantially; veritably; avowedly; abominably; detestably; extremely; illegally; nefariously; unfortunately; unluckily; openly; deliberately; maliciously; venomously; libelously; scurrilously; foully; slanderously.

CALUMNIOUS

adverbs

deliberately; inherently; naturally; habitually; unfortunately; unpleasantly; disagreeably; detestably; abominably; hatefully; malignantly; maliciously; poisonously; venomously; viciously; insinuatingly; slyly; subtly; scandalously; wilfully; dangerously; extremely; openly; foully; unforgivably.

CALUMNY

adjectives

gross; frequent; willful; barbarous; backwounding; transparent; private; flagitious; hideous; popular; superstitious.

verbs

accuse of—; asperse with—; characterize

156

by—; charge with—; diffuse—; invent—; propagate—; raise—; repudiate—; subject to—; utter—; —blights; —defames; —detracts; —imputes to; —injures; —libels; —misrepresents; —slanders.

(See slander, aspersion, accusation.)

CALVINISTIC

adverbs

rigidly; soundly; strictly; unyieldingly; inflexibly; faithfully; scrupulously; unbendingly; loyally; puritanically; chastely; punctiliously; literally; precisely; rigorously; unaffectedly; unimpeachably; frankly; openly; avowedly; sincerely; obstinately; stubbornly; obdurately; intolerantly; proudly.

CAMARADERIE

adjectives

careless; spirited; joyous.

CAMEL

adjectives

gloomy-eyed; crouching; fast; cream-colored; browsing; patient; fleet; miserable; baggage; fine-riding; beautiful; prodding; magnificent; kneeling; swift; sure-footed.

verbs

domesticate—; load—; mount—; train—; water—; —bolts; —consumes; —fasts; —gurgles; —jolts; —kneels; —nibbles; —rages; —roars; —shakes; —stores; —sweats; —thrives.

(See animal.)

CAMEO

adjectives

exquisite; precious.

CAMERA

adjectives

television; candid; clicking; heavy; leveled.

verbs

adjust—; arm with—; besiege with —s; conceal—; focus—; insert in—; level—; load—; operate—; pose before—; regulate —; sit before—; utilize—; —aids; —captures; —catches; —copies; —enlarges; —espies; —grinds out; —obtains; —pictures; —records; —registers; —reproduces.

CAMOUFLAGE

adjectives

pleasant; pious; shallow; discreditable; impenetrable; foolish.

CAMP

adjectives

hostile; dismantled; horrible; concentration; deserted; aboriginal; circumvallating; permanent; temporary; picturesque; fortified; turbulent; peaceful; comfortable; armed; spacious; attractive; modest; thriving; selected; opposite; lawless; antagonistic; divided; nightly; luxurious; chaotic.

verbs

arouse—; beleaguer—; besiege—; command —; concentrate—; conduct—; conduct to—; divide into —s; escort to—; pitch—; proclaim—; put out of—; quarter at—; split into —s; strike—; —busies; —buzzes; —hums; —rises; —swarms.

(See barracks.)

CAMP (v)

adverbs

ostentatiously; conveniently; permanently; temporarily; turbulently; lawlessly; nightly; luxuriously; strategically.

CAMPAIGN

adjectives

triumphant; ill-fated; successful; whispering; perfunctory; systematic; demographic; vigorous; anti-crime; collective; energetic; fruitless; gubernatorial; brilliant; tremendous; aggressive; virulent; victorious; independent; indiscriminate; plausible; preliminary; piratical; comprehensive; subtle; long; tedious; bloody; doggerel; wearisome; approaching; powerful; persistent; perfidious; journalistic; deliberate; devouring; lulled; preceding; critical; anti-feminist; amatory; mighty; brilliant; thrilling; worldwide; far-flung; intense; thorough; guerrilla; national; educational; money-raising; recruiting; secret; quiet; off-stage; complete; exacting; sanguinary; haphazard; extraordinary.

verbs

broaden—; carry on—; conduct—; embark on—; feature—; focus—; foster—; inaugurate—; initiate—; inspire—; intensify—; launch—; map out—; participate in—; plan —; plot—; promote—; push—; stir—; sway —; swing—; transcend—; wage—.

(See operation, contest, appeal.)

CAMPAIGN (v)

adverbs

vigorously; triumphantly; ill-fatedly; vaingloriously; perfunctorily; systematically; energetically; fruitlessly; brilliantly; gubernatorially; aggressively; virulently; independently; indiscriminately; perfidiously; comprehensively; tediously; educationally; extraordinarily; haphazardly.

(See operate.)

CAMPAIGNER

adjectives
agitated; ogling; leering; scheming; artful; active; seasoned.

CAMPER

adjectives
scattered (pl); unsuspecting.

CAMPFIRE

adjectives
forsaken; gleaming; rosy; flickering; bright; glowing; tiny; cozy; smoking; central.

CAMPUS

adjectives
dignified; attractive.

CAN

adjectives
highly-colored; discarded.

verbs
cap—; dent—; deposit in—; dump —s; grade—; heap —s; label—; litter with —s; manufacture—; package —s; penetrate—; put up in—; save in—; seal—; shape—; shelve—; —preserves; —protects; —rusts.
(See cup.)

CANADIAN

adverbs
staunchly; stoutly; shrewdly; indomitably; loyally; dauntlessly; stolidly; generously; cannily.

CANAL

adjectives
shining; picturesque; slender; enchanting; stagnant; inland; crude; sluggish; beautiful; tree-lined; intestinal; vast; network; practicable; intracoastal; alimentary; auditory; winding; lotus-paved; irregular; pestiferous; tortuous; marble-lined; glittering; terrestrial; ribbonlike; semicircular; shadowed; vestigial.

verbs
bank—; block—; border by—; bridge—; circle—; construct—; drain—; dredge—; fortify—; lay out—; line—; lock—; navigate —; obstruct—; project—; tow through—; —communicates; —connects; —conveys; —irrigates; —retains; —shortens; —unites.
(See channel, duct, passage.)

CANARD

adjectives
base; preposterous.

CANARY

adjectives
ephemeral; fluffy; fragile; gladsome; green-gold; restless; song-bursting; twittering.

verbs
—carols; —peeps; —trills; —tweets.
(See bird.)

CANCER

adjectives
malignant; hereditary; inoperable.

verbs
ascribe to—; control—; detect—; diagnose —; discover—; engraft—; examine for—; excise—; indicate—; lecture on—; localize —; recognize—; reveal—; sacrifice to—; suffer from—; suspect—; treat for—; —advances; —appears; —courses through; —develops; —disables; —eats away; —extends; —lodges; —lurks; —results; —spreads.
(See tumor, disease.)

CANCEROUS

adverbs
hopelessly; lamentably; malignantly; incurably; irremediably; morbidly; painfully; distressingly; inoperably; sorely; agonizingly; grievously; horribly; dolorously; frightfully; pitiably; woefully; tragically.

CANDELABRA

adjectives
myriad; tall; bronze; brilliant; huge; silver.

CANDENT

adverbs
glowingly; whitely; tropically; lambently; scintillatingly; flamingly; smolderingly; incalescently; intensely; fiercely; sulphurously; overpoweringly; intolerably; unendurably; incredibly.

CANDESCENT

adverbs
blazingly; dazzlingly; effulgently; brightly; radiantly; intolerably; gloriously; luminously; refulgently; resplendently; splendidly; magnificently; garishly; lustrously; vividly; genially; mildly; exceedingly; surprisingly; gratefully; agreeably; magically.

CANDID

adverbs
utterly; openly; honestly; innocently; simply; sincerely; artlessly; deliberately; resolutely; roughly; directly; downright; frankly; ingenuously; naively; naturally; plainly; unflatteringly; delicately; nakedly; soberly;

palpably; evidently; manifestly; truthfully; veraciously; bluntly; indulgently; particularly; scrupulously; unaffectedly; unnecessarily; inexcusably; faithfully; unreservedly; respectfully; incorruptibly; crudely; painfully; gaily; unfeelingly; characteristically; habitually; amazingly; humorously; unexpectedly; engagingly; alarmingly; charmingly.

CANDIDACY
adjectives
insurgent; unsuccessful.

verbs
announce—; avow—; back—; boost for—; campaign for—; criticize—; decide—; discuss—; interest in—; offer for—; promote —; propose—; protest—; reject—; rob of—; select for—; support—; work for—.

CANDIDATE
adjectives
potential; gubernatorial; legitimate; senatorial; aspiring; glamorous; receptive; prospective; rejected; unexceptionable; proper; eligible; formidable; leading; opposing; passive; alternative; presidential.

verbs
choose—; doom—; endorse—; favor—; groom—; handicap—; honor—; idealize—; squelch—; uphold—; —aspires to; —offers; —orates; —"slings mud"; —stumps; —thunders; - -triumphs.
(See contestant.)

CANDIED
adverbs
deliciously; delectably; lusciously; richly; densely; thickly; indissolubly; substantially; sweetly; fruitily; generously; agreeably; palatably; deceptively.

CANDLE
adjectives
dumb; newfangled; paraffin; shining; beeswax; flickering; brief; gigantic; guttering; meek; neglected; tall; ghastly; blessed; diminutive; melancholy; flaring; spent; cabbage-headed; half-burned; lighted; sputtering; waning; snuffed; long-wicked.

verbs
dip —s; extinguish—; mould —s; snuff—; —decorates; —drips; —flickers; —gutters; —illuminates; —melts; —shadows; —shines; —shrinks; —sputters; —stains; —tapers.
(See light, lamp.)

CANDLESTICK
adjectives
squat; slender; graceful.

CANDOR
adjectives
crude; unfailing; ingenuous; shameless; maidenly; winning; half-rebellious; friendly; perfect; pervading; utmost; gay; transparent; unwonted; incomparable; painful; dignified; unfeeling; fresh; apparent; characteristic; piercing; brotherly; stainless; endearing; illuminating; violent; good-humored; unashamed; unsuggestive; uncompromising; amazing; wholesome; spiritual; direct; heartfelt; vigorous; humorous; unexpected; courageous; perfect; devastating; engaging; openhearted; rustic; unruly; alarming; comical.

verbs
acclaim—; boast—; discourse with—; dispose toward—; express—; feign—; honor —; judge with—; radiate—; —brightens; —frees; —shines; —shocks; —strains; —surprises.
(See frankness, impartiality, fairness, sincerity.)

CANDY
adjectives
silk; atrocious; hard; lime; delicious; tempting; nutritious.

verbs
bribe with—; congeal into—; consume—; decorate—; feast on—; flavor—; hanker for—; immerse—in; inspissate—; proffer—; regale with—; thicken—; —appeals; —crystallizes; —sickens; —stales; —vanishes.
(See cake.)

CANE
adjectives
lithe; long; ebony; ivory-headed; silver-headed; Malacca; gold-headed; slender; impenetrable; light; flexible; leaded; jewelled; silver-topped; beribboned.

verbs
beat with—; brandish—; carve—; enamel —; flex—; flog with—; flourish—; jab with —; joint—; lean on—; notch—; poise—; sheathe—; tap with—; utilize—; —supports.
(See stick, staff, whip.)

CANINE
adjectives
affectionate; luckless.

159

adjectives
groveling.

CANKER

adjectives
vengeful; gnawing.

verbs
banish—; infect with—; slough—; spray—; —consumes; —corrupts; —decays; —depraves; —destroys; —develops; —devours; —discharges; —diseases; —eats; —envelops; —gnaws; —grows; —indisposes; —poisons; —pollutes; —rusts; —spreads; —tarnishes.
    (See cancer, ulcer, sore.)

CANKEROUS

adverbs
increasingly; injuriously; poisonously; corrosively; blightingly; irremediably; incurably; painfully; distressingly; troublesomely; pitiably; unfortunately.

CANNED

adverbs
perfectly; exquisitely; expertly; faultlessly; irreproachably; hygienically; scientifically; soundly; carefully; well; safely; home; prophylactically; guardedly.

CANNIBALS

adjectives
gigantic; raging.

CANNON

adjectives
least-accessible; monstrous; small; academical; clumsy; ugly; yawning; widely-sloping; terraced; prostrate; grumbling; booming; brazen-throated; improvised; boulder-choked; distant; useless; breaching; spiked; roaring; frowning; lateral; brazen; belching; thundering; hostile.

verbs
capture—; charge—; discharge—; level—; load—; man—; mount—; sight—; silence —; train—upon; —batters; —blazes away; —booms; —emits; —explodes; —menaces; —pounds; —recoils; —revolves; —roars; —rolls; —salutes; —throws; —thunders; —vollies.
    (See gun, weapon.)

CANNONADE

adjectives
tremendous; sullen.

adverbs
astonishingly; shrewdly; weirdly; uncommonly; infinitely; suavely; smoothly; adroitly; cleverly; diplomatically; artfully; subtly; cunningly; naturally; craftily; guilelessly; astutely; foxily; deeply; knowingly; politically; discreetly; intelligently; sharply; wisely; sagely; sagaciously; alertly; smartly.

CANOE

adjectives
stealthy; canvas-covered; capsized; frail; careening; racing; dug-out; birchen; lonely.

verbs
ballast—; capsize—; cruise in—; fashion—; guide—; handle—; launch—; level—; model —; navigate—; overturn—; propel—; race in—; right—; rig up—; sail—; stabilize—; steer—; trim—; twist—; waterproof—; weight—; —dips; —glides; —outsails; —rocks; —slips.
    (See boat.)

CANOEIST

adjectives
seasoned.

CANON

adjectives
hospitable; highest; continent; aesthetic; worthy; obtrusive; waterless; metrical.

CANONICAL

adverbs
strictly; highly; conformably; obtrusively; ecclesiastically; monastically; pontifically; illustriously; conventionally; formally; habitually; ordinarily; regularly; acceptably; rigidly; typically; uncompromisingly; evangelically; sacredly; prophetically; inviolably; expressly.

CAN OPENER

adjectives
maligned.

CANOPY

adjectives
moon-proof; damask; shifting; irremovable; drooping; arched; orb-like; moth-flitted; overhead; luminous; oblique; skyey; silken; flowery; crimson; celestial; velvet; azure; somber; verdant; umbrageous.

verbs
bracket—; couch under—; embroider—; hang out—; spread—; support—; suspend —; —circles; —covers; —decorates; —

hangs over; —hoods; —projects; —protects;
—shades; —shelters; —surmounts.
(See pavilion, tent.)

CANT

adjectives
specious; traditional.

CANTER

adjectives
clumsy; brisk; undeniable; preliminary.

CANTER (v)

adverbs
clumsily; briskly; carelessly; steadily;
spiritedly; half-heartedly; unevenly; monotonously; jouncingly; pleasurably; lazily.
(See trot.)

CANVAS

adjectives
mute; melancholy; billowing; snowy; smoke-
darkened; gigantic; towering; shimmering;
famous; important; dark-colored; mighty;
somber; rickety; defiled; broad; idly-flap-
ping; mimic; remarkable; inflammable.

verbs
bleach—; daub—; depict on—; display on
—; dye—; execute on—; garment in—; line
with—; live under—; portray on—; retain
on—; spread—; surface—; transfer to—;
weave—; —blinds; —filters; —protects; —
screens.
(See cloth, sail, tent, picture, painting.)

CANVASS

adjectives
frantic; extensive; national; house-to-house;
thorough; misleading; hotly-contested; electoral; industrious; effective.

CANYON

adjectives
deepening; lowland; tributary; carved; narrow; sharp; shallow; dreaded; deserted;
winding; mile-deep; color-flaming; hollow;
bare; hard; blind; frowning; weird; wind-
swept; somber; snow-clad; treeless; mist-
filled; nave-like; mystic; rocky-bottomed;
grand.

verbs
carve—; collect in—; delve in—; enter—;
erode into—; explore—; flow through—;
stream through—; traverse—; widen—; —
beautifies; —extends; —narrows; —skirts;
—traverses; —widens.
(See gorge, valley.)

CAP

adjectives
rakish; coon-tail; checked; grimy; shabby;
demure; bulging; peaked; close-fitting; vi-
sored; tall; shako-like; thin; plumed; gauze;
paltry; flaring; jaunty; blue-tasseled; night-
spangled; frilled; perforated; traditional;
funnel-shaped; lace; muslin.

verbs
adjust—; admire—; appear in—; clap—on;
crown with—; don—; fashion—; fling—;
hurl—in air; line—; pattern—; peak—; —
balloons; —blows off; —covers; —distinguishes; —fits; —perches; —protects; —
shades; —shields; —surrounds; —warms.
(See hat, cover.)

CAPABILITIES

adjectives
ultimate; brilliant; admitted; generous; endless.

verbs
admit—; apprehend—; ascertain—; boast
of—; confirm—; convince of—; demand—;
destroy—; display—; discover—; doubt—;
drain—; enlarge—; establish—; evince—;
examine—; exhibit—; gift with—; investigate—of; perceive—; possess—; recognize
—; reward—; strike one with—; trust in—
of.
(See ability, capacity, skill.)

CAPABLE

adverbs
unusually; brilliantly; remarkably; normally; generally; immensely; naturally; highly;
notably; efficiently; sufficiently; incredibly;
exceptionally; energetically; potentially; influentially; adroitly; cleverly; dexterously;
deftly; discreetly; expertly; ingeniously; indefatigably; tirelessly; intelligently; practically; skilfully; proficiently; felicitously;
handily; neatly; pleasantly; willingly; thoroughly; technically; shrewdly; entirely;
gratifyingly; prepossessingly; agreeably.

CAPACIOUS

adverbs
unusually; incredibly; extensively; extremely; sweepingly; magnificently; broadly;
splendidly; grandly; superbly; unbelievably;
wonderfully; marvellously; illimitably; infinitely; admirably; majestically; roomily;
enormously; remarkably; notably; famously;
renownedly; formidably; singularly; uncommonly; particularly.

adjectives
imitative; business; temporal; assimilative; remarkable; absorptive; negative; productive; private; normal; functional; boundless; superior; reserve; carrying; immense; phenomenal; histrionic; unbounded; equestrian; bestowed; fruitful; partisan; sovereign; native; fatal; individual; narrowest; physical; psychological; proper; everlasting; increasing; cubical; wage-earning; reputed; creative; intellectual; interpretative; notable; productive; automatic; honorary; earning; predatory; constitutional; dignified; uncommon; extensive; aggregate; daily; destructive; magical; executive; exceptional; innate; latent; automatic; enlarged; varying; inexhaustible; bear-like; extraordinary; tremendous; ultimate; human; seating; consulting; mental; social; official; business; threefold; spiritual; prehensile; advisory; endless; singular; considerable; utmost; marked; unique; stunted; amazing; unparalleled; infinite; limitless; incredible; strange; cold-blooded; meanest; inherent; natural; fertile; implanted; expert; unsuspected; sufficient; demonstrated; flexible; inborn; benevolent; hidden; varied; contrasted; formidable.

verbs
cultivate—; delineate—; demonstrate—; develop—; endow with—; engender—; enlarge —; exceed—; exert to—; expand—; gauge —; impair—; increase—; limit—; measure —; nourish—; overestimate—; reduce—; sharpen—; —dwindles; —wanes.

(See ability, talent, power, space, position, office.)

CAPE
adjectives (clothing)
dark; all-enveloping; velvet; cloth; dusky; ghostly; chestnut; graceful; small; fluttering.

CAPE
adjectives (land)
stupendous; huge; rocky; famous; grassy.

CAPER
adjectives
wild; queer; prancing; droll; weird; drunken; inexplicable.

verbs
cut —s; dance in —; execute—; frolic in —s; jump in —s; leap in —s; perform—; prance in—; run into—; skip in—; sport in—; twist in—.

(See prank, trick, leap, spring.)

adjectives
gleeful; lamb-like; idle.

CAPITAL
adjectives (city)
seething; delightful; mad; hospitable; national; inland; stricken; remote; proud; brilliant; sophisticated; intellectual; financial; provincial; faraway; critical; highland; ancient; gilded; sculptured; flowery; peerless.

CAPITAL
adjectives (financial)
ample; slender; insufficient; borrowed; local; surplus; invested; ready; maximum; accumulated; potential; enchanting; embellished; tolerable; available; abundant; organized; skittish; enlightened; unproductive.

verbs
accumulate—; amass—; calculate—; contribute—; convert into—; distribute—; employ—; exploit—; favor—; fix—; float—; furnish—; gain—; guarantee—; impair—; increase—; insure—; invest—; organize—; produce—; protect—; subscribe—; withdraw—; —earns; —finances.

(See money, wealth, stock.)

CAPITALISM
adjectives
regenerated; decadent; imperialistic; monopolist.

verbs
abuse—; attack—; base on—; berate—; condemn—; creep upon—; denounce—; deplore—; favor—; oppose—; overthrow—; prejudice against—; rebuild—; reform—; reject—; revive—; support—; vindicate—; —collapses; —concentrates; —evolves from; —exploits; —flourishes; —promotes; — possesses; —retards; —rules; —speeds up; — topples; —tyrannizes.

CAPITALIST
adjectives
foolish; old-style; hard-boiled; new-risen; timid; satanic; retired; world-famed; local; noted; universal; desirable; unregenerate; designing.

CAPITULATION
adjectives
dishonorable; unexpected; so-called; careful; generous.

162

CAPRICE

adjectives
cruel; revolting; monstrous; swift; boyish; accidental; magnificent; slightest; youthful; expensive; sudden; unaccountable; feminine; passing; innocent; common; irresistible.

verbs
act on—; depend on—; humor—; lead by—; leave to—; restrain—; subject to—; —determines; —fancies; —fixes; —forms; —governs; —guides; —turns.
(See whim, fancy, notion.)

CAPRICIOUS

adverbs
waywardly; whimsically; wantonly; playfully; captiously; unreasonably; amusingly; ridiculously; delightfully; irresistibly; strikingly; extravagantly; senselessly; humorously; cruelly; childishly; irresponsibly; unaccountably; girlishly; incorrigibly; intractably; curiously; foolishly; preposterously; nonsensically; drolly; comically.

CAPSULE

adjectives
compact; dehiscent; formidable; gelatine; handy; metallic; portable; soluble; transparent; unappetizing.

verbs
administer—; cover with—; dissolve—; dose with —s; enclose in—; form in—; heat—; medicate—; melt—; perforate—; seal in—; swallow—; —bursts; —contains; —cures; —envelops; —opens; —sheathes; —surrounds.
(See case.)

CAPTAIN

adjectives
turbulent; portly; doughty; gallant; dauntless; resourceful; inspiring; imperturbable; wily; bluff; honest; naval; brutal; steady; reliable; plump; rubicund; grave; calm; wigged; staff; blustering; youthful; sagacious; usurping; triumphant; modish; unwilling; unapproachable; senior; russet-coated; victorious; mutinous; self-sufficient; spectacular; valiant.

verbs
beseech—; betray—; commission—; commune with—; dread—; elect—; elevate to —; entreat—; promote to—; rank as—; raise to—; —assigns; —authorizes; —commands; —heads; —leads; —orders; —roars; —survives; —thunders; —upbraids.
(See leader, commander.)

CAPTIOUS

adverbs
disagreeably; offensively; irritatingly; needlessly; groundlessly; wilfully; unpleasantly; truculently; cantankerously; capriciously; whimsically; irresponsibly; provokingly; fitfully; contrarily; uncomfortably; excitably; petulantly; intolerably; unpardonably; irascibly; irritably; fretfully; inexplicably; fractiously; sarcastically; woefully.

CAPTIVE

adjectives
illustrious; beautiful; sullen-eyed; barbaric; slaughtered; hopeless; hapless; delighted; luckless; trapped; defenseless; willing; unhappy; devoted; cowardly; shamed; spent; princely; august.

verbs
acquit—; bind—; cage—; carry away—; chain—; deliver—; detain—; enslave; exchange —s; fetter—; free—; humble—; liberate—; mutilate—; restore—; slaughter —s; struggle with—; subdue—; take—; torture—.
(See prisoner.)

CAPTIVITY

adjectives
killing; limitless; perpetual; weakening; prolonged.

verbs
bring into—; cancel—; carry into—; counsel in—; dash into—; deliver from—; desolate in—; detain in—; dwell in—; enforce—; escape from—; feel—; hold in—; incarcerate in—; languish in—; lead into—; pine in—; resign to—; sell into—; shut in—; sink into —; subject to—; submit to—.
(See bondage, slavery.)

CAPTURE

adjectives
final; violent; rich; gallant; important; nefarious; imminent.

CAPTURE (v)

adverbs
triumphantly; previously; brilliantly; finally; violently; gallantly; nefariously; shrewdly; skillfully; dexterously; slyly; viciously; cruelly; wantonly.
(See apprehend, arrest, seize.)

CAR

adjectives
spectral; rheumatic; unobtrusive; high-

toned; high-priced; heavenly; short-lived; sumptuous; rushing; antiquated; magnificent; fast; refrigerator; private; outmoded; jangling; streamlined; swift; horse; electric; dull; faded; forward; triumphal; airborne; pellucid; impressive; frivolous; ill-smelling; clanging; luxurious; excellent; appointed; fine-looking; gay; resplendent; ancient; battered; touring; rattling; scraggly; ramshackle; decrepit; small; shabby; disreputable; armored; torpedo-shaped; queer; coffin-shaped; showy; motor; gaudy; rakish; spectral; death; twisted; crippled; expensive; charging; oncoming; hurtling; roaring; pursuing; departing; passing; jolting; bouncing; purring; lurching; brilliant; swinging; mud-splashed; full-length; close-parked; halted; gleaming; massive; roomy.

verbs
check—; convey in—; crowd—; crush beneath—; demolish—; draw—; fuel—; grease—; guide—; jaunt in—; load—; polish—; power—; proceed in—; ride in—; scramble from—; smash—; tow—; transport in—; tumble from—; wheel—; —backfires; —s collide; —s file by; —glides; —glistens; —groans; —hums; —purrs; —rattles; —serves; —skids; —skims; —speeds; —traverses; —whizzes by.
(See automobile.)

CAR
adjectives (railroad)
clanking; gliding; heavily-laden; obdurate; rattling; runaway; swaying; unmanned; unwieldy; weighty; trundling; creaking; brawling.

verbs
attach—; brake—; couple —s; derail—; design—; dispatch—; electrify—; equip—; gear—; haul—; hook on—; light—; load—; model—; number—; refrigerate—; shunt—; signal—; station—; streamline—; switch—; transport in—; —chugs along; —s collide; —rattles by; —rumbles past; —rusts.
(See coach.)

CARAVAN
adjectives
innumerable (pl); floating; assembled; angelic; formidable; long-winding; slow-crawling; trekking; vast; imposing; lonely; patriarchal; stately; sluggish.

verbs
arm—; attack—; burden—; convoy—; encounter—; engage—; equip—; guard—; guide—; halt—; head—; hire—; lead—;

route—; set upon—; tour in—; —assembles; —marches; —perishes; —sets forth; —starves; —travels; —traverses; —treks; —troops by; —wanders.
(See company, cart, wagon.)

CARAVANSARY
adjectives
frivolous; huge; pretentious; courtyard.

CARBOHYDRATES
adjectives
essential; tissue-building; fortifying; vital; woody.

verbs
analyze—; burn up—; characterize—; class as—; consist of—; consume—; contain—; depend on—; distribute—; form—; induce —; lack—; —benefit; —energize; —fuel; —occur in; —produce; —reveal; —serve as.
(See compound.)

CARBON
adjectives
amorphous; crystallized; free; elemental; ebon; smudgy; uncombined.

verbs
anaylze—; clean—; combine with—; compound with—; crystallize—; deposit—; filter with—; free—; give off—; illuminate —; produce—; reduce to—; —blackens; —condenses; —decolors; —joins with.
(See element.)

CARCASS
adjectives
bloodstained; bovine; flaccid; gross; swarming; fresh-bitten; floating; putrefying; snake-bitten; swollen; miserable; mutilated; handsome; lifeless; rascally; partly-devoured; warm; bleeding; frozen; corrupt; bloody.

verbs
bury—; cast out—; drape—; drop—; glut —; hide—; mutilate—; prostrate—; rend —; reveal—; scatter —s; suspend—; tear —; tread upon—; —decays; —decomposes; —disintegrates; —putrefies; —rots.
(See body, frame.)

CARD
adjectives (calling)
ill-judged; official; engraved; neatly-typed; attention-compelling.

CARD
adjectives (playing)
best; false; winning; shuffled; precious; worn; greasy; stacked.

verbs

arrange —s; box —s; cheat at —s; draw —; flash—; gather —s; introduce —s; mark —s; pack —s; perforate—; shuffle —s; stack —s; stake —s; stencil —s; throw up —s; trump—; wager on —s; —s allot; —designates; —slides; —slips; —warrants.

CARDINAL
(bird)

adjectives

brilliant-plumaged; crested; flitting; music-flooding; regal; scarlet-flashing; sun-reflecting; pine-homing.

verbs

cage—; tame—; —plumes; —whistles.
(See bird.)

CARE

adjectives

scientific; secret; degrading; unhappy; reverential; dull; business; public; sincere; harassing; artistic; dismal; ill-reputed; wasting; fastidious; considerate; domestic; humbler; stimulating; carping; patient; unquiet; paternal; medical; ministering; nice; meanest; gigantic; thoughtful; bounteous; sharp; fatherly; elaborate; watchful; timely; indefatigable; peculiar; jealous; anxious; cankering; institutional; painstaking; tender; sufficient; chary; honest; reverent; fearful; scrupulous; rankling; loving; never-ceasing; heavy; sleepless; grisly; meticulous; considerable; fostering; wrinkled; persistent; efficient; extreme; municipal; telltale; providential; sympathetic; ignoble; wearying; warlike; chief; overpowering; conscientious; earth-born; practical; untuned; unremitting; apparitional; scrutinizing; eating; arduous; fevered; conquered; alliterative; preventive; utmost; prodigious; perpetual; silent; commonplace; judicious; self-intrusted; mortal; same; knowing; vexing; heavy; particular; gnawing; magnificent; altruistic; reverent; pale; touching; loving; consumptive; excellent; shallow; pastoral; intrusive; daintiest; prudent; exaggerated; vigilant; infinite; special; unusual; foreboding; exacting; sinful; late; surgical; maternal; miserable; sheltering; sordid; rigid; pitying; colossal; intensive; queenly; distracting; peremptory; ancient; religious; studious; sedulous; solicitous; protective; hospitable; exquisite; admirable; tender; expert; rooted; squalid; searing; wrinkling; stern; ageless; minute; tireless; human; pressing; deliberate; visible; foolish; constant; inevitable; unctuous; inadequate; masterly; incessant; patriarchal.

verbs

abolish—; banish—; bend with—; bestow —upon; brood with—; charge with—of; choke with—; conduct with—; delegate—of; demand—; deride—; devote—to; discharge —s; disclaim—; drive away—; droop with —; drown—; dull with—; ease—; escape —; exempt from—; exercise—; foster with —; free from—; fret with—; harass with —; heal —s; intrust—of; kill —s; lavish— upon; lay aside—; lift —s; load with—; lose —s; merit—; observe—; oppress with —; overcome with—; perform with—; redouble—; relax—; release from—; rest from —; rout—; shake off—; share —s; soothe —s; sour with—; twist with—; unload —s; wash away—; waste with—; weigh down with—; wrack with—; wring with—; yoke with—; —ceases; —s chafe; —s consume; —s linger; —perplexes; —pursues; furrow with—.

(See concern, anxiety, worry, caution.)

CARE (*v*)

adverbs

particularly; hardly; assiduously; violently; chiefly; scientifically; reverentially; artistically; patiently; paternally; medically; bounteously; indefatigably; jealously; anxiously; painstakingly; tenderly; sufficiently; scrupulously; never-ceasingly; meticulously; efficiently; conscientiously; unremittingly; arduously; magnificently; providently; touchingly; prudently; exaggeratedly; surgically; maternally; religiously; studiously; sedulously; solicitously; hospitably; exquisitely; expertly; patriarchally; domestically.

(See worry.)

CAREER

adjectives

decent; brilliant; military; creative; sterile; medical; hard-working; subsequent; honorable; prosperous; notable; checkered; literary; wasted; remarkable; tremulous; serene; cinematic; philanthropic; ill-starred; unblemished; generous; victorious; adequate; kind; unsentimental; stormy; eventual; buoyant; editorial; distinguished; definite; uninterrupted; artistic; academical; parliamentary; changed; rough; terrible; desperate; horrible; riotous; laboring; dignified; forceful; wandering; martial; theatrical; inglorious; unwearied; conjugal; pale; rollicking; joyous; diplomatic; coarse; low; anti-social; recognized; remorseless; official; political; placid; dazzling; wild; agitated; tragic; unscrupulous; clerical; independent; legal; triumphant; mercantile; honest; professional; obscure; shameful; disastrous; unadvanced; unswerving; irresistible; journalistic; heavenly; active; normal; marvelous; termagant; bloody; picturesque; celibate; hapless; saintly; inspiring; fluctuating; celebrated; astonishing; story-book; startling; extraordinary; exceptional; amazing; incredible; meteoric; budding; illustrious; clean; vivid; noted; imposing; sensible; fine; assured; magnificent; promising; serious; versatile; invincible; famous; portentous; spectacular; dramatic; sensational; eventful; colorful; breathless; adventuresome; exciting; arduous; quick; tempestuous; mad; extravagant; challenging; tumultuous; controversial; erratic; servile; turbulent; disturbed; revolutionary; happy; rollicking; blithe; disappointing; lonely; hopeless; lively; active; busy; vicious; infamous; strange; tormented; brutal; enigmatic; seafaring; forensic; golfing; burdened; moneymaking; pleasurable; public; scholastic; college; peripatetic; discomforting; scientific; posthumous; brief; true; indecorous; sufficient; chosen; diverging; material; limited; glittering; fixed; fortuitous; penitential; subsequent; prone.

verbs
achieve—; aspire to—; blast—; carve out —; checker—; close—; commence—; crown —; date—; embark on—; embrace—; endanger—; enter upon—; enthrall by—; further—; jeopardize—; litter—; mar—; mark —; pursue—; renounce—; smash—; stunt —; terminate—; unfold—; wreck—.
(See achievement, course, life, profession.)

CAREFUL
adverbs
prudently; vigilantly; alertly; attentively; meticulously; extremely; particularly; intelligently; scrupulously; conscientiously; decorously; dutifully; obediently; admirably; thoughtfully; deliberately; ridiculously; significantly; comfortingly; considerately; warily; cautiously; absolutely; energetically; definitely; discreetly; wisely; singularly; strangely; sagac ously; expertly; nervously; unduly; characteristically; naturally; usually; laughably; uneasily; elaborately; unobtrusively; satisfactorily; exaggeratedly; habitually; fastidiously; solicitously; sedulously; unusually; infinitely; lovingly; prodigiously; indefatigably.

CARELESS
adverbs
inexcusably; nonchalantly; casually; gaily; airily; indecently; recklessly; wantonly;

vexatiously; irritatingly; amusingly; laughably; imprudently; indiscreetly; dangerously; perilously; significantly; noticeably; heedlessly; thoughtlessly; deliberately; indifferently; inconsiderately; unwarily; irresponsibly; absolutely; lazily; idly; unaccountably; inexplicably; impossibly; listlessly; languidly; defiantly; rebelliously; ostentatiously; flauntingly; stupidly.

CARELESSNESS
adjectives
aristocratic; criminal; elaborate; assumed; habitual; inveterate; idle; lovable; studied; superb; unpardonable; willful; culpable; deliberate.

verbs
berate—; breed—; condone—; countenance —; decry—; denounce—; inculcate—; inveigh against—; neglect in—; occasion—; punish—; regret—; resent—; utter in—; warn against—; wear an air of—; — disturbs; —worries.
(See neglect.)

CARESS
adjectives
condescending; complacent; fond; final; gentle; hasty; haughty; impulsive; impassioned; perfunctory; sympathetic; mesmeric; bitter-sweet; adolescent; dizzying; monotonous; turbulent; vicarious; exploratory; casual; mellowing; playful; sustained; infinite; indescribable; fierce; pussy-cat; rude; vague.

verbs
bestow —es on; cherish —es; countenance —es; delight in —es; encourage —es; favor with —es; fondle—; hunger for —es; intermix with —es; invite —es; long for —es; overwhelm with —es; ward off —; welcome —; —es allure; —es burn; —es cheer; —es endear; —es offend; —es soothe.
(See embrace, kiss, flattery.)

CARESS (v)
adverbs
endearingly; ecstatically; adoringly; sympathetically; warmly; lovingly; roughly; thrillingly; imploringly; affectionately; blissfully.
(See embrace, kiss, court.)

CAREWORN
adverbs
irritably; distressingly; intolerably; uncomfortably; dejectedly; sadly; anxiously; wretchedly; grievously; miserably; pitiably;

horribly; sorely; sorrily; heartbreakingly; unbearably; piteously; bitterly; dismally; hopelessly; unutterably; tragically; extremely; incredibly; gravely; outrageously; indescribably.

CARGO

adjectives
guarded; guilty; indifferent; precious; smuggled; surreptitious; undeclared; worthless.

verbs
burden with—; dampen—; discharge—; disinfect—; haul—; hoist—; import—; inspect —; insure—; land—; levy on—; load—; salvage—; ship—; tax—; transport—; underwrite—; —ballasts; —weighs.
(See freight, load, burden.)

CARNAL

adverbs
loosely; sensually; intemperately; luxuriously; voluptuously; grossly; shamelessly; wantonly; rakishly; bestially; erotically; indecently; self-indulgently; dissipatedly; intemperately; licentiously; coarsely; unbelievably; obscenely; evilly; sinfully; vilely; detestably; odiously.

CAROL

adjectives
gay; haunting; joyous; lively; merry; rustic; round; ancient; swelling; warbled.

verbs
bellow—; bless in—; burst into—; celebrate with —s; chorus—; compose—; dance to—; exercise—; flute—; hallow—; join in—; listen to —s; practise—; praise—; revive —; scream—; warble—; —cheers; —encourages; —expresses; —rings out; —sounds; —survives; —warms.
(See song, hymn.)

CAROUSE (v)

adverbs
hilariously; drunkenly; sordidly; squalidly; riotously; viciously; rollickingly; tumultuously; turbulently; wildly.
(See drink, celebrate.)

CARPENTER

adjectives
village; rare; retired; veteran.

verbs
employ—; hire—; —bevels; —chisels; —constructs; —designs; —frames; —hammers; —joins; —labors; —levels; —mea-sures; —molds; —mortises; —notches; —s organize; —pins; —rules; —sands; —saws; —smooths; —tenons; —tails; —wedges.
(See worker, workman.)

CARPET

adjectives
sumptuous; grassy; mossy; wind-woven; flaunty; matted; frayed; brilliant; swampy; varicolored; taupe; worn; dusty; odorous; dirty; heavy; gay; stair; soft; suspended; treacherous; patternless; fiber; deep-pile; thick; handsome; bright; eye-offending.

verbs
dance on—; design—; dust—; fringe—; kneel on—; litter—; market—; match—; patch—; prostrate on—; scour—; shampoo —; shred—; spread on—; strew on—; tack down—; warp—; weave—; —beautifies; —covers; —decorates; —protects; —shields; —slides.
(See fabric, rug.)

CARRIAGE
(manner)
adjectives
military; dashing; haughty; vigorous; graceful; violent; reckless; frank; toiling; unbending; indifferent; picturesque; internal; fierce; unpretentious; gentle; courteous; reverend; elegant; exquisite; superb; certain; sedate; fine; dignified; stately; soldierly; upright; erect; insolent; intelligent; swaggering; unwieldly; faulty; obstinate; headstrong; peculiar; sanctimonious.

CARRIAGE
(vehicle)
adjectives
imperial; rough; decent; elegant; horseless; lumbering; travelling; countless; handsome; heavy; painted; lurching; wooden-wheeled; ramshackle; musty; moldy; rickety.

verbs
bar—; burden—; dispatch—; draw—; fashion—; guard—; guide—; harness—; load—; ornament—; provide—; tow—; wheel out —; —accommodates; —bounces; —conveys; —jolts; —rattles; —rocks; —rolls; —rumbles; —sways; —transports; —winds its way.
(See car, vehicle, coach.)

CARRION

adjectives
foolish; unsavory; putrefied.

CARRY (v)

adverbs
imperfectly; occasionally; triumphantly;

habitually; surreptitiously; imperceptibly; valiantly; ultimately; infallibly; delicately; laboriously; unfalteringly; accommodatingly; unconsciously; jauntily; continuously; unanimously; infallibly; slavishly; penitently; ostentatiously.

(See convey, bear, transport.)

CART
adjectives
creaking; retreating; fatal; ungainly; heavy; laden; shabby; jaunty.

verbs
direct—; draw—; grease—; harness to—; harvest with—; license—; load—; mount —; operate—; peddle on—; pile in—; provide—; team—; traverse by—; wheel—; —clatters; —conveys; —creaks; —jolts; —looms; —pitches; —progresses; —rumbles; —wheels.

(See vehicle, truck.)

CARTOON
adjectives
animated; completed; contemporary; much-remarked.

CARTOON (*v*)
adverbs
derisively; animatedly; sarcastically; satirically; diplomatically; viciously; humorously; blisteringly.

(See picture, design.)

CARTOONIST
adjectives
ribald; clever.

verbs
—attacks; —caricatures; —characterizes; —colors; —conceives; —contributes; —copies; —crystallizes; —denotes; —designs; —distorts; —draws; —engages in; —exaggerates; —executes; —illustrates; —implies; —indulges in; —irritates; —lampoons; —misrepresents; —mocks; —offends; —prints; —qualifies; —represents; —sets forth; —supplies; —sways; —wields.

(See artist.)

CARTRIDGE
adjectives
blank; buck-shot; cylindrical; deadly; highly-charged; inflammable; trusty; hoarded.

verbs
arm with —s; belt —s; box —s; case —s; distribute —s; fit—; form into—; ignite—; insert—; load with—; provide—; replenish —s; shape—; store—; —bursts; —detonates; —explodes; —penetrates.

CARVE (*v*)
adverbs
curiously; richly; marvelously; elaborately; skillfully; exquisitely; delicately; ornately; cunningly; ingeniously; fantastically; medievally; wearily.

(See sculpture, engrave, fashion.)

CARVING
adjectives
elaborate; fantastic; relief; grotesque; intricate; salvaged; weatherworn; delicate; splendid; flat; ornamental; hand; exquisite; artistic; ill-favored; medieval.

verbs
adorn with—; auction off—; destroy—; discover—; display—; embellish with—; exhibit—; fret with—; ornament with—; skill in—; unearth—; —hardens; —lasts; —illustrates.

(See sculpture, art.)

CASCADE
adjectives
foaming; perpetual; shimmering; feathery; pearly; motionless; veritable; gushing; showy; dazzling; musical; enthusiastic; blonde; roaring; tossing; magnificent.

verbs
lose in—; surmount—; sweep over—; —churns; —descends; —erodes; —falls; —foams; —pours over; —roars; —rumbles; —thunders.

(See waterfall.)

CASCADE (*v*)
adverbs
sibilantly; foamingly; perpetually; shimmeringly; gushingly; dazzlingly; roaringly; magnificently; awesomely; spectacularly.

CASE
adjectives (box)
huge; packing; worn; oblong; odd-shaped; platinum; ponderous; concrete; jeweled; venerable-looking; tarnished.

verbs
buckle on—; ease—; frame in—; loose—; peel off—; strap on—; strip off—; unclasp —; —covers; —protects; —shields.

(See sheath, box, chest.)

CASE
adjectives (legal term)
arguable; trying; contested; noted; curious; pending; simple; celebrated; criminal; collateral; disputed; brilliant; trivial; hope-

less; analogous; unaccountable; hardened; pathetic; exceptional; idiopathic; inexplicable; celebrated; pressing.

verbs
advise upon—; assign to—; bring—to trial; clinch—; conduct—; confer on—; contend with—; dispose of—; expedite—; fashion—; frame—; handle—; injure—; judge—; peruse—; plead—; prejudice—; present—; prove—; recount—; rest—; reverse—; review—; support—; sway—; testify in—; try —; unravel—; —hangs fire; —proves.

CASE

adjectives (medical term)
virulent; incurable; chronic; grave; critical; abnormal; dangerous; surgical.

verbs
cure—; diagnose—; encounter—; improve —; isolate—; protract—; relieve—; remedy —; succumb to—; treat—; —occurs; —recovers; —yields.

(See disease.)

CASE

adjectives (situation)
flattering; excellent; exceptional; important; striking; clear; conspicuous; rare; factual; difficult; intricate; severe; complicated; overwhelming; diverse; notable; eminent; necessitous; simplified; weird; inevitable; outrageous; analagous; stubborn; notorious; absurd; inevitable; insoluble; unpardonable; convincing; speculative; twisted; discussed; common; definite; desperate; recent; important; laughable; isolated; sole; parlous; pathetic; extreme; unforeseen; aggravated; deceptive; illustrative; lamentable; specific; evident; authentic; perplexing; superfluous; blessed; parallel; handsome; falsified; battle-scarred; imaginary; unrecognized; well-prepared; remarkable; mournful; special; pitiful; innumerable (pl); supposititious; sporadic; selective (pl); extraordinary; meritorious; multifarious (pl).

CASEMENT

adjectives
clasping; ivied; shaded; rattling; glimmering; ill-shut; oriel; wide; magic.

CASH

adjectives
evanescent; ample; pitiless; unquestionable;

predatory; leaking; safe; cold; ambrosial; immediate.

verbs
amass—; appropriate—; check—; convert into—; demand—; discount for—; forward —; guard—; hoard—; involve—; register —; release—; secure—; transact with—; turn into—; —circulates; —flows through; —pours in.

(See coin, currency, money.)

CASKET

adjectives
precious; handsome; bronze; wrought; imposing; leaden; contrary; inlaid; glorious; draped; guiltless; scaly.

verbs
bank—; bless—; cache—; conceal—; decorate—; discover—; encrust—with; enrich— with; entrust—to; file past—; inter in—; lay in—; lower—; mourn at—; penetrate ; rob ; unearth—; unlock—, value—, —reveals.

(See box, chest, coffin.)

CAST

adjectives (drama)
capable; supporting; remarkable; insignificant; mythical; revengeful; fiery; fantastic; medieval; morbid; heterogeneous; desperate; undramatic; frivolous; stony.

verbs
allot to—; annoy—; applaud—; assemble —; assign to—; bestow on—; bring together —; choose—; coach—; congratulate—; direct—; dismiss—; dominate—; introduce—; manipulate—; provide—; recruit—; ruffle —; scan—; select—; train—; try out for—; —bows; —disbands; —impresses; —justifies; —mutilates; —performs; —produces; —rehearses; —renders.

(See actors.)

CAST

adjectives (glance)
pensive; pinkish; determined; wistful; meditative; wonted; somber; pale; mirthful; changeful.

CAST (v)

adverbs
rashly; humbly; weakly; demurely; bluntly; pensively; determinedly; wistfully; meditatively; somberly; mirthfully.

(See hurl, throw, fling.)

CASTANETS

adjectives
clicking; distant; jittering; rhythmic; noisy.

CASTAWAY

adjectives

lonely; assembled (pl); starving; lean; cadaverous; despairing; frantic; gaunt.

CASTE

adjectives

learned; distinct; priestly; inconvenient; sacerdotal; perpetual; ethic; transparent; time-honored.

verbs

ally with—; define—; distinguish—; forfeit —; form—; found—; isolate—; loathe—; organize—; preside over—; privilege—; qualify for—; restrict—; revile—; unite—; weld—; —aggregates; —collects; —confines to; —excludes; —groups; —practices; — inhabits; —resembles; —serves; —succumbs.
(See class, rank.)

CASTIGATION

adjectives

heartening; malicious; soul-deadening; deserved.

CASTLE

adjectives

ruined; haughty; baronial; ancient; Moorish; huge; grim; serviceable; razed; shimmering; inconvenient; ancestral; dream; medieval; moated; fairy; grandiose; princely; formidable; bastioned; ruined; cloud; stuccoed; enchanted; moldering; stupendous.

verbs

abide in—; assail—; bar—; besiege—; dominate—; dwell in—; fly to—; force—; ransack—; sack—; storm—; undermine—; —crumbles; —decays; —quakes; —shadows; —topples; —yields.
(See fortress, stronghold, mansion, building.)

CASTOR OIL

adjectives

disgusting; disguised; healing; malignant; nauseating; stomach-turning; skillfully-administered; repulsive; viscous.

verbs

administer— —; capsule— —; decoct— —; dose with— —; employ— —; express— —; inject— —; — —aggravates; — —cleans; — —induces; — —loosens; — —lubricates; — —nauseates; — —purges; — —relieves.
(See oil.)

CASUAL

adverbs

charmingly; nonchalantly; habitually; coolly; presumably; indeterminately; usually; provokingly; vexatiously; vaguely; perplexingly; unfortunately; undoubtedly; absolutely; positively; heartbreakingly; insufferably; intolerably.

CASUALNESS

adjectives

charming; practiced; hushed; lacerating; easy.

CASUALTY

adjectives

unforeseen; distressing; unlooked-for.

CAT

adjectives

clawing; long; tawny; enigmatic; gaunt; watchful; two-faced; ubiquitous; stray; sleek; despicable; huge; Persian; sinuous; predatory; singed; staid; spitting; plump; slinking; suspicious; cold; slow-witted; round-eyed; mewing; quick; harmless; contented; calculating; tiger; musing; lemon; sheltered; homeless; foiled; prudent.

verbs

pet—; stroke—; —arches; —claws; — climbs; —clutches; —darts; —devours; — laps; —leaps; —licks; —meows; —paws; — purrs; —preys on; —slinks; —sniffs; — sprawls; —springs; —washes.
(See animal, kitten.)

CATACOMB

adjectives

vaulted; literary; secret; large.

CATALOGUE

adjectives

descriptive; endless; illustrated; dry; melancholy; amplest; technical; diabolical; wearying; complete; seasonal; beautiful.

verbs

choose from—; clarify—; compile—; edit—; enter in—; index—; insert in—; issue—; list in—; order from—; prepare—; print —; publish—; set up—; —advertises; — confuses; —describes; —enumerates; —explains; —fascinates; —features; —lists; — offers; —pictures; —prices; —registers; — systematizes.
(See list, record.)

CATAPULT

adjectives

deadly; powerful; regulated; vicious; well-aimed.

verbs

discharge—; draw—; fire—; gear—; invent—; lay siege with —s; manipulate—; release—; storm with —s; —batters; —bombards; —damages; —harms; —hurls; —overcomes; —propels; —stones.
    (See cannon.)

CATARACT

adjectives

shining; superb; sounding; roaring; earthquaking; fiery; remorseless; smoky; pouring; opaque; tireless; foaming.

verbs

lose in—; spout —s; stem—; view—; —churns; —crashes; —dashes down; —descends; —falls; —flashes; —foams; —leaps; —pours over; —precipitates, —roars; —rumbles; —rushes over; —surges; —sweeps down; —wears away.
    (See waterfall, flood, cascade.)

CATASTROPHE

adjectives

tremendous; awful; imminent; historical; welcome; dire; impending; tragic; inevitable; general; calamitous; world-wide; ironical; picturesque; national; unexpected; crowning; unavertable; overwhelming; breath-taking; dreadful; unforeseen.

verbs

avert—; culminate in—; experience—; inflict with—; mourn—; plunge into—; result in—; rush to—; suffer—; survive—; —distresses; —looms; —overwhelms; —shocks; —threatens.
    (See disaster, misfortune.)

CATASTROPHIC

adverbs

tragically; unmitigatedly; disastrously; extremely; ruinously; ominously; significantly; appallingly; deplorably; staggeringly; unspeakably; extraordinarily; shockingly; absolutely; unfortunately; unluckily; calamitously; incredibly; gravely; direly.

CATCH

adjectives

meager; passionate; little; obstinate; remarkable; maximum; uncommon; attractive.

CATCH

adjectives   (fishing)

boasted; briny; exaggerated; gleaming; meager; modest; silvery; scaly; thrilling; traditional.

verbs

acquire—; bait—; devour—; display—; ensnare—; exhibit—; lure—; market—; net —; prepare—; prize—; relish—; scale—; transport—; value—; —amazes; —disappoints; —impresses; —increases.

CATCH (v)

adverbs

unceremoniously; impulsively; instinctively; convulsively; mechanically; red-handedly; charmingly; inadvertently; essentially; unerringly; passionately; obstinately; remarkably.
    (See seize, clasp, clutch.)

CATCHER

adjectives   (baseball)

adroit; alert; courageous; clumsy; befuddled; dependable; fumbling; unpredictable.

verbs

—blocks; —covers; —encourages; —fumbles; —misses; —muffs; —recovers; —signals; —steadies; —tags.

CATCHING

adverbs

highly; easily; dangerously; epidemically; pestilentially; unfortunately; acutely; widely; perilously; seriously; extremely; decidedly; unquestionably; astonishingly; frightfully; absolutely; remarkably; alarmingly; curiously; awfully; critically; definitely; fatally; positively.

CATCHY

adverbs

irresistibly; sweetly; indefinably; mysteriously; luckily; unutterably; powerfully; singularly; charmingly; engagingly; undeniably; bewitchingly; enchantingly; delightfully; daintily; smartly; jauntily; youthfully; tormentingly; teasingly; hauntingly; unexpectedly; surprisingly; genuinely; miraculously; luckily; unprecedentedly.

CATEGORICAL

adverbs

positively; undeniably; avowedly; broadly; certainly; emphatically; explicitly; formally; markedly; peremptorily; solemnly; reliably; authentically; axiomatically; evidently; manifestly; undoubtedly; indisputably;

irrefutably; solidly; soundly; unmistakably; uncomfortably; conclusively; gratefully; cheeringly; disturbingly; dogmatically.

CATEGORY
adjectives
amiable; poetic; astonishing; definite; separate; neat; depressing; reasonable; odious; scholastic.

verbs
add to—; bring into—; disagree with—; discard—; exclude from—; express in—; group in—; interest in—; list in—; recognize—; reduce to—; regard—; relegate to —; understand—; upset—; —consists of; —deals with; —derives from; —differs from; —includes; —represents.
(See class, division, condition, predicament.)

CATER (v)
adverbs
exclusively; delectably; democratically; professionally; amiably; commonly; stealthily; unaccountably.
(See provide, supply, furnish.)

CATERPILLAR
adjectives
bristly; evil-horned; fuzzy; harmless; inching; plushy; sojourning; whither-bent.

verbs
combat —s; cultivate —s; examine—; exterminate—; infest with —s; observe—; spray —s; teem with —s; —s abound; —s attack; —s bore into; —s collect; —crawls; —despoils; —devours; —emerges; —s gather; —hibernates; —s invade; —s molt; —s ravage; —secretes; —spins a cocoon.
(See insect.)

CATHEDRAL
adjectives
Gothic; Doric; staid; sleepy; dim; mystic; peaceful; medieval; miniature; quaint; magnificent; majestic; unfinished; elaborate; spacious; Roman.

verbs
approach—; congregate in—; construct—; design—; erect—; explore—; found—; glorv in—; hallow—; install in—; preside over —; pour from—; raise—; revere—; worship at—; —awes; —echoes; —impresses; —induces; —inspires; —looms; —shadows; —towers.
(See church, tabernacle.)

CATHOLIC
adverbs (general sense)
broadly; comprehensively; unusually; prevalently; magnanimously; remarkably; liberally; comfortably; generally; decently; sagaciously; intelligently; admirably; reasonably; generously; dependably; charitably; intellectually; discerningly; perceptively; obviously; manifestly; nobly; unselfishly.

CATTLE
adjectives
blooded; grazing; crazed; unkempt; roving; peaceful; scraggy; weak; driven; fine; drowsy; stolen; bedded; wild; long-horned; bartered; mottled; reclining; tainted; lazy; sweltered; murrained; domesticated; meanest; draught; thin.

verbs
corral—; dehorn—; exchange for—; infect —; market—; raise—; slaughter—; stampede—; tend—; tether—; —bellow; —freeze; —graze; —huddle; —low; —pasture; —plod; —roam; —stagger.
(See animal.)

CAUSATION
adjectives
natural; eternal; inevitable.

CAUSE
adjectives (agent or reason)
abundant; scattered (pl); obnoxious; specific; proximate; predisposing; pressing; apparent; fundamental; hopeless; unavoidable; immediate; prolific; duplicating; rational; dreadful; effective; underlying; mighty; noble; just; sacred; worthy; legitimate; endless; redeeming; supernatural; spectacular; apparent; assignable; faltering; secondary; physical; universal; growing; innocent; predominant; remote; unknown; scandalous; sensational; plausible; permanent; transient; fatal; potential; weighty; assignable; prominent; internal; erroneous; contributory; subjective; temperance; amorous; glorious; breaking; eternal; ultimate; paramount; unconscious; frequent; princely; philosophical; natural; mistaken; malignant; alleged; latent; discreditable; recorded; celebrated; sordid; economic; primeval; mitigating; constitutional; sensible; ennobling; determining; mechanical; infallible; propelling; hated; secondary; obvious; habitual; minute; idiotic; antecedent; justifiable; primal; creative; irritating; efficient; unkind; notable; unwitting; extraneous; lawful; unaccountable; identical; ex-

citing; worthy; immoral; functional; vanquished; multifarious (pl); impious; trivial; sublunary; artificial; ridiculous; everlasting; similar; righteous.

verbs

acquaint with—; advance—; allege—; appraise—; approach—; ascertain—; ascribe —to; assign—; attach—; attribute—to; concern with—; cure—; deal with—; debate—; declare—; define—; demonstrate—; determine—; discover—; display—; dwell upon —; eliminate—; eradicate—; estimate—; explain—; fathom—; inquire into—; judge —; laugh at—; obliterate—; obviate—; overcome—; perceive—; procure—; regard —; relieve—; remand—; remove—; report —; reveal—; reverse—; rue—; seek—; serve as—; state—; strike at—; suggest—; surmise—; suspect—; trace—to; weigh—; —prevails; —resides in.

(See reason, motive, source, origin.)

CAUSE

adjectives (aim, principle, movement)
adopted; alien; championed; espoused; glorious; lost; noble; sacred; undying.

verbs

adopt—; advocate—; approve—; betray—; bolster—; bow to—; champion—; cleave to —; contribute to—; defame—; desert—; devote to—; die for—; do ill to—; embrace —; encourage—; engage in—; enlist in—; espouse—; favor—; forsake—; further—; guide—; harm—; injure—; interpret—; justify—; labor for—; maintain—; misinterpret—; pay tribute to—; persecute—; plead—; praise—; promote—; rally to—; scorn—; serve—; speak for—; sponsor—; spurn—; struggle for—; suffer for—; sunder—; support—; transgress—; tread—under foot; unbraid—; vindicate—; withdraw from—; —perishes; —prospers; —suffers; —triumphs.

(See aim, principle, movement.)

CAUSE (v)

adverbs

inadvertently; noxiously; specifically; fundamentally; apparently; unavoidably; rationally; legitimately; supernaturally; spectacularly; physically; universally; predominantly; fatally; potentially; subjectively; eternally; ultimately; philosophically; malignantly; allegedly; mechanically; infallibly; unaccountably; artificially; righteously.

(See induce, effect.)

CAUSTIC

adverbs

bitterly; unpardonably; unreasonably; mildly; maliciously; hatefully; sharply; acrimoniously; cruelly; brutally; atrociously; resentfully; venomously; ominously; needlessly; incisively; sarcastically; ironically; cunningly; mercilessly; churlishly; unsparingly; perversely; abusively; uncivilly; intolerably; captiously; obnoxiously; unbearably; tauntingly; unwisely; malevolently; unwontedly; habitually; unwarrantably; disagreeably; unpleasantly.

CAUTION

adjectives

superfluous; common; vast; habitual; infinite; singular; subtle; inborn; abominable; timid; commendable; puerile; conscientious; wonted; just; extraordinary; prudent; preliminary; unholy; philosophic; extreme; losing; intended; vigilant; necessary; worldly; superior; redoubled, stealthy; reverent; niggardly; beneficent; utmost; curious; patriotic; friendless.

verbs

advise—; deaden—; exercise—; heed—; indicate—; inspire—; lessen—; motivate by —; necessitate—; perform with—; proceed with—; sound a note of—; throw—to the winds; —safeguards; —wanes.

(See prudence, care.)

CAUTIOUS

adverbs

discreetly; prudently; wisely; significantly; ludicrously; suspiciously; habitually; singularly; unnecessarily; timidly; extraordinarily; alertly; stealthily; curiously; strangely; oddly; outlandishly; sagaciously; expertly; deftly; foolishly; unwontedly; nervously; excitedly; idiotically; incomprehensibly; queerly; cravenly; faintheartedly; genuinely; unduly; inexplicably; laughably; characteristically; gravely; uneasily; extravagantly; elaborately; quietly; unobtrusively; undoubtedly; inherently.

CAVALCADE

adjectives

straggling; grim; martial; scampering; gorgeous; furbished; infinite; brilliant; large.

CAVALIER

adjectives

attentive; boyish; tall; gallant; bold; comely; free; sprightly; deformed; stout-hearted; effeminate; high-spirited; trusty; plumed; pretentious; victorious; arrogant; broken-down; gay; impecunious.

CAVALRY

adjectives

bedizened; best-mounted; thundering; foaming; dismounted; exploiting; dashing; irregular.

CAVE

adjectives

lonely; lovely; moonlit; dark; damp; stalactite; virtual; glistening; unexplored; enormous; ice; magical; winding; abandoned; unlighted; shore-cliff; fretted; destined; toothless; coral; forlorn; shadowy; unfathomed; tiny; deep; cold; yawning; unimagined; sapphire; vaulted; low-browed; monstrous; dewy; gloomy; spacious; coastal.

verbs

abandon—; bar—; block—; bury in—; crawl into—; creep into—; discover—; dwell in —; grope in—; harbor in—; inhabit—; issue from—; lodge in—; retire to—; roll from—; scoop out—; seal—; shelter in—; —echoes; —resounds.
(See hole, recess.)

CAVERN

adjectives

fairy-like; verdurous; dark; beautiful; marvelous; mysterious; ghostly; enormous; notchy; desolate; crystal; unfathomed; smudged; obscure; glaucous; horrid; smoky; dusky; ominous; spacious; tongueless; rifted; sparry; precipitous; gloomy; gelid; mossy; inaccessible; scorched; murmuring.

CAVERNOUS

adverbs

darkly; dimly; vastly; mysteriously; alluringly; deeply; dangerously; alarmingly; irresistibly; fantastically; gloomily; obscurely; duskily; murkily; sombrely; astonishingly; marvellously; frighteningly; indistinctly; strangely; terribly; hideously; formidably; awfully.

CAVITY

adjectives

dark; dungeon-like; hideous; conical.

verbs

cap—; dilate—; drain—; drill—; empty—; fill—; grind—; irrigate—; line—; obliterate —; tap—; treat—; —contains; —weakens.
(See hole, cave, hollow, excavation.)

CAVORT (v)

adverbs

blithely; friskily; gaily; spiritedly; joyously; sportively; grotesquely; gracefully; idiotically; pleasingly.

CEASE (v)

adverbs

functionally; abruptly; presently; suddenly; definitely; temporarily; prematurely; entirely; eventually.
(See discontinue, stop, refrain.)

CEDAR

adjectives

spicy; stunted; gray-sheathed; pyramiding; tall; slim; fantastic; distorted; stately; lordly; vast; majestic; somnolent; dark; mighty; drooping.

CEDE (v)

adverbs

superfluously; entirely; willingly; temporarily; outwardly; prematurely; partially.
(See surrender, relinquish, grant.)

CEILING

adjectives

beamed; frescoed; gorgeous; lofty; gilded; festooned; clouded; vault-like; fallen; damp; stained; crumbling; grimy; dirty; arched; slanting; sagging; dingy; domelike; moulded; ornamented; pictured; sloped; mirrored; reflecting.

CELEBRATE (v)

adverbs

hilariously; painfully; pompously; traditionally; obstreperously; appropriately; dissolutely; justly; discreetly; jubilantly; enthusiastically; dramatically; elaborately; barbarously; deliberately; raucously; gorgeously; nationally.
(See commemorate, observe.)

CELEBRATED

adverbs

locally; justly; universally; eminently; notably; illustriously; nationally; genuinely; rightfully; appropriately; brilliantly; remarkably; exceptionally; fitly; especially; particularly.

CELEBRATION

adjectives

discreet; jubilant; enthusiastic; centenary; forthcoming; final; dramatic; flourished; bicentenary; misconstrued; elaborate; decennial; gaudy; monster; roaring; barbarous; deliberate; raucous; gory; gorgeous.

verbs
arrange for—; climax—; deserve—; disturb
—; enter—; extol—; fete with—; hold—;
indulge in—; launch—; observe—; plan—;
retain—; —commemorates; —exhausts; —
honors; —overjoys; —surprises.
(See observance.)

CELEBRITY

adjectives
half-forgotten; rare; permanent; cosmopolitan; revered; glittering; dead; contemporary; available; innumerable (pl);
continental; immediate; literary; envious;
frustrated; fastidious; world-wide; posthumous.

CELERITY

adjectives
swift; amazing; deft; surprising; indescribable; dramatic; magical; characteristic;
reckless; miraculous; incredible; rounded;
admirable; ingenious

CELERY

adjectives
crunchy; crisp; green; curled.

CELL

adjectives
fungal; transition; sylvan; poor; mossy;
dermal; reflective; solitary; overcrowded;
photo-electric; filthy; drafty; narrow; tiny;
whitewashed; dingy; cement-floored; steel;
quiet; dreary; dismal; naked; cloistered;
eremitic; waxen; monastic; longitudinal;
convent; inmost; uncouth; unused; ambrosial; functional; albumenoid; wretched;
semi-transparent; prophetic; gloomy; uncomfortable; wind-rocked; message-sending;
tender; solemn; primordial; dungeon-like.

verbs
bind in—; brood in—; cloister in—; confine
in—; dwell in—; ensconce in—; force—;
gain—; imprison in—; lodge in—; pour
from—; range in—; remand to—; retire to
—; share—; store in—; track to—.
(See room, cavity, chamber.)

CELL

adjectives (biological)
amoebic; detached; enlarged; enemy; floating; gelatinous; malignant; normal; structural.

verbs
build —s; destroy —s; feed —s; motivate
—s; nourish —s; protect —s; regenerate
—s; renew —s; stimulate—; —s adhere to;

—s degenerate; —fulfills; —s increase; —s
multiply; —s perform; —shrivels; —specializes; —s store; —s work.
(See unit, compartment, blood.)

CELLAR

adjectives
dark; reeking; damp; fire-stopped; verminous; spacious; nether; dry; shallow; rat-
infested.

verbs
carpet—; convert—; cool in—; dampen—;
descend to—; drain—; emerge from—; enter by—; flood—; grope in—; inhabit—;
illumine—; lodge in—; stock in—; store in
—; —conceals; —extends.
(See basement, vault, room.)

CELLULOID

adjectives
brittle; explosive; flimsy; highly-inflam
mable; inexpensive; pretentious; shining;
showy.

verbs
compose of—; derive from—; employ—; encase in—; manufacture—; mould—; polish
—; press—; season—; shape—; stain—;
turn—; utilize—; —covers; —cracks; —
imitates; —protects; —serves as; —shields;
—shrivels.
(See material.)

CEMENT

adjectives
crack-proof; grayish; impenetrable; marble;
plastic; protecting; resisting; tested; unyielding.

verbs
apply—; blast—; bore into—; calcine—;
coat with—; compact—; compound—; crush
—; grind—; lay—; mix—; slake—; surface
with—; —adheres; —binds; —clinkers; —
crumbles; —dehydrates; —glues; —hardens;
—secures; —sets; —solidifies; —walls in.
(See mortar, plaster.)

CEMENT (*v*)

adverbs
firmly; securely; fixedly; perpetually; eternally; enduringly; permanently.
(See join, fasten.)

CEMETERY

adjectives
walled; tiny; bleak; dismal; weed-grown;
desolate; neighboring; pauper.

CENSER

adjectives
floral; coveted; gilded; flame-like; smoking.

CENSOR

adjectives
royal; strict; sternest; formidable; official; prejudiced; incompetent.

verbs
assign to—; elect—; escape —s; moderate for —s; offend —s; submit to —s; —approves; —bans; —bars; —blames; —clamps down; —condemns; —criticizes; —cuts out; —examines; —exercises; —guards; —grants; —inquires; —inspects; —investigates; —judges; —preserves; —prohibits; —reviews; —slashes; —supervises; —torments.
(See critic.)

CENSORIOUS

adverbs
sharply; mercilessly; ominously; destructively; needlessly; venomously; invidiously; viciously; unsparingly; churlishly; snappishly; obnoxiously; unpleasantly; disagreeably; remorselessly; relentlessly; dryly; roughly; rudely; cleverly; spitefully; sarcastically; maliciously; malevolently; bitterly; ruthlessly; uncompromisingly.

CENSORSHIP

adjectives
moralistic; strict; recent; rigid; vague; effective; religious; powerful; insidious; official; actual; iron; voluntary; rigorous.

verbs
announce—; clamp down—; concoct—; enforce—; establish—; exercise—; impose—; indicate—; institute—; pass—; practise—; submit to—; tighten—; —cuts; —militates; —outlaws; —prevails; —slashes; —supervises; —suppresses.
(See superintendence, revision, criticism, censure.)

CENSURABLE

adverbs
seriously; unquestionably; exceptionally; lamentably; deplorably; deservedly; justly; avowedly; properly; strictly; fairly; unfortunately; unhappily; unluckily; obviously; manifestly; plainly; conspicuously; grievously.

CENSURE

adjectives
moral; heavy-handed; violent; declamatory; implicit; critical; reluctant; ecclesiastical; perpetual; just; erroneous; undeserved; awful; lewd; implied.

verbs
avoid—; cringe under—; endure—; escape —; incur—; smart under—; wag one's tongue in—; —abates; —looms; —repels; —threatens.
(See blame, disapproval, criticism, revision, censorship.)

CENSURE (v)

adverbs
morally; violently; critically; reluctantly; ecclesiastically; perpetually; undeservedly; impliedly; scornfully; gravely; captiously; freely; scathingly.
(See reprove, rebuke, upbraid.)

CENSUS

adjectives
national; biennial; previous; rough; partial.

CENTER

adjectives
musical; inspiring; nervous; spiritual; cultural; permanent; intellectual; exclusive; allied; important; residential; veritable; principal; information; overpopulated; dead; banking; distributing; key; trading; financial; industrial; bustling; civic; business; urban; railroad; unique; metropolitan; important; steamship; legislative; exact; religious; commercial; smart; creative; harmonious; congested; prosperous; subtle; dazzling; storm; enlightened; fashionable; remote; accessible; strategic; tessellated; eternal; relative.

verbs
balance at—; collect at—; converge toward —; diffuse from—; draw to—; emerge from —; fall toward—; form in—; gravitate toward—; group in—; intersect at—; move toward—; occupy—; proceed from—; radiate from—; revolve around—; root in—; throw off—.
(See middle.)

CENTRAL

adverbs
conveniently; acceptably; appropriately; diplomatically; advantageously; exactly; comfortably; satisfactorily; relatively; approximately; strategically; practically.

CENTRALIZATION

adjectives
elaborate; rigorous; bureaucratic; political; absorbing; hierarchical.

CENTURY

adjectives
populous; modern; countless (pl); tempestuous; romantic; untold; preceding; myriad (pl); glorious; previous; unborn; hoary; present; noiseless; stormy; arduous; brilliant; successive (pl); amusing; senile.

verbs
endure for —ies; fade into —ies; gild—; measure in —ies; span —ies; roll into—; — abounds in; —creeps past; —draws to an end; —elapses; —unwinds.

CEREAL

adjectives
nourishing; tempting; whole-grain; steaming; golden-wheat; farinaceous.

verbs
bleach—; combine—with; consume—; cultivate—; diet on—; exploit—; moisten—; prepare—; produce—; refine—; steam—; sweeten—; —comprises; —flourishes; —furnishes; —nourishes; —provides; —stimulates; —strengthens; —supplies.
   (See grain.)

CEREBRUM

adjectives
divided; convalescent; convoluted; boiling; membrane-wrapped; throbbing; overlapping.

verbs
affect—; injure—; penetrate to—; —compacts; —comprises; —consists of; —controls; —files away; —forms; —is divided into; —is enveloped in; —presides over; —occupies; —overlaps; —regulates.
   (See brain.)

CEREMONIAL

adjectives
voodoo; elaborate; fitting; impressive; quaint; stately; insignificant; rich; tiresome; pompous; compulsive; enormous; insulting; cumbrous; wailing; magnificent; frivolous; burdensome; overpowering; curious.

CEREMONIOUS

adverbs
admirably; devoutly; elaborately; meticulously; punctiliously; appropriately; highly; decorously; reverently; traditionally; properly; conventionally; magnificently; splendidly; royally; barbarically; impeccably; reverentially; beautifully; irreproachably; majestically; extravagantly; wondrously; superbly.

CEREMONY

adjectives
preparatory; customary; lawful; scant; whimsical; decent; curious; fetish-like; a-nointing; approaching; diabolical; bloody; dedicatory; solemn; picturesque; ancient; hazardous; occult; impressive; religious; elaborate; tedious; appalling; venerable; appropriate; outrageous; stately; somber; reverent; enforced; time-consecrated; incongruous; peculiar; inauguration; imposing; formal; august; notable; gracious; futile; melancholy; fantastic; colorful; calm; dignified; punctilious; grim; savage; icy; painful; superstitious; primitive; undue; funeral; final; outward; ritualistic; appointed.

verbs
beautify—; bore with—; endure—; enrich —; observe—; officiate at—; preserve—; ritualize—; shorten—; stand on—; wed with —; —commemorates; —drags; —entails; —honors; —ruffles.
   (See rite, form, solemnity, formality, sacrament.)

CERTAIN

adverbs
actually; definitely; positively; absolutely; undeniably; assuredly; solidly; substantially; decisively; categorically; incontestably; irrefutably; conclusively; officially; plainly; indisputably; acceptably; unfortunately; unhappily; fortunately; luckily; humiliatingly; terribly; reasonably; comfortably; authoritatively.

CERTAINTY

adjectives
absolute; inevitable; old; humiliating; terrible; established; polite; painful; perfect; ultimate; unbreakable; considerable; simple; comfortable; practical; swift; astounding; reasonable; atrocious; dark; inevitable; instant; instinctive; automatic; positive; boyish; monumental; fierce; unerring; dead; towering.

verbs
accept as—; authenticate—; be born of—; confirm—; demonstrate with—; destroy—; inform of—; neglect—; postulate as—; ques-

177

tion—; surrender to—; venture on—; verge on—; —relieves; —satisfies.

(See confidence, assurance, conviction, fact, truth.)

CERTIFICATE

adjectives
gilded; original; engraved; baptismal; round; marriage; laudatory; authenticated; sales.

verbs
attest by—; bear—; collect —s; confirm—; counterfeit—; dispense—s; esteem—; forge —; furnish with—; garner—s; issue—; register—; revoke—; seal—; suspend—; witness—; —assures; —authorizes; —certifies; —guarantees; —licenses; —restricts; — specifies; —testifies.

(See declaration, document, testimony.)

CERTITUDE

adjectives
reasonable; fresh; inward.

CESSATION

adjectives
sudden; entire; instant; negative; good-humored; gradual; complete; premature.

CHAFF

adjectives
mocking; antiquarian; absurd.

verbs
bear up—; beat out—; drive away—; fan—; flay out—; gather—; pick from—; scatter—; separate from—; sift out—; weed out—; winnow—; wipe away—; —flies away.

(See straw.)

CHAFF (v)

adverbs
banteringly; unmercifully; considerably; mockingly; excessively; humiliatingly; boisterously; bitterly; coquettishly; hostilely; enigmatically; frivolously.

(See banter, ridicule, jest.)

CHAGRIN

adjectives
natural; evident; universal; jealous; bitter; secret.

verbs
arouse—; conceal—; devour by—; display —; excite—; feel—; meet with—; observe —; profess—; smile away—; steep in—;

touch with—; —daunts; —fumes away; — suffuses; —waxes.

(See mortification, vexation, humiliation, confusion.)

CHAIN

adjectives
linked; secular; leash; endless; indissoluble; unbroken; firm; lengthening; household; ponderous; rattling; long-worn; mesh; nocturnal; clanking; winding; golden; flowery; galling; resplendent; multitudinous (pl); massive; continuous; impressive; feudal; adamantine; ascending; everlasting; dangling; countless (pl); gleaming; indivisible; bolted; door; bloody; glittering; rosy; trembling; human; roaring; shrieking; howling; jingling; hateful; shameful; curious; will-forged; stout; giant; relentless; binding; restraining; damaging; mental; intangible.

verbs
affix—; bind in —s; bolt—; burst—; condemn to —s; dally with—; deliver from —s; drag in —s; draw—; encircle with—; encompass in—; fasten—; file—; hedge —s about; knit—; link in—; loose —s; manacle in —s; pluck off —s; shake off —s; smite at—; strive in —s; tangle—; tighten —; unravel—; untwist—; wreathe in —s; —clanks; —engirdles; —falls off; —fetters; —rattles; —yields.

(See bond, shackle.)

CHAIN (v)

adverbs
ingloriously; secularly; indissolubly; unbrokenly; firmly; ponderously; everlastingly; indivisibly; stoutly; bindingly; relentlessly; restrainingly; intangibly.

(See restrain, fasten.)

CHAIR

adjectives
rocking; lounge; slim; worm-eaten; leather; pillowed; straight; glowing; prominent; swinging; covered; over-stuffed; cane-seated; long-legged; solitary; classic; rickety; capacious; proffered; marble; cushioned; inhospitable; mahogany; rigid; magisterial; split-bottomed; professorial; confessional; narrow; Morris; substantial; dangling; exiguous; ornamental; adjustable; high; triumphal; anatomical; editorial; rustic; fragile; carved; tipped-back; mural; gilt; lower; vacant; cozy; heavy; upholstered; soft; comfortable; club; arm; formidable; easy; roomy; favorite; noble; battered; faded; untrustworthy; worn; invalid; dilapidated; uncertain; overturned; adjoining;

groaning.; clattering; reversible; swivel; basket; wing; Windsor; hideous; creaking; wicker; walnut; hickory; iron; horsehair; rattan; curule-back; expectant.

verbs
accept—; advance to—; appropriate—; bound from—; descend from—; drop into—; ensconce in—; hoist from—; jerk out of—; loll back in—; monopolize—; motion to—; occupy—; offer—; perch on—; plump into —; resign—; retire to—; shift in—; shrink back in—; sink in—; slump in—; snuggle in—; splinter—; sprawl all over—; straddle—; throne in—; tip—back; uprear in—.
(See seat, bench.)

CHAIRMAN
adjectives
temporary; anecdotal; prosy.

verbs
—adjourns; bangs; conducts; —delegates; —dismisses; —exercises; —occupies; —opens; —performs; —presides; —vetoes.
(See president.)

CHALICE
adjectives
cup-like; poisoned; silver; exuberant; sacred.

CHALLENGE
adjectives
visual; roguish; hoarse; loud; singing; heroic; silent; singular; provocative; sonorous; contemptuous; roistering; gay; feeble; stormy; direct; unsuccessful; peremptory; demoniac; concentrated; insolent; manifest; artistic; chivalrous; pert; mocking; puny; derisive; laughing; flippant; devil-may-care; malicious; sinister; menacing; truculent; fierce; wanton; snarling; angry; sharp; strident; stern; riotous; sweeping; tremendous; formidable; ringing; constant; perpetual; high-pitched; subtle; stimulating; reasonable; vague; unvoiced; startling; blue; definite; objective; hysterical.

verbs
arouse—; blaze—; cringe before—; debate —; defy—; deliver—; fling—; howl—; hurl —; ignore—; meet—; open to—; point—; read—; refuse—; ridicule—; scorn—; take up—; whistle—; —echoes; —rings; —resounds; —withers.
(See defiance, objection, exception, accusation, charge.)

CHALLENGE (v)
adverbs
egotistically; gruffly; justly; promptly; insolently; bravely; provocatively; sonorously; directly; peremptorily; demoniacally; pertly; mockingly; sinisterly; sternly; stridently; formidably; hysterically; definitely; startlingly; fiercely; wantonly; snarlingly.
(See defy, dare, brave.)

CHAMBER
adjectives
conjugal; aspiring; well-guarded; underground; silent; sordid; desolate; bare; nuptial; operating; comfortable; antique; mean; solitary; echoing; sepulchral; voluptuous; subterranean; subaqueous; privy; mystic; chill-looking; glorious; airy; accursed; ducal; treasure; mutilated; respective; chilling; uppermost; gloomy; dismal; unstable; haunted; untenanted; noble; repulsive; empty; crumbling; grimy; dusty; vault-like; lethal; burial; inner; low-ceilinged; tiny; circular; unexplored; spacious; lofty; gilded; confined; packed.

verbs
abide in—; array in—; attend—; build—; carve—; convey into—; dress up—; empty —; gather in—; hie to—; invite to—; retire to—; seal—; seep into—; withdraw into —; —echoes.
(See room, cell, hall.)

CHAMPAGNE
adjectives
effervescent; brisk; excellent; cool; dashing; sparkling; tingling; convivial; atmospheric; gurgling; winking.

verbs
age—; blend into—; bucket—; cask—; characterize—; christen with—; consume—; cork—; drown in—; flavor—; foul—; ice —; lose in—; mature—; mix—; produce—; proffer—; revel in—; sip—; steep in—; support by—; swill—; tap—; toast with—; uncork—; urge on with—; —arouses; —bubbles; —effervesces; —exhilarates; —ferments; —fizzes; —glitters; —inspires; —intoxicates; —matures; —numbs; —sparkles; —unsteadies.
(See wine, liquor.)

CHAMPION
adjectives
undistinguished; formidable; invincible; undoubted; avowed; opposing; proper; ardent; conspicuous; valiant; illustrious; celebrated; sturdy; solitary; devoted; victori-

ous; doughty; undaunted; energetic; stalwart; lusty; redoubtable; brave; resolute; determined; unswerving; uncompromising; foremost; self-admitted; noble; gaunt; royal; prospective; fanatical; loyal; strange; defeated; fearless; resistless.

verbs
acclaim—; applaud—; challenge—; combat—; condition—; crown—; defeat—; defy—; develop—; disable—; dispute—; fear—; hail—; laud—; overthrow—; present—; proclaim—; protect—; provide—; —appears; —competes; —contends; —defends; —engages; —maintains; —performs; —renders; —represents; —teaches; —trains; —upholds; —vanquishes.
(See defender, winner, hero, conqueror.)

CHAMPIONSHIP
adjectives
intrepid; intemperate; conjugal; hyper-enthusiastic; vigorous; notable.

CHANCE
adjectives
slim; fluctuating; lost; opening; opportune; miraculous; lifetime; calculable; divine; slight; desperate; matrimonial; sporting; robust; limited; faint; ironical; impossible; evil; unforeseen; additional; mere; slender; golden; reasonable; fighting; undue; exceptional; brilliant; precious; main; endless; favorable; fortunate; magnificent; good-sized; fair; happy; unlooked-for; convenient; pure; barest; slightest; remote; small; equal; unfortunate; desperate; fatal; frustrated; awful; unfair; hazardous; repeated; fortuitous; amazing; timely; unlimited; glamorous; impartial; full; incorruptible; individualized; complicated.

verbs
advance—; await—; blast —s; brood over —; dispose of—; forfeit—; grab at—; grasp —; imperil —s; intercept by—; invite—; jump at—; leap at—; lessen —s; mind—; muff—; obviate—; rush for—; scoff at—; seize—; shun—; spy by—; stake on—; subject to—; yield to—; —begets; —controls; —detains; —determines; —dies; —fades; —fails; —governs; —guides; —leads.
(See fortune, luck, possibility, hazard, risk, probability.)

CHANCELLOR
adjectives
great; fallen; iron.

CHANDELIER
adjectives
cut-glass; crystal; interesting; central; dazzling; immense; prism-fringed; brilliant; glistening.

CHANGE
adjectives
singular; momentous; subtle; logical; ministerial; definite; threatened; healthful; indescribable; amazing; innovational; perceptible; incestuous; personal; far-reaching; periodical; remarkable; random; striking; varying; gradual; fluctuant; refreshing; incessant; vindictive; rhythmic; continual; rapid; industrial; tragical; stupendous; extraordinary; infinitesimal; withering; physiological; molecular; fine; hideous; enjoyable; radical; ceaseless; generating; appreciable; agreeable; constant; profound; prelusive; frequent; cunning; coincidental; instantaneous; delicate; fearful; acceptable; painful; pathetic; alarming; implied; essential; numerous (pl); eternal; intermediate; never-ending; distressing; partial; genuine; far-reaching; healing; startling; elaborate; drastic; magical; notable; wholesome; comprehensible; monotonous; revolutionary; unaccountable; permanent; consolidating; accumulated; progressive; astonishing; unimportant; political; social; economic; structural; miraculous; obliterative; corresponding; desirable; succeeding; fundamental; constant; violent; geophysical; asthmatic; marked; sudden; degenerative; inexpedient; miserable; extensive; solar; mortal; impending; metamorphic; observable; electrical; agreeable; flattering; malignant; pathological; valuable; secular; lightning-like; fermentative; welcome; seasonal; noticeable; decided; verbal; pleasing; ceaseless; convulsive; panoramic; periodic; beneficent; numerable (pl); realized; much-needed; alleged; abrupt; necessary; sly; wide; complex; enduring; practical; problematic; undeniable; unvarying; tangible; quiet; kindliest; peaceful; noteworthy; magical; refreshing; propitious; vital; tactful; serious; dramatic; vast; thrilling; epoch-making; cataclysmic; arbitrary; doleful; terrific; saddening; inevitable; visible; kaleidoscopic; psychic; psychological; adolescent; bodily; daily; physical; technical; natural.

verbs
accomplish—; advance—; advise—; advocate—; anticipate—; await—; bemoan—; beset by —s; bless—; compel—; concede—; confirm—; contemplate—; debate—; deplore

—; destine for—; dread—; effect—; execute
—; exhort—; fathom—; frown upon—; hinder—; impart—; inaugurate—; indicate—;
induce—; mourn—; occasion—; oppose—;
perceive—; prescribe—; promise—; pronounce—; prophesy—; propose—; report—;
stir to—; suffer—; undergo—; warrant—;
work—; —accompanies; —arises from; —
equalizes; —modifies; —occurs; —perplexes.
(See variation, alteration, transition.)

CHANGE (v)
adverbs
accordingly; singularly; momentously; logically; definitely; healthfully; indescribably;
amazingly; perceptibly; personally; refreshingly; incessantly; industrially; tragically;
stupendously; infinitesimally; molecularly;
radically; appreciably; profoundly; instantaneously; acceptably; partially; eternally;
genuinely; drastically; momentously; magically; notably; wholesomely; permanently;
progressively, economically; miraculously;
desirably; fundamentally; electrically; pathologically; seasonally; undeniably; noticeably; unvaryingly; tangibly; propitiously;
vitally; arbitrarily; chemically; climatically; technically.
(See alter, shift, reform.)

CHANGEABLE
adverbs
bewilderingly; vexatiously; curiously; characteristically; constantly; impulsively; provokingly; giddily; fitfully; capriciously; inexcusably; wantonly; recklessly; carelessly;
injudiciously; ridiculously; fantastically;
temperamentally; dramatically; inconsiderately; selfishly; rashly; indiscreetly; unstably; outrageously; unbelievably; tactlessly; unwisely; shiftily; erratically; restlessly;
nervously; weakly; timidly; irresolutely;
irresponsibly; unreliably; unfortunately; deplorably; wilfully.

CHANNEL
adjectives
correct; proper; earthly; turbulent; precipitous; somber; legitimate; inconsequent; subterranean; intricate; dreaming; transparent; colossal; destined; practical; devious;
manifold; diplomatic; regular; sound; conservative; productive; selfish; fortuitous;
tranquil; oozy; funnel-like; free-flowing;
foaming; tortuous; contorted; rock; unmapped; river; slender; deepened; narrow; burrowed; boiling; miniature; uncounted; noisier; personal; ample; powerful; smiling;
artistic; sequestered.

verbs
deepen—; dredge—; explore—; flow into
—; narrow—; obstruct—; pilot through—;
slide into—; sound—; stray into—; swell
—; trench—; turn into—; waft across—;
—extends; —widens.
(See canal, avenue, route, stream.)

CHANNEL (v)
adverbs
deeply; subterraneously; intricately; deviously; diplomatically; contortedly; narrowly; mysteriously.

CHANT
adjectives
intoned; low; deep-toned; barbaric; monotonous; fragmentary; musical; frenzied;
rhythmical; sonorous; rude; solemn; wild;
pathetic; droning; mellow; melancholy; triumphant; virginal; wailing; aspirated; joyful; impassioned; antiphonal; liturgic; Gregorian; weird; doleful; guttural; nasal;
funeral; ominous; intellectual; wordless;
outlandish; obstreperous; pagan; tribal;
lachrymose; eerie.

verbs
accompany—; answer with—; compose—;
intone—; introduce—; mock—; mourn—; recite—; respond with—; sing—; take up—;
throw off—; troll—; uplift—; utter—; warble—; —celebrates; —consists of; —haunts;
—influences; —praises; —resounds.
(See song, melody.)

CHANT (v)
adverbs
angelically; barbarically; musically; monotonously; rhythmically; sonorously; solemnly; pathetically; mellowly; triumphantly;
wailingly; impassionedly; antiphonally; gutturally; ominously; outlandishly; obstreperously; lachrymosely.
(See intone.)

CHAOS
adjectives
stagnant; aboriginal; conquered; formless;
barren; shapeless; revolutionary; dark; living; wonderful; glaring; resulting; fierce;
cluttered; Stygian; boundless; black; idiotic;
financial; human; approaching; turmoiling;
whirring; tumultuous; leaden; primeval;
unintelligible; blank; entertaining; stimulating; appalling; ghastly; stricken; smothering; gloomy; hopeless; pathetic; bewildering; jumbled; indescribable; cultural; social; economic; industrial; political; primordial; age-long; blind; temporary; strident; ancient.

verbs

beset by—; build out of—; free from—; kindle—; plunge into—; produce—; resolve —; restore from—; rise out of—; survey—; swim through—; —arises; —confounds; —distresses; —overwhelms; —reigns; —roars; —rules; —threatens.

(See confusion, disorder.)

CHAOTIC

adverbs

fiercely; lamentably; uproariously; riotously; noisily; wildly; hysterically; tumultuously; turbulently; hopelessly; madly; distressingly; disturbingly; ominously; alarmingly; threateningly; perplexingly; confusedly; confusingly; indescribably; bewilderingly; pathetically; appallingly; idiotically; senselessly; needlessly; deplorably; unreasonably; unjustifiably; inconceivably; absurdly; perversely; unhappily.

CHAP

adjectives

wild; expensive; likable; sturdy; little; queer; good-looking; affable; lovable; facetious; fortunate; engaging; nice; clear-eyed; clever; capable; bully; jolly; handsome; slender; peaceable; decent-looking; shrewd; stout-hearted; sensible; fastidious; plucky; quiet; reserved; harmless; taciturn; undecided; irresolute; steady; unimpressive; callous; burly; massive; disappointed; solemn; roguish; belligerent; stocky; contriving; smirking; seagoing; oldish; well-mannered; polite; charming.

CHAPEL

adjectives

dimly-lighted; wattled; bare; dreary; lofty; exquisite; fragrant; ivied; unimposing; nonconformist; encircling; compulsory; ancient; carved; gilded; brown-tiled; quaint; old-fashioned; lapis lazuli; private; quiet; forgotten, white-spired; shabby.

verbs

consecrate—; dedicate—; enlarge—; establish—; found—; frequent—; gather at—; grant to—; install in—; maintain—; occupy —; perform in—; revere at—; summon to —; worship in—; —accommodates; —awes; —beckons; —enshrines; —serves; —solaces.

(See church.)

CHAPERON

adjectives

seedy; glowering; inadequate.

CHAPERON (v)

adverbs

conscientiously; inadequately; willingly; cheerfully; nominally; perfunctorily.

(See protect.)

CHAPTER

adjectives

tedious; individual; interesting; brilliant; stimulating; thrilling; solemn; miserable; immortal; spacious; singular; striking; morbid; unwritten; subsequent; supplementary; vivid; crisp; pleasant; debonair; racy; vivacious; fascinating; profoundly-illuminating; surprising; flaming; remarkable; crucial; satirical; provocative; circumspect; concluding; gloomiest; analogous; staccato; explanatory; didactic; drifting; detailed; secret.

verbs

arrange in—s; branch into—s; constitute—; contradict—; divide into—s; head—; introduce—; organize—; pen—; record in—; refer to—; section into—s; touch up—; —deals with; —depicts.

(See category, paragraph, story.)

CHARACTER
(quality, personality)

adjectives

vexatious; illustrious; first-rate; exceptional; celebrated; sheer; toothsome; prosy; composite; parasitic; private; fabulous; axiomatic; positive; nefarious; negative; munificent; salient; deleterious; stern; tempting; formal; reflective; sturdy; undecided; durable; substantial; apoplectic; cabalistic; melodramatic; provisional; indifferent; unscrupulous; vindictive; steadfast; estimable; personal; central; religious; fictional; finite; grasping; hollow; peculiar; composite; intrinsic; amiable; honest; uncelebrated; analogous; distinctive; intellectual; roving; liberal; alarming; feeble; notorious; pedestrian; sad; unspotted; moral; high-toned; daring; intense; diverse; frivolous; startling; half-obliterated; august; gallant; chivalrous; amazing; odious; elevated; heterogeneous; unwieldly; ridiculous; artistic; refulgent; elusive; absorbing; wanton; depraved; timid; trembling; unstable; virtuous; unsullied; robust; arduous; singular; dynamic; determinate; contrasting; beautiful; historical; vicious; interesting; inviolate; seductive; romantic; chameleon-like; miscellaneous; eccentric; arbitrary; powerful; clerical; defective;

murderous; unworthy; pristine; anecdotic; ferocious; sterling; spontaneous; ardent; presumptuous; headstrong; appealing; irresolute; lofty; sinister; luminous; feminine; extraordinary; contrary; eminent; acquired; general; goblin; complimentary; cold; passionless; checkered; obliterated; suspicious; unpractical; public; philological; simplest; primitive; prominent; unpleasant; minor; capricious; voluptuous; nobler; double; outward; antiquated; native; patriotic; deadly; improvident; accursed; external; ungainly; admirable; urgent; dubious; gloomy; melancholy; haughty; imperious; odd; domestic; massive; unique; dry; hard; assumed; fraudulent; heart-rending; exotic; self-reliant; bucolic; pacific; tempestuous; rightful; fictitious; random; complete; exhaustive; timely; idealistic; moral; unemotional; vigorous; epigrammatic; joyous; gentle; sacred; dissolute; flawless; reckless; genial; indelible; reigning; seasoned; lovable; indigenous; predominating; subordinate; unsavory; clean; natural; jovial; shallow; uninspiring; blackened; loquacious; homophonic; physiognomic; hermit; sensational; utilitarian; disturbing; hard-bitten; dwarfish; degrading; flabby; authoritative; jellyfish; picturesque; theocratic; tragic; fluctuating; literary; airy; modish; coquettish; desperate; incidental; colorful; irreproachable; vulgar; veritable; rugged; decorative; compendious; undefined; implacable; pontifical; imperfect; articulate; antithetical; legendary; opaque; tranquil; true; arid; mysterious; commanding; historical; surreptitious; observing; current; grandiose; gay; sympathetic; charming; functional; apathetic; vain; lyrical; nondescript; zigzag; explicit; inherited; statuesque; well-established; trivial; national; contemptible; hurried; hostile; material; accidental; vicious; doubtful; motley; congratulatory; enigmatical; prerogatived; external; abandoned; inviolable; vehement; monochromatic; uncommon; poisonous; sensuous; dicrotic; magnanimous; coherent; positive; semidivine; normal-sized; strenuous; affectionate; ethereal; disfiguring; irregular; forceful; idealistic; poetical; constipating; spiritual; grave; biographico-historical; proud; lying; submissive; many-sided; dutiful; upright; worthless; homely; humorous; insignificant; imperishable; gentlemanly; useful; abusive; decorous; indecisive; cosmopolitan; vague; dangerous; treasonable; atrocious; half-paternal; factitious; unsteady; shadowy; rude; wooden; impassioned; villainous; yielding; architectural; gross;

specific; conscientious; firm; hereditary; unimpeachable; sporting; harmonious; strong; contrasting; unnatural; dominant; special; bright; emphatic; desert; clear-cut; defined; handsome; stainless; collective; corporate; speculative; critical; eclectic; savory; loose; resolved; nebulous; advanced; impeccable; authentic; unblemished; rare; chosen; sophisticated; celestial; saint-like; docile; creditable; cute; attractive; virile; adamantine; curious; idiosyncratic; jaunty; bizarre; adventurous; comic; fantastic; silent; methodical; satisfied; staid; solidified; reticent; dull-witted; timorous; infantile; saturnine; soft; phlegmatic; vacillating; planless; traditionless; varied; racy; infamous; base; notorious; vengeful; unscrupulous; mercenary; obstinate; preposterous; racial; Mephistophelean; Puritan; hieroglyphic; seditious; quasi-public; figurative; youthful; semi-private; artificial; grave; cursive; specialized; representative; confidential; voluntary; individual; composite; intimate; interpolated; unequivocal; abnormal; unified; holy; incidental; deepest; ironic; realistic; abstract; contemporary; secondary; well-rounded; famous; well-known; picaresque; functionless; minor; queer; well-conceived; bygone; rough; Brobdingnagian; deliberate; light; splendid; principal; credible; ambitious; memorable; leading; burlesque; whimsical; quaint; flamelike.

verbs

alter—; analyze—; behold—; besmirch—; blacken—; brand—; breathe—; clear—; debase—; defend—; degrade—; denote—; detract from—; disclose—; display—; elevate—; embody—; emulate—; estimate—; express—; mask—; mold—; paint—; purify—; redeem—; reflect—; rehabilitate—; respect—; reveal—; slur—; traduce—; transform—; undermine—; warp—; —achieves; —breaks down.

(See constitution, nature, personality, temperament.)

CHARACTER
(role in drama or literature)

adjectives

biblical; dramatic; heroic; historic; legendary; mythological; fictional; personated; comic; tragic; contemporary.

verbs

assume—; compound—; conceive—; delineate—; depict—; differentiate—s; display—; distort—; draw—; interpret—; introduce—; invent—; juggle—s; merge into—; play—; portray—; produce—; roll into—; unfold—; —impresses; —represents; —symbolizes.

CHARACTERISTIC

adjectives

distinctive; prevalent; hereditary; congenial; essential; distinguishing; dominant; marked; personal; cheering; salient; general; diffusive; artistic; definite; admirable; farseeing; attractive; familiar; striking; swampy; psychical; unfailing; outstanding; individual; unmitigated; rife; recurring; external; commanding; visible; fundamental; praiseworthy; unsuspected; social; unique; national; spiritual; physical; emotional; peculiar; graceful; common; commendable; prudent; conspicuous; habitual; desirable; major; endearing; whimsical; useful; vicious; vulpine; supposed; reprehensible; tiresome; fictitious; radical; fatal; changeable; facial; group; racial; mental; climactic; local; rudimentary; tell-tale; complex; noticeable; great; unavoidable; inclusive; conceivable; differentiated.

verbs

abolish—; conceal—; disclose—; feign—; interpret—; manifest—; normalize—s; —appeals; —condemns; —differs; —distinguishes; —enhances; —heightens; —persists; —resembles.

(See trait, feature, attribute, quality, idiosyncrasy.)

adverbs

distinctly; particularly; superbly; singularly; specifically; specially; racially; inherently; definitely; typically; essentially; genuinely; truly; normally; significantly; notoriously; notably; touchingly; indelibly; intrinsically; substantially; practically; markedly; supposedly; presumably; ordinarily; naturally; fundamentally.

CHARACTERIZATION

adjectives

masterly; subtle; dramatic; first-rate; cursory; striking; curious; essential; accurate; contemptuous; intimate; convincing; appreciative; hopeful; delicate; musical; beneficent; genial; humorous; fine; readable; delightful; amazing; short; pithy; tricky; finely-etched; vivid; naive; exhaustive; spirited; shrewd; vigorous; sympathetic; penetrating; sharp; amusing; superb; hard-boiled.

CHARACTERIZE (v)

adverbs

justly; frivolously; positively; nefariously; negatively; substantially; provisionally; indifferently; amiably; honestly; distinctively; feebly; odiously; absorbingly; voluptuously; nobly; fraudulently; exotically; tempestuously; fictitiously; unsparingly; authoritatively; colorfully; irreproachably; vulgarly; sympathetically; charmingly; enigmatically; saturninely; villainously; seditiously; confidentially; intimately; ironically; realistically; credibly; whimsically; abnormally; quaintly; timorously; timidly; dynamically; romantically.

(See distinguish.)

CHARGE

adjectives

false; bayonet; untrue; competent; reiterated; swift; avaricious; substantiated; needy; specific; piebald; unlucky; excessive; gallant; ridiculous; unexpected; baleful; sensational; grievous; galloping; calumnious; tremendous; insulting; bloody; injudicious; precious; ignoble; generous; emotional; nominal; desperate; undiscriminating; exorbitant; modest; moderate; blasphemous; extortionate; spectacular; cruel; swift; impetuous; unburned; roaring; disgraceful; fluctuating; sole; typical; scrupulous; disputed; express; insurance; fair; immediate; humiliating; frivolous; warlike; motherly; boisterous; monstrous; quoted; atrocious; warehousing; bitter; additional; preposterous; ungrateful; unmerited; unnecessary; serious; mighty; cynical; horrible; defamatory; grotesque; homicide; criminal; dissenting; formal; groundless; trivial; indirect; swaggering; startling; accusing.

CHARGE
(accusation)

adjectives

absurd; civil; criminal; false; lying; specific; preposterous; unfounded; unjust; unsupported; unwarranted; substantial.

verbs

advance—; answer—; brand with—; brush aside—; conclude—; convey—; couch—; deny—; drone—s; fire—at; frame—against; incur—; justify—; lessen—s; level — at; lodge—s against; motivate—; prefer—s against; protest—; squash—s; refute—; repudiate—; splutter—s; spring—; suppress—; vindicate from—; voice—; —arises from; —rifles; —vexes; —wanes.

(See accusation, complaint.)

CHARGE
(duty, trust)

adjectives

burdensome; entrusted; costly; difficult; doubtful; inevitable; trying.

verbs

assign—; commit to—of; comprehend—; ease—; execute—; fail in—; fulfill—; impose—upon; obey—; perform—; release from—; resign—; shirk—; tend—.

(See duty, trust, custody, care, responsibility, management.)

CHARGE
(rush)

adjectives

driving; furious; concerted; blind; headlong; fruitless; onslaughting.

verbs

ambush—; block—; command—; cut down in—; dodge—; hasten to—; hinder—; lead—; precipitate—; rush to—; succumb to—; —conquers; —overcomes; —overwhelms; —succeeds; —surges; —surprises.

(See attack, assault.)

CHARGE (v)

adverbs

temporarily; strictly; bluntly; excessively; falsely; reiteratedly; specifically; ridiculously; unexpectedly; sensationally; calumniously; injudiciously; ignobly; exorbitantly; spectacularly; unscrupulously; bitterly; humiliatingly; unmeritedly; criminally; accusingly; groundlessly; startlingly; indirectly.

(See effort, impose, assault.)

CHARGEABLE

adverbs

conveniently; easily; indubitably; definitely; morally; officially; unquestionably; positively; absolutely; unfortunately; unluckily; inopportunely; legally; equitably; incontestably; explicitly; certainly; justly; properly; legitimately.

CHARGER

adjectives

foaming; wearied; stamping; restless.

CHARIOT

adjectives

black-lacquered; fiery; colliding; triumphal; colossal; four-horse; glossy; flaming; visionary; sumptuous; fierce.

verbs

arm—; depict—; display—; guide—; mount—; ornament—; rein—; —clanks; —conveys; —mows down; —overturns; —s parade; —rolls by; overthrow—.

(See vehicle, carriage.)

CHARITABLE

adverbs

humanely; amiably; benevolently; considerately; generously; lovingly; philanthropically; sympathetically; tenderly; unselfishly; bounteously; complaisantly; mercifully; blessedly; liberally; graciously; freely; tolerantly; unsparingly; munificently; bountifully; astonishingly; admirably; superbly; dependably; genuinely; sincerely; truly.

CHARITY

adjectives

moral; tender; intellectual; remedial; precarious; suffering; gracious; truest; indiscriminate; princely; spasmodic; grudging; blessed; uncommanded; impulsive; abused; mutual; easy-going; voluntary; unwise; pious; unpublished; natural; aggressive; casual; deadened; superb; neighborly; learned; false; estimable; impressive; endless; confining; rigid; forbidden; tender.

verbs

administer—; appeal to—; assist through—; beseech—; bind with—; contribute to—; entitle to—; influence—; interest in—; lack —; necessitate—; pour forth—; relieve through—; remove from—; subject to—; subscribe to—; temper with—; —alleviates; —ameliorates; —declines; —enables; —grows; —heals; —revives; —suffers from.

(See love, benevolence, tolerance, alms.)

CHARLATAN

adjectives

preying; industrial; accomplished; ingenious; barred; shameless; ambitious.

CHARM

adjectives

flattering; awakened; glittering; soothing; outward; unusual; rare; quiet; distinct; untitled; healing; substantial; paltry; artless; haunting; subtle; inexplicable; personal; awful; lovely; mysterious; indescribable; celestial; imputed; wintry; forbidden; central; veiling; increasing; unique; insinuating; lyric; melodious; superficial; irresistible; heathenish; zestful; home-like;

traditional; distinguished; peculiar; wonder-working; soul-subduing; terrible; inscrutable; voluptuous; conversational; unspeakable; immortal; fictitious; native; unholy; substantial; compact; nostalgic; understanding; piquant; ineffable; delicious; grave; sensitive; vast; inimitable; compelling; indefinable; feminine; quaint; extraordinary; unmodish; seductive; individual; radiant; unfailing; poetic; flirtatious; fastidious; genuine; literary; changeable; reigning; essential; vocal; chief; haunting; quieting; inherent; serene; external; insouciant; modest; striking; incommunicable; inexhaustible; naturalistic; lasting; singular; stately; appropriate; rugged; intrinsic; crowning; restful; picturesque; decorative; elfin; ripening; definite; ideal; sovereign; softening; alluring; nameless; ethereal; inner; dishevelled; potent; spontaneous; simple; flying; material; exotic; unflagging; bitter-sweet; rose-tinted; fatal; suffocating; wild; astonishing; graphic; piquant; varied; recognized; original; perennial; captivating; superlative; brilliant; peaceful; magic; wistful; shy; magnetic; elusive; merry; fleeting; revealing; compensating; persuasive; devastating; certain; ardent; innate; indigenous; unusual; florid; sedate; mature; ancient; lasting; unhurried; lazy; languorous; unsuspected; vexing; thoughtless; ugly; thwarted; melancholy; flexible; chemical; immortal; historic; gala; dimpling; professional; youthful; topographical; provocative; auroral; scenic; domesticated; infantile; old-fashioned; boyish; naive; languorous.

verbs
apply—; attain—; eclipse—; emanate—; enchant with—; endow with—; enhance—; exercise—; loose—; lend—; radiate—; reflect—; resist—; retain—; savor—; survey—s; underrate—; win with—; —appeals; —conquers; —disarms; —dissolves; —enslaves; —fades; —melts; —pervades; —wanes.
(See fascination, beauty, spell, incantation, attraction.)

CHARM (v)
adverbs
delectably; bewitchingly; artlessly; outwardly; angelically; hauntingly; inexplicably; subtly; uniquely; mysteriously; indescribably; celestially; lyrically; melodiously; superficially; irresistibly; peculiarly; conversationally; genuinely; essentially; vocally; inherently; insouciantly; modestly;

strikingly; alluringly; ethereally; spontaneously; exotically; unflaggingly; seraphically; piquantly; perennially; captivatingly; superlatively; magnetically; elusively; devastatingly.
(See fascinate.)

CHARMING
adverbs
indescribably; delightfully; bewilderingly; amazingly; unquestionably; wondrously; surprisingly; radiantly; ineffably; wholly; joyously; blithely; consciously; tormentingly; overwhelmingly; provokingly; unimaginably; mysteriously; graciously; gravely; youthfully; exotically; alluringly; downright; exquisitely; genuinely; ingenuously; incomparably; irresistibly; rapturously.

CHART
adjectives
imperfect; neat; workman-like; cosmographical; authoritative; unusual; tattered; triumphal; fever; mystic; customary.

verbs
ascertain by—; calculate by—; compile—; consult—; depend on—; issue—; publish—; refer to—; scan—; stud—with; survey—; utilize—; —assists; —benefits; —directs; —furnishes; —indicates; —informs; —outlines; —plans; —reveals; —supplements; —sustains.
(See map, charter.)

CHART (v)
adverbs
unobtrusively; imperfectly; invisibly; vaguely; neatly; cosmographically; customarily; professionally; expertly; skillfully.

CHARTER
adjectives
accepted; approved; disputed; adopted; granted; grand; rejected; ratified; restored; submitted; revitalized.

verbs
abolish—; grant—; issue—; renew—; revoke—; —allows; —expires; —legalizes; —permits; —privileges.
(See deed, document, lease, agreement, contract, right, immunity.)

CHARY
adverbs
thriftily; stingily; selfishly; closely; parsimoniously; penuriously; frugally; providently; unreasonably; prudently; singularly; superfluously; curiously; needlessly;

unpleasantly; coolly; discreetly; cautiously; guardedly; warily; meanly; sordidly; greedily; cannily.

CHASE

adjectives
spirited; exciting; invisible; emulous; piteous; desultory; vague; dull; panting; delicious; wild-goose; fruitless; protracted; mad; perpetual; hectic; stern; blissful; grim; hard; desperate; cruel; lengthy; weary; heartbreaking; frenzied; thrilling.

verbs
follow—; forsake—; plan—; prolong—; pursue—; refrain from—; swerve from—; undertake—; —ensues; —fatigues.
(See pursuit, hunt.)

CHASE (v)

adverbs
spiritedly, madly, perpetually; excitingly; desperately; cruelly; heartbreakingly; thrillingly; remorselessly; grimly.
(See pursue, track, hunt.)

CHASM

adjectives
bloody; fearful; unfathomable; infinite; azure; brazen; billowy; bottomless; immense; fateful; watery; formidable; chalk; sunlit; unaccountable; Alpine; narrow; roaring; remarkable; wide; rock-walled; wonderful; dizzy; precipitous.

verbs
break into—; bridge—; cross—; disrupt into—; hollow—; open into—; rend—; rut with—s; span—; —breaches; —divides; —extends; —gapes; —interrupts; —resounds; —slants; —yawns.
(See gulf, gap, opening.)

CHASTE

adverbs
delicately; artistically; architecturally; virtuously; incomparably; beautifully; modestly; incorruptibly; unaffectedly; tastefully; classically; supremely; marvellously.

CHASTEN (v)

adverbs
amply; awfully; unnecessarily; physically; publicly; ruthlessly; brutally; fiendishly; triumphantly; soullessly; odiously; lawfully; legally.
(See punish, whip, correct.)

CHASTISEMENT

adjectives
awful; earthly; unnecessary; literary; physical; maternal; public.

CHASTITY

adjectives
sacred; constant; spotless; cold; enforced; fruitless; habitual; pure; stainless; incomparable.

verbs
affect—; blemish—; dedicate to—; despoil—; enforce—; honor—; impose—upon; laud—; mar—; practice—; pretend—; seduce from—; suspect—of; testify to—; violate—; —extends; —prescribes.
(See purity, virtue.)

CHAT (v)

adverbs
vivaciously; confidentially; mirthlessly; desultorily; emptily; pleasantly; informally; comfortably; loquaciously; frivolously; incessantly; jovially; aimlessly; absurdly; nervously; garrulously; carelessly; constantly; superficially; inconsequentially; amiably.
(See talk, gossip.)

CHATEAU

adjectives
imposing; dilapidated; turreted; ruined.

CHATTER

adjectives
rapid; mirthless; empty; convulsive; frothy; furious; confidential; pleasant; informal; short; comfortable; lively; neighborly; slipshod; unexpected; vivacious; social; friendly; loquacious; backstairs; mere; idle; egotistical; gay; joyous; competent; frivolous; merry; subdued; precocious; incessant; jovial; aimless; absurd; nervous; irresponsible; rattle-brained; garrulous; careless; constant; superficial; indignant; inconsequential; unfailing; bootless.

CHATTER (v)

adverbs
exuberantly; incessantly; complacently; volubly; monotonously; blithely; woefully; excitedly; affably; obstreperously; vivaciously; querulously; unrestrainedly; perplexingly.
(See chat, talk, gossip.)

CHATTY

adverbs
interminably; sociably; hospitably; heartily; genially; cordially; intimately; casually;

happily; companionably; affably; cosily; gregariously; fluently; gabbily; garrulously; nonsensically; glibly; harmlessly; revealingly; cheerfully; dangerously; indiscreetly; venomously; maliciously; indiscriminately.

CHAUFFEUR

adjectives
recommended; liveried; fur-clad; peaceful; sleeping; uniformed; wary; practiced; able; expert.

CHAUVINISTIC

adverbs
pretentiously; bombastically; flauntingly; triumphantly; swaggeringly; magniloquently; boastfully; brassily; highly; obviously; absurdly; foolishly; vapidly; noisily; ostentatiously; blatantly; fantastically; ludicrously; ignobly; inanely; stupendously; splendidly; vaingloriously; airily; blithely; manifestly; impudently.

CHEAP

adverbs
absurdly; unreasonably; contemptibly; indifferently; miserably; pitifully; ridiculously; laughably; worthlessly; unspeakably; incredibly; amazingly; attractively; undoubtedly; indubitably; tolerably; passably; really.

CHEAT (v)

adverbs
perpetually; infernally; villainously; flagrantly; scandalously; vilely; cleverly; shrewdly; diplomatically.
(See defraud, trick.)

CHEATING

adjectives
infernal; villainous; tyrannical; risky; disguised; cowardly; flagrant; glorious; freeboot.

verbs
amount to—; associate with—; bar for—; condone—; convict of—; depose for—; dispose toward—; implicate in—; indict for—; obtain by—; practice—; tolerate—; —affects; —besmirches; —blemishes; —dishonors; —lowers; —mars.
(See fraud, deception, imposition, delusion.)

CHECK

adjectives
bank; thief-proof; signed; gigantic; cancelled; reversible; formidable; sublime; indispensable; distinct; invaluable; generous; salutary; health-giving; contrasting; wholesome; constitutional; temporary; perceptible; accurate; worn; pallid; deplorable; effective; absolute.

CHECK (v)

adverbs
cleverly; fortunately; powerfully; abruptly; temporarily; effectively; formidably; systematically; constitutionally; perceptibly; accurately; absolutely.
(See impede, curb, restrain.)

CHEEK

adjectives
apple-red; crimson; cherry-colored; ruddy; ruddled; flushed; burning; fat; flaming; glowing; pretty; scarlet; blushing; fevered; blazing; rosy; incarnadining; pale; tranquil; sallow; livid; pasty; pallid; ashen; death-like; wan; triangular; lean; sunburnt; tanned; mottled; ebony; smudged; singed; painted; downy; smooth; boyish; placid; fresh; cold; sweet; firm; amiable; withered; weather-beaten; wrinkled; leathery; haggard; careworn; wizened; wasted; darkened; hollowed; cavernous; sunken; emaciated; bony; heavy; forged; rough; unshaven; flabby; jelly-like; puffed; comfortable; plump; soft; sleep-flushed; icy; droopy; hard; marble; freckled; pockmarked; scarred; smarting; tremulous; pendent; upturned; unresponsive; wind-freshened; consumptive; sweat-damp; infantile; peachy; delicate-rounded; high; warm; transparent; wide; strong; protruding; mangy; prominent; sinister; bronzed; tender; sinewy; distended; damask; blanched; dimpled; unprofaned; marked; veined; unworthy; straining; melting; pellucid; brown; tear-stained; mantling; placid; waning; quivering; faded; smiling; furrowed; smutted; tear-sodden; pinched; rubicund; glowing; lank; clear; pink; flaccid; swarthy; untasted; shrunken; shaded; blanched; cracking; languid; bloodless; emaciated; waxen; virgin; harlot; kissing; delicate; changing; inflamed; sunny; white; yellow-cowslip; childish; worn; proud; jutting; silver; drawn; amiable; animated; peony-colored; pinched; haggard; unreluctant; blooming; freshening; massive; lifeless; purplish-mottled; carmine-colored.

verbs
blanch —s; brighten —s; color —s; cool —s; corrugate —s; daub —s; dimple —; empurple —s; fan —; flame —s; flush —s;

hollow —; lean on —; moisten —s; paint —s; pat —; puff —s; redden —s; smite —; stain —s; stream down —; swell —s; tint —; varnish —; waste —; wrinkle —; —s blush; —s burn; —s fade; —s glisten; —s glow; —s hang; —s pale.

(See **face**.)

CHEEKY

adverbs

pertly; brassily; insolently; impertinently; insufferably; offensively; impudently; brazenly; flippantly; shamelessly; unpleasantly; disagreeably; saucily; swaggeringly; arrogantly; audaciously; provokingly; terribly; odiously; ridiculously; presumptuously; daringly; detestably; abominably; unwarrantably; jauntily; unbecomingly.

CHEER
(shout of applause)

adjectives

national; tumultuous; ironical; forced; admiring; hysterical; loud; rousing; shrill; hearty; panting; frenzied; rippling; irrepressible; patient; thunderous; incomparable; immense; blithe; lofty; pathetic; heart-strengthening; daily; mingled; answering; encouraging; sunny; lusty; universal; undaunted; wedding; unanimous; ringing; triumphal; measureless; traditional; good; intimate; massive; whooping; vociferous; solemn; silvery; evil; melancholy; uncertain.

verbs

celebrate with —s; depart with —s; draw —; echo—; grudge—; hail—; incite to —s; judge by —s; kill —; lessen —s; participate in —; raise —; rejoice in —; thunder —; — abates; — ceases; — dies; — fades; — greets; —rouses; — sweeps; — wanes.

(See **applause, cheering**.)

CHEER (v)

adverbs

raucously; rabidly; lustily; wildly; vociferously; enthusiastically; heartily; jovially; mirthfully; tumultuously; hysterically; rousingly; shrilly; frenziedly; irrepressibly; thunderously; incomparably; encouragingly; undauntedly; unanimously; triumphantly.

(See **praise, applaud**.)

CHEERFUL

adverbs

habitually; pleasantly; naturally; irrepressibly; immensely; blithely; vociferously; placidly; serenely; vivaciously; charmingly; refreshingly; youthfully; casually; calmly; hilariously; maddeningly; vexatiously; merrily; jauntily; airily; exuberantly; heedlessly; bewilderingly; surprisingly; unexpectedly; strangely; oddly; unwontedly; exhilaratingly; contentedly; lightly; gladly; complacently; tolerably; genially; jovially; jubilantly; briskly; smilingly; winsomely; noticeably; perplexingly; unbelievably; extraordinarily.

CHEERFULNESS

adjectives

unabated; placid; imperturbable; undiminished; sparkling; consistent; weary; hysterical; natural; charming; growing; healthy; infectious; contagious; uncomplaining; pensive; constrained; forced; renewed; spasmodic; affected; perennial; usual; weird; desperate.

verbs

animate with—; conceal—; denote—; diffuse—; dispose toward—; exhibit—; exude—; feign—; fight with—; free with—; inspire—; invade with—; reflect—; regain—; restore—; revive—; season with—; temper with—; welcome—; —comforts; —eases; —encourages; —exhilarates; —pervades; —stimulates.

(See **optimism, buoyancy**.)

CHEERING

adjectives

earnest; frenzied; fresh; unusual; loud; vociferous.

verbs

accelerate—; conduct—; direct—; drown in—; encounter—; join—; lead—; promote—; repress—; —acclaims; —animates; —compliments; —dies down; —echoes; —encourages; —heartens; —enlivens; —gladdens; —greets; —indicates; —overwhelms; —resounds; —stimulates; —subsides; —swells; —welcomes.

(See **applause, ovation, cheer**.)

CHEERING

adverbs

reasonably; brightly; definitely; encouragingly; reassuringly; propitiously; comfortingly; helpfully; positively; unusually; finally; tolerably; moderately; fairly; somewhat; downright; wholly.

adverbs

dismally; grievously; unhappily; sorely; sadly; unpleasantly; disturbingly; utterly; horribly; drearily; piteously; woefully; deplorably; pathetically; needlessly; discouragingly; dishearteningly; hopelessly; desolately; oppressively; extremely; undeniably; unutterably; wretchedly; peculiarly; cruelly.

CHEERY

adverbs

sturdily; resolutely; brightly; consistently; charmingly; healthily; infectiously; ;contagiously; professionally; philosophically; spontaneously; loudly; serenely; placidly; courageously; confidently; reassuringly; hearteningly; encouragingly; valiantly; gallantly; refreshingly; pleasantly; cordially; attractively; delightfully; calmly.

CHEESE

adjectives

milk; pyramided; vintage; large; ripe; stale; mouse-eaten; rancid; dry.

verbs

coagulate into—; consume—; enclose—in; grate—; import—; introduce—; loaf—; manufacture—; market—; mix—; pack—; process—; refrigerate—; roll—; slice—; spread—; sprinkle with—; toast—; turn into—; —moulds; —ripens.

adverbs

achieve with—s; analyze—s; apply—s; compose of—; concentrate—; devise—; employ—; evaluate—; extract—; force by—s; impregnate with—; involve—; mix—; obtain—; precipitate—; prepare—; produce—; resist—; synthesize—; —accomplishes; —acidizes; —acts; —alkalizes; —alters; —attracts; —catalyzes; —s combine; —converts; —counteracts; —depends on; —neutralizes; —poisons; —preserves; —reacts; —transforms.
(See substance.)

CHEMICALS

adjectives

injurious; common; inexpensive; mixed; synthetic.

CHEMIST

adjectives

renowned; brilliant; ruthless; analytical; alleged.

adjectives

agricultural; pure; applied; industrial; theoretical.

CHERISH (v)

adverbs

secretly; mutually; innocently; piously; tenderly; reverently; fondly; unconsciously; vociferously; tenaciously.
(See protect.)

CHERISHED

adverbs

carefully; affectionately; absurdly; highly; sentimentally; tenderly; reverently; ardently; fondly; ridiculously; stoutly; passionately; truly; sincerely; genuinely; whimsically; lovingly.

CHERRY

adjectives

fermented; fiery; ripened; blushing; pale.

CHEST
(part of body)

adjectives

stalwart; barrel; bulging; professional; corded; massive; out-muscled; superb; self-confident; thick; plump; brawny; skinny; cadaverous; cavernous; puny; meager; bony; unathletic; feeble; narrow; broad; pigeon; deep-sprung; expanded; wizened; sagging; crushed; collapsed; heaving; hollow; battle-scarred; inflated; hairy; soldierly; portentous; chubby; excessive; vainglorious; ample; laboring; decorated; tattooed.

verbs

blow out—; contract—; crush—; deflate—; deform—; develop—; expand—; flatten—; inflate—; lock up in—; loosen—; massage—; pierce—; puff out—; rend—; seal in—; stretch—; thump—.

CHEST
(receptacle)

adjectives

lopsided; crammed; treasure; battered; scarred; wooden; nail-studded; rivetbound; stout; øaken; ironbound; corded; roped; brass-mounted; refrigerating; musty; capacious; ornate; plenteous; sacred; fireproof; ample.

CHEW (v)

adverbs

viciously; contentedly; placidly; hungrily; vigorously; continuously; tranquilly; normally; restrainedly; noisily; crushingly.
(See nibble, munch, crunch.)

adverbs

distinctly; smartly; fashionably; exceptionally; dramatically; fabulously; demurely; cleverly; artistically; stylishly; slenderly; effectively; correctly; trimly; conservatively; sparklingly; brilliantly; barbarically; expensively; conventionally; habitually; elegantly; quietly; handsomely; becomingly; intriguingly; appropriately.

CHICKADEE
(*titmouse*)

adjectives

black-capped; cheerful; lisping; flocking; lusty; evergreen-loving.

verbs

—carols; —chats; —chirps; —clings; —flits; —frolics; —hops; —preys on; —shrills; —somersaults; —whistles.
(See bird.)

CHICKEN

adjectives

cackling; snowy; browned; fragrant; smoking; drawn; rudimentary.

verbs

behead—; breed—; dine on—; excite—; exhibit—; fatten—; infest—; pen up—; prey on—; relish—; roast—; savor—; spice—; stuff—; —clucks; —flutters about; —gobbles up; —invades; —lays; —molts; —pecks; —perches; —scratches; —scurries; —squawks; —struts.
(See fowl, bird.)

CHICKENHEARTED

adverbs

notably; laughably; ridiculously; ludicrously; constitutionally; unwontedly; timorously; avowedly; shamefully; effeminately; dastardly; basely; solicitously; appallingly; astoundingly; wonderfully; amazingly; surprisingly; inexplicably; shockingly; fearfully; tenderly; obviously; disgracefully; outrageously; infamously; incurably.

CHIDE (*v*)

adverbs

scowlingly; mildly; severely; reprovingly; moderately; kindly; harshly; embarrassingly; vociferously; violently; sharply; shyly; intelligently; churlishly; mercilessly; legitimately; sternly.
(See admonish, censure, scold.)

CHIDING

adjectives

churlish; stormy; gallant; meaningful.

CHIEF

adjectives

indulgent; revered; supreme; prominent; gangster; powerful; local; native; usurping; polygamous; picturesque; murderous; mountain; desert; brigand; hereditary; indignant; deputed; reticent; patriarchal; despotic; venerable; artful; descendant; influential; kind; uncrowned; tribal; dominating; brave-hearted; gentle; generous; formidable; independent; invincible; responsible; crimson-stained.

verbs

advance to—; depose—; execute—; forsake—; guard—; hail—; hang—; idolize—; name—; oppose—; patronize—; rank as ; restore—, serve—; swerve from—; torture—; —commands; —inveighs; —leads; —orders; —rejoices.
(See head, leader, commander, captain.)

CHIEFTAIN

adjectives

feudal; bearded; putative; simple; desert; venerable; bandit; lifeless.

CHIFFON

adjectives

multitone; bright; filmy; sinuous.

CHILD

adjectives

delightful; charming; dutiful; cherubic; enchanting; divine; brilliant; bright; rosy; nice; capable; contented; accomplished; gifted; intelligent; respectable-looking; well-bred; supernatural; fun-loving; eager; exemplary; affectionate; studious; lovable; responsive; winsome; wistful-eyed; misty-eyed; golden-haired; fair-skinned; well-formed; comely; prepossessing; immaculate; prim; unnatural; normal; typical; average; growing; obedient; meek; humble; tactful; old-fashioned; subdued; repentant; contrite; tractable; tranquil; absorbed; silent; reflective; problem; sensitive; bewildered; shy; shrinking; artistic; emotional; unreasonable; nervous; high-strung; neglected; adorable; confused; sickly; delicate; frail; rickety; ragged; spindling; colorless; nondescript; angular; ugly; brutal; beastly; wretched; impertinent; rebellious; spoiled; spiteful; petted; precocious; audacious; impetuous; headstrong; heartbroken; prostrate; unhappy; miserable; forlorn; terrified; adored; admired; afflicted; frightened; greedy; wayward; unruly; exasperating; foolish; grown-up; offensive; refractory; obstreperous; monstrous; stubborn; obdurate; burdensome; unwitting; artless; retarded; stolid; annoying; slow-growing; defective; stupid; sturdy; pot-bellied; lean-faced; leggy; plain; thin; big-eyed; sallow; chubby-faced; regretful; toddling; prattling; wailing; screaming; sobbing; play-loving; beauty-loving; staring; frail; convalescing; engrossed; mere; weeping; casual; innocent; puzzled; venturesome; quizzical; adventurous; riotous; finicky; changeling; romantic; cockney; vaudeville; aristocratic; infant; drowsy; rash; loathed; unflinching; defective; culpable; pouting; petulant; conscientious; minor; wanton; dazed; eloquent; sanguine; forward; reticent; gallant; virtuous; vixenish; beaten; delightful; impious; crippled; exceptional; precious; churlish; talented; robust; engrossed; roguish; heaven-obscuring; loyal; turbulent; houseless; nurtured; tender; unborn; adolescent; simple; sole; heavenborn; cherished; complaining; blind; foolish; vagrant; comparative; scampering; weakest; credulous; guileless; merciless; illegitimate; sacred; fractious; proud; vivacious; burnt; pampered; abused; ambidextrous; healthy; unruly; passionate; undisciplined; self-willed; posthumous; fretful; imitative; melancholy; untutored; docile; migratory; princely; lily-shining; cunning; secretive; unmanageable; victorious; bewitching; sad-looking; riotous; unquenchable; wondrous; slumbering; veritable; eccentric; imaginative; flaxen-haired.

verbs

attend—; awaken—; bear—; befriend—; beget—; bereave—; bring forth—; build-up—; burden—; chastise—; cherish—; circumcise—; comprehend—; conceive—; correct—; debilitate—; deliver—; develop—; discipline—; disinherit—; dispossess ; educate—; emaciate—; embrace—; encourage—; exhort—; expose—; father—; fondle—; forsake—; govern—; harden—; inspire—; lull—; lure—; name—; nourish—; nurse—; oppress—; punish—; rear—; reassure—; remain—; restrain—; revive—; scold—; sire—; spoil—; teach—; tempt—; train—; trust—; understand—; wean—; whip—; —babbles; —clambers; —clamors; —contracts a disease; —dis-

obeys; —heeds; —moans; —pines; —rebels; —skips; —sobs; —strays; —struggles; —thrives; —wails; —weeps.

(See offspring, son, daughter, descendant, boy, girl, infant.)

CHILDHOOD

adjectives

earliest; amazing; seeming; narrow; nightmare-ridden; neglected; sheltered; imaginative; distorted; light-hearted; bleak; lonely; cheerless; spindle-legged; pathetic; precocious; inconsiderate; captious; mysterious; docile; blooming; unappreciative; serene; satisfied; joyous; humble; meditative; healthy; ripe; passive.

verbs

acquire in—; affect—; care for during—; conceive in—; dominate—; form during—; govern—; inculcate in—; learn in—; mould during—; preserve in—; recall—; rejoice in—; reminisce about—; restrict—; revert to—; teach in—; train in—; —contributes; —flees; —lapses; —ripens into; —strays.

(See infancy, youth.)

CHILDISH

adverbs

foolishly; disagreeably; utterly; unpleasantly; unexpectedly; shamefully; dreadfully; inexplicably; deliberately; unreasonably; ill-temperedly; pathetically; unbearably; wretchedly; senselessly; unaccountably; stubbornly; obstinately; horridly; ridiculously; sullenly; flagrantly; awkwardly; gawkily; unhappily; indecorously; outlandishly.

CHILDLIKE

adverbs

innocently; delightfully; simply; artlessly; guilelessly; naively; radiantly; joyously; charmingly; rosily; contentedly; lovably; meekly; adorably; foolishly; chubbily; wonderfully; bewitchingly; irresistibly; appealingly; utterly; touchingly; alluringly; unaffectedly; ingenuously; frankly; sweetly.

CHILDREN

adjectives

passive; fidgety; hostile; supersensitive; refractory; shy; obtrusive; irresponsible; prison; native; illegitimate; semi-hypnotized; bickering; gawky; mercurial; wondering; stoical; egotistical; unimaginative; pampered; promising; bright; worthy; wholesome; angelic; charming; marvellous; carefully-bred; blithe; laughing; rollicking; smiling; audacious; happy; playful; prankish; romping; sturdy; robust; lusty; noisy; clamoring; clattering; frantic; screaming; unkempt; ragged; verminous; unwashed; wide-eyed; stocky; golden-haired; long-legged; quaintly-garbed; chubby; enormous; gayly-dressed; tiny; naked; half-grown; thick-legged; growing; underweight; undernourished; sickly; imperfectly developed; abandoned; heartbroken; frightened; radiant; desolate; trembling; pale; unloved; uncared-for; hungry; homeless; irresponsible; healthy; syphilitic; motherless; restless; squabbling; homespun; true; shivering; bedazed; vagrant; heartless; degenerate; crippled; unruly; earnest-hearted; vexing; starry; promising; natural; unreasonable; unbridled; fiery-blooded; outcrying; myriad; notorious; ill-bred; vulgar; ill-favored; exquisite; fresh; white-faced; silent; insolent; smutty; hovering; pert; dirty; squalling; fretful; sycophantic; mischievous; destitute; glorious-eyed; maddened; strumous; garrulous; hilarious; delinquent; violent; erring; handicapped; unlettered; vociferous; cruel; neglected; veritable; vigorous.

CHILL

adjectives
horrid; penetrating; biting; shrinking; severe; mental; violent; curious; embarrassing; noticeable; hopeless; sharp; congestive; sudden; inexplicable; slight; damp; timid; dry; icy; bone-penetrating; deathly; vault-like; bitter; uncomfortable; balmy; growing; cold; increasing; dreadful; comfortless; shaking.

verbs
blow—; chatter with—s; experience—; expose to—; overcome by—; produce—; prolong—; quiver with—; run—; seize with—; sense—; shake with—; shiver with —; shudder with—; strike with—; survive —; treat for—; —accompanies; —affects; —creeps in; —depresses; —injures; —numbs; —penetrates.

(See sensation, cold.)

CHILL (*v*)

adverbs
bitingly; severely; violently; hopelessly; noticeably; sharply; suddenly; inexplicably; bitterly; increasingly; dreadfully; mortally; painfully.

CHILLY

adverbs
suddenly; inexplicably; curiously; slightly; uncomfortably; dreadfully; alarmingly; keenly; tremulously; visibly; uncommonly; unendurably; strangely; unaccountably; unpleasantly; dangerously; unusually; unwontedly; inexcusably; indefensibly.

CHIME

adjectives
musical; pathetic; dolorous; silvery; sweet-toned; unhurried; clear; jubilant; silver; soothing; unvaried; religious; faint; heavenly.

CHIME (*v*)

adverbs
drowsily; harmoniously; mischievously; dolorously; unhurriedly; jubilantly; soothingly; religiously; faintly; heavenly; musically, clearly.
(See ring.)

CHIMERICAL

adverbs
strangely; fantastically; grotesquely; wildly; eccentrically; erratically; quaintly; curiously; baselessly; foolishly; exceptionally; peculiarly; extraordinarily; unaccountably; extravagantly; preposterously; fabulously; dreamily; fancifully.

CHIMNEY

adjectives
rotten; smoking; natural; stubborn; ample; curious; spiraled; defective; tottering; stumpy; low; ungainly; blackened; ghostly; clustering; open-throated; sparkless; disused.

verbs
block—; blow down—; clean—; connect—; construct—; convey through—; dampen—; decorate—; design—; escape through—; extend—; fire—; inspect—; lodge in—; muffle—; obstruct—; pass through—; suck up—; support—; —breathes; —carries off; —diffuses; —discharges; —draws off; —exhales; —fumes; —leaks; —reeks; —smokes; —topples; —tumbles.
(See passage.)

CHIN

adjectives
out-thrust; curious; jutting; determined; provocative; elongated; significant; prominent; dominant; fighting; obstinate; aggressive; protruding; stubborn; molded;

prognathous; rounded; square; retreating; bulldog; cleft; portly; dimpled; daintily; shaped; clean-cut; aristocratic; triangular; pointed; strong; rounded; sensitive; delicate; demure; quivering; protesting; scrubby; stubbled; unshaven; bristly; sunken; curbed; callow; tremulous; weak; girlish; bevelled; unflinching; lowered; firm; heavy; mutinous; marred; bruised; impudent; receding; arrogant; trembling; dumpy; formless; patrician; slack-set; full; granite; gray-bearded; seamy; witching; clean-shaven; sagging; generous.

verbs
box—; caress—; chafe—; dimple—; dip—; double—; furrow—; guard—; hollow—; pillow—on; razor—; roughen—; smooth—; strike on—; stroke—; stubble—; tickle—; —juts out.
(See jaw.)

CHINA
(*country*)
adjectives
ancient; colorful; present-day; famine-cursed; tasteful.

CHINA
(*dish*)
adjectives
atrociously-patterned; colorful; decorated; egg-shell; fragile; glazed; mongrel; ancestral; mended; imported; lustered; lustrous; treasured; superb; rare; delicate; magnificent; glorious; exquisite; dainty.

verbs
bake—; carve—; decorate—; design—; exhibit—; fire—; glaze—; inherit—; lithograph—; manufacture—; model—; mold—; paint—; preserve—; print—; process—; produce—; trace on—; trim—; turn—; vitrify—; —attracts; —sparkles.
(See porcelain.)

CHINAMAN
adjectives
slant-eyed; sinister; innocent; cryptic.

CHIP
(*counter or disk in game*)
adjectives
accumulated; cashed-in; clicking; ivory; ominous; nested; red-and-blue; rattling; plastic; stacked.

verbs
accumulate—s; amass—s; ante—; calculate—; cash—s; mark—s; pile up—s; revalue—; toss in—; wager—; —s rattle; —s represent.

CHIP (*v*)
adverbs
laboriously; unweariedly; characteristically; disfiguringly; hurtfully; disastrously; idiotically; carelessly.

CHIPMUNK
adjectives
burrowing; chipping; conspicuous; beautifully-striped; darting; free-roving; fence-travelling; gleaming; marauding; scampering.

verbs
—chirps; —emerges; —ranges; —scurries; —stores.
(See squirrel, animal.)

CHIPPER
adverbs
blithely; heartily; gaily; cheerily; wholesomely; briskly; actively; ably; laughingly; light-heartedly; sunnily; smartly; alertly; energetically; happily.

CHIPS
(*fragments*)
adjectives
infinitesimal; coarse; falling; scattered; shapeless; raw; valueless.

verbs
break into—; chisel into—; chop into—; cut into—; fly into—; gather—; hack into —; hew into—; piece into—; separate into—; split into—; —accumulate; —clutter up; —fly; —gather; —strike.
(See fragment, piece.)

CHIRP (*v*)
adverbs
shrilly; disdainfully; rapturously; ecstatically; joyously; contentedly; obstreperously; cheerfully; maddeningly; noisily; incessantly; obtrusively; deafeningly; unendingly; subduedly; discordantly.
(See twitter.)

CHIVALRIC
adverbs
patriotically; loyally; fanatically; devotedly; fantastically; bigotedly; faithfully; chauvinistically; unnecessarily; showily; ostentatiously; genuinely; sacrificially; pi-

ously; religiously; ardently; zealously; uncompromisingly; impulsively; sincerely; sublimely; martially; fiercely; incorruptibly; staunchly; inviolably; excessively.

CHIVALROUS

adverbs

delicately; devotedly; politely; generously; magnanimously; innately; inherently; traditionally; racially; suavely; gallantly; civilly; pleasantly; ardently; fervently; courteously; extremely; gently; urbanely; smoothly; obsequiously; amiably; ceremoniously; attentively; blandly; ingratiatingly; pleasingly; tactfully.

CHIVALRY

adjectives

morbid; belated; unsullied; old-fashioned; rekindled; deficient; fantastical; poetic; latent; knightly; gay; misplaced; exaggerated; distant; feudal; religious; delicate; loyal; medieval; undaunted; vaulted; celestial; youthful; generous.

verbs

affect—; attend with—; attribute to—; awaken—; bend toward—; blind by—; celebrate—; charge with—; commend for—; confer on ; dispense with—; educate for —; encounter—; equip for—; institute—; knight for—; reward—; —constitutes; —decays; —dies; —flourishes; —flowers; —prevails; —survives.

(See gallantry, courtesy, bravery.)

CHLOROFORM

adjectives

colorless; ethereal-odored; insidious; penetrating; pungent; sickish-sweet; sleep-producing.

verbs

administer—; anesthetize with—; dissolve in —; dose with —; expose —; gelatinize —; inhale —; melt —; overcome with —; sniff —; solidify —; subject to —; — acts; — boils; — decomposes; — dissolves; — dulls; — eases; — lessens.

(See anaesthetic.)

CHOCK-FULL

adverbs

generously; utterly; satisfactorily; inconveniently; dangerously; sloppily; carefully; calculatedly; accurately; happily; luckily; absolutely; surprisingly; gratifyingly; entirely; brimmingly; nicely.

CHOCOLATE

adjectives

thick; creamy; burning; sugary; tasty; bitter; rancid; delicious.

CHOICE

adjectives

inevitable; sensible; indefensible; ideal; hasty; shrewd; ultimate; emotional; distinguished; alternate; definite; conscious; free; happy; mistaken; unlimited; fortunate; sympathetic; logical; wise; moral; wide; important; half-humorous; unrestricted; endless; arbitrary; uncorrupted; critical; unessential; irrelevant; nonsensical; ideal; solicitous; scrupulous; ghastly; admirable; satisfactory; premium; perfect; sturdy; bitter; loathed; boundless; random; unaccountable; injudicious; intelligent; first; deliberate; perfect; haphazard; excellent; doubtful; mercenary; dazzling; appropriate; resolute; righteous; prudent; haughty.

verbs

abide by —; applaud —; bind to —; commend —; conceal —; contend with —; delight in —; determine —; encourage —; envy —; extend —; favor —; guard —; indicate —; justify —; leave —; overrule —; regulate —; restrict —; widen —; yield to —.

(See alternative, option, preference, election.)

CHOICE

adverbs

unusually; exquisitely; valuably; indubitably; unquestionably; evidently; manifestly; incomparably; inimitably; singularly; particularly; inestimably; invaluably; exceptionally; alluringly; temptingly; exotically; incalculably; immeasurably; imposingly; infinitely; sumptuously; inexpressibly; utterly; absolutely.

CHOIR

adjectives

soothing; plumed; enraptured; chantry; surpliced; cathedral; full-throated; extraordinary; immortal; starry; constellated; matin; white-robed; angelic; sweet-voiced; ritual; dusky; captive; silent; mystic; pausing; shining; winged; invisible.

verbs

accompany —; coach —; compose —; conduct —; direct —; employ —; establish —; garb —; invite —; organize —; pitch —; regulate —; retain —; stimulate —; support

—; train —; — answers; —anthems; — carols; — chants; — croaks; — croons; — devotes; — invokes; — is situated; — performs; — practises; — rehearses; — renders; — resounds.

(See chorus, singers.)

CHOKE (v)
adverbs
horribly; fiendishly; murderously; hellishly; painfully; furiously; fatally; mortally; partially; savagely.

(See strangle, throttle.)

CHOLERA
adjectives
Asiatic; devastating; dread; horrible; life-snuffing; malignant; pestilential; spreading; impartially-dealing; ravaging.

verbs
afflict with —; arrest —; attack with —; cause —; control —; distinguish —; expose to —; inoculate against —; overcome —; prevent —; protect against —; quarantine —; recognize —; recover from —; resemble —; scourge with —; stamp out —; subdue —; subject to —; suffer from —; treat for —; — affects; — infects; — invades; — irritates; — occurs; — prevails; — ravages; — spreads; — subsides; — travels; — visits.

(See disease, epidemic.)

CHOLERIC
adverbs
inveterately; terribly; extremely; excitedly; irascibly; habitually; touchily; cantankerously; exceptionally; intolerably; dangerously; hotly; petulantly; restively; incorrigibly; inherently; incurably; alarmingly; irritatingly; unbearably; unreasonably; senselessly; miserably; unfortunately; ill-temperedly; plaguedly; waspishly; querulously.

CHOOSE (v)
adverbs
promiscuously; precisely; deliberately; unanimously; inevitably; fastidiously; invariably; sedulously; universally; constitutionally; tactfully; tastefully; unselfishly; sensibly; shrewdly; ultimately; emotionally; definitely; mistakenly; sympathetically; logically; morally; unrestrictedly; arbitrarily; critically; irrelevantly; nonsensically; scrupulously; admirably; unaccountably; injudiciously; haphazardly; appropriately;

resolutely; righteously; prudently; instinctively; finally; discreetly; speedily.

(See select, prefer.)

CHOP
adjectives
breaded; congealed; dripping; double; evenly-browned; fat; juicy; oozing; bony; shriveled.

verbs
broil —; butter —; devour —; digest —; dine on —; enjoy —; garnish —; grill —; heat —; pepper —; preserve —; relish —; roast —; salt —; savor —; season —; trim —; — burns; —simmers; — sizzles; — steams.

(See meat.)

CHOP (v)
adverbs
savagely; vigorously; ambitiously; hurriedly; leisurely; grimly; regularly; ineffectively; monotonously; continuously.

CHORAL
adverbs
melodiously; harmoniously; lyrically; fundamentally; originally; essentially; tunefully; euphoniously; symphoniously; orchestrally; effectively; splendidly; magnificently; sweetly; primarily; simply; elaborately; complicatedly.

CHORD
adjectives
harmonic; emotional; sympathetic; tender; responsive; peremptory; compassionate; triumphant; thunderous; preliminary; opening; impromptu; maddening; wailing; noisy; closing; sobbing; dreamy; dashing; nerve-racking; rare; vibrant; responsive; strong; broad; determined; familiar; answering; conscious; throbbing; susceptible; airy; sonorous; breaking; plenteous; liquid; sensitive; dominant.

verbs
pluck —; sound —; twang —; — charms; — shivers; — thrills; —trembles.

(See tendon, string.)

CHORE
adjectives
old-fashioned; bitter; small; domestic; weary.

verbs
dispatch —s; do —s; perform —s; plan —;
—s bind; —s devolve on; —s occupy; —s
settle on.
(See job, duty, task.)

CHORISTER
adjectives
impatient; poor; supercilious; monotonous.

CHORUS
adjectives
noisy; welcoming; general;-angry; fearful;
jangling; affirmative; derisive; obtrusive;
hallelujah; exhausted; tender; deafening;
hoarse; booming; familiar; whispering;
pessimistic; eerie; intricate; mighty; hair-
raising; shrill; musical-comedy; shrieking;
unending; recurrent; tuneful; abusive; masterly; jubilant; echoing; universal; horrend-
ous; solemn; jolly; deep; screaming; hideous; vernacular; subdued; unprecedented;
dirge-like; clamorous; wild; unfaltering;
multitudinous (pl); seasonable; seditious;
blasphemous; bibulous; mumbling; gleeful;
meaningless; ranting; discordant.

verbs
accompany —; coach —; collect —; conduct —; constitute —; flow from —; join in
on —; laugh in —; manage —; organize
—; pitch—; regulate—; repeat—; take
up —; train —; transpose —; utter —;
whine in —; — breaks out; — chants;
— executes; — harmonizes; — imitates; —
practices; — rehearses; — renders; — reports; — resounds; — revels; — revives;
— shrills; — spreads; — swells.
(See choir, song, refrain.)

CHRIST
adjectives
agonized; crucified; unheralded; infallible;
merciful; glorious; death-triumphant; pur-
ple-robed; sorrowing; thorn-crowned; unconquerable; comforting.

verbs
acknowledge —; apprehend —; beseech —;
bless —; bow before —; conform with —;
consecrate to —; contemplate —; deny —;
discern —; endow with —; esteem —; fight
for —; follow —; forsake —; herald —;
interpret —; preach —; preserve —; protect —; receive —; reject —; unveil —;
uphold —; — ascends; — bears; — heals;
— passes; — prophesies; — redeems; —
represents; — rises; — rules; — suffers;
— teaches; — toils.
(See God, Jesus.)

CHRISTIAN
adjectives
sincere; misguided; professing; preeminent; heartfelt; genuine.

CHRISTIAN
adverbs
devoutly; sincerely; ardently; fervently; devotedly; faithfully; humbly; meekly; piously; religiously; sanctimoniously; beatifically; joyously; blessedly; reverently; solemnly; benignly; honestly; genuinely; benevolently; mercifully; tolerantly; humanely;
charitably; obviously; unmistakably; plainly; evidently; openly; avowedly; professedly.

CHRISTIANITY
adjectives
admirable; dogmatic; muscular; mysterious;
primitive; sustained; sympathetic; profound.

verbs
conceive —; convert to —; cut off from —;
denote —; embrace —; exalt —; extirpate
—; follow —; found —; illustrate —; implant —; inculcate —; live in —; lose faith
in —; manifest —; obscure —; persecute
—; plant —; preach —; profess —; regard
—; reject —; restore —; spread —; support —; teach —; trace —; — concerns; —
embodies; — grows; — progresses; — redeems; — saves; — transcends; — triumphs.
(See religion, faith.)

CHRONIC
adverbs
avowedly; incurably; unfortunately; finally;
obstinately; stubbornly; lingeringly; mildly; firmly; deplorably; grievously; pitiably;
indubitably; manifestly; evidently; palpably; obviously; unquestionably; distinctly;
plainly; incontrovertibly; unmistakably.

CHRONICLE
adjectives
sensuous; pagan; commonplace; objective;
calm; gay; fascinating; detailed; lively;
scandalous; stirring; heroic; racy; salty;
wistful; tender; humorous; courageous;
mocking; faithful; vivid; massive; memorable; poignant; unique; gripping; incomparable; lofty; moving; human; vigorous;
episodic; broad-spoken; tedious; zestful;
medieval; tattered; factual; dusty; fast-
moving; personal; sententious; intimate.

197

verbs

accumulate in —; arrange —; compare —; compile —; complete —; compose —; devote — to; examine —; forge —; keep —; preserve —; recite —; refer to —; skeletonize —; — consists of; — contains; — contradicts; — conveys; — disposes; — determines; — embraces; — presents; — recollects; — registers; — reveals; — sets down; — treats of.

(See record, account, narrative, diary, history.)

CHRONICLER

adjectives

matter-of-fact; scandal-loving; contemporaneous.

CHRONOLOGICAL

adverbs

accurately; carefully; meticulously; fussily; absolutely; dependably; tolerably; infallibly; scrupulously; strictly; uncannily; unimpeachably; avidly; punctiliously.

CHRONOLOGY

adjectives

dismal; distilled; condensed; meaningful; mouldering; simple; uneventful; unvarnished; verified.

verbs

arrange —; ascertain —; base — on; check —; compare — with; correlate —; develop —; explain —; fix —; interest in —; preserve —; reckon —; settle —; telescope —; verse in —; — classifies; — computes; — depends on; — enumerates; — includes; — indicates; — measures; — provides; — records; — reveals; — survives; — traces.

(See science, time.)

CHRYSANTHEMUM

adjectives

huge; tawny; bronze; brave; pink; golden; great; pale; shaggy; yellow; calm.

CHUBBY

adverbs

adorably; sweetly; cheerily; buxomly; huskily; rosily; pleasantly; happily; cheerfully; sturdily; healthily; stoutly; laughably; ridiculously; lovably; admirably; ludicrously; stupidly; heavily; laughingly; gaily; blithely; bonnily; winsomely; handsomely; terribly.

CHUCKLE

adjectives

appreciative; affectionate; naive; long; delicious; humorous; benevolent; sepulchral; melancholy; mirthless; low; little; slow; deep; noiseless; vicious; gloating; evil; sneering; irreverent; exultant; gratuitous; ghastly; unpleasant; eerie; soft; childish; crazy; husky; shrewd; mild; elfish; asthmatic; inward; dry; communicative; contagious; cruel; palpitating; suppressed; sly; insulting; bitter; inward; prolonged; coarse; fearful; tremulous; joyous; grim.

CHUCKLE (*v*)

adverbs

inaudibly; casually; maliciously; gruffly; waggishly; inwardly; fearfully; hollowly; appreciatively; affectionately; naively; humorously; benevolently; sepulchrally; mirthlessly; noiselessly; gloatingly; sneeringly; irreverently; exultantly; gratuitously; unpleasantly; huskily; elfishly; contagiously; asthmatically; insultingly; bitterly; tremulously; joyously; grimly.

(See laugh.)

CHUMMY

adverbs

delightfully; helpfully; devotedly; intimately; sympathetically; companionably; affectionately; cordially; warmly; sincerely; heartily; amicably; affably; wonderfully; frankly; graciously; loyally; distinctly; enthusiastically; congenially; marvellously; unselfishly; staunchly; generously; steadfastly; courageously.

CHURCH

adjectives

venerable; impressive; calm; dignified; simple; famous; historical; imposing; ancient; hoary; handsome; exquisite; fashionable; enormous; frescoed; small; gray; loopholed; ivy-clad; colonial; belfry-towered; country; white-washed; fly-bitten; square-towered; parabolic; village; parish; dismal; silent; superfluous; competing; huddling; dedicated; pillaged; dissenting; buttressed; belfried; cathedral; sumptuous; ornate; friendly-looking; tremendous; dominating; ambitious; primitive; prosaic; barnlike; uncouth; spireless; gloomy; established; conservative; olive-green; sandstone; decent; remote; comprehensive; self-denying; laborious; unwearied; ancient.

verbs

assemble in —; baptize in —; christen in —; confirm in —; consecrate —; deface —; drift away from —; enrich —; establish —; esteem —; file into —; forsake —; gather in —; hie to —; interpret —; laud —; liberalize —; neglect —; orient —; present to —; ransack —; respect —; salute —; unite —; wed in —; worship in —; — absolves; — inspires; — molds; — moulders; — wanes.

(See temple, cathedral, chapel, tabernacle, sanctuary, congregation.)

CHURCH-GOERS

adjectives

austere; backbiting; backsliding; devout; earnest; dogmatic; fervent; grave; heaven-aspiring; hypocritical; morose; long-faced; puritanical; salvation-seeking.

verbs

appeal to —; appoint —; join —; patronize —; prevail on —; respect —; witness —; — abandon; — attend; — authorize; — band; — commune; — conform; —congregate; — contribute; — control; — convene; — criticize; — endow; — flow by; — grow; — ignore; — organize; — provide; — rally; — sneer; — stream past; — support.
(See congregation.)

CHURCHY

adverbs

devoutly; hypocritically; ostentatiously; sententiously; unctuously; devotedly; fashionably; unwearyingly; pompously; dramatically; dutifully; properly; appropriately; adequately; meticulously; punctiliously; obediently; piously; sentimentally; obsequiously; pharisaically; sanctimoniously; conscientiously; righteously; pretentiously.

CHURL

adjectives

drunken; seditious; sturdy; vulgar; brash; brazen.

CHURLISH

adverbs

inordinately; bluntly; sullenly; stupidly; basely; ruggedly; fantastically; awkwardly; offensively; unconsciously; unwittingly; artlessly; deliberately; colossally; detestably; insufferably; intolerably; unbearably; rudely; crudely; abominably; intentionally; shockingly; innately; boorishly; ignorantly; harshly; disagreeably; outrageously; indefensibly; vulgarly; brazenly; coarsely; brashly; brassily; contemptibly; shamefully.

CHURN (v)

adverbs

irrationally; viciously; vigorously; wildly; impressively; awesomely; grimly; tumultuously; thunderously; deafeningly.

CIDER

adjectives

piercing; tangy; aromatic; acid.

CIGAR

adjectives

smooth; mild; mellow;' vile; unlighted; butted; disheveled; half-smoked; aromatic; excellent; villainous; rank; rough; exotic; inevitable; refreshing.

verbs

box —; chew on —; clip —; clutch —; crave —; display —; extinguish —; flick —; grade —; import —; inhale —; insert —; manufacture —; mold —; object to —; pocket —; point ¡ produce —, proffer —; puff on —; pull at —; roll into —; shape —; smoke —; wave —; wrap —; yearn for —; — appeals; — burns; — glows.

CIGARETTE

adjectives

disconsolate; soggy; indispensable; lightly-fingered; monogrammed; bungled; unlighted; blended; acrid; quashed; dangling; proffered; pasty; formless; customary.

verbs

blend —s; carton —s; choke on —; consume —s; cough on —; discard —s; fumble for —; grade —; inhale —; mentholize —; moisten —; package —; perfume —; proffer —; purvey —; tip —; toast —; turn out —; wave —; — dies; — dries out; — fumes; — glows; — smoulders; — stales.

CIMMERIAN

adverbs

gloomily; darkly; vastily; expansively; extensively; terrifyingly; frightfully; luridly; sunlessly; tenebriously; umbrageously; obscurely; dimly; shadily; murkily; sombrely; stupendously; appallingly; hideously.

CINDERS

adjectives

besieging; blinding; blazing; cruel; drifting; catapulting; dusty; feathery; gritty; inky; murky; smudgy; sooty; sharp; stinging.

verbs
arrest —s; deposit —s; eject —s; form —s; pile —s; quench into —s; rake —s; reduce to —s; sift —s; throw off —s; turn to —; — die; — fly; — glow; — lodge; — pop; — sear; — smoulder.
(See coal, residue, ashes.)

CIPHER

adjectives
valueless; inextricable; constant.

CIRCLE

adjectives
conversational; social; illustrious; exclusive; gilded; artistic; political; aristocratic; literary; fashionable; wealthy; financial; wide; brilliant; well-bred; bigoted; select; limited; cheery; charmed; real; ideal; convivial; erratic; perfect; dim; pale; iron; eddying; disintegrated; blurred; broken; enclosing; great; sweeping; sturdy; charmed; intimate; executive; solemn; predestined; concentric; cosmopolitan; bizarre; widening; charred; ceremonial; ringing; collapsed; ever-enlarging; original; vicious; agricultural; splendid; decorative; leading; influential; distinguished; smartest; elastic; pleasant; closed; petty; educational; esoteric; polished; interior; operatic; ultrafashionable; awkward; extended; deep; ruddy; vast; walled; uninterrupted; conservative; privileged; noisy; wavering; pallid; giddy; curious; deft; professional; diplomatic.

verbs
accomplish —; assemble in —; bar from —; circumscribe —; cleave —; complete —; cut —; disband —; emit from —; form —; flutter in —; guard —; hallow —; inscribe —; insert in —; join —; lead into —; narrow —; pour in —; revolve —; round —; spin in —; swell —; trace —; — disintegrates; — widens.

CIRCLE (v)

adverbs
demurely; erratically; solemnly; wideningly; ceremonially; viciously; awkwardly; noisily; waveringly; curiously; treacherously.
(See surround.)

CIRCLED

adverbs
darkly; ominously; closely; gloriously; radiantly; strangely; completely; hopelessly; fatally; alarmingly; perplexingly; unexpectedly; suddenly; roseately.

CIRCUIT

adjectives
respectful; due; electric; unbroken; annual; elliptical; tedious; irregular; spacious; voltaic; short.

verbs
administer —; appoint to —; attach to —; complete —; discontinue —; divide into —s; enclose within —; form —; plug into —; regulate —; remodel —; retain —; ride —; supervise —; travel —; visit —; — comprises; — consists of; — prevails; — transmits.
(See district, course.)

CIRCUITOUS

adverbs
exasperatingly; terribly; needlessly; tediously; wearisomely; monotonously; vexatiously; undesirably; unsuitably; extremely; hopelessly; endlessly; sadly; tortuously; intricately; crookedly; deviously; disturbingly; distressingly; dangerously; suspiciously; obscurely; alarmingly; astonishingly; bewilderingly; wretchedly; unduly.

CIRCULAR

adjectives
inviting; descriptive; confidential; brief; significant; sluggish.

verbs
announce by —; display —; distribute —; lay out —; request —; shower —s; subscribe to —; summon by —; — advertises; — colors; — describes; — explains; — informs; — proclaims; — propagates.
(See communication, publication, letter.)

adverbs
perfectly; absolutely; symmetrically; artistically; ceremonially; originally; decoratively; significantly; smartly; fashionably; curiously; brokenly; naturally; elliptically; impressively; architecturally; theatrically; harmoniously.

CIRCULATE (v)

adverbs
immediately; greedily; continually; widely; extensively; briskly; industriously; limitedly; considerably; enormously; sluggishly; periodically; selectively; inadequately; effectively; normally.
(See disseminate, diffuse.)

CIRCULATION

adjectives   *(blood)*

abnormal; adequate; aroused; deficient; defective; engorged; impaired; lax; hindered; over-stimulated; rapid; sluggish; simulated; tonic.

verbs

aid —; carry on —; check —; constrict —; depress —; increase —; impair —; impede —; improve —; maintain —; obstruct —; overtax —; promote —; quicken —; quiet —; relieve —; restore —; speed up —; stimulate —; throw into —.

CIRCULATION
(newspaper,
adjectives   *magazine, etc.)*

amazing; limited; considerable; vast; enormous; select; huge; extensive; sluggish; periodical; suspended; defective; repressed; throttled; inadequate; effective; brisk; normal.

verbs

augment —; boost —; build —; double —; fix —; heighten —; increase —; lose —; maintain —; promote —; reduce —; — climbs; — drops; — gains; — jumps; — sags; — spurts; — wanes.

(See distribution, number, quantity.)

CIRCUMFERENCE
adjectives
extensive; vast; extreme; luminous.

CIRCUMJACENT
adverbs
closely; influentially; contributively; advantageously; interestedly; actively; importantly; anxiously; indivisibly; inseparably; consequentially; momentously; potently; authoritatively; closely; cooperatively; helpfully; serviceably; opportunely; concernedly; sympathetically; watchfully; warily; providently; alertly; heedfully.

CIRCUMLOCUTORY
adverbs
tiresomely; tediously; unnecessarily; amateurishly; monotonously; maddeningly; vexatiously; impossibly; undesirably; ineptly; unsuitably; extremely; excessively; incurably; incorrigibly; insistently; pedantically; pedagogically; academically; hopelessly; digressively; ramblingly; sadly; inexcusably; inefficiently.

CIRCUMSCRIBE (v)
adverbs
narrowly; severely; precisely; closely; rigorously; definitely; clearly; specifically.
(See confine, defense, limit.)

CIRCUMSPECTION
adjectives
exact; utmost; administrative; continual; pious; sly.

CIRCUMSTANCE
adjectives
dominant; antecedent; analogous; formal; favorable; encouraging; exceptional; fortunate; imagined; extenuating; mitigating; accompanying; hurried; external; altered; similar; actual; existing; ensuing; diverse; subsequent; attendant; concomitant; accessory; contingent; manifold; contributory; leading; collateral; expeditious; unfortunate; equivocal; droll; adventitious; novel; romantic; auspicious; pitiful; fortuitous; identical; peculiar; incredible; unsafe; interesting; faulty; minute; formidable; easy; irritable; providential; ridiculous; encumbered; isolated; painful; affluent; present; disastrous; striking; arduous; discouraging; obsolete; momentary; incidental; dreadful; unforeseen; unpropitious; disquieting; untoward; promiscuous; straitened; forgotten; extraordinary; mysterious; uncontrollable; suggestive; singular; suspicious; sordid; curious; comfortable; accidental; unbelievable; peculiar; unlucky; delicate; unpromising; adverse; differing; historical; accidental; evanescent; inexplicable; potent; varying (pl); ignoble; probable; embarrassing; trying; sordid; intellectual; advantageous; astonishing; iniquitous; distressing; trifling; disheartening; agreeable; brutal; reduced; domestic; precarious; impressive; remarkable; frivolous; perplexing; dramatic; diametric; moderate; prevailing; complicated; sensational.

verbs
ascribe to —; attend with —; depend on —; detail —; engender —; impress with —; meet —; overcome by —; ponder —; recount —; relish —; respond to —; rest on —; shape —; stress —; struggle against —; weigh —; — accompanies; — alarms; — alters; — arises; — determines; — forces; — hampers; — imputes; — prevents; — surrounds; — wavers; — yields.

(See condition, incident, cause, occurrence, situation, feature, environment.)

adverbs
sensationally; remarkably; insignificantly; trivially; favorably; temporarily; extenuatingly; aggravatingly; coincidentally; fortuitously; unpropitiously; unfavorably; suspiciously; adversely; adventitiously; critically; incidentally; contradictorily; corroboratively; reasonably; plausibly; speciously; credibly.

CIRCUS

adjectives
Jacksonian; bloody; tented; political; traveling; tinseled; three-ring.

verbs
admit to —; "ballyhoo" —; operate —; perform at —; stage —; yearn for —; — amuses; — blares; — displays; — engages; — enlivens; —entertains; — exhibits; — parades; — roams; — tours; — travels; — troups.
(See show.)

CITADEL

adjectives
celebrated; straw-built; unguarded; ancient; social; aerie; capitulated; impregnable; pensile; undefended.

verbs
attack —; bar from —; command —; construct —; erect —; establish —; evolve —; fortify —; man —; pour from —; retreat to —; scale —; siege —; storm —; — contains; — defends; — defies; — guards; — protects; — rises; — stores; — towers; — withstands.
(See fortress.)

CITATION

adjectives
corroborated; ample; apt; ludicrous; partial.

CITE (v)

adverbs
earnestly; partially; amply; aptly; accurately; authoritatively; relevantly; sensationally; fortuitously; strikingly.
(See quote, mention.)

CITIZEN

adjectives
belligerent; busy; esteemed; perspicacious; small-salaried; luckless; prosperous; distinguished; patched; individual; prejudiced; plodding; enlightened; enthusiastic; inde-finite; unworthy; substantial; intelligent; god-fearing; ordinary; peaceable; law-abiding; unoffending; disillusioned; callous; staid; home-loving; ornamental; defenseless; competent; simple; plain-speaking; public-spirited; conscious; active; conspicuous; callous; vile; half-starved; influential; venerable; indignant; average; private; generous; illustrious; cultivated; grave; respectable; admirable; eminent; cloaked; reputable; representative; loyal; worthy; useful; law-abiding; duteous; bespectacled; patriotic; well-known; honorable; lamented; mutinous; plain; simple; quiet; easygoing; innocent; tight-lipped; august; pugnacious; disgruntled; beleaguered; iron-bellied; wistful; regretful; ordinary; humble; average; mere; prosaic; typical; able-bodied; courageous; husky; young; stalwart; bibulous; sanguine; careless; selfish; blind; serious-minded; straight-thinking; reckless; conscientious; high-minded; foremost; valued; wealthy; prominent; leading; outstanding; revered; self-sacrificing; hard-working; progressive; zealous; loyal; kindly; honest; decent; cultured; altruistic; worthy; well-meaning; stolid; solid; independent; untrammeled; noble; exemplary.

verbs
conscript —s; disfranchise —; entitle as —; harangue —s; interview —; oppress —; privilege —; protect —; regiment —s; register as —; tax —; wheedle —s; —s assemble; —s demand; —s elect; — enjoys; — possesses; — protests; —s rally; —s vote; — vows.
(See individual, inhabitant.)

CITIZENRY

adjectives
outraged; humble; contented; greasy; dignified.

CITIZENSHIF

adjectives
national; commonplace; robust; conscientious.

verbs
accept —; acquire —; admit to —; apply for —; cancel —; confer — upon; declare —; deprive of —; desire —; divest of —; drop —; establish —; forfeit —; obtain —; refuse—; renounce—; revoke—; — confers; — entitles; — privileges; — protects.

adjectives

throbbing; bustling; seething; hustling; thriving; growing; brutal; busiest; wealthiest; progressive; unperturbed; huge; teeming; headlong; glorious; rushing; stirring; energetic; modern; flourishing; busy; enterprising; gay; laughing; lighthearted; sleeping; dead; quiet; wicked; free; sin-stained; wilted; worth-while; corrupt; ruined; content; intolerant; fanatical; smoldering; dull; murky; grimy; congested; drab; squalid; ugly; commonplace; worse-lit; widespreading; outermost; rich; influential; prosperous; conservative; trading; selfsame; shimmering; noble; thronged; unruly; cathedraled; melancholy; mighty; breathless; ruinous; humming; resplendent; coastal; swarming; fascinating; inspiring; sunken; deserted; gilded; distinguished; diversified; hopeful; distracted; mirthful; opulent; queer; glittering; long-shaped; peaceful; friendly, shivering, glamorous, lamplit; rock-built; annihilated; joyous; menacing; elegant; youthful; mansion-decked; ambitious; nether; imperial; titanic; restless; enchanted; pagan; pleasure; tropical; typical; slumbering; prospective; maritime; clustering; affrighted; melancholy; earth-commanding; advertised; drowned; wondrous; gorgeous; hard-boiled; powerful; a-wakened; isolated; industrious; ancient; crooked; tortuous; snakelike; rising; unhappy; undefended; cursed; commercial; voluptuous; plague-stricken; congested; wailing; spacious; vast; helpless; holocaust; pest-ridden; torpid; passive; dejected; garrisoned; well-washed; appreciative; ruined; constricted; thriving; decayed; masterful; wrought; luxurious; well-ordered; spirited; advancing; altar-decked; silenced; crowded; provincial; beleaguered; cordial; death-stricken; verdureless; once-famous; heathen; attractive; jeweled; well-watered; eternal; plague-stricken; negligent; vice-laden; spire-adorned; sin-compassed; rogue-haunted; monolithic; hapless; besieged; materialistic; nebulous; commercial; sin-burdened; austere; sunless; unrivalled; futuristic; enthralling; delightful; majestic; marvelous; fabulous; aspiring; great; lovable; desirable; coveted; fascinating; benignant; scintillating; proud; bright; fairest; naughty; impregnable; beautiful; staid; silent; moonlit; dream; lovely; colorful; gray-blue; snow-white; unique; grand; mysterious; adventurous; glittering; dying; buried; bombarded; monotonous; muffled; agate; polyglot; golden-doomed; appealing; infant; native; cosmopolitan; royal; tourist; shipbuilding; lake-girted; guardian; prehistoric; alabaster-like; holy; flat-roofed; oriental-looking; walled; medieval; legendary; industrial; pontifical; celestial; exotic; homogeneous; lurid; confused; incredible; burning; meticulous; leading; principal; vibrant; far-flung; populous; fortified; conquered; well-kept; ever-growing; sun-baked; parched-brown; gentle-mannered.

verbs

abide in —; adjoin —; annihilate —; approach —; assault —; banish from —; besiege —; burn —; congregate in —; corrupt —; crowd —; deface —; defend —; deluge —; depopulate —; desolate —; destroy —; doom —; encompass —; erect —; establish —; flank —; harbor in —; haunt —; huddle in —; impoverish —; inhabit —; inundate —; issue from —; lay siege to —; lay waste to ; march through —, migrate to —; mold —; oppress —; pen up in —; pillage —; pollute —; raze —; rule —; sack —; scatter through —; shake —; stake out —; steal over —; strike —; survey —; swallow up in —; take —; tarry in —; tax —; terrorize —; veer toward —; wall in —; war on —; warn —; — acclaims; — basks; — decays; — expands; — flourishes; — forges ahead; — hums; — reeks; — roars; — simmers; — sprouts; — straggles; — towers.

(See town, community.)

adverbs

extraordinarily; significantly; unexpectedly; surprisingly; undeniably; meticulously; deliberately; artificially; naturally; disagreeably; agreeably; discordantly; ostentatiously; inharmonoiusly; superciliously; arrogantly; pathetically; ludicrously; ridiculously; foolishly; awkwardly; busily; enterprisingly; prosperously; proudly; fashionably; grandly; incongruously.

adverbs

smoothly; coolly; correctly; properly; appropriately; scarcely; politely; affably; warmly; graciously; sweetly; fawningly; idly; nonchalantly; unexpectedly; suddenly; carefully; officiously; unctuously; blandly; obligingly; complacently; obsequiously; ingratiatingly; tactfully; diplomatically; sagaciously; wisely; necessarily; condescendingly; urbanely; decorously; fashionably;

punctiliously; meticulously; admirably; conventionally; stiffly; demurely; primly; precisely; cautiously; warily.

CIVILIAN

adjectives
meddlesome; covenanted; humdrum; conceited; wretched.

CIVILITY

adjectives
unforced; sad; cold; sweet; creeping; fawning; base; chill; ancient; restrained; interchanged (pl); impetuous; idle; unmeaning.

verbs
accept with —; act with —; answer with —; breed —; cherish —; conform to —; consider —; employ —; deny —; lack —; oblige with —; observe —; occasion —; preserve —; respect —; teach —; train in —; treat with —; want —; — befits.

(See courtesy, politeness.)

CIVILIZATION

adjectives
brutalized; luminous; distinctive; potential; perished; private; primitive; ancient; increasing; vast; varied; overvaunted; bloated; progressive; sophisticated; troubadour; moral; decadent; earthly; ordered; material; contemporary; turbulent; strange; advancing; complex; indigenous; mechanical; passionate; refined; higher; saturated; enlightened; decent; perilous; sick; alien; technical; crumbling; disintegrating; effete; bygone; older; long-vanished; artistic; archaic; forgotten; unique; extraordinary; so-called; cracked; industrial; megalopolitan; superficial; luxurious; urban; domestic; barbaric; aboriginal; agrarian; national; crude; fastidious; majestic; unrecorded; belligerent; chivalrous; selfish; solid; positive; pernicious; prosy; modern; curious; attendant; perfected.

verbs
blot out—; break down—; contribute to—; court—; cradle—; destroy—; doom—; extol—; flout—; found—; fuse—s; infect—; menace—; promote—; raise—; shame—; standardize—; threaten—; —advances; —asserts itself; —decays; —declines; —enslaves; —falls; —inflicts; —mars; —perishes; —progresses; —reverts to type; —sweeps onward; —wanes.

(See enlightenment, progress, refinement, advancement, culture.)

adverbs
richly; elaborately; gaudily; wretchedly; fully; scantily; shabbily; raggedly; poorly; luxuriously; carefully; carelessly; recklessly; absurdly; fashionably; ridiculously; ludicrously; grotesquely; honorably; unfashionably; garishly; wantonly; laughably; clownishly; seductively; gaily; gorgeously; glamorously; awkwardly; incongruously; outlandishly; expensively; cheaply; smartly; handsomely; drably; extravagantly; economically; tastefully.

CLAD (v)

adverbs
decorously; symbolically; grossly; imperfectly; fittingly; partially; scantily; scarcely; heavily; warmly; harmoniously.
(See dress.)

CLAIM

adjectives
additional; faint; ardent; extenuating; misleading; exaggerated; extravagant; curative; substantiated; indisputable; enormous; groundless; confidential; bitter; exclusive; plausible; intellectual; unquenchable; notorious; complacent; intolerable; advertising; hereditary; unjustifiable; unprophetic; slender; peculiar; sales; fraudulent; rhetorical; accumulating; valid; remaining; worthless; reproachful; respectable; illegal; embroidered; time-honored; extortionate; suitable; contested; obsolete; conflicting (pl); imperial; inexorable; insistent; professional; modest; abiding; prior; rival; inflated; fanciful; questionable; incredible; preposterous; unsavory; false; pecuniary; parental; royal; special; implacable; imperative; unusual; difficult; depreciating; relative.

verbs
adjust—; annul—; assert—; attest to—; base—on; cede—; combat—; confirm—; consider—; contradict—; debate—; defy—; demolish—; denounce—; deny—; dismiss —; dispose of—; dispute—; doubt—; establish—; exempt from—; expose—; forfeit—; honor—; iron out—s; justify—; lay—to; offset—; press—; protest—; reconcile—; record—; refute—; renounce—; retain—; shatter—; smile at—; stake out—; stultify—; substantiate—; support—; surrender—; verify—; waive—; —s diminish; —s dissolve.

(See pretension, demand. title. right.)

CLAIM (v)

adverbs
persistently; strenuously; confidently; assuredly; adroitly; falsely; boldly; vociferously; exorbitantly; ardently; exaggeratedly; groundlessly; unjustifiably; reproachfully; fraudulently; extortionately; inexorably; professionally; insistently; incredibly; legitimately; validly; fancifully; preposterously; implacably; imperatively.
(See assert, affirm, maintain.)

CLAIRVOYANT

adverbs
remarkably; unmistakably; mysteriously; unquestionably; marvelously; prophetically; mesmerically; hypnotically; naturally; extraordinarily; undeniably; absolutely; indisputably; incontestably; traditionally; inherently; palpably; infallibly; conclusively; phenomenally; triumphantly; evidently; manifestly; obviously; incredibly; astonishingly; astoundingly; startlingly.

CLAMBER (v)

adverbs
aimlessly; bravely; laboriously; ceaselessly; clumsily; unsteadily.
(See climb.)

CLAMMY

adverbs
unpleasantly; disagreeably; horridly; horribly; loathsomely; disgustingly; offensively; repulsively; hatefully; necessarily; distastefully; manageably; stickily; adhesively; cohesively; coldly.

CLAMOR

adjectives
full-voiced; ghastly; noisy; tremendous; hideous; hellish; impatient; violent; nerve-straining; deafening; general; mournful; never-ceasing; heart-warming; popular; raucous; frenzied; turbulent; orchestral; sudden; staccato; venomous; savage; ministerial; excited; wretched; smothered; deplorable; loud; ignorant; exacting; blind; vulgar; universal; confirmatory; persistent; dismal; querulous; fulsome; vague; virile; impertinent; muffled; uncontrollable; petty; frightful; selfish; national; thunderous.

verbs
cease—; ease—; fill with—; harken to—; lose in—; prolong—; raise—; vent—; — abates; —bursts forth; —deafens; —

drowns; —peals; —rings; —rumbles; — thickens; —wanes; —waxes.
(See uproar, tumult, din, racket.)

CLAMOR (v)

adverbs
dissentingly; noisily; vociferously; obstreperously; shrilly; hideously; hellishly; mournfully; raucously; frenziedly; turbulently; venomously; wretchedly; deplorably; persistently; dismally; querulously; fulsomely; impertinently; thunderously; uncontrollably.
(See bawl, roar.)

CLAMOROUS

adverbs
noisily; impatiently; surlily; angrily; happily; eagerly; hungrily; deafeningly; madly; frenziedly; suddenly; excitedly; wretchedly; blindly; persistently; anxiously; querulously; vaguely; uncontrollably; selfishly; restlessly; explosively; alarmingly; menacingly; hysterically; enthusiastically; ungovernably; significantly; fanatically; boisterously; jubilantly; joyously; shrilly; uproariously; ominously; importunately; appallingly; impressively; extraordinarily; unwontedly; urgently.

CLAN

adjectives
critical; prolific; original; feudal; clamorous; sturdy; romping; murderous; visionary; hostile; rival.

verbs
assemble—; associate with—; connect with —; descend from—; dissolve—; father—; found—; grace—; join—; lead—; muster —; organize—; prohibit—; represent—; rule—; trace—; unify—; —gathers; —marauds; —pillages; —plunders; —terrorizes.
(See tribe.)

CLANDESTINE

adverbs
romantically; furtively; sordidly; inviolately; strictly; necessarily; unhappily; guiltily; subtly; curiously; unsavorily; evasively; stealthily; slyly; skulkingly; terribly; miserably.

CLANG

adjectives
imperious; fearful; warning; horrid; windy; glad; melancholy; lingering; hol-

low; ecstatic; nonchalant; resounding; harsh; discordant; metallic; muffled; funereal; brassy; vibrating.

CLANG (v)
adverbs
discordantly; infernally; resonantly; imperiously; fearfully; horridly; hollowly; ecstatically; vibratingly; metallically; funereally; dismally.

CLANGOR
adjectives
mad; sudden; merry; deafening; reverberative; impatient.

CLANGOROUS
adverbs
madly; terrifyingly; violently; riotously; horribly; jubilantly; cheeringly; mournfully; funereally; sadly; alarmingly; warningly; menacingly; joyously; happily; joyfully; stirringly; thunderously; sweetly; softly; harmoniously; deeply; deafeningly; sonorously; melodiously; mellifluously; heartily; hearteningly.

CLANK
adjectives
steady; metallic; tiny; tinkling.

CLANNISH
adverbs
incurably; delightfully; loyally; incorrigibly; eternally; characteristically; inherently; sturdily; stoutly; noisily; quietly; devotedly; staunchly; dependably; truly; racially; locally; provincially; intrepidly; indomitably; intrinsically; dangerously; alarmingly; actively; definitely; vigorously.

CLANNISHNESS
adjectives
unconquerable; enforced.

CLAP
adjectives
friendly; frightful; genial.

CLAP (v)
adverbs
conclusively; vigorously; dutifully; noiselessly; unobtrusively; frightfully; thunderously; genially; enthusiastically; freely; monotonously; liberally; appreciatively; sympathetically; gratefully; welcomingly; ceaselessly.
(See applaud.)

CLARIFY (v)
adverbs
successfully; intellectually; admirably; miraculously; satisfactorily; completely; partially; painstakingly; generally; notably.
(See illumine, clear.)

CLARITY
adjectives
intellectual; painful; interpretative; unsurpassed; sparkling; aching; diamondlike; enervating; sickening; miraculous; admirable; fragrant; intense; sunlit; irrefutable; quiet; cold; crystal.

CLASH
adjectives
furious; threatened; explosive; angry; contemporaneous; rude; syncopated; sharp; memorable; initial; street; recurrent; joyous; violent; naval; brisk; soundless; bloody; metallic; muffled; inter-racial.

verbs
attack with—; avoid—; collide with—; embroil in—; engage in—; incite—; produce—; recoil from—; recount—; result in—; strike with—; —conflicts with; —echoes; —peals; —resounds; —shocks; —thunders; —warns.
(See crash, collision, opposition, noise.)

CLASH (v)
adverbs
unpleasantly; antagonistically; explosively; rhythmically; furiously; angrily; rudely; sharply; initially; recurrently; violently; muffledly; thunderously; intermittently; instinctively.
(See hurtle, crash, disagree.)

CLASHING
adverbs
unfortunately; unhappily; hostilely; inimically; contradictorily; unpropitiously; constantly; pugnaciously; truculently; ill-naturedly; contentiously; quarrelsomely; unnecessarily; ill-advisedly; hastily; antagonistically; foolishly; irritably; unreasonably; senselessly; miserably; hotly; frightfully; pathetically; vexatiously; bitterly; rudely; violently; frequently; furiously; crudely; sharply.

CLASP
(embrace)
adjectives
conventional; dewy; impulsive; uncoercive; warm; comforting; gentlemanly; gentle; confiding; cruel; lingering; eager; cold; firm; frantic; healthy; strong.

CLASP
(fastener)

adjectives
gilt; ornate; clicking.

CLASP
(general)

verbs
affix—; brace—; buckle—; cleave—; connect—; fit—; fumble with—; furnish with—; gird with—; hook—; join—; strain—; —bars; —embraces; —encircles; —fastens; —grasps; —insures; —interlocks; —overlaps; —secures.
(See hook, embrace, lock.)

CLASP (v)

adverbs
convulsively; deliberately; fondly; unprofitably; familiarly; sensually; hungrily; severely; frantically; impulsively; comfortingly; confidingly; cruelly; lingeringly; coldly; firmly, despairingly.
(See grasp, grapple, clutch.)

CLASS
(school)

adjectives
academic; attending; assembled; bespectacled; diligent; elementary; fixed; grade; grouped; graduating; freshman; intermediate; lecture; overworked; primer; primary; advanced; subdivided; unlimited.

verbs
address—; admit to—; attend—; change —es; conduct—; divide into—es; examine —; lecture—; limit—; promote—; raise—; rate—; unite—; —answers; —assembles; —choruses; —competes; —graduates; —recites; —reviews; —sings; —studies.

CLASS
(social)

adjectives
arrogant; unclaimed; ruthless; vast; emergent; ruling; history-conscious; leisure; spurious; laboring; useful; humble; technical; servile; degraded; generic; social; diversified; privileged; conflicting; piratical; consistent; submerged; collected; represented; traditional; dole-receiving; peaceful; better; vicious; inarticulate; dominant; rapid; various (pl); exclusive; despised; venal; conspicuous; liberated; opulent; irresponsible; possessionless; obnoxious; corresponding; lower; agrarian; distinct; noticeable; exploiting; vulgar; inferior; irreconcilable; wealthy; cultured;
upper; cultivated; best; preferred; conservative; industrial; intellectual; proletarian; illiterate; submerged; artisan; contented; prosperous; working; object; odious; mediocre; truant; rising; central; middle-aged; indivisible; appointive; chivalrous; holy; iron-bound; vigorous; skeptical; unimpassioned; economic.

verbs
arouse—; bow to—; consort with—; do away with—es; educate—; elevate—; enslave—; fix—; free—; level—; liberate—es; lower—es; separate—; stifle—; —es arise; —es gravitate; —idolizes; —predominates; —rebels.
(See caste, rank, order.)

CLASSIC

adjectives
perfumed; bristling; venerable; favorite; beloved; noblest; unforgettable; purest; intellectual; juvenile; immortal, rare.

CLASSICAL

adverbs
superbly; acceptably; admittedly; elegantly; easily; gracefully; readily; academically; artistically; chastely; correctly; felicitously; naturally; unaffectedly; modestly; unpretentiously; undoubtedly; deservedly; avowedly; pleasingly; aptly; appropriately; commendably; deservedly; admirably; laudably; universally; uniformly.

CLASSICISM

adjectives
capricious; cold; ethical.

CLASSICS

verbs
accept—; acquaint with—; assimilate—; associate with—; bar—; criticize—; delve into—; discuss—; edit—; educate in—; familiarize with—; favor—; forsake—; instruct in—; introduce to—; model on—; pertain to—; place among—; prefer—; quote—; regard—; revel in—; tabulate—; verse in—; —exemplify; —guide.
(See literature, history, biography, religion.)

CLASSIFICATION

adjectives
racial; minute; inexact; detailed; price; misleading; occupational; moral; lucid; compendious; social; principal; broad; fixed.

verbs

allocate—; arrange—; assign—; assume—; attempt—; confirm—; correct—; distinguish—; employ—; exclude—; exhaust—; formulate—; head—; lead—; observe—; place in—; question—; recognize—; reduce—; retain—; separate into—; subordinate—; systematize—; —allows; —orders; —permits.

(See arrangement, group.)

CLASSIFY (v)

adverbs

carefully; ignorantly; conveniently; racially; minutely; exactly; misleadingly; lucidly; compendiously; socially; broadly.

(See arrange.)

CLASSMATE

adjectives

erstwhile; condescending; fun-loving; heckling; parasitic; superiority-inflicting; snubbing; snobbish; unapproachable; whilom.

verbs

compete with—s; enroll with—s; hail—s; prompt—s; recognize—s; reunite with—s; tutor—; —advances; —chooses; —s clash; —cribs (colloq.); —disenrolls; —s elect; —fails; —"flunks"; —graduates; —s honor; —recites; —vacations.

(See member, student, companion, friend.)

CLASSROOM

adjectives

grimy; gloomy; stuffy; modern; noisy.

verbs

absent from—; "barge" into—; bustle into —; buzz through—; clutter up—; congregate in—; dismiss from—; disorder—; equip—; illuminate—; preside over—; retain in—; rule—; scurry through—; survey—; —clamors with; —hums.

(See room.)

CLATTER

adjectives

prodigious; city-bred; glib-tongued; authoritative; confused; subsided; metallic; hideous; delectable; rousing; ringing; harsh; sudden; rhythmic; wild; hysterical; swift; reverberating; castanet.

CLATTER (v)

adverbs

recklessly; dissonantly; prodigiously; confusedly; metallically; hideously; ringingly; harshly; wildly; hysterically; furiously; excitingly; rudely.

(See tramp.)

CLAUSE

adjectives

complicated; misleading; expatiatory; particular; introductory; compensatory; sweeping; glacial; insidious; qualifying; solemn; independent; appended; ambiguous; flexible; limiting; adjective; adverbial; noun; appositional; descriptive; secret; hidden.

verbs

actuate—; condemn—; cudgel—; denounce—; evade—; "fake"—; frame—; insert—; insist on—; introduce—; kill—; legalize—; motivate—; occasion—; order—; ponder—; question—; sacrifice—; rule against—; unearth—; violates—; —bars; —cedes; —denotes; —embodies; —governs; —guards against; —joins; —provides; —stipulates; —varies; —wills.

(See provision, article, part.)

CLAW

adjectives

grimy; hooded; bloody; scarifying; holy; ominous; nipping; powerful; burrowing; slimy; acute; prehensile; scaly; sheathed; quivering; dirt-encrusted; feeble; invisible.

verbs

arm with—s; clip—s; clutch in—s; grapple with—s; grasp in—s; grip in—s; hook in —s; lay hold with—s; pare—s; seize in—s; sharpen—s; snip off—s; strike with—s; try —s on; —s flash by; —s lacerate; —s miss; —s rend; —s rip; —s scrape; —s scratch; —s snatch; —s tear.

(See talon, nail, clutch, hand.)

CLAW (v)

adverbs

wildly; fiercely; bloodily; ominously; feebly; voraciously; hungrily; viciously; hatefully; fiendishly; frantically; frightfully; sadistically.

(See scratch.)

CLAY

adjectives

clammy; cradling; humble; barren; encumbering; painted; sun-baked; impure; rebellious; uncoffined; tenacious; senseless; fruitful; unconsecrated; well-trodden; unconscious; breathless; human; eventful; sodden; reddish; brittle; damp.

verbs

cart—; cast—; chisel—; cleave—; color—; compound—; daub with—; dry—; fashion of—; fire—; form of—; line with—; mix—; moisten—; mould—; paint—; plaster with

—; prepare—; refine—; rise from—; seal with—; shape with—; soil with—; temper —; tread into—; —cements; —hardens; —moulders; —pastes; —resists; —sinks; —succumbs; —wears.

CLEAN

adverbs
hygienically; immaculately; neatly; spotlessly; stainlessly; tidily; trimly; sweetly; refreshingly; satisfactorily; punctiliously; meticulously; fragrantly; wholesomely; healthily; fastidiously; exquisitely; scrupulously; surgically; personally; shiningly; glowingly; delightfully; gratefully; comfortably; perfectly; faultlessly; impeccably; consummately; neatly; sprucely; radiantly; superbly; incredibly; finically; fussily; fanatically; daintily; sturdily; acceptably; passably; indifferently; presumably; appreciably.

CLEAN (v)

adverbs
immaculately; scrupulously; ambitiously; superficially; fussily; diligently; indifferently; ostentatiously; industriously; scientifically; passably; thoroughly; generally; fastidiously; exquisitely; enviably; orally; spotlessly; surgically; aridly.
(See wash.)

CLEANING

adjectives
distinctive; scientific; effective; exclusive; passable; spasmodic; thorough; general.

CLEANLINESS

adjectives
sterile; sweet; life-saving; fastidious; exquisite; notable; enviable; oral; scrupulous; spotless; personal; surgical; nice; general; arid; sinewy.

verbs
advise —; emphasize —; enjoin —; extol —; honor —; lack —; maintain —; necessitate —; preach —; respect —; sacrifice —; teach —.
(See hygiene.)

CLEAR

adverbs
explicitly; intelligibly; definitely; graphically; unmistakably; beautifully; crystally; unsurpassably; remarkably; unequivocally; decisively; startlingly; essentially; terribly; extraordinarily; easily; smoothly; positively; definitely; absolutely; unquestionably;

obviously; plainly; categorically; incontestably; happily; comfortingly; satisfactorily.

CLEAR (v)

adverbs
tolerably; auspiciously; systematically; substantially; crystally; dramatically; poetically; unequivocally; limpidly; essentially; admirably; partially; annoyingly.
(See clarify, elucidate, explain.)

CLEAR-HEADED

adverbs
shrewdly; naturally; subtly; extremely; alertly; consciously; intentionally; discreetly; unexpectedly; infallibly; precociously; coldly; penetratingly; singularly; astoundingly; cleverly; astutely; craftily; profoundly; discriminatingly; manifestly; obviously; significantly; dangerously; alarmingly; perspicaciously; unwontedly.

CLEARING

adjectives
eloquent; unproductive.

CLEARNESS

adjectives
unaccustomed; ever-increasing; unsurpassable; agonizing; masterly; noonday; crystal; remarkable; sufficient; dramatic; admirable; diminished; poetic; crystalline; unequivocal; decisive; limpid; startling; essential; burning; horrible; nauseous; eerie; abominable; impulsive; calculating.

CLEATS

adjectives
longitudinal; transverse; rubber; football; leather; damaging; dangerous.

CLEFT

adjectives
unsunned; mossy; deep; gaping; vertical; narrow; steep.

CLEMENCY

adjectives
executive; merciful; benignant; gracious; bountiful; charitable; magnanimous.

verbs
allow —; beg —; display —; dispose toward —; exercise —; exhibit —; forgive in —; grant —; incline toward —; insure —; offer —; oppose —; promise —; recommend —; soften with —; suggest —; temper with —; — adds; — spares.
(See forbearance, mercy.)

CLEMENT

adverbs

mercifully; sympathetically; tolerantly; moderately; mildly; compassionately; humanely; understandingly; unexpectedly; piteously; charitably; ruthfully; sagaciously; wisely; discerningly; generously; benevolently; shrewdly; magnanimously.

CLENCH (v)

adverbs

convulsively; tightly; firmly; unrelentingly; severely; agonizingly; hopelessly; unceasingly; hysterically; tremblingly; abruptly; fearfully; genially; characteristically; appallingly; deftly; painfully.

(See clutch.)

CLERGY

adjectives

modest; fashionable; regional; corrupt; parochial; reverend; fanatical.

verbs

benefit by —; connect with —; distinguish —; divide —; exempt —; oust from —; persecute —; robe —; set apart —; support —; unfrock —; — advocates; — authorizes; — consecrates; — devotes; — embraces; — engineers; — ministers; — preaches; — privileges.

(See clergyman, minister.)

CLERGYMAN

adjectives

worthy; ordained; well-informed; influential; leading; superannuated; fussy; distinguished; eminent; disgraced; spineless; diffident; respected; deserving; unsuccessful; welcome; elderly; purring.

verbs

abide by —; bar —; confess to —; confide in —; delude —; ordain —; persecute —; qualify as —; revere —; — beseeches; — blesses; — delivers; — endeavors; — intones; — orates; — pleads; — preaches; — teaches; — voices; — waxes.

(See minister.)

CLERIC

adjectives

minor; prim; devout; righteous; exhorting; mild; inoffensive; shepherding; soul-directing.

CLERICAL

adverbs

monotonously; fastidiously; punctiliously; tediously; importantly; primarily; modest-ly; humbly; pompously; primly; precisely; fanatically; comically; unsuitably; slavishly; humbly; elegantly; gently; mildly; unassumingly; unpretentiously; ostentatiously; flauntingly; worthily; influentially; fussily; sedately.

CLERK

adjectives

shabby; confidential; delicate; officious; trustworthy; discreet; minor; embarrassed; assessing; unsympathetic; dispensing; efficient; obsequious; hard-working; quick-witted; gouging; small; studious; wise; lynx-eyed; vigilant; plodding; sneering; genial; generous; courteous; diligent; satisfactory; busy; conscientious; meticulous; orderly; dapper; impecunious.

verbs

advance —; discharge —; ordain —; promote —; retain —; — accounts; — announces; — collects; — corresponds; — documents; — enters; — greets; — rates; — records; — sells.

(See employee.)

CLEVER

adverbs

notably; strikingly; consummately; diabolically; slyly; fiendishly; peculiarly; artfully; marvellously; adroitly; incredibly; admirably; remarkably; dangerously; palpably; obviously; undeniably; suspiciously; neatly; matchlessly; craftily; masterfully; wonderfully; constitutionally; innately; instinctively; inherently; subtly; cunningly; capably; competently; proficiently; deftly; discreetly; handily.

CLEVERNESS

adjectives

notable; insolent; insinuating; satiric; striking; meretricious; considerable; consummate.

verbs

accompany with —; deceive with —; display —; envy —; exhibit —; market —; necessitate —; perform with —; question —; reward —; shed —.

(See skill, ingenuity.)

CLICK

adjectives

faint; whispered; resolute; dry; animated; soulless; jarring; indignant; responsive; metallic; sharp; hollow; emphatic; mysterious; mechanical; significant.

adverbs

teasingly; faintly; animatedly; indignantly; metallically; jauntily; gaily; significantly; spontaneously; mechanically; repeatedly; intermittently.

(See sound.)

CLIENT

adjectives

trembling; desirable; gilded; prospective; fair; courtroom; stolid; indifferent; obstinate; timid; whilom; unfortunate; parasitical; rich; likely; uninvited; much-injured; oppressed; distinguished.

CLIENTELE

adjectives

discriminating; conservative; distinguished; congenial; refined; select; restricted; discerning; diversified; financial; desirable; exacting; influential; fine.

CLIFF

adjectives

smooth; vertical; lofty; abrupt; ebony; frowning; iron-stained; black; distant; ochre; scarped; hoary; jutting; fringing; treacherous; honeycombed; populous; inaccessible; naked; formidable; perpendicular; snowy; desolate; picturesque; precipitous; ragged; rude; radiant; unexpected; perilous; buttressed; stupendous; abrupt; craggy; majestic; impending; fearful; steep; frosty; sheer; rugged; overhanging; reeking; implacable; cloudy; haughty; cloud-encircled; broken; great; colossal; lofty; gigantic; tremendous; high; mighty; towering; giant; barren; bald; bare; wild; tinted; tortuous; weathered; wind-worn; crumbling; jagged; crude; sinister; grotesque; fantastic; limestone; granite; rocky; thorn-clad; narrow; iron-walled; ferny; orchard-crowned; heavily wooded; forest-covered; icebound; broad; bold; receding; sculptured; sloping.

verbs

clamber up —; climb —; fall from —; overhang —; peer from —; reconnoiter —; scale —; skirt —; slither over —; suspend from —; throw from —; tumble from —; — looms up; — rises; — sinks.

(See crag, precipice.)

CLIMATE

adjectives

dry; marvelous; summer; outdoor; world-famous; incomparable; mild; kindly; inviting; pleasant; enervating; rugged; healthful; bracing; life-prolonging; gracious; superb; gentle; beneficent; maligned; semitropical; oppressive; delicious; glowing; balmy; invigorating; divers (pl); burning; listless; villainous; various (pl); boreal; hyperequatorial; bland; trying; exhausting; arctic; dry; sultry; severe; trick; tropical; exhilarating; salubrious; temperate; genial; frowning; delightful; subduing; smiling; perfect; year-round; propitious; equable; fittest; tranquil; ocean; lovely; stern; excellent; unbearable; bitter; forbidding; rigorous; harsh; rotten; poisonous; arid; high; wonderful; winter; southern; atmospheric; variable; capricious; altered; seasonal; coldest; humid; torrid; damp; changing.

verbs

accustom to —; adapt to —; ascribe to —; chart —; malign —; record —; seek —; succumb to —; — affects; — batters; — braces; — depends on; — destroys; —devastates; — discourages; — invigorates; — irritates; — enlivens; — prevails; — ravages; — restores; — revives; — sickens; — stimulates.

(See weather.)

CLIMAX

adjectives

characteristic; appalling; fit; momentous; glorious; culminant; unforgettable; sad; dramatic; exquisite; progressive; prepared; surprising; approaching; autumnal; frolicsome; disgraceful; ingenious; horrifying; grandstand; poignant; emotional; proper; unexpected; thunderous; oratorical; inevitable; marvelous; stupendous; glowing; inescapable; pulsating; deft; unsatisfactory; lightninglike.

verbs

abate at —; ascend to —; culminate in —; deduce —; delay —; delight in —; foreshadow —; hurtle to —; lax after —; postpone —; prelude —; prepare for —; rise to —; — dies; — excites; — interests; — occurs; — surprises.

(See culmination, extreme.)

CLIMAX (v)

adverbs

inevitably; appallingly; momentously; gloriously; unforgettably; dramatically; exquisitely; disgracefully; horrifyingly; poignant-

ly; emotionally; unexpectedly; oratorically; marvelously; stupendously; tragically; comically.
(See finish.)

CLIMB

adjectives

lewd; beastly; upward; breezy; steady; wonderful; sporty; muscle-racking; long; hard; uphill; winding; persistent; plodding; blistering; dizzy.

verbs

accomplish —; ascend —; attain —; boast of —; cease —; enjoy —; gird for —; mount to —; negotiate —; prepare for —; reconnoiter for —; scale —; spur to —; toil up —; — excites; — exhausts; — exhilarates; — fatigues; — thrills; — wearies.
(See ascent.)

CLIMB (v)

adverbs

nimbly; perversely; strenuously; reluctantly; desperately; lamely; steadily; ploddingly; dizzily; dexterously; skillfully; laboriously; unceasingly; determinedly.
(See clamber, scale.)

CLIMBER

adjectives

expert; social; respectable; superior; snobbish; repulsed; wonderful; ambitious; intrepid; mountain; indefatigable; aggressive.

CLIMBING

adjectives

hot; venturous; exhausting; tedious; fruitless; arduous.

CLIME

adjectives

serene; inclement; cloudless; delightful; sunless; inhospitable; blissful; celestial; rougher; torrid; pleasant; eastern; drear; hostile; sunny; glorious; radiant; changeful; distant; genial; unknown; capricious; fair; happy; scenic; southern; rigorous.

CLING (v)

adverbs

adhesively; tenaciously; desperately; blindly; credulously; firmly; faithfully; purposefully; heavily; persistently; timorously; affectionately; endearingly; invariably; exhaustingly.
(See hang.)

CLINIC

adjectives

public; impersonal; domestic; courtesy; private; convenient; indispensable.

verbs

admit to —; attach to —; attend —; conduct —; contribute to —; endow —; establish —; extol —; install —; institute —; maintain —; practise in —; subsidize —; support —; visit —; — adjusts; — administers; — advises; — cures; — diagnoses; — discovers; — investigates; — observes; — records; — specializes; — surveys; — tabulates; — treats.
(See school, instruction, institution.)

CLIP (v)

adverbs

fantastically; closely; raggedly; dexterously; evenly; painfully; skillfully; roughly.
(See trim.)

CLIPPER

adjectives

lofty; heavy; sparred; lean; graceful; swift.

CLIQUE

adjectives

irresponsible; campus; mutinous; ruling; esoteric; secret; nominating.

CLOAK

adjectives

leopard-skin; hooded; constitutional; bad-fitting; ludicrous; tattered; snatched; feathery; dusky; frieze; cardinal; ungathered; shimmering; girlish; sodden; voluminous; long; sweeping; tinseled; mantled; impervious; full.

verbs

bear under—; bury in—; drape—about; draw—; envelop in—; fashion—; fasten—; garment in—; line—; loose—; pluck off—; raise—; spread—; stain—; wrap in—; —conceals; —covers; —disguises; —hides; —hoods; —mantles; —masks; —protects; —secretes; —shelters; —warms.
(See coat, mask, garment, disguise.)

CLOAK (v)

adjectives

constantly; completely; ludicrously; shimmeringly; voluminously; sweepingly; imperviously; snugly; warmly; comfortably; parsimoniously.
(See conceal, mask.)

CLOCK

adjectives

brass-bound; clanging; unvarying; vigilant; ingenious; tall; glowing; synchronous; illuminated; noisy; chiming; solemn; dignified; pine; delirious.

verbs

read—; set—; wind—; —alarms; —chimes; —clangs; —s disagree; —fools; —gains; —heralds; —indicates; —knells; —lies; —misses; —rings; —strikes; —ticks off; —tolls; —trembles; —vibrates; —warns.
(See watch.)

CLOD

adjectives

finite; loamy; frozen; wormy; icy; kneaded; sluggish; plow-cloven.

CLOISTER

adjectives

shady; open; solemn; personal; dilapidated; mournful; monkish; restful; beautiful.

CLOISTERED

adjectives

conventionally; monastically; happily; willingly; voluntarily; perpetually; consecratedly; religiously; inviolably; piously; holily; devoutly; reverently; fervidly; eagerly; blessedly; prayerfully; securely; unassailably; safely.

CLOSE

adjectives

summary; speedy; rapid; long-expected; official; bloody; glorious; victorious; tragic; rollicking; undramatic.

CLOSE (v)

adverbs

securely; peremptorily; lazily; reluctantly; abruptly; grimly; instantly; spasmodically; virtually; unexpectedly; wistfully; hermetically; discreetly; summarily; officially; victoriously; tragically.
(See terminate, end.)

CLOSENESS

adjectives

furtive; essential; unwinking.

CLOSET

adjectives

well-filled; portable; glazed; stuffy; cedar; hall; dark; tiny; shallow; obscure.

verbs

air—; conceal in—; creep from—; crowd—; deposit in—; enclose in—; force—; hide in—; imprison in—; invade—; lock in—; occupy—; recess in—; repose in—; retire into—; retreat into—; rummage in—; seclude in—; secrete in—; shut in—; store in—; unlock—; ventilate—.
(See chamber, room, recess.)

CLOSE-TONGUED

adverbs

discreetly; prudently; wisely; judiciously; sagely; quietly; thoughtfully; reflectively; unusually; habitually; philosophically; astutely; cleverly; laconically; reticently; safely; invariably; cautiously; warily; circumspectly; loyally; smartly; consistently; shrewdly.

CLOT

adjectives

convenient; cohesive; fibrous; embolic; gelatinous; hardened; semisolid; stubborn.

verbs

coagulate in—; cohere in—; congeal into—; dissolve—; form—; mass in—; mat with —s; melt—; —cements; —checks; —hardens; —lumps; —stems.

CLOTH

adjectives

worsted; patented; irreproachable; beautiful; nonshrinkable; sturdy; long-fibred; handsome; silver-striped; imported; rugged; soft; subdued; fine-textured; rich; dressy; quality; cool; smart; suave; silky; smooth-textured; wool; long-wearing; summer; unfinished; featherweight; zephyrweight; superlative; firm; striped; twoply; knife-edge; durable; baize; painted; elegant; hair; spotless; brocaded; coarse; fluttering; thin; cotton; vile; greasy; trailing; polishing; draped; snowy; immaculate.

verbs

adorn—; bias—; cast—over; darn—; emerge from—; finger—; gather—; saturate—; shroud in—; spin—; strain through—; weave—; wrap in—; —adorns; —hangs; —indicates.
(See fabric, wool, silk, cotton, drapery, material.)

CLOTHE (v)

adverbs

comfortably; miserably; profusely; uniformly; irreproachably; beautifully; handsomely; coolly; smartly; suavely; spotlessly; coarsely; immaculately; vilely; seductively; temptingly; ravishingly; glamorously; appropriately; faultlessly; inappropriately; incongruously; formally; ordinarily; voluminously; hideously; drablv

(See dress, attire.)

CLOTHED

adverbs

richly; elaborately; gaudily; wretchedly; fully; scantily; shabbily; raggedly; luxuriously; carefully; elegantly; carelessly; recklessly; absurdly; fashionably; ridiculously; ludicrously; honorably; unfashionably; garishly; laughably; gaily; seductively; gorgeously; glamorously; rakishly; awkwardly; incongruously; outlandishly; expensively; cheaply; smartly; handsomely; drably; extravagantly; economically.

CLOTHES

adjectives

gay; seductive; feminine; tempting; gorgeous; ravishing; glamorous; bright; fluttering; sensible; fresh; clean; appropriate; harmonized; picture-book; well-cut; ready-made; fashionable; faultless; evening; unkempt; dusty; bedraggled; ragged; patched; town; shiny; stained; dirty; cast-off; inappropriate; lanky; ill-fitting; loose-hanging; awkward; free; incongruous; horrible; dreadful; deplorable; bizarre; rakish; gaudy; nobby; vivid; outlandish; astonishing; everyday; working; riding; queer; country; shabby; summer; immaculate; disordered; ordinary; patriarchal; expensive; swaddling; drenched; bespattered; mud-covered; formal; voluminous; Easter; foolish; smart; dependable; famous; individualized; well-tailored; fine; hand-tailored; comfortable; hideous; baggy; dowdy; string-colored; advertised; pepper-and-salt; drab.

CLOTHING

adjectives

ragged; tailored; travel-stained; indispensable; fastidious; tattered; cast-off; sad; nondescript; complicated; soiled; frayed; legal; dreadful; russet; mortal; small; scant; flashy; drenched; ruined; seedy; personal.

verbs

alter—; array in—; bare of—; cast off—; closet—; design—; discolor—; display—; divest of—; doff—; don—; fashion—; lack—; launder—; model—; outwear—;

penetrate—; purvey—; refurbish—; rend —; renew—; saturate—; store—; strip off—; style—; swaddle in—; tailor—; tatter—; vest in—; —allures; —belies; —chafes; —denotes; —expresses; —flutters; —masquerades.

(See dress, raiment, apparel.)

CLOUD

adjectives

slate-colored; puffy; snow-white; gray-blue; mauve; silver; opaline; dense; glittering; golden; crisp; hazy; bluish; sun-filled; dazzling; thin; misty; drifting; passing; hurrying; scattering; rolling; racing; soaring; flying; scudding; broken; rifted; wild; black; frayed; breaking; gritty; paunchy; blood-colored; bulbous; swollen; cumulus; dark; darkening; endless; sullen; rolling; disastrous; angry; menacing; thunder; lowering; heavy; shapeless; curtain; exemplary; leaking; massed; low-hanging; opaque; distant; tangible; unvarying; tiniest; wind-spun; mysterious; mountain; smoke; desolate; incandescent; moon; crimson; flitting; flaky; eternal; sanguine; wind-driven; mantling; dangerous; glimmering; wrinkled; coifing; airy; veiling; purple; fugitive; pasturing; delicate; radiant; coppery; eddying; foggy; melting; lachrymose; mournful; embattled; scattered; perpetual; thick; sun-rimmed; sacred; chariot; sunset; darksome; rainy; luminous; vast; severing; bursting; downpouring; sullen; brilliant; serrate; smothered; lurid; dull; restless; sundering; envious; massive; gilded; fleecy; flowing; hovering; fat; clammy; perturbed; poisonous; westward-stationed; murmurous; suffocating; interwoven; tear-laden; battlemented; dripping; many-folded; perceptible; pillared; inky; irrevocable; feathery; dusking; orange; infernal; sulphurous; amber; canvas; cinerous; wondrous; rosy; billowy; soft-gray; sable.

verbs

ascend to—s; aspire to—s; bivouac in—; checker with—s; cleave—s; clothe in—; curtain with—s; deck with—; descend from —; fan off—; float in—; gild—; lose in—; penetrate—; pierce—; ride upon—; sail on—; slip into—; vanish into—; withdraw into—; wreathe in—; —billows; —blankets; —blots out; —creeps up; —curls; —darkens; —descends; —dims; —discharges; —disperses; —drenches; —drifts; —flees; —freaks; —gushes; —hides; —hovers; —hurries; —lifts; —melts;

—menaces; —mottles; —mounts; —musters; —obscures; —obstructs; —overcasts; —overshadows; —s part; —s pockmark the sky; —races; —rebuffs; —s scatter; —screens; —scurries; —shrouds; —smoulders; —soars; —s stream by; —sweeps down; —swirls up; —threatens; —vanishes; —veils; —wanders; —weeps; —whitens; —wings by.

CLOUD (v)
adverbs
heavily; densely; hazily; mistily; rollingly; scuddingly; blackly; sullenly; disastrously; mysteriously; foggily; mournfully; sulphurously; luridly.
(See shade.)

CLOUDLESS
adverbs
gloriously; beautifully; brightly; brilliantly; dazzlingly; radiantly; sunnily; garishly; refulgently; pitilessly; mercilessly; hotly; breathlessly; happily; luckily; fortunately; joyously; splendidly; magnificently; enchantingly; pleasantly; delightfully; ravishingly; pleasurably; refreshingly; cheeringly; enjoyably; utterly.

CLOUDY
adverbs
mistily; darkly; rosily; densely; hazily; thinly; thickly; completely; partly; occasionally; wildly; gloomily; sullenly; dismaly; angrily; windily; mysteriously; suddenly; delicately; foggily; perpetually; brokenly; luridly; fleecily; suffocatingly; surprisingly; hopelessly; ominously; menacingly; discouragingly; faintly; muggily; dunly; distressingly; disturbingly.

CLOVER
adjectives
incarnate; scented; sweet-smelling; blooming; nodding; bee-calling.

CLOWN
adjectives
sweet; bungling; loutish; sad; yawning; brokenhearted; roguish; impudent; grimacing; rollicking; whimsical; appreciated.

verbs
play—; —antics; —burlesques; —caricatures; —entertains; —farces; —frolics; — grimaces; —jigs; —mimics; —pantomimes; —portrays; —somersaults; —taunts.
(See fool.)

CLOWN (v)
adverbs
professionally; hilariously; divertingly; sophisticatedly; loutishly; roguishly; impudently; grimacingly; rollickingly; whimsically.
(See jest.)

CLOWNISH
adverbs
roguishly; impudently; whimsically; comically; madly; foolishly; provokingly; everlastingly; incurably; teasingly; irresistibly; boorishly; waggishly; jocosely; roughly; innocently; merrily; blithely; joyously; boyishly; entertainingly; rowdily; indecorously; unbecomingly; extravagantly; horridly; amusingly; unwontedly; hilariously; habitually; delicately; deliberately; unceasingly; incessantly; tiresomely.

CLUB
(*society*)
adjectives
influential; literary; luxurious; attractive; sumptuous; social; enthusiastic; industrial; exclusive; permanent; flourishing; musical.

verbs
affiliate with—; associate with—; bar from—; "blackball" from—; charter—; contribute to—; form—; found—; house—; organize—; pledge to—; preside over—; —assembles; —benefits from; —convenes; —elects; —springs up.
(See organization, association.)

CLUB
(*weapon*)
adjectives
mossy; powerful; formidable; threatening; respect-inspiring; sturdy; purposeful.

verbs
arm with—; bat with—; batter with—; bear—; brandish—; carve—; clutch—; cudgel with—; exercise—; extend—; flog with—; flourish—; hurl—; rule with—; strike with—; subdue with—; submit to—; threaten with—; whirl—; wield—; yield to—.
(See cudgel, bat.)

CLUBFOOTED
adverbs
unfortunately; hopelessly; irremediably; crookedly; monstrously; hideously; slightly; pathetically; unmistakably; noticeably;

grotesquely; fantastically; outlandishly; miserably; wretchedly; helplessly; strangely; pitiably; woefully.

(See crippled.)

CLUCK (v)

adverbs

busily; anxiously; industriously; maternally; absorbedly; endlessly; cheerfully; fondly; pleasantly; unrestrainedly.

(See chatter.)

CLUE

adjectives

inescapable; priceless; vital; suggestive; recondite; fancied; elusive; definite; flawless; tangible; exhausted; magnificent; startling; surprising; bewildering; slender.

verbs

discover—; divulge—; efface—; follow up—; join—s; muddle up—; produce—; recognize—; scatter—s; strike upon—; tackle—; thread—s together; trace—; track down—; uncover—; unearth—; unravel—; yield—; —convicts; —crumbles; —guides; —indicates; —perplexes; —puzzles; — solves; —warns.

(See intimation, hint.)

CLUMP (v)

adverbs

aimlessly; monotonously; painfully; laboriously; tiredly; woefully; miserably; desolately; lachrymosely; loutishly; rudely.

(See thump.)

CLUMSINESS

adjectives

grotesque; intolerable; wasteful; massive; inexcusable; wanton; marked.

verbs

accentuate—; attend with—; decry—; display—; feign—; lack—; perform with—; ridicule—; simulate—; —annoys.

(See awkwardness.)

CLUMSY

adverbs

childishly; awkwardly; gawkily; inexpertly; adorably; provokingly; vexatiously; unconsciously; involuntarily; obviously; charmingly; ludicrously; ridiculously; laughably; cheerfully; momentarily; naturally; objectionably; unnecessarily; foolishly; unluckily; ungraciously; hopelessly; helplessly; bashfully; shyly; painfully.

CLUSTER

adjectives

superb; globular; kindling; luscious; indefatigable; delicate; shining; drowsy; dense; vivid; telltale; peaceful; gleaming; grapelike; many-branched; rich.

verbs

assemble in—; cultivate—; emerge from—; form in—; gather in—; group in—; halve —; join—; pluck—; swarm in—; tear—; unite in—; —collects; —droops.

(See group.)

CLUSTER (v)

adverbs

gayly; abundantly; luxuriously; lusciously; lovingly; globularly; delicately; gleamingly; richly; darksomely.

(See crowd.)

CLUTCH

adjectives

detaining; fibrous; ungainly; evil; frantic.

verbs

avoid—; clasp in—es; draw into—es; escape—; evade—; fasten— es; free from—; grasp in—es; grip in—; lock in—es; seize in—; snatch from—es; strive in—es; struggle in—es; trap in—es; wrench from—es.

(See grasp, grip, hold.)

CLUTCH (v)

adverbs

frantically; conclusively; desperately; instinctively; covetously; rapaciously; nervously; unconsciously; detainingly; vigorously; fiercely; fanatically.

(See grasp, grip.)

COACH

adjectives

ponderous; gilded; lazy; decayed; liveried; rolling; hackney; rumbling; gilt; clumsy; deserted; ancient; motor; imperial; rattling; elaborate; dingy; passenger; lurching.

verbs

alight from—; attend—; carve—; convey in—; draw—; gild—; hire—; jog along in—; journey in—; ornament—; travel in—; upset—; —approaches; —careens; —jolts; —jounces; —rumbles; —speeds on; —traverses.

(See carriage.)

COACHMAN

adjectives

superannuated; ridiculous; stiff; dignified; glossy; supercilious; liveried; crest-emblazoned.

COADJUTANT

adverbs

willingly; profitably; politically; conveniently; favorably; suspiciously; heartily; voluntarily; reluctantly; cheerfully; agreeably; confessedly; admittedly; avowedly; acquiescently; contentedly.

COAL

adjectives

dull; burning; glowing; red; roseate; glimmering; living; dying; soft; purloined; hard.

verbs

bake on—s; char—; devour—; fire—; fuel with—; heave—; ignite—; kindle—; lay on—s; power by—; quench—; rake—; scuttle—; transport—; —darkens; —emits gas; —glows; —soils.
(See carbon, ember.)

COALESCENT

adverbs

actually; easily; monotonously; valuably; scientifically; fortunately; probably; amazingly; surprisingly; indistinguishably; homologously; convertibly.

COAL FIELDS

adjectives

bleak; dreary; grime-shrouded; honeycombed; exhausted; abandoned; producing; pit-fallen; valuable; wealth-yielding; worked-out; anthracite; bituminous; lignite.

verbs

capture— —; cede— —to; conserve— —; control— —; dominate— —; employ in— —; exhaust— —; exploit— —; inherit— —; invade— —; replenish from— —; transport from— —; utilize— —; value— —; work— —; — —boom; — —extend; — —range; — —supply.

COALITION

adjectives

favorable; fresh; genuine; lasting; instantaneous; political; superfluous; tardy.

verbs

ally in—; blend in—; federate—; form—; fuse in—; improvise—; support—; unite in—; —aids; —connects; —forces; —insures; —offers.
(See alliance, union.)

COARSE

adverbs

disagreeably; abominably; intolerably; unbearably; basely; bluntly; carelessly; hideously; unutterably; stupidly; pathetically; odiously; blatantly; insufferably; awkwardly; boorishly; intentionally; deliberately; unpardonably; barbarously; indecorously; ribaldly; tawdrily; vulgarly; hoydenishly; rowdily; shockingly; heavily; horridly; monstrously; obtrusively; outlandishly; impossibly.

COARSENESS

adjectives

crass; disgusting; homely; hopeless; innate; gorgeous; humiliating; savage; revolting; provincial; vulgar; unvarying.

verbs

acquire—; alleviate—; display—; exhibit —; modify—; pardon—; polish off—; refine—; retain—; sand away—; smooth—; —embarrasses; —inflames; —irks; —irritates; —rasps; —vexes.
(See rudeness, vulgarity.)

COAST

adjectives

unguarded; rock-bound; frequented; desolate; craggy; foggy; adjacent; perilous; eerie; crystal; lowly; bold; sea; sandy; high; verdant; pathless; imperfect; shining; chalk; viny; inhospitable; picturesque; trimmed; rectangular; fateful; misty; extended; iron-bound; remarkable; rebelling; melancholy; weather-beaten; forlorn; murky; azure; colorful; historic; rough; deserted; irregular; dangerous; harborless; barren; indented; shallow; flat; tranquil; elongated; sun-kissed.

verbs

abide on—; batter—; blockade—; border —; depart from—; enlarge—; expel from —; fortify—; guard—; invade—; land on—; move up—; patrol—; pebble—; scout—; skirt—; spy—; travel along—.
(See shore, beach.)

COAT

adjectives

tattered; greasy; dirty; damaged; dusty; shiny; comfortable; dinner; expensive; heavy; shapeless; buttoned; tawny; rhythmic; striped; outer; flimsy; cloth; pajama; sopping; laced; collarless; soft; fleecy; fresh; clean; distinguished; simple; boxy; tailored; custom-made; threadbare; protective; stunning; immaculate; voluminous; enticing; frogged; magic; russet; fetching; fustian; holiday; shabby; smartest; useful; raglan.

verbs
clothe in—; design—; discolor—; divest of—; dry-clean—; embroider—; encase in—; fray—; gird with—; jacket in—; model—; peel off—; press—; provide—; ruin—; seam—; split—; strip off—; style —; tailor—; tatter—; weave—; —envelops; —glitters; —protects; —warms.
(See garment, overcoat.)

COAT-TAIL

adjectives
dangling; elongated; formal; flippant; funereal; restless; tentaculate; twisting; sweeping.

verbs
alter—; cling to—; embroider—; fray—; hoist—; line—; press—; rend—; shorten—; soil—; suspend from—; tatter—; tread on—; wrinkle—; —covers; —drags; —protects.
(See coat.)

COAX (v)

adverbs
irresistibly; tantalizingly; endearingly; slyly; treacherously; lewdly; sweetly; angelically.
(See persuade.)

COBWEB

adjectives
dusty; patterned; glittering; hanging; iridescent.

verbs
abound with—s; brush away—; capture in—; dart from—; elude—; enmesh in—; ensnare in—; entangle in—; entwine in—; evade—; fringe with—; lace with—; spin—; strain in—; struggle in—; weave —; —s gather; —hangs from; —traps.
(See web, net, snare, network.)

COCK

adjectives
belligerent; bullying; cavalier; calcarate; defiant; domineering; clarion-sounding; game; strutting; spur-brandishing; vainglorious; vanquishing; victorious.

verbs
breed—s; excite—; —announces the morn; —battles; —crows; —heralds the dawn; —pecks; —perches; —rages; —scurries; —struts.
(See fowl, bird, rooster.)

COCKNEY

adverbs
unmistakably; markedly; rowdily; frankly; honestly; loyally; toughly; helpfully; sturdily; stoutly; idly; unaffectedly; heartily; healthily; humbly; chaffingly; churlishly; sorrily; originally; raffishly; menially; clownishly.

COCKROACH

adjectives
defiant; glistening; horned; invading; inexpugnable; scurrying; ubiquitous; crackling; reddish-brown; filthy; vile; obscene; offensive; nasty; foul; abominable; beastly; repulsive; immodest.

verbs
abound with—es; bait—; crush—; detest—; exterminate—; plague with—; poison—; rid of—; spray—; —infests; —multiplies; —scuds; —scurries; —wanders.
(See insect.)

COCK-SURE

adverbs
calmly; confidently; deeply; professedly; unshakably; arrogantly; egotistically; positively; provokingly; determinedly; doggedly; happily; vainly; insolently; loquaciously; tranquilly; blandly; foolishly; swaggeringly; magnificently; smugly; brassily; brazenly; heedlessly; cavalierly; importantly; blusteringly.

COCKTAIL

adjectives
aromatic; relaxing; reassuring; shudder-producing; stimulating; sticky; welcome.

verbs
chill—; concoct—; dispatch—; down—; drain—; flavor—; ice—; join in—; level—; mix—; partake of—; soak up—; tolerate—; vary—; water—; —exhilarates; —intoxicates; —quickens; —stimulates; —warms.
(See drink, liquor, whiskey.)

COCOON

adjectives
dainty; clumsy; fragile; silken; bark-powdered; suspended; swinging; silver-grey; ovate; webby.

verbs
burst from—; emerge from— encase in—; enclose in—; envelop in—; flutter from—; raise from—; spin—; swathe in—; tend—; weave—; —expels; —flowers; —hatches.

(See envelop, case.)

CODE

adjectives
changing; rigid; moral; unwritten; ambitious; voluminous; detailed; accepted; logical; traditional; ruthless; peculiar; lasting; ancient; true; rigorous; artificial; strict; odious; professed; sexual; chivalrous; elaborate; social.

verbs
decipher—; draft—; elaborate—; enforce—; formulate—; guard—; honor—; impose—; intercept—; interpret—; jeopardize—; observe—; preserve—; protect—; relay—; respect—; sanction—; subject to—; translate—; —amends; —restricts; —systematizes.

(See system, law, legislation.)

COEFFICIENT

adverbs
clannishly; collusively; concertedly; unanimously; fraternally; companionably; collectively; jointly; amazingly; surprisingly; remarkably; notoriously; supremely.

COEQUAL

adverbs
evenly; symmetrically; adaptably; broadly; generously; good-humoredly; amiably; cooperatively; affably; placidly; serenely; scrupulously; carefully; contentedly; apparently; notoriously; easily.

COERCION

adjectives
vulgar; parental; ruthless; painstaking; deliberate; wily.

verbs
advocate—; apply—; bar—; control by—; drive to—; employ—; exercise—; gain by—; govern by—; irk by—; oppose—; rebel at—; resist—; resort to—; restrain by—; retain by—; separate by—; submit to—; —antagonizes; —inflames; —intimidates.

(See compulsion, force, restraint, constraint.)

COERCIVE

adverbs
illegally; substantially; disagreeably; officially; brutally; martially; enforceably; necessarily; forcibly; violently; inexorably; irresistibly; peremptorily; ruthlessly; cruelly; intolerably; authoritatively; unjustly; outrageously; unreasonably; unlawfully; unjustifiably; inauspiciously; injudiciously; openly; furtively; slyly; actually.

COFFEE

adjectives
steaming; strong; savory; weak; adulterated; delicious; best; morning; aromatic; muddy-looking; tepid; syrupy; finest; selected; black; rancid.

verbs
brew—; cultivate—; grind—; gulp down—; ice—; imbibe—; market—; percolate—; pound—; roast—; serve—; sniff—; sweeten—; tend—; tin—; wash down with—; yield—; —refreshes; —rouses; —stales; —stimulates; —wakens; —weakens.

(See tea, drink.)

COFFER

adjectives
depleted; hoarded; mouldy; grudging; opulent; overflowing; well-guarded.

verbs
bind—; burden—; burst—; bury in—; deposit in—; enrich—; force—; hoard in—; lay up in—; line—; ornament—; plunder—; preserve in—; ransack—; seal—; secure—; stuff—; suck—dry; swell—; treasure in—; —yields.

(See treasury.)

COFFIN

adjectives
insignificant; sumptuous; unlowered; precious; naked; flaming; rude; hard; misshapen; stately; large.

verbs
attend—; bear—; confine in—; decorate—; disinter—; encase in—; inter in—; mourn at—; remove from—; rest in—; rob—; seal—; sleep in—; stand around—; trail—; transport—; view—; weep at—; —receives; —sinks.

(See casket, case.)

COGITATE (v)

adverbs

gravely; deeply; absorbedly; perplexedly; abstrusely; abstractedly; studiously; frowningly; fixedly.

(See meditate, think.)

COGITATION

adjectives

gloomy; matrimonial; fragmentary; groping; manifold.

COIFFURE

adjectives

rustling; waved; elaborate; charming; conservative; monstrous; ingenious; gleaming; eccentric; affected; severe; elegant; sculptured.

COIL

adjectives

adamantine; tortured; lustrous; ceaseless; flat; irregular; steel; long; snakelike; hideous; opal; cumbrous; temporal; brilliant; mortal; collapsed; limp; shining; twisting

COIL (v)

adverbs

lavishly; ceaselessly; flatly; irregularly; hideously; cumbrously; limply; twistingly; intricately.

(See twist.)

COIN

adjectives

fair; bogus; deceptive; well-worked; unadulterated; glittering; nimble; ancient; valuable; artificial; rare.

verbs

assort—s; collect—s; convert into—; counterfeit—; deposit—; devaluate—; fashion —; hoard—s; melt—; mold—; mutilate—; pocket—; press—; stamp—; treasure—; uncover—; unearth—; value—; —circulates; —clinks; —depreciates; —represents; —wears thin.

(See cash, money, metal.)

COINCIDE (v)

adverbs

exactly; oddly; strangely; sardonically; singularly; amazingly; romantically; happily; fortunately; curiously; minutely; unexpectedly; tragically; occasionally; extraordinarily; crazily; closely.

(See agree.)

COINCIDENCE

adjective

strange; odd; singular; sardonic; happy; horrible; cruel; amazing; romantic; lucky; mere; crazy; curious; minute; unexpected; accidental; unusual; overdone; tragic; occasional; extraordinary; powerful; unfortunate; uncomfortable; suggestive.

verbs

discern—; discuss—; evidence—; illustrate—; involve—; marvel at—; report—; strike—; witness—; wonder at—; —amazes; —blends; —confounds; —occurs; —startles.

(See correspondence, agreement.)

COLD
(illness)

adjectives

harrassing; head; chest; bronchial; miserable; stubborn.

verbs

dispose toward—; down by—; engender—; expose to—; guard against—s; indispose by—; nurse—; predispose to—; resist—; subject to—; —lowers resistance; —strikes; —subsides; —weakens.

(See sickness.)

COLD
(weather)

adjectives

hostile; icy; intense; biting; deadly; stinging; cruel; casual; arctic; deathlike; encroaching; inescapable; bitter; paralyzing; freezing; wondrous; immense; retreating; purifying; interminable; midnight; piercing; stubborn; extreme; troublesome; ambient; heavy; penetrating; Stygian; monstrous.

verbs

blanket against—; brave—; chatter with—; endure—; expose to—; huddle in—; inure to—; paralyze by—; resist—; stem—; —abates; —bites; —blasts; —creeps in; —freezes; —nips; —persists; —pinches; —refreshes.

(See winter.)

COLD

adverbs

uncomfortably; intolerably; unfortunately; impossibly; frigidly; bitingly; piercingly; icily; wintrily; disagreeably; inconveniently; unpleasantly; uninvitingly; unluckily;

terrifically; dreadfully; frightfully; unnecessarily; dangerously; intensely; cruelly; penetratingly; increasingly; freezingly; nippily; perilously; unbearably.

COLD-HEARTED
adverbs
bitterly; unpleasantly; disturbingly; relentlessly; cruelly; outrageously; inhumanly; unsympathetically; terribly; dreadfully; incurably; habitually; temperamentally; constitutionally; obviously; manifestly; shamefully; unbelievably; astonishingly; actually; selfishly; naturally; inexplicably; fearfully; inexorably; uncharitably; unfortunately.

COLDNESS
adjectives
dewy; incisive; still; sudden; faithless; superficial; wintry; relentless; increasing; contemptuous; supreme; lofty; studied; mortified; intellectual; selfish; fancied; disdainful.

COLLABORATE (v)
adverbs
unreservedly; successfully; harmoniously; artfully; skilfully; imaginatively; superbly; brilliantly; startlingly; enthusiastically.
(See work, cooperate.)

COLLABORATION
adjectives
direct; efficient; permanent; enduring; spiritual.

COLLAPSE
adjectives
moral; constant; painful; cataclysmic; progressive; widespread; nervous; complete; disgraceful; simulated; eventual; imminent; inevitable; pretended; subsequent; tragic; alleged; disastrous.

verbs
fall into—; guard against—; hasten—; insure—; predict—; shrink in—; sink into—; verge on—; —discourages; presage—.
(See exhaustion, failure, ruin.)

COLLAPSE (v)
adverbs
utterly; invariably; tragically; partially; fatally; completely; ruinously; disastrously; fearfully; wretchedly; dramatically.
(See fall.)

COLLAPSIBLE
adverbs
conveniently; laughably; comically; dangerously; perilously; easily; cleverly; cunningly; neatly; handily; ingeniously; tidily; quickly; instantly; disastrously; momentarily; tragically.

COLLAR
adjectives
ermine; greasy; soft; fur; oppressive; enormous; clerical; obdurate; snug; upstanding; celluloid; muzzle; resplendent; faultless; diminutive; onerous.

verbs
crane at—; engrave—; fumble with—; harness in—; insert in—; jewel—; pleat—; ring with—; slip out of—; split—; strain at—; suspend from—; tug at—; —bands; —binds; —chains; —chokes; —encircles; —encompasses; —fetters; —ornaments; —restrains; —shrinks; —wreathes; —yields; —yokes.

COLLEAGUE
adjectives
word-compelling; melancholy; congressional; conscientious; efficient; critical; turbulent; immediate; peripheral; redoubtable; ardent; gifted; pagan; older; experienced; artful; disgruntled; atrabilious; professional; distinguished.

verbs
aid—; ally with—; assemble—s; associate with—; bow to—; cooperate with—; debate with—; emulate—; enjoin—; favor—; inveigle—into; lead—; sever from—.
(See associate, accessory, ally.)

COLLECT (v)
adverbs
painlessly; systematically; haphazardly; eagerly; privately; scientifically; gloriously; remarkably; exclusively; posthumously; dramatically; actively; cantankerously; indiscriminately; laboriously; sedulously; periodically; assiduously.
(See accumulate, group.)

COLLECTION
adjectives
wonderful; arresting; suggestive; pretentious; rare; attractive; ponderous; complete; expensive; priceless; weird; heterogeneous; haphazard; motley; vague; private; interesting; useful; fair; authentic; miscellaneous; entertaining; tolerable; ave-

rage; classified; individual; comprehensive; annotated; voluminous; scientific; varied; hideous; exciting; representative; enticing; adequate; imaginative; brilliant; extensive; world; superb; spring; advanced; copious; incongruous; considerable; notable; vast; glorious; remarkable; exclusive; thrilling; posthumous; original; magnificent; active; dramatic; infinite; zoological; cantankerous; startling.

verbs
accumulate—; amass—; delay—; display—; equal—; examine—; exhibit—; herd—; insure—; join—; lead—; mass—; prize—; raise—; rifle—; speed—; suspend—; treasure—; uncover—; unearth—; value—; yield—; —depicts; —symbolizes.
(See heap, group.)

COLLECTIVE
adverbs
effectively; efficiently; agreeably; typically; officially; undeniably; comprehensively; indivisibly; unanimously; substantially; broadly; indefinitely; locally; significantly; representatively; startlingly; surprisingly.

COLLECTIVE BARGAINING
adjectives
conciliatory; deferred; haggled; generalized; tactless; tolerant; prolonged; summary.

verbs
abolish— —; acclaim— —; achieve through — —; acquire— —; activate— —; base on— —; criticize— —; demand— —; discuss— —; drift into— —; employ— —; enjoy— —; exercise— —; forbid— —; object to— —; oblige by— —; oppose— —; organize— —; prohibit— —; recognize— —; restrict— —; support— —; — —enables; — —functions; — —improves; — —insures; — —involves; — —recognizes; — —secures; — —upholds.
(See negotiation.)

COLLECTOR
adjectives
ardent; modest; assiduous; insatiable; advanced; passionate; entranced; curious; enthusiastic; worthy; unceasing; discriminating; prominent; budding.

verbs
avoid—; evade—; rob—; waylay—; —accumulates; —acquires; —amasses; —assembles; —classifies; —compiles; —displays; —embezzles; —evades; —exhibits; —prizes; —recovers; —solicits; —sues; —values.

COLLEGE
adjectives
aggressive; liberal; commercial; general; aspiring; rival; venerable; electoral; denominational; junior; endowed.

verbs
administer—; attach to—; bar from—; charter—; enroll at—; establish—; father—; found—; incorporate—; invest—with; pursue in—; register at—; reopen—; respect—; restrict—; staff—; suspend from—; —accommodates; —conducts; —confers; —expels; —honors; —instructs; —lodges; —offers; —prepares.
(See school, university.)

COLLEGIATE
adverbs
ostentatiously; airily; knowingly; smartly; ridiculously; pompously; clannishly; arrogantly; thoroughly; strictly; proudly; determinedly; resolutely; correctly; faintly; laughably; properly; academically; actively; becomingly; unimpeachably; respectably; admirably; satisfactorily; duly; responsibly.

COLLISION
adjectives
fierce; monstrous; inevitable; chance; actual; violent; personal; fatal; frequent; successive; clear; serious; menacing; exciting; amusing; sudden; sharp; fateful; imminent; expensive.

verbs
avoid—; foresee—; insure against—; result in—; swerve from—; warn against—; —batters; —dashes; —destroys; —entangles; —impairs; —necessitates; —rends; —upsets.
(See clash, impact, conflict, encounter, shock.)

COLLOQUIAL
adverbs
informally; easily; admissibly; chattily; provincially; pleasantly; frankly; agreeably; comfortably; familiarly; sociably; ingenuously; childishly; simply; naturally; unceremoniously; unconventionally; recklessly; candidly; artlessly.

adjectives
prolonged; fruitful; serious; peaceful.

COLLUSIVE

adverbs
shrewdly; dangerously; illegally; astutely; fraudulently; surreptitiously; subtly; cleverly; craftily; cunningly; incontrovertibly; undeniably; unluckily; unfortunately; openly; abominably; unwisely; dishonestly; palpably; manifestly; essentially; substantially; deplorably; unhappily; artfully; inauspiciously; openly.

COLON
(part of body)

adjectives
distended; inactive; inflamed; impacted; sluggish; varicose.

verbs
abscess ; accumulate in—; block—; constrict—; distend—; drain—; excise—; flush—; force from—; incise—; inflame—; irrigate—; lubricate—; oil—; purge—; ulcerate—; wash—; irritate—.
(See intestine, bowel.)

COLONEL

adjectives
crusty; old; courtly; benign; gallant; cultured; rum-rotten.

COLONIAL

adverbs
strictly; authentically; architecturally; characteristically; distinctly; respectably; acceptably; accurately; admirably; attractively; boldly; originally; gallantly; charmingly; pleasantly; hospitably; spaciously; formally; beautifully; markedly; significantly; remarkably; conspicuously; faithfully; loyally; generously; broadly.

COLONIST

adjectives
pacific; early; hardy; patriotic; affluent; desperate; original; God-fearing; ever-encroaching.

COLONY

adjectives
abandoned; congenial; agricultural; depressing; independent; outlying; foreign; smart; wealthy; summer; colorful; wrangling; unique; devoted; robust; exempted; hale; dusky; tropical; proprietary; flour-

COLLOQUY

ishing; inheriting; remote; suburban; wretched; pretty; conquering; segregated; feeble; adjacent; dependent.

verbs
administer—; ban from—; cede to—; defend—; evict from—; free—; govern—; immigrate to—; launch—; maladministrate—; seize—; set up—; transfer to—; —flounders; —founders; —prospers; —rebels; —revolts; —riots; —smoulders; —wars on.
(See settlement.)

COLOR

adjectives
gorgeous; enchanting; rich; shining; clear; dazzling; uniform; subdued; gleaming; unheroic; quiet; faded; reticent; dull; canary; natural; artificial; exuberant; youthful; spirited; vibrant; kaleidoscopic; iridescent; full; lavish; live; vague; harmonious; piebald; sensuous; emotional; crude; raw; delicate; fragile; soft; false; basic; popular; rising; watery; gaudy; daring; welcome; flashy; isolated; normal; clean; complementary; solid; delightful; unwonted; radiant; dulled; hectic; thick; fatty; varied; dark; deep; decorative; brilliant; flying (pl); lustrous; subtle; intermediate; grimy; instrumental; tremendous; local; hideous; detestable; festive; staring; prismatic; heightened; glowing; incredible; warm; flickering; grinding; reassuring; unusual; new; water; factitious; equatorial; autumn; mellow; rapturous; ethereal; tender; faint; sickly; superb; crowded (pl); somber; profuse; motiveless; bright; exuberant; jumbled (pl); sleek; flamboyant; livid; solemn; sad; agreeable; riotous; pastel; summer; prominent; conventional; gay; seasonal; bold; plain; fluctuating; vigorous; orchestral; exquisite; dirty; garish; impregnated.

verbs
abhor—; accentuate—; alter—; array in—; assume—; bathe in—; bedeck with—; blend—; brush on—; burnish—; clothe in—; convey—; dash with—; deck in—; deprive of—; dim—; dip in—; disguise—; enamel with—; exhibit—; flush with—; grade—; indulge in—; invest with—; lend—; lose—; mix—; overcharge with—; paint in—; portray in—; retain—; shade—; sprinkle; steal—from; subdue—; sully—; tone—; touch with—; vary—; —arrests; —dazzles; —distinguishes; —ebbs; —emanates from; —enhances; —flames; —flow-

223

ers; —glares; —glows; —harmonizes; —heightens; —mingles; —mounts; —predominates; —runs rampant; —sickens; —soothes; —sparkles; mask—.
(See hue, blush.)

COLOR (v)

adverbs
amusingly; distinctly; faintly; unevenly; angrily; painfully; brilliantly; synthetically; violently; conspicuously; obscurely; exquisitely; highly; gorgeously; enchantingly; uniformly; vibrantly; iridescently; lavishly; emotionally; crudely; fragilely; gaudily; daringly; normally; decoratively; harmoniously; festively; incredibly; factitiously; flamboyantly; conventionally; exquisitely; garishly.
(See tint, tinge.)

COLORFUL

adverbs
gorgeously; strikingly; beautifully; garishly; gaudily; remarkably; famously; bizarrely; barbarically; incredibly; delicately; daintily; pleasantly; agreeably; artistically; splendidly; brilliantly; magnificently; superbly; flashily; gaily; cheerfully; strangely; impressively; extraordinarily; riotously; outlandishly; fantastically; extravagantly.

COLORING

adjectives
illusive; youthful; fanciful; mustard; vivid; admirable; tender; somber; warm; luxurious; genuine; motley; special; clear; mellow; rich; artificial; musical; radiant; gorgeous; deep; lustrous; neutral; delightful; flawless; appropriate.

COLORLESS

adverbs
monotonously; dully; cheerlessly; wanly; pallidly; neutrally; dismally; drearily; discouragingly; grievously; sorely; sadly; utterly; piteously; deplorably; pathetically; cruelly; wretchedly; singularly; oppressively; hopelessly; dishearteningly; needlessly; horribly; unpleasantly.

COLT

adjectives
frolicking; uncomely; dark; unhandled; youthful; awkward; wanton; unbroken; rough; handsome.

verbs
corral—; curb—; groom—; exercise—; loose—; mount—; stable—; —balks; —frisks; —gallops off; —grazes; —hurdles; —neighs; —pastures.
(See animal, horse.)

COLUMN
(architectural, military, etc)

adjectives
twisting; resistless; ascending; noble; tall; solid; marble; sturdy; dusty; massive; huge; vast; soaring; classic; stark; interpretative; warlike; somber; shattered; steel-clad; venerable; marching; flowered; lucrative; attacking; airy; perpendicular; crystal; slender; parallel; surging; monumental; vertebral; isolated; lofty; unending; advancing; ivory-shaped; vaporous; rostral; fragile; majestic; internal; spouting; graceful; gigantic; fantastic; glittering; luminous; rising; fluted; copulated; clustered.

verbs
ambush—; attach to—; construct—; destroy—; encircle—; erect—; file in—; head —; join—; line up in—; reinforce—; rule into—; shake—; shape—; shatter—; shield—; —crumbles; —marks; —supports; —swerves; —tapers; —vibrates; —winds.
(See line, post, shaft.)

COLUMN
(journalistic)

adjectives
mercurial; exciting; fascinating; informative; interpretative; hackneyed; inspiring; authoritative.

verbs
caption—; condense—; dash off—; devour —; edit—; evolve—; excerpt—; feature—; head—; limit to—; print—; publish—; rewrite—; syndicate—; title—; —berates; —conveys; —demeans; —interests; —inveighs against; —libels; —prejudices; —scandalizes.
(See writing, editorial.)

COMA

adjectives
deathlike; glassy-eyed; mild; rigid; trancelike; wide-staring.

verbs
affect with—; arouse from—; awake from—; emerge from—; fail in—; fall

into—; lapse into—; mutter in—; relieve—; sink into—; succumb to—.

(See unconsciousness, lethargy.)

COMB
(animal)
adjectives
cresting; crimson; defiant; flaunting; proudly-borne; imperial; nodding; superbly-curving; waggish.

verbs
adorn with—; curry—; develop—; ruffle—; serrate—; —crests; —matures; —protrudes; —waves.

(See crest.)

COMB (v)
adverbs
sleekly; briskly; dreamily; languidly; dexterously; effectively; left-handedly; gently.

(See brush.)

COMBAT
adjectives
frequent; ensuing; single; fierce; blood-stirring; aerial; chivalric; imaginable; beauteous; armed; hourly; historic; isolated; sportful; savage; noiseless; gladiatorial; primeval; mortal; feminine; caveman; merry; exciting; pitched; mimic; open-air; close; rude.

verbs
challenge in—; clash in—; collapse in—; crave—; dare—; disdain—; engage in—; face—; gird for—; heat—; incite to—; join in—; lay low in—; offer—; pledge to—; prick to—; view—; ward off—; —burns; —devastates; —rages; —seethes.

(See contest, battle, struggle, bout, contention.)

COMBAT (v)
adverbs
continually; effectively; fiercely; aerially; mortally; historically; savagely; gladiatorially; fatally; rudely; overwhelmingly; victoriously; thunderously; surgingly.

(See fight, struggle.)

COMBATANT
adjectives
successful; colossal; effective; unpropitious.

verbs
distinguish—; engage—; face—; fence with—; beat—; irk—; join—; lock with—; oppose—; overwhelm—; surround—; tri-

umph over—; unsnarl—s; —contends; —vanquishes; —wins.

(See contestant, fighter.)

COMBATIVE
adverbs
absurdly; ferociously; foolishly; noisily; unreasonably; immoderately; truculently; pugnaciously; irresponsibly; blatantly; insolently; openly; challengingly; daringly; teasingly; vexatiously; offensively; lamentably; unfortunately; quickly; boyishly; egotistically; vaingloriously; conceitedly; boldly; unpleasantly; disagreeably.

COMBINATION
adjectives
charming; rare; wonderful; striking; perfect; lovely; pretty; extraordinary; amazing; unusual; curious; grotesque; strange; foolish; occasional; lucky; strategic; simplest; unbeatable; agricultural; mental; brilliant; intricate; intellectual; exclusive; special; ecstatic; positive; possible; seasonable; solemn; subtle; gigantic; magnificent; extensive; weird; nutritive; synergistic; inexplicable; incongruous; pleasing; industrial; vigorous; ingenious; color; skillful; equilibrious; pernicious; bright; bold; distasteful; dramatic; compelling; illegal; fortunate; roomy; irresistible; unholy; dextrous.

verbs
achieve—; attain—; balk at—; capture—; conceal—; guard—; hide—; join—; justify—; lock in—; reveal—; seal—; warn against—; weld—; —conflicts; —strengthens; evolve—.

(See union, alliance, league, coalition.)

COMBINE (v)
adverbs
intricately; successfully; euphoniously; felicitously; skillfully; dexterously; chemically; wisely; shrewdly; gorgeously; charmingly; extraordinarily; strategically; grotesquely; agriculturally; mentally; intellectually; subtly; weirdly; inexplicably; incongruously; industrially; ingeniously; perniciously; dramatically; legally; irresistibly; unfortunately.

(See unite, merge.)

COMBUSTIBLE
adverbs
readily; dangerously; unfortunately; perilously; easily; alarmingly; dreadfully; unhappily; conveniently; temptingly; hazard-

ously; appallingly; advantageously; distressingly; unluckily; disastrously; sadly; direly; sorely; deplorably; inauspiciously; spontaneously; instantaneously; explosively.

COMBUSTION

adjectives
fitful; spontaneous; resultant; dire; disastrous; chemical; destructive.

verbs
accompany with—; destroy by—; excite to—; kindle to—; prevent—; produce—; protect against—; reduce by—; resist—; result in—; save from—; support—; throw into—; —consumes; —devours; —eats; —generates; —heats; —rages.
(See outbreak, disturbance.)

COME (v)

adverbs
laboriously; reluctantly; decently; prosaically; richly; undeniably; vividly; argumentatively; inevitably; fitfully; steadily; intermittently; confidently; rarely; voluntarily; briskly; warily; peaceably; archly; spasmodically; vehemently; distinctly; unquestionably; drunkenly; rapidly; silently; hopefully; swiftly; hesitatingly; deliberately; monotonously; sporadically; obliquely; seasonably; drowsily; wondrously; indiscriminately; assiduously; ponderously; slyly; jauntily.
(See arrive, approach.)

COMEDIAN

adjectives
eminent; slapstick; popular; audacious; acrobatic; facile.

COMEDIENNE

adjectives
eccentric; apt; world-renowned; clever; scintillating.

COMEDY

adjectives
brilliant; pleasing; charming; restrained; intelligent; rich; social; suave; earnest; ironic; clever; satirical; light; sardonic; fluffy; riotous; farcical; roaring; buoyant; high; tiresome; wry; ineffective; sickly; alleged; fantastic; absurd; lamentable; tragic; mournful; burlesque; macabre; amateur; romantic; artificial; plain; fancy; veritable; crisp; wary; lascivious; admirable; sentimental; slapstick; optimistic; frivolous; robust; complicated; poetic; eccentric.

verbs
applaud—; conclude—; dramatize—; enact—; indulge in—; perform—; present—; produce—; revel in—; write—; —burlesques; —characterizes; —delights; —depicts; —enlivens; —entertains; —lightens; —relishes; —satirizes.
(See play, drama, representation.)

COMELY

adverbs
altogether; sufficiently; surprisingly; bloomingly; rosily; ruddily; roughly; singularly; vividly; serenely; innocently; proudly; unconsciously; robustly; quietly; unspeakably; admirably; unexpectedly; charmingly; pleasantly; gracefully; jauntily; smartly; tidily; specially; pleasingly; attractively.

COMET

adjectives
splendid; wandering; refulgent; vagrant; thunder-toned.

verbs
analyze—; calculate—s; control—; describe—; discover—; distinguish—; — examine—; expel—; focus on—; identify—; interested in—; observe—; recognize—; regard—; separate from—; study—; witness—; —approaches; —burns; —deviates; —diminishes; —emits; —excites; —flashes; —influences; —speeds; —travels; —wanes.

COMFORT

adjectives
blessed; genial; gentle; thoughtful; priceless; bracing; cold; increased; dubious; poor; scant; miserable; physical; plush; velvety; spiritual; knee-deep; old-fashioned; modern; intellectual; home; comparative; measurable; smug; temporary; ordered; necessary; summer; easy; great; shirtsleeve; refreshing; jaunty; ideal; constant; breezy; smart; luxurious; every; physical; whispering; quiet; superior; social; superb; cheerful; supreme; extra; genuine; continental; casual; suffused; melancholy; rural; restful; urban; heavenly; untold; heating; scantiest; maximum; perpetual; swinish; joyous; fireside; filthy; mysterious; dispensing; material; exclusive; blissful; indisputable; needed.

verbs
afford—; augment—; delight in—of; deprive of—; derive—from; draw—from; fill with—; insure—; maintain in—; mini-

ster to—; rear in—; refuse—; restore—; scorn—; subsist in—; take—from; withhold—.

(See ease, solace, consolation, encouragement.)

COMFORTABLE
adverbs
altogether; pleasantly; utterly; finally; increasingly; physically; comparatively; immeasurably; snugly; happily; easily; refreshingly; luxuriously; quietly; socially; supremely; genuinely; mysteriously; blissfully; serenely; contentedly; unexpectedly; immensely; definitely; deliciously.

COMFORTER
adjectives
effectual; wayside; despairing; gorgeous; sympathetic; placating.

COMICAL
adverbs
absurdly; pleasantly; brilliantly; cleverly; ironically; riotously; uproariously; tiresomely; tediously; highly; effectively; fantastically; complexly; eccentrically; intentionally; deliberately; daintily; dazzlingly; hilariously; mercilessly; bitterly; fatuously.

COMMA
adjectives
checking; favored; interfering; interspersed; omitted; perfunctory; setting-off; indispensable; jutting; obstructing.

verbs
designate by—; dot with—s; invert—; mark with—; pause at—; punctuate with—; —clarifies; —denotes; —indicates; —interrupts; —punctuates; —separates.

(See mark, interval, pause, delay.)

COMMAND
adjectives
brisk; snarled; definite; sharp; stern; brusque; crisp; curt; despotic; peremptory; absolute; authoritative; unconditional; tyrannical; facile; supreme; independent; imperious; iron; deathless; masterly; fluent; unconcerned; stentorian; low-voiced; shouted; spoken; hoarse; shrill; raucous; sole; unified; urgent; last; hurrying; prompt; effective; divine; implied; incisive; suggestive; rudimentary; consequential; shaky; tactful; phenomenal; incomparable; geographical; instant; cold; lawful; unique; disguised; renewed; vigorous; immediate;

irregular; enthusiastic; instinctive; military; snapped; fierce; unlimited; laudable; pernicious; admirable; stifled; long-desired; rapturous; strenuous; intermingling; respective; just.

verbs
assume—; attend—; await—; bear—; boast—; comply with—; condescend to—; constitute—; defy—; execute—; fulfill—; lose—; obey—; release from—; relieve from—; relinquish—; respond to—; send forth—; stand ready at—; sway by—; thunder—; transgress—; understand—; waive—; —confuses; —enrages; —rings; —splits the air; —startles.

(See order, charge, mandate, authority, leadership, control.)

COMMAND (v)
adverbs
imperiously; authoritatively; intellectually; impatiently; laughingly; peremptorily; petulantly; definitely; brusquely; crisply; curtly; despotically; unconditionally; tyrannically; independently; stentorianly; hoarsely; shrilly; raucously; urgently; promptly; effectively; incisively; tactfully; phenomenally; incomparably; vigorously; immediately; enthusiastically; instinctively; fiercely; laudably; perniciously; justly.

(See order, direct.)

COMMANDER
adjectives
trusted; plucky; dashing; able; spectacular; immediate; insulted; victorious; regimental; immovable; illustrious; panic-stricken; fiery; respected; half-clad; venerable; renowned; indomitable.

verbs
appoint to—; exalt—; obey—; raise to—; rank as—; —assigns; —assumes; —authorizes; —campaigns; —controls; —directs; —disposes of; —exercises; —grants;— overrules; —pensions; —plans; —rules.

(See master, officer, captain, leader.)

COMMANDING
adverbs
harshly; fussily; sternly; briskly; definitely; sharply; crisply; curtly; despotically; peremptorily; authoritatively; imperiously; hoarsely; shrilly; raucously; urgently; incisively; tactfully; coldly; vigorously; enthusiastically; insultingly; offensively.

COMMANDMENT

adjectives

harsh; fussy; express; stern; abrupt; strait; unwritten; divine.

verbs

annul—; charge with—; delight in—; deliver—; disregard—; forbid by—; forsake—; fulfill—; hearken to—; neglect—; rebel against—; reject—; send forth—; transgress—; tremble at—; violate—; urge—

(See command, precept, law, order, warning.)

COMMEMORATE (*v*)

adverbs

jubilantly; appropriately; fitly; justly; splendidly; gloriously; annually; royally; simply; serenely; privately; publicly; passionately; sincerely.

(See celebrate.)

COMMEMORATIVE

adverbs

tenderly; reverently; publicly; appropriately; affectionately; permanently; nobly; deeply; triumphantly; faithfully; perpetually; graciously; worthily; adequately; suitably; gratefully; humbly; lastingly; enduringly; splendidly; magnificently; fittingly; beautifully; especially; impressively; felicitously.

COMMENCE (*v*)

adverbs

ceremoniously; busily; prosperously; daily; accustomedly; jocosely; meticulously; amiably; comfortably; conventionally; shrewdly.

(See begin, start.)

COMMENCEMENT

adjectives

elementary; prosperous; propitious; belated; annual; current.

COMMEND (*v*)

adverbs

grandiloquently; strongly; extravagantly; chiefly; emphatically; warmly; meritedly; flatteringly; heartily; fulsomely; boundlessly; scantily; meagerly.

(See recommend.)

COMMENDABLE

adverbs

altogether; especially; meritoriously; emphatically; particularly; eminently; unusually; unimpeachably; gloriously; admirably; worthily; highly; markedly; uncommonly; definitely.

COMMENDATION

adjectives

sorry; emphatic; extravagant; warm; merited; well-meant; gentle; widespread; worthy; hearty.

verbs

bestow—upon; consider—; convey—; deliver—; deserve—; discharge from—; express—; favor with—; flatter with—; gain—; regard—; respect—; silence—; solicit—; still—; value—; welcome with—; —abates; —ceases; —extols; —graces; —lauds; —praises; —recedes.

(See approbation, approval, praise, recommendation.)

COMMENSURATE

adverbs

exactly; appropriately; approximately; suitably; undeniably; properly; adjustably; tolerably; remarkably; meticulously; essentially; mathematically; scrupulously; carefully.

COMMENT

adjectives

favorable; approving; polite; appreciative; triumphant; grateful; important; significant; interesting; persuasive; sane; civilized; fretful; intelligent; shrewd; laconic; enlightening; cultured; prosaic; inappropriate; characteristic; dry; stumbling; trivial; bewildered; incoherent; wild; trite; open; gloomy; dubious; direct; vigorous; crisp; daring; pungent; scathing; sharp; penetrating; humorous; witty; jesting; facetious; upstart; quick; running; spontaneous; disgruntled; constant; exquisite; philosophic; speculative; editorial; cartoon; pamphleteering; country-wide; local; mental; printed; verbal; moralizing; censorious; detailed; curious; whispered; audible; casual; passing; critical; wistful; rare; contemporary; inane; enthusiastic; playful; cheerful; cynical; caustic; unsympathetic; perverse; churlish; uncomplimentary; endless; sour; abundant; cheering; quain; considerable; public; analytic; needless; inconsequential; musical; stupid; jocular; introductory; prophetic; skeptical; authoritative; enlivening; lavish; vulgar; resentful; acrimonious.

verbs

analyze—; arouse—; attach—; bear—; betray into—; challenge—; conceal—; cram with—; deride—; elicit—; evince—; evoke—; excite—; issue—; lavish—on; occasion—; provoke—; subject to—; underline—; —criticizes; —disconcerts; —elucidates; —enlightens; —flatters; —illuminates; —illustrates; —interprets; —penetrates; —squelches.

(See remark, observation, explanation.)

COMMENT (*v*)

adverbs

grumblingly; haughtily; admiringly; dryly; audibly; grimly; favorably; approvingly; politely; appreciatively; gratefully; significantly; interestingly; sanely; fretfully; intelligently; shrewdly; laconically; prosaically; inappropriately; characteristically; tritely; gloomily; dubiously; vigorously; crisply, pungently; scathingly; penetratingly; humorously; facetiously; spontaneously; philosophically; speculatively; editorially; locally; mentally; verbally; inanely; wistfully; playfully; cheeerfully; cynically; caustically; endlessly; sourly; cheeringly; quaintly; publicly; analytically; inconsequentially; stupidly; jocularly; drolly; flatteringly; prophetically; skeptically; authoritatively; lavishly; vulgarly; resentfully; acrimoniously; pityingly.

(See remark, observe.)

COMMENTARY

adjectives

significant; brilliant; sad; ironic; biting; pure; dazzling; binding; striking; authentic; curious; philosophic; keen; critical; rollicking; satiric; stressed; subtle; whimsical; penetrating; ludicrous; panoramic.

COMMENTATOR

adjectives

genial; philosophical; dramatic; unknown; hostile; political; inelegant; unseen.

COMMERCE

adjectives

nascent; enlarged; far-flung; unsullied; peaceful; flourishing; lawless; enhanced; expanding; international; vast; increasing; interstate; long-established; petty.

verbs

blockade—; derange—; develop—; encourage—; engage in—; hinder—; imperil—; insure—; interchange—; invade—; join in—; levy on—; negotiate—; open—; profit by—; protect—; regulate—; restrict—; route—; safeguard—; stimulate—; stint—; subsidize—; traffic in—; —dwindles; —flourishes; —transports; —wanes.

(See trade, business, intercourse, traffic, communication.)

COMMERCIAL

adverbs

sordidly; blatantly; profitably; readily; thrivingly; flourishingly; prosperously; productively; unaccountably; satisfactorily; fairly; openly; frankly; avowedly; uninterestingly; brilliantly; insistently; briskly; cheerfully; keenly; terribly; competently; thoroughly; dully; tediously; comically; actively; successfully; assiduously; energetically; shrewdly; craftily.

COMMERCIALISM

adjectives

blatant; camouflaged; high-powered.

COMMISERATION

adjectives

exaggerated; false; gentle; tender; light; regretful; sincere.

verbs

act in—; assist out of—; attend with—; behold in—; conceal—; defy—; deserve—; disdain—; distress with—; excite—; express—; feign—; lack—; pretend—; succumb to—; tear with—; tender—; wrack with—; wring with—.

(See compassion, pity, sorrow.)

COMMISSION

adjectives

perilous; permanent; promised; glorious; royal; simple; delicate; accredited; illicit; flattering; nonpartisan; legislative; eminent; joint; mixed; innocent; imaginary; unspoken; gabbling; much-desired.

verbs

accept—; appoint to—; assume—; authorize—; buy—; charge with—; confer—upon; delegate to—; deliver—; devise—; discharge—; dispatch—; empower—; entrust with—; execute—; tender--; undertake—; warrant—; —empowers; —instructs; —orders; —ranks; —specifies.

(See mission, delegation, errand, trust.)

229

adjectives
imperial; mouth-dripping; perfunctory; supercilious; unbending; bribe-swallowing; porcine.

COMMIT (v)
adverbs
consciously; irrevocably; unconsciously; habitually; sinfully; wilfully; rarely; solemnly; vilely; deliberately; unreservedly; fearlessly; criminally; treacherously; shrewdly; mysteriously; antagonistically; swiftly; veritably; vulgarly.
 (See assign, entrust.)

COMMITMENT
adjectives
careless; imaginary; solemn; revealed; judicial; official.

COMMITTEE
adjectives
advisory; influential; corresponding; reception; adjuvant; self-constituted; associational; intractable; select; prudential; vigilance; chagrined; strong; supreme; grand; advisory; special; executive; proper; socialistic; pacific; utilization.

verbs
appear before—; appoint to—; arm—; corral—; dominate—; hamstring—; head—; invent—; preside over—; set up—; taunt—; —advises; —bans; —bars; —condones; —denounces; —evinces; —favors; —functions; —proclaims; —retorts.
 (See group, board.)

COMMODIOUS
adverbs
sufficiently; adequately; advantageously; expediently; handily; serviceably; valuably; luckily; conveniently; pleasantly; appropriately; fortunately; splendidly; completely; excellently; spaciously; cheerily; comfortably; capaciously; extremely; admirably; roomily; particularly; suitably; uncommonly; exceptionally.

COMMODITY
adjectives
precious; agricultural; respected; unwanted; unctuous; valuable; opposite; essential; leading; vital; industrial; prized; necessary.

adjectives
culinary; evasive; vapid; conventional; tedious.

verbs
beautify—; enrich—; exalt—; express—; sink into—; soar above—; utter—; —bores; —fails to impress; —tires; —wearies.
 (See platitude, remark.)

adverbs
undeniably; insignificantly; trivially; indifferently; particularly; ridiculously; negligibly; cheaply; contemptibly; immaterially; miserably; pitifully; shabbily; wretchedly; distinctly; laughably; remarkably; surprisingly; stupidly; monotonously; prosaically.

COMMON-SENSE
adjectives
practical; supreme; salty; shrewd; courageous; hard-headed.

verbs
accept as— —; argue with— —; characterize by— —; demand— —; derive by— —; develop— —; display— —; endow with— —; evince— —; exhibit— —; forsake— —; judge with— —; lack— —; override— —; perceive with— —; require— —; violate— —; — prevails.
 (See judgment, understanding.)

COMMONWEALTH
adjectives
corrupted; co-operative; precarious; ancient; native; advanced; free; industrial; individual.

COMMOTION
adjectives
nervous; subdued; hurried; violent; sudden; faint; diurnal; inner; economic; mysterious; sad; strong; tremendous.

verbs
engage in—; excite—; quell—; quiet—; still—; throw into—; —agitates; —bristles; —confuses; —disorders; —irritates; —perturbs; —rages; —recurs; —rises;—stirs; —subsides; —terrifies.
 (See agitation, excitement, tumult, disturbance, turmoil, riot, stir.)

COMMUNE (v)

adverbs

spiritually; intimately; immortally; rapturously; ineffably; wordlessly; mentally; intellectually; constantly; socially; devoutly; worshipfully; divinely.

(See confer, converse.)

COMMUNICABLE

adverbs

highly; easily; perilously; alarmingly; dangerously; scarcely; freely; openly; secretly; rapidly; slyly; electrically; directly; conveniently; instantly; fearfully; frightfully; hardly; mysteriously; quickly; expeditiously; advantageously; expediently.

COMMUNICATE (v)

adverbs

duly; unknowingly; felicitously; thrillingly; formally; efficiently; gracefully; uniquely; swiftly; economically; rapidly; constantly; continuously; belligerently; garrulously; crudely; slyly; telepathically; directly; anonymously; sympathetically; confidentially; treacherously; conveniently; unreservedly; spiritually; clandestinely; telegraphically; precariously; domestically.

(See impart, transmit.)

COMMUNICATION

adjectives

efficient; sincere; graceful; rich; unique; swift; economical; rapid; easy; constant; continuous; belligerent; inarticulate; garrulous; profane; flimsy; crude; covert; sly; underhanded; world; visual; electrical; papal; aerial; interstate; telepathic; unrestricted; telltale; articulated; direct; anonymous; sympathetic; confidential; treacherous; depressing; convenient; unreserved; spiritual; slow-moving; pregnant; clandestine; evil; friendly; mercantile; unlimited; secure; radio; telegraphic; privileged; pretended; domestic; precarious.

verbs

break—with; contrive—; cut off—; deliver—; draw—; establish—with; exchange —s; interfere with—; reestablish—; relay—; scatter—; set up—with; stimulate—; —conveys; —expresses; —imparts; —informs; —proceeds from; —purports to; —requests.

(See intercourse, conference, correspondence, message, letter.)

COMMUNION

adjectives

immortal; rapturous; ineffable; friendly; wordless; mental; intellectual; intimate; untroubled; constant; social.

COMMUNISM

adjectives

lawless; isolated; outright; iconoclastic; jealous; possessive; intolerant.

verbs

advocate—; aspire to—; bow to—; combat—; decry—; denounce—; draw the line against—; embrace—; envision—; eradicate—; espouse—; flirt with—; incite to—; riddle with—; seethe with—; spread—; storm toward—; suppress—; taint with—; war on—; —abolishes; —derives from; —destroys; —equalizes; —menaces; —levels; —reconstructs; —undermines; —idealizes.

(See socialism.)

COMMUNIST

adjectives

subtle; unadulterated; rabid; confirmed; covert; active.

verbs

ban—; bar—; condemn—; denounce—; deport—; evict—; forbid—; harbor—; organize—s; recognize—; regulate—; reproach—; shelter—; style as—; —advocates; —agitates; —antagonizes; —exhorts; —expresses; —dreams; —influences; —opposes; —orates; —practices; —proclaims; —s riot; —struggles; —supports; —undermines; —vows.

(See socialist.)

COMMUNISTIC

adverbs

honestly; dangerously; sincerely; intrepidly; daringly; audaciously; enthusiastically; actively; furtively; slyly; openly; obviously; convincingly; absurdly; alarmingly; recklessly; inherently; appallingly; bitterly; outright; downright; thoroughly; entirely; subtly; deceptively; startlingly; surreptitiously.

COMMUNITY

adjectives

benighted; enlightened; forward; average; model; decent; beautiful; ideal; prideful; ambitious; busiest; enterprising; self-respecting; progressive; aggressive; sturdy; self-sustaining; comfortable; isolated; much-maligned; antagonistic; sprawling; ecclesiastical; overcrowded; treeless; civilized; closely-knit; urban; country; laboring; alien; polyglot; quiet; residential; pioneer; rural; sacred; tropical; industrial; monastic; conservative; organized; homogeneous; composite; enormous; fortresslike; curious; moral; congenial; guileless; self-supporting; hostile; opulent; veritable; seafaring; serene; drainageless; expanding; sober; scattered.

verbs
acquaint with—; beautify—; burden—; confine to—; dominate—; dwell in—; elevate—; establish—; expel from—; filter into—; forsake—; govern—; offend—; organize into—; pervade—; present to—; represent—; rule—; unite in—; —elects; —fosters; —levies; —shares; —supports.
(See city, town, village, public, society, association, people.)

COMPACT
adjectives
convenient; social; indissoluble; comfortable; voluntary; earthly; unwritten; imaginary; binding; favorable.

verbs
admit to—; authorize—; compose—; confirm—; contract—; draw up—; frame—; fulfill—; gather in—; join—; knit in—; plan—; ratify—; seal—; sign—; solemnize—; weld in—; —aids; —allies; —consolidates; —insures; —protects; —strengthens; —supports.
(See covenant, agreement, pact, treaty, contract.)

COMPANION
adjectives
beloved; wonderful; alluring; pleasant; charming; gentle; beautiful; popular; trusted; genial; attractive; true; faithful; devoted; wonted; burly; happy; thoughtful; useful; fit; illustrious; bosom; constant; intimate; inseparable; indefatigable; daily; gayest; jolly; jocose; meticulous; amiable; agreeable; lively; entertaining; droll; emaciated; pale; slim; young; feeble; stocky; lithe; rough; double-crossing; profligate; undesirable; sneering; doubtful; fickle; morose; weak; pitiable; gloomy; craven; irate; dispirited; tense; shrinking; prostrate; intellectual; drinking; mysterious; familiar; unsuspecting; grave; normal; authentic; eager; boon; ardent; engaging; quaking; environed; ghastly; polite; unique; troublesome; disappointing; lifelong; blithe; confederate; friendly (pl); semi-conscious; equivocal; spruce; subsidiary; often-tried.

verbs
associate with—; consort with—; engage—; entertain—; hire—; join—; lack—; lead—; long for—; reproach—; reunite with—; seek—; share with—; sway—; vie with—; —entertains; —escorts.
(See comrade, associate, ally.)

COMPANIONABLE
adverbs
pleasantly; agreeably; always; charmingly; unusually; genially; truly; faithfully; happily; thoughtfully; gaily; amiably; comfortably; entertainingly; curiously; politely; delightfully; inestimably; congenially; distinctly; unobtrusively; quietly; cheerfully; sociably; cosily; chattily.

COMPANIONSHIP
adjectives
genial; noble; voluntary; coarse; revered; endeared; creative; neighborly; thoughtful; indiscriminate; intimate; delightful; human; dull; honorable; dark; inestimable; mutual; helpful; satisfactory; refined; sympathetic; loving; mysterious; loyal; gay; humorous; pleasant; exclusive; friendly.

verbs
avoid—; break—; conceal—; crave—; delight in—; denounce—; desire—; hunger for—; invite—; join in—; lack—; limit—; lose—; maintain—of; object to—; seek—; win—; withdraw from—.
(See association, company, intimacy, fellowship, society.)

COMPANY
(*association, companionship*)
verbs
crave—; cultivate—; curse—; delight in—of; detest—; forbid—; forsake—; grace with—; miss—; placate—; refrain from—; regain—of; request—; sever from—; thrust into—of; woo—; —amuses; —bores; —departs; —dwindles; —entertains; —straggles in.
(See companionship.)

COMPANY
(*corporation*)
verbs
absorb—; bankrupt—; buy up—; charter—; consolidate—; defraud—; embezzle from—;

found—; incorporate—; manage—; merge—; reorganize—; ruin—; —branches out; —recovers; —profits; —survives.

(See corporation, firm.)

COMPANY
(general)
adjectives
subsidiary; lightheaded; respectable; assembled; scanty; ubiquitous; jocund; devout; treasonable; select; panic-stricken; choice; trading; merry; congenial; licentious; loathsome; saintly; high-born; agreeable; mysterious; villainous; ennobling; distinguished; defunct; brilliant; pleasant; enterprising; cosmopolitan; animated; suspecting; enchanting; glamorous; immortal; great; picturesque; unobtrusive; sympathetic; jovial; buoyant; refined; talented; detestable; rascally; infernal; wild; chartered; generating; transmission; gigantic; aggressive; forward-looking; reputable; commissary; projected.

COMPANY
(military division)
verbs
ambush—; assign to—; command—; desolate—; discontinue—; dispatch to—; divide into—ies; enlist in—; evolve—; forge—; head—; manoeuvre—; overtake—; partition—; separate—; spy on—; train—; —retreats; —traverses.

(See army, troops.)

COMPARABLE
adverbs
invidiously; scarcely; highly; easily; definitely; analogously; proportionally; relatively; homogeneously; interestingly; pertinently; distinctly; curiously; significantly; favorably; deservedly; worthily; excellently; appropriately; suitably; fittingly; properly; decently.

COMPARE (*v*)
adverbs
invidiously; egotistically; unavoidably; faithfully; favorably; unintentionally; approvingly; challengingly; odiously; metaphorically; significantly; caustically; classically; drolly; poignantly; dismayingly; conscientiously; directly; accurately; unfavorably; brutally; inevitably; aptly.

(See observe.)

COMPARISON
adjectives
vigorous; productive; challenging; odious; cost; metaphorical; insignificant; self-invited; curious; outworn; caustic; retrospective; classic; droll; poignant; dismaying; conscientious; direct; accurate; momentary; invidious; hateful; significant; unfavorable; brutal; strained; inevitable.

verbs
attempt—; bear—; belittle—; consider—; despair of—; despise—; disdain—; draw—; fail in—; flaunt—; illustrate—; institute—; invite—; judge—; lend to—; lose by—; place beyond—; ridicule—; scoff at—; stand—; subject to—; suffer by—; —brings out; —emphasizes; —measures; —parallels; —suggests.

(See illustration, simile.)

COMPARTMENT
adjectives
separate; concealed; rear; public; watertight.

verbs
coil in—; couch in—; decorate—; design—; distribute in—; divide in—; dwell in—; lay out—; occupy—; ornament—; panel—; partition into—s; prepare—; retain—; seal—; separate into—s; space—s; widen—; —accommodates; —adjoins; —allows; —permits.

(See section, chamber, part, division.)

COMPASS
adjectives
narrow; golden.

verbs
attract—; box—; manipulate—; navigate with—; observe—; plan with—; plot with—; suspend—; trust—; chart—; —describes; —deviates; —directs; —guides; —indicates; —informs; —leads; —limits; —marks; —measures; —pilots; —records; —routes; —safeguards; —surveys.

(See instrument.)

COMPASSION
adjectives
pitying; proud; deep; sincere; involuntary; august; womanly; delicate; angelic; bleeding; intolerable; melancholy; infinite; chivalrous; moving; affectionate; protective; scornful; profound; hurried; infallible; tender; faint; sweet; bored; dying; divine.

verbs
act in—; arouse—; conceal—; consume
with—; contain—; display—; excite—; express—; feign—; fill with—; melt in—;
minister with—; mourn in—; move to—;
plead for—; pretend—; reveal—; stir to—;
succor in—; take—upon; touch with—;
weep in—; wrack with—; wring with—;
—humanizes; —tempers.

(See commiseration, pity, sympathy,
mercy.)

COMPASSIONATE
adverbs
keenly; sympathetically; understandingly;
charitably; graciously; leniently; humanely;
mercifully; pityingly; tenderly; disarmingly; softly; utterly; gently; tolerantly; indulgently; mildly; magnanimously; comfortingly; effectively; deeply; sincerely;
delicately; infinitely; chivalrously; affectionately; profoundly; divinely.

COMPATIBLE
adverbs
easily; happily; felicitously; fortunately;
unusually; harmoniously; amiably; agreeably; pleasantly; joyously; obviously; essentially; manifestly; supremely; famously;
gracefully; opportunely; auspiciously; comfortably; amicably; extremely; unquestionably; unaccountably; surprisingly; fundamentally; notably.

COMPATRIOT
adjectives
assumed; grateful; affected.

COMPEL (*v*)
adverbs
flatly; ultimately; adroitly; reluctantly;
strategically; artfully; slyly; politely;
subtly; indirectly; truculently; legally; privately; troublesomely; economically; mysteriously; aggressively.

(See make, force.)

COMPENDIOUS
adverbs
remarkably; surprisingly; pleasingly; compactly; amazingly; laconically; tersely;
conveniently; exceedingly; expertly; inexpressibly; faultlessly; commendably; laudably; extraordinarily; strikingly; sensibly;
prudently; synoptically; concisely; neatly;
cleverly; adroitly; agreeably; usefully;
helpfully; advantageously.

COMPENDIUM
adjectives
astonishing; encyclopedic; similar.

COMPENSATE (*v*)
adverbs
adequately; amply; partially; grudgingly;
sufficiently; satisfactorily; financially; tolerably; pecuniarily; ultimately; abundantly;
solemnly; fully; barely; genially; nobly;
voluntarily; loyally.

(See pay, replace.)

COMPENSATION
adjectives
adjusted; ample; satisfactory; dwindling;
eternal; objective; financial; reassuming;
tolerable; pecuniary; abundant; fixed;
heartless; solemn; reasonable; adequate;
dynamic; ultimate.

COMPENSATORY
adverbs
satisfactorily; safely; securely; luckily;
happily; allowably; considerately; honorably; calculatingly; accurately; remuneratively; retroactively; highly; cleverly; acceptably; soundly; sensibly; wisely; adjustably; amply; financially; tolerably;
generously; reasonably; adequately; ultimately; prudently; sufficiently.

COMPETE (*v*)
adverbs
hotly; hilariously; unrestrainedly; unrestrictedly; freely; spectacularly; constructively; legitimately; ruinously; destructively; bitterly; actively; intensely; keenly;
strenuously; effectively; formidably; unprecedentedly; meaninglessly; individually; internally; domestically; internationally;
critically; primarily; unfairly; unequally;
aggressively; benevolently; basely; dishonorably; ruthlessly; hopefully; triumphantly.

(See contend, strive.)

COMPETENCE
adjectives
notable; cold; easy technical; hard; unruffled; modest; financial; mental; utmost;
professional; decent; occupational; bare;
sufficient.

verbs
allot—; amass—; bestow—upon; enlarge—;
exhaust—; fritter away—; furnish—; in-

herit—; insure of—; lack—; live off—; provide—; require—; rob of—; run through—; secure—; —dwindles; —suffices.
(See wealth.)

COMPETENT

adverbs
thoroughly; remarkably; highly; brilliantly; exceptionally; influentially; deftly; ingeniously; intelligently; proficiently; excellently; capably; discreetly; smartly; shrewdly; consummately; prepossessingly; undoubtedly; unquestionably; manifestly; completely; perfectly; notably; modestly; sufficiently.

COMPETITION

adjectives
unrestrained; unlimited; unrestricted; utterly unbridled; free; full; spectacular; unregulated; constructive; legitimate; ruinous; destructive; bitter; active; intense; keen; severe; sharp; heavy; strenuous; serious; effective; unprecedented; formidable; meaningless; puny; individual; world; internal; native; water-power; utility; truck; domestic; socialistic; international; critical; interstate; adjudicable; tangled; unwanted; constant; increased; enhanced; primary; counter; supplantive; unfair; unequal; hampering; foreign; savage; eager; formidable; pecuniary; marginal; benevolent; consequent; base; dishonorable; aggressive; harsh; ruthless; anarchical; hopeful; triumphal.

verbs
cripple—; curb—; discourage—; eliminate—; exclude—; face—; nurture on—; obliterate—; offer—; overcome—; promote—; reduce—; sharpen—; squelch—; stamp out—; stimulate—; suppress—; survive—; sustain—; —abates; —eases; —enlivens; —grinds; —steels; —tempers; —threatens.
(See rivalry, contention, strife.)

COMPETITIVE

adverbs
bitterly; actively; enthusiastically; brutally; ruinously; intensely; keenly; sharply; strenuously; formidably; primarily; savagely; appealingly; contentiously; pugnaciously; destructively; stimulatingly; rousingly; dangerously; cruelly; barbarously; desperately; mischievously; trickily; cunningly; shrewdly; deceptively; unfairly.

COMPETITOR

adjectives
insurgent; easygoing; formidable; alert; dangerous; cruel; honest; lame; veteran; motor; throat-cutting; husky; local; direct; active.

verbs
bankrupt—; defeat—; dispose of—; eliminate—; engage—; equal—; harass—; judge—; mass—s; outdistance—; outstrip —; rival—; suppress—; vanquish—; vie with—; —contests; —endeavors; —gains; —objects; —s organize; —retires; —stimulates.
(See contestant, opponent, rival, antagonist.)

COMPILATION

adjectives
intelligent; magnificent; handy; voluminous; exact; wretched; unoriginal; subsequent; important; systematic; hasty; valuable.

COMPLACENCY

adjectives
philosophical; bland; cynical; benign; pleased; yielding; melancholy; smug; superb; amiable; pleasant; light; foolish; placid; meek; oily; agreeable; affectionate.

verbs
announce with—; approach with—; breathe —; breed—; characterize—; display—; dwell in—; exhibit—; gain—; jolt out of—; observe with—; puncture—; rebuke—; receive with—; regard with—; resent—; satirize—; shake—; shock out of—; smile with—; —reigns.
(See satisfaction, serenity.)

COMPLACENT

adverbs
oddly; serenely; calmly; placidly; maddeningly; smugly; conceitedly; arrogantly; incredibly; imperturbably; vexatiously; pleasantly; comfortably; affably; blandly; gently; graciously; composedly; tranquilly; sedately; contentedly; cheerfully; entirely; good-humoredly; curiously; resolutely; admirably; justifiably.

COMPLAIN (*v*)

adverbs
shrewishly; bitterly; sorrowfully; dismally; audibly; feelingly; grievously; drawlingly; drearily; vehemently; respectfully;

peevishly; humorously; angrily; constantly; unjustly; ignorantly; pathetically; formally; jealously; frivolously; vexatiously; chronically; vigorously; dolefully.

(See grumble, murmur.)

COMPLAINT

adjectives

infantile; troublesome; vehement; loud; private; belated; frequent (pl); timid; alarming; mournful; loathsome; rash; angry; incipient; constant; fatal; unjust; prevalent; ignorant; fond; quavering; pathetic; distressing; formal; jealous; frivolous; dysenteric; pulmonary; vexatious; unintelligible; irritating; wailing; individual; public; chronic; paternal; vigorous; hoarse; well-founded; well-formed; pleasant; bitter; doleful; defensive; frenetic; praiseful; threnodic.

verbs

amend—; burden with—; complicate—; contract—; develop—; dismiss—; ease—; investigate—; issue—; lodge—against; mourn—; murmur—; pour out—; propogate—; renew—; rid oneself of—; set forth—; suffer—; swallow—; terminate—; usher in—; utter—; whisper—; withdraw —; —irritates; —s rain in; —recurs; —saddens; —wanes; —waxes.

(See grievance, lamentation, ailment, accusation, disease.)

COMPLAISANCE

adjectives

ready; affectionate; discreet; supple; sad; veiled.

COMPLAISANT

adverbs

amiably; benignly; kindly; warm-heartedly; indulgently; good-humoredly; benevolently; considerately; tenderly; accommodatingly; obligingly; sweetly; unaffectedly; comfortably; pleasantly; gravely; generously; happily; graciously; quietly; unobtrusively; remarkably; charmingly; gallantly; gently; urbanely; gracefully.

COMPLEMENTARY

adverbs

unusually; fortunately; remarkably; usefully; serviceably; happily; luckily; auspiciously; delightfully; pleasantly; absolutely; completely; entirely; thoroughly; mutually; opportunely; profitably; advantageously; conveniently; astonishingly; ingeniously.

COMPLETE

adverbs

absolutely; finally; happily; fortunately; luckily; satisfactorily; remarkably; unbelievably; magnificently; splendidly; extraordinarily; ideally; actually; delightfully; ceremonially; royally; formally; legally; officially; really.

COMPLETE (v)

adverbs

rapidly; swiftly; partially; gradually; skillfully; conventionally; finally; respectably; absolutely; delightfully; entirely; satisfactorily; casually; determinedly; superbly.

(See finish, perfect.)

COMPLETENESS

adjectives

unapproached; exhaustive; ethical; frightful; conventional; ruthless; respectable; final; round; absolute; firm; delightful.

COMPLETION

adjectives

apparent; advanced; divine; glorious; malevolent; plentiful; prophetic; stony; timely; unexpected; premature.

verbs

accomplish—; achieve—; attain—; await—; celebrate—; commemorate—; consent to—; desire—; expedite—; predict—; speed—; time—; —exhausts; —tires.

(See accomplishment, fulfillment, conclusion, end.)

COMPLEX

adjectives

repressed; haunting; sadistic; exceeding; flourishing; superior; vague; parlor; calamity; familiarity; modern; unreconciled; knitting; permanent; inferiority; narcissistic.

verbs

affect by—; analyze—; attribute to—; banish—; comprehend—; develop—; disentangle—; form—; indicate—; interpret—; involve—; nurture—; psychoanalyze—; relieve—; remove—; subject to—; understand—; unravel—; —chains; —consumes; —fetters; —seeks an outlet; arm with—.

(See complication, fear, influence.)

adverbs

bewilderingly; disturbingly; irritatingly; needlessly; seriously; embarrassingly; ambiguously; evasively; strangely; oddly; exceedingly; vaguely; astonishingly; bafflingly; unintelligibly; unnecessarily; tiresomely; painfully; harassingly; impossibly; intricately; perplexingly; confusingly; confoundedly; plaguedly; disconcertingly.

COMPLEXION

adjectives

flawless; clear; transparent; creamy; ivory; putty; sallow; apoplectic; pale; long; faded; unflushed; sanguine; fresh; ruddy; healthy; port-wine; choleric; beery; sunburnt; olive; sandy; swarthy; unnatural; delicate; dazzling; pleasant; muddy; blotchy; pretty; dark; ruined; shadowed; private; country; embrowned; coarse; variable; rubicund; jealous; florid; leaden; tanned; pallid.

verbs

beautify—; blemish—; blot—; change—; clear—; coarsen—; darken—; discolor—; dot—; inflame—; mar—; paint—; praise—; redden—; smirch—; tan—; tinge—; wither —; wrinkle—; —brightens; —freckles; —glows; —shines.

(See character, color, hue.)

COMPLEXITY

adjectives

astonishing; endless; infinite; ever-growing; abstract; ornate; serried; political; extraordinary; exciting; amazing; bewildering; differentiated; cosmic; baffling; increasing; technical.

verbs

attend with—; comprehend—; confine—; delve into—; disintegrate—; dispose of—; dissolve—; embrace—; evolve—; extricate from—; investigate—; involve—; reduce—; regard—; result in—; simplify—; solve—; sweep away—; —amazes; —discourages; —puzzles; —vanishes.

(See intricacy, complication, entanglement.)

COMPLIANCE

adjectives

immediate; faithful; servile; suave; entreating; implicit; infantile; calm; strict.

verbs

balk at—; betoken—; bow in—; coerce into—; demand—; desire—; enforce—; fall into—with; gain—; move to—; necessitate —; press for—; profess—; propose—; refuse—; request—; signify—; utter—; yield—.

(See submission, concession, acquiescence.)

COMPLIANT

adverbs

obligingly; gently; readily; willingly; vexatiously; slavishly; obsequiously; pleasantly; meekly; timidly; obediently; supinely; spinelessly; weakly; devotedly; passively; submissively; deferentially; affectionately; faithfully; loyally; unwillingly; rebelliously; sweetly; gladly; implicitly; childishly; calmly.

COMPLICATED

adverbs

hopelessly; senselessly; foolishly; necessarily; purposely; seriously; dangerously; ominously; sadly; perplexingly; embarrassingly; unavoidably; queerly; strangely; alarmingly; interestingly; disconcertingly; bafflingly; astonishingly; unintelligibly; ridiculously; confusingly; bewilderingly; desperately; painfully; plaguedly.

COMPLICATION

adjectives

serious; unseen; interesting; threatening; sad; annoying; embarrassing; military; endless; ingenious; delicate; everlasting; perplexing; indispensable; annoying; constant; dangerous; simple; psychological; dizzying; fresh; queer; added; social; imaginative; international; unforeseen.

verbs

avoid—; bar—; catch in—; develop—; free from—; guard against—; induce—; involve—; prevent—; result in—; solve—; suffer—; —abates; —arises; —endangers; —occurs.

(See complexity, entanglement, intricacy, confusion.)

COMPLICITY

adjectives

potential; secret; treacherous; eager; energetic; guilty; deceptive.

verbs

accuse of—; act in—with; charge with—; clear of—; convict of—; deal in—; free of—; imprison for—; involve in—; suspect of—; vindicate of—.

(See guilt.)

COMPLIMENT

adjectives
genial; pleasant; admirable; handsome; rare; high; generous; apt; polite; fervid; sincerest; respectful; justified; honest; delicate; smooth-tongued; high-flown; flowery; stilted; grudging; left-handed; fulsome; dubious; youthful; peculiar; unphilosophical; noncommittal; questionable; erudite; abstracted; subtle; appropriate; gentle; awkward; indirect; feminine; gratifying; truculent; stipulated; supreme; piquant; munificent; bombastic; professional; superlative; gallant; ephemeral; deferential; mawkish; double-barreled; formal; undeniable; sugared; two-edged; exaggerated; idle; well-turned; tactful; novel; affectionate; ghastly; hyperbolic.

verbs
accept—; acknowledge—; allow—; bestow—; deliver—; disdain—; expect—; extend—; favor with—; greet with—; imply—; pay—; present—; receive—; return—; turn—; —commends; —flatters; —pleases; —praises; —soothes.
(See greeting, remembrance, congratulation, praise.)

COMPLIMENT (v)

adverbs
warmly; genially; admirably; handsomely; rarely; highly; generously; aptly; fervidly; sincerely; justifiedly; delicately; stiltedly; grudgingly; fulsomely; dubiously; eruditely; subtly; appropriately; awkwardly; indirectly; gratifyingly; bombastically; supremely; piquantly; professionally; superlatively; gallantly; deferentially; mawkishly; formally; undeniably; exaggeratedly; idly; affectionately; hyperbolically.
(See praise.)

COMPLIMENTARY

adverbs
delightfully; flatteringly; gallantly; charmingly; politely; exaggeratedly; absurdly; smilingly; chivalrously; adoringly; pleasingly; highly; sincerely; appropriately; affectionately; truly; honestly; grudgingly; dubiously; questionably; subtly; gently; indulgently; pompously; supremely; deferentially; handsomely; lovingly.

COMPLY (v)

adverbs
promptly; strictly; willingly; gladly; partially; slavishly; humbly; irritably; non-chalantly; bitterly; sourly; grimly; carelessly.
(See agree, consent.)

COMPONENT

adjectives
essential; necessary.

adverbs
fundamentally; essentially; necessarily; indispensably; unavoidably; constitutionally; organically; vitally.

COMPOSE

adverbs
nominally; identically; wholly; partly; artistically; largely; simultaneously; incessantly; luckily; prolifically; abundantly; charmingly; picturesquely; didactically; pretentiously; ludicrously; vilely; monstrously; allegorically; monumentally; orchestrally; historically; fantastically; chorally; crudely; elaborately; vitally; gravely; dramatically; humorously; gracefully; creatively; realistically.
(See lull, calm.)

COMPOSER

adjectives
native; brilliant; voluminous; contemporary; eminent; operatic; productive; talented; anxious; instinctive; ultramodern; best-known; foremost; outstanding; exuberant; modernist; versatile; pharisaical; famous; hack; master; deft; practiced.

COMPOSITION

adjectives
decorative; didactic; careless; pretentious; ludicrous; tragic; vile; dishonorable; artistic; unwieldy; monstrous; secular; monumental; reposeful; allegorical; touching; fugitive; orchestral; historical; intensive; feminine; studied; capricious; fantastic; motley; choral; essential; elaborate; crude; important; vital; grave; dramatic; humorous; graceful; striking; aesthetic; creative; realistic.

verbs
adjust—; alter—; arrange—; compound—; deliver—; fashion—; form—; frame—; interpret—; order—; polish—; prepare—; print—; release—; reshape—; score—; toss off—; transpose—; versify—; vocalize—; —involves.
(See essay, story.)

COMPOSURE

adjectives

perfect; kind; gentle; magnificent; incomparable; unruffled; flintlike; utmost; splendid; absolute; unimpaired; astonishing; solemn; curious; labored; grave; hard; horrible; contemptuous; reticent; equable; uncanny; airy; mournful; melancholy; marble; seeming; insolent; extraordinary; austere; inflexible; strained; undisturbed; dogged; comparative; amiable; cruel; unshakable; affected.

verbs

blemish—; break—; enjoy—; feign—; handle with—; maintain—; mar—; meet with—; preserve—; recover—; regain—; settle in—; shake—; shock out of—; view with—; —disarms; —follows.

(See equanimity, serenity.)

COMPOUND

adjectives

hypothetical; monstrous; metallic; disastrous; ferrous; utmost; rankest; argenteous; thermoplastic; harmonious; complicated; deliquescent; linguistic; tantalizing; elaborate; ingenious; chemical; incongruous.

verbs

absorb—; analyze—; break down—; characterize—; combine in—; derive—from; devise—; dissolve—; form—; heat—; indicate—; make up—; meet—; mix—; prescribe—; stir—; stimulate—; unite in—.

(See mixture, combination.)

COMPREHEND (*v*)

adverbs

fully; perfectly; readily; rightly; intelligently; discriminatingly; partially; scientifically; deeply; accurately; generally; dispassionately; tardily; masterfully; instinctively.

(See grasp, understand.)

COMPREHENSION

adjectives

conspicuous; intelligent; calm; infant; social; absent; discriminating; untrained; perfect; martial; vast; human; growing; enlightened; scientific; deeper; accurate; easy; imaginative; adequate; general; faithful; quick; dispassionate; gathering; complete; unparalleled; tardy; masterly; instinctive; dawning.

verbs

achieve—; affect—; attain—; attempt—; benumb—; enlarge—; exhibit—; extend—; feign—; go beyond—; grasp—; include in—; lack—; listen with—; simulate—; stagger—; view with—; warp—; —dawns; —results in.

(See understanding, apprehension, knowledge.)

COMPREHENSIVE

adverbs

wonderfully; broadly; unusually; fortunately; cogently; liberally; tolerantly; tolerably; fairly; extremely; luckily; purposely; explicitly; advantageously; generously; admirably; delightfully; superbly; conspicuously; nobly; strikingly; unquestionably; impressively; astonishingly.

COMPRESS (*v*)

adverbs

firmly; severely; savagely; bitterly; tightly; angrily; powerfully; dramatically.

(See crowd.)

COMPROMISE

adjectives

expensive; unworthy; lean; sensible; timid; tolerable; workable; proposed; wise; self-sufficient; practical; judicious; tacit; occasional; dignified; negotiated; imaginable; ineffectual; prudent; pitiful; strange; cowardly; ultimate; wretched; curious; scorning.

verbs

accept—; achieve—; agree upon—; announce—; arrange—; arrive at—; attempt —; come to—; conclude—; consent to—; draw up—; effect—; extend—; maintain—; offer—; result in—; risk—; —adjusts; —decides; —recommends; —reconciles; —settles; —soothes.

(See agreement, settlement, promise.)

COMPROMISING

adverbs

unfortunately; possibly; alarmingly; leniently; sensibly; reasonably; opportunely; fearfully; timidly; timorously; bravely; courageously; senselessly; scandalously; recklessly; indiscreetly; curiously; indubitably; injudiciously; awkwardly; unluckily; evasively; unhappily; unwisely; shockingly; appallingly; rashly; appeasingly.

COMPULSION

adjectives

silent; irresistible; subtle; fascinated; armed; legal; restraining; unrecognized; physical; sad; temperamental; moral; strong; inescapable.

verbs

accept under—; act in—; appear under—; commit under—; confess under—; develop by—; devise by—; exercise—; involve—; obey under—; rebel at—; resist—; restrain by—; submit under—; wring out by—; —exculpates; —forces.

(See coercion, force, necessity, restraint, obligation.)

COMPULSORY

adverbs

disagreeably; hatefully; substantially; significantly; dangerously; disturbingly; implicitly; strictly; rigidly; hideously; flagrantly; wisely; sensibly; cruelly; detestably; odiously; wickedly; irksomely; arbitrarily; officially; locally; inescapably; fortunately; annoyingly; tediously; prosily; vexatiously; needlessly; ineffectively; irresistibly; silently; subtly; sadly; inexorably; stringently; peremptorily; terrifyingly; actually; authoritatively; absolutely; dominantly; imperiously; originally; sternly; necessarily.

COMPUNCTION

adjectives

slight; severe; grievous; motherly; evident; mathematical; natural; bitter.

COMPUTATION

adjectives

careful; sardonic; arithmetical; subsequent; moderate; impressive; ridiculous.

verbs

calculate—; check—; correct—; corroborate—; employ—; err in—; estimate—; fail in—; fall short of—; find by—; increase—; inspect—; prove—; reach by—; reckon—; scorn—; —accounts for; —differs; —helps; —indicates.

(See calculation, reckoning.)

COMPUTE (v)

adverbs

accurately; sketchily; carefully; arithmetically; mathematically; geometrically; impressively; ridiculously; statistically; scientifically.

(See calculate, estimate.)

COMRADE

adjectives

worthy; fastidious; gallant; benevolent; wounded; self-denying; placid; hackneyed; suffocated; inseparable (pl); little; garrulous; abiding; agreeable; wonder-loving; intellectual; exhausted; needy; sensible; merry; conforming; loyal; bickering; gluttonous.

verbs

aid—; applaud—; assist—; associate with —; betray—; forsake—; fraternize with—; gain—; march with—; protect—; share with—; shield—; treasure—.

(See companion, associate, mate.)

COMRADELY

adverbs

loyally; devotedly; sympathetically; cordially; warmly; helpfully; heartily; amicably; affably; frankly; distinctly; congenially; unselfishly; staunchly; generously; courageously; gallantly; agreeably; faithfully; gaily; comfortably; entertainingly; curiously; unobtrusively; quietly; sociably; chattily.

COMRADESHIP

adjectives

happy; warm; flattering; unconditional; spiritual; impossible; ceaseless; genuine; kindly; pleasant; tragic; deep-hearted; constant; simple; rare; international; lifelong; sympathetic; unspeakable.

CONCEAL (v)

adverbs

cleverly; effectually; criminally; partially; instinctively; feloniously; dexterously; deliberately; stupidly; ignorantly; guiltily; conscientiously; fearfully; scrupulously.

(See hide, suppress.)

CONCEALMENT

adjectives

expedient; ignorant; stupid; coarse; juggling; ladylike; watery.

verbs

appear from—; attempt—; disclose—; divulge—; effect—; intend—; lay bare—; necessitate—; offer—; place in—; reveal—of; seek refuge in—; suspect—; uncover—; veil in—; wrap in—.

(See secretion, seclusion, privacy.)

CONCEDE (v)

adverbs

deferentially; completely; unexpectedly; apologetically; willingly; generally; tactfully; frankly; generously; tamely; gently; freely; liberally.

(See yield, admit.)

CONCEIT

adjectives

devastating; quaint; mere; whimsical; colossal; comical; solemn; peculiar; lessening; sanguine; keen; erroneous; piteous; stupid; rational; boyish; staple; enigmatic; graceful; profound; doubtful; partial; presumptuous; lively; ingenious; gallant; noble; true; innocent; earthy; gross; fantastic; literary; passing; imperious; self-centered; melancholy; artificial; sickening; modest; fabulous; false; platonic; vain; immense.

verbs

bare—; cloud with—; deplore—; devour with—; display—; fill with—; humor—; puff up with—; rebuke—; shatter—; soak in—; swallow up by—; tickle—; wallow in—; ween—; —disgusts; —exaggerates; —inflames; —overestimates; —overvalues; —prejudices; —robs; —twists.

(See egotism, pride, vanity.)

CONCEITED

adverbs

harmlessly; ludicrously; solemnly; piteously; ridiculously; arrogantly; intolerably; stupidly; gracelessly; presumptuously; innocently; grossly; fantastically; offensively; imperiously; sickeningly; immensely; disgustingly; foolishly; inordinately; contemptibly; amusingly; ingenuously; artlessly; complacently; prodigiously; colossally; unconsciously; unwittingly; awkwardly; foppishly; simperingly; stagily; abominably; laughably; pathetically; noisily; theatrically; transparently; unreasonably; loftily; grandly; undeniably; extremely; palpably; remarkably; incredibly.

CONCEIVABLE

adverbs

scarcely; possibly; readily; easily; fantastically; reasonably; sensibly; hardly; barely; obscurely; oddly; grotesquely; faintly; ridiculously; probably; presumably; romantically; preposterously; theoretically; fancifully; appallingly.

CONCEIVE (v)

adverbs

wondrously; hastily; chastely; humbly; craftily; admirably; distinctly; harshly; instantly; empirically; artistically; ingeniously; effectually; erroneously; majestically; nobly; inspiringly; popularly; narrowly; uniquely; morally; politically; cynically; definitely; puerilely; sentimentally; liberally; nebulously; intellectually; romantically; unchristianly; traditionally; previously; exaltedly; dramatically; subjectively; aesthetically; musically; competitively; peculiarly; erroneously; vitiatedly; incongruously; spontaneously; idealistically; judicially; crudely; grandly; divinely; immaculately; sympathetically.

(See understand, imagine.)

CONCENTRATE (v)

adverbs

swiftly, mentally; logically; intensely; fruitfully; protractedly; deliberately; achingly; devoutly; exhaustively; grimly; intently; desperately; incessantly; persistently; passionlessly; impassionedly; carefully; ambitiously; wholly.

(See focus.)

CONCENTRATION

adjectives

mental; intense; logical; zestful; vague; dreamy; undue; fruitful; physical; protracted; deliberate; agonized; aching; devout; exhausting; grim; perpetual; desperate; implacable; administrative; deadly; intent; desired; completed; incessant; persistent; pronounced; impassioned; careful; gigantic.

verbs

affect—; cultivate—; direct—; gain by—; gather in—; lose in—; necessitate—; produce—; require—; strive for—; —collects; —empowers; —enables; —intensifies; —strengthens; —unifies.

(See condensation, contraction.)

CONCEPT

adjectives

cynical; ethereal; social; major; permanent; simple; beneficent; fundamental; negative; petty; platonic; economic; emotional; rational; mystical; anthropopsychic; consonant; abstract; steady; liberal; heroic; ridiculous; idiotic.

verbs

accept—; build up—; discard—; express—; form—; guard—; hallow—; idealize—; join in—; lose—; master—; produce—; reshape—; reverence—; symbolize—; —develops; —disappears; —fades; —grows.

(See idea, conception, thought, notion.)

CONCEPTION

adjectives

majestic; noble; lofty; proud; inspiring; popular; beautiful; imperial; powerful; daring; profound; accurate; just; coherent; ingenious; undiluted; curious; unique; narrow; haziest; raw; immature; moral; military; brilliant; mental; political; cynical; definite; puerile; sentimental; novel; liberal; fixed; abstract; easy; inward; general; nebulous; artistic; imaginative; intellectual; evolutionary; theologic; ethical; romantic; freer; objective; movie; arabesque; unchristian; utopian; traditional; previous; exalted; true; delicate; grotesque; distinguished; gross; crude; dramatic; sensuous; wildest; essential; subjective; aesthetic; musical; dynamic; faintest; fickle; competitive; physical; adequate; theoretical; ancient; poetic; original; admirable; peculiar; erroneous; vitiated; serviceable; advanced; incongruous; spontaneous; idealistic; hysterical; cherished; judicial; fabulous; dim; vague; crude; gracious; rival; radiant; grand; different; proper; divine; immaculate; sordid; dominant; sympathetic; continental.

CONCEPTION

verbs

accept—; acquire—; attain—; base—; blur—; broaden—; clarify—; classify—; color—; confuse—; derive—; destroy—; disrupt—; divorce from—; embody—; endow—; enlarge—; envisage—; exalt—; expound—; fulfill—; gain—; give—; ·implant—; inherit—; justify—; perfect—; ponder—; reflect—; rest on—; revise—; school in—; set aside—; translate—; —exists; —denotes; —forms; —prevails.

(See idea, notion, concept, impression, imagination.)

CONCERN
(business)

adjectives

pioneer; long-established; competing; successful; dominating; settled; private; commercial; ultra-respectable; prospective; pretentious.

CONCERN
(feeling)

adjectives

sweet; kindly; tender; mild; affectionate; anxious; eager; charitable; intense; human; sympathetic; pitying; agonizing; real; honest; deep; serious; grave; consuming; jealous; secondary; irritable; superfluous; dramatic; suprasensual; primary; personal; lifelong; general; vital; ever-pressing; mutual; patent; complex; terrestrial; interior; materialistic; temporal; immediate; flourishing; pressing; extreme; disquieting; ethical; soft; menial; waking; pàramount; nonchalant; hypochondriacal.

verbs

cause—; contemplate with—; create—; **de**monstrate—; detect—; ease—; engage—; excite—; feel—; feign—; frown with—; involve—; lift—; manifest—; neglect—; plead—; pretend—; question—; regard with—; relate with—; share—; throw into—; trouble with—; —vexes.

(See anxiety, care.)

CONCERN (v)

adverbs

feverishly; intelligently; intimately; immensely; intensely; principally; solely; tenderly; mildly; affectionately; humanly; anxiously; eagerly; charitably; sympathetically; gravely; consumingly; jealously; dramatically; mutually; patently; materially; disquietingly; ethically; passionately.

(See worry.)

CONCERNED

adverbs

deeply; anxiously; financially; nationally; personally; appallingly; vitally; scandalously; curiously; excitedly; nervously; strangely; unaccountably; justly; responsibly; unfortunately; uneasily; importantly; heavily; solicitously; inseparably; undeniably; painfully; seriously; gravely; primarily; materially; surreptitiously; secretly.

CONCERT

adjectives

classical; orchestral; spiritual; thrilling; indoor; monster; basic; charitable; home; impromptu.

CONCERTED

adverbs

effectively; influentially; efficiently; strongly; irresistibly; favorably; clannishly; irrepressibly; invincibly; alertly; thoughtfully; resolutely; vigilantly; guardedly; securely;

legally; legitimately; warrantably; justifiably; formidably; confidently; ably; authoritatively; adaptably.

CONCESSION

adjectives

radical; scandalous; surprising; trivial; veritable; voluntary; momentary; mutual; temporary; secret; valuable; unconscious; generous; dignified; minor; gracious; reciprocal; commercial; vital; unwise; unlimited; cowardly; benevolent; original; liberal; sufficient; pencil-making; political; unusual; unworthy.

verbs

accept—; allot—; allow—; appreciate—; claim—; demand—; exact—; execute—; exploit—; force into—; grant—; obtain—; receive—; refuse—; scorn—; submit to—; warrant—; yield—; —admits; —ameliorates; —fails; —infers; —mitigates.

(See privilege, right, favor, allowance.)

CONCILIATION

adjectives

harmonious; promoted; predetermined; unattainable; replete; voluntary; amiable; tender; lenient.

verbs

accept—; achieve—; attempt—; bring into—; declare—; dispute—; effect—; hope for—; offer—; open avenues of—; promote—; recommend—; strive for—; tease into—; welcome—; win—; —harmonizes; exhibit—.

(See reconciliation.)

CONCILIATORY

adverbs

hopefully; possibly; presumably; properly; justly; wisely; sagaciously; favorably; sensibly; reasonably; soundly; fairly; profoundly; craftily; subtly; shrewdly; deceptively; fortunately; decently; respectfully; generously; honestly; appropriately; judiciously; impressively; moderately.

CONCISE

adverbs

gratifyingly; remarkably; satisfactorily; surprisingly; pleasingly; pleasantly; briefly; compactly; crisply; laconically; tersely; conventionally; conveniently; exceedingly; curtly; pointedly; inexpressibly; faultlessly; commendably; laudably; extraordinarily; strikingly; necessarily; sensibly; wisely; prudently.

CONCLUDE

adverbs

sorrowfully; erroneously; inevitably; cynically; peremptorily; definitely; abruptly; pessimistically; tartly; amicably; summarily; jocosely; confidently; coolly; officially; triumphantly; contemptuously; reasonably; legitimately; brilliantly; theoretically; logically; humiliatingly; despairingly; irresistibly; obviously; rationally; preposterously; statistically; ultimately; fallaciously; tragically; hypothetically; misleadingly.

(See end, close.)

CONCLUSION

adjectives

official; generalized; conducive; triumphant; intelligible; contemptuous; doubtful; still; strict; legitimate; practical; definite; inevitable; vile; languid; painful; speculative; spiritualistic; solid; meager; practiced, satisfactory; reasonable; brilliant; virtuous; lurid; adventurous; foregone; theoretic; suitable; logical; compulsory; negative; ungracious; erroneous; murdering; palpable; bloody; humiliating; consolatory; dreary; preliminary; impotent; happy; sterile; demonstrated; scientific; auspicious; pregnant; valuable; horrible; devastating; despairing; portentous; irresistible; victorious; trivial; obvious; rational; abrupt; preposterous; statistical; ultimate; farcical; astonishing; surprising; fallacious; lame; subversive; opposite; tragic; hypothetical; critical; spooky; necessary; tricky; misleading.

verbs

accept—; admit—; arrive at—; base—on; bias—; bring to—; build—; carry to—; confirm—; crown—; deduce—; delude—; divine—; draw—; enunciate—; escape—; establish—; formulate—; induce—; influence—; jump to—; lead to—; march to—; perceive—; prejudice—; reach—; refute—; reinforce—; seek—; set down—; shake—; shape—; strengthen—; substantiate—; support—; sustain—; tolerate—; weigh—; win—; —fades; —follows.

(See decision, determination, deduction, completion.)

CONCLUSIVE

adverbs

satisfactorily; officially; doubtfully; legally; definitely; painfully; reasonably; ungraciously; positively; absolutely; decisively; arbitrarily; dogmatically; incontestably;

categorically; tyrannically; unmistakably; brutally; hopelessly; firmly; disagreeably; peremptorily; unconditionally; finally; uncannily; unalterably; happily.

CONCOCTION
adjectives
promoting; bitter; delicious; fatal; philanthropic; potent.

CONCOMITANT
adverbs
usually; habitually; naturally; presumably; probably; inevitably; recurrently; occasionally; reasonably; definitely; ordinarily; assuredly; undoubtedly; apparently; evidently; unavoidably; inescapably; painfully; unfortunately; strangely; miraculously; always; providentially; significantly; luckily; deliberately; designedly.

CONCORD
adjectives
never-ending; everlasting; universal; perfect; gentle; sweeping; jarring.

CONCOURSE
adjectives
fortuitous; gallant; immense; abusive; vast; numerous (pl); divine; affected; orderly; deep.

CONCRETE
adverbs
convincingly; satisfactorily; actually; explicitly; expressly; objectively; substantially; sensibly; perceptibly; representatively; appreciably; unequivocally; unmistakably; demonstrably; intelligently; decisively; intelligibly; comprehensibly.

CONCUR (v)
adverbs
entirely; amiably; directly; heartily; half-heartedly; diplomatically; affably; casually; tentatively; provisionally; privately; unboundedly; tranquilly.
(See agree.)

CONCUSSION
adjectives
hearty; fearful; tremendous; momentary; enormous.

CONDEMN (v)
adverbs
unjustly; unmercifully; irrevocably; universally; intentionally; mildly; mercilessly; unhesitatingly; petulantly; emphatically; unanimously; bitterly; publicly; unqualifiedly; unhesitatingly; blindly; severely; drastically; indignantly; barbarously; formally.
(See censure, blame.)

CONDEMNATION
adjectives
bitter; unqualified; sharp; public; critical; sweeping; unhesitating; blind; severest; vigorous; censorious; sorrowful; active; reverberating; drastic; unhesitating; iniquitous; unanimous; cruel; scornful; indignant.

verbs
announce—; deserve—; fall into—; judge —; launch—; merit—; procure—of; pronounce—; repent—; reproach with—; spare—; steep in —; —blames; —censures; —inflames; —libels; —slanders.
(See denunciation.)

CONDENSATION
adjectives
amazing; conjoined; hasty; literal; moderate; sensible; viscous.

verbs
effect—; hasten—; —compresses; —concentrates; —converts; —crowds; —eliminates; —hardens; —intensifies; —purifies; —reduces; —thickens; —vaporizes; —heats.
(See contraction.)

CONDESCEND (v)
adverbs
urbanely; graciously; ostentatiously; hypocritically; patronizingly; haughtily; languidly; stiffly; benignantly; amusingly; gently; amiably; magnanimously.
(See yield.)

CONDESCENSION
adjectives
gradual; ostentatious; hypocritical; patronizing; lofty; haughty; languid; stiff; graceful; benignant; edifying; condoling; infinite; good-natured; familiar; awful; terrifying; presidential; amusing; gentle; utmost; amiable; degrading.

CONDITION
adjectives
excellent; perfect; satisfactory; ideal; pathological; prepossessing; happy; blissful; remarkable; unusual; stringent; robust; righteous; tumbled; primitive; dilapidated; neglected; unsanitary; crowded; miserable; terrible; deplorable; woeful; pitiful; gloomy; below par; demoralized;

alarming; untidy; fatigued; distracted; productive; senile; mental; unsettled; financial; gaseous; ultimate; permanent; natural; relaxed; garrulous; hard; analogous; harsh; proper; normal; correct; genial; glamorous; inspiring; delectable; humane; contemporary; dangerous; chaotic; changing; temporal; local; grim; corrupt; pleasant; evil; unfavorable; quiet; working; early; stipulated; defined; varying; existing; hazardous; severe; embryonic; calamitous; operating; parlous; servile; underlying; rational; peculiar; degraded; wretched; degenerate; interesting; flowing; discouraging; artificial; erotic; fluctuating; adverse; slight; disabled; neglected; ill; molten; outward; altered; poisoned; responsive; ameliorated; inferior; industrial; abject; starving; infamous; foot; expressed; optical; grievous; flourishing; inchoate; ultimate; top-notch; depraved; unsightly; unbailed; distressing; threatening; unsatisfactory; disturbed; semi-barbarous; undated; prolonged; chronic; stagnant; delicate; incompatible; belligerent; vapory; hopeless; molecular; rigid; fluid; atmospheric; frightful; impaired; moribund; aeronautical; helpless; critical; social; intellectual; established; humblest; embarrassed; bruised; political; drooping; prostrate; arid; thriving; ragged; dreadful; introverted; muddy; complicating; traffic; subgrade; unique; cheeky; destitute; nourishing; visceral; taut; contrasting; inflammatory; amorphous; surrounding; climatic; hypnotic; healthy; antecedent; clogged; encumbered; sober; lamentable; crippled; acute; pecuniary; opposing; ignoble; temporary; famishing; incurable; elastic; seraphic; upset; identical; light; irritated; anguished; tubercular; gruelling; convulsive; befuddled; unhygienic; defenseless; spasmodic; morbid; equivalent; special; cold; heterogeneous; disordered; atomic; perilous; habitable; succulent; certain; unbearable; deterrent; cataleptic; humbler; prevailing; linguistic; odd; sophisticated; desolate; quick; ruinous; exhausted; disastrous; bewildering; desiccated; foolish; precise; replenished; humble; itching; depleted; slovenly; idyllic; impassable; negative; perplexed.

verbs
abolish—; accept—; accustom to—; adapt to—; affect—; aggravate—; alter—; ameliorate—; analyze—; appraise—; avoid—; benefit by—; better—; cavil—; check—; comply with—; comprehend—; conquer—;

consider—; contribute to—; convert—; cope with—; create—; depend on—; designate —; diagnose—; discover—; elucidate—; embrace—; encounter—; enter on—; eradicate—; exaggerate—; exemplify—; exempt from—; foresee—; fulfill—; govern—; heal—; ignore—; impose—; improve—; inform of—; investigate—; judge—; manifest—; mark—; neglect—; obviate—; portray—; prophesy—; protest—; recognize—; rectify—; regard—; regulate—; rejuvenate—; relieve—; remedy—; restore—; rule—; scorn—; simulate—; stabilize—; stipulate—; subject to—; submit to—; taint—; thrive on—; treat—; ward off—; welcome—; yield to—; —arises; —attends; —characterizes; —culminates in; —embitters; —ensues; —evolves; —indicates; —permits; —persists; —prevails; —provokes; —recurs; —reflects; —shifts; —spreads; springs from—; —threatens; —vanishes; —warrants; —yields to.

(See state, plight, situation.)

CONDITIONAL
adverbs
wisely; definitely; stringently; deplorably; properly; unfortunately; explicitly; reasonably; ungraciously; tersely; curtly; offensively; repugnantly; humiliatingly; auspiciously; trivially; favorably; rationally; surprisingly; trickily; equivocally; provokingly; treacherously; deviously; perplexingly; unacceptably; fantastically.

CONDONE (*v*)
adverbs
sentimentally; magnanimously; freely; sanctimoniously; unqualifiedly; humanely; broad-mindedly; intelligently; tenderly; affectionately; willingly; absolutely.

(See pardon.)

CONDUCIVE
adverbs
actually; essentially; significantly; distinctly; fundamentally; valuably; originally; splendidly; meritoriously; superbly; indubitably; definitely; expressly; enduringly; surprisingly; virtually; actively; serviceably; indispensably; profitably; indescribably; indisputably.

CONDUCT
adjectives
private; meritorious; exemplary; commendable; efficient; high; sane; civilized; plausible; consistent; circumspect; chivalrous; gallant; lazy; mannerless; unmanly; un-

ruly; annoying; indecorous; flagitious; instinctive; rebellious; licentious; abstemious; intemperate; editorial; criminal; theatrical; active; shameless; cruel; precipitate; fraudulent; inexplicable; barbarous; unyielding; daring; ungenerous; dishonest; peaceful; angelic; perverse; questionable; refractory; intolerable; neutral; patriotic; discreditable; irreproachable; disloyal; flagrant; flighty; analytical; unruly; outrageous; flamboyant; unethical; forward; arbitrary; obstreperous; bearish; boorish; courteous; perceptive; irascible; mad; depraved.

verbs
approve—; better—; correct—; decry—; denounce—; deprecate—; elevate—; emulate—; guide—; improve—; impugn—; influence—; interpret—; loathe—; pursue—; restrain—; shape—; —agitates; —conforms.
(See behavior.)

CONDUCT (*v*)
adverbs
inelegantly; rigidly; honorably; intelligently; prudently; improvidently; solemnly; marvelously; diligently; privately; secretly; commendably; efficiently; circumspectly; indecorously; rebelliously; licentiously; meritoriously; intemperately; editorially; criminally; theatrically; shamelessly; precipitately; fraudulently; barbarously; inexplicably; unyieldingly; daringly; dishonestly; peacefully; perversely; questionably; irreproachably; disloyally; analytically; unethically; arbitrarily; obstreperously; boorishly; courteously.
(See escort, lead.)

CONDUCTOR
(*electric*)
adjectives
central; extended; brass; faulty; fixed; insulated; metallic; prime; water-tight.

verbs
ground—; insulate—; pass through—; shield—; tape—; —carries; —conveys; —shocks; —transmits.

CONDUCTOR
(*escort or guide*)
adjectives
gifted; orchestral; philharmonic; natural; theatrical; amiable; poor; talented; celebrated.

verbs
tip—; uniform—; —accompanies; —collects; —directs; —escorts; —leads; —lectures; —motions; —signals; —guides.
(See guide, leader, escort.)

CONDUIT
adjectives
earthen; flood; secret; circuitous; transmitting; subterranean; water.

verbs
block—; bury—; clog—; connect—; drain—; force through—; issue from—; obstruct—; paint—; pipe through—; pour from—; pump through—; run through—; spout from—; —channels; —communicates; —conveys; —distributes; —freezes; —irrigates; —leads; —leaks; —protects; —rusts; —spouts; —transmits; —channels.
(See channel, canal, pipe, passage.)

CONE
adjectives
long; slender; truncated; symmetrical; veritable.

CONFECTION
adjectives
tasteless; mystic; sundry; delightful; cooked; appetizing; delicate.

CONFEDERATION
adjectives
absolute; powerful; vigorous; active; loyal.

CONFER (*v*)
adverbs
secretly; ostentatiously; freely; proposedly; hurriedly; briefly; privately; personally; officially; nationally; informally; ominously; endlessly; amicably; annually; softly; treacherously; rebelliously.
(See give, consult.)

CONFERENCE
adjectives
friendly; all-night; midnight; afternoon; dinner; proposed; rapid; hurried; whispered; brief; private; personal; long; wearisome; fateful; remarkable; regional; diplomatic; astronomical; family; official; arms; plenipotentiary; national; sad; radical; recent; emergency; worth-while; informal; preliminary; secret; ominous; homespun; amicable; endless; intended; extraordinary; soft; affable; casual; overheard; annual.

verbs

adjourn—; address—; break off—; bring before—; buckle down to—; close—; demand—with; dissolve—; gather in—; herald—; meet in—; preside over—; represent at—; resume—; sponsor—; urge—; —assembles; —collapses; —convenes; —discusses; —elects; —ensues; —formulates; —governs; —honors; —outlaws; —passes; —resolves; —rules.

(See consultation, assembly, meeting, council.)

CONFESS (v)

adverbs

ruefully; subsequently; truthfully; naively; timorously; hesitatingly; blushingly; penitently; candidly; gaily; blankly; humbly; frankly; affectionately; artlessly; shamefully; indiscreetly; unavailably; tacitly; touchingly; reciprocally; mortifyingly; abjectly; tearfully; belatedly; mysteriously; sincerely.

(See acknowledge, admit.)

CONFESSION

adjectives

tender; precious; eloquent; hopeful; naive; humble; honest; frank; full; complete; difficult; horrifying; shameful; deadly; indiscreet; voluptuous; phlegmatic; unavailing; liberal; honorable; tacit; plenary; revealing; bashful; touching; pitiful; reciprocal; soft; mortifying; abject; sham; constant; ecclesiastical; tearful; cool; belated; unconscious; mysterious; derisive; sincere; youthful; unsworn.

verbs

acknowledge—; beat out—; demand—; deny—; dictate—; drag out—; evidence—; force—; pour out—; record—; render—; repudiate—; rescind—; secure—; sign—; urge—; witness—; —absolves; —alleviates; —amends; —humbles; —humiliates.

(See statement.)

CONFIDANT

adjectives

intimate; faithful; special; ever-receptive; sympathetic.

CONFIDE (v)

adverbs

tearfully; languidly; apologetically; falteringly; timidly; loyally; genially; divinely; joyously; blithely; serenely; placidly; patriotically; arrogantly; spiritually; intellectually; unhesitatingly; profoundly; utterly; tactlessly; implicitly; tranquilly; pathetically; personally; charmingly; unsuspectingly; absolutely; unboundedly; complacently; wistfully.

(See trust. commit.)

CONFIDENCE

adjectives

gentle; sublime; fine; loyal; supreme; soft; wedded; divine; marvelous; ecstatic; gay; genial; joyous; blithe; touching; cheerful; certain; perfect; fullest; resolute; complete; boundless; utmost; limitless; inviolable; serene; calm; placid; sorry; silent; sober; patriotic; popular; renewed; immovable; easy; abiding; stern; arrogant; thrusting; spiritual; intellectual; infinite; presumptuous; invincible; unhesitating; sordid; utmost; assumed; strict; obliging; overweening; profound; veiled; restored; undiminished; buoyant; fullest; sincerest; utter; vanished; inspired; mutual; tactless; quiet; secure; fulsome; sketchy; unusual; industrial; heart-rending; tranquil; prophetic; pathetic; liberal; devilish; strong; superb; robust; shaken; animated; personal; imposing; charming; public; reminiscent; radiant; humble; preternatural; unsuspecting; absolute; unlimited; innocent; celebrated; unbounded; harassed; habitual; complacent; unreasonable; loving; admiring; snaring; heartfelt; unbroken; implicit; tender; childish; exaggerated; curious; sufficient; eager; wistful; vigorous; community; aboriginal.

verbs

beget—; betray—; blend in—; break—; breed—; buttress—; destroy—; dull—; dwell in—; earn—; enjoy—; establish—; evince—; evoke—; exchange—; express—; found in—; gravitate into—; honor with—; inspire—; interchange—; justify—; merit —; misplace—; mistrust—; reek—; regain—; register—; reject—; rejoice in—; renounce—; repose—in; restore—; root—in; shake—; share—; stimulate—; swear—; treat in—; undermine—; violate—; warrant—; weaken—; win—; —prevails; —soars; —wavers.

(See trust, faith, assurance, reliance.)

CONFIDENT

adverbs

absolutely; unreasonably; justifiably; egotistically; blatantly; extravagantly; gravely; seriously; shrewdly; assuredly; assuringly;

comfortably; comfortingly; sublimely; loyally; marvellously; genially; joyously; blithely; cheerfully; completely; calmly; placidly; quietly; serenely; imperturbably; sternly; presumptuously; overly; foolishly; fully; securely; unusually; tranquilly; impressively; charmingly; innocently; radiantly; unsuspectingly; habitually; complacently; curiously; encouragingly; courageously; egregiously; preposterously; rashly; absurdly; unjustifiably; unwarrantably; groundlessly; erroneously; profoundly.

CONFIDENTIAL

adverbs

strictly; necessarily; solemnly; terribly; mysteriously; portentously; ominously; seriously; vitally; stupendously; scrupulously; inviolately; momentously; significantly; essentially; intimately; sacredly; impressively; formidably; extremely; supremely.

CONFIGURATION

adjectives

geographical; tortured; certain; edifying; fundamental; classic.

CONFINE (v)

adverbs

exclusively; undeservedly; prudently; inexorably; mainly; remorselessly; necessarily; sedulously; comparatively; narrowly; continuously; irksomely.

(See restrict, restrain.)

CONFINEMENT

adjectives

solitary; respectful; prolonged; comparative; narrow; continuous; feverish; rigid; instant; irksome.

CONFIRM (v)

adverbs

speedily; stirringly; rapidly; strikingly; miraculously; unanimously; explicitly; concretely; abundantly; singularly; unexpectedly; instantaneously; amply; particularly.

(See affirm.)

CONFIRMATION

adjectives

complete; concrete; documentary; supplemental; splendid; singular; unexpected; instantaneous; unconscious; unexamined; fresh; particular; ample.

verbs

add the weight of—; ascertain—; authenticate—; dread—; establish—; inspect—; investigate—; maintain—; rejoice in—; sanction—; settle—; strengthen—; —assures; —convinces; —corroborates; —encourages; —fortifies; —legalizes; —proves; —ratifies; —removes doubt; —supports; —verifies.

(See ratification, proof.)

CONFLAGRATION

adjectives

frequent; devastating; disastrous; brilliant; nation-wide; mounting; enormous; widespread; delightful; amorous; raging; perpetual.

verbs

battle—; beat down—; contend with—; fight—; fan—; kindle—; prevent—; quell —; smother—; —blazes; —bursts out; —consumes; —deforests; —denudes; —dies; —envelops; —extends to; —menaces; —rages; —razes; —roars; —spreads; —threatens.

(See fire, blaze.)

CONFLICT

adjectives

triumphant; gigantic; stupendous; long; arduous; amorous; constant; eternal; ceaseless; sensational; heroic; dramatic; deliberate; determined; serious; severe; sharp; irrepressible; terrible; bitter; wasteful; violent; fierce; wanton; emotional; moral; general; visible; notorious; open; direct; external; coming; local; unfortunate; inevitable; sanguinary; approaching; irreconcilable; internal; civilized; irritating; unexpected; enormous; hopeless; impending; obstinate; fighting; deadly; desperate; immediate; disastrous; conscientious; earnest; class; bloody; obvious; unrelenting; savage; decisive; fiery; trying; mental; territorial; genial; protracted; brutal; decorous; tragic; linguistic; hopeless; commercial; hideous; armed; tumultuous; selfish; subjective; periodic; uncertain; psychic; intestinal.

verbs

avert—; avoid—; draw into—; elude—; end—; engage in—; experience—; explode in—; foment—; precipitate—; prolong—; provoke—; raise—; run into—; —bobs up; —bursts out; —consumes; —engulfs; —rages; —rends.

(See strife, battle, antagonism.)

CONFLICT (v)

adverbs

amorously; arduously; eternally; ceaselessly; sensationally; heroically; dramatically; deliberately; irresponsibly; violently; terribly; wantonly; emotionally; notoriously; morally; externally; locally; inevitably; irreconcilably; obstinately; desperately; disastrously; conscientiously; unrelentingly; savagely; decisively; mentally; commercially; tumultuously; subjectively.

(See interfere.)

CONFLUENCE

adjectives

riotous; harmonious; thickest; torrential; raging; seething; undistinguishable; peaceful; grateful.

CONFORM (v)

adverbs

tactfully; placidly; pusillanimously; complacently; docilely; strictly; entirely, rigidly; inflexibly; artistically; artificially; legally.

CONFORMATION

adjectives

athletic; peculiar; well-sculptured.

CONFORMITY

adjectives

complacent; pusillanimous; docile; strict; rigid.

CONFOUND (v)

adverbs

eternally; mysteriously; inexplicably; unspeakably; fathomlessly; gropingly; helplessly; inextricably

(See confuse.)

CONFRONT (v)

adverbs

bravely; indignantly; furiously; impudently; boldly; fearlessly; carelessly; brazenly; dramatically; theatrically; vociferously.

(See face, oppose.)

CONFUSE (v)

adverbs

paradoxically; wildly; deliberately; intricately; endlessly; inextricably; disastrously; emotionally; momentarily; infinitely; significantly; chaotically; intellectually; indescribably; feignedly; mentally; feverishly; socially; psychologically; mysteriously; purposely.

(See perplex, embarrass.)

CONFUSED

adverbs

delightfully; mysteriously; vaguely; perplexingly; hopelessly; strangely; comically; disastrously; completely; horribly; indescribably; visibly; manifestly; palpably; uproariously; tipsily; foggily; dazedly; rosily; brokenly; happily; incurably; pathetically; laughably; ridiculously.

CONFUSION

adjectives

joyous; cheerful; honest; orderly; multiple; endless; inextricable; strange; disastrous; hideous; sad; raging; wildest; lusty; deliberate; emotional; slight; flushed; misty; crimson; seeming; impersonal; peaceful; complete; topographical; blissful; momentary; deepening; infinite; picturesque; sweet; chaotic; irretrievable; tense; inextricable; hopeless; perpetual; crystalline; bosky; horrid; general; utter; utmost; ominous; significant; seeming; gibbering; dire; considerable; delightful; pretty; dreadful; studied; intellectual; speculative; indescribable; handsome; indistinct; tremendous; bubbling; multiform; feigned; visible; musical; whirling; mental; metaphysical; apparent; dusty; feverish; social; psychological; mysterious; manifold; crazy; melancholy; uproarious; disturbing; advertized; puzzling; commodious; vociferous; smiling.

verbs

afflict with—; boil with—; cover—; create—; deliver to—; eliminate—; embroil with—; fall into—; fill with—; flounder in—; grapple with—; heap—; lose in—; provoke—; retire in—; subdue—; subject to—; throw into—; weather—; work—; —aggravates; —ensues; —rises; —surrounds.

(See tumult, consternation, disorder, commotion, agitation, distraction.)

CONGEAL (v)

adverbs

instantaneously; readily; perfectly; partially; entirely; ultimately; normally; swiftly; rapidly; completely.

(See freeze.)

CONGENIAL

adverbs

completely; pleasantly; unusually; agreeably; charmingly; entertainingly; jovially; truly; happily; amiably; comfortably; curiously; delightfully; inestimably; distinctly;

unobtrusively; quietly; cheerfully; sociably; cosily; highly; exceedingly; unexpectedly; affably; unpretentiously; unaffectedly; artlessly.

CONGESTED

adverbs

hopelessly; inconveniently; dangerously; inordinately; needlessly; desperately; irremediably; impossibly; horribly; alarmingly; purposely; intentionally; stupidly; foolishly; senselessly; inextricably.

CONGESTION

adjectives

plethoric; cerebral; abnormal; prolonged; urban; slight; permanent.

verbs

accumulate—; clear—; heap in—; increase—; relieve—; —retards; —bars; —blocks; —crowds; —disorders; —hampers; —hinders; —impairs; —masses; —obstructs; —overcomes; —produces; —spreads; —weakens.
(See confusion.)

CONGLOMERATE

adverbs

ingeniously; heterogeneously; democratically; unmistakably; undeniably; utterly; curiously; interestingly; bewilderingly; confusedly; kaleidoscopically; staggeringly; internationally; unintelligibly; confusingly; diffusely; outlandishly; bizarrely; barbarically; inimitably; noisily; astoundingly; extravagantly; oddly; strangely.

CONGLOMERATION

adjectives

kaleidoscopic; multitudinous; staggering; curious; imperial.

CONGRATULATE (*v*)

adverbs

civilly; warmly; cordially; sincerely; dutifully; ceremoniously; facetiously; humbly; genially; volubly; effusively; solemnly; heartily; fulsomely; fiendishly.
(See sympathize.)

CONGRATULATIONS

adjectives

dutiful; abortive; ceremonious; facetious; humble; warmest; genial; voluble; solemn; heartiest.

verbs

acknowledge—; appreciate—; beam—; convey—; deliver—; deserve—; dismiss—; exchange—; express—; extend—; flood with—s; offer—; pay—; rejoice in—; return—; shower—; telegraph—; warrant—; wave away—; —gratify.
(See felicitation, sympathy.)

CONGRATULATORY

adverbs

pleasantly; dutifully; filially; grudgingly; ceremoniously; facetiously; happily; joyously; heartily; warmly; genially; jovially; jocosely; waggishly; proudly; solemnly; blessedly; rapturously; ecstatically; coolly; civilly; courteously; officially; politely; perfunctorily; obsequiously; unctuously; sententiously.

CONGREGATE (*v*)

adverbs

temptingly; silently; conservatively; piously; scantily; annually; triumphantly; sorrowfully; formally; diplomatically; dutifully.
(See gather.)

CONGREGATION

adjectives

motley; cultivated; dissolving; silent; dissenting; pious; foul; dispersing; scanty; sunburned; shaggy; staid; conservative.

verbs

assemble—; bless—; break up—; call—; come into—; cut off from—; distract—; gather—; offer to —; preach to—; rile—; sanctify—; separate from—; —breaks into song; —issues forth; —responds; —worships.
(See assembly, gathering.)

CONGRESS

adjectives

chaotic; international; bicameral; complaisant; musical; unique; legislative; filibustering.

verbs

discipline—; elect to—; empower—; importune—; prevail upon—; prod—; represent in—; seat in—; storm—; sway—; —adjourns; —appropriates; —assembles; —authorizes; —confers on; —confirms; —convenes; —debates; —deliberates; —designates; —dissolves; —frames; —func-

tions; —interviews; —lags; —legislates; —meets; —rebels; —reforms; —regulates; —rejects; —revises; —suspends; —taxes.
(See assembly, conference, legislature.)

CONGRESSMAN
adjectives
conspicuous; humorless; accomplished; grandiloquent; rabble-rousing; argumentative; glorified.

verbs
appeal to—; berate—; bribe—; criticize—; elect—; invite—; petition—; rally to—; reserve for—; run for—; select—; support—; —addresses; —men assemble; —men convene; —declines; —deliberates; —discusses; —filibusters; —introduces; —issues; —orates; —proposes; —protests; —questions; —represents; —signs; —withdraws.
(See legislator, senator, member.)

CONGRUITY
adjectives
separate; manifest; apparent; gratifying; practical; theoretical.

CONGRUOUS
adverbs
wholly; wonderfully; appropriately; nicely; exactly; accurately; entirely; aptly; adroitly; studiously; carefully; considerately; thoughtfully; becomingly; pertinently; relatively; agreeably; altogether; duly; happily; felicitously; opportunely; superbly; extraordinarily.

CONJECTURE
adjectives
whispered; frail; simple; stimulating; vague; languid; rational; bewildered; shrewd; right; straining; probable; plausible; sanguine; hurried; vacillating; speculative; half-hinted; serious; wild; cynical; fruitless; premature; alarming; vague.

verbs
absorb in—; base on—; cast—; conclude from—; form—; gather from—; infer from—; inject—; judge on—; offer—; propose—; scoff at—; scorn—; throw—; —guesses; —puzzles; —surmises.
(See guess, hypothesis, surmise, supposition, inference.)

CONJUNCTION
adjectives
successive; particular; clumsy; covert; helpful.

CONJUNCTURE
adjectives
fortunate; frequent; prodigious; delicate; straight; critical.

CONJURATION
adjectives
detestable; measured; spirited; inviolable; occult; mystic.

CONNECT (*v*)
adverbs
closely; organically; intimately; indissolubly; collaterally; innocently; eminently; honestly; inseparably; originally; exclusively; subtly; physiologically; remotely; unconsciously; persistently; matrimonially; adequately; lucratively; harmoniously; intellectually; surreptitiously; invisibly; uniformly; rigidly; profitably; vitally; perniciously; internationally.
(See join, link.)

CONNECTION
adjectives
reciprocal; physiological; closest; definite; remote; natural; intimate; unfathomable; unconscious; persistent; unbroken; illicit; valuable; influential; apparent; multifarious; judicious; matrimonial; fragmentary; uninterrupted; shameless; casual; obvious; adequate; touching; apparent; numerous; lucrative; remote; inevitable; mercantile; harmonious; manifold; intellectual; surreptitious; invisible; sole; florid; uniform; rigid; profitable; neat; positive; irregular; plausible; vital; pernicious; direct; deepwater; international; brief; genetic.

verbs
block—; break—; contract—with; disclaim —; dissolve—; establish—; fasten—; invalidate—; join in—with; link in—with; maintain—; mark—; mention in—with; prevent —; prohibit—; rend—; repudiate—; run in —with; sever—; snap—; —binds; —ties.
(See union, alliance, relationship, affiliation, association.)

CONNECTIVE
adjectives
social; iconoclastic; ineffectual; sturdy; tried.

CONNIVING
adjectives
petty; treasonable; clever; skillful; foxy; selfish.

CONNOISSEUR

adjectives
appreciative; true; profound; ogling; dramatic; amateur.

CONNOTATION

adjectives
biological; original; conventional; proper; sentimental; hazy.

CONQUER (v)

adverbs
technically; triumphantly; intellectually; eventually; honorably; personally; ultimately; romantically; basely; scientifically; partially; irresistibly.
(See **win.**)

CONQUEROR

adjectives
ultimate; sottish; roving; indigenous; vulgar; rapacious; satiate; daunted; virile; invisible; illustrious; single-handed; lesser.

verbs
hail—; herald—; honor—; overthrow—; proclaim—; welcome—; —acquires; —attains; —campaigns; —defeats; —enslaves; —gains; —invades; —masters; —overcomes; —pursues; —retreats; —subdues; —subjugates; —vanquishes; —wars.
(See **hero, army.**)

CONQUEST

adjectives
intellectual; territorial; illusory; unprovoked; honorable; vainglorious; continental; shameful; prophetic; industrial; imperial; personal; doubtful; amatory; remote; ultimate; easy; dazzling; barren; adventurous; romantic; material; barbarian; complete; base; air; unbroken; momentary; perpetual; fresh; hard-won; social; scientific; partial; furtive; rapid; notorious; feminine; irresistible; radical.

verbs
achieve—; acquire by—; crown—; effect—; enjoy the fruits of—; frustrate—; gain by—; herald—; inspire—; plunge into—; reap—; repel—; revel in—; revenge—; spread—; subdue by—; threaten—; win—; —captivates; —falters; —subdues; —subjugates; —succeeds; —stifles.
(See **victory, triumph.**)

CONSCIENCE

adjectives
smooth; haunting; latent; intellectual; padded; inflexible; insufferable; awakened; strenuous; quickening; guilty; drugged; beaten; stoned; sensitive; reproachful; artistic; obsessed; national; tender; obtuse; uneasy; straightforward; delicate; vast; floating; scientific; sensitive; capricious; filial; indulgent; fastidious; individual; obdurate; seared; well-seasoned; masterful; stricken; resolved; struggling; agonizing; heavy; unsilenced; proscriptive; renewed; peaceful; corrupted; condemning; fierce; judicial; worrying; ethical; aesthetic; perverse; poor; wounded; high; mute; alarmed; keen; free; super-developed; healthy; supreme; determined; clear; untroubled; twinging; aching; writhing; elastic; sluggish; bomb-proof; democratic; prickly; literary; celebrated; puritan; political; approving; private; childish.

verbs
alarm—; appeal to—; arouse—; cauterize —; compromise—; defile—; disburden—; ease—; examine—; fetter—; free—; invoke—; muffle—; offend—; pad—; purge —; quiet—; rectify—; rule by—; salve—; sear—; shake—; sour—; square—; suppress—; torment—; wake—; weaken—; wound—; wring—; —assails; —blames; —condemns; —convicts; —impels; —reproaches; —plagues; —prompts; —reproves; —slumbers; —tortures; —troubles; —twinges; —upbraids; —whispers.
(See **judgment.**)

CONSCIENTIOUS

adverbs
terribly; puritannically; extremely; rigorously; sternly; austerely; deeply; painfully; rigidly; stiffly; decorously; properly; unimpeachably; irreproachably; becomingly; stringently; dutifully; amenably; respectably; scrupulously; incorruptibly; courageously; lamentably; uncomfortably; ostentatiously; unnecessarily; carefully; foolishly.

CONSCIENTIOUSNESS

adjectives
exemplary; deep; historical; magnificent; stubborn; commendable; heroic.

CONSCIOUS

adverbs
fully; acutely; painfully; vividly; sharply; altogether; keenly; curiously; tinglingly; psychically; sorely; happily; uncomfortably;

wretchedly; pleasantly; rapturously; intensely; suddenly; poignantly; astutely; wholly; partially; slowly; wearily; actually; bitterly.

CONSCIOUSNESS
adjectives
full; private; inner; drowsier; ennobling; waking; joyous; veiled; guilty; perverted; bitter; instinctive; ever-abiding; susceptible; dawning; dim; proud; individual; well-founded; disagreeable; acute; living; unadmitted; amiable; gloomy; pleased; uplifting; mortifying; vivid; present; dreadful; despotic; widened; glad; glowing; impersonal; ineffable; half-bewildered; wordless; religious; glimmering; astonishing; sudden; joyful; intense; demure; collective; profound; transitory; shamefaced; lucid; reviving; inward; shaky; disintegrated; beatific; humble; native; growing; diffused; human; continental; pained; financial; class; political; social.

verbs
bestow—; bring to—; develop—; display—; drag to—; enfold—; indicate—; jar into—; lose—; obscure—; obsess—; percolate—; possess—; precede—; retain—; rub into—; seize with—; thrust into—; vanish from—; waken to—; —brings; —evolves.
(See sensation, feeling, intuition.)

CONSCRIPTION
adjectives
ruthless; established; legislated; mandatory; selective; indiscriminative.

CONSECRATE (v)
adverbs
specially; religiously; ceremoniously; hallowedly; reverently; formally; fittingly; impressively.
(See dedicate, hallow.)

CONSECRATED
adverbs
divinely; ecclesiastically; eternally; sacredly; early; devoutly; devotedly; faithfully; humbly; reverently; splendidly; conspicuously; avowedly; deeply; practically; notably; eminently; heroically; illustriously; piously; solemnly; gloriously; signally.

CONSECRATION
adjectives
immortal; pathetic; tragic; perpetual; ecclesiastical.

CONSECUTIVE
adverbs
conveniently; endlessly; monotonously; meticulously; punctiliously; carefully; accurately; impressively; rarely; handily; painstakingly; comfortably; accommodatingly; appropriately; properly; tediously; invariably; methodically; systematically; exactly; significantly; actually.

CONSENT
adjectives
unanimous; magnanimous; particular; ardent; tacit; grudging; reluctant; common; hard; general; cringing; mutual; unwilling; formal; personal; passive; generous; grumbling; effective; mournful; gracious.

verbs
announce—; batter into—; blush—; crave —; deny—; desire—; extend—; nod—; serve with—; suffer—; swear—; win—; wink—; write—; yield—.
(See acquiescence, compliance, approval, agreement.)

CONSENT (v)
adverbs
reluctantly; unwittingly; tacitly; handsomely; gloomily; instantly; sulkily; cheerfully; wisely; legally; unanimously; ardently; magnanimously; grudgingly; cringingly; mutually; unwillingly; formally; personally; passively; generously; mournfully; graciously; blandly.
(See agree, concur.)

CONSEQUENCE
adjectives
natural; territorial; eventual; disastrous; cruel; tremendous; necessary; self-evident; dramatic; dire; logical; inevitable; direct; lurking; ambushed; far-reaching; political; educational; perilous; unavoidable; permanent; favorable; momentous; sensational; serious; instantaneous; important; natural; surprising; paramount; probable; horrible; evil; debasing; fruitful; deplorable; certain; fatal; utmost; ethical; awful; unexpected; deepest; unforeseen; equivalent; temporal; invisible; viewless; heavy; mechanical; mischievous; injurious; dreadful; remoter; unshunned; catastrophic; desirable; possible; incalculable; wretched;

disagreeable; appalling; wonderful; beneficent; brilliant; obvious; patent; inescapable; vital; enormous; tragic; devastating; demoralizing; calamitous; unhappy; embarrassing; ultimate; physiological; emotional; social; financial; moral; risky; comical; small; foolish; involved; detailed; legal.

verbs
abide by—; appreciate—; avert—; balk at—; conceal—; dread—; deter by—; escape—; face—; ignore—; portray—; realize—; shun—; suffer—; torment by—; —ensues; —follows; —results in.
(See issue, result, outcome, importance, distinction, consideration.)

CONSEQUENTIAL
adverbs
evidently; ludicrously; ridiculously; arrogantly; pompously; stupidly; gracelessly; presumptuously; impressively; ostentatiously; grossly; fantastically; grotesquely; immensely; inordinately; amusingly; complacently; colossally; awkwardly; stagily; foppishly; laughably; theatrically; loftily; extremely; unbelievably; absurdly.

CONSERVATISM
adjectives
zealous; sprightly; stubborn; passionate; industrious; extreme; moderate; innate; disillusioned; smug; hearty; emotional.

verbs
abolish—; admire—; characterize by—; embody—; engender—; enliven—; epitomize—; hinder by—; practice—; preserve—; prod—; produce—; satisfy—; school in—; shrink from—; swerve from—; swing toward—; —crops up; —fears; —retains; —safeguards.
(See stability, conventionality.)

CONSERVATIVE
adjectives
uncompromising; extreme; staunchest; gruesome; obstinate; grim; sturdy; born; honest; cynical; stuffy; hidebound.

adverbs
incurably; tenaciously; consistently; obstinately; stubbornly; half-heartedly; permanently; solidly; stiffly; unchangeably; fixedly; firmly; immovably; resolutely; irrevoc-

ably; steadfastly; unalterably; inactively; quietly; passively; zealously; passionately; smugly; contentedly; pertinaciously; temperamentally.

CONSIDER (v)
adverbs
intrinsically; impartially; tenderly; duly; carnally; prospectively; lightly; maturely, accordingly; politically; honestly; anxiously; tentatively; dispassionately; seriously; previously; arithmetically; erroneously; respectfully; matrimonially; rationally; theoretically; belatedly; paternally; philosophically; delicately; momentously; sympathetically; unselfishly; posthumously; temporarily; shallowly; economically; sordidly; morally; optionally.
(See ponder, contemplate.)

CONSIDERABLE
adverbs
seriously; worthily; assuredly; notably; prominently; essentially; substantially; critically; imposingly; gravely; materially; remarkably; significantly; signally; vitally; momentously; impressively.

CONSIDERATE
adverbs
courteously; thoughtfully; tenderly; officiously; politely; deferentially; respectfully; appropriately; unusually; obsequiously; deliberately; generally; astutely; keenly; shrewdly; tenderly; mercifully; tolerantly; benevolently; charitably; generously; carefully; prudently; providently; hospitably; alertly; vigilantly; scrupulously.

CONSIDERATION
adjectives
theoretic; paternal; belated; distinguished; favorable; humanitarian; ethical; vital; special; tedious; individual; secondary; close; palpable; philosophic; calm; striking; delicate; tremendous; seeming; abstract; solemn; gracious; serious; momentous; indisputable; respectful; monetary; sympathetic; elusive; salient; important; unselfish; quiet; melancholy; ostensible; due; prime; obvious; mature; practical; minor; limited; partial; long; sedate; candid; fuller; posthumous; unspeakable; distracted; chivalrous; remote; keen; theoretical; various (pl.); confidential; thoughtful; reasoned; dominant; scanty; unhurried; careful; fatherly; triumphant; temporal; elaborate; predominant; common; ultimate;

judicial; weighty; practical; conscientious; difficult; half-hesitating; half-assenting; exclusive; enlarged; grateful; weightier; rational; unpleasing; regrettable; foregoing; strategical; valuable; distinguished; momentary; urgent; scant; earnest; fair; fascinating; finer; grave; profoundest; pragmatic; marked; primary; careful; tender; prudent; dispassionate; cool; logical; intelligent; sordid; false; shallow; selfish; money; economic; material; moral; liberal; collateral; painful; constant; immediate; accumulated; optional; theoretical; rough; personal.

verbs
analyze—; bar—; compel—; dally with—; demand—; extend—; fade from—; gain—; increase—; merit—; quit—; stifle—; view with—; —actuates; —impresses; —sways.
(See thought.)

CONSIGN (*v*)
adverbs
everlastingly; formally; customarily; tacitly; solemnly; definitely; willingly; commercially.
(See command, commit.)

CONSISTENCY
adjectives
muddy; smoothest; possible; fatal; unwavering; foolish; religious; external; unbroken; theoretical; chewy; conscious.

verbs
boil into—; depart from—; disrupt—; doubt—; establish—; give—to; induce—; practise—; preach—; preserve—; profess—; pursue with—; remain in—; return to—; sacrifice—; stand on—; vary in—; —habituates; —harmonizes.
(See harmony.)

CONSISTENT
adverbs
admirably; dependably; conscientiously; imperturbably; undisturbedly; invariably; equitably; monotonously; conformably; prosaically; agreeably; regularly; habitually; usually; uncompromisingly; queerly; unfailingly; properly; relatively; obstinately; unreasonably; reliably; altogether; courageously; unpleasantly; vapidly; extraordinarily; virtuously.

CONSOLATION
adjectives
bitter; inexpressible; profound; hollow; proudest; infallible; homely; tangible; mean; supreme; perfunctory; divine; substantial; wonderful; ironic; religious; orthodox; clumsy; feeble; abiding; inward; infinitesimal.

verbs
admit of—; convey—; derive—; dismiss—; dispense with—; grant—; impart—; offer —; rejoice in—; seek —; secure—; take— from; —ameliorates; —cheers; —comforts; —encourages; —mitigates; —recompenses; —relieves; —solaces; —soothes.
(See solace, comfort, relief, support.)

CONSOLE (*v*)
adverbs
profoundly; hollowly; infallibly, perfunctorily; divinely; substantially; ironically; religiously; clumsily; feebly; inwardly; infinitesimally; precipitately.
(See cheer, sympathize.)

CONSONANT
adjectives
concurring; mute; nasal; unaspirated; slurred; elided; rumbling; jarring; harsh; true.

CONSORT
adjectives
ill-fated; gentle; sovereign; hovering; poor; feeble; wasted.

CONSPICUOUS
adverbs
highly; creditably; distinctly; gloriously; intentionally; disagreeably; unpleasantly; vainly; personally; eminently; exaltedly; arrogantly; absurdly; foolishly; unwisely; politically; deliberately; elaborately; fashionably; garishly; gaudily; loudly; noisily; officiously; unfortunately; shamefully; awkwardly.

CONSPIRACY
adjectives
rebel; domestic; tacit; abortive; awkward; finespun; well-contrived; criminal; fraternal; elaborate; organized; ravishing; purported; irresistible; monstrous; political; dark; infamous; grim; pleasing; silent; popular; crackbrained; malevolent; nationwide; alley; fatal.

verbs
block—; charge with—; combine in—; conceal—; contrive—; convict of—; disclose—; discover—; excite—; foil—; hatch—; incite—; indict for—; instigate—; intrigue in—; involve in—; plot—; punish—; strengthen—; uncover—; unearth—; —brews; —damages; —fails; —flourishes; —injures; —ripens; —succeeds.
   (See plot, intrigue.)

CONSPIRATOR
adjectives
resident; audacious; crafty; baffled; chief; uneasy.

CONSPIRATORS
adjectives
capricious; criminal; fearful; illegal; implicated; fellow; mercenary; reprehensible; treasonable; plotting; seditious.

verbs
arm—; charge—; convict—; disclose—; execute—; expose—; foil—; hang—; join—; punish—; shield—; —chortle; —combine; —contrive; —devise; —engage; —intrigue; —plan; —plot.
   (See plotter.)

CONSTABLE
adjectives
discomfited; discredited; learned; unskilled; blustering; rural; overmaligned.

verbs
appoint—; arm—; authorize—; commit to—; consign to—; deputize—; elect—; empower—; enroll—; escape—; overrule—; rank—; serve as—; uniform—; —administers; —arrests; —enforces; —fines; —imprisons; —quells; —sells.
   (See officer, police.)

CONSTANCY
adjectives
infatuated; dangerous; unremitting; inviolable; unchangeable; admirable; true; inflexible; invincible; wonted.

verbs
admire—; amaze at—; attack—; attend with—; bear with—; boast of—; break—; commend—; conduct with—; endure with—; esteem—; exhibit—; inspire—; justify—; laud—; maintain—; occasion—; persist in—; praise—; require—; test—; tolerate with—; value—.
   (See faithfulness, stability, fidelity.)

CONSTELLATION
adjectives
golden; arched; bright; brilliant; shimmering.

verbs
appear in—; describe—; distinguish—; dominate—; examine—; form—; name—; obscure—; observe—; steer by—; stud with—; study—; treat of—; —awes; —burns; —embodies; —guides; —illuminates; —mystifies; —portrays; —reveals; —symbolizes.
   (See stars.)

CONSTERNATION
adjectives
unseen; general; overwhelming; considerable; mournful; visible; silent; inexpressible; comprehensible; unutterable; momentary; frightened.

verbs
betray—; feign—; fill with—; manifest—; overwhelm with—; prostrate with—; recover from—; shock into—; suppress—; terrify with—; terrorize with—; throw into—; —amazes; —confounds; —dismays; —falls; —incapacitates; —surprises.
   (See fear, terror, alarm, panic.)

CONSTIPATION
adjectives
intractable; chronic; stubborn; recurring; harrowing; drug-induced.

verbs
afflict with—; alleviate—; cure of—; doctor for—; dose for—; ease—; flush away—; intensify—; overcome—; produce—; relieve—; remedy—; treat—; warn against —; —hints at; —irks; —necessitates; —obstructs; —sets in.
   (See disease.)

CONSTITUENCY
adjectives
large; urban; foremost; urgent; enthusiastic.

CONSTITUENT
adjectives
enraptured; characteristic; parsimonious; material; chemical; valuable; necessary; saline; primal; eternal; colored; approved; irreducible; soluble; youthful; enlightened; influential.

analyze—; assemble—s; authorize by—s;
break into—s; determine—s; discern—;
distinguish—; gather—; lose—; obey—;
represent—s; —s assist; —s complain;
—s compose; —s diminish; —elects; —s represent.

(See part, element, ingredient.)

CONSTITUTE (v)

adverbs
singularly; legally; fairly; splendidly; remarkably; amorphously; magnificently;
physically; morally; peculiarly; delicately;
intellectually; undeniably.

(See compose, establish.)

CONSTITUTION
(general)

adjectives
frail; splendid; diseased; amorphous;
healthy; remarkable; strong; loose-jointed;
robust; magnificent; physical; moral; iron;
peculiar; vigorous; delicate; oligarchical;
paper; emotional; consolidated; rugged;
well-knit; feeble; glorious; powerful; provisional; permanent; liberal; imperial;
intellectual; ancient; sickly.

CONSTITUTION
(governmental)

adjectives
amended; consolidated; hammered-out;
botched-up; intrenched; framed; liberal;
oligarchical; standardized.

verbs
abandon—; abide by—; abuse—; adopt—;
alter—; amend—; clarify—; construe—;
defend—; draft—; embody in—; establish—; flaunt—; form—; found—; frame—;
improve—; interpret—; modify—; nullify—; ordain—; organize—; preserve—;
ratify—; ruin—; stabilize—; tamper
with—; twist—; violate—; —abolishes;
—decrees; —defines; —grants; —guides;
—limits; —prescribes; —prohibits; —provides; —regulates; —sets forth; —totters.

CONSTITUTION
(physical)

adjectives
amorphous; emotional; frail; iron; magnificent; powerful; robust.

verbs
benefit—; brace—; build up—; disturb—;
enervate—; exercise—; improve—; inherit—; invigorate—; overtax—; renew—;
revitalize—; revivify—; run down—;
shatter—; strain—; strengthen—; undermine—; weaken.

(See physique, structure. temperament,
character.)

CONSTRAIN (v)

adverbs
unquestionably; unnaturally; artificially;
severely; rigidly; commercially; embarrassedly; tyrannically; bitterly; formally;;
mercilessly.

(See compel, oblige.)

CONSTRAINT

adjectives
tyrannous; bitter; evident; mute; gloomy;
sorrowful; curious; formal; sharp; awkward; merciless; heavy; slight.

verbs
act under—; exercise—; lessen—; manifest—; occasion—; pale under—; prevent—; produce—; resist—; speak with—;
subdue—; tug at—; —binds; —checks;
—confines; —prohibits; —represses; —
tightens; —voices.

(See force, compulsion, pressure, restraint, restriction.)

CONSTRICT (v)

adverbs
rigorously; harmfully; icily; painfully;
automatically; physiologically; partially;
insufferably; intellectually.

(See compress, contract.)

CONSTRICTION

adjectives
harmful; icy; oppressive; deep; hampering; morbid; marked; express.

CONSTRUCT (v)

adverbs
hastily; diaphanously; patiently; rudely;
variously; studiously; ingeniously; dramatically; bizarrely; artistically; ruggedly;
flawlessly; primitively; durably; majestically; musically; substantially; solidly;
legitimately; technically; scientifically; rudely; crudely; enduringly; flimsily.

(See build, manufacture.)

adjectives

complicated; unsurpassed; improved; patented; rigid; rugged; initial; complex; flawless; exclusive; superb; famous; primitive; ingenious; harmonic; durable; imperfect; majestic; sublime; riveted; mistaken; institutional; pithy; exquisite; immediate; superior; flattering; constitutional; artful; custom-built; excellent; evasive; strained; questionable; peculiar; musical; dependable; substantial; shrewd; sturdy; malicious; dramatic; contemplated; solid; recent; steel-truss; highway; engineering; correct; worst; wrong; strict; illegitimate; charitable; technical; crude.

CONSTRUCTIVE

adverbs

helpfully; critically; definitely; remarkably; valuably; significantly; magnificently; sensibly; fundamentally; essentially; liberally; splendidly; creatively; clearly; saliently; strikingly; explicitly.

CONSTRUE (*v*)

adverbs

variously; maliciously; confusedly; shrewdly; erroneously; charitably.
(See interpret.)

CONSUL

adjectives

dignified; autocratic; duly-appointed; officiating; protective; prudent; self-important; artful; wily; fastidious.

verbs

appeal to—; appoint—; authorize—; beseech—; charge—with; choose—; elect—; name—; present—; recall—; receive—; retain—; slay—; withdraw—; —advises; —anticipates; —holds office; —promotes; —promulgates; —proposes; —protects; —rejects; —reports; —represents.
(See magistrate, representative, counselor.)

CONSULT (*v*)

adverbs

selfishly; philosophically; confidentially; timidly; vainly; distressingly; solemnly; informally; anxiously; earnestly; gravely; deliberately; privately; frequently; protractedly.
(See deliberate, discuss.)

adjectives

solemn; whispered; hasty; informal; mature; anxious; actual; serious; religious; rapid; timely; earnest; vociferous; short; grave; deliberate; private; frequent; brief; protracted; muffled.

verbs

advise—; assist at—; call—; confer in—; deliberate in—; demand—; follow—; go into—; meet in—; secure—; seek—; —advises; —concludes; —decides; —ensues; —exposes; —guides; —results in.
(See conference, council.)

CONSUME (*v*)

adverbs

annually; ravenously; leisurely; utterly; relatively; ultimately; unwarily; industrially; ferociously.
(See burn, destroy.)

CONSUMER

adjectives

desirable; hard-working; mortgaged; ultimate; humble; general; unorganized (pl.); unprotected; unwary; trusting; duped.

CONSUMMATION

adjectives

desirable; relentless; harmonious; supreme; fitting.

CONSUMPTION

adjectives

needful; cold; languorous; melancholy; domestic; laryngeal; pulmonary; equitable; conspicuous; old-fashioned; annual; food; slackening; residential; industrial; diminishing.

verbs

afflict with—; consume with—; contract—; cure—; infect with—; inherit—; predispose to—; smite with—; suffer with—; tend towards—; treat for—; waste away with—; —atrophies; —attacks; —decomposes; —destroys; —invalids; —lingers; —preys on; —rots; —takes a toll; —wreaks.
(See tuberculosis, disease.)

CONTACT

adjectives

friendly; richest; effective; stimulating; intimate; personal; close; casual; fleeting; intermittent; brief; abrupt; superficial; bitter; difficult; banal; brutish; human; nation-wide; diplomatic; domestic; prolonged; mere; necessary; constant; alert; accidental; sonorous; immediate; direct; uninterrupted; unrestricted; terrible; intellectual; social; osculatory; slight; unclean; extensive; miscellaneous; spontaneous; careless; rude; proffered; lawless; responsible.

verbs
abolish—; approve of—; balk at—; bring into—; conceal—; defile by—; enter into—; establish—; favor—; harbor—; join in—; lose—; maintain—; modify—; negotiate—; oppose—; profit by—; reestablish —; renew—; uncover—; vary—.
(See connection.)

CONTAGION
adjectives
rigid; terrible; deadly; delicious; virulent.

verbs
check—; convey by—; engender—; expose to—; guard against—; harbor—; isolate—; propagate by—; quarantine—; restrain—; spread—.
(See pestilence, plague. infection.)

CONTAGIOUS
adverbs
highly; dangerously; pestilentially; unfortunately; acutely; widely; perilously; seriously; extremely; exceedingly; decidedly; unquestionably; frightfully; absolutely; remarkably; alarmingly; curiously; awfully; critically; definitely; fatally; positively; notoriously.

CONTAIN (v)
adverbs
virtually; fully; partially; entirely; fittingly; snugly; amazingly; completely; substantially.
(See hold.)

CONTAINER
adjectives
transparent; airtight; offsize; metal; standardized; smart; huge.

CONTEMPLATE (v)
adverbs
objectively; actually; soberly; vaguely; philosophically; consciously; listlessly; curiously; absorbedly; dreamily; serenely; profoundly; rapturously; complacently; severely; plaintively.
(See meditate.)

CONTEMPLATION
adjectives
frowning; ravishing; precocious; listless; passing; will-less; curious; celestial; absorbed; deep; hopeless; cold; solitary; mystic; dreamy; serene; wondering; academic; narrow; unfettered; profound; continued; sundry; comprehensive; silent; lofty; spiritual; complacent; zealous; rapturous; lonely; steadfast; habitual; pleasurable; melancholy; selfish; leaden; severe.

verbs
absorb in—; arouse from—; drift in—; engross in—; hold in—; fall into—; lose in—; meditate in—; molest in—; rejoice in—; soar in—; steep in—; swathe in—; wrap in—; —beholds; —colors; —pictures; —reflects; —stirs.
(See reflection, thought, meditation.)

CONTEMPLATIVE
adverbs
deeply; thoughtfully; reminiscently; prophetically; studiously; closely; ponderingly; abstractedly; intelligently; philosophically; sagely; wisely; leisurely; thoroughly; habitually; pensively; anxiously; eagerly; curiously; queerly; oddly; coldly; academically; zealously; loftily; mysteriously; calmly.

CONTEMPORARY
adjectives
admirable; poetic; fiendish; celebrated; unanimous; skeptical; disillusioned; eminent; cheery; erudite; wholesome; northern; smaller; male.

adverbs
conveniently; embarrassingly; undeniably; obviously; certainly; unquestionably; evidently; curiously; admittedly; presumably; probably; possibly; supposedly; oddly; incontrovertibly; authentically; actually; categorically; authoritatively; ironically.

CONTEMPT
adjectives
inexplicable; beautiful; impersonal; concentrated; dignified; undisguised; supercilious; exaggerated; inexpressible; reckless; fierce; lofty; veiled; half-compassionate; uncharitable; faint; deprecating; emphatic; cynical; spendthrift; withering; utmost; considerable; unreasoning; infinite; ineffable;

indiscriminate; bitterest; thorough; profound; uncompromising; notable; alternate; characteristic; deep-rooted; loud; ironical; arrogant; irrepressible; supreme; utter; habitual; geniune; biting; absolute; irrevocable; noisy; blighting; ineffable; unequivocal; notable; paternal; grand; magnificent; eloquent; smiling; good-natured; factitious; unfeigned; ardent; courageous; illimitable; aristrocratic; lofty; cavalier; holy; highbred; cold; stern; skeptical; icy; scornful; gloating; exasperating; shocked; keen; apparent; thundering; hereditary; growing; sudden; shattering; inherited; sweeping; high-nosed; friary.

verbs
admit—; awake—; bear—; breed—; convey—; deserve—; disdain—; entertain—; excite—; fill with—; foster—; gesture—; hurl—; imply—; place in—; pour out—; profess—; provoke—; regard with—; shield from—; sigh with—; smile—; spurn—; tinge with—; treat with—; veil—; wither with—; —arises; —deepens; —dies; —flickers; —infuriates; —terrifies; —shrivels up.
(See disdain, scorn, derision.)

CONTEMPTIBLE
adverbs
abominably; odiously; detestably; hatefully; shockingly; unspeakably; despicably; invidiously; woefully; lamentably; noxiously; execrably; flagrantly; intolerably; incredibly; disgustingly; utterly; outrageously; horribly; inexpressibly; notoriously; infamously; glaringly; monstrously; wickedly; remarkably.

CONTEND (v)
adverbs
pedantically; strenuously; incredulously; physically; laboriously; forcefully; narrowly; fiercely; boldly; stoutly; optimistically; senselessly; shrewdly; ridiculously; acrimoniously; ironically; undeviatingly; vigorously.
(See oppose.)

CONTENT
adjectives
sufficient; scholarly; organic; prescribed; sociological; trusting; universal; infinite; spacious; final; anti-religious; deepest; intimate; nestling; incongruous; supreme; wondrous; wise; greedy; drowsy; dreamy; measureless; immortal; blissful; cubical;

infantile; scrutinized; radiant; adequate; muddy; gorgeous; endless; significant; melodic; shrewd; fluid; flinty; fermented; logical; corrupt; imbecile; unaggressive; protein; perfect; physical; sweet; scented; quiet; intellectual.

CONTENTION
adjectives
stout; brave; optimistic; bloody; senseless; ridiculous; fierce; unnatural; ravishing; rival; critical; acrimonious; basic; general; ironical.

verbs
abandon—; cast out—; contest—; dispute—; endorse—; illustrate—; justify—; match—; raise—; refute—; rend with—; support—; —lingers; —upsets.
(See strife, conflict, struggle, dispute, argument, dissension.)

CONTENTIOUS
adverbs
characteristically; incorrigibly; disagreeably; loftily; shrewdly; intelligently; stupidly; doggedly; foolishly; bitterly; unnecessarily; testily; mildly; impetuously; violently; mulishly; stolidly; abusively; unreasonably; habitually; hotly; offensively; absurdly; pretentiously; brazenly.

CONTENTMENT
adjectives
inward; homelike; childish; stolid; rapturous; sweet; complete; thoughtless; perfect; placid; domestic; rare; abiding; happy; odd; new; supreme; drowsy; ineffable; sleepy; sinking.

verbs
achieve—; attain—; bathe in—; desire—; destroy—; feign—; fill with—; pretend—; purr—; realize—; relax in—; resign in—; result in—; seek—; sigh in—; sink into—; smile with—; strive for—; struggle for—; swathe in—; view with—; yearn for—; —evades; —proceeds from.
(See satisfaction, happiness, gratification.)

CONTENTS
adjectives
valuable; varied; lively; treasurable; illuminating; deadly; gruesome; nauseous; horrific; strange; discursive; golden; heterogeneous; problematical; sluggish; terse.

verbs
add to—; assimilate—; dehydrate—; discharge—; eject—; empty—; expel—; gut of—; imbibe—; master—; **pound**—; rob of—; stir—; —escape.
(See ingredients.)

CONTEST
adjectives
unequal; remarkable; **obstinate**; decisive; interstate; animated; bloody; deadly; dread; formal; sanguinary; passionate; inevitable; pending; civic; naked; spirited; frightful; ceaseless; violent; diplomatic; jarring; dramatic; tremendous; culminating; emotional; costly; tedious; amicable; bitter; mighty; audacious.

verbs
attend—; "ballyhoo"—; cheer—; debate—; develop into—; dispute—; emerge from—; enter—; invite to—; lose—; prepare for —; relish—; renew—; strive in—; struggle in—; vie in—; win—; witness—; —awards; —excites; —proceeds.
(See tournament, competition, dispute, dissension.)

CONTEST (v)
adverbs
fiercely; energetically; gallantly; bitterly; unequally; remarkably; obstinately; decisively; animatedly; bloodily; passionately; inevitably; ceaselessly; violently; diplomatically; dramatically; amicably; audaciously.
(See oppose, dispute.)

CONTESTANT
adjectives
feeble; leading; vindicated; keen; rival; earnest; obstinate; invincible; indefatigable.

verbs
equip—; reduce—s; —achieves; —applies; —battles; —competes; —contends; —endures; —gains; —overcomes; —races; —rivals; —strains; —strives; —struggles.
(See competitor, rival.)

CONTINENCE
adjectives
absolute; vowed; eternal; inordinate; lofty; ascetic; monastic; impenetrable; inviolable.

CONTINENT
adjectives
rich; new; powerful; remote; sunken; commanding; unexhausted; sunny; undiscovered; virgin; unborn; unmapped; orbed; infinite.

verbs
abound on—; bound—; communicate with —; cover—; discover—; divide—; explore—; exploit—; govern—; inhabit—; populate—; rule—; sail for—; span—; speed across—; study—; tranquilize—; travel—; traverse—; wage on—.
(See land, country.)

CONTINGENCY
adjectives
remote; various (pl); fatal; imaginable; impossible; dangerous; unforeseen; future.

verbs
admit—; conceive—; consider—; contemplate—; exempt from—; expose to—; foresee—; forestall—; fortify against—; free from—; involve—; prepare for—; regard—; subject to—; —befalls; —occurs; —requires.
(See chance, possibility, accident, hazard.)

CONTINGENT
adjectives
various (pl); assorted (pl); fresh; obligatory; unlimited; valuable; denominated; incidental.

adverbs
accidentally; unexpectedly; fortuitously; unfortunately; presumably; casually; unluckily; advantageously; possibly; remotely; imaginably; gravely; distantly; presciently.

CONTINUANCE
adjectives
further; simultaneous; perpetual; dogged; indefinite.

verbs
balk at—; bore by—; detest—; forswear—; hinder—; insure—; lapse—; prohibit—; shrink from—; speed—; stay—; urge—; —adds; —confirms; —engulfs; —improves; —inculcates; —irks; —oppresses; —perfects; —preserves; —renders.

CONTINUATION

adjectives

sketchy; mirthful; interminable; ruthless; casual; fluent; moderate.

CONTINUE (v)

adverbs

presumptuously; relentlessly; calmly; uncomplainingly; dauntlessly; voluntarily; passionately; stealthily; triumphantly; obstinately; jerkily; thoughtfully; facetiously; affably; mercilessly; hopefully; defiantly; imperturbably; treacherously; blandly.

(See persevere.)

CONTINUITY

adjectives

historic; unbroken; inexplicable; long-sighted; strict; general; agreeable; grim.

CONTINUOUS

adverbs

maddeningly; providentially; monotonously; tiresomely; intolerably; incredibly; grimly; dangerously; indescribably; unbearably; alarmingly; frightfully; crazily; insufferably; solemnly; ruthlessly; appallingly; cleverly; dismally; noisily; provokingly; automatically.

CONTORT (v)

adverbs

misshapenly; facilely; inanely; horribly; capriciously; drolly; spasmodically; frantically; sinisterly; agilely; facially; sneeringly.

(See twist, wrench.)

CONTORTION

adjectives

deprecatory; wonderful; frightful; spasmodic; joyful; frantic; sneering; sinister; unsystematic; slight; facial; agile.

CONTOUR

adjectives

delicate; vertical; bodily; inviting; ground; vague; pleasing; facial; rugged; muscular; hard; skeletal; cranial; childish; chubby; snug; effeminate; pronounced; rounded; sharp; youthful; wasted; swinging; voluptuous; pert; harsh; smooth; girlish; sagging; exquisite.

CONTRABAND

adjectives

confiscated; exported; proclaimed; prohibited; seized; smuggled.

verbs

ban as—; carry—; confiscate—; deal in—; declare as—; destroy—; export—; forbid as—; forfeit—; import—; list as—; proclaim as—; prohibit as—; seize as—; smuggle—; supply—; traffic in—.

(See arms, supplies.)

CONTRACT

adjectives

fat; solemn; valid; conjugal; stamped; workable; favorable; vowed; true; signed; nullified; binding; huge; definite; gilt-edged; legal; repudiated; direct; airtight; substantial; advantageous; invariable.

verbs

abandon—; amend—; breach—; cancel—; celebrate—; cleave to—; depart from—; dispense with—; execute—; forfeit—; fulfill—; interpret—; jockey over—; jump—; land—; modify—; rebel at—; revoke—; term—; terminate—; violate—; void—; waive—; win—; —binds; —discloses; —expires; —holds; —implies; —specifies; —stipulates.

(See compact, agreement, arrangement, bargain, promise.)

CONTRACT (v)

adverbs

violently; vigorously; bindingly; definitely; legally; advantageously; substantially; physically; spasmodically; intermittently; solemnly.

(See narrow, shrink.)

CONTRACTION

adjectives

muscular; inevitable; continuous; sharp; deep; nervous; concentric.

verbs

allow for—; produce—; regulate—; tend toward—; —abbreviates; —apostrophizes; —condenses; —confines; —diminishes; —draws; —hampers; —lames; —limits; —narrows; —reduces; —restricts; —shortens; —shrinks.

(See condensation.)

CONTRACTOR

adjectives

certain; labor; alert; scheming; enriched; resourceful; purloining.

CONTRADICT (v)

adverbs
expressly; violently; inexplicably; constantly; embarrassingly; fatuously; flagrantly; mutually; bewilderingly; curiously; logically; extravagantly; vulgarly; boorishly; curtly; ill-manneredly; explicitly; directly.

(See say.)

CONTRADICTION

adjectives
violent; inexplicable; constant; embarrassing; slight; irreconcilable; moral; breathtaking; productive; idealistic; disruptive; imaginary; self-corroding; fatuous; accumulated; social; flat; absurd; apparent; flagrant; painful; notable; mutual; bewildering; amazing; curious; logical; affectionate; extravagant.

verbs
affirm—; brook—; claim—; deny ; discern—; encompass with—; endure—; forbid—; indulge in—; involve—; object to—; offset—; press—; profess—; prove—; reconcile—; solve—; sustain—; utter—; —irritates; —perplexes; —proposes; —yawns.

(See opposition, paradox, inconsistency.)

CONTRADICTORY

adverbs
strangely; oddly; naively; subtly; blatantly; inexplicably; embarrassingly; irreconcilably; disruptively; absurdly; flagrantly; pugnaciously; truculently; amazingly; curiously; apparently; obviously; palpably; illogically; bewilderingly; flatly; fiercely; directly; fatally; unbecomingly; defiantly.

CONTRAPTION

adjectives
happy; pleasing; refreshing; delicious; charming; excellent; attractive; pleasant; effective; interesting; encouraging; true; striking; vivid; marked; sharp; pronounced; momentous; notable; smashing; amazing; astounding; unbelievable; startling; surprising; puzzling; quaint; odd; curious; cruel; violent; prosaic; dismal; amusing; abrupt; ludicrous; deft; precise; tremendous; instructive; dramatic; intense; singular; gratifying; possible; ghastly; artificial; obvious; favorable; crazy; delightful; subtle; melancholy; piquant; gloomy; contemporaneous.

verbs
contemplate—; contrive—; design—; destroy—; devise—; employ—; extricate from—; immerse in—; interest in—; invent—; mesh in—; plan—; set up—; test—; work out—; —attracts; —envelops; —puzzles.

(See device.)

CONTRAST

adjectives
clear; exciting; flattering; bitter; brilliant; remote; poignant; startling; unfavorable.

verbs
accentuate—; cap—; disclose—; emphasize—; mark—; place in—; present—; resent—; revel in—; serve as—; strike—; study—; vow—; —glares; —grows; —interests.

(See comparison.)

CONTRAST (v)

adverbs
vividly; sharply; strangely; whimsically; bitterly; strikingly; violently; picturesquely; invidiously.

(See compare.)

CONTRIBUTE (v)

adverbs
materially; unceasingly; indirectly; voluntarily; considerably; cheerily; altruisticly; willingly; liberally; simultaneously; singularly; gloomily; voluminously; conspicuously; effectively; powerfully; notably; anonymously; originally; technically; fundamentally; uniquely; meritoriously; formidably; permanently; characteristically.

(See give, furnish.)

CONTRIBUTION

adjectives
important; notable; anonymous; epoch-making; significant; distinctive; voluminous; august; practical; passionate; magnificent; literary; original; technical; fundamental; valuable; unique; varying; copious; charming; worthy; liberal; heartfelt; generous; sole; fascinating; splendid; superb; meritorious; formidable; serious; permanent; solid; genuine; enduring; tangible; priceless; cultural; private; statesmanlike; creative; cooperative; definite; negligible; phantom; invigorating; timely; characteristic; startling; immediate.

verbs
begrudge—; collect—; deluge with—s; favor with—; gather—s; offer—; sacrifice—; solicit—; squeeze—out of; —exemplifies; —s pour in.
(See alms.)

CONTRIBUTOR
adjectives
distinguished; prolific; occasional; prospective; sparkling; anonymous; forgotten; flourishing; industrious; scholarly; well-remembered; frequent.

verbs
advertise for—s; appeal to—s; approach —s; back by—s; pay—; promise—; satisfy—; seek—s; serve as—; —aids; —endows; —furnishes; —raises; —rallies; —responds; —supports; —writes.
(See supporter.)

CONTRIBUTORY
adverbs
helpfully; advantageously; liberally; commercially; cooperatively; charitably; economically; encouragingly; generously; harmoniously; jointly; obligingly; originally.

CONTRITION
adjectives
veritable; authentic; apparent; heartfelt; warm; mock; pitiful; sudden; blind.

verbs
afflict with—; arise from—; break with—; bruise with—; display—; dissolve in—; exhibit—; languish in—; melt in—; pray in—; reduce to—; repent in—; sow—; strike with—; suffer—; wear with—; weep in—; —softens.
(See sorrow, remorse.)

CONTRIVANCE
adjectives
clumsy; mechanical; various (pl); discarded; ingenious; kindred; well-fitted; curious; perfect; mysterious; fun-making; excitement-arousing; dumpy; rickety; admirable; mock; peculiar; delightful; tricky; intricate; labor-saving; quaint; malignant.

CONTRIVE (v)
adverbs
ingeniously; cunningly; sedulously; curiously; cleverly; providentially; indirectly; scientifically; mechanically; mysteriously; intricately; malignantly; maliciously; viciously; bitterly; revengefully.
(See scheme, invent.)

CONTROL
adjectives
powerful; menial; supervisory; easy; heroic; thought; political; centralized; mysterious; transcending; absolute; repressive; automatic; effective; determined; collective; benevolent; inadequate; virtual; irremissible; remote; autonomous; inventory; democratic; effortless; rigorous; working; parental; precise; undisputed; production; autocratic; perfect; substantial; self-assumed; immediate; hypnotic; arbitrary; excellent; iron; firm; entire; permanent; complete; full; supreme; exclusive; nominal; limited; partial; hectic; craven; hateful; sinister; degrading; systematic; ordered; social; ancestral; merchandising; unjust; civilian; traffic; nerve; scientific; strong; external; silent; boundless; planned; private; growing; critical; steady.

verbs
acquire—; assume—; attest to—; centralize—; concentrate—; demonstrate—; divorce—; endanger—; entrust with—; establish—; exempt from—; exercise—; exert—; fight—; gain—; grab—; lose—; maintain—; manifest—; release—; respond to—; seek—; seize—; settle in—of; teach—; trick into—of; vest—in; win—; —changes hands; —rests with.
(See regulation, restraint, domination, command.)

CONTROL (v)
adverbs
absolutely; imperiously; arbitrarily; powerfully; heroically; politically; mysteriously; dictatorially; automatically; determinedly; benevolently; adequately; virtually; democratically; effortlessly; rigorously; autocratically; hypnotically; exclusively; nominally; partially; privately; critically; steadily.
(See regulate, restrain.)

CONTROVERSIAL
adverbs
highly; unfortunately; temptingly; inevitably; religiously; violently; tediously; painfully; excitably; vehemently; stupidly; obstinately; endlessly; bitterly; intricately; dangerously; traditionally; diplomatically; perplexingly.

CONTROVERSY

adjectives

perplexing; pending; long-standing; religious; violent; acrimonious; vehement; tedious; frequent; painful; external; important; bitter; political; sectarian; ferocious; exciting; pending; contemptible; heated; long; warm; drawn-out; endless; intricate; arduous; acrid; terrific; lively; scorching; threatening; dangerous; ancient; long-forgotten; legal; economic; international; diplomatic; clerical; parlor; silly; unfortunate; unexpected; waning.

verbs

appraise—; arouse—; avoid—; carry on—; clarify—; cut through—; dismiss—; engage in—; entangle in—; involve in—; judge—; occasion—; perpetuate—; plunge into—; precipitate—; shrink from—; stir up—; suppress—; sway by—; unleash—; view—; wage—; —arises from; —blasts; —convulses; —fizzles; —flares; —rages; —spits.

(See dispute, contention, debate, feud.)

CONTUMACIOUS

adverbs

stubbornly; stiffly; defiantly; hotly; tempermanentally; habitually; insufferably; intractably; unmanageably; uncontrollably; foolishly; ridiculously; mutinously; violently; restlessly; lawlessly; seditiously; ungovernably; openly; formidably; irreconcilably; alarmingly; dangerously; unaccountably; obstreperously; inveterately; malevolently; distressingly.

CONTUMELIOUS

adverbs

blatantly; absurdly; airily; egotistically; unpardonably; fantastically; insufferably; extremely; audaciously; flippantly; saucily; shamefully; bumptiously; brassily; offensively; provokingly: unpleasantly; disagreeably; intolerably; arrogantly; haughtily; unreasonably; senselessly; idiotically; unwisely; indiscreetly; imprudently.

CONTUSION

adjectives

severe; fatal; painful; serious; violet-hued; predominant.

verbs

acquire by—; anoint—; bandage—; cure—; dress—; infect—; inflame—; irritate—;

produce—; relieve—; suffer—; treat—; —bruises; —crushes; —enervates; —heals; —incapacitates; —injures; —swells.

(See bruise, injury.)

CONUNDRUM

adjectives

stock; baffling; fascinating; improvised; stale; original.

CONVALESCENCE

adjectives

tolerable; hard-won; adequate; drowsy; slow; uncertain; maddening.

verbs

affect—; delay—; doze through—; discharge from—; ease through—; interrupt—; nurse through—; regain during—; revive in—; shorten—; strengthen in—; treat during—; visit during—; while away—; —advances; —cures; —overcomes; —proceeds.

(See recovery, improvement.)

CONVALESCENT

adjectives

petulant; selfish; irritable; impatient; implacable; whining; whimsical.

adverbs

happily; fortunately; securely; finally; contentedly; easily; tolerably; slowly; painfully; actually; pleasantly; luckily; gratefully; thankfully; affably; normally; definitely; apparently; blessedly; cheerfully; charmingly; truly; presumably; undoubtedly; decisively.

CONVENIENCE

adjectives

domestic; timesaving; greater; money-saving; every; ultra-fashionable; incidental; notable; modern; homelike; foresighted; admirable; earliest; consequent; passing; delightful; added; safe; metropolitan; undoubted; tremendous; general.

verbs

adopt—; afford—; allow—; appreciate—; avail oneself of—; await—of; enjoy—; extend—; lack—; marry for—; offer—; pay for—; permit of—; possess—; require—; —comforts; —eases; —saves.

(See comfort, ease, opportunity.)

CONVENIENT

adverbs
particularly; comfortably; highly; properly; acceptably; admirably; marvelously; tremendously; safely; delightfully; exceptionally; perfectly; completely; incredibly; wholly; extraordinarily; singularly; suitably; duly; unusually; ingeniously.

CONVENT

adjectives
suppressed; measureless; once-famous; secluded; peaceful; cloistered.

CONVENTION
(custom)

adjectives
timid; operatic; faith-healing; classic; universal; social; civic; restricting; rigid; facile; poetic.

CONVENTION
(meeting)

adjectives
radical; national; projected; provincial; famous; cheap; wide-open; labor; advertising.

verbs
appoint to—; assemble in—; boycott—; brand—; cavort at—; control—; denounce—; elect at—; emanate in—; hold—; join—; meet in—; open—; preside at—; represent at—; run away with—; stage—; —abolishes; —adjourns; —alters; —bestows; —considers; —convenes; —nominates; —prepares; —proclaims.
(See meeting, conference, congress, council, assembly.)

CONVENTIONAL

adverbs
properly; formally; strictly; habitually; naturally; normally; ordinarily; positively; usually; uncompromisingly; typically; rigidly; stiffly; consistently; absurdly; needlessly; carefully; arrogantly; affectedly; shyly; bashfully; ostentatiously; pretentiously; pompously; meticulously; insistently.

CONVENTIONALITY

adjectives
pleasant; sterile; frigid; precise; ceremonious; cutting; supreme.

verbs
accept—; adhere to—; base on—; beat down—; blind by—; breach—; break—; break away from—; buttress by—; chal-

lenge—; contradict—; defer—; defy—; discard—; disregard—; drop—; flout—; follow—; hamper—; hate—; heed—; obey—; overthrow—; ridicule—; sacrifice to—; satirize—; shatter—; shelter—; smash—; subject to—; violate—; wall in by—; —allows; —determines; —hampers; —permits; —recognizes; —sanctions; —settles; —supports; —upholds.
(See custom, usage, habit, rule, form, practice.)

CONVERGE (*v*)

adverbs
sharply; suddenly; gradually; obviously; abruptly; unexpectedly; consequently; fatally; tragically; significantly.
(See approach.)

CONVERSANT

adverbs
thoroughly; intimately; slightly; fortunately; luckily; auspiciously; expertly; liberally; deeply; profoundly; shrewdly; reportedly; supposedly; reputably; ingeniously; cleverly; intelligently; capably; advantageously; consummately; perfectly.

CONVERSATION

adjectives
desultory; sedate; forcible; vapid; whispered; exquisite; subsequent; inane; trivial; informal; temporary; difficult; frank; touching; calm; natural; cheerful; animated; private; bristling; preliminary; thoughtful; philosophical; savory; embellished; unspecific; mysterious; idyllic; interminable; earnest; measured; gossip-riddled; filthy; reminiscent; considerable; agreeable; subdued; hurried; distracting; energetic; gentle; frivolous; sparkling; undertoned; low-voiced; real; heavenly; pleasant; enchanting; fascinating; egotistic; previous; appreciative; personal; direct; tumultuous; memorable; vivacious; amiable; improbable; intelligent; offhand; comfortable; inmost; casual; serious; bold; liberal; idle; scattered; curious; apparent; ribald; spicy; extravagant; delightful; interesting; sustained; passing; dramatic; diligent; sublimated; piquant; rational; select; easy; graceful; protracted; intimate; eager; edifying; mercurial; running; sportive; open; sociable; antiquarian; inimitable; brilliant; clear; persuasive; sympathetic; sane; coherent; amicable; enthralling; luminous; famous; witty; aphoristic; hilarious; amusing; bantering; facetious; smiling; light; explosive; spirited; lively;

sprightly; negligible; everyday; ordinary; aimless; drifting; languishing; flickering; scattered; intermittent; halting; jerky; wandering; lagging; jumbled; fitful; indefinite; elusive; spiritless; extended; inconclusive; timorous; wearisome; fatuous; insipid; lazy; lackadaisical; muttered; bold; impractical; pert; leery; hidebound; loud; superfluous; irate; embattled; hideous; concerting; coarse; obscene; illiterate; successful; dinner table; eyebrow; traveled; healthy; emotional; quiet; cultured; confidential; startled; amazing; conspicuous; condensed; brief; rapid; promiscuous; unblushing; spontaneous; sudden; chatty; general; developed; simple; polite; absorbed; imaginary; uninterrupted; harmless; dutiful; plausible.

verbs
address—to; conduct—with; connive at—; direct—; divert—; drag into—; dull—; engage in—; essay—; forego—; guide—; infuse into—; interrupt—; key—; lead into—; narrate—; nurture—; open—; overhear—; plunge into—; prolong—; refrain from—; rush into—; shatter—; shift—; shoulder—; snatch at—; suspend—; swing —back to; transcribe—; —breaks out; —drifts on; —evolves from; —flames; —flows; —languishes; —lapses; —palls; —precedes; —rambles; —ranges; —scintillates; —skips from; —streams away; —stumbles upon.
(See dialogue, intercourse, communication, conference, talk.)

CONVERSATIONAL
adverbs
amiably; stiffly; sociably; affably; pompously; garrulously; provincially; gruffly; laconically; informally; calmly; naturally; cheerfully; jovially; helpfully; unwontedly; agreeably; eagerly; gently; brilliantly; enchantingly; illuminatingly; fascinatingly; vivaciously; intelligently; comfortably; casually; seriously; idly; curiously; spicily; ribaldly; drunkenly; convivially; interestingly; dramatically; gracefully; intimately; graciously; wittily; amusingly; facetiously; happily; luckily; intermittently; abstractedly; fitfully; inconclusively; yawningly; insipidly; lazily; loudly; blatantly; noisily.

CONVERSATIONALIST
adjectives
fluent; elegant; absorbing; gifted; interesting; brilliant.

CONVERSE
adjectives
earnest; eager; grave; sagacious; purposeful; covert.

CONVERSE (v)
adverbs
vivaciously; fluently; freely; interestingly; agreeably; courteously; affably; desultorily; acrimoniously; sedately; inanely; trivially; informally; temporarily; frankly; touchingly; animatedly; privately; brilliantly; philosophically; mysteriously; distractedly; curiously; ribaldly; piquantly; rationally; dramatically; gracefully; mercurially; inimitably; persuasively; sympathetically; coherently; amicably; enthrallingly; hilariously; banteringly; aimlessly; pointlessly; intermittently; jerkily; laggingly; fitfully; indefinitely; fatuously; insipidly; timorously; superfluously; irately; emotionally; confidentially; promiscuously; spontaneously; politely; absorbedly; uninterruptedly; harmlessly; pointedly.
(See talk, chat.)

CONVERSION
adjectives
spiritual; infinite; romantic; tardy; religious; abrupt; imminent; vivid.

CONVERT
adjectives
proposed; immovable; enthusiastic; docile; devout; irrevocable.

verbs
baptize—; direct—; gather—s; guide—; lead—s; make—; preach to—; —accepts; —acknowledges; —changes; —embraces; —falls from grace; —forsakes; —gains; —professes; —rallies; —substitutes; —transfers.
(See disciple, follower.)

CONVERT (v)
adverbs
religiously; frequently; enthusiastically; sincerely; passionately; conscientiously; irresistibly; intellectually; rationally; unalterably; solemnly.
(See apply, use.)

CONVERTIBLE
adverbs
readily; easily; handily; economically; quickly; conveniently; instantly; serviceably; instantaneously; advantageously; ingeniously; deftly; dexterously; fortunately;

luckily; accommodatingly; adaptably; providentially; promptly; profitably; altogether; unquestionably; happily.

CONVEY (v)
adverbs
naturally; forcefully; exquisitely; imperceptibly; delicately; competently; peculiarly; luxuriously; privately; diplomatically; tactfully; ceremoniously.
(See carry, transport.)

CONVEYANCE
adjectives
miserable; competent; shaky; tenantless; impossible; peculiar; ornamental; creditable; luxurious; available; modern; private; usual.

verbs
construct—; convoy—; design—; draw—; drive—; escort—; guide—; lead—; load—; lubricate—; mechanize—; model—; pull—; power—; restrain—; transport in—; trust—; upset—; —rattles; —rumbles; —transmits.
(See carriage, vehicle.)

CONVICT
adjectives
political; pardoned; vital; wily; shivering; rat-faced; horrified; fear-dazed; filthy; degraded; villainous.

verbs
apprehend—; chain—; deliver—; execute—; expose—; free—; pardon—; parole—; punish—; rehabilitate—; reprieve—; sentence—; train—; transfer—; try—; —breaks jail; —confesses; —escapes; —invades; —offends; —prowls; —rebels; —reforms; —serves.
(See criminal, culprit, prisoner.)

CONVICT (v)
adverbs
invariably; circumstantially; insidiously; politically; villainously; sternly; intellectually; positively; unmistakably; deliberately; solemnly; theoretically; swiftly; secretly; overwhelmingly; legally.
(See condemn.)

CONVICTION
adjectives
arresting; passionate; humbling; doubtful; historic; conscientious; true; firm; perverse; random; instantaneous; stern; indefeasible; youthful; profound; rapturous; frail;

unsettled; irresistible; unshaken; widespread; deep; popular; honest; intellectual; inbred; esteemed; fixed; religious; coessential; subjective; sincere; rational; unalterable; vivid; calm; reasonable; extravagant; remote; positive; instinctive; unmistakable; steel; thorough; moral; antagonistic; internal; jocular; definite; persistent; deliberate; paternal; tried; innermost; solemn; intimate; unspoken; well-known; theoretic; extreme; socialistic; immediate; unutterable; prophetic; perfect; earnest; sober; clear; accepted; assured; lively; joyous; thrilling; exhilarating; lasting; steadfast; stubborn; ineradicable; unassailable; unsullied; unquestioning; independent; heroic; fierce; strong; intense; absolute; personal; individual; horrible; torturing; unaccountable; disagreeable; wild; grim; unfortunate; weary; pathetic; humanitarian; aesthetic; increasing; growing; light; odd; swift; overwhelming; comfortable; latent; naive; dawning; instinctive; secret.

verbs
accept with—; awaken to—; bring—; carry—; cherish—; develop—; express—; fire—; form—; guide by—; indoctrinate—; ingrain—; justify—; lack—; lay down with—; lead to—; profess—; reiterate—; rouse—; share—; stand by—; —accrues; —burdens; —deserts; —grows; —restrains; —springs; —wavers.
(See faith, belief.)

CONVINCE (v)
adverbs
demonstratively; despairingly; rationally; solemnly; reluctantly; unalterably; profoundly; stubbornly; firmly; thoroughly; passionately; conscientiously; irresistibly; honestly; intellectually; religiously; reasonably; positively; theoretically; overwhelmingly; secretly.
(See satisfy.)

CONVIVIAL
adverbs
warmly; extremely; hospitably; sociably; fraternally; cosily; gregariously; entertainingly; chattingly; hilariously; waggishly; uproariously; pleasantly; merrily; gaily; blithely; affably; highly; agreeably; sportively; facetiously; boisterously; noisily; obstreperously; jovially; lovingly; festively; heartily.

CONVIVIALITY

adjectives
dried; dead; joyous; infectious; communicable; sparkling.

CONVOCATION

adjectives
jocund; ecclesiastical; heterogeneous; noble; clamorous; political; incessant.

CONVOKE (v)

adverbs
legitimately; legally; formally; annually; flagrantly; solemnly; ceremoniously; perfunctorily.
(See call, gather.)

CONVOY

adjectives
lumbering; speeding; rushing; protective; unwelcome; sequestering.

CONVULSION

adjectives
popular; perilous; suicidal; gleaming; rare; burnished; hammered; tarnished; public; hysterical; spasmodic; passionate; sardonic; civic; fearful; ghastly; strong; horrid; freakish; dreadful; moral; amiable; seething; mighty; mad.

verbs
attend with—; pass through—; produce—; quiet—; shake with—; stiffen in—; treat for—; writhe in—; —arises from; —recurs; —seizes.
(See spasm, fit, paroxysm.)

COO (v)

adverbs
plaintively; murmurously; softly; romantically; gently; lovingly; affectionately; delicately.
(See whisper.)

COOING

adjectives
soft; melancholy; subdued; mournful; gentle; lullabied; hushed.

COOK

adjectives
outlandish; splendid; superb; excellent; peerless; lusty; furious; surprised; sleepy-eyed; excited; pious; covetous; studious; cursed.

COOK (v)

adverbs
excellently; arduously; outlandishly; superbly; peerlessly; unsurpassingly; appetizingly; deliciously; exotically; delicately; tastefully; experimentally.
(See prepare.)

COOKERY

adjectives
master; tasty; experimental; unpalatable; hopeless; praiseworthy.

COOKIES

adjectives
delicious; stale; fresh; newly-baked; holiday; refrigerator.

COOKING

adjectives
delicate; unsavory; hygienic; casual; indifferent; superb; incomparable.

verbs
delight in—; plan—; practise—; provide—; relish—; school in—; skill in—; teach—; turn to—; —invites; —tempts.

COOL

adverbs
refreshingly; comfortably; uncomfortably; suddenly; unusually; gratefully; sufficiently; extremely; somewhat; moderately; unexpectedly; surprisingly; luckily; unfortunately; unluckily; terribly; beautifully; delightfully.

COOL (v)

adverbs
rapidly; sufficiently; scientifically; nocturnally; professionally; autumnally; abnormally; mechanically.
(See chill.)

COOL-HEADED

adverbs
quietly; calmly; equably; dispassionately; gravely; imperturbably; moderately; patiently; wisely; serenely; stoically; tolerantly; judiciously; sensibly; habitually; temperamentally; luckily; provokingly; sanely; extremely; superbly; astutely; admirably; amazingly; cautiously; warily; discreetly.

COOLNESS

adjectives
alluring; masterful; grateful; soft; admirable; nocturnal; cynical; obstinate; pro-

fessional; smooth; twinkling; utmost; undisturbed; slumberous; dim; correct; apparent; matchless; welcome; sudden; autumnal; inhuman; sneering; delicious.

COOPERATE (v)
adverbs
alternately; enthusiastically; gladly; consciously; respectably; willingly; harmoniously; courteously; advantageously; wholesomely; benevolently; mechanically; agriculturally; heartily; voluntarily; sympathetically; spontaneously; successfully.
(See help, unite.)

COOPERATION
adjectives
peaceful; matchless; loyal; genuine; courteous; close; harmonious; wise; generous; advantageous; wholesome; benevolent; municipal; unwavering; active; constant; cordial; constructive; munificent; emotional; agricultural; merchandising; public; international; pontifical; hearty; voluntary; stabilizing; spontaneous; sympathetic; immense; universal; conscious; indispensable; successful; powerful.

verbs
act in—with; advocate—; balk at—; court—; develop—; display—; dispose toward—; effect—; enlist—; exhibit—; foster—; lack—; necessitate—; pledge—; practise—; result in—; stress—; teach—; urge—; work in—with; —helps; —overcomes; —produces; —saves.
(See action, participation.)

COOPERATIVE
adverbs
wonderfully; serviceably; ardently; energetically; intelligently; zealously; actively; overwhelmingly; ingeniously; skilfully; willingly; grudgingly; instantly; loyally; genuinely; wisely; generously; advantageously; benevolently; unwaveringly; cordially; munificently; heartily; spontaneously; immensely; indispensably.

COORDINATE (v)
adverbs
logically; rationally; physically; functionally; excellently; delicately; mentally; muscularly; exactly; definitely; skilfully.

COORDINATION
adjectives
rational; physical; functional; excellent; delicate; mental; local; muscular.

verbs
arrange—; display—; hamper—; impair—; improve—; involve—; lose—; obstruct—; perform with—; proceed in—; regulate with—; require—; study—; supervise—;

—effects; —pleases.
(See harmony.)

COP
adjectives
strutting; hidebound; bullying; pompous; brass-buttoned; mace-brandishing; dictatorial; obliging; humanitarian.

COPE (v)
adverbs
successfully; bravely; heroically; continually; prevailingly; stalwartly; fearlessly; surprisingly.
(See strive.)

COPIOUS
adverbs
overwhelmingly; lavishly; naturally; needlessly; amply; luxuriantly; abundantly; aboundingly; exuberantly; affluently; inexhaustibly; overpoweringly; prodigally; handsomely; excessively; wantonly; unreasonably; remarkably; inexpressibly; fabulously; extraordinarily; astonishingly; amazingly; particularly; wonderfully; staggeringly; surprisingly; unbelievably; marvellously; fortunately; profusely.

COPPER
adjectives
shining; old; burnished; simmering; gleaming; hammered; tarnished.

verbs
alloy—; coat with—; dissolve—; grub out—; heat—; line with—; mine—; mold—; oxidize—; process—; produce—; purify—; refine—; sheathe in—; smelt—; work in—; —conducts; —insulates; —occurs; —oxidizes; —resists.
(See metal.)

COPSE
adjectives
woven; thick; rambling; summer; luxuriant.

COPY
(general)

adjectives

spirited; modified; examined; literal; certified; advance; drab; uninteresting; exact; laborious; attested; feeble; unique; mimeographed; photostatic; burlesque; fair; fragmentary; engrossed; virtuous; identical; pale; lame; stray; questionable; fraudulent; plaster; unexpurgated.

COPY
(journalism)

adjectives

badly-typed; blue-penciled; interlined; intelligible; transcribed; thumb-worn; sadly-deleted; smudgy.

verbs

arrange—; butcher—; deride—; damage—; edit—; enliven—; expand—; improve—; lengthen—; outline—; overbalance—; overdo—; point up—; read—; rearrange—; review—; set—; shorten—; simplify—; tone up—; write—.
(See advertisement.)

COPY
(reproduction)

adjectives

authentic; accurate; flattering; pathetic; preposterous; sketchy; veritable.

verbs

alter—; attest—; bequeath—; change—; collect—ies; distribute—ies; embellish—; forward—; garnish—; guard—; mail—; pattern—; refer to—; retain—; rewrite—; sign—; transcribe—; translate—; witness —; —appears; —exemplifies; —imitates; —reproduces.
(See imitation, duplicate, pattern.)

COPY (v)

adverbs

accurately; silently; extensively; uninterestingly; literally; exactly; laboriously; uniquely; photostatically; fairly; fragmentarily; identically; fraudulently; faithfully.
(See reproduce, imitate.)

COPYRIGHT

adjectives

popular; valid; world-wide; ineffective; disregarded.

verbs

apply for—; assign—to; defeat—; grant—; infringe on—; invalidate—; reconvey—; renew—; take out—; violate—; —expires; —protects; —secures.
(See right, patent.)

COQUETRY

adjectives

spasmodic; childish; unconquerable; open; feeble; modest; shy; clumsy; graceful; unconscious; native.

COQUETTE

adjectives

laughing; cold-blooded; superannuated; natural; insolent; typical; attractive; little.

COQUETTE (v)

adverbs

saucily; laughingly; insolently; attractively; modestly; shyly; slyly; gracefully; endearingly; lovingly; temptingly; irresistibly; naturally; precociously; shamelessly.
(See flirt.)

COQUETTISH

adverbs

charmingly; shamelessly; wantonly; enchantingly; irresistibly; unconsciously; deliberately; intentionally; effectively; laughingly; coolly; defiantly; inherently; naturally; awkwardly; shyly; incorrigibly; incurably; gracefully; attractively; typically; provokingly; openly; shamefully; clumsily; exquisitely; consciously; demurely; adorably; captivatingly; bewitchingly; reprehensibly; ardently; zealously.

CORAL

adjectives

pearl-hued; polished; blushing; branching; intricately-structured; imperishable.

verbs

abound in—; bedeck in—; deposit—; distribute—; employ—; fashion of—; fish for—; form—; inlay with—; market—; obtain—; polish—; procure—; secrete—; tint—; touch with—; trade—; trim with—; utilize—; value—; —attaches to; —covers; —crusts; —decorates; —flourishes; —ornaments; —grows; prize—.

CORD

adjectives

long; dangling; spinal; tense; frayed; durable; vital; hempen; subtle; sensitive; encircling; creaking; tangled; silver; penny; taut.

verbs

attach by—; bind with—; bite—; break—; cast away—; cut asunder—; draw—; gnaw at—; knit—; lengthen—; loop—; loose—; pull—; sever—; sterilize—; strengthen—; tie—; wind—; —binds; —snaps.

(See string, chain.)

CORDIAL

adjectives

best; exhilarating; warming; stimulating; animating; revivifying.

adverbs

eagerly; spontaneously; graciously; sincerely; warmly; heartily; genially; politely; courteously; unwontedly; ostentatiously; obviously; unusually; pleasantly; agreeably; indulgently; civilly; affectionately; devotedly; intimately; quietly; sympathetically; freely; openly; amicably; frankly; gallantly.

CORDIALITY

adjectives

genial; apparent; unexpected; pleasing; intoxicating; unaffected; great; condescending; businesslike; warm; utmost; loud; unofficial.

verbs

display—; doubt—; exhibit—; fraternize with—; greet with—; hate with—; lack—; resent—; respect—; return—; strive in—; —beckons; —bespeaks of; —cheers; —comforts; —exhilarates; —induces; —warms.

(See sincerity, ardor, affection.)

CORE

adjectives

inmost; putrefied; burning; endearing; festering; hidden; vibrant.

verbs

bore into—; cut from—; destroy—; dig to—; eat at—; extract—; feed upon—; fill to—; imbed at—; loosen—; pare to—; putrefy at—; remove—; rot at—; sheathe —; stab to—; surround—; taste to—; touch to—; wring to—; —contains; —disintegrates; —remains; discard—.

(See heart.)

CORK

adjectives

popping; large; leaking; obstinate; unbudging.

CORN

adjectives

military; starving; unsickled; sprinkled; bounteous; strengthening; bladed; scanty; lusty; golden; bruised; dry; pungent; waving; tall; ripening; thriving; rustling.

verbs

blast—; consume—; feed on—; furrow—; gather—; grind—; harvest—; husk—; market—; parch—; pluck—; prepare—; reap—; sack—; scatter—; shell—; shock—; sift—; sow—; stack—; store—; strip—; thrash—; tread out—; wither—; wreathe in—; —blossoms; —ripens; —rustles; —shoots up; —sustains; —sways; —waves.

(See cereal, grain.)

CORNER

adjectives

favorite; accessible; comfortable; cozy; tranquil; quiet; hintermost; secluded; sheltered; sunny; shaded; obscure; murky; isolated; removed; remote; vine-covered; grassy; theological; neglected; wickedest; overstuffed; coolest; tight; ill-smelling; outward; twisting; propitious; genteel; adjacent; inconspicuous; awkward; unexpected; arbored; hooded; hazardous; farthest; dim; dark; squalid; somber; cooperative; unpretentious; neighboring; idle.

verbs

bevel—; cower in—; crouch in—; droop in—; dwell in—; emerge from—; fall in—; hinge—; move to—; obscure in—; pray in—; round—; sharpen—; sit in—; sulk in—; sweep in—; tuck in—.

(See niche.)

CORNFIELD

adjectives

waving; swaying; sweltering; immense; dense; luxuriant; exuberant; discouraged; struggling.

CORNICE

adjectives

ornamental; hand-wrought; elaborate; top-heavy; scrolled; jutting; overhanging.

adjectives
generous; filled; flowing; bounteous; redolent; replete; plenteous; expansive; well-assorted; full-variety; assuring.

COROLLARY

adjectives
necessary; reasonable; definite; consequent; maintained; sustained; abrupt; inevitable; eventual; invariable.

CORONATION

adjectives
earthly; princely; poetical; seraphic; triumphant; glorious; climacteric.

CORONET

adjectives
vast; jeweled; braided.

CORPORAL

adjectives
insignificant; stately; impressive; awkward; imposing; exacting; domineering.

CORPORATION

adjectives
prosperous; civil; remarkable; bloated; modern; soulless; giant; moneyed; world-renowned; flourishing; dummy; tremendous; prominent; large.

verbs
bankrupt—; build up—; charter—; combine in—; constitute—; control—; dominate—; form—; found—; head—; join in—; outlaw—; preserve—; rule— unite in—; —advertises; —branches out; —develops; —employs; —grows; —undersells.
(See company, firm, association.)

CORPS

adjectives
diplomatic; detached; meager; well-tried; judiciary; terrible; executive; attacking; admirable; celebrated.

verbs
assign to—; captain—; command—; enlist in—; form—; join—; lead—; organize—; quarter—; station—; uniform—; —assembles; —attacks; —charges; —combats; —encamps; —marches; —patrols.
(See army.)

adjectives
poor; little; galvanized; sundried; good-looking; bleeding; dripping; handsome; desiccated; mangled; unrecovered; mutilated; disfigured; peaceful; lovely; charred; shriven; bloated.

verbs
animate—; attend—; bear—; bury—; collect—s; desert—; destroy—; discover—; disinter—; dismember—; dispose of—; drag for—; exhume—; grapple for—; hide—; hunt—; identify—; inter—; lament—; lay out—; mourn—; preserve—; recognize—; regard—; restore—; strew with—s; stumble on—; trip over—; view—; —decays; —decomposes; —disintegrates; —putrefies.
(See remains, carcass.)

CORPULENT

adverbs
unfortunately; incredibly; unhappily; incurably; comfortably; contentedly; distressingly; absurdly; ridiculously; ludicrously; lamentably; sadly; blithely; joyously; dangerously; heavily; gracefully; admittedly; funnily; unreasonably; incorrigibly; irremediably; complacently; mournfully; dramatically; complainingly.

CORPUSCLE

adjectives
bulbous; life-bearing; oxygen-supplying; scavenging; striving; surging; vitally-laden.

verbs
divide into—s; furnish with—s; increase—s; lower—s; study—; tear down—; —acts; —attacks; —bursts; —destroys; —envelops; —immunizes; —provides; —reproduces; —resists; —splits; —wanders about.

CORRAL

adjectives
rickety; shabby; flaming; palisaded; guarded; over-crowded; incarcerating; confining.

verbs
accept—; acknowledge—; devise—; allow —; authorize—; counteract—; direct—; follow—; fumble for—; invite—; judge—;

modify—; need—; offer—; perform—; print—; refuse—; rejoice in—; resent—; subject to—; substitute—; superintend—; —amends; —improves; —neutralizes; —revises.

(See punishment, discipline.)

CORRECT
adverbs
strictly; formally; fashionably; habitually; ordinarily; positively; uncompromisingly; rigidly; stiffly; insistently; absurdly; carefully; arrogantly; affectedly; ostentatiously; pretentiously; pompously; meticulously; punctiliously; dependably; scrupulously; infallibly; uncannily; disturbingly; unimpeachably; mathematically; insatiably; avidly.

CORRECT (v)
adverbs
painstakingly; constructively; helpfully; sufficiently; harshly; courteously; agreeably; adequately; reasonably; grammatically; infallibly; tactfully; rudely; crudely; curtly; sincerely; obnoxiously.

(See right, reprove.)

CORRECTION
adjectives
courteous; agreeable; autograph; strong; uranographical; adequate.

verbs
accept—; acknowledge—; advise—; allow —; authorize—; counteract—; direct—; follow—; fumble for—; invite—; judge—; modify—; need—; offer—; perform—; print —; refuse—; rejoice in—; resent—; subject to—; substitute—; superintend—; —amends; —improves; —neutralizes; —revises.

(See punishment, discipline.)

CORRECTNESS
adjectives
reasonable; superb; grammatical; irreproachable; lavish; infallible; tactical; rigid.

CORRELATE (v)
adverbs
mutually; definitely; significantly; properly; seriously; exactly; statistically.

(See correspond.)

CORRELATION
adjectives
definite; significant; proper; serious; exact; high; statistical.

CORRESPOND (v)
adverbs
confidentially; exactly; extensively; commonly; spiritually; relatively; curiously; prominently; obviously; superficially.

(See correlate.)

CORRESPONDENCE
adjectives
extensive; poetical; contraband; mutual; clandestine; spurious; noteworthy; seditious; mere; frank; subsequent; spicy; voluminous; lifelong; irresponsible; varied; intimate; diplomatic; heated; imperishable; amatory; objectionable; spiritual; copious; cipher; empirical; commercial; glorious; ungrammatical; vivacious; indiscreet; desultory; relative; curious; sympathetic.

verbs
answer—; conduct—with; enter into—with; establish—with; express—with; file—; influence—; interchange—; invite—; maintain—; manage—; neglect—; open—with; receive—; renew—; return—; safeguard—; treat—; —communicates; —enlightens.

(See communication, intercourse, letter.)

CORRESPONDENT
adjectives
humble; prominent; eavesdropping; sympathetic; flattered; international; energetic; special; active; reliable; diplomatic; warshy; persistent; punctilious.

CORRIDOR
adjectives
vaulted; angling; lengthened; spacious; interminable; golden; gloom-shrouded; dreamland; solitary; labyrinthine; tortuous; majestic; deserted; dusty; footworn; myriad (pl); curtained; endless; sloping; bleak; thronged; polished; resounding; murky; circular; concrete; black; eerie.

verbs
brighten—; clatter in—; cross—; darken—; glimmer through—; guard—; light—; line—; narrow—; pass through—; patrol —; run through—; scrub—; shuffle along—; stroll in—; sweep—; traverse—; watch—; widen—; —connects; —joins; —links; —opens into; —resounds with; —unites.

(See gallery, passage, hall.)

CORRIGIBLE

adverbs

submissively; meekly; humbly; wisely; sensibly; sensitively; fortunately; luckily; happily; easily; willingly; reasonably; intelligently; impressibly; moderately; actually; genuinely; tolerably; surprisingly; unusually; probably; presumably.

CORROBORATE (v)

adverbs

substantially; partially; reliably; fully; undeniably; undoubtedly; convincingly; authentically.

(See confirm, support.)

CORROBORATIVE

adverbs

wholly; entirely; partially; satisfactorily; scarcely; collusively; unfortunately; shamefully; unhappily; completely; circumstantially; exactly; generally; authentically; absolutely; warrantably; intrinsically; significantly; impressively; precisely; authoritatively; credibly; inferentially; terribly; fortunately; substantially.

CORRODE (v)

adverbs

perniciously; morally; detrimentally; psychically; permanently; fatally; irreparably; irremediably.

(See consume.)

CORROSIVE

adverbs

poisonously; terribly; destructively; irreparably; injuriously; harmfully; wastefully; hopelessly; dangerously; perniciously; rankly; banefully; detrimentally; disastrously; ruinously; irremediably; undoubtedly; seriously; unquestionably; positively.

CORRUGATION

adjectives

delicate; microscopic; faint; threadlike; fluted; transverse; deep; shallow; intense; decided.

CORRUPT

adverbs

incredibly; loathsomely; utterly; infamously; secretly; notoriously; officially; politically; perniciously; basely; generally; grossly; crassly; abominably; shamelessly; openly; admittedly; detestably; odiously; execrably; scandalously; outrageously; darkly; maliciously.

CORRUPT (v)

adverbs

flagrantly; undesignedly; dishonorably; profoundly; incredibly; wondrously; loathsomely; utterly; infamously; notoriously; perniciously; basely; generally; systematically; satanically.

(See spoil, debase.)

CORRUPTION

adjectives

chronic; mercenary; medieval; chill; unparalleled; dishonorable; profound; incredible; wondrous; loathsome; utter; infamous; hidden; unhappy; ensuing; glossy; political; foulest; civic; official; business; notorious; pernicious; base; miry; monetary; general.

verbs

attend with—; befoul with—; charge with—; conceive in—; cripple by—; defend from—; deliver from—; denounce—; fall into—; fatten on—; feast on—; infect with—; loathe—; perish in—; practise—; preserve from—; rot with—; sow—; subject to—; taint with—; —blemishes: —breaks up; —contaminates; —decomposes; —depraves; —despoils; —destroys; deteriorates; —disintegrates; —dissolves; —extends to; —perverts; —putrefies; —undermines; —violates.

(See perversion, pollution, demoralization, dishonesty, decay.)

CORSET

adjectives

armor-plated; confining; curve-restricting; corrective; breath-expelling; gusseted; hampering; health-destroying; torturing; ironclad; stout; tightly-laced.

verbs

discard—; divest of—; encircle in—; fit—; lace—; loose—; pierce—; squeeze into—; tighten—; —binds; —covers; —molds; —narrows; —protects; —shapes; —stiffens; —smooths; —strangles; —straps; —supports.

COST

adjectives

trifling; nominal; moderate; inflated; minimum; enormous; appalling; excessive; prodigious; huge; average; comparative; fearful; spiritual; low; relative; ultimate; superfluous; prevailing; exorbitant; administrative; prime; inevitable; extra; classical; operating; additional; insignificant; evident; initial; proper; increasing; outrageous; haulage; aggregate.

verbs
absorb—; avoid—; bear—; calculate—; defray—; forfeit—; heighten—; incur—; maintain—; omit—; prate about—; rate—; reckon—; shave—; shoulder—; spare—; whittle down—; —astounds; —piles up; —soars; —varies; recoup—.
(See price, expense, loss.)

COSTLY

adverbs
enormously; appallingly; unreasonably; fearfully; outrageously; unusually; exorbitantly; absurdly; gorgeously; unwarrantably; senselessly; wickedly; elegantly; flagrantly; unbelievably; extremely; inestimably.

COSTUME

adjectives
charming; brilliant; fetching; clever; intriguing; perfect; gorgeous; colorful; nativity; ornamented; elaborate; unconventional; indelicate; inappropriate; convict-like; native; flamboyant; ballet; bizarre; theatrical; local; allegorical; crepepaper; abbreviated; authentic; gala; billowing; stiff; characteristic; gaudy; lavish; fantastic; lugubrious; variegated; rhetorical; exquisite; daring; singular; mournful; picturesque; old-fashioned; grotesque; embroidered; quaint; antique; swagger; flattering; jacketed; capricious.

verbs
array in—; attire in—; change—; deck in—; design—; devise—; disguise in—; divest of—; don—; embroider—; fashion—; launder—; mend—; model—; parade in—; pose in—; recognize—; tailor—; trim—; —dazzles; —enhances; —interprets; —symbolizes.
(See dress, garment, clothing.)

COSY

adverbs
comfortably; snugly; luxuriously; entertainingly; pleasurably; gratefully; refreshingly; sweetly; hospitably; cheerfully; companionably; heartily; intimately; socially; easily; confidentially; agreeably; pleasantly; truly; curiously.

COT
(cottage)

adjectives
hurdled; weed-inwoven; chimneyed; cozy; overgrown; rose-thatched; sheltered; unpretentious; picturesque; ivied; tenanted.

COT
(bed)

adjectives
iron; lowly; downy; snug; sleep-forbidding; lumpy; miserable; untidy; tumbled.

verbs
erect—; pounce on—; slumber on—; throw oneself upon—; toss on—; —creaks.
(See bed, couch.)

COTERIE

adjectives
half-serious; playful; philosophical; select; exclusive; cabal; formidable; numerous; assembled.

COTTAGE

adjectives
thatched; attendant; prim; peaceful; coquettish; straggling; green-shuttered; nestling; squat; smoke-grimed; vine-clad; secluded; luxurious; abandoned; modest; dim-lit; enchanted; attractive; cozy; ancient; rustic; authentic; pert; suburban; eerie; mysterious; gray; small; tidy; weathered; low; lovable; dream; midget.

verbs
abide in—; adorn—; brighten—; construct—; dot with—s; dwell in—; erect—; forsake—; furnish—; inhabit—; lease—; lodge in—; rent—; repair to—; shade—; shelter—; —cheers; —invites; —s line; —secludes.
(See house, hut, cabin, lodge.)

COTTON

adjectives
speckled; glorified; striped; absorbent; excellent; lovely; sheer; snowy; feathery.

verbs
apply—; bale—; clean—; clothe in—; cultivate—; dye—; export—; gin—; market—; pack with—; pad with—; pick—; prey on—; print on—; raise—; saturate—; sterilize—; swab with—; thread—; twist—; wad—; weave—; wrap in—.
(See cloth, thread.)

COUCH

adjectives

frosty; hollow; narrow; unruffled; fiery; uncurtained; rushy; slippery; nuptial; tortured; stony; bridal; resplendent; sumptuous; festal; luxurious; be-tumbled; eastern; rude; restless; soft; broad; low; big; grassy.

verbs

clamber on—; defile—; ensconce on—; exalt —; fling upon—; lie on—; recline on—; rest on—; roll off—; sprawl on—; stretch upon—; stuff—; upholster—; —invites; —tempts.

(See bed, sofa.)

COUCH (v)

adverbs

cautiously; gracefully; flatteringly; tactfully; fastidiously; expressively; diplomatically.

(See express.)

COUGH

adjectives

bad; monotonous; persistent; sinister; low; irritable; slight; little; sharp; tremendous; sepulchral; muffled; hectic; distressing; hacking; dubious; apologetic; troublesome; churchyard; shattering; discreet; annoyed; wheezing; timid; dismal; hollow; smothered; premonitory.

verbs

affect with—; afflict with—; bark—; characterize by—; contract—; dose—; ease—; relieve—; stifle—; subdue—; suffer with—; —attacks; —disturbs; —drowns; —expels; —expresses; —indicates; —irritates; —persists; —strangles; —warns; —weakens.

COUGH (v).

adverbs

incessantly; huskily; heavily; significantly; discreetly; agonizingly; apologetically; monotonously; persistently; sinisterly; sepulchrally; muffledly; hectically; hackingly; distressingly; troublesomely; exhaustingly; wheezingly; dismally.

(See sound.)

COUNCIL

adjectives

local; advisory; official; ecclesiastical; church; intermediate; undecided; lawful; executive; general; private; separated; motley; municipal; imposing; irresponsible; elective; legislative; wicked; common; maiden.

verbs

admit to—; appoint—; assemble—; bar from—; call—; command—; dismiss—; dissolve—; frame—; gather—; hear—; herald—; sit in—; summon—; —advocates; —bans; —condemns; —decrees.

(See assembly, cabinet.)

COUNSEL
(advice)

adjectives

profound; wise; simple; humane; sane; sweet; gratuitous; anxious; politic; grave; external; insidious; weighty; sworn; heartsome; friendly; erroneous; paternal; vigorous; stout-hearted; medical; expert; wholesome; diffident; ill; intelligible; divided; prudent; crooked; unanimous; lenient; spiritual; senseless; psychiatric; valorous; sage; distracted; appealing; infernal; misguided; financial.

verbs

accept—; amend—; ask—; bestow—; condemn—; decree—; denounce—; engage—; enter—; examine—; execute—; follow—; hearken unto—; hint—; implore—; lack—; lend—; mislead—; plead—; prize—; propose—; receive—; reject—; seek—; speak—; take—; —displeases; —guides; —prevails; —sways; deliver—; forsake—.

(See advice, admonition, consultation.)

COUNSEL
(attorney)

adjectives

opposing; experienced; prosecuting; leading; clever; learned; adroit; defending; burly.

COUNSEL (v)

adverbs

earnestly; sternly; wisely; simply; humanely; sanely; gratuitously; gravely; insidiously; weightily; erroneously; paternally; medically; expertly; prudently; senselessly; leniently; sagely; misguidedly; financially.

(See advice, admonish.)

COUNSELOR

adjectives

civil; general; prime; private; prophetic; worthy.

verbs

confer with—; confide in—; empower—; entrust with—; heed—; praise—; retain—; —advises; —advocates; —charges; —cross-examines; —deliberates; —demands; —devises; —insinuates; —instructs; —orates; —perjures; —persuades; —pleads; —plots; —practises; —proposes; —recommends; —schemes; —summarizes; —sums up.

(See lawyer, attorney.)

COUNT

adjectives

grieved; amorous; fraudulent; noble; bona-fide; unctuous; bogus.

COUNT (*v*)

adverbs

definitely; clearly; confidently; silently; legally; partially; entirely; trustingly; basically.

(See compute.)

COUNTENANCE

adjectives

pleasing; amiable; romantic; happy; polite; reverent; smiling; reckless; oval; sturdy; ponderous; eager; grotesque; alert; lugubrious; dejected; long; solemn; rueful; pathetic; idiotic; dull; expressionless; vacant; haughty; frank; serious; gracious; open; thin; simpering; bleeding; battered; convulsed; astute; ingenuous; keen; livid; pale; roseate; dark; clouded; impassive; smug; bland; remote; soft; ordinary; homely; harsh; rumpled; haggard; worn; savage; dirty; hated; evil; stern; brazen; truculent; sullen; grim; frowning; fearful; holy; large; patient; mobile; eloquent; moist; heavy; serenest; rubicund; cheerful; blooming; half-startled; vivacious; menacing; sardonic; animated; colorless; tragic; beaming; austere; whimsical; withered; undue; shiny; discontented; speaking; princely; saturnine; meager; changed; wan; melancholy; reserved; humorous; tranquil; placid; commanding; ruddy; striking; interesting; uncomely; troubled; pallid; malignant; incensed; scandalized; shriveled; truthful; overcast; saddened; branded; joyous; swarthy; repulsive; priestly; unveiled; hueless; watchful; elevated; triumphant; graceful; angry; ferocious; meditative; villainous; mottled; scarred; bloated; tragic; independent; apathetic; spirit-sighted; benignest; puzzled; sculptured; resolute; angelic; household; horror-stricken; familiar; belligerent;

blandest; quiet; sleepy; florid; meek; distorted; philosophic; martial; infantile; undenoted; piteous; ashen; marble; courageous; plain; superior; flushed; sallow; rueful.

verbs

agitate—; avert—; behold—; bury—in; change—; darken—; distress—; flush—; lift up—; pale—; sadden—; scan—; study—; unmask—; wrinkle—; —beams; —glares; —glowers; —glows; —rebukes; —resembles; —sharpens; —shines; —wavers.

(See face, appearance.)

COUNTERFEIT

adjectives

gross; specious; notorious; worthless; plausible; ostensible; cheap; clever; apish; vulgar; ingenious; tawdry.

verbs

accept—; beguile with—; circulate—; discover—; expose—; fashion—; forge—; identify—; mark—; pass—; reproduce in—; scout as—; stamp—; transform—; withdraw—; work—; —assumes; —copies; —deceives; —defrauds; —differs; —disguises; —imitates; —pretends; —resembles; —simulates.

(See imitation, copy.)

adverbs

grossly; speciously; notoriously; worthlessly; obviously; cleverly; adroitly; deftly; perfidiously; deceptively; cunningly; craftily; unscrupulously; artfully; skilfully; dexterously; ingeniously.

COUNTERMAND (*v*)

adverbs

dramatically; severely; unjustly; legally; treacherously; unexpectedly; rebelliously; effectively.

(See contradict, oppose.)

COUNTERPART

adjectives

precise; painful; unworthy; institutional; modern; earthly; exclusive; emotional; feminine; dense; stooped; elaborate; shrunken.

COUNTRY

adjectives

beloved; enchanting; interesting; advanced; aristocratic; conservative; quaint; small; peaceful; diminutive; weak; underdeveloped; backward; crude; great; mesa; plain; broken; art-producing; flourishing; mountainous; picturesque; cultivated; unrevealed; continental; twilight; desolate; extensive; open; nightmare; exotic; surrounding; drowsy; outlying; inefficient; dun; solitary; barren; sterile; inaccessible; agricultural; wasted; undulating; fainting; familiar; roadless; pine; principal; competing; swampy; illustrious; standardized; gracious; adoptive; thinly-settled; mysterious; semi-pastoral; neighboring; ravaged; habitable; promising; useless; indissoluble; watered; wooded; unexplored; rolling; songless; primitive; modern; poor; parsimonious; unhappy; secluded; peaceful; virgin; unspoiled; exquisite; rugged; arid; dry; dead; deserted; prairie; landscape; imperiled; proud; timbered; droll; level; populous; self-lifted; alpine; respective; lonesome; prosperous; fresh; civilized; undiscovered; fragrant; invaded; overcrowded; thankless; farming; ungraded; hard; unoffending.

verbs
assault—; benefit—; bleed—; bombard—; conquer—; depart from—; desolate—; despoil—; devastate—; distress—; dominate—; dumbfound—; exploit—; fortify—; free—; govern—; honor—; invade—; lay waste—; love—; march through—; plunge —into war; ravish—; repair to—; reverence—; return—; rouse—; ruin—; saddle —; salute—; scurry about—; serve—; travel—; unify—; —endures; —protects; —seethes; —tries.
(See territory, region, nation, state, kingdom, republic.)

COUNTRYMAN

adjectives
seditious; unpolished; rapacious; unhappy; erring; well-fed; suffering; petitionary; humble.

verbs
aid—; appeal to—; elevate—; entertain—; greet—; invite—; mold—; repatriate—; school—; subject—; unite—; uplift—; welcome—; —men aid; —men assemble; —men congregate; —men gather; —men rally; — rejoices.
(See citizen, farmer, peasant.)

COUNTRYSIDE
adjectives
remote; lonely; rolling; charming; picturesque; gossiping; peaceful; pleasant; suburban.

verbs
beautify—; defile—; denude—; depict—; describe—; devastate—; dot—; eulogize—; familiarize with—; haunt—; invade—; landscape—; paint—; plague—; preserve—; prowl about—; range—; roam—; scour—; storm—; terrorize—; unite against —; —abounds with; —echoes; —teems with.
(See country, land, farm, region.)

COUPLE

adjectives
sober; strolling; loving; inseparable; devoted; curious; ill-assorted; delectable; stately; venerable; plump; amorous; retiring; worthy; withered; happy; struggling; prudent; moneyless; elderly.

verbs
attach—; betroth—; bless—; conjoin—; connect—; dance in—s; divide—; divorce—, engage—; eye—; fasten—; halve —; join—; knit—; leash—; link—; loose—; pair—s; rend—; sever—; split—; tie—; troop in—s; unite—; yoke—.
(See partners.)

COUPLE (v)
adverbs
inevitably; normally; abnormally; hideously; logically; shrewdly; generally; poetically.
(See connect, joint.)

COUPON
adjectives
detachable; hoarded; interest-bearing; neatly-clipped; prepayment; significant; worthless; separable.

verbs
bear—; cash—; clip—; count—s; date—; detach—; identify—; issue—; present—; rate—; register—; save—; snip—; value—; —certifies; —claims; —promises; —represents.
(See certificate, ticket.)

COURAGE
adjectives
splendid; noble; peerless; sublime; superb; ardent; joyous; proud; frank; quiet; simple; patient; dogged; hot; fiery; fighting; wavering; oozing; rising; swelling; stony; unwonted; creative; philosophic; hereditary; moral; ratlike; steadfast; careless; impetuous; indomitable; shamed; unsurpassed; blended; brute; unflinching;

matchless; rare; moral; desperate; pitiful; undiminished; reawakening; husbanded; conscious; exalted; tremendous; tried; reviving; immortal; reckless; abundant; intelligent; ancient; stubborn; personal; devoted; unshaken; passive; sublime; incredible; admirable; habitual; steady; romantic; undismayed; drooping; magnificent; foolhardy; hopeful; animal; exceptional; imperious; placid; dignified; conspicuous; stand-up; renewed; native; undaunted; obdurate; revolutionary; worn; sober; knightly; unfailing; adamantine; audacious; heroic; passive.

verbs
acclaim—; applaud—; blend with—; boast—; bolster—; cultivate—; daunt—; equip with—; exhibit—; extol—; gain—; imbue with—; instill—; lose—; maintain—; manifest—; muster—; plant—; pluck up—; raise—; reflect—; renew—; require—; reveal—; rouse—; screw up—; shake—; shatter—; stiffen—; stimulate—; stir up—; strain—; strengthen—; strut with—; summon—; take—; temper—; whistle up—; —droops; —endures; —flags; —mounts; —rises; —runs high.

(See bravery, fortitude, heroism, valor.)

COURAGEOUS
adverbs
dangerously; rashly; temperamentally; alarmingly; fantastically; foolhardily; colossally; breath-takingly; terribly; admirably; dramatically; notoriously; crazily; strangely; singularly; amazingly; recklessly; unbelievably; foolishly; romantically; heroically; youthfully; boyishly; disconcertingly; extravagantly; splendidly; nobly; superbly; proudly; quietly; patiently; doggedly; enduringly; morally; steadfastly; impetuously; consciously; stubbornly; devotedly; personally; sublimely; habitually; magnificently; calmly.

COURSE
(direction)
adjectives
splendid; admirable; sedate; sagacious; reasonable; sensible; serpentine; winding; sinuous; dizzy; desultory; twisting; circuitous; irregular; roundabout; sanguinary; rich; airy; resistless; dangerous; extreme; disagreeable; meteoric; advisable; straight; secretive; indefensible; devious; speedy; politic; heedless; prudent; fixed; middle; needful; unexplored; comfortable; unenvious; erratic; alternative; traditional; lenient; stupid; evil; dreary; fatal; mild; tortuous; endowed; systematic; peevish; indirect; frail; zigzag; feverish; rigorous; magnanimous; decisive; stony; immutable; desperate; exemplary; circular; natural; prescribed; luminous; unsilent; prolonged; headlong; initiatory; arduous; hereditary; extreme; strange; motley; conquering; skyward; unscrupulous; uniform; impetuous; tangential; precarious; profligate; tardy; basalt; tearless; curvilinear; lusty; coercive; orderly; ambiguous; long; shady; rapid; endless; wheeling; intermitting; destined; practical; furious; fair; bloody; normal; excellent; spherical; tranquil; doubtful; victorious; aimless; uneventful; peculiar; respective; contrary; irresistible; economical; diurnal; swift; precipitate; majestic; preparatory.

verbs
advance—; alter—; appoint—; bend—; blow off—; chart—; check— commend—; conceal—; condemn—; continue in—; cut off from—; decide on—; denote—; determine—; dictate—; direct—; disturb—; drift in—; embark on—; fix—; follow—; hinder—; hold—; illumine—; impede—; interrupt—; lead—; leave to—; map—; mark—; modify—; order—; outrun—; persevere in—; pervert—; plot—; praise—; pursue—; rebuke—; resolve on—; return to—; reverse—; run—; set—; settle on—; shape—; shun—; steer—; stem—; stick to—; subdue—; swerve from—; travel—; tread—; turn—; upbraid—; veer from—; wander off—; wing—; —fluctuates; —runs; —shifts; —winds; —zigzags.

(See direction, line, conduct.)

COURSE
(study)
adjectives
advanced; logical; pedagogic; technical; rigorous; difficult; condensed.

verbs
abandon—; change—; choose—; complete—; comprise—; conduct—; cut—; deride—; divide into—s; elect—; emphasize—; establish—; evaluate—; finish—; flunk (colloq.)—; follow—; fulfill—; initiate—; model—upon; pursue—; renew—; revise—; set up—; speed up—; —equips; —intends to; —prepares.

COURSE (v)

adverbs

tortuously; swiftly; windingly; circuitously; sinuously; irregularly; deviously; erratically; impetuously; tranquilly; irresistibly; precipitately.

(See travel.)

COURT
(enclosed yard)

adjectives

cobbled; gravelly; dusty; muddy; noisy; paved; tiled; rubbish-filled; neglected; sunless; gloomy; discouraging.

verbs

approach—; besiege—; build—; cross—; fill—; guard—; measure—; pace—; retire to—; roof—; shut up in—.

COURT
(law)

adjectives

vested; open; stuffy; instituted; hospitable; primitive; voluntary; spiritual; temporal; silent; petrified; superior; imperial; gloomy; papal; punctilious; murky; merciless; respectable; sapient; strict; corrupt; packed; primitive; competent; inferior; international; circuit; criminal.

verbs

adjourn—; adjudicate in—; beseech—; blockade—; call into—; coerce—; defy—; dismiss—; exploit—; hale into—; haul into—; liberalize—; override—; overrule —; pack—; petition in—; preside over—; reform—; rejuvenate—; remake—; resort to—; revamp—; strangle—; submit to—; sway—; tamper with—; vow in—; —awards; —convenes; —fines; —grants; —impounds; —judges; —recognizes; —renders a decision; —restrains; —upholds.

(See tribunal, judge.)

COURT
(royal)

adjectives

ceremonious; tavern; ostentatious; revolutionary; dilapidated; ecclesiastical; spacious; cloistered; envious; weedy; pontifical; assiduous; ambitious; magnolia; pompous; gloomy; admirable; sportive; untidy; dripping; bosky.

verbs

break up—; dispatch to—; entertain at—; establish—; fete at—; forsake—; hold—;

honor at—; join—; muster—; open—; present at—; preside at—; station at—; —flourishes; —glories in.

COURT (v)

adverbs

lustfully; assiduously; steadfastly; absurdly; ostentatiously; subtly; romantically; devotedly; shyly; masterfully; wildly; incessantly; languidly; impetuously.

(See attract, woo.)

COURTEOUS

adverbs

exquisitely; deeply; quietly; deferentially; perfunctorily; thoughtfully; extravagantly; tenderly; formally; naturally; dangerously; scarcely; scantily; traditionally; languidly; lazily; grimly; cordially; outwardly; genuinely; provokingly; gracefully; particularly; charmingly; gravely; loftily; meticulously; punctiliously; unfailingly; inherently; reverently; suspiciously; unexpectedly; especially.

COURTESY

adjectives

matchless; perfect; fine; gentle; exquisite; spiritual; deep; quiet; understanding; deferential; insinuating; decent; stately; dignified; perfunctory; thoughtful; extravagant; strained; serious; benevolent; stolid; dissembling; unclean; tender; formal; condescending; studied; national; natural; dangerous; official; gracious; scant; neighborly; poor; traditional; senatorial; caressing; straining; languid; special; grim; pressing; obvious; common; cordial; outward; intolerable; particular; graceful; charming; impersonal; doubtful; princely; international; oily; obliging; grave; last; lofty; wayward; patient; rigid; genuine; meticulous; unfailing; cold; automatic; southern; foreign; mickle; inherent; utmost; unusual; sacred; measured; novel.

verbs

accord—; air—; allow—; deny—; deserve—; disdain—; greet with—; imbue with—; misplace—; offer—; overstrain—; praise—; respect—; return—; scorn—; show—; strain—; stress—; temper with—.

(See politeness.)

COURTIER

adjectives

hovering; splendid; decrepit; senile; veteran; garrulous; subtle; shrewd; wary; pompous; vainglorious; sapient; extravagant; absolute; gallant; dissipated; smirking; expectant; avaricious; eulogizing; gaudiest.

COURTSHIP
adjectives
strange; careful; subtle; devoted; romantic; shy; masterful; wild; long; gradual; unhappy; customary; incessant; orthodox; languid; harassed.

verbs
attend in—; chaperon—; conduct—; delight in—; flatter during—; involve in—; lengthen—; pay—; pledge in—; prolong—; pursue with—; reject—; respond to—; revel in—; rush—; sway by—; verse in—; —ends; —expires; —flags; —softens.
(See friendship.)

COUSIN
adjectives
worthy; philological; valiant; capricious; stalwart; pious; enormous; gentle; favorite; distant; pallid; bloody; aristocratic; impecunious; remote; loutish.

COVE
adjectives
fascinating; shallow; sunlit; quiet; wooded; eddying; drowsy; snug.

COVENANT
adjectives
sacred; solemn; binding; common; perpetual; broad; eternal.

verbs
agree upon—; alter—; annul—; break—; confirm—; declare—; defile—; destroy—; draw up—; ensure—; enter into—; establish—; forsake—; invert—; mind—; obey—; profane—; record—; respect—; sever—; stabilize—; stipulate in—; swear to—; transgress—; void—.

COVER
adjectives
fairest; ephemeral; glazed; dewy; precious; enameled; soiled; coarse; garish; friendly; illuminated; excellent; practical; floor; protective; grassy; underdone; loathsome; reversible; detachable; flimsy; inmost; frail; weedy; sorry; luxuriant; ghostly; variegated; conical.

verbs
attach—; clap on—; form—; improvise—; lift—; ornament—; raise—; remove—;
screw on—; slide—on; take to—; wrap in—; —clothes; —conceals; —defends; —encloses; —envelops; —hides; —hinges; —overlays; —overspreads; —projects; —protects; —rests upon; —screens; —shelters; —surfaces.
(See case, lid, canopy, roof, spread, shelter.)

COVER (v)
adverbs
instinctively; adequately; grotesquely; insufficiently; inadequately; exhaustively; partially; garishly; protectively; loathsomely; flimsily; fraily; luxuriantly; conically.
(See conceal, hide.)

COVET (v)
adverbs
burningly; obviously; lustfully; jealously; bloodthirstily; sinfully; viciously; insanely; instinctively; economically; vulgarly; basely; detestably; infamously.
(See crave.)

COVETED
adverbs
eagerly; highly; passionately; enviously; wickedly; earnestly; excitedly; justifiably; sinfully; fondly; impatiently; keenly; hungrily; greedily; desirously; wishfully; wistfully; insatiably; avidly; madly; ambitiously; rabidly; invidiously; jealously; yearningly; ardently; curiously; fervently.

COVETOUSNESS
adjectives
excited; justifiable; bloodthirsty; unholy; inordinate; eager; rapacious.

COW
adjectives
serene; spotted; fat; milch; gentle; gaunt; fractious; ambitious; sad; mooing; contented.

verbs
breed —s; feed —s; herd —s; infect —; inspect —; raise —; slaughter —; test —; —s graze; —s huddle; —s leap; —s lumber; —s pasture; —s plod; —s roam; —s trail.
(See cattle, animal.)

COWARD
adjectives
thrasonical; arrant; vulgar; miserable; hulking; base; egotistic; contemptible; mannish; notable; faithless; detestable; abject; conscienceless; crafty; blaspheming; blatant; devout; infernal; pale; infamous.

verbs
bar —; brand as —; denounce —; designate as —; develop into —; intimidate —; ostracize —; proclaim —; regale —; reproach —; slay —; sneer at —; stigmatize as —; taunt —; — faints; — falters; — fears; — flees; — pales; — pleads; — protects; — shakes; — shies; — slanders; — slinks; — trembles; — whimpers; — yields.

COWARDICE
adjectives
empty; servile; moral; ineffable; vilest; abject; unexpected; palpable; strange.

verbs
banish —; brand with —; breed —; charge with —; conceal —; curb —; denounce —; display —; exhibit —; feign —; flaunt —; flee in —; hide —; loathe —; mark —; overcome —; protest —; rage at —; soil with ; vindicate of —, — defiles; — demoralizes; — shames.
  (See timidity.)

COWARDLY
adverbs
abjectly; unexpectedly; vilely; feebly; shamefully; suddenly; basely; miserably; contemptibly; hideously; detestably; abominably; pitiably; notoriously; infamously; secretly; pathologically; helplessly; hopelessly; embarrassingly; pathetically; irremediably; consciously.

COWBELL
adjectives
jangling; battered; brassy; silvery; tinkling; musical; matutinal; vespertine.

verbs
attach—; hang on—; respond to—; tie on—; —clangs; —clanks; —dangles; — directs; —echoes; —greets; —jangles; — suggests; —sways; —swings; —tinkles; —tolls.
  (See bell.)

COWBIRD
adjectives
attending; herd-following; hoarsely-commenting; perching.

verbs
—crowds out; —gurgles; —intrudes; — warbles.
  (See bird.)

COWBOY
adjectives
elemental; daredevil; equestrian; bright; crooning; weather-beaten; saddle-hardened; hard-riding.

verbs
employ—s; quarter—s; —brands; —breaks horses; —breaks loose; —charges; —corrals; —drives; —herds; —lassoes; — mounts; —punches cattle; —ropes; —rounds up; —rustles; —stampedes; —trails; — whoops; —wrangles.

COWER (v)
adverbs
gloomily; weakly; shrinkingly; ignobly; basely; abjectly; servilely; palpably; pusillanimously; spinelessly.
  (See crouch, squat.)

COY
adverbs
timidly; diffidently; shyly; modestly; retiringly; bashfully; blushingly; humbly; nervously; demurely; primly; pleasantly; adorably; uneasily; engagingly; gracefully; captivatingly; delightfully; sweetly.

COYOTE
adjectives
gaunt; night-prowling; howling; sneaking; sly; wary; pusillanimous.

verbs
frighten by—s; trap—s; —s abound; —s attack; —s bark; —burrows; —s carry off; —cries; —destroys; —digs; —gallops; — hides; —howls; —infests; —inhabits; — laps; —lurks; —mangles; —prowls; — ranges; —screams; —scurries; —slinks; —sneaks; —s surround; —wails; —yaps; —yips; —yowls.
  (See animal.)

CRAB
adjectives
roasted; reluctant; soft-shelled; luscious; invading; semi-transparent; side-walking; scurrying; sodden; swiftly-moving.

verbs
broil—; capture—; catch—; devil—; roast —; steam—; —claws; —crawls; —weighs.

CRABBED
adverbs
bitterly; unnecessarily; unwarrantably; vexatiously; sourly; perplexingly; natural-

ly; innately; horribly; detestably; abominably; persistently; obnoxiously; unpleasantly; constantly; permanently; incurably; unreasonably; intractably; stubbornly; plaguedly; discourteously; rudely; uncivilly; tactlessly; coolly; pertly; obtrusively; snarlingly.

CRACK
(blow)

adjectives
sharp; smart; mannish; punitive; admonitory; disciplinary; surreptitious; vindictive; solar plexus; resounding.

CRACK
(fissure)

adjectives
shallow; minute; widening; seamy; ragged; fearful; devastating.

verbs
close—; fill—; peer through—; seal—; seep through—; shine through—; squeeze into—; stretch out—; trace—; widen—; —breaks; —bursts; —damages; —endangers; —gapes; —opens; —separates; —weakens; —widens; —yawns.
(See chasm, gap, opening.)

CRACKLE

adjectives
snapping; faint; sickening; brittle; cheery; warning; ominous; starchy; silken.

CRACKLE (v)

adverbs
cheerily; fiercely; industriously; faintly; sickeningly; furiously; threateningly.
(See sound.)

CRADLE

adjectives
tiny; earthen; equatorial; leafy; stony; hollow; procreant; clumsy; swaddling; unostentatious; animal-skin; rocking.

verbs
attend—; bar—; carry in—; decorate—; deck—; discard—; dream in—; fall from—; jig—; lull in—; mount—; nurture in—; repose in—; rest in—; rock—; shelter in—; sleep in—; snatch from—; stifle in—; sway—; swing—; unveil—; watch over—.
(See bed.)

CRADLE (v)

adverbs
comfortingly; endearingly; maternally; cozily; domestically.
(See bed.)

CRAFT
(boat)

adjectives
stately; leaky; weatherly; ponderous; ghostly; frail-looking; multitudinous (pl); tidy; ill-equipped; clumsy; unseaworthy; aging; tiny; speedy; graceful; small; trim; little; slow; toiling; disabled; staunch; makeshift; slender; strange-looking; waterlogged; ridiculous.

CRAFT
(skill)

adjectives
hellish; inexhaustible; vulpine; consummate; purloined; mechanical; extraordinary; manual; devilish; elfin; earthly; astonishing; slippery; subtle; inveterate; intervening; peaceful; ancient; coy; crude; indolent; pleasurable; strange-looking; diabolical; contentious; waterlogged.

verbs
apply—; beguile with—; counterfeit—; devote to—; display—; exhibit—; follow—; learn—; master—; perform with—; pursue—; skill in—; study—; trick with—; verse in—; —deceives; —occupies; —thrives.
(See skill, trade.)

CRAFTINESS

adjectives
uncanny; cold; weird; deft; astounding; practiced.

CRAFTSMAN

adjectives
expert; skilled; master; trained; seasoned; meticulous; experienced; sincere; able; erudite; polished; thoroughgoing; wandering; sedentary.

CRAFTSMANSHIP

adjectives
rare; unusual; exquisite; delicate; centuries-old; superb; authentic; progressive; skilled; custom.

CRAFTY

adverbs
suavely; subtly; urbanely; artfully; designingly; dangerously; commercially; alarmingly; suspiciously; extremely; singularly;

profoundly; unexpectedly; deftly; astutely; inscrutably; habitually; warily; cautiously; wisely; invariably; politically; deliberately; shamefully; fiendishly; expertly; horribly.

CRAG

adjectives

stupendous; bare; massive; far-distant; gray; lofty; inaccessible; steep; tottering; yellow; weathered; sustaining; overhanging; dense-wooded; fantastic; impregnable; rocky; mountain; shaggy; slippery; shrubless; jagged; splintered; accumulated; bald; jutting; morselled; whinstone; descendent; beetling; giant-snouted; lichen-covered; dizzy; gaunt; lordly; shredded; precipitous; storm-washed; airy.

verbs

ascend—; batter—; beat—; blow from—; catch on—; clasp—; cling to—; expose—; peer from—; precipitate from—; scale—; scan—; storm—; strand on—; swing from—; topple from—; —hinders; —juts out; —menaces; —slopes; climb—.
(See cliff, rock.)

CRAM (v)

adverbs

completely; reputedly; fully; intellectually; enormously ;swellingly; hoggishly; bestially.
(See crowd, squeeze.)

CRAMP

adjectives

agonizing; distressing; hindering; muscle-fettering; paralyzing; torturing; violent.

verbs

affect with—; alleviate—; cause—; contract with—; ease—; massage—; predispose to—; produce—; rack with—; seize with—; take with—; —agonizes; —attacks; —benumbs; —constricts; —extends; —incapacitates; —knots; —numbs; —pains; —paralyzes; —pinches; —restrains; —stiffens; —tortures.
(See pain.)

CRANE
(bird)

adjectives

eerie-sounding; frog-questing; mournful; shadowy; ungainly; voracious; eternally-wading.

verbs

—alights; —antics; —circles; —clowns; —croaks; —dances; —drifts down; —

evades; —hops; —leaps; —skips; —stalks over; —trumpets; —wades; —whoops.
(See bird.)

CRANK

adjectives

ridiculous; complete; usual; veritable; unenviable; decided.

CRANK (v)

adverbs

laboriously; sweatingly; difficultly; stiffly; energetically; spiritedly.
(See turn.)

CRASH

adjectives

ominous; incessant (pl); reverberating; thunderous; dazzling; successive (pl); hideous; simultaneous (pl); fearful; confused; heavy; blinding; railroad; grinding; tremendous; almighty; tumultuous; occasional; mighty; light; rolling; heart-shaking; impending; vicious; loud; fatal; resounding; dull; heavy; smashing; distant; disastrous; terrific; rending; ear-splitting; dangerous; sudden; hollow; rhythmic; splintering.

verbs

avert—; avoid—; escape—; produce—; witness—; —breaks; —bursts; —crushes; —dashes; —resounds; —ruins; —shatters; —shivers; —shocks; —smashes; —splinters; —thunders.
(See noise, collapse, ruin, failure.)

CRASH (v)

adverbs

sickeningly; haphazardly; ominously; incessantly; reverberatingly; thunderously; simultaneously; heavily; grindingly; tumultuously; rollingly; fatally; resoundingly; disastrously; terrifically; rendingly; ear-splittingly; hollowly; splinteringly.
(See collapse, smash.)

CRASSNESS

adjectives

unutterable; despicable; undescribable; hopeless; irritating; inane.

CRATER

adjectives

extinct; ancient; gaping; active; grass-covered; weed-grown; smoking; exhausted; submerged; cindery; cuplike; thundering; roaring; seething.

verbs

fly over—; form—; run from—; —boils; —bubbles; —discharges; —disgorges; —ejects; —emits; —erupts; —forms; —furrows; —hardens; —pours out; —roars; —rumbles; —seethes; —simmers; —smokes; —spouts; —throws up.

(See volcano.)

CRAVAT

adjectives

unknotted; voluminous; unkempt; nice; well-chosen; correct; becoming; flowing; resplendent.

verbs

admire—; color—; display—; knot—; purchase—; purvey—s; spot—; tie—; —adorns; —blazes; —encircles; —harmonizes; —muffles; —ornaments; —protects; —shields; —shocks.

(See tie, necktie.)

CRAVE (v)

adverbs

irresistibly; humbly; instinctively; insatiably; inordinately; intensely; earnestly; unappeasingly; incessantly; uncontrollably; violently; persistently; abnormally; vaguely; maternally; erotically; spiritually; insensately.

(See desire, want.)

CRAVEN

adjectives

stricken; confessed; marked; cowering; fearful; cringing; crass.

CRAVING

adjectives

intense; earnest; unappeasable; eager; incessant; uncontrollable; violent; persistent; tenacious; unbeautiful; spasmodic; frivolous; abnormal; maternal; unsatisfied; mysterious; endless; forbidden; sporadic; instinctive; premature; erotic; insatiable; cruel; vague; mastered; spiritual; insensate; intermittent.

verbs

annul—; appease—; conceal—; dispatch—; ease—; frown on—; harbor—; indulge—; master—; quell—; repress—; resist—; satisfy—; still—; stir up—; sublimate—; —overpowers; —seizes.

(See passion, appetite, hunger, desire, longing, leaning, entreaty.)

CRAWL (v)

adverbs

interminably; sluggishly; softly; wearily; tortuously; bestially; dejectedly; sorrowfully; toilingly; determinedly.

(See grovel, creep.)

CRAZE

adjectives

fashionable; dull; amusement; midsummer; newest; freakish; passing; temporary.

verbs

adopt—; denounce—; despise—; develop into—; fancy—; follow—; ignore—; inaugurate—; overcome—; succumb to—; —affects; —attracts; —dies; —fades; —flashes; —seizes; —spreads.

(See mania, caprice.)

CREAK (v)

adverbs

stridently; irritatingly; monotonously; continually; disturbingly; intermittently; rhythmically.

(See sound.)

CREAKING

adjectives

strange; cautious; imperceptible; massive; ear-teasing; inaudible.

CREAM

adjectives

rich; pure; oily; stainless; intellectual; vanishing; rejuvenating; penetrating; superb; cosmetic; dulcet; soothing; massage; unguent.

verbs

add—; anoint with—; apply—; beat—; churn—; convert—; dilute—; filter—; form—; gather—; mature—; mix—; moisten with—; pasteurize—; purify—; rub in—; separate—; serve—; skim—; sour—; spread—; stir—; sweeten—; whip—; —foams; —froths; —greases; —mantles; —rises.

CREAMERY

adjectives

spotless; inviting; appetizing; efficient; germ-proof; hermetic; ship-shape.

CREASE (v)

adverbs

deftly; readily; disgustingly; offensively; intolerably.

(See wrinkle.)

adverbs

obviously; artistically; unconsciously; independently; unexpectedly; painstakingly; artificially; fantastically; specially; fancifully; complicatedly; permanently; forcibly; harmoniously; uniquely; individually; abstractly; brilliantly; imaginatively; inferiorly; gigantically; intellectually; sublimely; beneficently; ceaselessly; figuratively; literally.

(See make, produce.)

CREATION

adjectives

huge; fantastic; special; foreordained; artistic; fanciful; witty; reflective; grave; complicated; primal; permanent; sculpturesque; forcible; surrounding; psychological; brute; harmonious; unique; individual; abstract; brilliant; dormant; pedigreed; rhythmical; coordinating; visible; ungalaly; imaginary; human; various; wide-reaching; evolutionary; artificial; immediate; divine; patented; rejuvenated; pendulous; previous; inferior; gigantic; poetical; violent; splendid; serio-comic; aboriginal; false; aerial; memorable; intellectual; infinite; approved; bountiful; special; sublime; beneficent; genial; warm; inanimate; travailing; catastrophic.

verbs

abolish—; behold—; condemn—; contradict —; counterfeit—; curse—; grasp—; illustrate—; improve—; inspire—; mar—; understand—; —collapses; —reflects.

(See world, universe.)

CREATOR

adjectives

responsible; unworthy; rival; benevolent; conscious; omnipotent.

verbs

betray—; consecrate to—; eulogize—; honor —; praise—; revere—; spring from—; worship—; —animates; —decrees; —divines; —empowers; —fashions; —grants; —moulds; —ordains; —originates; —produces; —reveals; —rules; —works.

(See God, inventor.)

CREATURE

adjectives

rare; likable; upstanding; honest-looking; lovable; admirable; brilliant; luscious; docile; glorious; winning; fine; great-hearted; fascinating; gentle; amiable; demure; marvelous; shy; thin; shortsighted; anemic; limitary; tiny; spiritless; forlorn; obscure; slipshod; ravishing; frugal; despicable; smitten; archaic; perennial; little; dull; yellowish-white; faithful-looking; foolish; struggling; furry; rational; perfect; smooth; pretty; plausible; absurd; doll-like; finite; delicate; sentimental; divine; web-footed; insensible; industrious; drugging; stricken; nasty; ill-bred; inconsequent; voracious; carnivorous; graceful; effeminate; singular; crawling; eyeless; fictitious; overflowing; threadbare; fantastic; bewildering; amphibious; pusillanimous; sensitive; hideous; perverse; desperate; inquisitive; silly; helpless; dependent; brutal; faithful; charming; loathsome; formidable; clear-eyed; harmless; fiery; frail; overgrown; carnal; phlegmatic; unhappy; purest; plainest; kind-hearted; magnanimous; artless; predatory; ever-interesting; nervous; timorous; blunt; pleasant; clambering; monstrous; indigenous; affectionate; sensible; cordial; loving; sweetest; dearest; stealthy; gregarious; insignificant; decrepit; two-fold; strenuous; easy; anxious; poor; unteachable; writhing; tortured; piteous; strange; romantic; sickly; faded; kindly; stout; untidy-looking; flowery; harlequin-like; ridiculous; glorious; foul; infinitesimal; hapless; reasonable; amendable; worthy; horned; love-maddened; coarse-grained; unwashed; flexible; noxious; hairless; diminutive; beastly; poor-spirited; unpolished; veiled; healthy-looking; governmental; discouraged; mendacious; precious; paltry; good-humored; vile; sagacious; dismal-looking; vagrant; nomadic; ferocious; primest; stupid; exquisite; grotesque; exotic; miserable; intellectual; irascible; insufferable; silk-clothed; obliging; goodly; inarticulate; new-made; natural; crooked; shameless; fawn-eyed; gigantic; bewitching; non-aggressive; fickle; thoughtful; grave; wistful; tolerable; human; fearful; sincere; cherubic; yearling; dainty; tallowy; slight; girlish; dawdling; beautiful; ravenous; injudicious; timid; sinful; driven; sweated; magnificent; doe-eyed; clinging; frenzied; heartless; ferocious-looking; impudent; fairest; mongrel; dying; wasted; vivid; earnest; grasping; sylphlike; fine-looking, gorgeous-looking; pretty; dark-eyed; spirited; handsome; elegant; dazzling; furtive; crafty; scheming; wily; baffling; uncanny; wise; cunning; uncouth; spineless; affrighted; gentle; meek-spirited; weak; weary; luckless; poor; humble; long-legged; gaunt; gangling; angular; ragged; emaciated; loose-jointed; lanky; cadaverous-faced; weird; strange; odd-looking; stodgy; porkish; kind; plump; flabby; huge; muscular; poised; self-confident; vital; energetic; big; forthright; hearty; blithe; buxom; sprightly; flippant; self-assured; capricious; sad; ugly; humdrum; stunted; strong-willed; stubborn; obstinate; queer-looking; humpbacked; passive; senseless; idiotic; silliest-looking; star-eyed; sinuous; beady-eyed; slim; bird-like; yellow-striped; half-wild; shy; feathered; migratory; feline; screeching; aquatic; lone; marsh; biting; crawling; forest; pathological; merry; wild; thankless; winged; troublesome; bloodthirsty; mangy-looking; broken; disintegrated; dirty; disheveled; unshorn; emaciated; filthy; ragged; detestable; menacing; primitive; worthless; undesirable; vicious-looking; tarnished; distressing; careless; wretched; half-blind; tottering; imaginary; mythical; fastidious; talkative; plain; huddle; two-legged; newly-evolved; vehement; gaudy; unvapory.

verbs
cage—; curse—; despise—; distress—; eye—; feed—; hunt—; hurt—; kill—; loathe—; oppress—; slay—; tame—; torture—; trap—; —echoes, —senses; —stirs; —walks.
(See being, animal.)

CREDENCE
adjectives
qualified; ready; partial; definite; unwarranted.

CREDENTIALS
adjectives
required; college; personal; time-tested; intellectual; valid; sufficient.

verbs
accept—; arm with—; bear—; check—; display—; doubt—; falsify—; forge—; forward—; honor—; investigate—; lose—; present—; provide with—; sign—; —attest to; —entitle; —reveal.
(See testimonial.)

CREDIBLE
adverbs
deeply; implicitly; actually; presumably; reliably; soberly; conceivably; certainly; assuredly; possibly; positively; impressively; fairly; reasonably; plausibly; probably; speciously; potentially; peradventurously; haply; obviously; unreservedly.

CREDIT
adjectives
unlimited; tentative; threatened; retirement; weakening; unquestioned; everlasting; cooperative; implicit; highest; fullest; personal; moral; comparative; small; unfailing; exhausted; practical; rescinded; domestic; long-term; foreign; extended.

verbs
accept—; accumulate—; ascribe to—; bolster up—; claim—; deserve—; expand—; extend—; favor with—; honor—; obtain —; redound—; rehabilitate—; secure—; share—; strain—; warp—.
(See confidence, trust, faith, prestige, influence.)

CREDIT (v)
adverbs
conveniently; ignorantly; tentatively; everlastingly; implicitly; fully; personally; morally; unfailingly; practically; locally; formally; unhesitatingly.
(See believe.)

CREDITABLE
adverbs
highly; altogether; admirably; becomingly; deservedly; duly; richly; splendidly; notably; eminently; conspicuously; remarkably.

CREDITOR
adjectives
importunate; inexorable; sourest; bloody; persistent; detaining; unfeeling.

verbs
avoid—; cajole—; dismiss—; escape—; evade—; hold off—; pay—; satisfy—; settle with—; —s rise; —assails; —demands; —depends; — descends upon; —s dwindle; —forces; —harasses; —importunes; —menaces; —stands; —sues; — threatens; —trusts.

CREDULITY
adjectives
good-natured; popular; heretical; human; great; unfathomable; reluctant; common; ignorant; curious; scornful; emotional; unshakable; grave; innocent.

verbs
appeal to—; assume—; attack—; bless with—; clothe in—; disguise—; invite—; lose—; preserve—; produce—; register—; remove—; strain—; tax—; transcend—; value—; —accepts; —aids; —astounds; —expires.
(See faith, belief.)

CREDULOUS
adverbs
good-naturedly; reluctantly; instantly; readily; gullibly; foolishly; thoughtlessly; unthinkingly; boyishly; eagerly; enthusiastically; fondly; blindly; innocently; gravely; stupidly; superstitiously; idiotically; laughably; guilelessly; artlessly; ingenuously; childishly; ardently; ignorantly.

CREED
adjectives
everlasting; common; rigid; narrow; respective (pl); noble; vulgar; delicious; confused; fashionable; senseless; rebellious; especial; ancient; healthful; soulless; hopeful; dominant; creative; polemic; cynical; procreative; strange; primeval; adopted; universal; heavenly.

verbs
accept—; adopt—; advance—; alter—; bind to—; displace—; fix—; follow—; formulate—; instill—; institute—; learn—; scoff at—; shake—; support—; subscribe to—; tangle—; teach—; —decays; —summarizes.
(See belief, faith.)

CREEK
adjectives
brawling; briny; winding; log-jammed; silvery; yearning; cheery; echoing; tortuous; emerald; dry; dirty; ice-fringed; dimpled; swollen; fresh-water; unruly; hidden; muddy; scanty; cool; pebbled; tiny; whispering; roaring.

verbs
bridge—; dam—; explore—; fish—; follow—; navigate—; paddle down—; span—; wade in—; —babbles; —bends; —branches off; —dances; —drenches; —gurgles; —harbors; —irrigates; —joins; —overflows; —penetrates; —sings; —twists; —widens; —winds.
(See brook, stream.)

CREEP (v)
adverbs
slyly; mechanically; noiselessly; timidly; cautiously; blindly; stealthily; piteously; meekly; invisibly; mysteriously; ultimately.
(See crawl, grovel.)

CREEPER
adjectives
blooming; luxuriant; spiky; parasitic; interlacing; indigenous; deciduous; poisonous; woody.

CREPE
adjectives
sheer; rayon; tailored; trim; crinkly; clinging; webby.

CRESCENDO
adjectives
rending; sudden; deafening; wild; gradual; muffled.

CRESCENT
adjectives
silvery; paling; sardonic; delicate; sharp; black; stormy.

verbs
adopt—as; attach—; carry—; carve—; decorate with—; design—; employ—; form —; mold—; ornament with—; rest upon—; shape—; trace—; —embellishes; —fades; —glimmers; —signifies; —symbolizes.

CRESS
adjectives
matted; mantling; pungent; tasty; crisp; fresh.

CRESSET
adjectives
blazing; burning; hanging; pendent; swinging; polished; shining; glowing.

CREST
adjectives
ferny; higher; snow-streaked; silver; flamelike; fire-tipped; glittering; ancestral; blazing; upturned; haughty; snowy; kindled; polished; gory; uncontrolled; crimson; golden; bald; towering; glimmering; turret; flaming; stainless; overhanging; compassed; princely; confused; proud; slide-scarred; knife-edged; cloven; tranquil; hissing; lofty; whitening; windy; cockatoo; mountain; jagged; distant.

verbs
affix—; bear—; brighten—; dance on—; elevate to—; erect—; fix—; helmet with—; let fall—; mount to—; plate with—; recognize—; seal with—; strike—; —bristles; —crowns; —droops; —ornaments; —plumes; —signifies; —symbolizes; —undulates; —waves; —wreathes.

(See comb, crown.)

CREVICE
adjectives
barren; rock; narrow; winding; snug; sunken; distant; mysterious.

CREW
adjectives
rollicking; skulking; pestilent; fiendish; motley; vulgar; lachrymose; revolutionary; enthusiastic; marauding; rebellious; persevering; well-organized; worthless; mumbling; rough-and-ready; scribbling; numerous; humorous; back-biting; unhallowed; horrid; dilapidated; whining; besotted; stammering; dispirited; orientallooking; strange; gaunt; merry; mutinous; gay; adventurous; rugged; coarse-fibred; indigent; stout; burly; handy; unruly; sleepy; ground; marooned; insubordinate; changing; sullen; annihilated; rascal; tiring; nefarious; madcap; banished.

verbs
address—; arouse—; assemble—; augment —; banish—; bestir—; captain—; capture —; command—; consult—; control—; curse—; direct—; dissemble—; engage—; enlarge—; exclude—; gather—; hire—; order—; organize—; oversee—; quarter—; rescue—; rule—; —accomplishes; —boards; —conspires; —embarks; —mans; —mutinies; —rebels; —revels.

(See crowd, company.)

CRIB
adjectives
lace-ruffled; comfortable; safeguarded; padded; wicker; swinging; basket.

CRICKET
adjectives
lusty; creaking; humming; chirping; drumming; incessant.

verbs
plague with—s; —chirps; —fiddles; —rubs; —sings; —shrills.
(See insect.)

adjectives
cherished; wretched; horrible; nameless; consummate; atrocious; conspicuous; inhuman; futile; prevailing; heinous; juvenile; unmilitary; sexual; solitary; hideous; unpardonable; darkest; inexplicable; absolute; flagitious; imputed; dreadful; reiterated; malicious; enormous; grave; legalized inexpiable; foul; dastardly; monstrous; locutionary; godless; devastating; cloistered; subsequent; gory; imaginable; heathenish; organized; earthly; unknowing; successful; petty; blackest; heartcrazing; flagrant; diversified; gloomy; aboriginal; perfect; crowning; greedy; calculated; cunning; unnatural; nefarious; infamous; barbarous; abominable; obscene; grisly; violent; gruesome; scandalous; brutal; fiendish; cowardly; ungrateful; hair-raising; unpunished; unsolved; unprevented; serious; professional; modern; vocal; attempted; conceivable; pitiful; incredible.

verbs
abet—; accuse of—; allege—; alleviate—; assail—; atone for—; avenge—; avoid—; betray—; breed—; cancel—; charge with —; check—; cloak—; condone—; contemplate—; contrive—; cover—; detect—; diminish—; divulge—; eradicate—; expiate —; extenuate—; fatten on—; grapple with —; hatch—; impute—to; involve in—; mark with—; perpetuate—; plot—; predispose to—; prosecute—; punish—; reconstruct—; restrain—; sentence for—; smash—; sully with—; suspect of—; taint with—; uncover—; urge—; witness—; —flourishes; —stains; —thrives.

(See offense, misdeed, sin, wrong.)

CRIMINAL
adjectives
irreclaimable; petty; condemned; roving; professional; notorious; dangerous; vicious; utter; conscienceless; piratical; organized (pl); runaway; calculating; confirmed; willful; visible; timorous; skulking; bloody; blackjacked; ruthless; hypothetical; potential; clever; perfect; experienced; frenzied; hardened; desperate; miserable; unfortunate; parricidal; adult; cinematographic; self-confessed; grotesque; incipient; enterprising; habitual; elusive; courageous; fleeing; daring.

verbs

apprehend—; arrest—; charge—; close in on—; coddle—; convict—; detain—; develop into—; harbor—; infest with—s; involve—; lash—; mark—; parole—; penalize—; point out—; pounce upon—; prosecute—; punish—; rehabilitate—; restrain—; retrieve—; round up—; sentence —; shame—; thwart—; —commits; —s congregate; —defies; —habituates; — haunts; —indulges; —plots; —reforms; —repents; —rifles; —schemes; —stalks; —swindles.

(See culprit, prisoner.)

adverbs

shockingly; outrageously; brutally; grossly; basely; iniquitously; despicably; abominably; pestilentially; accursedly; damnably; diabolically; infernally; noxiously; vilely; virulently; preposterously; corruptly; atrociously; viciously; profligately, scurvily, scandalously; heinously; fiendishly; incorrigibly; irreclaimably.

CRIMSON

adjectives

deepest; angry; dull; burning; fever; richest; russet; clear; glowing; spiritual.

CRINGE (v)

adverbs

humbly; servilely; slavishly; menially; brokenly; defeatedly; grotesquely; timorously.

(See cower, fawn.)

CRINKLE

adjectives

crisp; pleasant; laughing; traitorous; effacing; merry; mischievous.

CRIPPLE

adjectives

neglected; wealthy; awful; hopeless; deformed; grotesque; drab; grizzled; rag-wrapped; whining.

CRIPPLED

adverbs

hopelessly; helplessly; pitiably; deplorably; tragically; permanently; temporarily; crookedly; slightly; terribly; fearsomely; incredibly; pathetically; pitifully; cruelly; horribly; brutally; deliberately; curiously; strangely; sadly; painfully; dreadfully; indescribably.

CRISIS

adjectives

mighty; momentous; great; tremendous; supreme; fearful; serious; grave; domestic; legislative; intense; emotional; economic; agricultural; unprecedented; spiritual; psychological; political; industrial; national; moral; recurring; financial; banking; favorable; naive; interminable; contemporary; unquiet; distressing; religious; commercial; deplorable; revolutionary; majestic; peculiar; tragical; approaching; memorable; nervous; over-estimated; exciting; sternest; rapid; diplomatic; noisy; striking; desperate.

verbs

aggravate—; avert—; confront with—; cope with—; face—; handle—; improve—; lead up to—; mark—; precipitate—; provoke—; reach—; suffer—; toil over—; weather—; —besets; grips; grows, —indicates; —occurs; —passes; —wears off.

(See emergency, exigency.)

CRISP

adverbs

delicately; crunchily; frailly; deliciously; tastily; neatly; concisely; curtly; pithily; crumbly.

CRISPNESS

adjectives

buttery; crunchy; blanched; pleasant; refreshing; airy; invigorating; icy.

CRITERION

adjectives

economic; post-factum; inadequate; surer; whimsical; corresponding.

verbs

admit as —; allow as —; award on —; base on —; conclude by —; decide by —; distinguish as —; establish —; estimate by —; gauge by —; judge by —; mark —; measure by —; present —; produce —; reach —; represent —; test by —.

(See standard, rule, law, test.)

CRITIC

adjectives

superficial; facetious; astute; dramatic; generous; literary; interpretative; level-headed; penetrating; routine; quibbling; shortsighted; ingenious; unsparing; carping; exacting; fastidious; contemporary; music; unperceived; unknown; crabbed; inimitable; bitter; theatrical; vigorous; judicious; inimical; celebrated; fair-minded; aggressive; arrogant; opinionated; over-subtle; ignorant; self-constituted; amateur; thoughtful; passionate; clumsy; educational; creative; penetrating; textual; profound; robust; vicious; haughty; persistent; radical; alert; fearless; toilsome; impartial; snarling; invidious; discriminating; unfriendly; surly; grave; primitive; captious; malevolent; merciless; conscientious; competent; sincere; pure; serious; sober; sanguine; enthusiastic; tolerant; disinterested; keen; ablest; authoritative; master; indisputable; first-rate; leading; eminent; noted; outstanding; caviling; jaundiced; befuddled; sarcastic, cynical; pious; caustic; hostile; pertinacious; belligerent; gloomy; ill-disposed; lethargic; incipient; typical; exaggerating; blatant; incessant; thoroughgoing.

verbs
confound —s; silence —s; — appraises; — assails; — asserts; — attacks; — belittles; — blames; —s chatter; — disparages; — exalts himself; — gauges; — gloats; — interprets; — inveighs; — lauds; — opposes; — praises; — pronounces; — rails; — shuns; — snipes at; — weighs.
(See judge, censor.)

CRITICAL
adverbs
facetiously; astutely; generously; penetratingly; ingeniously; unsparingly; exactingly; fastidiously; crabbedly; bitterly; vigorously; judiciously; aggressively; ignorantly; thoughtfully; clumsily; gracelessly; creatively; viciously; haughtily; persistently; constructively; alertly; fearlessly; courageously; impartially; gravely; captiously; mercilessly; malevolently; conscientiously; keenly; authoritatively; tolerantly; ably; caustically; disagreeably; obnoxiously; unpleasantly.

CRITICISM
adjectives
adverse; favorable; brief; hostile; inductive; malevolent; shallow; argumentative; satisfactory; eerie; comparative; dramatic; querulous; harsh; exacting; withering; reverential; hazy; reprobative; numberless (pl); carping; sophistical; irritating; mordant; metaphysical; trenchant; depressing; cold; merciless; absurd; captious; comprehensive; loud; eager; detailed; negative; audible; severe; social; benevolent; injurious; rational; gentle; satiric; ungenerous; prejudiced; spasmodic; unintended; vigil-

ant; frank; dispassionate; scathing; watchful; cheery; acute; unsparing; sweeping; philosophical; loving; implicit; impartial; outside; caustic; sustained; literary; praiseless; biting; stimulating; musical; acrimonious; premature; qualifying; energetic; stupid; reflected; skeptical; unkind; affected; epigrammatic; candid; careful; intelligent; lucid; searching; healthy; salutory; expert; constructive; justified; corrective; witty; ironic; acrid; barbed; endless; lengthy; copious; vehement; stormy; murderous; libelous; bitter; faultfinding; peculiar; slurring; boorish; small-minded; sullen; stringent; factional; journalistic; partisan; aesthetic; presumptuous; subjective; implied; snobbish; retrogressive.

verbs
base — on; bow to —; chafe at —; dispense with —; distort —; draw —; elicit —; endure —; evoke —; expose to —; heap —; hurl —; indulge in —; justify —; pour forth —; provoke —; refrain from —; squelch —; stifle —; subject to —; welcome —; — cites; — confounds; — marks; — stirs; — takes root.
(See censure, judgment, examination.)

CRITICIZE (v)
adverbs
adversely; editorially; harshly; constructively; scoffingly; constantly; insidiously; fiercely; severely; rationally; malevolently; querulously; witheringly; reprobatively; irritatingly; trenchantly; depressingly; mercilessly; captiously; comprehensively; injuriously; impartially; caustically; acrimoniously; prematurely; energetically; candidly; stupidly; intelligently; searchingly; expertly; correctively; ironically; acridly; copiously; vehemently; libelously; slurringly; boorishly; presumptuously; subjectively; snobbishly.
(See censure, reprove.)

CRITIQUE
adjectives
elaborate; exquisite; instructive; poetical; preliminary; commendatory.

CROAK
adjectives
prophetic; monotonous; booming; empty; bellowing; rusty; harsh; discordant.

CROAK (v)

adverbs

tunelessly; roughly; discordantly; inauspiciously; prophetically; monotonously; sinisterly; nocturnally.

(See sound, complain.)

CROCKERY

adjectives

coarse; crudely-shaped; garishly-decorated; homely; humble; over-glazed; paunchy; porous.

verbs

advertise —; bake —; collect —; crack —; craze —; decorate —; display —; exhibit —; glaze —; mould —; paint —; place —; polish —; rattle —; shelve —; smash —; store in —; unearth —.

(See porcelain, china.)

CROCODILE

adjectives

rabbit-footed; slow-living; armored; slimy; stealthy; tearful; preying; slithering; death-dealing.

verbs

— ambles; — bathes; — cracks; — crunches; — crushes; — dives; — floats; —s herd; — invades; — lashes; — slithers; — snaps; — snorts; — splashes; — suns itself; — swims; — whips its tail.

(See reptile.)

CROCUS

adjectives

fatted; lusty; blooming; gay; adventurous; winter-defying; pioneer; spring-bannered.

CRONE

adjectives

withered; gaunt; old; haggard-visaged; dried-up.

CRONIES

adjectives

familiar; odious; bridge-playing; coarse-mouthed; illiterate; race-track; philandering.

CROOK

adjectives

dirty; filthy; loathsome; ordinary; obsequious; terrible; artificial; international; sneaking; whitecollar; capable.

CROOKED

adverbs

unstably; sinuously; jaggedly; darkly; indirectly; implicitly; covertly; cunningly; craftily; strategically; profoundly; diplomatically; shiftily; bafflingly; bewilderingly; insidiously; unscrupulously; disgracefully; perfidiously; treacherously; infamously; contemptibly; scurvily; disloyally.

CROON

adjectives

cheerful; plaintive; melodic; heart-touching; depth-sounding; hollow-ringing; weird; savage.

CROON (v)

adverbs

soothingly; harmoniously; comfortingly; pleasingly; gently; pathetically; sentimentally; romantically; maternally; cheerfully; plaintively; melodiously; touchingly.

(See sing.)

CROP

adjectives

catch; fateful; encouraging; anticipated; bumper; unmanufactured; ungathered; varied; abundant; sprouting; diminished; mildewed; uncertain; agricultural; plenteous; bountiful; scanty; customary; fast-ripening; phenomenal; profitable; huge; staple; immense; luxuriant; tender; supreme; worthless; superior; lavish; fodder; teeming; unfailing; annual; stunted; newly-planted; increased.

verbs

affect —; blast —; blight —; devastate —; devour —; harvest —; injure —; pluck —; produce —; reap —; salvage —; trample —; yield —; — fails; — flowers; —matures; — rustles; — shrivels; — sprouts; — withers.

(See harvest, fruit.)

CROSS

adjectives

customary; blazoned; glimmering; absolving; shameful; abhorred; momentary; reeking; planted; sunken; pastoral; radiant; scarlet; ebony; patient; cold; marble; enameled.

verbs

award —; bear —; curse —; deliver one to —; deny —; embrace —; endure —; erect —; fight for —; glory in —; hallow —; idolize —; kneel before —; mark with —; nail to —; plant —; sign with —; take up —; trust in —; uphold —; vow by —; wear —; worship at —; — leads; — saves; — signifies; — symbolizes.

adverbs

petulantly; perpetually; unreasonably; habitually; disagreeably; sullenly; morosely; gloomily; unbearably; pathetically; tragically; shockingly; waywardly; restively; glumly; crustily; cantankerously; brutally; sternly; forbiddingly; needlessly; graceless-/ly; unpardonably.

CROSS (v)

adverbs

freely; laterally; obliquely; boldly; accommodatingly; rapidly; devoutly; diagonally; inevitably; cautiously.

(See pass.)

CROSS-EXAMINATION

adjectives

merciless; extraordinary; lengthy; wearisome; pointless; inquisitive; three-cornered.

CROSSING

adjectives

memorable; deserted; careful; transpolar; smooth.

CROSSNESS

adjectives

accustomed; habitual; infectious; morbid; ascetic; acid; bitter; morose.

CROUCH (v)

adverbs

menacingly; sullenly; squatly; tensely; servilely; odiously; threateningly; alertly; aggressively.

(See squat, cringe.)

CROUPIER

adjectives

impassive; efficient; tight-lipped; spidery; inscrutable; grim.

CROW

adjectives

wandering; feeble; poaching; carrion; saucy; heavy-winged; boisterous; amazing; bold; startled; predatory; noisy; ragged; shrill.

verbs

domesticate —; hood —; snare —; tame —; throttle —; — annoys; — caws; — clamors; — claws; — fights; —s flock; — harms; — imitates; — isolates; — quarrels; —ravages; — robs; — roosts; — scours; — shrieks; —s swarm; — thieves; — uproots; — wrangles.

(See bird.)

CROW (v)

adverbs

triumphantly; derisively; harshly; loudly; feebly; saucily; boisterously; boldly; shrilly; monotonously; repeatedly; discordantly.

(See vaunt, brag.)

CROWD

adjectives

discordant; noisy; sportive; yelling; cosmopolitan; shouting; odd; oppressive; silent; rushing; eager; gaping; interminable; boisterous; passing; thick-pressed; promiscuous; voluble; madding; unreasonable; dark-robed; mercenary; miserable; streaming; heartless; hurrying; trembling; unabashed; mingled; surrounding; luckier; gossipy; village; horrid; gloomy; strangling; sympathetic; whispering; assembled; moving; motley; curious; excited; talented; discharged; enthusiastic; threatening; starry; tremendous; seething; scurrying; supper-hungry; still; gentlemanly; jocund; vulgar; dull-faced; self-controlled; dispersing; distinguished; colorful; indiscreet; serried; unfeeling; anxious; quiet; applauding; swirling; weary; malicious; tumultuous; buffeting; raucous; unnumbered; scattered; unhesitating; thickening; impatient; baser; patriotic; good-sized; advancing; watching; awful; jeering; gesticulating; angry; dense; outraged; idle; giddy; well-bred; debauching; surging; thinned; pitying; excited; laughing; unworthy; worthwhile; picturesque; ignoble; cheering; fickle; gazing; prostrate; reformed; exulting; incoming; thoughtless; visionary; sacrificial; virile; idealistic; helpless; ribald; wild-scrambling; myriad-tongued; thronging; dignified; merry; spiteful; purblind; suffering; brilliant; animated; somber; preoccupied; gay; drunken; handsome; glittering; friendly; well-behaved; orderly; healthy; complacent; awed; admiring; acclaiming; morbid; reverent; interested; sober-faced; tranquil; devout; convivial; attentive; hilarious; half-tipsy; roistering; thirsty; rollicking; mirthful; merry-making; congenial; jubilant; good-natured; vivacious; whimsical; smart; sophisticated; well-dressed; expensive; screaming; obstreperous; hooting; queer; enormous; hushed; tatterdemalion; hard-looking; tough; suspicious; quick-acting; realistic; bargaining; heterogeneous; listening; waiting; strolling; murmuring; chattering; milling; swarming; elbowing; lurching; shoving; swaying; eddying; writhing; turbulent; hustling; indifferent; bustling; hostile; challenging; troublesome; pestering; victorious; restless; blood-mad; quarrelsome; frenzied; frightened; wavering; panicky; bibulous; bourgeois; casual; residential; exultant; modern; ubiquitous; famished; impoverished; gaudy; vigorous; powerful; unreflective; increasing; critical; slow-moving; thawing.

verbs
bewilder —; bore —; cater to —; disassociate from —; disperse —; draw —; excite —; harangue —; key up —; plunge into —; steal among —; tower above —; wait with —; — assembles; — clusters; — collects; — dissolves; — gapes at; — gathers; — groans; — hoots; — jams; — jeers; — jostles; — lionizes; — mills about; — mutters; — packs into; — pours from; — presses; — retreats; — scurries; — seethes; — speculates; — stares; — storms; — surges; — swarms; — swerves; — throngs; — wavers.
(See multitude, throng, mob, horde.)

CROWD (v)
adverbs
uncomfortably; amiably; perplexingly; alertly; warmly; thickly; odiously; abundantly; desperately; discordantly; oppressively; boisterously; promiscuously; maddeningly; volubly; unreasonably; horridly; curiously; enthusiastically; vulgarly; colorfully; indiscreetly; tumultuously; buffetingly; raucously; impatiently; gesticulatingly; giddily; animatedly; somberly; complacently; admiringly; acclaimingly; morbidly; roisteringly; hilariously; rollickingly; mirthfully; congenially; vivaciously; obstreperously; suspiciously; listeningly; murmuringly; chatteringly; turbulently; indifferently; bustlingly; victoriously; exultantly; ubiquitously.
(See swarm.)

CROWN
adjectives
silken; crimson; golden; glittering; olive; thorny; kingly; giddy; accursed; treacherous; fruitless; glorious; admired; tufted; starry; molten; embellished; hemispherical; woven; brilliant; rejected; glistening; fadeless; celestial; hoary; clustering; bloomless; flaming; imperial; dread; piercing; blessed; laurel; tiny; jeweled; caplike; magnificent; discarded; pointed; long-expected; unused.

verbs
anoint —; aspire to —; bear —; bequeath —; blemish —; bless —; cast away —; claim —; conform to —; corrupt —; deliver

up —; deprive — of; deprive of —; disgrace —; disown —; encompass by —; gild —; inherit —; lay aside —; lift off —; merit —; offer —; pawn —; profane —; raise —; ransom —; refuse —; reject —; remove —; renounce —; repossess —; resign —; revere —; sear —; serve —; shave —; spurn —; tear off —; wear —; weave —; wreathe —; yield to —; yield up —; — flourishes; — rules; — shines.

CROWN (v)
adverbs
visibly; fittingly; spiritually; goldenly; glitteringly; gloriously; brilliantly; celestially; imperially; magnificently.
(See complete.)

CROWNING
adjectives
glorious; gorgeous; colorful; victorious; jubilant.

CRUCIFIX
adjectives
great; gaunt; ghastly; little.

CRUCIFY (v)
adverbs
miserably; horribly; barbarically; brutally; fiendishly; morally; literally; figuratively.
(See punish.)

CRUDE
adverbs
crassly; gracelessly; harshly; stiffly; awkwardly; barbarously; offensively; ignorantly; bashfully; intolerably; unluckily; baldly; unfortunately; offensively; coarsely; roughly; shiftlessly; quaintly; unsophisticatedly; ill-manneredly.

CRUDENESS
adjectives
honest; blunt; crass; vulgar; elemental; unsavory; natural; primitive.

verbs
abhor —; affect —; alter —; breed —; characterize by —; convert — into; correct —; cure of —; develop —; display —; exhibit —; loathe —; lose —; produce —; recoil from —; regard —; silence —; temper —; work —; — alarms; — annoys; — detracts; — shocks.

CRUDITY
adjectives
jocular; stylistic; frontier; obvious; careless; obsolete; sincere.

adjectives

blood-smeared; organized; unsparing; abysmal; complacent; fiendish; devouring; inhuman; strange; reckless; super-rogatory; amiable; wanton; lawless; innate; stern; execrable; ruthless; tyrannic; sinister; sovereign; hellish; ignorant; atrocious; thriving; intolerable; apparent; abominable; hideous; savage; existing; peculiar; dull; unimaginable; indescribable; unnecessary; foul; barbarous; malevolent; official; violent; devastating; seeming; narrow; incestuous; lecherous; unavenged; social; callous; irrational; insensate; instinctive; moody; excessive; insidious; unbridled; merciless; monotonous; shameful; needless; brutal; persistent; increasing; petty; continuous.

verbs

batter with —; boast of —; delight in —; display —; dispose to —; encounter —; exhibit —; govern with —; impose —; inflict —; manifest —; mask —; master with —; mitigate —; perpetuate —; practise —; prompt —; protect from —; provoke —; repent—; repress—; reproach for—; revel in —; revenge —; subject to —; suffer from —; tolerate —; yield to —; — distresses; — oppresses; — pains; —surpasses.

(See brutality, tyranny.)

adjectives

intrepid; involuntary; world; enchanting; southern; successful; rest-giving; romantic; difficult; strenuous; notable; delightful; varied; premier; attractive; wonderful.

verbs

anticipate —; direct —; embark on —; enjoy —; entertain on —; escort —; leave on —; navigate —; observe on —; operate —; organize —; plan —; promote —; relax on —; sail on —; travel on —; — accommodates; — attracts; — consists of; — embraces; — enthralls; — envelops; — furnishes; — includes; — inspires; — invigorates; — provides; — rests; — thrills.

(See voyage, journey, trip.)

adjectives

vigilant; protected; submersible; mighty; sojourning; tourist-laden.

adjectives

occasional; forsaken; paltry; stale; mouldy; hoarded; grudging; life-sustaining.

verbs

accept —; beg —; break into —s; brush away —; catch —; cover with —s; dress with —s; dry —; fall into —s; finger into —s; gather —s; mouth —s; pick up —; prepare with —s; reduce to —s; step on —; sweep away —s; thicken with —s; throw away —s; toss —s to.

CRUMBLE (v)

adverbs

coarsely; gradually; completely; totally; disastrously; fatally; finely; unexpectedly; thoroughly; partially.

(See decline, decay.)

CRUMBLING

adjectives

gradual; complete; ear-splitting; total; erosive; timely; pathetic.

CRUMPLE (v)

adverbs

viciously; rudely; roughly; destructively; pathetically; carelessly; hideously; slatternly.

(See smash.)

CRUNCH

adjectives

distinct; audible; sickening; clear; sharp; decisive; monotonous.

CRUNCH (v)

adverbs

hungrily; viciously; furiously; bestially; rapaciously; eagerly; greedily; distinctly; audibly; sickeningly; sharply.

(See eat.)

CRUSADE

adjectives

perennial; lifesaving; insane; emotional; organized; humanitarian; noble; pathetic; anti-crime.

verbs

assemble—; bless—; champion—; direct—; endorse—; engage in—; expedite—; inspirit—; instigate—; launch—; lead—; oppose—; organize—; plan—; prepare for —; support—; wage—; —advances; —

campaigns; —conquers; —crushes; —defeats; —defends; —endeavors; —realizes;
—revives; —succeeds; —undertakes; —
wrestles with.

(See enterprise, movement, warfare.)

CRUSADE (v)

adverbs
vaingloriously; actively; religiously; peren-
niàlly; insanely; emotionally; nobly; pathetically; gallantly; zealously; victoriously;
inspiredly.

CRUSADER

adjectives
gallant; overzealous; anti-vice; young;
medieval; valiant.

CRUSH (v)

adverbs
perfectly; deliberately; tenderly; softly;
completely; painfully; carelessly; nervously; rigorously; spiritually; overwhelmingly;
finally.

(See smash.)

CRUST

adjectives
favoring; scanty; stony; overpublicized;
upper; fruitful; flaky; external; treacherous; shallow; brittle; well-browned; flimsy;
hardened; fluted.

verbs
beg for—; break—; coat with—; compose
—; contract into—; cover with—; deposit
—; dissolve—; dry into—; feed—; form—;
gnaw—; harden into—; hide under—; line
with—; mass into—; munch—; penetrate
—; puncture—; render—; scrape—; season
—; slice—; —crumbles; —forms; —hardens.

(See casing, shell.)

CRUTCHES

adjectives
badly-worn; needed; helpful; tapping;
supporting; betraying; stout; taped.

CRY

adjectives
raucous; feeble; painful; melancholy; guttural; heartsick; cornered; shrill; sharp;
solitary; importunate; hoarse; choking;
satirical; earnest; furious; thrilling; unanimous; pathetic; protesting; strident; peevish; battle; human; broken; triumphant;
warning; petulant; wailing; plaintive;
bootless; simultaneous; responsive; similar;
distinct; suppressed; avenging; defiant;
boastful; inspiring; drunken; pitiful; long-
drawn; careless; passionate; supreme;
piercing; unending; desolate; discordant;
vociferous; prayerful; exultant; half-suppressed; half-demoniac; funeral; answering; terrified; inharmonious; impious;
aspiring; yapping; plausible; premature;
inevitable; harsh; ugly; shivering; stifled;
strangled; joyous; wild; unearthly; despairing; clamorous; sharp; hissing; death-
dealing; maniacal; piteous; amazed; comfortable; weird; impassioned; startling;
rallying; unceasing; solitary; untenable;
delirious; admiring; wrathful; everlasting;
universal; prevailing; farthest-sounding;
shuddering; inarticulate; gurgling; long;
half-hysterical; dirgelike; loud; incoherent;
perpetual; distressing; wrenching; sobbing;
agonizing; brief; happy; smothered; full-
mouthed; drawling; peculiar; fearful;
fierce; ribald; far-resounding; odious; ineffable; continuous; mocking; supplicating;
terrible; patriotic; noisy; dismal; expostulating; welcoming; ghastly; mutual; exulting; jubilant; ecstatic; joyful; delighted;
gladdening; naive; inspiriting; wistful;
stimulating; high; soft-noted; insistent;
clarion; squeaky; rasping; clangorous;
heart-chilling; babyish; heartbroken; dismayed; solemn; whimpering; breathless;
stricken; important; frenzied; frantic;
gulping; muffled; wanton; insulting; contemptuous; groaning; derisive; murder;
fiendish; horror-stricken; anguished; spiteful; barbaric; sighing; yearning; low; appealing; hysterical; entreating; ominous;
involuntary; frightened; haunting; elfin;
sporting; familiar; asinine; wheezy; wordless; destructive; fluttering; incessant;
scattered; hurtling; penetrating; vibrating;
soul-shaking; dolorous; mournful; provocative; revolutionary; multitudinous (pl).

verbs
echo—; flee at—; force out—; give ear to—;
hearken to—; heed—; let slip—; mock—;
raise up—; repeat—; roar—; take up—;
utter—; voice—; wring—from; —arouses;
—awakens; —bursts forth; —disturbs; —
fills; —jars; —resounds; —reverberates;
—rises; —scares; —shatters; —wanes.

(See outcry, exclamation, scream, shriek,
howl, lamentation, wail, plaint, yell.)

CRY (v)

adverbs
discordantly; querulously; reproachfully;
jealously; hoarsely; earnestly; inarticulate-

ly; heartbrokenly; dishearteningly; flippantly; vehemently; enthusiastically; persistently; piteously; sternly; passionately; jovially; tempestuously; haughtily; indignantly;
incoherently; irritably; energetically; contemptuously; exultantly; reprovingly; ringingly; gaily; disconsolately; unrestrainedly;
tauntingly; feverishly; peremptorily; tantalizingly; falteringly; mirthfully; spontaneously; sympathetically; stormily; unanimously; petulantly; wailingly; drunkenly;
passionately; piercingly; agonizingly; vociferously; jubilantly; ecstatically; inspirit-
ingly; solemnly; spitefully; sighingly; hysterically; involuntarily; ominously; wordlessly; incessantly; dolorously; yearningly;
bitterly; inwardly.
  (See wail, weep.)

CRYING
adjectives
harsh; endless; irrational; awkward; bitter; remorseful; stormy; furious.

CRYPT
adjectives
mournful; venerable; quiet; mossy; dismal; mouldy; time-honored; ancestral.

CRYPTOGRAM
adjectives
magic; involved; difficult; mysterious; puzzling; baffling; tortuous.

CRYSTAL
adjectives
shimmering; transparent; pellucid; celestial; strange; fluffy; slow-frozen; gleaming;
stinging; flashing; ice; diaphanous; needle-
like; lambent; glittering; perilous; quartz;
tempting; tremulous; fragile; long; jagged;
tiny; irregular.

verbs
adorn with—; aggregate into—; clear—;
concentrate in—; congeal into—; delve
for—; dig out—; discover—; dissolve—;
drip—s; freeze into—; gaze into—; mass
into—; melt—; quaff—; search—; —adheres to; —beams; —darkens; —shines;
—sparkles.
  (See glass.)

CUB
adjectives
self-willed; young; modest; helpless;
clumsy; awkward; closely-watched.

CUCKOO
adjectives
cowled; domineering; echoic; masterful;
unmaternal; melancholy; ravenous; usurping; vehement.

verbs
—calls; —chucks; —deposits; —ejects; —
flits; —mocks; —shrills; —shies away;
—surveys; —wheels.
  (See bird.)

CUDDLE (v)
adverbs
cozily; snugly; comfortably; lovingly; fondly; maternally; gently; affectionately;
tenderly.
  (See nestle.)

CUDGEL
adjectives
short; heavy; thick; bloody; bludgeoning;
murderous.

verbs
attack with—; awe with—; beat with—;
belabor with—; brandish—; combat with—;
cross—s; defend with—; resist—; scar
with—; shake—; smite with—; strike with
—; swing—; take up—; terrify with—;
wave—; wield—; —descends; —fells;
—stuns.
  (See club.)

CUE
(billiards)
adjectives
ash-wood; leather-tipped; nicely-balanced;
pliant; well-seasoned; tapering; graceful.

verbs
aim—; bridge—; chalk—; crack—; draw
with—; indicate with—; point—at; rest—
on; retip—; score with—; skill with—;
slide—; tip—; —slides; —bends; —slips;
—strikes; —warps.

CUE
(braid)
adjectives
carefully-braided; bristling; coiled; limp;
genteel; powdered; protruding; scrupulous.

verbs
braid into—; clip—; cut—; exhibit—; fashion—; plait—; powder—; roll—; tie into
—; twist into—; —dangles; —grows.

CUE
(signal)

adjectives

cryptic; answering; guiding; secret; suggestive; politic; strategic.

verbs

answer—; begin on—; enter on—; forget —; heed—; hint with—; mind—; miss—; muff—; pronounce—; remember—; speak —; signal with—; wait for—; whisper—; —arrives; —comes; —enables; —warns.
(See hint, suggestion, intimation.)

CUFF
(sleeve)

adjectives

sheer; possible; transparent; organdy; starched; immaculate; chafing; frilled.

CUISINE

adjectives

local; national; appetizing; exceptional; world-famous; perfect; excellent; tempting; distinctive; wholesome; unsurpassed; distinguished; tasty; matchless; splendid; finest; delicious; unrivaled; superlative; renowned.

CULMINATION

adjectives

over-ripe; dizzy; fitting; probable; ultimate; untimely.

verbs

ascend to—; attain—; bask in—; crown—; develop to—; display—; encourage—; establish—; form—; herald—; look forward to—; reach—; rise to—; speed—; take pride in—; urge—; —occurs; —takes place.
(See end.)

CULPRIT

adjectives

wretched; miserable; shameful; apprehended; confessed.

CULT

adjectives

capricious; ridiculed; emotional; diverse; aesthetic; sweet; love; sentimental; idiotic; nudist; moribund; moral; eminent; logical; exclusive; religious; bizarre; unconventional; secret; sinister.

verbs

adopt—; denounce—; despise—; develop—; embrace—; inaugurate—; join—; organize—; perpetuate—; succumb to—; take

up—; —affects; —attracts; —believes; — devotes; —fades; —interests; —practices; —spreads; —worships.
(See belief, system, ritual.)

CULTIVATE (v)

adverbs

diligently; extensively; sedulously; passionately; intensively; freely; generously; assiduously; fastidiously; systematically; intellectually; profitably; continuously.
(See work.)

CULTIVATION

adjectives

proper; intensive; fictional; continuous; hot-house; forced.

CULTIVATOR

adjectives

prosperous; sensible; practiced; apt; skilled; trained.

CULTURE

adjectives

snob; diligent; literary; rational; spiritual; high; musical; splendid; unprecarious; profound; virile; brilliant; superior; natural; substantial; polite; simple; harmonious; pronounced; untrammeled; mellow; older; mature; age-old; traditional; borrowed; inherited; acquired; vulgar; inferior; dangerous; national; warmed; raw; wide; universal; abundant; vast; considerable; intellectual; indigenous; cruel; pagan; autonomous; alien; civil; rounded; religious; exhilarating; prescriptorial; petty; nascent; curious; active.

verbs

absorb—; acquire—; assimilate—; attain—; borrow—; disparage—; fetter—; flout—; imbibe—; lack—; perpetuate—; propagate —; relegate—; retard—; shed—; spread —; stifle—; —broadens; —enhances; —enlightens; —improves; —polishes; —raises; —refines.
(See refinement, enlightenment, education.)

CULTURE (v)

adverbs

laboriously; diligently; naturally; abundantly; indigenously; spiritually.

CULTURED

adverbs

elaborately; ostentatiously; laboriously; diligently; painfully; highly; profoundly;

brilliantly; naturally; inherently; innately; widely; curiously; delightfully; consciously; obviously; unquestionably; tastefully; genuinely; unaffectedly; bookishly; aimlessly; methodically; scholastically; generally.

CUMBERSOME
adverbs
bulkily; ponderously; gravely; awkwardly; ungracefully; embarrassingly; unmanageably; vexatiously; impossibly; clumsily; massively; stiffly; grotesquely; fantastically; heavily.

CUNNING
adjectives
giddy; diabolical; cordial; tough; stalwart; gentle; sly; fiendish; premeditated; malicious; devilish; peculiar; infinite; instinctive; unconscious; revengeful; stealthy; artful; swift.

verbs
acquire through—; apply—; beguile with—; calculate with—; cheat with—; check—; cover—; deceive by—; devise by—; display—; dispose to—; employ—; entrap by—; excel in—; exercise—; exhibit—; expose—; frame with—; impart—; puff up with—; school in—; trick by—; work—; —hides; —deceives.
(See craft, deceit, trickery, skill, ingenuity.)

adverbs
diabolically; slyly; fiendishly; maliciously; adroitly; cleverly; adeptly; artfully; subtly; insidiously; dangerously; commercially; extremely; astoundingly; profoundly; deliberately; sagaciously; cautiously; carefully; invariably; habitually; incurably; astutely; customarily; ordinarily.

CUP
adjectives
bitter; enameled; verdant; tulip-tinted; silver; red; lacquer; lordly; gold-encrusted; pink-sprigged; intoxicating; crowning; delicate; inebriating; consecrated; lustrous-petaled; sapphire; thin; large; thimble-like; quivering; graceful; odd; vicious; little; demure; coveted; fragile; impersonal; hygienic; invigorating.

verbs
burnish—; drain—; drink—; fill—; finger —; overflow—; partake of—; pour—; quaff—; sip—; share—; steep in—; swell over—; taste—; wash—; win—; —con-

tains; —flows; —runs over; —sparkles; —steams.

CUPID
adjectives
wrestling; painted; devilish; effective; love-darting.

CUPIDITY
adjectives
native; personal; marked; avaricious; expressive.

CUPOLA
adjectives
gigantic; spherical; delicate; gilded; triumphant; towering; opulent.

CUR
adjectives
mean; mongrel; crooked; ragamuffin; contemptible; treacherous; bedraggled; crouching; worthless; cruel-hearted; impenetrable; mangy; carnal; half-starved; yelping.

CURATE
adjectives
perpetual; narrow; egotistical; impecunious; up-to-date; shuffling; pleasant; genial.

CURATIVE
adverbs
effectively; eventually; soothingly; pleasantly; safely; powerfully; speedily; valuably; mythically; infallibly; originally; rarely; expensively; heroically; strangely; miraculously; mysteriously; permanently; remarkably; fraudulently.

CURB (v)
adverbs
intentionally; beneficently; spasmodically; stringently; sternly; harshly; brutally; dictatorially; tyrannically.
(See stop.)

CURE
adjectives
renowned; timely; single; simple; sovereign; contemptuous; radical; drastic; fascinating; little; strange; natural; permanent; jagged; miraculous; efficacious; impersonal; so-called; immediate; alleged; prospective; instant; remarkable; sordid; accurate; elaborate; deepest; fraudulent.

verbs

accelerate—; accomplish—; advocate—; applaud—; apply—; approve—; effect—; hasten—; indicate—; perform—; produce —; proffer—; render—; seek—; trust—; work—; —follows; —results.

(See treatment, remedy.)

CURE (v)
adverbs

sufficiently; radically; permanently; miraculously; efficaciously; impersonally; immediately; remarkably; fraudulently; professionally; medically; presumably; partially; temporarily.

(See help.)

CURIOSITY
adjectives

high; sympathetic; logical; healthy; frank; profound; sublime; respectful; natural; reverent; indifferent; lively; breathless; instant; insatiable; passionate; intense; intelligent; vague; sedate; pregnant; half-ironic; mingled; eager; oblique; romantic; ardent; unhealthy; heartless; inflamed; intellectual; jealous; ethnological; indefatigable; laboratory; half-cunning; sheer; calculating; impertinent; kind; latent; amused; overwhelming; excited; persevering; overpowering; vacant; tremulous; typographical; rude; beneficial; blunt; morbid; prying; laudable; irresistible; imperious; unenvious; enlightened; gluttonous; languid; anthropological; idle; discontented; unobtrusive; innocent; frightened; contemptuous; unquenchable; ghoulish; sullen; regretful; literary; kindred; weak; mutual; obtrusive; ill-bred; endless; sharp; delighted; vulgar; childlike; indolent; unsated; gratified; evident; noble; unallayed; baffled; passionate; geographical; prejudiced; piqued; chastened; reluctant; persistent; polite; burning; malicious; cordial; professional; importunate; considerable; great; rampant; immense; inordinate; widespread; untiring; undiminished; penetrating; unappeased; quenchless; devouring; itching; momentary; passing; detached; mild; waning; small; faint; stirring; lazy; undisguised; growing; vast; objective; troubled; worried; timid; nervous; furtive; covetous; indecent; greedy; gruesome; avid; prurient; burdensome; leering; sinister; forbidden; impious; perverse; eclectic; visual; disoriented; titillating; gaping; startled; sudden; scared.

verbs

admit—; arouse—; awaken—; blame—; burst with—; cater to—; develop—; devour with—; display—; evince—; excite—; exhibit—; experience—; feed—; gratify —; manifest—; move by—; overcome—; pique—; practice—; prompt by—; repel—; repress—; satisfy—; seize with—; spur on by—; steam with—; —grows; —impels; —motivates; —prevails.

(See interest, thirst.)

CURIOUS
adverbs

incurably; meanly; inquisitively; intellectually; daringly; crassly; offensively; frightfully; gracelessly; grossly; maliciously; malevolently; unbearably; odiously; roughly; childishly; innocently; wonderingly; impertinently; impudently; unpardonably; inexcusably; hatefully; coarsely.

CURL
adjectives

soft; radiant; salt-wet; shining; drenched; sawdust; flat; vine; floating; countless (pl); short; upturned; sweeping; treasured; thick; mustache; twisted; moistened; lustrous; streaming; falling; disordered; luxuriant; clustering; smoky; stray; sunny; mutinous; glossy; careless; burnished; soft; copious (pl); copper-colored; white; blond; fluffy; gold; silky; black; brown; nut-brown; wire-gold; resolute; blue; massive; willful; protruding; tossing; doubtful; tight; glossy; loose; impracticable; tumbled; stubborn; fluttered; strange; powdered; damp; superabundant (pl); straggling; crisp; rolled; knotted; short; flaxen; corkscrew; dark; riotous; raven; unruly; fuzzy; dishevelled; dusty; gleaming; puffy.

verbs

admire—s; adorn with—s; assume—; arrange—s; clip—s; dress in—s; finger—s; fondle—s; form—s; promote—s; ribbon—s; shake—s; sun—s; tangle—s; tie into—s; twist into—s; wind into—s; —s attract; —s run riot; —s stream; —s wave.

(See hair.)

CURL (v)
adverbs

deftly; gracefully; riotously; indolently; systematically; scornfully; disdainfully;

charmingly; lustrously; luxuriantly; mutinously; carelessly; copiously; loosely; dishevelledly.

(See twist.)

CURRENCY

adjectives

spurious; immediate; auxiliary; new; crisp; special; separate; weak; universal; valueless; tropical.

verbs

accept—; adopt as—; coin—; counterfeit—; debase—; deflate—; depreciate—; exchange for—; guard—; honor—; inflate—; issue—; legalize—; rate—; recall—; stabilize—; stamp out—; tender—; value—; —changes; —wobbles.

(See money, coin.)

CURRENT

adjectives

friendly; irresistible; dangerous; treacherous; gentle; perilous; tricky; mighty; powerful; terrific; swift; racing; shifting; swirling; churning; weltering; streaming; air; glacial; tidal; descending; broad; undulating; steady; smooth; pulling; noiseless; skeptical; romantic; vital; philosophical; social; subtle; stinging; buoyant; fluvial; crystal; atmospheric; arduous; swollen; silver; favoring; conflicting; eddying; ceaseless; contrary; plunging; gushing; descending; mealy; clean; sweeping; lessening; warm; life; haze-enveloped; brown; greasy; running; rippling; timetossed; smooth; moisture-bringing; genial; wild; dreamy; alternating; unbroken; great; strengthened; brinish; galvanic; nauseous; cool; vicious; mazy; low-voiced; prattling; mysterious; permeating; fruity; twisting; lucent; contagious; intellectual; artistic; unseen; integrated; fatal.

verbs

allay—; attune to—; chart—; dam—; defile—; deviate from—; escape—; impede—; oppose—; retard—; ruffle—; stem—; —absorbs; —drives; —forces; —glides; —jets; —originates at; —pushes; —rolls on; —runs on; —shatters; —shifts; —springs from.

(See stream, movement, course.)

CURRICULUM

adjectives

rational; traditionary; academic; narrow; rigid; daily.

verbs

approve—; arrange—; balance—; complete—; constitute—; consult—; contemplate—; decide on—; detail—; fix—; investigate—; load—; offer—; outline—; pursue—; recommend—; regulate—; reject—; run through—; secure—; select—; supervise—; work out—; —covers; —embraces; —entails; —equips; —instructs in; —prepares for; —requires; —satisfies; —trains; —provides.

(See course, study.)

CURSE

adjectives

sobbing; vile; futile; snarling; unintelligible; fervent; dazzling; exasperated; muttered; bitter; great; hot; muffled; steamy; primal; intolerable; irritable; cunning; deep; valiant; haunting; sterile; well-hurled; dread; inevitable; long-forgotten; unutterable; sardonic; primeval; murmuring; blaspheming; shrieking; canceled; smothered; latent; fiendish; furious; primordial; abiding.

verbs

annul—; bait with—; blast—at; breathe—; bring—upon; cast—; croak—; dread—; endow with—; growl—; heap—s upon; hurl—at; mutter—; pronounce—; redeem from—; remove—; shake off—; smite with —; speak—; stifle—; swear—; taunt with —; voice—; wish—; woo—; —bodes ill for; —falls upon; —s pour out; —prevails; —stings.

(See denunciation, imprecation, oath.)

CURSE (v)

adverbs

endlessly; furiously; wrathfully; persistently; belligerently; bitterly; jovially; vulgarly; coarsely; blasphemously; unintelligibly; fervently; exasperatedly; hotly; intolerably; irritably; fiendishly.

(See swear.)

CURTAIL (v)

adverbs

sharply; considerably; drastically; harmfully; detrimentally; abruptly; unexpectedly; nominally; promptly.

(See reduce.)

CURTAILMENT

adjectives

prompt; drastic; unparalleled; harmful; sharp; detrimental.

CURTAIN

adjectives

falling; flapping; wavering; honey-colored; hotel-red; roseate; dirty; mud-brown; cloudless; azure; sinister; black; accordion-pleated; ruffled; embroidered; jeweled; gingham; crisp; bright; chintz; organdie; cretonne; gaily-colored; heavy; felt; wry; old; rich-toned; cheerful; skimpy; hanging; triangular; strong; final; gray; cloudy; dimity; wadded; clinging; billowy; improvised; sunshiny; undrawn; jonquil; silk; blue; light-pierced; dusky; exasperating; crimson; luminous; dazzling; impalpable; tawdry; convenient; sun-lace; formless; tattered.

verbs

adjust—; close—; draw—; drop—; emerge from—; fade behind—; hide behind—; lift—; lower—; peep through—; spread—; stretch out—; —flutters; —protects; —quivers; —shades; —sways.

(See drapery.)

CURTNESS

adjectives

semi-growling; autocratic; sudden; unfeeling; brusque; harsh; perfunctory.

CURTSY

adjectives

majestic; mock; graceful; delicate; practiced; bobbing; deferential.

CURVE
(bend as of a highway)

adjectives

gradually-descending; magnificent; unprotected; precipitous; graceful; sinuous; hairpin; wide-swung; continuous.

verbs

approach—; assume—; bank—; collide on —; crowd at—; dart around—; eliminate —; negotiate—; round—; screech around—; turn over on—; upset on—; warn of—; whiz round—; —confronts; —endangers; —hazards; —menaces; —obscures; —represents; —slants.

CURVE
(general)

adjectives

seductive; sensuous; luscious; ardent; entrancing; magnificent; graceful; exquisite; winsome; dizzy; dazzling; sweeping; bold; wide; scraped; scornful; disdainful; fleshy; opulent; slim; dignified; sensitive; close-coiled; easy; concave; sheltering; irregular; flat; hairpin; downward; lax; convex; subtle; symmetrical; gigantic; sheltered; painted; wavering; drooping; phosphate; additional; cuspidated; majestic; continuous; caustic; lineless; living; epicycloidal; precipitous; prudish; luxurious; aquiline; flowing; gracile; ceaseless; rich; tender; sweeping; alluring; yielding; self-sought; exquisite; glimmering.

CURVE
(line of deviation on a graph)

adjectives

double; reverse; reciprocal; transcendental; mechanical; radical; radial; peculiar.

verbs

construct—; describe—; generate—; interest in—; intersect—; obtain—; study—; trace—; transform—; —corresponds to; —degenerates; —envelops; —falls, —indicates; —recedes; —represents; —sinks.

(See deviation, line.)

CURVE (v)

adverbs

perceptibly; seductively; sensuously; entrancingly; magnificently; exquisitely; winsomely; sweepingly; boldly; abruptly; dangerously; sinuously.

(See bend.)

CUSHION

adjectives

pillow; rustling; elastic; silken; multicolored; bright-hued; thin; downy; soft; velvet; damask; faded; reclining; convertible; form-fitting; slippery; loose-seat; padded; ample; natural.

verbs

conceal with—; cover—; embroider—; fringe—; furnish with—; kneel on—; lay on—; loll on—; offer—; place—under; relax against—; repose on—; rest on—; sit on—; stuff—; —decorates; —eases; —graces.

(See pillow.)

CUSPIDOR

adjectives

stately; ill-placed; fanciful; vulgar; avoided; obstreperous; spattered.

CUSTODIAN

adjectives

possible; official; sole; faithless; temporary; definite.

CUSTODY

adjectives

safe; protective; temporary; court; jealous; zealous; watchful.

verbs

accept—of; acknowledge—of; advise—of; authorize—of; commit to—of; confine to—of; direct—of; preserve—of; resent—of; retain—of; subject to—of; —amends; —improves; —neutralizes; —protects; —rectifies; —restrains; —superintends.

(See care, imprisonment.)

CUSTOM

adjectives

august; precious; gracious; venerated; pleasant; sentimental; quaint; bizarre; effete; mutable; ancient; immemorial; time-honored; convenient; prudent; barbaric; pagan; primitive; yearly; native; austere; civilized; tribal; nightly; family; social; old-fashioned; southern; administrative; religious; accepted; wild; gay; universal; innocent; disinterested; reprehensible; contrasting; established; observed; prevailing; casual; frequent; habitual; recognized; classic; homogeneous; antiquated; unwonted; barbarous; charming; burial; pious; genteel; blind; stupid; laudable; national; long-continued; kingly; transient; excellent; preserved; ludicrous; prescribed; early; depraved; usual; infuriating; political; traditional; obsolete; enlightened; invariable; offensive; salutary; idiotic; well-known; uniform; familiar; reverent; exuberant; discrepant; monastic; praiseworthy; queer.

verbs

adhere to—; break—; cherish—; cling to—; conform to—; corrupt—; defend—; defer—; defy—; deprecate—; develop—; discharge—; establish—; esteem—; extenuate—; flout—; honor—; impose—; inaugurate—; maintain—; mar—; mock—; observe—; overlap—; overwhelm by—; respect—; retain—; reverence—; revert to—; revive—; run counter to—; stamp out—; —demands; —dictates; —governs; —intimidates; —narrows; —runs back to; —springs from; —stales; hamper by—.

(See usage, conventionality, practice, habit.)

CUSTOMARY

adverbs

scarcely; quaintly; queerly; graciously; pleasantly; conveniently; charmingly; stupidly; infuriatingly; idiotically; amusingly; locally; racially.

CUSTOMER

adjectives

potential; quondam; gay; prospective; tough; favored; fussy; cautious; flighty; lavish; famous; resident; difficult; hard; hideous; soldier; quick; hungry; capricious; disgruntled; excellent; grumpy; dark; lathered; noble; open-aired; profitable; residential; favored; satisfied; admiring; discriminating; picnic; slippery; famished; potential; passing; steady; destructive.

verbs

approach—; bargain with—; beckon to—; deal with—; encourage—; entice—; furnish —; guarantee to—; mulct—; refund to—; round up—s; satisfy—; seek—; smirk at—; tempt—; urge—; —bickers; —complains; —orders; —purchases; —responds; —selects; —s support; —s troop in.

(See purchaser, buyer.)

CUT

adjectives

sharp; sincere; substantial; long; ragged; vile; inelegant; vertical; tremendous; duck-bellied; delicate; fearful; whimsical.

verbs

bandage —; bathe —; bleed —; cleave —; disinfect —; dress —; incise —; infect —; inflict —; open —; salve —; sew —; stitch —; suffer —; suture —; treat —; wound with —; — divides; — heals; — pains; — penetrates; — removes; — separates; — severs.

(See wound.)

CUT (*v*)

adverbs

completely; exquisitely; cruelly; violently; deliberately; effectively; diagonally; summarily; snobbishly; obliquely; transversely; keenly; generously; heartlessly.

(See gash.)

CUTLASS

adjectives

gleaming; dripping; naked; sturdy; heavy; serviceable; dangling; undimmed.

verbs

arm with —; brandish —; carve with —; chop with —; dull —; flourish —; furnish with —; hew with —; sever with —;

sharpen —; shield from —; thrust —; wave —; wield —; work —; yield to —; — menaces; — pierces; — slashes; — slays.

(See sword, weapon.)

CUTLERY

adjectives

flashing; steely; keen-edged; ivory-handled; adaptable; concealed; cleverly-applied; sundering.

verbs

clean —; dent —; employ —; glaze —; grind —; harden —; inspect —; manipulate —; manufacture —; monogram —; place —; plate —; polish —; provide with —; require —; scour —; sharpen —; spread —; stain —; temper —; utilize —; — clatters; — glistens; — jingles; — resists.

(See instrument, tool.)

CYCLE

adjectives

irregular; uncharted; business; elemental; repetitious; past; never-failing; comprehensive; pleasant; distinct; imaginary; endless; unvarying; normal.

verbs

approve —; avert —; complete —; compute —; continue in —; end —; form —; move in —; obviate —; pass through —; recognize —; recur during —; regain during —; resume —; revolve in —; span —; study —; — gauges; — indicates; — possesses; — promises; — represents.

(See period.)

CYCLONE

adjectives

human; lurking; impending; destructive; periodic; seasonable; threatening; rumbling; whirling.

CYLINDER

adjectives

metal; stubby; rotary; inscribed; clay; reciprocating; wicker; unsymmetrical.

verbs

bolt —s together; bore —; compress in —; construct —; design —; employ —; grind —; insert in —; operate —; — circles; — contracts; — expands; — lags; — leaks; — revolves; — rolls; — rotates; — turns.

CYMBAL

adjectives

tinkling; brazen; clashing; vibrating; jubilant; sounding; heartful.

CYMBALS

adjectives

bronzed; clashing; tinkling; empty-sounding; gypsy; triumphant; traditional.

verbs

cast —; clash —; crash —; play on —; rub —; sound —; strike —; — clash; — echo; — quiver; — resound; — ring; — tinkle.

CYNIC

adjectives

unfeeling; bitter; cold-blooded; licentious; ferocious; unmoved; wandering; cruel; irreverent; sensual; intolerable; sated; singular; imperturbable; consistent; decided; admirable; cheery: depressed; despairing.

CYNICAL

adverbs

bitterly; harshly; gloomily; contemptuously; derisively; scornfully; sneeringly; disdainfully; morosely; witheringly; superciliously; pitifully; censoriously; abusively; scandalously; outrageously; dryly; cuttingly; disparagingly; insufferably; pompously; arrogantly; bumptiously.

CYNICISM

adjectives

prevalent; abstract; consummate; immeasurable; meretricious; searing; cold-blooded; bitter; new-found; grinning; smooth; ugly; sinister; unbearable; rough; infamous; arid; appalling; polished; selfish; philosophical; repellent; analytical; thin; querulous; apparent; disdainful; genial.

verbs

adopt —; attain —; base on —; clothe in —; condemn —; criticize —; dethrone —; display —; dispose of —; don —; exhibit —; exercise —; fall into —; fetter with —; imply —; indulge in —; ingrain —; mask —; provoke —; regard with —; ridicule —; uphold —; — cloaks; — develops; — emphasizes; — evolves; — flourishes; — outrages; — seeps in.

(See contempt, sarcasm, distrust, pessimism.)

CYPRESS

adjectives

towering; gigantic; bearded; hoary; patriarchal.

adjectives
absolute; perturbed; grieved; obstinate; mighty; omnipotent; craven; ruthless.

adjectives
masterful; frantic; neurotic; vainglorious; pride-eaten; ambitious; power-driven.

D

adjectives
giant; yellow; nodding; flaunting; vernal; coquettish.

DAGGER

adjectives
bloody; bronze; gold-hilted; curved; flint; short; heavy; gleaming; well-sharpened.

verbs
attack with —; blunt —; brandish —; conceal —; draw —; dull —; edge —; flourish —; hack with —; nuzzle —; pare with —; pluck with —; point —; reel under —; run — through; sharpen —; sheathe —; shoot —; speak —s; stab with —; threaten with —; thrust —; wave —; wield —; — inflicts; — nicks; — penetrates; — slays; — wounds.
(See knife, weapon.)

DAILY

adjectives (newspaper)
conservative; provincial; radical; yellow; blatant; local; syndicated.

DAINTINESS

adjectives
exquisite; fastidious; unwonted; inimitable; inborn; personal; superlative; luxurious; preening; faultless.

DAINTY

adjectives
carefully-prepared; prized; coveted; diet-robbing; sugared; tempting; toothsome.

verbs
allure by —; crave —; desire —; feed on —; pamper with —; prepare —; promise —; provide —; relish —; reward with —; share —; spice —; store —; surrender to —; — appeals; — delights; — pleases.
(See food.)

adverbs
fastidiously; exquisitely; subtly; extremely; gracefully; charmingly; girlishly; personally; faultlessly; fashionably; meticulously; primly; demurely; delicately; particularly; scrupulously; pleasingly; immaculately; sweetly; fragrantly.

DAISY

adjectives
white; buttercup-hued; English; innocent; unabashed; golden-hearted; question-eyed; love-telling.

verbs
adorn with —; arrange —ies; bear —ies; chain —ies; cultivate —ies; disclose —ies; gather —ies; grow —ies; pin —ies; pluck —ies; scatter —ies; trim with —ies; — blooms; — blossoms; —ies deck; —ies dot; — flowers; — folds; — lurks; — opens; — sleeps; —ies sprinkle; — winks.
(See flower.)

DALE

adjectives
smiling; piny; flowery; wooded; dark; fragrant; shadow-dappled.

verbs
abandon —; bedeck —; bloom in —; grow in —; haunt —; hide in —; inhabit —; retreat to —; roam in —; scatter through —; situate in —; speed over —; wander in —; — invites; — protects; — shelters; — slopes; — winds.
(See valley, dell, vale.)

DALLIANCE

adjectives
pleasant; silken; delightful; primrose; lunar; playful; gentle.

DALLY (v)

adverbs
dangerously; carelessly; playfully; indifferently; procrastinatingly; seductively.
(See delay, trifle.)

DAM (water)

adjectives
gracious; milky; restless; undermined; log; earth-filled; broken; frothy; noisy; gushing; beaver.

verbs
bank —; burst —; construct —; install —; level —; overflow —; pipe from —; reinforce —; sweep away —; — bars; — blocks; — breaks; — bridges; — confines; — controls; — discharges; — halts; — impounds; — irrigates; — leaks; — obstructs; — preserves; — prevents; — protects; — restrains; — supplies.
(See barrier.)

DAMAGE

adjectives

moral; irreparable; considerable; inestimable; permanent; malicious; substantial; sudden; serious; material; pecuniary; noticeable; characteristic; infinite; unspeakable; accidental; consequent; enormous; hidden; resultant; unliquidated; willful; unmistakable; punitive.

verbs

account for —; compute —; counteract —; countervail —; distress by —; forestall —; guard against —; inflict —; measure —; mitigate —; offset —; pay —s; receive —; recoup —; recover —; reveal —; survey —; sustain —; — flows from; — impairs.
(See destruction, injury, harm.)

DAMAGE (v)

adverbs

seriously; morally; irreparably; inestimably; permanently; maliciously; substantially; materially; noticeably; characteristically; infinitely; unspeakably; accidentally; consequently; enormously; resultantly; unmistakably; punitively; wilfully; revengefully; woefully; unscrupulously; savagely.
(See injure. hurt.)

DAMASK

adjectives

heavy; silk; crimson; mingled; traditional; imported; luxurious; gorgeous.

DAME

adjectives

coquettish; scented; imperious; high-nosed; resolute; fairest; rawboned; admiring; glowing; ruffled; peerless; keen-eyed; beauteous; antiquated; sinful; blooming; handsome; disdainful; solicitous; chaste; tissued; wanton; affrighted.

DAMNABLE

adverbs

utterly; odiously; completely; horribly; shockingly; profoundly; venomously; infernally; consummately; unnaturally.

DAMNATION

adjectives

eternal; relentless; utter; deep; everlasting; irretrievable; consummate.

DAMP

adjectives

murk; occidental; death; soothing; uncheerful; choking; senseless; sickly.

adverbs

slightly; clammily; chillingly; penetratingly; rawly; stuffily; noxiously; foggily; depressingly; inescapably; pestilentially; mistily; mysteriously; coldly; smotheringly; muggily; soggily; soddenly; icily; piercingly; frigidly.

DAMPNESS

adjectives

clammy; chilling; penetrating; stuffy; unctuous; consistent.

DAMSEL

adjectives

pulchritudinous; beauteous; young; calm-eyed; dainty; efficient; demure; frank; attractive; shrieking; lovelorn; stout; faery; comely; flounced; frail; frolicsome; officiating; citified; rubicund; haggling; distressed; dashing; misguided; hapless.

verbs

attend—; avow to—; captivate—; cherish —; court—; dishonor—; distress—; misuse—; nurture—; protect—; win—; woo—; —attracts; —blushes; —curtsies; —dreams; —droops; —faints; —frolics; —simpers; —twitters; —yearns.
(See woman, girl.)

DANCE

adjectives

rhythmic; divine; ingenious; frantic; wild; passionate; pulse-quickening; queer; eccentric; weird; mazy; absurd; freak; astonishing; grotesque; shambling; classic; old-fashioned; curious; square; folk; ritual; holiday; religious; moonlight; native; exotic; reveling; intricate; pompous; judicious; ballet; risque; characteristic; monopolized; fading; confident; scandalous; Moorish; bewitching; quaint; impish; carnal; exquisite; naked; overture; languid; fairy; mystic; howling; murdering; eternal; evening; amusing; sporadic; erotic; sunset; slow; serene; mirthful; astronomical; revolving; barbaric; spectacular; yearlong.

verbs

accompany—; assemble at—; attend—; blend with—; burst forth in—; contort in—; dress for—; embrace in—; escort to—; grace—; invite to—; join in—; lead off—; leave—; master—; open—; perfect—; perform—; polish—; popularize—; rejoice in—; render—; revel in—; study—; survey—; take part in—; vary—; weary of—;

—breaks; —circles; —enchants; —expresses; —interprets.
(See waltz, minuet.)

DANCE (v)

adverbs
frivolously; bewitchingly; gracefully; divinely; exquisitely; violently; vivaciously;
solemnly; triumphantly; angelically; strenuously; eccentrically; grotesquely; picturesquely; seductively; wantonly; gleefully;
incessantly; rhythmically; ingeniously; religiously; weirdly; shamblingly; ritually;
exotically; quaintly; impishly; carnally; exquisitely; serenely; mirthfully; barbarically;
spectacularly; skillfully; zestfully.

DANCE FLOOR

adjectives
deserted; pretentious; polished; gleaming;
inviting; seductive; mirror-smooth.

DANCE HALL

adjectives
common; tawdry; overcrowded; revolting; frivolous; forcibly-gay.

verbs
assemble at— —; attend — —; congregate
in— —; crowd— —; file into— —; frequent
— —; gather at— —; introduce to— —;
popularize— —; supervise— —; wander
around— —; — —appeals; — —breeds; —
—corrupts; — —offers; — —swarms with;
— —swelters.

DANCER

adjectives
merry; good; superb; delightful; graceful;
light; rhythmic.

verbs
applaud—; fete—; fire—; inspire—; train
—; —awes; —delights; —entertains; —executes; —exercises; —exerts; —expresses;
—interprets; —flies; —flutters; —frisks;
—glides; —s jostle; —leaps; —performs;
—personifies; —pirouettes; —pivots; —
practises; —prances; —s promenade; —
quivers; —registers; —springs; —suggests;
—wheels; —whirls.
(See acrobat.)

DANCING

adjectives
outlandish; outrageous; exquisite; convulsive; titillating; rhythmic; habitual; acrobatic; furious.

DANDELION

adjectives
straggling; common; autumnal; late-blown;
frost-braving; starry; fairy-seeded; omnipresent; humble.

DANDY

adjectives
amiable; professional; hypocritical; dapper;
ingratiating; surreptitious; superficial; perfumed; silk-stockinged.

DANGER

adjectives
ever-impending; imminent; looming; hidden; gathering; unseen; unknown; fancied;
mythical; inevitable; unceasing; vile; imaginary; indefinite; miserable; acute; extreme; august; constant; remote; significant; undiluted; discernible; obvious; immediate; overwhelming; inherent; grave;
pretended; apparent; approaching; potential; future; unavoidable; recurring; spicy;
unexampled; real; countless (pl).

verbs
admit—; avert—; avoid—; beset by—;
blind to—; brave—; confront with—; court
—; create—; demonstrate—; duck—; eliminate—; emphasize—; entail—; exaggerate
—; exempt from—; expose to—; face—;
flee—; foresee—; foretell—; free from—;
guard against—; harbor—; ignore—; increase—; incur—; indicate—; induce—;
involve—; laugh at—; lessen—; lie in—;
minimize—; overcome—; pluck from—;
ponder—; realize—; recognize—; remain
in—; risk—; scoff at—; scorn—; sense—;
shield from—; state—; stem—; taste—;
underestimate—; visualize—; weigh—;
wink at—; woo—; —attends; —impends;
—looms; —lurks; —subsides.
(See peril. hazard, risk.)

DANGEROUS

adverbs
secretly; imminently; mythically; inevitably; miserably; acutely; extremely; remotely; obviously; overwhelmingly; gravely; potentially; unavoidably; critically;
ominously; terribly; incredibly; horribly;
palpably; openly; manifestly; conspicuously.

DANGLE (v)

adverbs
mockingly; loosely; tantalizingly; irritatingly; erotically; teasingly; playfully.
(See hang.)

adverbs

effeminately; sartorially; extremely; elegantly; absurdly; smartly; importantly; expensively; brightly; exquisitely; trimly; sprucely; neatly; nimbly; alertly; gracefully; jauntily; nattily; consciously; swankily; sleekly; becomingly; ornamentally.

DARE (v)

adverbs

impiously; virtuously; dauntlessly; boisterously; foolhardily; courageously; impetuously; bravely; unhesitatingly.

(See defy, challenge.)

DAREDEVIL

adjectives

reckless; lovable; hopeful; invincible; adventure-seeking; conquering; amiable.

DARING

adjectives

moon-faced; virtuous; dauntless; remorseless; speculative; boisterous; foolhardy; harmonic.

adverbs

dangerously; rashly; temperamentally; fantastically; alarmingly; foolhardily; breathtakingly; colossally; terribly; dramatically; notoriously; crazily; strangely; singularly; shamefully; amazingly; recklessly; incredibly; unbelievably; foolishly; boldly; avidly; bravely; audaciously; romantically; vicariously; courageously; youthfully; boyishly; disconcertingly; extravagantly.

DARK

adjectives

perilous; fierce; haunted; shuddering; leafy; lugubrious; frosty; shadowed; impenetrable; ambrosial; silent; abysmal; peaceful; fragrant; creeping; intricate; tinkling.

adverbs

mysteriously; impenetrably; perilously; shudderingly; lugubriously; peacefully; abysmally; dismally; fragrantly; suddenly; appreciably; blessedly; fearfully; frightfully; alarmingly; intensely; totally; utterly; pitchy; eerily; unnaturally; bewilderingly; oppressively; increasingly; uneasily; thickly.

adverbs

obscurely; opaquely; murkily; partially; gloomily; unaccountably; perceptibly; inauspiciously; nocturnally; totally; utterly; unnaturally; bewilderingly; increasingly; bafflingly; prematurely; comparatively; mysteriously; generally; devouringly; fatefully; mercifully.

(See shade, obscure.)

DARKENING

adjectives

sudden; gradual; appreciable; perceptible; fathomless; ominous; unprecedented.

DARKNESS

adjectives

blank; blessed; friendly; cozy; deep; hampering; intense; total; opaque; utter; black; somber; pitchy; eerie; unnatural; bewildering; baffling; breathless; preternatural; environing; enveloping; oppressive; choking; stabbing; formless; deepening; increasing; reverberating; howling; Stygian; dense; dripping; silvery; velvety; scented; barbaric; leafy; mental; gross; eternal; uneasy; quiet; serene; abrupt; heavy; muffling; premature; comparative; outer; silent; chilly; blessed; mysterious; general; feudal; blind; lifting; gathering; stormy; horrible; abiding; smooth; fetid; midnight; regnant; fateful; cavernous; dumb; inmost; perennial; wormy; circumambient; thick; devouring; looming; brooding; revolutionary; gay; hot; desert; shadowy; fearful; horrid; merciful; hilltop; windy; marble; healing; unfathomed; priestly; chaotic; abysmal; impending; inwoven; double; lustrous; embarrassing.

verbs

abide in—; accustom to—; beam in—; burnish by—; burrow into—; cast into—; conceal in—; descend to—; disappear into—; discern in—; dispel—; distinguish in—; dread—; dwell in—; encompass by—; encounter—; engulf in—; enlighten—; glow through—; grope in—; haunt—; illumine—; keep in—; lapse into—; laugh at—; lose in—; peer into—; pierce—; plunge into—; prowl in—; pursue in—; remain in—; roam in—; scatter—; shine in—; sink into—; sparkle in—; stumble in—; survey—; toil in—; tread in—; wander in—; wrap in—; yield to—; —approaches; —blinds; —blots out; —broods; —deepens; —depresses; —descends; —devours; —eclipses; —embalms; —embraces; —encompasses; —endures; —enfolds; —ensues; —falls; —flees; —folds over; —gathers; —grows; —hides; —mantles; —melts; —obscures; —prevails; —robes; —shadows; —shrouds; —spreads; —steals upon; —surrounds; —swallows up; —terrifies; —thickens; —veils.

(See gloom, obscurity, shadow.)

DARKY

adjectives

rollicking; superstitious; stalwart; ragged; ingenious; septic-looking; magic-footed; tattered; greasy; cringing; blissful; wool-thatched.

DARLING

adjectives

spunky; plucky; extravagant; spoiled; over-indulged; pampered.

adverbs

utterly; adorably; sweetly; lovably; seductively; charmingly; captivatingly; enchantingly; bewitchingly; tenderly.

DART

adjectives

fiery; false; envenomed; swift; imperceptible; slender; sudden; goading; bullet-like; lightning; dribbling; sickening; spirit-quelling; singing; flaming; shining.

verbs

aim—; blunt—; blow—; brandish—; dash —; defend with—s; envenom—; feather—; flash—; interpose; remove—; poison—; polish—; shake—; shield from—; shoot—; spear—; tip—; thrust—through; —hisses by; —soars; —strikes; —whizzes by; —wounds.

(See missile, spear, shaft, weapon, arrow.)

DASH

adjectives

final; blind; despairing; fiery; flying; headlong; inadvertent; tremendous; meaningful; splendid; giddy; joyous; brilliant; surreptitious; eloquent; refreshing; gallant; rosy.

DASH (v)

adverbs

gently; aimlessly; turbulently; hurriedly; immediately; madly; blindly; inadvertently; despairingly; splendidly; joyously; gallantly; eagerly; anxiously; furiously; victoriously; unrestrainedly; violently.

(See hurl.)

DASHING

adverbs

showily; jauntily; gallantly; pretentiously; proudly; vainly; gorgeously; dramatically; theatrically; spectacularly; sumptuously; boldly; rashly; valiantly; pluckily; stoutly; audaciously; dauntlessly; confidently; fashionably; stylishly.

DATA

adjectives

curious; strange; one-sided; accompanying; available; existing; latest; relative; interesting; relevant; fascinating; convincing; accurate; basic; factual; important; significant; extensive; erroneous; obscure; modern; corrective; research; programmed; official; scientific; technical; merchandising; precise; recorded; necessary; incomplete; impeccable; authentic; intimate; historical; biographic.

verbs

accept—; accumulate—; analyze—; attest by—; authenticate—; catalogue—; collect —; elaborate—; furnish—; gather—; improve—; present—; produce—; study—; survey—; synthesize—; track down—; — indicate; —measure; —prove; —reveal; —show.

(See fact, information.)

DATE

adjectives

ineffective; arbitrary; fixed; exact; recent; ancient; prescribed; decisive; closing; historical; equivalent; significant; future; remote; immediate; memorable; subsequent; calamitous; lasting; endless; tentative; dark; dividing; equinoctial.

verbs

ascribe—to; assign—to; bear—; calculate —; cancel—; confirm—; denote—; determine—; extend—; fix—; forestall—; inscribe—; insert—; jot down—; limit to—; mark with—; reckon—; refer to—; require—; set—; specify—; —denotes; —expires.

(See time, duration.)

DATE (v)

adverbs

variously; significantly; recently; historically; tentatively; unquestionably; subsequently.

(See record.)

adjectives
unsightly; wretched; pitiful; artless; spattered; colorful.

DAUB (v)
adverbs
wretchedly; hideously; hatefully; amateurishly; carelessly; halfheartedly.
(See smear, soil.)

DAUGHTER
adjectives
loyal; considerate; true; dutiful; self-sacrificing; stubbornly-devoted; tiny; plump; brisk; pretty; beautiful; hardhearted; militant; rebellious; errant; irreconcilable; sedate; tomboy; virginal; debutante; spoiled; idolized; virtuous; modern; outspoken; tender; chaste; marriageable; repentant; gay; beldam; buxom; blithe; debonair; short; untutored; fragile; mangled; abominable; peerless; loving; expiring; flighty; uncultured.

verbs
adopt—; adore—; bear—; berate—; betroth—; bring forth—; chastise—; cherish —; conceive—; confer on—; delight in—; fondle—; long for—; market—; marry off—; mold—; pamper—; preach to—; present with—; nurse—; rear—; rebuke—; rejoice in—; reprimand—; seduce—; woo —; —elopes; —graces; —inherits; — pleads; —shames; —shocks.
(See child, girl, person, woman.)

DAUNTLESS
adverbs
heroically; courageously; recklessly; rashly; resolutely; splendidly; superbly; joyously; proudly; fiercely; morally; carelessly; impetuously; stubbornly; magnificently; exceptionally.

DAVENPORT
adjectives
sagged; restful; upholstered; comfortable; dumpy; deep.

DAWDLE (v)
adverbs
perversely; idly; languidly; tantalizingly; calmly; everlastingly; lightly; somnolently; lazily; lackadaisically; irritatingly; aimlessly.
(See dally.)

adjectives
calm; everlasting; lackadaisical; nonchalant; idle; purposeless.

DAWN
adjectives
black; crawling; opalescent; dirty; gray; thick; crimson; golden; pitiless; pearl; cool; false; dismal; cheerless; wet; pale; perfect; premature; faint; hushed; slow; tropical; clear; stormy; countless (pl); roseate; autumnal; northern; waking; hazy; kindling; crude; softly-breaking; radiant; wintry; savage; streaked; low; dappled; amorous; reddest; tender; noonday; bashful; tempestuous; joyful; azure; unmellowed; crepuscular; smothering; melancholy.

verbs
behold—; foretell—; front—; herald—; journey till—; precede—; rise at—; usher in—; wait for—; wake with—; warn of—; —arouses; —ascends; —blazons; —blushes; —breaks; —cheers; —creeps on; —flares; —flees; —flushes; —glimmers; —pierces; —ripens into day; —surges; —surprises; —steals over; —verges with.
(See daylight.)

DAWN (v)
adverbs
finally; abruptly; clearly; brilliantly; incisively; eerie; troubled; gorgeous; antiphonal; hazy; phosphorescent.
(See lighten.)

DAY
adjectives
adventurous; agreeable; arduous; alternate; anxious; auspicious; beautiful; brilliant; buoyant; broiling; blowing; bitter; bloody; blank; bygone; blissful; brave; burning; bright; bustling; boyhood; bountiful; battering; commendable; chaotic; cloudy; cool; crisp; calm; coronation; courageous; clear; checkered; capricious; cheerless; catechizing; corsair (pl); credulous; colorful; crowded; careless; canicular; vivid; carefree; dim; dayless; decisive; declining; dying; dull; disastrous; dismal; dramatic; drab; drizzling; dedicated; diviner; domestic; degenerate; dangerous; decadent; delightful; depression (pl); dark; dragging; dreary; dusty; despairing; distracting; dead; dumb; drowsy; dancing; eventful; empty; epochal; endless; expiring; everlasting; ensuing; eternal; enchant-

ed; enlightened; exciting; evil; exceptional; fateful; first; fatiguing; fatal; funeral; flourishing; former; festal; fragrant; fairy; frosty; foul; gentle; glorious; grinding; gloomy; gushing; garish; gallant; garden; golden; gay; glamorous; gambling; hectic; hot; holy; happy; hopeful; halcyon; honest; historic; humid; homesick; happy-go-lucky; innocent; illustrious; indelible; intercalary; ideal; idle; irretrievable; irreclaimable; interleaving; judgment; jocund; joyous; laborious; late; luckless; long; lively; lazy; limpid; lagging; lifeless; memorable; mysterious; miserable; melancholy; motionless; magnificent; monastic; muted; medieval; momentous; opulent; northern; noisy; newborn; natal; nuptial; neophyte; overbusy; old; opal-colored; proverbial; piercing; peevish; present; prosperous; preceding; proud; perfect; pretty; pleasant; pessimistic; pre-medieval (pl); postwar (pl); planless; phlegmatic; primitive; parsimonious; pilgrim; palmy; quondam; restful; rainy; recurring; reckoning; rosy; romantic; regal; raucous; roisterous; red-letter; ruminant; righteous; splendid; sultry; sunless; silent; soggy; silver; strenuous; summer; somnolent; sorry; smiling; sullen; sinking; sodden; scornful; solitary; serene; superb; solar; sordid; short; simple; somber; sinister; supplementary; sizzling; scorching; tiresome; slumberous; topsy-turvy; tumultuous; toil-stained; triumphal; tedious; temperamental; visionary; torrid; unreal; untroubled; unremembered; vanished; campaigning; victorious; vagabond; vacant.

verbs
appoint—; await—; bemoan—; behold—; bless—; busy—; cap—; cloud—; contemplate—; crown—; curse—; decree—; denounce—; dispose of—; divide—; drag out —s; ease—; enliven—; endure—; grace—; herald—; honor—; keep—; kill—; lament —; lose—; mar—; measure—; name—; observe—; peak—; record—; regret—; rejoice—; reminisce of—s; rest by—; rue—; rule—; save—; solemnize—; waste—; win—; —advances; —affords; —approaches; —breaks; —cheers; —closes; —comforts; —darkens; —dawns; —dazzles; —declines; —decreases; —dies; —drags by; —s elapse; —is born; —lags; —mounts; —oppresses; —peers forth; —races by; —saddens; —s shorten; —unfolds; —vanishes; —wanes; —waxes; —wears off.
(See time. age, generation.)

adjectives
glimmering; resplendent; glorious; joyous; gratifying; welcome; salutary; golden.

DAYLIGHT
adjectives
fading; burning; broad; wintry; sick; gray; haggard; dying; garish; partial; glimmering; adequate; diffused; beautiful; blessed; obscure; unnatural; scented; yellow; primrose.

verbs
employ—; keep in—; let in—; surrender to—; —appears; —approaches; —arouses; —breaks; —burns; —dawns; —dazzles; —dies; —diffuses; —discloses; —envelops; —fades; —filters through; —floods; —illumines; —pours in; —promises; —seeps in; —shines; —suffuses; unfolds, —vanishes; —wanes.
(See day, light. dawn.)

DAZE
adjectives
fatuous; open-mouthed; sodden; staggering; effacing; somnambulistic.

DAZED
adverbs
stupidly; unaccountably; genuinely; disturbingly; strangely; indescribably; fearfully; insuperably; depressingly; terribly; alarmingly; unreasonably; vaguely; uncomfortably; inexplicably; awkwardly;; extremely; helplessly; pitifully; tragically; sadly; hopelessly; dangerously.

DAZZLE (*v*)
adverbs
suddenly; glamorously; resplendently; purposely; bewilderingly; awesomely; blindingly; fatuously; hopelessly; fatally.
(See blind, bewilder.)

DEACON
adjectives
dutiful; long-faced; solemn; ruling; parsimonious; funereal-looking; sleek-haired; sin-denouncing.

adverbs
appoint—; elect—; ordain—; unfrock—; —administers; —admonishes; —advises; —assists; —attends; —awes; —baptizes; —christens; —collects; —disperses; —dis-

tributes; —performs; —prays; —preaches; —provides; —reproves; —serves; —supervises; —visits.
(See minister, elder, officer.)

DEAD

adjectives
stricken; unseen; illustrious; beloved; pitiful; humble; heroic; war; ghastly; gallant; moldering; enduring; sainted; venerable; imponderable; silent; turbaned; decaying; ungathered; coffined; spectral; pestilential; unconscious; restless; mighty; dearest; honorable; untimely; vulgar; faithful; precious; passionless; floating.

verbs
awaken—; bemoan—; blaspheme—; bury —; commemorate—; consort with—; curse —; defile—; disinter—; embalm—; entomb—; honor—; judge—; mourn—; number—; record—; reincarnate—; remember—; revive—; rise from—; rob—; — sleep on; —wither.
(See carcass, corpse.)

DEADLOCK

adjectives
hopeless; partial; growing; convenient; relentless; quarterless; fatal.

DEADLY

adverbs
disastrously; noxiously; virulently; exceptionally; irremediably; woefully; execrably.

DEAF

adverbs
totally; insufferably; irritatingly; vexatiously; annoyingly; pitiably; slightly; utterly; deplorably; lamentably; unfortunately; stubbornly; callously; deliberately; unhappily; pitifully; tragically; forlornly; desperately; moodily; lonesomely.

DEAL

adjectives
neighborly; momentous; shady; dirty; legitimate; ill-savored; unprotected; square; devised; financial; business; backstairs; important; great; vast; infinite; complete; skin; wandering; famished; sensational; new; tremendous; parlor; wonder; made-to-order; timed-to-the-minute; combination; bargain; smashing; pace-setting; thrilling.

verbs
arrange—; bargain—; benefit by—; carry on—; clinch—; close—; concoct—; disclose—; engage in—; engineer—; engross

in—; enter—; involve in—; participate in—; put over—; transact—; unfold—; —fizzles (colloq.); —promises.
(See transaction.)

DEAL (*v*)

adverbs
ceremoniously; promptly; ruthlessly; bountifully; primarily; heedlessly; discreetly; severely; summarily; zestfully; scientifically; munificently; adequately; rigorously; gratuitously; momentously; legitimately; financially; sensationally; thrillingly; persuasively; exclusively; competently; plainly; brilliantly.
(See negotiate, distribute.)

DEALER

adjectives
opulent; persuasive; ignorant; unscrupulous; keen; double; individual; antique; honest; retail; exclusive; plain; implement; competent.

DEALINGS

adjectives
hard; plain; decent; gracious; unauthorized; shrewd; double; quick; sharp; satisfactory; dishonest; high-minded; generous; rough; hazardous; strenuous; undiplomatic; wanton; unscrupulous; fair; nefarious; punctilious; extensive; business; wise; patient; highhanded; furtive; ruthless.

DEAN

adjectives
callous; pompous; incompetent; meticulous; impeccable; impinging; smug.

DEAR

adverbs
infinitely; adorably; admirably; delightfully; affectionately.

DEARTH

adjectives
barren; deplorable; notable; absolute; sickening; hapless; agreeable.

DEATH

adjectives
brave; beautiful; happy; glorious; heroic; gentle; gallant; calm; romantic; tranquil; painless; swift; reasonable; merciful; natural; appropriate; deliberate; certain; sure; untoward; early; premature; melancholy; tragic; baleful; lamented; instantaneous; quick; sudden; vicious; grappling; grisly; grim; horrible; ghastly; dreadful; beastly;

314

ignominious; slow; lingering; physical; spiritual; temporal; somatic; cool; enfolding; tearful; sleeping; silent; long; unified; inflexible; ensuing; imbecilic; latent; cruel; intellectual; partial; honorable; immediate; recent; deplored; radiant; shadow-like; diverse(pl); mysterious; uniform; delicious; ugly; moral; fearful; drowning; threatened; awful; gradual; merited; devouring; foreboding; impending; immortal; stalking; unlooked-for; tardy; covetous; bright; unspeaking; heartening; atrocious; disgraceful; adulterate; direful; slaughtering; humane; engrossing; sacrificial; unsubstantial; bloody; maternal; helpless; poetic; violent; affronted; unregretted; flaming; unnoticed; instant; sacred; everlasting; manly; glowing; timeless; malignant; agonizing; eternal; obscure; placid; present; golden; ultimate; approaching; protracted; unrewarded; subsequent; tithed; untimely; distressing; hideous; watery; senseless; dusty; accidental; sequent; tuberculous; occasional (pl); ominous; excruciating; voluptuous; shameful; dramatic; pale; wasted; miserable; princely; paralyzing; drier; opportune; delaying; stony; self-abased; sulphurous; overshadowing; unanticipated; propagating; strong; shrouded; scurvy; treacherous; fierce; unavoidable; unseen; mellow; loathsome; temporal; living.

verbs
administer—; announce—; apprise of—; avert—; bore to—; brood on—; cause—; cheat—; condemn to—; confirm—; contemplate—; dance with—; deliver from—; deserve—; designate—; devise—; dramatize —; endure—; evade—; exact—; experience —; expiate—; face—; feign—; frighten to —; gamble with—; give up to—; guard till; —harass to—; harry to—; hasten—; hunger for—; induce—; join in—; laugh at—; long for—; mete out—; mock—; mourn—; overcome—; persecute unto—; poise at the brink of—; pour—on; predestine to—; prepare for—; preserve from—; quail before—; recoil from—; repose in—; repulse—; rescue from—; result in—; revenge—; scorn—; seal with—; send to—; sentence to—; snatch from—; spare from—; spell—; spurt—; stay—; struggle against —; submit to—; suffer—; symbolize—; threaten with—; triumph over—; usher in—; ward off—; warrant—; welcome—; wreak—; yield to—; —alters; —claims; —clamors; —concludes; —dances; — dawns; —devours; —dogs; —embitters;

—engulfs; —ensues; —follows; —grieves; —grins; —harvests; —humbles; —intervenes; —invades; —lurks; —menaces; — parts; —reveals; —shades; —shadows; —spreads; —stalks among; —stings; — supervenes; —swallows up; —terminates; —triumphs; —vanquishes; —walks; — strikes.
(See extinction, destruction, slaughter, mortality.)

DEBASE (v)
adverbs
obscenely; miserably; shamefully; tragically; ruinously; unavoidably; irrevocably; irreparably; tyrannically.
(See degrade, humiliate.)

DEBASED
adverbs
grossly; abjectly; morally; perfidiously; treacherously; disgracefully; darkly; infamously; arrantly; vilely; contemptibly; shamefully; bestially.

DEBATABLE
adverbs
highly; unquestionably; definitely; obviously; profoundly; endlessly; turbulently; violently; critically; dangerously; excitingly; hotly; amusingly; readily; easily; reasonably; rationally; concretely; equivocally; hypothetically; precariously; speciously; logically.

DEBATE
adjectives
stormy; profound; mental; inward; parliamentary; foul; keen; acrimonious; notable; instructive; picayune; animated; interrupted; open; free; public; obstructive; lively; endless; prolix; fierce; impassioned; mock; lifelong; extemporaneous; considerable; political; epistolary; vigorous; newspaper; turbulent; organized; heated; disorderly; spirited; exciting; familiar;. long-winded; noisy; hot; brotherly; amusing; teleological; loud; dialetical.

verbs
admit to—; assemble for—; climax—; contend during—; deliberate on—; draw into —; engage in—; enter into—; indulge in—; involve in—; judge—; practise—; prepare —; resolve into—; settle—; subject to—; welcome—; wrangle during—; —concludes; —discusses; —revolves about.
(See dispute, controversy, combat, contest, discussion.)

DEBATE (v)

adverbs

abundantly; extensively; futilely; inwardly; profoundly; mentally; instructively; animatedly; openly; publicly; endlessly; fiercely; impassionedly; extemporaneously; considerably; politically; vigorously; turbulently; heatedly; spiritedly; noisily; hotly; amusingly; loudly; dialectically; acrimoniously; shrewdly.

(See argue, discuss.)

DEBATER

adjectives

cogent; convincing; tight-lipped; ready; interlocutory.

verbs

coach—; judge—; prepare—; train—; verse—; —argues; —assembles; —asserts; —assures; —cajoles; —concludes; —contends; —convinces; —declares; —discusses; —disputes; —engages; —gestures; —illustrates; —informs; —points out; —refers to; —refutes; —registers; —shouts; —voices.

(See speaker.)

DEBAUCH

adjectives

veritable; riotous; rudimentary; prolonged; unwonted; limitless; grisly; abnormal; drunken; secret; fictional.

DEBAUCHED

adverbs

pitiably; grossly; terribly; horribly; shamelessly; abjectly; lamentably; openly; shamefully; morally; disgracefully; infamously; notoriously; arrantly; vilely; contemptibly; bestially; voluptuously; wildly; dissolutely; brutishly; indecently.

DEBAUCHERY

adjectives

brutal; sensual; profligate; titled; coarse; truant; corrupt; perverse.

DEBILITY

adjectives

languid; attendant; general; extreme; congenital; nervous; spectral; physical.

DEBRIS

adjectives

accumulated; rock; floating; chaotic; fragmentary; sad; littered; hopeless.

verbs

emerge from—; crumble to—; fall amidst —; rise from—; scatter—; search—.

(See ruins, remains, fragments, rubbish.)

DEBT

adjectives

common; enormous; stale; ancestral; crushing; credit; impaired; recoverable; petty; immeasurable; incalculable; heavy; tremendous; huge; lawful; honest; long-standing; mounting; urgent; floating; discharged; everlasting; terrible; dubious; regulating; desperate; profound; gambling; unpayable, joint; countless; paltry.

verbs

abolish—; acknowledge—; amass—; assume —; cancel—; clear—; confront with—; contract—; die in—; discharge—; dissolve —; encumber with—; free from—; harass with—; incur—; overwhelm with—; plunge into—; repay—; repudiate—; scale down—; smart under—; swell—; unload—; wipe away—; —jumps; —rises; —soars.

(See obligation, liability.)

DEBTOR

adjectives

prodigal; luckless; shabby; insolvent; grateful; broken.

verbs

accommodate—; bind—; bond—; demand of—; die—; harass—; harry—; hound—; imprison—; insure—; jail—; limit—; oblige—; press—; release—; subject—; sue —; —abolishes; —appeals to; —borrows; —discharges; —falls delinquent; —promises; —reduces.

DEBUT

adjectives

operatic; successful; daring; startling; notable; eventual.

DEBUTANTE

adjectives

pretty; awkward; career-seeking; altarbound; dazzling; successfully-launched; expensive; luxury-seeking.

DECADE

adjectives

present; recent; stormy; independent; successive; mauve; ironical; past; coming; prosperous; legendary.

verbs
approach—; celebrate—; include in—; infuse in—; form in—; recall —s; recognize—; survive—; vanish with—s; —advances; —elapses; —ensues; —envelops; —flourishes.
(See period, time.)

DECADENCE
adjectives
pale; sentimental; brilliant; passionate; pathetic; fragrant; vegetating; mouldy.

verbs
abandon to—; arouse from—; awake from —; crumble into—; fall into—; incur—; lapse into—; prevent—; produce—; resist —; result in—; rise out of—; slide into—; steep in—; suffer—; threaten with—; —approaches; —beckons; —girdles; —sleeps in.
(See deterioration, decay.)

DECADENT
adverbs
cankerously; decrepitly; effetely; corrosively; corruptibly; irreparably; incurably; irremediably; lamentably; deplorably; pitifully; viciously; degenerately; corruptly; unbelievably; astoundingly; pitiably; hopelessly.

DECAY
adjectives
inevitable; melancholy; symbolic; premature; elegant; slow; mental; swift; physical; flamboyant; approaching; common; perpetual; integral; picturesque; unperceived; sensible; dry; gradual; inexorable; fatal; lichened.

verbs
accelerate—; arrest—; attack by—; bar—; conceal—; delay—; doom to—; exempt from—; fall into—; presage—; preserve from—; reek of—; resist—; subject to—; suffer—; —bores into; —sets in.
(See deterioration, decomposition, corruption.)

DECAY (v)
adverbs
fearfully; disastrously; inevitably; symbolically; prematurely; mentally; swiftly; physically; picturesquely; sensibly; inexorably; gradually; fatally; obviously; partially; invisibly.
(See rot, disintegrate.)

DECEIT
adjectives
charming; dreamlike; dear; radiant; adored; coquettish; remorseful; blind; beguiling; unprincipled; fatal.

verbs
abhor—; avoid—; breed—; commit—; conceal—; contrive by—; depart from—; dispose to—; dwell in—; indulge in—; intend—; nourish—; quit—; redeem from —; shroud—; suspect—; unearth—; utter —; wallow in—; work—; annoys; —counters; —falsifies; —flourishes; —harms; —irks; —misleads; —pricks; —tricks; reprove—.
(See fraud, deception. trick, stratagem, cheating.)

DECEITFUL
adverbs
inherently; naturally; habitually; characteristically; temperamentally; subtly; shrewdly; astutely; carefully; deliberately; insidiously; smoothly; fiendishly; maliciously; astoundingly; deftly; dangerously; insinuatingly; horribly; abominably; shamefully; daringly; surprisingly; unexpectedly; expertly.

DECEIVE (v)
adverbs
deliberately; grossly; palpably; bitterly; eternally; prodigiously; blackly; mightily; heartlessly; systematically; basely; purposely; vilely; villainously; treacherously.
(See mislead.)

DECEIVER
adjectives
systematic; heartless; gracious; seductive; gay; artful; politic; insidious; crafty.

DECENCY
adjectives
ordinary; sheer; conventional; common; mere; enforced; requisite; wanton; political; true; social; eminent; respectable; temperate; native; disregarded.

verbs
breed in—; conform to—; dress in—; dwell in—; execute with—; expect—; inject into—; insist on—; maintain—; manage with—; observe—; perform with—; practise—; pretend—; violate—; —befits; —flourish; —requires; outrage—.
(See propriety, modesty, decorum.)

DECENT

adverbs

decorously; utterly; entirely; honestly; modestly; admirably; habitually; conventionally; eminently; innately; inherently; notably; chastely; suitably; naturally; appropriately; unobtrusively; superbly; remarkably; essentially; palpably; obviously; extraordinarily; unaffectedly.

DECEPTION

adjectives

palpable; gross; downright; swaggering; detestable; obvious; systematic; pious; venial; innocent; intentional; harmless; inevitable; economic; relative; facial; deliberate; refined; universal.

verbs

apply—; avoid—; commit—; conceal—; devise—; dispose to—; expose—; fall into —; fear—; form—; imagine—; impose— upon; justify—; perform—; produce—; practice—; suspect—; unearth—; unfold—; —harms; —injures.

(See deceit, craft, cunning, trickery, fraud.)

DECEPTIVE

adverbs

palpably; grossly; detestably; obviously; cruelly; systematically; methodically; intentionally; purposely; maliciously; harmlessly; deliberately; childishly; innocently; teasingly; criminally; cleverly; astutely; adroitly; expertly; carefully; meanly; despicably; contemptibly; disgracefully; terribly.

DECIDE (v)

adverbs

adversely; conclusively; discreetly; positively; affirmatively; irrevocably; authentically; impartially; wisely; tentatively; peremptorily; glumly; confusedly; arbitrarily; simultaneously; impulsively; virtually; unanimously; eventually; conspicuously; grudgingly; favorably; magnanimously; sensibly; temperately; resolutely; unalterably; authoritatively; haphazardly; prematurely; precipitately; tactically; emphatically; spectacularly; promptly; theoretically; academically; technically; politically; speedily.

(See determine, resolve.)

DECISION

adjectives

favorable; comforting; sagacious; well-considered; careful; correct; perfect; prac-

tical; magnanimous; sensible; unfettered; unbought; accurate; straightforward; just; calm; temperate; final; irreparable; irrevocable; invincible; expectant; inexorable; peremptory; sweeping; important; resolute; unflinching; firm; unmistakable; unalterable; unchanged; authoritative; unbiased; weighty; momentous; august; arbitrary; vacillating; haphazard; premature; abrupt; precipitate; rapid; instant; hasty; intuitive; quick; swift; hair-trigger; dangerous; desperate; ruinous; illegal; adverse; judicial; critical; temporal; ticklish; major; iniquitous; unanimous; last-moment; applauded; perplexing; tactical; controlling; definite; profitless; cryptic; tentative; overt; successive; prompt; emphatic; due; unbalanced; disastrous; solemn; demurred; spectacular; supreme; indolent; instant; practical; ruling; belated; blamable; strict; impartial; theoretical; calculated; epoch-making; heart-searching; resolute; sudden; daring; executive; tremendous; resounding; academic; unwise; crushing; initiatory; technical; adverse; political; rumored; sundry (pl).

verbs

abide by—; accept—; acclaim—; adhere to—; analyze—; circumvent—; confirm—; contest—; dictate—; enforce—; execute—; greet—; hail—; hand down—; influence—; obey—; prejudice—; reach—; render—; reverse—; stiffen—; subject to—; submit to—; swing—; voice—; weigh—; —embroils; —favors; —foreshadows; invalidates; —takes place; —wavers.

(See settlement, conclusion, verdict.)

DECISIVE

adverbs

alarmingly; conclusively; definitely; scarcely; mercifully; fortunately; happily; favorably; comfortingly; practically; justly; irrevocably; inexorably; sweepingly; importantly; firmly; unmistakably; unalterably; authoritatively; authentically; weightily; augustly; intuitively; swiftly; desperately; critically; iniquitously; solemnly; tremendously; politically.

DECK

adjectives

hurricane; forward; promenade; white-scoured; bright; snowy; spotless; glistening; holystoned; sloping; inclining; reeling; pitching; slippery; slimy; unscrubbed; shattered; spacious; blazing; cluster-lighted; splinter-strewn; awninged; watery;

crowded; ghostly; creamy; tapered; wind-swept; ocean; long; great; open; comfortable; gay; sun; broad; shot-torn; shuddering; wave-set; steamer; stricken; bloody; unobstructed; wreckage-laden.

verbs
batter—; burst—; clear—; cover—; dash on—; glimmer on—; keep above—; lash—; lie on—; pace—; scatter on—; shatter—; splinter—; sprawl on—; stand on—; sun on —; toss on—; tramp—; view from—; wave from—; —extends; —runs.
(See platform. floor.)

DECLAMATION
adjectives
rhetorical; strident; stuttering; insipid; passionate; empty; facetious; sounding.

verbs
alter—; burst into—; compose—; dispute—; influence—; inspire—; publish—; render—; repeat—; set forth—; stir up—; thunder—; utter—; —embodies; —exacerbates; —expresses; —proves; —shocks; —stirs.
(See speech. oration, oratory.)

DECLAMATORY
adverbs
absurdly; effusively; unnecessarily; foolishly; ridiculously; ludicrously; amusingly; bombastically; pompously; arrogantly; pretentiously; stridently; passionately; fervently; emptily; facetiously; sententiously; laughably; piously; grandiloquently; floridly; preachily; pedantically; frothily; flashily; flamboyantly; blatantly.

DECLARATION
adjectives
culminating; remarkable; far-echoing; formal; droll; insulting; emphatic; public; appalling; passionate; blunt; voluntary; candid; downright; bold; determining; significant; official; profound; strong; solemn; superior; positive; vehement; frequent; rigid; important; absolute; distinct; undisguised; open; customary; fierce; friendly; supplementary; bitter; passionate; abasing; unmistakable.

verbs
adopt—; announce—; belie—; constitute—; decry—; dispute—; expound—; immortalize—; inspire—; introduce—; issue—; present—; proclaim—; publish—; set forth—; —contradicts; —embodies; —influences; —pleads; —proves; —shocks.
(See assertion, statement.)

DECLARATORY
adverbs
plainly; comfortingly; reassuringly; explicitly; clearly; analytically; broadly; substantially; literally; honestly; simply; significantly; intelligibly; authoritatively; formally; emphatically; bluntly; officially.

DECLARE (v)
adverbs
vociferously; formally; publicly; emphatically; passionately; bluntly; candidly; boldly; significantly; officially; solemnly; vehemently; absolutely; distinctly; openly; fiercely; bitterly; unmistakably; conceitedly; enthusiastically; pedantically; petulantly; grimly; virtually; impatiently; contemptuously; stoutly; hypocritically; privately; haltingly; inconclusively; antagonistically; formally; shamelessly; speciously; archly; hotly; earnestly; rapturously; severely; wrathfully; repeatedly; unanimously; solemnly.
(See affirm, state.)

DECLINE
adjectives
marked; considerable; general; ultimate; lingering; terrific; unquestionable; alarming; social; drastic; prolonged; accelerated; sad; subsequent; premature; short; dreary; unaccountable; hopeless; marked; incipient; ominous; partial; unprecedented; indubitable.

DECLINE (v)
adverbs
peremptorily; repeatedly; progressively; blandly; spinelessly; respectfully; steadily; gently; invariably; bluntly; querulously; rapidly; gravely; firmly; quietly; majestically; ultimately; alarmingly; socially; acceleratedly; subsequently; prematurely; drearily; unaccountably; hopelessly; ominously; partially; indubitably; unprecedentedly.
(See languish, bend.)

DECLIVITY
adjectives
slight; dread; gentle; abrupt; steep; obstructing.

DECOMPOSITION
adjectives
chemical; spontaneous; painful; tedious; rapid; erosive; timely.

319

verbs

crumble into—; fall into—; incur—; lapse into—; object to—; prevent—; produce—; resolve into—; result in—; slide into—; suffer—; threaten with—; undergo—; —abates; —continues; —distributes; —separates.

(See disintegration, decay.)

DECORATE (v)

adverbs

elaborately; exquisitely; profusely; picturesquely; garishly; inelegantly; charmingly; lavishly; gaudily; quaintly; splendidly; tastefully; mournfully; superfluously; sumptuously; superbly; festively; gorgeously; pictorially; richly; tastefully; delicately; ornately; ostentatiously; characteristically; formally; realistically; murally; scenically; fantastically; architecturally; grotesquely.

(See adorn, embellish.)

DECORATION

adjectives

coveted; incidental; pictorial; simulated; profuse; mistaken; disturbing; quiet; rich; new; superb; modern; regal; tasteful; delicate; contemporary; delightful; ornate; ostentatious; personal; excessive; last-moment; characteristic; silver; detailed; glaring; formal; realistic; eye-filling; sense-curdling; painted; elaborate; polychrome; mural; casual; sober; religious; lateral; lavish; unobtrusive; sparkling; scenical; stupendous; sculptural; simple; fantastic; costly; lifeless; colorless; architectural; molded; grotesque; subordinated.

DECORATIVE

adverbs

delicately; incidentally; properly; quietly; richly; superbly; regally; tastefully; delightfully; ornately; excessively; formally; elaborately; casually; soberly; lavishly; unobtrusively; pleasantly; agreeably; appropriately; graphically; picturesquely; romantically; unusually; beautifully.

DECORATOR

adjectives

prominent; competent; resourceful; professional; amateur; over-ambitious; aspiring; over-nice; classically-inclined.

DECOROUS

adverbs

becomingly; modestly; essentially; socially; strictly; scrupulously; carefully; invariably; habitually; ordinarily; dependably; politely; fashionably; punctiliously; conventionally; civilly; respectfully; reverentially; deferentially; ceremoniously; decently.

DECORUM

adjectives

external; stately; perfect; naughty; social; artistic; strict; pallid; unyielding; scrupulous; grave; public.

verbs

adhere to—; act with—; behave with—; cling to—; clothe in—; hedge by—; maintain—; mantle in—; nourish—; observe—; preserve—; require—; safeguard—; shed —; shock—; wallow in—; —lapses; —prevails; —restrains.

(See politeness, decency, propriety.)

DECREASE

adjectives

sagging; marked; dripping; noticeable; proportional.

DECREASE (v)

adverbs

imperceptibly; immeasurably; relatively; markedly; proportionally; noticeably; amazingly; astonishingly; tragically; fatally; woefully.

(See diminish, reduce.)

DECREE

adjectives

judgment; repealing; castigatory; omnipotent; law; august; tyrannical; eternal; emergency; royal; unalterable; unfathomable; divine; imperial; established; stern; oppressive; changeless; pitiless; unexecuted; irreversible; obnoxious; generous; paternal; laconic; primeval; absolute; extemporary.

verbs

adjust—; affirm—; alter—; annul—; bow to—; break—; carry out—; condemn—; confirm—; contest—; declare—; delay—; enforce—; favor—; issue—; mold—; obey—; oppose—; overleap—; proclaim—; promulgate—; repeal—; resist—; reverse —; revoke—; shape—; sign—; submit to—; sustain—; trample upon—; —banishes; —bans; —conscripts; —disposes of; —prohibits.

(See law, edict, mandate, ordinance, decision, rule.)

DECREE (v)

adverbs

irrevocably; tyrannically; legislatively; formally.

(See enact.)

DECREPIT

adverbs

helplessly; prematurely; dangerously; pitiably; hopelessly; pathetically; terribly; deplorably; heartbreakingly; hoarily; dodderingly; feebly; totteringly; crazily; incurably; weakly; lamentably; pitifully.

DECREPITUDE

adjectives

premature; dangerous; helpless; hampering; fretful; onrushing; subtle.

DEDICATE (v)

adverbs

pompously; respectfully; tacitly; solemnly; chiefly; wholeheartedly; sincerely; humbly; flatteringly; appreciatively; modestly; arrogantly; worshipfully.

(See consecrate, devote.)

DEDICATION

adjectives

handsome; nauseating; flattering; honorary; memorable; cursory; nominal.

DEDUCE (v)

adverbs

psychologically; rationalistically; unscientifically; logically; immediately; daringly; legitimately; profoundly; modestly; shrewdly.

(See conclude.)

DEDUCTIBLE

adverbs

immediately; legitimately; legally; logically; naturally; liberally; fortunately; ultimately; deceptively; possibly; unquestionably; inferentially; authentically; authoritatively; generously; substantially.

DEDUCTION

adjectives

immense; entomological; immediate; pure; sound; unverified; daring; trifling; logical; legitimate; profound; liberal; analogical; ultimate; false; bibulous; dipsomaniacal; modest; sagest; possible; hazardous; labored; spurious; genuine.

verbs

allow—; arrive at—; bear out—; claim—; confirm—; contemplate—; contradict—; debate—; decide on—; deny—; derive—; draw—; err in—; form—; reach—; reason —; secure—; —confuses; —follows.

(See demonstration, proof, inference.)

DEED
(general)

adjectives

sundry (pl); good; glorious; worthy; wise; brilliant; maniacal; meritorious; glamorous; notable; unforgettable; momentous; brave; courageous; heroic; mighty; doughty; rash; evil; dangerous; terrible; dishonest; desperate; inhuman; dirty; brutal; treacherous; violent; bloodthirsty; unholy; harsh; vainglorious; atrocious; silly; tacit; valiant; contemplated; passionate; unnatural; charitable; shameful; cursed; radiant; rueful; conspicuous; piteous; peaceful; wicked; hideous; masterful; execrable; heinous; bloody; lustful; chivalric; honorable; long; traitorous; virtuous; foulest; selfish; corrupt; unjust; steadfast; tragic; dastardly; magnanimous; historic; pious; truculent; knightly; disgraceful; manful; irrevocable; dragon; untried; lovely; sculptured; fiendish; lawless; persistent; deathless; fell; amazing; kindred; hazardous; darkest; venturous; stern; ill; unostentatious; precious; baleful; title; daring; horrible; barbarous; fearful; evil; remorseless; blazing; kind; sublime; caitiff; generous; wholesome; human; reckless; vile; abhorrent; loyal; pure; kingly; senseless; undying; grander; impeachable; noble; despicable; myriad (pl).

verbs

acclaim—; achieve—; answer for—; applaud—; ascribe to—; attempt—; bear out—; belittle—; blame—; bless—; boast of—; celebrate—; commemorate—; commend—; commit—; consent to—; contrive —; dare—; die in—; dignify—; dispense with—; dread—; emulate—; enshrine—; execrate—; glory in—; govern—; hallow—; honor—; incite to—; judge—; justify—; match—; noise—; perform—; please by—; proclaim—; promote—; recompense—; record—; relate—; resent—; render—; repent—; report—; reprove—; reward—; rue—; serve in—; shudder at—; sing of—s; spur to—; spurn—; void—; vouch for—; —awes; —flames; —indicates; —lives; —shames.

(See act. feat, performance, reality, exploit, achievement.)

adjectives

restless; violet; uncomprehensible; over-brimming; mystic; uncreated; populous; airy; avenging; waveless; unfathomable; glimmering; laughing; lonely; vasty; waiting; blue; windless; lethal; boundless; lower; muffled; sunnier; sacred; regal; quiet; lampless; charmed; wind-obeying; shuddering; dreary; tranquil; unsounded; dangerous; mid-sea; transparent; unclosing; immeasurable; presumptuous; unnatural; tempest-wrinkled; dark-blue; innumerable (pl); murmuring; voiceless; remorseless; finny; unapparent.

verbs

abound in—; ambush from—; cast into—; conceal in—; delve in—; draw into—s; fill—; gaze at—; hide in—; lower to—; pierce—; pursue through—; recede into—; thunder in—; venture from—; —engulfs; —resounds.

adverbs

abysmally; inscrutably; mysteriously; unfathomably; quietly; immeasurably; profoundly; immensely; dangerously; hideously; prodigiously; wondrously; obviously; enormously; astonishingly; marvellously; unutterably; fabulously; curiously; amazingly.

DEEPEN (*v*)

adverbs

insensibly; sufficiently; unconsciously; unfathomably; boundlessly; shudderingly; immeasurably; unnaturally; remorsefully.
  (See intensify.)

DEEP-SEATED

adverbs

intrinsically; inherently; stubbornly; obstinately; incurably; intensely; traditionally; customarily; racially; frequently.

DEER

adjectives

shy; brown; agile; astonished; stricken; shadowy; wounded; tame; antlered; plentiful; exquisite; graceful; sobbing; sleek; truant; fleet; swift.

verbs

chase—; follow—; herd—; lasso—; shelter —; skin—; rouse—; wound—; —bounds; —darts; —frequents; —haunts; —leaps; —roams; —sheds; —shies; —shuns; — treads; —treks.
  (See animal.)

adverbs

rustily; unrecognizably; terribly; hopelessly; unpardonably; inexcusably; irreparably; irremediably; frightfully; grimly; horribly; grossly; odiously; shockingly.

DEFAME (*v*)

adverbs

libelously; viciously; revengefully; wantonly; hatefully; treacherously; illegally; spitefully; ruinously.
  (See slander.)

DEFAULT

adjectives

glaring; notorious; serious; infinitesimal; covert; punishable.

verbs

arrest—; commit—; convict of—; expect—; expose—; force—; impose—; mend—; occasion—; pardon—; penalize—; practise—; punish—; record—; urge—; —deprives; —occurs.
  (See neglect, omission, failure, deficiency.)

DEFEAT

adjectives

avowed; acknowledged; tremendous; crushing; graceful; overwhelming; shameful; ignoble; humiliating; signal; bitter; gory; ugly; rudest; inevitable; ultimate; impending; intellectual; trivial; unconditional; vain; stinging; unwilling; serious; sheer; later; subsequent; disheartening; crowning; humble; expensive; insignificant; final; inglorious; decisive; utter; undisguised; damned; ignominious; logical; ridiculous; unexpected; smashing; dreadful; heartbroken; averted; telling; encompassed; paralyzing; creditable; pet; disastrous; spiritual; dispirited; irretrievable.

verbs

acknowledge—; administer—; bear—; brand with—; brood over—; contribute to —; court—; destine to—; doom to—; emerge from—; foredoom to—; foresee—; gesture—; go down in—; invite—; involve—; meet—; pave the way for—; suffer —; thrive upon—; visualize—; writhe at—; —encompasses; —shakes.
  (See repulse, loss, ruin.)

DEFEAT (*v*)

adverbs

incessantly; absolutely; successively; decisively; utterly; subsequently; exultantly;

crushingly; overwhelmingly; effectually; gloriously; shamefully; ignobly; humiliatingly; signally; bitterly; inevitably; ultimately; unconditionally; finally; ignominiously; logically; paralyzingly; disastrously; spiritually.

(See whip, thrash.)

DEFECT

adjectives

basic; vital; grave; serious; glaring; important; dominant; simple; secondary; minor; flagrant; fatal; unfortunate; psychic; functional; mental; mechanical; characteristic; uncorrected; possible; qualitative; latent; undeniable; structural; fair; abominable; constitutional; aggravated; concealed; palpable; inconspicuous; unexpected; temporary; manifold; serious; surface; complementary (pl); immense; obvious; capital; woeful; postural; inherent; radical; glaring; poetical; perilous; speculative.

verbs

analyze—; compensate for—; discover—; eliminate—; judge—; indicate—; make up for—; minimize—; produce—; rectify—; remedy—; shackle by—; spot—; stamp—; suffer from—; supply—; —impairs; —taints.

(See imperfection, blemish, fault, foible. flaw, shortcoming.)

DEFECTIVE

adverbs

unacceptably; unfortunately; grossly; carelessly; crudely; objectionably; provokingly; vexatiously; definitely; altogether; shamefully; outrageously; obviously; perceptibly; palpably; indefensibly; inexcusably.

DEFECTION

adjectives

contemplated; temporary; momentary; growing; relative; moral; impulsive.

DEFENDANT

adjectives

heroic; private; scared; frightened; worried; perjured.

verbs

accuse—; acquit—; aid—; attack—; bail—; befuddle—; bind—; challenge—; charge—; cross-examine—; discharge—; enjoin—; guard—; question—; represent—; restrain —; vindicate—; —answers; —attests; —

counters; —declares; —defies; —denies; —maintains; —perjures; —pleads; —resists; —swears; —vouches; —vows.

(See defender, champion, advocate.)

DEFEND (v)

adverbs

elaborately; vigorously; gallantly; warmly; strenuously; stoutly; formidably; spiritedly; desperately; principally; subtly; ardently; philosophically; valorously; sturdily; passively; staunchly; brilliantly; obstinately; eloquently; competently; courageously; vigorously; determinedly; impassionedly; sensationally; unexpectedly; heroically; spiritlessly; aggressively; effectually; mutually; instinctively; unfailingly; injudiciously; unapproachably.

(See guard, protect.)

DEFENDER

adjectives

ardent; lawful; impenitent; philosophical; bold; brave; valorous; uncompromising; stout; sturdy; staunch; unconquerable; clever; gallant; passive; sincere; brilliant; steadfast; obstinate; habitual; eloquent.

verbs

acclaim—; banish—; challenge—; charge —; deploy—s; drive out—; hail—; honor —; reward—; —assails; —averts; —counters; —forsakes; —guards; —protects; — repels; —restrains; —upholds; —wards off.

(See defendant, advocate, champion.)

DEFENSE

adjectives

spirited; competent; noble; brilliant; courageous; strong; formidable; valiant; vigorous; long; determined; unassailable; involuntary; bungling; impassioned; halfhearted; weak; sensational; awkward; compelling; half-amused; adequate; national; manufactured; critical; inartificial; organized; offensive; frenzied; conceivable; unexpected; steadfast; natural; dignified; rare; spiritless; obstinate; pretty; armed; heroic; plausible; aggressive; uncompromising; honest; sorry; effectual; questionable; uncouth; eloquent; moral; capital; elaborate; gallant; adamantine; projected; womanly; leisurely; prompt; powerful; compensatory; mutual; instinctive; self; unfailing; minute; anomalous; injudicious; unapproachable.

verbs

abandon—; achieve—; argue in—; arise in—; batter—; bolster—; build—; bungle —; buttress—; demolish—; employ—; imperil—; map out—; prepare—; propound —; rally—; reenforce—; rehabilitate—; rush to—; sharpen—; smash—; spring to—; stand in—; stiffen under—; survey—; throw up—; vow—; —breaks; —crumbles; —crumples; —interposes.

(See protection, plan.)

DEFENSELESS

adverbs

tragically; unhappily; pathetically; silently; horribly; suddenly; surprisingly; utterly; bitterly; sadly; unexpectedly; scandalously; shockingly; calamitously; fatally; ignominiously; ominously; mysteriously; inexplicably.

DEFENSIVE

adverbs

eagerly; humbly; hastily; skilfully; reluctantly; angrily; confusedly; openly; awkwardly; nervously; instantly; preposterously; unnecessarily; sufficiently; profoundly; tearfully; pathetically; incoherently; sheepishly; embarrassingly; miserably; slavishly; disgustingly; deeply; half-heartedly; honestly.

DEFER (v)

adverbs

suavely; unfeignedly; condescendingly; pleasantly; scrupulously; particularly; servilely; resentfully; punctiliously; ungrudgingly; habitually; admiringly; carelessly; sympathetically.

(See delay.)

DEFERENCE

adjectives

unfeigned; suave; condescending; pleasant; exceeding; scrupulous; blissful; unfailing; chivalrous; particular; bullying; servile; secret; resentful; respectful; awesome; self-restraining; punctilious; exquisite; due; apparent; ungrudging; utmost; habitual; admiring; careless; sympathetic.

verbs

acknowledge—; allow—; bestow—; bow in—; choose out of—; claim—; conduct with—; entitle to—; grant—; nod in—; pay—; proceed with—; render—; respect —; respond to—; tender—; transact with —; treat with—; yield—.

(See respect, regard.)

DEFERENTIAL

adverbs

charmingly; pleasantly; properly; respectfully; scrupulously; exceedingly; unfailingly; chivalrously; punctiliously; exquisitely; duly; apparently; habitually; carefully; courteously; delightfully; devotedly; loyally; modestly; affably; amiably; gallantly; ceremoniously; ingratiatingly; tactfully; dutifully; decorously; sweetly; cordially.

DEFIANCE

adjectives

calm; silent; rare; quiet; fine; daring; resolute; firm; gay; mirthful; drawling; roaring; fierce; raucous; shrill; blatant; willful; ruffian; snarling; monstrous; shamefaced; reckless; desperate; murderous; mock; sneering; indignant; open; curious; passionate; exhilarating; quivering; quotable; shrinking; cringing; thundering; puny; irritating; perceptible; sudden; nomadic; scornful; admirable; maledictory; frank; potential; nonchalant; hurt; robust; half-frightened; schoolgirlish; unrighteous; mute; bristling; mortal; contemptuous; solitary; mutual; bold; actual; successful; patient; implied; indomitable; still; suppressed; savage.

verbs

attempt—; breathe—; fling—at; foster—; glare—; greet with—; hurl—; quell—; scorn—; shout—; snort—; sponsor—; stand firm in—; throw—at; uphold—.

(See challenge, opposition, provocation, contempt, rebellion.)

DEFIANT

adverbs

calmly; rarely; silently; quietly; boldly; resolutely; firmly; blithely; fiercely; blatantly; shrilly; monstrously; desperately; mockingly; indignantly; openly; sullenly; curiously; strangely; irritably; frankly; mutely; moodily; indomitably; stubbornly; obstinately; inexplicably; justly; defensibly.

DEFICIENCY

adjectives

unavoidable; fatal; evident; mental; technical; previous; glaring; psychological; marked; organic; suprarenal; noticeable.

verbs

accentuate—; allow—; balance—; compensate for—; condone—; correct—; counteract—; detect—; manifest—; mend—; observe—; presage—; reveal—; supply—; weep for—; —glares; —occurs.

(See defect, imperfection, shortcoming, inadequacy.)

DEFICIENT

adverbs

fatally; evidently; mentally; technically; markedly; glaringly; noticeably; crudely; lamentably; unfortunately; sadly; miserably; pitifully; woefully.

DEFICIT

adjectives

genuine; increasing; successive; alleged; alarming; startling; unaccountable.

verbs

accumulate—; arrest for—; bear—; calculate—; estimate—; expose—; falsify—; finance—; force—; halt—; mend—; pile up—; protect against—; reveal—; stagger through—; suspect—; uncover—; wipe out —; —arises; —deprives; —dwindles; —occurs.

(See deficiency.)

DEFILE

adjectives

dark; tangled; lofty; wild; rugged; rocky; towering; mountain; dangerous.

DEFILEMENT

adjectives

solemn; majestic; zonal; constructive; compact; straggling.

DEFINE (v)

adverbs

boldly; closely; sharply; sufficiently; particularly; bluntly; precisely; explicitly; accurately; crudely; arbitrarily; exactly; interestingly; subjectively; objectionably; essentially; technically; vigorously; invidiously; imperfectly; objectively; brilliantly; informally; vaguely; scientifically.

(See interpret, limit.)

DEFINITE

adverbs

crisply; bluntly; accurately; arbitrarily; interestingly; sharply; oddly; objectionably; thoroughly; brilliantly; pleasingly; acceptably; comfortingly; intelligibly; conspicuously; reliably; dogmatically; officially; authoritatively; authentically; vividly; graphically; comprehensibly.)

DEFINITION

adjectives

accurate; crude; representative; arbitrary; abstract; exclusive; exact; precise; interesting; perfervid; subjective; sharp; clear-cut; objectionable; famous; preliminary; unchallenged; healthy; thoroughgoing; essential; positive; vigorous; technical; analogous; invidious; objective; brilliant; informal; vague; scientific; elastic; reasonable; serviceable; imperfect.

verbs

apply—; arrive at—; construct—; determine—; establish—; restrict—; search for —; stretch—; supply—; understand—; weaken—; —defines; —describes; —determines; —enlightens; —explains; —expresses; —fixes; —limits; —satisfies; —specifies; —unfolds.

(See explanation, description, comment, exposition, interpretation.)

DEFLATION

adjectives

sweeping; monetary; postwar; credit; vicious; severe; sharp; salient; encroaching.

verbs

guard against—; master—; prepare for—; produce—; prophesy—; protect against—; release—; remedy—; repair—; sink into—; —affects; —injures; —looms; —menaces; —occurs; —produces; —reduces; —remedies; —repairs; —ruins.

(See collapse.)

DEFORMED

adverbs

woefully; physically; hideously; sadly; monstrously; congenitally; pitiably; lamentably; mysteriously; inexpressibly; horribly; deplorably; wretchedly; distressingly; incurably; irremediably; sorrily; crookedly; grossly; gruesomely; repulsively; terribly.

DEFORMITY

adjectives

apoplectic; unexpressed; pockmarked; physical; mocking; hideous; monstrous; foul; passing; hereditary.

verbs

accentuate—; avert—; brace—; correct—; enhance—; fake—; guard against—; iron out—; minimize—; overcome—; prevent—; produce—; result in—; torture into—; twist into—; —disfigures; —distorts; —impairs; —recurs.

(See blemish, abnormality.)

DEFRAUD (v)

adverbs
deliberately; coolly; villainously; cleverly; knavishly; deceitfully; unsuspectingly; deftly; sagaciously; financially.
(See cheat.)

DEFRAY (v)

adverbs
individually; regularly; belatedly; tardily; unhesitatingly; handsomely; regally; completely.
(See pay.)

DEFT

adverbs
unusually; admirably; wondrously; enviably; nimbly; marvellously; amazingly; remarkably; consistently; harmoniously; socially; conversationally; felicitously; appropriately; intelligently; shrewdly.

DEFTNESS

adjectives
marvelous; amazing; remarkable; skillful; marked; noteworthy.

DEFY (v)

adverbs
haughtily; sullenly; recklessly; arrogantly; undauntedly; menacingly; calmly; resolutely; fiercely; raucously; blatantly; snarlingly; desperately; murderously; mockingly; passionately; frankly; nonchalantly; righteously; mutely; bristlingly; mortally; contemptuously; savagely.
(See challenge, dare.)

DEGENERACY

adjectives
deplorable; nervous; physical; dissolute; irreparable; abject.

DEGENERATE

adjectives
unmoral; lazy; pathological; hopeless; irretrievable.

adverbs
grossly; outrageously; poisonously; corruptly; viciously; brutally; shabbily; effetely; decrepitly; dangerously; hopelessly; helplessly; woefully; abjectly; disgracefully; infamously; contemptibly; shamefully.

DEGENERATION

adjectives
infectious; eventual; apparent; inflammatory; progressive.

DEGRADATION

adjectives
moral; physical; unmerited; hideous; absolute; habitual; excessive; concomitant; stunting; deep; present.

DEGRADE (v)

adverbs
hopelessly; materially; ruinously; morally; unmeritedly; hideously; absolutely; deeply; shamefully; disgracefully; humiliatingly.
(See debase, disgrace.)

DEGREE

adjectives
large; high; fullest; surpassing; extreme; maximal; marked; slightest; infinitesimal; limited; imperceptible; tiny; small; astonishing; extraordinary; remarkable; amazing; startling; unusual; singular; diverse; vulgar; moderate; disgraceful; unsatisfactory; disconcerting; appalling; pre-eminent; uncanny; rare; greatest; practicable; fair; irreparable; increasing; sufficient; corresponding; artificial; intolerable; advanced; superlative; requisite; microscopic; moderate; alarming; considerable; high; unprecedented; varying; feverish; lavish; passable; measurable; adroit; incalculable; slow; adequate; improbable; surpassing; admirable; pronounced; fine; incredible; unabated; evergrowing; remote; minute; awe-inspiring; comparative; diminished; unwonted; gentle; significant; valuable; modified; paramount; unparalleled; sublime; imposing; traditional; extravagant; shameless; certain; cunning; excessive; reasonable; notable; unusual; uncommon; successive; illuminating; unsolicited; impudent; ancient; striking; valued; least; coveted; honorary; impressive; academic; doctorate; transcendent; subordinate; multiform.

verbs
ascend by—s; attain by—s; award—; change by—s; coax by—s; confer—; elevate —; exalt—; honor—; improve by—s; intensify—; lead by—s; limit—; mark—s; match—; overrate—; raise—; respect—; sharpen by—s; suffice to—; turn by—s.
See extent, rank, amount, station, position, title.)

DEITY

adjectives
tutelar; heathen; sylvan; ubiquitous; innumerable (pl); patron; anthropomorphic; beneficent; temperamental; pagan; presid-

ing; vestal; glorious; gloomy; tremendous; graceful; accursed; vital; protecting; incarnate; ascended; impotent; inferior; patronymic; numerous (pl); disowned; injured; dangling; benevolent; oracular; contemporary; iron; dishonorable; solemn.

verbs
absorb in—; adore—; appease—; befit—; believe in—; break away from—; complain to—; conceive of—; create—; defy—; deny—; despise—; dethrone—; enthrone—; incense—; offend—; please—; pray to—; renounce—; signify—; worship—; —creates; —interposes.
(See God, divinity.)

DEJECTED
adverbs
inconceivably; hopelessly; mournfully; pitiably; incurably; incredibly; piteously; horribly; tragically; alarmingly; unbelievably; singularly; oddly; strangely; miserably; comically; unreasonably; ridiculously; youthfully; ostensibly; openly; glumly; disconsolately; moodily; heavily; ludicrously.

DEJECTION
adjectives
vague; querulous; profound; complete; utter; intense; bewildered; utmost; deep; miserable; spiritless; passionate; weary.

verbs
bow in—; bury in—; cast into—; forsake —; humiliate into—; imply—; lower into —; manifest—; register—; shroud into—; sink into—; succumb to—; sustain—; throw into—; —deepens; —envelops; —fells; —weakens; —provokes.
(See depression, melancholy, discouragement.)

DELAY
adjectives
considerable; majestic; lingering; enforced; useless; injurious; unaccountable; inexplicable; petty; incomprehensible; anterior; proverbial; infamous; extended; dull; dangerous; corresponding; avoidable; needless; tedious; prolonged; slight; long; hazardous; endless; disappointing; fatal; strange; enforced; irksome; heartbreaking; exasperating; unconscionable; grievous; amorous; vexatious; sweet; parliamentary; characteristic; innumerable (pl).

verbs
advise—; brook—; counsel—; effect—; eliminate—; entail—; importune—; necessitate—; obtain—; occasion—; produce—; promise—; rebel against—; subject to—; trace—; work—; —endangers; —hinders.
(See procrastination, obstruction.)

DELAY (v)
adverbs
immeasurably; unaccountably; injuriously; temporarily; unfortunately; unreasonably; painfully; enforcedly; uselessly; incomprehensibly; infamously; tediously; fatally; disappointingly; irksomely; heartbreakingly; exasperatingly; unconscionably; grievously; vexatiously; characteristically; amorously.
(See dally. postpone.)

DELECTABLE
adverbs
refreshingly; invitingly; appetizingly; delicately; excitingly; charmingly; alluringly; altogether; consistently; irresistibly; unusually; remarkably.

DELEGATE
adjectives
messenger; rural; assembled (pl); interested; legal; ardent; recusant; lone; autochthonous.

verbs
act as—; appoint—; commission—; depute —; employ—; engage—; entrust to—; instruct—; send—; —s assemble; —attends; —s confer; —s convene; —s determine; —exercises; —manages; —performs; —represents; —wearies; —yells.
(See deputy, substitute. representative.)

DELEGATE (v)
adverbs
expressly; successfully; impressively; formally; nominally; authoritatively.
(See order.)

DELEGATION
adjectives
hilarious; impressive; express; representative; pathetic; dependable; authorized; random; select.

verbs
address—; appoint—; assemble—; entrust to—; instruct—; sway—; —attends; —chants; —cheers; —confers; —convenes;

—journeys; —represents; —subscribes to; —supports; —switches to; —votes; —wearies.

(See committee.)

DELETERIOUS
adverbs

malignly; abominably; painfully; grievously; oppressively; noxiously; perniciously; dreadfully; horribly; exceptionably lamentably; woefully; extremely; incredibly.

DELIBERATE
adverbs

evidently; sagaciously; good-humoredly; coolly; duly; sagely; wisely; gravely; ominously; vexatiously; calmly; terribly; impressively; solemnly; consciously; exaggeratedly; cleverly; curiously; pleasantly; prudently; anxiously; courteously; quietly; intently; thoughtfully; particularly; attentively; observantly; carefully; craftily; smartly; skilfully; shrewdly; cautiously; warily; discreetly.

DELIBERATE (v)
adverbs

earnestly; sagaciously; coolly; good-humoredly; sagely; gravely; calmly; solemnly; skillfully; prudently; protractedly; slowly.

(See debate, consider.)

DELIBERATION
adjectives

evident; sagacious; mature; good-humored; cool; sage; equable; grave; terrible; immense; studied; calm; solemn; joint; unexampled; impressive; congressional; knowing; conscious; curious; pleasant; skillful; prudent; public; anxious; due; maddening; courteous; protracted; considerable; massive; cutting; slow; disdainful; anguished.

DELICACY
adjectives

proper; conceivable; lineal; respectable; penetrating; covert; autumnal; fastidious; unexpected; pastel; epicurean; unbounded; ephemeral; substantial; native; exquisite; subtle; spiritual; fine; false; piercing; esteemed; great; extreme; innate; special; instinctive; charming; graceful; imaginable; fine; artistic; manly; morbid; feminine; queenly; dreamlike; complicated; bashful; dangling; exquisite; tempting; infinite; international; raw; pompous; toothsome.

DELICATE
adverbs

exquisitely; incredibly; beautifully; airily; frailly; crisply; freshly; harmoniously; pleasingly; agreeably; sweetly; bewitchingly; daintily; delightfully; ravishingly; gracefully; artistically; richly; properly; fastidiously; ephemerally; subtly.

DELICIOUS
adverbs

altogether; inexpressibly; exquisitely; pleasantly; daintily; felicitiously; palatably; appetizingly; ambrosially; utterly; unexpectedly; pungently; spicily; fragrantly; richly; stimulatingly; lusciously; sweetly.

DELIGHT
adjectives

pure; chastened; true; sincere sacred; home-felt; ecstatic; rapturous; whimsical; jubilant; tittering; utter; sheer; keen; complete; subtle; bizarre; unexpected; unnatural; strange; surprised; awed; supreme; incredulous; wondering; noisy; clamorous; wild; unrestrained; frantic; perfervid; frenzied; ungovernable; unqualified; unending; immeasurable; inexhaustible; tremendous; inexpressible; ineffable; unspeakable; unholy; dumb; fiendish; scornful; malevolent; perverted; painful; fierce; infectious; malicious; vain; frustrated; untrammeled; unalloyed; unfailing; sensuous; passionate; Epicurean; sadistic; childish; gastronomic; boyish; businesslike; chief; generous; intimate; inborn; naive; paroxysmal; extravagant; exalted; rare; drooling; varied; abiding; ardent; insatiate; frank; impossible; anticipatory; redoubled; secret; incommunicable; emulous; riotous; perfumed; idiotic; comforting; flitting; continual; awed; perpetual; sensational; occult; barren; subsequent; deep; dull; mournful; wild; swift; infinite; solicitous; rarefied; siren; lasting; inward; calm; buoyant; sentimental; unfelt; bitter; false; seasonable; hurricane; inexplicable; perpetual; hourly; hysterical; stunned; malignant; surprised; unquiet; trenchant; callous; celestial; rude; intense; ever enduring; laughing; unequalled; gay; unutterable; exquisite; flagging; soft; inebriating; subsiding; delicate; royal; bubbling; vivid; undefined; delicious; taste-tempting; mingled; languorous; unconcealed; nebulous; vigorous; rapturous; wild-beast; fresh; immortal; inestimable; divine; true; savage; anticipatory; astonished; cordial; pretended; rich; impish; tremulous; spiteful; obvious; special; young; unmanaged; vicious; dreamy; innocent; unchecked; preposterous; genuine; rare; giggling; measureless; peculiar; silly; breathless; sweet; placid; unmixed; fair; warm; lingering; singular; musical; mutual; fragmentary; serious; composed; dissembled; temporal; wanton; whimsical; eager; animated; vague; sustained; audible; subdued; capricious; seductive; consummated; manifold (pl).

verbs
afford—; bathe in—; behold with—; derive —; drink in—; enjoy—; exalt—; express—; extol—s of; fall into with—; feed with—; feel—; fill with—; find—in; gaze with—; hail with—; hide—; inspire—; listen with —; mar—; mount in—; offer—; pour—; recall with—; redden in—; shiver with—; smile in—; snuff out—; spread—; submerge in—; taste—; teem with—; turn to—; turn—into; weep with—; win—; yield—; —comes; —flees; —fleets; — pierces; —shines; —tempers.
(See happiness, rapture, joy, entertainment, pleasure, satisfaction.)

DELIGHTFUL
adverbs
charmingly; whimsically; utterly; strangely; unexpectedly; supremely; immeasurably; ineffably; delicately; freshly; cordially; innocently; peculiarly; particularly; youthfully; sweetly; glamorously; enchantingly; pleasantly; gracefully; entertainingly.

DELINEATE (v)
adverbs
graphically; minutely; humorously; familiarly; truthfully; recognizably; unsurpassedly; impartially; satirically.
(See depict, describe.)

DELINEATION
adjectives
humorous; familiar; truthful; recognizable; subtle; unsurpassed; impartial.

DELINQUENCY
adjectives
seeming; imaginary; juvenile; egregious; blameworthy.

DELINQUENT
adverbs
criminally; woefully; viciously; indiscreetly; enormously; outrageously; censurably; reprehensibly; objectionably; villainously;

wretchedly; monstrously; loosely; unpardonably; inexcusably; carelessly; deliberately; indifferently; purposely; wantonly; wickedly; accidentally; shamefully; scandalously; disreputably; heedlessly; rashly; foolishly.

DELIRIOUS
adverbs
wildly; woefully; dangerously; alarmingly; crazily; violently; frantically; madly; feverishly; helplessly; critically; terribly; incoherently; oddly; strangely; hysterically; startlingly; uncontrollably; turbulently; distractedly; restlessly.

DELIRIUM
adjectives
mad; tossing; restless; extreme; raving; emotional; critical; blissful; confused; terrible; dreamy; prolonged; fierce; maniacal; insane.

verbs
break out into—; characterize—; dance in —; excite to—; haunt—; indicate—; induce—; murmur in—; produce—; quake with—; rave in—; seize with—; stimulate to—; suffer—; tremble with—; wander in—; —attacks; —exhausts; —impairs; —occurs.
(See insanity, hallucination, excitement, enthusiasm, rapture.)

DELIVER (v)
adverbs
simultaneously; conveniently; eloquently; solemnly; habitually; coldly; duly; consequently; sullenly; resolutely; impassionedly; volubly; hazardously; inarticulately; daily; promptly; tardily; reproachfully.
(See give, transfer.)

DELIVERANCE
adjectives
immediate; abrupt; miraculous; timely; tardy; gracious; hazardous.

verbs
achieve—; aid in—; arrange—; commemorate—; complete—; desire—; effect—; hope for—; offer—; order—; pray for—; rejoice in—; seek—; work for—; yearn for—; —liberates; —rescues; —sets free; —yields.
(See rescue, release, salvation.)

DELIVERER

adjectives

would-be; commanding; deliberate; graceful; intrepid; chance.

verbs

acclaim—; hope for—; pray for—; send—; thank—; welcome—; yearn for—; yield to—; —dispatches; —disburdens; —disposes of; —liberates; —orders; —rescues; —rids; —saves; —sets forth; —sets free; —surrenders; —releases.

DELIVERY

adjectives

resolute; voluble; impassioned; happy; complex; hazardous; inarticulate; measured; certified.

DELL

adjectives

bosky; mysterious; darksome; shaded; dreamy; labyrinthine; pathless; pastoral; narrow; hollow; diminutive; desolate; untrodden; resounding; budded; healthy; briery.

verbs

abandon—; bloom in—; frolic in—; grow in—; haunt—; hide in—; inhabit—; leap in—; perform in—; retire to—; retreat into—; ring through—; seek—; shelter in —; wander in—; —invites; —protects; —soothes; —winds.

(See valley, dale.)

DELUGE

adjectives

dawn-tinted; fiery; overflowing; binding; veritable; fearful; eternal; lawless; smothering; silvery; perfect; delectable; swashing; drowning; vapory.

verbs

bury under—; drown in—; escape—; fall before—; perish in—; pour—; release—; shower—; suffer from—; swell into—; vent—; —abates; —breaks loose; —confronts; —demolishes; —descends; —destroys; —floods; —harms; —occurs; —proceeds; —submerges; —sweeps away.

(See flood.)

DELUSION

adjectives

nightmare; cherished; fixed; superstitious; generous; grandiose; ignorant; insane; partial; monstrous; mental; shattered; anthropocentric; hollow; false; phantasmic; treasured; crazy; tenderhearted; unconquerable; pleasant; systematized; salutary; popular; miserable; long-detached; equal; mere; uncomfortable; plausible; stage; optical; pernicious; fond; empty; financial; neat; mocking; tragic; psychotic; somnolent.

verbs

cast out—; cure of—; destroy—; develop—; dismiss—; dissipate—; foster—; give up to—; guard against—; labor under—; share—; slip into—; suffer—; —exists; —misleads; —pursues.

(See illusion, deception, error, fallacy, hallucination.)

DELUSIVE

adverbs

cunningly; smoothly; insidiously; fallaciously; unfairly; starkly; inevitably; slyly; fraudulently; mendaciously; untruthfully; mistily; deceptively; ironically; strategically; incredibly; artfully; erroneously; dishonestly; perfidiously; unsoundly; trickily; treacherously; groundlessly; heretically; disingenuously; evasively; grimly.

DELVING

adjectives

curious; industrious; bibliographical; mental; scientific; relentless.

DEMAGOGUE

adjectives

consummate; selfish; irresponsible; fluent; political; inveterate; notorious; captious.

verbs

abandon to—; become the prey of—s; cultivate—; descend from—; despise—; play—; prove—; rule as—; stoop to—; —agitates; —appeals; —defends; —esponses; —fires; —influences; —leads; —obtains; —opposes; —orates; —panders; —suits; —sways; —undertakes.

(See politician, orator, leader.)

DEMAND

adjectives

ceaseless; incessant; insistent; constant; ever-increasing; rapid; mounting; growing; overwhelming; unabated; uncompromising; intransigent; persistent; obstinate; stern; strong; extreme; shouted; clamorous; roaring; exorbitant; modern; intermittent; inevitable; inescapable; irresistible; general; consistent; fluctuating; exigent; imperious; peremptory; vehement; exacting; outrageous; blustering; unfortunate; unjust; unfair; relentless; surly; impossible; arrogant; abnormal; excessive; enlarged; unlimited; important; normal; human; social; industrial; consumer; decorative; popular; peculiar; multitudinous (pl); ever-changing; diminishing; emotional; unique; concrete; embarrassing; sufficient; immediate; preparatory; half-resentful; half-appealing; urgent; brusque; imaginative; craving; immense; inadmissable; definite; worthy; unprecedented; voiced; authoritative; effectual; fanatical; earnest; unsatisfied; insidious; widespread; essential; renewed; complex; paternal; insulting; nervous; remorseless; uproarious; intense; importunate; voluntary; unreasonable; necessary; explicit; widening; infrequent (pl); temporary; never-ending; feverish; unheeded; logical; sternest; tremendous; live; nationwide; huge; terrific; steady; gigantic; additional; ridiculous; temporal; emphatic; exaggerated; transient; continuing; unconditional; audacious; progressive; monstrous; arbitrary.

verbs
accede to—; accomplish—; acquiesce in—; agree to—; attend—; besiege with—s; browbeat with—s; clarify—; comply with —; confront with—; create—; deny—; divine—; dwarf—; echo—; evoke—; fulfill —; grant—; ignore—; indulge—; meet—; obey—; parry—; press—; reiterate—; reject—; respond to—; satisfy—; stabilize —; supply—; thunder—; unite in—; utter —; voice—; wake to—; yield to—; — astounds; —diminishes; —grows.

(See requirement.)

DEMAND (v)
adverbs
vibrantly; savagely; gutturally; greedily; persistently; relentlessly; frantically; unreasonably; brusquely; exorbitantly; rapaciously; sternly; bluntly; ruthlessly; briskly; scornfully; triumphantly; indignantly; truculently; riotously; clamorously; impetuously; obviously; despairingly; exactingly; unanimously; staunchly; imperatively; ultimately; stridently; cruelly; arrogantly; unconscionably; assuredly; gruffly; hungrily; curtly; incessantly; uncompromisingly; definitely; arbitrarily; formally; imperiously; sharply; furiously; virulently.

(See order, request.)

DEMEANOR
adjectives
smiling; calm; dignified; unassuming; staid; modest; composed; sweet; gentlemanly; unruffled; gentle; majestic; lordly; torpid; hangdog; wild; cold; impassive: commonplace; surly; savage; ferocious; fickle; inscrutable; accustomed; somber; unflinching; immoral; peculiar; interested; punctilious; solemn; courtly; popular; menacing; comical; contemptuous; sober; widespread; coy; laughing; obtuse; offensive; quiet; proud; sanctified; subdued; violent; pompous; puritanical; tacit; sage; haughty; meditative; cheerful; courageous; undaunted; resolute; private; unbending; unusual; unostentatious; reserved; stately; confident; cringing; dispassionate; aggressive; turbulent.

verbs
adopt—; alter—; disdain—; disguise—; exhibit—; judge by—; maintain—; mask—; soften—; trust—; —changes; —expresses; —irritates; —registers; —shames; —signifies.

(See behavior, mien.)

DEMENTED
adverbs
idiotically; sadly; inexplicably; foolishly; witlessly; frenziedly; incoherently; oddly; strangely; wildly; distractedly; dangerously; alarmingly; peculiarly; woefully; hopelessly; deplorably; pitiably; startlingly; uncontrollably; ungovernably; pathetically; tragically; unaccountably; mysteriously; stupidly; feebly; confusedly; noticeably; palpably; obviously; unmistakably; perceptibly; plainly.

DEMISE
adjectives
speedy; approaching; early; inevitable; heroic; premature; sad; lamented; longawaited.

DEMOCRACY
adjectives
forward-looking; sham; industrial; passionridden; unlimited; enraged; semieducated; true; shrewd; humorous; multitudinous; kindly; economic; formidable; representative; pure; inclusive; rampant; qualified; experienced; financial; primitive; fierce.

verbs
attack—; betray—; contribute toward—; destroy—; foster—; imperil—; instill—;

jeopardize—; ordain—; preserve—; retain
—; satirize—; supplant—; sustain—;
threaten—; tread down—; —advances; —
degenerates; —elevates; —flourishes; —
functions; —levels; —marches ahead; —
prevails; —survives; —asserts itself.
(See government, people, republic.)

DEMOCRATIC

adverbs
marvellously; tolerantly; broadly; unusually; magnanimously; foolishly; admirably;
remarkably; embarrassingly; rampantly;
amusingly; extremely; eminently; notoriously; openly; liberally; impartially; high-
mindedly; violently; vociferously; unselfishly; charitably.

DEMOLISH (v)

adverbs
utterly; ruinously; brutally; cruelly; savagely; thoughtlessly; bestially; blood-
thirstily; uncompromisingly; fiercely.
(See destroy.)

DEMON

adjectives
heroic; insatiable; unabashed; devastating;
wrestling; fiery; angry; fragile; screaming;
monstrous; cruel; heartless; horrible; demoralizing; protecting; trap-door; satellite;
seeming; malignant; treacherous; avenging;
restraining.

verbs
attribute to—; call forth—; dismiss—;
drive out—; endow with—; exorcise—;
introduce—; possess—; rout—; sacrifice to
—; worship—; —controls; —destroys; —
disturbs; —dominates; —dwells in; —enters; —frightens; —haunts; —infests; —
inflicts; —inhabits; —leads; —prevails;
—rules; —surrounds; —wails.
(See devil, spirit.)

DEMONIAC

adverbs
screamingly; insatiably; fierily; angrily;
cruelly; monstrously; heartlessly; horribly;
malignantly; maliciously; treacherously; revengefully; venomously; excitably; feverishly; hysterically; wildly; frantically;
frenziedly; sensationally; dramatically;
bitterly; invidiously; ruthlessly; brutally;
atrociously; infamously; flagrantly; nefariously; viciously; grossly; infernally.

DEMONSTRATE (v)

adverbs
lucidly; tastefully; repeatedly; strictly;
abundantly; practically; phenomenally; experimentally; fully; conceitedly; conclusively; convincingly; substantially; triumphantly; abstractedly; forcefully; abstrusely; approximately; ocularly; precisely; visually;
cordially.
(See show, indicate.)

DEMONSTRATION

adjectives
patriotic; subtle; triumphant; abstract;
abstruse; forceful; approximate; corrupt;
dramatized; familiar; ocular; charitable;
grandiose; active; enthusiastic; attention-
compelling; simple; interesting; convincing; dynamic; startling; spot; irresistible;
sales-producing; breath-taking; quick; inspiring; emphatic; salivary; quadrennial;
amazing; rigorous; precise; rigid; noisy;
striking; visual; grand; superb; flattering;
riotous; dramatic; bitter; hostile; unfriendly; armed; elaborate; outward; cordial.

verbs
answer by—; apprehend—; crown—; defy
—; establish by—; harangue—; mar—;
offer—; stage—; subject to—; support—;
thwart—; understand—; —exposes; —
proves.
(See celebration.)

DEMONSTRATIVE

adverbs
readily; easily; triumphantly; forcefully;
dramatically; spectacularly; actively; enthusiastically; interestingly; convincingly;
startlingly; irresistibly; amazingly; noisily;
strikingly; flatteringly; elaborately; outwardly; cordially; heartily; offensively;
delightfully; charmingly; amiably; vexatiously; provokingly; foolishly; unbecomingly; unnecessarily; frankly; brazenly; boldly; ominously; markedly; conspicuously;
disagreeably.

DEMORALIZE (v)

adverbs
profoundly; partially; utterly; speedily;
swiftly; incredibly; socially; morally.
(See corrupt.)

DEMORALIZATION

adjectives
incredible; widespread; social; linguistic;
nervous.

verbs

aid in—; check—; guard against—; influence—; prevent—; produce—; protect from —; yield to—; —corrupts; —deprives; —destroys; —envelops; —lowers; —reduces; —seeps in; —unnerves; —weakens.
(See corruption.)

DEMURE

adverbs

affectedly; prudishly; coyly; timidly; shyly; delightfully; gravely; quietly; unaffectedly; conspicuously; deliberately; discreetly; tranquilly; placidly; soberly; submissively; harmoniously; meekly; cleverly; purposely; ostentatiously; unnaturally; stiffly; primly; puritanically; priggishly; bashfully; skittishly; admirably; attractively; alluringly; blushingly.

DEMURENESS

adjectives

stately; slumberous; timid; lofty; aloof; deceptive; becoming.

DEN

adjectives

careless; stifling; stuffy; dark; trackless; moldy; unsanitary; loathsome; steamy; horrible; hidden; dreary; turreted; fresh-dug.

verbs

abide in—; cast into—; confine to—; convert into—; crouch in—; drive from—; dwell in—; escape to—; habitate—; hibernate in—; hide in—; immure in—; lodge in—; lurk in—; nestle in—; pace—; retire to—; retreat to—; smoke out of—; stow in—; visit—; stray about—; —conceals; —hides; —reeks.
(See lair, cave, hut, retreat.)

DENIAL

adjectives

incredulous; amused; bold; vehement; armed; cynical; indignant; visual; arrogant; gracious; telegraphic; rigid; furious; steadfast; vigorous; smiling; disarming; chivalrous; utter; peremptory; quibbling; naive; positive; emphatic.

verbs

accept—; brook—; color—; conceal with —; counter—; evoke—; ignore—; lash out—; prepare—; rebut—; request—; resign to—; spurn—; storm—; —contradicts;

—discourages; —irks; —peeves (colloq.); —refuses; —refutes; —repulses; —wearies.
(See contradiction, refusal, restraint.)

DENIZEN

adjectives

long-eared; finny; astute; stately; furred; feathered; forgotten; permanent.

verbs

accept—; acquaint—; admit—; allow—; fill with—s; furnish with—s; grant to—; make—of; offer—; people with—s; populate with—s; privilege—; —dwells; —enjoys; —obtains; —occupies; —prospers; —settles.
(See inhabitant, citizen, native.)

DENOUEMENT

adjectives

curious; interesting; melodramatic; iridescent; tragic; crowning; premature.

DENOUNCE (v)

adverbs

vehemently; furiously; sternly; unsparingly; scoffingly; insultingly; bitterly; scathingly; obstreperously; violently; vociferously; witheringly; astoundingly; dramatically; vitriolically; mercilessly; roundly.
(See accuse.)

DENSITY

adjectives

sufficient; mean; different; tangled; repellent; depthless; frightful.

DENT

adjectives

sizable; slightest; permanent; cruel; hideous.

DENTIST

adjectives

ruthless; unfeeling; ultra-schooled; late-edition; glorified; hit-or-miss.

verbs

consult—; visit—; —anaesthetizes; —applies; —assembles; —caps; —closes; —drills; —examines; —extracts; —fastens; —files; —fills; —furnishes; —grinds; —inserts; —operates; —practises; —prepares; —preserves; —restores; —shapes; —treats.

DENUNCIATION

adjectives

withering; mystic; astounding; fiery; glib; unmerited; furious; spiteful; playful;

severest; loud; intemperate; sweeping; grand; impartial; effective; thorough; resounding; impassioned; dramatic; vitriolic; ominous; unsupported; combative; rabid; angry; utter; preliminary; filthy; violent; merciless.

verbs
announce—; authorize—; blast—; characterize by—; defy—; indulge in—; reiterate —; thunder—; tolerate—; —accuses; —affects; —alarms; —condemns; —deluges; —frightens; —humbles; —informs; —inveighs against; —punishes; —ruins; —scathes; —sears; —threatens; —warns; —weakens.
(See condemnation, accusation.)

DENUNCIATORY
adverbs
scarcely; dogmatically; scandalously; needlessly; strongly; bitterly; acrimoniously; jealously; enviously; inexcusably; scurrilously; abusively; profanely; execrably; thunderously; cruelly; caustically; harshly; ungraciously; ferociously; ruthlessly; sarcastically; dryly; severely; unsparingly; exceptionably; indefensibly; viciously; terribly.

DENY (v)
adverbs
hotly; unequivocally; promptly; absolutely; bitterly; indignantly; effectively; peremptorily; stoutly; inhospitably; crossly; cravenly; unselfishly; strenuously; passionately; categorically; justly; vehemently; flatly; shamelessly; arrogantly; disarmingly; positively; naively.
(See contradict, renounce.)

DEPART (v)
adverbs
voluntarily; peacefully; mysteriously; seriously; cheerfully; clandestinely; noiselessly; radically; precipitately; momentously; daringly; agitatedly; unprecedentedly; abruptly.
(See leave, quit.)

DEPARTMENT
adjectives
subsidiary; vast; systematized; countless (pl); elementary; remote; significant; drabbest; immense; irrational; beautiful; capable; experienced; vocational; public; vulgar; administrative; insular.

verbs
allot to—; assign to—; bestow upon—; boss—; branch into—s; break into—; close —; control—; convert—; create—; divide into—s; establish—; organize—; portion into—s; preside over—; regulate—; supervise—; —administers; —caters to; —handles; —practises.
(See part, division, section, branch.)

DEPARTURE
adjectives
clandestine; abrupt; refreshing; noiseless; instant; radical; precipitate; revolutionary; momentous; impending; mysterious; unannounced; impetuous; calm; imminent; immediate; rollicking; sudden; hurried; frank; frequent (pl); speedy; hasty; considerate; approaching; contemplated; daring; dinnerless; agitated; noticeable; exceptionable; controlled; compelled; maiden; expected; awaited.

verbs
arrive at—; assure of—; await—; enjoy—; facilitate—; fear—; laugh at—; notice—; occasion—; plan—; prepare—; regret—; speed—; spur to—; take—; —divides; —frees; —nears; —partitions; —saddens; —separates; —severs; —sunders; prevent—.
(See deviation, withdrawal, separation, death.)

DEPEND (v)
adverbs
utterly; unfailingly; exclusively; materially; completely; mathematically; virtually; ultimately; directly; perpetually; apparently; irksomely; fatuously; absolutely; haplessly.
(See lean, trust.)

DEPENDABILITY
adjectives
superb; absolute; steady; impeccably; invariable; inflexible.

DEPENDENCE
adjectives
utter; lifetime; helpless; indirect; apparent; perpetual; disgraceful; irksome; increasing; sure; fatuous; absolute; harmless; magnified; ultimate; humble.

DEPENDENT
adjectives
servile; wise; beggarly; penniless; mutual; weaker; helpless; hapless.

DEPENDENT

adverbs
pitifully; completely; partially; sadly; help-lessly; unhappily; grievously; sullenly; subserviently; servilely; fawningly; obse-quiously; hopelessly; desperately; wholly; meekly; touchingly; pathetically.

DEPICT (v)

adverbs
symbolically; aesthetically; dramatically; graphically; powerfully; deftly; starkly; episodically; vividly; mercilessly; shrewdly; realistically; fearlessly.
(See delineate, describe.)

DEPICTION

adjectives
episodic; merciless; stark; shrewd; real-istic; fearless; vivid.

DEPLETE (v)

adverbs
entirely; largely; physically; utterly; defi-nitely; swiftly; suddenly; fatally; woefully; financially.
(See exhaust.)

DEPLETION

adjectives
corresponding; physical; excessive; utter; definite; sudden; swift.

DEPLORABLE

adverbs
piteously; unwontedly; terribly; seriously; gravely; direly; especially; signally; dis-tressingly; wretchedly; exceptionably; bit-terly; dismally; woefully.

DEPLORE (v)

adverbs
sincerely; satirically; prophetically; loudly; tearfully; pitifully.
(See lament, regret.)

DEPORTMENT

adjectives
habitual; exigent; correct; laudable; ex-ceeding; proper; maidenly; fashionable; graceful; amiable; blameless; fine; un-expected; inexplicable; grave; incredible.

DEPOSIT
(general)

adjectives
superficial; alluvial; extensive; stratified; evanescent; coralline; affected; fertile; un-touched; inexhaustible; graphite; modest; fossiliferous; sacred; required; fabulous: immense; nominal; sedimentary; buttery; driftwood; precious; phosphate; turquoise; bank; large; unexpected.

DEPOSIT
(money or property)

adjectives
nominal; actual; legal; stipulated; optional; binding; good faith.

verbs
accumulate for—; bank—; collect—s; com-mit—to; deliver—; demand—; entrust with —; guard—; invest—; place—; pledge—; receive—; require—; restore—; return—; squander—; withdraw—; —benefits; —in-creases; —settles.

DEPOSIT (v)

adverbs
deliberately; daintily; noiselessly; hastily; superficially; extensively; inexhaustibly; evanescently; fabulously; immensely; un-expectedly.
(See place.)

DEPOSITOR

adjectives
luckless; frightened; hypothetical; poor; illiterate; ingenuous; middle class; unlo-cated; unfortunate; ultimate; robust.

DEPOT

adjectives
cavalry; temporary; commissary; indispens-able; prearranged; stationary.

DEPRAVED

adverbs
wickedly; shamelessly; grossly; outrageous-ly; corruptly; brutally; dangerously; awful-ly; hopelessly; woefully; abjectly; disgrace-fully; infamously; contemptibly; notorious-ly; shamefully; arrantly; dissolutely; in-decently; perfidiously.

DEPRAVITY

adjectives
precocious; moral; joint; vicarious; total; horrible; rude; contented; professional; humorous.

DEPRECATE (v)

adverbs
forcibly; timidly; periodically; modestly; markedly; increasingly; hurriedly; mildly; vigorously; pleadingly.
(See disapprove.)

DEPRECATION

adjectives

timid; hurt; pleading; periodic; modest; hurried; abysmal.

DEPRECATORY

adverbs

timidly; pleadingly; modestly; elaborately; unnecessarily; urgently; importunately; clamorously; solicitously; compassionately; sympathetically; tenderly; critically; abusively; accusingly; sarcastically; sharply; trenchantly; censoriously.

DEPRECIATION

adjectives

marginal; disastrous; marked; ever-increasing; substantial; radical; elaborate.

DEPRESS (v)

adverbs

particularly; fearfully; dreadfully; vaguely; obviously; acutely; drastically; economically; financially; industrially; spiritually; nationally; mentally; nervously.

(See lower.)

DEPRESSED

adverbs

alarmingly; dangerously; gloomily; incurably; inconceivably; incredibly; horribly; woefully; dismally; gravely; seriously; inconsolably; sadly; unreasonably; desperately; piteously; pitifully; tragically; wanly; unduly; unnecessarily; moodily; lamentably; darkly; wearily.

DEPRESSING

adverbs

sadly; alarmingly; needlessly; terribly; unreasonably; unaccountably; inexplicably; dreadfully; acutely; grimly; painfully; cursedly; grievously; unfortunately; sorely; unluckily; intolerably; tremendously; cruelly.

DEPRESSION
(business)

adjectives

prolonged; agricultural; successive (pl); mild; general; current; exaggerated; dreadful; evil; aching; acute; drastic; major; vast; long; business; economic; financial; industrial; national; world; price; severe.

DEPRESSION
(general)

adjectives

paralyzing; epidemic; enveloping; growing; inflation.

verbs

aggravate—; alleviate—; banish—; emerge from—; intensify—; mitigate—; offset—; plunge into—; prolong—; relapse into—; survive—; tackle—; thaw out—; weather —; —annihilates; —blights; —grips; —hits; —slashes.

(See dejection, melancholy, discouragement, despondency.)

DEPRESSION
(spirits)

adjectives

low; nervous; sundry (pl); sympathetic; frequent; spiritual; constant; mental.

DEPRESSION
(surface)

adjectives

sheltered; circumscribed; shallow; cup-like; deep; noticeable; amphitheatrical; saucer-like; extreme.

DEPRIVATION

adjectives

haphazard; stringent; total; ruinous; violent; vicious; indigent.

DEPTH

adjectives

generous; unguessed; shielding; protective; underlying; deceptive.

verbs

advance from—s; attain—; bear through —s; descend to—s; discover in—s; explore —s; foul in—s; gauge—; harbor in—; judge—; launch into—s; measure—; penetrate to—of; pitch to—s; preserve from—s; probe—s; raise from—s; reach—; reflect in—; repose in—; rise from—; scour—; search—; thrust into—; venture beyond—; —closes round; —covers; —embraces; —exceeds.

(See extent, measure.)

DEPTHS

adjectives

dizzy; profound; unfathomable; considerable; perpendicular; homely; crystalline; fertile; remorseless; tremendous; melancholy; nethermost; giddiest; slumberous; remote; hollow; blank; soundless; somber; seeming; distant; inmost; glassy; shadowed; abysmal; lost; awesome; limpid; unknown; cavernous; hideous; liquid; secret; aesthetic; hidden; wondrous; unexplored; lowest; unserviceable; passionless; sleeping; adverse; warm; darkest; pearly; evil;

unimagined; ghostly; annulling; prodigious; shapeless; voiceless; forest; folded; calm; reflective; slimy; cold; frozen; agitated; yawning; luminous; inaccessible; superhuman; insatiable; pathless; dewy; vast; music-haunted; wakening; clear; shameful; gloomy; abhorrent; nightmare; sylvan; subterranean; apparent; Stygian; secure.

DEPUTY

adjectives

dishonest; hateful; gun-toting; indolent; tense; amiable; strict; presumptive; pernicious; corrupt; radiant.

verbs

appoint—; authorize—; bribe—; corrupt —; depose—; elect—; employ as—; evade —; oust—; rebuke—; swear in—; —aids; —arrests; —assists; —enforces; —fines.
(See representative, agent, delegate.)

DERANGE (v)

adverbs

irreparably; seriously; mentally; functionally; extensively; sexually; mechanically.
(See confuse.)

DERANGED

adverbs

eccentrically; incoherently; madly; strangely; unaccountably; inexplicably; queerly; foolishly; dangerously; peculiarly; woefully; hopelessly; helplessly; deplorably; pitiably; lamentably; shockingly; uncontrollably; mysteriously; noticeably; obviously; unmistakably; perceptibly; terribly.

DERANGEMENT

adjectives

mental; extensive; functional; obstinate; obsessional; intermittent.

DERBY

adjectives

battered; cherished; perforated; shabby; broken; battle-scarred; aggressively-tilted; ancient; salvaged.

DERELICT

adjectives

human; moral; physical; sleeping; floating; wretched; barnacle-incrusted.

verbs

abandon—; defend—; desert—; discover —; lift—; observe—; pity—; reduce to—; relinquish—; seize—; —s assemble; —s

congregate; —drifts; —flounders; —s infest; —limps in; —s overrun; —suffers; —s swarm.

DERIDE (v)

adverbs

steadily; correspondingly; opprobriously; sourly; scornfully; lightly; ribaldly; coarsely; brutally; mercilessly; bitterly; loudly; boisterously; unsparingly; contemptuously; sharply; stingingly.
(See ridicule, jeer.)

DERISION

adjectives

mysterious; sour; scornful; light; ribald; unconquerable; coarse; brutal; merciless; filthy; bitterest; loud; boisterous; approving; pressed; uneasy; foul; unsparing.

verbs

bait with—; be in—; cackle in—; call forth —; chuckle in—; expose to—; express—; give vent to—; laugh in—; mock in—; open to—; ridicule in—; scorn—; sting by—.
(See ridicule, mockery, scorn, sarcasm.)

DERISIVE

adverbs

sharply; arrogantly; pompously; mockingly; sarcastically; cynically; offensively; officiously; disagreeably; unbearably; insufferably; mysteriously; sourly; lightly; blithely; airily; ribaldly; disrespectfully; coarsely; grossly; brutally; ignorantly; crudely; mercilessly; clumsily; bitterly; loudly; boisterously; enviously; foully.

DERIVATION

adjectives

remote; theoretical; unanswerable; grotesque; indirect; authentic.

DERIVATIVE

adjectives

direct; traceable; flattering; acknowledged; questionable.

verbs

accept—; confuse—; develop—; discover —; employ—; form—; gain—; generate—; market—; obtain—; process—; produce—; recognize—; reduce—; substitute—; use—; utilize—; —emanates from; —originates; —supplants.
(See product, word.)

DERIVE (v)

adverbs

recently; evidently; shamelessly; primarily; corruptly; ultimately; essentially; remotely; theoretically; grotesquely; endlessly.

(See obtain.)

DEROGATORY

adverbs

shamefully; enviously; bitterly; venomously; vengefully; maliciously; scandalously; disagreeably; peevishly; petulantly; falsely; slanderously; abusively; injuriously; shockingly; unreasonably; unwarrantably; indefensibly; vindictively; dreadfully; mercilessly; ruthlessly; openly; shamelessly; deliberately; viciously.

DERVISH

adjectives

demented; dancing; filthy; whirling; frenzied.

DESCEND (v)

adverbs

quickly; unexpectedly; noiselessly; sharply; gradually; hastily; giddily; benignly; impartially; laboriously; gracefully; fearsomely; pompously.

(See fall.)

DESCENDANT

adjectives

lineal; direct; eager; legitimate; homeward-flown; pure-blooded; glorious; degenerate; remote; immediate; impoverished; ill-starred; hybrid; presumed; winsome; indolent; guilty; genuine; unmixed.

verbs

acquire—; advertise for—; characterize—; extract—; leave—; nourish—; transmit to—; —s assemble; —belongs to; —carries; on; —s congregate; —s convene; —s gather; —s honor; —s inherit; —s respect; —s settle; —s spring from; —s wrangle over.

(See posterity, offspring, issue.)

DESCENT

adjectives

rapid; direct; steep; aristocratic; hasty; gradual; rocky; pitiless; precipitous; stately; deep; smooth; laborious; graceful; harsh; unblemished; ladderlike; armed; sheer; illustrious; dateless; artistic; pompous; actual; noble; maternal; barbarous; flashing; uninterrupted; royal; divine; fearsome; slow.

verbs

attempt—; balk at—; ease—; dread—; flow upon—; halt—; hazard—; hinder—; manage—; menace—; observe—; plan—; point for—; prepare—; prevent—; resume —; venture—; —dizzies; —frightens; —sharpens; —slopes.

(See fall, deterioration, slope, attack, raid.)

DESCRIBE (v)

adverbs

ludicrously; graphically; adequately; admiringly; pathetically; trippingly; accurately; derisively; justly; feelingly; expansively; compactly; comprehensively; elegantly; elaborately; felicitously; minutely; traditionally; eloquently; illuminatingly; succinctly; superlatively; subsequently; erroneously; fittingly; imperfectly; contemptuously; facetiously; impressionistically; boisterously; radiantly; glowingly; sentimentally; humorously; animatedly; verbally; uncensoredly; tersely; intimately; satirically; suggestively; enticingly; distortedly; imaginatively; realistically; vaguely; colorfully; briefly; essentially.

(See delineate, depict.)

DESCRIPTION

adjectives

facetious; minute; impressionistic; boisterous; admirable; exquisite; graphic; detailed; contemporary; radiant; entangled; magnificent; luminous; eloquent; adjectival; distinctive; impassioned; felicitous; faithful; elaborate; extended; racy; preceding; picturesque; punctual; lengthy; frivolous; leisurely; sublime; tolerable; restrained; appropriate; enthusiastic; illustrated; ludicrous; harrowing; truthful; accurate; glowing; sentimental; vivid; hopeless; humorous; animated; unpleasant; lucid; primitive; verbal; censored; admirable; unexcelled; pompous; threadbare; negative; terse; rhapsodical; intimate; pathetic; satiric; suggestive; enticing; distorted; savage; imaginative; authoritative; realistic; adequate; abridged; silent; magnificent; robust; vague; damning; flashing; colorful; complicated; recondite; brief; modest.

verbs

amend—; base—; baffle—; beggar—; color—; defy—; detail—; enter into—; fit—; limit—; paragon—; quote—; suit—; verify—; —centers; —clarifies; —colors; —combines; —delineates; —depicts; —

equals; —excels; —explains; —furnishes; —illuminates; —illustrates; —implies; —impresses; —introduces; —motivates; —paints; —pictures; —portrays; —presents; —provides; —suggests; —surpasses; —tires; —vivifies; —wearies.

(See portrayal, representation, definition.)

DESCRIPTIVE

adverbs
graphically; vividly; effectively; unusually; remarkably; facetiously; minutely; admirably; splendidly; magnificently; eloquently; faithfully; elaborately; extensively; racily; tolerably; appropriately; enthusiastically; ludicrously; accurately; humorously; intimately; savagely; authoritatively; adequately; vaguely; briefly; modestly; realistically.

DESECRATION

adjectives
impudent; attempted; wanton; impious; daring; inconoclastic.

verbs
accuse of—; admit—; confess—; criticize for—; enjoy—; ignore—; indulge in—; preserve from—; rear in—; sentence for—; spit—; suffer—; threaten—; —injures; —involves; —pains; —nauseates; —undermines.

(See violation.)

DESERT

adjectives
dreary; irreclaimable; flat; melancholy; rude; mountainous; rocky; burning; lifeless; alkaline; pathless; encompassing; arid; forbidding; reactionary; scorching; unspeakable; mysterious; dreadful; measureless; voiceless; bare; palpable; comfortless; vast; withered; desolated; uninhabitable; barren; waterless; open; grim; dangerous; cactus; sandy; silent; illimitable.

verbs
advance through—; border—; chart—; conceal in—; dwell in—; frequent—; gain—; inhabit—; lead into—; lose in—; patrol—; redeem—; retire to—; retreat to—; roam —; span—; swallow up by—; track—; wander in—; —envelops; —howls; —menaces; —parches; —threatens.

(See merit, reward, solitude, waste.)

DESERT (v)

adverbs
woefully; heartlessly; easily; virtually; basely; cruelly; impulsively; treasonably; wilfully; criminally; wantonly; finally.

(See forsake, abandon.)

DESERTED

adverbs
cruelly; criminally; hastily; shamefully; ingloriously; humiliatingly; mercilessly; ruthlessly; inhumanly; brutally; wickedly; iniquitously; scandalously; ignominiously; wantonly; inconsiderately; groundlessly; wilfully; deliberately; unhappily; ungratefully; wretchedly.

DESERTION

adjectives
contemplated; cruel; impulsive; treasonable; willful; proverbial; wholesale; criminal; wanton.

DESERVE (v)

adverbs
equally; notoriously; perpetually; fittingly; unreservedly; distinctly; eminently; wholeheartedly; undeniably.

(See merit.)

DESIGN
(intention)

adjectives
ultimate; honorable; base; fell; ill-conceived; rash; deadly; deep; evil; deliberate; stern; wicked; ostensible; malicious; oppressive; serious; importunate; hostile; ambitious; joyous; true-meant; immoral; misguided; criminal; evident; vile; matrimonial; disgusting; mischievous; far-reaching; avowed; traitorous; aggressive; lawful; villainous; perfidious; nefarious.

verbs
admit—; adopt—; approve—; arrange—; carry out—; conceive—; concur on—; declare—; discover—; disguise—; execute—; form—; frustrate—; harbor—; plan—; pursue—; relinquish—; settle on—; undertake —; —aims; —fails; —requires.

(See scheme, plan, purpose, project, intention.)

DESIGN
(pattern)

adjectives
authentic; immense; elaborate; inscrutable; constructive; fierce; beautiful; arabesque; border; intricate; sporting; famous; artist-

ic; ethical; fanciful; matchless; polychromatic; structural; well-known; conventional; monstrous; impractical; flowing; simple; graceful; anatomical; chevron; deliberate; heavy-duty; tentative; distinctive; exclusive; transitional; interior; conservative; unfathomable; palpable; engineering; harmonious; attractive; central; classical; crude; quaint; scientific; unintelligent; grotesque; aliform; vast; gorgeous; geometrical; efficacious; secular; smart; original; unusual; nautical; advanced; stitched; modern; staggering; unjust; superior; functional; systematic; wise; dramatic; compass; thoughtful; ingenious; feathery; engraved; mosaic; curious; huge; exotic; general; novel; tangled; cut; dried; gay; rational; brilliant; stunning; annulose.

verbs
arrange—; carve—; conceive—; contrive—; develop—; draw—; elaborate—; embellish; —embroider; —employ—; engrave—; execute—; hammer—; mark—; model—; paint —; plan—; prescribe—; sketch—; strike—; submit—; teach—; trace—; work—; —decorates; —denotes; —depicts; —improves; —ornaments; —represents; —signifies; —stresses.
(See pattern, ornament, sketch, model, representation.)

DESIGN (*v*)
adverbs
scientifically; properly; solely; exquisitely; seriously; admirably; specially; primarily; harmoniously; expressly; artfully; elaborately; charmingly; masterfully; skillfully; intricately.
(See intend.)

DESIGNATE (*v*)
adverbs
incriminatingly; innocently; erroneously; euphoniously; strictly; specifically; appropriately; felicitously; aptly; fittingly; properly; correctly.
(See identify.)

DESIGNATION
adjectives
appropriate; playful; substitutive; territorial; felicitous; apt; proudest; patrician; fitting; proper; correct.

verbs
appoint—; arrange—; arrive at—; decide —; denote—; describe—; determine—; indicate—; justify—; name—; point out—;

prepare for—; refuse—; search for—; — appeals; —serves.
(See mark, name, title, epithet, arrangement.)

DESIGNER
adjectives
experienced; noted; scenic; landscape; master; skilled; leading; functional.

DESIRABLE
adverbs
utterly; enchantingly; irresistibly; temptingly; alluringly; seductively; pleasantly; quietly; intensely; vaguely; darkly; acutely; inordinately; infinitely; genuinely; specially; absurdly; practically; conveniently.

DESIRE
adjectives
intense; longing; laudable; childish; sweet; gallant; brutal; extravagant; haughty; unextinct; fair; express; elevated; deferred; sensuous; corrupt; sentimental; customary; ardent; imperious; vague; earnest; devoted; prayerful; crushing; passionate; overpowering; innocent; noble; hearty; morbid; quaint; amiable; imperative; commendable; lifelong; insatiable; irresistible; confused; dark; furious; comfortable; cold; mistaken; automatic; lost; cordial; acute; unjust; scant; feeble; magnanimous; instinctive; slightest; warm; fond; faintest; inordinate; subtle; burning; infinite; sincere; countless (pl); selfish; conscientious; petty; frenzied; anxious; mad; implacable; consuming; inhibited; troublesome; deliberate; illimitable; excessive; benevolent; impatient; keen; pure; gnawing; restless; parching; unsatisfied; prevailing; quick; impetuous; known; longing; genuine; unlawful; subdued; strong; unacknowledged; high; insane; hot; dangerous; dominant; vehement; ungratified; dimmest; vain; proud; fiery; carnal; special; evident; unholy; torturing; inflamed; scattering; anxious; nervous; appeased; individual; egotistical; wolfish; bloody; ravenous; amorous; defrauded; emotional; covetous; honest; untamable; aimless; chaste; practical; feverish; mistaken; dwarfed; perceptible; wild; increasing; repressed; sacred; soft; delicate; wistful; sordid; ungenerous; laudable; lascivious; false; philanthropic; quenchless; unbaffled; phlegmatic; personal; boundless; loving; touching; lurking; popular; absurd; reasonable; senile; universal; apparent.

verbs
accomplish—; aggravate—; appease—; arouse—; attain—; awake—; balk—; beat with—; breed—; burn with—; cater to—; chasten—; cherish—; communicate—; conquer—; curtail—; eat up with—; entertain —; equal—; exercise—; experience—; exploit—; express—; feed—; flash—; gratify —; humble—; humor—; inflame—; inhibit—; instil—; intensify—; kindle—; lack —; languish in—; loose—; master—; melt into—; nourish—; obscure—; obsess with —; overbalance—; prompt—; provoke—; quell—; quench—; quicken—; quiet—; raise—; realize—; refine—; relinquish—; repress—; reward—; satisfy—; seethe with —; seize with—; sharpen—; smother—; subjugate—; sublimate—; submit to—; tangle—s; temper—; throttle—; thwart—; undermine—; yield to—; —consumes; — disquiets; —embodies; —endures; —fires; —hounds; —hungers; —impels; —motivates; —rules; —tortures; —urges on.

(See longing, craving. learning, wish, appetite, passion, impulse, request, aspiration.)

DESIRE (v)
adverbs
passionately; earnestly; ardently; eminently; obviously; insistently; presumably; unquestionably; particularly; intensely; consistently; unanimously; gallantly; extravagantly; brutally; sensually; customarily; imperiously; overpoweringly; nobly; heartily; morbidly; quaintly; insatiably; automatically; cordially; acutely; inordinately; burningly; infinitely; implacably; consumingly; benevolently; impatiently; gnawingly; genuinely; unlawfully; vainly; vehemently; carnally; torturingly; egotistically; ravenously; amorously; emotionally; chastely; delicately; wistfully; sordidly; ungenerously; lasciviously; boundlessly; touchingly; personally; absurdly.

(See want, wish.)

DESIROUS
adverbs
intensely; longingly; childishly; extravagantly; expressly; sentimentally; ardently; imperiously; earnestly; prayerfully; passionately; heartily; morbidly; insatiably; darkly; furiously; inordinately; sincerely; selfishly; madly; consumingly; troublesomely; impetuously; insanely; hotly; vehemently; proudly; anxiously; perceptibly; covetously; enviously; wistfully.

DESIST (v)
adverbs
abruptly; entirely; partially; completely; willingly; mutually; wisely; lazily; temporarily; subsequently; eventually; deliberately; totally.

(See stop, cease.)

DESK
adjectives
broad; secluded; ancient; battered; mahogany; flat; smooth; rickety; large; carved; Renaissance; polished; oak; dull; grimy; matutinal; reading; writing; spindle-legged; ransacked; roll-top.

verbs
anchor to—; beat—; clutter up—; cover—; dust—; dawdle at—; erect—; flank—; litter —; lock—; pad—; plop at—; rummage in—; seal—; smite—; stack on—.

(See table, stand, pulpit.)

DESOLATE
adverbs
grimly; utterly; profoundly; desperately; dreadfully; indescribably; singularly; supremely; bleakly; unutterably; tragically; bitterly; unbearably; intolerably; oppressively; appallingly; drearily; emptily; dismally; wildly; fearfully; perceptibly.

DESOLATION
adjectives
blazing; harsh; lifeless; utmost; dusty; grim; willful; utter; profound; dreadful; whispering; universal; wintry; careless; degraded; rightful; indescribable; chaotic; haunted; blank; unrevenged; fancied; barren; rapid; fresh; burlesque; weird; withered; mighty; icy; rocky; striking; heartsick; singular; immense; rugged; bleak.

verbs
behold—; blast—; bury in—; clothe with—; curse with—; decry—; doom to—; dwell in—; emerge from—; face—; fade into—; fall to—; inhabit—; lift from—; mourn—; repair—; —encroaches; —entombs; —overcomes; —overwhelms; —sets in.

(See loneliness, waste, region.)

DESPAIR
adjectives
absolute; pessimistic; calm; tragic; mute; mild; stolid; endless; unending; savage; dim; sick; grim; appalling; sudden; dismal; irremediable; human; dumb; crushed; whimsical; comfortless; comical; sham;

smothered; secure; beautiful; reluctant; inward; rash; deep; perplexed; spiritual; cold; keen; suppressed; rigid; abysmal; proud; solitary; rayless; sad; abhorred; sheer; errorless; black; reckless; pleased; utmost; mad; wild; lonely; scientific; blank; patient; speechless; passionate; pitiful; comfortless.

verbs

comfort in—; crush with—; doom to—; drive to—; end in—; engender—; fan into —; gasp with—; lift from—; lighten—; listen to—; plague with—; rack with—; rescue from—; save from—; seize with—; shake with—; sink in—; slump into—; spring from—; sweep away—; swoon in—; turn to—; unveil—; wring with—; yield to—; —chills; —grips; —grows; —hovers over; —poisons; —sets in; —settles in; —wells up; —withers; —wracks.

(See hopelessness, discouragement, despondency.)

DESPERADO
adjectives
slinking; sleepless; unarmed; bloodthirsty; ferocious; brutal; murderous; bestial.

DESPERATE
adverbs
tragically; wildly; mutely; savagely; helplessly; grimly; appallingly; suddenly; dismally; dumbly; comically; inwardly; proudly; madly; pitifully; fatally; frantically; cruelly; curiously; awfully; miserably; shockingly; fearfully; obstreperously; ungovernably; excitedly; hysterically; rashly; recklessly.

DESPERATION
adjectives
sheer; blind; melancholy; suicidal; frantic; sullen; utter; ruthless; momentary; stubborn; light-hearted.

DESPICABLE
adverbs
utterly; contemptibly; inexpressibly; shamefully; basely; terribly; outrageously; scandalously; notoriously; meanly; generally; incredibly.

DESPOND (v)
adverbs
daily; morbidly; deeply; profoundly; suicidally; utterly; sullenly; mournfully; tearfully; abnormally; unduly; unreasonably.
(See worry.)

DESPONDENCY
adjectives
temporary; morbid; deep; dire; frank; profound; suicidal; despairing; utter; pronounced; stifling; sullen; mournful.

verbs
beset with—; burden with—; chase—; create—; encourage—; envelop in—; express—; forbid—; indulge in—; labor under —; lament—; sink in—; throw into—; wallow in—; —darkens; —deforms; —depresses; —drowns; —envelops; —oppresses; —overcomes; —seeps in; —torments; —triumphs.

(See despair, depression, dejection.)

DESPONDENT
adverbs
temporarily; morbidly; deeply; direly; ominously; significantly; frankly; openly; admittedly; incurably; profoundly; suicidally; dangerously; alarmingly; desperately; sullenly; inexplicably; palpably; mournfully; habitually; ordinarily; inordinately; irremediably; pathologically; temperamentally.

DESPOT
adjectives
merciful; outraged; insulted; fierce; angered; petty; absolute; egotistic; monstrous; municipal; dangerous; predatory; benevolent; arrogant; small-souled; stern; hot-tempered; cruel; rank; vicious; iron-willed.

DESPOTIC
adverbs
relentlessly; ruthlessly; overbearingly; overwhelmingly; intolerably; imperiously; presumptuously; harshly; severely; oppressively; cruelly; obdurately; haughtily; insufferably; unreasonably; terribly; fearfully; dreadfully; incredibly; unwarrantably; dangerously; foolishly; barbarously; heartlessly; recklessly; outrageously; monstrously; viciously; benignly.

DESPOTISM
adjectives
unlimited; mild; barbarous; native; military; benign; agelong; ceremonious; astonished; combined (pl); absolute; irresistible; insupportable; irresponsible; capitalistic; reckless; heartless; rapacious; subsequent; iron.

verbs
adopt—; allay—; apply—; crush under—; establish—; exercise—; expose to—; form

—; free from—; guard against—; launch —; organize—; preserve from—; protect from—; relax—; submit to—; support—; surrender to—; throw off—; tolerate—; —compels; —controls; —enslaves; —governs; —limits; —restrains; —survives; —wills.

(See tyranny.)

DESSERT

adjectives
abbreviated; frugal; colorful; frozen; tempting; cold; delicious; nourishing; gay-looking; tiny.

DESTINATION

adjectives
mutual; secret; final; natural; appointed; moral; different; inevitable; deeper; suitable; proposed; outlandish; religious.

DESTINY

adjectives
false; manifest; impossible; loftiest; wondrous; unaccomplished; unhappy; auspicious; blighted; terrible; myriad (pl); precarious; transcendent; magnificent; deathless; resolute; outwitting; uncertain; circumvolving; inevitable; natural; moral; human; changing; common; momentous; eternal; desolate; future; sunless; noble; solemn; bright; inexorable; tragic; divine; high; evil; inherited; strange; evident; kindest; ultimate; proud; ill-starred.

verbs
abide by—; accept—; bless—; carve—; chart—; command—; condemn by—; evade —; expand—; fight out—; fulfill—; guide —; master—; mold—; pursue—; seal—; shape—; solve—; steer—; struggle with—; succumb to—; supervise—; ward off—; waylay—; work out—; —appoints; —awaits; —beats; —bewails; —carries out; —conspires; —decrees; —dogs; —dooms.

(See fortune, doom, fate, lot.)

DESTITUTE

adverbs
absolutely; sadly; utterly; helplessly; hopelessly; pennilessly; unquestionably; miserably; wretchedly; appallingly; comparatively; abjectly; astonishingly; peculiarly; distressingly; embarrassingly; horribly.

DESTITUTION

adjectives
absolute; utter; penniless; hopeless; abandoned; indigent.

verbs
abandon to—; avoid—; engulf by—; escape —; forsake to—; imply—; lift from—; leave in—; reduce to—; throw into—; verge on—; —approaches; —deprives; —increases; —menaces; —stalks.

(See poverty, want.)

DESTROY (v)

adverbs
deliberately; wantonly; ruthlessly; partially; foolishly; irreparably; frequently; simultaneously; eternally; ultimately; unwittingly; rigorously; utterly; effectually; thoughtlessly; universally; mutually; eventually; indiscriminately; consequently; lawlessly; practically; remorselessly; deliberately; inevitably; mercilessly; incalculably.

(See ruin, demolish.)

DESTROYER

adjectives
fierce; parasitic; brutal; plowing; ruthless; courteous; soulless.

DESTRUCTION

adjectives
sudden; instant; universal; wanton; daily; self; total; wild; brilliant; mutual; eventual; willful; indiscriminate; probable; consequent; miserable; practical; comprehensive; threatening; remorseless; deliberate; useless; apparent; utter; flashing; inconceivable; inevitable; ominous; merciless; incalculable; ultimate; sheer; wasting; lawless; necessary; subsequent.

verbs
attempt—; await—; behold—; bring on—; contemplate—; crumble into—; dash to—; deliver from—; ensure—; foredoom to—; incline to—; invite—; involve in—; lead to—; leap to—; lure to—; redeem—; rejoice in—; rescue from—; revel in—; revenge—; rush to—; seek—; send to—; shower—; smite with—; sweep with—; suffer—; thirst for—; woo—; work—.

(See ruin.)

DESTRUCTIVE

adverbs
appallingly; unnecessarily; drunkenly; hysterically; angrily; riotously; deliberately; designedly; wantonly; universally; widely; horribly; unbelievably; lethally; instantly; eventually; indiscriminately; probably; infallibly; remorselessly; inconceivably; ominously; mercilessly; incalculably; ultimately; wastefully; carelessly; thoughtlessly; needlessly; meanly; hatefully; systematically.

DESULTORY

adverbs

merely; irregularly; disconnectedly; lazily; quaintly; exasperatingly; fatally; carelessly; unsystematically; heedlessly; negligently; nonchalantly; indifferently; blithely; smilingly; wantonly; intolerably; imperturbably; vexatiously; unluckily; placidly; serenely; plaguedly.

DETACHMENT

adjectives

alert; hard; fierce; philosophic; lofty; cool; aloof; displayed; detailed; reserved; various (pl); ever-proceeding; beautiful; hastily-gathered; successive; indolent; numerous (pl).

DETAIL

adjectives

rich; decorative; sickening; harmonious; intimate; perturbing; enduring; incredible; visual; elaborate; irrelevant; minute; ornate; amusing; personal; trivial; luscious; troublesome; unpoetical; fictitious; superficial; architectural; repugnant; alarming; impeccable; sensuous; outstanding; conventional; authentic; characteristic; confusing; ingenious; harrowing; technical; tedious; cumbersome; painful; disgusting; exquisite; complete; distinctive; profound; vivid; profuse; charming; unimportant; commonplace; agonizing; remaining; ornamental; profligate; petty; admirable; picturesque; remarkable; significant; sharp; graphic; fervid; reliable; voluminous; appropriate; devastating; realistic; revolting; hateful; trifling; little; worrisome; vexatious; delicate; subtle; gossiping; brief; merest; dull; complicated; tiniest; circumstantial; grim; sordid; collateral; sufficient; loveliest; essential; unusual; perplexing; mean; unrevealed; cleverest; homely; domestic; biographical; scenic; endless; methodical; exact; statistical; clear; restless; hampering; subordinate; heterogeneous; vulgar; needless; topographical; pedantic; faultless; historical; meager; concise; irksome; dreary; myriad (pl).

verbs

array—s; authenticate—s; avoid—; chronicle—s; contribute to—; correlate—s; describe—s; dig out—s; dispense with—; divulge—; dwell upon—; enumerate in—; furnish with—s; grapple with—; grasp—; intersperse—s; marshal—s; master—s; memorize—s; note—s; observe—s; offer in—; parade —s; rehearse—s; relate—s; repeat—s; reveal—s; set forth—s; spare—s; study—s; suppress—s; thrash out—s; treat in—; underestimate—; unearth—; waive —; wrestle with —s; —s bewilder; —s bore; —s elude; —s enrich; —s leak out; —s weary.

(See particular, item, part.)

DETAIL (v)

adverbs

minutely; intimately; visually; elaborately; irrelevantly; amusingly; trivially; lusciously; poetically; superficially; significantly; conventionally; authentically; characteristically; tediously; completely; profusely; vividly; picturesquely; fervidly; voluminously; realistically; vexatiously; briefly; sordidly; endlessly; exactly; methodically; statistically; vulgarly; meagerly; irksomely; drearily.

(See narrate.)

DETAILED

adverbs

accurately; explicitly; clearly; meticulously; punctiliously; richly; horribly; intimately; incredibly; elaborately; minutely; amusingly; alarmingly; ingeniously; tediously; painfully; disgustingly; exquisitely; completely; vividly; graphically; admirably; remarkably; sharply; reliably; appropriately; realistically; hatefully; delicately; briefly; circumstantially; sordidly; unusually; cleverly; statistically; endlessly; exactly; clearly; needlessly; faultlessly; drearily; irksomely.

DETAIN (v)

adverbs

forcibly; unavoidably; successfully; honorably; ingloriously; vexatiously; outrageously; accidentally; unhappily.

(See keep, arrest.)

DETECT (v)

adverbs

easily; cleverly; shrewdly; casually; astutely; logically; artfully; slyly; brilliantly; scientifically; accidentally.

(See discover, uncover.)

DETECTION

adjectives

casual; successful; skillful; logical; artful.

verbs

avoid—; baffle—; elude—; escape—; evade —; fear—; flee—; frustrate—; hide from

—; stumble upon—; suffer—; —alarms; —discloses; —exposes; —informs; —reveals.

(See discovery, disclosure.)

DETECTIVE

adjectives
private; geological; dental; shrewd; competent; hard; luckless; district; burly; typical; tireless; great; heroic; unsympathetic.

verbs
baffle—; commission—; dispatch—; elude—; employ—; escape—; evade—; hire—; inform—; reward—; —accuses; —corners; —discloses; —discovers; —disguises; —dogs; —executes; —exposes; —guards; —hounds; —hunts; —inquires; —inspects; —investigates; —masks; —nabs; —observes; —protects; —pursues; —raids; —reveals; —runs down; —searches; —spies; —studies; —suspects; —tracks; —tracks down; trails, —uncovers; —unearths; —watches.

(See officer, police.)

DETENTION

adjectives
prolonged; honorable; inglorious; compulsory; vexatious; outrageous; accidental; unhappy.

DETERIORATE (*v*)

adverbs
sadly; horribly; physically; mentally; morally; bodily; inevitably; steadily; intellectually; lamentably; seriously; markedly.

(See impair.)

DETERIORATION

adjectives
physical; bodily; inevitable; mental; nervous; steady; intellectual; lamentable; serious; marked.

verbs
defend from—; detect—; employ in—; exaggerate—; preserve from—; pretend—; produce—; save from—; undergo—; —abates; —arises; —continues; —degenerates; —depresses; —destroys; —impairs; —injures; —seeps in.

(See corruption.)

DETERMINATION

adjectives
obvious; inflexible; intrinsic; great; zealous; steadfast; tireless; grim; deathly;
feverish; personal; supernatural; insistent; passionate; sudden; abrupt; settled; bounding; equal; fixed; prescient; mighty; harsh; forceful; intelligent; calm; accurate; cool; early; tangible; selfish; chronological; unwilling; stubborn; dogged; warm; uniform; indefatigable; judicial; desperate; controlling; unanimous; persistent; obstinate; invincible; unflinching; resolute; cold; immutable; precise; whole-souled; ruthless; iron; inexorable; pudgy; manifest; drunken; earnest; indomitable.

verbs
change—; equip with—; flash—; forge—; inspire—; hail—; obsess with—; plod along in—; quench—; reiterate—; reward—; sharpen—; strengthen—; struggle in—; —achieves; —triumphs; —wanes.

(See decision, resolution.)

DETERMINE (*v*)

adverbs
absolutely; happily; objectively; unanimously; shrewdly; passionately; accurately; precisely; resolutely; sternly; conclusively; immediately; unceremoniously; inflexibly; zealously; grimly; stubbornly; doggedly; invincibly; unflinchingly; ruthlessly; inexorably; manifestly; indomitably; largely.

(See decide.)

DETERMINED

adverbs
firmly; inordinately; immovably; irrationally; illogically; childishly; irrevocably; stubbornly; officially; mightily; finally; courageously; quietly; inexorably; harshly; feverishly; passionately; intelligently; calmly; coolly; selfishly; desperately; ruthlessly; drunkenly; crazily; earnestly; curiously; fatally.

DETEST (*v*)

adverbs
fundamentally; thoroughly; positively; unreasonably; infinitely; exaggeratedly; definitely; markedly; obviously; noticeably; unhallowedly; violently.

(See hate.)

DETESTABLE

adverbs
utterly; incredibly; unbelievably; hatefully; abominably; completely; flagrantly; viciously; deplorably; lamentably; diabolically; noxiously; terribly; generally; woefully; odiously; repulsively; despicably; intolerably; insufferably; horridly.

DETESTATION

adjectives
infinite; prolonged; exaggerated; definite; marked; noticeable.

DETHRONE (v)

adverbs
ignominiously; completely; shamefully; dishonorably; pusillanimously; courageously; cowardly; brutally; violently; forcefully.
(See usurp.)

DETONATION

adjectives
remote; mystic; continuous (pl); muffled; tremendous; furious; sharp; spasmodic.

verbs
accompany by—; attribute—to; enkindle—; fire—; muffle—; produce—; result in—; —echoes; —erupts; —expels; —occurs; —reports; —rips; —shocks; —stuns; —thunders; —uproots; —violates.
(See explosion.)

DETOUR

adjectives
weary; lightning; quick; disconcerting; unexpected; wrong; bumpy; long; roundabout; wretched.

DETRACTION

adjectives
timid; rude; subtle; uninitiated; aggravated.

DETRIMENT

adjectives
clogging; acute; raw; unbiased; grave; serious.

verbs
accept—; acquire—; admit—; burden with —; cause—; free from—; harbor—; incur —; load with—; repair—; replace—; suffer —; sustain—; —accrues; —affects; —harms; —impairs; —injures; —weakens.
(See injury, loss, damage, harm.)

DETRIMENTAL

adverbs
undeniably; economically; financially; physically; terribly; unluckily; intentionally; maliciously; designedly; substantially; enormously; incalculably; irreparably; irremediably; seriously; personally; disgracefully; unintentionally; incidentally; palpably; essentially; disastrously; woefully.

DEVASTATE (v)

adverbs
virtually; generally; appallingly; spiritually; systematically; aimlessly; heartlessly; fiendishly; tyrannically; viciously; ferociously; brutally.
(See ruin.)

DEVASTATING

adverbs
unimaginably; horribly; incredibly; ruinously; inhumanly; savagely; vastly; universally; viciously; sinfully; iniquitously; extensively; irremediably; irrevocably; irrecoverably; heinously; dismally; calamitously.

DEVASTATION

adjectives
cyclonic; general; appalling; forest; spiritual; systematic; aimless.

DEVELOP (v)

adverbs
precociously; enormously; advantageously; harmoniously; indirectly; majestically; copiously; riotously; subsequently; perfectly; logically; habitually; unexpectedly; definitely; independently; inordinately; exclusively; rationally; invariably; extraordinarily; tediously; arduously; irrationally; intricately; belatedly; artistically; culturally; muscularly; socially; economically; mentally; physically; deftly; imposingly; continuously; poetically; subsequently; coherently; vindictively; scientifically; progressively; morally; spectacularly; aesthetically; uniquely; deviously; legitimately.
(See complete, unfold.)

DEVELOPMENT

adjectives
extraordinary; astonishing; startling; amazing; rapid; meteoric; long; tedious; arduous; extravagant; irrational; intricate; vast; extensive; slow; evolutionary; gradual; belated; deliberate; hirsute; artistic; cultural; muscular; social; economic; modern; mental; physical; noble; high; deft; majestic; effective; logical; imposing; egregious; intellectual; secluded; surface; inferred; diversified; further; general; continuous; eventual; recent; poetic; subsequent; surprising; coherent; architectural; vindictive; enriching; compensatory; scientific; progressive; basic; disproportionate; laudable; harmonic; individual; impartial; strained; wholesome; previous; promising; technical; organic; moral; multifarious;

psychosexual; magnificent; glorious; institutional; consequent; thematic; peculiar; spectacular; recent; liturgical; safety; empiric; aesthetic; intensive; industrial; defective; external; remoter; unique; devious; expansive; legitimate; profligate; multiple (pl); arrested.

verbs
arrest—; attain—; await—; check—; contribute to—; encourage—; enfeeble—; evaluate—; foresee—; forestall—; foster—; hail—; hamper—; hasten—; hinder—; impair—; keep abreast of—; paralyze—; retard—; 'review—; revolutionize—; rush—; speed—; spur—; stimulate—; stunt—; trace—; undergo—; visualize—; witness—; —germinates from; —proceeds; —surges forward.
(See evolution, growth, expansion, enlargement.)

DEVIATE (v)
adverbs
unconventionally; grossly; materially; peculiarly; slightly; frequently; momentarily; anomalously; occasionally; abnormally; unaccountably; oddly; exceptionally; strangely; weirdly.
(See stray, wander.)

DEVIATION
adjectives
peculiar; slight; gross; material; frequent (pl); anomalous; momentary; occasional.

verbs
accept—; allow—; ascertain—; cause—; determine—; doubt—; eliminate—; govern —; measure—; observe—; recognize—; render—; suspect—; tend toward—; —destroys; —shocks; —strays; —varies.
(See variation, divergence, error.)

DEVICE
adjectives
ingenious; grotesque; elaborate; great; fertile; clockwork; amazing; safety; unworkable; wicked; stale; petty; crude; devious; clumsy; happy; shallow; rhetorical; patriotic; labor-saving; convenient; frugal; improved; successful; hard; simple; shrewd; cunning; artful; clever; magical; sundry (pl); sufficient; heraldic; alignment; desperate; quaint; local; singular; comfortable; playful; artificial; supreme; effective; ancient; symbolic; noble; ceremonial; makeshift; curious; economic; excellent;

scholastic; rotary; timesaving; automatic; protective; hazardous; discredited; suitable; chosen; favorite; optical; childish; treacherous.

verbs
abandon—; adopt—; affect—; contrive—; employ—; equip with—; finance—; hit upon —; invent—; launch—; manufacture—; patent—; resort to—; scorn—; utilize.
(See invention, scheme, strategem, symbol.)

DEVIL
adjectives
excellent; incarnate; unsympathetic; deceitful; poor; red; charming; imaginary; flaming; fever-scourged; cruel; stubborn; attractive; little; frisky; obstinate; greedy; latent; merry; destroying; exorcised; surly; eternal; good-looking; chained-up; burning; interior; tempting; mocking; malicious; foreign; raging; daring; conjuring.

verbs
bargain with—; cast out—; conquer—; conspire with—; contend with—; curb—; defy—; deny—; destroy—; drive out—; emancipate from—; exorcise—; expel—; flee from—; follow—; grapple with—; league with—; offend—; personify—; possess by—; preserve from—; "raise"—; rebuke—; resist—; sacrifice to—; scorn—; steer toward—; subject to—; take up with —; worship—; —betrays; —conjures; — deceives; —deludes; —ensnares; —enters; —entices; —harries; —mocks; —oppresses; —rules; —spurs; —tempts.
(See demon, spirit, evil.)

DEVILISH
adverbs
hatefully; inconceivably; iniquitously; irretrievably; incredibly; incorrigibly; atrociously; infernally; shockingly; manifestly; openly; exceptionably; horribly; outrageously; incurably; obdurately; stubbornly; nefariously.

DEVILTRY
adjectives
good-humored; inexhaustible; stock; petty; ineradicable.

DEVIOUS
adverbs
obscurely; circumbendibusly; sinuously; unfortunately; astutely; adroitly; unnecessarily; strangely; oddly; ominously; cur-

iously; provokingly; vexatiously; suspiciously; cleverly; cruelly; intricately; amazingly; confusingly; deliberately; craftily; sharply; fatally; obviously; inscrutably; perplexingly.

DEVISE (v)
adverbs

ingeniously; carefully; cunningly; peculiarly; subtly; specially; grotesquely; elaborately; crudely; deviously; clumsily; conveniently; frugally; shrewdly; sufficiently; comfortably; artificially; effectively; symbolically; economically; curiously; automatically; scholastically; hazardously; suitably; amazingly.
(See contrive, invent.)

DEVOLVE (v)
adverbs

wholly; unexpectedly; absurdly; startlingly; weightily; heavily; normally; politically; traditionally.
(See transmit.)

DEVOTE (v)
adverbs

exclusively; properly; faithfully; unstintingly; passionately; intensely; unreservedly; exclusively; civilly; fearlessly; zealously; earnestly; tenderly; uniquely; expressly; profoundly; religiously; patriotically; personally; mutually; humbly; doggedly; dumbly; blindly; obviously; absurdly; heroically; submissively; unselfishly; sentimentally; conscientiously; unswervingly; untiringly; recklessly; fervidly; deathlessly; assiduously; conjugally; unimpeachably; unobtrusively; agelessly; sublimely; patiently.
(See dedicate, consecrate.)

DEVOTED
adverbs

piously; profoundly; childishly; earnestly; personally; ardently; completely; humbly; mutually; doggedly; blindly; foolishly; queerly; absurdly; heroically; deeply; extremely; submissively; unselfishly; tenderly; sentimentally; exclusively; dangerously; conscientiously; genuinely; passionately; unswervingly; exquisitely; ostentatiously; conspicuously; reverently; staunchly; assiduously; fondly; unobtrusively; sublimely; patiently; openly.

DEVOTEE
adjectives

impious; reverent; average; enthusiastic; ardent; fresh; rabid; distinguished; meek; worshiping; religious; theosophic; highminded; indigent; true; congenial; servile.

verbs

attract—; gain—; interest—; victimize—; —s assemble; —clamors; —s congregate; —consecrates; —s convene; —dedicates; —denounces; —disparages; —esteems; — exhibits; —indulges in; —introduces; — offers; —practices; —pursues; —worships.
(See follower.)

DEVOTION
adjectives

profound; wearied; religious; patriotic; infantile; earnest; lifetime; studied; personal; detached; complete; humble; mutual; dogged; real; dumb; blind; open; queer; absurd; increased; heroic; wholehearted; obvious; deep; impious; discouraged; endless; extreme; continued; distant; submissive; unselfish; outdated; painful; tender; sentimental; spiritless; exclusive; dangerous; unceasing; conscientious; genuine; passionate; pure; unparalleled; unswerving; evening; exuberant; capable; angry; faithful; untiring; constant; unconditional; exquisite; ardent; disinterested; unostentatious; conspicuous; undiminished; reverent; speculative; reckless; consecrated; fervid; wifely; deathless; absolute; doglike; unfaltering; respectful; mystic; desperate; obsequious; chivalric; staunch; inextinguishable; cheerful; manly; bigoted; costliest; austere; solitary; unalterable; ceremonious; idyllic; efficient; assiduous; extemporary; conjugal; outstanding; abiding; unimpeachable; incessant; fondest; invisible; protective; unobtrusive; passing; nunlike; reunited; ageless; sublime; patient.

verbs

accept—; bestow—; cease—; command—; excite—; exploit—; extend—; favor with —; glorify—; interrupt—; lavish—upon; pay—; show—; tender—; —abates; — wanes; —warms.
(See zeal, allegiance, attachment, love, worship, adoration, fidelity, religion.)

DEVOUR (v)
adverbs

ravenously; omnivorously; voraciously; greedily; rapidly; utterly; brutally; fiendishly; hoggishly; bestially; rudely.
(See eat, consume.)

adverbs

profoundly; earnestly; completely; humbly; queerly; whole-heartedly; piously; submissively; unselfishly; unceasingly; reverently; conscientiously; faithfully; ardently; loyally; assiduously; unobtrusively; admirably; sincerely; solemnly; fervently; meekly.

DEW

adjectives

drenching; fragrant; cleansing; damp; dripping; murky; lethal; sparkling; heavy; melodious; filmy; glittering; glistening; warm; moonlit; starry; starlight; hoary; scented; gracious; moistening; quivering; spangled; prodigal; fiery; melancholy; ambrosial; new-dropped; fattening; ghastly; pestilent; gleaming; undried; cold; blinding; richer; unconcealing; sunlit; gathering; bitter; innocent; softest; melting; nocturnal; lingering; mellifluous; healing; falling; sickly; silvery.

verbs

bathe in—; bedabble with—; brush away—; deck with—; dip in—; dissolve in—; distill—; flower in—; sip—; spray with—; steep in—; sweep away—; wash with—; wet with—; —chills; —dabbles; —drenches; —drops; —falls; —freshens; —glistens; —moistens; —pearls; —refreshes; —revives; —spangles; —strengthens; —thickens; —twinkles.

(See moisture, tears, drop.)

DEXTERITY

adjectives

reasonable; digital; polite; amazing; bland; graceful; manual; unusual; marvelous; incredible; rapid; superior; wonderful; admirable; cool; indescribable; automatic; fatal.

DEXTEROUS

adverbs

reasonably; unusually; politically; blandly; amazingly; wonderfully; admirably; automatically; incredibly; dangerously; skilfully; particularly; consciously; proudly; ostentatiously; dramatically; expertly; felicitiously; discreetly; advantageously; acutely; shrewdly; scientifically; quickly; consummately; spectacularly; opportunely; astutely.

DIABOLIC

adverbs

inconceivably; iniquitously; incredibly; incorrigibly; atrociously; infernally; shock-ingly; manifestly; openly; flagrantly; exceptionably; horribly; outrageously; incurably; obdurately; stubbornly; nefariously; villainously; execrably; accursedly; inhumanly; ruthlessly.

DIABOLISM

adjectives

everlasting; widespread; apparent; marked; noticeable; flagrant.

DIADEM

adjectives

priceless; imperial; starry; kingless; stellated; royal; regal; ducal.

DIAGNOSE (v)

adverbs

precisely; accurately; exactly; correctly; medically; solemnly; bacteriologically; logically; scientifically; casually; conscientiously, astutely.

(See study.)

DIAGNOSIS

adjectives

exact; definite; bitter; unpromising; correct; medical; solemn; bacteriological.

verbs

conduct—; confirm—; embrace in—; form —; reach—; record—; study—; value—; weigh—; —assures; —determines; —discovers; —distinguishes; —errs; —identifies; —reveals; —warrants.

(See conclusion, judgment.)

DIAGRAM

adjectives

legible; clear; confused; graphic; explanatory; key; brief.

verbs

compose—; constitute—; draw—; examine —; exhibit—; experiment with—; improve —; mark—; measure—; outline—; produce —; —charts; —demonstrates; —directs; —illustrates; —points out; —represents; —symbolizes.

(See plan, outline, map, drawing, illustration.)

DIAL

adjectives

wavering; luminous; recessed; spacious; graduated; moss-grown; sun.

verbs

adjust—; affect—; center—; check—; discover by—; employ—; furnish with—; provide—; refer to—; set—; spin—; watch—; —aids; —counts; —describes; —directs; —indicates; —measures; —points to; —regulates; —revolves; —substantiates; —times.

(See compass, watch.)

DIALECT

adjectives
drawling; guttural; hinterland; crude; broad; garrulous; vulgar; handed-down; ancestral; forcible; unintelligible; strange; multiplying (pl); unpleasant; peculiar; nasal; native; authentic; queer; rural; overaccented; delicious; amorous; gibbering; purest; expressive; barbarous; quaint; untutored; hissing; unmusical.

verbs
adopt—; affect—; converse in—; drop—; influence—; interpret—; lay aside—; missound—; modify—; overcome—; recognize —; study—; understand—; —amuses; —confuses; —corrupts; —missounds; —retains; —vanishes.

(See language, speech.)

DIALOGUE

adjectives
fabulous; witty; short; solemn; natural; spontaneous; earnest; happy; hurried; vivid; delightful; tender; adequate; poetic; urbane; sparkling; final; mysterious; amusing; fast-paced; wooden; frothy; delicious; rapier-like; brilliant; imaginary; merry; wasted; feeble; dramatic; realistic; sustained.

verbs
carry on—; compile—; compose—; confine —to; contrive—; enter into—; entertain with—; inject into—; introduce in—; involve in—; launch into—; transcribe—; —animates; —concerns; —engrosses; —enlivens; —passes; —praises; —vivifies; interests in—.

(See conversation, talk.)

DIAMOND

adjectives
paste; oblong; spurious; illicit; sparkling; enormous; square-cut; pendent; blazing; icy; fair-sized; uncut; monstrous; starry; flashing; unlimited (pl); countless (pl); elemental; flaming; smuggled.

verbs
admire—; adorn with—; deck with—s; imbed—; mine—s; polish—; prize—; quarry

—s; set—; win—; yield—s; —crowns; —flames; —flashes; —gleams; —glimmers; —glistens; —glitters; —glows; —reflects; —scintillates; —sparkles.

(See gem, stone, jewel.)

DIAPHRAGM

adjectives
crude; concave; heaving; parchment; tough; bisecting.

DIARY

adjectives
careful; meteorological; intimate; manuscript; joyous; cryptic; copious; vigorous; authoritative; conscientious; well-kept; informal; informative; gossipy; risque; bold; revealing.

verbs
cherish—; enter in—; expose—; hide—; inscribe in—; jot in—; peep into—; prepare—; publish—; recollect by—; record in—; refer to—; repose in—; scan—; —collects; —contains; —covers; —notes; —observes; —relates; —reveals.

(See record, account, book, literature.)

DIATRIBE

adjectives
notorious; violent; revengeful; brutal; incessant.

verbs
break out in—; conclude—; direct—; erupt —; fire—; fulminate—; indulge in—; regret—; set off—; thunder—; utter—; vent —; —abuses; —arouses; —contributes; —exaggerates; —offends; —provokes; —shocks.

(See invective, tirade, discourse, discussion.)

DICE

adjectives
lucky; loaded; rattling; false; unfailing; irresistible; seductive.

verbs
bet on—; box—; cast—; cheat at—; gamble with—; jostle—; load—; lose by—; play with—; scatter—; shake—; shoot—; throw —; toss—; win at—; —clack; —clink; —decide; —fall; —rattle; —reveal; —settle; —topple; —turn.

adjectives
definite; unheeded; vicious; infernal; soundest; passionate; fascist.

DICTATE (v)
adverbs
amiably; simultaneously; personally; definitely; viciously; infernally; passionately; bestially; heartlessly; fiendishly; reasonably.
(See command.)

DICTATION
adjectives
aimless; laborious; imperious; rapid; accurate; careless.

DICTATOR
adjectives
military; musical; cruel; unseen; benevolent; philosophic; willful; occult; imperious; ranking; domestic.

verbs
appeal to—; develop into—; entrust—with; fall before—; follow—; name—; prate about—s; serve under—; succumb to—; —authorizes; —bans; —checks; —coerces; —crushes; —decrees; —exercises; —forbids; —forces; —fulminates; —governs; —orders; —prescribes; —rules; —tyrannizes; —violates; —wields.
(See tyrant, monarch, ruler.)

DICTATORIAL
adverbs
absolutely; politically; offensively; unashamedly; officiously; ostentatiously; imperially; regally; imperiously; cruelly; unwarrantably; disagreeably; needlessly; arrogantly; haughtily; superciliously; hatefully; carefully; obstinately; dogmatically; fanatically; fantastically; deliberately; insolently; saucily; impertinently; bumptiously; brazenly; shamelessly; presumptuously.

DICTATORSHIP
adjectives
absolute; military; political; proletarian; economic; stultifying; unashamed; irregular; temporary; household; bloody; mighty; inefficient; imperial; popular; literary; fruitless.

verbs
accept—; assume—; attempt—; create—; cultivate—; curtail—; elect to—; entrust—to; establish—; exercise—; install—; lust for—; repulse—; revolt against—; set up

—; serve under—; shake—; succumb to—; yield to—; —coerces; —compels; —crushes; —holds sway.
(See despotism, control, rule.)

DICTION
adjectives
stilted; meticulous; parietal; exquisite; tragic; dignified; metaphorical; illogical; artless; terse; elaborate; glowing; extravagant; loitering; poetic; racy; fashionable; classical; unadorned; overwhelming; peculiar; crabbed; bold.

DICTIONARY
adjectives
comprehensive; dusty; voluminous; exhaustive; unabridged; unusable; historical; universal; excellent; rhyming; biographical; scholarly; pronouncing; scriptural; phonetic; synonymic; grammatical; weighty; authoritative.

verbs
abridge—; compile—; consult—; edit—; enlarge—; have recourse to—; provide—; publish—; resort to—; revise—; —aids; —arranges; —classifies; —confirms; —contains; —decides; —defines; —determines; —informs; —interprets; —pictures; —verifies.
(See book.)

DICTUM
adjectives
energetic; famous; harsh; bold; brisk; final.

DIDACTIC
adverbs
tiresomely; tediously; wearisomely; monotonously; conceitedly; learnedly; instructively; endlessly; absurdly; egotistically; indefatigably; disagreeably; unpleasantly; ostentatiously; diffusely; preachily; sharply; academically; eruditely; expertly; bumptiously.

DIDACTICISM
adjectives
solemn; sugar-coated; obvious; patent; marked; unintelligent.

DIE (v)
adverbs
ultimately; unaccountably; wholly; utterly; valiantly; peacefully; sullenly; violently; gloriously; proudly; recently; providentially; stoically; pennilessly; invariably; hap-

lessly; blissfully; huskily; respectively; honorably; mysteriously; quiveringly; holily; abruptly; shamefully; accidentally; religiously; rebelliously; precipitately.

(See perish.)

DIET

adjectives

abstemious; starvation; daily; piscatory; ample; proper; modern; scant; mixed; varied; balanced; ordinary; exclusive; monotonous; nut; fastidious; invented; staple; nourishing; enriched; astringent; vitaminized; spurious; vegetarian; optimum; adequate; coniferous; correct; predominant; meat; peculiar; skimpy; rigid; sensible; intellectual; carnivorous; dangerous; strict; liquid; heavy.

verbs

adhere to—; adopt—; alter—; change—; commend—; complete—; compound—; discuss—; employ—; exclude from—; increase —; mix—; modify—; place on—; prescribe—; recover on—of; reduce—; regulate—; restrict—; spare in—; subsist on—; supplement—; vary—; yield to—; —cures; —influences; —nourishes; —reduces; —
(See fare, victuals. ration, food.)
stimulates; —supplies; —sustains.

DIETETICS

adjectives

compulsory; insipid; accessory; elementary; fundamental.

verbs

engross in—; instruct in—; interest in—; study—; —adapts; —cautions; —comprises; —cures; —defines; —extends to; —inquires; —observes; —prevents; —reforms; —regulates; —solves; —systematizes; —aids.
(See hygiene.)

DIFFER (v)

adverbs

radically; racially; decidedly; essentially; widely; profoundly; chemically; entirely; acutely; sharply; markedly; noticeably; perceptibly; infinitesimally; psychologically; mentally; religiously; gravely; appreciably; strikingly; palpably; vitally; significantly; fundamentally; philosophically; prodigiously; intrinsically; structurally.
(See disagree.)

DIFFERENCE

adjectives

sharp; marked; acute; honest; conscientious; noticeable; perceptible; decided; evident; inconsequent; infinitesimal; scant; slight; petty; racial; psychological; mental; religious; matrimonial; grave; insuperable; subtle; bitter; radical; simulated; conceded; actual; essential; utmost; striking; outstanding; profound; vast; appreciable; noteworthy; tremendous; palpable; calm; assignable; important; fresh; material; vital; sad; qualitative; pathetic; supreme; happy; minute; amazing; factional; original; significant; indefinable; supposed; superficial; magical; tribal; fundamental; irrepressible; deep-seated; philosophical; irreconcilable; prodigious; intrinsic; temporary; structural.

verbs

acquaint with—; appreciate—; bury—s; cancel—; compensate for—; correlate with —s; debate—; define—; determine—; discern—; discuss—; dread—; expose—; illustrate—; master—; notice—; obliterate—; observe—; reconcile—s; rest—s; settle—; smooth out—; —appears; —s arise; —s estrange; —s flare up; —prevents.
(See disagreement, discrimination, variation, inequality.)

DIFFERENT

adverbs

multifariously; incidentally; impertinently; harmlessly; objectionably; inadmissibly; unconformably; strangely; remotely; outlandishly; undeniably; palpably; essentially; grotesquely; disagreeably; pleasantly; obviously; inconceivably; discordantly; fantastically; exotically.

DIFFERENTIATE (v)

adverbs

legitimately; generously; elaborately; acutely; bluntly; properly; distinctly.
(See distinguish.)

DIFFERENTIATION

adjectives

subtle; elaborate; proper; acute; blunt.

DIFFICULT

adverbs

relatively; tremendously; overwhelmingly; formidably; unbelievably; supremely; seriously; administratively; physically; obviously; naturally; peculiarly; particularly;

strangely; curiously; conspicuously; alarmingly; patently; evidently; dishearteningly; impossibly; intricately; perplexingly; desperately.

DIFFICULTY

adjectives

immense; great; huge; tremendous; enormous; overwhelming; formidable; redoubtable; unbelievable; amazing; supreme; innumerable (pl); grave; serious; agrarian; domestic; emotional; administrative; technical; diplomatic; physical; economic; religious; appalling; financial; fiscal; evident; obvious; inherent; identical; underlying; insurmountable; vital; peculiar; practical; necessary; problematic; familiar; initial; insuperable; unpleasant; lamentable; invincible; conspicuous; unforeseen; functional; alarming; recurrent; endless; disheartening; relative; principal; censorship; bargaining; visual; baffling; impending; incredible; considerable; unprecedented.

verbs

adjust—; attend with—; belittle—; beset by—; breathe with—; clear up—; comprehend—; conclude—; confront with—; conquer—; contend with—; demonstrate—; double—; eliminate—; encounter—; escape —; estimate—; evade—; experience—; go to the root of—; grapple with—; grasp—; impose—; impress with—; iron out—; labor in—; minimize—; obliterate—; obviate—; pass—; perceive—; raise—; remedy—; rouse with—; shirk—; smooth away—; stir up—; strew with—; surmount—; weigh —; wrestle with; —ies accumulate; —ies arise; —grows out of; —intervenes; —looms; —persists.

(See obstacle, hindrance, quarrel, trouble.)

DIFFIDENCE

aajectives

delicate; rustic; becoming; excessive; amused; half-boyish; proper.

verbs

attack—; disperse—; enter into with—; indulge in—; lay aside—; manifest—; practise—; proceed from—; speak with—; teach —; —afflicts; —assails; —creeps over; —prevents; —shames; —submits to; —terrifies; —wounds.

(See bashfulness.)

DIFFIDENT

adverbs

delicately; provincially; becomingly; excessively; amusingly; laughably; ridiculously; needlessly; properly; nervously; anxiously; dreadfully; painfully; bashfully; blushingly; demurely; quietly; shyly.

DIFFUSE

adverbs

tiresomely; tediously; monotonously; vexatiously; endlessly; verbosely; copiously; circuitously; disagreeably; provokingly; pedantically; stupidly; dully; indirectly; interminably; prosily; maddeningly; notoriously.

DIFFUSE (*v*)

adverbs

naturally; delicately; excessively; wastefully; widely; copiously; freely; liberally; perplexingly.

(See scatter, disseminate.)

DIFFUSENESS

adjectives

rhythmical; excessive; expansive; limited; unshadowed; beaming; theoretical.

DIFFUSION

adjectives

wide; cultural; original; soft; vast; inexpressible; universal.

DIG

adjectives

sly; intentional; vicious; sarcastic; witty; humorous; retaliative.

DIG (*v*)

adverbs

laboriously; perseveringly; viciously; intentionally; purposively; industriously; indefatigably.

(See work, labor.)

DIGEST

adjectives

interesting; careful; considered; chronological; fact.

DIGEST (*v*)

adverbs

complacently; rapidly; internally; interestingly; carefully; chronologically; intelligently; mentally; cleverly; briefly.

(See absorb, classify.)

DIGESTION

adjectives

torpid; agreeable; disturbed; superb; sound; pure.

verbs

activate—; affect—; allay—; disturb—; govern—; impair—; improve—; interrupt —; promote—; regulate—; reinvigorate—; retard—; sour—; stimulate—; upset—.

(See health.)

DIGIT

adjectives

lone; disassociated; menacing; insignificant; discounted.

verbs

calculate—; count—; dismember—; divide into—s; decorate—; employ—; exercise—; express in—s; flex—; indicate—; memorize—; number—; ornament—; run into—s; sever—; spoil—s.

(See toe, finger, figure, number.)

DIGNIFIED

adverbs

properly; proudly; informally; graciously; simply; pleasantly; nobly; serenely; calmly; quietly; gravely; faultlessly; elaborately; coldly; indescribably; ridiculously; superbly; naturally; magisterially; matchlessly; sternly; impressively; incongruously; austerely; professionally; pompously; senselessly; gently; disagreeably; repellently; notoriously; augustly; fashionably; solemnly.

DIGNITARY

adjectives

honorable; famous; professional; local; robot; titular; learned.

DIGNITY

adjectives

proper; proud; upright; informal; happy; delicate; external; lofty; lauded; gracious; supreme; simple; majestic; pleasant; complacent; noble; robust; brave; serene; calm; quiet; grave; unwinking; studied; measured; faultless; immaculate; elaborate; sure; stilted; cold; severe; savage; impaired; faded; obedient; mysterious; social; impassive; indescribable; forensic; dashing; waddling; ridiculous; outraged; poised; trembling; spacious; potential; outward; stoical; superb; forced; unbroken; ageless; natural; silent; sententious; sad;

irresistible; magisterial; distant; matchless, undeserved; ill-timed; spiritual; patriarchal; wonted; smug; scholastic; gruesome; military; threatened; short-lived; stern; pious; panoplied; leisure-class; frowning; impressive; spectral; incongruous; white; celestial; mutilated; austere; professional; youthful; additional; senseless; mournful; sedate; pompous; mock; epic; inherent; insulted; gentle; careless; unprecedented; Wagnerian.

verbs

achieve—; cast off—; detract from—; develop—; discard—; dispose of—; enhance —; grope for—; halo in—; inject—; impair—; impart—; invest with—; lend—; maintain—; outrage—; preserve—; retain —; rob of—; shed—; shrug aside—; stress —; surpass—; sustain—; treat with—; vindicate—; win—.

(See eminence, honor, distinction.)

DIGRESS (*v*)

adverbs

irrelevantly; deviously; slightly; politically; fascinatingly; descriptively; boringly; dryly; interminably; illogically.

(See wander, deviate.)

DIGRESSION

adjectives

pleasing; slight; bitter; political; fascinating; irrelevant; unintegrated; wise; agreeable; descriptive; periodic (pl).

DIGRESSIVE

adverbs

vexatiously; endlessly; wordily; verbosely; diffusely; copiously; circuitously; disagreeably; provokingly; tiresomely; unintelligibly; pedantically; vaguely; stupidly; dully; ramblingly; indirectly; interminably.

DILAPIDATED

adverbs

terribly; wretchedly; miserably; sorely; pathetically; dreadfully; ruinously; hideously; outrageously; fantastically; shabbily; shockingly; inconceivably; greatly; inexpressibly; worthlessly.

DILAPIDATION

adjectives

general; wholesale; pathetic; ragged; tumble-down; remnantal.

DILATE (v)

adverbs

endlessly; visibly; abnormally; intolerably; unprecedentedly; continuously; unreasonably.

(See swell.)

DILATORY

adverbs

injuriously; uselessly; needlessly; vexatiously; irritatingly; senselessly; unaccountably; obstinately; stubbornly; dangerously; exasperatingly; unconscionably; characteristically; habitually; gravely; terribly; impertinently; indolently; stupidly; languidly; listlessly; inertly; slothfully; drowsily; dreamily; inexcusably; unpleasantly; gallingly.

DILEMMA

adjectives

economic; awkward; annoying; ancient; veritable; insoluble, cruel; moral; pitiful; agonizing; dire; frightful; doubtful; sentimental; unpleasant; terrible; desperate; inescapable; hopeless.

verbs

balk at—; drift into—; elude—; escape from—; extricate from—; face—; founder on—; grasp—; rescue from—; seize—; solve—; take—by the horns; —baffles; —confronts.

(See choice, predicament.)

DILIGENCE

adjectives

characteristic; sullen; unwearied; savage; conscientious; guilty; true; extraordinary; exceeding; utmost; duteous; scrupulous; tenderest; dire; indefatigable; persevering; dusty; yellow; unsparing; tireless; unwonted.

verbs

admire—; apply—; dispatch with—; display—; exercise—; exert—; note—; nourish —; repay—; report—; require—; reward —; rule with—; show—; summon—; —accomplishes; —persists; —pleases.

(See industry, care, application.)

DILIGENT

adverbs

extraordinarily; carefully; innately; studiously; assiduously; industriously; busily; constantly; doggedly; faithfully; loyally; indefatigably; conscientiously; exceedingly; duteously; scrupulously; tirelessly; habitually; trustworthily; energetically; pleasantly; surprisingly; zealously; devotedly; officiously; briskly; ostentatiously; conspicuously; diplomatically; astutely; shrewdly.

DIM

adverbs

mysteriously; obscurely; strangely; curiously; oddly; nebulously; dully; faintly; cloudily; confusingly; perplexingly; disturbingly; wretchedly; miserably; pallidly; imperceptibly; unaccountably; plaguedly; infernally; dreadfully.

DIM (v)

adverbs

perceptibly; scarcely; mystically; prematurely; dramatically; awesomely; effectively; abruptly; perceptibly.

(See darken, obscure.)

DIMENSION

adjectives

important; narrow; reduced; dominating; prodigious; mere; colossal; ideal; mathematical; basic; toylike; supernatural; hugest; portentous; relative; corporal; gigantic; stupendous; miniature; scanty; horizontal; volcanic; enormous; manageable; palatial; moderate; ambitious; noble; desired; imperial; spacious; confined; incompatible.

verbs

compute—; describe—; discover—; draw—; expand—; explore—; find—; furnish—; measure—; mistake—; reach—; reduce—; require—; speculate on—; supply—; take —; —bounds; —confuses; —exceeds; —represents; —shrinks.

(See magnitude, size, extent.)

DIMINISH (v)

adverbs

perceptibly; partially; proportionally; steadily; materially; insignificantly; sensibly; seriously; vastly; appreciably; intolerably; sensibly; continuously.

(See reduce, lessen.)

DIMINUTION

adjectives

appreciable; sensible; continuous; perceptible; subtle; covert; gradual.

DIMNESS

adjectives

mystic; lovely; gracious; unreal; chequered; shadowy; dreamlike; holy; religious; premature; vast; lonely; cobwebby; misty.

DIMPLE

adjectives

reluctant; fugitive; elusive; tantalizing; fleeting; impertinent; wanton; roguish; neighboring.

verbs

bait with—; break into—; depress into—; expose—; flash—; form—; hollow into—; laugh—; mark with—; part in—; practise —; repay in—; reveal—; smile—; —captivates; —dances; —delights; —lures; —smiles; —twinkles.

DIN

adjectives

terrible; infernal; sudden; outrageous; jocund; clanging; alarming; competing; wheezing; awful; chaotic; terrific; rude; discordant; horrible; chattering; general; ominous; exclamatory; ear-splitting; merry; lively; plaintive; deafening; ever-waxing; furious; vexatious; wild; humming; resounding; reverberating; echoing; shattering; intermittent; frightful.

verbs

diminish—; drown—; endure—; muffle—; penetrate—; raise—; silence—; tremble at —; —awakens; —blasts; —breaks; —dies away; —ensues; —fades; —hisses; —reverberates; —roars; —streams forth; —waxes louder.

(See noise, clamor, uproar, rattle.)

DINE (v)

adverbs

prodigally; sumptuously; ostentatiously; regally; piggishly; opulently; delectably; luxuriously; gaily; talkatively; impressively; miserably; simply; abundantly; belatedly; modestly; ceremoniously; diplomatically; formally.

DINER

adjectives

agitated; gay; talkative; Epicurean; gluttonous.

verbs

cook for—; entertain—; greet—; satiate—; suit—; welcome—; —indulges; —overeats; —relishes; —samples; —stuffs; —tastes; —tips.

DINGY

adverbs

bleakly; terribly; obscurely; gloomily; faintly; disagreeably; repulsively; hatefully; disgustingly; unpleasantly; monotonously; incredibly; pitiably; surprisingly; unexpectedly; discouragingly; hopelessly; inexcusably; dishearteningly; depressingly.

DINING-ROOM

adjectives

oak-paneled; charming; huge; typical; sweltering; cheerless; tapestried; dim; quiet; empty; resplendent.

DINNER

adjectives

impressive; princely; charming; old-fashioned; pleasant; elaborate; sumptuous; delicious; gala; respectable; cheerful; good; decent; tolerable; stupid; miserable; oppressive; masculine; state; simple; abundant; belated; expensive; modest; incredible; endless; savory; magnificent; wretched; melancholy; solitary; periodical; ceremonious; diplomatic; woman-cooked; desolate; doubtful; formal; midnight.

verbs

accompany at—; address at—; attend—; dance at—; dispatch—; drop in for—; enliven—; hobnob at—; invite to—; prepare—; relish—; revel at—; ring for—; sample—; savor—; serve—; spread for—; tear at—; —cools; —nourishes; —satisfies; —steams.

(See meal.)

DIP

adjectives

invigorating; exhilarating; morning; tallow; convulsive; curious.

DIP (v)

adverbs

heavily; abnormally; invigoratingly; exhilaratingly; convulsively; curiously; continuously.

(See lower.)

DIPHTHERIA

adjectives
malignant; mild; tentative; membranous; controlled; dread.

verbs
afflict with—; carry—; contract—; describe —; diagnose as—; doctor for—; immunize to—; infect with—; inoculate against—; isolate—; quarantine for—; recognize—; seize with—; succumb to—; suffer from—; treat for—; —attacks; —inflames; —rages; —ravages; —takes its toll.
(See disease.)

DIPLOMACY

adjectives
tortuous; wasted; secret; minute; private; unskilled; shrewd; consummate; formal; proper; misty; tricky.

verbs
acquire—; adjust with—; adopt—; boast —; conduct with—; control by—; cultivate —; destroy—; detect—; dole out—; employ—; encourage—; exert—; favor—; fit for—; found in—; gain by—; infiltrate—; instruct in—; introduce—; manage with—; necessitate—; negotiate—; propose—; school in—; suggest—; —achieves; —attains; —conceals; —reconciles; —smooths out; — wins.
(See tact, shrewdness, craft.)

DIPLOMAT

adjectives
clever; astute; seasoned; distinguished; veteran; wary; consummate; Oriental; skillful; traditional; old-style; career; formal; suave; scholarly; incredulous; eminent; deft; accomplished; practiced.

verbs
appoint—; employ—; entrust to—; introduce—; invest—with; privilege—; prove —; receive—; select—; —arranges; — conciliates; —conducts; —humors; — "joshes"; —manages; —proposes; — smooths; —suggests; —tricks.
(See ambassador.)

DIPLOMATIC

adverbs
subtly; cunningly; shrewdly; artfully; gravely; wisely; craftily; smoothly; suavely; cleverly; astutely; instinctively; habitually; skilfully; formally; deftly; adroitly; tactfully; profoundly; courteously; cannily; discerningly; nimbly; sagaciously; sagely; blandly; wisely; affably; calculatingly; strategically.

DIPLOMATIST

adjectives
career; cunning; unscrupulous; acute; supple; wary; tenacious; dexterous; decorated.

DIRECT

adverbs
delightfully; pleasantly; helpfully; comfortingly; charmingly; gratifyingly; satisfactorily; pleasingly; ingenuously; frankly; candidly; honestly; courageously; boldly; unequivocally; agreeably; surprisingly; conveniently; childishly; bluntly; sincerely; unaffectedly; unflatteringly; crudely, curiously; strangely.

DIRECT (*v*)

adverbs
vaguely; intelligently; generally; competently; practically; brilliantly; magnificently; disastrously; dangerously; legislatively; habitually; relentlessly; ultimately; academically; arbitrarily; ignobly; intellectually; intricately; eccentrically; hurriedly; curtly; calmly; frivolously; vigorously; automatically; vainly; verbally; uniformly; perseveringly; astutely; dramatically; independently; victoriously.
(See control, guide.)

DIRECTION

adjectives
unlooked-for; vague; intelligent; competent; general; steady; practical; brilliant; magnificent; indicated; careful; unified; cohesive; disastrous; dangerous; legislative; opposite; forbidden; habitual; desirable; inhibited; oblique; relentless; distinguished; succinct; ultimate; academic; retrograde; homeward; arbitrary; ignoble; businesslike; complicated; intellectual; intricate; low-toned; eccentric; crisp; voluble; concise; hurried; curt; calm; explicit (pl); contradictory; transversal; dazzling; frivolous; minute.

verbs
comply with—; determine—; divert from —; drift in—; err in—; face in—of; gaze in—; give—to; heed—; incline—; lack—;

observe—s; respond to—; reverse—; tend
in—of; train in—; transmit—s; turn in—;
—swerves; —wavers.
(See instruction, course. position.)

DIRECTNESS

adjectives
commendable; uncanny; bull-headed; downright; pleasing; brisk; characteristic; engaging; arrowlike; uncompromising;
simple; unstudied; brutal; revealing; clipped; unabashed; manly; military; impulsive; naive; brusque.

DIRECTOR

adjectives
capable; painstaking; regional; financial;
shadowy; honorable.

DIRGE

adjectives
mournful; wailing; beautiful; prophetic;
wrathful; death; funeral; undifferentiated;
weird.

verbs
chant—; compose—; intone—; introduce—;
moan—; occasion—; perform—; renew—;
sing—; soothe with—; sound—; utter—;
wail—; —commemorates; —laments; —
mourns; —saddens.
(See song, poem, music.)

DIRT

adjectives
stubborn; encrusted; soft; excess; sweaty;
grayish; imbedded; accumulated; unspeakable.

verbs
acquaint with—; breed in—; cast out—;
defile with—; fleck with—; fling to—; frolic
in—; grind into—; ingrain with—; originate from—; plant in—; pluck from—; pollute with—; scrape away—; search in—;
throw—; tread in—; wade in—; wallow
in—; wash away—; —accumulates; —adheres; —befouls; —clings; —soils.
(See earth, soil, filth, squalor.)

DISABILITY

adjectives
total; grim; physical; permanent; financial;
partial; inescapable.

verbs
attend with—; bring on—; complain of—;
cope with—; create—; cripple by—; emancipate from—; gloat over—; increase—;

labor under—; lessen—; remove—; stress
—; —paralyzes; —prevents; —restricts;
—tortures.
(See inability, incompetence, impotence,
weakness.)

DISABLE (v)

adverbs
totally; physically; permanently; financially; partially; inescapably; tragically; woefully; completely; entirely.
(See handicap.)

DISABLED

adverbs
tragically; oddly; sadly; utterly; strangely;
dangerously; grimly; totally; partially;
physically; mentally; irremediably; irrecoverably; lamentably; pitiably; deplorably;
pitifully; unnecessarily; helplessly; hopelessly; recently.

DISADVANTAGE

adjectives
distinct; physical; immense; tactical; serious; obvious; ungenerous; initial; economic; particular; individual; undue; painful; tremendous.

verbs
balance—; conceal—; confront with—; deprecate—; endure—; fight at—; hurdle—;
labor under—; place at—; overcome—;
regret—; sell at—; surmount—; tug at—;
uproot—; weight with—; —hinders; —
injures; —obstructs.
(See injury, loss, inconvenience, detri-
ment, drawback, hindrance.)

DISADVANTAGEOUS

adverbs
financially; socially; decidedly; distinctly;
physically; immensely; strategically; seriously; obviously; manifestly; unfortunately; economically; particularly; unduly;
painfully; tremendously; perniciously; disastrously; horribly; exceptionally; infernally; irremediably.

DISAGREE (v)

adverbs
spiritedly; violently; emphatically; excessively; unwittingly; vehemently; internally;
utterly; bitterly; acridly; reasonably; emotionally; rationally; spitefully; venomously.
(See differ, contradict.)

DISAGREEABLE
adverbs
pathetically; utterly; atrociously; outrageously; obviously; senselessly; unreasonably; unnecessarily; horribly; disgustingly; bitterly; deliberately; unintentionally; habitually; gravely; rankly; indecently; disrespectfully; odiously; painfully; unfortunately; unbearably; plaguedly; obnoxiously; dismally; shockingly; harshly; cruelly.

DISAGREEMENT
adjectives
vehement; internal; utter; bitter; acrid.

verbs
abandon—; attribute—to; avoid—; cancel —; cause—; engross in—; evade—; expose to—; feign—; indulge in—; live in—; overcome—; pacify—; remove—; settle—; —disgusts; —displeases; —offends; —vexes.
(See difference, contention, quarrel, dispute.)

DISAPPEAR (*v*)
adverbs
mysteriously; unaccountably; abruptly; miraculously; evanescently; unquestionably; gradually; totally; effectually; unexpectedly; irretrievably; virtually.
(See vanish, recede.)

DISAPPEARANCE
adjectives
unexpected; unexplained; irretrievable; inexplicable; sudden; gradual; virtual.

verbs
achieve—; credit—to; discover—; effect—; fear—; feign—; investigate—; solve—; witness—; —astounds; —baffles; —mystifies.
(See escape.)

DISAPPOINT (*v*)
adverbs
acutely; obviously; grievously; wretchedly; woefully; bitterly; continually; visibly; childishly; distinctly; overwhelmingly; inevitably; vaguely; deeply; poignantly; remorsefully; horridly; mutually; perpetually; cruelly; repeatedly.
(See frustrate, baffle.)

DISAPPOINTED
adverbs
sadly; hopelessly; bitterly; heartbreakingly; irrecoverably; obscurely; grievously; distinctly; overwhelmingly; obviously; manifestly; inexpressibly; vaguely; definitely; deeply; poignantly; horribly; woefully; repeatedly; disconcertingly; tragically; bleakly; senselessly; foolishly; pitiably; terribly; inconsolably; forlornly; miserably; wrtechedly; cruelly.

DISAPPOINTING
adverbs
cruelly; bitterly; harshly; sharply; overwhelmingly; unbearably; sadly; grievously; distinctly; inexpressibly; vaguely; woefully; searingly; pitiably; wretchedly; terribly; tragically; fearfully; definitely; deeply.

DISAPPOINTMENT
adjectives
minor; obscure; scathing; bitter; grievous; distinct; overwhelming; obvious; hurt; expressive; inevitable; resultant; burning; vague; outward; unhappy; deep; poignant; remorseful; unrepressed; horrid; woeful; classic; mutual; perpetual; cruel; melancholy; repeated; callous; demoniac.

verbs
adjust—; conceal—; deserve—; dole out—; entail—; feign—; oppress with—; preclude —; pretend—; produce—; shoulder—; sob —; soothe—; suppress—; taste—; —dampens; —ensues; —irks; —rankles; —saddens; —teaches; —wounds.
(See frustration, dissatisfaction, chagrin, misfortune, defeat.)

DISAPPROBATION
adjectives
express; strong; bitter; haughty; hesitant; ready; spontaneous.

DISAPPROVAL
adjectives
envious; ponderous; unmistakable; cold; emphatic; mounting; marked; absent-minded; prim; shocked; icy; unanimous; stern; distinct; tragic; wordless; consistent; harsh; lofty; undisguised; united; violent; ungracious; frigid.

verbs
anticipate—; earn—; indicate—; mask—; prompt—; quench with—; register—; relax —; signify—; snort—; storm—; vent—; —abates; —dampens; —descends; —oppresses; —silences; —vexes.
(See condemnation, censure.)

DISAPPROVE (v)

adverbs

distinctly; heartily; obviously; strongly; unmistakably; coldly; emphatically; primly; icily; unanimously; consistently; sternly; wordlessly; harshly; violently; ungraciously; frigidly.

(See criticize, grumble.)

DISARMAMENT

adjectives

effective; universal; unilateral; world-wide; wide-spread.

verbs

affect—; agree to—; approve of—; confer on—; demand—; disagree upon—; introduce—; join in—; propose—; secure—; urge—; —deprives; —divests; —promises; —reduces; —secures; —strips; —terrifies; —weakens.

DISASTER

adjectives

black; dreadful; messy; hideous; terrible; unmitigated; unbearable; cataclysmic; overwhelming; serious; stupendous; titanic; ultimate; irreparable; irretrievable; marital; economic; melodramatic; planetary; cosmic; social; family; metaphysical; political; commercial; matrimonial; personal; unforeseen; unaccountable; unprecedented; indefinable; dim; imaginary; merited; dire; instant; sheer; sad; fresh; grievous; increasing; appalling; sweet; financial; subsequent; irremediable; awful; ominous; ignominious; illimitable; apparent; widespread; impending; unmerciful.

verbs

circumvent—; court—; force into—; foredoom to—; head for—; investigate—; invite—; meet with—; obviate—; presage—; prophesy—; provoke—; rush into—; salvage from—; shield from—; sow the seeds of—; spell—; suffer—; threaten—; —befalls; —dogs; —impends; —jars; —overtakes; —overwhelms; —sweeps.

(See calamity, catastrophe, mishap, misfortune, accident.)

DISASTROUS

adverbs

overwhelmingly; wholly; irremediably; inexpressibly; horribly; politically; strategically; ruinously; dreadfully; hideously; cataclysmically; seriously; stupendously; ultimately; irreparably; economically; socially; unaccountably; direly; appallingly; financially; apparently; unmercifully; exceptionally; shockingly.

DISAVOW (v)

adverbs

explicitly; deservedly; modestly; completely; distinctly; partially; honestly; earnestly; heatedly; excitedly; repeatedly.

(See disclaim.)

DISAVOWAL

adjectives

distinct; modest; complete; craven; rash; deliberate.

DISBELIEF

adjectives

scornful; cynical; heartsick; raucous; stuttering; total.

verbs

acquire—; adjust—; alter—; assert—; attack—; conceal—; drift into—; express—; form—; hint—; mantle—; pretend—; strip of—; —angers; —annoys; —persists; —refuses; —vexes; —rejects.

(See doubt, distrust, incredulity, skepticism.)

DISC
(See disk)

adjectives

flat; brilliant; polished; keen; turned; crude.

DISCARD (v)

adverbs

ruthlessly; consequently; permanently; gradually; partially; entirely; carelessly; uncaringly; selfishly; obliviously; cruelly.

(See throw, reject.)

DISCERN (v)

adverbs

dimly; faintly; clearly; scornfully; acutely; truthfully; shrewdly; enlightenedly; keenly; jealously; raptly; suspiciously.

(See distinguish, see.)

DISCERNIBLE

adverbs

easily; scarcely; quickly; obscurely; dimly; clearly; plainly; eventually; humanly; amazingly; startlingly; fatally; distinctly; intuitively; dangerously; definitely; positively; momentarily; hardly.

DISCERNING

adverbs
notoriously; profoundly; deeply; sagaciously; judicially; philosophically; expertly; adroitly; cleverly; keenly; astutely; shrewdly; solidly; quickly; brilliantly; acutely; intelligently; ingeniously; discriminatingly; wisely.

DISCERNMENT

adjectives
shrewd; human; enlightened; acute; rapt; keen; jealous.

DISCHARGE

adjectives
watchful; judicious; successful; assiduous; instant; thunderous; conscientious; ignominious; offensive; immediate; luminous; electrical; profuse; vigilant; faithful; occasional; copious

verbs
absorb—; arrest—; check—; emit—; mop out—; purify—; stop—; suck out—; —burns; —drips; —gushes; —inflames; —irritates; —itches; —renews; —varies; —wanes.
(See firing, blast.)

DISCHARGE (v)

adverbs
instantaneously; intelligently; conscientiously; ingeniously; adequately; capably; briskly; faithfully; fully; punctually; judiciously; watchfully; assiduously; ignominiously; offensively; vigilantly.
(See remove, stop.)

DISCIPLE

adjectives
ardent; doubting; youthful; ignorant; inquiring; leading; prolific; uncritical; blunt; renowned; wholehearted; faithful; fervent; humble; patient; temporary; tractable; immediate; civil; primitive; hopeful; trusted.

verbs
accept—; address—; baptize—; cast out—; choose—; command—; distinguish—; instruct—; lead—; rebuke—; teach—; win—; —advances; —apprehends; —believes; —deserts; —establishes; —expounds; —fasts; —follows; —forsakes; —ministers; —prays; —propagates; —records; —understands.
(See convert, follower.)

DISCIPLINARIAN

adjectives
harsh; ferocious; stern; incompetent; ineffectual; strong-minded.

DISCIPLINE

adjectives
mental; hard; strict; unsympathizing; monastic; religious; stern; patient; firm; virtuous; gentle; effective; military; grim; iron; inflexible; rigorous; compulsory; irksome; inexorable; cellular; unfeeling; imaginative; infracted; systematic; painful; affectionate; heroic; moral; speculative; conventual; unrelenting; secret; peculiar; spasmodic; needful; unflagging; questioned; sound; absolute; perfect; modern; prudent; monastic; iron.

verbs
abate—; chafe under—; dread—; enforce —; fuse with—; impose—; maintain—; neglect—; preserve—; relax—; subject to —; wreck—; —deteriorates; —exacts; —falters; —loosens; —wavers; —weakens.
(See training, subjection, punishment, correction.)

DISCIPLINE (v)

adverbs
conscientiously; admirably; ardently; faithfully; patiently; strictly; morally; physically; rigorously; daily; harshly; severely; mentally; unsympathizingly; monastically; religiously; virtuously; gently; effectively; grimly; inflexibly; irksomely; inexorably; unfeelingly; conventionally; unflaggingly; soundly; prudently.
(See train, correct, punish.)

DISCLAIM (v)

adverbs
privately; modestly; excitedly; vehemently; repeatedly; violently; noisily; vigorously; grumblingly; eloquently; fluently; loudly; definitely; weakly; spiritedly; competently; aggressively; promptly; compellingly.
(See deny, renounce.)

DISCLOSE (v)

adverbs
immodestly; irreverently; recently; immediately; fully; shamelessly; modestly; staggeringly; gradually; startlingly; sensationally; diplomatically; dramatically; formally; monstrously; unflatteringly; ruthlessly.
(See reveal, expose.)

adjectives
important; staggering; startling; gradual; cumulating; sensational; diplomatic; dramatic; undeniable; flattering; wide; formal; monstrous.

verbs
anticipate—; guard against—; prepare for —; prevent—; publish—; view—; —accuses; —liberates; —menaces; —precipitates; —reveals; —shocks; —threatens; —unfolds; —yields; —shames.
(See revelation, exhibition, display, discovery.)

DISCOLORATION
adjectives
repulsive; mottled; superficial; unsightly; dark; obtrusive.

DISCOMFIT (*v*)
adverbs
completely; embarrassingly; humiliatingly; momentarily; comically; immediately; spitefully; playfully; calculatedly.
(See humiliate, defeat.)

DISCOMFITURE
adjectives
momentary; comical; old-fashioned; humiliating; nettled; barbed.

DISCOMFORT
adjectives
conscious; visible; emotional; acute; general; agitated; human; prudent; personal; slight; apparent; uncommon; steaming; petty; postprandial; myriad (pl); picturesque; indefinite; sordid; eerie; social; mental; heavy; unendurable; heated; hospitable.

verbs
allay—; alleviate—; chafe in—; chuckle at—; endure—; inflict—; remove—; return with—; share—; suffer—; —disheartens; —dismays; —forces; —grows; —leads; —pains.
(See uneasiness, distress, pain.)

DISCONCERTED
adverbs
embarrassingly; awkwardly; deeply; profoundly; visibly; obviously; painfully; amazingly; terribly; significantly; palpably; vaguely; momentarily; considerably; violently; unmistakably; inexplicably; inadvertently; hopelessly; desperately; irreparably; vexatiously; grievously; glumly; strangely; slightly; mysteriously; oddly.

DISCONSOLATE
adverbs
visibly; apparently; sadly; heavily; pathetically; pitiably; unreasonably; irrationally; appallingly; drearily; grimly; sullenly; resentfully; oddly; ostentatiously; gloomily; biliously; pitifully; profoundly; hopelessly; wearily; desperately; unbearably; unutterably; bitterly; touchingly; genuinely; pensively; mopishly; moodily; dully.

DISCONTENT
adjectives
heavy; economic; real; inevitable; chronic; moderate; prevalent; dreadful; weary; divine; habitual; sullen; desperate; patent; renewed; thoughtful; querulous; perpetual; brawling; thralled; epidemic; popular; vain; moody; gloomy; unruly; smoldering; muttered; latent; futile; growing; impious; sublime; audible; ancient; widespread; aggravating.

verbs
articulate—; awake—; calm—; curse in—; excite—; foment—; murmur—; mutter—; revolt in—; rumble—; seethe with—; sow —; spread—; —afflicts; —flames; —flares; —gathers; —impairs; —sours.
(See dissatisfaction, uneasiness.)

DISCONTINUE (*v*)
adverbs
peremptorily; permanently; temporarily; abruptly; gradually; suddenly; surprisingly; spectacularly.
(See cease, stop.)

DISCORD
adjectives
exquisite; gay; jarring; hidden; ludicrous; mournful; factional; international; jangling; grating; quavering; unmusical; melodious; bitter; unappeasable; striking; distressing; intestinal; inevitable; civic; fluctuant; causeless; lingering; fearful; multitoned.

verbs
accept—; breed—; clash in—; conquer—; correct—; fall to—; ferment—; foment—; hush—; intensify—; master—; overcome—; produce—; silence—; sow—; subject to—;

suffer—; swallow up in—; terminate in—; wipe out—; yield to—; —confounds; —destroys; —follows; —jars; —reigns; —strains.

(See dissension, disagreement, contention, strife, antagonism.)

DISCORDANCE
adjectives
bewildering; complicated; noisy; deafening; incipient; harsh; covert.

DISCORDANT
adverbs
bewilderingly; surprisingly; unexpectedly; unendurably; roughly; harshly; disagreeably; impossibly; intolerably; ludicrously; bitterly; ridiculously; oddly; strangely; exceptionally; shockingly; queerly; strikingly; distressingly; inevitably; racially; essentially; fundamentally; ideologically; unreasonably; distinctly; incongruously; incompatibly; terribly; irreconcilably.

DISCOURAGE (*v*)
adverbs
sepulchrally; entirely; distinctly; churlishly; wisely; heartbreakingly; pathetically; habitually; profoundly; deeply; unreasonably; ruthlessly; permanently.

(See depress, dishearten.)

DISCOURAGEMENT
adjectives
combined; heartbreaking; pathetic; habitual; profound; countless (pl).

verbs
conceal—; mask—; pretend—; produce—; register—; succumb to—; turn in—; yield to—; —abates; —chills; —dampens; —ensues; —hinders; —obstructs; —oppresses; —suppresses; —depresses.

(See despair, depression, dejection, obstacle.)

DISCOURSE
adjectives
admirable; amiable; gay; pleasant; amusing; instructive; didactic; short; humorous; ingenuous; stirring; amazing; connected; rambling; flagging; rhymed; romantic; eloquent; serious; excellent; pointed; identical; separate; vehement; fallible; intended; doctrinal; harmonic; correct; sweet; voluble; sharp; remarkable; fair; bold; moral; witty; common; erratic; profound; unsympathizing; venial.

verbs
admit in—; change—; comprehend—; control—; delight in—; deliver—; devour—; draw out—; enter into—; fill with—; interchange—; invite—; leave off—; open—; peruse—; publish—; render—; spice—; venture on—; waste—; —differs; —enchants; —ensues; —matures.

(See address, speech, dissertation, oration, conversation.)

DISCOURSE (*v*)
adverbs
pleasantly; accurately; prophetically; eloquently; abstrusely; incredibly; delightfully; confusingly; impressively; admirably; amiably; gaily; authoritatively; amusingly; instructively; didactically; ingenuously; humorously; stirringly; romantically; ramblingly; volubly; morally; unsympathetically.

(See speak, converse, lecture.)

DISCOURTEOUS
adverbs
churlishly; sullenly; bluntly; snarlingly; angrily; deliberately; offensively; truculently; hotly; ignorantly; intentionally; unwittingly; brutally; harshly; captiously; sulkily; pertly; saucily; repulsively; venomously; perversely; contemptibly; purposely; impudently; shamefully; crudely; roughly; impertinently; disgracefully; inherently; grossly; tactlessly; morosely; arrogantly; boldly; insolently; trenchantly; maliciously; contemptuously.

DISCOURTESY
adjectives
seeming; gross; prevalent; personal; rough; contemptuous.

DISCOVER (*v*)
adverbs
finally; subsequently; readily; traitorously; astoundingly; amazingly; spectacularly; startlingly; thrillingly; remarkably; stupendously; trivially; miraculously; scientifically; painfully; revolutionizingly; astonishingly; momentously.

(See disclose, ascertain.)

DISCOVERY
adjectives
cheery; delightful; heartening; pleasant; beautiful; astounding; amazing; startling; spectacular; interesting; thrilling; far-reaching; marvelous; remarkable; important; stupendous; paleontological; radical; grievous; awkward; trivial; disconnected; public; godlike; decorative; miraculous;

scientific; striking; painful; epoch-making; bold; notable; pristine; archaeological; grand; useful; initiatory; pictorial; revolutionary; glorious; mineral; laboratory; outward; astonishing; momentous; fatal; salutary; uncomfortable.

verbs

announce—; anticipate—; bring forth—; communicate—; conjure up—; corroborate —; culminate in—; discredit—; examine —; finance—; follow up—; hail—; honor —; lead to—; obtain—; pursue—; report —; stumble on—; verify—; —benefits; —discloses; —reflects; —sheds light on; —underlies.

(See detection, disclosure, revelation, exposure.)

DISCREDITABLE

adverbs

hideously; secretly; subtly; palpably; manifestly; evidently; sadly; terribly; calamitously; foully; abjectly; basely; shamefully; disgracefully; notoriously; scandalously; opprobriously; outrageously; shockingly; appallingly; pitifully.

DISCREET

adverbs

astutely; reasonably; habitually; safely; loyally; admirably; cautiously; warily; wisely; sagaciously; carefully; tremendously; invariably; rarely; absolutely; dependably; naturally; thoughtfully; considerately; oddly; superbly; shrewdly; craftily; marvelously; unerringly; consummately; prudently; vigilantly; cannily; scrupulously; sharply.

DISCREPANCY

adjectives

ironical; peculiar; irreconcilable; slight; curious; minute; embarrassing; minor; frightful; strange.

verbs

admit—; attribute—to; avoid—; clarify—; conceal—; detect—; exhibit—; expose—; harass by—; observe—; overlook—; produce—; remove—; reveal—; search for—; —displeases; —offends; —surprises; —worries.

(See variation, difference, disagreement.)

DISCRETION

adjectives

over-wide; limited; safe; heroic; admirable; tremendous; official; sufficient; arbi-

trary; peaceable; victorious; unshaken; expert; invariable; rare; absolute; wiser; unrestrained; undefined.

verbs

act with—; answer with—; defer in—; doubt—; employ—; exercise—; guide with —; lack—; leave to—; necessitate—; practise—; preserve with—; school in—; yield to—; —befits; —distinguishes; —separates.

(See prudence, wisdom, judgment.)

DISCRIMINATE (*v*)

adverbs

sharply; nicely; emotionally; mentally; infallibly; racially; carefully; rationally; fastidiously; intelligently; scrupulously; aesthetically; artistically; dramatically; unjustly; sagaciously.

(See distinguish, contrast.)

DISCRIMINATING

adverbs

keenly; carefully; cautiously; expertly; unusually; oddly; shrewdly; nicely; fastidiously; scrupulously; naturally; infallibly; habitually; critically; duly; wisely; sagaciously; impeccably; deeply; sharply; cleverly; thoughtfully; prudently; meticulously; delicately.

DISCRIMINATION

adjectives

nice; emotional; mental; infallible; racial; preconceived; careful; rational; fastidious; intelligent; scrupulous; due; innate; geographical; open; aesthetic; ineffable; unfair; impeccable; artistic; dramatic; unjust; laborious; sensory; sagacious; rare.

verbs

apply—; approve—; attempt—; avoid—; credit—; develop—; employ—; exercise—; imply—; lack—; note—; nourish--; pretend—; tolerate—; touch with—; —bites; —earns; —rewards; —separates; —succeeds; —vexes.

(See difference, distinction.)

DISCURSIVE

adverbs

tediously; garrulously; ramblingly; fascinatingly; interestingly; tiresomely; vexatiously; provokingly; illogically; irrelevantly; disputatiously; prosily; maunderingly; verbosely; digressively; effusively; frothily; palaveringly; chattily; tattlingly; senselessly; loquaciously; pratingly; preachily.

DISCUSS (v)

adverbs

animatedly; calmly; intellectually; glibly; heatedly; unreservedly; widely; exhaustively; seriously; despondently; enigmatically; gravely; academically; audibly; robustly; noisily; eagerly; languidly; critically; lucidly; penetratingly; brilliantly; masterfully; amiably; passionately; argumentatively; violently; vitriolically; challengingly; acutely; ethically; fruitfully; colorfully; extensively; elegantly; frankly; inconclusively; philosophically; protractedly; trivially; pertinently; acridly; reasonably; sympathetically; satisfyingly.

(See argue, debate.)

DISCUSSION

adjectives

lucid; penetrating; brilliant; popular; masterful; amiable; lively; doubtful; friendly; agreeable; noisy; heated; passionate; animated; spirited; brisk; keen; argumentative; violent; vitriolic; challenging; enthusiastic; acute; radical; voluble; calm; dignified; intelligent; serious; thoughtful; embittered; acrimonious; academic; nationwide; unofficial; earnest; curtailed; spicy; lusty; ethical; fruitful; cultural; colorful; intensive; critical; concise; detailed; prearranged; extensive; fiery; unexpected; current; everlasting; elegant; miserable; frank; preliminary; fair; complicated; inconclusive; philosophic; protracted; intolerable; scientific; squalid; productive; unprofitable; perpetual; trivial; free; speculative; excited; political; domestic; salutory; group; metaphysical; stormy; pertinent; theological; wearisome; idle; grave; acrid.

verbs

advocate—; avoid—; balk at—of; block—; break into—; center—upon; characterize —; cut short—; deserve—; dominate—; drag into—; enter—; evoke—; exclude from—; influence—; launch into—; merit—; open—; plunge into—; promote—; provoke —; refrain from—; sidetrack—; —enlightens; —informs; —follows; —opens up; —takes place.

(See debate, argument.)

DISDAIN

adjectives

condescending; supercilious; pardonable; chill; withering; pathetic; haughty; hightoned; quick; icy; cynical; aggressive; bitter; well-bred; invincible; lofty; aristocrat-ic; ineffable; proud; profound; incredulous; unutterable; constructive; uncharitable; scornful; vile; utmost; listless; cold; monotonous; immovable; unquenchable; contemptuous.

verbs

call in—; conceive—; confer—upon; convert to—; cool—; deserve—; disregard—; entertain—for; jeer in—; regard with—; reject with—; reply in—; reproach with—; retire in—; scan with—; sting with—; suffer —; taunt in—; treat with—; turn up one's nose in—; upbraid with—; view with—; wrinkle one's nose in—; —displeases; —embitters; —grows; —infuriates; —melts; —offends; —pierces; —swells; —vexes.

(See contempt, scorn, arrogance.)

DISDAIN (v)

adverbs

sneeringly; churlishly; superciliously; condescendingly; witheringly; icily; haughtily; cynically; bitterly; aristocratically; proudly; uncharitably; scornfully; coldly; contemptuously.

(See shame, scorn.)

DISDAINFUL

adverbs

arrogantly; foolishly; senselessly; fantastically; scornfully; youthfully; superciliously; pathetically; absurdly; ridiculously; ludicrously; laughably; haughtily; icily; loftily; aristocratically; proudly; profoundly; unutterably; uncharitably; humiliatingly; nonchalantly; coolly; bumptiously; blusteringly; brazenly; imperiously; insolently; flippantly; boldly.

DISEASE

adjectives

mental; malignant; lurking; prevalent; hideous; pestilential; casual; vague; infectious; incurable; mystifying; loathsome; obscure; virulent; contagious; incipient; insidious; organic; curious; communicable; subtle; fatal; childish; indigenous; inherent; devastating; corrupting; frightful; tropical; inexorable; dread; devilish; pulmonary; inveterate; epidemic; tumorous; lingering; unconquerable; chronic; bewildering; horrible; secondary; intercurrent; febrile; fungus; advanced; inflammatory; foul; sporadic; moral; constitutional; wasting; unique; well-feigned; long-extinct; progressive; unripe; nutritional; resultant; purulent.

verbs

accelerate—; afflict with—; aggravate—; alleviate—; arrest—; attribute—to; awaken —; battle—; beget—; bow down with—; breed—; carry—; characterize—; check—; combat—; communicate—; complicate—; contract—; control—; convey—; deal with —; detect—; diagnose—; disseminate—; efface—; eliminate—; engender—; eradicate —; exempt from—; expose to—; exterminate—; forestall—; fortify against—; foster —; harden to—; heal—; immunize against —; implant—; import—; induce—; infest with—; inherit—; intensify—; introduce—; isolate—; languish with—; master—; overcome—; predispose to—; recognize—; recover from—; rekindle—; relieve—; resist —; smite with—; stamp out—; succumb to—; suffer from—; transmit—; usher in —; ward off—; wrestle with—; —advances; —breaks out; —consumes; —declines; —destroys; —emaciates; —fastens itself upon; —flourishes; —gains a foothold; —hangs on; —lingers; —lurks; —manifests itself; —menaces; —plagues; —prevails; —progresses; —rages; —ravages; —runs rampant; —spreads; —springs up; —stalks; —strikes; —subsides; —threatens.

(See ailment, disorder, malady, pestilence, plague, epidemic.)

DISEASED

adverbs

horribly; unfortunately; appallingly; pitiably; cankerously; pitifully; pathetically; awfully; disgustingly; alarmingly; dangerously; mentally; hideously; incurably; irremediably; irrecoverably; infectiously; virulently; insidiously; organically; curiously; fatally; inherently; congenitally; frightfully; chronically; morally.

DISFAVOR

adjectives

absolute; mingled; high; stern; increasing; lasting; bitter.

verbs

bring into—; deserve—; dispense—; draw —of; earn—; experience—; fall into—; familiarize with—; incur—; mar with—; pour—; pretend—; regard with—; roar—; shower—; spread—; taste—; —affects; —attends; —handicaps; —hinders.

(See disapproval, dislike.)

DISFIGURED

adverbs

grotesquely; queerly; crookedly; horribly; strangely; fantastically; grossly; grimly;

hopelessly; terribly; shamefully; tragically; slightly; odiously; repulsively; pitifully; pathetically; comically; bitterly; deliberately.

DISGRACE

adjectives

hideous; concealed; unmitigable; bewailed; final; crying; sad; eternal; calamitous; nominal; intolerable; foul; invisible; pardonless; indelible; manifold; infinite; glorified; personal; continual; inescapable.

verbs

acknowledge—; augment—; betray—; bewail—; derive—; dishonor with—; dread —; experience—; fall into—; heap—upon; incur—; join in—; lay—upon; lie in—; reflect—; revenge—; rise from—; shrink from—; subject to—; suffer—; sustain—; —blemishes; —deprives; —mars; —shames; —undoes.

(See reproach, infamy, ignominy, disrepute, dishonor.)

DISGRACE (v)

adverbs

publicly; wrongfully; hideously; finally; eternally; calamitously; intolerably; infinitely; personally; wantonly; spitefully; intentionally; revengefully.

(See humiliate, shame.)

DISGRACED

adverbs

permanently; shamefully; terribly; odiously; horribly; sadly; calamitously; disastrously; eternally; momentarily; inexplicably; inescapably; palpably; personally; deeply; darkly; disreputably; notoriously; publicly; outrageously; pathetically; deservedly.

DISGRACEFUL

adverbs

outrageously; wickedly; infamously; scandalously; brutally; flagrantly; atrociously; criminally; dissolutely; foully; hideously; unmitigably; intolerably; indelibly; unforgettably; grossly; shamelessly; patently; palpably; unmistakably; utterly; inexpressibly.

DISGRUNTLED

adverbs

obscurely; bitterly; distinctly; obviously; visibly; openly; inevitably; vaguely; naturally; understandably; sorely; frankly; seriously; fiercely; silently; evidently; sullenly; quietly; wretchedly; miserably; fretfully; peevishly.

DISGUISE

adjectives
neutral; clever; absurd; thin; mystical; inanimate; terror-striking; strange; modest; filthy; effective; reverend; deceptive; extraordinary; impenetrable; customary; smiling; logical; credulous; troublesome; opaque; desperate.

verbs
assume—; attempt—; **cloak with—**; contrive—; counterfeit by—; deck in—; detect —; don—; invent—; lurk beneath—; penetrate—; pierce—; recognize—; see through —; strip off—; take refuge in—; throw off—; —alters; —conceals; —deceives; — disfigures; —masks; —misleads; —succeeds; —transforms.
(See pretense, **mask, cloak,** dress, costume.)

DISGUISE (v)

adverbs
perfectly; handsomely; cleverly; absurdly; thinly; mystically; strangely; effectively; deceptively; extraordinarily; slyly; logically; subtly.
(See **mask, cloak.**)

DISGUISED

adverbs
cleverly; absurdly; thinly; strangely; modestly; effectively; deceptively; extraordinarily; impenetrably; mysteriously; exactly; ridiculously; cryptically; furtively; stealthily; darkly; inviolately; secretly; palpably; harmlessly; falsely; fraudulently; unfairly; maliciously; artfully; perfidiously; mischievously; skilfully; comically; trickily; successfully; **completely.**

DISGUST

adjectives
implacable; sharp; vast; exasperated; angry; outraged; inherent; profound; creeping; shuddering; secret; icy; silent; honest; personal; evident; furious; intense; sheer; indignant; intolerable; weary; mingled; infinite; considerable; mutual; supreme; deep; sullen; philosophical; sickened; cruel; loathing; bewildered; excessive; previous; violent.

verbs
arouse—; assert—; attend with—; awake —; conquer—; control—; depict—; drown —; excite—; raise—; retreat in—; sicken in—; shun in—; shrug—; —deters; —dissuades; —nauseates; —offends; —wounds.
(See aversion, abhorrence, repugnance, distaste.)

DISGUST (v)

adverbs
presumably; thoroughly; implacably; profoundly; secretly; personally; evidently; intensely; intolerably; considerably; mutually; supremely; cruelly; loathingly; excessively; violently.
(See revolt, **offend.**)

DISGUSTED

adverbs
immeasurably; terribly; utterly; bitterly; painfully; intolerably; dreadfully; tremendously; exceedingly; morally; heartily; secretly; obviously; openly; sharply; profoundly; intensely; deeply; violently.

DISH

adjectives
humble; distinguished; glorious; different; tempting; delicious; time-honored; warmed-over; exotic; appetizing; delicate; fattening; sumptuous; velvet; lordly; rattling; tempting; priceless; savory; attractive; fascinating; toothsome; succulent; elaborate; unwholesome; economical; earthen; kingly; chafing; tasty; pewter; substantial; rich; sparkling; unornamental; fatal; fragile; glittering; nutritious; strange; clean; dirty; anomalous; conventional.

verbs
cover—; devour—; dip into—; eschew—; garnish—; hurl—; pile—; relish—; sauce —; scour—; serve—; smash—; sprinkle—; wipe—; —clatters; —nourishes; —rattles.
(See plate, platter, **cup,** food.)

DISHEARTEN (v)

adverbs
dismally; inwardly; decidedly; partially; purposely; unintentionally; completely; tragically; finally.
(See discourage, depress.)

DISHEARTENED

adverbs
profoundly; exceedingly; pathetically; deeply; remarkably; extremely; mysteriously; significantly; vaguely; completely; intense-

ly; utterly; miserably; wretchedly; wearily; finally; increasingly; signally; inexplicably; unaccountably; strangely; oddly; queerly.

DISHEVELED
adverbs
carelessly; negligently; wildly; merrily; laughably; shamefully; thoughtlessly; terribly; exceedingly; blithely; indifferently; untidily; recklessly; lazily; rudely; heedlessly; lumpishly.

DISHONEST
adverbs
instinctively; inherently; innately; naturally; characteristically; traditionally; slyly; racially; insidiously; invidiously; shrewdly; fiendishly; maliciously; astoundingly; trickily; surreptitiously; habitually; speciously; manifestly; essentially; abominably; detestably.

DISHONESTY
adjectives
rank; mercantile; unself-conscious; childlike; acquired.

verbs
accuse of—; conceal—; convict of—; cover —; deny—; dispose to—; expose—; renounce—; reveal—; tempt to—; uncover —; —colors; —defiles; —disgraces; — scars; —shames; —stains; —violates; — wanes.
(See fraud, cheating.)

DISHONOR
adjectives
whispered; partial; foul; ultimate; deathless; base.

verbs
bear—; bring into—; clothe in—; defile with—; die in—; meet with—; plague by—; pronounce—; root in—; sow—; stain with —; suffer—; tempt with—; tread down in—; undergo—; —blemishes; —blurs; — hounds; —lies.
(See insult, reproach, disgrace, disrepute.)

DISHONORED
adverbs
scandalously; distinctly; notoriously; infamously; publicly; permanently; unutterably; indelibly; irremediably; unforgettably; desperately; ignominiously; basely;

shamefully; unjustly; unfairly; opprobriously; foully; reportedly; allegedly; immeasurably; immensely.

DISILLUSION
adjectives
stupendous; postwar; chill; bitter; heartbreaking.

DISILLUSION (v)
adverbs
precipitately; cruelly; completely; politely; immodestly; frankly; unthinkingly; abruptly; fiendishly; shrewdly; wisely; foolishly.
(See free, liberate.)

DISILLUSIONED
adverbs
pitiably; miserably; wretchedly; sadly; suddenly; early; unhappily; unexpectedly; cruelly; bitterly; dismally; grimly; appallingly; tremendously; inconsolably; despairingly; hopelessly; heartbreakingly.

DISILLUSIONMENT
adjectives
cruel; unembittered; complete; furious; devastating; haughty; polite.

verbs
increase—; incur—; move to—; protect against—; reject—; suffer—; —ages; — banishes; —begets; —depresses; —descends; —disappoints; —displaces; —frees from; —rocks; —sets in; —settles over; —shatters; revenge—; —arouses.

DISINCLINATION
adjectives
intolerable; deep-rooted; definite; stubborn; unreasoning.

DISINFECTANT
adverbs
effectively; infallibly; powerfully; extremely; heroically; mildly; perfectly; soothingly; correctively; specifically; simply; safely; beneficially; advantageously; commendably; highly; essentially; intrinsically.

DISINFECTION
adjectives
efficient; rigorous; unstinted; disciplinary; punitive.

verbs
practise—; subject to—; —destroys; — guards against; —nauseates; —offends; —ousts; —overcomes; —prevents; —purifies; —rejects; —routs; —safeguards.

DISINHERITED

adverbs

unfairly; unfortunately; properly; unjustly; deservedly; unluckily; miserably; wretchedly; crushingly; summarily; audaciously; cruelly; deliberately; curtly; wrongfully; unwarrantably; inexcusably; unreasonably; inauspiciously; logically.

DISINTEGRATE (v)

adverbs

deliberately; steadily; relentlessly; rapidly; financially; slowly; hopelessly; mentally; socially; progressively; internally; abruptly; completely; locally.

(See crumble, decay.)

DISINTEGRATION

adjectives

rapid; financial; slow; relentless; hopeless; mental; social.

verbs

blast into—; break into—; control—; demand—; detach by—; effect—; expose to—; hasten—; influence—; produce—; tend toward—; undergo—; —blurs; —destroys; —modifies; —multiplies; —proceeds from; —reduces; —separates; —sets in.

(See decay, decomposition.)

DISINTERESTED

adverbs

personally; truly; neutrally; sufficiently; obviously; manifestly; satisfactorily; demonstrably; sternly; judiciously; honestly; undeniably; avowedly; acceptably.

DISK

(see disc)

adjectives

scintillating; whirling; rotating; advancing; menacing.

verbs

affix—; emerge from—; grind—; hollow—; hurl—; mount—; roll—; send—; shape—; shoot—; strike—; whirl—; —careens; — loops; —protects; —revolves; — rises; — rotates.

(See plate.)

DISLIKE

adjectives

profound; inordinate; violent; instinctive; active; malicious; deep; intense; maddening; involuntary; abnormal; innate; virulent; entire; fundamental; colonial; mu-

tual; haughty; peculiar; ardent; reasoned; expressed; incurable; foolish; irrational; everlasting; contemptuous; personal.

verbs

betray—; conceal—; consider with—; feed —; feign—; fume—; grow into—; harbor —for; impel by—; incur—; kindle—; mask —; regard with—; shudder with—; subject to—; warrant—.

(See distaste, repugnance, aversion, antipathy, hatred.)

DISLIKE (v)

adverbs

strongly; inherently; notoriously; heartily; profoundly; inordinately; violently; instinctively; maliciously; deeply; intensely; maddeningly; involuntarily; virulently; fundamentally; mutually; incurably; irrationally; personally; contemptuously; cordially.

(See disapprove, hate.)

DISLOCATE (v)

adverbs

dreadfully; fatally; tragically; calamitously; critically; severely; cruelly; devastatingly.

(See separate, dislodge.)

DISLOCATION

adjectives

serious; complex; cursory; temporary; tentative; remediable.

verbs

adjust—; bind—; cure—; exercise—; force —; impede—; involve—; place in—; prevent—; produce—; suffer—; submit to—; treat for—; —alarms; —pains; —swells.

(See displacement, disorder.)

DISLODGE (v)

adverbs

successfully; viciously; brutally; triumphantly; vigorously; severely; expeditiously; resolutely.

(See remove, eject.)

DISLOYAL

adverbs

shamefully; treacherously; perfidiously; disgracefully; extremely; secretly; publicly; boldly; cruelly; basely; subtly; bitterly; openly; unpardonably; incredibly; surprisingly; unexpectedly; eventually; shabbily;

tremendously; abjectly; unutterably; unscrupulously; infamously; contemptibly; ingloriously.

DISMAL

adverbs

drearily; drably; lonesomely; abjectly; disconsolately; irremediably; soddenly; sadly; wretchedly; excessively; irrecoverably; deeply; horribly; profoundly; incorrigibly; incurably; darkly; solemnly; anxiously; sombrely; despondently; fixedly; sullenly; heavily; dangerously; ominously; cheerlessly; intensely; terribly.

DISMAY

adjectives

incredulous; unutterable; direct; pale; goggle-eyed; stark; nameless; evident; vague; abject; dumb; genuine; dawning; dark; terrified; alarmed; extreme; mad; immeasurable; utter; indescribable; ineffable; panic-stricken.

verbs

contemplate—; cope with—; discover—; heap—; mitigate—; paralyze with—; read —; recoil in—; rout—; shake with—; spread—; swoon with—; view with—; —daunts; —defeats; —discourages; —engulfs; —threatens.

(See consternation, terror, alarm, fear.)

DISMAY (v)

adverbs

thoroughly; abjectly; dumbly; genuinely; extremely; immeasurably; utterly; indescribably; bullyingly.

(See alarm, frighten.)

DISMAYED

adverbs

unaccountably; deeply; profoundly; unreasonably; illogically; dreadfully; alarmingly; fearfully; incredibly; starkly; evidently; vaguely; abjectly; genuinely; terribly; extremely; immeasurably; significantly; utterly; indescribably; remarkably; notably visibly; wildly; bewilderingly.

DISMISS (v)

adverbs

reluctantly; summarily; finally; courteously; instantly; contemptuously; flatly; lightly; curtly; abruptly; harshly; ignominiously; impudently; brusquely; uncouthly.

(See discharge, banish.)

DISMISSAL

adjectives

contemptuous; harsh; ignominious; brusque; impudent; abrupt; summary; instant; immediate.

verbs

annul—; bow—; counsel—; demand—; denounce—; indicate—; justify—; order—; punish by—; request—; seek—; suffer—; threaten with—; urge—; wave—; —discourages; —liberates; —rectifies; —releases; —sets free.

(See discharge, removal.)

DISOBEDIENCE

adjectives

continued; alleged; filial; repeated; defiant; wilful; persistent.

verbs

construe as—; correct—; express—; fall into—; foster—; instigate—; nourish—; punish for—; reprimand for—; revenge—; rue—; subscribe to—; —annoys; —begets; —develops; —erupts; —irks.

(See defiance.)

DISOBEDIENT

adverbs

stubbornly; obstinately; impudently; impertinently; insolently; arrogantly; constantly; continually; haughtily; obdurately; peevishly; boldly; openly; flagrantly; invidiously; sullenly; morosely; carelessly; wildly; inexcusably; unduly; deliberately; consciously; flauntingly; laughingly; brazenly; allegedly; provokingly; extremely; dreadfully; rebelliously; resentfully; defiantly; restively; impatiently; resolutely.

DISORDER

adjectives

allergic; emotional; turbulent; careless; forlorn; homelike; miry; tousled; musty; unparalleled; wild; lawless; riotous; diffuse; frightful; inconsistent; tumultuous; frenzied; virulent; violent; considerable; moving; curing; gay; infectious; mental; prevailing; direst; accumulated; seeming; spasmodic; strange; degenerate; nutritional; infantile; grave; spiritual; underlying; momentary; current; shameful; neurotic; statistic; extreme; deep-seated; admired; contagious; curious; chaotic; physical; picturesque; complete; pleasant; inconceivable; ensuing; chronic; half-mended; infernal; indescribable; harlequinesque; nervous; radical; immaculate; moral.

verbs

accompany—; ascribe to—; benefit—; caution against—; fall into—; foment—; indicate—; introduce—; plague with—; produce —; relieve—; remedy—; remove—; rout—; spring from—; succumb to—; vanquish—; —surges ahead; —threatens.

(See confusion, chaos, disturbance.)

DISORDERLY

adverbs

remarkably; notoriously; turbulently; truculently; outrageously; noisily; flagrantly; violently; wildly; riotously; lawlessly; frightfully; gayly; uproariously; convivially; genially; laughingly; daringly; inconsiderately; indescribably; inconceivably; ungovernably; uncontrollably; curiously; contagiously; momentarily; mutinously; gravely; alarmingly; ominously; significantly; terrifyingly; tumultuously; tempestuously; viciously; extravagantly; excitedly.

DISPARAGEMENT

adjectives

caustic; cynical; systematic; ruthless; unsparing; merciless.

verbs

bring into—; commit—; deserve—; express —; hurl—; impose—; intend—; involve in—; justify—; lose by—; reproach for—; speak—; vilify with—; —annoys; —belittles; —degrades; —disgraces.

DISPASSIONATE

adverbs

imperturbably; provokingly; vexatiously; serenely; calmly; deeply; immovably; apparently; dreadfully; coldly; completely; carelessly; nonchalantly; discouragingly; utterly; singularly; stolidly; stonily; coolly; soberly; judicially; sagely; wisely; securely; tranquilly; placidly; philosophically; tolerantly.

DISPATCH

adjectives

calamitous; hostile; amazing; quick; marvelous; summary; rapid; convenient; diplomatic; hourly; insolent; elaborate; amended; swift; equal; vivid; detailed; telegraphic; simultaneous; importunate; important; explanatory; outspoken; uncensored; satisfactory; frequent (pl).

verbs

announce—; arrive with—; attend to—; cable—; carry—; convey—; deliver—; depart with—; hasten—; leave on—; obey—; order—; receive—; relay—; report—; rush —; seal—; send—; smuggle in—; speed—; transfer.

(See message, telegram.)

DISPATCH (v)

adverbs

mercifully; secretly; summarily; rapidly; diplomatically; insolently; telegraphically; swiftly; simultaneously; satisfactorily; frequently; conveniently; hastily.

(See send, forward.)

DISPEL (v)

adverbs

effectually; instantly; immediately; entirely; frankly; innocently; humanely; charmingly; testily.

(See withdraw, dissipate.)

DISPENSATION

adjectives

benign; critical; merciful; mysterious; special; divine; providential; heavenly; frugal; afflicting; artistic; favorable.

verbs

administer—; allow—; arrange—; claim—; conduct—; deliver—; deserve—; grant—; manage—; obtain—; order—; provide—; receive—; require—; reward with—; seek —; sue for—; undertake—; urge—; warrant—; —distributes; —pardons; —releases.

(See distribution, pardon, exemption.)

DISPENSE (v)

adverbs

vicariously; bountifully; gracefully; liberally; naturally; mercifully; divinely; providentially; frugally.

(See distribute, administer.)

DISPLACEMENT

adjectives

sympathetic; successive (pl); unmerited; slight; hazardous; careless; capacious.

verbs

indicate—; occasion—; order—; request—; seek—; set—; threaten with—; —disposes of; —embarrasses; —liberates; —occurs; —rectifies; —releases; —remedies; —shifts.

(See removal, discharge, dismissal.)

DISPLAY

adjectives

alluring; ceremonial; enviable; ostentatious; tawdry; unrivaled; garish; blatant;

enchanting; gorgeous; grisly; creditable; pitiful; emotional; lurid; audacious; glaring; splendid; obtrusive; amazing; magnificent; appropriate; lavish; legitimate; ludicrous; frequent (pl); color; thaumaturgic; remarkable; aggravating; autumnal; fabulous; breath-taking; triumphant; fanatical; heroic; pedantic; attractive; modern; gaudy; mass; beautiful; official; merciless; singular; wild; arresting; material; prominent; extraordinary; romantic; single-handed; elaborate; vast; brilliant; haunting; many-colored; prodigal; boasted; vulgar; maladroit; provocative; vivid; mere; admirable; barbarous; temporary; tasteful; profuse; superfluous; quixotic; childish; unfortunate; dazzling; fan-shaped.

verbs

abhor—; adorn—; arrange—; feed on—; furnish—; gape at—; nose among—s; prepare—; unfurl—; view—; wonder at—; —advertises; —appeals; —attracts; —describes; —exhibits; —explains; —expresses; —glitters; —represents; —unfolds.

(See exhibition, show.)

DISPLAY (v)

adverbs

pompously; flamboyantly; tastefully; magnificently; realistically; conspicuously; charmingly; habitually; refreshingly; equally; palpably; ostentatiously; vaingloriously; smartly; temptingly; vulgarly; eminently; lavishly; dazzlingly; entrancingly; alluringly; ceremonially; garishly; blatantly; pitifully; audaciously; legitimately; mercilessly; ludicrously; singularly; prodigally; temporarily; superfluously.

(See exhibit, expose.)

DISPLEASE (v)

adverbs

stupidly; purposely; markedly; unsophisticatedly; rudely; frankly; seriously; pettishly; ungenerously; lastingly; coldly; boorishly; carelessly; inadvertently.

(See anger, offend.)

DISPLEASED

adverbs

remarkably; extravagantly; extremely; uneasily; wearily; anxiously; miserably; unreasonably; unaccountably; sorely; heavily; horribly; vexedly; painfully; grievously; bitterly; cheerlessly; fiercely; savagely; markedly; visibly; openly; frankly; seriously; permanently; implacably; coldly;

alarmingly; dangerously; unspeakably; profoundly; deeply; inordinately; justly; rightly.

DISPLEASURE

adjectives

smothered; surprised; fierce; marked; sore; sovereign; unsophisticated; frank; everlasting; serious; noble; petty; ungenerous; lasting; cold; divine.

verbs

avoid--; conceal—; display—; dread—; heighten—; incur—; indicate—; languish in—; meet with—; occasion—; provoke—; risk—; shoulder—; signify—; snort—; —annoys; —irks; —mounts; —overwhelms.

(See dissatisfaction, vexation, dislike, resentment, disapproval.)

DISPOSE (v)

adverbs

carelessly; antagonistically; religiously; briefly; favorably; symmetrically; ornamentally; effectually; graciously; immediately; variously; gracefully; peaceably; coolly; effectively.

(See settle, adjust.)

DISPOSITION

adjectives

pacific; amenable; amiable; covetous; docile; morose; winsome; credulous; mercurial; bromidic; penurious; depraved; petulant; avaricious; peevish; jovial; bad; sweet; equable; contentious; balky; impetuous; fiery; angelic; vivacious; unyielding; confiding; cheery; vacillating; sunny; sullen; bitter; eager; cordial; raving; delicate; characteristic; generous; noble; litigious; rough; envious; well-oiled; jealous; vicious; masterful; dreamy; increasing; testamentary; passionate; princely; violent; chilly; humane; puerile; stubborn; contemplative; unconquerable; melancholy; inquisitive; affectionate; bloodthirsty; resolute; tractable; pious; dogged; ungodly; virtuous; commiserating; natural; excellent; romantic; kind; similar; charming; pliant; stupid; tame; grateful; tranquil; speculative; favorable; skillful; alert; neurotic; suitable; innate; ingenuous; friendly; adventurous; traitorous; faithful; indolent; eager; shirking; sociable; prevailing; incomprehensible; unpredictable; classic; combative; tunable; phlegmatic; peremptory; dangerous; buoyant; secret; magnificent; thoughtful; brooding; aesthetic; primitive; humane; amicable; irregular;

submissive; methodical; venomous; fantastical; timid; hereditary; restless; roving; retiring; imperious; absolute; noxious; further; hysterical.

verbs
abuse—; admire—; alter—; change—; complete—; consider—; contrive—; derange—; disguise—; evince—; excuse—; indulge—; inherit—; judge—; punish—; soften—; sour—; specify—; submit to—; touch—; view—; —comprehends; —inclines; —precipitates; —restores; —secures.
(See mood, will, propensity, inclination, tendency, temperament.)

DISPOSSESS (v)
adverbs
forcibly; legally; harshly; irregularly; doggedly; calmly; cruelly; selfishly.
(See eject, remove.)

DISPUTANT
adjectives
scientific; forensic; obstinate; moral; voiceless; excited.

DISPUTATION
adjectives
public; scholastic; private; learned; religious; doubtful; prodigious; wrangling.

DISPUTATIOUS
adverbs
troublesomely; immensely; tremendously; egregiously; elaborately; intricately; eccentrically; egotistically; loftily; superciliously; tyrannically; dogmatically; extremely; learnedly; academically; provokingly; disagreeably; unpleasantly; obtrusively; officiously; conceitedly; astutely; pugnaciously; hotly; captiously; churlishly; remarkably; marvellously.

DISPUTE
adjectives
doctrinal; theological; inevitable; learned; angry; bitter; dull; vain; laughing; demoralizing; serious; uncontrollable; pending; cold; international; academic; free; conceivable; long-standing; violent; notable; fierce; perpetual; territorial; fruitless; factional; leisurely.

verbs
adjudicate—; adjust—; arbitrate—; beguile into—; conciliate—; meditate—; quash—; quell—; solve—; suppress—; take part in—;
—arises; —bubbles; —evaporates; —flares up; —foreshadows; —overshadows; —rages.
(See discussion, contest, controversy, quarrel.)

DISPUTE (v)
adverbs
skillfully; acrimoniously; consciously; angrily; subsequently; inhumanly; successfully; publicly; privately; religiously; prodigiously; fiercely.
(See argue, wrangle.)

DISQUIET
adjectives
vague; emotional; constant; restless; growing.

DISQUIET (v)
adverbs
chiefly; solely; thoroughly; abruptly; subtly.
(See alarm, disturb.)

DISQUIETUDE
adjectives
serious; vague; mental; extreme.

verbs
arouse—; fear—; fill with—; infest with—; occasion—; pass with—; relay—; sow—; subject to—; trouble with—; view with—; wait with—; —alarms; —disturbs; —envelops; —spreads.
(See alarm, anxiety, fear, agitation.)

DISQUISITION
adjectives
political; clever; popular; lengthy; wordy; learned.

DISREGARD
adjectives
insane; cynical; reckless; defiant; persistent; total; unabashed; bland; pagan; brutal; generous; utter; blithe; calm; benevolent; selfish; cruel; jaunty; entire; drunken; astonishing; habitual; strange; superb; apparent; contemptuous; sublime; peremptory.

DISREGARD (v)
adverbs
incessantly; chronically; totally; utterly; contemptuously; insanely; cynically; recklessly; defiantly; persistently; totally; unabashedly; blandly; brutally; generously;

utterly; blithely; calmly; benevolently; recklessly; entirely; habitually; sublimely; peremptorily; selfishly.

(See ignore, overlook.)

DISREPUTABLE

adverbs
notoriously; infamously; exceedingly; generally; utterly; scandalously; opprobriously; fearfully; dissolutely; admittedly; villainously; grossly; drunkenly; coarsely; shamefully; horribly; remarkably; incredibly; unbelievably; abjectly; pitifully; ingloriously; shockingly; atrociously; viciously.

DISREPUTE

adjectives
(See disgrace.)

verbs
beget—; bring into—; clothe in—; cure of —; depart in—; disguise—; fall into—; ignore—; incur—; indicate—; instigate—; leave in—; return in—; vow—; —dampens; —excludes; —showers; —underlies.

(See disgrace, dishonor.)

DISRESPECT

adjectives
(See rudeness.)

verbs
augment—; bear—; disguise—; display—; free from—; manifest—; mention with—; nourish—; proceed from—; reprimand for —; smother—; stoop to—; suffer—; tolerate—; —indicates; —profanes; —troubles.

(See dishonor, rudeness.)

DISRESPECTFUL

adverbs
irreverently; boundlessly; utterly; blandly; recklessly; persistently; defiantly; totally; brutally; cruelly; entirely; impiously; jauntily; rashly; boldly; astonishingly; elaborately; ostentatiously; openly; habitually; chronically; strangely; particularly; peculiarly; contemptuously; disparagingly; derisively; ironically; rudely; bumptiously.

DISSATISFACTION

adjectives
unending; personal; prevailing; universal; seeming; increasing; evident; undifferentiated; rebellious; widespread.

verbs
anticipate—; be subject to—; beget—; conduct with—; confine—; exhibit—; experience—; express—; occasion—; overcome —; pretend—; smother—; veil—; —disquiets; —irks; —perplexes.

(See discontent, disapproval, displeasure.)

DISSATISFIED

adverbs
slightly; vaguely; wholly; strangely; entirely; increasingly; palpably; evidently; visibly; openly; sullenly; morosely; secretly; obviously; deeply; desperately; horribly; querulously; glumly; gloomily; austerely; sternly; implacably; crabbedly; perversely; continually.

DISSECT (*v*)

adverbs
mercilessly; tranquilly; scientifically; studiously; thoroughly; painstakingly; absorbedly.

(See cut, criticize.)

DISSEMBLE (*v*)

adverbs
politely; slyly; deeply; artfully; skillfully; ingeniously.

(See hide, conceal.)

DISSEMINATE (*v*)

adverbs
widely; unsparingly; insidiously; nationally; universally.

(See spread, circulate.)

DISSENSION

adjectives
considerable; frightful; irreconcilable; humiliating; internal; bitter; sharp; disastrous; factional; growing; intestinal; grave; turbulent; angry; perpetual.

verbs
brew—; crush—; excite—; halt—; incite —; instigate—; investigate—; review—; stir with—; —arises; —breaks out; —flares; —grows; —menaces; —tears; —threatens.

(See discord, strife, quarrel, contention, feud.)

DISSENT

adjectives
metaphysical; profound; internal; grave; effective; ignorant; ill-natured.

verbs

accept—; apprehend—; arouse—; constitute—; enter—; explain—; free of—; ignore—; interpose—; overlook—; question
—; tolerate—; trace—; voice—; —prevails;
—sunders.

(See disagreement, difference.)

DISSERTATION

adjectives

moral; illuminating; exhaustive; stilted;
learned; rhapsodic; elaborate; pedantic;
physiological; scholarly.

verbs

absorb in—; censor—; compose—; criticize—; dedicate—to; engage in—; launch
upon—; level—at; pause in—; prepare—;
study—; —carries; —concerns; —discusses;
—treats.

(See discourse, speech, lecture.)

DISSIMULATION

adjectives

polite; deft; practiced; splendid; skilled.

DISSIPATE (v)

adverbs

abruptly; partially; voluptuously; senselessly; reprehensibly; carelessly; excessively; incessantly; disgustingly; jovially;
recklessly; fashionably; tragically; thoughtlessly.

(See dispel.)

DISSIPATION

adjectives

voluptuous; senseless; reprehensible; careless; excessive; mild; incessant; besetting;
solitary; minor; disgusting; jovial; reckless; polished; recreative; fashionable.

verbs

consume by—; defy—; denounce—; engage
in—; imbibe in—; investigate—; lose in—;
practise—; relinquish—; squander in—;
warn against—; —corrupts; —endangers;
—enslaves; —grinds; —penalizes; —wears.

(See diversion, crime.)

DISSOLUTE

adverbs

frightfully; utterly; irretrievably; gracelessly; irremediably; boundlessly; wantonly; recklessly; grossly; wildly; shamelessly;
outrageously; perversely; irreclaimably;
senselessly; remarkably; grotesquely; manifestly; abysmally; lawlessly; disgracefully;
criminally; obdurately; heinously; gravely;
sensually; intemperately; rakishly.

DISSOLUTENESS

adjectives

frightful; reckless; ferocious.

DISSOLUTION

adjectives

impending; natural; continual; ultimate.

DISSOLVE (v)

adverbs

partly; mutually; mysteriously; harmlessly;
entirely; thoroughly; perfectly; experimentally.

(See melt.)

DISSONANCE

adjectives

excruciating; wild; unpleasant; barbarous;
weird; raucous; harsh.

DISTANCE

adjectives

hazy; mean; weary; legendary; celestial;
deepest; drowsy; magnificent; shooting;
dusty; tantalizing; spacious; untold; extreme; impossible; obscure; safe; unattainable; perihelion; zenith; infinite; considerable; entire; visible; cautious; respectful;
widening; exquisite; excessive; proportionate; inaccessible; twinkling; vast; unvarying; surlier; inscrutable; musket-shot; hail-
ing; limited; unknown; inadequate; supporting; remote; short; surprising; observing; terrible; uncertain; linear; measured;
delicate; mellow; dimmer; indefinite; required; insurmountable; discreet; sufficient;
pathless; beautiful; unapproachable; ever-
increasing; misty; retrospective; walking;
previous; assaulting; unbridgeable; riding;
running; dangerous; mean; enormous; indeterminate; broadening.

verbs

annihilate—; estimate—; fade in—; fall
at—; indicate—; mark—; measure—; proportion—; rise in—; span—; stand in—;
traverse—; —alienates; —enchants; —
lends; hold at—.

(See space.)

DISTASTE

adjectives

profound; sordid; intellectual; furious; extreme; scornful; cynical; patient; passionate; startling; evident.

verbs
banish—; bring into—; conceive—for; cultivate—for; develop—; dismiss—; excite—; express—; heal—; imply—; inherit—; nourish—; pamper—; possess—for; produce—; regard with—; relinquish—; rescue from —; view with—; —develops; —implies; —menaces.

(See aversion, dislike, antipathy.)

DISTASTEFUL
adverbs
horribly; deeply; profoundly; sordidly; intellectually; furiously; extremely; exaggeratedly; startlingly; shockingly; inordinately; extraordinarily; remarkably; immensely; dreadfully; evidently; manifestly; palpably; fundamentally; essentially; sickeningly; nauseatingly; sorrily; plaguedly; bitterly; grimly; frightfully.

DISTENSION
adjectives
pale; chronic; acute; pestilential; fatal; feminine.

DISTENTION
verbs
attend with—; blow into—; conceal—; fill to—; force into—; guard against—; imbibe to—; inflate to—; labor under—; prevent—; produce—; protect from—; —follows; —harms; —injures; —pains; —sunders.

(See expansion, inflation.)

DISTILL (v)
adverbs
imperceptibly; specially; powerfully; elaborately; delicately; experimentally; expertly; painstakingly.

DISTILLATION
adjectives
elaborate; strong; renewed; delicate; powerful.

DISTINCT
adverbs
particularly; cruelly; meticulously; precisely; exactly; easily; accurately; wonderfully; especially; clearly; emphatically; separately; effectively; powerfully.

DISTINCTION
adjectives
striking; pedantic; arresting; moral; sweeping; manifest; artificial; crude; material; considerable; supreme; theoretical;

grave; philosophic; fundamental; military; superfluous; arbitrary; ethical; social; exclusive; unreal; cruel; topographical; solid; trade; unusual; ancient; perceptible; unhappy; obvious; immediate; dubious; essential; man-made; additional; unique; sage; minor; threefold; nervous; racial; deep; literary; ephemeral; financial; singular; subtle; natural; sole; invidious; repugnant; family; color; worldly; coveted; grand; preeminent; unenviable; individual; popular; groundless; slender; fleeting; fanciful; frivolous; honorable; constitutional; sensible; moral; race; artistic; broad; innate; particular; careless; visible; inglorious.

verbs
achieve—; attain—; blur—; carry—; convey—; discern—; draw—; earn—; enhance —; grant—; hunger for—; level—; maintain—; obliterate—; obtain—; perceive—; perpetuate—; recognize—; reduce—; sense —; serve with—; trace—; uphold—; warrant—; yearn for—; yield—.

(See eminence, prominence, renown.)

DISTINCTNESS
adjectives
surprising; exquisite; sufficient; arbitrary; tragic; unmistakable; vivid; considerable; growing; luminous.

DISTINGUISH (v)
adverbs
curiously; logically; justly; pedantically; crudely; theoretically; philosophically; fundamentally; arbitrarily; obviously; uniquely; sagely; singularly; subtly; invidiously; unenviably; groundlessly; fancifully; frivolously; sensibly; morally; artistically; broadly; scientifically.

(See discriminate, discern.)

DISTINGUISHABLE
adverbs
easily; readily; generally; entirely; particularly; diversely; divergently; differentially; broadly; carefully; instantly; conveniently; immediately; altogether; separately; unmistakably; plainly; decidedly; satisfactorily; positively; definitely; absolutely; clearly.

DISTINGUISHED
adverbs
brilliantly; extraordinarily; internationally; academically; illustriously; notably; remarkably; admirably; matchlessly; profes-

sionally; prominently; nationally; supremely; impressively; splendidly; augustly; imperishably; ecclesiastically; heroically; immortally; honorably; enviably; eminently; strikingly; manifestly; singularly.

DISTORT (v)
adverbs
momentarily; painfully; fatally; obviously; ludicrously; hideously; fantastically; insanely; madly; jokingly; fiendishly
(See twist, misrepresent.)

DISTORTED
adverbs
wilfully; perniciously; purposely; deliberately; deceptively; visibly; obviously; clearly; palpably; frightfully; excessively; dreadfully; intentionally; falsely; adroitly; craftily; wickedly; academically; disputatiously; remarkably; fatally; elaborately; completely; partially; loosely; fantastically; grotesquely; grossly; harmfully; utterly; maliciously; astutely; cleverly.

DISTORTION
adjectives
pale; fatal; obvious; imbedded; elaborated; ludicrous; intentional; fantastic.

DISTRACTION
adjectives
infinite; compelling; manifold; powerful; sweet; skillful; extreme; artificial; material; innocent; bewildered; beneficial; endless; blind; great; cautious.

verbs
attend with—; avoid—; blind to—; condemn—; drive to—; fear—; justify—; labor under—; lock out—; occasion—; result in—; shut out—; view with—; —arises; —confuses; —diverts; —intercepts; —interrupts; —perturbs.
(See confusion, disorder.)

DISTRESS
adjectives
simulated; palpable; widespread; pecuniary; horrible; mental; mortal; violent; keenest; intellectual; obvious; sore; obstinate; poignant; genuine; fearful; hideous; fancied; sentimental; dark; blind; generalized; terrified; needless; supreme; spiritual; bitter; fatherless; sensitive; financial; painted; severe; extreme; pathetic; heart-

searching; recurrent; sharp; sublime; deep; chronic; painful; insupportable; bare; wide-eyed; cowering; dire; evident; unrelieved; supposed; public.

verbs
afflict with—; aggravate—; answer—; bawl —; behold in—; consume with—; counsel in—; deliver from—; embolden by—; expose to—; give rise to—; pity—; relieve—; soothe—; submit in—; suffer—; wait in—; wring with—; —afflicts; —crazes; —gnaws.
(See suffering, pain, misery, agony.)

DISTRESS (v)
adverbs
deeply; shockingly; mentally; triumphantly; dreadfully; palpably; pecuniarily; horribly; mortally; violently; obviously; sorely; poignantly; genuinely; fearfully; hideously; sentimentally; needlessly; recurrently; supremely; spiritually; chronically; painfully, insupportably; direly; publicly.
(See grieve, wound.)

DISTRESSING
adverbs
extremely; remarkably; awfully; painfully; sorely; profoundly; deeply; appallingly; horribly; gravely; shockingly; incredibly; unspeakably; unmentionably; mentally; violently; keenly; poignantly; genuinely; hideously; supremely; bitterly; insupportably; evidently; unutterably; intensely; seriously; starkly; uncommonly; acutely; fundamentally; unduly; immoderately; unusually.

DISTRIBUTE (v)
adverbs
genially; exclusively; uniformly; indecisively; judiciously; equally; geographically; geometrically; irregularly; indefinitely; equitably; plentifully; scientifically; socially; ultimately; unlimitedly; symmetrically; lavishly; visibly; wastefully.
(See allot, apportion.)

DISTRIBUTION
adjectives
wide; general; equitable; liberal; wasteful; scientific; social; impracticable; ultimate; uniform; respective; symmetrical; rude; democratic; extensive; unlimited; lavish; indiscriminate; geographical; high; low; visible.

verbs
arrange—; bless with—; comprehend—; control—; effect—; enjoy—; increase—;

influence—; mention—; prepare for—; prevent—; reject—; sanction—; urge—; —abates; —aids; —disposes; —enriches; —involves; —reduces.

(See arrangement, disposition.)

DISTRICT

adjectives

outlying; thinly-populated; fashionable; simple; rural; residential; industrial; swankiest; congested; pastoral; remote; congressional; newly-gained; urban; scenic; sanitary; fertile; squalid; arid; extensive; coterminous; financial; genial-hearted; native; affected; accessible; dispatching; productive; adjacent; tenement; various (pl); charming; malodorous; populous.

verbs

appoint to—; assign to—; comprise—; constitute—; control—; divide into—s; dwell in—; elect to—; hedge in—; inhabit—; manage—; occupy—; separate into—s; supervise—; vest in—; —affords; —embraces; —envelops; —includes; —takes in; —thrives.

(See region, tract, locality, territory, circuit.)

DISTRUST

adjectives

cynical; grim; profound; paternal; morbid; reserved; instinctive; lurking; painful; lessening; vigilant; vulgar; palpable; mutual; abiding; inward; deep; prejudicial; unreasonable; vague; dawning; marked; foul.

verbs

accuse of—; acquire—; approach with—; augment—; awaken—; breed—; earn—; entertain—; eye with—; foster—; incur—; intensify—; mark with—; regard with—; silence—; view with—; warrant—; —appears; —enters; —grows; —sprouts.

(See doubt, suspicion.)

DISTRUST (v)

adverbs

instinctively; heartily; constantly; unavoidably; cynically; profoundly; morbidly; painfully; vigilantly; palpably; mutually; abidingly; deeply; unreasonably; vaguely; markedly.

(See suspect, doubt.)

DISTRUSTFUL

adverbs

gravely; alertly; watchfully; constantly; grimly; altogether; positively; profoundly; chronically; habitually; temperamentally; morbidly; painfully; instinctively; intuitively; inwardly; secretly; openly; unreasonably; vaguely; suspiciously; obnoxiously; disagreeably; wisely; warily; quietly; prudently; faintly; uneasily; seriously; momentarily; anxiously; sagaciously; nervously; timidly; horridly; skeptically.

DISTURB (v)

adverbs

inwardly; particularly; wantonly; perceptibly; profoundly; permanently; materially; deeply; grievously; emotionally; functionally; mentally; mutually; exceptionally; powerfully; pathologically; intellectually; violently; electrically; psychically; internally; glandularly; rudely; unnecessarily; unpleasantly.

(See annoy, perturb.)

DISTURBANCE

adjectives

civil; spasmodic; organic; emotional; terrific; mutual; atmospheric; insurrectionary; functional; mental; exceptional; powerful; gastric; strange; pathological; magnetic; widespread; intellectual; violent; electrical; psychic; visual; emotional; internal; agitated; glandular; serious; rude; unnecessary.

verbs

accompany by—; aggravate—; allay—; attend with—; continue—; engender—; foment—; free from—; generate—; relieve —; suffer from—; —arises; —fizzles out (colloq.); —subsides.

(See tumult, confusion, commotion, uproar, clamor.)

DISTURBING

adverbs

faintly; vaguely; definitely; seriously; gravely; alarmingly; significantly; evidently; manifestly; irrationally; palpably; visibly; noticeably; unreasonably; needlessly; maliciously; meddlesomely; shockingly; turbulently; fussily; restlessly; excitably; hysterically; tantalizingly; bitterly; miserably; intolerably; horribly; unpleasantly; disagreeably; obnoxiously; exceptionally.

DISUSE

adjectives
(See neglect.)

verbs
cast into—; come into—; drop into—; excuse—; fall into—; lapse into—; lose by—; overcome—; parch by—; proceed from—; regret—; rot away in—; rouse out of—; rust from—; stifle by—; weaken by—; —affects; —deteriorates; —prevents; grows into—.
(See neglect.)

DITCH

adjectives
briny; oozy; impassable; rain-soaked; muddy; filthy; deep.

verbs
bog in—; fall into—; level—; mire in—; plunge in—; turn in—; —ensnares; —forms, —furnishes; —serves.
(See trench, channel.)

DITTY

adjectives
sea-going; hiccup; time-honored; popular; strident; amorous; doleful; woeful; sentimental; irrelevant.

verbs
carol—; compose—; dash off—; entertain with—; hum—; mourn—; mute—; pipe—; warble—; welcome with—; —amuses; —celebrates; —cheers; —flows; —lulls; —praises; —resounds.
(See air, poem, song, tune.)

DIVAN

adjectives
perfumed; pillowed; rickety; commodious; luxurious; resplendent; inviting; comfortable.

DIVE (*v*)

adverbs
spectacularly; gracefully; unerringly; precipitately; abruptly; harrowingly; thrillingly; bravely; courageously.
(See plunge, drop.)

DIVERGENCE

adjectives
(See deviation.)

verbs
allow for—; bridge—; check—; correct—; flow in—; follow—; generate—; illustrate —; increase—; intersect—; occasion—; produce—; question—; relate with—; test —; —affects; —arises; —diminishes; —occurs; —proceeds from; —separates; —widens.
(See deviation, disagreement, difference.)

DIVERGENT

adverbs
extraordinarily; resolutely; definitely; sharply; interestingly; disputatiously; positively; harshly; discordantly; disagreeably; uncongenially; incompatibly; inaptly; terribly; endlessly; pitiably; painfully; exceptionally; deliberately.

DIVERSE

adverbs
utterly; harmlessly; momentarily; intellectually; economically; mysteriously; inexplicably; sharply; markedly; remarkably; notably; acutely; perceptibly; gravely; insuperably; racially; subtly; essentially; strikingly; fundamentally; radically; appreciably; materially; amazingly; significantly; superficially; extremely; irreconcilably; prodigiously; temperamentally; intrinsically; completely.

DIVERSION

adjectives
social; congenial; harmless; pleasurable; staple; childish; constant; unending; favorite; momentary; contemporary; popular; infantile; intellectual; sturdy; innocent; outdoor; decorous; unique; languid; incidental; seasonable; healthful; economical; agreeable; mysterious; attacking; exquisite; exhilarating.

verbs
advocate—; allow—; amuse with—; conceive—; consider—; contrive—; employ—; engage in—; forget in—; invent—; look for—; need—; occupy with—; search for—; sprout—; suggest—; —attracts; —benefits; —entertains; —excites; —fatigues; —gratifies; —withholds.
(See amusement, recreation, entertainment, sport, relaxation, pastime.)

DIVERSITY

adjectives
delightful; continental; extraordinary; infinite; outward; merry; magnificent; grave; picturesque.

DIVERT (v)

adverbs

frequently; immensely; delightfully; extraordinarily; infinitely; outwardly; merrily; magnificently; pleasurably; childishly; constantly; intellectually; uniquely; healthfully; economically; agreeably; exquisitely; exhilaratingly.

(See turn, withdraw.)

DIVERTING

adverbs

deviously; erratically; circuitously; endlessly; delusively; sharply; cleverly; artfully; adroitly; skilfully; mysteriously; cunningly; deceptively; insidiously; trickily; meretriciously; wickedly; amusingly; entertainingly; playfully; sportively; clumsily; merrily; joyously; wittily; pleasantly; cheerily; roguishly.

DIVIDE (v)

adverbs

customarily; transversely; horizontally; conveniently; finely; subtly; wisely; evenly; longitudinally; miraculously; hopelessly; equally; formally; critically; scientifically; fatally; geographically; appropriately; arbitrarily; factionally; racially; unexpectedly; originally.

(See separate, sever.)

DIVIDEND

adjectives

illegitimate; substantial; reasonable; regular; generous.

verbs

advise of—; allot—; announce—; bear—; declare—; distribute—; draw—; invest—; mail—; obtain—; pay—; present—; promise—; report—; yield—; —s accrue; —s suffice; —s support; share in—.

(See portion, amount, money.)

DIVINITY

adjectives

anthropomorphic; ancient; omnipresent; scholastic; sylvan; jealous; false; actual; utter; strange; winged; favorite; sarcastic; dying; tutelar; polemical.

verbs

attain—; claim—; conceive—; concern—; embrace—; encounter—; express—; invoke —; manifest—; preach—; reflect—; reject —; unite in—; verse in—; —governs; — inspires; —rules; —stirs.

(See deity, God.)

DIVISION

adjectives

venereal; contending; formal; minutest; critical; various (pl); proposed; scientific; astonishing; equitable; isolated; distinct; fatal; assaulting; heroic; antecedent; primary; geographical; arbitrary; appropriate; factional; racial; unexpected; original.

verbs

arrange in—s; attempt—; avoid—; cement —; control—; distinguish—; draw from—; enforce—; establish—; form—; include in —; lead—; mark—; note—; number—; observe—; place in—; separate into—s; struggle for—; supervise—; zone—; — comprises; —consists of; —distributes; —widens.

(See distribution, part, section.)

DIVORCE

adjectives

salubrious; irregular; hateful; unwholesome; deadly; collusive; welcome; long-sought; publicized; worth-while; surprise; framed.

verbs

abuse—; agree to—; apply for—; approve of—; consent to—; contemplate—; declaim against—; favor—; grant—; involve in—; lament—; pronounce—; recognize—; resort to—; sanction—; stay—; sue for—; terminate in—; warrant—; —cleaves; — corrupts; —dissolves; —frees; —privileges; —separates; authorize—; prevent—; tolerate—.

(See separation, marriage.)

DIVORCED

adverbs

irrevocably; unhappily; unfortunately; frequently; regularly; unjustly; unluckily; grievously; rightfully; properly; legally; loosely; distinctly; justifiably; judicially; profitably; recently; correctly; felicitously; irreconcilably.

DIZZINESS

adjectives

swift; paralyzing.

verbs

attend with—; diagnose—; feign—; induce —; occasion—; overcome—; produce—; strike with—; sway in—; take with—; treat for—; —diminishes; —ensues; — envelops; —forewarns; —perplexes; —relaxes; --suggests.

(See giddiness, confusion.)

adverbs

hopelessly; suddenly; helplessly; dangerously; alarmingly; slightly; completely; blindly; dimly; confusedly; mistily; obscurely; glaringly; sickeningly; frightfully; fearfully; inadvertently; muzzily; abnormally; deliriously; incoherently; crazily; light-headedly; uncontrollably; oddly; curiously; strangely; queerly.

DOCILITY

adjectives

noiseless; submissive.

DOCK

adjectives

shipping; humming; dingy; ancient; wet; neat.

DOCKET

adjectives

(See calendar.)

verbs

appear on—; arrange—; cancel—; file—; inclose in—; mention in—; prepare—; produce—; rearrange—; run through—; seal —; search—; strike—; survey—; —authorizes; —contains; —dispenses with; —indicates; —revolves; preserve—.

(See calendar, list.)

DOCTOR

adjectives

young; learned; vivacious; resourceful; inscrutable; lauded; illustrious; indefatigable; old-fashioned; provincial; would-be; mellifluous; tall; capable; country; handpicked; easy-going; fashionable; distracted; badgered; reverend; worthy; murderous; talented; mystic; eminent; discreet; budding; regimental.

verbs

(See physician.)

DOCTRINAL

adverbs

rigidly; austerely; augustly; sternly; undeviatingly; absurdly; devoutly; strictly; tenaciously; persistently; insistently; consistently; wholly; conscientiously; meticulously; punctiliously; ceremoniously; ritualistically; dogmatically; obstinately; stubbornly; stiffly; dismally; fundamentally; zealously; abstractly; comfortably; placidly; primarily; horribiy.

adjectives

dismal; dangerous; fundamental; heretical; pernicious; incestuous; outworn; decided; zealous; positive; blessed; conflicting; revolutionary; mystical; audacious; subversive; traditional; exoteric; recondite; cold; abstract; sound; pleasant; sensational; elevated; valid; accursed; denominational; living; recurring; enlarging; rigid; evil; deliberate; vulgar; licentious; nefarious; blighting; barbarous; opposite; cherished; characteristic; unflinching; republican; unedifying; undefiled; devilish; dubious; hermeneutical; time-honored; orthodox; comfortable; vague; pregnant; imported; erroneous; traditive; evolutionary; heterodox; wildest; primary; essential; tantalizing; evangelical; shallow; bold; religious; horrible; sentimental; deistical; contrary; practical.

verbs

accept—; adhere to—; adopt—; advocate —; apply—; attack—; believe—; blaspheme—; bolster—; challenge—; commit to—; concur in—; define—; demolish—; derive—from; echo—; enunciate—; epitomize—; espouse—; expound—; illustrate—; immerse in—; impart—; inculcate—; invoke —; nullify—; obey—; pledge to—; practise—; preach—; promulgate—; propound —; put forth—; refer to—; reject—; sin against—; spread—; teach—; understand —; unite in—; —astounds; —confounds; —embraces; —governs.

(See teaching, belief, dogma, principle, precept.)

DOCUMENT

adjectives

genuine; routine; epic; intimate; tremendous; human; effective; dull; trustworthy; ethnological; authoritative; vivid; revealing; precious; obnoxious; colorless; official; controversial; immortal; fundamental; notable; living; ecclesiastical; diplomatic; temperate; extraordinary; unique; amazing; public; formidable; illuminating; brief; decorous; forceful; momentous; dangerous; pathetic; significant; rambling; equivocal; flimsy; finicky; noteworthy; singular; irreproachable; trenchant; unpublished; fatal; different-looking; authentic; ponderous; uncommon; insidious; iconographic; respective (pl); edifying.

verbs

arrange—; crowd with—s; cull from—;

draw up—; entrust with—; explore through —s; file—; inscribe in—; preserve—; produce—; refer to—; release—; scan—; seal —; search—; sign—; survey—; term—; value—; witness—; —asserts; —authorizes; —enlightens; —entitles; —informs; —points out; —proves; —records; —serves; —verifies.

(See paper, evidence, proof, record.)

DOCUMENTARY
adverbs
inescapably; genuinely; trustworthily; ecclesiastically; legally; amazingly; formidably; briefly; momentously; dangerously; significantly; irreproachably; fatally; ponderously; trenchantly; uncommonly; unexpectedly; surprisingly.

DODDERING
adverbs
tremulously; quaveringly; helplessly; feebly; pleasantly; uncertainly; hopelessly; desperately; decrepitly; wanderingly; erratically; confusedly; bewilderedly; pathetically; bravely; prematurely; nervously; besottedly; drunkenly; slowly; wearily.

DOG
adjectives
wistful; spineless; mauled; loutish; shambling; squat; well-shaped; mongrel; tubby; stray; wolf-like; well-bred; barking; marauding; placid; slinking; whipped; cringing; huge; lion-like; cross-grained; savage; vicious; sedate; beaten; avid; yelping; raging; inestimable; alien; clean; rabid; murderous; angry; hungry; handsome; stately; jubilant; worthless; gigantic; lean; gallant; happy; famished; miserable; reliable; frail; little; woolly; deep-chested; disgraceful-looking; couchant; myopic; demented; tawny; treacherous; panting; half-wolf; stripe-tailed; surly; brutal; stranger; accursed; unconscionable; patient; fierce; snapping; chivalrous; jovial; vagrant; atheistical; thievish-looking; voiceless; lame; sneaking; sad; craven; traitorous; thirsty; bipedal; gentlemanly; elderly; mangy; hellish; lounging.

verbs
cast to—s; coax—; crop—; cudgel—; lash —; soothe—; stone—; unleash—; whip—; —barks; —bays; —clambers; —crouches; —darts by; —dashes by; —depredates; — frisks; —gnaws; —growls; —herds; — howls; —invades; —laps; —licks; —limps; —lurks; —menaces; —performs; —points; —preys; —pursues; —retrieves; —skulks;

—slinks off; —snaps; —snarls; —strays; —tears; —trots away; —whimpers; —whines; —wrangles; —yelps; —yowls.

(See animal, puppy.)

DOGGED
adverbs
stubbornly; obstinately; boundlessly; excessively; resolutely; sullenly; morosely; pertinaciously; glumly; silently; irresistibly; obdurately; implacably; inveterately; bravely; heroically; endlessly; surprisingly; unexpectedly; mulishly; perversely; blindly; intractably; fanatically; wilfully; intrepidly; enterprisingly; fiercely; churlishly; grouchily; moodily; crustily; grumpishly.

DOGMA
adjectives
wide-rooted; delicate; dangerous; religious; deflating; dour; theological; pungent; narrow; entrenched; intolerant; pure; sheer; rash; inscrutable; fundamental; negative; sweeping.

verbs
abandon—; assert—; defend—: expound—; follow—; formulate—; impose—; inherit—; justify—; preach—; proclaim—; propound —; put forward—; question—; sanction—; save—; state—; teach—; —convinces; — denounces; —flourishes; —satisfies; — vanishes.

(See doctrine, principle.)

DOGMATIC
adverbs
unwarrantably; disagreeably; confidently; marvelously; unaccountably; egotistically; cruelly; harshly; severely; conceitedly; bumptiously; ecclesiastically; tyrannically; officially; inexorably; stiffly; dangerously; dourly; narrowly; fundamentally; purely; utterly; singularly; austerely; arrogantly; proudly; unyieldingly; solidly; absolutely; definitely; positively; fanatically; superficially; intolerantly; provincially; remarkably; fussily; peremptorily; emphatically; solemnly.

DOINGS
adjectives
hot-headed; habitual; subsequent; infinite; valiant; ill; sinister; factual.

DOLE
verbs
apply for—; apportion—; approve of—; deprive of—; dispense—; distribute—; di-

vide—; drop from—; entitle to—; impart —; issue—; reduce to—; reward—; relinquish—; subsist on—; —eases; —supports.
(See alms, charity.)

DOLEFUL

adverbs
habitually; temperamentally; utterly; ceaselessly; deeply; darkly; foolishly; unreasonably; vexatiously; needlessly; remarkably; singularly; oddly; oppressively; inarticulately; silently; immoderately; unutterably; fundamentally; extravagantly; dismally; abjectly; glumly; gloomily; lugubriously; dreadfully; biliously; horribly.

DOLL

adjectives
mature; gorgeous; absurd; rag; exquisite; mutilated; adorable; cherished; brainless; dancing; dressed-up; dilapidated; moonfaced; battered.

verbs
collect—s; display—; dress—; entertain with—; name—; present with—; repair—; sleep with—; tire of—; wind—; yearn for —; —attracts; —cheers; —dangles; — pleases; —satisfies; —simpers; —sleeps; —surprises; —walks.
(See toy.)

DOLLAR

adjectives
precious; shrunken; tangible; advertising; paltry; appreciating; solitary; minted; countless (pl); depreciating; inflated; purchasing.

verbs
adopt—; beg—; coin—s; count—s; counterfeit—; deflate—; devaluate—; earn—; fill with—; flash—; furnish with—; inflate—; issue—; lose—; mint—s; present with—; print—s; proffer—; rate—; reduce to—; reject—; relinquish—; soil—; tear—; value —; worship—; —s accrue; —adorns; — attracts.
(See money, coin.)

DOLTISH

adverbs
unutterably; strangely; dully; apathetically; singularly; oddly; curiously; unaccountably; inscrutably; abysmally; grotesquely; palpably; essentially; incurably; irremediably; callously; shockingly; soddenly; sullenly; vacuously; ridiculously; lumpishly; grossly; coarsely; direly; blandly; stupidly; stolidly.

DOMAIN

adjectives
temporal; spiritual; allied (pl); speckless; ancestral; rough-hewn; extended; unexploited; bleak; ecclesiastical; obscure; shifting; elastic; scanty; shattered; melancholy; eminent; imperial; unassailable; forbidden; flourishing; impenetrable; outlying; all-pervading; vast.

DOME

adjectives
golden; majestic; great; granite; shallow; saucer-like; gilded; blue-tiled; truncated; bell-shaped; silent; glorious; velvety; vaulted; star-fretted; tremulous; inevitable; isolated; monastic; gaping; observatory; firmamental; clustered; shadowy; ribbed; Moorish; towering; heaven-pointing; illuminated; porphyroid.

verbs
adorn—; ascend to—; cradle in—; decorate —; dwell in—; enlarge—; gild—; illuminate—; poise on—; round off in—; stud—; survey—; swell—; —arches; —attracts; —resounds; —revolves; —shields; —sparkles; —spreads; —totters.
(See roof, building.)

DOMESTIC

adverbs
incurably; delightfully; cozily; comfortably; exaggeratedly; elaborately; ostentatiously; blatantly; offensively; conspicuously; hopelessly; charmingly; narrowly; insistently; flamboyantly; proudly; absurdly; impressively; vexatiously; boundlessly; entirely; pretentiously.

DOMESTICITY

adjectives
smug; safe; dull; suburban; hard-won.

verbs
acquaint with—; avoid—; balk at—; dabble in—; eliminate—; escape—; feign—; glance into—; incur—; indulge in—; pretend—; school in—; swallow by—; trap by—; wallow in—; weary of—; wrap in—; —annoys; —appeals; —bores; —involves; —restrains; —shelters.
(See affair.)

DOMICILE

adjectives

luxurious; semi-detached; sumptuous; self-contained; sanctified; historic; commodious; tempting.

DOMINANT

adverbs

disturbingly; arrogantly; prominently; interestingly; strangely; substantially; emphatically; markedly; primarily; remarkably; vitally; virtually; dangerously; luckily; alarmingly; fortunately; unluckily; strongly; invincibly; inescapably; supremely; disagreeably; unpleasantly; officiously; selfishly; ruthlessly; inconsiderately; politically; unfortunately; insistently; manifestly; obviously; terribly; loftily; sternly; extraordinarily.

DOMINATE (v)

adverbs

atavistically; powerfully; effectively; tyrannically; overwhelmingly; sternly; inevitably; insistently; solely; persistently.

(See govern, control.)

DOMINATION

adjectives

lofty; overwhelming; hard; stern; cortical; banded; extraordinary; inevitable; insistent; sole; extended.

verbs

break away from—; condemn—; curse by —; dwell in—; enlarge—; enrich—; establish—; foster—; join—; subject to—; submit to—; suffer under—; trace—to; —compels; —inflicts; —reaps; —rules; —thrives.

(See control, dominion, rule, government, tyranny.)

DOMINEERING

adverbs

disagreeably; ridiculously; amusingly; tyrannically; unreasonably; characteristically; arrogantly; clownishly; persistently; airily; shockingly; politely; officiously; ludicrously; despotically; pompously; inherently; superciliously; loftily; insistently; sharply; detestably; offensively; naturally.

DOMINION

adjectives

sole; hereditary; dim; voracious; hard; unlimited; uncurbed; supreme; gross; drear.

verbs

control—; exercise—over; explore—; form —; gain—; grant to—; grasp—; inhabit—; integrate—s; procure—over; recognize—; rule—; rule with—; sever—from; sway—; yield to—; —comprises; —extends to; — obeys; —serves; govern—.

(See sovereignty, authority, nation, empire, kingdom.)

DONATE (v)

adverbs

munificently; generously; charitably; anonymously; amply; lavishly; splendidly; meagerly; grudgingly; complainingly.

(See give, contribute.)

DONATION

adjectives

generous; ample; munificent.

DONKEY

adjectives

laden; tiny; gray; straggling; diminutive; plodding; modest; gentle; omnipresent; neat-stepping; patient.

verbs

burden—; fetter—; lash—; lasso—; pasture —; tether—; water—; —ambles; —balks; —draws; —grazes; —hauls; —kicks; — pulls; —shies; —snorts.

(See animal, ass.)

DOOM

adjectives

impending; ultimate; irrevocable; ignominious; inescapable; dreadful; tragic; distant; thankful; inevitable; eternal; mysterious; dark; self-wrought; everlasting; inscrutable; stormy; graceless; fatal; approaching; imminent; perpetual; dubious; ultimate.

verbs

announce—; assign—; avoid—; bear—; bide—; consign to—; curse—; draw to—; dread—; fix—; fly to—; foresee—; foreshadow—; foretell—; hasten to—; move to—; near—; precipitate—; pronounce—; read—; revoke—; seal—; sound—; spell —; threaten—; —closes in; —impends.

(See judgment, fate, destiny.)

DOOM (v)

adverbs

irrecoverably; irrevocably; apparently; everlastingly; prophetically; ultimately; ignominiously; inescapably; dreadfully; tragically; inevitably; eternally; mysteriously; inscrutably; fatally; cruelly.

(See condemn, ruin.)

DOOMED

adverbs

irretrievably; finally; mortally; endlessly; terribly; ultimately; irrevocably; ignominiously; inescapably; dreadfully; tragically; inevitably; eternally; mysteriously; darkly; everlastingly; inscrutably; perpetually; unhappily; utterly; evidently; manifestly; fatefully.

DOOR

adjectives

massive; battered; paneled; reluctant; clamped; iron-bound; barricaded; heavy; monumental; lovely; sun-blistered; baffling; carved; solid; grilled; unyielding; bolted; humble; weather-beaten; cathedral; unlatched; ponderous; stout; studded; opening; squeaking; communicating; yawning; cringing; ancient; worm-eaten; hacked; clanging; front; fateful; mystic; perpetual; unfrequented; love-crowned; substantial; impervious; moldering; revolving; portcullis; lodge; postern; sloping; sliding; hospitable; intermediate; veiled; padded; unguarded; infernal; impalpable; paternal; mossy; adamantine; unhinged; arched; mountain; shattered; curtained; guilty; shrunken; dilapidated; feeble.

verbs

appear at—; arch—; attain—; bar—; barricade—; batter down—; beat down—; bolt—; clamor at—; command—; commune at—; darken—; defend—; encamp at—; escort to—; exclude from—; fling open—; force—; gather at—; glimmer through—; guard—; guide to—; hammer on—; hinge —; hover about—; jam—; peep through—; pry at—; repulse from—; slam—; steal through—; stream through—; tap on—; tarry at—; tend—; venture through—; —admits; —creaks; —groans; —squeaks; —yawns.

(See entrance, portal, gate, opening, doorway.)

DOOR-BELL

adjectives

(See bell.)

verbs

adjust—; answer—; attach—; connect—; hang—; press—; quiet—; ring—; sound—;

—announces; —chimes; —disturbs; —interjects; —interrupts; —jingles; —pierces; —warns.

(See bell.)

DOOR-KNOB

adjectives

(See knob.)

verbs

adjust—; attach—; fasten to—; force—; grasp—; handle—; hug—; jiggle—; manipulate—; mark—; move—; ornament—; palm—; release—; toy with—; try—; tug at—; turn—; soil—; —gives way; —turns.

(See handle, knob.)

DOOR-MAN

adjectives

hulking; hard-faced; resplendent; staring; ruthless; gigantic.

DOORWAY

adjectives

sheltered; stately; doorless; curtained; unpretentious; pilastered; time-stained; flamboyant; enticing; impressive; unsavory; sculptured.

verbs

admit through—; adorn—; darken—; embellish—; enter—; file through—; flutter past—; huddle in—; jostle into—; loom in—; observe from—; occupy—; open into —; ornament—; pursue through—; scamper through—; shadow—; —beckons; —divides; —exhibits; —invites; —separates.

(See door.)

DORMANT

adverbs

temporarily; transiently; healthily; momentarily; latently; passively; inertly; heavily; lethargically; inactively; mysteriously; importantly; smoulderingly; symbolically; impenetrably; inferentially; fortunately; naturally; quiescently.

DOSE

adjectives

minimum; enormous; nauseous; attenuated; curative; large; graduated (pl); tremendous; unpalatable; minute; occasional; nontoxic; potable; protective; moderate; monstrous; therapeutic; homeopathic.

verbs

adjust—; administer—; advocate—; apply —; calm with—; concoct—; decrease—;

increase—; inject—; ladle out—; measure—; portion out—; prepare—; prescribe—; reduce—; refuse—; regulate—; repeat—; suggest—; swallow—; —alleviates; —relieves; —suffices.

(See portion, draught, amount, medicine.)

DOTING

adverbs

foolishly; absurdly; inordinately; childishly; tenderly; ludicrously; tempestuously; frankly; proudly; significantly; ridiculously; openly; ostentatiously; fatuously; fervently; idolatrously; ardently; inarticulately; inexpressibly; madly; fervidly.

DOUBLE-FACED

adverbs

subtly; cunningly; insidiously; notoriously; infamously; surreptitiously; artfully; craftily; deceitfully; remarkably; dangerously; cleverly; alarmingly; distressingly; maneuveringly; plaguedly; adroitly; successfully; underhandedly; shrewdly; proverbially; manifestly; suavely; sanctimoniously.

DOUBT

adjectives

premonitory; wondering; casual; growing; reasonable; prudent; impending; recurring; faint; presumptuous; insinuating; audacious; uneasy; horrid; black; wistful; serious; disturbing; grisly; consuming; bitter; sickening; momentary; angry; torturing; cynical; passionate; formless; unmerited; nagging; insidious; mean; conflicting; anxious; painful; pecuniary; timid; sarcastic; considerable; solitary; lingering; inseparable; floating; paralyzing; melancholy; remorseful; hideous; sorrowing; thronging; rational; hopeless; jealous; tragic; unwelcome; injurious; dark; coquettish; blasphemous; unclaimed; childish; oft-repeated; religious; unanswerable; good-humored; constitutional; grave; fiendish; sagacious; cloudy; broken; desperate; earthly.

verbs

assail with—; attend with—; banish—; breed—; brush away—; burden with—; cast into—; chill with—; circulate—; clear up—; cloud with—; conceive—; convey—; crush—; defy—; dissipate—; dissolve—; eliminate—; entertain—; erase—; express—; falter in—; fight—; interpose—; occasion—; oppress with—; raise—; remove—; rend with—; resolve—; strike with—; sustain—; sweep away—; torture with—; trouble by—; voice—; wrap in—; wring

with—; —creeps in; —encompasses; —incenses; —lingers; —lurks; —overshadows; —prevails; —pursues; —springs up; —stabs; —taints.

(See uncertainty, distrust, disbelief, incredulity, skepticism.)

DOUBT (v)

adverbs

casually; growingly; reasonably; recurringly; seriously; disturbingly; consumingly; sickeningly; momentarily; formlessly; painfully; jealously; childishly; gravely; sagaciously; paralyzingly.

(See distrust, suspect.)

DOUBTER

adjectives

fastidious; sneering; puny.

DOUBTFUL

adverbs

altogether; reasonably; seriously; gravely; vexatiously; still; wholly; timidly; vaguely; hazily; bewilderingly; mysteriously; enigmatically; ignorantly; distractedly; nervously; uncertainly; embarrassingly; elusively; remarkably; singularly; inexplicably; oddly.

DOUGH

adjectives

tasteless; crisp.

verbs

cake—; knead—; leaven—; mix—; mould—; moisten—; prepare—; punch—; set—; shape—; sprinkle—; sweeten—; transform—into; work—; —ferments; —puffs; —rises.

(See mass.)

DOUGHNUT

adjectives

lunch-counter; sugary; forbidden.

DOVE

adjectives

crooning; staid; strengthless; mellow-mourning; lonely; sucking; milk-white; cooing; brooding; silver; snowy.

verbs

tame—; toy with—; —bills; —broods; —coos; —crouches; —grieves; —haunts; —moans; —mourns; —murmurs; —plains; —sails; —trembles; —trumpets; —tumbles; —walks.

(See bird.)

DOWAGER

adjectives
ugly; old; **decorous**; ill-tempered; amiable.

DOWDY

adverbs
indescribably; dismally; untidily; vaguely; shamefully; embarrassingly; pitiably; incredibly; unfashionably; inexcusably; indifferently; nonchalantly; blithely; carelessly; gloriously; laughingly; placidly; self-consciously; unconscionably; inordinately; unpardonably; vexatiously; downright; smudgily; grimily; lazily; obstinately; slouchily; gaily; negligently.

DOWER

adjectives
unconscious; fragrant; generous; sufficient; convenient.

DOWN

adjectives
solitary; dewy-glooming; callow; loaning; soft; undulating (pl); hushless (pl); beautiful; swelling (pl).

DOWNCAST

adverbs
terribly; unreasonably; needlessly; gloomily; glumly; inordinately; emphatically; dourly; sorely; irrationally; inexplicably; moodily; alarmingly; dangerously; incurably; inconceivably; incredibly; horribly; woefully; gravely; seriously; inconsolably; desperately; tragically; unduly; wearily.

DOWNFALL

verbs
anticipate—; approach—; bring about—; drag into—; escape—; expect—; experience—; fear—; guard against—; heed—; meet—; pitch to—; promise—; protect from —; recover from—; tumble to—; warn of—; —destroys; —engulfs; —teaches.
(See disgrace, ruin, destruction.)

DOWNPOUR

adjectives
torrential; thinning; increasing; steady; drenching; tropical.

DOWRY

adjectives
(See gift.)

verbs
agree upon—; amass—; assign—; assure of—; bestow—; demand—; endue with—;

furnish—; grant—; guarantee—; increase —; marry for—; pay—; present with—; provide—; return—; seek—; —compensates; —impoverishes; —satisfies; —shrinks.
(See endowment, **gift**, property, portion, reward.)

DOZE

adjectives
noontide; surreptitious; sudden; heavy; fitful; nightmare-ridden; comfortable; wakeful; uncomfortable.

DOZE (v)

adverbs
peacefully; slumberously; surreptitiously; fitfully; comfortably; wakefully; interminably; lazily.
(See sleep, **drowse.**)

DRABNESS

adjectives
colorless; external; bleak; blank.

verbs
clothe in—; compensate for—; conceal—; envelop by—; expel—; exude—; observe—; relieve—; shroud in—; throw off—; —depresses; —displeases; —drowns; —offends; —oppresses; —overwhelms; —seeps in; —suits.
(See dullness, monotony.)

DRAFT
(air)

adjectives
icy; adventurous; sparkling; severe; swift.

verbs
admit—; avoid—; breathe—; create—; draw—; expose to—; force—; guard against—; inhale—; place in—; prevent—; produce—; protect against—; shiver in—; sit in—; —effects; —enters; —escapes; —harms; —passes through.
(See current, air, breeze.)

DRAFT
(money)

verbs
address—; approve—; cash—; date—; defer—; draw—; honor—; pay with—; produce—; send—; tender—; wire—; write—; —enables; —orders; —suffices.
(See money.)

DRAG (v)

adverbs
painfully; listlessly; dejectedly; bodily;

heavily; tenderly; stubbornly; forcibly; despondently; unwillingly; sternly.

(See haul, trail, pull.)

DRAGON

adjectives
undulant; cave-hid; gilded; fabulous; swift; full-gorged; transfixed; ugly; hideous; murderous; Hydra-headed; green; monstrous; bloodthirsty.

verbs
beset by—; cast out—; confront by—; crush—; pacify—; prevail against—; rout —; slay—; strike at—; vanquish—; —claws; —destroys; —fumes; —guards; —hisses; —licks; —menaces; —ravages; —snorts; —spouts forth; —swallows up; —symbolizes; —tramples; —vanishes; —wails; —writhes.

(See monster, serpent.)

DRAIN

adjectives
(See ditch, pipe, trench.)

verbs
clog—; connect to—; consign to—; dig—; discharge in—; drop into—; employ—; enter—; flush—; furnish—; insert—; pour down—; —carries off; —clears; —preserves; —prevents; —serves; washdown—.

(See gutter, channel. trench, ditch, pipe.)

DRAIN (v)

adverbs
steadily; thoroughly; partially; unscrupulously; unsparingly; entirely; completely; painfully.

(See empty, exhaust, deplete.)

DRAMA

adjectives
spiritual; modern; languid; excessive; loquacious; moving; honest; courageous; stirring; sturdy; classic; dazzling; intense; irrepressible; successful; trivial; stark; high; spectacular; unpretentious; lyric; terrific; painful; crucial; ineffective; unsettled; sensational; hidden; sinister; comic; touching; grim; vivid; gloomy; tragic; dynamic; many-sided; homely; homespun; heartrending; agonizing; absorbing; daily; rousing; weird; romantic; enthralling; raw; elemental; episodic; moon-lit; grisly; moribund; terrestrial; breathless; turgid; far-flung; unrelenting; throbbing; intensified; psychological; adulterous; quiet; piquant; stupendous; thrilling; philosophical;

judicial; realistic; naturalistic; poetic; merciless; pitiless; constructive; decadent; fierce; historical; mimic; powerful; religious; impending; oft-rehearsed; voiceless; equestrian; potential; tragic; social; great; well-ordered; transpired; blustering; nefarious; well-arranged; celebrated; revolutionary; sublime; epic; passionate; vast; heroic; propaganda; depressing; exhilarating.

verbs
cast—; enact—; fashion—; foreshadow—; ground in—; intensify—; pervade—; portray—; recreate—; reform—; revive—; sense—; sketch—; spell—; take part in—; temper—; unfold—; —depicts; —electrifies; —stirs; —teeters; —unrolls.

(See play, composition, performance, tragedy, literature.)

DRAMATIC

adverbs
spectacularly; absurdly; impressively; extravagantly; emphatically; foolishly; ridiculously; laughably; profitably; undoubtedly; evidently; palpably; grotesquely; fantastically; unusually; admittedly; excessively; movingly; highly; lyrically; sensationally; weirdly; romantically; breathlessly; enthrallingly; quietly; psychologically; stupendously; marvellously; abundantly; thrillingly; mercilessly; historically; undeniably; powerfully; potentially; sublimely; epically; vastly; heroically; passionately; exhilaratingly; touchingly; immensely; intensely; boundlessly.

DRAMATIST

adjectives
celebrated; contemporary; deft; practiced; renowned; distinguished.

verbs
acclaim—; applaud—; condemn—; criticize—; inspire—; praise—; reward—; support—; sympathize with—; —composes; —conceives; —concocts; —entertains; —excels; —foreshadows; —implies; —motivates; —moves; —plans; —presents; —prevails; —relates; —stirs; —yields.

(See writer, playwright, author.)

DRAPE

adjectives
extreme; modified; easy; natural; smart; athletic; careless; fashionable; poised; proper; graceful.

DRAPE (v)

adverbs

artistically; sparingly; carelessly; archly; smartly; fashionably; properly; gracefully; gloomily; vividly; voluminously; richly; flutteringly; monotonously; fantastically; gorgeously; judiciously; dustily.

(See hang, adorn, cover.)

DRAPERY

adjectives

sweeping; gloomy; gleaming; damask; smoke-grey; vivid; chiffon; voluminous; sad; silvery; rich; orchid; taffeta; window; glistening; festooned; stifling; floating; filmy; sable; well-managed; snowy; fluttering; verdant; monotonous; undulant; translucent; sonorous; graceful; gorgeous; golden; diaphanous; flying; silken; judicious; soft; streaming; sooty; gauzy; fantastic; witching; ambulant; chintz; voile; dusty.

verbs

admire—; arrange—; clothe in—; cover with—; decorate with—; dress in—; festoon in—; fold—; furnish with—; hang—; model—; place—; select—; strip of—; suspend—; weave—; —adds —dresses; —enhances; —graces; —offsets; —ies part.

(See curtain, cloth, material.)

DRASTIC

adverbs

cruelly; intensely; inhumanly; emphatically; unscrupulously; pitifully; powerfully; intensely; virulently; poignantly; harshly; resolutely; immensely; strenuously; incisively; violently; desperately; brutally; trenchantly; strikingly.

DRAUGHT

adjectives

copious; literary; roaring; shallow; mellow; crystal; daring; refreshing; beneficial; delirious; frequent (pl); nectared; unpalatable; portentous; long; hearty; ample; fresh; considerable; acid; grateful; magic; liquorish; fiery; nut-brown; immortal; mingled (pl); fatal; assisted.

verbs

concoct—; down—; drain—; draw off—; empty—; finish in one—; imbibe—; mix—; order—; partake of—; rejoice in—; tap—; —effervesces; —foams; —quenches; —revives; —sates; —soothes; —suffices.

(See drink.)

DRAW (v)

adverbs

fiercely; reluctantly; passionately; mournfully; caressingly; silently; swiftly; contentedly; lazily; demurely; passively; haughtily; apprehensively; irresistibly; reproachfully; inevitably; hastily; affectionately; tenderly; symbolically; exquisitely; sophisticatedly; sketchily; grotesquely; impeccably; hideously; apologetically.

(See depict, sketch, pull.)

DRAWBACK

adjectives

tremendous; undeniable; numerous (pl); practical; definite.

verbs

accept—; anticipate—; control—; expect—; involve—; lack—; necessitate—; overcome —; produce—; pronounce—; refuse—; relax—; reveal—; weigh—; —diminishes; —hinders.

(See disadvantage, hindrance, defect.)

DRAWER

adjectives

secret; gilt-labelled; locked; hidden; stuffed; filled.

verbs

arrange in—; conceal in—; decorate—; discover in—; draw out—; examine—; explore —; fit in—; lock—; muss—; obtain from—; ornament—; rummage in—; search in—; wade through—s; —contains; —exposes; —reveals; —sticks; —swallows.

(See case, box.)

DRAWING

adjectives

water-color; modernistic; free-hand; magnificent; clever; amazing; delectable; symbolical; beautiful; holy; exquisite; sophisticated; sketchy; charcoal; crude; sturdy; grotesque; impeccable; bewildering; distinguished; detailed; icicle-like; naturalistic; hideous.

verbs

collect—s; embellish—; exhibit—; interest in—; model for—; pen—; pencil—; pose for—; praise—; produce—; scratch out—; sit for—; sketch—; study—; translate—; —attracts; —depicts; —imparts; —represents; —reveals; —symbolizes.

(See sketch, picture.)

adjectives

frescoed; honest; staid; spacious; marble-floored.

DRAWL

adjectives

tantalizing; unexcited; calm; level; lazy; musical; indistinct; mountain; innocent; maddening; affected; enchanting; slow; steady; masculine; comforting; pleasant; ingenious; listless; haughty; sardonic; husky; amusing; amiable; quiet; soft; confidential; high; emphatic.

verbs

acquire—; adopt—; affect—; catch—; copy—; correct—; employ—; inject—; mimic—; mumble—; recognize—; retain—; translate—; understand—; utter—; —fascinates; —intrigues; —irritates; —loiters; —pleases.

(See speech, utterance, accent.)

DRAWL (v)

adverbs

slowly; wearily; tantalizingly; lazily; musically; indistinctly; maddeningly; affectedly; enchantingly; steadily; comfortingly; pleasantly; listlessly; sardonically; huskily; amusingly; amiably; softly; calmly.

(See speak, sound.)

DRAWLING

adverbs

lazily; sleepily; indifferently; carelessly; drowsily; yawningly; insolently; arrogantly; stupidly; impudently; slowly; indistinctly; affectedly; listlessly; languidly; huskily; interminably; endlessly; tiresomely; slackly; slouchily; leisurely; deliberately; apathetically; dully; maunderingly; inarticulately; singularly; faintly; idly; inertly; dreamily; inexcusably.

DREAD

adjectives

despising; wondrous; superstitious; half-conscious; silent; mysterious; contagious; ignorant; sickening; apprehensive; maddening; unreasonable; secret; speechless; mysterious; lurking; shrinking; shadowy; slavish; inexplicable; haunting; unimaginable; nameless; inexpressible; morbid; somber; fresh; blank; irrational; racking; stark; mutual; constant; unnamed; obscene; unnatural; foolish; abnormal; salutary; oppressive; decorous; ill-defined; vague; shuddering; subconscious; feminine; incomprehensible; grinding; popular; nervous;

pious; unformulated; poignant; supernatural; recurrent; indefinable; unfathomable; overwhelming; inspiring.

verbs

attend with—; awaken—; cause—; cure of—; diagnose—; disguise—; dwell in—; hide in—of; induce—; nourish—; obsess with—; oppress by—; overcome—; produce—; provoke—; put away—; regard with—; relinquish—; ripen into—; shake with—; wrap in—; —causes; —dogs; —inspires; —overcomes.

(See fright, horror, terror, awe.)

DREAD (v)

adverbs

righteously; vaguely; habitually; superstitiously; ignorantly; apprehensively; unreasonably; secretly; speechlessly; shrinkingly; inexplicably; hauntingly; unimaginably; inexpressibly; morbidly; somberly; irrationally; starkly; mutually; constantly; unnaturally; foolishly; oppressively; vaguely; nervously; piously; poignantly; supernaturally; recurrently; indefinably; unfathomably; overwhelmingly.

(See fear, anticipate.)

DREADFUL

adverbs

unutterably; unspeakably; horridly; abominably; tragically; gloomily; incredibly; indescribably; absolutely; starkly; uncommonly; amazingly; astonishingly; cruelly; shockingly; startlingly; perniciously; damnably; disastrously; ruinously; arrantly; reprehensibly; execrably; irremediably; insupportably; appallingly; repulsively; abhorrently; sickeningly; calamitously; cataclysmally.

DREAM

adjectives

aerial; aching; amazing; ambitious; amusing; amethystine; angelic; antenatal; appalling; astonishing; attenuated; bad; baleful; balmy; beastly; beatific; beauteous; besetting; bewildering; bitter; blessed; blighting; blissful; botched; boyish; bucolic; captured; changing; chaste; cherished; childhood; clear; clouded; colored; confused; consecrating; constant; conversational; daring; crazy; dark; day-appearing; dazzling; dead; dearest; deep; delicate; delicious; delirious; delusive; depressed; disconnected; discordant; disjointed; disordered; distorted; distressing; disturbed; divine; dotard; doubtful; dreadful; ecstatic; drowsy; embodied; empty; enthralled; external; evil; exacerbated; exquisite; extraordinary; extravagant; exuberant; fabulous; faded; fairy tale; false; fanatical; fanciful; fancy; fantastic; favorite; fearful; feverish; fitful; flashing; flattering; fleeting; floating; fond; foolish; fragile; friendly; frightful; futile; ghastly; girlish; glorious; gloomy; golden; gorgeous; grandiose; grotesque; half-forgotten; half-remembered; hashish; hateful; haunting; hazy; hideous; horrible; horrid; horrifying; hovering; idle; idyllic; illusory; immortal; impossible; impressive; incommunicable; industrial; ineffaceable; ingenuous; insistent; inspiring; interlunar; interminable; intransitive; invisible; iridescent; jeweled; jostling; journeying; jocund; languorous; lasting; lethargic; liquored; lifelong; liberal-minded; living; loftiest; lotus-eating; lowly; luxurious; mad; maddening; magical; magnificent; melancholy; materialized, millennial; misty; mournful; mooning; morbid; nightly; nightmare; obliging; particular; pensive; perfectible; perishing; odorous; oppressive; ominous; painful; perpetual; persistent; picturesque; pipe; poetic; pompous; poor; preposterous; prophetic; quarrelsome; protracted; pure; quaint; quaking; qualm-filled; quarrelsome; quavering; queenly; quenchable; quick; quieting; querimonious; querulous; questionable; quirky; quizzical; remarkable; restless; resurrected; ridiculous; rocking-chair; romantic; rosy; senseless; sensual; significant; shameful; shattered; shivering; short-lived; sin-chastising; sprinkling; singular; sleepless; slow; smiling; solid; stern; strange; summer; sweet; symbolic; telepathic; tender; terrific; terrifying; thoughtless; topsy-turvy; torturing; transitory; trivial; troubled; tumultuous; unborn; uneasy; unmeaning; unpleasant; unquiet; unremembered; unshakable; unsubstantial; untold; vague; veritable; vernal; vicious; visionary; vivid; waking; wandering; waning; wavering; whirling; whiskey; whispered; wicked; winged; wildering; wildest; wistful; wretched; youthful; zestful.

verbs
awake from—; babble in—; blend in—; break—; calm—s; cast into—; conceive in—; create in—; delight in—; destroy—; dissipate—; exist in—; explain—; fade to —; fly away in—; foresee in—; forget—; fulfill—; glimpse in—; haunt—; hearken to—; indulge in—; interpret—; lose in—; nurse—; pass from—; perpetuate in—;

produce—; realize—; rule—s; shake off—; shatter—; sink into—; slumber in—; spin —; suffer in—; transform—; understand—; wander in—; —betokens; —crumbles; —disturbs; —flees; —flowers; —foretells; —haunts; —overpowers; —overshadows; —presages; —prophesies; —puzzles; —reveals; —signifies; —startles; —terrifies; —torments; —troubles; —warns.
(See illusion, reverie, fancy, fantasy, hallucination, vision.)

DREAM (v)
adverbs
unchastely; delectably; romantically; splendidly; confusedly; fondly; contentedly; ambitiously; amusingly; astonishingly; blissfully; dazzlingly; deliciously; deliriously; disconnectedly; drowsily; distressingly; dreadfully; ecstatically; emptily; evilly; exquisitely; extravagantly; exuberantly; fabulously; fanatically; fancifully; fleetingly; gloomily; gorgeously; grotesquely; horribly; inspiringly; interminably; maddeningly; magnificently; oppressively; pensively; perpetually; persistently; picturesquely; poetically; prophetically; ridiculously; romantically; senselessly; sensually; significantly; vividly; waveringly; zestfully; deliriously.
(See fancy, imagine.)

DREAMER
adjectives
egotistic; inefficient; preposterous; imaginative; languishing; impractical; hair-splitting; drowsy; pathetic; soppy; deep; blissful; solitary; delirious; superstitious; utopian; stony.

DREAMY
adverbs
languidly; somnolently; lazily; delightfully; terribly; wonderfully; slightly; deliciously; comfortably; cosily; amazingly; amusingly; inattentively; carelessly; abstractedly; beatifically; boyishly; constantly; irritatingly; naturally; habitually; inherently; provokingly; wistfully; wickedly; vaguely; yearningly; longingly; sweetly; strangely; tenderly; uneasily; thoughtlessly; sleepily; quaintly; remarkably; restlessly; perpetually; crazily; deeply; divinely; ecstatically; extraordinarily; fancifully; fantastically; foolishly; girlishly; gloriously; hatefully; idly; interminably; pensively.

DREARINESS

adjectives

mute; funereal; cacophonous; soporific; appalling; blank.

DREGS

adjectives

wretched; bitterest; painful; basest; final; bottom; last.

DRENCH (v)

adverbs

instantaneously; entirely; thoroughly; fully; fatally; refreshingly; repeatedly.

(See flood, overflow.)

DRESS

adjectives

fetching; charming; daring; motley; gay; luxurious; trim; exquisite; gorgeous; delicious; evening; sky-blue; conventional; simple; starched; stiff; immaculate; adorable; homely; conspicuous; sophisticated; gauzy; filmy; gleaming; dishevelled; faded; dirty; frumpy; torn; crumpled; rumpled; flecked; queer; shabby; tattered; muslin; voile; serge; bridal; ostentatious; proper; irreproachable; azure; alpaca; holiday; low-necked; traveling; brocade; silk; hand-embroidered; ceremonial; wedding; picturesque; metal; native; turquoise; satin; fringed; beaded; buckskin; fluttering; flowing; insufficient; favorite; voluminous; old-style; detailed; antediluvian; unpretending; flaunting; shaggy; scant; plain; sumptuous; tight-fitting; sober; decorous; splendid; fantastical; ecclesiastical; airy; clean; yellow; fresh; somber; different; good-looking; extraordinary; school-girlish; flowered; varicolored; trailing; made-over; soft; sheer; identical; suitable; frivolous; flame; nondescript; gaudy; dazzling; cute; vivid; wearable; outlandish; martial; orchestral; distinctive; well-made; exceptional; fashionable; tinted; gala; lively; rich; basic; bloody; negligent; obsolete; impeccable; tailored; elegant; romantic; loose; glittering; quaint; rainy day; ragged; olive-green; outdoor; red; tulle; ballerina; becoming; masculine; fitted; boyish; convenient; hideous; fleshly; enchanting; rustic; indecent; shiny; wretched; flattering; versatile; foppish; manly; similar; alluring; gingham; incomparable.

verbs

adorn—; ban—; complete—; delight in—; don—; fancy—; fray—; gather—es; hem—; iron—; long for—; pleat—; shorten—;

stitch—; straighten—; —befits; —clings; —rustles.

(See apparel, attire, gown, frock, clothing.)

DRESS (v)

adverbs

sparsely; impecuniously; exquisitely; ravishingly; punctiliously; fastidiously; extravagantly; flamboyantly; garishly; gaudily; flashily; uninvitingly; smartly; opulently; alluringly; superfluously; tastefully; picturesquely; gorgeously; expensively; impeccably; conservatively; fashionably; resplendently; somberly; foppishly; fantastically; drably; identically; ostentatiously; modestly; primitively; brilliantly; scrupulously; fetchingly; daringly; trimly; immaculately; dishevelledly; ceremonially; ecclesiastically; nondescriptly; distinctively; martially; obsoletely; negligently; rustically; shabbily; gallantly.

(See garb, attire, array.)

DRESSER

adjectives

consummate; flashy; top-notch.

DRESSING

adjectives

elaborate; court; surgical; decongestive; somber; passionate; undisciplined; artificial.

verbs

admire—; apply—; bedeck in—; change—; compliment—; complete—; concoct—; eat with—; occupy with—; prepare—; scrutinize—; serve with—; signal for—; soak through—; soil—; tear off—; wear—; —appeals; —eases; —preserves.

DRESSMAKER

adjectives

domestic; fashionable.

DRIFT

adjectives

pearly; scudding; glacial; pallid; irresistible; wind-swept; fallacious; wordy; imaginative; social; passing; intended; amoral; steaming; feathery; powdery; blinding; treacherous.

DRIFT (v)

adverbs

delightfully; quietly; naturally; casually; waywardly; lazily; smoothly; unconsciously; hopelessly; tranquilly; alternately; irresistibly; indecisively; purposelessly; scuddingly; glacially; fallaciously; blindly.

(See wander, deviate.)

DRIFTER

adjectives
shiftless; disgruntled; utter.

DRIFTWOOD

adjectives
dancing; scattered.

DRILL

adjectives
arduous; painful; sword; emergency; stiff; dusty; grammatical.

DRILL
(*instrument*)

verbs
attach—; man—; power—; sharpen—; sink —; yield to—; —beats out; —bores; — forces; —grinds; —plunges into; —strikes; —uncovers.

(See tool, machine.)

DRINK

adjectives
refreshing; useful; stimulating; seductive; sleepy; sparkling; zestful; hearty; robust; mellow; keen-tasting; acidulous; exhilarating; cooling; thirst-quenching; superb; delicate; delicious; appetizing; nutritious; soothing; innocuous; long-deferred; effervescent; frosty; fermented; hot; heady; tinkling; fiery; stiff; repulsive; steaming; choice; soft; wholesome; excellent; restorative; limpid.

verbs
abandon—; adulterate—; cool—; derive— from; err through—; ferment—; gulp—; ice—; indulge in—; offer—; rage with—; reek of—; regale with—; serve—; sour—; stagger with—; swallow—; thirst for—; —affects; —appeals; —assuages; —debauches; —depraves; —enslaves; —exhilarates; —intoxicates; —nourishes; — quenches; —refreshes; —satiates; —stimulates; —transforms; reel with—.

(See liquid, beverage, liquor, draught.)

DRINK (*v*)

adverbs
abstemiously; excessively; ravenously; plentifully; vilely; greedily; intemperately; copiously; thirstily; systematically; deeply;

convivially; bestially; insatiably; inconsolably; loyally; deliberately; injudiciously.

(See sip, imbibe.)

DRINKER

adjectives
lusty; confirmed; chronic; mean; deadly; fat; unforgivable; suspicious; intemperate; unhealthy; inured; obstinate; problem.

DRINKING

adjectives
conspicuous; hard; excessive; copious; free; easy; constant; injudicious.

DRIP (*v*)

adverbs
monotonously; drearily; steadily; ceaselessly; intermittently; maddeningly; torturingly.

(See drop, fall.)

DRIVE
(*campaign*)

adjectives
(See campaign.)

verbs
abandon—; abate—; captain—; conduct—; deadlock—; forsake—; hail—; inaugurate —; join—; lash into—; launch—; map out —; organize—; stage—; wage.

(See campaign, effort.)

DRIVE
(*general*)

adjectives
fashionable; beautiful; urban; weed-grown; gravel; jolting; scenic; cliff-skirting; magnificent; wood; curving; public; leaf-strewn; coquina; steep; winding; fatal; monster; determined; concentrated; concerted; organizational; solitary; conclusive; oppressive; phenomenal.

DRIVE
(*road*)

adjectives
(See road.)

verbs
amble along—; approach—; bar—; choke —; circle—; clear—; conceal—; crowd—; direct to—; emerge from—; enter—; follow —; gallop along—; hedge—; meet in—; park in—; patrol—; ramble along—; roll

along—; shout from—; skirt—; widen—; zoom into—; —beckons; —circles; —flanks; —winds; —zigzags.
(See road, avenue.)

DRIVE (v)
adverbs
ridiculously; irresponsibly; oppressively; tirelessly; tensely; erratically; heedlessly; blithely; electrically; masterfully; involuntarily; cautiously; leisurely; steadily; briskly; simultaneously; helplessly; tumultuously; precipitately; grimly; drunkenly; ineptly; furiously; irresistibly; contemptuously.
(See impel, propel.)

DRIVEL
adjectives
maudlin; meaningless; puerile; sentimental.

DRIVER
adjectives
addlebrained; grim; recumbent; cruel-visaged; skilled; trusted; insolent; sweating; wretched; reckless; superb; acrobatic; benumbed; drunken; inept; unlicensed.

verbs
apprehend—; blame—; convict—; direct—; employ—; fine—; hire—; jail—; license—; pay—; request—; summon—; tip—; trust —; —charges; —compels; —complies; — hails; —halts; —signals; —urges; arrest—.
(See engineer, operator.)

DRIZZLE
adverbs
driving; steaming; slow; spiritless; early-morning; fine; thick; cold; chill; falling.

DROLL
adverbs
entertainingly; laughably; naturally; racially; endlessly; remarkably; quaintly; oddly; deliciously; marvellously; piquantly; robustly; whimsically; fancifully; fantastically; grotesquely; genially; jeeringly; good-naturedly; spontaneously; chattily; sardonically; delightfully; coarsely; quietly; irrepressibly; irresistibly; playfully; unaccountably; inexhaustibly; effervescently; waggishly; facetiously; outlandishly.

DROLLERY
adjectives
broad; absurd.

DROMEDARY
adjectives
helmless; patient.

DRONE
adjectives
sonorous; teasing; supine; liturgic; stingless; luxurious.

DRONE (v)
adverbs
mechanically; somnolently; sonorously; monotonously; teasingly; maddeningly; dully; stupidly.
(See sound, idle.)

DRONING
adverbs
wearily; endlessly; prosaically; academically; pretentiously; incessantly; languidly; indifferently; leisurely; tiresomely; monotonously; intolerably; insufferably; unbearably; maddeningly; eternally.

DROOP
adjectives
discouraged; affectionate; pensive; pathetic; childish; weary; dissatisfied.

DROOP (v)
adverbs
gloomily; mournfully; cheerlessly; pathetically; languidly; dejectedly; alarmingly; tenderly; visibly; sleepily; pensively; wearily; tremulously.
(See fade, faint.)

DROP
(fall)
adjectives
sickening; sheer.

DROP
(liquid)
adjectives
minute; needle-like; pearly; crystal; myriad (pl); ambrosial; beady; glittering; blistering; infinitesimal; foolish; fresh; morning; congealed; twinkling; priceless; falling; tearful; insolent; bitterest; contiguous; bitter; ruddy; mournful; burning.

verbs
absorb—; add—; administer—; dispense —s; distil in—s; draw off—; drink—; dry —s; exude—; fall in—s; form—; give off —s; instill—s; mix with—s; moisten with —s; prepare—; save—; shed—; shower—; spill—; squeeze—; sweat—; wipe away—s;

—s appear; —s dampen; —s descend; —evaporates; —glitters; —issues from; —s stream from; —wets.
(See moisture.)

DROP (v)
adverbs
miraculously; swiftly; quietly; carelessly; listlessly; gently; significantly; tearfully; alarmingly; methodically; mournfully; lazily; heavily.
(See fall.)

DROPSY
adjectives
(See disease.)

verbs
affect with—; afflict with—; aggravate—; cure—; fall into—; incur—; relieve—; suffer from—; swell with—; treat for—; —appears; —arises; —destroys; —enlarges; —inflates; —overcharges; —pains.
(See disease.)

DROSS
adjectives
(See scum.)

verbs
allow for—; bloat with—; convert from—; dissolve into—; give off—; heap—; leave —; mass—; mix with—; mound—; purge of—; refine—; separate—; scum—; skim off—; —detracts; —floats; —remains.
(See impurity, waste, scum.)

DROUGHT
adjectives
devilish; burning; severe; prolonged; unparalleled; unprecedented; insatiate; scorching; extensive; continued; stagnant; extreme.

verbs
endure—; expose to—; flee—; prepare for —; prevent—; relieve—; subject to—; succumb to—; suffer from—; —burns; —continues; —descends; —destroys; —dries; —grips; —parches; —ravages; —ruins; —scorches; —sears.
(See heat.)

DROVE
adjectives
immense; countless.

DROWNING
verbs
avoid—; bewail—; escape—; guard against —; mark—; rescue from—; —bereaves; —takes its toll.

DROWSE (v)
adverbs
sorrowfully; deliciously; lazily; wearily; carelessly; comfortably; continually.
(See sleep.)

DROWSINESS
adjectives
overwhelming; overpowering; delicious; petulant; slight; bored; morbid.

DROWSY
adverbs
irresistibly; pleasantly; dully; deliciously; overwhelmingly; heavily; comfortably; cosily; warmly; fortunately; suddenly; fitfully; uncomfortably; inconveniently; overpoweringly; fatally; quietly; tranquilly; quietly; restfully; peacefully; drunkenly; pleasingly; mysteriously; startlingly; alarmingly; feverishly; hypnotically; dangerously; constantly; languorously; gradually; imperceptibly; idly; inertly; torpidly; lumpishly; dreamily; wearily.

DRUBBING
adjectives
(See beating.)

verbs
administer—; deserve—; earn—; expect—; impose—; inflict—; merit—; protect from—; punish with—; render—; scream under—; suffer—; threaten with—; undergo—; yield to—; —benefits; —cures.
(See beating.)

DRUDGE
adjectives
weary; household; casual; incessant; faithful; cautious; miserable; sickly; ordinary; domestic.

DRUDGE (v)
adverbs
monotonously; wearily; casually; incessantly; faithfully; miserably; domestically; deadeningly; depressingly; ceaselessly; degradingly; tediously; mechanically; unremittingly; grievously; unendingly; commercially.
(See work, labor.)

DRUDGERY

adjectives

tiresome; deadening; depressing; ceaseless; degrading; low; tedious; mechanical; grievous; unremitting; severest; formal; old-time; unending; initial; youthful; mercenary; pretty.

verbs

charge—to; condemn—; decline—; detail to—; earn by—; employ for—; expose to—; fade under—; fall into—; flee—; heap upon; impose—upon; perform—; punish with—; put to—; release from—; relieve —; require—; subject to—; toil in—; — chokes; —wearies; —wears.

(See toil, work, labor.)

DRUG

adjectives

opiate; antisyphilitic; spicy; ancient; various (pl); somniferous; impotent; fatal; injurious; valuable; convenient; officinal; nerve-exciting; deleterious; evil-smelling; subtle; incompatible; nauseous; diluted; obnoxious; illicit; habit-forming; powerful; futile; sleep-inducing; insidious; pernicious; deadly.

verbs

addict to—; administer—; apply—; diminish—; distribute—; employ—; inhale—; label—; peddle—; prescribe—; purvey—; recommend—; rely on—; saturate with—; smuggle in—; swallow—; traffic in—; treat with—; turn to—; —affects; —aids; — allays; —alleviates; —antidotes; —controls; —heals; —induces; —poisons; —purges; —scours; inject—.

(See narcotic, poison, potion.)

DRUGGED

adverbs

disgustingly; hopelessly; pleasantly; overwhelmingly; heavily; comfortably; overpoweringly; fatally; mysteriously; startlingly; shockingly; alarmingly; dangerously; languorously; gradually; imperceptibly; inertly; dreamily; injuriously; subtly; insidiously; wickedly; inhumanly; habitually; incidentally; accidentally; deliberately; cruelly.

DRUM

adjectives

deafening; rolling; cask-like; sullen; insistent; furious; sardonic; deep-throated; bellowing; exploding; jarring; perpetual; droning; boisterous; revolving; muffled; recruiting; thumping; unbraced; churlish; distant; weird; rattling; repeating; monotonous.

verbs

belabor—; hearken to—; muffle—; rattle—; sound—; strike up—; thump—; —beats; — booms; —murmurs; —rolls; —stirs; — thunders; —warns; —welcomes.

DRUM (v)

adverbs

fretfully; vigorously; deafeningly; sullenly; insistently; furiously; jarringly; perpetually; droningly; muffledly; thumpingly; weirdly; monotonously.

(See beat, pound.)

DRUMBEAT

adjectives

furious; rapid; swift; staccato; far-off.

DRUMSTICK

verbs

accept—; approve of—; beat with—; bless with—; covet—; dress—; examine—; eye —; favor—; pick at—; regard—; reject—; relish—; request—; select—; squabble for —; —appeals; —appeases; —attracts.

(See meat, food.)

DRUNK

adverbs

comically; gloriously; jovially; convivially; pleasantly; beastly; soddenly; happily; deliciously; unconsciously; heartily; vacuously; fatuously; ribaldly; funnily; smartly; deeply; sleepily; drowsily; tragically; helplessly; hopelessly; terribly; utterly; desperately; dangerously; fantastically; grotesquely; palpably; morosely; glumly; woefully; mournfully; lovingly; ridiculously; ludicrously; lamentably; deplorably; pitifully; truculently; quarrelsomely; amiably; magnificently; obnoxiously; furiously; boisterously; outrageously; noisily; chattily; dizzily.

DRUNKARD

adjectives

heavy; cursing; quarrelsome; hopeless; confirmed; amiable; uncouth; magnificent; congenital; half-stupefied; reformed; infatuated; habitual; unproductive; swinish; incorrigible; abandoned.

verbs

abhor—; apprehend—; commit—to; confine—; cure—; direct—; humor—; incense

—; lock up—; perplex—; punish—; steady —; stupefy—; treat—; —assails; —disturbs; —partakes; —raves; —reels; —revels; —shocks; —staggers; —teeters; —totters; —wavers.

DRUNKENNESS

adjectives
habitual; seasonal; babbling; intemperate; usual; perpetual; rash.

verbs
abuse in—; addict to—; chain in—; cure—; denounce—; extirpate—; feign—; frown on—; imbibe to—; overcome by—; prevent —; saturate into—; seize by—; simulate—; soak into—; treat for—; yield to—; —appalls; —destroys; —envelops; —harms.

DRY

adverbs
terribly; painfully; horribly; intolerably; unbearably; unprofitably; unproductively; treelessly; dustily; torridly; hopelessly; desperately; heartbreakingly; destructively; insupportably; feverishly; parchedly.

DRYNESS

adjectives
unhealthful; satirical; extreme; intolerable.

DUALITY

adjectives
antagonistic; apparent; incredulous; baffling; unbelievable; inescapable.

DUBIOUS

adverbs
momentarily; strangely; horribly; anxiously; painfully; oddly; ominously; curiously; embarrassingly; remarkably; terribly; openly; dreadfully; frightfully; vaguely; frankly; obscurely.

DUCK

adjectives
iridescent; gabbling.

verbs
—beats water; —dives; —quacks; —rests on the water; —wings; —whirls past; —whirs.
(See fowl, bird.)

DUCT

adjectives
non-functional; necessary; essential; much-used.

verbs
discover—; draw through—; follow—; form—; introduce—; mark—; meet—; observe—; pass through—; perfect—; retreat through—; tap—; —communicates; —contains; —conveys; —directs; —dispatches; —guides; —runs; —secretes; —transmits; —turns.
(See passage, canal, conduit, pipe, channel.)

DUE

adverbs
legally; officially; naturally; recently; inescapably; conveniently; properly; justly; fairly; rightfully; reasonably; warrantably; legitimately; indefeasibly; allowably; equitably; substantially; imperatively; morally; immediately; opportunely; unexpectedly.

DUEL

adjectives
single-handed; mortal; formidable; celebrated; straight-out; valiant; political; judicial; desperate; inevitable; fatal; violent; informal; impromptu; bloody; spectacular; protracted; farcical; grudging; grim; solemn; honor-prompted.

verbs
arrange—; challenge to—; demand—; enter —; excuse from—; fight—; practise for—; stab in—; succumb in—; vanquish in—; witness—; —acquits; —decides; —discharges; —ensues; —entrances; —scars; —settles; —tests.
(See combat, encounter.)

DUES

adjectives
ecclesiastical; ample; usual.

DUET

adjectives
lively; little; long; thrilling; sentimental.

DUGOUT

adjectives
primitive; shallow; damp; foul-smelling; wartime; protective.

DUKE

adjectives
gracious; mighty; renowned; comical; fierce; noble; worthless; compassionate; virtuous; fantastical; banished; necessitous; covetous.

DULL

adverbs
abysmally; indifferently; insensitively; stupidly; strangely; stolidly; apathetically; vacantly; vacuously; ridiculously; unnaturally; singularly; oddly; peculiarly; curiously; unaccountably; inscrutably; irritatingly; vexatiously; shockingly; callously; coldly; carelessly; hopelessly; unpardonably; inexplicably; intolerably; heavily.

DULLNESS

adjectives
mysterious; pardonable; intolerable; tired; heavy; lonely; narrow; legitimate; ungenial; unbelievable; desperate; utter; everyday; kindly; incipient; vacant.

verbs
bar—; consign to—; contemplate—; correct —; curse—; dread—; mark by—; possess —; ridicule—; shroud in—; stagnate in—; tolerate—; —bores; —castigates; —distresses; —endangers; —irks; —maddens; —overwhelms; —pervades; —provokes; —surrounds.
(See apathy.)

DUMB

adverbs
pathetically; tragically; completely; suddenly; abysmally; wondrously; amazingly; stupidly; breathlessly; surprisingly; mysteriously; unutterably; wordlessly; silently; reticently; inarticulately; voicelessly; inexplicably.

DUMPY

adverbs
ridiculously; sturdily; robustly; clumsily; ludicrously; grotesquely; strangely; oddly; peculiarly; dwarfishly; elfishly; compactly; stubbily; stockily; outlandishly; comically; tragically; curiously; unfortunately; brawnily; stalwartly; stoutly.

DUNES

adjectives
darkened; shifting; lonely; sea-cast; high; tufted; transverse; desolate; shadowy; sandy; blistering; roasting; waterless; uninhabitable.

DUNGEON

adjectives
airless; subterranean; underground; miserable; bleak; awful; villainous; pagan; priestly; gloomy.

verbs
air—; bind in—; burst—; cast into—; clap into—; commit to—; conceal in—; confine to—; doom to—; dwell in—; escape from —; fling to—; gather in—; guard—; hide in—; imprison in—; incarcerate in—; lock in—; mold in—; rescue from—; rot in—; solace in—; storm—; —harbors; —incarcerates; —reeks.
(See cell, prison, hole.)

DUPE

adjectives
confiding; fair; penitent; innocent; credulous; intended; egregious.

DUPLICATE

adjectives
original; reversed.

verbs
appear in—; deliver—; encounter—; enter —; file—; furnish—; grant—; order—; part with—; provide—; purchase—; reserve—; retain—; save—; send—; sign—; supply—; take in—; transfer—; transmit—; void—; —copies; —repeats.
(See copy, replica.)

DUPLICITY

adjectives
infinite; twofold; unconscious; unworthy; patent; obvious.

DURABILITY

adjectives
utmost; increasing.

DURATION

adjectives
blooming; indefinite; customary; variable; perpetual; uncertain; momentary; endless; irregular; probable; limitless; comprehensible.

verbs
allow for—; calculate—; depend on—; fade in—; forbid—; grant—; limit—; mark—; pass—; portion—; prepare for—; propose —; time—; —continues; —lasts, —restricts; —suffices; —terminates.
(See period, time, era.)

DUSK

adjectives
growing; premature; eternal; grateful; gathering; friendly; mournful; dolorous; rainy; wet; winter; moonlit; thickening; deepening; early; glittering; clear; whis-

pering; soft; sweet; mellow; warm; humid; cool; softening; glimmering; green; deep; blue; moon-silvered; breathing.

verbs
diminish in—; dip in—; grope through—; haunt—; retire at—; wait for—; —clouds; —descends; —drifts in; —dulls; —gives away; —harbors; —hovers; —obscures; —reveals; —shades; —shadows; —swallows; —thickens; —treads.
(See twilight, evening, darkness.)

DUSKY

adverbs
prematurely; eternally; mournfully; thickly; softly; sweetly; deeply; dimly; inkily; sombrely; dingily; murkily; obscurely; nebulously; gloomily; glimmeringly; fragrantly; weirdly; fearfully; frightfully; pleasantly; restfully; peacefully; shadily; coolly; drearily; forlornly; desolately.

DUST

adjectives
cosmic; yellow; shining; fainting; dying; trifling; impalpable; valiant; undisturbed; shapeless; dreadful; sodden; titillating; red; desert; thick; blue; gray; heavy; blinding; oppressive; choking; stagnant; siliceous; shameful; trodden; dedicated; honored; long-committed; animate; fine; staining; unlovely; lonely; garnered; historical; rolling; scentless; murderous; material; injurious; sleeping; brown-colored; leveled; sunny; sunlit; suffering; kindred; burning; dim; scanty; feathery; illumined; senseless; slumbering; delicate; sacred; tawny; crumbling; vile; powdered; invisible; atomic; whirling; torturing; atmospheric; spiraling; hatred; stirred; gritty; smelly; filthy; parched; wayside; pervading; dissipating; mounting; precious; learned; flaming; uncontrolled; floating; undivided.

verbs
beat—; cake with—; carpet with—; clot with—; clothe in—; crumble to—; decompose into—; drag down to—; fall into—; filter—; form into—; go down in—; grovel in—; impregnate with—; issue from—; kick up—; lift from—; mar with—; mix with—; moulder in—; parch with—; reduce to—; remand to—; repose in—; return to—; roll in—; scatter—; scrape off—; scuff through—; shake off—; shower—; smite—; soil with—; spring from—; stamp —; stir up—; trail in—; tread in—; turn to—; write in—; —beclouds; —chokes; —clings to; —creeps in; —gathers; —permeates; —settles; —shrouds; —thickens.
(See ashes, powder, rubbish, earth.)

DUST (v)

adverbs
furiously; animatedly; industriously; vigorously; listlessly.
(See clean, polish.)

DUSTY

adverbs
disagreeably; intolerably; parchedly; painfully; uncomfortably; impalpably; dreadfully; terribly; abominably; unbearably; heavily; blindingly; oppressively; chokingly; shamefully; vilely; grittily; hatefully; filthily; pervasively; untidily; grossly; carelessly.

DUTIFUL

adverbs
carefully; beautifully; painfully; meticulously; punctiliously; assiduously; ostentatiously; passionately; pretentiously; obviously; scrupulously; devotedly; affectionately; primly; precisely; constantly; marvellously; sternly; officiously; efficiently; terribly; actively; energetically; publicly; submissively; competently; anxiously; solicitously; respectfully; politely; courteously; austerely; diplomatically; mechanically; grimly; piously; dully; rigorously; odiously; fondly; constantly; unfailingly.

DUTY

adjectives
irksome; self-assumed; unpleasant; imperative; simple; stern; domestic; humanest; arduous; boring; differential; obnoxious; official; expedient; obvious; religious; paternal; stooping; manifold (pl); bounden; inescapable; unending; inefficient; inviolable; particular; useful; terrible; serious; wide-reaching; unloved; indispensable; colorless; ever-esteemed; active; humbler; costuming; civic; social; pedagogic; creative; vexatious; nerve-racking; constitutional; public; appropriate; disagreeable; sad; monotonous; weary; dangerous; exhausting; exacting; uncongenial; painful; respective; definite; foolish; routine; submissive; competent; obstructionary; forcible; hardest; responsible; laborious; barbarous; conjugal; onerous; anxious; sickening; perilous; special; competent; childlike;

charitable; additional; ministerial; necessary; paramount; rental; far-off; pleasurable; professorial; momentous; military; eternal; vile; devotional; peremptory; respectful; easy; polite; generous; melancholy; intimate; principal; filial; unforgotten; imperious; eventual; matutinal; major; discriminating; blockading; wifely; incumbent; austere; consular; immediate; habitual; noble; irresistible; sworn; diplomatic; protective; distasteful; lowliest; fearful; unfamiliar; mechanical; tyrannous; slothful; solemn; earthly; grim; cursed; dull; high; pious; repugnant; homely; harsh; unhappy; rigorous; derelict; multifarious (pl); stern-voiced; nebulous; odious; manifest; tripartite.

verbs

assign—; assume—; attend to—; charge with—; comply with—; consign—to; define —; discharge—; disengage from—; encroach on—; engross in—; fail in—; fulfill—; impose—on; inculcate—; infringe on—; lessen—; meet—; neglect—; obey—; perform—; perish in—; pledge to—; pursue—; relieve of—; repudiate—; restrain by—; scrap—; shirk—; shoulder—; slacken in—; stand firm on—; stress—; surrender —; swerve from—; teach—; transgress—; —allows; —binds; —embraces; —enjoins; —impels; —inspires; —permits; —presses; —pricks on; —slackens; —weighs.

(See responsibility, business, work, obligation. function.)

DWARF
adjectives
deformed; rickety; stirring.

verbs
employ—; engage—; harbor—; gift—with; jeer at—; ridicule—; —antics; —busies; —carries off; —chuckles; —climbs; — covers; —dances; —hobbles; —hops; — mimics; —performs; —prances; —struts.
(See animal, manikin, clown.)

DWARFED
adverbs
hopelessly; mysteriously; grotesquely; fantastically; irremediably; unhappily; unfortunately; unluckily; singularly; oddly; strangely; queerly; sturdily; clumsily; elfishly; compactly; stockily; outlandishly; tragically; curiously; stalwartly; stoutly; pathetically; pitifully.

DWELL (v)
adverbs
luxuriously; languidly; pleasurably; laughingly; principally; impatiently; spaciously; lingeringly; occasionally; affectionately; impecuniously; inharmoniously; eternally; gloomily; artfully; gratefully; royally; unostentatiously; sedately; uncouthly; dismally; humbly; indefinitely.
(See live, abide.)

DWELLER
adjectives
dullest; admirable; planned; distinguished.

DWELLING
adjectives
planned; steadfast; isolated; ancestral; royal; prolonged; primitive; pretentious; ancient; snow-enveloped; forgetful; undisturbed; clustered; rustic; unostentatious; habitable; rapturous; odorous; sedate; time-stained; ambitious; tranquil; dismantled; rambling; uncouth; dismal; neglected; blank; underground; graceful; comfortable; humblest; stately; lovely; impressive; obscure; fabulous; patriarchal; communal; quaint; red-tiled; lacustrine; frail; abandoned.

verbs
assign to—; choose—; confine to—; decorate—; destroy—; enter—; erect—; fire—; flood—; grace—; lay waste—; move into—; occupy—; preserve—; purchase—; raze—; renovate—; restore—; retire to—; return to—; surround—; ventilate—; —appeals; —crumbles; —harbors; —invites; —shelters.
(See house, residence, abode.)

DWINDLE (v)
adverbs
amazingly; alarmingly; partially; insensibly; rapidly; markedly; obviously; scarcely; abruptly; logically; tragically; fatally.
(See decrease, diminish.)

DYE
adjectives
angry; synthetic; crimson; vegetable; progressive; autumnal.

DYNAMIC
adverbs
admirably; energetically; responsibly; socially; fortunately; acceptably; helpfully; usefully; stimulatingly; interestingly; actively; progressively; commercially; powerfully; effectively; efficiently; mightily.

400

DYNAMITE

adjectives

potential; swift; powerful.

verbs

arm with—; attack with—; blast with—; charge with—; contain—; convert into—; employ—; experiment with—; fire—; ignite —; mine with—; prepare—; shell—; test —; touch off—; —blasts; —blows up; — damages; —destroys; —disrupts; —explodes; —rends; —shakes; —shatters; — threatens; —uproots; —wrecks.

(See explosive, powder.)

DYNAMO

adjectives

(See motor.)

verbs

acquaint with—; employ—; examine—; exhibit—; operate—; provide—; ruin—; study—; —aids; —converts; —deposits; —excites; —generates; —induces; —purrs; —revolves; —rotates; —supplies; —transforms.

(See machine, generator, motor.)

DYNASTY

adjectives

reigning; unoffending; remote; trembling; continuous; unbroken; imperial; semifeudal.

verbs

begin—; carry on—; cut short—; denounce —; found—; inaugurate—; maintain—; overthrow—; perpetuate—; rear—; —declines; —rules; —stems.

(See race, government, sovereignty.)

E

adverbs

extremely; youthfully; girlishly; boyishly; childishly; unspeakably; inordinately; suspiciously; significantly; admirably; wonderfully; industriously; energetically; actively; alarmingly; adorably; ardently; fervidly.

EAGERNESS

adjectives

apologetic; utmost; excessive; passionate; extraordinary; manifest; restrained; childish; youthful; intelligent; dashing; sheer; liberal; hasty; hawk-eyed; feverish; fatal; diffident; fresh.

verbs

burn with—; conceal—; cure of—; display —; impart—; incite—; instil—; intensify —; moderate—; possess—; pursue with—; resist—; satiate—; stimulate—; temper—; —irritates; —devours; —exasperates; — maddens; —vexes.

(See impatience, fervor, intensity, zeal, ardor, impetuosity.)

EAGLE

adjectives

ravening; screaming; conquering; stuffed; rampant; princely; soaring; immense; gilded; empty; famished; symbolical; home-building.

verbs

cage—; exalt—; shelter—; —attacks; — braves; —captures; —circles; —clasps; — cleaves sky; —climbs; —destroys; —drives home; —drops; —eyes; —falls; —floats; — hawks; —hooks; —inspires; —moults; — preys on; —robs; —sails; —screams; — sights; —signifies; —soars; —surveys; — sweeps; —swoops; —symbolizes; —terrorizes; —thieves; —watches; —wheels; — zooms.

(See bird.)

EAR

adjectives

sensual; perked; dull; deaf; dozing; treacherous; attentive; unconscious; reasonable; good; licentious; thrifty; unheeding; help-less; eager; attending; sickly; pregnant; vouchsafed; kindest; external; deafened; listless; acute; greedy; reluctant; quick; sympathetic; large; cultivated; sensitive; passionate; gentler; foreboding; practiced; tesselated; apprehensive; furry; blushing; thievish; instinctive; loathing; listening; flapping; velvet; pleased; willing; public; sweet; enthusiastic; charmed; pendulous; living; dreaming; gorgeous; lobe-shaped; bewitched; trembling; ravished; waiting; dying; married; sickly; savage; aged; favorable; idle; insensible; untutored; modest; patient; inner; general; outwearied; kissed; fortified; fancy; inquisitive; royal; expectant; shuddering; reeling; mortal; unaccustomed; thoughtful; startled; proper; uninitiated; astonished; raptured; erect; impaired; innumerable (pl); flat; ill-developed; silken; uncultivated; ample; honest; grateful; aching; middle; cupped; drooping; constant; wakeful; sealed; vexed; burning; haughty; world; unwearied; uneducated; pointed; fainting; lewd; startled; straining; close-lying; public; couchant; senseless; inaudible; sylvan; favorable; leaning; hooded; untaught; silky; delicate; close-set; dainty; fine; gracious; velvety; well-set; quick; exact; sharp; critical; appreciative; alert; keen; cocked; intent; vigilant; cabbage; flabby; cauliflower; prominent; angular; preposterous; bruised; ungladdened; thick; long-lobed; enormous; stiff; droll; outstanding; uncomprehending; unattuned; unresponsive; cynical; inhospitable; unfailing; musical; irritated; entranced; thrilled; welcoming; delighted; shell-like; modern; royal; jeweled; ringing; jaunty; aloof; gullible; frisky; unjaded; well-trained; wiggly; tweaked; pert; questioning; hopeful.

verbs

abuse—; attune—to; beat against—; bend —; block—; box—; charm—; cleanse—; cock—; crop off—; deceive—; delight—; depend on—; din into—; drain—; dull—; gain—; impart to—; incline—; insert in—; irrigate—; lend—; lodge in—; meet—; muffle—; mutilate—; prick—forward; rend —; resound in—; strike—; twitch—; weary —; whisper in—; wiggle—; —s betray; —s buzz; —s devour; —discharges; —rings; —throbs; —tingles; stuff—.

(See head, ear-drum.)

EAR-DRUM

verbs

affect—; attack—; burst—; fall upon—; incise—; infect—; inflame—; injure—; meet—; perforate—; pierce—; rupture—; shatter—; split—; strike—; stun—; treat—; wound—; —admits; —pains; —protects; —vibrates.

(See membrane, ear.)

EARLY

adverbs

unusually; exceptionally; conveniently; amply; unnecessarily; remarkably; uncomfortably; unpleasantly; gloriously; appropriately; sufficiently; ridiculously; needlessly; opportunely; comfortably.

EARN (v)

adverbs

professionally; determinedly; lawfully; honestly; criminally; astoundingly; rapidly; drudgingly.

(See gain, procure.)

EARNEST

adverbs

enthusiastically; seriously; unusually; truly; zealously; fervently; ridiculously; habitually; eagerly; graciously; cordially; resolutely; desperately; tenaciously; inflexibly; unusually; extremely; gravely; solemnly; remarkably; indubitably; incredibly; emphatically; heartily; passionately; deeply.

EARNESTNESS

adjectives

simple; fixed; grave; intense; eager; conscientious; impressive; tragic; passionate; beseeching; aggressive; perpetual; burning; profound; characteristic; devout; somber; cold; honest; forgetful; dogged; taciturn; habitual; mighty; sanctified; mournful; solemn; downright; visible.

verbs

adopt—; allege—; begin with—; conduct with—; declare in—; endeavor with—; enter in—; express—; feign—; inculcate—; indicate—; instil—; pledge—; supplicate with—; touch by—; watch with—; —recommends; —secures.

(See ardor, sincerity, seriousness.)

EARNINGS

adjectives

scanty; exiguous; individual; fabulous; present; undistributed; sky-rocketed; hard-won; slender; stabilized.

EAR-PHONE

verbs

attach—; bag—; bank—; collect—; curtail—; demand—; distribute—; enhance—; increase—; invest—; merit—; mortgage—; pledge—; save—; withdraw—; withhold—; —accrue; —decline; —recompense; —top.

(See wage, salary, pay.)

EAR-PHONE

verbs

adjust—; clamp on—; display—; furnish—; mislay—; pick up with—; require—; seek—; speak into—; —aids; —amplifies; —assists; —benefits; —clarifies; —communicates; —relieves; —rescues.

EARTH

adjectives

social; fructifying; plashy; stony; melancholy; calcareous; sunburned; verdant; daedal; thirsty; kindly; unviolated; groaning; fragrant; porous; frozen; transformed; sullen; gloomy; arching; molten; voluble; gaping; laboring; green-girt; hostile; distraught; disembowelled; chapped; unconsidered; spherical; moist; gaunt; wounded; awakening; bare; native; spongy; gladdened; powdered; delightful; frostbound; renovated; shocked; shackled; perennial; messy; reconciling; nursing; synthetic; dull; prosaic; barren; despised; hungry; sanguine; encumbering; clodded; faithless; unawakened; arid; pendulous; easeful; wearied; sun-spangled; unyielding; virgin; mangled; filial; consecrated; turfless; frost-crisped; horrible; ancient; parched; sordid; absorbent; unmoistened; alluvial; stagnant; troubled; patient; various-mingled (pl); sinful; profiting; beleaguered; teeming; life-giving; habitable; darkened; spacious; healthy; odorous; unsinning; narrowing; menaced; lawful; burying; beauteous; faded; deep; peopled; trembling; desolate; indubitable; sleepy; bright; red; ashy; black; devastated; ordinary; shaken; fresh-turned; primeval; tenacious; widened; savage; fainting; fresh-plowed; chafed; harsh; central; pleasant; reluctant; silvery; waiting; finished; substantial; ridgy; imminent.

verbs

beautify—; blast—; bless—; bore into—; cling to—; command—; crawl upon—; create—; creep upon—; deface—; depart from —; explore—; fertilize—; gain—; grovel on—; inhabit—; inherit—; landscape—; mantle—; paw—; perish from—; plant—; plow—; pluck from—; rake—; reign on—;

replenish—; return to—; scatter over—; scorch—; scour—; sink into—; swoop to—; till—; tramp over—; trample—; veil—; wrestle with—; —abounds with; —blooms; —flowers; —heaves; —moulders; —nourishes; —quakes; —revolves; —sustains; — swallows up; —teems; —throbs; —trembles; —whirls; —renews.

(See world, globe, ground, soil, land.)

EARTHLY

adverbs

sordidly; selfishly; meanly; mercenarily; ungenerously; temperamentally; habitually; gracelessly; incredibly; basely; grossly; inconceivably.

EARTHQUAKE

adjectives

unusual; slumbering; murderous; all-devouring; disastrous; tremendous; submarine.

verbs

behold—; flee from—; record—; warn of—; —blights; —blots out; —crumbles; —destroys; —devastates; —jars; —razes; — reduces; —rends; —ruins; —rumbles; — shakes; —shatters; —subsides; —takes toll; —thunders; —topples; —wrecks.

(See tremor, shock, vibration.)

EASE

adjectives

amateur; blessed; ignoble; rakish; natural; light-hearted; tolerable; considerable; somnolent; charming; comparative; consequent; luxurious; extraordinary; miraculous; frivolous; insidious; rhythmic; dreamy; muscular; dignified; stately; material; solid; democratic; loose; astonishing; affluent; slothful; masterly; bloodless; constant; reckless; beauteous; cross-legged; disastrous; inglorious; cool; chivalric; deceptive; apparent; corrective; extreme; graceful; tranquil.

verbs

couch at—; court—; dwell in—; enhance—; enjoy—; envy—; interpose—; lack—; leap with—; live at—; loll in—; perform with—; procure with—; recline in—; rest at—; sacrifice—; seek—; spend in—; vault with—.

(See comfort, luxury.)

EASE (v)

adverbs

appreciably; greatly; partially; materially; markedly; miraculously; apparently; ostensibly; gracefully.

(See alleviate, soothe.)

EAST

adjectives

blustering; incandescent; lucid; purpling; blushing; blank; mummied; eyeless; fervid; mournful; bloodless.

EASY

adverbs

unusually; incredibly; remarkably; ridiculously; perfectly; comfortably; fairly; distinctly; definitely; naturally; conveniently; absolutely; suspiciously; unquestionably.

EAT (v)

adverbs

inordinately; leisurely; fastidiously; barbarously; enormously; bestially; heartily; regularly; hurriedly; swiftly; wolfishly; insufficiently; ravenously; incontinently; excessively; sparingly; plentifully; noisily; irrevocably; surreptitiously; swinishly; gluttonously.

(See consume, devour.)

EATABLE

adverbs

safely; deliciously; lusciously; definitely; perfectly; conveniently; unquestionably; wholesomely; avowedly; warrantably; assuredly; properly.

EATING

adjectives

mass; impudent.

verbs

abstain from—; coax into—; consider—; consume in—; exhaust by—; forbid—; reduce—; refrain from—; stimulate—; —appeases; —benefits; —bolsters; —encourages; —exhilarates; —fattens; —nourishes; —produces; —reassures; —revives; —satiates.

(See food, feeding.)

EAVES

adjectives

overhanging; lofty; dripping; gargoyled; sheltering.

adjectives
reduced; constant; alternate.

EBB (v)
adverbs
constantly; alternately; markedly; noticeably; scarcely; partially; wholly; entirely; slowly; tragically; fatally; rapidly.
(See flow, 'move.)

EBONY
adjectives
grizzled; flowing.

EBULLIENT
adverbs
effervescently; gushingly; violently; hysterically; outrageously; turbulently; riotously; obstreperously; naturally; excitedly; stormily; ungovernably; uncontrollably; terribly; highly.

EBULLITION
adjectives
youthful; sulphurous; trifling; present.

ECCENTRIC
adjectives
genial; amazing.

adverbs
highly; outlandishly; ostentatiously; fantastically; oddly; offensively; incurably; proudly; flagrantly; peculiarly; inexplicably; inscrutably; temperamentally; egotistically; exasperatingly; comically; pitiably; unfortunately; abnormally; wantonly; singularly; unaccountably; extravagantly; insanely; capriciously; whimsically; uncomfortably; unusually.

ECCENTRICITY
adjectives
gentle; hopeless; individual; amiable; violent; drunken; troublesome; benevolent; ghastly; moderate; asinine.

verbs
acquire—; adopt—; affect—; allow—; attribute to—; betray—; blame on—; condemn—; develop—; feign—; govern—; laugh at—; mimic—; overlook—; palliate —; pardon—; produce—; ridicule—; sense —; stray into—; tolerate—; —amuses; —offends; —perplexes.
(See oddity, idiosyncrasy.)

adverbs
highly; completely; sacredly; judicially; lawfully; legally; reverently; strictly; soundly; literally; evangelically; faithfully; positively; infallibly; irrefutably; dogmatically; authoritatively; doctrinally; authentically; officiously; reverently; fanatically; deeply; devoutly.

ECHO
adjectives
death-groan; congenial; sonorous; eternal; faint; stunning; distorted; awaking; heartbreaking; softened; jovial; dreary; drumming; startling; sullen; melodious; unimpressive; woodland; respectable; evasive; sparse; prophetic; sharp; metallic; trashy; reverberating; resonant; hovering; wearisome; laughing; ringing; deep-resounding; high; multiplied; somnolent; battling; vibrant; obedient; mad; bellowing; wheezing; wild; tragic; mocking; haunting; silvery; reminiscent; trembling; slumbering.

verbs
evoke—; listen for—; prolong—; silence—; stir—; voice—; —answers; —breaks; — dies away; —fades; —hurls back; —repeats; —resounds; —returns; —reverberates; —rings; —roars; —shrills; —sings out.
(See sound, voice.)

ECHO (v)
adverbs
buoyantly; contemptuously; piously; responsively; cheerily; ominously; dubiously; joyously; anxiously; heartily; falteringly; stupidly; congenially; sonorously; faintly; heartbreakingly; jovially; drearily; sullenly; melodiously; evasively; prophetically; metallically; reverberatingly; wearisomely; ringingly; vibrantly; obediently; hauntingly; mockingly; reminiscently; tremblingly.
(See reverberate, resound.)

ECLIPSE
adjectives
mysterious; swift; dismal; temporary; absolute; ominous.

verbs
identify—; observe—; predict—; record—; study—; suffer—; throw into—; —blinds; —cloaks; —clouds; —darkens; —deprives; —dims; —extinguishes; —hides; —intercepts; —intervenes; —obscures; —occurs; —overcasts; —screens; —shadows.
(See darkness.)

ECLIPSE (v)

adverbs

exultantly; mysteriously; swiftly; dismally; temporarily; absolutely; ominously; skillfully; treacherously; eventually; partially; entirely; scarcely; finally; triumphantly.

(See surpass, excel.)

ECONOMICAL

adverbs

properly; methodically; systematically; carefully; frugally; stingingly; successfully; highly; overly; habitually; admirably; utterly; wonderfully; remarkably; pitifully; practically; shrewdly; thriftily; parsimoniously; selfishly; unnecessarily; shabbily; ungenerously; sordidly; miserably; necessarily; wisely; cheerfully; churlishly.

ECONOMICS

verbs

affect—; alter—; apply—; attack—; control—; deal with—; determine—; devote to—; employ—; experiment with—; govern —; improve—; manage by—; observe—; regulate—; school in—; specialize in—; understand—; —assumes; —discerns; —flourishes; —regards; —serves.

(See science.)

ECONOMIST

adjectives

professional; orthodox; political; academic.

ECONOMY

adjectives

vulnerable; rugged; centralized; reasonable; regimental; actual; domestic; scrupulous; excessive; benign; solitary; desperate; smooth-running; careful; ultimate; numerous (pl); political; drastic; niggardly; expensive; operating; utmost; satisfying; random; ready; careful; capitalistic; animal; internal; democratic; rigid; spiritual; unequalled; household; strictest; outstanding; supernatural; gasoline; false; agricultural; physical.

verbs

betray—; decree—; denounce—; disparage —; effect—; encourage—; favor—; hail—; ignore—; instil—; maintain—; necessitate —; observe—; plan—; practise—; promote—; require—; sacrifice—; systemize—; tighten—; undertake—s; —assures; —preserves; —saves.

(See management, frugality, thrift.)

ECSTASY

adjectives

sheer; delicate; mounting; artistic; tingling; silent; trembling; insane; voluble; bedazzled; boundless; untaught; brainless; anguished; mingled; delicious; spiritual; quiet; simulated; inexpressible; wonderful; unquestioned; consuming; momentary; wonderful; gentle; heaven-breathed; stolen; spontaneous; restless; modern; awed; undivided.

verbs

blast—; blunt—; burst into—; emerge from —; enthrall in—; experience—; flow in—; flutter in—; glow with—; increase—; indulge in—; inspire—; quiver with—; recall in—; respond to—; swoon in—; throw into —; tingle in—; transport into—; tremble with—; wake to—; —dissolves; —excites; —flushes; —pervades; —pulsates; —rules; —stirs.

(See bliss, happiness, delight, rapture, joy, enthusiasm.)

ECSTATIC

adverbs

rapturously; happily; unrestrainedly; blissfully; youthfully; blessedly; delightfully; extravagantly; preposterously; romantically; enthusiastically; fervently; eagerly; passionately; deeply; thrillingly; breathlessly; glowingly; hysterically; significantly; obviously; charmingly; ravishingly.

ECZEMA

verbs

exude from—; pick at—; rub—; salve—; suffer from—; treat—; x-ray—; —burns; —cracks; —discharges; —excretes; —inflames; —irritates; —itches; —pains; —smarts; —spreads; —stings; —tingles; —torments.

(See disease.)

EDDY

adjectives

whirling; murmuring; brilliant; wild; twisting; nervous; blue; boiling; curled; dimpling.

EDDY (v)

adverbs

irresistibly; whirlingly; murmuringly; wildly; twistingly; boilingly; dimplingly; ceaselessly; monotonously; dangerously; rapidly; sickeningly.

(See whirl, swirl.)

EDGE

adjectives

shadowed; sharpened; upturned; natural; outermost; foaming; thin; extremest; trembling; distinctive; cord; jutting; keen; cruel; marshy; raveled; cutting; frayed; frowsy; smooth-quarried; relentless; perilous.

verbs

bevel—; blunt—; crimp—; double—; drive to—; dull—; escape—; file—; flounder on—; heave over—; round—; set on—; sharpen—; slip from—; smite with—; smooth—.

(See border, verge, boundary.)

EDIBLE

adverbs

safely; undeniably; deliciously; lusciously; wholesomely; healthfully; delightfully; warrantably; refreshingly; daintily; agreeably; palatably; pleasantly; acceptably; appetizingly; definitely; highly.

EDICT

adjectives

late; strict; fearful; imperial; royal.

verbs

decry—; denounce—; enforce—; frame—; fulfill—; impose—; infringe on—; introduce —; invalidate—; issue—; legalize—; nullify—; proclaim—; revoke—; spurn—; support—; —bans; —corrects; —declares; —reforms; —stands; —subjugates.

(See decree, mandate, proclamation, ordinance.)

EDIFICATION

verbs

break down—; contribute to—; contrive—; demolish—; destroy—; dismantle—; dispense—; inspire—; justify—; profane—; promote—; prompt—; provide—; ravage—; ruin—; scoff at—; deserve—.

(See enlightenment, education, instruction, improvement.)

EDIFICE

adjectives

gaunt; holy; ramshackle; massive; timeworn; solid; sumptuous; humble; sacred; ghostly; enchanted; shattered; spiritual; historic; august; vast; splendid; stately; public; imposing; spacious; social; heathen; elaborate; ecclesiastical.

verbs

convert—; demolish—; destroy—; dismantle —; erect—; modernize—; profane—; raise —; ravage—; raze—; renovate—; ruin—; —collapses; —crumbles; —moulders; —topples.

(See building, structure, house.)

EDIT (v)

adverbs

skillfully; artfully; exquisitely; originally; hastily; voluminously; sympathetically; crudely.

(See prepare, check.)

EDITION

adjectives

revised; voluminous; choice; camouflaged; pirated; limited; reprint; enormous; successive (pl); telescoped; exquisite; lavish; rare; illustrated; muggier; original; ornamented; annotated; abridged; cherished; privately-printed.

verbs

amend—; annotate—; arrange into—; change—; collect—s; conceive—; copyright —; correct—; criticize—; examine—; exhaust—; favor—; furnish—; illustrate—; issue—; mend—; order—; prepare—; print —; publish—; quote from—; revise—; —abounds with; —corrects; —informs; —surpasses.

(See issue, work, book, publication, copy.)

EDITOR

adjectives

vituperative; country; important; cable-desk; guileless; pugnacious.

verbs

consult—; employ—; —arranges; —conceives; —condemns; —conducts; —criticizes; —describes; —details; —exposes; —expunges; —inserts; —manages; —pens; —plans; —prepares; —publishes; —refuses; —relates; —revises; —scorns; —selects; —suggests; —supervises.

(See journalist, publisher.)

EDITORIAL

adjectives

conspicuous; calumnious; rousing; occasional; learned; rattling; fearless.

verbs

censor—; commend—; compose—; contribute—; criticize—; grind out—; popularize —; prepare—; revise—; set up—; venture

—; word—; —embarrasses; —exonerates; —exposes; —insinuates; —intimates; —recounts; —relates; —shocks; —suggests; —unloads.
(See article, writing.)

adverbs
reliably; officially; responsibly; ridiculously; sagely; egotistically; unquestionably; notoriously; flatteringly; astutely; adroitly; obviously.

EDITORIALIZE (v)
adverbs
elatedly; pompously; calumniously; learnedly; fearlessly; ponderously; fanatically; oracularly; languidly; pathetically.
(See write, talk.)

EDUCATE (v)
adverbs
simultaneously; properly; insensibly; imperfectly; adequately; superficially; genteelly; rigorously; bookishly; progressively; classically; technically; intensively; practically; liberally; musically; undisciplinedly; systematically; formally; artistically; legitimately; aesthetically; religiously; snobbishly; methodically; scholastically; primitively; physically; idealistically; vocationally; competently.
(See instruct, teach.)

EDUCATION
adjectives
bookish; purposive; self-acquired; intellectual; progressive; priggish; aimless; technical; elementary; spiritual; mass; classical; advanced; intensive; practical; inevitable; meager; imperfect; precarious; previous; liberal; musical; systematic; military; evolutionary; formal; invigorating; confused; undisciplined; barren; wasteful; superficial; artistic; legitimate; adequate; aesthetic; wider; practicable; far-reaching; preparatory; humane; specific; religious; methodical; labored; compulsory; scholastic; primitive; interior; physical; positive; idealistic; vocational; regular; rudimentary; competent.

verbs
achieve—; broaden—; deny—; dominate—; enforce—; foster—; furnish—; glean—; influence—; laud—; liberalize—; neglect —; promote—; retard—; —biases; —broadens; —cultivates; —develops; —enlightens; —forms; —spreads.
(See culture, enlightenment, development, training.)

EDUCATIONAL
adverbs
highly; unusually; inconceivably; uncommonly; delightfully; alarmingly; formidably; distressingly; monotonously; agreeably; helpfully; tiresomely; necessarily; advantageously; acceptably; slightly.

EERIE
adverbs
uncommonly; uncannily; supernaturally; dreadfully; terribly; unusually; singularly; oddly; curiously; queerly; unnaturally; inexplicably; remarkably; frightfully; appallingly; gruesomely; grotesquely; undeniably.

EFFACE (v)
adverbs
rapidly; gradually; partially; entirely; totally.
(See obliterate, cancel.)

EFFECT
adjectives
similar; profound; influential; immediate; harmonious; beneficent; picturesque; pernicious; reactionary; ventriloquial; verbal; visible; fleeting; nutritive; continuous; external; displeasing; fearful; biologic; adverse; soothing; equal; singular; enormous; contractile; tragic; radiant; emotional; designed; salutary; useful; sinking; palpable; excellent; demoralizing; perceptible; social; festive; elegant; stimulating; smooth; modern; ultimate; tonic; fatal; harmful; cumulative; spacious; stunning; disastrous; probable; deterrent; dying-duck; powerful; atmospheric; characteristic; putrefactive; indirect; heavenly; grotto; depressing; electrical; sustained; pronounced; hypnotic; particular; recreational; prejudicial; recurrent; stabbing; continuous; important; enervating; naturalistic; exhilarating; varied; striking; outdoor; lamplight; remote; psychological; honest; combined; dreadful; decisive; charming; fair; gabardine; rejuvenating; theatrical; plaster; gravitating; dramatic; wondrous; devastating; incredible; summary; injurious; impressive; permanent; secondary; enchanting; artistic; malevolent; pathetic; accumulating; sedative; rare; extrinsic; detrimental; contrary; harmonic; metrical; rhythmical; astringent; prismatic; incomparable; startling; hardening; deleterious; decorative; supreme; paralyzing; bewildering; debasing; tranquillizing; luminous; strange; uncanny; stiffening; mechanical; striped; harsh; moral; architectural; broadening;

finished; unfailing; entrancing; orchestral; inspired; instantaneous; vivid; stormy; considerable; alkalizing; deteriorating; similar; preternatural; appreciable; marvellous; outrageous; racial; metrical; subversive; chromatic; maleficent; invigorating; ordinary; pyramidical; noble; depressing; thrilling; noticeable; rude; sinister; intended; massed; bracing; detectable; geophysical; brilliant; persuasive; enduring; distinguished; terrestrial; healthful; reciprocal; dampening; unfortunate; oratorical; regulating; tremendous; solemn; awful; polyphonic; unreal; unifying; distinctive; exotic; practical; flowered; composite; desired; invigorating; lasting; pompous; preservative; curative; magical; peculiar; unusual; textural; gratifying; subsequent; smartest; manifested; propitious; astounding; touching; suave; inevitable; twilight; dynamical; preponderant; secular; baneful; momentary; prized; destructive; dignified; perishing; thermometric; tragic; marked; binding; bizarre; half-veiled; required; scanty; baleful; exquisite; minute; kaleidoscopic; resultant; disintegrating; powerful; rhetorical; possible; absurd; mere; healing; imposing; tingling; fructifying; crushing; organ; luxurious; correspondent; errant; surprising; subtle; delicate; legitimate; acoustical; ill; variegated (pl); narcotic; nugatory; elevating; comic; deadly; sculptural; outward; happy; calamitous.

verbs

accentuate—; achieve—; analyze—; attain —; banish—; comprehend—; conceive—; counteract—; curse—; demonstrate—; destroy—; disturb—; elicit—; escape—; evaluate—; exercise—; exert—; gauge—; heighten—; ignore—; lessen—; mar—; mark—; match—; minimize—; mitigate—; neutralize—; notice—; observe—; obviate —; occasion—; offset—; predict—; prevent—; recapture—; record—; rehearse—; remove—; rob of—; speculate on—; strive for—; suffer from—; time—; trace—; visualize—; weaken—; witness—; —endures; —persists; —wears off.

(See result, realization, end, aim.)

EFFECT (v)

adverbs

speedily; insidiously; skillfully; advantageously; simultaneously; satisfactorily; unconsciously; tremendously; promptly; periodically; profoundly; perniciously; beneficently; externally; fearfully; adversely; soothingly; singularly; emotionally; percep-

tibly; demoralizingly; ultimately; fatally; harmfully; powerfully; characteristically; recurrently; continuously; remotely; decisively; theatrically; devastatingly; incredibly; injuriously; permanently; malevolently; pathetically; supremely; bewilderingly; debasingly; mechanically; unfailingly; racially; depressingly; curatively; gratifyingly; propitiously; dynamically; subtly; comically; calamitously.

(See accomplish, achieve.)

EFFECTIVE

adverbs

satisfactorily; highly; pleasantly; undeniably; profoundly; remarkably; sufficiently; powerfully; extremely; adequately; serviceably; practically; unusually; tremendously; admittedly.

EFFECTIVENESS

adjectives

theatric; amazing; histrionic; architectural; outstanding; dramatic; general; pictorial; decorative; haphazard; marvelous; maximum.

verbs

attain—; attend with—; augment—; direct with—; dispose with—; employ—; execute with—; follow with—; function with—; impair—; increase—; mar—; operate with —; prevent—; produce—; pursue with—; treat with—; weaken—; —accomplishes; —comforts; —decides; —produces; —rectifies; —renders.

(See efficiency, power.)

EFFECTUAL

adverbs

thoroughly; consummately; elaborately; perfectly; finally; immediately; felicitously; fortunately; highly; completely; absolutely; altogether; utterly; surprisingly.

EFFEMINATE

adverbs

disgustingly; unfortunately; unpleasantly; disagreeably; pitiably; fearfully; weakly; nervously; softly; languidly; horribly; extremely; timidly; infirmly; remarkably; vexatiously.

EFFERVESCENT

adverbs

highly; unusually; delightfully; amusingly; sparklingly; frothily; ebulliently; energetically; enthusiastically; excitedly; irrepressibly; restlessly; violently; mercurially; tempestuously; impulsively; curiously; remarkably; excessively; foolishly.

EFFETE
adverbs
horribly; lamentably; pitiably; tragically; unfortunately; deplorably; undeniably; remarkably; significantly; unsubstantially; uselessly; emptily; hopelessly; obviously.

EFFICACIOUS
adverbs
(See efficient.)

EFFICACY
adjectives
untamable; proved; constitutional; feeble.

EFFICIENCY
adjectives
calm; bustling; normal; productive; awkward; chaotic; devastating; vaunted; pedagogical; modest; maximum; extreme; technical; superior; industrial; impaired; top; outstanding; administrative; dreadful; physical; individual; creative; working; up-to-date; antiseptic; defensive; stolid; executive; incredible; added; increased; slender; swift; cleansing; expanding.

verbs
achieve—; admit—; assimilate—; demand —; destroy—; discharge with—; display—; effect—; enforce—; exhibit—; impair—; increase—; lack—; prove—; rate—; weaken—; —produces; —promotes; —saves.
(See ability, power.)

EFFICIENT
adverbs
remarkably; unusually; obviously; busily; incredibly; completely; sensibly; wisely; officiously; pleasantly; gracefully; politely; irritatingly; ostentatiously; horribly; satisfactorily; skilfully; expertly; cleverly; adroitly; ingeniously; shrewdly; ably; invaluably; surprisingly; unbelievably; uncommonly.

EFFIGY
adjectives
silent; grotesque; gilded; insensible; clumsy; crowned; sceptered; pompous; full-length; sad; recumbent; ghastly; transfixed; rueful; granite.

verbs
bear—; burn—; carry—; damn in—; display—; draw in—; dress up—; execute in—; hang in—; mount—; prepare—; —copies; —depicts; —destroys; —dramatizes; —illustrates; —portrays; —represents; —ridicules.
(See image, figure.)

EFFORT
adjectives
sheer; obvious; ceaseless; insane; sporadic; powerful; convulsive; belated; manful; stringent; fanatical; bitter; renewed; daring; conciliatory; overt; pitiful; thwarted; ponderous; childish; rash; humble; feeble; emotional; culminating; futile; creditable; clumsy; persistent; crowning; strained; zealous; individual; abortive; desperate; unscrupulous; constrained; infantile; frantic; untiring; slightest; reasonable; laborious; fragmentary; prolonged; wasted; proud; unsuccessful; painful; indomitable; stupendous; superior; strenuous; sustained; conscious; concentrated; active; stern; Herculean; visible; pictorial; vigorous; charitable; automatic; dynamic; heroic; mightiest; literary; concerted; willful; strong; intermittent; bounding; mental; feverish; immense; utmost; tentative; paramount; extra; oracular; extant; superhuman; conversational; languid; consecutive; tireless; unionized; wearisome; insufferable; historical; fruitless; human; best; spasmodic; persevering; editorial; effectual; baffled; irrelevant; determined; vague; misdirected; rash; sincere; spontaneous; notable; crude; violent; vain; inadequate; collective; immense; energetic; perilous; organized; powerful; undue; conceivable; formidable; periodic; praiseworthy; pioneering; never-ceasing; continued; self-denying; willing; exhausting; arduous; constructive; moral; fitful; creative; initial; expiratory; bizarre; rain-making; remedial; serious; apparent; sober; sympathetic; painstaking; offensive; special; colloquial; ridiculous; everlasting; sedulous; anxious; united; patient; plastic; maiden; pathetic; dutiful; generous; repetitive; financial; belated; poetic; obstinate; volunteer; co-operative; communal; religious; appropriate; published; unremitting; diligent; supreme; avowed; expired; earnest; enforcement; passionate; future; pretentious; evident; bluffing; murderous; barren; sublimest; kindly; sincere; vexed; ambitious; operatic; courageous; unwise; individual; unflinching; restraining.

verbs

belittle—; bend—; berate—; cheer—; compensate for—; concentrate—; coordinate—s; counter—; crown—; decry—; dwarf—; endorse—; enlist—s; entail—; exert—; expend—; fail in—; focus—s on; galvanize—; garble—; glorify—; hamper—; impede—; intensify—; justify—; key up for—; lend—; mock—; nullify—; quicken—; redouble—; repay—; repel—; reward—; scotch—; spare—; squander—; slacken—; stir to—; succumb to—; suppress—; suspend—; thwart—; —attains; —bears fruit; —exhausts.

(See attempt, endeavor, exertion.)

EFFRONTERY

adjectives

calculated; humorous; brazen; incredible; unabashed; hardy; vulgar; matchless.

EFFULGENT

adverbs

radiantly; glaringly; sparklingly; scintillantly; shimmeringly; dazzlingly; luminously; lustrously; unbelievably; remarkably; brilliantly; garishly; splendidly; brightly; incredibly; unexpectedly; showily; gaudily; flashily; tremendously.

EFFUSION

adjectives

amatory; tender; pathetic; vocal; gymnastic; osculatory; lyrical; rich; boisterous; copious; labored; characteristic; reducing; irrepressible; unnecessary; vaporing; hypocritical; merry; hypercritical.

EFFUSIVE

adverbs

garrulously; lavishly; chattily; enthusiastically; explosively; excessively; needlessly; ridiculously; foolishly; inappropriately; unpleasantly; comically; endlessly; noticeably; amusingly; overly; absurdly.

EGG

adjectives

pendent; ostrich; whipped; fried; poached; scrambled; hot.

verbs

addle—; beat—; burst from—; coddle—; crate—s; deposit—; emerge from—; gather —s; germinate in—; guard—s; hatch from —; hunt—; impregnate—; incubate—; market—; nest—; originate in—; poach—;

puncture—; scramble—; sit on—; snatch—; spring from—; start from—; whip—; — brings forth; —curdles; —produces.

EGO

adjectives

exaggerated; inflated; restless; exalted; hard; poised; fretted; bubbling; monarchical; suppressed; assertive.

verbs

bolster up—; commiserate—; excite—; express—; foster—; gratify—; inflate—; pervert—; reflect—; satiate—; satisfy—; soothe —; submerge—; understand—.

(See personality, individuality.)

EGOISM

adjectives

sullen; puppyish; dramatic; tyrannical; justifiable; elemental; narrowing; unlimited; psychopathic; holy, sublime, sentimental; comfortable; collective; passionate; colossal; animal; narcissistic.

EGOTISM

adjectives

outrageous; instinctive; explicable; monstrous; intense; superb; stultifying; passionate; blustering; savage; solid; immense; baseless; absurd; ruthless; unselfish; indecent; vivacious; supreme; undisguised; magnanimous; friendly; dreary; compound; naive; absolute; slightest; importunate; young; cultivated; placid.

verbs

allow—; annihilate—; apologize for—; avoid—; banish—; brand—; criticize—; excuse—; justify—; pardon—; pierce—; produce—; recommend—; resist—; —absorbs; —bores; —dominates; —irks; — occupies; —offends.

(See conceit, vanity, self-esteem.)

EGOTIST

adjectives

diseased; sentimental; offensive; supreme; turbulent; hateful; fantastic; sheer; unmalleable; harmless; power-hungry.

EGOTISTICAL

verbs

shamefully; arrogantly; absurdly; outlandishly; palpably; obviously; highly; profoundly; inexcusably; ponderously; blatantly; boastfully; vaingloriously; ridiculously;

noisily; curiously; unashamedly; disagreeably; offensively; foolishly; extremely; habitually; incredibly; blindly.

EJACULATE (v)
adverbs
sarcastically; faintly; incredulously; blankly; feelingly; sententiously; forcefully; vigorously; caustically; admiringly; joyfully; fiercely; piously; angrily; indelicately; hollowly; muffledly.
(See exclaim, call.)

EJACULATION
adjectives
customary; heartfelt; fervent; profane; pious; startled; angry; indelicate; religious; barbarous; hushed; hollow; muffled.

EJACULATORY
adverbs
violently; ridiculously; needlessly; noisily; importantly; egregiously; highly; arrogantly; blatantly; suddenly; startlingly; shockingly; ludicrously; stertorously; vociferously; monstrously; immensely; outlandishly.

EJECT (v)
adverbs
forcibly; copiously; abruptly; vigorously; determinedly; suddenly.
(See discharge, expel.)

ELABORATE (v)
adverbs
minutely; successfully; eloquently; ingeniously; ridiculously; pompously; ramblingly; fully.
(See develop, perfect.)

ELABORATE
adverbs
extremely; excessively; unnecessarily; arduously; egregiously; incredibly; ostentatiously; ingeniously; skilfully; intolerably; preposterously; fearfully; unduly; inappropriately; suitably; ceremoniously; oddly; singularly; significantly; pompously; laboriously; marvellously; beautifully.

ELABORATION
adjectives
ingenious; quaintest; ridiculous; polychronic; productive.

ELASTIC
adverbs
conveniently; expediently; comfortably; immensely; extremely; marvelously; resiliently; sturdily; wonderfully; powerfully; effectively; adequately; diplomatically; buoyantly; springily; notably.

ELASTICITY
adjectives
molecular; virtual; joyous; dangerous.

verbs
acquire—; calculate—; depend on—; deprive of—; lessen—; limit—; lose—; recover—; remove—; require—; return by—; strain—; stress—; test—; —overcomes; —resists; —restores; —varies.

ELATED
adverbs
unduly; hysterically; strangely; oddly; curiously; highly; naturally; ecstatically; rapturously; proudly; quietly; properly; unusually; brightly; enthusiastically; triumphantly; merrily; exultantly; confidently; pertly; priggishly; smugly; dramatically; boastfully; indescribably; irrepressibly.

ELATION
adjectives
short-lived; undue; cruel; hysterical; strange.

ELBOW
adjectives
bony; touching; angular; fat; massive; crooked; dimpled; immaculate; hard; inert.

verbs
brace—; cap—; extend—; fit on—; fracture—; jab with—; join—; jostle with—; move—; nudge with—; pad—; prop on—; raise—; rest on—; skin—; strain—.
(See joint, arm.)

ELDER
adjectives
disillusioned; itinerant; unsuspecting; ruling; grumpy.

verbs
appeal to—; assemble—s; burlesque—; consult—; entreat—; exhort—; gather—s; grieve—; heed—; honor—; ordain—; persuade—; respect—; revere—; succeed—; worry—; —advises; —counsels; —decrees; —heads; —interposes; —judges; —officiates; —pardons; —presides over; —punishes; —rebukes; —warns.
(See deacon, minister, ruler.)

412

adverbs
respectably; unquestionably; soberly; reliably; safely; pleasantly; comfortably; graciously; sourly; augustly; gravely; admittedly; frightfully; depressingly; incurably.

ELECT (v)
adverbs
unanimously; tacitly; spontaneously; subsequently; optionally; popularly; municipally; decisively; willingly; virtually.
(See choose, select.)

ELECTION
adjectives
farcical; obligatory; ensuing; local; optional; subsequent; degrading; frank; popular; financial; municipal.

verbs
announce ; campaign for—; climax—; conduct—; doom—; gain—; inveigh against—; merit—; nullify—; officiate at—; postpone—; propose—; revoke—; riot at—; stay—; swing—; —installs; —results in.
(See vote.)

ELECTIONEER (v)
adverbs
blatantly; flatteringly; obviously; humorously; pompously; volubly; wheedlingly; politically; masterfully; passionately; journalistically.
(See plan, campaign.)

ELECTIVE
adverbs
freely; unconditionally; fortunately; highly; frankly; wisely; generously; broadly; extensively; liberally; tolerantly; widely.

ELECTRICITY
adjectives
dynamical; spiritual; galvanic; wondrous; helpful; servant-like; static.

verbs
activate—; apply—; charge with—; communicate by—; conduct—; connect—; conserve—; consume—; develop—; direct—; discharge—; employ—; generate—; harness —; induce—; measure—; resist—; supply —; transmit—; utilize—; wire for—; —circulates; —emanates from; —flows; —magnetizes; —radiates from; —shocks; —vitalizes.

adjectives
tasteful; sartorial; unusual; impaired; gracious; extreme; solid; stately; sculptured; cheerless; superficial; concise; unfailing; luxurious; voluptuous; sovereign; chill; refining; quiet; palatial; simple; futile; dainty; urban; indescribable; modish; restrained; decorous; envied; dark; classic; restless; certain; bright; supercilious; inborn; airy; rustic; rich; cautious; inherent; chaste; subdued; austere; correct; lazy; shabby; social; verbal; defiant; peculiar; pristine.

verbs
abandon—; arrange with—; behave with —; breed in—; demonstrate—; destroy—; detest—; display—; dress with—; effect—; indulge in—; instruct in—; polish with—; surrender to—; treasure—; tutor in—; yield to—; —charms; —graces; —impresses; —prevails; —wins.
(See refinement.)

ELEGANT
adverbs
tastefully; graciously; quietly; indescribably; modishly; richly; chastely; naturally; unerringly; exquisitely; quaintly; discriminatingly; correctly; superbly.

ELEGY
adjectives
Sapphic; biblical; funeral; lamenting; somber; pastoral.

ELEMENT
adjectives
instinctive; structural; romantic; automatic; subtle; personal; opposing; radical; mutable; flavoring; incongruous; rare; hereditary; picturesque; lawless; thinkable; lymphatic; volitional; aesthetic; disproportionate; jarring; conservative; fragmentary; chemical; undefined; necessary; nationalistic; ominous; simple; discordant; valuable; discrepant; professional; poetic; complex; unalloyed; salient; airy; fighting; unlikely; limpid; primal; negligible; essential; various (pl); devouring; lurking; perverse; dramatic; exhilarated; commonest; dissolving; dreadful; unchained; recessive; liberal; unimaginative; diviner; mercantile; physic; criminalistic; regressive; nutritional; denominative; ambient; basic; ancient; uncanny; lesser; heterogeneous; individual; maltreated; unobstructed; conflicting; sensual; insignificant; cultivated;

honest; inflammable; primordial; cheerful; chalky; fantastic; simplest; positive; dominant; pitiless; **divergent**; **pagan**; **lawless**; inextinguishable; repeated; elliptic; seasonal; melancholy; **ungenial**; desirable; erotic; distinct; furious; vitamin; **mineral**; dissatisfied; prim; grim; sufficient; sensitive; minority; moral; decisive; sedate; opaque; disturbing; contradictory; **connate**; supernatural; determining; sound; hostile; visible; ultimate; fundamental; irreconcilable; bodily; contending; ideal; artistic; divers (pl); permanent; diversifying; natural; serenest; primary; untamed; eternal; incompatible; principal; unloosed; glorious; subtle; **insane**; **comic**; burning; lazy; humorous; **slow**; **speculative**; vital; harmless; food; **important**; valuable; mysterious; emotional; backsliding; infelicitous; restful; venal; subjective; neutralizing; metaphysical; dimorphous; cultured; celestial; alien.

verbs
coalesce—s; constitute—; disintegrate—; fathom—; inject—; introduce—; master—; mix—; nourish—; play to—; **rouse**—; stress—; submerge—; surrender—; symbolize—; unearth—; unite—s; —disturbs; —pervades; —predominates.
(See ingredient, constituent.)

ELEMENTAL
adverbs
distinctly; obviously; **simply**; powerfully; irresistibly; purely; **absolutely**; solely; manifestly.

ELEMENTARY
adverbs
clearly; purely; sheerly; singularly; simply; exclusively; **woefully**; amazingly; lamentably; unfortunately; significantly; gravely; momentously; **seriously.**

ELEMENTS
(*weather*)
verbs
bar—; barricade against—; combat—; conquer—; contend with—; struggle with—; yield to—; —destroy; —deteriorate; —determine; —disintegrate; —flash; —fret; —govern; —rust; —wreck.
(See earth, air, fire, **water**.)

ELEPHANT
verbs
anger—; arouse—; climb on—; domesticate —; mount—; spear—; train—; travel upon —; —bathes; —batters; —charges; —

draws; —flings; —hisses; —lumbers; — performs; —rages; —rams; —remembers; —roars; —runs amuck; —spears; —tosses; —trumpets.
(See **animal**.)

ELEVATE (*v*)
adverbs
morally; perceptibly; **proudly**; correspondingly; scarcely; partially.
(See raise, lift.)

ELAVATED
adverbs
reputably; **highly**; estimably; honorably; majestically; eminently; unusually; consciously; nobly; gloriously; immensely; remarkably; uncommonly; notably; famously; conspicuously; illustriously; splendidly; brilliantly; prominently; sacredly.

ELEVATION
adjectives
corresponding; proud; displeased; moral.

ELEVATOR
adjectives
special; **arch**; **fast**; **slow**; decorated; express.

verbs
accelerate—; block—; burden—; **control**—; crowd—; disable—; employ—; enter—; file out of—; install—; jam—; jostle in—; level—; man—; manipulate—; operate—; overload—; pour from—; retard—; ring for—; signal—; station at—; **stream from** —; —ascends; —descends; —drops; —facilitates; —hoists; —hums upward; —plunges; —transfers; —zooms.
(See platform, aeroplane.)

ELF
adjectives
happy; semi-respectable; sportive; **cunning**; troublesome; perverse; bad; imperturbable; vagrant; scribbling.

ELFISH
adverbs
delicately; **mischievously**; **sportively**; cunningly; perversely; vagrantly; uncannily; weirdly; impishly; undeniably; laughably; **amusingly**; **naturally.**

ELIGIBLE
adverbs
legally; capably; competently; wholly; **unusually**; highly; undeniably; exceptionally;

socially: becomingly; conveniently; obviously; evidently; admirably; financially.

ELIMINATE (v)
adverbs
completely; utterly; entirely; abruptly; virtually; outrageously; tyrannically; courageously; completely.
(See separate, remove.)

ELIXIR
adjectives
wondrous; imperious; youth-giving; immortal; nectarous; divine.

ELLIPSE
verbs
bound by—; circle in—; course—; cut into —; define; —describe—; disfigure—; draw —; execute—; fashion—; form—; shape into—; sketch—; wheel in—; —belts; — entertains; —frames
(See circle.)

ELM
adjectives
hedgerow; overshadowing; lofty; spindling; immemorial; vaulted; ancient; graceful; sighing.

verbs
entwine—; rock—; trim—; —branches; — flowers; —groans; —nods; —protects; — quivers; —shades; —sheds; —shelters; — stirs; —tapers; —towers; —waves.
(See tree.)

ELOPE (v)
adverbs
blithely; lovingly; spiritedly; clandestinely; surreptitiously; furtively; secretly; slyly; stealthily; impetuously.
(See run, flee.)

ELOQUENCE
adjectives
manly; grand; bold; persuasive; gloomy; transcending; bitter; melodic; florid; voluble; wheedling; candid; political; impressive; native; seductive; caustic; hardy; stately; indignant; impersonal; sonorous; patriotic; solemn; resistless; cold; clear; pathetic; silent; denunciative; masterful; masculine; insidious; solid; flatulent; astonishing; awful; touching; imperishable; impetuous; religious; native; saucy; audacious; attractive; brilliant; passionate; luminous; clarion-like; convincing; additional; parliamentary; journalistic; fiery;
rich; insinuating; supreme; consummate; rude; unstudied; lofty; picturesque; simple; fervent; abusive; prompt; gorgeous; sublime; worthy; copious; popular; ecclesiastical.

verbs
breathe out—; burst out in—; disregard—; drown in—; endow with—; prompt—; resist—; utter—; woo with—; —acquits; — colors; —flowers; —flows from—; —glitters; —induces; —moves; —pierces; — strikes; —sways.
(See speech, fluency, elegance, utterance.)

ELOQUENT
adverbs
powerfully; marvelously; incisively; impressively; dramatically; vigorously; sensationally; briiliantly; pleadingly; pithily; loftily; sublimely; touchingly; vehemently; passionately; exceptionally; astonishingly; attractively; highly; uncommonly; simply; consummately; irresistibly; persuasively.

ELUCIDATE (v)
adverbs
graphically; clearly; extensively; thoroughly; patiently.
(See describe, explain.)

ELUDE (v)
adverbs
exasperatingly; continually; slyly; ingeniously; cleverly; repeatedly; irritatingly.
(See evade, avoid.)

ELUSIVE
adverbs
cunningly; deceptively; insidiously; trickily; meretriciously; fraudulently; cleverly; artfully; abominably; evasively; adroitly; subtly; treacherously; archly; unbelievably; highly; alarmingly; singularly; terribly.

ELYSIAN
adverbs
delectably; beatifically; ecstatically; divinely; rapturously; ravishingly; seraphically; sweetly; celestially.

EMACIATED
adverbs
pitiably; outrageously; scandalously; miserably; shakily; wirily; sparely; gauntly; haggardly; tenuously; shockingly; terribly; unusually; wretchedly; unwarrantably; shamefully.

EMANATION

adjectives
divine; miasmal; primitive.

EMANCIPATION

adjectives
bourgeois; unconditional; prospective.

EMBALM (v)

adverbs
carefully; elaborately; skillfully; marvelously; artfully; professionally.
  (See preserve.)

EMBALMING

adjectives
elaborate; marvelous; skilled.

EMBARGO

adjectives
silly; alternative; virtual.

verbs
adopt—; apply—; assail—; authorize—; clap on—; condemn—; counter—; declare —; effect—; employ—; enforce—; impose —; instigate—; justify—; lift—; patronize —; proclaim—; propose—; support—; threaten—; urge—; —checks; —hinders; —restrains; —starves.
  (See hindrance, impediment, injunction, restraint.)

EMBARK (v)

adverbs
gleefully; sadly; joyfully; formally; unmolestedly; freely; tardily; eventually; hastily.
  (See begin, venture.)

EMBARKATION

adjectives
businesslike; unmolested.

EMBARRASS (v)

adverbs
disconcertingly; satirically; startlingly; perceptibly; sadly; slyly; perplexingly; visibly; painfully; . pecuniarily; secretly; acutely; considerably; strangely.
  (See harass, shame.)

EMBARRASSED

adverbs
singularly; curiously; oddly; strangely; profoundly; awkwardly; deeply; shamefully; shyly; financially; socially; distressingly; painfully; publicly; secretly; timidly; occasionally; vaguely; slightly; greatly; horribly; visibly; angrily; acutely; considerably; helplessly; hotly.

EMBARRASSMENT

adjectives
visible; flattering; painful; evident; pecuniary; nervous; tingling; angry; secret; acute; considerable; strange.

verbs
betray—; blush in—; conceal—; contribute to—; ease—; flush in—; guard against—; lead to—; manifest—; pardon—; relieve—; —hinders; —prevents; —silences.
  (See chagrin, perplexity.)

EMBASSY

adjectives
overburdened; heaven-like; loving.

EMBELLISH (v)

adverbs
peculiarly; handsomely; profusely; tastefully; poetically; artistically; architecturally; rhetorically; flamboyantly; gaudily; beautifully; lavishly.
  (See adorn, ornament.)

EMBELLISHED

adverbs
ornately; tastefully; gaudily; crudely; garishly; beautifully; artistically; gorgeously; smartly; showily; unnecessarily; highly; extravagantly; excessively; richly; gayly; daintily; elegantly; chastely; simply.

EMBELLISHMENT

adjectives
poetical; artistic; architectural; rhetorical.

EMBER

verbs
blanket—s; conceal beneath—; fan—; feed —s; heap on—s; heat on—s; poke—s; quench—s; rake—s; roast in—s; stir—s; strew over—s; toast on—s; —blazes; —burns; —s comfort; —dies; —expires; —flames; —glows; —heats; —s sleep; —smoulders; —s warm; —chars.
  (See coal, ashes, cinders.)

EMBERS

adjectives
rose-red; burnt-out; glowing; smoldering; latent; dying; dangerous; pale; dim; fading; glimmering; throbbing; slumbering; raked; inextinguishable; feeble; ruddy; ashen-gray; blue; crumbling; smoky.

EMBITTERED

adverbs

deeply; permanently; irremediably; unfortunately; justifiably; hopelessly; irrecoverably; secretly; profoundly; morbidly; sullenly; unhappily; strangely; naturally; pathetically; violently; savagely; dejectedly; desperately.

EMBLAZON (*v*)

adverbs

vividly; richly; weirdly; brilliantly; astonishingly; colorfully.

(See adorn, shine.)

EMBLAZONED

adverbs

gorgeously; colorfully; artistically; brilliantly; wonderfully; marvelously; ceremonially; magnificently; splendidly; sumptuously; dramatically, richly; glitteringly; brightly; highly.

EMBLAZONING

adjectives

dim; fiery; weird; astonishing.

EMBLEM

adjectives

talismanic; portentous; ecclesiastical; gorgeous; hieroglyphical; conventional; mortuary; graven-lined; masonic; sepulchered.

verbs

bear—; bedeck with—s; distinguish with —s; engrave—; enrich with—s; insert—; reward with—; select—; scrutinize—; vie for—; —attests; —denotes; —expresses; —flutters; —indicates; —represents; —suggests; —symbolizes; —testifies.

(See representation, symbol, sign, badge.)

EMBLEMATIC

adverbs

characteristically; truly; ecclesiastically; gorgeously; splendidly; highly; remarkably; particularly; obscurely; appropriately; suitably; graphically; felicitously; extraordinarily; uncommonly; manifestly.

EMBODIMENT

adjectives

stirring; organic; adequate; striking; rough.

EMBODY (*v*)

adverbs

satisfactorily; stirringly; organically; strikingly; adequately; roughly; successfully; convincingly.

(See combine, form.)

EMBRACE

adjectives

clinging; maddening; bearlike; straining; wordless; rapturous; mute; passionate; quiet; transparent; pure; warm; turbulent; meek; fervid; hard; stimulating; emotional; sorrowing; soothing; fierce; strict; firm; chill; rugged; silent; romantic; locked; welcoming; timid; tight; tepid; kind; lank; stormy; stiff; clumsy.

verbs

avert—; avoid—; blush at—; break—; check—; clasp in—; delight in—; enclose in—; force—; gather in—, lock in—; resist—; seek—; shelter in—.

(See clasp.)

EMBRACE (*v*)

adverbs

tenderly; blithely; lasciviously; licentiously; cheerfully; responsively; affectionately; warmly; fitfully; passionately; voluntarily; devoutly; boldly; clingingly; maddeningly; wordlessly; rapturously; emotionally; mutely; turbulently; sorrowfully; soothingly; fiercely; firmly; ruggedly; romantically; timidly; tepidly; clumsily; stormily.

(See caress, clasp.)

EMBRASURE

adjectives

gloomy; mighty.

EMBROIDER (*v*)

adverbs

dexterously; delicately; ecclesiastically; strangely; brilliantly; artfully; skillfully; fantastically.

(See sew, ornament.)

EMBROIDERY

adjectives

brilliant; sad; glittering; ecclesiastical; fancy; eyelet; cross-stitch; lace; delicate.

EMBROILMENT

adjectives

bloody; wearisome; needless; furious.

verbs

abort—; disengage—; enclose—; examine
—; form—; hatch—; kill—; nourish—;
shape—; stifle—; stimulate—; surround—;
—develops; —dwells in; —enfolds; —impresses; —matures; —occupies; —originates; —ripens.

(See germ, beginning.)

EMERALD

adjectives

living; veined; encrusted; sparkling; striking; great; square; exquisite.

verbs

adorn with—; cover with—s; delight in—;
favor—; guard—; lure with—; purchase
—; secrete—; value—; —crowns; —dazzles;
—gleams; —glimmers; —glitters; —scintillates; —shines.

(See jewel, gem, diamond.)

EMERGE (v)

adverbs

dramatically; noiselessly; coolly; gradually;
luminously; transcendingly; reluctantly;
mystically; shyly; abruptly; unmistakably.

(See rise, come.)

EMERGENCY

adjectives

fearful; prolonged; sudden; fiscal; threatening; temporal; frequent;. peculiar; unexpected; popular; pressing; unusual; serious;
desperate; international.

verbs

anticipate—; bow to—; challenge—; confront with—; cope with—; ease—; face—;
guard against—; handle—; iron out—;
lessen—; meet—; resign to—; rise to—;
—arises; —exists.

(See crisis, exigency, necessity.)

EMETIC

verbs

act as—; administer—; does with—; employ
—; prescribe—; suggest—; swallow—; —
aids; —corrects; —counteracts; —cures; —
empties; —excites; —induces; —produces;
—prostrates; —remedies; —stimulates.

(See medicine, laxative, enema.)

EMIGRANT

adjectives

unfortunate; greenhorn; bewildered; aggressive.

EMIGRATION

verbs

admit—; advocate—; assist—; campaign
for—; dodge—; embark on—; halt—; occasion—; prevent—; record—; shift—; stir
—; undertake—; —drifts; —flows; —
lapses; —relieves; —streams; —trickles.

(See exodus, departure, immigration.)

EMINENCE

adjectives

lofty; intellectual; grassy; bright; conspicuous; crested; humble; narrowed; specific;
abrupt; sudden; immediate; gentle; incontestable; commanding; inland; archaeological; practicable; affected; sacred; cliffy;
deserted; professional; unblemished; gigantic; noble.

verbs

ascend to—; assume—; attain—; command
—; deserve—; elevate to—; enjoy—; enthrone in—; hope for—; merit—; perch
in—; rise to—; shoot to—; surpass in—;
tower in—; worship—.

(See distinction, fame.)

EMINENT

adverbs

notably; internationally; ecclesiastically;
politically; socially; distinctly; illustriously;
splendidly; proudly; conspicuously; honorably; deservedly; brilliantly; famously.

EMISSARY

adjectives

paid; secret; trustworthy; discreet.

verbs

assign—to; dispatch—; employ—; entrust
with—; interview—; send—; —announces;
—carries; —communicates; —conveys; —
corresponds; —furnishes; —imparts; —implies; —informs; —performs; —pries; —
promotes; —relays; —reports; —represents;
—scouts; —spies.

(See agent, messenger, ambassador.)

EMISSION

adjectives

non-luminous; watery.

EMOLUMENT

adjectives

stipendiary; unearned; colossal; untaxable.

verbs

calculate—; consider—; deny—; deprive
of—; derive—; earn—; enjoy—; forfeit—;

obtain—; pocket—; produce—; reap—; receive—; return—; seek—; —amends; —atones for; —comforts; —compensates; —improves; —rewards; —satisfies.

(See advantage, gain, profit.)

EMOTION

adjectives
poignant; intellectual; enthusiastic; touched; pent-up; gentle; repressed; inscrutable; barbaric; profound; blushing; conflicting; fierce; dark; complex; vague; vindictive; turbulent; painful; dominant; disturbing; desirable; private; desperate; kindled; human; extraordinary; petty; ardent; suitable; exulting; tremulous; generous; primitive; perfect; sudden; passionate; unquiet; joyful; parental; unmaidenly; chivalric; opposite; irrevocable; decadent; violent; indescribable; timid; charitable; passive; transient; repentant; trembling; contending; diverse; tumultuous; untried; sensitive; irrepressible; scornful; rapid; lively; mingled; suppressed; distinct; contradictory; intricate; dead; keen; sincere; adult; unstable; overwhelming; evident; patriotic; quivering; natural; intense; irreproachable; educated; anguished; elusive; corresponding; religious; tender; similar; singular; gushing; innocent; inner; spontaneous; aesthetic; genuine; hot-headed; silent; excited; immature; shallow; cheap; neat; compelling; inelastic; visible; awe-inspiring; incomprehensible; strong; sham; momentary; adulterated; sociable; inward; intimate; surcharged; acute; sustained; sympathetic; wandering; rebellious; compassionate; catholic; outward; tragic; burning; awakened; volcanic; uncontrollable; ineffable; synthetic; perverted; antagonistic; distressful; frozen; deepest; inmost; swelling; ill-concealed; pleasing; vehement; undisciplined; unfathomable; dumb; subdued; passion-hued; haggard; inexpressible; encompassing; unrestrained; facile; full-fledged; causeless; primal; deadened; inwrought; honest; confused; incomparable; personable; incongruous; incredible; indefinable; devastating; vivid; depressive; overpowering; simultaneous; old-fashioned; mysterious; unearthly; ultimate.

verbs
appeal to—; arouse—; awaken—; batter down—; betray—; blunt—; cherish—; choke—; conquer—; control—; cover—; curb—; disentangle—s; experience—; express—; falsify—; feign—; hide—; kindle —; lavish—on; move with—; overflow with

—; palpitate with—; play with—; prompt by—; pulsate with—; quake with—; quiver with—; register—; respond to—; restrain —; still—; suppress—; sway with—; toy with—s; tremble with—; vanquish—; vent —; whip up—; wrench by—; wring with—; —s clash; —s conflict; —governs; —recurs; —s riot; —seizes; —surges; —vacillates.

(See feeling, sensation, passion, perturbation, agitation.)

EMOTIONAL

adverbs
peculiarly; deeply; ardently; unstably; eagerly; warmly; quickly; strongly; obviously; fervently; uncontrollably; ungovernably; impetuously; impulsively; hysterically; unsteadily; remarkably; inherently; naturally; expressively; violently; highly; unusually.

EMOTIONALISM

adjectives
crude; seething; accursed; florid.

EMPEROR

adjectives
illustrious; reigning; ambitious; ardent; haughty; tyrannical.

verbs
admire—; assassinate—; attend—; bow to —; cringe before—; crown—; fete—; guard —; hail—; huzza—; pledge to—; present to—; succeed—; wait upon—; —addresses; —conquers; —decrees; —dismisses; —pardons; —receives; —rules; —subdues.

(See king, monarch.)

EMPHASIS

adjectives
lingering; menacing; stubborn; marked; terrific; daring; allowable; improper; extravagant; dreadful; indignant; prodigious; fretful; passionate; prevailing; serious; trivial; joyous; sufficient; ethical; victorious; appealing; artistic; attenuated; sarcastic; flattering; languid; tantalizing.

verbs
bear—; convey—; express with—; focus upon—; lay—upon; lose—; mark—; note—; observe—; require—; shift—; voice—; —accentuates; —affirms; —delivers; —forces; —imbeds; —implies; —impresses; —inculcates; —insists; —instils; —points; —sharpens; —stresses.

(See stress, force.)

EMPHASIZE (v)

adverbs

significantly; repeatedly; effectively; victoriously; graciously; boastfully; adequately; menacingly; stubbornly; markedly; daringly; improperly; extravagantly; indignantly; fretfully; passionately; seriously; trivially; sufficiently; appealingly; artistically; tantalizingly.

(See stress, impress.)

EMPHATIC

adverbs

stubbornly; terribly; fretfully; joyously; aggressively; boldly; loftily; truculently; extravagantly; impudently; insolently; audaciously; arrogantly; blandly; confidently; sweepingly; dogmatically; astoundingly; autocratically; despotically; imperiously; monstrously; presumptuously; preposterously; rashly; blatantly; sarcastically.

EMPIRE

adjectives

calm; powerful; mighty; disintegrating; formidable; distracted; extensive; audacious; vain; populous; consolidated; celestial; peerless; permanent; veritable; effeminate; far-reaching; full-fledged; supernatural; gentle; colonial; barbaric; mercantile; spiritual.

verbs

bind—; bound—; build—; carve—; cement —; command—; conquer—; consolidate—; create—; destroy—; dictate—; disentangle —; divide—; forsake—; found—; govern —; invade—; overthrow—; police—; rock —; rule—; seek—; shake—; spread through —; unite—; wreck—; yoke—; —dwindles; —extends; —falls; —perishes; —ranges; —sickens; —staggers.

(See state, nation, dominion, sovereignty, kingdom.)

EMPLOY (v)

adverbs

habitually; conspicuously; vigilantly; anxiously; faithfully; uselessly; frequently; thriftily; steadily; methodically; profitably; gainfully; vigorously; skillfully; magically; unceasingly; temporarily; advantageously; peacefully; sparingly; incessantly; hazardously; individually; occasionally; domestically; legitimately; remuneratively; suitably; figuratively; ingloriously; systematically; actively.

(See use, work.)

EMPLOYEE

adjectives

conscientious; rank-and-file; valued; prudent; salaried; unionized.

verbs

agitate—s; assign—to; coerce—; command —; discard—; dismiss—; dock—; engage —; engross—; enroll—; intimidate—; manage—s; misuse—; regulate—s; supervise —s; —s demand; —exerts; —obeys; —s organize; —s recess; —s strike.

(See worker, workman, laborer, clerk.)

EMPLOYER

adjectives

philosophic; recusant; apprehensive; prospective; banded (pl).

verbs

demand of—; persuade—; picket—; plead with—; seek—; —acquires; —advertises; — assigns; —controls; —disposes; —economizes; —engages; —fires; —hires; —locks out; —pities; —procures; —provides; — refuses; —regulates; —supervises; —sympathizes; —tyrannizes; —understands.

(See master, owner, manager.)

EMPLOYMENT

adjectives

unconscious; hazardous; individual; occasional; domestic; legitimate; remunerative; regressive; useful; suitable; skillful; congenial; responsible; continuous; money-making; figurative; seasonable; inglorious; obvious; temporary; lucrative; profitable; regular; diverse; military; justifiable; creative; systematic; gainful; mercantile; initial.

verbs

acquire—; apply for—; assign—; avoid—; carry on—; devote to—; evade—; fit for—; insure—; necessitate—; offer—; procure—; pursue—; receive—; regulate—; reject—; seek—; stabilize—; stimulate—; throw out of—; —fluctuates; —maintains; —occupies; —preserves; —satisfies.

(See occupation, vocation, calling, business, profession, trade, job.)

EMPRESS

adjectives

chimerical; power-drunk; haughty.

EMPTINESS

adjectives

divine; ultimate; horrid; echoing; civilized; gnawing; spiritual; wide; desolate; bleak; blank; black; void; gaping; yawning.

EMPTY (v)

adverbs

surreptitiously; completely; partially; automatically.

(See deplete, exhaust.)

EMPTY

adverbs

hopelessly; deplorably; lamentably; desperately; completely; almost; obviously; visibly; dreadfully; desolately; bleakly; startlingly; awfully; dismally; unbelievably; palpably; contemptibly; unhappily; unfortunately; wretchedly.

EMULATION

adjectives

literary; perpetual; generous; envious.

EMULSION

adjectives

light; sensitive; suspended; cloudy.

ENACT (v)

adverbs

comparatively; gravely; legally; prohibitively; legislatively; socially; illegitimately; dictatorially; forcefully; dogmatically.

(See perform, accomplish.)

ENACTMENT

adjectives

statutory; prohibitive; legislative; social; revolutionary; legal.

ENAMEL

adjectives

tinted; lucid; brittle; brilliant.

ENAMOURED

adverbs

crazily; besottedly; wholly; rapturously; blindly; immensely; ecstatically; ardently; passionately; idolatrously; fervidly; deeply; inordinately; absorbingly; perilously; dangerously; absurdly; hopelessly; helplessly.

ENCHANT (v)

adverbs

magically; ravishingly; sweetly; uniquely; mysteriously; powerfully; fantastically; mystically; passionately.

(See charm, fascinate.)

ENCHANTED

adverbs

utterly; delightfully; marvellously; oddly; perfectly; curiously; unquestionably; irresistibly; openly; avowedly; completely.

ENCHANTING

adverbs

delightfully; charmingly; seductively; bewitchingly; girlishly; youthfully; marvellously; radiantly; daintily; exquisitely; courteously; divinely; gracefully; brightly; chivalrously; politely; attentively; urbanely; ingratiatingly; genially; extremely; curiously; oddly; uncommonly.

ENCHANTMENT

adjectives

grave; sweet; rapt; unique; age-old; powerful; mysterious; perpetual; varied; divine; social; heightened; drear; cool; true; aristocratic; gloomy; mystic.

verbs

brew—; cast—; drink in—; endow with—; exercise—; gaze with—; invest with—; lend—; respond to—; steep in—; succumb to—; touch with—; view with—; —allures; —assails; —beguiles; —bewitches; —captivates; —charms; —cloaks; —delights; —enraptures; —enslaves; —expires; —fascinates; —fetters; —influences; —overpowers; employ—.

(See charm, fascination.)

ENCOMIUM

adjectives

unjust; warm; eulogistic; heaped-up (pl).

ENCOUNTER

adjectives

loose; strange; accidental; constant; fierce; ordinary; bloody; murderous; romantic; amiable; strong; awkward; fatal; vile; pugilistic; sharp; chivalrous; previous; bitter.

verbs

anticipate—; avoid—; calculate—; **clash** in—; confess to—; contemplate—; dare—; engage in—; experience—; expose to—; fear —; flush from—; intend—; join—; launch —; match in—; plan—; relate—; risk—; shrink from—; shun—; venture—; welcome—; —follows; —unsteadies.

(See meeting, collision, contest, conflict, battle.)

ENCOUNTER (v)

adverbs

repeatedly; proudly; frequently; occasionally; obliquely; cheerfully; unexpectedly; fearlessly; accidentally; murderously; romantically; amiably; awkwardly; fatally; chivalrously; bitterly.

(See meet, confront.)

ENCOURAGE (v)

adverbs

smoothly; openly; jovially; tremendously; sympathetically; willingly; specially; genially; unduly; adroitly; enormously; affectionately; consistently; wordlessly; unceasingly; remotely; cordially; professionally.

(See aid, assist.)

ENCOURAGEMENT

adjectives

enormous; lifelong; affectionate; consistent; wordless; unceasing; remote; slender; managerial; cheerful; cordial; melancholy; fresh; misplaced.

verbs

afford—; impart—; lend—; rally to—; thrive on—; —animates; —cheers; —comforts; —enlivens; —exhilarates; —heartens; —impels; —incites; —induces; —inspires; —kindles; —promotes; —prompts; —reassures; —restores; —stimulates.

(See help.)

ENCOURAGING

adverbs

cheerily; genially; gravely; enormously; affectionately; immensely; highly; silently; cordially; sincerely; resolutely; decisively; impulsively; discreetly; deliberately; helpfully; amicably; confidently; enthusiastically; reassuringly; sympathetically; actively; genuinely; exceptionally; prudently; thoughtfully; reliably.

ENCROACH (v)

adverbs

steadily; progressively; unconsciously; brazenly; perpetually; aggressively; belligerently; martially; pugnaciously.

(See trespass, intrude.)

ENCROACHMENT

adjectives

noteworthy; perpetual.

verbs

justify—; observe—; prevent—; rant against—; recognize—; resent—; resist—;

revenge—; seize by—; tolerate—; wrest by—; —arouses; —deprives; —disables; —irritates; —offends; —outrages; —perils; —robs; —violates.

(See intrusion, invasion.)

ENCUMBER (v)

adverbs

perilously; hopelessly; monstrously; tragically; fatally; tyrannically; viciously; pathologically.

(See hinder, impede.)

ENCUMBRANCE

adjectives

vast; hopeless; monstrous.

verbs

accept—; attach—; discharge—; dispel—; divest of—; free from—; load with—; master—; struggle with—; suffer—; —annoys; —burdens; —clogs; —complicates; —embarrasses; —hampers; —harasses; —hinders; —impedes; —obstructs; —oppresses; —presses; —restrains.

(See load, burden, hindrance, impediment.)

ENCYCLOPEDIA

adjectives

skeptical; exhaustive; character; walking; biographical; all-inclusive.

verbs

appear in—; compile—; comprehend—; consult—; discover in—; edit—; employ—; refer to—; require—; scan—; —comprises; —educates; —enlightens; —explains; —illustrates; —informs; —instructs; —specifies; —teaches.

(See book.)

END

adjectives

dreary; practical; extreme; definite; private; lofty; selfish; ambitious; sordid; common; remote; swanlike; unsavory; equivocal; inexorable; surprising; personal; muchcoveted; teleological; adequate; ornamental; technical; ulterior; contingent; unpitied; desirable; special; worthier; appointed; hideous; latter; petty; sad; professed; untimely; abhorred; economical; wretched; radiant; conscious; tapering; immortal; futile; spiritual; individual; chief; shameful; ephemeral; extravagant; lifeless; blunt; preconceived; ultimate; gracious; disastrous.

verbs
accomplish—; achieve—; attain—; bend to
—; catch—; constitute—; continue until—;
contrive—; discern—; draw to—; endure
to—; fear—; fulfill—; further—; hasten—;
indicate—; justify—; maintain till—; obtain—; pause at—; pray for—; progress
toward—; pursue—; push to—; put to—;
scorn—; serve—; sever—; sleep till—;
stave off—; subserve—; waste—; welcome
—; work out—.

(See purpose, intention, aim, object, goal.)

END (v)
adverbs
invariably; eloquently; feebly; amicably;
mournfully; abruptly; fatally; badly; tragically; comically; sorrowfully; dramatically;
coldly; virtually; intelligibly; disastrously;
breathlessly; inevitably; miserably; ultimately; insignificantly; ominously; appropriately; abruptly; gradually; poetically;
swiftly.

(See finish, stop.)

ENDANGER (v)
adverbs
seriously; frequently; foolishly; absurdly;
carelessly; jauntily; bravely; ridiculously.
(See imperil, risk.)

ENDEARMENT
verbs
address—to; cajole with—s; caress in—;
coax with—s; court with—s; exhibit—; feast
on—; flatter with—s; fondle in—; pat with
—; refrain from—s; secure—of; serenade
with—s; utter—; wheedle with—s; whisper
—s; woo with—s; —annoys; —s charm;
—flatters; —pleases.
(See caress, affection, love.)

ENDEAVOR
adjectives
enthusiastic; painstaking; deformed; vain;
apparent; infinite; earnest; tenacious;
mournful; incessant; rash; awful; patient;
desperate; passionate; humane; utmost;
high; speedy; organized; fruitless; fair;
stern; honest; unsuccessful; ceaseless; beneficent; personal; therapeutic; urgent; self-
protective; strenuous; fierce; psychoanalytic; sanctified; junior; charitable; dead;
suicidal; dull; strong; philanthropic; continuous; decorative; intellectual; foolish.

verbs
bless—; conceal—; direct—; dwarf—; emulate—; encourage—; exert in—; extend—;

forestall—; forsake—; frustrate—; inspire
—; lessen—; oppose—; plan—; put forth—;
renew—; smile on—; struggle in—; —contributes; —ennobles; —helps; —sweeps
away.

(See attempt, effort, struggle.)

ENDEAVOR (v)
adverbs
scrupulously; vainly; forcefully; energetically; constantly; primarily; inadequately;
feebly; conscientiously; fruitlessly; unconsciously; gravely; heroically; ineffectually;
eternally; enthusiastically; painstakingly;
apparently; earnestly; tenaciously; mournfully; incessantly; patiently; desperately;
passionately; humanely; strenuously; charitably; intellectually; foolishly.

(See try, strive.)

ENDING
adjectives
insignificant; ominous; tragic; gigantic;
physical; abrupt; fittest; appropriate; gradual; beautiful; soft; poetic; swift.

ENDLESS
adverbs
horribly; apparently; almost; irritatingly;
hopelessly; vexatiously; terrifyingly; incalculably; maddeningly; fabulously; unendurably; fearfully; frightfully.

ENDORSE (v)
adverbs
enthusiastically; tentatively; legally; legitimately; criminally; dishonestly; optimistically.

(See approve, agree.)

ENDORSEMENT
adjectives
enthusiastic; tentative.

verbs
(See indorsement.)

ENDOW (v)
adverbs
richly; invariably; exceptionally; wisely;
lavishly; liberally; speedily; suitably; splendidly; mentally; spiritually; hypocritically;
naturally; intellectually; physically; rarely;
uncommonly.

(See give, donate.)

ENDOWMENT

adjectives

mental; spiritual; intrinsic; hypothetical; natural; decorative; intellectual; physical; rare; literary; uncommon.

verbs

assure of—; bequeath—to; bestow—upon; confer—upon; deserve—; furnish—; grant —; inherit—; lavish—on; leave—to; obtain —; present—; provide—; secure—; settle —on; solicit—; stipulate—; vest—; wheedle —; will—; —eases; —enriches; —provides for; —rescues; —supports.

(See bounty, gift, money.)

ENDURABLE

adverbs

scarcely; grimly; barely; hardly; philosophically; stoically; tolerably; heroically; reasonably.

ENDURANCE

adjectives

dignified; calm; physical; marvelous; pained; resolute; unparalleled; silent; heroic; unlimited; patient; passive; superhuman; moral; stout; brave.

verbs

attain—; bear with—; discipline to—; enhance—; harden—; impose on—; limit—; prolong beyond—; replenish—; tax—; torment beyond—; —conquers; —ebbs; — fades; —fails; —surpasses; —sustains; — terminates; —wanes.

(See persistence, fortitude, patience, forbearance.)

ENDURE (v)

adverbs

placidly; firmly; coldly; irksomely; everlastingly; impatiently; consciously; simply; daily; permanently; dignifiedly; heroically; naturally; intellectually; physically; passively; morally; stoutly; bravely.

(See suffer, bear.)

ENEMA

verbs

employ—; endure—; inject—; introduce—; order—; prepare—; prescribe—; recommend—; resort to—; urge—; —aggravates; —aids; —appeases; —comforts; —eases; —enervates; —exasperates; —infuriates; — purges; —quickens; —relieves; —soothes; —weakens.

(See medicine, laxative, emetic.)

ENEMY

adjectives

approaching; spiteful; transalpine; routed; hereditary; partisan; scrupulous; fearful; generous; retreating; domestic, vanquished; damaging; embittered; pernicious; confiding; political; patient; sagacious; faithful; malarial; sworn; potential; stern; cruel; legendary; mysterious; invisible; avowed; discomfited; malicious; vigilant; treacherous; intrenched; formidable; destructive; prejudiced; pleasant; bigoted; subtle; legionary; inveterate; aggressive; contemptuous; external; visionary; fanatical; unfair; bitter; self-reliant; resolute; common; skulking; service; ferocious; pregnant; imaginary; alien; courageous; loathed; penniless; rival; devouring; butchering; lurking; malignant; exposed; deadly; cunning; unrelenting; panic-stricken; implacable; erstwhile; exasperated; indefatigable; insidious; ruthless; vehement; vindictive.

verbs

acquiesce to—; ambush—; annihilate—; approach—; baffle—; beleaguer—; betray to —; charge—; chase—; confront—; crush—; cultivate—; curse—; deliver—; demoralize—; destroy—; disarm—; eliminate—; elude—; engage—; enslave—; entrap—; erase—; excoriate—; exterminate—; face—; fall into the hands of—; foil—; forgive—; harass—; hold—at bay; hurl back—; intercept—; inveigh against—; judge—; massacre—; mislead—; mollify—; negotiate with—; outstrip—; overpower—; overwhelm—; prey upon—; provoke—; persecute—; pursue—; rage at—; reproach—; reveal—; rid of—; scatter—; slay—; smite —; subdue—; survey—; trap—; vanquish —; yield to—; —clamors; —conspires; — falls; —invades; —launches; —lures; — lurks; —plots; —retires; —retreats; — slanders; —withdraws; overthrow—.

(See adversary, antagonist, foe, opponent, rival, competitor.)

ENERGETIC

adverbs

spasmodically; courageously; consistently; actually; indefatigably; gloriously; conspicuously; monumentally; phenomenally; creatively; colossally; stupendously; patiently; strikingly; laboriously; magnificently; spectacularly; breath-takingly; supremely; impressively; valorously; indomitably; nervously; joyously; formidably; prodigiously;

fitfully; restlessly; tremendously; appallingly; suspiciously; excitedly; disturbingly; normally; abnormally.

ENERGETICS

adjectives
metaphysical; speculative; philosophic.

ENERGY

adjectives
active; indomitable; wonted; untiring; feverish; progressive; torrential; resistless; undiminished; imperfect; newborn; constructive; cheering; felicitous; nervous; twofold; contortionary; difficult; joyous; murderous; characteristic; wondrous; abundant; lagging; formidable; surpassing; stern; resolute; boundless; uncommon; impressive; superhuman; vigorous; untamable; repressed; cumulative; imparted; latent; prevailing; overmastering; enormous; sustained; rebellious; dynamic; mysterious; creative; deceptive; tireless; youthful; fervid; patient; inexhaustible; biological; triumphant; collective; relentless; inherent; passionate; vital; vehement; available; unfaltering; invincible; exhaustless; multiform; tameless; undivided; flagging; due; never-ceasing; dampened; stormy; hopeful; tidal; liquid; administrative; striking; unabated; incalculable; intellectual; volcanic; intrepid; convulsive; destructive; sleepless; tremendous; expansive; prodigious; long-discordant; presidential; unmeasured; enlightened; hollow; despairing; impetuous; spiritual; terrible; native; productive; indefatigable; mastering; excited; reposing; diligent; discursive; overflowing; manly; radiant; well-directed; unparalleled; potential; pathetic; mechanical; unaided; concentrated; rapid; fitful; industrious; subtle; compulsive; throbbing; unwearying; distorting; hypothetical; dulled; intensive; dauntless; dashing; hopeful; ridiculous; biting; fiery; reckless; grim; capacious; rank; incomparable; magnetic; useful; unimpeded; subatomic; desperate; ruthless; vivid; searching; reserve; marked; superfluous; wasteful; dogged; restless; impartial; restricted; ultimate; scientific; electric; kinetic; mental; singular; superabundant; structural; moral.

verbs
absorb—; bend—toward; build up—; center —; conserve—; consume—; control—; convert into—; dedicate—to; demand—; derive —from; develop—; devote—to; discharge —; dissipate—; display—; drain—; endow with—; exhibit—; expend—; fill with—;

flood with—; focus—upon; fritter away—; gather—; increase—; liberate—; organize —; provide—; relax—; renew—; release —; resuscitate—; retard—; reward—; smother—; spend—; squander—; store up —; tax—; transform—; transmit—; unleash—; unlock—; utilize—; waste—; — deteriorates; —flags.

(See force, power, vigor, strength, zeal.)

ENERVATING

adverbs
undeniably; terribly; unfortunately; dangerously; unbelievably; alarmingly; deplorably; definitely; horribly; strangely; oddly; visibly; hopelessly; deeply.

ENFEEBLED

adverbs
pitiably; miserably; wretchedly; hopelessly; irremediably; visibly; apparently; manifestly; outrageously; cruelly; extraordinarily; curiously; nervously; languidly; unquestionably; ominously; mysteriously; horribly; inexplicably.

ENFEEBLEMENT

verbs
brace—; fortify—; give way to—; guard against—; incur—; invigorate—; languish in—; produce—; relax in—; resist—; sustain—; totter in—; —cramps; —deprives; —drains; —impoverishes; —prevents; — reduces; —saps; —unhinges.

ENFORCE (v)

adverbs
rigorously; arrogantly; rigidly; stringently; steadily; strictly; promptly; obstinately; sufficiently; aggressively; roughly; nominally; doggedly; painstakingly.

(See force, compel.)

ENFORCEMENT

adjectives
vigorous; sufficient; rough; rigid; aggressive.

ENGAGE (v)

adverbs
professionally; professedly; obviously; industrially; industriously; controversially; earnestly; actively; pitifully; extensively; variously; picturesquely; successfully; continuously; seriously; actively; willingly; exclusively; amicably; hotly; demurely;

jointly; bindingly; allegedly; partially; obstinately; bloodily; pecuniarily; indecisively; intensively.

(See pledge, indulge.)

ENGAGEMENT

adjectives
binding; alleged; partial; bloody; obstinate; quasi-voluntary; pecuniary; long-standing; memorable; indecisive; pressing; wordy; professional.

verbs
agree upon—; announce—; anticipate—; arrange for—; attend—; break—; cancel—; celebrate—; contract—; defer—; desire—; enroll—; free from—; fulfill—; liberate from—; obtain—; prolong—; release from —; terminate—; —affiances; —betroths; —binds; —pairs; —pledges; —surprises.

(See betrothal, promise.)

ENGAGING

adverbs
irresistibly; charmingly; captivatingly; youthfully; delightfully; pleasantly; adorably; sweetly; gracefully; winningly; interestingly, fascinatingly; amiably; quietly; modestly; pertly; saucily; lovingly; attractively; enchantingly; unusually; artlessly; innocently; indefinably; extraordinarily; singularly.

ENGINE

adjectives
locomotive; palpitating; lifeless; mutilated; cruel; deadlier; mysterious; inanimate; atmospheric; fettered; awesome; devilish; asthmatic; rotary; monstrous; phenomenal; ubiquitous.

verbs
coal—; cool—; develop—; devise—; fuel—; lubricate—; muffle—; oil—; pilot—; repair—; —backfires; —batters; —buzzes; —chugs; —clatters; —coughs; —dies; —drives; —drones; —racks; —recoils; —roars; —snarls; —sputters; —throbs; —transforms; —utilizes; —wavers.

(See machine, mechanism.)

ENGINEER

adjectives
painstaking; consulting; self-styled; distinguished; research; topographical.

verbs
consult—; employ—; require—; —alters; —arranges; —bridges; —computes; —constructs; —contrives; —designs; —devises; —invents; —manages; —measures; —plans; —performs; —schemes; —suggests; —supervises; —undertakes.

(See driver, operator, manager.)

ENGINEERING

adjectives
automotive; unrivaled; chemical; civil; electrical; mechanical.

ENGLAND

verbs
ally with—; defame—; defend—; govern —; honor—; integrate—; invade—; journey to—; maim—; reign over—; represent—; revere—; rule—; —acclaims; —bleeds; —endures; —honors; —laments; —triumphs; —vanquishes.

(See country, democracy, republic, monarchy.)

ENGLISH

adjectives
clipped; civilized; thoughtful; simple; fatuous; rhythmic; plain; rough.

verbs
accent—; analyze—; comprehend—; converse in—; correct—; corrupt—; criticize—; falter in—; improve—; interpret—; polish —; purify—; render in—; rhyme—; speak —; study—; translate—; —changes; —derives from; —develops; —evolves.

(See language, literature.)

ENGRAVE (v)

adverbs
delicately; handsomely; daintily; indelibly; exquisite; curious; extraordinary; reproduced; vivid; delicate; deft; skillful.

(See carve, imprint.)

ENGRAVING

adjectives
exquisite; curious; extraordinary; reproduced; vivid; delicate; deft; skillful.

ENGROSS (v)

adverbs
constantly; deeply; chiefly; earnestly; wholly; entirely; sympathetically; entirely; passionately; successfully.

(See absorb, occupy.)

ENHANCE (v)

adverbs
enormously; vastly; radically; inexpressibly; fascinatingly; consequently; attractively.
(See increase, magnify.)

ENIGMA

adjectives
inexplicable; incomprehensible.

verbs
deal in—s; disclose—; dissect—; dissolve—; explain—; express in—; investigate—; question—; ransack—; screen in—; scrutinize—; shroud in—; solve—; —baffles; — conceals; —mystifies; —perplexes; —puzzles; —seals.
(See riddle, mystery, puzzle.)

ENIGMATIC

adverbs
bewilderingly; vexatiously; obscurely; inscrutably; oddly; curiously; peculiarly; singularly; precariously; bafflingly; unaccountably; infernally; unreasonably; inexplicably; unnecessarily.

ENJOIN (v)

adverbs
peremptorily; rudely; dictatorially; harshly; sternly; firmly; casually.
(See command, forbid.)

ENJOY (v)

adverbs
intensely; habitually; unconsciously; sagaciously; contemplatively; languidly; poignantly; acutely; hugely; profoundly; keenly; wholesomely; amazingly; vastly; tranquilly; tremendously; passively; evanescently; maliciously; mentally; meditatively; feverishly; indolently; mischievously; voluptuously; trivially; domestically; serenely; aesthetically; innocently; personally; wholeheartedly; imaginatively; idly; unpretentiously; heartily; reasonably; consciously; contemplatively.
(See gratify, like.)

ENJOYABLE

adverbs
thoroughly; utterly; occasionally; always; keenly; profoundly; heartily; immensely; altogether; delightfully; luxuriously.

ENJOYMENT

adjectives
republican; evanescent; passive; malicious;

mental; meditative; different; full; feverish; stately; immediate; indolent; rapt; healthy; affected; frequent; novel; separate; mischievous; voluptuous; perfect; unwonted; trivial; unmolested; prosperous; domestic; serene; sublunary; aesthetic; surfeited; lazy; suppressed; joint; innocent; personal; whole-hearted; imaginative; idle; aimless; gluttonous; amused; refined; open; mystical; tranquil; solid; solitary; statutory; unpretentious; keen; hearty; animal; civil; wholesome; evident; reasonable; frank; conscious; exclusive; contemplative.

verbs
afford—; bless with—; charge with—; covet—; crave—; derive—; desire—; detract from—; forestall—; grasp—; indulge in—; interrupt—; lead to—; limit—; manifest—; prove—; pursue—; quench—; savor with—; scatter—; seize—; share—; spoil —; subdue—; temper—; —engrosses; — monopolizes; —occupies; —palls; —refreshes.
(See pleasure, entertainment, delight, satisfaction, happiness.)

ENLARGE (v)

adverbs
unboundedly; quickly; dangerously; abnormally; unduly; gradually; continuously; threateningly.
(See expand, broaden.)

ENLARGEMENT

adjectives
remarkable; gradual; ignorant; undue; continuous.

verbs
advocate—; attempt—; check—; curb—; curtail—; demand—; influence—; justify—; limit—; necessitate—; plan—; prepare—; prevent—; procure—; promote—; regulate —; require—; restrain—; restrict—; strangle—; strive for—; survey—; warrant —; —absorbs; —enhances; —exalts; —improves.
(See increase, extension, development, expansion, growth.)

ENLIGHTENMENT

verbs
communicate—; direct—; express—; furnish —; impart—; need—; occasion—; plan—; plead for—; present—; prompt—; seek—; shed—; signify—; strive for—; supply—; support—; suppress—; taste—; —acquaints;

—assists; —awakens; —edifies; —exhilar-ates; —progresses; —revives.
(See wisdom, advancement.)

ENMITY
adjectives
secret; everlasting; oblivious; lifelong; passionate; irreconcilable; unwarrantable; stolid; intense; dark.

verbs
abolish—; allay—; disarm—; drown—; earn—; enact through—; express—; frown upon—; ground on—; harbor—; incite—; incur—; nurse—; overcome—; perceive—; place—between; ponder—; set—between; sow—; vanquish—; —abates; —breaks; —separates; —severs; —splits.
(See hostility, ill-will, opposition, antagonism, hatred, animosity.)

ENNUI
adjectives
listless; eternal; mortal.

verbs
affect with—; bore with—; curse with—; die of—; divert—; feel—; overcome—; produce—; resent—; save from—; signify—; subdue—; suffer from—; taste—; weary with—; wrap in—; —abates; —attacks; —bereaves; —despairs; —dethrones; —grows; —is born; —palls; —vexes; —victimizes; —weights.
(See weariness, languor.)

ENORMOUS
adverbs
incredibly; preposterously; inordinately; tremendously; fabulously; astonishingly; absolutely; extraordinarily; indescribably; positively; frightfully; alarmingly.

ENQUIRE (*v*)
adverbs
innocently; hopefully; continually; persistently; annoyingly; repeatedly; fervently.
(See ask, question.)

ENRAPTURED
adverbs
obviously; utterly; inordinately; particularly; strangely; surprisingly; completely; deeply; indubitably; wonderfully; mysteriously; highly; avowedly.

ENRICH (*v*)
adverbs
prodigiously; delectably; abundantly; magnificently; elaborately; immensely; ultimately; considerably; ornately.
(See adorn, embellish.)

ENRICHMENT
adjectives
resultant; minor; ornate.

ENROLLMENT
verbs
check—; dismiss from—; enter in—; erase from—; inscribe in—; list—; mark—; merit —; place on—; qualify for—; record in—; refer to—; register in—; seek—; view—; —acknowledges; —approximates; —certifies; —embodies; —increases; —notes.
(See record.)

ENSCONCE (*v*)
adverbs
snugly; firmly; comfortably; safely; cozily; warmly; domestically.
(See sit, repose.)

ENSEMBLE
adjectives
impressive; rustic; harmonious; neighborhood.

ENSIGN
adjectives
national; armorial; fluttering.

verbs
cheer—; guard—; humble—; lift up—; march under—; plant—; protect—; raise—; rally round—; salute—; scatter—; shred—; spread—; tatter—; unfurl—; —advances; —blazes; —flutters; —signifies; —symbolizes; hang up—.
(See standard, flag.)

ENSLAVEMENT
verbs
cast into—; decry—; deliver from—; denounce—; drive into—; free from—; hamper by—; liberate from—; prevent—; quit —; reduce to—; release from—; repel—; return to—; submit to—; throw into—; —deprives; —disgusts; —hinders; —restrains; —stifles; —subjugates.
(See bondage, subjugation, subjection, slavery.)

ENTANGLE (v)

adverbs

inextricably; equally; unnecessarily; thoroughly; fatally; tragically; unfortunately; matrimonially; domestically; ceaselessly; rashly.

(See tangle, involve.)

ENTANGLEMENT

adjectives

inextricable; unnecessary.

verbs

avoid—; charm into—; extricate from—; inveigh into—; knit—; lure into—; prevent —; remove—; risk—; snare in—; unfold—; unravel—; trap in—; weave—; —complicates; —confuses; —distresses; —embarrasses; —embraces; —impedes; —implicates; —involves; —pains; —perplexes; escape—.

(See intricacy, complication, tangle.)

ENTER (v)

adverbs

gradually; inconspicuously; presumptuously; peremptorily; calmly; belligerently; triumphantly; obtrusively; intimately; minutely; hurriedly; intelligently; gratefully; optimistically; promptly; controversially; casually; ceremoniously; boldly; unlawfully; pompously; abruptly; simultaneously.

(See penetrate, insert.)

ENTERPRISE

adjectives

profitable; amazing; legitimate; individual; heterogeneous; successful; commercial; regional; dignified; lofty; voluntary; economic; vulgar; protracted; inadequate; stupid; philanthropic; characteristic; romantic; fresh; monumental; desperate; year-round; unscrupulous; blameless; ill-starred; magnanimous; daring; equal; vivid; manly; costly; co-operative; active; chimerical; honorable; venturesome; formidable; uncertain; serviceable; perilous; glorious; prodigious; productive; fabulous; nautical; mundane;- infernal; gigantic; prominent; dangerous; hazardous; brilliant; illegal; crusading; charitable; appalling; audacious; inviting; indomitable; laudable; imaginative; delicate.

verbs

abandon—; arm for—; consider—; display —; embark on—; endanger—; enlist in—; enroll in—; exploit—; finance—; hazard—; imperil—; initiate—; manage—; partake in—; persist in—; risk—; stimulate—; struggle in—; swear to—; undertake—; venture on—; —fails; —flourishes; —prospers; —requires; —succeeds; —thrives.

(See project, task, work, undertaking.)

ENTERPRISING

adverbs

unusually; amazingly; daringly; laudably; brilliantly; prodigiously; cleverly; skilfully; alertly; smartly; energetically; marvelously; wonderfully; astutely; zealously; strenuously; earnestly; oddly; briskly; vigorously; indefatigably; industriously; diligently; intrepidly; confidently; uncommonly; competently.

ENTERTAIN (v)

adverbs

momentarily; seriously; pretentiously; fabulously; jovially; charmingly; extensively; lavishly; sumptuously; gravely; royally; tolerably; gaily; steadily; hospitably; vaguely; ponderously; uniformly; erroneously; rudely; incessantly; boisterously; casually; cleverly; musically; laboriously; incidentally; sparklingly; fitfully.

(See amuse, divert.)

ENTERTAINER

adjectives

talented; professional; terrified; master.

verbs

acclaim—; announce—; applaud—; boo—; deride—; encore—; encourage—; engage—; heckle—; hire—; hiss—; order—s; produce —; provide—; seek—s; supply—s; —amuses; —bores; —delights; —diverts; —enlivens; —exhibits; —performs; —pleases; —practises; —wearies.

(See hostess, actor.)

ENTERTAINING

adverbs

brilliantly; pleasantly; highly; agreeably; racily; undoubtedly; unusually; charmingly; elaborately; distinctly; delightfully; cleverly; gallantly; amusingly; wittily; sportively; hilariously; roguishly; noisily; admirably; impressively; merrily; comically; ridiculously.

ENTERTAINMENT

adjectives

charming; rude; hospitable; society; elaborate; endless; incessant; boisterous; casual; youthful; distinguished; amateur; critical; mutual; princely; diversified;

clever; friendly; dramatic; musical; honorable; momentary; laborious; sumptuous; guest; evening; varied; sparkling; incidental.

verbs
accord—; afford—; announce—; applaud—; approve of—; buy—; desire—; furnish—; guarantee—; lack—; perceive with—; prepare—; produce—; provide—; seek—; stage—; supply—; surprise with—; —annoys; —bores; —delights; —diverts; —enlivens; —interests; —pleases; —tires; —wearies.
(See performance, amusement, delight, diversion, enjoyment, recreation, hospitality.)

ENTHRALLED
adverbs
irresistibly; utterly; completely; wondrously; mysteriously; rapidly; rapturously; ecstatically; blissfully; strangely; deeply.

ENTHRONE (v)
adverbs
solemnly; grandly; ceremoniously; magnificently; pompously; regally; spectacularly.
(See raise, elevate.)

ENTHUSIASM
adjectives
rash; increasing; unbounded; fanatical; heartiest; warm; passionate; noisy; generous; ill-judged; romantic; voluble; girlish; glowing; exaggerated; weakening; boundless; fervent; ubiquitous; academic; rapt; unrestrained; passing; patriotic; polemical; rousing; gushing; uncontrolled; uncommon; positive; lyric; religious; intense; irrepressible; beautiful; delirious; vapid; proud; popular; impetuous; smoldering; healthy; altruistic; fierce; contagious; usual; greedy; human; available; misguided; rapturous; solemn; latent; unreflecting; honest; dwindled; instant; wild; frantic; temporary; buoyant; fervid; virginal; virtuous; genuine; inexhaustible; boyish; sweet; joyous; earnest; hearty; lofty; flamboyant; divine; common; contagious; actual; infectious.

verbs
admire—; arouse—; awaken—; beam with —; beget—; chill—; dampen—; dim—; display—; evoke—; express—; feed—; fire with—; halt—; imbue with—; impart—; inspire with—; muster—; pour forth—; rationalize—; respond to—; rouse—; share —; spend—; suppress—; sustain—; tolerate

—; vibrate with—; —blazes; —blinds; — bubbles; —flags; —flows; —melts away; — pales; —penetrates; —perishes; —rises; —spreads; —subsides; —wanes; —waxes.
(See zeal, ecstasy, eagerness, earnestness, ardor, fervor, passion.)

ENTHUSIAST
adjectives
prominent; dreaming; zealous; culpable; martial; religious; inconsiderate; baffled; harebrained; romantic.

ENTHUSIASTIC
adverbs
unusually; sincerely; delightfully; keenly; profoundly; actively; immediately; zealously; glowingly; passionately; fanatically; warmly; generously; girlishly; fervently; childishly; loudly; boundlessly; raptly; intensely; irrepressibly; beautifully; impulsively; impetuously; fiercely; instantly; wildly; sweetly; joyously; infectiously; extravagantly; strikingly; ardently; exceptionally.

ENTITLE (v)
adverbs
unquestionably; incorrectly; legally; fully; completely; thoroughly; clearly.
(See justify.)

ENTITY
adjectives
abstract; operative; self-acting.

ENTRAILS
adjectives
massy; palpitating; intolerable.

ENTRANCE
adjectives
clairvoyant; auspicious; reputed; complicated; triumphant; unperturbed; hospitable; bricked-up; ceremonious; stormy; sudden; ragged; dirty; fitting; changeful; bursting; unobserved; sheltered; adjacent; brilliant; noisy; swaggering.

verbs
bar—; block—; camouflage—; circle—; clog —; command—; conceal—; convey to—; direct to—; disdain—; effect—; fight for—; flank—; forbid—; forsake—; gain—; guard —; lead to—; obtain—; penetrate—; procure—; reject—; win—; force—.
(See access, door, entry, gate, introduction, opening.)

ENTRANCED

adverbs

perfectly; enthusiastically; utterly; irresistibly; naturally; obviously; noticeably; visibly; delightfully; ecstatically; happily; rapturously; wholly; irrecoverably.

ENTRANT

verbs

admit—; assign—; award to—; file—; herd —s; insert—; introduce—; judge—; limit —s; privilege—; receive—; register—; require—; reward—; select—; welcome—; —s compete; —s flow past; —influences; — participates; —subscribes to.

(See beginner, applicant, competitor.)

ENTREAT (v)

adverbs

civilly; brokenly; pathetically; frankly; patronizingly; earnestly; tenderly; sighingly; fondly; urgently; reproachfully; persistently; humbly; noisily.

(See plead, urge.)

ENTREATY

adjectives

earnest; fond; urgent; boisterous; reproachful; persistent; hospitable; humble; previous; repeated (pl).

verbs

allow—; answer—; comply with—; consent to—; grant—; harass with—ies; hawk—ies; heed—; protest—; rebuff—; recite—; repulse—; resist—; tender—; tolerate—; vex with—; yield to—; —irritates; —persuades; —requests.

(See request, petition, appeal.)

ENTREE

verbs

anticipate—; arrive at—; await—; ban—; choose—; demand—; give—to; gulp—; limit—; prepare—; prevent—; procure—; provide—; refuse—; relish—; select—; serve—; value—; —tempts.

(See dish, food.)

ENTRENCH (v)

adverbs

firmly; safely; protectively; defensively; deeply; securely.

(See intensify, fortify.)

ENTRY

adjectives

forcible; partial; abrupt; official; illegal; discursive; triumphant; burglarious; grandiloquent; mere; magnificent.

verbs

cancel—; certify—; duplicate—; file—; inscribe—; insert—; jot down—; limit—s; note—; post—; record—; register—; reject—; solicit—ies; strike out—; tabulate ies—; welcome—; wipe out—; —s flood.

(See entrance, access, hall.)

ENVELOP (v)

adverbs

thickly; gaseously; materially; impenetrably; nebulously; obscurely.

(See surround, inclose.)

ENVELOPE

adjectives

gaseous; rigid; material; impenetrable.

verbs

address—; assign to—; enclose in—; fold —; gum—; knife—; pen—; seal—; stamp —; tear—; wrap in—; —bears; —confines; —contains; —covers; —encases; —protects; —surrounds.

(See wrapper, case, sheath.)

ENVELOPMENT

adjectives

nebulous; curious; obscure; ungrateful.

ENVIABLE

adverbs

utterly; eminently; vaguely; intensely; apparently; obviously; highly; undeniably; uncommonly; invidiously.

ENVIRONMENT

adjectives

unnatural; accidental; fictitious; cultural; gay; friendly; refined; smart; spiritual; stately; refreshing; restricted; unambitious; ideal; hostile; economic; early; playhouse; suitable; specific; luxurious; pseudo-social; moral; fitting; cooling; healthful; unsuited; niggardly; native; unfavorable; frontier; unusual; human; felicitous; musical; nationalistic; physical; fertile; limited.

verbs

adjust to—; alter—; control—; create—; dominate—; endure—; escape from—; fit—; harmonize with—; lift from—; modify—; shape—; share—; —corrupts; —exerts; —influences; —moulds; —shapes; — strengthens; —weakens.

(See surroundings, circumstances, conditions.)

adjectives
immediate; sheltered; picturesque; straggling.

ENVY

adjectives
petty; daggered; jealous; vile; powerless; ghoulish; malignant; poignant; pardonable; bitter; secret; gnawing; public; private; strenuous; illiberal; mixed; unnatural; sharp; sick-bed.

verbs
arouse—; awaken—; conceal—; discipline —; evoke—; excite—; exempt from—; express—; fill with—; incite—; incur—of; infect with—; move by—; murmur—; occasion—; provoke—; raise—; regard with—; sicken with—; stab with—; —blazes up; —convulses; —envelops; —inflames; —narrows; —prejudices; —swells; —threatens.
(See malice, desire, jealousy.)

ENVY (v)

adverbs
secretly; sincerely; pettishly; jealously; vilely; powerlessly; ghoulishly; malignantly; bitterly; gnawingly; privately; unnaturally; painfully.
(See suspect, desire.)

EPHEMERAL

adverbs
fleetingly; wondrously; transiently; shiftily; sadly; precariously; tantalizingly; vexatiously; transitorily; evanescently; mortally; perishably; briefly; heartbreakingly.

EPIC

adjectives
peopled; magnificent; grand; unscrupulous; extant; future; literary; counterfeiting; ponderous; medieval; pietistic; eternal; heroic; familiar; lengthy.

adverbs
traditionally; fabulously; nationally; racially; universally; nobly; significantly; majestically; splendidly; dramatically; tragically; brilliantly; deathlessly; imperishably; timelessly; sweepingly; consummately; amazingly; highly; magnificently; staggeringly; incomparably; grandly.

EPICURE

adjectives
jovial; classical; facetious; cultured; suave; fastidious; precise.

EPICUREAN

adverbs
fastidiously; delicately; luxuriously; sensuously; indulgently; daintily; discriminatingly; greedily; highly; openly; manifestly; intemperately; voluptuously; rakishly; wildly; inordinately; lamentably; extremely; deliberately; avowedly.

EPIDEMIC

adjectives
veritable; dangerous; disastrous; prevailing; periodical; acute; terrible; infectious.

verbs
approach—; constitute—; curtail—; eradicate—; fend against—; inoculate against—; succumb to—; —appears; —breaks out; —consumes; —devastates; —lingers; —prostrates; —rages; —ravages; —sweeps; —swells; —wanes.
(See disease, plague, cholera, smallpox.)

adverbs
locally; universally; currently; recently; sweepingly; commonly; prevalently; generally; infectiously; contagiously; noxiously; pestilentially; virulently; unfortunately; diffusively; dangerously; disastrously; periodically; acutely; terribly; curiously; obscurely; inexplicably; mysteriously.

EPIDERMIS

verbs
affect—; apply to—; blemish—; dab—; damage—; daub—; flay—; form—; impair —; infect—; injure—; mar—; repair—; restore—; salve—; scratch—; shed—; smear on—; —coats; —covers; —defends; —encases; —peels; —tans; —regenerates.
(See skin.)

EPIGRAM

adjectives
sparkling; feeble; biting.

verbs
abound in—s; compose—; enjoy—; indulge in—; inscribe—; master—; recite—; resent —; translate—; vent—; —charms; —condenses; —debases; —expresses; —irks; —points out; —provokes; —puzzles; —revenges; —satirizes; —stings; —consists of.
(See saying, poem, writing.)

EPIGRAMMATIC

adverbs
facetiously; waggishly; sententiously; laconically; crisply; curtly; neatly; quaintly;

pithily; concisely; summarily; wittily; cruelly; harshly; sarcastically; clownishly; drolly; jocosely; playfully; smartly; consciously; vexatiously; endlessly.

EPISODE

adjectives
impressive; dramatic; colorful; ludicrous; tragical; unsavory; extraordinary; pungent; exciting; wearing; pathetic; undignified; magnificent; ugly; continental; momentous; stirring; detached; mystical; peaceful; quixotic; picturesque; unforeseen; human; moving; trivial; soul-stirring; unfinished.

verbs
arrange—s; brood upon—; continue—; dramatize—; finish—; interject—; interpose—; introduce—; involve in—; number —s; recount—; refer to—; relate—; repeat —; resume—; —climaxes; —concerns; — crops up; —embraces; —entertains; —implicates; —intervenes.
(See incident, event, occurrence, action, story.)

EPISTLE

adjectives
famous; closely-written; absurd; tearful; heartfelt; imperial; business; monotonous; gracious; elegant; maternal; perplexing.

verbs
address—; compose—; delay—; deliver—; dispatch—; inspire—; laud—; pen—; prepare—; seal—; —aims at; —communicates; —consoles; —conveys; —declares; —explains; —indites; —instructs; —links; — relates; —reunites; —reveals; —strays; — wanders; —waxes.
(See letter, communication, writing.)

EPITAPH

adjectives
lying; mournful; pompous; uxorious; chiseled; inordinate; pitiable; simple; celebrated; original; dusty; sly; faithful; ancestral; wise; fitting; appropriate; irreverent.

verbs
bestow—on; compose—; conceive—; define —; deliver—; deserve—; hang—on; incorporate in—; inscribe—; interpret—; judge —; merit—; render in—; —adorns; —de-

scribes; —familiarizes; —glitters; —glorifies; —honors; —records; —reflects; — slanders; —vulgarizes.
(See inscription.)

EPITHET

adjectives
deranged; obnoxious; profane; insulting; deprecatory; opprobrious; polite; repeated; contumelious; endearing; courteous; balanced; fatal; significant.

verbs
answer—; apply—; bandy—s; bestow— upon; christen with—; comprehend—; convey—; design—; employ—; fix—; glory in—; indulge in—; justify—; originate—; pelt with—s; rain—s; represent with—; scatter—s; stuff with—s; —belongs; —designates; —disgraces; —justifies; —qualifies; —signifies; —terms.
(See phrase, expression, adjective, designation.)

EPITOMIZE (*v*)

adverbs
successfully; wittily; artfully; completely; shrewdly.
(See summarize, discuss.)

EPOCH

adjectives
geological; brilliant; colonial; misguided; glacial; legendary; memorable; impersonal; agitated; eventful; warfaring; climacteric; barbarous; revolutionary; haunted; chronological; antique; pagan.

verbs
begin—; commemorate—; create—; divide into—s; enhance—; form—; indicate—; inherit from—; mark—; open—; outlive—; refer to—; remember—; venerate—; — declines; —embraces; —glides on; —impresses; —produces; —provides; —survives.
(See period, era, time.)

EPOCHAL

adverbs
distinctly; significantly; markedly; notably; unforgettably; shamefully; brilliantly; memorably; legendarily; fabulously; imperishably; matchlessly; startlingly; stupendously; incalculably.

EQUABLE

adverbs
comfortably; pleasantly; dependably; naturally; happily; habitually; inherently; se-

renely; faultlessly; monotonously; reliably; drearily; methodically; agreeably; fairly; vexatiously; always; enviably.

EQUAL

adverbs
fairly; satisfactorily; agreeably; monotonously; symmetrically; broadly; practically; reasonably; legitimately; lawfully; admittedly; avowedly; synonymously; sufficiently; apparently; obviously; manifestly; evidently; incontestably.

EQUALITY

adjectives
rude; cozy; perfect; social; moral; legitimate; large; unrestricted; eternal; condescending.

verbs
abuse—; acquire—; admit—; approach—; assert—; assume—; attain—; demand—; denounce—; deny—; destroy—; disturb—; endow with—; maintain—; plead—; practice—; prate about—; prevent—; proclaim —; refuse—; require—; —breeds.
(See equilibrium, right, fairness, justice.)

EQUANIMITY

adjectives
astonishing; cool; unruffled; suave.

verbs
admire—; accept with—; approve—; bear with—; command—; concede with—; demonstrate—; digest with—; disregard with —; dwell in—; endure with—; justify—; keep in—; maintain—; possess—; recommend—; recover—; require—; restore—; suffer with—; swallow with—; wonder at —; —continues; —impresses; —persists; —surprises.
(See composure, serenity.)

EQUATION

adjectives
quadratic; personal; explanatory.

EQUILIBRIUM

adjectives
natural; balanced; unstable; happy; atmospheric.

verbs
attain—; check—; correct—; display—; exhibit—; gain—; guard—; illustrate—; maintain—; preserve—; restore—; threaten—.
(See balance, proportion.)

EQUIPAGE

adjectives
lumbering; huge; gilded; sumptuous; sufficient; somber.

EQUIPMENT

adjectives
technical; complete; optional; brilliant; recreational; obsolete; extensive; standard; defective; scanty; scientific; physical; inadequate; vocal; motorized; primitive; superior; ample; necessary; mental; intellectual.

verbs
acquire—; allot—to; complete—; contrive —; devise—; guard—; install—; modernize—; provide—; repair—; shield—; transport—; utilize—.
(See outfit, apparatus.)

EQUIPOISE

adjectives
boasted; unusual; vaunted.

EQUITABLE

adverbs
wisely; reasonably; duly; plainly; profoundly; prudently; rationally; sensibly; providently; expediently; justly; impartially; honorably; fairly; squarely; lawfully; legally; allowably; absolutely; legitimately; properly; scrupulously; punctiliously.

EQUIVALENT

adjectives
thermal; fair; modern; universal; financial; precise.

adverbs
meticulously; convertibly; tantamountly; avowedly; broadly; currently; customarily; regularly; naturally; wontedly; mathematically; genuinely; officially; strictly; basically; precisely; materially.

EQUIVOCAL

adverbs
vexatiously; irritatingly; purposely; intentionally; ambiguously; craftily; subtly; adroitly; cleverly; dubiously; debatably; insecurely; vaguely; mysteriously; ticklishly; obscurely; untrustworthily; unreliably; provokingly; cunningly; unfairly; artfully; fraudulently; perfidiously; insincerely; highly.

adjectives

crude; garish; showy; industrial; uninspired; commercialized; brief; comparative; colonial; illuminated; vamp; cultural.

verbs

acclaim—; announce—; enhance—; gild—; glorify—; hallow—; mark—; open—; symbolize—; typify—; usher in—; vulgarize—; —advances; —dawns; —emerges; —passes.

(See period, epoch, time.)

ERASURE

adjectives

lineal; untidy; unsightly; careless; blotchy; neat; nearly-invisible.

ERECT

adverbs

sturdily; staunchly; bravely; gallantly; loftily; firmly; grandly; rigidly; boldly; admirably; conspicuously; consciously; stiffly; proudly; imperiously; arrogantly.

ERECT (v)

adverbs

loftily; firmly; grandly; staunchly; toweringly; eloquently; triumphantly.

(See build, raise.)

ERECTNESS

adjectives

firm; conscious; natural; easy; military.

EROSION

verbs

activate—; check—; occasion—; overcome —; prevent—; produce—; protect from—; risk—; subject to—; —damages; —disintegrates; —endangers; —occurs; —strains; —weakens.

(See destruction, decay, acid.)

EROSIVE

adverbs

dangerously; wastefully; distressingly; disturbingly; unprofitably; harmfully; disastrously; detrimentally; deplorably; irremediably; inexpediently; increasingly; unfortunately; unnecessarily; grossly; outrageously; appallingly.

EROTIC

adverbs

amorously; tenderly; seductively; ardently; captivatingly; unduly; notably; particularly; interestingly; rapturously.

adjectives

mysterious; arrogant; uncouth; discouraging; slightest; reluctant; urgent; mournful; stumbling; futile; various (pl); wondrous.

verbs

accept—; administer—; bear—; commission for—; consent to—; discharge—; dispatch on—; execute—: fail in—; fake— (colloq); feign—; journey on—; send on—; speed on—.

(See mission, commission, communication.)

ERRANT

adverbs

incurably; nonchalantly; carelessly; incorrigibly; irresponsibly; gaily; happily; rapturously.

ERRATIC

adverbs

irregularly; habitually; characteristically; provokingly; unreliably; strangely; curiously; inscrutably; irresponsibly; inconsiderately; naturally; restlessly; mercurially; vagrantly; incurably; inveterately; fitfully; whimsically; capriciously; contrarily; uncomfortably; foolishly; inconsistently; marvelously; terribly.

ERRONEOUS

adverbs

tragically; purposely; carelessly; fallaciously; materially; foolishly; illogically; deceptively; intentionally; blunderingly; misleadingly; slightly; altogether; dreadfully; unpardonably.

ERROR

adjectives

manifest; inextricable; fatal; capital; successful; intellectual; deep-seated; common; vulgar; sweet; silly; trivial; apparent; gross; earthly; popular; strange; destructive; outstanding; biting; feeble; shallow; weak; mountainous; egregious; universal; ignoble; bare; venial; tactical; childish; unavoidable; curious; annoying; unguessed; statistical; innumerable (pl); scientific; serviceable; crumbling; pernicious; wild; warm; fantastic; glaring; opposite; chronic; dietetic; pleasing; previous; petty; profound; matrimonial; irretrievable; infinite; fundamental; unwelcome; counter; haughty; serious; damned; tempest-winged; typographical; monstrous; unfortunate; irremediable.

verbs
abound in—s; acknowledge—; adhere to—; aggravate—; atone for—; befog—; betray into—; build on—; cast out—; chafe at—; claim—; combat—; conquer—; correct—; counteract—; debate—; detect—; dispel—; escape—; expiate—; expose—; fall into—; forsake—; involve in—; lead into—; learn from—; lift above—; minimize—; neutralize—; overrule—; produce—; rebuke—; rectify—; reduce—; regret—; reject—; relinquish—; remove—; retrieve—; root in—; rue—; sense—; uncover—; unveil—; utter —; vanquish—; war against—; ward off—; wrestle with—; —contaminates; —deludes; —destroys; —impedes; —misleads.
(See fault, blunder, mistake, inaccuracy.)

ERUDITION
adjectives
mock; scholarly; extraordinary; specious.

verbs
abuse—; admire—; demand—; demonstrate —; denote—; digest—; employ—; exhibit —; feign—; freight with—; indicate—; judge—; justify—; oppress—; regard—; represent—; require—; —gratifies; —impresses.
(See knowledge, learning, wisdom.)

ERUPT (v)
adverbs
prematurely; terrifically; violently; prodigiously; volcanically; thunderously; crashingly; blindingly.
(See burst, explode.)

ERUPTION
adjectives
ruddy; cutaneous; memorable; terrific; copious; violent; prodigious; simultaneous; volcanic.

verbs
break forth in—; fear—; force—; hinder—; occasion—; prevent—; subject to—; —appears; —bursts; —discharges; —ejects; —emits; —harms; —issues forth; —occurs; —overwhelms; —shatters; —showers; —spreads.
(See outbreak, outburst.)

ESCAPADE
adjectives
suspicious; political; rash; youthful; drunken.

ESCAPE
adjectives
miraculous; precious; destitute; momentary; trivial; ignoble; impossible; marvelous; perilous; ultimate; hairbreadth; extraordinary; hair-raising; strong.

verbs
aid—; allow—; assist in—; attribute—to; conceal—; conspire—; cut off—; desire—; despair of—; effect—; enable—; guard against—; hinder—; insure—; investigate —; permit—; prevent—; scorn—; shun—.
(See flight, excuse, evasion.)

ESCAPE (v)
adverbs
exultantly; miraculously; temporarily; narrowly; easily; resolutely; audaciously; incessantly; barely; momentarily; ignobly; marvelously; perilously; ultimately; extraordinarily; hair-raisingly.
(See flee, elude.)

ESCORT
adjectives
military; proper; honorary; lounging; insufficient; barbaric.

verbs
accept—; attend in—; choose—; command —; desire—; employ—; form—; invite—; require—; serve as—; —abandons; —accommodates; —accompanies; —conducts; —conveys; —deserts; —guides; —lectures; —manages; —nurses; —protects; —serves; —supervises.
(See guard.)

ESCORT (v)
adverbs
tumultuously; barbarically; formally; ceremoniously; grandly; magnificently; regally; royally; gaily.
(See attend, follow.)

ESPIONAGE
adjectives
ostentatious; stealthy; cleverly-concealed; sympathetic.

ESPOUSE (v)
adverbs
obstinately; warmly; passionately; rabidly; ardently; rashly; impatiently; sincerely; treacherously.
(See undertake, assume.)

ESPOUSER

adjectives
ardent; rabid; rash; impatient.

ESSAY

adjectives
satirical; controversial; historical; critical; introductory; moral; discursive; provocative; delightful; notable; apathetical; celebrated; detached; literary; elaborated; sublime; fragmentary; informative; admirable; kindred; penetrating; classical; enlightening; presumptuous; remarkable.

verbs
abandon—; accept—; agree with—; attack —; caption—; compose—; criticize—; discuss—; elaborate—; judge—; laud—; offer —; praise—; prepare—; preserve—; propound—; —attempts; —encourages; —expresses; —implies; —meditates on.
(See composition, endeavor, attempt, effort, exposition.)

ESSAYIST

adjectives
critical; classical; aggressive.

ESSENCE

adjectives
seductive; intentional; tenfold; concrete; lasting; solitary; everlasting; spiritual; subtle; carnal; divine; congenial; electric; enduring; singular; ethereal; poetic; meager; heavenly; invisible; articulate; omnipresent; distinct; penetrative; volatile; rubylike; thin; fiery; winged; glassy; sensuous; impalatable; immutable.

verbs
apply—; convey—; counterfeit—; cover with—; distil—; exhale—; extract—; flavor with—; instil—; perfume with—; prepare —; preserve—; procure—; resign—; rub in—; sprinkle—; steep in—; —nauseates; —penetrates; —pervades; —refreshes; — sickens; —sinks in.
(See substance, perfume, odor, scent.)

ESSENTIAL

adjectives
salient; vital; food; absolute; minimum; basic.

verbs
ascertain—; cloud—; constitute—; deprive of—; destroy—; discern—; dispense with —; establish—; lack—; master—; obstruct —; overlook—; prove—; require—; restore —; strain—; suppress—; understand—; withhold—; —necessitates; —represents; — vanishes.
(See element, principle, quality.)

ESSENTIAL

adverbs
highly; absolutely; cardinally; emphatically; gravely; momentously; vitally; fundamentally; primarily; signally; significantly; urgently; extraordinarily; inordinately; seriously; utterly; peculiarly; unusually.

ESTABLISH (v)

adverbs
infallibly; conclusively; firmly; pompously; ultimately; solidly; definitely; indispensably; officially; permanently; triumphantly; incontestably; sufficiently; extensively; formally; rudely; splendidly; ancestrally; palatially; administratively.
(See show, prove.)

ESTABLISHED

adverbs
permanently; enduringly; stably; inviolately; thoroughly; immemorially; traditionally; generally; commonly; familiarly; conventionally; socially; regularly; officially; long; recently; firmly; easily; legally; emphatically; inescapably.

ESTABLISHMENT

adjectives
monastic; modest-looking; productive; immense; rude; conventional; splendid; primitive; odorous; penal; permanent; consular; separate; extensive; palatial; domestic; immediate; select; ancestral; manufacturing; ultimate; princely; meat-curing; administrative; costly; respectable-looking.

verbs
attack—; bar from—; conduct—; dictate —; enlarge—; evict from—; found—; guard—; hallow—; join—; legalize—; maintain—; nurture—; offend—; patronize—; set up—; superintend—; underwrite —; —crumbles; —fails; —flourishes; — prospers.
(See organization, institution.)

ESTATE

adjectives
manorial; residuary; intestate; unencumbered; landed; ancestral; precarious; competent; distressed; dark; scanty; fabulous;

feudal; impoverished; ecclesiastical; paltry; low; poor; outlying; hushed; sublunary; pretentious; unspeakable; meager; strange; uncorrupted; seignorial.

verbs
administer—; auction off—; charge to—; confiscate—; disable—; dissipate—; doom —; fall from—; fritter away—; lease—; maintain—; mortgage—; reapportion—; rent—; scorn—; settle—; shift—; tax—; —declines; —prospers; —shrinks.
(See property, possessions.)

ESTEEM

adjectives
great; rising; profound; exalted; proudest; racial; envious; impious; general; bright; favorable; sincerest.

verbs
command—; conceal—; deserve—; drop from—; enjoy—; entertain—; forfeit—; gain—; grow in—; hide—; hold in—; increase—; lose—; regard with—; value—; win—; —cools; —fades; —grows.
(See regard, respect, honor, favor, worth, opinion, value.)

ESTEEM (*v*)

adverbs
particularly; profoundly; racially; generally; sincerely; logically; enviously.
(See respect, honor.)

ESTIMABLE

adverbs
entirely; generally; highly; profoundly; undeniably; creditably; unimpeachably; obviously; worthily; dreadfully; respectably; dully; extremely; priggishly.

ESTIMATE

adjectives
impartial; production; exact; sanguine; contemptuous; accurate; accepted; modest; conservative; rough; truer; provisional; respectful; private; critical; utmost; exaggerated; judicious; reasonable; professional; slighting; undue; exaggerated; fallacious; moderate; current; contradictory; erroneous; inadequate; fantastic; theoretical; lightning.

verbs
accept—; arrive at—; attempt—; beggar—; calculate—; compute—; correct—; denounce —; entertain—; exaggerate—; extend—;

forward—; govern—; harbor—; offer—; reach—; reel off—s; sway—s; —agrees; —coincides; —differs; —errs; —falls short; —indicates.
(See computation, calculation, value.)

ESTIMATE (*v*)

adverbs
conservatively; variously; accurately; critically; approximately; authoritatively; unhesitatingly; wildly; unerringly; calculatingly; fallaciously; erroneously; inadequately; fantastically; theoretically; professionally; provisionally; worthily.
(See value, appraise.)

ESTIMATION

adjectives
worthy; reverend; excessive; ludicrous; ungalled; avowed; exalted; aristocratic.

ESTRANGED

adverbs
pitiably; altogether; tragically; pathetically; curiously; inexplicably; mysteriously; oddly; silently; obviously; evidently; coldly; hatefully; temporarily; deeply; permanently; stubbornly; relentlessly; visibly; idiotically; astonishingly; lamentably.

ESTRANGEMENT

adjectives
transient; political.

verbs
bear—; brood over—; complete—; incur—; mourn—; pine in—; prevent—; rebel against—; sink in—; submit to—; suffer—; —agonizes; —burns; —dejects; —depresses; —desolates; —disheartens; —isolates; —oppresses; —pains; —wearies.

ETCH (*v*)

adverbs
vividly; powerfully; movingly; delicately; skillfully; artfully; dexterously; strikingly.
(See draw, sketch.)

ETCHING

adjectives
powerful; delicate; moving.

ETERNITY

adjectives
self-enshrined; dead; endless; shoreless; present; measureless; indivisible; dreadful; tiny.

verbs
accept—; believe in—; dwell in—; endure for—; foretaste—; glimpse—; leave to—; pass through—; probe—; prolong to—; reach—; reveal—; seems—; sing of—; spend in—; wander through—; —effaces; —exists.

(See immortality.)

ETHER

adjectives
luminiferous; finer; limpid; luminous; elastic; celestial; boundless; subtle.

verbs
administer—; apply—; float in—; put under —; sleep under—; spray—; —anaesthetizes; —affects; —deadens; —diminishes; — dims; —dissolves; —drowns; —dulls; — moderates; —numbs; —palls; —reduces; —stupefies.

(See anaesthetic.)

ETHEREAL

adverbs
daintily; airily; insubstantially; lightly; buoyantly; incredibly; delicately; vivaciously; whimsically; blithely; gracefully; sportively; inexpressibly.

ETHICAL

adverbs
punctiliously; meticulously; highly; systematically; unfailingly; ostentatiously; laboriously; carefully; naturally; habitually; professionally; strictly; rigidly; happily; gracefully; politely; diplomatically; marvellously; conscientiously; dutifully; amenably; absolutely.

ETHICS

adjectives
professional; inflexible; strict; dreary; government; ministerial; legal; cheerless; bad; heightened.

verbs
adopt—; consider—; control by—; digest—; discourse on—; embrace—; exhort—; impose by—; improve—; instruct in—; involve—; judge—; live up to—; obligate by—; observe—; rebel against—; rely on—; test—; versed in—; —directs; —guides; — provides; —raises.

(See science, rules, philosophy.)

ETIQUETTE

adjectives
fixed; punctilious; stiff; established; courtly; exclusive; rigid.

verbs
apply—; conduct with—; educate in—; impose by—; inform on—; judge by—; loosen —; observe—; polish—; practise—; prescribe—; require—; study—; transact with —; transgress—; —bans; —demands; — forbids; —improves; —obliges; —prohibits; —tames; —ties.

(See code, rules, decorum.)

EULOGISTIC

adverbs
sententiously; sincerely; properly; suitably; regularly; duly; smugly; sanctimoniously; hypocritically; highly; impressively; dramatically; immeasurably; unnecessarily; sonorously; artfully; brilliantly; magnificently; admirably; splendidly; unctuously; sycophantically; speciously; fulsomely.

EULOGIZE (v)

adverbs
unctuously; flamboyantly; effusively; lavishly; flatteringly; deceptively; slyly; treacherously; deceivingly.

(See laud, praise.)

EULOGY

adjectives
barren; unmeasured; artful; embarrassed; swallowing; lengthened; brilliant; indiscriminating; sorry; glowing; sounding.

EUPHEMISTIC

adverbs
cleverly; artfully; adroitly; ironically; sarcastically; wittily; smoothly; humorously; plausibly; pompously; rhetorically; merrily; teasingly; neatly; felicitously; pleasantly; inoffensively.

EUPHONY

adjectives
gushing; sheer.

EUROPE

verbs
communicate with—; denounce—; embattle —; embroil—; introduce in—; invade—; ring through—; rock—; rule—; sail for—; seize—; shock—; tour—; unite—; —allies with; —arms; —copies; —envies; —ex-

ports; —imitates; —imports; —quakes; —repudiates; —seethes; —simmers; —stands; —voices; —wars.
(See continent.)

EVACUATION

adjectives
copious; sanguinolent; alvine.

verbs
advocate—; authorize—; command—; compel—; deplore—; direct—; facilitate—; force—; impose—; insist on—; prepare—; prescribe—; promote—; resist—; submit to —; suggest—; withdraw in—; —relinquishes; order—.
(See withdrawal, discharge.)

EVADE (v)

adverbs
gracefully; studiously; partially; slyly; treacherously; cleverly; dexterously.
(See avoid, shun.)

EVALUATION

adjectives
clinical; clear.

EVANESCENT

adverbs
flittingly; impermanently; briefly; ephemerally; precariously; transiently; transitorily; perishably; mortally; sadly.

EVANGELISTIC

adverbs
ardently; zealously; sincerely; earnestly; successfully; eagerly; persistently; fervently; devotedly; fervidly; passionately; assiduously; solemnly; happily; joyously; enthusiastically; rapturously; superbly; intensely; unwearyingly; devoutly.

EVASION

adjectives
elaborate; endless; dexterous; pitiful; terror-stricken; treasonable; sly .

verbs
addict to—; criticize—; decry—; detect—; employ—; endure—; forbid—; force—; frustrate—; practice—; require—; shift in —; shuffle in—; stammer in—; suspect—; trouble with—; wrap in—; —assists; —shelters.
(See subterfuge.)

EVASIVE

adverbs
unfortunately; disturbingly; deliberately; undesirably; ambiguously; equivocally; distressingly; offensively; insultingly; suspiciously; undeniably; quibblingly; perplexingly; bewilderingly; obscurely; mysteriously; seriously; irritatingly; stolidly; vaguely; disagreeably; insidiously; significantly; stupidly; unwisely; objectionably; cunningly; cleverly; adroitly.

EVE

adjectives
autumn; dew-glistening; sealing; keener; momentous; thoughtful; dewy; ghostly; deepening.

EVENING

adjectives
lingering; tranquil; happy; occasional; curious; long; fatal; autumnal; cold; frosty; red; triumphant; sad-colored; ravishing; chilly; awkward; bacchanal; bridal; calm; swift-falling; unfortunate; deepening; sorrowful; unillumined; bronzed; sleepy; balmy; eventful; golden; peaceful; imperial; ensuing; purple; gusty; premature; sober; dewy; ghostlike; dull; shadowy; memorable; grateful; languorous; bygone; dusky; hectic; delirious; warm; muggy; uncomfortable; cheerful; amazing; preceding; quiet; starry; harmonic; roseate.

verbs
approach—; await—; chill—; cloud—; crown——; draw toward—; gild—; hush—; last till—; occupy—; overcast—; ramble through—; return at—; rift—; rise at—; solemnize—; still—; sup at—; toil till—; usher in—; —approaches; —closes; —cools; —declines; —dies; —dims; —fades; —falls; —flies; —reposes; —shades; —sobers; —steals on.
(See twilight, dusk.)

EVENNESS

adjectives
velvet; insipid; boring; smooth; pleasant.

EVENT

adjectives
solemn; unbeatable; important; comprehensive; festival; outward; outstanding; sensational; trivial; huge; memorable; extraordinary; tragic; thrilling; embarrassing; disgusting; headline; contemporary; gigantic; strange; sweet; perturbing; crowning; subsequent; tremendous; strik-

ing; confused; fortunate; true; fierce; natural; unlooked-for; obscene; preposterous; dignified; sublime; momentous; inescapable; ultimate; startling; dramatic; pivotal; exciting; deplorable; celestial; mysterious; fateful; propitious; supreme; remarkable; future; sinful; minutest; detectable; stormy; dark; hurried; bizarre; unforeseen; stirring; fortuitous; unexpected; tempestuous; miraculous; boding; melancholy; overshadowing; succeeding; naked; recurrent; domestic; insignificant; humiliating; hastened; intermediate; calamitous; historical; previous; disastrous; happy; current; impolite; pin-point; dire; dreadful; preventable; antecedent.

verbs
acclaim—; applaud—; ascribe—to; attend—; beget—; commend—; detail—; dramatize—; explain—; fashion—; forecast—; foresee—; govern—; interpret—; mark—; narrate—; ponder—; predict—; presage—; rehash—; resume—; rue—; scan—; seize upon—; shape—; stamp—; view—; witness —; —commemorates; —confuses; —evolves; —portends; —represents; —results in; —underlies.

(See occurrence, incident, episode, consequence, issue, fortune.)

EVICT (v)
adverbs
raucously; sternly; heartlessly; coldly; cruelly; dictatorially; vigorously; harshly; peremptorily; abruptly; legally; forcefully; formally.

(See expel, dispossess.)

EVICTION
adjectives
harrowing; tragic; pitiful; heartless.

EVIDENCE
adjectives
silent; fearful; happiest; overwhelming; corroborative; further; official; tangible; repeated; spectroscopic; additional; damnatory; damaging; multiplied; irrefutable; confirmatory; circumstantial; diagnostic; documentary; substantial; signal; stronger; moral; noisy; convincing; incontrovertible; concrete; inadmissible; marked; apocryphal; explicit; abundant; bibliographical; contemporaneous; irrelevant; customary; secondhand; definite; palpable; visual; unmistakable; authentic; touching; effectual; white-spotted; legendary; sufficient; internal; contemporary; speechless; striking; ex-

traordinary; certain; conspicuous; gratifying; remarkable; scientific; faintest; absolute; unassailable; revealing; external; pragmatic; ungarbled; trustworthy; material; corrected; hearsay; impressive; factual; ample; cumulative; manifest; undoubted; lawful; modest; conclusive; positive; indubitable; unanswerable; unexceptionable; incontestable; breathing; experimental; reasonable; truthful; overt; concentrated; supporting; decisive; hopeful; notable; unconscious; considerable; undeniable; direct; usual; unerring; outward; archaeological; satisfactory; unequivocal; presumptive.

verbs
accept—; accumulate—; adduce—; alter—; amass—; base on—; confirm—; confront with—; contradict—; corroborate—; credit —; deduce—; deny—; destroy—; digest—; emphasize; examine; falsify—; ferret out—; gaze on—; interpret—; invoke—; offer—; overrate—; overrule—; parade—; perjure—; produce—; proffer—; recite—; regard—; reject—; review—; ruin—; search for—; seek—; sift—; submit—; substantiate—; sum up—; team with—; transcend—; unearth—; verify—; weigh—; yield to—; —collates; —damns; —discloses; —piles up; —supports; —sustains; —warrants.

(See fact, testimony, proof, demonstration.)

EVIDENT
adverbs
fearfully; overwhelmingly; irrefutably; convincingly; substantially; explicitly; unmistakably; sufficiently; strikingly; materially; conclusively; undeniably; flagrantly; easily; plainly; clearly; glaringly; reasonably; shamefully; outrageously; pitifully; dangerously; plaguedly; perilously; fortunately.

EVIL
adjectives
once-abounding; attendant; besetting; multiplied (pl); alleged; cave-keeping; substantial; dreadful; terrible; secret; manifest; necessary; infinite; inevitable; heaviest; familiar; scandalous; restless; trifling; unseen; remediable; impending; incalculable; desperate; unsubduable; imminent; weakheaded; manifold (pl); partial; temporary;

crying; accursed; ominous; future; thirsty; iniquitous; imaginary; approaching; unavoidable; abstract; moral; fixed; ruthless; necessary; human; accumulated; insidious; immeasurable.

verbs
abhor—; abolish—; abstain from—; aggravate—; alleviate—; ameliorate—; atone for—; avoid—; banish—; beset by—; besmirch with—; blind to—; breed—; cast out —; combat—; compensate for—; cope with —; counteract—; counterbalance—; cure—; deliver from—; denounce—; deplore—; dispose to—; dwell in—; effect—; eradicate—; evince—; exempt from—; fortify against —; imply—; insinuate—; intend—; intensify—; lapse into—; loathe—; master—; mitigate—; overcome—; persist in—; personify—; promote—; punish—; repent—; stir up—; strike at—; submit to—; suffer—; symbolize—; tackle—; tempt with—; uncover—; unite against—; uproot—; —befalls; —degrades; —menaces; expose to—; resist—.
(See wickedness, sin, iniquity, disaster, misfortune, reverse, injustice, wrong, affliction.)

adverbs
cruelly; flagrantly; hatefully; dangerously; mischievously; violently; irretrievably; inconceivably; poisonously; viciously; iniquitously; shamefully; incredibly; brutally; incorrigibly; atrociously; infernally; shockingly; woefully; sadly; villainously; irremediably; scandalously; manifestly; openly; avowedly; exceptionally; obnoxiously; disastrously; detestably; diabolically; perniciously; basely; irrevocably; horribly.

EVINCE (v)
adverbs
noticeably; markedly; unmistakably; obviously; sickeningly; partially; undoubtedly.
(See show, indicate.)

EVOLUTION
adjectives
regressive; rapid; uninterrupted; accelerated; lingual; mental; inevitable; intricate; uncertain; social; orderly; pious; masterly; creative; deliberate; mystic; eternal; cosmic; daring; terrestrial.

verbs
climb in—; complete—; confirm—; effect—; examine—; influence—; manifest—; observe—; produce by—; represent—; resolve by—; roll in—; speed up—; support —; verify—; —lifts; —progresses; —ripens; —spreads; —transmits; —unfolds.
(See development, growth.)

EVOLVE (v)
adverbs
scientifically; illogically; rapidly; perpetually; acceleratedly; mentally; intricately; uncertainly; splendidly; creatively; mystically; socially; daringly.
(See develop, complete.)

EWE
adjectives
mild-faced; fulsome.

EXACT
adverbs
infallibly; unimpeachably; strictly; literally; rigorously; scrupulously; painstakingly; punctiliously; mathematically; scientifically; unerringly; meticulously; authentically; absolutely; dependably; terrifyingly; uncannily; monotonously; essentiallly; astonishingly; impartially; ostentatiously; manifestly; graphically; astonishingly.

EXACT (v)
adverbs
rigidly; inexorably; harshly; cruelly; legally; painfully; strictly; formally.
(See demand, extort.)

EXACTION
adjectives
dictatorial; tyrannous.

EXACTITUDE
adjectives
graphic; conscientious; mathematical; clear-cut; scrupulous.

EXACTNESS
adjectives
scrupulous; close; ironical; crystalline; literal; elaborate; legal; unfailing; painful; technical; historical; mathematical.

EXAGGERATE (v)
adverbs
monstrously; sensationally; absurdly; vaingloriously; recklessly; grossly; amusingly;

crudely; grotesquely; rhetorically; journalistically; palpably; virulently; turbulently.
(See lie, magnify.)

EXAGGERATION
adjectives
sensational; cruel; striking; reckless; pardonable; gross; reactionary; amusing; crude; grotesque; rhetorical; passionate; journalistic; delicious; intense; palpable; rowdy; virulent; turbulent.

verbs
addict to—; anticipate—; blame—; confess —; decry—; guard against—; mark by—; reduce—; relate with—; represent—; ridicule—; sneer at—; tolerate—; warn of—; —adds; —amuses; —entertains; —harms; —misleads; —offends; —overwhelms.
(See overstatement.)

EXALT (v)
adverbs
boundlessly; loftily; indefinitely; religiously; mystically; sentimentally; blissfully; joyfully; spiritually; vividly; feverishly; impassionedly; hysterically.
(See magnify, elevate.)

EXALTATION
adjectives
religious; mystic; essential; sentimental; blissful; joyful; spiritual; high; nervous; vivid; dreamy; curious; feverish; impassioned; personal; unimaginable; mesmeric; perfect; harmonic.

EXALTED
adverbs
eminently; highly; conspicuously; notably; distinctly; gloriously; illustriously; splendidly; proudly; honorably; imposingly; majestically; wonderfully; remarkably.

EXAMINATION
adjectives
blind; impromptu; oral; minute; dispassionate; separate; unprejudiced; astute; unimpassioned; thoughtful; perfunctory; microscopic; critical; accurate; detailed; severe; competitive; censorial; elaborate; premarital; unsparing; stiff; fruitless; preventative; periodic; careful; searching; verbal; expert; posthumous; simultaneous; hasty; anatomical; exacting; unbiased; cooler; tedious; cursory; hostile; placid; frequent (pl); monotonous; brusque; caustic; judicial; meticulous; subsequent; systematic.

verbs
compete in—; conduct—; cram for—; crib in—; fail in—; flunk—; merit—; pass—; perform—; prepare for—; resort to—; select by—; subject to—; submit to—; summon for—; tackle—; undergo—; urge—; waive—; —discloses; —proves; —reveals.
(See scrutiny, investigation, search, review, autopsy, inquiry, test.)

EXAMINE (v)
adverbs
minutely; curiously; critically; superficially; studiously; gravely; closely; attentively; expertly; subsequently; ostensibly; hastily; rigorously; briefly; blindly; dispassionately; separately; astutely; perfunctorily; thoughtfully; microscopically; severely; competitively; premaritally; unsparingly; fruitlessly; preventatively, periodically; verbally; expertly; posthumously; simultaneously; anatomically; unbiasedly; tediously; cursorily; hostilely; placidly; monotonously; brusquely; caustically; judicially; meticulously; systematically; subsequently.
(See scrutinize, inspect.)

EXAMPLE
adjectives
pernicious; glaring; magnificent; picturesque; genuine; colorful; notorious; admirable; subsequent; fond; familiar; notable; remote; fatal; stirring; savage; disastrous; illustrious; shining; encouraging; extreme; servile; debasing; effective; melancholy; comparative; innumerable (pl); legible; elaborate; excellent; cruelest; supreme; imitated; striking; foremost; tardy; ultimate; enlightening; noble; unique; analogous; uncommon; impressive; attainable; painful; recorded; vicious; vindictive; concrete; classic; splendid; pathetic; judicious; morbid; eloquent; conspicuous; astounding; contagious; flagrant; haphazard; executive; pregnant; high-poised; rare; instructive; formidable; heroic; valuable; patriotic.

verbs
afford—; cite—; cull—; display as—; emulate—; encourage—; enumerate—s; exhibit —; follow—; glorify—; imitate—; interpret—; make—of; pattern on—; unearth—; view—; —defiles; —illustrates; —incites; —proves; —verifies.
(See instance, sample, specimen, model, illustration, precedent.)

EXASPERATING

adverbs

dreadfully; unbearably; intolerably; oddly; vexatiously; intentionally; unwittingly; innocently; terribly; tormentingly; naughtily; raspingly; bitterly; savagely; relentlessly; ungovernably; unusually; occasionally.

EXASPERATION

adjectives

religious; renewed; increased; inner; sardonic; frequent; intense; sudden; continual; increasing; incessant.

verbs

account for—; bear—; dispose to—; enrage with—; forbear—; incense with—; increase —; incur—; inflict—; irritate to—; load with—; occasion—; plot to—; remedy—; shiver with—; subject to—; torment to—; vent—; —disposes; —explodes; —harms; —wells up.

(See anger, irritation, provocation.)

EXCAVATION

adjectives

abandoned; lone; gaping; desolate.

verbs

direct—; discover during—; employ in—; engage in—; examine—; forbid—; place—; plan—; prevent—; require—; tunnel—; unearth in—; watch—; —divulges; —exposes; —impairs; —lays bare; —progresses; —reveals; —ruins.

(See cavity, hole.)

EXCEED (v)

adverbs

frequently; illegally; surprisingly; splendidly; astonishingly; notably; memorably; wildly.

(See transcend, surpass.)

EXCEL (v)

adverbs

unexpectedly; conspicuously; immeasurably; peculiarly; intrinsically; individually; comparatively; marvelously; surpassingly; materially; unusually; trivially; matchlessly; supremely; dramatically; genuinely; consistently; exceedingly.

(See surpass, transcend.)

EXCELLENCE

adjectives

highest; intrinsic; exceeding; compensatory; artistic; rare; individual; comparative; marvelous; unobtrusive; eternal; surpassing; minor; architectural; material; unapproached; unusual; trivial; matchless; supreme; dramatic; acoustic; professional; peerless; genuine; unrivaled; unvarying; known; consistent; unsurpassed; dateless; superior; self-made; brand-new.

EXCELLENCY

adjectives

reverend; moral.

EXCELLENT

adverbs

dependably; consistently; consciously; reliably; obviously; evidently; palpably; incomparably; matchlessly; surprisingly; brilliantly; artistically; genuinely.

EXCEPTION

adjectives

notable; memorable; violent; trifling; marked; conspicuous; solitary; occasional; delightful; important; innumerable (pl); rare; possible; inexcusable; honorable.

verbs

answer—; appeal for—; ban—; bar—; declare—; defend—; demand—; examine —; expose to—; justify—; lodge—; produce—; protect—; provide—; rule—; state —; take—to; —appears.

(See objection, omission.)

EXCEPTIONAL

adverbs

undoubtedly; highly; indubitably; conspicuously; delightfully; notably; famously; memorably; inimitably; peculiarly; eccentrically; fantastically; exotically; outlandishly; grotesquely; unconventionally.

EXCESS

verbs

accumulate—of; addict to—; burn—; eliminate—; gather—; protest—; rebuke—; refrain from—; remove—; reject—; regret —; reprove—; scatter—; spread—; waste —; —disgraces; —intoxicates.

(See extravagance, surplus, residue, intemperance.)

EXCESSES

adjectives

poor; mad; factional; deplorable; utmost; sanguinary; hideous; extravagant; intolerable; morbid; dangerous; clumsy; mischievous; wildest; witty; persistent; loathsome; personal; dreadful; careless; strained.

EXCHANGE

adjectives

typical; significant; inevitable; dexterous; mute; mutual; unauthorized; solemn; sympathetic; friendly; intimate; immediate; whispered.

verbs

agree on—; allow—; authorize—; counteract—; demand—; dote on—; give in—; grant—; lose through—; operate—; permit —; plan—; procure—; profit by—; promote —; reject—; return in—; solicit—; win—.
(See trade, traffic.)

EXCHANGE (*v*)

adverbs

mutely; significantly; dexterously; solemnly; sympathetically; intimately; immediately.
(See accept.)

EXCHANGEABLE

adverbs

readily; easily; conveniently; equitably; allowably; obviously; scarcely; legally; hardly; adaptably; commercially; negotiably; reciprocally; properly; warrantably; necessarily; assuredly.

EXCITABILITY

adjectives

morbid; rabid; easy; choleric.

EXCITABLE

adverbs

terribly; abnormally; easily; highly; uncommonly; unusually; temperamentally; naturally; habitually; unfortunately; absurdly; childishly; ridiculously; oddly; curiously; strangely; mysteriously; slightly; disturbingly; painfully; dangerously; significantly; extremely; excessively; outlandishly; uncontrollably; ungovernably; wildly; fussily; inexplicably; deplorably.

EXCITATION

adjectives

unnatural; noticeable; spiritual; frenzied; marked.

EXCITE (*v*)

adverbs

strongly; mutinously; painfully; sedulously; intensely; fiercely; supernaturally; wildly; vivaciously; pleasurably; contagiously; artificially; tremulously; exhaustingly; bound-lessly; terrifically; preternaturally; sensuously; coarsely; riotously; scandalously; hilariously; hectically; intellectually.
(See arouse, stimulate.)

EXCITEMENT

adjectives

intense; fierce; vast; fascinated; fevered; constant; glowing; supernatural; wild; vivacious; pleasurable; abated; contagious; considerable; gradual; turbulent; aggressive; remorseful; stirring; flushed; perpetual; overpowering; artificial; tremulous; insolent; solemn; strong; hasty; feeble; exhausting; innocent; bubbling; dangerous; pale; adventurous; subdued; joyous; composed; avid; pleasant; tense; probable; peculiar; delicious; momentary; nervous; deep; delirious; emotional; gross; diseased; uncontrollable; sheer; cerebral; contemporary; unprovoked; healthful; frantic; involuntary; frenzied; boundless; high; extraordinary; smothered; terrific; preternatural; sensuous; coarse; perpetual; inconceivable; drawled; riotous; scandalous; hilarious; correspondent; suppressed; mental; hectic; painful; veritable; previous; neutral; intellectual; revolutionary.

verbs

arouse—; avoid—; buzz with—; calm—; conceal—; contain—; crave—; eliminate—; flash—; flush with—; guard against—; induce—; respond to—; rock with—; seethe with—; sense—; stir to—; suppress—; thirst for—; thrive on—; wheeze with—; —blazes; —dies away; —fades; —leaps high; —shines in one's eyes; —smolders; —subsides; —surges.
(See perturbation, commotion, agitation, stimulation.)

EXCLAIM (*v*)

adverbs

wildly; curiously; breathlessly; softly; thoughtfully; boisterously; fiercely; delightfully; acidly; admiringly; jovially; facetiously; angrily; incredulously; distressfully; bitterly; enthusiastically; solemnly; blankly; saucily; triumphantly; impulsively; testily; gleefully; savagely; boastfully; regretfully; profanely; tragically; piteously; sharply; reproachfully; anxiously; ostentatiously; disappointedly; unadvisedly; fervently; joyously; rapturously; faintly; audibly; stifledly; abruptly; ardently; helplessly; enthusiastically; frantically; shockedly; gutturally.
(See ejaculate, shout.)

EXCLAMATION

adjectives

joyous; rapturous; passionate; angry; fiery; furious; half-suppressed; faint; nervous; incoherent; mourning; audible; half-articulated; impatient; stifled; abrupt; homely; ardent; helpless; enthusiastic; sharp; frantic; indistinct; vivid; pleased; assenting; guttural; shocked.

verbs

burst out in—; drown—; elicit—; emit—; heed—; mark with—; mouth—; pour forth —; pronounce—; protest with—; startle by—; suppress—; utter—; —delights; — expresses; —pains; —resounds; —surprises.
(See outcry, utterance, cry.)

EXCLAMATORY

adverbs

dramatically; absurdly; ludicrously; needlessly; unnecessarily; noisily; violently; offensively; vexatiously; loudly; cholerically; angrily; enthusiastically; blatantly; conspicuously; boldly; urgently; impressively; ridiculously; gustily; coarsely; grossly; sympathetically; terribly; frightfully.

EXCLUDE (*v*)

adverbs

strictly; vigorously; expressly; deliberately; entirely; cautiously; jealously; utterly; rigorously; persistently.
(See omit, prevent.)

EXCLUSION

adjectives

stereotyped; utter; impolitic; studied; strictest; rigorous; perpetual; persistent.

EXCLUSIVE

adverbs

socially; discriminatingly; absurdly; wisely; necessarily; snobbishly; proudly; haughtily; carefully; significantly; purposely; designedly; unreasonably; offensively; formally; officially; safely; rigidly; ridiculously.

EXCLUSIVENESS

adjectives

scornful; fastidious.

EXCOMMUNICATION

verbs

banish to—; brood over—; delay—; demand—; denounce—; deplore—; deserve—; fulminate—; incur—; prevent—; prohibit —; pronounce—; rebel against—; repent—;

restrain—; sentence to—; submit to—; suffer—; threaten with—; —ejects; —excludes; —exiles; —expels; —interdicts; — separates; —shuts out.
(See separation, expulsion.)

EXCRESCENCE

adjectives

preternatural; hideous; annoying; ugly.

EXCRETION

adjectives

wasteful; useless; diminished.

verbs

encourage—; expel during—; facilitate—; halt—; necessitate—; observe—; occasion —; prevent—; produce—; promote—; provoke—; reduce—; require—; stimulate—; suppress—; throw out in—; —cleanses; — exhausts; —occurs; —pains; —purges.
(See discharge.)

EXCRUCIATING

adverbs

terribly; unbearably; visibly; obviously; piteously; unnecessarily; inexpressibly; dreadfully; appallingly; insufferably; insupportably.

EXCURSION

adjectives

amatory; vague; opportune; equestrian; pedestrian; novel; episodical; periodical; rural; provincial; preliminary; piratical; involuntary; compulsory; sporting; restless; predatory; hunting; sketching; torch-light.

verbs

anticipate—; arrange—; delight in—; depart on—; embark on—; escape on—; join —; organize—; plan—; prevent—; start on —; take—; undertake—; venture on—; enjoy—.
(See journey, trip, expedition.)

EXCUSABLE

adverbs

easily; readily; scarcely; hardly; apparently; plausibly; fairly; barely; legitimately; defensibly; reasonably.

EXCUSE

adjectives

apparent; plausible; sheepish; sufficient; audible; penitent; ominous; coy; lawful; puerile; crazy; fair; generous; bare; specious; voluble; cleanly-coined; deft; bashful;

dingy; unblushing; flimsy; useful; **reasonable**; truthful; ready; legitimate; good; slightest; time-honored; inept; fabricated; unspeakable.

verbs
accept—; beg for—; condone—; defend with—; demand—; denounce—; furnish—; hatch—; invent—; judge—; offer—; plead —; pray for—; present—; produce—; propose as—; request—; require—; seek—; seize on—; shape—; —absolves; —acquits; —amends; —exonerates; —explains; —infuriates; —justifies; —patches up; —releases; —suffices; —vindicates.
(See plea, reason, apology.)

EXCUSE (v)
adverbs
ostensibly; pleasantly; apparently; plausibly; sheepishly; audibly; penitently; ominously; coyly; speciously; volubly; deftly; reasonably; ineptly.
(See forgive, pardon.)

EXECRATION
adjectives
terrible; half-smothered; frantic.

EXECUTE (v)
adverbs
imperfectly; faithfully; unquestionably; intensively; beautifully; simultaneously; brilliantly; stoutly; momentously; bureaucratically; thoroughly; successfully; duly; splendidly; unremittingly; vigorously; summarily; gracefully; practically; skillfully; admirably; knowingly; linguistically; economically; rudely; justifiably; secretly; intrepidly; imposingly; crudely; magnificently.
(See administer, perform.)

EXECUTION
adjectives
linguistic; efficient; imperfect; economic; justifiable; rude; supreme; secret; immediate; intrepid; unrivaled; imposing; brilliant; hopeful; bloody; crude; magnificent; vigorous; facile.

verbs
await—; cite—; condemn to—; delay—; deliver over to—; demand—; enforce—; entrust—to; escape—; obstruct—; postpone —; reprieve from—; risk—; stay—; warrant—; witness—; —expiates.
(See performance, accomplishment, death.)

EXECUTIVE
adjectives
able; industrial; admirable; signal; energetic; insignificant; high-powered; tyrannical; overbearing; pompous.

adverbs
responsibly; highly; legally; carefully; cautiously; supremely; imperiously; authoritatively; royally; municipally; arbitrarily; masterfully; imposingly; efficiently; brilliantly; magnificently; splendidly; vigorously; intrepidly; unquestionably; proudly; effectively.

EXECUTOR
adjectives
literary; financial; grasping; efficient.

EXEMPLARY
adverbs
admirably; famously; notably; conspicuously; illustriously; effectively; elaborately; supremely; strikingly; nobly; impressively; uncommonly; uniquely; splendidly; eloquently; heroically; valuably; dramatically.

EXEMPLIFICATION
adjectives
historic; unostentatious; significant.

EXEMPLIFY (v)
adverbs
richly; strikingly; effectively; vaingloriously; historically; significantly; unostentatiously; perfectly.
(See illustrate, prove.)

EXEMPT
adverbs
legally; officially; notably; explicitly; expressly; wisely; craftily; fortunately; adroitly; cleverly; politically; absolutely; automatically; unaccountably; mysteriously; happily; luckily; inexplicably; radiantly.

EXEMPTION
verbs
acquire—; beg—; command—; demand—; enjoy—; grant—; merit—; plead—; procure—; protest—; purchase—; renounce—; select for—; —debars; —excludes; —frees; —removes; —unburdens.
(See immunity. freedom, privilege.)

EXERCISE

adjectives

unwearied; bodily; vigorous; appropriate; pedestrian; social; sinister; manly; vacation; habitual; arbitrary; daily; princely; exhilarating; useless; ruthless; mechanical; conscientious; active; simple; unlawful; righteous; well-planned; equitable; monotonous; generous; virtuous; intelligent; fatiguing; effortless; unbiased; perpetual; delectable; injudicious; joyous; constant; conscious; graceful; unwonted; painful; divine; continued; utmost; preposterous; efficient; courtly; mental; gymnastic; unremitting; insufficient; unquestionable; enlightened; nocturnal; ecstatic; memorial; devilish; gentle; graduated; strenuous; mere; internal; plentiful; violent; muscular; recreative; intellectual; anteprandial.

verbs

adapt—to; apply—; assign—to; carry out —; delight in—; deprive of—; diminish—; forego—; graduate—; indulge in—; neglect —; perform—; practise—; recommend—; refrain from—; repeat—; restrict—; resume; —develops; —enlivens; —exhilarates; —tires.

(See act, action, activity, exertion, practise, drill, use.)

EXERCISE (v)

adverbs

diversely; exclusively; violently; ruthlessly; bodily; unweariedly; vigorously; appropriately; socially; habitually; uselessly; mechanically; delectably; joyously; painfully; gymnastically; unremittingly; insufficiently; mentally; nocturnally; muscularly; strenuously; recreatively.

(See exert, apply.)

EXERT (v)

adverbs

strenuously; vocally; undoubtedly; vigorously; unscrupulously; prodigiously; assiduously; incredibly; desperately; extraordinarily; laudably; incessantly; courageously; productively; vainly; unusually; seriously.

(See exercise, apply.)

EXERTION

adjectives

unaccustomed; equivalent; utmost; strenuous; prodigious; assiduous; redoubled; incredible; vigorous; individual; useless; unremitted; desperate; extraordinary; violent; fresh; intrepid; laudable; incessant; supernatural; polite; diurnal; courageous; fortunate; physical; mental; ceaseless; laborious; unusual; productive; ungracious; vain; joint.

verbs

abhor—; break under—; carry—of; delay —; hinder—; increase—; kindle—; manifest—; produce by—; render—; resist—; reveal—; rouse to—; stimulate to—; waste —; —agitates; —aggravates; —fags; —fatigues; —restores; —taxes.

(See effort, struggle, endeavor.)

EXHALATION

adjectives

ammoniacal; mephitic; ceaseless; foggy; loathsome; unwholesome; noxious.

EXHAUST (v)

adverbs

stertorously; utterly; finally; financially; totally; seemingly; mutually; racially; ruthlessly; practically; physically; spiritually.

(See deplete, prostrate.)

EXHAUSTED

adverbs

utterly; well-nigh; pitiably; shockingly; alarmingly; pathetically; portentously; ludicrously; laughingly; feebly; wheezily; grievously; faintly; perceptibly; visibly; unusually; naturally; obviously.

EXHAUSTION

adjectives

worn; mutual; racial; nervous; sheer; ruthless; practical; physical; spiritual.

verbs

approach—; carry on to—; collapse in—; cure—; diminish—; discuss to—; drain to—; drop in—; induce—; occasion—; produce—; reach—; recuperate from—; reduce to—; succumb to—; tax to—; —destroys; —enervates; —ensues; —incapacitates; —perils; —prostrates.

(See fatigue, weariness.)

EXHIBIT

adjectives

studious; mercantile; bulky; archaeological; educational; pitiable; admirable; startling; doleful; representative.

EXHIBIT (v)

adverbs

immodestly; markedly; unexpectedly; pretentiously; shamelessly; obscenely; gratuitously; glaringly; curiously; muscularly; conspicuously; educationally; persuasively; studiously; representatively.

(See show, display.)

EXHIBITION

adjectives

retrospective; permanent; positive; invidious; wholesale; detailed; spectacular; amazing; spontaneous; portentous; barefaced; frequent (pl); incomparable; theatrical; fanciful; competitive; foremost; remarkable; pitiable; noticeable; notable; comic; degrading; disgusting; enormous; colonial; spirited; creditable; outstanding; florid; symbolical.

verbs

acclaim—; applaud—; appreciate—; bill—; boycott—; display—; inspect—; participate in—; sponsor—; throng—; witness—; —amuses; —astounds; —commemorates; —draws; —entertains; —fascinates; —instructs; —opens; —profits.

(See display, spectacle, show.)

EXHILARATE (v)

adverbs

vivaciously; briskly; momentarily; strangely; voluptuously; joyously.

(See excite, cheer.)

EXHILARATING

adverbs

tremendously; immensely; vigorously; wonderfully; boundlessly; highly; buoyantly; briskly; hilariously; vivaciously; sparklingly; radiantly; splendidly; superbly; surprisingly; astoundingly.

EXHILARATION

adjectives

brisk; inexplicable; momentary; elated; strange; voluptuous; joyous.

verbs

burst into—; dampen—; defer—; discourage—; enliven by—; flush in—; impart—; inspire—; kindle—; leap in—; move to—; produce—; refrain from—; repress—; skip in—; stimulate—; subdue—; suppress—; —animates; —frisks; —rollicks; —sparkles.

(See stimulation, gladness, cheer.)

EXIGENCY

adjectives

unexpected; various (pl); present.

verbs

adapt to—; contribute to—; create—; ease —; escape—; judge—; labor under—; meet —; relieve—; rise to—; satisfy—; stress—; subject to—; tolerate—; —claims; —demands; —necessitates; —pinches; —presses; —requires; —threatens.

(See necessity, demand, need, emergency.)

EXILE

adjectives

needy; administrative; imperious; melancholy; lifelong; scarred; cynical; penniless; wandering; impudent; multitudinous (pl); outlandish; prejudiced; lasting; pensive; political; communal; venturous; vagabond; involuntary; indiscriminate.

verbs

abandon to—; authorize—; banish into—; cast into—; condemn to—; die in—; doom to—; dwell in—; endure—; enter—; escape —; flee from—; follow into—; force into—; imprison in—; languish in—; liberate from —; recall from—; release from—; relegate to—; retire to—; shut in—; waste in—; —depresses; —saddens; —veils.

(See banishment, expulsion.)

EXILED

adverbs

miserably; pitiably; wretchedly; desolately; unjustifiably; deservedly; homelessly; forlornly; ignominiously; shamefully; savagely; lamentably; unhappily; shockingly; mercilessly; permanently.

EXIST (v)

adverbs

beggarly; parasitically; uninterruptedly; contemporaneously; naturally; impecuniously; cheerlessly; amicably; smoothly; gracefully; individually; primitively; socially; bodily; irregularly; animally; grossly; amiably; miserably; thoughtlessly; meagerly; spiritually; imperiously; carelessly; contemplatively; exaltedly; desolately; torpidly; lifelessly; narrowly; rudely; tranquilly; virtuously; drably; romantically; separately.

(See live, continue.)

adjectives

smooth; carefree; graceful; refined; individual; primitive; savage; reasoned; ordered; social; bodily; irregular; well-regulated; illusive; animal; dreamlike; feeble; gross; amiable; theoretical; political; obscure; intrinsic; objective; miserable; universal; thoughtless; meager; spiritual; waking; eternal; harmonious; future; contained; independent; imperious; dominating; substantial; fractional; careless; contemplative; complicated; sad; precarious; imaginary; distracted; poetical; whole; peaceful; horrible; tangible; exalted; desolate; schizophrenic; divided; wretched; spectral; general; common; artistic; warped; torpid; lifeless; unostentatious; destructive; ephemeral; secluded; charmed; congenial; tormented; dissipated; petty; restless; humdrum; semi-monastic; infantile; determined; untarnished; secular; actual; intra-uterine; mere; restrained; narrow; genuine; inevitable; stormy; moribund; inscrutable; superficial; dubious; perennial; rude; adolescent; unreal; unending; wasted; self-fixed; country; tranquil; bright; virtuous; pampered; unsympathizing; vulgar; drab; long-forgotten; material; beneficent; treacherous; triumphant; undisciplined; tropical; pleasurable; honorable; romantic; unnecessary; indolent; diversified; untroubled; separate; beauteous.

verbs

admit—of; animate—; annihilate—; contemplate—; dedicate—to; demonstrate—of; deny—of; determine—; disbelieve—; dispute—; drag out—; eke out—; grant—; guide—; heighten—; ignore—; imperil—; invigorate—; justify—; loathe—; obliterate—; pop into—; preserve—; recognize—; rule—; shape—; shatter—; struggle for—; suspect—of; sustain—; threaten—; uproot —; verify—; —bores; —continues; —wearies.
(See reality, fact, life.)

adjectives

eccentric; clear; funnel-shaped; joyful; mysterious; hurried.

verbs

bar—; barricade—; burst from—; chain —; dramatize—; emanate from—; excrete through—; file from—; give—; issue from —; padlock—; perceive—; scorn—; search

for—; sigh for—; trickle through—; witness —; —discharges; —effuses; —ejects; —erupts; —expels.
(See passage, doorway.)

adjectives

dramatic; wholesale; gradual.

verbs

consent to—; encounter—; force—; plan—; overtake—; speed—; start—; trace—; —abates; —attains; —commences.
(See departure, emigration.)

adverbs

completely; partially; fully; satisfactorily; entirely; unconditionally; impartially.
(See pardon, acquit.)

adverbs

completely; honorably; recently; wholly; justly; happily; luckily; fortunately; easily; glibly; smoothly; craftily; publicly; properly; rightfully; legally; entirely; unquestionably; unconditionally.

adverbs

insanely; intolerably; terribly; extremely; frightfully; criminally; illegally; preposterously; inordinately; egregiously; fantastically; outrageously; outlandishly; crazily; flagrantly; grossly; incredibly; enormously; prodigiously; amazingly; glaringly; appallingly.

adjectives

illustrious; tiny; rare.

adverbs

progressively; rapidly; limitlessly; sufficiently; continually; sanely; monstrously; ingeniously; lustily; adroitly; tremendously; marvelously; subsequently; intellectually; ephemerally; explosively; economically; industrially; muscularly; noisily; inevitably; imperially; poisonously; chaotically.
(See dilate, enlarge.)

adjectives

treeless; sealike; dreary; tranquil; sunny; shadowless; still; boundless; undulating; great; prodigious; shining; broad; vast;

trackless; bare; uncharted; endless; prairie-like; glassy; barren; pale; serene; berg-filled; measureless; limitless; windless.

EXPANSION

adjectives
transcendent; fanlike; marvelous; tremendous; subsequent; intellectual; cruel; ephemeral; vital; free; explosive; economic; prodigious; temperamental; industrial; reflex; muscular; important; noisy; amazing; ill-directed; inevitable; major; rapid; imperial; conceivable; healthful; chaotic; enormous.

verbs
advocate—; check—; confine—to; cover—; curtail—; demand—; evince—; force—; influence—; justify—; limit—; nip—; plan —; prevent—; regulate—; speed up—; strangle—; suppress—; terminate—; —continues; —ends; —follows.
(See enlargement, increase, extension, development.)

EXPANSIVE

adverbs
conveniently; adaptably; broadly; signally; remarkably; wonderfully; incredibly; exceptionally; naturally; amply; roomily; spaciously; capaciously; comfortably; amazingly.

EXPATRIATION

adjectives
instant; delayed; enforced; prolonged.

EXPECT (v)

adverbs
confidently; unreasonably; half-heartedly; gloomily; romantically; anxiously; vaguely; plainly; apparently; breathlessly; presumptuously; blissfully; sanguinely; ardently; benevolently; vainly; mystically; fondly; rationally; erroneously; impossibly; evidently; extravagantly; tremulously; hourly.
(See anticipate, hope.)

EXPECTANCY

adjectives
reasonable; shuddering; dread; eager; lounging; tranquil; wistful; vigilant; anxious; homeless.

EXPECTANT

adverbs
happily; joyously; mysteriously; excitedly; hysterically; passionately; thrillingly; unreasonably; impatiently; ardently; keenly; eagerly; charmingly; joyfully; fervently; anxiously; crazily; madly; nervously; confidently; vainly; hopefully.

EXPECTATION

adjectives
blissful; confident; sanguine; harrowing; exorbitant; pecuniary; ardent; benevolent; florid; vain; reasonable; appreciative; mystic; fondest; remote; rational; continual; erroneous; future; protracted; exaggerated; impossible; evident; sure; tremulous; delightful; brilliant; ulterior; anxious; hopeful; hourly; indefinite; visionary; commensurate; extravagant; distant.

verbs
await with—; blast—; confirm—; darken —; encourage—; excite—s; fall short of—; fulfill—; gamble in—; glow with—; prolong —; quiver with—; shine in—; thwart—; torment with—; warrant—; whirl in—; —becomes; —fails; —grows; —perishes; —shrinks.
(See anticipation, prospect, hope.)

EXPECTORATE (v)

adverbs
nauseously; excessively; disgustingly; continually; foully; filthily.
(See spit, expel.)

EXPECTORATION

adjectives
excessive; sustained.

verbs
diminish—; discharge in—; effect—; eject in—; eliminate in—; emit in—; encourage —; evict in—; excrete in—; expel in—; forbid—; hack with—; increase—; interrupt—; promote—; retch in—; warn against—; —clears; —disgorges; —dislodges.
(See sputum, spit, saliva.)

EXPEDIENCE

verbs
balance—; base on—; befit—; charge with —; conform to—; consider—; consult—; doubt—; employ—; necessitate—; require —; resort to—; sacrifice to—; suit—; —controls; —embarrasses; —guides; —perplexes; —rules; —silences; —violates.
(See utility, propriety.)

EXPEDIENT

adjectives

seducing; astute; unlawful; financial; dangerous; temporary; favorite; happy; simple; unworthy; desperate; fertile; splendid; shifty; sensible; customary; physical; various (pl); effective; readiest.

adverbs

politically; immediately; wisely; necessarily; strategically; properly; undoubtedly; opportunely; luckily; eminently; ingeniously; indisputably; astutely; dangerously; temporarily; boldly; roughly; cleverly; subserviently; usefully; adaptably.

EXPEDITION

adjectives

implemented; conquering; disastrous; maritime; elaborate; dangerous; Odyssean; hostile; filibustering; nervous; suicidal; successful; predatory; brazen; particular; nefarious; exploring; favorite; notable; rescue; zoological; costly; memorable; punitive; much-vaunted; perilous; sanguine; swiftest; abortive.

verbs

command—; defer—; endanger—; fit out—; guard—; hasten on—; head—; organize—; overwhelm—; prepare—; set forth on—; sponsor—; spur—; support—; undertake—; venture on—; —claims; —cruises; —discloses; —discovers; —sights; —uncovers; —winters.
(See journey, excursion, enterprise.)

EXPEDITIOUS

adverbs

earnestly; smartly; briskly; alertly; eagerly; intently; resolutely; vigorously; actively; energetically; uncommonly; highly; miraculously.

EXPEL (v)

adverbs

brutally; unceremoniously; painfully; peremptorily; summarily; abruptly; heartlessly; formally.
(See banish, eject.)

EXPEND (v)

adverbs

usefully; lavishly; prodigally; unwisely; honestly; modestly; extravagantly; frugally; annually; prudently; unreasonably; unfortunately; judiciously.
(See employ, consume.)

EXPENDITURE

adjectives

increasing; modest; lavish; unstinted; extravagant; frugal; loose; annual; prudent; unreasonable; prodigal; corresponding; large; undue; unfortunate; speediest; nervous; judicious; equivalent.

verbs

afford—; approve—; check—; deplore—; furnish—; grudge—; incur—; invest in—; involve—; pare down—; provide for—; purvey—; recruit—; require—; restrict—; return—; —acquires; —amounts; —crushes; —drains; —exhausts; —impoverishes; —purchases.
(See outlay, expense, payment.)

EXPENSE

adjectives

useless; prodigal; major; extreme; ruinous; extraordinary; minimum; profitless; miscellaneous; crushing; enormous; improper; maintenance; inescapable; considerable; financial; operating; imperial; advertising; personal; monstrous; trifling.

verbs

advance—; appropriate for—; defray—; dread—; entail—; increase—; incur—; involve—; necessitate—; pay—; pool—; rate —; save—; slice—; spare—; survey—; trim—; —arises; —galls; —increases; —rises; —weighs.
(See cost, expenditure, outlay.)

EXPENSIVE

adverbs

tremendously; absurdly; unreasonably; ridiculously; excessively; dreadfully; cruelly; inordinately; extremely; enormously; inevitably; inconceivably; naturally; inexpressibly; impossibly; uselessly; ruinously; foolishly; exorbitantly; extortionately; illegally; criminally; extravagantly; wastefully; abominably; amazingly; immoderately; outrageously.

EXPERIENCE

adjectives

early; expensive; novel; dreamy; profound; tragic; deadly; purifying; diversified; trying; literate; mystical; unpleasant; salient; glorious; colorful; jarring; transitory; throbbing; absolute; tedious; major; bitter; inductive; unique; considerable; personal; vigilant; spiritual; preparatory; ripe; universal; uniform; various (pl); unguessable; deplorable; practical; exceptional;

accumulated; anticipatory; horrid; disgraceful; blind; dangerous; invariable; salutary; deep-reaching; thrilling; unfavorable; memorable; financial; satisfying; professional; manifest; initial; exhaustive; confident; vulgar; perplexing; architectural; distressing; worldly; gradual; vast; crushing; fatal; intellectual; enormous; deceptive; sensory; funny; ludicrous; private; evolutionary; rich; unfortunate; sacred; extensive; infallible; disillusioning; unalterable; costly; waking; deep; versatile; amorous; augmented; collegiate; exhilarating; bitter; reportorial; traumatic; unmatched; fascinating; pioneering; imperfect; agonizing; preliminary; aesthetic; direful; dismal; analytic; hereditary; veridical; fateful; rough; pathogenic; droll; public; bitter-sweet.

verbs
accumulate—; achieve—; analyze—; attain —; cite—; continue—; deduce from—; derive—; discolor—; diversify—; enjoy—; exaggerate—; furnish—; gain—; grow out of—; marshal—; narrate—; prepare—; reject—; relate—; relive—; review—; seek —; survive—; tax—; understand—; undertake—; unfold—s; unify—s; utilize—; — delights; —discloses; —embitters; —enriches; —fathers; —guides; —harrows; — teaches; —unnerves; —verifies; —warns.
  (See experiment, proof, practice, knowledge.)

EXPERIENCE (*v*)
adverbs
alternately; tediously; profoundly; tragically; mystically; gloriously; colorfully; uniquely; spiritually; variously; uniformly; practically; deplorably; horridly; financially; professionally; manifestly; fatally; intellectually; ludicrously; privately; unalterably; exhilaratingly; dismally; fatefully; drolly; accidentally.
  (See endure, suffer.)

EXPERIENCED
adverbs
amazingly; smartly; cunningly; adeptly; adroitly; carefully; skilfully; unusually; competently; proficiently; ingeniously; masterfully; eminently; impressively; scarcely; broadly; profoundly.

EXPERIMENT
adjectives
lengthy; innumerable (pl); vagrant; happily-conceived; foregoing; weak; partial;

cheap-money; exploded; extensive; hypnotic; ethical; unpleasant; rigid; awkward; transoceanic; trifling; memorable; vulgar; instructive; promising; crude; telepathic; gainful; unsought; hazardous; opposite; rash; inductive; vaunted; soon-abandoned; leading; momentous; complicated; supplementary; socialistic; definite; social; important; dangerous; innocent; philosophical; graceful; good-natured; analytical; disastrous; ingenious; interesting; costly; trustworthy; exhaustive; agricultural; continuous; lateral; doubtful; unfailing; amusing; preliminary; practical; revolutionary; wild; pedagogical; endless; tremendous; colossal; meticulous; interminable; absurd; mad; conclusive; cautious; daring; radical; crucial; ignoble; tentative; atrocious; laboratory; epochal; gigantic; novel; singular; misguided; deplorable; ignorant; clumsy; ill-advised.

verbs
benefit by—; conduct—; contrive—; design —; doom—; embark on—; engage in—; indulge in—; interpret—; perform—; prove by—; submit to—; tolerate—; —fails; — fares; —saddens; —suggests; —yields.
  (See trial, attempt, test.)

EXPERIMENT (*v*)
adverbs
indefatigably; extensively; hypnotically; awkwardly; memorably; vulgarly; instructively; crudely; gainfully; hazardously; rashly; inductively; complicatedly; definitely; dangerously; philosophically; exhaustively; agriculturally; continuously; amusingly; practically; interminably; absurdly; cautiously; daringly; radically; crucially; ignobly; tentatively; ignorantly; ill-advisedly; clumsily.
  (See try, test.)

EXPERIMENTAL
adverbs
definitely; avowedly; fantastically; openly; extensively; crudely; boldly; dangerously; exhaustively; wildly; amusingly; absurdly; madly; cautiously; clumsily; awkwardly; courageously; adventurously; expensively; heroically; tentatively.

EXPERIMENTATION
adjectives
zealous; clinical; persistent; rigid; controlled.

EXPERT

adjectives

distinguished; eminent; authentic; technical; nautical; transplanted; moral; monetary; illumination; industrious; irrigation; undisputed; tight-mouthed; acknowledged; accomplished; high-salaried; acoustical; competent; independent; manufacturing; efficiency; decoding; practical; able; two-fisted; qualified; outstanding; self-appointed.

verbs

acclaim as—; affront—; applaud—; cope with—; demand—; develop into—; employ —; flatter—; judge by—; nominate—; regard as—; require—; trust—; try—; —conquers; —criticizes; —excels in; —judges; —manages; —masters; —practises; —scowls.

(See specialist, master.)

adverbs

skilfully; obviously; reasonably; unusually; ably; adroitly; capably; competently; technically; mechanically; deftly; efficiently; handily; ingeniously; inventively; smartly; masterfully; proficiently; readily; oddly; curiously; professionally; admirably; prodigiously; uncommonly; miraculously; surprisingly.

EXPIATION

adjectives

tragic; particular; penitential; complete.

EXPLAIN (v)

adverbs

proudly; patiently; quaintly; amply; candidly; plausibly; speciously; prefatorily; redundantly; superfluously; passionately; comprehensively; adequately; essentially; partially; definitely; solemnly; carefully; sulkily; presently; sufficiently; hesitatingly; casually; paradoxically; tenderly; technically; voluntarily; minutely; undauntedly; elaborately; effectively; inaudibly; lengthily; immaterially; confusedly; ingeniously; laboredly; immediately; incongruously; philosophically; sympathetically; volubly; competently; psychologically; invaluably; tardily; apologetically; illogically; concisely; facetiously; fundamentally; comically; prosaically; disarmingly; lamely; casually; haltingly.

(See interrupt, elucidate.)

EXPLANATION

adjectives

plausible; inaudible; immaterial; lucid; hesitating; dreaded; comprehensive; confused; ingenious; satisfactory; labored; immediate; mechanistic; unreserved; fantastic; dynamic; vivid; philosophical; disjointed; incongruous; sympathetic; voluble; abbreviated; competent; adequate; scientific; rational; palliative; indiscreet; pathological; glib; specious; consequent; blind; various (pl); psychological; paralyzing; muddled; invaluable; tardy; groundless; half-true; apologetic; supreme; parenthetical; useless; attempted; flimsy; illogical; overwhelming; blithe; clarifying; concise; simplifying; aesthetic; petulant; facetious; fundamental; reasonable; common-sense; comic; struggling; tedious; elaborate; prosaic; matter-of-fact; air-tight; fictional; disarming; diluted; casual; lame; halting.

verbs

amplify—; bear—; clarify—; clear—; comprehend—; condemn—; confirm—; defy—; devise—; drown out—; elaborate—; emerge with—; frame—; fumble for—; grasp—; muddle—; offer—; stammer—; swallow—; tender—; wind up—; yield—; —clarifies; —involves; —rests on; —simplifies.

(See exposition, solution, interpretation, key.)

EXPLANATORY

adverbs

satisfactorily; aptly; effectively; sufficiently; definitely; clearly; lucidly; acceptably; liberally; roughly; carefully; crudely; artfully; skilfully; adroitly; sagely; wisely; craftily; sincerely; genuinely; plausibly; ingeniously; vividly; graphically; competently; glibly; discreetly; tardily; flimsily; fundamentally; intelligently; elaborately; casually; lamely.

EXPLETIVE

adjectives

muttered; raucous; exasperated; choice; foul-mouthed; energetic; unmeaning.

EXPLICIT

adverbs

elaborately; clearly; fully; succinctly; tersely; curtly; definitely; undeniably; unusually; highly; oddly; unnecessarily; needlessly; carefully; meticulously; strangely; curiously; noticeably; graphically; broadly; dogmatically; officially; imperiously; decisively; formally; solemnly; ominously.

EXPLODE (v)

adverbs
indignantly; successfully; prematurely; squarely; sharply; terrifically; volcanically; frightfully; violently; tremendously; initially; deafeningly; horribly; titanically; dreadfully; disastrously; catastrophically.

(See burst, erupt.)

EXPLOIT

adjectives
boldest; illustrious; quick-witted; antique; ludicrous; memorable; heroic; jocular; gigantic; engineering; dread; phenomenal; daring; dashing; transcendent; brilliant; decisive; hazardous; exuberant; unmatched; imagined; valorous; news; psychic; hair-raising; atrocious; spectacular.

verbs
achieve—; boast of—; close—; conceive —; design—; dream of—; perform—; plot —; recount—; resent—; set forth—s of; share in—; succeed in—; witness—; view —; —reverberates.

(See deed, act, feat, achievement.)

EXPLOIT (v)

adverbs
unethically; arrogantly; fully; indefensibly; ruthlessly; profitably; assiduously; cleverly; industrially; competitively; agriculturally; capitalistically; unreasonably; hideously; nationally; unscrupulously.

(See persecute, oppress.)

EXPLOITATION

adjectives
competitive; pagan; agricultural; middleman; capitalistic; reasonable; hideous; coastwise; national.

verbs
accomplish by—; achieve through—; carry on—; conduct—; consider—; curtail—; decry—; denounce—; delve into—; expose to —; frown on—; instigate—; investigate—; prohibit—; prosper through—; renounce—; resist—; reveal—; view—; —agitates; — enriches; —impoverishes; —ransacks; — reigns.

(See employment, utility, profit.)

EXPLORATION

adjectives
titanic; celebrated; linguistic; nocturnal; unproductive; extensive; arctic; authentic; geographical; daring; world-girdling; fervid; perilous; exhaustive; exotic.

verbs
absorb in—; conduct—; deserve—; discover by—; discuss—; frustrate—; instigate—; plan—; prepare for—; relate—; resume—; subscribe to—; tire of—; undertake—; — ascertains; —determines; —discloses; —inquires; —investigates; —proves; —reveals.

(See search, examination, investigation.)

EXPLORE (v)

adverbs
intelligently; carefully; completely; morbidly; zealously; undauntedly; adventurously; intrepidly; untiringly; scientifically; methodically.

(See examine, search.)

EXPLORER

adjectives
enterprising; zealous; undaunted; adventurous; literary; fortunate; intrepid; untiring; hardy; scientific.

EXPLOSION

adjectives
premature; sharp; terrific; volcanic; frightful; violent; intermittent; numbing; tremendous; deplorable; initial; deafening; magnificent; strange; horrible; dreadful; rending; staccato; titanic; disastrous; gigantic; soul-shattering; catastrophic.

verbs
augment—; forestall—; investigate—; produce—; threaten—; —alarms; —casts out; —damages; —discharges; —drives out; — ejects; —emits; —erupts; —jars; —reports; —rocks; —scars; —shatters; —shocks; — showers; —sunders; —thunders; —violates.

(See outburst, discharge, detonation.)

EXPLOSIVE

verbs
employ—; play with—; toy with—; threaten with—; touch off—; warn of—; —alarms; —blows off; —bursts; —damages; —detonates; —discharges; —drives out; —ejects; —erupts; —jars; —rocks; —shatters; — shocks; —showers; —thunders; —violates.

(See gunpowder, dynamite.)

adverbs
dangerously; reportedly; ominously; alarmingly; highly; unusually; allegedly; undeniably; notoriously; abominably; hazardously; perilously; precariously; ticklishly; terrifically; frightfully; tremendously; horribly; disastrously; easily; readily.

EXPLOSIVENESS

adjectives

volatile; choleric; ready.

EXPONENT

adjectives

able; distinguished; outstanding; scholarly; preeminent; quasi-authoritative; skilled; sole; impressive; faithful; philosophical.

EXPORT

verbs

allow—s; ban—; boycott—s; confiscate—s; deal in—s; demand—s; dispose of—s; dump —s; exchange—s; halt—s; levy against—s; license—s; minimize—s; permit—s; produce for—; reduce—s; restrain—; ship—s; speculate in—s; stimulate—; suspend—; tax—s; underwrite—s; value—s; —s decline; —s rise.

EXPORTER

verbs

bargain with—; communicate with—; consult—; exchange with—; impose on—; license—; order from—; purchase from—; remit to—; restrain—; subsidize—; tax—; —deals in; —demands; —disposes of; —dumps; —invests; —produces; —speculates; —values.

EXPOSE (v)

adverbs

shamelessly; unequivocally; unblushingly; reputedly; blasphemously; fearlessly; dangerously; conspicuously; piteously; improperly; sufficiently; ultimately; virtually; subsequently; unwisely; shrewdly; partially; lucidly; subtly; thrillingly; incautiously; graphically; relentlessly; ruthlessly; definitely; imprudently; inevitably.

(See denounce, accuse.)

EXPOSITION

adjectives

comprehensive; simply written; progressive; ever-varying; precise; lucid; striking; suitable; masterly; contemporaneous; courteous; erroneous; chronological; classic; sound; scientific; clear; serious; accurate; amusing; brilliant; pretentious; concise; skillful; enthusiastic; daring; illuminating; consummate; distinguished; subtle; straightforward; ethnographical; thrilling; well-reasoned; graphic; sane; forcible; passionate; lucid; fresh.

verbs

arrange—; attend—; conduct—; display at —; enter into—; finance—; hearken to—; interpret—; launch into—; present at—; prohibit—; publish—; recount—; render—; report—; show at—; view—; —advocates; —awes; —confuses; —explains; —expounds; —interests.

(See display, exhibition, essay, composition, explanation.)

EXPOSITORY

adverbs

clearly; drearily; dully; endlessly; dismally; wearily; droningly; lucidly; intelligibly; unusually; definitely; admirably; agreeably; needfully; suitably; skilfully; soundly; accurately; acceptably; artlessly; realistically; critically; wonderfully.

EXPOSTULATE (v)

adverbs

softly; fiercely; petulantly; madly; mildly; wrathfully; amicably; frantically; frankly.

(See protest, remonstrate.)

EXPOSTULATION

adjectives

mad; mild; wrathful; lingering; amicable; frantic; frank.

EXPOSURE

adjectives

horrible; projected; undue; serviceable; fatal; bleak; inevitable; imprudent; fearless; initial; earnest; intelligent; courageous; sociological; wanton; definite; ominous; startling; sensational; ruthless; unremitted; incautious; cruel; relentless; blatant.

verbs

anticipate—; deserve—; entail—; escape—; guard from—; lay open to—; prohibit—; protect from—; sentence to—; subject to—; suffer from—; view—; —deprives; —discloses; —displays; —divulges; —endangers; —expels; —reveals; —shames.

(See disclosure, revelation.)

EXPOUND (v)

adverbs

repeatedly; grimly; clearly; gravely; quaintly; mystifyingly; incomprehensibly; patiently.

(See explain.)

EXPRESS

adjectives

roaring; aerial; limited; endless.

EXPRESS (v)

adverbs

audibly; cordially; admirably; resignedly; lightly; precisely; visually; optimistically; poetically; pointedly; metaphorically; significantly; inelegantly; openly; peevishly; wittily; independently; frivolously; accurately; obviously; submissively; vaguely; delicately; urgently; exquisitely; eloquently; privately; succinctly; indignantly; mildly; figuratively; adequately; bluntly; repeatedly; inadequately; gratefully; forcibly; voluntarily; lucidly; ingenuously; courteously; pithily; whimsically; graphically; stupidly; placidly; felicitously; affably; affectedly; angelically; animatedly; arrogantly; appropriately; arbitrarily; benevolently; blandly; buoyantly; capriciously; caressingly; characteristically; calculatingly; contemptuously; creatively; deceptively; delicately; demurely; diabolically; dubiously; ecstatically; equivocally; ferociously; formidably; genially; grammatically; gravely; grimly; grotesquely; humorously; forbiddingly; impassionedly; indescribably; indignantly; instinctively; introspectively; journalistically; jovially; knowingly; legitimately; loftily; lugubriously; luminously; majestically; martially; meekly; melodiously; memorably; metaphysically; charmingly; mirthlessly; mutinously; momentarily; nobly; nonsensically; nostalgically; owlishly; patriotically; peculiarly; pedantically; pensively; pessimistically; petulantly; pitifully; plaintively; portentiously; radiantly; recklessly; sardonically; saturninely; savagely; secretively; sheepishly; shrewdly; sinisterly; smugly; solemnly; soothingly; sourly; superbly; spiritedly; spontaneously; sternly; strainedly; submissively; sullenly; synonymously; technically; transparently; treasonably; tritely; truculently; ultimately; uniformly; vicariously; viciously; vindictively; vivaciously; vividly; volubly; warily; wistfully; wryly; yearningly.

(See say, utter.)

EXPRESSION

adjectives

adequate; affable; affected; agonized; airy; alchemistical; all-conquering; altered; amazed; ambiguous; angelic; animated; anxious; apologetic; appalled; appealing; appraising; appropriate; arbitrary; arrogant; artistic; assertive; astonished; austere; banal; beatific; belligerent; benevolent; bewildered; bitter; blameless; bland; bleak; broken; brutish; buoyant; cabalistical; calm; capricious; careless; caressing; ceremonious; characteristic; charming; chastened; chivalric; calculating; comical; commanding; conciliatory; confidential; consecrated; conspicuous; consummate; contemplative; contemptuous; contended; contrite; countless (pl); courteous; creative; criminal; crystalline; cunning; curious; dazed; deceptive; deliberate; delicate; demoniac; demonstrative; demure; depressed; despairing; diabolic; disagreeable; disdainful; distasteful; dolorous; dithyrambic; dogged; dominant; dramatic; dreamy; dubious; dumb; ear-pleasing; eager; earnest; ecstatic; elegant; embossed; emotionless; emphatic; encouraging; equivocal; etherealized; exalted; evanescent; expectant; exterior; facial; faintest; fanglike; faraway; far-off; felicitous; feline; ferocious; fervent; fiendish; fierce; figurative; fine; fixed; fleeting; forbidding; forced; forlorn; formidable; freezing; frequent; frightened; frowning; frustrated; fundamental; furtive; genial; gentle; gladsome; glazed; gloomy; glorified; graceful; grammatical; grave; grim; habitual; grotesque; grouchy; haggard; half-absorbed; half-articulate; half-humorous; half-downright; half-pathetic; half-hearted; half-indulgent; half-suspicious; hangdog; happy; hard; hard-set; haunting; heartbroken; hearty; hereditary; homely; honest; hopeless; horrible; horrid; hospitable; humorous; ideal; idiotic; idyllic; ill-natured; imaginative; imbecilic; immobile; impassioned; imploring; implied; impressive; incidental; incredulous; indescribable; indignant; indirect; infinite; injured; inquiring; inscrutable; instinctive; intense; intent; introspective; jolly; journalistic; jovial; joyous; kindly; knowing; lackluster; legitimate; listening; listless; literary; lofty; lovable; lucid; lugubrious; luminous; majestic; malign; martial; martyrlike; maudlin; meaningful; meek; melancholy; melodious; memorable; menacing; merry; metaphysical; mirthless; moody; momentary; moral; mutinous; mysterious; mystic; noble; noncommittal; nonsensical; nostalgic; noteworthy; odd; ominous; open; outward; owlish; plain; pleasing; pantomimic; particular; passionate; patriotic; peculiar; pedantic; peevish; pensive; perfect; periphrastic; perplexed; pessimistic; petulant; physiognomic; pithy; pitiful; placid; plaintive; plastic; pleasant; poetic; poignant; popular; portentous; predatory; preoccupied; prim; professional; proper; provoking; prose; puzzled; quaint; quarrelsome; queer; questioning; quiet; quizzical; radiant; rapt; rare; rebuked; reckless; relaxed; remarkable; repelling; resentful; resolute; respective; rueful; sagacious; sad; sarcastic; sardonic; saturnine; saucy; savage; secretive; self-concentrated; seraphic; serio-comic; serious; set; severe; sharp; sheepish; shocked; shrewd; sicklied; significant; sincere; singular; sinister; slight; slow; sly; smileless; smug; soft; softened; solemn; soothing; sorrowful; sour; ·spacious; superb; spirited; spontaneous; sprightliest; stealthy; stern; stony; strained; structural; submissive; subtle; sulky; sullen; surprised; sweet; synonymous; taut; technical; tender; tense; theoretical; thoughtful; thought-saving; thwarted; tragic; transparent; treasonable; trite; triumphal; triumphant; troubled; truculent; ultimate; unanimous; unbelieving; unbounded; uncompromising; unelaborated; unconscious; uneasy; unfit; unforgettable; unguarded; uniform; unmoved; unstudied; unusual; upright; vacant; vague; various (pl); vehement; venomous; vibratory; vicarious; vicious; victorious; vindictive; violent; virtuous; visual; vivacious; vivid; voluble; warlike; warm; wary; wavering; well-bred; whimsical; wild; wily; wistful; woebegone; wondering; wordless; worn; worried; wry; yearning.

verbs
achieve —; assume —; crave —; cry out for —; cultivate —; distort —; divest of —; efface —; fathom —; fix —; limit —; recollect —; stifle —; strive toward —; struggle for —; translate —; understand —; wear —; — congeals; — plays; — settles.
  (See utterance, statement, assertion.)

EXPRESSIVE
adverbs
clearly; particularly; distinctly; emphatically; beautifully; especially; wonderfully; accurately; powerfully; effectively; cruelly; remarkably; sympathetically.

EXPRESSIVENESS
adjectives
mobile; pregnant.

EXPULSION
adjectives
pathetic; forcible; virtual.

verbs
accept—; anticipate—; criticize—; demand —; employ —; face —; favor —; inflict —;

influence —; order —; promote —; punish with —; resign to —; secure —; suffer —; threaten with —; welcome —; — benefits; — corrects; — shames.
  (See discharge, dismissal.)

EXPURGATED
adverbs
mercilessly; unnecessarily; relentlessly; priggishly; carefully; zealously; absurdly; needlessly; hopelessly; inanely; ridiculously; primly; spinsterishly; puritanically; mawkishly; properly.

EXQUISITE
adverbs
daintily; charmingly; enchantingly; delicately; matchlessly; remarkably; beautifully; utterly; delicately; airily; incredibly; wonderfully; gracefully; harmoniously; richly; melodiously.

EXTEMPORANEOUS
adverbs
genuinely; sincerely; honestly; obviously; rigidly; strictly; avowedly; artlessly; spontaneously; crudely; thoughtlessly; carelessly; delightfully; impulsively; manifestly.

EXTEMPORIZE (v)
adverbs
jocosely; freely; humorously; artfully; skillfully; clumsily; cleverly; shrewdly.
  (See improvise.)

EXTEND (v)
adverbs
spaciously; understandingly; beseechingly; widely; liberally; skillfully; infinitely; beneficently; enormously; generously; gradually; laterally; additionally; internationally; invitingly.
  (See lengthen, project.)

EXTENSION
adjectives
infinite; enormous; generous; ideal; dangerous; gradual; further; lateral; additional; international; widest.

verbs
advocate —; check —; confine —; curtail —; grant —; justify —; influence —; limit

—; nip —; open —; permit —; plan —;
plead for —; prevent —; regulate —; strangle —; terminate —; — accommodates; —
eases.
(See increase, addition, expansion, enlargement.)

EXTENT

adjectives
dangerous; uncivil; unjust; perceptible; amazing; probable; unprecedented; monstrous; considerable; far-reaching; reasonable; enormous; vast; unusual; boundless; solemn; important; limitless; sufficient; immense; greater; fearful; astonishing; satisfying; bewildering; disproportionate.

verbs
ascertain —; carry to —; consider —; define —; estimate —; exercise to —; limit —; occupy to —; reach —; recognize —; rule — of; serve —; understand —; — alarms; — allures; — consists; — forces; — reduces.
(See amount, size, magnitude, degree.)

EXTERIOR

adjectives
impenetrable; rustic; indifferent; fearless; attractive; commonplace; grave; showy; valorous; calm; amphibious; passive; listless; visible; expansive; impassible; quiet; soft; cold; stolid.

EXTERMINATE (v)

adverbs
ruthlessly; gradually; certainly; speedily; inevitably; totally; subsequently; entirely; cruelly; blindly; finally.
(See destroy, remove.)

EXTERMINATION

verbs
attempt —; banish to —; demand —; drive into —; end in —; engage in —; guard against —; plan —; prevent —; prophesy —; protect against —; pursue to —; repel —; war on —; warn against —; — destroys; — drives out; — eliminates; — extirpates; — forces out; — reduces; — rids.

EXTINCTION

adjectives
final; certain; hurried; speedy; inevitable; total; subsequent.

verbs
blot into —; decay into —; demand — of; deplore —; doom to —; flicker into —; guard against —; meet —; mourn —; plan —; prevent —; suffocate into —; surrender to —; threaten with —; warn against —; witness —; yield to —.
(See destruction, extermination.)

EXTINGUISH (v)

adverbs
instantly; temporarily; instantaneously; abruptly; promptly; rudely; hastily; swiftly.
(See destroy, remove.)

EXTOL (v)

adverbs
frequently; highly; loudly; continually; flatteringly; lavishly; shrewdly; purposely; ostensibly; sincerely.
(See exalt, praise.)

EXTORT (v)

adverbs
soullessly; miserly; graspingly; meanly; exorbitantly; usuriously; heartlessly.
(See wring, force.)

EXTORTION

adjectives
oppressive; multiplied (pl); baffled; criminal.

EXTORTIONATE

adverbs
criminally; highly; illegally; terribly; absolutely; positively; unbelievably; cruelly; harshly; tyrannically; greedily; rapaciously; sordidly; meanly; ravenously; insatiably.

EXTRACT

adjectives
liquid; liberal; embryonic; subsequent; garbled; glandular; misquoted.

verbs
administer —; copy —; deduce —; derive —; discharge —; distil —; draw forth —; elicit —; employ —; evolve —; issue —; obtain —; prepare —; quote —; view —; — finishes; — flavors; — represents.
(See essence, selection.)

EXTRACT (v)

adverbs
freshly; imperfectly; wilfully; liberally; subsequently; glandularly; erroneously; illegally.
(See draw, select.)

EXTRACTION

adjectives
oral; foreign; noble.

EXTRANEOUS

adverbs
unessentially; relatively; definitely; obviously; naturally; discordantly; exotically; curiously; strangely; mysteriously.

EXTRAVAGANCE

adjectives
fine; reckless; ostentatious; unusual; tasteless; absurd; oratorical; rough; gorgeous; favorite; complete; unwarrantable; incipient; lavish; wasteful; senseless; frightful; old-time; wicked; imaginable; utmost; elegant; profligate; forensic; bromidic; unjustified; flagrant.

verbs
check —; cloak in —; consort with —; court —; criticize —; guard against —; indulge in —; involve in —; regret —; rue —; sacrifice to —; smack of —; stimulate —; supply —; warn against —; — corrupts; — destroys; — drains; — fetters; — impoverishes; — inflames; — reigns; — shocks.
(See waste, excess.)

EXTRAVAGANT

adverbs
wantonly; foolishly; madly; rapturously; lavishly; happily; drunkenly; wildly; blithely; wickedly; improvidently; fantastically; outrageously; vulgarly; proudly; ostentatiously; extremely; absurdly; ridiculously; pompously; outrageously; gayly; inordinately; exceedingly; incredibly; magnificently; splendidly; gorgeously; recklessly; fully; senselessly; flagrantly; immensely.

EXTREME

adjectives
absurd; delirious; fantastic; spiritualistic; unhealthy; uttermost; strenuous; blunt; precise; calculable; dangerous; glorious; exhaustive.

verbs
avoid—; delight in—; dress in—; drive to —; employ—; endure—; leap to—; moderate—; proceed to—; reach—; run to—; shun —; temper—; twist to—; warn against—; —begets; —blinds; —confuses; —destroys; —disturbs; —endangers; —maddens.
(See excess.)

EXTREMITY

adjectives
dire; sensuous; dread; ultimate; desperate; furthest; remotest.

EXUBERANCE

adjectives
glorious; effervescent; fantastic; brash; floral; prodigal; fitful; incondite; brisk.

verbs
attest by—; avoid—; burst into—; correct —; drain of—; exhaust—; hide—; indulge in—; inject—; lessen—; play with—; repress—; spoil—; steep in—; suppress—; teem with—; —astonishes; —overflows.
(See abundance, luxuriance, excess.)

EXUBERANT

adverbs
gloriously; fantastically; profusely; prodigally; excessively; inordinately; uncommonly; oddly; immensely.

EXUDE (*v*)

adverbs
aromatically; disgustingly; vilely; sickeningly; freely; abnormally gradually.
(See discharge, flow.)

EXULT (*v*)

adverbs
vauntingly; openly; enthusiastically; triumphantly; boastfully; happily; gloatingly; drunkenly.
(See rejoice, triumph.)

EXULTANT

adverbs
loudly; noisily; proudly; pompously; splendidly; magnificently; quietly; deeply; childishly; triumphantly; happily; incredulously; boastfully; humbly; rapturously; ecstatically; incoherently; profoundly; joyously; jubilantly; elatedly; delightedly; immensely; exceedingly; remarkably.

EXULTATION

adjectives
vaporous; justifiable; fierce; savage; childish; honest; incoherent; facetious; wonted; sublimest; raptured; menacing; splendid.

EYE

verbs
affix to—; avert—; bat—; bathe—; blear—; blink—; cast —s upon; catch—; cloud—; cock—; darken—; dazzle—; delude—; di-

late—; dim—; divert—; examine—; extract from—; feast —s upon; glue —s upon; goggle—s; inflame—; intrigue—; irrigate —; irritate—; moisten—; narrow—s; offend —; paste—s on; pin—s on; pucker up—s; rivet—s on; roll—s; screw up—s; shadow —s; shield—s; snag—; soften—s; soothe—s; stagger—; strain—s; suffuse—; tear—s away; test—; tire—s; veil—s; —s acquiesce; —s beam; —s blaze; —s brood; —s bulge; —s challenge; —s climb; —s dance; —s devour; —discerns; —s drift; —s drink in; —embraces; —s fall; —s flash; —s flicker; —s flinch; —s glare; —s gleam; —s glint; —s glitter; —s glow; —s kindle; —penetrates; —s plead; —probes; —s protrude; —s redden; —rests upon; —roams; —roves; —scans; —scorns; —scrutinizes; —shines; —smarts; —s smoulder; —s snap; —s sparkle; —s squint; —s study; —s swell; —s swim; —s twinkle; —s twitch; —s water; —s waver; —s widen; —s beseech.
(See sight.)

EYE (v)

adverbs
wistfully; piercingly; candidly; keenly; curiously; suspiciously; boldly; challengingly; squarely; critically; sternly; pathetically; attentively; thoughtfully; timidly; painfully; hungrily; contemptuously; unwaveringly; inquisitively; significantly; frigidly; derisively; moodily; covetously; soulfully; bleakly; dispassionately; fastidiously; stonily; sullenly; darkly; insatiably; beseechingly; alertly; mischievously; inquiringly; absently; abstractedly; amazedly; ardently; arrogantly; benignly; bestially; bewilderedly; bewitchingly; earnestly; enviously; intently; lovingly; piteously; intelligently; pleadingly; heavily; humorously; formidably; gaily; glassily; glintingly; glitteringly; maudlinly; joyously; mysteriously; professionally; raptly; sheepishly; steadfastly; studiously; superficially; uncritically; vacantly; watchfully; wisely; wolfishly; wonderingly; wordlessly; venomously.
(See watch, observe.)

EYEBALLS

adjectives
fierce; searing; burning; gorgeous; dead; bugle; rolling; protruding; swimming; staring; dilated; half-eaten.

EYEBROW

verbs
arch—s; cock—; corrugate—s; darken—s;

jet—s; knit—s; pluck—s; quirk—; raise—; slant—s; thin out—s; tidy up—s; —s beetle; —s curve; —s shag.

EYEBROWS

adjectives
bushy; shaggy; fierce-looking; supercilious; calm; haughty; broad-arched; peaked; high; pencil-line; sandy; mastic-darkened; solemn; prominent; raised; tangled; thick; curved; heavy; bristly; stiff; silky; delicate; wispy; perfect; bent; drawn; uneven; surprised; sardonic; elevated; uplifted; bold; gloomy; mismated; boyish; languid; ginger; thin; proud; twitching; pepper-and-salt; disapproving.

EYELASHES

adjectives
sooty; dusky; mascaraed; artificial; tear-drenched; dense; dark-fringed; thick; long; sopping; dark; uplifted; beaded; blinking; sandy; absurd; beautiful; long-lashed; heavily-fringed.

verbs
bat—; clip—; lift—; —brush; —droop; —flash; —flatter; —flicker; —flutter; —fringe; —glisten; —guard; —quiver; —repose; —shade; —shimmer; —sleep; —sweep; —veil.

EYELIDS

adjectives
quivering; quiet; swollen; shaken; withered; heavy; drooping; long-fringed; broad; worn-off; fluttering; wrinkled; straight-cut; languid; trembling; waxen; bronze; bluish; opaque; leaden; tired; limp; hanging; half-closed; narrowed; closed; shriveled; lazy; tremulous; thin; pain-wrenched.

verbs
drop—; fringe—; kiss—; lift—; raise—; squeeze—; wag—; weigh—down; —ache; —droop; —fall; —flutter; —quiver: —sleep; —slumber; —twitch.

EYES

adjectives
able; abnormal; absent; accusing; abstracted; aching; actual; admirable; adorable; adoring; adulterated; adventure-seeking; aesthetic; affrighted; affronted; agate; age-dimmed; agonized; age-blue; alien; all-seeing; alluring; almond; altered; amazed; amber-colored; ambitious; amiable; amorous; amused; angered; anguished; ani-

mated; anxious; apathetic; appealing; appraising; appreciative; apprehending; approving; archeological; ardent; arrogant; ash-rimmed; assailing; assenting; astonished; astounded; attentive; attractive; august; austere; authoritative; autumn-leaf; avaricious; averted; avid; awakened; awe-inspiring; azure-tinted; baby-blue; bad; baffling; bagged; baleful; bashful; battered; battle-aged; battle-lighted; beadlike; beady; beady-bright; beaming; beautiful; beauty-loving; beetling; bemused; benignant; bent; beseeching; bestial; bewildered; bewitching; bilberry; big; bilious; bland; blazing; blue; bleak; bleared; blissful; blood-injected; bloodshot; bodeful; bold; bonny; boring; boundless; bovine; bright; brightened; brimming; brooding; brown; bruised; brown-flecked; bulbous; bulging; burrowing; bursting; button; calculating; calm; candid; canny; capricious; careless; cat-like; cautious; cavernous; celestial; challenging; chance-met; changeable; charmed; chaste; chastening; childish; cheerful; chilly; chocolate-brown; civic; clear; clever; clinging; close-set; closing; clouded; coal-black; cold; colorless; color-loving; commanding; commemorative; commiserating; compassionate; compelling; concealed; concerned; condemnatory; confused; congested; contemplative; contemptuous; contracted; contumelious; conventional; convivial; convulsed; cool; countless; courageous; covert; covetous; craving; created; critical; crumpling; crystal-clear; cunning; curious; cynical; dancing; dangerous; dark-fringed; dark-lashed; death-darting; darkness-dazed; darting; dazzled; deadly; deceiving; decorous; deep; deep-circled; deep-curtained; deep-set; deep-socketed; deep-sunk; defenseless; defiant; dejected; deliberating; delighted; delightful; demanding; demon; demure; deprecating; derisive; descriptive; desolate; despair-glazed; despairing; devastating; devilish; devouring; dewy; dilated; directing; discerning; discolored; discomfited; discontented; discovering; disdainful; disillusioned; dispassionate; dissatisfied; displeased; disquieting; dissecting; dissipated; distasteful; distempered; distended; distracting; distressed; disturbed; divining; dizzy; dog-true; doubtful; dovelike; downcast; dramatic; down-dropped; dreadful; dream-shrouded; dream-swept; dreamy; dreary; drink-filmed; drooping; drowsy; dry; dull; dusky; dying; eager; eagle; eagle-gray; eagle-

keen; earnest; educated; effective; effeminate; eloquent; eluded; embittered; emerald-green; empty; enameled; enamored; enchanted; energetic; enigmatic; enlarged; enlivening; enormous; enthralled; entranced; envious; epiphyseal; evasive; ever-lusterless; ever-moving; ever-questing; evil; examining; excited; expanding; expectant; expiring; expert; expressionable; expressive; extraordinary; exulting; faded; failing; fainting; fairer; faithful; falcon; familiar; far-gazing; far-off; farseeing; far-sighted; fascinated; fastened; fastidious; fatal; fatherly; fathomless; fatigue-dimmed; favoring; fear-filled; feminine; fear-glazed; fear-laden; fearful; fearless; feeble; ferocious; ferret; feverish; fidgety; fierce; fiery; filmed; finding; fine-wrought; fishlike; fishy; fixed; flashing; flat-blue; fleshy-looking; flickering; flinty; flowerlike; flustered; fluttering; foolish; forbidden; foreboding; foreign; forgiving; formidable; formless; foul; frank; freezing; fresh; fretful; fright-filled; frightened; frosty; frowning; frozen; furious; furtive; galled; gamesome; gay; gazelle; gemlike; gentle; ghastly; gifted; gimlet; gin-cleared; girlish; glad; glaring; glassy; gleaming; glimmering; glinting; glittering; gloating; globular; glorious; glossy; glowering; glowing; glutton; goggling; golden; golden-brown; good; grave; gray; gray-steel; great; greedy; gross; grotesque; groveling; guarded; guiding; guileless; guilty; gypsy; habituated; haggard; hale; half-closed; half-defiant; half-repentant; half-shut; half-veiled; happy; harassed; hardened; haughty; haunting; hawk-brown; hazel; healthy; heart-broken; heart-reaching; heartless; heart-sick; heated; heavenly; heavy; heavy-lidded; heedless; hollow; honest; hooded; horny; horrified; hostile; housewifely; hovering; human; humble; humid; humorous; hyacinth-blue; hungry; hunted; hurt; hypnotic; hypnotized; ice-blue; icy; idealistic; ill-omened; immobile; immortal; impartial; imperious; implacable; imploring; impudent; incandescent; incredulous; incensed; incurious; indifferent; indignant; indolent; indomitable; indulgent; inebriate; inexorable; inexperienced; inferior; inflamed; innocent; innumerable; insolent; inquiring; inquisitive; insane; inscrutable; insipid; insistent; intelligent; intent; interrogating; intricate; intriguing; introspective; intrusive; intuitional; inventive; inward; inward-turning; iris-blue; jade; jaded; irradiant;

462

jaundiced; jewel; jolly; joy-filled; joyous; joy-pronouncing; keen; keen-puckered; kind; kindled; knowing; kohl-rimmed; laboring; lackluster; lackadaisical; lambent; landlubber; languid; languorous; large; lascivious; lashless; laughing; leaden; lecherous; leering; lenient; level; lidless; life-darting; lifted; light; limpid; lingering; liquid; listless; livid; living; loathing; lodestar; lofty; longing; lovable; love-deep; love-laden; love-lit; love-weary; loving; lucent; lurid; lumpy; lurking; lusterless; lustrous; lynx; madonna; magisterial; magnificent; mahogany; malevolent; malicious; malignant; mangling; martial; masculine; maternal; mature; maudlin; mean; medicinable; meditating; melancholy; melting; memory-ridden; menacing; microscopic; merciless; merry; meteor; mild; military; milky; miraculous; miscast; mischievous; miserable; mismatched; mistaking; misty; mocking; modest; moist; moistened; Mongolian; monstrous; moody; mortal; mortified; motionless; mottled; mournful; murderous; muddy-brown; musing; musty; mutinous; myopic; myriad; mysterious; mystical; mystifying; naked-bladed; narrow; national; neighboring; normal; observant; observing; obsidian; offering; ogling; onyx; opal; opaque; opening; oriental; outraged; outstanding; outward; overflowing; overhanging; overstrained; oxlike; owlish; pain-dimmed; pain-filled; pain-lashed; painful; pale; pale-blue; pallid; pansy-blue; pansy-dark; passing; passionate; paternal; patient; peacock; peeping; peering; peevish; pellucid; penetrating; pensive; perceiving; peremptory; perspicuous; persuasive; perverse; philosophical; phoenix; piercing; piglike; pious; piteous; pitying; placid; plaintive; pleading; pleasant; poetic; polished-looking; pondering; preoccupied; ponderous; popping; porcine; possessive; pouchy; powerful; practiced; pragmatic; predatory; probing; prodigious; profane; professional; prominent; prompting; prophetic; protecting; protuberant; proud; provocative; public; puffed; punished; purblind; pure; purged; purple; prying; puzzled; querulous; questioning; quick; quick-lifted; quick-shifting; quiet; quizzical; radiant; raccoonlike; raging; random; rapt; ratlike; ratty; ravenous; ravished; realmless; rebel; rebelling; rebuking; red-rimmed; reddened; reflecting; reflective; reluctant; remarkable; remote; reproachful; resplendent; retrospective; reverent; reverted; revengeful; rheumy; richest; rival; riveting; roaming; roguish; rolling; romantic; rose-colored; round; roving; ruddy; ruddy-brown; rueful; rust-colored; sad; saddened; sagacious; sanguine; sarcastic; sardonic; satiated; saturnine; saucy; savage; scandalized; skeptic; scornful; scowling; screwed-up; scrutinizing; sea-blue; sea-gray; sea-green; sea-spent; searching; searchlight; seductive; seeing; selfsame; sensible; seraphic; sere; serene; serious; serpent; shaded; shadow-nurtured; shadowed; shadowy; shifting; sharp; sheepish; shifty; shimmering; shining; shrewd; shrinking; shrouded; shy; sibylline; sidelong; sightless; silent; silly; single; sinister; skeptical; sky-blue; skyey; slant; slate-colored; slaty; sleep-sodden; sleepless; sleepy; slight; slitty; sly; small; smart; smarting; smiling; smoke-blue; smoldering; snake; snapping; sober; sodden; soft-winged; solemn; solicitous; solitary; sorrowing; soul-telling; soulful; soulless; sour; sparkling; speaking; spectacular; speculating; speculative; spell-set; spirit-beaming; sphered; splendid; sprightly; sprouting; stainless; starlike; staring; spirit-thrilling; stark; starry; starting; steady; steadfast; stealthy; steaming; steel; steel-bright; steel-cold; stinging; steely; stern; stony; stormy; strained; strange; straying; streaming; striking; strong; studious; stupefied; subtle; subdued; sud-filled; suffering; suffused; sullen; sulky; sulphurous; sultry; sunken; sun-clear; sun-dazzled; sunshiny; superb; superficial; surprised; surveying; suspicious; sweeping; swimming; swollen; sympathetic; Tarquin; taunting; tawny; tear-blurred; tearful; tear-marred; tear-ridden; tear-wet; telescopic; telltale; tempestuous; tender; terrible; terrifying; terror-glazed; threatening; terrorized; terror-stricken; thankful; tiger; thirsty; thoughtful; tigerish; time-dimmed; timorous; tiny; tip-tilted; tired; tired out; tolerant; tormented; tormenting; tortured; topaz; touching; town-bred; trained; traitorous; tranquil; tremendous; transcendent; transparent; zinc-colored; tremulous; triumphal; triumphant; trouble-strained; truant; truculent; true; trustful; trustless; twinkling; unabashed; unaccountable; unaccustomed; unaided; unaltering; unbelieving; unannointed; unavoided; unblended; unblinded; unblinking; uncanny; uncaptious; uncertain; unclouded; uncomprehending; unconscious; uncritical; uncultivated; uncurious; undaunted; uneasy; unencumbered; unemotional; unenlightened; unenvious; unfathomable; unflickering; unflinching; unfriendly; uninitiate; unkind; unlearned; unnatural; unoperated; unpitying; unpredictable; unpleasant; unpracticed; unprejudiced; unprepossessing; unpresumptuous; unresponsive; unrevealing; unrewarded; unscrupulous; unseeing; unshackled; unshaded; unsmiling; unsophisticated; unspeakable; unsullied; unsuspecting; untamed; unterrified; untrained; untutored; untroubled; unusual; unwearied; unworldly; upbraiding; upraised; upturned; ugly; urgent; vacant; vacuous; velvet-soft; vague; veering; veiled; veilless; veiny; velvety; vengeful; venomous; vigilant; violet-blue; virgin; visionary; visionless; vivid; vulgar; wailing; waiting; wander-

ing; wanton; war-wearied; waxen; warning; wary; washed; wasted; watchful; watery; weak; weary; weasel; weather; weeping; welkin; whimsical; well-known; well-spaced; wicked; wide; wide-open; wild; willful; wincing; winking; wintry; wise; wistful; wolfish; wonderful; wondering; wondrous; wood-nymph; wordless; worldly-wise; worn; worried; worshipped; wrathful; wretched; yellow; yielding; youthful; zestful.

EYESIGHT

adjectives

partial; unsealed; failing; precious; weakening; impaired; inefficient; palsied; neglected.

F

FABLES

adjectives

comic; antique; contextual; wretched; trivial; impious; vivid; gorgeous; romantic; traditional; prehistoric; fantastic.

FABRIC

adjectives

political; attractive; sturdy; fine-wearing; ultra-smart; notable; practical; choicest; worsted; ideal; pure; wool; superb; tropical; rich; wearable; soft; exclusive; easy-draping; hard-finished; select; popular; excellent; mellowed; non-shrinkable; favored; summer; luxurious; wonderful; wear-packed; good-looking; sparkling; cool; expensive; original; sensational; iridescent; shivered; delicate; tinted; lustrous; gaudy; spangled; colorful; lightweight; soft-textured; quality; comfortable; easy-fitting; long-living; neutral color; rugged; famous; firm; extraordinary; lovely; apparent; hairy-surfaced; casual; unsubstantial; imported; cobweb; resilient; massive; durable; stately; identical; novelty; sheer; gossamer; distinctive; social; impregnated; misty; symmetrical; textile; clinging; accentuated; husky; brawnier; loomed; patterned.

verbs

construct—; fashion—; frame—; plan—; rebuild—; renovate—; spin—; supply—; threaten—; weave—; —awes; —endures; —inspires; —tatters.

(See cloth.)

FABRICATE (*v*)

adverbs

ingeniously; cleverly; hypocritically; plausibly; affectedly; falsely; maliciously; slyly; traitorously; convincingly.

(See devise, construct.)

FABRICATION

adjectives

wholesale; feeble; delicious; clumsy.

FABULOUS

adverbs

foolishly; extravagantly; egregiously; terribly; abominably; absurdly; laughably; outlandishly; whimsically; maliciously; fantastically; outrageously; mythically; ironically; perversely; romantically; utterly; manifestly; openly.

FACADE

adjectives

exquisite; unlovely; venerable; florid.

FACE

adjectives

absorbed; accusing; aggrieved; adored; aged; aghast; aging; agitated; agonized; alert; alluring; amazed; amiable; amused; flabby; angelical; angry; anguished; angular; animated; anxious; apathetic; apprehensive; approving; arresting; aquiline; arch-female; aristocratic; arrogant; artificial; ascending; ascetic; ashen; assiduous; astonished; astounding; attentive; attractive; audacious; auroral; austere; automaton; averted; awe-swept; awful; babyish; begrimed; baleful; barren; battered; beaming; beardless; beauteous; beefy; beloved; benevolent; benign; benignant; beseeching; besmeared; bestial; bewildered; bewitching; biddable; big; big-boned; big-featured; black; blackened; black-eyed; blanching; bland; blank; blear-eyed; blind; blissful; blistered; blithe; bloated; blood-faint; bloodless; bloodstained; bloodthirsty; bloody; blossomy; blubbering; blue-white; blurred; blushing; bold; bony; boulder-colored; boyish; bright; broad; broad-cheeked; brooding; brown; bruised; brutal; brutish; bucolic; burning; businesslike; cadaverous; calloused; calm; cameo; candid; capable; carbonadoed; careless; cavernous; careworn; carved-bone; cast-iron; celestial; chagrined; chalklike; changing; charitable; charming; charred; chastened; cheated; cheerful; cherubic; childlike; choleric; chubby; clammy; clawed; clean-cut; clean-shaven; clear-cut; clever; close; clouded; coarse; cold; cold-creamed; collapsed; colorless; combative; comely; comfortable; comical; commanding; complaining; complicated; composed; condemning; confident; congealed; congested; consumptive; contorted; contracted; convulsed; copper-bronzed; coppery; cordial; corpselike; corrugated; country-looking; cowardly; crafty; craggy; creamy-white; crude; cruel; crystal; cunning; curious; cynical; cynically-lined; dainty; daring; dark; darkened; dark-huddled; dazed; deadly; deadly-white; dead-white; death-like; deathly-pale; death-marked; debauched; deceptive; deep-lined; deeply-marred; dejected; delicate; delicately-formed; delicately-modeled; delighted; demure; delightful; denunciatory; despairing; despotic; determined; devilish; dewy; diffident; dignified; dimpled; dirty; disagreeable; disapproving; discolored; discontented; disdainful; disfigured; disillusioned; dismal; disordered; dissipated; distinct; distinguished; distorted; distracted; disturbed; doleful; dour; downcast; dowdy; drained; dreadful; dreary; dripping; droll; drooped; drowsy; dryad; dubious; dull; dusky; dust-colored; eager; earnest; easy-mannered; effeminate; elfin; eloquent; elusive; emaciated; embarrassed; eminent; enchanting; encrimsoned; energetic; enigmatic; enormous; enraptured; erstwhile; ethereal; ever-changing; everlasting; ever-welcome; evil; exceeding; expectant; exposed; expressionless; expressive; exquisite; eyeless; familiar; faded; fainting; fair; faithful; fallen; famine-stricken; famous; fanatical; fascinating; fat; fatigued; fatuous; fawning; fear-contorted; fearless; ferret-like; fervent; fiery; fighting; filled; fine; fixed; flabby; flamboyant; flat; flattened; flattered; fleshless; fleshy; flinty; flowerlike; flower-tinted; fond; foolish; forbidding; forced; foreign; formed; forsaken; forward; frail; frank; fraternal; freckled; fresh; friendly; frightened; frightful; froglike; frosted; furious; frosty; frozen; full; full-charged; furrowed; furtive; fuzzy; gamin; gaping; gaunt; gay; genial; ghastly; ghastly-pale; gigantic; girlish; gleaming; glistening; glittering; gloating; glory-beaming; glowing; glum; gnarled; gnomish; godlike; golden; good-humored; grotesque; good-natured; grained; granite; granite-gaunt; granite-hewn; grateful; grave; great; greenish-hued; grim; grinning; groping; gross-bloated; gruesome; guileless; gypsy; haggard; hair-fringed; hairless; half-averted; half-shrinking; half-haunted; handsome; hapless; happy; harassed; hard; hard-boiled; hard-muscled; harsh-featured; haughty; hate-clouded; hawklike; hearty; healthy-looking; heart-shaped; heated; heavenly; heat-flushed; heavy; helpless; heroic; hideous; hideously-scarred; well-bred; high-cheekboned; high-spirited; hirsute; hollow; holy; homely; honest; horrible; horror-stricken; hostile; huddled; humble; humorous; hungered; hungry; hunted; husklike; hypocritic; icy; idiotic; ignominious; illuminated; immemorial; immortal; immovable; impassive; imperial; imperious; imperturbable; impish; implacable; imploring; impudent; incredulous; indifferent; indignant; indomitable; ineffable; ineffectual; inelegant; inexorable; inexpressible; inexpressive; infant; infantine; inflamed; infuriated; ingenious; innocent; innumerable (pl); inoffensive; inscrutable; intellectual; intelligent; interesting; intrepid; irregular; irritable; isolated; ivory; jolly; jovial; keen-featured; kill-joy; kind; kindling; kindly; lampblack; large; lantern-jawed; laughing; lean-cheeked; leathery; leering; lemon-yellow; lifeless; little; lined; lineless; line-old; listening; listless; lively; livid; loathsome; locked; long; long-chinned; lordly; lovable; lovely; loving; gay; lowering; luminous; lustrous; majestic; malarial; malicious; malignant; maniacal; manly; mantling; marble; marred; martial; martyr; masklike; masked; massive; meager; meek; melancholy; memorable; merciless; merrier; mild; mirth-lit; miserable; mistrustful; mobile; mocking; modeled; motionless; monstrous; moon-colored; moonlike; moon-shaped; motherly; mottled; mottled-red; mournful; mud-besmeared; much-desired; muddy; mummied; murderous; muscular; mutilated; mutinous; mysterious; naked; nervous; neurotic; noble; noncommittal; noseless; objective; nutcracked; observant; obtuse; oil-smeared; oil-streaked; oily; olive; ominous; open; oval; overcast; pain-chiseled; pain-distorted; painted; pale; pansy-shaped; pallid; parchment; passionate; passionless; pasty; pasty-white; patient; patrician; peaceful; peaked; peerless; peaked; pearly; peasant; peevish; pensive; perfect; perfectly-formed; perished; perpendicular; perspiring; pert; pictured; phantom-like; piggish; pimply; pinched; piquant; piteous; pitiable; pitying; pitted; placid; plain; plaintive; pleasant; pleasing; plump; pock-marked; poetic; pointed; poker; porcelain-tinted; potent; powdered; powerful; precipitous; predestinate; premature; prematurely-aged; prevaricating; pretty; prison-pale; proud; puckered; pudding; pudgy; puffed; puffy; pugnacious; puny; purple-colored; putty-colored; puzzled; quaint; queenly; quiet; quivering; rabbity; radiant; rage-torn;

466

rage-twisted; rain-drenched; rapt; ratlike; ravaged; rebellious; reckless; red; refined; reflective; relentless; reproachful; resigned; resolute; respectable; responsive; restless; reticent; retributive; retrospective; reverent; reversed; ridged; rigid; roguish; rose-petal; rose-tinted; rosebud; rosy; roughly-hewn; round; rubicund; ruddier; rueful; rustic; ruthful; sad; sagacious; saintly; sallow; salt-stung; sanguine; sardonic; satanic; saturnine; saucy; scandalized; scapegrace; scared; scarlet; scarred; scheming; scholarly; scornful; scowling; scraggly; scratched; scrawny; screech-owl; seamed; scrutinizing; searching; seared; sedate; self-assured; selfless; sensitive; sensual; sentimental; serene; serious; serpent; serpentine; set; shaded; shamed; shameful; sharp-featured; sharply-angled; shaven; shining; shocked; shockingly disfigured; shrewd; shrouded; sick-looking; sickly; sightless; silent; silly; simpering; simple; sin-scarred; sinister; slant-eyed; sleek; sly; small; smashed; smiling; smile-lit; smirking; smoke-begrimed; smooth; smooth-coated; smooth-pale; smudged; smutted; snarling; sneering; sober; soft; soldierly; sorrow; somber; sorrowful; sorrowing; sorry; spare; sparkling; speaking; spectral; spirited; spiritual; splotched; staring; spongy; square; stark; square-jawed; square-jowled; startled; startling; steadfast; steady; steaming; stern; still; stolid; stone; stony; storm-beaten; stout; straight; straight-featured; strenuous; straightforward; strained; stubbly; streaming; stricken; striking; subdued; strong; strong-featured; stupid; sublime; sulky; sullen; sun-bitten; sun-browned; sunburned; sun-darkened; sun-scorched; sunken; sunny; surly; suspicious; swarthy; sweat-marked; sweat-streaked; sweating; sweet; tabid; tallow; swollen; tanned; tawny; tear-dabbled; tearful; tear-stained; tear-streaked; tear-wet; teary; tender; tense; terrible; thin; thoughtful; threatening; tight; tightening; tight-lipped; tight-skinned; tilted; time-stained; time-worn; timid; tired; toothless; tortured; tough; towering; tragic; tranquil; transfigured; transformed; transparent; triumphant; treacherous; troubled; trunkless; twisted; twittering; ugly; unabashed; unbelieving; unconscious; uncouth; uncovered; underhung; uneasy; unforgetful; unfriendly; unhealthy; unintellectual; unkempt; unlighted; unlined; unmoved; unpenciled; unreadable; unrejoicing; unremembering; un-

shaven; unscathed; unsmiling; unspoiled; unsunny; unsympathetic; untroubled; unwashed; unwithered; unworldly; unworried; unwrinkled; uplifted; uptilted; upturned; upward; vacant; vacuous; varnished; vanished; vapid; varying; veiled; vellum-colored; vicious; villainous; vindictive; virginal; vivacious; vulturish; waning; wan; washed; wayward; waxen; weak; weather-beaten; weather-stained; weather-worn; wedge-shaped; wee; weird; well-cut; well-featured; well-groomed; well-known; well-remembered; whimsical; whiskered; white; wicked; whitewashed; wide-eyed; wine-flushed; winsome; winter-blighted; wiry; wistful; withered; wizened; woebegone; woeful; wolfish; womanly; wonder; wrinkled; wooden; working; worn; worried; wrathful; wry; yearning; young; youthful; yeoman-built; arch; delicately-cut; frolic; lean; sleeping; slender.

verbs

animate—; blanch—; contort—; distort—; draw—; flush—; furrow—; illumine—; mop —; obscure—; pinch—; pucker up—; puff up—; read in—; scrutinize—; stamp—with; submerge—; suffuse—with; tense—; wrinkle—; —beams;— bleaches; —blooms; —brightens; —charms; —clouds; —creases; —darkens; —fascinates; —flames; — gleams; —glows; —lights up; —pales; — purples; —relaxes; —resembles; —smarts; —whitens.

(See countenance, features.)

FACE (v)

adverbs

haughtily; resolutely; squarely; undauntedly; challengingly; listlessly; courageously; indomitably; unflinchingly; immovably; accusingly; agitatedly; alluringly; animatedly; amiably; apathetically; apprehensively; arrogantly; ashenly; audaciously; bewitchingly; austerely; callously; chastenedly; cherubically; comically; composedly; cordially; cynically; despotically; determinedly; diffidently; disdainfully; disillusionedly; distractedly; dolefully; dourly; drearily; dubiously; eloquently; energetically; enigmatically; fanatically; fatuously; fawningly; guilelessly; humbly; hypocritically; idiotically; impassively; imperiously; imperturbably; impishly; implacably; imploringly; incredulously; indifferently; intrepidly; majestically; maniacally; martially; meekly; miserably; mutinously; neurotically; obtusely; ominously; passionately; passionlessly; pertly; priggishly; piquantly; piteously; potently; precipitously; prematurely; radiantly; rebelliously; raptly; recklessly; relentlessly; reticently; reverently; roguishly; ruefully; schemingly; selflessly; sensually; sentimentally; serenely; smirkingly; sneeringly; stubbornly; tenderly; tensely; tragically; treacherously; uncouthly; unintellectually; unsmilingly; unsympathetically; wistfully; woefully; wrathfully.

(See meet, confront.)

FACETIOUS

adverbs
comically; waggishly; entertainingly; inappropriately; unseasonably; happily; merrily; youthfully; smartly; unfortunately; fantastically; quick-wittedly; nimbly; clownishly; jovially; convivially; whimsically; amusingly; pleasantly; foolishly; banteringly; teasingly; drolly; fatuously; remarkably.

FACETIOUSNESS

adjectives
grave; sparkling; cheery; dull; unwitty.

FACETS

adjectives
sparkling; gleaming; well-cut.

FACIAL

adjectives
refreshing; hasty; stimulating; cleansing.

FACILE

adverbs
skilfully; dexterously; extremely; unusually; cleverly; adroitly; artfully; neatly; ingeniously; felicitously; deftly; smartly; expertly; capably; competently; intelligently; enthusiastically; eagerly; earnestly; amenably; heartily; glibly; conveniently; pliantly; smoothly.

FACILITATE (*v*)

adverbs
readily; necessarily; skillfully; automatically; unsurpassingly; commercially; mechanically; briskly; unfailingly; completely.

(See advance, hasten.)

FACILITIES

adjectives
housekeeping; intermediate; clinical; educational; characteristic; technical; limitless;

equal; extra; modern; recreational; convenient; marvelous; unmatched; complete; astonishing; culinary; superior; abundant; inadequate; merger; available; unsurpassed; banking; admirable; improved; mechanical; surprising; fatal; elaborate; telegraphic; musical; subsequent; terminal; rapid-transit; existing; sanitary; commercial.

FACILITY

verbs
abuse —; accomplish with —; afford —; break down —; compose with —; contribute to —; hinder —; impede —; increase —; learn with —; manage with —; perform with —; permit of —; prove —; provide —; utilize —; wipe out —; — accelerates; — lightens; — lubricates.

(See ease.)

FACSIMILE

adjectives
diminished; alleged.

FACT

adjectives
mere; ugly; unassorted (pl); stark; unvarnished; statistical; unpalatable; vital; ultimate; iron; serious; gratifying; timely; curious; salient; undoubted; indisputable; astonishing; surprising; marvelous; miraculous; magnificent; confounding; unheard-of; singular; extraordinary; incredible; unforeseen; rarest; private; enviable; subtle; outstanding; isolated; well-established; simple; unfortunate; significant; smallest; natural; cosmic; accomplished; psychological; grim; historic; lamentable; practical; dominant; sordid; illuminating; governing; eternal; insuppressible; inexplicable; remarkable; systematizing; ineluctable; conceded; multifarious (pl); straight-from-the-shoulder; scientific; interesting; striking; noteworthy; accepted; inexorable; cruel; prosaic; hard; sprightly; inescapable; persistent; settled; essential; contradictory; embellished; deniable; stubborn; fundamental; revolting; unanswerable; disgraceful; unrelated; concomitant; intriguing; optical; naked; undeviating; instructive; damaging; changing; fluid; amazing; full; free; cold; startling; elemental; important; demonstrated; unconventional; permanent; visible; notorious; well-ascertained; brutal; preliminary; relevant; bitter; admitted; melancholy; deplorable; embodying; memorable; bare; palpable; unquestionable; authenticated; cardi-

nal; incontrovertible; worthy; final; ultimate; absolute; graphical; quiet; special; patent; unsuspected; unguessed; reasonable; architectural; dark; mysterious; concrete; palpitating; delightful; irresistible; delicious; unimpugnable; analogous; sinful; well-known; conspicuous; clear; distinct; firm; passionless; impartial; noticed; meticulous; illuminating; scanty; inert; vivid; tremendous; previous; exact; formidable; unconnected; first; empirical; acoustical; external; perpetual; bald, encouraging; physical; plain; ascertained; convincing; horrific; central; negative; basic; tangible; indubitable; geological; suggestive; trivial; rudimentary; clenching; acquired; outward; adduced; inconvenient; major; self-evident; commonplace; verifiable; supreme; actual; positive; sheer; apparent; acknowledged; ethical; diverting; sober; unpleasant; disturbing; unpoetic; tragic; queer; fantastic; colorful; fabulous; notable; stirring; buried; laborious; discovered; overwhelming; exhaustive; multitudinous (pl); detailed; hazy; confusing; experimental; paradoxical; observed; challenging; superficial; immaterial

verbs
accept —; account for —; accumulate —s; allude to —; amplify —; apprise of —; array —s; ascertain —; ascribe — to; assail —; assemble —s; attest to —; awake to —; bear out by —; belittle —; bemoan —; blind to —; blur —; bring — to light; bring home —; certify —; cite —; collate —; color —; confirm —; conform to —; confront with —; construe —; cram with —s; credit —; debate —; deduce —; demonstrate —; deny —; deplore —; digest —; disclose —; disentangle —s; disguise —; distort —; divulge —; dodge —; embrace —; emphasize —; establish —; evidence by —; exhaust —s; exploit —; expound —; face —; found on —; garble —s; generalize —s; glean —s; grant —; grapple with —; grasp —; harp on —; ignore —; impress with —; interpret —; juggle —s; master —; misconstrue —; misrepresent —; mull over —s; obscure —; oppose —; outweigh —; overlook —; override —; ponder —; question —; recapitulate —s; reconcile —s; refute —; regale with —s; rehash —s; represent as —; rest upon —; run counter to —; sift —s; stress —; stud with —s substantiate —; suppress —; trace — to; transform —s; unearth —; verify —; weigh —; wrestle with —; —s co-

here; — dawns; — depresses; — disquiets; — illustrates; — looms; — sinks in; —startles; — supports; — verifies.
(See truth, act, incident, statement.)

FACTION
verbs
attach to —; avoid —; combine —s; criticize —; defend —; disturb —; divide into —s; extinguish —; join —; maintain —; rend into —s; run into —s; sort into —s; split in —s; spread —; support —; suppress —; unite —s; — abandons; — declines; — dictates; — disperses; — springs from.
(See party, opposition.)

FACTIONS
adjectives
fluctuating; petty; discordant; embittered; wretched; defeated; turbulent; atrocious; execrable; fierce; mischievous; warring; hostile; rival; musical; exasperated; oligarchical; various; aristocratic; contending; internal; respective; opposing; imprisoned; reconciling.

FACTOR
adjectives
selective; dietary; prominent; etiological; potent; growth; various (pl); significant; vital; psychological; unfortunate; inestimable; additional; causative; determining; indispensable; compensating; prime; intellectual; dependable; encouraging; underlying; distinct; astounding; contributory; fundamental; outside; limiting; legendary; inherited; unquestioned; environmental; important; practical; dominant; industrial; external; material; essential; responsible; decisive; narcissistic; ecclesiastical; obvious; negligible; despised; dangerous; racial; geographical; constitutional; constant; motivating; all-pervasive; avoidable; incalculable.

verbs
belittle —; consider —; coordinate —s; embrace —; establish —; influence by —; limit —s; ponder —; reckon —; reveal —; unravel —; weigh —; —s converge; — determines; — emerges; —looms; —s militate against; — predisposes; — dominates.
(See element, constituent, influence, cause.)

FACTORY
adjectives
besieged; enormous; noisy; irrepressible.

verbs
boycott —; conduct —; control —; convert —; destroy —; dispose of —; equip —; erect —; establish —; examine —; improve —; inspect —; maintain —; man —; manage —; observe —; picket —; promote from —; strip —; supervise —; — employs; — idles; — produces; — specializes in.

(See plant, mill, shop, building.)

FACULTY
adjectives
contemplative; divine; unworn; ruling; bounded; healthful; bigoted; domestic; artful; visualizing; ready; rational; corporeal; biased; imaginative; perceptive; distinct; trained; reasoning; intellectual; remarkable; scientific; benumbed; integral; honorable; unimpaired; sterner; reciprocal; courageous; practised; departmentalized; balancing; glorious; winged; natural; rare; unique; primary; worldly; efficient; sublimest; wondrous; higher; dormant; aesthetic; elaborative; human; visual; imitative; cardinal; potential; awakened; penetrating; governing; administrative; spiritual; critical; cogitative; analytical; abnormal; treacherous; moral; finite; antipodal; comparative; common; creative; inventive; uncanny; obstinate; acute.

verbs
arouse —; assist —; collect —s; concentrate —ies; cultivate —ies; dazzle —; develop —ies; dull —ies; endow with —; exercise —; exhibit —; hamper —; impair —; manifest —; rally —ies; reclaim —; recruit —ies; retain —; strain —; strengthen —; stupefy —; waste—ies; — decays; — enables.

(See power, capacity, ability, skill, talent.)

FAD
adjectives
commendable; expensive; dietary; crazy; innocent; passing.

verbs
addict to —; adopt —; advocate —; annihilate —; attribute — to; conceive —; condemn —; criticize —; cultivate —; deter —; dispose to —; frown on —; gibe at —; indulge in —; nourish —; produce —; pursue —; ridicule —; start —; warn against —; — exaggerates; — passes; — seizes; — spreads; — sprouts.

(See fancy, fashion, hobby, whim.)

FADE (v)
adverbs
partially; gracefully; strangely; autumnally; hauntingly; dismally; inevitably; corporeally; depressingly; tragically; lingeringly.

(See droop, decay.)

FAGGED
adverbs (fagged-out)
utterly; inexpressibly; dangerously; alarmingly; haggardly; gauntly; hopelessly; irrecoverably; lamentably; pitiably; wretchedly; miserably.

FAGGOT
adjectives
wintry; blazing; ashy; glazing.

FAIL (v)
adverbs
miserably; tragically; unquestionably; ridiculously; deplorably; essentially; deservedly; constantly; conspicuously; unwittingly; signally; lamentably; ignominiously; eventually; despicably; grievously; partially; scholastically; abjectly; habitually; inexplicably; indefensibly.

(See decline, deteriorate.)

FAILING
verbs
aggravate —; alter —; anticipate —; apprehend —; breed —; brood over —; compensate for —; deserve —; detect —; discover —; establish —; excuse —; exploit —; forgive —; incur —; mention —; pardon —; produce —; promote —; supply —; — enfeebles; — overtakes.

(See fault, foible, shortcoming, failure, deficiency, infirmity, defect.)

adverbs
indubitably; visibly; hopelessly; shockingly; feebly; weakly; languidly; decrepitly; desolately; shakily; perceptibly; manifestly; patently; conspicuously; noticeably; rapidly; inevitably; finally; slowly; obviously; avowedly; brokenly; wretchedly; pitifully; undoubtedly; languishingly; hopelessly; fatally; incurably; infirmly; strangely.

FAILINGS
adjectives
radical; common; inherited; proudest.

adjectives
impending; eventual; despicable; grievous; pathetic; distressed; architectural; expensive; wasteful; baking; partial; corresponding; miserable; irritating; repeated; dismal; celebrated; melancholy; appalling; foredoomed; regretted; vacillatory; consecutive (pl); preliminary; scholastic; abject; pitiable; sensible; ignominious; hideous; frantic; predestined; lamentable; mental; conspicuous; habitual; heroic; inexplicable; unhappy; indefensible; depressing; sudden; gigantic; pioneering.

verbs
ameliorate —; avert —; brood over —; court —; face —; foredoom to —; foretell —; grapple with —; indemnify against —; insure against —; offset —; overcome —; precipitate —; predict —; punish —; view as —; — disheartens; — dismays; — impends; — invalidates; — looms.
(See bankruptcy, neglect, short-coming, failing.)

FAINT
verbs
anticipate —; avert —; fall into a —; feign —; fight off —; produce —; recover from —; revive from —; rouse from —; simulate —; sink in —; stay —; treat for —; — confuses; — depresses; — enfeebles; — ensues; — weakens.
(See fit, paroxysm, convulsion.)

adverbs
woefully; terribly; incredibly; illegibly; powerlessly; visibly; noticeably; conspicuously; obviously; wretchedly; helplessly; dangerously; alarmingly; dreadfully; mysteriously; strangely; oddly; curiously; wearily; breathlessly; drowsily.

FAINT (v)
adverbs
ostensibly; charmingly; abruptly; unexpectedly; calculatingly; intermittently; designingly.
(See despond, fade.)

FAINTNESS
adjectives
present; humiliating.

adjectives
fashionable; cruel; slumbering.

adverbs
invariably; honestly; beautifully; equitably; always; indubitably; incontestably; legally; scrupulously; meticulously; carefully; dutifully; cautiously; discreetly; reasonably; surprisingly; astutely; logically; sensibly; expediently; providently; admirably; pleasantly; grudgingly; primarily; tolerably; exceptionally; satisfactorily; remarkably; generously; strictly; rigidly; impartially.

FAIR-GROUNDS
adjectives
populous; spacious; frequented.

FAIRNESS
adjectives
supposed; scrupulous; pretended.

verbs
assail —; bestow with —; dispute —; doubt —; exhibit —; judge —; necessitate —; repay —; reward —; seek —; violate —; yield to —; — pleases.
(See justice, impartiality, honesty.)

FAIRY
adjectives
adventurous; pitiless; rough; omnipotent; venturous; good; fiendish.

verbs
transform into —; —ies array; — assumes; — charms; — circles; — dances; — darts; — enchants; — flits; — frisks; — frolics; — gambols; — hies away; — inhabits; — leaps; — meddles; —revels; — scampers; — sings; — tricks; — trips; — warbles.
(See angel, spirit.)

FAIRYLAND
adjectives
vague; misty.

FAITH
adjectives
abiding; indestructible; consolatory; sublime; gladder; scrupulous; passionate; mutual; ripening; childlike; obliterated; obliged; nobler; inflexible; implicit; efficient; pure-eyed; grim; unbounded; whimsical; plighted; sturdy; radiant; joyful; religious; rising; unbroken; rational; potential; blind;

unquestioning; manly; lesser; unfeigned; humble; trusting; unfailing; utter; undying; secure; absolute; conflicting (pl); fervid; melancholy; sincere; optimistic; earnest; all-absorbing; heartier; devouring; habitual; immaculate; lofty; unwavering; sacramental; supreme; dumb; helpless; good; willing; generous; unalterable; unshaken; true; fugitive; orthodox; public; exulting; purblind; quickened; implied; heart-enrooted; inviolate; stalwart; tardy; obedient; blighting; impious; feeble; down-sunken; deathless; customary; active; shattered; sinless; material; profound; infirm; honorable; transcendent; barren; simple; steadfast; plural (pl).

verbs
apostatize from —; break — with; cling to —; confirm —; dampen —; endure with —; exhibit —; found upon —; forsake —; fortify —; inculcate —; inspire —; invalidate —; justify —; maintain —; manifest —; mould —; persecute for —; pervert —; pin — in; preach —; proclaim —; profess —; purge —; reawaken —; reiterate —; retain —; rivet — in; shake —; share —; sway by —; voice —; — melts away; — perishes; — quickens; — stands; — survives; — wavers.
(See assurance, belief, conviction, confidence, trust.)

FAITHFUL
adverbs
affectionately; loyally; duly; honorably; scrupulously; rigidly; deeply; grimly; resolutely; sturdily; undeviatingly; joyously; blindly; humbly; utterly; absolutely; optimistically; earnestly; heartily; unwaveringly; unalterably; inviolately; steadfastly; actively; flatteringly; abjectly; punctiliously; meticulously; actively; simply; unaffectedly; candidly; openly; incorruptibly; uncommonly.

FAITHFULNESS
adjectives
utter; assertive.

verbs
believe in —; build —; cherish —; create —; demand —; display —; encourage —; justify —; necessitate —; overshadow —; praise —; prove —; rely on —; require —;

reward —; suspect —; try —; — falls; — shines; — supports; — trusts.
(See loyalty, fidelity, constancy, allegiance, devotion.)

FAITHLESS
adverbs
shamelessly; terribly; abominably; timorously; basely; faint-heartedly; brazenly; coolly; openly; obdurately; detestably; execrably; audaciously; perversely; hypocritically; evasively; artfully; perfidiously; cunningly; insidiously; surreptitiously; dreadfully; unbelievably; unexpectedly; direly; disastrously; shamefully.

FAKE
verbs
conceive—; contrive—; denounce—; detect —; divine—; expose—; father—; inspire—; invent—; palm off—; perform—; plan—; plunder with—; practice—; regard as—; reveal—; shape—; taboo—; uncover—; work—; —deceives; —entrances; —fascinates; —fools; —perturbs.
(See swindle, sham, deceit.)

FALL
adjectives
tremendous; jade-green; weary; graceful; repeated (pl); preceding; virtuous; sloping; gleaming; deadliest; intertangled; bubbly; clattering; answering; melodious; dying; instantaneous; uncropt; thundering.

verbs
(See autumn.)

FALL (v)
adverbs
ultimately; noiselessly; subsequently; perpendicularly; insensibly; involuntarily; supinely; disdainfully; melodiously; resistlessly; unceasingly; inertly; precisely; incoherently; unwittingly; leisurely; dreamily; violently; intermittently; disconcertingly; fitfully; ponderously; thunderingly.
(See drop, descend.)

FALLACIOUS
adverbs
deeply; grossly; utterly; obviously; sorrily; patently; manifestly; wretchedly; clumsily; grotesquely; fantastically; absurdly; oddly; scientifically; deliberately; speciously;

egregiously; horribly; laughably; flimsily; nonsensically; evasively; blunderingly; deceptively; intentionally; perversely; shamefully.

FALLACY

adjectives
glittering; discarded; deepest; gross; sophistical; pathetic; discovered.

verbs
accept—; admit—; challenge—; correct—; demonstrate—; denounce—; discover—; disperse—ies; disprove—; explode—; rationalize—; reveal—; ridicule—.
(See delusion, error, deception, misconception.)

FALLIBILITY

adjectives
extreme; obvious; apparent.

FALLIBLE

adverbs
precariously; embarrassingly; obscurely; timidly; indecisively; vaguely; occasionally; foolishly; weakly; inconclusively; deceptively; speciously; carelessly; casually; remarkably; frequently; bewilderingly; blithely; thoughtlessly; inconsequentially; impulsively; untenably.

FALLING

adjectives
unconscious; swift; desperate.

FALLOW

adverbs
aridly; unfruitfully; unprofitably; naturally; carelessly; shiftlessly; passively; inactively; unproductively; purposely; improvidently; rudimentally; roughly; calmly; tentatively; temporarily; deliberately; advisedly; provisionally; wisely.

FALSE

adverbs
subtly; stiffly; crudely; inelegantly; crassly; grotesquely; laughably; ridiculously; awkwardly; outlandishly; stagily; cleverly; ingeniously; obviously.

FALSEHOOD

adjectives
practised; flattering; incredible; base; clumsy; downright; palpable; grotesque; blushing; deliberate; infamous; pardonable; ingenious; cheerful; illusive; hidden; hypocritical; conventional; fawning; tortured; twisted.

verbs
accept—; admit—; avoid—; challenge—; confess—; demonstrate—; denounce—; disprove—; explode—; refrain from—; utter —; —dishonors; —pervades; —reeks; —sours; —taints.
(See lie, counterfeit, mistake, error.)

FALSENESS

adjectives
glittering.

FALSETTO

adjectives
tender; querulous; mincing; anxious; senile.

FALSIFIER

adjectives
wretched; conscienceless; insidious; adept.

FALSIFY (v)

adverbs
mystifyingly; abundantly; basely; prodigiously; incredibly; clumsily; palpably; grotesquely; deliberately; infamously; ingeniously; hypocritically; fawningly.
(See misrepresent, distort.)

FALTER (v)

adverbs
technically; abruptly; quaveringly; meekly; habitually; agedly; feebly; unattractively; repeatedly; recurrently; absurdly; ridiculously.
(See tremble, hesitate, waver.)

FAME

adjectives
fabulous; dying; boundless; imperishable; philosophic; volatile; hallowed; bastard; genuine; partial; lawful; glorious; prophetic; academic; inferior; abstract; soaring; shouting; patrimonial; monumental; artistic; tremendous; spotless; matchless; immense; unqualified; illustrious; extensive; prodigious; horrible; imaginary; eternal; posthumous; spurious; stainless; spreading; vague; inordinate; legal; faultless; immortal; nascent; worthy; untainted; sinister; international; equal; envious; additional; dead; serial; unpolluted; lifelong; enduring; deadly-purchased; dingy; long.

verbs
achieve—; acquire—; amass—; covet—; dazzle with—; destine to—; establish—; exalt to—; recapture—; renounce—; secure —; snatch at—; vault to—; —expands; — glows; —reaches; —rests on; —waxes.

(See renown, reputation, eminence, glory, notoriety.)

FAMILIAR
adverbs
thoroughly; intimately; wholly; cordially; affably; unceremoniously; informally; heartily; conversantly; entirely; highly; accessibly; courteously; perfectly; completely; habitually; wontedly; long; companionably; chattily; sociably; suavely; blandly; graciously; tactfully; genially; openly; publicly; avowedly; remarkably; undoubtedly; somewhat.

FAMILIARITY
adjectives
growing; sentimental; impertinent; legitimate; insolent; becoming; affectionate; misdirected; easy; sheer; hourly; dear; curious; intimate; democratic; personal; sweet; profane.

FAMILY
adjectives
sorrowing; aristocratic; human; peaceable; imperial; citrus; helpless; defenseless; hereditary; unnurtured; well-governed; ancient; illustrious; immediate; distinguished; ever-growing; affluent; respectable; numerous; aristocratic; discriminating; exaggerating; impecunious; influential; wellordered; harmonious; attractive; pious; august; aghast; impoverished; meritorious; indigent; regal; talented; jarring; proud; national; wrangling; mignonette; well-regulated; homeless; powerful; intimate; decayed; short-lived; close-mouthed; stiffnecked; divided; frugal; brawny; destitute; increasing; lively; handsome; chivalrous; patrician.

verbs
contribute to—; dominate—; evict—; head —; hold—together; inspire—; join—; maintain—; respect—; reunite—; rule—; stir—; warp—; —flourishes; —overflows; —quarrels; —unites; —wrangles.

(See clan, tribe.)

FAMINE
adjectives
impending; desperate; **pining; consuming;** fearful; feverish.

verbs
bring—; die in—; **expose to—; incur—;** keep—at bay; lament—; perish in—; recover from—; suffer—; threaten with—; —attacks; —besieges; —blights; —clings; —devastates; —distresses; —ensues; —frustrates, —punishes; —prevails; —ravages; —reduces; —subdues.

(See destitution.)

FAMISHED
adverbs
incredibly; dreadfully; shamefully; abominably; unbelievably; utterly; starvingly; actually; haggardly; gauntly; horribly; shockingly; startlingly; heartbreakingly; emaciatedly; hungrily; insatiably; breathlessly; pitiably; awfully; murderously; terribly.

FAMOUS
adverbs
illustriously; brilliantly; notoriously; terribly; internationally; prodigiously; tremendously; distinctly; gloriously; honorably; deservedly; ingloriously; ignobly; horribly; imperishably; splendidly; politically; proudly; nobly; undeniably; remarkably; reputably; signally; amazingly.

"FAN"
(devotee)
verbs
breed—s; collect—s; produce—s; supply—s; —acclaims; —applauds; —attends; — cheers; —s congregate; —s flock to; —indulges in; —is addicted to; —praises; — pursues; —s rally; —responds; —"roots" for; —s turn out.

(See fanatic, devotee.)

FAN
(implement)
adjectives
cooling; breezy; whirling; flirting; feather; winnowing.

verbs
employ—; install—; regulate—; —agitates; —airs; —blasts; —blows; —buzzes; — cools; —churns; —creates a draft; —drives; —eases; —refreshes; —relieves; —revol-

ves; —rotates; —supplies; —urges; —ventilates; —whizzes.
(See propeller.)

FAN (v)

adverbs
coolingly; breezily; whirlingly; refreshingly; pleasingly; irritatingly; maddeningly; furiously; feverishly.
(See cool, ventilate, rouse.)

FANATIC

adjectives
revolutionary; religious; unflinching; murderous; vegetarian; sour; crazed; recognized; unbalanced; miserable; vicious; passionate.

verbs
combat—; control—; enlist—; inflame—; intoxicate—; oppose—; ridicule—; scorn—; transform into—; —accomplishes; —s band; —charms; —explodes; —fevers; —imagines; —infects; —inveighs against; —kindles; —prates; —prattles; —rants; —stirs; —undermines; —uproots.

FANATICAL

adverbs
intolerantly; illiberally; narrowly; provincially; wildly; madly; insanely; terribly; unfortunately; fantastically; outrageously; outlandishly; unreasonably; stupidly; crazily; ribaldly; eccentrically; sharply; deeply; earnestly; fervently; fervidly; zealously; feverishly; hysterically; ungovernably; excitably; deliriously; moodily; dangerously; dreadfully.

FANATICISM

adjectives
ignorant; remorseless; arrogant; insupportable; growing; unbridled; harsh; contemptible; lamented; religious.

verbs
control—; delude by—; display—; evince—; express—; fire with—; heat with—; incline to—; incur—; inflame with—; manifest—; overwhelm by—; persecute for—; plant the seed of—; tolerate—; —disqualifies; —drains; —exaggerates; —ferments; —governs; —impresses; —inhibits; —intoxicates; —overdoes; —prejudices; —prohibits; —rends; —stimulates; —sunders; —terrifies.
(See intolerance, superstition.)

FANCIER

adjectives
sensitive, professional.

FANCIFUL

adverbs
gloriously; illusively; abstractly; fantastically; notionally; delusively; chimerically; phantasmagorically; romantically; fugitively; whimsically; momentarily; imperishably; extravagantly; deceptively; insubstantially; fabulously; inventively; voluptuously; comfortingly; ecstatically; ardently; playfully; wildly; grotesquely; absurdly; ludicrously; laughably; ridiculously; beautifully.

FANCY

adjectives
passing; distorted; subjective; sportive; delicate; religious; bubbling; enthusiastic; deluding; school-girl; ingenious; boundless; superstitious; starry; virgin; quainter; tenderer; changeful; fond; disturbed; poetical; stray; youthful; difficult; ungrateful; irritable; popular; flesh-imprisoned; wild; prodigal; subtle; shadowy; groundless; ridiculous; childish; morbid; curious; vagrant; wayward; thick-coming (pl); fluttering; riotous; trustworthy; fermenting; exquisite; languid; incipient; airiest; feeble; preposterous; lingering; sudden; busy; extravagant; fickle; romantic; correlated; luxuriant; restless; quaint; hopeless; hypochondriacal; cruel; angry; later; odd; gushing; fecund; timorous; sweet; strange; voluptuous; gentle; mystical; insistent; long-faded; quick-springing; torpid; ardent; credulous; rambling; captious; wheeling; playful; giddy; unfirm; crude; disordered; unreciprocated; fastidious; irregular; excited; distempered; ever-veering; pardonable; unearthly; waking; fragrant; flying; footless; viewless; fugitive; worthless; delicious; violent; gloomy; wild-looking; mere; weak-hinged; scheming; frivolous; hideous; thoughtful; unsettled; whimsical; diseased; quavering; extraordinary; idolatrous.

verbs
breed—; build with—; catch—; chime with —; cure of—; crystallize—; dally with in —ies; draw upon—; excite—; fit—; free from—; indulge in—; lead by—; press upon —; reject—; restrain—; —conceives; —

flees; —flickers; —ies gather; —pursues; —
—reigns; —roams; —rushes; —travels; —
—wakes; —wanders.

(See fantasy, conceit, whim, caprice.)

FANCY (v)

adverbs

chimerically; erroneously; subjectively; enthusiastically; boundlessly; superstitiously;
tenderly; poetically; ridiculously; childishly;
morbidly; waywardly; romantically; voluptuously; frivolously; whimsically; idolatrously.

See imagine, dream.)

FANDANGO

adjectives

shuffling; mad; whirling; wild.

FANFARE

adjectives

dying; sounding; glorious; wild; raucous.

FANGS

adjectives

sharpened; bloody; poisoned; harpy; particular; mimic; dripping; unseen; enormous; knotted; viewless.

verbs

bury—in; display—; escape—; expose—;
imbed—; insert—; shed—; strike with—; —
drive at; —fold back; —gnaw; —pass into;
—penetrate; —perforate; —pierce; —poison; —puncture; —spike.

(See claw, talon, nail.)

FANTASTIC

adverbs

illusively; deliciously; wildly; queerly; sadly; vainly; strangely; oddly; curiously;
mysteriously; romantically; whimsically;
extravagantly; fabulously; divertingly;
playfully; grotesquely; absurdly; ludicrously; laughably; horribly; ridiculously; unreasonably; irrationally.

FANTASY

adjectives

satirical; utopian; errant; delirious; babbling; wild; causeless; bewildering; vivid;
sinful; incestuous; conjectural; winged;
shadowy; scant; hideous; blasphemous;
guiltless; sinuous; shaping; aboriginal;
gracious; hateful; cherished; ingenious;
cosmic; unconscious.

verbs

delight in—; devise—; express in—; frame
in—; flutter in—; imagine in—; live in—;
project—; retreat into—; scatter—; soar in
—; stray in—; travel in—; view—; wander
in—; —attracts; —beckons; —gallops; —
hovers; —melts away; —roams; indulge
in—.

(See image, illusion, fancy, dream, phantasy, caprice.)

FAR

adverbs

incredibly; fabulously; outlandishly; outrageously; remotely; inaccessibly; impossibly;
immeasurably; fantastically; wearily; extremely; surprisingly; dangerously; disturbingly; discouragingly; heartbreakingly;
terribly; lamentably; pitifully; incalculably.

FARCE

adjectives

coarse; physical; ghastly; gayest; moral;
boisterous; solemn; gigantic; social; bawdy;
glorious; brisk.

FARCICAL

adverbs

comically; laughably; ridiculously; ludicrously; fantastically; outlandishly; noisily;
boisterously; uproariously; racily; ribaldly;
coarsely; satirically; genially; socially;
brilliantly; crudely; gayly; solemnly; gloriously; hilariously; spectacularly; luminously; nonsensically; extravagantly; preposterously; senselessly; ironically; cleverly;
waggishly; facetiously; merrily; jocosely;
whimsically; drolly; bombastically; irresistibly; tremendously.

FARE

adjectives

monotonous; dainty; palatable; delicious;
sumptuous; heavenly; primitive; meager;
frugal; unwholesome; humble; ambrosial;
acceptable; penitential; bounteous; monastic; substantial.

FARE
(passage money)

verbs

calculate—; call for—; demand—; deposit
—; extend—; forfeit—; furnish—; mislay
—; necessitate—; produce—; reduce—;
reject—; remit—; request—; require—; supply—; take up—.

(See money, amount, price.)

FARE (v)

adverbs

sumptuously; disastrously; monotonously; deliciously; primitively; penitently; bounteously; substantially; monastically.

(See live, suffer.)

FAREWELL

adjectives

stern; ceremonious; affectionate; cheerful; fervent; edifying; wifely; remaining; inimitable; sublime; reluctant; mock; secret; fantastical; dilated; hasty; tender; thundering; summary; courteous; sobbing; heart-breathed; horrible; silent; mute; long; touching; mechanical.

verbs

anticipate—; bid—; bless at—; deter—; express—; mourn—; pour out—; prolong—; regret—; remember—; shorten—; take—; wave—, weep—; —depresses, —distresses, —ensues; —pains; —saddens; —terminates.

FAR-FETCHED

adverbs

laboriously; ridiculously; ineptly; irrelevantly; absurdly; ludicrously; unfortunately; clumsily; outlandishly; discordantly; inappropriately; pointlessly; senselessly; foolishly; studiously; sedulously; speciously; vapidly; inanely; stupidly; doltishly; remarkably; vacuously; childishly.

FARM

adjectives

stud; hospitable; deserted; scattered; exhausted; allodial; collective; extensive; productive; diversified; isolated; fruitful; well-cultivated.

verbs

abandon—; cultivate—; dwell on—; equip —; establish—; forsake—; grow on—; inhabit—; labor on—; leave—; maintain—; overrun—; raise on—; settle on—; till—; transform—; vacation on—; —deteriorates; —employs; —furnishes; —nestles; —produces; —provides; —supplies.

(See land, tract, district.)

FARMER

adjectives

incautious; florid; peasant-like; hard-handed; embattled; prosperous; stricken; indifferent; sheep; border-line; enlightened; sinewy; gentleman; close-fisted; liberal-hearted; disingenuous; venturesome; stout; industrious; plodding.

verbs

grubstake—; subsidize—; tax—; —cultivates; —fertilizes; —flourishes; —furrows; —garners; —gathers; —harvests; —hoes; —labors; —markets; —ploughs; —prunes; —reaps; —slaves; —sows; —spades; —thrives; —tills; —plucks.

(See countryman, peasant.)

FARM-HOUSE

adjectives

pleasant; smiling; comfortable-looking; stout.

verbs

abandon—; care for—; conceal—; describe —; dwell in—; erect—; gather in—; locate —; long for—; renovate—; restore—; search for—; surround—; threaten—; welcome—; yearn for—; —deteriorates; —nestles; —stands; retire to—.

(See dwelling, building, house.)

FARMING

adjectives

speculative; diversified; intensive; fertile; scientific.

FASCINATE (v)

adverbs

bewitchingly; enchantingly; inexplicably; infinitely; absurdly; irresistibly; singularly; carnally; voluptuously; dangerously.

(See charm, enchant.)

FASCINATED

adverbs

inexpressibly; inordinately; incomprehensibly; radiantly; innocently; incredibly; marvellously; artlessly; unconsciously; utterly; thoroughly; completely.

FASCINATING

adverbs

adorably; attractively; bewitchingly; charmingly; inexpressibly; dazzlingly; radiantly; innocently; designedly; intentionally; cleverly; incredibly; undeniably; marvellously; inordinately; dangerously; winningly; artlessly; unconsciously; utterly; highly; thoroughly; teasingly; smartly; consciously; craftily; seductively; completely.

FASCINATION

adjectives

painful; potent; enchanting; dread; charming; horrible; occult; absorbing; inexplicable; perilous; acute; infinite; tremulous; inexhaustible; ominous; youthful; absurd; irresistible; singular; divine; wild; carnal; indefinable; wonderful; dangerous; shuddery; personal.

verbs

apply—; cast—; employ—; lie under—; overcome—; prevent—; resist—; succumb to—; surrender to—; sweep on by—; tantalize with—; withstand—; yield to—; —attracts; —binds; —compels; —draws; —freezes; —haunts; —impels; —masters; —overpowers; —perils; —prevails.

(See enchantment, charm, influence, attraction.)

FASCISM

adjectives

distinct; aggressive; insidious; power-drunk; efficient; masterful; stultifying.

verbs

admit to—; establish—; infect with—; inspire—; join—; oppose—; smack of—; succumb to—; support—; yield to—; —advocates; —aims at; —attacks; —campaigns; —controls; —crushes; —deprives; —embodies; —enforces; —girds its loins; —organizes; —ousts; —prohibits; —regulates; —revolts; —riots; —violates; —welds.

(See movement.)

FASHION

adjectives

convincing; casual; improving; scimitar; belated; futile; paternal; masterly; promising; authentic; sumptuous; peculiar; sinister; bourgeois; summery; changing; refreshing; military; charming; comical; vigorous; cold-blooded; casual; coat; outstanding; debonair; dress; sensational; gay; important; hurried; righteous; tawdry; wicked; pernicious; bygone; graceful; latest; effeminate; aesthetic; school-boy; regal; exclusive; foolish; beastly; fickle; mythical; tragic; fine; quaint; excellent; picturesque; debased; florid; symbolic; polluted; seemly; obedient; faultless; orderly; jovial; delicate; hearty; squalid; metropolitan; expensive; liberal; excited; impulsive; infantine; unstudied; unostentatious; accepted; surly; taciturn; shifting; smart; early; appealing; distinctive; formless; hellish; malignant; piquant; self-respecting; desultory; unbecoming; perfect; coordinating; candid; straightforward; corduroy; fantastic; rare; oriental; prevailing; serious; high-and-mighty; outlandish; simple; superficial; identical; classic; perpendicular; intrusive; orthodox; rude; bungling; haphazard; obvious; offensive; primitive; phlegmatic; soldierly; dramatic; feminine; fanciful; diverting; characteristic; feeble; brilliant; stimulating; fastidious; clownish; enervating; window-shutter; democratic; brutal; halting; obsolete; fugitive; literary; noble; obstinate; materialistic; unceremonious; ornate; reckless; romantic; humblest; patriarchal; gossipy; chatty; forced; upstart; plain; childish; united; inconvenient; awkward; listless; vague; antique; bovine; lavish; merciless; beneficent; contradictory; womanly.

verbs

accommodate—; anticipate—; appraise by —; attune to—; balk at—; create—; decree —; follow—; influence—; purvey—; rule—; set—; style—; —derives from; —dies out; —endures; —fades; —flickers out; —prevails; —roots in.

(See mode, method, usage, style.)

FASHION (*v*)

adverbs

primitively; crudely; superbly; flawlessly; deftly; tenderly; meticulously; delicately; comically; sensationally; gaily; perniciously; aesthetically; quaintly; picturesquely; symbolically; unostentatiously; fantastically; rudely; haphazardly; offensively; dramatically; characteristically; fastidiously; democratically; ornately; awkwardly.

(See style, make.)

FASHIONABLE

adverbs

completely; occasionally; enthusiastically; seriously; carefully; entirely; thoroughly; uncommonly; extraordinarily; habitually; conventionally; decorously; highly; modishly; socially; conformably; stylishly; jauntily; conspicuously; resolutely; determinedly; exquisitely; foppishly; flirtatiously; pretentiously; famously; notoriously; splendidly; reputably; eminently; imposingly; impressively; inveterately.

478

FAST

adverbs
incredibly; expeditiously; smartly; actively; mercurially; nimbly; remarkably; amazingly; marvellously; miraculously; unaccountably; intolerably; breathlessly; dangerously; alarmingly; hazardously; bewilderingly; terrifically; insanely; inordinately; immoderately; immeasurably; incalculably.

FAST (v)

adverbs
stubbornly; continually; frequently; tediously; determinedly; fatally; fanatically; rigorously; monastically; severely.
(See starve, abstain.)

FASTEN (v)

adverbs
securely; attractively; firmly; gaily; fastidiously; competently; snugly; closely; permanently; temporarily.
(See fix, secure.)

FASTIDIOUS

adverbs
inordinately; extravagantly; daintily; precisely; primly; exquisitely; neatly; habitually; punctiliously; rigidly; strictly; rigorously; arbitrarily; admirably; marvellously; meticulously; priggishly; delicately; captiously; censoriously; scrupulously.

FASTIDIOUSNESS

adjectives
aristocratic; complete; extreme; studied.

FASTNESS

adjectives
forest; wild; remote; unillumined; mountain; inaccessible; rugged; desolate; solitary.

FASTS

adjectives
frequent; bitter; tedious; hunger-strike.

FAT

adjectives
twofold; juicy; rancid; waxy; resinous; insoluble; additional; indigestible.

verbs
accrue—; accumulate—; acquire—; compose of—; devour—; digest—; emulsify—; fight against—; grow—; guard against—; live on—of; overcharge with—; prevent—; produce—; provide—; provoke—; put on —; reduce—; ridicule—; store up—; supply —; —blossoms; —forms; —nourishes; —sizzles.
(See flesh.)

adverbs
inexpressibly; unhappily; incredibly; incurably; laughably; lamentably; comfortably; contentedly; distressingly; absurdly; ridiculously; ludicrously; sadly; joyously; dangerously; heavily; gracefully; admittedly; funnily; unreasonably; incorrigibly; complacently; complainingly; mournfully; dramatically; pathetically; gracelessly; shapelessly; waddlingly.

FATAL

adverbs
unhappily; unfortunately; lamentably; deplorably; grievously; inevitably; presumably; usually; heartbreakingly; obscurely; darkly; strangely; oddly; curiously; mysteriously; unaccountably; irresistibly; inexorably; violently; mercifully; inescapably.

FATALISM

adjectives
vulgar; stubborn; reckless; hysterical; inevitable.

FATALISTIC

adverbs
inveterately; unshakably; implicitly; soberly; staunchly; confidently; incorrigibly; positively; gloomily; delusively; dispassionately; stubbornly; fantastically; calmly; unreasonably; irrationally; unfathomably; vaguely; actually; absurdly; destructively; insanely; credulously; securely; doctrinally.

FATALITY

adjectives
irresistible; all-powerful; inexorable; stark; strange; ironical.

FATE

adjectives
indulgent; tempted; solemn; inexorable; ultimate; special; pure; untoward; unchallenged; relentless; kindly; subsequent; uncommon; cruel; bitter; ignominious; blind; baffling; cramping; tragic; hostile; fixed; adverse; obedient; precious; unenviable; inevitable; awful; varied (pl); incumbent; obdurate; dismal; probable; narrower; tear-compelling; fairest; obliging; uncer-

tain; evil; chequered; vanquished; whimsical; dedicated; happy; pursuing; favoring; deplorable; melancholy; endangered; ungentle; oracular; fabled; vulgar; worldly; harsh; indifferent; ruthless; unconscious; impending; proper; insensate; hapless; thwarting; sundering; monarchial; horrible; undoubted; ample; leafless; ungracious.

verbs
accept—; challenge—; cloud—; confront by —; dodge—; fulfill—; hinge on—; impose by—; mould—; outwit—; preside over—; prophesy—; resign to—; scoff at—; seal—; share—; work out—; —crushes; —deals; — destines; —engulfs; —fashions; —hangs; — moulds; —orders; —pushes; —singles out; —tortures.
(See destiny, necessity, doom, death.)

FATED
adverbs
blindly; adversely; inexorably; inevitably; imperiously; relentlessly; inauspiciously; ominously; portentously; luckily; auspiciously; resistlessly; direly; blessedly; obscurely; propitiously; unluckily; unpropitiously.

FATHER
adjectives
doting; implacable; prosaic; crusading; reverend; illustrious; active; improvident; bustling; electioneering; mitered; groveling; virtuous; joyful; ill-tempered; fond; dreadful; peevish; noble; ghostly; banished; honored; earthly; obdurate; hilarious; strenuous; formidable; vain; hollow; heartless; persecuted; imperial; uncowled; stricken; avaricious; spendthrift; unsuspecting; benignant; narrow-praying; blustering; indulgent; worthy; irate; grimy; jaunty; tender; scholarly; venerable; adoptive; remorseful; impecunious; avaricious; dissolute; judicious; temporal; deceiving; autocratic.

verbs
adopt —; adore —; ape —; idolize —; obtain —; owe to —; respect —; revere —; — advises; — aids; — allows; — assents; — corrects; — declares; — guards; — guides; — maintains; — moulds; — neglects; — nourishes; — pampers; — permits; — pets; — presents; — prevents; — pro-tects; — punishes; — restrains; — scolds; — spoils; — supports; — thrashes.
(See parent, ancestor, author, mother.)

FATHERLAND
adjectives
icebound; heavenly; pleasant; memorable.

FATHERLESS
adverbs
unhappily; forlornly; unluckily; unfortunately; helplessly; drearily; desolately; miserably; wretchedly; pitiably; disconsolately; haplessly; deplorably; cheerlessly; dismally; obviously.

FATHERLY
adverbs
dutifully; indulgently; severely; gently; unnecessarily; quietly; wisely; proudly; providently; lovingly; generously; warmly; humanely; benevolently; sympathetically; comfortingly; amiably; lovingly; graciously; complaisantly; bounteously; benignly; mercifully; magnanimously; tenderly; warmly; softly; accommodatingly; usefully; considerately.

FATHOMLESS
adverbs
abysmally; profoundly; mysteriously; vastly; quietly; shudderingly; drearily; tranquilly; dangerously; immeasurably; incalculably; voicelessly; terrifyingly; inscrutably.

FATIGUE
adjectives
industrial; wild; insidious; extreme; expressed; decreased; unexplainable; excessive; pure; dangerous; painful; mental; undue; alcoholic; sheer; deep; unparalleled; harsh; dreamy; curing; resultant; intolerable; unwonted.

verbs
allay —; alleviate —; avoid —; correct —; dispel —; droop in —; eliminate —; endure —; induce —; inure to —; lessen —; measure —; produce —; recover from —; recuperate from —; — daunts; — dulls; — ensues.
(See exhaustion, weariness.)

FATIGUED

adverbs
inexpressibly; alarmingly; desperately; extremely; excessively; immeasurably; remarkably; inexplicably; painfully; mentally; physically; inordinately; deeply; intolerably; utterly; terribly; seriously; haggardly; gauntly; frightfully; mysteriously; unreasonably; quickly.

FATUITY

adjectives
parental; unspeakable; apparent.

FATUOUS

adverbs
unspeakably; tiresomely; foolishly; vacuously; inanely; idiotically; senselessly; absurdly; waggishly; terribly; preposterously; egregiously; intolerably; emptily; nonsensically; bombastically; pompously; absurdly; vaguely; insignificantly; ordinarily; habitually; frivolously; inconsequentially; endlessly; wearily; plaguedly.

FAUCET

adjectives
defective; rushing; singing; whistling; mixing; shining; dripping.

FAULT

adjectives
inherited; earthly; unforgivable; social; existing; distinctive; unbelievable; beastly; serious; cold; rankest; vile; outfacing; innumerable (pl); grave; glaring; inherent; headstrong; potent; grossest; unpardonable; undeserved; evident; grievous; universal; punishable; irremediable; apparent; brilliant; contrasted; unexpiable; venial; gracious; unwilling; prime; rash; technical; shunning; pernicious; excusable; tragic; illfavored.

verbs
accept —; atone for —; beset by —; burden with —; compensate for —; confess —; conquer —; denounce —; disclose —; evince —; excuse —; find —; flay —; guard against —; iron out —s; lapse into —; lay — on; overlook —; spare —; subdue —; — blemishes; — glares; — mars.
(See error, mistake, offense.)

FAULTLESS

adverbs
perfectly; incredibly; utterly; marvellously; inexpressibly; obviously; manifestly; immaculately; superbly; splendidly; absolutely; fashionably; rarely; technically; ineffably; remarkably; completely; theoretically; comparatively; exquisitely; overwhelmingly; matchlessly; morally; mechanically; artistically; unapproachably; unbelievably.

FAULTY

adverbs
technically; mechanically; obviously; provokingly; undeniably; intentionally; designedly; purposely; unfortunately; reprehensibly; grievously; inexcusably; unpardonably; irremediably; curiously; strangely; grossly; frightfully; slightly; unfortunately; strategically; absurdly; stupidly; cruelly; ludicrously; horribly.

FAVOR

adjectives
distinguished; heavenly; fairy; generous; sweet; fashionable; unmistakable; dissembled; supreme; gracious; royal; political; special; childish; imperial; ephemeral; trifling; scientific; singular; flattering; divine; equivalent; princely; preferential; ecclesiastical; gastronomical; private.

verbs
bask in —; bestow —; beg —; bid —; compete for —; confer — on; court —; curry — with; deny —; design —; dispense —s; efface —s; entertain — of; fall out of —; flow in — of; meet with —; seek —; win —; yield —s; — fattens.
(See kindness, benefit, advantage.)

FAVOR (*v*)

adverbs
patently; particularly; manifestly; fruitlessly; universally; unduly; corruptly; incidentally; uncannily; generously; sweetly; politically; childishly; ephemerally; scientifically; singularly; gastronomically; ecclesiastically; privately.
(See support, encourage.)

FAVORABLE

adverbs
highly; profoundly; obviously; certainly; sweetly; cordially; sincerely; undoubtedly; unqualifiedly; unconditionally; heartily; enthusiastically; immediately; graciously; singularly; flatteringly; publicly; unmistakably; considerately; openly; remarkably; marvelously; auspiciously; zealously; actively; altogether.

adjectives

universal; overwhelming; particular; exclusive; profligate; prime; especial; eternal; general; reigning; indulged; current; perennial; summer; envious; unquestioned.

verbs

acclaim—; admire—; bestow on—; cheer—; choose—; cultivate—; deny—; grant—; gratify—; mark as—; receive—; regard as —; respect—; reveal—; shine on—; —effaces; —requests; —tumbles; —wins.

(See companion, associate, friend, etc.)

adverbs

undeniably; obviously; universally; currently; apparently; enviably; curiously; strangely; unreasonably; openly; offensively; flauntingly; pleasantly; attractively; socially; companionably.

FAVORITISM

adjectives

personal; opposing; apparent; political; annoying.

FAWN

adjectives

sportive; tender; new-roused; nursling; startled; leaping; gamboling; gentle.

FAWN (v)

adverbs

obsequiously; servilely; tenderly; sportively; gently; calculatingly; schemingly; slyly; traitorously; impiously.

(See flatter, cringe.)

FAWNING

adverbs

unctuously; fulsomely; servilely; humbly; slavishly; flatteringly; cringingly; abjectly; basely; meanly; obsequiously; pliantly; subtly; sycophantically; shamelessly; artfully; craftily; shrewdly; pretentiously; knavishly; deceitfully; unscrupulously; openly; unashamedly; deferentially; submissively.

FEALTY

adjectives

unswerving; lifelong; forsworn.

adjectives

jealous; stark; harrowing; palpitating; phantasmal; mutual; sneaking; conjectural; prodigious; womanly; unaccustomed; indefinable; hideous; chilling; mingled; wonted; ghoulish; political; sweeping; degrading; irrational; surging; sharp; chasmed; mortal; deadly; supernatural; troubling; unnerving; predominant; anguished; superstitious; unspoken; ghastly; servile; abysmal; lingering; clutching; lurking; fretful; foolish; bashful; childlike; oppressive; nagging; maiden; rising; exaggerated; pet; selfish; trembling; horrible; incredible; reverential; unreasonable; haunting; depressive; pathological; scrupulous; spiritual; morbid; ghostly; prudent; dreadful; lessening; natural; vague; numbing; perpetual; general; feminine; hurtful; impatient; premonitory; growing; momentary; various (pl); nameless; slight; pious; never-buried; secret; recanting; specific; universal; strange; excessive; holy; bloodless; slavish; inextinguishable; age-old; terrible; physical; conflicting; faint-footed; prophetic; grim; pale-hearted; pleasing; devouring; tormenting; pitiable; distressing; tender; gloomy; distracted; idiotic; incomprehensible; continual; groundless; petrified; nervous; helpless; anxious; savage; primitive; uneasy; unutterable; remorseless; unaccountable; respectful; inexpressible; unnamed; shuddering; startling; trivial; shivering; yearning; dark; paltry; mysterious; dominant; crushing; scarce-hidden.

verbs

allay—; banish—; beset by—; bespeak—; brush aside—; counteract—; curtail—; dismiss—; dispel—; dissipate—; drown—; eliminate—; entertain—; eradicate—; evoke —; express—; foster—; ground—upon; harbor—; harness—; impregnate—; ingrain—; inspire—; intensify—; justify—; modify—; nourish—; obliterate—; petrify with—; play on—; quake with—; quell—; quiet—; rule by—; rout—; scoff at—; share—; shiver with—; soothe—; subdue—; surmount—; vanquish—; —blights; —chills; —clutches; —coerces; —dominates; —drives; —evaporates; —fetters; —hounds; —insinuates itself; —lurks; —materializes; —melts; —motivates; —numbs; —obsesses; —overshadows; —prevails; —preys upon; —racks; —subsides; —takes possession.

(See dread, terror, apprehension, dismay, consternation, fright, anxiety.)

FEAR (v)

adverbs

unjustifiably; instinctively; inexpressibly; grossly; unreasoningly; jealously; harrowingly; irrationally; superstitiously; abysmally; oppressively; exaggeratedly; unreasonably; hauntingly; pathologically; morbidly; momentarily; secretly; excessively; pitiably; distressingly; incomprehensibly; groundlessly; inexpressibly; mysteriously.

(See dread, apprehend.)

FEARFUL

adverbs

indefinably; childishly; unusually; unwontedly; nervously; superstitiously; fretfully; foolishly; bashfully; incredibly; unreasonably; morbidly; prudently; dreadfully; naturally; vaguely; perpetually; momentarily; constantly; namelessly; secretly; slightly; excessively; strangely; terribly; prophetically; grimly; tormentingly; pitiably; distressingly; tenderly; gloomily; idiotically; incomprehensibly; groundlessly; helplessly; anxiously; uneasily; unutterably; unaccountably; inexpressibly; shudderingly; shiveringly; darkly; coldly; mysteriously; timidly; queerly; curiously; starkly; timorously; genuinely; suspiciously; significantly.

FEARLESS

adverbs

unquestionably; utterly; curiously; oddly; unnaturally; habitually; temperamentally; always; bombastically; boastfully; pretentiously; ostentatiously; apparently; avowedly; allegedly; amazingly; incredibly; confidently; boldly; valiantly; intrepidly; calmly; serenely; quietly; courageously; firmly; doggedly; resolutely; determinedly.

FEASIBLE

adverbs

easily; smoothly; clearly; undeniably; practically; apparently; oddly; entirely; completely; unbelievably; patently; palpably; manifestly; possibly; scarcely; hardly; conceivably; perhaps; uncertainly; doubtfully.

FEAST

adjectives

solemn; artistic; annual; sinful; memorable; sumptuous; continuous; constant; horrible; royal; ample; joyful; Lucullan; endless; sacrificial; accustomed; pagan; popish; marshaled; rural; movable; fashionable; bountiful; convent; princely; wondrous; funeral; impious; nobler; inimitable; superfluous; triumphal; Saturnalian; sunborn; purveying; vernal; reasonable.

verbs

anticipate—; bless—; cater at—; celebrate with—; crown—with; destine for—; enjoy —; enter—; entertain at—; gather for—; gorge at—; hold—; honor at—; invite to—; join in—; partake of—; plan—; prepare—; rejoice at—; —cheers; —commemorates; —gratifies; —refreshes.

(See entertainment, repast, anniversary.)

FEAST (v)

adverbs

convivially; recklessly; annually; triumphantly; bountifully; gluttonously; unstintedly; sumptuously; memorably; idolatrously; lavishly.

(See dine, eat, gratify.)

FEASTING

adjectives

mutual; swinish.

FEAT

adjectives

notable; merchandising; piteous; prodigious; additional; superhuman; inconsiderable; extraordinary; curious; noble; herculean; elaborate; pugilistic; haughty; brilliant; spectacular; dashing; marvelous; warlike; magic; miraculous; incomparable.

verbs

acclaim—; accomplish—; advertise—; applaud—; duplicate—; emulate—; enact—; enjoy—; equal—; exploit—; gasp at—; perfect—; perform—; practise—; praise—; recount—; regale with—; watch—; work—; —awes; —dazzles; —delights; —displays; —enthralls; —pleases; —punctures.

(See act, performance, deed, exploit, achievement.)

FEATHER

adjectives

flying; rumpled; motionless; courteous; superincumbent; molted; decorative; draggled; animated; varicolored (pl); lofty; silky; mottled; drooping; variegated (pl).

verbs

adorn with—; attach—; bristle with—s; clothe with—s; cover with—s; crop—s; decorate with—s; deck with—s; display—s; exhibit—s; fledge with—s; furnish—s; molt —s; ornament with—s; pick—s; pluck—; plume with—s; preen—s; provide—s; ruffle —s; rumple—s; rustle—s; shake—s; smooth —s; strip of—s; wave—; wear—s; —floats; —tickles.

(See ornaments.)

FEATURE
(of the face)

verbs

age—s; blur—s; characterize—s; cheat of —; cloak—s; cloud—s; contort—s; define —s; discern—s; ·distinguish—s; inherit—; mark—; obliterate—s; scar—; sketch—; weary—; —s beam; —s express; —s glare; —s glisten; —s gloom; —indicates; —s pucker up; —s shine.

(See shape, form, face.)

FEATURE
(part)

verbs

acclaim—; applaud—; appraise—; bar—; conceal—; detect—; eliminate—; embody—; evince—; execute—; incorporate—; negate —; plan—; present—; preserve—; recognize—; schedule—; strike at—.

(See item, characteristic, point.)

FEATURE (v)

adverbs

exclusively; faultlessly; consistently; animatedly; monotonously; characteristically; classically; conspicuously; disastrously; decorously; distinctively; distortedly; dominatingly; eloquently; graphically; harmoniously; irrationally; legitimately; offensively; picturesquely; piquantly; perennially; specifically; dominantly.

(See portray, delineate.)

FEATURES

adjectives

active; added; additional; advanced; agitated; agreeable; air-cooling; alabaster; altered; amazing; angular; angelic; animated; anxious; aristocratic; aquiline; arrogant; ascetic; attractive; astonishing; automatic; awkward; battered; bearded; bearish; bold; beauteous; benevolent; benignant; bewitching; bizarre; bloated; brightest; blurred; bronzed; Caesarean; calm; characteristic; charming; chiseled; clean-cut; classical; clear-cut; clearly-chiseled; coarse; comely; comfortable; commonplace;

composed; concealed; conforming; conspicuous; constructive; contorted; convenient; convulsed; corpselike; correct; craggy; crowning; ·daring; dark; decorated; decorous; delicate; delightful; desirable; desperate; determined; detestable; difficult; disastrous; distinctive; distinguishing; distorted; distressing; divers; diversified; dominant; dripping; dominating; dusky; eager; ebon; eloquent; effective; elongated; embarrassing; embrowned; engrossing; entrancing; essential; epic; evil; exasperating; exceptional; exclusive; expansive; exploitational; expressive; exquisite; extraneous; extraordinary; fabric; fair; familiar; fascinating; ferocious; fervent; fierce; fine; finely-cut; firm; flawless; flexible; flowerlike; forbidding; fundamental; gaunt; gay; genial; gentle; geologic; glorious; graphic; grave; haggard; handsome; hand-tailored; harmonious; hawk-like; haughty; healthful; heavy; high; high-priced; homely; hueless; humorous; immovable; important; impassive; impressive; indelible; indistinguishable; ineffable; inherited; innocent; insensible; insipid; intellectual; interesting; iron; intriguing; irrational; kindly; lamentable; large; leading; lean; legitimate; light; long; lovely; majestic; malignant; marked; massive; medieval; melancholy; mild; minor; mobile; mocking; modern; molded; monstrous; natural; neat; new; noble; notable; noteworthy; noticeable; objectionable; offensive; operating; occult; oppressive; original; ornamental; outstanding; pain-drawn; pain-seamed; pallid; passionless; particular; passionate; patented; patrician; peaked; perplexing; peculiar; perennial; persisting; personal; physical; picturesque; piquant; pivot-turning; placid; plastic; positive; pock-marked; poignant; practical; predominant; prevailing; prominent; protective; proscriptive; quality; questionable; quivering; quizzical; rare; recognized; recreational; recurring; redeeming; refined; regular; remarkable; restful; revolting; rigid; rough; rugged; sad; safety; saggy; salient; saturnine; scapegrace; scenic; scowling; sculptured; sensational; Semitic; semi-constructional; sensitive; serious; severe; shrunken; significant; sharp; singular; sinister; slumbering; small; smiling; socialistic; softened; sophisticated; sordid; sorry; sport; special; specific; splendid; square; stain-preventing; stellar; sterile; stern; striking; strategic; strong; structural; style; suffering; sunken; superior; swarthy;

swollen; symmetrical; tanned; thoughtful; tightly-drawn; ugly; unaffected; uncertain; ineloquent; unique; unmistakable; unrevealed; unshaven; unsightly; unusual; upraised; useful; valuable; visible; varied; vital; vivid; wasted; weazened; welcome; well-balanced; well-cared-for; well-cut; well-marked; well-proportioned; worn-out.

FECUNDITY
adjectives
incredible; mental; artificial.

FEDERAL
adverbs
impressively; inescapably; finally; predominantly; imperiously; authoritatively; officially; imperatively; compulsively; autocratically; decisively; conclusively; grandly.

FEDERATION
adjectives
loose; irksome; compact.

verbs
accomplish—; ally with—; condense into—; contract—; dismember—; establish—; form —; join—; organize—; propose—; readjust —; unite—; —advocates; —authorizes; — campaigns; —controls; —delegates; —despairs; —develops; —manages; —performs; —supports.
(See league, alliance, association, union.)

FEE
adjectives
ceremonious; unpredictable; hateful; wandering; prodigious; undeserved.

verbs
accept—; augment—; beg for—; bill—; calculate—; command—; demand—; entitle to —; execute—; expect—; fatten on—; fix—; grant—; hold in—; incur—; limit—; merit —; perform for—; procure—; promise—; refuse—; require—; rob of—.
(See payment, reward, wage.)

FEEBLE
adverbs
pitiably; lamely; hunchedly; forlornly; lugubriously; pleasantly; comfortably; placidly; admittedly; distressingly; passively; plaintively; touchingly; helplessly; utterly; frequently.

FEEBLENESS
adjectives
infantine; boyish; inherent; gathering; negligent; accustomed.

verbs
commit to—; conceal—; convince of—; cure —; degenerate into—; delight in—; fall in —; feign—; guard against—; imply—; indicate—; inflict—; loathe—; minimize—; mourn—; pity—; produce—; resist—; ridicule—; —afflicts; —deters; —prevents.
(See debility, weakness, infirmity.)

FEED (*v*)
adverbs
serenely; omnivorously; sumptuously; gluttonously; continually; artfully; carefully; delicately; dietetically; scientifically; consistently; regularly, beneficially; sparingly.
(See nourish, subsist.)

FEEDING
adjectives
careful; destructive; faithful; delicate; worthy; fast.

verbs
abstain from—; administer—; anticipate—; attempt—; call for—; crown—with; encourage—; force—; gorge in—; invite to—; join in—; manage—; partake of—; plan—; prepare—; provide—; regulate—; rely upon —; serve—; surfeit—; supervise—; — chokes; —nourishes; —refreshes; —satiates; govern—.
(See food, eating.)

FEEL (*v*)
adverbs
instinctively; genuinely; sweetly; exquisitely; amiably; turbulently; reverently; maternally; triumphantly; graciously; exuberantly; vindictively; poetically; spontaneously; tyrannically; morbidly; mutually; congenially; compassionately; philanthropically; vehemently; profoundly; spiritually.
(See touch, grope, handle.)

FEELING
adjectives
grateful; peculiar; deep-souled; instinctive; undiminished; sensitive; partisan; genuine; suppressed; subdued; pragmatic; sweet; exaggerated; repressed; empty; artistic; exquisite; amiable; ardent; selfish; con-

gealed; sad; vague; solemn; painful; exasperated; intuitive; strange; sickening; horrible; ineffable; bitter; ancient; feudal; passionate; regenerated; turbulent; dreadful; reciprocal; lofty; high-wrought; bewildered; unmistakable; soapy; reverent; excited; cognate; sacred; anti-clerical; preponderant; triumphant; imaginative; sublime; gracious; expansive; tender; profound; humble; vindictive; apparent; inward; unshared; poetic; spontaneous; remorseful; strangled; exuberant; tight; revolted; morbid; hostile; tyrannical; pent-up; shamed; kindly; grosser; evident; aesthetic; enthusiastic; unfounded; overcharged; mutual; subconscious; rancorous; remorseful; diminished; absurd; universal; annoying; intense; haughty; strange; telltale; fantastic; congenial; burning; dim; compassionate; appreciative; philanthropic; suspicious; ruffled; discordant; queer; ripened; awesome; uneasy; sick; half-ironical; half-superstitious; affectionate; dysphoric; nervous; innermost; mingled; maternal; erroneous; poignant; acute; stilted; upleasant; differentiated; unfilial; immoral; rarest; uncanny; overburdened; potent; unworthy; felicitous; vehement; complicated; dormant; fortified; taut; strained; dissimilar; mercenary; jealous; devotional; democratic; unhappy; wounded; pious; fancied; resultant; superior; uncomfortable; profound; mightiest; domestic; warm; hangdog; worn-out; ill; benevolent; indescribable; restless; blissful; liberal; selfish; holiest; lingering; contrary; half-defined; resentful; noble; national; subtler; ungovernable; amicable; subordinate; individual; refreshing; genial; embarrassed; lethargic; unspeakable; sincere; kindred; tight-throated; breathless; repressed; energetic; martial; honest; playing; heady; oldish; forlorn; uncertain; spiritual.

verbs

abate—; analyze—; awaken—; capture—; cherish—; deaden—; disturb—; divulge—; engender—; evince—; evoke—; excite—; experience—; express—; foster—; gratify —; guard—; harbor—; hide—; impart—; inflame—; inhibit—; injure—; instill—; manifest—; mask—; modify—; outrage—; pen up—; petrify—; probe—; provoke—; quicken—; regard with—; reveal—; rouse —; soothe—; stir up—; strain—; strengthen —; subdue—; suffuse with—; tamper with —; tinge—; vent—; voice—; wound—; —

blossoms; —dominates; —envelops; —explodes; —impends; —impresses; —overpowers; —overwhelms; —persists; —pervades; —pours from; —rests upon; —runs high; —subsides.

(See sensation, emotion, sentiment, consciousness, conviction.)

FEET

adjectives

tender; multitudinous; dancing; delicate; pattering; marshy; scuffing; indolent; industrious; accursed; reluctant; whispering; undelaying; dainty; wicked; wanton; unwearied; aimless; overlarge; charming; rugged; untrammelled; twinkling; trampling; faltering; restless; uncertain; racing; dimpled; fear-sped; clammy; golden; errant; daring; blistered; webbed; tripping; willing; strolling; straddling; small; silvery; marshalled; angel; dangling; swift; flying; aristocratic; slender; tortured; erring; distorted; impious; unshod; wary; bare; romping; glorious; shuffling; noiseless; stumbling; wandering; shod; trembling; claw; moccasined; scurrying; cautious; hurried; shoe-encased; churlished; infinitesimal; desultory; approaching; substantial; windy; hastening; airy; grappling; morning-winged; mournful; running; consecrated; staggering; myriad; veined; spreading; peaceabiding; wayward; bleeding; rushing; careless; adroit; feathery; bruised; radiant; big; muddy; charging; dirty; countless; silent; aching; echoing; shrivelled; calloused; sagging; desperate; lagging; leaden; wild; timorous; ivory-channeled; skipping; eager; jumping; cursed; stealthy; faultless; tiny; swirling; swift; frenzied; nimble; ample; heroic; huge; tottering; none-too-steady; unsure; immovable; obstinate; halting; dragging; indifferent; sweaty; ragged; graceless; slipshod; deformed; crippled; swollen; faltering; arched; slim; elongated; narrow; cloven; squared; padded; innumerable; slippered; heavily-shod; sandaled; velvet; clay; piggish; clattering; thudding; hobbled; stockinged; satined; rubbered; thumping; pounding; wandering; scampering; stamping; marching; little; shuffling; naked; parched; outraged; uncivilized; trusting; tireless; wary; bound; tangled; unseen; departing; protruding; unguided; educated; prodding; frantic; creeping; booted; thick; mad; clawing; immortal; fetter-incumbered; plundering.

adverbs
calculatingly; slyly; cleverly; expressly; treacherously; artfully; skillfully; deftly; fawningly; dissolutely; roguishly; knavishly.
(See pretend, simulate, assume.)

FEINT

adjectives
preliminary; solitary; diplomatic.

FELICITATION

verbs
accept—; acknowledge—; anticipate—; bestow—; compliment with—; delight in—; enjoy—; exchange—; express—; extend—; greet with—; incur—; inspire—; offer—; present—; produce—; promote—; pronounce—; receive—; return—; thank for—; —pleases.
(See congratulation.)

FELICITOUS

adverbs
auspiciously; opportunely; happily; supremely; superbly; grandly; splendidly; inexpressibly; undeniably; altogether; consummately; utterly; singularly; unexpectedly; harmoniously; delightfully; rapturously; extremely; unusually; uncommonly.

FELICITY

adjectives
earthly; engaging; exalted; supreme; expressional; uninterrupted; singular; eternal; true; pastoral; curious; domestic; Arcadian.

FELLOW

adjectives
chuckle-headed; absurd; lovable; tainted; jolly; sturdy; brash; lusty; amiable; scurvy; woodland; underbred; fine-spoken; clever; clean-living; intelligent; tractable; generous; light-hearted; industrious; bustling; common-looking; gaunt; ill-visaged; jovial-looking; loathsome; riotous; unrefined; honorary; guileless; robustious; muffled; massive; great-shouldered; muscled; lewd; merry; manly; sharp; amiable-looking; impudent; feeble; noble; pestilent; funniest; good-natured; hearty; broad-faced; dapper; fierce; valiant; cunning; admirable; wiry; sallow; enviable; heartless; worthless; indignant; craggy-faced; gnomish; odd; unaccountable; fluctuating; irresolute; voluble;

slender; prattling; hilding; captious; **hale**; hard-bitten; big; handsome; back-slapping; rollicking; villainous; good-hearted; easygoing; devil-may-care; kindly; lawless; open-hearted; brilliant; gentle-mannered; plausible; unthoughtful; innocent; sneaking; talkative; enthusiastic; unstudious; vulgar-looking; officious; engaging; swarthy; smock-faced; coal-blackened; florid; prettier; magnificent-looking; gallant; hulking; meager; verdant; brawny; stale; licentious; white-bearded; hatchet-faced; sheepish; awkward; respected; desperate; foppish; bluff; blunt; indiscreet; self-assured; conceited; celestial; melancholy; abominable; beetle-browed; powerful; marvelous; witty; eloquent; prodigious; fine; staring; inexorable; ghostly; disgruntled; capricious; insignificant; simpering; intelligent; courageous; good-humored; roguish; ignorant; noisy; unweighing; notable; good; dull; vicious; dissolute.

FELLOWSHIP

adjectives
sweet; pleasant; superficial; close-linked; accursed; generous.

verbs
admit—; build up—; enjoy—; enter into—; entitle to—; honor—; instil—; obtain—; necessitate—; participate in—; receive in—; refuse—; reject—; renounce—; separate from—; share in—; shatter—; unite in—; —honors; —predominates.
(See companionship, association.)

FELON

adjectives
acquitted; larcenous

FELONIOUS

adverbs
dastardly; outrageously; contemptibly; obviously; openly; heinously; infamously; basely; grossly; shamelessly; scandalously; brutally; atrociously; scurvily; diabolically; terribly; frightfully; horridly; insanely; venomously; fiendishly.

FELT

adjectives
faded; clean.

FEMALE

adjectives
buxom; irresponsible; elderly; frivolous; elegant; delicate; sour-faced; anemic; hys-

teric; shivering; tattered; bewildered; unimpeachable; upholstered; parthenogenetic; large; desirable; muscular; unattached; angular; firm-faced; formidable; grim.

FEMININE

adverbs

daintily; sweetly; delightfully; ravishingly; ineffably; seductively; bewitchingly; charmingly; lovably; utterly; provokingly; wantonly; weakly; dependently; irritatingly; clingingly; comfortingly; gracefully; graciously; altogether.

FEMININITY

adjectives

stigmatized; collective; rampant; disquieting; flagrant; desirable.

FENCE

adjectives

woven-wire; straggling; distorted; elaborate; bushy; pitiless; verbal; locust; split-rail; hurdle; whitewashed; spiritual; weather-beaten.

verbs

break through—; construct—; erect—; fortify with—; hurdle—; jump—; leap—; level —; provide—; repair—; skirt—; straddle —; surround with—; —bars; —defends; — deters; —encloses; —guards; —hinders; — limits; —partitions; —protects; —repels; — restricts; —screens; —shields; —wards off; —yields.

(See defence, wall.)

FENCE (v)

adverbs

deftly; skillfully; artfully; vigorously; expertly; professionally; fascinatingly; mentally; courageously; intelligently; arrogantly.

(See evade, shift.)

FENDER

verbs

attach—; bump—; clod—; crack—; damage —; dent—; run into—; rust—; secure—; splash—; split—; spray—; streamline—; strike—; —s collide; —guards; —prevents; —protects; —rattles; —shimmies; — squeaks; —vibrates.

FERMENT

adjectives

putrid; foreign; alcoholic; microscopic; anarchistic; violent; subtle; tumultuous; active; political; irresistible.

FERMENT (v)

adverbs

putridly; alcoholically; microscopically; violently; subtly; tumultuously; politically; irresistibly; actively.

(See decay, excite.)

FERMENTATION

adjectives

vinous; offensive; natural.

verbs

agitate to —; control —; employ —; excite to —; give rise to —; hinder —; incur —; occasion —; produce —; subject to —; suffer —; undergo —; work —; — aids; — results; — sours; — subsides.

(See decomposition, transformation.)

FERN

adjectives

discolored; luxuriant; water-loving; minute; exquisite; metallic; lacelike; sprouting.

FEROCIOUS

adverbs

savagely; inexpressibly; cruelly; diabolically; unspeakably; atrociously; brutally; pretentiously; comically; dutifully; unduly; mercilessly; ruthlessly; inhumanly; malevolently; coldly; unnaturally; unbelievably; stonily; barbarously; heinously; utterly; uncommonly; unutterably.

FEROCITY

adjectives

gloomy; deft; reckless; uncommon; brutal; diabolic; dull; pitiless; cruel; vigilant; admirable; frightful; unmitigated; martial; senseless; terrific; moist; clammy; mad; hair-raising; ill-concealed; blazing; incredible; unlimited; ungovernable; lurid; smoldering.

verbs

abate —; display —; escape —; fire with —; generate —; incur —; inflame to —; occasion —; ponder —; provoke to —; recover from —; salve —; shake with —; subdue —; — alarms; — blights; — destroys; — frightens; — overwhelms; — terrifies.

(See cruelty, fury.)

FERRY

adjectives

improvised; antiquated; electric.

FERTILE

adverbs

creatively; productively; luxuriantly; abundantly; fruitfully; teemingly; richly; plenteously; inexhaustibly; incredibly; remarkably; superbly; amazingly; incomparably; matchlessly; satisfactorily; surprisingly; naturally; highly; completely.

FERTILITY

adjectives

triumphant; personal; exuberant; teeming; superior; incredible; inexhaustible; dauntless; absolute; amazing; singular; improved; intellectual; unrivaled; incomparable.

FERTILIZER

verbs

advocate —; apply —; broadcast —; employ —; enrich with —; gorge with —; introduce —; purchase —; stock with —; supply —; — enhances; — enriches; — generates; — replenishes.

FERVENT

adverbs

warmly; sincerely; ardently; zealously; eagerly; significantly; earnestly; actively; utterly; heartily; fanatically; uncommonly; remarkably; contagiously; piously; magnetically; eloquently; feverishly; passionately; youthfully; dynamically; intensely; tremendously; solemnly; amazingly.

FERVID

adverbs

intensely; emotionally; contagiously; infectiously; feverishly; nervously; peculiarly; oddly; curiously; abnormally; strangely; glowingly; hotly; impressively; rapturously; breathlessly; zealously; absorbingly; fanatically; impetuously; magnificently.

FERVOR

adjectives

contagious; inward; renewed; religious; superficial; unprecedented; magnetic; disinterested; eloquent; undiminished; poetic; feverish; lurid; intolerable; passionate; revolutionary; equinoctial; meridian; devotional; exalted; involuntary; racy; youthful; vain; primitive; nationalistic; dynamic; patriotic; blazing; fascinating; emotional; intense; defensive; animated; tremendous; artificial; lyric; solemn; romantic; prophetic; loving; simple; noontide.

verbs

arouse —; bridle —; cool —; execute with —; fill with —; flush with —; inflame with —; instil —; join with —; pitch to —; quench —; replace —; shape with —; starve —; sweat with —; waste —; — animates; — boils; — blazes; — glows; — rages; — torments.

(See ardor, intensity, zeal, enthusiasm.)

FESTAL

adverbs

delightfully; joyously; charmingly; companiably; chattily; convivially; noisily; happily; jovially; gregariously; magnificently; splendidly; brilliantly; sparklingly; sumptuously; highly; elaborately; extravagantly; uproariously; unexpectedly; ineffably; tumultuously; excitedly; inexpressibly; innocently; spontaneously; exultantly; radiantly; supremely; highly.

FESTER (v)

adverbs

malignantly; hideously; horridly; disgustingly; fatally; repeatedly; continually; agonizingly; hatefully; devastatingly.

(See pain, suffer.)

FESTIVAL

adjectives

solemn; religious; torchlight; domestic; magnificent; sumptuous; nocturnal; carousing; democratic; annual; circling; memorial; high; brilliant; recurring; community; notorious; extravagant; licentious; elaborate; holiday; clamoring; grandiose.

FESTIVE

adverbs

hilariously; boisterously; uproariously; informally; happily; gaily; gloriously; utterly; absurdly; ineffably; blithely; irrepressibly; merrily; unaccountably; unexpectedly; noisily; magnificently; intimately; spontaneously; radiantly; tumultuously; inexpressibly.

FESTIVITY

adjectives

brilliant; boisterous; final; compelled; holiday; maudlin.

FESTOONS

adjectives
scalloped; looping; flung; graceful; ethereal.

FETE (v)

adverbs
ceremonially; blithesomely; handsomely; joyfully; magnificently; . sumptuously; annually; memorially; brilliantly; notoriously; extravagantly; elaborately; grandiosely.

(See celebrate, feast.)

FETID

adverbs
offensively; rankly; horridly; unbearably; mustily; suffocatingly; impossibly; unspeakably; abominably; noisomely; terribly; disagreeably; frightfully; malodorously; foully; strongly; grossly; pestilentially; unwholesomely; perniciously; poisonously; extremely; inconceivably.

FETISH

adjectives
popular; patriotic; exploded; carved; wooden; much-loved.

FETTER

verbs
chain with —s; clap into —s; commit to —s; escape —s; fasten —s; free from —s; hobble in —s; impose —s; load with —s; loose —s; release from —s; relieve of —s; relinquish —s; secure —s; shackle with —s; shake off —s; — binds; — checks; — confines; — constrains; — guards; — hinders; — prevents; — restrains; — restricts; — tortures; — vexes.

(See bond, shackle, chain.)

FETTERS

adjectives
gratuitous; triple; brazen; rose-blossom; adamantine; galling; unmeasured; creed-imposed; riven; fleshly.

FEUD

adjectives
fatal; fresh; bitter; fruitful; private; lasting; internal; dismal; revamped; primeval; mutual; tribal; relentless; grim; long-standing; age-long; nasty; murderous; deadly; domestic; personal; ancient; futile; hereditary.

verbs
activate —; arouse —; beget —; carry on —; clash in —; convert into —; declare —; enjoy —; entangle in —; inflame into —; instigate —; interrupt —; justify —; prevent —; rankle into —; renew —; root out —; — agitates; —continues; — disturbs; — flares up; — originates; compete in —.

(See strife, hostility, enmity, animosity, bitterness, quarrel.)

FEUDALISM

verbs
abhor —; bring under —; check —; convert into —; incline to —; influence —; overthrow —; practise —; recognize —; reject —; subject to —; support —; — bridles; — clutches; — deprives; — originates; — persists; — reduces; — stultifies; — survives; — treads on; — tyrannizes.

(See system.)

FEUDATORY

adjectives
mutinous; disaffected; tyrannical.

FEVER

adjectives
contagious; eruptive; ravenous; rheumatic; cruel; irregular; low; violent; fitful; prevalent; swamp; intermittent; bilious; high; malignant; unhallowed; infectious; splenic; rapid; raging; morbid; gnawing; malarial; typhus; envious; puerperal; riotous; obvious; tortured; lurking; deadly; perpetual; acute; childbed; hunting; burning; inflammatory; slow.

verbs
accompany by —; allay —; attend with —; characterize by —; come down with —; contract —; control —; develop —; heighten —; induce —; predispose to —; reduce —; retard —; transmit —; — burns; — consumes; — continues; — devours; — grips; — heats; — infects; — persists; — rages; — smoulders; — subdues.

(See excitement, disease.)

FEVERISH

adverbs
cruelly; violently; terribly; highly; extremely; obviously; dangerously; alarmingly; uncomfortably; fearfully; deliriously; acutely; dreadfully; hysterically; deplorably; burningly; restlessly; wildly; unusually; uncommonly; curiously; peculiarly.

FEW

adjectives

unscornful; far-visioned; desperate; favored; comparative; privileged; hateful; chosen.

FEW

adverbs

remarkably; extremely; strangely; lamentably; significantly; deplorably; miserably; wretchedly; fortunately; happily; curiously; mercifully; presumably.

FIASCO

adjectives

mountainous; official.

FIBER

adjectives

fleecy; pusillanimous; secret; ancestral; civic; resonant; ligneous; crude; tough; tenacious; delicate; flaccid; genuine; spiritual; moral; quivering; unexperienced; twisting; intellectual; sensitive; coarser; maguey.

FIBRE

verbs

bind with —; compose of —; connect —s; consist of —; develop —; draw into —; exhibit —; furnish with —; join —; knot —; produce —; rig with —; shred —; stretch —; swathe in —; twist —; weave —; — connects; — girdles; — hangs; — links.

FIBRIN

adjectives

coagulated; increased; exudative.

FICKLE

adverbs

disgustingly; uncertainly; unstably; mercurially; changeably; irresolutely; capriciously; whimsically; unfortunately; remarkably; exceedingly; sensationally; undependably; unhappily; deplorably; habitually; temperamentally; irresolutely; erratically; waywardly; terribly.

FICTION

adjectives

luxuriant; native; sensational; convenient; evasive; romantic; serious; bold; mythological; improbable; extravagant; picturesque; conventional; monstrous; short-lived; distinguished; unmitigated; frothy; introspective; current; sentimental; contemporary.

verbs

cast away —; compose —; condemn —; consume —; criticize —; desire —; devise —; distinguish from —; embroider —; prefer —; produce —; reject —; relate —; select —; steep in —; turn into —; — charms; — confuses; — copies; —delights; — diverts; — enchants; — informs; — influences; — instructs; — interests; — pleases; — poisons; — transports; — unwinds.

(See story, novel, narrative, myth.)

FICTITIOUS

adverbs

harmlessly; allegedly; avowedly; undoubtedly; whimsically; nonsensically; suppositiously; extravagantly; probably; grotesquely; fantastically; ironically; obviously; manifestly; ingeniously; romantically; preposterously; utterly; surprisingly; completely; hypothetically; dreamily; innocently; wildly.

FIDDLE

adjectives

nocturnal; uncivilized.

FIDDLER

adjectives

diligent; rascal; rollicking; peripatetic.

FIDELITY

adjectives

conjugal; eye-taking; doglike; unswerving; undying; utmost; undeviating; eternal; scrupulous; minute; marvelous; assured; realistic; rigid; inviolable; subtle; flawless; dull; unwavering; long-tried; intense; reverent; sober; unblemished; sorrowful; lifelike; profound; historic; pastoral; diving; true-hearted; noteworthy; everlasting.

verbs

abuse —; appreciate —; arouse —; bestow —; buy —; depend on —; endow with —; entwine with —; exact —; incur —; instil —; nourish —; rivet —; shake —; strengthen —; support with —; swear —; threaten —; violate —; — endears; — endures; — palls; — perishes.

(See faithfulness, loyalty.)

FIDGET (v)

adverbs

uneasily; unceasingly; impatiently; painfully; embarrassedly; unpleasantly; secretly; fruitlessly; suppressedly.

(See move, stir, jump.)

adverbs

suspiciously; terribly; unnecessarily; annoyingly; vexatiously; uneasily; uncomfortably; fussily; officiously; clamorously; excitably; hysterically; foolishly; impatiently; irrepressibly; curiously; peculiarly; oddly; odiously; strangely; significantly; atrociously; unpleasantly; extremely; needlessly.

FIELD

verbs

capture —; clothe —; crop —; deplete —; dominate —; double —; encumber —; entrench —; fence —; invade —; litter —; lord over —; pioneer —; plod across —; preempt —; replenish —; sow —; tap —; tramp across —; usurp —; wall —; — extends; — lies; — slumbers; — stretches.

(See meadow, land.)

FIELDER

(*baseball or cricket*)

verbs

contract for —; fire —; hire —; release —; trade —; — catches; — chases; — covers; — drops; — fields; — holds out; — juggles; — misjudges; — muffs; — races; — runs; — slides; — slips; — snares; — spears; — sprints; — steals; — stops; — returns; — traps; — whips.

(See player, athlete.)

FIELDS

adjectives

gray-green; emerald; frost-bitten; whitened; glistening; ripened; sun-parched; windswept; sparse; billowing; fertile; soft; wet; untrodden; picturesque; stubble; rolling; tremendous; uncrowded; virgin; untouched; fruitless; crimsoned; bloody; drowned; molding; barren; swamped; useful; conquered; disturbed; tented; grazing; plowed; fragrant; archaeological; fenceless; weedy; spring; amaranth; aesthetic; desolate; rain-gullied; swelling; smoky; blossoming; wanton; hunting; encompassing; uncarved; well-dressed; twilight; fallow; unchartered; productive; silken; wintry; remnant; subterranean; feathered; extensive; beautiful; economic; poisonous; illimitable; tobacco-jetted; hard-fought; coal; industrial; deserted; joyless; sedgy; abandoned; untried; magnetic; interpretative; somber; azure; languishing; stricken; teeming; sequestered; electrostatic.

adjectives

despiteful; foul; stout; incarnate; shivering; father; consummate; possessing; kindred; infernal; abandoned; impetuous; cursed; lubber; human; delicate; malignant; viewless; glaring; sneering.

FIENDISH

adverbs

unspeakably; inexpressibly; uncommonly; brutally; incomprehensibly; unthinkably; odiously; atrociously; heinously; flagrantly; outrageously; outlandishly; grotesquely; inscrutably; barbarously; coldly; stonily; diabolically; inhumanly; unnaturally; defiantly; ominously; ungovernably; uncontrollably; insatiably.

FIERCE

adverbs

implacably; incredibly; intentionally; barbarously; cruelly; ungovernably; impetuously; vehemently; uproariously; brutally; outrageously; fantastically; abruptly; uncontrollably; savagely; irrepressibly; sarcastically; dreadfully; bitterly; explosively; irately; blusteringly; relentlessly; pitilessly; remarkably; amazingly.

FIERCENESS

adjectives

unscrupulous; brutal; suppressed; dramatic; intense.

FIG

adjectives

luscious; large; tasty; over-ripe.

FIGHT

adjectives

inextricable; unflinching; miscellaneous (pl); portentous; isolated; murderous; desultory; bloody; furious; sublimated; ensuing; serious; trench; unavailing; arduous; heavy; futile; ever-losing; factional; running; desperate; winning; memorable; successful; strenuous; tumultuous; showdown; sea-convulsing; manful; vulturous; incessant; dreadful; unequal; dubious; mortal; bitter.

verbs

accept —; augur —; conduct —; evade —; gird for —; lack —; participate in —; reopen —; rouse to —; schedule —; show —;

stage —; wage —; witness —; —embitters; — grows; — rages; — wanes; — waxes; pledge to —; precipitate —.

(See strife, struggle, battle, conflict, combat.)

FIGHT (v)
adverbs

murderously; desultorily; furiously; unavailingly; memorably; strenuously; manfully; dubiously; mortally; viciously; vaingloriously; stolidly; simultaneously; rebelliously; gallantly; doggedly; magnificently; sanguinarily; ostentatiously; vindictively.

(See combat, battle, struggle.)

FIGHTER
adjectives

infuriated; stubborn; considerable; effective; unimaginable; undisciplined; malicious; fearless; reputed; aggressive; ruthless.

verbs

cheer —; condition —; cow —; cuff —; goad —; hack —; incite —; sponge —; spur —; urge —; — bangs; — beats; — bruises; — clinches; — cuts; — dances; — dodges; — drops; — ducks; — feints; — flinches; — jumps; — practises; — punches; — reels; — retreats; — sags; — skips; — slams; — slips; — tallies; — taps; — whacks; — winces.

FIGMENT
adjectives

seductive; idle; imaginative.

FIGURE
verbs

accept —s; bandy —s; cite —s; compile —s; delineate —s; deluge with —s; juggle —s; publish —s; quote —s; scribble —s; splotch —s; —s claim; —s pour in; — soars.

(See digit, number, amount.)

FIGURE
(*general*)
adjectives

able; absurd; advancing; allegorical; aged; alluring; ample; appealing; ardent; arrestive; athletic; august; battered; belligerent; beloved; benignant; bent; bestial; blue-clad; blurred; bony; bouncing; bulky; buoyant; buxom; cherubic; clever; cloyed; colorful; colossal; comfortable; comical; comparative; compelling; conspicuous; contorted; cool; cosmopolitan; courtly; cowering;

crabbed; credible; crouched; crumpled; curious; dainty; dark; dashing; defenseless; defiant; dejected; demure; departing; desolate; dignified; dim; diminutive; discreet; dismal; distinguished; distorted; dominant; domineering; dramatic; draped; drawn; dressed; dwarfed; eager; elegant; emaciated; emblematical; enameled; enchanting; energetic; enigmatic; enormous; epauletted; erect; eternal; excited; exquisite; exuberant; famous; fatigued; fashionable; fawning; flat; flexible; foregoing; forlorn; formless; frail; fragmentary; full-grown; furtive; gagged; gallant; gaunt; geometric; ghastly; girlish; glowing; gorilla-like; grandiose; grappling; grave; grotesque; heroic; growing; haloed; heavy; horrid; huddled; hurrying; ideal; imperious; incalculable; independent; indifferent; indistinguishable; inert; influential; innocent; inscrutable; insignificant; interesting; international; irridescent; irrelevant; jaunty; kneeling; lagging; lawless; lax; leading; lean; legendary; limping; literary; lithe; little; lost; lumbering; lurid; lurking; magnetic; majestic; marvelous; masculine; massive; mean; melancholy; memorable; menacing; minor; mocking; miserable; misshapen; monosyllabic; motionless; mountainous; mournful; muffled; mummy-like; mythic; naive; national; nautical; neglected; negligible; nervous; noble; notable; nude; odious; ominous; ornamental; osseous; outlandish; outstanding; pale; panting; pathetic; perfect; petite; pinched; picturesque; pitiful; plastic; pliant; podgy; poetic; poignant; portentous; powerful; preserved; principal; prominent; prone; prostrate; puny; quadrilateral; quaint; quivering; quixotic; rapid; rare; reclining; recumbent; reeling; related; respected; resplendent; retreating; ridiculous; rigid; romantic; rounded; rustic; salient; sardonic; sauntering; semi-legendary; shaking; shameless; shapeless; shrewd; silent; shrinking; shriveled; shuddering; shrouded; silhouetted; sinister; sluggish; skinny; sleek; smart; sob-shaken; solitary; somber; spiritless; sprawled; spry; stalwart; stiff; stocky; stolid; stooping; straight; stricken; strong; stunted; stupendous; sunburned; superb; supple; svelte; swaying; sylphlike; symbolical; tabulated (pl); talented; tatterdemalion; tense; thickset; tottering; unattractive; tragic; tremendous; trim; truculent; turbulent; typical; uncouth; uniformed; unique; unkempt; unobtrusive; veiled; venerable; vigorous;

vestlike; wasted; weak; well-loved; well-molded; whirling; white-clad; wild; winsome; wiry; wizened; wooden; worthy; tall; wretched; writhing; young; radiant; quaking; queenly; quiet.

FIGURE
(physique)
verbs
blur—; conceal—; corset—; develop—; enhance—; forge—; guard—; illuminate—; jeopardize—; nurture—; silhouette—; uncoil—; visualize—; —looms; —s mill; —symbolizes; —writhes.
(See shape, form.)

FIGURE (v)
adverbs
conspicuously; deliberately; absurdly; prominently; allegorically; appealingly; belligerently; benignantly; colorfully; comically; domineeringly; dramatically; irrelevantly; fashionably; grandiosely; lawlessly; luridly; mythically; negligibly; picturesquely; portentously; ornamentally; saliently; typically; unobtrusively.
(See calculate, contrive.)

FILE
(catalogue or cabinet)
verbs
arrange in—; assemble in—; catalogue—; clean—; destroy—; dig into—; feed—; go through—; lodge in—; prepare—; preserve in—; pull from—; rank in—; refer to—; search—; store in—; wade through—; —aids; —arranges; —facilitates; —separates.
(See list, catalogue, collection, cabinet.)

FILE
(general)
adjectives
endless; extensive; newspaper; glittering; moldering; lengthening; four-ranked; successive (pl); straggling; droning.

FILE
(tool)
verbs
employ—; slide—; yield to—; —abrades; —evens; —finishes; —glazes; —gnaws; —grates; —grinds; —nicks; —polishes; —reduces; —removes; —restores; —scratches; —sharpens; —smooths; —wears down.

FILE (v)
adverbs
sedately; painstakingly; noiselessly; endlessly; monotonously; stragglingly; patiently; ceaselessly; solemnly; incessantly.
(See smooth, cut, walk.)

FILIBUSTER (v)
adverbs
bombastically; wordily; vigorously; exasperatingly; venomously; repeatedly; uncontrollably.
(See hinder, prevent, argue.)

FILL (v)
adverbs
adequately; creditably; efficiently; generously; amply; faultlessly; cleverly; partially; greedily; graciously; constantly; skillfully; exclusively; scantily; systematically.
(See satisfy, occupy.)

FILLING
adjectives
continuous; systematic; adequate.

FILM
(camera)
adjectives
color; sooty; celluloid; supersensitive; exposed; iridescent.

FILM
(covering)
adjectives
transitory; glossy; sanguine; adherent; shadowy; permanent; half-drawn; base; clogging.

verbs
break—; cover with—; emerge from—; penetrate—; remove—; —dims; —envelops; —floats; —forms; —grows; —hides; —hinders; —obscures; —prevents.
(See membrane, cover.)

FILM
(picture)
verbs
acclaim—; applaud—; ban—; bar—; censor—; criticize—; cut—; develop—; enjoy —; expose—; feature—; guard—; legalize —; manipulate—; preview—; rave about—; —burlesques; —satirizes; —portrays.

494

FILTH

adjectives
squalid; undiluted.

verbs
abhor—; collect—; detest—; drag through
—; expose—; fling—; forbid—; gather—;
live in—; loathe—; purge of—; reek with
—; remove—; revolt at—; shun—; suffer
—; swarm with—; wallow in—.
   (See dirt.)

FILTHY

adverbs
grossly; coarsely; unspeakably; incredibly;
grotesquely; horribly; abominably; grimily;
foully; beastly; offensively; slovenly; squalidly; unpardonably; inexcusably; unreasonably; needlessly; hideously; unwarrantably;
piteously; pitiably; deplorably; outlandishly; wretchedly; singularly; exceptionally;
extraordinarily.

FIN

verbs
cut off—s; course with—s; cruise with—s;
employ—s; injure—; insert—s; paddle with
—s; support with s; swim with s;   s
flap; —s flip; —s lash; —s navigate; —s
project; —s propel; —s steer.

FINAL

adverbs
tragically; conclusively; heartbreakingly;
egotistically; pompously; acrimoniously; officially; irrevocably; ultimately; catastrophically; elaborately; hopelessly; decisively; absolutely; definitely; unmistakably; inevitably; unchangeably; unimpeachably; dogmatically; authoritatively; authentically;
clearly.

FINALE

adjectives
ludicrous; wonderful.

verbs
approach—; compose—; encore—; enjoy—;
perfect—; play—; rehearse—; render—; —
completes; —concludes; —delights; —disposes of; —ends; —pleases; —terminates;
—winds up.
   (See end, conclusion.)

FINALITY

adjectives
unmistakable;   consecrated;   unshakable;
helpless; brutal.

FINANCE (*v*)

adverbs
niggardly; soundly; scientifically; ceremoniously; pragmatically; ingenuously; professionally; unscrupulously; unethically; ingeniously.
   (See provide, manage.)

FINANCES

adjectives
declining; pitiful; low; unsound; prospective.

verbs
accumulate—; amass—; clear up—; conceal—; deplete—; destroy—; drain—; imperil—; manipulate—; patch up—; pervert
—; provide—; rally—; shake—; strain—;
—accrue; —accumulate; —dwindle.
   (See income, revenue, funds.)

FINANCIAL

adverbs
inescapably; naturally.

FINANCIER

adjectives
unscrupulous; accurate.

verbs
beseech—; curb—; employ—; provide—;
ruin—; —accomodates; —accumulates; —
amasses; —collects; —conducts; —controls;
—demands; —deposits; —invests; —judges;
—levies; —manages; —operates; —persuades; —recruits; —secures; —supports;
—swindles.
   (See manager.)

FIND

adjectives
consequent;   definite;   important;   right;
ghastly.

FIND (*v*)

adverbs
inevitably; eventually; invariably; conclusively; ultimately; locally; intuitively; distinctly; frequently; officially; promptly; con-
sequer *y*; definitely.
   (See acquire, attain, discover.)

FINDING

adjectives

malicious; specific; pertinent; scientific.

verbs

chance on—; consider—; determine—; elucidate—; endorse—; examine—; expose—; furnish—; inquire about—; inspect—; labor for—; observe—; owe—to; pay for—; pick up—; preserve—; procure—; produce—; provide—; reveal—; supply—; view—; — aids; —clarifies; —reveals.

(See discovery.)

FINE

verbs

anticipate—; agree upon—; condemn to—; evade—; exact—; execute—; exempt from —; impose—; incur—; lament—; levy—; obtain—; pass—on; pronounce—; remit—; settle—; subject to—; suffer—; —compensates; —punishes; —reduces; —releases; —restrains.

(See penalty, money, sum, payment.)

FINE (v)

adverbs

heavily; unscrupulously; punitively; legally; unethically; maliciously; cruelly; sternly.

(See dispossess, punish, attack.)

FINERY

adjectives

metropolitan; priceless; grotesque; worthless; gaudy; tawdry; verdant; shimmering; bright; thin; elaborate; ruinous; scarlet; barbaric; natural.

verbs

addict to—; adorn in—; appreciate—; bedeck in—; clothe in—; crave—; deck in—; decorate in—; degenerate into—; display—; dress in—; envy—; exhibit—; indulge in—; observe—; prefer—; sport (colloq.)—; view —; —amazes; —attracts; —impresses; —consoles.

(See ornament, splendor.)

FINES

adjectives

enormous; aggregate; unfair; wholesale.

FINGER

verbs

beckon with—; bend—; cramp—; cut—; distend—; drum with—; extend—; level—

at; prick—; snap—s; —s clutch;—s fly; —s fumble with; —s hover near; —s twist; —s twitch.

(See digit, thumb, hand.)

FINGER (v)

adverbs

significantly; nervously; delicately; tremulously; feverishly; tremblingly; intimately; lingeringly; caressingly; fumblingly; rheumatically; lustfully; authoritatively; cannily; agilely.

(See handle, touch.)

FINGERNAIL

verbs

bite—; break—; chew—; claw with—; clean —; clip—; cream—; dig with—; employ—; excavate with—; file—; jag—; manicure—; polish—; round—; shape—; split—; trim—; —s attract; —s scratch; —s shine.

FINGERNAILS

adjectives

rose-tinted; pointed; unimpeachable; untidy; long; sharp; shiny-rouged; talon-like; crooked; yellow; polished.

FINGERS

adjectives

guiding; tapering; prisoned; tremulous; uncut; slim; deft; searching; exquisite; listless; merciless; dimpled; slender; artistic; patient; careless; knotted; dewy; numbed; icy; outstretched; fevered; imitative; sharp; clumsy; nimble; skilled; ferocious; plastic; hushing; bloody; trembling; unresisting; needle-marked; guiding; interlacing; chubby; jeweled; pointed; weary; marble; radiant; horny; gloved; ineffectual; groping; invisible; ghostly; pensive; accusing; sensitive; solicitous; shaking; reverent; lily; grubby; bruised; flitting; dextrous; lingering; fairy; waxen; talented; intimate; tense; rosy; unseen; cruel; pale; bony; moistened; lean; nervous; quick; grimy; courageous; forced; benumbed; dirty; benign; rapid; transparent; shriveled; brown; coral-tipped; rosy-nailed; soft; rose-tinted; vigorous; premonitory; amethyst; skeleton; effacing; pinching; clutching; tenacious; solemn; iron; glowing; choppy; mortal; beckoning; swathed; royal; pilfering; sudden; microscopic; wasted; barky; unraised; nicotine-stained; false; hungry; catechising; heavily-ringed; uncontrolled; gentle; caressing; limp; lax; hesitating; idle; pitying;

beguiling; chilled; awkward; ready; cautious; scorched; imperative; feeble; fluttering; disengaged; itching; indignant; warning; denunciatory; admonitory; busy; exploring; cold; prying; covetous; searching; blundering; greedy; mischievous; playful; meddling; offensive; slight; thieving; usurious; exploratory; tapping; snatching; gripping; fumbling; grasping; emphasizing; stiff; rheumatic; tendril-like; skinny; fleshy; blunt-tipped; thick; ruthless; plump; lustful; felonious; deadly; predatory; sinewy; powerful; rough; agile; smudgy; soiled; dingy; square; flat; stubby; freckled; curled; strong; spatulate; arched; huge; crooked; firm; authoritative; steady; experienced; well-groomed; manicured; quick; canny; excited.

FINGER-TIPS
adjectives
reverent; slim; caressing; calloused; semiconscious; warm; sensitive; chill; gentle.

FINICKY
adverbs
frivolously; idly; inanely; uncommonly; absurdly; unreasonably; ludicrously; primly; priggishly; vexatiously; bumptiously; loudly; unnecessarily; intolerably; tiresomely; inordinately; extravagantly; elaborately; pitifully; ridiculously; shabbily; amazingly.

FINISH
adjectives
elaborate; high; literary; permanent; pictorial; sleek; glace; gleaming; harmonious; artistic; lustrous; meticulous; smooth; ill-conceived; warm; mellow; oratorical; scholarly; surface; admirable; exquisite; attractive; interior; rare; delicate; subtle.

verbs
acquire—; adorn with—; anticipate—; await—; design—; destroy—; exhibit—; lay —; mar—; obtain—; plan—; polish to—; prepare—; produce—; provide—; restore —; select—; —perfects.
(See perfection.)

FINISH (v)
adverbs
uniformly; leisurely; deliberately; neatly; minutely; solemnly; abstractedly; hurriedly; elaborately; lustrously; meticulously; exquisitely; delicately; subtly.
(See complete, end.)

FINISHED
adverbs
perfectly; unquestionably; irrevocably; recently; satisfactorily; smoothly; politely; irremediably; finally; consummately; highly; definitely; unfortunately; beautifully; fundamentally; exquisitely; wonderfully; amazingly; faultlessly; cleverly; ingeniously; expertly; artistically; elaborately; splendidly.

FINITE
adverbs
materially; inevitably; essentially; mortally; lamentably; fitly; tragically; appropriately; evanescently; merely; transitorily; passingly; humanly.

FIRE
adjectives
scattering; withering; blasting; raging; scorching; penal; scared; continuous; purging; oracular; crimson; cheerful; incessant; smoldering; suicidal; contagious; dormant; enfilading; unquenchable; horrid; eternal; dullest; answering; celestial; heavenly; constant; heavy; ethereal; gnawing; latent; cozy; untoward; baleful; closest; starry; aromatic; blinding; plumed; combined (pl); elemental; fearful; liquid; inextinguishable; rolling; long-suffering; barbed; singular; permeating; blinking; fruitless; accustomed; lambent; all-consuming; volcanic; ardent; innumerable (pl); central; lively; unfathomed; insatiate; mirrored; living; destructive; well-directed; unwonted; pulsating; cordial; sweet; slumbering; murderous; impetuous; undermining; swift; mystic; golden; unapparent; unavailing; mocking; molten; soul-scorching; subtile; ruddy; capricious; cleansing; solar; blazing; terrific; plucky; feeble; strange; electric; corrosive; tempestuous; powerless; conflicting; thrifty; deadly; flaming; beamless; dusky; twilight; overwhelming; tremulous; soft; unspotted; grim; roaring; intolerable; lurid; well-directed; effective; flickering; baser; raking; devastating; tempering; azure; deep; spiritual; restless; steady; opalescent; remorseless; avenging; divine; nightly; slow; pale; fresh-lit; instantaneous; animating; vestal; monumental; branding; hallowed; turf; boisterous; pernicious; ancestral; incipient; unhallowed; galling; solitary; musketry; unhealthful; ravenous; wild; disastrous; immortal; wandering; smokeless; ceaseless; considerable; impassioned; appalling; magic; incense; illumin-

ating; sea-coal; immeasurable; unearthly; velvet; dead; drowsy; desultory; extraordinary; insignificant; languid; freezing; diverging; chaster; commingling; subterranean; parental; mortal; specifical; waning; unslackened; merry; fanatical; respective; elfin; spiral; conquering; theologic; everlasting; fluttering; hoarded; dreadful; open; hot-burning; council; actual; covered; hectic; kindly; combined; prophetic; shafted; impatient; inward; sleeping; mad; suppressed; bright; flashing; purifying; undivided; amber; sheathing; lightless; fierce; sprightly; vaporous; telling; crackling.

verbs
assail with—; concentrate—; douse (colloq.) —; extinguish—; feed—; intensify—; lower—; quench—; rake—; replenish—; revive—; smother—; stoke—; torture with—; vent—; witness—; yield to—; —breaks out; —consumes; —crackles; —devastates; —devours; —flashes; —gnaws; —leaps; —menaces; —rages; —ravages; —razes; —reaches out; —roars; —scorches; —shrivels; —slakes down; —smolders; —snaps; —sputters; —whips through.
(See blaze, flame, conflagration.)

FIRE (v)
adverbs
electrically; witheringly; blastingly; scorchingly; incessantly; fearfully; destructively; lethally; murderously; perniciously; mortally; fiercely; shatteringly; devastatingly.
(See explode, burn, blaze.)

FIREFLY
verbs
capture—; welcome—; —blinks; —cheers; —emits; —flames; —flashes; —flickers; —glimmers; —glitters; —glows; —illuminates; —lights; —scintillates; —shimmers; —spangles; —sparkles; —twinkles; —winks.
(See insect.)

FIRELIGHT
adjectives
flickering; wan; lifeless; bright; glaring; warm; drab; dull.

verbs
behold—; emit—; neglect—; observe—; provide—; quench—; —blinks; —casts; —cheers; —flames; —flashes; —flickers; —

gleams; —glimmers; —glows; —illuminates; —rages; —sparkles; —transmits; —twinkles; —warms; —warns.
(See light.)

FIREPLACE
adjectives
rustic; capacious; radiant; immense; stone; clean-swept; spacious; desolate; high; cheery; white-tiled.

verbs
congregate around—; crackle in—; delight in—; gather 'round—; lounge around—; nestle near—; pave—; provide—; rejoice 'round—; toast at—; —blinks; —cheers; —furnishes; —glimmers; —heats; —illuminates; —welcomes.

FIREWORKS
verbs
arrange—; attack with—; cast—; celebrate with—; charge with—; dedicate with—; design—; display—; execute—; exhibit—; honor with—; prepare—; present—; start —; —appear; —burn; —conclude; —cover; —disturb; —excite; —explode; —harm; —represent; —spark; —splutter.

FIRING
verbs
attend to—; commence—; halt—; inspire—; instigate—; lead to—; minimize—; perceive —; prepare for—; prevent—; prohibit—; require—; restrain—; slacken—; start—; subject to—; warn against—; —ceases; —destroys; —ruins; —wanes.
(See attack.)

FIRM
adjectives
salvaging; futile; magnanimous; munificent; enterprising; business; successful; mercantile; bankrupt.

verbs
alter—; associate with—; bankrupt—; designate—; establish—; head—; indict—; join —; manage—; supervise—; —advises; —agrees; —delivers; —dissolves; —engages; —perishes; —promotes; —sells; —solicits; —trades; —transacts.
(See partnership, corporation, company.)

adverbs
stably; dependably; securely; safely; sufficiently; satisfactorily; immovably; obdu-

rately; stubbornly; severely; wisely; care
fully; affectionately; paternally; desperate
ly; sullenly; relentlessly; pitilessly; curious·
ly; remorselessly; primly; priggishly; offi·
cially; professionally; vexatiously; unnec·
essarily; resolutely; decisively; emphatic·
ally; remarkably; singularly; particularly;
uncommonly.

FIRMAMENT
adjectives
beautiful; boundless; darkling; airy; star-
spangled; full-arched; starry; azure; cloudless; aerial; spacious; frosty; all-encircling;
unquestionable; rolling; economic; overcast;
pellucid; twinkling; terrestrial; expectant.

FIRMNESS
adjectives
desperate; gloomy; relentless; curious; remorseless; fatal; necessary; exemplary;
practical; miscalled; fresh; equal; temperate; unexampled, futile.

FISH
adjectives
fin-twinkling; fiery; armored; magnificent;
surface; fatted; voracious; darting; glistening; golden; artificially-grown; live; game;
broiled; diminutive; silly; slim; silvery;
tawny; iridescent; sodden; much-comforted;
playful; meddlesome; mystical; speckled;
bony; lacelike; cartilaginous; salmonoid;
shining; putrid; floating; edible; brain-
giving.

verbs
abound in—; catch—; cure—; drag for—;
feed—; harbor—; limit—; plant—; prepare
—; raise—; shred—; steam—; yield—; —
darts off; —deposits eggs; —flashes past; —
flops about; —hovers near; —inhabits; —
schools; —spawns; —squirms; —swoops
past.

FISH (v)
adverbs
intently; contentedly; placidly; somnolently;
abstractedly; ruminatively; enthusiastically;
skillfully; professionally; devotedly.
  (See search, seek.)

FISHERMAN
verbs
ban—; enthrall—; license—; permit—; tantalize—; tempt—; —anchors; —angles; —
attempts; —baits; —casts; —catches; —
collects; —courts; —displays; —disturbs;

—elicits; —enthuses (colloq.); —hauls in;
—hooks; —nets; —occupies; —pulls; —
snaps; —strives; —struggles with; —supplies; —trawls.

FISHERMEN
adjectives
energetic; skillful; stalwart; unsuccessful;
professional; lowly; ideal; shabby; devoted;
rude.

FISHING
verbs
acclaim—; ban—; bar—; contemplate—;
control—; employ in—; offer—; permit—;
popularize—; prevent—; rely on—; supervise—; thrive on—; tutor in—; —bores; —
disturbs; —diverts; —entertains; —lags; —
pleases; —supplies; —supports; —tests; —
tires; —yields.
  (See sport.)

FIST
adjectives
clenched; rocklike; parental; fat; helping;
husky; tense; skillful; clumsy; practised;
dimpled; huge; solid; hamlike; giant;
heavy; ample; pudgy; iron; hard-knuckled;
useful-looking; great; raw; calloused;
knotted; gnarled; vengeful; angry; furious;
shaking; defiant; rage-driven; smashing;
whirling; swinging; pounding; thudding;
closed; hairy; doubled; impotent; knuckle-
torn; rock-laden; mailed; choking; eager:
oxlike.

verbs
bandage—; box with—; clasp in—; clench
—; close into—; conceal in—; dodge—;
double into—; drive with—; feint with—;
fight with—; flourish—; fold into—; grasp
with—; injure—; lay on with—; shake—;
strike with—; swing—; wield—; —clutches;
—crushes; —descends; —grips; —shoots
out; —staggers.
  (See hand (colloq. for fist.)

FISTICUFFS
adjectives
childish; brutal; scientific.

FIT
adjectives
fainting; plethoric; smooth; trim; excellent;
slenderizing; violent; immoderate; jealous;
snug; periodical; poetic; painful; dreadful;
melancholy; sullen; apoplectic; hysterical;

natural; morose; economical; perfect; permanent; wild; suave; comfortable; superior; proper; lasting; soft; custom; superb; correct; assured.

verbs

ail with—; anticipate—; attack with—; burst into—; check—; convulse in—; cure of—; fall into—; fear—; master—; scream in—; seize with—; shake with—; sweat in —; take with—; throw into—; treat for—; —exhausts; —possesses; —seizes; —wracks.
(See spasm, convulsion, paroxysm.)

adverbs

remarkably; splendidly; magnificently; capably; competently; expertly; skillfully; amazingly; opportunely; conveniently; appropriately; brilliantly; robustly; sturdily; gratifyingly; pleasantly; unusually; marvelously.

FIT (v)

adverbs

snugly; exquisitely; adorably; peculiarly; permanently; specifically; curiously; delicately; smoothly; periodically; economically; superbly.
(See adorn, wear.)

FITFUL

adverbs

erratically; irregularly; capriciously; vexatiously; undependably; unsystematically; haltingly; changeably; inconstantly; terribly; oddly; restlessly; waywardly; fantastically; whimsically; captiously; inconsistently; surprisingly; unpleasantly; disturbingly.

FITNESS

adjectives

practical; vital; exquisite; highest; personal; harmonious; absolute; visible.

FIX

adjectives

awkward; monetary; erroneous; frightful; dreadful.

FIX (v)

adverbs

hypnotically; firmly; arbitrarily; unalterably; inherently; accurately; steadily; steadfastly; ingeniously; rigidly; awkwardly; momentarily.
(See fasten, secure, arrange.)

FIXED

adverbs

irrevocably; firmly; irresistibly; finally; resolutely; permanently; unalterably; inevitably; immovably; persistently; immutably; steadfastly; obstinately; ineradicably; irretrievably; indelibly; traditionally; officially; absolutely; inviolately.

FLABBERGASTED

adverbs

wondrously; breathlessly; mysteriously; unutterably; unspeakably; utterly; completely; helplessly; confusingly; confoundedly; obviously; embarrassingly; peculiarly; entirely; ludicrously; comically; pitiably.

FLABBY

adverbs

uselessly; pliably; flexibly; limply; malleably; inadequately; slackly; helplessly; hopelessly; wretchedly; miserably; terribly; disgustingly; vexatiously; dreadfully.

FLAG

adjectives

rippling; hoisted; wind-swayed; tattered; crimson; insulted; back-blown; radiant; saucy; faltering; drooping; enchanted; movable; fluttering; enormous; quadrangular; constabulary; tricolored; shameful; lozenge-shaped; scoured; ominous; hearth; withered; common; many-colored; gaudy; simplest; easiest; veranda; garish; unfurled; hostile; invincible; draped; precious; historic.

verbs

accept—of; bear—; crowd 'round—; display—; elevate—; extend—; flaunt—; guard—; half-mast—; haul down—; hoist —; jeopardize—; level—; moor—; nail—; pay homage to—; rally 'round—; unfurl—; wave—; —ascends; —cheers; —descends; —flutters; —symbolizes; —unfurls; —whips in the breeze.
(See banner, ensign.)

FLAGRANT

adverbs

arrantly; notoriously; patently; strikingly; incredibly; unconcealably; scandalously; publicly; grossly; atrociously; indecorously; indiscreetly; iniquitously; nefariously; reprehensibly; shamelessly; unconscionably; exceptionally; emphatically; indefensibly; wickedly.

FLAIR

adjectives

vicious; promotional; remarkable; definite; noticeable.

FLAKES

adjectives

lazy; starry; quivering; fervent; wandering; hoariest; ash; thick-descending; jetty; crackling; crunchy; flavor-packed; discolored; sun-ripened; delicately-browned; whole-wheat; tender; luscious; flying; snow; wavering; radiant; whirling; white; mated; blinding; elfish.

verbs

blow—; break into—; chip off—; cover with—; cut into—; dress in—; fall in—; peel in—; powder with—; scale—; scrape into—; separate into—; silver with—; spread with—; strip into—; —descend; —fly; —pave.
(See fragment, chip.)

FLAMBOYANT

adverbs

conspicuously; openly; ostentatiously; brazenly; daringly; audaciously; floridly; sonorously; pompously; egotistically; rhetorically; bombastically; flashily; noisily; terribly; marvelously; uproariously.

FLAME

adjectives

vivid; dancing; flapping; unshapely; lean; bursting; unresting; pitiless; candle; hungry; fever; solar; sunny; fragrant; cheerful; inward; pointed; dying; lambent; livelier; spiritual; devouring; sacrificial; quickening; unconsuming; conscious; immediate; celestial; dull; low-lit; pure; changeless; ruddy; sulphurous; polluted; generous; inferior; floating; rival; innocent; sacred; showering; mutual; enormous; heavenly; self-divided; restless; pale; earnest; pallid; elusive; ethereal; many-colored; irregular; guiding; quick; darting; stiller; variegated; white; ardent; tired; leaping; noiseless; flickering; lawless; wasting; writhing; hurrying; subtle; penetrating; torturing; amorous; evangelic; lurid; vital; feeble; blue; scarlet; greenish; luminous; dreadful; incandescent; vengeful; empyreal; midnight; heavenward; sudden; irregular; joyful; inexorable; springing; clearest; delusive; intermittent; chastening; accustomed; outrageous; withering; purer; livid; authentic;

spiral; cold; radiant; captive; flashing; baleful; inextinguishable; mumuring; rapid; quenchable; serpent; seraphic; furious; ill-dissembled; all-absorbing; sullen; wrathful; prismatic; loyal; purple; liquid; bickering; deep-red; mounting; embracing; peaceful; creeping; unshelterable; blessed; vestal; transported; avenging; breathing; oxyhydrogen; tossing; productive; lustral; coral; powerful; imagined; internal; ceaseless; roaring; unchanging; unimprisoned; silver; gigantic; lustrous.

verbs

burst into—; deliver up to—; dim—; extinguish—; feed—; kindle—; spout—; spray with—; —blisters; —breathes; —chars; —consumes; —crackles; —curls; —devours; —flickers; —hovers over; —leaps; —licks; —overcomes; —plays; —rages; —ravages; —roars; —spreads; —spurts; —subdues; —subsides; —trembles; wanes, —wavers.
(See fire, blaze.)

FLAME (v)

adverbs

gorgeously; vividly; lambently; spiritually; sacrificially; ruddily; dartingly; writhingly; amorously; inextinguishably; unquenchably; sullenly; wrathfully; furiously; mountingly; ceaselessly; lustrously.
(See blaze, burn.)

FLANK

adjectives

bleeding; belathered; vertical; universal; monstrous; cavernous; bulging; heaving; towered.

FLANNEL

adjectives

spotless; tawdry; immaculate; easily-cleaned; rough.

FLAP (v)

adverbs

aimlessly; incessantly; irritatingly; monotonously; lustily; carelessly; impotently; characteristically.
(See beat, flutter, quiver.)

FLARE (v)

adverbs

vividly; repeatedly; luminously; torridly; heatedly; destructively; celestially; ethereally; balefully; blindingly; luridly.
(See flicker, dazzle, blaze.)

adjectives

incessant; vicious; simultaneous (pl); continual (pl); temporary; vivid; rapid; illuminating; serpentine; forked; lurid; brilliant; sardonic; momentary; fiery; intellectual; blinding; deafening; free; intolerable; luminous; long-lingering; quick; eager; impetuous; sulphurous; flambeaux; electric; astonishing; meteoric; rhythmic; quivering; kaleidoscopic; sublime; downward; opalescent; white; clean-cut; fitful.

verbs

create—; criticize—; develop into—; disclose—; display—; fire—; produce—; rebound in—; repeat—; ridicule—; shoot—; strike with—; wait for—; —appears; —arouses; —astounds; —attracts; —blazes; —bursts; —directs; —displays; —disturbs; —exposes; —flares; —flaunts; —flouts; —gleams; —ignites; —illumines; —indicates; —occurs; —passes over; —relinquishes; —reveals; —signals; —spurts; —vanishes; —violates.

(See blaze, gleam.)

FLASH (v)

adverbs

briefly; brilliantly; gloriously; vindictively; instantaneously; irresistibly; fiercely; restlessly; intermittently; radiantly; lambently; simultaneously; serpentinely; luridly; electrically; meteorically; kaleidoscopically; opalescently; fitfully.

(See sparkle, gleam.)

FLASH-LIGHT

verbs

douse (colloq.)—; employ—; necessitate—; replenish—; resort to—; supply—; —beams; —blinks; —brightens; —dazzles; —exposes; —flickers; —floods; —glares; —glimmers; —guides; —illuminates; —reflects; —reveals; —shines; —spots; —uncovers.

(See light.)

FLASH-LIGHT (*photography*)

verbs

anticipate—; ban—s; bar—s; blink at—; conceal—; employ—; guard against—; jump at—; permit—; pose for—; protect from—; refuse—; —enrages; —explodes; —illumines; —interrupts; —irritates; —pops; —reveals; —scares; —startles; —surprises.

(See flash.)

adverbs

pretentiously; gaudily; garishly; flauntingly; daringly; highly; wonderfully; cheaply; grossly; coarsely; attractively; ornately; smartly; pompously; gorgeously; indecorously; unbecomingly; rudely; provincially; outlandishly; fantastically; grotesquely; dreadfully; horribly.

FLASK

adjectives

supernal; primitive; tapering; liquor; pocket-size.

FLAT

adverbs

monotonously; tiresomely; vapidly; disagreeably; invariably; intolerably; uninterestingly; wearily; tediously; endlessly.

FLATS

adjectives

dangerous; vile; sumptuous; inhospitable; cluttered; crowded; sewage-polluted; fertile; streaming; occidental; windowed; various; tenement; lurid.

FLATTER (v)

adverbs

obsequiously; fondly; grossly; hugely; slavishly; unduly; artfully; immeasurably; prettily; cunningly; adeptly; adroitly; deftly; coyly; treacherously; deceptively; coarsely; egregiously; sleekly; fatuously; expertly.

(See compliment, praise.)

FLATTERED

adverbs

happily; blushingly; pleasantly; rosily; smilingly; highly; pleasingly; delightfully; convivially; excitedly; jubilantly; artlessly; inordinately; uncommonly.

FLATTERER

adjectives

impudent; cunning; defective; adept; adroit.

FLATTERY

adjectives

coarse; temporizing; sordid; graceful; innumerable (pl); gross; egregious; judicious; servile; friendly; unconscious; grateful; sleek; supple; dulcet; cautious; fatal; infinite; verbal; blazoned; expert; delicate; commonplace.

verbs

abhor—; accept—; addict to—; conceal with
—; court—; detest—; endure—; expand
under—; fall for—; feed with—; fool by—;
savor of—; steel to—; succumb to—; thick-
en with—; withstand—; yield to—; —deceives; —soothes; —tricks.

(See adulation.)

FLAUNT (v)

adverbs

arrogantly; insultingly; saucily; pertly; exasperatingly; tantalizingly; maliciously;
subtly; coyly; mortifyingly.

(See parade, show.)

FLAVOR

verbs

acclaim—; adulterate—; affect—; create—;
detect—; dislike—; extract—; marvel at—;
mask—; protect—; retain—; scent—; smell
—; —appetizes; —burns out; —delights; —
dies; —rivals; —stales.

(See taste, savor.)

FLAVOR (v)

adverbs

delectably; delicately; exotically; appetizingly; pungently; inimitably; matchlessly;
characteristically; originally; temptingly;
palatably; exhilaratingly; toothsomely; incomparably.

(See season, taste.)

FLAVORING

verbs

add—; dislike—; employ—; impart—; inject—; lack—; mix with—; necessitate—;
savor—; season with—; select—; spice with
—; taste—; try—; —enhances; —flatters;
—pleases; —stings; —teases.

(See extract, spice, etc.)

FLAVORS

adjectives

marvelous; exotic; luscious; appetizing;
oleaginous; pleasant; juicy; spirited; unapproachable; delicate; aristocratic; pungent;
inimitable; distinctive; exclusive; minty;
matchless; characteristic; delicious; intellectual; imaginative; full-bodied; treacherous;
international; original; satisfying; grand;
extra-fresh; odorous; acrid; individual;
abominable; faint; infused; sublime; palatable; tender; supreme; exhilarating; delicious; native; tempting; subtle; apparent;
mellow; reminiscent; unique; mild; tangy;

toothsome; peculiar; balanced; smoky; dry;
hearty; popular; unusual; fine; criminal;
appetizing; old-time; incomparable; clinging.

FLAW

adjectives

foul; inherent; blemishing; inscrutable; apparent; age-old; inherited.

verbs

accept—; conceal—; consider—; constitute
—; detect—; develop—; discern—; discover
—; eradicate—; exempt from—; free from
—; guard against—; hide—; jade with—s;
overcome—; —blemishes; —mars; irons out
—.

(See defect, blemish, imperfection, fault,
crack.)

FLAWLESS

adverbs

perfectly; incredibly; marvelously; utterly;
unbelievably; delicately; simply; tastefully;
chastely; obviously; superbly; splendidly;
absolutely; technically; ineffably; completely; comparatively; exquisitely; matchlessly;
artistically.

FLEE (v)

adverbs

incontinently; instinctively; peremptorily;
precipitately; timorously; tremulously; impetuously.

(See run, abandon.)

FLEECE

adjectives

delicate; silky; plenteous; warm.

FLEECY

adverbs

warmly; softly; comfortingly; comfortably;
incredibly; genuinely; agreeably; pleasantly; tenderly; sleekly; smoothly; shaggily;
delightfully; snugly; delicately.

FLEET

verbs

antiquate—; assemble—; assign to—; command—; dispatch—; expand—; increase—;
mobilize—; observe—; order—; recondition
—; —anchors; —blockades; —celebrates;
—cruises; —exhibits; —files in; —journeys;

—migrates; —navigates; —passes; —performs; —plies; —sails; —shifts; —ships; —speeds; —travels.

(See squadron, navy.)

adverbs

incredibly; nimbly; gracefully; marvelously; splendidly; remarkably; expeditiously; smartly; actively; lightly; mercurially; inordinately; unwontedly; naturally; unusually; surprisingly; amazingly; trippingly.

FLEETING

adverbs

impermanently; evanescently; mortally; transiently; transitorily; perishably; quickly; temporally; illusively; elusively; sadly; unhappily; ephemerally; pitifully; terribly.

FLEETNESS

adjectives

sleek; eager; easy; unapproachable; swift.

FLEETS

adjectives

allied; provisional; myriad; trade; mimic; royal; confederate; formidable; cumbrous; grim; multitudinous; death-dealing.

FLESH

adjectives

mortifying; famished; fever-stricken; palatable; cumbrous; festering; quivering; lank; unsavory; overroasted; flower-tinted; soft; pink; sun-bronzed; ivory; pale; waxen; bruised; shuddering; swollen; dusty; exhausted; putrefying; carrion; miserable; half-cooked; pierced; mad; attractive; common; living; sweet; tender; transfigured; dead; redundant; yielding; warm; lumpy; scalded; mangled; tainted; wrinkled; ample; muscular; decrepit; quaky; firm; human; crawling; swooping; swelling; slippery; sensitive; blooming; decaying; rebellious; seraphic; gangrenous; overwearied; quick; aching; adhering; mutinous; torn; elaborate; dressed; sinful; avaricious.

verbs

accumulate—; chafe—; char—; crucify—; denounce—; derive from—; flavor—; gain —; gather—; grind—; inject into—; market —; mutilate—; produce—; reduce—; waste —.

(See meat, fat.)

FLESHY

adverbs

mortifyingly; cumbrously; comfortably; burdensomely; embarrassingly; dreadfully; inordinately; dangerously; amiably; miserably; wretchedly; clumsily; awkwardly; strangely; warmly; stockily; alarmingly; heavily; hideously; shockingly; wholesomely; merrily; nonchalantly; cheerfully.

FLEXIBLE

adverbs

conveniently; adaptably; suitably; appropriately; diplomatically; agreeably; pliantly; tractably; complaisantly; affably; pleasantly; indulgently; easily; manageably; smoothly; fortunately; properly.

FLICKER

adjectives

curious; small; tiny; rapid; abrupt; unseen.

verbs

emit—; observe—; reduce to—; repeat—; shake with—; vibrate in—; —annoys; — dies out; —disturbs; —flames; —mottles; — remains; —warms; —warns; —wavers.

(See light.)

FLICKER (v)

adverbs

inscrutably; involuntarily; fitfully; rapidly; incessantly; repeatedly; mysteriously; interminably.

(See flutter, waver.)

FLIER

verbs

employ—; examine—; exhaust—; inform—; license—; overtake—; strain—; test—; — achieves; —accomplishes; —ascends; —attempts; —charts; —circles; —controls; — descends; —dips; —endures; —lands; — loops; —manipulates; —navigates; —operates; —perceives; —pilots; —somersaults; —speeds; —takes off; —transports; — zooms.

(See aviator, aeroplane.)

FLIES

adjectives

lazy; insolent; gilded; unfortunate; shrivelled; swarming; glittering; incautious; stinging; vicious; bothersome.

FLIGHT

adjectives

pattering; comely; droning; fagging; impetuous; wheeling; gay; labored-looking; ceaseless; joyous; temporary; cankerous; vehement; tireless; unreturning; bold; poetic; rhythmic; self-same; erratic; hysterical; epochal; prolonged; intertwined; nuptial; mocking; impeded; principal; common; angry; unjust; disguising; pretended; ignominious; airy; troublesome; perceptible; humanitarian; risky; mediocre; freshening; industrious; frolic; promiscuous; illuminated; tremendous; precipitate; untried; aery; lagging; filmy; fleeting; rapturous; fearful; perilous; howling; ambitious; imperial; interminable; ponderous; winding; higher; unwearied; intrepid; hurried; undulating; unbounded; upward-hovering; never-ending; impudent; swift; rickety; tremulous; transitory; wide; worn; persistent; cloistered; cowardly; voluptuous; orderly; annual; unsustained; measureless; distant.

verbs

accomplish—; accustom to—; attempt—; depart in—; drop in—; hasten in—; impede —; lose in—; mount in—; move to—; observe—; plan—; pursue in—; record—; resume—; retreat in—; sally forth in—; scatter—; soar in—; witness—; —exhausts; —fails.

(See journey, trip.)

FLIGHTY

adverbs

comically; wantonly; cheerfully; happily; merrily; charmingly; vexatiously; curiously; deliriously; strangely; oddly; queerly; alarmingly; dangerously; insanely; whimsically; wildly; capriciously; fantastically; lightly; drunkenly; heedlessly; thoughtlessly; carelessly; inadvertently; remarkably; utterly.

FLIMSY

adverbs

absurdly; airily; vaguely; tenuously; unreasonably; nonsensically; foolishly; slightly; ridiculously; miserably; wretchedly; contemptibly; pitifully; unmanageably; unserviceably; objectionably.

FLING

adjectives

overhand; disdainful; senseless; disjointed; surreptitious; ill-natured.

FLING (v)

adverbs

mechanically; dramatically; fiercely; jauntily; simultaneously; impetuously; violently; harshly; carelessly; savagely; tauntingly; disdainfully; ill-naturedly; contemptuously; extravagantly.

(See hurl, cast.)

FLINTS

adjectives

stubborn; clattering; brittle; steely.

FLIPPANCY

adjectives

extravagant; friendly; verbal; studied; marked; open; definite; disgusting.

FLIPPANT

adverbs

impertinently; carelessly; insouciantly; audaciously; daringly; brazenly; charmingly; attractively; giddily; heedlessly; jauntily; saucily; unblushingly; shamelessly; wantonly; unduly; disrespectfully; comically; inappropriately; unbecomingly; inopportunely; youthfully; glibly; smartly; inconsiderately; sacrilegiously; terribly.

FLIRT

adjectives

saucy; harmless; wild.

FLIRT (v)

adverbs

blatantly; shamelessly; saucily; wildly; outrageously; unconscionably; boldly; coyly; shyly; immodestly; voluptuously; arduously; impassionedly; trivially; desultorily.

(See coquette, love.)

FLIRTATION

adjectives

sly; anonymous; literary; unworthy; miserable; pleasant; hit-and-run; trivial; desultory; detached; discreet; swift; arduous; meaningful; mere; summer; unimpassioned.

verbs

arouse—; arrest—; cease—; coach—; commit—; continue—; delight in—; express in —; interrupt—; overlook—; recount—; regard as—; renew—; school in—; tease in —; —deceives; —excites; —grows; —inspires; —invites; —involves; —stimulates.

adverbs

innocently; harmlessly; amusingly; designedly; resolutely; definitely; systematically; assiduously; sedulously; charmingly; noticeably; curiously; oddly; habitually; seductively; irresistibly; coquettishly; philanderingly; merrily; openly; obviously; palpably; whimsically; engagingly.

FLIT (v)

adverbs

errantly; feverishly; vaguely; joyously; tantalizingly; momentarily; casually; ephemerally; temporarily.

(See flutter, fly.)

FLOAT (v)

adverbs

nebulously; airily; buoyantly; lazily; gracefully; listlessly; majestically; drowsily; delicately; miraculously; gorgeously; lumberingly; glitteringly.

(See move, billow, creep, drift, hover.)

FLOATS

adjectives

gossamer; lumbering; horse-drawn; glittering; beautiful; papier-mache; river; gorgeous; glorious.

FLOCK

adjectives

close-pinned; golden; crowding; divided; trembling; scattered; endless; fleecy; blood-bought; patriarchal; afflicted; nibbling; snowy; browsing; timorous; homeward; clustering; healthful; pictorial; benighted.

verbs

appeal to—; call on—; care for—; guide—; journey in—; manage—; muster—; preach to—; supervise—; travel in—; —assembles; —congregates; —flees; —gathers; —journeys; —occupies; —supports; —swarms.

(See pack, group, herd, congregation.)

FLOCK (v)

adverbs

protectively; reposefully; timorously; clusteringly; pictorially; benightedly; habitually; characteristically; seasonally.

(See assemble, crowd.)

adjectives

intoxicating; impetuous; sluggish; vitreous; soaking; mighty; torrential; creeping; short-lived; devastating; human; babbling; untamable; spring; savory; copious; shoreless; seething; passing; brackish; fearful; crystal; maddened; foaming; phenomenal; raging; steaming; shining; redundant; weltering; unfathomable; shaded; disastrous; shallow; uncurling; surging; horned; isle-fretted; moon-lit; breaking; all-destroying; advancing; overflowing; post-glacial; drenching; shedding; glowing; turbid; sparkling; storied; wondrous; full; eternal; main; wasteful; lashing; fiery; glassy; urgent; tranquil; azure; furious; unbroken; frigid; ice-imprisoned; tropical; roaring; all-engulfing; gathering; clearest; fretful; unwelcome; poured-out; eddying; vaporous; theoretic; wandering; widespread.

verbs

abate—; ameliorate—; check—; dam—; guard against—s; halt—; mitigate—; recoil from—; stem—; swirl with—; unloose—; —cripples; —devastates; —inundates; —overwhelms; —recedes; —submerges; —sweeps away.

(See deluge.)

FLOOD (v)

adverbs

fatally; partially; impetuously; torrentially; devastatingly; untamably; copiously; seethingly; foamingly; phenomenally; ragingly; disastrously; drenchingly; sparklingly; furiously; roaringly; eddyingly.

(See overflow, submerge, drench.)

FLOOR

adjectives

watery; dark-stained; polished; topmost; unpretentious; sanded; desolate; glassy; olive; opalescent; light; stained; glittering; gleaming; seedy; oaken; translucent; sinking; mosaic; drafty; musty; gritted; amethystine; spotless; desert-yellow; charred; cloudy; slimy; draughty; well-swept; untrodden; mirrored; clammy; brazen; tremulous; expansive; diamond-paved; planet-powered; dilapidated; brick; herbless; carpetless; conscious; vaster; threshing; blazing; shining; scholastic; marble; iron-bound; tessellated; tiled.

verbs

board—; cement—; crowd—; inlay—; joist —; lay—; litter—; nail to—; polish—; rest on—; root to—; scrape—; shellac—; slip on—; splinter—; strew—; swab—; tread on —; varnish—; warp—; wax—; —collapses; —creaks; —rots; —sags; —supports.

(See surface, platform.)

FLORID

adverbs

ruddily; uncommonly; dangerously; alarmingly; healthily; intensely; freshly; blowzily; warmly; wholesomely; unusually; remarkably; oddly; habitually; unwontedly; naturally.

FLOUNDER (v)

adverbs

bewilderingly; haphazardly; awkwardly; comically; clumsily; helplessly; wretchedly.

(See stumble, struggle.)

FLOUNDERING

adjectives

haphazard; ignoble; awkward; laughable.

FLOUR

adjectives

ill-mixed; unadulterated; unbolted; bleached.

verbs

bag—; barrel—; bin—; bleach—; brush off —; cover with—; employ—; grade—; grind into—; manufacture—; mill—; mix with—; obtain—; pulverize into—; reduce to—; select—; sift—; sprinkle—; triturate into—; —dusts; —whitens.

(See cereal, powder.)

FLOURISH

adjectives

ornamental; periodic; sudden; joyous; eloquent; graceful; festive; indignant; brazen.

FLOURISH (v)

adverbs

chiefly; luxuriously; gloriously; vigorously; periodically; gracefully; festively; brazenly; heartily; boisterously.

(See thrive.)

FLOURISHING

adverbs

highly; uncommonly; remarkably; prosperously; successfully;· sturdily; steadily; in-

dubitably; certainly; materially; apparently; evidently; manifestly; splendidly; magnificently; obviously; fortunately; luckily; deservedly; extremely.

FLOUT

adjectives

wounding; brash; resounding.

FLOW

adjectives

inward; sonorous; cheerful; increasing; intermitting; eternal; long-accustomed; dual; lurid; spontaneous; irrepressible; beneficent; sluggish; restless; maladjusted; seething; social; dolorous; endless; lateral; never-ending; excessive; constant; boisterous; agreeable; continuous; metrical; wavy; taintless; melodious; uneventful; quiescent; exuberant; imaginative; babbling; enclasping; incessant; gracious; balanced; rhetorical; unceasing; rippling; perpetual; lyrical; literary; everlasting.

verbs

accelerate—; bar—; check—; control—; dam—; diminish—; direct—; increase—; induce—; lessen—; prevent—; produce—; re-establish—; reiterate—; restrain—; still —; stimulate—; —advances; —ceases; —progresses.

(See stream, current, outpouring, fluency, abundance.)

FLOW (v)

adverbs

diffusely; noiselessly; divergently; tortuously; incessantly; lazily; mutely; sluggishly; inevitably; serenely; spontaneously; vehemently; placidly; seethingly; melodiously; quiescently; babblingly; rhetorically; perpetually; lyrically.

(See move, pass, float.)

FLOWER

verbs

arrange—s; array—s; awaken—s; bear—s; blanket with—s; crush—; cultivate—s; cull —s; fertilize—s; gather—s; landscape with —s; pluck—; press—; putter among—s; strew with—s; surround with—s; trample —; —s beckon; —s bob; —s cascade; —s cluster; —droops; —s drink in; —emerges; —fades; —nods; —ravishes; —shrivels; —springs up; —sways in the breeze; —unfolds; —withers; —waves.

(See blossom, plant, rose, lily, etc.)

FLOWER (v)

adverbs

resplendently; fragrantly; consummately; opulently; transiently; garishly; pendulously; wantonly; fugitively; vernally; deathlessly; luxuriantly; autumnally; vernally. (See blossom, bloom.)

FLOWERS

adjectives

fragrant; spicy; graven; inwrought; constellated; starry; drooping; withering; consummate; tender; venturesome; wasted; amassing; wave-reflected; hybrid; thirsting; flamelike; wilting; carven; modest; spangled; variable; tissued; varicolored; opulent; delicate; pearling; transient; venomous; exotic; shy; climbing; homely; balmy; bewailing; garish; budding; laughing; uncropped; prim; thriving; fresh; expanded; dewy; perishable; sculptured; sweet; maiden; transitory; unfolding; unpretentious; satisfactory; pendulous; mystic-passion; wanton; fugitive; brilliant; rootless; storm-marred; busy; wilted; unthroned; immeasurable; infinite; scattering; manifold; sweet-tipped; festal; precious; thorny; summer-swelling; gazing; fair-named; visionary; indomitable; sanguine; waxen; multicolored; richly-colored; brightly-hued; frost-white; gorgeous; faded; fragile; printless; clustering; choicest; curious; crocus; wayside; artificial; unfolded; beauteous; tinted; tributary; achromatous; welcome; air-sown; mysterious; glowing; helpless; sweet-smelling; vernal; fullest; big; gallant; splashy; shaded; deathless; moisture-loving; classic; new-bloomed; unblown; heaven-plated; soft-breathing; incense-mingling; snow-white; changing; scented; meanest; fairest; pressed; foolproof; heartier; hand-planted; unperishing; promiscuous; luxuriant; earthly; autumnal; votive; ligulate; new-sprung; fantastic; torn; dissimilar; saffron; silvery; languishing; thread-hung; barren; uncourted; flourishing; enameled; discriminating; cleftborn; belated; sculptured; innocent; unconscious; prolific; resting; crimson-petalled; woodland; departed; chief; goodly; angel-missioned; breathing; stately; golden-hearted; overflowing; wordlike.

FLOWERY

adverbs

absurdly; ridiculously; bombastically; pompously; egotistically; importantly; blatantly; ornately; elaborately; ludicrously; bumptiously; sonorously; sententiously; egregiously; outlandishly; fantastically; inordinately; senselessly; preposterously; extravagantly.

FLUCTUATE (v)

adverbs

feverishly; violently; transiently; perceptibly; normally; cyclically; seasonally; economically. (See waver, vary.)

FLUCTUATION

adjectives

violent; silken; alternate; transient; considerable.

FLUENCY

adjectives

extreme; rare; deplorable; inexhaustible; sweet; inimitable; impressive; illimitable.

verbs

acquire—; administer with—; declaim with —; deliver with—; discharge with—; dispatch with—; emit—; exhibit—; express with—; flow with—; increase—; orate with —; pen with—; proceed with—; promote—; recite with—. (See ease.)

FLUENT

adverbs

amazingly; surprisingly; admirably; consistently; enviably; gracefully; readily; naturally; habitually; easily; felicitously; rhythmically; delightfully; wonderfully; strikingly; splendidly; eloquently; impressively.

FLUFFY

adverbs

delightfully; delicately; deliciously; warmly; softly; smoothly; remarkably; surprisingly; correctly; comfortably; comfortingly; deeply; amazingly; genuinely; uncommonly; extremely; distinctly; completely; lightly.

FLUID

adjectives

innumerable (pl); life-giving; gummy; intoxicating; subtle; vapid; sizy; scarce; lacteal; germinating; dark-hued; amber-colored; opaque; overabundant; turbid; electric; illusive; bleaching; unwholesome; precious; drinkable; vital; inky; incompressible; ethereal.

verbs

absorb—; consume—; discharge—; drain—; draw off—; effuse—; employ—; expel—; exude—; generate—; inject—; introduce—; secrete—; spill—; tap—; —circulates; —stains.

(See liquid, liquor, gas.)

FLUIDITY

adjectives

noticeable; linguistic; remarkable.

FLURRY

adjectives

undeniable; smiling; spiteful; abortive; pinwheel; angry.

FLUSH

adjectives

hectic; bloomy; unwonted; happy; momentary; blackish; brick-red; dull-red; fiery; gentle; helpless; fading; rosy; mahogany; perceptible; embarrassed; uneasy; novel; irritated; delicate; angry.

verbs

arouse—; cover with—; emit—; glow with —; overcome—; produce—; provoke—; redden into—; robe with—; subdue—; suffuse with—; —allures; —animates; —ebbs; —exasperates; —mantles; —overspreads; —throbs; —veils.

(See glow, blush, excitement, bloom.)

FLUSH (v)

adverbs

painfully; faintly; violently; delicately; miserably; singularly; passionately; transparently; hectically; unwontedly; rosily; perceptibly; embarrassingly; angrily.

(See blush, glow, thrill.)

FLUSHED

adverbs

extremely; drunkenly; feverishly; excitedly; apoplectically; alarmingly; dangerously; significantly; shyly; embarrassingly; ruddily; rosily; violently; angrily; furiously; madly; insanely; terribly; dreadfully; inordinately; frightfully; unnaturally; unusually.

FLUSTERED

adverbs

nervously; awkwardly; clumsily; significantly; helplessly; pitifully; weakly; terribly; agitatedly; hopelessly; ineptly; distractedly; distressingly; comically; absurdly; unreasonably; distinctly; undoubtedly; unwontedly; merrily; gloriously; drunkenly; tipsily.

FLUTE

adjectives

meditative; pastoral; oaten; perpendicular; enchanted; breathing.

verbs

dance to—; employ—; finger—; ornament —; pipe—; pitch—; practise on—; render on—; scale—; sound—; tootle on—; transpose on—; —blends; —cheers; —complains; —enraptures; —harmonizes; —shrills; —utters; —whines; —whistles.

FLUTTER

adjectives

unconscious; faint; indescribable; continual; perpetual; gay; sleek.

FLUTTER (v)

adverbs

recurrently; lightly; tremulously; gently; wantonly; ominously; convulsively; persistently; gaily; indescribably

(See tremble, fluctuate.)

FLY

adjectives

aggressive; officious; untrapped; pestering; stuttering; intolerable.

verbs

abandon to—ies; bar—ies; guard from—ies; harbor—ies; protect from—ies; screen off —ies; torture with—ies; —ies breed; —buzzes; —ies crawl; —drones; —glitters; —ies infest; —lays eggs; —lights on; —plagues; —settles; —torments; —ies swarm.

(See insect.)

FLY (v)

adverbs

professionally; gracefully; undauntedly; breath-takingly; basely; fantastically; cheerily; intrepidly; instinctively; precipitately; characteristically; swiftly; unerringly.

(See soar, flee.)

FLYER

adjectives

feathered; unsuccessful; dare-devil; intrepid; courageous; fearless; inimitable; daring; great; world-wide; seasoned; professional; careful; negligent; lawless; nerveless.

FOAM

adjectives
tainted; snow-soft; circumambient; ocean; fantastic; dashing; driven; creamy; panting; loose; wasteful; pale; fleet; lacteal; rainbow-colored; sea; rolling; fragile; salt; sweet; flamelike; delicious; wind-tossed; yeasty; fleecy; border; crested; carded; moonlit; seething; springtide; surging; uneasy; luminous; enchanted; twinkling; cruel; crawling; constellated; barren; sparkling; wild.

verbs
aggregate—; beat to—; boil to—; break into —; cover with—; crest with—; emit—; ferment—; fill with—; fleck with—; toss off—; —bubbles; —drips off; —effervesces; —floats; —froths; —gurgles; —issues from; —reams; —scuds; —smothers; —streaks; —washes.
(See froth.)

FOCUS

adjectives
constant; sharp; blurred; careful; precise; accurate.

FOCUS (*v*)

adverbs
sharply; precisely; accurately; deftly; skillfully; blurredly; scientifically; exactly.
(See concentrate, adjust.)

FOE

adjectives
prostrate; headless; murderous; mortal; prejudiced; vanquished; imaginary; spectral; intestinal; foreign; malicious; private; prevailing; ruthless; fierce; inveterate; exhausted; ghastly; remorseless; embodied; overweening; fallen; formidable; mailed; bigoted; blushing; contemptible; sensuous; inferior; daring; wily; ribald; wicked; sternest; unseen; countless (pl); implacable; victorious; ferocious; bitter; monstrous; invading; immortal; inexorable; mental; invisible; effective; heartless; treacherous; insolent; despicable; ubiquitous; stubborn; blaspheming; deadliest; cunning; contending; faint; blood-seeking; hereditary; lurking; bitterest; over-confident; one-time; hellish; persistent; dark; encircled; external; mocking; unexpected; savage; alert; hostile; ironclad; captured; defeated; cowering; principal; dastardly.

verbs
curse—; defy—; denounce—; disarm—; discover—; dislodge—; embolden—; grapple with—; halt—; inflame—; inflict on—; inveigh against—; overwhelm—; persecute—; puzzle—; reconcile—; subdue—; vanquish —; —advances; —approaches; —assaults; —attacks; —falls; —looms up; —strikes.
(See enemy, adversary, opponent, antagonist.)

FOG

adjectives
transparent; antarctic; autumnal; dank; treacherous; opalescent; thick; black; rolling; gray; heavy; white; pea-soup; dense; chill; contagious; low-lying; relentless; increasing; germ-laden; midsummer; silent; drooping; blinding; impenetrable; miasmal; curling; dismal; decided; wall-like; opaque; blanketing; heartless.

verbs
cut—; dispel—; disperse—; dissipate—; emerge from—; fathom—; grope in—; penetrate—; —abates; —blankets; —clears; —creeps up; —devours; —fades; —lifts; —settles on; —swallows up; —wraps around.
(See mist, haze, darkness.)

FOGGY

adverbs
mysteriously; unluckily; unfortunately; thickly; slightly; lightly; strangely; alarmingly; fearfully; dangerously; frightfully; impossibly; darkly; impenetrably; muddily; hazily; vaporously; wetly; mistily; nebulously; murkily; uncommonly; opaquely.

FOIBLE

adjectives
harmless; amiable; pitiable; laughable; pleasant; cheery; understandable.

verbs
acknowledge—; correct—; cure of—; detect —; disclose—; discover—; entail—; expose—; inherit—; observe—; overcome—; perceive—; produce—; resent—; reveal—; ridicule—; screen—; tempt—; —appears; —arises; —hinders; —irritates; —results.
(See fault, failing, weakness, defect, frailty.)

FOIL

adjectives
glistening; glittering; gleaming; sharp; glinting; swift.

adjectives
enchanting; mazy; misty; snapping; secret; drowsy; brazen; caressing; snowy; floating; dimpled; thick; amorous; effeminate; ample; vaporous; voluminous; wind-flowing; loosened; deep-shadowed; clammy; becoming; sweeping; glistening; filmy; radiant; horizontal; fatal; strangling; gold-fringed; overhanging; graceful; meaningless; pinching; shivering; unapproachable.

FOLD (v)

adverbs
tensely; neatly; unconsciously; ostentatiously; quaintly; placidly; threateningly; wearily; voluminously; tenderly.
(See embrace, clasp.)

FOLDER

adjectives
descriptive; illustrated; well-printed; lucid; advertising.

verbs
arrange in—; assemble in—; attach to—; collect in—; destroy—; distribute—s; go through—; lodge in—; pass out—s; place in—; pore over—; prepare—; preserve in —; pull from—; refer to—; search in—; store in—; —advertises; —contains; —discloses.
(See catalogue, record.)

FOLIAGE

adjectives
cloudy; profuse; scattering; sapless; admirable; gracious; feathered; fresh; brilliant; luxuriant; delicate; evanescent; tropical; polished; gorgeous; golden; bright; tinted; silvery; bluish-gray; tender; scarlet; autumnal; shining; clustering; wasted; observable; sunny; dense; colored; fiery; blunt; curly; knotted; entangled; massive; dropping; ruddy; fresh; rustling; scant; softened; umbrageous; dying; intervening; voluminous; graceful; ornamental; protecting; overhanging; disease-resistant; impenetrable; screening; glossy.

verbs
admire—; bear—; behold—; decorate with —; don—; drench—; refresh—; shed—; shower—; sprout—; welcome—; yield—; —abounds; —adorns; —appears; —bathes; —blooms; —dies; —rustles; —shadows; —surrounds; —trembles.
(See leaves.)

adjectives
illuminated; ponderous; rare; inestimable; unhandy.

FOLK

adjectives
quick-witted; trivial; cross-tempered; quarrelsome; finical; guileful; guarded; suspicious; anxious; furtive; purposeful; true-hearted; famished; complacent; eavesdropping; ordinary; old-fashioned; showy; shadowy; placid; unexcitable; wee; shepherd; pert; novelty-loving; scribbling; fashionable; timorous; humble; hard-working; religious; peaceful; indigenous; unwieldy; slow; heavy; pale; prosperous; happy; furtive; cunning; hysterical; well-mannered; reaping; invincible; marooned; congenial; worthy; bourgeois; plain.

FOLKS

verbs
amuse—; enjoy—; please—; study—; visit —; —abide by; —adhere to; —admit; — cherish; —cleave to; —cling to; —congregate; —flourish; —follow; —frolic; —gambol; —gather; —inherit; —instil; —persevere; —resent; —revel.
(See people, nation, family, relatives.)

FOLLOW (v)

adverbs
instinctively; abjectly; trustfully; inevitably; irresistibly; reverently; wistfully; obsequiously; relentlessly; heedlessly; slavishly; reluctantly; unswervingly; gallantly; mechanically; traditionally; dutifully; dumbly; placidly; mutely; logically; religiously; grudgingly; undeviatingly; automatically; implicitly; doggedly; devoutly; diligently; sedulously.
(See chase, pursue.)

FOLLOWER

verbs
attract—s; beget—s; beguile—; conduct—; dictate to—; direct—; exhort—; fascinate —; gather—s; goad—; instruct—; retain—; secure—s; spurn—s; woo—s; —accepts; — accompanies; —admires; —assists; —imitates; —obeys; —practises; —s preserve; —serves.
(See disciple.)

FOLLOWERS

adjectives

heterogeneous; heretical; despairing; immediate; unruly; conservative; obsequious; faithful; diffident; egregious; wayworn; insuperable; sincerest; discontented; favorite; influential; scattered; stout-hearted; deluded.

FOLLOWING

adjectives

prodigious; tremendous; overbearing; unnatural; popular; huge; national; inspired.

verbs

guide—; instruct—; retain—; secure—; spurn—; whip up—; —adheres; —attends; —disbands; —pursues.
(See follower.)

FOLLY

adjectives

sheer; ludicrous; violent; prostrate; wilful; gratuitous; vain; shouting; stupendous; industrious; crowning; derogatory; egregious; serious; rash; present; deplorable; superfluous; sordid; idiotical; capricious; incurable; human; sentimental; disastrous; daring; amiable; pernicious; extreme; enormous; impious; obvious; ingrained; youthful (pl); amorous; harmless; pretty; wild; glaring; covert; pretentious; incredible; ridiculous; countless (pl); flagrant; repudiated; irritating; repented; repeated; absurd; intermittent (pl).

verbs

accuse of—; balk at—of; commit to—; decry—; deplore—; discern—; emancipate from—; fall into—; flatter into—; guard against—; lure into—; mitigate—; regret —; ridicule—; rue—; run after—ies; scorn —; uncover—; vex with—; work—.
(See foolishness, indiscretion, absurdity, infatuation.)

FOMENTATIONS

adjectives

copious; generous; applied; restful; unexpected.

FOND

adverbs

foolishly; unutterably; inordinately; infatuatedly; undyingly; obsequiously; genuinely; unwontedly; particularly; remarkably; childishly; extremely; tenderly; mawkish-

ly; warmly; filially; dutifully; enthusiastically; intensely; spasmodically; ludicrously; demonstratively; temperately; tempestuously; gratefully; impulsively; respectfully; passionately; sincerely; beautifully; frankly; proudly; violently; sentimentally; deeply; heart-warmingly; gratifyingly; temperately; innately; essentially; confessedly; ridiculously; ostentatiously; understandably; justly; devotedly; incongruously; professedly; obviously; palpably.

FONDNESS

adjectives

thoughtful; foolish; maternal; exaggerated; inordinate; unutterable; inbred; infatuated; undying; obsequious; undiscriminating; genuine; unwonted; particular; remarkable; regal; evident; childish; solicitous; usual; extreme; gruesome; hoarded; faithful; unusual; tender; mawkish; precocious.

FOOD

adjectives

unwholesome; essential; wholesome; synthetic; spiritual; health; celestial; unsating; best; marvelous; intellectual; digestible; exceptional; repulsive; abundant; nutritious; natural; precious; unscrupulous; untasted; leathery; toothsome; heedful; unusual; attractive; delicious; inferior; unsavory; highly-spiced; concentrated; smoking; inedible; nectar; canned; adulterated; medicinal; palatable; enjoyable; protective; satisfying; superb; substantial; desirable; piscatorial; frosted; frozen; tonic; out-of-season; obnoxious; packaged; non-fattening; tempting; accustomed; rejuvenating; cheapest; sharp-tasting; execrable; inadequate; concentrated; well-cooked; raw; fundamental; automatic; elaborate; ambrosial; plenteous; delectable; scanty; superb; assimilated; vitalizing; luscious; world-famous; choice; dainty; tasty; good; fine; appetizing; excellent; splendid; inspired; insufficient.

verbs

absorb—; accumulate—; anoint—; assimilate—; bolt—; brown—; consume—; contaminate—; convey—; crave—; deprive of —; devitalize—; dilute—; dispense—; dole out—; expel—; flavor—; forage for—; freight—; masticate—; munch—; order—; partake of—; peptonize—; predigest—; prescribe—; puke—; purvey—; ration—; refine—; requisition—; restrict—; season—; shovel down—; snatch at—; sniff—; subsist on—; vomit—; withdraw—; wolf—; —agrees with; —decreases; —ferments; —irritates; —putrefies; —sustains; —upsets.

(See nourishment, nutriment, meat, bread, rations, victuals, viands, refreshments.)

FOOL

verbs
appear like—; play the—; prove oneself a —; put the—upon; remain—; ridicule—; suspect oneself—; think one a—; turn—; —apes; —beckons; —capers; —complains; —counterfeits; —disregards; —diverts; —dotes; —gambols; —ignores; —jests; —lets slip; —mistakes; —possesses; —prates; —preaches; —sidles; —mocks.

(See idiot, clown.)

FOOL (v)

adverbs
amiably; ignorantly; wantonly; pitifully; blindly; hatefully; vulgarly; tediously; clumsily; unfeelingly; ungratefully; venomously; deliberately; sportively; shallowly.

(See deceive, trick.)

FOOLERIES

adjectives
bygone; humorous; insouciant.

FOOLHARDY

adverbs
ignorantly; youthfully; boldly; ridiculously; absurdly; sadly; recklessly; fecklessly; carelessly; daringly; desperately; rashly; idiotically; preposterously; indiscreetly; extravagantly; imprudently; childishly; dangerously; terribly; senselessly.

FOOLING

adjectives
gracious; admirable; airy; flippant.

FOOLISH

adverbs
ridiculously; absurdly; ludicrously; unreasonably; insanely; extravagantly; idiotically; ineptly; inanely; irrationally; childishly; stupidly; blatantly; brainlessly; fatuously; injudiciously; rashly; simply; weakly; altogether; supremely; senselessly; fantastically; manifestly; grossly; pathetically.

FOOLISHNESS

adjectives
potent; drunken; colossal; unspeakable.

verbs
awaken—; cast aside—; confess—; convert into—; criticize—; forsake—; govern by—; grieve over—; ignore—; indicate—; persuade to—; practise—; pretend—; provide —; reprimand—; resent—; ridicule—; rue —; shape—; sneer at—; suffer for—; —amuses; —befits; —persists; —smarts; —tempts; prevent—.

(See folly, absurdity; imprudence, indiscretion.)

FOOLS

adjectives
calf-like; luckless; flatulent; simple-minded; amiable; bleating; superstitious; superannuated; ignorant; weak-minded; poor; dappled; wanton; blind; pitiful; blasted; badgering; family; dull; impractical; incapable; honest; besotted; blundering; hateful; crack-brained; veritable; tuneful; precious; misguided; puling; pale; scrawny; wretched; vulgar; allowed; frantic; proud; tedious; witty; clumsy; gullible; strait-laced; soft; dull-eyed; shallow; learned; sweeter; unfeeling; inconstant; damnable; ungrateful; hairy; accursed; motley; officious; positive; brazen; venomous; yawning; consummate; obstinate; conspicuous; fond; deliberate; contemplative; rash; patient; scoundrelly.

FOOT

adjectives
wandering; blistered; emphatic; itching; fiery; stealthy; mutilated; inaudible; noiseless; crushing; punctilious; spurning; feathered; ponderous; restless; fearful; godlike; diminutive; forgetful; cautious; unresisting; swelled; slight; slender; bounding; maladjusted; individual; tentative; struggling; cloven; careless; investigating; nimble; fairy; exquisite; shapely; tiniest; beautiful; small; bare; dangling; naked; extended; sensitive; sandaled; exploring; large-booted; gout-ridden.

verbs
ail—; bandage—; bare—; brace—; chafe —; control—; drum—; elevate—; expose—; injure—; journey on—; lame—; lay—on; massage—; plant—; plunk (colloq.)—; scramble to feet; shod—; shuffle feet; spring to feet; stagger to feet; stamp—; trample under—; wander on—; —aches; —drags;

—pounds; —presses; feet scurry; —sinks in; —soils; feet slacken their pace; —treads on; —trips; —lags; —marks; feet patter.

FOOTFALL
adjectives
lightest; stealthy; pattering (pl).

FOOT-HILLS
adjectives
desolate; barren; uninhabitable.

FOOTHOLD
adjectives
meager; scant; precarious; tentative.

verbs
acquire—; apply—; climb by—; contrive—; devise—; effect—; employ—; gain—; grab —; lose—; manage—; necessitate—; recover—; relax—; release—; warrant—; —agonizes; —enables; —saves.
(See support, hold.)

FOOTING
adjectives
insecure; surer; friendly; uncertain; indispensable; equal; solid; unsteadfast; treacherous; unsteady.

FOOTLIGHTS
verbs
crave—; diminish—; employ—; hover at —; reach—; require—; —attract; —color; —deceive; —divert; —emblazon; —enhance; —flash; —flatter; —flood; —glare; —illumine; —shine; —soften; —suffuse.
(See light, stage, theater.)

FOOTMAN
adjectives
servile; stiff-necked; powder-headed; select.

FOOT-NOTE
adjectives
humble; elusive; helpful; necessary.

FOOTPRINTS
adjectives
fading; fiery; veritable; dim; blurred; blood-stained; halting.

FOOTSTEP
verbs
anticipate—; characterize—; dim—; identify—; listen for—; muffle—; obliterate—;

pad—; recognize—; trace—; tread in—; —destroys; —exposes; —lags; —mars; —marks; —patters; —presses; —resounds; —reveals; —sinks in; —soils; —surprises; —warns; anticipate—.
(See step.)

FOOTSTEPS
adjectives
ringing; impartial; martial; harmless; pattering; plainer; faltering; retreating; ethereal; cautious; shuffling; early; tranquil; hastening; hurried; tottering; hallowed; errant; unwary; coming; paternal; trembling; visiting; rapid; parting; softened; rustling; foul; light; bounding.

FOOTSTOOL
adjectives
radiant; battered; comfortable.

FOOTWAY
adjectives
grass-grown; discernible; winding.

FOOTWEAR
adjectives
superior; expensive; exclusive; comfortable.

FOP
adjectives
priggish; suave; conceited; bold; overdressed; rash; silk-stockinged.

FOPPERIES
adjectives
exaggerated; indescribable; undesirable; unthinkable.

FOPPISH
adverbs
effeminately; fashionably; gallantly; preposterously; foolishly; ludicrously; absurdly; senselessly; conceitedly; ostentatiously; showily; flauntingly; jauntily; blithely; habitually; outlandishly; outrageously; disgustingly; pretentiously; proudly; pridefully; detestably; offensively; abominably.

FORAGING
adjectives
criminal; adept; clumsy; exploratory.

FORAYS
adjectives
occasional; frequent; sudden; ill-starred; remorseless; endless.

FORBEARANCE

adjectives

friendly; generous; unusual; wonderful; abounding; systematic; passive; unexpected; affectionate; good-natured; gentle.

verbs

admire—; commend—; conduct with—; end—; endure with—; excel in—; extort—; feign—; indulge in—; justify—; laud—; learn—; occasion—; practise—; praise—; pretend—; submit with—; suffer—; treat with—; —surprises.

(See patience, mercy, indulgence, tolerance.)

FORBID (*v*)

adverbs

specifically; ostentatiously; positively; dogmatically; rudely; pugnaciously; reluctantly; vehemently.

(See restrain, hinder, prevent.)

FORBIDDING

adverbs

sternly; disagreeably; unreasonably; unpleasantly; wryly; frightfully; gracelessly; grossly; grimly; shockingly; roughly; repulsively; monstrously; horridly; haggardly; dreadfully; odiously; appallingly.

FORCE

adjectives

tangential; orthogonal; material; automatic; selling; striving; provisional; elastic; diminished; perturbative; brainless; all-compelling; intensified; organizing; victorious; quickening; despoiling; radial; disturbing; insurgent; expeditionary; ethical; considerable; available; dramatic; hoplite; campaigning; resistless; influential; chemical; odious; cumulative; inadequate; powerful; imperious; sufficient; tremendous; superior; crushing; irresistible; apogee; vital; antagonistic; extraordinary; deadly; imperial; sullen; enduring; overwhelming; thwarting; civilizing; working; financial; deterring; conflicting; enormous; deterrent; molecular; static; latent; incomprehensible; invading; opposing; mechanical; insuperable; inorganic; vast; mental; formidable; unvarying; headlong; superior; intense; artistic; demoralized; meditative; self-formed; scattered; unguided; blind; striking; social; constant; besieging; threatening; protective;

centrifugal; centripetal; objective; spiritual; ignoble; unwieldy; retarding; natural; frictional; universal; concentrated; entire; spontaneous; operant; devitalizing; permanent; virile; efficient; blasphemous; exuberant; attacking; unrestrained; creative; excessive; electro-motive; well-disciplined; human; reverberating; impelling; synthetic; injurious; swelling; explosive; negative; indivisible; malevolent; instrumental; reactionary; fivefold; overpowering; subterranean; repellent; auxiliary; comparative; insignificant; genuine; meager; potent; fearful; harnessed; terrible; unknown; frontier; outnumbered; selective; cohesive; divided; frightful; calculable; fluid; disturbing; controlling; muscular; superhuman; physical; ameliorative; unaided; brute; tragic; moral; missionary; numerical; defending; living; nervous; passionate; innovating; armed; all-pervading; compulsory; disheartened; elemental; original; lacking; famished; available; hostile; demoniac; peculiar; bodily; uncommon; magnetic; mere; undiminished; pneumatic; lifting; terrifying; supplementary; persuasive; domestic; ascensional; revolting; overmastering; equivalent; driving; deep; remedial; vegetative; sheer; dubious; competent; incisive; generative; unrelenting; sacred; quiet; unmerciful; educational; dynamic; almighty; omnipresent; effectual; wavering; plastic; dumbgazing; supernatural; unrestricted; destructive; reliable; tractive; emotional; multiple; caressing; illustrative; ethereal; subversive; masterful; philosophical; colonial; unseen; international; furious; economic; wavewhirled; gravitating; sustaining; mercenary; much-needed; propulsive; undeniable; motley; subtle; ceaseless; bull-like; sales; uniformed; unpitying; elevatory; inherent; royal; obstructive; dominant; great; contending; innate; imperious; constructive; psychological; exigent; exhausted; prevalent; warring; primal.

verbs

absorb—; accelerate—; acquire—; assail by —; combat—; concentrate—s; defy—; diminish—; discipline—s; dislodge by—; divert —; employ—; focus—upon; join—s; gather —s; generate—; hamper—; harmonize—s; harness—; impede—; intensify—; let loose —s; marshal—s; mass—s; muster—s; neutralize—; nullify—; rally—s; react upon with—; recruit—s; resist—; resort to—; stymie—; suspend—; suppress by—; transmit—; triumph over—; utilize—; weaken—; —s battle; —s engulf; —impels; —s motivate; —subdues; —subsides; —s underlie; —s war.

(See energy, power, strength.)

FORCE (v)
adverbs
deliberately; instinctively; ruthlessly; offensively; gradually; automatically; dramatically; antagonistically; financially; ignobly; spontaneously; blasphemously; malevolently; potently; demoniacally; incisively; dynamically; psychologically; odiously.

(See oblige, compel.)

FORCEFUL
adverbs
impressively; immensely; unwontedly; admirably; intensely; ably; dynamically; potentially; persuasively; vigorously; invincibly; sublimely; eloquently; influentially; strikingly; effectively; effectually; energetically; intentionally; deliberately; trenchantly; vehemently; violently; sensationally; boldly; passionately; vividly.

FORD
adjectives
practicable; convenient.

FOREARMS
adjectives
wiry; sinewy; hairy.

FOREBEARS
verbs
admire—; claim—; commemorate—; extol —; honor—; inherit from—; invent—; judge—; receive from—; uphold—; venerate—; wean away from—; —achieve; —accomplish; —found; —inspire; —instil; —lead; —migrate; —produce; —settle; —suffer.

(See ancestors.)

FOREBODING
verbs
arouse—; assail by—; cast aside—; disperse—; fly from—; heed—; realize—; relate—; ridicule—; —advises; —betokens; —divines; —foretells; —oppresses; —overhangs; —prophesies; —signifies; —warns.

(See apprehension, anticipation, prognostication.)

FOREBODINGS
adjectives
vague; gloomy; dismal; unfavorable; cynical; sorrowful; dim; retroactive; chilling; undefinable; wretched; sinister; grim; inexplicable; incorrect.

FORECAST
adjectives
judicious; vivid; conservative; surprising; accurate; exultant; enlightened; broad; prophetic; provident.

verbs
abide by—; arise from—; believe—; commend—; flout—; heed—; inquire of—; provide—; read—; rectify—; ridicule—; study —; trust—; —advises; —anticipates; —dejects; —indicates; —predicts; —promises; —warns.

(See prophecy, estimate.)

FOREFATHERS
adjectives
crusading; physical; pioneering.

FOREFINGER
adjectives
absolute; gnarled; coercive; swarthy; grimy; argumentative; slim; beckoning; pointed; long; flapping; thick; blunt; admonitory; crooked; mocking.

FOREHEAD
adjectives
flaming; tattooed; unfretful; expanded; marble; smooth; swarthy; luminous; tanned; pale; pallid; mantling; frowning; mountainous; square; fretted; bulging; lofty; spacious; jutting; powerful; branded; fabled; dusky; livid; ample; dirty; well-developed; unsustained; knobby; somber; tranquil; exquisite; disfigured; shaped; wide; massive; cloudless; wrinkled; deep-grooved; damp; moist; perspiring; mean; calm; burning; towering; bold; throbbing; princely; well-shaped; fine; narrow; aristocratic; intelligent; brainy; anxious; receding; unbashful.

verbs
cloud—; distinguish by—; furrow—; knot —; mop—; raise—; scar—; —wrinkles; —puckers; —pulsates; —throbs.

(See face, head.)

adverbs

harmlessly; objectionably; inadmissably; unconformably; strangely; remotely; irrelevantly; outlandishly; undeniably; ostentatiously; palpably; essentially; obviously; disagreeably; inconceivably; relatively; discordantly; impertinently; fantastically; exotically; intrusively; inimically; disinterestedly; extraneously.

FOREIGNER

adjectives

high-born; cursed; invading; enlightened; hated; distinguished.

verbs

accept—; admit—; allow—; Americanize—; beguile—; deport—; enhance—; entertain —; examine—; limit—s; lodge—; naturalize—; reject—; school—in; smuggle in—s; welcome—; —s colonize; —s crowd; —s intrude; —s settle in.

(See alien.)

FORERUNNER

adjectives

elegant; early; indigenous.

FORESEE (*v*)

adverbs

dimly; timorously; morbidly; clairvoyantly; vividly; mysteriously; supernaturally; unerringly.

(See anticipate, prepare, foretell.)

FORESIGHT

adjectives

shrinking; patriotic; economic; fiery; sagacious; divine; prudent; keen.

FOREST

adjectives

dull; motionless; intricate; illimitable; isolated; teak; aboriginal; virgin; lonely; primeval; ilex; adjacent; unawakened; green-haired; trackless; preservable; cathedral-vaulted; thick-studded; favoring; natural; solemn; tropical; impenetrable; solitary; mildew; uncleared; enchanted; rank; moon-illumined; great; silent; desolate; interminable; incense-bearing; magnificent; fragrant; murmuring; umbrageous; blackened; sun-filled; flaming; black; golden; tinted; unspoiled; moaning; boundless; thicketed; still; thick; rude; untrodden; dripping; shadowed; unwilling; mel-

ancholy; somber; tangled; pine-carpeted; infinite; tantalizing; hazy; unbroken; coniferous; panther-peopled; odorous; stretching; hoary; intervening; matted; immense; majestic; fast-darkening; surrounding; dreary; leafless; silver-powdered; limitless; disenchanted; unsurveyed; thrifty; unwholesome; girdling; trackless; frowning; consuming; scathed; ancient; encircling; mighty; massy; monotonous; luxuriant; sleeping; uncouth; miniature; black-bearded; encroaching; slumberous.

verbs

conserve—s; denude—s; deplete—; dot with —s; entangle in—; fell—; guard—; harbor in—; infest—; invade—; jeopardize—s; level—; patrol—; poach in—; preserve—; raze—; skirt—; thin out—; wipe out—; —abounds in; —encircles; —extends; —flourishes; —ranges; —whispers.

(See jungle.)

FORETELL (*v*)

adverbs

portentously; sensationally; uncannily; clairvoyantly; accurately; unerringly.

(See predict, portend, foresee.)

FORETHOUGHT

adjectives

divine; anxious; endless; deliberate.

verbs

commend—; decide with—; discipline to—; employ—; exercise—; exhibit—; indulge in —; mark by—; necessitate—; note for—; praise—; provide—; save by—; submit to —; urge—; —assures; —determines; —enables; —impedes; —influences; —obviates; —overcomes; —prepares; —reaps.

(See consideration, prudence, precaution.)

FORFEIT

adjectives

unredeemable; profitless; vain.

verbs

call—; demand—; exact—; impose—; incur—; lose—; offer—; pay—; penalize with —; punish with—; redeem—; remit—; subject to—; take—; —clears; —deprives; —redeems; —releases; —ruins.

(See fine, penalty.)

FORFEIT (v)

adverbs

automatically; legally; irrevocably; inevitably; provisionally; nominally.

(See fine, pay.)

FORGE

adjectives

gleaming; sounding; flashing.

FORGE (v)

adverbs

laboriously; dexterously; artfully; audaciously; deliberately; daringly; subtly.

(See force, push.)

FORGERY

adjectives

literary; flimsy; deliberate; audacious.

FORGET (v)

adverbs

mercifully; promptly; speedily; momentarily; eternally; wantonly; deliberately; conveniently; prudently; flagrantly.

(See ignore, neglect, overlook.)

FORGETFUL

adverbs

lamentably; carelessly; idly; inattentively; senilely; agedly; hopelessly; deplorably; unfortunately; conveniently; tactfully; forgivingly; gracefully; irritatingly; provokingly; vexatiously; incurably; helplessly; nervously; weakly; treacherously; sadly; terribly; inexcusably; criminally; tragically.

FORGETFULNESS

adjectives

conceivable; dull; momentary; frank; heavenly; atrocious; slumberous; unkind; eternal.

FORGIVE (v)

adverbs

graciously; magnanimously; indulgently; meekly; heartily; mutually; patiently; solemnly; cordially; spiritually.

(See excuse, acquit.)

FORGIVENESS

adjectives

infinite; mutual; implored.

FORGIVING

adverbs

gracefully; indulgently; wisely; discreetly; wholly; tolerantly; tactfully; generously; graciously; infinitely; nobly; magnanimously; charitably; benignly; unexpectedly; surprisingly; chivalrously; gallantly; affably; extremely.

FORGOTTEN

adverbs

sadly; altogether; unhappily; conveniently; cold-heartedly; unfeelingly; wretchedly; unpardonably; inexcusably; carelessly; brutally; thoughtlessly; mercilessly; selfishly; ungratefully; thanklessly; friendlessly; desolately; forlornly; miserably; disconsolately; appallingly; shockingly.

FORK

adjectives

gesticulating; triple; excoriated; soft; tender; furrowy; vibrating; tuning.

verbs

barb with—; brandish—; cast with—; convey on—; draw with—; hook with—; impale on—; jab with—; lift—; pursue with —; stab with—; —pierces; —prongs; —spears; —transfers.

(See knife.)

FORLORN

adverbs

lonesomely; terribly; pitiably; pathetically; uncommonly; utterly; listlessly; silently; glumly; resignedly; profoundly; weirdly; singularly; immensely; blankly; unutterably.

FORM

adjectives

absurd; active; acute; admirable; adorable; aesthetic; aggravated; airy; ample; analogic; angular; antique; apparent; archaic; archangelic; architectural; artistic; athletic; attenuated; barbarous; barest; beastlike; beautiful; bent; bestial; bewildering; bewitching; birdlike; blanketed; blasting; bleeding; bliss-inspiring; bloated; bounding; boyish; briefest; brigand-like; broken; buckskin-clad; burly; changing; charming; chaste; childish; chronic; circular; clamorous; classic; clothed; codified (pl); collectible; colloidal; comely; commanding; compact; complicated; concentrated; conciliatory; concrete; condensed; constitutional; contrary; convenient; conventional; corrupted; countless (pl); creeping; crowded; crumpled; cultivated; cumulative; curvilinear; debasing; cylindrical; dainty; decrepit; desired; definite; democratic; detailed; determinate; diabolic; diluted; disguised; disrobed; dissolving; distressing; distribution; durable; earliest; ecstatic; elastic; elegant; elliptic; emasculated; erect; ephemeral; epistolary; equitable; established; erroneous; eventual; exaggerated; express; expurgated; exquisite; faded; fair; faltering; famished; fan-shaped; fantasmalike; fantastic; faultless; feigned; feminine; fiery; flawless; flitting; floral; fluid; fragile; fruitful; gallant; fundamental; garbled; gaseous; gigantic; gasping; gaunt; geometrical; ghostly; glancing; gleaming; gloomy; glorious; glowing; gnarled; graceful; goodly; graceless; grandiose; granular; graphic; greyhound-like; groaning; guileless; handsome; harmless; harmonic; heavenly; herculean; heroic; historic; horrible; huddled; hulking; human; hungry; hurrying; ill-clad; imposing; improvisational; incoherent; inconvenient; indirect; individual; indurate; inert; inexorable; infantile; ingenious; intimate; instrumental; intricate; irritated; jovial; jostling; kicking; languid; lanky; lifeless; long; low; magnified; majestic; malignant; mainfold; manly; mantled; maritime; metrical; microscopic; milder; mitigated; moderate; modified; moldering; monophonic; monumental; motionless; motley (pl); moving; mundane; myriad; mythologic; native; never-shifting; needleshaped; obese; offensive; oligarchic; operatic; organic; outward; palpable; palatable; particular; pathetic; permanent; plastic; pliant; poetic; pompous; portly; prescribed; pretentious; printed; pristine; prone; proper; prostrate; protesting; proverbial; provincial; puerile; puerperal; pure; quantitative; quivering; rebellious; recitative; recumbent; regular; related; reluctant; repugnant; respectful; retiring; rhythmic; robust; rigid; sardonic; scholastic; semicircular; semi-elliptical; senseless; serpentine; shadowy; shaky; shapely; simple; shivering; shriveled; shrouded; sinking; shrunken; singular; skeleton; slender; slim; smug; slouching; slumping; spare; spectral; spheroidal; spiritualized; squalid; staggering; standard; startling; stately; stiff; strange; strong; structural; struggling; stunted; subsumed; suffering; suitable; superb; swallow-tailed; symmetrical; tall; tapering; technical; tedious; theistic; thickening; thin;

tiny; titanic; tortuous; tottering; towering; traditional; transient; typical; unadulterated; unblemished; undulating; undying; unhealthy; unimaginable; unintelligible; united; unmatched; unnatural; unphonetic; unremembered; unsubstantial; unusual; vacant; valuable; vaporous; varied; vast; veiled; venerable; vicarious; villanelle; virulent; visible; visionary; warlike; wasted; wedge-shaped; weird; well-balanced; willowy; feeble; coherent; wolflike; wooden; writhing; conversational; peculiar; pedagogic; peerless; phantom.

verbs
accept—; adhere to—; assume—; conventionalize—; develop—; distort—; enhance —; evince—; gain—; insist on—; jeopardize—; lend—to; model on—; pattern—; retain—; scoff at—; standardize—; —embraces; —sways.

(See method, ritual, style, model.)

FORM (*v*)

adverbs
voluntarily; theoretically; successively; gracefully; dexterously; expeditiously; inadvertently; prematurely; originally; insensibly; ultimately; delicately; collectively; ingeniously; durably; aesthetically; constitutionally; cumulatively; democratically; diabolically; ephemerally; erroneously; fantastically; geometrically; grandiosely; majestically; organically; symmetrically; tortuously.

(See shape, mould.)

FORMAL

adverbs
extremely; unusually; officially; strictly; conventionally; dogmatically; ritualistically; legally; ecclesiastically; absolutely; undeviatingly; explicitly; solemnly; ceremoniously; curiously; gracefully; splendidly; brilliantly; terribly; awesomely; punctiliously; meticulously; particularly; needlessly; coldly; unnecessarily; foolishly.

FORMALITY

adjectives
concluding; statuesque; affected; stiff; precise; professional; imposing; architectural; stately; icy; tired; tiring; degrading; rigid; joyless.

verbs
adopt—; break—; conduct with—; conform to—; discard—; dress in—; don—; ease—;

encase in—; end—ies; endure—; engage in —; execute with—; exercise—; insist on—; observe—ies; perform—ies; peach—ies; preserve—ies; relax—; require—; school in —; shed—; shun—; —corsets; —exasperates; —retards; —stifles; —preserves.

(See conventionality, ceremony.)

FORMATION
adjectives
geological; humanistic; proper; peculiar; meteoric; tertiary; harmonic; crude; various (pl); fantastic; shaft-like; remarkable; delusional; delicate; inanimate; slow.

verbs
abet —; aid —; bar —; check —; conceal — of; discover —; divest of —; emerge from —; precede —; prevent —; shake —; sponsor —; suppress —; whip into —; — breaks; — divides; — splits; — takes place.

(See arrangement, development.)

FORMULA
adjectives
mathematical; moral; abstract; original; magical; aphoristic; invariable; devotional; bristling; perfected; barren; creative; dead; noble; majestic; definite.

verbs
accept—; apply—; apprise of—; bungle—; change—; coin—; compound—; compute—; devise—; employ—; evolve—; express in—; falsify—; fetter by—; fulfill—; reduce to—; simplify—; utilize—; work from—; —clarifies; —curbs; —states.

(See rule, form, prescription, principle, ritual.)

FORMULATE (v)
adverbs
peculiarly; scientifically; enterprisingly; academically; skillfully; dexterously; crudely; professionally.

(See plan, prepare.)

FORMULATION
adjectives
academic; scientific; definite; crude.

FORSAKE (v)
adverbs
reluctantly; unnaturally; disastrously; faithlessly; shamefully; churlishly; unfeelingly.

(See abandon, quit, leave.)

FORSAKEN
adverbs
desolately; lamentably; desperately; helplessly; shockingly; utterly; unhappily; coldheartedly; unfeelingly; wretchedly; miserably; appallingly; friendlessly; mercilessly; unpardonably; thoughtlessly; cruelly; brutally; disconsolately; dreadfully; pitifully.

FORT
adjectives
outlying; improvised; grim; silent; impregnable; well-garrisoned; deserted; strategic; hidden; camouflaged.

FORTIFICATION
adjectives
wasted; noble; remarkable; permanent; extensive; grim; stupendous; medieval; tremendous; useless; antiquated.

verbs
arm —; assail —; charge —; erect —; fire on —; maintain —; march to —; necessitate —; plan —; provide —; require —; shatter —; — defends; — guards; — overlooks; — preserves; — protects; — repels; — shields; — surrounds; — yields.

(See castle, stronghold.)

FORTIFY (v)
adverbs
unwaveringly; speedily; stalwartly; mysteriously; testily; crudely; powerfully; permanently; grimly; medievally; antiquatedly; extensively.

(See defend, guard, protect, resist.)

FORTITUDE
adjectives
Christian; matchless; admirable; uncomplaining; unpretentious; placid; remarkable; surprising; stoic; unshakable; intestinal; sustained; physical; iron; enduring; calm; extraordinary; sufficient; stolid.

verbs
admire —; arm with —; bear with —; commend —; conduct with —; consider —; endure with —; excel in —; exhibit —; laud —; mark by —; occasion —; practice —; praise —; require —; summon —; tolerate with —; treat with —; — amazes; — surprises.

(See courage, endurance, strength.)

520

FORTRESS

adjectives

level; mighty; permanent; improvised; baronial; gloomy; island; feminine; garrisoned; inaccessible; dismantled; frowning; seductive; insulated; frost-locked; grim; walled; magnificent; medieval; ragged; beleaguered; rock-bound; impregnable; isolated.

FORTUITOUS

adverbs

curiously; obviously; luckily; presumably; casually; wholly; comically; inexplicably; mysteriously; admittedly; ludicrously; certainly; providentially; frequently; purportedly; evidently; luckily; awkwardly; pleasantly; tragically; undependably; uneasily; uncertainly; opportunely; ironically; favorably; conveniently.

FORTUNATE

adverbs

blessedly; splendidly; politically; incidentally; moderately; luckily; unwontedly; propitiously; systematically; regularly; uniformly; brilliantly; inherently; triumphantly; inexpressibly; inscrutably; signally; notoriously; unaccountably; unwarrantably; significantly; mysteriously; immensely; marvellously; ultimately; enviably; conveniently; ingeniously; accidentally; reasonably; highly; extremely; happily; fairly; auspiciously; luckily; providentially; remarkably; unusually; consistently; gratifyingly; pleasantly; agreeably; fittingly; delightfully; appropriately.

FORTUNE

adjectives

fairer; munificent; fallen; rude; adverse; cursed; blessed; varying; colossal; competent; considerate; gracious; splendid; political; forlorn; individual; shattered; ample; stupendous; unparalleled; equal; favorable; blind; moderate; stormy; good; fitful; frowning; drooping; public; invulnerable; tottering; wretched; rare; fluctuating; enormous; crooked; humbled; squandered; dire; subsequent; brilliant; indulgent; inconstant; princely; changing; gloomy; wild; patrimonial; narrow; fierce; keen; adventurous; sunny; superior; promising; dissipated; extraordinary; desperate; fouler; spiritual; broken; prodigious; relenting; signal; hostile; unconfirmed; fretted; sure; disastrous; dependent; ultimate; doubtful; waning.

verbs

accumulate —; amass —; bemoan —; bewail —; dissipate —; establish —; fall into —; garner —; hazard —; mend —; net —; prophesy —; reap —; recoup —; replenish —; restore —; retrieve —; stake — on; struggle for —; tempt —; wipe away —; wreck —; —s ascend; —s crash; — ebbs; — fails; — favors; — flows; — melts away.

(See chance, fate, destiny, estate, possessions, success, wealth.)

FORWARD (v)

adverbs

conscientiously; progressively; unselfishly; magnanimously; munificently; disastrously; ultimately.

(See advance, send.)

FORWARDNESS

adjectives

intrusive; brusque; brash.

FOSSIL

adjectives

Paleozoic; contained; stone-pervaded; mammalian; minute; significant.

FOSTER (v)

adverbs

cunningly; gradually; effectually; deliberately; diligently; cordially; subtly; diabolically; treacherously; philosophically.

(See support, promote.)

FOULNESS

adjectives

horrid; Stygian; dank; miasmic.

FOUNDATION

adjectives

massive; explanatory; moral; splendid; well-laid; unorthodox; rational; permanent; slender; substantial; antiquated; shifting; virtual; respectable; monstrous; dangerous; durable; treacherous; solid; floating; everlasting; enviable; philosophic; sufficient; economical; lasting; broad; crumbling; reciprocal; thrilling; slenderizing.

verbs

build —; correct —; deprive of —; dig at —; erect —; founder at —; ground on —; jeopardize —; lay —; protect —; ruffle —; sap —; shake —; strike at —; undermine —; — crumbles; — remains; — shudders; — stands; — supports.

(See base, basis, principles.)

FOUNDER

adjectives
traditional; energetic; patient; spiritual.

FOUNDLING

adjectives
helpless; undernourished; scantily-clad.

FOUNT

adjectives
sapphire; never-failing; continual; perennial; babbling; sacred; consecrated; youth-giving.

FOUNTAIN

adjectives
paved; wide-spreading; inexhaustible; burning; searchless; trickling; foul; ancient; perennial; bitter; many-voiced; spouting; celestial; ever-filling; welling; untainted; fresh; life-sealed; gurgling; weedy; pleasant; fire-laden; reedy; living; perpetual; hillside; fiery; soulless; bubbling; distant; sporting; earthly; fresh; ceaseless; gushing; unlocked; unfailing; lightning; cool; ablutionary; flashing; geyserlike.

verbs
admire —; choke —; illuminate —; — bubbles; — dances; — flings; — floods; — gleams; — gurgles; — gushes; — plays; — sallies; — scintillates; — sings; — sparkles; — splashes; — spouts; — sprinkles; — spurts; — twinkles; — weeps.
(See spring, brook, spray.)

FOUNTAIN-PEN

verbs
feed —; fill —; illustrate with —; pocket —; press on —; regulate —; reserve in —; store in —; transcribe with —; uncap —; — blotches; — drips; — leaks; — scratches; — spills; — stains.
(See pen.)

FOWL

adjectives
domestic; plump; glossy; long-billed; gluttonous; winged; screaming; sea; poor; miserable; ravenous; fearful; wild; skinny; sapless; lagging; ungainly; succulent; lean.

verbs
behead —; boil —; breed —s; call —; catch —; devour —; feed —s; house —s; roast —; serve —; shoo —; snare —; steal —; — cackles; — crows; —s flock; —s gather; — pecks; — scratches.
(See hen, rooster, bird, chicken, turkey, duck, etc.)

FOX

adjectives
stealthy; caverned; cunning; loping; sly; sleek; slinking.

verbs
chase —; ensnare —; farm —; pursue —; raise —es; skin —; trap —; — burrows; — claws; — darts; — digs; — displays; — excavates; — fools; — leaps; — outwits; — preys on; — roams; — tricks.
(See animal.)

FOXY

adverbs
naturally; cautiously; shrewdly; artfully; abominably; treacherously; trickily; subtly; sharply; evasively; skilfully; adroitly; astutely; deceptively; cunningly; unexpectedly; profoundly; unusually; diplomatically; insidiously; deplorably; unfortunately; strategically; commercially; financially; cannily.

FOYER

adjectives
bare; grotesque; sumptuous.

FRACAS

verbs
bridle —; curb —; describe —; enjoy —; enter —; indulge in —; inflame to —; inquire into —; instigate —; interrupt —; invite —; involve in —; occasion —; prevent —; produce —; quell —; raise —; referee —; — annoys; — irritates; — subsides; — unnerves.
(See fight, brawl, uproar, disturbance.)

FRACTION

adjectives
insignificant; minute; undue; slender; mixed.

verbs
break into —s; denote —; diminish to —; dispense with —; dispute —; divide into —s; dwindle to —; express —; include —;

indicate —; instruct in —s; measure by —; observe —; piece into —s; reduce to —; — irks; — puzzles.

(See fragment.)

FRACTIOUS
adverbs
unmanageably; irritatingly; distressingly; undeniably; notoriously; uncontrollably; ungovernably; abominably; detestably; petulantly; highly; utterly; terribly; peculiarly; singularly; oddly; queerly; churlishly; excitably; snappily; captiously; cantankerously; restively; intolerably; utterly.

FRACTURE
verbs
cast —; compound —; depress —; examine —; expose —; fasten —; incur —; inflict —; prevent —; produce —; recognize —; reconcile —; reduce —; splice —; splint —; support —; x-ray —; — divides; — heals; — mends, — shocks; — splits; — splinters; — unites.

(See rupture, breach.)

FRAGILE
adverbs
delicately; infirmly; weakly; languidly; increasingly; terribly; totteringly; tremulously; decrepitly; defensely; flimsily; nervously; frightfully; shakily; hopelessly; irremediably; uncommonly.

FRAGMENT
adjectives
unrelated; expurgated; enormous; intelligible; welcome; warlike; sparkling; numberless (pl); cumbrous; colossal; tattered; insignificant; scattered (pl); hissing; weary; whirling; clattering; chaotic; shattered; quarried; incoherent; isolated; misty; artless; halting; detached; ill-smelling; connected; cometary; heterogeneous; massive; indubitable; massy; rough; curious; countless (pl); weary; fancy; important; disjointed; grand; beauteous; sculptured; pitiful; brilliant; restless; exquisite.

verbs
break into—s; cast into—s; cherish—s; conceal—s; discard—s; excise—s; extract—s; gather up—s; hack into—s; preserve—s; reduce to—s; retain—s; rip into—s; scatter —s; splinter into—s; strew—s; tear into—s; —embarrasses; —s fill; —projects; —s scatter.

(See part, portion, piece, remnant, chip.)

FRAGRANCE
adjectives
fruity; heady; worldly; delicious; favorite; faint; clinging; delightful; ardor-awakening; sweet; visible; strong; tea; delicate; full-blown; nocturnal; powerful; cloverlike; midsummer; ambrosial; breathing; wholesome; odorous; salty; diffusing; fog; subtle; autumnal; exotic; worldly; unmatched; feverish; ineffable; homelike; dewy; aromatic; spicy; manifold; healthful; nutlike; honied; evanescent; blended; provocative; woody; sense-dissolving; embodied; balmy.

verbs
admire—; anoint with—; delight in—; diffuse—; emit—; exude—; fill with—; gather —; inhale—; savor—; share—; veil in—; yield—; —assaults; —clouds; —edifies; — floats; —outlasts; —permeates; —pleases; —scents; —stirs.

(See sweetness, odor, perfume, scent, smell.)

FRAGRANT
adverbs
pleasantly; spicily; redolently; sweetly; pungently; arrestingly; refreshingly; seductively; pleasingly; alluringly; strongly; delicately; faintly; exquisitely; enchantingly; charmingly; overpoweringly; overwhelmingly; delectably; intoxicatingly; lingeringly; exotically; romantically; evanescently.

FRAIL
adverbs
terribly; pitifully; unusually; increasingly; nervously; feebly; decrepitly; languidly; defenselessly; helplessly; hopelessly; appallingly; shockingly; miserably; wretchedly.

FRAILTY
adjectives
human; decorous; female; universal; patent; obvious; apparent; inexcusable.

verbs
admit—; condemn—; confess—; crush—; cure—; disguise—; draw—; fall into—; hide—; inherit—; overcome—; play on—; remove—; reveal—; seek—; surrender to —; tempt—; tolerate—; treat—; —s cheat; —shames.

(See weakness.)

adjectives

consistent; wasted; mortal; lordly; narrow; thrilling; graceful; universal; spreading; comfortable; lean; becoming; ebonite; tottering; decrepit; unhelpful; nerveless; ponderous; imposing; corporal; unbreathing; stalwart; elastic; weary; lank; long-limbed; grateful; smitten; impassioned; growing; iron; sinful; kindred; anxious; well-knit; wretched; ultimate; chilled; feeble; inexplicable; racked; bent; gilded; blanket-covered; spiritless; huge; husky; faltering; tortured; powerful; pain-worn; portly; delightful; luminous; gaunt; slender; fine; massive; reluctant; dying; arabesque; unlovely; large; meager; hardy; well-proportioned; trembling; oddest; tuneful; irksome; emaciated; attentuated; vigorous; buxom; vital; mystic; uneasy; moldering; unpleasant; perforated; unresisting; shriveled; goodly; measured; spare; matchless; hardy; ethereal; unearthly; daring; vandal; delicate; physical; shrunken; magnificent; seductive; vast; rugged; muscular; vigorous; sky-scraper; flexible; gigantic; stocky; osseous; thick-set; hard; light; wiry; loose; stolid; weak.

verbs

adjust—; brace—; construct—; dissolve—; enclose in—; enter into—; fashion—; fence with—; fix to—; lodge in—; move—; overthrow—; place in—; regulate—; set in—; set up—; shape on—; weave on—; —arises; —collapses; —s differ; —shuts out; —stretches.

(See structure, case.)

FRAME (v)

adverbs

brilliantly; picturesquely; substantially; inexplicably; vaguely; gracefully; imposingly; luminously; seductively.

(See devise, contrive, plan.)

FRAMEWORK

adjectives

rigid; skeletal; essential.

FRANCHISE

adjectives

elective; tangible; legal; limited.

verbs

acquire—; admit to—; advocate—; bequeath —to; deprive of—; enjoy—; establish—; exercise—; forbid—; grant—; invest with

—; limit—; possess—; purchase—; renew —; restore—; seek—; sell—; violate—; — benefits; —empowers; —exempts; —privileges; —protects.

(See right, exemption, freedom.)

FRANK

adverbs

delightfully; charmingly; bitterly; cruelly; attractively; distressingly; unusually; characteristically; sarcastically; crudely; appallingly; refreshingly; inordinately; artlessly; innocently; ingenuously; plainly; guilelessly; unaffectedly; apparently; strikingly; naively.

FRANKNESS

adjectives

manly; irrevocable; perfect; natural; cordial; timid; placid; virtuous; medical; absolute; inestimable; unsophisticated; superfluous; careless; unprepossessing; engaging; simple; uncomplimentary; brotherly; military; hearty; beautiful; intimate; indolent; imperious; brisk; medieval; sardonic; straightforward; youthful; uninhibited; repellent; naive; savage; genial; painful.

verbs

admit—; confess with—; declare with—; experience—; inflict—; meet with—; occasion—; permeate with—; relish—; require —; return—; reveal—; —annoys; —cuts; —disquiets; —hurts; —mortifies; —nettles; —offends; —pains; —pricks; —ruffles; — stings; —wounds.

(See candor, fairness, liberalism.)

FRANTIC

adverbs

irritably; passionately; distractedly; feverishly; hysterically; nervously; wildly; eccentrically; crazily; fanatically; incoherently; insensately; rabidly; starkly; acutely; desperately; uncontrollably; irrepressibly; unappeasably; ungovernably; terribly; pitifully; frightfully.

FRATERNAL

adverbs

genially; convivially; generously; warmly; indulgently; closely; remotely; intimately; congenially; harmoniously; tranquilly; dependably; quietly; remarkably; securely; comfortably.

FRAUD

adjectives

unremitting; shameful; presumable; wretched; economic; mercenary; pious; gigantic; petty; manifest; glaring; meditated; flagrant; barefaced.

verbs

beguile with—; commit—; cover—; declaim against—; design—; detect—; discern—; draw into—; engage in—; execute—; impose—upon; indulge in—; glory in—; lament—; perceive—; perpetrate—; practise —; prevent—; punish—; rectify—; reveal —; suspect—; taint with—; uncover—; unearth—; —amuses; —deceives; —dejects; —enables; —provokes; —ruins; —succeeds.

(See deception, deceit, trick, dishonesty, cheat, swindle.)

FRAUDULENT

adverbs

criminally; obviously; manifestly; apparently; openly; flagrantly; subtly; artfully; shrewdly; cleverly; adroitly; sharply; smartly; miserably; indefensibly; basely; grossly; knavishly; villainously; disgracefully; ignominiously; meanly; shabbily; unscrupulously; extremely; infamously; notoriously; surreptitiously.

FRAY

adjectives

deadly; fair; bloody; lawless; late; obstinate; youthful; horrid; clamorous; devilish; holy; mimic; thundering; insidious; nefarious.

verbs

charge into—; clash in—; commence—; crush in—; curb—; describe—; indulge in —; inquire into—; instigate—; interrupt—; involve in—; occasion—; plunge into—; raise—; referee—; —boils; —disperses; —frightens; —irritates; —unnerves; —disturbs.

(See fracas, combat, fight, commotion.)

FREAK

adjectives

grotesque; sudden; disgraceful; wanton; fashionable; unaccountable; fierce; impossible; peculiar.

FREAKISH

adverbs

outlandishly; ostentatiously; manifestly; absurdly; shamelessly; intentionally; disgustingly; inexcusably; laughably; idiotically; teasingly; tormentingly; erratically; eccentrically; fantastically; whimsically; particularly; wantonly; waywardly; uncomfortably; frivolously; terribly; unexpectedly.

FRECKLES

verbs

bleach—; conceal—; discern—; encourage —; mark with—; produce—; remove—; spangle with—; sprinkle with—; —cover; —dapple; —discolor; —dot; —embarrass; —mar; —spot; —stain; —variegate.

FREE

adverbs

gloriously; joyously; happily; independently; finally; utterly; completely; absolutely; unconditionally; irrepressibly; irresponsibly; gaily; blithely; merrily; unaccountably; gladly; jubilantly; incredibly; fortunately; luckily; unbelievably; unexpectedly.

FREE (v)

adverbs

ultimately; eventually; legally; economically; filially; unrestrainedly; magnanimously; unquestionably.

(See liberate, release.)

FREEDOM

adjectives

incomparable; bold; unbounded; perfect; unquestioned; unnoticed; personal; newly-regained; unchecked; untrammeled; licentious; perpetual; untamed; unbridled; annihilating; determined; brave; practical; deserving; airy; courtly; subjective; reverent; half-bashful; half-saucy; hopeless; complete; comparative; dignified; economic; accustomed; refined; filial; spotless; exceptional; intellectual; unbroken; unrestrained; priceless; dearly-bought; bloody; unwonted.

verbs

achieve—; advocate—; alienate—; announce—; assert—; break for—; confer-on; curb—; curtail—; deprive of—; encroach on—; expand with—; exult in—; flutter to—; guarantee—; hamper—; heighten—; impair—; imperil—; infringe on—;

menace—; relinquish—; resign—; retain—; strive for—; suppress—; surrender—; thrill in—; trample—; wed to—.
(See liberty, independence, ease, frankness.)

FREEZE (v)
adverbs
nightly; seasonally; spectrally; glacially; dangerously; tragically; formidably; permanently.
(See congeal, chill.)

FREEZING
adjectives
unexpected; bulk; seasonal; costly; artificial.

FREIGHT
adjectives
human; perishable; superannuated; additional; weary; animate; precious.

verbs
bear—; charge for—; convey by—; deduct for—; deposit—; despatch by—; export—; handle—; hold up—; load—; pay—; protect —; store—; transport by—; —s collide; —costs; —weighs.
(See cargo, load, transportation.)

FRENZIED
adverbs
deliriously; joyously; madly; wildly; excitedly; feverishly; insanely; fanatically; violently; completely; pathetically; jealously; inexpressibly; appallingly; alarmingly; dangerously; abnormally; incurably; deplorably.

FRENZY
adjectives
astonishing; fanatical; violent; selfish; poetic; complete; pathetic; maddening; full; jealous; dread; untimely; dreadful; inexpressible.

verbs
anticipate—; attack in—; dart with—; drive to—; fall into—; fight with—; imbue with —; incur—of; indulge in—; inflame to—; infuriate to—; inspire—; lash into—; plunge into—; provoke—; roll in—; salve —; seize with—; shake with—; shriek in—; strike with—; subject to—; throw into—; unloose—; —alarms; —descends; —disturbs; —seizes.
(See agitation, fury, madness, enthusiasm, fanaticism.)

FREQUENCY
adjectives
determinate; disheartening; distasteful; persistent; increasing; nervous.

verbs
commit with—; condemn—; diminish—; displease with—; encourage—; endure—; enjoy—; impose with—; increase—; justify—; occur with—; necessitate—; reduce—; relax—; repeat with—; return with—; vary—.
(See speed.)

FREQUENT
adverbs
annoyingly; disturbingly; unnecessarily; unusually; recurrently; monotonously; tiresomely.

FREQUENT (v)
adverbs
intermittently; habitually; persistently; carelessly; rashly; daringly; unconventionally; customarily.
(See visit.)

FRESH
adverbs
delightfully; unquestionably; genuinely; lusciously; deliciously; lately; exquisitely; excellently; capitally; superlatively; inimitably; admirably; pleasantly; agreeably; wonderfully; marvelously; emphatically; perfectly.

FRESHNESS
adjectives
original; enviable; dewy; lyrical; immortal; permeating; morning; faded; dreadful; youthful; infinite; cool; guaranteed; astonishing; clean; abounding; genial; delicate; sweet; unsunned; soothing; bracing; glorious; frosty; gay; perennial; breezy; elastic; vernal; odorous; wholesome.

FRET (v)
adverbs
pettishly; childishly; morbidly; irritatingly; unreasoningly; unintelligently; abnormally; pathologically.
(See vex, irritate, tease, annoy.)

FRETFUL
adverbs
whiningly; peevishly; complainingly; nervously; spitefully; feverishly; pathetically; unfortunately; unbearably; intolerably; sullenly; restlessly; capriciously; jealously; ap-

pallingly; shockingly; surprisingly; unreasonably; foolishly; needlessly; groundlessly; sadly; unwisely; shrewishly; querulously; cantankerously; restively; perversely; terribly; captiously.

FRIABLE

adverbs
desirably; admirably; sufficiently; satisfactorily; duly; frangibly; impalpably; wonderfully; astonishingly; surprisingly; superbly; splendidly; adequately; amply.

FRIAR

adjectives
coarse; unreverend; unhallowed; bungling; mendicant; saucy; true; meddling; frantic; humble; pious.

FRICTION

adjectives
constant; incessant; insufficient; sectional; cheerful; spiritual; unnecessary; destructive; laborious; tidal; continual; unpleasant.

verbs
expose to—; ignite by—; prophesy—; suffer —; sustain—; transmit—; undergo—; — agitates; —blisters; —chafes; —corrodes; —develops; —endangers; —grates; —polishes; —resists; —rubs; —scrubs; — smooths; —stings; —tingles; —torments; — wears away.
(See resistance.)

FRIEND

adjectives
indefatigable; well-meaning; circumspect; valued; discriminating; influential; wonderful; feathered; familiar; perfidious; neglecting; faithless; thankless; all-seeing; political; social; frank; loyal; impressionable; impetuous; fiery; sworn; intimate; gracious; genial; impartial; democratic; discouraging; unprofitable; disinguished; disinterested; ardent; benignant; charitable; obliging; light-hearted; disapproving; enthusiastic; serviceable; congenial; dexterous; hollow; affectionate; distressful; devoted; indiscreet; candid; bubbling; esteemed; immediate; marvelous; illustrious; indisposed; courtly; unfortunate; lasting; solid; lifelong; profligate; distant; utmost; roistering; tyrannous; ancient; medieval; timid; loving; acquainted; unflinching; high-toned; imaginary; lawless; ecclesiastical; sable; caressing; inconstant; confidential; honorable; quondam; bleating; censorious; de-parted; much-lamented; scrutinizing; numerous (pl); timorous; magnanimous; mute; amiable; philanthropic; treacherous; absent; traitorous; consumptive; blushing; hospitable; lazy; valuable; firm; velvet; festive; veteran; sweet; judicious; coolest; biteless; inebriated; unselfish; inestimable; gentle; spirited; puissant; officious; powerful; epicurean; banished; bosom; inseparable; obliging; staunch; long-sustaining; beloved; worthy; trusty; conservative; liberal; secret; nameless; common; late-embarked; warmest; true; literary; importunate; merry; dissipated; vindictive; benevolent; strong; creditable; rival; family; steadfast; unswerving; unrepentant; provoking; pock-marked; middle-aged; satirical; reasonable; particular; virtuous; modest; long-tried; long-known; gossiping; courageous; unwavering; sympathizing; questioning; suspicious; unconditional; choice; well-tried; false; sad; well-advised; irritable; gifted; prying.

verbs
accept as—; accost—; affront—; alienate —; berate—; betray—; cast away—; concede to—; exasperate—; exempt—s; favor —; forsake—; harbor—; idolize—; join—; lack—; let down—; muster—s; part with—; protect—; sacrifice—; succor—; sustain—; take leave of—s; value—; vex—s; wish—; yield to—; —consoles; —s drift away; — lends a hand; —prevails; —stands by; — supports.
(See associate, ally, companion, favorite.)

FRIENDLINESS

adjectives
patronizing; beaming; familiar; ignoble; truest; genuine; curious; paternal; effusive; heavenly.

FRIENDLY

adverbs
disarmingly; consistently; unquestionably; essentially; extremely; gratifyingly; courteously; placidly; gravely; smilingly; cordially; helpfully; quietly; remarkably; palpably; ostentatiously; condescendingly; singularly; charmingly; genuinely; sincerely; unaffectedly; naturally; delightfully; politely; openly; heartily; scrupulously; loyally; enchantingly; engagingly; altogether.

527

FRIENDSHIP

adjectives
platonic; distinguished; diplomatic; remarkable; acknowledged; disinterested; traditional; proffered; supercilious; partisan; equal; hereditary; warmest; informal; subsidiary; steadfast; deathless; ardent; resistless; lasting; ancient; problematical; practical; confidential; ill-assorted; heaping; tranquil; precious; intimate; true; poetic; intellectual; pure; lifelong; three-cornered; expedient; serviceable; loyal; commercial; estranged; deep; benevolent; unreturned; familiar; generous; dignified; cordial; warm; patronizing; profound; casual; adoring; unusual; strict; fragile; ominous; well-known; inseparable; unquenchable; passionate; restful; sober; youthful; energetic; bosom; offered; exquisite; literary; ancient; protracted; expansive.

verbs
accept—of; attain—of; bask in—; cultivate —; destroy—; disrupt—; encourage—; endanger—; enhance—; foster—; gain—of; hold out the hand of—; jeopardize—; kill—; manifest—; taint—; voice—; —blossoms; —cools; —fades; —flowers; —ripens.
(See affection, attachment, amity, intimacy, devotion.)

FRIEZE

adjectives
professional; magnificent; dignified.

FRIGHT

adjectives
perfect; whispered; sudden; supernatural; helpless; violent; overwhelming; quivering; collective; intolerable; morbid.

verbs
blanch with—; conceal—; convulse in—; cower in—; crouch in—; die of—; exhaust with—; harrow with—; hesitate in—; impel by—; quake with—; quiver with—; recoil in—; shake with—; start in—; subject to—; sweat with—; take—; thrill with —; throw into—; tremble with—; —abates; —freezes; —paralyzes; —petrifies; —slackens; —shocks; shiver with—.
(See alarm, fear, dismay, terror, consternation.)

FRIGHTEN (*v*)

adverbs
genuinely; horribly; supernaturally; violently; morbidly; collectively; intolerably; overwhelmingly; instinctively; devilishly; nefariously; insidiously.
(See alarm, terrify.)

FRIGHTFUL

adverbs
hideously; awfully; shockingly; appallingly; grimly; unspeakably; inexpressibly; incalculably; indescribably; peculiarly; particularly; utterly; insupportably; cruelly; brutally; grimly; uncommonly.

FRIGID

adverbs
obnoxiously; calmly; arrogantly; bitterly; languidly; impassively; phlegmatically; unemotionally; indifferently; callously; imperturbably; unconcernedly; maddeningly; discourteously; abominably; insufferably.

FRINGE

verbs
adorn with—; bear—; border with—; deck with—; drape—; edge with—; finish with —; hang by—; knot—; ravel—; rip—; suspend—; swing—; toy with—; —beautifies; —dances; —dangles; —fascinates; —quivers.
(See border.)

FRINGES

adjectives
fleecy; raveling; icy; angry-looking; luxuriant; amber; penumbral; straggling; outermost; solid; mysterious; cotton; ball; scalloped; hand-knotted; luminous; sleek; tattered; tasseled; delicate.

FRIPPERY

adjectives
feminine; tawdry; meretricious.

FRISK (*v*)

adverbs
joyously; gaily; laughably; unconventionally; youthfully; wantonly; scandalously; thoughtlessly; dissipatedly.
(See leap, skip, frolic.)

FRISKING

adjectives
joyous; carefree; unconventional; animal.

FRISKY

adverbs
youthfully; childishly; vivaciously; nimbly; happily; blithely; smartly; eagerly; delightfully; charmingly; interestingly; buoyantly;

jauntily; airily; lightsomely; brightly; joyously; sportively; gleefully; trickily; jocosely; exultantly; jubilantly; irrepressibly; exhilaratingly; indescribably; playfully.

FRIVOLITY

adjectives
scholastic; Gallic; irresponsible; scandalous.

verbs
attack—; beckon in—; celebrate with—; condemn—; denounce—; discard—; display —; exhibit—; pretend—; prevent—; repudiate—; ridicule—; —amuses; —attracts; —excites; —flourishes; —irks; —vexes.
(See frolic, fun.)

FRIVOLOUS

adverbs
wildly; foolishly; entertainingly; absurdly; gaily; blithely; idly; childishly; utterly; senselessly; lightly; ridiculously; ludicrously; capriciously; fantastically; giddily; wantonly; freakishly; blatantly; extravagantly; nonsensically; vacantly; hilariously.

FROCK

adjectives
smartest; charming; sheerer; gleaming; silver; filmy; close-fitting; icy; twice-turned; chic; dowdy.; spangled; gayest; refreshing; fashionable.

verbs
adore—; alter—; arrange—; compliment on —; design—; discard—; dislike—; display —; don—; envy—; fit—; injure—; purchase—; renovate—; select—; slip into—; yearn for—; —attracts; —becomes; —befits; —exposes; —flatters; —reveals; —slenderizes.
(See garment, gown, dress, robe.)

FROG

verbs
can—s; farm—s; persecute—s; —blinks; —burrows; —croaks; —damages; —dips; —s disperse; —dives; —evolves; —excavates; —jumps; —leaps; —snatches; —swims; —trills.
(See animal.)

FROGS

adjectives
croaking; reasonable; vulgar.

FROLIC

adjectives
carnal; lively; midnight.

verbs
bridle—; curb—; enter into—; gambol at —; gather for—; indulge in—; interrupt—; invite to—; observe—; provide—; reprimand—; revel at—; savor—; subdue—; suffer for—; —amuses; —delights; —tempts.
(See merriment, sport, prank, fun.)

FROLIC (v)

adverbs
boyishly; gleefully; jocundly; winsomely; exuberantly; sportively; blithesomely; drunkenly.
(See leap, skip, play.)

FROLICSOME

adverbs
genially; gaily; gleefully; vivaciously; irrepressibly; mirthfully; hilariously; noisily; boisterously; laughingly; merrily; jovially; joyously; brightly; lightly; delightedly; happily; jauntily; immensely; immeasurably; infectiously; pleasantly; playfully; waggishly; amazingly.

FRONDS

adjectives
dark; sempiternal; pinnate; magnificent; beauteous; waving; hoving.

FRONT

adjectives
formidable; starry; atheist; willing; bastionlike; undaunted; proud; defying; bold; blazoned; blushless; time-stained; ivory; immediate; pompous; ardent; honorable; confident; veneered; gallant.

verbs
bound—; direct to—; display—; edge—; erect—; enter—; face—; forge to—; form at—; furnish—; limit—; move to—; pertain to—; place at—; provide—; scale—; situate at—; skirmish on—; station at—; unite—; —crumbles; —extends; —shields.
(See rear.)

FRONTIER

verbs
charge—; command—; defend—; dispatch to—; extend—; guard—; inhabit—; invade —; repel at—; scale—; settle on—; shun—; situate on—; station at—; thrust to—; unite

—; —advances; —bounds; —limits; — presses forward; —recedes; —resists; — shifts; —surrounds.
(See border, boundary.)

FRONTIERS

adjectives
narrow; indefensible; remotest; flexible; dangerous; maritime; rude; guarded; expanding; constraining.

FROST

adjectives
flowery; white; radiant; pondering; wondrous; make-believe; ceaseless; wintry; dazzling; crackling; sharp; keen; relentless; singeing; killing; envious; autumn; audacious; piercing; blighting; withering; fettering; bitter; heavy; gray; iridescent; chilly; hard; snapping; untimely; hoar.

verbs
form—; hang with—; lace with—; trace with—; —bites; —chills; —covers; —damages; —decorates; —descends; —designs; —draws; —etches; —falls; —glimmers; — glistens; —glorifies; —injures; —lingers; —nips; —projects; —settles on; —sharpens; —silvers; —sprays; —transforms.
(See snow.)

FROSTY

adverbs
sharply; refreshingly; bitterly; appetizingly; freshly; bleakly; bitingly; nippingly; terribly; cruelly; destructively; slightly; invigoratingly; delightfully.

FROTH

adjectives
sudden; flowery; flying; idlest.

verbs
agitate to—; beat to—; boil to—; break into—; churn up—; cover with—; crest with—; emit—; ferment to—; fleck with—; shake into—; toss off—; —bubbles; — creams; —effervesces; —floats; —foams; — gurgles; —issues from; —reams.
(See foam.)

FROTHY

adverbs
lightly; airily; volatilely; thickly; effervescently; sparklingly; lusciously; fizzily; deliciously; genuinely; attractively; invitingly.

FROWN

adjectives
ominous; ireful; discontented; blackening; mournful; rumorous; bitter; puzzled; chilling; feudal; gloomy; sternest; habitual; steady; churlish; crusty; fastidious; gathering; old-fashioned; restrained; drunken; petulant; searching; angry; pedantic; unfeeling; charming; fleeting; deep-furrowed.

verbs
assume—; blemish with—; contract in—; cringe before—; disclose—; display—; form —; incur—; observe—; overcome—; perceive—; rebuke with—; relax—; suppress —; wrinkle into—; —belies; —commands; —corrugates; —creases; —deters; —expresses; —intimidates; —punishes; —reprimands; —terrorizes.
(See scowl.)

FROWN (v)

adverbs
sullenly; belligerently; blackly; wrathfully; inauspiciously; reprovingly; dismally; majestically; ferociously; austerely; ominously; mournfully; bitterly; sternly; habitually; churlishly; petulantly; uncongenially.
(See scowl.)

FROWZY

adverbs
carelessly; roughly; inexcusably; neglectfully; dreadfully; miserably; nonchalantly; wretchedly; merrily; cheerfully; indifferently; unconcernedly; inordinately; terribly; excitedly.

FRUGAL

adverbs
carefully; necessarily; thriftily; cautiously; warily; watchfully; ostentatiously; habitually; naturally; amazingly; cooperatively; inherently; meanly; sensibly; providently; moderately; parsimoniously; admirably; intelligently; judiciously.

FRUGALITY

adjectives
ostentatious; necessary; apologetic; helpful; customary; habitual; native.

verbs
bare—; commend—; conceal—; conduct with—; display—; endure—; expose to—; found—; justify—; mark—; occasion—;

practise—; praise—; reduce to—; relieve—; require—; resent—; resign to—; reveal—.
(See economy, thrift.)

FRUIT

adjectives

forbidden; copious; unavailing; immediate; fairy; delicious; grateful; acid; just; divine; mellow; pulpy; ambrosial; monthly; teeming; autumnal; fuller; beatific; wholesome; fragrant; delightful; deciduous; luscious; bitter; discordant; blessed; apparent; bleeding; sacred; proper; gushing; clustering; golden; compensating; disastrous; ruddy; detested; glorious; exotic; immortal; alluring; natural; noble; fresh; cordial; panting; wandering; fairest; legitimate; sun-ripened; vigorous; personal; pouting; celestial; cherished; ripe; fallacious; unknown; blushing; sole; mellow; seasonal; proper; wind-tossed; choicest; dazzling; tolerable; ornamental; sprouting; ripe-cheeked; remarkable; nectarine; oversized; divinest; flesh-colored; rotten; wormy.

verbs

attack—; bear —; blight—; blossom into—; consume—; damage—; develop into—; diet on—; gather—; load with—; partake of—; produce—; reap—; relish—; replenish with —; savor—; serve—; spray—; store—; yield—; —abounds; —delights; —rots; —satiates.
(See crop, harvest.)

FRUITFUL

adverbs

profitably; satisfactorily; unusually; prolifically; luxuriantly; admirably; genuinely; copiously; abundantly; teemingly; sparsely; apparently; ordinarily; remarkably; sufficiently; surprisingly; plentifully; richly; uberously.

FRUITFULNESS

adjectives

mellow; uncommon; tropical.

FRUITION

adjectives

instant; tantalizing; unalloyed; ceaseless.

FRUITLESS

adverbs

grievously; disappointingly; inconsequentially; terribly; disconcertingly; ruinously; unfortunately; unluckily; wretchedly; miserably; pitiably; pathetically; naturally; inevitably; irremediably; sadly; dreadfully.

FRUMPISH

adverbs

crabbedly; morosely; perversely; moodily; sulkily; intolerably; utterly; doggedly; grumpily; peevishly; crustily; inscrutably; vaguely; sourly; unreasonably; habitually; usually; disagreeably

FRUSTRATE (v)

adverbs

effectually; treacherously; legitimately; vindictively; jealously; subtly; basely; temporarily.
(See prevent, defeat, disappoint.)

FRUSTRATION

verbs

avoid—; balk at—; condemn—; curb—; denounce—; endure—; hurdle—; overcome—; resent—; subdue—; suffer—; —baffles; —circumvents; —defeats; —deters; —harms; —hinders; —injures; —interrupts.
(See failure, defeat, disappointment.)

FRYING-PAN

verbs

adhere to—; blacken—; brandish—; cleanse —; dent—; employ—; escape—; grease—; mix in—; necessitate—; place in—; polish —; scour—; —clatters; —jangles; —rattles; —shines; —sizzles.
(See pan.)

FUEL

adjectives

premium; inflammable; volatile; self-sustaining; exhausted; available; solid; fresh.

verbs

acquire—; burn—; employ as—; fill with—; furnish—; ignite—; necessitate—; obtain—; produce—; replenish—; require—; select—; supply—; —explodes; —flames; —heats; —illumines; —inflames; —sustains.
(See wood, coal, etc.)

FUGITIVE

adjectives

gallant; young; suppliant; mangled; royal; solitary; panting; sole; wretched; stricken; returning; frenzied.

verbs

conceal—; deter—; endanger—; espy—; harbor—; nab—; prevent—; protect—; pur-

sue—; search for—; shelter—; track down
—; —absconds; —deserts; —escapes; —
flees; —hides; —journeys; —wanders.
(See prisoner.)

adverbs
elusively; shyly; evasively; remotely; evanescently; transiently; ephemerally; etheral-
ly; nebulously; perishably; mortally; temporally; transitorily; unhappily; sadly; unfortunately; tormentingly.

FULFILL (v)
adverbs
magnificently; admirably; conscientiously;
abundantly; moderately; approximately;
swiftly; blindly; ultimately; immutably;
adequately; partially.
(See accomplish, complete.)

FULFILLMENT
adjectives
adequate; abundant; mere; rigid; speedy;
partial.

verbs
accomplish—; allow—; anticipate—; attain
—; attempt—; concede—; defeat—; effect
—; execute—; express—; grant—; perform
—; pray for—; predict—; promote—; reach
—; supply to—; yearn for—; —completes;
—disappoints; —satiates; —satisfies.
(See accomplishment, realization.)

FULL
adverbs
moderately; satisfactorily; sufficiently; completely; fortunately; gloriously; abundantly; measurably; adequately; liberally; generously; pleasantly; agreeably.

FULLNESS
adjectives
quiet; flaring; swelling; grim; apparent;
arduous; generous; lavish; flaccid; abounding; messy; eloquent; all-excluding; immeasurable; molded.

FUMBLE (v)
adverbs
casually; nervously; drunkenly; clumsily;
fruitlessly; tremulously; ineffectually; absurdly; pedantically.
(See blunder, flounder, miss, stumble.)

FUME (v)
adverbs
indignantly; sulphurously; poisonously; unendurably; odoriferously; exasperatedly; angrily; wrathfully; blatantly; prodigiously.
(See rage, bluster.)

FUMES
adjectives
noxious; greasy; odoriferous; resinous; unendurable; earthly; unkindly; poisonous;
fishy; devilish; disagreeable; sulphurous.

verbs
bear—; blow—; disperse—; discharge—;
emit—; exhale—; fill with—; flood with—;
give off—; inhale—; scent—; send forth—;
spray with—; —creep out of; —mantle; —
overcome; —pass off; —perfume; —please;
—preserve; —rise; —smother; —stifle; —
vanish.
(See vapor, smoke.)

FUN
adjectives
spirited; capital; innocent; fairy; hilarious;
practical; legitimate; gentle; monstrous;
genuine; nonsensical; boisterous; monotonous; tremendous; bitter; nasty; ill-timed;
painful.

verbs
carouse in—; create—; drown—; entertain
with—; exclude—; indulge in—; play for—;
poke—at; pretend in—; spare—; —amuses;
—ceases; —cheers; —diverts; —enlivens;
—grows; —relaxes; —wearies.
(See frolic, joke, mirth, gayety, merriment, amusement.)

FUNCTION
adjectives
ministerial; vital; legitimate; valuable; useful; manifold (pl); ritualistic; perverted;
nerve; judicial; impaired; aesthetic; beneficent; natural; economic; animal; normal;
consular; religious; executive; cherished; intellectual; pitiable; hospitable; cognitive;
imitative; precise; sacerdotal; essential; basest; appropriate; principal; civilian; impaired; numerous (pl); social; obsolete; inescapable; diminished; proper; primary; indispensable; frightful; spiritual; gracious;
ecclesiastical; sociological; diversified (pl);
imperfect; varied (pl); episcopal.

verbs

abuse—; arrest—; associate with—; block —; centralize—; check—; delegate—to; discharge—; embarrass—; energize—; exercise —; fulfill—; impair—; improve—; invest with—; magnify—; perform—; preserve—; promote—; regulate—; resume—; restore—; subserve—; vest—in; —s overlap one another.

(See duty.)

FUNCTION (*v*)

adverbs

automatically; efficiently; biologically; splendidly; sluggishly; elaborately; ministerially; beneficently; economically; indispensably; spiritually.

(See perform, discharge.)

FUND

verbs

abscond with —s, abuse—; administer—; advance —s; allocate —s; allot —s; appropriate —s; audit—; bolster—; campaign for —s; deplete—; divert from—; draw from —; embezzle —s; endow with—; juggle —s; misappropriate —s; muster —s; pool —s; seek —s; solicit —s; stretch —s; struggle for —s; supplant—; swell—; utilize—; —benefits; —dwindles; —increases; —s roll in.

(See money, capital.)

FUNDAMENTAL

adverbs

definitely; indispensably; radically; significantly; essentially; ineradically; inherently; intrinsically; virtually; substantially; absolutely; fairly; basically; undeniably.

FUNDAMENTALS

verbs

cleave to—; cling to—; deviate from—; doubt—; exhaust—; implant—; inculcate—; inform in—; instruct in—; interfere with—; involve—; necessitate—; preserve—; recognize—; regard—; reiterate—; rely on—; require—; revere—; subject to—; submit to—; sway from—.

(See essential, rule, principle, law.)

FUNDS

adjectives

stabilization; exhaustless; contingent; accumulated; unlimited; reserve; insurance; pegging; special; slush; inexhaustible; char-

itable; needed; unlimited; unequalled; tremendous; misused; supplemented; baffling; available; endowment; meager; misappropriated.

FUNERAL

adjectives

leafy; lugubrious; genteel.

verbs

announce—; arrange—; ease—; eulogize at —; expend on—; follow—; reign at—; mourn at—; observe—; officiate at—; preside at—; proceed at—; toll at—.

(See death.)

FUNEREAL

adverbs

solemnly; lugubriously; quietly; reverently; murmurously; depressingly; gloomily; disconsolately; dismally; gravely; heavily; horribly; oppressively; sadly; dully; mournfully; cheerlessly; frightfully; lamentably; dolefully; incredibly; unnecessarily; absurdly; extremely; inordinately.

FUNGUS

adjectives

decayed, dismal.

verbs

cover with—; divest of—; neglect—; nourish—; —chokes; —corrupts; —damages; —encrusts; —enervates; —flourishes; —gathers; —harms; —injures; —invades; —kills; —overruns; —penetrates; —poisons; —ripens; —spreads; —rots.

(See plant.)

FUNNY

adverbs

hilariously; laughably; excruciatingly; uproariously; comically; wholesomely; divertingly; delightfully; drolly; drily; quaintly; entertainingly; merrily; facetiously; smartly; extravagantly; ridiculously; fantastically; whimsically; outlandishly; extremely; exceedingly.

FUR

adjectives

shimmering; sleek; rich; warm; glossy; jet; ruffled; luxurious; silk-soft; semiprecious; camouflaged; prickly; ice-covered; tawny; sumptuous; imitation; expensive; woolly; fuzzy.

verbs

adjust—; clothe in—; deck with—; display —; dress in—; encase in—; face with—; fluff—; hunt for —s; line with—; muffle in —; ornament with—; sheathe in—; strip of —; stroke—; trade in —s; trim with—; value—; wrap in—; —encircles; —envelopes; —flies; —protects.

(See coat, skin, hair.)

adverbs

senselessly; sullenly; suddenly; intolerably; hotly; justly; obviously; foolishly; ridiculously; dangerously; alarmingly; terribly; dreadfully; coldly; genuinely; uncontrollably; passionately; violently; sternly; implacably; unjustly; inordinately; insanely; naturally; ludicrously; unnaturally; curiously; oddly; strangely; unappeasably; recklessly; inconsiderately; blindly; savagely; jealously; indescribably; tragically; absurdly; hysterically; inanely; idiotically; groundlessly; boisterously; desperately; murderously; fearfully; frightfully; fiercely; truculently; diabolically; brutally; needlessly; horribly.

FURLOUGH

adjectives

delightful; precious; desired; short; happy.

verbs

absent on—; authorize—; beg—; concede—; defer—; demand—; earn—; favor with—; forbid—; grant—; leave on—; license—; obtain—; order—; overstay—; permit—; refuse—; request—; restrict—; return from —; take—; warrant—.

(See vacation.)

FURNACE

adjectives

fiery; sacred; untiring; molten; smelting.

verbs

bake in—; cast into—; dry in—; feed—; fire —; fuel—; install—; issue from—; operate —; rake—; start—; supply—; tap—; tend —; —burns; —converts; —emits; —exhales; —heats; —sighs.

(See stove.)

FURNISH (v)

adverbs

abundantly; defectively; meanly; gaudily; bizarrely; adequately; scantily; sumptuously; tastefully; exquisitely; luxuriously; rudely; drably; modernistically.

(See provide, supply.)

FURNITURE

adjectives

scanty; enduring; somber; haircloth; simple; meager; hand-made; custom-made; time-worn; elegant; unfriendly; commodious; ecclesiastical-looking; space-saving; antique; luxurious; rude; best-styled; massive; costly; dim; drab; incidental; hideous; rickety; bulky; modernistic; streamlined.

verbs

appoint—; arrange—; clutter with—; cover —; damage—; decorate—; design—; equip with—; fill with—; inherit—; nick—; outfit with—; overcrowd with—; place—; polish —; possess—; scratch—; select—; stock with —; store—; van—; —fits; —harmonizes; —matches; —suffices.

(See equipment, outfit, chair, table, etc.)

FUROR

adjectives

bacchic; devilish; raucous; riotous; frenzied.

FURROW

adjectives

sounding; foul; fat; unmeaning; roaring; mucky; silvery; sonorous; fruitless; shining; rectangular; dry-drawn; unthrifty; vertical.

FURTIVE

adverbs

craftily; adroitly; cleverly; uncommonly; habitually; suspiciously; strangely; oddly; curiously; warily; evasively; mysteriously; cryptically; whisperingly; needlessly; significantly; unduly; cautiously; extremely; remarkably; particularly.

FURY

adjectives

domestic; utmost; irresistible; civil; unappeasable; suppressed; violent; tempestuous; warlike; unabated; reckless; undiminished; exasperated; empty; whirling; drink-engendered; satiate; direful; fierce; concentrated; snake-locked; everlasting; fighting; manifest; indiscriminate; inconsiderate; uncontrolled; steelhearted; perfect; hellish; exterminating; blistering; blindfold; mineral; revolutionary; mad; governable; bestial; increasing; unreasoning; sparkling; unbridled; coming; sudden; implacable; chaotic; overpowering; disappointed; savage; unchained; vindictive; obvious; concentrated; pretty; jealous; unrelenting; indescribable; blind; incarnate; tragic.

verbs

blast with—; conceal—; dignify—; drive to —; encounter—; engender—; fan—; fly into —; gaze in — at; mutter in—; rage in—; roar in—; seethe with—; simmer with—; vent—; whip into—; work into—; —abates; —increases; —lets down; —subsides.

    (See anger, rage, passion, frenzy, excitement.)

FUSE

adjectives

unreliable; burning; hissing; short; time.

FUSILLADE

adjectives

murderous; fierce; random; furious; brutal; bloody; merciless.

verbs

discharge—; emit—; keep up—; pour—; protect from—; rain—; run from—; shower —; spout—; swear—; warn of—; withstand —; —assaults; —butchers; —ceases; —executes; —levels; —massacres; —mows down; —shatters; —terrorizes.

    (See volley, barrage.)

FUSION

adjectives

fiery; graceful; necessary; remarkable.

FUSS

adjectives

indignant; noisy; quarrelsome; sudden; nasty; unspeakable.

FUSSY

adverbs

needlessly; tiresomely; irritatingly; restlessly; excitedly; foolishly; ineptly; unduly; eternally; noisily; annoyingly; feverishly; briskly; officiously; uneasily; twitteringly; naggingly; abominably; detestably; unbearably; remarkably; intolerably; hatefully.

FUTILE

adverbs

lamentably; invariably; unfortunately; deplorably; helplessly; unluckily; unhappily; feebly; weakly.

FUTILITY

adjectives

clumsy; apparent; sweet; fantastic; magnificent; obvious; patent; accepted.

verbs

battle with—; bemoan — of; break in—; contend with—; curse—; dispose of—; evade—; fritter into—; lapse into—; lose in —; manifest—; object to—; recognize—; reduce to—; result in—; screen—; strike at —; while away in—; —appears; —confronts; —conquers; —dies.

    (See uselessness, worthlessness.)

FUTURE

adjectives

ever-better; magnetic; blest; naturalistic; impending; imminent; immediate; luminous; physical; immortal; distant; impossible; eternal; financial; promising; boundless; uncertain; commercial; brilliant; infinite; interesting; cruel; ruthless; secure; dubious; dim; black; significant; controlling; happy; measureless; hopeless; cheerful; supramundane; heterogeneous; somber; altered; terrestrial; fantastic; invisible; far-stretching; friendless; permanent; real; gloomy; glorious; unlimited; profitable; assured; lurid; long-time; cosmopolitan.

verbs

anticipate—; blast—; chart—; cloud—; despair of—; endanger—; entrust to—; explore —; fear for—; figure out—; forecast—; foretell—; gamble away—; gaze into—; glance into—; guide—; hope for—; jeopardize—; lay — open; menace—; mortgage —; overshadow—; peer into—; project into —; prophesy—; read—; risk—; save for—; secure—; stake — on; view—.

    (See outlook.)

G

GABLE

adjectives
sculptured; towering; fantastic; peaked.

GADGET

adjectives
life-saving; lethal; noise-making; education-al.

GAIETY

adjectives
fictitious; unfeigned; served; wild; airy; fortunate; exuberant; uncanny; bounding; fatigued; inward; forced; brilliant; charming; facile; heedless; social; jaded; seeming; careless; prevalent; nimble; leaden; affectionate; bewitching; sparkling; teasing; surface; delirious; animating; exhausting; false; spurious; customary; ironical; childlike; mock; embarrassed; tempered; alternate; enticing; unearthly; wholehearted.

verbs
(See gayety.)

GAIN

adjectives
glorious; immense; sure; intellectual; eternal; substantial; capital; selfish; adequate; personal; speculative; happy; immediate; indubitable; obvious; fruitful; fallacious; indicated; unhallowed; qualitative; scanty; treacherous; pecuniary; proper; equivalent; territorial; untold; mystic; appreciable; unjust; corporate; hopeless.

verbs
accomplish—; acquire—; begrudge—; claim —; content with—; count—; derive—; dissipate —s; forego—; promise—; register—; seek—; serve for—; spurn—; struggle for —; yield—; —astonishes; —benefits; —decreases; —increases; —mounts; —outweighs.
(See profit, advantage.)

GAIN (v)

adverbs
vastly; legally; lawfully; ethically; deservedly; definitely; unquestionably; incredibly; consistently; incessantly; singularly; sub-stantially; gloriously; immensely; speculatively; indubitably; unhallowedly; pecuniarily; territorially; subtly.
(See profit, win.)

GAINFUL

adverbs
amazingly; securely; certainly; magically; mysteriously; unexpectedly; productively; surprisingly; admirably; luckily; fortunately; happily; providentially; adequately; curiously; valuably; oddly; legally; definitely; unquestionably; incredibly; gloriously; immensely; subtly; pecuniarily; financially; singularly.

GAIT

adjectives
staid; swinging; rolling; stooping; shuffling; awkward; majestical; unremitted; aerie; true; haggard; lofty; shambling; weary; gentle; traveling; unnatural; pacing; common; ponderous; rapid; stately; princely; habitual; heavy; feeble; swaggering; musing; measured; lumbering.

verbs
change—; fix—; go at—; hobble in—; limp in—; lumber in—; mimic—; mock—; practise—; quicken—; recognize—; settle down to—; shift—; slacken—; slow up—; solemnize—; stagger in—; steady—; stumble in—.
(See walk, step.)

GALAXY

adjectives
splendid; cooperative; successive (pl).

GALE

adjectives
treacherous; spicy; approaching; lurid; angry; shrieking; tearing; frantic; passing; sunrise; dreadful; furious; boisterous; merry; heavy; southern; viewless; favoring; odor-scented; cold; wet; carping; keel-compelling; sinking; coming; mocking; pleasant; heroic; terrific; strenuous; destroying; freshening; gracious; shadowy; rising; balmy; sighing; reveling.

verbs
buck—; combat—; encounter—; —abates; —accelerates; —arises; —blusters; —carries away; —damages; —disperses; —fans; —fumes; —lashes; —rages; —rampages; —

536

riots; —screams; —shrieks; —stiffens; —sweeps away; —violates; —whips up; —wreaks.

(See breeze, current, wind, tempest.)

GALL

adjectives
burning; soul-tormenting; hypercritical.

GALLANT

adjectives
open-handed; trim; gay; pleasant-spoken; boisterous; high-spirited; faultless; chivalric.

adverbs
splendidly; valorously; heroically; courteously; unwontedly; unusually; consistently; habitually; inherently; intrepidly; fearlessly; boldly; courageously; resolutely; adventurously; bravely; audaciously; firmly; confidently; daringly; dangerously, pluckily, fiercely; doughtily; urbanely; suavely; dutifully; blandly; graciously; obsequiously; ingratiatingly; immeasurably.

GALLANTRY

adjectives
generous; uncouth; delicate; desperate; sheepish; wonted; conspicuous; boyish; distinguished; rare; calm; consistent; premature; excessive; imputed; timeless; self-conscious; overdone; elaborate; natural; practical; noticeable.

verbs
accost with—; applaud—; attend with—; bear with—; behave with—; breathe—; conduct with—; court with—; deck in—; defend with—; display—; escort with—; exaggerate—; exchange —s; exhibit—; lay aside—; mock—; premeditate—; rejoice in —; —captures; —steals away; —wins.

(See bravery, courage, heroism, chivalry, prowess.)

GALLERY

adjectives
elliptical; gilded; elaborate; dirty; immense; encircling; frequented; extensive; whispering; formal; gracious; classical; ignorant; subterranean; loaded; starlit; vaulted.

verbs
assemble in—; exhibit in—; guide through —; hang in—; lounge in—; occupy—; par-

ade through—; play to—; proclaim from—; rail—; set up in—; speak from—; subdue —; support—; visit—; —edifies; —heckles; —hushes; —surrounds.

(See corridor, balcony, audience.)

GALLOP

adjectives
thunderous; false; perilous; rapid; soundless; clattering; morning; daily; historic; breathless.

GALLOP (v)

adverbs
furiously; picturesquely; gallantly; stiffly; thunderously; swiftly; perilously; clatteringly; breathlessly.

(See run, trot.)

GALLOWS

verbs
bring to—; cheat—; condemn to—; conduct to—; correct on—; deliver from—; deserve —; erect—; escape—; execute on—; hang on —; inflict—; punish on—; reprieve from—; save from—; sentence to—; threaten with —; —cures; —tames; —terrifies; —terrorizes.

(See gibbet.)

GAMBLE (v)

adverbs
habitually; inveterately; suavely; besottedly; professionally; foolhardily; passionately; improvidently.

(See risk.)

GAMBLER

adjectives
passionate; ready; riverboat; incarnate; prodigious; professed; besotted; adept; inveterate; skilled; sleek; suave.

GAMBLING

verbs
abhor—; bewail—; campaign against—; cheat at—; defraud at—; degenerate into—; denounce—; hedge in—; play at—; rail at —; resist—; resort to—; risk in—; shackle to—; share in—; speculate in—; stake for —; thrive on—; trap in—; wager on—; — destroys; —disgraces; —dismembers; — harms; —preys on; —relaxes; —ruins; — wrecks.

(See game.)

GAMBOLS

adjectives

wanton; noisy; joyous; insufferable; dainty; uncouth; frolicsome; pleasant; childish.

GAME

adjectives

mocking; dangerous; toilsome; impious; heroic; risky; thrilling; open; intricate; formidable; tedious; shut; attractive; daily; mimic; impassioned; unmeaning; poetic; lawful; Olympic; card; disappearing; contested; skillful; endless; arrayed; high-powered; intellectual; bickering; strenuous; political; national; cordial; nobler; entrancing; tight; overtime; professional; heated.

verbs

announce—; cheat in—; dabble at—; emerge from—; enjoy—; enliven—; enthuse (colloq.) over—; feature—; follow—; improve —; indulge in—; invent—; join in—; judge —; master—; practise—; referee—; quarrel at—; score—; share—; strive in—; view—; witness—; —amuses; —contents; —cripples; —delights; —diverts; —entertains; —enthralls; —excites; —stales; —tires; —wanes; —wearies.

(See contest, recreation, sport.)

GAME
(*animals*)

verbs

bag—; cherish—; destroy—; ensnare—; enthrall by—; exterminate—; follow—; preserve—; prey upon—; relish—; rouse—; search for—; stalk—; trap—; view—; —abounds; —flees; —flourishes; —thrives; pursue—.

(See animal.)

GAMESOME

adverbs

amusingly; enliveningly; briskly; smartly; energetically; divertingly; happily; entertainingly; unusually; marvellously; enthusiastically; airily; blithely; buoyantly; exhilaratingly; hilariously; delightfully; jauntily; jovially; merrily; playfully; rollickingly; roisteringly; waggishly.

GAMESTER

adjectives

vehement; embryo; experienced; common; desperate; lukewarm.

GANG

verbs

associate with—; attract—; break up—; control—; disperse—; form—; head—; hire —; join—; lead—; manage—; regulate—; reprimand—; supervise—; —dissipates; —gathers; —meets; —operates; —separates; —troops in.

(See group, band, company, crew, crowd, squad.)

GANG-PLANK

verbs

(See gangway.)

GANGRENE

verbs

affect with—; cure—; decompose with—; defile with—; heal—; infect with—; lop off —; occasion—; result in—; seize with—; treat for—; —begins; —corrupts; —endangers; —pains; —oozes; —sets in; —spreads.

GANGSTER

verbs

accuses—; apprehend—; battle—; consort with—; employ—; round up—; rub out—; track down—; —bribes; —foments; —"hides out"; —intimidates; —maltreats; —murders; —s operate; —s organize; —revenges; —smuggles; —snuffs out; —terrifies; —terrorizes; —wounds.

(See thief.)

GANGWAY

verbs

ascend—; assemble at—; climb—; confine to—; crowd—; enter by—; file down—; hoist—; leave by—; lower—; pass down—; raise—; rush up—; stream down—; stride up—; take up—; —accommodates; —extends; —bridges.

(See platform.)

GAP

adjectives

wide; appalling; unbridgeable; tremendous; invisible; innumerable (pl); perceptible; ghastly; apparent; long; conversational; glaring.

verbs

break into—; bridge—; cut—; discover—; enter—; escape through—; form—; mend —; notch into—; open into—; pass through

—; patch—; span—; stop—; wear into—;
—diminishes; —heals; —interrupts; —separates; —unites; —widens.
(See passage, breach.)

GARAGE
verbs
direct to—; equip—; grease at—; inspect
at—; maintain—; operate—; paint at—;
polish—; repair in—; stock—; store in—;
wash at—; —distributes; —furnishes; —
harbors; —itemizes; —services; —supplies;
manage—; weld at—.

GARB
adjectives
fantastic; offensive; splendid; angelic; penitential; puritanical; sacred; dazzling; holiday; traditional; eccentric; shaggy; fleshy;
severe; brighter; half-clerical; ecclesiastical; curious; symbolic; rustic; pompous;
mourning; disordered; humble; shapeless;
picturesque; antique; chronic; somber.

GARB (v)
adverbs
immaculately; spectacularly; fantastically;
puritanically; eccentrically; ecclesiastically;
symbolically; rustically; drably; somberly;
modestly.
(See clothe, array, dress.)

GARBAGE
verbs
accumulate—; complain of—; destroy—;
discard as—; disintegrate—; dispose of—;
dump—; heap—; incinerate—; litter with
—; object to—; separate—; sterilize—;
strew with—; utilize—; —contaminates; —
decomposes; —fertilizes; —menaces.
(See waste.)

GARBLED
adverbs
hopelessly; senselessly; sadly; ridiculously;
vexatiously; incoherently; wildly; deliberately; carelessly; ignorantly; disastrously;
indescribably; intentionally; maliciously;
dishonestly; unfairly; cunningly; adroitly;
mischievously; terribly; inexcusably; indefensibly; horribly.

GARDEN
adjectives
colonization; mellowing; exotic; luxuriant;
bowery; celebrated; fateful; private; curious; aquatic; countless (pl); tranquil; radiant; delicious; odorous; fabled; spacious;

desolate; ample; rustic; walled; extensive;
seedy; orchard; ravaged; shady; tiny;
broken; terraced; revived; alluring; vigorous; suburban; enchanted; sequestered; neglected; stately; weedless; beautiful; untidy;
hanging; sunny; formal; productive; magnificent; illuminated; rock; delightful;
dainty.

verbs
cultivate—; delve in—; fence—; fringe—;
girdle—; hedge in—; plan—; plot—; preserve—; putter in—; rejoice in—; sow—;
sprinkle—; stroll through—; till—; tour—;
transplant to—; wall in—; water—; —delights; —flourishes; —thrives.
(See yard.)

GARGLE
verbs
advise—; advocate—; apply—; bathe with
—; dilute—; employ—; prepare—; require
—; treat with—; wash with—; —cools; —
eases; —heals; —relieves.
(See liquid, preparation.)

GARISH
adverbs
cheaply; glitteringly; unpleasantly; surprisingly; unexpectedly; intensely; crudely; discordantly; inharmoniously; rudely; monstrously; obtrusively; pretentiously; pompously; spectacularly; dramatically; unbecomingly; ridiculously; intensely; preposterously.

GARLAND
adjectives
funereal; live; jeweled; lovely; immortal; leafy; beauteous; victorious.

verbs
bear—; compete for—; crown with—; deck
with—; display—; festoon with—s; lay—;
mantle with—; reward with—; set—upon;
swathe in—; wind—; —adorns; —decorates.

GARMENT
adjectives
drenched; banqueting; tattered; ordinary;
sacerdotal; wretched; voluminous; trailing; coarse; operating; dignified; delicate;
fragile; sober; mortal; perennial; discarded; stage; bridal; transparent; necessary;
glittering; rustic; vaporous; shabby; shapeless; magic; exquisite; clean; flimsy; seductive; upper; radiant; charity; appropriate;
superb; snowy; sweeping; fluttering; flat-

tering; luxurious; handsome; custom; cool; elegant; exclusive; poisoned; untimely; imperial; dusty; modest; everlasting.

verbs
admire—; damage—; design—; dishevel—; display—; dye—; envy—; exhibit—; fashion—; fumigate—; injure—; model—; repair—; sew—; shroud in—; strip off—; sweat in—; weave—; yearn for—; —attracts; —befits; —clings to; —flatters; —reveals.

(See dress, coat, gown.)

GARNISHED

adverbs
tastefully; beautifully; generously; gayly; colorfully; invitingly; attractively; pleasingly; decoratively; becomingly; gorgeously; showily; simply; lusciously; deliciously; elaborately; cleverly; laboriously; ingeniously; unbelievably.

GARRET

verbs
accumulate in—; ascend to—; betake to—; conceal in—; deposit in—; evict from—; furnish—; heap in—; hoard in—; inhabit —; lodge in—; mount to—; preserve in—; remove to—; renovate—; reserve in—; search in—; stock in—; store in—; stow away in—; —garners; —projects; —totters.

(See attic, room.)

GARRISON

adjectives
intrusive; ample; large; floating; stalwart; retreating; slender; beleaguered; sturdy; strong; well-manned.

verbs
assault—; beset—; besiege—; bombard—; build—; charge—; erect—; fire upon—; invade—; maintain—; march upon—; quarter in—; reinforce—; station at—; threaten—; —defends; —guards; —shields; —surrenders; —withdraws.

(See fortification.)

GARRISON (v)

adverbs
sturdily; feebly; inadequately; stalwartly; smartly; prodigiously; effectually; adeptly.

(See supply, furnish.)

GARRULITY

adjectives
senile; unflagging; increased; nauseous; feminine; usual; boring; customary.

GARRULOUS

adverbs
endlessly; tediously; happily; chattily; genially; illuminatingly; knowledgeably; tiresomely; toothlessly; cacklingly; ribaldly; merrily; nauseatingly; unusually; habitually; highly; inescapably; incorrigibly; ponderously; monotonously; feverishly; excitedly; mumblingly.

GAS

adjectives
illuminating; foul; lethal; vivifying; incandescent; subtle; insidious; continuous; nebulous; congealed; fermenting; beneficent; transmuted; superseded; liquefied; mystery; deadly; noxious; injurious; rarefied; offensive; healthful.

verbs
accumulate—; battle—; bottle—; burn—; develop—; exhale—; guard against—; inhale—; isolate—; overcome by—; saturate with—; —asphyxiates; —emerges; —escapes; —expands; —flows; —fouls; —lifts; —poisons; —rises; —seeps in; —fuels.

(See oxygen.)

GASH

adjectives
deep; ghastly; fearful; fatal; abominable; hideous; deadly; murderous; bloody.

GASH (v)

adverbs
mortally; deeply; fatally; abominably; hideously; murderously; fearfully; savagely; fiendishly; diabolically.

(See slash, cut, tear.)

GASP

adjectives
convulsive; painful; long; grieving; struggling; broken; terrific; fitful; gurgling; last.

GASP (v)

adverbs
incredulously; breathlessly; unintelligibly; audibly; convulsively; fitfully; dramatically; brokenly; startlingly.

(See pant, breathe.)

GATE

adjectives

rusty; unclosed; churlish; inexorable; curtained; yawning; swinging; wooden; steel; decorated; awful; moon-lit; spectral; monumental; thronged; fast-locked; characteristic; facile; infernal; adamantine; massive; mosque; million-dollar; forbidden; figured; eastern; widest; celestial; huge; planched; applauding; painted; hospitable; silent; folding; sculptured; gorgeous; occidental; shadowy; postern; seaward; enchanted; grim; guarded; wicket; latched.

verbs

admit at—; bar—; beat against—; besiege —; fling open—; furnish—; guard—; knock on—; latch—; mend—; pass through —; repair—; storm—; swing on—; —bars; —hangs; —prevents.

(See opening, entrance, door.)

GATEWAY

adjectives

dilapidated; massive; secluded; crumbling; decorated; illumined.

GATHER (v)

adverbs

methodically; unpretentiously; seditiously; amiably; posthumously; tenderly; laboriously; noiselessly; cautiously; comprehensively; assiduously; formally; gaily; annually; riotously; raucously; exclusively.

(See assemble, congregate, accumulate.)

GATHERING

adjectives

informal; gay; insufficient; considerable; quiet; blind; assiduous; fashionable; indignant; annual; uncultured; democratic; eclectic; prompt; distinguished; noisy; unruly; riotous; unusual; raucous; notable; select; exclusive.

verbs

address—; arrange—; call—; collect into—; compose—; disperse—; dissipate—; enrage —; govern—; guide—; lead—; prevent—; provoke—; pull—; sway—; swell—; threaten—; —buzzes; —clamors; —contributes; —crowds; —impresses; —murmurs; — packs; —proposes; —views.

(See assembly, crowd.)

GAUDY

adverbs

unusually; unutterably; terribly; shockingly; extravagantly; oddly; gracelessly; unexpectedly; ridiculously; childishly; preposterously; horribly; offensively; disgustingly; unpleasantly.

GAUGE

verbs

adjust—; affect—; apply—; attach—; devise—; employ—; examine—; refer to—; test—; —advances; —ascertains; —determines; —fluctuates; —limits; —marks; — measures; —mounts; —notes; —records; — registers; —safeguards; —warns.

(See measure, standard.)

GAUGE (v)

adverbs

accurately; scientifically; correctly; skillfully; professionally; logically; mentally.

(See measure, estimate.)

GAUNT

adverbs

forbiddingly; haggardly; crookedly; unbelievably; terribly; awfully; unpleasantly; disagreeably; touchingly; miserably; portentously; wretchedly; ominously; alarmingly; horribly; uncommonly; meagerly; wanly; pallidly.

GAUZE

adjectives

theatrical; motionless; artful; vague; dappled; filmy.

verbs

apply—; bandage with—; brace with—; clean—; disinfect—; guard with—; join with—; sterilize—; strain through—; support with—.

(See fabric, silk.)

GAVEL

verbs

administer—; bang—; beat with—; drum —; employ—; hammer with—; heave—; inflict with—; knock—; rap with—; sound —; strike with—; —entreats; —hushes; — interferes; —interrupts.

(See hammer.)

GAWKY

adverbs

incredibly; pitiably; ludicrously; absurdly; inexcusably; sadly; utterly; remarkably;

clownishly; deliberately; pretentiously; comically; grotesquely; outlandishly; sensationally; theatrically; stupidly; heavily; **youthfully.**

GAY

adverbs

gracefully; boyishly; lightly; cheerfully; inexpressibly; racily; blithely; airily; saucily; proudly; carelessly; joyously; confidently; buoyantly; mystically; fantastically; devilishly; dashingly; artlessly; disarmingly; refreshingly; fashionably; racially; playfully; wantonly; roguishly; bewitchingly; engagingly; radiantly.

GAYETY

verbs

beget—; blush with—; commend—; displace—; eclipse—; feign—; flush in—; imbue with—; indulge in—; release—; revive —; rollick in—; thirst for—; unloose—; wreathe in—; yield to—; —blazes; —bubbles up; —cheers; —refreshes; —reigns; —ripples; —wearies.

(See merriment, fun, frolic, sport, liveliness, vivacity.)

GAZE

adjectives

uncertain; tributary; penetrating; mute; orphaned; relentless; quiet; kindred; probing; inquiring; abstracted; presumptuous; loving; searching; uncomplaining; earnest; averted; steady; enraptured; somber; maternal; inspiring; animated; shrewd; level; answering; admiring; bright; intent; compelling; concentrated; modest; steadfast; unwinking; calm; large; curious; living; dark; keen; vulgar; shrinking; piercing; hostile; disembodied; fervid; trained; appalling; complacent; unrestricted; astonished; lecherous; universal; dimmed; commanding; patient; long; prying; magic; painful; strained; imploring; ardent; melancholy; motionless; malevolent; questioning; different; tender; impartial; rapt; sullen; passionate; disdainful; reverent; magisterial; drowsy; mild; fixed; undeviating; yearning; enamored; ferret-like.

verbs

avoid—of; fix—on; quail beneath—; screen from—; shun—; stand at—; strain—toward; turn—upon; wilt beneath—; wince beneath—; writhe under—; —chills; —falls; —falters; —pierces; —searches; —wanders.

(See look, stare, glare.)

GAZE (v)

adverbs

vacantly; indifferently; inquiringly; deliberately; mournfully; impassionedly; trustfully; steadfastly; searchingly; furtively; blankly; defiantly; wistfully; dreamily; intently; sympathetically; impertinently; apprehensively; menacingly; disconsolately; reflectively; piercingly; keenly; obtrusively; insinuatingly; mockingly; beseechingly; profanely; piteously; perplexedly; meditatingly; yearningly; shrewdly; lecherously; ardently; malevolently.

(See look, stare.)

GEAR

adjectives

new-fashioned; dainty; dangerous; diminishing; adamantine; shapeless; bloody; military.

verbs

change—; connect—s; damage—s; drive in —; equip with—; fit with—; grease—; lock—; provide—; put into—; repair—; reverse—; rip—; strip—s; throw into—; —grinds; —s mesh.

(See equipment, mechanism.)

GEAR (v)

adverbs

adequately; delicately; mechanically; intricately; complicatedly; highly; scientifically.

(See prepare.)

GELATINE

verbs

abhor—; box—; coat with—; contain—; convert into—; contaminate—; dissolve—; garnish—; mold—; prepare—; relish—; serve—; shape—; utilize—; —preserves; —shakes; —shimmies; —trembles; —wobbles.

GEM

verbs

adorn with—s; collect—s; cut—; discover —; display—; engrave—; fashion—; girdle with—s; mine for—s; polish—; prize—; unearth—; value—; weigh—; —delights; —glistens; —glitters; —illuminates; —scintillates; —spangles.

(See stone, jewel, emerald, diamond, **ruby**, etc.)

542

GEMS

adjectives

sparkling; infusorial; twinkling; expensive; superb; flashing; shining; glittering; oracular; priceless; dainty; sunborn; reflecting; radiant; costly; animated; burnished; brilliant; carven.

GENEALOGY

verbs

admit—; commend—; dig up—; insert in—; interest in—; investigate—; mark—; note in—; praise—; reckon—; record—; register—; trace—; view—; —enumerates; —exhibits; —proves; —verifies.

(See record.)

GENERAL

adverbs

admittedly; broadly; surprisingly; necessarily; astonishingly; mysteriously; inexplicably; naturally; unaccountably; unwarrantably; fortunately; illimitably; sweepingly; inclusively; significantly; evidently; amazingly; dreadfully.

GENERAL
(army)

adjectives

politic; intrepid; merciful; permanent; commanding; grim; skilled; knowing; trained; clever; bungling; immortal; cruel; brash; stubborn; brutish; worsted; incipient; respective (pl); sagacious; shelved.

verbs

commission as—; decorate—; promote to—; respect—; salute—; —accuses; —administrates; —authorizes; —castigates; —commands; —conducts; —controls; —disposes of; —entrusts; —exercises; —leads; —maltreats; —orders; —plans; —posts; —quarters; —supervises; —terrorizes.

(See officer, commander, leader, chief.)

GENERALITIES

adjectives

polite; vague; inane; solemn; inept; illogical; meaningless.

GENERALITY

verbs

agree on—; arrive at—; avoid—; comment on—; comprehend—; confine to—s; deal in —s; descend from—s; evade—; guide—s; judge—; limit to—s; propound—; question —s; relegate to—s; resort to—s; restrain —s; skip—s; sound—s; stress—s; test—.

(See statement.)

GENERALIZATION

adjectives

easy; mystic; embracing; fantastical; scientific; hazardous; metaphysical; unsupported.

GENERATE (*v*)

adverbs

spontaneously; swiftly; sturdily; corruptly; endlessly; ceaselessly; intemperately; prolifically.

(See produce, reproduce, propagate.)

GENERATION

verbs

activate—; beget—; compute—; expose to —; glorify—; introduce—; laud—; praise —; reckon—s; remove from—; urge—; —arises; —s cherish; —s gather; —s heap; —s inherit; —involves; —s issue from.

(See period, time, age.)

GENERATIONS

adjectives

modest; innumerable; spontaneous; remote; sturdy; pompous; extremest; corrupt; countless; endless; coming; rising; future; spirited; existing; depraved; succeeding; frustrated; spurious; perished; analytical; tongueless; false; illiterate; whole; experimental; aesthetic; ceaseless; previous; intemperate; traveling.

GENERATOR

verbs

drive—; employ—; operate—; simplify—; —alternates; —converts; —draws; —heats up; —produces; —revolves; —rotates; —whines; —whirs; —winds.

(See machine, apparatus, dynamo.)

GENEROSITY

adjectives

impetuous; impulsive; unwonted; eager; judicious; amazing; consummate; pious; trustful; unparalleled; scornful; fond; divine; hearty; bitter; lavish; hospitable; celestial; careless; unquestioning; understandable; widespread; designing; dastardly.

verbs

admit—; bestow with—; commend—; credit —; distrust—; endow with—; exceed in—; expose—; flatter—; indulge—; owe to—; practise—; praise—; reveal—; rival—; shower with—; subscribe with—; temper with—; —bribes; —delights; —deprives; —drains.

(See benevolence.)

GENEROUS

adverbs

sincerely; quixotically; fantastically; ostentatiously; publicly; extremely; altruistically; charitably; benevolently; instinctively; distinctly; spontaneously; lavishly; extravagantly; habitually; truly; genuinely; amazingly; notably; essentially; magnificently; splendidly; essentially; unselfishly.

GENIAL

adverbs

pleasantly; courteously; affably; amiably; heartily; merrily; jovially; altogether; consistently; resolutely; fraternally; comfortingly; charmingly; cordially; delightfully; engagingly; marvelously; extraordinarily; unusually; habitually; conspicuously.

GENIALITY

adjectives

frank; shrewd; artificial; suave; hearty; boyish; artistic; feigned; real; soothing; effervescent; everlasting; annoying.

verbs

accustom to—; bask in—; diffuse—; flush with—; light up with—; practise—; receive with—; smile with—; welcome with —; —animates; —cheers; —delights; —endears; —exhilarates; —inspires; —warms.
(See cordiality, cheerfulness, warmth.)

GENIUS

adjectives

consummate; presiding; intellectual; inherent; interpretative; evil; unique; sublimest; engineering; sheer; ardent; sceptered; acute; fanciful; eloquent; bounding; sartorial; extraordinary; executive; untutored; unfettered; renovated; amiable; universal; persistent; various (pl); rare; decorative; sardonic; prodigious; military; solemn; solitary; gloomy; dramatic; inventive; erratic; hereditary; singular; fresh; organizing; malignant; incredible; financial; disciplined; obscure; recessive; rich; evident; peculiar; diabolical; culinary; assured; stupendous; poetical; veritable; commanding; mathematical; autocratic; superior; musical; misdirected; unclarified; intrepid; dormant; harsher; precocious; strange; brightest; gigantic; statesmanlike; vigorous; feminine; inventive; meditative; political; desultory; unique; pining; irritated; artificial; middling; majestic; maiden; innate; contriving; sullen; capricious; saturnine; fertile; legislative; bountiful; puissant; tutel-

ary; individual; creative; special; ethnic; massive; fiery; lofty; true; masterly; evil; mature; adroit; tragic; predominant; mundane; characterized.

verbs

acclaim—; attain—; befriend—; endow with—; exhibit—; inspire—; marvel at—; nourish—; nurture—; produce—; recognize —; starve—; tincture—with; trifle with—; waste—; worship—; —aspires to; —creates; —enlightens; —produces; —fructifies; —glows; —ripens; —triumphs.
(See talent, power, creator, artist.)

GENTEEL

adverbs

proudly; nobly; aristocratically; inherently; genuinely; truly; admittedly; tenaciously; handsomely; elegantly; impressively.

GENTILITY

adjectives

brave; stripped; plated; faded; shabby; penniless; sham; decayed; decadent; worn; worked; noticeable .

verbs

bear with—; borrow—; claim—; confute—; convey—; counterfeit—; cultivate—; degrade from—; diffuse—; exhibit—; expel—; patronize—; pursue—; recognize—; reveal —; stand on—; vanquish—; —decays; —enhances; —fades; —graces.
(See dignity, politeness, elegance, refinement.)

GENTLE

adverbs

considerately; sympathetically; indulgently; remarkably; particularly; affably; curiously; compassionately; mercifully; understandingly; softly; tolerantly; calmly; forbearingly; patiently; gravely; quietly; serenely; complaisantly; politely; ingratiatingly; amazingly.

GENTLEMAN

adjectives

worthy; dignified; conservative; old-fashioned; prosy; antique; majestic; country; whiskered; eligible; aristocratic; credulous; digressive; gallant; decorous; opulent; polished; decrepit; unusual; chivalrous; superannuated; curious; studious; lovely; legal-looking; vacuous-looking; benevolent; eccentric; elderly; ceremonious; fastidious;

544

venerable; scholarly; valiant; flippant; loyal; downright; reverend; inane; decayed; clerical; suave; heedless; sober; fat; landed; frayed; frail; silk-stockinged.

verbs
admire—; bear like—; be born—; behave like—; conduct like—; define—; denote—; disguise as—; educate as—; grace—; mellow into—; pass for a—; perfect—; produce—; respect—; transform into—; welcome—; —considers; —forbears; —honors; —reproaches; —respects; —submits; —sympathizes; —understands.

GENTLENESS
adjectives
stately; infinite; intelligent; supreme; caressing; surface; unassuming; deprecating; wonted; unbelievable; tender; heartfelt.

GENTLEWOMAN
adjectives
shrewd; virtuous; fresher; dainty; elegant.

GENTRY
adjectives
landed; minor; cocked-hat; light-fingered.

GENUINE
adverbs
unquestionably; veritably; obviously; manifestly; unimpeachably; indubitably; essentially; authentically; incontestably; substantially; inimitably; invaluably.

GEOGRAPHY
verbs
add to—; confuse—; familiarize with—; perfect—; refer to—; resort to—; subdue—; verse in—; —defines; —describes; —explains; —informs; —reveals; —treats of.
(See science.)

GERM
verbs
check—s; combat—; crawl with—s; destroy—; detect—; disseminate—s; eliminate—s; fall prey to—; filter—s; harbor—; identify—; infect with—; infest with—; isolate—; resist—; sow—s; track down—; transmit—; —inhabits; —invades; —lodges in; —migrates; —multiplies; —strikes; —thrives.
(See disease.)

GERMICIDE
verbs
advocate—; disinfect with—; employ—; flush with—; fumigate with—; wash with—; —allays; —arrests; —cleans; —cures; —destroys; —evaporates; —exterminates; —heals; —overpowers; —prevents; —purifies; —rids; —routs; —sterilizes.
(See disinfection.)

GERMS
adjectives
natural; fruitful; virulent; organic; pernicious; fundamental; floating; delicate; vegetable; infant; marauding; infectious; prolific; insidious.

GESTICULATE (v)
adverbs
violently; ludicrously; dramatically; expressively; suavely; gleefully; impatiently; sweepingly; airily; affectedly; ecstatically; significantly; authoritatively.
(See gesture.)

GESTURE
adjectives
wild; authoritative; mental; ponderous; conciliatory; magnificent; ungoverned; convulsive; dreadful; despairing; angry; spontaneous; imploring; eloquent; generous; affectionate; threatening; pitying; ferocious; airy; truculent; dignified; dramatic; expressive; vulgar; romping; abrupt; symbolic; fine; impetuous; helpless; parting; joyous; excited; gentle; sweeping; negative; impatient; uncouth; insolent; respectful; tentative; violent; spasmodic; careless; grateful; absurd; polite; gleeful; animated; significant; vehement; arbitrary; regal; emphatic; heroic; deprecatory; faint; pretty; chivalrous; spectacular; interrogatory; emotional; superstitious; childish; renunciatory; magnanimous; effective; imperceptible; furious; inexplicable; disparaging; frivolous; courtly; menacing; frail; analyzing; pioneering; possessive; benignant; scarce; wide; graceful; invincible; masterful; quick; noble; imperious.

verbs
accompany with—s; ape—; emphasize with—; employ—; execute—; express by—; indulge in—; imitate—; mix with—; moderate—s; motion with—; note—; perform—; record—; refuse—; restrict—s; ridicule—; speak with—s; signify by—; —s express; —s harmonize.
(See motion, posture.)

GESTURE (v)

adverbs

wildly; ponderously; magnificently; convulsively; despairingly; spontaneously; generously; ferociously; truculently; vulgarly; symbolically; uncouthly; animatedly; vehemently; regally; emphatically; spectacularly; menacingly; benignantly; imperiously; masterfully.

(See gesticulate.)

GEYSER

verbs

—blows off; —boils; —bubbles; —darts; —ejects; —emits; —erupts; —explodes; —gurgles; —gushes; —jets; —plays; —pours; —relaxes; —ruins; —shoots; —snorts; —spouts; —spurts; —swells; —throws off.

(See spring, fountain.)

GHASTLY

adverbs

incredibly; unbelievably; inexpressibly; horribly; awfully; fearfully; shockingly; portentously; appallingly; monstrously; formidably; weirdly; terribly; utterly.

GHOST

adjectives

sheeted; gigantic; livid; lofty; gliding; glowing; drab; pale; frighted; silvery; collaborating; sweet; songless; pathetic; slender; reflected; mad; aimless; restless; peaceful; infernal; beckoning; disturbed; pensive; pious; haunting; handsome; graphical; headless; shrouded; honest.

verbs

give up—; harbor—; perceive—; raise—; shape—; speak to—; —beckons; —cries; —flits; —follows; —glares; —haunts; —howls; —points; —prowls; —pursues; —returns; —scares; —shadows; —stalks; —torments; —vanishes; —visits.

(See apparition, phantom, spirit, shade, soul.)

GHOSTLY

adverbs

weirdly; alarmingly; immaterially; spectrally; uncannily; appallingly; mysteriously; inscrutably; horribly; terribly; inexplicably; comically; strangely; curiously; oddly; unbelievably; remarkably; singularly.

GIANT

adjectives

mental; financial; rich; juicy; shock-headed; glorious; massy; mysterious; petrified; supernormal; stupendous; genial; peaceable; useless; pastoral; deformed; hideous; monstrous.

verbs

conquer—; crush—; dread—; flee from—; grapple with—; mount—; overthrow—; quell—; wrestle with—; —heaves; —inhabits; —menaces; —overpowers; —overwhelms; —roars; —shoulders; —terrifies; —threatens; —tramples.

(See monster.)

GIBBER (v)

adverbs

ghoulishly; drunkenly; disgustingly; idiotically; aimlessly; inanely; unintelligibly; insanely.

(See chatter, jabber.)

GIBBET

adjectives

shameful; gloomy; intellectual; menacing; ancient; unused; life-snatching.

verbs

chain to—; condemn to—; conduct to—; deserve—; erect—; escape—; execute on—; gaze at—; punish on—; save from—; send to—; sentence to—; suffer—; tie to—; —frightens; —glooms.

(See gallows.)

GIBE

adjectives

rude; insolent; stinging; jocose; exultant; nasty; bitter; raucous; friendly.

GIDDINESS

verbs

anticipate—; bring on—; condemn—; cure —; delight in—; faint with—; fall in—; incur—; occasion—; repent—; stagger with —; swim with—; tolerate—; whirl with—; —bewilders; —confuses; —creeps over; —envelops; —infuriates; —maddens; —ruins; —vexes.

(See dizziness.)

GIDDY

adverbs

wildly; heedlessly; distractedly; carelessly; dreamily; happily; rapturously; blithely;

capriciously; wantonly; deliriously; incoherently; foolishly; irresolutely; irresponsibly; amazingly; reprehensibly; erratically; fitfully; fantastically; unstably; freakishly; waywardly; captiously; frivolously.

GIFT

adjectives

charming; lasting; valuable; expensive; mental; worthless; poetic; lovely; heavenly; worth-while; exceptional; inalienable; practical; satirical; equal; especial; divine; conversational; ample; promised; fragile; higher; festive; peaceful; myriad (pl); fair; genuine; lyrical; hospitable; innate; pious; glozing; distinctive; versatile; gracious; sacramental; brilliant; healing; compensating; acceptable; wonderful; appropriate; sweet; random; suitable; melancholy; unavailing; entrusted; transcendent; golden; youthful; fecund; rare; graceful; clever; placating; superlative; godlike; lyrical; trifling; sponsorial; unique; prophetic; precious; pure; cankering; free; mysterious; ineffable; cherished; imitative; peerless; wondrous; oratorical; clever; dangerous; matchless; propitiatory; social; costly; formidable; different; spicy.

verbs

apologize with—; bestow — upon; cherish—; cultivate—; endow with—; enhance —; exercise—; favor with—; grant—; honor with—; lavish —s upon; offer—; proffer—; scorn—; surprise with—; value—; —delights; —elates; —enriches; —impresses; —obligates; —persuades; —s pour in.

(See present, endowment, talent, benefaction, contribution.)

GIFTED

adverbs

brilliantly; unusually; wonderfully; magnificently; notably; consummately; peculiarly; expertly; intellectually; eminently; admirably; illustriously; aptly; conspicuously; extraordinarily; supremely; uncommonly; highly.

GIGANTIC

adverbs

incredibly; stupendously; tremendously; unbelievably; inexpressibly; colossally; prodigiously; overwhelmingly; terrifyingly; appallingly; marvellously; terribly; astonishingly; astoundingly.

GIGGLE

adjectives

rich; girlish; antiquated; sudden; nervous; loud.

verbs

burst into—; convulse in —s; cure of —s; degenerate into —s; laugh in —s; set into —s; suppress—; throw into —s; utter—; — annoys; —bores; —disgusts; —disturbs; — interrupts; —sickens; —sparkles; —tickles; —wearies.

(See laugh.)

GIGGLE (v)

adverbs

nervously; hysterically; self-consciously; intermittently; abruptly; explosively; coquettishly; alluringly.

(See snicker, titter.)

GILD (v)

adverbs

radiantly; lavishly; artfully; tastefully; professionally; superfluously; richly; ornamentally.

(See cover, color.)

GILL

verbs

breathe with—; close—; cuff—; draw into —; expand—; furnish with—; stroke—; inhale through—; strain—; —absorbs; — admits; —flaps; —inhales; —quivers; —receives; —sucks; —swells.

GIN (liquor)

adjectives

meditative; sullen; accursed.

verbs

abstain from—; denature—; distill—; imbibe—; legalize—; loathe—; reek of—; resist—; —destroys; —dulls; —grogs; —inebriates; —influences; —intoxicates; —overcomes; —regales; —seduces.

(See liquor.)

GIRAFFE

verbs

anger—; arouse—; cage—; exhibit—; lasso —; pet—; train—; —ambles; —batters; — browses; —forages; —gallops; —s herd; — kicks; —plucks; —roams; —straddles.

(See animal.)

adjectives

sylvan; docile; unaffected; much-courted; cuddlesome; dear; delightful; stricken; robust; athletic; country; serving; frowzy; wishy-washy; tawdry; expensive; clumsy; urgent; watchful; passionate; anserine; adolescent; elegant; slim; confiding; artful; sensible; true; scrawny; giddy; sweet; gentle; beautiful; ornamental; casual; suitable; frail; sympathetic; light; colored; timbrel; ambitious; radiant; exotic; truthful; semi-wild; utilitarian; blushing; alluring; unregulated; debilitated; loitering; singsong; impecunious; trembling; dependent; sullen; charming; pluckiest; dainty; sober; uneducated; freckle-faced; worthless; industrious; ridiculous; swarthy; sophisticated; vigorous; decent; virtuous; enthusiastic; patrician; perverse; unruly; willful; flippant; comely; awkward; sad; shiftless; peevish; commonplace; emotional; suicidal; coquettish.

verbs

betroth—; bud into—; consort with —s; —beguiles; —blushes; —charms; —dances; —giggles; —loves; —lures; —mystifies; —pouts; —prates; —smiles; —sulks.

(See infant, child, youth, damsel.)

GIRTH

adjectives

generous; broad; immense; cumbersome; muscular; spanless; bountiful.

GIST

verbs

convey—; define—; deviate from—; explain —; follow—; glimpse—; overlook—; phrase —; sum up—; translate—; understand—; wade through—; —deals with; —denotes; —lies in; —necessitates.

(See substance, core. essence.)

GIVE (v)

adverbs

exclusively; grudgingly; charitably; benevolently; abundantly; grumblingly; discriminately; spontaneously; magnificently; methodically; unsparingly; discreetly; conscientiously; periodically; impartially; infallibly; subsequently; wantonly; invariably; ultimately; intentionally; substantially; prodigally; legitimately.

(See bestow, accord, grant.)

adjectives

undiscerning; venerable; judicious; Indian.

GLACIER

adjectives

grinding; upended; extinct; immense; unnamed; glistening.

verbs

climb—; consolidate into—; cross—; form —; melt—; press into—; slide into—; warn of—; —chokes; —confronts; —creeps; —derives from; —drifts; —glistens; —glitters; —glows; —lodges; —sparkles.

(See stream, ice, snow.)

GLAD

adverbs

genially; laughingly; wholly; definitely; heartily; truly; genuinely; wholeheartedly; amazingly; pathetically; childishly; sincerely; radiantly; delightedly; enthusiastically; profoundly; quietly; visibly; boundlessly; solemnly; exceedingly; gloriously; rapturously; hysterically; excitedly; serenely.

GLADE

adjectives

rustling; steep; hopeful; enchanted; shaded; woodland; mossy; purple; shadowy; umbrageous; sheltered; tropic.

GLADNESS

adjectives

tender; whimsical; quiet; visionary; subdued; visible; sunny; hidden; bursting; boundless; solemn; ignorant; maniacal; exceeding; glorious; unfeigned; abrupt; tranquil; immortal; effervescent; sober; ebullient.

verbs

bring on—; cloak in—; comprehend—; couch in—; crush—; derive — from; deserve—; dispense—; emit—; enliven with —; exude—; flush with—; occasion—; overwhelm—; quell—; radiate—; send out—; trample—; —confuses; —enhances; —speaks.

(See delight, exhilaration, joy, pleasure.)

GLAMOROUS

adverbs

seductively; delightfully; undeniably; beautifully; gloriously; irresistibly; peculiarly; utterly; adorably; charmingly; exotically;

wantonly; girlishly; deliberately; carefully; calculatingly; immeasurably; inconceivably; incomparably; naturally; purposely; cleverly; bewitchingly; unconsciously; darkly; brilliantly; entrancingly.

GLAMOUR

adjectives

harmless; romantic; laughing; longing; sophisticated; midnight; theatrical; lingering; pictorial; extraneous; fortuitous.

verbs

capture—; create—; deck in—; dim—; invest with—; recapture—; sacrifice—; savor —; surround with—; win with—; yield to —; —allures; —attracts; —awes; —bewitches; —charms; —dazzles; —deceives; —deludes; —enchants; —entrances; —fades; —fascinates; —magnetizes; —stirs; —wears off.

(See charm, enchantment, fascination, glory, spell.)

GLANCE

adjectives

tender; sidelong; mirthful; dreamy; wistful; mechanical; furtive; fierce; maternal; reproachful; hasty; keen; languid; quick; pitying; uneasy; mingled; oblique; timid; mischievous; departed; pure; half-inviting; flaming; penetrating; vindictive; imploring; comprehensive; passing; interrogatory; approving; satisfying; chastened; sinister; deep; hostile; malevolent; tranquil; curious; apologetic; crawling; mortal; wild; expressive; mournful; fantastical; unseeing; fiery; covert; careless; bridling; suspicious; clear; significant; inquiring; admiring; rapid; errant; frightened; unintercepted; single; heartfelt; nervous; wandering; absorbing; baleful; annihilating; superficial; farewell; dull; bird; momentary; vertical; frank; casual; contemptuous; supplicating; conciliatory; fleeting; expectant; indolent; genuine; sudden; sharp; malign; critical; heavy; meteor; furious; meaning; steady; hurried; meager; backward; irresistible; exquisite; surprised; evil; dubious; compassionate; venomous; irresolute; proud; soulful; swift; pleading; expiring; confused; cold; mild; satanical; luminous; ripened; abstracted; frowning; murderous; incidental; saucy; ominous; wondering; beseeching; appealing.

verbs

bestow — upon; cast — upon; detect at a—; flash—; intercept—; quail beneath—; rivet —upon; shift—; shoot — at; steal — at; survey at—; —chills; —falters; —pricks; — rests on; —strays.

(See look, gleam, glimpse, flash.)

GLANCE (v)

adverbs

curiously; complacently; suspiciously; furtively; rebelliously; piercingly; cursorily; indifferently; disconsolately; disdainfully; involuntarily; contemptuously; critically; reproachfully; apprehensively; surreptitiously; wistfully; inquisitively; significantly; tenderly; malignantly; covertly; casually; instinctively; passionately; imperiously; intuitively; dubiously; deferentially; maliciously.

(See beam, gleam, glitter.)

GLAND

adjectives

lymphatic; dormant; secretive; master; lively; sex; ineffective; swollen; abnormal.

verbs

affect—; block—; graft—; inflame—; reduce—; reinvigorate—; transplant—; —controls; —enlarges; —functions; —indurates; —opens into; —pours forth; —produces; —responds; —secretes; —suppurates; —swells.

(See organ.)

GLARE

adjectives

savage; bright; burning; furious; warning; ghastly; gaudy; blinding; blistering; sun; dull; interested; meteoric; dancing; kingly; fearful; fiery; pale; lurid; ruddy; rifted; wild; frozen; desert; awful; brazen; blank; merciless; yellow; chill.

verbs

bask in—; bate—; cast—; destroy with—; fix—; incur—; ignore—; mark—; observe —; relieve—; remove—; shade—; shine with—; —angers; —blinds; —dazzles; — exposes; —lights; —reveals.

(See light, look, gaze, splendor.)

GLARE (v)

adverbs

ferociously; comically; fiercely; scowlingly; balefully; resentfully; vindictively; hostilely; stonily; remorselessly; oddly; blazingly.

(See frown, stare.)

adjectives

undersized; sapphire; frosted; gleaming; spilled; parenthetical; arid; iridescent; bifocal; misted; delicate; preparatory; smoky; sumptuous; watery; tarnished; steaming; shattered; spattering; neglected; molten; poor; distorted; stained; cobwebbed; superstitious; irregular; untasted; social; translucent; medieval; brimming; swirled; rimmed; uncolored; inverted; dimpling; opaque.

verbs

brandish—; blow—; cast—; chip—; clink —s; color—; cover with—; crack—; drain —; engrave—; etch on—; file—; fondle—; frame with—; glaze with—; grind—; mold —; nick—; pulverize—; shape—; shatter—; split—; stain—; —s clash; —s clatter; —s clink.

(See crystal, mirror.)

GLAZE

adjectives

dreamy; monotonous; sincere; defiant; granite; iridescent; thin; death.

GLEAM

adjectives

rare; momentary; occasional; varied (pl); silvery; dazzling; diabolic; sorrowful; cool; phosphorescent; portentous; troubled; lurid; livid; fiery; brilliant; distant; convex; dull; new; hateful; crafty; starry; subdued; unpleasant; sulphurous; metallic; stray; elusive; polar; waning; pallid; summer; flickering; bountiful; bright; ruddy; spasmodic; pale; alluring; determined; ineffectual; faint; vagrant; tearlike; broken; wilder; solitary; opaline; visionary; formless; evanescent; greasy; angry; illusive; moon-lit; splendid.

verbs

behold—; cast—; diffuse—; emit—; flare into—; flash—; light up with—; obscure—; reflect—; send—; shoot—; spread—; — blazes; —dazes; —dazzles; —flickers; — glitters; —illuminates; —pales; —shimmers; —shudders; —sparkles; —twinkles.

(See light, flash, beam, ray.)

GLEAM (v)

adverbs

weirdly; unnaturally; ominously; tigerishly; obscurely; fitfully; dangerously; momentarily; dazzlingly; diabolically; phosphorescent-

ly; portentously; sulphurously; pallidly; spasmodically; flickeringly; evanescently; illusively.

(See shine, glow.)

GLEE

adjectives

rapturous; malicious; unconscious; strange; noisy; defying; childish; uncouth; unbidden; counterfeited; fiendish; sparkling; tumultuous; pelting; innocent; laughing; intemperate; venturous; chortling.

verbs

advance with—; bubble with—; condemn—; dance in—; display—; exhibit—; exude—; feign—; flaunt—; grin with—; increase—; jump in—; laugh with—; leap in—; occasion—; plunge into with—; rub the hands in—; sport with—; titter in—; turn into—; —envelops; —infects; —spreads.

(See mirth, gayety, merriment, joy.)

GLEEFUL

adverbs

blithely; enthusiastically; infectiously; innocently; happily; irresistibly; completely; naturally; elatedly; triumphantly; joyously; light-heartedly; merrily; hilariously; sportively; utterly; openly; laughingly; noisily; effervescently; ecstatically; wholesomely; habitually.

GLEN

adjectives

peaceful; shadowy; shrubby; narrow; unfrequented; mountain; leafy; woody; silent; obscurest; darkened; solitary; shaded; sunless.

GLIB

adverbs

blandly; smoothly; cleverly; adroitly; deceptively; astutely; suspiciously; blatantly; suavely; socially; professionally; unctuously; fluently; nimbly; easily; felicitously; dexterously; affably; complaisantly; urbanely; civilly; politely; ingratiatingly; entertainingly; persuasively; resourcefully; amazingly; extraordinarily; strikingly.

GLIBNESS

verbs

admire—; beget—; criticize with—; deliver with—; impede—; judge by—; mistrust—; perform with—; practise—; praise—; proceed with—; speak with—; unfold with—;

utter with—; —charms; —deceives; —delights; —impresses; —misleads; —oils.
(See fluency.)

GLIDE (v)
adverbs
smoothly; gracefully; unobtrusively; serenely; majestically; sinuously; noiselessly; dreamily.
(See slide, slip.)

GLIMMER
adjectives
misty; fading; uncertain; ghostly; pale; gleaming; dying; quivering; ignorant; confused; faint; quiet; pallid.

GLIMMER (v)
adverbs
dimly; phosphorescently; spasmodically; intermittently; evanescently, uncertainly; pallidly; gaily; mistily.
(See gleam, shine.)

GLIMPSE
adjectives
intriguing; touching; vivid; interesting; incidental; electric; vague; marvelous; amusing; faint; transient; picturesque; tempting; comforting; occasional; tantalizing; leafy; fleeting; delicious; shadowy; shimmering; cautious; prophetic; furtive; chilly; flashing; unveiled; mysterious; passing; murky; desired.

verbs
afford—; catch—; deny—; detect at—; drink in—; flash—; hope for—; obtain—; prevent—; procure—; win—; yearn for—; yield—; —dazzles; —delights; —glimmers; —glitters; —perforates; —reveals; —shimmers; —shines.
(See flash, glance.)

GLINT
adjectives
moiled; rigid; ravishing; fiery; murderous; nasty; wicked.

GLINT (v)
adverbs
suspiciously; antagonistically; brutally; angrily; murderously; wickedly; fiendishly; viciously; vindictively.
(See gleam, flash, glitter.)

GLISTER
adjectives
faint; ruddy; scornful; spotless.

GLITTER
adjectives
prismatic; gilded; steely; intense; jeweled; scaly; fiery; mercurial; dangerous; sinister; streaked; sarcastic; dull; wandering; pristine; weary; effeminate; blinding; ghastly; opulent; gaudy.

GLITTER (v)
adverbs
lustrously; prismatically; intensely; mercurially; sinisterly; coldly; devilishly; blindingly; opulently; gaudily.
(See sparkle, gleam, flash.)

GLOAT (v)
adverbs
spitefully; hilariously; selfishly; pettishly; triumphantly; hatefully; jealously; vindictively; morbidly; victoriously.
(See covet, lust, ogle.)

GLOBE
adjectives
terrestrial; habitable; ponderous; gorgeous; spotty; gluey; heavenly; stupendous; terraqueous; bewildering; celestial; native; many-mortaled; whirling; spinning; careening.

verbs
circle—; circumnavigate—; consult—; discern on—; employ—; fill—; form into—; girdle—; perfect—; refer to—; revolve—; rotate—; suspend—; —defines; —describes; —explains; —points; —represents; —rolls; —rotates; —spins; —whirls.
(See ball, sphere, earth, world.)

GLOBULAR
adverbs
amazingly; overwhelmingly; stupendously; astonishingly; astoundingly; totally; inconceivably; boundlessly; extraordinarily; unprecedentedly; strangely; unwontedly; surprisingly; singularly.

GLOBULES
adjectives
teeming; swarming; insignificant; minute; porous.

adjectives

congregated; dark; ascetic; deepening; shady; solemn; hopeless; malodorous; partial; anxious; lingering; additional; thick; funereal; desponding; murkier; dishwater; moving; gathering; chilly; fixed; slumbrous; melancholy; impenetrable; somber; sacred; grateful; ceaseless; minister; surrounding; forest; eternal; atmospheric; unromantic; perpetual; sepulchral; profound; pregnant; damp; warm; divine; convent; azure; woven; settled; sullen; dungeon; foreboding; sympathetic; twilight; wintry; intensified; lurid; coiled; starving; unavailing; heavy; persistent; dreary; pervasive; darkling; glowing; unobtrusive; dangerous; conventional; glorious; coppery; verdurous; gorgeous; adamantine; arched; natal; cheerless; silent; sable; oppressive; dank; languid; prairie; utter; ethereal; delicate; sheer; blighting; roseate; abnormal; rich; curtained; sibylline; haunting; stained; shadowed; Stygian.

verbs

assimilate—; cast upon—; detach from—; dispel—; envelop in—; exude—; harbor—; overcome—; overhang with—; overwhelm with—; pierce—; wrap in—; —assails; —deepens; —dwells on; —oppresses; —pervades; —settles on; —thickens.

(See darkness, obscurity, melancholy, sorrow, misfortune, despondency, dejection.)

GLOOMY

adverbs

abjectly; helplessly; depressingly; incurably; inconceivably; hopelessly; incredibly; piteously; horribly; tragically; unbelievably; singularly; unreasonably; miserably; needlessly; comically; ridiculously; ostensibly; obviously; desperately; heavily; sadly; mournfully; moodily; pensively; sulkily; inconsolably; desolately; disconsolately; dismally; gravely; woefully; glumly; wanly; unnecessarily; irritatingly.

GLORIFY (v)

adverbs

insanely; enthusiastically; boisterously; lovingly; martially; sumptuously; posthumously; eternally; physically; radiantly; ancestrally; feudally; imperially; romantically; regally; matchlessly; barbarically.

(See praise, adore.)

adverbs

effulgently; brilliantly; splendidly; superbly; unexpectedly; martially; inestimably; radiantly; proudly; regally; ecstatically; peculiarly; matchlessly; supremely; barbarically; distinctly; solemnly; sublimely; remarkably; eminently; imperishably; transcendently.

GLORY

adjectives

ghastly; martial; gaping; reflected; sumptuary; posthumous; fainter; semblance; coeternal; inevitable; liquid; elemental; sudden; butchered; native; physical; inner; athletic; shining; paternal; short-lived; earthly; radiant; proud; ancestral; gentle; false; golden; pristine; endless; evolving; hirsute; mild; celestial; eclipsed; incipient; abandoned; lustrous; living; feudal; spectacular; insubstantial; universal; passive; imperial; romantic; artistic; transient; setting; crimson; western; lineal; lasting; regal; undulating; naked; meridian; peerless; ebbed; imperishable; meteoric; shadowy; flaming; ecstatic; boasted; crowning; supernal; floral; lambent; heroic; scenic; promised; unclouded; unknown; peculiar; unclasped; matchless; lesser; barbaric; original; untasted; quiet; everlasting; pinnacled; bloody; departing; concentrated; sole; inestimable; imaginary.

verbs

accentuate—; bask in—; blaze in—; blind to—; crown with—; debilitate—; dissipate —; elect to—; encircle with—; elevate to —; extol—; flaunt—; mark for—; participate in—; reflect—; revel in—; reward with—; raise to—; shed—; —passes; —shines; —suffuses; revivify—.

(See honor, fame, renown, pomp, splendor, grandeur, praise.)

GLOSS

adjectives

opaque; ultimate; faultless; brilliant; shining; raven; stimulating; firm.

GLOVE

adjectives

frosted; leathern; long; slim; cloth; fringed; greasy; primrose; easy; cheveril; snug-fitting; warm; worn.

GLOW

adjectives
lurid; phosphorescent; rainbow; pallid; vinous; rich; fitful; silvery; ruby; vague; starry; full; strong; suffusing; warm; chastened; dim; joyous; transparent; luminous; dreamy; brilliant; soft; scorching; fiery; mystical; pectoral; molten; original; reflected; white; youthful; inward; comfortable; feverish; unaccustomed; sunset; faint; summer; somber; evening; latent; wavering; conscious; clustering; earthly; fearful; hectic; tropic; genial; emotional; refracted; refulgent; ethereal; blessed; hideous; sorrowing; tremulous; seraphic.

verbs
agitate to—; burn to—; clothe in—; emit—; feel—; heat to—; kindle—; pale—; quench —; quicken to—; shade—; suffuse with—; —brightens; —captivates; —cheers; —declines; —deepens; —flushes; —guides; — illuminates; —irradiates; —lights up; — radiates; —scorches; —shines; —subsides; —warms.
(See flush, animation, ardor, warmth.)

GLOW (v)

adverbs
morosely; intensely; luminously; nebulously; sardonically; auspiciously; mellowly; perceptibly; luridly; phosphorescently; mystically; vaguely; ruddily; feverishly; genially; hectically; ethereally; tremulously; seraphically.
(See shine, beam.)

GLOWING

adverbs
radiantly; softly; dimly; perceptibly; brilliantly; splendidly; gorgeously; endlessly; magnificently; sumptuously; constantly; ineffably; lustrously; phosphorescently; vividly; brightly; intensely; resplendently; marvellously; luridly; richly; fitfully; joyously; transparently; whitely; faintly.

GLUM

adverbs
dismally; incurably; stupidly; cheerlessly; immovably; terribly; hopelessly; lugubriously; darkly; anxiously; despondently; curiously; profoundly; heavily; drearily; dangerously; dreadfully; abnormally; significantly; silently; unreasonably; sulkily; mopishly; strangely; disconsolately; exasperatingly.

GLUT (v)

adverbs
swinishly; brutishly; disgustingly; inordinately; madly; unrestrainedly; ravenously.
(See gorge, eat.)

GLUTTONOUS

adverbs
unbelievably; insanely; disgustingly; repulsively; strangely; crudely; grossly; hungrily; greedily; voraciously; extremely; excessively; wolfishly; inordinately; recklessly; dangerously; extravagantly; horribly; horridly; ravenously; insatiably; offensively; revoltingly; abominably; incredibly.

GNARLED

adverbs
roughly; ruggedly; scraggily; crookedly; sturdily; agedly; stumpily; robustly; massively; tenuously; thickly; rheumatically; gauntly; wirily.

GNASH (v)

adverbs
incessantly; frenziedly; horribly; furiously; fiercely; hungrily; fiendishly; dreadfully; insanely.
(See rage, fume, storm.)

GNAW (v)

adverbs
hungrily; ravenously; furiously; madly; brutishly; bestially; vigorously; ferociously; famishedly.
(See chew, bite.)

GOAD

adjectives
insistent; galling; sharp; inexorable.

GOAL

adjectives
veiled; ultimate; luminous; common; glittering; incentive; stimulating; selfsame; receding; unreachable; refined; successive (pl); utmost; mortal; illusory; desired; tertiary; inevitable; traditional; amaranthine; mysterious; hard-gained; fictitious.

verbs
achieve—; attain—; bar—; cherish—; defeat—; effect—; forge forward—; gain—; guard—; hamper—; move toward—; propel toward—; realize—; strive for—; surmount to—; sway from—; swerve from—; swing from—; touch—; push toward—.
(See end, aim, destiny, mark.)

GOAT

adjectives
romantic; silky; browsing; sure-footed; metamorphosed; mutinous; sacrificial.

verbs
domesticate—; clip—; exercise—; fleece—; herd—s; pasture—; shear—; stall—; tether —; —attacks; —butts; —forages; —grazes; —leaps; —pastures; —supplies; —yields.
(See animal.)

GOBLET

adjectives
knobbed; embossed; smoke-colored.

GOD
(*divine being*)

adjectives
faultless; unalterable; sacred; immortal; stern; everlasting; deathless; compassionate; ever-living; serene; inspiring.

god
(*idol*)

adjectives
monstrous; extemporal; bestial; goat-nursed; stalwart; unappeasable; bleating; victim-nourished; appeasable; defiant; contending; drunken; fire-robed; distant; tinseled; winged; capricious; exasperated; petty; crumbled; artificial; blinded; associate; banished; inexorable; unsolicited; false; materialized; frivolous; deposed; auxiliary.

verbs
banish—; beseech—; blaspheme—; defy—; deify—; discover—; exalt—; herald—; implore—; invoke—; placate—; propitiate—; recognize—; reveal—; revere—; revile—; vow before—; worship—; wrestle with—; —commands; —grants; —guides; —illumines; —judges; —ordains; —prevails.
(See deity, divinity, idol, ruler, creator, Jesus Chirst.)

GODDESS

adjectives
libidinous; voluptuous; impending; fickle; glorious; loving; beauteous.

GODLESS

adverbs
horribly; impiously; perversely; fanatically; recklessly; avowedly; sacrilegiously; blasphemously; profanely; heartbreakingly; graciously; obstinately; obdurately; unhappily; irrationally; unreasonably; immovably; openly; skeptically; materially; agnostically; faithlessly; indifferently.

GODLIKE

adverbs
wondrously; peerlessly; angelically; seraphically; undeniably; charitably; sweetly; piously; virtuously; humbly; beatifically; consecratedly; spiritually; reverently; purely; incredibly; utterly.

GODLY

adverbs
beautifully; devotedly; humbly; piously; reverently; consistently; devoutly; actively; justly; remarkably; eminently; notably; transcendently; earnestly; zealously; illustriously; wondrously; consecratedly; faithfully.

GOLD

adjectives
fraud-accumulated; burnished; sculptured; transparent; crystal; molten; wrought; mealy; fretted; refined; virgin; bright; hard-earned; rusted; intense; gleaming; mossy; dominant; vaporous; tested; gravel; supple; gaudy; damning; barbaric; powdered; sterilized; coronation; beaten; clearest; drowned; countless; vile; richest; hoarded; stamped; fluid; fairy; blowing; musty; shimmering; iridescent; cloudy; streaked; shining; fragrant; faint; floral; glittering; ruined; banked; clean; coarse; ruddy.

verbs
alloy—; amass—; beat out—; bless with—; bribe with—; delve for—; desire—; dig for —; discover—; emboss with—; hammer—; harden—; heap—; hide—; hoard—; load with—; melt—; mine—; pan—; plot for—; roll—; salvage—; search for—; separate—; spurn—; squander—; thirst for—; treasure —; —blinds; —chains; —charms; —clinks; —corrupts; —curses; —degenerates; —glitters; —glistens; —occurs; —sparkles.
(See metal, element, treasure.)

GOLF

verbs
compete in—; concentrate on—; contend at —; enjoy—; gamble at—; improve—; pair off in—; practise—; tie in—; score in—;

—beguiles; —diverts; —engrosses; —entertains; —excites; —exerts; —interests; —wearies.
(See sport, game.)

GOLF COURSE
verbs
compete on—; construct—; cover—; design —; develop—; extend—; form—; idle on —; open—; operate—; visit—; wander over —; —attracts; —beckons; —stretches.

GONG
adjectives
clangorous; dreadful; sounded; resonant; echoing.

verbs
clash—; drum on—; hammer—; hearken to —; strike—; —alarms; —assembles; —calls; —clanks; —clatters; —deafens; —resounds; —reverberates; —signals; —sounds; —summons; —surprises; —thunders; —vibrates.
(See bell.)

GOOD
adjectives
indifferent; supreme; possible; garnered; public; tender; unimagined; infinite; irreconcilable; celestial; chief; ultimate; timely; final; permanent; common; spiritual; sovereign; unmitigated; worldly; satiating; everlasting; unchanging; weak; universal.

verbs
accept—; admire—; approve of—; ascertain—; augur—; commend—; devote to—; distinguish by—; endorse—; expound—; favor—; invite—; laud—; nullify—; offer —; relish—; repay—; reward—; welcome —; —benefits; —merits; —pleases; —profits; —prospers.
(See advantage, benefit, virtue, welfare.)

adverbs
exceptionally; wonderfully; incontrovertibly; undeniably; absolutely; faultlessly; commercially; spiritually; materially; supremely; innately; naturally; inherently; essentially; unusually; uncommonly; consistently; fairly; completely; unquestionably; intrinsically; genuinely; pricelessly; unutterably.

GOOD-HUMORED
adverbs
delightfully; pleasantly; genially; merrily; jovially; immensely; unfailingly; invariably; wholesomely; amazingly; marvelously; patiently; visibly; notably; remarkably; indulgently; considerately; graciously; generously.

GOODNESS
adjectives
mantled; wholesome; innate; inherent; natural; hearty; infinite; adorable; undeserved; essential; true; full; awful; delicious; breathing; invisible; unusual; universal; tasty; obedient; hypocritical.

GOODS
adjectives
glittering; worldly; perishable; unwanted; transitory; worthless; non-durable; treasured.

GOOD-WILL
verbs
abuse—; cultivate—; dispense—; earn—; enjoy—; evoke—; favor with—; foster—; further—; gain—; grant—; inculcate—; inherit—; merit—; obtain—; pay with—; permit—; procure—; promote—; regard with —; seek—; sell—; solicit—; speak with—; spread—; win—; work for—; —privileges; —wanes.
(See reputation, favor.)

GOOSE
verbs
—attacks; —braves; —cackles; —captures; —circles; —clasps; —cleaves sky; —climbs; —destroys; —dives; —drives; —drops; —eyes; —floats through; —hawks; —hooks; —moults; —perches; —preys on; —robs; —sails; —screams; geese sever themselves; —sights; —soars; —sweeps.
(See bird.)

GOPHER
verbs
—burrows; —devastates; —digs; —honeycombs; —scuds.
(See animal.)

GORE
adjectives
stiffened; gladiatorial; sacred; dusky; quivering; unheeded; stagnant; hideous.

GORGE

verbs

cut—; descend into—; dig—; enter—; furrow—; hollow—; scoop out—; scour—; skirt—; traverse—; wear—; —bends; —confronts; —deepens; —extends; —frightens; —slopes.

(See canyon.)

GORGE (v)

adverbs

unrestrainedly; hungrily; ravenously; brutishly; swinishly; nauseously; habitually; insatiably; immoderately.

(See glut, eat.)

GORGEOUS

adverbs

brilliantly; splendidly; magnificently; uncommonly; unusually; dazzlingly; resplendently; superbly; supremely; glitteringly; vividly; richly; harmoniously; imposingly; impressively; extravagantly; inordinately; strikingly.

GORGES

adjectives

twisting; shadowy; picturesque; sunlit; wondrous; narrow; deep; unscaled; roaring; windy; desolated; immediate; mountainous; intricate; melting; protected; tremendous; rock-fanged.

GORILLA

verbs

—challenges; —chews; —cries; —crushes; —drums; —entertains; —nurses; —rages; —raids; —roars; —rushes; —shies; —tears; —terrifies; —wanders.

(See animal.)

GORY

adverbs

unspeakably; horribly; murderously; distressingly; wretchedly; hideously; abominably; beastly; grossly; awfully.

GOSPEL

adjectives

political; radiant; fiery; bitter; gradual; everlasting; healing; long-repeated; time-worn; helpful.

verbs

carry—; crusade—; decry—; denounce—; explode—; herald—; narrate—; preach—;

propagate—; propound—; spread—; transmit—.

(See truth, story, narrative, tale, teachings, Bible, Scriptures.)

GOSSIP

adjectives

habitual; savory; baseless; interested; slanderous; mighty; idle; laggard; good-natured; dashing; careless; ubiquitous; censorious; drowsy; cheerful; impertinent; agreeable; withering; contemporaneous; neighborhood; useful; whispered; undercover; vulgar; insignificant; malicious; scandalous; social; ugly.

verbs

cackle—; center—on; circulate—; deal out —; exchange—; feed on—; indulge in—; interchange—; interest in—; ladle out—; savor—; sputter—; whisper—; —buzzes; —floats about; —libels; —maligns; —slanders.

(See rumor.)

GOSSIP (v)

adverbs

gregariously; inanely; incautiously; inimically; indiscreetly; loquaciously; baselessly; habitually; slanderously; censoriously; impertinently; witheringly; vulgarly; maliciously; jealously; enviously; treacherously.

(See talk, rumor, tattle.)

GOVERN (v)

adverbs

inharmoniously; dictatorially; paternally; intricately; nobly; tyrannically; bureaucratically; autocratically; democratically; plutocratically; ruthlessly; despotically; aristocratically; ephemerally; legitimately; perfidiously; constitutionally; prudently.

(See rule, control.)

GOVERNMENT

adjectives

hard up; executive; tyrannical; municipal; patriarchal; long-lived; authoritarian; radical; shameful; jealous; odious; provincial; paternal; stable; supernatural; ruthless; despotic; representative; aristocratic; free; unprosperous; ephemeral; puppet; vacillating; irresponsible; legitimate; mushroom; acknowledged; ill; deceased; consular; perfidious; industrious; consolidated; constitutional; orderly; imperial; dangerous; respective; monarchial; central; moral; provisional; prudent; autonomistic; conservative; totalitarian; bankrupt.

verbs
abuse—; balance—; castigate—; centralize —; control—; corrupt—; criticize—; defraud—; hoodwink—; jeopardize—; lose faith in—; maintain—; obliterate—; plot against—; preserve—; reverence—; revolt against—; surrender—to; undermine—; upbraid—; usurp—; —capitulates; —cooperates with; —crumbles; —functions; — launches; —regulates; —subsidizes; —succors; —teeters; —thrives.

(See administration, authority, management.)

GOVERNOR

adjectives
sturdy; testy; saucy; assiduous; unerring.

verbs
appoint—; criticize—; draft for—; honor—; impeach—; nettle—; nominate for—; override—; remove—; welcome—; —abuses; — administers; —admonishes; —allows; —authorizes; —s confer; —consents; —controls; —s convene; —executes; —heads; —oppresses; —pilots; —represents; —reprieves; — resides at; —rules; —steers; —vetoes; — visits.

(See master, ruler, guardian.)

GOWN

adjectives
fragile; star-sprinkled; long; flowing; tattered; curtailed; goodly; fluttering; sleeveless; sophisticated; rusty; glamorous; enticing; dull; flapping; saffron; flounced; ruffed; rustling; conventional; silk; close-fitting; sacred; furred; soiled; waxen; lowcut.

verbs
admire—; damage—; design—; don—; exhibit—; fashion—; fit—; model—; repair—; sew—; shed—; tread on—; yearn for—; — becomes; —exposes; —flatters; —flows; — flutters; —reveals; —ripples; —s vary.

(See dress, robe, garment.)

GOWN (v)

adverbs
exquisitely; tastefully; dully; ecclesiastically; spectacularly; gaily; strikingly; vividly; richly; ornately.

(See dress, garb.)

GRAB (v)

adverbs
ruthlessly; despotically; fanatically; autocratically; selfishly; brutishly; vulgarly; nefariously; offensively.

(See seize, clutch, grasp.)

GRACE

adjectives
exquisite; petitionary; tempting; homicidal; impartial; luxuriant; aerial; fruitless; reviving; crowning; singular; refined; supple; literary; lasting; gleaming; natural; apt; gloomy; nameless; strengthening; ineffable; quiet; soft; fluent; tranquil; tolerable; precise; wild; resolute; majestic; lazy; vigorous; inward; flexuous; nobler; sovereign; supreme; jocund; infant; caressing; redeeming; animating; gentle; negligent; perceptible; restoring, extreme; fugitive; melancholy; manly; extenuating; demure; bewildering; boundless; matchless; youthful; inexplicable; happy; evolvent; lingering; saving; ideal; summer; irresistible; extraordinary; antique; old-fashioned; loathsome; condescending; insinuating; chivalrous; swaying; sufficient; outward; pardoning; habitual; infinite; feminine; musical; living; rude; lascivious; languished; fugitive; jaunty; superb; careless; celestial; needful; easy; sinuous; divine; touching; subtle; good; peculiar; maiden; classical; awkward; virginlike; golden; regal; languid; invigorating; charming; courtly; ravishing; unconscious; casual; heavenly; winsome; winning; poetic; tactful; fraternal; sweetest; mundane; tragic; abounding; fastidious; heroic; hopeless; girlish; perfect; cordial; righteous; pastoral; serious; calm; stately; lordly; truer; lurid; celestial; slow; modern; airy; eloquent; simple; sportive; hidden; stupendous; breezy; beauteous; social; pitying; fleeting; coy; capricious; inimitable; facile; undulating; human; inferior.

verbs
admire—; approach—; attain—; commend —; conduct with—; divest of—; endow with —; exhibit—; express with—; form with—; imitate—; invoke—; lend—; move with—; possess—; serve with—; —attracts; —distinguishes; —charms.

(See favor, kindness, mercy, prayer, beauty, love.)

adverbs
amiably; pleasantly; unusually; definitely; slenderly; skillfully; wonderfully; delightfully; uncommonly; naturally; habitually; instinctively; exquisitely; singularly; aptly; ineffably; quietly; softly; lazily; supremely; extremely; superbly; matchlessly; youthfully; irresistibly; extraordinarily; ineffably; carelessly; charmingly; unconsciously; felicitously; unaffectedly; attractively; quaintly.

GRACELESS

adverbs
harshly; stiffly; awkwardly; crudely; offensively; grotesquely; bluntly; carelessly; appallingly; rudely; clumsily; shockingly; inexcusably; viciously; lawlessly; indecorously; incorrigibly; indiscreetly; obdurately; stubbornly; indefensibly; shamefully; obstinately; frightfully; terribly.

GRACIOUS

adverbs
charmingly; delightfully; indulgently; cordially; courteously; unusually; consistently; habitually; exceedingly; sincerely; warmly; hospitably; eagerly; amenably; heartily; suavely; ceremoniously; obsequiously; deferentially; attentively; unctuously; ingratiatingly; benevolently; kindly; considerately; unusually.

GRADATION

adjectives
subtle; organic; beautiful; cold; fractional; manifest; intermediate; ravishing; insensible; rapid; minute; infinitesimal.

GRADE

adjectives
laborious; convenient; intermediate; successive (pl); correct; seasonal; lower.

verbs
approve—; branch into —s; classify —s; compare —s; criticize—; delineate —s; enter—; examine—; organize—; promote—; recognize—; skip—; withdraw—; —guarantees; —indicates; —promises; —satisfies.
(See degree, step, rank, division.)

GRADE (v)

adverbs
legitimately; fairly; delicately; skillfully; laboriously; scholastically; provisionally; academically; nominally.
(See calculate, estimate.)

adverbs
progressively; comparatively; intentionally; purposely; significantly; wisely; designedly; necessarily; inevitably; imperceptibly; slowly; inexpressibly; extremely; sensibly; intelligently; subtly; insidiously; cleverly; deliberately; shrewdly.

GRADUATE

verbs
assemble —s; confer on—; congratulate —s; employ—; enlist—; examine—; fete—; gift —; honor—; laud—; pose as—; praise—; present to—; privilege—; train—; —completes; —excels in; —harks back; —qualifies; —understands.
(See student.)

GRADUATE (v)

adverbs
creditably; subsequently; formally; ultimately; eventually; respectfully.
(See win, finish.)

GRAFT

adjectives
foreign; niggling; vigorous; huge; amazing; regular; stupendous; successful.

verbs
devise—; employ—; induce—; introduce—; support—; yield to—; —accomplishes; —attracts; —begets; —flourishes; —instils; —interests; —intrigues.
(See fraud.)

GRAIN

adjectives
burdening; natural; waving; distinct; fine; springing; gathered; sprouting; garnered; hardy; scanty; coarse; vintage; pungent; generous; well-ripened; rustling; indigenous.

verbs
bag—; cast — to; char—; collect—; distill from—; feed on—; ferment—; gather—; glean—; harvest—; injure—; plant—; prepare—; prize—; reap—; sow—; stack—; yield—; —fattens; —flourishes; —invites; —nourishes; —ripens.
(See seed, crop.)

GRAMMAR

verbs
abide by—; abuse—; conform to—; criticize —; disregard—; fumble with—; heed—; judge—; master—; obey—; observe—; rel-

ish—; violate—; —concerns; —confuses; —demands; —explains; —informs; —ordains; —rules.

(See rhetoric.)

GRAND

adverbs

impressively; imposingly; magnificently; infinitely; sublimely; majestically; augustly; eminently; superbly; illustriously; ineffably; essentially; fundamentally; resplendently; remarkably; transcendently.

GRANDEUR

adjectives

wild; political; religious; weird; imposing; solemn; primitive; tantalizing; gloomy; inherent; contemplative; tumultuous; superior; ancient; superlative; labored; monotonous; human; venerable; sustained; shadowy; rough; solitary; husbanded; superficial; desolate; poetic; magnificent, severe, false; massive; hideous; infinite; melodious; pristine; architectural; sarcastic; deceitful; dilapidated; original; savage; civic; sublime; dreary.

verbs

abate—; acquaint with—; borrow — from; contemplate—; debase—; discipline—; emulate—; equal—; exhibit—; intimate—; love —; parade—; perceive—; reduce—; ridicule—; rise in—; sacrifice—; stagger by—; touch with—; witness—; —diminishes; —expands; —impresses; —impels; —soars.

(See display, splendor, elegance.)

GRANITE

adjectives

unhewn; barren; straited; enduring; everlasting; defiant; cumbersome.

verbs

build on—; carve from—; chip—; crack—; demolish—; hammer—; hew from—; lay—; mix—; pave with—; pierce—; quarry—; shatter—; smooth—; spike—; split—.

(See rock, stone.)

GRANT

adjectives

authentic; fairest; legislative; definite.

GRANT (v)

adverbs

liberally; tacitly; exclusively; subsequently; courteously; grudgingly; graciously; originally; readily; fairly; legislatively; definitely.

(See allow, permit.)

GRAPE

adjectives

shrivelled; luscious; choicest; ripened; celestial; rare; intoxicating; blossoming; autumn; noble; sweet; rich; sour.

GRAPES

verbs

abound with—; bag—; bear—; crate—; gather—; glean—; harvest—; mash—; seed —; skin—; squash—; suck—; —hang; —ripen; —ferment.

(See fruit.)

GRAPPLE

adjectives

iron; death; watchful; painful; damaging; bruising.

GRAPPLE (v)

adverbs

frantically; painfully; bruisingly; fiercely; vigorously; methodically; firmly.

(See clutch, seize.)

GRASP

adjectives

relaxing; iron; monstrous; bitter; prosperous; slender; weak; oblique; unrelaxing; stiffening; consumptive; immature; godlike; unaccommodating; intuitive; conscious; fearful; warm; tenacious; hot; masculine; cordial; prophetic; mental; timorous; vigorous; incisive; childish; octopus-like; passionate; dying; despotic; encyclic; double; fevered.

verbs

beguile into—; carry off in—; crush in—; elude—; entice into—; evade—; gain—; loosen—; relax—; release—; shake from—; wrest from—; yank (colloq.) from—; —bruises; —pains.

(See grip, embrace.)

GRASP (v)

adverbs

frantically; avariciously; selfishly; rudely; firmly; convulsively; cordially; impetuously; tightly; loosely; greedily; unrelaxingly; tenaciously; passionately; despotically.

(See seize, clutch.)

adjectives

tangling; waving; succulent; full-grown; pure; lush; new; long; gentle; fruitful; comfortable; pleasant; dull; starved; trampled; straggling; luxuriant; cut; dry; reedy; dripping; wiry; gaunt; shaven; parched; associated; pinched; nutritious; tedded; flowering; scented; aromatic; delicate; wilted; mossy; rank; russet; aquatic; ornamental; bladed; inland; silent; tumbled; hindering; peopled.

verbs

clip—; crop—; fence off—; mow—; pasture on—; plow through—; sow—; sprinkle—; tread on—; —beautifies; —blankets; —carpets; —cloaks; —covers; —creeps up; —dots; —flows; —pushes up; —spreads; —springs up; —trembles.

(See herb, plant, hay, pasture.)

GRASSHOPPER

verbs

exterminate—; plague with—s; swarm with —s; —alights; —chews; —chirrups; —s damage; —leaps; —limps; —races; —reposes on; —secretes; —sings; —sips; —skips; —s strip; —vaults; —wings.

(See insect.)

GRATE

adjectives

gaping; glowing; abhorred; ponderous; old-fashioned.

GRATE (*v*)

adverbs

harshly; unendurably; roughly; irritatingly; exasperatingly; monotonously; continually; ceaselessly; repeatedly.

(See rub, irritate.)

GRATEFUL

adverbs

utterly; heartily; thankfully; sincerely; pathetically; significantly; inexpressibly; curiously; oddly; volubly; openly; obviously; extremely; inordinately; delightedly; embarrassingly; overwhelmingly; speechlessly; extravagantly; genuinely.

GRATIFICATION

adjectives

refined; instant; external; personal; aesthetic; innocent; pretty; natural; sensual;

speechless; solitary; idle; perfect; vilest; profound; correspondent; intellectual; emotional.

verbs

afford—; anticipate—; bestow—; consider with—; crave—; derive—; experience—; express—; incur—; indulge in—; observe with—; obtain—; offer—; receive—; — attends; —recompenses; —satisfies.

(See satisfaction, pleasure, reward.)

GRATIFIED

adverbs

extremely; highly; uncommonly; happily; proudly; pleasantly; inordinately; ineffably; visibly; noticeably; naturally; marvellously; wonderfully; overwhelmingly; volubly; shyly; utterly; inexpressibly.

GRATIFY (*v*)

adverbs

lustfully; sexually; aesthetically; profoundly; adequately; personally; sensually; intellectually; emotionally; innocently.

(See please, indulge.)

GRATITUDE

adjectives

admiring; endless; intense; natural; virtuous; innocent; deep; passionate; permanent; respectful; noble; erring; bewildered; elementary; pathetic; tender; meek; universal; heartfelt; devout; profound; earnest; fervent; reverent; patriotic; humble; genuine; characteristic; everlasting; sincere; simple.

verbs

acknowledge with—; earn—of; exact—; expect—; express—; feel—; reject—; return in—; reward with—; thrive on—; touch with—; —embarrasses; —humiliates; —justifies; —overflows; —pains.

(See appreciation, adoration, affection.)

GRATUITOUS

adverbs

unexpectedly; surprisingly; acceptably; generously; pleasantly; unnecessarily; cordially; genially; graciously; tactfully; helpfully; impulsively; incredibly.

GRAVE

adjectives

prehistoric; volcanic; nameless; humble; grassy; putrid; innocent; artless; shallow;

desolate; nobler; trodden; sullen; yawning; unmarked; liquid; triumphant; ecstatic; dishonored; burning; solitary; watery; tenantless; sacred; ocean; unblessed; pauper; heaving; insatiate; curtained; scented; bloody; untimely; populous; dusky; mimic; new-made; gloomy; hastily-dug; forgotten; gaping; unmade; dismal; destitute; obscure; dreary; mattress; close-set; stone; inglorious.

verbs
bequeath to—; confine to—; couch in—; hound to—; lie in—; loot—; lower into—; mourn over—; pillage—; pray at—; rest in—; shudder in—; sleep in—; slumber in—; snatch from—; tear open—; turn in —; unearth—; weep at—; wrest from—; —reconciliates; —silences; —snatches; — swallows.
(See tomb, death.)

adverbs
habitually; critically; alarmingly; preternaturally; profoundly; intensely; extremely; frightfully; indescribably; essentially; incalculably; downright; emphatically; cruelly; shockingly; inconceivably; momentously; signally; eventfully; pregnantly; impressively; urgently; solemnly; saliently; portentously; grievously; deplorably; insupportably; disastrously; exceptionally.

GRAVEYARD

adjectives
various (pl); silent; ancestral; country; populous.

GRAVITATE (v)

adverbs
naturally; habitually; paradoxically; customarily; ominously; affectionately; supernaturally; awfully; specifically.
(See attract, sink.)

GRAVITATION

adjectives
irresistible; mutual; pervading; touching; constant.

GRAVITY

adjectives
mock; fantastic; portentous; comic; habitual; sustained; becoming; superb; accustomed; unusual; ominous; dreamless; amused; paradoxical; affectionate; sudden; heavy; elaborate; melancholy; supernatural; dark; colder; awful; attentive; abundant; specific; technical; pompous; frowning; affected.

verbs
challenge—; mitigate—; preserve—; recover—; repel—; robe in—; —alters; — attracts; —directs; —draws; —exercises; —forces; —increases; —influences; —produces; —restricts; —tends.
(See seriousness, solemnity, importance.)

GRAY

adjectives
smiling; salt; mottled; austere; soft; ashen; joyless; fallow; bluish; uncertain; subtle; dark; pearly; dappled; warm; smart; dim; gleaming.

GRAYNESS

adjectives
spring; arrested; dense; spectral; grim; premature; recurring; whitish.

GRAZE (v)

adverbs
peacefully; contentedly; ruminatively; habitually; ceaselessly; monotonously; beneficially.
(See feed.)

GREAT

adverbs
supposedly; naturally; unaffectedly; apparently; fairly; substantially; essentially; fundamentally; downright; immeasurably; incalculably; pleasantly; surprisingly; incredibly; marvellously; wonderfully; amazingly; unusually; singularly; admittedly; undeniably; distinctly; illustriously; reputably; conspicuously; eminently; brilliantly; famously; locally; nationally; internationally; splendidly; sublimely; deservedly; transcendently; memorably; remarkably; unassumingly.

GREATNESS

adjectives
false; intellectual; enduring; moral; natural; ingenuous; true; simple; affected; immeasurable; veiled; esteemed; imperial; patent; corresponding; undiminishable; deserved; apparent; recognized.

561

verbs

achieve—; advertise—; attain—; bestow—upon; contemplate—of; envy—; expatiate on—; gain—; inspire—; perceive—; pursue—; reach—; seize—; sweep into—; thrust—upon; —affects; —appeals; —elevates; —fetters; —serves; —torments.

(See magnitude, eminence, distinction, importance, seriousness.)

GREED

adjectives

pulpit; inordinate; disappointed; reckless; instinctive; intrenched; insatiable; rapturous; internecine; misapplied; misdirected; methodical; physical; miserly.

verbs

clog with—; curse with—; devour with—; indulge—; loathe—; occasion—; overcome with—; prey upon—of; quench—; resent—; satiate—; torment with—; vanquish—; —annoys; —chokes; —deforms; —drags; —drains; —repels; —shames; —sickens; —stints; —tempts.

(See avarice.)

GREEDY

adverbs

inordinately; covetously; avidly; ravenously; insatiably; voraciously; incurably; incorrigibly; strangely; instinctively; painfully; embarrassingly; irreclaimably; hopelessly; shamelessly; perpetually; appallingly; shamefully; scandalously; indecently; brazenly; palpably; unmistakably; obviously; openly; manifestly.

GREEK

verbs

accent—; decipher—; interpret—; laud—; smatter—; translate—; utter—.

(See language, literature.)

GREEN

adjectives

shimmering; woodsy; opaque; dense; diversified; aqueous; resonant; luxuriant; dull; quiet; waving; pale; varied; feathery; delicate; wanton; pistache; exquisite; emerald; dim; faint; mossy; luminous; malachite; leaping; neutral; festive; luscious; slimy; lesser; consecutive; tender; tainted; translucent; glossy; arbute; rusty; delicious; willow; fresher; serpent; turquoise.

GREENERY

adjectives

tangled; moist; varying; well-kept.

GREET (*v*)

adverbs

affably; jovially; charmingly; affectionately; cordially; effusively; ardently; sympathetically; benignly; blandly; genially; brusquely; civilly; fraternally; perfunctorily; hilariously; boisterously.

(See hail, accost, address.)

GREETING

verbs

accost with—; address—to; approach with —; embrace in—; evoke—; exchange—s; express—; ignore—; meet with—; nod—; return—; salute with—; shun—; —arouses; —surprises; —welcomes.

(See salutation, salute, welcome, compliment.)

GREETINGS

adjectives

cordial; civil; playful; absent; kindly; usual; respectful; undemonstrative; paschal; fraternal; joyous; spasmodic; innumerable; sad; perfunctory; affable; effusive; hospitable; hilarious; daily; neighborly; flustered; boisterous; inaudible; affectionate; holiday; warm; mutual; unspoken.

GREGARIOUS

adverbs

jovially; socially; politically; companionably; incurably; heartily; naturally; instinctively; inherently; pleasantly; hospitably; freely; sociably; healthily; wholesomely; briskly; unusually; normally.

GRENADE

verbs

charge with—; catapult—; employ—; fire —; flee from—; fling—; hurl—; roll—; —assaults; —bursts; —dispenses; —explodes; —s harass; —injures; —maims; —levels; —s terrorize; —wounds.

(See bomb, shell.)

GRENADIER

adjectives

gallant; grim; warlike; various (pl); pleasant; gaudy; eye-pleasing.

GRIDIRON
(colloq. for football field)

verbs

battle on—; clash on—; compete on—; condition—; construct—; cover—; design—; excel on—; injure on—; meet on—; pack —; subsidize—; swarm—; witness on—; — attracts; —extends; —beckons; —lies.

(See field, battlefield.)

GRIEF

adjectives

reproachful; national; silent; burning; irremediable; hysterical; immoderate; hopeless; purposeless; needless; passionate; private; strong; sincere; idle; truer; beauteous; half-smothered; poignant; chastening; successive (pl); domestic; lasting; overwhelming; elegiac; endless; casual; unutterable; remorseful; hateful; proud; sudden; mortal; inconsolable; innocent; conjectured; barren; sacred; sentimental; angry; deeper; selfish; lighter; paroxysmal; unmanly; stark; arbitrary; single; withered; fettered; ancient; vanished; callous; uncontrollable; compensated; inward; perished; cloudy; unavailing; fundamental; relentless; utmost; forecasted; wayward; bitter; eternal; touching; present; household; greatest; genuine; pure; young; excessive; second; extravagant.

verbs

assail with—; assuage—; bring to—; confide—in; disguise—; drown—; emerge from —; fight—; overcome by—; overwhelm with —; rush into—; smite with—; stifle—; submerge—; —abates; —lessens; —overwhelms; —spends itself.

(See sorrow, sadness, anguish, distress, tears.)

GRIEVANCE

adjectives

intense; industrial; undoubted; lofty; maritime; maudlin; intolerable; eternal; permanent; serious; heartfelt; deep; deadly.

verbs

adjust—; air—; allege—; arbitrate—; bound with—; conceal—; detail—; exploit —; iron out—; outline—s; recount—; voice —; yield to—; —justifies; —warrants.

(See wrong, injustice, resentment, complaint.)

GRIEVE (v)

adverbs

perpetually; obstinately; silently; unfeignedly; hysterically; immoderately; hopelessly; passionately; poignantly; endlessly; remorsefully; uncontrollably; bitterly; touchingly; genuinely; excessively; extravagantly.

(See lament, mourn.)

GRIEVOUS

adverbs

deplorably; lamentably; sadly; piteously; distressingly; intolerably; appallingly; horribly; unaccountably; unwarrantably; irremediably; unutterably; uncontrollably; bitterly; touchingly; genuinely; grimly; sorely; cruelly; inexpressibly; inordinately; terribly.

GRILLING

verbs

conduct—; cringe from—; criticize—; denounce—; dread—; escape—; overdo—; resent—; suffer—; tense for—; withstand—; wrestle with—; yield to—; —exposes; — irritates; —reveals; —threatens.

(See questioning, examination, inquiry, inquisition.)

GRIM

adverbs

horribly; terribly; cruelly; bitterly; unutterably; unaccountably; unwarrantably; acutely; austerely; brutally; cynically; morosely; perversely; discourteously; sullenly; unceremoniously; impolitely; horridly; sternly; severely; depressingly; oppressively; heavily; forlornly; frightfully; irredeemably.

GRIMACE

adjectives

admiring; mocking; mental; fantastic; convulsive; furious; comical; passing; sour; droll; cold; dissatisfied; idiotic; wry; harrowing.

GRIMACE (v)

adverbs

facetiously; fiercely; humorously; dourly; mockingly; fantastically; convulsively; furiously; drolly; idiotically; wryly.

(See leer, sneer, smirk, scowl.)

adverbs

inexcusably; unspeakably; merrily; laughably; nonchalantly; carelessly; offensively; hopelessly; inevitably; momentarily; repulsively; irretrievably; laughingly; smudgily; dustily; darkly; grotesquely; fantastically; outlandishly; shamelessly; unconcernedly; coolly; indifferently; unashamedly.

GRIN

adjectives

tigerish; noble; wooden; homely; amused; cast-iron; broad; triumphant; insolent; sardonic; lewd; specious; jubilant; ingenuous; incredible; mocking; leering; sympathetic; understanding; unmitigated; lopsided; sheepish; saucy; fiendish; doubtful; relieved; affable; sly; horrible; courageous; infectious; whimsical; saturnine.

verbs

attempt—; break into—; broaden into—; conceal under—; expand in—; force—; manage—; master—; muster—; provoke—; restrain—; salute with—; smother—; stab with—; wear—; wrinkle into—; —creases; —delights; —embarrasses; —fades; —lurks; —recurs; —widens; —wreathes.
(See smile, smirk.)

GRIN (v)

adverbs

genially; wistfully; bashfully; flatteringly; sheepishly; affably; stupidly; skeptically; amiably; sympathetically; complacently; impudently; derisively; ironically; toothlessly; ruefully; fulsomely; tantalizingly; wryly; broadly; engagingly; craftily; lewdly; jubilantly; ingenuously; saturninely.
(See smirk, laugh, smile.)

GRIND
(colloq. for drudgery)

verbs

abhor—; avoid—; coach—; detest—; enforce—; labor on—; necessitate—; perform at—; plod at—; reduce to—; toil away at —; —crushes; —exacts; —harasses; —prepares; —oppresses; —sharpens; —torments; —wearies; —wears down.
(See drudgery, labor, work.)

GRINNING

adverbs

foolishly; facetiously; fatuously; vacuously; vacantly; cheerfully; happily; mischievously; teasingly; pertly; tormentingly; suavely; blandly; indulgently; slyly; broadly; triumphantly; jubilantly; sheepishly; joyously; sympathetically; mockingly; elaborately; openly.

GRIP
(grasp)

adjectives

tight; paralyzing; momentary; firm; muscular; nervous; burning; remorseless; herculean; frantic; throttling; fiendish; intellectual.

verbs

loosen—; relax—; release—; —pains; —reassures; —slips; —strains; —wearies.
(See clutch, grasp.)

GRIP
(colloq. for valise)

verbs

clasp—; clutch—; fit into—; grab—; insure —; load in—; seize—; stow—; —wearies.
(See satchel, bag.)

GRIP (v)

adverbs

fervently; licentiously; momentarily; nervously; remorselessly; frantically; fiendishly; vigorously; selfishly; figuratively.
(See seize, grasp.)

GRIPE

adjectives

convulsive; mincing; communicated.

GRIT
(sand)

adjectives

blinding; parching; grinding; unpleasant; rough.

verbs

brush away—; conceal—; dissolve—; fill with—; free of—; gather—; scour with—; sieve—; sift—; slip on—; sprinkle with—; strain off—; sweep away—; wash away—; —chokes; —impairs; —injures; —irritates; —scratches.
(See sand.)

GRITTY
(plucky)

adverbs

pluckily; sturdily; stoutly; resolutely; indomitably; firmly; courageously; spunkily.

GRITTY
(sandy)

adverbs

roughly; harshly; coarsely; crudely; grossly; impossibly; uselessly; desirably; friably; suitably; properly; unduly; terribly; remarkably; extremely; uncommonly; excessively.

GRIZZLED

adverbs

wintrily; crabbedly; hoarily; dingily; sadly; gently; gloriously; patriarchally; fabulously; honorably; proudly; mellowly; vainly.

GROAN

adjectives

rheumatic; tortured; deep; indignant; expiring; solemn; ghastly; frequent (pl); fierce; thrilling; smothered; unutterable; subdued; loud; bubbling; agonizing; dying; heartrending; deadly; dismal; passionate; unsolaced; convulsive; self-accusing; mirthful; gurgling; heavy; mortifying; unwilling; bitter; penitential.

verbs

blanket—; convulse with—; drown—; emit —; murmur—; restrain—; stifle—; utter—; —distresses; —disturbs; —haunts; —rends; —resounds; —subsides.

(See moan, sigh, sound.)

GROAN (*v*)

adverbs

audibly; painfully; agonizingly; dreadfully; inwardly; bitterly; involuntarily; unutterably; heartrendingly.

(See moan, complain, scream.)

GROOM

adjectives

diminutive; natty; surly; envious; unpolished; sturdy; surfeited; industrious; bashful; nervous; worried.

GROOM (*v*)

adverbs

foppishly; tastefully; immaculately; nattily; handsomely; fittingly; appropriately; decoratively; impressively.

(See dress, brush.)

GROOMED

adverbs

perfectly; carefully; immaculately; recently; lately; meticulously; punctiliously; primly; starchily; fastidiously; fashionably; especially; obviously; manifestly; freshly; radiantly; sophisticatedly; remarkably; elaborately.

GROOVE

adjectives

habitual; prosaic; uncongenial.

verbs

excavate—; fall into—; flow in—; force along—; furrow—; hollow out—; lapse into —; lie in—; mark with—; obstruct—; provide—; rust in—; sink into—; slide in—; throw out of—; travel in—.

(See channel, rut, routine, course.)

GROPE (*v*)

adverbs

futilely; blindly; vaguely; wildly; ineffectually; dazedly; mentally; uncertainly.

(See feel, search.)

GROSSNESS

adjectives

intermingled; material; mortal; swinelike.

GROTESQUE

adverbs

outlandishly; fantastically; clownishly; elaborately; ornately; abnormally; eccentrically; monstrously; singularly; oddly; curiously; exceptionally; egregiously; unusually; extraordinarily; queerly; unconsciously; capriciously; whimsically; extravagantly; barbarically; horribly; uncommonly; immeasurably; unnaturally; absurdly; ridiculously; ludicrously; highly.

GROTTO

verbs

adorn—; construct—; excavate—; exhibit—; ornament—; nestle in—; retreat to—; — beautifies; —delights; —displays; —echoes; —pleases; —shades; —solaces.

(See cave, recess, cavity.)

GROUCH

verbs

irritate—; nurse—; serve—; tolerate—; — complains; —deplores; —frets; —frowns;

—growls; —grumbles; —laments; —moans; —roars; —scowls; —wails; —whines.
(See anger, bitterness, ferocity.)

GROUND
(earth)

adjectives

analogical; habitual; ticklish; enchanted; avowed; crinkled; soggy; slightest; shaky; tedious; rugged; fragrant; difficult; sanctified; vantage; unexpressed; sterile; dry; azure; emotional; vulgar; tainted; solid; interesting; attractive; plausible; pastel; teeming; scientific; spacious; moaning; moral; delicate; callous; bordering; hallowed; innate; wounded; cultivated; fissured; commanding; incontrovertible; common; terraced; happy; conceded; illogical; dangerous; practical; rough; insufficient; good; bloody; reasonable; haunted; holy; treacherous; proper; thirsting; technical; theological; sluttish; slippery; burning; vivid; eudaemonistic; trampled; adequate; sanctified; superior; extensive; shuddering; filthy; familiar; untouched; unmarked; spawning; various (pl); debatable; heartless; quaking; reigning; cleared; obscure; ridgy; aesthetic; desolate; plain; ornamented; intuitive; neutral; remoter; grassy; subjective; dwelling; dewy; irregular; consecrated; excellent; tenable; dubious; sole; base; sectional; tufty; objective; highest; waste; alien; precise; casting.

verbs

assign—to; carpet—s; cast to—; congest—s; cultivate—; encamp on—s; gain—; parch —; plod over—; plow—; shift—; spade—; stand—; strew—; trample—; tread—; work —; writhe on—.
(See earth, soil, land, clay, dirt.)

GROUNDLESS

adverbs

nonsensically; flimsily; foolishly; absurdly; undeniably; palpably; obviously; patently; manifestly; maliciously; inconclusively; inconsistently; irrationally; unreasonably; inexcusably; unscientifically; unwarrantably; delusively; fallaciously; illogically; untrustworthily; unsubstantially; intentionally; deliberately; deceitfully; malignly; perversely; disastrously; ruinously; ridiculously.

GROUNDS
(reasons)

verbs

afford—for; attack on—; maintain—; object on—.
(See reason, consideration, premise, motive, inducement.)

GROUNDWORK

verbs

accomplish—; add to—; depend on—; enhance—; exhibit—; expand—; finish—; form—; hurry—; lay—; manage—; perform —; plan—; spurn—; supervise—; undermine—; —benefits; —precedes.
(See basis, foundation.)

GROUP

adjectives

ancillary; afflicted; exclusive; oncoming; limited; select; co-ordinated; ethnic; personified; heterogeneous; non-listening; cultural; pedimental; garrulous; chattery; valid; specialized; waning; geographical; parental; enthusiastic; civic; statuesque; spurious; flitting; sparse; straggling; considerable; loitering; vocational; remarkable; federated; unscrupulous; racial; efficient; distinct; sympathetic; lethargic; careless; weird; complete; dominant; diversified; overlapping; huddled; gesticulating; noisiest; lazy; divers (pl); representative; congenial; curious; listless; clustering; odious; humiliated; stalwart; grotesque; irregular; silent; lounging; intramural; brilliant; singular; denominational; allegorical; fearful; impressive; loquacious; detached; emblematic; spectacular; hedgehog; jovial; executive; jeering; sullen; craning; militant; prolific; controlling; anarchical; indispensable; producing; tractable; mournful; isolated; sobbing; pressure; elaborate; hostile; molecular; negligible; decorative.

verbs

assemble in—; belong to—; break with—; cluster in—; collect in—; compose—; divide into—s; disperse—; draft—; form—; gather —; huddle in—; lead—; scatter in—; segregate—s; split into—s; stand in—; work in —; —congregates; —co-operates; —gathers; —roves; —s spring up; —survives; — thins; —visions; —wanes; —yields.
(See crowd.)

GROUP (v)

adverbs
systematically; logically; categorically; picturesquely; vocationally; carelessly; representatively; congenially; elaborately; decoratively.
(See cluster, crowd.)

GROUPINGS

adjectives
picturesque; molecular; effective; attractive; fundamental; confused; huddled; fragmentary; photographic.

GROUSE

verbs
bag—; pelt—; retrieve—; roast—; —alights; —bellows; —booms; —cackles; —clucks; —dodges; —drums; —flutters; —glides; —grumbles; —haunts; —hides; —hoots; —roves; —ruffles; —rustles; —scratches; —scurries; —squats; —struts; —thumps; —thunders.
(See bird.)

GROVE

adjectives
shadowy; inviolate; sacred; melancholy; Elysian; lofty; haunted; celestial; primeval; pathless; fringed; boundless; musical; hoary; warbling; thriving.

GROVEL (v)

adverbs
obsequiously; humbly; servilely; slavishly; flatteringly; abjectly; debasingly; shamelessly.
(See cringe, fawn.)

GROW (v)

adverbs
tremendously; luxuriously; abundantly; proportionately; sensibly; vigorously; culturally; inevitably; formidably; abnormally; densely; miraculously; infinitely; ulcerously; wantonly; pendulously; phenomenally; intellectually; malignantly; tropically; vernally; spiritually.
(See increase, develop.)

GROWL

adjectives
meaning; significant; warning; low; audible; indignant; guttural; angry; friendly; fierce.

verbs
break into—; charge with—; emit—; enrage to—; incur—; mutter—; reiterate—; restrain—; stifle—; utter—; arouses; —s drown; —eclipses; —reverberates; —rises from; —terrifies; —terrorizes; —thunders; —vibrates.
(See rumble, complaint, roar, grunt.)

GROWL (v)

adverbs
ominously; pugnaciously; disapprovingly; menacingly; furiously; warningly; audibly; ferociously; formidably; irascibly; surlily; gutturally.
(See grumble, snarl.)

GROWTH

adjectives
coarse; sturdy; vigorous; rock-loving spontaneous; miraculous; arborescent; continuous; ulcerous; wanton; rooted; pendulous; phenomenal; inoperable; luxuriant; ghostly; stunted; monstrous; perpetual; stupendous; morbid; cancerous; unpleasant; intellectual; remarkable; tropical; unconscious; parasitic; healthy; native; scanty; incessant; record; evolutionary; puny; unexampled; developmental; unequal; hasty; mushroom; successive (pl); intervening; unbroken; astounding; endless; vital; rapid; sterile; outward; nutritious; proper; innate; funguslike; differenial; continuous; enormous; plant; malignant; sudden; psychic; unabated; contorted; wayside; vernal; marked; knotty; tremendous; arrested; constant; fateful; lush; spiritual; secular; unkept; strong; millennial; bushy; dense.

verbs
augment—; check—; control—; foster—; govern—; hinder—; induce—; promote—; stunt—; suppress—; thwart—; retard—; strengthen—; witness—; —commences; —develops; —swallows up.
(See development, increase, extension, enlargement.)

GRUDGE

adjectives
private; personal; economic; ancient; bitter.

verbs
annul—; avenge—; bear—; brush aside—; bury—; cherish—; engender—; harbor—;

incur—; lay aside—; nurse—; owe—; pursue—; relinquish—; resent—; warrant—; —troubles; —vexes.

(See malice, hatred, antipathy, rancor, enmity, resentment.)

GRUESOME

adverbs
horribly; cadaverously; horridly; unbearably; forbiddingly; squalidly; frightfully; grimly; grossly; monstrously; odiously; repulsively; shockingly; appallingly; intolerably; dreadfully; impossibly; inconceivably; unspeakably; inexpressibly; indescribably; preposterously; exceedingly.

GRUFF

adverbs
unnecessarily; intolerably; uncivilly; discourteously; needlessly; naturally; habitually; unfortunately; deliberately; unconsciously; rudely; grossly; sullenly; churlishly; intentionally; discouragingly; reluctantly; professionally; bluntly; curtly; captiously; moodily; abusively; boorishly; sarcastically; crudely; clumsily; snarlingly; venomously; significantly; surprisingly; particularly; remarkably.

GRUMBLE (v)

adverbs
captiously; discontentedly; pessimistically; forebodingly; cantankerously; vindictively; monotonously; gloomily.

(See growl, snarl.)

GRUNT

adjectives
complacent; mingling (pl); peculiar; roaring; occasional; satisfied; whining; disdainful; rebellious; startled; long; swinish.

verbs
acquiesce with—; answer with—; concede with—; manage—; resent—; snort—; suffer—; understand—; tolerate—; —annoys; —disturbs; —irritates; —s subside.

(See growl.)

GRUNT (v)

adverbs
audibly; complacently; peevishly; contemptuously; swinishly; disdainfully; rebelliously; appreciatively; approvingly.

(See croak, mumble, bray, stammer.)

GUARANTEE

adjectives
sufficient; money-back; sensational; satisfaction; iron-clad; official; further; serious; perpetual; limited; broken; vague; unfulfilled.

verbs
accompany with—; afford—; apply for—; base—on; break—; chain to—; consider—; demand—; enforce—; enter into—; forfeit —; fulfill—; propose—; test—; utilize—; witness—; —assures; —secures; —suffices.

(See security, reparation, insurance, protection, safeguard, safety.)

GUARANTEE (v)

adverbs
solemnly; unconditionally; unethically; unequivocally; scrupulously; fully; reliably.

(See promise, pledge.)

GUARD

verbs
arouse—; assign—to; bait—; conceal—; decoy—; deride—; double—; eject—; escape —; evade—; flank with—s; hail—; limit —; mount to—; muster—; post—; rile—; stand on—; station—; —manhandles; —patrols; —seizes; —s swarm; —s swarm round.

(See sentry, patrol.)

GUARD (v)

adverbs
closely; jealously; adequately; warily; zealously; rigidly; exclusively; circumspectly; sedulously; dependably.

(See defend, watch.)

GUARDED

adverbs
cautiously; carefully; watchfully; constantly; warily; discreetly; prudently; vigilantly; respectfully; affectionately; tenderly; devotedly; reverently; piously; punitively; sternly; skillfully; successfully; effectively; adroitly; cleverly; subtly; heavily; inefficiently; carelessly; insufficiently; perfectly; scrupulously; pitilessly; faithfully; temporarily; currently; elaborately; invincibly.

GUARDIAN

adjectives
ghostlike; gloomy-winged; particular; faithful; wary; fearless; dissembling; glistering; zealous; legal; appointed; temporary; greedy.

568

verbs

appoint—; choose—; commit to—; employ —; entrust—; necessitate—; respect—; — administers; —defends; —executes; —governs; —guides; —manages; —performs; —preserves; —protects; —supervises; —watches.

(See guard, defender, keeper.)

GUARDS

adjectives

pitiless; dependable; provost; vigilant; dust-choked; abdominal; imperturbable; scrupulous; inexorable; affrighted; angelic; advanced; obsequious; fearful.

GUESS

adjectives

admirable; happy; accepted; shrewd; instinctive; various (pl); ridiculous, worst, elaborate; wild.

verbs

attempt—; base—on; calculate—; chance—; estimate—; form—; hazard—; measure—; necessitate—; vary—; venture—; weigh—; withdraw—; —amazes; —coincides; —deceives; —rescues.

(See conjecture, surmise, supposition, speculation.)

GUESS (v)

adverbs

shrewdly; instinctively; profoundly; cleverly; skillfully; miraculously; intuitively; luckily; unerringly.

(See imagine, suppose.)

GUEST

adjectives

illustrious; forward; flirting; solitary; plebeian; gathering (pl); sparing; ungreeted; adoring; applauding; agreeable; telltale; long-awaited; welcome; neglected; lovelorn; parting; delightful; fastidious; distinguished; elegant; congenial; kingly; tedious; unexpected; taciturn; believing; late; surreptitious; terrible; unloved; continual; invited; straggling; boisterous; sour; involuntary; princely; glorious; entranced; sundry (pl); favorite; dreaded; shipwrecked; tolerated; frivolous; sybaritic; celestial; crowding; transient; honored; monster; mortal.

verbs

arrange—s; circulate among—s; delight—s; escort—; fete—; honor—; lodge—; prepare for—; regale—; speed—; —s assemble; —departs; —s mill about; —returns; present —.

(See visitor, friend.)

GUFFAW (v)

adverbs

coarsely; boisterously; crudely; obstreperously; sardonically; ribaldly; vulgarly; rudely; unrestrainedly; frivolously; drunkenly.

(See laugh.)

GUIDANCE

adjectives

tactful; energetic; vocational; celestial; continuous; psychiatric; genial; economic; perverse; fresh; cheering; altruistic.

verbs

bring under—of; commit to—; direct—of; entrust to—of; manage—; necessitate—; observe—; operate under—; relinquish—; remove—; resist—; respect—; supervise—; teach by—; —controls; —influences; —preserves; —protects; —trains.

(See protection, patronage, direction.)

GUIDE

verbs

commit to—; employ—; exhort—; provide —; —climbs; —conducts; —controls; —courses; —directs; —explains; —indicates; —influences; —leads; —lectures; —manages; —pilots; —plans; —points out; —rambles; —supervises; —tests; —trains.

(See conductor, pilot.)

GUIDE (v)

adverbs

fearlessly; intelligently; insensibly; tactfully; genially; altruistically; competently; intrepidly.

(See steer, conduct.)

GUIDES

adjectives

magnetic; careless; portly; trustworthy; baldpated; impassive; unerring; competent; powerful; greasy; spiritual; trusty; loving; infallible; intrepid; mysterious; sun-swart; foolhardy.

verbs

admit to—; elect to—; impede—; organize —; regulate—; supervise—; support—; — aids; —benefits; —controls; —dispenses; — educates; —exhibits; —honors; —offers; — pursues.

(See association, fraternity, society, corporation, brotherhood.)

GUILE

adjectives

political; baleful; false; innocent; spiritual; fatal; venerable; smooth; sweet.

GUILELESS

adverbs

unaffectedly; apparently; delightfully; incredibly; refreshingly; touchingly; childishly; wonderfully; manifestly; charmingly; ravishingly; surprisingly; unbelievably; ingenuously; youthfully; unquestionably; candidly.

GUILT

adjectives

mutual; accessorial; exultant; hideous; apparent; open; inexpiable; stubborn; frustrate; tyrannic; supposed; bounteous; admitted; dread; enormous; ineffable; occulted; imputed; traitorous; murderous; uneasy; multiplied; heinous; miserable.

verbs

accept—; adduce—; ascertain—; betray—; blush with—; conceal—; exhibit—; experience a sense of—; expose—; hide—; incur —; induce—; measure—; prove—; repudiate—; reveal—; shoulder—; take—; uncover—; —attends; —dishonors; —shames.

(See sin, offense, wrong, crime.)

GUINEA-PIG

verbs

breed —s; dissect—; experiment with—; inject into —s; propagate —s; test —s.

(See animal.)

GUISE

adjectives

altered; secret; abstracted; fitting; festal; mortal; novel; startling; attractive; celestial; compellent; lowly; truthful; human; opalescent; reputable; gentler; murky; artful; silken; modern; winning.

adjectives

accustomed; tinkling; roaring; vigilant; humming; strumming; vibrant.

verbs

accompany with—; brush—; employ—; finger—; feet—; handle—; peck—; pick on—; pluck—; provide—; serenade with—; string —; strum—; tune—; twang—; —delights; —harmonizes; —moans; —throbs; —tinkles.

(See banjo.)

GULF

adjectives

voracious; winding; foaming; starlit; yawning; impassable; remoter; deep; tragic; unfathomable; roaring; pebbly; fiery; envious; breaking; starry; mystic; mediate; azure.

verbs

bridge—; deepen into—; dip into—; span—; —absorbs; —confronts; —hides; —opens; —roars; —separates; —sweeps.

(See chasm, separation, whirlpool, bay, vortex.)

GULL

adjectives

curving; circle; flannel; flapping; laughing; fading; strenuous; notorious; gleaming.

verbs

—barks; —bullies; —chatters; —s colonize; —darts; —fishes; —floats; —s flock; —s fraternize; —s prey on; —rends the air; — robs; —roves; —sails; —screams; —shrills; —skims; —soars; —squalls; —swoops; — wails; —wheels; —wings out to sea.

(See bird.)

GULLIBLE

adverbs

credulously; foolishly; weak-mindedly; dully; inanely; weakly; thoughtlessly; blindly; unthinkingly; easily; disastrously; unfortunately; fatuously; vacuously; childishly; superstitiously; confidently; exceptionally; obviously; manifestly; absurdly; ridiculously; idiotically; imprudently; indiscreetly; witlessly; brainlessly; amazingly; unexpectedly.

verbs

excavate—; force along—; form—; furrow
—; hollow into—; rise from—; scramble up
—; straddle—; —deepens; —extends; —
graduates; —opens.

(See gorge, channel, hollow, gutter,
ditch, gulf.)

GULP (v)

adverbs

noisily; disgustingly; hungrily; vulgarly;
eagerly; nauseously; rapaciously; ravenously.

(See swallow, eat.)

GUM

verbs

barrel—; consume—; dissolve—; glue with
—; harden into—; secrete—; spread—; utilize—; twist—; yield—; —issues from; —
preserves; —prevents; —stiffens.

GUMS

adjectives

enormous; toothless; odorous; lucid; precious; aromatic.

GUN

adjectives

honeycombed; squirrel; strong; pneumatic;
murdering; resounding; hungry; rapid-fire;
threatening; crackling; truculent; booming;
resonant.

verbs

brave —s; cover with—; deflect—; jab—at;
level—at; loose—at; man —s; mount—;
muster —s; notch—; sheathe—; sight—;
train—on; whip out—; —barks; —belches
fire; —blazes away; —bombards; —booms;
—s clatter; —demolishes; —enfilades; —
glints; —grumbles; —jams; —pours; —
roars; —rumbles; —spits; —spurts; —thunders; —volleys; —whines.

(See rifle, cannon, musket, pistol.)

GUN-FIRE

verbs

attack with—; break into—; charge with—;
dodge—; flee from—; order—; rake with
—; retreat from—; spatter with—; —assaults; —breaks loose; —crackles; —damages; —destroys; —disperses; —explodes;
—reverberates; —tears up; —terrorizes.

(See firing, bombardment, fusillade,
shots, volley.)

verbs

agitate—; blast with—; charge with—; compound—; discharge—; inflame—; kindle—;
reek with—; store—; —detonates; —explodes; —flashes; —smokes.

(See ammunition, dynamite, explosive.)

GURGLE

adjectives

slobbery; liquid; rich; childish; thick; horrible; oozing.

GURGLE (v)

adverbs

drearily; monotonously; pleasantly; musically; melodiously; ceaselessly; perpetually;
spasmodically.

(See hiss, ripple, whisper.)

GUSH (v)

adverbs

copiously; spontaneously; terrifically; roaringly; richly; impetuously; foamingly; unrestrainedly; loquaciously.

(See rush, flow.)

GUSHING

adverbs

elaborately; volubly; fluently; foolishly; effusively; sentimentally; ecstatically; rapturously; joyously; inanely; absurdly; ridiculously; inconsequently; excitedly; nervously;
warmly; racily; breathlessly; hysterically;
impressively; pretentiously; ostentatiously;
showily; unpleasantly; offensively; uncommonly; habitually; constantly; impetuously;
vivaciously; tiresomely; endlessly; interminably.

GUST

adjectives

chill; fitful; hot; unusual; violent; fierce;
stormy; buffeting; extreme; passionate; sudden; scented; eddying; angry.

GUSTO

adjectives

culinary; geyserish; racy; joyous; wholesome; great; inartistic; rare; sardonic;
hearty; solemn.

verbs

discharge in—; drag in—; drift down—;
furrow—; jostle into—; lodge in—; recline
in—; slope to—; stream down—; sweep into
—; wear away—; —carries away; —irrigates; —drains;.

(See channel, ditch, groove.)

adverbs

deeply; brokenly; inarticulately; pleasantly;
heavily; outlandishly; exotically; grotesquely; absurdly; mockingly; thickly; hesistant-
ly; distinctly; extremely; undisguisedly; surprisingly.

H

HABIT

adjectives

moral; ferocious; mental; celestial; tranquil; quasi-religious; barbarian; sedentary; unclean; desultory; unrestrained; invariable; systematic; social; separate; idle; economical; sober; contrary; old-fashioned; disconcerting; lifelong; healthful; steady; taciturn; lifetime; precious; established; estranged; unsettled; long-existing; philosophical; popular; spendthrift; cleanly; incurable; religious; offensive; courteous; innate; sidewalk; ill; parti-colored; vulgar; devilish; aquatic; fixed; personal; priceless; dissolute; important; peculiar; cherished; sociable; outdoor; baneful; migratory; industrious; indelicate; retrospective; steady; gregarious; exasperating; tutored, psychological; fastidious; immoral; virtuous; asthmatic; intense; wandering; acquired; uncanny; vicious; comparative; harmless; injurious; prevalent; confirmed; spending; abominable; feminine; deadly; expensive; drinking; mating; unsightly; bloodcurdling; unhygienic; pernicious; voracious; proper; degrading; unproductive; intemperate; honorable; natural; unfortunate; orderly; watchful; flabby; dainty; epicurean; cherished; virile; judicious; ineradicable; purgative; disputatious; busy; convivial; frugal; industrious; temperate; ascetic; studious; nascent; leisurely; hurtful; depraved; mean; intoxicating; careless; fatal; constant; inexcusable; incompatible; physical; silly; dreadful; disgusting; beguiling; autocratic; sluggish; roving; debauched; evil; remorseless; ingrained; domestic; active; awkward; licentious; luxurious; extravagant; artificial; dishonest; mourning; filthy; untoward; piscatory; unmanageable; corrupt; slovenly; indolent; humble; simple; unfixed; dietetic; stylish; unassuming; sordid; demure; synthetic; deliberate; daring; terrible; worse; improvident; intellectual; watchful; unconscious; detestable; dangerous.

verbs

acquire—; adopt—; assume—; break up—; breed—; check—; contract—; cultivate—; deplore—; develop—; discard—; dissolve —; diverge from—; eradicate—; establish —; fall into—; gain—; inculcate—; induce —; indulge in—; instill—; protest against —; pursue—; regulate—; relinquish—; renounce—; set up—; teach—; unlearn—; upset—; —accustoms; —binds; —compels; — loses its hold; —persists; —roots; —takes possession.

(See custom, practice, inclination.)

HABITATION

adjectives

devoted; personal; moving; crude; squalid; humble; peaceful; dismal; commodious; isolated.

HABITUAL

adverbs

idly; disconcertingly; incurably; deliberately; carefully; peculiarly; traditionally; inherently; harmlessly; unfortunately; automatically; ineradicably; studiously, dreadfully; awkwardly; dangerously; methodically; prosaically; conveniently; unconsciously.

HACKNEYED

adverbs

tiresomely; boresomely; ineffectively; tritely; prosaically; typically; bookishly; learnedly; academically; pedantically; professionally; banally; conventionally; pedagogically; unctuously; sententiously; wearisomely; stupidly; monotonously; flatly; terribly; dully.

HAEMOGLOBIN

verbs

break down—; combine with—; count—; destroy—; enrich—; gain in—; lessen—; measure—; study—; —circulates; —conveys; — crystallizes; —dispenses; —oxidizes; —provides.

HAG

adjectives

unseemly; edentate; withered; repulsive; blear-eyed; hideous; ferocious; wretched; wicked; secret; black; midnight.

HAGGARD

adverbs

terribly; alarmingly; surprisingly; pitiably; pathetically; fearfully; unwontedly; extremely; frightfully; mysteriously; significantly; distressingly; disturbingly; gauntly; shockingly; appallingly; wearily; uncommonly; singularly; strangely; cruelly.

HAIL

adjectives

continuous; lashing; sonorous; pearly; sulphurous; incessant; cursing; dreadful.

verbs

deluge with—; escape—; pour—; send down —; shower with—; volley—; —assails; —chills; —descends; —desolates; —falls; —pierces; —ravages; —shatters; —spatters; —stones; —tattoos; —whistles round.

(See rain, snow.)

HAIL (v)

adverbs

exultingly; rapturously; imperatively; enthusiastically; resoundingly; boisterously; thunderously; obstreperously; vigorously.

(See salute, accost.)

HAIR

adjectives

abnormal; abominable; abounding; abundant; agglutinated; alluring; amber; amorous; ash-blonde; ash-colored; asthetic; auburn; back-blown; backward-streaming; bad; battling; beautiful; bleached; blowing; blond; blue-black; bobbed; boyish; braided; brick-colored; bright; bristling; brittle; bronzed; brunette; brushed; bushy; carefully-brushed; careless; carroty; chestnut; close-curling; close-cut; close-trimmed; clustering; coal-black; coiled; colored; copious; coppery; corn-colored; correct; cottony; crinkly; crisp; crownless; cumbersome; curled; dabbled; dark; dazzling; dewy; disarranged; dirty; discolored; disheveled; disordered; drab; dressed; dripping; drowning; dull; dusky; dusty; dyed; ebon; effulgent; elaborately-dressed; electrified; erect; entangled; excessive; faded; fair; falling; fiery; filthy; fine; finespun; flamelike; flattened; flaxen; flecked; floating; flowing; fluffy; fluttering; flying; forlorn; frizzed; frowzy; fussy; fuzzy; garlanded; glamorous; gleaming; glinting; glittering; glorious; glossy; golden; gorgeous; gray; graying; greasy; grimy; grizzled; haggard; hard; harsh; hay-colored; hazel; heavy; helmeted; hempy; henna; hoary; honey-colored; horrent; horrible; horrid; impeccable; impetuous; incredible; iron-gray; jet; jet-black; jeweled; kinky; knotted; lambent; lank; lifeless; light; limp; long; loosening; loose-waved; lovely; luminous; lustrous; luxuriant; mahogany; marcelled; marvelous; massive; matted; metallic; mis-dressed; misty; mortal; mouse-colored; muddy; mussed; mustard-colored; neat; neglected; nut-brown; objectionable; oily; odorous; over-bleached; overgrown; overlong; pale; palled; pallid; palsied; parted; pendulous; perfumed; plaited; plentiful; plastered; pomaded; poppied; portentous; powdered; precious; prematurely-gray; prim; princely; problematical; prodigious; profuse; puffed; queenly; quiet; radiant; ragged; raven; ravishing; rebellious; reddish; reddled; refractory; reverend; ribboned; rich; riotous; rippling; romantic; rough; ruffled; rumpled; russet; rusty; sandy; satiny; scant; scattered; scented; scorched; scraggly; sculptured; shadowy; shaggy; sheeny; shining; shingled; short; short-cropped; silken; silver-gilt; silvery; sleek; slender; slicked; sluttish; smoky; smoothed; smothering; snowy; soft; soggy; spiky; spilling; sprouting; starchy; steel-gray; stiff; stiff-looking; straggly; straight; straw-colored; streaked; subtle; streaming; strength-giving; stringy; strong; stubbly; stubby; sun-blanched; sunny; sun-bleached; sustaining; swart; sylvan; swarthy; sweaty; taffy; tangled; tawny; thick; tidy; time-hallowed; tiny; tousled; tow-colored; tumbled; turbulent; twining; twisted; two-toned; unbound; uncompromising; unconquered; uncurled; undone; undulating; unhealthy; unkempt; unkinked; unmanageable; unruly; untidy; unwashed; usurping; vegetable; velvety; venerable; vibrant; vivid; voluminous; waved; wavy; waxed; well-brushed; well-known; weltering; wet; wild; wind-blown; wind-rumpled; wind-whipped; wiry; wondrous; wreathless; youthful; zephyr-blown; burnished.

verbs

arrange—; beribbon—; braid—; curl—; deck—; discipline—; dishevel—; fluff out—; glue down—; groom—; ruffle—; rumple—; train—; whisk back—; —bristles; —frames; —gleams; —glistens; —glows; —luxuriates; —projects; —ripples; —shimmers; —shines; —straggles; —waves.

(See beard, whiskers, curls.)

HALCYON

adverbs

gently; calmly; peacefully; gratefully; delightfully; gloriously; enviably; agreeably; providentially; happily; sunnily; smoothly; charmingly; blissfully; comfortably; beatifically; cloudlessly; unbelievably; refreshingly; felicitously; miraculously; incomparably.

adverbs

delightfully; sturdily; stoutly; vigorously; vivaciously; cheerily; healthily; soundly; hardily; robustly; ordinarily; vibrantly; exuberantly; remarkably; incredibly; exceptionally; unwontedly; enthusiastically; unbelievably; cheerfully.

HALF-HEARTED

adverbs

obviously; unconcealedly; openly; frankly; manifestly; curiously; indifferently; timidly; indecisively; lazily; indolently; insolently; capriciously; indeterminately; irresolutely; phlegmatically; languidly; nonchalantly; carelessly; inattentively; imperturbably; extraordinarily; inexplicably; unaccountably; irresponsibly; insouciantly; vexatiously; lackadaisically; noticeably; conspicuously.

HALL

adjectives

moody; boundless; cerulean; pillared; gilded; naked; windy; dimly-lighted; spacious; brilliant; low-browed; gaslit; upper; festal; voiceless; lofty; hospitable; marble-paved; ancestral; ancient; unillumined; dusky; enormous; capacious; shallow; subterranean; barrel-vaulted; main; oak-lined; paternal; palatial; roofless; lonely; ample; gloomy; ethereal.

verbs

appropriate—for; assemble in—; convert—into; gather in—; grace—; jam—; loiter in —; occupy—; receive in—; transact in—; preside over—.

(See building, room, auditorium, passage, entry.)

HALLOW (v)

adverbs

traditionally; solemnly; formally; religiously; pompously; perfunctorily.

(See reverence, bless.)

HALLUCINATION

adjectives

visionary; engendering.

verbs

abolish—; dispose to—s; entertain—s; expel—; molest with—; produce—; suffer—s; wander into—; welter in—; wrap in—; —

annoys; —arises; —envisions; —harasses; —hounds; —preys upon; —suggests; —sweeps away; —worries.

(See delusion, illusion.)

HALLWAY

adjectives

frigid; austere; narrow.

HALO

adjectives

majestic; radiant; glistening; hollow.

verbs

award—; crown with—; display—; fashion —; form—; garland with—; invest with—; spread—around; suspend—; weave—; —appears; —blinks; —encircles; —encompasses; —girdles; —glorifies; —hovers over; —radiates; —surrounds; —wreathes.

(See glory, circle, light.)

HALT

adjectives

panting; dead.

verbs

bring to—; call—; come to—; command—; earn—; fall to—; induce—; merit—; necessitate—; plead for—; sound—; stumble to —; urge—; —refreshes; strengthens; —vivifies.

(See truce.)

HALT (v)

adverbs

abruptly; irresolutely; awkwardly; instantaneously; jarringly; completely; permanently.

(See stop, cease.)

HAMLET

adjectives

scattered (pl); rude; nameless; obscure; favored; humble; huddled; disheveled; insignificant.

HAMMER

adjectives

ponderous; polished; deafening.

verbs

beat with—; clasp—; crush with—; drive with—; employ—; flourish—; guide—;

575

labor with—; rap with—; shape with—; smite with—; strike with—; swing—; tap with—; wield—; —injures; —menaces; —suffices.

(See gavel, club, hatchet.)

HAMMER (v)
adverbs
untiringly; repetitiously; energetically; deafeningly; maddeningly; industriously; monotonously; vigorously; thunderously.

(See beat, pound.)

HAMMOCK
adjectives
concealing; leafy; creaking.

verbs
bear in—; cradle in—; ensconce in—; hang in—; hide in—; loll in—; nest in—; relax in—; rest in—; shroud in—; sling—across; slip into—; suspend—; turn into—; —holds; —swings; —upsets.

(See bed, couch.)

HAMPER (v)
adverbs
disastrously; tragically; purposely; fatefully; seriously; painfully; cruelly; superfluously.

(See impede, restrain.)

HAND
verbs
aspire to—of; beckon with—; callous—; clap—s; clasp in—; clench—; denote with —; employ—; extend—; flex—; flick—; flourish—; gain—of; indicate with—; join —s; paralyze—; proffer—; pump—; spread —; splint—; tender—; wring—; —quivers; —trembles; —twitches.

(See palm, claw, fingers, marriage.)

HANDCLASP
adjectives
latticed; fluid; fervent.

HANDFUL
adjectives
paltry; unshackled; comparative; thorny; scanty; scattered; promiscuous.

HANDICAP
adjectives
difficult; generous; cruel; troublesome; personal.

verbs
burden with—; compensate for—; gain—; impose—; insist on—; load with—; offset—; overcome—; require—; resent—; suffer under—; survive—; —alters; —equalizes; —evens; —hampers; —penalizes; —reduces.

(See disadvantage.)

HANDICAP (v)
adverbs
hopelessly; heavily; physically; psychically; spiritually; economically; maritally.

(See hinder.)

HANDKERCHIEF
adjectives
glaring; necktie; napkin; shabby; scandalous; unclean; tear-stained; immaculate; wadded.

verbs
adorn—; border—; display—; embroider—; expose—; fringe—; monogram—; perfume —; pocket—.

(See cloth, silk, linen.)

HANDLE
adjectives
knob; lever; hollow; detachable; composition; substantial.

verbs
clasp—; clutch—; deprive of—; fly off—; grab—; grasp—; grip—; hold by—; manage—; manipulate—; nab—; operate—; snatch—; twist—; —controls; —protrudes; —regulates.

(See knob.)

HANDLE (v)
adverbs
effectively; dexterously; summarily; severely; rudely; technically; awkwardly; individually; arbitrarily; competently; urgently; suavely; adroitly; skillfully.

(See manipulate, touch.)

HANDLING
adjectives
masterly; ill; indecisive; adroit; clever; rough; technical; dexterous; unexceptionable; guileful; skillful.

adjectives

able; accursed; accomplished; achieving; active; admonishing; aged; affectionate; agile; agitated; aggressive; airy; almighty; ambitious; angelic; applauding; aristocratic; armed; arresting; artistic; atrocious; audacious; automatic; avaricious; awkward; balmy; barbarous; bare; beautiful; beckoning; begrimed; bejeweled; beneficent; benumbed; beseeching; bewildered; black; branded; black-gloved; blanched; bleeding; blistered; blithe; bloodless; bloody; blundering; bony; botanic; bounteous; bountiful; brawny; broad; bronzed; brown; bruised; brutal; bungling; burning; callous; capable; careless; caressing; casual; cautious; cemented; chafed; chamois-gloved; chapped; charitable; cheap; cheery; chill; chilly; childish; chopped; chubby; clammy; clapping; clasping; clawing; clawlike; clean; clenched; clever; cold; clinched; clumsy; clutching; coarse; comforting; colossal; confident; conscious; considerate; consoling; cordial; craven; cringing; crooked; cunning; curative; cushionlike; dainty; damaging; darting; deadly; deeply-tanned; defiling; deft; deformed; delegated; delicate; deprecating; despairing; despoiling; detaining; dexterous; diamond-ringed; disguised; dirty; dimpled; discolored; disdainful; disengaged; disrobing; divine; dogmatic; dolllike; dominating; dreadful; drooping; drink-shaken; dubious; dying; eager; eclipsing; eloquent; emaciated; emphatic; enameled; enchanting; energetic; envious; erudite; ever-open; ever-awakening; excellent; execrable; expensive; experienced; expert; explanatory; exploring; exquisite; extended; eye-instructed; fair; facile; failing; fairy; faithful; false; faltering; fanless; fastidious; fatigued; favoring; fearless; feeble; ferocious; fevered; fidgety; fiery; filthy; fine; firm; flabby; flaccid; flattering; flawless; fleshless; fleshy; flexible; floury; fluttering; foam-white; folded; foraged; frank; frantic; fratricidal; freckled; free; frenzied; friendly; fumbling; furtive; fussy; gaunt; gauntleted; generous; gentle; gesticulating; girlish; gloating; glorified; gloved; glowing; gnarled; gorilla; gracious; grasping; graspless; greasy; green; grimy; groomed; groping; grubby; guiding; hairy; hallowed; hamlike; hammerhard; handsome; hanging; hard; hardpalmed; hasty; hateful; healthful; hearty; heavy; heavy-veined; heedless; helpful; helping; high; hollowed; holy; honest; honored; horny; hospitable; hovering; huge; human; humble; hurried; icy; idle; ignoble; immaculate; immediate; immense; immortal; impatient; imperious; impious; imploring; impulsive; incarnadined; inconsequent; indignant; indiscriminate; indolent; indomitable; ineffective; inexperienced; infant; innocent; innocuous; inquisitive; insistent; instinctive; instrumental; intelligent; interpretative; intractable; intruding; invisible; iron; irresolute; irresponsible; irreverent; ivory; jerking; jeweled; kindly; knotted; knuckled; labor-calloused; lacerated; lacerating; lame; languid; lavish; lax; lean; leathery; legible; lemon-scented; lenient; dishpan; wise; liberal; limp; listless; lithe; little; locked; lone; long; long-fingered; long-stretched; long-taloned; loose-hanging; lordly; loving; lustful; mailed; magnetic; malicious; malignant; manacled; manicured; manipulating; martial; massive; masterly; maternal; meager; menacing; merciful; mere; mighty; ministering; miscalculating; mittened; moist; molded; motionless; mottled; mournful; much-ringed; murderous; munificent; nameless; narrow; neighborly; nerveless; nervous; nestling; niggardly; nimble; noiseless; numbed; offending; old-looking; olive; outdoor; outflung; outstretched; pale; pallid; palsied; pampering; parched; parricidal; passive; patrician; peaceful; persistent; persuasive; pierced; pious; pitiless; placid; plastic; plenty-dropping; plump; poised; portraying; powder-blackened; powerful; practiced; pragmatic; praying; presumptuous; priestly; prim; primitive; prodigal; profane; proffered; prompt; proper; protective; providential; providing; pudgy; puffy; pulpy; pure; quavering; quizzical; rash; rapacious; raw; reassuring; reaching; reckless; relaxed; remorseless; relentless; reluctant; resolute; respectful; responsive; restless; restraining; reverent; rheumatic; rigid; rigorous; ringed; ringless; robust; rose-leaf; rose-petal; rosy; rough; royal; rude; ruinous; ruthless; sacred; sacrilegious; sallow; satiny; saving; sceptered; scheming; scholarly; scornful; sculptured; searching; seared; severe; sinless; shadowy; shaking; shapely; shattered; shiny; shriveled; shuddering; signaling; sin-avenging; sinew-swelled; sinewy; skeleton; skillful; slack; slender; slim; slimy; slippery; slow; sly; small; smooth; smudgy; snowy; soaked; soft; soiled; solid; soot-grimed;

staying; steady; stealthy; stiffened; stodgy; stout; straggling; straining; strange; strengthening; strong; stubby; subtle; sudden; suing; sunburned; supine; supple; supplicating; supporting; sure; surreptitious; sustaining; swarthy; swollen; sympathetic; tactful; tainted; tampering; tanned; tapering; tear-dampened; tempestuous; tender; thick; thievish; thin; threatening; throttling; tied; tight-clasped; timid; tiny; tiring; titanic; toil-hardened; toilworn; toiling; torn; trained; translucent; transparent; treacherous; trembling; tremendous; tremulous; trusting; tugging; twitching; tyrannous; unaided; uncertain; unclasped; unconscious; uncovered; unequal; unerring; unfamiliar; unfettered; ungainly; ungloved; ungrudging; uninhibited; unlineal; unresisting; unresponsive; unseen; unskilled; unsparing; unsteady; unswerving; untrained; untrembling; unvenerable; unwilling; uplifted; upstretched; useful; uselesslooking; usurious; valorous; victorious; viewless; vigorous; violent; vital; vulgar; wan; wandering; wanton; warm; warning; warring; wasted; water-shriveled; wavering; waxlike; weather-browned; welcoming; well-bred; well-cared-for; wellformed; well-shaped; willing; withered; work-hardened; lifeless; working; workmarked; wounded; work-soiled; wrapped; wrinkled; wretched; clear; soothing; upraised; spider; sprawling; sprightly; vandalous; vast; veined; venerated.

HANDSOME
adverbs
dazzlingly; gloriously; intangibly; matchlessly; fiercely; surprisingly; sullenly; compellingly; richly; darkly; duskily; cruelly; stormily; vitally; singularly; imposingly; impressively; proudly; sternly; triumphantly; resplendently; glowingly; startlingly; regally; glamorously.

HANDWORK
adjectives
painstaking; plodding; patient; deft.

HANDWRITING
adjectives
sprawling; attested; unmistakable; feeble; quavering; distinctive; intelligent; inelegant; bold; clear; poor; scrawly; uncultivated; crabbed.

verbs
admire—; alter—; counterfeit—; decipher —; develop—; forge—; judge—; recognize —; —fascinates; —flourishes; —reveals; —wavers.
(See writing.)

HANDY
adverbs
extremely; providently; conveniently; exceptionally; remarkably; carefully; delightfully; cleverly; unusually; perfectly; uncommonly; thoughtfully; noticeably; incomparably; serviceably; advantageously; practically; appropriately; readily; ingeniously; miraculously.

HANG (v)
adverbs
fatefully; debatably; imminently; dolefully; fondly; precariously; waveringly; indecisively; tenderly; listlessly; stubbornly; conspicuously; breathlessly; lankly; disconsolately; doggedly; flaccidly.
(See lynch, execute.)

HANGINGS
adjectives
leafy; wholesale; sumptuous; inflammable.

HAPHAZARD
adverbs
casually; carelessly; indolently; informally; adventitiously; incidentally; nonchalantly; indifferently; fortuitously; delightfully; abominably; terribly; atrociously; reprehensibly; joyously; merrily; irresponsibly; gloriously; dreadfully; inconveniently.

HAPPEN (v)
adverbs
opportunely; propitiously; auspiciously; allegedly; subsequently; historically; spontaneously; mysteriously; logically; promptly.
(See occur, befall.)

HAPPENINGS
adjectives
alleged; accidental; subsequent; historical; ordinary; spontaneous; vital; invented; unbelievable; strenuous; mysterious.

HAPPINESS
adjectives
boundless; excited; fireside; tranquil; resultant; connubial; crowning; legitimate; incomparable; wild; overwhelming; keen;

grave; peaceful; celestial; passive; humble; supreme; human; cheap; vulgar; true; romantic; buoyant; puerile; subsequent; unproductive; unclouded; scant; pure; golden; glowing; earthly; mutual; secret; rapturous; eternal; visionary; unexpected; highest; solid; unexcelled; redundant; unutterable; radiant; sublunary; sublime; unappreciated; dizzy; surface; delusive; temporal; exquisite; soft; personal; dear; strange; domestic; virulent; poor; neighborly; pastoral; exalted; joyous; healthy; close-woven; superhuman.

verbs

achieve—; assail—of; bar from—; betoken —; breathe—; conceal—; convert to—; derive—from; destroy—; extract—from; hamper—; inhale—; jeopardize—; overrate—; predestine to—; promote—; recapture—; rescue—; salvage—; shut out—; stake everything on—; strive for—; struggle for —; tend toward—; voice—; void—; yield —; —endures; —evades; —fades; —lingers; —reposes in; —touches; —visits; — wanes.

(See prosperity, gladness, delight, pleasure, bliss, joy, comfort, enjoyment, satisfaction.)

HAPPY

adverbs

radiantly; beamingly; beautifully; bonnily; curiously; rosily; smilingly; ridiculously; openly; innocently; childishly; shyly; modestly; frankly; brightly; rapturously; excitedly; tranquilly; quietly; incomparably; wildly; keenly; overwhelmingly; supremely; secretly; unutterably; joyously; ecstatically; ineffably; profoundly; tenderly; deliriously; breathlessly.

HARANGUE

adjectives

mere; soporific; seditious; inflammatory; tempestuous; conciliatory; soldierly; unintelligible; coherent; explanatory; fiery; belligerent.

HARANGUE (v)

adverbs

bombastically; vehemently; seditiously; tempestuously; unintelligibly; coherently; fiercely; belligerently; vigorously.

(See orate, address.)

HARASS (v)

adverbs

consistently; grievously; ceaselessly; perpetually; maddeningly; irksomely; irritatingly; exasperatingly; incessantly.

(See distress, persecute, trouble.)

HARASSMENT

adjectives

ceaseless; perpetual.

HARBOR

adjectives

immense; sun-splashed; sunlit; little; green-bordered; earthly; exposed; secret; miniature; landlocked; fortified; blue; restless; mountain-bound; all-creating; bustling; glassy; neutral; matchless; noble; placid; sheltered; fair; unrivaled.

verbs

admit to—; afford ; anchor in—; assign to—; blockade—; drift to—; lie in—; lodge at—; obtain—; put into—; seek—; set out of—; slip into—; —accommodates; —conceals; —protects; —quarters; —shelters.

(See refuge, haven, shelter, retreat.)

HARD

adverbs

stonily; wilfully; unyieldingly; pitilessly; obdurately; unrelentingly; unrepentantly; inexorably; stubbornly; obstinately; mulishly; doggedly; perversely; fanatically; resolutely; determinedly; unmercifully; cruelly; maliciously; vengefully; implacably; bitterly; sternly; unreasonably; manifestly; palpably; undeniably.

HARDEN (v)

adverbs

glacially; excessively; immoderately; perpetually; scientifically; methodically; mechanically.

(See season, invigorate.)

HARDIHOOD

adjectives

slipshod; reckless; barbaric; desperate.

HARDNESS

adjectives

iron; steely.

verbs

allay—; arm with—; crust with—; deliver from—; dissemble—; inure to—; incur—;

loathe—; overcome—; penetrate—; produce
—; rub off—; shed—; suffer—; —defends;
—endures; —protects; —resists.
  (See difficulty, harshness, cruelty, severity.)

HARDSHIP
adjectives
continued; increasing; inevitable; nameless;
physical; appreciable; incredible; tremendous; unnecessary; unexpected; early; unre-
pining.

verbs
allay—; alleviate—; ameliorate—; bear—;
bow under—; condemn to—; ease—; endure
—; entail—; evade—; groan under—; impose—; inflict—; learn through—; oppress
with—; share—; suffer—; taste—; tolerate
—; torment with—; —anguishes; —destroys; —discourages; —presses.
  (See privation, injury, affliction, adversity, trouble, pain.)

HARDY
adverbs
resolutely; intrepidly; courageously; stoutly; sturdily; robustly; boldly; fortunately;
indubitably; obviously; indefatigably; dependably; strongly; staunchly; vigorously;
stalwartly; inexhaustibly; courageously;
audaciously; pluckily; wonderfully; irresistibly; astonishingly; prodigiously.

HARE
adjectives
purblind; timorous; fluffy; flying.

HARLEQUIN
adverbs
erratically; capriciously; changeably; mercurially; kaleidoscopically; vagrantly; waywardly; fleetingly; nimbly; swiftly; fleetly;
trippingly; stagily; dramatically; spectacularly; comically; trickily; lightly; clownishly; jocosely; waggishly; fabulously; entertainingly; laughingly; mockingly.

HARM
adjectives
sullen; bodily; enormous; substantial; tremendous; imminent; delicious; irreparable;
incalculable; chief; outward; serious; personal.

verbs
anticipate—; avert—; commit—; correct—;
counterbalance—; forgive—; heed—; inflict
—; lament—; offset—; prevent—; protect
against—; rectify—; remedy—; render—;
resent—; ruminate upon—; save from—;
suffer—; sustain—; weigh—; —afflicts; —
angers; —distresses; —pains; —threatens.
  (See injury, damage, evil, wrong.)

HARMFUL
adverbs
terribly; immediately; ultimately; distinctly;
admittedly; obviously; maliciously; venomously; deliberately; innocently; unconsciously; ignorantly; intentionally; purposely; irrevocably; irremediably; calamitously; disastrously; dreadfully; outrageously; atrociously; perniciously; exceptionably; deplorably; uncommonly; frightfully; immeasurably; incalculably.

HARMLESS
adverbs
innocently; distinctly; assuredly; avowedly;
obviously; manifestly; definitely; altogether;
utterly; comparatively; allegedly; perfectly; impeccably; virtually; substantially;
practically; negligibly; essentially; presumably; reasonably; assuredly.

HARMONIOUS
adverbs
agreeably; fortunately; sweetly; luckily; unquestionably; happily; felicitously; unbelievably; unexpectedly; sociably; ineffably; cordially; heartily; obviously; manifestly; sincerely; highly; entirely; uncommonly; remarkably; particularly; delightfully; serenely; exquisitely; seraphically; gloriously; inexpressibly.

HARMONY
adjectives
ingenious; distinguished; plaintive; serene;
subtle; thrilling; ringing; sublime; unutterable; amiable; developed; divine; ravishing; inner; absolute; complete; whirlwind;
primal; undisturbed; entire; methodical;
perfect; ethereal; general; incomparable;
celestial; angelic; pre-established; exquisite; multitudinous (pl); many-sounding;
unbroken; heavenly; household; deceiving;
liquid; delightful; peculiar; inarticulate;
eternal; discordant; canarylike; complicated; blatant; enchanting; weird; insured;
glorious; limitless; soft; subdued; inexpress-

ible; aerial; unconjectured; color; intoxicating; far-linked; elemental; impromptu; autumnal; wonderful; rugged; lugubrious; consonant; palatable; chiseled.

verbs
admire—; beget—; bind into—; cement—; compose into—; destroy—; dispose toward —; insure—; maintain—; melt into—; stress —; strike—; weave in—; work in—; — charms; —delights; —emanates from; — enchants; —grows; —pervades; —prevails; —smooths.
(See friendship, agreement, peace, consistency.)

HARP
adjectives
murmuring; piano; neglected; cunning; mysterious; sullen; reproofless; impaled; aeolian; smitten; solemn; sounding; sweet; tuneful.

verbs
flow from—; marry to—; pitch—; string—; strum—; touch—; tune—; waken—; welcome—; —chimes; —disarms; —enervates; —entrances; —pleases; —reverberates; — rings out; —sings; —sleeps; —soothes; — thrills; —trembles; —whispers.
(See guitar, banjo.)

HARP (v)
adverbs
exclusively; repetitiously; irksomely; naggingly; inexorably; bitterly; moodily; venomously; groundlessly; sullenly.
(See persist, repeat.)

HARPING
adjectives
constant; mysterious; celestial.

HARROW (v)
adverbs
mercilessly; cruelly; superfluously; gratuitously; sadistically; grimly.
(See wound, distress, torture.)

HARSH
adverbs
dreadfully; needlessly; unnecessarily; bitterly; inexplicably; austerely; irritably; discourteously; forbiddingly; irritatingly; inexcusably; deliberately; maliciously; incredibly; unreasonably; vengefully; disconcertingly; tyrannically; despotically; dogmatically; imperiously; authoritatively; terribly; uncompromisingly; stubbornly; cruelly; unmitigatedly; mercilessly.

HARSHNESS
adjectives
terrible; stubborn; momentary; sinister; mellowed.

verbs
apply—; assail with—; avoid—; clash with —; correct—; creak with—; pardon—; resent—; resist—; rub with—; shed—; subdue—; taste—; temper—; thunder—; — arises from; —displeases; —grates; —sours.
(See severity, cruelty, hardness.)

HARVEST
adjectives
terrible; reaped; pecuniary; costly; easy; sorrowful; rich; bounteous; promising; uncertain; preposterous; golden; ripened; abundant; heavenly; full; fair; millennial; hidden; glorious; unshared; full-sheaved.

verbs
bear—; celebrate—; enrich—; gather—; glean—; heap—; house—; invite to—; mar —; promise—; reap—; rear—; ruin—; sickle—; toil in—; treasure—; —cheers; — contents; —glows; —graces; —repays; — rewards; —satisfies; —wearies.
(See crop, yield, product, reward, fruit, proceeds, result, return.)

HASTE
adjectives
heedless; breathless; duteous; delirious; phantom; disciplined; desperate; unseemly; wrathful; fiery; undue; hot; wild; indecent; purblind; unscrupulous; lamentable; eager; irreverent; barbarous; clumsy; nervous; noiseless; mad; frantic; reckless; uncivil; feverish; deadly; frenzied; disgraceful; rash; ruthless; moderate; dread; incredible; unusual; straining; over-credulous; tremulous; generous; noticeable.

HASTEN (v)
adverbs
instinctively; obsequiously; anxiously; vastly; materially; dutifully; nervously; unscrupulously; irreverently; frantically; uncivilly; feverishly; incredibly; tremulously.
(See urge, hurry.)

HASTY

adverbs

disgracefully; inexcusably; rudely; unforgivably; shamefully; hysterically; impetuously; impulsively; ridiculously; unnecessarily; unfortunately; madly; insanely.

HAT

adjectives

drab; shiny; tomato-colored; glazed; straw; rusty; soiled; silk; glossy; discolored; sleek; napless; chocolate; absurd; shabby; ordinary; archaic; hereditary; beaver; crownless; conical; jaunty; battered; distinguished; befeathered; beribboned; broad-brimmed; sugar-loaf; hard; high; cocked; cavernous; flattish; stunning; featherweight; felt; rush; high-crowned; flopping; dilapidated; fantastic; misshapen; much-worn; coquettish; beguiling; casual; slouched; formless; distinctive; fashionable; devastating; smart; shovel; horrible; becoming; plumed; infinitesimal; shapeless; dun-colored; soft; fetching; flowered; slouch; dishpan-shaped; delicate; battered; cunning.

verbs

clap on—; cock—; deck—; design—; discard—; display—; doff—; don—; fancy—; fashion—; plume—; scorn—; shed—; sport (colloq)—; tide—; tip—; trim—; wave—; —awes; —flatters; —s fly; —perches; —protects; —reposes on; —shocks; —teeters.
  (See cap, helmet.)

HATCHET

verbs

brandish—; crush with—; drive—into; employ—; flourish—; hew with—; knock down with—; sharpen—; smite with—; split with —; 'strip with—; strike with—; threaten with—; wield—; yield to—; —cuts; —destroys; —lacerates; —menaces; —severs; —splits; —subdues; —wounds.
  (See axe, hammer, club, bat, gavel.)

HATE

adjectives

high-strung; prejudiced; vigorous; counterfeiting; morbid; malevolent; racking; vanquished; constant; hideous; sectional; murderous; savage; steadfast; individual; groveling; immortal; deadly; inflexible; unfilial; grudging; envious; despotic; lodged; impious; heavy; ancestral; sullen; ill-dissembled; consuming; unrelenting; strong; bitter; mutual; irrevocable; quenchless; shameful; successful; unspoken; misbegotten; unmistakable; supernatural; vehement.

HATE (v)

adverbs

perniciously; implacably; cordially; insatiably; invariably; vindictively; jealously; instinctively; mutually; passionately; inflammably; politically; irrepressibly; unconquerably; groundlessly.
  (See detest, dislike.)

HATED

adverbs

utterly; abominably; repugnantly; mortally; intolerably; impossibly; incredibly; completely; shockingly; detestably; disgustingly; insufferably; horribly; terribly; odiously.

HATEFUL

adverbs

bitterly; utterly; unspeakably; odiously; offensively; completely; abominably; disgustingly; insufferably; intolerably; horribly; terribly; shockingly; profoundly; uncommonly; intensely; unnaturally; curiously; passionately; venomously; infernally; furiously; consummately.

HATER

adjectives

reputed; persistent.

HATRED

adjectives

native; innate; instinctive; internal; caustic; patient; deadly; profound; intense; bitter; rancorous; mutual; unaffected; unnatural; unsleeping; hidden; curious; lifelong; strong; ineradicable; passionate; moody; fierce; obscure; inextinguishable; revolutionary; inflammable; virtuous; vigorous; apparent; venomous; smiling; inexorable; immodest; antique; ancient; fanatical; unleavened; hearty; national; raw; implacable; political; irrepressible; partisan; nauseous; jealous; racial; infernal; base; active; indurated; color; perfidious; relentless; furious; vindictive; violent; unconquerable; baffled; undying; consuming; groundless.

verbs

allay—; appease—; breed—; cherish—; conceal—; deepen—; depict—; deplore—; endure—; excite—; focus—upon; incite to —; justify—; kindle—; manifest—; nourish—; nurse—; placate—; regard with—; quicken—; scatter—; shower with—; stir up—; summon—; sustain—; turn to—; voice—; —blazes; —bubbles; —convulses; —embitters; —festers; —impels; —lingers; —maligns; —stings; —subsides; —ravages; —rends; —sunders; —wanes; —waxes.

(See abomination, animosity, antagonism, contempt, enmity, hostility, indignation, jealousy.)

HAUGHTINESS
adjectives
staring; unconscious; self-approving.

HAUGHTY
adverbs
arrogantly; deliberately; pompously; absurdly; unreasonably; unnecessarily; offensively; ridiculously; egotistically; insolently; bumptiously; imperiously; superciliously; impertinently; shamefully; laughably; swaggeringly; presumptuously; contemptuously; .contemptibly; justifiably; atrociously; extremely; unusually.

HAUL (v)
adverbs
economically; daily; professionally; customarily; speedily; laboriously; vigorously; painfully; lumberingly.

(See pull, draw, drag.)

HAUNCHES
adjectives
powerful; cold.

HAUNT
adjectives
genteel; childhood; authenticated; private; familiar; hideous; reptile; undergraduate; classical; cheerful; frequent; gay; frightful; native; brightened; strange; indigenous; delightful; swampy; deserted; weary; unaccustomed; popular; picturesque; mysterious; public; garden; melodious; shaded; inaccessible.

HAUNT (v)
adverbs
bewitchingly; lecherously; dejectedly; privately; hideously; frightfully; indigenously; mysteriously; bewilderingly.

(See persecute.)

HAVEN
adjectives
windless; beauteous; spacious; commodious; sheltered; wished.

verbs
admit to—; afford—; bar from—; conceal in—; enter—; establish—; flee to—; lodge —; retreat to—; seek—; —accommodates; —consoles; —protects; —quarters; —shelters; —solaces; —supports; —welcomes.

(See harbor, shelter, refuge, retreat, asylum.)

HAVOC
verbs
anticipate—; come to—; create—; cry—; decry—; fortify against—; pass into—; play —; practise—; repair—; resist—; survey—; witness—; work—; wreak—; —confounds; —distresses.

(See destruction, waste, ruin.)

HAWK
verbs
—alights; —attacks; —dashes; —destroys; —dodges; —floats; —glides; —gyrates; —pounces on; —preys on; —prowls about; —sails; —scans; —screams; —screeches; —seizes; —severs; —skims; —soars; —somersaults; —squeals; —sweeps down; —twists; —swerves; —swoops; —wheels around; —whistles.

(See bird.)

HAWKER
verbs
license—; patronize—; —advertises; —attracts; —babbles; —barks; —barters; —bears; —bellows; —carries; —disposes of; —cries; —expatiates on; —jabbers; —plies; —prates about; —rants about; —rattles off; —spiels; —travels; —vends; —wanders.

(See merchant, salesman.)

HAY
adjectives
nutritious; crisping; new-mown; fragrant; sun-scorched; fresh; half-tanned.

verbs
basket—; bundle—; cart—; cock—; conceal —; consume—; fork—; hook—; load—; market—; mow—; pitch—; preserve—; rake —; press—; spade—; stack—; store—; toss —.

(See grass.)

adjectives
high-shouldered; proverbial.

HAZARD

adjectives
structural; lessened; unreasonable; reduced; glorious; industrial; temporary; human; intrinsic; specified; extreme; blind; skidding; physical; tremendous; awful; extraordinary; perilous; dust.

verbs
avoid—; **dally with**—; dare—; doubt—; eliminate—; expose to—; face—; incur—; obviate—; overcome—; preserve from—; risk—; run—; stand—; stake on—; venture —; view—; —allures; —endangers; —obstructs; —perils; —threatens.

(See chance, risk, danger, peril, stake.)

HAZARDOUS

adverbs
extremely; recklessly; perilously; presumably; obviously; manifestly; unreasonably; gloriously; tremendously; awfully; extraordinarily; mysteriously; ominously; alarmingly; terribly; attractively; alluringly; notoriously; undeniably; adventurously; exceedingly; strangely.

HAZE

adjectives
blossomy; luminous; suspended; soft; emotional; hueless; silver; blue; purple; smoke; gauzy; transparent; waterish; golden; mellowing; murky; burning; yellow; soft; faint; autumnal; amber; glittering; diaphanous; fictitious; Indian Summer; nebulous; iridescent; mournful; dim; gray; damp; misty; penumbral; somnolent; fluid; shimmering; reddish; sumptuous; moonlit; drowsy; vanishing; undefinable; deepening; shining; tremulous; glimmering; noontide; languorous.

verbs
clear—; disappear in—; falter in—; grope in—; lose in—; mingle with—; penetrate—; —develops; —dims; —encompasses; —lifts; —frosts; —hangs; —hovers over; —melts; —mists; —obscures; —rests on.

(See vapor, smoke, mist, fog, obscurity, clouds.)

adverbs
dangerously; obscurely; dimly; incredibly; curiously; oddly; strangely; queerly; peculiarly; particularly; unpleasantly; unintelligibly; incomprehensibly; intentionally; deliberately; perilously; vexatiously; darkly; nebulously; uncertainly; foggily.

HEAD

adjectives
abominable; aching; acknowledged; addled; administrative; aggressive; ambitious; ample; antique; apprehensive; ashen; aspiring; asymmetrical; attentive; auburn; auspicious; averted; bald; bandaged; banished; battered; bedraggled; beautiful; beloved; bent; bewildering; blameless; blighted; blunt; bobbed; bowed; boyish; braided; brainless; bright; bristling; bruised; bullet; burnished; bursting; bushy; cavernous; classic; clean; clean-swept; clear; close-clipped; clumsy; coiffed; collective; comely; common; confused; copper; country; cowering; craven; cropped; crowned; crumpled; crushed; curious; curling; cursed; dark; dastardly; deathless; defending; deathlike; defenseless; defiant; delicate; delightful; desperate; devoted; diminished; disordered; dispirited; distant; dizzy; doll-like; downcast; downy; drooping; drowsy; drunken; dusky; early-silvering; elegant; elegantly-wigged; elfin; elongated; enticing; erect; executive; extravagant; fanciful; fascinating; fast-whitening; feathered; feeble; fine; finely-molded; firm; flame-red; flattened; flaunted; flaxen; fleshy; flowerless; forked; forlorn; frizzled; frowzy; gasping; ghastly; gleaming; glossy; golden; golden-mouthed; good-natured; gossipy; graceful; graduated; grizzled; grotesque; hairless; hairy; handsome; happy; haughty; heaven-saluting; heavy; heavy-jawed; heavy-jeweled; helmeted; helpless; henna; hideous; high-held; hoary; hooded; hopeless; horny; horrible; horrid; huge; hunted; ignorant; immortal; impassioned; imperial; imperious; impotent; impressive; impudent; impulsive; inclined; incongruous; inert; inexperienced; inquisitive; intellectual; intelligent; intermediate; intervening; iron-gray; irregular; irrevocable; joyful; keen; kingly; kinky; knavish; languid; large; learned; leonine; limp; lingering; little; living; logical; lofty; lolling; long; long-haired; lowered; low-lying; magnificent; mangled; massive; meek; melancholy; menacing; mighty; military; mob-

capped; molded; mossy; mottled; mountainous; muddy; mummylike; nightcapped; nodding; obsequious; obtuse; old; oval; ovate; overhanging; overheated; packed; palsied; pantomime; patchily-bald; patchy; patriarchal; patrician; pendent; pensive; periwigged; pictured; picturesque; plebeian; plumy; poetic; powdered; practical; presumptive; pretty; prostrate; proud; remarkable; queenly; racking; regal; responsible; restless; retracted; reverend; ridiculous; rolling; romantic; round; rude; saintly; satiny; saucy; sculptured; seemingly-devoted; sensible; shaggy; shaken; shamed; shapely; shameless; shaven; shiny; shrunken; sickly; silken; simple; sleek; sleeping; sleepless; slender; slightly-bald; small; smooth; snowy; sorrow-bowed; sovereign; spaniel; specular; spiritual; splendid; sprouting; square; stained; stately; steady; steaming; steel-hard; stupid; sturdy; suave; subtle; sufficient; sumptuous; sun-baked; sun-bleached; sunburned; tangled; thorny; thick-curled; thorn-crowned; throbbing; tilted; titled; titular; tombless; tonsured; tormenting; tossing; tousled; tremendous; troublesome; turbaned; twisted; ugly; uncovered; uncrowned; undishonored; unhonored; unkempt; unmellowed; unprotected; unshaven; unsuspecting; upheld; uptilted; upturned; veiled; venerated; virile; virtual; vivacious; vulgar; wabbling; wagging; weak; weary; weird; well-balanced; well-bleached; well-constructed; well-formed; well-poised; well-proportioned; well-shaped; whimsical; white-wigged; wigged; wobbly; woolly; yoke-encumbered; youthful.

verbs
adorn—; balance on—; bare—; bob—; bow —; cock—; crown—; erect—; hang—; incline—; involve—; pillow—; pound—; raise —; split—; surge to—; tilt—; wag—; waggle—; —buzzes; —protrudes; —reels; — sings; —spins; —swims; —throbs.
    (See skull, mind, crown.)

HEADACHE
adjectives
frightful; agonizing; excruciating; satisfactory; attendant; racking; incessant; violent; splitting; insidious.

verbs
aggravate—; allay—; alleviate—; assail with—; attack with—; banish—; confine with—; cure—; dispose of—; ease—; groan with—; incur—; mitigate—; relieve—; remedy—; soothe—; subdue—; subject to—; temper—; throb with—; treat for—; —ensues; —indisposes; —prostrates; —returns; —weakens; —yields to.
    (See pain.)

HEADDRESS
adjectives
gleaming; horned; immense.

HEADING
adjectives
cabalistic; comprehensive; general; definite.

HEADLAND
adjectives
graceful; misty; picturesque.

HEADLIGHT
adjectives
dazzling; blinding; blinking.

verbs
adjust—; dim—; extinguish—; focus—; regulate—; shun—; turn on—; —beams; — blinds; —dazzles; —flares; —flickers; — glares; —gleams; —illuminates; —penetrates; —reflects; —reveals; —shimmers; — shines.
    (See light.)

HEADLINE
verbs
consult—; garner —s; hush down —s; pop into —s; scan —s; —alarms; —amazes; — announces; —asserts; —attracts; —awakens; —blares; —blazes; —blazons forth; — discloses; —disquiets; —hints; —misleads; —proclaims; —reports; —s protest; —suggests; —screams (colloq.); —shrieks; (colloq.).

    (See title, advertisement, announcement, proclamation.)

HEADQUARTERS
adjectives
harried; military; ecclesiastical.

verbs
assume — at; convey to—; direct from—; dispatch to—; inhabit—; move into—; operate from—; order from—; repair to—; report to—; respect—; transact at—; —an-

nounces; —bars; —conceals; —decrees; — harbors; —issues; —reinstates; —shelters.
(See quarters, center, residence, house.)

HEADSTRONG
adverbs
stubbornly; wilfully; indomitably; doggedly; obdurately; obstinately; absurdly; ridiculously; unreasonably; violently; untractably; cantankerously; unmanageably; ungovernably; uncontrollably; persistently; inveterately; habitually; dreadfully; frightfully; inherently; incorrigibly; hopelessly; invincibly; sturdily; extremely.

HEAL (v)
adverbs
marvelously; miraculously; permanently; temporarily; superficially; medically; scientifically.
(See cure, repair.)

HEALING
adjectives
divine; sovereign; transient; miraculous.

HEALTH
adjectives
accustomed; decayed; comely; hardy; declining; failing; rude; tolerable; inexhaustible; robust; rustic; shattered; delicate; fundamental; glowing; particular; ever-uncertain; buxom; departing; saving; comparative; sweet; virile; ruddy; rose-tinted; vibrant; summer; absolute; universal; buoyant; positive; vigorous; precarious; glorious; moral; trying; blasted; flagrant; lonely; redundant; informing; frail; invigorating; dynamic; impaired; feeble; infirm; inexhaustible; exuberant; reacquired; required; physical; drunken; mental.

verbs
bankrupt—; battle for—; brace—; bubble with—; confer — upon; cultivate—; deprive of—; deteriorate in—; drain upon—; drink —; enjoy—; entrust—; foster—; hazard—; impair—; imperil—; improve—; influence —; injure—; insure—; lower—; maintain —; promote—; preoccupy with—; recapture —; restore to—; sacrifice—; sap—; shatter —; strive for—; sustain—; undermine—; —breaks; —continues; —fails; —improves; —suffers.
(See welfare, prosperity, strength.)

HEALTHFUL
adverbs
presumably; allegedly; bracingly; invigoratingly; restoratively; curatively; notoriously; reputably; famously; distinctly; remarkably; wonderfully; demonstrably; manifestly; evidently; undeniably; marvellously; unquestionably; extremely.

HEALTHY
adverbs
robustly; normally; unusually; admirably; wonderfully; fortunately; tolerably; fundamentally; comparatively; altogether; completely; buoyantly; vigorously; radiantly; gloriously; exuberantly; sturdily; happily; constitutionally; remarkably; excellently; magnificently; splendidly.

HEAP
adjectives
moldering; promiscuous; mountainous; tumbled; contorted; dismaying; enormous; undistinguishable; solemn; compost; wretched; writhing; convulsed; bony; wind-driven; sprawled; silvery; shapeless; lifeless; apparent; hoarded; inextricable; despicable.

verbs
accumulate into—; amass—; cast into—; collect in—; cone—; form—; gather into—; level—; lie in—; load into—; pile up—; relegate to—; rise in—; stand in—; store up—; throw into—; —grows; —overwhelms; —rises.
(See pile, mass.)

HEAP (v)
adverbs
massively; promiscuously; impartially; confusedly; profusely; indiscriminately; contortedly; convulsively; shapelessly; inextricably.
(See pile, accumulate.)

HEAR (v)
adverbs
accidentally; distinctly; occasionally; keenly; inevitably; audibly; dumbly; unconsciously; subconsciously; perpetually.
(See listen, perceive.)

HEARER
adjectives
eloquent; complacent; indefatigable; critical; attentive.

verbs

attract—s; bore —s; convince —s; crave—; enchant—; impress—; inflame—; inform—; instruct—; interest—; move—; obtain—; preach to—; tire—; weary—; —assents; —complies; —heeds; —judges; —learns; —listens; —perceives.

(See audience, listener, spectator.)

HEARING

adjectives

respectful; impaired; defective; harsh; distinct; impartial; favorable; younger.

verbs

accede to—; bar from—; block—; crave—; defer—; dull—; favor with—; grant—; judge—; prejudice—; preside at—; question —; rant at—; sustain—; weaken—.

(See meeting, investigation.)

HEARKEN (v)

adverbs

wistfully; respectfully; expectantly; eagerly; nervously; excitedly; cautiously; instinctively.

(See hear, perceive, listen.)

HEART

adjectives

abysmal; aching; adulterate; affectionate; affection-starved; agitated; alien; alienated; anguished; animated; anxious; ardent; arid; attentive; barren; bursting; base; beating; beauty-broken; beauty-loving; beclouded; beefy; befuddled; besotted; bewildering; black; bland; blank; blazoned; bleeding; blighted; boding; bounding; brave; breaking; breathless; broken; brute; bucklered; burdened; burning; bursting; busy; callous; careless; cheerful; cheering; cheery; childlike; clamorous; cold; compassionate; conscious; conservative; constant; constricted; contented; contrite; coreless; corrupted; courtly; covetous; cowardly; critical; crushed; dark; darkened; dauntless; dazzling; dead; deceitful; dedicated; defying; delicate; delighted; desolate; despairing; disappointed; discontented; diseased; divided; dormant; double; doubting; drained; dreary; drowsy; dull; duteous; eager; echoing; ecstatic; editorial; effeminate; emptied; enchanted; encouraged; energetic; entranced; erring; ever-beating; everlasting; exacting; excited;

fainting; faithful; false; famished; famous; farseeing; fascinated; faultless; fearful; fecund; feeble; feminine; fevered; fiendish; fierce; fiery; firm; fleshy; flinty; wrung; fluttering; foolish; forestalled; forever-shattered; fragrance-laden; frail; frank; freer; fretted; frightened; frostbound; frosted; frowning; frozen; gallant; general; generous; gentle; genuine; girlish; gleeful; graceless; grateful; gravel; grieved; guileless; half-snared; hammering; happy; haughty; heavenly; heavy; heedless; hereditary; heroic; hidden; humanitarian; humble; hungering; hurrying; hushed; idolatrous; impassioned; impious; impressionable; improvident; impulsive; inconstant; indecent; individual; indolent; indurated; inmost; inner; innocent; intense; irritable; joyous; kind; kindling; kindred; laboring; lacerated; laggard; languid; laughing; lavish; leaden; life-giving; light; lively; living; lofty; lonely; long, long-enduring; long-pent; long-wandering; longing; loudly-beating; love-pampered; loving; low; low-hushed; maddening; manful; manly; marble; mean; meditative; merry; mighty; moist; mourning; mountain; moved; mysterious; mystic; naked; noble; obdurate; open; oppressed; orphaned; outraged; overburdened; overflowing; overfull; overladen; overworked; pained; palpitating; passionate; paternal; pearly; penitent; pent; perfect; perplexed; perturbed; perverse; pinched; pious; pitiless; pitying; plighted; poisoned; poor; popish; popular; poverty-stricken; private; profane; profound; propelled; prophetic; proud; pulsating; puny; pure; pusillanimous; quaking; queenly; queer; quenched; quick-beating; quick-breathed; quickened; rapt; rapture-filled; ravaged; rebellious; reckless; relenting; repressed; responsive; restless; returning; reverent; riotous; rising; rocky; rough; royal; rude; rugged; rusting; saddened; satisfied; scented; scheming; scorching; seated; self-accusing; sensitive; shadowy; shallow; sheer; shuddering; sickly; sincere; sinewy; singing; single; sinking; slight; slow; smitten; smothered; softened; solitary; somber; sore; sorrowful; spotless; stagnant; stainless; stalwart; starry; steadfast; sterner; still-renewed; stirring; stony; stout; straitened; stricken; strong; struggling; stubborn; sturdy; suffocating; sullen; sunny; superstitious; susceptible; swelling; sweltering; sympathetic; tavernlike; tempest-tossed; tender; terrified;

thankful; thoughtless; thought-propelled; throbbing; thumping; tortured; tossed; towering; trembling; tremulous; troubled; trusting; tumultuous; turbulent; tyrannous; unassisted; uncaged; unconjectured; undivided; uneasy; unfettered; unfortified; unfrozen; unguarded; universal; unmoved; unpurchasable; unquickened; unquiet; unselfish; unsophisticated; unsuspecting; untutored; unwavering; unworn; unyielding; upright; vacant; veritable; virgin; wakening; wandering; warm; wasting; waxing; wayward; weak; weary; well-contented; well-disposed; wicked; widowed; wild; wintry; withering; womanly; wooing; wordless; worldly; worried; worshipping; wounded; wretched; yearning; zealous.

verbs
appeal to—; beguile—; chill—; depress—; dilate—; ease—; engage—; enshrine in—; furrow—; gather—; gladden—; harden—; hug to—; lay open—; melt—; mend—; pluck at—; pour out—; smite—; stab to—; stimulate—; take to—; warm—; wring—; —awakens; —betrays; —bleeds; —blinds; —contracts; —craves; —expands; —fails; —hungers; —jumps; —misgives; —overflows; —palpitates; —pines; —pounds; —prompts; —quakes; —races; —responds; —sinks; —softens; —swells; —throbs; —ticks; —yearns.
(See essence, core, pulse, organ, affection, passion, courage, strength.)

HEARTBEAT
adjectives
tumultuous; vexing.

HEARTBREAK
adjectives
terrible; human.

HEART DISEASE
verbs
convalesce from— —; correct— —; cure of — —; examine for— —; incur— —; indicate— —; recover from— —; resist— —; suffer from— —; treat— —; — —degenerates; — —dilates; — —menaces; — — pains; — —ravages; — —subsides.
(See disease, sickness, malady.)

HEARTH
adjectives
blazing; domestic; lonely; imperial; glit-

tering; familiar; heavenly; glowing; inmost; desolated; tiled; hospitable; altar; ancestral; dreary; lowly; sordid.

HEARTLESSNESS
adjectives
cruel; perfect; undisguised; criminal.

verbs
bare—; brook—; conceal—; deny—; excuse —; steep in—; wither into—; —bites; — contrives; —crushes; —dejects; —despairs; —embitters; —lurks; —murders; —pains; —strikes; —wounds.
(See cruelty.)

HEARTY
adverbs
sincerely; enthusiastically; graciously; spontaneously; warily; impressively; rapturously; eagerly; cordially; impetuously; impulsively; openly; splendidly; sympathetically; devotedly; cheerily; jovially; entirely; exceptionably; extremely; unusually; noticeably; conspicuously; especially.

HEAT
adjectives
primitive; intense; intercepted; parching; hardening; dulling; destructive; resisting; sulphurous; automatic; self-regulating; unifying; genial; ordinary; subterranean; excessive; steaming; shimmering; white; fervent; gray; heartburning; yellow; incandescent; dancing; breathless; blood-red; imminent; midday; prickly; internal; sweltering; fierce; subtle; central; controlled; oppressive; tempered; incarnate; scalding; blistering; ferocious; feverish; heroic; fortunate; visceral; vague; withering; imperial; scorching; restless; blinding; tremulous; torturous; masculine; radiant; deadly; incremental; defying; infernal; furious; palpable; saturating; wet; devoted; overpowering; polished; rash; false; aching; clean; efficient; dependable; effortless; healthful; boisterous; instant; steady; terrestrial; boiling; unspeakable; tropical; love-devouring; uniform; intolerable; bristling; generous; luminous; beneficial; glowing; perpendicular; savage; unendurable; suffocating; kindly; animal; brooding; fantastic; sickening; fierce; quivering; stifling; freezing; stimulating; intolerable; exceptional; fluent, temperate; extreme; concentrated; continuous; expensively-produced; transmuted; burning.

verbs

apply—; bask in—; control—; foment—; generate—; maintain—; measure—; raise —; regulate—; relieve—; sustain—; swelter in—; swoon from—; transform into—; treat with—; utilize—; —blights; —blisters; —encompasses; —escapes; —evolves; —parches; —scorches; —stifles; —subsides.

(See fire, flame.)

HEAT (v)

adverbs

fiercely; intensely; destructively; sulphurously; automatically; excessively; subtly; oppressively; witheringly; scorchingly; palpably; blisteringly; tropically; intolerably; beneficially; suffocatingly; concentratedly.

(See warm.)

HEATH

adjectives

flowery; vast; uncultivated; blasted; magnificent; pastoral; bleak; tottering; menacing; stultifying; ugly; murky; dismal.

verbs

clip—; crop—; cut—; grow—; plant—; roof with—; tend—; thatch with—; utilize —; —abounds; —banks; —blazes; —flourishes; —flowers; —perfumes; —stretches.

(See land, area, plant, flower.)

HEATHEN

adjectives

benighted; tiresome.

HEATHENISH

adverbs

shamelessly; cruelly; deliberately; grossly; ignorantly; savagely; brutally; barbarously; unconscionably; inordinately; terribly; dreadfully; unbelievably; inexpressibly; atrociously; shamefully; brazenly; ostentatiously; openly; crudely; blindly; darkly; coarsely; rudely; brutishly; shockingly; appallingly.

HEAVE (v)

adverbs

bodily; fulsomely; breathlessly; spasmodically; tumultuously; intermittently; laboriously; oppressively.

(See throw, lift.)

HEAVEN

adjectives

frosty; righteous; luminous; cloudless; precipitating; overhanging; bounteous; transfigured; untrod; starry; sublunar; clear; subjugated; high; bending; miniature; smiling; avenging; tranquil; angry; broad; firmamental; unfolding; swelling; bending; unrelenting; gladsome; spangled; insulted; unpavilioned; troubled; merciful; unimagined; clear-eyed; naked; unclouded; pitying; crystal; hollow; influent; frowning; slumberless; impenetrable; jealous; deepening; unimaginable; sweet; vaulty; cloudless; piteous; encompassing; unpitying; remote; glorious; star-deserted; crystalline; unobstructed; immeasurable; middle; material; warm-colored; pinky-purple; bland; placid; stainless; sick; scoffing; propitious; flaming; deaf.

verbs

abide in—; ascend to—; bless in—; conduct to—; contemplate—; deny—; depart for—; depict—; descend from—; dwell in—; enthrone in—; gain—; long for—; look up to —; offend—; prepare for—; prevail in—; rail at—; reign in—; reside in—; rest in—; rise to—; seek—; steal into—; transport to—; trust in—; visit in—; win—; —s dazzle; —s look down; —s open; —promises; —radiates.

(See paradise, sky, Providence, God.)

HEAVENLY

adverbs

delectably; ecstatically; divinely; utterly; altogether; consummately; ineffably.

HEAVINESS

adjectives

unaccustomed; palpable; dreamy; lifeless; curious; embraced; languid; singular; deceptive; moody.

verbs

augment—; burden with—; cast—over; counterbalance—; discard—; drowse under —; dump—; enter with a sense of—; lament —; seize with—; shed—; —angers; —dejects; —displeases; —enrages; —manifests; —oppresses; —saddens; counterpoise—.

(See weight, gravity, sadness, despondency, dejection.)

aajectives
tumultuous; needless; intermittent.

HEAVY

adverbs
grievously; financially; painfully; economically; unwarrantably; dreadfully; pitifully; gravely; unendurably; increasingly; unnecessarily; inescapably; seriously; insufferably; dangerously; unusually; strangely; unfortunately; cumbrously; monstrously; oppressively; aggravatingly; vexatiously; unjustly; tragically; embarrassingly.

HECKLER

verbs
"bounce" out—; court—; encounter—; oust —; remove—; subdue—; —annoys; —bests; —bothers; —catechizes; —chastises; —contends; —derides; —examines; —irks; — irritates; —plagues; —questions; —scolds; —teases; —wrangles.
(See pest, audience.)

HECTIC

adverbs
feverishly; terribly; tensely; excitably; emotionally; crucially; breathlessly; hysterically; impetuously; poignantly; thrillingly; violently; hotly; angrily; decidedly; bitterly; intensely; peculiarly; curiously; strangely; queerly; extremely; inexplicably; unaccountably; unwarrantably; unusually.

HEDGE

adjectives
lofty; wayside; impenetrable; rustic; decorative; thorny; prickly; flowery.

HEED

adjectives
prudent; accurate; immediate; absent.

HEED (v)

adverbs
carefully; scrupulously; painstakingly; anxiously; prudently; cautiously; instinctively; characteristically; habitually.
(See attend, notice, regard.)

HEEDLESS

adverbs
provokingly; intolerably; inherently; habitually; thoughtlessly; incorrigibly; stupidly; nonchalantly; indifferently; wilfully; obstinately; stubbornly; sadly; grievously; cruelly; pathetically; unwisely; foolishly; frivolously; inexcusably; recklessly; rashly; dangerously; deplorably; lamentably; incurably; shockingly; frightfully.

HEEL

adjectives
hindermost; unmesmerized; official; wavering; hoofed; despotic; miry; flying; cloven; heavy.

verbs
blister—; click—s; clutch at—s; cool—s; crush with—; drive—into; hang up by—s; squat on—s; trample beneath—; —s clatter; —s kick up dust.
(See foot, end, bottom.)

HEIFER

adjectives
illustrious; languid; breathing.

HEIGHT

adjectives
level; pinnacle; considerable; winged; excessive; unsuspected; glimmering; definite; prayerful; azure; wooded; extreme; odorous; pernicious; opposite; embattled; sequestered; serene; gigantic; hoary; mountain; empty; dizzy; commanding; tiptoeing; entrenched; glittering; extravagant; windworn; crystal; preposterous; towering; dark; craggy; moon-bewildering; garden; considerable; grand; sunlit; yonder; streamriven; fixed; heavenly; immortal; fantastic; mounting; reachless; impressive; matchless; panoramic; helpless; immeasurable; divine; daring; obvious; empyreal; utmost; heroic; lofty; bristling; perilous; superb; dusky; eloquent; slippery; desolate; gleaming; barren; sovereign; immense; barometric; melancholy; distant; emerald; rocky; stately; adverse; unscalable; noble; massy; sunscorched; bleak; appointed; waxen; grassy; historic; fortified; starry-headed; inordinate; difficult; full; gray; grave; rugged; precipitous; supernal; financial.

verbs
ascend to—; attain—; attempt--; average —; depend on—; descend—; discover—; fall from—; gain—; mount—s; raise to—; reach—s; rise to—; scale—; set on—; situate on—; soar to—; view from—; — amazes; —slopes down.
(See altitude, stature, eminence, zenith, summit.)

HEINOUS

adverbs

atrociously; abominably; diabolically; criminally; brutally; shamefully; basely; feloniously; flagitiously; flagrantly; deliberately; foully; villainously; viciously; wickedly; incalculably; iniquitously; immeasurably; inexpressibly; grossly; shamelessly; indecently.

HEIR

adjectives

spiritual; immediate; unexpected; lineal; natural; indolent; unwitting; blissful; legitimate; recognized; lavish; contentious; beauteous; joyous; adopted; prodigal; illustrious; peasant-born; true; spendthrift; gilded; impatient.

verbs

apportion to—s; bear—; bequeath to—; curse—; endow—; enrich—; extort from—; guard—; impose on—; nominate—; present with—; prey on—s; tax—s; will to—; yearn for—; —acquires; —is entitled to; —overjoys; —succeeds.

(See offspring, child.)

HELL

adjectives

pitiless; multitudinous; impious; dismal; high-vaulted; yawning; gratuitous; incipient; tangible; monster-teeming; ever-burning; social; inevitable; fabled; jealous; fearsome; inextricable; earth-consuming.

verbs

boil in—; burn in—; chain in—; condemn to—; damn to—; deliver from—; descend to—; doom to—; dwell in—; embark for—; escape—; lead to—; parch in—; plunge into—; punish in—; purify in—; sink in—; torment in—; torture in—; —breaks loose; —devours; —flames; —gapes; —scorches; —shadows; —threatens.

(See torment, torture, flame.)

HELLISH

adverbs

barbarously; fiendishly; inhumanly; inexpressibly; unutterably; indecently; abysmally; accursedly; basely; flagitiously; nefariously; enormously; monstrously; outrageously; obscenely.

adjectives

thronging; prosperous; passive; obedient.

verbs

abandon—; control—; course—; ease—; govern—; handle—; lash to—; menace—; manipulate—; meddle with—; mind—; operate—; order to—; post at—; slander—; steer at—; wrestle with—; —cares; —directs; —guides.

(See wheel, guidance, helmet, pilot, guide, command; control, administration.)

HELMET

adjectives

pith; vicious-looking; fire; leather; superb; spiked; conical; flat-topped; glittering.

verbs

arm with—; attire in—; balance—; bear—; break through—; furnish—; open—; pad—; penetrate—; pierce—; polish—; provide—; supply—; top with—; —clanks; —crowns; —defends; —prevents; —protects; —reflects; —resists; —rests on.

(See hat.)

HELP

adjectives

indispensable; senseless; agreeable; distinct; explanatory; simple; invaluable; adventitious; slender; ever-present; effective; sympathetic; availing; unbiased; beneficial; relative; mutual; timely; injurious.

verbs

afford—; clamor for—; consent to—; furnish—; invoke—; obtain—; present—; procure—; profit by—; promise—; provide—; purchase—; refuse—; render—; seek—; —ameliorates; —amends; —augments; —benefits; —delivers; —extricates; —relieves; —remedies.

(See aid, assistance, remedy, relief, succor, co-operation, support.)

HELP (v)

adverbs

chivalrously; effectually; materially; cheerfully; perversely; personally; generously; precipitately; leisurely; adventitiously; sympathetically; beneficially; mutually.

(See aid, assist, alleviate.)

HELPFUL

adverbs

ingratiatingly; amiably; delightfully; obsequiously; ostentatiously; pompously; unspeakably; amazingly; providentially; accommodatingly; cordially; willingly; eagerly; courteously; habitually; unusually; significantly; heartily; resolutely; dutifully; civilly; servilely; loftily; exceedingly; extremely; gravely; graciously; charmingly; freely; gruffly; roughly; awkwardly; childishly; lovingly; affectionately; skillfully; politely; bluntly; generously; splendidly; surprisingly.

HELPFULNESS

adjectives

patient; cordial; mutual; unassuming.

HELPLESS

adverbs

pitiably; weakly; incurably; intentionally;
gloomily; abjectly; depressingly; desolately;
inconceivably; ludicrously; comically; horribly; woefully; dismally; gravely; seriously; inconsolably; sadly; desperately; obviously; unreasonably; piteously; tragically;
actually; absolutely.

HELPLESSNESS

adjectives

silent; ignominious; sudden; revealed; unconscious; utter; galling; bitter.

verbs

accuse of—; alleviate—; attack—; conceal
—; degenerate into—; discover—; grieve
over—; increase—; lament—; relieve—;
remedy—; retire into—; ridicule—; scorn
—; sink into—; —amazes; —angers; —
crushes; —despairs; —distresses; —oppresses.
  (See weakness.)

HELPMATE

adjectives

devoted; feeble; imperious.

HELTER-SKELTER

adverbs

horribly; laughingly; hilariously; precipitately; confusedly; boisterously; joyously;
triumphantly; hastily; breathlessly; impetuously; riotously; tumultuously; uproariously; madly; wildly; inordinately; extraordinarily; tempestuously; happily.

HEMISPHERIC

adverbs

broadly; surprisingly; expansively; extensively; liberally; hospitably; comprehensively; increasingly; generously; magnanimously; necessarily; commonly; strangely; designedly; intentionally; significantly; preferably.

HEMORRHAGE

verbs

arrest—; check—; control—; delay—; diminish—; excite—; induce—; prevent—; produce—; repress—; risk—; stem—; succumb
to—; suffer—; treat—; —ceases; —diminishes; —endangers; —ensues; —gushes; —
pours; —recurs; —spouts.
  (See discharge, bleeding, blood.)

HEN

adjectives

scrawny; rained-on; cackling; maternal;
speckled; teeming (pl); unsung; matronly-
minded.

verbs

  (See chicken, bird.)

HERALD

adjectives

pale; perfect; tempestuous; flame-tongued;
sad-faced.

HERB

adjectives

winged; aromatic; tender; fragrant; artificial; vivid; bespangling; poisonous; tufted; enchanted; beneficial; culinary; trodden; baneful; pungent; grassy.

verbs

administer—; collect—s; crop—s; cultivate
—s; devour—; feast on—s; feed on—s; flav-
or with—s; garnish with—s; gather—s;
market—s; overgrow with—s; prescribe—s;
yield to—; —abounds; —cures; —flowers;
—stimulates; —withers.
  (See plant, grass.)

HERBAGE

adjectives

sprouting; autumnal.

HERCULEAN

adverbs

distressingly; arduously; obscurely; obviously; evidently; notably; desperately; formid-

ably; toilsomely; laboriously; operosely; stoutly; gigantically; hardily; overwhelmingly; robustly; irresistibly; inexhaustibly; wirily; unconquerably; invincibly; astonishingly; remarkably; inexpressibly; admirably; wondrously; enormously; onerously; extraordinarily; tremendously.

HERD

adjectives
bellowing; stolid; fear-crazed; vulgar; weanling; scaly; meager; wild; wanton; maddening; weaponless; turbulent; servile; careless; drooping; wandering; innumerable (pl); untamable; countless (pl); incomparable; quiet; gentle; sarcastic; nightmare; diminishing; woolly; profane; galloping; tempting.

verbs
abandon—; assemble in—; associate with—; break—; breed in—; cluster in—; congregate in—; control—; destroy—; drive—; gather in—; guard—; join—; lead—; mingle among—; prey on—; rule—; single out of—; slaughter—; stall—; stampede—; —lows; —grazes; —perishes; —ranges; —treks.
(See rabble, crowd, flock.)

HEREDITARY

adverbs
supposedly; probably; definitely; questionably; sadly; unfortunately; allegedly; highly; occasionally; decidedly; basically; intrinsically; invariably; naturally; ineradicably; lamentably; possibly; undoubtedly.

HEREDITY

adjectives
contaminated; established; epileptic; definite; patent.

verbs
boast of—; claim—; degenerate from—; disparage—; doubt—; envy—; interest in —; praise—; renounce—; revere—; revile —; scorn—; stain—; trace—; transmit by —; —burdens; —constrains; —decays; —governs; —heightens; —influences; —instills; —polishes; —weakens.
(See ancestors, birth, father.)

HERESY

adjectives
literary; passing; downright.

verbs
abhor—; accuse of—; confess—; create—; curb—; dare—; defeat—; denounce—; destroy—; excommunicate for—; incur—; interpret as—; protest—; renounce—; revenge —; ridicule—; scan—; shake off—; work—; —denies; —enrages; —mocks; —offends; —scoffs; —taints; —tolerates.

HERETIC

verbs
approve—; burn—; consider—; curb—; denounce—; deprive—; disapprove of—; disperse—s; ignore—; lament—; punish—; regard—; reject—; ridicule—; scoff at—; tolerate—; weed out—s; —denies; —disbelieves; —disobeys; —disregards; —enrages; —mocks; —offends; —preaches; —professes.

HERETICS

adjectives
obstinate; upstart; vile; gruff; brash.

HERITAGE

adjectives
national; rich; common; splendid; precious; deathless; destined; princely; classic; inalienable; unexpected; useless; noble; sempiternal; dramatic.

verbs
acquire—; administer—; allot—; bequeath —; bestow—; bless—; cherish—; claim—; curse—; devolve—; endow—; entitle to—; envy—; execute—; extort—; govern—; present—; preserve—; provide—; reserve—; shear of—; stipulate—; transmit—; —devolves; —overjoys; —provides.
(See inheritance, birthright, estate.)

HERMIT

adjectives
stalwart; genial; lesser; lone; withered; solitary.

HERO

adjectives
unambitious; grotesque; noble; ghostly; beauteous; self-made; admirable; laureled; wonder-working; overbearing; martyred; spiritual; chivalrous; scatterbrained; ornithological; fettered; picturesque; classic; omnipresent; unassuming; stalwart; fabulous; incompetent; energetic; honored; renowned; contemporary; mythic; legendary; vulgar; gentle; immaculate; doughty; stout;

worthy; transcendental; portentous; immortal; barbarous; discomfited; erring; illustrious; incomparable; splendid.

verbs
acclaim—; admire—; cheer—; decorate—; distinguish—; emulate—; enhance—; esteem —; glorify—; hail as—; honor—; identify oneself with—; indebt to—; pity—; respect —; reverence—; shoulder—; supplant—; sympathize with—; venerate—; worship—; —achieves; —braves; —conquers; —courts; —deserves; —excels in; —fades; —regales; —rescues; —rises; —suffers; —withers.
(See champion, character, actor, God.)

HEROIN
verbs
addict to—; analyze—; confiscate—; crave —; derive—from; dissolve—; dose with—; drug with—; forbid—; import—; ingest—; inject—; insufflate—; smuggle—; subject to —; —allays; —anaesthetizes; —depresses; —enslaves; —numbs; —relieves; —victimizes.
(See narcotic, drug.)

HEROINE
adjectives
persecuted; peerless; sentimental; fallen; durable; revengeful.

verbs
acclaim—; identify oneself with—; worship —; —beguiles; —bewitches; —blushes; — captivates; —charms; —enchants; —enraptures; —entrances; —fascinates; —gladdens; —ravishes; —shrinks; —suffers; — transports; —wins.
(See character, hero.)

HEROISM
adjectives
volcanic; unmatched; reckless; romantic; foredoomed; cowering; potential; fierce; intolerant; dauntless; latent; melodramatic; ostentatious; vulgar; showy.

verbs
abate—; aim at—; commend—; conduct with—; contemplate—; crown with—; display—; emulate—; extol—; frown upon—; illustrate—; imitate—; laud—; perform—; reflect—; reward—; sacrifice to—; —dazzles; —glorifies; —merits; —sparkles.
(See valor, courage, bravery, fortitude.)

HERON
verbs
—calls; —circles; —colonizes; —croaks; — fishes; —flaps; —gossips; —impales; — roosts; —shies away; —snaps up; —soars; —squawks; —wades; —wings.
(See bird.)

HERONS
adjectives
long-necked; crested; great; night; long-beaked; stately; graceful.

HESITANCY
adjectives
strange; grave; characteristic; reserved; courteous; apparent; awkward; blushing.

HESITANT
adverbs
capriciously; captiously; uncertainly; reluctantly; doubtfully; stammeringly; changeably; indecisively; timidly; weakly; irresolutely; deliberately; falteringly; waveringly; feebly; tormentingly; infirmly; unsteadily; tremulously; significantly; fearfully.

HESITATE (*v*)
adverbs
fatally; ominously; dubiously; thoughtfully; inexplicably; imperceptibly; timorously; characteristically; coquettishly; momentarily.
(See vacillate, falter.)

HESITATION
adjectives
sensitive; obvious; imitative; painful; surprised; charming; inexplicable; imperceptible; timorous; controlled; characteristic; awkward; coquettish; momentary; ineloquent.

verbs
banish—; conceal—; decry—; deny—; grieve over—; lament—; pretend—; reproach—; shrink in—; stagger in—; stammer in—; tear with—; —confounds; —endangers; —frustrates; —haunts; —loses; — perplexes; —prevents; —shames; —tortures; —embarrasses.
(See doubt, uncertainty.)

HEW (*v*)
adverbs
roughly; bravely; ambitiously; vigorously; industriously; stalwartly; robustly; untiringly.
(See cut, sever.)

HIDE

adjectives

tawny; spotted; shaggy; strange-colored; swarthy; horny; silken; callous; precious; crafty; withered; tanned.

HIDE (v)

adverbs

effectually; obscurely; modestly; instinctively; completely; craftily; skillfully; subtly; avariciously.

(See conceal, mask, cloak.)

HIDEBOUND

adverbs

inordinately; deplorably; unfortunately; stubbornly; obstinately; oddly; curiously; provincially; narrowly; dogmatically; intolerantly; fanatically; immovably; inflexibly; perversely; tenaciously; doggedly; mulishly; ungenerously; terribly; notably; notoriously.

HIDEOUS

adverbs

outrageously; inordinately; extraordinarily; unbearably; grossly; terribly; indescribably; starkly; grotesquely; immoderately; monstrously; piteously; cruelly; shockingly; dreadfully; pathetically; horribly; repulsively; inexpressibly; appallingly.

HIDEOUSNESS

adjectives

naked; unshaped; outward; grim; gross.

HIDING-PLACE

adjectives

primeval; undisturbed; criminal; undiscovered; discreet.

HIERARCHY

adjectives

lofty; definite; centralized; disciplined; administrative; apostolical.

HIGH

adverbs

eminently; prominently; gigantically; monstrously; terrifyingly; incredibly; inordinately; supremely; toweringly; enormously; immensely; infinitely; astonishingly; essentially; extraordinarily; fabulously; preposterously; prodigiously; unsuitably; impossibly; confoundedly; frightfully; horribly; immeasurably; incalculably; delightfully; gloriously; marvellously; particularly; pecu-

liarly; dangerously; perilously; hazardously; singularly; strikingly; woefully; cruelly; awfully; wonderfully; miraculously.

HIGHBORN

adverbs

aristocratically; nobly; notably; gently; undeniably; obviously; evidently; unmistakably; unquestionably; proudly; consciously; illustriously; eminently; admittedly; palpably; undeniably; avowedly; allegedly; probably.

HIGHNESS

adjectives

imperial; incredible; unspeakable; breathless.

HIGH-SPIRITED

adverbs

unusually; delightfully; infectiously; ineffably; happily; radiantly; irrepressibly; hilariously; boisterously; blithely; merrily; mirthfully; teasingly; mockingly; contagiously; charmingly; immeasurably; ardently.

HIGHWAY

adjectives

crooked; invisible; leaf-hung; imperial; dusty; dubious; traffic-crowded; smooth; sleek; arterial; tree-lined; panoramic.

verbs

block—; cruise on—; drive along—; follow —; frequent—; keep to—; laud—; motor along—; patrol—; perceive—; protect—; roll along—; stream down—; traverse—; tread—; —connects; —divides; —endures; —gleams; —leads to; —winds.

(See road, thoroughfare, way.)

HIGHWAYMAN

verbs

apprehend—; defend against—; execute—; hang—; overtake—; protect from—; pursue—; resist—; —appropriates; —deprives of; —escapes; —frequents; —frightens; —gorges on; —plagues; —preys upon; —terrorizes; —victimizes.

(See robber, thief.)

HILARIOUS

adverbs

uproariously; merrily; heartily; noisily; infectiously; contagiously; enthusiastically; effervescently; audaciously; mischievously; intensely; uncommonly; deliriously; unbecomingly; convulsively; irrepressibly; unmanageably; irresponsibly; joyously; blithely; enviably; delightfully; sociably; foolishly; nonsensically; senselessly; consummately; utterly; unrestrainedly; uncontrollably; youthfully; magnificently; jubilantly; inexplicably; warrantably; gleefully.

HILARITY

adjectives
audacious; mischievous; intense; reckless; increasing; delirious; unbecoming; misdirected.

verbs
attempt—; conceal—; conduce to—; enliven to—; excite to—; feign—; flush with—; inspire—; overcome with—; provoke—; reduce—; season with—; spend in—; temper —; —brightens; —diverts; —fades; — flows; —palls; —pours from; —seizes; — solaces; —tires; —wanes; —wearies.
(See mirth, glee, gayety, jollity.)

HILL

adjectives
gleaming; moon-tortured; green-clad; emerald; autumn-tinted; moon-swept; dense; verdured; moonlit; silver; verdant; radiant; silent; shimmering; bright; stony; tawny; soft; rolling; gentle; peak; shadowed; scarred; rock-ribbed; primeval; neighboring; dripping; innocent; reverberating; ferny; naked; forest-cinctured; long-contested; alluring; picturesque; arid; delicious; slanting; soilless; heathery; dry; parched; savage; desolate; ghastly; treeless; volcanic; lower; square-topped; uprooted; eternal; full-grassed; lavish; granite; terraced; breezy; heaped; ever-changing; windy; environing; many-faced; vine-covered; overhanging; massive; bare; steep; incomparable; squalid; encompassing; disturbed; sequestered; pastoral; haughty; bald; bleak; commanding; breezy; ancient; folded; pulpy; conical; cup-shaped; quaking; parched; steadfast; skirting; everlasting; undulating; opprobrious; huge; inferior; barren; disconsolate; invisible; chalk; low-lying; alluvial; rolling; smooth; dawning; wooded; remote; defiant; eternal; silent; dominating; romantic; pestilent; rhododendron; distant; thicketed; sunny; dusty; windy; colored; precipitous; echo-giving; sun-baked; classical; retiring; cindery; pine-clad; spotless; milken; swelling; carven; monumental; forked; savage; timbered; rocky; rock-ribbed; answering; ice-clad; templed; leaping; heathery; pastoral; reeking; distorted; detached; high; utmost; flowery; populous; bustling; fertile; bedimmed; dreary; dark; cloud-capped; sun-kissed; umbrageous; misty; lowering; superb; billowy; consecrated; sterile; craglike; dewy; trembling.

verbs
ascend—; cap—; clear away—; coast down —; crown—; descend—; dwell in —s; heap into —s; observe from—; peep over—; retreat to —s; scale—; settle in —s; stray to —s; survey from—; toil up—; tumble down —; —arises; —charms; —s dot; —s encroach; —s entrance; —flanks; —s greet; —interposes; —shades; —shadows; mount —.
(See heap, mountain.)

HILLOCK

adjectives
scattered (pl); mortal; isolated; palmy; snowy.

HILLSIDE

adjectives
exposed; rounded; blackened; placid; flower-starred; pine-plumed; swelling; sunburned; slippery; sloping; stony; rocky; steep.

verbs
belt—; conceal in—; conduct to—; devastate —; frequent—; inhabit—; mount—; outline —; ravage—; roam—; rove—; settle on—; stream down—; survey—; —blooms; — charms; —flowers; —slopes.
(See hill, bank.)

HILLTOP

adjectives
arduous; breezy; grassy; sun-begoldened.

HIND

adjectives
loitering; heartless.

HINDER (*v*)

adverbs
unendurably; insurmountably; irritatingly; tremendously; irksomely; painfully; burdensomely.
(See retard, obstruct.)

HINDRANCE

adjectives
outward; tremendous; insurmountable.

verbs
condemn—; contribute—; decry—; endure —; erect—; grieve over—; lament—; object to—; overcome—; present—; provide—; remove—; —embarrasses; —frustrates; —objects; —perplexes; —perturbs; —prevents; —threatens.

(See obstruction, obstacle, interruption, delay, restraint, disadvantage.)

HINGE
verbs
attach with—; bind with—; hang on—; join with—; lift off—; lubricate—; manipulate on—; nail—; pin—; pivot on—; prop on—; rest on—; revolve on—; swing on—; turn on—; —groans; —supports; —unites; —yields.

(See joint.)

HINGES
adjectives
rusty; rusted; pregnant; musical.

HINT
adjectives
significant; practical; private; curious; advantageous; prompt; dark; rude; lavish; sundry (pl); ineffectual; equivocal; grotesque; doubtful; oblique; vague; suggestive; friendly; occult; elusive; unintelligible; insinuated; intimated.

verbs
afford—; catch—; comprehend—; contemplate—; convey—; derive — from; heed—; ignore—; infer—; interpret—; perceive—; proffer—; provide—; respond to—; seek—; seize on—; suggest—; weigh—; —distresses; —implies; —indicates; —insinuates; —promises.

(See intimation, insinuation, suggestion.)

HINT (v)
adverbs
barely; delicately; obscurely; wickedly; privately; bashfully; significantly; curiously; vaguely; suggestively; unintelligibly.

(See intimate, imply.)

HIPPOPOTAMUS
verbs
—ambles; —bathes; —charges; —crushes; —damages; —dives; —floats; —s herd; —puffs; —scoops; —sinks; —snorts; —submerges; —splashes; —swims; —tramples.

(See animal.)

HIPS
adjectives
supple; spacious; smooth; rounded; flabby; powerful; streamlined; swaying; bolstered; slim; sinewy; snake-like.

HIRELING
adjectives
sanguinary; base.

HISS
verbs
deride with—; disapprove with —s; dread —; drive away with —s; emit—; express in —; greet with—; ignore—; inject—; overhear—; revile with—; scorn with—; utter —; voice in—; whisper—; —drowns; —disparages; —disturbs; —heckles.

(See sound, noise.)

HISS (v)
adverbs
menacingly; vehemently; venomously; sibilantly; spitefully; viciously.

(See whisper, sound, sing.)

HISTORIAN
adjectives
eloquent; contemporary; romancing; hostile; elegant; fact-grubbing; ecclesiastical; celebrated; apt.

HISTORIC
adverbs
minutely; authoritatively; authentically; accurately; specifically; allegedly; avowedly; evidently; obviously; verifiably; graphically; scarcely; valuably; splendidly; eminently; significantly; serviceably; admirably; indubitably; undeniably.

HISTORICAL
adverbs
slightly; suggestively; traditionally; pleasantly; entertainingly; reminiscently; extravagantly; crudely; accurately; extraordinarily; dully; monotonously; tiresomely; artistically; thrillingly; graphically; entirely; instructively; nostalgically; broadly; generally; altogether; closely.

HISTORY
adjectives
administrative; thrilling; painful; fashion; family; significant; ecclesiastical; contemporary; much-revised; educational; diplo-

matic; stormy; dazzling; tragic; informal; revolutionary; fateful; detailed; typographical; limited; subsequent; pertinent; simple; painstaking; scathing; episodical; future; institutional; human; lamentable; uneventful; monumental; inglorious; noble; pathetic; spiritual; artistic; chronological; natural; eminent; curious; remote; consecutive; authentic; sacred; profane; feigned; forgotten; informative; terrible; impartial; tumultuous; confused; picturesque; incontrovertible; financial; commercial; secret; ancestral; copious; accurate; narrative; inductive; impartial; venerable; social; governmental; international; aesthetic; piteous; wondrous; separate; tender; eventful; glorious; wretched; wisdom-woven; tribal; invaluable; naval; religious; prejudiced; conjectural; school; unrecorded; benevolent; problematical; winged; eventful; gradual; fragrant; subsequent; early; economic; anecdote; magnificent; musical; political; dignified; literary; exhaustive; fantastic; subsequent; authoritative.

verbs
burrow into—; "debunk"—; delve into—; derive from—; dig through—; exhibit in—; expatiate on—; falsify—; garnish—; glean from—; informalize—; modify—; record—; recount—; review — of; shape—; suppress —of; telescope—; trace—; unfold—of; — dates back to; —enchants; —enshrines; — extends to; —recurs; —reflects; —throws light upon.
(See narrative, tale, story, book, account.)

HISTRIONIC
adverbs
attractively; technically; alluringly; seductively; extravagantly; spectacularly; ludicrously; dramatically; absurdly; brilliantly; splendidly; inexpressibly; unexpectedly; illustriously; magnificently; competently; melodramatically; ably; tragically; operatically; stagily; stupendously; sensationally; incurably; immensely; pleasantly; exaggeratedly; uncommonly; remarkably; fantastically.

HIT
verbs
acclaim as—; anticipate—; applaud—; chance—; effect—; gain—; obtain—; pray

for—; pronounce—; provide—; score—; strike—; —astonishes; —delights; —enriches; —reveals; —surprises.
(See blow, success, stroke, victory, triumph.)

HIT (*v*)
adverbs
severely; viciously; repeatedly; injuriously; cruelly; brutally; vigorously.
(See strike, beat, pound.)

HITCH (*v*)
adverbs
unconsciously; impatiently; unexpectedly; clumsily; mechanically; automatically.
(See fasten, attach.)

"HITCH-HIKER"
verbs
accommodate—; arrest—; bar —s; convey —; dispose of—; forbid—; maroon—; outlaw—; pick up—; prohibit—; —attacks; — begs; —"bums"; —bunks (colloq.); —"chisels"; —clambers aboard; —dodges; —s dot; —freights; —legs; —signals; —tramps; —thumbs.

HIVE
adjectives
scandalous; prolific; considerable; overloaded; nest.
verbs
board in—; crowd—; destroy—; forsake—; gather in—; inhabit—; issue from—; locate in—; lodge in—; occupy—; store in—; swarm to—; watch over—; —busies; —buzzes; —houses; —shelters; —teems; —worships.
(See swarm, crowd, bees, box, home.)

HOARD (*v*)
adverbs
avariciously; jealously; niggardly; meanly; fanatically; selfishly; desperately.
(See store, accumulate.)

HOARSE
adverbs
curiously; strangely; alarmingly; dangerously; fearfully; inexplicably; speechlessly; stridently; harshly; coarsely; raucously; unpleasantly; gruffly; angrily; sepulchrally; deeply; gratingly; terrifyingly; suddenly; uncommonly; extraordinarily; remarkably; discordantly; terribly; horribly; excruciatingly.

HOARY

adverbs
venerably; patriarchally; ripely; perfectly; snowily; gracefully; distinctly; majestically; gloriously; honorably; splendidly; conspicuously; grandly; nobly.

HOAX

verbs
accept—; conceive—; contrive—; denounce —; espy—; frame—; impose — upon; manufacture—; perpetrate—; plan—; practise —; reveal—; spring—; vend—; —amuses; —deceives; —mystifies; —ridicules; —succeeds; —scares; —victimizes.
(See deception, joke, trick.)

HOBBLE (*v*)

adverbs
painfully; feebly; laboriously; miserably; slowly; waveringly; falteringly.
(See limp, falter, walk.)

HOBBLING

adverbs
ineffectually; lamely; quietly; forlornly; wretchedly; limply; stumblingly; brokenly; distressingly; grievously; woefully; slowly; painfully; awkwardly; cumbrously; dreadfully; pathetically; sadly; uncomfortably; sturdily; crookedly; gayly; mournfully.

HOBBY

adjectives
dominant; fascinating.

verbs
advocate—; allow—; dabble in—; devote to —; excel at—; favor—; indulge in—; permit—; pursue—; ride—; school in—; suggest—; sympathize with—; tinker with—; trifle with—; —amuses; —delights; —diverts; —enthralls; —occupies; —relieves.
(See occupation, interest, vocation, topic, plan, pursuit.)

HOBNOB (*v*)

adverbs
jovially; fraternally; loquaciously; extravagantly; boisterously; democratically.
(See associate, mingle.)

HOG

adjectives
goaded; ill-bred.

verbs
auction —s; breed —s; exhibit—; fatten—; market—; pen—; roast—; slaughter—; stable—; stick—; —devours; —farrows; —grunts; —hobbles; —snorts; —squeaks; —squeals; —wallows; —yields.
(See animal, pig.)

HOLD (*grip*)

adjectives
spiritual; demoniac; tenacious; vise-like; passionate; careless; fragile; imploring; pocket.

verbs
bar—; break—; catch—; correct—; divert —; emerge from—; escape—; evade—; force—; gain — on; knit—; loose—; maintain—; mend—; obtain—; seize—; take—; —slips; —supports; —yields.
(See grasp, grip, authority, power, stronghold, refuge.)

HOLD (*ship*)

verbs
assemble in—; ballast—; cache in—; chain in—; conceal in—; condemn to—; confine to —; couch in—; hide in—; lock in—; provide—; replenish—; stock in—; store in—; stow in—; stuff—.
(See interior, prison.)

HOLD (*v*)

adverbs
stubbornly; desperately; proudly; tenaciously; securely; frenziedly; obstinately; inviolably; jealously; staunchly; tenderly; tremulously; deferentially; permanently; stoutly; hungrily; tentatively; gingerly; dexterously; automatically; diplomatically.
(See grasp, clutch.)

HOLDING

adjectives
large; theoretical; allotted.

"HOLDUP"

verbs
abet—; appropriate in—; curb—; deprive in —; escape—; execute—; frustrate—; plague with —s; protect from—; reduce —s; resist —; surprise in—; —appalls; —terrorizes.
(See assault, robbery.)

HOLE

adjectives
huge; nest; shallow; halfway; effective; deep; ragged; obvious; death-spitting; oc-

casional; furtive; treacherous; dull; ghastly; obscure; ominous; vast; circular; expansive; inmost; gaping.

verbs
bore—; burrow—; conceal—; drill—; drive —; escape—; excavate—; hollow—; lurk in —; perforate—; pick —s; pierce—; plant in —; plug—; rot in—; sink into—; smother in —; thrust into—.

(See opening, cavity, pit, flaw, defect, hollow.)

HOLIDAY
adjectives
enforced; universal; conventional; invigorating; golden; pastoral; piecemeal; summer; sunshine; sparkling.

HOLINESS
adjectives
pharisaical; penitential; assumed; outward.

verbs
brighten with—; cherish in—; commend—; dedicate to—; diffuse—; dispose to—; dwell in—; glow with—; manifest—; possess—; seek—; share—; shroud in—; touch with—; violate—; —beautifies; —charms; —glorifies; —inspires; —purifies.

(See sanctity, piety, sacredness, purity.)

HOLLOW
verbs
bellow through—; blow through—; bore—; depress—; enclose—; excavate—; fashion—; occupy—; rest in—; shape—; shelter in—; sink into—; thrust into—; —interposes.

(See cavity, depression, channel, basin, valley, hole.)

HOLLOWNESS
adjectives
dreadful; echoing.

HOLLOWS
adjectives
fleshless; intricate; unsuspected; desolate; windless; curving; curdled; starved; fearful; marshy; dreadful; dampish; arid; delicate; wide; cloudy; gaping; grassy.

HOLY
adverbs
reverently; sacredly; divinely; altogether; consummately; perfectly; utterly; eternally; gloriously; infinitely; celestially; spiritually; ineffably; majestically; triumphantly; solemnly; consecratedly.

HOMAGE
adjectives
poor; devoted; disinterested; glorious; reluctant; decorous; regal; unpurchasable; lowly; dreadful; wild; respectful; spontaneous; corporate; due; assiduous; grateful; humble; instinctive; loyal.

verbs
acknowledge—; bow in—; demand—; do—; kneel in—; offer—; owe—; present—; profess—; render—; renounce—; submit to—; swear—; yield — to.

(See respect, deference, obeisance, loyalty.)

HOME
adjectives
kitchen; inn; lodge; nest; suitable; well-ordered; contemporary; devout; rustic; frugal; veritable; industrial; blazing; discriminating; earthly; deep-thatched; undiscovered; devastated; deep-sea; kindred; humble; hereditary; antiquated; exclusive; delegated; desolate; charming; handsome; eternal; secluded; cheerful; terrestrial; stately; gay; cool; inviting; vast; ancestral; unfathomable; peaceful; tainted; remote; simple; material; fond; sheaf-gathered; commodious; sumptuous; unpretentious; reeking; love-guarded; sordid; trim-built; stainless; convenient; historic; palatial; sullen; cloudy; sylvan; silent; distinguished; year-round; fine; perfect; holiday; ideal; primeval; airy; wanton; antenatal; sheltered; chaotic; glory; flooded; peasant; spacious; uninhabitable; artistic; eternal; comfortable; resplendent; imperiled; tiny; congenial; dismantled; annihilated; defenseless; orthodox; dainty.

verbs
abide at—; admire—; banish from—; bless —; cleave to—; cut loose from—; dream of —; escort—; evict from—; flee from—; frequent — of; install in—; lodge at—; long for—; lounge at—; master—; nurse in—; prefer—; preserve—; prize—; provide—; repair to—; sequester in—; survey—; tie to —; troop—; uproot from—; wander from —; welcome—; —beckons; —charms; — cheers; —comforts; —delights; —eases; — protects; —shelters.

(See abode, house, residence, dwelling.)

600

HOMELESS

adverbs

miserably; wretchedly; desolately; pitiably; cruelly; bitterly; unhappily; incredibly; unfortunately; unluckily; forlornly; pitifully; deservedly; naturally; oddly; curiously; particularly; outrageously; desperately; dreadfully; hopelessly; helplessly; lonesomely; friendlessly; inconceivably; unbelievably; definitely; ironically; disconsolately; dismally; drearily.

HOMELY

adverbs

forbiddingly; awkwardly; clumsily; frightfully; gracelessly; gauntly; haggardly; horribly; monstrously; shockingly; undeniably; simply; plainly; manifestly; curiously; unaffectedly; strangely; dully; avowedly; undisguisedly; outlandishly; indifferently; uncommonly; oddly; cheerfully; sturdily; imperturbably; wholesomely; pleasantly; unconcernedly.

HOMESICK

adverbs

actually; seriously; evidently; manifestly; signally; dangerously; alarmingly; fearfully; frightfully; truly; irrecoverably; desperately; extraordinarily; naturally; slightly; extremely; comprehensibly; bitterly; ruefully; sorely; insatiably; woefully; miserably; sadly; wretchedly; appallingly; shockingly; critically; unaffectedly; irremediably; unaccountably; terribly.

HOMESICKNESS

adjectives

drear; desperate; dread; supportable; nostalgic; prolonged; pronounced.

verbs

affect with—; conceal—; control—; doom to —; intensify—; moan in—; waste in—; yield to—; —afflicts; —arises; —depresses; —eats; —fatigues; —mars; —recurs; —saddens; —steals over; —troubles; —wracks.

(See nostalgia, sadness.)

HOMILY

verbs

address—; ascribe — to; attribute—; compose—; cultivate—; deliver—; excel in—; issue—; preach—; pronounce—; —awes; —bores; —edifies; —explains; —impresses; —moralizes; —pursues; —tires; —wearies.

(See sermon, discourse.)

HONEST

adverbs

absolutely; naturally; sincerely; honorably; morally; downright; altogether; completely; ingenuously; innately; inherently; unreservedly; habitually; constitutionally; virtuously; courageously; bravely; fearlessly; candidly; impartially; fairly; faithfully; sometimes; usually; spasmodically; incorruptibly; loyally; punctiliously; meticulously; respectably; reputably; scrupulously; trustworthily; conscientiously; frankly; inviolably; stainlessly; staunchly; uprightly; utterly; strictly; basically; unimpeachably; fundamentally; essentially; unshakably; apparently.

HONESTY

adjectives

basic; unimpeachable; unquestioned; belated; savage; strict; intrinsic; childlike; shakable; tribal; crystal; rigid; sham; confirmed; intellectual; surface; apparent.

verbs

approve—; assert—; boast of—; conduct with—; consider—; corrupt—; depend on—; desire—; inspect—; instill—; praise—; proclaim—; require—; respect—; test—; trust —; try—; undermine—; violate—; —repays; —rewards; —shines.

(See integrity, sincerity, fairness.)

HONEY

adjectives

pure; limpid; thick; flavored; fine; fermented; amber; sweet; nectareous.

HONEYSUCKLE

verbs

attire in—; bear—; cultivate—; naturalize —; ripen—; shower—; suck—; —attracts; —beautifies; —blooms; —clings; —clutches; —crawls; —creeps; —entwines; —exudes; —flowers; —garlands; —glorifies; —scents; —wreathes.

(See flower, plant, shrub, vine.)

HONOR

adjectives

dropsied; chivalrous; grave; cleansed; distinguished; well-earned; disinterested; enduring; foolish; royal; material; artistic; literary; scientific; sensitive; unprecedented; worldly; assaulted; blushing; academic; unviolated; unending; proffered; divine; proclaiming; professional; questionable; murdered; high; hereditary; especial; bridal; double; unsullied; primitive; imposing; petty; immortal; moral; worthy; blushing; liberal; empty; posthumous; fading; false; unblemished; sunny; perpetual; troublesome; maiden; special; unwonted; proud; dangerous; unsolicited; unexpected; long-transmitted; diplomatic; low-declined; conspicuous; haughty; civic; reverent; jealous; innumerable (pl); scrupulous; dangerous; platonic; strict; dimmed; unpretending; doubtful; sacred; slight; actual; mother-city.

verbs
accord—; assail—; attest to—; avenge—; bestow—; clothe with—; confer—upon; covet—; heap—; invoke—; lavish—; outrage —; pay—; preserve—; reflect upon—; sacrifice—; satisfy—; sell—; solicit—; stain—; steal—; sully—; vie for—; walk away with —; —overjoys.
(See esteem, respect, chastity, virtue, glory, reverence, reputation, dignity.)

HONOR (*v*)
adverbs
chastely; scrupulously; undeviatingly; academically; uniquely; faithfully; royally; materially; artistically; scientifically; scholastically; professionally; perpetually; posthumously; diplomatically; formally.
(See revere, esteem, respect.)

HONORABLE
adverbs
reputably; supposedly; allegedly; unshakably; irreproachably; sincerely; strictly; fundamentally; naturally; basically; dependably; reliably; altogether; innately; virtuously; fearlessly; intrepidly; courageously; impartially; incorruptibly; loyally; carefully; apparently; utterly; staunchly; scrupulously; meticulously; remarkably; notably; notoriously; illustriously; eminently; utterly.

HOOD
adjectives
riven; purpled; drooping.

HOODLUM
(*colloq.*)
breed—s; chastise—; denounce—; disperse —s; punish—; shelter—; warn—; —annoys; —absconds; —baffles; —damages; —drifts;

—dodges; —escapes; —evades; —s gang —s gather; —harms; —snatches; —threatens.
(See gangster, robber, thief, criminal.)

HOOF
verbs
caulk—s; file—s; muffle—s; paw with—s; protect—s; shoe—s; stamp—s; trim—s; —s clang; —s clank; —s clatter; —s clink; —s drum; —s furrow the ground; —s pound; —s roar; —strikes; —thuds.
(See foot.)

HOOFS
adjectives
stamping; cloven; devilish; edged; delicate; ironshod; flying; plunging; unshod; clattering; clumsy; galloping; clanging; rattling; death-dealing; heavy; awkward.

HOOK
adjectives
nail; peg; rusty; anchoring.

verbs
arm with—; angle with—; bait with—; bend with—; capture with—; cast—; drag with—s; draw—; grapple with—; grasp with—; hang on—; raise with—s; seize with—; snare with—; suspend from—; —catches; —cuts; —links; —penetrates; —secures; —snags.
(See clasp, snare, trap, pin.)

HOOT
adjectives
terrified; clanging.

HOOT (*v*)
adverbs
disconsolately; dismally; dolefully; scoffingly; monotonously; eerily; mockingly; jeeringly.
(See deride, denounce, shout.)

HOP (*v*)
adverbs
nimbly; agilely; gaily; swiftly; lightly; sportively; merrily.
(See jump, frisk, bound.)

HOPE
adjectives
ardent; debarred; lingering; honest; deathless; best; sustaining; tremendous; awakened; buried; presumptuous; unearthly; fond;

sole; latent; fiery; buoyant; visionary; absurd; unacknowledged; dead; darkened; false; trusting; unbounded; flowering; roseate; strained; sanguine; groveling; unraveled; indefatigable; twin-born; beautiful; inexperienced; baffled; extravagant; winged; frustrated; high-hearted; generous; departing; dauntless; quenchless; ripening; pale-cheeked; blighted; reverent; perfect; deceptive; patient; half-revealed; smallest; wildest; renewed; gray-haired; inspiriting; troublous; faltering; bursting; dazzling; holy; glorious; wandering; reactionary; lingering; flickering; dying; ardent; heartfelt; improbable; ruined; faded; freshening; blasted; fair; reasonable; trembling; increasing; slender; toppling; absolute; indefinite; dull; atrocious; vague; half-rallied; fruitless; parched; fervent; unchristian; untransmitted; histrionic; definite; decaying; broken; submissive; withered; forlorn; confident; earthly; full; fluttering; savage; pure; budding; tranquil; ultimate; shattered; vague; dreamy; inhaling; celestial; boundless; barren; thrilling; stubborn; ambitious; tortured; dear; flattering; sweet; delusive; feeble; troubled; hovering; unworthy; impossible; natural; blessed; disappointed; prophetic; bright; raised; vain; realized; fallacious; dawning; gaudy; vulgar; future; delicious; exultant; brilliant; odious; perpetuating; latent; polite; desperate; famished; appointed; rekindled; reckless; improbable; countless (pl); yearning; feverish; joyous; sleeping; pathetic; obedient; spacious; intenser; perpetual; confiding; remote; innocent; grim; philosophic; cheerful; unheeded; supreme; trusting; undying; abandoned; inconsistent; earnest; greedy; blossoming.

verbs
afford—; attain—; base—on; blast—; blight —; center—s in; cherish—; cling to—; console with—; crush—s; culminate in—; dash —s; defer—; delude with—; discourage—; divest of—; entertain—; exaggerate—; fall from—; falsify—; flush with—; frustrate—; fulfill—; hatch—; hold out—; impart—; infuse—; inspire—; justify—; kindle—; pin —s on; prompt—; relinquish—; restore—; rouse—; splinter—; stimulate—; substantiate—; undermine—; voice—; —blossoms; —collapses; —deserts; —exalts; —flickers; —glimmers; —is born; —leaps high; — lingers; —looms; —mounts; —perks up; —

sinks; —springs; —stirs; —vanishes; — wanes; realize—.
(See trust, reliance, expectation, optimism, anticipation.)

HOPE (v)
adverbs
vainly; fervidly; philosophically; optimistically; piously; fondly; desperately; fervently; devoutly; irresistibly; ardently; deathlessly; presumptuously; reverently; fallaciously; fruitlessly.
(See pray, desire, wish.)

HOPEFUL
adverbs
joyously; mysteriously; unaccountably; pleasurably; excitedly; hysterically; passionately; thrillingly; unreasonably; impatiently; ardently; keenly; eagerly; charmingly; joyfully; fervently; patiently; gloriously; fairly; increasingly; stubbornly; naturally; exultantly; pathetically; philosophically; earnestly; crazily; presumptuously; fondly; absurdly; reverently; extraordinarily.)

HOPEFULNESS
adjectives
desperate; perennial; gentle; indulgent.

HOPELESS
adverbs
probably; apparently; unfortunately; pitiably; wretchedly; miserably; forlornly; utterly; desperately; disconcertingly; insuperably; absolutely; calmly; tragically; bitterly; stolidly; grimly; appallingly; secretly; blankly; speechlessly; frantically; utterly; extremely; undeniably; obviously; manifestly; finally; frightfully.

HOPELESSNESS
adjectives
utter; cruel; black; dark; despairing.

verbs
bow down by—; complain of—; confront with—; doom to—; fret over—; groan with —; incline to—; lose in—; overcome—; paralyze with—; recognize—; reflect—; shroud in—; weight with—; —afflicts; —agonizes; —anguishes; —burdens; —clouds; —deadens; —desolates; —deters; —discourages; —saddens; —submerges; —weakens.
(See despair, despondency, pessimism, sadness.)

adjectives

miserable; motley; implacable; maddened; antlike; gray; conquering; impious; existing; vandal; rabble; elfish; veteran; rebellious; bleeding; barbarian; retreating; moving; turbulent; infuriated; undisciplined; roving.

verbs

accumulate—; congregate—; gather in—; spring from—; —bands; —concentrates; —congests; —crowds; —crushes; —disbands; —disperses; —dwells; —flocks; —floods; —howls; —migrates; —mills about; —packs; —roams; —scatters; —stampedes; —strays; —swarms; —throngs; —thunders; —wanders.

(See crowd, swarm, pack, throng, multitude.)

HORIZON

adjectives

heavy; landscape; flushed; solar; soft; endless; ruddy; glowing; magnificent; dim; open; historical; sunny; misty; tinted; dull; dusky; hazy; mother-of-pearl; contracted; lost; dreadful; vaporous; moral; circling; wide; intellectual; mental; imperial; boundless; ever-receding; expanding; far-off.

verbs

blacken—; broaden—; emerge from—; enlarge—; expand—; hesitate on—; loom on —; obscure—; open—; survey—; widen—; —beckons; —broadens; —embraces; —lightens; —recedes.

(See line, range, border, boundary.)

HORN

adjectives

toppling; dolorous; signaling; heavenly; masked; crescent; pellucid; sultry; impatient; lusty; sullen; formidable; barbarous; monstrous; cruel; long; twanging; curving; gilded; distinct; insistent; audacious; clangorous.

verbs

bear—; defend with—; develop—; drive—s into; impale on—s; loose—s; pierce with—; pinion down with—; —butts; —drills; —s endanger; —s frighten; —s gore; —s lance; —s prick; —s punch; —s puncture; —s rip; —s spike; —s threaten; —s wound.

(See antler, pin, point.)

HORNET

verbs

arouse—s; provoke—s; —attacks; —basks in; —bites; —hums; —s infest; —inflicts; —s nest; —perforates; —pierces; —pricks; —regurgitates; —riots; —s swarm.

(See wasp, bee, insect.)

HORRIBLE

adverbs

grimly; unexpectedly; surprisingly; naturally; inevitably; dismally; alarmingly; awfully; frightfully; tremendously; unforgettably; unspeakably; inexpressibly; abhorrently; sickeningly; nauseatingly; unbearably; intolerably; incredibly; wildly; gruesomely; dreadfully.

HORRID

adverbs

disgustingly; repulsively; shockingly; appallingly; offensively; abominably; atrociously; intolerably; unbearably; hideously; frightfully; unbelievably; incredibly; peculiarly; outrageously; unaccountably; positively; unendurably; insufferably; uncommonly; unduly.

HORRIFIED

adverbs

utterly; amazingly; dreadfully; astoundingly; blankly; startlingly; breathlessly; wordlessly; appallingly; indescribably; fearfully; inexpressibly.

HORROR

adjectives

profound; damp; amused; attendant; alien; gentle; bragging; ignorant; scaly; untold; speechless; weary; blank; cloudy; congenial; superstitious; instinctive; unmitigated; invariable; distant; pious; ridiculous; accumulated; gloomy; hovering; incredulous; indescribable; quaint; formless; dismal; pursuing; sleepy; blank; misbegotten; fantastic; grisly; inseparable; supernumerary; unspeakable; stunned; anxious; nameless; ghastly; large-eyed; inconvenient; silent; inconceivable; insuperable; peculiar; infinite; tragic; cold; pungent; unimaginable; affected; incredible; dreary; unaccountable; shadowy; grim; journalistic; stunned; burlesque; incumbent; inactive; uncouth; utter; imaginary; positive; irrational; piercing; unfeigned; frightful; inexorable; intolerable; bloody; distant; mingled (pl); pale; unburied; childlike.

verbs
banish—; chill with—; conceal—; depict—; enhance—; expose—; freeze with—; ponder over—; recoil in—; reconstruct—; rise to the height of—; strike—; survey—; transfix with—; view with—; witness—; — grows; —strikes.
(See fear, dread, consternation.)

HORSE
adjectives
mustang; livestock; startled; dozing; hot; unbroken; riderless; steaming; petrified; winged; prancing; enchanted; massive; heavy; plodding; unwilling; spurred; vicious; docile; broken-down; unweaned; ghostly; pack; chubby; unmanageable; mettlesome; reluctant; well-broken; spirited; redoubtable; outspent; sorry; maniacal; generous; light-limbed; restive; bang-tailed; great-limbed; true; beautiful; foam-flecked; mottled; moth-eaten; dilapidated; straining; stalking; solemn; ramping; slender; rawboned; sweating; plow; blazed-faced; well-breathed; arrogant; unafraid; fiery; exhausted; weary; bony; dispirited; disemboweled; jibbing; drooping; jaded; foam-lipped; indifferent; admirable; harrowed; blooded; plunging; corn-stuffed.

verbs
bed down—; corral—; breed—s; currycomb —; guide—; harbor—; hobble—; jockey—; lash—; leap from—; mount—; pace—; rein in—; round up—s; saddle—; spur—; stable —; straddle—; tether—; tumble off—; — balks at; —bolts; —bucks; —canters; — capers; —caracoles; —champs at the bit; —dances; —falls to feeding; —founders; — hurdles; —neighs; —paws; —plods; — prances; —quivers; —races; —rears; — shies; —shivers; —snorts; —tramples; — trots; —vaults; —veers; —wheels; — whickers; —whinnies.
(See colt, animal, mare.)

HORSEBACK
verbs
canter on—; charge on—; convey by—; excel on—; exhibit on—; gallop in on—; journey on—; joust on—; mount—; race on—; sport on—; traverse on—; trot on—; vault on—.
(See horse.)

HORSEMAN
adjectives
brave; coated; mystic; unwary; gallant; solitary; admirable; steel-clad; headless; unhorsed.

verbs
—men assemble; —bestrides; —breeds; — charges; —coaches; —controls; —exhibits; —fancies; —flogs; —halts; —lashes; —manages; —mounts; —performs; —pets; — plods; —rears; —reins in; —spurs; — strokes.
(See rider, cowboy, soldier.)

HORSEMANSHIP
adjectives
consummate; daring; showy; superb.

HOSE
adjectives
stout; dusty; russet; silken; gossamer; diaphanous; cotton; worsted; shrunken.

HOSE
(conduit)
verbs
burst—; couple—; drench with—; pump through—; sprinkle with—; water with—; —bursts; —conducts; —conveys; —showers.
(See pipe.)

HOSIERY
adjectives
unsatisfactory; beautiful; sheer; cobwebby.

verbs
don—; draw on—; mend—; rip—; roll—; shed—; snag—; snap—; —fades; —glistens; —runs.

HOSPITABLE
adverbs
graciously; warmly; delightfully; cordially; generously; bounteously; liberally; munificently; splendidly; magnificently; freely; handsomely; pleasantly; sociably; happily; merrily; heartily; jovially; genially; urbanely; companionably; informally; gregariously; immensely; courteously; enthusiastically; exuberantly; inordinately; good-naturedly; unobtrusively; lavishly; quietly; genuinely; charmingly; wholeheartedly.

HOSPITAL
adjectives
contemporary; improvised; convalescent; dingy; special; cheerless; contagious.

HOSPITALITY

adjectives

courteous; sailorlike; effusive; uncommon; exuberant; mellowed; proverbial; rival; discreet; lasting; stinted; princely; elegant; undiscriminate; thankful; rural; good-natured; dignified; generous; professional; profuse; reluctant; wonted; hearty; cordial; unobtrusive; cheerful; genial; unwearying; lavish; quiet; warm; surpassing; genuine; old-time; luxurious; hearty; charming; homelike; famous; unique; cordial; warmhearted; incredible; gracious; reluctant; extempore; southern; wholehearted.

verbs

dispense—; enjoy—; maintain—; offer—; practise—; provide—; repay—; reward—; ruffle—; share—; warm with—; —blossoms; —charms; —cheers; —dwindles; — eases; —flourishes; —flows; —relieves.

(See entertainment, generosity, friendship.)

HOST

adjectives

dejected; ungracious; disagreeable; heavenly; secondary; routed; subtle; benignant; tragic; starry; affable; reluctant; straggling; new-found; genial; angelic; crusading; illimitable; shadowy; numerous; overweening; inseparable; chafing; kind; legionary; indignant; embattled; celestial; spangled; assaulting; heathen; conquering; amiable; heavenly; pensive; battle-broken; visionary; countless; smiling; ranting; ill-fated; motley; square; swarthy; ethereal; tombless; venerable; frugal; innumerable; hurrying; mustering; frank; miserable; prospective; glorified; radiant; niggardly; weary; generous; bewildered.

verbs

besiege—; honor—; praise—; —amuses; — appears; —approves; —befriends; —bids; —charms; —comforts; —delights; —enlivens; —flatters; —greets; —plans; —presides; —provides; —relieves; —welcomes.

(See entertainer, actor, friend.)

HOSTESS

adjectives

temporary; noble; popular; impromptu; attentive; exuberant; lavish; ambitious; small; fat; good-natured; fair; charming; gracious; air; amiable; tidy; buxom.

HOSTILE

adverbs

coldly; politely; secretly; surreptitiously; inscrutably; openly; candidly; absurdly; hatefully; malevolently; venomously; maliciously; viciously; ominously; portentously; villainously; inscrutably; inexplicably; irreconcilably; antagonistically; dangerously; alarmingly; curiously; strangely; oddly; queerly; unreasonably; irrationally; exceptionally; tragically; inconveniently; irrevocably; horribly.

HOSTILITY

adjectives

determined; quiet; small; quenched; implacable; slumbering; languid; perpetual; unexpressed; sudden; smiling; unnecessary; undiluted; expensive; alert; expectant; uncompromising; indecent; provoking; bitter; unintermitting; implacable; innate; jealous; frequent (pl); wily; deadly; concealed; smoldering; methodical; intuitive; evident; legislative; defensive; interfering; neighborly; unprofitable; fanatical.

verbs

arouse—; break—s; cease—; encourage—; engage in—s; enter—s; evince—; excite—; fan—; incur—of; loose—s; renew—s; suspend—s; temper—; view with—; —frightens; —grows.

(See enmity, animosity, opposition, warfare, anger.)

HOT

adverbs

devilishly; horribly; unbearably; unusually; remarkably; abnormally; feverishly; unnaturally; angrily; dangerously; apparently; unseasonably; strangely; intolerably; sufficiently; scarcely; inordinately; queerly; peculiarly; curiously; unfortunately; oppressively; swelteringly; stiflingly; bakingly; blazingly; suffocatingly; intensely.

HOTEL

adjectives

superb; smart; first-class; fine; famous; quiet; dignified; luxurious; distinguished; friendly; notable; favored; complete; beachfront; residential; delightful; attractive; skyscraper; seaside; centrally-located; modern; perfect; cheerful; warm; inviting; traditional; unique; outstanding; swanky; distinguished; exclusive; apartment; ambitious; wooden; cozy; commercial; resort;

small; provincial; rambling; frame; vermin-infested; temperance; convenient; grand; comfortable; charming; nice; hospitable; cosmopolitan; well-kept; well-organized; innumerable (pl); glamorous.

verbs
convene at—; dwell at—; inhabit—; loll in—; patronize—; retain at—; stow away in—; —accommodates; —caters to; —comforts; —delights; —employs; —flourishes; —offers; —provides; —serves; —welcomes; —furnishes.

(See inn, house, building, tavern.)

HOUND

adjectives
overrash; cadaverous; lean; ugly; couchant; degenerate; long-eared; deepmouthed; patient; fox; aged; hot; scent-snuffing; baffled; phenomenal; howling; licking; fawn-colored; thirsty-looking; cunning; toothless; graceful.

verbs
pat—; quiet—; unleash—; whip—; —bays; —dashes by; —growls; —s harry; —howls; —points; —pursues; —snarls; —tears; — whines; —yelps; —yips.

(See dog, animal.)

HOUR

adjectives
accustomed; additional; agonizing; all-glorious; amazing; appointed; arid; atoning; awful; baleful; bitter; black; bleak; blessed; blighted; blue-eyed; bounteous; brawling; breakfast; breathless; brief; bright; calm; captive; careful; cheerless; closing; cloudless; comfortless; coming; conditioned; confident; consecrated; countless (pl); cramped; critical; crucial; customary; darkened; darkling; dawning; definite; delicious; designated; desirable; disastrous; discouraged; dolorous; dread; dreadful; dream-haunted; dreaming; dreary; drinking; dull; dusky; early; eerie; elected; ensuing; enthusiastic; eventful; evil; exciting; fair; famished; fatiguing; favored; fearful; fervent; feverous; flaming; forbidden; forgetful; forlorn; forsaken; fragrant; fruitful; generous; gentle; giddy; gleeful; gloom-clad; glutted; gory; gradual; hallowed; happy; hateful; hazy; heavenly; heavy; heinous; heterogeneous; hushed; hustling; hypnotic; idle; illuminating; imperious; impossible; impressionable; impressive; inaus-

picious; incessant; industrious; inevitable; instant; interminable; jocund; jovial; joyful; jubilant; laborious; languorous; lasting; lazy; leisure; lingering; lonely; long; luckless; lyric; meet; melancholy; memorable; merciless; meridian; merry; midnight; moonlit; mortal; mourning; murderous; natal; new-fledged; niggard; noteless; nuptial; old; optional; pallid; particular; parting; passing; peaceful; perilous; placid; pleasant; precious; precise; prefixed; prescribed; promised; rare; regretful; regulated; retributive; rosy-fingered; sacred; sauntering; secret; serene; serious; shadowed; shiny; short; sleepless; slow-paced; social; soft; solemn; somber; sorrowful; spent; splenetic; starless; stormy; strange; suffering; sunny; sunset; superincumbent; supreme; surviving; swift; tedious; thorny; thoughtful; thrilling; torturing; tranquil; transient; treacherous; trembling; tremulous; troublous; trysting; twilight; unbearable; unborn; unconscionable; unfortunate; unlucky; unnatural; unreturning; unseasonable; unsuspecting; untroubled; usual; valuable; vast; vehement; vesper; voluptuous; wakeful; wasted; weary; wedlock; weird; weeping; white-robed; wholesome; wild; wonted; working; wretched.

verbs
appoint—; budget—s; consume—s; count —s; crowd—; devote—s to; employ—; fix —; fritter away—s; kill—s; laze away—s; note—; postpone—; read—of day; reckon —; regulate—s; set—; —approaches; —s crawl by; —s drag; —elapses; —s fly; —s lag; —s ripen; —strikes; —s wear on.

(See time, occasion.)

HOUSE

adjectives
mansion; miserable; enchanting; cat-encumbered; solitary; scattered (pl); gloomy; dilapidated; true; pretentious; archetypal; echoing; painted; battlemented; imperial; ambitious; dignified; quaint; religious; gaunt; comfortable; straggling; disreputable; showy; imaginative; practical; reminiscent; adjacent; shiftless; austere; aristocratic; poultry; gliding; modest; tile-roofed; haunted; burnished; conspicuous; illustrious; farm; gnarled; jolly; deserted; squatty; lonely; first-run; widespreading; rayless; darksome; crafty; magnificent; ancestral; lofty; supply; substantial; idyllic; shamble; economical; town; continental;

shell-pitted; giddy; shabby; pillaged; lady-like; shameful; dower; blithe; ugly; hallowed; powerful; low-browed; inviting; tenement; triangular; terraced; humble; wretched; wattled; dull; lucrative; untenantable; paltry; inconvenient; dreamy; ruined; ducal; ill; country; dismantled; useless; gay; gambling; naughty; celestial; neat; treasure; festive; warm; jovial; sunny; luxurious; embellished; pharmaceutical; comfortable-looking; log; dwelling; tremendous; unpeeled; well-insulated; mobile; trembling; gay-roofed; little; popular; swarming; stuccoed; irregularly-scattered (pl); handsome; respectable; bleak; hospitable; ill-furnished; filthy; dirty; isolated; thatch-roofed; cane; respected; faltering; unobtrusive; ancient; narrow; flimsy; reigning; royal; desolate; fair; vast; treasure; identical; tumble-down; boxlike; unquiet; crowded; parental; eery; model; lodging; commodious; stately; unreal; excellent; pretentious; swell-front; shutterless; old-fashioned; once-fashionable; clattering; adobe; ranch; sheltering.

verbs
adorn—; bedizen—; billet in—; demolish—; design—; ensconce in—; inhabit—; model —; pattern—; refurbish—; renovate—; sanctify—; shatter—; tenant—; undermine —; waddle into—; —hushes; —looms; —nestles; —springs up.
(See building, abode, home.)

HOUSE (v)
adverbs
luxuriously; warmly; faithfully; imperially; quaintly; disreputably; practically; shiftlessly; austerely; aristocratically; hospitably; magnificently; economically; shabbily; commodiously; pretentiously.
(See shelter, protect.)

HOUSEHOLD
adjectives
ducal; decorous; quiet; turbulent; tyrannical; literary; minute.

HOUSEKEEPER
adjectives
active; manifest; procrastinating.

HOUSEKEEPING
adjectives
modern; efficient.

HOUSEWIFE
adjectives
fastidious; primitive; chaste; querulous; busy; lazy.

HOUSING
adjectives
better; overcrowded; low-cost; planned; government-supported.

HOVEL
adjectives
poverty-stricken; ruinous; lowly; wretched

HOVER (v)
adverbs
perpetually; perilously; caressingly; ceaselessly; expectantly; eagerly; protectingly; lovingly.
(See flutter, linger.)

HOWL
adjectives
long; loud; piteous; increasing; reverberate; unearthly; occasional; barbaric; tumultuous; deep; wild; ghastly; triumphant; angry; prolonged; fearful; dismal; lugubrious.

verbs
break into—; muffle—; prolong—; subdue —; unleash—; utter—; —arises; —astonishes; —breaks out; —distresses; —frightens; —penetrates; —pierces; —rends; —rips through; —terrifies; —confuses.
(See cry, wail, noise.)

HOWL (v)
adverbs
dismally; incessantly; bleakly; victoriously; gruesomely; sickeningly; heart-rendingly; ironically; blatantly; eerily.
(See roar, wail.)

HOWLING
adjectives
melancholy; weird; ear-rending.

HOYDENISH
adverbs
gaudily; boisterously; coarsely; noisily; conspicuously; flauntingly; blatantly; publicly; shamelessly; barbarously; boorishly; remarkably; lamentably; extravagantly; queerly; unfortunately; horribly; indecorously; monstrously; indecently; terribly; outlandishly; outrageously; wantonly; ri-

baldly; particularly; shabbily; provincially; shockingly; uncivilly; extremely; horribly; inexcusably.

HUBBUB
adjectives
chaotic; universal; confused; inarticulate.

HUDDLE
adjectives
low; confused.

verbs
band in—; concentrate in—; congregate in —; crowd in—; crush in—; emerge from—; flock in—; gather in—; lie in—; mingle in —; move in—; throng in—; tumble into—; spring from—; swarm in—; —confuses; — disperses; —writhes.
  (See group, crowd.)

HUDDLE (v)
adverbs
pathetically; sluggishly; comfortably; protectingly; snugly; patiently; instinctively; dolorously.
  (See crouch, pack, crowd.)

HUE
adjectives
intense; stone; tender; undecided; vivid; varied (pl); native; prismatic; exuberant; deathly; roseate; unalterable; ashy; glorious; brimstone; golden; somber; autumn; ghastly; celestial; pallid; pronounced; rainbow; healthy; firm; unshimmering; kindred; slaughterous; predominating; faint; myriad (pl); intense; unwithering; sad; blended; heavenly; tawny; universal; melodious; tempting; chameleon; damask; sulphurous; manifold (pl); livid; pallid; pure; lovely; somber; curious (pl); virgin; sublimer; azure; florid; ghastly; voluptuous; enchanting; homely; lurid; brassy; sightly; rich; fair; unwashed; fading; sunburned; evanescent; normal; unnatural; brilliant; predominant; wild; unpropitious; delicate; unfading; charming; different; changing; sanguine; decided; dazzling; doubtful; generous; washed-out; nondescript; aerial; shifting; burnished; iridescent; gorgeous; undying; kaleidoscopic; twilight; various (pl).

verbs
blend—s; dab—; daub with—; dim—; dip into—; enhance—; flush—; mix—; paint—;
smear—; stroke—; teem with—; —brightens; —delights; —enchants; —fades; —glows; —melts; —merges.
  (See color, shade.)

HUG
adjectives
affectionate; exemplary; ecstatic.

HUG (v)
adverbs
brazenly; amorously; affectionately; ecstatically; lustily; brutishly; stalwartly; tenderly; voluptuously; lasciviously.
  (See clasp, grip, embrace.)

HUGE
adverbs
remarkably; bulkily; monstrously; awkwardly; stupendously; grossly; grotesquely; queerly; impossibly; overwhelmingly; ponderously; prodigiously; sensationally; unusually; formidably; unduly.

HULK
adjectives
lumbering; shallow; unprizable; lifeless.

HULL
adjectives
polished; rough; swift; graceful.

verbs
confine to—; discard—; divest of—; enrobe in—; equip with—; fashion—; shed—; shell —; swathe in—; wrap in—; —armors; — covers; —encases; —encompasses; —encrusts; —envelops; —hides; —protects; — reverberates.
  (See frame, blanket.)

HUM
adjectives
busy; murmurous; beelike; soft; bubbling; hideous; endless; peaceful; lily-muffled; dolorous; distant; discordant; hoarse; pleasant; sonorous; faint; musical; drowsy.

verbs
endure—; heed—; ignore—; join in—; muffle—; perceive—; raise—; subdue—; — attracts; —bothers; —charms; —delights; —disturbs; —plagues; —waxes.
  (See murmur.)

HUM (v)

adverbs
tremulously; blithely; discordantly; hoarsely; sonorously; drowsily; musically; melodiously; monotonously.

(See drone, buzz, croon.)

HUMAN

adjectives
frail; feeble; fallible.

adverbs
charitably; generously; sympathetically; compassionately; kindly; tenderly; lovingly; mercifully; graciously; understandingly; intelligently; gently; uncommonly; remarkably.

HUMANE

adverbs
benevolently; tenderly; intelligently; consistently; dependably; charitably; comfortingly; considerately; graciously; warmly; mercifully; philanthropically; altruistically; patriotically; generously; leniently; admirably; wonderfully; actively; naturally; habitually.

HUMANITARIAN

adverbs
constructively; altruistically; benevolently; beneficently; public-spiritedly; generously; sincerely; actively; compassionately; effectively; admirably; superbly; magnificently; nobly; worthily; eminently; immensely; intensely; definitely; broadly.

HUMANITY

adjectives
enslaved; misshapen; outraged; frail; struggling; downtrodden; common; kindred; communal; exalted; suffering; unexpected; active; frank; sturdy; armed; heated; rugged; semi-tropical; multiform; profound; natural; polluted; redeemed; despairing; glorious; rekindled; warm; adorned; consistent; chained.

verbs
claim for—; contemplate—; contribute to—; educate—; enrich—; exhibit—; found on —; imitate—; regard—; observe—; pity—; portray—; prompt by—; relieve—; rely on —; rule—; stir—; uplift—; —inclines; — mitigates; —restrains.

(See mankind, human nature, compassion, tenderness, kindness, benevolence, civilization, world.)

HUMAN NATURE

verbs
appeal to—; attribute to—; benefit—; bewail—; characterize—; contemplate—; lament—; observe—; regard—; rely on—; scrutinize—; subjugate—; —balks at; —behaves; —evolves; —pursues; —responds; —revolves.

(See character, disposition, temperament, constitution, mankind, humanity.)

HUMBLE

adverbs
quietly; unusually; sincerely; modestly; shyly; timidly; obsequiously; submissively; abjectly; astoundingly; timorously; unassumingly; guiltily; demurely; devoutly; reverently; solemnly; gravely; consecratedly; penitently; contritely; sadly; unexpectedly; unnecessarily; extremely.

HUMBLE (v)

adverbs
abjectly; painfully; utterly; profoundly; unmeritedly; shamefully; sadistically; vindictively.

(See debase, humiliate.)

HUMBLENESS

adjectives
whispering; profound.

HUMBUG

adjectives
solemn; intolerable; sleek; hypocritical; dishonest.

HUMDRUM

adverbs
flatly; dully; stupidly; uninterestingly; monotonously; intolerably; usually; habitually; conspicuously; laboriously; tediously; prosily; dismally; wearisomely; tiresomely; prosaically; endlessly; interminably; baldly; disgustingly; ponderously; heavily; impossibly; curiously; unbearably.

HUMID

adverbs
suffocatingly; sultrily; horribly; dreadfully; frightfully; unusually; uncommonly; highly; extremely; excessively; damply; muddily; soggily; reekingly; drippingly; oppressively; uncomfortably; relatively; remarkably; surprisingly.

adjectives
oppressive; rotten; dense; unusual; relative; **extreme**; unwholesome; uncomfortable.

HUMILIATE (v)
adverbs
bitterly; horribly; ineffably; profoundly; spitefully; hatefully; jealously; enviously; treacherously.

(See humble, debase, shame.)

HUMILIATED
adverbs
extremely; deeply; profoundly; intolerably; shamefully; unnecessarily; needlessly; intentionally; deliberately; cruelly; bitterly; painfully; brutally; publicly; utterly; direly; sorely; deplorably; scandalously; outrageously; inexcusably; unforgivably; criminally; shockingly; basely; terribly; dreadfully.

HUMILIATION
adjectives
painful; jovial; utter; imagined; frequent; just; ineffable; anticipated; profound; deep; unmerited; subsequent.

verbs
bow in—; break in—; deserve—; end in—; expose to—; incur—; inure to—; invite—; go down in—; kneel in—; overcome with—; pretend—; purchase by—; resign to—; sink in—; submit to—; suffer—; walk in—; —humbles; —shames; —tortures.

(See mortification, dishonor, ignominy.)

HUMILITY
adjectives
proud; abrupt; deep; profound; singular; matchless; laughable; egotistic; mock; vast; mild; utmost; true; provoking; apparent; shamed; cringing; honest; servile; false; respectable; marked; passionate.

verbs
accept with—; affect—; breathe—; commend —; feign—; fill with—; gown in—; practice—; relish—; submit with—; walk with —; —contents; —satisfies; —tempers.

(See modesty, humiliation.)

HUMMING
adjectives
gentle; intermittent; audible; drowsy.

verbs
—beaks; —chirps; —flits; —hops; —hums; —skims about.

(See bird.)

HUMOR
adjectives
gay; ironic; wonted; **savage; drawling**; malicious; lively; cantankerous; dismal; sportive; piquant; homely; arrogant; mingled; delighted; good; robust; devastating; oppressive; mixed; clumsy; puppy; whimsical; tender; resistless; genial; boisterous; bubbling; caustic; pestilent; parched; jeering; grave; playful; unhappy; gentle; satirical; headstrong; frank; companionable; unaccountable; secondhand; good-natured; capricious; obliging; black; little; melancholy; arresting; pleasant; ponderous; audacious; grim; true; spleeny; splenetic; cynical; acrid; biting; fertile; irresistible; lordly; proper; sarcastic; racy; inexhaustible; overwhelming; excellent; charming; fiery; delightful; vile; morbid; insolent; grotesque; fantastical; broad; quizzical; seditious; grave; holiday; unruffled; sly; subtle; bawdy; effervescent; ironic; fickle; reigning; buoyant; ebullient; ill-concealed; quaint; impatient; serious; flattering; irrepressible; admirable; sneering; ready; quiet; wholesome; fireside; mocking; reckless; testy; bitter; coarse; choice; sectional; ill; unconfined; sanguine; unfailing; trading; gossiplike; querulous; careless; salty; unquarrelsome; sardonic; irregular; universal; exquisite; farcical; Rabelaisian; aqueous; comparative; limited; pitiless; painful; acute; sullen; toplofty; spontaneous; sulphurous; meditative; burlesque; irreverent; unhappy; bizarre; corresponding.

verbs
appreciate—; attempt—; bar—; color with —; conceive—; delight in—; disdain—; execute—; indulge in—; milk dry of—; regale with—; sense—in; subdue—; subtilize—; tame—; —abates; —bores; —eases; —effervesces; —enlivens; —flashes; —flows; —palls; —pales; —penetrates; —ruffles; —scintillates; —shines through; —wanes; —wears thin.

(See disposition, mood, caprice, whim, fancy, fun, mirth, merriment, play.)

HUMOR (v)

adverbs

patronizingly; slyly; indulgently; consciously; ironically; maliciously; whimsically; grotesquely; fantastically; subtly; mockingly; coarsely; sardonically; irreverently.

(See laugh, giggle.)

HUMOROUS

adverbs

smartly; sharply; habitually; temperamentally; wittily; unusually; uncommonly; delightfully; pleasantly; keenly; charmingly; entertainingly; divertingly; waggishly; robustly; lustily; gustily; noisily; boisterously; outrageously; irrepressibly; spontaneously; naturally; broadly; cleverly; brilliantly; whimsically; merrily; comically; wonderfully; endlessly; uncommonly; highly; amazingly; unfailingly.

HUNCH

verbs

believe in—; consider—; contemplate—; deal in —s; follow—; heed—; indulge in—; inspire with—; mark—; observe—; pursue —; stake on—; submit to—; trust—; —implies; —hints; —proves; —suggests.

(See impression, belief.)

HUNCHBACKED

adverbs

unfortunately; pitiably; incurably; slightly; crookedly; grotesquely; terribly; dreadfully; nonchalantly; gallantly; bravely; extremely; possibly.

HUNGER

adjectives

coarse; alleviated; gaunt; gluttonous; deep; ravening; healthful; vulturous.

verbs

abate—; abolish—; appease—; excite—; expire from—; faint in—; press by—; quiet—; risk—; satiate—; satisfy—; spur on by—; stave off—; suffer—; weaken by—; —irritates; —predisposes; —threatens; —vexes.

(See craving, desire, appetite, famine.)

HUNGRY

adverbs

insatiably; terribly; slightly; greedily; pitiably; incessantly; habitually; extremely; unspeakably; alarmingly; ravenously; eagerly; seriously; gauntly; cadaverously; gluttonously; healthily; wolfishly; impatiently; avidly; wistfully; curiously; strangely; irritably; awfully; restlessly; fretfully.

HUNK

adjectives

substantial; seditious; luscious; juicy; flavorful.

HUNT

adjectives

fruitless; scavenger; vengeful; man.

HUNT (v)

adverbs

mercilessly; patiently; anxiously; fruitlessly; enthusiastically; intrepidly; passionately; wantonly; humanely; daringly.

(See seek, search, pursue.)

HUNTER

adjectives

venerable; winged; passionate; unsuccessful; novice; persistent; pugnacious; gold; lifelong; unthinking; wanton; humanity; outstanding; fair-weather; daring; intrepid.

HUNTING

adjectives

purposed; realistic.

HURDLE

verbs

balk at—; brace—; break—; construct—; erect—; fence with—; fly over—; fortify with—; gain—; jump—; leap over—; spring over—; stride—; take—; vault—; —bars; —encloses; —obstructs; —topples.

(See barrier, frame, fence.)

HURL (v)

adverbs

viciously; heedlessly; relentlessly; vigorously; boisterously; stalwartly; prodigiously; thunderously; flagrantly; tempestuously.

(See fling, cast.)

HURRICANE

adjectives

untamed; furious; aimless; tempestuous; lightning.

verbs

cast away by—; dread—; encounter—; perish in—; report—; wallow in—; —bedevils; —breaks; —bursts; —ceases; —confuses; —destroys; —devastates; —falls upon; —

612

overthrows; —persecutes; —rages; —ravages; —rends; —riots; —shrieks; —sweeps; —takes toll; —violates; —whirls.

(See storm, tempest, typhoon, snow, blizzard.)

HURRIED
adverbs
unfortunately; carelessly; inefficiently; urgently; nervously; harassingly; terribly; intensely; monstrously; foolishly; ineptly; excitedly; feverishly; hysterically; restlessly; violently; wildly; irrepressibly; impolitely; uncivilly; discourteously; boorishly; ungraciously; furiously; breathlessly; desperately; unduly; indecently; unscrupulously; clumsily; madly; noticeably; visibly; obviously.

HURRY
adjectives
monstrous; national; raging; frivolous; hot.

HURRY (*v*)
adverbs
nervously; merrily; conservatively; gallantly; furtively; tremulously; precipitately; anxiously; madly; feverishly; mechanically; blindly; confusedly.

(See hasten, dispatch.)

HURT
adjectives
unbandaged; real; painful; dull; deep; permanent; growing; bodily; mortal; nagging; aroused.

HURT (*v*)
adverbs
grievously; hideously; deeply; permanently; acutely; bodily; fatally; superficially; incurably.

(See injure, damage, wound.)

HURTFUL
adverbs
mischievously; intentionally; deliberately; innocently; unconsciously; dreadfully; perniciously; maliciously; obnoxiously; legally; disastrously; venomously; villainously; exceptionably; deplorably; pitiably; lamentably; wretchedly; sadly; reprehensibly; confoundedly; hopelessly; purposely; irremediably; dangerously; alarmingly; seriously; hopelessly; desperately; unusually; incredibly.

HURTLE (*v*)
adverbs
recklessly; swiftly; spectacularly; gloriously; furiously; blazingly; daringly; fiercely.

(See throw, hurl.)

HUSBAND
adjectives
frigid; itinerant; shiftless; distraught; love-selfish; unworthy; allowing; truant; worthless; war-blinded; unfaithful; affianced; attached; exacting; impecunious; obstinate; unhopeful; disgruntled; cynical; captive; coarse; instructive; ill; indolent; divorced; heavy; uxorious; precise; devoted; appreciative; scandalous; imaginary; bereaved; cruel; cantankerous; wild; noble; generous; dissipated; irascible; maddening; distracted; ingenious; indignant; fiery; stolid; jealous.

verbs
abide with—; attend—; chide—; divorce—; nag—; obtain—; rebuke—; respect—; serve —; submit to—; —abandons; —chastises; — defends; —deserts; —domineers; —heads; —lords over; —philanders; —rebukes; — represses; —reprimands; —reproves; — rules; —supports.

(See master.)

HUSBANDRY
adjectives
prolific; animal; skilled; economical.

HUSH
adjectives
sudden; expectant; breathless; dread; timeless; primeval; windless; unbreathing; evening; instinctive; religious; all-pervasive; awed; deadly; starlight; deep; peculiar; grim; instant.

verbs
command—; demand—; enforce—; expect —; impose—; pierce—; procure—; reduce to—; restore—; seek—; split—; spread—; welcome—; —calms; —charms; —deepens; —delights; —disturbs; —ensues; —hangs heavy; —invades; —pervades; —rules.

(See stillness, silence, quiet.)

HUSH (*v*)
adverbs
significantly; breathlessly; instinctively; peculiarly; cautiously; temporarily; abruptly.

(See silence, repress, suppress.)

adverbs

solemnly; reverently; quietly; quickly; unusually; wonderfully; swiftly; inordinately; uncommonly; gloomily; irritably; suddenly; breathlessly; instinctively; deeply; profoundly; grimly; instantly; particularly; peculiarly; curiously; queerly; horribly; oddly; infinitely; strangely; temporarily; momentarily; eternally.

HUSK

adjectives

scholastic; fruitless; bearded; wrinkled.

HUSKY
(strong)

adverbs

vigorously; robustly; mightily; powerfully; sturdily; stoutly; irresistibly; incontestably; inexhaustibly; stubbornly; soundly; magnificently; splendidly; remarkably; brutally; immensely; prodigiously; evidently; incredibly; obviously; manifestly; palpably; surprisingly; matchlessly.

HUSKY
(voice)

adverbs

faintly; deeply; murmurously; languorously; hoarsely; softly; audibly; throatily; seductively; seriously; dreadfully; terribly; deliberately; stagily; whisperingly; melodiously; musically; raucously; brutally; sepulchrally; hollowly; permanently; temporarily; purposely; alarmingly; amazingly; fearfully; slightly.

HUSSY

adjectives

cantankerous; brazen; brash; loud-mouthed.

HUSTLE (v)

adverbs

unceremoniously; precipitately; abruptly; undignifiedly; characteristically; breathlessly; enthusiastically.
   (See hurry, hasten.)

HUSTLING

adverbs

restlessly; constantly; fitfully; zealously; noisily; happily; everlastingly; ceaselessly; cheerily; actively; energetically; assiduously; diligently; earnestly; eagerly; excitedly.

adjectives

unaired; mud-walled; abandoned.

HYBRID

adverbs

undeniably; obviously; cheaply; miserably; indiscriminately; palpably; manifestly; peculiarly; singularly; unaccountably; noteworthily; fantastically; unfashionably; professedly; quaintly; promiscuously; heterogeneously; openly.

HYDROGEN

adjectives

nascent; carbureted.

HYENA

verbs

—attacks; —battles; —barks; —carries away; —crushes; —devours; —feeds on; —inhabits; —laughs; —overpowers; —preys on; —scavenges; —stalks.
   (See animal.)

HYGIENE

verbs

deride—; heed—; improve—; instruct in—; obey—; practise—; preach—; prescribe—; promote—; scorn—; verse in—; violate—; —defends; —extends to; —guards against; —preserves; —prevents; —resists; —sustains.
   (See science, health, cleanliness.)

HYGIENIC

adverbs

wonderfully; satisfactorily; unusually; unquestionably; commendably; appreciably; safely; warrantably; authoritatively; properly; duly; appropriately; securely; perfectly; completely; agreeably; prophylactically; sanitatively; sanitarily; usefully; remarkably; wholesomely; avowedly; allegedly; matchlessly; superbly; supremely; acceptably; splendidly.

HYMN

adjectives

celestial; anguished; tuneful; joyful; measured; ceaseless; wrathful; pious; solemn; undying; ancient; impassioned; nuptial; appropriate; choral; swelling; pretty; dreadful; metaphorical; edifying; impious; vernal; sentimental; angelic; warbled; exulting.

verbs

adore with—; arrange—; carol—; chant—; compose—; express in—; honor with—; hum —; quote—; rehearse—; whistle—; worship with—; —bursts forth; —delights; —extols; —glorifies; —honors; —praises; —resounds; —thanks.

(See song, composition, poem, music.)

HYPERBOLE

adjectives

eloquent; extravagant; original.

HYPNOTIC

adverbs

mysteriously; scientifically; strangely; professionally; amateurishly; allegedly; curiously; oddly; inscrutably; questionably; incredibly; supposedly; probably; possibly; slightly; incontrovertibly; dreadfully; fearfully; alarmingly; frightfully; highly; uncommonly; curatively; helpfully; experimentally; dangerously; terrifyingly; marvellously; ominously.

HYPNOTISM

verbs

advocate—; approve of—; consent to—; deride—; induce—; inject—; interest in—; fall into—; place under—, practise—; resist —; submit to—; succumb to—; treat by—; utilize—; witness—; —amends; —cures; — influences; —intrigues; —relieves.

(See sleep, spell.)

HYPOCHONDRIAC

adverbs

gloomily; dismally; incurably; unfortunately; miserably; sadly; distressingly; alarmingly; disturbingly; fanatically; insensately; unreasonably; irrationally; pitiably; blankly; abjectly; despondently; heavily; biliously; dreadfully; grimly; lamentably; lugubriously; inordinately; senselessly; helplessly; hopelessly; desperately; surprisingly.

HYPOCRISY

adjectives

smooth; habitual; adjusted; smug; unsleeping; transparent; coarse; blustering.

verbs

accuse of—; befog with—; blanket in—; clothe in—; couch in—; denounce—; despise —; detest—; discern—; explode—; feed—; oil with—; protest—; prove—; purge of—;

repent—; steep in—; trick by—; —beguiles; —deceives; —disgusts; —frames; —veils.

(See insincerity, pretence, sham, affectation, trickery.)

HYPOCRITE

adjectives

honest; mealy-mouthed; vamped-up; cruising; canting; consummate; sharp; pompous; oily; lowborn.

verbs

denounce—; despise—; detect—; detest—; discern—; expose—; purge—; —affects; — beguiles; —binds; —blinds; —deceives; — disgusts; —feeds; —feigns; —oils; —poisons; —pretends; —tricks; —veils.

(See liar, snob.)

HYPOCRITICAL

adverbs

shamefully; obviously; palpably; evidently; scandalously; notoriously; infamously; outrageously; atrociously; undependably; faithlessly; disloyally; sanctimoniously; openly; falsely; contemptibly; atrociously; abominably; detestably; flagrantly; artfully; insincerely; evasively; flatteringly; ingeniously; perfidiously; craftily; shrewdly; basely; dangerously; terribly.

HYPOTHESIS

adjectives

problematical; unreal; rationalistic; unverified; monstrous; creative; metaphysical; untenable; tentative; scientific; cherished; inaccurate; superficial; unlikely.

verbs

accept—; advance—; apply—; argue on—; build up—; condemn—; consider—; deduce —; demonstrate—; depend on—; deride—; dispute—; draw—; evolve—; frame—; put forth—; reason by—; rest on—; state—; work on—; wreck—; —assumes; —embraces.

(See theory, supposition, assumption, information, fact.)

HYPOTHETICAL

adverbs

thinly; disguisedly; obviously; manifestly; usually; cleverly; shyly; serviceably; usefully; dubiously; vaguely; obscurely; precariously; supposably; academically; presumptively; stimulatingly; probably.

adjectives
military; imminent; continual; giggling.

verbs
augment—; blaze into—; convulse with—; excite to—; goad to—; indicate—; indulge in—; laugh in—; overcome—; prevent—; produce—; remedy—; restrain—; soothe—; struggle in—; subject to—; —attacks; —bubbles; —disturbs; —hovers near; —occurs; —presses; —wrecks.
(See nervousness, excitement, anger.)

adverbs
wildly; foolishly; remarkably; unreasonably; rabidly; loudly; nervously; intentionally; habitually; conveniently; profitably; contemptibly; provokingly; pitiably; unduly; insufferably; deliberately; miserably; helplessly; incoherently; capriciously; erratically; uncontrollably; ungovernably; incurably; incorrigibly; disconcertingly; distressingly; dreadfully; deliriously; furiously; passionately; angrily; fanatically; violently; uncommonly; highly.

I

ICE

adjectives

enchanted; tinkling; never-melting; thick-ribbed; confounded; congealed; treacherous; translucent; cerulean; gathered; perennial; anchor; polished; liquefied; crevassed; cushioned; crashing; everlasting; grinding; blue-white; glittering; phosphorescent; pellucid; transparent; overwhelming; drifted.

verbs

chip—; congeal to—; crush—; engulf in—; scar—; scrape—; shave—; sheet with—; smooth—; thaw—; tong—; —barricades; —blocks; —clinks; —drifts; —gleams; —glistens; —jams; —shimmers; —shines.
(See diamond, light, snow.)

ICEBERG

adjectives

glittering; sharp; jagged; ghostly; colossal; murderous; silent; ominous.

ICE-BOAT

adjectives

dainty; swift; wind-swept; dashing; gliding.

ICE-DRIFT

adjectives

heavy; ruinous.

ICICLE

adjectives

pendent; petrified; callous; living.

verbs

chip—; flow from—; —crashes; —s decorate; —drips; —endangers; —gleams; —glistens; —glitters; —shimmers; —shines; —suspends from; —thaws; —s weight.

ICINESS

adjectives

calm; bitter; calculated.

ICING

adjectives

rich; creamy; sparkling; sugar.

ICONOCLASTIC

adverbs

terribly; habitually; temperamentally; brutally; critically; harshly; inconsiderately;

impiously; evilly; cruelly; dreadfully; unreasonably; wantonly; deliberately; irreverently; atheistically; disrespectfully; blasphemously; profanely; idiotically; egotistically; unintelligently; pretentiously.

ICY

adverbs

terribly; unbearably; significantly; horribly; unexpectedly; perilously; dangerously; hazardously; fearfully; impossibly; remarkably; peculiarly; curiously; hideously.

IDEA

adjectives

abiding; absorbing; abstract; adequate; admirable; aggressive; amazing; antiquated; approximated; artistic; ascetic; associated; attractive; bare; baseless; basic; beautiful; blasphemous; bold; brilliant; casual; charming; clashing; cherished; chimerical; classical; clear; cognate; cold; commanding; complete; confused; concrete; confined; conflicting; concluding; congealed; contemporary; contemptible; contrasting; conventional; crafty; critical; crude; cryptic; delicious; delirious; democratic; despicable; destructive; determinate; devouring; dim; disastrous; distinct; divergent; divine; dominant; dynamic; economical; educational; elementary; elevating; embryo; empty; endearing; entangled; entire; erroneous; essential; evolutionary; exaggerated; excellent; explicit; explosive; extraordinary; faintest; false; fantastic; fashionable; fastidious; fixed; flattering; fleeting; forward-moving; fundamental; funny; geographical; graceful; grandiose; grotesque; habitual; hazy; heathen; heroic; immature; impalpable; impolitic; impure; inane; inconceivable; inconvenient; industrial; ingenious; innate; insane; irruptive; jolly; literary; lofty; ludicrous; malicious; manifest; meditative; melodic; miscalled; mistaken; momentary; monarchic; musical; moral; money-making; nascent; nebulous; new; noble; notorious; novel; obvious; oft-repeated; opulent; original; pastoral; patentable; perfect; philosophical; picturesque; platitudinous; plebeian; poetical; ponderous; popular; preconceived; preposterous; prevailing; previous; primitivistic; private; profit-making; progressive; puzzling; quaint; radical; rational; realized; remote; repressed; retrogressive;

revolutionary; romantic; selling; sensational; sentimental; singular; sketchy; slightest; snob; sound; speculative; spiritual; spontaneous; spurious; stable; startling; sterling; stern; stimulating; striking; structural; sufficient; suggested; synthetic; systematic; tasteful; tempting; terrible; theologic; theoretical; traditional; tranquilizing; tutelary; twisted; ugly; unhappy; underlying; undesired; unexpected; unfulfilled; uninteresting; universal; unjust; unsound; vagrant; vague; vaporous; varied (pl); vile; well-grounded; whimsical; widespread; womanish; wonderful.

verbs

absorb—; amplify—; apprehend—; assemble—s; assimilate—s; balk at—; boil down —; brood upon—; cherish—; clarify—; color—; communicate—to; conceive—; concentrate on—; conform to—; contribute—; convey—; crystallize—; cultivate—; curb —; deride—; devote to—; disclose—; discredit—; dispel—; dissociate—from; divest of—; divulge—; elaborate on—; embed—in; endorse—; entertain—; entrench—; envisage—; evolve—; explode—; exploit—; expound—; favor—; fertilize—; formulate —; foster—; grasp—; grope for—; guard —; hail—; harbor—; hatch—; hit upon—; illuminate—; illustrate—; imbue with—; implant—; impose—; impregnate with—; incubate—; inculcate—; inspire—; interchange—s; invest with—; jot down—; launch—; modify—; mold—; mull over—; nourish—; obliterate—; obsess with—; overflow with—; patent—; pervert—; pioneer with—; play with—; ponder—; pounce upon —; promote—; promulgate—; pursue—; rally to—; recoil from—; refute—; reject —; relish—; repudiate—; retain—; reverse —; revive—; root—in; scoff at—; scorn—; set forth—; spike—; sprout—; stifle—; sum up—; superimpose—; suppress—; surrender to—; sustain—; symbolize—; toy with—; unfold—; visualize—; —clings; —s crowd; —dominates; —emanates from; —emerges; —endures; —flashes upon; —germinates; —haunts; —incorporates; —is born; —lurks; —matures; —permeates; —persists; —pops up; —predominates; —prevails; —progresses; —seeps in; —springs from; —takes shape; —wells up; embody in—; instil—; master—.

(See thought, opinion, design, plan, project, conception, impression, apprehension, ideal, belief, theory.)

verbs

assimilate—; betray—; cherish—; cling to —; consecrate to—; cultivate—; defend—; depart from—; elevate—s; embody—; exemplify—; extol—; forsake—; foster—; further—; imbue with—; inculcate—; ingrain—; inspire—; instill—; maintain—; mutilate—; nourish—; nurse—; owe to—; personify—; play havoc with—; preserve—; sacrifice to—; satisfy—; shatter—; shape—; symbolize—; weld to—; worship—; —aims at; —binds; —inspires; —permeates; —rests upon; realize—.

(See model, pattern, standard.)

adverbs

chimerically; dreamily; fantastically; perfectly; impossibly; extravagantly; romantically; preposterously; notionally; unsubstantially; whimsically; vaporously; entertainingly; emphatically; beautifully; charmingly; emptily; nebulously; speculatively; ridiculously; vaguely.

IDEALISM

adjectives

crystallized; poetical; romantic; moral; altruistic; impulsive; abstract; soaring; poignant.

verbs

breathe—; clothe in—; decry—; dwell in—; encourage—; found on—; inculcate—; marvel at—; nurse—; prate about—; sacrifice to—; temper with—; value—; voice—; tinge with—; —affirms; —compensates; —denies; —hampers; —melts; —reigns; —teaches; —transcends.

(See honesty, confidence, faith, trust.)

IDEALIST

adjectives

unconscious; rash; fatuous.

verbs

chain—; criticize—; delude—; disenchant —; disillusion—; enthrall—; frustrate—; hamper—; —cherishes; —contemplates; —despises; —dreams; —envisions; —regards; —sacrifices; —speculates on; —values.

(See poet, writer, philosopher, artist, author.)

IDEALITY

adjectives

refined; poetic; muzzy; confused; muddled.

IDEALS

adjectives

chivalrous; romantic; fatal; perfect; undigested; adequate; false; poetic; elevating; sublime; temperate; vague; educational; cherishing; retrograde; fanciful; picturesque; exalted; abstract; empty; ultimate; spiritual; collective; theoretical; factitious; racial; intangible; entrancing; complete; visionary; industrial; literary; ascetic; divine; unfulfilled; tutelary; cherished; degrading; distant; bric-a-brac; noble; affecting; unavowed; unclean; ethical; secret; antiquated; stern; unattainable.

IDENTIFICATION

adjectives

imputed; obliterated; spurious.

IDENTIFY (*v*)

adverbs

unconsciously; mystically; irrevocably; peculiarly; . mechanically; ecclesiastically; prominently; nominally.

(See recognize, ascertain.)

IDENTITY

adjectives

concealed; conscious; obliterated; substantial; separate; sweet; veritable; undiscovered; revealed; fictitious.

verbs

assure of—; conceal—; convince of—; demand—; determine—; discourage—; doubt —; establish—; forfeit—; grope for—; lose —; merge—with; preserve—; recognize—; reveal—; seek—; substantiate—; suggest—; suspect—; —leaks out; —perplexes; prove—.

(See similarity, individuality, accuracy.)

IDIOCY

adjectives

sublimest; teeth-chattering; morbid; impertinent.

IDIOM

adjectives

delicate; racial; succinct; racy; vulgar; national; quaint; absurd.

verbs

approve of—; cherish—; excel in—s; express in—; familiarize with—; interpret—; maintain—; repeat—; speak in—; translate

—; transmit in—s; —amuses; —confuses; —differs; —glows; —perplexes.

(See expression, phrase, speech, dialect, jargon, word, thought.)

DIOSYNCRASY

adjectives

personal; morbid; sickly; separate.

verbs

ban—; dispense with—; foster—; humor—; imitate—; indulge in—; inherit—; parade —s; permit—; protest—; question—; restrain—; ridicule—; tolerate—; transmit—; understand—; warrant—; wonder at—; — embarrasses; —perplexes; —puzzles.

(See eccentricity, characteristic, habit.)

IDIOT

adjectives

mad; contemplative; congenial; insolent; blinking; sloppy; sentimental; monumental; stargazing; optimistic; notorious.

verbs

bar—; behave like—; conceal—; content—; control—; guard—; incarcerate—; lament —; manage—; mistrust—; play—; please —; shelter—; tolerate—; treat—; witness —; —amuses; —blinks; —dotes on; —giggles; —mistakes; —misunderstands; — ogles; —stares.

(See fool, imbecile, dunce, lunatic.)

IDIOTIC

adverbs

pathetically; hopelessly; incurably; congenitally; insolently; monumentally; crazily; purposely; maddeningly; utterly; foolishly; infatuatedly; rashly; recklessly; simply; childishly; nonsensically; blatantly; dully; extravagantly; grossly; idly; inappropriately; injudiciously; obtusely; ridiculously; senselessly; unwisely; stolidly; stupidly; spoonily.

IDLE

adverbs

vexatiously; languidly; lazily; slothfully; constitutionally; preferably; naturally; habitually; obesely; contemptibly; selfishly; sleepily; delightfully; continually; obstinately; stupidly; deliberately; torpidly; stubbornly; irresponsibly; reprehensibly; inexcusably; unduly; remarkably; strangely; unusually; dreadfully.

IDLE (v)

adverbs

frivolously; disreputably; intellectually; listlessly; aimlessly; wantonly; blissfully; degenerately; disgracefully; talkatively.

(See trifle, loaf.)

IDLENESS

adjectives

disgraceful; good-night; busy; unwilling; chatty; disreputable; intellectual; enforced; compulsory; conscientious; ancient; shapeless; elegant; rapturous; summer; absent; fatal; listless; sheer; aimless; settled; inert.

verbs

avoid—; banish—; denounce—; dread—; excuse—; hatch in—; maintain in—; pillow in—; repose in—; reproach—; revel in—; shake off—; stagnate in—; thrive in—; wallow in—; waste in—; —beguiles; —breeds; —demoralizes; —destroys; —harms; —poisons; —rusts; —shames; —tempts; —wearies.

(See indolence, futility.)

IDLER

adjectives

luxurious; busy; dependent; shiftless; studied; practiced.

IDOL

adjectives

burning; particular; subterraneous; lifeless; baser; grim; brass; vile; well-painted; matinee; youthful; gross; shapeless; gilded; bewitching; celebrated.

verbs

bless—; bow before—; cast down—; chant to—; clasp—; found—; mock—; offer to—; profane—; prostrate before—; renounce—; sacrifice to—; serve—; worship—; —embodies; —represents.

(See image, representation, effigy, notion, fallacy, hero, altar.)

IDOLATROUS

adverbs

fanatically; foolishly; infatuatedly; fatuously; inordinately; fantastically; extravagantly; irrationally; fervently; ridiculously; absurdly; oddly; passionately; superstitiously; credulously; bigotedly; wildly; enthusiastically; rabidly; grossly; inconceivably; blindly.

IDOLATRY

adjectives

social; long-upheld; popular; passionate; bloody; religious; foolish; enthusiastic.

IDOLIZE (v)

adverbs

inordinately; foolishly; lovingly; adoringly; passionately; madly; religiously; fervently; faithfully; fanatically.

(See adore, worship.)

IDYLLIC

adverbs

blissfully; romantically; sentimentally; rapturously; ecstatically; fancifully; extravagantly; inexpressibly; indescribably; beautifully; marvelously; utterly.

IGNITE (v)

adverbs

spontaneously; abruptly; dangerously; spectacularly; swiftly; furiously; startlingly; brilliantly; mechanically.

(See kindle, excite, rouse, burn.)

IGNOBLE

adverbs

basely; undeniably; surprisingly; despicably; unbelievably; horribly; contemptibly; grossly; consciously; deliberately; innately; naturally; inexpressibly; hopelessly; notoriously.

IGNOMINIOUS

adverbs

shamefully; contemptibly; ingloriously; scandalously; abjectly; arrantly; shockingly; dreadfully; terribly; unmentionably; outrageously; obscurely; inexpressibly; unbelievably; humbly; vaguely.

IGNOMINY

adjectives

imputed; complete; undesired.

verbs

arise from—; base on—; bear—; bow in—; confess to—; cover with—; crumble into—; endure—; eradicate—; fall into—; hide in —; reveal—; rise above—; spring from—; subject to—; suffer—; veil—; —chains; —degrades; —dishonors; —pursues.

(See disgrace, dishonor, infamy, defeat.)

IGNORAMUS

adjectives

splendid; hopeless; obvious; posturing.

IGNORANCE

adjectives

presumptuous; simple; personal; intelligent; self-loved; brutal; complete; deplorable; widespread; absolute; prevailing; singular; guilty; primitive; genteel; amazing; gross; fatuous; pure; universal; mingled; sheer; miraculous; timid; sanctified; blissful; faithless; desperate; profound; admirable; modest; entire; woeful; unpained; learned; crass; barbaric; swirling; helpless; disconcerting; honest; deep; extreme; violent; popular; general; culpable; intense; daring; dense; blind; humble; spotless; impertinent; naked; glooming; united; intellectual; polished; manifold; feigned; maidenly; perpetual; childish.

verbs

alienate through—; bare—; betray—; brand —; breed—; conceal—; condemn—; confess —of; deplore—; emancipate from—; expose —; forgive—; foster—; lapse into—; mock —; nurture—; remain in—; remedy—; scoff at—; shroud in—; tolerate—; yield to—; —blinds; —darkens; —deforms; —prejudices; —shames.
(See stupidity, foolishness, illiteracy.)

IGNORANT

adverbs

hopelessly; blissfully; dully; abjectly; absurdly; shamefully; utterly; merrily; stupidly; crassly; stolidly; contentedly; obviously; terribly; criminally; inexcusably; unfortunately; deplorably; curiously; strangely; grossly; woefully; painfully; helplessly; deeply; culpably; amazingly; uncommonly.

IGNORE (v)

adverbs

snobbishly; blandly; blatantly; antagonistically; scornfully; contemptuously; sneeringly; uncivilly; impudently.
(See snub, disregard.)

ILL

adjectives

oppressive; infinite; unmitigated; cruel; invisible; obscure; vindictive; false; malign; financial; cureless; sundry (pl); swooning; foulest; specific; dreadful; violent; approaching; virulent; knowing; earthly; willing; matchless; economic; hastening; invented.

verbs

banish—; better—; correct—; decry—; defend from—; destroy—; endure—; expatiate on—; feign—s; foreshadow—s; grieve over —; incur—; number—s; occasion—; remedy —; suffer—; unravel—; work—s; —s befall; —s beset; —s confront; —s disappear; —s distress; —s imperil; —shadows.
(See evil, misfortune, disease, pain.)

ILL

adverbs

seriously; desperately; slightly; temporarily; violently; honestly; strangely; fatally; mortally; naturally; extremely; cruelly; incurably; terribly; irrecoverably; unhappily; unfortunately; woefully; recently.

ILL-BRED

adverbs

boorishly; crassly; grossly; downright; unbelievably; notoriously; shamelessly; terribly; unbearably; offensively; barbarously; cruelly; intolerably; shamefully; deplorably; lamentably; woefully; obnoxiously; extremely; dreadfully; curiously; obviously.

ILLEGAL

adverbs

notoriously; admittedly; obviously; dangerously; trickily; shamelessly; vaguely; obscurely; flagrantly; perilously; riskily; openly; daringly; audaciously; villainously; viciously; flagitiously; shamefully.

ILLEGALITY

adjectives

obvious; apparent; declared; widespread.

verbs

censor—; charge—; conceal—; condemn—; criticize—; cure of—; deal with—; espy—; foster—; oppose—; permit—; protest—; punish—; rectify—; taint with—; tolerate —; war on—.
(See crime, dishonesty.)

ILLEGIBLE

adverbs

utterly; quasi; entirely; hopelessly; shamefully; vexatiously; carelessly; childishly; purposely; intentionally; deliberately; agedly; scrawlingly; indecipherably; pompously; unfortunately; unluckily; crampedly; deplorably; woefully; strangely; unusually; habitually; uncommonly; feebly.

ILLEGITIMATE

adverbs

nefariously; criminally; obviously; admittedly; horribly; cruelly; woefully; deliberately; dangerously; riskily; hazardously; audaciously; daringly; heinously; extremely; curiously; flauntingly; flagrantly; shamelessly; hopelessly; notoriously.

ILLIBERAL

adverbs

fanatically; narrowly; bigotedly; stingily; meanly; basely; selfishly; cruelly; parsimoniously; sordidly; uncharitably; necessarily; temperamentally; innately; naturally; habitually; prejudicially; provincially; dogmatically; stupidly; unreasonably; penuriously; shabbily; exceedingly; remarkably; notoriously.

ILLICIT

adverbs

criminally; obviously; shamefully; furtively; stealthily; perilously; ignominiously; strangely; desperately; contemptibly; horribly; cruelly; dangerously; fearfully; unaccountably; terribly.

ILLITERACY

adjectives

pitiful; undesirable; brutish; inert.

verbs

campaign against—; conceal—; condemn—; curse with—; excuse—; hide—; induce—; judge—; nourish—; plead—; rectify—; reform—; remedy—; ridicule—; shroud in—; test—; tolerate—.

(See ignorance, blunder, error, stupidity.)

ILLITERATE

adverbs

boorishly; shamefully; provincially; hopelessly; helplessly; innocently; unduly; lazily; slothfully; shamelessly; surprisingly; unexpectedly; woefully; deplorably; amazingly; utterly; remarkably; unreasonably; inexplicably; pitiably; sadly; completely; barbarously; terribly.

ILL-MANNERED

adverbs

unpardonably; unforgivably; crudely; sensationally; boorishly; exceptionally; woefully; pitifully; ignorantly; hopelessly; offensively; curiously; strangely; inexplicably; oddly; surprisingly; terribly; amazingly; inordinately; inexcusably; utterly; positively; unbearably; unendurably; ungraciously; flagrantly; boisterously.

ILL-NATURED

adverbs

peevishly; fretfully; meanly; unbearably; innately; naturally; constitutionally; curiously; strangely; inexplicably; oddly; querulously; viciously; brutally; maliciously; slanderously; obviously; dreadfully; implacably; harshly; sternly; unutterably; completely; irremediably.

ILLNESS

adjectives

deadly; wearisome; passing; desperate; pernicious; chronic; prolonged; unsuspected; fatal; exhausting; disabling; frequent (pl); trifling; acute; separate; particular; severe; protracted; slow; gradual; wearing; dangerous; absolute; serious; violent; hopeless; lingering.

verbs

attend with—; combat—; contract—; convalesce from—; cure—; diagnose—; exempt from—; guard against—; hinder by—; induce—; recuperate from—; report—; succumb to—; suffer—; —abates; —debilitates; —enfeebles; —prostrates; —seizes; —weakens.

(See disease, malady, sickness, ailment, complaint, indisposition.)

ILLOGICAL

adverbs

strangely; absurdly; vexatiously; alarmingly; dangerously; ridiculously; ominously; perilously; irrationally; terribly; deliberately; ignorantly; shortsightedly; unstably; trickily; speciously; inordinately; irritatingly; wildly; viciously; particularly; dreadfully; uncommonly; impulsively; evasively; foolishly.

ILLUMINATE (v)

adverbs

singularly; brilliantly; gloriously; vividly; feebly; sparklingly; indirectly; partially.

(See brighten, adorn.)

ILLUMINATION

adjectives

full; softened; glorious; public; burning; phosphoric; faintest; brilliant; secondary; partial; competent; rude; veritable; indirect.

ILLUMINE (v)

adverbs

clearly; vividly; brilliantly; fully; faintly; publicly.

(See adorn, brighten.)

ILLUSION

adjectives

self-imposed; transparent; phantasmagorical; egregious; optical; innocent; grave; desired; ambrosial; childlike; brief; gorgeous; fantastic; strange; dramatic; auditory; kindred (pl); terrifying; momentary; sacred; brilliant; vague; exquisite; romantic; beloved; concrete; shattered; spectral; charming; dazzling; sweet; pleasing; multiplied (pl).

verbs

awaken from—; beguile with—; cherish—; complete—; create—; cultivate—; destroy —; dispel—; dispose of—; dissolve—; entertain—; extirpate—; harbor—; illustrate —; maintain—; mask—; prolong—; shatter—; strip of—; suffer—; sweep away—; triumph over—; uncover—; wander in—; — blinds; —crumbles; —haunts; —lulls; — persists; —prevails; —robs; —stupefies.

(See misconception, delusion, hallucination, idea, fallacy.)

ILLUSIVE

adverbs

fancifully; imaginarily; romantically; ideally; whimsically; extravagantly; fabulously; notionally; insubstantially; visionarily; fantastically; phantasmally; spectrally; imaginatively; chimerically; wildly; singularly; preposterously; absurdly; unreasonably; ridiculously; irrationally.

ILLUSTRATE (v)

adverbs

profusely; copiously; adequately; abundantly; humorously; liberally; vividly; lavishly; dramatically; admirably; splendidly; graphically; superbly; instructively; vivaciously; curiously; decoratively.

(See draw, engrave, describe.)

ILLUSTRATION

adjectives

suppositious; striking; sublime; graphic; prophetic; amusing; practical; accompanying; superb; helpful; gorgeous; excellent; plentiful; delightful; crude; sufficient; fearful; extreme; lithographic; sketchy; notable; instructive; apt; vivacious; curious; profuse; inimitable; elaborate; occasional; decorative; interesting; irrelevant; concrete; dreamy; brilliant; cogent; vivid; dramatic; fair; typical; forcible; modest; touching; well-known; supreme; elusive; descriptive; pleasant; puerile; exotic; magnificent.

verbs

afford—; commend—; criticize—; design—; display—; draw—; embellish—; exhibit—; lend to—; popularize—; pour forth—s; — adorns; —attracts; —caricatures; —depicts; —emphasizes; —exemplifies, —explains; glorifies; —indicates; —interests; —proves.

(See comparison, example, picture, sketch, photograph.)

ILLUSTRIOUS

adverbs

splendidly; brilliantly; distinctly; broadly; orably; famously; proudly; unimpeachably; generally; conspicuously; imperishably; hon-deservedly; enviably; nobly.

ILL-WILL

verbs

bear—; derive—; display—; haunt by—; incite—; incur—; infect with—; level—at; mock with—; moderate—; nourish—; poison with—; regard with—; repent—; resent—; scorn—; —barks; —bites; —blinds; — chills; —curdles; —disturbs; —lashes.

(See malice, hatred, antipathy, resentment, rancor, grudge.)

IMAGE

adjectives

dead; latest; fixed; dull; mimic; remembered; faint; delusive; watery; sacred; mental; faithful; concise; imperial; wavering; colossal; familiar; pathetic; discreet; wandering; visionary; helpless; fallen; blurred; falsest; contrasted; imperfect; radiant; licentious; agreeable; vague; tissued; thronging (pl); sweetest; tremulous; reduced; indistinct; sainted; idolatrous; teasing; rude; carved; graven; serene; sublime; heavenly; impassive; bronze; waxen;

scattered (pl); flying; livid; exact; unsculptured; spitting; distorted; monstrous; confused; hampered; lovely; mysterious; visible; newborn; ludicrous; perceptible; royal; peace-bearing; magnified; graceful; wonder-working; wrinkled; heroic; constant; effective; fallen; luminous; palpitating; deathlike; fantastic; delicate; pleasant; vivid; poetical; horrible; foul; votive; reflex; compendious; dreamlike; artificial; subordinate; molten.

verbs

bow before—; call up—; carve—; confront with—; conjure up—; convey—; distort—; efface—; etch—; evoke—; evolve—; exalt —; focus—; perpetuate—; picture—; preserve—; project—; reflect—; reject—; retain—; scorn—; stamp—; summon—; transform—; transmit—; —blooms; —gleams; —glimmers; —represents; —terrifies.

(See imitation, representation, conception, idea, figure, statue, hallucination, picture.)

IMAGERY

adjectives

mental; external; woven; obscene; metaphorical; definite; amorphous; oriental; passionate; childish; vivid; pensive; carven; sculptured; learned; wondrous; colorful; glowing; inapplicable.

IMAGINABLE

adverbs

scarcely; easily; readily; horribly; illusively; barely; possibly; hardly; dimly; vaguely.

IMAGINARY

adverbs

undoubtedly; probably; highly; possibly; unquestionably; assuredly; vexatiously; pitiably; hypothetically; supposedly; illusively; definitely.

IMAGINATION

adjectives

luxuriant; emotional; proud; copious; splendid; morbid; ardent; vivid; exacting; realizing; kindling; atavistic; inquisitive; teeming; creative; youthful; pure; retired; somber; poetic; sympathetic; rustic; capricious; irreverent; kindly; lively; indolent; veracious; astounding; exuberant; glorious; fertile; constructive; powerful; sanest; diseased; dim; contemporaneous; heated; restless; headlong; respective; fond; sluggish;

cultivated; warm; historic; disorderly; ardent; ribald; popular; foul; cumulative; daring; tensest; fruitful; disordered; morbid; pure; solitary; retired; limitless; salty; fever-driven; agile; plastic; epic; hyperbolical; inventive; apt; quick; gifted; robust; defective; delicate; irrepressible; unconfinable; dire; dark; mortal; heated; distempered; boyish; idealizing; burning; jaded; penetrating; scientific; riotous; melancholic.

verbs

ballast—; capture—; check—; confine—; confound—; curb—; develop—; distort—; drift in—; dull—; enslave—; exercise—; fire—; flow from—; inflame—; infuse into —; kindle—; nurture—; parade before—; pursue in—; revel in—; seize—; spur—; stagger—; stain—; stimulate—; stretch—; tax—; transcend—; breaks loose—; —elucidates; —envisages; —pictures; —recoils; —runs away; —soars; —vaults.

(See conception, image, fancy, fantasy, vision, mind, brain, power.)

IMAGINATIVE

adverbs

highly; wildly; violently; unstably; obviously; creatively; inventively; usefully; inconsistently; untrustworthily; romantically; admirably; wonderfully; remarkably; brilliantly; artistically; extremely; deeply; beautifully; inordinately; fearfully; dangerously.

IMAGINE (v)

adverbs

optimistically; poetically; nobly; vainly; fondly; swiftly; vividly; vaguely; naively; emotionally; morbidly; ardently; capriciously; irreverently; indolently; exuberantly; heatedly; sluggishly; daringly; irrepressibly; scientifically; riotously.

(See dream, suppose, fancy.)

IMAGININGS

adjectives

vain; bilious; untutored; profound; fervid; horrible; chimerical; fertile; mystic; audacious.

IMBECILE

adjectives

financial; inept; vacuous; egregious.

IMBECILITY

adjectives

vehement; congenital; wonted; cheerful; incurable.

verbs

confirm—; contemplate—; contend against —; cure—; curse with—; foster—; lament —; punish—; reduce to—; shelter—; sustain—; verge on—; —confounds; —damages; —endangers; —irks; —itches; —maddens; —provokes.

(See foolishness, feebleness, stupidity.)

IMBED (*v*)

adverbs

deeply; firmly; permanently; snugly; concretely; securely.

(See bury.)

IMDIDE (*v*)

adverbs

copiously; sympathetically; insensibly; generously; freely; liberally; unstintingly.

(See drink, absorb, assimilate.)

IMBIBING

adjectives

generous; profuse; ravenous insatiate.

IMBUE (*v*)

adverbs

thoroughly; deeply; wholesomely; morally; naturally; insidiously; tacitly; psychologically.

(See impress, tinge.)

IMITATE (*v*)

adverbs

ludicrously; successfully; fearlessly; superfluously; inimitably; consciously; effectively; exquisitely; preposterously; authentically; creditably; slavishly; palpably; obviously.

(See impersonate, simulate, copy.)

IMITATION

adjectives

literal; unintentional; corrupt; preposterous; considerable; cunning; sorry; dead; wretched; lifeless; authentic; cheap; mortifying; makeshift; exaggerated; showy; flattering; excellent; creditable; sickly; curious; slavish; miserable; laughable; clumsy; accurate; effective; vociferous; direct; narrative; palpable; elaborate; obvious; apish.

verbs

alter—; condemn—; disguise—; praise—; recognize—; reduce to—; savor of—; — borrows; —defaces; —falters; —feeds on; —injures; —mimics; —models; —ransacks; —resembles; —steals.

(See copy, counterfeit, parody.)

IMITATIVE

adverbs

cleverly; skillfully; brilliantly; adroitly; expertly; unconsciously; deliberately; preposterously; fantastically; cheaply; admiringly; derisively; laughably; accurately; effectively; devotedly; affectionately; extraordinarily; perfectly; apishly; absurdly.

IMITATIVENESS

adjectives

selective; sycophantic; vigilant; wary.

IMITATOR

adjectives

literal; servile; accidental; circumspect.

IMMACULATE

adverbs

usually; perfectly; extraordinarily; completely; admirably; wonderfully; amazingly; utterly; faultlessly; consummately; sprucely; neatly; tidily; daintily; delicately; nattily; beautifully; pleasantly; attractively; wondrously; indescribably; entrancingly.

IMMATERIAL

adverbs

vaguely; definitely; admittedly; palpably; ephemerally; transiently; momentarily; temporarily; wholly.

IMMATURE

adverbs

ridiculously; disgustingly; rosily; appealingly; helplessly; delicately; shyly; absurdly; hopelessly; sweetly; wretchedly; crudely; surprisingly; coarsely; roughly; thoughtlessly; shiftlessly; terribly; unsuitably; unfortunately; preposterously; unbelievably; miserably; painfully; awkwardly; adorably; gawkily; feverishly; obviously; noisily; blithely; inexpressibly; markedly; dully; ingeniously; garrulously; incredibly.

IMMENSITY

adjectives

vast; involved; sublime; actual; unfriendly; unknowable; roofless; increate.

IMMERGE (v)

adverbs
partially; abruptly; wholly; suffocatingly; fatally; protectively; instinctively.
(See plunge, dip.)

IMMERSION

adjectives
continuous; partial; total.

IMMIGRANT

verbs
assimilate—s; awe—; bar—s; check—s; confuse—; distress—; finance—s; limit—s; perplex—; puzzle—; reduce—s; refuse—; shelter—; succor—; —Americanizes; —s crowd to; —lands; —settles.
(See alien, foreigner, stranger.)

adverbs
indiscriminately; transiently; recently; outlandishly; awkwardly; bewilderingly; conspicuously.

IMMIGRATION

adjectives
indiscriminate; limited.

verbs
assimilate—; ban—; check—; control—; curtail—; discourage—; finance—; govern —; harbor—; influence—; limit—; permit —; reduce—; restrict—; stimulate—; —distresses; —fluctuates; —shifts; —slackens.
(See invasion, penetration.)

IMMINENT

adverbs
immediately; terribly; ominously; perilously; dangerously; significantly; portentously; dreadfully; woefully; alarmingly; suddenly; fatally; gloomily; dismally; actually; inevitably; inescapably.

IMMOBILE

adverbs
stiffly; rigidly; curiously; absolutely; oddly; strangely; inexplicably; sternly; severely; altogether; stolidly; implacably; inimically; harshly; stubbornly; stupidly; phlegmatically; skeptically; uncomprehendingly; silently; statically.

IMMOBILITY

adjectives
intelligent; skeptical; perfect; awe-inspiring; deathly; masklike.

IMMODERATE

adverbs
foolishly; fantastically; palpably; wildly; inexcusably; hysterically; woefully; notoriously; inanely; distressingly; grievously; miserably; grossly; astoundingly; singularly; outlandishly; glaringly; fundamentally; naturally; innately; habitually; unfortunately.

IMMODEST

adverbs
dreadfully; inordinately; reprehensibly; wantonly; seductively; alluringly; shamefully; terribly; inexcusably; unpardonably; naturally; always; spitefully; unconsciously; deliberately; thoughtlessly; alarmingly; coarsely; grossly; crassly; brazenly; flagrantly; notoriously; offensively; horribly.

IMMODESTY

verbs
accuse of—; array in—; chasten—; decry—; denounce—.
(See coarseness, obscenity.)

IMMOLATE (v)

adverbs
religiously; selflessly; traditionally; customarily; perfunctorily; cruelly; barbarically.
(See sacrifice.)

IMMOLATION

adjectives
determined; enforced.

IMMORAL

adverbs
grossly; openly; audaciously; daringly; obstinately; insufferably; crassly; flagrantly; heinously; terribly; obviously; extraordinarily; blithely; carelessly; incurably; unwarrantably; iniquitously; criminally; viciously; brazenly; scandalously; infamously; notoriously; sadly; atrociously; brutally; despicably; incorrigibly; malevolently; obdurately.

IMMORALITY

adjectives
coarse; cruel; wanton; flagrant; ugly; blatant; obvious; evident; daring; reprehensible; impenitent; hardened; hopeless; notorious; gross; boundless.

IMMORTAL

adverbs

divinely; gloriously; ineffably; immemorially; sublimely; sacredly; illustriously.

IMMORTALITY

verbs

achieve—; admit—; allege—; assure of—; commune with—; crown with—; deny—; destine to—; dwell in—; earn—; escape to —; flourish in—; rejoice in—; seek—; win —; —degrades; —endures; —exempts.

(See infinity, permanence, stability, sanctity, holiness.)

IMMOVABLE

adverbs

obstinately; stubbornly; altogether; completely; stiffly; firmly; stably, permanently; fixedly; inveterately; indestructibly; quietly; tenaciously; mulishly; inexorably; doggedly; wilfully; inertly; dogmatically; horribly; sternly; harshly; obdurately.

IMMUNE

adverbs

naturally; happily; fortunately; luckily; freely; properly; warrantably; authoritatively; legally; exceptionably; constitutionally; presumptively; duly; legitimately.

IMMUNITY

adjectives

national; glorious; happy; tolerable; various (pl); just; precarious; comparative.

verbs

acquire—; break—; confer—upon; enjoy—; favor with—; grant—; guarantee—; hope for—; induce—; observe—; preserve—; prove—; purchase—; test—; —exempts; —frees; —lasts.

(See exemption, freedom.)

IMMUTABLE

adverbs

divinely; sacredly; naturally; celestially; spiritually; permanently; securely; timelessly; marvelously.

IMP

adjectives

impudent; squabbling; mercurial; sturdy; unmerciful.

IMPACT

adjectives

modulated; joyous; sharp; abrupt; physical.

verbs

calculate—; prepare for—; prevent—; resist —; —communicates; —destroys; —drives; —impresses; —jams; —pinions; —presses; —rends; —resounds; —shatters; —splits; —stamps; —vibrates; —violates; —wedges.

(See collision, force, contact, blow.)

IMPAIR (v)

adverbs

palpably; seriously; disastrously; permanently; superficially; fatally; dangerously; cruelly.

(See ruin, injure, weaken.)

IMPALPABLE

adverbs

evanescently; transitorily; ephemerally; vaporously; nebulously; vexatiously; tormentingly; evasively; intangibly; teasingly; curiously; oddly; alluringly; altogether.

IMPART (v)

adverbs

concisely; confidentially; abundantly; secretly; trustingly; tacitly; freely; uninhibitedly.

(See communicate, give, grant, disclose.)

IMPARTIAL

adverbs

thoroughly; carefully; judicially; meticulously; particularly; admirably; properly; scarcely; cautiously; punctiliously; affectionately; paternally; grudgingly; cleverly; astutely; craftily; sagaciously; wisely; reasonably; prudently; keenly; sharply; shrewdly; perfectly; discreetly; considerately; politically; moderately; faithfully; scrupulously; conscientiously.

IMPARTIALITY

adjectives

editorial; historic; deliberate; absolute; pretended; imperial; known; magnanimous; perfect.

verbs

approve of—; commend—; conduct with—; depart from—; encourage—; favor with—; feign—; judge with—; maintain—; observe —; perform with—; practice—; praise—;

prescribe—; preserve—; profess—; seek—; stamp with—; submit to—; veer from—; witness with—; —assures.

(See fairness, justice, equity.)

IMPASSABLE

adverbs

utterly; completely; undeniably; obviously; clearly; obstinately; desperately; hopelessly; incontrovertibly; admittedly; evidently; manifestly.

IMPASSIONED

adverbs

rapturously; ecstatically; ardently; fervently; feverishly; utterly; sublimely; eloquently; fervidly; amorously; gloriously; vehemently; wildly; fiercely; enthusiastically; fanatically; eagerly; impulsively; impetuously; irrepressibly; excitedly; utterly; violently; foolishly; vainly.

IMPASSIVE

adverbs

stoutly; phlegmatically; stupidly; dully; stolidly; apathetically; neutrally; quietly; serenely; provokingly; resolutely; deliberately; frightfully; alarmingly; dreadfully; ominously; portentously; deaflly; blindly; obtusely; obdurately; languidly; indifferently; uncommonly; deeply; carelessly; callously; imperturbably; maddeningly.

IMPATIENCE

adjectives

intolerable; nervous; polyglot; vehement; thwarted; balked; obvious; angry; insolent; feverish; languishing; demonstrative; rash; surprised; ungovernable; helpless; ill-concealed; unreasonable; singular; restless; filial; enraged; domineering; passionate; ferocious; repressed; uncalculating; rude; burning; subdued; bored; irritating; fidgety.

verbs

betray—; burn with—; calm—; chastise—; crack with—; detect—; dispose toward—; enrage with—; fever with—; prance with —; rage in—; remedy—; sheathe—; spur on by—; struggle with—; warn against—; —amazes; —angers; —grasps; —irritates; —stings; control—.

(See restiveness, restlessness, uneasiness, nervousness.)

IMPATIENT

adverbs

peevishly; fretfully; wildly; violently; vehemently; nervously; unduly; peckishly; vexatiously; surprisingly; inexcusably; incorrigibly; irritatingly; provokingly; feverishly; habitually; always; unpardonably; eagerly; happily; rapturously; childishly; inordinately; extremely; oddly; curiously; strangely; remarkably; unaccountably; inexplicably; unreasonably; disagreeably; unnecessarily.

IMPEACHMENT

adjectives

unfair; soft; withering; amusing.

verbs

acquit of—; anticipate—; carry—; clamor for—; conduct—; demand—; expose to—; justify—; lament—; prevent—; proceed to —; remove by—; suggest—; —disqualifies; —shames; —suspends.

(See accusation, arraignment, trial, arrest.)

IMPECCABLE

adverbs

admittedly; wholly; notoriously; altogether; clearly; exceptionally; consciously; unquestionably; utterly; notoriously; virtuously; incomparably.

IMPECUNIOUS

adverbs

wretchedly; pitiably; admittedly; obviously; terribly; woefully; uneasily; desperately; evidently; manifestly; strangely; curiously; destitutely; distressingly; embarrassingly; alarmingly; hopelessly.

IMPEDE (*v*)

adverbs

unaccountably; tragically; purposely; premeditatedly; totally; partially; mechanically.

(See hinder, obstruct.)

IMPEDIMENT

adjectives

sundry (pl); formidable; sluggish; occasional; visible; unaccountable.

verbs

admit—; bear—; breed —s; brush aside—; correct—; cure—; curse—; hurl aside—; pass—; remove—; resist—; —chains; —constrains; —delays; —disconcerts; —hinders; —irritates; —obstructs; —petrifies; —restrains; —restricts; —strangles; —vexes.

(See obstruction, hindrance, obstacle, difficulty, bar, barrier, encumbrance.)

IMPEL (v)
adverbs
blindly; steadily; simultaneously; instinctively; naturally; normally; sexually; emotionally; subconsciously.

(See drive, urge, incite.)

IMPENETRABLE
adverbs
dimly; darkly; densely; thickly; massively; absolutely; utterly; strangely; mysteriously; altogether; terribly; fearfully; blindly; unaccountably; solidly; pathlessly; inscrutably; hopelessly, defiantly; stubbornly; definitely; manifestly.

IMPERATIVE
adverbs
vitally; essentially; fundamentally; urgently; pressingly; harshly; severely; austerely; arbitrarily; absolutely; legally; tyrannically; strictly; rigidly; uncompromisingly; inexorably; dreadfully; highly.

IMPERCEPTIBLE
adverbs
altogether; definitely; materially; infinitesimally; miserably; comparatively; almost; unaccountably; impalpably; evanescently; nebulously; vaporously; obscurely; fuzzily; curiously; symbolically; inferentially; covertly.

IMPERFECT
adverbs
crassly; grossly; carelessly; obviously; manifestly; inexplicably; disastrously; wretchedly; unsatisfactorily; defectively; sketchily; crudely; disgustingly; annoyingly; inexcusably; hopelessly; unbelievably.

IMPERFECTION
adjectives
hateful; technical; degrading; moral.

verbs
alter—; complain of—; conceal—; criticize —; detect—; expose—; gloat over—; mani-

fest—; note—; observe—; perceive—; remove—; reveal—; view—; x-ray for —s; —blemishes; —mars.

(See deficiency, fault, blemish, defect, flaw, shortcoming.)

IMPERIAL
adverbs
arrogantly; dogmatically; haughtily; regally; magisterially; domineeringly; royally; grandly; splendidly; pompously; proudly; beneficently; dictatorially; generously; cruelly; authoritatively; tyrannically; bossily; fussily; absolutely; supremely; magnificently; boldly.

IMPERIL (v)
adverbs
outrageously; recklessly; foolhardily; gallantly; thoughtlessly; intrepidly, daringly.

(See endanger, risk.)

IMPERIOUS
adverbs
disagreeably; regally; ridiculously; amusingly; tyrannically; arbitrarily; unreasonably; arrogantly; clownishly; airily; shockingly; unwarrantedly; officiously; ludicrously; despotically; hatefully; pompously; inherently; superciliously; loftily; haughtily; proudly; sharply; offensively; naturally; rudely; grossly.

IMPERIOUSNESS
adjectives
mighty; apparent.

IMPERISHABLE
adverbs
gloriously; lustrously; solemnly; splendidly; sublimely; eminently; magnificently; memorably; brilliantly; immutably; unchangeably; forever; grandly; astonishingly; incomparably.

IMPERSONAL
adverbs
coldly; vaguely; ineptly; indifferently; politely; disagreeably; evasively; nonchalantly; casually; frigidly; disinterestedly; vexatiously; unpardonably; horribly; detestably; broadly; sweepingly; generally; arrogantly.

IMPERSONATE (v)

adverbs

inimitably; jocosely; vulgarly; lewdly; dexterously; shrewdly; artfully; histrionically; adequately; fancifully; phlegmatically.

(See represent, assume.)

IMPERSONATION

adjectives

heroic; scattered (pl); inadequate; succeeding; fanciful; phlegmatic.

IMPERTINENCE

adjectives

light; stunning; intrusive; damned; chirping; superb; delicate; female; fond; idiotic; preposterous.

IMPERTINENT

adverbs

grossly; ignorantly; foolishly; senselessly; inanely; unreasonably; disrespectfully; deliberately; crudely; purposely; intentionally; subtly; furtively; openly; flagrantly; defiantly; stupidly; unfortunately; idiotically; preposterously; astoundingly; blithely; outlandishly; crassly; brazenly; blatantly; ostentatiously; rudely; superciliously; saucily; pertly; bumptiously; shamelessly; boisterously; swaggeringly; terribly.

IMPERVIOUS

adverbs

tightly; snugly; callously; securely; satisfactorily; scientifically; hermetically; hopelessly; entirely; utterly; manifestly; reportedly; allegedly; actually; genuinely.

IMPETUOSITY

adjectives

characteristic; jocose; vehement; sinewy; flamboyant; irresistible.

verbs

attack with—; bear—; bridle—; check—; curb—; flame with—; mistrust—; obey—; overcome—; reply with—; repress—; rush into with—; subdue—; suppress—; —blunders; —endangers; —forces; —spurs; —tempts.

(See eagerness, passion, enthusiasm, exuberance, violence.)

IMPETUOUS

adverbs

foolishly; wildly; childishly; rashly; recklessly; thoughtlessly; inconsiderately; uncontrollably; violently; blithely; merrily; happily; precipitately; dangerously; generously; delightfully; enchantingly; engagingly; astonishingly; uncommonly; highly; roughly; boisterously; explosively; stormily; noisily; vivaciously; restlessly; indiscreetly; wantonly; adventurously; dreadfully.

IMPETUS

adjectives

accumulated; momentous; logical; considerable; enormous; great; fresh; intellectual; moral; united; desired.

verbs

acquire—; add—; bridle—; curb—; gather —; mistrust—; receive—; repress—; rush with—; struggle for—; —carries; —destroys; —directs; —forces; —overcomes.

(See momentum, impulse, incentive, stimulus.)

IMPIETY

adjectives

pure; natural; heinous; filial; negative; sacrilegious.

IMPIOUS

adverbs

dreadfully; disrespectfully; reprehensibly; irreverently; scornfully; terribly; scoffingly; deliberately; purposely; insultingly; inordinately; extraordinarily; ostentatiously; unforgivably; offensively; audaciously; frowardly; waywardly; blasphemously; profanely; unspeakably; infamously; astoundingly.

IMPLACABLE

adverbs

hopelessly; terribly; appallingly; shockingly; horribly; inexorably; harshly; sternly; severely; amazingly; suddenly; temperamentally; pitilessly; remorselessly; ruthlessly; cruelly; stolidly; immovably; uncommonly; remarkably; notoriousiy.

IMPLANT (v)

adverbs

deeply; vigorously; insidiously; skillfully; artfully; scientifically; artificially; subconsciously.

(See instill, plant.)

IMPLEMENTS

adjectives

martial; agricultural; trashy; crude; homemade; medicinal; fantastic; facile; ungainly; gainly.

IMPLICATE (v)

adverbs
rashly; vaguely; tacitly; socially; treacherously; shamefully; premeditatively; thoughtlessly; spitefully.
(See involve, entangle.)

IMPLICATION

adjectives
materialistic; covert; historical; moral; practical; far-reaching; small; tacit; social.

verbs
convey—; deny—; detect—; detest—; dodge —; fathom—; involve—; judge—; justify —; lament—; leave to—; pale at—; prove —; —confuses; —disturbs; —entangles; — entwines; —hints; —infers; —irritates; — shocks.
(See suggestion, entanglement, deduction, inference.)

IMPLICIT

adverbs
allusively; inferentially; expressly; subtly; secretly; doctrinally; indirectly; covertly; understandably; carefully; profoundly; cunningly; diplomatically; artfully.

IMPLORE (v)

adverbs
piteously; heartrendingly; beseechingly; plaintively; fruitlessly; ceaselessly; noisily; blatantly; repetitiously.
(See beg, entreat.)

IMPLY (v)

adverbs
obviously; virtually; suggestively; meaningfully; vaguely; slanderously; slyly.
(See signify, infer.)

IMPOLITE

adverbs
unbelievably; subtly; deliberately; ignorantly; crudely; awkwardly; unintentionally; purposely; inexcusably; habitually; always; cruelly; appallingly; shockingly; uncivilly; imprudently; indiscreetly; unfortunately; offensively; distastefully; openly; intentionally; superciliously; arrogantly; boisterously; roughly; noisily; grossly; brazenly; flagrantly.

IMPORT
(meaning)

adjectives
sinister; serious; mystic; peaceful; physiological; enormous; direful; violent; spiritual; immediate; ominous; mysterious; weighty; reliable; hideous.

verbs
bear—; contemplate—; convey—; discern—; doubt—; overlook—; question—; value—; weigh—; —amazes; —baffles; —betokens; —disconcerts; —implies; —indicates; —interests; —involves; —perplexes; —states.
(See meaning, purport, signification, importance, significance.)

IMPORT
(trade)

adjectives
vast; domestic; agricultural; mineral; excisable; dutiable.

IMPORT (v)

adverbs
exclusively; professionally; domestically; agriculturally; annually; legally.

IMPORTANCE

adjectives
paramount; distressing; incalculable; portentous; relative; pressing; subordinate; considerable; direct; practical; outstanding; primary; unworthy; vital; supreme; unspeakable; signal; slight; moral; overwhelming; valetudinarian; genuine; artistic; fictitious; decisive; intrinsic; comparable; rising; overstrained; anticipatory; preeminent; consequent; infinite; tremendous; historic; utmost; overshadowing; trifling; negligible; lingering; transcendent; commercial; strategic; proportionate; significant; requisite; enormous; commanding; vast; honorable; commercial; secondary; endless; profound; glowing; fundamental; grave; vanishing; conspicuous; apparent; absolute; mighty; plenary; immense; major; increasing; exaggerated; sufficient; exceptional; constitutional; far-reaching; perpetual; startling; cultural; infinitesimal; true; evident; ultimate; radical.

verbs
accentuate—; amplify—; assume—; attach —to; belittle—; bolster up—; convey—; detract from—; diminish—; dwarf—; enhance —; exaggerate—; feign—; imbue with—;

manifest—; minimize—; overemphasize—; overestimate—; overrate—; overwhelm with —; puff out with—; rob of—; signify—; stress—; swell with—; underestimate—; underrate—; weigh—of.

(See value, consequence, worth.)

IMPORTANT
adverbs
highly; urgently; gravely; seriously; materially; scarcely; terribly; extraordinarily; mysteriously; secretly; implicitly; unusually; personally; internationally; immeasurably; incalculably; ominously; vitally; genuinely; infinitely; tremendously; historically; commercially; exceptionally; peculiarly; particularly; oddly; astonishingly; profoundly.

IMPORTS
(merchandise)
verbs
blockade—; curtail—; affect—; gain in—; increase—; levy on—; restrict—; stimulate —; tax—; —dwindle; —recede; —wane.

(See merchandise, wares.)

IMPORTUNATE
adverbs
persistently; endlessly; teasingly; provokingly; annoyingly; vexatiously; harrassingly; bothersomely; indiscreetly; incredibly; inappropriately; inconsiderately; inveterately; clamorously; unpleasantly; disagreeably; obnoxiously; piteously; pathetically; dreadfully; uncommonly; highly.

IMPORTUNE (v)
adverbs
shamelessly; rapturously; irritatingly; persistently; pressingly; incessantly; ceaselessly.

(See implore, beg.)

IMPORTUNITIES
adjectives
precluded; trivial; renewed.

IMPORTUNITY
verbs
ease—; endure—; experience—; indulge in —; labor under—; relax—; restrain—; sacrifice to—; satisfy—; suffer—; yield to—; —annoys; —chafes; —clamors; —goads; —irks; —irritates; —pains; —torments; —troubles.

(See insistence, urge, demand.)

IMPOSE (v)
adverbs
inordinately; wilfully; deliberately; tyrannically; disgracefully; legally; tactlessly; selfishly; thoughtlessly.

(See command, enjoin.)

IMPOSING
adverbs
splendidly; brilliantly; tremendously; magnificently; sublimely; incomparably; undeniably; satisfactorily; carefully; sensationally; dramatically; solemnly; remarkably; grandly; nobly; significantly; eminently; signally; immensely; enormously.

IMPOSITION
adjectives
tyrannical; disgraceful; illegal; tearful.

verbs
agree to—; avert—; avoid—; bar—; burden with—; enforce—; escape—; inflict—; levy—; necessitate—; overcome—; pay—; punish with—; refuse—; subject to—; suffer—; suspect—; —irks; —irritates.

(See abuse, tax, oppression, burden.)

IMPOSSIBILITIES
adjectives
wild; apparent; utter; undesired.

IMPOSSIBILITY
verbs
accomplish—; achieve—; admit—; argue—; attempt—; consider—; contemplate—; fret over—; hurdle—; lessen—; master—; overcome with—; remove—; render—; stress—; strip of—; wander in—; —chafes; —torments.

IMPOSSIBLE
adverbs
highly; probably; practically; altogether; presumably; allegedly; obviously; manifestly; evidently; naturally; hopelessly; desperately; wildly; utterly; absurdly.

IMPOSTOR
adjectives
privileged; crafty; latent; artistic; ignorant; vile; wretched.

IMPOTENCE
adjectives
peevish; terrorized; pitiful; glaring; languishing; unstable.

632

verbs

afflict with—; betray—; bewail—; denounce —; expose—; feel—; feign—; grieve over —; incur—; jibe at—; reduce to—; —agonizes; —displeases; —limits; —provokes; —restrains; —shames; —torments.

(See weakness, deficiency, fatigue, inefficiency.)

IMPOVERISHED

adverbs

somewhat; pitiably; ruinously; slightly; altogether; utterly; considerably; hopelessly; helplessly; incredibly; grievously; embarrassingly; distressingly; indigently; terribly; wretchedly; unfortunately; unbelievably; immeasurably.

IMPOVERISHMENT

verbs

conceal—; descend to—; discover—; dread —; endure—; further—; grind to—; inflict —; reduce to—; relieve—; steep in—; suffer —; tax to—; wallow in—; —attends; —distresses; —embitters; —scorches.

(See poverty, distress, need, privation.)

IMPRACTICABLE

adverbs

absurdly; terribly; notionally; absolutely; utterly; foolishly; manifestly; obviously; desperately; hopelessly; formidably; awkwardly; perplexingly; completely.

IMPRECATION

adjectives

dreadful; articulated; profane; elaborate; good-natured; loud; tumultuous; petulant; solemn; unprecedented.

verbs

abuse with—s; blacken with—; blast with —; crush with—; curse with—; fling—at; hurl—at; lash out—; mutter—; perish under —; pour out—; scorn—; shower—; whip with—; wilt under—; —frightens; —outrages; —pains; —stings.

(See oath, curse, denunciation.)

IMPREGNABILITY

verbs

attack—; beat at—; condemn—; defy—; deny—; derive—from; lessen—; overcome —; prove—; threaten—; —assures; —counteracts; —deteriorates; —discourages; —obstructs; —perishes; —represses; —repulses; —resists; —withstands.

(See strength, toughness, tenacity, security.)

IMPRESS (v)

adverbs

deeply; immensely; tremendously; vividly; profoundly; indelibly; forcibly; pitilessly; unduly; disagreeably; strikingly; palpably; vehemently; painfully; emotionally; humorously; solemnly; mysteriously; charmingly; austerely; superficially; fraudulently; spiritually; permanently.

(See affect.)

IMPRESSION

adjectives

vivid; mysterious; external; erroneous; weak; correct; tremendous; optimistic; exchanged (pl); charming; curious; chilling; half-preternatural; hoarse; dual; instantaneous; ineffaceable; misleading; ludicrous; sprawling; artistic; pleasant; immediate; violent; indelible; favorable; austere; cultural; false; lasting; explicable; earliest; subtle; majestic; feeble; deep; imperfect; unanalyzed; current; superficial; dissimilar; severest; half-farcical; painful; ungainly; prominent; suitable; profound; undiscernible; confused; intelligible; surface; repellent; powerful; momentary; unwelcome; mistaken; uneasy; desolate; penetrating; firm; childhood; sensual; journalistic; consequent; perceptible; private; acoustic; lively; dominant; outward; nameless; needful; orderly; illusory; delightful; divine; vague; amusing; ill-founded; fraudulent; faint; obscure; distinct; sincere; irresistible; all-pervading; antecedent; awful; reverent; indefinable; absolute; personal; grotesque; unmistakable; dangerous; maximum; chief; cheerful; undiscernible; spiritual; superstitious; comparative; prevalent; permanent; credulous; scarlike.

verbs

absorb—; analyze—; communicate—; confirm—; convey—; correct—; create—; crystallize—; deepen—; discount—; dissipate—; dull—; efface—; evoke—; formulate—; gain—; give rise to—s; interpret—; jumble —; justify—; record—; reproduce—; sharpen—; soften—; stamp—; strengthen—; sum-

marize—s; sum up—; sustain—; translate
—; verify—; weaken—; —fades; —flickers
out; —persists; —prevails; —seeps in.
   (See effect, result, picture, action, achievement.)

IMPRESSIVE
adverbs
tremendously; splendidly; touchingly; deeply; uncommonly; oddly; incredibly; surprisingly; majestically; royally; powerfully;
profoundly; unmistakably; sincerely; affectingly; overwhelmingly; mysteriously; inexplicably; strangely; subtly; vaguely; immensely.

IMPRINT (v)
adverbs
deeply; indelibly; permanently; artistically;
strongly; professionally; skillfully.
   (See print, stamp, mark.)

IMPRISON (v)
adverbs
temporarily; unjustly; legally; permanently; tyrannically; harshly; perpetually.
   (See confine, restrain.)

IMPRISONMENT
adjectives
ignorant; severe; subsequent; prolonged;
dreary; unjust; tyrannical; perpetual.

verbs
cast into—; condemn to—; confine to—;
doom to—; frown upon—; inflict—; justify
—; lament—; release from—; resort to—;
sentence to—; suffer—; —bridles; —deprives; —deters; —divests; —gags; —
scandalizes.
   (See restriction, prison.)

IMPROBABLE
adverbs
altogether; entirely; curiously; palpably;
highly; wholly; naturally; presumptively.

IMPROMPTU
adverbs
awkwardly; obviously; delightfully; enchantingly; diffidently; undisguisedly; spontaneously; gracefully; altogether; evidently;
warmly; cordially; sincerely; wholly;
charmingly.

IMPROPER
adverbs
shockingly; altogether; terribly; wantonly;
carelessly; insolently; impudently; highly;
inappropriately; offensively; flagrantly; defiantly; obstinately; ignorantly; bumptiously; recklessly; rashly; indiscreetly; imprudently; vexatiously; disagreeably; unpleasantly; wildly; incorrigibly; dreadfully;
subtly; vaguely.

IMPROVE (v)
adverbs
markedly; rapidly; tremendously; suitably;
infinitely; unquestionably; artificially; verbally; gradually; admirably; progressively;
intellectually; definitely.
   (See enhance, gain.)

IMPROVEMENT
adjectives
artificial; needed; pronounced; astonishing;
invariable; substantial; admirable; ecclesiastical; religious; theoretical; decorative;
laudable; salutary; effective; urban; progressive; noteworthy; sensible; revolutionary; eternal; intellectual; sensational; definite; industrious; profitable; corresponding;
outstanding; internal; general; countless;
continual; objective; perceptible; beneficial;
concrete; perpetual; proposed; acoustic;
mutual.

verbs
acclaim—; adopt—; applaud—; campaign
for—; depart for—; evince—; experience—;
institute—; manifest—; mark—; note—; observe—; pioneer—; promote—; push—;
register—; restrict—; retard—; subject to
—; undertake—; venture—; win—; yield—.
   (See reform, recovery.)

IMPROVIDENT
adverbs
lamentably; unfortunately; culpably; hopelessly; incorrigibly; vexatiously; tragically;
unbearably; impossibly; heedlessly; recklessly; rashly; thoughtlessly; inattentively; negligently; arrantly; flagrantly; cruelly; brutally; shiftlessly; injudiciously; wildly; impulsively; senselessly; culpably.

IMPROVISE (v)
adverbs
freely; dexterously; artistically; roughly; crudely; professionally; brilliantly.
   (See extemporize, perform.)

adverbs

hastily; visibly; obviously; cleverly; skillfully; experimentally; oddly; instantly; adroitly; comically; adequately; successfully; impulsively; brilliantly; splendidly; marvellously; crudely; dexterously.

IMPRUDENT

adverbs

incorrigibly; hopelessly; altogether; carelessly; heedlessly; wantonly; strangely; wastefully; defiantly; disagreeably; rashly; recklessly; desperately; wildly; flagrantly; curiously; obstinately; utterly; precariously; indiscreetly; adventurously; dreadfully; astonishingly; uncommonly; highly.

IMPUDENCE

adjectives

overbearing; shameless; brazen; amazing; useless; passable; increasing; unbounded; bland; stupefying; happy; uncommon; magniloquent; interrupting.

IMPUDENT

adverbs

disgustingly; obstinately; stubbornly; stolidly; incurably; incorrigibly; oddly; strangely; curiously; noticeably; visibly; openly; flagrantly; noisily; boisterously; ostentatiously; recklessly; rashly; insolently; snobbishly; arrogantly; hopelessly; offensively; disagreeably; insufferably; heedlessly; wantonly; ignorantly; deliberately; purposely; terribly; astoundingly; surprisingly; habitually; occasionally; always.

IMPULSE

adjectives

peculiar; sudden; abrupt; unconscious; bibulous; burning; mad; perverse; speculative; visionary; violent; admirable; kindly; generous; irresistible; poetical; unintelligent; mutual; wandering; malignant; choice; successive (pl); lively; kinesthetic; changing; mighty; repressed; spontaneous; august; inward; dreadful; confiding; grateful; rash; strong; suspended; dramatic; subtle; pleasurable; lyrical; natural; deepest; simpler; animating; maddening; national; mysterious; creative; popular; simultaneous; senseless; unanimous; intensified; headlong; sonorous; inexplicable; selfsame; involuntary; overmastering; fierce; missionary; repressed; deep-reaching; celestial; morbid; immortal; disturbing; frustrated; blind; vital;

governing; patriotic; analytic; upward; primary; chivalrous; wondrous; initial; common; romantic; instinctive; primitive; powerful; lightning; consecutive; intensifying; restless; motivating; piquant; unreasoning; singular; cordial; original; separate; drunken; obscure; latent; aristocratic; unguarded; indescribable; isochronous; unequaled; unprecedented; boisterous; warm; regular; excitable; westward; varying (pl); recurrent; uncontrollable; mastering; transcendent; catlike; electric; artistic; praiseworthy.

verbs

arouse—; block—; blunt—; choke—; control —; cultivate—; curb—; deaden—; destroy —; direct—; eradicate—; exercise—; exhaust—; follow—; impart—; manifest—; obey—; perform on—; respond to—; restrain—; sense—; sidetrack (colloq.)—; stifle—; subordinate—; suppress—; yield to—; —departs; —overwhelms; —persists; —rends; —sweeps over; —travels.

(See motive, incentive, impetus, ambition, desire.)

IMPULSIVE

adverbs

charmingly; utterly; habitually; temperamentally; innately; obviously; incorrigibly; wildly; enchantingly; alarmingly; extraordinarily; unstably; undependably; unreliably; indescribably; interestingly; dangerously; flightily; lamentably; deplorably; terribly; incredibly; imprudently; indiscreetly; bewitchingly; enthusiastically; irresistibly; heedlessly; adventurously; fanatically.

IMPURE

adverbs

definitely; positively; terribly; unfortunately; lewdly; indelicately; grossly; crassly; brazenly; indecently; foully; immodestly; obscenely; coarsely; lamentably; deplorably; meretriciously.

IMPURITY

verbs

cleanse of—; contaminate with—; defile by —; expel—; fling forth—; free from—; guard against—; inhale—; pollute with—; prevent—; purge of—; rid of—; swarm with—; tempt to—; —corrupts; —s deluge; —detracts from; —enters; —offends; —spreads.

(See dirt, filth, pollution, infection, squalor.)

adjectives
unworthy; injurious; scandalous.

IMPUTE (v)

adverbs
generally; erroneously; fallaciously; lavishly; speciously; injuriously; scandalously; unworthily; slanderously; viciously; vindictively.

(See charge, attribute.)

INABILITY

adjectives
sheer; restless; obvious; consequent; patent.

verbs
accept—; afflict with—; certify as to—; conceal—; dwell on—; judge—; observe—; overcome—; recognize—; regard—; remove —; respect—; —disqualifies; —distresses; —disturbs; —limits; —pains; —restrains; —restricts; —shames.
(See inefficiency, incompetence, helplessness, weakness, impotence, stupidity.)

INACCESSIBLE

adverbs
hopelessly; almost; desperately; altogether; presumably; allegedly; reportedly; remotely; utterly; incredibly; maddeningly; lamentably; preposterously; deplorably; positively; definitely; terribly; incredibly; tragically.

INACCURACY

adjectives
demoniac; unintentional; slight; gross.

verbs
calculate—; conceal—; condemn—; contain —s; correct—; couch in—; criticize—; curse —; deal in—; detect—; observe—; overlook—; plague with—s; prove—; rectify—; suffer—; —astonishes; —overwhelms.
(See error, blunder, mistake, misconception.)

INACCURATE

adverbs
lamentably; unacceptably; definitely; scientifically; mathematically; hopelessly; culpably; criminally; deliberately; slyly; utterly; slightly; fallaciously; mendaciously; purposely; carelessly; incautiously; calculably; positively; craftily; subtly; vaguely; bewil-

deringly; unbelievably; erroneously; accidentally; blunderingly; deceitfully; illusively; nefariously; egregiously.

INACTION

adjectives
unaccustomed; dreadful; silent; fruitless; enforced; inevitable; prolonged.

INACTIVE

adverbs
necessarily; helplessly; tragically; unfortunately; preferably; habitually; naturally; temperamentally; lamentably; unhealthfully; unluckily; lazily; languidly; torpidly; idly; indolently; sleepily; indifferently; lumpishly; passively; unintelligently; terribly; incredibly; hopelessly; undependably; unreliably; unhelpfully; sluggishly; vexatiously; disagreeably; cruelly; selfishly.

INACTIVITY

adjectives
sluggish; hopeless; enforced; protracted.

INADEQUACY

verbs
compensate for—; cure—; curse—; demonstrate—; denounce—; inveigh against—; observe—; overcome—; refer to—; regard—s; suffer from—; —chafes; —distresses; — hampers; —hinders; —limits; —overwhelms; —pains; —plagues; —restrains; —restricts; —tortures; —undermines; — vexes.
(See lack, deficiency, need, deficit.)

INADEQUATE

adverbs
hopelessly; entirely; lamentably; deplorably; miserably; wretchedly; cruelly; bitterly; wholly; utterly; disproportionately; deliberately; incredibly; stingily; criminally; iniquitously; mercilessly; ruthlessly; grievously; pitifully; altogether.

INADMISSABLE

adverbs
legally; socially; conventionally; altogether; definitely; positively; usually; highly; objectionably; inconveniently; unfortunately; unluckily; exceptionally.

INADVERTENT

adverbs
unfortunately; negligently; forgetfully; carelessly; inexcusably; unintentionally; la-

mentably; gracelessly; dreamily; reprehensibly; thoughtlessly; absently; disconcertingly; altogether.

INADVISABLE
adverbs
highly; altogether; utterly; wholly; completely; prudently; commercially; financially; personally; socially; locally; expediently; positively.

INANE
adverbs
fatuously; foolishly; witlessly; utterly; unconscionably; senselessly; hopelessly; vexatiously; curiously; irritatingly; disagreeably; impossibly; tenuously; vaguely; vacuously; thoughtlessly; absently; irrationally; flimsily; contemptibly; uselessly; futilely; oppressively; ridiculously.

INANITY
adjectives
oppressive; mythological; expressional.

INAPPLICABLE
adverbs
hopelessly; entirely; unserviceably; distressingly; ridiculously; wretchedly; outlandishly; discordantly; incongruously; inappropriately; unseasonably; definitely; utterly; disappointingly; vexatiously; ineptly; unfortunately; unluckily.

INAPPROPRIATE
adverbs
distinctly; deplorably; unfortunately; reprehensibly; subtly; dimly; sadly; definitely; indecorously; irreverently; wantonly; terribly; deliberately; unconsciously; tragically; comically; unbecomingly; inaptly; offensively; vexatiously; awkwardly; embarrassingly; highly; exceptionally; objectionably; inconveniently; immeasurably; remarkably; flagrantly; absurdly; ridiculously; wildly; altogether; senselessly; ludicrously; entirely; completely; discordantly; oddly; curiously; hilariously; incongruously; exceptionally; extremely; distressingly; dreadfully.

INARTICULATE
adverbs
unfortunately; diffidently; shyly; awkwardly; timidly; gruffly; ridiculously; ludicrously; extremely; taciturnly; heavily; stammeringly; tremulously; stiffly; gawkishly; sil-

ently; laconically; curtly; reticently; reservedly; gravely; bewilderingly; strangely; unwisely.

INARTISTIC
adverbs
grossly; crudely; childishly; amazingly; remarkably; strangely; unbelievably; painfully; cruelly; loudly; garishly; tawdrily; cheaply; blatantly; forbiddingly; shapelessly; crookedly; gracelessly; stiffly; awkwardly; clumsily; hideously; frightfully; horribly; shockingly; gaudily.

INATTENTION
adjectives
sheer; consequent; impolite; trivial.

INATTENTIVE
adverbs
rudely; disagreeably; visibly; obviously; significantly; dreamily; drowsily; remarkably; heedlessly; mindlessly; impolitely; insolently; arrogantly; superciliously; scornfully; learnedly; impertinently; openly; distractedly; vacantly; absently; vacuously; negligently; vexatiously; defiantly; provokingly; extremely.

INAUDIBLE
adverbs
almost; unfortunately; miraculously; pleasantly; intentionally; deliberately; painfully; distressingly; irritatingly; provokingly; disappointingly; unnecessarily; carelessly, mumblingly; confusedly; faintly.

INAUGURATE (*v*)
adverbs
ceremoniously; jubilantly; ostentatiously; enthusiastically; triumphantly; festively.
(See install, begin.)

INAUSPICIOUS
adverbs
deplorably; direly; dreadfully; grievously; ominously; portentously; lamentably; pitifully; signally; woefully; wretchedly; miserably; oppressively; sadly; curiously; definitely; desperately; extremely.

INCANTATION
verbs
bewitch with—; chant—; charm with—; defy—; moan—; mouth—; mutter—; mumble—; pour forth—; practise—; ridicule—;

whisper—; —amuses; —beseeches; —cures; —enchants; —exorcises; —summons; recite —.

(See song, magic, sound, melody, tune, air, harmony, ballad, poem.)

INCAPABLE

adverbs

helplessly; desperately; pitiably; languidly; ineptly; stupidly; grossly; arrantly; carelessly; terribly; provokingly; woefully; utterly; extremely; obviously; embarrassingly; miserably; wretchedly; unserviceably; hopelessly; clumsily; doltishly; vapidly; obtusely; deliberately; feignedly; undisguisedly; frankly.

INCAPACITY

adjectives

permanent; social; innate; ruinous; witless; confessed.

INCARNATION

adjectives

blameless; critical; astonishing; previous; distributive.

INCAUTIOUS

adverbs

definitely; undoubtedly; wildly; vexatiously; alarmingly; perilously; tragically; dangerously; terribly; recklessly; rashly; absurdly; unreasoningly; irresponsibly; unwittingly; doltishly; stupidly; foolishly; senselessly; amazingly; witlessly; youthfully; unpardonably.

INCENSE

adjectives

grateful; lavish; mystic; rare; impatient; delicate; hoarded; perpetual; dreadful; hallowed; stale.

verbs

bear—; breathe—; offer—; pray with—; scatter—; scent with—; suffuse with—; — ascends; —clouds; —curbs; —fumigates; — mists; —perfumes; —permeates; —pervades; —rises; —rolls; —smokes; —sweetens.

(See perfume, breath, fragrance, odor, aroma, spice, flowers.)

INCENTIVE

adjectives

noblest; renewed; conceivable; external; powerful; perpetual; high; especial.

verbs

arouse—; crush—; design as—; restore—; smother—; —beckons; —encourages; —excites; —induces; —inflames; —influences; —inspires; —prevails; —provokes; — springs from; —spurs; —stirs; —sways.

(See ambition, motive, inducement, provocation, influence, inspiration.)

INCESSANT

adverbs

intolerably; unbearably; mysteriously; garrulously; needlessly; maddeningly; vexatiously; curiously; oddly; incredibly; torturously; tormentingly; painfully; agonizingly; plaguedly; infernally; peculiarly; crazily.

INCH

adjectives

furthest; shuddering; single; available; proverbial; last.

INCIDENT

adjectives

tragic; astonishing; romantic; fictitious; cheery; comic; marvelous; simultaneous; moving; thrilling; well-connected; pleasing; dramatic; principal; ludicrous; trifling; amusing; terrifying; noteworthy; curious; related; significant; humorous; minutest; absurd; disturbing; long-forgotten; developing; ignoble; cruel; well-invented; chief; burlesque; dreadful; historic; picturesque; maddening; outstanding; shameful; illustrative; fruitful; illuminating; creditable; affecting; noticeable; distorted; unimportant; stirring; weird; dramatic; unrelated; spectacular; poetic; expected; traumatic; petty; noble; innocent; nonsensical; absurd; frightful; monotonous.

verbs

ascribe—to; climax—; compile—s; devise—; found on—; illustrate—; lead up to—; misinterpret—; narrate—; record—; relate—; shudder at—; vivify—; —demonstrates; — exasperates; —exposes; —occurs; —reveals.

(See event, circumstance, occurrence, episode.)

INCIPIENT

adverbs

mildly; indeterminately; fortunately; apparently; obviously; definitely; luckily; manifestly.

INCISION

adjectives

deep; unauthorized; curving; external.

INCISIVE

adverbs

clearly; sharply; acrimoniously; maliciously; sarcastically; cruelly; bitterly; scornfully; inquisitively; strangely; remarkably; quickly; painfully; terribly; needlessly; harshly; severely; sternly; questioningly; gruffly; intensely; acutely; caustically; vigorously; impressively; autocratically; magisterially; piercingly; poignantly; fanatically.

INCITE (v)

adverbs

deliberately; treacherously; spitefully; vindictively; artfully; slyly; dangerously; perversely; intentionally; maddeningly; passionately; violently; overwhelmingly; excessively.

(See stimulate, arouse.)

INCLEMENT

adverbs

stormily; disastrously; severely; harshly; roughly; forbiddingly; incredibly; remarkably; surprisingly; unexpectedly; unnecessarily; unreasonably; injudiciously; needlessly; frigidly; bitterly; keenly; coldly; austerely; relentlessly; arbitrarily; tyrannically; cruelly; mercilessly.

INCLINATION

adjectives

undue; irresistible; religious; conspicuous; matrimonial; sensual; jaunty; treacherous; particular; respectful; haughty; profound; courteous; natural; mutual.

verbs

acquire—; beget—; endow with—; evince —; follow—; gratify—; obviate—; oppose —; repress—; restrain—; sharpen—; smother—; stifle—; stimulate—; suppress—.

(See desire, tendency, propensity, aim.)

INCLINE

adjectives

wicked; slow; stony; flinty.

INCLINE (v)

adverbs

significantly; beneficently; unconsciously; tolerantly; favorably; seriously; piously; respectfully; benevolently; philosophically; naturally; diversely; subconsciously; affectionately; viciously; peaceably; wickedly.

(See slope, lean.)

INCLOSE (v)

adverbs

completely; darkly; securely; snugly; safely; oppressively; mechanically; thoroughly; lovingly.

(See surround, circumscribe.)

INCLOSURE

adjectives

delicious; little; dark; circular; large; grassy; mosque; square; walled; utilitarian.

INCLUDE (v)

adverbs

ultimately; parenthetically; implicitly; fundamentally; specifically.

(See comprehend, inclose.)

INCLUSIVE

adverbs

broadly; generally; promiscuously; indiscriminately; democratically; comprehensively; pleasantly; agreeably; satisfactorily; sufficiently; astonishingly; diplomatically; courteously.

INCOHERENCE

adjectives

colossal; maddening; affectionate; intentional.

INCOHERENT

adverbs

stammeringly; inarticulately; timidly; nervously; hysterically; wildly; feverishly; tragically; chokingly; sobbingly; sorrowfully; sadly; eagerly; enthusiastically; excitedly; frantically; frenziedly; fanatically; insanely; screamingly; bewilderingly; hopelessly; perplexingly; extremely; helplessly; strangely.

INCOME

adjectives

slender; living; taxable; ample; modest; lowered; comfortable; net; retirement; moderate; steady; gratifying; definite; diminished; precarious; subsequent; substantial; national; slim; meager; inadequate; unimpaired; dependable; prosperity; nice; splendid; profitable; cash; good; daily.

verbs

aid—; augment—; budget—; control—; curb—; curtail—; derive — from; devastate—; diminish—; divert from—; expand —; fritter away—; glean—; invest—; reduce—; stabilize—; tax—; —fluctuates; —oscillates; —rises; —wanes.

(See profits, revenue, proceeds, salary, wages.)

INCOMPATIBLE

adverbs

frankly; hopelessly; admittedly; evidently; manifestly; innately; temperamentally; unusually; admittedly; unfortunately; unluckily; violently; sadly; bitterly; acutely; stupidly; signally; remarkably; irreconcilably; openly; strangely; dreadfully; irremediably; highly.

INCOMPETENCE

verbs

cure—; decry—; denounce—; diminish—; display—; eliminate—; exclude—; maim with—; object to—; overcome—; remedy—; remove—; —arises; —corrupts; —cramps; —cripples; —hampers; —hinders; —prevails; —unnerves; —weakens.

(See inefficiency, inability, stupidity, dullness, carelessness.)

INCOMPETENT

adverbs

incredibly; hopelessly; irremediably; idly; lazily; stupidly; doltishly; immeasurably; unfortunately; ignorantly; frankly; surprisingly; unexpectedly; unmitigably; maddeningly; provokingly; presumably; allegedly; possibly; utterly; amazingly; terribly; uncommonly.

INCOMPREHENSIBLE

adverbs

incoherently; unreasonably; unnecessarily; unusually; highly; evasively; delusively; deliberately; utterly; vexatiously; perplexingly; inscrutably; mysteriously; symbolically; provokingly; unaccountably; curiously; uncomfortably; cryptically; embarrassingly.

INCONGRUITIES

adjectives

careless; apparent; pitiful; inexplicable; curious.

INCONGRUITY

verbs

abolish—; commit—; detect—; perceive—; rectify—; sense—; smile at—; utter—; —arises; —denotes; —fouls; —glares; —inconveniences; —interferes; —intrudes.

(See discord, sin, wrong, discrepancy, error, mistake.)

INCONGRUOUS

adverbs

ridiculously; fantastically; utterly; grotesquely; painfully; awkwardly; embarrassingly; completely; strangely; oddly; curiously; crudely; pitifully; inexplicably; mysteriously; unpleasantly; unhappily; unreasonably; flimsily; discordantly; inharmoniously; inartistically; noticeably; terribly; highly.

INCONSEQUENTIAL

adverbs

foolishly; utterly; senselessly; inanely; manifestly; legally; quite; evasively; trivially; absurdly; ridiculously; wretchedly; quibblingly; illusively; speciously; inordinately; unusually; obviously.

INCONSIDERABLE

adverbs

altogether; modestly; miserably; comparatively; practically; pitiably.

INCONSIDERATE

adverbs

thoughtlessly; selfishly; cruelly; crassly; constantly; harshly; surprisingly; terribly; pitiably; wretchedly; miserably; ignorantly; carelessly; hideously; bitterly; inexcusably; unpardonably; grossly; flagrantly; noticeably; notoriously; naturally; characteristically; utterly; uncharitably; inadvertently; heedlessly; rashly; recklessly; ruthlessly; impulsively; impetuously.

INCONSISTENCY

adjectives

curious; astounding; allowable; charming; political; apparent; innocent; uncommon; feminine.

verbs

accuse of—; argue—; charge—; despise—; display—; exhibit—; frown on—; imply—; observe—; practise—; prove—; unfold—; wonder at—; —confounds; —contradicts; —distresses; —irks; —perplexes; —vexes.

(See discord, stupidity.)

INCONSISTENT

adverbs

unfortunately; manifestly; carelessly; heedlessly; illogically; indiscreetly; dangerously; embarrassingly; politically; expediently; habitually; strangely; ridiculously; annoyingly; provokingly; perilously; horribly; fantastically; utterly; highly; uncommonly; provokingly; unreliably; unstably; impulsively; vaguely; preposterously; egregiously; stupidly; blatantly; injudiciously; astoundingly.

INCONSOLABLE

adverbs

bitterly; miserably; utterly; sadly; mournfully; desolately; uncommonly; manifestly; evidently; unhappily; hopelessly; dismally; lamentably; dreadfully; drearily; ruefully; disconsolately; forlornly; desperately; pitiably; pathetically; hysterically; tragically.

INCONSPICUOUS

adverbs

timidly; diffidently; shyly; busily; usually; habitually; preferably; naturally; deliberately; vaguely; quietly; obscurely; discreetly; wisely; modestly; unassumingly; unaffectedly; meekly; sweetly; gracefully; serenely; contentedly.

INCONSTANT

adverbs

notoriously; flagrantly; blithely; recklessly; ruthlessly; pitilessly; carelessly; reprehensibly; obviously; curiously; habitually; temperamentally; highly; egregiously; inordinately; unfortunately; unstably; unreliably; dreadfully; gaily; restlessly; erratically; capriciously; waywardly; incorrigibly.

INCONVENIENCE

adjectives

least; possible; accidental; immediate: unnecessary; mutual; supposed.

verbs

abuse with—; avert—; bemoan—; hurdle—; ignore—; lead to—; observe—; rectify—; remedy—; spare—; submit to—; suffer—; —arises; —interferes; —torments.

(See disadvantage, drawback, handicap, trouble, misfortune.)

INCONVENIENT

adverbs

highly; seriously; embarrassingly; provokingly; irritatingly; utterly; troublesomely; awkwardly; unseasonably; financially; expensively; inconsiderately; extremely; unmanageably; terribly; curiously; hideously.

INCORRECT

adverbs

shamefully; carelessly; unfortunately; incautiously; idly; viciously; deliberately; intentionally; evasively; mendaciously; criminally; unaccountably; inexcusably; foolishly; inconsistently; speciously; troublesomely; hopelessly; wretchedly; intentionally; erroneously; fallaciously; obviously; manifestly; deceitfully; infamously; cruelly; indefensibly.

INCORRIGIBLE

adverbs

presumably; altogether; utterly; deplorably; manifestly; evidently; allegedly; notoriously; tragically; wretchedly; stubbornly; obdurately; mulishly; perversely; waywardly; obstinately; hopelessly; terribly; viciously; impenitently; gracelessly; heartbreakingly; unspeakably; portentously.

INCREASE

adjectives

corresponding; apparent; abnormal; ultimate; prodigious; anticipated; rational; periodical; sporadic; inevitable; goodly; relative; imperceptible; unprecedented; unexampled; happy; subsequent; sharp; considerable; marked; progressive; definite; commensurate; concomitant; enormous.

verbs

anticipate—; calculate—; check—; cite—; compute—; decree—; derive — from; entitle to—; estimate—; occasion—; order—; promote—; rejoice in—; reward with—; stimulate—; urge—; welcome—; yield—; — cheers; —enthuses (colloq.).

(See addition, expansion, growth, reward.)

INCREASE (v)

adverbs

materially; alarmingly; acutely; enormously; perseveringly; notably; perceptibly; grotesquely; grossly; enormously; noticeably; infinitely; relentlessly; boundlessly; perpetually; proportionably; stupendously; manifestly; abnormally; rationally; sporadically; commensurately; concomitantly.

(See multiply, enlarge, extend.)

INCREDULITY

adjectives

concealed; total; impertinent; angry; pathetic; complete; petulant; polite.

verbs

arouse—; convert to—; display—; dispose to —; expose to—; ignore—; incur —; indicate —; prompt—; receive with—; remove—; study with—; —distresses; —irks; —robs; —vexes.

(See amazement, disbelief, distrust, confusion, surprise, perplexity, wonder.)

INCREDULOUS

adverbs

blindly; youthfully; suspiciously; openly; distrustfully; skeptically; doubtfully; frankly; laughingly; amusedly; teasingly; blasphemously; scoffingly; gracelessly; impolitely; rudely; ignorantly; totally; impertinently; angrily; pathetically; comically; politely; petulantly.

INCREMENT

adjectives

unearned; substantial; annual.

INCRIMINATING

adverbs

definitely; positively; manifestly; unquestionably; incontrovertibly; unfortunately; unexpectedly; unanswerably; tragically; implicitly; gravely; seriously; dangerously; alarmingly; ominously; dreadfully; inescapably; profoundly; momentously.

INCULCATE (v)

adverbs

weightily; firmly; vigorously; forcefully; unforgettably; vividly; skilfully; academically.

(See implant, impress.)

INCUR (v)

adverbs

legitimately; thoughtlessly; indulgently; lamentably; excessively; superfluously.

(See assume, accept.)

INCURABLE

adverbs

definitely; positively; grievously; altogether; presumably; supposedly; allegedly; hitherto; lamentably; deplorably; tragically; pur-

portedly; wretchedly; unhappily; unfortunately; hopelessly; essentially; normally; usually; fundamentally; unluckily.

INCURSIONS

adjectives

dangerous; nocturnal; savage; hostile.

INLEBTED

adverbs

deeply; insolvently; embarrassingly; seriously; hopelessly; helplessly; gravely; heavily; slightly; pleasantly; increasingly; everlastingly; enormously; tremendously; unbelievably; gratefully; thankfully; personally; profoundly; inextricably.

INDECENT

adverbs

horribly; slightly; tremendously; altogether; somewhat; utterly; flagrantly; boisterously; carelessly; recklessly; viciously; offensively; shamelessly; broadly; grossly; publicly; unbelievably; inexcusably; inexpressibly; culpably; vilely; villainously; grossly; outrageously; basely; insufferably; criminally; perniciously; nefariously; heinously.

INDECIPHERABLE

adverbs

strangely; exotically; mysteriously; altogether; almost; evidently; deliberately; purposely; unfortunately; horribly; oddly; outlandishly; hopelessly; dimly; faintly; presumably; supposedly; sadly; provokingly; bewilderingly; perplexingly; disconcertingly; maddeningly; vexatiously; disappointingly; unaccountably; inscrutably; enigmatically; fantastically.

INDECISION

adjectives

ludicrous; chronic; momentary; fatal; gentlemanlike; habitual; costly; temporary; customary.

INDECISIVE

adverbs

evasively; waveringly; hesitantly; timorously; feebly; weakly; timidly; provokingly; maddeningly; abjectly; habitually; always; uncertainly; perplexingly; bewilderedly; irresolutely; variably; capriciously; unstably; mercurially; fitfully; unreliably; strangely; curiously; unaccountably; inexplicably; unpleasantly; disagreeably; indolently.

INDECOROUS

adverbs

unintentionally; flagrantly; rashly; impudently; irreverently; outlandishly; outrageously; deliberately; fantastically; disagreeably; unpleasantly; unacceptably; boorishly; crassly; grossly; rudely; stupidly; coarsely; impolitely; discourteously; habitually; intentionally; gracelessly; awkwardly; terribly; oddly; strangely.

INDEFATIGABLE

adverbs

sturdily; stoutly; robustly; apparently; evidently; manifestly; inordinately; surprisingly; astoundingly; astonishingly; unexpectedly; marvellously; almost; pluckily; indomitably; manfully; actively; zealously; nimbly; strenuously; resolutely; busily; restlessly; amazingly; marvellously; miraculously; unbelievably.

INDEFINITE

adverbs

exasperatingly; politically; sagaciously; evasively; delusively; craftily; maddeningly; bewilderingly; perplexingly; preposterously; crudely; cruelly; bitterly; weakly; timorously; viciously; vaguely; deliberately; vexatiously; embarrassingly; foggily; casually; mysteriously; obscurely; enigmatically; distressingly; inordinately; inscrutably; terribly; highly.

INDELICATE

adverbs

conspicuously; gracelessly; shamefully; immodestly; grossly; rudely; wantonly; improperly; openly; defiantly; boorishly; intrusively; coarsely; indecorously; unsympathetically; obtusely; impertinently; unbecomingly; loudly; boisterously; obscenely; foully; viciously; villainously; flauntingly; flagrantly; terribly; inexcusably; incorrigibly; unbelievably.

INDEPENDENCE

adjectives

sturdy; industrial; patrimonial; constitutional; proud; aggressive; inexorable; supreme; cherished; characteristic; fearless; modest; virtual; personal; mental; extraordinary; immediate; daring; lofty; rough; uncouth; insolent; wrathful; virtual; unsurpassed; leisurely; saucy; harmonic; masterful; inflexible.

verbs

afford—; assert—; assume—; boast—; breed—; cherish—; defend—; encroach on —; enjoy—; favor—; inspire—; maintain —; preserve—; prize—; quell—; relish—; respect—; restore—; revel in—; safeguard —; share—; strive for—; suppress—; taste —; undermine—; —increases; —irritates.

(See strength, freedom, liberty, privilege, power, security, individuality.)

INDEPENDENT

adverbs

immeasurably; delightfully; selfishly; resolutely; manfully; openly; arrogantly; rightfully; freely; happily; boldly; courageously; tenaciously; fortunately; luckily; nationally; fearlessly; intrepidly; extraordinarily; inordinately; miraculously; unbelievably; marvellously; affluently; comfortably; absolutely; entirely.

INDEX

adjectives

refractive; flattering; classified; elaborate; cephalic; prosaic; analytical; unusable; helpful.

INDIAN

adjectives

bronze-skinned; wily; athletic; dark-looking; garrulous; stealthy; keen-sighted; cigar-store.

verbs

govern —s; overcome —s; tutor —s; — dances; —fishes; —s flourish; —hunts; —s maraud; —s pillage; —s plunder; —s roam; —scalps; —shrieks; —slays; —squats; — trails; —vanishes; —s war; —whoops.

(See savage, native, barbarian.)

INDICATE (*v*)

adverbs

fairly; specifically; definitely; broadly; irresistibly; unmistakably; forcibly; conclusively; accurately; vaguely; tersely; vividly.

(See designate, signify.)

INDICATION

adjectives

suspicious; surface; perceptible; powerful; vouchsafed; definite; convincing; genuine; obvious; smiling; picturesque; cold; peculiar; sufficient; unmistakable; syntactic; conjectural.

verbs

afford—; await—; derive — from; exaggerate—; follow—; forsake—; heed—; measure —; neglect—; note—; observe—; reduce—; respect—; —denotes; —enlightens; —hints; —implies; —misleads; —promises; —signifies.

(See evidence, symptom, sign, manifestation.)

INDICTMENT

adjectives

extraordinary; blistering; quashed.

verbs

advocate—; demand—; dismiss—; draw up —; endorse—; ignore—; justify—; launch into—; oppose—; plead—; present—; propose—; protest—; quash—; suffer—; suspend—; upset—; witness—; —engrosses; — shames.

(See accusation, charge.)

INDIFFERENCE

adjectives

polished; apparent; entire; lordly; chilling; nodding; forced; Olympian; dreadful; blind-walled; perfect; suicidal; semi-barbarized; luxurious; exquisite; moral; complete; purposeless; immense; lofty; offhand; careless; calm; public; artless; gallant; simulated; nonchalant; discouraging; utter; singular; profound; stolid; drunken; lethargic; negligent; gloomy; cold-blooded; passive; hardened; stony; supreme; evident; listless; curious; delightful; disdainful; callous; unteachable; reckless; criminal; affected; studied; proud; political; wandering; cynical; mere; uncomfortable; affable; heartbreaking.

verbs

attain—; bare to—; buttress with—; case in —; commend—; cultivate—; cure of—; ice with—; feign—; lure by—; maintain—; mourn—; profess—; regard with—; shed—; signify—; slight by—; —chills; —depresses; —dulls; —torments.

(See apathy, carelessness, impartiality.)

INDIFFERENT

adverbs

dully; stupidly; strangely; stolidly; apathetically; vacantly; ridiculously; singularly; oddly; peculiarly; curiously; unaccountably;

irritatingly; vexatiously; shockingly; callously; coldly; carelessly; hopelessly; unpardonably; inexplicably.

INDIGENT

adverbs

pitiably; constantly; seriously; tragically; pathetically; needlessly; shiftlessly; lazily; idly; impecuniously; miserably; wretchedly; helplessly; hopelessly; strangely; mysteriously; unaccountably; unwarrantably; incomprehensibly.

INDIGESTION

verbs

anticipate—; develop—; dose for—; fume with—; induce—; palliate—; reap—; seize with—; sow—; suffer from—; —agonizes; —attacks; —crucifies; —indisposes; —tortures; —vanishes; —wracks.

(See sickness, disease, pain.)

INDIGNANT

adverbs

horribly; wildly; violently; mildly; justly; righteously; deeply; loudly; boisterously; drunkenly; foolishly; profoundly; justifiably; dangerously; properly; silently; alarmingly; furiously; resentfully; inordinately; absurdly; foolishly; needlessly; unaccountably; unusually; unwarrantably; unappeasably; implacably; sternly; harshly; stonily; irrecoverably; vengefully; bitterly; sorely; sadly; grievously.

INDIGNATION

adjectives

virtuous; unrelaxed; unmitigable; righteous; mollified; noble; repressed; rising; natural; speechless; furious; pent-up; tempered; sincere; loyal; moral; capacious; overwhelming; expressive; popular; utmost; hearty; tumultuous; superb; becoming; impotent; uncommon; foaming; dignified; satirical; passionate; warm; astonished; violent; cruel; fiery.

verbs

blow up in—; burn with—; curb—; dread —; embitter by—; experience—; heap— upon; incense with—; move to—; mantle—; overflow with—; pour out—; quench—; restrain—; rock with—; rouse—; scorn—;

shock into—; shriek—; snort with—; swell with—; vent—; —blinds; —effervesces; — glows; —mounts; —waxes.

(See anger, violence, contempt, fury, rage, wrath, resentment, passion.)

INDIGNITY

adjectives

excessive; various (pl); supposed; glaring; sensible; amusing; intolerable; harsh; fresh; egregious.

verbs

ignore—; nurse—; persecute with—s; prompt—; punish—; restrain—; revenge—; subject to—; submit to—; suffer—; —aggravates; —heats; —inflames; —kindles; — riles (colloq.); —stings; —vexes; —nettles.

(See insult, injury, offense, outrage, contempt.)

INDIRECT

adverbs

perplexingly; disturbingly; distressingly; intricately; needlessly; absurdly; circumbendibusly; deliberately; evasively; irritatingly; atrociously; maliciously; unhappily; unnecessarily; circuitously; craftily; nefariously; artfully; adroitly; astutely; outrageously; outlandishly; insidiously; shiftily; ingeniously.

INDISCREET

adverbs

amazingly; gravely; dreadfully; dangerously; compromisingly; thoughtlessly; heedlessly; carelessly; youthfully; awkwardly; unsophisticatedly; unconsciously; rashly; recklessly; imprudently; innocently; harmlessly; impulsively; stupidly; incomprehensibly; surprisingly; egregiously; idiotically; senselessly; ridiculously; madly; unbelievably; strangely; curiously; inexpressibly.

INDISCRETION

adjectives

manifest; culpable; racy; childish; abominable; lamentable.

verbs

abandon—; absolve from—; assail—; commit—; conceal—; conduct with—; curb—; curtail—; mar by—; mute—; rationalize—;

repent—; soil with—; suffer for—; —reflects; —scandalizes; —shames; —tempts.

(See error, mistake, recklessness, foolishness, act.)

INDISPENSABLE

adverbs

vitally; fundamentally; essentially; presumably; supposedly; allegedly; purportedly; curiously; oddly; strangely; utterly; emphatically; imperatively; unquestionably; absolutely.

INDISPOSITION

adjectives

casual; slight; physical.

verbs

aggravate—; correct—; detain by—; evince —; increase—; induce—; irritate—; recover from—; rectify—; sweeten—; —confines; —deters; —hampers; —hinders; — interrupts; —repels; —restricts; —tantalizes; —vexes.

(See reluctance, unwillingness, aversion, illness.)

INDISPUTABLE

adverbs

curiously; altogether; legally; officially; authoritatively; evidently; palpably; manifestly; oddly; mysteriously; professedly; scientifically; mathematically; technically; strangely; incomprehensibly; positively; absolutely; truly.

INDISTINCT

adverbs

curiously; unfortunately; deliberately; intentionally; inaudibly; purposely; bewilderingly; confusedly; chaotically; dimly; faintly; remotely; vexatiously; unsatisfactorily; unacceptably; fantastically; miserably; wretchedly; lamentably; grievously; deplorably; disagreeably; unexpectedly; mysteriously; carelessly; obscurely; vaguely; sadly.

INDIVIDUAL

adjectives

happy-looking; erratic; numerable; jocular; distinguished; determinate; obscure; coatless; dismal; intelligent; unchanged; transfigured; progressive; independent; self-centered; disciplined; tattered; troublesome; reasonable; bellicose; enfeebled; conservative; irresponsible; thinking; noxious; adventurous; acquisitive; privileged; enthusiastic; laborious; intoxicated; gifted; uncommon; dignified; arrogant; vanishing; unworthy; ill-conducted; beef-faced; unlucky; scant-haired; hardy; amoral; fearless; quiet-spoken; remarkable; enterprising; under-slung; myriad (pl); peculiar; famed; delightful; relaxed, maladjusted; hesitant; harmonious; unprepared; unhappy; perverse.

verbs
bequeath to—; characterize—; depend on—; direct to—; dwarf—; ignore—; incense—; insulate—; intrude on—; isolate—; mold—; shape—; support—; —achieves; —strives.
   (See person, being.)

INDIVIDUALISM
adjectives
rugged; blind; intense; excessive; pioneering; exaggerated; ruinous; obtrusive.

INDIVIDUALITY
adjectives
separate; abstract; persistent; piquant; genuine; characteristic; pronounced; intense; well-equipped; powerful; indolent; decided; magnetic; distinct.

verbs
assert—; cherish—; contrive—; crush—; desert—; distinguish by—; divest of—; efface—; enlarge—; impart—; inspire—; justify—; lose—; maintain—; mold—; preserve—; reflect—; respect—; retain—; sacrifice—; season with—; shield—; submerge —; sustain—; throttle—.
   (See personality, independence, strength, freedom, liberty, power, security.)

INDOLENCE
adjectives
lifeless; alternate; listless; habitual; regal; dreamy; inert; bland; easy; lackadaisical.

verbs
avoid—; banish—; bask in—; breed—; deplore—; dispose to—; overcome—; pillow in —; reproach—; revel in—; shake off—; stagnate in—; stretch in—; strangle by—; wallow in—; waste in—; —demoralizes; — destroys; —ensnares; —rusts.
   (See idleness, apathy, lethargy, procrastination.)

INDOLENT
adverbs
lackadaisically; delightfully; abominably; atrociously; comfortably; drowsily; lazily; deplorably; meretriciously; inexcusably; inherently; constitutionally; obstinately; gaily; blithely; contentedly; immovably; slothfully; feebly; wisely; vexatiously; maddeningly; restfully; peaceably; peevishly; quietly; serenely; brilliantly; mentally; unpardonably; unforgivably; selfishly; heavily; torpidly; stubbornly; inconsiderately; amazingly; thoughtlessly.

INDOMITABLE
adverbs
sturdily; resolutely; determinedly; surprisingly; unexpectedly; marvelously; invincibly; vigorously; staunchly; stubbornly; heroically; gallantly; bravely; boldly; courageously; habitually; hardily; irresistibly.

INDORSE (v)
adverbs
enthusiastically; unwittingly; unsuspectingly; legitimately; laconically.
   (See attest, approve, confirm.)

INDORSEMENT
adjectives
peremptory; terse; enthusiastic; ill-natured; laconic; premature.

verbs
authorize—; carry—; examine—; necessitate—; note—; pen—; question—; refuse—; require—; respect—; seek—; sign—; transfer by—; witness—; —confirms; —sanctions.
   (See approval, sanction, ratification.)

INDUCE (v)
adverbs
automatically; involuntarily; effectively; strongly; fawningly; cleverly; slyly; immorally; patiently.
   (See influence, persuade, urge.)

INDUCEMENTS
adjectives
soul-sustaining; flattering; principal.

adverbs
coin—; contrive—; decline—; frame—; hold out—; ignore—; offer—; repeat—; —

determines; —influences; —motivates; —persuades; —procures; —sways; —urges.

(See incentive, motive, stimulus, provocation.)

INDUCTIONS
adjectives
absolute; reflective; subsequent; logical; dangerous.

INDULGE (*v*)
adverbs
excessively; fallaciously; incontinently; unscrupulously; moderately; incessantly; passionately; heartily; luxuriantly; habitually; viciously; sensually; immorally.

(See gratify, satisfy, allow.)

INDULGENCE
adjectives
idle; habitual; passing; social; partial; expensive; pampered; rare; caustic; plenary; legal; vicious; indeterminable; unseasonable; vile; unrestrained; sensual; excessive; prolonged; maternal; classic; immoral; pitying; polite; complaint; further; unaesthetic.

verbs
abstain from—; beg—; check—; curb—; curse—; feast on—; grant—; humor with—; live in—; permit—; practise—; reproach for—; share in—; temper—; tempt to—; treat with—; wallow in—; yield to—; —fattens; —gratifies; —shackles; —weakens.

(See gratification, luxury, sin, crime, wickedness, violence.)

INDULGENT
adverbs
unfortunately; over; unhappily; lazily; carelessly; spasmodically; intermittently; tenderly; lovingly; unwisely; sympathetically; sadly; idly; thoughtlessly; unluckily; short-sightedly; foolishly; vacuously; affectionately; graciously; complacently; serenely; good-naturedly; tolerantly; torpidly; benevolently; warmly; humanely; ridiculously; excessively; uncommonly.

INDUSTRIALIST
verbs
enrich—; organize—; protect—; rouse—; satisfy—; spur—; support—; urge—; —achieves; —derives; —directs; —governs; —labors; —plies; —plods; —pushes; —submerges; —supplies; —yields to.

(See boss, executive, banker, farmer, manager.)

INDUSTRIOUS
adverbs
painfully; perseveringly; dependably; unremittingly; energetically; actively; carefully; constantly; temperamentally; characteristically; busily; reliably; amazingly; unusually; uncomplainingly; happily; cheerfully; unwaveringly; invariably; uniformly; persistently; insistently.

INDUSTRY
adjectives
domestic; ignorant; large; indefatigable; honest; urban; diversified; pious; prodigious; persistent; purposeless; scheduled; languid; necessitous; productive; peaceable; incomparable; much-vexed; myriad-shaped; indigenous; extraordinary; untiring; vast; growing; refining; charming; laudable; seasonal; unwearied; promising; middling; patient; technical; all-absorbing; mingled; damnable; unflagging; depression-born; unfaltering; modest; native; skilful; adoring; subsidized; persistent; unaided; predominating; dark-armed.

verbs
blossom into—; bulwark—; chastise—; cow—; cripple—; dislocate—; dominate—; evolve into—; father—; fortify—; foster—; gag—; merge—s; modernize—; organize—; paralyze—; prod—; reconstruct—; regulate—; rejuvenate—; resurrect—; retard—; revitalize—; revive—; sovietize—; speed up—; stimulate—; subsidize—; threaten—; tie up—; —booms; —buzzes; —collapses; —flourishes; —languishes; —perks up; —rallies; —squirms.

(See business, company, manufacture, trade, profession, enterprise, pursuit, vocation.)

INEFFECTIVE
adverbs
tragically; pitifully; surprisingly; disappointingly; utterly; wholly; strangely; suddenly; finally; painfully; curiously; singularly; unluckily; occasionally; feebly; weakly; tiresomely; languidly; stodgily; pitiably.

INEFFICIENCY
verbs
affirm—; characterize by—; condemn—; couch in—; degenerate to—; execute with—; observe—; plague with—; rectify—; relapse

into—; remove—; suffer from—; —accounts for; —bankrupts; —impoverishes; —scandalizes; —ruins; overlook—.

(See carelessness, stupidity, indifference.)

INEFFICIENT
adverbs
tragically; hopelessly; pitiably; miserably; wretchedly; helplessly; feebly; provincially; ignorantly; ineptly; clumsily; awkwardly; nervously; bashfully; shyly; self-consciously; inexpertly; crudely; grossly; flagrantly; crassly; surprisingly; harmlessly; dreadfully.

INELEGANT
adverbs
crudely; slightly; uncommonly; highly; gracelessly; awkwardly; boorishly; garishly; stiffly; rudely; inartistically; roughly; gaudily; grotesquely; artificially; vulgarly; coarsely; remarkably; unbelievably; incredibly.

INEPT
adverbs
stupidly; frightfully; foolishly; vacuously; terribly; comically; unfortunately; incompetently; miserably; wretchedly; senselessly; painfully; embarrassingly; unserviceably; lamentably; deplorably; pitiably; dreadfully.

INEQUALITIES
adjectives
inevitable; seeming; shameless; mountainous; irritating; supplementary; patent; sensible; glaring; gross; parallactic; slight; planetary.

INEQUALITY
verbs
complain of—; conduce to—; consider—; detect—; dispute—; frown on—; grieve over—; lament—; observe—; occasion—; owe to—; reconcile—; rectify—; treat with —; —glares; —shocks· —unbalances.

(See injustice, inferiority.)

INERT
adverbs
passively; dully; drowsily; heavily; indolently; lethargically; noddingly; quietly; sluggishly; stupidly; torpidly; dreamily; idly; lazily; lumpishly; sleepily; motionless-

ly; somnolently; apathetically; callously; habitually; unusually; uncommonly; phlegmatically; unconcernedly; imperturbably.

INERTIA
adjectives
gross; somber; amiable; ordinary; insurmountable.

verbs
display—; fall into—; force—; lull into—; overcome—; reform—; shed—; stimulate—; subject to—; suspend—; weary of—; while away in—; —consumes; —dulls; —prevents; —resists; —weakens.

(See indolence, idleness.)

INEVITABLE
verbs
accept—; bow to—; buck—; condone—; defer—; foresee—; foretell—; ignore—; predict—; prophesy—; resign to—; resist—; submit to—; yield to—.

(See fate.)

adverbs
tragically; embarrassingly; naturally; terribly; certainly; fatally; lamentably; fortunately; happily; awfully.

INEXCUSABLE
adverbs
wholly; altogether; entirely; manifestly; naturally; shamefully; hopelessly; flagrantly; scandalously; unfortunately; unluckily; irremediably; absolutely; admittedly; gravely; seriously.

INEXHAUSTIBLE
adverbs
boundlessly; generously; abundantly; luxuriantly; gorgeously; happily; naturally; apparently; miraculously; fortunately; surprisingly; evidently; marvelously; inexplicably; mysteriously; curiously; oddly; utterly; strangely; copiously; exuberantly; lavishly; gratefully; pleasantly.

INEXORABLE
adverbs
terribly; unfeelingly; unsympathetically; brutally; stiffly; severely; hard-heartedly; stonily; coldly; utterly; unreasonably; unaccountably; inexplicably; pitilessly; merci-

lessly; scornfully; pitiably; miserably; craftily; rigidly; uncompromisingly; austerely; haughtily; cruelly; tyrannically; imperiously; unsparingly; puritanically; authoritatively.

INEXPEDIENT
adverbs
palpably; obviously; awkwardly; inconveniently; embarrassingly; perplexingly; intricately; vexatiously; disconcertingly; bewilderingly; obstructively; objectionably; viciously; manifestly; utterly; clearly; painfully; glaringly; grossly; senselessly; terribly; grotesquely.

INEXPENSIVE
adverbs
surprisingly; amazingly; curiously; naturally; gratifyingly; delightfully; fortunately; conveniently; attractively; prudently; unexpectedly; cleverly; luckily; agreeably; pleasingly; remarkably; quite; comparatively.

INEXPLICABLE
adverbs
altogether; fantastically; utterly; strangely; inscrutably; mysteriously; peculiarly; mystifyingly; obscurely; darkly; capriciously; captiously; wantonly; impulsively; curiously.

INFALLIBILITY
verbs
acquire—; admit—; assure of—; boast of—; confirm—; confute—; deride—; doubt—; judge—; overrate—; praise—; promise—; prove—; puff up with—; reveal—; strain —; tempt—; test—; witness—.
(See skill, judgment, ability, ingenuity.)

INFALLIBLE
adverbs
unctuously; smugly; pompously; arrogantly; sapiently; sagaciously; practically; usually; consciously; reputably; notoriously; admittedly; apparently; supposedly; avowedly; bumptiously; maddeningly; gallingly; offensively; ostentatiously; proudly; blusteringly; swaggeringly; curiously.

INFAMOUS
adverbs
scandalously; vilely; notoriously; unjustly; unutterably; inexpressibly; grossly; crassly; brazenly; wickedly; odiously; atrociously; unbelievably; incredibly; ingloriously; un-

mentionably; shamefully; arrantly; shockingly; outrageously; pitifully; atrociously; shabbily; fantastically; uncommonly; deplorably.

INFAMY
adjectives
unutterable; callous; clumsy; vilest; perpetual; crushing; immortal.

verbs
bear—; blot out—; brand—; challenge—; consign to—; deface with—; denounce—; doom to—; endure—; hold up to—; incur—; infer—; inflict—; mire with—; scar with —; suffer—; work—; —disgraces; —pains; —shames; stain with—.
(See disgrace, dishonor, shame, scandal.)

INFANCY
adjectives
smiling; philologic; unlearned; fretting; cherub; innocent; dauntless; endless; careless; slumbering; unpracticed; mewling.

verbs
cloud—; develop in—; emerge from—; extend—; form in—; foster from—; guide through—; impress in—; mould in—; nourish in—; nurse in—; plead—; regress to—; soothe in—; terrorize in—; train in—; utter in—; —precedes; —unfolds.
(See childhood.)

INFANT
adjectives
well-educated; squalling; bewildered; undipped; unvaccinated; sucking; clay-faced; blue-lipped; baptized; conventional; miraculous; swaddling; ragged; hungry; mute; speechless; suffering; sentient; premature; trustful; vigorous.

verbs
christen—; cradle—; cuddle—; govern—; guard—; guide—; pamper—; quell—; soothe—; suckle—; swaddle—; swathe—; wean—; —bawls; —chatters; —howls; —mewls; —prattles; —pukes; —scampers about; —squalls.
(See child, baby.)

INFANTRY
adjectives
redoubtable; intrenched; disciplined; unsupported; trampling; well-armed; spiritless.

verbs

collect—; distress—; snipe at—; —advances; —assails; —besieges; —charges; —defends; —guards; —harries; —invades; —maneuvers; —marches; —mops up; —parries; —peppers; —presses; —reconnoiters; —retreats; —shields; —storms; —strikes; —wars on.

(See army, regiment, soldier.)

INFATUATION

adjectives

judicial; sad; incomprehensible; girlish.

verbs

besot with—; blame—; blind with—; deride —; fire by—; free from—; infect with—; overcome by—; provoke—; resist—; suffer —; stun by—; —dazzles; —dopes; —overwhelms; —perturbs; —ruffles; —ruins; —sharpens; —thrills.

(See love, charm, passion, tenderness.)

INFECTION

adjectives

diphtheritic; acute; common; respiratory; wide-spread; bacterial; innocent; recurrent; severe.

verbs

breathe—; combat—; cope with—; contract —; convey—; diagnose—; eradicate—; escape—; expose to—; exterminate—; immunize against—; incise—; introduce—; localize —; predispose to—; purge of—; risk—; scatter—; transmit—; —derives from; —enters; —lingers; —ravages; —spreads.

(See disease, malady, plague.)

INFECTIOUS

adverbs

highly; dangerously; easily; alarmingly; uncommonly; definitely; positively; portentously; slightly; supposedly; allegedly; probably; surprisingly; remarkably; particularly; acutely; seriously; gravely; fearfully.

INFER (*v*)

adverbs

hastily; carelessly; vaguely; unfoundedly; unreasonably; absurdly; rationally; irresistibly; confidently.

(See imply, gather, deduce.)

INFERENCE

adjectives

decisive; ruinous; vague; astounding; pathological; unfounded; unreasonable; bare; typographical; absurd; rational; charitable; irresistible; justifiable; sharp.

verbs

accept—; argue—; condemn—; conclude—; consider—; deduce—; derive—from; dispute—; draw—from; indulge in—s; justify —; pour out—s; resent—; respect—; scoff at—; scorn—; —implies; —indicates; —insinuates; —troubles.

(See opinion, thought, conclusion, consequence.)

INFERENTIAL

adverbs

probably; carelessly; naturally; logically; ruinously; vaguely; obscurely; incontrovertibly; soundly; unreasonably; absurdly; fallaciously; shrewdly; undeniably; covertly; obviously.

INFERIOR

adverbs

hopelessly; comparatively; pitifully; manifestly; palpably; shockingly; appallingly; terribly; unmistakably; oddly; curiously; patently; apparently; greatly; dreadfully; mentally; physically; essentially; materially; utterly; inexplicably; unaccountably; unacceptably.

INFERIORITY

adjectives

decent; mental; intellectual; alleged; admitted.

verbs

burden with—; conceal—; consider—; curse —; detect—; experience—; fret over—; lament—; prove—; overcome—; suffer—; —anguishes; —cramps; —gnaws; —shames; —stings; —vexes.

(See complex, inequality, injustice, mediocrity.)

INFERNO

adjectives

gasoline; raging; lurid; hot; white.

INFEST (*v*)

adverbs

horribly; pestiferously; peculiarly; grossly; luxuriantly; unpleasantly; extraordinarily; perniciously; fatally.

(See overrun, haunt, annoy.)

adjectives
perilous; professed; stalwart.

INFIDELITY

adjectives
foolish; matrimonial; religious.

verbs
admit—; blot with—; commit—; confess—; flaunt—; inspire—; motivate—; repent—; reproach for—; sully with—; —dejects; —desolates; —destroys; —disgraces; —dishonors; —poisons; —stains; —taints; —threatens.
(See unfaithfulness, treachery, sin.)

INFILTRATION

verbs
advocate—; consider—; curb—; fill by—; halt—; introduce by—; lead to—; observe —; permeate through—; receive—; travel by—; —alarms; —breeds; —endangers; —preserves.
(See penetration.)

INFINITE

adverbs
gloriously; spiritually; divinely; ineffably; vastly; mysteriously; impenetrably; boundlessly; immensely; incomprehensibly; fearfully; occultly; unknowably; inexpressibly; incalculably; unapproachably; unfathomably; immeasurably.

INFINITY

verbs
ascend into—; dwell in—; infringe on—; lead to—; measure—; pattern—; range in —; represent—; understand—; yield to—.
(See eternity.)

INFIRM

adverbs
decrepitly; weakly; languidly; brokenly; defenselessly; helplessly; pitiably; unbelievably; horribly; lamentably; pathetically; nervously; powerlessly; shakily.

INFIRMITIES

adjectives
physical; hideous; besetting; divine; mortal; unique; growing; venial; deplorable; quotidian; speedy.

verbs
bare—; bear—; brace—; discover—; escape —; lament—; linger in—; master—; pretend—; relieve—; suffer—; trample on—; —blights; —constrains; —desolates; —despairs; —enfeebles; —gnaws; —relents; —restrains.
(See weakness, feebleness, illness, disease.)

INFLAME (v)

adverbs
superficially; fatally; excessively; chronically; temporarily; painfully; treasonably.
(See provoke, excite.)

INFLAMMABLE

adverbs
highly; criminally; uncommonly; easily; dangerously; seriously; illegally; hazardously, perilously; probably; indubitably; instantly; terribly; extremely.

INFLAMMATION

adjectives
excessive; fatal; chronic.

verbs
allay—; avert—; check—; clear up—; confine—; diminish—; excite—; indicate—; palliate—; reduce—; relieve—; subdue—; undergo—; —abates; —accompanies; —extends to; —proceeds; —ravages; —sustains.
(See infection, sore, ulcer, pain.)

INFLATION

verbs
advocate—; authorize—; block—; border on —; condemn—; criticize—; distrust—; head for—; predict—; propose—; puff by—; resort to—; spike—; suffer—; threaten—; veer from—; —benefits; —devaluates; —dilates; —distends; —enhances; —swells.
(See expansion, prosperity, depression, success.)

INFLEXIBLE

adverbs
rigidly; obdurately; stiffly; arrogantly; austerely; autocratically; brutally; strictly; imperiously; domineeringly; tyrannically; sharply; rigorously; hardly; haughtily; inexorably; peremptorily; severely; uncompromisingly; unsparingly; sternly; hatefully; notoriously; intolerably; heartbreakingly; obstinately; tenaciously; resolutely; de-

terminedly; stubbornly; unreasonably; consistently; immovably; indomitably; unflinchingly.

INFLICT (v)

adverbs

thoughtlessly; painfully; cruelly; heavily; superfluously; unpleasantly; perniciously.

(See impose, strike.)

INFLUENCE

adjectives

prevailing; inspirational; disintegrating; brutalizing; powerful; benignant; incalculable; tidal; starry; tyrannical; fructifying; sinister; corrosive; parental; controlling; good; withering; gentler; similar; malevolent; baneful; potent; intimate; political; soft; corrupt; personal; iron; sullen; defiant; hypnotic; restless; formative; considerable; disorganizing; maleficent; variable; appealing; cogent; malign; permanent; mephitic; evil; favorable; insidious; pathetic; depressing; scathing; consequent; important; solemn; educational; disastrous; restraining; controlling; enormous; gentle; diminishing; inhibiting; compelling; helpful; mesmeric; mysterious; deadly; healing; persuasive; warping; demoniac; sober; useful; fair; stabilizing; decisive; overgrown; beauteous; internal; unquestioned; uncanny; court; mellow; moonlight; human; morbid; fierce; undue; wide; partisan; precious; magical; reviving; environmental; divine; hypnotic; genial; disciplinary; evangelical; adverse; favorable; prodigious; conservative; calamitous; censorial; baleful; demoralizing; ultimate; subtle; revolutionary; wholesome; destined; dispiriting; sobering; extensive; marked; destructive; foreign; soothing; vague; reassuring; mitigated; pernicious; gracious; jangling; exhilarating; sympathetic; refining; prenatal; stupefying; quickening; heinous; softening; enlightening; literary; guiding; imponderable; predisposing; invigorating; moral; repressing; ethnographical; incalculable; territorial; desolating; broadening; omnipotent; overgrown; weakening; irritating; lasting; liberal; credible; spreading; tremendous; single; sinister; poetical; disquieting; profound; invariable; witching; dominating; unconscious; balmiest; hasty; compensating; ultimate; environing; secret; disturbing; proportional; steadying; damping; unperceived; dwarfing; ennobling; corrupting; subtle; secondary; political; immense;

beneficent; various (pl); salutary; vast; transcendent; despotic; commanding; trivial; sovereign; civilizing; protective; nerve-depleting; subjective; potential; blighting; wide-spread; many-mingled; reflex; problematical; sacred; sweet; transitory; misleading; ethical; marvelous; awful; antecedent; beneficial; unmindful; pernicious; jealous; vivifying; magical; subsequent; unexampled; infinite; invasive; emotional; soothing; tranquilizing; blasting; benumbing; propitious; aesthetic; toughening; gladdening; immediate; suggestive; carnicular; lost; predominating; underhand; materializing; mollifying; all-embracing; unconditional; mitigating; restraining; icy; moderating; celestial; superlative; narrowing; inaugurating; perceptible.

verbs

arrest—; bow to—; broaden—; come under —of; cramp—; curb—; diffuse—; exercise —; exert—; fall under—; impose—; infuse —; labor under—; lend—; manifest—over; measure—; multiply—; paralyze—; preserve from—; press—; promote—; reflect—; resist—; spread—; stem—; subject to—; survive—; wield—; yield to—; —bends; — corrupts; —declines; —extends to; —prevails; —reigns; —sways; —undermines; — wanes.

(See control, sway, prestige, persuasion, authority, strength, power.)

INFLUENCE (v)

adverbs

profoundly; powerfully; significantly; phenomenally; subsequently; adversely; unduly; vitally; strikingly; insensibly; unwillingly; remotely; benignantly; brutalizingly; parentally; malevolently; banefully; hypnotically; depressingly; exhilaratingly; despotically; jealously; morbidly; restrainingly.

(See induce, compel.)

INFLUENTIAL

adverbs

highly; remarkably; mysteriously; darkly; extremely; generally; peculiarly; politically; financially; notoriously; ominously; dangerously; alarmingly; helpfully; socially; nationally; sagaciously; powerfully; disastrously; enormously; quietly; calmly; tremendously; profoundly; artfully; immensely; persuasively; craftily; openly; obviously; palpably; manifestly; inexplicably; unaccountably; marvelously; wisely; secretly.

adjectives
vast; miraculous; steady.

INFORM (v)
adverbs
tremulously; blandly; personally; authoritatively; gruffly; unequivocally; officially; credibly; curtly; superficially; confidentially; comprehensively; fallaciously; dogmatically.

(See instruct, notify.)

INFORMAL
adverbs
graciously; intimately; delightfully; carelessly; charmingly; elaborately; deliberately; artfully; intentionally; happily; sweetly; pleasantly; amiably; agreeably; enchantingly; surprisingly; naively; remarkably; attractively; naturally; oddly; unexpectedly; heartily; cordially; diplomatically; exceedingly; habitually.

INFORMALITY
adjectives
pleasant; admirable; well-bred; delightful; charming.

INFORMATION
adjectives
instructional; imparted; common; broiling; miscellaneous; superficial; authentic; precise; vague; coordinating; scanty; solid; criminal; practical; household; substantial; summarized; trustworthy; factual; accurate; elusive; genuine; scientific; encouraging; inviting; astounding; exact; useful; further; detailed; comprehensive; false; up-to-the-minute; startling; practical; reliable; usable; behind-the-scenes; understandable; fallacious; gloomy; invaluable; superfluous; curious; anterior; accumulated; tabulated; profit-building; current; comparative; restricted; dogmatic; fascinating; unpleasant.

verbs
abound in—; absorb—; accumulate—; acquire—; authenticize—; bear—; buttress—; clamor for—; compile—; contribute—; convey—; coordinate—; correlate—; derive—; dig out—; digest—; dispense—; disseminate—; distort—; divulge—; elicit—; falsify —; garner—; glean—; impart—; misinterpret—; plead for—; prod for—; pump for —; relay—; rely on—; retail—; solicit—;

summon—; suppress—; tabulate—; thirst for—; unburden oneself of—; utilize—; verify—; volunteer—; vouchsafe—; wheedle—; withhold—; worm—; yield—; —embodies; —leaks out.

(See knowledge, intelligence, data, facts, understanding, wisdom, science, statistics.)

INFRACTION
verbs
accuse of—; chastise for—; condemn—; detect—; fine—; harass by—; lament—; overlook—; penalize—; plague with—s; suffer —.

(See breach, error, violation, infringement.)

INFREQUENT
adverbs
painfully; frigidly; usually; remarkably; vexatiously; probably; luckily; fortunately; gratifyingly; uncertainly; erratically; undeniably; mysteriously; inscrutably; happily; negligibly.

INFRINGEMENT
verbs
abet—; allege—; curb—; enjoin—; observe —; protest—; punish—; resent—; restrain —; rue—.
(See violation, breach, infraction.)

INFUSION
adjectives
organic; putrescible; imperceptible; sterilized; steeped; imaginable; dormant.

INGENIOUS
adverbs
cleverly; artfully; skilfully; unusually; notably; famously; remarkably; adroitly; particularly; artistically; diplomatically; admirably; amazingly; marvelously; helpfully; extremely; capably; intelligently; unbelievably; exceedingly; dexterously; expertly; deftly; resourcefully; smartly; shrewdly; incredibly.

INGENUE
adjectives
raw; artless; guileless.

INGENUITY
adjectives
considerable; mechanical; inventive; misguided; speculative; wonderful; naive;

fiendish; subtle; puerile; interwoven; productive; devilish; unbetrayed; calumnious; extraordinary; conjectural.

verbs
acknowledge—; conceive by—; defy—; demand—; display—; employ—; excel in—; encourage—; endow with—; exercise—; feign—; invent by—; observe—; profit by —; strain—; swathe in—; tax—; witness—; —conquers; —triumphs.
(See infallibility, skill, ability, genius.)

INGENUOUS
adverbs
youthfully; openly; childishly; pleasantly; unsuspectingly; candidly; naturally; sincerely; innocently; honestly; frankly; bluntly; marvellously; unusually; unexpectedly; utterly; exceedingly; extraordinarily; surprisingly; amazingly; strikingly; astonishingly; miraculously; unaffectedly.

INGRATIATING
adverbs
deliberately; skilfully; artfully; politically; purposely; pleasantly; craftily; disgustingly; abjectly; insidiously; invidiously; diplomatically; amiably; curiously; elaborately; obsequiously; ceremoniously; suavely; gently; courteously; urbanely; gallantly; unctuously; blandly; cordially; affably; civilly; extremely.

INGRATITUDE
adjectives
occasional; habitual; horrible; foul; base.

verbs
brood over—; complain of—; denounce—; expose to—; suffer—; taint with—; treat with—; wipe out—; —barbs; —bites; —bruises; —oppresses; —pains; —pierces; —provokes; —shames; —thrives; —undermines.
(See oppression, infidelity, treachery, selfishness.)

INGREDIENTS
adjectives
healing; costly; dry; delicious; sifted; accidental; sweetening; unintelligible; prominent; basic; malicious; principal; choicest; modern; balanced; seething; pernicious; commonplace; poisonous; necessary; muddy; nutritive; nourishing.

verbs
adjust—; analyze—; calculate—; concoct of —; denounce—; discover—; gather—; measure—; memorize—; mix—; note—; prepare —; produce—; reduce—; separate—; skimp on—; test—.
(See parts, elements, materials.)

INHABIT (v)
adverbs
thinly; comfortably; successively; wretchedly; swarmingly; solely; misguidedly; placidly; domestically; humbly.
(See abide, dwell, live.)

INHABITANTS
adjectives
strange; glorious; unmolested; unobtrusive; aboriginal; intimate; permanent; larger; wretched; respective; awe-struck; diverse; fortunate; cordial; respectable; unambitious; rustic; brawny; feathered; defenceless; plague-stricken; tender; placid; amazed; pious; ancient; wretched; swarming.

verbs
confer on—; consider—; entitle — to; grant to—; privilege—; regulate—; rule—; urge —; —attend; —benefit; —complain; —congregate; —dwell; —enjoy; —frequent; —organize; —rejoice; —revolt; —rise; —tenant; —welcome.
(See individual, native.)

INHALE (v)
adverbs
audibly; deeply; luxuriously; spasmodically; gaspingly; sharply; agonizingly; laboriously.
(See breathe.)

INHARMONIOUS
adverbs
unpleasantly; inexplicably; annoyingly; disastrously; inexcusably; unreasonably; utterly; freqeuntly; mysteriously; obscurely; unnecessarily; strangely; disgustingly; fearfully; ominously; significantly; unbelievably; oddly; curiously; extremely.

INHERENT
adverbs
disturbingly; ineradicably; indubitably; obviously; manifestly; fortunately; happily; palpably; deeply; essentially; fundamentally.

INHERIT (v)

adverbs
legally; unexpectedly; spectacularly; dramatically; nominally; traditionally; customarily; fortunately.
(See receive, possess, derive.)

INHERITANCE

adjectives
dismal; fairest; fallen; ill-starred; astounding; storied; entailed; occasional; moderate; racial.

verbs
administer—; bequeath—; bless with—; come into—; confirm—; derive—from; divide—; enjoy—; entitle to—; forfeit—; forsake—; grant—; lay claim to—; portion—; preserve—; profit by—; relinquish—; restore to—; scatter—; squander—; succeed to —; tax—; —enriches; —falls to.
(See legacy, estate, money, property, profits.)

INHIBITION

verbs
detect—; express—; harass by—; incur—; persecute with—; proceed from—; remove —; suffer—; sympathize with—; veil—; vent—; —arrests; —disappears; —haunts; —plagues; —restrains; —restricts; —torments; —tortures.
(See restraint, fear, complex, restriction.)

INHOSPITABLE

adverbs
strangely; rudely; uncivilly; inexcusably; curiously; coldly; unpardonably; deliberately; openly; ostentatiously; purposely; discourteously; oddly; inexplicably; unaccountably; miserably; wretchedly; terribly; gruffly; brusquely; roughly; distinctly; unsociably; churlishly; ungraciously; forbiddingly; extremely; unforgettably; peculiarly; remarkably; significantly.

INHUMAN

adverbs
brutally; brutishly; curiously; incredibly; savagely; unbelievably; strangely; deliberately; barbarously; cruelly; ferociously; atrociously; ruthlessly; relentlessly; fiendishly; fantastically; viciously; diabolically.

INIMICAL

adverbs
essentially; radically; fundamentally; altogether; naturally; antagonistically; malevolently; maliciously; secretly; mysteriously; inexplicably; unaccountably; strangely; unreasonably; obviously; oddly; unexpectedly; palpably; manifestly; significantly; sadly; violently; spitefully; constitutionally; ominously; dangerously.

INIMITABLE

adverbs
altogether; remarkably; utterly; incomparably; peerlessly; brilliantly; perfectly; artistically; preciously; peculiarly; delightfully; faultlessly; avowedly; reputedly; presumably.

INIQUITIES

adjectives
conjugal; juvenile; aged; crowning; manifest.

INIQUITOUS

adverbs
atrociously; unbelievably; inexpressibly; unspeakably; obscenely; heinously; invidiously; egregiously; inordinately; exceptionally; unmentionably; diabolically; grievously; irremediably; banefully; criminally; unwarrantably; immorally; unimaginably; viciously; nefariously; malevolently; impiously; unconscionably; basely; vilely; savagely.

INIQUITY

verbs
acquit of—; bring forth—; cleanse of—; cling to—; conceive of—; confess—; defile with—; delight in—; disclose—; drown in —; forgive—; foul with—; perish in—; punish for—; purge of—; rebuke—; redeem from—; reveal—; steep in—; taint with—; turn from—; work—; —flourishes.
(See sin, wickedness, abomination, crime.)

INITIATE (v)

adverbs
festively; ceremoniously; dramatically; annually; imaginatively; originally; forcefully; beneficently.
(See begin, instruct, introduce.)

INITIATION

adjectives
practical; exceptional; unwilling; elementary; baptismal.

adjectives

unusual; private; unfettered; individual; untrammeled; unparalleled; aggressive; independent; popular.

verbs

cripple—; crush—; curb—; demonstrate—; develop—; display—; encourage—; exhibit —; imbue with—; kill—; manifest—; observe—; praise—; provoke—; reward—; —activates; —yields.

(See originality, ability, skill, genius, proficiency.)

INJECT (v)

adverbs

hypodermically; intravenously; insidiously; spitefully; slyiy; salaciously; maliciously; medically; scientifically; methodically.

(See put, introduce, insert, interject.)

INJUDICIOUS

adverbs

thoughtlessly; senselessly; foolishly; indiscreetly; imprudently; childishly; heedlessly; vengefully; ignorantly; unintentionally; unfortunately; sadly; disastrously; blindly; rashly; impulsively; impetuously; adventurously; heedlessly; inexpediently; recklessly; wantonly; stupidly; ridiculously; absurdly.

INJUNCTION

adjectives

solemn; serious; conflicting; sternest; strict; vehement; permanent; pretty; curt; tacit; restraining; temporary.

verbs

apply for—; consecrate—; deny—; enforce —; grant—; hand down—; justify—; obey —; refuse—; suspend—; sustain—; —bans; —bars; —blocks; —restrains; —restricts; — ties up.

(See action, order, instructions, command, requirement.)

INJURE (v)

adverbs

severely; dangerously; wilfully; critically; incurably; shockingly; permanently; unwittingly; atrociously; wantonly; gravely; internally; materially; irreparably.

(See damage, hurt, wound.)

adjectives

atrocious; potent; wanton; conscious; protracted; sinister; dreaded; serious; widespread; multiplied; repeated; grave; previous; internal; incredible; permanent; material; mental; disabling; irreparable; incalculable.

INJURIOUS

adverbs

distinctly; presumably; definitely; positively; irremediably; slightly; surprisingly; distressingly; unintentionally; indiscreetly; mysteriously; maliciously; deliberately; desperately; highly; perniciously; seriously; destructively; tragically; outrageously.

INJURY

verbs

avenge—; bewail—; compensate for—; entail—; expose to—; inflict — upon; insure against—; occasion—; preserve from—; proclaim—; receive—; recover from—; recuperate from—; resist—; suffer—; sustain—; work—; —cripples; —outrages; —restricts; —unnerves.

(See wound, damage, wrong, outrage, mischief, pain, injustice.)

INJUSTICE

adjectives

murderous; temporary; wanton; cruel; tyrannic; abominable; cruelest; flagrant; social; crowning; peculiar; horrible; artistic; shocking; unspoken; treacherous; inherent; unintentional; immemorial; atrocious; gross.

verbs

accept—; attack—; belabor—; bewail—; brood over—; cite—; crush with—; decry —; denounce—; detect—; eliminate—; extirpate—; impose—; inflict—; lament—; inveigh against—; persist in—; reek of—; remedy—; sense—; shrink from—; swallow —; wallow in—; work—.

(See inequality, injury, unfairness, grievance, wrong.)

INK

adjectives

corroding; potent; sympathetic; invisible.

verbs

battle with—; blacken with—; blot with—; cloud with—; color with—; dilute—; dip into—; drip—; eject—; expel—; reservoir

—; smear—; smirch with—; —blurs; —spatters; —spots; —stains.
(See paint.)

INMATES
adjectives
temporary; cowering; exasperating; feeble-minded; querulous; miserable-looking; destitute; licentious; unhappy; mad.

INN
adverbs
dwell in—; establish—; frequent—; keep—; lodge in—; maintain—; put up at—; repair to—; reside in—; sojourn at—; stop at—; —accommodates; —houses; —invites; —provides; —quarters; —warms; —welcomes.
(See hotel, home, apartment, tavern.)

INNOCENCE
adjectives
harmless; loveliest; virgin; extreme; spotless; intrinsic; recognized; inviolable; unsuspecting; helpless; strange; fulsome; unabashed; childish; deliberate; despairing; injured; elaborate; pretended; starry; lofty; conscious; departed; primitive; heavenly; gentle; hapless.

verbs
assert—; betray—; commend—; despoil—; feign—; guard—; hallow—; immortalize—; jeopardize—; maintain—; plead—; prey on —; protest—; prove—; seduce—; smile in - -; vindicate—.
(See purity, simplicity, sincerity.)

INNOCENT
adverbs
delightfully; childishly; naturally; legally; sweetly; presumably; girlishly; charmingly; playfully; beautifully; helplessly; apparently; manifestly; palpably; irresistibly; gently; essentially; virtuously; positively; artlessly; sincerely; unaffectedly; ingenuously; frankly; admirably; unbelievably; happily; refreshingly; naively; touchingly; wonderfully; alluringly; graciously; ravishingly; exquisitely; alluringly; adorably.

INNOCUOUS
adverbs
utterly; advantageously; valuably; unobjectionably; vacuously; inoffensively; negligibly; presumably; probably; wholesomely; safely; undoubtedly; definitely.

INNOVATION
adjectives
striking; political; unquiet; distasteful; ghastly; outward; unauthorized; startling; tyrannical; interesting; radical; endless; inexpedient; recent; countless (pl).

verbs
champion—; clamor for—; curb—; demand —; disapprove of—; discourage—; favor—; plan—; protest against—; resist—; sprout —; stay—; suspect—; welcome—; —attracts; —improves; —revolutionizes; encourage—.
(See change, improvement, style, fashion, movement.)

INNUENDO
adjectives
unspoken; malicious; biting; salacious.

verbs
convey by—; employ—; indulge in—; insinuate by—; interpret—; utter—; —annoys; —hints; —implies; —intimates; —libels; — peeves (colloq.); —puzzles; —slanders; — suggests.
(See insinuation, suggestion.)

INOCULATE (v)
adverbs
successfully; scientifically; experimentally; automatically; prudentially.
(See protect, insert, introduce, inject.)

INOFFENSIVE
adverbs
utterly; safely; negligibly; warrantably; assuredly; surely; completely; wholly; avowedly; indubitably; satisfactorily; fairly; probably; quietly; amiably; diplomatically; wisely; sagaciously; discreetly.

INOPERATIVE
adverbs
provokingly; vapidly; vexatiously; hopelessly; idly; lately; legally; harmlessly; untenably; wholly; utterly.

INOPPORTUNE
adverbs
awkwardly; embarrassingly; vexatiously; wholly; singularly; peculiarly; financially; politically; commercially; disastrously; unfortunately; presumably; socially; signally;

seriously; unfortunately; unluckily; inexpediently; inaptly; clumsily; stupidly; foolishly; terribly; sadly; miserably; wretchedly.

INQUIRE (v)
adverbs
solicitously; perfunctorily; boldly; mischievously; curiously; sarcastically; diligently; concernedly; incredulously; laconically; superficially; placidly; ominously; bluntly; officially; passionately; skeptically; apprehensively; dolorously; innocently; curtly.

(See ask, seek, question.)

INQUIRER
adjectives
individual; diligent; curious; historical; philosophical; profane.

INQUIRY
adjectives
investigational; liberal; audacious; vindictive; studious; calm; dispassionate; laconic; rigorous; extensive; horrified; breathless; minute; confidential; particular; skeptical; recent; diligent; patient; successful; urgent; sarcastic; apprehensive; exacting; troubled; cold; sanctioned; sleepy; dolorous; fruitless; competent; respectful; troublesome; subsequent; eager; physical; point-blank; thorough; sincere; innocent; direct; discreet; pertinent; scientific; suave; vain; solid; indefinite; tentative; strict; sad; accurate; unthinking; suspicious; sarcastic; mild; hospitable; formal; curt; brisk; brash.

verbs
bombard with—s; conduct—; deter—; institute—; meet—; occasion—; overwhelm with —s; press—; provoke—; pursue—; push—; renew—; repeat—; reply to—; resume—; subject to—; waive—; —discloses.

(See question, investigation, research, examination.)

INQUISITION
adjectives
tyrannous; ceaseless; imperious; bootless; comfortable; solemn; merciless; cruel.

verbs
demand—; escape—; fall foul of—; justify —; launch—; occasion—; propose—; search by—; suggest—; sweep by—; —explores; —irks; —proves; —reviews; —trespasses.

(See investigation, inquiry, research.)

INQUISITIVE
adverbs
inordinately; offensively; curiously; oddly; persistently; maliciously; meddlesomely; tiresomely; offensively; venomously; innocently; harmlessly; miserably; distressingly; unpardonably; inexcusably; discourteously; unforgivably; dangerously; significantly; alarmingly; intellectually; scientifically; intrusively; pryingly; mysteriously; egregiously; openly; expertly; officiously; relentlessly; impolitely; boundlessly; insatiably.

INQUISITORS
adjectives
delegated; persecuting; mealy-mouthed; death-dealing.

INROADS
adjectives
destructive; perpetual; frequent; constant; serious; casual; blighting.

INSANE
adjectives
wildly; slightly; probably; mildly; presumably; avowedly; violently; slightly; permanently; periodically; pathetically; tragically; recently; allegedly; notoriously; dangerously; pitiably; miserably; hopelessly; irremediably; irrecoverably; dreadfully; incurably; utterly; deliriously; fanatically; eccentrically; hysterically; incoherently; distressingly.

INSANITY
adjectives
true; warlike; intellectual; temporary; dire; pious; incipient; incurable; speculative; hysterical; harmless; systematic; delusional; hereditary.

verbs
anticipate—; banish—; border on—; condemn to—; correct—; detect—; discern—; drive to—; hush—; lament—; lead to—; observe—; plead—; produce—; sense—; simulate—; subdue—; suffer—; thrust into —; treat—; —desolates; —imprisons; —seizes; overcome—.

(See mania, madness, frenzy, delirium.)

INSATIABLE
adverbs
greedily; voraciously; miserably; shamelessly; hungrily; terribly; pitiably; rapacious-

ly; unbelievably; curiously; strangely; grossly; avidly; covetously; cravingly; sordidly; openly; manifestly.

INSCRIBE (v)
adverbs
lightly; erroneously; appropriately; decoratively; legibly; hieroglyphically; tenderly; officially; historically.
(See imprint, write.)

INSCRIPTION
adjectives
analogous; trilingual; sham; inappropriate; monumental; absorbing; cuneiform; simple; lofty; horizontal; decorative; legible; duplicate; flattering; mural; libelous; hieroglyphical; ominous; effaced.

verbs
bear—; carve—; chisel—; decipher—; engrave—; furnish—; mark—; pen—; place —; study—; survey—; trace—; word—; —adorns; —commemorates; —dedicates; —denotes; —heads; —indicates; —records; —reminds.
(See record, handwriting, monument, document.)

INSCRUTABLE
adverbs
mysteriously; oddly; hopelessly; curiously; impenetrably; altogether; strangely; utterly; unaccountably; wholly.

INSECT
adjectives
individual; venomous; luminous; aculeate; industrious; blundering; coral; silken-winged; bloated; noisome; dormant; swarming; glittering; populous; all-devouring; melodious; gorgeous; countless (pl); injurious; ubiquitous; energetic; acquisitive; sweet; throbbing; mottled; destructive; painless; annoying; voracious; multitudinous (pl).

INSECTS
verbs
allure—; breed—; combat—; exterminate—; feed on—; hunt—; lure—; net—; overrun with—; trap—; —annoy; —buzz; —demolish; —devour; —dismantle; —distress; —fertilize; —hum; —nest; —pest; —plague; —pupate; —ravage; —sap; —settle on; —swarm; —swirl; —undergo a metamorphosis; —creeps.
(See individual insects.)

INSECURE
adverbs
pitiably; alarmingly; distressingly; fearfully; hopelessly; flimsily; embarrassingly; awkwardly; vaguely; bewilderingly; precariously; dangerously; carelessly; inexcusably; critically; ominously; perilously; curiously; dreadfully; horribly; undeniably; fatally; continuallly; wearily; professionally; pathetically; apprehensively; uncomfortably; anxiously; tormentingly; grievously; financially.

INSENSIBLE
adverbs
curiously; stolidly; dully; apathetically; sluggishly; languidly; torpidly; utterly; callously; indifferently; phlegmatically; drowsily; somnolently; sleepily; stupidly; dazedly; obtusely; lethargically; imperturbably; inattentively; unconcernedly; unbelievably; incredibly.

INSEPARABLE
adverbs
affectionately; insistently; physically; scientifically; technically; financially; politically; logically; commercially; naturally; cohesively; firmly; solidly; tenaciously; securely; legally; authoritatively; officially; warrantably.

INSERT (v)
adverbs
parenthetically; expressly; daily; meticulously; formally; officially; logically; derogatorily.
(See inject, interject.)

INSIDIOUS
adverbs
peculiarly; subtly; dangerously; alarmingly; appallingly; cunningly; shrewdly; terrifyingly; particularly; shockingly; ominously; uncomfortably; deceptively; surreptitiously; elusively; fraudulently; slyly; profoundly; cleverly; artfully; astutely; shabbily; wickedly; perfidiously; shamefully; trickily.

INSIGHT
adjectives
clearer; intuitive; vivid; profound; spiritual; rare; true; mythic; penetrating; partial; uncanny; sympathetic; psychological;

pathetic; keen; intellectual; comprehensive; steady; sagacious; curious; imaginative; prophetic; dramatic; clearest; scientific; objective; valid; mature; mystic.

verbs
acquire—; endow with—; flash—; follow with—; furnish with—; gain—; give—; lack—; obtain—; possess—; ripen into—; understand through—; —comprehends; —discerns; —fathoms; —penetrates; —perceives; —rewards; —searches.
(See understanding, wisdom.)

INSIGNIA
adjectives
distinguishing; military; graceful.

INSIGNIFICANCE
adjectives
paltry; essential; sallow; miserable; puny.

verbs
bury in—; crouch in—; dwindle into—; fade into—; pale into—; plunge into—; reduce to—; ridicule—; scorn—; sink into—; spring from—; suffer—; —engulfs; —prostrates; —swallows.
(See obscurity, seclusion, trifle, oblivion.)

INSIGNIFICANT
adverbs
altogether; negligibly; admittedly; avowedly; inconsequentially; weakly; pitifully; contemptibly; ridiculously; vaguely; absurdly; fatuously; inanely; pathetically; terribly; ultimately.

INSINCERE
adverbs
woefully; curiously; obviously; strangely; indubitably; palpably; hopelessly; arrantly; evidently; shamefully; transparently; absurdly; slyly; evasively; pretentiously; flatteringly; cruelly; insidiously; bitterly; clearly; unmistakably; grossly; dreadfully.

INSINCERITY
verbs
abhor—; charge with—; clog with—; condemn—; detect—; embroider with—; engage in—; falsify with—; incline toward—; witness—; —adulterates; —deceives; —disgraces; —disguises; —distorts; —forfeits; —shames.
(See unfaithfulness, treachery, deception, hypocrisy.)

INSINUATE (*v*)
adverbs
brazenly; slanderously; coyly; pointedly; delicately; calumniously; offensively; adroitly; covertly; reticently; outrageously.
(See imply, hint, suggest.)

INSINUATION
adjectives
calumnious; conscientious; adroit; slanderous; covert; nasty; reticent; evil; unguarded; offensive; outrageous; terrible; unfortunate; slow.

verbs
contemplate—; dare—; defeat—; deliver—; dispose of—; omit—; perceive—; weigh—; wince at—; —alludes; —creeps in; —hints; —implies; —informs; —instills; —shocks; —suggests.
(See accusation, innuendo, intimation, suggestion, hint.)

INSIPID
adverbs
stupidly; feebly; unusually; habitually; naturally; hopelessly; tiresomely; vacuously; fatuously; colorlessly; vexatiously; tediously; prosaically; dully; doltishly; inertly; passively; phlegmatically; listlessly; lackadaisically; recklessly; uninterestingly; monotonously; depressingly; unbearably.

INSIPIDITY
adjectives
conventional; slumbrous; stereotyped.

INSIST (*v*)
adverbs
hotly; glowingly; indignantly; belligerently; stolidly; perversely; deliberately; pedantically; resolutely; pointedly; pertinaciously; disobligingly; uniformly; emphatically; vehemently; strenuously; obstinately; blandly; sternly; eloquently.
(See urge, persist, press.)

INSISTENCE
adjectives
stern; steadfast; deliberate; important; melancholy; eloquent; perpetual; pathetic; stereotyped.

verbs
assert with—; increase—; relax—; require —; silence—; steel against—; stick with—;

—annoys; —conquers; —determines; —irks; —relents.

(See persistence, determination, intensity, perseverance.)

INSISTENT
adverbs
vexatiously; tiresomely; intolerably; annoyingly; captiously; peevishly; cruelly; tyrannically; discourteously; violently; disagreeably; unpleasantly; hospitably; generously; aggressively; inescapably; urgently; embarrassingly; pestiferously; cantankerously; distressingly; dictatorially; resolutely; firmly; tenaciously; obstinately.

INSOLENCE
adjectives
haughty; increasing; disobedient; smiling; beefy; studied; ferocious; displeasing; gigantic; personal; insane; wanton; flat-faced; mutinous; puffed.

INSOLENT
adverbs
unbearably; atrociously; arrogantly; proudly; haughtily; arrantly; inordinately; egregiously; intolerably; ridiculously; unpardonably; disrespectfully; terribly; flippantly; pertly; saucily; crudely; grossly; abusively; outrageously; outlandishly; scandalously; loudly; brazenly; crassly; bumptiously; imperiously; highly; audaciously; inexcusably.

INSOLVENT
adverbs
pitiably; suddenly; finally; pathetically; unfortunately; admittedly; hopelessly; sorrowfully; desperately; deeply; unluckily; unhappily; impecuniously; embarrassingly; ruinously; unaccountably; inexplicably; mysteriously; curiously; incredibly; needlessly.

INSOMNIA
verbs
afflict with—; conquer—; correct—; ease—; grapple with—; labor under—; release—; subject to—; suffer—; —hinders; —interferes; —provokes; —stupefies; —unnerves; —weakens.

(See disease, pain.)

INSOUCIANT
adverbs
inconsiderately; blithely; giddily; dizzily; heedlessly; dreamily; gaily; cheerily; carelessly; unconcernedly; imperturbably; recklessly; rashly; serenely; calmly; heartily.

INSPECT (v)
adverbs
intently; circumspectly; fastidiously; judiciously; rigidly; periodically; personally; cursorily; cautiously; painstakingly.

(See examine, investigate.)

INSPECTION
adjectives
immediate; rigid; bare; painstaking; periodic; cursory; cautious; personal.

INSPIRATION
adjectives
passionate; fatal; unmistakable; fresh; happy; healthier; subtle; verbal; sudden; heroic; divine; adequate; overpowering; mystic; elevated; dramatic; inward; maternal; incarnate; mighty; unbiased; natural; irrepressible; sustaining; struggling; feeblest; laborious; ennobling.

verbs
conflict with—; derive—from; exhaust—; foster—; gain—; kill—; presage—; pray for—; preserve—; restore—; suppress—; whisper—; —cheers; —flags; —rallies; —seizes; —visits; —wells from.

(See enthusiasm, fervor, influence, genius.)

INSPIRE (v)
adverbs
religiously; divinely; nocturnally; unceasingly; invariably; passionately; fatally; happily; subtly; verbally; heroically; mystically; dramatically; maternally; irrepressibly; feebly; laboriously; tenderly.

(See kindle, arouse, rouse, animate.)

INSTABILITY
adjectives
emotional; molecular; psychic; permanent; mental.

verbs
aggravate—; betray—; buttress—; condemn—; convey—; deplore—; detect—; judge—; lament—; lead to—; observe—; reflect on—; reform—; support—; survey —; —irks; —threatens.

(See weakness, impotence.)

adverbs
magnificently; ceremoniously; regularly; comfortably; formally; scientifically; modernistically; charitably; governmentally; legislatively; dictatorially.

(See establish, place.)

INSTALLMENT

verbs
administer—; commend—; consent to—; direct—; glorify—; herald—; honor by—; influence—; inspire—; invite to—; observe—; occasion—; perform—; plan—; preside at —; seek—; view—; —climaxes; witness—.

(See payment.)

INSTANCE

adjectives
contradictory; isolated; individual; noteworthy; wonderful; abundant; well-authenticated; striking; inconsiderable; parallel; continued; dramatic; precise; memorable; far-famed; admirable; melancholy; conspicuous; arresting; notable; forcible; unfortunate; characteristic; splendid; abortive; comparable; notorious; tragic; recorded; solitary; unrelated; typical; worthy; particular; extreme; delightful; present; illustrious; rare; undeniable; remarkable.

verbs
afford—; cite—; contradict—; demand—; dispute—; experience—; furnish—; multiply —s; offer—; point out—; provide—; quote —; ridicule—; solicit—; study—; —exemplifies; —illustrates; —indicates; —proves; —reminds.

(See example, illustration, precedent.)

INSTANT

adjectives
unseasonable; luminous; approaching; flashing; terrible; fleeting; single; breathless; fatal; swift.

verbs
accomplish in an—; convey in—; depart for —; emerge in—; flicker out in—; pause for —; separate for—; —passes; —presses.

(See moment, hour, time.)

INSTIL (*v*)

adverbs
ridiculously; subtly; insidiously; cleverly; slyly; perfidiously; covertly; mystically; paternally; scholastically.

(See introduce, impress, implant.)

INSTINCT

adjectives
poetic; indefinable; impulsive; hereditary; faithful; natural; holy; warm; brutal; prophetic; profoundest; subtle; dramatic; vague; combative; protective; military; proper; religious; beneficent; noble; aesthetic; conservative; inherited; artistic; self-preserving; denied; invisible; maternal; unerring; refined; gentle; deepest; semi-barbaric; perverted; animal; sterile; amorphous; conservative; universal; deep-rooted; formal; ennobled; delicate; driving; human; heroic; grosser; native; transcendental; tameless; sympathetic; long-dormant; disorderly; journalistic; monastic; social; irresistible; fine; quality; predominating; provident; spiritual; tender; wonderful; mechanical; prudential; fiery; grateful; innate; sudden; scientific; imperative; sure; trained; superhuman; speculative; irrrelevant; snob; groping; gregarious; terrible; herd; independent; fortunate; selective; kindly; unconscious; purest; common; iconoclastic; logical; racial; brutal; derogatory.

verbs
cloud—; control—; curb—; develop—; endow with—; follow—; gratify—; numb—; obey—; offend—; pander to—; rely on—; repress—; rouse—; stir—; succumb to—; suppress—; thwart—; violate—; —deceives; —guides; —impels; —motivates; —persists; —s war within.

(See impulse, desire, skill, nature.)

INSTITUTION

adjectives
frail; cherished; extraordinary; charitable; religious; popular; temporary; essential; instrumental; professional; venerable; august; notable; existing; ecclesiastical; sacerdotal; preparatory; necessary; time-honored; infant; remarkable; major; peculiar; sundry (pl); aristocratic; feudal; fiduciary; diverse (pl); flourishing; ancient; dignified; free; popular; bestial; inevitable; liberal; respective; lauded; social; distinctive; dominant; economic; benevolent; perfidious; bureaucratic; long-established; various (pl); abhorrent; moneyed; powerful; notorious; parochial; superb; monstrous.

verbs
abolish—; acclaim—; bar from—; charter —; commit to—; confirm—; discard—; endow—; grant to—; herd in—s; lampoon—;

maintain—; patronize—; support—; undermine—; —crumbles; —flourishes.

(See establishment, club, society, school.)

INSTRUCT (v)

adverbs

peremptorily; urgently; artistically; solemnly; forcefully; adequately; laconically; ethically; clinically; parochially; tediously; theoretically; intellectually; facetiously; vaguely; academically; formally; inspirationally; diligently.

(See teach, command, direct.)

INSTRUCTION

adjectives

adequate; hurried; scattered; bloody; laconic; inevitable; careful; explicit; brave; ethical; botanical; clinical; stimulative; parochial; official; minute; thoughtful; elementary; theoretical; intellectual; facetious; pleasurable; cabled; hazy; vague; religious; tedious; classroom; parliamentary.

verbs

abide by—; attend to—; authorize—; comply with—; conform to—; contravene—; counsel—; deluge with—; desire—; disqualify for—; follow—; hearken to—; impart—; lack—; overwhelm with—s; prescribe—; profit by—; radio—; refuse—; —corrects; —guides.

(See teaching, information, education.)

INSTRUCTOR

adjectives

clerical; capable; competent; sober; sordid; reticent.

INSTRUMENT

adjectives

physical; master; keyboard; gracious; godlike; negotiable; outstanding; dictating; grand; musical; ingenious; expensive; unfit; precision; potent; rude; glorious; philosophical; penitent; facile; perfect; rough; extraordinary; noble; exceptional; component; heavenly; murderous; incomprehensible; spellbound; blunt; passive; unconscious; compact; scorned; supple; astronomical; serviceable; quaking; dental; cunning; greedy; sacred; tolerable; immediate; graceful.

verbs

contaminate—; contrive—; devise—; employ—; encase—; fashion—; forge—; guard —; hamper—; hinder—; introduce—; lubricate—; manipulate—; obstruct—; perform with—; project—; resist—; utilize—; yield to—.

(See tool, utensil, method, document, machine.)

INSTRUMENTAL

adverbs

definitely; helpfully; necessarily; admittedly; covertly; secretly; furtively; openly; proudly; ostentatiously; usefully; diabolically; benevolently; obscurely; inscrutably; valuably; serviceably; fortunately; capably; competently.

INSUBORDINATE

adverbs

insufferably; unbearably; intolerably; recklessly; rashly; brazenly; sullenly; subtly; openly; unaccountably; deliberately; arrantly; accidentally; purposely; unconsciously; unpardonably; hopelessly; grossly; crassly; flagrantly; slyly; audaciously; mutinously; seditiously; treacherously; incredibly; restively; impatiently; egregiously; amazingly; dangerously; childishly; senselessly.

INSUBORDINATION

adjectives

sharp; colonial; criminal; flagrant; rank.

INSUBSTANTIAL

adverbs

terribly; hopelessly; tragically; nebulously; imaginatively; dreamily; pitifully; wretchedly; airily; tenuously; vaguely; dimly; altogether; blankly; obviously; utterly.

INSUFFERABLE

adverbs

utterly; disagreeably; incredibly; altogether; haughtily; boisterously; rudely; arrantly; grossly; crassly; crudely; boorishly; arrogantly; swaggeringly; scornfully; loudly; maliciously; slanderously; invidiously; importunately; abhorrently; odiously; generally.

INSUFFICIENT

adverbs

pitiably; tragically; wretchedly; altogether; stingily; parsimoniously; unbelievably; evidently; palpably; ungenerously; thoughtlessly; piteously; miserably; criminally; incredibly; shockingly; appallingly; awfully.

INSULAR

adverb

incredibly; happily; safely; securely; narrowly; narrow-mindedly; bigotedly; fanatically; contentedly; smugly; dogmatically; stupidly; surprisingly; naturally; peacefully; complacently; inordinately; rustically; provincially.

INSULT

adjectives

harsh; unfeeling; endurable; rash; crowning; biting; personal; cruel; grossest; veiled; monstrous; fresh; mortal; stinging; deadly; persistent; dire; supposed; petty.

verbs

avenge—; barb with—; bawl—; brook—; condone—; decry—; endure—; exchange —s; fling—at; hurl—at; ignore—; shout—; suffer—; take affront at—; —grieves; — infuriates; —libels; —rebuffs; —slanders; pardon—.
(See outrage, offense, wrong.)

INSULT (v)

adverbs

scurrilously; desperately; vilely; impudently; grossly; brazenly; outrageously; sullenly; wantonly; unendurably; monstrously.
(See affront, abuse, offend.)

INSULTING

adverbs

horribly; unpardonably; intolerably; unbearably; insufferably; boorishly; cruelly; subtly; covertly; sneeringly; cynically; ironically; openly; deliberately; intentionally; inexcusably; coarsely; grossly; publicly; superciliously; impudently; flagrantly.

INSUPPORTABLE

adverbs

altogether; evidently; manifestly; fantastically; obviously; heavily; tragically; pitiably; wretchedly; lamentably; indubitably; visibly; shockingly; pitifully; physically; painfully; grievously; finally; oppressively; tormentingly.

INSURANCE

verbs

collect—; consider—; examine for—; obtain —; pay—; prefer—; refuse—; regulate—; transfer—; value—; undertake—; under- write—; —guarantees; —indemnifies; —invests; —lapses; —provides; —reassures; —safeguards.
(See security, guarantee.)

INSURE (v)

adverbs

prudentially; customarily; rashly; paradoxically; conventionally; conservatively; liberally.
(See protect, assure.)

INSURGENTS

verbs

accede to—; beat down—; check—; disperse —; inflame—; kindle—; quell—; repel—; repulse—; rout—; stir—; subdue—; —arise; —conspire; —demand; —dictate; —intrigue; —occupy; —oppose; —overthrow; —plot; —revolt; —spring up; —tyrannize.
(See enemy, rebel, foe, rival, competitor.)

INSURMOUNTABLE

adverbs

heavily; oppressively; appallingly; manifestly; admittedly; apparently; perplexingly; bafflingly; absurdly; desperately; seriously; gravely; unfortunately; curiously; altogether; legally; disconcertingly; embarrassingly; awkwardly; cruelly.

INSURRECTION

adjectives

muting; wide-spread; hopeless; subsequent; servile; absurd; serious; laughable; domestic.

verbs

check—; conspire—; crush—; encourage—; engage in—; excite—; finance—; foment—; head—; inflame—; instigate—; kindle—; plot—; quell—; resist—; restrain—; support—; suppress—; —alarms; —breaks out; —bursts forth; —dismays; —endangers; — menaces; —sweeps away; —threatens.
(See revolution, rebellion, fight.)

INTACT

adverbs

blessedly; luckily; fortunately; incredibly; happily; visibly; safely; securely.

INTANGIBLE

adverbs

evanescently; undeniably; practically; dimly; vaguely; obscurely; fleetingly; provokingly; legally; foggily; indeterminately; temporally; darkly; unintelligibly; naturally; mysteriously; faintly.

INTEGRITY

adjectives

territorial; constitutional; innate; unimpeachable; sturdy; delicate; unassailable; sterling; unbending; unquestioned; determined; administrative; incorruptible; moral; transparent; intellectual; perfect; stubborn; stern; indisputable.

verbs

blemish—; breed—; commend—; doubt—; esteem—; impair—; laud—; maintain—; note—; preserve—; question—; require—; reserve—; retain—; reward—; root in—; taint—; test—; trust—; sacrifice—; vow—.

(See honesty, virtue, truth, sincerity.)

INTELLECT

adjectives

cultured; keen; expanded; happy; considerable; godlike; high; stern; jaded; powerful; sluggard; prostrated; ruthless; unclouded; benighted; noble; restless; unguided; comprehending; austere; elevated; sluggish; brilliant; ordinary; lofty; inferior; articulate; frightened; active; provincial; haggard; fertile; ripening; profound; undying; imperial; superior; aroused; cultivated; crudest; discerning; prepared; meddling; humble; cold; resourceful; human; shadowy; penetrating; colossal; wavering; uninformed; grasping; singular; mightiest; reasoning; many-sided; stagnant; refined; stirring; seraphic; all-subtilizing; amazing; constructive; massive; eternal.

verbs

balance—; cobweb—; cultivate—; destroy —; dissipate—; distort—; educate—; enlarge—; enthrone—; excel in—; expand—; impair—; judge—; perfect—; reflect—; shake—; sharpen—; stunt—; train—; weigh —; —comprehends; —deteriorates; —discerns; —enslaves; —revolts; —speculates.

(See brain, mind, understanding, intelligence.)

INTELLECTUAL

adverbs

proudly; blatantly; swaggeringly; consciously; brilliantly; immensely; keenly; sharp-

ly; shrewdly; astutely; highly; profoundly; seriously; soberly; cleverly; solidly; alarmingly; incredibly; gravely; heavily.

INTELLIGENCE

adjectives

earliest; remorseless; keen; patient; banded; reassuring; native; alarming; sluggish; subtlest; extreme; swift; alert; shrewd; melancholy; luminous; elusive; mysterious; afflicting; morbid; restless; human; vulgar; musing; diagnostic; presiding; matrimonial; conscious; coherent; welcome; obvious; informed; supreme; unwonted; infinite; unexpected; hideous; magnified; detached; unfailing; lofty; meanest; mediocre; wide; untutored; vivid; concentrated; prophetic; polished; quick; weakened; precocious; unclouded; creative; clear; rapid; rarefied; omniscient; cheering; passive; divine; sympathetic; disagreeable; crushing; cold; hard; penetrating; astounding; musical; sharp; sad; singular; diseased; supreme; bizarre; energetic; pure; sagacious.

verbs

approach with—; assert—; bow to—; brim with—; dim—; dull—; endow with—; exercise—; gamble on—; impart—; mock—; radiate—; register—; reveal—; sharpen—; subjugate—; —controls; —dominates; — governs.

(See ability, intellect, insight, mind, wisdom, talent.)

INTELLIGENT

adverbs

unwontedly; keenly; patiently; naturally; alarmingly; subtly; extremely; swiftly; alertly; shrewdly; mysteriously; vigilantly; restlessly; consciously; obviously; supremely; unexpectedly; unfailingly; infinitely; broadly; loftily; vividly; prophetically; creatively; precociously; clearly; omnisciently; cheeringly; sympathetically; divinely; disagreeably; coldly; penetratingly; warmly; astoundingly; singularly; sagaciously; apparently; cleverly; profoundly; fairly; thoughtfully; politically; discriminatingly; manifestly; exceedingly; significantly.

INTELLIGIBLE

adverbs

wholly; fairly; hardly; easily; surprisingly; scarcely; explicitly; instantly; graphically; unmistakably; strikingly; barely; clearly.

verbs
abstain from—; addict to—; atone for—; avoid—; betray—; burst with—; cure—; drown in—; err through—; fall into—; forego—; indulge in—; outlaw—; rack by —; sink into—; slide into—; —burns; — clouds; —defaces; —degenerates; —dissipates; —reigns; —sickens.

(See drunkenness, excess, debauchery, wickedness.)

INTEMPERATE

adverbs
foolishly; fatally; recklessly; dangerously; rashly; unaccountably; senselessly; extravagantly; voluptuously; luxuriously; wildly; rakishly; drunkenly; dreadfully; occasionally; habitually; notoriously; absurdly; preposterously; dissolutely; indiscreetly.

INTEND (v)

adverbs
characteristically; primarily; virtually; incalculably; originally; complimentarily; ostensibly; wantonly; subtly; unquestionably; maliciously; tyrannically; amiably; cruelly; dictatorially; loyally; jocularly; irreverently.

(See design, propose.)

INTENSIFY (v)

adverbs
vividly; inordinately; furiously; dramatically; emotionally; subjectively; morbidly; infinitely; fiercely; tragically; gloriously.

(See aggravate, emphasize, magnify.)

INTENSITY

adjectives
intermediate; decreasing; dreadful; lyrical; savage; scorching; barbarous; varying; unsurpassable; dramatic; clear; severe; low; unequal; mystical; emotional; subjective; white-faced; waning; morbid; infinite; desired; fierce; bare; dramatized; tragic; peculiar; heightened; glorified.

verbs
denote—; exhibit—; glow with—; increase —; live with—; measure—; note—; observe —; register—; relax—; revive—; slacken —; —grows; —overcomes; —strains; — taxes; —tires; —trebles; —wanes.

(See energy, force, strength, power, zeal.)

INTENT

adjectives
deliberate; wicked; mad; late; charitable; swift; amorous; bad; fierce; conscious; absurd; unlawful; evil; original; sublime; obvious; malicious.

adverbs
curiously; strangely; absently; wholly; abstractedly; oddly; deeply; eagerly; deliberately; carefully; wisely; impressively; earnestly; seriously; closely; resolutely; diplomatically; considerately; thoughtfully; critically; studiously; markedly; vigilantly; flatteringly; raptly; breathlessly; zealously; uncommonly.

INTENTION

adjectives
serious; deliberate; immoral; especial; tyrannous; docile; murderous; honorable; ulterior; honest; supposable; amiable; emotional; benignant; cordial; cruel; benevolent; wicked; wise; avowed; hospitable; definite; travelling; alleged; evil; dictatorial; loyal; earthly; original; industrial; festive; greedy; hostile; fixed; charitable; unconscious; evident; speculative; objective; cold; calculated; liberal; apparent; pacific; testamentary; treacherous; profound; matrimonial; suicidal; warlike; irreverant; jocular; private.

verbs
burst with—; cancel—; communicate—; conceal—; declare—; deny—; disavow—; disclaim—; err in—; impede—; miscarry—; misconstrue—; mistake—; proclaim—; purify—; reaffirm—; reiterate—; relinquish—; stick to—.

(See plan, aim, desire, purpose.)

INTERACTION

adjectives
ethical; unsuspected; incessant; harmonious.

INTERCEPT (v)

adverbs
subtly; dexterously; slyly; treacherously; inimically; jealously; hatefully; selfishly; zealously; perfidiously.

(See seize, take, prevent.)

INTERCHANGE

adjectives
healthful; interesting; provident; sweet; so-

cial; savage; constant; wearisome; pleasant; mutual; rapid; unfettered.

INTERCOURSE

adjectives

sexual; amicable; continual; free; frigid; convivial; pleasant; innocent; mutual; beautiful; intimate; unrestrained; sweet; genial; delightful; formal; beneficial; unhappy; courteous; social; personal; vile; intimate; habitual; commercial; unreserved; constant; diplomatic; friendly; frequent; intellectual.

verbs

abstain from—; avoid—; bind by—; carry on—; discontinue—; employ—; encourage —; engage in—; limit—; open—; overindulge in—; prevent—; prohibit—; refrain from—; relax—; stimulate—; survey—; — balances; —debilitates; —declines; —increases.

(See communication, commerce, conversation, traffic, transaction.)

INTERDICT (v)

adverbs

solemnly; formally; legally; tyrannically; dictatorially; officially; religiously.

(See restrain, repress.)

INTEREST

verbs   (attention or concern)

absorb—of; accentuate—; alienate—; attach — to; awaken—; betoken—; catch—; cultivate—; dim—; display—; distract—; eclipse —; elicit—; engage—; enlist—; evoke—; excite—; exude—; feed—; feign—; focus—; inspire—; intensify—; kill—; kindle—; lend —; manifest—; muster—; note with—; pique—; quicken—; recapture—; regain—; revive—; rivet — upon; share—; smother—; stimulate—; sustain—; switch—; whip up —; —abates; —s bind; —centers on; — deepens; —ebbs; —endures; —fades; — flags; —mounts; —palls; —picks up; — wanes; engross—.

(See concentration, attention, vigilance.)

INTEREST

adjectives   (general)

far-flung; special; national; religious; commercial; personal; passing; indulgent; individual; detached; momentous; property; selfish; minority; friendly; complicated; irresistible; affected; benevolent; primary; historic; philanthropic; superstitious; restrained; exorbitant; busy; final; jarring;

well-meant; equal; presbyterian; literary; pecuniary; mercantile; great; attentive; missionary; extreme; evident; general; popular; genuine; lively; mournful; careful; bosom; paradoxical; private; growing; central; probable; pathetic; worldly; fraternal; universal; renewed; confessed; touching; paramount; amused; sudden; indifferent; satirical; feverish; certain; philosophic; intelligent; lasting; considerable; painful; respective; appalling; intense; thoughtful; overrated; immense; absorbing; surpassing; ultimate; connected; warm; widespread; national; stealthy; furtive; insistent; proprietary; vital; languid; energetic; diverse; bibliographical; thrilling; ennobling; peculiar; intellectual; overmastering; economic; vital; theoretical; active; gloomy; bankrupt; principal; endless; suave; urgent; sustained; human; racial; keenest; direct; jealous; discriminating; tepid; shadowy; languid; overmastering; contemporaneous; extraordinary; exclusive; philosophical; characteristic; surpassing; aesthetic; childish; anthropological; particular; enduring; extraneous; antiquarian; truant; exaggerated; crowning; inimical; lofty; revived; enormous; satisfying; undisturbed; parochial; medieval; ancient; awesome; neverceasing; student; sectional; humanitarian; public-spirited; diminished; real; sincere; insatiable; courteous; pathological; unutterable; coincidental; deepest; involved; expressional; inexhaustible; controlling; active; exceptional; long-nursed; wistful; faintest; unconquered; vaguest; passionate; grim; chauvinistic; lukewarm; vested; ethical; interwoven; compounded; dark; conflicting; perfunctory; elusive; persistent; particular; academic; world-wide; critical; heightened; potential; imperialist; affectionate; ignorant; domestic; alarmed; burning; solicitous; stirring; sordid; discriminating; perplexing; antipodal; lingering; dissimilar (pl).

INTEREST
(financial)

verbs

affect—; amass—; cater to—; cherish—; control—; defend—; enlarge—; enumerate —; fortify—; foster—; merge—; promote —; regulate—; represent—; safeguard—; strengthen—; subverse—; unite—s of; weld —s of; —s flourish; —s overlap; —s prosper.

(See business, advantage, good, benefit.)

INTEREST
(money)
verbs

bear—; borrow on—; calculate—; charge —; claim—; compound—; entitle to—; fix —; figure—; forfeit—; obtain—; reckon—; request—; return—; subtract—; —accrues; —compensates; —taxes.

(See amount, sum, money, profit.)

INTEREST (v)
adverbs

proportionately; consistently; particularly; profoundly; excessively; keenly; genuinely; ingeniously; intensely; moderately; religiously; commercially; selfishly; affectionately; benevolently; philanthropically; paradoxically; jealously; philosophically; passionately; perfunctorily; academically; potentially; solicitously.

(See concern, excite.)

INTERESTING
adverbs

thrillingly; absorbingly; breathlessly; specially; historically; extremely; generally; genuinely; intensely; vitally; economically; extraordinarily; particularly; pathologically; vaguely; curiously; keenly; charmingly; strangely; attractively; pleasantly; engrossingly; marvelously; especially.

INTERFERE (v)
adverbs

boisterously; materially; consciously; energetically; unreasonably; irrationally; officiously; arrogantly; providentially; destructively; judicially; jealously; enviously; vindictively.

(See conflict, intermeddle, intervene.)

INTERFERENCE
adjectives

slightest; untimely; impertinent; feeble; ill-judged; arrogant; avoidable; unwarranted; providential; destructive; judicial; intolerant; mutual; optical; hostile; unexpected; unauthorized; supernatural; jealous; imperative; humane; watchful; hot; outside; needless; powerful.

verbs

brook—; counteract—; encounter—; inveigh against—; justify—; oppose—; overcome—; provoke—; refrain from—; resent—; restrict—; tolerate—; withdraw—; —agitates; —blocks; —chokes; —clogs; —disheartens; —distresses; —hinders; —impedes; —meddles; —retards.

(See opposition, collision, intervention, resistance, hostility, obstacle.)

INTERIOR
adjectives

distinctive; ambitious; distinguished; sumptuous; superb; opaque; domestic; webby; capacious; unmodified; colonial; costly; austere; musty; dusty; wretched; pierced.

verbs

acquaint with—; advance into—; creep into —; display—; enter—; harmonize—; invade —; line—; lose in—; penetrate—; press into —; pry into—; push into—; situate in—; withdraw into—; worm into—; —awes; —impresses; —unfolds.

(See jungle, recess, middle, center.)

INTERJECT (v)
adverbs

bitingly; devoutly; unexpectedly; harshly; abruptly; piercingly; rudely; coarsely; fiercely; wittily; indignantly; unreasonably; nervously; ferociously; instructively; irritatingly.

(See inject, insert.)

INTERLINE (v)
adverbs

warmly; richly; comfortably; luxuriously; expensively; matchlessly; ornamentally.

INTERLOCUTOR
verbs

employ—; —acquaints; —amuses; —announces; —asserts; —communicates; —corrects; —explains; —expresses; —informs; —instructs; —interferes; —interposes; —introduces; —intrudes; —leads; —prompts; —opens; —outlines.

(See speaker, debater, actor, clown.)

INTERLUDE
adjectives

strange; musical; brief; charming; circling; underworld; calm.

INTERMENT
adjectives

pious; showy; honorable.

INTERMINGLE (v)

adverbs

gregariously; grotesquely; democratically; unrestrictedly; swarmingly; offensively; perpetually; extraordinarily.

(See mingle, mix.)

INTERMISSION

adjectives

seasonable; lucid; irregular (pl); much-needed.

INTERMIXTURE

adjectives

occasional; subtle; helpful.

INTERPOSE (v)

adverbs

unwillingly; deftly; providentially; mercifully; mysteriously; deliberately; fortunately; designedly; vainly; aggressively; zealously; blankly.

(See intervene, interrupt.)

INTERPOSITION

adjectives

deft; timely; providential; renewed; merciful; divine.

INTERPRET (v)

adverbs

literally; objectively; narrowly; allegorically; sympathetically; intelligently; boldly; unfavorably; adequately; superficially; metaphysically; speculatively; offensively; poetically; charitably; mythologically.

(See translate, construe, render.)

INTERPRETATION

adjectives

superficial; corresponding; metaphysical; polyphonic; diverse (pl); legal; rabbinical; speculative; conflicting; mental; probable; ingenious; thoughtful; offensive; fascinating; authoritative; understandable; subtle; mystic; poetic; mythological; imperfect; lyric; base; musical; scriptural; allegorical; inexperienced; uncharitable.

verbs

abuse—; accept—; advance—; broaden—; contemplate—; correct—; deduce—; evolve —; hand down—; infer—; lend—; misconstrue—; misquote—; offer—; reiterate—; reject—; question—; scorn—; —mutilates; —signifies.

(See conception, explanation, idea.)

INTERPRETER

adjectives

urbane; euphuistical; noble; zealous; penetrating; coarse; apt; false; picturesque.

INTERROGATE (v)

adverbs

sumptuously; rudely; impudently; roughly; impishly; boldly; formally; characteristically; frankly; pompously; fraternally; authoritatively.

(See question, examine.)

INTERROGATION

adjectives

incredible; fresh; impish; wondering.

INTERRUPT (v)

adverbs

rudely; joyously; hastily; frequently; blatantly; judiciously; indignantly; earnestly; conveniently; peremptorily; momentarily; irrelevantly; abruptly; vaguely; temporarily; prematurely; spasmodically; repetitiously.

(See interpose, obstruct, retard.)

INTERRUPTION

adjectives

frequent; serious; spasmodic; jarring; abrupt; stern; absolute; continual; palpable; reasonable; momentary; temporary; unseemly; extraordinary; external.

verbs

attempt—; beg—; forgive—; hinder with —; tolerate—; welcome—; wince at—; witness—; —angers; —disturbs; —infringes; —provokes; —severs; —thwarts.

(See pause, rudeness, impudence, delay.)

INTERSPERSE (v)

adverbs

widely; thoroughly; comfortably; regularly; conveniently; occasionally; methodically.

(See mix, scatter, distribute.)

INTERTWINE (v)

adverbs

inextricably; elaborately; amorously; delicately; endlessly; complexly; haphazardly; artfully; skilfully; curiously.

(See entangle, twine, wind.)

INTERVAL

adjectives

slender; irregular; fitting; considerable;

feeding; torpid; measured; painful; equidistant; suitable; stated; frequent (pl); wide; fathomless; varying (pl); tranquil; rapid; indeterminate; endless; rare; twilight; reasonable; precious; dreadful; starless; recurring; lucid; mystical; harmonic; immeasurable; brief; stipulated; enormous; ensuing; conceivable; stolen; lesser; unflattering; spasmodic; long.

verbs

administer at—s; bridge—; consider in—; designate at—s; doze at—s; fill—; fritter away—; grant—; increase—s; pause for—; regulate—s; review—; sleep at—s; span—; —annoys; —delays; —separates; —vanishes.

(See space, pause, distance.)

INTERVENE (v)

adverbs

actively; impetuously; diabolically; miraculously; demoniacally; indiscreetly; venomously; slyly; paternally; hatefully; habitually; jealously.

(See interpose, interrupt.)

INTERVENTION

adjectives

armed; miraculous; indiscreet; diabolical; perpetual; untoward; demoniacal.

verbs

appeal for—; approve of—; consider—; decry—; denounce—; deplore—; employ—; exercise—; frame—; grant—; necessitate—; plead for—; seek—; terminate—; —aids; —annoys; —impedes; —interrupts; —irks; —relieves; —wanes.

(See opposition, interference, resistance.)

INTERVIEW

adjectives

satisfactory; valuable; confiding; affecting; complicated; unauthorized; interesting; clandestine; frequent; stormy; remarkable; painful; expressive; tussling; unchaperoned; vesper; transient; short-sighted; frank; preliminary; childish; protracted; brief; unexpected; psychoanalytic; parting; unsatisfactory; disastrous.

verbs

allow—; chronicle—; conclude—; confine—to; demand—; draw into—; elicit in—; endure—; evade—; grant—; obtain—; promise—; publish—; report—; request—; seek

—; shirk—; terminate—; transpire at—; —degrades; —reveals; —tires; —wearies.

(See discussion, talk, conversation, conference.)

INTERVIEW (v)

adverbs

genially; professionally; confidentially; journalistically; daily; secretly; clandestinely; politically.

(See question.)

INTERWEAVE (v)

adverbs

artfully; intimately; mysteriously; dexterously; laboredly; elaborately; delicately; ornamentally; richly; intricately.

(See weave, intermingle.)

INTERWEAVING

adjectives

labored; dexterous; endless; elaborate; delicate.

INTESTINE

verbs

afflict—; attach to—; attack—; block—; clog—; constrict—; distend—; ferment in—; penetrate—; poison—; puncture—; obstruct—; putrefy in—; strangle—; twist—; —absorbs; —adheres; —coils; —discharges; —functions; —kinks; —mats; —provides.

INTIMACY

adjectives

annoying; agreeable; increasing; pleasant; peculiar; apparent; unfriendly; amorous; unseemly; lifelong; affectionate; curious; surprised; seeming; daily; closest; sudden; true; delicious; clandestine; immemorial; homely; rare; patronizing; embarrassed; mutual.

verbs

attempt—; brook—; court—; crush—; desire—; display—; draw back from—; enjoy—; enter with—; establish—; forbid—; question—; poison—; press into—; relax—; resist—; ripen into—; solicit—; strike up—; —arises; —mitigates; —reveals; —springs up.

(See friendship, fellowship, companionship, love, tenderness.)

adverbs

exceptionally; reprehensibly; curiously; inordinately; strangely; charmingly; closely; unusually; uncommonly; pleasantly; affectionately; embarrassingly; oddly; sweetly; confidentially; particularly; peculiarly; singularly; artlessly; cordially; devotedly; companionably; agreeably; gently; graciously; unbecomingly.

INTIMATE (v)

adverbs

bitterly; silently; darkly; distinctly; simultaneously; tacitly; mystically; officially; unpleasantly; slyly; diabolically; delicately; plausibly.

(See hint, indicate.)

INTIMATION

adjectives

slightest; evident; injurious; mystical; official; silent; scattered; delicate; subjective; free; previous; unpleasant.

verbs

acknowledge—; advance—; contemplate—; dare—; furnish—; heed—; perceive—; ridicule—; seek—; weigh—; —creeps in; —denotes; —hints; —indicates; —informs; —interests; —leaks out; —notifies; —suggests.

(See accusation, innuendo, hint, suggestion, implication.)

INTIMIDATE (v)

adverbs

illegally; jealously; forcefully; unfairly; fiercely; ferociously; ruthlessly; formidably; economically; physically; deliberately; rudely.

(See frighten, scare, threaten.)

INTIMIDATED

adverbs

brutally; constantly; illegally; criminally; unquestionably; evidently; horribly; cruelly; tyrannically; daily; perceptibly; ignorantly; ridiculously; spinelessly; terribly.

INTOLERABLE

adverbs

absolutely; painfully; finally; naturally; odiously; grievously; oppressively; grimly; abhorrently.

adjectives

fierce; unchecked; ecclesiastical; fiery; narrow; marked; wicked.

verbs

accuse of—; attend with—; campaign against—; deplore—; indicate—; observe—; overcome—; provoke to—; show—; suffer from—; —scorns; —shames; —treads on; —vitiates.

(See fanaticism, wickedness.)

INTOLERANT

adverbs

harshly; sternly; austerely; fretfully; rigidly; dogmatically; professionally; narrowly; ignorantly; generally; inexcusably; unduly; unpleasantly; disagreeably; terribly; inconsistently; strangely; extremely; conspicuously; arrogantly; superciliously; emphatically; stubbornly; obdurately; unyieldingly; cruelly; bitterly; provincially; fanatically; doctrinally; mulishly; doggedly; impatiently; fiercely; officially.

INTONATION

adjectives

pitying; different; soft; searching; ascending; calm; genuine; limpid; liquid; sweet; steadfast; wilful; contemptuous; languorous; asthmatic; nasal; characteristic; bellowing; lazy; nervous; guttural; perceptible; muffled.

INTONE (v)

adverbs

sanctimoniously; languorously; sepulchrally; melodiously; sweetly; gutturally; monotonously; characteristically.

(See speak, recite, sing.)

INTOXICATION

adjectives

subduing; complete; serene; habitual; partial; sweet; giddy; prolonged; utter; helpless.

INTRACTABLE

adverbs

perversely; incorrigibly; provokingly; vexatiously; unbearably; intolerably; stubbornly; wilfully; offensively; defiantly; utterly; doggedly; stolidly; wildly; capriciously; uncontrollably; cantankerously; mulishly; pitifully; violently; obstinately; scandalously;

sullenly; waywardly; formidably; hopelessly; restively; peevishly; churlishly; inveterately; narrow-mindedly.

INTRENCH (v)
adverbs
strongly; safely; securely; inviolably; firmly; strategically; protectively.
(See encroach, invade, entrench.)

INTREPID
adverbs
valorously; gallantly; chivalrously; boldly; feignedly; conversationally; swaggeringly; boastfully; audaciously; spunkily; resolutely; determinedly; heroically; valiantly; pluckily; marvellously; remarkably; uncommonly; adventurously; firmly; apparently; stoutly.

INTRICACY
verbs
comprehend—s; conceal in—s; conduct through—s; cut off—s; ease—; enmesh in —s; entangle in—s; involve—s; lessen—; map out—s; overcome—; probe—s; understand—; unravel—s; —bewilders; —complicates; —perplexes; —puzzles.
(See complication, complexity, tangle, confusion, obstruction.)

INTRICATE
adverbs
perplexingly; obscurely; obstructively; hopelessly; strangely; unduly; embarrassingly; objectionably; needlessly; terribly; deliberately; tortuously; subtly; awkwardly; formidably; provokingly; unnecessarily; clumsily.

INTRIGUE
adjectives
romantic; genuine; peaceful; violent; perpetual; criminal; sinuous; revolutionary; paltry; scandalous; sordid; ambitious; political; continental; double; indefatigable; dynastic; sacrilegious; abortive; tortuous; poor; clever; private.

verbs
bristle with—; conspire—; detect—; enjoy —; expose—; fall into—; infuse—; involve in—; meddle with—; plot—; plunge into—; share in—; stimulate—; uncover—; unearth —; —accomplishes; —deceives; —embarrasses; —mystifies.
(See adventure, plot, scheme, mystery.)

INTRODUCE (v)
adverbs
deliberately; simultaneously; ceremoniously; advantageously; casually; decorously; mischievously; commercially; conventionally; perfunctorily; unblushingly; orchestrally; formally.
(See present, insert, commence.)

INTRODUCTION
adjectives
preliminary; basic; promiscuous; impressive; appreciative; conventional; appropriate; perfunctory; coveted; improbable; wearisome; illicit; unblushing; depressing; orchestral; embarrassing; formal; labored.

verbs
contribute to—; crave—; demand—; manoeuvre—; plan—; prefix—; refuse—; survey—; wangle—; —agitates; —comments on; —communicates; —delights; —eulogizes; —explains; —makes known; —prepares; —presents.

INTRODUCTORY
adverbs
pleasantly; favorably; agreeably; courteously; smoothly; graciously; cordially; eulogistically; approvingly.

INTROSPECTION
adjectives
cold; morbid; pitiless.

INTROSPECTIVE
adverbs
curiously; unwontedly; unfortunately; unduly; overly; oddly; habitually; naturally; highly; sorrily; ominously; dangerously; morbidly; sensitively; pitifully; moodily; incurably; deplorably; lamentably; absurdly; miserably; incorrigibly; inveterately.

INTRUDE (v)
adverbs
presumptuously; bumptiously; rashly; irksomely; startlingly; irritatingly; exasperatingly; selfishly; jealously; obnoxiously; perpetually; pompously; impertinently; forcibly; abruptly; unwontedly.
(See obtrude, invade, encroach, intrench.)

INTRUDER

adjectives

base; peaceful; queenly; friendly; troublesome; miserable; solitary; murderous; burglarous.

verbs

dislodge—; dispose of—; eject—; evict—; ignore—; object to—; punish—; warn—; —disrupts; —encroaches; —forces; —infringes; —invades; —oversteps; —transgresses; —trespasses; —usurps.

(See robber, thief, villain, intrusion, invader, enemy.)

INTRUSION

adjectives

pompous; foul; resented; impertinent; forcible; involuntary; pale; swift; abrupt; noisy; hated; unwonted; rude.

verbs

deplore—; embitter by—; enter by—; excuse —; inform of—; loathe—; observe—; prevent—; protect from—; refuse—; threaten —; —disturbs; —pains; —violates; resent—.

(See intruder.)

INTRUSIVE

adverbs

obnoxiously; provokingly; annoyingly; uncommonly; meddlesomely; inexcusably; discourteously; inquisitively; amazingly; pertly; insolently; rudely; miserably; insidiously; abominably; maliciously; crudely; ignorantly; disgustingly; tiresomely; terribly; grossly; brazenly; persistently; unpardonably; troublesomely.

INTRUST (v)

adverbs

particularly; subsequently; willingly; tacitly; faithfully; confidently; authoritatively; cautiously; legislatively; medically; economically; pecuniarily; financially.

(See confide, commit.)

INTUITION

adjectives

divinest; deepest; pure; unerring; special; sensible; extraordinary; mysterious; half-desolate; womanly; instinctive; judicious.

INTUITIVE

adverbs

amazingly; marvellously; miraculously; naturally; uncommonly; highly; unusually; impulsively; vaguely; unscientifically; absurdly; inconsequently; notoriously; psychically; distinctly; infallibly; strangely; oddly; curiously; fantastically; unbelievably; astonishingly; incredibly; inconsequentially.

INVADE (v)

adverbs

ruthlessly; perilously; outrageously; ferociously; heartlessly; monstrously; totally; unnaturally; belligerently; bellicosely; illegally.

(See encroach, intrench, trespass.)

INVADER

adjectives

ruthless; ferocious; upstart; heathen; petty; expelled; filthy; ragged.

verbs

battle—; beat back—; drive off—; expose to —; harass—; repel—; resist—; vanquish—; withstand—; —assaults; —eludes; —encroaches; —entrenches; —infringes; —intrudes; —penetrates; —ravages; —violates.

(See enemy, intruder, army, troops, soldiers, multitude, robber.)

INVALID

adjectives

habitual; brave; gallant; bedridden; incurable; reeling; bawling; hopeless; feverish; nervous; marked; secluded; chronic; weak; despairing; comfortable; eager.

verbs

comfort—; delight—; discharge—; encourage—; entertain—; exhaust—; pension—; raise—; render—; report—; shelter—; treat —; visit—; —despairs; —recovers; —struggles.

adverbs

untenably; undeniably; groundlessly; absurdly; fallaciously; evasively; deceptively; cunningly; deplorably; legally; unluckily; unfortunately; inoperatively; spuriously; meretriciously.

INVALIDISM

adjectives

temporary; cruel; continual; increasing; nervous; chronic.

INVALIDITY

adjectives

established; judicial; utter; obvious.

INVALUABLE

adverbs

inestimably; extremely; marvellously; pricelessly; unusually; incredibly; astoundingly; wonderfully; indubitably; notoriously; distinctly; manifestly; prodigiously; extraordinarily; inexpressibly; unconscionably; unbelievably.

INVARIABLE

adverbs

incredibly; wonderfully; surprisingly; comfortingly; steadily; consistently; amazingly; warrantably; essentially; fundamentally; intrinsically; monotonously; habitually; drearily; tiresomely; hatefully; conventionally; agreeably; prosaically; typically; doctrinally; deliberately; wisely; purposely; designedly.

INVASION

adjectives

meditated; atrocious; premature; rebel; fratricidal; pioneer; advancing; contaminating; unauthorized; hostile; apparent; lawless; threatened; long-continued; air.

verbs

avert—; curb—; defend against—; deplore —; fight—; inform of—; plan—; persist in —; protect from—; repel—; resist—; stage —; stem—; suffer—; threaten—; yield to—; —destroys; —embitters; —succeeds.

(See raid, aggression, infringement, encroachment, violation.)

INVECTIVE

adjectives

indignant; opprobrious; unreasonable; furious; insulting; bitter; indiscriminate; coarsest; classical; fierce; witty; heated.

verbs

burst into—; deluge with—s; discharge—; drench with—; express in—; flay with—; fling—at; hurl—at; pour forth—; provoke —; rail—; rain—s; roar—; shoot at—; suffer—; shower—s; volley—s at; —angers; —denounces; —embitters.

(See sarcasm, abuse, oath.)

INVEIGH (*v*)

adverbs

censoriously; violently; bitterly; spitefully; vindictively; cantankerously; treacherously;

acrimoniously; acidly; blasphemously; insidiously; sternly; roughly; ruthlessly; ferociously.

(See censure, reproach, rail.)

INVENT (*v*)

adverbs

deftly; creatively; infernally; matchlessly; diabolically; inexhaustibly; sensationally; dangerously; maliciously; technically; fantastically; poetically; prodigally; marvelously; spectacularly; singularly.

(See devise, contrive, discover, originate.)

INVENTION

adjectives

matchless; sad; infernal; stupendous; neoteric; diabolical; dangerous; exorbitant; gymnastic; multitudinous (pl); fervid; inexhaustible; florid; sensational; proposed; dangerous; numerous (pl); distributive; sheer; malicious; divine; technical; melodic; considerable; labor-saving; arbitrary; modern; fantastic; admirable; plausive; poetic; harassing; breath-taking; greatest; perfected; prodigal; modistic; topical; feeble; honest; marvelous; remarkable; sensational; patented; amazing.

verbs

accelerate—; beget—; commemorate—; contrive—; devise—; exploit—; introduce—; laud—; paralyze—; perfect—; seek—; stumble on—; submit—; suppress—; —eases; —enlightens; —improves.

(See discovery, patent, device, stratagem, improvement.)

INVENTIVE

adverbs

cleverly; amazingly; ingeniously; skilfully; wonderfully; expertly; surprisingly; profitably; scientifically; extraordinarily; conveniently; handily; crudely; curiously; shrewdly; broadly; expediently; fortunately; necessarily; unusually; uncommonly; highly; resourcefully; magnificently; dexterously; unbelievably; deftly; competently; capably; delightfully; fortunately; luckily; inexhaustibly; admirably.

INVERSION

adjectives

unnatural; monstrous; total.

INVERT (v)

adverbs

confusingly; perplexingly; complicatedly; abnormally; eccentrically; characteristically; humorously; habitually.

(See reverse, turn, overthrow.)

INVEST (v)

adverbs

fraudulently; annually; temporarily; forcibly; financially; shrewdly; austerely; astutely; strategically; judiciously; modestly; initially.

(See clothe, dress, surround.)

INVESTIGATE (v)

adverbs

promptly; personally; intensively; duly; vigorously; anatomically; tediously; assiduously; tranquilly; legislatively; analytically; diligently; intellectually; comprehensively; judicially; conclusively; abstractly; inquisitively; physiologically; methodically; aimlessly.

(See examine, inquire, probe.)

INVESTIGATION

adjectives

vast; anatomical; tedious; empiric; unprejudiced; eager; assiduous; futile; patient; tranquil; personal; cautious; legislative; analytical; literary; diligent; shouldered; racial; intellectual; careful; clinical; elaborate; journalistic; contemporary; comprehensive; judicial; hostile; rigorous; subsequent; conclusive; minuter; abstract; introspective; inquisitive; empirical; embarrassing; physiological; methodical; aimless.

verbs

carry on—; conduct—; contribute to—; dismiss—; exhaust—; facilitate—; institute—; ponder—; promise—; submit to—; summarize—; throttle—; yield to—; —brings to light; —concentrates; —convinces; —discloses; —drags; —indicates; —reveals; —wearies.

(See inquiry, examination, research, inquisition.)

INVESTMENT

adjectives

sound; gilt-edged; attractive; healthy; strategic; permanent; lifetime; elaborate; comparative; conservative; judicious; defence-less; economical; individual; modest; initial; desirable; careful; extraordinary; substantial; definite.

verbs

convert—; derive from—; discourage—; gain by—; impair—; necessitate—; preserve —; profit by—; pyramid—; represent—; sacrifice—; safeguard—; sell out—; subscribe to—; —accumulates; —crashes; —diminishes; —skyrockets (colloq.).

(See stocks, shares, bonds, property, interest, money.)

INVESTORS

adjectives

institutional; individual; hypothetical; multitudinous; thoughtful; painstaking.

INVIGORATE (v)

adverbs

artificially; scientifically; medically; alcoholically; mentally; physically; emotionally; beneficially; hurtfully; detrimentally.

(See animate, encourage.)

INVIGORATING

adverbs

pleasantly; highly; refreshingly; definitely; notoriously; conspicuously; unquestionably; wholesomely; fortunately; infallibly; gratefully; unexpectedly; surprisingly; strangely; marvellously; curiously; wonderfully; permanently; gloriously; progressively; restoratively; incredibly; miraculously; splendidly; remarkably; magnificently.

INVINCIBLE

adverbs

sturdily; stoutly; amazingly; unexpectedly; proudly; notoriously; conspicuously; surprisingly; preposterously; incredibly; genuinely; apparently; evidently; manifestly; curiously; strangely; oddly; fantastically; indomitably; insuperably; doggedly; stubbornly; obstinately; mightily; powerfully; splendidly; magnificently; irresistibly; mysteriously; unbelievably.

INVISIBLE

adverbs

mysteriously; curiously; strangely; incredibly; oddly; fantastically; designedly; provokingly; disappointingly; vexatiously; minutely; mistily; foggily; mystically; significantly.

adjectives

colorful; specific; long-standing; cordial; smart; flattering; outright; friendly; cheerful; implied; indefinite; actual; unanswered; clamorous; open; unexpected; sinister; original; unauthorized; pressing; liberal; hearty; perpetual; vague; inescapable.

verbs

answer—; besiege by —s; decline—; dine by —; draft—; ignore—; issue—; limit—; long for—; prepare—s; present—; prize—; procure—; —allures; —amuses; —delights; —flatters; —gladdens.

(See summons, call, question.)

INVITE (v)

adverbs

cordially; formally; frequently; graciously; peculiarly; forcibly; daintily; vociferously; specifically; flatteringly; originally; nominally; suavely; fatally; ostensibly.

(See ask, induce, summon, call.)

INVITING

adverbs

charmingly; delightfully; pleasantly; coolly; refreshingly; warmly; cordially; hospitably; marvellously; unexpectedly; attractively; bewitchingly; cordially; cheerfully; heartily; politely; comfortably; lusciously; delectably; alluringly; temptingly; irresistibly; wonderfully; surprisingly.

INVOCATION

adjectives

brief; unknown; sweet; solemn.

INVOKE (v)

adverbs

eloquently; ardently; solemnly; incessantly; reverently; briefly; earnestly; verbally; monotonously.

(See pray, beseech, beg.)

INVOLVE (v)

adverbs

markedly; shockingly; tragically; unfathomably; inextricably; hopelessly; abstrusely; problematically; ultimately; tremendously; scandalously.

(See implicate, include, entangle, embarrass.)

verbs

acclaim—; appreciate—; boast—; charge—; demand—; doubt—; estimate—; mistrust—; relax—; respect—; shake—; strain—; test —; threaten—; —defends; —sustains; — irks.

(See strength.)

INVULNERABLE

adverbs

proudly; ominously; happily; fortunately; consciously; remarkably; strongly; obviously; manifestly; completely; supposedly; presumably; apparently; allegedly; securely; safely; tenably; snugly; confidently.

IODINE

verbs

apply—; antidote—; disinfect with—; inject —; impregnate with—; paint with—; smear —; tint with—; treat with—; —poisons; —relieves; —safeguards; —sterilizes.

(See chemical, antiseptic, medicine.)

IRASCIBLE

adverbs

insufferably; highly; hotly; moodily; cholerically; capriciously; inexplicably; temperamentally; habitually; naturally; inexcusably; unreasonably; illogically; snappishly; querulously; contentiously; excitably; restively; uncommonly; rudely; captiously.

IRATE

adverbs

dangerously; alarmingly; highly; unusually; terribly; inexplicably; extremely; fearfully; sullenly; silently; noisily; tempestuously; unreasonably; savagely; senselessly; moodily.

IRE

adjectives

political; vengeful; patriot; noble; raging; avenging.

verbs

appease—; arouse—; assuage—; avert—; awake—; draw—of; dread—; ferment—; flush with—; fume with—; glow with—; moderate—; pale with—; provoke to—; shake with—; sharpen—; shelter from—; slake—; subdue—; —effervesces; —erupts; —riots.

(See anger, rage, wrath, passion, vexation, temper.)

IRIDESCENT

adverbs

shimmeringly; beautifully; amazingly; uncommonly; gloriously; splendidly; magnificently; delicately; daintily; flashily; curiously; oddly; marvellously; inexplicably; unexpectedly; attractively; highly; uncommonly.

IRKSOME

adverbs

tediously; wearily; heavily; distastefully; monotonously; dully; stupidly; vaguely; unpleasantly; dismally; drearily; oppressively; onerously; laboriously; vexatiously; provokingly; formidably; grievously; bitterly.

IRON

adjectives

adamantine; crushing; hot; assimilated; magnetized; tempered; redcoated; stubborn; rusted.

verbs

alloy with—; cast—; employ—; forge—; gird with—; hammer—; lathe—; magnetize —; mold—; plate with—; polish—; puddle —; roll—; shackle in—; shod with—; smelt —; utilize—; weld—; —clangs; —corrodes; —grates; —masters; —rusts.

(See metal, steel.)

IRONICAL

adverbs

bitterly; suddenly; justifiably; calmly; sarcastically; shrewdly; terribly; insolently; acidly; keenly; scoffingly; sneeringly; mockingly; tauntingly; teasingly; cleverly; perspicaciously; astutely; inscrutably; unduly; rudely; disagreeably; offensively; openly.

IRONY

adjectives

discordant; malignant; secret; terrible; masterly; characteristic; calm; strange; fearless; melancholy; subtle; laughing; delicate; enchanting; quaint; unconscious; wanton; unpleasing; fine; gentle; trivial; dramatic; civilized; somber; delicious; amiable; tragic.

verbs

afford—; aim at—; convey—; exhibit—; imply—; pierce with—; prick with—; recognize—; relish—; stress—; suggest—; suspect

—; tinge with—; wince at—; —amuses; — barbs; —cuts; —nips; —penetrates; —rebukes.

(See sarcasm, satire, ridicule, mockery.)

IRRADIATION

adjectives

intense; imponderable; hidden; compulsory.

IRRATIONAL

adverbs

pathetically; portentously; absurdly; ridiculously; senselessly; stupidly; irascibly; fallaciously; crazily; preposterously; extravagantly; alarmingly; strangely; oddly; unwontedly; impulsively; evasively; nonsensically; obstinately; foolishly; incredibly.

IRRECLAIMABLE

adverbs

hopelessly; tragically; legally; virtually; lamentably; deplorably; altogether; presumably; allegedly; shamefully; viciously; impenitently; defiantly; recklessly; unfortunately; unluckily; lucklessly; wickedly; unconscionably; conclusively; apparently; manifestly.

IRRECOVERABLE

adverbs

desperately; hopelessly; lamentably; unfortunately; sadly; unhappily; utterly; presumably; probably; allegedly.

IRREDEEMABLE

adverbs

hopelessly; strangely; cruelly; officially; unluckily; legally; authoritatively; curiously; mysteriously; probably; definitely; unquestionably; incontrovertibly; absolutely.

IRREGULAR

adverbs

shamefully; disgracefully; furtively; openly; strangely; deplorably; cruelly; dangerously; secretly; unfortunately; terribly; slightly; gravely; seriously; suspiciously; egregiously; highly; utterly; wildly; lamentably; unpardonably; inexcusably; unsatisfactorily; unacceptably; disagreeably; disgustingly; indiscreetly; imprudently; unhappily.

IRREGULARITIES

adjectives

technical; faint; odd; quaint; exasperating; clumsy; rugged; fatal; ruddy.

IRREGULARITY

verbs

acknowledge—; adjust—; admit—; commit
—; condone—; detect—; disperse—; file
down—; generalize—s; lament—; magnify
—; note—; penalize—; perform—; relent—;
rue—; —debars; —disqualifies; —impedes.

(See abnormality, error, mistake, wrong,
oversight.)

IRRELEVANCE

adjectives

boring; inextricable; apparent; complete;
established.

IRRELEVANT

adverbs

disturbingly; vexatiously; insolently; suddenly; shrewdly; sadly; purposely; deliberately; hopelessly; uselessly; unserviceably;
impracticably; impertinently; nonchalantly;
casually; coolly; outlandishly; inappropriately; incongruously; exceptionally; oddly;
unreasonably; foolishly; inanely; ridiculously; absurdly; unbelievably.

IRRELIGIOUS

adverbs

outlandishly; irreverently; curiously; terribly; unpardonably; conspicuously; flagrantly;
inconceivably; sadly; flauntingly; inveterately; offensively; quietly; stolidly; stubbornly; immovably; impiously; grievously;
irremediably; atheistically; indifferently; ostentatiously; dreadfully; strangely.

IRREMEDIABLE

adverbs

evidently; unluckily; grievously; sadly; unfortunately; presumably; possibly; apparently; hopelessly; forlornly; curiously; singularly; extraordinarily; peculiarly; particularly; avowedly; significantly; heartbreakingly; queerly; incomprehensibly.

IRREPARABLE

adverbs

curiously; hopelessly; oddly; strangely; unfortunately; unluckily; bitterly; cruelly; dismally; absolutely; apparently; obviously;
manifestly; indubitably; palpably; haplessly; unhappily; distressingly; disturbingly;
grievously.

IRREPRESSIBLE

adverbs

obstreperously; riotously; uproariously; cur-

iously; vexatiously; alarmingly; obviously;
wantonly; mischievously; garrulously; independently; absolutely; offensively; restlessly;
boisterously; noisily; feverishly; hysterically; violently; hot-headedly; fanatically; impulsively; disagreeably; unbecomingly;
strangely; blatantly.

IRREPROACHABLE

adverbs

notoriously; consistently; conspicuously; generally; altogether; unquestionably; wholly;
presumably; emphatically; positively; incontrovertibly; ineffably; assuredly; warrantably; securely; acceptably; implicitly; impressively; probably.

IRRESISTIBLE

adverbs

charmingly; delightfully; utterly; absolutely; wholly; fascinatingly; inexhaustibly; altogether; persuasively; indomitably; argumentatively; logically; consciously; personally; oddly; singularly; powerfully; attractively; strangely; evidently.

IRRESOLUTE

adverbs

feebly; timidly; indecisively; weakly; singularly; senselessly; strangely; particularly;
incredibly; foolishly; pliantly; hesitantly;
infirmly; capriciously; whimsically; lamentably; oddly; captiously; nervously; restively; stupidly; unwisely; noticeably; dreadfully; timorously; tremulously; warily.

IRRESPONSIBLE

adverbs

gaily; blithely; insouciantly; nonchalantly;
wantonly; hopelessly; singularly; deplorably; curiously; outlandishly; fantastically;
oddly; strangely; vexatiously; unpleasantly; maddeningly; wildly; heedlessly; utterly; painfully; incorrigibly; alarmingly; dangerously; intolerably; palpably; sadly; incredibly; inveterately; temperamentally; incurably; obviously.

IRREVERENT

adverbs

impiously; flagrantly; offensively; unforgivably; rudely; grossly; crudely; thoughtlessly; unbecomingly; painfully; unutterably;
unspeakably; arrantly; invidiously; insolently; terribly; crassly; brazenly; senselessly;
utterly; blasphemously; sacrilegiously; deliberately; singularly; peculiarly; carelessly;

unpardonably; ignorantly; boorishly; insultingly; outrageously; scandalously; shamefully; egregiously; irremediably.

IRREVOCABLE
adverbs
lamentably; terribly; disastrously; ruinously; calamitously; hopelessly; desperately; sadly; lamentably; horribly; tragically; seriously; gravely; legally; pitiably; validly; indelibly; unintentionally; patently; inexorably; fortunately; happily.

IRRIGATION
adjectives
minute; plenteous; land-saving; colonic.

IRRITABILITY
verbs
control—; exaggerate—; fan—; lament—; manifest—; observe—; plague to—; rouse to —; salve—; stimulate—; —annoys; —lessens; —pains; —vexes.

(See irritation.)

IRRITABLE
adverbs
silently; resentfully; extremely; evidently; horridly; fiercely; violently; bitterly; absurdly; senselessly; foolishly; unreasonably; increasingly; slightly; definitely; hotly; furiously; mightily; unbearably; intolerably; grievously; sorely; ludicrously; plaguedly; annoyingly; wretchedly; miserably; distinctly; unfairly; deeply; easily; unhappily; comically; unjustly; ill-temperedly.

IRRITATE (v)
adverbs
unduly; nervously; perpetually; exasperatingly; sharply; temporarily; psychologically; physically; childishly; needlessly; excessively; superfluously.

(See provoke, vex, annoy, offend.)

IRRITATION
adjectives
stifled; puerile; deep-seated; concealed; nervous; perpetual; passing; burning; infinite; teasing; increasing; private; lulling; sharp; temporary; psychological; childish; consequent; needless; excessive.

verbs
allay—; alleviate—; arouse—; augment—; bear—; check—; convey—; endure—; excite —; expose to—; express—; fume with—;

master—; relieve—; respond to—; se with—; stimulate—; stir up—; subject t thunder—; —bursts forth; —ferments lashes; —subsides.

(See pain, anger, impatience, vexa temper, irritability.)

ISLA
adjectives
extensive; weedy; barren; fragrant; glac polished; sea-girt; adjacent; desolate; s ing; marshy; imaginary; rugged; l swampy; ill-fated; oozy; barricaded; cluded; moraine; river-girt; bare; co floating; uninhabited; beautiful; verda glittering; serene; wretched; industrial; canic; antique; irregular; classical; s ile; rocky; roaming; substantial; dism sun-drenched; southern; romantic; v table; uttermost; jeweled; remote; l sacked.

verbs
banish to—; batter—; bombard—; desol —; encompass—; infest—; isolate—; n roon on—; overrun—; populate—; plunc —; rule—; settle on—; sight—; strand —; strew with —s; stud with —s; surrou —; survey—; take root on—; winter on— —blooms; —chains; —s dot; —enchants; flowers; —overlooks; —shelters; —swarr with; —veers off; —yields.

(See land, shore.)

ISL
adjectives
oozy; lofty; desolate; peaceful; flat bloomy; mystic; shady; weeping; volcanic low; wooded; hateful; pumice; bee-pasturing; tributary; foamless; outlying; execrable; high-favored; storm-encompassed.

ISOLATE (v)
adverbs
pathetically; voluntarily; effectively; dismally; advisedly; temporarily; virtually; morally; politically; physically; formidably; geographically; financially; economically; legally.

(See segregate, separate.)

ISOLATED
adverbs
somewhat; lamentably; fortunately; happily; necessarily; cruelly; bitterly; preferably; remotely; terribly; relatively; comparatively; desolately; drearily; singularly;

oddly; curiously; particularly; strangely; deliberately; unwillingly; inconveniently; inhospitably; snugly; safely; securely; unsociably.

ISOLATION
adjectives

moral; lonely; luxurious; infinite; blank; self-centered; studied; prompt; sectional; moribund; lofty; exposed; sheltered; physical; stupendous; selfish; desolate; deliberate; absolute; anguished; formidable; self-perceived; geographical; awful; magnificent; economic; financial; terrible.

verbs

advocate—; bear—; condemn to—; contemplate in—; delight in—; dread—; dwell in —; expel into—; meditate in—; penetrate —; procure—; punish by—; resign to—; retire into—; risk—; shake from—; suffer —; wrap in—.
(See privacy, solitude, loneliness, seclusion, retirement.)

ISSUE (*v*)
adverbs

spuriously; portentously; anonymously; particularly; publicly; officially; politically; controversially; triumphantly; victoriously; colorfully; significantly.
(See result, terminate, proceed.)

ISSUE
adjectives

sequent; political; momentous; controversial; great; fruitful; genuine; fundamental; ethical; indirect; unlimited; clear; dearest; profuse; precarious; degenerate; precise; vital; moral; abundant; tragic; confused; doubtful; remarkable; fascinating; colorful; basic; supreme; stupendous; irrelevant; insignificant; luckier; proposed; proud; concrete; adverse; felicitous; unlucky; immeasurable; tremendous; happy; disinherited; discussable; uncertain; dreadful; coming; involved; wartime; particular; recent; national; unforeseen.

verbs

analyze—; ban—; clarify—; confuse—; crystallize—; debate—; decline—; determine —; dismiss—; dodge—; dramatize—; duck —; dwarf—; elaborate on—; entangle—; evade—; force—; forego—; gloss over—; inject—; judge—; obliterate—; outlaw—; prejudice—; scrutinize—; set forth—;

sharpen—; side-step—; speed—; split on—; state—; subordinate—; swamp—; tackle—; terminate—; —burns; —s conflict; —emerges; —involves.
(See outcome, result, consequence, question, point.)

ITCHING
adjectives

considerable; intense; profuse; excessive; unbearable.

verbs

affect with—; aggravate—; allay—; cure —; ease—; increase—; relieve—; remedy —; renew—; soothe—; wash—; —annoys; —attends; —indicates; —maddens; —tickles; —torments; —vexes.
(See disease, pain, torment, torture.)

ITEM
adjectives

important; inconspicuous; imperative; various (pl); replacement; indispensable; popular; rarest; fascinating; seasonable; considerable; middling; crucial; drab; related; restricted; associated; central; profit; essential; outstanding; lively; unpretentious; derogatory.

verbs

calculate—s; charge—; check—; classify—; compute—s; enter—; enumerate—s; exempt —; muster—s; note—; plow through—s; register—; specify—; total—s; —tempts.
(See amount, details.)

ITERATION
adjectives

monotonous; caressing; deliberate.

ITINERANT
adverbs

irresponsibly; necessarily; compulsively; happily; willingly; recklessly; pleasantly; profitably; adventurously; extravagantly; vagrantly; politically; lazily; vapidly; inanely; foolishly; vigilantly; nomadically; erratically; restlessly; vexatiously; peculiarly; outlandishly; whimsically; expensively; grievously; piteously; interestingly; fascinatingly; thrillingly; attractively; amazingly; unaccountably; idly.

verbs

approve—; arrange—; contemplate—; describe—; draw up—; follow—; measure—; plan—; prepare—; refer to—; study—; — delights; —informs; —mentions; —proposes.

(See program, plan, project, scheme.)

IVORY

adjectives

waxen; tinted; delicate; rose-ensanguined; carved.

adjectives

clinging; poison; variegated; linked; wandering; climbing; embowering.

verbs

crown with—; direct—; train—; —bowers; —canopies; —clasps; —climbs; —clings; — creeps; —curls; —decorates; —feeds on; —hangs; —hides; —jackets; —leaps; — nods; —twines; —twists; —wanders; — wreathes.

(See plant, flower, vine.)

J

JAB (v)

adverbs

viciously; repeatedly; verbally; savagely; bitterly; ferociously; brutally; vindictively; malignantly.

(See thrust, poke, dig.)

JABBER (v

adverbs

bestially; perpetually; enthusiastically; excitedly; cheerfully; effusively; idiotically; loquaciously.

(See talk, babble, chatter.)

JACKDAW

verbs

tame—; —babbles; —cackles; —caws; — chatters; —clacks; —flits; —frequents; — gabbles; —gossips; —hops; —imitates; — jabbers; —steals; —thieves.

(See bird.)

JACKET

adjectives

undress; soft; bright; embroidered; wadded; silk; familiar; long; reversible; ill-fitted; clumsy.

verbs

adorn—; box in—; conceal under—; divest of—; don—; emerge from—; fortify with —; fray—; stain—; tatter—; utilize—; — preserves; —protects.

(See coat, overcoat, cloak.)

JADE

adjectives

veriest; outworn; brazen-faced; veined; unruly; tired.

JADED

adverbs

wearily; exhaustedly; gaspingly; tiredly; haggardly; uncommonly; gauntly; entirely; finally.

JAGGED

adverbs

angularly; dangerously; roughly; ruggedly; sharply; crookedly; obliquely; curiously; fearfully; perilously; strangely; hazardous-ly; terribly; ominously; frightfully; unpleasantly; painfully; disagreeably; horridly; hideously; distressingly.

JAIL

adjectives

fantastic; infernal; distasteful; pleasant; comfortable.

verbs

break—; clamp in—; clap into—; commit to—; confine to—; deliver from—; deposit in—; detain in—; dwell in—; free from—; guard—; imprison in—; incarcerate in—; languish in—; parole from—; patrol—; release from—; secure in—; slap into—; — confines; —corrects; —penalizes; —rehabilitates.

(See prison.)

JAM

adjectives

absolute; fearful; traffic; inextricable.

JANGLE (v)

adverbs

crudely; dissonantly; inharmoniously; irritatingly; blatantly; exasperatingly; ceaselessly; hideously.

(See clang, clash.)

JAR

adjectives

dripping; giddy; subsequent; intestinal; mortal; endless; importunate; tempestuous; family-sized; inharmonious; treble.

JAR (v)

adverbs

rudely; terrifically; tempestuously; roughly; disastrously; mysteriously; awkwardly; economically.

(See jolt, shock, grate.)

JARGON

adjectives

wretched; broken; unscientific; courtly; meaningless; commonplace; unintelligible; barbarous; infernal; pitiful; busy.

verbs

babble—; chatter—; despise—; interpret—; master—; prate—; ring with—; translate

—; —confounds; —confuses; —delights; —grates; —perplexes; —prevails.

(See language, dialect, slang, speech.)

JAUNDICE

verbs

afflict with—; induce—; occasion—; tincture with—; treat for—; —appears; —deranges; —discolors; —disquiets; —distresses; —torments; —worries; —attacks.

(See disease.)

JAUNDICED

adverbs

biliously; querulously; regrettably; unhappily; incurably; slightly; jealously; evidently; visibly; clearly; unmistakably; highly; fulvously; inferentially; prejudicially; blindly; provincially; narrowly; fanatically; dogmatically; stupidly; illiberally; terribly.

JAUNT

adjectives

pleasure; summer; daring; mental.

JAUNTY

adverbs

blithely; carelessly; buoyantly; fashionably; delightfully; smilingly; nonchalantly; wholesomely; charmingly; lightly; brightly; insouciantly; laughingly; swaggeringly; heedlessly; wantonly; happily; rollickingly; saucily; comically; ludicrously; whimsically; cheerfully; gaily; gleefully; airily; heartily; joyously; playfully; sportively; marvelously; effervescently; jubilantly; remarkably.

JAW

adjectives

set; prominent; stern-set; grinning; outstanding; poisonous; delicate; mastic; bloody; protruding; resolute; aristocratic; firm; square-cut; pugilistic; marble; powerful; massive; protuberant; horrible; ponderous; unshaven; hollow; underhanging; infernal; poor; weasel; monstrous; champing; brutal; malevolent; grim; ravening; snarling; mighty; square-set; strong; clamped; industrious; determined; dogged; hard; iron; formidable; heavy; immense; bulging; clean-cut; elastic; inflexible; locked; lean; recessive; foaming; loose; distended; uplifted; pikelike; scarred; flaring; gaping; yawning; snapping; triangular; pier-

like; haggard; beefy; flabby; jutting; projecting; lower; prognathous; combative; fighting; sagged; drooping; hanging; fallen; sharp; tense.

verbs

brace—; click—s; crack—; fracture—; tear with—s; wire—; work—s; —s clasp; —s close; —s crunch; —s crush; —drops; —s embrace; —s foam; —gapes; —juts out; —sags; —s snap; —s tighten.

(See teeth.)

JAY

verbs

—destroys; —hops; —mimics; —s mob; —pipes; —preys on; —scolds; —screams; —shies; —tears; —teases.

(See bird.)

JAZZ

verbs

beat out—; blare—; bridle—; entertain with—; inspire—; mute—; record—; repress—; revolt against—; seethe with—; sprinkle with—; trumpet—; welcome—; —agitates; —arouses; —batters; —cradles; —evolves from; —predominates; —reigns; —rushes.

(See music, melody, song, noise.)

JEALOUS

adverbs

inordinately; insanely; madly; wildly; furiously; violently; slightly; somewhat; justly; reasonably; naturally; intensely; venomously; pitiably; pathetically; unutterably; vengefully; supposedly; allegedly; probably; suspiciously; miserably; wretchedly; groundlessly; unbearably; insufferably; wonderfully; basely; disgracefully; contemptibly; foolishly; dangerously; deplorably; unbearably.

JEALOUSY

adjectives

insensate; fond; green-eyed; intense; self-harming; dangerous; popular; continual; savage; lively; maternal; mutual; inventive; instinctive; furious; narrow; mad; excessive; exaggerated; needless; lurking; smoldering; petty; miserable; frantic; unreasonable; improvident; habitual; acute; sensitive; active; selfish; fiercest; exalted; self-betraying; watchful; rare; retrospective; sentimental; malignant; factional; alternating; blinding; naive; overwrought; commercial; rancorous; undefined.

verbs

abhor—; arouse—; beget—; conceal—; cure
—; curse with—; dread—; extinguish—;
fire—; incur—; nourish—; occasion—;
overcome—; squirm in—; strangle—; —
blasts; —corrodes; —dictates; —disturbs;
—frustrates; —grips; —harms; —magnifies; —pains; —perverts; —poisons; —subsides; —torments; —tortures; —wanes.

(See suspicion, distrust, curiosity, selfishness.)

JEER

verbs

cripple with—; deride with—; flog with—;
flout with—; incur—s of; inflict—; heat
with—s; pelt with—s; punish with—s; scorn
—s; silence—s; stone with—s; —bruises; —
disconcerts; —mocks; —perturbs; —taunts;
—unnerves; —upsets.

(See taunt, ridicule, derision, sneer, laughter.)

JEER (v)

adverbs

scornfully; sardonically; vindictively; sarcastically; enviously; bitterly; spitefully;
acrimoniously; acidulously.

(See mock, ridicule.)

JEERING

adverbs

scornfully; irreverently; disrespectfully;
contemptuously; derisively; cruelly; bitterly; savagely; mockingly; insultingly; outrageously; superciliously; sarcastically;
basely; tauntingly; dreadfully; tormentingly.

JEOPARDIZE (v)

adverbs

recklessly; rashly; foolhardily; absurdly;
superfluously; idiotically; madly; passionately; deliriously.

(See risk, imperil, endanger.)

JERK (v)

adverbs

spitefully; instinctively; desperately; ludicrously; furiously; intermittently; ignominiously; frantically; mechanically; repetitiously; violently.

(See twitch, snatch.)

JERKY

adverbs

unnaturally; abnormally; lamentably; miserably; deplorably; pitiably; incurably; reg-

ularly; strangely; spasmodically; convulsively; suddenly; inexplicably; curiously;
fitfully; recurrently; restlessly; singularly;
peculiarly; surprisingly; woefully; frightfully.

JEST

verbs

beware of—s; enjoy—; fashion—; flash—s;
glean—s; harass with—; interpret—s; refine—; repeat—; season with—; share—;
speak in—; suppress—; time—; —affronts;
—amuses; —cures; —delights; —pains; —
ridicules; —slings; —taunts.

(See joke, witticism, parody, satire.)

JEST (v)

adverbs

indelicately; indecently; subtly; amiably;
recklessly; satirically; slanderously; scurrilously; wittily; boisterously; unrestrainedly; foolishly.

(See joke, clown, fool.)

JESTER

verbs

appreciate—; encourage—; humor—; maintain—; retain—; —aims; —attempts; —
directs; —diverts; —entertains; —excites;
—indulges; —jokes; —makes game of; —
makes merry; —makes sport of; —provokes;
—treats.

(See clown, actor.)

JESTING

adverbs

roguishly; mischievously; broadly; teasingly; tormentingly; merrily; banteringly;
waggishly; facetiously; playfully; comically;
frivolously; whimsically; airily; idly.

JESUS

verbs

accept—; behold—; betray—; blaspheme—;
crown—; crucify—; follow—; forsake—;
glorify—; hallow—; invest—with; proclaim
—; reject—; —bleeds; —comforts; —cures;
—forgives; —heals; —reigns; —rises; —
saves; —suffers; —weeps.

(See Christ, God.)

JETS

adjectives

silvery; sparkling; glittering; branching;
augmenting.

JEWEL

adjectives
dull; cloudy; glistening; glittering; sparkling; sullied; dumb; barbaric; treasured; molten; rich; costly; heavenly; gleaming; glowing; burnished; eternal; graceful; propitious; best; fluid.

verbs
begem with—; box—; collect—s; display—; exhibit—; insure—; mount—; offer—; pawn —; retrieve—; set with—s; stud with—s; swathe in—s; value—; —adorns; —awes; —s bedeck; —dazzles; —flashes; —gleams; —glistens; —glitters; —ornaments; —sparkles.

(See gem, diamond, gold, pearl, ruby.)

JEWELER

verbs
—adorns; —deals in; —decorates; —determines; —estimates; —furnishes; imports; —inscribes; —mounts; —prices; —prizes; —purveys; —sets; —values; —vouches for; —insures.

(See merchant.)

JEWELRY

adjectives
abundant; delicate; ponderous; glimmering; subtlest; starry; resplendent.

JILT (v)

adverbs
senselessly; brazenly; cruelly; heartlessly; capriciously; frivolously; selfishly; disgracefully.

(See flirt, coquette.)

JINGLE

adjectives
petulant; spasmodic; clear; discordant; pleasant; foolish.

JINGLE (v)

adverbs
melodiously; musically; petulantly; spasmodically; discordantly; gaily; genially; pleasantly; propitiously.

(See ring, resound.)

JOB

adjectives
rapid; life-toning; craftsmanlike; daily; tedious; practical; identical (pl); thankless; nefarious; constricting; definitive; dirty; difficult; bungling; advertising; hack-writing; unpleasant; needless; remodeling; political; surrealistic; executive; assured; thorough; faultless; royal.

verbs
abandon—; abolish—; apply for—; attack —; buckle down to—; bungle—; chuck—; contemplate—; cut out for—; decry—; despatch to—; equip for—; fumble at—; harness to—; jeopardize—; land (colloq.)—; nail—; quail at—; register for—; swing into—; tackle—; threaten—; undertake—; usurp—; wangle—; —fazes (colloq.); — materializes.

(See position, work, situation, employment, engagement.)

JOCOSE

adverbs
facetiously; waggishly; convivially; playfully; whimsically; foolishly; fatuously, pleasantly; drolly; clownishly; banteringly; quick-wittedly; humorously; fantastically; teasingly; whimsically; quibblingly; entertainingly; happily; naturally; cheeringly.

JOCULAR

adverbs
immensely; always; habitually; entertainingly; genially; amiably; charmingly; divertingly; dependably; heartily; wholesomely; good-naturedly; characteristically; amusingly; agreeably; waggishly; broadly; banteringly; comically; drolly; dryly; whimsically; facetiously; merrily; pleasantly.

JOCULARITY

adjectives
nervous; perplexed; forced; mock.

JOCUND

adverbs
pleasantly; wittily; archly; cheerfully; amusingly; heartily; irrepressibly; blithely; admirably; imperturbably; consistently; naturally; charmingly; lustily; noisily; boisterously; incomparably.

JOG (v)

adverbs
monotonously; ceaselessly; cheerfully; automatically; conventionally; dismally; uneventfully; tediously; arduously; toilsomely.

(See shake, push, jar, jolt.)

JOIN

adverbs
enthusiastically; obsequiously; slavishly; matrimonially; lustily; indissolubly; devoutly; mechanically; temporarily; snugly.
(See add, annex, knit.)

JOINT

adjectives
diminishing; stiffened; distorted; affected; enlarged; stubborn; firm-knit.

verbs
bandage—; cement—; connect at—; dislocate—; displace—; fit—; form—; hinge—; lay—; limber up—; lubricate—; mend—; nodulate—; shake out of—; strengthen—; support—; sustain—; turn on—; —creaks; —squeaks.
(See bone.)

JOKE

adjectives
rude; matter-of-fact; practical; outrageous; affectionate; oft-repeated; grave; crowning; pathetic; sly; obscene; indelicate; cynical; mocking; foolish; fermented; repressed; bibliomaniacal; deplorable; mutual; uncountable (pl); endless; inopportune; wonderful; delicious; off-color; miserable; particular; impish; questionable; horrible; priceless.

verbs
censor—; exchange—s; flash—; guffaw at —; interpret—; laugh at—; perpetrate—; refine—; report—; retail—s; season with —; share—; swap (colloq.)—s; time—; understand—; —affronts; —amuses; —caps; —climaxes; —delights; —offends; —pains; —stings; —wears thin.
(See jest, witticism, parody, satire.)

JOKER

adjectives
absolute; loud-tongued; misused.

JOLLITY

adjectives
innocent; unrestrained; frenzied; youthful.

verbs
arrest—; dampen—; dip in—; enjoy—; feed —; immerse in—; occasion—; overcome with—; prolong—; relent—; repent—; share

—; split in—; steep in—; yield to—; —exhausts; —inebriates; —palls; —prevails; —wanes.
(See fun, mirth, merriment, relaxation, recreation, laughter.)

JOLLY

adverbs
immensely; invariably; consistently; heartily; wholesomely; delightfully; tremendously; inveterately; indomitably; constitutionally; naturally; habitually; unusually; uncommonly; extravagantly; exceedingly; unsuitably; blithely; merrily; sportively; teasingly; tormentingly; mockingly; inopportunely; roguishly; unquenchably; whimsically; exuberantly; mischievously; impishly; marvelously.

JOLT

adjectives
staggering; nasty; gigantic; painful.

JOLT (v)

adverbs
heavily; crunchingly; staggeringly; terrifically; thunderously; rudely; destructively; disastrously.
(See shock, grate, jar.)

JOLTING

adjectives
unendurable; incessant.

JOURNAL

adjectives
musical; vivacious; naked; satirical; enterprising; independent; distinguished; inflated; pompous; veracious.

JOURNALIST

adjectives
well-informed; eminent; cultured; conscientious; flamboyant; inspired; death-defying; disreputable; able; irresponsible; brilliant; prolific.

verbs
bribe—; condemn—; congratulate—; criticize—; fear—; hire—; —awes; —composes; —corrupts; —describes; —edits; —expounds; —humanizes; —itemizes; —publishes; —reports; —serves; —sums; —vulgarizes.
(See writer, reporter, publisher, editor.)

adjectives

frightful; tedious; dreaded; proposed; fruitless; interesting; expeditious; fatiguing; fatal; costly; weary; innumerable (pl); arduous; self-appointed; unspeakable; dismal; unsteady; stately; longing; measureless; long; foggy; subsequent; daily; harrowing; troubled; wearisome; leisurely; evangelizing; extended; unexpected; uneventful; triumphant; adventurous; shorter; rumored; aimless; perilous; sentimental; celebrated; plodding; memorable; romantic; toilsome; infinite; mysterious; accursed; triumphal; pleasant; homeward.

verbs

accompany on—; break—; contemplate—; embark on—; enjoy—; plan—; proceed on —; quicken—; set out on—; shape—; undertake—; —benefits; —fatigues; —interests; —pleases; —tires; —wearies

(See trip, tour, voyage.)

JOURNEY (v)

adverbs

tediously; fruitlessly; fatiguingly; fatally; arduously; dismally; daily; harrowingly; leisurely; uneventfully; triumphantly; aimlessly; perilously; memorably; romantically; triumphally.

(See travel, tour.)

JOURNEYINGS

adjectives

tiresome; constant; endless; costly.

JOVIAL

adverbs

immensely; extremely; heartily; wholesomely; amusingly; cordially; warmly; teasingly; companionably; sociably; convivially; happily; pleasantly; comfortably; familiarly; amiably; freely.

JOY

adjectives

earth-born; malignant; fiendish; serene; spirit-piercing; unreasoning; intense; sounding; ineffable; tumultuous; material; inexpressible; deceitful; exultant; domestic; vernal; secret; insecure; temporary; concentrated; inward; unbelieving; early; awkward; cradle; pretty; profound; unchecked; immortal; innumerable (pl); hearty; guilty; furious; deluding; fierce; thankful; transient; palpable; rapturous; strange; frank; unsubstantial; unbidden; grateful; youthful; deep; innocent; parental; deluding; lasting; spontaneous; superabundant; benevolent; eloquent; insidious; savage; unsuppressed; strained; increasing; mutual; triumphant; corroding; shivering; brief; embodied; overborne; sheer; wonderful; passionate; voluptuous; chastised; sober; unchecked; passionless; indistinct; heavenly; reviving; lively; presented; common; unappreciated; gentle; truant; boisterous; exulting; wild; celestial; overwhelming; plenteous; aching; general; quiet; unimaginable; ghastly; restrained; expectant; lustful; holy; exquisite; submissive; monumental; lovely; worldly; universal; passing; attainable; petty; dangerous; doubtful; unprecedented; incommunicable; tender; true; withered; acute; fleeting; artistic; beguiled; sharp; natural; wretched; thronged; unutterable; solemn; diversified; infant; curious; unmingled; abiding; murmuring; inconceivable; unmitigated; gushing; homely; unbodied; tranquil; flawless; majestic; equable; sedate; taintless; blustering; boundless; Lethean; amazed; delirious; incredulous; life-giving; purest; wordless; ill-natured; costlier; bridal; keen-witted; mild; suffused; refined; barbaric; human; overmastering; deepest; religious; radiant; breathless; narrow; thrilling; mixed; constant; vivid; explosive; animal; comforting; never-fading; lofty; stolen; unmingled; heartfelt; supreme; palpitating; eager; disguised; unbounded; hideous; abstract; perennial; eternal; prolonged; beatific; social; hackneyed; intoxicating; equal; filial; stern; fretful.

verbs

anticipate—; awaken—; blight—; conceal —; dampen—; derive—; experience—; extinguish—; forego—; impart—; intoxicate with—; leap for—; revel in—; snatch—; swoon with—; throw into a paroxysm of—; veil—; —floods the soul; —mounts; —riots in his eyes; —rises.

(See fun, mirth, merriment, happiness, pleasure, rapture.)

JOYFUL

adverbs

triumphantly; victoriously; magnificently; splendidly; brilliantly; naturally; exceedingly; marvelously; wonderfully; elatedly; exuberantly; overwhelmingly; quietly; secretly; proudly; humbly; gratefully; thankfully; utterly; speechlessly; unspeakably; inexpressibly; ineffably; rapturously; ecstatically; obviously; visibly; openly; professedly; apparently; downright; decidedly; infinitely; immeasurably; properly.

JOYOUSNESS

adjectives
symbolic; trustful; subdued.

JUBILANT

adverbs
naturally; marvellously; duly; triumphantly; happily; unspeakably; loudly; deeply; noisily; exultantly; boisterously; clamorously; immoderately; hilariously; vivaciously; spiritedly; tremendously; emphatically; riotously; turbulently; tumultuously; appropriately; hearteningly; utterly; unusually; noticeably; visibly; unconcealedly; secretly.

JUBILEE

adjectives
fierce; careless; wildly-celebrated.

JUDGE

adjectives
existing; rash; self-appointed; sagacious; equitable; discriminating; sympathetic; competent; imaginary; sole; honorable; terrible; ruthless; fitting; elective; dyspeptic; supreme; eminent; worthy; rightful; ecclesiastical; upright; learned; fastidious; capable; brutal; wicked; finicky; frowning; dispassionate; wanton; constitutional; capital; shrewd; disinterested; favorable.

verbs
appeal to—; appear before—; appoint—; elect—; impeach—; oust—; —administers; —admonishes; —assigns; —authorizes; — awards; —condemns; —deliberates; —determines; —grants; —hears; —holds; —investigates; —outlaws; —pardons; —penalizes; —presides; —pronounces; —sentences; —weighs.

(See president, umpire, congressman, senator.)

JUDGE (v)

adverbs
summarily; harshly; rigidly; rashly; righteously; wrathfully; hastily; cursorily; superficially; sentimentally; sagaciously; discriminatingly; equitably; competently; ruthlessly; ecclesiastically; learnedly; fastidiously; brutally; wickedly; wantonly; consti-

tutionally; disinterestedly; impartially; inflexibly; objectively; adversely; shallowly.

(See decide, discern, discriminate, consider.)

JUDGMENT

adjectives
solid; impartial; casual; profound; unerring; veritable; astonishing; declamatory; primitive; clearest; unfavorable; unimpeachable; scornful; verdant; aesthetic; historical; stern; intellectual; inappropriate; solemn; melodious; capricious; moral; subtle; snap; considered; artistic; sound; healthy; noble; fundamental; manifest; perverted; educated; critical; righteous; biased; discriminating; unflattering; jealous; ripe; tolerant; affectionate; cold; inflexible; popular; calm; awful; invaluable; depraved; unbiased; sober; silent; ready-made; disciplined; erroneous; imitative; military; discretionary; irritating; full-grown; burning; superior; qualitative; withering; adverse; objective; masculine; exulting; poetic; shallow; strict; true; interested; brawling; temperate; kindly; false; settled; unstable; dispassionate; rash; presentative; tautological; individual; unmerciful; reformed; lame; tried; admirable; enlightened; harsh; synthetic; advanced; maturer; ablest; retributive; cooler; strong; simple.

verbs
confirm—; derange—; distort—; endorse—; enfeeble—; exercise—; formulate—; impair —; impose—; impugn—; influence—; interfere with—; modify—; obtain—against; pass—; pervert—; pronounce—; render—; reverse—; ripen—; stimulate—; suspend—; temper—; venture—; voice—; waive—; warp—; withhold—; —affirms; —coerces; —impels.

(See decision, decree, sentence, verdict, opinion.)

JUDICIAL

adverbs
gravely; seriously; discreetly; officially; scarcely; pompously; magisterially; sagaciously; competently; capably; honorably; equitably; calmly; ruthlessly; cruelly; serenely; discriminatingly; supremely; eminently; fastidiously; coldly; deliberately; brutally; dispassionately; shrewdly; disinterestedly; impartially; splendidly; wonderfully.

JUDICIARY

adjectives
elective; appointive; corrupt; effective; independent.

JUDICIOUS

adverbs
remarkably; admirably; unusually; surprisingly; carefully; thoughtfully; soberly; sensibly; discreetly; keenly; acutely; astutely; discerningly; profoundly; considerately; uncommonly; wisely; habitually; temperamentally; dependably; reliably; comfortingly.

JUG

verbs
crack—; drain—; mold—; replenish—; seal —; shape—; shatter—; sterilize—; stew in —; store in—; —preserves; —protects; — tapers.
(See glass.)

JUGGLE (v)

adverbs
dexterously; skillfully; marvelously; professionally; verbally; grotesquely; spectacularly.
(See manipulate, handle.)

JUGGLING

adjectives
grotesque; verbal; remarkable.

JUICE

adjectives
concocted; helleboric; resinous; vegetable; rich; natural; savory; precious; rare-flavored; cooling; sweetened; vilesome; gastric; autumnal; acrid; necessary; fermented; joyful; bilious; ruddier; inspissated; gelatinous; pungent; viscous; aerial; nectarian.

verbs
derive—from; dilute—; draw off—; drink —; express—; extract—; flavor with—; moisten with—; relish—; save—; secrete—; squeeze out—; strain—; suck—; suffuse—; tap—; wring out—; —dries; —drips—; exudes; —flows; —intoxicates; —oozes.
(See liquid, water, fluid, solution.)

JUICY

adverbs
lusciously; deliciously; palatably; sufficiently; scarcely; slightly; satisfactorily; sufficiently; delightfully; wonderfully; remark-

ably; surprisingly; unexpectedly; drippingly; soppingly; terribly; delectably; extremely.

JUMBLE

adjectives
absurd; sad; wearisome; confused; incoherent.

JUMBLED

adverbs
hopelessly; terribly; intricately; miscellaneously; heterogeneously; miserably; unsystematically; promiscuously; chaotically; carelessly; confusedly; inexcusably; indefensibly; hastily; perplexingly; distressingly; disconcertingly; indiscriminately; indistinguishably; erratically; wantonly; dreadfully; impossibly; unimaginably; desperately; inextricably; frightfully; messily.

JUMP

adjectives
daring; awkward; high; corkscrew; vehement.

JUMP (v)

adverbs
nimbly; lightly; lumberingly; daringly; threateningly; smartly; gingerly; awkwardly; precipitately; rashly; gallantly; gracefully; thoughtlessly; agilely.
(See hop, spring, bound.)

JUMPY

adverbs
strangely; curiously; nervously; hysterically; foolishly; inanely; ostentatiously; painfully; shockingly; incurably; appallingly; helplessly; hopelessly; desperately; pitifully; stupidly; childishly; fearfully; unreasoningly; irremediably; pathetically; tragically.

JUNCTURE

adjectives
present; alarming; dangerous.

JUNGLE

adjectives
encroaching; hobo; steaming; unhealthy; uninhabited; vibrant; familiar; artificial; impenetrable; misty.

verbs
abandon in—; beat—; clear—; conceal in—; creep through—; cultivate—; desert—; explore—; guide through—; hack through—;

infest—; inhabit—; invade—; lose in—; overhang with—; penetrate—; tangle in—; thread through—; trudge through—; —enmeshes; —hems in; —looms; —swamps; —terrifies.

(See woods, thicket, forest.)

JUNK

adjectives
toy; majestic; gaudy; bright.

verbs
cart—; collect—; consume—; convert—; deal in—; discard—; dispose of—; eject—; employ—; enlist—; exhume—; fill with—; peddle—; refuse—; sack—; salvage—; sweep away—; utilize—.
(See rubbish, mess, sewage, waste.)

JURISDICTION

adjectives
reciprocal; exclusive; consular; provisional; military; constitutional; doubtful; competent; ecclesiastical; conflicting (pl).

verbs
abolish—; arrive within—; assume—; demand—; exempt from—; exercise—; extend —; free from—; include in—; infringe on —; invade—; limit—; relax—; resent—; subject to—; submit to—; vest—in; —embodies; —empowers; —extends.
(See authority, power.)

JURIST

adjectives
ermined; impartial; eminent; able; robed.

JURY

adjectives
absurd; impartial; swayed; emotional; prejudiced.

verbs
address—; appoint—; bribe—; challenge—; charge—; intimidate—; lay before—; panel —; plead with—; submit to—; summon—; swear in—; —acquits; —ballots; —conducts; —considers; —decides; —deliberates; —discharges; —haggles; —indicts; —meditates; —judges; —recommends; —retires; —takes oath; —withdraws.
(See tribunal, committee, hearers, court, judge.)

JUST

adverbs
undeniably; absolutely; impartially; admittedly; admirably; profoundly; unerringly; veritably; astonishingly; clearly; unimpeachably; uncommonly; unusually; appropriately; sternly; solemnly; soundly; nobly; fundamentally; righteously; coldly; tolerantly; strictly; temperately; dispassionately; entirely; manifestly; substantiallv; roughly; terribly; frightfully; remarkably.

JUSTICE

adjectives
distributive; poetical; passionless; ridiculous; temperate; biased; manifest; remarkable; substantial; inordinate; exemplary; swordless; armed; dreadful; summary; strictest; reasoned; eternal; stern; ultimate; resolute; unfailing; knavish; irascible; poetic; distorted; impartial; criminal; universal; rough-handed; wild; even-handed; scanty; presiding; sparing; perfect; divine; social; retributive; conservative; inflexible; vindictive; moral; common; private; ample; striking; strict; tardy; conceded; recompensive; bare; drowsy; immovable; equal; exact; slow; cruel; tied-up.

verbs
achieve—; administer—; advance—; defeat —; deny—; despair of—; dispense—; do — to; elude—; execute—; hamper—; imperil —; insure—; mete out—; obstruct—; paralyze—; preserve—; render—; taint—; thirst for—; trample—; —evolves; —grows; —hinges on; —rests.
(See righteousness, right, virtue, purity, truth.)

JUSTIFIABLE

adverbs
eminently; splendidly; scarcely; expediently; entirely; legally; morally; unquestionably; substantially; fundamentally; essentially; possibly; supposedly; presumably; apparently; sufficiently; reasonably; plausibly; barely; advantageously.

JUSTIFICATION

adjectives
substantial; abundant; gradual; creative; theoretical.

JUSTIFY (v)

adverbs
completely; amply; definitely; sufficiently; reasonably; righteously; unmistakably; manifestly; undoubtedly; substantially; abundantly; theoretically.

(See excuse, absolve, warrant.)

JUT (v)

adverbs
prodigiously; precipitately; sharply; abnormally; prominently; frightfully; dangerously.

(See protect, protrude.)

K

adverbs

variably; restlessly; changefully; colorfully; shiftily; perilously; unstably; waveringly; interestingly; dizzily; artfully; terribly; surprisingly; amazingly; incredibly; perplexingly; mysteriously; queerly; inconveniently; oddly; dreadfully; uncertainly.

KANGAROO

verbs

—balances; —carries; —expels; —fights; —gnashes; —hops; —jumps; —pouches; —races; —nibbles.

(See animal.)

KEEN

adverbs

intelligently; unwontedly; sharply; acutely; naturally; subtly; extremely; shrewdly; sensibly; mysteriously; obviously; supremely; unfailingly; infallibly; prophetically; precociously; penetratingly; astoundingly; singularly; uncannily; sagaciously; wisely; apparently; obviously; profoundly; thoughtfully; exceedingly.

KEENNESS

adjectives

hereditary; uncanny; catlike.

KEEP (v)

adverbs

perniciously; charitably; surreptitiously; deliberately; shamelessly; tenderly; sedulously; discreetly; stubbornly; courteously; religiously; undeviatingly; ceaselessly; perpetually; inevitably; ostentatiously; jealously.

(See preserve, celebrate, observe, maintain.)

KEEPER

adjectives

pernicious; charitable; inquisitive.

verbs

appoint—; dodge—; elude—; escape—; install—; evade—; —abandons; —administers; —attends; —chastises; —controls; —governs; —guards; —inspects; —preserves; —prosecutes; —pursues; —retains; —scans; —snatches.

(See manager, guardian.)

KEEPING

adjectives

watchful; devoted; perfect.

KEN

adjectives

inscrutable; human; widest.

KENNEL

adjectives

loathsome; dubious; extensive; ghostly.

KERCHIEF

adjectives

bleached; pale; square-drooping.

KETTLE

adjectives

prophetic; simmering; melting; steaming.

verbs

beat—; brew in—; brush—; drain—; polish —; replenish—; scour—; scrub—; stew in —; strike—; strum on—; —chirps; —gleams; —hisses; —hums; —simmers; —sings; —trills; —whistles.

(See caldron, pot, tub, vat.)

KEY

adjectives

crystal; romantic; feeble; excellent; foreboding; tentative; strategic; interrogative; ponderous; unwieldy; tingling; massy.

verbs

belt —s; fit—; force—; fumble with—; inject—; grope for—; insert—; jangle—; mislay—; pocket—; ram — into; respond to—; —s clank; —s jingle; —s rattle.

KEY (music)

adjectives

rigid; plaintive; tender; sad; minor; cracking.

KEYBOARD

adjectives

console-like; magic; complicated; master.

verbs

belabor—; caress—; dance on—; finger—; journey over—; perform on—; pounce upon

—; recite on—; render on—; run along—; skip over—; trip along—; work—; — gleams.

(See instrument, banjo, piano.)

KEYNOTE

verbs
elaborate on—; fire—; hit—; introduce—; reach—; recognize—; reveal—; seek—; sound—; strike—; touch—; —arouses; —attracts; —excites; —impresses; —interests; —stirs.

(See point, policy, idea.)

KEYSTONE

adjectives
indispensable; all-supporting.

KICK

adjectives
mighty; harmless; ceremonious.

KICK (v)

adverbs
affectionately; profanely; unmercifully; brutally; furiously; spasmodically; carelessly; frantically; simultaneously; unceremoniously; savagely; clumsily; murderously; madly; viciously; vindictively; ferociously.

(See oppose, resist, recoil.)

KID

adjectives
healthy; irresponsible; squalling.

KIDNAPPER

verbs
apprehend—; contact—; negotiate with—; prosecute—; pursue—; —abducts; —decoys; —delivers; —demands; —directs; —entices; —frightens; —lures; —operates; —snatches; —spirits away; —surveys; —threatens.

(See thief, robber, murderer.)

KIDNEY

adjectives
hard-worked; distressing; paining.

verbs
belt—; block—; congest—; dilate—; engorge —; impair—; inflame—; obstruct—; pad—; support—; —enlarges; —excretes; —filters; —floats; —fuses; —moves; —swells.

(See bladder, liver, organ, intestines.)

KILL (v)

adverbs
incessantly; simultaneously; accidentally; designedly; uselessly; intentionally; instantly; wantonly; ferociously; brutally; pitilessly; insanely; savagely; basely; sportively.

(See murder, slay, assassinate.)

KILLER

adjectives
tyrannical; pitiless; brutal; mad.

KILLING

adjectives
merciless; unrestricted; unsolved.

verbs
atone for—; avenge—; conceal—; confess —; contrive—; indulge in an orgy of—s; lament—; observe—; perform—; plan—; resent—, revenge—, stifle—, uncover—; unearth—; warrant—; witness—; —awes; —incenses; —infuriates; —offends; —puzzles; —shocks.

(See murder, slaughter, massacre, assassination.)

KIN

adjectives
blood; nearest; surviving.

KIND

adjectives
refractory; voracious; abstracted; unexpected; corresponding; literal; positive; unworthy; fraternal; direst; various (pl); wondrous; honey-gathering; tingling; haphazard; curious; mortal; fascinating; heavier; weakest; baser; unlike; particular; noblest; sprightliest; restless; elaborate; expensive; barbarous; branching; peculiar; indifferent; unsatisfied; awful; lonesome; effectual; defensive; increasing; adventurous; equivocal.

adverbs
graciously; generously; hospitably; helpfully; unexpectedly; extremely; exceedingly; habitually; naturally; indulgently; gently; mistakenly; thoughtfully; lovingly; unaffectedly; effusively; officiously; sincerely; cordially; unspeakably; unusually; uncommonly; openly; apparently; noticeably; unselfishly; sympathetically; amiably; affably; unwontedly; considerately; humanely; complaisantly.

KINDLE (v)

adverbs

patiently; skillfully; daily; purposely; premeditatively; punctually; swiftly; spectacularly; vividly.

(See ignite, burn, inflame, rouse.)

KINDLINESS

adjectives

tranquil; clear; close-fisted; proverbial; eager; unaffected; sincere; comfortable.

KINDNESS

adjectives

gracious; ostentatious; undiminished; manifest; systematic; sickening; honey; paternal; sneaking; fraternal; mysterious; selfsame; indulgent; mistaken; loving; thoughtful; false; mellow; anxious; maddening; touching; like; present; patient; generous; fair; subtle; covetous; usurious; impersonal; marked; quizzical; proffered; grave; considerable; lukewarm; cruel; extreme; homely; exceeding; benevolent; natural; indolent; remorseful; hospitable; commended; native; cordial; unbought; forbearing; apparent; untaught.

verbs

bestow—upon; bless with—; confer—; enslave by—; extend—; overflow with—; render—; scatter—; trust—; —charms; —comforts; —conquers; —converts; —enriches; —gladdens; —melts; —shines; —soothes.

(See tenderness, tolerance, charity.)

KING

adjectives

maleficent; deposed; uncrowned; shameful; tributary; wily; grisly; besieging; cautious; guarded; crafty; lofty; apostate; bereaved; loving; nominal; bonanza; well-intentioned; penitent; harlot; veritable; anointed; uxorious; lawful; captive; prostrate; rightful; boastful; mythological; guileless; pious; colorless; blameless; lottery; faithless; untamed; sanguine; unwholesome; resplendent; fangless; landless; provincial; incredulous; fratricidal; licentious; dissimulating.

verbs

acknowledge—; anoint—; consort with—s; crown—; dethrone—; exile—; forsake—; guard—; honor—; praise—; respect—; serve—; —abdicates; —administers; —awes; —commands; —governs; —reigns; —rules; —surveys.

(See monarch, queen, god, ruler.)

KINGDOM

adjectives

infernal; peasant; teeming; animal; mineral; island; watery; moss-hung; hereditary; unconquerable; petty; stout; little; enchanting; enduring; dull; vassal.

verbs

banish from—; conquer—; divide—; forsake —; govern—; grant—; infect—; inhabit—; invade—; overthrow—; partition—; reign over—; renounce—; resign—; rule—; serve —; skirt—; split—; subdue—; —embraces; —extends; —ranges.

(See kingship, realm, monarchy, jurisdiction, dominion, empire.)

KINGLY

adverbs

undeniably; admittedly; consciously; notably; admirably; strikingly; astonishingly; superbly; estimably; magnificently; splendidly; consummately; expertly; aristocratically; nobly; unimpeachably; judiciously; benevolently; resplendently; absolutely; authoritatively; influentially; supremely; autocratically.

KINGSHIP

verbs

abdicate—; abolish—; accept—; bestow—upon; forsake—; honor—; invest—with; ordain to—; propose—; respect—; survey—.

(See kingdom.)

KINSHIP

adjectives

emotional; spiritual.

KINSMEN

adjectives

distinguished; lamented; honorable; moldering.

KISS

adjectives

salt; sterile; spiritlike; melancholy; squandered; multiplied (pl); successive (pl); bought; barren; piteous; breathless; rapturous; wafted; indulgent; passionate; energetic; perfunctory; burning; glowing; implacable; ungiven; farewell; hot; silent;

fleeting; mute; deep-drawn; fruitful; horizontal; cancerous; treacherous; lovely; sisterhood; famished; tempting; punctuating; loving; holy; sovereign; furious; honeyed; guileless; humbled; fervent; furtive; impassioned; ardent; rarely-tempered; admiring; compassionate; serio-comic; reverent; vigorous; abstracted; random; sincere; airy; moist; reassuring; iron; eager; hasty; laughing; latter; timorous; broken; delicious.

verbs
bestow—upon; blow—; blush at—; brush—; cement with—; cling in—; dab—; dot with —; pluck—; press—; print—upon; promise with—; resist—; sever—; smother with—s; snatch—; steal—; taste—; tempt with—; wed in—; yield—; —disturbs; —enraptures; —entrances; —pecks; —quenches; —subdues; —thrills.
(See caress, embrace.)

KISS (v)
adverbs
passionately; resoundingly; reverently; clumsily; violently; tenderly; airily; ravenously; earnestly; brazenly; soberly; intimately; exultantly; crudely; tantalizingly; fondly; perfunctorily; devoutly; dutifully; vivaciously; mutely; timorously.
(See caress, salute, embrace.)

KISSING
adjectives
voluptuous; continual; heated; promiscuous; ignominious; passioned.

KITCHEN
adjectives
commodious; fragrant; detached; reeking; itinerant; greasy; pretty; well-designed.

verbs
avoid—; consign to—; convey from—; drudge in—; equip—; inspect—; loiter in —; preside over—; retire to—; rule—; scrub—; slave in—; survey—; sweat in—; toil in—; work in—; —enslaves; —gleams; —shines; —smells of.
(See home, room, shop, factory, laboratory.)

KITES
adjectives
carrion; marauding; ravenous.

KITTEN
adjectives
imaginary; striped; playful; impish.

verbs
pet—; stroke—; —amuses; —antics; — basks; —capers; —diverts; —frisks; — frolics; —gambols; —laps; —meows; — plays; —romps; —toys with.
(See cat, puppy, lamb, baby, calf.)

KNACK
adjectives
mechanical; instinctive.

KNAVE
adjectives
cowardly; luckless; unthrifty; lunatic; base; poor; gallant; false; arrant; jealous; decayed; shrewd; ingenious; foolish; rascally; whoreson; beetle-headed; flap-ear; misshapen; pestilent, foul-mouthed; calumnious; scurvy; railing; wrangling; thin-faced; fantastical; doting; sooty; veritable; sinful.

KNAVERY
verbs
brew—; check—; condemn—; confess—; curb—; despise—; escape—; frustrate—; observe—; resist—; shun—; suffer—; suspect—; unfold—; witness—; yield to—; — jars; —shocks; —tempts.
(See wickedness, villainy, vice, crime.)

KNAVISH
adverbs
arrantly; downright; notoriously; grossly; consummately; egregiously; abominably; atrociously; villainously; viciously; infamously; daringly; wickedly; brazenly; extraordinarily; outrageously; monstrously; unbelievably; sinfully; terribly; insufferably; unscrupulously; insidiously; ingloriously; lawlessly; disreputably; scandalously; incorrigibly; shamelessly; astoundingly

KNEAD (v)
adverbs
savagely; industriously; vigorously; laboriously; mechanically; experimentally; patiently; wholesomely; furiously.
(See fashion, massage, mould, mix.)

KNEE
adjectives
guiding; shaking; shaken; bended; knotted; twinging; naked; rocky; suppliant; feeble;

mailed; pliant; trembling; faltering; up-gathered; relentless; silken; immaculate; sagged; well-molded; sagging; bony; flaccid; tottering; wobbly; weak; exposed; bare; numb; stalwart; buckling; jutting; drawn-up; clasped; scratched; dimpled; enticing.

verbs
bend—; beseech on—s; bow—; brace—; bruise—; climb on—; drop on—; entreat on —s; fall upon—; flex—; implore on—; sink to—; smite—; supplicate on—; —s buckle; —s fold; —s sag; —s weaken.

KNEEL (v)
adverbs
heavily; laboriously; devoutly; submissively; reverently; blindly; prayerfully; imploringly; meekly; religiously; adoringly .
(See surrender, bend.)

KNELL
adjectives
doleful; perpetual; inevitable.

KNIFE
adjectives
ill-directed; harmful; murderous; crooked; keen; burning; long; two-edged; broad; sharp-pointed; naked; big; tempered; curved; brass-handled; blunt; hatchetlike; pointless; whetted; blood-stained.

verbs
brandish—; carve with—; clasp with—; fling—; flourish—; hack with—; heave—; hone—; hurl—; pare with—; pocket—; sheathe—; slash with—; slay with—; stab with—; thrust—; whirl—about.
(See sword, stiletto.)

KNIGHT
adjectives
moralizing; valiant; dauntless; adventurous; tender-smelling; solitary; gallant; cheerful; virgin; sinful; dissembling; blended; belted; irreverent; greasy; assailing; tight-lipped; stalwart; particular; fabled; dubbed; brave.

KNIGHTLY
adverbs
dauntlessly; intrepidly; courteously; gallantly; invariably; habitually; splendidly; superbly; magnificently; generously; chivalrously; distinctly; eminently; nobly; bene-

volently; delightfully; charmingly; pleasantly; affably; uncommonly; unusually; exceptionally.

KNIT (v)
adverbs
indefatigably; industriously; vigorously; busily; exquisitely; laboriously; patiently; domestically; artistically; beneficially; healthfully; swiftly; monotonously.
(See tie, unite, join, weave.)

KNITTING
verbs
abandon—; admire—; busy with—; commend—; concentrate on—; display—; enjoy —; exhibit—; instruct in—; interrupt—; observe—; occupy with—; survey—; teach —; unravel—; —annoys; —bores; —contents; —delights; —fascinates; —satisfies; —takes form.
(See work.)

KNOB
adjectives
battered; rusty; bent; twisted; turning.

verbs
adjust—; affix—; force—; furnish—; grasp —; grope for—; handle—; jiggle—; locate —; manipulate—; move—; raise—; shake —; turn—; —juts out; —opens; —resists; —submits.
(See handle.)

KNOCK
adjectives
welcome; jarring; thundering; timid; hesitating; parlous; cheerful; imperative; timorous; hard; unwonted; resounding.

KNOCK (v)
adverbs
sharply; clamorously; deliberately; accidentally; respectfully; irritably; resoundingly; unwontedly; thunderously; echoingly; startlingly.
(See rap, clash, beat, strike.)

KNOLL
adjectives
neighboring; sandy; moon-lit; wooded; treeless; timber-covered; rising; verdant.

KNOT
adjectives
inextricable; mystic; intricate; unsuccess-

ful; curious; murderous; true-love; shaggy; salient; writhing; snaky; sagest; feathered.

verbs
curl into—; disentangle—; do up in—; draw into—; form—; knit into—; loop into—; loose—; secure with—; unravel—; untwine —; weave into—; —assures; —mystifies; —perplexes; —puzzles.

KNOTTED

adverbs
dreadfully; tightly; nervously; angrily; inextricably; roughly; strangely; queerly; loosely; carelessly; deliberately; unevenly; jaggedly; hopelessly; terribly; untidily; indiscriminately; mischievously; maliciously; incurably; irreparably; perniciously; vexatiously; inexcusably.

KNOW (v)

adverbs
precisely; intimately; distinctly; intuitively; authoritatively; affectionately; grimly; casually; graciously; jocularly; abstractly; instantaneously; superficially; alliteratively; imperfectly; officially; familiarly; presumably; academically; traditionally; personally; fallaciously.

(See apprehend, realize, understand, ascertain, recognize.)

KNOWLEDGE

adjectives
technical; subtle; painful; pleasurable; experimental; distinct; tinctured; hearsay; extensive; intuitive; slight; detailed; repugnant; profound; dark; uncanny; sudden; acquired; human; systematic; psycho-analytic; copious; elementary; unique; well-known; definite; fuller; academic; intimate; precise; rudimentary; prodigious; barren; bookish; extemporary; unimparted; uncertain; critical; boundless; accurate; specialized; exhilarating; unwelcome; superior; guilty; dangerous; swift; unrelated; superficial; miraculous; worldly; unutterable; imperfect; substantial; immense; preliminary;

fluent; growing; untimely; proficient; inestimable; complete; improved; practical; symbolic; consummate; masterful; extraordinary; previous; satisfying; medieval; organized; theoretical; advanced; wearisome; crafty; instinctive; varied; seeming; increased; thorough; lawful; inexhaustible; phenomenal; accumulated; comprehensive; preternatural; gradual; learned; unerring; scientific; definite; clearer; objective; special; lesser; naturalistic; adequate; hard-won; competent; masculine; shrewd; natural; deeper; desecrated; inherited; cynical; rapidly-acquired; delivering; deep-fetched; limited; dread; defective; positive; indisputable; fallacious; educational; gossipy; colloquial; all-embracing; traditional; questionable; acquired; laborious; working; premature; verified; superfluous; meager; personal; astronomic; contemptuous; inward; actual; earthly; secure; rooted; fiendish; fascinating; up to the-minute; priceless, happiest; nobler; inferior; well-founded; momentary; unrivaled.

verbs
absorb—; accumulate—; acquire—; apply —; arm with—; assimilate—; attain—; augment—; broadcast—; confront with—; contribute to—; convey—; cultivate—; derive —; digest—; disavow—; disseminate—; draw upon—; employ—; enlarge—; enrich with—; equip with—; evince—; evolve—; exhibit—; expand—; extend—; feed with—; flash—; flaunt—; grope for—; illuminate with—; impart—; imply—; obscure—; pool —; prize—; promulgate—; purchase—; record—; retain—; retard—; safeguard—; soak up—; spread—; thirst for—; treasure —; utilize—; yearn for—; —enlightens; —boils down to.
(See learning, facts, information, understanding, wisdom.)

KNUCKLE

adjectives
bleeding; white; pudgy; bruised; skinned; swarthy; abraded; brass.

L

LABEL

adjectives
progressive; registered; bothersome.

verbs
affix—; destroy—; investigate—; note—; require—; scan—; seal with—; slap on—; stamp—; —attests; —clings; —describes; —designates; —indicates; —represents.
(See mark, stamp, notice, badge, trademark.)

LABEL (v)

adverbs
legally; sarcastically; laconically; carelessly; perfunctorily; cursorily; painstakingly; methodically; decoratively; attractively; concisely; symbolically; fantastically; characteristically.
(See classify, mark.)

LABOR

adjectives
enormous; arduous; sedentary; colossal; persevering; unskilled; lofty; conscientious; praiseworthy; enlightened; earnest; patient; painful; fastidious; graver; uplifting; exhausting; toilsome; unceasing; intellectual; self-imposed; initiatory; faithful; incredible; useless; indefatigable; ceaseless; reproachful; assiduous; unsparing; manual; wonderful; immense; manifold; ill-paid; unimaginable; attendant; unremitting; nocturnal; incessant; endless; grievous; journalistic; intermittent; wearisome; strenuous; unrequited; exploited; loving; sleepless; sweated; diligent; untiring; confining; unceasing; steadfast; imperative; degraded; superfluous; insurgent; inconceivable; fantastic; bucolic; herculean; honorable; skilled; mighty; guiltless; daring; infinite; moderate; effective; congenial; smoke-grimed; gratuitous; united; earnest; unbroken; painstaking; influential; powerful; culinary; unselfish; historical; interrupted; successive (pl); backbreaking; previous; subordinate; organized; active; unwearying; vilified; productive; tremendous; exacting; harsh; aspiring; patient; painful; tedious; ideal; untasked; convict; dreadful; rural; additional; sylvan; pleasant; astrological;

oppressed; wonted; tutorial; symbolical; evasive; menial; ever-successful; short-lived; literary; coarse; ferocious; professional; ministerial; heartbreaking.

verbs
absorb in—; bleed (colloq.)—; discipline—; enslave—; free from—; mar—; necessitate —; organize—; placate—; prohibit—; recompense—; recuperate from—; regulate—; reward—; stimulate—; supplement—; surmount—; thrive upon—; undertake—; —profits; —reaps; —supports; —sustains.
(See work, workers, task, industry, toil, production.)

LABOR (v)

adverbs
systematically; incessantly; indefatigably; assiduously; unmercifully; industriously; vigorously; tirelessly; prodigiously; diligently; tumultuously; arduously; fastidiously; unsparingly; gratuitously; congenially; productively; exactingly; unwontedly; tutorially; symbolically; menially; ferociously; professionally.
(See work, toil, drudge.)

LABORATORY

adjectives
destructive; stupendous; metallurgical.

verbs
dissect in—; emit from—; employ in—; establish—; experiment in—; inspect—; investigate in—; lecture in—; manufacture in—; prepare in—; rig out—; stock—; test in—; tinker in—; turn out of—; verify in —; work in—; —discloses; —nauseates; —reeks of; —discovers.
(See kitchen, shop, factory.)

LABORER

adjectives
diverting; solitary; bucolic; devoted; potential; agricultural; diligent; luckless.

LABORIOUS

adverbs
extremely; oppressively; intricately; objectionably; unexpectedly; surprisingly; unremittingly; sedulously; overwhelmingly; enormously; immensely; painfully; incred-

ibly; grievously; strenuously; fantastically; moderately; dreadfully; pleasantly; wholesomely; backbreakingly; elaborately; wearisomely; terribly; undeniably; unbelievably.

LABYRINTH
adjectives
slimy; close; mighty; vast; trackless; burning; weary; watery; aboreal; inextricable.

LABYRINTHINE
adverbs
intricately; hopelessly; perplexingly; curiously; queerly; alarmingly; amazingly; dreadfully; surprisingly; mysteriously; dangerously; perilously; complexly; sinuously; tortuously; troublesomely; circuitously; vexatiously; terrifyingly; ominously.

LACE
adjectives
tawdry; exquisite; cream; supernumerary (pl), billowing; meandering; delicate; passementerie; erring; fluttering; elaborate; tarnished; creamy; tinted.

LACE (v)
adverbs
tightly; suffocatingly; fashionably; injuriously; oppressively.
(See fasten, tie, bind.)

LACERATION
verbs
incur—; inflict—; occasion—; soothe—; sterilize—; stitch—; suture—; tourniquet—; —appals; —bares the bone; —distresses; —heals; —horrifies; —inflames; —pains; —scars; —shocks; —throbs; —tortures.
(See wound, injury, pain, cut.)

LACK
adjectives
pretended; noticeable; all-round; deplorable; disorderly; overwhelming; impressive; plentiful; definite; obvious.

verbs
atone for—; bare—; bemoan—; compensate for—; confess—; decry—; disclose—; imply —; perceive—; recognize—; recompense for —; remedy—; sense—; suffer—; supply—; suspect—; —crushes; —disgraces; —handicaps; —humbles; —irks; —offends; —ostracizes; —saddens.
(See inadequacy, need, want.)

LACK (v)
adverbs
lamentably; puzzlingly; vainly; essentially; wretchedly; sorely; utterly; sadly; deplorably; definitely; obviously; tragically; dramatically.
(See need, want.)

LACKADAISICAL
adverbs
nonchalantly; ostentatiously; obviously; foolishly; sentimentally; romantically; languidly; dreamily; inanely; provokingly; drunkenly; stupidly; crazily; pretentiously; foppishly; vainly; unnaturally; artificially; languishingly; heavily; terribly; gravely; thoughtfully.

LACKEY
adjectives
saucy; liveried; silk-stockinged.

LACONIC
adverbs
meagerly; unsatisfactorily; emphatically; disappointingly; vexatiously; habitually; tersely; drily; drolly; crisply; curtly; comprehensively; summarily; trenchantly; curiously; oddly; officially; arrogantly; cynically; laudably; neatly; compactly; sententiously; professionally; provokingly; remarkably; wonderfully; notably; famously; uncommonly; highly; amazingly; incredibly; effectively.

LACONISM
adjectives
formal; concise; annoying; notable.

LACQUERS
adjectives
decorative; shiny; protective; gaudy; bright.

LAD
adjectives
malicious; lethargic; raw; daring; sober; gallant; joyous; vigorous; singular; loutish; fine; gentlemanly; valiant; painstaking; capable; ambitious; blithe; sensitive; sweet; rosy; mad; delirious; promising; struggling.

LADDER
adjectives
petal-woven; corded; rude; commodious; symbolical; palpable; golden; heavenly.

verbs
ascend—; clamber up—; drop from—; employ—; extend—; hoist—; leap up—; mount —; rung—; scale—; scramble up—; shake —; shift—; support—; teeter on—; —aids; —bridges; —conveys; —dizzies; —totters; travel up—.
(See steps, stairs.)

LADY

adjectives
demure; spare; grave; worthy; estimable; double-dealing; venerable; generous; gallant; out-sized; perennial; gracious; blushing; haughty; pitiful; excellent; accomplished; wretched; audacious; quick-fingered; quick-witted; quick-eyed; sacred; horny-handed; virtuous; sweet; innocent; good-natured; courageous; beauteous; incredulous; celestial; disloyal; hopeful; miserable; conventional; decorous; well-mannered; dejected; soft-spoken; square-faced; starched; profound; interested; autocratic; languid; well-brought-up; masterful; delicate; high-bred; pink-cheeked; reverend; vixenish; colossal; dignified; elderly; flustered; skeptical; diminutive; blameless; giddy; charming; gentle; fortunate; little; chubby; prudent; pleasant-spoken; exotic; sentimental; thrice-fair; pleasant-spirited; desolate; poor; wrong; chic; acidulated; chaste; agreeable; prepossessing; illustrious; elegant; glittering; ingenuous; favorite; metallic; solicitous; pearly-robed.

LADYLIKE

adverbs
oppressively; exquisitely; absurdly; delightfully; overwhelmingly; fastidiously; foolishly; agreeably; pleasantly; graciously; comically; modestly; demurely; coyly; decorously; genteelly; formally; properly; fashionably; appropriately; conventionally; aristocratically; politely; courteously; ostentatiously; stylishly; elegantly; ceremoniously; stiffly; awkwardly; pretentiously; affably; complaisantly; charmingly; enchantingly.

LAG

adjectives
cultural; common; noticeable.

LAGOON

verbs
approach—; cover—; cross—; describe—; enclose—; enter—; form—; observe—; open into—; row in—; sail in—; separate—; skirt—; swim in—; —appears; —beckons; —extends; —invites.
(See lake, bay, pond.)

LAIR

adjectives
frigid; equatorial; shaggy; rosy; dreadful; jungle; deathless.

verbs
conceal in—; corner in—; discover—; dwell in—; ensconce in—; enter—; expose—; harbor in—; lodge in—; nestle in—; recline in—; repose in—; retreat to—; reveal—; track to—; uncover—; venture upon—; —comforts; —reeks; —shelters.
(See den, refuge, retreat.)

LAKE

adjectives
shimmering; tranquil; climbing; lily-mantled; darkling; grassy; azure; misty; stagnant; placid; bitter; weedy; far-reaching; encircling; shattered; picturesque; forest-bosomed; crystal; encompassing; starry; lovely; seething; translucent; calm-flowing; rumored; universal; parent; sleeping; lucid; contrasted; burning; smiling; argent; glittering; airy; lonely; ruffled; liquid; mirrored; fringed; dazzling; noble; dusky.

verbs
angle in—; cast into—; encompass—; fish in—; navigate—; ramble by—; row on—; sail—; shade—; sight—; skim over—; skirt —; slip into—; surround—; waft across—; —affords; —dazzles; —gleams; —glimmers; —laps; —mirrors; —reflects; —ripples; —shimmers; —spangles; —winks; —yawns.
(See lagoon, river, stream, bay, pond, sea.)

LAMB

adjectives
bleating; parti-colored; sinful; sacrificial; silly; twinned; heaven-sent.

verbs
brand—s; cuddle—; fatten—s; market—; roast—; sacrifice—; slaughter—; —baas; —bleats; —capers; —frisks; —frolics; —gambols; —grazes; —nuzzles; —prances; —symbolizes.
(See kitten, calf, sheep, animal, baby, puppy, cat.)

LAMBENT

adverbs

delicately; gently; flickeringly; effulgently; flashingly; gloriously; steadily; luminously; phosphorescently; shimmeringly; softly; recurrently; lustrously; scintillatingly; unusually; peculiarly; strangely.

LAMENT

adjectives

constant; loud; inevitable; lugubrious; passionate.

LAMENT (*v*)

adverbs

dolorously; pitifully; pathetically; eternally; morbidly; passionately; lugubriously; quaveringly; tearfully; abnormally; hysterically; affectionately.

(See weep, wail, grieve.)

LAMENTABLE

adverbs

altogether; downright; pitiably; bitterly; sorely; direly; utterly; exceptionally; shockingly; appallingly; horribly; unusually; extremely; fearfully; frightfully; tragically; wretchedly; indescribably; sadly; absolutely; unspeakably; inexpressibly; singularly.

LAMENTATION

adjectives

piteous; moderate; importunate; frantic; grand; purposeless; loud; diabolical; silent; sublime; quavering; burlesque.

verbs

censure—; deplore—; fill with—; forego—; forestall—; regret—; restrain—; staunch—; stifle—; utter—; wail in—; —arises; —ceases; —encompasses; —haunts; —increases; —rends the air; —resounds; —weakens.

(See tears, sadness, grief, sorrow.)

LAMP

adjectives

flickering; wharf; quenchless; fragrant; incandescent; glimmering; respectable; acetyline; blear; trembling; mirrored; tawdry; frail; light-giving; intoxicating; ill-trimmed; wasting; pendulous; failing; rain-splashed; glow-worm; festooned; slow-sliding; meteoric; impudent; innumerable (pl); classic; sleepy; street; eternal; oil-dried; fluorescent; midnight; smoky; outburnt; shaded; reading; bronze; copper; shining;

winking; flashing; soft; colored; tiny; sputtering; gas; oil; luminous; twinkling; vital; studious; flaring; kindled; dewy.

verbs

blast—; deck with—s; extinguish—; grope for—; quench—; restore—; strangle—; suspend—; switch on—; —beautifies; —blinds; —brightens; —cheers; —comforts; —directs; —enhances; —fails; —flickers; —glimmers; —glows; —mellows; —reveals; —shines; —silhouettes.

(See light, candle, flame, fireworks, match, sunshine, twilight, spark.)

LANCE

adjectives

ill-headed; gleaming; thirsty; leafy; quivering; strong; shivered; rusted; splintered; unused.

verbs

cast—; charge with—s; harpoon with—; shatter—; slay with—; spear with—; splinter—; stab with—; thrust—; wield—; —cripples; —defends; —disfigures; —injures; —maims; —pierces; —scratches; —shivers; —splinters; —splits; —threatens; —wounds.

(See spear, sword, stiletto.)

LAND

adjectives

brawny-breasted; weather-beaten; tempting; wide; uninhabited; fruitful; radiant; rolling; toiling; devastated; depreciated; desolate; swampy; bleeding; cultivated; uncharted; intolerant; sylvan; eloquent; unshorn; exhausted; delightful; twilight; favored; death-polluted; dying; delectable; woeful; venerable; alluvial; granitic; barren; arable; heavenly; sickly; dewy; contiguous; pastoral; sun-soaked; virgin; enchanted; ceded; broad; monotonous; flat; factious; romantic; quaggy; guilty; boggy; habitable; sterile; forbidden; allodial; lifeless; gasping; sheltering; delicious; forsaken; debatable; enlightened; guileless; dirty; mortgaged; dawning; smiling; genial; sullen; scorched; superior; unhappy; untraveled; chivalric; gracious; inspirational; wretched; time-stricken; foreign; extreme; sprightly; listening; neighboring; untilled; goodly-growing; fertile; fallen; long-promised; hostile; springtime; sinless; disburdened; dipping; defenceless; unappropriated; wilderness; unoccupied; well-contented; watered; dependent; curtained; ruined; gentler;

sorrow-stricken; shadowy; hazy; ice-prison-ed; white; useless; beautiful; vacation; placid; tight; upheaved; sculptured; aesthetic; undulous; dim; vast; tranquil; irrigable; rich; blatant; fabled; misty; scrubby; furrowed; shadowless; antique; divers (pl); unseated; high-cost; touch-and-go; sluggish; marshy; fettered; hollow; bustling; native; derelict; waste; heath; many-tinted; boundless; prosperous; bountiful; invisible; timeless; sodden; unexplored; unconcerned; financial; fairy; luxuriant; exhaustless; desirable; agricultural; surrounding; night-enfolded; spiritual; unknown; gullied; middling; hereditary; distant; alien; dismembered; stubble; blossoming.

verbs

apportion—; bargain for—; cede—; claim —; cleanse—; corrupt—; cultivate—; darken—; defile—; denude—; despoil—; dower —; engulf—; enrich—; exploit—; fertilize —; inhabit—; inherit—; lease—; link—; nurse—; plow—; portion—; purge—; rule —; scour—; sow—; squat on—; sweep—; till—; vest—s in; —abuts; —adjoins; — yields.

(See earth, soil, ground, farm.)

LANDHOLDER
adjectives
wealthy; pampered; heavily-taxed; frugal.

LANDING
adjectives
rude; haphazard; prosaic; steamboat; three-point; perfect; fatal; forced.

verbs

anticipate—; bar—; contemplate—; effect—; forestall—; hinder—; hope for—; impede —; limit—; meet at—; prepare for—; prohibit—; salute—; superintend—; survey—; swoop to—; view—.

(See platform, finish.)

LANDLADY
adjectives
callous; slipshod; overpositive; shrieking; untrained; half-distracted; miserly.

LANDLORD
adjectives
absentee; lonely; liberal; grasping.

LANDMARK
adjectives
ghostly; tall; treasured; celebrated; obliterated; ancient; historical; well-kept; awe-inspiring.

LANDSCAPE
adjectives
ideal; imaginative; volcanic; broad; wet; dreary; reposeful; shadowy; manifold (pl); glorious; delicate; gliding; desolate; dismal; rolling; inspiring; autumnal; harmonious; limited; extravagant; bewildered; poetical; suggestive; naked; receding; twilight; motionless; mystic; glimmering; colored; austere; stupendous; delicious; ungenial; ravaged; forbidding; bitter; peaceful; perfect; winter; untrodden; melancholy; impressive; serious; shivering; imposing; large; dreamy; terrestrial; hoary; lunar; hazy; sunlit; glowing; variegated; pastoral; scarred; vernal; withered; dim; embrowned; distant.

verbs

clutter—; contemplate—; denude—; desecrate—; design—; dot—; enhance—; exhibit—; gaze on—; gild—; glorify—; integrate—; intersperse—; perfect—; photograph—; regard—; scrutinize—; shade—; tinge—; view—; —charms; —delights; — educates; —gratifies; —spreads; —stretches.

(See country, countryside, view, scene, picture, scenery.)

LAND-SLIDE
adjectives
fashion; fatal; crushing; spectacular.

LANE
adjectives
dark; solitary; hedgerowed; grassy; seaward; rambling; turfy; cattle-haunted; leafy; pleached; neighboring; winding; miry; isolated; infrequent; sandy; rectory; bowery; dirty; rutty; hollow; shaded; forest; high-walled; quiet; deep-shaded.

verbs

adhere to—; bolt down—; clear—; follow —; labor up—; lurk in—; mantle—; pause in—; rest in—; scamper down—; shade—; shadow—; shun—; skirt—; tarry in—; veer from—; —diverges; —flanks; —meanders; —spirals; —swerves; —twists; —wanders; —winds.

(See road, alley, passage, path, street, thoroughfare, walk.)

LANGUAGE

adjectives
various (pl); symbolical; evasive; abusive; well-known; clear; understandable; simple; clarified; easy; peculiar; profane; psychoanalytic; lovely; figurative; neighboring; luminous; ungracious; graceless; energetic; ominous; satirical; adopted; subservient; impassioned; rhythmical; strenuous; lucid; emphatic; precise; noble; judicious; conversational; similar; amicable; forcible; violent; unseemly; flexible; musical; refined; primitive; wide-spread; copious; metrical; native; expressive; unmistakable; worthy; passionate; maternal; extinct; warming; dead; universal; reviling; elegant; opprobrious; inoffensive; biblical; scrupulous; classical; provincial; concise; sublime; appropriate; nervous; unintelligible; official; elaborate; stilted; bombastic; temperate; winning; cordial; sensible; semibarbarous; mystic; glowing; tart; strong; persuasive; inadequate; provocative; hearty; lustful; animated; rude; decorous; uncensored; remarkable; felicitous; colloquial; declarative; emotional; melodious; informal; striking; paradoxical; imaginative; contemptuous; coarse; embellished; pleasurable; impossible; vehement; rugged; vigorous; idiomatic; austere; traditional; high-flown; hidden; spiritual; characteristic; artificial; lifeless; sacred; colorless; symbolic; euphonious; literary; immoderate; festive; impious.

verbs
abuse—; bolt—; broaden—; clothe in—; command—; corrupt—; decipher—; decode —; defile—; interpret—; manipulate—; master—; mold—; mutilate—; purify—; restrict—; revive—; strangle—; vitalize—; vulgarize—; —abounds in; —bears witness; —bristles with; —flows; —lilts; —survives.
(See speech, dialect, slang, jargon.)

LANGUID

adverbs
listlessly; dreamily; lazily; idly; deliberately; deliciously; softly; blissfully; unwontedly; delightfully; pensively; thoughtfully; wearily; mildly; strangely; unusually; peculiarly; alarmingly; ominously; oddly; dispiritedly; dejectedly; indifferently; indolently; inertly; uncommonly; woefully; significantly; particularly; constitutionally; objectionably; exasperatingly; provokingly; inveterately.

LANGUISH (v)

adverbs
piteously; idly; gradually; pathetically; sickly; wanly; pensively; wearily; dreamily; amorously; listlessly; unwontedly; blissfully; lazily; agonizingly; passionately; ceaselessly; lovingly.
(See pine, droop, faint, weaken.)

LANGUOR

adjectives
increasing; ladylike; apparent; wearisome; delicious; gentle; delightful; pensive; passionless; restive; melancholy; sensuous; dreamy; amorous; unwonted; listless; gracious; soft; blissful; divine; mortal; exceeding; lazy.

verbs
complain of—; depress into—; diffuse—; droop in—; exhibit—; exude—; fall into—; perceive—; relieve—; shake off—; sink into —; sway with—; —arrests; —floats over; —oppresses; —pervades; —spreads.
(See lassitude, exhaustion, weariness.)

LANKY

adverbs
unbelievably; comically; ludicrously; increasingly; awkwardly; clumsily; bashfully; haggardly; hungrily; terribly; pathetically; woefully; weedily; gauntly; slenderly; extremely; preposterously; fantastically; impressively; dreadfully; inexpressibly; curiously; laughably; particularly; peculiarly; strangely.

LANTERN

adjectives
port-colored; multicolored; treacherous; exquisite; smoky; ill-smelling.

LAP

adjectives
flowery; mossy; verdant; commodious; soft; inviting.

LAP (v)

adverbs
greedily; thirstily; affectionately; hungrily; fawningly; cringingly; ingratiatingly.
(See lick, eat.)

LAPSE

adjectives
careless; temporary; momentary; single; liquid; deplorable; smooth; strong; venial;

occasional; incredible; atrocious; enormous; soothing; sad; moral; melancholy; abrupt.

verbs
attribute—to; dispel—; emerge from—; expose to—; fall into—; glide into—; recover from—; sink in—; slip into—; spend—; suffer—; vacate—; —avails; —decays; flow into—.

(See mistake, error, indiscretion.)

LAPWING
adjectives
wanton; swift.

LARCENY
adjectives
petit; grand; mammoth.

LARDER
verbs
deposit in—; drain—; exhaust—; hang in —; invade—; load—; purge—; raid—; replenish—; resort to—; sack—; stock—; store in—; tap—; —abounds in; —conserves; —gratifies; —overflows; —preserves.

(See stock, supply, store.)

LARGE
adverbs
extremely; incalculably; incredibly; immeasurably; preposterously; exceedingly; particularly; overwhelmingly; infinitely; enormously; monstrously; prodigiously; astoundingly; marvelously; remarkably; notoriously; uncommonly; immoderately; inordinately; signally; strikingly; amazingly; tremendously; immensely; comparatively; incomparably; imposingly; formidably; sensationally; unusually; amply; satisfactorily; sufficiently.

LARK
adjectives
veritable; merry; late; full-throated; mounting; morning; winging.

verbs
—carols; —chants; —chimes; —chirrups; —circles; —composes; —s congregate; —s flock; —heralds the dawn; —improvises; —instills; —molts; —ravishes; —sharps; —showers melody; —shrills; —slurs; —sprinkles notes; —squats; —startles; —strains; —trills; —whistles.

(See bird.)

LASH
adjectives
drooping; burning; sweeping; sooty; dark; arrowy; invisible; sleepy; scattered (pl); fluttering; glistening; torturing; flickering; stinging; inky; silky; languid; bristly; downcast; molten; delicate; pale; long; flaxen; biting; verbal.

LASH (v)
adverbs
viciously; furiously; frenziedly; maniacally; vilely; brutally; sadistically; murderously; madly.

(See whip, scold, beat, punish.)

LASHING
adjectives
ominous; merciless; cruel; interrupted; crippling; bloody; bitter; mad; furious; fierce; frenzied; maniacal.

verbs
bemoan—; bestow—upon; cringe under—; crucify with—; denounce—; experience—; gloat over—; inflict—; suffer—; wince at —; writhe under—; yield to—; —angers; —convulses; —cows; —infuriates; —maddens; —subdues; —tortures.

(See scolding, punishment, beating.)

LASS
adjectives
prettiest; lowborn; morbid; enticing; dark-eyed; bouncing; tidy-looking; flat-faced; modest; buxom; bewitching; pleasant; vivacious; smiling.

LASSITUDE
adjectives
despairing; general; poppied; speechless; languorous; drowsy; dreamy; hopeless.

verbs
combat—; depress into—; diffuse—; droop into—; exhibit—; induce—; perceive—; remedy—; shake off—; sink into—; tie with —; yield to—; —arrests; —envelops; —floats over; —flows over; —oppresses; —pervades; —spreads; —takes hold.

(See languor, exhaustion, weariness, fatigue.)

LAST (v)
adverbs
interminably; unendurably; unreasonably; briefly; unconsciously.

(See endure, continue, remain.)

adjectives
clinking; welcoming.

LATE

adverbs
extremely; horribly; preposterously; hideously; terrifyingly; alarmingly; significantly; dreadfully; intentionally; deliberately; carelessly; unfortunately; disastrously; calamitously; nonchalantly; lazily; inconsiderately; strangely; curiously; understandably; habitually; inexcusably; unpardonably; inexplicably; ungraciously; excusably; justifiably; unavoidably; apologetically; incredibly; vexatiously; unluckily; inordinately; terribly; uncommonly.

LATENESS

adjectives
preposterous; repeated; excusable.

LATENT

adverbs
imperceptibly; mysteriously; inferentially; implicitly; unsuspectedly; darkly; confusingly; mistily; indistinguishably; astoundingly; unhappily; impenetrably; unfortunately.

LATHER

adjectives
sudsy; brushless; shaving; foamy; plentiful; softening.

verbs
agitate to—; beat up—; burst into—; confect—; enjoy—; exercise into—; form—; give—; mix into—; sponge with—; swathe in—; thrash up—; wash in—; whip into—; work up—; —agrees with; —bubbles; —cleanses; —foams; —fortifies; —froths; —gushes; —overflows; —penetrates; —purifies; —refreshes; —sinks deep; —sputters; —stimulates; —tingles.
(See cream, soap, foam, froth.)

LATIN

verbs
acquaint with—; deliver in—; discourse in —; express in—; honor—; interpret—; mumble—; recite—; spout—; translate—; vent—; —bewilders; —confuses; —conveys; —dismays; —distracts; —flourishes; —revives; —stumps (colloq.).
(See dialect, language, literature.)

adjectives
utmost; boundless; beloved; heliographical; medieval.

LATTICES

adjectives
stormy; antique; caged.

LATTICEWORK

adjectives
quaint; artistic; delicate.

LAUD (*v*)

adverbs
flatteringly; fawningly; foolishly; extravagantly; sincerely; fervently; enthusiastically; passionately; exaggeratedly.
(See sing, praise, celebrate.)

LAUDATORY

adverbs
fawningly; flatteringly; admiringly; politically; unctuously; officially; ostentatiously; fulsomely; subtly; appreciatively; blatantly; lavishly; sincerely; moderately; humbly; unnecessarily; reluctantly; eloquently; heartily; solemnly; warmly; profusely; effusively; highly; excessively.

LAUGH

adjectives
scornful; cackling; incredulous; wild; abrupt; gruesome; childish; simple; gay; subdued; hoarse; low; relieved; inaudible; approving; forced; rippling; mild; familiar; horrid; distracted; funny; hard; little; tremulous; unpleasant; wheezy; triumphant; irritating; crackling; gentle; noisy; spiteful; uneasy; jeering; sarcastic; mocking; eerie; sinister; terrible; unmelodious; hearty; arch; frightful; constrained; blunt; malicious; sweet; vain; ringing; young; enchanting; trifling; suppressed; loud; evil; coarse; chuckling; fierce; jovial; silent; slight; cheery; rapturous; polite; merry; choked; melodious; careless; clumsy; gibing; cold; gurgling; startling; humorous; tinkling; boisterous; wild; impish; fearsome; bitter; drunken; sweet; mirthless; meaningful; fiendish; bubbling; wicked; harsh; ironical; taunting; tuneful; carnivorous; hysterical; delicious; silver; horse; self-conscious; childlike; joyous; grating; gasping; throaty; deep; hearty; good-humored; half-desperate; discordant; brit-

tle; characteristic; woeful; roguish; irritable; rattling; complacent; derisive; convulsive; hospitable; mingled (pl); sardonic; sonorous; supercilious; astonished; penitent; rueful; angry; sobbing; weak; musical; tittering; bursting; ghostly.

LAUGH (v)

adverbs

incredulously; gruesomely; tremulously; triumphantly; irritatingly; spitefully; jeeringly; sarcastically; triflingly; jovially; boisterously; humorously; impishly; drunkenly; mirthlessly; fiendishly; gratingly; discordantly; complacently; convulsively; sardonically; sonorously; superciliously; musically; croakingly; gleefully; mordantly; uproariously; jauntily; ruefully; derisively; significantly; ironically; constrainedly; sheepishly; unquenchably; grimly; idiotically; dramatically; jubilantly; exultantly; reassuringly; gustily; insolently; immoderately.

(See roar, giggle, snicker, titter.)

LAUGHABLE

adverbs

ludicrously; comically; monstrously; ironically; absurdly; quaintly; delightfully; uncommonly; moderately; scarcely; heartily; frankly; amusingly; prankishly; pleasantly; rousingly; stimulatingly; cleverly; admissibly; outlandishly.

LAUGHTER

adjectives

silent; delighted; thistle-down; immoderate; boisterous; mingled; shrill; subdued; uncontrolled; resonant; restrained; refreshing; rude; discordant; ill-natured; smothered; derisive; inward; mocking; deluded; resolute; hearty; artificial; soft; wild; hysteric; cackling; lifeless; zealous; delicious; high-pitched; murmurous; joyous; careless; frank; wholesome; meaningless; lovely; honest; unbelted; babbling; intellectual; faltering; Homeric; irreverent; rapid; irresistible; internal; confident; everlasting; hysterical; rippling; childish; unholy; sincerest; rollicking; bitter; mortal; intermingling; wilder; beery; innocent; immortal; foolish; free; bubbling; silvery; sudden; scary; throaty; excessive; gushing; hoarser; treble; shallow; fairy; savage; riotous; inheld.

verbs

break into—; burst into—; check—; constrain—; convulse in—; dimple in—; draw —; elicit—; enjoy—; evoke—; excite—; explode in—; flood with—; forgive—; join in —; occasion—; provoke—; raise—; reel in—; refrain from—; repress—; roar with —; rock with—; roll in—; scorn—; split with—; stifle—; stab with—; suppress—; swallow—; tumble into—; turn to—; wrinkle into—; —dances; —delights; —distorts; —ebbs; —explodes; —fizzles out (colloq.); —flows; —jars; —jets; —punctures; —quivers; —resounds; —rings out; —spills from; —warms; —wins.

(See mirth, grin, smile, merriment, snicker.)

LAUNCH

verbs

anchor—; appoint—; buffet—; endanger—; navigate—; propel—; repair—; slap—; view from—; —capsizes; —chugs; — circles; —courses; —cruises; —dances in; —drifts; —glides; —noses past; —ploughs; —rocks; —steams; —transports.

(See boat, tugboat, motor-boat, ship, steamer, schooner, yacht, vessel.)

LAUNCH (v)

adverbs

simultaneously; ceremoniously; auspiciously; vigorously; politically; enthusiastically; formally; diplomatically.

(See start, begin.)

LAURELS

adjectives

congregated; unsunned; untwined; bright; barren; fadeless; windless; unplucked; mingling.

verbs

acquire—; bestow—; blast—; crown with —; display—; envy—; garnish with—; look to—; merit—; reap—; regain—; repose on —; rest on—; retire on—; reward with—; seek—; snatch—; —delight; —enhance.

(See medal, prize, reward, trophy, crown.)

LAVA

adjectives

disintegrated; fluid; naked; incandescent; basaltic; massed; molten; smoking.

verbs

discharge—; disgorge—; drool—; emit—; pour—; puke—; spew—; —boils; —bubbles; —bursts; —courses down; —crushes; —deluges; —devastates; —envelops; —erupts; —expands; —flows; —gurgles; —inundates; —issues from; —oozes; —overflows; —percolates; —ravishes; —solidifies; —streams from; —swoops down.

(See water, mortar, liquid, plaster, bullet.)

LAVISH
adverbs

astoundingly; extravagantly; exceedingly; overwhelmingly; regally; royally; ridiculously; exorbitantly; profusely; disgustingly; inordinately; needlessly; unnecessarily; ostentatiously; proudly; pompously; wastefully; improvidently; thriftlessly; foolishly; inanely; witlessly; idiotically; generously; charitably; benevolently; benignly; amiably; graciously.

LAVISH (v)
adverbs

impulsively; vainly; extravagantly; regally; royally; affectionately; tenderly; passionately; adoringly; liberally; immoderately; recklessly.

(See spend, bestow.)

LAVISHNESS
adjective
glittering; sparse; regal.

LAW
adjectives

immutable; sacred; penal; violated; stringent; fundamental; impartial; salutary; comprehensive; valid; international; eternal; sumptuary; important; traditional; inexorable; remedial; flagitious; changeless; singular; angry; constricting; physical; standing; secular; unwritten; common; mild; conciliatory; criminal; invariable; certain; efficacious; unfailing; adequate; inoperative; severest; bloody; existing; conscription; never-to-be-formulated; geometric; organic; unspectacular; non-corporation; bogus; supreme; primitive; scientific; radiant; antiquated; prohibitory; uniform; rigorous; hideous; undiscriminating; drastic; continuous; all-building; recorded; subjective; severe; inescapable; biting; benignant; unconstitutional; sharp; evident; economic; oppressive; empirical; righteous; anatomic; deathless; conservation; mun-

dane; beneficent; harsh; sumptuary; ceremonial; querulous; sanguine; chancery; rigid; outraged; unequal; civil; social; hidden; substantive; obnoxious; mortal; stern; slavery-fashioned; ungracious; admirable; dramatic; academic; irreversible; active; indwelling; immovable; murderous; primal; unwieldy; tyrannical; blind; furious; unreasoning; crude; complex; clumsy; fiery; brutal; underlying; strictest; sordid; indiscreet; fantastical; expiring; ridiculous; restraining; proposed; express; protective; ultimate; martial; fallible; human; intolerant; preadjusted; physiological; clocklike.

verbs

amend—; administer—; apply—; array against—; bow to—; challenge—; circumvent—; clarify—; codify—; comply with—; comprehend—; conform to—; defy—; denounce—; dispute—; disregard—; dodge—; draft ; elude—, enact—; enforce—; expound—; flout—; forge—; forsake—; frame —; grind out—s; heed—; impose by—; infringe—; instigate—; interpret—; invoke—; mock—; modify—; nullify—; promulgate—; rail against—; ratify—; repeal—; repudiate —; resist—; run afoul of—; stiffen—; subject to—; supersede—; supplant—; suspend —; sustain—; systematize—; tamper with —; tighten—; transgress—; uphold—; — broadens; —clamps down; —curbs; —decrees; —defines; —differentiates; —empowers; —isolates; —prescribes; —relaxes; —restricts; —sanctions; —stipulates.

(See bill, statute, ordinance, regulation, edict, decree, mandate, rule, legislation.)

LAW-ABIDING
adverbs

carefully; duly; cautiously; respectfully; reputably; generally; habitually; usually; remarkably; always; scarcely; voluntarily; conscientiously; ordinarily; publicly; obviously; uniformly; invariably; obediently; willingly; passively; actively; faithfully; loyally; devotedly; superbly; consistently; customarily; exceptionally; notably.

LAWFUL
adverbs

definitely; expressly; explicitly; officially; ordinarily; prescriptively; properly; duly; acceptably; admissibly; equitably; constitutionally; downright; completely; fundamentally; authentically; singularly; emphatically; unquestionably; unimpeachably; currently; altogether.

LAWLESS
adverbs
dangerously; alarmingly; youthfully; heedlessly; daringly; audaciously; lamentably; deplorably; openly; actively; defiantly; insurgently; seditiously; restively; insubordinately; mutinously; rebelliously; tumultuously; treasonably; incorrigibly; persistently; obstinately; incredibly.

LAWLESSNESS
adjectives
rash; irresponsible.

verbs
assail—; condemn—; condone—; countenance—; crush—; decry—; denounce—; infest with—; reform—; suffer—; survive—; subscribe to—; yield to—; —breaks out; —fascinates; —grinds; —offends; —oppresses; —reigns; —spreads; —sullies.

(See crime, vice, anarchy, communism, wickedness, sin.)

LAWN
adjectives
dewy; grassy; upland; smooth; squared; summery; sunny; carpetlike; sun-baked; unkempt; dew-besprinkled; russet; spacious; sleek; sun-bathed; well-kept; flowered; shadow-chequered; wintry; sun-soaked; moon-lit; thick; velvety.

verbs
adorn—with; besprinkle—; border—; design —; fence in—; gird—; hedge in—; injure —; mow—; pluck from—; romp on—; shadow—; sprinkle—; tread—; —beautifies; —carpets; —clothes; —creeps; —extends; —flowers; —slopes.

(See grass, field, garden.)

LAWSUIT
adjectives
vexatious; improper; ugly; ruinous; prolonged; endless; trumped-up; expensive.

verbs
avoid—; bear—; condemn—; contest—; drop—; elude—; encounter—; incur—; institute—; judge—; propose—; saddle with —; subpoena for—; support—; wrangle

over—; —confounds; —drags; —harasses; —perplexes; —tires; —wearies.

(See litigation, suit, case, prosecution.)

LAWYER
adjectives
crooked; gray-haired; briefless; solemn-faced; shyster; contemporary; constitutional; struggling; well-trained; prominent; competent; sharp; cunning; tricky; conceited; supercilious; dignified; profound; learned; callow; bullying; quick-witted; capable; unconventional; eccentric; eminent; good; skinflint; rascally; kindly.

verbs
employ—; retain—; —addresses; —advocates; —appeals; —battles; —blusters; —cavils; —charges; —confounds; —cross-examines; —defends; —expounds; —interprets; —litigates; —objects; —outwits; —pleads; —pounds; —practises; —queries; —questions; —quibbles; —shifts; —solicits; —strives; —wrangles.

(See orator, congressman, senator, attorney.)

LAX
adverbs
surprisingly; inscrutably; mysteriously; deliberately; criminally; negligently; leniently; indulgently; lamentably; incomprehensibly; regrettably; terribly; disastrously; calamitously; scandalously; outrageously; atrociously; dangerously; ominously; carelessly; languidly; lazily; indifferently; unusually; unwontedly; habitually; inexcusably; noticeably; obviously; apparently; dreadfully.

LAXATIVE
verbs
addict to—s; advocate—; dose with—; employ—; necessitate—; order—; require—; resist—; resort to—; suggest—; —abuses; —cleanses; —cures; —dispels; —eases; —loosens; —purges; —relieves; —unloads.

(See medicine, enema, remedy.)

LAXITY
adjectives
social; moral; parental.

LAYERS
adjectives
peripheral; thin; successive; innumerable;

reflecting; stratified; conglomerate; favorable; superficial; aerial; saline; serrated.

LAYMEN

adjectives
impertinent; unhallowed; incompetent; unpracticed.

LAYS

adjectives
embroidered; melodious; deathless; mirthful; mystic.

LAZINESS

adjectives
intense; mental; incorrigible; lifelong; noticeable.

LAZY

adverbs
unbelievably; deliciously; delightfully; utterly; incurably; inexcusably; openly; flauntingly; nonchalantly; blithely; carelessly; admittedly; vauntingly; intensely; mentally; incorrigibly; horribly; selfishly; inconsiderately; ungraciously; curiously; unpardonably; impudently; blatantly; flagrantly; insufferably; unbearably; lethargically; languidly; heavily; lumpishly; inertly; dreamily; sleepily; drowsily; terribly; provokingly.

LEA

adjectives
windy; russet; flowery; darkening; emerald; shadowed; rich; calm.

LEAD

adjectives
hissing; murderous; dull; unencumbered; smoke-blackened; merciless; proper.

verbs
cast—; expose—; fuse—; melt—; mine—; refine—; sheet—; smelt—; solder—; treat with—; unearth—; weight with—; —corrodes; —poisons; —softens; —tarnishes.
(See metal, iron, steel.)

LEAD (v)

adverbs
deceitfully; gallantly; boldly; intrepidly; triumphantly; victoriously; mercilessly; ceremonially; dexterously; ultimately; fatefully; enterprisingly; illustriously; imagin-

atively; reluctantly; gallantly; despotically; fanatically; energetically; intelligently; unscrupulously; nominally; ecclesiastically; incomparably; supremely.
(See command, direct, guide.)

LEADER

adjectives
enterprising; illustrious; reluctant; doubtful; foremost; cavalry; political-minded; creative; imaginative; naive; eminent; come-by-chance; spiritual; fanatical; party; befeathered; distinguished; despotic; conspicuous; prudent; prominent; submissive; insurgent; acknowledged, subjugated; ascetic; inspiring; quality; moderate; unquestioned; energetic; intelligent; self-constituted; unscrupulous; popular; typical; halting; patriot; nominal; revolutionary; adored; ecclesiastical; incomparable; brilliant; knightly; liberal; natural; recognized; crestfallen; typical, supreme.

verbs
adhere to—; distinguish—; emulate—; engage—; flock to—; gather 'round—; pattern on—; rally 'round—; support—; trust—; —arises; —commands; —conducts; —controls; —directs; —fires; —guides; —harangues; —influences; —marshals; —pilots; —presides; —unites; —voices.
(See minister, clergyman, boss, manager, official.)

LEADERSHIP

adjectives
lamentable; vital; accepted; inspired; vigorous; skillful; unchallenged; fashion; undisputed; intelligent; consummate; compensating; careful; aggressive; heroic; daring; recognized; judicious; palsied.

verbs
anticipate—; assume—; commend—; compete for—; crave—; favor—of; follow—; flourish under—; grant—to; offer—; overthrow—; prosper under—of; recognize—; rely on—; require—; settle—; stress—; strive for—; succeed to—; sustain—; trust to—; yield to—.
(See command, direction, guidance, protection, patronage.)

LEAF

adjectives
dancing; folded; garrulous; delicate; weary; laurel; latest; rueful; retuse;

voluminous; withered; minutest; rustling; medicinal; sleeping; braided; tender; plaited; glossy; primordial; peopled; drifted; vibrant; blushing; flattering; needlelike; drooping; notched; lanceolate; stirring; succulent; heedless.

LEAFAGE
adjectives
rustling; spreading; luxuriant.

LEAGUE
adjectives
united; endless; weary; hostile; moribund; nuptial; immeasurable; remarkable; unconscious; stormy.

verbs
ally with—; appeal to—; associate with—; band into—; crack—; criticize—; enter—; excite—; join—; renounce—; resuscitate—; —assists; —confers on; —defends; —safeguards; —sanctions; —shelters; —threatens; —unites.
  (See society, club, organization, union, association.)

LEAGUE (v)
adverbs
inseparably; nuptially; protectively; firmly; perpetually.
  (See combine, unite, associate.)

LEAK
verbs
block—; bare—; choke—; dam—; detect—; drill—; indicate—; master—; plug—; repair—; riddle with—s; seal—; spring—; —drains; —frightens; —gapes; —sinks; —weakens; —yawns.
  (See hole, gap, flow.)

LEAKY
adverbs
dangerously; intentionally; slightly; unconscionably; uselessly; inconsequentially; suspiciously; mysteriously; ominously; treacherously; apparently; wastefully; terribly; unfortunately; miserably; extremely; fearfully; increasingly; wretchedly.

LEAN (v)
adverbs
slumberously; placidly; mechanically; gracefully; slantingly; wearily; impulsively; perilously; listlessly; indolently; dizzily; confidentially.
  (See incline, recline, slope, tend, depend.)

LEAP
adjectives
imperious; breezy; astonishing; demoniacal; sudden; flying; rash; concealed; vigorous; mortal; quick; tremendous; horrid; queer; bold; gathered.

verbs
admire—; attempt—; calculate—; complete—; dare—; endeavor—; observe—; perfect—; practice—; rebound from—; record—; venture—; —amazes; —awes; —impresses.
  (See feat.)

LEAP (v)
adverbs
lissomely; simultaneously; blithely; sure-footedly; frolicsomely; nimbly; spryly; boisterously; perilously; demoniacally; boldly; vigorously; swiftly; agilely.
  (See jump, spring, bound.)

LEARN (v)
adverbs
aptly; brilliantly; instinctively; normally; precociously; scientifically; pedagogically.
  (See acquire, attain, master, obtain.)

LEARNER
adjectives
incipient; reputed; polite; awkward; brilliant.

LEARNING
adjectives
typical; harsh; crabbed; abstruse; unorganized; worldly; barren; superficial; serviceable; detrimental; optimistic; polite; philosophic; higher; extensive; carnal; varied; introvertive; inconsiderable; subtle; radiant; classical; supposed.

verbs
consume—; digest—; drink in—; feed on—; foster—; impart—; lack—; overestimate—; revive—; shun—; stamp out—; swallow—; test—; underestimate—; value—; wonder at—; —crowns; —discerns; —enlightens; —flourishes; —intoxicates; —penetrates; —polishes; —serves; —shines; —sobers; —speeds; —upbraids.
  (See knowledge, wisdom, facts, information, understanding.)

LEASE
verbs
approve—; cancel—; comply with—; de-

ndition—s;   ; ignore
fracture—;   study—;
n—s; reveal   —guar-
hen—; trust   atisfies;
rotrudes; —s
-s twitch; —s   agree-

LEGACY

'ASH

nal; precious;   n—;
                      —
                ts;

nticipate—; be-
ourt—; deprive
fritter away—;   R
—; partition—;
ndles; —enrich-

oney, wealth, in-

LEGAL

admittedly; un-
authoritatively;
antably; presump-
peachably; equit-
perly; securely.

LEGEND

itionary; fanciful;
; marvelous; prim-
ble; diffused; epic;
ntemporary; medie-
; puissant; fictitious;
nal.

nfute—; demolish—;
—; discard—; dispel
oider—; emerge from
ate—; interpolate—;
e—; peruse—; —at-
m; —persists; —por-

yth, lie, narrative.)

LEGENDARY

acceptably; admittedly;
y; romantically; fanci-

---

shifting; shivering; shimmering; frosted;
glittering; withered; dewy; arching; glossy;
listening; rustling; crumpled; brilliant; interlaced; ripened; dentated; glistering;
crystal; frost-crisped; close-shut; pounded;
suspended; motionless; pendant; lusty; sere;
implicated; delicate; clustering; scented;
amorous; soft; silken; summer; verdant;
healing; fading; painted; falling; crowded;
velvet; rejected; sweet; barren; yellowing;
crimson; brazen; lapping; shining; russet;
serrated; fingery; languid; twinkling;
silent; retuse; dying; drifted; mantling;
blanched; steaming; sweeping; wind-tossed;
flaming; tiny; soiled; age-worn; vellum;
tremulous; hardy; gay; autumn; burning;
polished; dark; copious; mottled; sweet-
fern; wintry; fanlike; agitated; coarse;
grasslike; lucent; twining; fair; false;
bruised; remembered; swarth; sodden; porcelain; unwritten; many-tinted; beauteous;
drooping; wild; somber; parti-colored; joyous.

verbs

bedew—; decorate with—; flush—; gather
—; scatter—; shed—; sprout—; thatch with
—; tinge—; —blazon; —blend; —drift
down; —droop; —float down; —flutter;
—mat; —overspread; —quiver; —redden;
—rustle; —shade; —shower down; —swirl;
—tremble; —unfold; —wave; —whisper;
wilt; —wither.
(See foliage, plant.)

LECTURE

ctives

ving; inaugural; compulsory; scientific;
minable; wide-spread; celebrated; did-
boring; ill-attended.

late—; attend—; concoct—; deliver
struct by—; preach—; profit by—;
—; —admonishes; —asserts; —as-
—attracts; —confounds; —interests;
xes; —rebukes; —reprimands; —
es; —stirs; —uplifts.
esson, speech, address, narration,
; oration.)

LECTURE (*v*

graphically; eruditely; vivid
; scientifically; interminably;
boringly; inspiringly; inspir
quently.
ldress, discourse, speak.)

LEDGE

adjectives

shaven; dangerous-looking; slippery; narrow; pine-clad; overhanging; rocky; dirty-backed; solid; basalt; shaded; craggy; projecting; bare; inaccessible; shelving.

verbs

clamber up—; cleave to—; cling from—; hover on—; hug—; lean from—; peer over —; pitch from—; scale—; teeter on—; totter on—; tumble from—; —gives way; — juts; —projects; —protrudes.

(See edge, ridge, shelf, reef.)

LEECH

verbs

apply—; breed—es; employ—; fatten—; — absorbs; —adheres; —bleeds; —clings; — cures; —draws; —evacuates; —extracts; —heals; —relieves; —remedies; —sticks; — sucks.

(See parasite, physician, doctor.)

LEER

adjectives

impudent; jealous; complacent; silly; half-triumphant; roguish; fawning; malignant.

LEER (v)

adverbs

obscenely; idiotically; spitefully; impudently; murderously; despicably; sardonically; jealously; complacently; malignantly; fawningly; roguishly.

(See look, sneer, glance, stare.)

LEERY

adverbs

slightly; altogether; artfully; cunningly; trickily; warily; guardedly; cleverly; suspiciously; diplomatically; strategically; cautiously; prudently; deliberately; discreetly; coolly; habitually; cannily; charily; politically; vigilantly; dependably; uncommonly; carefully.

LEG

adjectives

xcellent; bowed; rickety; timber; gouty; aceful; sturdy; bandy; lower; convulsed; ckinged; shapely; long; fluted; sinewy; wny; spindle; incased; thin; shivering; some; amputated; thread-like; leaden; lar; bony; pitiful; tiny; slender; knot-cked; jagged; hairy; gaitered; love-eful; bulging; slim.

verbs

admire—; bow—s; brace—;
elevate—; expose—; fetter—s
massage—; peer at—s; reel o
—; straddle with—s; streng
—s; —s entwine; —s fly; —p
sag; —supports; —s taper; —
weary.

(See foot, knee.)

adjectives

supplemented; limited; perso
unexpected; hereditary.

verbs

administer—; allocate—; a
queath—; contemplate—; c
of—; direct—; envy—;
grant—; inherit—; parcel-
provide—; reckon—; —dw
es.

(See estate, property, m
heritance, resources.)

adverbs

entirely; incontrovertibly;
questionably; allowably;
duly; prescriptively; war
tively; absolutely; unin
ably; constitutionally; pr

adjectives

fearful; golden; trad
facile; splenetic; heroic
eval; shadowy; service
fading; picturesque; c
val; confusing; profane
interminable; conventio

verbs

blast—; carry on—; c
destroy—; detach from
—; dispose of—; embr
—; exploit—; exten
lampoon—; perpetua
tests to; —grows fr
trays.

(See story, tale, m

adverbs

wholly; vestigially;
daringly; inventivel

712

fully; ingeniously; purportedly; theoretically; notionally; fairly; authentically; presumably; doubtfully; probably; highly; vaporously; heroically; picturesquely; pleasantly.

LEGIBILITY
verbs
admire—; appreciate—; approve—; commend—; demand—; desire—; emblazon—; esteem—; extol—; heighten—; increase—; praise—; prize—; regard—; recommend—; value—.

LEGIBLE
adverbs
clearly; perfectly; gratifyingly; pleasantly; crudely; altogether; neatly; plainly; easily; distinctly; definitely; precisely; graphically; unmistakenly; scrawlingly; hieroglyphically; eventually; pleasingly; extremely; immediately; satisfactorily.

LEGION
adjectives
gallant; ragged; puissant; well-disciplined; iron-breasted; scouring; locust; swarthy; victorious; invincible.

verbs
array in—; assemble—; decimate—; direct —; fill with—s; follow—; gather—; overthrow—; secure—; sustain—; unite in—; —congregates; —defends; —drifts; —engages; —flocks —participates; —serves; —strives.
(See army, crowd, association, enemy.)

LEGISLATE (v)
adverbs
precipitately; shrewdly; beneficently; malignantly; oppressively; economically; socially; constitutionally; perniciously; ecclesiastically; appropriately; arbitrarily; unscrupulously.
(See effect, enact.)

LEGISLATION
adjectives
oppressive; economic; sumptuary; social; preferential; intemperate; critical; unconstitutional; pernicious; injurious; ecclesiastical; educational; dangerous; absolute; remedial; appropriate; defunct; amendatory; arbitrary; refined; adverse; unscrupulous; undesirable; vindictive; class.

verbs
acclaim—; admire—; broaden—; enact—; enforce—; influence—; invalidate—; jam—through; lobby for—; motion for—; pile up —; propose—; sanction—; schedule—; sponsor—; stifle—; strangle—; sustain—; urge —; veto—.
(See law, bill, statute, ordinance, regulation.)

LEGISLATIVE
adverbs
augustly; imposingly; strictly; exclusively; oppressively; coolly; impersonally; absolutely; scrupulously; impartially; finally; irrevocably; wisely; providentially.

LEGISLATOR
verbs
criticize—; elect—; invest—with; nominate —; —attempts; —authorizes; —s convene; —deliberates; —devises; —interprets; —judges; —moves; —proposes; —propounds; —serves.
(See congressman, senator, politician, statesman.)

LEGISLATURE
verbs
appoint to—; nominate for—; recommend to—; —affirms; —appropriates; —confirms; —defeats; —deliberates; —dismisses; —enacts; —frames; —overrules; —passes; —propounds; —reveals; —revokes; —suspends; —congregates; —convenes.
(See congress, parliament, legislator, government.)

LEGITIMATE
adverbs
wholly; unquestionably; substantially; plainly; unqualifiedly; unimpeachably; authoritatively; authentically; genuinely; verily; allowably; unconditionally; justly; absolutely; duly; properly; completely; rightly.

LEISURE
adjectives
scant; elegant; extreme; endowed; practicable; sour; patient; graceful; multitudinous; everlasting; abundant; fallow; infinite; precious; tranquil; unbroken; spiritual; ample; dignified; literary; sufficient; unholy; superfluous; holiday; dilettante; calm; machine-created; wasted.

verbs

bankrupt of—; beautify—; burden with—; court—; devote—to; discipline—; dispense with—; employ—; enjoy—; fill—; indulge at —; occupy—; pursue at—; rejoice in—; retire into—; revel in—; reward with—; steal —; wallow in—; weary of—; —civilizes; —delights; —enriches; —entombs; —polishes.

(See time.)

LEMON

verbs

bear—s; box—s; crate—s; cultivate—; express from—; extract from—; flavor with —; gather—s; harvest—s; pack—s; peel—; pickle in—; pierce—; scent with—; ship—s; sort—s; squeeze—; wrap—; —clings; — puckers; —ripens.

(See fruit.)

LEND (v)

adverbs

grudgingly; conveniently; conditionally; gracefully; innocently; legitimately; unscrupulously; willingly; gratuitously.

(See accommodate, assist, furnish.)

LENDER

adjectives

legitimate; money; licensed; unscrupulous.

LENGTH

adjectives

learned; barbarous; apparent; extortionate; manlier; abbreviated; intolerable; variable; irregular; average; ludicrous; unaltered; extreme; considerable; unconscionable; enormous; interminable; majestic; pellucid; lamentable; shameful; immoderate; standard; ancient; unwieldy; startling; weary; apportioned; slender; infinite; wondrous; measured; treacherous; vine-clad.

LENGTHEN (v)

adverbs

indefinitely; ludicrously; unconscionably; interminably; immoderately; infinitely; disproportionately.

(See extend, stretch.)

LENGTHY

adverbs

interminably; intolerably; tiresomely; monotonously; unbelievably; endlessly; ramblingly; reminiscently; diffusely; effusively; wretchedly; miserably; wearisomely; unconscionably; ludicrously; sadly; terribly; shamefully; incredibly; inexcusably.

LENIENT

adverbs

habitually; conveniently; indulgently; affectionately; spasmodically; considerately; mercifully; courteously; hospitably; graciously; weakly; supinely; deliberately; gently; calmly; absent-mindedly; nervously; pacifically; reasonably; blandly; purposely; lamentably; unduly; wisely; helpfully; disgustingly; feebly; temperately; tolerantly; complaisantly; compassionately; humanely; exceedingly.

LENITY

adjectives

half-contemptuous; half-calculated; sufficient; vaunted; customary; assumed; apparent.

LENS

adjectives

immense; photographic; concave; shadowy; convex; powerful.

LEOPARD

verbs

bag—; creep up on—; ensnare—; infest with—s; skin—; trap—; —attacks; —barks; —charges; —claws; —climbs; —depredates; —devours; —drags off; —lies in ambush; —pounces; —preys on; —pulls down; — rages; —roars; —screams; —seizes; — slaughters; —slinks; —springs; —stalks; — steals upon; —wails; —infests.

(See animal, lion, tiger.)

LEPER

verbs

ban—; bar—; cleanse—; cure—; heal—; incarcerate—; isolate—; purge—; quarantine—; restore—; segregate—; shelter—; — befouls; —begs; —contaminates; —defiles; —infects; —stigmatizes; —suffers; —taints,

(See beggar, invalid, parasite.)

LEPROUS

adverbs

fatally; tragically; horribly; unfortunately; miserably; wretchedly; infirmly; incurably; pitiably; morally; mortally; indubitably; dreadfully.

LESION

adjectives

local; organic; mechanical; healed.

LESSEN (*v*)

adverbs

abnormally; scientifically; beneficially; mechanically; gradually; agreeably; appreciably.

(See diminish, reduce, decrease.)

LESSON

adjectives

crowning; salutary; rude; strategical; humiliating; valuable; distasteful; sacred; deathless; wholesome; exemplary; object; copious; pioneer; curious; striking; stern; impressive; instructive; ethical; important; noble; outstanding; painful; baneful; tremendous; fruitful; needful; hard; silent.

verbs

assign—; deliver—; experience—; expound —; imply—; inculcate—; instill—; memorize—; preach—; project—; rebel at—; recite—; spice—; yield—; —penetrates; —rebukes; —reprimands; —sinks in.

(See lecture, talk, speech, moral.)

LETHARGY

adjectives

intellectual; torpid; icy; blind; pleasant; patriarchal; complete; apparent; inglorious; passive; utter.

verbs

arouse from—; breed—; descend into—; fade into—; fall into—; fix in—; lie in—; lift from—; mumble in—; overcome—; —attacks; —blinds; —chokes; —envelops; —hinders; —paralyzes; —restrains; —seduces; —seizes; —stupefies.

(See languor, weariness, fatigue, exhaustion, lassitude.)

LETTER

adjectives

rare; deprecatory; terrible; much-discussed; anonymous; unfeeling; complimentary; entertaining; amusing; exhaustive; innumerable; confidential; charming; loathsome; vitriolic; insolent; threatening; overbearing; pensive; seditious; amiable; commendatory; pitiful; subjoined; promised; obliging; impassioned; strange; incoherent; obscure; incomprehensible; bulky; pattern; civil; simple-minded; subsequent; obnox-

ious; elementary; discursive; nonsensical; dead; unfriendly; repentant; passionate; adulatory; indiscreet; ill-spelled; runic; affectionate; shameful; orderly; menacing; luminous; feigned; curt; immediate; interminable; pithy; gilt; full; convincing; esteemed; accusing; interesting; specific; deep-cut; reprehensive; pastoral; brief; terse; condensed; emphatic; exculpatory; beautiful; eloquent; touching; conspicuous; good; unjust; delicious; sweet; patient; wise; tender; painful; abusive; round-robin; often-recurring; chance-preserved; introductory; burning; generous; handsome; mystical; explanatory; racy; exquisite; slanderous; ill-written; libelous; crafty; brusque; unsound; stilted; pleading; naive; denunciatory; easy-flowing; inevitable; long; reproachful; sparkling; enigmatical; depressing; assisting; condemnatory; faded; fatal; clandestine, ridiculous; agreeable; hasty; impudent; enthusiastic; unauthenticated; taunting; dedicatory; chatty; kind-hearted; cheery; journalistic; happy; timely; conclusive; effective; admonitory; indignant; spiteful; pathetic; dainty; memorable; sad; begging; witty; misguiding; resounding; fascinating; inquisitive; occasional; compromising; laconic; needless; unfinished; genuine; obedient.

verbs

append to—; bear—; besiege with—s; bombard with—s; censor—; communicate by—; convey—; deluge with—s; devise—; devour —; dictate—; frame—; peruse—; post—; scribble—; seal—; skim through—; speed—; suppress—; welcome—; —acquaints; —assures; —breathes; —cheers; —commends; —commissions; —consoles; —conveys; —expatiates; —gushes; —imparts; —links; —s pour in; —reveals; —unites.

(See communication, note, correspondence, message, telegram.)

LEVEL

adjectives

portentous; maintenance; conversational; unlovely; vulgar; conciliating; preeminent; remunerative; childish; artistic; unending; windy; desirable; reflecting; usual; varying; harmless; unmeaning; humdrum; common; ordinary.

verbs

attain—; defile—; degrade to—; destroy—; discover—; drain—; elevate to—; find—;

715

gain—; hold—; jump to—; lie within—; maintain—; mark—; preserve—; raise above—; reduce to—; regress to—; sink to —.

(See height, depth, altitude, summit, mark.)

adverbs
meticulously; exactly; monotonously; conveniently; smoothly; endlessly; uniformly; tiresomely; changelessly; drearily; continuously; symmetrically; roughly; unevenly; ruggedly; fairly.

LEVER

verbs
adjust—; apply—; brace—; heave out with —; jack with—; manipulate—; yank (colloq.)—; —disembowels; —dislodges; — elevates; —expels; —lifts; —overthrows; —pries open; —raises.
(See handle, bar.)

LEVITY

adjectives
incorrigible; enervate; uncanonical; responsive; unpardonable; superficial; dreadful; careless; shameful; bitter; exquisite; undesirable; foolish; unnecessary; unbecoming; surface.

LEVY

adjectives
forced; undisciplined; successive (pl).

LEWD

adverbs
ribaldly; boisterously; inexcusably; gustily; evilly; immodestly; shamelessly; wantonly; habitually; inexplicably; unaccountably; unwarrantably; hilariously; terribly; ostentatiously; unscrupulously; crudely.

LIABILITY

verbs
account for—; admit—; burden with—; clog with—; confess—; display—; exempt from —; free from—; impose—; limit—; load with—; meet—; relieve of—; saddle with —; shoulder—s; —cramps; —deters; — disheartens; —hampers; —impedes; —imposes; —obligates; —oppresses; —shackles; —weighs.
(See trouble, responsibility, misfortune, reverse, debt, obligation.)

LIABLE

adverbs
criminally; undeniably; unfortunately; financially; morally; legally; unhappily; fatally; inescapably; inevitably; embarrassingly; deeply; inconveniently; properly; ethically; prescriptively.

LIAR

adjectives
congenial; false-hearted; designing; monstrous; virtuous; probable; political; prophesying; beneficent; notorious; endless; generous.

verbs
accuse—; avoid—; condemn—; criticize—; despise—; judge—; punish—; reprimand—; reproach—; shame—; spurn—; support—; —beguiles; —blinds; —contrives; —convinces; —deceives; —devises; —forges; — fumbles; —invents; —libels; —raves; —relates; —slanders; —stabs; —violates.
(See criminal robber, thief, hypocrite, quack.)

LIBATION

adjectives
wonted; copious; devout.

LIBEL

adjectives
infamous; poisonous; criminal; seditious; scandalous; outrageous; intentional; anonymous; atrocious.

verbs
accuse of—; contradict—; convict of—; denounce—; disprove—; forge—; incur—; institute—; introduce—; oppose—; publish—; rebut—; serve—; sue for—; —accuses; — alleges; —assails; —charges; —declares; —defames; —discredits; —implies; — slanders.
(See slander, rumor.)

LIBERAL

adverbs
naturally; habitually; generally; always; extremely; charitably; considerately; lavishly; thoughtfully; ostentatiously; grudgingly; calculatingly; carelessly; unwarrantably; improvidently; moderately; bountifully; generously; munificently; handsomely; unwisely; unselfishly; thoroughly; unfailingly; dependably.

adjectives
militant; enlightened; extreme; journalistic.

verbs
absorb—; adopt—; advocate—; convert to —; criticize—; crusade for—; cultivate—; endanger—; exercise—; inculcate—; interpret—; plant—; plead for—; restrain—; scorn—; stifle—; stimulate—; unite in—; weaken—; —affords; —aims at; —emerges from; —involves; —prevails; —thrives.
(See democracy, freedom, socialism, communism, movement.)

LIBERALITY
adjectives
unstinted; decent; unbounded; mutual; enlarged; patriotic.

LIBERATE (*v*)
adverbs
promptly; magnanimously; industrially; philosophically; politically; temporarily; economically; nobly; rationally; partially; subversively.
(See free, release, deliver.)

LIBERTY
adjectives
elemental; unwarrantable; glorious; philosophical; wild; popular; hard; political; natural; temporary; unrestrained; sanctioned; economic; industrial; religious; ignoble; pagan; secure; atheistic; unequalled; unbridled; headstrong; false; stormy; intermittent; universal; rational; partial; subversive; adored; masculine; excessive; perfect; lyric; dearly-bought.

verbs
abdicate—; champion—; concede—; confiscate—; conspire against—; defend—; deprive of—; encroach upon—; enjoy—; forsake—; grant—; imperil—; infringe upon —; invade—; jeopardize—; maintain—; prate of—; purchase—; sacrifice—; scorn —; sequester—; shackle—; spurn—; suppress—; suspend—: taint—; threaten—; violate—; —crumbles; —perishes; —vanishes.
(See rights, freedom, privilege, independence.)

LIBRARY
adjectives
provincial; extensive; circulating; immense;

somber; reference; astronomical; valuable; comprehensive; well-balanced; technical.

verbs
bequeath to—; browse in—; bury in—; cherish—; confine to—; drink from—; endow—; enrich—; establish—; labor in—; refer to—; repose in—; resort to—; revel in—; shelve in—; subscribe to—; —circulates; —collects; —entombs; —feeds; — fines; —lends; —nourishes; —preserves; — records; —safeguards; —stores.
(See book, literature.)

LIBRETTOS
adjectives
innocuous; unappealing; poetical; complete.

LICENSE
adjectives
passionate; poetic; uncontrolled; mocking; wanton; warrantable; unpunished; unchecked; transport; boldest; amplest; unbridled; graceful; roving; ignoble; extraordinary; democratic; driving; vending.

verbs
abuse—; acknowledge—; concede—; deny —; display—; draw—; enjoy—; forge—; grant—; inspect—; obtain—; observe—; practise under—; require—; revoke—; withdraw—; —authorizes; —permits; —protects; —vouches.
(See right, privilege.)

LICENSE (*v*)
adverbs
legally; medically; authoritatively; officially; nominally; wantonly; properly.
(See permit, authorize.)

LICENTIOUS
adverbs
unwarrantably; riotously; ungovernably; dissolutely; wickedly; despicably; contemptibly; terribly; disgustingly; viciously; unimaginably; dreadfully; unexpectedly; villainously; wildly; rakishly; deplorably; lamentably; unforgivably.

LICENTIOUSNESS
adjectives
unbridled; evil; uncurbed; repeated.

verbs
campaign against—; check—; curb—; defend—; denounce—; explode—; harbor—;

impute to—; inflict—upon; regret—; taste
—; tolerate—; tumble into—; witness—;
—irks; —occurs; —offends; —prevails; —
reigns; —vexes.

(See wickedness, vice, sin.)

LID

adjectives
just-raised; placid; translucent; drooping;
long; sly; flaming; veinous; opaque; blue-
veined; drowsy; flower-soft; fringed; unsullied; squinted; lower; eternal; coarse;
triangular-shaped; low; wrinkled; conscious; timorous; heavy.

verbs
clamp—on; clap—on; fit—; force—; overlay—; plant—on; pry—off; seal—; tap—;
tighten—; —conceals; —preserves; —prevents; —protects; —resists; —restrains; —
screens; —yields to.
(See cover, canopy.)

LIE

adjectives
glittering; vicious; monkey-faced; vivid;
spectral; glib; painted; plausible; sin-born;
wanton; endless; improbable; consoling; intolerable; libelous; deadliest; drowsing;
diplomatic; ungentlemanly; organized; conventional; filthy; original; convincing; blaspheming; preposterous; gracious; sustained; surpliced; costly; pious; calm; quaint;
shameless; damnable; dumb; helpless; glorious; puny; rotten; absurd; magnificent;
unnumbered; iniquitous; measured; poisonous; deliberate; purchased.

verbs
acknowledge—; censure—; condemn—; condone—; confess to—; decry—; detect—;
evolve—; promulgate—; propagate—; reject—; rend—; reveal—; spill—s; uncover
—; utter—; —blackens; —cheats; —cloaks;
—defrauds; —dishonors; —falsifies; —fetters; —frees; —perplexes; —swindles.

(See crime, statement, falsehood, misre-
presentation.)

LIE (v)

adverbs
nervelessly; slothfully; smoothly; perversely; atrociously; malignly; glibly; supinely;
profusely; portentously; outrageously; mutely; composedly; plausibly; wantonly; libelously; preposterously; shamelessly; iniquitously.
(See fabricate, misrepresent.)

LIEUTENANT

adjectives
lion-hearted; self-important; selected.

LIFE

adjectives
abhorred; abject; abnormal; abstract; aboriginal; abundant; academic; active; act-
ion-craving; affluent; agonized; agreeable;
agricultural; all-embracing; altruistic;
amazing; ambrosial; angelic; antecedent;
antenatal; artificial; ascetic; astonished;
austere; bad; beneficent; benevolent; blameless; blithe; blooming; boulevard; bountiful; bright-eyed; broad; broken; brute;
bubbling; buoyant; busy; bygone; bird-
cage; cankerous; carefree; careful; changing; charmed; civic; civilized; cloistral;
cold-blooded; collective; college; colorful;
commercial; commonplace; communal; concentrated; consistent; constant; contemplative; contemporary; contemptuous; convenient; convulsive; cordial; corporate; cosmic;
country; crescent; cruel; crystal; cultivated;
cultured; darkened; darkling; darting;
deadening; decorous; deep-bosomed; defaced; delightful; democratic; demonstrable; deplorable; desultory; devouring;
diffusive; diminished; diplomatic; disastrous; discontented; disfigured; dishonored;
disjointed; disposed; dissipated; dissolute;
distasteful; distracted; dividing; double; domestic; doubtful; dull; dusky; dutiful; easy-
going; eccentric; economic; effete; effective;
effeminate; elemental; emancipated; embittered; emotional; enlarging; ennobling;
ephemeral; equal; erotic; equivocal; essential; eternal; eventful; existing; exotic; expanding; external; extinguished; exuberant;
exultant; factitious; familiar; farcical;
farmyard; fascinating; fashionable; fast-
fleeing; fast-withering; fettered; feudal;
feverish; fictionized; flabby; flickering;
floating; flourishing; foreign; fragrant;
free; friendless; frisking; frivolous; frugal;
fruitful; fugitive; fullest; genuine; gushing;
grimy; groovelike; gypsy; half-revealed;
hapless; hard-working; harmless; healthful;
helpful; hideous; hoary; high-pressure;
homely; honest; human; humdrum; hygienic; ideal; idyllic; imagined; imaginative;
immortal; impatient; impeccable; imper-

fect; imperiled; imperishable; impish; incarnate; increasing; independent; individual; indulgent; industrious; infantile; informal; inglorious; inherent; inner; innermost; insect; unsociable; integrated; intellectual; intense; interior; intimate; irresponsible; irregular; joyless; kindly; knowable; laborious; large; licentious; lifeless; liquid; listless; literary; livable; loathed; long; low; lush; lusterless; luxurious; magnanimous; many-sided; married; material; maximum; meditative; melancholy; mental; meteoric; middle-married; milder; millennial; mingled; mirthful; miserable; modest; monastic; monotonous; moral; mortal; moving; multitudinous (pl); mythological; namby-pamby; nervous; nobler; nomadic; objectless; obscure; old-maidish; ordinary; orgiastic; outer; out-of-town; outside; paltry; palpitating; pampered; parasitic; parental; peaceful; perilous; permeating; perverted; phenomenal; pioneer; plausible; pleasant; plenteous; practical; precarious; prevailing; priceless; private; progressive; prosperous; prosaic; provincial; prudent; pseudo-social; psychical; public; pulsating; pulseless; pure; quickening; radical; rampant; realistic; redundant; regular; rejuvenated; reproductive; renovated; restive; restless; retired; revolutionary; rhythmical; rollicking; rough; roving; ruddy; rural; sacred; sacrificial; scandalous; scanty; secluded; secret; secular; sedentary; sensuous; sequestered; serene; sheltered; shifting; shudderable; simpering; simple; singing; single; skilful; sky-wedded; sleeping; slow-moving; sluggish; smiling; smug; snug; sobered; social; solitary; sophisticated; spiritual; spontaneous; sportive; starved; steady; sterile; stimulating; straggling; strenuous; studious; subsequent; sunless; sunlit; supersensual; sustaining; sweet; swinish; tangled; temperate; tempestuous; tender; terrestrial; thin-spun; thoughtless; thwarted; toilsome; torpid; tortured; tragic; tramping; tree; trite; troubled; tumultuous; turbulent; tyrant; unambitious; unassuming; unbearable; unceasing; unchanging; unconventional; uncircumscribed; undeniable; unendurable; undistinguished; uneventful; unjaded; unprofitable; unprosperous; unrealized; unresisting; unsatisfactory; unseen; unseparable; unsettled; unsightly; unsophisticated; unstable; upright; useful; urban; various (pl); vagrant; vicious; veritable; vigorous; vile; virtuous; wagering; wandering;

warm; wasted; wayside; wayward; well-lost; wholesome; wild; winged; wistful; womanly; wonted; workless; worldly; worthless; worthy; wretched; youthful; action-filled; adequate; adventurous.

verbs

abbreviate—; alter—; bare—of; beautify —; blight—; blot out—; burst into—; carve —; challenge—; cling to—; commence—; comprehend—; conceive—; consecrate—to; cope with—; dedicate—to; degrade—; delve into—; depict—; deplete—; detach from—; devote—to; devour—; disorganize—; dissipate—; diversify—; drag out—; drain of—; embitter—; endanger—; endow with —; enhance—; ennoble—; equip for—; erase—; exemplify—; face—; flash into—; flinch from—; foreshorten—; foster—; fritter—away; galvanize into—; gamble—on; immerse in—; insulate against—; intercede for—; interpret—; intrude upon—; invade—; isolate—; jeopardize—; maim—; maintain—; manifest—; mar—; mend—; mock—; mold—; muddle through—; nourish—; oppress by—; pay with—; permeate —; plunge into—; portray—; probe—; prolong—; race through—; radiate—; rebuild —; reconstruct—; rekindle—; resuscitate —; retire from—; revel in—; routinize—; shock into—; skim through—; snuff out—; squander—; stake—on; submerge—; sum up —; sustain—; taste—; terminate—; thirst for—; tranquilize—; trifle away—; uplift —; vitiate—; warp—; weigh—; —blossoms; —buzzes by; —disintegrates; —ebbs; —evolves; —flowers; —flows; —hangs; — —s intertwine; —persists; —pulsates; — quickens; —rallies; —surges; —trudges on; —unfolds; —withers.

(See career, existence.)

LIFELESS

adverbs

dully; inactively; languidly; inertly; lazily; idly; torpidly; quiescently; silently; actually; heavily; passively; sluggishly; unusually.

LIFETIME

verbs

concentrate in—; curtain—; devote—to; endure—; fill—; guide through—; pledge—; pour into—; record—; seek—; spend—; spin —; strive—; stumble through—; terminate —; withstand—; wrap in—; —grinds; — slides by; —wearies.

(See time, age, century.)

LIFT (v)

adverbs

momentarily; stalwartly; vigorously; feebly; reverently; instinctively; responsively; daintily; involuntarily; alertly; simultaneously; perceptibly; stealthily.

(See elevate, raise, support.)

LIGAMENT

verbs

rupture—; sever—; strain—; strengthen—; stretch—; suture—; tear—; tie—; treat—; —attaches; —binds; —connects; —couples; —extends; —fastens; —joins; —reinforces; —supports; —unites.

(See muscle, cord, tie, bond.)

LIGATURE

verbs

apply—; —arrests; —binds; —checks; —clamps; —collapses; —compresses; —constricts; —contracts; —curbs; —heals; —remedies; —restrains; —squeezes; —stems; —strangulates.

(See bandage, tape.)

LIGHT

adjectives

accusing; adequate; advancing; all-beholden; all-surprising; altering; amber; ample; amusing; angelic; angry; approaching; arrowy; artificial; ashy; attractive; auroral; austral; available; baleful; beacon; becoming; bewildering; blinding; blinking; blissful; blithe; burning; borrowed; bright; broken; brutal; calm; celestial; center; chalky; changeless; chastening; chatoyant; cheering; clear; cloudless; collateral; comforting; confused; congealed; contrasting; cool; coppery; coruscating; crystal; curious; dancing; danger-dissipating; dark; dawning; dazzling; day; deadly; deceitful; deceptive; deep; defiant; delusive; departing; despairing; despondent; dewy; dim; diaphanous; diffused; dirty; discernible; disheveled; distant; distressing; divine; doubtful; dreadful; dreamy; dry; dusky; dying; earliest; effulgent; elfin; enlivening; enkindling; emerging; emitting; erroneous; emotional; eternal; evening; everlasting; evermoving; factitious; fading; faint; fair; falling; fanning; feeble; featureless; filtered; fitful; flaming; flaring; flash; flashing; flighty; fluctuating; fluttering; fuller; garish; gas; gentle; ghastlier; ghostly; gladsome; glancing; glaring; glazed; gleaming; gleamy; glimmering; glorious; glowing; gradual; hallowed; hard; harnessed; harsh; hateful; hazy; heavenly; holy; hovering; illimitable; immortal; imperfect; inaudible; incandescent; indefinite; indistinct; ineffable; inexorable; influential; inner; innumerable (pl); inquisitive; insolent; intellectual; interfused; internal; intrinsic; inward; irreligious; joyous; laborious; leaning; legendary; lessening; lesser; liquid; literary; livid; lofty; lonelier; lovely; luminous; lunar; lurid; malicious; marquee; melancholy; mellow; melting; meridian; meteor; midday; mingling; ministering; minute; mobile; momentary; morning; mourning; murderous; murky; myriad (pl); mysterious; naked; native; nebulous; nocturnal; northern; obscured; odor-giving; opalescent; opposing; patient; pecuniary; peerless; perpetual; petulant; phantasmal; phantom; phosphorescent; piercing; pitiless; planetary; poisoned; political; primogenital; prismatic; propitious; pure; purging; quivering; rackless; rational; ravishing; reflected; remoter; restored; returning; revealing; rising; roseate; rough; ruddy; rush; rushing; sanctioned; sanguine; satisfactory; sacred; scattered (pl); serious; sectarian; serene; sevenfold; shaping; shadowing; shifting; shimmering; shining; shrouded; sickly; slanting; smoky; smothered; soft; solar; solitary; sparkling; stagnant; starry; steady; steely; straggling; streaming; strengthened; subtle; sudden; suffering; sullen; sulphurous; summer; sunset; swimming; tempered; tender; terrific; time-wasting; timid; transmitted; transparent; tremulous; trembling; uncanny; unaccustomed; unapproached; twinkling; uncertain; unclouded; uncreated; undivided; undoubted; undulating; undying; unenvied; unfading; unfavorable; unnatural; unpitying; unsettled; unshadowed; unshaken; unsifted; unspeakable; untainted; unwavering; unwelcome; unwilling; upspringing; vacillating; valiant; varied; vehement; victorious; wandering; waning; warming; wave-divided; wavering; weak; weeping; weird; welcoming; well-diffused; well-loved; wishing; wistful; wondrous; worldly; zigzag.

verbs

adjust—; bathe in—; blot out—; centralize —; douse (colloq.)—; extinguish—; flood with—; focus—upon; glory in—; grope for —; kindle—; muffle—; obscure—; radiate —; refract—; rejoice in—; shed—upon; shield from—; soften—; wreathe in—; —

720

blazes; —blinds; —blinks; —creeps in; —
dances; —dazzles; —diffuses; —dwindles;
—exposes; —fades; —filters in; —flares;
—flickers; —gleams; —glitters; —glows;
—illumines; —penetrates; —pierces; —seeps
in; —stabs; —streams in; —streaks; —
twinkles; —wanes; —wavers; —wells
from; —winks.
(See lamp, candle, flame, fireworks, match,
sunshine, spark.)

adverbs
insignificantly; extremely; exceedingly; unusually; uncommonly; unbelievably; airily;
buoyantly; brilliantly; garishly; pallidly;
faintly; indifferently; passably; tolerably;
ordinarily; scarcely; manageably; conveniently; happily; jauntily; briskly; brightly;
cheerfully; surprisingly; bewilderingly;
comfortably; gloriously; mysteriously; unaccountably.

LIGHT (v)
adverbs
brilliantly; spectacularly; visibly; adequately; scantily; partially; gracefully; blindingly; cheerfully; exquisitely; vividly.
(See illumine, illuminate, ignite.)

LIGHTEN (v)
adverbs
blazingly; blindingly; dreadfully; terrifyingly; vividly; explosively; spectacularly.
(See flash, illuminate.)

LIGHT-HEARTED
adverbs
cheerfully; exhilaratingly; genially; good-
humoredly; naturally; temperamentally;
laughingly; optimistically; roguishly; briskly; blithely; brightly; buoyantly; bonnily;
hilariously; youthfully; hopefully; jauntily;
jubilantly; winsomely.

LIGHTNESS
adjectives
imaginative; graceful; innumerable (pl);
dry; extreme; cheerful; exquisite; boyish;
sheer; buoyant; inexpressible.

LIGHTNING
adjectives
blind; parching; internal; wicked; uncom-
municated; consuming; volcanic; unleashed; lovelier; poisonous; irreversible; silent;
mercy-winged; congregated; artificial;
naked; sheet; baleful; arrowy; reverber-

ating; restless; glaring; keener; livid;
harmless; nimble; diffused; yoked; indirect;
vivid; deadly.

verbs
—bolts; —chars; —cleaves; —dances; —
darts; —demolishes; —destroys; —flames;
—flashes; —flickers; —glows; —ignites; —
illumines; —illuminates; —plays; —rends;
—reveals; —streaks; —terrifies; —wreaks;
—zigzags.
(See light, lamp, storm, thunder, spark,
tornado, typhoon, wind, hurricane.)

LIKE (v)
adverbs
scarcely; extremely; metaphorically; universally; faithfully; persistently; constantly;
mutually; momentarily; superficially.
(See fancy, approve, choose.)

LIKELY
adverbs
fairly; somewhat; plausibly; reasonably;
speciously; hardly; perhaps; questionably;
undoubtedly; dependably; positively.

LIKENESS
adjectives
striking; unaltered; unsubstantial; intrinsic;
rude; tangible; graphic; distorted; hideous;
speaking; inaccurate; mysterious; generic;
grotesque; immortal; mutual; faithful; famous; executed; momentary; consistent; family; rudimental; mute; persistent; phantasmal.

LILIES
adjectives
lazy; sculptured; unsullied; lolling; slumbrous; gleaming; water; waxen; vast; ineffable; fair; pure; languid; pale; sere;
mystic; robust; careworn; wind-sown.

LILY
verbs
attire in—; bear—; blight—; crown with
—ies; cultivate—ies; stain—; sully—; tint
—; —blushes; —ies clothe; —droops; —
fades; —ies fester; —flourishes; —glistens;
—heaves; —nods; —symbolizes; —unfolds;
—withers.
(See flower, plant.)

LIMB
adjectives
vast; swollen; rigid; unshapely; weary;

wan; trembling; unnatural; withered; un-broken; willing; fervid; coarse-featured; uncouth; unfettered; mangled; gouty; child-ish; sturdy; knotted; writhing; arching; leafless; half-frozen; scabby; severe; toss-ing; leprous; shivering; pulsed; oily; cord-ed; stiffened; languid; immovable; unhewn; shrunken; painful; degraded; gangling; puny; little; putrefying; chafed; feeble; naked; denuded; burning; helpless; droop-ing; sinewy; long-laboring; jaded; massive; thin; weather-beaten; charred; loving; queenly; bare; crippled; paralytic; distort-ed; wreathing; gentle; tawny; tender; wondrous; supplemental; mutilated; deli-cate; bending; shuddering; exquisite; lithe; agile; artificial; palsied; aged.

verbs

amputate—; bare—; brace—; char—; cramp—; deform—; develop—; drag—; employ—; exercise—; fracture—; inject into —; paralyze—; strain—; torture—; —shrinks; —supports; —withers.

(See leg, foot, body, elbow.)

LIME-LIGHT

verbs

avoid—; bask in—; crave—; earn—; emerge from—; extinguish—; fade from—; gain—; glory in—; quench—; seek—; steal —; throw into—; —dazzles; —glows; —notorizes; —publicizes; —smoulders; —wanes.

(See fame, publicity, notoriety, renown, reputation.)

LIMES

adjectives

arching; quiet-leaved; bitter; ripened.

LIMIT

adjectives

narrow; rigid; geographic; predetermined; municipal; severe; definite; maximum; ut-termost; extended; lazy; ultimate; treaty; broad; hallowed; corporate; judicious; nar-rowest; practicable; confined; ancient; ut-most; wiser; extreme; true; insurmountable; fenceless; transcending; glimmering; con-stitutional; remotest; legitimate; sanctified; certain; whimsical; original; modest; sensi-ble; reasonable; appointed.

LIMIT (v)

adverbs

grammatically; rigidly; definitely; consti-tutionally; narrowly; infinitely; scientific-ally; inescapably; practically; mathematic-ally; morally; fastidiously.

(See confine, restrict, circumscribe.)

LIMITATIONS

adjectives

spheric; rigid; constitutional; reasonable; proper; narrow; hereditary; infinite; in-ner; scientific; inevitable; immediate; self-imposed; mortal; finite; inescapable; prac-tical.

verbs

abandon—; acknowledge—; amend—; cir-cumscribe—; circumvent—; discern—; dis-pel—; dispute—; enforce—; escape—; est-ablish—; extricate from—; impose—; pre-scribe—; subject to—; transcend—; —bar; —bridle; —check; —confine; —constrain; —curb; —expire; —fetter; —incarcerate; —repress; —restrain; —restrict; —yoke.

(See restriction, restraint, limit.)

LIMITED

adverbs

indescribably; legally; unfortunately; strict-ly; viciously; exclusively; unchangeably; necessarily; conveniently; rigidly; ridicul-ously; wickedly; inexcusably; traditionally; conventionally; legislatively; excessively; absurdly; wisely; imperiously; irrevocably.

LIMITLESS

adverbs

incredibly; expansively; awesomely; ter-ribly; broadly; generously; inexpressibly; unutterably; incomprehensibly; fearfully.

LIMITS

verbs

act with—; authorize—; bind by—; compress—; define—; exceed—; extend—; fall within—; indicate—; lift—; measure —; narrow—; order—; overstep—; sanc-tify—; slip over—; sound—; transgress—; urge to—; —bar; —constrain.

(See bounds, restraint, restriction, scope, limitations.)

LIMP

adverbs

languidly; wearily; lankly; soggily; wetly; sadly; hopelessly; helplessly; absurdly;

laughably; feebly; powerlessly; flabbily; pliantly; flimsily; ludicrously; drunkenly; breathlessly; utterly; ridiculously.

LIMP (v)

adverbs

laboriously; painfully; sorely; hideously; piteously; pathetically; feebly; jadedly; wanly; uncouthly; repulsively.

(See hobble, walk, falter.)

LIMPID

adverbs

beautifully; transparently; coolly; serenely; clearly; pellucidly; innocently; trustingly (eyes); ripplingly; translucently.

LINE

adjectives

fine; skirmish; untutored; soft; flowing; harmonious; never-ceasing; demolished; graceful; melodic; undulating; depending; transparent; rippling; continuous; scientific; collateral; advancing; extended; capricious; oblique; sounding; intertwisted; impromptu; important; imaginary; beautiful; impregnable; policy; gleaming; opposing; exiled; converging; occasional; legitimate; feeling; half-illegible; pencil-traced; tighter; sensuous; emphatic; inspiring; minute; fleeting; never-varying; fringing; sharpened; youthful; subtle; insuperable; agitated; endless; divergent; special; curving; dainty; never-relaxing; flexible; roaring; sensitive; equinoctial; curling; flimsy; absolute; straight; feudal; suave; dignified; body-traced; crisp; wide; well-proportioned; smart; smart-draping; distinguished; tapering; easy; exclusive; distinctive; vulnerable; ravaged; sonorous; unbroken; monastery; bread; uneven; ragged; cramped; parallel (pl); eccentric; sleepless; irregular; pathetic; wabbling; quivering; ensuing; paternal; wavering; decided; eastward; fringing; fortified; etched; shapely; style; constricting; exterior; remotest; rent; successive (pl); slim; stirring; insolent; decisive; mystic; long; urbane; broad; tedious; swagger; classic; apostolic; complete; swinging; transcontinental; surging; stunning; weight-bearing; traditional; characteristic; honied; poetic; circumvallating; radial; moral; interconnecting; natural; jeweled; slender; wanton; rambling; trim; immortal; smart-tailored; ever-lengthening; stubborn; sleek; sun-tempting; back; dauntless; luxuriant; unreturning; fantastic; momentous; placid; solemn; noiseless; intertangled; infinitesimal; oblique; shoddy; eloquent; narrative; witty; preparatory; hypothetical; impassioned; unpunctuated; inimitable; telegraphic; harsh; effective; circling; competing; bristling; faint; intrenched; brilliant; vanquished; horizontal; cabalistic; sinuous; preconcerted; completed; well-defined; stateliest; unfading; glittering; never-ending; allied; quaint; experimental; nodal; prosaic; radiating (pl); trimmer; industrial; intellectual; heroic; improvised; illustrious; admirable; hard; grim; humble; imitative; ghostly; foul; swelling; touching; foolish; connecting; imperiled; unpolished; bobbing; unrelated; brief; plumb; slimmer; compact; simple; unconquered; vocal; holy; therapeutic; theoretic; charging; ferocious; thought-tracked; genealogical; sublime; fleshly; surging; dividing.

verbs

alternate—s; blur—; delineate—; derive—from; eradicate—; extend—; foul—; fracture—; intersect—; overrun—; scale—; thread—; trace—; warp—; wipe out—s; —bounds; —s coincide; —deviates; —digresses; —dips; —grades; —graduates; —limits; —parallels; —progresses; —s radiate from; —refracts; —represents; —straggles; —swerves; —veers; —verges; —wobbles.

(See mark, boundary, outline, route, road.)

LINEAGE

adjectives

ancient; imperial; injured; honorable.

LINEAMENTS

adjectives

haughtiest; stricken; pallid; striking; noble; dead; hideous; mental; exaggerated; warworn; strong; sculptured; impertinent; personal; shifting.

LINED
(wrinkled)

adverbs

deeply; humorously; scowlingly; ripely; puckeringly; agedly; patriarchally; terribly; significantly.

LINEN

adjectives

blood-clotted; snowy; dubious; age-yellowed; spotless; filthy; foul; stout; dainty; immaculate; embroidered; outward-surging; convent.

verbs

array in—; attire in—; bleach—; brocade
—; carbonize—; card—; comb—; disentangle—; drape—; dress—; embroider—;
fringe with—; garb in—; gird in—; grade
—; hackle—; hank—; ret—; soak—; spin
—; vest in—; warp—.

(See cloth, silk, velvet.)

LINGER (*v*)

adverbs

tenderly; affectionately; vaguely; monotonously; boringly; obtrusively; wearily; confusedly; regretfully; perilously; idly; irresolutely; indecisively.

(See loiter, saunter.)

LINGUIST

adjectives

skilled; ready; manifold; comparative; accomplished; brilliant; celebrated.

LINIMENT

verbs

administer—; apply—; drench with—; yield
to—; —cools; —limbers; —mollifies; —palliates; —relaxes; —relieves; —restores; —
soothes.

(See medicine, iodine, tonic, remedy, ointment, salve.)

LINING

verbs

strip of—; stud with—; —chafes; —coats;
—crusts; —inflames; —jackets; —pads; —
preserves; —sheathes; —wads.

(See cloth, silk, velvet, wrapper.)

LINK

verbs

cement—; dissolve—; fuse—; partition into
—s; pivot on—; rend—; sever—; solder—;
sunder—; terminate—; —affiliates; —allies;
—bridges; —cleaves; —coincides; —communicates; —correlates; —facilitates; —fetters; —hinges; —leagues; —shackles; —
spans; —unites; —leashes.

(See chain, bond, tie, ring, union, part,
ligament, ligature.)

LINK (*v*)

adverbs

indissolubly; inextricably; rhythmically; inevitably; inseparably; perpetually; incessantly; slanderously; humorously; incongruously; incompatibly.

(See join, connect, unite.)

LINKS

adjectives

intervening; thought; special; connecting;
accustomed; mystic; clay-cold; adamantine;
successive; breezy.

LINNET

verbs

—collects; —s flock; —mimics; —pipes; —
warbles.

(See bird.)

LINOTYPE

verbs

dump—; ink—; melt—; print from—; set—;
trim—; —assembles; —casts; —clanks; —
composes; —distributes; —facilitates; —
stereotypes; —transcribes.

(See type, metal.)

LION

adjectives

tameless; tawny-bearded; prisoned; rampant; jagged-jawed; wondrous.

verbs

encounter—; rouse—; slay—; —attacks; —
carries off; —claws; —creeps upon; —devours; —drags off; —forages; —glares;
—growls; —menaces; —paws; —preys on;
—purrs; —rages; —rampages; —roams; —
roars; —rolls over; —slaughters; —springs;
—stalks; —stretches; —tears; —yawns.

(See animal, tiger, leopard.)

LIONIZE (*v*)

adverbs

bizarrely; enthusiastically; customarily; fraternally; hospitably; jovially; congenially;
sportively; agreeably.

(See glorify, adore, exhibit, display.)

LIPS

adjectives

kissing; bridled; bearded; ripe; marble;
burning; dimpled; fervent; rosy; trembling;
quivering; seldom-parted; seductive; pendulous; curdled; ruddy; seeking; tender; sensitive; clear-cut; blistering; coward; carmine; glowing; loving; gaping; languid;
wet; rosy; pallid; sinful; placid; downdrawn; brazen; dewy; blanched; swollen;
bold; parching; flaccid; pursed; tightened;
generous; thin; gummed-up; villainous;
straight; pale; discolored; unpainted;
roughed; pinched; dry; rosebud; ruby;
whitening; crystal; shiny; coral; wide;

over-red; livid; bloodless; velvet; blanched; cerise; lead-colored; flower-petal; sardonic; projecting; compressed; unbreathing; protruding; heavy; half-open; full; purpled; flower-soft; traitorous; dainty; milk-fed; loose; eloquent; scornful; curse-laden; icy; mute; opened; stern; set; fevered; fettered; fleshless; babbling; mortal; ample; living; warm; sealed; eased; tired; willing; gifted; insatiable; sinuous; unseen; mobile; contorted; angel; squandering; innocent; imperial; firm; uncaressing; love-enkindled; luscious; appreciative; hueless; perjured; voluptuous; lifeless; dying; republican; wax-red; grim; nectared; bristled; mocking; unfettered; gnarled; miserable; careless; winning; girlish; sallow; frothing; lax; slight; haughty; proud; retracted; sad; voiceless; severed; curled-up; flashing; skinny; full; incense-breathing; sensuous; intertwisted; carved; calm; pure; thirsty; grosser; guarded; writhing; drooping; obsequious; shrunken; puckered; slanderous; relaxing; half-pouting; crooked; pendulous; mellow; prehensile; meager; tortured; honeyed; unclosed; averted; starved; covetous; convivial; unclean; well-cut; ineffectual; scorched; passionate; leopard; lily; stammering; infant; panting; cracked; stifling; rapid; chiseled; milkless; wrinkled; long-silent; devout.

verbs
compress—; depress—; excoriate—; glue—; gnaw—; lock—; parch—; pucker—; purse —; seal—; smack—; sully—; thin—; tumble from—; wring from—; —beguile; —curl; —falter; —pout; —proclaim; —profane; — protrude; —quiver; —scorn; —snarl; — stir; —thin; —tremble; —writhe; —yield.
(See mouth.)

LIQUID
adjectives
malodorous; viscous; foul; limpid; combustible; sparkling; denser; anesthetizing; lifeless; ecstatic; rosy; plain; noxious; queer-looking; seminal; unliquidating; colorless; swarming; consecrated; putrid; opaque.

verbs
charge—; chill—; dabble in—; deluge with —; dilute—; discharge—; drain—; draw off —; exude—; gargle—; gulp—; imbibe—; immerse in—; infiltrate—; inject—; precip-

itate—; spout—; squirt—; steep in—; strain —; submerge—; tap—; —babbles; — gurgles; —ripples; —saturates.
(See water, fluid, liquor, beverage, drink.)

LIQUOR
adjectives
amber; muddy; intoxicating; crimson; fuming; pleasant; drowsy; rebellious; sparkling; grand; spiritual; hateful; nectarial; exquisite; stimulating.

verbs
abstain from—; age—; carouse with—; compound —; dilute—; distill—; ferment—; grade—; imbibe—; overindulge in—; perfume—; reek of—; reel with—; restrict—; stamp—; sublimate—; sweeten—; tax—; traffic in—; —inebriates; —stupefies.
(See whiskey, brandy, beer, ale, wine.)

LISP (v)
adverbs
affectedly; mincingly; insipidly; captivatingly; emulously; irritatingly; annoyingly; sibilantly.
(See utter, talk, speak.)

LISSOME
adverbs
slenderly; daintily; youthfully; girlishly; beautifully; attractively; unusually; uncommonly; delightfully; softly; yieldingly; tenderly; gracefully; charmingly.

LIST
adjectives
inexhaustible; extensive; provisional; authoritative; stupendous; representative; eligible; pompous; voting; growing; metrical; interminable; fatal; appalling; shining; gratifying; alarming; casualty; diversified; abbreviated; annotated; prescribed; protesting; mere; certain; inexorable; illegitimate.

verbs
approve—; audit—; check—; circularize—; compile—; delete—; enroll in—; extend—; investigate—; muster—; rattle off—; recapitulate—; review—; supplement—; swell—; —accounts; —calendars; —catalogues; — computes; —declines; —dwindles; —enumerates; —indexes; —measures; —polls; — recedes; —registers; —schedules; —scores; —sums up; —wanes.
(See schedule, sum, amount, account, record, statistics, statement, program.)

LISTEN (v)

adverbs

apprehensively; indulgently; intently; attentively; dreamily; compassionately; piously; obediently; intelligently; impassively; reflectively; languidly; aimlessly; sympathetically; interminably; gratifyingly; raptly.

(See attend, heed, hearken, obey.)

LISTENER

adjectives

attentive; sympathetic; untutored; intelligent; chance; anxious; uninitiated; puzzled; radiant; discriminating; unprejudiced; admiring; individual; laconic; impassive; wondering; mute; rapt; unobtrusive; defiant; close; trembling.

verbs

admonish—; bar—; bore—; enchant—; entrance—; inform—; reproach—; rouse—; spellbind—; —absorbs; —bends an ear; —s chorus; —considers; —eavesdrops; — grasps; —hearkens; —heeds; —pricks up his ears; —regards; —senses; —wearies.

(See audience, congregation, hearer, visitor, guest, crowd.)

LISTLESS

adverbs

provokingly; languidly; inertly; lazily; dully; carelessly; heedlessly; indifferently; irritatingly; vexatiously; arrogantly; obviously; visibly; unaccountably; inexplicably; insufferably; impolitely; discourteously; insolently; inconsiderately; helplessly; drowsily; distractedly; dreamily; terribly; amazingly; surprisingly; dreadfully.

LITERAL

adverbs

painfully; punctiliously; insufferably; legally; meticulously; intolerably; ostentatiously; professionally; officiously; unctuously; learnedly; academically; boresomely; unduly; unnecessarily; mercilessly; ruthlessly; unimaginatively; prosaically; mathematically; correctly; severely; uncompromisingly; curiously; exaggeratedly; awfully; uncommonly.

LITERATURE

adjectives

vigorous; national; contemporary; classical; related; city-bred; romantic; descriptive; illustrated; tinted; creative; imperishable; vernacular; inventive; satirical; critical; superficial; current; periodical; obscene; extensive; mainstream; complete; forensic; personal; ancient; primitive; social; significant; majestic; disciplined; prolific; imaginative; vitalized.

verbs

acclaim—; appreciate—; assail—; bar—; censor—; create—; criticize—; dabble in—; delve into—; evaluate—; execute—; foster —; haunt—; interpret—; nurse—; patronize —; relish—; revaluate—; sanctify—; stabilize—; unify—; —charms; —communicates; —conveys; —enlightens; —delights; —enraptures; —eternizes; —expresses; —immortalizes; —incites; —informs; —inspires; —portrays; —provides; —redeems; —reveals; —stimulates; —transfuses; —transports.

(See art, story, biography, newspaper, press, essay, fiction, poetry, writing, book, magazine.)

LITIGATION

adjectives

expensive; sufficient; recent; weary; furious; prolonged; bitter.

verbs

appeal—; clinch—; discharge—; dispose of —; dispute—; evidence—; execute—; judge —; speed—; support—; —apprehends; — arraigns; —clashes; —distrains; —drags; —embroils; —impeaches; —indicts; —jars; —prosecutes; —squabbles.

(See lawsuit, case, suit (law), argument, verdict, results, decision, settlement.)

LITTER

adjectives

sable; terrible; intellectual; huge.

LITTER (v)

adverbs

confusedly; untidily; sloppily; haphazardly; disheveledly; obtrusively.

(See scatter, separate, intersperse.)

LITTLE

adverbs

precious; confoundedly; pitiably; inconsequentially; remarkably; miserably; cruelly; incredibly; inadequately; infinitesimally; wretchedly; blessedly.

LIVE
(alive)

adverbs

actively; mentally; amazingly; animatedly; perilously; briskly; eagerly; mysteriously; sensitively; energetically; spiritually; fiercely; unmistakably; joyously; secretly; keenly; spiritedly; emotionally; intellectually; persistently; tragically; enterprisingly; exuberantly; vigorously; undeniably; restlessly; substantially; strongly; warmly; wretchedly; vivaciously; vitally; acutely; flourishingly; impatiently; tenaciously; exultantly; resolutely; happily.

LIVE (v)

adverbs

lavishly; dangerously; originally; expansively; improvidently; actively; profligately; opulently; ostentatiously; excessively; inconsequentially; affluently; gloriously; immortally; significantly; luxuriously; fantastically; penuriously; pretentiously; sumptuously; dissolutely; harmoniously; religiously; precariously; blithely; exclusively; spiritually; economically; abstemiously; scandalously; barbarously; monotonously; strenuously.

(See exist, abide, dwell.)

LIVELIHOOD

adjectives

meager; humble; bare; reputable; honest.

verbs

acquire—; afford—; bereave of—; command —; derive—from; draw—from; earn—; furnish—; gain—; grub—; insure—; maintain—; offer—; procure—; reap—; scrape together—; strip of—; yield—.

(See living, support, sustenance, income, wages, salary.)

LIVELINESS

verbs

animate with—; frolic in—; manifest—; radiate—; sparkle in—; stimulate—; —cheers; —effervesces; —elates; —enlivens; —exhilarates; —gladdens; —inspirits; —perks up.

(See animation, action, activity, vivacity, life.)

LIVELY

adverbs

immensely; joyously; noisily; naturally; unwontedly; unbelievably; briskly; gloriously; conspicuously; strikingly; fitfully; abnormally; dramatically; ostentatiously; ridiculously; singularly; habitually; disturbingly; pleasantly; refreshingly; enchantingly.

LIVER

adjectives

unchaste; torpid; spotted.

verbs

afflict—; attack—; congest—; damage—; derange—; disorganize—; impair—; infect —; —deteriorates; —discharges; —ejects; —excretes; —expels; —functions; —lodges; —purifies; —secretes; —shrivels.

(See bladder, organs, heart, kidney.)

LIVERY

adjectives

silver; reclusive; religious; gorgeous; cunning; destined; sober; bare; showy; beauteous; humble; drab-colored; gilded; royal; special.

LIVES

adjectives

best-regulated; scandalous; infinite; sedentary; weary; frivolous; deplorable; millennial; constricted; barbarous; valueless; luxurious; fateful; uncultivated; eventful; precious; regimented; craven; misplaced; strenuous; acceptable; fashionable; worthy; stunted; solitary; unnumbered; pale; virgin; disordered; imaginative; carnivorous; intermittent; lawless; divided; brutish; monotonous.

LIVESTOCK

verbs

auction off—; brand—; confine—; corral—; deal in—; free—; insure—; obliterate—; pasture—; shelter—; stable—; tend—; tether—; water—; —grazes; —sickens; —stampedes; —tramples; —wanders.

(See cow, horse, cattle, oxen, mule, sheep, lamb.)

LIVID

adverbs

terribly; hideously; terrifyingly; painfully; awfully; gruesomely; darkly; dreadfully; ashenly; coldly.

LIVING

adjectives

riotous; monotonous; concentrated; fruitful; flourishing; luxurious; scandalous; enjoyable; precarious; lucrative; gracious; contemporary; successful; happy; reckless; useful; dissipated; sufficient; vicarious; fat; independent; complicated; healthier; clean; ascetic; cheap; moderate; contented; strenuous; satisfactory; pleasurable; honorable; generous; primitive; scanty; quiet; fine; inexpensive; congenial; restful; wasteful.

verbs
acquire—; afford—; derive—from; earn—; eke—; fend for—; furnish—; gain—; garner—; glean—; offer—; simplify—; wrest —from.
(See livelihood, support, sustenance, income, wages, salary.)

LIZARD
verbs
—burrows; —claws; —crawls; —dives; — erects; —flies; —frequents; —invades; — paddles; —poisons; —preys upon; —reproduces; —sheds; —slithers; —suns itself; — swims; —whips its tail; —wounds; — wriggles.
(See reptile, animal, snake.)

LOAD
adjectives
bounteous; dark; weary; precious; concentrated; work; moaning; dead-weight; groaning; grievous; cumbrous; harsh; life-compelling; monstrous; tremendous.

verbs
ameliorate—; augment—; bear—; bend under—; bow by—; collect—; discharge—; droop under—; strap—on; support—; weigh —; —burdens; —clogs; —encumbers; — hampers; —impedes; —oppresses; —overwhelms; —restrains; —weakens.
(See burden, weight, pressure.)

LOAF (v)
adverbs
contentedly; idly; improvidently; dreamily; disgracefully; drunkenly; corruptly; enjoyably; congenially; wastefully.
(See dawdle, lounge, loiter, loll.)

LOAM
adjectives
fresh; woodland; tenacious; yielding; smeared.

LOAN
adjectives
brief; willing; stagnant; inadequate; exorbitant.

verbs
acknowledge—; advance—; amortize—; confer—upon; contract—; contribute—; extend—; facilitate—; float—; force—; grant —; inveigle—; launch—; obtain—; pledge —; press—; procure—; raise—; solicit—; subscribe—; —gratifies; —indebts.
(See debt, money, funds, payment.)

LOATHSOME
adverbs
unspeakably; abominably; disgustingly; mortally; sickeningly; insufferably; intolerably; uncommonly; impossibly; utterly; completely; horribly; repulsively; detestably; shockingly; hatefully.

LOATHING
adjectives
indignant; deepest; instinctive; enormous.

LOBBY
adjectives
commodious; magnificent; new; busy; quiet; economical; impressive; appointed; cheerful; furnished; luxurious.

verbs
appropriate—; decorate—; frequent—; lounge in—; pace—; page in—; retire to —; retreat to—; throng—; wait in—; — connects; —echoes with; —resounds; — swarms.
(See hall, corridor, passage, room.)

LOCAL
adverbs
apparently; allegedly; merely; luckily; strongly; unquestionably; evidently; emphatically.

LOCALITY
adjectives
affected; attractive; residential; memorable; isolated; miserable.

verbs
acclimate to—; annihilate—; assign to—; canvass—; examine—; explore—; fix—; in-

habit—; investigate—; mold to—; scan—; scour—; search—; seek—; select—; sever from—; shift—; view—; —militates.

(See territory, region, neighborhood, vicinity, district.)

LOCATE (v)

adverbs
systematically; centrally; conveniently; precisely; picturesquely; distinctly; matchlessly; conveniently; strategically; geographically.

(See place, establish.)

LOCATION

adjectives
pleasant; choice; favored; unexcelled; preferred; ideal; unique; matchless; convenient; superb; beautiful; quiet; splendid; particular; strategic; changing; available; interesting; hazardous; advantageous; geographical; outstanding; efficient; mythical; industrial; peculiar; unrivaled.

LOCK
(hair)

adjectives
unkempt; curling; raven; clustering; flowing; luxuriant; thin; dangling; straggling; whitened; crisped; snaky; golden; recalcitrant; massy; obstinate; bushy; truant; glossy; sunny; intertwining; straying; shining; tumbled; dense; shaggy; well-groomed; shorn; stiff; flat; dripping; hoary; clustering; sparse; unruly; fearful; floating; silken; careless; scanty; disheveled; plaited.

LOCK
(mechanical)

adjectives
shattering; languid; crude; mitered; profuse; keyhole; intricate; burglar-proof.

verbs
adjust—; design—; force—; jimmy—; pick —; set—; tamper with—; test—; unbar—; withdraw—; —clasps; —clicks; —embraces; —repulses; —resists; —responds; —seals; —secures.

(See bolt, bar.)

LOCK (v)

adverbs
discreetly; cautiously; prudently; mechanically; automatically; modestly; suspiciously; covetously; staunchly.

(See fasten, fix, secure.)

LOCOMOTIVE

verbs
board—; derail—; dismount from—; fuel —; propel—; —chugs; —halts; —hammers; —overtakes; —pants; —puffs; —screeches; —shrieks; —shuffles; —speeds; —sputters; —stammers; —steams; —traverses; —wails; —wheezes; —whizzes.

(See train, engine.)

LOCUST

verbs
crush—; exterminate—s; —bores; —burrows; —s cloud; —cymbals; —destroys; —drones; —drums; —s migrate; —molts; —s plague; —rasps; —rattles; —sings; —sucks; —s swarm; —s symphonize; —undergoes; —s descend.

(See insect, grasshopper.)

LODGE

adjectives
ivy-covered; rude; supreme; nightly; country; hunting.

verbs
abandon—; charter—; confine to—; enjoy —; invite to—; luxuriate in—; occupy—; organize—; repose in—; reside at—; retire to—; retreat to—; vacate—; —accommodates; —comforts; —harbors; —shelters; —solaces.

(See club, home, residence, society, room.)

LODGE (v)

adverbs
snugly; firmly; fatally; temporarily; miserably; congenially; uniquely; conveniently; strategically; advantageously; industrially; permanently.

(See stay, remain, abide.)

LODGING

adjectives
inferior; hard; primitive; comfortable; barren.

verbs
afford—; assure of—; demand—; engage—; enjoy—; find—; furnish—; grant—; guarantee—; inquire into—; lease—; offer—; procure—; scorn—; secure—; seek—; warrant—; —delights; —refreshes; —shames.

(See shelter, refuge, room, rest, repose, sanctuary.)

LOFTY

adverbs

arrogantly; notoriously; incalculably; ridiculously; eminently; majestically; exaltedly; impressively; imposingly; proudly; toweringly, incredibly; tremendously; imperiously; strangely; ludicrously.

LOG

adjectives

smoldering; inanimate; unhewn; hollowed; flaming; back; blazing; hickory; yule; drunken; senseless; floating; ostensible; patent; moldered.

verbs

batter with—; bear—; char—; fire—; hew —; ignite—; kindle—; poke—; stir—; toast over—; vault—; —chills; —flames; —fuels; —glows; —seethes; —smokes; —smoulders.
(See club, wood, flame, fire, board, timber.)

LOGIC

adjectives

unerring; remorseless; persistent; energetic; soundest; dangerous; delightful; rigorous; symbolic; feminine; erstwhile; convincing; uncharitable; unanswerable; aesthetic; dispassionate; vast; cruel; hasty; imperfect; triumphant; inexorable; simple; compelling; pitiless; easy; strict; subtle; inevitable; unyielding; blundering; naked; suicidal.

verbs

condemn—; defy—; demonstrate—; endorse —; govern by—; indicate—; judge—; lame —; practise—; question—; reduce to—; refute—; require—; review—; warp—; ween from—; —analyzes; —annihilates; —convinces; —deduces; —determines; —dictates; —evolves; —prevails; —solves; —speculates.
(See reason, theory, accuracy.)

LOGICAL

adverbs

entirely; historically; skilfully; unfailingly; admirably; justly; remarkably; inevitably; unerringly; alarmingly; inexorably; fearfully; inescapably; undeniably; amazingly; uncommonly; wholly.

LOINS

adjectives

unknown; frozen; supple; girt; proper.

LOITER (v)

adverbs

undecidedly; jauntily; lackadaisically; tantalizingly; idly; luxuriously; persistently; excessively.
(See loaf, dawdle, lounge, loll.)

LOLL (v)

adverbs

luxuriantly; idly; listlessly; carelessly; wearily; impassively; frivolously; wantonly.
(See lounge, loaf, dawdle.)

LONE

adverbs

desolately; noticeably; distinctly; prominently; tragically; cheerlessly; remotely; intensely; solitarily; terribly; remarkably; uniquely; dreadfully.

LONELINESS

adjectives

supreme; visionary; abstracted; infinite; mossy; tragic; bowery; unutterable; oppressive; indescribable; multitudinous; infinitesimal; appalling; palatial; dreary; empty; bitter; unbearable; intolerable.

verbs

abate—; assuage—; conceal—; decry—; dissipate—; drive away—; evince—; fear—; guard against—; heighten—; overcome—; ravage by—; shroud in—; stress—; succumb to—; —accompanies; —assails; —engulfs; —envelops; —penetrates.
(See seclusion, solitude, isolation, dullness.)

LONELY

adverbs

strangely; unbelievably; unaccountably; naturally; oddly; forlornly; unbearably; unendurably; unnecessarily; distressingly; portentously; infinitely; tragically; unutterably; bitterly; intolerably; drearily; appallingly; indescribably; inexpressibly; pitiably; irremediably; pathetically; cruelly.

LONESOME

adverbs

dismally; reminiscently; gloomily; serenely; lazily; jealously; unhappily; terribly; intensely; peevishly; fretfully; drearily; supremely; absurdly; inexpressibly; grievously; hopelessly; pathetically; deservedly; unexpectedly; remarkably; curiously; dimly; vaguely; startlingly; extremely.

730

LONG

adverbs

extraordinarily; endlessly; interminably; monotonously; unbearably; ridiculously; excessively; remarkably; singularly; extremely; unbelievably; unnecessarily; sufficiently; tediously; inexcusably; unserviceably; unconscionably; incredibly; diffusely; tiresomely; wearily; terribly; curiously; unaccountably; unwarrantably.

LONG (*v*)

adverbs

nostalgically; impassionedly; wildly; sentimentally; fondly; inexplicably; fruitlessly; morbidly; restlessly; irresistibly; insatiably; singularly; inexpressibly; lingeringly; buoyantly; irrationally.

(See yearn, crave.)

LONGEVITY

verbs

contribute to—; derive—; endure—; enjoy —; entail—; evoke—; forestall—; hinder—; increase—; induce—; invest with—; procure—; produce—; provoke—; secure—; shatter—; —enfeebles; —results.

(See health.)

LONGING

adjectives

wild; nostalgic; vain; impassioned; sympathetic; premature; indefinite; wholesome; satisfied; strange; unpenetrated; mad; hopeless; immortal; musical; fond; earnest; unconscious; unchaste; new-born; inexplicable; vague; anxious; unceasing; indefinable; passionate; animal; earliest; patent; potent; half-deadly; half-voluptuous; persistent; bitter; fruitless; diseased; morbid; innermost; undefined; restless; ungratified; irresistible; painful; cruel; insatiate; ceaseless; upward; uncontrollable; faded; singular; doglike.

verbs

abate—; conceive—; devour by—; fulfill—; gratify—; hatch—; live in—; quench—; respect—; sate—; satisfy—; suffer—; upfoot—; —burns; —destroys; —gnaws; —palls; —tantalizes; —tears at.

(See desire, yearning, craving, nostalgia.)

LOOK

adjectives

absent; agonized; alabaster; appealing; alert; amorous; animated; approving; arch; ardent; artless; attenuated; backward; bantering; beaming; beguiling; beseeching; bewildered; bitter; black; brazen; bleached; brown; bullying; burning; careworn; colorless; comic; compassionate; complacent; comprehensive; conjunctive; contemptuous; contented; counterfeit; critical; cross; crystal; cunning; curious; cursory; damp; dazed; deadly; deep; defiant; dejected; delicate; delirious; demure; deserted; despairing; desperate; despondent; dim; discontented; disdainful; dismal; dissipated; dissembling; distasteful; disturbed; doubting; downcast; drawn; dreamy; droopy; dubious; dying; elusive; enthralling; envious; expectant; exultant; fair; faraway; far-off; fearful; fear-stunned; flashing; frequent (pl); frightened; furtive; gentle; gloomy; glowering; glum; good; gracious; grateful; grave; grieved; guileless; haggard; half-laughing; hanging; haunting; heartbroken; helpless; honest; hopeless; hostile; hunted; hurried; hurt; icy; impertinent; imploring; indignant; innocent; inquiring; inscrutable; intelligent; intent; intimidating; irreverent; jaunty; keen; kind; knowing; languid; latent; lean; lingering; loftiest; longing; lowering; luminous; melancholy; melodramatic; merry; mild; mischievous; momentary; moody; mute; mysterious; naughty; obdurate; oblique; occasional; ogling; ominous; open; outdoor; pale; pathetic; penetrating; perplexed; phantasmal; piercing; pitiful; plaintive; pleading; predatory; preoccupied; prepossessing; prolonged; provocative; puzzled; queenly; queer; questioning; quick; quizzical; rakish; reluctant; resigned; reverend; riveted; robust; rueful; roguish; rowdy; rugged; sad; saucy; scared; scornful; scowling; searching; seeking; seraphic; serene; serious; shy; shamed; sidelong; significant; silky; silly; smart; soft; somnambulistic; sorrowful; sour; spectral; speculative; speechless; spiteful; sprightly; startled; steady; staunch; stealthy; stereotyped; stiff-necked; strained; stricken; stunned; sulky; sullen; surprised; suspicious; swift; swarthy; sweetest; tearful; thick; timely; threatening; timid; tired; tranquil; truculent; unfathomable; unflinching; ungentle; unguarded; united; unrestful; unseeing; unusual; vacant; valiant; vexed; vindictive; vivid; waiting; wan; weak; weather-beaten; welcoming; wild; whimsical; wistful; wise; withering; woebegone; wonderful; wondering; worn; worshipful; yearning.

verbs
acclaim with—; belie—; conceal—; confuse
—; evade—; flash—; manufacture—; quail
before—; shoot—; snatch—; sneak—; sour
—; —challenges; —cows; —probes; —rebukes; —scorches; —shines; —wanes; —
wavers; —withers.
(See glance, gaze, scrutiny, glimpse.)

LOOK (v)
adverbs
amorously; beseechingly; cursorily; compassionately; demurely; disdainfully; impertinently; dubiously; haggardly; reverently;
ominously; pathetically; provocatively; in-
timidatingly; roguishly; seraphically; speculatively; vacantly; vindictively; witheringly; uncomprehendingly; covertly; sagaciously; stonily; meditatively; disconsolately; ferociously; ponderingly; wistfully; raptly;
keenly; frivolously; mockingly; sheepishly;
woefully; querulously; significantly; incredulously.
(See gaze, glance, stare.)

LOOM
adjectives
rustling; webless; creaking; interwoven;
ages-old; wooden; handicraft; triumphant;
primitive; magic; precious.

LOOM (v)
adverbs
ominously; thunderously; portentously;
threateningly; impressively; belligerently;
direly; stupendously; awesomely.
(See shine, rise, appear.)

LOOSE
adverbs
dangerously; fearfully; oddly; inexplicably;
perilously; hazardously; distinctly; insecurely; inexcusably; terribly; accidentally; mysteriously; undeniably; unstably; carelessly;
incautiously.

LOOSEN (v)
adverbs
radically; sufficiently; comfortably; medically; beneficially; healthfully; scientifically;
partially.
(See free, separate, unfasten.)

LOOT
verbs
appropriate—; bag—; bicker over—; con
ceal—; divide—; embrace—; feed on—;

forage for—; gather—; nab—; parcel—;
plunder for—; pocket—; ransack for—; sack
for—; scramble for—; smuggle—; snap up
—; snatch—; strip of—; suckle on—; vie
for—; wean on—.
(See spoils, plunder, graft.)

LOQUACIOUS
adverbs
interminably; wildly; garrulously; chattily;
maliciously; undeniably; highly; endlessly;
inanely; glibly; clackily; flippantly; tiresomely; insufferably; amusingly; vexatiously; incredibly; hysterically; verbosely; repetitiously; dreadfully; amazingly; strangely; nonsensically.

LOQUACITY
adjectives
irrepressible; nervous; unlimited; noticeable.

LORD
(*gentleman*)
adjectives
stalwart; pampered; truant; absolute; predestined; rapacious; dread; native; gracious; illustrious; dethroned; worthy; courteous; brindled; merry; distressed; mocking;
sovereign; faithless; new-trothed; filthy;
scurvy; unworthy; unnatural; self-complacent; honored.

LORD
(*divine being*)
verbs
accept—; beseech—; bow to—; cherish—;
exalt—; invoke—; offer unto—; praise—;
pray to—; supplicate—; worship—; —
anoints; —bestows; —controls; —heals; —
judges; —masters.
(See God, Christ, Jesus.)

LORDLY
adverbs
arrogantly; insufferably; naturally; imposingly; impressively; absurdly; ridiculously;
ludicrously; magnificently; splendidly; magnanimously; majestically; distinctly; notoriously; eminently; conspicuously; superciliously; imperiously; incredibly; proudly;
laughably; curiously.

LORE
adjectives
slothful; poetic; listless; childlike; astrolo-
gic; legendary; idle; mythical; sublimest;
exhaustless; technical; nauseous; immortal;

deceptive; inmost; shining; civilizing; gentlest; lascivious; mystic; legal; golden; preternatural; eternal; divinest.

verbs
acquire—; arm with—; banish—; comprehend—; delve into—; exaggerate—; gather —; ignore—; initiate into—; instruct in—; master—; perpetuate—; preserve—; steep in—; strip of—; substantiate—; unearth—; —deludes; —impresses; —misleads; —survives.
(See legend, tale, story, wisdom, learning.)

LOSER
verbs
condole—; declare—; deprive—; deride—; dispossess—; draw—; jeer—; renounce—; ridicule—; spot—; sympathize with—; —beseeches; —blunders; —complains; —deplores; —discards; —fails; —falls; —grumbles; —laments; —pledges; —prates; —protests; —sacrifices.
(See failure.)

LOSS
adjectives
consequent; wasteful; proportional; total; threatened; mournful; irreparable; considerable; excessive; disastrous; serious; unendurable; continual; awakened; prospective; infinite; intolerable; vague; frightful; heavy; trifling; financial; tragic; fearful; trivial; melancholy; sickening; crushing; shocking; inconsiderable; dear; moisture; perceptible; slight; petty; gainful; immeasurable; ultimate; imminent; undetectable; aggregate; lamentable; moneyed; irretrievable; tremendous; frightful; complete; appalling; preventable; numerical; maiden; partial; positive; anticipated; grievous.

verbs
absorb—; attribute—to; bemoan—; brood over—; cloak—; compensate for—; concede —; counterbalance—; curtail—; deplore—; grieve over—; incur—; lament—; lighten—; mourn—; occasion—; offset—; outweigh—; recoup—s; redress—; regard—; reimburse —; repent—; report—; retrieve—; smart under—; suffer—; sustain—; swallow—; —anguishes; —maddens; —s mount; —shames; —s soar.
(See bankruptcy, defeat, failure, misfortune.)

LOST
adverbs
irrecoverably; irretrievably; recently; altogether; forever; temporarily; lamentably; deplorably; utterly; strangely; curiously; terribly; unfortunately; incredibly; miserably.

LOT
adjectives
adjacent; adventurous; vacant; disreputable; enviable; dreary; toilsome; cheerless; loose-living; human; picturesque; unfortunate; homely; future; worthless; scrubby; uncomfortable; cloudless.

verbs
administer—; apportion—; assign—; bequeath—to; cast—s; deplore—; detail—; dispense—; distribute—s; draw—s; elect by —; embrace—; parcel—; partition—; remedy—; sacrifice—; share—; throw—in with.

LOTION
adjectives
creamy; soothing; cool; pleasant; unguent.

verbs
bathe with—; dilute—; dissolve in—; gargle —; immerse in—; saturate with—; steep in —; vend—; —beautifies; —heals; —perfumes; —purges; —purifies; —refreshes; —repairs; —repels; —soothes.
(See ointment, salve, soap.)

LOUD
adverbs
boisterously; terribly; crashingly; fearfully; impressively; unbelievably; clamorously; deafeningly; tumultuously; infernally; uncommonly; strangely; unnecessarily; unduly; appallingly; shockingly; thunderously; tempestuously; shrilly; objectionably; explosively; unmistakably; insufferably; unbearably.

LOUD-SPEAKER
verbs
boom through—; muffle—; suppress—; thunder through—; —amplifies; —bellows; —blares; —blasts; —deafens; —discharges; —grates; —produces; —shrieks; —startles; muzzle—.
(See bugle, bagpipe, trumpet.)

LOUNGE

verbs

assemble in—; dawdle in—; decorate—; dillydally in—; gather in—; idle in—; loaf in—; loiter in—; loll in—; relax in—; retire to—; saunter into—; skulk in—; slouch in—; —soothes; —swarms.

(See bedroom, room, chair, apartment.)

LOUNGE (v)

adverbs

idly; disconsolately; unambitiously; lasciviously; slothfully; trivially; comfortably; shamelessly; sensually.

(See recline, rest.)

LOUNGERS

adjectives

cultivated; suave; beach; dingy-looking.

LOUT

adjectives

foolish; gross; clumsy; lazy.

LOVABLE

adverbs

entirely; charmingly; delightfully; bewilderingly; bewitchingly; fascinatingly; indescribably; inexpressibly; unusually; uncommonly; tenderly; graciously; sweetly; attractively; engagingly; amiably; enchantingly; captivatingly; irresistibly; genially; heartily; ingratiatingly; adorably.

LOVE

adjectives

abiding; absorbing; abstract; adulterous; all-absorbing; all-discerning; ambitious; animal; animated; approving; ardent; arduous; artless; baffled; barbaric; barefaced; beholding; betrayed; bleeding; blissful; boundless; bounteous; brave; brittle; brotherly; burning; calculating; casual; celestial; changeful; changeless; changing; chasing; childlike; chastising; chivalrous; clandestine; condemned; coerced; comely; common; comprehensive; condescending; confessed; confiding; connubial; consanguine; consenting; consoling; condemned; conventional; corrupt; costly; courtly; cunning; cutting; dear; deathless; debasing; debatable; deep-buried; deepening; deep-rooted; deep-seeing; depraved; descending; despised; despiteful; dire; disgusting; distilling; divine; domestic; duteous; earnest; earthly; eloquent, embittered; emblematic; endearing; enduring; enlightened; ennobl-

ing; enthusiastic; equal; entrancing; erring; everlasting; exacting; exceeding; faddist; faithful; faithless; false; fantastical; fastidious; fathomless; faultless; feigning; fervent; festering; filial; florid; flustered; foolish; forgiving; forgotten; fostering; fraternal; frustrated; genuine; glorified; great; hapless; hard-believing; heavenly; heavy; hereditary; holy; highest; hoarded; hollow; heroic; honest; honor-loving; hopeless; humble; humiliated; hungry; illicit; imagined; immoderate; immortal; immune; impetuous; inborn; inbred; incalculable; inestimable; inexpressible; inextinguishable; inextricable; infinite; instinctive; intense; intellectual; intimate; invincible; irradiating; jealous; languid; lavish; lessening; lifelong; lively; light; limitless; living; long-suffering; lordliest; loveless; loveliest; luminous; manly; masterful; matchless; maternal; meek; melancholy; meritorious; militant; misguided; mother; mutual; mystical; nameless; nascent; newborn; never-wearying; new-found; noble; noiseless; obdurate; obscure; obsequious; one-sided; overmastering; painful; palsied; paltry; pardonable; parental; passionate; pathetic; perennial; persistent; philosophic; physical; pigeon; platonic; potential; pounding; predominating; proffered; primal; profound; prosperous; protecting; provident; public; puerile; pure; purifying; rational; real; reasonable; reassuring; recovering; redeeming; redoubtable; relenting; remorseful; rending; renouncing; repentant; repudiated; responsive; resurgent; reunited; reverent; romantic; sacrificial; satiated; selfish; self-renouncing; sensual; sensuous; sentimental; sham; shamed; shameless; shining; shy; silent; sin-destroying; sinful; sleepless; spiritual; spontaneous; steadfast; stilled; stimulated; stirring; strong; stupendous; sustaining; sweet; sweet-suggesting; tamed; tender; thankful; thoughtful; thwarted; tragic; tranquil; transient; transparent; true; true-confirmed; trusting; truthful; unalterable; unavailing; unbecoming; unbounded; unchanging; unconquerable; undying; unconscious; unexaggerated; unfashionable; unfathomable; unfocused; unfortunate; universal; unlawful; unmanly; unpropitious; unqualified; unquestioned; unreasonable; unregarded; unrelenting; unrequited; unrestful; unreturned; unruly; unsatisfactory; unselfish; unspoken; untaught; unutterable; unvowed; unwed; valiant; vigorous; violent; virtue; virtuous; visionary;

vivacious; vivid; wandering; wanton; warped; wasted; wasteful; weakening; welcoming; well-deserved; well-earned; well-known; well-quitted; willing; wilting; wonder-filling; wondrous; wonted; worst; worthiest; wrenching; wronged; yearning; youthful; zealous.

verbs

abide in—; arm with—; awaken—; cultivate—; enthrone in—; excite—; feign—; fire with—; forsake—; fulfill—; idealize—; inculcate—; instill—; insure—; lavish—upon; overflow with—; overshadow—; pine for—; proffer—; profess—; recapture—; reject—; revive—; ripen into—; scorn—; shatter—; smite with—; strangle—; sublimate—; —anguishes; —burns; —chastens; —dawns upon; —enchains; —endures; —ennobles; —illumines; —inspires; —reigns; —seizes; —smites; —tortures; —vanishes; —wells up; —wounds.

(See passion, tenderness, friendship, affection, devotion, infatuation.)

LOVE (v)

adverbs

irretrievably; immortally; fondly; passionately; instinctively; engrossingly; disinterestedly; possessively; ardently; inordinately; uniquely; jealously; profoundly; devotedly; virtuously; violently; exquisitely; heroically; exclusively; utterly; unrequitedly; illicitly; carnally; steadfastly; mawkishly; abstractly; adulterously; arduously; artlessly; boundlessly; blissfully; celestially; casually; clandestinely; connubially; corruptly; deathlessly; debasingly; fantastically; fastidiously; fathomlessly; feigningly; fervently; festeringly; inexpressibly; languidly; masterfully; parentally; philosophically; physically; zealously; platonically; rationally; romantically; sensually; sensuously; spiritually; spontaneously; sustainingly; transiently; unfathomably; vigilantly.

(See like, admire, adore.)

LOVELINESS

adjectives

solitary; perennial; attractive; boasted; female; soft; budding; informing; surpassing; vernal; uncommon; evanescent; shamed; enchanting; exquisite; ineffable; radiant; virgin; pensive; fragile; lustrous; unnoticed; luminous; chaste; uncultivated; exceeding; passing; twofold; sheer; pristine; inner; genuine; ethereal; breath-taking;

moral; unaccountable; unthrifty; winning; supernal; superb; imperious; sensuous; placid; scattered; petite; tempestuous; modest; incomparable; stately; mild; exalted; opulent; conventional.

verbs

admire—; adorn with—; appreciate—; bloom in—; cultivate—; deface—; devour —; flaunt—; garment in—; glow with—; mar—; praise—; preserve—; sully—; taint —; —charms; —dazzles; —enchants; —endures; —glitters; —haunts; —hypnotizes; —shines; —surpasses.

(See beauty, grace, charm, splendor.)

LOVELY

adverbs

charmingly; adorably; indescribably; utterly; delicately; gracefully; delightfully; absorbingly; artlessly; exquisitely; gently; softly; ineffably; enchantingly; radiantly; breath-takingly; unutterably; sweetly; genuinely; superbly; incomparably; incredibly; completely.

LOVER

adjectives

tender; considerate; laggard; betrothed; melancholy; disconsolate; romantic; passionate; despairing; hot; beseeching; universal; entwined (pl); advanced; weary; ardent; triumphant; meek; changing; newly-plighted; lifelong; patriarchal; listening; whispering; greatest; fond; ethereal; accepted; estranged; impassioned; tragic; redeeming; remorseful; starved; hesitating; loathsome; lowly; memorable; enthusiastic; forsaken; notable; subtle; clinging; faithful; monastic; unhappy; distracted; true; flaming-breasted; truant; sleepless; sempiternal; pattern; fearful; credulous; youthful.

verbs

anger—; deceive—; exact from—; excite—; inflame—; renounce—; reward—; ridicule —; sting—; —beams; —blesses; —capers; —caresses; —desires; —devotes; —dotes upon; —dreams; —frets; —muses; —reflects upon; —repents; —reveres; —s rift; —sacrifices; —sighs; —thirsts; —treasures; —woos; —yearns; —yields.

(See suitor, sweetheart, admirer, friend.)

LOVING

adverbs

ardently; tenderly; exceedingly; excessively; ostentatiously; proudly; fervently; adoringly; idolatrously; infatuatedly; passionately; rapturously; yearningly; wistfully; coquettishly; flirtatiously; excitedly; sweetly; seductively; devotedly.

LOW

adverbs
inconceivably; extremely; abysmally; exceedingly; uncomfortably; peculiarly; mysteriously; alarmingly; curiously; inconveniently; unnecessarily; unduly; impossibly; terribly; disagreeably; unpleasantly.

LOWER (v)

adverbs
mechanically; cautiously; appreciably; materially; economically; charmingly; coyly; tremulously; bestially.
(See reduce, drop, depress, diminish, fall.)

LOWLY

adverbs
childishly; inconceivably; sweetly; humbly; surprisingly; modestly; plainly; humbly; unpretentiously; unaffectedly; marvellously; admirably; wondrously.

LOYAL

adverbs
unaffectedly; genuinely; unquestionably; unimpeachably; sincerely; utterly; undeviatingly; sturdily; stoutly; faithfully; constantly; devotedly; unswervingly; negatively; positively; incredibly; reliably; dependably; steadily; militantly; patriotically; obediently; eagerly; ardently; meticulously; tremendously; utterly; uncommonly; steadfastly.

LOYALTY

adjectives
unswerving; instinctive; recovered; fastidious; stanch; inflexible; unconditional; fresh; religious; willing; unflinching; enthusiastic; savage; indestructible; mistaken; human; habitual; obstinate; fervent; filial; tenacious; intense; racial; quixotic; passionate; clan; true; ardent; alternate; unwavering; devoted; unchanging; affectionate; vaunted; basic; stubborn.

verbs
acknowledge—; attend with—; awaken—; chain by—; command—; discharge with—; exact—; fix—; follow with—; inspire—; overcome—; owe—; pledge—; profess—; protest—; prove—; retain—; reward—;

shift—; stress—; submit with—; sustain—; —ennobles; —flames; —prevails.
(See faithfulness, devotion, love, faith, zeal.)

LUBBERLY

adverbs
heavily; awkwardly; ridiculously; laughably; absurdly; good-naturedly; unmanageably; inconveniently; unfortunately; terribly; lazily; massively; lumpishly.

LUBRICANT

verbs
enlist—; feed—; inject—; react to—; —benefits; —clears; —eases; —facilitates; —frees; —lightens; —nourishes; —promotes; —quickens; —relieves; —smooths; —speeds; —unclogs; —waxes.
(See oil, soap, lather.)

LUBRICATE (v)

adverbs
thoroughly; seasonally; periodically; mechanically; systematically; annually.
(See facilitate.)

LUCID

adverbs
unusually; beautifully; satisfactorily; transparently; clearly; vividly; brilliantly; splendidly; especially; peculiarly; oddly; brightly; curiously; particularly; distinctly; luminously; delightfully; amazingly; astonishingly.

LUCK

adjectives
imaginable; ragged; blundering; unmerited; hard; monumental; good; ill; incredible; unearned; foolish.

verbs
ascribe to—; bemoan—; beset by—; bewail —; deplore—; earn—; encounter—; face —; fall into—; stake on—; trust to—; —attends; —befalls; —chases; —deals; —deserts; —disheartens; —ebbs; —favors; —mocks; —pursues; —singles out; —soars.
(See chance, fortune, risk, misfortune, reverse.)

LUCKLESS

adverbs
wretchedly; miserably; always; consistently; unfortunately; habitually; markedly; notoriously; distinctly; positively; unhap-

pily; conspicuously; disastrously; calamitously; deplorably; lamentably; constantly; altogether; pitiably; dreadfully; uncommonly.

LUCKY

adverbs

always; inexplicably; auspiciously; fortunately; inherently; blessedly; shrewdly; deservedly; adroitly; triumphantly; advantageously; inexpressibly; deucedly; remarkably; surprisingly; inscrutably; notoriously; unaccountably; unwarrantably; mysteriously; strangely; oddly; curiously; immensely; cleverly; admirably; wonderfully; miraculously; marvellously; ingeniously; conveniently; boastfully; surpassingly; accidentally; reasonably; assuredly; casually; incidentally; unexpectedly; blessedly.

LUCRATIVE

adverbs

commendably; admirably; enviably; commercially; happily; duly; naturally; distinctly; definitely; astonishingly; surprisingly; mysteriously; measurably; incalculably; moderately; immensely; tremendously; exceedingly; pleasantly; immoderately; unexpectedly; satisfactorily; profitably; advantageously; curiously; unbelievably.

LUDICROUS

adverbs

immoderately; grotesquely; fantastically; curiously; uproariously; extravagantly; monstrously; whimsically; quaintly; outlandishly; eccentrically; preposterously; drolly; contemptibly; decisively; strangely; irresistibly; inconceivably; amazingly; intensely; unexpectedly; marvellously; inordinately.

LUGUBRIOUS

adverbs

miserably; wretchedly; inconsolably; determinedly; ostentatiously; funereally; gloomily; ridiculously; inordinately; uncommonly; terribly; unbearably; absurdly; unreasonably; pompously; showily; dreadfully; solemnly; demurely; grimly; disconsolately.

LULL (v)

adverbs

deliciously; magically; miraculously; momentarily; intermittently; sweetly; melodiously; maternally; affectionately.

(See hush, subside.)

LULLS

adjectives

reverberate; hopeless; magic; intermittent.

LUMBER (v)

adverbs

ponderously; heavily; monotonously; peacefully; stupidly; phlegmatically; lifelessly; solidly; soddenly; stolidly; passionlessly.

(See move, walk, stagger.)

LUMINARY

adjectives

legal; heavenly; glorious; kindliest.

LUMINOUS

adverbs

brilliantly; gloriously; effulgently; radiantly; splendidly; magnificently; phosphorescently; resplendently; scintillantly; shimmeringly; intermittently; steadily; beautifully; remarkably; intensely; extremely; unusually.

LUMPISH

adverbs

stupidly; dully; awkwardly; stolidly; boorishly; ignorantly; incredibly; remarkably; fantastically; terribly; inertly; drowsily; heavily; listlessly; languidly; lazily.

LUMPS

adjectives

rude; painful; lifeless; restive; solid; phlegmatic; deformed; soft; persistent; translucent; sympathetic; painless; obstinate; helpless; sodden; monstrous.

LUNATIC

adjectives

criminal; privileged; harmless; wild; rough.

adverbs

wildly; unmanageably; ungovernably; violently; absurdly; uproariously; ravingly; frenziedly; drunkenly; deliriously; daftly; fanatically; fantastically; strangely; curiously; unaccountably; irresponsibly; suddenly; frantically; dreadfully.

LUNCH

adjectives

well-balanced; belated; frugal; costly; convivial; substantial; suitable; abundant; half-wrapped; cold.

LUNCH (v)

adverbs

frugally; convivially; substantially; abundantly; swiftly; fraternally; hospitably; gaily; appetizingly; insatiably.

(See eat, dine.)

LUNCHEON

adjectives

grim; enormous; hilarious; sacrilegious; scant; well-attended.

verbs

conclude—; cram in—; design—; digest—; honor at—; indulge in—; savor—; scorn—; tender—; welcome to—; —appeals; —beguiles; —cheers; —contents; —inaugurates; —lubricates; —nourishes; —satisfies; —tempts.

(See supper, dinner, breakfast, meal, food, repast.)

LUNG

adjectives

prodigious; spongy; bursting; choked; skeleton; delicate; iron.

verbs

collapse—; compress—; congest—; deflate —; enter—; envelop—; examine—; infect —; inflate—; perforate—; scar—; solidify —; spot—; traverse—; waste—; —decays; —expands; —heaves; —labors; —retracts; —rots; —shrivels.

(See balloon, chest.)

LURCH (v)

adverbs

drunkenly; crazily; perilously; dizzily; rashly; abruptly; sensually; fatally; comically.

(See stagger, sway, roll.)

LURE

adjectives

constant; obvious; velvet.

verbs

bait—; betray into—; expose to—; follow —; inveigle into—; manoeuvre—; risk—; spread—; succumb to—s; swindle by—; —attracts; —beguiles; —deceives; —deludes; —enchants; —ensnares; —entices; —tempts; —tricks; —victimizes.

(See bait, temptation.)

LURE (v)

adverbs

delusively; obscenely; lustfully; coyly; lasciviously; sexually; sensually; joyously; suavely; wantonly.

(See tempt, attract.)

LURID

adverbs

sensationally; disgracefully; terribly; remarkably; reprehensibly; inordinately; comically; ridiculously; gloomily; dismally; awfully; repulsively; obscurely; deeply; dingily; faintly; ruddily; oddly; strangely; peculiarly.

LURK (v)

adverbs

slyly; obscurely; insidiously; deceptively; treacherously; diabolically; instinctively; viciously; grimly.

(See prowl, steal, stalk.)

LUSCIOUS

adverbs

remarkably; admirably; particularly; delectably; deliciously; pleasantly; attractively; invitingly; agreeably; acceptably; gratefully; daintily; delicately; appetizingly; sweetly; richly; peculiarly; uncommonly; unusually.

LUSH

adverbs

abundantly; luxuriantly; amazingly; unusually; particularly; freshly; refreshingly; remarkably; juicily; marvellously; admirably; attractively.

LUST

adjectives

short-sighted; careless; burning; monstrous; ruffian; healthy; mad; hurtful; amberscented; mute; melancholy; sordid; ignoble; worldly; hellish; alien; decrepit; devilish; unnatural; exceeding; inbred; vile; evercraving; coarse; concupiscible; greedy; fleshy; intemperate; tyrannous; ominous; drunken.

verbs

abhor—; cater to—; cool—· conquer—; couch in—; extinguish—; intoxicate with—; loathe—; melt in—; quench—; resist—; satiate—; sink in—, —blemishes; —burns; —

consumes; —corrupts; —decays; —defiles; —frenzies; —maddens; —massacres; — overthrows; —ruins; —scandalizes.

(See wickedness, sin, abomination, iniquity.)

LUST (v)

adverbs
obscenely; insatiably; devilishly; ceaselessly; monstrously; madly; mutely; sordidly; ignobly; unnaturally; vilely; pervertedly; concupiscibly; intemperately; intoxicatedly; ominously.

(See desire, long.)

LUSTER

adjectives
joyless; exceeding; collective; dazzling; sparkling; added; undiminished; feeble; refreshing; smooth; vitreous; glossy; dull; intolerable; classic; freshening; full; subdued; feverish; transient, ethereal, brilliant; iridescent; penetrating; timid; ancient; soft; purer; growing; spectral; hoary; starry; nebulous; pearly; antique; welcome; sulphurous; natural; hungry; original.

LUSTY

adverbs
remarkably; robustly; vigorously; unusually; enviably; sturdily; exceptionally; extraordinarily; amazingly; notoriously; dependably; luckily; fortunately; incredibly; surprisingly.

LUTE

adjectives
short-stringed; warbling; enfeebling; fragile; long-neglected; ravishing.

LUXURIANCE

adjectives
tropical; unchanged; prodigal; rank; wild.

verbs
abate—; attire in—; burst forth in—; cushion in—; display in—; feed on—; indulge in—; prune—; ransack—; soak in—; surrender to—; taste—; wallow in—; —diffuses; —enslaves; —entices; —flourishes; —inebriates; —overwhelms.

(See wealth, luxury.)

LUXURIANT

adverbs
abundantly; unusually: tropically; amazing-

ly; uncommonly; exceptionally; unbelievably; naturally; surprisingly; profitably;. amply; satisfactorily; richly; incalculably; advantageously; opportunely.

LUXURIATE (v)

adverbs
blissfully; joyously; exaggeratedly; carnally; sentimentally; drunkenly; wantonly; profanely; riotously; boastfully.

(See lavish, bestow.)

LUXURIOUS

adverbs
delightfully; pleasantly; agreeably; actually; unexpectedly; amazingly; indescribably; unconscionably; inordinately; extravagantly; gratifyingly; comfortably; refreshingly; enjoyably; enchantingly; cheerfully; blissfully; extraordinarily; incredibly; elaborately; expensively; gorgeously; happily.

LUXURY

adjectives
refined; lapping; useless; unfailing; sublime; elaborate; costly; leafy; swinish; expensive; voluptuous; hateful; sordid; manly; easy; light; innocent; prejudicial; incommunicable; colossal; subtle; multiform; unusual; gorgeous; invalid; higher-priced; rare; harmless; accustomed; profuse; wanton; superfluous; unequaled; almost-forgotten; cramping; attendant; sleek; pagan; indecent; unnecessary; sensual; idle; unobtrusive; quiet; secluded; modern.

verbs
afford—; bless with—; contemplate—; couch in—; crave—; diffuse—; dispense with—; intoxicate with—; lack—; loll in—; nurse in —; pamper with—; revel in—; steal—; swathe in—; thirst for—; —cushions; — hinders.

(See luxuriance, wealth.)

LYMPH

adjectives
pellucid; transparent; lava.

verbs
absorb by—; discharge—; dissolve in—; extract—; exude—; inject in—; secrete—; —

assimilates; —attenuates; —coagulates; —deteriorates; —dilutes; —escapes; —flows; —percolates; —streams.

LYNCH (v)

adverbs

madly; ferociously; bestially; insanely; swiftly; horrifyingly; sadistically; heartlessly; cruelly; tigerishly.

(See kill, murder, hang, punish.)

LYRE

adjectives

slumberous; sparkling; sweet-toned; tuneful; darling; lascivious.

LYRICAL

adverbs

sweetly; smoothly; tunefully; fluently; unusually; completely; utterly; curiously; softly; gently; clearly; enchantingly; fascinatingly; euphoniously; pleasantly; agreeably; roughly; perfectly; crudely; correctly; harmoniously; remarkably; magnificently; splendidly.

LYRICS

adjectives

poignant; rural; conventional; occasional; studied; dramatic; satirical; infrequent; sentimental.

M

MACHIAVELLIAN

adverbs

shrewdly; craftily; unbelievably; astutely; wickedly; colossally; designingly; subtly; arrantly; dreadfully; archly; crookedly; evasively; viciously; dangerously; alarmingly; curiously; fearfully; insidiously; nefariously; invidiously; profoundly; cleverly; notoriously; deceptively; heinously.

MACHINATE (v)

adverbs

diabolically; politically; unscrupulously; subtly; insidiously; perfidiously; treacherously; ambitiously.

(See plot, scheme.)

MACHINATIONS

adjectives

sublime; subtlest; insidious; political; perfidious.

MACHINE

adjectives

unmoral; cosmic; efficient; propaganda; specialized; vending; merciless; infernal; admirable; memorial; vast; fantastic; protected; ponderous; domestic; cranky; undependable; ill-omened; senseless; electrical; slow; expensive; leased; extraordinary; radical; omnipresent; colossal.

verbs

abolish—; clog—; construct—; control—; demonstrate—; exalt—; fuel—; humanize —; install—; lubricate—; master—; meter —; putter with—; sublimate—; subordinate —; tamper with—; tinker with—; transmute —; worship—; —accommodates; —clicks; —enslaves; —functions; —roars; —rumbles; —stamps.

(See engine, apparatus, instrument, drill, elevator, generator, dynamo, mechanism.)

MACHINE-GUN

verbs

nest—; place—; set up—; —bellows; — blasts; —chatters; —deafens; —drums; — fulminates; —mows down; —mutters; — rakes; —raps; —rat-tat-tats; —rends; —

retaliates; —reverberates; —rolls; —spatters; —tattoos; —yammers (colloq.); — crackles.

(See gun, cannon, pistol, revolver, rifle.)

MACHINERY

adjectives

physical; warlike; experimental; elaborate; agricultural; complicated; economical; tireless; arbitration; internal; domestic; suspended; educational; cumbrous; subtle; stupendous; disinterested; specialized; budgetary; commonplace; dread; multiplied; comprehensive; unified; irrigating; newfangled.

MAD

adverbs

incoherently; fanatically; hopelessly; incurably; pathetically; violently; distractedly; bewilderedly; frantically; insanely; suddenly; periodically; hysterically; wildly; tragically; irrecoverably; irremediably.

MADMAN

verbs

arouse—; chain—; coddle—; confine—; cudgel—; enchain—; enkindle—; fetter—; harness—; immure—; imprison—; incarcerate —; infuriate—; isolate—; liberate—; manacle—; overpower—; perturb—; pinion—; pique—; restrain—; shackle—; subdue—; yoke—; —dotes; —drivels; —flames; — foams; —fumes; —gibbers; —leers; — rages; —rambles; —raves; —scowls.

(See fool, idiot.)

MADNESS

adjectives

feigned; apparent; inexplicable; amorous; sweet; mingled; incipient; mysterious; strange; mob; tender; autumnal; supernatural; solemn; studied; sacred; solitary; cruel; voluntary; midsummer; centrifugal; harmonious; moody; utter; suicidal; decided; sad; merry; drunken.

verbs

cloud with—; feign—; ramble in—; rave in —; —aberrates; —afflicts; —deranges; — diseases; —disorders; —embroils; —infects;

—invalidates; —possesses; —ravages; —seizes; —shatters; —taints; —unbalances; —undermines; —warps.

(See frenzy, insanity, stupidity, delirium, hysteria, mania.)

MAELSTROM
verbs
circumvent—; sweep into—; —agitates; —boils; —buffets —churns; —circulates; —drenches; —flings; —foams; —gyrates; —jets; —revolves; —rolls; —spouts; —threatens; —trundles; —whirls.

(See whirlpool, rain, river, turmoil, torrent, waves.)

MAGAZINE
adjectives
short-lived; humorous; independent; reputable; liberal; entertaining; lively; all-around; popular; foremost; smart; fast-growing; up-to-date; progressive; incipient; sectarian; well-storied; short-story.

verbs
censor—; contribute to—; dip into—; disseminate—s; extol—; glean from—; hawk —s; launch—; linotype—; peruse—; rack —s; sanction—; scan—; set up—; —accounts; —blazes; —chronicles; —circulates; —condenses; —delineates; —depicts; —digests; —polls; —promulgates; —records; —reports; —reviews; —summarizes; —supports.

(See literature, newspaper, press, publication, book, story, volume.)

MAGIC
adjectives
supernatural; practised; foul; peculiar; curative; traditional; subtle; powerful; sheer; wild; all-subduing; aimless; lush.

verbs
conjure up by—; contrive—; exercise—; influence by—; practise—; reek of—; skill in —; —bedevils; —bewitches; —casts spells; —divines; —enchants; —exorcises; —fascinates; —forecasts; —foretells.

(See incantation, trick, miracle, manipulation.)

MAGIC
adverbs
bewilderingly; occultly; cleverly; subtly; amazingly; undeniably; wondrously; miraculously; curiously; strangely; unbelievably; wickedly; ascendan ly; weirdly; cabalistically; mystically; mysteriously; slyly; obviously; presumably.

MAGISTERIAL
adverbs
officiously; ostentatiously; authoritatively; arrogantly; superciliously; offensively; vexatiously; sternly; severely; harshly; cruelly; tyrannically; rigidly; unnecessarily; ridiculously; absurdly; gravely; solemnly; droningly; coldly; strictly; intolerably; overbearingly; imperiously; pretentiously; stiffly; magnificently; ceremoniously; arbitrarily.

MAGISTRATE
adjectives
unmeriting; proud; violent; teasing; lawful; principal; inferior; directing; venal; elective; civil; presiding; stipendiary.

verbs
commit to—; impeach—; plead with—; vest in—; —acquits; —administers; —arbitrates; —arraigns; —assigns; —authorizes; —commands; —concedes; —deprives; —determines; —dispenses; —empowers; —exempts; —exonerates; —grants; —judges; —pronounces; —prosecutes; —restrains; —reviews; —sanctions; —sentences; —summons.

(See judge, consul, legislator, governor, president.)

MAGNANIMITY
adjectives
delicate; unbounded; peaceable; critical; rough; splendid; unlimited.

MAGNANIMOUS
adverbs
unusually; dependably; conspicuously; wonderfully; remarkably; unexpectedly; surprisingly; delightfully; beneficently; magnificently; utterly; habitually; unwontedly; unselfishly; generally; loftily; chivalrously; admirably; generously.

MAGNETIC
adverbs
highly; strongly; amazingly; surprisingly; delightfully; attractively; charmingly; unusually; powerfully; potently; preponderantly; influentially; persuasively; temptingly; irresistibly; unaccountably; immensely; extremely; remarkably.

MAGNETISM

adjectives
permanent; terrestrial; animal; proudest; universal.

MAGNIFICENCE

adjectives
mournful; profuse; calculated; theatrical; oriental; solid; fancied; barbaric; gorgeous; stern; multiplied; tawdry; ephemeral; pristine; unquestionable; snowy; lavish; incredible; wide-spread; somber.

MAGNIFICENT

adverbs
splendidly; gorgeously; grandly; sumptuously; brilliantly; gaudily; regally; extraordinarily; remarkably; marvelously; ceremonially; majestically; pompously; formally; highly; unspeakably; beautifully; elegantly; overwhelmingly; stupendously; colossally; resplendently; richly; imposingly; sublimely; matchlessly; impressively.

MAGNIFY (*v*)

adverbs
stereoptically; enormously; stupendously; gloriously; theatrically; barbarically; audaciously; scientifically; mechanically; prodigiously.
(See enlarge, exaggerate, augment.)

MAGNITUDE

adjectives
enhanced; prodigious; audacious; infinite; imposing; sensible; intermediate; considerable; swelling.

verbs
amplify—; comprehend—; extend—; heighten—; limit—; reduce—; restrict—; swell to —; —abates; —diminishes; —soars.
(See dimension, extent, greatness, measurements.)

MAGPIE

verbs
molest—; persecute—; tame—; —amuses; —chatters; —cheeps; —scolds; —shies; — steals; —talks; —thieves.
(See bird.)

MAHOGANY

adjectives
massive; rich; heavy; clumsy.

MAID

adjectives
unwilling; thoughtless; imprudent; poor; lowly; sentimental; lovelorn; wronged; meek; graceful; chariest; expiring; cleaner; sun-swart; deflowered; wretched; deceitful; sprightly, dark-tressed; loud-screaming; ungrateful; uncommon; guileless; kind; virtuous; fasting; blooming; lurking; milking; volatile; butterfly; kittenish; old; heavenly; stainless; recreant; pretty; chaste; simple; buskined; confiding; serving; stately; pale; impassioned; virginal; orphaned; fair; cruel; careless.

MAIDEN

adjectives
modest; guileless; simple; barefoot; dimpled; timid; white-veiled; sainted; homekeeping; cherry-cheeked; rosy-lipped; burlesque; gleeful; toddling; pastoral; dejected; snow; movie-mad; timid; willful; loosegirdled; affectionate; hapless; orbed; pale; avaricious; virtuous; rigid; decked; broadbacked; unfortunate; bright-eyed; enamored.

MAIDENHOOD

adjectives
delectable; stainless; frank; lean; profaned; blooming.

MAIDENLY

adverbs
demurely; coyly; sedately; shyly; decorously; becomingly; modestly; blushingly; rosily; suitably; properly; sweetly; graciously; conventionally; attractively; quietly; serenely; bashfully; appropriately.

MAIL

adjectives
glittering; ubiquitous; outgoing; departed; brisk.

verbs
assemble—; bag—; bear—; certify—; classify—; collect—; communicate by—; consign to—; convey—; defraud by—; distribute—; flood—; fly—; insure—; loot—; plunder—; register—; rifle—; transmit by—.
(See message.)

adjectives

troubled; unfathomable; whitening; infinite; boundless; molten; azure; pulseless; tideless; billowed; murmuring; immeasurable; moaning.

MAINTAIN (v)

adverbs

stubbornly; willfully; inexorably; unreservedly; automatically; gallantly; scrupulously; peremptorily; diabolically; resolutely; unblushingly; stoutly; intensely; ignorantly; vigorously; inflexibly; normally; agreeablv; perpetually; progressively; jealously; adequately.

(See claim, sustain, support, affirm.)

MAINTENANCE

adjectives

continued; scanty; perpetual; fitting; progressive; standing; adequate; jealous.

MAIZE

adjectives

tall; spiky; twinkling; sun-loving; ripening; towering; tasseled.

MAJESTIC

adverbs

splendidly; gloriously; brilliantly; imposingly; solemnly; ceremonially; augustly; sublimely; impressively; grandly; formally; pompously; superbly; imperially; loftily; sumptuously; gorgeously.

MAJESTY

adjectives

essential; ghostlike; wonted; collective; impressive; angered; sluggard; unfamiliar; sheer; serene; characteristic; conscious; outraged; awful; singular; tranquil; dreadful; comparable; gentle; vigorous; tropical; sweet; rare; commanding; overshadowing; apparent; unspeakable; glittering; unascended; inaccessible; colossal; shadowy; mutilated; certain; dispelled; clouded; unshakable; rayless; ineffable; grotesque; ethereal; swarthy; dramatic; imperious; pastoral; sublime; somber.

MAJORITY

adjectives

overwhelming; popular; hostile; legislative; phenomenal; vast; handsome; compact; emphatic; bare; preponderant; ignorant; enlarged.

MAIN

verbs

attain—; bow to—; endow witn—; gain—; increase—; pile up—; poll—; purchase—; reach—; render—; sway—; swell—; —balances; —carries; —determines; —exceeds; —overtops; —overwhelms; —predominates, —prevails; —surpasses.

(See generality, age, minority, multitude, throng, crowd.)

MAKE (v)

adverbs

powerfully; eventually; inevitably; ultimately; unquestionably; crudely; obviously; inadvertently; advisedly; persistently; unwittingly; unhesitatingly; temporarily; subsequently; superbly; indiscriminately; laboriously; lawfully; delicately; scientifically.

(See create, compose, invent, manufacture.)

MAKESHIFT

adverbs

cleverly; ingeniously; obviously; carelessly; shiftlessly; adroitly; permanently; clumsily; awkwardly; evidently; dexterously; smartly; handily; pitifully; crudely; presumably; miserably; wretchedly; comically; suitably.

MAKE-UP

verbs

apply—; blanch under—; disguise with—; renew—; represent by—; strip of—; —ages; —alters; —clogs; —colors; —embellishes; —ornaments; —smudges; —tones.

(See paint, color, disguise, mask, pose, pretense, sham.)

MALADIES

adjectives

putrid; incurable; terrible; relievable; organic; infinite; still-clinging; kindred; mortal; deadly; grievous; past-cure; corporeal; painful; expensive; pestiferous; reparable.

MALADJUSTMENT

adjectives

serious; temperamental; deep-seated.

MALADROIT

adverbs

absurdly; unexpectedly; ridiculously; laughably; comically; ludicrously; surprisingly; inexpertly; clumsily; awkwardly; shyly; bashfully; deliberately; purposely; intentionally; helplessly; pitiably; miserably; wretchedly; hopelessly; oddly; stupidly; obtusely; gawkily; embarrassingly; shockingly; uselessly.

MALADY
verbs
afflict with—; aggravate—; allay—; arrest —; communicate—; contract—; control—; diagnose—; eradicate—; expose to—; immunize against—; infest with—; inherit—; isolate—; recognize—; succumb to—; withstand—; —consumes; —lingers; —menaces; —prostrates; —reasserts itself.

(See ailment, disease, infection, illness, sickness.)

MALE
adjectives
monstrous; inexhaustible; art-shy; dominant; rival; smug.

verbs
attract—; lure—; —begets; —fertilizes; — fructifies; —fuses; —generates; —husbands; —implants; —impregnates; —incorporates; —infuses; —preserves; —procreates; — propagates; —sires; —unifies.

(See parent, father.)

MALEDICTION
adjectives
profane; patting; bitter; hearty; muffled.

verbs
address with—s; bluster—; call down—; fulminate—; invoke—; thunder—; utter—; —abuses; —anathematizes; —clamors; — curses; —denounces; —execrates; —scolds; —threatens.

(See curse, slander, denunciation.)

MALEVOLENT
adverbs
viciously; vengefully; savagely; terribly; brutally; sternly; harshly; incredibly; mercilessly; relentlessly; ruthlessly; unspeakably; desperately; villainously; alarmingly; dangerously; notoriously; infamously; criminally; actively; nefariously; inordinately; utterly; incurably; inescapably; heinously; dreadfully; rancorously; spitefully; barbarously; bitterly.

MALICE
adjectives
burning; insane; fairy; devilish; venomous;

ancient; fiendish; sportful; serpent; deepest; diabolical; ingenious; crafty; partisan; womanly; warm; dancing; genial; cold-blooded; ferocious.

verbs
bear—; betray—; breed—; excite—; express —; harbor—; impel to—; impute to—; incite—; intend—; provoke—; recoil from—; regard with—; rile to—; sense—; shudder at—; sow—; tinge with—; view with—; wreak—upon; —embitters; —harasses; — hardens; —harries; —molests; —ripens.

(See bitterness, grudge, ill will, envy, anger, rage, violence, wrath.)

MALICIOUS
adverbs
flagrantly; dangerously; violently; irretrievably; inconceivably; poisonously; abominably; accursedly; perniciously; viciously; basely; deplorably; diabolically; disastrously; dreadfully; exceptionally; grievously; hatefully; venomously; violently; manifestly; subtly; irremediably; irrevocably; immeasurably; villainously; sadly; woefully; shockingly; cruelly; infernally; atrociously; incredibly; shamefully; iniquitously.

MALIGN
adverbs
ominously; portentously; dangerously; undeniably; disastrously; calamitously; ruinously; venomously; poisonously; treacherously; ruthlessly; relentlessly; slanderously; incredibly.

MALIGNANT
adverbs
openly; deliberately; studiously; hatefully; curiously; incorrigibly; evilly; desperately; outrageously; cruelly; bitterly; harshly; venomously; truculently; atrociously; dangerously; poisonously; abominably; perniciously; disastrously; exceptionally; grievously; subtly; sadly; woefully; shockingly; infernally.

MALIGNITY
adjectives
impure; incredible; factious; fiendish; drunken; elaborate; devilish.

MAMMALS
adjectives
branch-building; aquatic; ungulate.

MAMMOTH

adverbs

colossally; gigantically; incredibly; unbelievably; inconceivably; immeasurably; monstrously; incalculably; mythically; stupendously; toweringly; overwhelmingly.

MAN

adjectives

able; acclaimed; alert; ambitious; amiable; anile; arbitrary; armed; austere; available; avaricious; bad; bald; bearded; beetle-browed; bemused; benevolent; benighted; bibulous; big-waisted; bizarre; blind; bloody; boastful; bony; boorish; boyish-looking; brawny; brilliant; broken; broken-hearted; burly; business; cadaverous; cannon-voiced; carefree; careful; carnal; celebrated; charming; chipper; coming; commercial; compassionate; completed; condemned; conscientious; contemplative; corpulent; corruptible; cultivated; cumbersome; cunning; cynical; dapper; dauntless; deathless; decorous; defeated; deep-dimpled; difficult; dilatory; disappointed; disengaged; disinterested; dissipated; double-chinned; dull; dumb; dusky; dynamic; easy-going; eccentric; effeminate; egotistic; elemental; eloquent; emancipated; embarrassed; energetic; enterprising; entertaining; envious; envisaging; estimable; exact; excellent; exceptional; exemplary; experienced; fair-haired; family; famous; fat; fierce; fine-looking; fine-shaped; firm; fit; flaunting; florid; formidable; fractious; frail; frivolous; frustrated; full; full-rigged; function-free; fussy; gallant; general; genial; godless; gossiping; graceless; great-hearted; gregarious; half-naked; handicraft; hard-fisted; hard-working; hawk-headed; headless; heavy-built; heroic; highbred; hoary; homely; honest; hooked-nose; hospitable; hot-tempered; huge; human; humorous; hungry; husky; idle; ill-instructed; ill-natured; illustrious; imperious; impertinent; impious; incomparable; incredible; incurious; indefatigable; indispensable; industrious; influential; informed; ingrateful; inner; inscrutable; intemperate; intrepid; irate; isolated; jolly; jovial; key; kind; knowing; lank; large; lawless; lean; lettered; literary; little; lonely; lovable; magnificent; magnified; married; masterless; mediocre; meditative; meek; merciful; merry; middle-aged; mild-appearing; mild-mannered; mincing; moaning; modest; much-experienced; mustached; myopic; myriad-

wrinkled; mysterious; narrow-minded; new-married; niggardly; noble; obstinate; olive-skinned; omnivorous; overconfident; over-sexed; pallid; pampered; patriarchal; petrified; phenomenal; plain-spoken; phlegmatic; plighted; politic; poorly-dressed; pragmatical; premature; primitive; prominent; proper; propertied; prospering; prudent; pushing; puzzled; quiet; rapid-fire; rational; ready; red-eyed; reflective; repentant; reticent; rich; riddled; rising; rough-looking; round; ruthless; sad; sane; saturnine; savage; seafaring; selfish; self-helping; self-isolated; self-made; self-poised; sensitive; sensual; sharp-eyed; sharp-witted; shock-headed; silent; silly; simple-minded; sinful; sleek; sleight-of-hand; smoking; sober; society; soft-voiced; sound; spoiled; spotted; square-set; squat-figured; staunch; steel-sinewed; stocky; strange; strange-voiced; stray; studious; successful; sullen; sunburned; superior; supple; sure-poised; sweaty; taciturn; talented; tempestuous; tender-hearted; toothless; tormented; ugly; unabashed; unabsolved; unadaptable; unbookish; unbreakable; unburied; uncompanionable; unfortunate; ungrateful; universal; unlettered; unquestioning; unrepentant; unrevolving; untidy; untutored; upright; useless; wayfaring; well-conditioned; wealthy; well-informed; well-proportioned; whimsical; witless; wind-swept; wiry; wise; worthy; vague; wretched; vain; vigorous; virtuous; yellow-visaged; voluptuous; youthful.

MANACLE

adjectives

mortal; menacing; hampering.

verbs

bind with—; clamp on—; don—; fetter with —; forge—; —bridles; —checks; —confines; —constrains; —controls; —curbs; —handcuffs; —prohibits; —restrains; —restricts; —secures; —shackles; —tethers.

(See fetter, restraint.)

MANAGE (v)

adverbs

economically; dexterously; effectively; humanely; judiciously; exclusively; bunglingly; artistically; ingeniously; peremptorily; governmentally; politically; systematically; conservatively; prudently; profitably; incompetently; adroitly; admirably.

(See conduct, supervise, administer, handle.)

adverbs

easily; smoothly; carefully; thriftily; commercially; financially; scarcely; altogether; strategically; subtly; strangely; readily; diplomatically; unexpectedly; quietly; tractably; tactfully.

MANAGEMENT

adjectives

municipal; marvelous; topsy-turvy; duped; frightened; conservative; generous; consolidated; wise; dietary; bungling; systematic; operative; prudent; profitable; admirable; good; adroit; clumsy; wasteful; incompetent; group; capable; vigorous.

verbs

acquire—; administer—; charge with—; conduct—; contrive—; control—; decry—; demean—; denounce—; direct—; enact—; guide—; manipulate—; master—; qualify for—; shift—; skill in—; superintend—; —negotiates; —transacts.

(See direction, government, economy, conduct, charge, legislature, owner, manager.)

MANAGER

adjectives

dexterous; peremptory; unyielding; operatic.

verbs

install—; —directs; —governs; —heads; —helms; —inspects; —orders; —oversees; —pilots; —regulates; —steers; —superintends; —supervises; —surveys; —threatens.

(See boss, industrialist, employer, superintendent, leader, management, owner.)

MANDATE

adjectives

constitutional; official; illegal; tragic; scholastic; royal; titular.

verbs

cite—; comply with—; enact—; issue—; lay down—; prescribe—; remand—; seal—; yield to—; —appoints; —bids; —commands; —controls; —decrees; —deposes; —directs; —dictates; —enjoins; —imposes; —ordains; —proclaims; —summons; —orders.

(See law, measure, decree, edict, command, warrant, regulation, ordinance, order, summons.)

adjectives

flowing; tossing; dripping; luxuriant; braided; hanging; illimitable; plaited; leonine; sudden; flaring.

verbs

brush—; corrugate—; crumple—; gnarl—; knot—; roughen—; ruffle—; rumple—; seize by—; stroke—; toss back—; —adorns; —crests; —droops; —erects; —flows; —fringes; —ripples; —shags.

(See hair, mustache, whiskers, plumage, beard.)

MANEUVER

adjectives

adroit; loving; little; ingenious; thrilling; sordid; political; important; inexplicable; pernicious; odious; shabby; perfunctory; legal; sensational; innocent; dishonest; decisive; skillful; polished; ticklish; ladylike; bold; engineering; intricate.

verbs

achieve—; circumvent—; commit—; contrive—; design—; detail—; enact—; evolve —; execute—; expedite—; organize—; outline—; participate in—; perform—; perpetrate—; practise—; project—; propose—; sanction—; systematize—; transact—; —conceals; —juggles; —temporizes.

(See method, strategy, tactics, subterfuge, trick, move.)

MANEUVER (v)

adverbs

skillfully; adroitly; ingeniously; thrillingly; dexterously; perfunctorily; legally; sensationally; decisively; diplomatically; boldly; rashly; daringly; intricately.

(See plan, scheme.)

MANFUL

adverbs

boldly; bravely; confidently; courageously; firmly; gallantly; hardily; intrepidly; sturdily; pluckily; resolutely; spunkily; valorously; nobly; honorably; virtuously; dauntlessly; splendidly; indomitably; stoutly; venturesomely; venturously; admirably.

MANGLE (v)

adverbs

hideously; shamefully; murderously; ruthlessly; savagely; bestially; brutishly; insanely; stupidly; outrageously; sordidly; perniciously.

(See torture, tear.)

MANHOOD

adjectives

generous; neglected; ripe; moral; sober; prosperous; blasted; pitiless; riper; stormy; toilworn; debonair; relentless; martial; remorseless; civilized; sturdy; vigorous; returning.

MANIA

adjectives

sad; dreadful; melancholy; fantastic; undoubted; infernal.

verbs

amount to—; control—; obsess with—; —abates; —attacks; —crazes; —deludes; —deranges; —enthuses (colloq.); —excites; —fades; —impassions; —rages; —wanes.

(See madness, insanity, frenzy, hysteria, delirium.)

MANIAC

adjectives

religious; raving; fettered; gesticulating; fugitive.

verbs

arouse—; chain—; confine—; enchain—; fetter—; harness—; imprison—; incarcerate—; isolate—; liberate—; overpower—; restrain—; shackle—; subdue—; —flames; —foams; —fumes; —howls; —leers; —rages; —rambles; —raves; —scowls.

(See madman.)

MANIFEST

adverbs

unwisely; conspicuously; demonstrably; distinctly; explicitly; boldly; strikingly; publicly; fortunately; unluckily; brazenly; shamefully; pitifully; alarmingly; fearfully; clearly; glaringly; plainly.

MANIFEST (v)

adverbs

obscurely; plainly; vividly; predominantly; broadly; speciously; exclusively; strenuously; universally; frankly; ingenuously; externally; exaggeratedly; conspicuously; whimsically; outwardly; directly; morbidly; physically.

(See reveal, show.)

MANIFESTATION

adjectives

incipient; exaggerated; contemporaneous; external; remarkable; terrestrial; temporary; visible; startling; conspicuous; moderate; astounding; fiery; impolitic; practical; imperial; special; whimsical; extraordinary; outward; historical; tawdry; distinct; decrepit; amplified; direct; recorded; morbid; external; troublesome; extravagant; physical.

verbs

discourage—; overshadow—; ponder—; render—; suppress—; —alludes to; —attests; —bears out; —conveys; —discloses; —evidences; —expresses; —implies; —indicates; —proves; —purports; —reveals; —signifies; —suggests; —symbolizes.

(See indication, evidence, display, disclosure, demonstration.)

MANIKIN

verbs

drape on—; photograph—; view—; —demonstrates; —depicts; —displays; —exhibits; —illustrates; —imitates; —impersonates; —mimics; —models; —parades; —personifies; —projects; —represents.

(Seee model.)

MANIPULATE (v)

adverbs

delicately; deceptively; dexterously; mysteriously; tactfully; secretly; adroitly; technically; surgically; automatically; mechanically; conservatively; deftly.

(See operate, handle.)

MANIPULATION

adjectives

secret; delicate; adroit; technical; surgical; mechanical; automatic; localized; conservative; deft.

verbs

absorb in—; admire—; circumvent—; contrive—; disparage--; employ—; execute—; necessitate—; observe—; practise—; refrain from—; resort to—; skill in—; transact—; —exercises; —stimulates.

(See magic, strategy, trick, mischief, management, treatment.)

adjectives

menaced; married; miserable; unregenerate; redeemed; beauteous.

verbs

admonish—; apprize—; beguile—; benefit—; confer on—; edify—; enlighten—; humanize—; immortalize—; judge—; liberate—; present to—; raise—; trace—; —achieves; —deifies; —evolves; —progresses; —wars on; —worships.

(See civilization, world, family, population, race, society.)

MANLINESS

adjectives

ancient; rugged; ripening; native; barbarous.

MANLY

adverbs

boldly; sturdily; admirably; wonderfully; stoutly; robustly; courageously; valiantly; gallantly; pluckily; resolutely; confidently; adventurously; heroically; fiercely; staunchly; candidly; splendidly.

MANNA

adjectives

animal; celestial; hidden; unexpected; heavenly.

MANNER

adjectives

absorbing; abstracted; acceptable; accessible; accustomed; acquiesced; affable; affectionate; aggressive; agitated; aimless; alarming; altered; ambiguous; amicable; amplest; apologetic; appropriate; approved; argumentative; aristocratic; arrogant; artificial; artist-like; assuming; astonishing; attitudinizing; authoritative; awkward; bantering; barbarous; base; bizarre; blackguardly; bland; bookish; boyish; brotherly; brusque; brutal; buoyant; burlesque; businesslike; calm; candid; casual; caustic; cautious; charming; chatty; cheap; chilling; circuitous; classical; clerkly; cogitating; collected; commodious; compendious; complacent; comprehended; confidential; connected; consummate; continuous; conventional; coquettish; cordial; corporate; correct; correctional; courteous; courtly; cowardly; creditable; crushing; cunning; customary; dainty; dazzling; debonair; deceptive; deferential; defying; delicate; delightful; depraved; deranged; derisive; derivative; despiteful; desultory; detached; dictatorial; different; diffident; dignified; discovered; discreditable; disdainful; disillusioned; disagreeable; derogatory; disquieting; distinctive; distressful; dreadful; earnest; elegant; embarrassed; enchained; enchanted; endearing; engaging; engrossed; entertaining; enviable; erratic; exasperating; exceptional; exhaustive; expressive; extraordinary; fantastic; fawning; festive; filial; finished; formal; forthright; frank; friendly; frugal; gallant; gentle; glaring; gleeful; greedy; guilty; guileless; gross; haphazard; harmonious; haughty; hearty; heavy; heedless; heroic; hideous; hospitable; hurried; identical; illiberal; imitating; immortal; impatient; impeccable; imperfect; imperturbable; imploring; incomparable; incomprehensive; incongruous; independent; indescribable; indispensable; indolent; inexplicable; ingenious; ingratiating; inimitable; insinuating; insolent; insulting; interesting; intimate; intolerant; intricate; invidious; invincible; irreproachable; irreverent; irritated; joyless; kind; kingly; lamblike; languid; laughing; lawabiding; legitimate; lethargic; lifelike; loathed; longing; ludicrous; maidenly; majestic; manufactured; masonic; masterful; meek; meditative; metaphorical; methodic; modern; modest; monotonous; muffled; musing; native; negligent; obsessive; obstinate; odd; offensive; orderly; ordinary; orthodox; outrageous; particular; overbearing; patronizing; peerless; peculiar; perfunctory; persuasive; pert; pettish; picaresque; piquant; piteous; plausible; poetic; polished; polite; pompous; positive; pragmatic; precise; premature; prepossessing; priestlike; profitless; promiscuous; proper; propitiatory; prosy; protesting; provoking; punctilious; quiet; rational; rattling; realistic; reasonable; reckless; refreshing; reluctant; repulsive; respectable; rough; roundabout; rustic; ruthless; satisfactory; saucy; savage; self-reliant; selfsame; sensational; sententious; sentimental; serene; shoddy; signal; silken; similar; simplified; simulated; sketchy; soft; slovenly; social; solemn; spectacular; spurious; stainless; suave; sublime; substantial; suitable; summary; sumptuous; supercilious; superficial; superlative; systematic; tactful; tender; terrifying; theoretical; thoughtful; touching; two-fold; triumphant; tumultuous; typical; unaccountable; unaffected; unassuming; uncompromising; undemonstrative; undiscriminating; un-disguised; unemotional; unenthusiastic; un-even; uneventful; unforgettable; ungrac-ious; unique; unmistakable; unobtrusive; unofficial; unostentatious; unprecedented; unpremeditated; unprincipled; unprofitable; unreserved; unsightly; unswerving; un-usual; unwavering; uproarious; urbane; warning; warring; wholesome; winning; vivacious; youthful; laughable.

verbs

affect—; acquire—; adopt—; ape—; corrupt —s; embolden—; evolve—; flaunt—s; in-culcate—s; modify—; recover—; revitalize —; revolt against—s; tolerate—; transform —; —bullies; —cools; —enrages; —s root in; —shocks; adapt—.

(See behavior, air, method, style, manner-ism, vogue, mode, mien, means.)

MANNERISM
adjectives
inscrutable; developing; humiliating; mus-ical; romantic; severe; compulsive; obstrep-erous.

verbs
abandon—; accentuate—; addict to—; affect —; caricaturize—; conventionalize—; en-dow with—; fall into—; inherit—; jeer at —; mimic—; mock—; ridicule—; satirize —; sustain—; —dandifies; —exemplifies; —individualizes; —simpers.

(See manner, eccentricity, style, method.)

MANNERLY
adverbs
inherently; naturally; carefully; beautifully; pleasantly; agreeably; studiously; unaffect-ed|y; ostentatiously; always; scarcely; bare-ly; urbanely; suavely; smoothly; affably; gallantly; chivalrously; obsequiously; re-spectfully; humbly; unctuously; blandly; gracious|y; genially; heartily; modestly; quietly; unfailingly; ceremoniously.

MANNIKIN
adjectives
flesh-hinged; mortal; god-driven; mechanic.

MANSION
adjectives
cheerless; mossy; determinate; ostentatious; commodious; moldered; noble; desolate; ex-ecutive; hospitable; dim; fatigued; reticent; old; feudal; happy; elegant; studious; soli-tary; heavenly; blissful; rich-chambered; eterna|; sun-mellowed; stout; substantial; white-pillared; gloomy; dolorous; marble; noisy; aristocratic; baronial; shut-up; palat-ial; intricate; stately; extensive; stormy; steady; temple like; beautiful; decorated; colonnaded; antiquated; fragile.

verbs
convert—; dwell in—; haunt—; inhabit—; modernize—; occupy—; permeate—; redec-orate—; remodel—; renovate—; reside in —; restore—; —awes; —houses; —inspires; —quarters.

(See castle, structure, palace, residence, house, apartment.)

MANTLE
adjectives
judicial; imperial; furred; motley; verdant; somber; russet; silver; curious; sable; in-visible; ermine; many-colored; grassy; flowery; stained; autumn.

MANUAL
adjectives
comprehensive; illustrated; constructive; in-formative; training; exquisite; helpful; complete.

MANUFACTURE (v)
adverbs
exclusively; prosperously; rudely; synthetic-ally; coarsely; reputably; legally; success-fully; preeminently.

(See make, create, invent, compose.)

MANUFACTURER
adjectives
coarsest; recalcitrant; obdurate; prominent; exclusive; reputable; preeminent; alert; successful.

MANUSCRIPT
adjectives
maltreated; moldered; crabbed; blazoned; lost; delusive; illuminated; scrawly; cunei-form; origina|; religious; written; quaint; typed; rare; valuable; long-penned.

verbs
acknowledge—; approve—; attest—; com-pile—; cull—; decipher—; decline—; edit —; engross in—; polish—; publish—; re-ject—; rewrite—; scratch out—; scrawl—; scribble—; transcribe—; witness—.

(See story, novel, message, romance, theme, thesis, volume.)

adjectives

density; topographical; previous; rude; accurate; road; aerial; changing.

verbs

design—; draft—; scale—; sketch—; —acquaints; —apprizes; —charts; —communicates; —conveys; —delineates; —describes; —details; —directs; —enlightens; —estimates; —guides; —imparts; —informs; —pilots; —portrays; —represents; —specifies.

(See chart, diagram, outline, plan.)

MARAUDER

adjectives

sanguine; terrible; ferocious; licentious; burglarious; deadly; stealthy.

MARBLE

adjectives

mottled; blended; breathing; variegated; wrought; remarkable; chill; polished; synthetic; lusterless; ponderous; snowy; chiseled; cold; imitation.

MARCH

adjectives

torturing; severe; fruitless; tedious; silent; famous; dreary; rapid; forced; cautious; circuitous; toilsome; dreadful; disorderly; victorious; bloody; irresistible; hobbling; retrograde; triumphant; arduous; dramatic; confused; slow; glorious; stealthy; measureless; marvelous; magnificent; unprecedented; stately; prolonged; endless; ordered; steady; stormy; victorious; general; monotonous.

verbs

command—; direct—; extend—; force—; renew—; resort to—; retard—; review—; steal—on; —advances; —circuits; —deviates; —parades; —precedes; —rambles; —shuffles; —straggles; —veers; —wends; —zigzags.

(See charge, advance, action, move, attack.)

MARCH (v)

adverbs

pompously; triumphantly; steadily; tirelessly; leisurely; endlessly; menacingly; circuitously; stalwartly; uninterruptedly; briskly; morosely; intrepidly; aimlessly; ignomin-iously; fruitlessly; cautiously; irresistibly; arduously; dramatically; magnificently; monotonously.

(See advance, walk.)

MARCHER

verbs

—advances; —jogs; —journeys; —normalizes; —patrols; —plods; —proceeds; —promenades; —rambles; —roves; —salutes; —saunters; —shuffles on; —strolls; —struts; —threads his way; —tramps; —treads; —trudges.

(See traveler, tourist, passenger.)

MARE

adjectives

striking-looking; nervous; high; infuriated; whinnying; placid; brood; riderless; sleek; calico; thoroughbred.

verbs

break ; bridle—; check—; curb—; curry—; groom—; mount—; rein in—; —bares; —balks; —canters; —conveys; —foals; —gallops; —hurdles; —neighs; —prances; —shies; —trots; —whinnies.

(See horse, colt, mule, donkey. ass, pony.)

MARGIN

adjectives

invisible; flowery; satisfactory; embarrassing; narrowing; refreshing; substantial; distinct; sedgy; slight; regular.

MARGINAL

adverbs

broadly; safely; dangerously; insecurely; permissibly; perilously; riskily; hazardously.

MARINER

adjectives

shipwrecked; ancient; sunswart; chartless; faint-hearted; cowering; cautious; ingenious; homesick; deft; seaworthy.

MARK

adjectives

destructive; decisive; gracious; distinguished; well-founded; separate; dreadful; wedge-shaped; venerable; evident; conspicuous; special; privy; unobtrusive; peculiar; visible; imperceptible; external; transient; deepened; brilliant; delicate; guiding; aimless; unchanging; indelible; tiny.

verbs
bear—; better—; detect—; hold—; over-
shoot—; recognize—; regard—; scale—;
scrutinize—; surpass—; toe—; —attests to;
—betokens; —brands; —characterizes; —
denotes; —directs; —guides; —identifies;
—indicates; —periods; —ranks; —relates
to; —signalizes; —signifies; —symbolizes;
—symptomizes.

(See goal.)

MARK (*v*)

adverbs
distinctly; gratefully; delicately; unalterably; conspicuously; dismally; boldly; indelibly; obviously; destructively; venerably;
privately; peculiarly; imperceptibly; externally; aimlessly; brilliantly.

(See brand, stamp, indicate.)

MARKET

adjectives
immediate; limited; glutted; rising; alternative; volume; extensive; matrimonial;
prominent; inchoate; essential; public; prosperous; domestic; non-competitive; bristle;
eager; growing; wide; open; huge; blooming.

verbs
barter in—; bear—; bottle up—; bull—;
congest—; deflate—; dominate—; dump on
—; flood—; glut—; invest in—; job in—;
kill—; negotiate in—; overload—; procure
—for; purvey at—; quote—; ravage—;
speculate in—; stabilize—; survey—; swamp
—; tax—; trade in—; traffic in—; transact
at—; underbid—; vend in—; —booms; —
fluctuates; —oscillates; —sags; —slumps.

(See exchange, trade, business, speculation, store, merchandise.)

MARKETABLE

adverbs
permanently; highly; seasonably; readily;
easily; scarcely; always; occasionally; fad-
dishly; uncertainly; remarkably; positively;
currently; advantageously; profitably; opportunely; extremely; unusually; stably;
durably; steadily; invariably; conveniently;
fortunately.

MARRIAGE

adjectives
mercenary; reckless; indissoluble; heterodox; cradle; wealthy; international; immediate; advantageous; previous; unhappy;
crude; dubious; ungentle; placid; conjectural; unworthy; bogged; subsequent; ill-
starred; spiteful; wondrous; fat; ceremonious; intelligent; dubious; possible; ideal;
continual; intended; somber; imprudent;
hasty; impending; private; ensuing; repented; plural; honorable; brilliant; acceptable;
sudden; monstrous; morganatic; uncertain;
consanguineous; impecunious; impromptu;
loveless; convenient; derogatory; ill-match-
ed; idiotic; imprudent; impetuous; necessary.

verbs
absolve—; annul—; attend—; bless—; cement—; consummate—; contract—; dissolve
—; ensure—; give in—; indicate—; precipitate—; romanticize—; sancitfy—; sanction
—; terminate—; undermine—; —materializes; —sanctifies; —unites; plunge into—.

(See hand, wedding, nuptial, union, matrimony.)

MARROW

verbs
chill to—; convey through—; freeze—; inculcate in—; infect—; ingrain in—; moisten
with—; suppurate—.

(See blood, being, bone, soul.)

MARRY (*v*)

adverbs
inadvertently; subsequently; advantageously; eventually; hastily; shamefully; recklessly; indissolubly; dubiously; congenially;
spitefully; ceremoniously; imprudently; honorably; morganatically; lovelessly; impecuniously; conveniently; imprudently; impetuously.

(See espouse, wed.)

MARSH

verbs
bog down in—; drain—; dwell in—; flourish
in—; infest—; inhabit—; mire in—; rehabilitate—; sink in—; slough in—; thrive in
—; —breeds; —contaminates; —inundates;
—menaces; —reeks; —stagnates; —submerges.

(See island, peninsula, swamp, valley,
jungle, forest.)

MARSHAL

adjectives
provost; undaunted; fiery; daunted.

MARSHAL (v)

adverbs
sternly; vigorously; militaristically; undauntedly; patriotically; dutifully; gallantly.
(See arrange, adjust, settle.)

MARSHES

adjectives
malarial; pestiferous; inhospitable; dreary; fever-haunted; deadly; venomous; unmarshlike; treacherous; desolate; steaming.

MART

adjectives
humming; considerable; desperate; imperceptible; prosperous.

MARTIAL

adverbs
splendidly; brilliantly; gorgeously, portentously; ominously; dominantly; belligerently; contentiously; predominantly; magnificently; noisily; grimly; subtly; ostentatiously; deliberately; offensively; fearfully; daringly.

MARTIN

verbs
—aids; —arrays; —attacks; —banks; —s colonize; —s journey; —migrates; —pierces; —preys on; —rounds; —scratches; —skims; —smooths; —spreads.
(See bird, swallow.)

MARTYR

adjectives
ancient; unheralded; exulting; patient; resolute; selfish; grave; unpractical; fiery; sainted; magnanimous; crucified.

MARTYRDOM

adjectives
heroic; disdainful; uplifting; voluntary; long-sought.

MARVEL

adjectives
admiring; fantastic; infinite; accomplished; dreamlike.

verbs
accomplish—; admire—; behold—; gape at —; paint—; stand aghast at—; —amazes; —astonishes; —astounds; —awes; —baffles; —bewilders; —dazes; —dazzles; —dumb-founds; —electrifies; —fascinates; —flabbergasts (colloq); —overwhelms; —strikes dumb; —stuns; —stupefies; —staggers.
(See wonder, beauty, radiance, splendor, mystery, success.)

MARVEL (v)

adverbs
secretly; fantastically; infinitely; mutely; impassively; joyously; candidly.
(See wonder, amaze.)

MASK

adjectives
servile crescentlike; grisly; laughing; smiling; newest; impenetrable; lifeless; impassive; theatrical; acquired; hideous; wanton; deceitful; well-trained; sun-expelling; dainty; waxen; placid; tragic; changing; child-faced; stately.

verbs
adjust—; cloak with—; doff—; emerge from —; fashion—; —beguiles; —blinds; —conceals; —deceives; —deludes; —depicts; —disguises; —eclipses; —lures; —portrays; —veils; don—.
(See cloak, disguise, make-up, masquerade.)

MASK (v)

adverbs
partially; cunningly; demurely; servilely; impassively; wantonly; deceitfully; daintily; tragically; deceptively; treacherously; hideously; ironically; slyly.
(See disguise, hide, veil, masquerade.)

MASON

verbs
employ—; hire—; —achieves; —blocks; —carves; —chips; —chisels; —constructs; —drills; —erects; —fabricates; —forges; —frames; —heaves; —hews; —lugs; —models; —molds; —rears; —shoulders; —sunders.
(See worker, workman.)

MASONRY

adjectives
roofless; arched; delicate; beautiful.

MASQUERADE

adjectives
brilliant; glittering; ghastly; savage; phantom; speaking; ironic; ghostly.

verbs

attend—; organize—; plan—; reveal—; — bamboozles (colloq.); —beguiles; —blinds; —cloaks; —conceals; —counterfeits; —curtains; —decoys; —deludes; —diverts; — eclipses; —enlivens; —hoodwinks; —lures; —masks; —muffles; —mystifies; —relaxes; —screens; —secretes; —shades; —shrouds; —stifles; —suppresses; —veils.

(See mask, disguise, misrepresentaion, dance, sham.)

MASQUERADE (v)

adverbs

bizarrely; brilliantly; savagely; ironically; enthusiastically; spectacularly; joyously; ceremonially; formally; perfunctorily.

(See mask, hide, veil, disguise.)

MASS
(general)

adjectives

heterogeneous; midnight; bucking; regimented; gloomy; immense; agitated; promiscuous; frowning; withered; helpless; physical; mighty; confused; prosaic; frantic; vulgar; ever-moving; phalanxed; unmanaged; specious; aggregate; straggling; celebrated; clinking; homogeneous; inert; buttressed; tangled; wrestling; ungrateful; disloyal; neutral; spheroidal; somber; animated; woolly; ponderous; oscillating; floating; bloated; crashing; continuous; seething; chaotic; heaving; solid; desiccated; melancholy; pulplike; discouraging; whirling; remarkable; gigantic; fermenting; tumultuous; imposing; gummy; ill-defined; nebulous; rushing; roaring; irresistible; flickering; whale-like; luminous; continuous; immeasurable; indiscriminate; glowing; gross; steely; leaping; sinking; cutting; amorphous; bristling; repugnant; insensible; dark; impending; unbroken; burnished; entangled; pinnacled; conglomerate; gigantic; agitated; restless; incoherent; inarticulate; quivering; resplendent; rough; packed; incandescent; unyielding; accumulating; inanimate; successive (pl); tough; leathery; somber; indistinct; charred; gelatine.

MASS
(lump, assemblage, heap, etc.)

verbs

accumulate—; aggregate—; bulk—; cement in—; cluster in—; compile—; constitute—; crush—; disintegrate—; dissolve—; embody

—; focus in—; heap in—; integrate—; lump in—; measure—; muster—; scrape—; verge in—; —expands; —ferments; —rises; — soars; —swells; —thickens; —towers; — transcends.

(See dough, generality, crowd, amount, heap.)

MASS
(religion)

verbs

administer—; anthem—; attend—; bow at —; chant—; chorus—; devote to—; give praise at—; kneel at—; mumble—; perform —; worship at—; —glorifies; —invokes; — offers; —salvages; —uplifts.

(See church, rite, ceremony, sacrament.)

MASSACRE

adjectives

atrocious; brutal; indiscriminate; cruel; fierce; horrid; dreadful; treacherous; wholesale; judicial; bloody .

verbs

decry—; denounce—; execute—; expire in —; frown on—; lust for—; perpetrate—; plot—; rebuke for—; reproach for—; resign to—; succumb in—; yield to—; —despatches; —enrages; —ensanguines; —incenses; —rages; —scandalizes; —scars; —stains; —threatens.

(See bloodshed, killing, murder, assassination, slaughter, violence.)

MASSAGE

adjectives

invigorating; stimulating; scientific; frictional; healing.

verbs

—enlivens; —exhilarates; —invigorates; — limbers; —quickens; —refreshes; —regenerates; —relaxes; —relieves; —soothes; —smooths; —ungnarls.

(See remedy, medicine, liniment, masseur.)

MASSAGE (v)

adverbs

industriously; actively; invigoratingly; stimulatingly; scientifically; healingly; beneficially.

(See rub, knead.)

MASSES
(general)

adjectives

singular; vapory; quadrangular; comet-shaped; thunderous; dusky; cosmic; exultant; dense; congested; multitudinous; surging; accumulated; struggling; huddled; flame-shaped; crushing; impenetrable; enormous; enthusiastic; metallic; hurrying; disorderly; grateful; cross; incensed; vast; bold; fleeing; irregular; illiterate; listening; glittering; shadowy; dusky; dull; huge; menacing; obedient; luminous.

MASSES
(people)

verbs

benefit—; cajole—; deride—; educate—; enkindle—; enslave—; exhort—; exploit—; ferment—; inflame—; indoctrinate—; lift —; move—; rally—round; subjugate—; submerge—; sway—; tread on—; weld—; —erupt; revolt; —seethe.

(See public, population, multitude, mob, society, throng, crowd.)

MASSEUR

verbs

train—; —comforts; —eases; —kneads; —manipulates; —massages; —pats; —pounds; —quiets; —rectifies; —rubs; —spanks.

(See massage.)

MASSIVE

adverbs

enormously; awkwardly; stupendously; impossibly; overwhelmingly; grotesquely; strangely; ponderously; grossly; monstrously.

MAST

adjectives

staggering; derrick-like; ripened; tapering; straining; naked; raking; towering; broken; snapped.

verbs

clamber up—; erect—; lash to—; lower—; nail to—; raise—; rig—; sail before—; spring—; step—; strain—; —creaks; —extends; —rises; —splinters; —supports; —sustains; —sways.

(See post, beam.)

MASTER

adjectives

imperious; profound; lurid; disloyal; captious; contemporary; testy; intriguing; sweet; urban; provincial; absolute; clouted; majestic; unrighteous; supreme; former; money; dish-faced; prayer; inglorious; independent; exasperating; unsuccessful; tyrannical; foremost; inward; school; mystic; industrial; noble; undisputed; accepted; perturbed; indignant; formidable; marvelous; proficient; blithe; shrewd; unworthy; injudicious; intractable; manful; jovial.

verbs

acknowledge—; appeal to—; attend—; betray—; bow to—; conspire against—; emulate—; enjoin—; follow—; salute—; serve —; supersede—; —authorizes; —censures; —controls; —directs; —disciplines; —enslaves; —governs; —guides; —judges; —lashes; —oversees; —rewards; —rules; —supervises.

(See expert, husband, commander, employer.)

MASTER (v)

adverbs

skillfully; imperiously; profoundly; absolutely; majestically; tyrannically; undisputedly; formidably; marvelously; proficiently; shrewdly; jovially; injudiciously; dictatorially.

(See handle, rule, command.)

MASTERPIECE

adjectives

ambitious; fair; exquisite; crisp; vivid; brief; restrained; unequaled; unsurpassed; literary; involuntary; eminent; symphonic; heroic.

verbs

acclaim—; accomplish—; achieve—; applaud—; appreciate—; cast—; chance upon —; contemplate—; emulate—; esteem—; examine—; extol—; hail as—; interpret—; laud—; match—; pay tribute to—; praise —; reproduce—; rival—; study—; transcribe—; value—; work—; —excels; —depicts; —portrays; —reposes in; —surpasses; —survives; —transcends.

(See picture, photograph, portrait, painting, model, plan, statue.)

adjectives

unrivaled; intelligent; barbarous; seductive; technical: imperfect; physical; complete.

verbs

aim at—; assay—; assert—; assume—; attain—; command—of; crown with—; dispute—; distinguish by—; exercise—; gain —; maintain—; match—; perform with—; prove—; regain—; relinquish—; spur to—; strive for—; struggle for—; surpass—; wield—; —awes; —dominates; —prevails; —sways.

(See perfection, proficiency, skill.)

MATCH
(fire)

verbs

apply—; dip—; extinguish—; ignite—; impregnate—; quench—; scratch—; smother —; tip—; touch off—; —chars; —devours; —dies; —enkindles; —flickers; —fuses; — glows; —incinerates; —simmers; —singes; —smoulders; —sputters.

(See lamp, light, flame, fire.)

MATCH
(general)

adjectives

brilliant; unwise; brief; ordinary; shameful; suitable; mad; rich; honorable; championship; unholy; inappropriate; love.

MATCH
(parallel, mate, boot, etc.)

verbs

arrange—; challenge to—; compete i -; contest—; enter—; judge—; negotiate—; officiate at—; promote—; prove—for; regulate—; scorn—; spurn—; view—; witness —; —corresponds; —duplicates; —mirrors; —parallels; —pairs; —resembles.

(See bout, fight, race (sport), contest.)

MATCH (v)

adverbs

equally; boldly; madly; rashly; foolhardily; brilliantly; unwisely; honorably; shamefully; improvidently.

(See oppose, challenge, defy, dare.)

MATE

adjectives

trembling; truant; incongruous; all-beautiful; nested; afflicted; vile; sincere; sweet; shivering; unloved; lovely; unkind; brooding; equal; imprudent; inharmonious; beauteous.

verbs

abandon—; choose—; compete for—; desert —; discard—; divorce—; espouse—; estrange from—; forsake—; guard—; join —; protect—; quit—; relinquish—; renounce —; vie for—; —matches; —parallels; —resembles.

(See comrade, husband, wife, friend.)

MATERIAL
(general)

adjectives

biographical; suggestive; front-page; illustrative; corrosive; supplementary; ennobling; inexhaustible; complex; delicate; gauzy; acoustical; intellectual; suitable; biblical; health; preserved; objectionable; documentary; infinite; mournful; hilarious; extensive; tangible; concentrated; factual; authoritative; vast; repressed; anthropological; exquisite; impressionable; ample; outside; moraine; underworld; heterogeneous; mailable; muscle-building; copious; rustable; combustible; superfine; prepared; quality; misleading; rubberlike; tenacious; unpromising; noble; rugged; infantile; washable; special; volatile; polished; positive; elastic; unformed; nutritive; discordant; packaging; cool; raw; molten; protective; illustrative; septic; superlative; conglomerating; basic; rude; superfluous; durable; versatile; abrasive; miraculous; abundant; unimpeachable; picturesque; inorganic; fragmentary; coarse; scanty; shining; intractable; disjointed; choicest; insulating; mulch; thematic.

MATERIAL
(information)

verbs

absorb—; accumulate—; amass—; arrange —; array—; assemble—; assort—; catallogue—; collect—; compile—; concentrate on —; delve into—; digest—; disseminate—; gather—; glean—; group—; jot down—; marshal—; muster—; rake up—; reduce—; sift—; simplify—; treat—; unify—.

(See knowledge, facts, science, copy, information, wisdom.)

MATERIAL
(matter)

verbs

allot—; amass—; apportion—; assemble—; consume—; derive—from; drain—; exhaust —; expend—; garner—; heap—; lay in—; load—; manipulate—; measure—; order—; reserve—; sift—; squander—; stock with—; store—; waste—; —fritters away.

(See cloth, drapery, ingredients, supply, food, merchandise.)

adverbs

grossly; flagrantly; selfishly; highly; essentially; vitally; fundamentally; gravely; eminently; indispensably; crassly; seriously; urgently.

MATERIALISM

adjectives

ruthless; dialectical; advanced; practical; lifeless; brutal; unreligious; coarse; scientific; crass.

verbs

absorb by—; accentuate—; cloak—; degenerate into—; disparage—; infest with—; lapse into—; shrink from—; sink into—; tend to—; transmute—; —blasphemes; — desecrates; —doubts; —hardens; —perverts; —profanes; —questions; —scorns; — wanes.

(See modernism, paganism, atheism, realism.)

MATERNAL

adverbs

fondly; fiercely; tenderly; solicitously; possessively; obsessively; jealously; proudly; comfortingly; unduly; naturally; habitually; admirably; charmingly; sweetly; placidly; serenely; imperturbably; dominantly; indulgently; good-humoredly; warmly; softly; bounteously; generously; providently; curiously; thoughtfully.

MATERNITY

verbs

anticipate—; arouse—; balk at—; delight in —; endear to—; exalt—; guard—; impair —; overwhelm by—; prepare for—; prevent —; pride in—; recognize—; train for—; — bores; —nauseates; —secures.

MATHEMATICS

verbs

advance by—; apply—; base on—; compile by—; demonstrate—; depend on—; dispute —; fathom by—; ferret out by—; formulate —; introduce—; —computes; —disciplines; —educes; —enthralls; —sharpens; —solves; —systematizes; —trains; —verifies; — weighs.

(See science, logic, solution, problem.)

MATING

adjectives

auspicious; seasonal; beneficial; integral.

MATRIARCHAL

adverbs

venerably; insistently; tyrannically; gently; tenaciously; uncommonly; highly; imperiously; oddly; naturally; unyieldingly; obviously; irrevocably; proudly; haughtily.

MATRIMONY

verbs

abhor—; blast—; cloud—; commit to—; consent to—; dissolve—; embark on—; entice into—; evade—; reconcile to—; sacrifice to —; scorn—; spurn—; surrender to—; — circles; —exacts; —knits; —mars; —preserves; —shackles; —survives; —torments; —unites.

(See marriage, wedding, nuptials, union.)

MATRON

adjectives

substantial; sober; ancient; stately; ailing; bulky; sharp-faced; fluttering; dignified; sober-suited; modest; pedantic; gracious; haughty.

verbs

appoint—; tip—; train—; vest in—; —administers; —assists; —cradles; —furnishes; —inspects; —manages; —obliges; —presides —reinforces; —resides; —serves; — superintends; —supervises; —supplies.

(See servant, housekeeper, wife.)

MATRONLY

adverbs

pleasantly; proudly; unexpectedly; charmingly; admirably; sedately; demurely; comfortably; serenely; imperturbably; undeniably; sweetly; graciously; happily; gently; tranquilly; placidly; remarkably.

MATTER

adjectives
subject; specific; triturated; perfunctory; doleful; heterogeneous; inconsequential; unimportant; spiritual; combustible; urgent; prudential; luminous; worldly; esoteric; indigent; trivial; imminent; spiritual; superficial; heavy; calcareous; internal; fixed; fluid; humid; dry; unctuous; crude; hard; soft; simple; veiny; compound; similar; organical; imponderable; extraneous; controversial; inevitable; critical; unpalatable; speculative; jesting; granular; erupted; exterior; analogous; ample; essential; brute; country; mineral; weighty; pertinent; waste; baser; suspended; countless (pl); theoretical; pecuniary; impending; critical; putrid; encrusted; tarry; bare; nitrogenous; stony; regrettable; indolent; protuberant; empty; forgotten; ecclesiastical; inert; testamentary; suspended; mighty; graver; inexhaustible; commonplace; relevant; remote; subtle; indifferent; inflammable; financial; earnest; hideous; abstruse; fascinating; temporal; coloring; worthy; woody; perishable; money; unattainable; carbonaceous; artistic; grave; morbid; cognate.

verbs
adjust—; aggravate—; brood over—; clinch —; deal with—; debate—; deliberate—; discuss—; dispute—; elucidate—; expedite—; forsake—; go to the root of—; inquire into —; judge—; mince—s; ponder—; press—; report—; shape—; simplify—; smooth—; visualize—; weigh—; —drifts; —engages; —engrosses; —|ingers; —pertains to.
(See business, affair, event, question, problem.)

MATTRESS

verbs
construct—; fluff—; handle—; hollow—; hump—; launder—; lug—; pad—; quilt—; stitch—; strain—; stuff—; tuck under—; tuft—; —comforts; —cushions; —eases; — molds; —pits; —refreshes; —supports.
(See bed, pillow.)

MATURE

adverbs
suddenly; undeniably; admirably; sensibly; sagaciously; sturdily; responsibly; unexpectedly; remarkably; curiously; strangely; surprisingly; reasonably; sufficiently; presumably; scarcely; thoroughly; progressively; strikingly; completely; fully; obviously; fairly; terribly; precociously; indescribably; gratifyingly; wisely; emotionally; physically; appallingly; supposedly; intellectually; unquestionably.

MATURITY

adjectives
fairest; complete; precocious; ripened; mysterious; surprising; hypothetical; indescribable; emotional; warm; rapid; cold; respectable; serene; luxuriant; sumptuous; buxom.

verbs
abide till—; approach—; attain—; grow in —; impede—; merge into—; settle into—; tarry—; undergo—; —charms; —limits; — mellows; —ripens; —subdues; —sweetens; —teaches; —transforms.
(See development.)

MAUDLIN

adverbs
drunkenly; foolishly; senselessly; incoherently; intoxicatedly; joyously; merrily; crazily; utterly; stupidly; oddly; disgustingly; hopelessly; helplessly; egregiously; heavily; tipsily; gloriously; comically; shamefully; happily; irresponsibly; excitedly; hysterically.

MAUVE

adjectives
soft; pale; brilliant.

MAXIM

adjectives
horrible; favorite; terse; common; sublime; wholesome; elevated; political; shrewd; sagacious; execrable; salutary; ethical; moral; polite; profane; semibarbarous.

verbs
apply—; coin—; comprehend—; condense into—; consider—; defend—; draw from—; interpret—; invoke—; mold—; observe—; propose—; retain—; speculate on—; weigh —; —concludes; —directs; —embodies; — guides; —philosophizes; —relates to.
(See adage, proverb.)

MAXIMUM

verbs
assign—; attain—; calculate—; conduct to —; distend to—; establish—; reach—; record—; test—; strain—; strike—; weigh—; —bears; —corresponds; —limits.
(See amount, average, degree, position, status, limit.)

MAZE

adjectives

quaint; murmuring; surging; tangled; institutional; flitting; uncouth; moon-loved; flowery; backward; vague; hopeless; musky-circled; mirthful; tortuous; statistical; mystic; intriguing; shadowy; winding; insane; bewitching; laborious; shifting; curious; intoxicating.

verbs

crack—; dissolve—; entangle in—; extricate from—; grope through—; guide through—; immure in—; retrace—; struggle through —; submerge in—; wander in—; weave—; —bewilders; —confounds; —confuses; — entwines; —perplexes; —puzzles; —twists; —winds; —wreathes.

(See mystery, perplexity, problem.)

MEADOW

adjectives

romantic; grassy, intervening; frost-flowered; luxuriant; bloody; fruitful; slushy; starry; outlying; tender; enameled; smooth; saturated; dewy; serene; mountain; sheltered; bright; undulating; extensive; quaint; parched; dim-seen; damp; open; homely; scorching; laughing; swelling; rolling; billowy; unmown; emerald.

verbs

amble through—; crop—; cultivate—; drench—; dress—; luxuriate in—; mow—; paint—; parch—; pasture in—; plough—; prance in—; romp in—; stain—; —blooms; —extends; —invites; —scents; —slopes.

(See field, grass, flowers, plant, country, lawn.)

MEAGRE

adverbs

pitifully; scantily; miserably; wretchedly; pitiably; deplorably; lamentably; pathetically; unnecessarily; unaccountably; unreasonably; criminally; stingily; meanly; cruelly; bitterly; hopelessly; desperately; incredibly; unbelievably; meretriciously; skimpily; contemptibly.

MEAL

adjectives

supplementary; sunset; ominous; scanty; small; floating; satisfying; well-balanced; belated; abominable; miserable; vegetable; frugal; hearty; hasty; elaborate; slender; indigested; sumptuous; savory; lavish; hot; jovial; quick; homelike; sailor-cooked; quiet; infantile; dismal; miraculous; assured; plenteous; solitary; luxurious; economical; accustomed; superb; delectable; tempting; perfect; appetizing; famous; marvelous; generous; tasty; home-cooked; thrilling; abundant.

verbs

beg—; consume—; despatch—; dispose of —; enhance—; lubricate—; relish—; savor —; snatch—; terminate—; —nourishes; — proceeds; —sustains; —tempts.

(See dinner, luncheon, food, breakfast, supper.)

MEALY-MOUTHED

adverbs

insufferably; perversely; pretentiously; humbly; deceitfully; mendaciously; perfidiously; hypocritically; cunningly; insidiously; treacherously; invidiously; trickily; meretriciously; atrociously; abominably; satirically; inconceivably.

MEAN

adverbs

abominably; terribly; stingily; viciously; maliciously; horribly; incredibly; inordinately; unbelievably; brutally; cruelly; bitterly; greedily; shamefully; despicably; outrageously; disgracefully; treacherously; selfishly; jealously; enviously.

MEANING

adjectives

mysterious; common; inexpressible; pathetic; doubtful; mythical; majestic; secondary; imploring; earnest; ominous; ambiguous; solemn; veiled; gentle; odious; candid; double; true; remote; ultimate; uncertain; specific; significant; obvious; generous; wicked; eucharistic; fearful; undecipherable; patriotic; platonic; heavenly; universal; philosophical; shrunken; painful; lawful; mean; historic; symbolic; irresolute; serious; deadly; unmistakable; plain; dark; intelligible; cloudy; abstruse; legitimate; moral; profound; folded; hideous; concrete; precise; borrowed; infinite; intellectual; spiritual; unaffected; unattractive; huge; hybrid; cryptic; secular; sexual; incredible; second; elusive; considerable; instant; involved; vague; express; accumulated; vital.

verbs

absorb—; adulterate—; apprehend—; ascribe—to; bestow—upon; clarify—; comprehend—; discover—; elaborate on—; elucidate—; embody—; extricate—from; grasp —; illustrate—; imply—; impregnate with —; pervert—; ponder—; reflect upon—; seek—; sum up—; translate—; weigh with —; wresle with—; attach—to.

(See reason, significance.)

MEANS

adjectives

iniquitous; effective; downright; legitimate; solid; extraordinary; vociferous; plunging; continuous; ample; systematic; peaceful; prying; drastic; efficient; radical; clumsy; hygienic; scantiest; slender; superficial; rapid; showy; artificial; honorable; comfortable; undue; subtle; unlawful; effectual; vast; superior; remote; mysterious; unexplained; considerable; subservient; further; highhanded; useful; indispensable; occult; earthly; inarticulate; mechanical; pecuniary; approved; devious; gigantic; accidental; instrumental; faint; conflicting; realistic; blessed; inadequate; extremest; practicable; readiest; apparent; double; abundant; unrestrained; speediest; lavish; quick; individual; moderate; miraculous; flagitious; potent; valuable; creditable; instinctive.

verbs

adopt—; attain—; contrive—; desire—; devise—; employ—; find—; invent—; meditate on—; outline—; resort to—; secure—; supplant—; suggest—.

(See agency, method, way, manner, policy.)

MEASLES

verbs

afflict with—; attack with—; convey—; develop—; dispose to—; immunize to—; isolate—; stud with—; usher in—; —abates; —blotches; —endangers; —erupts; —fades; —infects; —invades; —patches; —spreads; —stains; —weakens.

(See sickness, malady, disease, smallpox.)

MEASURE
(general)

adjectives

effectual; dictatorial; decisive; mystic; unconstitutional; delightful; harsher; faltering; aesthetic; star; buskined; domestic; extreme; classical; diminished; good; considerate; large; hostile; rustic; merriest; precautionary; equal; discriminatory; infinite; quaint; drastic; pending; intemperate; judicious; repressive; defiant; puretoned; irregular; solemn; unattainable; compulsory; undeserved; hygienic; conservative; corrective; preventive; radical; contemptuous; potent; energetic; conciliatory; violent; pernicious; tempestuous; sinister; undaunted; scant; retaliatory; large; fluctuating; rhythmical; brimming; galloping; tuneful; vigorous; airy; stringent; generous; just; final; unexpected; accurate; weightiest; flowing; unrhymed; stately; financial; sweeping; inevitable; hostile; ample; aggressive; individual; tyrannical; dusty; highhanded; swelling; smallest; compromise; dulcet; preliminary; prompt; satisfactory; boundless; sterilizing; sufficient; proposed; doubtful; desperate; tedious; irregular; considerate; quantitative; rude; severe; vulgar; hasty; lavish; strained; pacific; debated; stark; concentrated; burning; central; centuried; organic; diverse (pl); eugenic; suitable; disciplinary; ruinous; emergency; corresponding; undreamed; contestable; gracious; bold; oppressive.

MEASURE
(legislation, course.)

verbs

adopt—; advance—; advocate—; block—; combat—; defy—; effect—; enact—; enforce—; execute—; exert—s; force—through; install—; institute—; introduce—; outlaw—; pilot—; promote—; promulgate —; reject—; repass—; resort to—; subscribe to—; suggest—; threaten with—s; — affords relief; —clamps down on; —corrects; —embodies; —embraces; —evolves from.

(See bill, law, rule, ordinance, statute, mandate.)

MEASURE (v)

adverbs

scientifically; mechanically; accurately; consciously; effectually; constitutionally; aesthetically; mystically; classically; equally; intemperately; judiciously; financially; individually; tediously; quantitatively; lavishly; radically.

(See gauge, rule, estimate.)

760

adjectives

micrometrical; accurate; geodetic; refined.

verbs

adopt—; appraise for—; ascertain—; calculate—; cling to—; collect—; confirm—; deduce—; derive--; determine—; estimate —; probe—; reckon—; report—; review—; sound—; stipulate—; —allow; —coincide with.

(See magnitude, size, dimension.)

MEAT

adjectives

lean; sizzling; homely; substantial; immortal; choleric; wretched; corrupted; unctuous; miserable; wholesome; manufactured; perishable; fatty; generous; preserved; tainted.

verbs

abstain from—; broil—; brown—; carve—; consume—; crave—; dispatch—; dive into —; dress—; dry—; extract from—; grill—; grind—; inspect—; market—; parch—; pickle—; prepare—; refrigerate—; roll—; salt—; savor—; shred—; store—; tenderize —; tub—; weigh—; —ages; —deteriorates; —putrefies.

(See flesh, game, food, stew.)

MECHANIC

adjectives

shrewd; roused; expert; trained; competent; skilled.

MECHANICAL

adverbs

cleverly; ingeniously; dexterously; marvelously; dully; automatically; altogether; accurately; conveniently; advantageously; profitably; precisely; unerringly.

MECHANISM

adjectives

literal; extremely delicate; intricate; lifeless; wondrous; dexterous; primary; gorgeous; elaborate; inanimate; greasy; interior; insensate; unconscious; instrumental.

verbs

acquaint with—; analyze—; approve—; construct—; design—; develop—; explain—; improve—; inspect—; install—; invent—;

operate—; substitute—; tamper with—; tinker with—; understand—; —eases; —performs; —specializes; —speeds.

(See gear, engine, machine, dynamo, apparatus.)

MEDAL

verbs

accord—; award—; bestow—; cast—; confer—; decorate with—; engrave—; favor with—; grant—; honor with—; inscribe on—; jingle—s; mold—; present with—; prize—; strike—; —commemorates; —distinguishes; —encourages; —records; —represents; —signifies; —symbolizes.

(See laurels, trophy, badge, memorial, reward.)

MEDDLESOME

adverbs

vexatiously; irritatingly; maliciously; incredibly; unaccountably; maddeningly; in curably; offensively; unpleasantly; disagreeably; unbelievably; busily; officiously; unpardonably; intrusively; invidiously; atrociously; inexcusably; curiously; inquisitively; inveterately; unscrupulously; incorrigibly; grievously.

MEDIA

adjectives

sympathetic; turbid; diffracting; fluctuating.

MEDICATION

adjectives

pre-anesthetic; proper; penetrating; soothing.

MEDICINAL

adverbs

warrantably; highly; splendidly; advantageously; incidentally; profitably; strangely; oddly; beneficially; opportunely; properly; admirably; wonderfully; extraordinarily; amazingly; surprisingly; unaccountably; extremely; acceptably; uncommonly; usefully.

MEDICINE

adjectives

loathed; cooling; sudorific; preventive; multiplying; domestic; reform; heavenly; native; proprietary; astringent.

verbs

administer—; anoint with—; dispense—; endorse—; gulp down—; instil—; measure—; overdose with—; prescribe—; reject—;

specialize in—; swallow—; verse in—; —allays; —alleviates; —palliates; —purges.

(See iodine, emetic, enema, laxative, liniment.)

MEDIOCRE
adverbs
hopelessly; indefensibly; undeniably; stupidly; dully; stodgily; uninterestingly; boresomely; tediously; monotonously; crudely; crassly; inexcusably; unaccountably; surprisingly; amazingly; terribly; unexpectedly; unwarrantably; awkwardly; provincially; tiresomely; dreadfully; pitiably; miserably; wretchedly.

MEDIOCRITY
adjectives
solemn; witless; practiced; superlative.

verbs
allow—; approve—; attain—; avoid—; condemn—; cringe in—; criticize—; disparage —; lift from—; respect—; —begets; —endures; —eclipses; —perseveres: —starves; —subjugates; —succeeds.

(See inferiority.)

MEDITATE (v)
adverbs
pensively; gloomily; seriously; morbidly; sedately; dispassionately; bitterly; wilfully; restlessly; whimsically; religiously; serenely; monotonously; characteristically; habitually.

(See muse, ponder, reflect, think.)

MEDITATION
adjectives
profound; portentous; heavenly; important; threadbare; silent; devout; thoughtless; restless; solemn; pensive; starred; whimsical; crude; fearful; plotting; holy; rapid; sullen; lofty; numerous (pl); serene; reconstructive; continual.

verbs
abide in—; absorb in—; bathe in—; build in—; discern through—; draw from—; fall into—; fix in—; immerse in—; neglect—; recall in—; recess in—; recline in—; shroud in—; spend in—; steep in—; wander in—; weave in—; wrap in—; —ensures; —nurses; —solaces; —strengthens.

(See contemplation, thought, philosophy, reflection, reverie.)

MEDITATIVE
adverbs
gravely; quietly; habitually; temperamentally; strangely; naturally; seriously; soberly; deeply; profoundly; studiously; reminiscently; remarkably; unduly; thoughtfully; inscrutably; solemnly; earnestly; dangerously; pensively; wistfully; philosophically; pointedly.

MEDIUM
adjectives
congenial; diaphanous; sympathetic; fleeting; meteoric; tangible; appropriate; accurate; ethereal; desirable; suitable; pictorial; cooling; proselytizing; surrounding; reliable; graphic; inaccurate; just; ridiculous; interpreting; ambient; pulsing; circulating; supporting; favored; laborious.

MEEK
adverbs
gently; quietly; submissively; modestly; humbly; supplicatingly; serenely; disgustingly; obsequiously; unnecessarily; provokingly; stupidly; miserably; wretchedly; tragically; passively; tranquilly; patiently; placidly; philosophically; gracefully; sedately; demurely; contentedly.

MEEKNESS
adjectives
proud; subdued; female; reverent; swaggering.

MEET (v)
adverbs
coincidentally; accidentally; nocturnally; surreptitiously; forcibly; casually; unwaveringly; tacitly; traditionally; solemnly; memorably; convivially; temperately; fraternally.

(See confront, encounter.)

MEETING
adjectives
turbulent; commonplace; accidental; pleasant; pietistic; traditional; conducive; friendly; solemn; merry; accidental; fortunate; momentous; revival; immediate; memorable; fictitious; soul-trying; convivial; midweek; agitated; temperance; memorial; factious; revolutionary.

verbs

address—; anticipate—; arrange—; ban—; convoke—; devise—; dwell on—; enjoy—; forecast—; foster—; plan—; plot—; promote—; shun—; —brightens; —charms; —delights; —excites; —pains; —quickens; —rekindles; —revives; —sharpens; —thrills; —unites.

(See convention, conference, hearing, assembly, appointment, encounter.)

MELANCHOLY

adjectives

gentle; tranquil; appropriate; natural; funereal; vague; delicious; dull-eyed; hungry; deep; tired; congenital; silent; soft; waning; quiet; gloomy; faithful; inviting; mild-eyed; sweetest; moral; vague; forbidding; bovine; resolute; rude; touching; moody; lovely; customary; profound; savage; constitutional; young; sentimental; somber; depressing.

verbs

charge with—; chase away—; conceal—; discern—; dissipate—; merge into—; sink into—; succumb to—; suffer—; —oppresses; —perks up; —shadows; —touches.

(See gloom, depression, dejection, mood, sadness.)

adverbs

alarmingly; unduly; incurably; stupidly; moodily; churlishly; sullenly; strangely; naturally; inherently; temperamentally; dangerously; doggedly; extraordinarily; inordinately; gloomily; heavily; cheerlessly; unhappily; lugubriously; mournfully; solemnly; dismally; lamentably; glumly; pensively; grimly; desolately.

MELLOW

adverbs

lusciously; delectably; pleasantly; agreeably; softly; richly; naturally; ripely; charmingly; benevolently; harmoniously; melodiously; sweetly; gorgeously; delicately; progressively; groggily; perfectly; adequately; sufficiently; amazingly; surprisingly; astonishingly; unexpectedly.

MELODIOUS

adverbs

delicately; exquisitely; triumphantly; enchantingly; thrillingly; convivially; boomingly; companionably; agreeably; plaintively; ecstatically; sweetly; liltingly; gracefully; meltingly; unutterably; strangely; soothingly; blissfully; lightly; lingeringly; saucily; hauntingly; catchingly; rollickingly; romantically; softly.

MELODRAMA

adjectives

virtuous; cheap; sentimental; exciting; underdone; celebrated; morbid; bloodcurdling.

verbs

applaud—; climax—; compose—; descend to—; dress in—; engage in—; formulize—; hiss—; impassion—; introduce—; lean toward—; overrate—; pattern—on; rehearse—; revive—; ridicule—; sink into—; —appeals; —bores; —exaggerates; —inspires; —intrigues; —lags; —thrives; —thrills; —touches.

(See play, opera, magic, pantomine, performance, tragedy, trick, act, comedy.)

MELODY

adjectives

celestial; untutored; strenuous; cloying; minstrel; delightsome; uplifted; faint-toned; venomed; wild; joyous; wondrous; beguiling; triumphant; exquisite; delicate; ravishing; stirring; vagrant; organic; harmonic; enchanting; sweetest; heavenly; thrilling; booming; siren; high; sky-born; congenial; conjuring; ancient; plaintive; unfailing; untaught; agreeable; liquid; chastened; efflorescent; breaking; consoling; unintelligible; symmetrical; ecstatic; oblivious; unearthly; hireling; nerve-dissolving; elegant; fresh; enchanted; delicious; pathetic; characteristic; rhythmic; facile; inspired; sustained; superabundant; acquired; original; sweet; lilting; exalted; stately; terrible; distinct; enervating; immortal.

verbs

air—; chant—; chorus—; compose—; drench in—; drown—; hum—; imprison—; improvise—; join in—; lilt to—; modulate—; wheedle—out of; —gratifies; —haunts; —heralds; —lingers; —rings out; —soars; —wanes.

(See chant, air, jazz, incantation, song, refrain.)

MELT (*v*)

adverbs

indistinctly; indefinably; silently; exquisitely; scientifically; methodically; deliciously; sweetly; appetizingly.

(See dissolve.)

MEMBER

verbs

admit—; coerce—; collaborate with—s; defend—; elect—; entertain—; honor—; invite —; limit—s; register—; —attends; —s band; —benefits; —charters; —contributes; —s convene; —heeds; —s incorporate; —organizes; —s rally; —undertakes; —votes.

(See faculty, classmate, congressman.)

MEMBERS

adjectives

prominent; mutinous; respectable; superfluous; consistent; confidential; eligible; eminent; numerous; obscure; vivacious; distinguished; myriad; mateless; influential; sundry; impecunious; self-respecting; illustrious; discordant; efficient; able; honorable; daring; exemplary; acceptable; conspicuous; representative; worthy; significant; right-thinking; learned; excitable; geometric; noxious; surviving; discredited; objectionable; disjointed; privileged; fat; sturdy; self-respecting; honest; erratic; devout; subsidiary; law-abiding; amiable; nicely educated; infatuated; disaffected; insubordinate; sundry (pl); corporeal; oracular; useless; unruly; violent; arbitrary; pronounced; cherished.

MEMBERSHIP

adjectives

distinguished; enormous; compulsory; unstable.

verbs

admit to—; desire—; discontinue—; elect to—; forfeit—; increase—; invite to—; limit —; register—; renew—; seek—; tabulate —; usher in—; vote on—; —concentrates; —expires; —includes; —requires; —terminates.

MEMBRANE

adjectives

previous; feather-covered; thin; gauzelike.

verbs

affect—; incise—; irritate—; perforate—; puncture—; shed—; soothe—; stretch—; swell—; thicken—; ulcerate—; —atrophies; —bulges; —erodes; —lines; —ruptures; —vibrates; —wastes.

(See film, eardrum.)

MEMENTO

adjectives

painful; ever-changing; grave; appropriate; melancholy; lovely; sacred.

MEMORIAL

adjectives

cypress; suitable; tender; dubious; frail; worthy; peevish; poetic; sculptured; faded; dogmatic; energetic; living.

verbs

address—; bestow in—; carve—; contribute to—; dedicate—; draw up—; endow—; engrave—; erect—; inscribe—; merit—; petition for—; raise—; —commemorates; —credits; —describes; —glorifies; —honors; —perpetuates; —portrays; —preserves; —recounts.

(See medal, trophy, monument.)

MEMORIES

adjectives

comfortless; tragic; ungracious; hurting; multicolored; muscular; grateful; faithful; hateful; pious; projected; rustling; suggestive; prompt; retentive; feeble; thronging; lamentable; long-to-be-cherished; conscious; color; unshaken; magnificent; unwelcome; artificial; white-lipped; sightless; puissant; vivid; surprising; ineffable; distinct; jarring; royal; incomparable; healthiest; disastrous; seductive; encyclopedia; disordered; glistening; usurious; aching; retributive; vindictive; solemn; ludicrous; blessed; confused; melodious; agreeable; natural; delightful; uncanny; bellicose; dark; animated; passionate; primeval; delicious; immortal; gay; infamous; ballad; dear; capacious; personal; living; impressive; vital; sacred; withered; sorrowful; pleasant; trifling; haunting; drowsy; fragrant; cherished; gossipy; atrocious; submerged; vapid; remorseful; tenacious; prodigious; amused; lingering; bright; stirred; sluggish; human; personified; resplendent; biographical; vague; fleeting; half-forgotten; endearing; dusty; eventful; fragmentary; weary; exhausted; deadly; deficient; precious; unbreathed; overwhelming; ghostlike; distorted; honored; detailed; time-fraught; everlasting; mutual; unfading; hereditary; intimate; lofty; public; blurred; rueful; embarrassed; unaccountable; imperfect;

bitter; accurate; emergent; grisly; musical; phenomenal; inevitable; priceless; unconscious; amazing; lurid; dormant; warming; enticing.

MEMORY
(faculty of remembering)
verbs
blur—; bury in—; cloud—; commit to—; drug—; dull—; engrave upon—; escape—; explore—; impair—; imprint on—; quote from—; strike—; coruscates; —paints; —pictures; —retains; —wanders.

(See mind, brain, consciousness, intellect.)

MEMORY
(reminiscence)
verbs
awaken—ies; blot out—; brood over—ies; cherish—; cling to—; dim—; dispel—; elucidate—; erase—; evoke—ies; freshen—; hallow—; honor—; haunt—; live in—; nurse—; nurture—; obliterate—; refresh—; revive—; shun—; suppress—; swap—ies; toy with—; treasure—; venerate—; —fades; —gnaws; —lingers; —pains; —surges; —survives.

(See remembrance, recollection.)

MEN
adjectives
vainglorious; succeeding; smooth-shaven; trampled; deft; glowing-eyed; up-and-doing; fashion-minded; fallible; able-bodied; orthodox; cringing; soft-conscienced; clear-witted; pusillanimous; decayed; banished; laconic; traitorous; hackneyed; sated; childless; huge-limbed; best-informed; best-tempered; insensate; ruling.

MENACE
adjectives
triple; significant; constant; mingled; dismal; ever-fearful; ominous; positive; deadly; feeble; dangerous; international; wrathful; crushing; serious; perpetual; fierce; terrible; transparent; owl-eyed; enticing; subdued; black.

verbs
avert—; banish—; conceal—; constitute—; denounce—; eradicate—; fear—; guard against—; harbor—; inveigh against—; invoke—; level—; share—; stamp out—; uncover—; ward off—; —endangers; —jeopardizes.

(See threat, peril, danger.

MENACE (v)
adverbs
seriously; portentously; ominously; dismally; dangerously; perpetually; fiercely; blackly; morally; seductively.

(See threaten, portend.)

MENAGE
verbs
adopt—; attach to—; bully—; conduct—; govern—; head—; install in—; involve—; join—; manage—; occupy—; recommend—; regulate—; superintend—; supervise—; support—; visit—; —bickers; —delights; —disperses.

(See home.)

MEND (v)
adverbs
appreciably; exquisitely; deftly; dexterously; cleverly; artfully; radically; expertly; artistically

(See repair, patch, improve.)

MENDACIOUS
adverbs
wickedly; venomously; spitefully; vengefully; maliciously; hatefully; viciously; notoriously; infamously; openly; shamelessly; treacherously; dangerously; trickily; craftily; arrantly; undeniably; brazenly; slyly; surreptitiously; atrociously; deplorably; lamentably; oddly; unaccountably; terribly; deliberately; shrewdly; meretriciously.

MENDACITY
adjectives
conscienceless; bugbear; deliberate; habitual; disreputable.

MENIAL
adverbs
odiously; basely; meanly; humbly; obsequiously; cringingly; pliantly; terribly; unaccountably; obediently; subserviently; obscurely; boorishly; pitiably; miserably; wretchedly; churlishly; incredibly.

MENSTRUATION
verbs
arrest—; delay—; disorder—; endure—; establish—; force—; induce—; perform—; retard—; stimulate—; suffer during—; suppress—; —ceases; —commences; —distresses; —exhausts; —fatigues; —impoverishes; —pains; —pauses; —strains.

adjectives

subconscious; practical; assumed; criminal; twisted; careless; subnormal; unbalanced.

verbs

burden—; check—; clog—; contemplate—; contribute to—; develop—; endow with—; exhaust—; furnish with—; impede—; limit —; nourish—; perfect—; relax—; repair—; strain—; tax—; tug at—; undermine—; — evolves from; —flags; —slackens.

(See brain, faculty, cleverness, brilliance, talent.)

MENTION

adjectives

special; passing; honorable; casual; fleeting; complimentary; occasional; copious; nonchalant.

verbs

deserve—; earn—; forbid—; merit—; peeve at (colloq.)—; report—; —alludes to; — describes; —disgusts; —excites; —inflames; —offends.

(See repetition, notice, remark, statement, utterance.)

MENTION (*v*)

adverbs

secretly; umbrageously; incidentally; mincingly; modestly; casually; nonchalantly; ominously; slanderously; slyly; inadvertently.

(See tell, reveal, relate, advise, expose.)

MENU

adjectives

proper; prescribed; balanced; convalescent; varied; nourishing.

verbs

alter—; approve—; arrange—; check—; compose—; consult—; dispatch—; glean from—; plan—; relish—; serve—; vary—; —appeals; —catalogues; —details; —lists; —nourishes; —offers; —prices; —suggests; —sustains; —tempts.

(See program, list.)

MERCANTILE

adverbs

highly; profitably; successfully; propitiously; negotiably; speculatively; stably; regularly; admirably; advantageously; prosperously; usefully; preeminently; obviously.

MERCENARY

adverbs

stingily; sordidly; basely; penuriously; greedily; deliberately; openly; obviously; manifestly; amazingly; surprisingly; selfishly; shamelessly; avowedly; miserably; wretchedly; blandly; frankly; ungenerously; rapaciously; avariciously; palpably; outrageously; inconsiderately; harshly; extortionately; churlishly; unbelievably; uncommonly.

MERCHANDISE

adjectives

timely; fashionable; quality; heterogeneous; exclusive; styled-right; jointed; seasonable.

verbs

assess—; bargain for—; catalogue—; claim —; close out—; convey—; dispense—; endow with—; evaluate—; hawk—; invest in —; liquidate—; overstock with—; peddle —; purchase—; purvey—; retail—; sacrifice—; salvage—; surrender—; turn over —; underwrite—; wholesale—.

(See imports, material, supply.)

MERCHANT

adjectives

respected; shaggy; successful; affluent; prudent; timorous; independent; prominent; sagacious; enterprising; prosperous; staid; sensible; clear-eyed; retired.

verbs

bargain with—; patronize—; —auctions; — deals in; —dispenses; —disposes of; — hawks; —jobs; —markets; —negotiates; — profits; —purveys; —puts under the hammer; —realizes a profit; —retails; —speculates; —traffics in; —transacts; —vends; —wholesales; —undersells.

(See hawker, jeweler, banker.)

MERCIFUL

adverbs

abundantly; benevolently; benignly; suddenly; habitually; kindly; generously; surprisingly; unaccountably; gravely; happily; fortunately; moderately; remarkably; exceedingly; compassionately; wondrously; uncommonly; infinitely; tenderly.

MERCILESS

adverbs

cruelly; bitterly; terribly; ruthlessly; pitilessly; relentlessly; stonily; sanctimoniously; rigidly; unfeelingly; hard-heartedly; maliciously; basely; incredibly; immovably; unspeakably; coldly; vengefully; unsparingly; tyrannically; sternly; abominably; barbarously; brutally; savagely; uncommonly; habitually.

MERCURIAL
adverbs
blithely; capriciously; delightfully; captivatingly; nimbly; actively; captiously; wantonly; cheerfully; changefully; inconstantly; craftily; unpredictably; problematically; perplexingly; irrationally; unreasonably; vivaciously; fascinatingly; temperamentally; unstably; merrily; erratically; waywardly; vagrantly; restlessly; nomadically; lightly; interestingly; casually.

MERCURY
verbs
administer—; anoint with—; drain—; inject —; scale—; —ascends; —contracts; —corrodes; —descends; —estimates; —expands; —gauges; —graduates; —impends; —measures; —poisons; —sublimates; —threatens; —warns.
(See chemical, medicine, thermometer, barometer.)

MERCY
adjectives
intellectual; wondrous; holy; tender; weak-eyed; ill-judged; noble; infinite; crowning; marvelous; common; eternal; devilish; saving; scant; lawful; hopeless; imperial; wonted; mutual; single; pardoning; gentle.

verbs
beg—; crown with—; dispose toward—; excite—; exercise—; extend—; favor with —; forbear out of—; grace with—; grant —; howl for—; implore—; invoke—; judge with—; lack—; lend—; plead for—; recommend—; rejoice in—; soften in—; sue for —; supplicate—; temper with—; tender—; throw upon—of; vouchsafe—; win—; — relents; —restrains; —spares; —thaws; — yields.
(See forbearance, grace, clemency, compassion, pity.)

MERETRICIOUS
adverbs
abominably; atrociously; unmentionably; dreadfully; unspeakably; pretentiously; shamelessly; bawdily; spuriously; indecor-

ously; coarsely; grossly; barbarously; outlandishly; monstrously; horridly; painfully; shockingly; particularly.

MERGE (v)
aaverbs
gradually; perpetually; conveniently; artfully; artistically; unconsciously; completely; superficially.
(See absorb, swallow.)

MERIT
adjectives
unusual; intrinsic; eminent; neglected; spectacular; unpopular; respective; artistic; patient; peculiar; multifarious; remarkable; comparative; indignant; solid; bashful; starving; toilworn; injured; mute; relative; ostensible; supereminent; accumulated; palpable; scientific; telling; strongest; transcendent; distinctive; technical; allsufficient; literary; aesthetic; striking; humbled; uneven; prime; essential; rare; tangible; productive; singular; doubtful; weaker; lap-dog; cardinal; noticeable; satisfying; conspicuous.

verbs
attain—; authorize—; award—; claim—; command—; confer—upon; detract from—; discuss—s; disclaim—; disclose—; dispute —; emulate—; entitle to—; esteem—; exhibit—; impute—to; judge—s; mark with —; overrate—s; rate—; reward with—; rival—; sanction—; test—; value—; vie for—; vindicate—; warrant—.
(See reward, advantage.)

MERIT (v)
adverbs
modestly; genuinely; justly; unquestionably; substantially; incalculably; ostensibly; justifiably; intrinsically; eminently; aesthetically; essentially; conspicuously.
(See deserve, earn.)

MERITORIOUS
adverbs
highly; uncommonly; manifestly; admirably; marvelously; unusually; laudably; exceptionally; splendidly; magnificently; indubitably; satisfactorily; estimably; appreciably; commendably; extremely.

MERRIMENT

adjectives

spasmodic; boisterous; continual; misplaced; hollow; apparent; considerable; tricksy; inward; thoughtless; sympathetic; ill-timed; quavering; rustic; mocking; chilling; joyous; merciless; excited; openhearted; adventurous; disproportional; infinite.

verbs

contribute to—; disport with—; feign—; frolic in—; frown on—; occasion—; regale with—; rejoice in—; reproach for—; revel in—; romp in—; —amuses; —brightens; —cheers; —convulses; —dies; —drives away care; —eases; —enlivens; —entertains; —flows; —palls; —perks up; —relaxes; —solaces; —titillates.

(See frolic, humor, glee, gayety, laughter, jollity, joy, fun.)

MERRY

adverbs

blithely; happily; mischievously; childishly; excitedly; madly; bewitchingly; ecstatically; joyously; naturally; habitually; inherently; mysteriously; noisily; boisterously; apparently; infinitely; hilariously; facetiously; jovially; genially; convivially; sportively; extremely; delightfully; fascinatingly; comically; drolly; briskly; exceedingly.

MESH

adjectives

mysterious; golden; tangled; guilty; glittering; shattered; legal; airy.

verbs

avert—; construct—; dangle in—; drain through—; elude—; entangle in—; extricate from—; interlace—; thread through—; weave—; —cages; —deceives; —ensnares; —fences off; —nets; —nonpluses; —perplexes; —puzzles; —sifts; —traps.

(See chain, complication.)

MESS

adjectives

nasty; dreadful; horrible; entire; filthy; viscid; savory; unholy; utmost; jovial; hoggish.

verbs

adulterate—; blend—; brew—; concoct—; entangle in—; ferment—; hash—; jumble into—; knead—; pound to—; reduce to—; shuffle into—; unravel—; —complicates; —

confuses; —disarrays; —disorders; —embarrasses; —litters; —muddles; —perplexes; —ruffles; —rumples.

(See junk, rubbish, waste.)

MESSAGE

adjectives

effective; divine; heartfelt; urgent; eternal; lucid; affectionate; turbulent; diabolical; true; expressive; unheeded; heated; spurred; dusty; private; precious; loving; telegraphic; sociological; farewell; verbal; pertinent; leaden; conciliatory; unanswered; assuring; rebukeful; laconic; distinct; luminous; terse; cryptic; hurried; alarming; instant; pitying; mysterious; speechless; heavenly; jubilee; anticipated; thrilling; crumpled; civil; rock-hewn; flattering; peevish; horrid; universal; vaunting; insurgent; faltering; ringing.

verbs

authenticate—; bear—; cable—; charge with—; communicate—; confirm—; convey —; decipher—; despatch—; dictate—; entrust—to; flash—; impart—; interpret—; issue—; narrate—; relay—; report—; signal—; telegraph—; transmit—; —informs; —rings; —stirs; deliver—.

(See errand, dispatch, letter, mail, manuscript.)

MESSENGER

adjectives

celestial; gracious; convenient; pure; winged; mindful; bonded; dusky; mourning; surly; arbitrating; angelic; trustworthy; distempered; shining; impatient; giddy; mystical; special; courageous; strong; churlish; guiltless; awe-stricken; wing-footed; breathless; welcome; better.

verbs

appoint—; assign—; consign to—; delegate —; dispatch—; —apprizes of; —bears; —communicates with; —confirms; —conveys; —declares; —delivers; —embarks; —forwards; —heralds; —imparts; —informs; —races; —reports; —reveals; —speeds; —transfers; —wings.

(See apostle, angel, emissary, delegate.)

MESSY

adverbs

abominably; dreadfully; hopelessly; unnecessarily; unduly; needlessly; confusedly; chaotically; intricately; confoundedly; untidily; shapelessly; irreducibly; inexcusably; unpardonably; unusually; inexplicably; unwarrantably; unspeakably; carelessly; filthily; crazily; surprisingly; extremely; indescribably.

METAL

adjectives

barren; engraving; sonorous; basic; combustible; glittering; mystical; precious; serviceable; non-tarnishable; best-tempered; burnished; invaluable; well-wrought; twisted; gleaming.

verbs

alloy—; assay—; cast—; congeal—; decarbonize—; engrave—; excavate—; hammer out—; model in—; mold—; prospect for—; refine—; render—; sheathe in—; smelt—; stamp—; strike—; value—; weld—; —corrodes; —expands; —oxidizes; —preserves.

(See lead, copper, coin, gold, iron, mineral.)

METAPHOR

adjectives

far-fetched; abundant; developed; suggestive; consistent; bucolic; striking.

verbs

abound with—s; apply—; employ—; —allegorizes; —alludes to; —collates; —colors; —compares; —contrasts; —depicts; —identifies; —illuminates; —illustrates; —likens; —parallels; —personifies; —portrays.

(See figure, word, phrase, paragraph, simile.)

METEOR

adjectives

disastrous; new-forged; unexpected; lurid; ominous; alarming; sudden; wandering; large; mighty; scarlet; cloud-encircled; descending; unctuous; deceitful.

METEORIC

adverbs

luridly; alarmingly; startlingly; swiftly; gloriously; incredibly; glowingly; splendidly; brilliantly; unbelievably; inconceivably; curiously; abruptly; miraculously; strangely; amazingly; astonishingly.

METER
(*instrument*)

adjectives

mystic; unconventional; inaccurate; dainty.

verbs

check—; feed—; flood—; —allots; —appoints; —apportions; —appraises; —assesses; —assizes; —compounds; —dispenses; —estimates; —graduates; —measures; —portions; —plumbs; —probes; —proportions; —records; —scales; —values.

(See barometer, thermometer, mercury.)

METHOD

adjectives

opposite; economical; selfsame; ingenious; inductive; haphazard; peaceful; laborious; scrupulous; numberless; hustling; indirect; exalting; novel; honorable; elaborate; summary; unostentatious; artistic; deductive; radio; unnatural; advantageous; clumsy; gruesome; commercialized; painless; convenient; statistical; authoritarian; getting; instinctive; conservative; picturesque; substantial; unique; dangerous; antiseptic; photographic; modern; up-to-the-minute; unsurpassed; therapeutic; orthodox; old-fashioned; lucid; prudent; time-honored; patented; scientific; sweet; objective; tentative; wholesome; plating; monstrous; philosophical; primitive; factory; despotic; imperturbable; feasible; transient; advertising; suitable; vociferous; unceremonious; naturalistic; lawful; evasive; subjective; preposterous; superstitious; accepted; surreptitious; particular; thoughtful; subversive; dilatory; peculiar; realistic; comely; inferior; outworn; analytic; amazing; humane; unpretending; histrionic; mystical; foolish; political; exclusive; dogmatic; equitable; ever-changing; descriptive; revolting; slack; peaceable; costly; doctrinal; appropriate; shrewd; false; ideal; autographic; financing; simplified; parliamentary; reproductive; pedantic; dictatorial; administrative; mild; barbarous; ignominious; collaborative; time-tried; indistinguishable; desultory; efficacious; inconsequent; injudicious; obsolescent; intuitive; glamorous; subtle; prosodic; avowed; current; fixation; enlarged; straightforward.

verbs

abandon—; abuse—; adopt—; advocate—; antedate—; ape—; apply—; conceive—; condemn—; design—; develop—; devise—; discard—; discover—; employ—; evolve—; exploit—; formulate—; introduce—; justify —; modify—; probe—; propose—; pursue

—; reform—; repudiate—; resort to—; revolutionize—; supplant—; supplement—.
(See procedure, process, fashion, manner.)

METHODICAL
adverbs
carefully; habitually; inherently; dependably; reliably; warrantably; overly; punctiliously; meticulously; outlandishly; comically; absurdly; rigidly; painfully; vexatiously; admirably; laudably; naturally; systematically; pleasantly; disagreeably; incredibly; unduly; uncomfortably; terribly.

METICULOUS
adverbs
carefully; painfully; disagreeably; uncomfortably; unduly; curiously; extremely; admirably; laudably; unfailingly; systematically; outlandishly.

METRICAL
adverbs
cleverly; pleasantly; melodiously; carefully;
smartly; cunningly; ingeniously; delightfully; tunefully; skillfully; harmoniously; enchantingly; mellifluously; artfully.

METROPOLIS
adjectives
exciting; throbbing; expectant; dazzling;
holiday; commercial; perfume; mystical;
huge; monstrous.

METTLE
adjectives
invincible; unimproved; scientific.

METTLESOME
adverbs
highly; vivaciously; animatedly; boldly; undauntedly; dauntlessly; cheerfully; sturdily;
actively; pluckily; courageously; spiritedly;
gayly; uncommonly; remarkably; notoriously; commendably; obviously; unusually;
energetically; strenuously; vigorously; intensely; restlessly; ungovernably; uncontrollably; audaciously; valiantly; adventurously.

MEW (v)
adverbs
plaintively; sympathetically; maternally;
shrilly; vociferously.
(See cry, wail.)

MICROPHONE
verbs
adjust—; announce through—; broadcast
through—; confront—; perform before—;
—amplifies; —clarifies; —communicates
with; —conveys; —enables; —intensifies; —
magnifies; —transmits.
(See loudspeaker.)

MICROSCOPE
verbs
adjust—; contemplate through—; discern
through—; employ—; examine under—;
focus—; glance into—; incline—; observe
under—; peep through—; peer into—; rivet
upon—; scrutinize through—; squint through
—; view through—; —augments; —detects;
—distinguishes; —enables; —enlarges; —
exaggerates; —magnifies; —reveals.
(See telescope.)

MICROSCOPIC
adverbs
minutely; infinitesimally; incredibly; curiously; ingeniously; unbelievably; amazingly; imperceptibly.

MIDDLE
verbs
ascertain—; assemble in—; balance in—;
cast in—; cleave in—; cling to—; concentrate in—; contract in—; converge on—;
designate—; focus on—; intersect in—; narrow toward—; proceed from—; situate in
—; split in—; taper toward—; —averages;
—centralizes; veer toward—.
(See interior, surface, center, bottom.)

MIDDLE-AGED
adverbs
hopelessly; permanently; persistently; miserably; wretchedly; doggedly; pertinaciously;
arthritically; rheumatically; pleasantly;
hoarily; venerably; patriarchally; wirily;
delightfully; obviously; youthfully.

MIDNIGHT
adjectives
impenetrable; fierce; profoundest; sedentary; sleek; beautiful; drear; blackest.

MIDSHIPMAN
verbs
amuse—; appoint—; consign—to; convey—;
delegate—; furlough—; promote—; school

—; train—; —crams; —embarks; —hoists; —marches; —plies; —promenades; — rooms; —sails; —tours.

(See sailor, officer, soldier.)

MIEN

adjectives
stately; gallant; placid; sullen; distant; spirited; haughty; conciliating; graceful; awe-inspiring; impressive; dejected; war-like; thoughtful; majestic; haggard; awk-ward; portentous; joyless; free; daring; noble; solemn; lofty; bold; withering; somber; undaunted; royal.

verbs
alter—; amend—; assume—; contemplate —; convert—; devise—; disguise—; eye—; influence—; modify—; present—; repose—; —awes; —conveys; —distresses; —disturbs; —enhances; —glares; —glows; —inspires; —menaces; —sours; —threatens.

(See demeanor, air, aspect, manner.)

MIGHT

adjectives
eternal; transparent; royal; truehearted; imposing; congregated; individual; withered; conquering; irresistible; apparent; fancied; divine; austere; intimate; unimaginable; ravenous; spacious; towering; resistless; delicious; outworn; borrowed; restless; wholesome; human; overmastering; brutal.

MIGRATION

adjectives
voluntary; forcible; autumnal; barbaric; instinctive.

MILD

adverbs
harmlessly; pleasantly; serenely; compassionately; reasonably; urbanely; blandly; suavely; affably; genially; tolerantly; complaisantly; leniently; judiciously; discreetly; diplomatically; carefully; placidly; imperturbably; philosophically; sedately; demurely; patiently; unctuously; graciously; ingratiatingly; winningly; tactfully.

MILDNESS

adjectives
resigned; mellow; incomparable; delicate.

MILE

verbs
advance—; clear—; detour—; estimate—; extend—; lag—; march—; progress—; pursue—; race—; recede—; total—s; trail for —s; trek—; withdraw—; —s drag; —s separate; —s weary.

(See distance.)

MILEAGE

adjectives
railroad; tire; maximum; gasoline; trip.

MILES

adjectives
dusky; tortuous; uncheered; weary; glistening; merry; laborious; geographical; delectable; glittering; appalling; snow-covered.

MILITARIST

adjectives
battering; greedy; professional; grasping; bloodthirsty; heartless.

MILITIA

adjectives
uniformed; hurrying; insubordinate.

verbs
arm—; arouse—; call out—; drill—; encounter—; enlist in—; discipline—; maintain—; muster—; qualify for—; recall—; regulate—; round up—; train—; —combats; —defends; —guards; —interferes; — mobilizes; —patrols; —pickets; —repels.

(See army, navy, regiment, soldier, troops.)

MILK

adjectives
tepid; acidophilus; skimmed; innocent; pulpy; metabolized; putrid; sour.

verbs
absorb—; administer—; churn—; concentrate—; condense—; contaminate—; curdle —; deprive of—; dilute—; draw—; extract from—; flavor—; pasteurize—; predigest—; rear on—; sip—; skim—; sour—; subsist on—; substitute—; taint—; thicken—; wean on—; —nourishes; —sustains.

(See food, cream.)

adjectives

neighboring; clanking; slander; mortgaged; social; busy; penetrating; muffled.

verbs

design—; establish—; guard—; manage—; operate—; picket—; report to—; set up—; speed up—; stock—; supervise—; —composes; —constructs; —frames; —manufactures; —organizes; —produces; —shuts down; —unionizes.

(See factory, shop, business, company, laboratory.)

MILL (v)

adverbs

eddyingly; riotously; alarmingly; tumultuously; disorderly; boisterously; actively.

(See reduce, crush.)

MILLION

adjectives

hardy; countless; shatterproof; mildewed; dark.

MILLIONAIRE

adjectives

senatorial; practical; decrepit; radical; amiable; myopic; eccentric; dirty-handed.

MIME

adjectives

mechanic; deft.

MIMIC (v)

adverbs

skillfully; audaciously; sardonically; sedulously; aptly; deftly; professionally; irritatingly; exasperatingly; roguishly.

(See mock, imitate.)

MINARETS

adjectives

slender; delicate; candle-extinguisher.

MINCE (v)

adverbs

primly; exaggeratedly; fastidiously; fashionably; wantonly; affectedly; delicately.

(See walk, step.)

MIND

adjectives

agitated; iron; conclusive; grosser; trained; thrifty; astute; observing; unbalanced; liberal; logical; far-seeing; poetic; subtle;

self-assured; conniving; contented; invisible; taintless; zealous; capricious; towering; feminine; swift; virtuous; shallow; untutored; courageous; languid; downcast; discriminating; controlling; well-trained; creative; philosophical; illustrious; pulverized; wavering; versatile; earthly; uncomplex; illuminated; earnest; weak; effeminate; careless; mortal; anxious; troubled; unthinking; terrestrial; dispassionate; exalted; elegant; reluctant; sympathetic; backward-looking; vigorous; romancing; ingenuous; tranquil; thoughtful; vulgar; twisted; imaginative; expanding; longing; pensive; unclean; virgin; sublimest; youthful; unconventional; flexible; restless; lethargic; conservative; apprehensive; erring; educated; enlightened; impressible; golden; distracted; lofty; inventive; disordered; undebauched; meditative; invoking; irritated; silly; fractional; preoccupied; giant; pure; soaring; gifted; exploring; ill-trained; independent; active; disburdened; ingenious; colossal; turbulent; callous; affrighted; cultivated; inattentive; exasperated; infinite; writhing; queasy; well-purged; honest; charming; quivering; unconquerable; wooing; ennobling; supersensitive; glowing; speculative; disciplined; scientific; slick; freckled; unfolding; infected; patriarchal; resourceful; unfettered; uninitiated; rude; mute; healthy; determined; mighty; realistic; abject; selfish; learned; far-reaching; devious; discriminating; plastic; brilliant; medieval; flurried; upright; respective; managerial; critical; priggish; sanguine; deferential; mercantile; superstitious; gullible; twofold; finite; percipient; grasping; mournful; wayless; reproductive; docile; theorizing; deliberating; unregenerate; reverential; unhinged; wounded; drunken; unaffected; fatuous; retentive; savage; inhospitable; self-formed; unrebellious; desecrated; diseased; sensitized; keen; serious; frivolous; infinite; robust; dissipated; intuitive; medical; canny; narrow; tabloid; deft; solitary; ductile; undergraduate; scholarly; unclouded; cheerful; nature-loving; idle; devotional; prying; high-sailing; immortal; eternal; petulant.

verbs

addle—; agitate—; assail—; attune—to; baffle—; banish—; bend—; bewilder—; broaden—; burden—; condition—; corrode —; corrupt—; convey to—; cultivate—; debauch—; delude—; depress—; detach—; dethrone—; disabuse—; disorient—; dispel from—; distort—; divert—; drug—; ease —; emancipate—; enfeeble—; engrave on —; enslave—; explore—; fertilize—; fetter —; filter into—; focus—on; harass—; haunt —; inflame—; impress on—; lodge in—; muddle—; plant in—; penetrate—; permeate —; pervade—; pop into—; rankle in—; reproach—; seep into—; shackle—; sharpen —; stamp on—; steel—; stimulate—; torture —; unbalance—; unbare—; unburden—; unhinge—; unsettle—; warp—; weigh in—; wrench—; —conceives; —dallies; —darts back; —deteriorates; —dictates; —disturbs; —dwells upon; —dwindles; —evolves; —envisages; —masters; —pictures; —probes; — reels; —roams; —seethes; —succumbs; — wanders; —wars.

(See consciousness, brain, imagination, head, intellect, memory.)

MINDFUL

adverbs

considerately; graciously; observantly; attentively; thoughtfully; affectionately; solicitously; tenderly; compassionately; carefully; discreetly; warily; prudently; providently; courteously; admirably; remarkably; sweetly; delightfully.

MINE

adjectives

gnomed; torched; fathomless; well-developed; abandoned; vast; rich; enwombed; exhaustless; hydraulic; inexhaustible.

verbs

abandon—; bore into—; burrow into—; cede —s to; confine in—; descend into—; emerge from—; excavate—; exhaust—; extract from —; gouge—; lower into—; operate—; ravage—; scoop from—; seal—; spring—; survey—; tunnel—; work—; —extends; —yields.

(See vein, earth, ground.)

MINER

verbs

asphyxiate—; confine—; disinter—; lower —; trap—; —bores; —burrows; —descends; —digs; —emerges; —excavates; —extracts; —gropes; —saps; —scoops; —shafts; — strikes; —tunnels; —uncovers; —unearths.

(See mole.)

MINERAL

adjectives

mortal; rare; vitreous; insignificant; tooth-building; essential.

verbs

abound in—s; alloy—; assay—; drill for —s; examine—; excavate—; extract—; prospect for —s; refine—; reveal—; scoop out —; uncover—; unearth—; utilize—; value —; —nourishes.

(See lead, metal, copper, gold, iron.)

MINGLE (*v*)

adverbs

democratically; promiscuously; inextricably; discreetly; affectionately; conspicuously; bizarrely; ostensibly; curiously; blasphemously; curiously; heterogeneously; profanely.

(See associate, mix.)

MINGLING

adjectives

rough; melancholy; charming; strange; promiscuous.

MINIATURE

adverbs

delicately; curiously; fragilely; incredibly; valuably; exceptionally; uncommonly; exotically; quaintly; fantastically; fashionably; modishly; pricelessly; expensively; exquisitely; matchlessly; incomparably.

MINIMUM

adjectives

irreducible; unimportant; smallest.

MINION

adjectives

pliant; sleek; dainty; luxurious; saucy; mindless.

MINISTER

adjectives

weak; debile; empyreal; nonconformist; accredited; formidable; efficient; gracious; sullen; shortsighted; puppet; irritated; gentle; misty; mournful; thoughtful; merciful; respective; refractory; shifty; retired; influential; unprincipled; powerful; grave; obstinate; right-hand.

verbs

appoint—; charge—with; invest—with; ordain—; —chastens; —cheers; —conducts; — converts; —consoles; —corrects; —dissents;

—executes; —imparts; —influences; —meditates; —offers; —officiates; —prays; —performs; —preaches; —rebukes; —reflects; —serves; —tames; —worships.

(See elder, deacon, leader, clergy, rabbi.)

MINISTERIAL
adverbs
gravely; authoritatively; officially; urbanely; suavely; blandly; unctuously; officiously; judicially; solemnly; pompously; professionally; considerately; subserviently; affably; genially; sympathetically; formidably; graciously; gently; influentially; courteously; ostentatiously; pleasantly; agreeably; sternly; cautiously; warily; wisely; admirably; wonderfully; acceptably; curiously.

MINISTRATION
adjectives
unfaltering; kindly; feminine; servile; pulpit; sleuthing; merciful.

MINISTRY
adjectives
maternal; pestilential; virgin; corrupt; tyrannical; radiant; hopeless; arduous; gracious; angelic; stated; bright-winged; incompetent; dictatorial.

verbs
acquaint with—; appoint to—; execute—; forsake—; fulfill—; invest—; obey—; ordain by—; plunge into—; retire from—; suspend from—; train for—; —assents; —chastens; —corrects; —meditates; —officiates; —performs; —rebukes.

(See cabinet, congress, management, government, church, legislature.)

MINK
verbs
dress in—; exhibit—; farm—; market—; prize—; skin—; value—; —burrows; —digs; —dives; —excavates; —inhabits; —shies; —swims.

(See animal, fur.)

MINOR
verbs
advise—; counsel—; cradle—; dictate to—; direct—; govern—; guard—; guide—; instruct—; manage—; model—; mold—; nourish—; prompt—; shape—; sustain—; —anticipates; —assumes; —attains; —matures; —ripens into.

(See child, boy, girl, youth.)

MINORITY
adjectives
enlightened; considerable; miserable; optimistic; aggressive; loud; troublesome; excitable; strong; substantial; intelligent; zealous; fanatic; hopeless; sulky; cultured.

verbs
bind—; defeat—; deprive—; dispense with —; eliminate—; emerge from—; oppress—; organize—; overrun—; overthrow—; tyrannize—; weed out—; —bows to; —engages; —fights; —opposes; —sacrifices; —struggles; —suffers; —thins.

(See childhood, majority, alien, foreigner.)

MINSTRELSY
adjectives
college; crude; barbaric.

MINUET
verbs
compose—; create—; excel at—; fancy—; form—; hum—; lead—; popularize—; step —; walk—; —amuses; —bewitches; —charms; —delights; —dignifies; —fascinates; —flourishes; —graces.

(See dance, waltz.)

MINUTE
verbs
(See moment.)

MINUTE
adverbs
infinitesimally; incredibly; embryonically; microscopically; unbelievably; imperceptibly; extremely; invisibly; undiscoverably; unimaginably; immeasurably; incalculably; inconceivably.

MINUTES
adjectives
joy-absorbing; leaden; immortal; thievish; exquisite; marvelous; soft; miserable; hopeless; breathless; tumultuous; golden; long-cold; precious; weary; interminable; searching; copious; unoccupied; fleeting.

MINUTES
verbs *(notes)*
depict in—; elaborate on—; enter into—; examine—; extract from—; jot down—; present—; record—; refer to—; report—;

submit—; —describe; —enlighten; —preserve; —recall; —refresh; —retain; —retrace; —specify; —sum up.

(See entry, notes, description, record,
item.)

MIRACLE

adjectives
culinary; celestial; numerous (pl); unfathomable; perpetual; incomprehensible; financial; inscrutable; established; blessed;
midnight; infinite; recorded; tenderest; gracious; medieval; year-born.

verbs
accept—; accomplish—; achieve—; ascribe
—to; behold—; confirm—; contradict—;
credit—; deny—; display—; divine—; foretell—; gape at—; hail as—; marvel at—;
prophesy—; render—; work—; —astounds;
—baffles; —bewilders; —convinces; —inspires; —mystifies; —dumbfounds; —unfolds; —violates.

(See magic, wonder, surprise, mystery)

MIRACULOUS

adverbs
unbelievably; incredibly; remarkably; wonderfully; solemnly; breath-takingly; divinely; indubitably; warrantably; manifestly;
assuredly; unfathomably; inscrutably; extraordinarily; strangely; marvelously; mysteriously; ineffably; stupendously; astoundingly; unquestionably.

MIRAGE

adjectives
holy; distorted; sound; floating; vapory;
exquisite.

verbs
blink at—; chase—; contemplate—; paint—;
reveal—; speculate on—; view—; —confuses; —dazzles; —deludes; —disperses; —
dissolves; —fades; —flickers; —hoodwinks;
—lifts; —looms; —melts away; —resembles; —shifts; —tantalizes; —vanishes.

(See maze, sight, view, vision, ghost.)

MIRE

adjectives
tenacious; puddled; lamp-reflecting; sensual; foul; sucking.

verbs
cast into—; drag through—; plunge in—;
sink in—; spatter in—; splash in—; stumble

in—; struggle through—; trample in—;
tread in—; wallow in—; —absorbs; —contaminates; —engulfs; —reeks; —sullies; —
swallows.

(See mud, swamp, marsh, dirt.)

MIRROR

adjectives
lie-consuming; spacious; distorting; wavering; retroscope; disposed; silver; gleaming;
magic; crystal; glorious; tarnished; liquid;
blurred; level; innumerable (pl); convex;
concave; enchanted; fleckless; frameless;
unflattering; detachable.

verbs
address—; behold in—; consult—; discern in
—; espy in—; flash in—; inspect in—; observe in—; panel—; polish—; peep in—;
perceive in—; spangle with —s; stare in—;
view in—; —exposes; —flickers; —glimmers; —magnifies; —reflects; —reveals; —
shimmers.

(See glass, reflection, water.)

MIRROR (v)

adverbs
skillfully; distortedly; waveringly; magically; liquidly; flatteringly; realistically; unfalteringly.

(See reflect, revert.)

MIRTH

adjectives
heart-easing; profane; painful; affected;
musing; careless; prolific; uproarious; sunburnt; roguish; petulant; buck-shrieked;
innocent; sacred; simple; festal; unquenchable; saturnine; sympathetic; immeasurable;
violent; tragical; resounding; boisterous;
heathenish; uncouth; harmless; whimsical;
fictitious; twinkling; Olympian; pagan; melodious; guiltless; desperate; undissembled;
hollow; ill-timed; suppressed; Philistinic;
dynamic; quaint; impish; ungrateful; cryptic; exuberant; frolic; rural; hysterical;
meditative; unconfined; dignified; pretended; marvelous.

verbs
bar—; bathe in—; choke with—; convulse
with—; disguise in—; elicit—; feign—;
flood with—; glide into—; light up with—;
provoke—; repent—; repress—; reprove—;
shake with—; sparkle with—; wreathe in
—; —bubbles; —eases; —ripples; —solaces;
—swells; —trespasses; —vexes.

(See joy, glee, fun, laughter, hilarity, humor.)

MIRTHFUL
adverbs
irrepressibly; hilariously; boisterously; noisily; scintillatingly; entertainingly; uproariously; blithely; gaily; merrily; playfully; comically; mischievously; roguishly; effervescently; indescribably; youthfully; happily; significantly.

MISANTHROPIC
adverbs
dreadfully; hatefully; cynically; unhappily; miserably; wretchedly; strangely; unaccountably; painfully; stupidly; obdurately; obstinately; fanatically; bitterly; morosely; moodily; cruelly; unreasonably; queerly; incorrigibly.; vexatiously; lugubriously; curiously; oddly; anti-socially; unbearably; insufferably; intolerably; unfortunately.

MISAPPREHENSION
verbs
flounder in—; incur—; labor under—; lament—; sense—; —addles; —agitates; —bewilders; —confounds; —confuses; —deludes; —distorts; —embarrasses; —muddles; —perplexes; —tortures; —twists.
(See misunderstanding, uncertainty, shame, suspense, misconception.)

MISBEHAVE (v)
adverbs
notoriously; ceaselessly; profanely; impishly; unregenerately; drunkenly; fatuously; intolerably; maliciously; wantonly; mortifyingly; wilfully.
(See act, conduct.)

MISCARRIAGE
verbs
agitate to—; avert—; brood over—; convalesce from—; deplore—; incite—; provoke —; succumb to—; ward off—; —bereaves; —disappoints; —disconcerts; —disheartens; —frustrates; —robs; —undermines; — weakens.
(See abortion, failure, mistake, indiscretion, blunder, unhappiness.)

MISCELLANEOUS
adverbs
discouragingly; confusingly; perplexingly; promiscuously; carelessly; hopelessly; delightfully; strangely; unsystematically; un-methodically; curiously; oddly; deliberately; untidily; indiscriminately; typically; characteristically.

MISCHIEF
adjectives
desperate; secret; direst; enormous; desultory; intolerable; tormenting; malicious; wanton; mortifying; anticipated; supernatural; irreparable; impish; private; willful; stomachic.

verbs
actuate—; conceive—; confess—; contrive —; devise—; dog with—; instigate—; molest with—; plague with—; rectify—; share in—; work—; —agitates; —befalls; —besets; —disorganizes; —distresses; —enrages; —grates; —harasses; —hatches; — incenses; —piques; —provokes; —rankles; —ruffles; —torments; —trails.
(See injury, harm, damage, offense, oppression, trouble.)

MISCHIEVOUS
adverbs
incorrigibly; innocently; delightfully; teasingly; harmlessly; viciously; deliberately; childishly; merrily; thoughtlessly; maliciously; vengefully; terribly; intolerably; vexatiously; maddeningly; deliberately; studiously; craftily; shamefully; desperately; secretly; furtively; wantonly; irreparably; impishly; elfishly; purposely; wilfully; openly; defiantly; obstinately; persistently; perniciously; noxiously; naughtily; unbearably; poisonously.

MISCONCEPTION
adjectives
dangerous; huge; unworthy; singular; complete; dreadful; harmful; definite; deliberate; studied.

verbs
dissipate—; expose to—; flounder in—; scent —; twist in—; —addles; —agitates; —bewilders; —confounds; —confuses; —deludes; —distorts; —embarrasses; —endangers; —muddles; —perplexes; —torments; —tortures.
(See error, inaccuracy, fallacy, illusion, misapprehension.)

MISCONDUCT

adjectives

intentional; prankish; private; flagrant; alleged; violent; open.

MISCONSTRUE (v)

adverbs

persistently; chronically; inevitably; recurringly; intentionally; profoundly; wilfully; tragically; cavalierly.

(See distort, twist, change.)

MISCREANT

adjectives

loathsome; meaner; apprehended; vile.

MISDEED

verbs

actuate—; boast—; confess—; confine—to; harass with —s; hatch—; lament—; molest with —s; repent—; rue—; share in—; — annoys; —distresses; —dogs; —enrages; — grates; —incenses; —piques; —rankles; — ruffles.

(See crime, deed, offense, conduct.)

MISDEMEANOR

adjectives

trifling; unlawful; ingenious.

MISER

verbs

abhor—; detest—; hiss—; scoff at—; scorn —; torment—; —accumulates; —acquires; —begrudges; —broods; —covets; —endures; —fears; —grasps; —hoards; —pinches; — sacrifices; —scants; —skins; —starves; — stints; —wrests.

MISERABLE

adverbs

wretchedly; unutterably; poignantly; visibly; helplessly; desolately; uncommonly; dismally; lonesomely; heavily; gloomily; drearily; hopelessly; disconsolately; forlornly; abjectly; dejectedly; downright; singularly; peculiarly; bitterly; cruelly; unwontedly; fretfully; sorely; oddly; incurably; intensely.

MISERLY

adverbs

inherently; incurably; basely; selfishly; crazily; stupidly; horribly; avariciously; penuriously; unaccountably; perniciously; mendaciously; sordidly; unspeakably; churlishly; greedily; rapaciously.

MISERY

adjectives

untried; unrelieved; sticky; disintegrating; life-deserting; unutterable; gnawing; shadow-vested; motionless; piercing; dim; beauteous; poignant; past; selfish; eternal; uncounted; quiet; consequent; human; tyrannical; vicious; frightful; splendid; lonely; far-off; helpless; slow; unspeakable; seething; extremest; intolerable; parasitical; petty; fictitious; attendant; remediless; lessening; dumb; appalling; deserved.

verbs

allay—; alleviate—; assuage—; augment—; deplore—; escape—; heighten—; lighten—; moan in—; moderate—; mollify—; reduce —; relieve—; repent in—; rid of—; shelter —; spare—; steep in—; waste away in—; —diminishes; —disheartens; —eases.

(See anguish, distress, ache, pain.)

MISFORTUNE

adjectives

unwonted; impending; domestic; terrible; irreparable; vital; serious; human; constant; private; possible; grave; crushing; prevailing; dire; especial; cursed; signal; admitted; unparalleled; lone.

verbs

bear—; beset by—; bow beneath—; endure —; lament—; plunge into—; remedy—; rise above—; shake off—; sob—; suffer—; triumph over—; —afflicts; —assails; —befalls; —blasts; —burdens; —distresses; —gnaws; —harrows; —heckles; —nips; —outstrips; —overtakes; —sleeps; —sours.

(See ill, evil, loss, disappointment, calamity, catastrophe, adversity, affliction, disaster.)

MISGIVINGS

adjectives

serious; shamed; dim; conscientious; restless; nervous; grave; strange; profound; sceptical; ominous.

verbs

admit—; entertain—; excite—; fence with —; flinch beneath—; harbor—; hesitiate from—; inspire—; overwhelm by—; shrink in—; wrap in—; wince beneath—; —alarm; —awe; —cloud; —creep over; —disquiet; —haunt; —overwhelm; —prey on; —strike; —torment; —weigh.

(See anxiety, solicitude, worry, apprehension.)

MISGUIDED

adverbs

utterly; unfortunately; wilfully; deliberately; perniciously; unutterably; unhappily; perversely; inconsiderately; foolishly; tragically; lamentably; deplorably; woefully; sadly.

MISHAP

adjectives

untoward; dire; industrial; unavoidable; preventable; serious.

verbs

allay—; avert—; avoid—; bridge—; culminate in—; curtail —s; dodge—; guard from—; labor under—; minimize —s; mourn —; secure from—; share—; succumb to—; —botches; —swallows; —swamps.

(See disaster, accident, misfortune, catastrophe, adversity.)

MISINFORMED

adverbs

lamentably; perfidiously; sadly; bitterly; cruelly; wilfully; deliberately; treacherously; unhappily; unfortunately; maliciously; purposely; peculiarly; unwittingly; erroneously; blindly; stupidly; unwittingly; deceitfully; craftily.

MISJUDGE (v)

adverbs

utterly; artlessly; pathetically; perniciously; grossly; deplorably; irritatingly; ludicrously; awkwardly.

(See decide, judge.)

MISLAY (v)

adverbs

inadvertently; accidentally; artlessly; senselessly; singularly; absently; disastrously; deliberately; carelessly; obtusely.

(See misplace.)

MISLEAD (v)

adverbs

deliberately; treacherously; intentionally; evilly; murderously; unwontedly; perniciously; cruelly; irrationally.

(See decline, cheat.)

MISPLACE (v)

adverbs

thoughtlessly; carelessly; absently; casually; unconsciously; unfortunately.

(See mislay.)

MISREPRESENT (v)

adverbs

grossly; vindictively; unjustly; scandalously; intentionally; artfully; hatefully; villainously; falsely; hypocritically.

(See distort, falsify.)

MISREPRESENTATION

adjectives

gross; willful; flagrant; specious; singular; monstrous; calculated.

verbs

deceive with—; decry—; denounce—; detect—; disclose—; fall victim to—; fathom —; interpret—; refute—; sense—; suffer from—; —aggravates; —amplifies; —deludes; —distorts; —dupes; —exaggerates; —falsifies; —magnifies.

(See lie, fallacy, deception.)

MISS (v)

adverbs

accidentally; coincidentally; seriously; narrowly; dreadfully; tragically; unavoidably; preventably.

(See omit, overlook.)

MISSHAPEN

adverbs

cruelly; bitterly; miserably; pitiably; horribly; unspeakably; pitifully; lamentably; woefully; pathetically; accidentally; congenitally; permanently; unfortunately; unluckily; awkwardly; clumsily; helplessly; hopelessly; irremediably; grotesquely; fantastically; outlandishly; peculiarly; sadly; tragically; crookedly; gauntly; forbiddingly; grossly; frightfully.

MISSILE

adjectives

divine; deadly; terrifying; ineffectual; innocent; squashy; living; unremitting; rebounding; speedy; well-directed.

verbs

arm with—s; assail with—s; direct—; discharge—; fire—; fling—; hurl—; pelt with —s; scatter—s; shoot—s; —shakes; —stabs; —stings; —stuns; —s torment.

(See dart, weapon, arrow, bullet, stone, shot, spear.)

MISSING

adverbs

tragically; hopelessly; irrecoverably; sadly;

blankly; starkly; undeniably; presumably; supposedly; avowedly; unmistakably; mysteriously; strangely; suspiciously; curiously; altogether; allegedly; shockingly; startlingly; disconcertingly; perplexingly.

MISSION
adjectives
intuitive; blushing; world-wide; fruitless; terrestrial; proposed; divine; unearthly; honorable; great; arduous; delicate; merciful; avowed; vicarious; perilous; momentous; indefinite; sublime; apostolic; secret; diplomatic; peaceful; dubious; memorable; celestial; loftiest; subsequent; novel; cultural; consequential; hardy; noble.

verbs
accept—; authorize—; charge with—; confide—to; deter—; entrust with—; equip for —; fulfill—; gain—; hamper—; hasten—; hinder—; impose—upon; journey on—; perform—; proceed on—; reveal—; select for —; speed—; undertake—.
(See errand, commission, purpose, object, view, trust.)

MISSIONARY
adjectives
itinerant; devoted; intelligent; adroit; shabby; gentle; eloquent; conscientious.

MISSPELL (v)
adverbs
habitually; intentionally; grossly; carelessly; absently; humorously; stupidly; inanely.
(See spell.)

MISSTATE (v)
adverbs
unblushingly; ungenerously; intentionally; artfully; shrewdly; legally; solemnly; cynically; characteristically; humorously; monstrously; eccentrically.
(See distort, falsify, misrepresent.)

MISSTATEMENT
adjectives
willful; unconsidered; ungenerous; planned; leading.

MIST
adjectives
azure; horrid; genial; shimmering; jealous; thin; fragrant; friendly; shrouding; sulphurous; sickening; contaminating; matutinal; morning; undistinguishable; sea-green; starry; dark; whirling; damp; parting; chronic; impenetrable; chilly; indistinct; blinding; luminous; feudal; jeweled; coral; semilucent; opaline; silvery; golden; happy; drenching; rolling; tenuous; square; unwholesome; gleamy; amber; malarial; driving; winged; amorous; earth-born; overhanging; radiant; flaky; descending; opal; heavy; glamorous; impalpable; drifting; odorous; murky; lowering; shifting; stultifying; hoary; rising; northern; ghastly; tremulous; midnight; visionary; feeble.

verbs
emerge from—; falter in—; flounder in—; swathe in—; —befogs; —blinds; —blurs; —clears; —clings about; —darkens; —deepens; —disperses; —encircles; —enfolds; —enshrouds; —envelops; —hangs over; —hides; —lifts; —obscures; —rises; —surrounds; —veils; —wraps.
(See fog, haze, clouds, smoke, spray, steam, vapor.)

MISTAKE
adjectives
grievous; pernicious; curious; strange; dreadful; frightful; pitiful; gross; slight; desperate; fatal; unfortunate; administrative; doltish; tactical; cardinal; traffic; capital; absurd; stupid; deplorable; irritating; felicitous; unavoidable; ludicrous; contradictory; horrible; awkward; petty; tragic; initial; natural; miraculous; cruel; pathetic; military.

verbs
account for—; avoid—; bare—; blush at—; commit—; convince of—; eradicate—; minimize—s; obscure—; observe—; obviate—; overlook—; pardon—; plunge into—; rectify —; regard—.
(See lapse, inaccuracy, fault, falsehood, error, incongruity, indiscretion, blunder.)

MISTAKE (v)
adverbs
grievously; grossly; perniciously; curiously; desperately; doltishly; absurdly; felicitously; ludicrously; tragically; pathetically.
(See misunderstand.)

MISTAKEN
adverbs
grossly; curiously; stupidly; senselessly; perversely; stubbornly; awfully; frightfully; blindly; tragically; emphatically; griev-

779

ously; pitiably; desperately; absurdly; ridiculously; pathetically; horribly; outrageously; manifestly; doggedly; preposterously.

MISTREAT (v)
adverbs
brutally; cruelly; sadistically; evilly; heartlessly; callously; pervertedly.
(See abuse, misuse.)

MISTREATMENT
verbs
bear—; beset by—; bow beneath—; bridle —; brood on—; burden by—; confess to—; endure—; fear—; harass with—; harrow by—; heap—upon; lament—; resent—; revenge—; subdue by—; subject to—; suffer —; —distresses; —embitters; —enrages; — frustrates; —incenses; —numbs; —wrecks.
(See abuse, pain, torture.)

MISTRESS
adjectives
gentle; mature; worthless; doting; fair; merry; accomplished; rare; gracious; white-handed; fine; queenly; slowly-fading; exacting; sovereign; indulgent; flaming; deserted; dread; petty; proud; dainty; virtuous; mischievous; brilliant; coquettish.

verbs
attend—; chain to—; desert—; devote to—; discard—; escort—; harbor—; maintain—; restrain—; serve—; squire—; stray to—; support—; —enslaves; —escapes; —submits.
(See lover, sweetheart, master, matron, friend.)

MISTRUSTFUL
adverbs
prudently; discreetly; habitually; temperamentally; chronically; insolently; anxiously; cautiously; intolerantly; insufferably; uncomfortably; darkly; subtly; sharply; absurdly; jealously; apprehensively; nastily; instinctively; suddenly; vaguely; inwardly.

MISTY
adverbs
strangely; terribly; obscurely; dimly; nebulously; cloudily; smokily; oddly; curiously; extremely; mysteriously; deliberately; dangerously; surprisingly; astonishingly;

perplexingly; frightfully; ominously; intensely; alarmingly; abominably; fragrantly; impenetrably; heavily; gloomily; dismally; drearily; vaporously; frostily; foggily.

MISUNDERSTAND (v)
adverbs
deliberately; obtusely; idiotically; illogically; doltishly; pathetically; characteristically; normally.
(See mistake, disagree.)

MISUNDERSTANDING
adjectives
mutual; future; ever-recurring; chronic; inevitable; costly.

verbs
apologize for—; avert—; avoid—; bridge —; conquer—; cope with—; decry—; eradicate—; expose to—; fear—; grapple with —; guard from—; iron out—; risk—; smooth over—; —alarms; —endangers; — excites; —incites.
(See misapprehension, misconception, controversy, disagreement.)

MISUSE (v)
adverbs
brutally; crudely; ruinously; ungenerously; pitilessly; insensately; irrationally; grievously.
(See mistreat, abuse.)

MITE
adjectives
wee; musical; round-bellied; microscopic.

MIX (v)
adverbs
experimentally; inextricably; confusingly; intimately; determinedly; marvelously; discreetly; curiously; ludicrously.
(See associate, mingle.)

MIXED
adverbs
hopelessly; indiscriminately; perplexingly; delightfully; frightfully; incongruously; artfully; cleverly; beautifully; unbelievably; exasperatingly; vexatiously; curiously; mysteriously; grotesquely; disastrously; advantageously.

MIXTURE

adjectives

singular; strange-looking; flecked; hybrid; curious; whimsical; miscellaneous; bright; prodigious; ineffable; fascinating; effervescent; elemental; incongruous; racemic; unbalanced; incoherent; aromatic; piquant; heavy; paradoxical; greasy; sticky; complicated; engaging; fiery; impotent; confused; irrational; ragged; conglomerate; messy.

verbs

administer—; apply—; boil—; compound—; dilute—; drain—; emerge from—; garnish —; saturate—; stir—; swallow—; —coagulates; —hardens; —simmers; —thickens.

(See compound, medicine, chemical, solution.)

MOAN

adjectives

tender; sullen; insidious; enchanted; solemn; untimely; dying; peevish; stifled; weird; faint; alternate; pathetic; broken; everlasting; repentant; languid; lovely; wailing; low; perpetual; sobbing; desolate; shivering; harmonious; angry; doleful; occasional; harsh; short; mortal.

verbs

emit—; endure—s; muffle—; silence—s; stifle—; swell—s; throttle—; tolerate—; —chills; —disquiets; —escapes the lips; —gnaws; —pierces; —rends; —stirs; —weighs; —wrenches.

(See groan, sigh, whine, sob, cry.)

MOAN (*v*)

adverbs

dolefully; spasmodically; lugubriously; disconsolately; heartrendingly; fitfully; tremulously; grievously; pathetically; tragically; agonizingly; appallingly; distractedly; desolately; weirdly; inarticulately.

(See groan, mourn, lament, complain.)

MOANING

adjectives

dismal; thunderous; weird; desolate; inarticulate; faint.

MOB

adjectives

pitiless; patriotic; reactionary; lawless; furious; heartless; hostile; bewildering; bawling; swaying; union; emotion-charged; insensate; grinning; unruly; irrationalized;

numerous; surging; distracted; great; mere; clumsy; hot-headed; fickle; ignorant; sadistic; immense; savage; supreme; angry; disorganized; noisy; mingled; infuriated; inflammable; riotous.

verbs

attract—; confront—; frustrate—; harangue —; inflame—; restrain—; sway—; —clamors; —disperses; —heckles; —huzzas; —jeers; —lynches; —pelts; —riots; —swarms; —storms; —withdraws.

(See crowd, masses, multitude, public, throng.)

MOBILE

adverbs

advantageously; curiously; skilfully; ingeniously; suddenly; sadly; variably; inconstantly; curiously; beautifully; handily; splendidly; conveniently; unstably; capriciously; erratically; unsteadily; waywardly; actively; vagrantly; captiously; nomadically.

MOCK (*v*)

adverbs

sneeringly; heartlessly; derisively; vindictively; sardonically; blandly; hollowly; jeeringly; cynically; impotently; despicably; maliciously.

(See mimic, imitate.)

MOCKERY

adjectives

hollow; unreal; solemn; unsubstantial; empty; cynical; standing; ghastly; forced; impotent; hideous; sardonic; bland.

verbs

bear—; endure—; expose to—; ignore—; persecute with—; provoke—; regret—; roast in—; —agonizes; —discomposes; —disconcerts; —disheartens; —humiliates; —mortifies; —rankles; —ruffles; —saddens; —wearies; —weighs upon; —wounds.

(See irony, derision, banter, sarcasm, ridicule.)

MOCKING

adverbs

hideously; hatefully; laughingly; teasingly; disrespectfully; tauntingly; sarcastically; skilfully; artfully; dramatically; scornfully; entertainingly; rudely; ironically; chaffingly; derisively; insufferably; vexatiously; unbearably; intolerably; disagreeably; unpleasantly; offensively; contemptuously; cruelly; unpardonably; sardonically.

MOCKINGBIRD

verbs
admire—; prize—; —copies; —grieves; —defends; —cackles; —imitates; —jests; —jibes; —mews; —mimics; —pours forth; —scoffs; —shakes music; —shrieks; —utters; —wails; —whistles.
(See bird.)

MODE

adjectives
compact; varying; simpler; desultory; perfected; sagacious; happy-go-lucky; sentimental; singular; adequate; proscribed; equivocal; subconscious; prevailing; pompous; uncivilized; feudal; indispensable; scenical; disagreeable; equitable; progressive; frizzling; questionable; hospitable; artless; peculiar; fleeting; ostentatious; ruinous; expeditious; mercenary; hygienic; languid; cheap; irregular; capricious; enjoyable; ultra-modern; ingenuous; ingenious.

verbs
accept—; approve—; burlesque—; conform to—; consent to—; deride—; endorse—; fix—; govern by—; observe—; overdo—; pattern—; prefer—; protest—; revive—; subscribe to—; —disfigures; —enslaves; —succumbs.
(See fashion, manner, mannerism, vogue, standard, trend.)

MODEL

adjectives
exclusive; stunning; venerable; hallucinatory; dressy; hanging; rustic; unique; classical; mechanical; mangled; conservative; casual; inspired; swagger; straight-line; jigger; uniform; unthrifty; worldly; fancy; lacy; stylish; slim.

verbs
borrow from—; construct—; copy—; depart from—; design—; devise—; draw up—; erect—; emulate—; evolve—; explain from —; follow—; imitate—; improve—; mould —; pattern on—; perfect—; refer to—; reproduce—; serve as—; shape—; —embodies; —represents.
(See example, ideal, design, classics, manikin, masterpiece.)

MODEL (v)

adverbs
deliberately; artistically; sedulously; mechanically; imitatively; conservatively; uniformly; uniquely; fashionably.
(See mould, fashion, shape.)

MODERATE

adverbs
sensibly; admirably; judiciously; sagaciously; wisely; acceptably; reasonably; altogether; frugally; prudently; discreetly; thriftily; modestly; singularly; astonishingly; cautiously; notoriously.

MODERATION

adjectives
false; illogical; genial; equal; due; classical; sworn; practiced; remarkable; notable.

verbs
advise—; caution—; confine to—; counsel —; cultivate—; inure by—; prefer—; prescribe—; prize—; recline in—; seat in—; taper to—; treasure—; treat in—; —calms; —combats; —contents; —sobers; —subdues; —suffices; —tempers.
(See conservatism, caution, temperance, restraint.)

MODERN

adverbs
fashionably; stylishly; acceptably; satisfactorily; sufficiently; delightfully; progressively; refreshingly; presumably; warrantably; conveniently; screamingly; attractively; noticeably; incongruously.

MODERNISM

verbs
accent—; bind in—; cater to—; challenge —; combat—; define—; defy—; diffuse—; dispense with—; evolve—; fashion in—; favor—; immerse in—; temper—; touch with—; welcome—; resist—; —amazes; —attracts; —enhances; —excites; —impresses; —prevails; —refreshes; —transforms.
(See materialism, religion, philosophy, socialism.)

MODEST

adverbs
extremely; girlishly; engagingly: charmingly; peculiarly; becomingly; naturally; fool-

ishly; ridiculously; touchingly; adorably; absurdly; comically; demurely; delicately; decently; decorously; admirably; attractively; pleasingly.

MODESTY

adjectives

shaking; womanly; delicate; singular; maidenly; pleasing; extreme; daring; beauteous; virgin; innate; incredible; hypocritical; unassuming; characteristic; austere; bashful; becoming; habitual; marital; ill-placed; boastful; cold; false; indignant; artful.

verbs

bait with—; counterfeit—; deport with—; discern—; extinguish—; feign—; inculcate —; personify—; recommend—; respect—; veil in—; violate—; wrap in—; —charms; —compels; —enjoins; —guards; —heightens; —hides; —padlocks; —restrains; —shuns; —survives.

(See decency, constraint, bashfulness, humility, purity, reserve.)

MODIFICATION

adjectives

slow; serious; substantive; profound; tiny; prescribed.

verbs

publish with—s; require—s; smooth into—; sober into—; undergo—; vary by—; —appeases; —deviates; —diverges; —hushes; —mollifies; —satisfies; —smothers; —softens; —subdues; —tempers; —tones down.

(See alteration, change, transition, variation.)

MODIFY (*v*)

adverbs

deferentially; partially; essentially; substantially; subsequently; drastically; profoundly; intrinsically; dogmatically.

(See adjust, limit.)

MODISH

adverbs

fashionably; extremely; remarkably; amazingly; oddly; delightfully; attractively; alluringly; temptingly; expensively; extravagantly; absurdly; unexpectedly; stylishly; unusually; uncommonly; astoundingly; daintily; tastefully; elegantly; conventionally; presentably; punctiliously; meticulously; showily; gaudily; quietly; acceptably.

MODULATE (*v*)

adverbs

exquisitely; mellifluously; coherently; harmoniously; musically;

(See adapt, adjust.)

MODULATION

adjectives

indiscriminate; learned; incoherent; inharmonic; mellifluous; surprising.

verbs

accord—; effect—; introduce—; perceive—; resign to—; value—; —delights; —enchants; —finishes; —flatters; —harmonizes; —pleases; —represses; —shades; —soothes; —subdues.

(See accent, adjustment, music, quiet.)

MOILS

adjectives

dynastic; imperial; far-flung; terrestrial.

MOIST

adverbs

excessively; extremely; unpleasantly; disagreeably; dangerously; unfortunately; satisfactorily; sufficiently; disastrously; continually; humidly; oppressively; soggily; swampily; conveniently; productively.

MOISTURE

adjectives

perpetual; heavenly; oppressive; suspicious; refreshing; needed; precipitated; genial; bounteous; dark; filthy; fated; destructive; pleasant; over-much; scant.

verbs

absorb—; boil away—; charge with—; condense into—; dabble in—; deprive of—; diffuse—; dim with—; emit—; exude—; inject —; precipitate—; restrain—; saturate with —; sponge with—; sprinkle with—; suck—; vaporize—; wring from—; —dampens; — irrigates; —refreshes; —seeps in.

(See dew, liquid, water, spray, vapor.)

MOLASSES

adjectives

dark; sorghum; fermented; tasty; rubber-like.

MOLD

adjectives

inflexible; heroic; delicate; vulgar; primitive; ethereal; determined; giant; virtuous;

rude; splendid; human; precision; wintry; gentle; beauteous; hollowed; arbitrary; muscular; different; dark; fresh; mossy; earthly; decaying; mortal; massive.

verbs
(See mould.)

MOLE

verbs
run down—; skin—; —burrows; —devastates; —destroys; —digs; —emerges; —excavates; —menaces; —preys on; —scoops; —shovels; —tunnels; —vacates.
(See animal, miner.)

MOLECULE

adjectives
blundering; organic; asymmetric; infinitesimal.

verbs
blast—; break down—; detect—; dissociate into—s; ionize—s; split—; store in—; weigh —; —attracts; —bombards; —charges; —clings; —collides; —composes; —fascinates; —s group; —s pair off; —puzzles; —retains; —s unite.
(See corpuscle, element.)

MOLLIFIED

adverbs
considerably; mercifully; reasonably; quietly; finally; ultimately; gradually; wholly; gently; visibly; eventually; happily; luckily; fortunately; presumably; somewhat; slowly; greatly; perceptibly; admittedly.

MOMENT

adjectives
decisive; spiteful; uncertain; voluptuous; critical; silent; lyrical; ludicrous; tragic; disagreeable; pictorial; appalling; musing; inspired; leisure; awful; microscopical; infinite; extraordinary; propitious; enlightened; proud; willful; little; heavier; immortal; delightful; high-tide; opportune; prolonged; gravest; radiant; usurped; bitter; highest; prearranged; charming; sulky; brisk; solemn; intuitive; giddy; whirling; supreme; omnipotent; inauspicious; unguarded; precise; culminating; single; blemished; gayest; rare; cantabile; shining; psychological; undecided; spellbound; earliest; vital; dreamy; affected; briefest; dramatic; heartrending; occasional; embittering; cooler; appointed; pleasant; illuminated; wak-

ing; breathless; hungry; ardent; lessened; important; flashing; crucial; theoretical; fading; poignant; fleeting; fateful; exalted; miraculous; pregnant; hostile; erotic; affectionate; necessary; sunny; impressive; reconciling; precise; tense; leisure; staggering; lofty; intimate; startled; inspirational; futile; practical; careless; sardonic; skinned; intent; delightful; lonely; golden; memoried; particular; few (pl); confused; swift; bold; brief; natal; troubled; deplorable; awful; sickening; inexpressible; tingling; cheerless; unnecessary; sunny.

verbs
acclaim—; anticipate—; consume in—; endure—; pause for—; relish—; seize—; snatch—; squeeze—dry; —flits by; —thrills; —troubles.
(See flash, instant, time.)

MOMENTOUS

adverbs
gravely; seriously; importantly; signally; unutterably; immensely; relatively; overwhelmingly; singularly; peculiarly; particularly; impressively; imposingly; strangely; mysteriously; secretly; inscrutably; exceptionally; infinitely; decisively; historically; tremendously; transcendently; insuperably; incomparably.

MOMENTUM

verbs
accumulate—; acquire—; defy—; gain—; lend—to; repel—; resist—; submit to—; withstand—; —batters; —butts; —drives; —impels; —increases; —prods; —shoves; —thrusts.
(See impetus, speed, force, velocity.)

MONARCH

adjectives
constitutional; magnanimous; affable; determined; degenerate; incompetent; conquering; pretentious; maddening; riotous; insolent; absolute; presumptuous; generous; rash; romantic; throned; deposed; new-crowned; ambitious; irrepsonsible; disheveled; unwilling; potent; forest; progressive; luxurious; unengaging; crumpled; affable; sensual; effeminate; puissant; opulent; sagacious; ill-starred; mighty; legendary; capricious; barbarous; factious; turbulent.

verbs

ape—; attack—; attend—; behead—; crown —; depose—; enthrone—; laud—; overthrow—; rebel against—; rule—; submit to—; —abdicates; —compels; —domineers; —imposes; —liberates; —misrules; —oppresses; —ordains; —reigns; —succeeds to; —surveys; —tramples; —yields.

(See emperor, dictator, king, monarchy, nobility, royalty.)

MONARCHY

adjectives

limited; restored; feudal; hereditary; absolute; constitutional; restricted; centralizing; flourishing; undisputed; despotic; serviceable; liberal; free; kingless.

verbs

attack—; destroy—; discontinue—; dispute —; establish—; head—; overthrow—; restore—; revive—; revolt against—; rout—; submit to—; survey—; tolerate—; —compels; —crumbles; —crushes; —falls; —imposes; —oppresses; —taxes; —treads on; —tyrannizes.

(See kingdom, monarch.)

MONASTERY

adjectives

vast; deserted, ruinous; secluded; flourishing.

verbs

cloister in—; conceal in—; desert—; enter —; exile in—; explore in—; foster in—; ramble through—; resort to—; retire to—; retreat to—; seclude in—; sequester in—; shut up in—; supervise—; —charms; —cowls; —disciplines; —embraces; —grants sanctuary; —harbors; —shelters; —soothes; —taboos.

(See prison, seclusion, religion.)

MONEY

adjectives

funded; depreciated; considerable; precious; reluctant; scattering; hoarded; dirty; cheaper; irredeemable; fraudulent; limp; grimy; paper; pin; parental; cold; hard; well-meant; flat; speculator; embezzled; continental; forfeited; worthless; counterfeit; inflated.

verbs

amass—; apportion—; bestow—upon; bilk of—; cling to—; coin—; counterfeit—; covet —; devalue—; divert—from; divest of—; exact—; expend—; extort—; fritter away —; hoard—; importune for—; lavish—upon; mulct of—; pile up—; pilfer—; plunk down—; pocket—; raise—; rake in—; restore—; revaluate—; risk—; salt away (colloq.)—; scrape together—; squander—; utilize—; wheedle—from; wring—from; —dribbles away; —dwindles; —flows in; —melts away.

(See investment, currency, fund, dollar, legacy, coin, cash, capital, inheritance.)

MONGREL

adverbs

despicably; basely; indubitably; indiscriminately; confoundedly; nondescriptly; peculiarly; anomalously; funnily; quaintly; fantastically; undeniably; contemptibly; ridiculously; remarkably.

MONGRELS

adjectives

sycophantic; engaging; brindled; dirty; swinelike.

MONK

adjectives

fanatical; ascetic; tonsured; preaching; cloistered; patient; persecuting; indifferent; excommunicated; abominable; lecherous.

MONKEY

adjectives

horrible-looking; meddling; misanthropic; withered-up; howling; cautious; monocled; grinning; manlike.

verbs

—antics; —s band together; —bounds; —capers; —climbs; —clings; —collects; —cuffs; —entertains; —fascinates; —fights; —frets; —grieves; —grimaces; —grins; —hangs; —howls; —imitates; —laughs; —leaps; —quarrels; —resembles; —scratches; —screams; —squeals; —swings; —tears; —warns; —wheels; —whines.

(See animal, ape.)

MONOCLE

verbs

adjust—; affix—; blink through—; discern through—; dislodge—; employ—; examine through—; fasten—; finger—; flip—; lurk behind—; peer through—; squint through—; tack—to; —dangles; —falls; —hangs from; —magnifies; —screws into.

(See spectacles, telescope, microscope.)

MONOLOGUE

adjectives

indignant; drowsy; inimitable.

MONOPOLIZE (v)

adverbs

selfishly; greedily; pretentiously; dictatorially; craftily; vigorously; legally.

MONOPOLY

adjectives

unlimited; sectional; unified; virtual; national; natural; insidious; wicked; wasteful; wretched; proposed.

verbs

bag—; break down—; confer—upon; denounce—; enjoy—; foster—; free from—; infringe on—; possess—; promote—; protest—; resent—; secure—; —controls; — enriches; —fetters; —gags; —masters; — prices; —reaps; —smothers.

(See power, authority.)

MONOTONE

adjectives

solemn; enchanting; dolorous; maddening; chanting; soothing; weirdly-spoken; mumbling; eternal; indistinguishable.

MONOTONOUS

adverbs

drearily; tediously; dreadfully; boresomely; endlessly; dismally; cheerfully; dully; intolerably; wearily; unbearably; unendurably; garrulously; ponderously; uninterestingly; repetitiously; unvaryingly; vapidly; irksomely; flatly; drowsily; droningly; prosily.

MONOTONY

adjectives

apparent; routine; unused; extreme; inescapable; desolate; endless; gray; maddening; studious; unvarying; fatiguing; deadening; dull; machine-like; unnatural; exasperating; inevitable; tedious; slumberous; loathsome; lazy; painful; hideous; dreary; dreadful; tiresome; wearisome; smooth; objectless.

verbs

allay—; beguile—; bewail—; curse—; deplore—; distract—; emerge from—; endure —; extinguish—; inflict with—; intensify—; object to—; overcome with—; relieve—; repose in—; sink into—; usher in—; while away—; yawn through—; —abates; — bores; —depresses; —drags; —threatens; —tires; —wearies.

(See drabness, oppression, pain, tedium, boredom.)

MONSTER

adjectives

patient; carniverous; insatiable; sprawling; strong-limbed; grim; hardhearted; unfeeling; cruel; devouring; insatiate; uncouth; slimy; fabled; wallowing; colossal; steaming; papyral; formidable; Briarean; slumbering; vile; modern; entangled; furry; hydra-headed; diabolical; pestilent; grotesque; accursed; eerie; quaint; pediculous.

verbs

abound with—s; beget—; condemn to—; dread—; fear—; overcome—; quell—; satiate—; subdue—; tame—; —coils; —devours; —frightens; —horrifies; —howls; — looms; —offends; —roams; —spouts; —terrifies; —terrorizes.

(See giant, beast, dragon, barbarian, animal; savage; villain; brute.)

MONTH

adjectives

healing; memorable; sweet; dreary; anxious; withered; story-book; ensuing; tedious; corresponding; brief; silent; wintry; tempestuous; treacherous; stretched; gentle; much-abused; crabbed; meager.

verbs

attain in—; endure—; enjoy—; estimate —s; extend—; finish—; indicate—; mark—; pass—; remain—; spend—; survive—; tide over—; waste—; —elapses; —fades; —separates.

(See time, week, year.)

MONUMENT

adjectives

imperishable; wondrous; vast; sarcophagus-like; wasting; lasting; worthy; enduring; extant; venerable; deathless; tawny; stately; strange; gigantic; divine; living; everlasting; endless; colossal; marble; notorious; mysterious; charred; sepulchral; immemorial; pompous; majestic; equestrian; mighty; impressive; lofty; surviving; splendid; kindred; obvious; conspicuous; public.

verbs

boast—; dedicate—; deface—; earn—; elevate—; engrave—; erect—; gild—; inscribe on—; restore—; —adorns; —commemorates; —endures; —glorifies; —immortalizes; —perpetuates; —preserves; —records; —represents; —signifies; —symbolizes; —towers.

(See inscription, trophy, memorial, statue, tomb.)

MONUMENTAL

adverbs

overwhelmingly; stupendously; massively; unbelievably; colossally; gigantically; incomparably; vastly; matchlessly; prodigiously; tremendously; inexpressibly.

MOOD

adjectives

similar; changing; characteristic; grateful; unwavering; rarest; ungentle; furtive; discontented; beguiling; half-dreaming; selfless; mysterious; exquisite; guileful; musing; uncertain; affectionable; wrathful; fantastic; willful; dominant; intemperate; adventurous; morbid; exuberant; genial; articulate; irregular; parleying; silent; ironic; lifelong; rebellious; imperious; bewildered; genial; chaffing; comfortable; freakish; reminiscent; impassioned; subjective; absonant; pensive; unimagined; enchanted; sprightly; sullen; impetuous; rebel; extinguished; mirthful; penitential; disagreeable; wrought-up; thoughtful; receptive; habitual; depressed; philosophic; merry; sentimental; misprized; fear-stricken; romantic; sanguine; pliant; dreamy; exacting; concurrent; raging; beneficial; rapid; garrulous; favorable; variable; placid; wayward; respectful; contemplative; stern; sarcastic; working; expectant; flippant; steadfast; affable; mournful; despondent; indifferent; submissive; idea-less; senseless; frantic; shallow; evanescent; presageful; central; morbid; gruesome; demagogic; indispensable; humane; hysterical; inquisitorial; capricious; alien; jealous; melancholy; habitual; impious; reflective; facetious; chastened; philosophic; anti-radical; religious; docile; hasty; loitering; artificial; successive (pl); dreaded; ascetic; intense; uneven; kindly; changeful; icy; mandatory; shuddering; springtime; berserk; conciliatory; permissive; shifting; minor; angelic; unfavorable.

verbs

combat—; communicate—; crystallize—; defer to—; depict—; dispel—; fathom—; fix —; govern by—; induce—; interpret—; jolt out of—; kindle—; lighten—; overstrain—; rage in—; recall—; reflect—; shock out of —; soothe—; submit to—; succumb to—; sustain—; temper—; voice—; wrap in—; yield to—; —presages; —prevails; —strikes; —vanishes.

(See disposition, melancholy, feeling, emotion.)

MOODY

adverbs

captiously; ominously; sullenly; bitterly; cynically; alarmingly; seriously; unaccountably; occasionally; unreasonably; perplexingly; morbidly; fearfully; portentously; significantly; dangerously; unusually; capriciously; irascibly; fretfully; perversely; glumly; grimly; frequently; rarely; seldom; doggedly; intractably; intolerably; insufferably; unendurably.

MOON

adjectives

envious; filmy; brilliant; full-orbed; Orient; airless; queenly; angry; infantine; misty; fleeting; morning; gibbous; sphered; wintry; melancholy; inconstant; smiling; carven; curved; semi-tropic; lifeless; crescent; triumphant; flying; tranquil; stormy; softer; waxing; prying; dying; mourning; bloody; setting; languorous; red; distorted; pale; cold; waning; mellow; sleepless; listening; harvest; laboring; dying; solitary; shining; hollowed; blazing; marvelous; climbing; broad; sickle; gracious; jealous; watery; fruitless; coined; fair; overcast; wandering; shrouded; slow; haunting; desolate; naked; belated; lingering; sacred; horned; large-lighted; tranquil; smiling; withered; changeless; overwhelming; beauty-seeking; temperamental; winter; unassuming; peeping; summer; round; intense; luminous; full; cruel; yellow; green; harvest; marigold; honey-colored; arctic; hazy; lucent; slow; silvery; frosted; apple-shaped; purple; sad; climbing.

verbs

behold—; encircle—; fringe—; gaze at—; obscure—; veil—; view—; —barges (colloq.); —beams; —blushes; —brightens; —climbs; —dances; —dies; —dips into; —drifts beyond; —emerges; —enamors; —enchants; —gleams; —glimmers; —glows; —impassions; —mellows; —peeps out; —reigns; —sails over; —scowls; —shimmers; —silvers; —sinks; —voyages; —wanes; —waxes.

(See sun, stars, clouds, sky.)

MOONBEAM
adjectives
opalescent; dim; blended; sluiced; cold; quivering; misty; mellow.

verbs
shed—; wash by—; —brightens; —dances; —dazzles; —drips; —enchants; —floods; —glimmers; —hallows; —kisses; —illumines; —mantles; —shrouds; —silvers; —sparkles; —sweeps; —swells; —trembles; —whitens.

(See ray, light, radiance, spark, sunshine, sunlight, twilight, moonlight.)

MOONLIGHT
adjectives
glinting; gentle; sickly; bleached; mellow; liquid; rich; down-slanting; mystical; cold; dewy; molten; golden; pleasant; pale; bubbling; magnificent; generous; weird; streaming; faint; white; muffled; fitful; ribboned; sacred; harvest; painted; vivid; glistening; tropic; autumn; sallow; milky; tremulous; slanting.

verbs
bathe in—; drip—; shroud in—; wash by—; —casts spell; —checkers; —enchants; —illuminates; —kindles; —streaks; —streams in; —swathes; —sweeps; —unveils; —wanes.

(See moonbeam.)

MOONSHINE
adjectives
white; sweet; silvery.

MOONSTRUCK
adverbs
crazily; outlandishly; queerly; fantastically; giddily; foolishly; bewilderingly; ridiculously; undoubtedly; hazily; foggily; daftly; incoherently; deliriously; unstably; heedlessly; witlessly.

MOOR (v)
adverbs
primitively; safely; permanently; seasonally; cautiously; habitually; prudently.

(See fasten, fix.)

MOORING
adjectives
sheltered; primitive; diplomatic.

verbs
anchor to—; attach to—; break—; cable to —; command—; direct—; drag from—; drive from—; drop from—; hinder—; quit —; secure—; shackle to—; slacken—; slip —; swing at—; wreck in—.

(See post.)

MOOSE
verbs
bait—; breed—; exhibit—; experiment with —; lure—; pet—; plague with—; stalk—; stuff—; trap—; —climbs; —frightens; —haunts; —hurries; —infects; —infest; —munches; —nibbles; —runs; —scurries; —shies; —squeals; —shuns; —digs.

(See animal, deer.)

MOPE (v)
adverbs
glumly; dismally; gloomily; morbidly; despondently; romantically; drearily; pallidly; sadly; abnormally.

(See sulk, brood.)

MORAL
adjectives
fearful; strictest; obtrusive; intellectual; pretty; austerest; admirable; latent; righteous; public; fallible; obvious; creditable; immovable; political; abstract; philosophical.

adverbs
chastely; sternly; strictly; rigidly; uncompromisingly; intolerantly; righteously; self-consciously; proudly; apparently; self-righteously; preachily; ostentatiously; blatantly; presumably; avowedly; virtuously; remarkably; astonishingly; tiresomely; unbelievably; sanctimoniously; unctuously; blandly.

MORALE
verbs
acclaim—; assail—; break down—; destroy —; fortify—; impair—; instill—; lower—; shatter—; stimulate—; strengthen—; —ascends; —descends; —sinks; —wanes.

(See nerve, courage, strength, valor, spirit, virtue.)

MORALIST

adjectives

rigid; fashionable; futile; shallow; pretending; dissembling; confirmed.

MORALITY

adjectives

provincial; austere; puritanical; strait; trite; wholesome; creditable; restrictive; hereditary; flabby; intolerant; rigorous; fastidious; semi-religious; predominant; collar-and-wrist-band; Christian; political; true; scrupulous; marital; speculative.

verbs

abandon—; cant—; contemplate—; develop —; discard—; elevate—; guard—; inspire —; instruct—; observe—; regulate—; revive —; stimulate—; sustain—; uphold—; white-wash (colloq.) —; —crumbles; —decays; — elevates; —enlightens; —improves; —protects; —raises.

(See virtue, purity, integrity, righteousness, honor, truth.)

MORALIZE (v)

adverbs

jocosely; piously; monotonously; religiously; paternally; irritatingly; indefatigably.

(See preach, teach.)

MORALS

verbs

annihilate—; communicate—to; compromise —; corrupt—; destroy—; disapprove of—; disregard—; draw—from; emancipate—; improve—; influence—; outrage—; point to —; —degenerate; —deteriorate.

(See lesson, ethics, habit, ideals.)

MORASS

adjectives

drear; dismal; frightful.

verbs

deluge—; dip in—; drain—; emerge from —; immerse in—; penetrate—; plunge into —; soak in—; steep in—; swamp in—; swash through—; wallow in—; wander into —; —bogs; —engulfs; —mires.

(See mire. swamp, marsh.)

MORBID

adverbs

profoundly; abnormally; distressingly; forlornly; dangerously; inordinately; preposterously; crankily; incurably; miserably; pathetically; pitiably; vexatiously; unreasonably; outlandishly; outrageously; disagreeably; intolerably; terribly; irrationally; ominously; horribly.

MORN

adjectives

cloudy; radiant; rosy; returning; balmy; fateful; lily-wristed; incense-breathing; hallowed; double-pillowed; unsullied; gaudy; summer; delusive; valorous; propitious; immortal; breaking; weeping; spring; lagging; misty; struggling; smiling; dismal; endless; gusty; silent; vernal; new-made; awful; refluent; radiant; silver-flecked; blooming; apocalyptic.

MORNING

adjectives

cold; sunless; identical; dreary; propitious; yellow-robed; amber; splendid; dazzling; breezeless; vapory; absorbing; historic; invigorating; precious; faultless; memorable; uneventful; cruel; glorious; listless; duncolored; bridal; dull; delicious; quiet; sullen; dreadful; raw; lurid; misty; clear; shining; perpetual; fresh; auspicious; soft; sharp; frosty; hoary; merry; pallid; portentous; drear; foggy.

verbs

herald—; usher in—; wash—; —ascends; — awakens; —beckons; —blooms; —breaks through; —checkers; —crowns; —dawns; —drones along; —glimmers; —is born; — rises; —shrouds; —smiles; —tints; —uncurtains; —unfolds.

(See dawn, day, afternoon, evening, time.)

MOROSE

adverbs

dismally; incorrigibly; unreasonably; unaccountably; pathetically; unbearably; horribly; crabbedly; cantankerously; churlishly; boorishly; ominously; inordinately; uncommonly; outrageously; inexcusably; rudely; uncivilly; impolitely; ungraciously; inexplicably; inscrutably; silently; suddenly; irascibly; perversely; restively; intractably; implacably; sourly; immovably.

MORPHEUS

verbs

court—; invoke—; resist—; yield to—; — approaches; —caresses; —conquers; — cradles; —delights; —deludes; —enfolds;

—develops; —harasses; —lulls; —purifies; —rejuvenates; —shades; —smooths; —soothes; —strokes; —treads; —weaves.
(See sleep, rest, slumber, lethargy.)

MORSELS
adjectives
tantalizing; epicurean; picturesque; luscious; piquant; nauseous; locutionary; exquisite; petty; piteous; succulent; lawn-wrapped; hungry; delicious; tempting; inviting-looking.

MORTAL
adjectives
contemporary; melancholy; great; rough; rapid; reason-boasting; wretched; sacred; scarcest; meekest; ordinary; venturesome; wee; worn.

MORTALITY
adjectives
indued; miserable; international; enormous; human; waning; dull; recreant; allotted; normal; sad; massed (pl); heaven-oppressed.

verbs
abate—; account for—; constitute—; control—; lower—; rate—; —alarms; —ascends; —decimates; —descends; —effaces; —increases; —piles up; —staggers; —varies; —wanes.
(See death, murder, plague, slaughter, suicide.)

MORTAR
verbs (vessel)
abrade—; beat in—; comminute in—; crumble in—; crunch in—; crush in—; granulate in—; grind in—; pound in—; powder in—; pulverize in—; rasp in—; reduce in—; stamp in—; triturate in—.

MORTGAGE
verbs
assign—; borrow on—; cancel—; confirm—; contract—; convey—; discharge—; foreclose—; fulfill—; grant—; lift—; melt into—; pay off—; undertake—; —assures; —burdens; —devours; —guarantees; —insures; —saps; —warrants.
(See loan, payment, bond, obligation, debt.)

MORTGAGE (*v*)
adverbs
hopelessly; rashly; improvidently; optimistically; lucklessly.
(See loan.)

MORTIFICATION
verbs
bear—; blush in—; cast into—; color in—; flush in—; hang in—; spare—; stoop in—; submit to—; swallow—; —confuses; —destroys; —crushes; —frustrates; —pains; —sobers; —treads on; —vexes.
(See chagrin, shame.)

MORTIFIED
adverbs
needlessly; horribly; shamefully; cruelly; unreasonably; extremely; humiliatingly; pitifully; naturally; exceedingly; terribly; unnecessarily; unaccountably; inexplicably; modestly; searingly; shockingly; bitterly; sorely.

MOSAICS
adjectives
golden; elaborate; curious; rare; radiant; glorious.

MOSQUITOES
verbs
devour by—; exterminate—; infest with—; spray—; —annoy; —buzz; —disquiet; —draw; —extract; —feast on; —infest; —pester; —plague; —poison; —puncture; —serenade; —suck; —swarm.
(See insects, fly.)

MOSS
adjectives
downy; fragrant; bright; idle; quaggy; silvered; creeping; branched; tender; sea-colored; hanging; velvetlike; bannered; spongy; furred; moldering.

MOTH
adjectives
soft; startled; resurrected; damage-wreaking.

verbs
singe—; snatch at—; —blights; —contaminates; —destroys; —deteriorates; —devours; —flutters; —gnaws; —harasses; —hovers about; —impairs; —s infest; —injures; —s plague; —preys on; —ravages.
(See insects, butterfly.)

adjectives

provident; prudent; glorious; peasant; impatient; frail; beautiful; admirable; pious; doting; mahogany-colored; tedious-working; bereaved; commonplace; potential; infuriated; jealous; indulgent; frowzy; venerable; melancholy; famishing; earthly; vigorous; aggressive; elemental; insatiate; spirited; celestial; prolific; strong-armed; authentic; incestuous; delicate; bountiful; over-fatigued; querulous; imaginary; virgin; green-girdled; sorrowing; devoted; foolish; widowed; subtle; deft; spiteful; adopting; altruistic; unnatural.

verbs

anchor—; cherish—; cling to—; deliver of —; devote to—; hound—; obey—; —bears; —cradles; —conceives; —embraces; —fondles; —forsakes; —nourishes; —nurses; — protects; —punishes; —rears; —rocks; — sacrifices; —suckles; —weans.

(See father, nurse, parent, woman.)

MOTHERLY

adverbs

affectionately; graciously; affably; comfortably; indulgently; gently; sympathetically; understandingly; intelligently; charmingly; unfailingly; tenderly; lovingly; wisely; altogether; admirably; wondrously; marvellously; incomparably; eagerly; happily; joyously; pleasantly; agreeably; good-naturedly; tolerantly; warmly; amiably; complacently; imperturbably; serenely; calmly; quietly; wholesomely.

MOTION

adjectives

ceaseless; visible; measured; dignified; airy; quivering; legal; alternative; perpetual; hesitating; subtle; delighted; stable; inconstant; measureless; appealing; chopping; lulling; spiral; captivating; slow; irregular; sickening; uncertain; nautical; natural; wavy; rapid; mighty; apparent; musical; mincing; proximate; dreamlike; hingelike; graceful; flickering; undulous; mechanic; arresting; awkward; lifelike; ceaseless; obvious; orbital; well-ordered; elliptic; parabolic; intended; revolving; sensible; relative; gyratory; convulsive; gentle; vibratory; dreary; slow; lateral; giddy; planetary; faltering; diurnal; reciprocating; retrograde; scythelike; liquid; horizontal; parallactic; warm; constant; gliding; light-

ning; heavy; rhythmic; astonished; comparative; metallic; erratic; primitive; increasing; habitual; rapturous; universal; admired; inward; feeble; delicious; extravagant; insectlike; unnumbered (pl); tiring; abrupt; veritable; molecular; atomic; nimble; many-valued.

verbs

arrest—; constrain—; express—; ferment into—; guide—; impel—; lose—; practise —; quell—; regulate—; restrain from—; restrict—; retard—; set into—; slide into—; sustain—; whirl into—; —agitates; —expresses; —saps.

(See gesture, flicker, action, movement.)

MOTIONLESS

adverbs

suddenly; silently; warily; breathlessly; strangely; curiously; oddly; watchfully; noiselessly; frightfully; incredibly; absolutely; utterly; statuesquely; unbelievably; miraculously; stealthily; scrupulously; cautiously; prudently; discreetly; secretly.

MOTION PICTURE

verbs

(See "movie.")

MOTIVE

adjectives

chivalrous; tragic; corrupt; predominant; incidental; ambitious; attributed; selfish; altruistic; kind; underlying; commercial; corrupt; worthy; interested; ignoble; greedy; intrusive; conscientious; plausible; priceless; principal; lofty; invented; ostensible; colonial; unmixed; misleading; professional; perplexing; secondary; high; generous; explanatory; interesting; complicated; auxiliary; disinterested; evil; urgent; improper; hedonistic; differing; compelling; imputed; ulterior; patriotic; melodic; inferior; mercenary; fatal; upright; pure; commanding; sufficient; keen; guiding; impugning; impelling; dominant; identical; basilar; ruling; potent; laudable; understandable; cryptic; bread-and-butter; segmented; sculptured; hidden; scarce-known.

verbs

abolish—; acknowledge—; appreciate—; assign—for; attribute—to; destroy—; impute —to; mock—; obscure—; ponder—; probe into—; recognize—; review —s; reward—;

weigh—; —actuates; —governs; —impels; —induces; —inspires; —prompts; —stimulates; —sways.

(See cause, grounds, incentive, impulse, inducement.)

MOTOR

adjectives

creaking; coughing; inactive; compression; oil-driven; whirring; undependable; wheezing.

verbs

accelerate—; choke—; fuel—; recondition —; stall—; —balks; —coughs; —drones; — fails; —fouls; —gasps; —hums; —purrs; —roars; —rasps; —rattles; —splutters; — steams; —whines.

(See generator, machine, engine, propeller.)

MOTORBOAT

verbs

anchor—; buffet—; moor—; test—; throttle —; —bobs; —capsizes; —chugs; —churns; —coughs; —drifts; —heads; —noses for; —splutters; —spurts; —sputters; —whisks; —whizzes; —zooms.

(See launch, ship, tugboat, yacht, vessel, steamer.)

MOTORCYCLE

verbs

straddle—; throttle—; —blasts; —breezes by; —chokes; —chugs; —coughs; —leans; —roars; —shoots by; —splutters; —sputters; —whisks away; —whizzes by; —wriggles; —zigzags.

(See automobile, taxi, motor.)

MOTTO

verbs

adopt—; apply—; coin—; condense into—; design—; devise—; digest—; heed—; inscribe—; misstate—; phrase—; quote—; recite—; recognize—; relish—; sing forth—; —emphasizes; —exalts; —glorifies; —provides; —signifies; —stresses; —symbolizes.

(See poetry, epigram, proverb, parable, saying.)

MOULD

verbs

adjust—; bake in—; cast—; cleave to—; conform to—; design—; drain into—; oil—;

pattern—; pour into—; press—; set in—; shape—; —cools; —fashions; —frames; — hardens; —imitates.

(See form.)

MOULD (v)

adverbs

exquisitely; trimly; faultlessly; subtly; realistically; professionally; deftly; skillfully; artistically; symmetrically; sensuously; voluptuously; meretriciously.

(See model, fashion, shape.)

MOULDY

adverbs

dangerously; deeply; poisonously; infectiously; rottenly; putridly; rankly; rancidly; offensively; grossly; noxiously; injuriously; terribly; riskily; presumably; apparently; extremely; obviously; manifestly.

MOUND

adjectives

pious; countless; rural; hideous; grass-grown; craggy; conical; sorrow-laden; shapeless; pyramidal; solitary; moldering.

MOUNT

adjectives

lofty; sloping; tireless; mimic; apocalyptic; flame-fringed; spectacular.

MOUNT (v)

adverbs

reluctantly; magnificently; awkwardly; perpetually; gradually; rigidly; reluctantly; mechanically; reticently; stealthily; spectacularly.

(See ascend, rise.)

MOUNTAIN

adjectives

shimmering; bare; cold; eroded; rugged; dizzy; faraway; wintry; forested; beacon-lighted; multitudinous; glacier-laden; pine-encircled; adamantine; dominating; spirit-haunted; cultivated; plain; melancholy; moonlit; steep; uncouthly-cut; beholding; inaccessible; lifeless; precipitous; gloomy; lifeless; variegated; flaring; relentless; soft-looking; enchanted; heaven-reaching; timberless; worshipful; huge; new; craggy; misty; fractured; snowy; moody; severed; tremendous; intervening; prickly; glittering; ruddy; delectable; remote; offensive; jagged; rude; slumbering; overhanging; pensive; eagle-baffling; ice-crowned; terraced;

round-topped; sharp-peaked; redoubtable; messy-looking; environing; tumbling; scarlet; morning; disintegrated; barren; symmetrical; volcanic; vast; everlasting; verdant; fabled; naked; sentinel; scarped; unscaled; windless; towering; colorless; ancient; timbered; gloomy; ponderous; prodigious; unique; weltering; steepy; circumjacent.

verbs
abandon—; ascend—; carve—; circumvent —; fortify—; furrow—; level—; plow through—; reconnoitre—; scale—; straddle —; trudge up—; —awes; —hinders; —looms up; —obscures; obstructs; —overawes; —shadows; —stands sentinel; —towers.
(See hill, bank, peak, precipice, tower.)

MOUNTAINEERS
adjectives
mythic; benighted; hardy; intractable; redoubtable; wary.

MOUNTAINOUS
adverbs
gloriously; hazardously; terribly; magnificently; splendidly; gorgeously; gloomily; disastrously; impenetrably; densely; impassably; scenically; steeply; bleakly; tremendously; perilously; dangerously; attractively; invitingly; alluringly; adventurously; notoriously; presumably.

MOURN (v)
adverbs
pathetically; sincerely; touchingly; nationally; primitively; tragically; barbarically; oppressively; jealously; querulously; unnaturally; piously.
(See grieve, regret, lament.)

MOURNER
adjectives
flap-mouthed; pensive; desolate; sorrowful; heartbroken.

condole—; console—; sympathize with—; —s attend; —despairs; —s file out; —laments; —grieves; —rends; —s respect; —screams; —sheds; —sobs; —suffers; —wails; —weeps; —groans.

MOURNFUL
adverbs
desolately; forlornly; dismally; drearily; hopelessly; helplessly; bitterly; sadly; tragically; pitiably; unutterably; unspeakably; unbearably; grievously; profoundly; irremediably; disagreeably; uncomfortably; shockingly; cruelly; gloomily; grimly; disconsolately; inconsolably; plaintively; querulously; resentfully; rebelliously.

MOUSE
adjectives
smallest; monstrous; realistic; scampering.

verbs
attract—; bait—; corner—; panic—; pursue —; snare—; stir—; trap—; —burrows; —cowers; —disturbs; —dodges; —gnaws; —nibbles; —ransacks; —rifles; —rummages; —scampers; —scurries; —scuttles; —whisks.
(See animal.)

MOUSTACHE
verbs
adorn with—; coil—; cultivate—; curl—; dye—; finger—; nourish—; pluck at—; roll —; ruffle—; smooth—; stroke—; trim—; twirl—; twist—; wax—; wipe—; —bristles; —charms; —curls; —droops; —gleams; —trembles; —wilts.
(See mane, beard, whiskers, curls.)

MOUTH
adjectives
smiling; deep; innocent; loud-ringing; mobile; enraged; foamy; sweet; rosy; impressive; good-humored; loving; alkaline; irritable; deathful-grinning; funnel-shaped; compressed; fine; sensuous; musty; winsome; cooing; dimpled; tender; relaxed; generous; unpampered; prudent; extraordinary; wide; wry; foul; brazen; cavernous; resolute; lascivious; delicate; frothy; churning; handsome; full; firm; querulous; ascetic; yawning; coral; ravishing; facile; perilous; puckered; toothless; rabbit; baby; branching; sulky; acid; gaping; arch; eloquent; unmelodious; bloodless; voluble; glad; expressive; economical; breathless; slobbering; serious; savage; insistent; sardonic; purposeful; shapeless; hungry; furnace; munching; painted; heavy; vermilion; distended; luscious; wrinkled; cruel; modeled.

verbs
convey to—; froth at—; honey—; introduce into—; irritate—; padlock—; paint—; pout

—; proceed from—; pucker up—; seal—; screw up—; sponge—; smite on—; swab—; —droops; —hardens; —lures; —quirks; — quivers; —relaxes; —tightens; —twitches; —utters.

(See lips, face, opening.)

MOVABLE

adverbs
conveniently; easily; handily; adjustably; cleverly; comfortably; appropriately; serviceably; usefully; freely; readily; lightly; adaptably; conformably; curiously.

MOVE

adjectives
ill-planned; latest; strategic; opening; vulnerable; subordinate; rusty; eccentric; hostile; brilliant; ambitious; fancy; stultifying.

verbs
abet—; alternate —s; attempt—; calculate —; concede—; determine—; devise—; encourage—; guard—; limit —s; speculate on —; study—; undertake—; —captures; —deceives; —misleads; —tricks.

(See march, maneuver, movement.)

MOVE (v)

adverbs
gracefully; automatically; perceptibly; sinuously; precariously; simultaneously; involuntarily; caressingly; violently; rashly; spasmodically; cautiously; deftly; impatiently; rhythmically; profoundly; visibly; sedately; invisibly; fearsomely; serenely; unintelligibly; blithesomely; drearily; stealthily; dubiously; erratically; sluggishly; obliviously; agilely; phelegmatically; passively; invincibly; warily; strategically; abortively; brusquely; tremulously; timorously; martially.

(See step, walk.)

MOVEMENT
(action, change of position, etc.)

verbs
accentuate—; accomplish—; attempt—; avoid—; cease—; control—; diminish—; effect—; enliven—; facilitate—; hamper—; impede—; induce—; minimize—; necessitate—; practise—; repeat—; restrain from —; restrict—; reverse—; —agonizes.

(See current, motion, move.)

MOVEMENT
(campaign)

verbs
actuate—; annihilate—; applaud—; ban—; block—; combat—; cripple—; criticize—; defeat—; dominate—; endorse—; engage in —; engineer—; facilitate—; father—; fling into—; found—; frustrate—; govern—; inaugurate—; initiate—; involve in—; launch —; mask—; promote—; quell—; rally to—; sponsor—; support—; —coagulates; —collapses; —commences; —culminates in; —dies; —flourishes; —originates in; —penetrates to; —springs from; —suffers; —symbolizes; —wanes.

(See crusade, fascism, innovation, cause.)

MOVEMENT
(general)

adjectives
anxious; contemplated; spasmodic; commendable; romantic; recent; involuntary; strategical; deliberate; planetary; wild; busy; complicated; passionate; graceful; revolutionary; impulsive; metallic; rude; unobtrusive; important; erratic; impatient; abortive; alternative; careless; rhythmic; bustling; wandering; uncapturable; delicate; pending; retrograde; offensive; flank; convulsive; scooping; life-sustaining; contemplated; self possessed; messianic; living; hostile; rebellious; particular; painful; cooperative; bridling; incessant; aesthetic; willowy; celestial; intentional; philanthropic; turbulent; fitting; silent; wasteful; insurrectionary; muscular; imperceptible; dexterous; soothing; foregoing; extensive; composite; clicking; nautical; masterly; terrorist; kneading; responsive; flexible; religious; insensible; tremulous; brusque; grandiose; silly; subsequent; slinking; crushing; fantastic; unconvulsive; guillotine-like; discerning; serpentine; energetic; circumspect; vigorous; recreation; zigzag; interdependent; lyrical; supple; agonized; timorous; hazardous; calm; cabalistic; springy; free; desultory; syncopated; enveloping; unanticipated; blithe; glacial; martial; present; cyclic; toss-over.

MOVER

adjectives
prime; mortal; fairest; unseen.

"MOVIE"

verbs
censor—; construct—; cram—with; direct —; film—; howl at—; inspire—; prevent—;

produce—; repress—; review—; romp through—; —amuses; —appeals; —attracts; —conveys; —depicts; —entertains; —excites; —refreshes; —surges; —thrills.

(See film, play, story.)

MUCOUS

verbs

cast out—; discharge—; eject—; emit—; excrete—; expel—; exude—; secrete—; —drains from; —emanates from; —issues; —lubricates; —moistens; —oozes.

(See secretion, discharge.)

MUD

adjectives

gurgling; oozing; sticky; flung; black; tenacious; dragging; poisonous; treacherous; viscous; sluggish; slimy; clinging; great; ancient; sloshing; hopeless; frozen; fertilizing; dense; respectable; spattered; caked; dried; jellylike.

verbs

bake—; bathe in—; bespatter with—; bog in—; cake—; dabble in—; daub with—; emerge from—; flounder in—; lodge in—; mire in—; plod through—; roll in—; sling —; spatter with—; steep in—; swash through—; wade through—; wallow in—; —cakes; —gurgles; —spatters· —sucks.

(See mire, dirt, filth, swamp, marsh.)

MUDDLE

adjectives

appalling; miserable; vicious; intricate; indescribable.

MUDDLED

adverbs

hopelessly; strangely; unfortunately; helplessly; mysteriously; vaguely; comically; tragically; disastrously; completely; horribly; indescribably; obviously; unmistakably; visibly; manifestly; dazedly; brokenly; pathetically; inexpertly; laughably; foolishly; greatly.

MUDDY

adverbs

untidily; deeply; impassably; horribly; distressingly; grimily; thickly; turbidly; foully; disagreeably; unpleasantly; inconceivably; unexpectedly; astonishingly; impossibly; dangerously; obstructively; swampily; quaggily.

MUFFLED

adverbs

dimly; obscurely; deliberately; unpleasantly; closely; furtively; stealthily; carefully; warily; softly; inaudibly; sepulchrally; confidentially; evasively; tremulously; curiously; peculiarly; faintly; cautiously.

MUGGY

adverbs

unpleasantly; disagreeably; humidly; damply; soggily; suffocatingly; smotheringly; breathlessly; unhealthily; duskily; dimly; obscurely; strangely; remarkably; extremely; peculiarly; confusingly; foggily; mistily; warmly; intolerably; distressingly.

MULE

adjectives

burdened; unshod; bare-backed; toil-enduring; snail-paced; flea-bitten; fruit-laden; sure-footed; lagging; jaded; opinionative; jingling; patient.

verbs

burden—; fetter—; guide—; manage—; rein—; tether—; water—; —balks; —s caracole; —carries; —endures; —groans; —hauls; —haunches; —kicks; —pulls; —shies; —snorts; —strains; —wearies.

(See mare, livestock, animal, donkey.)

MULISH

adverbs

doggedly; intractably; intolerably; disagreeably; unpleasantly; obstinately; sullenly; stubbornly; defiantly; dogmatically; immovably; inflexibly; obdurately; perversely; sulkily; stiffly; tenaciously; waywardly; wilfully; determinedly; obstreperously; remarkably; notoriously; inveterately; confoundedly; terribly.

MULLIONED

adverbs

artistically; elegantly; richly; elaborately; gorgeously; splendidly; magnificently; beautifully.

MULTIPLY (v)

adverbs

ceaselessly; prodigiously; exceedingly; miraculously; alarmingly; lustily; mathematically; beneficially; wantonly; deliberately; disconcertingly.

(See increase, enlarge.)

adjectives

vast; breathless; productive; feathered; rude; assembled; furious; buzzing; pleased; barbarous; flocking; lessening; tawny; infuriated; anarchic; immense; applauding; dripping; straggling; carven; hushed; pestilence-stricken; considerable; interminable; prostrate; polluting; thronging; picturesque; kindred; shadowy; overawed; blissful; soaring; promiscuous; babbling; dauntless; heavenly; superfluous; inextinguishable; captive; blind; panting; white-robed; distracted; unthoughtful; dizzy; potent; joyous; clamorous; trampled; groaning; adoring.

verbs

assail—; condemn—; convert—; convey to —; despise—; enthrall—; govern—; harangue—; inspire—; move—; rouse—; rule —; scorn—; —blasphemes; —congregates; —flees; —gathers; —masses; —swarms; —throngs; —worships.

(See crowd, invader, horde, legion, masses, mob.)

MUM

adverbs

discreetly; prudently; wisely; carefully; decently; reliably; securely; sagely; sagaciously; taciturnly; laconically; reticently; quietly; calmly; resolutely; determinedly; uncommunicatively; cautiously; warily; loyally; judiciously; considerately; courteously; shrewdly; judiciously; sensibly; discerningly; remarkably; deliberately; significantly.

MUMBLE (v)

adverbs

inarticulately; vaguely; bashfully; gruffly; querulously; idiotically; roughly; monotonously; irreverently; formidably; outlandishly; grotesquely; gruesomely.

(See mutter, utter.)

MUMMERY

adjectives

ghostly; profane; present; unmeaning.

MUNCH (v)

adverbs

placidly; cozily; contentedly; dreamily; greedily; famishedly; toothlessly; insatiably.

(See chew, nibble, eat.)

adjectives

obsequious; sham; ring-ridden; patriotic.

MUNIFICENT

adverbs

lavishly; surprisingly; astonishingly; bountifully; extravagantly; incredibly; wastefully; abundantly; bounteously; unimaginably; excessively; preposterously; ostentatiously; exorbitantly; inordinately; magnificently; philanthropically; pompously; notably; charitably.

MURDER

adjectives

cold-blooded; wanton; complicated; anarchic; mightiest; mortal; contested; high-handed; potential; unparalleled; unprovoked; foul; direful; nihilistic; sacrilegious; treacherous; willful; judicial; deliberate; various (pl); ruthless; gruesome.

verbs

atone for—; avenge—; contrive—; cover—; exalt—; execute—; expiate—; perform—; perpetrate—; plan—; plot—; punish—; redeem—; relish—; repent—; reveal—; revenge—; —awes; —confuses; —scandalizes; —terrifies.

(See killing, assassination, massacre, mortality.)

MURDER (v)

adverbs

pitilessly; deliberately; foully; treacherously; inhumanly; wantonly; unprovokedly; direfully; sacrilegiously; gruesomely; ruthlessly; irrationally; sadistically.

(See kill, butcher.)

MURDERER

adjectives

cowardly; viperous; notorious; guilty; cursed; egregious; bloody.

verbs

apprehend—; curse—; execute—; glorify—; hunt—; incarcerate—; inspire—; net—; overtake—; overwhelm—; pardon—; penalize—; reproach—; reveal—; sate—; sentence—; spot—; stain—; terrify—; —contrives; —flees; —stifles.

(See assassin, kidnapper, robber, thief.)

MURDEROUS

adverbs

savagely; cruelly; vengefully; brutally; insanely; fiercely; strangely; alarmingly; dangerously; ominously; dreadfully; portentously; unmistakably; presumably; stealthily; fearfully; enormously; undeniably; incontestably.

MURKY

adverbs

strangely; unaccountably; curiously; dimly; smokily; faintly; obscurely; darkly; duskily; thickly; dangerously; alarmingly; ominously; frighteningly; unseasonably; gloomily; dismally; drearily; dankly; somberly; mistily; muggily; dingily; awfully.

MURMUR

adjectives

awed; sad; long-pent; softer; prolonged; exacting; rapid; prophetic; perpetual; crunching; splashing; faint; applauding; tender; portentous; thrilling; pervading; mimic; sullen; startling; depreciating; powerless; homely; monotonous; rustic; singing; inarticulate; gurgling; hasty; pleasing; shallow; wailing; drowsy; self-contemptuous; hurtful; satisfying; ominous; inarticulate; deepening; mournful; foreboding; whispering; lulling; popular; confused; gentle; kindling; querulous; broken; hushed; perturbed; irrepressible; plaintive; dissentient; cheerful; reverent; hollow; melodious; sympathetic; elusive; low; formidable.

verbs

break—; breathe—; buzz with—s; emit—; melt into—; restrain—; smother—; soften into—; stifle—; still—; subdue—; —floats; —flows; —perturbs; —pervades; —ripples in; —trickles through.
(See hum, sigh, sob.)

MURMUR (*v*)

adverbs

demurely; complacently; involuntarily; dreamily; drowsily; ceaselessly; whimsically; despondently; moodily; plaintively; apologetically; ruefully; ecstatically; dolefully; hoarsely; deprecatingly; languorously.
(See whisper, mutter.)

MUSCLES

adjectives

well-strung; saddle; noble; flaccid; facial; intestinal; sagging; important; massive; fatigued; aching; expressive; quivering; strengthened; painful; wild; bulging; sturdy; smashing; sledge-hammer; important; strained; swelling; gnarled; swollen; weary; prominent.

verbs

bring—into play; contract—; control—; distort—; embed in—; employ—; enlarge—; exercise—; exert—; expand—; flex—; govern—; incise—; inflame—; invigorate—; limber—; lodge in—; massage—; reeducate —; rejuvenate—; relax—; stiffen—; swell —; tense—; tone up—; weaken—; —atrophy; —bulge; —degenerate; —knot; —quiver; —ripple; —support; —twitch.
(See ligament, body, tendon.)

MUSCULAR

adverbs

amazingly; incredibly; robustly; sturdily; brawnily; athletically; wonderfully; unusually; uncommonly; remarkably; vigorously; powerfully; wirily; admirably; wondrously; soundly; tremendously; invincibly; unbelievably; unconquerably.

MUSE (*v*)

adverbs

pensively; dolefully; romantically; affectionately; nostalgically; irrelevantly; disconsolately; regretfully.
(See meditate, ponder, reflect.)

MUSES

adjectives

mournful; worst-humored; inspiring; gentle; dreamy; dauntless; humanizing.

MUSEUM

adjectives

local; desolate; veritable; admirable; provincial; miniature.

verbs

assemble in—; bequeath to—; congregate in —; dedicate—to; donate—; endow—; exhibit in—; flock to—; guide through—; muster in—; pack—; ransack—; refer to—; store in—; stream through—; —accumulates; —aggregates; —amasses; —collects; —compiles; —displays; —inspires; —preserves; —sponsors.

MUSIC

adjectives

unregarded; undying; orchestral; barbaric;

instrumental; contemporary; pianoforte; virginal; classical; charming; polyphonic; effective; sparkling; picturesque; elegiac; tragic; sonorous; higher; symphonic; concerted; random; intellectual; homophonic; starry; potential; excellent; secular; voluptuous; low; molten; bold; incidental; mechanized; martial; negroid; jocund; sweet; sinewy; brilliant; torrential; melancholy; mournful; heady; graceful; exquisite; grotesque; vocal; echoing; surging; nationalistic; dumb; ethereal; prismatic; deep-sweet; transporting; melting; evening; tinkling; shrill; steady; enchanted; worthy; unearthly; lively; reeling; dancing; ecclesiastical; liturgical; discordant; seraphic; sensuous; sacred; repining; contrapuntal; roaring; unutterable; half-delirious; pensive; chamber; gay; lilting; mere; persuasive; complex; outlandish; glad; contemporary; preluding; tawdry; delicious; hushed; sparkling; tantalizing; deathless; cadent; sobbing; measureless; brassy; meretricious; triumphant; soul-awakening; grinding; mewling.

verbs
mingle with—; ring with—; set to—; silence —; soften—; strum out—; sway to—; —awakens; —beats; —blares; —charms; —clashes; —electrifies; —elevates; —ensnares; —enthralls; —fascinates; —floats from; —humanizes; —kindles; —lessens; —moans; —mourns; —pauses; —rolls; —sobs; —soothes; —subsides; —swells; —throbs; —tingles; adapt—; drink in—.
(See hymn, modulation, jazz, song, melody.)

MUSICIAN
adjectives
erudite; excellent; graceful; temperamental; foreign-bred; self-taught; skilled; indignant; impertinent; capable; endowed; contemporary; airy; authoritative; eminent; talented; influential.

verbs
acclaim—; accord—; applaud—; encourage —; entreat—; inspire—; welcome—; —bows; —charms; —delights; —dreams; —enchants; —expresses; —interprets; —loosens; —moves; —pours; —renders; —soothes; —speaks; —strays; —thrills.
(See artist.)

MUSKET
adjectives
old-fashioned; smoky; percussion; ancient; unused.

verbs
arm with—; bear—; combat with—; discharge—; employ—; enlist—; force from—; provide—; repel with—; retaliate with—; salute with—; shoulder—; storm with—; wield—; —crackles; —flashes; —glitters; —rattles.
(See gun, pistol, machine gun, rifle.)

MUSLIN
adjectives
saffron; superior; unbleached; spotless; cream-tinted.

MUSSY
adverbs
inexcusably; unpleasantly; untidily; inexplicably; unnecessarily; unaccountably; senselessly; carelessly; shiftlessly; confusedly; chaotically; troublesomely; vexatiously; irritatingly; intolerably; disagreeably; inchoately; incidentally; casually; improvidently; wastefully; inconsiderately.

MUSTACHE
adjectives
cream-colored; tobacco-stained; thick; immature; stiff; iron-gray; jaunty; white; budding; sprouting; sandy; swooping; dashing; curling; tawny; twirled; waxed; indomitable; walrus; sleek; slight; silken; well-trimmed; disdainful; grizzled; blond; silver-streaked; fierce; pepper-and-salt; weedy.

MUSTANG
verbs
retreat before—; break—; breed—s; bridle —; captivate—; check—; confine—to; consign—to; corral—; domesticate—; entrap —; restrain—; round up—s; spur—; stable —; tame—; tether—; —roves; —shies; —wanders.
(See horse.)

MUSTARD
verbs
anoint with—; cultivate—; flavor with—; grind—; mix—; plaster—on; prepare—; relish—; savor—; season with—; smear—;

798

spice with—; spoon—; spread—; —bites; —flatters; —heightens; —sharpens; —stings.
(See salt, spice.)

MUTES

adjectives
obedient; congenital; deaf; wistful.

MUTILATION

verbs
conceal—; fear—; lament—; mend—; punish by—; recover from—; resort to—; sentence to—; suffer—; —attends; —blemishes; —blights; —defaces; —deforms; —deprives, —disfigures; disables; —handicaps; —pains; —shocks; subject to—.
(See laceration, sabotage, injury, violence.)

MUTINOUS

adverbs
uncontrollably; ungovernably; tumultuously; rebelliously; turbulently; uproariously; unmanageably; riotously; chaotically; dangerously; ominously; portentously; intensely; terribly; alarmingly; doggedly; sullenly; brutally; sternly; murderously; seditiously; truculently; wildly; restlessly; disturbingly; oddly; uneasily; secretly.

MUTINY

adjectives
abortive; famous; practical; incited; exciting; long-planned.

verbs
attempt—; commit—; conspire—; draw into —; encounter—; inspire—; instigate—; invite—; overcome—; quash—; quell—; quench—; rise in—; rouse to—; seethe with —; snuff out—; suppress—; —roars; — smashes; —strikes; —threatens; —unfolds.
(See revolution, rebellion, insurrection.)

MUTTER

adjectives
incessant; drowsy; articulate; growling; low.

MUTTER (v)

adverbs
threateningly; despairingly; incoherently; mournfully; huskily; inaudibly; fitfully; defiantly; savagely; grimly; indistinctly; incessantly; drunkenly; thickly; bestially.
(See murmur, utter.)

MUTTERING

adjectives
internal; magic; bewildered; instant; habitual; unpleasant; inane; drear; visceral.

MUZZLE

adjectives
outstretched; creamy; glittering; shiny; gleaming.

verbs
burst—; clap on—; disengage—; emerge from—; impose—; jam on—; link—; require—; secure—; —checks; —controls; — curbs; —gags; —masks; —prevents; —represses; —restrains; —restricts.
(See brake, collar.)

MYRIADS

adjectives
phantom; propagated; humbler; countless; breathing; swarming; misty.

MYSTERIOUS

adverbs
altogether; strangely; perplexingly; uncomfortably; distressingly; unutterably; occultly; inscrutably; mystically; preposterously; pretentiously; unreasonably; foolishly; unnecessarily; vaguely; cryptically; inordinately; unfathomably; impenetrably; indefinitely; darkly; inviolately; evasively; queerly.

MYSTERY

adjectives
sweet; solemn; unsolved; bewildering; mighty; durable; inscrutable; profound; dread; artistic; baffling; overpowering; woodland; unaccountable; venerable; incarnate; hateful; fashionable; ridiculous; inevitable; unfolded; delicate; gray; unanswerable; ecstatic; unborn; worshipful; embarrassing; unexplored; mild; bearded; abstruse; labyrinthine; sacred; solemn; prime; sublime; peculiar; subtle; unfathomable; hungering; occult; sensational; painful; brooding; wingy; domestic; indescribable; deluding; juggling; physical; shrouding; selfsame.

verbs
absorb in—; cloak in—; comprehend—; concoct—; confront with—; deepen—; delve into—; dispel—; dissipate—; elucidate—; encompass by—; envelop in—; explore—ies of; fathom—; ferret out—; heighten—; init-

iate into—; penetrate—; plumb—; ponder —; reveal—; shroud in—; solve—; unlock —; unravel—; unveil—; wrap in—; — baffles; —prevails; —surrounds.

(See marvel, miracle, enigma, secret, maze.)

MYSTIC

adverbs
casually; vaguely; mysteriously; obscurely; precariously; unintelligibly; unfathomably; inscrutably; curiously; strangely; oddly; queerly; nebulously; symbolically; darkly; inferentially; impenetrably; covertly; magically; incomprehensibly.

MYSTICISM

adjectives
mellow; spiritual; sensuous; dramatic; philosophical.

verbs
achieve—; capitulate to—; chatter—; cloud by—; contemplate—; dabble in—; derive from; devour—; entertain with—; immerse in—; involve—; poison by—; rationalize—;

ridicule—; speculate on—; steep in—; wallow in—; —deludes; —pervades; —perverts; —poses as.

(See magic, doctrine, belief.)

MYTH

adjectives
nature; heroic; solar; ancient; aboriginal; domestic.

verbs
blast—; conceive—; dispel—; dissipate—; eradicate—; explode—; give rise to—; narrate—; preserve—; shatter—; strangle—; trace—; —antedates; —deals with; —develops; —evolves from; —explains; —grows; —portrays; —reflects; —relates; —reverberates; —survives; —wanes.

(See legend, fiction, story.)

MYTHOLOGICAL

adverbs
fabulously; fantastically; fancifully; presumably; probably; supposedly; speculatively; presumptively; preposterously; presumably; remotely; fantastically; groundlessly; purely; authentically; authoritatively; altogether; wholly.

N

NAG (v)

adverbs

shrewishly; maddeningly; unceasingly; monotonously; repetitiously; bitterly; acrimoniously; offensively; vehemently; viciously; diabolically.

(See tease, torment.)

NAIL

adjectives

tapering; cruel; brass-headed; sulphurous; diamond; slim; sturdy; bent; rusty.

verbs

cast—; clip off—; drive—; fabricate—s; fasten with—; hammer—; impale on—; mend with—; pound in—; secure with—; strike—; stud with—s; suspend from—; thump—; whack—; —impinges; —pierces; —rivets; —splinters.

(See fang, claw, pin, rivet, point, hook.)

NAIVE

adverbs

charmingly; unexpectedly; ingenuously; quaintly; childishly; incredibly; pitifully; pathetically; absurdly; ridiculously; laughably; ludicrously; unaccountably; inexplicably; surprisingly; sweetly; obviously; overwhelmingly; plainly; disarmingly; delightfully; refreshingly; cheerfully; unsuspiciously; utterly.

NAKED

adverbs

shamelessly; distressingly; pitiably; pathetically; grievously; scandalously; miserably; utterly; painfully; shockingly; horribly; wretchedly; deplorably.

NAKEDNESS

adjectives

primitive; sad; uncomely; cherubic; utter.

NAMBY-PAMBY

adverbs

hopelessly; feebly; pathetically; vexatiously; irritatingly; absurdly; unutterably; disgustingly; reprehensibly; ridiculously; deplorably; incurably; naturally; inherently; detestably; nervously; incomprehensibly; surprisingly; spinelessly; submissively; pliantly.

NAME

adjectives

republican; specious; altered; immortal; ambitious; fictitious; high-sounding; low; humble; feigned; aristocratic; charming; potent; endearing; opprobrious; musical; spotless; sacred; unworthy; blighted; generic; prosaic; gentle; uncommon; lasting; mystic; glorious; uncomfortable; interchangeable (pl); fashionable; bucolic; revolting; disreputable, creditable; naked; baptismal; beloved; honored; untarnished; hapless; worthless; ill; fair; mellifluous; doubtful; sonorous; imperial; servant; ancient; deathless; charitable; all-adored; stainless; ragged; abominable; deferential; saucy; everlasting; meaningless; ungentlemanly; hateful; illustrious; dreadful; flattering; inappropriate; grotesque; sheltering; hieroglyphic; long-living; distinguished; imposing; significant; unforgettable; deep-cut; humorous; childish; almighty; noble; unpronounceable; imperishable; respected; contemptuous; complaining; beauteous; musical; impious; wonted; graceless; inconspicuous; revered; phantom; soft; foremost; idolized; lustrous; poisonous; unblemished; influential; important; excellent; famous; good; euphonious; exact; renowned; nightbegotten; authoritative; lofty; florid; vaunting; cherished; latinized; assumed; characteristic; family; poetic; suggestive; incongruous; wounded; borrowed; unsoiled; botanical; eminent; alluring; international; classical; inviolable; inoffensive; impressed; heroic; patrician; objectionable; half-mocking; haughtier; shining; fashionable.

verbs

adopt—; append—to; apply—to; assume—; attach interest to—; bear—; besmirch—; bestow—upon; blaspheme—; brand—; coin —; conjure with—; couple—s of; deprecate —; dignify—; dismiss—; divulge—; glorify —; identify with—; inscribe—; link—with; perpetuate—; preserve—; reveal—; scrawl —; stain—; thunder—; usurp—; venerate —; —blazes; —bobs up; —conveys; —derives; —embodies; —implies; —recurs; —shines; —strikes terror; —suggests.

(See title, character, reputation.)

NAME (v)

adverbs

speciously; ambitiously; fictitiously; humbly; aristocratically; musically; generically; prosaically; mystically; mellifluously; sonorously; deferentially; significantly; contemptuously; characteristically; offensively; heroically; haughtily; originally; appropriately; promptly.

(See entitle, designate.)

NAMELESS

adverbs

obscurely; curiously; remotely; ingloriously; unhappily; humbly; meekly; strangely; unfortunately; ignominiously; purposely; sadly; significantly; necessarily; abjectly; opprobriously; pathetically; diplomatically; strategically.

NAPKIN

verbs

edge—; fold—; fringe—; gather—; hold —; monogram—; mop with—; ring—; soil —; sponge with—; tuck—; utilize—; whip open—; wrinkle—; —assures; —catches; —protects; —safeguards.

(See handkerchief, cloth, towel.)

NARCOTICS

verbs

abstain from—; addict to—; control—; distribute—; drowse under—; inhale—; inject —; load with—; peddle—; purvey—; smuggle—; specialize in—; swallow—; trade in —; traffic in—; warn against—; —corrupt; —defile; —degenerate; —deteriorate; —ease; —induce; —menace; —poison; —ravage; —stultify; —wreck.

(See drug, heroin, medicine.)

NARRATE (v)

adverbs

bizarrely; absorbingly; vividly; romantically; grippingly; dramatically; movingly; deftly; tensely; vigorously; artfully; prosaically.

(See tell, recite, relate.)

NARRATION

adjectives

dramatic; bare; vivid; gripping; moving; swift; sure; deft; skilled; breathless.

verbs

blend into—; color—; commend—; discuss —; embellish—; enter into—; introduce into

—; publish—; recite—; recount—; rehearse —; resume—; set forth in—; state in—; —delights; —depicts; —enchants; —enthralls; —portrays; —reveals; —unfolds.

(See lecture, story, tale.)

NARRATIVE

adjectives

dry; boasting; comprehensive; epical; enticing; shocking; contemporary; lugubrious; disjointed; digested; romantic; autobiographical; superficial; sober; poetical; imaginative; touching; dramatic; tragic; vivid; melodramatic; sacred; graphic; connected; superb; splendid; fictitious; thrilling; faithful; concise; mirthful; chequered; trustworthy; serious; earnest; authentic; metrical; truthful; personal; descriptive; persuasive; fantastic; voluminous; incredible; celebrated; present; masterly; supernatural; painful; pathetic.

verbs

acclaim—; blend into—; commend—; complicate—; condense—; embellish—; enliven —; impair—; interlard—; introduce in—; peruse—; recount—; set forth in—; spice —; strew throughout—; sum up—; —delights; —enchants; —flows; —portrays; —strikes; —unfolds.

(See fiction, lecture, legend, anecdote, story, tale.)

NARROW (v)

adverbs

appreciably; markedly; abruptly; perilously; impracticably; strikingly.

(See reduce, contract.)

NARROW

adverbs

impossibly; terribly; unbelievably; remarkably; painfully; inconveniently; inexplicably; outlandishly; stingily; frugally; parsimoniously; absurdly; ridiculously; perilously; hazardously; dangerously; inexcusably; outrageously; shockingly; terrifyingly; uselessly; unserviceably; curiously; undesirably; vexatiously; perplexingly; uncommonly.

NARROW-MINDED

adverbs

stubbornly; intolerably; intractably; obdurately; wilfully; incurably; incorrigibly; persistently; fanatically; perniciously; obstinately; hopelessly; mulishly; incomprehensibly; inveterately.

adjectives
ignoble; puritanic; old-fashioned; mental; moral; unexpected.

NASTY

adverbs
squalidly; obscenely; indelicately; disgustingly; offensively; repulsively; odiously; disagreeably; unnecessarily; unpardonably; indecently; loathsomely; nauseatingly; diabolically; terribly; sickeningly; unhealthfully; pestilentially; dangerously; unsanitarily.

NATION

adjectives
powerful; puissant; guarded; shopkeeping; delivered; advanced; expectant; friendly; regenerated; dusky; surrounding (pl); liberated; disenchanted; grateful; altruistic; respective; warring; neighboring; restless; energetic; impressionable; civilized; happy; peaceable; wretched; impoverished; delusive; motley; swarming; greedy; aggressive; magnificent; resolute; impudent; unpolished; conquered; diverse; unsubdued; maritime; capitalist; woeful; eminent; scientific; long-suffering; declining; raw; mercantile; gentle; moral; uncivilized; stunned; helpless; leaderless; loyal; barbarous; brave; vigorous; ignorant; incredulous; benighted; sacred; homogeneous; burdened; stricken; unfriended; ambitious; progressive; wild; corrupted; exceptional; callous; courageous; brave; enslaved; eager; fickle; ill-assorted; ancient.

verbs
awaken—; blanket—; compensate—; convulse—; envelop—; filch from—; further—; incite—; inflame—; jolt—; liberate—; menace—; realign—; seduce—; terrorize—; trample—; —decays; —embarks on; —quakes; —retaliates; —rises; —s vie for.
(See folk, country, empire, public.)

NATIONAL

adverbs
strongly; ardently; narrowly; broadly; strictly; eagerly; fervently; intensely; devotedly; fiercely; zealously; indifferently; enthusiastically; sharply; selfishly; actively; admirably.

NATIONALISM

adjectives
intense; spiritual; ardent; growing; evident; forced; powerful.

verbs
advocate—; base on—; breed—; cultivate —; defend—; encourage—; favor—; foster —; institute—; justify—; maintain—; prate of—; prescribe—; respect—; seethe with—; steep in—; threaten—; value—; —characterizes; —comforts; —shields; —smooths.
(See democracy, atheism, socialism, independence.)

NATIONALITIES

adjectives
dominant; jarring; divers; healthy; autonomous.

NATIONALITY

verbs
annihilate—; cast off—; characterize—; color—; denote—; deny—; describe—; distinguish—; efface—; extinguish—; ferret out—; protest—; renounce—; threaten—; —pains; —vanishes.
(See heritage, nation.)

NATIVE

adverbs
unquestionably; genuinely; happily; indigenously; unaffectedly; frankly; plainly; obviously; advantageously; contentedly; indubitably; conveniently; warrantably.

NATIVES

adjectives
frightened; superstitious; credulous; bedizened; grinning; influential; energetic; polygamous; well-connected; indifferent; effeminate; nondescript; bronzed; free-born; wretched; exiled; unprejudiced; guileless; predatory; genuine; belated.

verbs
astonish—; commend—; dispute with—; encounter—; fraternize with—; interrogate—; scuffle with—; —adhere; —adopt; —fashion; —inhabit; —merit; —populate; —praise; —rear.
(See inhabitant, Indian, negro, peasant.)

NATURAL

adverbs
essentially; inherently; artlessly; honestly; ingenuously; openly; unaffectedly; spontane-

ously; simply; frankly; naively; cordially; delightfully; suddenly; altogether; refreshingly; touchingly; wondrously; charmingly; ravishingly; unbelievably; graciously; innocently; alluringly; childishly; guilelessly; youthfully; pleasantly.

NATURALIST

adjectives
well-known; inoffensive; abstracted; wise.

verbs
appeal to—; unfold to—; —breeds; —classifies; —collects; —conserves; —examines; —exhausts; —fathoms; —gazes on; —invades; —investigates; —marvels at; —observes; —preserves; —reflects; —studies; —tabulates; —treasures; —treks; —verifies; —worships.

(See scientist, philosopher.)

NATURALIZATION

verbs
approve—; await—; consider—; deny—; desire—; dispute—; encourage—; gain—; merit—; prepare for—; protest—; qualify for—; question—; seek—; undergo—; —commends; —ensues; —insures; —privileges.

(See citizenship.)

NATURE

verbs
attune to—; conform to—; defy—; endow by —; master—; mirror—; observe—; portray —; reflect—; rely on—; return to—; struggle with—; subdue—; supplant—; take refuge in—; wring from—; —allures; —arrays; —bestows; —decrees; —exacts; —imposes; —molds; —paints; —plays; —rejoices; —sanctions; —shapes; —stages; —thwarts; —unfolds; supplement—.

(See instinct, God, life, convention, conventionality.)

NATURE

adjectives (*character*)
abject; able; adventurous; affectionate; agitating; angelic; animate; arduous; arrogant; artistic; awakening; awed; belated; beneficent; binding; boisterous; blind; blithesome; bloody; blunt; brooding; brute; bubbling; buoyant; calculating; calm; cantankerous; cautious; capricious; celestial; chivalrous; clinging; cold; combative; communicable; complicated; composite; conceited; concentrated; confiding; conscientious; con-servative; contracted; contradictory; contrary; controversial; corporeal; craven; creating; cruel; crumbling; cursed; cynical; daring; darkening; dazzled; definite; delicate; delightful; desperate; determined; diabolical; dictatorial; difficult; diligent; dismal; disordered; distasteful; diversified; domineering; dual; dynamic; easygoing; ecclesiastical; elemental; elevated; emotional; enduring; encouraging; engrossing; erratic; essential; everlasting; evil; exacting; exaggerating; exclusive; exhilarating; expansive; exquisite; external; extraordinary; false; fastidious; fearless; fiendish; fiery; finite; forbearing; forbidding; formidable; frank; friable; frivolous; functional; generous; gloomy; gracious; half-savage; great; gross; hardy; harmonious; harsh; hateful; haughty; hazardous; heaven-born; hereditary; heretical; hidden; hideous; highstrung; honest; honorable; horrible; hostile; human; illustrious; hysterical; immaterial; immutable; imperfect; imperious; impetuous; imperturbable; impracticable; inanimate; incomprehensible; incongruous; indigenous; infectious; infinite; inherent; inmost; inorganic; inscrutable; inspired; intellectual; intense; internal; interpretative; intimate; intrinsic; introspective; intuitive; invertebrate; kind; irritable; latent; lavish; leonine; light; living; lofty; lovable; luxuriant; maimed; magnetic; marked; martial; mean; material; mechanical; melancholy; mid-summer; mercurial; merry; mild; mischievous; miraculous; mismade; moral; murky; mute; mysterious; neutral; niggard; noble; obscure; observant; omnipotent; onerous; operative; opposed; opulent; oracular; ostentatious; outward; painful; paradoxical; parallel; parsimonious; passionate; patriotic; peculiar; pecuniary; personal; phantasmagorical; planetary; playful; pliant; poetic; polished; popular; populous; precise; praiseworthy; prime; primitive; private; probable; prodigal; profaning; prophetic; protracted; proud; quarrelsome; quick; radiant; rash; rational; reasonable; recalcitrant; receptive; recondite; religious; reluctant; restless; retiring; revengeful; rude; sanguine; sardonic; savage; seasonal; self-effacing; self-sacrificing; sensitive; sensuous; sentient; sentimental; severe; shallow; shrinking; silent; sluggish; social; sordid; soldierly; sorry; sound; specific; spiritual; spiteful; spoiled; spontaneous; sterling; stifled; strong; struggling; subordinate; sturdy; subtle; sunny; sympathizing;

swampy; tangible; teaching; temperate; tenacious; thoroughgoing; timid; transitional; transitory; trite; trivial; truthful; ultimate; unadvanced; unblemished; uncompromising; uncultivated; undisciplined; unending; unfatherly; ungentlemanly; ungracious; unique; universal; unoffending; unpoetic; unpredictable; unprofessional; unrepentant; unselfish; unsociable; unstable; untaught; untractable; untrained; upright; vacant; vague, vain; vehement; vengeful; virile; vital; vivacious; voiceless; volatile; volcanic; voluntary; voracious; vulgar; wary; weak; weighty; well-derived; wild; willful; winged; wiry; wistful.

verbs
alter—; ascertain—; bewail—; crush—; determine—; disfigure—; dwarf—; elevate—; flaunt—; indicate—; manifest—; mold—; offend—; recognize—; sate—; temper—; — prompts.
(See character, quality.)

NAUGHTY
adverbs
roguishly; mischievously; childishly; disagreeably; thoughtlessly; embarrassingly; slyly; furtively; innocently; unbearably; maliciously; surprisingly; unwontedly; unusually; vexatiously; remarkably; perversely; incorrigibly; curiously; uncommonly; extremely; scampishly; prankishly; gracelessly.

NAUSEA
verbs
escape—; excite—; induce—; loathe—; relieve—; overcome with—; remedy—; sate to —; seize with—; shock into—; stifle—; suffer—; —agonizes; —disgusts; —dispirits; —grieves; —wearies.
(See vomiting, disgust, resentment, hatred.)

NAUSEOUS
adverbs
terribly; uncommonly; disagreeably; offensively; unnecessarily; unpardonably; unbearably; grievously; painfully; bitterly; obnoxiously; mortifyingly; intolerably; appallingly; hatefully; hideously; insufferably.

NAUTICAL
adverbs
correctly; properly; appropriately; unquestionably; completely; admirably; wildly; charmingly; brightly; nattily.

NAVAL
adverbs
strictly; gloriously; strongly; invincibly.

NAVIGATE (*v*)
adverbs
precariously; professionally; deftly; skillfully; seasonally; intrepidly; daringly; fearlessly; disastrously.
(See sail, guide, steer.)

NAVIGATION
adjectives
celestial; uninterrupted; protracted; widespread; ocean.

NAVY
adjectives
auxiliary; unexploring; dauntless; protective; strong; fearless; well-manned; undersized; great.

verbs
enlist in—; equip—; maintain—; modernize —; volunteer for—; —defends; —manoeuvres; —patrols; —practises; —recruits; — safeguards; —schools; —trains; —transports; —yields.
(See militia, fleet, army.)

NEAR
adverbs
intimately; advantageously; conveniently; pleasantly; agreeably; handily; surprisingly; remarkably; unexpectedly; ominously; unfortunately; happily; luckily; opportunely; profitably.

NEARNESS
adjectives
immediate; familiar; unknown; breathless.

NEAT
adverbs
painfully; pleasantly; incorrigibly; particularly; remarkably; incomparably; curiously; intolerably; placidly; extremely; admirably; perfectly; habitually; incurably; uniformly; immaculately; daintily; exquisitely; jauntily; attractively; spotlessly; miraculously.

NEATNESS
adjectives
expectant; chilly; unusual; indescribable; extreme; miraculous; meticulous; incomparable.

verbs

cluster into—; cover with—; —beautify; —charm; —decorate; —embellish; —enchant; —enhance; —fascinate; —illuminate; —mantle; —mass; —mist; —patch; —powder; —thicken; —whirl.

(See stars, clouds.)

NEBULOUS

adverbs

vaguely; dimly; obscurely; umbrageously; foggily; mistily; faintly; confusingly; bewilderingly; vaporously; unfathomably; dangerously; hazardously; alarmingly; perplexingly; unpleasantly; extremely.

NECESSARY

adverbs

strictly; hardly; scarcely; entirely; absolutely; completely; undeniably; obviously; definitely; manifestly; unquestionably; financially; economically; apparently; cruelly; unfortunately; unluckily; bitterly; imperatively; unavoidably; tragically; embarrassingly; terribly.

NECESSITY

adjectives

prime; humiliating; absolute; economic; empowered; stern; imperative; sheer; pecuniary; obvious; irresistible; physical; crying; urgent; relative; material; highborn; deplored; indispensable; mathematical; righteous; pressing; time-honored; everyday; unalterable; inexorable; immutable; dire; expressive; practical; military; objective; cruel; dread; inevitable; invincible; belittling; strict; immediate; vicious; temporary; factitious; mortifying; fatal; unavoidable; logical; desperate; burning; fancied; superfluous; metaphysical; domestic; implacable; unyielding; marvelous; physiological; hypothetical; tragic; bitter; apparent; startling; household; amazing; fast-selling; feminine; clever; business; daily; money-saving.

verbs

argue—; feel—; fortify by—; illustrate—; impel by—; inspire by—; minister to—; obviate—; ponder—; preclude—; relieve of—; skimp on —s; urge—; yield to—; —abates; —arises; —cements; —compels; —forces; —pinches; —s pop up; —presses.

(See fate, emergency, exigency, compulsion, requirement, want, need.)

adjectives

beguiling; withered; distended; ivory; stiffening; corrigible; mottled; humbled; misshapen; glossy; feminine-looking; naked; graceful; gaunt; sinewy; glowing; gleaming; chic; square; distressful; shimmering; stately; snowy; athletic; scalloped; dry-skinned; nervous; wrinkled; thin; flattered; arching; queenly; silly; well-turned; sleek; jeweled; enameled.

verbs

adorn—; arch—; bow—; button at—; clutch by—; crane—; decorate—; dislocate—; exercise—; furbish—; jerk—; massage—; powder—; sever at—; wreathe—; yoke by—.

NECKTIE

verbs

adjust—; criticize—; examine—; knit—; knot—; loosen—; pattern—; print—; spot —; stripe—; weave—; yank (colloq.)—; —blazes; —exaggerates; —flames; —impresses; —infuriates; —matches; —overwhelms; —shocks.

(See cravat, handkerchief.)

NECTAR

verbs

bathe in—; draw — from; drown in—; nourish with—; relish—; secrete—; seek—; sink in—; spout—; suck—; tongue—; —cools; —delights; —intoxicates; —oozes; —gratifies; —steams.

(See sweetness, liquid, beverage, drink.)

NEED

adjectives

individual; imperative; critical; profound; fundamental; airy; spiritual; specialized; self-existing; genuine; unnumbered (pl); warranted; changing; pressing; burning; dubious; desperate; emergency; tragic; primitive; dreadful; urgent; future; spiritual; action-shaping; absolute; obvious; perpetual; definite; private; increasing; artless; shameful; dearest; psychic; extravagant; sorest; inexorable; diverse; economic; home; preliminary; intellectual; emotional; distinct; supreme; pervading; particular; deepest; practical; cruel; bitter; degrading; corporate; quiet.

verbs

anticipate—; ascertain—; awaken to—; beget—; bend to—; conceal—; define—; eliminate—; enunciate—; evince—; emphasize —; express—; meet—; minimize—; minister to—; portray—; reveal—; satisfy—; serve —; smother—; study—; supplant—; supply —; suppress—; survey—; torture by—; voice—; —arises; —dictates; —presses.

(See lack, impoverishment, inadequacy, exigency, necessity, want, poverty.)

NEED (v)
adverbs

direly; imperatively; horribly; desperately; sorely; urgently; critically; fundamentally; spiritually; genuinely; tragically; inexorably; economically; degradingly.

(See lack, require, want.)

NEEDLE
adjectives

magnetic; shining; cambric; trembling; glancing.

verbs

case—; direct—; dodge—; draw—through; grope for—; magnetize—; mend with—; ply —; polish—; prick with—; stick with—; thread—; tug at—; work with—; —designs; —flies; —penetrates; —perforates; —punctures.

(See pin, point.)

NEEDLESS
adverbs

utterly; apparently; altogether; absurdly; obviously; wholly; ridiculously; manifestly; inconsequentially.

NEEDY
adverbs

desperately; undoubtedly; warrantably; tragically; pitiably; pathetically; pitifully; hopelessly; helplessly; surprisingly; avowedly; lamentably; extremely; distressingly; unfortunately; sadly; strangely; unaccountably; obscurely; unquestionably; wretchedly; miserably; inexpressibly.

NEFARIOUS
adverbs

incomparably; abominably; diabolically; extremely; incredibly; unfathomably; wildly; deplorably; dangerously; unconscionably; grossly; scandalously; malevolently; reprehensibly; gracelessly; shamelessly; monstrously.

NEGATIVE
adjectives

strange; audacious; emphatic; startled; definite; clear.

adverbs

feebly; hopelessly; fortunately; luckily; unquestionably; emphatically; flatly; peremptorily; blankly; virtually; completely; incontrovertibly; discouragingly; distressingly; unhappily; unexpectedly; avowedly; allegedly; presumably; probably.

NEGLECT
adjectives

habitual; ostentatious; unintentional; willful; deplorable; hideous; high-spirited; comparative; loving; disdainful; intended; culpable; apathetic; predestined; monstrous; infamous; total.

verbs

atone for—; breed—; charge with—; complain of—; convict of—; die of—; goad by —; pardon—; rescue from—; suffer—; throw into—; wither in—; —corrodes; — damages; —endangers; —harms; —injures; —insults; —rusts; —saps.

(See failure, default, carelessness.)

NEGLECT (v)
adverbs

habitually; ostentatiously; deplorably; hideously; wilfully; disdainfully; apathetically; monstrously; infamously; totally; shamefully; slovenly; impudently; improvidently.

(See ignore, disregard.)

NEGLIGENCE
adjectives

studied; sluggard; tonsorial; official; unwonted; thoughtless; military; criminal; occasional; gross; repeated; lazy; intermittent.

NEGLIGIBLE
adverbs

comparably; comparatively; altogether; somewhat; scarcely; shamefully; ignominiously; infamously; insignificantly; ridiculously; contemptibly; politically; socially; financially.

NEGOTIATE (v)

adverbs

craftily; astutely; ingeniously; zealously; diplomatically; solemnly; tactfully; separately; commercially; internationally.

(See treat.)

NEGOTIATIONS

adjectives

premature; pending; platonic; commercial; proposed; concurrent; abortive; temporal; complex; long-drawn-out; matrimonial; solemn; friendly; mercantile; secret; peace.

verbs

advocate—; assemble for—; bolt—; carry on—; commence—; depart from—; enter into—; favor—; open—; reopen—; renew —; suspend—; terminate—; —bore; —fail; —falter; —flounder; —succeed; —tire; — weary.

(See collective bargaining, meeting, conference.)

NEGRO

adjectives

tattered; superb; shiftless; accused; harassed; free; diligent; music-loving; melodious.

verbs

auction—es; deal in—es; educate—; emancipate—; lynch—; sympathize with—; tolerate—; understand—; uplift—; whip—; — chants; —coaxes; —es congregate; —contorts; —stomps; —"trucks"; —worships.

(See native, denizen, inhabitant.)

NEIGHBOR

adjectives

uncharitable; formidable; reticent; congenial; toxophilitic; pretentious; anarchist; near; marvelous; influential; good; overbearing; backbiting; stout-shouldered; barbarian; amiable; peaceable; civilized; weaker; territorial; inquisitive; frivolous; infidel; gaping; charitable; calculating; dangerous; wingless; good-natured; barbarous; parallel; singular; perfidious; miserly; pleasant; companionable; afflicted; gossipy; enisled.

verbs

acknowledge—; associate with—; bicker with—; consort with—s; denounce—; drive out—; hedge—; respect—; rouse—s; sanctify—; scandalize—s; wrangle with—; —s band; —befriends; —complains; —contends; —gossips; —imposes; —quarrels; — rivals; —visits.

(See friend, woman, enemy.)

NEIGHBORHOOD

adjectives

audacious; fashionable; moneyed; residential; frequented; immediate; disreputable; malodorous; adjoining; noisome; deteriorating; gruff.

verbs

arouse—; attract to—; avoid—; crowd—; denounce—; drive from—; explore—; huddle in—; inflame—; master—; preserve—; rule—; scandalize—; shun—; visit—; — appeals to; —bands together; —befriends; —congregates; —petitions.

(See locality, section, city, village, town, district.)

NEIGHBORLY

adverbs

actively; heartily; generously; wonderfully; agreeably; delightfully; helpfully; sincerely; sociably; extremely; unwontedly; incredibly; amicably; chattily; hospitably; gregariously; companionably; remarkably; heart-warmingly.

NEPHEW

adjectives

warming; prodigal; chubby; scapegrace; celebrated; spurious; disinherited.

NERVE

adjectives

firm; strained; tingling; marble; gustatory; languid; irritable; underlying; shaky; delicate; tremulous; sensitive; ragged; gentle; taut; excellent; iron; curious; auditory; miraculous; invisible; sciatic; wailing; harassed; shattered; vibrating; overstrained; optic; inconceivable; adamantine; shrinking; uncertain; tender; overstrung; revolutionary; high-strung; pneumogastric; exhausted; jangled; shuddering; silent; excitable; sympathetic; physical; oversusceptible; overwrought.

NERVELESS

adverbs

pitiably; helplessly; ineffectually; incompetently; curiously; pathetically; distressingly; miserably; wretchedly; ineptly; pitifully; limply; strangely.

NERVES

verbs

addle—; calm—; constrict—; deaden—; desensitize—; dilate—; disturb—; drag at—; exhaust—; fray—; impinge upon—; irritate —; involve—; jangle—; jolt—; jar—; numb —; pad—; relax—; sever—; shatter—; shock—; soothe—; steady—; stimulate—; strain—; tranquilize—; unstring—; — bristle; —jump; —respond; —snap.

NERVOUS

adverbs

highly; uncommonly; extremely; significantly; pitifully; hysterically; feverishly; unnecessarily; strangely; absurdly; ridiculously; guiltily; curiously; physically; secretly; apparently; timidly; bashfully; childishly; exceedingly; pitiably; pathetically; ludicrously; sadly; touchingly; laughably; miserably; alarmingly; ominously; unfortunately.

NERVOUSNESS

adjectives

concealed; excessive; mere; feverish; subtle.

verbs

allay—; decline into—; enhance—; manifest —; overcome—; overpower—; remedy—; scoff at—; spring from—; suffer from—; — confuses; —debilitates; —deprives; —distresses; —disturbs; —enervates; —enfeebles; —shakes; —strains; —weakens.
(See hysteria, impatience, sickness.)

NERVOUS SYSTEM

verbs

derange— —; ease— —; excite— —; flow through— —; govern— —; guard— — from; impair— —; nourish— —; overwork — —; stimulate— —; strain— —; support — —; tax— —; — —collapses; — — cramps; — —links; — —recovers; — —responds.

NEST

adjectives

drowsy; clamorous; broodless; deserted; eternal; central; quiet; mossy; watery; northern; unmaternal; hungry; enlightened; pensile; well-built; shattered; windless; distant; balmy; spicy; sheltered; warm; cozy.

verbs

camouflage—; construct—; deposit in—; discover—; disturb—; expose—; hollow out —; huddle in—; incubate in—; isolate—; lodge in—; perch in—; pillage—; protect —; pry into—; quit—; retire to—; rob—; scoop out—; swing—; tree—; —comforts; —cradles; —shelters.
(See home, shelter, hole, hive. lair, refuge.)

NESTLE (v)

adverbs

snugly; cozily; domestically; tenderly; drowsily; warmly; affectionately.
(See cuddle.)

NET

adjectives

fishing; anchored; elastic; weblike; impassable; inescapable; closely-woven.

verbs

bag with—; capture in—; cast—; confine in—; construct—; dip—; dredge with—; dry—; fish with—; knit—; lower—; pay out —; repair—; secure with—; slip through— spin—; spread—; stretch—; sweep into—; swim into—; trap in—; trawl with—; — drifts; —ensnares; —entangles.
(See trap, snare, mesh, network.)

NETTLE (v)

adverbs

intolerably; exasperatingly; maddeningly; spitefully; vengefully; cruelly; formidably; bitterly.
(See provoke, irritate.)

NETWORK

adjectives

gigantic; ramified; endless; ingenious; complicated; broadcasting; national; social.

verbs

bind into—; chain into—; construct—; control—; convey over—; extend—; hook up on —; incorporate—; interfere with—; join—; localize—; present over—; tie up with—; unravel—; weave—.
(See system, net.)

NEUROSIS

verbs

accentuate—; classify—; despise—; dispel —; explain—; group—es; ignore—; pronounce—; resist—; shake—; stem—; suffer from—; usher in—; —attacks; —cripples; —exists; —irritates; —nags; —obsesses; — persists; —upsets.
(See complex, disease, sickness.)

NEUROTIC

adjectives

advanced; compulsive; unfortunate; life-long; hapless.

adverbs

undeniably; vexatiously; hopelessly; pathetically; absurdly; helplessly; incurably; intolerably; miserably; wretchedly; lamentably; needlessly; unfortunately; exceedingly; curiously; deplorably; incomparably; cursedly; deucedly; conveniently; disgustingly.

NEUTRAL

adverbs

resolutely; dependably; altogether; strictly; rigidly; infallibly; sagaciously; wisely; carefully; cautiously; unimpeachably; sincerely; honorably; respectfully; deliberately; determinedly; indifferently; alertly; judiciously; intelligently; interestedly; evasively; necessarily; pluckily; stoutly; conveniently; steadily; unwaveringly; irreproachably.

NEUTRALITY

adjectives

stern; hostile; selfish; benevolent; malevolent; political; blameless; precarious; armed; maintained; difficult.

verbs

advocate—; break—; commend—; disrupt —; enjoy—; express—; favor—; foreswear —; infract—; maintain—; observe—; pledge—; preserve—; profess—; propose—; renounce—; respect—; uphold—; violate—; —balances; —continues; —endangers; —gratifies.

(See attitude, position.)

NEWCOMERS

verbs

befriend—; criticize—; denounce—; fend off —; judge—; limit—; mold—; pity—; quarrel with—; repel—; snub—; suspect—; train —; wrangle with—; —band; —impress; —invade; hedge—.

(See foreigner, alien, stranger.)

NEWLYWEDS
(colloq.)

verbs

davise—; bless—; caution—; endow—; fete —; fetter—; mock—; serenade—; sever—; —beam; —blush; —cherish; —clasp; —coo;

—dream; —flush; —honeymoon (colloq.); —nest; —rejoice; —repent.

(See lover, sweetheart, husband, wife, suitor.)

NEWS

adjectives

lamentable; alarming; distasteful; inevitable; ill; current; pleasant; inestimable; cheerful; especial; unwelcome; electrifying; disastrous; positive; serious; fresh; irrelevant; dire; long-expected; glorious; interpretative; astonishing; dreadful; vengeful; amazing; definite; startling; fashionable; comparative; distressing; encouraging; exciting; reassuring; deplorable; stupefying; blackest; domestic; panic; inside; sharp; ominous; hopeful; unacceptable; uncertain; unsatisfactory; major; vital; ghastly; significant; condensed; below-the-surface; latest; accurate; fevered; world; heartbreaking.

verbs

bear—; bound into—; broadcast—; bruit about—; comb for—; crop into—; disseminate—; dominate—; edit—; falsify—; flash into—; glean—; greet—; hail—; impart—; overshadow—; purvey—; relay—; scan—; scream—; sift—; spot—; suppress—; verify —; —blazes; —breaks; —fades; —filters through; —stuns; —trickles in.

(See report, word, rumor, message, telegram.)

NEWSPAPER

adjectives

enterprising; disloyal; daily; influential; sensational; leading; matrimonial; conservative; weekly; contemporaneous.

verbs

blazon on—; clip from—; comb—; creep into—; crumple—; deliver—; hawk—s; peddle—s; peruse—; pore over—; purvey—s; scan—; scoop—; skim through—; supplement—; syndicate—; —campaigns; —circulates; —devotes to; —functions; —suppresses.

(See literature, magazine, periodical, publication, press.)

NEWSPAPERMAN

adjectives

astute; hateful; well-respected; enterprising; bold.

verbs

crowd— —; dash to— —; drift to— —; enjoy— —; mill through— —; pack— —; plunge into— —; stream through— —; taxi 'round— —; tour— —; — —astonishes; — —bewilders; — —clutches; — —enchants; — —excels; — —excites; — —irritates; — —pains; — —sparkles; — —thrills; — —towers; — —unfurls.

(See city.)

NIBBLE (v)

adverbs

tantalizingly; daintily; teasingly; cautiously; intermittently; shyly; coyly.

(See munch, bite.)

NICE

adverbs

extraordinarily; particularly; wonderfully; scrupulously; punctiliously; meticulously; invariably; incomparably; unsurpassably; unquestionably; apparently; obviously; manifestly; admirably; unusually; inherently; exquisitely; marvellously; altogether; remarkably.

NICETY

adjectives

peculiar; critical; professional; scrupulous; utmost; painful.

verbs

accomplish with—; acknowledge—ies; appreciate—; delight in—ies; demonstrate —ies; educate in—ies; express with—; frame in—; manage with—; question—; require—; stand upon—; verse in—ies; — prevails; —ies serve for; offend—ies; operate with—.

(See precision, efficiency, skill, tact.)

NICHE

adjectives

comfortable; murky; opposite; appropriate; temporary.

verbs

assign—; attain—; carve out—; claim—; contrive—; crack—; decorate—; dig—; examine—; fill—; find—; gain—; hew—; hollow out—; molest—; occupy—; place in—; select—; sink into—; —protects.

(See corner, place.)

verbs

adopt—; assume—; bear—; bedevil with—; bestow—upon; brand with—; coin—; contrive—; define—; dub with—; earn—; incur—; —adheres; —annoys; —clings; — labels; —mocks; —sticks; —survives; — vexes.

(See name, title.)

NICKNAME (v)

adverbs

aptly; sneeringly; vindictively; viciously; scoffingly; slurringly; hatefully; fraternally; jovially; humiliatingly; facetiously.

(See entitle, designate.)

NIGGARDLY

adverbs

grossly; unreasonably; meanly; basely; unutterably; inconsiderately; greedily; unnecessarily; disgustingly; penuriously; sordidly; crassly; unbelievably; terribly; shabbily; despicably; contemptibly; wretchedly; overwhelmingly; unutterably; absurdly.

NIGHT

adjectives

mantling; naked; hopeless; perpetual; long; tedious; dull; brooding; frosty; waxing; restless; feverish; deepening; cloudless; moonlight; stark; unspeakable; cloud-hung; sleepless; hideous; sweating; dim; darksome; sultry; fatal; unfathomable; eternal; earth-shaking; wretched; lyric; carved; impelling; precarious; bespangled; congenial; weary; anxious; noiseless; cheerless; tempestuous; brilliant; magic; tortuous; fearsome; gusty; wakeful; wassail; tolerable; large-eyed; silvery; desolate; romantic; watchful; deep-winding; utter; stifling; memorable; broad-winged; difficult; previous; star-studded; lingering; bridal; stagnant; extended; revolving; abysmal; peerless; summer; capped; subtle; serene; somber; cooling lustrous; light; bottomless; fragrant; dewy; profound; departing; shining; dreamless; drizzly; unalienable; heaviest; glimmering; soft; agate; tourmaline; glass-clear; overcast; milky; ghastly; black; impenetrable; perfumed; smiling; pale; live; black-frost; sable; lurid; moonless; slowly-gathering; eyeless; raving; blessed; eventful; prolonged; irksome; unlanterned; unsocial; stormy; gradual; unseeing; ugly; laboring; fashionable; clear; pallid; bright; golden; sweet-smelling; obscure; dumb;

lingering; limitless; inky; star-silent; earthly; moon-mad; hushed; crimeful; enchanting; divine; shadowy; moonshiny; comfortless; merciless; feeding; pitchy; vaporous; interlunar; supperless; identical; ecstatic; fateful; careful; dreaming; dreary; illstarred; sweltering; gathering; festival; breathless; humorous; black-faced; azure; auspicious; polar; grim; notable; voluptuous; sightless; lonely.

verbs

contemplate—; fritter away—; lapse into—; lurk in—; pierce—; repose at—; sink into —; —blankets; —calms; —clouds over; — creeps up; —curtains; —depresses; —descends; —drags; —engulfs; —enshrouds; — envelops; —inspires; —mantles; —oppresses; —reigns; —robs; —shades; —tiptoes; — veils; —wanes; —waxes; —yawns.

(See evening, twilight, darkness, dusk.)

NIGHTINGALE

adjectives

wakeful; unenvying; tempestuous; triumphant; full-throated; voluptuous; importunate; undying; beauteous.

verbs

—anthems; —bewails; —bursts out; — chants; —charms; —cheers; —complains; —courts; —crowds; —delights; —enchants; —hurries; —lullabies; —mourns; —pierces; —precipitates notes; —pours forth; —ravishes; —shies; —sings out woe; —sobers; — thrills; —transports; —trills; —utters; — vocalizes; —wails; —warbles.

(See bird.)

NIGHTMARE

adjectives

horrifying; preposterous; fiendish; racking; catapulting; portentous; indistinguishable; intolerable; weird; half-vanishing; hideous; weary; eyeless; horrible; financial; veritable.

verbs

beset with—; conceive in—; convulse in—; fancy in—; free from—; imagine in—; picture in—; plunge into—; sink into—; toss in —; unloose—; —alarms; —chokes; —distresses; —settles on; —strains; —strangles; —suffocates; —terrifies; —tortures; — weighs.

(See menace, dream, vision, delusion.)

NIMBLE

adverbs

actively; alertly; unbelievably; surprisingly; remarkably; miraculously; noticeably; obviously; amazingly; unusually; lightly; deftly; adroitly; cleverly; smartly; expertly; peculiarly; incredibly; dexterously; wondrously; briskly; vigilantly.

NIPS

adjectives

fatal; surreptitious; powerful; piercing.

NITROGEN

verbs

combine with—; derive—from; expel—; extract—; furnish with—; manufacture—; market—; mix with—; obtain—; reveal—; store—; temper with—; unite—with; —dilutes; —evaporates; —extinguishes.

(See chemical, acid, mixture, solution.)

NOBLE

adverbs

naturally; quietly; innately; aristocratically; genuinely; truly; admittedly; tenaciously; inherently; actually; elegantly; splendidly; unaffectedly; avowedly; unquestionably; essentially; eminently; grandly; imposingly.

NOBILITY

adjectives

rapacious; transcendent; conspicuous; dubious; mental; latent; impoverished; inherent; austere; powerless; factious; outraged; certain; pervading.

verbs

acknowledge—; attract—; conceal—; crown with—; display—; enhance—; forfeit—; glory in—; honor—; meet—; rouse—; seat among—; smack of—; steep in—; —characterizes; —distinguishes; —enriches; — graces; —outlives; —pedigrees; —shines.

(See aristocracy, gallantry, monarch, splendor, supremacy.)

NOBLEMAN

adjectives

needy; veritable; self-respecting; impoverished; fiery; dissolute; sporting; eminent.

NOBLENESS

adjectives

natural; native; quiet; free; inborn; innate.

NOBLES

adjectives

violent; hereditary; thoughtful; dissolute; dense; emigrant; malevolent; indolent; faithful; prudent; high-taught; philosophic; dastard; rapacious; cushioned; factious; arrogant; haughty; speculative.

NOD

adjectives

jolly; little; swaggering; impertinent; approving; placid; gracious; wrenlike; imperceptible; insinuating; impatient; laconic; emphatic.

NOD (*v*)

adverbs

sagely; comprehendingly; vehemently; incisively; crisply; dreamily; benignly; solemnly; drowsily; assuringly; significantly; pensively; urbanely; affably; energetically; complacently; sagaciously; affirmatively; rhythmically; positively; assentingly; jovially; philosophically; speculatively.

(See bow, bend.)

NOISE

verbs

ban—; contribute to—; eliminate—; emit—; endure—; exclude—; guard against—; intensify—; reproduce—; resound with—of; saturate with—; simulate—s of; suppress —; —abates; —s blend; —confuses; —hampers; —hinders; —shuffles; —stuns; —subsides.

(See crash, howl, hiss, din, clash, roar.)

NOISELESS

adverbs

completely; warrantably; avowedly; allegedly; reasonably; absolutely; reputably; incredibly; remarkably; mysteriously; magically; unbelievably; peculiarly; furtively; stealthily; solemnly; awfully; alarmingly.

NOISES

adjectives

sharp; pattering; unfamiliar; rustling; shuffling; sniffling; appalling; sundry; booming; audible; ejaculatory; creaking; thunderous; cowing; ruder; sympathetic; tempestuous; rattling; increasing; frightful; pitiful; snivelling; humming; sinister; melancholy; shattering; prodigious; discordant; stringed; croaking; meaningless; buzzing; roaring; barbarous; sullen; sufficient; continuous; humming; guttural; distant;

singular; dangling; whirring; clumping; ripping; rumbling; loud; damnable; whining; impetuous; swishing; confused; unique; unexplained; confounded; midnight; murmuring; shrill; distinct; sudden; subtler; unexpected; startling; unbelievable; objectionable; doubtful; rushing; softest; ill-resounding; slightest; diabolical; unmeaning; vulgar; outside; explosive; deafening; violent; grating; cool; chirping; jocund; fiendish; spiteful; terrifying; dull; unseemly; vague; harsh; unearthly; everlasting; ceaseless.

NOISY

adverbs

clamorously; vociferously; restlessly; uproariously; happily; childishly; screamingly; thunderously; stentoriously; lustily; ribaldly; naturally; boisterously; oddly; unwontedly; curiously; hoydenishly; audaciously; excitedly; hysterically; wildly; intolerably; provokingly; habitually; uncontrollably; ungovernably.

NOMADIC

adverbs

naturally; inherently; nonchalantly; happily; blithely; habitually; voluntarily; periodically; erratically; aimlessly; restlessly; adventurously; profitably; stubbornly; incurably; incorrigibly; remarkably; curiously; strangely; elusively; extraordinarily; recklessly; indefatigably; merrily.

NOMINAL

adverbs

considerately; altogether; merely; absurdly; obviously; curiously; usually; conventionally; conveniently; generously; deliberately; purposely; prudently; intentionally; deceptively; circumspectly; discreetly; simply.

NOMINATE (*v*)

adverbs

unanimously; jubilantly; independently; modestly; spontaneously; aptly; democratically; thunderously.

(See name, designate.)

NOMINATION

adjectives

spontaneous; caucus; predetermined; independent; unanimous.

verbs

acquiesce in—; aim at—; arrange—; authorize—; confer—upon; control—; court—; decline—; favor—; limit—s; offer for—; propose—; refuse—; reject—; rejoice in—; second—; seek—; —gratifies; —honors.

(See vote, selection, suggestion.)

NONCHALANCE

adjectives

trenchant; enticing; exasperating; debonair; knavish; affected; exquisite; suave; easy; practiced; deft.

verbs

affect—; assume an air of—; feign—; harden into—; listen with—; penetrate—; prefer—; pretend—; prick—; subdue—; tire of—; —crusts; —impresses; —interests; —irks; —nauseates; —pervades; —provokes; —tantalizes.

(See indifference, carelessness, silence.)

NONCHALANT

adverbs

habitually; blithely; indifferently; arrogantly; superciliously; inherently; naturally; usually; remarkably; studiously; deliberately; ominously; cleverly; intentionally; resolutely; charmingly; attractively; apparently; apathetically; coolly; disinterestedly; carelessly; significantly; decidedly; peculiarly; strangely; wonderfully; uncommonly; unwontedly.

NONDESCRIPT

adverbs

inexplicably; noticeably; conspicuously; curiously; strangely; oddly; hopelessly; unaccountably; unutterably; carelessly; defiantly; needlessly; fantastically; grotesquely; eccentrically; exceptionally; monstrously; singularly; peculiarly.

NONSENSE

adjectives

unmitigated; victorious; fatuous; continued; puerile; idiotic; nimble; incomprehensible; tawdry; driveling; nostalgic; undiluted; inexcusable; intelligible; licentious; good-natured; delicious; unadulterated; abject; frothy; palpable; amusing; blasted; airy; ridiculous; pleasant; absolute; blatant; extravagant; aristocratic.

verbs

dare—; denounce—; disapprove of—; disfavor—; emit—; frown on—; quibble in—; relish—; reproach for—; scoff at—; spare —; swallow—; tolerate—; wrap in—; —clouds; —confuses; —eases; —perplexes; —prevails; —revolts; —romps; —shames; —stigmatizes.

(See absurdity, folly, stupidity.)

NONSENSICAL

adverbs

fantastically; whimsically; utterly; delightfully; completely; charmingly; pleasantly; freakishly; fancifully; quaintly; oddly; wildly; drolly; frivolously; foolishly; absurdly; preposterously; inordinately; wholly.

NOOK

adjectives

sunny; lovely; shadow-haunted; sunnier; shady; obscurest; sequestered; narrow; fleshly; winding; advantageous; cobwebby; sheltered; trysting; secluded; unfrequented; leafy; studious.

NOON

adjectives

drowsy; stainless; calm; summer; joyous; burning; breezy; celestial; ardent; melting; languid; shadeless; sultry; glorious; blue-skied; liquid; sweet; clean; fiery.

NORMAL

adverbs

fairly; wholly; scarcely; altogether; comfortably; admirably; wholesomely; comfortingly; practically; finally; happily; fortunately; luckily; allegedly; avowedly; delightfully; apparently; manifestly.

NOSE

adjectives

aquiline; simple; aggressive; inquisitive; waggling; genial; flexible; innocent; arrogant; astute; weird; rueful; ferret; unerring; pudgy; rubicund; pink; blushing; cherry; streaming; crimson; sunburned; reddened; lavendar-tinted; handsome; diabolic; pug; microscopic; Grecian; fiat; saddle; endless; protruding; intrepid; hooked; well-cut; pointed; arched; showy; little; sensitive; depressed; impertinent; thin; delicate; sharp; meager; twitching; peeled; ruby; exceptional; scornful; typical; flabby; pendulous; enormous.

verbs
cock up—; crinkle—; flatten—; impact in—;
sniff up—; spray—; squinch—; thumb—;
tweak—; wrinkle—; —bleeds; —curls; —
quivers; —streams; —twitches.

(See nostrils, nozzle.)

NOSEY

adverbs
intolerably; despicably; obnoxiously; incurably; incorrigibly; inquisitively; childishly;
harmlessly; maliciously; unbearably; dangerously; ominously; alarmingly; odiously;
hatefully; poisonously; invidiously; insatiably; intrusively; inordinately; mischievously; impertinently; rudely; officially; singularly; unbelievably; unwarrantably; horribly; inescapably.

NOSTALGIA

verbs
aggravate—; bewail—; crush—; cure of—;
deplore—; dread—; ease—; endure—; expect—; foster—; hamper by—; induce—; infect with—; lament—; satisfy—; suffer from
—; —discontents; —harrows; —impels; —
preys upon; —weighs.

(See homesickness, loneliness, seclusion,
sadness.)

NOSTRILS

adjectives
overdelicate; slight; distended; dilated;
quivering; tremulous; dullest; creased;
straining; sensitive; wide; huge.

verbs
affront—; assail—; clog—; dilate—; discharge from—; irrigate—; lift—; obstruct
—; paint—; protect—; spray—; titillate—;
—quiver; —tremble.

(See nose.)

NOTABLE

adverbs
universally; nationally; internationally;
splendidly; extraordinarily; distinctly; conspicuously; unusually; extremely; illustriously.

NOTE
(*music*)
adjectives
low; full-chested; cool; musical; gracious;
flutelike; recognizable; hopeful; pensive;
imitative; piping; hoarser; varied (pl);
discordant; penetrative; cultural; eternal;

mocking; tender; accenting; plaintive; triumphant; vibrant; resounding; rambling;
piercing; profound; deepest; sentimental;
brooding; mingled (pl); rich; husky; shrill;
screech-owl; tingling; simpering; soft;
shaken; complaining; dominant; long-
drawn; wretched; whimpering; sweeter;
prelusive; grieving; mournful; pleasing;
soaring; tuneful; teasing; despairing; cocked-hat; golden; tinkling; tentative; air-feed-
ing; fundamental; voluminous; confused;
rapturous; wondrous; echoing; pealing;
gentle; blending; herald; dirgelike; grandest; warbling; wailing; full; liquid; subduing; resulting; momentary; rasping;
trembling; rising; sustained; melodious; un-
tunable; drowsy; rare; faltering; metallic.

verbs
chant—; emit—; hit—; inject—; peal—;
pitch—; scale—s; soften—; sound—; stress
—; strike—; thump—; utter—; wail—;
warble—; —dies away; —reverberates; —
shrills; —trembles; —weakens.

(See tone.)

NOTE
(*writing*)

adjectives
fundamental; melting; kindly; mirthful; occasional; ironical; dangerous; congratulatory; courteous; cordial; little; ardent; personal; copious (pl); piercing; crisp; crackling; joyous; subdued; pathetic; loud; tragic; triumphant; brief; hasty; quaint; wild;
livelier; sweet; authoritative; changed; satirical; despairing; menacing; endless; pervading; disjointed; expiring; impulsive;
warning; insistent; vexed; additional; indefinable; lesser; curious; unexpressive;
noble; contemporary; special; optimistic;
jubilant; blithest; spry; rebellious; improvised; erudite; admirable; incontrovertible;
curt; potent; definite; pleasing; precious;
sweet; agreeable; nimble; mental; queer;
tense; confidential; illegible; wild; proper;
mighty; jeering; choked; depreciated; animated; timid; funeral; authentic; illustrative; tonic; national; short; perfunctory;
hieroglyphic; tender; scholarly; warning;
flourishing; elaborate; significant; alternate;
purer; premonitory; dissentient; impulsive;
unmeasured; ironical; bubbling; exquisite;
neat; culminating; voluble; flattering;
merry; heedful; perjured; marginal; wary;
centrifugal; wandering; liked; recurrent;
penciled; promissory; inspiring; soiled; de-

scriptive; disconnected; exultant; greatest; impassioned; salutary; prefatory; desultory; fragmentary; hurried· jocund; coaxing; brief; official; kindly· confusing; infallible; unsealed; prophetic; consecutive (pl); simultaneous; dominant; brisk; monotonous; twisted; cursory.

verbs

append—; attest to—; blunt—; deliver—; direct—; dispatch—; interpret—; peruse—; point—at; scrawl—; tender—; veil—in; —elucidates; —engrosses; —explains.

(See message, letter, comment, explanation.)

NOTE (v)

adverbs

consciously; faithfully; vaguely; mirthfully; personally; triumphantly; authoritatively; satirically; curiously; eruditely; perfunctorily; impulsively; ironically; marginally; impassionedly; fragmentarily; officially; prophetically; simultaneously.

(See record, comment.)

NOTED

adverbs

nationally; unusually; brilliantly; splendidly; conspicuously; universally; nationally; locally; happily; curiously; remarkably; famously; singularly; prominently; eminently; fabulously; tremendously; reputably.

NOTEWORTHY

adverbs

distinctly; remarkably; illustriously; undoubtedly; singularly; extremely; unusually; gratifyingly; conspicuously; altogether; admittedly; emphatically; predictably.

NOTHINGS

adjectives

pronounced; airy; empty; pointless; merciful; seeming; sublime; invulnerable; poetical.

NOTICE

adjectives

hypercritical; appreciative; timely; repeated; forbidding; incidental; threatening; attentive; sympathetic; numerous (pl); disparaging; palpable; advance; favorable; sweet; obituary; previous; smiling; appropriate; perceptible; casual; parting; scanty; scrawled; commonplace; hasty.

verbs

bill—; court—; draw—; escape—; observe —; peer at—; review—; scrutinize—; —advises; —attracts; —beckons; —discloses; —enlightens; —imparts; —informs; —instructs; —interests; —intimates; —mentions; —points out; —prescribes; —specifies; —warns.

(See mention, announcement, advertisement, label.)

NOTICE (v)

adverbs

curiously; pityingly; dispassionately; pathetically; graphically; emphatically.

(See observe, see, recognize.)

NOTICEABLE

adverbs

glaringly; shamefully; brazenly; decidedly; singularly; curiously; uncommonly; strikingly; surprisingly; painfully; miserably; shockingly; pitiably; blatantly; distressingly; eminently; prominently; inescapably.

NOTIFY (v)

adverbs

portentously; officially; formally; nominally; sympathetically; appropriately; customarily.

(See tell, inform.)

NOTION

verbs

adopt—; cling to—; convey—; disprove—; distort—; embrace—; entertain—; entrench —; explode—; express—; gather —s; inculcate—; inherit—; justify—; retain—; ridicule—; scoff at—; tolerate—; —misleads; —persists.

(See caprice, conception, idea, opinion, view.)

NOTIONAL

adverbs

strangely; eccentrically; quaintly; fantastically; oddly; grotesquely; capriciously; captiously; remarkably; vexatiously; intolerably; unpredictably; undependably; unreliably; erratically; freakishly; egregiously; inordinately; provokingly; painfully; restlessly; nervously; feverishly; fussily; troublesomely; extremely.

NOTIONS

adjectives

moral; preposterous; inadequate; craziest;

pretty; settled; current; disparaging; odious; patriotic; tolerable; vaguest; baby; sudden; dangerous; modern; eerie; fictitious; illusory; elaborate; predestinarian; vergent; contradictory; diametric; opposed; basic; sensual; distinct; nonsensical; amiable; hateful; obscure; silly; chivalrous; inapplicable; fallacious; mistaken; blind; fabulous; confused; cheerful; half-blown; superstitious; rationalistic; idolatrous; glimmering; exaggerated; rudimentary; faint; vehement; pious; preconceived; feeble; pregnant; previous; monstrous; persistent; economical; dreamy; elementary; idealistic; false; excusable; frugal; civilized; ridiculous; cranky; definite; eccentric; strange; fantastic; crude; conceivable; erroneous; imperfect; ghoulish; half-assimilated; strained; conventional; imbecile; dictator; vitiated; childish; unformed.

NOTORIETY

adjectives
newspaper; despised; unpleasant; criminal; unenviable; public; scandalous; romantic; infamous; melancholy.

verbs
achieve—; acquire—; avoid—; burden with —; delight in—; devote to—; exult in—; flaunt—; heap—on; hunt—; labor under—; outshine—; raise to—; seek—; wallow in—; —attracts; —bridles; —decomposes; —enthrones; —glorifies; —overshadows; —palls; —shames.
(See limelight, fame, publicity, renown, reputation.)

NOTORIOUS

adverbs
nationally; generally; locally; unhappily; illustriously; shamefully; brilliantly; eminently; disgracefully; egregiously; splendidly; magnificently; universally; politically; infamously.

NOURISH (v)

adverbs
beneficially; healthfully; maternally; affectionately; sympathetically; substantially; spiritually.
(See nurture, feed, foster.)

NOURISHING

adverbs
incredibly; notably; admittedly; curiously; altogether; wholesomely; pleasantly; invigoratingly; healthfully; highly; uncommonly; exceptionally; extremely; strangely; admirably; notably; noticeably; strikingly; remarkably; substantially.

NOURISHMENT

adjectives
delicious; tasty; concentrated; virtual; sympathetic; necessary; proper; spiritual; healthy; substantial; daily.

verbs
administer—; beg—; decline—; deny—; deprive of—; draw—from; furnish—; gulp down—; impart—; inject—; lack—; offer —; provide—; refuse—; request—; resist—; supply—; volunteer—; —builds up; —comforts; —restores; —satiates.
(See food, nutrition, meal.)

NOVEL

adjectives
powerful; cherished; gifted; historical; pretty; lurid; liberal; daring; surging; trifling; psychological; well-contrived; mysterious; admirable; humorous; meritorious; successful; crude; indecent; imitative; masterly; engrossing; melancholy; improbable; sensational; popular; ambitious; episode; brilliant; ingenious; well-made; subtle; profound; contemporary; fast-moving; dramatic; frank; sympathetic; conventional; distinguished; social; florid; sentimental; slipshod; inflated; proletarian; romantic; biographical; jejune; fine; light; sex-free; sentimental; absorbing; exotic; diverting; comprehensive; vivid; accurate; late; experimental; original; convincing; readable; excellent; magnificent; moving; interesting; pleasant; glowing; enjoyable; grand; fascinating; early; stirring; famous.

verbs
acclaim—; applaud—; clamor for—; climax —; construct—; contemplate—; copyright—; create—; denounce—; devour—; embark on —; engross in—; interpret—; introduce—; peruse—; plan—; portray in—; scribble—; weave into—; —appears; —centers about; —deals with; —depicts; —enthralls; —evolves; —portrays; —reveals; —treats of; —unfolds.
(See fiction, book, manuscript, story, tale.)

NOVELIST

verbs
applaud—; berate—; criticize—; laud—; —

alters; —characterizes; —compares; —composes; —complains of; —copies; —creates; —dedicates; —depicts; —describes; —details; —dictates; —imagines; —indites; —insinuates; —narrates; —pens; —portrays; —rearranges; —relates; —retires; —rewrites; —satirizes; —scribbles; —sets forth; —unfolds.

(See poet, author, journalist, writer, artist.)

NOVELTY

adjectives

solemn; realistic; perfect; myriad (pl); startling; latest; dazzling; ever-changing; puzzling; divine; semi-tropical; constant.

verbs

clamor for—; create—; discard—; exhaust —; indulge in—; invent—; laud—; marvel at—; praise—; quicken with—; seek—; spur on by—; wonder at—; —amuses; —captures; —charms; —dazzles; —delights; —disquiets; —diverts; —entrances; —impresses; —palls.

(See change, innovation, originality, oddity.)

NOVICE

adjectives

anxious; musing; humble; beautiful; bashful.

verbs

advise—; befriend—; discipline—; discourage—; enlighten—; impress—; improve—; instruct—; order—; prime—; train—; —botches; —bungles; —conquers; —drills; —familiarizes; —fumbles; —imitates; —labors; —masters; —practises; —profits; —qualifies.

(See beginner, amateur, apprentice.)

NOXIOUS

adverbs

disastrously; calamitously; terribly; shockingly; appallingly; admittedly; notoriously; irremediably; pestillentially; virulently; inevitably; notably.

NOZZLE

verbs

adjust—; affix—; block—; clog—; dam—; direct—; flow from—; grease—; insert—; introduce—; manipulate—; obstruct—; ooze

from—; regulate—; screw on—; service—; —emits; —projects; —protrudes; —spouts; —spurts.

(See nose, pipe, tube.)

NUCLEUS

adjectives

unyielding; convenient; unrivaled; solid.

NUDE

verbs

admire—; adorn—; dismiss—; divest to—; enfold—in; examine in—; expose—; glance at—; model in—; parade in—; pose in—; sanction—; scorn—; strip to—; study—; survey—; undrape to—; —astonishes; —defames; —disgusts; —horrifies; —revolts; —shocks.

(See body, figure, painting, sculpture, statue, drawing.)

adverbs

chastely; innocently; artistically; embarrassingly; shamelessly; distressingly; pitiably; pathetically; grievously; scandalously; sadly; miserably; utterly; painfully; completely; shockingly; wretchedly; horribly; seductively; alluringly; unconsciously; beautifully; deplorably; entirely.

NUISANCE

adjectives

prodigious; insufferable; unmitigated; civic; intolerable; rejected; everlasting; universal.

verbs

abate—; bear—; beset by —s; eliminate—; endure—; exterminate—; harass with —s; harrow with —s; inflict with —s; inveigh against—; overcome—; rectify—; upbraid —; —chafes; —distresses; —encumbers; —irks; —irritates; —offends; —pains; —plagues; —smarts; —weighs on.

(See annoyance, pest, plague, condition.)

NULL

adverbs

abeyantly; absently; baselessly; fabulously; unreally; unsubstantially; inanely; groundlessly; ethereally; airily; visionarily; actually; ridiculously.

NUMB

adverbs

alarmingly; completely; fortunately; blessedly; mercifully; unaccountably; suddenly; occasionally; apathetically; appallingly; surprisingly; pathetically; pitiably; strangely; curiously; oddly; remarkably; inertly; unconcernedly; callously; portentously; ominously; heartlessly.

NUMBER
verbs
affix — to; allot—; ascertain—; check—; conjecture—; decimate —s; demonstrate with —s; deplete —s; dwarf in—; inscribe with —; limit—; memorize—; recall—; recite —s; repeat—; run over —s; select—; — dwindles; —shrivels; —wanes.
(See figure, quantity, amount.)

NUMBER (v)
adverbs
correspondingly; overwhelmingly; countlessly; adequately; prodigiously; extravagantly; increasingly; definitely; interminably; mystically; proportionally; lavishly.
(See count, figure.)

NUMBERS
adjectives
countless; reasonable; considerable; sufficient; requisite; undiminished; fluctuating; unmitigated; incalculable; overwhelming; adequate; infinite; unequal; quantum; subsequent; superior; indeterminate; prodigious; extravagant; stipulated; certain; gentle; qualified; useless; singular; overpowering; gratifying; depleted; unwieldy; immense; actual; unknown; incredible; increasing; harmonious; laggard; jocund; definite; preponderating; fuller; respectable; rhythmic; untold; lofty; superfluous; goodly; augmented; possible; greatest; previous; uncountable; conceivable; scanty; unending; interminable; unvanquishable; diminutive; mystic; comparative; small; mournful; unavoidable; substantial; unrecorded; fiery; choral; fearful; proportional; lavish (pl).

NUMBNESS
adjectives
mental; fortunate; complete; vibrant; deadly; stealthy.

verbs
affect with—; create—; incur—; massage—; overcome with—; receive—; remedy—; — creeps over; —deadens; —dulls; —enfeebles; —hardens; —hibernates; —impairs; — ossifies; —paralyzes; —stupefies.
(See paralysis.)

NUNS
adjectives
undedicate; uncloistered; self-loving; chanting; holy; sincere.

NUPTIALS
verbs
assemble for—; attend—; bless—; celebrate —; consummate—; defer—; discharge—; gather for—; mar—; officiate at—; perform —; plan—; rehearse—; simplify—; solemnize—; —climax; —impress; —join; —symbolize; —unite.
(See marriage, matrimony, wedding.)

NURSE
adjectives
devoted; sedulous; mercenary; sole; hireling; avid; sapient; foul; exemplary; heroic; smart; bustling.

verbs
employ—; notify—; recruit —s; register—; train—; —administers; —allays; —alleviates; —assuages; —attends; —bathes; — cajoles; —cheers; —comforts; —consoles; —dresses; —eases; —massages; —refreshes; —reports; —salves; —smooths; — soothes.
(See mother, doctor, physician.)

NURSE (v)
adverbs
assiduously; devotedly; sedulously; avidly; heroically; maternally; gratuitously; affectionately; sympathetically.
(See attend, tend.)

NURSERY
adjectives
potent; airy; exquisite; huge; profitable.

NURTURE (v)
adverbs
delicately; exquisitely; tenderly; solicitously; appropriately; intellectually; spiritually; lovingly; selflessly.
(See nourish, foster, feed.)

NUTRIMENT
adjectives
appropriate; slight; elemental; intellectual.

verbs
administer—; advise—; digest—; double--; furnish—; infuse with—; lack—; necessitate—; offer—; order—; refuse—; resist—;

rob of—; savor—; spurn—; —aids; —a-
mends; —appeals; —brightens· improves;
—promotes; —refreshes; —renews.

(See nourishment, nutrition.)

NUTRITION

verbs
deprive of—; draw—from; furnish—; improve—; lack—; limit—; maintain—; necessitate—; obtain—; offer—; pervert—; promote—; provide—; refuse—; regulate—;
retard—; scorn—; spurn—; supply—; —absorbs; —comforts; —utilizes.

(See nourishment, food, nutriment.)

NUTRITIOUS

adverbs
unusually; wonderfully; remarkably; exceptionally; pleasantly; agreeably; singularly;
curiously; scientifically; admittedly; warrantably; delightfully; usefully; extraordinarily; properly; substantially; usefully; valuably; inexpensively; wholesomely; healthfully; conveniently; extremely.

NYMPH

adjectives
slim; skilful; inebriated; ambrosial; attending; woodland; gaudy; jeweled.

verbs
—s array; —awes; —cheers; —charms; —
dances; —delights; —frolics; —gambols; —
gladdens; —graces; —inspires; —meanders;
—rejoices; —roams.

(See fairy, angel, saint.)

820

O

OAK

adjectives

stunted; branched; gnarled; ancestral; enormous; hoary; gouty; rugged; knotted; heaven-delighting; deciduous; mossy; well-worn; monumental; perforated; stern; leafless; doting; twisted; sturdiest; massive; polychromed; stiff.

verbs

beam with—; cleave to—; fell—; moss—; timber with—; —braves; —commands; —crowns; —defies; —droops; —endures; —flourishes; —outlasts; —protects; —reigns; —roofs; —rules; —spreads; —stretches; —towers.

(See tree.)

OAR

adjectives

gliding; cautious; skimming; stalwart; busy; groaning; flashing; ponderous; muffled; paddling; suspended; lingering; laborious; golden; dipping; lazy; languid; rhythmic.

verbs

arm with—; drag—; heave—; manipulate —; paddle with—; ply with—; propel with —; splinter—; steer with—; stroke—; tug on—; —brushes; —cuts; —dips; —furrows; —impels; —splashes; —stirs; —sweeps.

(See paddle.)

OASIS

verbs

come upon—; dwell on—; encounter—; guide to—; refresh at—; seek—; sight—; welcome—; —attracts; —cheers; —delights; —invigorates; —nourishes; —relieves; —renews; —restores; —soothes; —strengthens.

(See fountain, safety, security.)

OATH

adjectives

grating; simultaneous; strange; furious; blood-curdling; infringed; binding; imperial; solemn; dreadful; round; sacred; pretty; horrible; slippery; sailor; continental; protesting; frantic; furious; new-found; consecrating; mouth-filling; royal; fearsome; rude; knightly; deadly; dismal; blistering; raucous; bold-beating; favorite; meaningless; soul-confirming; tremendous; angry;

ingenious; inviolable; bombastic; ancient; solemn; confounding; unfeigned; innocent; brave; deep; little; bellowing; muttered; iron-clad; sacramental.

verbs

administer—; break—; cast—; flay with—; hiss—; launch—at; hurl—; repudiate—; spit out—; subscribe to—; utter—; —breaks from; —consummates; —solemnizes; —s stream from; —symbolizes; —vows; falsify under—.

(See curse, invective, ban, imprecation.)

OBDURATE

adverbs

sternly; stubbornly; incorrigibly; implacably; terribly; harshly; roughly; callously; mulishly; cantankerously; grossly; tenaciously; sullenly; perversely; dreadfully; shockingly; dogmatically; austerely; stiffly; uncompromisingly; tyrannically; puritanically; cruelly; bitterly; unaccountably; unbearably; intolerably.

OBEDIENCE

adjectives

military; implicit; hallowed; mechanical; true; fractional; infallible; divine; prompt; strict; characteristic; punctilious; scrupulous; instinctive; faithful; universal; rigid; unquestioning; weary; filial; instant; compliant; blind; passive; voluntary; plausible; slavish; transitory; hideous; docile; reverential.

verbs

abjure—; approve—; coerce into—; demand —; dispute—; enforce—; enslave by—; exact—; feign—; owe—to; profess—; reduce to—; submit in—; suffer—; train to—; yield —; —binds.

(See submission, obeisance.)

OBEDIENT

adverbs

highly; altogether; unfailingly; meekly; submissively; devotedly; affectionately; absurdly; promptly; always; scarcely; deferentially; respectfully; reverently; piously; ridiculously; readily; compliantly; obsequiously;

unctuously; ostentatiously; diplomatically; obviously; stupidly; doltishly; grudgingly; implicitly; meticulously; surprisingly; painstakingly; strictly; passively; grudgingly.

OBEISANCE

adjectives
graceful; surly; humble; profound; ironical; flattering.

verbs
approve—; bow in—; feign—; owe—; pay —; sacrifice to—.
   (See homage, obedience, reverence, allegiance, devotion.)

OBESE

adverbs
alarmingly; uncomfortably; comically; tragically; unnecessarily; ridiculously; indescribably; clumsily; dangerously; ominously; significantly; grossly; awkwardly; embarrassingly; lumpishly; unhappily; unfortunately; unbelievably; peculiarly; strangely; dropsically; unaccountably; inherently.

OBESITY

verbs
brood over—; dread—; eat into—; fear—; lament—; overcome—; reduce—; remedy—; repress—; resist—; threaten with—; —alarms; —astounds; —dejects; —depresses; —encumbers; —endangers; —hinders; — irks; —restrains; —restricts.
   (See stoutness.)

OBEY (*v*)

adverbs
dully; unquestioningly; hypnotically; reluctantly; mechanically; implicitly; systematically; involuntarily; infallibly; filially; punctiliously; scrupulously; rigidly; passively; voluntarily; slavishly; docilely; reverentially.
   (See comply, heed.)

OBJECT

adjectives
salient; varied (pl); beloved; conspicuous; well-defined; practicable; spiritual; compassionable; irrelevant; tender; unworthy; contrary; opaque; warlike; foreign; venerable; slipping; benevolent; charitable; repressed; commanding; dark; uncouth; pear-shaped; dreadful; immediate; humanitarian; isolated; chimerical; hideous; accidental; ulterior; characteristic; manifest; fruitful;

darling; concealed; staple; primary; animated; imperfect; half-seen; principal; determinate; sensuous; loathsome; nobler; far-distant; beneficent; desired; frequent (pl); inanimate; forlorn; ornamental; definite; closest; supernatural; impersonal; gruesome; express; homely; prominent; unoffending; acceptable; exclusive; specific; interesting; commonplace; innumerable (pl); solitary; innocent; cardinal; celestial; terrific; natural; secondary; enigmatical; unappetizing; sausage-like; engrossing; incompatible; shining; rugged; sensible; objectionable; visible; baser; sufficient; noteworthy; ostensible; memorable; avowed; sublime; absorbing; pure; visual; alluring; baleful; infamous; remarkable; transparent; repulsive; dusky; legitimate; tangible; dispassionate; praiseworthy; respective; incommunicable; worthy; sole; indifferent; outward; distinct; obtrusive; demagogical; personified; requisite; laudable; engaging; supreme; important; honorable; distinguishing; death-dealing; central; vital; striking; shapeless; petty; sparse; impressive; unreasoning; particular; ludicrous; external; conceivable.

verbs
achieve—; acquaint with—; **aim at—**; attain —; consecrate to—; contemplate—; embrace —; endorse—; expose—; frustrate—; glorify—; labor for—; oppose—; perceive—; pursue—; represent—; reveal—; serve—; —hinders; —interposes; —interrupts; —obstructs.
   (See aim, end, view, goal, objective, mission, purpose.)

OBJECT (*v*)

adverbs
strenuously; gruffly; pointedly; perversely; incompatibly; legitimately; passionately; dogmatically; unreasonably; graciously; ludicrously; fruitlessly; snobbishly; ultimately; sturdily; singularly.
   (See oppose, disapprove.)

OBJECTION

adjectives
fatal; forcible; futile; insuperable; overt; plausible; critical; insurmountable; principal; gracious; embarrassing; feeble; strenuous; snobbish; ultimate; trivial; various (pl); rooted; violent; further; sturdy; depressing; ingenious; incompetent; singular.

verbs

anticipate—; brush aside—; cease—; disparage—; entertain—; justify—; meet—; outbalance—; overcome—; provoke—; put forward—; reply to—; surmount—; temper —; voice—; —arises; —enlarges; —impedes; —wilts.

(See challenge, exception, opposition, interference.)

OBJECTIONABLE

adverbs
positively; highly; uncommonly; remarkably; unutterably; altogether; definitely; violently; singularly; particularly; personally; professionally; exceptionally; socially.

OBJECTIVE

adjectives
definite; ostensible; constructive; vicious; avowed; economic; clear; precise.

verbs
acclaim—; achieve—; advance upon—; applaud—; back—; complete—; conceal—; deny—; honor—; menace—; surrender—; threaten—; conquer—.

(See object, purpose, goal, mission.)

OBLIGATION

adjectives
financial; solemn; filial; reciprocal; cruel; divine; irksome; contractual; sacred; eternal; inexpressible; mystic; mutual; superadded; maturing; unlucky; pecuniary; deep; universal; external; tacit; parental; religious; corresponding; solemn; effectual.

verbs
accept—; acknowledge—; balk at—; bind by—s; discharge—; disregard—; evade—s; free from—s; fulfill—; impose—; incur—; perform—; place under—; release from—; repudiate—; satisfy—; shirk—; stud with —s; transfer—.

(See bond, debt, mortgage, payment, loan.)

OBLIGATORY

adverbs
dreadfully; rigorously; inescapably; legally; morally; financially; sadly; stringently; rigidly; unfortunately; sternly; inflexibly; appallingly; strictly.

OBLIGE (v)

adverbs
flatteringly; gushingly; reluctantly; infinitely; financially; mutually; morally.

(See please, accommodate.)

OBLIGING

adverbs
pleasantly; amiably; generously; graciously; infallibly; unfailingly; willingly; immediately; gladly; helpfully; expertly; considerately; politely; courteously; tactfully; cordially; heartily; genially; cheerfully; happily; instantly.

OBLITERATE (v)

adverbs
instantaneously; completely; abruptly; wholly; cruelly; dictatorially.

(See efface, blot, remove.)

OBLIVION

adjectives
dusty; complete; mute; utter; dark; sweet; keen; blank.

verbs
accept—; bask in—; bury in—; cast into—; consign to—; doom to—; drag from—; emerge from—; fade into—; flounder in—; gain—; join in—; merit—; overtake—; seek —; sink into—; speed to—; threaten with—; yield to—.

(See insignificance, failure, obscurity.)

OBLIVIOUS

adverbs
vexatiously; carelessly; indifferently; ungratefully; thanklessly; abstractedly; dreamily; drowsily; selfishly; inconsiderately; egotistically; stupidly; apathetically; completely; unfeelingly; utterly; inexcusably; unpardonably; grossly; heartlessly; blindly; coolly; curiously; rudely.

OBNOXIOUS

adverbs
entirely; highly; uncommonly; extremely; deeply; odiously; reprehensibly; unnecessarily; manifestly; curiously; disastrously; exceptionably; detestably; abominably; deliberately; bitterly; shockingly; appallingly; frightfully; unbearably.

OBOE

verbs
finger—; pitch—; render on—; scale—; solo

on—; sound—; tune—; —beseeches; —
buzzes; —chants; —confounds; —hums; —
mourns; —penetrates; —pleads; —wails;
—whispers.
(See bagpipe.)

OBSCENE

adverbs

frightfully; illegally; unimaginably; filthily; terribly; ribaldly; grossly; coarsely; offensively; disgustingly; hatefully; shamefully; lewdly; suggestively; intolerably; broadly; wantonly; meretriciously; abominably;
particularly; unexpectedly; unwarrantably.

OBSCENITY

verbs

besmirch by—; censure—; decry—; denounce—; deplore—; devour—; disapprove
of—; escape—; foul by—; gorge on—; indulge in—; loathe—; pardon—; repent—;
revel in—; wallow in—; —defiles; —nauseates; —offends; —perishes; —revolts; —
shocks; —stains; —violates.
(See immodesty, sin, perversion, abomination, corruption.)

OBSCURE

adverbs

lamentably; altogether; curiously; inconveniently; darkly; murkily; cloudily; foggily;
mistily; dimly; confusingly; bewilderingly;
unintelligibly; unfortunately; unluckily; unaccountably; unnecessarily; unsatisfactorily;
vaguely; mysteriously; remarkably; vexatiously; disappointingly.

OBSCURE (v)

adverbs

mysteriously; gloomily; puzzlingly; artfully;
purposely; cunningly; hopelessly; patently;
diplomatically; politically.
(See darken, eclipse.)

OBSCURITY

adjectives

patient; habitual; deep; obscene; comparative; elusive; humble; ever-deepening; impenetrable; dark; polite; hopeless; smooth;
dense; unmerited.

verbs

bury in—; doom to—; drag from—; drive
into—; drown in—; exile to—; face—; fade
into—; languish in—; perplex with—;
plunge into—; retire into—; return to—;
sink into—; slip into—; —shields; —veils.
(See darkness, gloom, insignificance, oblivion.)

OBSEQUIOUS

adverbs

blandly; suavely; unctuously; professionally; exceptionally; deferentially; humbly; ingratiatingly; submissively; cringingly; tactfully; curiously; oddly; strangely; unaccountably; slavishly; servilely; abjectly;
significantly; mysteriously; pliantly; inexplicably; pitiably; lamentably; sadly; eagerly; reverentially; ceremoniously; unnecessarily.

OBSERVANCE

adjectives

sacred; rigorous; over-curious; strict; puritanical; ceremonious; mute; ritual; superstitious; cordial; religious; cheerful; meticulous; faithful; devout.

verbs

advise—of; advocate—of; celebrate in—;
comply with—; demand—; direct—; exact
—; extend—; fulfill—; inspire—; join in—;
necessitate—; preclude—; relish—; sponsor
—; —aids; —obligates; —satisfies.
(See celebration, anniversary, fulfillment)

OBSERVANT

adverbs

keenly; aptly; expertly; skilfully; intelligently; acutely; sharply; critically; terribly;
dreadfully; alarmingly; officiously; impertinently; impudently; offensively; vexatiously; carefully; watchfully; cautiously; attentively; remarkably; noticeably; alertly;
prudently; thoughtfully; meticulously; amusingly; unusually; punctiliously.

OBSERVATION

adjectives

necessary; specific; dispassionate; punctilious; silent; unaided; personal; quiet; continued; searching; accurate; direct; common; shrewd; watchful; pertinent; judicious; questioning; satirical; surface; natural; homely; penetrating; insignificant; detached; outward; celestial; phrenological;
objective; tentative; cursory; august; trifling; encouraging; friendly; consistent; curious; delicate; loving; sufficient; extensive;
facetious; astronomical; glib; unlimited;
minute; childish; conflicting (pl); discrim-

inating; detailed; mere; abstract; meridional; restless; wondrous; quiet; sundry (pl); original; loose; vague; keen; assiduous; controlled; humorous; insufficient; subsequent; faulty; practiced; meteorological; disconcerted.

verbs
bias—; bolster—; confirm—; elude—; enlarge—s; escape—; exchange—s; guide—s; offer—; record—s; report—; resume—; shun—; voice—; —authenticates; —confirms; —discloses; —reveals; —shocks; — stuns.

(See view, remark, conversation, opinion.)

OBSERVE (v)
adverbs
alertly; philosophically; astutely; slyly; profoundly; significantly; oracularly; sagaciously; parenthetically; studiously; complacently; autobiographically; wistfully; bluntly; impartially; religiously; skeptically; scrupulously; cordially; composedly; spontaneously; infallibly; sentimentally; primly; systematically; punctiliously; shrewdly; pertinently; judiciously; tentatively; facetiously; meteorologically.

(See notice, see.)

OBSERVER
adjectives
stupefied; hasty; wise; phlegmatic; casual; expert; superficial; extraterrestrial; philosophic; silent; attentive; vigilant; practiced; sympathetic; distinguished; rocking-chair; dispassionate; devoted; unprejudiced; uninitiated; scientific; inattentive; careful; careless; numerous; keen-eyed; sagacious; disinterested; unconscious; constant; slight; ignorant; sharp; experienced; political; deliberate; energetic; sarcastic; inexpert; impartial; hasty; indignant.

verbs
admit—s; allow—s; attract—s; confine—s to; deceive—; delude—; limit—s; mislead —; permit—s; present to—s; surprise—s; — beholds; —comprehends; —concentrates; — concludes; —contemplates; —s crowd; — detects; —meddles; —notes; —relishes; — surveys; —views; —witnesses.

(See witness, individual, public.)

OBSESSION
verbs
actuate—; assail by—; beset by—; fret

over—; molest with—; plague by—; —annoys; —bedevils; —discomposes; —disquiets; —distresses; —disturbs; —grasps; —grates; —haunts; —hovers over; —inhabits; —inspires; —persecutes; —plagues; —ruffles; —seizes; —tortures; —vexes; — weighs.

(See prejudice, delusion, daydream, idea, hallucination, illusion, nightmare.)

OBSTACLE
adjectives
insuperable; unforeseen; hideous; apparent; tremendous; insurmountable; appalling; usual; effectual; recognized; hopeless; formidable; technical; trifling; prodigious; imaginary; unseen; serious; fatal; stubborn; frightful; infrequent (pl); specific; unexpected; artificial; successful; puny; impending; considerable; practical; impassable; solid-looking; stupendous; petty.

verbs
anticipate—; brush aside—; circumvent—; cut through—; encounter—; gauge—; interpose—; level—; meet with—; overcome—; remove—; surmount—; vanquish—; — arises; —hinders; —restrains; —restricts; —thwarts.

(See bar, impediment, hindrance, difficulty, interference, trouble.)

OBSTINACY
adjectives
senile; dogged; brutal; sheer; wrong-headed; inveterate; hellish; lawless; sufficient; desperate; gentle; suicidal; natural; surprising; misdirected; inflexible; unyielding; invincible; somber.

verbs
adhere with—; attack by—; break—; fatigue—; fight with—; harden into—; induce —; maintain—; narrow into—; rebuke—; relent—; repent—; steel with—; stiffen in —; —conquers; —disconcerts; —endures; —inflames; —perseveres; —persists; —petrifies; —resists; —smothers; —sulks.

(See stubbornness, opposition, antagonism, hostility.)

OBSTINATE
adverbs
doggedly; wilfully; inflexibly; stubbornly; astonishingly; disagreeably; dangerously; incorrigibly; surprisingly; naturally; wonderfully; unexpectedly; implacably; stern-

ly; brutally; inveterately; desperately; habitually; obnoxiously; obdurately; viciously; dreadfully.

OBSTREPEROUS
adverbs
unmanageably; ungovernably; uncontrollably vexatiously; intolerably; habitually; always; altogether; annoyingly; shamefully; mischievously; roguishly; teasingly; tormentingly; violently; wildly; boisterously; viciously; desperately; outrageously; stormily; strangely; unaccountably; unwarrantably; unbelievably; indescribably.

OBSTRUCT (v)
adverbs
deliberately; premeditatedly; doggedly; desperately; unyieldingly; pettishly; formidably; stupidly; forcibly; strenuously; economically; viciously.
(See oppose, retard.)

OBSTRUCTION
adjectives
artificial; mere; insurmountable; blank; formidable; cold; frequent; acute.

verbs
accumulate into—; attempt—; clear away —; complain of—; devise—; localize—; mourn—; offer—; pierce—; purge of—; suffer—; treat—; —arrests; —bars; —clogs; —hinders; —interposes; —resists; —restrains; —shuts out; —stems; —thaws; —delays.
(See impediment, bar, barrier, hazard, hindrance.)

OBTAIN (v)
adverbs
legally; effectually; unethically; surreptitiously; rapaciously; honorably; selfishly; uncharitably; legitimately; singularly; disgracefully; unceremoniously.
(See gain, procure.)

OBTAINABLE
adverbs
recently; currently; conveniently; easily; readily; inexpensively; probably; certainly; assuredly; warrantably; possibly; scarcely; hardly; barely; measurably; later.

OBTRUDE (v)
adverbs
inconsiderately; impudently; irrelevantly,

voluntarily; forcefully; vigorously; selfishly; bluntly; formidably.
(See intrude, encroach.)

OBTRUSIVE
adverbs
inconveniently; irritatingly; pestiferously; inquisitively; impertinently; rudely; inexcusably; boorishly; innocently; mischievously; constantly; miserably; vexatiously; unpardonably; bluntly; meddlingly; meddlesomely; grossly; indecorously; unbecomingly; shockingly; surprisingly; oddly; impolitely; pertly; rudely; inconsiderately; ignorantly; discourteously.

OBTUSE
adverbs
pitiably; terribly; unbelievably; unimaginably; incurably; boorishly; rudely; incomprehensibly; inordinately; shockingly; inexpressibly; callously; stupidly; heavily; stolidly; doltishly; dully; unusually; uncommonly.

OBTUSENESS
adjectives
mental; moral; monumental; colossal; apparent.

OCCASION
adjectives
innocent; ceremonial; last-mentioned; rare; various (pl); utmost; ample; dire; approaching; long-expected; abundant; subsequent; memorable; numerous (pl); lugubrious; insignificant; gala; separate; auspicious; festal; appropriate; trivial; extraordinary; momentous; impressive; everyday; obvious; picturesque; solemn; world-famous; little-known; grand; festival; ordinary; virtuous; sacred; proudest; notable; exceptional; peculiar; unprecedented; joyful; speedy; multiple; fateful; celebrated; infrequent; mellow; critical.

verbs
afford—; commemorate—; contrive—; feast on—; hunger for—; observe—; offer—; present—; rise to—; seduce by—; seek—; seize —; snatch—; spurn—; —demands; —merits; —prompts; —slips by; —warrants.
(See hour, opportunity, occurrence.)

adverbs

mysteriously; annoyingly; confusingly; bewilderingly; unmistakably; marvellously; undeniably; indubitably; abstrusely; darkly; impenetrably; incomprehensibly; inscrutably; obscurely; vaguely; unfathomably; perplexingly; puzzlingly; disturbingly; peculiarly; strangely.

OCCUPANT

adjectives

voiceless; sheeted; tossing; imaginary; solitary; primitive; sparse.

verbs

confine—; cradle—; discharge—; eject—; evict—; expel—; intrude on—; oust—; remove—; retain—; —s abandon; —admits; —appropriates; —departs; —establishes; —s gather; —nestles; —s pack; —roosts; —s stream from; —tenants; —withdraws.

(See inhabitant.)

OCCUPATION

adjectives

final; praiseworthy; trivial; illegal; congenial; intellectual; agreeable; youthful; earnest; disastrous; hellish; intense; unquiet; beloved; indispensable; triumphant; enviable; sedentary; remunerative; arduous; hazardous; breadwinning; productive; monotonous; strenuous; absorbing; profitable; dignified; various; useful; restful; savory; untidy; joint; undesirable; favorite; degrading; menial; brutalizing; solitary; prosaic; doubtful; unimportant; nightly; chief; ignoble.

verbs

absorb in—; chain to—; cherish—; choose —; comprehend—; despise—; employ in—; engage in—; escape—; follow—; lack—; postpone—; practise—; profit by—; pursue —; qualify for—; seek—; shun—; train for —; —contents; —enthralls; —interests; — rusts; —wearies.

(See business, calling, course, hobby, employment, work.)

OCCUPY (*v*)

adverbs

extensively; variously; solely; incessantly; densely; assiduously; intermittently; profoundly; temporarily; arduously; triumph-

antly; congenially; intellectually; hazardously; monotonously; strenuously; profitably; menially; prosaically; ignobly.

(See keep, hold, possess.)

OCCUR (*v*)

adverbs

perpetually; sporadically; coincidentally; propitiously; phenomenally; historically; contemporaneously; miraculously; incredibly; circumstantially; preternaturally; distressingly; fortuitously; deplorably; marvelously.

(See happen, befall.)

OCCURRENCE

adjectives

striking; unusual; shadowy; historical; contemporaneous; miraculous; incredible; biennial; similar; inexplicable; menstrual; determined; alleged; trifling; circumstantial; preternatural; untoward; distressing; supernatural; disgraceful; fortuitous; frequent; shocking; deplorable; unnoticed; joyful; marvelous; unforeseen.

verbs

advertise—; anticipate—; compile—s; count —s; edit—; endure—; experience—; impute —to; meet with—; narrate—; note—; record—; report—; —brings to light; —interrupts; —supervenes; —surprises.

(See course, affair, event, episode, adventure, incident.)

OCEAN

adjectives

treacherous; salt-waved; wild; wreckstrewn; gushing; measureless; distant; dancing; purpling; leaden; madfoam; mighty; voluminous; darkling; momentary; moaning; sanguine; neglected; freshening; circumfluous; turbulent; wasteful; blue; winter; hungry; gleaming; tempestuous; shoreless; wine-dark; surging; charmed; lifeless; bursting; unresting; tossing; illimitable; tumultuous; homeless; boundless; unconfined; ethereal; wasteful; unruffled; infinite; close-lying; yearning; cheerless; boiling; chafed; small-sized; bottomless; mimic; glaucous; vast; calm; unfruitful; resistless.

verbs

brave—; cradle in—; girdle—; harness—; launch on—; —booms; —bubbles; —buffets; —flashes; —foams; —grumbles; —hammers at; —heaves; —lashes; —leaps; —lulls; —

moans; —murmurs; —pitches; —plays; —
ravages; —resounds; —rolls; —shoulders;
—sighs; —smiles; —spumes; —surges; —
swells; —tosses; —washes; —whispers.
(See sea, waves, breakers.)

ODD

adverbs
decidedly; inexplicably; grotesquely; fantastically; unfortunately; positively; extraordinarily; uncommonly; disagreeably; offensively; unpleasantly; awkwardly; comically; boorishly; outlandishly; barbarously;
shamefully.

ODDITY

adjectives
individual; numerous (pl); definite.

verbs
appreciate—; deride—; display—; exhibit
—; marvel at—; reveal—; ridicule—; scoff
at—; scorn—; stare at—; tolerate—; value
for—; —amuses; —astounds; —awes; —
bewilders; —decorates; —dumbfounds; —
flabbergasts (colloq.); —startles; —strikes.
(See eccentricity, novelty.)

ODDS

adjectives
overwhelming; rushing; confounding; fearful; moderate; tremendous; worthless; conceivable; formidable; reckless; highest.

verbs
acquire—; approve—; calculate—; demand
—; discourage—; enjoy—; justify—; play
—; reckon—; reduce—; refuse—; request
—; submit to—; —despair; —increase; —
prevail; —protect.
(See disadvantage, advantage.)

ODE

adjectives
imperishable; turgid; lofty; mortal; patriotic; celebrated.

ODIOUS

adverbs
extremely; uncommonly; extraordinarily;
detestably; abominably; atrociously; unusually; flagrantly; egregiously; intolerably;
incredibly; shockingly; disgustingly; particularly; singularly; peculiarly; monstrously.

ODOR

adjectives
sickening; objectionable; universal; savory;
mingled; musty; offensive; reconciling;
mysterious; undefinable; charnel; thick;
mephitic; delicious; exquisite; peculiar; indescribable; characteristic; prison; vague;
influent; delicate; undesirable; dreamy;
sweet-scented; succulent; fragrant; keen-
edged; greasy; sweetish; spicy; strange;
pervading; fugitive; single-flower; dry; arrowy; autumn; champac; rich; vigorous;
nightly; butyric; body; mystical; dewy;
faint; cloying; perspiration; sweaty; sulphurous; suffocating; poisonous; disagreeable; unsanitary; national; underarm;
subtlest; sour; soft; pungent; balsam;
charming; dainty; languishing; heavy;
grateful; soul-dissolving; aromatic; fecund;
breezy; chafed; durable; evil; intoxicating;
ambrosial; insufferable; subtle; noxious;
distinctive; embarrassing; pleasant.

verbs
combat—; detect—; diffuse—; efface—; emit
—; exhale—; impregnate with—; inhale—;
retain—; snuff up—; waft in—; —assails;
—s commingle; —emanates; —floats from;
—greets; —invigorates; —mingles; —pervades; —sickens.
(See aroma, incense, essence, fragrance,
smell, stench.)

OFFEND (*v*)

adverbs
mortally; inevitably; desperately; deeply;
morally; spiritually; socially; personally.
(See wound, affront, hurt.)

OFFENDED

adverbs
mortally; heinously; grievously; continually;
slightly; deeply; irreparably; gravely; definitely; unreasonably; senselessly; bitterly;
sorely; grievously; frightfully; distressingly; mightily; dangerously; hotly; obviously;
openly; ludicrously; extremely; absurdly;
foolishly; unfortunately; throughout.

OFFENDER

adjectives
inveterate; hardened; banished; desperate;
misguided; repeating.

verbs
apprehend—; chastise—; detain—; fine—;
forgive—; pardon—; penalize—; punish—;

828

reform—; resent—; restrict—; reveal—; subject—to; try—; —commits; —displeases; —infringes; —transgresses.

(See loser, criminal, thief, robber.)

OFFENSE

adjectives
criminal; indecent; mortal; dire; flagrant; heinous; aggravated; imputed; trivial; penitentiary; deliberate; actual; supreme; vile; grievous; giddy; voluntary; heavy; continual; superficial; dismissed; similar; odious; impeachable; primitive; slightest; unpardonable; vicious; enormous; grave; excruciating; rank.

verbs
bewail—; commit—; condone—; countenance—; decry—; denounce—; excuse—; fear —; indict for—; lash for—; palliate—; penalize—; punish—; rue—; uncover—; —besmirches; —debases; —defaces; —disgraces; —involves; —libels; —slanders.

(See crime, insult, guilt, misdeed.)

OFFENSIVE

verbs
act on—; assume—; choose—; detail—; dispose to—; launch—; occupy—; plan—; rely on—; take up—; —aggravates; —batters; —drives; —grapples; —harries; —instigates; —invades; —presses; —storms; —strikes.

(See aggression.)

adverbs
distinctly; strikingly; conspicuously; highly; terribly; unexpectedly; boorishly; impertinently; cruelly; bitterly; amazingly; monstrously; daringly; deliberately; purposely; intentionally; unpardonably; inexcusably; execrably; abominably; disagreeably; unnecessarily; unwarrantably; disgracefully; shamefully; aggressively.

OFFER

adjectives
repeated; palliative; munificent; magnificent; friendly; coherent; intelligent; special; introductory; liberal; amazing; low-priced; unusual; dubious; engaging; particular; disinterested; magnanimous; outstanding; singular; remarkable; unique; combination; inexpensive; generous; hospitable; private; testimonial; unprecedented; polite; irresponsible; spectacular; ridiculous; positive;

greatest; free; no-risk; demonstrator; smashing; money-making; quick-starting; astounding; trial; startling; genuine.

verbs
accept—; advance—; avail oneself of—; bombard with—s; consider—; decline—; disdain—; entertain—; hawk about for—s; invite—s; jump at—; present—; press—; propose—; propound—; refuse—; reject—; renew—; resent—; solicit—s; spurn—; tender—; waive—; withhold—; —entices; —satisfies.

(See bid, bribe, gift, opportunity, proposition.)

OFFER (v)

adverbs
generously; exclusively; zealously; gratuitously; voluntarily; tentatively; stolidly; temptingly; facetiously; magnanimously; obtrusively; munificently; liberally; dubiously; disinterestedly; uniquely; unprecedentedly; demonstratively; genuinely.

(See bid, propose.)

OFFERING

adjectives
bounteous; princely; freewill; mortuary; exceptional; votive; propitiatory; imposing; annual; rustic; odious; magnificent; appropriate; polluted; sensational; great; strange; intelligent; purest; definite; acceptable; feeble; faithful; worthy; never-fading; extraordinary; remarkable.

OFFICE
(general)

adjectives
imperial; holy; ill; drafty; administrative; magnificent; paneled; imposing; nobler; elective; unpretentious; kind; breviary; basest; oldest; established; beneficent; executive; menial; subordinate; domestic; melancholy; appointed; choked; modest; distinct; turbaned; charitable; required; lofty; invidious; courteous; truer; permanent; pious; sceptered.

OFFICE
(place of business)

verbs
abandon—; assign to—; clerk in—; collect at—; conduct at—; establish—; glower around—; head—; inquire at—; lodge in—; pour into—; supervise—; transact at—;

transfer—to; usher into—; —buzzes; —dispenses; —drones; —employs; —functions; —hums; —operates.

(See room, building, place.)

OFFICE
(position, duty, etc.)

verbs

abolish—; abuse—; assume—; catapult into —; chain to—; dawdle in—; elevate to—; entitle to—; fill—; hoist into—; hound out of—; induct into—; oust from—; perform —; qualify for—; railroad out of (colloq.) —; resign—; retire from—; slide into—; soar to—; undertake—.

(See capacity, position, job, duty, service.)

OFFICER

adjectives

estimable; rebellious; ranking; administrative; courageous; handsome; gallant; high-minded; energetic; health; faithful; adroit; unscrupulous; sagacious; ragged; efficient; straggling; presiding; preventive; regimental; prefectual; cautious; conservative; consular; arrogant; slothful; executive; subordinate; treacherous; astute; sensitive; embarrassing; resisting; staff; audacious; senior; liberal; peevish; pelting; petty; accomplished; downhearted; hard-working; harassed; mortal; vigilant; competent; superior; liaison; newly-fledged; glaring; unblushing; confidential; native; eminent; forceful; high-spirited; subaltern; disobedient.

verbs

appoint—; consult—; court-martial—; elect —; empower—; refer to—; resist—; —administers; —admonishes; —assembles; —attends; —authorizes; —chastises; —commands; —conducts; —directs; —disbands; —inspects; —records; —serves.

(See constable, deacon, midshipman, detective, commander, general.)

OFFICIAL

adjectives

cruel; incompetent; distinguished; bureaucratic; incorruptible; fearless; intelligent; mere; salaried; corrupt; negligent; faithless; amiable; dignified; foreign; blustering; unappreciative; overdriven; energetic; aesthetic; suspicious; obstinate.

verbs

appoint—; consult—; direct—; elect—; huddle with—s; invest—with; rebuke—; refer to—; serve as—; staff with—s; —administers; —advocates; —s assemble; —attends; —authorizes; —blusters; —chastises; —conducts; —directs; —inspects; —judges; —orders; —presides; —summons.

(See leader, ambassador, legislator, congressman, governor, magistrate, president.)

adverbs

undeniably; admittedly; avowedly; assuredly; obviously; evidently; manifestly; authentically; authoritatively; absolutely; reliably; dependably; solemnly; actually; indubitably; unmistakably; odiously; irresistibly; cruelly; sternly; responsibly; imposingly; shockingly; studiously; weightily.

OFFICIOUS

adverbs

pompously; disagreeably; offensively; foolishly; absurdly; ridiculously; unwarrantably; unnecessarily; proudly; meddlesomely; impertinently; unbecomingly; ceremoniously; ingratiatingly; magisterially; unpleasantly; strangely; egotistically; busily; actively; zealously; smartly; expertly; persistently; ardently; restlessly; alertly.

OFFSPRING

adjectives

precocious; illegitimate; turbulent; new-fledged; frightened; hideous; speckled; spot-.ed; numerous; unfilial; valiant; inferior; diminutive; sole; resulting; fatherless; groveling; motherless.

verbs

bestow—upon; bless with—; enjoy—; idolize—; issue—; mother—; present with—; produce—; promise—; rear—; transmit to —; yearn for—; —blossom; —burden; —comfort; —delight; —gather; —inherit; —torment.

(See fruit, child, heir, brood, generation, descendant.)

OGLE (v)

adverbs

flirtatiously; affectedly; amorously; lasciviously; voluptuously; lustfully; unblushingly; immodestly; brazenly; coyly.

(See look, stare.)

adjectives
volatile; subtle; raw; golden; unbleached; soothing; midnight; rich; rugged; chemic.

verbs
adulterate—; anoint with—; disseminate—; distil—; distribute—; drill for—; drive by —; extract—; feed—; force—; flush—; fuel with—; lubricate with—; market—; power with—; press—from; prospect for—; pump —; refine—; saturate with—; spout—; —accumulates; —drips; —flows; —seeps through; —smooths.
(See lubricant, fuel.)

OILY

adverbs
unpleasantly; dangerously; surprisingly; admirably; satisfactorily; sufficiently; extremely; uncommonly; significantly; wonderfully; unfortunately; treacherously; hazardously; evenly; mildly; pleasantly; soothingly.

OINTMENT

verbs
absorb—; advocate—; apply—; assimilate —; dose with—; dress with—; plaster—on; prepare—; smear—on; —assuages; —cleanses; —corrects; —draws; —eases; —palliates; —relieves; —remedies; —restores; —salves; —soothes.
(See balm, liniment, lotion, salve.)

OLD

adverbs
genuinely; unquestionably; decrepitly; incredibly; truly; apparently; evidently; obviously; deceptively; smartly; graciously; genteelly; absurdly; beautifully; proudly; valuably; unbelievably.

OLD-FASHIONED

adverbs
ridiculously; charmingly; sedately; sweetly; laughably; eccentrically; obstinately; consistently; serenely; placidly; hopelessly; carelessly; indifferently; pricelessly; whimsically; fantastically; grotesquely; shabbily; innocently; deliberately; intentionally; absurdly; barbarously; unpleasantly; embarrassingly; unconcernedly; nonchalantly; unashamedly; pleasantly; unpretentiously.

adjectives
ill; auspicious; prophetic; fearful; unfavorable; parlous; favorable; happy; pleasant; cheery.

OMINOUS

adverbs
unmistakably; significantly; disturbingly; distressingly; sadly; prophetically; alarmingly; unpleasantly; dismally; markedly; noticeably; drearily; fearfully; terribly; heartbreakingly.

OMISSION

adjectives
voluntary; merciful; insidious.

verbs
check—; frown on—; discover—; incur—; lament—; object to—; observe—; overcome —; protest—; rectify—; scoff at—; supply —; —detracts; —irks; —magnifies; —resounds; —scandalizes; —shocks.
(See default, error, mistake.)

OMIT (*v*)

adverbs
premeditatedly; accidentally; tragically; pointedly; voluntarily; mercifully; insidiously; hazardously; rashly; cavalierly.
(See ignore, disregard.)

ONE

adjectives
unsubstantial; eclectic; lisping; heterogeneous; irresistible; delicate; reluctant; silent; memorable; uncivil; awe-inspiring.

ONEROUS

adverbs
unusually; remarkably; uncommonly; formidably; embarrassingly; objectionably; tremendously; grievously; cruelly; unexpectedly; perplexingly; bewilderingly; desperately; irksomely; unaccountably; surprisingly; singularly.

ONLOOKERS

adjectives
uncomprehending; unsophisticated; silent; innocent; conspiring.

ONRUSH

verbs
check—; elude—; instigate—; master—; stem—; —breaks; —deluges; —issues from;

—stampedes; —swamps; —sweeps by; —
tramples.

(See onslaught.)

ONSET

adjectives
spiteful; insidious; thunderous; brilliant;
impetuous; unyielding; intellectual.

ONSLAUGHT

adjectives
ubiquitous; furious; unscrupulous; merciless; ludicrous; savage; direct; hasty;
rapid; murderous.

verbs
anticipate—; check—; curb—; dread—; escape—; fear—; flee from—; fortify against
—; prompt—; stem—; subdue—; succumb
to—; surrender to—; weather—; witness—;
—destroys; —horrifies; —overpowers; —
terrorizes.

(See assault, attack, onrush.)

OPALESCENT

adverbs
brilliantly; wonderfully; unusually; colorfully; marvelously; beautifully; uncommonly; splendidly; magnificently; barbarically;
remarkably; singularly; peculiarly; particularly; oddly; attractively; gorgeously;
wondrously; amazingly.

OPAQUE

adverbs
inconveniently; absolutely; satisfactorily;
necessarily; completely; hazily; muddily;
cloudily; vaporously; mysteriously; strangely; admirably; disappointingly; smokily;
bafflingly; perplexingly; bewilderingly.

OPEN

adverbs
invitingly; mysteriously; conveniently; comfortably; advantageously; yawningly; widely; constantly; continually; evidently; palpably; apparently; indulgently; allowably;
legally; officially; hospitably; unconditionally; currently; generously; broadly; liberally; helpfully.

OPEN (v)

adverbs
rarely; partially; tempestuously; listlessly;
conveniently; drowsily; automatically; hap-

hazardly; incautiously; beneficently; cautiously; unwarily; modestly; invitingly; portentously; prematurely; symmetrically.

(See reveal, unfold.)

OPEN-HANDED

adverbs
lavishly; extravagantly; liberally; indulgently; foolishly; senselessly; considerately;
graciously; benevolently; wastefully; munificently; thoughtfully; freely; hospitably;
incomparably; particularly; generously; indiscriminately; diplomatically; strategically;
kindly; amazingly; affluently; eminently.

OPEN-HEARTED

adverbs
generously; liberally; charitably; magnanimously; always; dependably; reliably; consistently; indulgently; cordially; candidly;
sincerely; frankly; artlessly; unaffectedly;
notably; conspicuously; remarkably; splendidly; magnificently; lavishly.

OPENING

adjectives
portentous; moderate; auspicious; friendly;
arched; chiseled; ambitious; proffered;
numerous (pl); advantageous; premature;
crescent; smaller; high-placed; symmetrical.

verbs
await—; desire—; enter—; intersperse with
—s; miss—; neglect—; observe—; present
—; scuttle through—; seize—; seek—; spurn
—; widen into—; —affords; —discloses; —
narrows; —offers; —promises; —reveals.

(See chasm, gate, door, opportunity,
chance.)

OPERA

verbs
applaud—; aspire to—; attend—; compose
—; conceive—; enjoy—; fancy—; patronize
—; perform—; produce—; subscribe to—;
—allures; —attracts; —captivates; —delights; —diverts; —enamors; —enchants;
—enraptures; —enthralls; —fascinates; —
flourishes; —thrills.

(See melodrama, theatre, play, music,
drama.)

OPERATE (v)

adverbs
onerously; insidiously; mechanically; scientifically; injuriously; skillfully; deftly; effectually; primarily; economically; mystically;

legitimately; viciously; defensively; legally; rhythmically; laboriously; logically; mentally; physiologically; physically; psychologically; disastrously; malignantly; surgically; hygienically.

(See manipulate, manage, handle.)

OPERATION
(general)

adjectives

gradual; primary; difficult; economical; subsequent; celestial; offensive; excessive; gas-wasting; low-gear; efficient; costly; wasteful; expensive; powerful; military; mythic; decisive; ultimate; justifiable; hazardous; expeditious; elaborate; legitimate; vicious; fiscal; industrial; diversified; important; active; gigantic; divine; successful; ceaseless; defensive; relentless; fiery; smooth; business; authentic; undisturbed; unlimited; hygienic; rhythmic; immediate; distinct; vandalic; intermediate; sequential; imperceptible; proposed; tremendous; preliminary; laborious; logical; mental; mining; primitive; brilliant; unprecedented; disastrous; delicate; malignant; surgical; exploratory.

verbs

absorb in—; assimilate in—; coordinate—s; curtail—; demonstrate—; employ—; execute —; expand—; expedite—; facilitate—; frustrate—; mask—; paralyze—; promote —; repeat—; subject to—; suspend—; transact—; —renews.

(See action, activity, process.)

OPERATION
(surgical)

verbs

advocate—; contraindicate—; convalesce from—; entail—; perform—; recover from —; recuperate from—; repeat—; submit to —; undergo—; witness—; —allays; —alleviates; —restores; —revitalizes; —scars.

(See abortion, procedure, surgery.)

OPERATIVE

adverbs

skilfully; profitably; actively; serviceably; wonderfully; successfully; eminently; conspicuously; amazingly; expertly; deftly; smoothly; dexterously; adroitly; cleverly; usefully; advantageously; currently; locally; incessantly; apparently; evidently.

OPERATOR

verbs

hinder—; recommend—; —controls; —despatches; —effects; —engages in; —executes; —handles; —investigates; —manipulates; —observes; —performs; —plies; —undertakes; —wields.

(See agent, engineer.)

OPIATE

verbs

addict to—s; administer—; inject—; —allays; —alleviates; —anaesthetizes; —balms; —eases; —lulls; —narcotizes; —numbs; —paralyzes; —restrains; —soothes; —tranquillizes.

(See narcotic, drug.)

OPINION

adjectives

conflicting; erroneous; well-founded; preconceived; weightier; fallacious; dispassionate; vulgar; triumphant; optimistic; imperfect; admitted; inconsistent; weening; lagging; mistaken; unequivocal; dissenting; unanimous; immediate; liberal; hard; essential; vain; decorous; ill; misguided; diverse (pl); presumed; clashing; effeminate; half-fabulous; intolerant; hideous; confirmed; candid; desponding; contrary; universal; progressive; plausible; singular; golden; hasty; conciliating; humble; discretional; true; temperate; speculative; undisguised; transient; present-day; contradictory; avowed; realistic; political; extravagant; dwarfed; emancipated; conservative; non-evolutionary; valueless; damning; exaggerated; expert; imperious; religious; public; unbiased; high; antagonistic; unsought; prevailing; adverse; atheistical; critical; reprehensible; authoritative; sincere; unasked; well-informed; monstrous; forceful; swollen; individual; inmost; revolutionary; false; editorial; dissenting; confidential; exalted; adulterated; awed; eccentric; contemptuous; mighty; expressed; implied; prevalent; rash; established; light.

verbs

abandon—; adhere to—; air—; alter—; assert—; base—on; bow to—of; cling to—; coincide with—; concur in—; condemn—; confirm—; controvert—; convert from—; convey—; crystallize—; defend—; dispute —; echo—; embody—; enforce—; formulate —; further—; justify—; modify—; muzzle —; offer—; moderate—; modify—; prepare

—; proclaim—; qualify—; reconcile —s; reflect—; rescind—; reserve—; retain—; shade—; shape—; submit—; subscribe to—; utter—; venture—; voice—; —carries weight; —s clash; —s conflict; —crystallizes; —s differ; —s diverge; —fluctuates; —hinges upon; —prevails.

(See idea, belief, inference, judgment.)

OPINIONATED
adverbs
insufferably; conceitedly; selfishly; egotistically; pompously; arrogantly; domineeringly; dogmatically; bigotedly; narrowly; ridiculously; senselessly; absurdly; foolishly; stubbornly; doggedly; doltishly; intolerably; decidedly; unbearably; unreasonably; offensively; blatantly; brazenly; rudely; grossly; crassly.

OPIUM
verbs
drowse under—; smoke—; smuggle—in; steep in—; trade in—; traffic in—; —allays; —assuages; —benumbs; —blunts; —deadens; —dulls; —enslaves; —mitigates; —palliates; —poisons; —stimulates; —stuns; —stupefies; —subdues.

(See opiate, narcotic, drug.)

OPOSSUM
verbs
—adheres to; —anchors to; —claws; —clings; —feigns; —grips; —licks; —mounts; —pouches; —preys on; —rolls; —seizes.

(See animal.)

OPPONENT
adjectives
formidable; political; honorable; strenuous; extreme; partizan; imaginary; worthy: determined; agile; masterful; malignant; foremost; fervent; energetic; prominent; unsympathetic.

verbs
capitulate to—; conquer—; discredit—; elude—; oust—; overwhelm—; rebuff—; —antagonizes; —condemns; —contends; —contests; —defends; —disputes; —maintains; —objects; —proposes; —resists; —struggles; —yields to.

(See foe, enemy, competitor, antagonist, adversary.)

OPPORTUNE
adverbs
delightfully; seasonably; fortunately; luckily; happily; conveniently; surprisingly; unexpectedly; felicitously; amazingly; particularly; providentially; extraordinarily; splendidly; unusually.

OPPORTUNITY
adjectives
plausible; perennial; exhaustible; golden; favorable; meager; extraordinary; superior; rare; magnificent; abundant; scanty; splendid; spacious; speedy; momentary; favorable; precarious; innumerable (pl); awaited; vast; long-coveted; ample; wasted; tempting; social; characteristic; natural; pleasing; crude; infinite; unusual; propitious; selling; notable; trial; sensational; golden; astounding; money-making; amazing; wonderful; big; superlative; masculine; heaven-sent; ill-annexed; limitless; glorious; boundless; final; well-used; early; convenient; adequate; enervating; indulgent; unequalled; decisive; generous; sorrowful; promising; indefinite; admirable; shrewd; unscrupulous; neglected; educational; irresistible; unsurpassed; growing; attractive; favorable; genuine; lifetime; astonishing; unparalleled; matchless; extra-money; new; profit; surprising; enviable; business; exceptional; non-competitive; grand; greatest.

verbs
afford—; anticipate—; avail oneself of—; awake to—; curtail—for; drain of —s; enlarge —s for; extend—; grasp—; heed—; ignore—; impoverish—for; jump at—; offer —; respond to—; seize—; sense—; snatch —; —beckons; —blooms; —fades; —flees; —knocks; —presents itself; —recurs.

(See occasion, opening, chance, possibility.)

OPPOSE (v)
adverbs
conscientiously; violently; stubbornly; diametrically; stoutly; virulently; fiercely; gallantly; obstinately; vigorously; ardently; clamorously; persistently; militantly; zealously; strenuously; cantankerously; radically; determinedly; avowedly; prematurely; fatally; maliciously; seditiously; redoubtably; vainly.

(See resist, combat.)

adverbs

violently; bitterly; subtly; fundamentally; persistently; racially; openly; politically; outspokenly; frankly; candidly; vindictively; fanatically; traditionally; formidably; irreconcilably; relentlessly; utterly; strangely; oddly; ironically; inexplicably; patently; palpably; significantly; basically; alarmingly; unaccountably; unwarrantably; immoderately; unflaggingly; powerfully; unmistakably.

OPPOSITE

adverbs

diametrically; directly; almost; exactly; incompatibly; antagonistically; hostilely; inimically; strangely; mysteriously; contrastingly; oddly; emphatically; curiously.

OPPOSITION

adjectives

cantankerous; uncompromising; radical; persistent; violent; reasonable; serious; determined; slow; powerful; considerable; downright; vigorous; astounding; avowed; rousing; direct; positive; liberal; open; strenuous; peevish; fictitious; bitter; stiffer; virulent; diametric; premature; filibustering; striking; skillful; bloody; fatal; malicious; ticklish; seditious; scholarly; vindictive; parliamentary; frightful; continual; redoubtable; brawling; vain; fierce.

verbs

align with—; antagonize—; anticipate—; batter down—; brook—; browbeat—; confront—; deter—; dispel—; encounter—; incite to—; manifest—; mow down—; mystify—; overcome—; persevere against—; provoke to—; pummel—; raise—; revive—; stimulate—; stir—; vanquish—; —clamors; —melts away; —stiffens.

(See objection, hostility, antagonism, defiance, interference.)

OPPRESS (v)

adverbs

sorely; sternly; vigorously; viciously; ruthlessly; odiously; dictatorially; unremittingly; cruelly; spiritually; rigidly; hideously.

(See persecute, aggrieve.)

OPPRESSION

adjectives

military; ruthless; discomfited; proud; ungrateful; ungracious; needless; odious; iron; long; indefinable; dismal; heavy; unbounded; subordinate; systematic; unremitting; super-inhuman.

verbs

bear—; chain to—; crumble under—; decry —; resist—; sacrifice to—; shake off—; slay by—; struggle with—; tyrannize wtih—; —chafes; —controls; —crushes; —destroys; —frustrates; —hushes; —masters; —ravages; —reigns; —silences.

(See burden, cruelty, tyranny, depression, imposition.)

OPPRESSIVE

adverbs

heavily; unbearably; intolerably; insufferably; dismally; cruelly; barbarously; bitterly; tyrannically; heartbreakingly; gallingly; domineeringly; savagely; brutally; inhumanly; drearily; ruthlessly; needlessly; systematically; incredibly; incomparably; grievously; obnoxiously; shockingly; appallingly; frightfully; odiously; tragically.

OPPRESSOR

verbs

boycott—; chastise—; crumble under—; defy —; denounce—; despise—; fear—; inveigh against—; loathe—; master—; resist—; —chains; —confiscates; —crushes; —despoils; —destroys; —dominates; —enforces; —enslaves; —exterminates; —fetters; —gags; —horrifies; —hushes; —inflicts; —intimidates; —misrules; —oppresses; —outrages; —persecutes; —reigns; —restricts; —rules; —silences; —spies; —suppresses; —terrorizes; —tramples; —tyrannizes; —victimizes.

(See tyrant, dictator.)

OPTIMISM

adjectives

slothful; radiant; placid; sober; incurable; misguided; bourgeois; innate; superb; baseless; unfailing; shallow; feeble; horrible; extravagant; militant; strident; undue; hollow; pretended.

verbs

bolster by—; crown with—; dispel—; feign —; pretend—; voice—; yield to—; —blinds; —cheers; —comforts; —cools; —encourages; —glows; —impresses; —penetrates; —pierces; —prevails; —stimulates; —warms.

(See hope, cheerfulness.)

adverbs

joyously; mysteriously; unaccountably; unreasonably; pleasurably; thrillingly; impatiently; ardently; charmingly; crazily; radiantly; superbly; unduly.

OPTION

verbs

abandon—; acquire—; assign—to; execute —; exercise—; purchase—; reject—; share —; specify in—; utilize—; vote on—; —expires; —guarantees; —insures; —provides; —relinquishes; —reserves; —seduces; —tempts.

(See choice, alternative, preference.)

OPULENCE

adjectives

lazy; undemocratic; approaching; unearned; sinful.

OPULENT

adverbs

amazingly; incredibly; fantastically; fabulously; magnificently; splendidly; monstrously; unbelievably; superbly; unsurpassably; incomparably; marvellously; miraculously; curiously; inexplicably; enviably; admirably; gloriously; contentedly; complacently.

ORACLE

adjectives

godlike; riddling; received; heathen; sublime; prescient; stalking; ambiguous; literary; ancient; mendacious; burning; commanding.

ORACULAR

adverbs

shrewdly; sapiently; wisely; alarmingly; frequently; confidently; dogmatically; blusteringly; solemnly; piously; mystically; seriously; gravely; soberly; reverentially; portentously; suddenly; remarkably; reputably; allegedly; avowedly.

ORATE (v)

adverbs

vaingloriously; verbosely; melodramatically; sonorously; pontifically; seditiously; facetiously; traitorously; thunderously; inspiringly; monotonously; ornately.

(See speak, talk.)

adjectives

powerful; sham; eloquent; passionate; infantile; panegyrical.

verbs

blurt out—; comprehend—; criticize—; deliver—; dispute—; frame—; garnish—with; plan—; pour forth—; recite—; render—; spout—; —declaims; —decries; —exhorts; —expounds; —harangues; —incites; —inflames; —informs; —impassions; —sways.

(See declamation, address, discourse, lecture, speech, sermon.)

ORATOR

adjectives

natural; sand-lot; soapbox; idiosyncratic; stay-at-home; brilliant; political; revolutionary; loud-voiced; distinguished; classical; impassioned; effective; discerning; patriotic; genuine.

verbs

distinguish—; introduce—; —addresses; —arouses; —berates; —bombards; —charms; —declaims; —defends; —delivers; —disquiets; —enchants; —enthralls; —fulminates; —gesticulates; —hurls; —incites; —inflames; —mouths; —pleads; —rants; —raves; —spellbinds; —wields.

(See lawyer, demagogue, attorney, congressman, legislator, minister.)

ORATORICAL

adverbs

splendidly; magnificently; emphatically; eloquently; pompously; bombastically; dramatically; comically; absurdly; vainly; egotistically; ridiculously; unctuously; laughably; needlessly; unreasonably; ludicrously; effectively; impressively; imposingly; brilliantly; ardently; passionately; patriotically; grandiloquently.

ORATORY

verbs

amplify—; burst into—; delight in—; excel in—; judge—; pour—; thunder—; —burns; —enchants; —flows from; —floods; —glitters; —glorifies; —hypnotizes; —impassions; —impresses; —persuades; —streams from; —sways; —thaws; —touches.

(See declamation, orator, talk, speech.)

836

adjectives

huge; brilliant; radiant; glaring; shining; freezing; cold; lifeless; sightless; multitudinous (pl); ruined; piercing; prominent; numerous (pl); intelligent; sickly; serene; mounting; fatal; flaming; parent; unfathomable; wan; planetary; mysterious; small; arch; restless; ruddy; whirling.

ORBIT

adjectives

implicated; moral; common; planetary; definite; independent; lurid; respective; mathematical; elliptic.

ORCHARD

adjectives

abounding; blooming; sappy; starry; fantastic; ravaged; new-planted; wind-swept; dripping; festive; beauteous; aromatic.

verbs

blight—; cultivate—; enclose—; fertilize—; frost—; harvest—; irrigate—; plan—; protect—; prune—; rob—; stock from—; tour —; —blooms; —blossoms; —supplies; —yields.

(See crops, farm, tree, fruit.)

ORCHESTRA

adjectives

errant; magnificent; revamped; mammoth; itinerant; nationally-known; broadcasting; favorite; popular; unrivaled; recording.

verbs

direct—; follow—; guide—; lead—; strike up—; uniform—; —accompanies; —attunes to; —beats time; —blares; —charms; —delights; —enchants; —expresses; —greets; — improvises; —pipes; —performs; —sweeps a chord; —tweedles.

(See band, music, musician.)

ORCHESTRAL

adverbs

splendidly; magnificently; tunefully; harmoniously; delightfully; gorgeously; impressively; sonorously; resoundingly; grandly; superbly; brilliantly; dazzlingly; richly; triumphantly.

ORDEAL

adjectives

painful; dreadful; crucial; tremendous; numbing; perilous; premature; coming; fiery.

verbs

bear—; doom to—; endure—; flinch from —; fortify for—; resign to—; submit to—; suffer—; tolerate—; undergo—; wince at—; —agitates; —chastens; —ensues; —proves; —shatters; —sobers; —tests; —verifies.

(See suffering, pain, torture.)

ORDER
adjectives (*command*)

peremptory; positive; executive; advance; admirable; divers (pl); liberal; rigid; rarest; extortionate; patriarchal; frantic; vast; abstract; existing; suspicious; preliminary; hostile; spiritual; convulsive; promised; imperative; social; secondary; inferior; sweeping; subsequent; additional; imminent; allied; urgent; superior; makeshift; established; showy; actual; thundering; relenting; conflicting; visible; alphabetical; preposterous; determinate; successive (pl); obstructing; provident; retaliatory; metropolitan; explicit; sinister; treasonable; logical; half-conscious; handsome; privileged; elegant; restricted; marching; spacious; chronological; switchback; notorious; noiseless; unfilled; agrarian; positive; retrograde; tessellated; fraternal; strategic; ill-conceived; sealed; beneficent; contrary; preconcerted; opposite; pretty; gallant; supplementary; internal; welcome; probable; injunction; excellent; shocking; meek; florid; melting; previous; intellectual; gracious; malignant; complacent; lucid; auspicious.

verbs

accept—; comply with—; disregard—; establish—; execute—; flash—; issue—; maintain—; modify—; obey—; preserve—; receive—; record—; rescind—; restore—; violate—; whip into—; —bans; —bars; —compels; —decrees; —hampers; —manifests itself; —reigns.

(See command, commandment, injunction, mandate, discipline.)

ORDER
(*organization, system, arrangement*)
adjectives

requisite; subsequent; existing; cloistered; festive; favored; valiant; venerable; celestial; vexatious; congenial; imperative; etern-al; slender; ethereal; chronological; outward; symmetrical; mystic; eerie; rude; admirable; lower; reiterated; petty; social; solemn; beneficial; dubious; private; revised; economic; different; financial; lofty; honorable; privileged; patrician.

verbs
adhere to—; annihilate—; ape—; bury—; challenge—; establish—; fit into—; institute —; perpetuate—; rage against—; undermine —; —passes; —pervades.

(See arrangement, class, system, government.)

ORDER
verbs (*sales*)
book —s; boost (colloq.)—; confirm—; consign—to; fill—; lose—; overwhelm with —s; procure—; realize—; reject—; ship—; solicit—s; swamp with—s; —s filter in; — grosses; —s mount; —nets; —s pour in; —s slacken.

(See purchase, sales.)

ORDER (*v*)
adverbs
peremptorily; explicitly; indiscriminately; treacherously; bluffly; reluctantly; insolently; sternly; quaintly; imperiously; congenially; pettishly; dubiously; economically; malignantly.

(See command, dictate.)

ORDERLY
adverbs
satisfactorily; unusually; wonderfully; remarkably; particularly; always; altogether; admirably; regularly; uniformly; scrupulously; meticulously; habitually; unwontedly; uncommonly.

ORDINANCE
adjectives
oppressive; divine; surrendered; solemn; secession; ill-starred; detested.

verbs
administer—; cite—; codify—; confirm—; enact—; enforce—; formulate—; frame—; promulgate—; remand—; transgress—; violate—; —commands; —decrees; —directs; —enjoins; —imposes; —legalizes; —ordains; —prescribes.

(See edict, decree, law, legislation, mandate.)

adjectives
useful; good-looking; metallic; massy; pavonine; vermilion-colored; rich; precious; manganese; iridescent; rough.

ORGAN
adjectives (*general*)
full-toned; deep-throated; vital; bodily; singular; discordant; lovely; mysterious; visual; sensual; improper; charming; delicate; deep-laboring; digestive; unique; damaged; sentient; rudimentary; reproductive; respiratory: administrative; generative; ardent; delegated; virile; olfactory.

ORGAN
verbs (*of the body*)
affect—; attack—; cleanse—; congest—; derange—; enliven—; impair—; inflame—; invade—; irrigate—; irritate—; nourish—; tone up—; tune—to; vitalize—; —atrophies; —decays; —functions; —recuperates.

(See heart, kidney, etc.)

ORGANISM
adjectives
finished; vital; political; alert; courageous; aggressive; social; diverse (pl); vegetable; precious; terrific; mysterious; living; active; sensuous; enfeebled; specific; composite; elaborate; molded; unicellular.

verbs
constitute—; culture—; examine—; stain—; study—; —attacks; —excretes; —flourishes; —functions; —invades; —poisons; —reproduces.

(See bacteria, embryo, germ.)

ORGANIZATION
adjectives
inadequate; active; magnificent; complete; accurate; hierarchical; ecclesiastical; farflung; rudimentary; resounding; various (pl); producing; worthy; efficient; sweetly-functioning; secret; farsighted; vital; underlying; scientific; unified; matchless; constitutional; laborious; elaborate; competitive; well-drilled; distributing; independent; eleemosynary; internal; quasi-benevolent; quasi-military; odious; gigantic; monolithic; associational; nervous; abstinence; chartered; well-formed; stupendous; marvelous; militant; mammoth.

verbs
disband—; dominate—; effect—; encourage
—; endow—; envision—; evolve—; foster
—; initiate—; penetrate—; perfect—; preside over—; revive—; sponsor—; subsidize
—; suppress—; weaken—; —expands; —
functions; —s merge.
(See club, league, establishment.)

ORGANIZE (v)
adverbs
admirably; politically; seditiously; treacherously; radically; delicately; efficiently; constitutionally; independently; militantly.
(See arrange, form.)

ORGANIZED
adverbs
highly; carefully; secretly; skilfully; recently; elaborately; simply; surreptitiously; admirably; independently; complexly; regularly; methodically; systematically; strategically; cleverly; intelligently; masterfully; fully; efficiently; marvellously; incomparably.

ORGY
adjectives
bloodiest; speculative; disgusting; emotional; verbal; loathed; sex; lustful; pagan;
midnight; disgraceful; nocturnal; drunken;
sinful; degrading.

verbs
carouse in—; feast in—; indulge in—;
plunge into—; recoil from—; revel in—;
submerge in—; wallow in—; welter in—;
—debauches; —gratifies; —intoxicates; —
nauseates; —palls; —revolts; —wearies.
(See merriment, sin, drunkenness.)

ORIGIN
adjectives
volcanic; unpolished; humble; supernatural;
psychogenic; variant; remote; doubtful;
genial; miraculous; accidental; bourgeois;
genetic; overseas; subjective; celestial;
moral; racial; contractual; recent; classical;
obscure; communal; antique; ultimate; legendary; fiery; modern; ignoble; common;
recent; soulless; synthetic; childish; germinal; historical; illegitimate; plebeian; proximate; abnormal; evolutionary; medieval.

verbs
ascribe—to; derive—from; mist—; outline
—; owe—to; question—; reveal—; shroud—

in; trace—; uncover—; —explains; —revolves about.
(See birth, beginning, cause, source.)

ORIGINAL
adjectives
select; authenticated; uncertain; vivid.

verbs
alter—; conceive—; copy—; counterfeit—;
create—; design—; deviate from—; diverge
from—; duplicate—; exhibit—; fabricate—;
imitate—; modify—; outdo—; overshadow
—; parallel—; prize—; reproduce—; treasure—.
(See model, duplicate, copy.)

ORIGINALITY
adjectives
everyday; characteristic; fixed; refreshing;
unconscious; ignorant; reckless; intellectual;
prophetic; notable; illiterate; absolute; con-
tra-distinguished; transcendent; inspired.

verbs
dispense with—; encourage—; exercise—;
foster—; gain—; induce—; inspire—; lack
—; require—; reward—; stifle—; stimulate
—; stress—; urge—; value—; want—; —attracts; —flourishes; —merits.
(See initiative, novelty, ability, talent.)

ORIGINATE (v)
adverbs
artificially; primevally; mysteriously; exclusively; authenticatedly; germinally; volcanically; celestially; legitimately; normally;
mythically.
(See begin, start.)

ORNAMENT
adjectives
foliated; literary; lovely; sweet; insipid;
conspicuous; enviable; heraldic; wealthy;
feather-inlaid; glittering; distinguished; appropriate; elaborate; characteristic; beseem-
ing; wonted; vacant; simple; trifling; sculptured; complicated; meretricious; showy;
fatal; bedecking; gold-embossed; historic;
desirable; delightful; barbaric.

verbs
convert into—; discard—; fashion—; flourish—; strip off —s; —beautifies; —s bedeck;
—bedizens; —decorates; —embellishes; —

emblazons; —enriches; —furbishes; —garnishes; —gilds; —glitters; —spangles; —trims.

(See finery, feather, design, button, bead, braid.)

ORNAMENT (v)
adverbs
grotesquely; gaudily; tastefully; decoratively; profusely; insipidly; conspicuously; appropriately; elaborately; simply; meretriciously; barbarically.

(See decorate, embellish.)

ORNAMENTAL
adverbs
gracefully; pleasantly; delightfully; artistically; unusually; highly; remarkably; tastefully; unbelievably; delicately; structurally; gaudily; floridly; cheaply; richly; scarcely; beautifully; clumsily; daintily; conspicuously; appropriately; barbarically; exotically; impressively; smartly; gorgeously; particularly; noticeably; expensively.

ORNAMENTATION
adjectives
whimsical; graceful; bristling; riotous; hideous; rich; floral.

ORNATE
adverbs
absurdly; unusually; surprisingly; remarkably; highly; uncommonly; peculiarly; curiously; unexpectedly; unwontedly; gaudily; smartly; flashily; richly; gorgeously; splendidly; colorfully; magnificently; brilliantly; architecturally; conspicuously; strangely; attractively; gracefully.

ORPHAN
adjectives
frail; exotic; white-faced; helpless; lonely; homeless.

ORTHODOX
adverbs
regularly; highly; unusually; rigidly; strictly; sternly; severely; uncompromisingly; intolerantly; dogmatically; bigotedly; narrowly; admirably; reverently; consistently; conventionally; conformably; invariably; conspicuously; unyieldingly; soundly; faithfully; truly.

OSCILLATION
adjectives
electric; gorgeous; vibrating; rushing.

OSTENTATION
adjectives
inelegant; mourning; isolated; minor; vain; ironical; brusque.

OSTENTATIOUS
adverbs
deliberately; significantly; purposely; sagaciously; impressively; absurdly; foolishly; egotistically; pompously; blatantly; noisily; arrogantly; dramatically; spectacularly; ridiculously; showily; ludicrously; cheaply; disgustingly; habitually.

OSTRACISM
verbs
deserve—; endure—; live down—; merit—; result in—; —banishes; —castigates; —crushes; —deprecates; —disparages; —excludes; —estranges; —exiles; —outlaws; —reprimands; —secludes; —sequesters; —shuts out.

(See banishment, obscurity.)

OUTBREAK
adjectives
incipient; sporadic; curious; periodical; rebellious; dusky; unexpected; vehement; audible; occasional.

verbs
aggravate—; alleviate—; down—; excite—; foment—; fulminate in—; incite—; instigate—; irritate to—; launch—; mitigate—; provoke—; quell—; quench—; suppress—; —disunites; —embroils; —foams; —fumes; —gushes; —razes; —scorches; —shocks; —thunders; —vents.

(See rebellion, revolution, eruption.)

OUTBURST
adjectives
sudden; restrained; warrantable; wild; spontaneous; mutinous; emotional; overwhelming; eloquent; rash; sacred; passionate; jolly; lyrical; unprecedented; thunderous; tempestuous; national; petulant; swift; sincere; hysterical; thoughtless.

verbs
excite—; plague to—; quell—; quiet—; staunch—; —boils; —discharges; —drains; —distracts; —effervesces; —emanates; —

840

evacuates; —fevers; —flushes; —gushes; —heats; —issues; —oozes; —perturbs; —rages; —storms; —strains; —wears away.
(See explosion, eruption, attack, onslaught.)

OUTCAST

adjectives
nameless; wretched; houseless; miserable; scathed; diseased; destitute; blighted; reprobated; shamefaced; wronged; ragged.

OUTCAST

adverbs
pitiably; reprehensibly; deservedly; viciously; wretchedly; miserably; wrongfully; pathetically; pitifully; shamefully; disgracefully; ingloriously; disreputably; scandalously; unfortunately; forlornly; desolately; obscurely; humiliatingly; cruelly.

OUTCOME

adjectives
eventual; useless; sublime; strangest; felicitous; unlucky; fatal.

verbs
announce—; anticipate—; blight—; contemplate—; declare—; determine—; doom—; effect—; endanger—; foresee—; predestine —; predict—; preordain—; prophesy—; temporize—; threaten—; —disappoints; —hinges on; —staggers; forestall—.
(See issue, consequence, result, effect.)

OUTCRY

adjectives
passionate; hysterical; absurd; violent; indignant; pitiful; diabolical.

verbs
bawl—; bellow—; mingle with—ies; minimize—; muffle—; restrain—; squeal—; still —; suppress—; whoop—; —bewails; —bursts forth; —clamors; —deafens; —deplores; —dies; —fades; —laments; —scandalizes; —wrings at; raise—; stifle—.
(See cry, exclamation, howl, noise)

OUTFIT

adjectives
colorful; spring; luxurious; pert; demure; effective; queer.

verbs
accoutre in—; array in—; attire in—; divest of—; don—; drape—; equip with—; gear

in—; invest in—; prepare—; refurbish—; renew—; rig in—; slip on—; strip off—; trap in—; —enrobes; —envelops; —mantles.
(See coat, overcoat, jacket.)

OUTFLOW

verbs
breast—; check—; contend with—; control —; cope with—; curb—; dam—; filter—; gauge—; oppose—; resist—; restrain—; restrict—; stem—; —drains; —effuses; —endangers; —exudes; —gushes; —spouts; —sweeps away.
(See flow, outpouring.)

OUTGROW (v)

adverbs
manifestly; prolifically; unrestrictedly; prodigiously; abundantly; abnormally.
(See surpass, grow.)

OUTLANDISH

adverbs
extraordinarily; surprisingly; strikingly; ridiculously; boorishly; doltishly; heathenishly; meretriciously; oddly; monstrously; indecorously; particularly; shockingly; uncivilly; absurdly; egregiously; unaccountably; singularly; unpleasantly.

OUTLAW

adjectives
excommunicated; renegade; tattered; dauntless.

OUTLAW (v)

adverbs
legitimately; legally; socially; morally; spiritually; economically; timorously; passionately; traditionally.
(See interdict, renounce.)

OUTLAY

verbs
absorb—; account for—; allow for—; appropriate for—; atone for—; audit—; exhaust—; expend—; fleece of—; garble—; invest—; recoup—; recover—; redeem—; rehabilitate for—; reimburse for—; remit—; restore—; retain—; reward—; subsidize—; —bleeds (colloq.); —drains; —indebts.
(See expenditure, expense, money, payment, profit.)

adjectives

manipulative; convenient; retail; common; satisfactory; obscure; constructive; agreeable; sufficient; emotional; noblest; stupendous.

verbs

bore—; bare—; clog—; crave—; drain—; drill—; effuse from—; emanate from—; exude from—; furnish—; gain—; leak from —; perforate—; plug—; provide—; puncture—; seek—; stem—; strive for—; — gapes; —yawns.

(See hole, chasm, opening.)

OUTLINE

adjectives

vague; sublime; cathedral-like; stubbly; shadowy; rude; circular; precise; fine; picturesque; distinct; rolling; faint; graceful; flowing; delicate; charming; crude; undefined; rugged; misty; harsh; unmistakable; broad; melodic; geographical; analytical; tentative; ghastly; soft; rounded; noble; majestic; irregular; angular; spirited; intellectual; arrowlike; imperfect; depressed; monotonous; lambent.

verbs

analyze—; blot out—; conceive—; diagram —; discern—; draft—; draw—; fashion—; launch into—; organize—; plan—; prepare —; scrutinize—; sketch—; stencil in—; trace —; —abstracts; —abbreviates; —condenses; —contracts; —digests; —guides; —represents; —reviews; —shortens; —skims over; —summarizes.

(See figure, line, map, diagram, sketch.)

OUTLINE (*v*)

adverbs

scholarly; studiously; purposefully; precisely; vaguely; delicately; rudely; crudely; unmistakably; geographically; intellectually; monotonously.

(See sketch, draw.)

OUTLOOK

adjectives

cosmopolitan; confident; savage; philosophic; passionate; desolate; tolerant; humorous; sectional; unwarped; disheartening; superb; model; fundamental.

verbs

alter—; blacken—; broaden—; convert—; darken—; dim—; foster—; modify—; narrow—; overcast—; reverse—; shade—; transform—; widen—; —brightens; — cheers; —disheartens.

(See future, hope.)

OUTPOURING

adjectives

unstudied; passionate; spontaneous; fervent; morbid; unsearchable.

verbs

erupt in—; escape—; evade—; quell—; restrain—; restrict—; stem—; —cools; —diminishes; —eases; —endangers; —immerses; —quenches; —ravages; —relieves; —roars; —swells; —weakens.

(See flow, outflow.)

OUTPUT

adjectives

prolific; excessive; profitable; mechanical; steady.

verbs

amplify—; augment—; decrease—; develop —; diminish—; dwarf—; enlarge—; expand —; govern—; halt—; market—; restrict—; stem—; treble—; utilize—; —climbs; —declines; —depreciates; —dwindles; —ebbs; —overloads; —shrinks; —subsides; — wanes; swell—.

(See production, crops, proceeds, product.)

OUTRAGE

adjectives

intolerant; unparalleled; dreadful; treacherous; uncivil; flagrant; atrocious; hideous; living; frantic; vile; miserable; brutal; cowardly; highhanded; ungentlemanly; rancorous; incredible.

verbs

absolve of—; acquit of—; avenge—; brand as—; commit—; condone—; countenance—; decry—; denounce—; disparage—; fulminate against—; incite—; inflict—; perpetrate —; punish—; —aggrieves; —blights; — debases; —despoils; —fans; —infuriates; — perverts; —stigmatizes.

(See injury, indignity, insult, atrocity.)

OUTRAGE (*v*)

adverbs

grossly; foully; treacherously; flagrantly;

atrociously; hideously; brutally; sexually; rancorously; incredibly.

(See offend, encroach.)

OUTRAGEOUS
adverbs
barbarously; despicably; incredibly; atrociously; intolerably; insufferably; appallingly; shockingly; execrably; dreadfully; unimaginably.

OUTSKIRTS
verbs
avoid—; circumvent—; direct to—; flank—; fortify—; hover on—; stretch to—; swerve to—; —border; —edge; —encompass; —extend; —parallel; —range; —surround.

(See boundary, border, barrier, edge, line.)

OUTSPOKEN
adverbs
unfortunately; unhappily; unwisely; foolishly; unpleasantly; displeasingly; absurdly; injudiciously; impolitically; indiscreetly; recklessly; pertly; impertinently; disrespectfully; rudely; boorishly; uncivilly; ignorantly; carelessly; brusquely; bluntly; disagreeably; roughly.

OUTSTRIP (v)
adverbs
masterfully; physically; mentally; economically; legally; vigorously; swiftly; overwhelmingly.

(See surpass, outgrow.)

OUTWEIGH (v)
adverbs
enormously; tremendously; markedly; indubitably; characteristically; personally.

(See exceed, surpass.)

OUTWIT (v)
adverbs
cunningly; subtly; deftly; slyly; dexterously; treacherously; nimbly.

(See defeat, surpass, cheat.)

OVARY
verbs
dislocate—; displace—; fertilize—; fructify —; impregnate—; inflame—; operate on—; remove—; sterilize—; —atrophies; —dis-

charges; —distends; —enlarges; —functions; —generates; —germinates; —reproduces; —secretes; —shrivels; —swells.

(See organ.)

OVATION
adjectives
perfect; tremendous; significant; thunderous; enthusiastic.

verbs
rejoice in—; render—; shout—; tender—; voice—; —acclaims; —cheers; —clamors; —gratifies; —honors; —rewards; —rings; —thunders.

(See cheering, celebration, triumph.)

OVERBEARING
adverbs
insufferably; pompously; arrogantly; egotistically; selfishly; tyrannically; importantly; domineeringly; intolerably; disagreeably; imperiously; superciliously; shockingly; appallingly; despicably; contemptibly; impertinently; extremely; presumptuously; terribly.

OVERCOAT
adjectives
heavy; worn; woolly.

verbs
array in—; divest of—; don—; fray—; huddle in—; model—; patch—; peel off—; penetrate—; shed—; tailor—; —assures; —fends off; —guarantees; —insulates; —insures against; —protects; —shelters; —wards off.

(See coat, jacket, outfit, clothing.)

OVERCOME (v)
adverbs
physically; militantly; vigorously; passionately; stoutly; defiantly; mentally; legally; energetically.

(See conquer, master.)

OVERFLOW
adjectives
natural; periodic; kind; spontaneous; simple.

OVERFLOW (v)
adverbs
naturally; prodigiously; periodically; seasonally; spontaneously.

(See flood, fill, pervade.)

OVERGROWN

adverbs

hopelessly; sadly; luxuriantly; weedily; irremediably; irrecoverably; shiftlessly; carelessly; neglectfully; terribly; desperately; irreparably; curiously; inexplicably; unfortunately; unrecognizably.

OVERHEAD

verbs

augment—; charge to—; cover—; cut—; lighten—; meet—; —ascends; —descends; —mounts; —staggers; —swamps.

(See expense, sum, amount, profits.)

OVERHEAR (v)

adverbs

inadvertently; innocently; accidentally; coincidentally; unflatteringly; tragically; fatally; thoughtlessly

(See hear.)

OVERLAP (v)

adverbs

richly; amply; largely; statistically; unavoidably; repeatedly; harmoniously.

(See encroach.)

OVERLOADED

adverbs

tremendously; shamefully; terribly; pathetically; pitiably; dangerously; alarmingly; disastrously; ruinously; dreadfully; unwisely; foolishly; absurdly; wretchedly; unfortunately; imprudently; awfully; bitterly; intolerably; unbearably; cruelly.

OVERLOOK (v)

adverbs

obligingly; tacitly; magnanimously; sullenly; naturally; selfishly; unfeelingly; delicately.

(See neglect, disregard, ignore.)

OVERPOWER (v)

adverbs

vigorously; physically; brutally; lustfully; cruelly; dictatorially; bestially.

(See conquer, overcome.)

OVERRATE (v)

adverbs

grossly; carelessly; confidently; egoistically; mistakenly; fatally; intellectually; morbidly.

(See exaggerate.)

OVERRUN (v)

adverbs

destructively; overwhelmingly; prodigiously; atrociously; brutally; victoriously; pugnaciously; seasonally; periodically.

(See invade, trespass.)

OVERSIGHT

adjectives

unparalleled; unwary; imprudent.

OVERSTATEMENT

verbs

avoid—; concoct—; foist—upon; purvey—; resort to—; —amplifies; —beguiles; —cheats; —colors; —decoys; —deludes; —embroiders; —exaggerates; —heightens; —libels; —lures; —magnifies; —meshes; —misleads; —strains; —stretches; —swindles.

(See exaggeration.)

OVERTHROW (v)

adverbs

decisively; victoriously; illegally; brutally; vindictively; petulantly; mutinously; unrestrainedly; tempestuously; seditiously; passionately; diabolically.

(See overpower, defeat.)

OVERTONE

adjectives

attendant; objectionable; pathetic; brisk.

OVERTURE

adjectives

diplomatic; unfeeling; ineffectual; delicate; joint; friendly.

OVUM

verbs

develop—; discharge—; exude—; fertilize—; impregnate—; secrete—; —enlarges; —generates; —germinates; —reproduces; —unites with; —yields.

(See egg, cell.)

OWE (v)

adverbs

fatally; hopelessly; tragically; fatefully; morally; spiritually; stupendously.

(See obligate.)

OWL

adjectives

moping; staring; melodious; vile; great; horned; nocturnal; clamorous; uncouth.

verbs

—attacks; —bodes; —bolts; —circles; —clamors; —claws; —devours; —flutters; —glides off; —grasps; —hisses; —hoots; —mocks; —perches; —pounces on; —protests; —prowls; —reigns; —sails; —sallies forth; —scans; —screams; —screeches; —shrieks; —skims along; —stares; —wails; —whistles; —explores.

(See bird.)

OWN (v)

adverbs

privately; rightfully; legally; legitimately; originally; enthusiastically; gratefully; luxuriously; selfishly.

(See have.)

OWNER

adjectives

rightful; truculent; same; enthusiastic; untutored; original; favored; dishonest; unfortunate; legitimate.

verbs

divulge—; fine—; indemnify—; levy against —; tax—; —assents; —auctions; —bans; —bars; —disputes; —enlarges; —evicts; —leases; —lodges; —mortgages; —occupies; —prohibits; —renovates; —rents.

(See manager, management, employer.)

OWNERSHIP

adjectives

enthusiastic; beneficial; undisputed; municipal; implied; multiple.

adjectives

stately; primitive; well-fed; fattened.

verbs

burden—; employ—; fetter—; harness—; load—; tether—; water—; yoke—; —balks; —carries; —charges; —gores; —halts; —hauls; —pulls; —rages.

(See buffalo, livestock, animal, bull, cow.)

OXEN

adjectives

patient; meek-eyed; broad-foreheaded; long-suffering.

OXYGEN

verbs

absorb—; administer—; combine with—; curtail—; dissolve—; employ—; extract—from; lack—; liberate—; prepare—; require —; supply—; unite with—; —invigorates; —restores; —resuscitates; —saves; —sustains; —sterilizes.

(See gas, chemical, medicine, tonic.)

OYSTERS

verbs

can—; consume—; crush—; cull—; cultivate—; dislodge—; dry—; farm—; fatten —; grade—; harvest—; irritate—; market —; prey upon—; rake for—; replant—; scallop—; scrape for—; shuck—; stew—; transplant—; —anchor to; —bob around; —imbed; —spawn.

P

adjectives

tranquil; unperturbed; swift; stealthy; measured; rapid; restless; incredible; stately; heedless; moderate; breakneck; jaunty; sluggish; hopping; sauntering; furious; precipitate; brisk; dashing; lively; deliberate; even; slow; sentry-like; inoffensive; ragged; eager; divers (pl); tremendous; quick; petty; trembling; evenly-geared; jubilant; killing; portly; quickened; moderate; feverish; terrific.

verbs

allay—; ease—; hold—; maintain—; quicken—; regulate—; set—; slacken—; smooth —; sustain—; —devours; —tires; —wearies.

(See step, gait, speed, stride.)

PACE (v)

adverbs

stormily; excitedly; moodily; meditatively; restlessly; furiously; tranquilly; heedlessly; sluggishly; deliberately; jubilantly; feverishly.

(See walk, amble, step.)

PACIFIC

adverbs

resolutely; calmly; serenely; assiduously; consistently; diplomatically; earnestly; definitely; urgently; quietly; inherently; naturally; insistently; harmoniously; amicably; reassuringly; marvellously

PACIFIST

verbs

defend—; denounce—; oppress—; persecute—; support—; —abstains; —advocates; —arbitrates; —argues; —decries; —hinders; —minimizes; —preserves; —proclaims; —refuses; —resists; —shrinks from.

(See coward.)

PACIFY (v)

adverbs

seductively; profoundly; artfully; domestically; prudently; diplomatically; politically; rationally.

(See calm, appease.)

PACING

adjectives

restless; mechanic; captive; nervous.

PACK

adjectives

damned; crumpled; lathered; baying; clamorous; weighty.

verbs

hunt with—; loose—; muster—; whistle for —; —attacks; —congregates; —defends; — deluges; —disbands; —disburses; —flocks; —gathers; —pursues; —roams; —rushes; —scatters; —storms; —strays; —surges; — throngs; —troops; —unites; —wanders.

(See crowd, flock, herd, hive, horde.)

PACK (v)

adverbs

suffocatingly; densely; scientifically; compactly; tastefully; professionally; deftly; artfully; medically.

(See bundle, wrap.)

PACKAGE

adjectives

convenient; cumbersome; deceptive; enormous; economical; nifty; seductive; bridal; sundry; airtight.

verbs

bear—; bow under—; burden with—; cart —; clutch—; dispatch—; haul—; heap—s on; load with—s; lug—; relieve of—; stoop under—; —weighs; —weights.

(See bundle, parcel.)

PACT

adjectives

futile; defensive; warning; unenforceable; joint; worthless.

verbs

abide by—; acclaim—; bind by—; challenge —; conclude—; confine—to; disregard—; fear—; guard—; implement—; inveigh against—; join—; negotiate—; regard—; scrap—; sustain—; violate—; —allies; — insures; —strengthens; —unites; —weakens.

(See treaty, accord, agreement, bargain, compact, covenant, lease.)

adjectives

shielding; smooth; thick; soothing.

PADDLE

verbs

chastise with—; dip—; drag—; guide with
—; ply—; propel—; strain at—; thwack
with—; whack with—; —brushes; —dabbles; —flays; —ploughs; —slides; —smacks;
—spanks; —steers; —strikes; —sweeps.
  (See oar.)

PADDLE (v)

adverbs

noiselessly; desperately; skillfully; deftly;
indefatigably; arduously; unerringly; intrepidly.
  (See row, propel.)

PADLOCK

adjectives

stout; jingling; burglar-proof; trusty.

PAGANISM

adjectives

aesthetic; poetic; devoted; honest; extreme.

verbs

convert from—; degenerate to—; denounce
—; exterminate—; meddle in—; oppose—;
practise—; relinquish—; revert to—; sink
to—; succumb to—; —blends; —blinds; —
destroys; —fancies; —fetters; —outrages;
—sacrifices; —worships.
  (See atheism, materialism.)

PAGE

adjectives

barren; blistered; storied; long-faded; rattling; historic; fervid; idle; dog-eared;
glorious; written; interesting; voluminous;
intricate; pregnant; sparkling; colorful;
fascinating; provocative; illuminated; labored; naughty; saucy; discolored; classic;
poetic; stone; vivacious; succeeding; remote; various (pl); precise; glowing; loitering; impish; vivid; blank; sleepy; luminous; scornful; pretty; knavish; ingenious;
unopened; title; lying; wondrous; bare-
kneed; boy scout; well-reputed; wormy;
crumbling; long; emblazoned; ample; penciled; large-margined.

verbs

bind—s; charge—with; flick—; flip—; fray
—; peruse—s; ponder—; reel off—s; skim

over—s; sprinkle—s with; stream across—s;
—cumbers; —sparkles; splash across—s.
  (See sheet, paper, book, copy, advertisement, picture, text.)

PAGEANT

adjectives

idle; dismal; unsubstantial; extensive; imposing; woeful; inspiring; melodious; martial; ostentatious; magnificent; doleful;
colorful; insubstantial; crumbling; fond;
warlike; motley; gleamy; proud.

verbs

acclaim—; applaud—; solemnize—; stage
—; view—; witness—; —colors; —commemorates; —delineates; —depicts; —glitters;
—impresses; —portrays; —predicts; —signifies; —symbolizes; —traces; —wends.
  (See celebration, demonstration, parade,
spectacle.)

PAGEANTRY

adjectives

adventurous; colorful; antique; ostentatious.

PAGODAS

adjectives

delicate; gilded; slender.

PAIL

adjectives

clicking; brimming; immense.

PAIN

adjectives

racking; sharp; gnawing; tolerable; sympathetic; straining; sleepless; hard-feat-
ured; rankling; long-stifled; terrible; labor;
passing; dull; keen; lonely; stinging; sacrificial; momentary; unbearable; excruciating; impotent; subtle; passionate; scrupulous; yearning; convulsive; intense; severe; lifelong; wise; palpitating; accusing;
secret; willing; ceaseless; ecstatic; unrepentant; divine; sublime; wriggling; fearful; utmost; molten; mortal; pure, exquisite; poisonous; poignant; aromatic; vile;
violent; pleasurable; hopeless; soothing
extraordinary; infinite; unendurable; bur
ing; rheumatic; helpless; perpetual; quiv
ing; full-blown; unmitigated; mutual; ir
rupting; incestuous; fierce; numbing;
gish; peculiar; gratuitous; distorted;
led (pl); penitential; morbid; li
tingling; throbbing; unlanguaged;
ated; enduring; cancerous; jeal

treme; long-drawn; travail; immediate; sweet; aching; transforming; courteous; accepted; recreant; acute; soul-racking; perceivable; hidden; needless; conquering; retributive; anticipated; bodily; afflicting; frightful; remorseful; tender; despairing; positive; stabbing; uncommon; voluntary; eternal; agonizing; heartfelt; longing; unsuccessful; grammatical; stifled; vague; cruel; melancholy; tortuous; frenzied.

verbs

accompany by—; aggravate—; allay—; alleviate—; assuage—; attend by—; combat —; deaden—; deprave with—; experience —; give rise to—; inflict—; intensify—; mark by—; mitigate—; occasion—; pant from—; relieve—; report—; seize with—; soothe—; stifle—; still—; subdue—; throb with—; writhe in—; —abates; —agonizes; —departs; —distracts; —extends to; — flashes up; —gnaws; —gripes; —hammers; —lancinates; —persists; —racks; —radiates from; —shoots; —stabs; —subsides.

(See headache, ill, ache, agony, injury, torture, pang, irritation.)

PAIN (v)

adverbs

acutely; intolerably; excruciatingly; poignantly; unendurably; gratuitously; stabbingly; cruelly; agonizingly.

(See hurt, torture.)

PAINFUL

adverbs

distressingly; terribly; intolerably; slightly; dreadfully; noticeably; apparently; excruciatingly; pitiably; unexpectedly; rackingly; intensely; acutely; extraordinarily; extremely; inordinately; unavoidably; moderately; bitterly; grievously; uncomfortably; unaccountably; pathetically; tremendously; deucedly.

PAINLESS

verbs

...ly; marvellously; miraculously; ostenavowedly; allegedly; unbelievably; ...y; comfortably; wonderfully; amaz...credibly; veritably; unaccountably; ...ly.

PAINSTAKING

adverbs

carefully; cautiously; meticulously; strikingly; surprisingly; unexpectedly; deftly; expertly; unusually; habitually; inordinately: unnecessarily; patiently; conscientiously; diligently; remarkably; admirably; consistently; unfailingly; courteously.

PAINT

adjective.

plastic; formidable; war; congealed; melodious; filmy; gaudy; lasting.

verbs

blend—; daub—on; scrape—; smear—; — brightens; —covers; —crusts; —emblazons; —enamels; —enriches; —faces; —fades; — gilds; —glosses; —peels; —preserves; — protects; —sheathes; —sheens; —smudges; —tinges; —tints; —veneers; —waterproofs.

(See complexion, hue, shade, color, ink, make-up.)

PAINT (v)

adverbs

gaudily; sensuously; exquisitely; realistically; artistically; consummately; garishly; formidably; atrociously; professionally; eminently; decoratively.

(See sketch, picture.)

PAINTER

adjectives

impressionist; squalid; supreme; ragged; decorative; itinerant; celebrated; eminent; perpetual; methodical; inexhaustible; extreme; distinguished; peripatetic; atheist; embattled; contemporary; continuous; sanguinary; experienced.

verbs

acclaim—; honor—; model for—; —blocks in; —caricaturizes; —chalks out; —dashes off; —delineates; —depicts; —designs; — enamels; —illustrates; —portrays; — scratches out; —shades; —silhouettes; — sketches; —squares out; —symbolizes; — traces.

(See sculptor, poet, artist, writer, painting.)

PAINTING

adjectives

gracious; barbaric; portrait; ornamental; gaudy; noteworthy; contemporary; immortal; elaborate; effective; labial; delicate; graceful; freakish; unpurchasable; priceless.

verbs
acclaim—; applaud—; authenticate—; copy —; dash off—; embellish—; exhibit—; illuminate—; illustrate—; prize—; value—; —depicts; —personifies; —portrays; —represents; —symbolizes.

(See picture, pattern, sketch, photograph, masterpiece, canvas.)

PAIR

adjectives
pensive; incestuous; assorted; canniest; trusting; happy; inseparable; immense; innocent; elegant; gorgeous; excitable; newly-married; epic; spindle; bereaved; newly-hatched; illustrious; imprudent; wedded; paltry; particular; ill-sorted; lively.

PALACE

adjectives
bridal; magnificent; enchanted; primeval; high-roofed; rural; floating; pleasure; gorgeous; spacious; fantastic; crystal; celestial; colonnaded; sumptuous; ducal; proud; shingle; pretentious; medieval; diminutive; golden-bright; imperial; domed; ethereal.

verbs
assemble in—; barricade—; besiege—; fortify—; guard—; inhabit—; lease—; lodge in—; loot—; plunder—; quarter in—; ransack—; renovate—; retreat to—; sojourn at —; tenant—; —dazzles; —looms; —towers; —yields.

(See house, castle, abode, dwelling, home, mansion.)

PALATABLE

adverbs
extremely; unusually; unexpectedly; delightfully; delectably; lusciously; surprisingly; remarkably; altogether; deliciously; daintily; tastily; toothsomely; pleasantly; definitely.

PALATE

adjectives
effeminate; unperverted; vitiated; crude; gratified; spoiled; censorious.

verbs
cleave to—; harden—; jade—; malform—;

reeducate—; refine—; soften—; tempt—; tickle—; —acclaims; —revolts; —savors; —tempts.

(See taste, appetite.)

PALATIAL

adverbs
gorgeously; splendidly; surprisingly; dazzlingly; brilliantly; luxuriously; overwhelmingly; impressively; imposingly; proudly; magnificently; richly; sumptuously; extraordinarily; magically; superbly; pretentiously; unexpectedly.

PALAVER

adjectives
shameless; windy.

PALE

adverbs
ghastly; horribly; inexplicably; ominously; distressingly; alarmingly; significantly; dangerously; suddenly; strangely; curiously; oddly; sadly; disturbingly; naturally; unnaturally; significantly; unaccountably; noticeably; timidly; nervously; fearfully; apprehensively; remarkably; uncommonly.

PALENESS

adjectives
marble; pastry; deadly; natural; livid; pained; unnatural; grisly.

PALETTE

adjectives
crowded; radiant; glowing.

PALFREY

adjectives
superb; good; small; dainty.

PALISADE

adjectives
gothic; nature-hewn; impregnable.

PALL

adjectives
leaden; fearful; lurid; fleecy; universal; velvet; dark; motionless.

verbs
cast—over; —cloaks; —descends; —disgusts; —enshrouds; —mantles; —nauseates; —subdues; —veils.

(See gloom, darkness, dusk, haze, night.)

PALLET

adjectives
curtainless; wretched; hard.

PALLOR

adjectives
lovely; pasty; chalky; bloodless; petal; luminous; deepening; wan; translucent; ashen; shadowy; ivory; dusky; swarthy; ghastly; moon-lighted; deadly; first-communion.

PALM

adjectives
sweating; ennobling; blistered; labor-hardened; calloused; sentry-like; occasional; branded; virginal; delicate; satin; sudden-moistured; sheltering; upreared; sympathetic; grimy; horny; feathery; white-gloved; slanted; scooped; paddling; moon-lit; verdant; solitary; ashen-colored; graceful; itching; lifeless; gorgeous; supplicating; thrilling; gauntleted; extended; meaningful; open.

verbs
clench—; clinch in—; clutch in—; cover—; cross—with; cup—; grasp in—; read—; retain in—; transfer to—; —itches; —unfolds.
(See hand.)

PALMY

adverbs
altogether; wondrously; happily; desirably; marvellously; miraculously; affluently; luckily; prosperously; agreeably; buoyantly; providentially; unexpectedly; strikingly; unbelievably; exhilaratingly; hopefully.

PALPITATION

adjectives
violent; horrible; blissful; skyey.

PALSIED

adverbs
tragically; venerably; hopelessly; miserably; pitiably; obviously; manifestly; irremediably; shakily; wretchedly; crookedly; infirmly; ingloriously; resentfully; helplessly; pathetically; completely.

PAMPHLET

adjectives
successive; controversial; truth-telling; ironical; little; allegorical; belligerent; scurrilous; libellous; seditious; descriptive.

verbs
circulate—; comment on—; criticize—; digest—; disseminate—s; edit—; issue—; peruse—; publish—; scatter—s; spread—s; —advertises; —discusses; —proclaims.
(See book, catalogue, magazine, publication, periodical.)

PAN

adjectives
greased; brimming; heated.

verbs
blacken—; brandish—; churn in—; grease —; liquefy in—; melt in—; rinse—; roast in—; scar—; scour—; scrape—; —seethes; —simmers; —steams; —whistles.
(See dish, kettle, pot, frying-pan.)

PANACEA

verbs
ascribe to—; brand as—; denounce—; deprecate—; disparage—; introduce—; offer —; proffer—; propose—; scoff at—; scorn —; seek—; sneer at—; spring—; suggest—; —corrects; —cures; —heals.
(See plan, remedy.)

PANE

adjectives
dingy; rain-streaked; twinkling; small; sparkling; quaint; clouded; dim-streaming; greenish; half-translucent; unbreakable.

PANEL

adjectives
worm-fence; complete; horizontal; brick-like.

PANG

adjectives
sweet; jealous; brutal; death; irresistible; abiding; bitter; maddening; acute; morbid; unceasing; still-varying; sharp; fierce; personal; short; impossible; throbbing; deep; joyful; vivid; intolerable; faint; vacant; wasting; icy.

verbs
endure—; —convulses; —cramps; —cuts; —deceives; —deludes; —excruciates; —misleads; —pierces; —shoots through; —tortures; —twinges.
(See pain, ache, affliction, agony, anguish, torture.)

adjectives
terror-stricken; evident; commercial; guilty; precocious; long-feared; uncontrollable; intense; motionless; bewildered; sudden; memorable; subterranean; prevailing; widespread; needless.

verbs
fall into—; flinch in—; flutter in—; halt—; hesitate in—; overcome with—; overwhelm by—; provoke—; quiver in—; result in—; shudder in—; sink into—; stampede in—; survive—; throb in—; throw into—; tremble in—; —deepens; —descends upon; —ensues; —hangs over; —overpowers; —seizes; —spreads.
(See alarm, fright, terror, fear, horror, consternation.)

PANICKY

adverbs
extremely; intensely; absurdly; reasonably; naturally; significantly; astonishingly; suddenly; terribly; nervously; timidly; bashfully; shyly; unaccountably; inexplicably; amazingly; strangely; curiously; unreasoningly; unnecessarily; unfortunately; avowedly; ominously; unluckily.

PANIC-STRICKEN

adverbs
unfortunately; nervously; groundlessly; hysterically; needlessly; terribly; helplessly; utterly; suddenly; horribly; disastrously; appallingly; unaccountably.

PANORAMA

adjectives
surprising; miserable; long-anticipated; characteristic; misty; brilliant; magnificent; limitless; beautiful; moving; specious; glamorous; colorful.

verbs
luxuriate in—; mar—; perceive—; revel in —; shade—; survey—; view—; —awes; —bewitches; —blends; —delights; —enchants; —flows; —gratifies; —impresses; —spreads; —unfolds; —unrolls.
(See landscape, view, picture.)

PANT (v)

adverbs
breathlessly; voluptuously; hoarsely; excitedly; eagerly; exhaustedly; prodigiously.
(See gasp, puff.)

PANTHER

verbs
lasso—; trap—; —attacks; —charges; —claws; —dodges; —glides; —hisses; —leaps; —paws; —rolls over; —scratches; —skulks; —slinks; —snarls; —springs; —tears; —yowls.
(See leopard, animal.)

PANTING

adjectives
voluptuous; hoarse; grievous.

PANTOMIME

adjectives
tongueless; ambiguous; careless; indifferent; shadowy; expressive.

verbs
convey in—; dash off—; denote by—; emphasize—; entertain with—; excel at—; exhibit—; represent in—; signify by—; —amuses; —diverts; —dramatizes; —expresses; —mimics; —outrages; —suggests.
(See drama, magic, comedy, opera, actions, melodrama.)

PANTOMIME (v)

adverbs
animatedly; vigorously; expressively; artistically; suggestively; professionally; obscenely.
(See gesture, gesticulate.)

PANTS
(*colloq.*)

adjectives
striped; invisible; distinct; tight-fitting.

verbs
alter—; cuff—; divest of—; don—; drape —; hitch up—; patch—; refurbish—; repair—; tailor—; —bag; —flare; —fray; —shriek; —tatter.
(See trousers, coat, suit.)

PAPER

adjectives
pulpy; fluttering; patient; infamous; sensitized; provincial; evening; coppery; impecunious; scented; note; diplomatic; several (pl); fragile; influential; country; old-fashioned; fancy; state; special; descriptive; dreadful; illustrated; inconvertible; white; conventional; respectable; moist; marginal; fly-specked; critical; captured; astounding; humorous; thick; ministerial; mammoth;

precious; chancery; incriminating; exclusive; crumpled; unauthenticated; suspicious; anti-regicide; lithographic; admirable; melancholy; short-lived; neatly-folded; scribbled; motley; snowy; stained; discolored; metropolitan; rag; nice; charred; sundry (pl); notable; transmitted; unsafe; precarious; lined; obnoxious; printed; velvet; brittle; clean; dusty; depreciated; mold-rotten; bond.

verbs
crumple—; deliver—; fiddle with—; glance at—; glaze—; pelt with—; plunge into—; rustle—; score—; search through—; strew with—; —bristles; —circulates; —editorializes; —flutters.
(See sheet, newspaper, article, book.)

PARABLE
verbs
construct—; couch in—; familiarize with—; inculcate by—; interpret—; narrate—; recite—; sum up—; unfold—; value—; —convinces; —describes; —edifies; —moralizes; —teaches.
(See proverb, adage, story, saying, moral, motto.)

PARACHUTE
verbs
bale out with—; dangle on—; float on—; fold—; foul—; inspect—; knot—; leap with —; pack—; patch—; provide with—; repair —; rig—; tug at—; twist—; —checks; —entwines; —expands; —protects; —resists; — safeguards; —settles; —tangles; —unfolds.

PARADE
adjectives
empty; imposing; dusty; unlicensed; halted; spectacular; bizarre; noisy; drunken.

verbs
climax—; display in—; exhibit in—; flock to—; inspect—; marshal—; muster—; organize—; prink for—; review—; stage—; witness—; —blazes; —files; —glitters; — protests; —surges; —winds.
(See celebration, pageant, demonstration, spectacle.)

PARADE (v)
adverbs
spectacularly; ostentatiously; rebelliously;

aimlessly; imposingly; drunkenly; obstreperously; clamorously; militantly; imposingly.
(See display, show, flaunt.)

PARADISE
adjectives
flower-enameled; painted; pagan; undefiled; terrestrial; youthful; undreamed-of; lively.

verbs
anticipate—; bask in—; breathe—; deny—; deprive of—; drive from—; envision—; glory in—; loll in—; promise—; relish—; surpass—; taste—; transform into—; wallow in—; —enchants; —enraptures; —enthralls; —harbors.
(See heaven, utopia.)

PARADOX
adjectives
cruel; painful; dampening; apparent; permissible; curious; audacious; perpetual; distressing; frivolous; subtle; hideous.

verbs
admit—; afford—; conceive—; confront with —; contemplate—; induce—; involve—; maintain—; propound—; prove—; savor of —; scorn—; skirt—; speculate on—; utter —; —conflicts; —contradicts; —mystifies; —perplexes; —puzzles.
(See statement, lie, truth, contradiction.)

PARADOXICAL
adverbs
strangely; inexplicably; obscurely; ironically; slightly; curiously; particularly; uncommonly; perplexingly; problematically; inscrutably; oddly; preposterously; fantastically; enigmatically; extremely.

PARAGON
adjectives
seeming; earthly; vertical; princely.

PARAGRAPH
adjectives
scandalous; scurrilous; inky; injurious; editorial; priceless; linking; pregnant; pathetic; illuminating; offensive; striking; long; trenchant; involved; complicated; overlong; transitional; brisk.

verbs
aggregate —s; amass —s; arrange in —; confine to—; connect—s; constitute—; couch

in—; divide into —s; indent—; partition into —s; phrase—; quote—; recast—; recount—; stumble upon—; —communicates; —deals with; —embodies; —expresses.

(See sentence, words, thought, statement.)

PARALLEL
adjectives
fitting; astonishing; close; fanciful; fortunate; striking.

verbs
approximate—; attempt—; collate—; contribute—; destroy—; draw—; extend in—; fix —; furnish—; identify—; model—; observe —; render—; tilt—; —balances; —conspires; —copies; —emulates; —reflects.

(See line, comparison.)

PARALLEL (v)
adverbs
precisely; strikingly; coincidentally; astonishingly; fancifully.

(See compare.)

PARALYSIS
adjectives
hysterical; creeping; intellectual; definite; magical; virtual; infantile; numbing.

verbs
affect with—; detect—; feign—; labor under —; languish in—; stun into—; suffer—; — benumbs; —blunts; —creeps upon; —cripples; —deadens; —deprives; —disables; — disqualifies; —halts; —incapacitates; — palls; —sears; —shatters; —silences.

(See disease, lethargy, laziness, stagnation, numbness.)

PARALYZE (v)
adverbs
intellectually; momentarily; permanently; magically; hypnotically.

(See stun, shock.)

PARALYZED
adverbs
completely; partially; unhappily; pitiably; hopelessly; lamentably; curiously; strangely; unaccountably; tragically; helplessly; decrepitly; incurably; irremediably; irrecoverably; pathetically; miserably; wretchedly; apparently; obviously.

PARAPET
adjectives
substantial; rugged; gilded; glistening; silvery; military; gun-studded; ominous; warlike; bloody.

PARAPHRASE
adjectives
harmonic; unique; ingenious; stilted; silly; worthless.

PARAPHRASE (v)
adverbs
skillfully; satirically; ingeniously; uniquely; harmoniously; smoothly; studiously.

(See quote, say.)

PARASITE
adjectives
harmless; business; tiny; formidable; smiling; smooth; detested; destructive; plant; social.

verbs
breed—; detest—; infest with —s; maintain —; nourish—; plague by —s; serve—; tend —; —absorbs; —attaches; —burrows into; —draws; —exacts; —fattens on; --flatters; —frequents; —lodges in; —penetrates; — robs; —sucks; —depends on.

(See cockroach, fly, mosquito, tramp, bugs, leper, leech.)

PARASITIC
adverbs
miserably; submissively; slavishly; helplessly; sycophantically; dependably; subserviently; obsequiously; inexplicably; obscurely; inscrutably; strangely; pitiably; contemptibly; amazingly; singularly; needlessly; pusillanimously; feebly; disgustingly; distressingly; hatefully; odiously; incomprehensibly.

PARASOL
verbs
extend—; hide behind—; poke—; spread—; tilt—; twirl—; —bobs; —caps; —conceals; —defends; —guards; —protects; —screens; —shades; —shields; —shelters; —veils.

(See umbrella, shade, cane.)

PARCEL
adjectives
youthful; bulky; untied; mysterious; clumsy; heavy.

verbs

accumulate —s; agglomerate —s; assort —s; deal out—s; deliver—; dispense—s; distribute—s; dole out—s; fumble—; group—s; heap—s; jumble—s; mislay—; mete out—s; rake up—s; share—s; —s litter; —s scatter; —tumbles.

(See bundle, package.)

PARCHED

adverbs

miserably; hopelessly; pitifully; cruelly; unprofitably; wretchedly; feverishly; bitterly; aridly; hotly; terribly; strangely; dreadfully; uncommonly; dangerously; alarmingly; distressingly; ruinously; disastrously; awfully.

PARCHMENT

adjectives

worthy; yellowed; valuable.

PARDON

adjectives

remorseful; free; present; unconditional; long-sought; welcome; humble.

verbs

accept—; beg—; buy—; crave—; expect—; grant—; implore—; invoke—; purchase—; refuse—; seek—; —absolves; —conciliates; —condones; —heals; —placates; —propitiates; —purges; —ransoms; —repairs; —reprieves; —whitewashes (colloq.).

(See forgiveness, mercy, relief, dispensation.)

PARDON (v)

adverbs

magnanimously; benignly; unconditionally; freely; indulgently; leniently.

(See acquit, forgive, excuse.)

PARDONABLE

adverbs

reasonably; justly; expediently; fairly; altogether; innocently; scarcely; wholly; understandably; somewhat; hardly; obviously; palpably; clearly; undoubtedly; undeniably; definitely.

PARENTAGE

adjectives

illegitimate; worshipful; angelic; obscure; unknown; verified.

PARENTHETICAL

adverbs

significantly; curiously; importantly; carelessly; noticeably; insignificantly; strangely; inexplicably; unaccountably; deliberately; intentionally; cleverly; deftly; informatively; illuminatingly; casually; pointedly; contemptuously; markedly.

PARENTS

adjectives

unnoticed; natural; evolutionary; dissenting; heroic; stubborn; obdurate; conscientious; frantic; imaginary; stern; careworn; reluctant; distressed; doting; honored; forward; narrow-minded; divine; harsh; vaporing; royal; jolly; lovable; perfect; splendid; health-minded; astonished; indignant; unloving; unscrupulous; grasping; ignorant.

verbs

forsake—; honor—; obey—; reassure—; respect—; revere—; revolt against—; —advise; —bless; —comfort; —discipline; —enlighten; —instruct; —judge; —provide; —punish; —restrain; —train; —tutor; —warn.

(See father, mother, husband, wife.)

PARISH

adjectives

humble; quiet; tiny; beautiful.

PARK

adjectives

permanent; pavilion; urban; extensive; spacious; odious; well-kept; dismantled; wooded; adjacent; artificial; moon-lit; umbrageous; city; cool.

verbs

caper in—; carouse in—; dally in—; disport in—; enclose—; frequent—; frisk in—; frolic in—; gambol in—; holiday in—; inhabit —; rake—; romp in—; tend—; weed—; —amuses; —beguiles; —bores; —diverts; —tires; —wearies.

(See country, field, grass, lawn, garden, meadow.)

PARLANCE

adjectives

theatrical; dramatic.

PARLIAMENT

adjectives

insular; empiric.

verbs

attend—; call—; conduct—; consult—; dissolve—; invest in—; petition—; represent in —; request—; summon—; sway—; —advises; —appropriates; —assembles; —convenes; —debates; —discusses; —frames; —imposes; —levies.

(See congress, senate, meeting, board, legislature, commission.)

PARLIAMENTARY

adverbs

highly; strictly; rigidly; regularly; curiously; pointedly; uncommonly; noticeably; rigorously; formally; unquestionably; impressively; overwhelmingly; magnificently; undeviatingly; splendidly; ceremoniously; gorgeously; scrupulously; meticulously; carefully.

PARLOR

adjectives

wainscoted; fire-lit; ample; long; darkened.

verbs

arrange—; chat in—; confer in—; convene in—; converse in—; deck—; entertain in—; frame—; furnish—; invade—; prepare—; receive in—; retire to—; shoo from—; squire into—; stuff—.

(See room, apartment.)

PARODY

adjectives

mocking; excellent; clever; discerning.

verbs

comment on—; decipher—; elucidate—; lend to—; snigger at—; translate—; —amuses; —caricatures; —distorts; —enrages; —exposes; —mimics; —mocks; —perverts; —ridicules; —roasts; —scoffs; —strains; —twits.

(See ridicule, writing, comedy, joke, jest.)

PAROLE

verbs

acquire—; advise—; advocate—; authorize —; dismiss on—; earn—; forfeit—; foster —; frame—; free on—; grant—; liberate on—; petition for—; plead for—; request—; sanction—; seek—; violate—.

(See pledge, promise, vow, agreement.)

PAROXYSM

verbs

cast into—; choke back—; curb—; discharge in—; fear—; kindle—; mitigate—; provoke to—; quiver with —s; restrain—; suffer—; throw into—; vent in—; —bursts; —disturbs; —explodes; —flares; —frightens; —froths; —incapacitates; —recurs; —rushes; —weakens.

(See convulsion, explosion, recklessness, violence.)

PARROT

adjectives

intrepid; spoiled; well-trained; confounded; petted; loud; mocking.

verbs

cage—; capture—; pamper—; pelt—; teach —; train—; —amuses; —attacks; —claws; —copies; —entertains; —imitates; —mimics; —mocks; —pecks; —perches; —senses; —squawks; —strokes; —whistles.

(See bird.)

PARRY (ψ)

adverbs

adroitly; deftly; skillfully; professionally; agilely; lithely; invincibly.

(See avert, evade, prevent.)

PARSLEY

verbs

chop—; cultivate—; deck with—; dot with —; dry—; grind—; sprig with—; sprinkle with—; —adorns; —crowns; —decorates; —dresses; —flavors; —garnishes; —seasons; —tones; —tops.

(See vegetable, herb, plant.)

PARSON

adjectives

bibulous; licentious; sociable; agreeable; careless; half-starved; unlucky; serious; sedate; lovable; diligent.

PARSONAGE

adjectives

country; unconventional; pure; generous; commodious; comfortable.

PART

adjectives

tragic; constituent; pompous; closely-fitted; moving; disconsolate; balancing; affected; integral; drossy; prime; splendid; significant; remote; authoritative; confused; convivial; eastern; pendulous; dissimilar; initial; sensitive; intimate; symbolical; animate; imaginative; tender; essential; distinguished; energetic; conspicuous; swaggering; moneyed; plump; outer; considerable; leading; prominent; decisive; manful; susceptible; formative; timely; striking; negative; tropical; immense; stubborn; uncourteous; oratorical; sequestered; active; subordinate; barbarous; relevant; invaluable; coloristic; abiding; incalculable; prudent; injurious; airy; speculative; theoretical; arid; generous; working; corresponding; aspiring; appropriate; reflex; innermost; understandable; related; declining; conventional; substantial; cumbrous; active; respectable; uttermost; metaphysical; slavish; various (pl); prefatory; effective; creditable; corresponding; over-stately; brilliant; evanescent; hindmost; worshipful; legitimate; retrenched; low; discreet; comedy; wondrous; fundamental; subsequent; external; virtuous; inherent; precipitous; inseparable; singular; choice; dominating; arduous; painful; brute; honorable; amiable; generous; sovereign; obnoxious; worthy; component; outward; membranous; mirthful; serious; vulgar; contiguous; incombustible; unsettled; vulnerable; pleasant; unprofitable; important; pathetic; virtuous; analogous; impertinent; midland; outlying; dissipated; vital; structural; treacherous; adjacent; retired; uninteresting; personal; formal; shady; loud-sounding; individual; restricted; inglorious; ghostly; romantic; impressive; desolate; sudden; prodigious; disjointed; inaccessible; disheartening; intrepid; lamentable.

verbs
accept—; acclaim—; balk at—; convey—; enact—; exaggerate—; live—; master—; perform—; render—; reproduce—; scorn—; sink into—; slip into—; treat—; wangle—; —affords; —allows.
(See lines, detail, character, scene.)

PART (v)
adverbs
despairingly; amicably; haughtily; meekly; convivially; pathetically; formally; romantically; lamentably.
(See divide, separate.)

PARTAKE (v)
adverbs
enthusiastically; joyously; convivially; cheerfully; gratefully; hungrily; ceremoniously; festively; fraternally.
(See share, participate.)

PARTIAL
adverbs
disgracefully; shamefully; illegally; unconstitutionally; openly; palpably; unfortunately; cruelly; bitterly; inexplicably; unjustifiably; unaccountably; miserably; wretchedly; prejudicially; unfairly; unjustly; obviously; openly; defiantly; perversely; curiously; strangely; amazingly.

PARTIALITY
adjectives
parental; sectarian; excessive; overweening; laudable; patent; noticeable.

verbs
avoid—; criticize—; entertain—; gain—; investigate—; lavish—; repel—; report—; shrink from—; —alienates; —distorts; —dotes; —forejudges; —incenses; —irritates; —provokes; —riles (colloq.); —shocks; —warps; —woos.
(See conviction, bias, prejudice.)

PARTICIPANTS
adjectives
interesting; prime; actual; leading.

verbs
cheer—; desire—; goad—; identify—; limit —; reckon as—; register—; seek—; test—; —assemble; —contest; —demonstrate; —enter; —labor; —share; —train; —vie for.
(See contestant, athlete.)

PARTICIPATE (v)
adverbs
willingly; jovially; energetically; heartily; enthusiastically; prominently; futilely; vigorously.
(See share, partake.)

PARTICIPATION
adjectives
undivided; active; human; futile; amateur.

verbs
anticipate—; incapacitate for—; join in—; prepare for—; revel in—; share in—; train for—; vie for—in; welcome—.
(See indulgence, enjoyment, association.)

PARTICLES
adjectives
granulated; seething; invisible; divine; irritating; scattering; constituent; colliding;

shining; impalpable; ultimate; invading; material; distinguishing; great; fruitful; harmful; discoloring; ignoble; gelatine.

PARTICULAR
adverbs
painfully; terribly; absurdly; meticulously; ridiculously; gruffly; scrupulously; conscientiously; extremely; considerately; dependably; reliably; vigilantly; unimpeachably; rigorously; scientifically; curiously; punctiliously; fastidiously; exactingly; inordinately; vexatiously; assiduously; unpleasantly; disagreeably; dreadfully; curiously; unnecessarily; distressingly; nervously; fussily; obnoxiously.

PARTICULARITY
adjectives
circumstantial; undue; over-luxurious.

PARTICULARS
adjectives
unexperienced; remarkable; multiplex; obvious; unnoticed.

verbs
adhere to—; afford—; contemplate—; disregard—; embody—; ignore—; inspect—; omit —; overlook—; mark—; record—; revise—; scan—; slight—; skim—; skip over—; slur —; —absorb; —explain.
(See details, information, facts.)

PARTING
adjectives
gracious; various (pl); undemonstrative; dreadful; present; frivolous; solemn; sweet; sorrowful.

PARTISAN
adjectives
zealous; extreme; undue; conscientious; conspicuous; immovable; long-dreaded; hated; factious.

adverbs
absurdly; rigidly; bigotedly; narrow-mindedly; dogmatically; oddly; strenuously; industriously; actively; thoughtlessly; witlessly; senselessly; unwaveringly; strongly; steadily; stubbornly; obstinately; zealously; confidently; inflexibly; mulishly; resolutely; incomparably.

PARTISANSHIP
adjectives
virulent; verified; insincere; fervid; honest; preposterous.

PARTITION
adjectives
saucer-shaped; unwarranted.

PARTNER
adjectives
semirecumbent; full; dignified; equal; junior; thick-skinned; rock-ribbed; dreadless; erudite; criminal; desperate.

verbs
admit—; couple with—; desire—; forsake —; heed—; require—; silence—; trust—; —agrees; —consults; —contemplates; —debates; —dissolves; —divides; —haggles; —joins in; —profits; —severs; —shares; —squabbles; —s unite.
(See ally, associate, brother, colleague, companion.)

PARTNERSHIP
adjectives
everlasting; effective; lifelong; endless.

verbs
annul—; cement—; combine in—; compose —; dissolve—; inaugurate—; pry apart—; seek—; sever—; undo—; —concurs; —conduces to; —confederates; —cooperates; —conspires; —requires; —seconds; —unites; —withstands.
(See friendship, alliance, company, corporation, society, firm.)

PARTRIDGE
verbs
domesticate—; flush—; startle—; —airs; —amuses; —beats; —bellows; —bills; —captivates; —challenges; —darts; —explores; —feigns; —s flush; —flutters; —glides; —jerks; —nods; —ranges; —roves; —rumbles; —scratches; —squeals; —steals.
(See grouse, bird, bob-white.)

PARTY
(general)
adjectives
assorted; hostile; revolutionary; serenading; tomahawk; staged; raiding; scalping; jovial; retiring; ill-starred; surprise; house; united; scattered; corrupt; fanatical; sectional; wild; antagonistic; dominant; quilting; lively; merry; traveling; singular;

857

constituted; detached; visionary; invisible; unbiased; exclusive; pleasure; desperate; contracting; foraging; conversation; lawless; luckless; straggling; skulking; disaffected; obtruding; reconnoitering; augmenting; rustic; storming; contending; shipwrecked; skirmishing; covering; excursion; dominant; fatigue; contending; misguided; marching; victorious; select; harmonious; ecclesiastical; scouting; reactionary; inimitable; litigating; all-day; paralyzing; imperial; informal; assaulting; fashionable; defenseless; radiant; bounding; invincible; discontented; amused; aggrieved; torchlight; zealous; ridiculous; joyous; especial; tramping.

PARTY
verbs (*political*)
appraise—; bolt—; cleave to—; consolidate —; dominate—; override—; purge—; rejuvenate—; scatter—; serve—; split—; supplant—; support—; wreck—; —advocates; —cleans house; —collapses; —declines; —flounders.

(See group, gang, following, faction.)

PARTY
verbs (*social*)
attend—; augment—; enliven—; fancy—; flock to—; invite to—; regale—; —amuses; —beguiles; —bores; —cheers; —disgusts; —diverts; —entertains; —palls; —solaces; —wearies.

(See meeting, theatre, ball, entertainment.)

PASS
adjectives
dolorous; desolate; silly; inaccessible; mountain; ragged; permissive; stupendous; perpendicular; gleaming.

PASS (*v*)
adverbs
translucently; invariably; harmoniously; deliberately; meekly; obliquely; placatingly; economically; wistfully; triumphantly; consciously; tediously; successively; victoriously; irresolutely; sedately; serenely; jauntily; leisurely; dolorously.

(See move, advance.)

PASSAGE
adjectives (*general*)
easy; pathetic; painful; palatial; sparred; tortuous; favorable; rickety; half-remembered; dimly-lighted; hazardous; objection-

able; latticed; random; secret; perilous; octave; well-concealed; impassable; wading; sloping; striking; arched; dark; particular; prosperous; speedy; matted; neglected; furious; poetical; disputed; exquisite; descriptive; remarkable; sensational; slippery; precarious; vaulted; circuitous; unedifying; abrupt; narrow-paneled; tedious; practicable; romantic; vivid; characteristic; sumptuous; ill-quoted; brilliant; gloomy; subterranean; stormy; despised; hackneyed; purple; redundant; rhetorical; brief; narrow; thorough; roomy; stirring; significant; secret; political; swift; honey; winding; awful; laudatory; adulatory; untrammeled; disjointed; perihelion; certain; frequent; glowing; oratorical; walled-up; impossible; scorching; alternate; lyric; musical; amorphous; melodious; rumbling; dramatic; instantaneous; treacherous; imaginative; arduous; elevated; lofty; impressive; sublime.

PASSAGE
(*literary*)
verbs
acclaim—; applaud—; analyze—; blend —s; cite—; delete—; erase—; interpret—; paraphrase—; quote—; —castigates; —expunges; —glows; —reveals; —stings.

(See paragraph, thought, sentence, portion, section, quotation, selection.)

PASSAGE
verbs (*way, avenue*)
accomplish—; bar—; block—; clog—; constrict—; emerge from—; fence in—; gain—; guard—; impede—; jeopardize—; offer—; protect—; quicken—; restrict—; safeguard —.

(See way, access, approach, lobby, exit, corridor, hall.)

PASSENGERS
adjectives
hurrying; unhappy; protesting; hooded; unsuspecting; stealthy; horror-struck; bustling; belated; frivolous; churlish; distinguished; fastidious; half-rate.

verbs
accommodate—; amuse—; assign—to; assure—; bore—; comfort—; enchant—; entertain—; enthrall—; escort—; excite—; guide—; reassure—; reveal to—; tire—; transport—; —fret; —fume; —idle; —tour; —thread; —weary.

(See marcher, audience, gathering.)

adjectives

absorbing; acrimonious; afflicting; aimless; angry; ardent; autobiographical; awakened; black; blazing; bestial; base; bad; bitter; bittersweet; blended; boisterous; bottomless; boyish; brutal; burning; bursting; busy; capital; certain; chivalrous; choleric; coarse; comfortable; concentrated; conflicting; contending; contrary; corrosive; damnable; dark; deadly; deathly; deceased; deep; deforming; degrading; delicious; deluding; democratic; departed; determinate; devastating; diabolical; dimmed; distempered; disturbing; divine; earthly; electric; elemental; enduring; energetic; engendered; engrossing; enthusiastic; envied; errant; erratic; eternal; everlasting; evil; exacerbated; exceeding; exciting; exquisite; extraordinary; exultant; fantastical; favorite; fervent; fierce; fitful; flaming; foaming; foul; frantic; frivolous; frozen; frustrated; fugitive; fundamental; futile; gambling; generous; gnawing; gross; guilty; half-accomplished; headlong; hidden; heavenly; high; hurtful; hopeless; human; humble; honest; idealistic; idealized; idiotic; ignoble; illicit; imprudent; inborn; incestuous; indignant; infernal; inflammable; insatiable; instinctive; intellectual; intense; intermediate; invisible; involuntary; ireful; irregular; irrepressible; irresistible; jealous; kindred; lasting; lawless; licentious; loving; lurid; lustful; master; masterful; merry; mischievous; morbid; mortal; mutinous; mutual; newfound; noble; obtuse; original; outrageous; overmastering; overt; overwhelming; palemouthed; pallid; partisan; patriotic; pent-up; personate; petty; philanthropic; pitying; preceding; present; prevailing; primal; primitive; private; prosperous; pseudo; radical; raging; rare; rash; religious; repressed; requisite; romantic; rude; ruling; selfish; secondary; silent; sophisticated; sordid; sore; sorry; southern; spectral; speechless; stifled; stirred; stormy; strange; subdued; strong; struggling; sudden; superior; suppressed; swelling; swift; tender; tempestuous; towering; thoughtful; thronging (pl); thwarted; torrid; tragic; tranquil; transient; transitory; triumphant; troubling; true; turbid; tyrannous; unaccustomed; unbridled; unchecked; undying; ungovernable; unhallowed; universal; unnoted; unprofitable; unregulated; unrequited; unsoothed; unsuspected; untainted; untamed; untrained; untried; unwise; unwomanly; unworthy; variable; vehement; vengeful; veritable; vindictive; violent; virile; wanton; warning; wayward; wild; worried; worst; youthful; zealous; exaggerated.

verbs

animate with—; arouse—; boil with—; bridle—; cherish—; declare—; distort with—; enchain by—; evoke—; extinguish—; fly into—; gratify—; impel by—; intensify—; nourish—; pledge to—; quicken with—; reciprocate—; redden with—; respond to—; restrain—; revive—; share—; unleash—; vanquish—; vent—; —consumes; —cools; —inflames; —rules; —seethes; —simmers; —tortures.

(See impetuosity, craving, appetite, ire, enthusiasm, emotion, infatuation, love, indignation.)

PASSIONATE

adverbs

amorously; angrily; cholerically; lovingly; uncontrollably; ungovernably; inordinately; uncommonly; innately; inherently; naturally; notoriously; warmly; ardently; enthusiastically; zealously; earnestly; violently; excitably; captiously; querulously; moodily; mercurially; violently; furiously; impulsively; irrepressibly; strangely.

PASSIVE

adverbs

strangely; apathetically; curiously; disgustingly; provokingly; incomprehensibly; dully; inertly; sluggishly; bluntly; inertly; doltishly; lazily; vexatiously; indolently; obediently; subserviently; hopelessly; servilely; submissively; pliantly; imperturbably; stoically; placidly; meekly; stupidly; stolidly; carelessly.

PASSIVITY

adjectives

despondent; disposed; dejected; dreamy; lazy; inert; stolid; unwavering; slumbrous; dull; dead.

PAST

adjectives

romantic; sorrowful; vanished; voiceless; foolish; monstrous; accumulated; remote; wintry; complacent; immemorial; stormy; immeasurable; gracious; artificial; dim; scarred; remorseless; dark; sinful; mischievous; precious; turbulent; receding; spectral; mysterious; irrevocable; blighted;

ducal; unfathomed; inexorable; changeless; bitter; rough; emotional; ungentle; ambiguous; unrelenting; long-distant; disputable; restored; embalmed; irreproachable; hideous; well-filled; boundless; unrelenting; unhallowed; glorious; ungracious; pathetic; picturesque; melancholy.

verbs
clarify—; decipher—; dip into—; discern—; enrich—; evoke—; grope in—; penetrate—; plumb—; recapture—; recreate—; reflect on —; regret—; relive—; resurrect—; shake off —; —fades; —haunts; —survives; —vanishes.
(See memories, future, life.)

PASTE

adjectives
milk-white; slippery-looking; lackluster; sticky; gelatinous.

PASTEL

adjectives
luscious; summer; gleaming; white.

PASTIME

adjectives
favorite; youthful; kindred; risky; innumerable (pl); gentlemanlike; delightful; brawling; gracious; light; refreshing; uncanonical.

verbs
absorb in—; advocate—; enjoy—; indulge in—; lack—; seek—; —amuses; —cheers; —diverts; —eases; —enlivens; —entertains; —recreates; —solaces; —soothes.
(See game, amusement, diversion.)

PASTOR

adjectives
ungracious; scholarly; zealously; flabby.

verbs
appoint—; ordain—; serve as—; submit to —; venerate—; —administers; —attends to; —consoles; —converts; —guides; —ministers; —negotiates; —pleads; —prays; —preaches; —protects; —rebukes; —reconciles; —rules; —sways; —sympathizes with; —teaches; —visits.
(See minister.)

PASTORAL

adverbs
sweetly; pleasantly; refreshingly; admirably; gently; firmly; mildly; agreeably; pleasingly; acceptably; comfortingly; helpfully; delightfully.

PASTRY

verbs
bolt—; crunch—; despatch—; do honor to —; feast on—; garnish—; gormandize—; knead—; leaven—; munch—; nibble—; roll —; top off with—; —appeals; —attracts; —fattens.
(See food, etc.)

PASTURE

adjectives
recumbent; poisonous; perpetual; sodden; naked; bleak; browsed; boulder-strewn; flowery; pleasant; neighboring; undulous; reeky; stony; verdant; coarse; scant; silver-shrouded.

verbs
abound in—; browse in—; conserve—; devour—; feast on—; feed on—; gnaw—; graze on—; patch—with; plow—; roam—; scrape—; survey—; wander on—; —extends; —fattens; —spreads.
(See grass, field, meadow.)

PAT (v)

adverbs
reassuringly; benignly; affectionately; comfortingly; approvingly; awkwardly; mechanically; caressingly; paternally.
(See tap, caress.)

PATCH

adjectives
vivid; broken; ugly; thrifty; phosphorescent; superficial; numerous (pl); insignificant; single.

PATCH (v)

adverbs
laboriously; awkwardly; deftly; eccentrically; thriftily; superficially; geometrically; pathetically.
(See repair, mend.)

PATE

adjectives
lean; understanding; ponderous; learned; bald; shiny.

PATENT

adjectives
valuable; formal; longed-for; secret.

verbs
grant—; infringe—; limit—; permit—; request—; restrict—; secure—; seek—; — authorizes; —blocks; —clinches; —empowers; —excludes; —expires; —favors; — guards; —pends; —protects; —seals; — vouchsafes.

(See invention, license, right, privilege.)

adverbs
glaringly; openly; plainly; unmistakably; conspicuously; undisguisedly; lawfully; notoriously; freely; safely; securely.

PATERNAL

adverbs
kindly; generously, indulgently, fondly; graciously; proudly; awkwardly; considerately; liberally; clumsily; benevolently; amiably; genially; complacently; complaisantly; tenderly; humanely; benignantly; ad monishingly; warningly; pompously; noisily; actively; virtuously; hilariously; autoeratically; domineeringly; absurdly; amusingly; happily.

PATERNALISM

adjectives
beneficient; beauteous; true.

verbs
advocate—; assume—; attempt—; contemplate—; induce—; propose—; wield—; — administers; —cements; —dominates; — governs; —preserves; —protects; —regulates; —reigns; —supplies.

(See power, action, care, control, government.)

PATERNITY

verbs
anticipate—; consider—; doubt—of; establish—of; forfeit—; hail—; impose—; respect—; revere—; spare—; venerate—; welcome—; —awes; —burdens; —comforts; —honors; —inspires; —salutes.

(See right, descent.)

PATH

adjectives
hollow-worn; pragmatic; steep; hillocky; obliterated; slippery; murmuring; gleaming; damp; luring; zigzag; fringed; twilight; winding; bushy; slender; straitened; adventuresome; hidden; trodden; dissimilar (pl); pleasant; unknown; upward; tempting; circumterrestrial; wild; lone; joyous; numerous (pl); rustling; sinuous; mountain; impracticable; bridle; predetermined; readier; pebbly; tortuous; desolated; endless; outgoing; dusk-shrouded; perilous; silvery; sacred; golden; green-bordered; hazardous; thorny; rough; pleasant; destructive; intricate; unstable; primrose; haughty; delicate; fairylike; factious; grave; beaten; fatal; enticing; pretty; gloomy; overgrown; dreary; chequered; dubious; flashing; conventional; inaccessible; solitary; untried; arduous; blustering; eccentric; homeward; radiating; frequented; lowly; shadowy; perpendicular; stone-flagged; artistic; tiny; intersecting; graveled; destined; somber; labyrinthine; acclivous; giday; narrow; paved; devious; peaceful; lonesome; pilgrim; darkling; firm; desolate; downward; gravel; doctrinaire; difficult; insecure; shelving; intermediate; climbing; uncharted; converging; unconscious; enchanted; weary; precarious; shady; thankless; triumphal; right; dark; curved; comfortless; coincident; parabolic.

verbs
bury—; choose—; cut—; deck—; depart from—; discern—; establish—; inveigle into —; map out—; reflect—; smooth—; strew —; —allures; —beckons; —diverges; — entices; —invites; —swerves; —veers; — winds.

(See lane, road.)

PATHETIC

adverbs
touchingly; unusually; uncommonly; pitiably; infinitely; altogether; poignantly; deeply; grievously; appallingly; shockingly; oddly; immeasurably; heartbreakingly; extraordinarily; dreadfully.

PATHLESS

adverbs
terrifyingly; alarmingly; appallingly; shockingly; perplexingly; bewilderingly; confusingly; dangerously; perilously; hazardously; unaccountably; hopelessly; boundlessly; distressingly; calamitously; disastrously; formidably; forbiddingly; ruggedly; impassably; impermeably; impenetrably.

PATHOS

adjectives

infinite; poignant; anxious; half-baked; puerile; sharp; exquisite; melodious; thin; instant; ever-present; intense; sobbing; despairing; expressible; grim; deep; extraordinary; celestial; stern; unfathomable.

verbs

bear—; catch—; endure—; experience—; harbor—; taste—; —affects; —agitates; —dwells; —impresses; —infects; —mantles; —moves; —palpitates; —pierces; —produces; —responds; —shakes; —warms.

(See sadness, unhappiness, suffering, affliction, sorrow, pity, sympathy, passion.)

PATHWAY

adjectives

murmurous; flinty; aerial; swaying; perilous; persistent; segmental; historic; radiant; shadowy; lightning; immemorial; predestined; rocky; lush; overhung; blind; corkscrew; crooked.

PATIENCE

adjectives

human; placid; simple; courteous; uncomplaining; untiring; gracious; pathetic; musing; chaotic; mild; commendable; inexhaustible; heavenly; self-restrained; melancholy; characteristic; strict; infinite; well-established; boundless; admirable; resigned; creditable; unwearying; haggard; struggling; unconscious; genial; elastic; deliberate; long-suffering; tender; saintly; helpless; mock; dogged; counseled; unwearied; bitter; cruel; unexampled; sad; heroic; serene; gentle; endless; trustful; precious; laboring.

verbs

cultivate—; employ—; entail—; exercise—; exhaust—; manifest—; necessitate—; require—; strain—; try—; —dwindles; —fails; —trays; —wears thin.

(See forbearance, perseverance, endurance, fortitude.)

PATIENT

adjectives

bedridden; unruly; noble; satisfied; reluctant; lucrative; passionate; individual; indignant; docile; fever; diabetic; ill; psychopathic; rheumatic; recalcitrant; susceptible; paranoiac; resolved.

verbs

caution—; discharge—; examine—; exhaust —; guard—; hospitalize—; incapacitate—; inspire—; irritate—; nauseate—; refresh—; relieve—; restore—; resurrect—; sponge—; tide—over; —expectorates; —rallies; —recovers; —relapses; —responds to.

adverbs

unbelievably; incredibly; sweetly; gently; imperturbably; uncomplainingly; quietly; serenely; wisely; sagaciously; indulgently; genially; tenderly; affectionately; expertly; persistently; indefatigably; placidly; courteously; charmingly; habitually; infinitely; unwearyingly; doggedly; resolutely; amazingly; uncommonly.

PATRIARCH

adjectives

hoary; dusky; aged; seafaring; aboriginal; venerable.

PATRIARCHAL

adverbs

properly; appropriately; proudly; arrogantly; domineeringly; imperiously; undeniably; uncommonly; incurably; haughtily; tyrannically; immensely; delightfully; amiably; indulgently; unforgettably; venerably; unyieldingly; obviously; obstinately; tenaciously; insistently; jealously; stubbornly.

PATRICIAN

adverbs

undeniably; innately; inherently; naturally; unmistakably; truly; genuinely; dominantly; proudly; palpably; obviously; evidently; manifestly; undeniably; nobly; conspicuously; eminently; exaltedly; renownedly; splendidly.

PATRIOT

adjectives

ardent; virtuous; sterling; devoted; zealous; epistolary; venerable; misguided; sturdy; prejudiced; worthy.

PATRIOTIC

adverbs

splendidly; curiously; ostentatiously; undeniably; nobly; unselfishly; genuinely; magnificently; grandly; unusually; inherently; truly; unquestionably; quietly; natural; ly; devotedly; conventionally; ardently; actively; assiduously; intelligibly; thoughtful-

862

ly; discriminatingly; wisely; sagaciously; alertly; vigilantly; altruistically; uncommonly; highly; extraordinarily.

PATRIOTISM
adjectives
fainting; flamboyant; haughty; devoted; pious; religious; uncompromising; engendering; impulsive; vigorous; irrepressible; serious; ardent; epidemic; sincere; jealous; disinterested; fearless; heroic; individual; fervent; sublime.

verbs
acclaim—; advocate—; applaud—; breed—; burst with—; choke—; develop—; exploit —; extinguish—; feign—; guard with—; harbor out of—; inflame with—; inspire—; justify—; kindle—; lampoon—; tear between—.

(See Americanism, love, devotion, loyalty.)

PATROL
verbs
elude—; evade—; maintain—; push through —; —guarantees; —guards; —insures; — paces; —protects; —safeguards; —scours; —traverses.

(See guard, sentry.)

PATROL (v)
adverbs
systematically; vigilantly; ceaselessly; cautiously; periodically; hourly; perpetually.

(See watch, march, protect.)

PATRON
adjectives
gentle; influential; munificent; august; fostering; unbidden; imperial; contemptuous; mighty; passing; perpetual.

PATRONAGE
adjectives
condescending; titled; continued; liberal; constant; increasing; political; admiring; generous; extensive; lucrative; obsequious; advised; loyal; proprietary; aldermanic.

verbs
cherish—; dispense—; enjoy—; extend—; foster—; gain—; seek—; solicit—; swell—; withdraw—; --abets; —advances; —aids;

—benefits; —bolsters; —cheers; —feeds; — influences; —nourishes; —overrides; — succors.

(See guidance, support, encouragement, aid, leadership, protection.)

PATRONIZE (v)
adverbs
deferentially; liberally; advisedly; lucratively; loyally; extensively; habitually.

(See encourage, favor, promote.)

PATRONIZING
adverbs
arrogantly; unduly; insufferably; intolerably; unbearably; intolerantly; pompously; haughtily; overbearingly; absurdly; comically; ludicrously; laughably; foolishly; ridiculously; inanely; terribly; fatuously; loudly; noisily; objectionably; provokingly; disagreeably; unpleasantly; obnoxiously; unreasonably; strangely; incredibly.

PATTERN
adjectives
curious; significant; exclusive; intricate; delicate; existing; original; distinctive; ornamental; complex; decorative; pronounced; wondrous; ageless; accurate; complicated; tasteful; metrical; tremulous; frigid; animal; primitive; blotchy; mental; shadow; effective; whimsical; comprehensive; unknown; arbitrary; geometrical; experimental; mosaic; balanced; agricultural; unpretentious; running; ever-present; schizoid; wanted; rich; vivid; starched; perfect; unconventional; operatic; rudimentary; tawdry; aesthetic; ideal; inconspicuous; characterful; scroll; serene; architectural; everlasting; colorful; new; striped; neat; smart; diversified; selective; beautiful; unususal; quiet; spring; stimulating; popular; plaid; plumage; subdued; dark; striking; artificial; attractive; exclusive; fabric; sprightly; authentic; young-blooded; lacy.

verbs
cling to—; comply with—; conform to—; copy—; devise—; follow—; improve upon —; infringe on—; knit—; mark—; observe —; surpass—; trace—; transcend—; violate —; weave—; —baffles; —exemplifies; — guides; —illustrates; —indicates; —regulates; —represents; —simplifies.

(See copy, ideal, design.)

PATTERN (v)

adverbs

exquisitely; exclusively; intricately; delicately; accurately; whimsically; geometrically; vividly; unconventionally; authentically.

(See copy, model, imitate.)

PATTY

adjectives

solid-looking; overdone; tiny.

PAUNCH

verbs

cram—; develop—; distend—; fill—; gorge —; heave—; load—; pamper—; reduce—; simulate—; stuff—; wad—; —craves; —encumbers; —expands; —gnaws; —protrudes.

(See belly, abdomen, stomach, intestines.)

PAUSE

adjectives

slow; awkward; haunting; appreciable; unconscious; normal; week-end; effect-collecting; thoughtful; cogitative; awful; terrible; pensive; ominous; brief; perceptible; discontented; reminiscent; deep; melancholy; decided; musing; appalling; stifling; suitable; inexplicable; humming; solemn; reticent; doubtful; grateful; considerable; frequent (pl); rapturous; transitory; uncomfortable; eternal; determined; respectful; transient; convenient; ensuing; natural; thrilling; present; discreet; wild-swan; habitual; rhetorical; painful; eloquent.

verbs

abstain from—s; destroy—; incur—; observe—; supply—; waste in—; —arrests; —emphasizes; —ensues; —falls; —halts; —hovers; —hushes; —impresses; —interposes; —interrupts; —intervenes; —persists; —suspends.

(See interruption, interval, lapse.)

PAUSE (v)

adverbs

reflectively; dramatically; reminiscently; instinctively; irresolutely; briefly; delicately; meaningfully; diffidently; lingeringly; ominously; deliberately; pensively; solemnly; discreetly.

(See waver, stop.)

PAVEMENT

adjectives

solitary; unsafe; brick; untrodden; rag-strewn; billowy; shady; deserted; dappled; grass-grown; firmamental; circular; insufficient; damp; marble; noiseless; dimly-lighted.

PAVILION

adjectives

vast; silk; glimmering; sumptuous; luminous; arabesque; gay.

verbs

decorate—; flock to—; garnish—; gather in—; ornament—; throng—; —accommodates; —encloses; —harbors; —protects; —rings; —rises; —shades; —shelters; —spreads; —swarms; —swelters.

(See canopy, tent, building.)

PAW

adjectives

tremendous; searching; tactile; bony; moist; unhallowed; horny; bloody.

PAW (v)

adverbs

fitfully; ineptly; vaguely; savagely; brutishly; clumsily; roughly; searchingly; lustfully.

(See stroke, strike.)

PAY

adjectives

sour; retirement; exorbitant; retroactive; scanty; meager; back; advance.

verbs

acquire—; attach—; claim—; crave—; cut —; derive—; deserve—; draw—; entitle to—; exact—; insist on—; merit—; raise—; restore—; solicit—; yield—; —accrues; —compensates; —defrays; —rewards; —squares (colloq.).

(See earnings, payment, profits, wages, money.)

PAY (v)

adverbs

moderately; handsomely; grudgingly; bounteously; heavily; cheerfully; annually; punctually; roundly; scantily; meagerly; exorbitantly.

(See compensate, reward.)

PAYMENT

adjectives

iniquitous; vicarious; substantial; convenient; easy; permanent; equivalent; coming; political; stipulated; benefit; preliminary; monthly; annual.

verbs

acknowledge—; afford—; await—; cease—; collect—; default—; deserve—; disburse—; evade—; reap—; recover—; refund—; resume—; suspend—; —discharges; —effaces; —pains.

(See pay, profits, wages.)

PAYROLL

verbs

add to—; anticipate—; calculate—; disburse—; distribute—; draw—; guard—; hold up (colloq.)—; insure—; pare down—; prepare—; protect—; reduce—; rob—; survey—; trim—; —increases; —mounts; —surpasses.

(See funds, profits, earnings.)

PEACE

adjectives

intellectual; bitter; profound; durable; dishonorable; unbroken; joyous; healthy; tolerable; enduring; industrial; internal; lovely; lasting; honorable; long-lost; heavenly; mellow-eyed; ineffable; dictated; passionate; meek-eyed; unresting; domestic; rapturous; neighborhood; absolute; unaccustomed; ignominious; settled; endless; everlasting; fruitful; speedy; temporary; ripening; universal; permanent; humiliating; eternal; deep; constant; indescribable; taunting; supplicated; unruffled; uneven; unsuspecting; treacherous; sweet; pale; ultimate; sinless; patched-up; barbaric; prudent; shameful; blissful; perpetual; honeyed; unbroken; inner; wealthy; silken; advantageous; luxurious; infinite; unspeakable; happy; ancient; sacred; poetic; unfluctuating; especial; external; repugnant; intimated; serene; balmy; profound; technical; ignoble; endurable; spiritual; windless; exquisite; riteless; incomparable; shining; fraternal; utter; immemorial; well-earned; pastoral.

verbs

achieve—; agitate for—; assure of—; botch —; breed—; compel—; crusade for—; destroy—; disrupt—; endanger—; enthrone —; further—; herald—; impose—; maintain—; menace—; negotiate—; prate about —; promote—; restore—; risk—; serve—; spurn—; sue for—; symbolize—; threaten

—; unsettle—; upset—; vouchsafe—; —pervades; —prevails; —reigns.

(See harmony, amity, friendship, quiet, tranquillity.)

PEACEABLE

adverbs

inherently; naturally; continuously; resolutely; placidly; mildly; tranquilly; habitually; determinedly; inoffensively; serenely; calmly; imperturbably; unimaginably; curiously; racially; soberly; blandly; unbelievably; uncommonly; reasonably.

PEACEFUL

adverbs

beatifically; serenely; happily; blessedly; rapturously; amiably; pleasantly; contentedly; unbelievably; delightfully; entrancingly; remarkably; gloriously; perfectly.

PEACOCK

verbs

—preens; —prides himself; —stalks; —strides; —strolls; —struts.

(See bird.)

PEAK

adjectives

pinnacled; singular; volcanic; dazzling; furrowed; rounded; perilous; lambent; herbless; snowy; rugged; airy; fierce; savage; glistening; bristling; glittering; isolated; barren; angular; mountain; celestial; gigantic; lofty; successive (pl); precipitous; single; steeple-like; sunlighted; abrupt; ermine-clad; pathless; frowning; craggy; unique; brumal; jagged; environing (pl); rock; multitudinous (pl); scalped; snow-patched; fantastic; snow-covered; solstitial.

verbs

ascend—; cap—; climb—; cuff—; culminate in—; push to—; rise to—; scale—; sharpen—; —commands; —crowns; —heightens; —hovers; —juts; —points; —projects; —rears· —soars; —tapers; —tops; —towers.

(See mountain, tower, hill, top, point, summit.)

PEAL

adjectives

silvery; yawning; merry; angry; repeated; strange; fearful; terrific; dismal; tuneful;

full-hearted; paschal; joyous; hideous; solemn; spasmodic; tremendous; thrilling; dreadful.

PEAL (v)

adverbs

melodiously; softly; gently; gaily; joyously; festively; merrily; angrily; terrifically; solemnly; spasmodically.

(See echo, resound, reverberate.)

PEANUTS

verbs

blanch—; chop—; clean—; consume—; crush—; cultivate—; dig up—; dry—; express from—; extract from—; hawk—; hurl —at; munch—; package—; ripen—; roast —; salt—; shell—; steam—.

PEAR

adjectives

yellow; waxen; withered; mellowing; hoary; blushing; frozen.

PEARLS

adjectives

oriental; ungathered; lustral; barbaric; shimmering; pink; glistening; creamy; iridescent; liquid; imitation; intermingled; sleepy; enormous; carven; inlaid; snowy; pellucid; perfect; melting; glittering.

verbs

collect—; covet—; cultivate—; deposit—in; dissolve—; dive for—; drill—; embellish with—; fish for—; imitate—; polish—; prize —; string—; value—; yield—; —adorn; — decorate; —enhance; —glitter; —ornament.

(See jewel, gem, diamond.)

PEARLY

adverbs

iridescently; beautifully; incredibly; exquisitely; sumptuously; opalescently; frostily; intensely; richly; gorgeously; sweetly; delicately; daintily; incredibly; marvelously; miraculously; creamily; consummately; indescribably; ineffably.

PEARS

verbs

bear—; blight—; box—; bruise—; can—; cook—; crate—; gather—; grade—; infect —; market—; pare—; pluck—; preserve—;

select—; serve—; spray—; stew—; wrap—; —cluster; —decay; —exude; —ripen; — rot; —thrive.

(See fruit, apple.)

PEAS

adjectives

dwarf; delicate; wild.

verbs

box—; can—; crate—; cultivate—; gather —; grade—; harvest—; injure—; plant—; process—; refrigerate—; row—; scoop up —; separate—; shell—; ship—; wash—; — germinate; —mature.

(See vegetables.)

PEASANTS

adjectives

unspoiled; passionate; raw; rude; jubilant; squalid; white-bearded; wretched; shelter-seeking; hopeless; gentle; naked; vindictive; insurgent; healthy-looking; well-dressed; trilingual; downtrodden; distrustful; hard-faced; unforgiving; self-assertive; universal; swarthy; enterprising; bewildered; unlettered; grimy; prating; honest-hearted; ruddy-cheeked; uncultivated.

verbs

agitate—; aid—; appease—; banish—; dominate—; enslave—; exile—; tyrannize over—; —assemble; —clamor; —herd; — economize; —immigrate; —rebel; —revolt; —toil; —uprise; —weary.

(See natives, countryman, farmer, worker, alien, foreigner.)

PEBBLES

adjectives

dewy; rounded; polished; sun-kissed; hard-flung; clean; colored.

PECCABLE

adverbs

unfortunately; unhappily; admittedly; unwontedly; naturally; unquestionably; pitifully; helplessly; probably; alarmingly; outrageously; undeniably; exceptionably; miserably; wretchedly; recklessly; irremediably.

PECULIAR

adverbs

racially; highly; distinctly; definitely; quaintly; strikingly; remarkably; curiously; oddly; highly; outlandishly; exotically; unaccountably.

PECULIARITY

adjectives

petty; salient; social; seasonal; manifold; awful; definite; well-known; humorous; quaint; minute; arbitrary; marked; intellectual; striking; mental; sectional.

PECUNIARY

adverbs

distinctly; exclusively; wholly; avariciously; fortunately; undeniably; definitely; conveniently; opportunely; luckily.

PEDAGOGICAL

adverbs

unmitigatedly; absolutely; definitely; pedantically; wholeheartedly; monotonously; tediously; loudly; blatantly; opinionatedly; patiently; studiously; meticulously; wisely; tiresomely; intelligently; boresomely; mildly; resolutely; ostentatiously; vainly; egotistically; priggishly; pompously; humbly; modestly; pretentiously; self-consciously; self-righteously; emphatically; insistently; dogmatically; proudly; impossibly.

PEDAGOGUE

adjectives

groveling; admirable; gross; stupid; harassed.

PEDANT

adjectives

sand-blind; miserable; fiery; academic; forward; wrangling.

PEDANTIC

adverbs

unmistakably; unshakably; tiresomely; insufferably; proudly; intolerably; ostentatiously; self-righteously; insistently; vexatiously; primly; assertively; confidently; solemnly; sharply; monotonously; incurably; absurdly; unwarrantably; scrupulously; consciously; punctiliously; unbearably; meticulously.

PEDANTRY

adjectives

display—; encrust with—; engender—; ridicule—; savor of—; scorn—; shake off—; —affects; —concludes; —disgusts; —dogmatizes; —obtrudes; —overestimates; —overacts; —poses; —prejudices; —presumes; —proceeds from; —repels.
(See learning, vanity.)

PEDDLER

adjectives

itinerant; flesh; pavement; unscrupulous; stentorian.

PEDESTAL

adjectives

elevated; formal; equal.

verbs

adorn—; bestride—; construct—; erect upon —; mount on—; ornament—; prop on—; repose on—; rest on—; topple from—; totter on—; —affords; —bases; —bolsters; —maintains; —supports; —sustains.
(See base, support, foundation.)

PEDESTRIAN

adjectives

belated; faulty; dust-covered; tall; muscular; travel-stained; raw-boned; successful; ardent; jay-walking

verbs

accord to—; assist—; block off—s; educate —; endanger—; hamper—; injure—; signal —; warn—; —co-operates; —crosses; —disobeys; —dodges; —evades; —observes; —tires; —tours; —travels; —wearies.

PEDIGREE

adjectives

unbroken; feudal; proud.

PEEP

adjectives

fair; momentary; hasty.

PEEP (v)

adverbs

shyly; slyly; shrinkingly; daringly; audaciously; modestly; coyly; flirtatiously.
(See peer, look.)

PEER

adjectives

painstaking; puissant; contemporary; penniless; wrong-incensed; gentle; lustrous; witty; notorious; impecunious; favorite.

PEER (v)

adverbs

earnestly; intently; timidly; curiously; cautiously; anxiously; fearfully; furtively; surreptitiously; slyly.
(See peep, look.)

PEERAGE

verbs

bestow—upon; congratulate—; convoke—; create—; entitle—to; forfeit—; influence—; limit—; privilege—; represent—; —adheres; —controls; —convenes; —honors; —serves.

(See aristocracy, nobility.)

PEEVISH

adverbs

unspeakably; unreasonably; unwarrantably; terribly; disagreeably; unfortunately; unpleasantly; horribly; uncommonly; habitually; naturally; querulously; feverishly; childishly; fretfully; captiously; obstinately; incurably; acrimoniously; vexatiously; intolerably; insufferably; unaccountably; inexplicably; curiously; strangely; oddly; significantly; brusquely; snappishly; embarrassingly; humiliatingly.

PEG

adjectives

rustic; wooden; unfitted.

verbs

bind to—; dangle from—; drive—; hammer —; hang on—; hitch to—; insert—;. pin with—; pound—; repose on—; tie to—; whittle—; —catches; —fastens; —holds; —projects; —protrudes; —supports; —sustains.

(See nail, hook.)

PELICAN

adjectives

rangy; large-billed; awkward.

verbs

—fishes; —gorges; —plunges; —secretes; —seizes.

(See bird.)

PELLUCID

adverbs

beautifully; admirably; unusually; wonderfully; marvellously; delightfully; incomparably; unsurpassably; limpidly; surprisingly; pricelessly; extraordinarily; inimitably; exquisitely; incomparably; peculiarly.

PEN

adjectives

educated; guided; gifted; severe; unbiased; inexhaustible; spiteful; brilliant; shy; inex-pressive; horrible; abler; plaguy; ill-natured; ready; fascinating; vile; enigmatic; substantial; facile; untrained; sprightly; blithesome; humorous; truant; burning; barbarous; dreadful; lucid; inadequate; young; passion-guided; trenchant.

verbs

dip—; exercise—; grasp—; poise—; pour from—; probe—into; scrawl with—; whisk —across; wield—; —assails; —comes to life; —exposes; —falters; —libels; —sears; —unfolds; —voices.

(See fountain-pen, writer, author, pencil.)

PEN (v)

adverbs

obscurely; trenchantly; spitefully; inexhaustibly; brilliantly; expressively; fascinatingly; enigmatically; facilely; passionately.

(See record, compose, write.)

PENAL

adverbs

unnecessarily; cruelly; bitterly; justly; correctively; exceptionally; acidulously; inordinately; egregiously; excessively; mildly; ineffectively; formally; terribly.

PENALIZE (v)

adverbs

ironically; severely; rigorously; painfully; barbarously; harshly; stringently.

(See punish, discipline.)

PENALTY

adjectives

tremendous; painful; mad; inescapable; grievous; similar; severe; proportionate; efficient; enrolled; suitable; spiritual; barbarous; fearful; easy.

verbs

accept—; assert—; assess—; balk at—; condemn to—; decry—; escape—; entail—; evade—; exact—; impose—; inflict—; levy —; pay—; —atones; —recompenses; —rehabilitates.

(See forfeit, fine, punishment, indictment.)

PENANCE

adjectives

fearful; secret; atrocious; purgatorial; easy; spiritual; barbarous; suitable; amorous; cruel; harsh; solemn; hearty; superstitious; severe; lingering; true-hearted; honest.

PENCHANT

verbs

admit—; avoid—; cling to—; eschew—; excite—; exhibit—; incur—; indulge—; —burns; —devours; —disgusts; —irritates; —horrifies; —lusts; —riles (colloq.).

(See desire, inclination, attraction.)

PENCIL

adjectives

stubby; artistic; energetic; mechanical; unsharpened; blunt; coarse.

verbs

clasp—; depict with—; draw with—; drum with—; poise—; scribble with—; sharpen —; tip—; —copies; —dashes off; —delineates; —inscribes; —jots; —marks; —outlines; —scrawls; —scurries; —sketches; —tattoos; —tints.

(See pen.)

PENDANT

adjectives

quaint; inflamed; haughty.

verbs

display—; fashion—; flourish—; hook—; strip off—s; suspend—; —attracts; —bobs; —dazzles; —dangles; —decks; —enhances; —flaps; —fringes; —hangs; —impresses; —ornaments; —swings; —weights.

(See drop, jewel, gem.)

PENDENT

adverbs

terribly; perilously; hazardously; dangerously; decoratively; attractively; delicately; daintily; lustrously; dazzlingly; brilliantly; curiously; strangely; grotesquely; fantastically; quaintly; strikingly.

PENDULOUS

adverbs

heavily; clumsily; awkwardly; corpulently; uncertainly; flabbily; dangerously; indeterminately; wabblingly; loosely; unbecomingly; curiously; strangely.

PENDULUM

adjectives

ponderous; large; rhythmic.

verbs

adjust—; hook—; —controls; —dances; —maintains; —oscillates; —pulsates; —regulates; —rocks; —suspends; —swaggers; —

swings; —tick-tocks; —vibrates; —wags; —waves.

PENETRATE (*v*)

adverbs

accurately; accidentally; decisively; freely; scientifically; discerningly; gradually.

(See pierce, bore, affect.)

PENETRATING

adverbs

curiously; deeply; warrantably; peculiarly; particularly; remedially; soothingly; alleviatingly; surprisingly; remarkably; strikingly; incredibly; unusually; uncommonly; acutely; shrewdly; intelligently; keenly; sharply; discerningly; cleverly; sagaciously; profoundly; incisively; impressively; unfailingly; highly.

PENETRATION

adjectives

profound; calm; accurate; usual; subtle; intuitive; bland; noiseless; perfect; uncanny; characteristic; instinctive; partial; infallible; tender; masterly; sympathetic.

verbs

attempt—; block—; escape—; evade—; force—; induce—; pretend—; resist—; unite by—; wonder at—; —awes; —discerns; —discriminates; —gores; —shoots; —uncovers; —yawns.

(See infiltration.)

PENINSULA

verbs

approach—; fortify—; guard—; inhabit—; near—; overrun—; surround—; view—; watch—; —adjoins; —beckons; —extends; —lengthens; —projects; —protrudes; —reaches; —ranges; —stretches.

(See marsh, island, land.)

PENITENCE

adjectives

haggard; pale; celestial; pathetic; anxious; prescribed.

PENITENT

adverbs

deeply; sincerely; sorrowfully; painfully; naturally; contritely; meekly; humbly; embarrassingly; truly; unduly; ruefully; obviously; evidently; manifestly; pitiably; confessedly; terribly.

PENNILESS

adverbs

pitiably; undeniably; finally; terribly; sadly; frightfully; dreadfully; ruefully; laughably; merrily; blithely; carelessly; nonchalantly; miserably; wretchedly; helplessly; hopelessly; vexatiously; embarrassingly; obviously; humiliatingly; manifestly; actually; evidently; strangely; inexplicably; unaccountably; purposely; intentionally; adroitly; cleverly; resolutely.

PENNY-WISE

adverbs

cleverly; carefully; penuriously; thriftily; cannily; shrewdly; capriciously; extravagantly; wastefully; absurdly; unreasonably; ridiculously; improvidently; lavishly; inconsistently; recklessly; ludicrously; incongruously.

PENSION

adjectives

contributory; liberal; retiring; literary; subsidiary; old-age.

verbs

assign—; authorize—; bestow—upon; derive —from; establish—; exact—; fix—; forfeit —; grant—; merit—; proffer—; provide—; request—; reserve for—; retire on—; welcome—; yield—; —assists; —enables; —encourages; —supports; —sustains.

(See pay, payment, allowance, subsidy.)

PENSIVE

adverbs

abstractedly; incongruously; strangely; silently; absent-mindedly; sweetly; quietly; soberly; anxiously; remotely; dreamily; ruefully; mournfully; dully; deeply; gravely; solemnly; happily; contentedly.

PENTHOUSE

verbs

decorate—; enjoy—; establish in—; furnish —; inhabit—; occupy—; offer—; philander on—; provide—; renovate—; view from—; —allures; —appeals; —attracts; —caps; —crowns; —delights; —enchants; —overlooks; —tops.

(See tower, apartment, roof.)

PENURIOUS

adverbs

intolerably; terribly; necessarily; pitiably; meanly; basely; incomprehensibly; inexplic-

ably; unreasonably; unpardonably; suspiciously; suddenly; inherently; naturally; inconveniently; conspicuously; strangely; incorrigibly; greedily; irremediably; unreasonably; disagreeably; unnecessarily; needlessly; unaccountably; niggardly; miserly; inexcusably; stingily; crustily; gruffly; wretchedly; avariciously; uncommonly; extremely; absurdly; miserably; sordidly.

PENURY

adjectives

cold; hard; frosty; tedious; unvanquishable; sordid; forgetful; utter; gripping; miserable.

verbs

burden by—; conceal—; fear—; feign—; reduce to—; resist—; survive—; —afflicts; —aggrieves; —deprives; —distresses; —embarrasses; —harasses; —irks; —narrows; —necessitates; —pains; —weighs upon.

(See poverty, want, destitution.)

PEOPLE

adjectives

aboriginal; abused; accursed; adventurous; affectionate; agile; alert; amiable; amused; aristocratic; aspiring; astounding; austere; aware; barbaric; benevolent; benighted; bent; border; brave; brusque; bustling; celebrated; charitable; chivalrous; civilized; cold; common; commonplace; communicative; congenial; congregated; conquering; constructive; contemplative; conventional; credulous; cruel; cultivated; debonair; decadent; decent; defenseless; degraded; deluded; democratic; desperate; devoted; diminutive; discontented; distinguished; discriminating; dissipated; distinct; doglike; distressed; egotistical; elbowing; eminent; energetic; enervated; enslaved; enfranchised; engrossing; enlightened; enterprising; erect; estimable; excited; everlasting; expatriated; extravagant; factious; fanciful; fashionable; fertile; fastidious; fickle; filthy; frenzied; fun-loving; friendless; friendly; frivolous; gaily-dressed; gay; generous; gloomy; grateful; great; growing; high-minded; homogeneous; humble; humdrum; hurrying; idolatrous; illiterate; impoverished; impulsive; inarticulate; indestructible; indignant; industrious; infatuated; inflamed; infuriated; insane; intense; kind-hearted; interesting; jealous; law-loving; kindly-faced; laboring; learned; liberty-loving; light; lighter; litigious; lively; malicious;

martial; materialistic; mediocre; merry; milling; miserable; modest; missionary-minded; money-making; nice; much-praying; mysterious; neighboring; niggardly; noble; nomadic; notable; noteworthy; obscure; oppressed; outrageous; overfed; packed; panic-stricken; peace-loving; panting; paradoxical; pastoral; peculiar; pediatric; perfect; persistent; persuadable; pessimistic; picturesque; pious; polished; polite; poor; poorly-dressed; practical; precise; prehistoric; preposterous; primitive; progressive; prominent; proud; provoking; quarrelsome; refined; reflective; restless; rich; rigid; rude; rugged; rushing; sagacious; sanguine; seafaring; selfish; sensible; self-seeking; semi-literate; sensitive; sentimental; servile; shabby; shade-loving; sightless; sleek; snobbish; smart; sober; social-minded; solitary; sore; sovereign; special; started; startled; stiff; strange; strong; stupid; sturdy; stylish; supine; substantial; suffering; sufficient; superior; superstitious; swollen; terror-stricken; thoughtful; tempted; thinking; tiresome; thoughtless; timid; tranquil; turbulent; ulcerous; unambitious; unclassical; uncouth; uncultivated; uncultured; unfortunate; unnatural; unobtrusive; unpoetic; unpolished; unreasonable; unreasoning; verbose; vigilant; vigorous; virile; virtuous; visiting; volatile; weak; well-dressed; well-informed; wholesale; wise; wonderful; wondering; worthless; young.

verbs
chide—; color—; conciliate—; corral—; denounce to—; depict—; fraternize with—; instigate—; jolt—; liberate—; outsmart (colloq.)—; portray—; regiment—; tyrannize over—; —arise; —flock to; —gather 'round.; —rally to; —revolt; —sanction.
(See English, folk, race, tribe, nation, persons, community.)

"PEP"
verbs
gain—; inject—; lack—; —gains; —brightens; —buoys; —cheers; —emboldens; —endures; —enthuses (colloq.); —glows; —fosters; —impresses; —infects; —inspires; —palls; —reassures; —tingles; —wanes; —warms.
(See energy, power, zeal, vigor.)

PERAMBULATION
adjectives
glad; stealthy.

PERCEIVABLE
adverbs
easily; readily; completely; manifestly; instantly; openly; immediately; perfectly; remarkably; strikingly.

PERCEIVE (v)
adverbs
vividly; tangibly; dimly; sagely; tremulously; instinctively; vaguely; distinctly; superficially.
(See discern, observe.)

PERCENTAGE
adjectives
unknown; doubtful; high.

verbs
calculate—; check—; compute—; cut—; deduct—; demand—; derive—; draw—; exact —; extract—; fix—; reduce—; stabilize—; yield—; —abates; —ascends; —exceeds; —mounts; —staggers.
(See amount, sum, proportion, part, rate, quantity.)

PERCEPTIBLE
adverbs
dimly; readily; scarcely; easily; cruelly; bitterly; instantly; immediately; finally; distinctly; conspicuously; plainly; clearly; mistily; hardly.

PERCEPTION
adjectives
triumphant; keen; dimmest; acute; quick; startling; single; ominous; honest; innate; intuitive; vivid; sharp; intellectual; mental; artistic; sudden; passive; dreamlike; accurate; exquisite; prodigious; vague; confused; sentimental; simultaneous; mystic; infallible; subtle; extra-sensory; spiritual; cloud; sure; steadfast; moral; awful; luminous; interior; penetrating; practical; human.

verbs
attain—; blind—; blunt—; clarify—; display—; dull—; heighten—; stimulate—; warp—; —adjusts; —aids; —appreciates; —apprehends; —fathoms; —matures; —scans; —warns.
(See eye, feeling, sensation.)

PERCH
adjectives
convenient; incongruous; precarious; lofty.

PERCH (v)

adverbs

conveniently; precariously; loftily; importantly; securely; gracefully; daringly.

(See sit, place.)

PERDITION

adjectives

everlasting; bottomless; eternal.

verbs

condemn to—; consume to—; —annuls; —batters; —blasts; —blots out; —confounds; —crashes; —crumbles; —demolishes; —desolates; —devastates; —devours; —engulfs; —eradicates; —overwhelms; —perplexes; —prostrates; —swamps.

(See hell, ruin, destruction.)

PEREMPTORY

adverbs

disagreeably; proudly; dictatorially; extremely; unnecessarily; arrogantly; emphatically; bumptiously; incisively; cuttingly; unwarrantedly; officially; formally; coldly; sharply; sternly; severely; trenchantly; unfortunately; offensively; unwisely; deliberately; habitually; unconsciously.

PERENNIAL

adverbs

conveniently; dependably; delightfully; satisfactorily; reliably; imperishably; comfortably; durably; happily; fortunately.

PERFECTION

adjectives

absolute; delicate; abnormal; classic; spontaneous; aesthetic; time-softened; infinite; divine; optical; fashionable; rare; strained; technical; ineffable; trim; studied; flattering; pure; balanced; complete; supreme; ravishing; final; theoretical; comparative; prosperous; exquisite; unlimited; overwhelming; matchless; constant; minute; moral; true; mechanical; imaginable; artistic; pure; tailored; unapproachable.

verbs

achieve—; acquire—; admire—; approximate—; attain—; disclaim—; emulate—; gain—; invest with—; lack—; mature to—; realize—; ripen to—; sacrifice—to; seek—; strive for—; transcend—; vie for—; —clinches; —crowns; —eludes; —saturates; —seals.

(See beauty, mastery, precision, accuracy.)

PERFIDIOUS

adverbs

dreadfully; treacherously; habitually; racially; inherently; terribly; seditiously; personally; highly; uncommonly; unforgivably; manifestly; cruelly; barbarously; savagely; dangerously; sadly; undeniably; disloyally; untrustworthily; dastardly; basically; horribly; wickedly; deliberately.

PERFIDY

adjectives

armed; household; unspeakable; calculated.

PERFORM (v)

adverbs

unwittingly; gallantly; energetically; creditably; pleasantly; dramatically; conscientiously; theatrically; gratuitously; brilliantly; capably; faithfully; methodically; scrupulously; publicly; effectively; zealously; punctually; rigorously; harmoniously; superlatively; exceptionally; consummately.

(See accomplish, execute, play, act.)

PERFORMANCE

adjectives

relative; theoretical; undignified; smooth; eager; zealous; arduous; singular; dependable; punctual; proved; pirated; exhibition; indubitable; silent; rigorous; maximum; choice; splendid; shoddy; slipshod; pantomimed; effective; harmonious; superficial; sensational; spectacular; laudable; charity; magnanimous; humdrum; incisive; top; charitable; superlative; decennial; periodic; scrupulous; sparkling; exceptional; ill-considered; splendid; faithful; vigorous; painstaking; proper; careless; innocuous; astonishing; fearless; brazen; discreditable; irresponsible; graceful; improper; superb; middling; subsequent; persuasive; impressive; remarkable; brilliant; magnificent; consummate.

verbs

acclaim—; affect—of; applaud—; broadcast —; direct—; engage in—; infuse into—; inject into—; key—; laud—; render—; reward for—; sponsor—; stage—; suspend—; witness—; —involves; —thrills.

(See feat, deed, entertainment, melodrama, play.)

PERFORMER

adjectives

accomplished; creditable; gratuitous; exact.

PERFUME

adjectives

delicate; sweet; enchanted; native; well-re-membered; swooning; drowsy; overpower-ing; excellent; faint; melodic; exquisite; powerful; delectable; floating; rhetorical; soft; pungent; intoxicating; haunting; filthy; lingering; rich; poisoned; attractive; dead; exotic.

verbs

anoint with—; dab—; distill—; douse with —; drench with—; emit—; exude—; haunt by—; inhale—; recognize—; reek with—; saturate in—; spray with—; steep in—; waft—; —clings; —delights; —exudes; —floods; —nauseates; —offends; —oppresses; —overcomes; —overwhelms; —pervades; —pleases; —scents; —tints.

(See aroma, essence, incense, fragrance.)

PERFUME (v)

adverbs

exquisitely; exotically; sweetly; delectably; intoxicatingly; hauntingly; richly; lingering-ly; voluptuously.

(See scent.)

PERFUNCTORY

adverbs

arrogantly; smugly; carelessly; disagree-ably; unpleasantly; unpardonably; indiffer-ently; apathetically; heedlessly; incautious-ly; mechanically; thoughtlessly; coolly; un-concernedly; coldly; hastily; inexcusably; inexplicably; unaccountably; horribly; cruel-ly; unfeelingly.

PERIL

adjectives

approaching; utmost; manifold; sundry (pl); imminent; extreme; extraordinary; real; vague; instant; personal; probable; attendant; vegetable; serious; formidable; growing; imaginary; nimble; incredible; be-setting; innumerable (pl); unavoidable; deadly; slight; weird; ever-recurring; en-compassing; great; unexpected.

verbs

anticipate—; brave—; chance—; dare—; defy—; encounter—; expose to—; face—; hazard—; incur—; rescue from—; risk—; steel against—; survive—; terrify by—; ven-ture—; warn of—; —endangers; —jeopar-dizes; —menaces; —oppresses; —threatens.

(See hazard, danger, menace, risk.)

PERILOUS

adverbs

notoriously; notably; undeniably; obviously; terribly; ghastly; miserably; peculiarly; in-fernally; undisguisedly; unutterably; mortal-ly; bitterly; dreadfully; extremely; inordin-ately; ominously; mercilessly; prodigiously.

PERIOD (time)

adjectives

secluded; adequate; successive (pl); tortur-ed; immediate; postwar; remote; unlimited; towering; prehistoric; immature; dismal; prolonged; engine-creating; brief; chrono-logical; pivotal; corresponding; severe; dangerous; characteristic; distinct; critical; definite; mental; extended; smiling; frivol-ous; traditional; respective; well-defined; pretentious; momentous; dark; potential; bubble; rude; vigorous; stirring; long; glamorous; creative; controversial; dead; spiritual; modern; specified; variable; bril-liant; devastating; limited; fruitful; disturb-ed; predetermined; unquiet; unmoral; cor-rupt; medieval; immense; pagan; formative; melancholy; calamity; measurable; pretty; reasonable; considerable; conversational; sidereal; productive; eventful; glorious; previous; lurid; palmy; contagious; glacial; noteworthy; tickling; indefinite; nebulous; typical; anomalistic; sluggish; provincial; impressionable; chaotic; comfortable; pro-scribed; transition; flourishing; definite; pioneering; congested; amusing; long-for-gotten; genial; happy; tranquil; expired; stated; moot; shameful; fecund; wondrous; discreditable; creative; probationary; trying.

verbs

characterize—; conclude—; inaugurate—; launch—; perpetuate—; personify—; plunge into—; shorten—; usher in—; —achieves; —advances; —consumes; —dawns; —dies; —elapses; —embarks; —embraces; —ex-pires; —flows; —glides; —intervenes; —terminates.

(See era, epoch, age, cycle, decade, gener-ation.)

PERIODIC

adverbs

regularly; fortunately; reliably; depend-ably; wisely; ordinarily; invariably; infal-libly; officially; necessarily; duly.

873

adjectives
fledgling; exoteric; esoteric; short-lived; spectacular; fireside; sarcastic; unread.

verbs
dispense—; disseminate—; distribute—; edit —; found—; hawk—; heap —s; hoard —s; launch—; publish—; preserve—; refer to—; scan—; subscribe to—; treasure—; —advertises; —amuses; —delights; —diverts; —illustrates; —informs.
(See newspaper, magazine, publication.)

PERISH (v)

adverbs
desolately; miserably; simultaneously; ignominiously; inevitably; agonizingly.
(See die, decay.)

PERISHABLE

adverbs
highly; uncommonly; unfortunately; remarkably; unluckily; extravagantly; unhappily; particularly; peculiarly; terribly; dreadfully; wastefully; undesirably; inordinately.

PERJURY

adjectives
false; flat; atrocious; cunning; extraordinary.

PERKY

adverbs
roguishly; smartly; saucily; stylishly; fashionably; irresistibly; tomboyishly; quaintly; fascinatingly; interestingly; piquantly; pleasantly; modishly; charmingly; ingeniously.

PERMANENCE

adjectives
historic; unnatural.

verbs
ascertain—; confirm—; establish—; guarantee—; intensify—; retain—of; sense—; threaten—; —drags; —endures; —evaporates; —fades; —flickers; —perseveres; —persists; —protracts; —totters; —weathers.
(See immortality, stability.)

PERMANENT

adverbs
comfortably; securely; admirably; assuredly; warrantably; unquestionably; fortunately; safely; reasonably; steadfastly; unchangeably; durably; inescapably; legally.

adverbs
expressly; generously; always; scarcely; socially; officially; intimately; obviously; evidently; patently; unconditionally; reportedly; reputedly; apparently; unquestionably; manifestly; definitely; explicitly; palpably; luckily; fortunately.

PERMISSION

adjectives
abstracted; unsolicited; verbal; express; requisite; reluctant; willing.

PERMIT (v)

adverbs
unsolicitedly; verbally; expressly; reluctantly; graciously; lazily; incidentally; promiscuously; readily; gratuitously; stolidly; magnanimously.
(See allow, consent.)

PERORATION

adjectives
justly-admired; noble; sprawling.

PERPETRATE (v)

adverbs
cruelly; fiendishly; illegally; vilely; wickedly; lustfully; crudely; murderously.
(See commit, accomplish.)

PERPLEX (v)

adverbs
facetiously; amazingly; sorely; painfully; cunningly; slyly; verbally; mentally.
(See bewilder, confuse.)

PERPLEXING

adverbs
unaccountably; disturbingly; genuinely; indescribably; strangely; fearfully; insuperably; dishearteningly; depressingly; terribly; vexatiously; alarmingly; unreasonably; uncomfortably; vaguely; subtly; awkwardly; stubbornly; extremely; secretly; annoyingly; exasperatingly; inexplicably.

PERPLEXITY

adjectives
inevitable; great; dim; insoluble; unexplained; sad; natural; painful; unrighteous; mingled; hopeless; dangerous; broken-hearted.

verbs
conceal—; flounder in—; grapple with—;

grope in—; hesitate in—; relieve—; tremble in—; unravel—; view with—; —bewilders; —bothers; —burdens; —confuses; —darkens; —embarrasses; —enmeshes; —entangles; —hounds; —muddles; —nets; —overwhelms; —weaves.

(See amazement, incredulity, bewilderment, uncertainty, complication.)

PERSECUTE (v)
adverbs
mercilessly; relentlessly; odiously; pettishly; determinedly; whimsically; remorselessly; senselessly; bitterly; unjustly; repeatedly; unflaggingly; doggedly; incredibly; unfalteringly.

(See oppress, torment.)

PERSECUTION
verbs
bewail—; criticize—; fear—; influe—; intensify—; intimidate by—; resist—; single out for—; subject to—; suffer—; temper—; —aggrieves; —dispirits; —grinds; —harasses; —haunts; —pains; —offends; —oppresses; —outrages; —tramples; —weighs.

(See oppression, tyranny.)

PERSECUTOR
adjectives
odious; petty; subtle; religious; domestic; determined; unjust; whimsical; cold-hearted; systematic; unmerited; remorseless; senseless; merciless; relentless; languid; fiery; bitter; imperial; miserable; actual; repeated.

PERSEVERANCE
adjectives
unflagging; relentless; tugging; resolute; dogged; steady; indefinite; incredible; majestic; patient; indomitable; scheming; unfaltering; mechanical.

verbs
acclaim—; acquire by—; instil—; reward —; tax—; wed to—; yield to—; —buckles down; —clings; —devotes; —drives; —falters; —fights; —persists; —plods; —plunges.

(See insistence, patience, persistence.)

PERSEVERE (v)
adverbs
steadily; pluckily; characteristically; unflaggingly; relentlessly; resolutely; doggedly;
incredibly; indomitably; unfalteringly; mechanically.

(See continue, persist.)

PERSEVERING
adverbs
resolutely; tenaciously; stubbornly; patiently; gently; mildly; irritatingly; vexatiously; tiresomély; monotonously; wildly; obstinately; mulishly; endlessly; unremittingly; singularly; oddly; peculiarly; awfully; commendably; admirably; terribly; conspicuously; doggedly.

PERSIFLAGE
adjectives
insolent; witty; swift; bantering.

PERSIST (v)
adverbs
archly; insubordinately; doggedly; undauntedly; audaciously; vigorously; stubbornly; enthusiastically; logically; relentlessly; ardently; faithfully; inextinguishably; triumphantly; morbidly; unreasonably.

(See persevere, continue.)

PERSISTENCE
adjectives
marked; ardent; unabated; culpable; faithful; indomitable; cruel; inextinguishable; wonderful; tiresome; patient; triumphant; appalling; morbid; further; uncomplaining; wearisome; adequate; unreasonable.

verbs
dog with—; instil—; tax—; —achieves; —attacks; —continues; —drags; —endures; —fades; —gains; —palls; —survives; —wanes.

(See application, insistence, perseverance.)

PERSISTENT
adverbs
vexatiously; disagreeably; inescapably; unpleasantly; obnoxiously; admirably; remarkably; uncommonly; highly; tiresomely; ardently; passionately; amazingly; incredibly; unreasonably; doggedly; determinedly; obstinately; stubbornly; maddeningly; insufferably; terribly.

PERSON
adjectives
acidulated; acrid; affected; apprehensive; arbitrary; argumentative; arrogant; attrac-

875

tive; bald-headed; bandy-legged; benevolent; blind; blunt; bold; brazen; brokenhearted; captious; capricious; captivating; charming; chivalrous; clear-headed; comely; commanding; compassionate; conceivable; consoling; consumptive; contemplative; conventional; corpulent; courteous; critical; crotchety; cunning; cute; deformed; delicate; democratic; designing; devout; diabolic; diminutive; disagreeable; discontented; discriminating; domestic; distinguished; divine; double; dubious; easygoing; effeminate; eloquent; erect; eminent; entertaining; estimable; firm; excessive; exotic; fastidious; florid; flourishing; fortunate; frecklefaced; frivolous; garrulous; gentle; ghastly; ghostly; gracious; great; grotesque; grizzily; handicapped; hearty; hard-looking; heavenly; heavy; hook-nosed; humorous; hump-shouldered; ignoble; ignominious; illustrious; imaginary; immense; impeccable; impertinent; impious; inconsiderate; indecorous; indolent; industrious; inelegant; influential; informed; ingenious; inimitable; inquisitive; insignificant; insolvent; just· instructed; intelligent; joking; little; knowledged; laughing; legendary; loquacious; malevolent; malicious; massive; masterly; matching; matter-of-fact; meaner; meek; menacing; mild; milk-livered; mocking; modern; moody; morbid; morose; mortified; namby-pamby; nervous; neurotic; never-smiling; nondescript; normal; obedient; obnoxious; obstinate; obstreperous; obvious; occult; odious; officious; ogreish; ordinary; original; outlandish; outrageous; outwitted; zeal-filled; overbearing; overmastering; overt; overweening; pale; pampered; passable; perfect; perfidious; perjured; persevering; phantasmal; phenomenal; phlegmatic; prejudiced; presumptuous; private; prime; profane; proper; prosperous; pugnacious; punctilious; reckless; reflecting; regular; reputable; respectable; reticent; rude; sacred; scientific; sedate; self-effacing; self-indulging; selfish; selfless; sensitive; sentimental; skilled; slim; slippery; small; smiling; solid; sophisticated; stricken; striking; stuffy; stupid; sublime; substantial; superior; susceptible; talkative; sympathetic; thinking; tiresome; traitorous; unaccountable; unapproachable; unauthorized; uncongenial; uncouth; undesirable; unenterprising; unobtrusive; unpeaceable; unruly; useless; unskilled; unvalued; unwieldy; vindictive; unworthy; venerable; veracious; versatile; virtuous; volatile;

wall-eyed; well-disposed; well-dressed; well-informed; well-intentioned; willful; wild; wily; witty; wordy; worldly; worthy; outstanding; young; assertive; fictitious.

PERSONABLE
adverbs
altogether; charmingly; unusually; uncommonly; highly; remarkably; obviously; undeniably; delightfully; pleasahtly; definitely; emphatically; fortunately; admirably; irresistibly; singularly; particularly; completely.

PERSONAGE
adjectives
trusty; eminent; silent; respectable; shabby; grimy; despondent; bitter; pallid; muselike; prominent; venerable; radiant; expansive; leading; all-compelling; allegorical; luminous; historical; leathery; filmy; showy; complex; singular; tutelary; fictitious; arrogant; noble; pompous; exalted; illustrious; subsidiary; favorite; powerful; gnarled; cynical; romantic; miraculous; tragic; nude; stalwart; whimsical; honorable; formidable; poetical; important; tremendous; fine; comely; worthy; ruddy; royal; unimportant; distinguished; sordid; strange-looking; shadowy; august; sympathetic.

verbs
conceal—; esteem—; honor—; introduce—; uncover—; —attracts; —awes; —enhances; —fosters; —graces; —impresses; —inspires; —overwhelms; —thrills.
(See individual, person, character.)

PERSONAL
adverbs
intimately; pleasantly; graciously; undeniably; particularly; unusually; remarkably; highly; uncommonly; specifically; significantly; unpleasantly; definitely; emphatically; obviously; curiously; manifestly; evidently; cruelly; flatteringly; bitterly.

PERSONALITY
adjectives
vivid; perfect; tenuous; fascinating; self-determining; judicial; calumnious; melancholy; unreasonable; erratic; projected; winning; fictitious; operatic; strong; abounding; poetic; vital; charming; intuitive; forceful; robust; integrated; recognizable; eminent; endowed; imaginative; meditative; potent; intense; aggressive; unimpaired;

distinct; agreeable; austere; vigorous; delightful; sinister; conscious; dignified; courteous; general; amiable; unfettered; exciting; dual; sure-fire; predominating; dramatic; arresting; exquisite; variegated; inward; unlicensed; curious; intense; embarrassed; aloof; conspicuous; dominant; big; vibrant; dynamic; powerful; attractive; winning; glowing; composite; serene; underlying; ostensible; unique; thorough; childlike; miserable; wholesome; firm; definite; recurrent.

verbs
absorb in—; build—; destroy—; develop—; disintegrate—; distort—; divest of—; electrify—; enhance—; enrich—; evolve—; lack —; radiate—; relapse into—; shed—; stamp —; stimulate—; submerge—; veil—; vitalize—; warp—; —matures; —s merge; — splits.

(See character, individuality, ego.)

PERSONIFICATION
adjectives
restful; dumpy; shadowy; tremendous.

PERSONNEL
verbs
alter—; charge—with; criticize—; enhance —; increase—; limit—; reduce—; retain—; superintend—; supervise—; train—; —assists; —inspects; —manages; —merits; — strikes; —votes.

(See staff, employees.)

PERSPECTIVE
adjectives
theatrical; artificial; monotonous; accurate; wide; historical; brilliant; scornful; infinite; dim; calm; true; enchanting; celestial; vast; soft; permanent; clear; interminable; deep; remarkable; boundless; artistic.

verbs
adjust—; broaden—; check—; clarify—; contemplate—; depend on—; develop—; gain—; influence—; lack—; maintain—; narrow—; reduce—; —assumes; —astonishes; —clears; —differs; —matures; —warps.

(See outlook, view, position.)

PERSPICACIOUS
adverbs
unusually; keenly; shrewdly; uncommonly; highly; brilliantly; astutely; penetratingly; subtly; craftily; warily; cleverly; undeni-

ably; uncommonly; sharply; sagaciously; wisely; quietly; observantly; gravely; signally; amazingly; marvellously.

PERSPIRATION
adjectives
violent; perpetual; clammy; profuse; excessive; flabby; cold; healthy; copious; odorous.

verbs
bathe in—; check—; drench with—; effuse —; excrete—; exude—; induce—; promote —; —annoys; —beads; —breaks from; — dampens; —drains; —escapes; —filters; — flows; —glistens; —gushes; —oozes; — purges; —reeks; —saturates; —streams from; —trickles.

(See sweat.)

PERSPIRE (v)
adverbs
profusely; perpetually; clammily; excessively; copiously; odorously; disgustingly; nauseatingly.

(See sweat, discharge.)

PERSUADE (v)
adverbs
readily; ultimately; tactfully; forcibly; vigorously; firmly; unobstructively; eloquently; argumentatively; soothingly.

(See convince, induce, urge.)

PERSUASION
adjectives
different; forcible; vigorous; firm; fanciful; deep; kind; parental; instinctive; womanly; melancholy; powerful; unobstructive; eloquent; persistent; argumentative; intimate; undoubting; kindly; soothing; demagogic.

verbs
advocate—; exercise—; possess—; rely upon —; resort to—; yield to—; —baits; —bewitches; —convinces; —entices; —forces; — impresses; —influences; —overcomes; — overwhelms; —seduces; —tames; strive for —.

(See belief, influence.

PERSUASIVE
adverbs
smoothly; irresistibly; graciously; cordially; sternly; suavely; politely; overpoweringly; passionately; enthusiastically; ardently;

overwhelmingly; subtly; insinuatingly; ingratiatingly; imperceptibly; forcibly; violently; loudly; crassly; disagreeably; pleasantly; completely.

PERT
adverbs
saucily; prettily; roguishly; mischievously; brazenly; impudently; insufferably; suddenly; trickily; archly; wantonly; insolently; rudely; flippantly; frivolously; idly; boldly; amazingly; daringly; naughtily; glibly; smartly.

PERTINACITY
adjectives
savage; playful; relentless; unprecedented; unwavering.

PERTINENT
adverbs
opportunely; advantageously; gravely; curiously; significantly; admirably; commendably; undeniably; profitably; happily; remarkably; unexpectedly; strikingly; helpfully; serviceably; usefully; fortunately; harmoniously; critically.

PERTURB (*v*)
adverbs
irritably; mentally; habitually; mutually; emotionally; superficially; impatiently; pathetically.
(See excite, disturb, agitate.)

PERTURBATION
adjectives
irritable; curious; mental; observed; habitual; internal; planetary; mutual; past; lunar; evident.

verbs
bear—; cool—; endure—; experience—; ferment—; inflict—; provoke—; shake with —; smart under—; wince in—; writhe in —; —chafes; —chokes; —enrages; —infects; —inflames; —jolts; —shakes.
(See excitement, emotion, disturbance.)

PERTURBED
adverbs
naturally; slightly; deeply; inwardly; secretly; obviously; visibly; incomprehensibly; shockingly; inordinately; extremely; curiously; strangely; painfully; pathetically; gravely; seriously; helplessly; subtly; absurdly; momentarily; terribly.

PERUSAL
adjectives
candid; careful; calm; submissive; cool; studied.

PERUSE (*v*)
adverbs
studiously; exhaustively; intensely; candidly; calmly; coolly; professionally; determinedly; imaginatively; sympathetically.
(See read, scan.)

PERVADE (*v*)
adverbs
intimately; intensely; foully; insidiously; curiously; morbidly.
(See penetrate, pierce, affect.)

PERVASIVE
adverbs
strangely; utterly; offensively; unpleasantly; disagreeably; delightfully; agreeably; fragrantly; pleasantly; pungently; aromatically; alarmingly; dangerously; deliberately; ominously; suddenly; terribly; sweetly; nauseatingly; acridly.

PERVERSE
adverbs
obstinately; wilfully; stubbornly; intractably; ungovernably; sadly; dreadfully; doggedly; waywardly; wantonly; purposely; deliberately; captiously; capriciously; inexplicably; inscrutably; unexpectedly; uncommonly; malignantly; hatefully; spitefully; fearfully; irritatingly; vexatiously; viciously; mischievously; incorrigibly.

PERVERSION
adjectives
horrible; abominable; monstrous; palpable; sexual; wilful.

verbs
practise—; resort to—; uncover—; unravel —; —abuses; —blemishes; —corrupts; — decimates; —defiles; —distorts; —impairs; —infects; —misdirects; —misleads; — poisons; —warps; —weakens; —misinterprets.
(See abuse, obscenity, corruption.)

adjectives
elaborate; hidden; curious.

verbs
brave—; condemn—; endure—; inflict—upon; temper—; treat with—; yield to—; —aggrieves; —angers; —astonishes; —chafes; —checks; —inflames; —insults; —irks; —jars; —provokes; —resists.
(See obstinacy, stubbornness.)

PERVERT (*v*)

adverbs
odiously; horribly; abominably; monstrously; palpably; wilfully; sexually.
(See debase, falsify.)

PESSIMISM

adjectives
sour; melancholy; polite; morbid; counterbalancing.

verbs
balance—; droop in—; infuse—; propagate—; remedy—; ridicule—; shake off—; warrant—; wilt under—; yield to—; —crushes; —dampens; —dashes; —dejects; —depresses; —despairs; —disconcerts; —dishcartens; —preys upon; —prostrates; —reigns; —represses; —saddens; —shadows; —shrouds; —weighs upon; —withers.
(See hopelessness, cynicism.)

PESSIMIST

adjectives
confirmed; polite; genial; deliberate.

verbs
desolate—; doom—; paralyze—; —clouds; —doubts; —complains; —condemns; —cowers; —disconcerts; —disheartens; —flinches; —funks; —grumbles; —laments; —poisons; —quails; —shies; —suspects.

PESSIMISTIC

adverbs
incorrigibly; incurably; deliberately; apparently; stubbornly; obstinately; horribly; unaccountably; gloomily; moodily; mournfully; miserably; wretchedly; intolerably; disgustingly; woefully; pitiably; unreasonably; morbidly; superstitiously; absurdly; foolishly; ridiculously.

adjectives
domestic; vicious; uninvited; injurious; destructive; lifelong.

verbs
chastise—; eradicate—; extirpate—; —annoys; —inflicts; —molests; —nettles; —offends; —piques; —plagues; —preys upon; —racks; —rankles; —riles (colloq.); —ruffles; —scourges; —torments; —tries; —vexes.
(See nuisance, disease, plague, insect, parasite.)

PESTIFEROUS

adverbs
intentionally; purposely; cantankerously; deliberately; wantonly; persistently; continually; unbearably; meanly; maliciously; venomously; woefully; wretchedly; miserably; curiously; strangely; intolerably; disgustingly; capriciously; naggingly, mischievously; trickily; annoyingly; oddly; wilfully.

PESTILENCE

adjectives
buoyant; great; hateful; occasional; infidel; life-poisoning; spreading; instinctive; infectious; tropical; air-borne.

verbs
breed—; confine—to; ease—; free from—; remedy—; succumb to—; suffer—; survive—; —abuses; —affects; —aggrieves; —breaks out; —devastates; —endures; —oppresses; —outrages; —pains; —prostrates; rages; —ravages; —swamps; —tramples; —victimizes.
(See contagion, disease, plague.)

PET

verbs
caress—; cater to—; cherish—; court—; cradle—; cuddle—; embrace—; favor—; fondle—; hug—; indulge—; maul—; pamper—; patronize—; praise—; serve—; spoil —.
(See child, baby, kitten, puppy.)

PETALS

adjectives
beauteous; flaming; plumy; richly-tinted; smoldering; faded; rich; plucked-out; dusky; yielding; nipped; rained; gauzy; scriptured; drenched; drifting.

verbs

bag—; dry—; gather—; lacerate—; pluck —; press—; tear—; tint—; —adorn; —blanket; —cup; —drop; —open; —shower; —spread; —strew; —unfold; —wilt.

(See flower, plant, leaf.)

PETITION

adjectives

suitable; begging; respectful; vain; bare; urgent; signed; lengthy; eloquent; specific; unanswered; discarded.

verbs

address—; deny—; enter—; evoke—; file —; press—; repeat—; resort to—; seek in —; solicit—; —appeals to; —s beset; —demands; —pleads; —protests; —supplicates.

(See appeal, application, entreaty.)

PETITION (v)

adverbs

fruitlessly; legally; urgently; lengthily; eloquently; specifically; vainly; slavishly; humbly.

(See entreat, pray.)

PETTICOAT

adjectives

balloon; kilted; elegant; lace-trimmed; braided; ankle-length; old-fashioned; billowy.

PETTINESS

adjectives

ironical; quaint; usual; needless.

PETTISH

adverbs

fretfully; peevishly; annoyingly; nervously; feverishly; childishly; jealously; impossibly; unbearably; intolerably; persistently; miserably; curiously; unwontedly; uncommonly; extremely; dreadfully; absurdly; impishly; wretchedly; forlornly.

PETTY

adverbs

frivolously; meanly; insignificantly; ridiculously; contemptibly; miserably; absurdly; childishly; pitiably; curiously; singularly; particularly; extraordinarily; extremely; terribly.

PETULANCE

adjectives

charming; impatient; cowardly; pathetic; habitual; lasting; proud; angry; pouting; becoming.

PETULANT

adverbs

unusually; abnormally; feverishly; nervously; hysterically; fretfully; wantonly; mischievously; crossly; captiously; habitually; naturally; strangely; oddly; intolerably; inexcusably; curiously; incorrigibly; disagreeably; unpleasantly; obnoxiously; hatefully; wistfully; whiningly.

PEW

adjectives

high-backed; respectable; dusty; uncomfortable; crowded; unused.

verbs

allocate—s; array in—s; commit to—; cram —; cushion—; direct to—; enter—; fill—; kneel in—; occupy—; perch in—; rent—; reserve—; scan from—.

(See place, seat, bench, compartment.)

PHALANX

adjectives

martial; invincible; cunning.

PHANTASIES

adjectives

guilty; childish; unconscious; elaborate; horrid; weird; distempered.

PHANTASY

verbs

coin—; concede—; conjure up—; devise—; dream—; efface—; excogitate—; fabricate —; improvise—; invent—; picture—; strike —; suggest—; —crumbles; —delights; —deludes; —dissolves; —fades; —floats; —passes.

(See picture, vision, image, illusion, delusion.)

PHANTOM

adjectives

sceptered; lurid; ghostly; formless; dismal; ugly; transparent; horrible; ignoble; glorious; charming; terrible; impudent; holy; melancholy; faithless; summer; granite;

pale; fair; cloudy; colossal; secular; recurring; august; prodigious; pleasurable; deceitful; monstrous; solemn; benignant; dark; simulated; majestic; midnight.

verbs
banish—; devise—; ogle at—; observe—; picture—; spy—; stare at—; —appears; —departs; —dissolves; —evaporates; —fades; —glares; —leers; —looms; —melts away; —passes; —retires; —vanishes.
(See apparition, ghost, vision.)

PHASE
adjectives
various (pl); intimate; personal; extreme; pioneering; ethical; sectional; curious; transitional; manifold (pl); subtle; intermediate; dramatic; conciliating; increasing; unavoidable; varying; unknown; disinterested; ever-changing; important, precise; enthusiastic; nascent; indispensable; interesting; vehement; exceptional; strenuous; submerged; characteristic; delicate; dreadful; periodic; gibbous; special; renewed; pathetic; romantic; significant; peculiar; diversified (pl).

verbs
alter—; assume—; discover—; enjoy—; explore—; exhibit—; form—; interpret—; investigate—; labor through—; master—; pry into—; recognize—; restore—; shape—; undo—; view—; —determines; —melts; —passes; —shifts.
(See condition, state, aspect.)

PHEASANT
verbs
domesticate—; flush—; hunt—; —beats; —bellows; —bills; —challenges; —crows; —feigns; —flutters; —glides; —haunts; —jerks; —pants; —roves; —rumbles; —rustles; —scratches; —steals; —struts; —thumps; —thunders; —whirs.
(See fowl, bird.)

PHENOMENA
adjectives
singular; neutral; visible; manifold; historical; sensible; mental; moral; capricious; multitudinous; brilliant; hypnotic; naked; ordinary; sundry; chromatic; scientific; degrading; spiritualistic; subjective; perplexing; interesting; bowling; entrancing; phonetic; characteristic; absurd; hopeful; remote; impressive; extraordinary; sublime;

universal; curious; ambiguous; social; linguistic; transitory; remarkable; unprecedented; striking; continuing; nervous; natural; capital; disturbing; electrical; kindred; unrelated; sporadic; physical; rare; volcanic; analogous; ingenious; mysterious; poetical; psychic; ghastly; monstrous; psychasthenic; expressional.

PHENOMENAL
adverbs
amazingly; incredibly; strangely; oddly; unbelievably; curiously; particularly; extremely; extraordinarily; abnormally; inexplicably; surprisingly; indubitably; matchlessly; superhumanly; superbly; extravagantly; fantastically; grotesquely; magnificently; splendidly; brilliantly; unutterably; indescribably; mysteriously; strikingly.

PHENOMENON
verbs
account for—; adduce—; aggravate—; belittle—; clarify—; elucidate—; exhibit—; explain—; exploit—; marvel at—; observe —; study—; stumble upon—; uncover—; view—; witness—; —amazes; —deludes; —excites; —indicates; —interests; —proves.
(See sight, miracle, fact, event.)

PHILANTHROPIC
adverbs
nobly; ostentatiously; sincerely; generously; admirably; commendably; unusually; notably; admittedly; consistently; dependably; lavishly; cordially; graciously; benignantly; magnanimously; broadmindedly; charitably; amiably; considerately; bounteously; altruistically; naturally; genuinely.

PHILANTHROPIST
adjectives
pretended; distinguished; irresponsible; long-headed; misguided; sundry (pl); disinterested; paralytic; generous; sanguine; supposed.

PHILOSOPHER
adjectives
pragmatic; classical; political; contemporary; quietistic; talkative; pompous; mystic; awe-stricken; physical; amiable; sourgrape; constitutional; disputative; logical; advanced; grave· weary; deistic; famous; dramatic.

verbs
comprehend—; dispute—; —applies; —asserts; —assists; —concludes; —contemplates; —dreams; —guides; —idealizes; —instructs; —observes; —perceives; —perfects; —proves; —records; —regulates; —restores; —searches; —speculates; —studies; —transcends.

(See idealist, naturalist, scientist.)

PHILOSOPHICAL
adverbs
distinctly; notably; comfortably; consistently; brilliantly; wisely; soundly; serenely; imperturbably; calmly; quietly; sagaciously; comfortingly; gravely; temperately; coolly; thoughtfully; placidly; composedly; tranquilly; deeply; profoundly; intelligently; conspicuously; extraordinarily; consummately.

PHILOSOPHIZE (v)
adverbs
sardonically; eloquently; sagely; politically; pompously; mystically; amiably; logically; gravely; ironically; fatalistically.

(See reason, predict.)

PHILOSOPHY
adjectives
inadequate; high; unruffled; healthful; stoical; occult; organized; clammy; comfortable; false; satisfactory; prudential; flippant; half-sportive; shameless; characteristic; educational; primitive; economic; synthetic; seductive; active; natural; fashionable; mental; terrible; positive; classical; calm; fruitful; natural; unoriginal; eclectic; speculative; fatalistic; cruel; worldly; mature; rude; democratic; sustaining; close-webbed; subtle; unprincipled; ruthless; flexible; pessimistic; reminiscent; archaic; seeming; mystical; stern; cynical; droll; lenient; enlightened; ancient; ultra-radical; social; growing; scholastic; coherent; ethnic; haughty; specious; obtrusive; self-centered; intellectual; authentic.

verbs
air—; bespeak—; condemn—; cultivate—; dismiss—; dispense—; dress out—; elaborate—; embody—; emit—; enshrine—; epitomize—; evolve—; execute—; exemplify—; expound—; formulate—; frame—; imbue with—; indulge in—; oppose—; outline—; postulate—; quote—; rear on—; set forth—; shape—; share—; sift—; sum up—; voice —; —consoles; —edifies; —pervades.

(See ethics, modernism, psychology, knowledge, wisdom, thought.)

PHLEGMATIC
adverbs
apathetically; dully; temperamentally; naturally; habitually; constantly; irritatingly; impossibly; vexatiously; incredibly; strangely; curiously; racially; maddeningly; oddly; imperturbably; indifferently; stoically; impassively; heavily; coldly; callously; hopelessly; incurably; dreadfully; inexplicably; stolidly; stupidly.

PHOSPHORESCENT
adverbs
mysteriously; brilliantly; strangely; curiously; frightfully; unexpectedly; terrifyingly; iridescently; magically; conveniently; advantageously; alarmingly; weirdly; fantastically; grotesquely; evanescently; serviceably; magnificently; splendidly; luridly; glowingly; amazingly.

PHOTOGRAPH
adjectives
existing; cherished; superb; appropriate; candid; telescopic; luxurious; insouciant; instantaneous; mammoth; irrelevant; dramatic; large; clear; intimate; vivid; gripping; rare; distinctive; beautiful; portrait; brilliant; enlarged.

verbs
blur—; enlarge—; exhibit—; expose—; frame—; illustrate with—; pose for—; request—; shade—; shadow—; snap—; superimpose on—; tint—; —adorns; —catches; —depicts; —fades; —flatters; —lies; —pleases; —reflects.

(See illustration, masterpiece, picture, sketch, portrait.)

PHOTOGRAPHER
adjectives
straggling; traveling; famous.

verbs
patronize—; shield from—; train—; —arranges; —s cluster about; —decorates; —drapes; —endeavors; —exposes; —focuses; —operates; —practises; —rejects; —selects; —shades; —shadows; —snaps; —solicits; —tints; —views.

(See artist.)

882

PHOTOGRAPHY

adjectives
professional; instantaneous; distinguished.

verbs
apply—; dabble in—; practise—; study—; utilize in—; —advances; —aids; —attracts; —awes; —captures; —impresses; —improves; —prints; —progresses.
(See science, art.)

PHOTOPLAY

adjectives
swift-moving; hilarious; serious.

PHRASE

adjectives
witty; explicit; ill; fantastic; tragic; poisonous; pompous; exclamatory; characteristic; vivid; musical; impressive; commanding; scriptural; glib; expressive; striking; occult; holiday; pedantic; appropriate; subtle; historic; cold; ringing; invariable; redoubled; banal; polished; recondite; learned; idiomatic; canting; studied; varying (pl); euphemistic; penetrative; useful; circuitous; handled; labored; judicial; modern; specific; introductory; depressed; hackneyed; catchy; authority-bearing; indispensable; superfluous; euphonious; overworked; courtly; sharp; isolated; sonorous; ingenious; allusive; convenient; homely; stereotyped; adulating; incoherent; perfect; sarcastic; technical; detached; silvery; obnoxious; ecstatic; metaphysical; vivid; familiar; poetic; poignant; grandiloquent; rabbinical; audacious; honeyed; theological; trivial; celebrated; sacred; pensive; plaintive; prolegomenous; empty; well-worn; suspicious; fanciful; eloquent; vibrant; comfortable; pungent; parliamentary; painful; vague; choice; polite; editorial; vile; swinish; ejaculatory; charming; dark; terrible; painted; inapplicable; high-sounding.

verbs
cling to—; create—; cull—; echo—; employ —; enunciate—; mouth—; omit—; pelt with —s; quibble over—; stumble over—; toss —s at; —enchants; —escapes; —falls upon; —haunts; —intrigues; —illustrates; —originates in; —scalds; —signifies; —springs from.
(See epithet, idiom, metaphor, idea, thought.)

PHRASE (v)

adverbs
subtly; concretely; colloquially; tersely; poetically; redundantly; explicitly; fantastically; vividly; scripturally; glibly; appropriately; euphemistically; ingeniously; obnoxiously; technically; fancifully; pungently; editorially.
(See style, express.)

PHRASEOLOGY

adjectives
accustomed; unhappy; diabolical; realistic; ordinary; commonplace.

PHRASING

adjectives
odd; Ciceronian; intelligent.

PHYSICIAN

adjectives
reluctant; renowned, departing; conscientious; competent; helpful; sagacious; incredulous; understanding; distinguished; eminent; respectable; tolerable; observant; overzealous; consecrated; conservative.

verbs
assist—; communicate with—; confer with —; confound—; consult—; inform—; —administers; —counsels; —decrees; —devotes to; —diagnoses; —examines; —guards; —prescribes; —pronounces; —recommends; —rules; —serves; —warns.
(See teacher, nurse, doctor.)

PHYSIOGNOMY

adjectives
unequivocal; faded; capacious.

PHYSIQUE

adjectives
infinitesimal; ungraceful; delicate; insignificant.

verbs
admire—; approve—; cramp—; endanger —; enfeeble—; esteem—; harden—; improve—; mold—; praise—; reduce—; strain —; strengthen—; vivify—; —deteriorates; —sustains; —toughens.
(See constitution, body.)

PIANIST

adjectives
phenomenal; admirable; fascinating; sleepy.

adjectives

grimy; little; tinkling; mechanical; grand; untuned; hideous.

verbs

attune to—; bang on—; beat—; caress—; finger—; instruct on—; perform on—; pound—; practice on—; scale—; strike—; strum on—; —deafens; —distracts; —enchants; —expresses; —peals; —rends; —resounds; —tinkles

(See keyboard, harp, music, banjo.)

PIAZZA

verbs

commit to—; enjoy—; festoon—; meet on —; overhang—; paint—; repose on—; rest on—; retire to—; screen—; shade—; —attracts; —cools; —delights; —refreshes; — spreads.

(See pavilion, porch, courtyard.)

PICK

verbs

brandish—; drive—; dull—; implant—; inject—; plunge—; ram in—; twist—; wield —; —chips; —chops; —cleaves; —cracks; —disperses; —eliminates; —gashes; — hacks; —loosens; —minces; —pierces; — rips; —severs; —shatters; —splinters; — slits; —strikes; —sunders; —uproots; — wrenches.

(See hatchet, axe, knife, tool.)

PICK (v)

adverbs

hastily; painfully; captiously; contentiously; aimlessly; obediently; precariously; laboriously; cautiously; mercifully; argumentatively; democratically; shrewdly.

(See select, choose.)

PICNIC

adjectives

perpetual; prolonged; never-ending; impromptu.

PICTORIAL

adverbs

conveniently; serviceably; highly; beautifully; advantageously; profitably; usefully; altogether; intelligibly; graphically; effective-ly; entertainingly; amusingly; accurately; appropriately; suitably.

PICTURE

adjectives

naturalistic; consistent; coordinated; exaggerated; kaleidoscopic; flaming; ineloquent; amorous; portrait; furry; spectacular; muscular; alert; surreptitious; delicate; dazzling; smiling; luminescent; casual; gay; authentic; elucidating; heavenly; amusing; handsome; paltry; striking; charming; improbable; tender; colored; ineffectual; vivid; conventional; scandalous; arresting; constant; wide; unchanged; forbidding; fascinating; living; veracious; touching; poetic; idyllic; affecting; ensemble; monotonous; pathetic; sacred; classical; religious; unrelated; tragic; philanthropic; dramatic; imaginary; lifeless; vitalized; tone; far-spreading; intimate; varied; dreary; unattractive; entrancing; ludicrous; truthful; well-painted; jumbled; provocative; lurid; moderate; radiant; dumb; black; horrible; finished; idealized; breathing; accurate; lively; grim; etched; mental; deplorable; incomparable; fresh; gilt; moving; notable; comprehensive; imposing; ghastly; emblematic; melancholy; crimson; degrading; allegorical; verbal; coherent; lovely; world-famous; unusual; illuminating; creamy; colorful; outstanding; nature; marvelous; remarkable; alluring; suggestive; candid; contemporaneous; immortal; gloomy; delightful; fleeting; cloud; inimitable; priceless; resplendent; bright; stark; impressive; retinal; choice; instantaneous; incredible; unique; interesting; distinct; decorative; imaginary; blurred; depressing; rhetorical; crude; symmetrical; bewitching; hideous; commercial; glowing; realistic; ghostly; unforgettable; fantastic; penitentiary; composite; dreamy.

verbs

animate—; ban—; blur—; cherish—; clarify —; complicate—; conjure up—; convey—to; delineate—; digest—; distort—; dominate —; embellish—; evoke—; execute—; exhibit—; fade from—; fashion—; harmonize with—; intersperse with—s; mar—; obliterate—; relish—; reproduce—; shade—; shadow—; transmute—; —contrasts with; —depicts; —materializes; —reveals; —revolves around; —unfolds; focus upon—.

(See image, impression, film, canvas, illustration, masterpiece, drawing.)

PICTURE (v)

adverbs

vividly; authentically; artistically; brilliantly; faithfully; eloquently; effectually; scandalously; speculatively; fatalistically; ruthlessly; mystically; cynically; speciously; intellectually.

(See draw, sketch.)

PICTURESQUE

adverbs

highly; uncommonly; magnificently; splendidly; undeniably; wildly; unusually; brilliantly; delightfully; grotesquely; fancifully; fantastically; stupendously; immensely; graphically; singularly; uniquely; oddly; gorgeously; superbly; imposingly; resplendently; sublimely; incomparably; unsurpassably; indescribably; unutterably.

PICTURESQUENESS

adjectives

elaborate; undeniable; vivid; superficial; startling; professional; sublime.

PICTURING

adjectives

dreamy; historical; sumptuous.

PIDDLING

adverbs

absurdly; trivially; vexatiously; idly; foolishly; insignificantly; inconsequentially; horribly; senselessly; stupidly; childishly; preposterously; nonsensically; wastefully; inexcusably; witlessly; ineptly.

PIE

adjectives

silken; leathery-looking; delicious; half-demolished; chattering; browned; fresh; tasty; luscious; steaming.

PIECES

adjectives

inanimate; charming; accessory; exhibitionistic; historical; isolated; perilous; truncated; distinctive; lush; suitable; fugitive; exquisite; impressive; singular; eloquent; dangerous; pendent; crooked; inferior; nimble; complicated; bizarre; honest; vivid; unexpected; ponderous; majestic; solemn; sordid; three-piled; imposing; curious; scientific; adventurous; shaped; bold; atrocious; complex; florid; pathetic; obvious; priceless; detached; merited; miscellaneous; miscreant; neglected; striking; conspicuous;

abject; ignoble; deplorable; dilated; volatile; visionary; popular; choral; fruitful; prodigious; gorgeous; wanton; instrumental; floral; character; infernal; sour; heavy-looking; grease-enveloped; first-rate; mere; abominable; delicate; dominating.

verbs

aggregate—; amass—; batter to—; cement —; clutch—; crack into—; crumble into—; crush to—; disintegrate into—; gather—; integrate—; mold—; portion—; smash to—; split into—; unite—; —constitute; —crash; —scatter.

(See chip, fragment.)

PIER

adjectives

elaborate; compound; tropical; much-used.

verbs

anchor at—; buffet—; construct at—; dock at—; destroy—; enclose—; land at—, lash to—; miss—; moor to—; nuzzle into—; offer —; pound—; reserve—; spray—; wash away—; —extends; —projects; —protects; —stretches.

(See landing.)

PIERCE (v)

adverbs

effectually; fatally; mortally; accurately; deeply; ruthlessly; ferociously.

(See stab, bore.)

PIERCING

adverbs

sharply; keenly; acutely; discerningly; accusingly; unpleasantly; disagreeably; unwontedly; incomparably; significantly; suddenly; painfully; uncomfortably; deliberately; astutely; craftily; cunningly; sagaciously; subtly; inescapably.

PIETY

adjectives

deadened; intense; ingrained; filial; quaint; strait; fervent; practical; scrupulous; unaffected; idiotic; humble; punctual; consistent; tempered; intentional; parenthetical; systematic; individual; infant; celestial; instructed.

verbs

commend—; display—; exhibit—; favor—; feign—; influence—; instil—; laud—; practise—; prefer—; pretend—; protest—; re-

semble—; respect—; revere—; —cheers; —
converts; —excels; —inspires; —shields.
　(See holiness, patriotism, sanctity, kindness, virtue.)

PIG

adjectives

gaping; fastidious; enormous; impious;
cadaverous; good-natured; kicking.

verbs

auction—; exhibit—; fatten—; graze—;
market—; pen—; slaughter—; stable—;
tend—; trough—; —gobbles up; —grunts;
—hobbles out; —snorts; —squeals; —
stumbles; —swarms; —wallows.
　(See hog, cattle, cow, ox.)

PIGEON

adjectives

nimble; plumaged; monogamous; carrier;
useful; homing; well-trained.

verbs

drive—s; capture—; market—s; net—s;
tame—s; —broods; —consumes; —coos; —s
darken; —darts; —s flock; —flushes; —
flutters; —gluts; —incubates; —nestles; —
strays.
　(See bird.)

PIGGISH

adverbs

horribly; brazenly; crassly; grossly; openly;
sadly; unashamedly; greedily; rapaciously;
voraciously; noisily; terribly; unbelievably;
boldly; hoydenishly; brutally; gluttonously;
insatiably; selfishly; naturally; inherently;
incorrigibly; inexpressibly; definitely.

PIG-HEADED

adverbs

immovably; stupidly; resolutely; implacably; obdurately; stolidly; incurably; inherently; naturally; temperamentally; obstinately; steadily; inexorably; senselessly; unreasonably; distinctly; unmistakably; cruelly; foolishly; absurdly; inanely; pertinaciously; contumaciously; truculently; offensively.

PIGMENT

adjectives

brilliant; bright; waterproof.

verbs

apply—; approve—; combine—; deposit—;
employ—; infuse—; insert—; mix—with;
secrete—; —blends; —colors; —constitutes;
—enhances; —harmonizes; —imbues; —
tinges; —tints.
　(See paint, color.)

PILE

adjectives

smoldering; vast; honest; unaffected; scholarly; dignified; heterogeneous; monumental; towering; amorphous; sumptuous; colossal; rambling; immense; enormous; unintelligent; gigantic; blazing; aspiring;
proud; gothic; voluptuous; chaotic; sunny;
frothy; venerable; gloomy; wretched.

verbs

accumulate—; amass—; disperse—; erect—;
heap—; knock down—; level—; mow down
—; squash—; rummage through—; scatter
—; spread—; strew—; upset—; —topples;
—totters; —towers; —tumbles; —wanes.
　(See heap, fortune, money.)

PILE (v)

adverbs

methodically; indiscriminately; commercially; toweringly; heterogeneously; monumentally.
　(See heap, accumulate.)

PILGRIM

adjectives

travel-weary; true-devoted; humble; adoring; devout; earnest; forlorn; fanatical;
passionate; disconsolate; white-robed; ambulant.

PILGRIMAGE

adjectives

perilous; nightly; sentimental; mocking; annual; holy; poetical; earthly; reverential;
earned; pious; connubial; stormy; unwilling; long-promised; useless; macabre;
angry; weary; zealous; previous; peaceful;
inspiring; maiden; amorous; enforced.

PILL

adjectives

gilded; bitter; curative; magic.

PILLAR

adjectives

lasting; well-deserving; fiery; shrinking;
fluted; rocky; cloudy; towering; immovable;

crossed; crowded; decapitated; beauteous; fantastic; shining; vine-clad; unconscious; tottering; petrified; glistening; massive; lone; huge; gigantic; lofty.

PILLORY

verbs
condemn—; deserve—; expose on—; sentence to—; undergo—; whip on—; writhe on—; —agonizes; —disciplines; —enrages; —frightens; —inflicts; —pains; —rebukes; —threatens; —tortures.
(See punishment, torture.)

PILLOW

adjectives
pretty; fringed; skimpy; seaweed; hard; deaf; feverous; unsolaced; dream-haunted; coal; nut-brown; sleepless; downy; humble; tossed; lacy; comforting; nightmared.

verbs
bury in—; grovel in—; heave—; knead—; mash—; prop up with—s; raise on—s; rearrange—; recline on—; relax on—; repose on—; sink into—; support on—; tarry on—; —comforts; —embeds; —envelops; —hushes; —lulls; —supports; —yields.
(See mattress, bed, cushion.)

PILOT

adjectives
desperate; sagacious; visiting; sublime; competent; wartime; licensed; lightning; skilled.

verbs
—communicates with; —conducts; —governs; —guides; —manages; —navigates; —occupies; —prescribes; —regulates; —sounds; —steers; —weathers.
(See guide, helm.)

PILOT (*v*)

adverbs
daringly; courageously; intrepidly; gallantly; desperately; sagaciously; competently.
(See direct, guide, steer.)

PIMPLES

verbs
break into—; dot with—; eradicate—; pinch —; salve—; squeeze—; treat—; —blotch; —bunch; —deface; —disfigure; —embarrass; —emboss; —mar; —speckle; —spread; —sprout; —swell; —undermine.
(See blemish.)

PIN

verbs
affix with—; attach with—; bristle with—s; jab with—; join with—; load with—s; locate—; mark with—; plant—; secure with —; tuck in with—; —barbs; —connects; —encloses; —fastens; —lodges; —penetrates; —pricks; —scratches; —stabs; —unites.
(See bolt, hook, horn, needle, nail.)

PIN (*v*)

adverbs
securely; tidily; firmly; mercilessly; relentlessly.
(See fasten, fix.)

PINCH

adjectives
emphatic; warning; relishing; gentlemanly; record; consecutive (pl); imperial; hurting.

PINCH (*v*)

adverbs
approvingly; emphatically; warningly; playfully; facetiously; cruelly; spitefully; coyly.
(See squeeze, oppress.)

PINCHED

adverbs
miserably; wretchedly; shamefully; woefully; pitiably; pitifully; sadly; haggardly; gauntly; embarrassingly; terribly; helplessly; unusually; unbelievably.

PINE

adjectives
tossing; pillared; mountain; unpolished; longing; runty; serried; lofty; scrubby; gnarled; wind-swept; odorous; immortal; venerable; swaying; gloomy; scattered; palpitating; vocal; dark; unwavering; parasol; scathed; legendary; rocking; storm-battered; pitchy; quick-growing; fragrant; passionless; blackening; glimmering; glutinous.

verbs
hew—; house under—s; —arches; —exudes; —fans; —graces; —moans; —overspreads; —purrs; —rises; —shadows; —shelters; —sighs; —sings; —tips; —tosses; —towers; —waves; —nods.
(See tree.)

PINE (*v*)

adverbs
miserably; secretly; homelessly; incessantly;

ceaselessly; tragically; woefully; morbidly.
(See long, yearn.)

PINING
adjectives
endless; homeless; heartfelt; secret; lonely.

PINION
adjectives
regal; outworn; borrowed; stooping; joyful; daring; downy; soft-tinted; lightning-braided; fearless; delighted; dusky; trembling; celestial; unimpeded; swanlike; silver; timorous; exultant.

PINK
adjectives
pearl; silver; sparkling; shell; salmon; rose; orchid; delicate; frothy; arresting; translucent; soft; raspberry; light; chalk; lavender; childish; gaudy; pathetic.

PINNACLE
adjectives
far-shadowing; massive; queer; eccentric; silent; lofty; lonely; snow-girt; mountainous; skyey.

verbs
achieve—; adorn—; ascend to—; attain—; descend from—; reach—; set on—; —caps; —crowns; —culminates; —juts; —ornaments; —projects; —rises; —supports; —terminates; —tops; —towers
(See tower, height, zenith, summit, peak, spire.)

PIONEER
adjectives
laboring; primal; rugged; celebrated; veritable; hardy; courageous; daring; undaunted; adventurous; venturous.

verbs
accoutre—; arm—; hark back to—; immortalize—; inure—; ridicule—; —blazes; —braves; —confronts; —conquers; —dares; —endures; —envisions; —equips; —faces; —foresees; —plods; —primes; —rigs.
(See colonist, explorer.)

PIONEER (v)
adverbs
daringly; loyally; laboriously; courageously; undauntedly; intrepidly; vainly; ruggedly; boisterously.
(See brave, defy, dare.)

PIOUS
adverbs
painfully; primly; sedately; priggishly; disgustingly; hypocritically; sincerely; truly; reverently; pharisaically; self-righteously; ostentatiously; suddenly; conveniently; judiciously; astutely; honestly; pretentiously; apparently; manifestly; evidently; strangely; unwontedly; habitually; temperamentally; keenly; remarkably; notably; distinctly; meekly; ardently; fervently; humbly; intensely.

PIPE
(conduit, etc.)
verbs
attach—; block—; clog—; couple—; explore—; flow through—; insert—; join—; lay—; pass through—; pour into—; stream through—; weld—; —bursts; —carries off; —connects; —conveys; —discharges; —emits; —expands; —freezes.
(See hose, conduit, nozzle, duct, drain.)

PIPE
(general)
adjectives
light; short-stemmed; precious; fragrant; rustic; peace; malodorous; masculine-looking; amber; mellow; rich; ripe; giant; fluted; accursed; golden; affluent; seductive; earthen; pastoral; generous; lascivious; faithful; gleeful; smoke-blackened; organ; wide-stopped; foul.

PIPE
(smoking)
verbs
addicted to—; clean—; crust—; draw on—; enjoy—; mislay—; mouth—; pack—; pocket —; scrape—; stuff—; suck on—; —cakes; —cheers; —eases; —fumes; —glows; —mellows; —solaces; —soothes.
(See tobacco, cigar, cigarette.)

PIPING
adjectives
mellow; sad; loud; mild; harmonious; sweet.

adjectives

peculiar; quaint; subtle; original; charming; becoming.

PIQUANT

adverbs

saucily; tartly; racily; gaily; charmingly; delightfully; amazingly; highly; entertainingly; interestingly; sharply; pointedly; amusingly; uncommonly; fascinatingly; vigorously; incisively; impressively; pithily; curiously; smartly; distinctly; arrestingly; catchily.

PIQUE

adjectives

momentary; private; definite; petty; pouting.

verbs

—abashes; —aggravates; —crushes; —disgraces; —enrages; —humbles; —humiliates; —irks; —irritates; —mortifies; —provokes; —rankles; —riles(colloq.); —ruffles; —stirs; —strikes; —treads; —vexes; —wounds.
(See anger.)

PIRACY

adjectives

governmental; undiscovered; intellectual; organized.

PIRATE(v)

adverbs

ruthlessly; mercilessly; ferociously; dangerously; notoriously; openly.
(See rob, steal, plunder.)

PIRATES

adjectives

ruthless; smiling; merciless; benevolent; ferocious; uncouth; notable; sanctimonious; wrangling; gallant; notorious; bloody; modern.

verbs

execute—; punish—; resist—; —capture; —chase; —conceal; —confiscate; —cruise; —dare; —despoil; —hang; —murder; —pillage; —ply; —plunder; —rove; —scour; —scuttle; —smuggle; —torture; —venture; —violate.
(See robber, criminal, highwayman.)

verbs

arm with—; brandish—; click—; fear—; flourish—; impound—; load—; snatch—; —cracks; —discharges; —frightens; —kills; —pops; —reports; —rings out; —scares; —sounds; —spits fire; —threatens; —volleys; —wounds.
(See gun, machine-gun, musket.)

PIT

adjectives

fiery; bottomless; infernal; ghastly; fathomless; charnel; abysmal; enchanting; round; stupendous; blazing; murky; sepulchral.

verbs

bore—; burrow—; delve into—; drill—; excavate—; explore—; hollow out—; mine from—; pitch into—; plug—; plunge into—; scoop—; seal ; sound—; —gapes; —traps; —undermines; —yields.
(See hole, opening.)

PITCH

adjectives

extreme; creative; alarming; sharp; overstrained; heightened; uncommon; dolorous; breezy; seething; extraordinary; ruinous; varied; nervous.

PITCH(v)

adverbs

drunkenly; plaintively; alarmingly; seethingly; nervously; craftily; professionally: unruffledly; prodigiously; rashly.
(See hurl, toss, throw.)

PITCHER
(baseball)

adjectives

all-time; great; clever; smooth; easy-working; jerky; wary; unruffled; valuable; undependable; wild; nerveless; crafty.

verbs

bench—; relieve—; —balks; —blazes; —hurls; —nips; —retires; —strikes; —tightens; —toes the slab; —whips; —winds up; —zips; —burns; —controls; —delivers; —fans.
(See player, athlete, fielder.)

PITCHER
(crockery)

adjectives

emptied; handleless; capacious.

adverbs

unhappily; distressingly; woefully; grievously; remarkably; uncommonly; disturbingly; undeniably; unusually; indescribably; singularly; extraordinarily; exceedingly.

verbs

avoid—; beset with—; chase into—; conceal—; encounter—; inveigle into—; lure into—; perceive—; perish in—; rescue from—; save from—; suspect—; tumble into—; warn of—; —captures; —ensnares; —overpowers; —surprises; —traps; cover —.

(See ambush, trap, pit.)

adverbs

pungently; drily; drolly; remarkably; smartly; absurdly; amusingly; cleverly; wonderfully; amusingly; trenchantly; paradoxically; scintillatingly; brilliantly; wittily; facetiously; curtly; quaintly; humorously; expressively; inimitably; incomparably; succintly.

adverbs

shockingly; terribly; definitely; deplorably; grievously; miserably; deservingly; truly; intensely; unspeakably; immeasurably; singularly; especially; particularly; peculiarly; unusually.

adverbs

gently; comfortingly; mildly; wisely; intelligently; sympathetically; helpfully; compassionately; sweetly; indulgently; tolerantly; mercifully; leniently; immensely; unusually; humanely.

adverbs

coldly; cruelly; sternly; implacably; unappeasably; stoically; bitterly; immovably; terribly; horribly; unbelievably; callously; stubbornly; apathetically; mercilessly; inexorably; woefully; ruthlessly; inexcusably; incalculably; incredibly; inexplicably; unaccountably; dreadfully.

adjectives

slender; remaining; contemptible; meager; trifling; bare; worthless; welcome.

verbs

acquire—; allot—; allow—; beg—; derive—; dole out—; donate—; drain—; draw—; exist on—; live on—; provide—; solicit—; yield—; —contents; —suffices.
(See wages, earnings, money, dole.)

adjectives

anxious; wondering; contemptuous; melancholy; inexpressible; faded; divine; fluttering; sacred; supplicating; confident; thrilling; scornful; indulgent; misapplied; self-forgiving; infant; ineffable; inner; painful; grave; double; treble; strenuous; unsuspected; tender; infinite; shocked; subtle; languid; affectionate; unutterable; pathetic; immense; foolish; solemn; unfortunate; respectful; anguished; unspeakable; reverent; vanquished; little; careless; continued; skinless; natural; human; divine; profound; angelic; malignant; amazed; indignant; spurious; unrighteous.

verbs

betray—; claim—; eye with—; feign—; implore—of; persecute without—; regard with —; shadow with—; stir to—; submerge in —; waste—on; wrap in—; yield to—; —dries up; —expires; —grips; —moves; —smites; —touches; —tortures.
(See compassion, mercy.)

adverbs

genially; politely; urbanely; genteely; unexpectedly; impressively; fortunately; luckily; pleasantly; surprisingly; tolerantly; mercifully; blandly; indulgently; reasonably; moderately; thoughtfully.

adjectives

vile; scurrilous; screaming.

verbs

affix—; circulate —s; diffuse —s; disperse —s; display on—; disseminate —s; emblazon with—s; post—; publish—s; set up—; —advertises; —announces; —attracts; —broaches; —heralds; —propagates; —screams; —tempts.

(See announcement, advertisement, notice.)

PLACE

adjectives

friendly; delightful; homelike; ideal; comfortable; mournful; war-torn; shrineless; prosperous; logical; halting; unsanctified; tenable; rough; important; joyous; pathless; contrary; prominent; incompatible; rival; lonely; bearable; distinctive; important; dormant; well-chosen; unwholesome; strange; lofty; perilous; objectionable; vulnerable; conspicuous; exalted; native; dwelling; outraged; burial; odd; gloomy; strategic; alleged; ruinous; nestling; shocking; enviable; supreme; sheltered; estimable; noisome; jubilant; wonted; blithe; permanent; wonderful; armed; mossy; foremost; straggling; appointed; seething; knotty; extensive; ancestral; ultimate; floral; popular; accustomed; nocturnal; resting; glorious; unexpected; breeding; venerable; ill-ventilated; foul-smelling; principal; flame-lit; despicable; craggy; prominent; amusing; waste; monastic; undisputed; unbelieving; desert; cozy; distinguished; suitable; subordinate; ill-omened; desolate; legitimate; unsearchable; important; dilapidated; beautiful; historic; pleasant; precarious; ineffable; slippery; well-ordered; tender; garish; big; ghostly; horrible; authentic; undisturbed; colonized; assigned; appropriate; unexpected; forsaken; special; free; easy; ostentatious; genial; fascinating; necessary; distinct; secondary; private; desecrated; hideous; flowery; cherished; noble; holy; definite; rightful; shallow; honorable; inaccessible; hackneyed; provisioned; customary; cheerless; dainty; humble; respective; sacred; shady; sequestered; wretched; parasitic; urbanized; calculated; prominent; languorous; tenement; wondrous; commodious; enormous; typical; predicted; gorgeous; exclusive; considerable; leafy; dreadful; separated; churlish; melancholy; ticklish; impudent; worthy; doleful; far-off; possible; impassible; evident; fearsome; especial; accessible; depressing; horrid; out-of-the-way; green-watered; abiding; enchanted; well-assured; cheerless; retired; window-barred; unique; rude; benighted; equal; convenient; homely; adequate; sacred; remote; proper; tumbledown; miserable; strange; beautiful; subordinate; desired; envied; decided.

verbs

depart from—; disclose—; dislodge from—; empty—; enjoy—in; fall into—; hold—; occupy—; relegate to—of; retain—; seek—; situate in—; snoop about—; transfer from —; usurp—; vacate—.

(See spot, room, locality, space, position, building, town, city.)

PLACE (v)

adverbs

voluntarily; precisely; unwittingly; obligingly; publicly; unreservedly; poetically; honorably; superficially; temporarily; conspicuously; recklessly; judiciously; impulsively; impersonally; tenderly; logically; objectionably; vulnerably; exaltedly; depressingly; accessibly; uniquely; rudely; subordinately.

(See establish, locate.)

PLACID

adverbs

immovably; sweetly; generously; vexatiously; serenely; terribly; imperturbably; fortunately; singularly; particularly; habitually; temperamentally; coolly; resolutely; stoically; philosophically; demurely; submissively; sedately; icily; patiently; remarkably; unexpectedly; surprisingly.

PLACIDITY

adjectives

spiritual; austere; frozen; eternal.

PLAGIARISM

adjectives

phenomenal; criminal; audacious; discovered; unintentional; obvious; deliberate; barefaced; bald.

verbs

accuse of—; resort to—; —apes; —borrows; —emulates; —mirrors; —models; —parallels; —patterns; —poaches; —purloins; —simulates; —sponges; —steals.

(See theft, dishonesty.)

PLAGUE

adjectives

destroying; wasting; ordaining; abhorrent; prevalent; devastating; immedicable; grasshopper; noxious; virulent; noisome; vile; deadly; dreaded; remorseless; incurable.

verbs

conquer—; control—; disperse—; guard against—; inoculate against—; —breaks out; —creeps through; —decimates; —descends upon; —rages; —ravages; —slays; —swoops upon; —traverses; —wanes.

(See curse, contagion, disease, infection.)

PLAIN

adjectives
alluvial; dewy; pool-studded; olive-plumed; alluring; torrid; fluctuating; capacious; friendless; brown; sunburnt; smiling; vast; barren; central; abounding; twilight; pensive; mournful; sterile; murderous; ravaged; sunny; harvest-shining; upland; high; delightful; skirting; rugged; rocky; celestial; sandy; trackless; melancholy; comforting; circumfluous; featureless; wan; infernal; illimitable; stubborn; ravished; wide-stretching; idol-burdened; rainy; billowy; fertile; cultivated; extensive; terraced; pastoral; variegated; desolate; prostrate; half-dreary; semibarren; extensive; ethereal; tilted; elevated; semibarbaric; sun-dried; dusky; grassy; placid; cactus; happy; watered; ivory; verdurous; unsheltered; empty; tawny; shimmering; ringing; joyous; delicious; immitigable; flower-paved; smiling; sultry; horrible; boundless; grassless; treeless; long; deep; sandy; wide; deluged; native; chequered; somber; iridescent; sun-blistered; moonlit; pensive; windswept; dazzling; fruitful; burning; ringing (pl); shadowed; immortal; horizon-bounded; stubble; dust-beclouded; undulating; extensive; cattle; classic; redolent; broad; dreary; narrow; soaring; temperate.

verbs
cultivate—; dwell in—; follow—; frequent —; inhabit—; level into—; overlook—; people—; roam—; scan—; till—; travel—; wander over—; —extends; —rolls; —stretches; —unfolds; —unrolls.

(See battlefield, valley, country, land, prairie.)

PLAIN

adverbs (*unadorned*)
emphatically; undeniably; pleasantly; hopelessly; significantly; severely; inartistically; monotonously; invariably; chastely; rigorously; unaffectedly; gracelessly; awkwardly; unfortunately; frightfully; hideously; curiously; singularly; horribly; forbiddingly.

PLAIN

adverbs (*clear*)
delightfully; distinctly; graphically; singularly; curiously; brilliantly; obviously; ad-

mirably; conveniently; vividly; unmistakably; extraordinarily; commendably; unusually; extremely; ingeniously.

PLAINNESS

adjectives
rigorous; emphatic; dignified; studious; elaborate; becoming; neat.

PLAIN-SPOKEN

adverbs
fearlessly; bluntly; gruffly; courageously; embarrassingly; irritatingly; dangerously; unwisely; foolishly; senselessly; imprudently; indiscreetly; impoliticly; injudiciously; inexpediently; harshly; offensively; absurdly; ineptly; exasperatingly; awkwardly; harshly; ungraciously; extremely; uncommonly; amazingly; outrageously.

PLAINT

adjectives
pathetic; doleful; somber; noisy.

verbs
breathe—; cease—; detect—; endure—; heave—; reiterate—; renew—; sob—; suppress—; throat—; utter—; whine—; —bursts; —distresses; —fades; —greets; —melts; —moves; —wearies.

(See cry, complaint.)

PLAINTIFF

verbs
allot—; award to—; vest in—; —accuses; —alleges; —appeals; —asserts; —blames; —brands; —challenges; —charges; —contends; —claims; —demands; —denounces; —exacts; —implicates; —imputes; —lodges; —prevails; —reproaches; —waives.

(See defendant, lawyer.)

PLAINTIVE

adverbs
deeply; querulously; tearfully; whiningly; mutteringly; sorrowfully; exasperatingly; sadly; pitifully; endlessly; exceedingly; lamentably; superfluously; unduly; monotonously; obscurely.

PLAN

adjectives
architectural; hazy; delectable; comprehensive; ill-contrived; parricidal; revolution-

ary; extempore; logical; homely; deferred; startling; intricate; makeshift; deliberate; concerted; showy; ambitious; feasible; cherished; immediate; tentative; denominational; trivial; careful; elaborate; insecure; sundry (pl); inscrutable; execrable; frugal; mercenary; eternal; complicated; primitive; frantic; oft-advanced; definite; extended; weird; detailed; welfare; harmonious; enthusiastic; proved; insurrectionary; simple; daring; grandiose; unproductive; long-concealed; tyrannical; far-trumpeted; solid; subtle; clean-cut; different; merchandising; unbelievable; profit-sharing; odd; cooperative; sensational; thrilling; guaranteed; confidential; startling; unusual; powerful; business; stimulating; certified; mail-order; exclusive; helpful; money-making; sales; new; easy; amazing; premium; business-building; selling; unique; coupon; original; complete; astounding; trade; starting; consistent; uttered; foolish; futile; extensive; complex; ultra-modern; vacation; treacherous; rational; intimate; exclusive; pensive; equitable; sagacious; low; time; payment; quixotic; indivisible; cohesive; philanthropic; meritorious; respective; apparent; eternal; widespread; treadmill; miscarried; nefarious; strict; consecutive; first-mentioned; coercive; expensive; melodramatic; best-laid; far-seeing; earnest; educational; strategic; standard; maternal; passioned.

verbs
abandon—; adopt—; advance—; analyze—; bolster—; broach—; buttress—; clarify—; concoct—; contemplate—; crystallize—; defeat—; design—; detail—; devise—; discard —; disclose—; divulge—; draft—; embark upon—; enact—; endorse—; engross in—; evolve—; expound—; foil—; formulate—; frame—; hatch out—; improvise—; inaugurate—; junk—; launch—; map out—; mull over—; obstruct—; pattern—on; promulgate —; propound—; ratify—; revamp—; reveal —; revise—; rout—; sidetrack—; snag—; sponsor—; submit—; terminate—; thwart —; upset—; veto—; withdraw—; —advocates; —s coincide; —crumbles; —embraces; —fizzles; —matures.
(See idea, itinerary, intention.)

PLAN (v)
adverbs
fantastically; subtly; magnificently; purposefully; zealously; methodically; tentatively; divinely; deliberately; meticulously; competently; cunningly; daintily; systematically; gloriously; architecturally; comprehensively; intricately; primitively; harmoniously; tyrannically; sensationally; confidentially; sagaciously; philanthropically; meritoriously; nefariously; strategically.
(See scheme, contrive.)

PLANE
adjectives
realistic; conversational; convex; experimental; inclined; reconnoitering; fast; luxurious; powerful; ascending; vertical; emerald; transport; swift; passenger; streamlined; metal; mail; tri-motored.

verbs
bail out of—; bank—; contact—; fuel—; hop (colloq.)—; license—; maroon—; navigate —; pilot—; throttle—; —bores up; —drones; —flashes over; —gleams; —gyrates; — swoops; takes off; —taxies out; —twists; —whirs; —wings; —zooms.
(See aeroplane.)

PLANET
adjectives
leaden; populous; wheeling; sin-ridden; vexatious; bawdy; glorious; household; ill; sleepy; turbulent; beautious; virginal; glittering; bruised; influential; perturbed; riming; dead; many-mortalled; spinning; sunless; careering.

PLANK
adjectives
grimy; raw; rotting; sturdy; proposed; political; fastened.

PLANNING
adjectives
adroit; unassuming; constructive; thoughtful; tedious; haphazard.

PLANT
adjectives
experimental; sapient; showy; microscopic; companionless; indigenous; remote; thorny; umbelliferous; greedy; naturalized; obstinate; efficient; marsh; vigorous; leguminous; set; aquatic; insectivorous; luxuriant; aromatic; hardy; celebrated; frost-nipped; reduction; wrinkled; branched; parasitic; intruding; stemless; yielding; ill-assorted (pl); infusorial; characteristic; ornamental; enchanting; liliaceous; baccate; happy; esculent; fragrant; nutritious; ignoble; in-

harmonious; succulent; rank; potted; sun-scorched; dwarf; gaudy; umbrageous; established; trailing; rubbed; redolent; long; water; drooping; wind-fertilized; herbaceous; exotic; native; neglected; curious; conventionalized; ballast; submerged; flowering; unsuccessful; ramshackle; precious.

verbs

cultivate—; develop—; hedge—; nurse—; perpetuate—; pollenize—; propagate—; prune—; scatter —s; strangle—; tend—; trim—; uproot—; vitalize—; —bears; —branches; —droops; —emerges; —flourishes; —flowers; —goes dormant; —puts forth; —roots in; —shoots up; —sprouts; —thrives.

(See bulb, herb, ivy, flower, bud, vine, grass.)

PLANT (v)

adverbs

triumphantly; solidly; immovably; advantageously; indigenously; vigorously; aquatically; luxuriantly; characteristically; ornamentally; nutritiously; succulently; conventionally.

(See establish, set.)

PLANTATION

adjectives

flourishing; tidewater; well-managed; substantial-looking; communal; artistic; super-abundant; rich.

PLANTER

adjectives

eccentric; remote; poverty-stricken; brusque; affluent; large-scale.

PLANTING

adjectives

permanent; spring; high-growing; experimental.

PLAQUE

verbs

border—; decorate—; exhibit—; figure—; hang—; inscribe on—; insert—; polish—; preserve—; reburnish—; reveal—; study—; unveil—; —acclaims; —commemorates; —honors; —inspires; —ornaments; —shines.

(See metal, ornament.)

PLASH

adjectives

appalling; muffled; startled; noisy.

PLASTER

adjectives

pale-hued; sovereign; peeling; moldering.

verbs

apply—; bedaub with—; cast—; dab—; daub—; mix—; repair—; smear—; spread —; stir—; surface—; —adheres; —cements; —cracks; —crumbles; —crusts; —cures; —encases; —faces; —hardens; —overlays; —surfaces; —survives.

(See paste, paint, cement.)

PLATE

adjectives

special; deep; piping-hot; untouched; burdensome; leaden; circular; photographic; burnished; rimless; elastic; lustrous.

verbs

arrange —s; chip—; cram—; lick—; load —; mar—; retrieve—; scour—; shatter—; stack —s; —crashes; —gleams; —s harmonize; —rotates; —shatters; —shines.

(See dish, disk, platter.)

PLATEAU

adjectives

inhospitable; remote; rock-strewn; undulating; extensive; endless; bare; high.

verbs

ascend to—; cover—; culminate in—; form —; traverse—; view from—; —awes; —extends; —fascinates; —inspires; —rises; —skirts; —stretches.

(See mountain, land, plain.)

PLATFORM

adjectives

movable; desolate; aggressive; rampart; terraced; portico; splintered; mosque; skeletonized; party.

verbs

ascend to—; construct—; crowd—; declaim from—; design—; entertain from—; erect —; flit across—; gather 'round—; jam—; help up—; leap upon—; pace—; perform on —; reveal—; squat on—; straggle over—; —extends; —harbors; —projects; —protects; —rises; —shelters.

(See deck, stage, floor.)

PLATITUDE

adjectives
pompous; sugared; old; theoretic; stale; worthless.

verbs
avoid —s; condemn—; excuse—; fall into —; hide under—; indulge in—; prate —s; take refuge in—; twaddle in—; —bores; —depresses; —dulls; —exasperates; —irks; —lulls; —tires; —vexes; —wearies.
(See proverb, maxim.)

PLATONIC

adverbs
coolly; strictly; altogether; supposedly; perhaps; utterly; amiably; studiously; sedately; thoughtfully; contemplatively; philosophically; calmly; tranquilly; stoically; soberly; demurely; presumably; dispassionately; disinterestedly; decorously; decently; honestly; virtuously; ridiculously; chastely.

PLATONISM

adjectives
delicate; refined; desirable; unsatisfactory.

PLATTER

adjectives
hideous; huge; well-filled; curious.

verbs
arrange —s; garnish—; glean from—; load —; replenish—; stack —s; support—; —crashes; —gleams; —shatters; —sizzles.
(See dish, plate.)

PLAUDITS

adjectives
anticipated; derogatory; noisy; sincere; deserved.

PLAUSIBILITY

adjectives
solemn; delusive; remote; scant; minute.

verbs
admit—; allow—; bear out—; commend—; convince of—; demonstrate—; doubt—; gloss over—; harbor—; lend—; maintain—; mince—; overestimate—; plead—; warrant —; —defends; —enables; —reconciles.
(See sincerity, integrity.)

PLAUSIBLE

adverbs
scarcely; altogether; extremely; manifestly; reasonably; highly; glibly; apparently; craftily; adroitly; pretentiously; remotely; deceptively; evasively; subtly; cleverly; remarkably; indisputably.

PLAY

adjectives (*general*)
amorous; much-performed; immortal; informal; infant; unfair; melodramatic; morality; careless; idle; fitful; miracle; steady; dignified; devilish; painful; boisterous; prismatic; swift; touching; tempestuous; superficial; fantastic; foul; hampered; harmless; firing; delightful; blithe; imaginative; heedless; stately; heroic; illimitable; desperate; unmatched; prophetic; varying; vivid; frivolous; stodgy; unusual; freak; ceaseless; deft; interminable; tragic; somber; witless; ambitious; wretched; immoral; mutual; brawling; rousing; petty; thin; diplomatic; meaningless; jocund; contemporary; clever; dublous, radical; cut-and-thrust; clumsy; uncontrollable; well-arranged; rapid, supernatural.

PLAY

verbs (*theatrical*)
acclaim—; attend—; commend—; criticize —; revive—; sponsor—; stage—; —bores; —charms; —diverts; —endears; —grips; —holds forth at; —impresses; —intrigues.
(See comedy, humor, opera, movie, melodrama, performance, game, sport, recreation, exercise, fun, amusement.)

PLAY (*v*)

adverbs
fervidly; cleverly; amorously; informally; boisterously; tempestuously; witlessly; blithely; frivolously; immorally; idly; brawlingly; jocundly; clumsily; angelically; capriciously; fantastically; seductively; incomparably; demurely; caressingly; adroitly; recklessly; melodiously; diligently; exquisitely.
(See frolic, romp.)

PLAYED-OUT

adverbs
altogether; finally; pitiably; entirely; miserably; helplessly; pathetically; needlessly; strangely; curiously; wretchedly; alarmingly; completely; undoubtedly; sincerely; utterly.

PLAYER

adjectives
sturdy; accurate; wandering; steely-finger-

ed; ardent; comprising; incompetent; impecunious; phenomenal; orchestral; strolling; professional; inspired; skilled; shrewd; nonchalant.

verbs
cast —s; cheer —s; encore—; "razz"—; recruit —s; spur —s on; star—; subsidize —s; —amuses; —charms; —delights; —dramatizes; —emotes; —enacts; —endears; —entertains; —impresses; —magnetizes; —overacts; —portrays; —redeems; —rehearses; —supports.
 (See athlete, actor, musician, etc.)

PLAYFUL
adverbs
rapturously; delightfully; teasingly; ecstatically; happily; amiably; annoyingly; sportively; friskily; amusingly; brightly; vivaciously; archly; coltishly; childishly; amazingly; frolicsomely; merrily.

PLAYFULNESS
adjectives
dignified; reverent; impetuous; elephantine; overburdened; half-serious; quizzical; ferocious; satirical; buoyant; effervescent.

PLAYGROUND
adjectives
endless; city; needed; crowded; well-equipped.

PLAYING
adjectives
unwitting; coloratura; brilliant; ingenious.

PLAYMATE
adjectives
sweet; desirable; agreeable; well-matched (pl); boisterous.

PLAYTHING
adjectives
broken; coarse; colored.

PLAYWRIGHT
verbs
acclaim—; award to—; criticize—; honor —; laud—; recognize—; —caters to; —composes; —contributes; —creates; —designs; —dramatizes; —impresses; —formulates; —offers; —thrives.
 (See dramatist, artist, writer, author.)

PLEA
adjectives
suggestive; eloquent; dastard; masterly; eternal; half-stifled; unmoral; impassioned; specious; irrational; pettifogging; ingenious; common; special; confederate.

verbs
address—; anticipate—; endorse—; file—; heed—; impair—; justify—; necessitate—; oppose—; press—; protest—; put aside—; respond to—; satisfy—; support—; witness —; —penetrates; —softens; —touches; —urges.
 (See apology, allegation, excuse, prayer.)

PLEAD (v)
adverbs
eloquently; persuasively; convincingly; vehemently; indignantly; ostensibly; earnestly; brokenly; meekly; despairingly; touchingly.
 (See beg, entreat.)

PLEADING
adjectives
patient; fervent; humble; vain; disinterested; impassioned; guilty; incessant.

PLEASANT
adverbs
consistently; extremely; essentially; sweetly; gratifyingly; courteously; placidly; gravely; unfailingly; graciously; smilingly; cordially; quietly; remarkably; ostentatiously; singularly; charmingly; genuinely; sincerely; unaffectedly; jocosely; whimsically; playfully; facetiously; delightfully; maturely; politely; waggishly; openly; heartily; humorously; scrupulously; enchantingly; engagingly; altogether; urbanely; obligingly; good-humoredly; fearlessly; furtively.

PLEASANTRIES
verbs
banter—; dally with—; enjoy—; exchange —; feast on—; perpetuate—; school in—; sport—; —cheer; —delight; —divert; —ease; —engage; —entertain; —impart; —solace; —titillate.
 (See banter, jest.)

PLEASANTRY
adjectives
indigestible; familiar; humoristic; formal; uncouth; ill-timed; fluent; bland; coarse; colloquial.

PLEASE (v)

adverbs

graciously; exceedingly; bewitchingly; inwardly; graciously; instinctively; aesthetically; fleetingly; sensuously; momentarily; blithely; grossly; legitimately; voluptuously; frankly; thrillingly; salaciously.

(See cheer, satisfy.)

PLEASED

adverbs

highly; graciously; exceedingly; momentarily; inordinately; frankly; openly; obviously; extremely; uncommonly; happily; proudly; ineffably; naturally; visibly; noticeably; marvellously; overwhelmingly; utterly; inexpressibly.

PLEASURABLE

adverbs

entirely; delightfully; hilariously; refreshingly; utterly; extremely; surprisingly, unexpectedly; strikingly; acceptably; measurably; moderately; actually; charmingly; splendidly; distinctly.

PLEASURE

adjectives

childish; fleeting; wanton; fearful; personal; supreme; playful; sensual; distinct; extraordinary; faithless; uninterrupted; gross; noisy; birdlike; frank; exalted; sweet; uninstructive; cordial; wild; pensive; agonizing; domestic; private; glorious; cruel; profligate; darling; innocent; unnecessary; tranquillizing; worthy; quiet; infinite; dizzy; sportsmanlike; fantastic; firm; rife; stern; fashionable; youthful; illicit; deceiving; tasteless; sheer; wingless; palling; malicious; guilty; multitudinous (pl); forbidden; grievous; untold; earth-born; selfish; peculiar; girlish; dangerous; melancholy; divine; delicate; ferocious; malignant; headlong; unrevealed; solid; unspeakable; tickling; strange; inoffensive; sensible; quickening; prodigious; infantile; warm; refined; gentle; glittering; curious; sweet; wincing; honest; personal; toiling; unmixed; eternal; giddy; voluptuous; indescribable; puerile; gracious; sensitive; unalloyed; unfeigned; mean; proud; exquisite; idle; profound; monotonous; joint; visible; vivid; scanty; unglorious; sincere; smoking; legitimate; pulsing; mischievous; frank; unabating; questionable; thrilling; frequent (pl); inexpressible; false; compensating; tenfold; primary; royal; grim; mysterious; proper;

simple; hollow; luxurious; profound; petty; monotonous; growing; delicious; dreadful; heartfelt; wholesome; unmeasured; persisting; perishing; agitating; secret; alluring; attendant; calm; celestial; varied; blithe; queer; perpetual; singular; base; harmless; avid; unearned; unreproved; infinite; intellectual; sunny; momentary; solemn; fiendish; mournful; unblinking; costless; kind; evident; prickling; bygone; faint; positive; piquant; sensuous; secondary; melancholy; ecstatic; vicious; malicious; macabre; unremembered; perverse; pure; alien; mere; silent; admirable; unadulterated; fermenting; unsubstantial; dissolute; intense; undisguised; natural.

verbs

addicted to—; afford—; bask in—; dampen —; derive—from; deprive of—; drink up—; enhance—; experience—; forego—; heighten —; indulge in—; partake of—; prolong—; pursue—; rejoice in—; relish—; resign—; sacrifice—; smile in—; squirm in—; taste —; weary of—.

(See gratification, happiness, gladness, delight, enjoyment.)

PLEBEIAN

adverbs

altogether; distinctly; unexpectedly; surprisingly; naturally; inevitably; terribly; pathetically; loudly; roughly; meanly; vexatiously; indecorously; unendurably; singularly; strangely; oddly; overwhelmingly; hopelessly.

PLEDGE

adjectives

sacred; temperance; tender; written; decided; solemn; terse; uncompromising; positive; eternal; uttered; indefinite; uncertain; reliable; unredeemed; noble.

verbs

accept—; administer—; contract—; enter into—; exact—; forfeit—; honor—; offer—; pawn—; redeem—; repudiate—; respect—; subscribe to—; undertake—; violate—; — assures; —binds; —commits; —guarantees; —secures; —ties; —warrants.

(See covenant, agreement, promise.)

PLEDGE (v)

adverbs

solemnly; mutually; enthusiastically; sacredly; tenderly; uncompromisingly; eternally;

definitely; reliably; nobly; nominally; gallantly.

(See promise, assure.)

PLENTIFUL

adverbs

reasonably; unexpectedly; presumably; luxuriantly; scarcely; lavishly; abundantly; adequately; exuberantly; profusely; sufficiently; immeasurably; incalculably; providentially; mercifully; fortunately; luckily; opportunely; auspiciously; happily.

PLENTY

adjectives

admired; wanton; boarded; wasted; unused.

verbs

bless with—; bristle with—; desire—; obtain —; produce—; reign in—; scatter—; shower —; swim in—; wallow in—; wish for—; —abounds; —flows; —teems.

(See abundance, affluence.)

PLIABLE

adverbs

conveniently; opportunely; reasonably; extremely; scarcely; fortunately; luckily; hardly; somewhat; adaptably; suitably; easily; advantageously; comfortably; readily; usefully; measurably; moderately; adequately; remarkably; marvellously; uncommonly.

PLIGHT

adjectives

lamentable; forsaken; sorry; ill; admirable; evil; pathetic; patient; chronic; grievous; shameful; pitiable; dolorous; sad; doleful; sorrowful; unfortunate.

verbs

betray—; exploit—; favor—; foster—; muse on—; reduce to—; swear to—; vow to—; — alarms; —assures; —binds; —contracts; —depresses; —guarantees; —puzzles; — secures; —shocks.

(See condition, predicament, state.)

PLOD

adjectives

painful; prosaic; barefoot.

PLOD (*v*)

adverbs

contentedly; monotonously; wearily; tire-

lessly; mechanically; ceaselessly; prosaically; steadily; dejectedly; stupidly.

(See tramp, trudge.)

PLODDING

adverbs

patiently; insistently; steadily; doggedly; stubbornly; stolidly; uncomplainingly; laboriously; resolutely; determinedly; admirably; commendably; hopefully; resignedly; firmly; staunchly; unwaveringly; tenaciously; perseveringly; undauntedly; unswervingly; courageously

PLOT

adjectives

exaggerated; formidable; comprehensive; dramatic; sandy; insidious; tyrannical; thin; thickening; naughty; grassy; murderous; lurid; audacious; inhuman; marshy; detestable; ill-omened; unfrequented; complicated; daisied; infernal; precious; horrible; pretty; fertile; neglected.

verbs

abet—; concoct—; construct—; cook up (colloq.)—; crush—; disclose—; entangle—; fancy—; found—on; frill—; garnish—; get wind of—; harmonize—; hatch—; implicate —; invent—; nip—; plunge into—; resolve —; spring—; summarize—; unmask—; weave—; —derives from; —generates; — smacks of.

(See argument, intrigue, conspiracy.)

PLOT (*v*)

adverbs

devilishly; maliciously; grimly; infernally; diabolically; formidably; insidiously; tyrannically; audaciously; inhumanly; detestably; perniciously; traitorously; seditiously.

(See scheme, machinate.)

PLOTTER

verbs

exile—; uncover—; —circumvents; —concocts; —contrives; —designs; —devises; — frames; —hatches; —intrigues; —manoeuvres; —overreaches; —schemes; —stoops; — undermines; —snatches

(See conspirator.)

PLOUGH (*v*)

adverbs

extensively; seasonally; laboriously; deeply; annually.

(See dig, labor.)

PLOVER

adjectives
graceful; scudding; snowy-winged.

PLOW

adjectives
flying; sulky; useful; ancient; improved.

verbs
employ—; equip with—; —bites; —breaks; —cuts; —delves; —digs; —furrows; —grooves; —intrudes; —loosens; —prepares; —uncovers; —wedges; —weeds.

PLUCK

adjectives
invincible; gallant; amazing; redoubtable; unusual; gigantic; great; noticeable.

PLUCK (v)

adverbs
petulantly; surreptitiously; courageously; agitatedly; idiotically; industriously; thievishly; haphazardly.
(See pick, pull.)

PLUCKY

adverbs
unbelievably; unusually; resolutely; naturally; inherently; habitually; remarkably; marvellously; uncommonly; amazingly; courageously; recklessly; determinedly; gallantly; valiantly; intrepidly; undauntedly; stoutly; manfully; tenaciously; indomitably.

PLUG

verbs
cram—into; drive—into; insert—; remove —; tap—; —bars; —blocks; —chokes; —dams; —obstructs; —prevents; —resists; —seals; —stuffs; —traps.
(See stopper.)

PLUG (v)

adverbs
tightly; effectually; firmly; completely; wholly; satisfactorily; efficiently.
(See plod, work.)

PLUMAGE

adjectives
splendid; fantastic; rich-colored; peculiar; rustling; lacy; glossy; entrancing; iridescent; black; glistening; glittering; ribboned; rosy; light; fluttersome; brilliant; demure; unmatchable.

verbs
adjust—; admire—; bear—; bunch—; display—; preen—; prime—; ruffle—; rumple —; smooth—; —adorns; —bedecks; —decorates; —embellishes; —glitters; —nods; —ornaments; —tufts.
(See mane, feather.)

PLUMBING

verbs
approve—; condemn—; criticize—; demolish—; display—; examine—; improve—; install—; lack—; modernize—; renovate—; repair—; sanction—; tear—down; wrench —apart; —sanitizes.
(See pipe.)

PLUME

adjectives
idle; stooping; dancing; waving; funeral; fantastic; sunny; bronze; striped; straining; advanced; rustling; sable; fancy; shining; magnificent; gay; dripping, resinous; fiery; snowy; graceful; shaken; tossing.

PLUMP

adverbs
delightfully; desirably; commendably; terribly; pleasantly; admirably; childishly; overly; unhappily; chubbily; stalwartly; strappingly; thumpingly; extraordinarily; remarkably; charmingly; daintily; rosily; exquisitely; pleasingly.

PLUMPNESS

adjectives
appreciable; unwanted; stodgy; awkward; pleasant.

PLUNDER

adjectives
nefarious; hideous; indiscriminate; winged; licentious; accumulated; plentiful; barbarous; piratical.

verbs
abstain from—; abhor—; acquire—; bag—; commit—; conceal—; convey—; locate—; seize—; share—; smuggle—; submit to—; transfer—; uncover—; —despoils; —ravages; —strips.
(See bribery, loot.)

PLUNDER (v)

adverbs
rapaciously; flagrantly; nefariously; hide-

ously; indiscriminately; barbarously; piratically; lustfully; dictatorially.
(See rob, steal.)

PLUNGE
adjectives
occasional; desperate; constant (pl); useless; despised; sounding.

PLUNGE (v)
adverbs
rashly; daringly; heavily; wildly; impetuously; determinedly; fiercely; violently; desperately.
(See dive, fall, drop.)

PLURALIST
adjectives
splendid; blatant; unblushing.

PLURALITY
verbs
abandon—; amass—; attract—; attribute—to; elect by—; pile up—; question—; require—; secure—; seek—; solicit—; stem—; —chooses; —decides; —determines; —expresses; —follows; —judges; —patronizes.
(See vote, majority, multitude.)

PLUSH
adjectives
moth-eaten; restful.

PLY (v)
adverbs
industriously; constantly; intermittently; diligently; vigorously; ambitiously; unweariedly; indefatigably.
(See work, apply.)

POCKET
adjectives
greedy; sagging; redundant; ragged; attenuated; hidebound; closed; warm; well-filled.

verbs
accumulate in—; button—; charge—with; conceal in—; deposit in—; dig in—; dislodge from—; draw from—; extract from —; fumble in—; grope in—; joggle in—; line—s; quarter in—; tuck in—; —bulges; —jingles; —swells.
(See basket, reservoir, hold.)

POD
verbs
bruise—; crack—; empty—; split—; —binds; —conceals; —defends; —discloses; —encases; —encloses; —enfolds; —faces; —guards; —preserves; —protects.
(See cover.)

POEM
adjectives
poisonous; excellent; patriotic; fantastic; tiny; ancient; typical; conventional; dramatic; simple; mystical; admirable; sentimental; immortal; negligible; genealogical; centenary; lyrical; remarkable; non-dramatic; epic; licentious; heroic; narrative; noble; painful; artificial; humorous; divine; devotional; unified; pastoral; deeply-felt; rare; imperishable; elegiac; Homeric; abiding; commemorative; mere; quizzical; contemplative; puerile; didactic; striking; elegant; personal; impressive; brief; historical; unequal; elevated; preposterous; faulty; primitive; laudatory; symphonic; curious; insipid; amatory; soulless; philosophical; dainty; unpopular; psychological.

verbs
acclaim—; appreciate—; chorus—; create —; evolve—; peruse—; rewrite—; work into—; —amuses; —appeals; —commemorates; —conveys; —depicts; —diverts; —echoes; —expresses; —flows; —inspires; —invokes; —rings; —romances; —sings; —transfuses; —voices.
(See poetry, hymn, ballad, incantation, ditty, epigram, romance, sonnet, dirge, ballad.)

POESY
adjectives
perennial; heaven-bred; inspired.

POET
verbs
acclaim—; appreciate—; award to—; chide —; criticize—; immortalize—; interpret—; laud—; quote—; recognize—; —beautifies; —builds; —chants; —commemorates; —composes; —contributes; —designs; —eternizes; —experiences; —expresses; —impresses; —laments; —offers; —redeems; —rimes; —scans; —sings; —teaches; —thrives; —versifies.
(See author, artist, creator, idealist, novelist.)

POETIC

adverbs

distinctly; delightfully; musically; rhythmically; deeply; melodiously; abstrusely; notably; sublimely; pleasantly; exquisitely; ingeniously; unexpectedly; truly; eloquently; vigorously; passionately; glowingly; impressively; fancifully.

POETRY

adjectives

pastoral; clear; academic; allegorical; visionary; smooth; respectable; lyrical; essential; faulty; satirical; joyful; dramatic; descriptive; subservient; romantic; charlatan; tragic; epic; devotional; delicate; meditative; riotous; spiritual; imaginative; impassioned; bewildering; elder; tender; highmannered; dreamy; austere; barbarous; glorious, mournful; vague; original.

verbs

conceive—; cultivate—; deliver—; like—; interpret—; mold—; resort to—; toy with —; —charms; —conveys; —delights; — eases; —elevates; —enchants; —endures; —flourishes; —humanizes; —inspires; — narrates; —reflects; —reveals; —softens; — soothes; —springs from.

(See literature, poem, story, sonnet, etc.)

POETS

adjectives

derivative; lofty; erotic; impecunious; contemporary; Ionian; notable; capricious; romantic; quick-conceiving; prominent; sublime; spontaneous; true; subtle; worthy; distinguished; satirical; celebrated; philosophical; tragic; well-known; spasmodic; scurrilous; ecclesiastical; saturnine; laureled; descriptive; sensitive; earnest; prattling; exquisite; synthetic; budding; specific; denominated; authentic; secular; pining; humorous; amorous; lyrical; peasant; ingenious; heathen; isolated; playful; religious; illustrious; mature; esteemed; vernacular; psychic; classical.

POIGNANT

adverbs

intensely; sharply; singularly; curiously; strangely; inscrutably; unexpectedly; apparently; manifestly; painfully; smartly; remarkably; strikingly; unbearably; trenchantly; vividly; suddenly.

POINT
(*feature, issue, question, etc.*)

verbs

admit—; allow—; attend to—; carry—; concede—; debate—; dispose of—; dodge—; drive home—; dwell on—; emphasize—; grant—; illustrate—; interrogate—; labor —; miss—; pursue—; reinforce—; rule on —; settle—; stress—; sympathize on—; — illustrates; —s interlock.

(See angle, feature, issue.)

POINT
(*general*)

adjectives

standard; essential; peevish; standing; transitional; original; sore; favorable; vulnerable; geographical; objective; delicate; varying; vindictive; fundamental; advantageous; knotty; statistical; luminous; trivial; weighty; crucial; rallying; superficial; physical; culminating; controverted; dazzling; desired; fiery; inconsiderable; sentimental; thorny; unsavory; noteworthy; narrow; mooted; burning; converging; unguarded; significant; well-selected; worldly; practical; inhuman; chivalric; principal; systematic; pivotal; assailable; prominent; equinoctial; strategic; contrary; suggestive; radiant; favorable; slippery; salient; aesthetic; artistic; remote; material; corrective; designated; matrimonial; elevated; indecomposable; critical; exposed; statistical; disputed; changeless; home-coming; pathetic; conceded; preconceived; minute; projecting; crowning; bitter; unimportant; knotty; decisive; sandy; epigrammatic; rallying; preliminary; characteristic; supreme; saturation; absurd; terminal; contentious; dubious; heterodox; unendurable; stagnant; impressive; dangerous; intangible; inappreciable; restricted; cardinal; determinable; ludicrous; speculative; ample; technical; yawning.

POINT (*v*)

adverbs

triumphantly; mysteriously; significantly; timidly; conclusively; mournfully; excitedly; scornfully; directly; peevishly; ludicrously.

(See indicate, designate.)

POINTED

adverbs

cruelly; barbarously; hatefully; bitterly; caustically; sarcastically; unmistakably; personally; meanly; maliciously; venomously;

impolitely; viciously; intentionally; deliberately; rudely; roughly; ungraciously; bluntly; brusquely; dogmatically; significantly;
curtly; crisply; sententiously; bitingly; incisively; impressively.

POINTLESS
adverbs
pitifully; feebly; inanely; fatuously; inconsequentially; insignificantly; monotonously;
ponderously; banally; trivially; vaguely;
flatly; insipidly; endlessly; foolishly; vacuously; ridiculously; intolerably; tiresomely;
absurdly.

POISE
adjectives
calm; serene; contemplative; aristocratic;
swerveless; exquisite; intellectual; aloof;
physical; domineering; admirable; culminating; coquettish; calculating; mental; dangerous; sturdy; equal.

verbs
acquire—; admire—; affect—; attain—;
envy—; exhibit—; lack—; maintain—;
practise—; recover—; regard with—; restore—; school in—; shatter—; value—; —
assures; —conquers; —controls; —impresses;
es; —polishes; —tones
(See equilibrium, ease, balance, stability.)

POISE (v)
adverbs
serenely; delicately; calmly; daringly; exquisitely; coquettishly; rashly; courageously;
undauntedly.
(See balance, pose.)

POISON
adjectives
bottom; virulent; simmering; consuming;
offensive; infusing; unseasonable; vanquished; occidental; insidious; intoxicating; infidel; rank; putrefactive; deadly; corrosive;
inorganic; delicious; innocuous; slow-work-
ing.

verbs
absorb—; antidote—; assimilate—; control
—; counteract—; distil—; eliminate—; excrete—; exude—; impregnate with—; infect
with—; inject—; neutralize—; reek with—;
—accumulates; —circulates; —ravages.
(See germicide, venom, drug.)

POISON (v)
adverbs
insidiously; murderously; premeditatively;
maliciously; organically; corrosively; intoxicatingly; basely; diabolically.
(See kill, murder.)

POISONOUS
adverbs
mildly; slightly; fatally; dangerously; mortally; alarmingly; seriously; dreadfully;
noxiously; maliciously; venomously; viciously; pestilentially; curiously; unexpectedly;
singularly; miserably; manifestly; obviously; invariably.

POKE (v)
adverbs
coyly; tantalizingly; brutally; warningly;
cautiously; teasingly; facetiously; delicately;
humorously; amorously.
(See thrust, excite.)

POLE
adjectives
boreal; slender; curtained; terrestrial; resonant; telephone; splintered; austral.

POLEMIC
adjectives
staunch; commonplace; bitter; ruthless.

POLICE
adjectives
adequate; lynx-eyed; executive; ubiquitous;
ornamental; interested; ineffective; rustic;
ingenious; indignant.

verbs
commend—; detail—to; evade—; tangle
with—; —accost; —apprehend; —clash; —
corner; —escort; —espy; —intimidate; —
patrol; —protect; —raid; —regulate; —
scout; —trace; —track down; —trail; —
trap; —warn.
(See detective, constable.)

POLICY
adjectives
obvious; parsimonious; aggressive; tyrannous; questionable; conservative; enlightened; peace; paltry; time-honored; ecclesiastical; dilatory; prudent; insidious; comprehensive; inconsistent; foreign; cherished;
let-alone; well-defined; vacillating; broad;
immediate; reasonable; ruinous; cruel; attractive; shameful; honorable; intricate;

liberal; magnanimous; intriguing; devious; public; vicious; dissimulating; beneficent; straightforward; emancipation; subsequent; hostile; medium; prevailing; handsome; odious; maritime; ostensible; shortsighted; Fabian; relentless; habitual; abhorrent; all-important; oppressive; unsound; studied; sound; earnest; logical; determined; rigid; dominant; alternate; consistent; strategic; uniform; alterant; unwavering; reactionary; evasive; effective; crafty; exclusive; kindred; taxing; fiscal; unadulterated; national; increasing; effective; committal; economic; constant.

verbs

abandon—; adhere to—; adjust—; adopt—; advance—; alter—; amend—; chart—; cling to—; defend—, define—; denounce—; dictate—; dominate—; draft—; effectuate—; embark on—; endorse—; enforce—; excoriate—; execute—; expound—; fashion—; forge—; formulate—; frame—; frown upon —; inaugurate—; initiate—; institute—; justify—; modify—; orient—; overhaul —ies; propound—; pursue—; reflect—; resolve—; reverse—; shape—; sponsor—; — embitters; —hinges on; —prevails; —wobbles.

(See principle, theory, course, prudence, procedure.)

POLISH

adjectives

patrician; massive; gleaming; sleek; high.

POLISH (v)

adverbs

painstakingly; superficially; vigorously; industriously; gleamingly; glitteringly; highly; splendidly.

(See rub, smooth.)

POLISHED

adverbs

fashionably; smoothly; suavely; urbanely; socially; smugly; aristocratically; expertly; adroitly; graciously; extraordinarily; admirably; remarkably; incomparably; unsurpassably; matchlessly; splendidly; gorgeously; magnificently; brilliantly; conspicuously; arrogantly; delightfully; charmingly; commendably; elegantly; unctuously; blandly; gravely; affably; gallantly; ingratiatingly.

POLITE

adverbs

dutifully; punctiliously; meticulously; particularly; excessively; deliberately; resolutely; determinedly; naturally; graciously; amiably; delightfully; properly; carefully; cautiously; nervously; awkwardly; clumsily; reluctantly; chivalrously; gallantly; ingratiatingly; suavely; smoothly; urbanely; unctuously; adroitly; formidably; scrupulously; ridiculously; absurdly; remarkably; courteously; obsequiously; affably.

POLITENESS

adjectives

exaggerated; veneered; formidable; pretty; unwavering; hollow; unwearying; determined; freezing; cold; ironical; oriental; indefatigable; grave; affected; insolent; oily; strained; scrupulous; refined; icy.

verbs

applaud—; breach—; conform to—; commend—; enjoy—; exhibit—; laud—; practise—; praise—; struggle with—; —appeals; —conciliates; —pleases; —polishes; —refines.

(See civility, courtesy, gallantry.)

POLITICAL

adverbs

artfully; shrewdly; strategically; craftily; subtly; obviously; manifestly; naturally; keenly; cleverly; necessarily; cunningly; deeply; profoundly; intriguingly; slyly; insidiously; astutely; adroitly; sensibly; judiciously; prudently; soberly; warily; watchfully; expediently; inveterately; wisely; cannily.

POLITICIAN

adjectives

practical; artful; budding; shrewd; designing; unguided; unfledged; malevolent; noisy; timorous; kid-gloved; cunning; ordinary; mechanical; vulgar; hoary; practical; cynical; peanut; conservative; corrupt; cheap; astute; impecunious; unprincipled; redoubtable; superficial; radical.

verbs

corrupt—; oust—; pay tribute to—; support —; —addresses; —administers; —conducts; —contrives; —controls; —directs; —governs; —manages; —orates; —orders; — panders to; —presides; —solicits; —steers.

(See boss, demagogue, legislator.)

POLITICS

adjectives

contemporary; inculcating; domestic; fundamental; partisan; sentimental; crooked; fading; corrupt; practical; economic; financial; moral; befuddled; stormy; puzzled.

verbs

bury in—; dabble in—; delve in—; immerse in—; inveigh against—; meddle with—; muddle in—; participate in—; plunge into —; prostitute—; retire from—; shun—; steer clear of—; tangle with—; verse in—.

(See government, management, affairs, business.)

POLITY

adjectives

primitive; well-ordered.

POLL.

adjectives

taxable; voting; straw; nation-wide.

POLLEN

adjectives

wind-blown; insect-borne; widespread.

verbs

carry—; diffuse—; disperse—; disseminate —; dust with—; gather—; issue—; sensitize to—; shed—; sprinkle—; strew—; — drifts; —fertilizes; —germinates; —scatters; —seeds; —sows.

POLLS

verbs

bribe at—; crowd—; entice to—; flock to—; guard—; herd to—; preside at—; rally to —; regulate—; station at—; swamp—; visit —; —protect; —register.

POLLUTED

adverbs

foully; utterly; slightly; poisonously; unnecessarily; infamously; noticeably; visibly; obviously; manifestly; evidently; mysteriously; criminally; dangerously; alarmingly; seriously; pestilentially; odiously; distressingly; illegally; horribly; abominably.

POLLUTION

adjectives

horrible; fat; moral; abhorrent; waterside.

verbs

befoul with—; complain of—; expose to—; labor under—; reproach for—; —brands; — corrupts; —defaces; —defiles; —degrades; —disgraces; —harms; —impairs; —infects; —mars; —offends; —overshadows; —pillages; —saps; —scathes; —shames; —stains; —sullies; —taints.

(See impurity, corruption.)

POLYGAMY

adjectives

praiseworthy; desirable; indiscriminate; outlawed.

POMP

adjectives

painted; regal; mournful; cumbrous; long; worthless; warlike; stately; disposed; solitary; disproportionate; unprecedented; episcopal; vain; bloody; apparent; vulgar; embarrassing; infinite; dazzling; decorative; moving; papistical; liturgical; inimitable; long-drawn; despotic; bloodless; visionary; wonted; wind-blown; solemn; superfluous; contented.

verbs

affect—; display—; exhibit—; relax—; relish—; sacrifice to—; —attracts; —awes; — blazons; —dazzles; —flaunts; —glitters; — sparkles; —splashes; —wearies.

(See display, splendor, magnificence.)

POMPOSITY

adjectives

affable; rollicking; attenuated; affected; bloated; unspeakable.

POMPOUS

adverbs

insufferably; ludicrously; self-righteously; absurdly; gorgeously; officiously; ridiculously; noisily; swaggeringly; affectedly; ostentatiously; blatantly; grandiloquently; splendidly; boastfully; showily; superbly; pettily; dramatically; spectacularly; remarkably; amazingly; drolly; comically; preposterously; crassly.

POND

adjectives

steel-bright; misty; mill; midsummer; fowl; clear; circular; tranquil; darksome; shining; bottomless.

verbs

dabble in—; deposit in—; dive in—; fish in —; immerse in—; merge into—; plunge into—; wade in—; —accumulates; —beautifies; —graces; —laps; —ripples; —sparkles; —washes.

(See lake, water, lagoon.)

PONDER (v)

adverbs

silently; meditatively; sagely; monotonously; seriously; patiently; perplexedly; morbidly; moodily; closely; reverently; meekly; darkly; philosophically.

(See think, reflect, muse.)

PONDEROUS

adverbs

seriously.; weightily; gravely; momentously; heavily; mightily; clumsily; awkwardly; impressively; crudely; formally; stiffly; stupidly; dully; flatly; tiresomely, monotonously; prosaically; intolerably; strangely; insipidly; pointlessly; singularly; incomparably; inexpressibly.

PONTOON

verbs

attach—; employ—; equip with—; lower —; moor to—; travel on—; —buoys; —carries; —enables; —floats; —guards against; —holds; —indicates; —insures; —saves; —supports; —sustains.

(See bridge, boat.)

PONY

adjectives

restless; thin; woebegone.

verbs

breed—ies; corral—ies; curry—; guide—; lash—; mount—; saddle—; tether—; tumble off—; —balks; —bolts; —canters; —capers; —paws; —prances; —shies; —trots; —whinnies.

(See horse, colt, mare.)

POODLE

adjectives

wretched; shaved; frolicsome.

POOL

adjectives

rank; glistening; gloomy; palm-edged; stagnant; seething; sullen; slumbrous; slimy; motionless; mirrorlike; broad; willowy; glassy; tepid; rippling; little; whirling; pebbled; dreaming; malarial; shadowed; mottled; shining; iridescent; scintillating; deep; amber; limpid; quiet; flowing; silent; brimming; oblivious; placid; swirling; loathsome; polished; spacious; outdoor; wholesome; dimpled; indicated; narrow; foaming; transparent; reedy; fish; frog; frozen; smooth.

verbs

chlorinate—; construct—; crowd—; dip into —; drain—; house—; plunge into—; splash in—; wade in—; —delights; —glistens; —invites; —laps; —ripples; —shimmers; —simmers; —sparkles; —tempts; dive into—.

(See river, lake, pond.)

POOR

adjectives

fancy; solitary; wily; nameless; neighboring; grateful; undeserving; unattended; shamefaced; neglected; sickly.

adverbs

miserably; wretchedly; deplorably; lamentably; pitiably; pitifully; helplessly; hopelessly; strangely; amazingly; remarkably; terribly; incredibly; unfortunately; unhappily; uncommonly; unusually; embarrassingly; uncomfortably; horribly; desperately; awfully.

POPE

verbs

bow before—; consult—; defy—; support—; visit—; —addresses; —administers; —appeals to; —beads; —blesses; —controls; —governs; —interviews; —officiates; —orates; —prays; —reprimands; —sanctions; —secludes; —supplicates.

(See minister, king.)

POPLAR

adjectives

attendant; showery; huge; shuddering; feathery; towering.

POPPY

adjectives

foolish; scarlet; bloody; flaming; crumpled; memorial.

POPULACE

adjectives

murmurous; giddy; barbarous; infuriated; squalid; malcontent; insolent; virtuous; excited; noisy; irritable.

adverbs

amazingly; incredibly; deservedly; surprisingly; strikingly; particularly; incomparably; unexpectedly; undeniably; manifestly; obviously; definitely; distinctly; evidently; widely; personally; politically; professionally; unmistakably; uncommonly; highly; socially; locally.

POPULARITY

adjectives

contemporary; formidable; respectful; facile; ageless; world-wide; unbounded; amazing; tremendous; zooming; prewar; illogical; apparent; corresponding; increasing; glaring; undeniable; universal; widespread; fickle; assured; fading; undetermined.

verbs

achieve—; attain—; begrudge—; bolster—; hinder—; jeopardize—; reduce—; reinstate —; ride to—; risk—; soar to—; spring into—; suffer—; sweep into—; —declines; —recedes; —tumbles; —wanes.

(See fame, glory, greatness.)

POPULATE (v)

adverbs

thickly; densely; teemingly; sparsely; turbulently; squalidly; swarmingly; homogeneously; animatedly; urbanly.

(See inhabit.)

POPULATION

adjectives

scattered; floating; indolent; communicative; teeming; wage-earning; bucolic; industrious; curious; inflammable; resident; indigenous; migratory; proper; crowded; ancient; coming; stunted; haggard; lifeless; varied; predatory; sparse; strenuous; adventurous; squalid; turbulent; rebellious; surplus; predominant; intractable; hostile; miserable; swarming; aboriginal; motley; much-slaughtered; abstemious; shifting; enormous; nomadic; supplicating; homogeneous; submissive; sufficient; voting; dense; warlike; sluggish; energetic; active; workless; rustic; animated; agricultural; urban.

verbs

control—; decimate—; harbor—; immunize —to; increase—; oppress—; scourge—; teem with—; —ascends; —decreases; —dwindles; —expands; —mounts.

(See masses, mankind.)

adverbs

uncommonly; definitely; distinctly; overly; congestedly; thickly; problematically; inconveniently; perplexingly; particularly; unpleasantly; unmanageably.

PORCELAIN

adjectives

unglazed; transparent; rare; imported.

verbs

bake—; cast—; decorate—; dip—; finish—; form—; glaze—; mold—; paint—; polish—; prize—; scour—; shape—; shatter—; smooth—; value—; —gleams; —graces; —shines.

(See china, crockery.)

PORCH

adjectives

vine-clad; spacious; sculptured; flowery; dripping; dingy; shrouded; glass-enclosed; jutting; rude; classic; shaded.

PORCUPINE

verbs

anger—; frighten—; —arches; —baffles; —bristles; —climbs; —clings; —defends; —erects; —inflicts; —preys on; —rattles; —rolls into a ball; —rushes; —scares off; —sticks; —wounds.

(See animal.)

PORE (v)

adverbs

painfully; industriously; studiously; bookishly; academically; scholastically; ambitiously.

(See study, ponder.)

PORES

adjectives

subtile; serried; drained-out; minute; clotted; stopped; non-functioning; enlarged; ugly; fine.

verbs

block—; choke—; cleanse—; clog—; contract—; enlarge—; escape from—; filter through—; flow from—; issue from—; obstruct—; penetrate—; plug—; purge—; —discharge; —effuse; —exude; —ooze; —open.

(See skin, hole, opening.)

PORK

verbs

barbecue—; condemn—; cure—; devour—;
dine on—; examine—; freeze—; garnish—;
gobble up—; gnaw—; infect—; inspect—;
nibble—; prepare—; putrefy—; relish—;
roast—; salt—; sandwich—; serve—.
   (See meat.)

POROUS

adverbs

unfortunately; unsalably; inconveniently;
unluckily; objectionably; unserviceably;
advantageously; intentionally; purposely;
curiously; singularly; manifestly; minutely;
scientifically; plainly.

PORT

adjectives

alluring; tropical; princely; delectable;
centuried; heavenly; intervening; broad-
brimmed; broad-armed; tranquil; convenient; favorite; neighboring; unfrequented;
swaggering; blockaded; difficult; hostile;
much-used.

PORTABLE

adverbs

easily; readily; luckily; conveniently; completely; inexpensively; compactly; invisibly;
inconspicuously; particularly; comfortably;
lightly; handily; appropriately; serviceably;
suitably; instantly.

PORTALS

adjectives

flashing; forbidden; frowning; mysterious;
ancient; time-beaten; ruby-colored; massy;
gorgeous; somber; subterranean; welcoming; subtle; outer-most; sparkling; gloomy;
shadowy; oaken; statue-crowned; ogival;
wrought; open; swinging; creaking.

verbs

block—; choke—; crash—; cross—; crowd
—; enter—; file from—; filter through—;
gain—; invite through—; issue from—;
obstruct—; secure—; swarm about—; throw
open—; —gape; —welcome; —yawn.
   (See door, entrance.)

PORTEND (v)

adverbs

gloomily; darkly; unfavorably; banefully;
dolefully; evilly; stormily; symbolically;
ominously; prophetically; direly.
   (See foretell, predict.)

PORTENT

adjectives

unmistakable; vast; fiery; baneful; worse;
doleful; evil.

verbs

disregard—; fear—; realize—; recognize—;
—depresses; —disconcerts; —disturbs;
—frightens; —indicates; —looms; —oppresses; —promises; —perplexes; —puzzles;
—shadows; —shrouds; —warns.
   (See warning, meaning.)

PORTENTOUS

adverbs

heavily; grievously; sadly; ominously;
gravely; seriously; critically; imminently;
unmistakably; direly; solemnly; oddly; significantly; particularly; oddly; dangerously;
immensely; sorely; manifestly; frightfully;
tremendously; alarmingly; dreadfully; momentously; deeply; profoundly; calamitously.

PORTER

adjectives

suppliant; dark; drowsing; fat; oily; station; slovenly; obsequious; neat; industrious; heavily-laden.

PORTICO

adjectives

antique; classic; gaunt; unfinished; huge.

PORTION

adjectives

dense; important; ascending; priceless; descending; prodigal; hearty; healthful; considerable; flourishing; prescribed; plenteous; energetic; edible; introductory; cascading; dim; minute; mobile; speculative;
residual; petty; various (pl); regenera-
tive; generous; chasm-like; valuable; untouched; inviting; vast; integral; tolerable;
lofty; broad; compensated; dangerous; uncovered; equitable; unexplored; submerged;
astonishing; large; continued; remote; silvery; disinterested; alloted; soluble; superficial; protruding; substantial; picturesque;
fleshy.

verbs

allot—to; allow—; break into—s; carve
into—s; deal—s; distribute—s; divide

907

into—s; dole out—s; integrate—s; mete out—s; sample—; share—; stint—; —appeases; —protrudes; —satiates.

(See share, inheritance, quota.)

PORTION (v)

adverbs

fairly; equitably; substantially; prodigally; magnanimously; arbitrarily.

(See share, divide.)

PORTLY

adverbs

inexpressibly; unhappily; incredibly; incurably; laughably; lamentably; comfortably; contentedly; distressingly; absurdly; ridiculously; ludicrously; sadly; joyously; dangerously; heavily; funnily; complacently; complainingly; mournfully; dramatically; pathetically; shapelessly; waddlingly.

PORTRAIT

adjectives

undisputed; ancestral; unfavorable; satirical; penned; unequaled; poetical; gallery; posthumous; deathlike; faded; dark; coarse; staring; notable; vivid; authentic; mezzotint; sharp; vulgar; inimitable; somber-toned; characteristic; spirited; initial; pathetic; unlifelike; gloomy; brilliant; vigorous; distinct; demure; alluring; late; realistic; whole-length; somber; painstaking; delectable; carnationed; rubicund; hard-favored; accurate; sympathetic; untouched.

verbs

admire—; adumbrate—; delineate—; detail—; display—; dress up—; embellish—; hang—; obscure—; pose for—; prepare—; shade—; shadow—; sit for—; sketch—; unveil—; —adheres to; —copies; —depicts; illustrates.

(See masterpiece, painting, picture.)

PORTRAITURE

adjectives

idealized; truthful; moral; rigid.

PORTRAY (v)

adverbs

magnificently; graphically; vigorously; ironically; accurately; vividly; objectively; nebulously; sharply; pathetically; alluringly; realistically; somberly; sympathetically; poetically.

(See picture, paint.)

PORTRAYAL

adjectives

truthful; sympathetic; single-scene; heart-warming; objective; realistic; ethical; ever-fresh.

verbs

achieve—; applaud—; commend—; criticize—; detail—; draw—; enjoy—; practise—; rehearse—; render—; review—; —characterizes; —delights; —depicts; —describes; —relates; —recounts; —unfolds.

(See description, portrait.)

POSE

adjectives

quiet; easy; dignified; habitual; theatrical; traditional; professional; unmistakable; ridiculous; deliberate; conventional; individual; classic; charming; hieratic; autocratic; swan-like; lordly; stiff; heroic; ultimate; hereditary; effective; obsequious; countless (pl).

verbs

affect—; animate—; assume—; carve—; cast—; fashion—; hold—; imitate—; maintain—; overdo—; regard—; ridicule—; shape—; strike—; —appeals; —attitudinizes; —caricaturizes; —characterizes; —copies; —impresses.

(See attitude, posture.)

POSE (v)

adverbs

professionally; importantly; strikingly; statuesquely; dignifiedly; ridiculously; deliberately; classically; autocratically; heroically; obsequiously.

(See balance, poise.)

POSITION

adjectives

absurd; admirable; advantageous; alphabetical; altered; ambiguous; amiable; angular; anomalous; arduous; anonymous; argumentative; artistic; aristocratic; asinine; attributive; awkward; belligerent; brilliant; broad; choice; commanding; compensating; conducive; competitive; conspicuous; consular; contrasting; coveted; creditable; defensive; cramped; crouching; dangerous; definite; degraded; delicate; deplorable; dependent; desirable; desperate; despondent; desultory; detestable; dignified; different; disagreeable; dreadful; dominant; ecclesiastical; elevated; embarrassing; eminent; enviable; envious; erroneous; essential; exalted; exasperating; executive; exposed; extraordinary; fatiguing; fiscal; formidable; fortified; genial; geographical; grand; gratifying; grotesque; handy; hardy; hated; homeless; honorable; idiotic; ignominious; illustrious; imperial; important; impoverished; impregnable; inartistic; insignificant; indefensible; insular; intact; intellectual; interesting; intermediate; irksome; irretrievable; isolated; legal; lucrative; literary; lofty; long-continued; lower; luxurious; masked; mercurial; military; modest; natural-minded; obscure; oceanic; odious; official; opposite; painful; peculiar; perilous; permanent; perplexing; picturesque; pivotal; poised; precarious; precise; premier; prominent; reclining; recognized; reconnoitered; recumbent; relative; relaxed; remarkable; resolute; respectable; responsible; risky; retired; secluded; semi-reclining; serious; shifting; social; solid; stationary; sophisticated; startle; strained; strong; strategic; subordinate; subservient; substantial; superfluous; supreme; tedious; technical; tenable; theological; theoretical; thoughtful; threatening; transitional; unambitious; unassailable; uncivil; uncomfortable; unconscious; unendurable; undistinguishable; unequivocal; unfashionable; unfavorable; unique; unlovely; unquestioned; unrivaled; unsupported; unstable; untenable; unworthy; virulent; weak; wicked; worldly; ' worth-while; wretched.

verbs
acquire—; alter—; aspire to—; challenge—; check—; clarify—; complicate—; compromise—; consolidate—; damage—; defend—; demote—; dignify—; elevate to—; indicate—; jeopardize—; jockey for—; justify—; maintain—; maneuvre for—; regain —; reiterate—; restore—; resume—; retain—; shift—; solidify—; struggle for—; surrender—; survey—; usurp—; wrest — from; —attracts; —reimburses
(See job, situation, rank, status.)

POSITIVE
adverbs
disagreeably; aggressively; boldly; emphatically; truculently; extravagantly; insolently; audaciously; arrogantly; offensively; blandly; calmly; confidently; astoundingly; monstrously; preposterously; rashly; blatantly.

POSSESS (*v*)

adverbs
legally; intellectually; incontestably; legitimately; intrinsically; originally; potentially; proudly; territorially; undisputedly; conclusively; hereditarily; tranquilly; hazardously; uniquely; enduringly; formally; nominally.
(See own, occupy.)

POSSESSIONS

adjectives
forcible; territorial; illegal; undisturbed; valuable; new; substantial; colonial; uncontrolled; priceless; exclusive; peaceful; dear; steady; imperishable; complete; undisputed; insolent; miserable; calm; vast; limited; overbearing; humble; prized; conclusive; hereditary; earthly; distant; cool; unassisted; narrow; tranquil; cherished; profitable; unquestioned; rightful; kindred; hazardous; naive; small; unique; scenic; remarkable; defiling; precious; enduring; formal; comparative; demoniacal; masterly; favored.

verbs
accrue—; auction off—; command—; cull—; enjoy—; entangle—; estimate—; expand—; forfeit—; gain—; gather—; harbor—; inherit—; liquidate—; mislay—; procure—; reap—; recover—; redeem—; restore—; savor—; value—.
(See estate, assets, fortune, property.)

POSSESSIVE

adverbs
rapturously; ardently; devoutly; jealously; selfishly; fanatically; abnormally; strangely; curiously; maternally; uncommonly; peculiarly; singularly; incorrigibly; foolishly; senselessly; unfortunately; overly; desperately; ridiculously; comically; unpleasantly; embarrassingly; highly; devotedly.

POSSESSOR

adjectives
original; potential; successive (pl); privileged; peaceful; boastful; proud.

POSSIBILITY

adjectives
limping; limitless; remote; easy; dramatic; profit; abstract; contingent; dismal; moneysaving; opulent; honest; transcendent; tremendous; horrid; far-reaching; awful; flexible; domestic-social; undiminished;

mental; generous; evolutional; fearful; charming; plausible; iridescent; future; subsequent; divine; envisioned; improbable; extravagant; rhythmic; unfathomable; serene.

verbs
afford—; appreciate—; bolster—; broach—; comprehend—; deny—; determine—; diminish—; disclose—; dissipate—; embroider—; entertain—; envisage—; exhaust—; exploit —; explore—; face—; jump at—; open—; preclude—; raise—; realize—; reject—; ridicule—; rule out—; —appeals to; —dawns upon; —looms; —lurks in; —pales.
(See chance, contingency, potentiality.)

POST
(place)
adjectives
strategic; arduous; worthless; perilous; impregnable; respective; important; significant; established; permanent; fortified; newly-created; farthest; diplomatic; faint; unbodied; lucrative; sedulous.

verbs
abandon—; assign to—; banish to—; confine to—; establish—; join—; locate—; occupy —; relinquish—; settle at—; station at—; strengthen—; vacate—; —discharges; —lodges; —mobilizes; —quarters.
(See position, situation, job, place, support.)

POST (v)
adverbs
ostentatiously; publicly; secretly; strategically; perilously; intermittently; permanently; periodically; diplomatically.
(See mail, send.)

POSTER
adjectives
frigid; salacious; safety.

verbs
circulate —s; diffuse —s; disseminate —s; plaster with —s; publish —s; —advertises; —advocates; —announces; —blazons; —broaches; —flourishes; —hawks; —heralds; —noises about; —proclaims; —promulgates; —trumpets.
(See placard, advertisement, announcement, notice.)

POSTERITY
adjectives
grateful; unloving; forgetful; unworried.

verbs
bequeath to—; hand down to—; record for —; —commemorates; —condemns; —defaces; —disgraces; —emulates; —exhumes; —glorifies; —honors; —inherits; —outshines; —pales; —perpetuates; —reflects; —reproaches; —reveres; —shames; —sullies; —surpasses; —traces.
(See descendants, family, offspring.)

POSTHUMOUS
adverbs
ironically; unfortunately; tardily.

POSTPONE (v)
adverbs
indefinitely; vaguely; arbitrarily; discreetly; regularly; permanently; temporarily; ultimately; disappointingly; formally.
(See delay, defer.)

POSTPONEMENT
adjectives
indefinite; unwelcome; regular; long-awaited.

POSTSCRIPT
adjectives
lengthy; apologetic.

POSTURE
adjectives
lifeless; bending; studious; stooping; unusual; healthful; spiritual; reclining; graceful; squatting; thoughtful; ungainly; abject; limp; suggestive; impressive; absurd; inelegant; sitting; unmalicious; faulty; easy; painful; incorrect; recumbent; unmanly; supplicating; favorable; poor.

verbs
acquire—; affect—; alter—; assume—; correct—; derange—; fix—; improve—; maintain—; remedy—; ridicule—; shift—; study —; —apes; —characterizes; —impresses; —mars; —tires.
(See gesture, attitude, pose.)

POSTURING
adjectives
dramatic; virile.

POSY

adjectives
fragrant; pretty.

POT

adjectives
earthenware; tea; unusual; molded; glazed; oddly-shaped.

verbs
blacken—; hook—; immerse in—; label—; load—; preserve in—; replenish—; scour—; scrape—; scrub—; —adorns; —boils; —dangles; —glistens; —seethes; —simmers.
(See caldron, kettle.)

POTATION

adjectives
sparkling; nightly; plentiful; spirituous; bubbling; joyous.

POTATO

adjectives
underdone; mashed; baked; frozen; scalloped; sweet; fried; eyeless.

POTENCY

adjectives
tragic; changeful; extraordinary; supernatural; changeful; outstanding; intense; remarkable; long-lived.

POTENT

adverbs
unexpectedly; surprisingly; fatally; peculiarly; singularly; incredibly; amazingly; moderately; scarcely; unusually; commendably; influentially; politically; personally; admittedly; officially; effectively; sufficiently; uncommonly; adequately; overwhelmingly; satisfactorily.

POTENTATE

adjectives
prodigal; rebel; pitiless; powerful; crowned; wealthy; temporal; illustrious; peerless; dread; prudent; wicked.

POTENTIALITY

adjectives
scattered (pl); lasting; remarkable; latent.

verbs
choke—; confer—; cripple—; develop—; discover—; double—; exhaust—; exploit—;

force—; lame—; maim—; muzzle—; realize—; recognize—; shatter—; silence—; strangle—; strengthen—; suppress—; utilize—; weaken—.
(See power, possibility.)

POTION

adjectives
bittersweet; direful; deadly; narcotic; soporific.

verbs
concoct—; dose with—; drain—; gulp down—; lap up—; mix—; quaff—; sip—; swallow—; swig—; swill—; toss off—; wash down—; —nauseates; —palliates; —relieves; —remedies; —restores.
(See dose, medicine, poison, liquid.)

POTTERY

adjectives
shattered; valuable; unusual; native; handmade.

POUCH

adjectives
capacious; gorgeous; bulging.

POULTICE

verbs
apply—; pat on—; smear—; surround with —s; treat with—; —allays; —alleviates; —balms; —comforts; —cures; —eases; —foments; —mitigates; —palliates; —refreshes; —relieves; —remedies; —soaks; —soothes.
(See salve, ointment.)

POUNCE (*v*)

adverbs
viciously; vindictively; furiously; instantaneously; murderously; diabolically; formidably; belligerently.
(See jump, dash.)

POUND

adjectives
scant; full; generous.

POUND (*v*)

adverbs
obstreperously; tirelessly; vigorously; lustily; bestially; vociferously; thunderously.
(See beat, strike.)

POUR (*v*)

adverbs
unceasingly; incessantly; liberally; hospit-

ably; effusively; unstintingly; hysterically; liquidly; melodiously; insatiably.

(See flow, stream.)

POUT (v)

adverbs

pettishly; sulkily; prettily; coyly; petulantly; tearfully; despondently.

(See sulk, scowl.)

POVERTY

adjectives

pinching; appalling; relative; hated; imaginary; benumbing; absolute; comparative; inevitable; abject; astonishing; squalid; wretched; genteel; peculiar; hard-working; deepening; irremediable; everlasting; low; continual; lifelong; haughty; distressful; speedy; extreme; general; worthless; utter; honorable; contorted; consequent; disgraceful.

verbs

abhor—; abolish—; accept—; banish—; boast of—; drive off—; outwit—; plead—; prolong—; suffer—; —callouses; —degrades; —dogs; —fetters; —oppresses; —overtakes; —pursues; —ravages; --stalks; —stigmatizes.

(See destitution, impoverishment, need, penury.)

POWDER
(general)

adjectives

smokeless; bronze; ordered; resultant; odorless; moistened; deadly; notorious; fetid; capsulated; dictatorial; heavy; inferior; murderous.

verbs

apply—; dab in—; dip in—; dust with—; prink with—; reduce to—; smear—; spread —; touch up with—; —beautifies; —conceals; —embellishes; —glorifies; —harmonizes; —improves; —mellows; —perfects; —pretties; —primes; —soothes; —tricks; —whitens.

(See make-up, dust, gunpowder.)

POWDER (v)

adverbs

fashionably; flirtatiously; glamorously; exaggeratedly; fascinatingly; bewitchingly; enchantingly.

(See perfume, scent.)

adjectives

abiding; abrogating; abrupt; absent; absolute; absorbing; abundant; active; advancing; adverse; afflicted; all-consuming; allegorizing; all-embracing; allied; all-inhering; amazing; ample; alternative; amorous; analytic; ancestral; ancient; antipathetic; apostolic; appalling; appointing; arbitrary; arch-angelic; architectural; argumentative; assertive; assumed; autocratic; belligerent; autonomous; balanced; beneficent; bestial; blessed; blighted; boasted; braking; boundless; brilliant; budding; buying; capricious; catapulting; celestial; centralizing; chameleon-like; coercive; chemic; civil; clairvoyant; cloven; coming; clerical; colossal; colonizing; comic; commanding; communicative; complete; compelling; composing; compulsive; concentrated; concocted; confederated; confident; confirming; conscious; considerable; consequent; consistent; constitutional; constructive; contending; contingent; contracting; corporate; cosmic; conversational; cosmetic; creative; critical; crowned; curative; curious; deepening; dangerous; defensive; delegated; deliberative; delicate; delightful; denuding; departed; desolate; despotic; destructive; developed; dictatorial; discretional; discerning; disorderly; disturbing; divine; dominant; dormant; driving; dramatic; dulled; dynamic; earning; earth-prisoned; ecclesiastical; educational; effulgent; elastic; elemental; emotional; enchanted; enhanced; energizing; enlarged; enormous; exceeding; erosive; ever-dreaded; evident; exalted; exceptional; excessive; exchangeable; executive; exhaustive; existing; expansive; exorbitant; explosive; extemporaneous; extraordinary; facile; fangless; fatal; far-reaching; fatherly; feeble; feudal; fertilizing; fierce; filial; financial; first-rate; flawless; flexible; formative; full; formidable; fraudulent; frightful; fundamental; generative; generous; genial; genuine; gigantic; godlike; heartfelt; granted; graphic; grasping; growing; guiding; hateful; healing; heavy; high; heavenly; heroic; hidden; hypnotic; imaginative; immature; immeasurable; immediate; immense; immortal; imperial; impossible; imperialist; implied; inborn; incomprehensible; indefinite; individual; indomitable; industrial; inexplicable; inevitable; infective; infernal; infinite; influential; ingrained; inherent; insensate; inimitable; inner; insensible; insubordinate; intellectual; intelligent; intermittent; interposing; intoxicating; intrinsic; intuitive; inutile; invalid; inventive; inveterate; invincible; invisible; irresistible; irresponsible; jealous; judicial; just; keen; kindly; kingly; lasting; latent; lawless; learning; legal; legislative; lifting; limited; linguistic; living; lordly; lubricating; luminous; luxurious; magical; magnetic; magnifying; maiming; malevolent; malign; marvelous; massive; mastering; mature; mental; mesmeric; microscopic; mighty; miraculous; monarchical; mon-eyed; moral; motive; mortal; murderous; muscular; narcotic; musical; myriad (pl); mysterious; necessary; necromantic; nefarious; obnoxious; nominal; nutritive; objurgatory; occult; omnipotent; omnipresent; ominous; omniscient; oratorical; oracular; organizing; original; overmastering; oxidizing; overwhelming; paramount; parliamentary; particular; passive; patient; patriarchal; peaceable; peculiar; penetrating; perceptive; pernicious; personal; perilous; periodical; persuasive; plastic; poetic; poisonous; political; potential; practical; preponderant; prevailing; primal; primordial; productive; profit; projectile; prolific; proper; prophetic; protecting; psychologic; public; purchasing; purging; quickening; rare; rational; reasoning; reckless; recumbent; recognized; recuperative; regal; relentless; remarkable; remorseless; renewed; reparative; reportorial; reserve; repulsive; requisite; resisting; restless; restrained; resultant; ripening; rival; revolutionary; rounded; royal; ruling; ruthless; sardonic; satanic; scant; secular; scathing; secret; seductive; seer-like; seething; self-dependent; selfish; self-realizing; self-restraining; sinister; selfsame; self-succeeding; silky; singular; sinless; siren; slow-moving; sole; speculative; sophisticated; spiritual; spontaneous; sprightly; springing; stagnant; startling; stimulating; sufficient; subtle; substantial; sullen; superior; superhuman; supernal; supernatural; supreme; surcharged; surging; surpassing; surprising; sustained; sweet; technical; temporal; terrible; thunderous; tranquil; transcendental; transforming; transporting; tremendous; tumultuous; twofold; tyrannous; ultimate; unappealable; unappeased; unborn; unbounded; uncanny; unconscious; undoubted; unexpected; unearthly; unequaled; unfettered; unfamiliar; unhallowed; uninviting; united; universal; unjust; unlimited; unmeasured; unprecedented; unrivaled; un-

qualified; unrestricted; unseen; unsightly; unspent; unsuspected; untried; unusual; unwearied; unwomanly; uplifting; urgent; utmost; vague; versatile; various (pl); vested; vibrant; victorious; violent; vital; vitalizing; waning; warlike; wearied; wondrous; worsted; worn; smooth; sufficient; self-sustaining.

verbs

abuse—; achieve—; animate with—; ascertain—; bask in—; bid for—; bolster—; bulwark by—; centralize—; check—; climb to —; clip—; clothe in—; confer—upon; consolidate—; crave—; curb—; curtail—; delegate—to; deprive of—; derive—from; dilute —; diminish—; disseminate—; dissipate—; dwarf—; elect to—; endow with—; enhance —; entrust with—; evince—; exercise—; exhaust—; fathom—; fatten on—; forfeit —; generate—; grant—; harness—; impair —, impart—to; impute—to; intensify—; intoxicate with—; lodge—in; lust for—; manifest—; nullify—; offset—; paralyze—; radiate—; regain—; resent—; restrict—; sap —; seize—; sense—; shake—; shear of—; stem—; strip of—; strive for—; surrender —; thirst for—; transmit—; unleash—; undermine—; usurp—; vest—in; vote into —; wield—; worship—; —decays; —declines; —resides in; —wanes; —waxes; —withers.

(See authority, influence, predominance, faculty, force, energy.)

POWERFUL

adverbs

inscrutably; amazingly; omnisciently; dangerously; dreadfully; unbelievably; vigorously; spiritually; influentially; irresistibly; indomitably; intensely; resolutely; acutely; cruelly; brutally; trenchantly; materially; commercially; socially; politically; universally; incredibly; terribly.

POWERLESS

adverbs

pitiably; desperately; hopelessly; inefficiently; altogether; remarkably; deplorably; unhappily; ineptly; awkwardly; clumsily; timorously; terribly; lamentably; miserably; wretchedly; incredibly; curiously; oddly; singularly; pathetically; stupidly; astoundingly; utterly.

913

PRACTICABILITY

adjectives

concrete; definite; inherent.

PRACTICABLE

adverbs

immediately; usefully; serviceably; opportunely; overwhelmingly; completely; happily; fortunately; conveniently; scientifically; easily; definitely; distinctly; particularly; unexpectedly; strikingly; remarkably; amazingly; luckily; sensibly; profitably; valuably; absolutely; reliably; dependably; positively.

PRACTICAL

adverbs

thoroughly; sensibly; wisely; usefully; commendably; particularly; admirably; fortunately; altogether; sagaciously; splendidly; happily.

PRACTICE

adjectives

ascetic; bayonet; cynical; lucrative; objectionable; lewd; diversified; tedious; competitive; time-honored; arduous; adulterous; traditional; wanton; long; vile; base; private; constant; nefarious; enthusiastic; ancient; shameless; magical; pernicious; assiduous; pagan; treasonable; normal; engineering; recognized; cunning; dangerous; corrupt; horrible; forensic; prevalent; monopolistic; augmented; ungentleman-like; consulting; unvarying; sedulous; ruined; extensive; actual; unique; psychoanalytic; questionable; contrary; licentious; deliberating; consequent; insidious; eminent; degrading; active; flourishing; present; superstitious; robust; irregular; choir; hateful; religious; fascinating; attendant; idolatrous; polygamous; unnatural; universal; prejudiced; comprehensive; revolutionized.

verbs

abandon—; acquire by—; addict to—; adhere to—; adopt—; neglect—; observe—; oppose—; perpetuate—; repress—; resort to—; restrict—; revive—; sanction—; —involves; —survives.

(See habit, conventionality, custom, exercise, performance.)

PRACTICE (v)

adverbs

spontaneously; discordantly; surreptitiously; diligently; vigorously; ambitiously; industriously; assiduously; professionally; sedulously; competitively; privately; forensically; periodically.

(See exercise, train, apply.)

PRACTITIONER

adjectives

successful; unqualified; ardent; ignorant; medical; mercenary.

PRAIRIE

adjectives

bleak; naked; blessed; spacious; teeming; carpeted; flowery; unbroken; corn-bladed; stubble-lined; wild; beautiful; short-turfed; great; undulating; sun-browned; verdant; rolling; broken; shaking.

verbs

course—; dwell on—; inhabit—; retire to—; ride—; roam—; traverse—; trek across—; view—; wander over—; wend across—; —blazes; —bores; —confronts; —extends.

(See plain, valley.)

PRAISE

adjectives

voluble; artless; sincere; partial; vain; moderate; humble; lavish; benignant; ignoble; love-pervaded; perfect; unstinted; aggressive; thriftless; expiatory; copious; unnecessary; untimely; reluctant; cynical; muted; awful; unmerited; unspoken; lofty; eloquent; elicited; unstinted; dolesome; passive; hearty; ill-considered; unworthy; unacceptable; deserved; solemn; ceaseless; partial; enthusiastic; unsought; warm; profane; silent; everlasting; unceasing; flattering; grudging; immortal; endless; virtuous; mingled; profuse; judicious; hollow; unqualified; melodious; implied; veiled; eternal; effusive; great; absent; fair; unbroken; lavish; excessive; exaggerated; intemperate; high; undeserving; compulsory.

verbs

administer—; apportion—; aspire to—; bestow—upon; bloom under—; capture—; deny—; desist from—; earn—; entitle to—; excite—; exhaust—; heap—upon; inspire—; justify—; pour out—; proclaim—; shower —upon; sing—; sum up—; swamp with—; —diminishes; —warms.

(See glory, approbation, compliment, adulation, commendation, applause.)

PRAISE (v)

adverbs

extravagantly; effusively; voluntarily; universally; judiciously; fulsomely; sincerely; flatteringly; rhapsodically; volubly; goldenly; immoderately; lavishly; benignantly; unstintedly; copiously; eloquently; intemperately.

(See extol, laud.)

PRAISEWORTHY

adverbs

deservedly; meritoriously; unusually; admirably; admittedly; conspicuously; modestly; highly; uncommonly; remarkably; exceptionally; undoubtedly; genuinely; highly; singularly; immensely; extremely; impressively; signally; unimpeachably; matchlessly; incomparably.

PRANCE (v)

adverbs

spiritedly; mincingly; vigorously; picturesquely; madly; freakishly; sportively.

(See cavort, spring.)

PRANK

adjectives

hoyden; mad; fruitless; common; wily; extravagant; gamesome; humorous; idle; freakish; youthful.

verbs

anticipate—; beguile with—s; concoct—; dodge—; indulge in—; relish—; smother—; —amuses; —disgusts; —diverts; —irks; —seduces; —tires; —traps; —tricks; —vexes.

(See frolic, joke, jest.)

PRANKISH

adverbs

mischievously; roguishly; teasingly; persistently; unexpectedly; incorrigibly; playfully; innocently; foolishly; absurdly; merrily; persistently; ludicrously; idly; frivolously; remarkably; cleverly; ingeniously.

PRANKSTER

verbs

chastize—; dodge—; evade—; forestall—; rebuke—; reprimand—; reproach—; —beguiles; —concocts; —contrives; —disports; —entertains; —wearies.

(See clown, fool, jester.)

PRATE (v)

adverbs

idiotically; foolishly; maliciously; vindictively; spitefully; boastfully; sacreligiously.

(See talk, chatter.)

PRATING

adjectives

solemn; continuous; noisy; bothersome.

PRATTLE

adjectives

winsome; foolish; intermittent.

PRATTLE (v)

adverbs

vapidly; artlessly; childishly; inanely; coyly; winsomely; foolishly; jejunely; insipidly.

(See talk, chatter, babble.)

PRAY (v)

adverbs

fervently; earnestly; distractedly; conspicuously; solemnly; humbly; devoutly; audibly; passionately; effusively; dumbly; supplicatingly; tremulously; blasphemously; inarticulately; wordlessly; virtuously; fruitlessly; sepulchrally.

(See entreat, beg.)

PRAYER

adjectives

idle; fervent; audible; professional; passionate; effectual; effusive; little; soft; prattled; sobbing; boding; priestly; dumb; nightly; chanted; humble; unuttered; dying; melting; weak; pious; supplicating; creditable; stated; conscious; bootless; earnest; perpetual; weekly; specious; poor; hearty; masticated; wistful; sublime; tremulous; common; granted; sunrise; contemptible; insane; trembling; blasphemous; pattered; morning; awed; inarticulate; wordless; fair; consecrating; virtuous; sepulchral; long-groaned; puling; reluctant; grateful; voluble; thankful; vociferated; wrestling; high-blooded; unlawful; true; pagan; fruitless; pleading; hallowing.

verbs

address—; avert by—; attend—; blend in —; bless in—; bow in—; chant—; console by—; fall down in—; fulfill—; grant—; intone—; kneel in—; offer up—; rattle off —s; unite in—; utter—; —beseeches; —

deifies; —entreats; —glorifies; —importunes; —petitions; —reconciles; —supplicates.

(See benediction, mass, entreaty, confession.)

PREACH (v)

adverbs

unctuously; eloquently; rabidly; narrowly; militantly; independently; sonorously; sanctimoniously; sublimely; vociferously; tiresomely; zealously; austerely; itinerantly.

(See speak, advise, teach.)

PREACHER

adjectives

dissenting; eloquent; judicious; tiresome; poor; dark-lantern; moonlight; fiery; zealous; austere; ordinary; misguided; eminent; opposition; devoted; itinerant; traveling; understanding.

PRECARIOUS

adverbs

obviously; naturally; unduly; admittedly; necessarily; terribly; painfully; gravely; awfully; fearfully; alarmingly; grievously; frequently; peculiarly.

PRECAUTION

adjectives

commendable; polite; absolute; sure; obvious; ordinary; oratorical; futile; former; due; extraordinary; well-known; sensible; businesslike; lifesaving; vigilant; utmost; absurd; remarkably; sanitary; superfluous; vital; undue; attentive.

verbs

advocate—; disregard—; employ—; enforce —; exercise—; heed—; necessitate—; neglect—; observe—; omit—; snelve—; suggest —; urge—; view with—; —assures; —arms; —guards; —preestablishes.

(See caution, care.)

PRECAUTIONARY

adverbs

carefully; punctiliously; meticulously; laudably; strangely; unfailingly; vigilantly; warily; significantly; oddly; ominously; portentously; momentously; unusually; surreptitiously; secretly; furtively; quietly; thoroughly; strikingly.

PRECEDENT

adjectives

laudable; rigorous; historical; auspicious; social; romantic; inappropriate; mighty; semi-barbaric.

verbs

afford—; bolster by—; break—; concede to —; defeat—; establish—; follow—; govern by—; invoke—; quote—; refer to—; shatter —; shun—; suffer from—; —controls; —determines; —enslaves; —justifies; —regulates; —rules.

(See custom, authority.)

PRECEPT

adjectives

repeated; benevolent; mild; excellent; civil; sage; strange; abstruse; divine; averaged; dull; moral; traditional; innumerable (pl); sublime.

verbs

advocate—; authorize—; compile—s; disobey—; dispense—; entrust—; formulate—; fulfill—; issue—; promulgate—; sanction—; submit to—; violate—; —decrees; —dictates; —forbids; —imposes; —instructs; —limits; —ordains; —orders; —prohibits; —requests; —requires; —restrains; —restricts.

(See order, principle, teaching, commandment, instruction.)

PRECINCT

adjectives

attractive; holy; warm; hallowed; consecrated; awful; sordid; local.

PRECIOUS

adverbs

unusually; adorably; remarkably; pricelessly; unreasonably; incredibly; singularly; curiously; altogether; unbelievably; understandably; uncommonly; amazingly; fantastically; immensely; immeasurably; incalculably.

PRECIPICE

adjectives

frowning; dizzy; granite; vertical; dread; superb; hanging; wooded; tremendous; beetling; cloven; rimmed; slippery; ivy-covered; stupendous.

verbs

careen down—; clamber up—; cling to—; hang on—; hazard—; risk—; scan—; slide down—; survey—; teeter on—; venture on —; —blocks; —cuts off; —endangers; —engulfs; —jeopardizes; —imperils; —swallows.

(See cliff, mountain.)

PRECIPITATION
adjectives
complete; extraordinary; daily.

PRECIPITOUS
adverbs
steeply; impossibly; dangerously; riskily; alarmingly; terribly; terrifyingly; incredibly; unreasonably; unspeakably; deucedly; murderously; roughly; icily; tremendously; impressively; imposingly; magnificently; superbly; splendidly; grandly; incalculably; immeasurably; dizzily; stupendously.

PRECISE
adverbs
overwhelmingly; absolutely; dependably; scrupulously; ridiculously; infallibly; remarkably; uncannily; meticulously; mechanically; monotonously; invariably; deliberately; unimpeachably; rigidly; mathematically; scientifically; carefully; particularly; painstakingly; rigorously; insatiably; avidly; necessarily; punctiliously; compellingly; impartially; uniformly.

PRECISION
adjectives
academic; calm; classical; scientific; unerring; rigorous; exquisite; passionate; inflexible; finical; rapid; utmost; careless; nauseating; antique; mechanical; geometrical; marvelous; rhythmic; remarkable; military; delighted; mathematical; melancholy; masterly; convincing; grammatical; admirable; meticulous; faithful; deadly; tolerable; delicate; sufficient; faultless; austere; overwhelming.

verbs
achieve—; applaud—; commend—; demonstrate—; denote—; disclose—; display—; evince—; exhibit—; lack—; manifest—; reveal—; urge—; —assures; —clarifies.

(See accuracy.)

PRECOCIOUS
adverbs
amazingly; remarkably; smartly; keenly; unusually; unpleasantly; disagreeably; impertinently; imprudently; knowingly; pert-ly; offensively; saucily; boldly; flippantly; bumptiously; obtrusively; oddly; incredibly; uncommonly; surprisingly.

PRECONCEPTION
adjectives
profound; definite; sentimental; unusual.

PREDATORY
adverbs
cruelly; rapaciously; voraciously; uncommonly; naturally; savagely; maliciously; wantonly; ravenously; barbarously; incorrigibly; piratically; cleverly; ungovernably; reprehensibly.

PREDECESSORS
adjectives
resourceful; superstitious; illustrious; ghostly.

verbs
commemorate—; emulate—; excel—; inherit from—; outshine—; succeed—; surpass—; trace—; —advise; —bequeath; —construct; —design; —floor; —found; —frame; —record; —will to.

(See ancestor.)

PREDICAMENT
adjectives
distressing; piteous; unhappy; mechanical; desperate; awkward; terrible.

verbs
alleviate—; avoid—; disentangle—; enjoy —; evade—; labor through—; manage—; risk—; sentimentalize—; shroud—; tackle —; unravel—; view—; —confronts; —distresses; —embarrasses; —flusters; —restrains; —shames.

(See dilemma, embarrassment, position, problem, situation.)

PREDICT (v)
adverbs
prophetically; confidently; correctly; lugubriously; mournfully; dismally; darkly; complacently; boldly; astrologically; miraculously.

(See foretell, portend.)

PREDICTION
adjectives
sure-fire; warlike; aristocratic; past; off-

hand; dominant; scientific; dismal; astrological; thunderous; poetical; overconfident; remarkable.

verbs

base—on; cast—; challenge—; divine—; justify—; upset—; venture—; verify—; —augurs; —betokens; —bids; —bodes; —excites; —foreshadows; —foretells; —forewarns; —heralds; —indicates; —portends; —precurses; —presages; —prognosticates; —promises; —prophesies.

(See prognostication, prophesy.)

PREDILECTION

adjectives

perverse; striking; traditional; broad-headed; ancient; well-understood.

PREDISPOSITION

adjectives

eternal; obvious; hereditary.

PREDOMINANCE

adjectives

oppressive; hoar; acknowledged; humorous; imperious; definite.

verbs

acquire—; assert—over; attain—; challenge —; gain—; garner—; spread—; —assures; —influences; —leads; —overbears; —overpowers; —overrides; —outweighs; —pervades; —prevails; —rages; —roots in; —succeeds.

(See power.)

PREDOMINANT

adverbs

rightfully; authoritatively; eminently; officially; regularly; imperiously; proudly; offensively; regally; electively; admittedly.

PREEMINENCE

adjectives

distinguished; dignified; established; unquestionable; intellectual.

verbs

acquire—; attain—; crave—; crown with—; culminate in—; demand—; reach—; shadow —; —eclipses; —glorifies; —inflates; —outbalances; —outstrips; —outweighs; —precedes; —prevails; —transcends; —whips.

(See fame, prominence, eminence, excellence.)

PREFACE

adjectives

hilarious; forcible; well-composed; epigrammatic.

PREFER (v)

adverbs

vastly; personally; infinitely; particularly; politically; individually; overwhelmingly; unaccountably; emotionally.

(See choose, pick.)

PREFERABLE

adverbs

decidedly; altogether; slightly; definitely; unquestionably; commercially; sensibly; practically; artistically; indubitably; genuinely; popularly; politically.

PREFERENCE

adjectives

personal; particular; exaggerated; political; individual; calculated; affectional; premature; overwhelming; unaccountable; definite.

verbs

acquire—; allow—; determine—; express—; exercise—; fix—; harbor—; indulge in—; list—; mark—; muse over—; offer—; permit—; poll—; select—; shout—; single out —; —culls; —decides; —elects; —espouses; —fancies.

(See choice, alternative.)

PREGNANCY

verbs

detect—; determine—; evade—; examine for—; fear—; generate in—; incur—; induce—; prevent—; procreate in—; produce —; suggest—; yield in—; —alters; —ensues; —increases; —irritates; —multiplies; —nauseates.

PREJUDICE

adjectives

antique; arrogant; feudal; vile; personal; violent; popular; abandoned; tender; ingrained; sectional; unworthy; virulent; vulgar; unflinching; established; unreflective; aristocratical; tainted; logical; conservative; superficial; pious; unconscious; tribal; present; frivolous; patrician; ignorant; senile; unreasonable; miserable; political; tenacious; sexual; bitter; undue; absorbing; intense; inveterate; imperial; unfounded; entrenched; fierce; social; furious; insular; religious; economic; invincible; superstitious.

verbs

arouse—; awaken—; beget—; beset with—; break down—; combat—; defy—; dictate by—; emancipate from—; erase—; exploit —; lampoon—; nourish—; oust—; pander to—; preach—; purge of—; shed—; subserve—; survive—; —distorts; —flourishes; —influences; —persists; —poisons; —shades; —vanishes; —undermines; —weakens.

(See bias, obsession, hate, judgment, opinion.)

PREJUDICE (v)

adverbs

hopelessly; personally; violently; sectionally; vulgarly; aristocratically; logically; unconsciously; ignorantly; irrationally; sexually; socially; inveterately; religiously; economically; superstitiously; politically.

(See injure, hurt.)

PREJUDICED

adverbs

unreasonably; unfavorably; affectionately; indulgently; viciously; maliciously; unfortunately; happily; absurdly; jealously; enviously; unfairly; narrowly; senselessly; terribly; doctrinally; politically; mischievously; indelibly; wrongfully; provincially; fanatically; outrageously; dreadfully; hopelessly.

PREJUDICIAL

adverbs

strongly; unfavorably; criminally; highly; incontrovertibly; definitely; fanatically; outrageously; scandalously; obviously; manifestly; evidently; wrongly; secretly; perniciously; disastrously; exceptionably; grievously; horribly; reprehensibly; inadvisably; unpardonably.

PRELATE

adjectives

haughty; fatuous; foreign; pampered; reverend; gallant; distinguished; princely; shrewd.

PRELIMINARY

adjectives

mysterious; invariable; essential; valuable; inevitable; indispensable.

verbs

anticipate—; arrange—; engage in—; miss —; observe—; settle—; stage—; view—;

—allays; —appeals; —entertains; —heads; —introduces; —leads; —precedes; —prefixes; —ushers in; —bridges; —prepares.

(See introduction, opening, ceremony, preface, prelude.)

PRELUDE

adjectives

fatal; mellow; formal; unpretentious; necessary.

PREMATURE

adverbs

unfortunately; unwisely; thoughtlessly; senselessly; recklessly; ineptly; clumsily; maladroitly; unskilfully; foolishly; imprudently; indiscreetly; disastrously; undiplomatically; inexpediently; calamitously; ill-advisedly; treacherously; sadly.

PREMEDITATED

adverbs

criminally; admittedly; wickedly; brutally; savagely; mischievously; outrageously; scandalously; maliciously; carefully; furtively; conclusively; unanswerably; inferentially; manifestly; cruelly; obviously; nefariously.

PREMISE

adjectives

false; petty; inconceivable; assumed; fundamental; unsound; unexamined; insufficient; academic; specific; cardinal.

verbs

assume—; bank on—; contradict—; depend on—; discuss—; endorse—; establish—; examine—; follow—; guard—; impair—; oppose—; question—; ratify—; rebut—; rely on—; stand upon—; support—; uphold —; verify—.

(See proposition, assumption, supposition, hypothesis.)

PREMONITORY

adverbs

distinctly; formidably; terribly; inferentially; fearfully; thoughtfully; surreptitiously; obviously; manifestly; unmistakably; woefully; horribly; coldly; cruelly; fortunately; subtly; significantly; gravely; deliberately; generously; fraternally; helpfully; suggestively; threateningly.

PREOCCUPATION

adjectives

smiling; intellectual; harassed; religious.

verbs

arouse from—; bury in—; cloud in—; distract from—; erase—; examine in—; immerse in—; interrupt—; necessitate—; notice—; observe—; scan in—; seal in—; view with—; —entertains; —reflects; —revises; —shrouds.

(See reverie, lethargy.)

PREOCCUPY (*v*)

adverbs

incessantly; intellectually; religiously; studiously; ambitiously; vigorously; clerically; mentally.

(See absorb, occupy.)

PREPARATION

adjectives

ineffectual; anatomical; excellent; nervous; proprietary; essential; initial; frantic; skillful; painstaking; elaborate; manifold; active; warlike; energetic; constant; secret; formidable; impartial; adequate; virtuous; mercurial; vigorous; imperfect; extensive; pain-killing; mighty; scientific; healthful; food; scant; minute; needful; intellectual; effectual; incessant.

verbs

advocate—; demand—; drill in—; justify—; lack—; plunge into—s; —aids; —arms; —arrays; —edifies; —enlightens; —expounds; —familiarizes; —grounds; —implants; —introduces; —organizes; —tunes.

(See qualification, training.)

PREPARATORY

adverbs

gravely; soberly; sadly; woefully; horribly; carefully; cautiously; completely; happily; rapturously; ecstatically; excitedly; frenziedly; heartbrokenly; hastily; deliberately; unwillingly; reluctantly; wildly; eagerly; anxiously; surreptitiously; resolutely; gallantly; thoughtfully; quietly; noisily; serenely; calmly; generously; ardently; piously; reverently; prayerfully.

PREPARE (*v*)

adverbs

amicably; gallantly; delectably; professionally; tastefully; manifestly; gravely; gratuitously; previously; independently; vigorous-

ly; sedulously; duly; amply; privately; cautiously; ceremoniously; wilfully; effectually; elaborately; energetically; formidably; minutely.

(See fit, provide, adapt.)

PREPARED

adverbs

well; badly; completely; scarcely; hardly; wonderfully; remarkably; eminently; fully; admirably; competently; fairly; barely; fortunately; skilfully; carefully; generously; altogether; unusually.

PREPONDERANCE

adjectives

undue; tremendous; noticeable; unquestioned.

PREPONDERANT

adverbs

heavily; unfairly; beneficially; influentially; dangerously; increasingly; politically; socially; dreadfully; unfortunately; imperiously; currently; tellingly; authoritatively; curiously; outrageously; naturally.

PREPOSSESSION

adjectives

personal; sudden; unfortunate; religious; unfavorable.

PREROGATIVE

adjectives

entrenched; personal; enviable.

verbs

allow—; assert—; authorize—; challenge—; demand—; disqualify—; entitle to—; exact—; extend—; grant—; insist on—; merit —; relax—; usurp—; violate—; wield—; —arrogates; —encroaches; —infringes.

(See privilege, right.)

PRESCIENCE

adjectives

slumberous; indistinct; passionate; hollow; unresisted; mystic.

PRESCRIBE (*v*)

adverbs

punctiliously; wisely; sagely; variously; preposterously; exclusively; legally; specifically; medically; medicinally; methodically.

(See order, advise.)

PRESCRIPTION

adjectives
favorite; exclusive; specific; deep-rooted; legal; unfailing; definite; mystic; age-old.

verbs
acquire—; addict to—; adhere to—; concoct —; dispense—s; fill—; follow—; formulate —; issue—; mix—; order—; recommend—; require—; write—; —alleviates; —eases; —instructs; —palliates; —relieves; —remedies; —soothes.
(See formula, medicine, direction.)

PRESENCE

adjectives
portly; reassuring; immediate; comely; inconspicuous; instant; palpitating; hateful; pale; glorious; visible; posthumous; gracious; protecting; unfamiliar; distinct; august; imposing; resplendent; singular; semiluminous; important; haunting; noiseless; royal; wondrous; palpable; ruddy; tranquil; effulgent; eternal; masked; universal; intolerant; abhorred; grim; imperial; impressive; ignoble; threatened; culprit; enchanting; maternal; detected; solemn; chastening; visionary; transforming; protecting; admirable; close; tender; celestial; gaunt; ramshackle; habitual; blighted; stately; passionate; continual; dreadful; perpetual; animate; pervading; abrupt; excellent; unrecognized; mortal; declared; commanding; dignified; unauthorized; unwelcome; striking; majestic; private; blessed; divine; invisible; engaging; stately; handsome; shadowy; cheering; unconjectured; gentle; combined.

verbs
acknowledge—; advertise—; announce—; ascertain—; conduct into—; detect—; enjoy—; mark—; reveal—; tolerate—; usher into—; —disturbs; —evokes; —impresses; —irritates.

PRESENT

adjectives
immediate; solid; magnificent; spontaneous; elegant; appropriate; ever-fleeting; eternal; realistic; substantial; grief-shadowed; reluctant; alien; visionary; stormy; placid.

verbs
accept—; acknowledge—; bedeck—; beribbon—s; bestow—s upon; conceal—; decline —; guard—s; lavish with—s; offer—; pres-

ent with—; solicit—; tender—; view—s; —dazzles; —excites; —flatters; —pleases; reconciles; —s shower upon; —stems; dispense—s.
(See gift.)

adverbs
inappropriately; unsuitably; inconveniently; fortunately; happily; conveniently; opportunely; always; seldom; occasionally; objectionably; embarrassingly; unwarrantably; unfortunately; ever; constantly; unexpectedly; auspiciously; generously; considerately; graciously.

PRESENT (v)

adverbs
modestly; formally; humbly; appropriately; reluctantly; satirically; adequately; realistically; brazenly; providentially; ethically; imploringly; casually; repeatedly; materially.
(See give, offer, introduce.)

PRESENTATION

adjectives
technical; diligent; elaborate; artistic; condensed; demon; superb; graphic; ruddy; attractive; dispassionate; illustrative; terse; farewell.

verbs
acknowledge—; administer—; anticipate—; beg for—; favor with—; ignore—; postpone —; propose—; refuse—; reject—; seek—; welcome—; withhold—; —accords; —bestows; —conciliates; —introduces; —reveals.
(See introduction.)

PRESENTIMENT

adjectives
fearful; cold; apt; uneasy; vague; unquiet; undefinable; decisive; guilty.

verbs
argue—; harbor—; heed—; laugh down—; ridicule—; —aggravates; —augurs; —betokens; —bids; —bodes; —disturbs; —excites; —foreshadows; —foretells; —forewarns; —grows; —precurses; —troubles; —visits; —presages.
(See anticipation, apprehension, fear.)

PRESENTMENT

adjectives
counterfeit; vague; forceful; definite.

PRESERVATION

adjectives

perfect; inflexible; miraculous; exquisite; unbelievable.

PRESERVE (v)

adverbs

miraculously; mercifully; unbelievably; marvelously; sagaciously; permanently; painfully; laboriously; durably; prudently; immortally; perpetually.

(See keep, save.)

PRESERVED

adverbs

carefully; reverently; thriftily; skilfully; duly; richly; fortunately; luckily; meticulously; punctiliously; cautiously; perfectly; miraculously; exquisitely; incredibly; well; permanently; inviolately; safely; secretly; doggedly; sacredly; divinely; mysteriously; inexplicably; magnificently; splendidly.

PRESIDENT

adjectives

honorable; unqualified; wearied.

verbs

consult—; impeach—; inaugurate—; induct as—; —addresses; —adjourns; —administers; —advises; —appoints; —berates; —conducts; —controls; —directs; —drives; —governs; —orates; —orders; —pilots; —presides: —rules; —sanctions.

(See official, chairman, judge, magistrate, executive, legislator.)

PRESS

adjectives

fluctuating; sensational; hostile; radical; daily; periodical; increasing; indefatigable; groaning; gagged; obnoxious; printing; vigilant; militant; bourgeois; respective; converted; brick; clashing; illustrated.

verbs

affiliate with—; divulge to—; gag—; meddle in—; regale—; ruffle—; tumble from—; —alludes to; —argues; —denounces; —discusses; —howls; —screams; —shouts; —spits out; —whirls.

(See literature, magazine, newspaper.)

PRESS (v)

adjectives

sorely; tenderly; vigorously; convulsively;

affectionately; emotionally; hotly; forcibly; desperately; courteously; cautiously; vigilantly; militantly.

(See compress, crowd.)

PRESSING

adverbs

strangely; curiously; immediately; insistently; persistently; inconveniently; instantly; inescapably; direly; embarrassingly; unduly; imperatively; absorbingly; desperately; gravely; critically; significantly; inordinately; portentously; momentously; ominously; peculiarly.

PRESSURE

adjectives

systolic; lingering; diplomatic; lateral; injurious; fierce; unreasoning; excessive; fluid; common; great; stupendous; aggressive; warm; angry; burning; teasing; atmospheric; irresistible; inevitable; convulsive; mechanical; extreme; sympathetic; cordial; normal; persistent; social; tremendous; superincumbent; opposing; diminished; insupportable; delicate; immense; inconstant; uniform; organized; undue; pecuniary; artificial.

verbs

alleviate—; apply—; counteract—; ease off—; employ—; exert—; expose to—; halt—; obliterate—; submit to—; succumb to—; subject to—; wobble under—; work under—; yield to—; —diminishes; —increases; —welds.

(See load, stress, force, power.)

PRESTIGE

adjectives

mysterious; personal; intellectual; frantic; national; original; unprecedented; considerable; glorious; battered; military; relative; enormous; extended; weighty; external.

verbs

acquire—; aspire to—; augment—; capitalize—; crack—; enhance—; enjoy—; extend —to; gain—; guarantee—; impair—; lessen —; lower—; preserve—; revive—; rival—; solidify—; threaten—; weaken—; —declines; —jumps.

(See influence.)

PRESUMABLE

adverbs

readily; reasonably; altogether; sensibly;

credibly; scarcely; hardly; barely; naturally; legally; easily; appropriately; particularly; circumstantially; wholly.

PRESUME (v)
adverbs
unblushingly; boldly; conceitedly; petulantly; insolently; arrogantly; insistently; pettishly.
(See assume, dare.)

PRESUMPTION
adjectives
subsequent; general; arrogant; insistent;
petulant; insolent; fundamental; unwarranted; scientific.

PRESUMPTUOUS
adverbs
impertinently; ungraciously; offensively;
conspicuously; boldly; audaciously; self-
importantly; inexcusably, boorishly; uncivilly; disrespectfully; irreverently; brazenly;
ignorantly; flippantly; obnoxiously; atrociously; unpardonably; egregiously; surprisingly; crassly; strikingly; arrogantly; recklessly; indiscreetly; imprudently; unbelievably; daringly; youthfully; obstinately; challengingly; obstreperously; foolishly; senselessly.

PRESUPPOSE (v)
adverbs
arrogantly; confidently; selfishly; carelessly; egotistically; independently.
(See assume, presume.)

PRETEND (v)
adverbs
satirically; childishly; deliberately; extravagantly; chimerically; groundlessly; idiotically; irrationally; sportively.
(See simulate, feign.)

PRETENDER
adjectives
sole; cowled; contemptible; royal.

PRETENSE
adjectives
specious; elaborate; cunning; slight; vile;
selfish; theatrical; plausible; vain; boyish;
transparent; empty; offensive; innocent;
weary; unfounded; scorned; boastful; mere;
false; insincere; melancholy; listless; emotional.

verbs
abandon—; accuse of—; afford—; assume
—; avoid—; breed—; concoct—; criticize
—; don—; eradicate—; fabricate—; garb
in—; inveigh against—; justify—; offer—;
penetrate—; pierce—; possess—; relax—;
ridicule—; simulate—; strip of—; wallow
in—; —awes; —deceives; —disguises;—distorts; —encroaches; —masks; —minces;
—misbecomes; —misrepresents; —ornaments; —overacts; —overcharges; —perverts; —poses; —strains; —transgresses.
(See disguise, hyprocisy, sham, affectation,
subterfuge, deception.)

PRETENSION
adjectives
groundless; ladylike; extravagant; capital;
chimerical; present; unreasonable; aesthetic;
arrogant; modish; aristocratic; lofty; faint;
supernatural; obnoxious; serious; military;
specific; rational; foolish; intellectual; genealogical; medieval; additional.

verbs
(See pretense.)

PRETENTIOUS
adverbs
foppishly; stiltedly; mincingly; simperingly;
stagily; abominably; absurdly; ridiculously;
ludicrously; laughably; disgustingly; pathetically; pompously; arrogantly; noisily;
elaborately; cunningly; cleverly; theatrically; transparently; offensively; boastfully; harmlessly; unreasonably; loftily; unnecessarily; fantastically; artlessly; amusingly;
prodigiously; colossally; tediously; stiffly.

PRETEXT
adjectives
specious; trifling; vulgar; plausible; worthy; reasonable; friendly; convenient; insignificant.

PRETTINESS
adjectives
bewildering; unearthly; verbal; slim;
youthful; stiff; fantastic; painted.

PRETTY
adverbs
innocently; delightfully; rosily; childishly;
seductively; alluringly; unbelievably;
charmingly; undeniably; naturally; artlessly; unaffectedly; sweetly; unusually; bewitchingly; altogether; remarkably; strik-

ingly; unexpectedly; fascinatingly; wholesomely; radiantly; glowingly; unconsciously; pertly; smartly; artfully; particularly; uncommonly; matchlessly.

PREVAIL (v)
adverbs
ultimately; universally; unanimously; dominantly; uniformly; normally; imperiously; appallingly; annoyingly; turbulently.
(See rule, dominate.)

PREVALENCE
adjectives
marked; imperious; overwhelming; appalling; strong; everlasting; annoying.

PREVALENT
adverbs
widely; generally; currently; recently; naturally; disastrously; unfortunately; inexplicably; significantly; unhappily; unaccountably; ideologically; deucedly; blightingly; destructively; oddly; fashionably; transiently; momentarily; temporarily; insignificantly; briefly; formidably.

PREVENT (v)
adverbs
permanently; effectually; effectively; forcibly; admirably; cautiously; methodically; automatically; mechanically; scientifically; medically.
(See avert, hinder, thwart.)

PREVENTION
verbs
effect—; employ—; investigate—; —averts; —baffles; —blankets; —chokes; —cramps; —disconcerts; —disheartens; —dooms; —encounters; —hampers; —impedes; —nips; —stifles; —thwarts.
(See obstruction, hindrance, impediment.)

PREVENTIVE
adjectives
continual; effectual; admirable; extraordinary.

adverbs
highly; successfully; presumably; helpfully; usefully; actively; moderately; prudently; remarkably; uncommonly; usually; supposedly; credibly; possibly; unquestionably; sometimes.

PREY
adjectives
miserable; finny; helpless; predestined; unexhausted; lawful; accustomed; fair; universal; shattered; specious; legitimate; unambitious; stern; silent; yielding; righteous; reluctant.

verbs
attack—; corner—; descend on—; ensnare—; evade—; fall—to; grasp—; lurk for—; mangle—; pursue—; reconnoiter—; strike—; wrestle with—.
(See victim.)

PRICE
adjectives
unbelievable; prohibitive; exorbitant; heavy; minute; prevailing; comparative; minimum; sacrifice; advancing; rising; prehistoric; dirt-cheap; bottom; wholesale; sensational; competitive; amazing; fabric; specific; cash; low; proportionate; remarkable; sale; moderate; original; ridiculous; extreme; countless (pl); fractional; irresistible; bewildering; unheard-of; insufficient; trivial; possible; popular; basic; fantastic; reasonable; modest; imposing; absurd; attractive; bargain; reduced; exceptional; stiff; outrageous; unjustifiable; frightful; diurnal; internal; history-making; reserve; proportionate; remunerative; fabulous; interesting; impressive; modest; astonishing; anniversary; advertised; democratic; thrifty; wholesale; onerous; money-saving; pleasant; consistent; unusual; national; phenomenal; singular; characteristic; factory-to-you; impressive; astounding; concrete; idle; introductory; retail; disproportionate; losing.

verbs
bolster—; command—; demur at—; depress—; enhance—; fix—; haggle over—; hoist—; inflate—; reduce—; slash—; threaten—; —falls; —fluctuates; —flurries; —shoots up; —soars; —tumbles.
(See cost, amount, fee, tax, expense, value, charge, worth.)

PRICE (v)
adverbs
sensationally; attractively; reasonably; exorbitantly; modestly; economically; prohibitively; ridiculously; outrageously; fabulously; competitively; sensationally; disproportionately.
(See value.)

924

adverbs

curiously; absolutely; sacredly; definitely; presumably; almost; altogether; sensationally; fantastically; immeasurably; incalculably; naturally; inimitably; superbly; magnificently; indescribably.

PRIDE

adjectives

absurd; adoring; amorous; arrogant; angry; aristocratic; barbarous; bounded; boyish; bubbling; calm; careful; bulldog; carnal; childish; civic; coeval; cold; commendable; competitive; conscious; considerable; contiguous; considerate; contemptible; craggy; daring; counterfeit; dark; defiant; delicious; demon; despairing; determined; disappointed; dormant; drooping; emulated; evident; excessive; exultant; fair; false; fantastical; fatuous; fiendish; fiery; firm; flattered; flowery; foamy; foolish; full-blown; garish; gay; generous; gentle; golden; gracious; grim; guiltless; hasty; haughty; heroic; hidden; high-blown; high-bred; holy; honest; housewifely; hurt; hypocritic; ignorant; imperial; inconsistent; indescribable; indomitable; inordinate; insolent; intellectual; interminable; intolerable; laudable; just; justifiable; legitimate; lingering; local; lofty; lovely; loyal; maiden; martial; masculine; matchless; maternal; melancholy; mingled; moderate; modest; monarchal; moral; morning; mortal; mortified; motley; much-vaunted; narrow; national; noble; obdurate; obstinate; offended; overweening; overwhelming; pardonable; particular; patrician; patriotic; personal; pertinacious; philosophic; piqued; piscatorial; pleasing; plunging; positive; pouting; prim; provincial; proper; purple; rapturous; reassuring; reflected; regal; ruthless; restless; reprehensible; retrospective; sad; sanctimonious; satisfactory; saucy; serpent; school-taught; secret; self-torturing; self-complacent; self-conscious; sensitive; shallow; sheltered; short-lived; signal; silent; single; snobbish; sober; special; spirited; splendid; spotless; stoic; stainless; stranded; stubborn; subdued; stupid; subtle; summer; sweet; tampering; tender; thankless; theatric; touchy; tyrannic; unendurable; ungenerous; unmixed; unsuspected; unvanquished; unwonted; vainglorious; vicarious; voluptuous; welling; wicked; worldly; womanly; wounded; wretched.

verbs

awaken—; beam with—; bloat with—; conceal—; flush with—; fortify—; glow with —; gratify—; humble—; injure—; lacerate —; pocket—; preserve—; reflect—; repress —; restrain—; rouse—; ruffle—; salve—; sting—; stir—; swallow—; swell with—; — animates; —armors; —bloats; —revolts; — supports.

(See conceit, vanity, arrogance, self-esteem.)

PRIEST

adjectives

solemn; white-robed; ministering; venerable; full; dull; frocked; persecuting; attendant; ash-smeared; long-haired; eagle-taloned; half-mad; wandering; native; pretended; sandaled; renegade; officiating; treacherous; unyielding; shameful; stout; rustic; rich; homey; luxurious; solitary; adorned; incensed; idolatrous; little; high; chanting; smooth-tongued; easy-living.

verbs

cloister—; confess to—; ordain—; —admonishes; —addresses; —attends; —baptizes; — blesses; —chants; —confirms; —consecrates; —converts; —fines; —genuflects; —hallows; —imposes; —instructs; —intercedes; —ministers to; —orders; —sanctifies; — serves; —supplicates.

(See minister, clergyman, clergy.)

PRIESTHOOD

adjectives

royal; idolatrous; self-constituted.

PRIESTLY

adverbs

reverently; devoutly; gently; sternly; helpfully; carefully; tolerantly; dutifully; fervently; admirably; estimably; zealously; ardently; diligently; earnestly; unfailingly; consistently; irreproachably.

PRIG

adjectives

sapless; offensive; hopeless; unsocial; obnoxious; well-meaning.

PRIGGISH

adverbs

intolerably; disagreeably; self-righteously; ostentatiously; uncomfortably; deucedly; unbearably; hatefully; immeasurably; unbelievably; miserably; unpleasantly; atrociously; inflexibly; pretentiously; awfully; suddenly; inveterately; incurably; offensively.

adverbs
demurely; sedately; coyly; naturally; disagreeably; incurably; shyly; unsophisticatedly; pleasantly; uncomfortably; innocently; attractively; suddenly; unexpectedly; unaccountably; singularly; remarkably; amazingly; inscrutably; distinctly; self-consciously; bashfully; unnecessarily; needlessly; unfortunately; crudely; virtuously; prettily.

PRIMACY
adjectives
hierarchal; archangelic; established.

PRIME
adjectives
dancing; dominant; golden; autumnal; refulgent; blooming; young; luxuriant; lusty; early; unvalued.

PRIMITIVE
adverbs
unexpectedly; impossibly; intolerably; beautifully; unfashionably; stylishly; restfully; strikingly; pathetically; incredibly; curiously; grotesquely; fantastically; dramatically: spectacularly; uncomfortably; entertainingly; interestingly; singularly; hopelessly; undesirably; quaintly; sweetly; fearfully; miserably; comfortably; happily.

PRIMROSE
adjectives
full-faced; colored; fragrant; meaningful.

PRINCE
adjectives
sovereign; ambitious; praiseworthy; covetous; sagacious; pious; illustrious; merciful; faithful; humane; religious; upright; worthy; trained; petty; imperious; ecclesiastical; independent; chivalrous; tyrannical; scrupulous; economical; democratic; dethroned; barbarian; reigning; renowned; pusillanimous; arbitrary; sweet; auspicious; confiscating.

PRINCELY
adverbs
gorgeously; magnificently; lavishly; splendidly; brilliantly; regally; superbly; nobly; incredibly; indescribably; unutterably; un-

imaginably; immeasurably; imperiously; absolutely; graciously; gallantly; distinctly; imposingly; impressively; genuinely.

PRINCESS
adjectives
sanctimonious; enchanted; long-despoiled; extravagant; disinherited; meddlesome; overfrivolous.

PRINCIPAL
adjectives
skilled; deft; practiced; renowned; respected.

PRINCIPALITY
adjectives
ecclesiastical; autonomous; tributary; scanty.

PRINCIPLE
adjectives
political; fundamental; moral; poetical; infallible; unsuspected; applicable; acknowledged; essential; immortal; revolutionary; rigid; guiding; ultimate; wholesome; just; competitive; cantilever; inductive; mistaken; common; immutable; particular; thoughtful; sexual; strict; eternal; underlying; false; animating; incorporating; vital; involved; party; maleficent; despotic; sacred; religious; uniform; methodological; architectural; patriotic; latent; antagonistic; vigorous; virtuous; odious; death-bringing; pervading; evolutionary; anti-centralizing; active; chemical; unimpeachable; humanitarian; first; vicious; internal; untrue; inductive; mischievous; settled; rational; human; leading; exhausted; distorted; one-term; critical; intuitive; basic; ruling; durable; adverse; honorable; beautifying; abandoned; intelligible; simple; commonsense; fixed; cooperative; rudimental; scientific; irreconcilable; immaterial; preposterous; philosophical; artistic; cardinal; warlike; favorite; sound; unquestionable; established; high; proper; enlightened; better; novel; demonstrative; sound; self-exploding; moving; dynamic; ethical; phonetic; elementary; unjust; spirited; uniform; dazzling; racial; germinal.

verbs
abhor—; accept—; adhere to—; apply—; base on—; commit to—; comprehend—; compromise—; concur on—; contravene—; deduce—; dispute—; dissect—; embody; — embrace—; endorse—; enunciate—; espouse —; establish—; exemplify—; expound—;

extend—; formulate—; grasp—; illustrate —;inculcate—; infract—; infuse—; instill —; invest with—; invoke—; obscure—; oppose—; pledge to—; proclaim—; promulgate —; refute—; reiterate—; safeguard—; steep in—; trample—; unfold—; utilize—; vaunt —; vindicate—; violate—; —decays; —justifies; —triumphs; —underlies.

(See dogma, doctrine, fundamental, formula, essential, law, rule, policy.)

PRINT

adjectives   (*ink*)
vivid; monotone; riotous; conspicuous; well-penetrated; impartial.

PRINT

verbs   (*news*)
break into—; compose—; creep into—; dash off—; decipher—; draw up—; impress—; scan—; summarize—; type—; —arouses; —blazons; —broaches; —circulates; —diffuses; —engrosses; —enlightens; —exposes; —heralds; —proclaims; —reports; —reveals; —rumors.

(See press, newspaper, news.)

PRINT

adjectives   (*picture*)
unframed; bright; false; colored; sticking; beauteous.

verbs
appreciate—; auction —s; brighten—; collect —s; color—; design—; frame—; imitate —; prize—; select—; study—; value—; —adorns; —attracts; —depicts; —embellishes; —harmonizes; —portrays; —suspends.

(See photograph, picture, painting.)

PRINT (v)

adverbs
slanderously; anonymously; indelibly; elegantly; professionally; impartially; irritatingly; sensationally; boldly; seditiously; scandalously; flatteringly.

(See publish.)

PRINTER

adjectives
enterprising; active; energetic; skilled; deft.

verbs
engage—; prepare for—; —arranges; —bundles; —composes; —copies; —effaces; —

errs; —inscribes; —issues; —measures; —presses; —publishes; —rushes; —sets up; —stains; —transcribes; —types.

(See publisher.)

PRISM

adjectives
refracting; colorful; revolving; perfect.

PRISMATIC

adverbs
gorgeously; iridescently; colorfully; beautifully; magnificently; magically; mysteriously; unbelievably; splendidly; phenomenally; gloriously; awesomely; unexpectedly; strikingly; matchlessly; brilliantly; dazzlingly; bewilderingly; fascinatingly; stunningly; astoundingly.

PRISON

adjectives
expensive; nonsensical; windowless; verbal; polluted; model; various (pl); wiry; medieval; repulsive; gloomy; twilight; squalid; voluntary; glittering; millennial; gilded; unsanitary.

verbs
cast into—; commit to—; languish in—; pine in—; rot in—; scuttle into—; throw into—; —bars; —cloisters; —confines; —encages; —gags; —harbors; —immures; —incarcerates; —paroles; —rehabilitates; —releases; —restrains; —yokes.

(See jail, dungeon, imprisonment, monastery, pillory.)

PRISONER

adjectives
panting; pardoned; life; sullen; self-made; incestuous; affable; emaciated; affable; defiant; careless; high-hearted; unfortunate; well-dressed; distinguished; disheartened; virtual; unprincipled; pale; wounded; linked; sorrowful; feathered; miserable; desperate.

verbs
arraign—; brand—; charge with—; denounce—; exonerate—; guard—; herd —s; incriminate—; indict—; liberate—; lodge—; prosecute—; release—; reproach—; restrain —; saddle—; slur—; stigmatize—; taunt—; twit—; vindicate—; —confesses; —implicates.

(See convict, captive, criminal.)

PRIVACY

adjectives

modified; necessary; outraged; perfect; absolute; tumultuous; defended; domestic; actual; comparative; boudoir; long-enjoyed; pleasing; desirable.

verbs

bottle up in—; couch in—; creep into—; demand—; deny—; destroy—; draw into—; embrace—; enjoy—; ensconce in—; infringe on—; impinge upon—; retire to—; rob of—; ruffle—; seclude in—; sink into—; yearn for —; —buries; —curtains; —fences; —mystifies; —puzzles; —repels; —shrouds.

(See concealment, isolation, seclusion, secrecy.)

PRIVATE

adverbs

strictly; necessarily; diplomatically; securely; safely; supposedly; sacredly; presumably; delightfully; furtively; secretly; particularly; confidentially; officially; intimately; appropriately; mysteriously; inviolably; surreptitiously; reticently; stealthily; pleasantly; happily; fortunately.

PRIVATION

adjectives

rigorous; material; signal; melancholy; revolting; ascetic; inevitable; personal; utmost; bitter; cruel; severe.

verbs

bear—; beget—; conceal—; endure—; experience—; expose to—; incur—; inflict—; meet with—; steel against—; suffer—; undergo—; —agitates; —agonizes; —chafes; —gnaws; —grates; —hinders; —pinches; —purifies; —racks; —smothers; —tortures.

(See hardship, impoverishment, poverty.)

PRIVILEGE

adjectives

royal; peculiar; ancient; valuable; additional; sublime; honorable; desolating; unrestricted; glorious; inestimable; immemorial; treasured; admirable; feudal; obsolete; cut-and-dried; antique; abused; fleeting; exclusive; exceptional; distinguishing; retirement; further; social; franking; chartered; undoubted; ancient; sovereign; accepted; cherished; irresistible.

verbs

abuse—; accord—to; assert—; bestow—upon; claim—; confer—upon; deprive of—; destroy—; encroach on—; extend—to; forego—; grant—; jeopardize—; overstep—; seek—; share—; strip of—; surrender—; wangle—; —enables; —expires.

(See independence, exemption, liberty, right.)

PRIVILEGED

adverbs

highly; especially; unfairly; fortunately; unaccountably; mysteriously; peculiarly; particularly; uniquely; inexplicably; financially; curiously; politically; socially; unusually; deservedly; indulgently; graciously; affectionately; freely; aristocratically; unconditionally; legally; duly; constitutionally; prescriptively; absolutely; properly.

PRIZE

adjectives

priceless; glittering; scarlet-bound; choice; coveted; easy; useless; savory; hard-earned.

verbs

acquire—; award—to; bestow—upon; capture—; collect —s; derive—; draw—; earn —; forfeit—; gain—; glean —s; merit—; obtain—; offer—; reap —s; reward with—; value—; win—; —allures; —enriches; —tempts.

(See laurels, medal.)

adverbs

inordinately; exceptionally; morbidly; casually; affectionately; ardently; exaggeratedly; memorably.

(See value, esteem.)

PRIZE-FIGHTER

verbs

—blocks; —bounds; —clinches; —counters; —dances; —ducks; —feints; —fouls; —groans; —hooks; —jabs; —launches; —levels; —pile-drives; —puffs; —skips; —smashes; —spars; —stabs; —stalls; —shadow-boxes; —trains; —unleashes; —uppercuts; —weakens; —whirls; —winds.

(See fighter, boxer.)

PROBABILITY

adjectives

inconceivable; golden; human; inherent; precarious; imminent.

verbs
consider—; contemplate—; erase—; evaluate
—; ground on—; ignore—; invest with—;
point to—; seek—; snort at—; speculate on
—; study—; trace—; —diminishes; —implies; —fathers; —justifies; —tempts.

(See chance, opportunity, possibility.)

PROBABLE
adverbs
highly; circumstantially; scarcely; hardly;
barely; naturally; extremely; confidently;
apparently; reasonably.

PROBATION
adjectives
healthful; troubled; temporary.

PROBATIONARY
adverbs
wisely; prescriptively; experimentally; naturally; sensibly; venturesomely; fortunately; virtually; luckily; distinctly; undoubtedly.

PROBE (v)
adverbs
secretly; deeply; curiously; morbidly; surgically; deftly; searchingly.

(See examine, investigate.)

PROBLEM
adjectives
sufficient; invincible; insolvable; residue;
important; age-old; perplexing; harassing;
abstruse; complicated; puzzling; criminal;
psychological; lifelong; farming; everyday;
pretty; metaphysical; decorative; vital; serious; ultimate; speculative; surgical; menacing; technical; arduous; executive; ethical;
comparative; easy; confusing; vast; terrifying; moral; unsolved; dramatic; tremendous; duplex; profound; acute; specific;
changing; individual; challenging; intricate; mathematical; deep; basic; striking;
personal; contemporary; social; workable;
troublesome; transportation; intellectual;
urgent; practical; vexatious; conflicting;
integral; defined; passionless; terrible;
graphic; discouraging; weighty; insoluble;
delicate; great; rising-hour; unanswerable;
rapid; accumulating; mooted; childish; evolutionary; economic; doleful; original; stupendous; pressing; uncontrollable; abstract;
orientation; individual; connected; vexing;
philosophic; veiled; shopping.

verbs
absorb in—; aggravate—; analyze—; approach—; attack—; boil down—; circumvent—; come to grips with—; complicate—;
confront with—; constitute—; contemplate
—; cope with—; deal with—; detour—; dismiss—; dispose of—; dissect—; dodge—;
engross in—; envisage—; expound—; face
with—; focus on—; formulate—; grapple
with—; high-light—; illuminate—; labor
over—; master—; meditate on—; misconceive—; outline—; ponder—; pose—; precipitate—; propound—; restate—; shed light
on—; smooth out—; solve—; struggle with
—; survey—; tackle—; wrestle with—; —s
baffle; —bedevils; —s beset; —embraces;
—looms; —narrows down to; —plagues; —
ruffles; —vexes.

(See riddle, matter, mathematics, predicament.)

PROBLEMATICAL
adverbs
ticklishly; delicately; altogether; precariously; distinctly; fearfully; critically; definitely; painfully; disturbingly; unusually; nicely; obscurely; intricately; perplexingly; curiously; singularly; disconcertingly; vexatiously; plaguedly; extremely.

PROCEDURE
adjectives
characteristic; momentous; amiable; peaceful; unprovoking; abstract; simple; obstinate; intellectual; mystical; well-established;
critical; specific; analytic; scandalous; energetic; wonted; tiresome; practical; routine;
educational; emergency; complicated.

verbs
adopt—; alter—; bear—; condemn—; conduct—; devise—; discharge—; disrupt—;
enact—; execute—; handle—; justify—;
manage—; open—; participate in—; practise—; shape—; study—; suggest—; terminate—; transact—; wind up—; —awes; —
bores; —"clicks".

(See transaction, process, routine, usage.)

PROCEED (v)
adverbs
softly; moderately; nonchalantly; systematically; circuitously; divergently; solemnly;
resolutely; vigorously; majestically; awk-

wardly; monotonously; cautiously; methodically; inquisitorially; suspiciously; summarily; critically; amiably; characteristically.

(See advance, progress.)

PROCEEDING

adjectives

rash; solemn; revolutionary; factious; ominous; hot; comely; furious; cumbrous; inquisitorial; cautious; ungrateful; odious; perfect; characteristic; momentous; customary; tumultuous; suspicious; mean; false; summary; manifest; violent; mere; negligent; offensive.

PROCEEDINGS

verbs

annul—; avoid—; conclude—; conduct—; denounce—; disturb—; institute—; legalize —; threaten—; —betray; —bore; —commence; —drag; —tire; —undo; —weary.

(See investigation, action.)

PROCEEDS

adjectives

pecuniary; astounding; unexpected; small.

verbs

deliver—; derive—; devote—to; draw—; inherit—; net—; pay—; procure—; raise—; realize—; reap—; secure—; swell—; treasure—; yield—; —accrue; —accumulate; produce—.

(See income, profit.)

PROCESS

adjectives

administrative; beautifying; combustion; tedious; abrasion; continuing; lucrative; doubtful; elaborate; same; dreary; exclusive; refining; expert; improved; unequivocal; cognitive; delicate; wrapping; ingenious; carving; artificial; evident; fundamental; cultural; glaucomatous; quick-freezing; digestive; tentative; clarifying; fertilizing; subjective; summary; manufacturing; simple; unconscious; intertwined; elementary; pleasant; logical; inductive; volitive; culinary; exacting; continuous; just; cream-choking; regular; inflammatory; obscure; complicated; mental; ricocheting; wasteful; technical; careful; expressive; circumrotary; punitive; reproductive; pressure; patented; sluggish; merciless; inflationary; remedial; primitive; monotypic; dynamic; fascinating; predictable; complex; artful; essential; physical; aquatint; haphazard; phy-

siological; secret; scientific; expensive; oriental; concentrated; painful; embarrassing; minor; bleaching; ordinary; coercive; democratic; purifying; informal; improved; incubating; involuntary; curbing; evolutionary; learning; laborious; uncertain; orderly; rational; inevitable; chemical; diabetic; synthetic; unique; extensive; blood-atonement; new-discovered; searching; creative; psychological; cyanide; deleterious; beneficient; educational; actual; organic; ineradicable; stultifying; variegated; miraculous; deliberate; artistic; torturing; gradual-reduction; persuasive; developed; exasperating; needless; natural; familiar; enlightened; subsequent; chastening; enormous; suitable; morbid.

verbs

accelerate—; advocate—; clarify—; develop —; disclose—; engross in—; facilitate—; hinder—; perfect—; prolong—; push—; regulate—; reject—; retard—; revamp—; reverse—; simplify—; subject to—; terminate—; undergo—; —evolves through; —fabricates; —refines.

(See operation, method, procedure.)

PROCESSION

adjectives

melancholy; pompous; bright; proud; solemn; dim; spangle-clad; funeral; timely; triumphal; torch-light; dull; spontaneous; gaudy; unnoticed; monkish; phantom; festal; unending; ant-like; stately; impressive; historic; parading; demure; triumphant; endless; dripping; religious; sacrificial; white-robed; imposing; mournful; motley; pensive; uniformed; sad; priestly; continuous; rustling; pale; picturesque; straggling; slow; lamentable; penitential; votive.

verbs

arrange—; disconcert—; interpose—; interrupt—; review—; —ambles; —attracts; — blazons; —bowls along; —courses; —displays; —files by; —glides by; —jogs; — paces; —plods; —shuffles; —struts; —trots; —wends.

(See parade, expedition, excursion, marchers, pageant.)

PROCESSIONAL

adverbs

gorgeously; ceremoniously; ceremonially; reverently; harmoniously; magnificently; splendidly; brilliantly; pretentiously; decoratively; decorously; joyously; triumphantly; conventionally; patriotically; mournfully; quietly; majestically; gravely; properly; appropriately.

PROCLAIM (v)
adverbs
formally; proudly; publicly; triumphantly; ostentatiously; loquaciously; boisterously; exuberantly; boldly; enthusiastically; seditiously; exultantly; solemnly.
(See announce, publish.)

PROCLAMATION
adjectives
celebrated; artful; supplementary; seditious; atrocious; insidious; magniloquent; flowery; preliminary; stirring; exultant; solemn; defiant; brilliant; plain-speaking; feeble.

verbs
authorize—; emit—; issue—; post—; prepare—; promulgate—; publish; recite—; —announces; —blazons; —broaches; —circulates; —diffuses; —disseminates; —heralds; —spreads; —surprises.
(See ban, edict, headline, announcement, notice.)

PROCLIVITY
adjectives
hopeless; sentimental; dangerous; insidious.

verbs
denounce—; endow with—; limit—; promote—; redound to—; temper—; warp—; —affects; —bends; —bids; —conduces; —disposes; —enables; —gravitates; —inclines; —predisposes; —tends; —verges.
(See tendency, inclination, propensity.)

PROCRASTINATION
verbs
addict to—; remedy—; —cools; —defers; —delays; —endangers; —irks; —irritates; —postpones; —prorogues; —protracts; —retards; —stalls; —staves off; —suspends; —waives; —wearies.
(See delay, indolence.)

PROCURE (v)
adverbs
legally; lustfully; lasciviously; salaciously; seasonally; carnally; periodically; sentimentally.
(See acquire, obtain, achieve.)

PRODIGAL
adjectives
good-natured; niggardly; rehabilitated; unconscionable; returning; prodigious; guilty; sinful; wicked; selfish.

adverbs
wastefully; reprehensibly; foolishly; wantonly; dissolutely; sadly; unthriftily; blithely; recklessly; rashly; lavishly; senselessly; thoughtlessly; selfishly; extravagantly; needlessly; immensely; witlessly; absurdly; ridiculously; wickedly; inordinately; unhappily.

PRODIGALITY
adjectives
boundless; reckless.

PRODIGIOUS
adverbs
incredibly; inordinately; amazingly; unbelievably; unaccountably; immeasurably; incalculably; strikingly; miraculously; uncommonly.

PRODIGY
adjectives
flashing; unique; infant; valorous; accompanying; juvenile; extraordinary; necromantic.

PRODUCE
adjectives
scanty; rude; dark; peaceful.

PRODUCE (v)
adverbs
prolifically; lavishly; magically; legitimately; enthusiastically; artificially; characteristically; infallibly; generously; systematically; wantonly; dramatically; luxuriantly; agriculturally; indigenously.
(See generate, yield.)

PRODUCER
adjectives
potential; multitudinous (pl); independent; rich.

PRODUCT
adjectives
national; advertised; fundamental; better; uncrystallizable; commercial; vegetable; salable; sole; glandular; seasonable; staple; meager; pharmaceutic; morphine; accepted; appetizing; attractive; abundant; delicious; wholesome; poisonous; natural; lusty; re-

sultant; non-perishable; noble; choice; dubious; abundant (pl); pristine; spontaneous; admired; extant; filthy; humble; phantastic; extraordinary; good; sensational; amazing; fast-selling; quality; rare; useful; guaranteed; liked; wanted; diversified (pl); allied (pl); abrasive; amphibious; definite; superstandard; multiform (pl); delectable; menacing; insidious; basic; efficient; amalgamated; recent; superior; barbarous; unforced; representative; marvelous; luxurious; dutiable; unpalatable; uniform; miraculous.

verbs
acclaim—; clamor for—; consume—; contribute to—; convert—; degrade—; deposit —; evolve—; finish—; handle—; market—; purvey—; retail—; transform—; transport —; utilize—; waste—.
  (See fruit, crop, harvest, output.)

PRODUCTION
adjectives
attractive; quantity; continuous; figure; indigenous; abortive; rhythmical; luxuriant; deep; earned; increased; labored; earnest; aggregate; mechanical; dramatic; chief; finished; varied; conventional; prolific; industrial; assembly-line; plastic; digestible; commercial; poetical; intensive; economic; spontaneous; carnal; appropriate; estimated; curtailed; dramatic; celebrated; aboriginal; vegetable; interrupted; momentary; capacity; crude; intelligent; monstrous; multifarious; maximum; agricultural; dewless; artificial; elaborate; faultless; isolated; immortal; composite; stimulated.

verbs
absorb—; accelerate—; ascribe—to; augment—; bolster—; boom—; cancel—; control—; curtail—; delay—; determine—; disrupt—; doom—; expand—; guide—; hamper—; measure—; quadruple—; rehearse —; scuttle—; simplify—; sponsor—; stimulate—; suspend—.
  (See output, product.)

PRODUCTIVE
adverbs
unusually; amazingly; strikingly; miraculously; conveniently; opportunely; profitably; commercially; surprisingly; sensationally; spectacularly; satisfactorily; adequately; highly; fortunately; experimentally; scientifically; naturally; famously; eminently; remarkably; uncommonly.

PROFANATION
adjectives
proposed; foul; ruinous; picturesque; menaced; lingering; definite; calculated; monstrous.

PROFANE
adverbs
irreverently; brazenly; openly; blasphemously; perversely; sacrilegiously; scoffingly; intolerably; terribly; godlessly; indefensibly; inexcusably; scandalously; wickedly; offensively; indecorously; scurrilously; luridly; startlingly; horribly; unspeakably; abominably; hideously; unbecomingly; shrilly; noisily; mutteringly; unutterably; impossibly; impiously; shamelessly.

PROFANE (v)
adverbs
obscenely; blasphemously; raucously; vulgarly; uncouthly; villainously; barbarously; diabolically.
  (See violate, debase.)

PROFANITY
adjectives
inarticulate; smothered; delicate; picturesque; time-honored; extraordinary; unbelievable; purposeless; shocking; disgusting; unmanly; stubborn; raucous; unnecessary; deliberate.

PROFESS (v)
adverbs
ignorantly; ostentatiously; impulsively; boldly; gaily; carelessly; obstreperously; vainly; vigorously; shamelessly; enthusiastically.
  (See admit, claim, avow.)

PROFESSION
adjectives
peaceful; rich; dissimilar (pl); dramatic; sacred; lettered; universal; knavish; solemn; kind; respectable; lucrative; clerical; shining; hard-working; shady; pacific; stupid; grave; educated; destined; medical; fraternal; chivalrous; preserved; inherited; honorable; paternal; private; noble; remunerative; knowing; earnest; obvious; elaborate.

verbs

commit to—; contract—; devote oneself to —; engage in—; enter—; fill—; follow—; honor—; overcrowd—; ply—; practise—; prosecute—; prosper in—; pursue—; struggle in—; undertake—; —adjures; —binds; —employs; —engages; —exacts; —obligates; —occupies.

(See calling, employment, industry, law, teaching.)

PROFESSIONAL

adverbs

strictly; scarcely; hardly; highly; expertly; self-consciously; ridiculously; absurdly; suddenly; incredibly; pretentiously; obscurely; insistently; consistently; supposedly; emphatically; assertively; dogmatically; formally; solemnly; conspicuously; unmistakably; prodigiously; ostentatiously.

PROFESSIONALISM

verbs

acquire—; commit to—; denounce—; discontinue—; display—; don—; drop—; exhibit —; practise—; shroud in—; study—; —annoys; —attends; —exacts; —irks; —irritates; —proselytes; —ties; —wearies.

PROFESSOR

adjectives

renowned; theorizing; mournful; dogmatizing; world-famed; controlling; volunteer; unsympathetic; eminent; assiduous; miserable; braintrust; unemployed; unlearned; grave; wizened; wise; absent-minded; kindly; knowing; eccentric; research; modest; masterful.

PROFICIENCY

adjectives

speedy; practical; established; technical; similar; obvious; palpable; notable; demonstrated.

verbs

acquire—; commend—; demand—; gain—; maintain—; misapply—; perceive—; possess —; praise—; profess—; realize—; recognize—; —accomplishes; —conquers; —defeats; —lags; —masters; —outflanks; —overcomes; —prevails; —succeeds; —triumphs; —weathers.

(See mastery, skill, ability, power.)

PROFICIENT

adverbs

obviously; unmistakably; marvelously; amazingly; emphatically; unfailingly; miraculously; singularly; curiously; indubitably; skilfully; expertly; remarkably; unsurpassably; matchlessly; profoundly; dexterously; deftly; felicitously; confidently; cunningly; admirably; commendably; consummately.

PROFILE

adjectives

sloping; inquisitive; clean-cut; architectural; Roman; sable; coin-clear; melancholy; aquiline; energetic; bold; flawless; regular; delicate; fine; vapid; athletic; Grecian; Nordic; gaunt; grisly; smooth; fetching; sagging; gripping; romantic; grim; noble; criminal.

PROFIT

adjectives

generous; quick; sensational; large; cash; clear; general; liberal; tremendous; amazing; steady; spot-cash; repeated; enormous; real; old-fashioned; staggering; unlimited; startling; additional; volume; big; daily; handsome; easy; distributed; potential; competitive; personal; substantial; immense; mutual; divided; moderate; reinvested; small; healthy; material; extortionate; sharp; singular; prospective; present; estimated; inconceivable; colossal; immediate; slender; honest; regular; individual; speculative; utmost; increasing; absolute; illicit; pecuniary; monetary; usurious; abnormal.

verbs

account for—; amass—; ascertain—; assure of—; consume—; create—; derive—from; eat—; educe—; eliminate—; evolve—; net —; pocket—; preclude—; reap—; retain—; spell—; squeeze—; swell—; —accrues; — booms; —evaporates; —lures; —materializes; —piles up; —s rise; —shoots from.

(See income, gain, emolument, pay, money.)

PROFIT (*v*)

adverbs

sensationally; liberally; enormously; potentially; competitively; personally; moderately; materially; colossally; pecuniarily; usuriously; abnormally.

(See gain, benefit.)

PROFITABLE

adverbs

highly; unusually; commercially; financially; professionally; remarkably; surprisingly; amazingly; inordinately; extraordinarily; extremely; unexpectedly; scarcely; hardly; altogether; socially; secretly; mysteriously; shadily; peculiarly; strangely.

PROFLIGATE

adjectives

despairing; lecherous; hopeless; debauched; drunken; unsocial.

verbs

admonish—; chastise—; condemn—; convert from—; punish—; rebuke—; reform—; reproach—; scald—; —brutalizes; —corrupts; —demoralizes; —deviates; —errs; —lapses; —offends; —sins; —slips; —strays; —transgresses; —trespasses; —sinks.

(See scoundrel, villain, criminal.)

PROFOUND

adverbs

mystically; abstrusely; obscurely; pedantically; eruditely; theologically; provokingly; prosaically; gravely; admittedly; politically; sagaciously; distinctly; shrewdly; keenly; astutely; rationally; impartially; thoughtfully; perspicaciously; oracularly; impressively; amazingly; inscrutably; doctrinally.

PROFUSE

adverbs

wonderfully; uncommonly; delightfully; unexpectedly; surprisingly; amazingly; curiously; strangely; exuberantly; luxuriantly; profitably; overly; wastefully; extravagantly; foolishly; senselessly; abundantly; amply; unsparingly; wickedly.

PROFUSION

adjectives

utmost; sheer; lavish; tempting; sumptuous; vernal; incalculable; happy; thick; ostentatious; glossy; luxuriant; extraordinary; disorderly; gothic.

PROGENY

adjectives

little; ungracious; twin-born; vigorous; numerous; enslaved; multiplied.

PROGNOSTICATION

adjectives

gloomy; financial; anguished; supernatural.

verbs

cast—; contemplate—; ignore—; justify—; —augurs; —betokens; —bids; —calculates; —discerns; —excites; —foreshadows; — foretells; —forewarns; —heralds; —points to; —precurses; —predicts; —presages; — promises; —senses; —signifies; —worries.

(See foreboding, prediction, forecast, prophecy.)

PROGRAM

adjectives

rigorous; coherent; laborious; inviting; commercial; aggressive; sponsored; balanced; serious; comprehensive; reading; great; fiction; economical; diagnosed; voluntary; relief; constructive; abstergent; seductive; varied; modernization; entertaining; aesthetic; exhaustive; ultra-professional; systematic; selfsame; sustaining; peace; nationwide; educational; social.

verbs

adhere to—; adopt—; attack—; bowl over —; carry out—; defer—; design—; devote to—; elaborate on—; embark on—; endorse —; evaluate—; evolve—; expand—; familiarize with—; formulate—; initiate—; institute—; integrate—; launch—; map out—; modify—; oppose—; outline—; participate in—; pound away at—; sketch—; submit—; supervise—; swamp—; thread through—; vary—; view—; —embraces; —languishes.

(See itinerary, list, menu.)

PROGRESS

adjectives

educational; marvelous; amazing; unbroken; moral; physical; successful; beneficent; actual; material; phenomenal; torturing; excellent; painful; joyous; eventful; social; obvious; mechanical; sufficient; luxurious; artistic; enormous.

verbs

abate—; achieve—; arrest—; blight—; block—; check—; control—; curb—; curtail —; expedite—; extend—; facilitate—; halt —; herald—; hinder—; impede—; imperil —; indicate—; insure—; keep abreast of—; mark by—; measure—; promote—; record —; retard—; survey—; trace—; yield to—.

(See advance, advancement, civilization, development, growth.)

PROGRESS (v)

adverbs

exultantly; boldly; methodically; spectacularly; enormously; swiftly; tardily; phenomenally; socially; mechanically; artistically; markedly.

(See advance, proceed.)

PROGRESSION

adjectives

audacious; endless; constant; harmonic; chromatic; upward.

PROGRESSIVE

adverbs

naturally; unusually; exceptionally; satisfactorily; ambitiously; pseudously; slowly; dependably; reliably; steadily; amazingly; happily; remarkably; startlingly; incredibly; unbelievably;. unexpectedly; highly; gratifyingly; solidly; substantially; brilliantly; undeniably.

PROHIBITION

adjectives

virtual; positive; perpetual; reiterated.

verbs

annul—; defy—; denounce—; deplore—; dispute—; enforce—; ignore—; laud—; support—; undermine—; uphold—; urge—; —debars; —forbids; —restrains; —restricts; —revokes; —smothers; —suppresses; —taboos.

(See taboo, embargo, ban, edict.)

PROHIBITIVE

adverbs

meanly; unhappily; unwisely; sordidly; racially; inordinately; senselessly; foolishly; viciously; strictly; sternly; legally; officially; authoritatively; narrowly; dogmatically; imperiously; unwarrantably; unfairly; narrow-mindedly; ineptly; antagonistically; disagreeably; unconscionably; unnecessarily; groundlessly; wisely; necessarily; warily; vigilantly; shrewdly; carefully; financially; prescriptively.

PROJECT

adjectives

ambitious; titanic; resettlement; juvenile; cherished; philosophical; cunning; sublime; modified; unrealized; reclamation; cumbersome; wild; murderous; audacious; brilliant; stupendous; immense; rehabilitation; relief; works; national.

verbs

abandon—; broach—; dedicate—; develop—; discard—; discourage—; expand—; formulate—; horn in on—; incubate—; launch—; lose in—; plan—; quash—; turn down—; —centers upon; —collapses; —goes awry; —marches to completion; —takes shape.

(See idea, design, enterprise.)

PROJECT (v)

adverbs

stereoscopically; distinctly; obtrusively; naively; infinitesimally; sharply; fantastically; ruggedly.

(See extend, jut, protrude.)

PROJECTILE

verbs

bolt—; cast—; discharge—; drive—; emit—; expel—; fire—; heave—; hurl—; pitch—; propel—; shoot—; sling—; toss—; —darts; —forces; —impels; screams by, —whistles.

(See bomb, bullet.)

PROJECTION

adjectives

rugged; blunted; infinitesimal; gnomonic; jutting; far-reaching; sharp.

PROLETARIAT

verbs

assail—; debar—; denounce—; grind—; incite—; restrain—; restrict—; smother—; stir—; support—; suppress—; trammel—; tyrannize over—; —defies; —degrades; —inflames; —labors; —rises; —revolts; —strikes.

(See bourgeoisie, foreigner, alien, peasant, worker, employer.)

PROLIFIC

adverbs

unusually; highly; distinctly; healthily; sadly; happily; fortunately; amazingly; normally; uncommonly; surprisingly; remarkably; undeniably.

PROLOGUE

adjectives

symphonic; learned; explanatory; necessary; useless; space-filling.

PROLONG (v)

adverbs

indefinitely; unduly; agonizingly; perpetually; embarrassingly; tantalizingly; excessively.

(See lengthen, extend.)

PROMENADE

adjectives
mental; solitary; public; sociable; daily; amorous; fashionable.

PROMINENCE

adjectives
political; literary; excessive; high; rocky; dominating; naked; especial; extraordinary; historical; disturbing; modest.

verbs
attain—; bounce into—; burst into—; deplore—; drag up to—; elevate to—; expose to—; hoist to—; jump into—; lift to—; merit—; mount to—; soar to—; —awes; —commands; —crowns; —exalts; —heightens; —mantles; —perches; —weighs.

(See distinction, fame, eminence.)

PROMINENT

adverbs
unusually; questionably; brilliantly; impressively; wickedly; boldly; audaciously; officially; officiously; curiously; strangely; inexplicably; noticeably; conspicuously; brazenly; eminently; gorgeously; gloriously; radiantly; rightfully; majestically; splendidly; memorably; illustriously.

PROMISCUITY

verbs
condemn—; denounce—; drift into—; refrain from—; shrink from—; suffer—; — agitates; —brews; —corrupts; —deranges; —diffuses; —disorders; —entangles; —reduces; —ruffles; —rumples.

(See indifference, mixture.)

PROMISCUOUS

adverbs
strangely; inexplicably; unaccountably; naturally; inevitably; democratically; significantly; necessarily; shamefully; reprehensibly; embarrassingly; unmanageably; unexpectedly; obviously; complexly; indiscriminately; casually; fortuitously; accidentally.

PROMISE

adjectives
optimistic; heartfelt; significant; solemn; dormant; fertile; considerable; whispered; liberal; maudlin; tremendous; firm; indefin-

ite; conservative; drunken; rash; cheerful; exceptional; remorseful; valiant; unbreakable; vernal; flattering; cheering; gracious; false; definite; scant; pathetic; tacit; doubtful; unredeemed; brilliant; deceiving; high; express; faithful; unfulfilled; light; haughty; scorching; stout-limbed; implied; nugatory; imperial.

verbs
avail oneself of—; carry out—; clutch—; dangle—; dispense—s; elicit—; enforce—; extort—; extract—; fulfill—; gain—; ignore—; issue—; nullify—; puncture—; redeem—; violate—; void—; —binds; —s clash; —electrifies; —implies; —materializes; —pledges; —sanctifies.

(See bond, contract. covenant, compromise, pledge.)

PROMISE (*v*)

adverbs
blithely; solemnly; vehemently; punctually; devoutly; cheerfully; blandly; speciously; optimistically; liberally; maudlinly; graciously; flatteringly; tacitly; lightly.

(See pledge, assure.)

PROMISING

adverbs
brilliantly; altogether; hopefully; unquestionably; remarkably; uncommonly; highly; splendidly; indubitably; auspiciously; distinctly; definitely.

PROMONTORY

adjectives
beaked; eminent; sea-beaten; keen-faced; salubrious; hoary; rock-girt; remote; mountainous; rugged; wooded; high; moon-bathed; venerable.

PROMOTE (*v*)

adverbs
infrequently; essentially; subsequently; wisely; swiftly; promptly; tardily; gratuitously; insidiously; seditiously; skillfully; ambitiously.

(See advance, encourage.)

PROMOTER

adjectives
zealous; doughty; enterprising; high-pressure; genial; sports; deft; skilled.

adjectives
picturesque; swift; deserved; lineal; gratuitous; prompt.

verbs
award—; deserve—; favor—; foster—; gain—; merit—; reward by—; secure—; seek—; —ameliorates; —betters; —bolsters; —brightens; —cheers; —elevates; —encourages; —enhances; —enriches; —invigorates; —smooths.
(See progress, advancement.)

PROMPT

adverbs
dependably; reliably; punctiliously; surprisingly; meticulously; carefully; always; curiously; significantly; suspiciously; courteously; considerately; graciously; cheerfully; politely; ingratiatingly; wisely; usually; unfailingly; pleasantly; gratifyingly.

PROMPTING

adjectives
imperious; deep-seated; inner; physiological; base; quiet; serious; definite.

PROMPTNESS

adjectives
absolute; self-satisfied; incredible; well-meant; characteristic; soldierly; utmost; unexampled; noncommittal; deliberate; practiced; remarkable.

PRONOUNCE (v)

adverbs
whimsically; unanimously; syllabically; solemnly; unhesitatingly; emphatically; impressively; weightily; definitely; academically.
(See speak, utter.)

PRONOUNCEMENT

adjectives
weighty; impressive; scientific; definite; startling.

verbs
authorize—; await—; circulate—; issue—; post—; prepare—; promulgate—; publish —; relay—; spread—; —blazons; —broaches; —diffuses; —disseminates; —heralds; —proclaims; —rings out.
(See proclamation, announcement.)

adjectives
careful; defective; smooth; facile; slipshod; hasty; inaccurate; local; improper; incorrect; antiquated; slovenly; lip-lazy; faulty; outlandish; uncouth; arbitrary; accepted.

verbs
accentuate—; alter—; aspirate—; bark—; clarify—; correct—; criticize—; detect—; drawl—; drown—; improve—; lament—; mangle—; mutter—; practise—; ridicule—; swallow—; —confuses; —perplexes.
(See accent, utterance.)

PROOF

adjectives
absolute; remarkable; experimental; confirming; ample; undeniable; refined; positive; indisputable; incontestable; irrefragable; actual; traditional; palpable; vulgar; abundant; similar; conclusive; distinct; documentary, lucid; secondary; innate; strenuous; tangible; irresistible; gratifying; strict; historical; convincing; incompatable; forcible; presumptive; convenient; melancholy; corroborative; perpetual; decisive; indubitable; gallery; ocular; bedrock; added; definite; practical; sufficient; triumphant; divine; dingy; authentic; shadowy; exemplary; formal; continuing; quick; legal; hourly; insidious; cruel; doubtful; dramatic; concrete; phenomenal; childhood.

verbs
advance—; cite—; demand—; demonstrate —; devise—; dig—; digest—; draw—; establish—; evince—; prepare—; question—; reflect upon—; seek—; strike at—; —checks; —leaks; —s multiply; —settles; —substantiates;.—verifies.
(See argument, evidence, confirmation.)

PROPAGANDA

adjectives
sedulous; sentimental; insidious; insistent; commercial; primitive; blatant; suicidal; incessant; educational; systematic; subversive; sinister; treacherous; political.

verbs
assail—; bedevil with—; denounce—; deny —; direct—at; dispute—; disseminate—; distrust—; doubt—; found on—; grind out —; impregnate with—; ignore—; mask—; pump—into; question—; release—; swallow —; weave—; —bewilders; —convinces; —

deceives; —edifies; —enlightens; —exploits; —familiarizes; —ignites; —implants; —impresses; —inculcates; —inflames; —misinforms; —misrepresents; —pervades; —perverts; —staggers; —startles; —threatens; —undermines.

(See message, doctrine, lie.)

PROPAGATE (v)

adverbs

peacefully; seditiously; agriculturally; radically; cunningly; audaciously; seasonally.

(See increase, reproduce.)

PROPEL (v)

adverbs

vigorously; swiftly; deftly; skillfully; leisurely; brilliantly; valiantly; daringly; rashly.

(See drive, force, impel.)

PROPELLOR

verbs

jerk—; rake—; start—; tug—; yank (colloq.)—; —arouses; —actuates; —calms; —drives; —forces; —halts; —hushes; —impels; —lashes; —revolves; —rotates; —spins; —urges; —whirs; —whizzes; —wrenches.

(See motor, fan.)

PROPENSITY

adjectives

martial; bad; edifying; cruel; feline; gregarious; bucaneering; degraded; mischievous; piscatorial; unsuspected; social; vulgar; erratic; indignant; unconscious; amorous; remarkable; noteworthy; unusual.

verbs

denounce—; gratify—; promote—; temper —; tempt—; —affects; —bends; —bids; —conduces; —disposes; —fancies; —gravitates; —inclines; —tends; —thirsts; —verges.

(See inclination, disposition, proclivity.)

PROPER

adverbs

conventionally; socially; altogether; acceptably; legally; punctiliously; carefully; cautiously; anxiously; graciously; courteously; politely; deferentially; respectfully; reverently; quietly; serenely; laboriously; easily; becomingly; demurely; correctly; unfailingly.

PROPERTY

adjectives

toxic; consular; medicinal; sonorous; outcropped; curative; beneficial; stimulating; private; extensive; desired; elaborate; inalienable; injurious; historical; magnetic; virgin; intellectual; inherent; structural; mechanical; business; essential; surplus; immense; profitable; defunct; physical; admirable; tonic; virtuous; airy; violent; ultimate; poisonous; permanent; living; distinctive; landed; deliquescent;˙ exclusive; health-giving; contested; luminous; papal; adjacent; unpredictable; ice-melting; acid-resisting; agreeable; specific; absolute; phonetic; substantial; acoustic; immutable; unentailed; nutritious; clinging; ancestral; existing; emollient.

verbs

acquire—; allocate—; assess—; confiscate—; deplete—; deprive of—; destine to—; destroy—; exalt—; expropriate—; fence—; guard—; inherit—; insure—; levy on—; liquidate—; retain—; saddle—; squander—; transfer—; —abuts; —includes.

(See estate, legacy, asset, inheritance, possessions.)

PROPHECY

adjectives

unpleasing; vaunting; bitter; humbler; gloomy; drunken; backward-glancing; optimistic; retrospective; impassionate; mad; imposing; painful; fanciful; ominous; dogmatic; numerous (pl); enkindling; maiden; pessimistic; apocalyptic; omnipresent; sanguine; fulfilled; inspired; prospective.

verbs

divine—; fulfill—; ignore—; mock—; scoff at—; sustain—; —augurs; —betokens; —bodes; —excites; —forecasts; —foreshadows; —foretells; —heralds; —points to; —precurses; —predicts; —presages; —promises; —warns.

(See forecast, prediction, foreboding, prognostication.)

PROPHET

adjectives

maddening; dumb; twice-tongued; fiery; courageous; master; disbelieved.

PROPHETIC

adverbs

wildly; hysterically; gravely; seriously;

oracularly; crazily; soberly; gloomily; cynically; sagely; reflectively; thoughtfully; alarmingly; ominously; gloriously; optimistically; groundlessly; profoundly; deeply; boldly; reasonably; sanely; sadly; pessimistically; wishfully; hopefully; sagaciously; intelligently; far-seeingly; perspicaciously; curiously; strangely; startlingly; highly; audaciously.

PROPITIATE (v)

adverbs

flatteringly; servilely; artfully; fawningly; cunningly; shrewdly; timidly; earnestly; studiously.

(See pacify, calm, soothe.)

PROPITIOUS

adverbs

pleasantly; agreeably; seriously; altogether; happily; delightfully; fortunately; opportunely; appropriately; graciously; pleasingly; advantageously; unusually; uncommonly; providentially; entirely; encouragingly; supposedly; singularly; particularly; especially.

PROPORTION

adjectives

cyclonic; impressive; modelled; splendid; respectable; portentous; heavy; exact; cavernous; tremendous; symmetrical; incredible; extensive; luxurious; heroic; sublime; ignoble; overwhelming; exaggerating; classic; inverse; geometrical; colossal; impudent; sizable; gigantic; enormous; proper; monstrous; rotund; sturdy; massive; divine; direct; balanced; faultless; increasing; staggering; unbelievable; inconsiderable; excessive; diminishing; relative; regal; varying; huge; ethical; progressive; majestic; large; meager; just; prodigious; consistent; constituent; pyramid; distinct; major; aldermanic; artistic; slender; clumsy; rude; due; far-reaching; equal; robust; national; vibrating; horrible.

verbs

allot—; allow—; amass—; assign—; assume —s; attain—s; consign—s; contort—; deal —s; deform—s; dispense—s; divide into—s; dole out—s; evaluate—s; indicate—s; misshape—s; preserve—s; retain—s; twist—s; warp—.

(See equilibrium, percentage, size, extent, degree, dimensions, share.)

PROPORTION (v)

adverbs

delicately; exquisitely; admirably; femininely; correctly; superbly; symmetrically; luxuriously; geometrically; massively; regally; meagerly; clumsily; rudely; equally; prodigiously.

(See divide, adjust, apportion.)

PROPORTIONATE

adverbs

fairly; justly; carefully; correspondingly; diplomatically; agreeably; satisfactorily; respectively; congruously; consistently; admissibly; felicitously; acceptably; quantatively; relatively; distinctly; impartially; equitably; laudably; legally; regularly.

PROPOSAL

adjectives

friendly; romantic; infamous; unique; alternative; oral; impracticable; ridiculous; lame, flattering; foolhardy; audacious; ambitious; crackpot; definite.

verbs

accept—; adopt—; argue—; back—; block —; carry out—; commend—; condemn—; denounce—; deride—; dismiss—; entertain —; explode—; heed—; inspire—; oppose—; pooh-pooh—; raise—; reject—; sanction—; submit—; support—; turn down—; vitiate —; withdraw—; —emanates from; —excites; —falls through.

(See bid, proposition, offer, deal, transaction, plan, suggestion, scheme.)

PROPOSE (v)

adverbs

spontaneously; seriously; dogmatically; originally; deliberately; impiously; insidiously; theoretically; philosophically; untenably; ominously; flatteringly; conditionally; passionately.

(See offer, discourse.)

PROPOSITION

adjectives

equitable; due; plausible; theoretical; unintelligible; tough; preposterous; brutal; solemn; definite; businesslike; philosophical; attractive; abstract; meaningless; untenable; ominous; mannerly; distasteful; marvelous; undeniable; dynamical; moneymaking; fundamental; flattering; conditional; general; novel; true; palpitating; astounding.

verbs
acclaim—; applaud—; balk at—; convey—; dedicate—; deliver—; demonstrate—; engage in—; entertain—; fancy—; immerse in—; jeopardize—; lay down—; misconstrue—; reject—; relate—; support—; —allures; —invites; —tempts.

(See offer, proposal, bid, deal.)

PROPOUND (v)
adverbs
academically; philosophically; theoretically; argumentatively; dispassionately; conditionally.

(See offer, propose.)

PROPRIETARY
adverbs
proudly; legitimately; comically; possessively; justly; graciously; absurdly; properly; pompously; ostentatiously; conspicuously; blatantly; ridiculously; modestly; anxiously; watchfully; responsibly; vigilantly; disagreeably; unctuously; suavely; smoothly; blandly; rapturously.

PROPRIETOR
adjectives
affluent; genial; antiquarian; ecclesiastic.

PROPRIETY
adjectives
unconscious; editorial; peculiar; established; equal; perfect; complacent; eminent; dramatic; rigid; obvious; sacred; dreamy.

verbs
adhere to—; admire—; befit—s; conform to—; contravene—s; fulfill—s; impose—; incur—; justify—s; observe—; respect—; satisfy—; suit—; undermine—; —becomes; —binds; —exacts; —obliges; —prescribes; —requires; —saddles.

(See decorum, convenience, decency.)

PROSAIC
adverbs
hopelessly; consciously; dully; flatly; tediously; unimaginatively; monotonously; stupidly; tiresomely; endlessly; unconsciously; pretentiously; pitiably; miserably; vacuously; inanely; diffusely; heavily; drearily; impossibly; terribly.

PROSE
adjectives
rhythmical; impassioned; polyphonic; news-paper; idealistic; strenuous; poetical; rhyming; lucid; glittering; immortal; artistic; famous; dull; heroic; harmonious; sinewy; uncerebral; hard-hitting; straight-from-the-shoulder; extensive; physical; humorous; conventional; flashing; elaborate; measured; conversational; dreamy; grand; mingled; salable; vigorous; poetic; puissant; supple; mellifluous; swift; masculine.

verbs
acclaim—; analyze—; compose—; contemplate—; dwell on—; enjoy—; —abounds in; —amplifies; —bores; —describes; —dilates; —discusses; —protracts; —rambles; —repeats; —swells; —thrills; —wearies.

(See poetry, writing, story, style.)

PROSECUTE (v)
adverbs
actively; recklessly; fearlessly; relentlessly; vindictively; diabolically; legally; spitefully; energetically; impassionedly; repulsively.

(See sue.)

PROSECUTION
adjectives
vigorous; persistent; inevitable; victorious; unceasing.

verbs
avert—; avoid—; demand—; endure—; escape—; evade—; file—; lodge—; order —; prefer—; risk—; suffer—; —brands; —implicates; —saddles; —slanders; —slurs; —stigmatizes; —weighs against.

(See lawsuit, suit (legal), arrest.)

PROSPECT
adjectives
dusky; melancholy; near; gloomy; smiling; brilliant; immediate; favorable; calm; peaceful; hideous; extreme; prosperous; tempting; flattering; consolatory; dazzling; brightening; adjacent; flaming; delightful; honorable; turbulent; bare; feeble; glorious; coveted; varying; bright; scanty; better; dismal; inexpressible; unobstructed; dim; gleaming; domestic; shadowy; repulsive; tempting; spacious; ineffable; glittering; blighted; bleak; dreary; embarrassing; glorious; cheering; depressing; grim; substantial; gay; happy; pleasing.

verbs
bait—; blanch at—; cripple—; dash—;

deter by—; eliminate—; entertain—; gaze at—; guard—; harbor—; insure—s; jeopardize—; open—; relinquish—; relish—; sustain—; tremble at—; —lures; —ponders; —speculates; —tempts; —s wane; —yields.
(See future, expectation, view, outlook, chance.)

PROSPER (v)
adverbs
materially; privately; personally; abundantly; excessively; illusively; financially; economically; miraculously; spectacularly.
(See thrive, gain, benefit.)

PROSPERITY
adjectives
material; public; infectious; rapid; nourishing; crass; common; supposititious; deserved; private; ever-increasing; riotous; exemplified; apparent; unexampled; abundant; excessive; fair illusive; sensual; worldly.

verbs
annihilate—; attain—; attribute—to; boom into—; boost—; build—; climb to—; contribute to—; enhance—; enjoy—; experience —; foster—; guarantee—; hamper—; induce—; promote—; re-establish—; retard —; revive—; share in—; —continues; —intoxicates; —permeates; —stems from; —vanishes.
(See boom, happiness, health, inflation.)

PROSPEROUS
adverbs
happily; comfortably; fortunately; extremely; pleasantly; gratifyingly; agreeably; surprisingly; serenely; enviably; snugly; sufficiently; fabulously; independently; tremendously; conspicuously.

PROSTITUTION
verbs
attack—; censor—; drift into—; eradicate —; extirpate—; lapse into—; suffer—; suppress—; wipe out—; —contaminates; —corrupts; —debauches; —defiles; —degrades; —depraves; —discolors; —embitters; —impairs; —mangles; —pollutes; —vitiates; —warps.
(See crime, sin, corruption.)

PROSTRATE (v)
adverbs
reverently; humbly; weakly; fawningly; cringingly; servilely; nervously; speechlessly; utterly.
(See overthrow, overpower, defeat.)

PROSTRATION
adjectives
nervous; servile; indolent; extreme; inanimate; utter.

PROTECT (v)
adverbs
adequately; legally; permanently; chivalrously; amply; unequivocally; honorably; sedulously; sacredly; nominally; automatically; scientifically; parentally; financially; dubiously.
(See defend, guard.)

PROTECTED
adverbs
tenderly; completely; unusually; remarkably; warmly; heavily; affectionately; ardently; carefully; cautiously; vigilantly; constantly; officially; unnecessarily; distinctly; deliberately; strangely; covertly; secretly; openly; successfully; always; legally.

PROTECTION
adjectives
positive; permanent; extra; especial; effectual; benign; immediate; invaluable; inadequate; satisfactory; maximum; parental; sublime; atrocious; mutual; lubricant; efficient; all-around; adequate; momentary; blow-out; generous; fancied; financial; sad-visaged; scanty; extended; gracious; indifferent; humiliating; warm; dubious; inexpensive; weatherproof.

verbs
afford—; bestow—upon; deny—; furnish—; gain—; grant—; insure—; legalize—; maintain—; seek—; sustain—; —assures; —eases; —preserves; —safeguards.
(See guidance, leadership, patronage.)

PROTECTOR
adjectives
guilty; desirable; sole; staunch; potent; courageous.

PROTEIN

adjectives
concentrated; coagulating; necessary.

verbs
absorb—; advocate—; assimilate—; burn—;
class as—; consume—; digest—; disintegrate—; inject—; lack—; necessitate—;
utilize—; —builds; —corrects; —regulates;
—strengthens.

(See food, carbohydrates, starch, sugar,
calorie.)

PROTEST

adjectives
indignant; feeble; ineffective; vigorous;
humble; passionate; persistent; comic; vociferous; courageous; somber; ancient; incautious; startled; religious; earnest; emphatic; living; masculine; voluble; vehement; inarticulate; shouted; shocked; hurt;
stubborn; half-scornful; howled; feigned;
energetic; unavailing; timid; manly; undersigned; respectful; harassing; passionate;
fiery; undignified; noisy; unwelcome.

verbs
anticipate—; arouse—; awaken—; brush
aside—; dismiss—; echo—; elicit—; explode
in—; file—; give rise to—; growl in—;
grumble—; howl in—; ignore—; issue—;
laugh away—; lodge—; maintain—; override—; provoke—; register—; rise in—;
scowl—; storm in—; summarize—s; voice
—; waive—; —emanates from; —infuriates; —s pour in; —flames forth.

(See complaint, grievance, objection,
answer.)

PROTEST (v)

adverbs
drawlingly; vehemently; rebelliously; solemnly; sullenly; violently; keenly; earnestly; lustily; fiercely; indignantly; suavely;
energetically; passionately; feebly; extravagantly; ungraciously; formally; persistently.

(See remonstrate, expostulate.)

PROTESTANT

verbs
oppress—; persecute—; —accedes; —acknowledges; —approves; —attends; —contradicts; —criticizes; —demurs; —flays;
—opposes; —persecutes; —practices;
—preaches; —protests; —questions; repudiates; —worships; —endorses.

(See church-goers.)

PROTESTANTISM

verbs
approve—; confirm—; convert to—; endorse
—; practice—; preach—; promise—; —accedes to; —acknowledges; —contradicts;
—demurs; —denies; —differs; —envelops;
—flays; —involves; —protests; —questions;
—repudiates.

(See religion, Christianity, protest.)

PROTESTATION

adjectives
passionate; jittery; grateful; shrieking;
roaring; injurious; characteristic; solemn;
extravagant; earnest; amorous.

PROTESTING

adjectives
pure; earnest; vigorous.

PROTRACTED

adverbs
unendurably; endlessly; foolishly; tragically; unhappily; purposely; wickedly; painfully; tiresomely; drearily; unbearably; miserably; wearily; hopelessly; inexplicably;
unaccountably; deliberately; purposely; intentionally; distressingly; viciously; lengthily; interminably; unendurably.

PROTRUDE (v)

adverbs
puffily; abnormally; flabbily; unusually;
hideously; disgustingly; prominently; exaggeratedly.

(See jut, project, extend.)

PROTUBERANCE

adjectives
horny; auricular; bulging; dimpled; elliptical; flabby; unusual; unsightly.

PROTUBERANT

adverbs
extremely; crookedly; pitiably; seriously;
gravely; noticeably; conspicuously; prominently; bulbously; tumorously; alarmingly;
dreadfully.

PROUD

adverbs
absurdly; arrogantly; boyishly; coldly; contemptibly; defiantly; excessively; fatuously;

foolishly; haughtily; honestly; rightfully; indescribably; inordinately; justly; moderately; pardonably; rapturously; regally; saucily; secretly; snobbishly; splendidly; stubbornly; stupidly; subtly; tenderly; unendurably; ungovernably; wretchedly; essentially.

PROVE (v)

adverbs
lucidly; axiomatically; irrefutably; conclusively; incontrovertibly; incontestably; ultimately; indubitably; abundantly; substantially; experimentally; undeniably.
   (See verify, corroborate.)

PROVERB

adjectives
enigmatical; prudential; silly; ungracious; bold; quaint; untruthful; well-worn. notable.

verbs
apply—; comprehend—; condense into—; contract into—; formulate—; frame—; jewel with—s; memorize—; recall—; refute—; value—; —directs; —embodies; —impresses; —instructs; —moralizes; —prescribes; —sparkles; —teaches; —warns.
   (See adage, maxim, motto, epigram.)

PROVIDE (v)

adverbs
graciously; hospitably; duly; suitably; abundantly; sparely; properly; liberally; adequately; specifically; copiously; expressly; indulgently.
   (See furnish, supply.)

PROVIDENCE

adjectives
beneficent; special; divine; shocking; indulgent; inscrutable; innocent; adverse; over-ruling.

verbs
beseech—; depend on—; meditate on—; ponder—; rely on—; —blesses; —creates; —decrees; —elects; —glorifies; —governs; —interposes; —intervenes; —justifies; —ordains; —predestines; —sanctifies; —smiles upon; —upholds.
   (See Heaven, God.)

PROVIDENT

adverbs
carefully; cautiously; habitually; generously; thriftily; cannily; scarcely; adequately; satisfactorily; lavishly; extravagantly; proudly; ostentatiously; noticeably; famously; notoriously; wisely; sagaciously; intelligently; admirably; commendably; unfailingly; prudently; considerately; thoughtfully; sensibly; elaborately.

PROVIDENTIAL

adverbs
divinely; fortunately; blessedly; highly; undoubtedly; unmistakably; curiously; mysteriously; strangely; happily; opportunely: auspiciously; gloriously; beneficently.

PROVINCE

adjectives
neighboring; fruitful; extensive; specific; outcrying; petitioning; ostensible; archiepiscopal; opulent; diverse; singular; discordant; subjugated; baffling; petty; dreaded; remote; invaded; turbulent; outlying; detailed; slender; idle; nugatory; qualificatory; stupendous; contradictory; tinned; illiberal; constitutional; suitable; severe; manipulated; complex; uncertain; antimanipulation; miraculous; adequate; obnoxious; ample; sweeping; stringent; institutionalized; standard; highly-important; scanty; illogical.

verbs
banish to—; border—; divide into—; dwell in—; edge—; encroach on—; extend—; inhabit—; lay waste—; occupy—; retire to—; rule—; settle in—; skirt—; tax—; tyrannize over—; visit—; —extends; —harbors; —trades.
   (See jurisdiction, kingdom, territory.)

PROVINCIAL

adjectives
uncouth; remote; daring; simple; single-minded; hopeless; ignorant; narrow.

adverbs
narrowly; utterly; hopelessly; boorishly; coarsely; bluntly; brusquely; remarkably; naturally; undisguisedly; illiberally; stupidly; credulously; awkardly; outlandishly; bashfully; self-consciously; strikingly; noticeably; unexpectedly; obviously; markedly.

PROVISION

verbs

adhere to—s of; annul—; balk at—; contemplate—; decry—; disregard—; enforce —; evade—; exempt from—; heed—; ignore—; incorporate—; infract—; insert—; inveigh against—; nullify—; sanction—; violate—; —amends; —augments; —compels; —eases; —elaborates on; —embodies; —wobbles.

(See clause, amendment, preparation, law.)

PROVOCATION

adjectives

abundant; severe; inscriptional; random; slight; mild.

verbs

agitate—; arouse to—; avoid—; electrify—; enkindle—; evoke—; fan—; foment—; impassion—; inflame—; irritate—; sharpen—; —boils; —disturbs; —fumes; —rages; —seethes; —simmers.

(See defiance, exasperation, hatred, stimulus, incitement.)

PROVOKE (*v*)

adverbs

wrathfully; unwittingly; deliberately; libelously; despicably; needlessly; unduly; abundantly; calculatingly; tremendously; maddeningly; irritatingly.

(See displease, incite, offend.)

PROVOKING

adverbs

particularly; intolerably; naughtily; mischievously; intentionally; deliberately; teasingly; disagreeably; foolishly; seriously; constantly; unbearably; uncommonly.

PROW

adjectives

beaked; glistening; pitch-black; pushing; unremembering; steadfast; reinforced; sharp; shining; gleaming.

PROWESS

adjectives

confirmed; mortal; martial; exploitative; memorable; amatory; mental; bodily; spiritual.

verbs

admire—; diminish—; display—; expose—; necessitate—; obscure—; reveal—; "tout"—;

—beards; —braves; —dares; —defies; —emboldens; —encourages; —defies; — overcomes; —overwhelms; —reassures; —shocks; —ventures.

(See gallantry, power, strength, bravery, valor.)

PROWL (*v*)

adverbs

nefariously; nocturnally; satanically; thievishly; viciously; slyly; characteristically; hellishly; perniciously; rapaciously; fiendishly; mutely.

(See wander, search, sneak.)

PROWLER

adjectives

vicious; thieving.

PROXIMITY

adjectives

welcome; perilous; tantalizing; suspicious.

PRUDE

adjectives

grave; waning; strict.

verbs

avoid—; condemn—; deride—; detest—; ostracize—; ridicule—; scandalize—; — affects; —attitudinizes; —bores; —irritates; —overacts; —patronizes; —poses; —simpers; —sneers; —vexes.

PRUDENCE

adjectives

habitual; rational; tottering; honorable; premeditated; calm; worldly; diplomatic; wise; uniform; traditional; mutual; slow.

verbs

acclaim—; applaud—; bolster with—; cherish—; employ—; endorse—; exercise—; extol—; ignore—; practise—; preach—; violate—; —assures; —cautions; —dictates; — forestalls; —gains; —guards; —prepares; —warns.

(See caution, forethought, consideration.)

PRUDISH

adverbs

ridiculously; comically; awkwardly; provincially; inherently; narrowly; fanatically; provokingly; vexatiously; annoyingly; affectedly; senselessly; ostentatiously; formally; stiffly; obdurately; puritanically; absurdly; ludicrously.

PSYCHOLOGY

verbs

apply—; approve—; delve into—; digest—; dominate—of; employ—; endorse—; illustrate—; involve—; lack—; practise—; —aids; —appreciates; —comprehends; —conceives; —copes with; —evolves; —fathoms; —meditates; —realizes; —studies; —understands.

(See philosophy, science.)

PUBERTY

verbs

anticipate—; attain—; confirm—; digest—; embrace—; reach—; recognize—; reveal—; —arms; —creeps upon; —despairs; —encourages; —envelops; —generates.

(See age, maturity, period.)

PUBLIC

adjectives

receptive; intellectual; alienated; fun-loving; disinterested; aroused; palpitating; surfeited; reverent; morbid; sentimental; trusting; enlightened; gullible; motoring; enduring; theatergoing; authentic; multifarious; indignant; mad; fighting; promiscuous; unorganized; indifferent; jaded; yearning; heartless; blameless; ungrateful; cynical; avid; acquiring; enlightened; attentive; fickle; exacting; ignorant; modern; credulous; importunate; consuming; investing; uneducated.

verbs

appeal to—; beguile—; captivate—; cater to —; deceive—; defraud—; divert—; enlighten—; foist on—; impress—; incite—; scan —; shrink from—; shun—; slip over on—; snare—; swindle—; —applauds; —flocks to; mystify—; present to—.

(See individual, community, masses, mob, nation, observer.)

PUBLICATION

adjectives

illegitimate; ultimate; laborious; conspicuous; wretched; facile; disreputable; posthumous; popular; unrivaled; vigorous; art; fastest-growing; unusual; interesting; outstanding; illustrated.

verbs

achieve—; advertise—; censor—; edit—; emit—; forge—; hatch—; prepare for—;

reach—; restrain—; sanction—; suspend—; translate—; —blazons; —broaches; —circulates; —edifies; —relates.

(See edition, magazine, newspaper, periodical.)

PUBLICITY

adjectives

unwanted; unfavorable; undesirable; immediate; wholesome; unsparing; unpleasant; humiliating; vague; unsavory; national; wide-spread; long-sought.

verbs

achieve—; attain—; avoid—; balk at—; court—; decry—; elude—; favor with—; gain—; leash—; maneuver for—; release—; screen from—; shower with—; shrink from —; shun—; submit to—; suffer—; sustain—; yearn for—; —celebrates; —engulfs; —fames; —glares.

(See limelight, notoriety, fame.)

PUBLIC OPINION

verbs

arouse—; consolidate—; count on—; crystalize—; excite—; formulate—; inspire—; mobilize—; muster—; prize—; rely on—; seek —; suppress—; sway—; value—; —alters; —approves; —condemns; —decides; —denounces; —sanctions; —scorns; —selects; —speculates; —tempers; —vetoes.

(See opinion, belief, sentiment.)

PUBLISH (v)

adverbs

posthumously; exclusively; surreptitiously; libelously; fraudulently; extensively; anonymously; boldly; advantageously; voluminously; compulsorily; seditiously.

(See print, announce, circulate.)

PUBLISHER

adjectives

unscrupulous; ungenerous; august; influential; heroic.

verbs

consult—; entreat—; —advertises; —edits; —emits; —heralds; —proclaims; —rejects; —rushes; —sanctions; —weans.

(See journalist, editor, printer.)

PUCKER (v)

adverbs

resentfully; coyly; teasingly; attractively; quaintly; sweetly; amorously.

(See crease, purse, wrinkle.)

PUDDING

verbs

bake—; cool—; dish—; flavor—; garnish —; mix—; mold—; relish—; serve—; spoon —; steam—; stir—; sweeten—; —curdles; —delights; —graces; —hardens; —tempts; —thickens.

(See cake, food, dessert.)

PUDDLE

adjectives

dirtiest; muddy; slopping; ugly.

PUERILE

adverbs

pitiably; inexplicably; frivolously; ridiculously; unfortunately; fatuously; inanely; trivially; surprisingly; hopelessly; vacuously; ineptly.

PUFF (v)

adverbs

prodigiously; violently; meditatively; reminiscently; pensively; breathlessly; laboredly.

(See blow, pant.)

PUGILISTIC

adverbs

skilfully; notoriously; famously; truculently; quarrelsomely; insistently; contentiously; argumentatively; expertly; eagerly; enthusiastically; zealously; unwarrantably; sturdily; stoutly.

PULL

adjectives

dreadful; energetic; vigorous; hearty; vicious; necessary.

PULL (v)

adverbs

rapidly; laboriously; vigorously; violently: unconscionably; irresistibly; energetically; frantically; tremulously; viciously; forcibly; heartily.

(See draw, haul.)

PULP

verbs

assay—; beat to—; compose of—; convert —; crush to—; derive from—; obtain—; pound to—; reduce to—; strain through—; test—; tread to—; —adheres; —fattens; — fills; —lines; —stuffs.

(See powder, mass.)

PULPIT

verbs

adorn—; ascend to—; climb to—; encrust— with; erect—; face—; orate from—; preach from—; support—; thunder from—; —attracts; —condemns; —decries; —denounces.

(See desk, platform, rostrum.)

PULSATE (v)

adverbs

rhythmically; markedly; regularly; periodically; throbbingly; violently; flutteringly; feverishly; turbulently; passionately; tremulously; hectically.

(See beat, throb.)

PULSE

adjectives

choral; throbbing; violent; new; bounding; fluttering; burning; ineradicable; languid; feverish; accelerated; rapid; quickened; chaster; pounding; arrested; fleshy; heightened; possible; turbulent; passionate; purple; haggard; energetic; hurried; leaping; firm; wearied; generous; tremulous; immortal; dormant; thrilling; hectic; emotional; inward; audible.

verbs

accelerate—; flag—; quicken—; record—; slow—; stir—; whip up—; —beats; — bounds; —drums; —flows; —flutters; — leaps; —responds; —slackens; —surges; — throbs.

(See stream, flow, vibration.)

PUMP

verbs

elevate—; handle—; labor with—; man—; manipulate—; operate—; require—; work —; —compels; —draws; —eases; —empowers; —enables; —fathoms; —forces; —presses; —pulls; —raises; —rectifies; —squirts; —sucks.

PUN

adjectives

arrant; copious; irresistible; unnecessary; stringing; weak; stupid; childish.

946

PUNCH

adjectives *(blow)*
essential; crisp; sinewy.

PUNCH

verbs *(drink)*
drain—; flavor—; ladle—; relish—; replenish—; savor—; serve—; sip—; soak in—; spike—; steep in—; swill—; thirst for—; —befuddles; —flows; —inebriates; —lushes; —quenches; —refreshes.

(See liquor, beverage, wine.)

PUNCTILIOUS

adverbs
overly; carefully; deferentially; ceremoniously; formally; conventionally; officially; meticulously; especially; peculiarly; infallibly; unbendingly; remarkably; particularly; uncommonly; highly; terribly.

PUNCTUAL

adverbs
usually; seldom; scarcely; infallibly; unfailingly; resolutely; painfully; ostentatiously; disagreeably; satisfactorily; notoriously; noticeably; quietly; serenely; pleasantly; unusually; coolly; habitually; pompously; deferentially; ceremoniously; respectfully; ingratiatingly; singularly.

PUNGENT

adverbs
spicily; pleasantly; arrestingly; refreshingly; strongly; faintly; overpoweringly; richly; attractively; aromatically; sharply; penetratingly; bitterly; hotly.

PUNISH *(v)*

adverbs
indiscriminately; summarily; barbarously; cruelly; justly; nominally; sparingly; vindictively; officially; exemplarily; ignominiously; ingeniously; atrociously.

(See discipline, penalize.)

PUNISHMENT

adjectives
dreadful; supplementary; inhuman; penitentiary; helpless; corporal; vindictive; servile; severe; direful; ignorant; eternal; adequate; express; impending; barbarous; everlasting; official; fitting; permanent; frightful; exemplary; summary; ignominious; brave; insufferable; ingenious; pleasing; dreadful.

verbs
administer—; condemn to—; enforce—; evade—; inflict—upon; mete out—; prohibit—; rain—upon; rebel against—; reserve—for; risk—; subject to—; suffer—; undergo—; —abates; —atones; —frightens.

(See lashing, discipline, torture, torment, penalty.)

PUNY

adverbs
feebly; miserably; whiningly; undoubtedly; obviously; manifestly; evidently; admittedly; unfortunately; wretchedly; pitifully; deplorably; incomparably; lamentably; shamefully; incurably; incredibly; strangely; unaccountably; hopelessly; discouragingly.

PUPIL

verbs *(eye)*
damage—; enlarge—; examine—; exercise—; expose—; film—; harm—; impair—; injure—; mar—; mist—; pierce—; strain—; —contracts; —dilates; —responds.

(See eye.)

PUPIL

adjectives *(general)*
apt; docile; individual; dilated; illustrious; ill-omened; interesting; ungifted; alert; unpromising; expressionless; unwilling; incapable; progressive; precocious; impressionable; desired; bewildered; diligent; apathetic; steely.

PUPIL

verbs *(student)*
chastise—; encourage—; entertain —s; examine —s; grade —s; graduate—; impart to—; inculcate in—; instil in—; instruct—; limit —s; prepare—; question—; reprimand—; —competes; —comprehends; —crams (colloq.); —demonstrates; —flunks (colloq); —grasps; —passes; —responds; —surpasses; —understands.

(See student.)

PUPPET

adjectives
gyrating; mere; painted; exceeding; skilled; gesticulating.

verbs
carve—; dress up—; employ—; enjoy—; manipulate—; represent by—; —amuses; —

947

capers; —delights; —depicts; —diverts; —enacts; —entertains; —frisks; —impersonates; —mimics; —mocks.
(See clown, doll.)

PUPPY

adjectives

contumacious; playful; hydrophobic; pleasant; tiny; helpless.

verbs

abandon —s; coax—; cuddle—; cudgel—; drown—; leash—; lose—; pet—; play with —; soothe—; train—; whelp —s; whip—; —annoys; —barks; —capers; —darts by; —frolics; —licks; —performs; —pursues; —whimpers; —whines; —yelps.
(See dog, animal, pet.)

PURCHASE

adjectives

remarkable; ill-considered; enforced; judicious; special; important; systematic; infinitesimal; fortunate; careless; opportune.

verbs

cart —s; charge—; check —s; collect —s; deliver—; dispose of—; gather —s; glean —s; inveigle into—; limit —s; mislay—; pile up —s; procure—; redeem—; ship—; weigh—; —s accrue; —loads.
(See merchandise, bundle, parcel, package.)

PURCHASE (v)

adverbs

substantially; advantageously; hypothetically; unwittingly; judiciously; systematically; shrewdly; astutely.
(See buy, acquire, secure.)

PURCHASER

adjectives

careless; persistent; potential.

verbs

advertise for—; allure —s; assure—; deceive—; net—; please—; satisfy—; tempt —; —charges; —complains; —demands; —dispenses; —markets; —patronizes; —procures; —selects; —shops.
(See buyer, customer.)

PURE

adverbs

perfectly; 100%; 99%; chastely; incredibly; warrantably; singularly; incredibly; unsur-

passably; incomparably; consummately; immaculately; spotlessly; absolutely; unadulteratedly; innocently; childishly; devoutly; virtuously; artlessly; genuinely; utterly.

PURGATIVE

adjectives

powerful; stimulating; violent; bitter.

verbs

addict to—s; avoid—s; employ—; —clarifies; —defecates; —expurgates; —filters; —flushes; —frees; —purges; —purifies; —racks; —refines; —removes; —scours; —sifts; —strains; —washes; —weeds.
(See sedative, medicine, remedy, enema.)

PURGATIVE

adverbs

thoroughly; warrantably; successfully; safely; remedially; necessarily; scientifically; naturally; unfailingly; genuinely; receptably.

PURITANICAL

adverbs

painfully; primly; sternly; unyieldingly: inflexibly; unbendingly; rigidly; priggishly; sedately; quietly; stoically; gravely; severely; strictly; austerely; obviously; silently; rigorously; harshly; seriously; learnedly; justly; fairly; ascetically; precisely; forbiddingly; dourly; inexorably; uncompromisingly; stiffly; dreadfully.

PURITANISM

verbs

advocate—; crusade against—; enshrine in —; inflict—; inspire—; practise—; suffer—; tolerate—; —condemns; —consecrates; —narrows; —oppresses; —reveres; —rules; —sanctifies; —simplifies; —smiles; —stints; —tramples.
(See protestantism, christianity.)

PURITY

adjectives

ethical; intellectual; womanly; classical; spotless; rare; pristine; absolute; racial; inexpressible; moral; unconscious; seraphic; touching; delicate; original; infinite; exalted; crystal; coldest; celestial; quiet; immaculate; perfect; impious; comparative; scholastic; sinless; earnest; extreme; displayed; conscious; personal; cherished; political; naked; sufficient; singular; snow-white.

verbs

achieve—; admire—; advocate—; attain—; defile—of; incur—; procure—; recommend —; revere—; select—; stain—; taint—; violate—; —awes; —eliminates; —pervades; —satisfies.

(See justice, holiness, innocence, chastity; modesty, morality.)

PURPLE

adjectives

imperial; intense; darkling; dun; regal; pansy; visual; tenderest; livid; rich; ruddy; soft; pale.

PURPORT

adjectives

dramatic; mystical; true; dim.

PURPOSE

adjectives

hellish; undefined; cosmic; syndicating; ambitious; fell; sinister; experimental; better; dire; sworn; pious; excellent; sacramental; critical; reference; avowed; moral; studied; persistent; communal; speculative; lofty; dramatic; practical; underlying; beneficent; voiceless; contrary; serious; artistic; specific; resolute; definite; high; honorable; constant; malignant; reasoned; deliberate; sufficient; laudable; primary; productive; exalted; menial; avowed; large; grim; unchanging; resurging; unswerving; ungenerous; broken; multitudinous (pl); keener; sternest; breeding; sugar-coated; ephemeral; rational; boundless; unaccomplished; restrained; unfathomed; dark; consuming; patient; altruistic; decorative; finite; defensive; distinct; hostile; aggressive; genuine; benevolent; energetic; earnest; common; essential; disinterested; ultimate; sole; poetical; finical; forlorn; flighty; infallible; willful; orbed; insurrectionary; notable; rugged; robust; tragic; humane; philosophical; unheeded; didactic; patriotic; double; extraneous; aesthetic; unchaste; intramural; visual; tolerable; ruthless; noble; corrupt; ulterior; salutary; public; histrionic; educational; patent; malicious; life; manifest; introductory; express; pernicious; heroic; inhospitable; visible; awkward; deadly; theoretical; unvarying; weighty; fraudulent; prudent; propagandist; temporary; deceptive; immediate; precautionary; domestic; abandoned; unsettled; luxurious; salubrious; iron; negative; unlawful; proper; fixed; diabolical; eternal; obstinate; pure;

commercial; industrial; therapeutic; pacific; enduring; divine; microscopic; apposite; doubtful; especial; colloquial; admirable; dumb; insuperable; ineradicable; ostensible; selfsame; infirm; half-formed; prime; economic.

verbs

achieve—; adhere to—; attain—; contrive for—; convey—; crystallize—; defeat—; disclose—; divert from—; divine—; extract —from; fulfill—; galvanize into—; inspire by—; intend for—; interpret—; overcloud —; pursue—; serve—; stiffen—; subserve —; swerve from—; thwart—.

(See end, aim, effect, intention, mission, object, objective.)

PURR (*v*)

adverbs

amiably; demurely; cozily; domestically; comfortably; contentedly; drowsily.

(See murmur, whisper.)

PURSE

adjectives

well-filled; borrowed; evading; slow; slender; humble; yawning; long; cunning; shut; over-gorged; privy.

verbs

clasp—; cling to—; conceal—; consign to —; decorate—; dent—; draw from—; fatten —; fumble in—; lose—; mislay—; pocket—; relinquish—; replenish—; snap—; snatch—; stuff—; suit—; swell—; —accrues; —amasses; —bulges; —flashes.

(See wallet, bag, pocket.)

PURSE (*v*)

adverbs

coyly; squeamishly; fastidiously; cunningly; aristocratically.

(See pucker, wrinkle, crease.)

PURSUE (*v*)

adverbs

adventurously; remorselessly; indefatigably; warily; energetically; lustfully; relentlessly; lasciviously; invariably; resolutely; diligently; doggedly; ardently; stolidly; blandly; sedulously; mechanically; strenuously; zealously; imprudently.

(See chase, follow, seek.)

adjectives

peaceful; immediate; hot; relentless; systematic; agricultural; innocent; intellectual; vigorous; dissipated; artistic; serious; exciting; studious; active; business; industrial; intimate; profitable; unjust; scuffling; professional; energetic; strenuous; relentless; sedentary; brilliant; weird; furious; peaceful; laboratory; vulgar; cultural; dangerous; unique; zealous; eager; imprudent; mercantile; athletic; worthy; hardy; wearisome; military; sluggish; sordid; sylvan; amphibious; lawful; honorable; compulsory; happy; invigorating; dogged; humble; lucrative; ardent; serious; irreparable; useless; rabid; favorite; scientific; ultimate; unavailing; instant; severer; evident; swift; illegitimate; blind; delusive; scholarly; idealistic; sedulous; disordered; engrossing; elevating; uninterrupted; vile; prompt; fascinating; passionate.

verbs

abandon—; avert—; avoid—; contemplate —; devote to—; distract from—; dog in—; engage in—; engross in—; enter—; follow in—; hinder—; hound in—; obstruct—; press—; prevent—; rush in—; spurn—; —annoys; —irks; —threatens.

(See hobby, industry, profession, quest, occupation, business, chase.)

PUS

verbs

cough up—; discharge—; drain—; eject—; emit—; expel—; fester—; localize—; produce—; —befouls; —contaminates; —defiles; —escapes; —exudes from; —fills; —forms; —offends; —oozes from; —pollutes; —reeks; —smears; —spatters; —sullies.

(See saliva.)

PUSH

adjectives

warning; vigorous; desperate; significant; determined; zealous.

verbs

climax—; necessitate—; require—; resist—; —boots (colloq.); —casts; —discharges; —drives; —expels; —favors; —forces; —heaves; —hurls; —impels; —jerks; —launches; —pitches; —startles.

(See charge, attack.)

adverbs

cautiously; sententiously; uncompromisingly; unceremoniously; adroitly; instinctively; vigorously; presumptuously; superciliously; unfalteringly; rudely; laboriously; mechanically.

(See shove, impel.)

PUSILLANIMOUS

adverbs

pitiably; insufferably; unhappily; miserably; wretchedly; shamefully; timorously; pitifully; contemptibly; atrociously; meanly; inexplicably; strangely; remarkably; disgracefully; basely; incredibly; hopelessly; disgustingly; pathetically.

PUTTY

verbs

apply—; case with—; coat with—; dab on —; lay—; mold—; plaster—; press—; reduce to—; smear—; spread—; squeeze—; —cements; —conceals; —covers; —faces; —holds; —pastes; —sticks.

(See mortar, plaster, cement.)

PUZZLE

adjectives

inexplicable; provocative; insolvable; fascinating; frightening; baffling.

verbs

disclose—; disentangle—; dissolve—; explain—; extricate—; popularize—; present —; reveal—; scramble—; solve—; study—; unfold—; unravel—; untie—; —baffles; —entertains; —involves; —irks; —irritates; —mystifies; —perplexes.

(See trick, riddle, problem, perplexity.)

PUZZLED

adverbs

strangely; terribly; bewilderingly; bafflingly; bitterly; cruelly; utterly; embarrassingly; painfully; obscurely; profoundly; seriously; completely; admittedly; confusingly.

PUZZLING

adverbs

sadly; naturally; hopelessly; dangerously; seriously; unreasonably; alarmingly; depressingly; unaccountably; disturbingly; genuinely; strangely; indescribably; fearfully; dishearteningly; maddeningly; unusually; terribly; vexatiously; vaguely; definitely; uncomfortably; subtly; awkwardly; extremely; annoyingly; exasperatingly; inexplicably.

Q

verbs

betray—; detect—; father—; patronize—; warn of—; —bamboozles (colloq.); —bilks; —cajoles; —deceives; —dupes; —ensnares; —fakes (colloq.); —gammons; —gulls; — hoaxes; —lures; —outwits; —traps.

(See liar, hypocrite, quackery.)

QUACKERY

verbs

denounce—; expose—; practice—; prevent —; support—; worship—; —cheats; —circumvents; —contaminates; —corrupts; — debases; —deludes; —pretends; —swindles; —tricks.

(See quack.)

QUAFF (v)

adverbs

deeply; unhesitatingly; thirstily; eagerly; fraternally; jubilantly.

(See drink, sip.)

QUAGGY

adverbs

hopelessly; impassably; undesirably; soggily; dangerously; uselessly; abominably; strangely; irremediably; unsalably; unfortunately; squashily; swampily; occasionally; seasonally.

QUAIL

verbs

domesticate—; flush—; —barks; —bills; — cruises; —feigns; —flushes; —flutters; — glides; —haunts; —jerks; —nods; —roves; —rumbles; —rustles; —scratches; — squeals; —struts; —tattoos; --trills; — thumps; —thunders; —yelps.

(See bird, bob-white, partridge.)

QUAINT

adverbs

delightfully; demurely; altogether; deliciously; exceptionally; extraordinarily; uncommonly; exotically; unfashionably; enchantingly; attractively; whimsically; bewitchingly; charmingly; pleasantly; alluringly; unusually.

QUAINTNESS

verbs

cultivate—; enjoy—; instil—; notice—; overdo—; practise—; reveal—; ridicule—; —appeals; —attracts; —becomes; —blooms; —deceives; —delights; —intrigues.

(See strangeness, beauty.)

QUALIFICATION

adjectives

inner; original; sterilizing; eminent; remotest; conventional; special; indispensable; scientific.

verbs

arm with—; contemplate—; disclaim—; discount—; dispute—; endow with—; ignore —; impugn—; increase—; seek—; tax—; vouch for—; weigh—; —adapts; empowers; —enables; —fits; —strengthens; —warrants.

(See power, endowment, essential.)

QUALIFIED

adverbs

competently; capably; entirely; unusually; exceptionally; singularly; well; wonderfully; acceptably; suitably; especially; particularly; incomparably; proficiently; technically; felicitously; obviously; evidently; manifestly; peculiarly; marvelously.

QUALIFY (v)

adverbs

patently; eminently; severely; admirably; splendidly; nominally; scientifically; medically; conventionally.

(See limit, modify, restrict.)

QUALITY

adjectives

absorptive; abstract; adaptive; academic; acoustical; adhering; administrative; aesthetic; affectionate; affrontive; allotted; analytical; anecdotal; antipyretic; appealing; ardent; aristocratic; artistic; atmospheric; authoritative; available; average; blended; blooming; blossom-like; brilliant; cardinal; characteristic; charming; childlike; companionable; chivalric; considerable; contradictory; cooking; correspondent; dependable; daredevil; decorative; deepreaching; deep-rooted; demonstrable; desirable; despised; determining; developmental; diagnostic; disciplinary; disinfectant; distinctive; divine; dogged; distinguished; dramatic; driving; dubious; educational; effective; electric; elusive; embracing; emollient; emotional; empty; enduring; energetic; entrancing; essential; ethical; evident; exasperating; exceptional; fabric; faithless; famous; fertilizing; fatal; feminine; filtering; fine; first; flawless; fleshy; floating; flowery; food; free-lathering; friendly; generous; genial; gentlemanly; genuine; good; gracious; guaranteed; handmade; haunting; health-giving; high; honest; imaginary; imperturbable; indubitable; inefficient; inestimable; infectious; inferior; inherent; inherited; innate; inoperative; insulative; intellectual; integral; intrinsic; introspective; invigorating; lasting; laughable; literary; luxurious; lyrical; machine-like; magnificent; masculine; maternal; maximum; mellow; melodic; mental; militant; minimum; mixing; moral; mordant; musty; mysterious; narcotic; national; nightmare; noble; noticeable; nutritious; objectionable; occult; opiate; outstanding; outward; overlooked; pagan; passive; pedigreed; peculiar; personal; pervasive; physical; pictorial; picturesque; practical; predominant; preeminent; preternatural; prime; primest; profuse; protective; provocative; pulsating; pregnant; pungent; real; realistic; redeeming; relaxing; reliable; remarkable; representative; restraining; robust; romantic; saccharine; ruder; rugged; sachet; sensational; sedative; serious; shameless; sheer; shimmering; showy; singular; slurred; smooth; social; spiritual; sterling; statuesque; sterner; steely; subtle; strengthening; studious; stylistic; subordinate; superior; superlative; syllogistic; tangible; temperamental; tempered; top; toxic; unbeatable; uncertain; unexpected; unfailing; unfitting; unfostered; uniform; united; universal; unreasoning; unquestioned; unsatisfactory; unsought; unsuitable; unsurpassed; untiring; unusual; varied (pl); venomous; vibrating; vital; warlike; wearing; whimsical; windy; womanly; wondrous; zestful; workmanlike; worthy; wretched.

verbs
appraise—; appreciate—; ascribe—to; define—; determine—; discern—; display—; divest of—; endow with—; evaluate—; extol—; impair—; impart—; improve—; inherit—; intensify—; maintain—; recognize

—; refine—; revere—; sacrifice—; share—; temper—; underrate—; —eludes; —predominates.
(See essence, attribute, characteristic, nature.)

QUALM

adjectives
conscience; sudden; bitter; unwonted.

verbs
arouse—; challenge—; incur—; justify—; raise—; register—; satisfy—; suffer—; — abashes; —alarms; —deprives; —frightens; —harrows; —hinders; —impedes; —lingers; —obstructs; —swerves; —unnerves.
(See scruple, fear, misgiving.)

QUANTITY

adjectives
exhaustless; immense; insufficient; unprecedented; unknown; indefinite; changeable; limited; astonishing; enormous; normal; unlimited; illustrative; dumb; untold; abstract; excessive; staggering; substantial; greater; surface; commercial; vast; goodly; monstrous; arbitrary; sufficient; minus; measurable; negligible; distorted; useless; unmanageable; surprising; considerable; incredible; generous; equivalant; adequate.

verbs
accumulate—; amass—; ascertain—; collect —; distribute—; estimate—; gather—; issue —; lessen—; limit—; measure—; muster— of; rake up—; reduce—; regulate—; — dwindles; —masses; —mounts; —soars; — transcends.
(See dose, amount, total, sum.)

QUARANTINE

verbs
demand—; enforce—; escape—; necessitate—; require—; repulse—; resist—; warrant—; —assures; —elapses; —excludes; —fences; —forbids; —houses; — isolates; —protects; —restrains; —restricts.
(See isolation, taboo, ban, boycott.)

QUARREL

adjectives
frequent (pl); monkish; unjust; petty; equivalent; theological; incipient; warranted; dignified; violent; private; intestine;

jealous; holy; comic; ancient; sudden; sharp; false; splendid; empty; continual; wretched; pretty; ecclesiastical; inconsequential; wrongful.

verbs
arouse—; deplore—; evoke—; lament—; patch up—; pick—; provoke—; regret—; repent—; sow—; stir up—; —breaches; —disconcerts; —embitters; —ensues; —gratifies; —rages; —sours.
(See brawl, dissension, disagreement, dispute.)

QUARREL (v)
adverbs
shamelessly; heatedly; pettishly; impertinently; theologically; jealously; acrimoniously; bitterly; squalidly; hatefully; vindictively.
(See dispute, disagree, wrangle.)

QUARRELSOME
adverbs
disagreeably; hotly; offensively; obstinately; abusively; stubbornly; irritatingly; violently; needlessly; nervously; excitably; unnecessarily; bitterly; foolishly; truculently; brutally; intolerably; unsufferably; disputatiously.

QUARRY
verbs
bait—; beguile—; contemplate—; corner—; draw—; gain on—; hole up—; investigate —; offer—; play for—; pursue—; risk—; speculate on—; tree—; vie for—; —delights; —lures; —tempts.
(See prey, victim.)

QUARTERS
adjectives
commodious; limited; exalted; charming; squalid; pleasant; deficient; distant; unsavory; fair; dingy; desolate; fashionable; moderate; heated; precise; comfortable; light-housekeeping; desponding; authoritative; ruined; cramped; ransacked; sumptuous; immigrant; bourgeois; treacherous; humble; unknown; cheerless.

verbs
assign to—; defile—; establish—; invade—; investigate—; locate—; lodge in—; picket

—; pitch—; plant—; post—; remove—; report to—; retire to—; set up—; situate—; station at—; take up—; vacate.
(See barracks, place, position, headquarters.)

QUAVER (v)
adverbs
tremulously; weakly; sickeningly; peculiarly; characteristically.
(See shake, tremble, quiver.)

QUAVERING
adverbs
anxiously; diffidently; despairingly; apprehensively; despondently; dismally; dreadfully; nervously; restlessly; solicitously; terribly; tremulously; agedly; eagerly; stammeringly; wearily; abjectly; timidly.

QUEEN
adjectives
refulgent; haughty; fairy; pale; papist; fiend-like; gracious; love-sick; mob-led; stately; legitimate; buxom; helmeted; amorous; crownless; well-intentioned; dark; peerless; uncrowned; crafty; potent.

verbs
attend—; crown—; escort—; guard—; honor—; pamper—; revere—; salaam before —; serve—; squire—; —abdicates; —appeals to; —ascends; —assigns; —commends; —dazzles; —orders; —punishes; —reigns; —rewards; —rules; —symbolizes.
(See king, monarch, ruler.)

QUEER
adverbs
outlandishly; terribly; exotically; egregiously; alarmingly; singularly; abominably; mysteriously; unaccountably; suddenly; dreadfully; ominously; fantastically; uncommonly; extraordinarily; comically; grotesquely; exceptionally; unwontedly; hopelessly; incurably; incorrigibly.

QUEERNESS
verbs
deride—; develop—; incur—; overlook—; permit—; pose—; relieve—; remedy—; ridicule—; study—; tolerate—; —baffles; —creeps into; —infringes; —perplexes; —surprises; —violates.
(See oddity.)

QUELL (v)

adverbs

effectually; forcefully; momentarily; outwardly; effectively; vigorously; legitimately; officiously; legally; demonstrably; brutally.

(See suppress, subdue, crush.)

QUERIES

adjectives

valued; amusing; superstitious; unfortunate; idiotic; sceptical; excellent; everlasting; clattering; desperate; fantastic.

QUERULOUS

adverbs

hatefully; uneasily; restlessly; exceptionally; habitually; extremely; insufferably; disagreeably; pitiably; pitifully; endlessly; crabbedly; morosely; moodily; lonesomely; unhappily; perversely; crossly; sulkily; understandably; helplessly.

QUERY (v)

adverbs

sharply; deprecatingly; deliberately; romantically; significantly; stubbornly; breathlessly; anxiously; curtly; scornfully; perplexedly.

(See question, ask, inquire.)

QUEST

adjectives

chivalrous; eternal; unsuccessful; lawful; terrible; hopeless; contrarious; eager; uncertain; original; evangelical; adventurous; furious; vain; winged; doubtful; childish; selfsame.

verbs

abandon—; aim—at; engage in—; follow—; join in—; justify—; tire of—; value—; —allures; —beguiles; —demands; —eludes; —escapes; —evades; —leads; —requires; —tempts; —wearies.

(See pursuit, journey, trip, adventure.)

QUESTION

adjectives

compound; innocent; prying; rhetorical; debatable; embarrassing; unvoiced; historic; ultimate; comprehensive; unthinkable; controversial; probing; tentative; pointblank; covert; perfidious; insidious; awkward; searching; identification; artless; incisive; unconscious; sad; vermicular; brute; philosophical; theological; touching; vexed; burning; tabooed; academic; angry; contemptuous; essential; clamorous; suspicious; physical; irrational; prompt; diverse; fundamental; trying; improper; gloomy; immodest; muttered; delicate; difficult; mooted; incessant; pertinent; hideous; intelligent; abstract; stale; celebrated; troublesome; long-pending; dreadful; social; unsettled; idle; constant; bald; agonized; piercing; present; impertinent; deciding; prominent; insolent; disputed; pressing; affable; ambiguous; germane; stern; unanswerable; dormant; sensible; sorrowful; inconvenient; serious; brusque; vital; disencumbered; horrible; frenzied; large; unsuitable; transit; profound; intricate; irritating; imminent; teasing; explosive; argumentative; innumerable (pl); reasonable; concrete; cheerless; ill-bred; cogent; momentous; political; financial; humanitarian; national; absurd; relevant; foregoing; technical; barbed; perennial; multiplying; combustive; tantalizing; beggarly; tremendous; peculiar; perfect; natural; broader; ironical; much-discussed; steep; pending; motherly; untiring; numberless (pl); pregnant; eternal; banal; lustier; dynastic; constitutional; abstruse; unsettled; ever-burning; confidential; ethical; austere; vexatious; economic; insolvable; rude; insatiate; complex; perplexing; basic; uneasy; frivolous; speculative; customary; blunt; trick; similar; exhaustive; civil; religious.

verbs

adjudicate—; bar—; bear upon—; bombard with—s; brood over—; complicate—; comprehend—; confront with—; constitute—; cope with—; darken—; debate—; deluge with—s; dispute—; elucidate—; evade—; face—; fire—at; fling—at; focus on—; formulate—; frame—; go to the heart of—; grapple with—; hammer with—s; hurl—at; open to—; parry—; ply with—s; ponder—; propound—; raise—; revive—; shelve—; shy away from—; solve—; split on—; submit—to; throw light upon—; touch upon—; voice—; wrestle with—; —agitates; —arises; —elicits; —embarrasses; —hangs fire; —involves; —looms; —obtrudes upon; —plagues; —pops up; —poses itself; —relates to; —revolves itself; —rings out; —simmers; —vexes.

(See issue, matter, problem, inquiry, questioning.)

QUESTION (v)

adverbs

importunately; cryptically; audaciously; curiously; vaguely; incredulously; blankly; ruefully; sarcastically; sophistically; prefatorily; minutely; impudently; reluctantly; tactfully; innocently; clamorously; delicately; improperly; sternly; brusquely; momentously; technically; ironically; banally; abstrusely; confidentially; speculatively; bluntly; exhaustively.

(See query, inquire.)

QUESTIONABLE

adverbs

highly; morally; controversially; argumentatively; distinctly; darkly; uncomfortably; naturally; particularly; legally; ticklishly; undeniably; mysteriously; inferentially; conventionally.

QUESTIONAIRE

verbs

circulate—; compile—; conduct—; contemplate—; distribute—; grapple with—; induce from—; infer from—; issue—; mark —; propound—; reply to—; return—; score —; —aids; —decides; —enables; —forecasts; —inquires; —interrogates; —investigates; —irks; —puzzles; —requests; —reveals; —settles.

(See application, petition, appeal.)

QUESTIONING

adjectives

continual; suicidal; interminable; inward; prudent; over-curious.

verbs

avert—; arraign for—; conduct—; dodge —; investigate—; pursue—; refuse—; review—; —agitates; —analyzes; —canvasses; —delves into; —demands; —elicits; —ferrets out; —overhauls; —probes; — pumps; —ransacks.

(See grilling.)

QUEUE

verbs

arrange—; braid—; clip—; dress—; tug at—; twist—; weave—; wind—; wrap—; —attracts; —hangs; —jiggles; —trails; —suspends; —sways; —swings.

(See braid, hair, tail.)

QUIBBLING

verbs

avoid—; brush aside—; check—; detest—; endure—; ignore—; incur—; suffer—; —annoys; —betrays; —deceives; —eludes; —evades; —glosses over; —hampers; — hinders; —irks; —provokes; —shuffles; —taxes; —vexes.

(See evasion, excuse.)

QUICK

adverbs

devilishly; surprisingly; alarmingly; incredibly; wonderfully; efficiently; normally; abnormally; extremely; cruelly; mentally; maliciously; diabolically; remarkably; duteously; feverishly; ordinarily; expertly; impulsively; mercifully; comically; uncomfortably; breathlessly; perilously; marvelously; unaccountably; luckily; astonishingly; dangerously; unbelievably.

QUICKNESS

adjectives

surprising; dizzy; devilish; irresolute.

QUICK-WITTED

adverbs

remarkably; astonishingly; nimbly; commercially; socially; disturbingly; incredibly; simply; admirably; sparklingly; scintillatingly; wonderfully; enviably; scintillantly; naturally; habitually; unsurpassably.

QUIESCENCE

verbs

arouse from—; endure—; lull to—; maintain—; quell to—; snub into—; —abides; —charms; —envelops; —flows; —hushes; —persists; —pleases; —stagnates.

(See lethargy, quiet, repose.)

QUIESCENT

adverbs

temporarily; luckily; fortunately; significantly; customarily; peculiarly; seasonally; remarkably; ominously; naturally; silently; immovably; usually.

QUIET

adjectives

dimmed; remarkable; restful; absolute; undisturbed; restoring; rural; subduing; penitential; endless; dull; luxurious; reverent; lifeless; ominous; domestic; graceful; aimless; formidable; passive; idealic; pastoral; peaceful; enforced.

verbs
brook—; envelop in—; insure—; reduce to
—; stir from—; wrap in—; —allays; —appeals; —appeases; —calms; —cools; —governs; —lulls; —maddens; —pervades; —
quells; —reigns; —smooths; —soothes.
 (See hush, silence, rest, repose, quiescence,
peace.)

adverbs
utterly; particularly; carefully; absurdly;
cautiously; furtively; stealthily; considerately; attentively; courteously; graciously;
pensively; anxiously; deliberately; dreamily; satisfactorily; temporarily; significantly;
miraculously; calmly; astonishingly; sullenly; moodily; gloomily; awesomely; terrifyingly; alarmingly; suspiciously; significantly; mysteriously; appallingly; uncommonly.

QUIETNESS
adjectives
inviolable; unobtrusive; external; extreme;
pensive; subdued.

QUIETUDE
adjectives
surprising; comforting; unusual; extraordinary; sartorial.

QUILL
adjectives
tuneful; enchanted; porcupine; many-colored; tinkling; venal.

QUIT (v)
adverbs
reluctantly; sadly; dejectedly; eventually;
hastily; abruptly; impetuously; significantly;
gloomily; mysteriously; consequently.
 (See cease, stop.)

QUIVER
adjectives
solemn; convulsive; subtle.

QUIVER (v)
adverbs
nervously; exasperatedly; wantonly; abnormally; violently; sluggishly; markedly; excitedly; passionately.
 (See shake, tremble, quaver.)

QUIVERING
adjectives
mysterious; gentle; anxious.

adverbs
nervously; tremulously; helplessly; feverishly; pathetically; pitiably; miserably;
visibly; angrily; grievously; timidly; af-
frightedly; curiously.

QUIZ (v)
adverbs
narrowly; closely; methodically; thoroughly; perfunctorily austerely; vexatiously;
rudely; speculatively; civilly; sternly; abstrusely.
 (See question, banter.)

QUOTA
adjectives
assigned; respective; insignificant.

verbs
acquire—; allot—; apportion—; attain—;
cede—; deal—; derive—; divide—; endow
—; fulfill—; furnish—; impose—; pledge
—; portion out—; present—; raise—; receive—; subscribe—; supply—; yield—.
 (See portion, share, part.)

QUOTATION
verbs
apply—to; bejewel with—s; comprehend—;
condense into—; contract into—; eschew—;
fling—at; frame—; memorize—; ooze—s;
pepper with—s; recall—; refer to—; value
—; —directs; —embodies; —exemplifies;
—illustrates; —impresses; —instructs; —
prescribes; —sparkles; —teaches; —warns.
 (See saying, maxim, proverb, passage.)

....QUOTATIONS
adjectives
biblical; poetical; irreverent; copious; innumerable; modest; half-remembered; seasonable; habitual; felicitious; capital; garbled; illustrative; multifarious.

QUOTE (v)
adverbs
copiously; philosophically; widely; extensively; oracularly; preeminently; plaintively; magnanimously; ardently; biblically;
poetically; habitually; felicitously; illustra-
tively; multifariously; aptly; erroneously.
 (See repeat, extract.)

R

verbs
induct—; ordain—; —authorizes; —blesses; —communes; —confirms; —consecrates; —officiates; —performs; —preaches;—ritualizes.

(See minister, priest, teacher.)

RABBIT

adjectives
juicy; misplaced; tasty.

verbs
domesticate—; dress—; experiment with —s; fence out—; pen—; pet—; shoot—; skin—; —bounds off; —burrows; —crouches; —devastates; —digs; —flashes by; —hops; —jumps; —leaps; —nibbles; —plagues; —scampers away; —scurries; —subsists on.

(See animal, pet.)

RABBLE

verbs
arouse—; class with—; concentrate—; court—; dispel—; disperse—; exclude—; harangue—; mingle with—; pander to—; restrain—; rout—; silence—; sway—; —assembles; —congregates; —masses; —mobs; —rules; —rushes; —storms; —surges; —throngs.

(See mob, crowd, proletarian.)

RABID

adverbs
insensately; wildly; unaccountably; dangerously; appallingly; fanatically; eccentrically; terribly; hysterically; downright; curiously; insatiably; violently; bitterly; absurdly; crazily; relentlessly; unbelievably; appallingly; shockingly; incredibly.

RACE
(competition)

verbs
accelerate—; approve—; clinch—; compete in—; contend in—; enter—; judge—; observe—; oppose in—; outdistance in—; postpone—; promote—; protest—; wager on—; —enlivens; —enraptures; —excites; —fascinates; —petrifies; —revives; —thrills.

(See match, game, contest.)

RACE
(general)

adjectives
severed; vengeful; sacerdotal; antipathetic; bloody-minded; fading; earth-born; alien; idle; girdled; amphibious; literary; infinite; indestructible; civilized; chequered; wasted; kindred; blissful; canine; impromptu; solid; tenacious; energetic; fecund; teeming; hectic; fallen; separate; radiant; golden; high-born; beauteous; touchy; savage; warlike; blind; blundering; knightly; proverbial; brave; despicable; barbarous; desperate; well-marked; swarming; obstinate; lascivious; titanic; lawless; hardy; thrifty; ethereal; jocund; elimination; inscrutable; uncultivated; wild; human; contemptible; singing; indigenous; glorious; sturdy; godly; best; fierce; studious; invincible; ill-fated; breathless; oppressed; melodious; long-lived; valiant; sullen; ancient; reprobated; intractable; dominant; unfortunate; subjugated; dwarfish; noble; incapable; aggressive; miserable; bounding; degraded; volatile; well-known; perished; magnificent; frolicsome; dusky; inveterate; unreturning; interesting; ghostly; short-distance; primitive; purblind; domestic; polished; courageous; stoical; decorative; semi-civilized; headlong; gentle; aboriginal; high-hearted; timid; proud; shining; inoffensive; illustrious; pitiless; invalid; unconverted; cultural; hostile; fickle; ruling; backward; impious; antediluvian; rudest; obstacle; delicate; nurtured; greedy; contested; untrustworthy; hard; beastly; vagrant; malignant; feverish; wise; shadowy; interloping; buxom; cognate; active; consequent; awkward; depraved; self-opinionated.

RACE
(nationality)

verbs
characterize—; conquer—; detest—; distinguish—; exterminate—; limit—; mark—; perpetuate—; purify—; sow—; strengthen —; study—; uplift—; —ebbs; —evolves; —perishes; —prospers; —subsists; —vanishes; —wanes.

(See breed, mankind, strain, nationality.)

RACE (v)

adverbs

tirelessly; vengefully; lawlessly; awkwardly; gloriously; invincibly; boundingly; frolicsomely; courageously; greedily; feverishly; spectacularly.

(See run, scamper, flee.)

RACIAL

adverbs

inherently; strongly; naturally; inseparably; peculiarly; inescapably; indestructibly; tenaciously; proverbially; gloriously; distinctly; significantly; fiercely; dominantly; proudly.

RACK

adjectives

fierce; low-trailing; cruel; commercialized; money-lending; corporeal.

RACKET

adjectives

noisy; gloomy; theatrical; vicious; favorite; flourishing; terrible; resounding.

verbs

—breaks; —clacks; —clashes; —crashes; —deafens; —dins; —drowns; —drums; —penetrates; —pierces; —resounds; —roars; —rumbles; —shakes; —snaps; —splits; —stuns; —thunders.

(See clamor, noise.)

RACY

adverbs

breezily; pungently; pithily; smartly; curiously; brilliantly; pleasantly; boldly; eloquently; piquantly; trenchantly; vigorously; unusually; amazingly; interestingly; arrestingly.

RADIANCE

adjectives

serene; glaring; rapturous; full; ruddy; variegated; clear; reflected; pale; milder; celestial; fathomless; indistinct; farewell; calm; soft; uniform; transitory; subdued; blinding; seraphic; secret; growing; orange; indescribable; mailed; tenderest; warm; flooding; sickly; prismatic; marvelous; bewildering; downcast; fantastic.

verbs

beam with—; blemish—; cloud—; dim—; dull—; eclipse—; extinguish—; glow with —; obscure—; overshadow—; shed—; —blazes; —enchants; —enhances; —flames; —gilds; —gleams; —glistens; —graces; —illuminates; —overspreads; —sparkles; —sublimates; —surrounds; —enlightens.

(See moonbeam, happiness, brilliance.)

RADIANT

adverbs

gloriously; splendidly; conspicuously; noticeably; visibly; happily; joyously; triumphantly; rapturously; ecstatically; jubilantly; exultantly; blissfully; contentedly; serenely.

RADIATOR

verbs

adjust—; bask near—; polish—; throttle—; —affords; —assures; —comforts; —diffuses; —glows; —parches; —scorches; —singes; —simmers; —warms.

RADICAL

adjectives

avowed; univalent; unreasonable; ill-balanced.

verbs

—contaminates; —corrupts; —demoralizes; —disparages; —fulminates; —harangues; —heckles; —ignites; —impairs; —pillories; —poisons; —pollutes; —raves; —taints; —undermines; —vituperates; —anathematizes; —cankers; —condemns.

(See anarchist, socialist, communist.)

adverbs

boldly; daringly; definitely; distinctly; deeply; thoroughly; uncompromisingly; sweepingly; appallingly; necessarily; downright.

RADIO

verbs

broadcast over—; communicate by—; filter into—; toy with—; tune down—; —amplifies; —bears; —blares forth; —bleats; —booms; —clarifies; —contacts; —conveys; —deafens; —disconcerts; —facilitates; —hums; —proclaims; —receives; —transmits; —unites.

(See loud-speaker.)

RAFT

adjectives

well-banded; fatal; formidable; ruined; prodigious; timber.

verbs

climb to—; crowd—; hoist on—; lap—; lash to—; punt—; rig—; slap—; smack—; support on—; sway—; threaten—; —bobs; —dips; —floats; —guides; —rocks; —transports; —troughs.

(See boat.)

RAFTER

adjectives

smoke-stained; gloomy; slender; resonant; skeleton.

verbs

bear on—; bestride—; hang from—; recline on—; repose on—; rest on—; straddle—; —abuts; —affords; —aids; —bolsters; —maintains; —s ring; —snaps; —supports; —sustains; —underprops; —upholds.

(See beam, timber, board.)

RAGE

adjectives

withering; impetuous; towering; foaming; tacit; guilty; fresh; grievous; righteous, inarticulate; impotent; extreme; cold; merciless; appeasing; disappointed; breathless; gloomy; punic; outflung; murderous; sudden; affectionate; haughty; divine; fierce; animal-like; mightier; furious; resolute; violent; pernicious; appertaining; indescribable; white-hot; unwonted; quick; hostile; unmitigated; sparkling; baffled; generous; unintelligible; silken; tremendous; ceaseless; prophetic; elemental; kindling; stormy; relentless; recurrent; concentrated; mental; pitiful; explosive; instantaneous; trembling; hard-favored; heathen; noble; female; overmastering.

verbs

blind with—; bluster in—; enkindle—; explode in—; fan—; fire with—; flush with—; fly into—; foment—; fume with—; glower with—; inflame with—; justify—; lash into—; pour out—; quiver with—; rouse—; shriek in—; snort with—; sputter with—; storm in—; thunder in—; tremble with—; vent—; work into—; —boils over; —effervesces; —ferments; —seethes; —smolders; —spends itself; —surges; —transports; —vanishes.

(See fury, indignation, anger, impatience, ire.)

RAGE (v)

adverbs

inwardly; magnificently; incessantly; mo-

mentarily; tremendously; fearfully; furiously; dangerously; fiercely; impetuously; foamingly; inarticulately; impotently; murderously; perniciously; unintelligibly; elementally; explosively; mentally.

(See storm, fume.)

RAGGED

adverbs

terribly; carelessly; pitiably; negligently; pathetically; impossibly; irregularly; disgracefully; contemptibly; shabbily; appallingly; shamefully; shockingly; unnecessarily; heedlessly; blithely; gleefully; hoydenishly; tomboyishly; nonchalantly; pitifully; deliberately; mischievously.

RAGING

adverbs

furiously; violently; tempestuously; angrily; resentfully; virulently; helplessly; stormily; hysterically; needlessly, deliriously; fanatically; feverishly; brutally; fiercely; tyrannically; madly; uncontrollably; bitterly; savagely; rabidly; uselessly; terribly; shockingly.

RAGS

adjectives

smelly; picturesque; grotesque; flattened; clean; slanting; riddled.

verbs

apparel in—; array in—; deck in—; discard —; divest of—; don—; envelop in—; sheathe in—; shun—; swaddle in—; swathe in—; vest in—; —humble; —humiliate.

(See clothing, raiment, apparel.)

RAID

adjectives

intrepid; mutual; memorable; bridge-burning; cavalry; unjustifiable; dreadful; marauding; foraging; rebel; murderous; copious (pl); conducted; similar; swift.

verbs

anticipate—; check—; engineer—; launch—; parry—; plan—; repel—; repulse—; resist —; retaliate for—; shield from—; stem—; —aims at; —assails; —attacks; —beleaguers; —besieges; —harries; —provokes; —saps; —storms; —thrusts at; —violates; —whips.

(See invasion, attack.)

959

RAID (v)

adverbs

lawlessly; intrepidly; memorably; unjustifiably; maraudingly; treacherously; rebelliously; murderously; cunningly; devastatingly; swiftly; belligerently.

(See attack, seize.)

RAIL

adjectives

shattered; sanded; twisted; continuous; purgatorial.

verbs

erect—; grasp—; —barricades; —bars; —checks; —circumscribes; —confines; —encloses; —fences; —fringes; —girdles; —protects; —restrains; —safeguards; —skirts; —terminates; —withstands; —restricts.

(See fence, barrier, barricade.)

RAIL (v)

adverbs

fretfully; bitterly; acrimoniously; acidly; sarcastically; devastatingly; witheringly; relentlessly; pitifully; plaintively; monotonously; copiously.

(See censure, reproach, upbraid.)

RAILROAD

adjectives

infant; pioneered; subtransatlantic; state-owned; opulent; efficient; necessary: well-run.

verbs

plan—; route—; sanction—; tear up—; utilize—; —advertizes; —covers; —enables; —extends; —facilitates; —guarantees; —insures; —invades; —opens; —prospers; —solicits.

RAIMENT

adjectives

snowy; gallant; gay; flying; shining; sumptuous; predestined; scanty.

verbs

admire—; cast off—; divest of—; don—; perk—; remove—; strip of—; swaddle in—; —clothes; —covers; —drapes; —enrobes; —flatters; —laps; —mantles; —muffles; —sheathes.

(See apparel, clothing.)

RAIN

adjectives

drizzling; drenching; summer; impalpable; fiery; mizzling; misty; melting; crushing; silent; blistering; inconceivable; frozen; lukewarm; quiet; dismal; frequent (pl); generous; gusty; recent; fertilizing; sudden; prodigious; hearty; long; continued; cold; abundant; driving; rapid; soft; violent; vernal; invisible; falling; pattering; roaring; passionate; autumn; pouring; swirling; incessant; heavy; pelting; pitiless; quickening; singing; sterile; substantial; windy; mellowing; plenteous; thick; sooty; gusty; healing; love-cast; irised; refreshing; unabated; sheeted; continual; dim; lashing; undecided; sweetest; snow-soft; emerald; chilling; immortal; biting; silver; frozen; constant; superannuated; reluctant; veritable; unprecedented; fitful; uninterrupted; dreary; heaven-sent; swishing.

verbs

brave—; dodge—; —blights; —crescendos; —dashes against; —deluges; —drenches; —drums; —gurgles; —gushes; —inundates; —jets; —lashes; —moistens; —patters; —pelts; —rattles; —relents; —roars; —slithers off; —spatters; —spurts; —teems; —threatens; —thuds; —wanes; —ripples; —trickles.

(See hail, shower, sleet, storm.)

RAIN (v)

adverbs

dismally; heavily; monotonously; desultorily; drizzlingly; prodigiously; abundantly; violently; vernally; patteringly; roaringly; pitilessly; unabatedly; fitfully; unprecedentedly.

(See shower, pour.)

RAINBOW

adjectives

momentary; live; wonderful; myriad (pl); glorified; ephemeral; wondrous; emerald.

RAINY

adverbs

unusually; uncommonly; extraordinarily; terribly; torrentially; softly; dreamily; drowsily; thunderously; drizzlingly; windily; gustily; unfortunately; unluckily; disappointingly; opportunely; seasonally; fortunately; providentially; strangely; gloomily; dismally; drearily; pleasantly; agreeably; lightly; suddenly.

RAISE (v)

adverbs

corruptly; insolently; deferentially; instinctively; eloquently; unscrupulously; defiantly; delicately; significantly; impressively; mechanically; expressively; daintily; warningly; majestically; deliberately; quizzically.

(See lift, elevate.)

RAKE

verbs

drag—; draw—; employ—; tug at—; —dredges; —eliminates, —extricates; —gathers; —grubs; —refines; —scratches; —smoothes; —unearths; —uproots.

RAKE (v)

adverbs

thoroughly; searchingly; painstakingly; questioningly; inquiringly.

(See gather, search.)

RAKISH

adverbs

wildly; recklessly; dissolutely; madly; blithely; gaily; hilariously; idly; merrily; boisterously.

RALLY (v)

adverbs

faithfully; gallantly; ardently; instinctively; fiercely; courageously; heartily.

(See collect, recover.)

RAMBLE (v)

adverbs

garrulously; blindly; monotonously; ceaselessly; maddeningly; purposelessly; pointlessly.

(See stroll, stray.)

RAMBLING

adverbs

pleasantly; quaintly; comfortably; leisurely; irregularly; idly; wantonly; happily; freely; interestingly; endlessly; aimlessly; capriciously; erratically; casually; artlessly; quietly; effortlessly; errantly; desultorily; vagrantly; blissfully.

RAMPANT

adverbs

roughly; obstreperously; uncontrollably; ungovernably; predominantly; buoyantly; no-

ticeably; expansively; singularly; remarkably; naturally; spontaneously; insuppressibly; unmanageably; merrily.

RAMPART

verbs

array on—; batter—; communicate with—; erect—; fret—; pass along—; patrol—; penetrate—; storm—; strengthen—; surmount—; —bulwarks; —defends; —protects; —resists; —surrounds; —unites.

(See defense, fortification, barricade.)

RAMSHACKLE

adverbs

deplorably; hopelessly; discouragingly; challengingly; dingily; dismally; interestingly; inexpensively; terribly; comically; brightly; charmingly; fascinatingly; merrily; curiously; scandalously; completely; rattily; incredibly; manifestly.

RANCID

adverbs

sourly; bitterly; acridly; odoriferously; obviously; outrageously; impossibly; disgustingly; hopelessly; shamefully; mustily; nauseatingly; uselessly; terribly; disagreeably; noticeably; evidently; vexatiously; miserably; undisguisably; visibly.

RANCOR

adjectives

unmitigated; violent; unrelenting; smothered.

verbs

arouse—; betray—; burst with—; defy—; harbor—; inflict—; protest—; repress—; unloose—; wreak—upon; —abuses; —blasts; —embitters; —irritates; —pierces; —shakes; —snarls; —sours; —stabs.

(See grudge, animosity, ill-will, bitterness.)

RANCOROUS

adverbs

unreasonably; senselessly; maliciously; venomously; relentlessly; incorrigibly; outrageously; shamefully; atrociously; dangerously; naturally; alarmingly; fearfully; singularly; insufferably; extraordinarily; violently; fanatically; uncontrollably.

RANGE

adjectives

considerable; extensive; narrow; point-blank; cruising; indicated; effective; enormous; massy; limited; encyclopedic; far-stretching; irregular; cloud-capped; snowy; interminable; billowy; unbounded; easy; flanking; infinite; widened; teeming; formidable; fluid; inexhaustible; vaster; ancient; longitudinal; wonted; unactive; colossal; icy.

verbs
amplify—; ascertain—; broaden—; encompass—; enlarge—; expand—; extend—; localize—; magnify—; narrow—; restrict—; scan—; spread—; sweep—; widen—; —fluctuates; —oscillates; —soars; develop—.
(See horizon.)

RANK
adjectives
high; foremost; crowding; honorable; illustrious; scholarly; serried (pl); unbroken; dense; poetical; bending; unwearied (pl); superior; wasting; preeminent; hostile (pl); distinguished; swaying (pl); teeming (pl); glittering (pl); myriad (pl); titled; depleted (pl); innumerable (pl); obscurest; riddled (pl); stalwart (pl); regular; inferior; extinguished; culinary; extrinsic; intermediate; exhausted (pl); shattered (pl); disordered (pl); relative; jeweled; stately; immortal; intellectual; melancholy; interminable; mournful; rightful; respective; enveloping (pl); princely; gathering (pl); delicate; swelling (pl); fastfalling (pl); equal; riven (pl); reeling (pl).

verbs
accredit—; achieve—; acquire—; ascend to —; aspire to—; assign to—; break—s; denote—; desert—s; divest of—; earn—; eject from—s; elevate to—; forfeit—; honor—; praise—s; promote to—; reduce to—s; respect—; scatter—; shatter—s; signal—s; solidify—s; split—s; swell—s; win—; —dignifies; —eclipses; —glorifies; —outshines; —surpasses; —transcends.
(See degree, grade, caste, class, position.)

RANK (v)
adverbs
deservedly; poetically; obscurely; relatively; intellectually; rightfully; aristocratically; humbly.
(See classify, group.)

RAP (v)
adverbs
smartly; vigorously; authoritatively; viva-ciously; persistently; furiously; tempestuously.
(See knock, thump.)

RAPACIOUS
adverbs
furtively; terribly; wickedly; scandalously; outrageously; shamefully; greedily; ravenously; insatiably; rabidly; ungovernably; uncontrollably; madly; monstrously; abominably; detestably; peculiarly; astonishingly; unbelievably; uncommonly.

RAPID
adverbs
unbelievably; effortlessly; invisibly; increasingly; mercifully; crazily; expertly; distressingly; painfully; breathlessly; impetuously; perilously; unaccountably; surprisingly; astonishingly; moderately; dangerously; lightly.

RAPIDITY
adjectives
incredible; fair; sufficient; inconceivable; fearful; marvelous; feverish; facial; dexterous; appalling; lightning; extraordinary; extreme; disconcerting; amazing; racial.

RAPIER
verbs
brandish—; evade—; fence with—s; flourish—; parry—; sheathe—; thrust with—; wield—; —lacerates; —penetrates; —pierces; —sheds.
(See sword, lance.)

RAPTURE
adjectives
ultimate; transient; holy; lasting; random; wounding; blissful; pure; speechless; dizzy; boundless; exquisite; heartfelt; divine; mute; radiant; heavenly; guilty; honest; fervid; careless; secret; rhetorical; mysterious; imaginative; maniacal; enveloping; unreasoning; serene; romantic; fading; suppressed; ecstatic; tumultuous.

verbs
breathe in—; cherish—; dilate with—; evoke—; exalt in—; excite—; exclaim in—; express—; feast on—; move to—; muse in —; regard with—; smite with—; speak in —; touch with—; tremble in—; —bewitches; —entrances.
(See ecstasy, delight, delirium, bliss, joy.)

adverbs

supremely; blessedly; truly; idiotically; ineffably; charmingly; unforgettably; enormously; dreamily; innocently; mysteriously; ecstatically; tumultuously; curiously; openly; childishly; rosily; ridiculously; shyly; frankly; excitedly; tranquilly; wildly; unutterably; joyously; tenderly; deliriously.

RARE

adverbs

unusually; valuably; singularly; inimitably; remarkably; pricelessly; incalculably; immeasurably; fantastically; amazingly; unbelievably; momentously; signally; marvelously; incredibly.

RASCAL

adjectives

merry; glaring; bald-pated; meddlesome; lying; barren; mean; consummate; muddymettled; mercenary; stretch-mouthed; designing; tawny; lovable; scheming; vile; unmitigated; dishonest; cony-catching; villainous; worthless.

RASCALLY

adverbs

mischievously; outrageously; outlandishly; incorrigibly; unmanageably; fearfully; maliciously; boyishly; trickily; craftily; shamefully; smoothly; atrociously; detestably; insidiously; contemptibly; singularly; appallingly; reprehensibly; treacherously; dishonestly; unregenerately; inveterately; bitterly; hatefully.

RASH

verbs

afflict with—; attribute—to; break into—; daub on—; produce—; solve—; swab—; treat—; —confines; —disappears; —effloresces; —erupts; —fades; —indicates; — irritates; —patches; —plagues; —speckles; —spreads; —subsides.

(See sore, boil.)

adverbs

adventurously; indiscreetly; imprudently; audaciously; unfortunately; wilfully; inconsiderately; foolishly; thoughtlessly; inadvertently; ignorantly; heedlessly; intrepidly; wantonly; desperately; misguidedly; flippantly; absurdly; preposterously; alarmingly; unaccountably; fearlessly.

adjectives

noble; unguided; weakest; stretched; general.

verbs

prevent—; protest—; repent—; rue—; warn against—; —breaks; —chances; —destroys; —endangers; —ignores; —irks; —provokes; —risks; —suffers; —ventures; —vexes; — wrecks.

(See recklessness, audacity.)

RASP (*v*)

adverbs

harshly; unmelodiously; atrociously; discordantly; gratingly; exasperatingly.

(See grate, file, offend.)

RAT

verbs

experiment on—s; exterminate—s; infest with—s; plague with—s; poison—s, rid of —s; trap—; —burrows; —digs; —excavates; —s frequent; —gnaws; —haunts; — infects; —nibbles; —penetrates; —pillages; —preys on; —ravages; —roves; —scampers; —scurries; —thrives.

(See animal.)

RATE

adjectives

prevailing; reasonable; high; proud; annual; special; low; surprising; respectable; comparable; amazing; expense; balancing; unusual; moderate; stipulated; incredible; differential; fluctuating; minimum; unconscionable; interest; usurious; legal; astounding; tremendous; alarming; reckless; standard; present; noble; rapid; overwhelming; attractive; fearful; death; furious; marvelous; trifling; enormous; modest; prodigious; nominal; unvarying; right; sensible; economical; remarkable; daily; weekly; monthly; thrifty; considerate; extreme; agreeable.

verbs

apply—; assess—; assign—; calculate—; command—; compute—; demand—; deprecate—; determine—; estimate—; fix—; impose—; proportion—; reduce—; slash—; stabilize—; standardize—; subject to—; tax —; —appraises; —corresponds to; —evaluates; —fluctuates; —prevails; —skyrockets; —varies.

(See tax, amount.)

RATE (v)

adverbs

soundly; harshly; disagreeably; furiously; wrathfully; discordantly; scorchingly.

(See appraise, estimate, value.)

RATIFICATION

verbs

fight for—; hinder—; submit for—; —admits; —alters; —attests; —authenticates; —certifies; —concerns; —corroborates; —endorses; —evinces; —indicates; —involves; —recognizes; —seals; —subverts; —upholds; —verifies.

(See approval, confirmation, indorsement.)

RATIFY (v)

adverbs

wisely; amicably; agreeably; ostentatiously; solemnly; internationally.

(See confirm, sanction.)

RATIONAL

adverbs

intelligently; philosophically; soundly; academically; intuitively; sensibly; perfectly; psychologically; coldly; irresistibly; fairly; cosmically; inferentially; elementally; profoundly; fundamentally; presumptively; penetratingly; discernibly; contemplatively; doctrinally; spiritually; innately; ideologically; speculatively; consciously; soberly; speciously; logically; persuasively; convincingly; conclusively.

RATIONS

adjectives

insufficient; deficient; regulation; delicious; balanced; emergency; abundant; scant; half; magic; particular; starvation; wartime.

verbs

allot—; carve—; cast—; consume—; crave —; cut—; deal—; distribute—; divide—; mete out—; parcel—; portion out—; reduce —; replenish—; share—; supply—; —appease; —relieve; —sate; —satisfy; —strengthen.

(See food, diet, supplies.)

RATTLE
(general)

adjectives

remote; sudden; tempestuous; globular; unheeded; peremptory; pulsing.

RATTLE
(toy)

verbs

chew—; employ—; —amuses; —appeases; —attracts; —clashes; —crashes; —delights; —diverts; —entertains; —fascinates; —interests; —pleases; —subsides; —tinkles.

(See toy, noise, racket.)

RATTLE (v)

adverbs

cacophonously; crisply; peremptorily; tempestuously; rudely; abruptly; irritatingly.

(See clatter, prattle.)

RAUCOUS

adverbs

noisily; curiously; hoarsely; blatantly; boisterously; disagreeably; uncommonly; unusually; unpleasantly; sepulchrally; rudely; raspingly; stertoriously; distinctly; horribly; obnoxiously; unnaturally; offensively; piercingly; peculiarly; curiously; strangely; intolerably; indescribably.

RAVAGES

adjectives

fearful; excessive; increased.

verbs

curb—; preserve from—; stay—; succumb to—; suffer—; —blemish; —blight; —cripple; —damage; —debase; —decimate; —deface; —defile; —desecrate; —disfigure; —embitter; —mutilate; —overwhelm; —prostrate; —ruin; —swamp.

(See damage, injury.)

RAVE (v)

adverbs

senselessly; rapturously; idiotically; drunkenly; fearfully; ominously; furiously; insanely; feverishly; pathetically; passionately; romantically; ecstatically; tumultuously.

(See rage, storm.)

RAVEN

adjectives

presaging; colored; somber; croaking; ominous.

verbs

—attacks; —beaks; —bellows; —bodes; —carries off; —croaks; —destroys; —flits; —kills; —pesters; —plagues; —prates; —preys on; —thieves.

(See bird, crow.)

RAVINE

adjectives

sandy; wooded; picturesque; stained; impenetrable; gaunt; difficult; luminous; inaccessible; bushy; rough; burning; steep; rocky; numerous (pl); precipitous.

RAVISH (v)

adverbs

violently; brutally; lustfully; lasciviously; fearfully; viciously; criminally; grossly; sordidly; passionately; bestially; sickeningly.
(See enchant, transport.)

RAVISHING

adverbs

incomparably; delectably; enchantingly; unbelievably; happily; inexpressibly; transportingly; rapturously; ecstatically; divinely; matchlessly; radiantly.

RAW

adverbs

awkwardly; grotesquely; repulsively; unbelievably; angularly; oddly; ludicrously; deplorably; strangely; fantastically; amusingly; pathetically; distressingly; terribly; horribly; grievously; ridiculously; singularly; queerly; drolly; curiously; painfully; crudely; coarsely; thoughtlessly; ignorantly.

RAY

adjectives

solar; deathless; fresh; glaring; dewy; ripening; cheering; evening; gilded; funeral; cosmic; oblique; pounding; visual; scattered (pl); darting; medullary; primary; blushing; early; unrefracted; discomforting; potent; castrated; glowing; lingering; celestial; penetrating; redoubled; luminous; mystic; changing; level; converging; chance; fiery; actinic; tender; unclouded; purest; lurid; overflowing; dimmer; sunny; reviving; dull; fervent; blood-red; transverse; propitious; genial; occasional; beauteous; rising; gladdening; enlivening; killing; hospitable; eternal; controlled; dauntless; diverging; slanting; everlasting; angry; piercing; sportive; parent; heavenly; splendid; dismembered; bewildering; indifferent; curative; reflected; glimmering; dissolving; vertical; illusive; liquid; angelic; streaming; orient; misty; silver; frozen; pensive; radiating; derived; sickly; unwelcome; jubilant; rapid; scorching; dim.

verbs

bend—; diffuse—; dim—; emit—; expose to—; focus—upon; obscure—; shed—; shield from—; shoot—; throw—; —dances; —dazzles; —s diverge; —illuminates; —penetrates; —pierces; —plays upon; —reveals; —shimmers; —streams from.
(See beam, gleam, moonbeam, light.)

RAZOR

verbs

blunt—; brandish—; dull—; employ—; grind—; hone—; nick—; sheathe—; stroke —; strop—; whet—; wield—; —denudes; —incises; —smooths.
(See knife, blade.)

REACH

adjectives

desolating; endless; sighing; automatic; utmost; extended; boundless; upper; illimitable; giddiest; naughty; sandy; vast; arid; easy; keen; timid; wistful, trackless.

REACH (v)

adverbs

promptly; simultaneously; automatically; impulsively; conveniently; timidly; ultimately; rapturously; greedily; vainly; wistfully.
(See touch, strike.)

REACT (v)

adverbs

discreditably; instantaneously; adversely; strangely; abnormally; divergently; feverishly; violently; passionately; intuitively; romantically; physically; logically; blindly.
(See resist, recoil, oppose.)

REACTION

adjectives

energetic; painful; emotional; necessary; feverish; varied; premature; strong; disastrous; consumer; unequivocal; fatigued; violent; protective; inevitable; deep-seated; vigorous; unexpected; natural; photochemical; uncomfortable; passionate; intuitive; impulsive; instantaneous; chemical; antagonistic; romantic; infantile; chronic; physical; barbarous; pleasant; artificial; individual; astounding; logical; sympathetic; dramatic; blind; unromantic; sanguinary.

verbs

awaken—; control—; defeat—; determine —; emphasize—; evaluate—; excite—; experience—; foresee—; forestall—; induce—;

observe—; produce—; promote—; provoke
—; repute—; reverse—; study—; suffer—;
test—; —astounds; —ensues; —sets in; —
warns.

(See answer, reply, response.)

REACTIONARY
adverbs
commendably; dangerously; manifestly; defiantly; openly; curiously; inexplicably; unaccountably; unreasonably; lamentably;
stimulatingly; progressively; energetically;
ominously; favorably; admirably; politically; irresolutely; unreliably; antagonistically;
painfully; astonishingly; reprehensibly; undependably.

READ (v)
adverbs
omnivorously; perpetually; insipidly; profoundly; nonchalantly; listlessly; attentively; extensively; drowsily; assiduously; advisedly; monotonously; genially; voraciously; habitually; casually; industriously; stimulatingly; desultorily; promiscuously; surreptitiously; haltingly; sporadically; judiciously.

(See peruse, scan, study.)

READABLE
adverbs
instantly; easily; readily; pleasantly; fascinatingly; entertainingly; delightfully; interestingly; scarcely; barely; instructively;
highly; uncommonly; remarkably; singularly; definitely; distinctly; plainly; unusually.

READER
adjectives
eager; intelligent; constant; everyday; enthusiastic; serious; gentle; phenomenal;
browsing; sagacious; assiduous; casual; insatiable; captious; extensive; persistent; dilettante; confused; unsuspecting; continental; absorbed; negligent; omnivorous; copy;
discriminating; stumbling; uncomprehending; fastidious; indefatigable; industrious;
prudish; voracious; ponderous; innocent;
voluminous; ardent; attentive; arid; rapid;
faulty; lifelong.

verbs
absorb—; acquaint—; amuse—; divert—;
edify—; enlighten—; entertain—; guide—;
inform—; instruct—; lay before—; outrage
—; persuade—; tickle—; train—; —appreciates; —browses; —comprehends; —cons;

—consumes; —criticizes; —delights; —
delves into; —dips into; —discerns; —enjoys; —gleans; —imbibes; —masters; —
peruses; —plunges into; —pores over; —
refers to; —scans; —thumbs; —wades
through; —apprehends.

(See student, scholar, pupil.)

READINESS
adjectives
dreary; extreme; stubborn; belligerent;
astonishing; sulky; useful; disconcerting.

READING
adjectives
essential; constructive; fascinating; stimulating; available; up-to-date; quick; intelligent; delightful; laborious; choral; extensive; assiduous; coarse; prodigious; random; absorbing; hurried; entertaining; tedious; monotonous; desultory; required; attentive; surreptitious; promiscuous; flighty;
diverting; irregular; dreary; dull; omnivorous.

verbs
assign—; coach in—; comment on—; define
—; enjoy—; expound—; improve—; interpret—; recite—; render—; study—; translate—; unfold—; unravel—; wade through
—; —acquaints; —delights; —edifies; —entertains; —serves; —yields.

(See story, lesson, interpretation, book.)

READJUSTMENT
adjectives
heroic; fundamental; sharp; comprehensive;
difficult.

verbs
advocate—; demand—; effect—; intensify
—; measure—; necessitate—; undergo—;
—accommodates; —adapts; —balances; —
copes with; —countervails; —equalizes; —
evens; —levels; —matches; —poises; —restores; —satisfies; —trims.

(See change, adjustment.)

READY
adverbs
resolutely; instantly; finally; recently; altogether; promptly; eagerly; intrepidly; warily; vigilantly; alertly; evidently; providently; prudently; painfully; carefully;
scrupulously; always; unfailingly; heroic-

ally; gallantly; formidably; fortunately; luckily; opportunely; reasonably; sensibly; practically; almost.

REAL

adverbs
intensely; fantastically; oppressively; tangibly; vividly; mercilessly; horribly; dangerously; vitally; painfully; starkly; solidly; hideously; grossly; crudely; temporally; mundanely; appallingly; hauntingly; monotonously; ponderously; eternally; sordidly; inexorably; basically; sternly; terribly; gloriously; glamorously; crassly; crudely; humanly; demonstrably; substantially; graphically; stubbornly.

REALISM

adjectives
wounding; decadent; gripping; graphic; unflinching; pure; gross; unshrinking; unpitying; surprising; lifelike; nauseating; inartistic; crude; bare.

verbs
advocate—; compromise—; conform to—; delve into—; dip into—; establish—; examine—; imbibe—; practise—; touch—; transcend—; composes—; —divests; —enthrones itself; —portrays.
  (See science, philosophy, psychology, reality, art.)

REALIST

adjectives
destitute; uncompromising; sumptuous; selective; skilled.

REALISTIC

adverbs
dramatically; spectacularly; utterly; unusually; undeniably; distinctly; admirably; notoriously; commendably; surprisingly; unexpectedly; astonishingly; intensely; vividly; mysteriously; incredibly; mercilessly; dangerously; beautifully; delightfully; happily; entertainingly; interestingly; unsurpassably; incomparably; faithfully; startlingly; appallingly.

REALITY

adjectives
grim; sordid; intense; fantastic; naked; oppressive; tangible; passionate; beneficient; clamant; vivid; living; ideal; typical; blunt; mysterious; infinite; waking; existing; sober; practical; elusive; commonplace; accidental; fearful; unfathomable; clear; conceived; spiritual; concrete; exacting; vulgar; fictitious; specific; merciless; peremptory; subtle; nautical; glassy; horrid; stern; dangerous; vital; painful; stark; solid; gloomy; beneficent.

verbs
bear—; convey—; deal with—; descend to —; divorce from—; endure—; enslave to —; escape—; evade—; face—; flee from—; gain—; gloss over—; grasp for—; ground on—; obscure—; pursue—; question—; return to—; spare—; varnish—; wrap in—.
  (See realism.)

REALIZATION

adjectives
hideous; evident; uninterrupted; vivid; devotional; bitter; dawning; living; piteous; stabbing; poseful; shocking; exact; eternal; dark.

verbs
achieve—; anticipate—; attain—; demand —; effect—; fancy—; jar into—; jolt into —; labor under—; register—; strive for—; struggle for—; —completes; —crowns; —dawns; —dazes; —discharges; —fulfills; —grows upon; —perfects; —strikes; —stuns.
  (See effect, fulfillment.)

REALIZE (v)

adverbs
sickeningly; nervously; instinctively; emphatically; dimly; speedily; vividly; vaguely; faintly; gloriously; partially; feebly; happily; piteously; stabbingly; shockingly.
  (See achieve, complete.)

REALM

adjectives
sterile; populous; empty; untrodden; mysterious; free; rival; sleepy; blissful; boundless; wealthy; sunnier; historic; airy; glorious; unsubstantial; masculine; interminable; intellectual; famous; impenetrable; ancient; loftier; starry; flowery; shuddering; conquered; unproductive; capricious; captivating.

verbs
conquer—; command—; control—; dominate —; dwell in—; explore—; govern—; inhabit

—; invade—; locate—; master—; misrule
—; occupy—; overrun—; preside over—;
seize—; sway—; visit—.
 (See kingdom, region, province.)

REAP (v)
adverbs
meritoriously; vigorously; seasonally; happily; gratefully; handsomely; rightfully.
 (See gather, collect.)

REAR
verbs
bring up—; construct—; dog—; guard—;
join—; lay—; —closes; —concludes; —determines; —ends; —finishes; —follows; —
lags; —nullifies; —shadows; —skirts; —
terminates; —trails; —treads.
 (See front, back.)

REAR (v)
adverbs
viciously; dangerously; skittishly; wildly;
blindly; capriciously; materially; domestically; shelteredly; innocently.
 (See raise, elevate.)

REARMAMENT
verbs
advocate—; condemn—; demand—; forbid
—; hinder—; limit—; permit—; plan—;
question—; reduce—; refuse—; repress—;
request—; restrain—; restrict—; sanction
—; —abuses; —agitates; —brews; —despairs; —endangers; —incenses; —protects.
 (See armament.)

REASON
(general)
adjectives
sensible; valid; potent; indignant; individual; sufficient; sentimental; unshackled; imperceptible; legal; intelligent; physical;
holy; sound; artistic; abundant; mere;
naked; alleged; supposed; cogent; religious;
punitive; exquisite; abstract; shattered; intangible; weighty; passive; mournful; root;
indisputable; ostensible; aesthetic; public;
human; satirical; unknown; contradicting;
inclusive; cold; improbable; crying; philosophic; prosaic; irresistible; calm; special;
prudential; earthly; sovereign; obscure:
honest; sharp; convincing; sententious; fundamental; liberal; impossible; precise; obvious; justifying; mysterious; firm; foremost; dawning; immense; powerful; natural; plain; unconscious; manly; hamper-

ing; insufficient; overwhelming; carnal; indefinable; inexplicable; righteous; cool; immortal; definite; odious; respectable; trivial; weightiest; evident; hollow; inscrutable; sober; apparent; occult; willful; eternal; bright; pure; practical; benevolent;
painful; plausible; logical; absurd; conceivable; organic; pompous; ethnological; inexperienced; unselfish; patent; specious; ultimate; pressing; simple; palpable.

REASON
(grounds, argument, etc.)
verbs
adduce—; advance—; analyze—; assign—
for; bolster—; cite—s; conceal—; convey—;
cook up—; debate—; discern—; draw—
from; elicit—; evidence—; feign—; omit—;
outline—s; overstep—; summarize—; —explains; —looms; —motivates; —underlies.
 (See excuse, grounds, cause.)

REASON
(intellectual, faculty, common-sense, logic)
verbs
appeal ,to—; base on—; derange—; employ
—; evince—; impregnate with—; invoke—;
supplant—; —crumbles; —determines; —
dictates; —impels; —ordains; —prevails;
—totters; —wanders; —yields to.
 (See logic, intellect, sense, sanity.)

REASON (v)
adverbs
coherently; inconsistently; persuasively: solemnly; dialectically; deductively; logically;
ridiculously; deviously; ineffectually; intelligently; circuitously; validly; sentimentally;
cogently; prosaically; sententiously; plausibly; speciously.
 (See argue, debate.)

REASONABLE
adverbs
intelligently; philosophically; soundly; academically; intuitively; sensibly; perfectly;
psychologically; coldly; fairly; cosmically;
inferentially; elementally; essentially; profoundly; fundamentally; presumptively;
penetratingly; discernibly; contemplatively;
doctrinally; spiritually; theologically; ideologically; speculatively; consciously; soberly; spaciously; logically; persuasively; convincingly; conclusively.

adjectives
accurate; habitual; profound; lawless; admirable; acute; careful; painstaking; deft; clever.

REASONING
adjectives
seductive; sober; secular; immethodized; speculative; unstable; judicial; vicious; hypothetical; inductive; erroneous; stern; calm; infantile; physiological; precocious; scientific; deliberate; sustained; fallacious; syllogistic; abstract; explicit; conclusive; logical.

REASSURANCE
adjectives
peaceful; hopeful; tremendous; slender.

REASSURING
adverbs
completely; comfortingly; genially; judicially; gravely; amiably; wisely; pleasantly; indulgently; graciously; smpathetically; understandingly; encouragingly; helpfully; hopefully; optimistically; considerately; affectionately; warmly; hospitably; pleasantly; mildly; earnestly; enthusiastically; confidently; definitely; distinctly.

REBEL (v)
adverbs
vindictively; heartily; hatefully; intellectually; patriotically; desperately; blindly; abortively; mutely; hopelessly; technically.
(See revolt, defy, resist.)

REBELLION
adjectives
technical; appeasing; incipient; perpetual; gigantic; extensive; righteous; seething; violent; open; unqualified; hurt; blind; abortive; memorable; vain; mute; persistent; universal; manifest; hopeless; futile.

verbs
abet—; confine—; finance—; fire—; foment —; incite to—; intensify—; liquidate—; plan—; plot—; plunge into—; quash—; quell—; repress—; restrain—; set down—; threaten with—; uncover—; verge on—; — breaks out; —perishes; —seethes; —stirs; —undermines.
(See insurrection, mutiny, revolution.)

adverbs
sullenly; doggedly; drearily; unhappily; bitterly; incorrigibly; incurably; unmanageably; sadly; justly; rightfully; intelligently; sensibly; wildly; cruelly; insensately; furiously; violently; uncontrollably; cantankerously; atrociously; detestably; unreasonably; justifiably; naturally; woefully; stubbornly; obstinately; desperately; dangerously; ominously; unfortunately; unluckily; unwisely; finally; instantly; resentfully; angrily; secretly; quietly.

REBELS
adjectives
intellectual; patriotic; incorrigible; vile; contending; repentant; desperate.

verbs
exile—; punish—; restrict—; silence—; — arise; —arm; —betray; —conspire; —corrupt; —defy; —infringe upon; —intrigue; —mutiny; —plot; —resist; —strike; —violate; —withdraw.
(See insurgents, opponent.)

REBUFF
adjectives
unforeseen; stupid; rude; unsympathetic; studied; complete; deserved.

verbs
cower before—; impel—; incur—; render —; resist—; sense—; smart under—; undergo—; withhold—; —chills; —crushes; — cuts; —insults; —jostles; —raps; —reviles; —revolts; —scandalizes; —shocks; —slaps; —smarts; —snubs.
(See insult, defeat, rebuke, refusal.)

REBUFF (v)
adverbs
superciliously; sneeringly; rudely; aristocratically; impertinently; proudly; vindictively.
(See resist, repulse, repel.)

REBUFFED
adverbs
definitely; unreasonably; distinctly; neatly; saucily; arrogantly; needlessly; unwarrantably; insolently; impudently; impertinently; unnecessarily; undeservedly; unaccountably; startlingly; surprisingly; properly; deservedly; properly; politely; adroitly; in-

geniously; subtly; disconcertingly; promptly; urbanely; suavely; uncivilly; unceremoniously; sharply; definitely; officially; blandly.

REBUILD (v)
adverbs
patiently; vigorously; hopefully; courageously; repeatedly; gloriously; imitatively.
(See build, repair.)

REBUKE
adjectives
pertinent; merited; grave; whispered; sour; stinging; artless; delicate; savage; frightened; stern; uncompromising; paternal; dignified; proud; smart; standing; sulphurous; scornful; sad; promptest.

verbs
administer—; endure—; imply—; offset—; submit to—; suffer—; thrust—at; —abashes; —corrects; —disconcerts; —hurts; —maddens; —silences.
(See rebuff, reprimand, ridicule.)

REBUKE (v)
adverbs
indignantly; priggishly; sternly; pertinently; gravely; stingingly; paternally; sulphurously; scornfully; briskly; curtly; cuttingly; incisively.
(See admonish, censure, reprove.)

REBUKED
adverbs
sternly; harshly; unreasonably; unaccountably; undeservedly; constantly; recently; saucily; officially; seriously; gravely; ominously; publicly; openly; quietly; deservedly; properly; naturally; necessarily; woefully; rudely; ungraciously; unwarrantably; unjustly; cruelly; wantonly; subtly; loudly; furiously; brusquely; bluntly; rudely; unforgivably; unforgettably.

RECALCITRANT
adverbs
cantankerously; habitually; always; disagreeably; unpleasantly; offensively; politically; obnoxiously; detestably; despicably; unfailingly; obstinately; stubbornly; unreasonably; unaccountably; naturally; stupidly; boorishly; doggedly; singularly; peculiarly; presumptuously; bumptiously.

RECALL (v)
adverbs
vividly; affectionately; palpably; momentarily; distinctively; perpetually; bitterly; vaguely; greedily; idly; passionately.
(See annul, retract.)

RECEIVE (v)
adverbs
courteously; precisely; graciously; affably; reluctantly; hospitably; opportunely; glowingly; morosely; willingly; scornfully; consciously; mournfully; credulously; gratuitously; supinely; indiscriminately; haughtily; cordially; royally; ceremoniously; frostily.
(See accept, take.)

RECEIVERSHIP
verbs
accept—; anticipate—; avoid—; demand—; enter into—; fall into—; grant—; lapse into—; repel—; resist—; save from—; succor from—; verge on—; —embarrasses; —safeguards; —satisfies; —terminates.
(See bankruptcy.)

RECEPTACLE
adjectives
sacred; unsightly; unworthy; hideous; secret; hidden.

RECEPTION
adjectives
unfriendly; sumptuous; canine; flattering; popular; suitable; favorable; enthusiastic; affectionate; honorable; courteous; critical; problematical; ceremonious; unprejudiced; instant; general; cordial; wonderful; traditional; frosty; grand; stormy; official; magnificent; bloody; court; extraordinary; welcome; royal; friendly; sympathetic; hospitable; tame; sullen.

RECEPTIVE
adverbs
intelligently; astonishingly; brilliantly; attentively; eagerly; ardently; gratefully; thankfully; utterly; actively; pleasantly; helpfully; sharply; keenly; particularly.

RECESS
adjectives
fathomless; remotest; dark; dim; glowing; tangled; innermost; profound; various (pl); mystic; grassy; appalling; cool; capacious; intimate; little-known; soul-haunting; shy; shady.

verbs

deny—; enjoy—; grant—; lull in—; pre-scribe—; suggest—; welcome—; —affords; —allays; —disburdens; —dispels; —eases; —refreshes; —relaxes; —relieves; —reviv-ifies; —vents.

(See rest, vacation, pause.)

RECESSION

adjectives

financial; business; widespread; nation-wide; gripping.

RECIPE

verbs

adhere to—; attempt—; clip—; commend—; devise—; follow—; interpret—; necessitate —; refer to—; scan—; seek—; study—; —acquaints; —eases; —edifies; —enlightens; —guides; —informs; —prevents; —satisfies; —suggests.

(See formula, method.)

RECIPROCAL

adverbs

agreeably; pleasantly; accommodatingly; publicly; readily; systematically; contract-ually; interchangeably; helpfully; sympa-thetically; openly; reluctantly; eagerly; proportionally; satisfactorily; conveniently; advantageously; profitably.

RECITAL

adjectives

bolting; warm; light; summary; amusing; quaint; dejected; tedious; dispassionate; in-structive.

verbs

narrate—; rehearse—; render—; sum up—; unfold—; —edifies; —enchants; —enlight-ens; —enthralls; —entrances; —inspires; —pictures; —portrays; —recounts; —relates; —unravels.

(See performance, concert, speech, poem.)

RECITATIVE

adverbs

crooningly; endlessly; effectively; monoton-ously; raucously; huskily; dully; unmelod-iously; comically; hilariously; clownishly; curiously; dramatically; melodiously; rhy-thmically; qauintly; dramatically; incompar-ably; strangely; pleasantly.

RECITE (v)

adverbs

drolly; faithfully; feelingly; passionately; ardently; quaintly; instructively; repetit-iously; monotonously; drearily.

(See relate, repeat.)

RECKLESS

adverbs

desperately; daringly; audaciously; blithely; merrily; hilariously; bitterly; cruelly; incon-siderately; thoughtlessly; heedlessly; de-liberately; optimistically; wickedly; discon-certingly; improvidently; extravagantly; exceedingly; fantastically; outlandishly; outrageously; grotesquely; ostentatiously; spectacularly; dramatically; wildly; indis-creetly; financially; commercially; political-ly; personally; inexcusably; insensately; angrily; furiously; jealously; pitiably.

RECKLESSNESS

adjectives

wanton; stubborn; unfelt; lavish; uncalcu-lating; staid; fastidious; daring; fatal; gallant.

verbs

admonish—; protest—; repent—; rue—; tempt—; tolerate—; warn against—; —de-stroys; —endangers; —exposes to; —ig-nores; —irritates; —provokes; —risks; —suffers; —ventures; —wrecks.

(See audacity, indiscretion.)

RECKONING

adjectives

annual; lunar; dreadful; final; false; dead; swift.

verbs

confuse—; demand—; discharge—; dis-count—; estimate—; ignore—; probe—; value—; weed out of—; —accounts for; —acquits; —balances; —clarifies; —dis-honors; —fathoms; —nullifies; —repays.

(See account, computation, calculation, consideration.)

RECLINE (v)

adverbs

lazily; somnolently; cozily; comfortably; swinishly; calmly; artlessly; unambitiously.

(See rest, relax.)

RECLUSE

adjectives

literary; curious; poetical; sanctified; churlish; venerable; staid.

RECOGNITION

adjectives

abbreviated; instant; reverent; warmest; rigid; deserved; continuous; momentary; enforced; long-awaited; critical; unbroken; increasing; welcome; cold; unmistakable; faint; intelligent; courteous; legislative; mutual; dismayed; admiring; tacit; grateful; orderly; affectionate; public; sole; formal; emphatic; full; familiar; premature; clouded; flattering; hard-won.

verbs

accord—; alter beyond—; arouse—; concede—; confer—; demand—; evade—; escape—; extend—; gain—; lose—; merit—; permit—; prompt—; receive—; refuse—; struggle for—; suggest—; win—; —confirms; —corroborates; —recalls.

(See fame, greatness, position.)

RECOGNIZABLE

adverbs

easily; readily; distinctly; unfailingly; instantly; unmistakably; singularly; manifestly; memorably; unforgettably; peculiarly; particularly; positively; transparently; conspicuously; glaringly; unconcealably; strikingly; remarkably.

RECOGNIZE (v)

adverbs

distinctly; instinctively; definitely; universally; formally; frankly; deservedly; coldly; courteously; mutually; affectionately; tacitly; formally; publicly; prematurely.

(See distinguish, acknowledge.)

RECOIL

adjectives

vicious; impetuous; silent; tardy; nervous.

RECOIL (v)

adverbs

instinctively; involuntarily; modestly; impatiently; impetuously; nervously; abruptly; abnormally; tremblingly.

(See react, shrink.)

RECOLLECT (v)

adverbs

agreeably; humiliatingly; delightfully; hate-fully; gratefully; remorsefully; vaguely; uneasily; romantically; painfully; affectionately.

(See remember, recall.)

RECOLLECTION

adjectives

nightmare; agreeable; humiliating; delightful; grateful; hateful; glorious; contemptuous; dark; stern; remorseful; vanished; importunate; dim; vague; sweet; eternal; uneasy; romantic; sudden; simultaneous; humbling; distinct; melancholy; painful; accurate; faithful; perfect; tangled; livelier; pleasant; dormant; vivid; hazy; blissful; ungracious; cloudy; affectionate.

verbs

attempt—; betray—; crowd—s; drown—; escape—; evade—; hallow—; hinder—; obliterate—; prompt—; seek—; shudder at —; sink into—; stimulate—; stir—; suggest —; urge—; verify—; —dawns; —dims; —fades; —refreshes.

(See memory, remembrance, reminiscence.)

RECOMMEND (v)

adverbs

conscientiously; respectfully; unreservedly; cordially; urgently; expressly; unanimously; confidently; unhesitatingly; vigorously; earnestly; aptly; eloquently; subtly; emphatically; consistently.

(See suggest, commend, praise.)

RECOMMENDATION

adjectives

definite; additional; nimble; sweet; subtle; novel; emphatic; hesitating; sound; impolitic; consistent.

verbs

carry out—; confer—; consult—; demand—; gain—; glean—s; incorporate—s; offer—; sketch—s; —advises; —advocates; —favors; —flatters; —glows; —impresses; —informs; —refers to; —reports; —suggests.

(See commendation, approval, approbation, reference.)

RECOMMENDED

adverbs

highly; enthusiastically; favorably; well; exceptionally; unconditionally; earnestly;

justly; readily; acceptably; thoughtfully; unreservedly; strongly; eminently; explicitly; expressly.

RECOMPENSE
adjectives
godlike; solid; immortal; earnest; noblest; friendly; generous; exciting; abundant; insufficient; scant.

RECONCILABLE
adverbs
easily; readily; scarcely; hardly; wholly; partially; entirely; logically; reasonably; sensibly; naturally; fortunately; pleasantly; amiably; generously; amicably; fortunately; consistently.

RECONCILE (*v*)
adverbs
peremptorily; briefly; conveniently; permanently; forgivingly; touchingly; dramatically; logically; philosophically.
(See adjust, settle.)

RECONCILIATION
adjectives
perfect; convenient; short-lived; sweet; lasting; generous; forgiving.

verbs
arrange—; declare—; draw—; effect—; exact—; gain—; refuse—; seek—; —allays; —appeases; —heals; —hushes; —pacifies; —placates; —renews; —restores; —settles; —smooths; —squares.
(See conciliation, peace, reunion.)

RECONDITION (*v*)
adverbs
efficiently; professionally; thoroughly; permanently; periodically.
(See renew, repair.)

RECONNOITRE (*v*)
adverbs
audaciously; slyly; dutifully; courageously; cautiously; brazenly.
(See examine, inspect.)

RECONSIDER (*v*)
adverbs
hastily; subsequently; consequentially; meditatively; contemplatively; reflectively; serenely.
(See review, contemplate.)

RECONSTRUCTION
adjectives
orderly; benign; inartistic; voluntary.

verbs
advise— facilitate—; necessitate—; retard —; —converts; —corrects; —cures; —heals; —recoups; —rectifies; —redresses; —refreshes; —reinforces; —rights.
(See repairs, improvement, change.)

RECORD
adjectives
attainable; successful; enviable; reliable; long; indispensable; unsavory; scriptural; manifold (pl); authenticated; mystical; honorable; engrossed; splendid; imperfect; woeful; forlorn; formless; faithful; creditable; distinguished; chronological; continuous; vivid; subtlest; illustrious; unapproachable; earliest; historic; stenographic; boasted; bristling; erroneous; lingering; shameful; surprising; trivial; fond; illustrated; contemporary; parliamentary; voluminous; damning; priceless; definite; terse; cold; literal; comparable; accurate; individual; progressive; glorious; formal; lasting; tabulated; valuable; supernatural; available; confessed; trustworthy; indelible; notarial; pathetic; dumb; accumulated; aggregated; official; flawless; unpretending; artistic; clinical; imperishable; enthralling; factual; romantic; commendable; tragic; exemplary; phenomenal; heraldic.

verbs
achieve—; afford—; assemble—s; best—; blast—; bolster—; catalogue—s; compare —s; compile—s; delve into—s; divulge—; establish—; filch from—s; hang up—; illuminate—; inscribe—; live up to—; obliterate—; pound out—; pore over—s; probe —s; produce—; top—s; —s set forth; —s vary.
(See chronicle, archives, list, reputation.)

RECORD (*v*)
adverbs
faithfully; accurately; precisely; amusingly; regularly; minutely; authentically; industriously; impassively; uninterruptedly; scripturally; mystically; creditably; chronologically; vividly; subtly; historically; graphically; trivially; voluminously; literally; formally; flawlessly; clinically; factually; commendably; phenomenally.
(See note, reserve.)

RECORDED

adverbs

duly; accurately; carefully; meticulously; indelibly; graphically; intricately; officially; memorably; secretly; punctiliously; promptly; instantly; immediately; beautifully; realistically; photostatically; precisely; faithfully; legally; methodically; systematically; lovingly; vividly; completely.

RECOVER (v)

adverbs

mechanically; sufficiently; extraordinarily; miraculously; swiftly; speedily; tardily; moderately; fortunately; gradually; spectacularly; normally.

(See repair, restore.)

RECOVERY

adjectives

slow; gradual; rapid; ultimate; languid; spontaneous; happy; noble; spectacular; permanent; extraordinary; receding.

verbs

anticipate—; attribute—to; effect—; envisage—; expedite—; facilitate—; fumble with—; hasten—; hinder—; impede—; insure—; jeopardize—; promote—; retard—; speed—; stimulate—; —cheers; —ensues; —follows.

(See improvement, convalescence, restoration.)

RECREANT

adverbs

detestably; incredibly; shamefully; grossly; meanly; stubbornly; disgracefully; blasphemously; fearfully; infirmly; infamously; tortuously; insidiously; ignominiously; knavishly; unworthily; gracelessly; irreclaimably; unconscionably; basely.

RECREATION

adjectives

stimulating; intellectual; sweet; healthful; inexpensive; joyous; subsidiary; luxurious; innocent; solitary; wholesome; mutual; constructive.

verbs

arrange—; enjoy—; indulge in—; plan—; provide for—; seek—; —amuses; —beguiles; —bores; —cheers; —diverts; — drags; —enlivens; —entertains; —palls;

—relaxes; —revivifies; —tires; —wearies.

(See game, entertainment, jollity, diversion, amusement.)

RECRIMINATION

adjectives

mutual; bitter; incessant; cruel; repeated (pl).

RECRUDESCENT

adverbs

fortunately; surprisingly; advantageously; profitably; startlingly; strangely; luckily; opportunely; periodically; conveniently; fortuitously; resurgently; providentially; blessedly.

RECRUIT (v)

adverbs

intelligently; forcefully; faithfully; mainly; militaristically; martially; haphazardly.

(See furnish, raise.)

RECRUITS

adjectives

clownish; manifold; raw; unwilling; well-drilled; flustered; trustworthy; intelligent; unarmed; discouraged.

verbs

attract—; contribute—; furnish—; initiate —; lure—; tempt—; —advance; —assist; —attend; —brace; —cheer; —expedite; — fortify; —prop; —protect; —reenforce; — rescue; —steel; —sustain; —vivify.

(See volunteers, soldier.)

RECTITUDE

adjectives

extreme; utter; absolute; conscious; primeval; aesthetic; strict; self-styled.

RECTOR

adjectives

lisping; stern; devout; earnest; pious.

verbs

consult—; support—; unfrock—; —administers; —admonishes; —announces; —conducts; —crusades; —directs; —governs; —guides; —ministers; —orates; —preaches; —prepares; —prescribes; —presides; — supervises.

(See minister.)

RECTUM

verbs

abscess—; act on—; cleanse—; dilate—; distend—; flush—; inflame—; inject into—; irritate—; plug—; purge—; support—; terminate in—; trouble—; —extends.

(See bowels.)

RECUPERATE (v)

adverbs

expectedly; normally; beneficently; placidly; markedly; tardily; extendedly; passively; entirely.

(See rally, improve.)

RECUPERATIVE

adverbs

highly; strongly; vigorously; happily; fortunately; wholesomely; healthfully; sturdily; slowly; steadily; quietly; incredibly; luckily; carefully; successfully; patiently; resolutely; calmly; undeniably.

RECUR (v)

adverbs

successively; intermittently; constantly; insanely; sporadically; unexpectedly; infrequently; abruptly; irritatingly; explosively.

(See return, restore.)

RECURRENCE

adjectives

infrequent; delicate; sweet; constant; emphatic; intermittent; noisy; angry.

verbs

anticipate—; endure—; insure against—; prepare for—; suffer—; survive—; —bores; —drums; —redoubles; —refreshes; —renews; —resumes; —revolves; —rings; —shocks; —surprises; —wearies.

(See frequency, occurrence, repetition.)

RED

adjectives

deep; bloody; hectic; ruby; flamingo; latest; blazing; shimmering; livid; angry; tuneful; vivid; cochineal; unnatural; bright; orange; gleaming; rich; velvety; rosy; lifeless; brightish; monochromatic; fiery; gaudy; eye-closing; garish.

REDDEN (v)

adverbs

hotly; coyly; blushingly; shyly; modestly; timidly; enthusiastically; visibly; furiously; feverishly; indignantly.

(See flush, blush.)

REDEEM (v)

adverbs

ultimately; promptly; spiritually; subsequently; everlastingly; honorably; faithfully.

(See recover, rescue.)

REDEEMABLE

adverbs

currently; locally; immediately; fortunately; conveniently; profitably; undoubtedly; warrantably; fairly; easily; proportionally; lucratively; admissibly; unquestionably; legally; definitely; contractually; readily.

REDEMPTION

adjectives

ultimate; everlasting; foul; prompt; subsequent; spiritual; complete.

REDNESS

adjectives

shimmering; dewy; startling; rheumy.

REDOLENT

adverbs

pungently; spicily; sweetly; fragrantly; deliciously; delightfully; pleasantly; aromatically; refreshingly; suggestively; woodsily; surprisingly; lingeringly; strongly; highly; uncommonly.

REDRESS

adjectives

adequate; instant; warlike; immediate.

REDS
(communists)

verbs

support—; suppress—; —advocate; —agitate; —aggravate; —band; —forfeit; —idealize; —inflame; —instigate; —invade; —pillage; —plot; —promise; —resist; —revolt; —riot; —strike; —undermine.

(See communist, anarchist.)

REDUCE (v)

adverbs

materially; sharply; correspondingly; emphatically; deliberately; necessarily; rigorously; substantially; markedly; radically; drastically.

(See diminish, lower.)

adjectives
substantial; successive (pl); inexplicable; tremendous; marked; enormous; proper; radical; honest; ample; drastic; smashing; equitable; perpetual; scant.

REED

adjectives
jungle; pastoral; balmy; stiff; solacing; bruised; swampy; bending; unsustaining; plaited; vocal; whispering; silvery.

REEF

adjectives
submerged; hidden; sunken; encircling; subterranean; lisping; bluff; leering; scowling; frowning; darkling; dangerous; black-browed.

verbs
avoid—; cast upon—; drift to—; drive upon—; doom to—; founder on—; lash—; pound—; shatter on—s; thunder on—; —descends; —extends; —menaces; —ranges; —stretches; —threatens.
(See beach, rocks, shore.)

REEK (v)

adverbs
foully; alcoholically; vilely; powerfully; nauseatingly; disgustingly.
(See smoke, smell.)

REEL (v)

adverbs
visibly; weakly; drunkenly; dizzily; abruptly; sickeningly; swayingly.
(See stagger, sway.)

REFER (v)

adverbs
sarcastically; ironically; indelicately; pointedly; caustically; vaguely; satirically; unequivocally; sneeringly; sagaciously; affectionately; cursorily; contemptuously; pertinently; hilariously; obscurely; vaguely.
(See allude, hint, intimate.)

REFERENCE

adjectives
contemptuous; satisfying; constant; complimentary; barren; innumerable (pl); pathetic; pertinent; bibliographical; polite; solitary; never-ending; unmistakable; figurative; hilarious; documentary; mutual; offhand; obscure; touching; specific; sudden; sly; gratifying; vague; slighting.

verbs
avoid—to; demand—s; furnish—s; heed—; request—s; seek—s; vouchsafe—s; weigh—s; —compliments: —concerns; —counsels; —flatters; —instructs; —justifies; —mentions; —pertains to; —prescribes; —relates to; —satisfies; —suggests; —warns.
(See allusion, recommendation, mention, hint, record.)

REFINEMENT

adjectives
vital; technical; conscious; artistic; subtle; structural; utmost; high; intellectual; fresh; inventive; studied; nameless; classic; elaborate; sophistical; characteristic; delicate; accentuated; expert; exquisite; distilled; soft; false; incidental.

verbs
cultivate—; discern—; infuse—; profit by —; touch with—; weigh—; —ameliorates; —discriminates; —distinguishes; —enhances; —enriches; —graces; —improves; —mellows; —mitigates; —polishes; —promotes; —sifts.
(See elegance, civilization, refinement, culture.)

REFLECT (v)

adverbs
calmly; meditatively; sparklingly; contemplatively; cannily; piously; pensively; moodily; morbidly; somberly; grimly; opportunely; serenely; ingenuously; cynically; bitterly; miserably; delicately; philosophically; coherently; candidly; logically.
(See mirror, revert.)

REFLECTION

adjectives
delicate; vivid; surface; opposite; dreadful; somber; sagacious; gloomy; grave; unpleasant; sobering; impersonal; colorless; mature; injurious; sage; passionate; solemn; admirable; unbroken; wicked; judicious; interesting; cheering; dazzling; rusty; satirical; rich; best; philosophic; melancholy; bitter; careful; subtle; calm; unconscious; dim; perturbed; mortifying; unquiet; dancing; rosy; perplexing; drowsy; powerful; spectral; shortest; profound; brooding; dis-

tracting; nostalgic; silvery; recurring; homely; disagreeable; agitating; adequate; philosophical; coherent; assuring; heartshaking; candid; prosaic; continuous; harrowing; disturbing; splendid; logical.

verbs
absorb in—; air—; bolster by—; bury in—; console with—; emerge from—; feign—; immerse in—; sustain by—; veil in;—; wrap in—; —calms; —convinces; —flatters; —mirrors.
(See consideration, contemplation, image, study, meditation.)

REFLECTIVE
adverbs
philosophically; lazily; idly; pensively; wistfully; actively; alertly; keenly; gravely; seriously; earnestly; studiously; deeply; profoundly; aimlessly; restfully; quietly; calmly; serenely; gloomily; pessimistically; sadly; happily; pleasantly; peacefully; unwontedly; habitually.

REFORM
adjectives
obstinate; headlong; subsequent; constitutional; valuable; great; liberal; beneficent; mimetic; effectual; important; educational; ideological; dietary; phonetic; baronial; simultaneous; rigid; radical; feverish; temperance; energetic; imposed; rational.

verbs
adapt to—; adopt—; advocate—; approve —; deal with—; dramatize—; effect—; enforce—; facilitate—; formulate—; initiate —; institute—; labor for—; overemphasize —; proffer—; propose—; stalemate—; — overtakes; —slogs along; —surges over.
(See improvement, change, amendment.)

REFORM (*v*)
adverbs
speedily; constitutionally; beneficently; educationally; ideologically; radically; temperately; energetically; rationally.
(See convert, change.)

REFORMER
adjectives
hardy; prison; ardent; pugnacious; theoretical; phonetic; joy-killing; meretricious; disorderly; impetuous; respectable; temperance.

verbs
—advocates; —ameliorates; —betters; — corrects; —cultivates; —directs; —doctors; —eases; —foists upon; —fosters; —mends; —prates; —promotes; —purifies; —rants; —relieves; —remedies; —reorganizes; — repairs.
(See apostle, minister.)

REFRACTORY
adverbs
hopelessly; uncommonly; highly; remarkably; incredibly; incomparably; unmanageably; stubbornly; doggedly; mulishly; obstinately; obdurately; contumaciously; naturally; incorrigibly; desperately; uncontrollably; stiffly; perversely; disobediently; impertinently; mischievously; vexatiously; intolerably; inscrutably; inexplicably; unreasonably; embarrassingly; atrociously.

REFRAIN
adjectives
everlasting; drear; wild; unmeaning; recurring; plaintive; irreverent; sadder; wearisome; constant; weird.

verbs
chant—; chorus—; drum—; endure—; join in on—; paraphrase—; renew—; resume—; shout—; sing—; —bores; —refreshes; —revolves; —hinges; —rings; —shocks; —surprises; —survives; —tires; —wearies.
(See chorus, melody, verse, song.)

REFRAIN (*v*)
adverbs
prudently; deliberately; purposely; pointedly; sagely; resolutely; cautiously; wisely.
(See restrain, check, curb.)

REFRESH (*v*)
adverbs
deliciously; delectably; periodically; deliberately; potently; seasonally; hospitably.
(See renew, restore, revive.)

REFRESHED
adverbs
delightfully; wholly; unbelievably; completely; permanently; momentarily; temporarily; pleasantly; helpfully; heartily; incredibly; surprisingly; unexpectedly; visibly; noticeably; evidently; marvelously; miraculously; curiously; mysteriously; highly; amazingly; deeply; profoundly; unmistakably.

REFRESHING

adverbs

healthfully; wholesomely; thoughtfully; delightfully; pleasantly; interestingly; surprisingly; strikingly; gloriously; vigorously; restfully; peacefully; quietly; extremely; deliciously; coolly; comfortably; graciously; keenly; hospitably; invigoratingly; sharply; simply; wholly.

REFRESHMENTS

adjectives

delicate; potent; invigorating; apparent; elaborate; suitable; cool; nightcap; delicious; edible; smoky; surprising; delectable.

verbs

afford—; gorge on—; relish—; —appeal; —appease; —cheer; —comfort; —console; —delight; —invigorate; —quench; —repair; —restore; —revive; —sate; —stimulate.
(See food, luncheon.)

REFUGE

adjectives

hunted; walled; sheltered; flimsy; comforting; grateful; soothing; time-honored; secret; unavailing; temporary; modest; blessed; permanent.

verbs

abandon—; afford—; erect—; establish—; find—; grant—; hide in—; offer—; provide —; seek—; threaten—; uncover—; yield—; —assures; —comforts; —conceals; —defends; —preserves; —protects; —secures; —shelters; —shrouds.
(See shelter, protection, lodging, haven, nest, home.)

REFUGEE

adjectives

repatriating; testy; penniless; favorite; sick; unwelcome.

verbs

aid—; harbor—; overtake—; prosecute—; pursue—; search for—; shelter—; succor—; —s abandon; —absconds; —departs; —eludes; —endeavors; —escapes; —evades; —flees; —migrates; —s pour into; —s retreat; —trudges.
(See prisoner, criminal, fugitive.)

REFUSAL

adjectives

frightened; explicit; peremptory; persistent; periodic; positive; obstinate; varied; resolute; decided; energetic; melodramatic; kind; courteous; flat; gracious; contemptuous.

verbs

confront with—; consider—; ignore—; incur —; issue—; rehearse—; —contravenes; —declines; —denies; —depresses; —irks; —nullifies; —oppresses; —rebuffs; —revokes; —saddens; —squelches; —stays; —suppresses.
(See denial, dissent, rebuff, repulse.)

REFUSE (v)

adverbs

curtly; tacitly; mutinously; courteously; obdurately; scornfully; sternly; doggedly; positively; arbitrarily; inexorably; austerely; snobbishly; flatly; emphatically; sullenly; steadfastly; scrupulously; peremptorily; indignantly; spitefully; prudently; persistently; contumaciously; vehemently; delicately; unequivocally; haughtily; honorably; characteristically; invariably; habitually; graciously.
(See deny, repulse.)

REFUTATION

adjectives

serious; violent; sincere; practical; labored; complete; adequate.

REFUTE (v)

adverbs

undeniably; indisputably; violently; completely; adequately; laboredly; spectacularly; rudely.
(See question.)

REGAL

adverbs

gloriously; grandly; majestically; brilliantly; gorgeously; splendidly; magnificently; sumptuously; ceremonially; ceremoniously; processionally; incredibly; pompously; proudly; superbly; appropriately; suitably; marvelously; incomparably; unsurpassably; uncommonly; resplendently; eminently; consummately; mightily; imposingly; impressively; richly.

REGALE (v)

adverbs

pleasingly; boisterously; affluently; convivially; ostentatiously; hospitably; sumptuously; joyously; fraternally.

(See entertain, feast, gratify.)

REGARD

adjectives
cordial; affectionate; cold; platonic; reverential; eloquent; glorious; general; rueful; intense; delicate; mutual; prudential; due; profound; deepening; repulsive; wearisome; scrupulous; conscientious; sagacious; unalterable; popular; infantine; undue; deep; heartiest; faint; austere; pure; candid; tender; habitual; indispensable; religious; charitable; critical; decorous; slightest; deliberate.

verbs
acquire—; bear—; command—; entertain—; feign—; gain—; inspire—; observe with—; recognize—; relax—; signalize—; solicit—; win—; —arises from; —distinguishes; —flatters; —glorifies; —honors; —outshadows; —shines.

(See favor, esteem, deference, attention.)

REGARD (v)

adverbs
contemptuously; patiently; affectionately; passionately; ruthlessly; lewdly; practically; fondly; narrowly; enviously; attentively; pensively; appraisingly; solemnly; severely; pugnaciously; skeptically; vindictively; curiously; hopelessly; maliciously; ruefully; cordially; platonically; reverentially; sagaciously; austerely; candidly; tenderly; religiously; decorously.

(See observe, consider, heed.)

REGARDFUL

adverbs
deferentially; carefully; considerately; graciously; ingratiatingly; respectfully; punctiliously; meticulously; diplomatically; cautiously; vigilantly; warily; shrewdly; keenly; watchfully; mindfully; attentively; highly; profoundly; alertly; courteously; unfailingly.

REGENERATION

adjectives
political; physical; successful; spiritual; remarkable.

REGIME

adjectives
fascist; competitive; acid-neutralizing; san-

guinary; scandalous; despotic; complete; dominant; established; totalitarian; royalistic; democratic; memorable; tyrannical.

verbs
abolish—; control—; denounce—; discredit —; enjoy—; encroach on—; establish—; influence—; introduce—; labor under—; overthrow—; relax—; shape—; support—; sway —; tolerate—; —alters; —dictates; —exercises; —overawes; —usurps.

(See reign, rule, government, power.)

REGIMEN

adjectives
better; strict; unruly; careful; systematic.

REGIMENT

adjectives
ragged; red-coated; magnificent; opinionated; various (pl); redoubtable; crack; splendid.

verbs
distribute—; locate—; lodge—; quarter—; —advances; —assembles; —attacks; —concentrates; —disbands; —flocks; —focuses on; —gathers; —overspreads; —pitches; —retreats; —separates; —throngs .

(See brigade, infantry, militia, soldier.)

REGIMENTED

adverbs
overly; bureaucratically; dangerously; hopelessly; strictly; helplessly; terribly; ominously; unconsciously; frankly; unwillingly; insidiously; alarmingly; unsuspectingly; portentously; deliberately; significantly; disastrously; tyrannically; despotically; calamitously.

REGION

adjectives
devastated; tenuous; remote; spiritual; considerable; untraversed; indiscriminate; saturnine; shadowy; equatorial; ugly; raw; dreaded; airy; desolate; dreary; caudal; mountainous; fertile; wild; antique; inland; nobler; ionized; humid; lonely; unfooted; icy; enchanting; dense; inspiring; equinoctial; interesting; grazing; sequestered; burning; afflicted; constellated; empyreal; disputed; mystical; sterile; ravaged; subterranean; celestial; frontal; arid; unknown; reflecting; barbarous; purer; inferior; boundless; embryonic; hospitable; romantic; idyllic; prolific; unexplored; neigh-

boring; condensed; immense; atmospheric; forest; extensive; infernal; crooked; habitable; healthy; industrial; untrod; low; lumbar; cardiac; gloomy; wooded; enchanted; picturesque; blooming; tropical; imperiled; agricultural; rarefied; adjacent; hypogastric; limited; uncultivated; fruitful; exhausted; semibarbarous; lacustrine; insulated; bleak; ill-defined; thrilling.

verbs
bound—; divide—; dominate—; dwell in —; endow—with; evacuate—; fortify—; infest—; inhabit—; invade—; locate in—; mark—; migrate to—; occupy—; rule—; settle in—; skirt—; visit—.
 (See field, country, district, locality, valley, plain.)

REGRET
adjectives
pious; undersigned; relentful; idle; unspeakable; fond; tender; contrite; indignant; mingled (pl); continued; passionate; bitter; serious; unmeaning; dead; keenest; constant; deep; hopeless; meek; vain; frantic; proud; repentant; immeasurable; formal; torturing; sweet; sensible; vague; wistful; inextinguishable; immense; sincere; unfeigned; momentary; endless; unhappy; fierce; subsequent; inexpressible; restless; fundamental; maudlin; unequivocal; unavailing.

verbs
accept—s; betoken—; bewail in—; cherish —; convey—s; croak—s; express—; lament —s; offer—s; plague with—s; send—s; —s chafe; —s confuse; —s disappoint; —s disconcert; —s dishearten; —s humiliate; — oppresses; —saddens; —s vex.
 (See sorrow, grief, misery.)

REGRET (v)
adverbs
audibly; pitifully; officially; deeply; bitterly; exceedingly; mournfully; piously; fondly; passionately; keenly; vainly; inexpressibly; vaguely; wistfully; maudlinly; unequivocally; unavailingly.
 (See deprecate, deplore.)

REGULAR
adverbs
strictly; sternly; horribly; chastely; systematically; methodically; altogether; painfully; strangely; artificially; stiffly; formidably;

unnaturally; formally; legally; detestably; beautifully; curiously; perfectly; unnecessarily; conveniently; surprisingly; marvelously.

REGULARITY
adjectives
chronological; vulgar; mechanical; absolute; commonplace; surprising; comparative; rhythmic; accustomed; unfailing; faultless; bashful; monotonous; clock-like.

verbs
acquire—; adjust to—; chime in—; drum with—; fall in—; form with—; level to—; maintain—; perform with—; range in—; sustain—; —conforms to; —offsets; —wearies.
 (See consistency, harmony, persistence.)

REGULATE (v)
adverbs
stringently; socially; solely; mechanically; scientifically; bureaucratically; autonomously; dictatorially; tyrannically; austerely.
 (See direct, control.)

REGULATIONS
adjectives
existing; labeling; influential; arbitrary; stupid; special; conflicting; cast-iron; elaborate; stringent; complicated; administrative; admirable; sanitary; military; martial; hostile; celebrated; barbarous; inviolable; local; wide-spread; federal; civic.

verbs
adopt—; approve—; bar by—; block—; comply with—; conform to—; control by—; decry—; defy—; denounce—; enforce—; govern by—; legislate—; impose—upon; improve—; promulgate—; provide—; revise —; submit—; sustain—; violate—.
 (See legislation, bill, arrangement, law, mandate, rule.)

REHABILITATE (v)
adverbs
completely; entirely; refreshingly; spectacularly; miraculously; superficially.
 (See restore, renew, revive.)

REHEARSE (v)
adverbs
incessantly; harmoniously; perfunctorily; dutifully; painstakingly; faithfully.
 (See practice, say.)

adjectives

transient; dismal; passionate; present; illustrious; imperial; unbreathing; subsequent; reasoning; secure; inexorable; abdicated; horrid; preceding; unsurpassed; liberal; unmolested; remotest; prosperous; gaudy; troublous; happy.

verbs

force—; limit—; overthrow—; submit to—; suffer under—; terminate—; undermine—; tolerate—; usurp—; —chafes; —contents; —dictates; —symbolizes; —trammels; —tramples on; —treads upon; —tyrannizes.

(See regime, government, dominion.)

REIGN (v)

adverbs

imperially; inexorably; liberally; prosperously; tyrannically; lustfully; beneficently; imperiously; supremely; austerely; contemporaneously; gloriously; royally.

(See govern, rule.)

REIMBURSE (v)

adverbs

appreciatively; satisfactorily; fully; generously; financially; liberally; unstintingly.

(See repay, avenge.)

REINDEER

verbs

bag—; domesticate—; exhibit—; mount—; preserve—; stalk—; team—; —draws; —herds; —inhabits; —migrates; —retreats; —scrapes; —sheds; —shies; —traverses.

(See animal, deer.)

REINFORCE (v)

adverbs

substantially; materially; firmly; enormously; strategically.

(See aid, assist.)

REINFORCED

adverbs

strongly; firmly; unbreakably; suddenly; necessarily; conveniently; advantageously; completely; appropriately; suitably; substantially; enormously; materially; providentially; immensely; opportunely; duly.

REINFORCEMENT

adjectives

enormous; seasonable; material; welcome; momentary; unexpected.

adjectives

commanding; jingling; loosened; leathern; dangling.

verbs

check with—; control—; discard—; dress—; grasp—; grease—; hand over—; jerk on—; knot—; loop—; master—; pluck at—; relax —; release—; respond to—; rustle—; saw with—; slap with—; spank—; take over—; tangle—; yank (colloq.)—; —check; —control; —dangle; —direct.

(See bit.)

REITERATE (v)

adverbs

incessantly; substantially; emphatically; characteristically; monotonously; maddeningly; intermittently.

(See repeat.)

REJECT (v)

adverbs

summarily; scornfully; disdainfully; scoffingly; unconditionally; overwhelmingly; airily; petulantly; incontinently; contemptuously; utterly; haughtily; stubbornly; indignantly; peremptorily; flatly; unanimously; sullenly; brusquely; bluntly; pointedly.

(See refuse, repulse.)

REJECTION

adjectives

sullen; intellectual; subsequent; pointed; blunt; brusque.

REJOICE (v)

adverbs

convivially; immoderately; festively; hilariously; exultantly; openly; gleefully; enthusiastically; spontaneously; impulsively; fraternally.

(See cheer, exult.)

REJOICED

adverbs

greatly; highly; uncommonly; radiantly; gloriously; proudly; triumphantly; splendidly; exultantly; elatedly; naturally; genuinely.

REJOICING

adjectives

endless; enthusiastic; excited; ravenous; spontaneous; surface; incessant; half-hearted.

adverbs

reverently; hilariously; uproariously; riotously; loudly; quietly; calmly; deeply; profoundly; thoughtfully; boisterously; triumphantly; gayly; merrily; happily; rapturously; wildly; enthusiastically; hysterically; excitedly; exuberantly; madly; tumultuously; heartily.

REJOIN (*v*)

adverbs

ultimately; laughingly; daringly; stingingly; passionately; flippantly; curtly; pointedly; tartly; quaintly; tardily; shrewdly; bitterly; sympathetically; reluctantly; icily; haughtily; calmly; musingly.

(See reply, answer.)

REJOINDER

adjectives

laughing; daring; stinging; passionate; flippant; curt; pointed; tart; clever; quaint; sad; usual; nasty; tardy.

REJUVENATION

verbs

buy—; draw—from; induce—; quaff—; retard—; seek—; —aids; —cures; —eludes; —rallies; —reanimates; —rectifies; —redresses; —repairs; —stimulates; —thrills.

(See youth, health, cure, remedy.)

RELAPSE

adjectives

subsequent; moral; fatal; momentary; swift; sure; unavoidable; inevitable.

verbs

anticipate—; deplore—; fall into—; incur —; lament—; preclude—; sink into—; slide into—; undergo—; verge on—; warn against—; —occurs; —recoils; —retrogrades; —reverts to.

(See recurrence.)

RELATE (*v*)

adverbs

mirthfully; speciously; variously; tediously; succulently; incredibly; intimately; gravely; confidently; graphically; sympathetically; monotonously.

(See tell, narrate.)

RELATED

adverbs

closely; remotely; intimately; personally; officially; scarcely; materially; inescapably;

obviously; naturally; circumstantially; conditionally; accidentally; casually; incomprehensibly; practically; obviously; manifestly; conveniently.

RELATIONS

adjectives

brotherly; hostile; uninterrupted; definite; long-dreaded; exacting; intimate; selfish; delicate; ecclesiastical; wretched; harmonious; pedagogic; causative; domestic; truthful; evident; sublimest; unbroken; genial; agreeable; confiding; pacific; veiled; peculiar; paternal; filial; diplomatic; untried; blessed; typical; mysterious; unobtrusive; sympathetic; conjugal; occult; amicable; prejudiced; nominal; friendly; necessary; supernatural; uncaressing; unsympathizing; dynamical; independent; complex; current; healthful; antagonistic; marital; coetaneous; incestuous; distinct; parallel; causal; scandalous; far-reaching; frank; simultaneous; cordial; piquant; amiable; perverse; confidential; innumerable; organic; mutual; fixed; uniform; established; determinate; passional; external; feudal; conflicting; unnatural; sex; altruistic; mathematical; antenuptial; consistent; symbolic; industrial; decorative; subsequent; clerical; strained.

verbs

achieve—; bear—with; break off—; cement —; cloud—; cripple—; deny—with; disturb —; entertain—with; establish—; facilitate —; govern—; harmonize—; ignore—; maintain—; mar—; preserve—; reestablish—; sever—; sharpen—; shun—; smooth—; strain—; suppress—; sustain—; —bind; —cool; —prevail; —tie.

(See relationship, affairs, connection.)

RELATIONSHIP

adjectives

intimate; unconventional; confidential; harmonious; hierarchical; personal; simple; monotonous; illicit; family; intelligible; intellectual; domestic; healthful; closer; sympathetic; marked; economic.

RELATIVES
(*kin*)

adjectives

distant; harmless; elderly; endangered; illustrious; erring; reluctant; interfering; interested; portly; unsympathetic; departing; circumspect; disagreeable; unpleasant.

verbs
characterize—; claim—; endure—; link—; plague with—; reconcile—; support—; —assemble; —bicker; —commemorate; —congregate; —convene; —criticize; —drift; —honor; —implore; —intrude; —pester; —quarrel; —recount; —report; —sanction; —trace.

(See friend, family.)

RELATIONSHIP

verbs
affect—; claim—; comprehend—; criticize —; discern—; draw from—; endure—; enter into—; expose—; form—; intrude on—; mar—; probe—; prove—; report—; sanction—; sever—; split—; terminate—; warp —; —associates; —binds; —comforts; —involves; —links.

(See alliance, connection, affiliation, relation.)

RELAX (v)

adverbs
momentarily; restfully; contentedly; totally: completely; beneficially; healthfully; blissfully; drowsily; refreshingly.

(See slacken, rest.)

RELAXATION

adjectives
acquiescent; complete; attendant; humanizing; universal; momentary; amused; necessary.

verbs
attain—; conduce toward—; loll in—; lounge in—; participate in—; practice—; seek—; —alleviates; —arouses; —calms; —composes; —modifies; —pacifies; —palliates; —quiets; —refreshes; —rests; —smoothes; —stills; —subdues; —tempers; —tranquilizes; —wastes.

(See diversion, jollity, recreation.)

RELAXED

adverbs
pleasantly; mentally; idly; momentarily; suddenly; wholly; delightfully; restfully; rarely; serenely; lazily; irresponsibly; unwontedly; surprisingly; comfortably; fortunately; beautifully; finally; drowsily; dreamily; satisfactorily; refreshingly; unbelievably; miraculously; curiously.

RELEASE

adjectives
impassioned; speedy; merciful; ultimate; eventual; anticipated; unaccountable; long-sought.

verbs
attempt—; beg for—; grant—; hinder—; permit—; procure—; sanction—; schedule for—; secure—; withhold—; —absolves; —acquits; —clears; —exonerates; —frees; —unbars; —unclogs; —unlooses.

(See bail, deliverance, discharge.)

RELEASE (v)

adverbs
unconditionally; instantaneously; blamelessly; consequently; subsequently; deftly; ultimately; unaccountably.

(See free, acquit.)

RELENT (v)

adverbs
graciously; grudgingly; tardily; beneficently; remorsefully; partially; smilingly.

(See yield, repent.)

RELIANCE

adjectives
affectionate; rugged; implicit; noble; sober; loving; just; calm; pretended; reciprocal; manly; centering; imbecilic; humble.

verbs
cherish—; consider—; doubt—; foster—; place—in; presume—; produce—; prove—; rest on—; shake—; trust—; —buoys; —encourages; —impresses; —inspires; —persuades; —satisfies.

(See hope, confidence, assurance, trust.)

RELIC

adjectives
antediluvian; hoary; visible; lacustrine; precious; melancholy; holy; fascinating; pathetic; prehistoric; sartorial; exquisite; venerable; sacred; unmistakable; quaint; supposed; amusing; incensing; celebrated; curious; archaeological; unseemly; tender; quivering; cherished; moldering.

RELIEF

verbs
administer—; afford—; derive—from; experience—; extend—; gain—; gasp with—;

grant—; hail—; heave a sigh of—; indulge —; mark by—; seek—; speed—; voice—.
(See help, aid, assistance, consolation.)

RELIEF
(charity, dole.)

verbs

apply for—; infringe upon—; promote—; slash—; —allays; —assuages; —cheers; —comforts; —disburdens; —eases; —encourages; —insures; —mitigates; —remedies; —solves; —smooths; —sustains.
(See payment, dole, charity.)

RELIEF
(general)

adjectives

consequent; speedy; hysterical; parochial; intense; joyous; beautiful; inevitable; delighted; complete; permanent; temporary; marked; distinct; regular; pronounced; infinite; immediate; effective; actual; spiritual; pretended; considerable; delicious; partial; decided; mean; instant; scant; sheer; welcome; urgent; national; decorative; reliable.

RELIEVE (v)

adverbs

tactfully; effectually; painlessly; ultimately; intensely; temporarily; spiritually; partially; economically; nationally.
(See alleviate, lessen.)

RELIGION

adjectives

scurvy; ritual; rudimentary; concentrated; positive; fierce; absurd; austere; profane; constructive; inaccessible; sanguinary; powerful; fervent; blessed; unalterable; irrevocable; distinct; revealed; peaceful; maudlin; professed; easy-minded; blatant; doctrinal; gripping; saving.

verbs

adopt—; attack—; cast aside—; cherish—; corrupt—; defile—; define—; devote to—; discredit—; embrace—; formulate—; inculcate—; interpret—; profess—; renounce —; ridicule—; side-track—; stamp out—; traduce—; venerate—; —comforts; —consoles; —elevates; —fetters; —influences; —moulds; —nourishes; —paralyzes; —perishes; —prevails; —purges; —purifies; — sanctifies; —sways; —unifies; —wanes.
(See devotion, faith, worship, Christianity, modernism.)

RELINQUISH (v)

adverbs

silently; nobly; gallantly; magnanimously; voluntarily; completely; reluctantly; philosophically; gloomily; unselfishly; logically.
(See surrender, waive, cede.)

RELISH

adjectives

savory; exciting; peculiar; anticipatory; derisive; insatiable; unwonted; evident; higher; callous; complacent; keen; savage; added; natural; acquired.

RELISH (v)

adverbs

heartily; appreciatively; intellectually; spicily; pungently; enjoyably.
(See enjoy, taste.)

RELUCTANCE

adjectives

resentful; sullen; unfeigned; fierce; reverent; unaffected; infinite; pretty; lingering; natural; insurmountable; shuddering; evident; double; general; untamed; curious; studied.

verbs

assume—; complain of—; dispel—; employ with—; feign—; harbor—; imply—; incite —; incur—; invite—; overcome—; prompt —; stifle—; —baits; —provokes; —resists; —restrains; —sharpens; —tantalizes; — whets.
(See distaste, aversion, unwillingness, repugnance, dislike.)

RELUCTANT

adverbs

inexplicably; terribly; visibly; evidently; sternly; inflexibly; unyieldingly; palpably; manifestly; strangely; harshly; morosely; undeniably; resentfully; unpleasantly; discourteously; impolitely; sullenly; uncivilly; roughly; unaffectedly; naturally; curiously; superstitiously; timidly; shyly; bashfully; fearfully; timorously; senselessly; sensibly; wisely; thoughtfully; profoundly; secretly; oddly; peculiarly; significantly; particularly; uncommonly.

RELY (v)

adverbs

implicitly; exclusively; chiefly; trustfully;

faithfully; tacitly; affectionately; reciprocally; soberly; humbly; calmly.

(See depend, trust.)

REMAIN (v)

adverbs

constantly; hopefully; tensely; determinedly; indefinitely; courageously; voluntarily; impassively; motionlessly; tranquilly; inflexibly; wilfully; permanently; peacefully.

(See stay, linger.)

REMAINS

adjectives

mangled; undemolished; mutilated; honored; numerous; jagged; august; fossilized; dreary; lifeless; insensible; imperishable; charred; mortal; architectural; heterogeneous; comic; disinterred; dingy; scattered; petrified; colorless; archaeological.

verbs

cart away—; conceal—; consign—to; cremate—; disinter—; dispose of—; dissect—; embalm—; entomb—; exhume—; expose—; honor—; inter—; mummify—; rescue—; ship—; trace—.

(See ashes, debris, dust, corpse, remnants.)

REMARK

adjectives

laughing; bantering; automatic; delighted; editorial; pregnant; noncommittal; ill-bred; futile; felicitous; stinging; harsh; preliminary; taunting; fertile; disparaging; commonplace; inaccurate; terse; hasty; vicious; candid; malicious; concluding; immortal; cryptic; appreciative; unpremeditated; enigmatical; unexpected; profound; brittle; opprobrious; deprecatory; chance; sententious; derogatory; outspoken; complimentary; incidental; tomfool; satiric; material; boorish; insubordinate; sage; insolent; coarse; cheerful; desultory; treasonable; merry; philosophic; withering; sarcastic; drunken; significant; casual; illuminating; laconic; feeble; caustic; pat; obscure; verbal; simultaneous (pl); surly; skeptical; mischievous; philosophical; egotistical; independent; special; characteristic; graceful; frolicsome; priceless; careless; indiscreet; prelusory; slurring; ejaculatory; animated; scintillating; epithetical; facetious; deathless; calescent; disputed; trivial; acrimonious; disgusting; critical; allusive; appropriate; judicious.

verbs

ban—; bar—; comprehend—; couch—; deliver—; digest—; drop—; emit—; exchange—s; insert—; occasion—; open—s; poise—; preface—; propose—; punctuate—; repress—; —deprecates; —disparages; —embitters; —falls; —indicates; —issues from; —interrupts.

(See mention, comment, observation, statement.)

REMARK (v)

adverbs

gratuitously; banteringly; ambiguously; anxiously; dryly; wittily; significantly; dispassionately; disparingly; illogically; mendaciously; casually; emphatically; judicially; modestly; complacently; affably; ruefully; vigorously; inquisitively; confidently; whimsically; indifferently; exuberantly; pathetically; sympathetically; sententiously; contemptuously; cynically; deftly; laconically; demurely; pointedly; wistfully; tenatively; caustically; editorially; pregnantly; noncommittally; felicitously; disparagingly; viciously; candidly; appreciatively; boorishly; obscurely; acrimoniously; allusively; appropriately; judiciously; skeptically; egotistically.

(See comment, assert.)

REMEDIABLE

adverbs

easily; fortunately; luckily; quickly; immediately; supposedly; probably; expensively; distinctly; definitely; manifestly; now; altogether; undoubtedly.

REMEDY

adjectives

worthless; potent; favorite; time-tested; present; similar; valuable; misbranded; fraudulent; mythical; accepted; manifold (pl); rational; insidious; infallible; palliative; celebrated; universal; unavailing; irrational; precious; radical; ancient; drug; original; effective; fruitless; costly; extreme; innocent; heroic; futile; makeshift.

verbs

advocate—; apply—; concoct—; denounce—; employ—; furnish—; grope for—; hail—; persevere with—; prescribe—; propose—; provide—; recommend—; rely upon—;

seek—; —alleviates; —eases; —palliates; —purges; —relieves; —soothes.
(See cure, liniment, laxative, purgative, medicine.)

REMEDY (v)
adverbs
concurrently; similarly; rationally; fraudulently; traditionally; heroically; medically; beneficially; miraculously.
(See cure, heal.)

REMEMBER (v)
adverbs
vividly; mechanically; graphically; sorrowfully; remorsefully; irrelevantly; dimly; subconsciously; vaguely; passionately; generously; superstitiously; gratefully; fondly; affectionately; morbidly; eternally; mournfully; involuntarily.
(See recollect, recall.)

REMEMBRANCE
adjectives
pleasant; affectionate; clear; lasting; loving; proud; grateful; fond; dull; discourteous; intuitive; melancholy; morbid; gray; desolate; yielding; burning; fevered; ennobling; ineffaceable; lively; personal; deep; triumphant; tender; ancestral; undimmed; foul; mournful; eternal; faithful; ignominious; listening; evil; gracious; involuntary; stern; worthiest; slow; honorable; sufficient; unwelcome; fading; delighted; constant; kindly; grateful; vivid; lifelong.

verbs
con—; bear in—; honor—; incite—; indulge in—; prompt—; retain—; rivet in—; suggest—; —commemorates; —diverts; —fades; —flatters; —impresses; —renews; —stings; —wanes.
(See memory, compliment, recollection, reminiscence.)

REMIND (v)
adverbs
relentlessly; grimly; persistently; poignantly; irksomely; demurely; accusingly; irrationally; determinedly; vigorously; vividly; pleasantly; personally; tenderly; painfully; laughingly; spitefully.
(See recall.)

REMINDER
adjectives
grim; curious; visible; painful; neat; tangible; pitiful; laughing; continual.

REMINISCENCE
adjectives
agreeable; uncomfortable; indistinct; haunting; glorified; vulgarized; distinguishable; tender; historical; pleasing; vague; barren; commonplace; crisp; humorous; incoherent; divine; fascinating.

verbs
awaken—; delight in—; dispel—; embarrass by—; enjoy—; indulge in—; interpose —; prolong—; revel in—; review in—; steep in—; veil—; —cheers; —colors; —consoles; —delights; —s flood; —warms; interrupt—.
(See remembrance, recollection, memory.)

REMINISCENT
adverbs
delightfully; happily; tiresomely; unendingly; crisply; humorously; divinely; fascinatingly; vaguely; pleasingly; tenderly; gloriously; teasingly; incoherently; uproariously; convivially; genially; embarrassingly; surprisingly; foolishly; deliriously; garrulously; unsteadily; wistfully; feebly; constantly.

REMISS
adverbs
apologetically; confessedly; admittedly; terribly; unpardonably; gravely; seriously; heedlessly; nonchalantly; criminally; tragically; inexplicably; unaccountably; strangely; curiously; unconsciously; unintentionally; carelessly; hopelessly; sorely; unacceptably; frequently; negligently; indifferently; atrociously.

REMNANTS
adjectives
sufficing; laggard; straggling; placable; salvaged; shrunken; scorched; enduring; shattered; discarded; miserable; pathetic; quaint; wretched; fugitive; lingering; greater; saving.

verbs
bag—; cherish—; collect—; conceal—; consume—; gather—; heap—; leave—; market —; offer—; piece—; proffer—; salvage—;

scatter—; store—; utilize—; value; —disappear; —survive.

(See fragment, residue, piece, remains.)

REMONSTRANCE
adjectives
passionate; energetic; rash; urgent; mutinous; bitter; temperate; tender; lukewarm; childish; indignant; peaceful; final; earnest; useless; obvious; eloquent; angry; rational; resentful.

REMONSTRATE (v)
adverbs
waggishly; vainly; rudely; incessantly; earnestly; calmly; passionately; energetically; mutinously; bitterly; tenderly; childishly; eloquently; rationally; resentfully.

(See protest, expostulate.)

REMORSE
adjectives
useless; sisterly; gnawing; fictitious; bitter; unconfessed; light; violent; vile; abrupt; unceasing; dull; poignant.

verbs
burden with—; confess—; depress by—; experience—; incite—; overcome with—; overwhelm with—; palliate—; relieve—; shake with—; shroud in—; smite with—; sober by—; suffer—; tinge with—; wrap in—; —colors; —devours; —humbles; —maddens; —overwhelms; —racks; —shatters; —subdues; —stirs; —surges within; —undermines.

(See contrition, regret, qualm, repentance.)

REMORSEFUL
adverbs
naturally; admittedly; openly; manifestly; miserably; tardily; wretchedly; pitiably; pitifully; pathetically; tragically; immeasurably; terribly; sorely; significantly; sincerely; sobbingly; weakly; duly; penitently; contritely; deeply; profoundly.

REMOTE
adverbs
coldly; distantly; proudly; shyly; timidly; arrogantly; superciliously; intellectually; absent-mindedly; abstractedly; philosophically; naturally; dreamily; discourteously; deliberately; resolutely; gravely; unsocially; inscrutably; mysteriously; vexatiously; gruffly; gravely; judiciously; absurdly.

REMOTENESS
adjectives
romantic; apparent; comparative; patent.

REMOVAL
adjectives
successful; prompt; repeated; forcible; swift.

verbs
advocate—; allow—; balk at—; compel—; delay—; demand—; ease by—; entail—; hamper—; hinder—; impede—; instigate—; order—; recommend—; rejoice in—; resist —; upset by—; —alters; —annoys; —confuses; —disturbs.

(See dismissal, displacement, withdrawal, change.)

REMOVE (v)
adverbs
dexterously; clumsily; skillfully; cautiously; surreptitiously; slyly; permanently; temporarily; forcefully; promptly; swiftly.

(See transfer, withdraw.)

REMUNERATIVE
adverbs
providentially; extravagantly; sufficiently; fairly; justly; adequately; highly; satisfactorily; surprisingly; astoundingly; remarkably; gratifyingly; incredibly; opportunely; finally; profitably; scarcely; duly; advantageously; usefully; fantastically: richly; uncommonly.

RENAISSANCE
verbs
anticipate—; characterize—; contribute to —; create—; foster—; hail—; instigate—; pertain to—; promote—; prompt—; terminate—; voice—; —alters; —flourishes; —produces; —reforms; —renews; —restores; —reveals; —revivifies; —stimulates; —unfolds.

(See birth, revival, restoration.)

RENDER (v)
adverbs
passively; powerfully; exquisitely; peculiarly; necessarily; infallibly; barely; charmingly; admirably; poetically; realistically; artistically.

(See repay, restore.)

RENDERING

adjectives

realistic; photographic; elusive; exquisite; independent; artistic.

RENDEZVOUS

adjectives

picturesque; favorite; charming; famous; appointed; storied; legendary; modern.

RENEW (v)

adverbs

modernistically; periodically; auspiciously; mysteriously; generously; harmoniously; incessantly; wholly; reverently; seasonally.

(See repair, restore.)

RENOUNCE (v)

adverbs

dogmatically; courageously; boldly; rashly; lawfully; faithlessly; virtually; eternally; voluntarily; passionately; shamelessly; explicitly; frankly.

(See reject, disclaim.)

RENOVATED

adverbs

perfectly; pleasingly; usefully; delightfully; acceptably; inexpensively; skilfully; marvelously; astoundingly; amazingly; opportunely; duly; attractively; newly; recently; properly; appropriately; lately; cleverly; artistically; substantially; admirably; satisfactorily; beautifully.

RENOWN

adjectives

splendid; posthumous; unfulfilled; ancient; chaste; temporary; contemporary; godlike; provincial; unspeakable; wide-spread; notorious.

verbs

accept—; accredit—; achieve—; acquire—; cherish—; feign—; gain—; glean—; radiate—; reflect—; respect—; rise to—; sing —; win—; —glorifies; —overshadows; —overwhelms; —shines; —spoils.

(See glory, fame, limelight, distinction, notoriety.)

RENT

adjectives

great; ragged; artificial; ghastly; economic; reconciling; preposterous; numerous (pl); outrageous.

RENUNCIATION

adjectives

passionate; shameless; sublime; frank; perfect; explicit.

REORGANIZATION

adjectives

intensive; careful; economic; periodical; necessary.

REPAIR (v)

adverbs

temporarily; hastily; haphazardly; amply; ceaselessly; extensively; technically; judiciously; medically.

(See restore, mend.)

REPAIRED

adverbs

obviously; recently; badly; handsomely; adroitly; secretly; visibly; skilfully; beautifully; marvelously; completely; aptly; expensively; reasonably; extensively; shoddily; ably; expertly; ingeniously; wonderfully; unnoticeably; perfectly; patently; imperceptibly; exquisitely; awkwardly; clumsily; sufficiently; satisfactorily.

REPAIRS

adjectives

extensive; judicious; necessary; expensive; technical; obvious; happy.

verbs

effect—; resume—; undergo—; view—; —ameliorate; —bolster; —compensate; —convert; —enhance; —purge; —rectify—; redeem; —refresh; —relieve; —remedy; —restore; —strengthen.

(See reconstruction, improvement.)

REPARATIONS

verbs

cancel—; demand—; forego—; liquidate—; offer—; refuse—; repudiate—; review—; —acknowledge; —appease; —atone; —correct; —indemnify; —pacify; —recompense; —redeem; —redress; —requite; —restore; —reward; —satisfy.

(See insurance, atonement, restoration.)

REPARTEE

adjectives

insulting; clever; humorous; colloquial; icy; restless; victorious; spicy; sparkling; witty.

verbs

banter—; engage in—; excel in—; furnish —; prolong—; quicken—; school in—; stimulate—; suffer—; surpass in—; —amuses; —arouses; —beguiles; —cheers; —delights; —diverts; —entertains; —excels; —frisks; —romps; —scintillates; —sparkles; —wanes.

(See answer, banter, reply.)

REPAST

adjectives

unsavory; sumptuous; cannibal; nocturnal; precious; disgusting; substantial; satisfying; ridiculous; extravagant; delicious; tumultuous.

verbs

crave—; devour—; donate—; gorge—; invite to—; partake of—; prepare—; relish—; spread—; wash down—; yield to—; —allays; —appeases; —attracts; —nourishes; —quells; —sates.

(See eating, luncheon, feast, meal, food.)

REPAY (v)

adverbs

promptly; severely; cheerfully; lavishly; amply; faithfully; conscientiously; legally; graciously.

(See reimburse, avenge.)

REPEAL

verbs

abolish—; advocate—; agitate for—; authorize—; celebrate—; demand—; desire—; discard—; favor—; fight—; induce—; overrule—; permit—; promote—; recommend—; reverse—; sanction—; seek—; welcome—; —ameliorates; —cheers; —dissolves; —gladdens; —improves; —nullifies; —relieves.

(See dismissal, displacement.)

REPEAL (v)

adverbs

expressly; totally; legally; harshly; dogmatically; unanimously; promptly.

(See retract, recall.)

REPEAT (v)

adverbs

idiotically; tediously; foolishly; maliciously; vindictively; icily; incredulously; insistently; vaguely; fatuously; insultingly; emphatically; peevishly; multitudinously; stubbornly; mechanically; simultaneously; musingly; fluently; deprecatingly; monotonously; interrogatively; authoritatively; aimlessly; tenderly; musically.

(See reiterate.)

REPEATED

adverbs

endlessly; monotonously; emphatically; frequently; necessarily; tediously; whiningly; sullenly; unbearably; tiresomely; foolishly; maliciously; garrulously; senselessly; accurately; erroneously; imprudently; indiscreetly; secretly; confidentially; cruelly; derisively; unfortunately; unluckily; malevolently; scoffingly; deliberately; treacherously; surreptitiously; slyly; intelligibly; audibly; authoritatively; ominously; significantly.

REPEL (v)

adverbs

obstinately; stubbornly; vigorously; forcefully; courageously; staunchly; determinedly; gallantly.

(See oppose, repulse.)

REPENT (v)

adverbs

religiously; remorsefully; bitterly; genuinely; submissively; sincerely.

(See regret, grieve.)

REPENTANCE

adjectives

genuine; unavailing; bitter; submissive; generous; deep; sad; shamefaced; deathbed; sincere; sullen.

verbs

burden with—; confess—; experience—; feign—; incite—; overcome with—; wrap in—; —appeases; —condones; —humbles; —oppresses; —overwhelms; —pacifies; —palliates; —relieves; —shrouds; —sobers; —subdues; —tinges.

(See remorse, contrition, regret.)

REPERTOIRE

verbs

acclaim—; acquire—; announce—; applaud —; arrange—; balance—; choose—; enact —; enlarge—; exhaust—; expand—; include in—; increase—; list—; plan—; practice—; rehearse—; round out—; —covers; —delights; —embraces; —engages; —includes; —unfolds.

(See program, plan, list.)

adjectives

insane; mannered; verbal; constant; monotonous; wholesale; frequent; musical; maddening; fine; unmeaning; steady; endless; broken; emphatic; undulating; useless; decorative; injudicious; vague; tragic; idiotic; deadly; suasive; meaningless; diverting; explanatory; forceful.

verbs

clamor for—; demand—; endure—; influence—; justify—; permit—; request—; stifle —; suffer—; survive—; threaten—; —bores; —emphasizes; —impresses; —irritates; —prolongs; —recalls; —refreshes; —teaches; —tires; —wearies.

(See mention, recurrence.)

REPLACE (v)

adverbs

surreptitiously; effectively; effectually; faithfully; graciously; promptly; intelligently; skillfully.

(See repay, restore.)

REPLICA

verbs

commend—; compare—; criticize—; prepare —; produce—; —adheres to; —appears; —attracts; —condenses; —copies; —deceives; —duplicates; —follows; —recalls; —reproduces.

(See duplicate, copy.)

REPLY

adjectives

suitable; lackadaisical; unexpected; frank; modest; judicial; unembarrassed; shameless; monosyllabic; disrespectful; short; temperate; haughty; elaborate; silly; immediate; ungracious; good-humored; noncommittal; guarded; discouraging; cold; pettish; memorable; gracious; categorical; contemptuous; impatient; ready; biting; caustic; tart; scornful; unmoved; intelligent; inarticulate; incoherent; tactful; tremulous; humble; proper; audible; chaffing; austere; obvious; correct; negative; preoccupied; conclusive; stumbling; impromptu; sound; impertinent; garbled; distorted; satisfactory; politic; magnanimous; chilling; languid; impressive; idiotic; chary; pungent; consolatory; evasive; angry; emphatic; unanimous.

verbs

calculate—; contemplate—; demand—; deign—; elicit—; evoke—; mutter—; overhaul—; probe—; propose—; provoke—; rejoin—; —acknowledges; —affirms; —alleviates; —answers; —clarifies; —clears; —determines; —explains; —informs; —interrogates; —rebuts; —refutes; —satisfies; —solves.

(See answer, response, retort, repartee.)

REPLY (v)

adverbs

evasively; solemnly; tonelessly; affirmatively; crisply; bitingly; equivocally; impertinently; promptly; auspiciously; grimly; dolefully; defiantly; wistfully; mechanically; elusively; falteringly; gravely; archly; laboriously; hilariously; dubiously; incoherently; inexorably; tremulously; petulantly; casually; tensely; modestly; placidly; jocosely; listlessly; cautiously; musingly; dejectedly; reflectively; mordantly; haughtily; serenely; maliciously; decisively; acrimoniously; pensively; meekly; dryly; sententiously; laconically; pettishly; ambiguously; indulgently; monosyllabically; temperately; noncommittally; magnanimously; pungently; emphatically.

(See answer, respond.)

REPORT

adjectives

verbatim; exact; unbiased; unanimous; distant; illustrated; first-hand; stimulating; clear; understandable; supplementary; complete; unconfined; successive (pl); dependable; inflammatory; untruthful; precise; flattering; plausible; gratifying; preliminary; press; energetic; sly; insidious; formal; official; partial; detailed; inaccurate; dazzling; hearsay; critical; archeological; suppressed; statistical; disheartening; neat; reassuring; ardent; vague; alarming; typical; regular; aggregated; voluble; orderly; condensed; annual; authentic; snobbish; veracious; written; admirable; pestiferous; outspoken; hopeless; voluminous; sensational; elaborate; shocking; frightened; thundering; commercial; reverberating; varying; random; astounding; enthusiastic; exaggerated; published; confused; pretentious; stenographic; unwelcome; explicit.

verbs

allay—s; append to—; bungle—; challenge —; chronicle—s; circulate—; confirm—;

corroborate—; counteract—; deluge with —s; draw up—; echo—; evaluate—; fudge —; indorse—; pigeon-hole—; prepare—; qualify—; render—; scoff at—; shelve—; summarize—; transmit—; verify—; wind up —; —bears out; —bolsters; —discloses; — emanates from; —embodies; —persists; — recommends; —spreads.

(See fame, account, news, rumor, record.)

REPORT (v)
adverbs
faithfully; precisely; currently; alarmingly; capably; officially; adversely; duly; glumly; graciously; verbally; insidiously; formally; partially; critically; archeologically; statistically; reassuringly; vaguely; volubly; annually; authentically; veraciously; sensationally; reverberatingly; exaggeratedly; pretentiously; stenographically.

(See announce, describe.)

REPORTER
adjectives
rushing; mere; prying; realistic; inquisitive; disreputable; disgruntled; clever; skilled.

verbs
besiege by—s; hush up—s; loathe—s; muffle —s; stifle—s; —alludes to; —announces; —s beleaguer; —s descend upon; —disguises; —eavesdrops; —expresses; —fences; —hints; —imparts; —imposes; —interviews; —intimates; —libels; —mentions; — mobs; —prowls; —reserves; —reviews; — "scoops"; —slanders; —specifies; —tips off; —withholds.

(See journalist, detective, writer.)

REPORTING
adjectives
franker; alert; candid.

REPOSE
adjectives
soothing; calm; innocent; serene; undisturbed; sullen; delicious; charmed; noble; blissful; final; comforting; grave; irksome; profitless; chronic; supreme; mental; stolid; permanent; scornful; effeminate; statuesque; long-coveted; profound; peaceful; solemn; comparative; orbed; unreached; vile; languorous; dreamy; passionless; weak; healthful; everlasting; fathomless; equivocal; intellectual; infamous; exquisite; last; rheumatic; particular; spacious; exasperating;

deep; echoless; fitful; indolent; placid; dull; sweet; dignified; complete; stupid; prolonged; cultivated; studied; momentary; outward; grave-like; grim; stern; thoughtful; reason-wrought; voluptuous.

verbs
advocate—; disturb—; dwell in—; indulge in—; seek—; while away in—; —energizes; —frees; —lulls; —preserves; —refreshes; —relaxes; —relieves; —rests; —soothes; — stagnates; —stems; —vivifies.

(See composure, rest, sleep, quiet, peace.)

REPOSE (v)
adverbs
lazily; soothingly; calmly; serenely; sullenly; deliciously; effeminately; profoundly; passionlessly; rheumatically; placidly; momentarily; voluptuously.

(See rest, relax.)

REPOSEFUL
adverbs
pleasantly; sweetly; oddly; calmly; serenely; unusually; gratefully; duly; dully; prosaically; quietly; lazily; blissfully; deliciously; soothingly; somnolently; drowsily; dreamily; idly; languidly; listlessly; deliberately; heavily; silently; immovably; incredibly; unexpectedly; utterly; happily.

REPREHENSIBLE
adverbs
lamentably; undeniably; openly; flagrantly; particularly; unpardonably; admittedly; miserably; shamefully; wretchedly; curiously; unwarrantably; uncommonly; highly; utterly; exceptionally; gravely; indiscreetly; unconscionably; inordinately; terribly.

REPRESENT (v)
adverbs
copiously; faithfully; magnificently; initially; beneficently; allegorically; fantastically; diagrammatically; materially; adequately; speciously; personally; orally; substantially; symbolically; conventionally; fictitiously; ludicrously; realistically.

(See portray, depict.)

REPRESENTATION
adjectives
oral; adequate; easily-understood; hallucinatory; pasteboard; hearty; disproportionate; concrete; animated; distinct; substantial; graphic; definite; direct; diplomatic; count-

less (pl); urgent; decennial; striking; vigorous; symbolic; democratic; renewed; just; faithful; pictorial; mental; material; fraudulent; proportioned; august; mere; earnest; specious; tolerable; abstract; wild; conventional; mimic; dramatic; one-sided; untruthful; harmonious; factual; fictitious; softened; sensuous; ludicrous; natural; unfair; realistic; archaic.

verbs

carve—; comprehend—; deprive of—; dress up—; mold—; rehearse—; yield to—s; —alludes to; —betokens; —depicts; —describes; —designates; —enlightens; —illustrates; —indicates; —informs; —points out; —portrays; —signifies; —symbolizes; —typifies.
(See description, comedy, design, reproduction, art, portrayal, drama.)

REPRESENTATIVE

adjectives

dwarfed; local-minded; fitting; dazzling; mentionable; assembled (pl); accredited: prominent; cold; correct; tremulous; striking; exemplary; placement; shy; awkward; authorized; diplomatic; surviving; lineal; avowed; arrogant; cold-brained; brilliant; fraudulent; traveling.

verbs

accredit—; apportion—s; antagonize—; delegate—; interchange—s; obligate—; replace —; —bandies; —calls; —commutes; —introduces; —offers; —reciprocates; —redeems; —retaliates; —serves; —solicits; —supersedes; —supplants.
(See consul, delegate, agent, deputy.)

adverbs

typically; truly; fairly; justly; altogether; officially; authoritatively; adequately; satisfactorily; substantially; diplomatically; tolerably; unfairly; scarcely; hardly; entirely; accurately; concisely; legally; uncommonly; warrantably; specifically; appropriately; singularly; functionally; appointively.

REPRESS (v)

adverbs

sternly; tyrannically; stoically; impatiently; amiably; severely; dictatorially; dogmatically; rudely; ruthlessly; systematically.
(See restrain, suppress.)

REPRESSED

adverbs

cruelly; naturally; morbidly; sternly; severely; harshly; unduly; pitiably; successfully; immediately; barbarously; opportunely; promptly; effectively; pitiably.

REPRESSION

adjectives

prompt; impartial; intense; sublime; self; particular; sexual; severe; definite.

REPRIMAND

verbs

expose to—; inflict—; load with—s; protest —; resist—; submit to—; subject to—; taunt with—s; —accuses; —anathematizes; —annoys; —cavils; —condemns; —corrects; —deprecates; —disparages; —execrates; —lashes; —rebukes; —reproaches.
(See rebuke, blame, censure, reproach.)

REPRIMAND (v)

adverbs

rigorously; sternly; publicly; officially; severely; sharply; violently; paternally; judicially.
(See reproach, scold.)

REPRINT (v)

adverbs

popularly; widely; multitudinously; perpetually; extensively; accurately; legally; faithfully.
(See print, reproduce.)

REPRISAL

adjectives

prompt; legitimate; indiscriminate; fearful; legal; swift; deadly; unerring.

verbs

anticipate—; breast—; check—; deserve—; draw—; elicit—; face—; fear—; grapple with—; offer—; provoke—; return—; stifle —; suppress—; visit—upon; —caps; —climaxes; —confronts; —dismays; —exchanges; —strikes; —subdues.
(See retaliation, punishment, penalty.)

REPROACH

adjectives

sorrowful; violent; constant; continual; disgustful; subtle; unutterable; thick-tongued; serious; bitter; ingenuous; mute; passionate; galling; unjust; mild; smiling; dumb; tacit; mystic; selfish; fierce; self; mingled; undeserved; angry; generous.

verbs

attach—to; cast—upon; disfavor—; expose to—; fling—at; imply—; justify—; overwhelm with—; resist—; support—; warrant —; —blots; —corrects; —cuts; —disgraces; —implicates; —reflects; —slurs; —sullies; —upsets.

(See blame, dishonor, disgrace, censure, disapproval.)

REPROACH (v)

adverbs

passionately; bitterly; abusively; violently; sorrowfully; subtly; mutely; gallingly; tacitly; fiercely; undeservedly; ungenerously; selfishly.

(See reprimand, scold.)

REPROACHFUL

adverbs

mildly; gently; softly; harshly; cruelly; moderately; sternly; severely; unforgivingly; hatefully; atrociously; intolerably; openly; publicly; secretly; abusively; immoderately; unnecessarily; needlessly; violently; vehemently; loudly; vociferously; vengefully; vituperously; unfairly; brutally; offensively; terribly; inflexibly; outrageously; arrantly; unwarrantably; pitilessly; viciously; gravely.

REPROBATE

adjectives

thorough; degenerate; notorious; malicious; energetic; self-styled.

REPRODUCE (v)

adverbs

superbly; scrupulously; perfectly; voluntarily; plastically; authentically; quaintly; historically; adequately; slavishly; mechanically; painstakingly; accurately; elaborately.

(See imitate, portray.)

REPRODUCTION

adjectives

plastic; authentic; quaint; historic; incessant; adequate; slavish; mechanical; subsequent; painstaking; accurate; elaborate.

REPROOF

adjectives

tacit; stinging; distinct; sour.

REPROVE (v)

adverbs

acridly; smartly; harshly; sternly; vigorously; bitterly; stingingly; tacitly; mutely; violently; verbally; expressly; explicitly; furiously; spiritedly.

(See reprimand, reproach.)

REPTILE

adjectives

venomous; hideous; characteristic; scaly; croaking; fishy; abhorrent; snakish; ugly; useful; groveling.

verbs

—coils; —consists; —contorts; —crushes; — encircles; —entwines; —glides; —lashes; —lies in wait; —meanders; —poisons; — slithers; —springs; —squeezes; —squirms; —strains; —strikes; —swirls; —swishes; — tightens; —twists; —undulates; —warns; — wounds; —writhes.

(See crocodile, alligator, lizard, snake.)

REPUBLIC

adjectives

model; visionary; peaceful; progressive; long-lived; rebellious; well-ordered; popular.

verbs

administer—; approve—; betray—; control —; disrupt—; dominate—; establish—; form—; govern—; organize—; override—; preserve—; preside over—; revolt against —; rule—; sway—; tolerate—; undermine —; wreck—; —relaxes; —triumphs.

(See country, democracy, government, state.)

REPUDIATE (v)

adverbs

instinctively; utterly; wholly; violently; faithlessly; unreservedly; flatly; ultimately.

(See reject, renounce.)

REPUGNANCE

adjectives

unforeseen; loathing; secret; invincible; sentimental; horrible; undefinable; strong; real; deep-seated.

verbs

allay—; arouse—; assuage—; avoid—; bear —; conceive—; dispel—; entertain—; excite —; feign—; incur—; mitigate—; mollify—;

overwhelm—; recoil from—; withdraw in
—; —estranges; —intrudes; —palls; —riles
(colloq.); —shocks.

(See disgust, dislike, opposition, antipathy,
inconsistency, aversion.)

REPULSE

adjectives

virtual; bloody; severe; brisk; complete.

verbs

encounter—; —abduces; —chases; —dashes;
—dispels; —hurtles; —impedes; —impinges; —jerks; —jogs; —prods; —pushes;
—resounds; —slaps; —spurs on.

(See defeat, refusal, rebuff, denial.)

REPULSE (v)

adverbs

briskly; stoutly; stalwartly; successfully;
sharply; readily; unceremoniously; severely;
violently.

(See repel, reject.)

REPULSION

adjectives

reciprocal; lively; utter; mutual; instinctive; deadly; bitter; indescribable; singular;
remarkable.

REPUTATION

adjectives

freshest; popular; rising; senseless; local;
unassailable; well-earned; murdered; magnificent; swollen; formidable; subverted;
enviable; commonplace; civic; evanescent;
posthumous; untarnished; immature; artistic; unblemished; literary; mushroom; exceptional; wounded; established; merited;
spotless; exaggerated; reverend; enduring;
undue; skittish; slender; bubble; unquestioned; professional; priceless; outstanding;
terrible; pious; vile; tender; savory; damaged; fabulous; poetic; lamentable.

verbs

achieve—; acquire—; belie—; blacken—;
build—; carve—; destroy—; enhance—; enjoy—; establish—; injure—; jeopardize—;
justify—; mar—; mature—; merit—; outlive—; prostitute—; protect—; rival—; sacrifice—; save—; stake—on; —blooms; —
languishes; —precedes; —precludes; —
spreads; —swells; —withers.

(See fame, name, character, distinction,
honor, notoriety, glory.)

REPUTE

adjectives

grave; ill; considerable; honorable; doubtful; prominent; local; scientific; charitable;
provincial; high.

REQUEST

adjectives

conflicting; unusual; continual; commonplace; inopportune; dying; special; urgent;
humble; whispered; emphatic; unreasonable; unconsidered; universal; pointed.

verbs

accede to—; acquiesce in—; assail with—s;
bombard with—s; comply with—; convey—;
dodge—; grant—; gratify—; heed—; justify—; meet—; pester with—s; repeat—;
swamp with—s; urge—.

(See desire, entreaty, application, appeal,
demand.)

REQUEST (v)

adverbs

urgently; haughtily; earnestly; fawningly;
emphatically; reluctantly; graciously; ultimately; insistently; particularly; reasonably; humbly; importunately.

(See ask, beg, entreat.)

REQUIRE (v)

adverbs

passionately; urgently; perpetually; vitally;
imperatively; strictly; reasonably; ethically;
personally; physically; medically; aesthetically.

(See exact, want, demand.)

REQUIRED

adverbs

legally; inescapably; naturally; technically;
inexorably; peremptorily; recently; authoritatively; officially; arbitrarily; tyrannically; dogmatically; reasonably; rigorously;
rigidly; absolutely; socially; conventionally;
prescriptively; lawfully; openly; duly; constitutionally; decently; traditionally.

REQUIREMENTS

adjectives

postnatal; eminent; classic; reasonable; relative; ethical; basic; collective; exacting;
hygienic; traditional; rigorous; technical;
strictest; human; personnel; specific; professional; complex; certain; maximum; minimum; residential; absolute; physical; rhythmic; aesthetic; sanitary; imperative.

verbs

check—; comply with—; condemn—; dispense with—; draw up—; fulfill—; furnish —; justify—; lack—; meet—; necessitate—; occasion—; offer—; overlook—; point out —; produce—; raise—; remove—; respect —; supply—; tabulate—; violate—; —apply to; —call for; —demand; —impede.

(See demand, injunction, necessity.)

REQUISITE

adjectives

regular; prime; definite; essential; indispensable.

REQUITAL

adjectives

humble; ungenerous; unworthy; poor; scant; fair; satisfactory.

RESCUE

verbs

aid in—; dash to—; deplore—; clog—; cumber—; expedite—; hamper—; hasten—; hinder—; impede—; interrupt—; obstruct—; perform—; pray for—; retard—; speed—; —delivers; —discommodes; —embarrasses; —preserves; —relieves; —saves.

(See deliverance, release.)

RESCUE (v)

adverbs

nobly; heroically; triumphantly; gallantly; stalwartly; rashly; boldly; courageously.

(See save, release.)

RESEARCH

adjectives

vigilant; philosophical; indefatigable; antiquarian; abstract; hydrological; subsequent; perpetual; relentless; celestial; original; brilliant; infinite; useless; enthusiastic; conscientious; scientific; extensive; microscopical; commercial; philological; bold; ingenious; effective; exhaustive; photographic; valuable; painstaking; patient; profound; deliberate; sociological; mysterious; laborious; masterly; comprehensive; stellar; ceaseless; critical; historical; malignant; archaeological; tireless; multitudinous (pl); psychoanalytic; obscure; profitable.

verbs

commence—; conduct—; direct—; engage in —; enter upon—; instigate—; launch—; maintain—; promote—; publish—; stimulate —; —analyzes; —awakens; —contributes; —culminates in; —determines; —discloses; —enlightens; —enriches; —exposes; —explores; —fathoms; —ferrets out; —imparts; —peers; —reveals.

(See inquiry, investigation, inquisition, study.)

RESEMBLANCE

adjectives

intricate; mimetic; enchanted; successful; extraordinary; fancied; natural; striking; faraway; vague; distant; self-evident; divine; partial; mysterious; close; protective; inaccurate; defensive; aggressive; capital; inexplicable; recognizable; unexpected; startling.

verbs

accentuate—; approximate—; assimilate—; bear—; detect—; discern—; evoke—; kindle —; savor of—; sharpen—; —amazes; —astounds; —disturbs; —moves; —shocks; —smites; —stirs; —strikes.

(See similarity, identity.)

RESEMBLE (v)

adverbs

strikingly; curiously; precisely; particularly; spectacularly; adequately; protectively; recognizably; startlingly; mysteriously; markedly; superficially.

(See favor.)

RESENT (v)

adverbs

forcibly; morbidly; vehemently; bitterly; subconsciously; indignantly; sternly; passionately; humorously; secretly; mutely; violently; keenly; fiercely; murderously; disdainfully; sullenly.

(See disapprove, begrudge.)

RESENTFUL

adverbs

angrily; dangerously; bitterly; passionately; sullenly; bluntly; sadly; cruelly; venomously; maliciously; vengefully; acrimoniously; violently; vociferously; strangely; unaccountably; unreasonably; insatiably; stubbornly; implacably; unappeasably; openly; secretly; fantastically; obviously; manifestly; evidently; furiously; irascibly; truculently; uncommonly; ominously; disastrously; permanently.

RESENTMENT

adjectives

terrible; increasing; admiring; individual; implacable; obstinate; dull; furious; keen; angry; impulsive; blind; half-sore; animal; fierce; intense; murderous; incipient; vigorous; sturdy; hot; disdainful; momentary; jealous; brooding; bitter; impotent; sagged; hasty; spirited; sullen; hard; viperish; astonished; impatient; additional; passionate; protecting; personal; desperate; general; generous; just; fancied.

verbs

arouse—; call forth—; cherish—; display—; engender—; evoke—; excite—; exhibit—; fill with—; flood with—; kindle—; reflect with—; shake off—; smother—; stir up—; —flares; —is born; —melts; —mounts; —wells; —yields to.

(See grudge, ill-will, anger, grievance.)

RESERVATION

adjectives

mental; explicit; express; common-sense; forest; experimental; heedful; definite; specific.

RESERVE

adjectives

scholarly; cash; considerable; substantial; emotional; chaste; appreciable; haughty; preliminary; habitual; dignified; sullen; mistrustful; maidenly; stately; sorrowful; stern; cold; unsympathizing; timberland; stubborn; approaching; singular; natural; compulsory; lawful; precious; womanly; ungenerous; freezing; naive; analytical; mysterious; alkaline; impenetrable; defective; delicate; mutual; watchful; critical.

verbs

break down—; deplete—; discard—; emerge from—; ignore—; inspire—; intensify—; penetrate—; pierce—; prick—; retain—; —cloaks; —conceals; —covers; —masks; —melts; —mystifies; —piques; —protects; —secludes.

(See aloofness, modesty, reticence, restraint, shyness, diffidence, fund.)

RESERVE (v)

adverbs

expressly; shrewdly; delicately; covetously; exclusively; faithfully.

(See retain, restrain.)

RESERVED

adverbs

quietly; demurely; sedately; characteristically; habitually; naturally; inherently; discreetly; strategically; prudently; wisely; gravely; judicially; arrogantly; proudly; shyly; bashfully; unduly; unfortunately; extremely; strangely; curiously; oddly; placidly; serenely; coyly; timidly; mysteriously; extraordinarily; sensibly; vexatiously.

RESERVOIR

adjectives

tapering; immense; ducal; copious; sheltered; inexhaustible.

verbs

construct—; dam—; exhaust—; flow from —; form—; inspect—; replenish—; tax—; —accumulates; —collects; —preserves; —reserves; —stores; —yields.

(See supply, tank.)

RESIDENCE

adjectives

episcopal; commodious; costly; palatial; comfortable; handsome; peculiar; official; ungarnished; stately; enlarged; wretched; permanent; seasonal; picturesque; temporary; monastic; ambitious; baronial; paternal; suitable; prolonged; sumptuous; modest.

verbs

establish—; frequent—; guard—; lack—; maintain—; neglect—; occupy—; regulate —; secure—; take up—; view—; invite to—.

(See home, establishment, mansion, dwelling.)

RESIDENT

adjectives

influential; distinguished; valued; temporary; permanent.

RESIDENTIAL

adverbs

pleasantly; strictly; expensively; exclusively; desirably; aristocratically; swankily; modestly; primarily; wholly; assuredly; delightfully; scrupulously; unmistakably; quietly; peacefully; agreeably.

RESIDUE

adjectives

harmful; visible; sweetest; solid; miserable; final; greasy; gummy; soapy; mournful.

verbs
bag—; consume—; cherish—; conceal—; discard—; gather—; heap—; "junk"—; leave—; offer—; proffer—; retain—; salvage—; scatter—; scrap—; store—; utilize —; value—; —disperses; —survives.
(See ashes, excess, cinders, remnant.)

RESIGN (*v*)
adverbs
reluctantly; voluntarily; nominally; officially; cheerfully; piously; fatalistically; irrevocably; philosophically; wearily.
(See abdicate, withdraw.)

RESIGNATION
adjectives
fatalistic; grim; virtual; dreamy; melancholy; serene; unsurprised; meek; patient; irrevocable; perverted; conscious; apparent; unwilling; quiet; infinite; philosophical; appalling; angelical; unhappy; spiritless; youthful; sorrowful; perfect; pathetic; tacit; passive; somber; gentle; mournful; despondent; voluntary; wearied; gloomy.

verbs
announce—; anticipate—; bewail—; compel —; decline—; deplore—; grant—; lament —; offer—; order—; present—; regret—; tender—; weigh—; —alters; —confuses; — disappoints; —disconcerts; —humbles; — mortifies.
(See surrender, retirement.)

RESIGNED
adverbs
philosophically; passively; quietly; scarcely; hardly; apathetically; resolutely; grimly; meekly; apparently; perfectly; shamelessly; appallingly; incredibly; eventually; obviously; strangely; humbly; pathetically; obediently; submissively; pliantly; weakly; calmly; imperturbably; stolidly; stupidly.

RESILIENT
adverbs
satisfactorily; unusually; highly; extraordinarily; smoothly; appreciably; pleasantly; desirably; adequately; extremely; conveniently; surprisingly; suitably; buoyantly; advantageously; uncommonly.

RESIST (*v*)
adverbs
stubbornly; vigorously; skillfully; dexterously; passively; blusteringly; modestly; stern-ly; heroically; effectively; violently; stoutly; physically; insurmountably; feebly; resolutely.
(See oppose, withstand.)

RESISTANCE
adjectives
rust; permanent; unexpected; forcible; popular; stern; unyielding; strenuous; heroic; prompt; amazing; pretended; successful; prolonged; stubborn; indignant; glorious; increased; warlike; crushed; desperate; enfeebled; stout; substantial; sad; perceiving; vague; militant; fierce; faint; humble; bold; incredulous; keener; tenacious; ineffectual; organized; gladiatorial; countervailing; rationalized; unlawful; unconscious; determined; patriotic; creditable; passive; severest; awed; earnest; coy; physical; meditating; stagnated; obstinate; rugged; hopeless; insurmountable; armed; feeble; resolute; vain; appreciable; angry.

verbs
acquire—; batter down—; break down—; build—; compensate for—; crush—; deplete —; determine—; encounter—; exercise—; harden for—; increase—; lower—; meet with—; prolong—; rationalize—; reduce—; stiffen—; weaken—; —collapses; —cracks; —lessens; —melts away.
(See antagonism, strength, opposition, hostility.)

RESOLUTE
adverbs
courageously; doggedly; stubbornly; intrepidly; gallantly; staunchly; persistently; immovably; steadily; unwaveringly; stoutly; dauntlessly; obstinately; cruelly; bitterly; determinedly; tragically; pluckily; tenaciously; indomitably; sadly; fanatically; dogmatically; ungenerously; inexorably; relentlessly; admirably; commendably; earnestly; zealously; enthusiastically; confidently; heroically; amazingly; remarkably; terribly.

RESOLUTION
adjectives
constitutional; settled; defiant; dogged; sensible; inflexible; virtuous; submissive; deliberate; jaunty; unanimous; daring; restless; generous; thoughtful; robust; gloomy; stern; tremendous; determined; austere; firm; immense; rash; obituary; indomitable; undaunted; desperate; philosophical; bold; early; stubborn; energetic; impulsive;

concurrent; invincible; passionate; dangerous; joint; vigorous; loyal; essential; satisfactory; freighted; fierce; unalterable; chivalrous; sacred; evanescent; memorable; momentous; gathering; congressional; pious; irrevocable; wise; courageous; godly; determined; heroic; imprudent; epic; unchangeable; queer; decisive.

verbs
abandon—; acclaim—; adhere to—; adopt —; applaud—; bolster—; convey—; crystalize into—; draft—; formulate—; fortify—; introduce—; prime with—s; shake—; stiffen —; uphold—; weaken—; —s pour in; —s strengthen.
(See decision, determination, bill, law.)

RESOLVE
adjectives
absolute; strained; secret; deliberate; fearless; rash; added; stern; desperate; virtuous; firm; deeper; mental; pertinacious; iron; concluding; excellent; courageous; calm; dominant; high; wise; terrible; unswerving; dauntless; mortified; inflexible; feeble-framed.

RESOLVE (v)
adverbs
ultimately; prudently; mentally; rationally; solemnly; privately; unanimously; stubbornly; inflexibly; deliberately; impulsively; fiercely; chivalrously; momentously; imprudently.
(See determine, dissolve.)

RESONANT
adverbs
pleasantly; deeply; unusually; harmoniously; surprisingly; marvellously; admirably; distinctly; hollowly; agreeably; strikingly; peculiarly; curiously; remarkably.

RESORT
adjectives
strict; brilliant; cold; lowest; fair; pleasure; attractive; little; embryonic; mountain; seasonal; favorite; fashionable; expanding; imposing, dissolute; habitual; desperate; summer; mundane; complete; seashore; family; self-contained; beach; delightful; best-loved; premier; world-famous; wonderful.

verbs
crowd—; fill—; frequent—; infest—; retire to—; repair to—; swamp—s; —advertises; —appeals; —attracts; —consoles; —delights; —eases; —offers; —refreshes; —strengthens.
(See hotel, refuge.)

RESOUND (v)
adverbs
thunderingly; discordantly; tremendously; dreadfully; awesomely; thunderously; reverberatingly.
(See peal, reverberate.)

RESOURCEFUL
adverbs
ingeniously; amazingly; skilfully; conveniently; fortunately; luckily; unusually; miraculously; incredibly; inventively; cleverly; adroitly; expediently; expertly; handily; adaptably; deftly; intelligently; felicitously; happily; particularly; manifestly; unfailingly; naturally; inimitably.

RESOURCES
adjectives
natural; decorative; perpetual; ever-present; fertile; meager; spiritual; financial; utmost; therapeutic; magnificent; manifold; productive; unfailing; mineral; artistic; boundless; reasonable; enormous; gigantic; technical; infallible; visual; limited; despairing; legitimate; exhausted; immense; physical; cyclopedic; immeasurable; temporal; material; healing; military; diplomatic; delightful; sole; insignificant; colossal; extensive; vast; tremendous; dramatic; strategic; privileged; unfailing; endless; slender; pecuniary; ready; adequate; scanty; prodigious.

verbs
assemble—; augment—; cast upon—; concentrate—; cultivate—; deplete—; develop —; employ—; encourage—; exhaust—; expend—; fortify—; impair—; liquidate—; mobilize—; paralyze—; squander—; strain —; tap—; tax—.
(See finances, assets, property, means.)

RESPECT
adjectives
exalted; regretful; greatest; idolatrous; reverential; utmost; impassive; continued; affectionate; proper; astonished; wholesome; compassionate; graceful; self; dignified; profound; temporal; haughty; deferential; pitying; punctilious; merited; apologetic;

indignant; unfeigned; listening; mutual; essential; delicate; tender; unqualified; grudging; devout; reluctant; important; high; lasting; credulous; weak; infinite; indescribable; extorted; extreme; considerate; habitual; corresponding; scant; diminished; genuine; remarkable; enormous; undefinable; unbounded; ambiguous; regretful; increased; expensive; constant; dutiful; particular; astonishing; popular; thoughtful; pusillanimous; diffident; marked.

verbs
broaden into—; command—; compel—; deepen—; deserve—; draw—; earn—; engender—; entitle to—; forfeit—; heighten —; impair—; inspire—; insure—; merit—; pay—s; preserve—; reflect—; retain—; train in—; violate—; win—.
(See esteem, deference, honor, homage, admiration, respectability.)

RESPECT (v)
adverbs
scrupulously; sympathetically; intuitively; universally; deferentially; punctiliously; unfeignedly; mutually; reluctantly; genuinely; unboundedly; dutifully; wholesomely; markedly; affectionately.
(See revere, esteem.)

RESPECTABILITY
adjectives
decent; indisputable; bourgeois; unshadowed; worldly; irreproachable; unimpeachable; unblemished; private; undeniable; obvious; dignified; spotless; triumphant; suburban; utilitarian.

verbs
acquire—; assume—; claim—; cleave to—; confer—; crown with—; don—; emulate—; feign—; gain—; preserve—; reflect—; renounce—; sacrifice—; shed—; wear—; — dignifies; —distinguishes; —elevates; — flourishes; —narrows; —restricts; —stifles.
(See respect.)

RESPECTABLE
adverbs
highly; eminently; decently; notably; unimpeachably; undeniably; obviously; admirably; extremely; admittedly; uncommonly; estimably; oppressively; painfully; ostentatiously; self-righteously; flauntingly; indisputably; scarcely; supposedly; pleasantly; harmlessly.

RESPECTFUL
adverbs
deferentially; ingratiatingly; servilely; slavishly; enthusiastically; affectionately; genuinely; sincerely; devotedly; devoutly; piously; reverently; graciously; gravely; flatteringly; amiably; courteously; politely; attentively; earnestly; ardently; nonchalantly; casually; significantly; solemnly; filially; dutifully; ardently; officiously; diplomatically; subserviently; gracefully; pleasantly; agreeably; hospitably; exceedingly; chivalrously; significantly; overwhelmingly; habitually.

RESPIRATION
adjectives
momentary; diminished; violent; labored; artificial.

verbs
clog—; disorder—; embarrass—; force—; govern—; heighten—; impede—; increase —; involve—; labor—; persevere with—; record—; stimulate—; sustain—.
(See breath, breathing.)

RESPITE
verbs
appeal for—; consume—; cut short—; demand—; enjoy—; grant—; seek—; spend —; —arrests; —delays; —elapses; —interrupts; —intervenes; —overjoys; —refreshes; —rescues; —stems; —tides over.
(See delay, rest, suspension, pause.)

RESPOND (v)
adverbs
royally; affably; felicitously; brilliantly; generously; curtly; brusquely; pertly; acridly; sarcastically; reluctantly; enigmatically; passionately; imperturbably; grimly; nervously; enthusiastically; patriotically; gallantly; genially; humorously; suitably; affectionately; ambiguously; felicitously; crabbedly; boisterously; sententiously; tardily.
(See reply, answer.)

RESPONSE
adjectives
unpalatable; affectionate; eager; astounding; loving; blessed; unfavorable; ready; gloomy; generous; cordial; patriotic; emotional; appropriate; feminine; immediate; popular; copious; instinctive; evident; oracular; verbal; ambiguous; sympathetic;

characteristic; hearty; felicitous; instantaneous; beauteous; tremendous; typical; accurate; crabbed; calm; quick; liquid; untimely; boisterous; remote; passive; enthusiastic; shallow; brutal; joint; sententious; rough.

verbs

avert—; awaken—; bark—; bolster—; call forth—; convey—; correlate—s; determine —; elicit—; evoke—; force—; gain—; guard—; hail—; invite—; level—at; mumble—; mutter—; provoke—; question—; quicken—; restrain—; welcome—; —dismays; —encourages; —gladdens; —heightens; —lessens.

(See answer, echo.)

RESPONSIBILITY

adjectives

executive; unending; fearful; pecuniary; colossal; immense; sacred; dubious; painful; divided; individual; incidental; administrative; gravest; moral; serious; dreadful; direct; frightful; tremendous; numerous (pl); weighty; corresponding.

verbs

absolve from—; awaken to—; assume—; bear—; cast off—; charge with—; confer—; deviate from—; delegate—; discard—; disregard—; dodge—; dread—; entail—; evade—; expand—; face—; impose—; incur—; inherit—; involve—; lighten—; meet—; obviate—; overburden with—; realize—; relieve of—; saddle with—; shield from—; shift—; shirk—; shoulder —; shrink from—; shy away from—; tackle—; undertake—; —devolves upon; —exacts; —presses; —reposes in; —rests on.

(See duty, charge.)

RESPONSIBLE

adverbs

admittedly; personally; individually; fearfully; unfortunately; entirely; directly; criminally; legally; accidently; voluntarily; peculiarly; indisputably; terribly; undoubtedly; officially; allegedly; indirectly; certainly; partially; reliably; sincerely; heavily; altogether; perfectly; safely; gravely; seriously; unhappily; completely; tragically; frightly; tremendously; naturally; incidentally; temporarily; permanently; momentarily; duly; morally; financially; deeply; carefully; wholly.

REST

adjectives

ecstatic; listless; ignoble; needful; saintly; unutterable; heavy-laden; comfortable; peaceful; common; prolonged; life-preserving; spacious; everlasting; fitting; unadulterated; grave; wholesome; predestined; eternal; tumultuous; sullen; gracious; mental; refreshing; frequent; happy; placid; noontide; recumbent; interminable; absolute; perpetual; balmy; breathless; comparative; saintly.

verbs

abstain from—; advocate—; afford—; deserve—; desist from—; enjoin—; enjoy—; fold in—; refrain from—; terminate—; —comforts; —delays; —eases; —invigorates; —refreshes; —rejuvenates; —relaxes; —relieves; —renews; —slackens; —soothes; —stagnates; —unburdens.

(See delay, pause, respite, sleep.)

REST (*v*)

adverbs

ultimately; unsoundly; implicitly; perpetually; philosophically; impassively; ostentatiously; placidly; serenely; firmly; securely; listlessly; eternally; interminably.

(See relax, stop, repose.)

RESTAURANT

adjectives

celebrated; exclusive; world-famous; exotic; modest; open-air; low-ceilinged; clattering; bustling; unpretentious; dingy; little; lighted; gay; bright; modern; excellent; glamorous; diverting; exciting; fine; distinctive; air-cooled; moderate; colorful; fashionable; renowned.

verbs

inspect—; license—; rig up—; —advertises; —appeals; —attracts; —caters to; —delights; —employs; —patronizes; —plans; —pleases; —prepares; —offers; —solicits; —specializes.

(See hotel, tavern, inn.)

RESTFUL

adverbs

quietly; pleasantly; agreeably; beautifully; unusually; lazily; moderately; comparatively; entirely; wholly; extremely; singularly; curiously; peculiarly; incomparably; unspeakably; gratefully; strangely; simply; irresponsibly; unutterably; refreshingly; ineffably; inexpressibly; unbelievably; easily; invitingly; irresistibly; dreamily; drowsily; safely; miraculously; marvelously; soporiferously.

RESTITUTION
adjectives
quantitative; hopeless; spiritual; complete.

RESTIVE
adverbs
strangely; oddly; unmanageably; naturally; hopelessly; incurably; pathetically; obstinately; constantly; pitiably; understandably; helplessly; painfully; impatiently; nervously; feverishly; fractiously; reluctantly; openly; visibly; unconcealably; undisguisedly; unhappily; wretchedly; extraordinarily.

RESTLESS
adverbs
noticeably; visibly; hopelessly; actively; energetically; painfully; undisguisedly; ostentatiously; impolitely; inattentively; feverishly; nervously; heedlessly; strangely; curiously; significantly; oddly; unpleasantly; disagreeably; sullenly; unhappily; impatiently; physically; inordinately; extraordinarily; inexplicably; unaccountably; unreasonably; seriously; alarmingly; dangerously; irritably; vexatiously; anxiously; uncomfortably; disquietingly; distressingly; disturbingly.

RESTLESSNESS
adjectives
morbid; incessant; fevered; undulating; covert; pallid; inexplicable; repining; abrupt; unsteady; mercurial; infinite; ragged.

verbs
allay—; appease—; breed—; brook—; calm —; endure—; foment—; master—; overcome—; repress—; suffer—; toss in—; undergo—; yield to—; —chafes; —distresses; —fumes; —grips; —pains; —rages; —tears; —torments.
(See impatience, agitation, excitement, delirium, uneasiness, discontent.)

RESTORATION
adjectives
joyful; tranquil; refreshing; prompt; speedy; cleansing.

verbs
authorize—; direct—; discuss—; inspire—;

lament—; order—; plead for—; repel—; resist—; sanction—; —appeases; —converts; —corrects; —enhances; —humbles; —improves; —pacifies; —repairs.
(See revival, reconstruction.)

RESTORATIVE
adverbs
pleasantly; effectively; successfully; usually; safely; definitely; distinctly; notably; prescriptively; supposedly; agreeably; dependably; reliably; actively; powerfully; adequately; satisfactorily; remarkably; highly.

RESTORE (v)
adverbs
accurately; unquestionably; ultimately; genuinely; miraculously; subsequently; skillfully; dexterously; faithfully; medically; speedily; promptly.
(See repair, renew.)

RESTRAIN (v)
adverbs
vigorously; voluntarily; gently; firmly; forcibly; narrowly; unreasonably; judiciously; legally; lawfully; tyrannically; artificially; irksomely; rigidly; vexatiously; oppressively; benevolently; commercially.
(See repress, suppress.)

RESTRAINED
adverbs
cautiously; discreetly; prudently; warily; austerely; patiently; judicially; wisely; carefully; politely; courteously; absurdly; unduly; stiffly; cruelly; determinedly; deliberately; resolutely; significantly; unusually; habitually; ominously; portentously; extraordinarily; strangely; singularly; oddly; unaccountably.

RESTRAINT
adjectives
parental; irksome; conventional; apparent; moral; strange; needful; artistic; uncommon; dignified; perceptible; strict; noble; outrageous; necessary; comparative; intense; rigid; practiced; wearisome; dry; grim; compelled; severe; professional; heroic; determined; habitual.

verbs
burst—; compel—; deplore—; dispel—; enforce—; exercise—; forge—; impose—; insist upon—; loosen—; necessitate—; relax

1001

—; require—; resist—; throw off—; —binds; —burdens; —checks; —controls; —curbs; —despairs; —gags; —intensifies; —melts.

(See constraint, embargo, denial, inhibition, limitation.)

RESTRICT (v)
adverbs
parentally; irksomely; grimly; rigidly; severely; selfishly; ascetically; maddeningly; pettishly.

(See restrain, limit.)

RESTRICTIONS
adjectives
commercial; narrow; arbitrary; quantitative; impassable; oppressive; benevolent; diet; unreasonable; sharp; judicious; enforced; vexatious; regulatory; rigid; irksome; artificial; tyrannical.

verbs
abolish—; advocate—; disregard—; establish—; impose—; lift—; maintain—; subject to—; surmount—; throw off—; tighten —; yield to—; —ban; —chafe; —check; —destroy; —doom; —embrace; —forbid; —hedge in; —inhibit; —limit; —prohibit; —restrain; —stifle.

(See limits, inhibition, restraint, limitations.)

RESULT
adjectives
historical; admirable; indecisive; promising; exquisite; barren; declared; discouraging; magnificent; half-starving; pernicious; tangible; observed; ripe; immediate; ultimate; substantial; gratifying; disastrous; outstanding; intractable; astounding; brilliant; amazing; dazzling; astonishing; consistent; momentous; pertinent; involuntary; deducible; decorative; splendid; detrimental; creditable; bewildering; positive; triumphant; natural; unfailing; pecuniary; moral; estimated; salubrious; winning; direct; beneficial; effective; calculated; appreciable; proportional; invariable; tangible; vociferated; hilarious; multitudinous (pl); casual; primary; encouraging; unobserved; crowning; fatal; necessary; naked; tardy; advantageous; lasting; honest; ambrosian; excellent; revealing; satisfactory; successful; inevitable; unanticipated; quantitative; accomplishing; speculative; unbelievable; pitiful; conclusive; startling; re-

markable; wonderful; abundant; extraordinary; profitable; therapeutic; agreeable; notable; satisfactory; desirable; intelligible; practical; confusing; fine; disappointing; outward; sifted; unquestionable; scientific; identical; valuable; accurate; infallible; marvelous; capital; auspicious; typical; startling; memorable; obvious; competent; educative; sweeping; surprising; rapid; partial; ethereal; expectable; living; prosperous; extreme; salutary; established; fruitful; equivocal; riotous; happy; comic; deferred; important; verified; feverish; exhausting; logical; gradual; factitious; disheartening; contradictory; traceable; ludicrous; demoralizing; delightful; damaging; chastening; beneficent; valid; sentimental; required; secondary; unreliable; compromising; unified; legitimate; stupendous; deplorable; fearful; net.

verbs
accept—; accomplish—; achieve—; anticipate—; assay—; attain—; cap—; challenge —; claim—; confirm—; decry—; discredit —; embody—; envisage—; evaluate—; falsify—; forecast—; garner—s; predict—; sum up—s; tally—s; trace—s; visualize—; yield—s; —s accrue; —s attend; —s justify.

(See consequence, effect, issue, outcome.)

RESULT (v)
adverbs
fatally; invariably; inevitably; appreciably; ludicrously; damagingly; demoralizingly; legitimately; deplorably; astonishingly; proportionally; infallibly.

(See terminate, end.)

RESUME (v)
adverbs
reluctantly; haughtily; diligently; placidly; traditionally; complacently; cheerily; voluntarily; uncomplainingly; blandly; customarily.

(See begin, start.)

RESURRECTION
adjectives
artificial; joyful; queer; summer; spiritual.

verbs
anticipate—; arrange for—; escape—; evade—; inspire—; mold—; plan—; prom-

ise—; seek—; shape—; stay—; suggest—; support—; warn of—; —restores; —threatens.

(See renaissance, restoration, revival.),

RETAIN (v)

adverbs

invariably; indefinitely; selfishly; voluptuously; basely; gloriously; righteously.

(See hold, keep, reserve.)

RETAINER

adjectives

taciturn; gorgeous; confidential; faithful; marshaled.

verbs

beckon—; chastise—; despatch—; discharge —; flout—; order—; recommend—; reprove —; suffer—; —accompanies; —aids; —arranges; —attends; —betrays; —confronts; —eases; —endures; —refers; —serves.

(See following, servant, matron.)

RETALIATE (v)

adverbs

revengefully; viciously; vindictively; pitilessly; treacherously; poisonously; hatefully; despicably; violently; insidiously; traitorously.

(See repay, avenge.)

RETALIATION

adjectives

pitiless; provoking; youthful; treacherous; angry.

verbs

avert—; draw—; grapple with—; ignore —; incur—; invite—; offer—; overlook—; smother—; threaten with—; withstand—; —avenges; —harms; —inflames; —kicks; — pierces; —rankles; —repulses; —revenges; —stems; —stings.

(See punishment, revenge, discipline, penalty.)

RETARD (v)

adverbs

mechanically; deliberately; inevitably; cautiously; expediently; automatically.

(See hinder, obstruct.)

RETENTION

adjectives

undue; stubborn; corresponding; enforced.

RETENTIVE

adverbs

highly; unusually; phenomenally; miraculously; extraordinarily; marvelously; astonishingly; amazingly; unbelievably; incredibly; conveniently; curiously; peculiarly; singularly; particularly; incomparably.

RETICENCE

adjectives

noble; diplomatic; exaggerated; introspective; masterly; strict; womanly; haughty; dignified; excessive; dogged; cautious; judicious.

verbs

couch in—; discard—; lapse into—; penetrate—; pierce—; shroud in—; sink into—; —blinds; —cloaks; —conceals; —curtains; —envelops; —masks; —mystifies; —perplexes; —puzzles; —screens; —veils; —withholds.

(See modesty, reserve, aloofness.)

RETICENT

adverbs

austerely; needlessly; absurdly; naturally; habitually; unnecessarily; highly; curiously; unreasonably; sensibly; singularly; oddly; peculiarly; unduly; taciturnly; foolishly; disagreeably; noticeably; unfortunately.

RETINUE

adjectives

glittering; brilliant; imperial; numerous (pl); copious; radiant; perilous.

RETIRE (v)

adverbs

timidly; cautiously; snobbishly; unwillingly; meekly; modestly; deferentially; shamefacedly; noiselessly; discreetly; decently; voluntarily; precipitately.

(See retreat, withdraw.)

RETIREMENT

adjectives

voluntary; imminent; short; quiet; suspicious; comparative; peaceful; secular; close; unobtrusive; romantic; precipitate; sweet; monastic; ostentatious; beloved; temporary.

verbs

creep into—; draw into—; drive into—; emerge from—; forego—; hasten—; hold in —; loathe—; remain in—; resist—; shame into—; shut into—; sink into—; slate for —; surrender to—; —abjures; —bores; — cuts off; —deprives; —stagnates.

(See isolation, resignation, retreat, seclusion.)

RETIRING

adverbs

unusually; shyly; timidly; studiously; habitually; naturally; diffidently; unsocially; inhospitably; reticently; taciturnly; forbiddingly.

RETORT

adjectives

gruff; famous; skillful; impulsive; scornful; spirited; readiest; instant; severest; stinging.

verbs

draw—; fire—; parry—; provoke—; —acknowledges; —appeases; —clinches; —confutes; —crushes; —defeats; —determines; —explains; —irks; —leaps to one's lips; — parries; —rebuts; —solves; —shatters; — silences; —verifies.

(See answer, reply, response, repartee.)

RETORT (v)

adverbs

sharply; curtly; absurdly; shrewdly; effectively; acrimoniously; comically; resentfully; spiritedly; caustically; facetiously; scurrilously; waspishly; petulantly; gruffly; stingingly.

(See respond, reply.)

RETRACT (v)

adverbs

pusillanimously; timidly; ultimately; cautiously; fearfully; ignominiously; hastily; dishonorably; despairingly.

(See recall, disavow.)

RETREAT

adjectives

tardy; ignominious; hasty; immediate; subterranean; verdant; hospitable; bloody; sacred; timely; final; hurried; sunless; precipitate; reckless; swift; panic-stricken; dignified; grateful; epic; flurried; chosen; beloved; circuitous; masterly; lonely; secluded; orderly; crippled; hasty; base; ultimate; snug; double-quick; disastrous; cavernous; rural; gracious; foul; ruinous; secure; serene; secret; favorite; despairing; soft; honorable; glorious.

verbs

advocate—; beat—; censure—; chase into —; drive into—; fall back in—; flee in—; force into—; hasten—; move in—; occasion —; order—; shrink in—; sound—; withdraw in—; —averts; —defeats; —saves.

(See retirement, isolation.)

RETREAT (v)

adverbs

cringingly; ignominiously; precipitately; irrationally; coquettishly; cravenly; disastrously; ruinously; serenely; honorably; despairingly; pusillanimously.

(See retire, withdraw.)

RETRENCH (v)

adverbs

financially; cautiously; conservatively; sensibly; enforcedly; periodically; disastrously; shrewdly.

(See lessen, limit.)

RETRIBUTION

adjectives

trenchant; severest; utmost; tardy; righteous; bloody; just; speedy.

verbs

anticipate—; award—; defy—; deserve—; fear—; ignore—; measure—; reap—; resist —; reveal—; sow—; —amends; —atones; —harries; —evens; —retaliates; —revenges; —upbraids.

(See justice, compensation, punishment, penalty.)

RETROACTIVE

adverbs

fortunately; disastrously; luckily; happily; opportunely; expediently; legally; wisely; unconditionally; unexpectedly; acceptably.

RETROSPECT

adjectives

widening; melancholy; drowsy; foregoing; deep; briefest; gratifying; entertaining

RETROSPECTIVE

adverbs

lamentably; curiously; tiresomely; unprofitably; unfortunately; dismally; stagnantly; stubbornly; sorrowfully; obstinately; fearfully; incorrigibly; incurably; inveterately.

adjectives

ordinary; periodical; honorable; tedious; successive (pl) ; infallible; pecuniary; physical; exuberant; inevitable; speedy; visible; reassuring; adequate; alleged; impending; bountiful; unprofited; scant; monetary; diminishing; abundant; circling; material; peaceful; tangible; swift; beggarly; immediate; imperfect; fortuitous.

verbs

anticipate—; deter—; foresee—; forestall—; foretell—; hamper—; hinder—; narrate—; observe—s; predict—; presage—; recount —s; relate—; resume on—; —s echo; — overjoys; —pleases; —s pour in; —redoubles; —renews.

(See harvest, report, profit, reply.)

RETURN (*v*)
adverbs

periodically; seasonally; sardonically; traditionally; habitually; customarily; testily; dubiously; deliberately; unceremoniously; subsequently; expeditiously; reluctantly; incessantly; triumphantly; fortuitously; infallibly; tediously; honorably.

(See recur, repay.)

REUNION
adjectives

chaotic; select; plotting; prominent; formal; ultimate; happy.

verbs

arrange—; attend—; band in—; bring about—; clasp in—; delay—; effect—; embrace in—; entwine in—; gather in—; invite to—; participate in—; plan—; —embodies; —interests; —overjoys; —recalls; —renews; —unites.

(See meeting, gathering, union.)

REVEAL (*v*)
adverbs

penetratingly; candidly; vividly; graphically; immodestly; daringly; traitorously; partially; concisely; deplorably; spaciously; strikingly; unmistakably; fluently; injudiciously; dismally; painfully; courageously; supernaturally.

(See disclose, expose.)

adjectives

lurid; nightly; bestial; heavy-headed; profligate.

REVELATION
adjectives

astonishing; unexpected; lightning; sickening; fluent; divine; deathlike; injudicious; ultimate; startling; veritable; awful; curious; vivid; unsuspected; successive (pl) ; celestial; appalling; dismal; unforeseen; cool; judicial; painful; incessant; intimate; supernatural; guarded; frightful; amazing; courageous.

verbs

color—; deplore—; fear—; inspire—; interpret—; prod to—; resist—; —admits; — awes; —bares; —concedes; —corrects; — disburdens; —discloses; —divulges; —embarrasses; —enlightens; —exposes.

(See disclosure, exposure, discovery.)

REVELER
adjectives

joyous; lusty; bright; profane; unconventional.

REVELRY
adjectives

wild; gay; wanton; drunken; rustic; wildest; ardent.

REVENGE
adjectives

dire; luscious-toothed; unlearned; sworn; desperate; frightful; implacable; passionate; undisturbing; stinging; delicate; meaningless; bloody; fierce; prophesied; timid; meditated; swift; secret; spiteful; just; wild; refined; doubtful; sweet.

verbs

aggravate to—; avert—; contrive—; evoke —; incur—; itch for—; provoke to—; restrain—; suppress—; vow—; wreak—; — angers; —confuses; —enrages; —evens; — exasperates; —flares; —foams; —grinds; — infuriates; —stings.

(See retaliation, vengeance, hatred, hate.)

REVENGE (*v*)
adverbs

diabolically; ingeniously; logically; direly;

frightfully; implacably; passionately; swiftly; secretly; spitefully; deliberately.

(See avenge, retaliate.)

REVENUE

adjectives

confiscated; royal; overflowing; advertising; surplus; princely; accruing; requisite; gross; expected; present.

verbs

acquire—; apportion—; bear—; boost (colloq.)—; claim—; derive—; dissipate—; draw—; expend—; forfeit—; gain—; increase—; invest—; possess—; produce—; promise—; seek—; spend—; untie—; yield —; —accrues; —dribbles in.

(See income, money, profit, wages.)

REVERBERATE (v)

adverbs

raucously; thunderously; overwhelmingly; threateningly; portentously; musically; crashingly; clangingly; deafeningly.

(See resound, peal.)

REVERBERATING

adverbs

dimly; loudly; thunderously; resonantly; faintly; distantly; strangely; hollowly; sepulchrally; frightfully; fearfully; dully; rumblingly; mournfully; dolefully; madly; jubilantly; triumphantly; wildly.

REVERBERATION

adjectives

rocking; surly; crashing; clanging; thunderous; deafening.

REVERE (v)

adverbs

religiously; blindly; adoringly; idolatrously; spiritually; physically; fanatically.

(See honor, respect.)

REVERENCE

adjectives

professed; increasing; unquestioning; profound; easy; infinite; worshipful; mystical; devotional; meek; habitual; involuntary; superstitious; apprehensive; pious; subdued; peculiar; grateful; serious; high; honest; dutiful; awed; defensive; unaffected; instinctive; forward; personal; wanting; servile; special; religious; nominal; implicit; instant; better-proportioned; overgreat; inexpressible; filial.

verbs

arouse—; bear—; bestow—; cherish—; command—; dedicate in—; deserve—; entertain —; evince—; feign—; inculcate—; ingrain —; inspire—; kneel in—; observe with—; pay—; present—; produce—; question—; win—; —edifies; —elevates; —enshrines; —overawes.

(See awe, honor, adoration, respect, obeisance.)

REVERENCE (v)

adverbs

devoutly; unquestionably; profoundly; infinitely; mystically; superstitiously; piously; dutifully; religiously; servilely; filially; inexpressibly.

(See venerate, revere.)

REVERENT

adverbs

respectfully; devoutly; piously; quietly; silently; duly; becomingly; fittingly; sincerely; deeply; profoundly; noticeably; commendably; visibly; carefully; habitually; inherently; truly; unusually; worshipfully; unaffectedly; unobtrusively; implicitly.

REVERIE

adjectives

dreamful; embowered; abstracted; absorbed; voluptuous; pensive; sublime; scornful; perplexed; anxious; gloomy; celestial; silent; uneasy; brief; delicious; motionless; pleasant; indignant; indefinable; blissful; intoxicating; unconscious; fantastic; enamored.

verbs

absorb in—; awake from—; base on—; bask in—; compose—; crack—; drift into—; engage in—; envelop in—; fall into—; fashion—; float into—; imbibe in—; indulge in —; intoxicate with—; lapse into—; lose in —; pursue in—; recall in—; rouse from—; shroud in—; sink into—; start from—; steep in—; —attains; —dances; —exalts; —promises; —reflects; —revolves; —sustains.

(See dream, meditation.)

REVERSE

adjectives

occasional; ominous; appalling; disastrous; catastrophic.

verbs
allay—; bear—; compare—s; contend with
—s; encounter—s; lament—; mitigate—;
shoulder—; suffer—; teach—; —annuls; —
cancels; —damages; —deposes; —depresses; —dissolves; —overrides; —saddles.

(See misfortune, calamity, defeat, adversity.)

REVERSE (v)
adverbs
dramatically; automatically; mechanically;
strategically; desperately; strikingly; appreciably.

(See invert, overthrow.)

REVERSIBLE
adverbs
conveniently; adaptably; fittingly; appropriately; easily; readily; comfortably; advantageously; usefully; serviceably; quickly; instantly; smartly; handsomely.

REVERSION
adjectives
far-off; natural; certain; inevitable.

REVERT (v)
adverbs
normally; customarily; traditionally; historically; instinctively; naturally; inevitably.
(See return, recur.)

REVIEW
adjectives
balanced; impartial; crisp; accurate; honest; unbiased; news; up-to-the-minute; annual; embracing; enthusiastic; competent;
prejudiced; financial; artistic; dispassionate; critical; sweeping; elaborate; exhaustive; strict; dignified; prodigal; learned;
lumbering; involuntary; copious; philosophical; adulatory; brief; flippant.

verbs
march in—; pass in—; —blasts; —censures;
—commends; —criticizes; —discusses; —exposes; —fatigues; —honors; —lauds; —
scorches; —suggests; —surveys; —treats
of; —unfolds.
(See analysis, study, parade, survey, examination.)

REVIEW (v)
adverbs
appreciatively; courteously; briefly; cursorily; formally; perfunctorily; critically; im-

partially; accurately; unbiasedly; annually;
competently; dispassionately; elaborately;
exhaustively; philosophically; acrimoniously.
(See reconsider, contemplate.)

REVISED
adverbs
recently; cleverly; handsomely; advantageously; profitably; wisely; ably; considerably; skilfully; satisfactorily; appropriately; acceptably; broadly; somewhat; ingeniously; capably; completely; substantially;
carefully; admirably.

REVISION
adjectives
substantial; patient; endless; downward;
quarrelsome; slight; careful; desperate.

verbs
advise—; advocate—; balk at—; complete
—; consider—; guide—; meditate on—; note
—; pass—; prepare—; publish—; survive
—; —astonishes; —condenses; —corrects;
—improves; —seasons; —suppresses .
(See censorship, change, correction, alteration.)

REVIVAL
adjectives
neo-classic; poetic; impetuous; incidental;
literary; religious; romantic; wide-spread.

verbs
assume—; attempt—; costume—; deserve—;
display—; hiss—; justify—; merit—; necessitate—; rejoice over—; retard—; wish for
—; —commences; —exhausts; —confuses;
—reawakens; —refreshes; —regains.
(See resurrection, renaissance.)

REVIVE (v)
adverbs
popularly; neo-classically; seasonally; poetically; religiously; spectacularly; dramatically; athletically; spiritually; physically.
(See restore, rally.)

REVOLT
adjectives
successful; meditated; wide-spread; minor;
projected; healthy; tentative; mental; incoherent; energetic; personal; inconsistent.

REVOLT (v)
adverbs
traitorously; viciously; vigorously; vindic-

tively; successfully; tentatively; abortively; unanimously; bloodlessly; violently; periodically; socially; ineffectively; inevitably.

(See rebel, shock.)

REVOLTING

adverbs
hideously; grossly; inordinately; extraordinarily; extremely; abominably; atrociously; nauseatingly; incredibly; unspeakably; detestably; unutterably; inexpressibly; particularly; strangely; painfully; appallingly; shockingly; grimly; unbearably.

REVOLUTION

adjectives
anomalistic; bloodless; veritable; successive (pl); interior; public; complete; impending; synodic; radical; dynastic; incarnate; social; industrial; sidereal; inevitable; ineffective; orbital; hideous; violent; solemn; proletarian; periodic; fickle; salutary.

verbs
betray—; consummate—; chronicle—; crush —; drive to—; engineer—; foment—; forestall—; hail—; hatch—; instigate—; justify —; launch—; map—; plunge into—; promote—; resist—; shatter—; sponsor—; spur —; stamp out—; stave off—; subdue—.

(See anarchy, insurrection, mutiny, outbreak, rebellion.)

REVOLUTIONARY

adverbs
ominously; completely; moderately; incredibly; genuinely; dangerously; alarmingly; fearfully; dreadfully; significantly; pointedly; appallingly; shockingly; grimly; restively; ungovernably; uncontrollably; riotously; mutinously; unsubmissively; insurgently; sullenly.

REVOLVE (*v*)

adverbs
incessantly; mechanically; automatically; perpetually; periodically; sidereally; synodically.

(See roll, spin.)

REVOLVER

verbs
conceal—; confiscate—; discharge—; display —; draw—; juggle—; oil—; pack—; pocket

—; prohibit—; snatch—; —barks; —frightens; —peppers; —protects; —reassures; —spatters; —spits fire.

(See machine-gun, gun, weapon, pistol.)

REVULSION

adjectives
bitter; rapid; extraordinary; violent; desperate.

verbs
develop—; direct—; encounter—; fall into —; incur—; meet with—; recover from—; shake off—; suffer—; —dizzies; —evolves; —overturns; —shocks; —spins; —uncoils; —whirls.

(See disgust, aversion, repugnance, dislike, sickness.)

REWARD

adjectives
comprehensive; particular; swift; dazzling; palpable; sufficient; material; slender; momentary; temporal; flat; ample; adequate; rich; destined; utmost; arbitrary; tangible; sure; due; coveted; political; just; crowning; pecuniary; monetary.

verbs
assign—; assure of—; confer—; contend for —; gather—; increase—; merit—; offer—; post—; promise—; reap—; scorn—; strive for—; woo—; —blesses; —decorates; —inspires; —recompenses.

(See merit, laurel, fee, dowry, medal, prize.)

REWARD (*v*)

adverbs
munificently; lavishly; graciously; handsomely; fitly; amply; abundantly; dazzlingly; monetarily; financially; tangibly; politically; pecuniarily.

(See offer, compensate.)

RHAPSODIZE (*v*)

adverbs
furiously; bombastically; vigorously; oratorically; maddeningly; eloquently; superfluously.

(See improvise, recite, play.)

RHAPSODY

adjectives
extravagant; romantic; incoherent; mystical.

adjectives
subtle; empty; heavenly; florid; full-voiced; ambitious; glowing; exuberant; judicial.

verbs
adhere to—; condemn—; consider—; exhibit —; frame—; hammer—into; heed—; indulge in—; inspect—; unmask—; lecture in —; obey—; observe—; polish—; refurbish —; school in—; steep in—; —confuses; —convinces; —expresses; —impresses; —influences; —languishes; —persuades.

(See style, prose, art, eloquence, elegance, oratory.)

RHEUMATIC
adverbs
painfully; gallantly; laughingly; embarrassingly; helplessly; hopelessly; desperately; permanently; incurably; extremely; obviously; manifestly; irremediably; crookedly; unfortunately; terribly; slightly; somewhat; distressingly; undoubtedly; noticeably; woefully.

RHEUMATISM
verbs
afflict with—; endure—; inflict with—; mitigate—; salve—; suffer from—; —attacks; —confines; —irks; —irritates; —lames; —locates; —pains; —racks; —ravages.

(See disease, pain.)

RHINOCEROS
verbs
cage—; capture—; —batters; —charges; —defends; —drowses; —feeds; —gores; —inflicts; —inhabits; —preys on; —puffs; —rams; —roams; —snorts; —waters.

(See animal.)

RHYME
adjectives
pairing (pl); lofty; feverish; uncouth; ruder; golden; bootless; tender; efficacious; ringing; visionary; facile; feminine; careless; nondescript; ever-varying; nobler; meaningless; accepted; refluent; scornful; fettered; unbaptized; brawling; rollicking; emblazoned; unmoving; frozen; nursery; euphonious; mournful; initiative; silvery; innocent; dangerous.

RHYTHM
adjectives
blithe; tantalizing; tenderest; doggerel; accelerated; settled; trotting; vibrating; visual; seductive; intriguing; wailing; sensuous; fluctuating; mighty; rowdy; dull; monotonous; incisive; abrupt; regulated; insinuating; characteristic; maddening; graceful; perfect; rustic; vehement; whirring; exquisite; maudlin; tragic; jarring; primal; natural; pulsating; throbbing; harmonious.

verbs
abuse—; accelerate—; accent—; attune to —; break—; dash into—; depend on—; derive—; determine—; lose—; measure—; regulate—; sing in—; set to—; stress—; sway to—; "swing" to—; synchronize—; —charms; —descends; —flows; —harmonizes; —persists; —reigns.

(See swing, flow.)

RIBALD
adverbs
coarsely; comically; hilariously; disgustingly; grossly; indecently; uproariously; boisterously; shockingly; appallingly; crassly; brazenly; blatantly; flagrantly; openly; notoriously; infamously; inexcusably; unpardonably; villainously; deliberately; impudently; shamelessly; shamefully; daringly.

RIBALDRY
adjectives
public; raucous.

RIBS
adjectives
overweathered; internal; irregular; glistening.

verbs
adhere to—; cling to—; crack—; crush—; develop—; divide into—; grate—; injure—; knuckle—; poke—; rend—; smash—; stick to—; stuff—; —brace; —compose; —extend; —frame; —protect; —snap; —support.

RICH
adverbs
moderately; affluently; opulently; comfortably; unbelievably; incredibly; immeasurably; incalculably; magnificently; mysteriously; suddenly; unquestionably; extremely; secretly; unimaginably; surreptitiously; exceedingly; sumptuously; abundantly marvelously.

adjectives

boundless; inherent; ineffectual; unsearchable; manifold; exceeding; intellectual; generous; singular; countless; heavy; unbelievable; fabulous; inordinate; enormous; undreamed-of; superfluous.

verbs

accumulate—; acquire—; administer—; amass—; bestow—; command—; covet—; desire—; despise—; draw—; enjoy—; estimate—; gather—; overwhelm with—; pile up—; possess—; spurn—; store—; treasure —; trust—; worship—; wring—; —abound; —content; —corrupt; —endanger; —enslave; —flow; —govern; —hinder; —serve.

(See affluence, wealth, money, income.)

RICHNESS

adjectives

inexhaustible; vivid; mellow; smooth; changing; vibrant; gilded; decorative; amazing; singular; exceeding; medieval.

RICKETY

adverbs

absurdly; comically; dangerously; fearfully; amusingly; extremely; hazardously; impossibly; alarmingly; curiously; noisily; perilously; laughably.

RID (v)

adverbs

effectually; permanently; ultimately; completely; logically; thoroughly; scientifically.
(See dispose.)

RIDDLE

adjectives

fustian; psychological; diplomatic; puzzling; insoluble; unread; inscrutable; miserable; torturing.

verbs

compose—; construct—; contrive—; couch in—s; desire—; dissolve—; evolve—; guess —; interpret—; propose—; propound—; record—; resolve—; solve—; speak in—s; weave—; —amuses; —diverts; —perplexes; —puzzles; —torments; —vexes; —yields.

(See enigma, puzzle, problem, mystery.)

RIDE

adjectives

dusty; daring; subsequent; starry; desper-

ate; tedious; delightful; tireless; midnight; fabled.

verbs

accept—; enjoy—; extend—; gain—; hasten —; invite for—; promise—; solicit—; terminate—; "thumb"—; —bores; —delights; — refreshes; —thrills; —tires; —wearies; — diverts.

(See trip, journey, tour.)

RIDE (v)

adverbs

thunderously; swiftly; triumphantly; furiously; victoriously; gallantly; blindly; leisurely; wildly; proudly; blithely; ruthlessly; roughly; desperately; dashingly; daringly; gracefully; decisively; superbly.

(See move, travel.)

RIDER

adjectives

consummate; heavy; gallant; superb; unmovable; dashing; expert; audacious; warlike; daring; decisive; groomless; graceful.

verbs

bear—; carry—; equal—; obey—; throw—; train—; unnerve—; —charges; —dismounts; —drags; —drives; —joggles; — lashes; —mounts; —pats; —reigns; — soothes; —spurs; —tires; —travels; — vaults; —wearies; —whips.

(See horseman.)

RIDGE

adjectives

cruciform; melancholy; woody; parallel; hummocky; hog-backed; wind-swept; barren; perpendicular; tremendous; mountain; formidable; lofty; precipitous; loosened; ice; craggy; gentle; encircling; shaggy; commanding; uncultivated; sunken; extended; crowned; hillocky.

verbs

climb to—; dance on—; discern—; dread—; drive to—; dwarf—; form—; fortify—; quit—; —beams; —caps; —chains; —crests; —elevates; —rises; —runs; —stretches; — tempts.

(See bank, range, mountain, hill.)

RIDICULE

adjectives

stinging; comic; raucous; merciless; personal; angry; bitter; traditional; abusive; sarcastic; scathing; biting.

verbs
bear—; defy—; expose to—; fear—; heap —; indulge in—; move to—; overcome—; resort to—; share—; subject to—; sustain—; taste—; turn to—; —bites; —checks; —cuts; —disgraces; —embarrasses; —embitters; —enrages; —pains; —smothers; —storms; —strips.

(See **banter, jeer,** irony, mockery, derision.)

RIDICULE (*v*)

adverbs
ruthlessly; sarcastically; cruelly; tenderly; spitefully; stingingly; raucously; mercilessly; angrily; bitterly; abusively; bitingly; scathingly.

(See mock, jeer.)

RIDICULOUS

adverbs
foolishly; absurdly; unreasonably; laughably; palpably; crazily; extravagantly; irrationally; childishly; stupidly; grotesquely; blatantly; whimsically; gaily; airily; intentionally; injudiciously; recklessly; weakly; senselessly; nonsensically; grossly; manifestly; rashly; unwisely; pathetically.

RIFLE

adjectives
leather-cased; handled; speckless; omnipresent; unwieldy; pneumatic; handsome; new; grimy; deathdealing; express; crackling; dreaded.

verbs
arm with—; brandish—; bristle with—s; conceal—; discharge—; examine—; fear—; inspect—; point—; provide with—s; shoulder— ;—crackles; —frightens; —gleams; —mows down; —speaks.

(See gun, machine-gun, musket.)

RIFT

adjectives
horrid; savage; gusty; keen; little; widening; convenient.

verbs
fill—; lament—; span—; —appears; —breaches; —brews; —disjoins; —disunites;

—gapes; —heals; —overhangs; —rends; —rips; —ruptures; —separates; —splits; —widens.

(See breach, gap.)

RIGHT

adjectives
outward; authoritative; individual; inalienable; hereditary; unrestricted; colonial; prescriptive; litigious; indefeasible; peculiar; legal; belligerent; relative; legitimate; marital; sacred; inviolable; unquestionable; undisputed; natural; respective; concrete; undoubted; exclusive; purchased; immemorial; substantial; inestimable; municipal; injured; prime; invaded; inborn; constitutional; derivative; inherent; obedient; vanquished; common; riparian (pl); conceded; poetical; autonomic; conjugal; functional; vested; unquestioned; beautiful; proprietary; antique; terrible; illimitable; civil; perfected; manorial; executive; formal; sable-vested; shameful; feudal; covenanted; immutable; invulnerable; unalterable; abstract; ecclesiastical; unclaimed; statutable; possessory; proprietary; lucrative; impugned; questionable; absolute; vital; senescent; uncontested; divine; irrevocable; provincial; vindicated.

verbs
abolish—; accord—; acknowledge—; arrogate—; assert—; assume—; cherish—; clamor for—; concede—; confer—; confiscate—; curtail—; defend—; deprive of—; derive—; dispose of—; dispute—; disregard —; earn—; embody—; encroach on—; establish—; exercise—; forfeit—; grant—; impair—; infringe upon—; insure—; invade —; invest with—; prate of—s; preserve—; protest—; relinquish—; remand—; respect —; restore—; retain—; revoke—; safeguard—; surrender—; suspend—; suppress —; terminate—; transgress—; undermine —; uphold—; urge—; vindicate—; violate —; vouchsafe—; waive—; win—; wrest—; — resides with; —triumphs.

(See liberty, license, franchise, **justice,** privilege, authority, prerogative.)

RIGHTEOUS

adverbs
rigidly; sincerely; consciously; utterly; completely; uprightly; inherently; carefully; ostentatiously; austerely; undeviatingly; strictly; painfully; ostensibly; incredibly; apparently; overly; dutifully; duly; unduly;

pretentiously; manifestly; pharisaically; uncompromisingly; stiffly.

RIGHTEOUSNESS
adjectives
divine; inherent; ungodly; final; spotless; haughty; imputed.

verbs
forsake—; found on—; garb in—; hunger for—; judge in—; maintain—; observe with —; proclaim—; thirst for—; uphold—; —advances; —exalts; —falters; —flourishes; —rewards; —withstands; —yields; impute —.

(See justice, good, virtue, purity.)

RIGID
adverbs
stiffly; painfully; terribly; dreadfully; stonily; bleakly; uncompromisingly; intolerably; woefully; coldly; harshly; austerely; cruelly; bitterly; sternly; severely; brutally; ungenerously; narrow-mindedly; dogmatically; tyrannically; puritanically; doctrinally; intolerantly.

RIGOR
adjectives
utmost; merciless; logical; decisive; religious; protracted; grizzly; coveted; unsparing; remorseless; pedantic.

RIGORS
verbs
allay—; alleviate—; ease—; endure—; enforce—; fear—; feel—; ferment—; guard against—; preserve from—; relax—; resist —; shelter from—; smart under—; survive —; temper—; —affect; —distress; —harden; —reduce.

(See difficulty, trouble, obstacle, severity, harshness.)

RILL
adjectives
narrow; wandering; babbling; dancing; tinkling; solitary; winding; sylvan; clear; fuming; glancing; gushing; waking; frosted; limpid; rebounding; singing; summer; flowing; purling; classic.

RING
adjectives
metallic; ducal; marriage; granite; tinkling; jubilant; carved; babyish; magnificent; diamond; diurnal; dry; subtle; typic;

glittering; rhythmic; betrothal; determined; watery; wondrous; closing; luminous; superb; old; scaly; mournful; insistent; diverting; contorted; stifling; clustering; lubricous; tense; monumental; familiar; sinister; dancing; flat; oval; solid; great; massive; dingy; continuous; concentric (pl).

verbs
admire—; appraise—; bedeck with—s; finger—; mislay—; restore—to; return—; tinkle—s; value—; —adorns; —binds; —dazzles; —encircles; —espouses; —imitates; —gleams; —glimmers; —glitters; —recalls; —seals; —sparkles; —weds.

(See diamond, jewel, gem.)

RING (*v*)
adverbs
incessantly; musically; harshly; dolefully; drowsily; monotonously; feebly; impatiently; blithely; resonantly; piercingly; metalically; vigorously; jubilantly; tinklingly.

(See resound, chime.)

RIOT
adjectives
prodigal; noiseless; bloody; subsequent; prison; licentious; golden; wild; senseless; springtide; transient.

verbs
deplore—; describe—; expose to—; incite to—; instigate—; pitch into—; provoke—; quash—; quell—; subdue—; suppress—; —bursts forth; —disorders; —ensues; —jeopardizes; —protests; —strikes; —upsets; —violates.

(See commotion, revolution, strike, disturbance, turmoil, violence.)

RIOTERS
verbs
calm—; condemn—; disperse—; incite—; pardon—; punish—; quell—; restrain—; suppress—; —agitate; —aggravate; —attack; —clamor; —demand; —harry; —pillage; —plunder; —ravage; —storm; —transgress.

(See striker, anarchist, terrorist, communist, scab.)

RIOTOUS
adverbs
dangerously; alarmingly; boisterously; seditiously; mutinously; disgracefully; inordinately; extraordinarily; strangely; uncon-

trollably; ungovernably; murderously; insensately; wildly; violently; vociferously; grimly; daringly; defiantly; tumultuously; seditiously; uproariously; terribly; sullenly.

RIPE

adverbs

finally; quite; entirely; altogether; lusciously; deliciously; completely; satisfactorily; perfectly; unexpectedly; pleasantly; sufficiently; extremely; unduly; evidently.

RIPEN (v)

adverbs

seasonally; wholesomely; deliciously; normally; luxuriantly; goldenly; succulently.

(See develop, complete.)

RIPPLE (v)

adverbs

idly; sleekly; liquidly; bubblingly; luminously; gildedly.

(See wave, sway.)

RIPPLES

adjectives

glad; silvery; purled; innumerable; foamy; moon-lit; timid; minute; bubbling; passing; luminous; breeze-ridden; transparent; sun-gilt; liquid.

verbs

agitate—; blow—; flow in—; form—; mark by—; observe—; smooth—; —fascinate; —glisten; —ruffle; —shimmer; —subside; —undulate; —wash.

(See wave, billow, breaker.)

RIPPLING

adverbs

merrily; cheerfully; pleasantly; clearly; smoothly; pleasantly; sparklingly; flashily; plashily; happily; blithely; brightly; brilliantly; laughingly; quietly; audibly; noisily.

RISE

adjectives

meteoric; successful; sufficient; miraculous; unprecedented; phenomenal; important; thermometric; nocturnal; gradual; corresponding; extraordinary; unpredictable; speedy.

verbs

anticipate—; check—; deplore—; forestall —; gauge—; heighten—; mount—; predict —; produce—; stem—; stimulate—; tremble

on—; —advances; —ceases; —continues; —frightens; —indicates; —profits; —thrills.

(See beginning, advance, progress, increase.)

RISE (v)

adverbs

dizzily; abruptly; majestically; airily; militantly; reluctantly; unanimously; gradually; mysteriously; solemnly; impulsively; leisurely; ceremoniously; conspicuously; deliberately; involuntarily; lingeringly; reverently; obediently; perpendicularly; instinctively; amiably; meteorically; phenomenally; unpredictably.

(See arise, ascend.)

RISK

adjectives

imminent; tremendous; operative; alarming; infinite; serious; continual; unaccustomed; canine; known; desirable; considerable; unjustifiable; extraordinary.

verbs

accept—; assume—; avoid—; balk at—; court—; decry—; diminish—; entail—; exclude—; expose to—; free from—; guard against—; harbor—; increase—; incur—; involve—; justify—; lessen—; obviate—; preclude—; preserve from—; question—; undergo—; underwrite—.

(See danger, chance, hazard, speculation.)

RISK (v)

adverbs

alarmingly; unjustifiably; rashly; heroically; needlessly; considerably; superfluously.

(See endanger, imperil.)

RISKY

adverbs

dangerously; ominously; perilously; alarmingly; hazardously; definitely; peculiarly; particularly; immensely; incalculably; admittedly; unwarrantably; unfortunately; always; manifestly; extremely; uncommonly; commercially; altogether; notoriously; obviously; gravely; seriously; inescapably; unavoidably; undeniably; inordinately; unaccountably; immeasurably; incalculably; desperately; appallingly; hideously; pitiably; fearfully; tragically; adventurously; distinctly.

adjectives

superstitious; purifying; pleasing; funeral; sanguinary; sensual; true; sacramental; courtly; bloody; pagan; nuptial; connubial; ecclesiastical; abominable; sacred; gorgeous; dismal; mysterious; wanton; barbaric; religious; gloomy; hideous; ceremonial; blessed; ancient; obnoxious; various (pl); horrid; preparatory; repulsive; propitiatory; gentle; solemn.

verbs

adhere to—; celebrate—; follow—; ignore —; institute—; observe—; perform—; prolong—; refrain from—; relinquish—; retain—; stage—; value—; —consists of; — honors; —impresses; —symbolizes.
(See ceremony, function, ritual.)

RITUAL

adjectives

social; captivating; visible; complicated; artistic; elaborate; burdensome.

verbs

adhere to—; adopt—; attempt—; attend—; elaborate—; evolve—; instruct in—; mumble—; observe—; offend by—; perform—; prepare for—; recite—; supply—; suspend —; —animates; —beautifies; —celebrates; —colors; —dignifies; —sanctifies; —symbolizes.
(See form, formula, rite, ceremony, function.)

RITUALISTIC

adverbs

elaborately; ceremonially; reverently; extravagantly; unusually; highly; profoundly; peculiarly; particularly; exotically; mysteriously; strangely.

RIVAL

adjectives

insolent; mutinous; unworthy; formidable; ribald; potent; irresistable; disagreeable; intolerable; vexatious; insolent; celebrated; successful; gallant; richer; traditional; guiltless; powerful; fallen; testy; scheming; hostile; confiding; incredible; favorable; importunate; circumstanced; angry; covetous; dangerous; strenuous; worthy; patriotic; distinguished; hopeless; domestic; rising; hated.

verbs

appraise—; defy—; emulate—; encounter —; excel—; oust—; outlast—; restrain—; shoulder aside—; surpass—; tolerate—; trail—; —aspires; —bewails; —s clash; — competes; —contends; —disputes; —equals; —excels; —glares; —opposes; —pursues; —s scramble; —spars; —squares off; — strives; —vies.
(See enemy, competitor, contestant, antagonist, insurgent.)

RIVALRY

adjectives

female; impious; dawning; fierce; ruthless; malignant; generous; unwitting; amiable; professional; ambitious; jealous; passionate; keen; sectional; kindly; municipal; bloody; inherent; dangerous; eager; bitter.

verbs

confess—; create—; eliminate—; endure—; engage in—; forbid—; forsake—; intensify —; promote—; subordinate—; —confronts; —continues; —divides; —intervenes; —separates; —subsides; —wanes; —threatens.
(See competition, enmity, opposition, antagonism.)

RIVER

adjectives

channeled; raucous; solemn; foaming; noble; unfranked; chafing; brimming; crystal; narrowed; exulting; far-off; pelting; babbling; ringing; racing; saturnine; rapid; fruitful; leaping; clear; deep-banked; booming; limpid; swollen; abominable; rushing; rife; turbid; ruinous; slow; noiseless; flowing; remarkable; ironical; encroaching; torrential; murmuring; roaring; peculiar; majestic; spectral; winding; mighty; darkening; unfordable; full-grown; peaceful; sunlit; meandering; cheerful; pebble-paved; immense; wandering; turbulent; incorrigible; glassy; brattling; capricious; hurrying; sparkling; resplendent; sobbing; weariest; useless; failing; reflecting; royal; quiet; doubling; hesitating; white-robed; subterranean; trickling; golden; unbridged; whirling; solitary; speeding; sluggish; mystic; subsiding; salmon-thronged; soft-flowing; ever-deepening; imaginary; freshening; frozen; long; gray; swanlike; impassable; hissing; swift; silent; sweet-voiced; hard-working; historic; mocking.

verbs

breast—; bridge—; divert—; emerge from
—; ford—; ply—; plunge into—; stock—;
—abounds in; —babbles; —batters; —
bawls; —chatters; —churns; —eddies; —
flows; —foams; —frets; —glides; —glitters; —growls; —gurgles; —laps; —laughs;
—leaps; —loiters; —meanders; —murmurs;
—races; —rises; —roars; —sallies; —stirs;
—subsides; —swells; —threads.

(See liquid, stream, brook.)

RIVET

verbs

beat—; bind with—; bucket—; force—;
hammer—; heat—; insert—; join with—;
loose—; secure with—; set—; strain—; —
braces; —s clatter; —clinches; —fastens;
—projects; —secures; —tightens; —unites;
—welds.

(See nail, link, bond, fetter, band.)

RIVULET

adjectives

merry; shady; woodland; shrunken; clear;
babbling; noisy; tinkling; cheerful; glittering; ever-joyous; melancholy; widely-wan-
dering.

ROAD

adjectives

endless; beaten; unfrequented; homeward;
arduous; gliding; country; grass-grown;
monotonous; impassable; lifeless; miry;
shady; sunny; winding; smiling; serpentine; misty; worthless; conventional; parched; dusty; corduroy; superb; dilapidated;
wood; rutty; rugged; vicinal; circuitous;
white; sand; sun-splashed; tortuous; steep;
hilly; silver; swarming; mended; half-defined; romantic; turfy; unguarded; lake-
side; starless; forsaken; military; thorny;
fated; unknown; coral-bordered; red; rut-
ted; surest; moon-lit; wrong; disused; miraculous; chocolate-colored; holy; intricate;
dreary; elevated; bumpy; glaring; subtler;
dubious; frozen; shaded; heavenly; indistinguishable; interminable; various (pl);
treacherous; miserable; smoother; level;
macadamized; translucent; narrow; sinuous; weary; unfamiliar; dappled; scenic;
uneven; undulating; zigzagging; ready;
unbroken.

verbs

bank—; bounce over—; clock—; clog—;
deviate from—; diverge from—; infest—;

jog along—; jounce over—; level—; patrol
—; plod along—; skim along—; slog over
—; skirt—; surface—; trudge along—; —
ambles; —s converge; —meanders; —s radiate from; —rambles; —swarms; —sweeps
along; —wanders; —wearies; —winds.

(See avenue, highway, lane, drive.)

ROADSIDE

verbs

bank—; beautify—; border—; carpet—;
defile—; dot—; fall to—; follow—; grace
—; lie along—; lodge on—; plant—; sprawl
over—; strew—; tramp—; tread—; view
from—; —appeals; —borders; —charms.

(See countryside, field, land.)

ROADSTER

adjectives

asthmatic; resplendent; low-slung; sport;
sleek; swift; streamlined; battered; shiny.

verbs

sport (colloq.)—; —bounces along; —careens; —chugs; —gleams; —glitters; —
hurtles; —performs; —rattles; —rolls a-
long; —slows up; —speeds; —sputters;
—spurts; —thrills; —whirs; —whizzes.

(See car, automobile.)

ROAM (v)

adverbs

casually; freely; leisurely; carelessly; buoyantly; lightly; circuitously; extensively.

(See wander, stray.)

ROAR

adjectives

deep; incessant; snarling; perpetual; majestic; indistinguishable; ebbing; shutter-
like; swelling; quavering; continuous;
dreadful; cannon-like; living; sullen; endless; incredible; hoarse; subdued; solemn;
baffled; hideous; unremitting; drumming;
deepening; heavy; monotonous; gusty; painful; distressed; awful; massive; sealike;
enormous; universal; stifled; muffled; deafening; dull; suppressed; confused; moaning; intermittent; tremendous; gesturing;
wildest; mingled; simultaneous; prolonged;
suggestive; vague; wavering; unceasing;
full-throated; dry; wild; triumphant; angry; steady; tumultuous; high-keyed; crackling; appalling.

verbs
deafen by—; imitate—; muffle—; restrain
—; suppress—; swell into—; utter—; —
blasts; —deafens; —disembowels; —drowns
out; —echoes; —enrages; —excites; —
frightens; —horrifies; —interrupts; —pains;
—rends; —splits the air.

(See noise, sound, uproar, thunder, rumble.)

ROAR (v)

adverbs
thunderously; awesomely; terrifically;
brutally; imperiously; vigorously; unremittingly; incessantly; incredibly; hoarsely;
hideously; deafeningly; triumphantly; tumultuously; appallingly; full-throatedly.

(See bellow, boom.)

ROB (v)

adverbs
systematically; professionally; slyly; insidiously; successfully; nocturnally; brazenly;
boldly; impudently.

(See plunder, steal.)

ROBBER

adjectives
nocturnal; bloody; prowling; brutalized;
successful.

verbs
apprehend—; deliver from—; incarcerate
—; —s congregate; —s conspire; —depredates; —despoils; —divests; —dodges; —
evades; —filches; —guts; —s infest; —s
invade; —loots; —marauds; —pilfers —
pillages; —plucks; —plunders; —purloins;
—ranges; —ransacks; —rifles; —sacks; —
strips; —tricks.

(See burglar, bandit, hoodlum, intruder,
liar, offender.)

ROBBERY

verbs
addict to—; commit—; conceal—; contrive
—; discover—; escape—; fear—; implicate
in—; interrupt—; mourn—; perform—; perpetrate—; plot—; punish—; report—; reveal—; uncover—; —impoverishes; —occurs; —strips.

(See "holdup", plagiarism, theft, plunder.)

ROBE

adjectives
canonical; luxuriant; tattered; tinsel; foot-
catching; flowing; flaunting; gossamer;
trailing; glistening; magnificent; operatic;
fantastic; painted; outspread; snowy; unconfined; sable; virgin; brocaded; spotless;
ceremonial; gorgeous; shimmering; conventional; somber; glittering; unreverent; sacerdotal; festive; priestly; woven; sweeping;
brilliant; dripping; cerulean; incomplete;
freckled; princely; transitory; ducal; officious; ruddy; royal; close-fitting; blood-
stained; transparent; vestal; musty; ample;
saffron; mortal; festal; gold-trimmed;
shroudlike; delicate; bridal; pompous;
little.

verbs
array in—; bestow—upon; cast off—; clothe
in—; disguise in—; doff—; don—; embroider—; fold—; huddle in—; gather—; invest
—; line—; strip of—; —beautifies; —enfolds; —envelops; —flows; —glorifies; —
heightens; —streams; —trails.

(See frock, blanket, gown, clothing.)

ROBE (v)

adverbs
magnificently; luxuriantly; fantastically;
spectacularly; ceremonially; conventionally;
sacerdotally; ecclesiastically.

(See shroud, cloak.)

ROBIN

verbs
befriend—; welcome—; —announces
Spring; —booms; —braves; —busies; —
cheers; —chirrups; —cocks; —darts; —
defies; —digs; —flutters; —hops; —moults;
—pokes; —snaps up; —swoops; —soars.

(See bird.)

ROBUST

adverbs
sturdiiy; splendidly; stoutly; healthily; vigorously; wholesomely; magnificently; enviably; admirably; stockily; brawnily; physically; amazingly; heartily.

ROCK (v)

adverbs
paternally; maternally; desolately; disconsolately; dizzily; patiently; tenderly.

(See sway, vacillate.)

ROCKET

verbs
bombard with—s; discharge—; display—;
eject—; fire—; fuse—; ignite—; project—;
propel—; set off—; signal with—; spark—;

touch off—; —bursts; —darts; —endangers; —hurtles; —illumines; —s scatter; —showers; —sizzles; —terrifies; —vanishes; —zooms.

(See bullet, shot, projectile.)

adjectives
bare; torpid; porphyritic; hospitable; darker; native; volcanic; craggy; glistening; fantastic; dazzling; picturesque; chalky; friable; jagged; sheltering; single; naked; ragged; spiritual; adamant; shelving; ancient; steep; sun-heated; rough-hewn; lichen-covered; fissured; cloven; miraculous; calcareous; low-browed; irresistable; living; igneous; perilous; precipitous; enwombed; sharp; splintered; riven; gaunt; flinty; stubborn; dun-colored; wave-encircled; disintegrated; inhospitable; sheer; tempest-beaten; submissive; sublime; traitorous; shadowing; jutting; steadfast; tidal; silver-fretted; impregnable; vine-clad; imperishable; hanging; unmistakable; merchant-marring; tall; cruel; burly-shouldered; shapeless; mantel-like; sea-beaten; shivering; wave-lapped; noticeable; senseless; sacrificial; gloomy; ice-bound; grass-covered; fearful; storied; incumbent; shining; rooted; cavernous; gneissic; sedimentary; genial; humid; monumental; ashy; mossy; projecting; massive; sparkling; sliding; peaked; curved; hoary; smitten; vaulted; churning; multitudinous; rigid; cream-colored; conspicuous; onlooking; echoing; unhewn; frowning; sullen; high-ascending; field; galled; kelp-covered; storm-drenched; cliffy; rugged; overhanging; wrinkled; glaciated; highest; insensible; basaltic; raging; serrated; time-stained; underlying; dangerous; dreary; weed-hung.

verbs
avoid—; bivouac on—; blast—; carve from —; crack—; crush—; dash against—; direct—; dislodge—; fear—; heap—; hew—; hurl—; quarry—; run upon—; shatter on —; split—; strike—; surmount—; —batter; —bound; —crest; —disintegrate; —erode; —fortify; —girdle; —hurtle; —jut; —project; —stud; —tower.

(See crag, reef, stone, granite, cliff.)

adverbs
painfully; arduously; extremely; impass-

ably; roughly; dangerously; exceedingly; incredibly; unexpectedly; surprizingly; amazingly; terribly; perilously.

adjectives
chastening; pastoral; bayonet; mystic; avenging; radiant; metallic; sharpest; transparent; sin-avenging; uplifted; gubernatorial; merciless.

adjectives
unconscionable; poor; drunken; damnable; false-hearted; cunning; dissentious; wenching; cowardly; fair-haired; little; consummate; unmitigated; tedious; pestilent; loitering; complete; overweening.

verbs
accuse—; apprehend—; deal with—s; denounce—; discomfit—; distrust—; punish —; quell—; rebuke—; reproach—; —baits; —beguiles; —deceives; —designs; —deviates; —devises; —entices; —fools; — "foxes"; —lures; —shirks; —swindles; — tricks.

(See robber, scoundrel, profligate.)

adverbs
mischievously; comically; lovably; rascally; innocently; merrily; teasingly; tormentingly; actively; ingeniously; inveterately; incurably; incorrigibly; naturally; wantonly; secretly; trickily; craftily; knavishly; particularly; villainously; peculiarly; singularly; notoriously.

adverbs
noisily; playfully; mirthfully; boisterously; capriciously; boldly; waggishly; wantonly; uproariously; sportively; prankishly; absurdly; inordinately; swaggeringly; boastfully; fantastically; outlandishly; blusteringly; tumultuously; turbulently; bombastically; merrily.

adjectives
inquisitorial; crucial; subordinate; inglorious; dominating; important; restricted; decisive; benevolent; influential; essential; pessimistic; responsible; unsavory; villainous; significant; prominent; destined; tremendous; suitable; self-imposed.

acclaim—; adopt—; animate—; bolster—;
color—; convey—; denounce—; enact—;
ennoble—; exploit—; extol—; fill—; fire—;
illuminate—; immortalize—; jade—; over-
act—; portray—; renounce—; romp through
—; spice—.
(See part, character.)

ROLL

adjectives

luscious; harsh; delicate; lumbering;
bloody; uncanny; condescending; mystic;
mathematic; rhythmic.

ROLL (v)

adverbs

heavily; furiously; enchantingly; impetuously; luxuriously; dangerously; exultantly;
fiercely; smoothly; sluggishly; lumberingly;
rhythmically.
(See whirl, revolve.)

ROLLICKING

adverbs

blithely; gaily; happily; frivolously; hilariously; boisterously; laughingly; divertingly; entertainingly; loudly; comically; clownishly; cheerfully; buoyantly; recklessly;
jauntily; vivaciously; noisily; gleefully;
sportively; joyously; mirthfully; jubilantly.

ROMANCE

adjectives

picaresque; somber; fictitious; touching;
rooted; veritable; synthetic; bottled; budding; unknown; boyish; chivalrous; brilliant; spirited; pure; ennobling; pastoral;
degenerate; headlong; elegant; passionate;
singular; stormy; tempestuous; tawdry; interminable; enthralling; nautical; mawkish; comic; tragic; prose; prodigal; charming; audacious; fiery; insipid; colorless;
cosmopolitan; fantastic; habitual; metrical;
blighted; discursive; wild; bloody; hazy;
sentimental.

verbs

color with—; crave—; culminate in—; delve
into—; denude of—; divest of—; dull—;
embalm—; enact—; guard—; nurture—;
permeate with—; repudiate—; taste—; tinge
with—; wreck—; —blinds; —blooms; —
blossoms; —conceives; —dissolves; —fades;
—flourishes; —flowers; —glows; —illuminates; —soars; —transports; —uplifts.
(See love, passion.)

ROMANTIC

adverbs

incurably; naturally; venturously; adventurously; unusually; absurdly; incorrigibly;
extravagantly; wildly; fantastically; sentimentally; imaginatively; picturesquely; incredibly; singularly; oddly; boldly; recklessly; whimsically; capriciously; magnificently; brilliantly; daringly; splendidly.

ROMP (v)

adverbs

sportively; boisterously; gaily; enthusiastically; irresistibly; intoxicatedly; pastorally;
amorously; rustically.
(See play, frolic.)

ROOF

adjectives

matted; distant; pyramidal; multitudinous;
(pl); consecrated; crumbling; picturesque;
gabled; timbered; weather-toned; unpretentious; terraced; milky; huddling; leafy;
sloping; brook-eaved; irregular; gambrel;
fantastic; embowered; purple-peaked; projected; moonwashed; slanting; majestical,
radiant; high-pitched; verdant; branching;
fretted; permanent; blackening; wavy; crystal; graceful; arched; high-peaked; man-
sard; lowly; vaulted; flowery; sagging;
ragged; thatched; dusky; mountainous;
atrocious; long; movable; waving; collapsing; great; massive.

verbs

examine—; ornament—; paint—; patch—;
pierce—; provide—; repair—; ruin—; shatter—; test—; thatch—; vault—; —affords;
—crests; —extends; —leaks; —projects; —
shades; —sheds; —shelters; —slants.
(See cover, ledge, dome.)

ROOK

verbs

—builds; —caws; —clamors; —flocks; —s
jangle; —mounts; —plunders; —pours
forth; —s quarrel; —s swarm; —torments;
—s wrangle.
(See bird.)

ROOM

adjectives

vaulted; modest; furnished; peaceful; shadowy; secluded; bleak; spacious; well-swept;
neighboring; immaculate; reading; sunny;
abutting; luxurious; desolate; well-proportioned; charming; livable; warmed; fire-

proof; light; slashing; ink-smelling; paper-littered; commodious; crowded; midnight; frescoed; tobacco-scented; emergency; colorless; haunted; utmost; wide; spiritual; dismal; disordered; habitable; cheerless; sunlit; saddening; sundry (pl); comfortable; wretched; gracious; octagonal; beam-roofed; rectangular; barny; squalid; scanty; generous; pleasant; drafty; poverty-stricken; plaster-dropping; adjoining; shabby; large; clean; dim; sick; dingy; dreary; dimly-lit; fencing; tranquil; guest; tolerable; stiff; moon-lit; immense; solitary; low-ceilinged; dark; uncarpeted; low; smoke-filled; banqueting; unattractive; remote; awesome; foul; polluted; elegant; slant-roofed; earthly; dull; musty; handsome; sunny; raftered; airy; upper; quaint; mirror; projection; squalid; air-conditioned; uncomfortable; sordid; stuffy; charming; dormer-windowed; gloomy; darkening; lonely; eerie; cozy; smart; impressive; intimate; restful; remarkable; delightful; ultramodern; homelike; perfect; unusual; beautiful; exquisite; appointed; outside; tasteful; attractive; livable; modern; sleeping; well-planned; inexpensive; appealing; excellent; faultless; amazing; fine; great; decorated; becoming; sound-proof; bright; oversize.

verbs
air—; bar—; barge into (colloq.)—; bundle out of—; bunk in—; burst into—; bustle out of—; confine to—; clutter—; darken—; direct to—; flank—; fresco—; furnish—; jam —; mass in—; pace—; pop into—; repair to—; saunter into—; scuttle from—; seclude in—; slip from—; stalk out of—; stump out of—; sweep from—; ventilate—; —buzzes; —invites.

(See classroom, lounge, lobby, cell, hall, chamber, apartment, bedroom, kitchen, office.)

ROOMY
adverbs
delightfully; charmingly; pleasantly; comfortably; satisfactorily; acceptably; unnecessarily; spaciously; magnificently; adequately; amply; pleasantly; luxuriously; agreeably; conveniently.

ROOSTER
verbs
behead—; exhibit—; fatten—; pen up—; wire in—; —flutters about; —gobbles up;

—invades the hennery; —molts; —pecks; —perches; —scratches; —squawks; —struts; —waxes indignant.
(See fowl, hen.)

ROOTS
adjectives
nocturnal; grasping; aerial; ulcerating; lurid; mucilaginous; insipid; antique; vigorous; nutritious; fibrous; giant; unsearchable; musty; inconsiderable; extraneous; spreading; wasting; parched; bulbous; sexless; powdered; moss-cushioned; orbed; goodly; gnarled; deep-lying; aromatic; venerable; cooling; fantastic; palatable; homeliest; vile; corrugated; babbling; wiry; old; uptorn; clasping; social; severed.

verbs
affix to—; choke—; dig to—; enrich—; feed —; fertilize—; ground—; grub among—; involve—; kill—; manure—; nourish—; stimulate—; uncover—; unearth—; —absorb; —bury in; —canker; —function; —go deep; —insinuate themselves into; —moor to; —project above; —supply; —thrust.
(See stem, cause, source, plant.)

ROPE
adjectives
graceful; greasy; hempen; rag; dangling; fatal; dragging; efficacious; innumerable (pl); rescuing; improvised; rain-bleached.

verbs
attach—; bind with—; braid—; cast—; haul on—; knife—; lay—; plait—; secure with—; snag—; strain—; tighten—; tug—; twist—; wind—; —binds; —chafes; —entwines; —fastens; —girdles; —secures.
(See cable, cord, string, chain.)

ROSE
adjectives
transient; fading; refreshing; quaint; distinctive; colorful; full-blown; fresh-blown; belated; wild; damask; dusty; shaken; panting; white-petaled; golden-centered; imperial; bubbled; winter; transcendent; amorous; fossil; glimmering; glowing; flowerless; newborn; burning; snowy; branching; delicate; blooming; embroidered; autumnal; countless (pl); fragrant; blushing; deeper; victorious; heavenly; living; immeasurable; wide-hearted; queenliest; virgin; magic; late.

verbs

bear—; crown with—s; gather—s; hawk —s; infect—s; pluck—; prize—; strew with —s; strip—; —adorns; —blooms; —blossoms; —blushes; —buds; —charms; — fades; —flames; —glows; —lingers; —perfumes; —perishes; —strews; —survives; — trembles; —withers; prune—.

(See flower, plant.)

ROSTRUM

verbs

adorn—; advance toward—; appeal from—; ascend—; assemble on—; erect—; exhort from—; glide into—; harangue from—; mount—; orate from—; pace—; speak from —; —quakes; —tremors.

(See pulpit, platform, stage.)

ROSY

adverbs

beautifully; charmingly; bewitchingly; blushingly; bloomingly; buxomly; happily; shyly; bashfully; modestly; hopefully; artlessly; naturally; sweetly; innocently; childishly; laughingly; healthfully; wholesomely; pleasantly; prettily.

ROTE

adjectives

rapt; aesthetic; rhythmal.

ROTTEN

adverbs

utterly; uselessly; ruinously; abominably; unfortunately; disgustingly; unserviceably; unusably; disastrously; disgustingly; dangerously; hopelessly; indescribably.

ROTUND

adverbs

amusingly; prosperously; becomingly; perfectly; healthily; laughably; ludicrously; slightly; somewhat.

ROUGH

adverbs

unpleasantly; extremely; uncommonly; disagreeably; unevenly; jaggedly; unusually; peculiarly; strangely; curiously; stiffly; harshly; rockily; unexpectedly; surprisingly; distressingly; uncomfortably; dreadfully; intolerably.

adjectives

diurnal; dutiful; mazy; ambitious; tedious; unheroic; lucent; subsequent; monotonous; merciful; heathen; airy; weary; terrible; unfailing; luminous; solemn; frequent; periodical; ceaseless; dizzy; mortal; daily.

ROUSE (v)

adverbs

abruptly; violently; startlingly; dutifully; daily; faithfully; harshly; habitually; instinctively.

(See arouse, excite.)

ROUTE

adjectives

circuitous; rigorous; diversified; branching; baffled; river; caravan; slow; laborious; disused; shorter; sylvan; convenient; quaint; ignominious; extensive; unobstructed; unusual; principal; roundabout; dangerous; pilgrim; time-honored; rebellious; wanton; practicable; meandering; direct; devious; passable; regular; profitable; common; traditional; elusive; untried.

verbs

assure of—; chart—; choose—; clog—; conceive—; course—; cover—; deviate from—; direct to—; enter by—; follow—; invade —; memorize—; reconnoiter—; seek—; signify—; survey—; travel—; traverse—; — diverges; —entrances.

(See line, channel, road, course.)

ROUTE (v)

adverbs

completely; devastatingly; ignominiously; wholly; rebelliously; ruthlessly.

(See direct, plan.)

ROUTINE

adjectives

irksome; obscure; home; pleasure-seeking; foul; mechanized; ostentatious; systematic; hack; ordinary; laborious; slavish; dull; dreary; pleasant; wearisome; habituated; professional; indolent; systematized; monotonously; hated; soul-degrading; regular.

verbs

acquaint with—; adhere to—; adopt—; chafe under—; discharge—; eliminate—; endure—; establish—; fix—; identify with —; lift from—; mire in—; perform—; quit

—; reduce to—; relax—; settle into—; sink
into—; —bores; —dulls; —encases; —rusts;
—stagnates; —wears.
(See rule, conventionality, habit, custom.)

ROW

adjectives
parallel; endless; bowing; everlasting; cour-
tesying; straggling; interminable; legioned;
branchy; pale; tranquil; burnished; flaring;
monotonous; serried; formal; answering;
tenement; impenetrable; lusty; tremendous;
dreadful; numberless (pl); venerable.

verbs
arrange in—s; break—; disrupt—; draw
from—; emerge from—; file in—; fix—;
mark in—; mow down—; rank in—; realign
—; reinforce—; station in—; string in—s;
verge from—; —dazzles; —impresses; interrupt—.
(See line, series.)

ROW (v)

adverbs
strenuously; energetically; industriously; heroically; monotonously; tirelessly; vigorously; victoriously.
(See paddle, propel.)

ROWDY

adverbs
uncommonly; indecorously; uncivilly; intolerably; disagreeably; coarsely; boorishly;
outlandishly; disreputably; shamefully; opprobriously; arrantly; shockingly; appallingly; disturbingly; outrageously; scandalously; boisterously; audaciously; uncontrollably; inherently; deliberately; daringly;
naturally; incorrigibly; insufferably; blusteringly; defiantly.

ROYAL

adverbs
magnificently; splendidly; brilliantly; gorgeously; gloriously; imperiously; dominantly; imperially; arrogantly; proudly; authoritatively; absolutely; superbly; grandly;
augustly; magnanimously; justly; majestically; sumptuously; munificently; lavishly;
extravagantly.

ROYALISTS

adjectives
triumphant; ardent; passionate; staunch;
erratic; economic; loyal.

verbs
exterminate—; favor—; inspire—· oust—;
overthrow—; repel—; resist—; restore—;
—adhere; —advance; —deplore; —flee; —
progress; —support; —yield.
(See nobility, aristocracy, peerage.)

ROYALTY (v)

verbs
ascribe to—; assume—; desert—: fear—;
imitate—; inherit—; mingle with—; pretend
—; profane—; regain—; regard—; relinquish—; support—; suspect—; treat as—;
usurp—; worship—; —departs; —functions;
—oppresses; —privileges.
(See royalists, monarch, aristocracy,
peerage.)

RUB (v)

adverbs
briskly; frantically; industriously; vigorously; mechanically; incessantly; injuriously; maddeningly; furiously; skillfully.
(See polish, massage.)

RUBBISH

adjectives
worthless; dripping; fragmentary; inconceivable; unutterable; intelligent-sounding;
hypocritical; delightful; sea-drifted; noxious; mental.

verbs
cart—; cast—; clutter with—; consign to—;
dig in—; dispose of—; haul—; heap—;
mingle with—; object to—; reject as—; relegate to—; remove—; sweep away—;
trample on—; —offends; —reeks; —stains
(See junk, dust, debris, filth, dirt.)

RUBY

verbs
adorn with—ies; appraise—; blemish—;
crust with—ies; cut—; deck with—ies; distinguish—; imitate—; polish—; prize—; set
—; tinge—; value—; —blazes; —flushes; —
gleams; —glitters; —glows; —sparkles;
—ies stud.
(See gem, jewel, ornament, stone.)

RUDDERLESS

adverbs
hopelessly; helplessly; flounderingly; pathetically; desolately; forlornly; woefully; unfortunately; aimlessly; sadly; powerlessly;
unhappily.

adverbs

coarsely; ignorantly; bitterly; boorishly; naturally; characteristically; inexcusably; unnecessarily; vulgarly; unintentionally; indefensibly; awkwardly; particularly; contemptibly; inordinately; unwittingly; colossally; shockingly; drunkenly; churlishly; disrespectfully; impudently; mischievously; moodily; morosely; coolly; unpardonably; unpleasantly; disagreeably; deliberately; boisterously; offensively; unconsciously; artlessly; insufferably; innately; unceremoniously.

RUDENESS

adjectives

downright; ineffaceable; apparent; equal; barbarous.

verbs

betray into—; encounter—; forgive—; loathe—; palliate—; pardon—; soften—; subject to—; tolerate—; —appears; —irks; —offends; —provokes; —shames; —springs from; —unveils; —vexes.

(See barbarism, coarseness, disrespect.)

RUDIMENTS

verbs

acquire—; convey—; detect—; drill in—; embellish—; furnish—; inculcate—; ingrain —; instruct in—; master—; pick up—; nourish—; receive—; reduce to—; teach—; tutor in—.

(See knowledge, elements, idea, principles, essentials.)

RUEFUL

adverbs

forlornly; terribly; pathetically; sorrowfully; dismally; desolately; hopelessly; pitiably; drearily; darkly; helplessly; miserably; wretchedly; unspeakably; strangely; distressingly.

RUFFIAN

adjectives

burly; black-looking; solitary; sordid; staring; shy; young; true; malignant-looking; miserable; swaggering; madcap; cowardly; unprincipled.

RUFFLE (v)

adverbs

truculently; frivolously; jocosely; boisterously; placidly; violently; deliberately.

(See pucker, wrinkle.)

RUFFLES

adjectives

triple; full; frivolous; atheistic; shirred; hemmed; double-picot.

verbs

arrange in—; draw into—; gather—; iron out—; press into—; smooth—; —adorn; —decorate; —droop; —enhance; —frill; —ornament; —sag; —trim; —wilt.

(See wrinkle, braids, lace, fringe.)

RUG

adjectives

thick; sumptuous; brilliant; luxurious; shaggy; lustrous; reversible; valuable.

verbs

beat—; cushion—; dye—; fold—; pattern—; place—; roll—; shampoo—; tack—; trip over—; weave—; —covers; —protects; —shields.

(See carpet.)

RUIN

adjectives

rambling; picturesque; dustless; temporary; irremediable; financial; dismantled; mossy; calamitous; magnificent; silent; remarkable; undistinguished; smoldering; mental; glorious; partial; treasured; weed-covered; irretrievable; blood-stained; accumulated; wild; reeking; moldering; twisted; hungry; venerable; ivy-wreathed; hideous; final; complete; crumbling; barricaded; fragmentary; unsightly; blazing; dirty; scattered; undecipherable; frowning; majestic; pathetic; chaotic; promiscuous; deathless; piteous; impending; smoking; sudden; graceful; sprawling; private; melancholy; sandswept; stark; gloomy; mournful; hopeless; discreditable; black.

verbs

avert—; batter to—; behold—; brood over —; bury in—; drag to—; drift to—; escape —; expire in—; fall to—; foresee—; hide —; mourn—; prophesy—; reduce to—; reflect—; repair—; rescue from—; restore—;

secure from—; shield from—; speed—; verge on—; —impends; —threatens.

(See defeat, downfall, destruction.)

RUIN, (v)

adverbs

irreparably; miserably; utterly; ruthlessly; ingeniously; traitorously; vindictively; vengefully; irretrievably; irremediably; hideously; calamitously; financially; economically; politically.

(See overthrow, destroy.)

RULE

adjectives

artificial; bayonet; dynastic; brutal; declaratory; invariable; fixed; prescribed; odalisque; stipulated; mistaken; cut-and-dried; military; benign; uncivil; arbitrary; elaborate; melodic; beneficent; ethical; absurd; dictatorial; disciplinary; rigid; capricious; chivalrous; parliamentary; vexatious; drastic; paternal; classical; meticulous; strict; unavoidable; eligibility; violent; aristocratic; supposititious; abstemious; cardinal; orthodox; accepted; general; long; brutal; fundamental; special; redtape; stern; authentic; mob; maiden; enlightened; inflexible; convenient; infallible; profitable; respected; eventful; municipal; sceptral; awful; definite; adequate; unfailing; clogging; ancient; austere; common; operose; vigorous; iron-clad; equitable; inviolable; contradictory; inexorable; conventional.

verbs

abandon—; abide by—s; adhere to—; apply—; ascertain—; chafe under—; challenge —; cleave to—; conform to—; devise—; disregard—; enforce—; establish—; fix—; formulate—; ignore—; impose—; lay down —; liberalize—; memorize—; observe—; prescribe—s; reiterate—; revise—; subject to—; submit to—; sum up—; violate—; yield to—; —decrees; —fetters; —hampers; —prevails; —regulates; —stipulates.

(See ethics, routine, law, decree, formula, fundamental, method.)

RULE (v)

adverbs

imperiously; indomitably; despotically; munificently; cunningly; democratically; implicitly; arbitrarily; capriciously; brutally; conventionally; inexorably.

(See dominate, govern, influence.)

RULER

adjectives

predominant; ruthless; beneficent; incapable; effete; venerated; constitutional; influential; absolute; distant; despotic; discredited; ecclesiastical; sagacious; moneyed; dynastic; unscrupulous; successive (pl).

verbs

acclaim—; advise—; bless—; bow to—; crown—; dethrone—; dictate to—; exile—; ordain—; praise—; trust—; yield to—; — abdicates; —administers; —authorizes; — commands; —controls; —defends; —divines; —heads; —judges; —manages; — respects.

(See king, God, sovereign, dictator.)

RULING

verbs

abide by—; adhere to—; amend—; anticipate—; authorize—; comprehend—; correct —; decry—; ignore—; justify—; manufacture—; post—; presage—; question—; refer to—; sustain—; threaten—; uphold—; warrant—; —decrees; —forbids; —menaces; —prohibits.

(See regulation, announcement, decision, proclamation, amendment.)

RUMBLE

adjectives

confused; formidable; endless; throbbing; subterranean; dull; low; incessant; terrifying; mysterious.

verbs

dull—; emit—; muffle—; prolong—; scorn —; utter—; —arouses; —breaks; —bursts; —clashes; —cracks; —dins; —disturbs; — drowns out; —issues from; —rends; —resounds; —rolls; —travels.

(See growl, roar, echo, noise, thunder.)

RUMBLE (v)

adverbs

portentously; ominously; threateningly; resoundingly; reechoingly; formidably; mysteriously; terrifyingly; incessantly; intermittently.

(See reverberate, resound.)

RUMOR

adjectives

absurd; perennial; malicious; persistent; untimely; hideous; vague; traditionary; convincing; pitiful; faint; insane; wild;

universal; exciting; contradictory; apparent; wildest; dreadful; false; ghastly; painful; splintered; sinister; fake; baseless; scandalous.

verbs
brand as—; bruit about—; buzz with—; confirm—; deny—; discount—; disprove—; explode—; foster—; further—; give rise to—; lend color to—; manufacture—; overshadow—; promulgate—; ridicule—; scotch —; seethe with—; set afloat—; set to rest —; suppress—; track down—; —blossoms; —buds; —carries weight; —circulates; — flies; —gains ground; —grows; —hints at; —menaces; —persists; —seeps out; — spreads; —startles; —suggests.
(See libel, gossip, news, secret, report, lie.)

RUMOR (v)
adverbs
ridiculously; absurdly; perennially; maliciously; persistently; falsely; baselessly; slyly; scandalously; vindictively.
(See circulate, spread.)

RUMPUS
(colloq)
verbs
denounce—; design—; devise—; endure—; loathe—; muffle—; plan—; quell—; restrain —; stir up—; suffer—; suppress—; —disconcerts; —distracts; —diverts; —enrages; —horrifies; —terminates in; —vexes.
(See fight, brawl, quarrel, wrangle, disturbance, fracas.)

RUN (v)
adverbs
refractorily; blindly; obediently; efficiently; deliberately; capriciously; noiselessly; infallibly; smoothly; greedily; spontaneously; tortuously; frantically; riotously; violently.
(See hasten, scamper.)

RUPTURE
adjectives
final; violent; irreducible; sudden; inexplicable; public.

verbs
acquire—; avert—; brace—; complete—; cure—; develop—; excite—; hint at—; incur—; induce—; suffer—; —breaches; —

discloses; —ensues; —severs; —strangulates; —weakens.
(See fracture, discord, dissension, breach.)

RURAL
adverbs
delightfully; charmingly; pleasantly; refreshingly; expensively; invitingly; attractively; advantageously; desirably; gratifyingly; appropriately; conveniently; spaciously; invigoratingly; healthfully; wholesomely; admirably; commendably; enviably; enjoyably; dismally; drearily; inconveniently; undesirably; shabbily.

RUSE
adjectives
innocent; favorite; desperate; ready-witted; clever.

verbs
contrive—; detect—; design—; devise—; elude—; evade—; plan—; plant—; suggest —; —ambushes; —baits; —beguiles; —distracts; —diverts; —ensnares; —lures; — succeeds; —tempts; —traps; —tricks; — waylays.
(See trick, hoax, subterfuge, stratagem.)

RUSH
adjectives
headlong; swift; hectic; precipitate; despairing; violent; blowing; flying; impulsive; engulfing; shrieking; blossomy; trampling; sickening; steady; titanic; madder; furious; pounding; rioting; never-ending; nodding; tumultuous; veritable; memorable; impetuous; recurrent; mighty; soft; chilly; onward; slimy.

verbs
attempt—; avert—; check—; control—; curb—; discharge—; foresee—; halt—; predict—; prophesy—; stem—; —abates; — carries along; —drives; —forces; —impels; —overcomes; —overwhelms; —severs; — strains; —surges; —swells; —sweeps; — traps.
(See attack, charge.)

RUSH (v)
adverbs
tumultuously; deliberately; powerfully; incoherently; blindly; irrepressibly; unceremoniously; impetuously; violently; recklessly; madly; sickeningly; precipitately.
(See press, hurry.)

adjectives
devouring; killing; protective.

RUSTIC

adjectives
boorish; austere; impudent; honest; patient; egregious; simple.

adverbs
artlessly; shabbily; quaintly; boorishly; bluntly; rudely; clownishly; cheaply; remotely; inconveniently; uncomfortably; undesirably; intolerably; roughly; clumsily; outlandishly; unattractively.

RUSTLE

adjectives
silken; delicate; indefinable; slow; occasional; sad; uncertain; attractive.

verbs
emit—; muffle—; produce—; restrain—; suppress—; —arouses; —attracts; —bestirs; —discloses; —distracts; —disturbs; —falls; —issues; —perturbs; —reveals.
(See sound, hum, murmur, whisper.)

adverbs
ruinously; unserviceably; unusably; horribly; impossibly; dangerously; unfortunately; terribly; singularly; extremely; hopelessly; uselessly; worthlessly; disagreeably.

RUT

verbs
approach—; avoid—; bounce over—; cut—; deplore—; drift into—; erode—; excavate —; groove—; heed—; hollow out—; lumber along—s; pursue—; settle into—; sink into —; wear—; —deepens; —disgraces; —envelops.
(See groove, hole, channel, track, habit.)

RUTHLESS

adverbs
atrociously; viciously; maliciously; vengefully; bitterly; cruelly; barbarously; brutally; ferociously; malevolently; venomously; outrageously; unbelievably; unimaginably; nefariously; wickedly; unutterably; strangely; unaccountably; inherently; terribly; shockingly; appallingly; astonishingly; horribly.

S

adjectives
hilted; gilded; cruel; clashing; gleaming.

SABOTAGE

verbs
accomplish—; advocate—; charge with—; convict of—; disclose—; frustrate—; resort to—; thwart—; uncover—; unveil—; —cripples; —delays; —destroys; —disorganizes; —hinders; —impedes; —injures; —obstructs; —violates.
(See mutilation, destruction, delay.)

SAC

verbs
clog—; dilate—; distend—; impair—; incise —; irritate—; lodge in—; obliterate—; penetrate—; pierce—; rupture—; tap— ;—contracts; —discharges; —encloses.

SACK

verbs
bear—; convey in—; dip into—; emerge from—; forage with—; hoist—; mend—; plunge into—; transport in—; twill—; weave—; —yields.
(See basket, box, case.)

SACRAMENT

verbs
administer—; deny—; observe—; partake of—; receive—; take—; —baptizes; —betokens; —binds; —canonizes; —christens; —confirms; —consecrates; —dedicates; —imposes; —impresses; —obligates; —ordains; —pledges; —promises; —ritualizes; —sanctifies; —seals; —signifies; —symbolizes.
(See ceremony, rite, benediction, matrimony.)

SACRED

adverbs
unutterably; inviolably; personally; universally; traditionally; locally; racially; curiously; inexplicably; affectionately; solemnly; carefully; augustly; impressively; genuinely; nationally; peculiarly; inordinately; unaccountably; inscrutably; mysteriously.

SACREDNESS

verbs
attach—to; blaspheme—; blemish—; despoil —; encroach on—; enshrine in—; esteem—; infringe upon—; mar—; preserve—; revere —; sense—; taint—; tamper with—; venerate—; violate—; —consecrates; —hallows; —glorifies; —secludes; —sets apart.
(See holiness, religion, benevolence, justice, integrity, sanctity, piety.)

SACRIFICE

adjectives
useless; prodigious; vicarious; living; idle; bloodless; fatal; patriotic; willing; personal; ruinous; superstitious; supreme; approaching; fearful; easy; tremendous; enormous; severe; ghastly; dreadful; exposed; inevitable; virtuous; appropriate; unimaginable; necessary; saving; sweeping; deliberate; unprofitable; mock; undue; eucharistic; economic; gratifying; numberless (pl); heroic; searching.

verbs
bemoan—; decry—; dramatize—; entail—; impose—; involve—; modify—; occasion—; offer—; ritualize—; submit to—; suffer—; undergo—; —absolves; —atones for; —compensates; —deifies; —deprives; —exemplifies; —expiates; —hallows; —purges; —purifies; —sanctifies; —sheds; —shrives; —symbolizes.
(See atonement, loss.)

SACRIFICE (v)

adverbs
repentantly; deliberately; economically; heartlessly; wantonly; shamefully; bloodlessly; patriotically; superstitiously; heroically; personally; supremely; fatally.
(See surrender.)

SACRILEGE

verbs
brand with—; commit—; deplore—; —blasphemes; —curses; —defiles; —desecrates; —injures; —insults; —offends; —outrages; —profanes; —reviles; —scandalizes; —violates.
(See sin, crime, vice.)

adverbs

habitually; naturally; inherently; incurably; lonesomely; curiously; unaccountably; heedlessly; inconsolably; inexplicably; awfully; profoundly; anxiously; deplorably; grievously; piteously; pathetically; pensively; ostentatiously; plaintively; dreamily; uncommonly; ominously; strangely.

SADDLE

verbs

break to—; cling to—; cushion—; ease from —; grip—; hop into—; ornament—; pad—; perch on—; polish—; rub—; slip from—; stir in—; straddle—; stud—; sway in—; sweep from—; swing into—; tear from—; vault into—.

(See seat ,chair.)

SADNESS

adjectives

settled; deadly; unmannered; uncultivated; treasured; great; real; simple; lyrical; pensive; inexpressible; wintry; shady; mild; sober; pleasing; unfathomable; unrecumbent; sudden; unbidden; clinging; preposterous; penetrating; thrilling; primeval; tender; good; prophetic; breathed; silent; mortal; humorous; painful; moody; haunting; profound; grateful; quaintest; utter; galling; compassionate; exquisite.

verbs

afflict with—; bow in—; brood in—; dispel —; exude—; incline toward—; induce—; mope in—; occasion—; —dampens; —deepens; —dejects; —depresses; —disheartens; —downcasts; —envelops; —hangs over; — pains; —pervades; —prevails; —racks; — rends; —seizes; —sheathes; —shrouds; — sobers; —touches; —weighs upon; —wrings.

(See grief, melancholy, homesickness, nostalgia, pathos.)

SAFARI

verbs

equip—; fit out—; gear—; guide—; organize—; outfit—; rig up—; —beats a path; —breaks camp; —explores; —fatigues; — films; —halts; —hunts; —records; —takes the trail; —thrills; —trails; —traverses; — treks; —uncovers.

(See expedition.)

adverbs

fortunately; luckily; happily; thankfully; comparatively; fairly; altogether; reasonably; supposedly; presumably; probably; forever; finally; ultimately; gratefully; relatively; permanently.

SAFEGUARD

verbs

adopt—; dispense with—; employ—; inspect —; offer—; prescribe—; preserve—; promote—; sweep away—; —affords; — bridles; —exempts; —flanks.; —insures; — protects; —reassures; —screens; —shelters; —shields; —shrouds; —wards off.

(See guard, protection.)

SAFETY

adjectives

precious; maximum; greatest; inglorious; comparative.

verbs

advance with—; advocate—; afford—; campaign for—; contrive for—; dwell in—; endanger—; engender—; enhance—; foster—; further—; hazard—; heighten—; insure—; jeopardize—; menace—; preach—; promote—; reduce—; risk—; scurry to—: threaten—.

(See security, protection, stability.)

SAG (*v*)

adverbs

concavely; dilapidatedly; hideously; mournfully; partially; weakly; abruptly; markedly; weakly.

(See sink, yield.)

SAGA

verbs

compose—; edit—; narrate—; publish—; relate—; treasure—; unfold—; —depicts; —entertains; —fascinates; —glories in; — honors; —interweaves; —intrigues; —perishes; —portrays; —recites; —recounts; — sings of; —stirs; —grips.

(See adventure, book, story, narrative.)

SAGACIOUS

adverbs

shrewdly; drolly; drily; eminently; dependably; notably; reputably; maturely; unusually; unexpectedly; strangely; coolly; marvelously; admirably; surprisingly; sharply; astutely; keenly; uncommonly; unfailingly.

SAGACITY

adjectives

superior; strange; clear-sighted; undimmed; shrewd; political; commercial; cool; crafty; mortal; unerring; marvelous; equal; practical; consummate; characteristic.

SAGE

verbs

acclaim—; consult—; venerate—; —counsels; —decrees; —foresees; —foretells; —predicts; —prescribes; —proclaims; —pronounces; —prophesies; —visions.

(See philosopher, scientist, master, counselor.)

adverbs

perceptibly; discerningly; profoundly; shrewdly; reputedly; notably; remarkably; unusually; uncommonly; extraordinarily; estimably; learnedly.

SAGES

adjectives

literary; rapt; puissant; honored; ancient; pungent; blundering; venerable; martyred; dusty; august; life-taught; hoary; erudite; analytical; cautious.

SAIL

verbs

cross—s; distend—; draw—; expand—; hoist—; lash—; lower—; puff out—; reef —; reenforce—; rig—; shorten—; slack—; stain—; strain—; stretch—; strike—; unfurl—; whip—; —billows; —booms; —dips; —droops; —flaps; —flutters; —propels; —shudders.

(See canvas, cloth.)

SAIL (v)

adverbs

peacefully; pensively; majestically; adventurously; prosperously; invincibly; gracefully; longitudinally; deftly; serenely.

(See embark, navigate.)

SAIL-BOAT

verbs

(See ship.)

SAILING

adjectives

emotional; gossiping; deft; smooth; superior; skilled; adept; seaworthy; landlubber-ly; graceful; accomplished; notable; crowded; intermittent; regular; spasmodic; announced; final; expected.

SAILOR

adjectives

shanghaied; storm-driven; outlandish-looking; swarthy; stray; apparent; sufficient; roistering; unwary; gesticulating; skillful; slow; homesick; roving; practical; drenched; mahogany-faced; stalwart; practised; trained; experienced; dissolute; debauched.

verbs

drill—s; elevate—; maroon—; quarter—s; —charts; —departs; —embarks; —fares; —guides; —mutinies; —navigates; —provisions; —voyages; command—; court-martial—; decorate—.

(See midshipman, soldier.)

SAILS

adjectives

bellying; cunning; swelling; gliding; roaring; snowy; vapory; drifting; flashing; slanting; rising; whitening; winglike; tattered; dead-leaf; slippery; riddled; flapping; torn; noisy; useless; sere.

SAINT

adjectives

criticizing; mounting; imaged; elder; loveliest; sublimest; particular; honored; toiling; felicitous; heavenly; apostolic; propitious; invisible; canonized; shoddy; glorious; beatified; latest; espoused; guardian; mortal; pastoral; mild-eyed; earthly; sentimental; pagan; reviling; lost; martyred; impolluted.

verbs

acclaim—; address—s; canonize—; esteem —; exalt—; glorify—; hail as—; hallow—; honor—; importune—; invoke—s; martyr —; persecute—; placate—s; prostrate before—; reverence—; supplicate—s; venerate—; worship—.

(See God, hero, angel, idol.)

SAINTED

adverbs

recently; devoutly; ceremoniously; ritualistically; deservedly; happily; piously; solemnly; formally; ceremonially; publicly; magnificently; officially; ecclesiastically.

SAINTLY

adverbs

downright; incredibly; drolly; sincerely; punctiliously; piously; ostentatiously; absurdly; unnecessarily; incongruously; excessively; stiffly; genuinely; extraordinarily; comically.

SALACIOUS

adverbs

unnecessarily; disagreeably; unreadably; abominably; detestably; loosely; disgustingly; coarsely; grossly; indecently; dreadfully; inordinately; highly.

SALADS

adjectives

excellent; tempting; crisp; cold; floating; bitter; green.

SALARY

adjectives

picayune; admirable; weekly; meager; terrific; substantial; moderate; tiny; exceptional; scanty; stated; adequate; unearned.

verbs

attach—; deprive of—; draw—; fix—; invest—; reap—; restore—; shear—; slash —; withhold—; —compensates; —fluctuates; —recompenses; —redresses —remunerates; —rewards.

(See income, livelihood, earnings, wages.)

SALES

adjectives

thrilling; spectacular; periodic; miscellaneous; insignificant; summer; sensational; sluggish; private; dynamic; previous; widespread; current.

verbs

advertise—; advise—; advocate—; balk at —; bolster—; climax—; close—; contrive—; disclose—; double—; facilitate—; force—; interfere with—; jeopardize—; kill—; prohibit—; promote—; push—; restrict—; stimulate--; unearth—; —accelerate; —decline; —diminish; —drop; —dwindle; — ebb; —jump; —rise; —soar; —spurt; — toboggan.

(See trade, traffic, purchase.)

SALESMAN

adjectives

traveling; live; direct; aggressive; real; well-paid; slick; super-annuated; invaluable; able; unusual; persuasive; well-dressed; suave; sleek; pleasant.

verbs

commission—; drill—; employ—; engage—; organize—; stall—; teach—; train—; — arouses interest; —beguiles; —colors; — convinces; —creates; —demonstrates; — enables; —exhibits; —explains; —interviews; —lures; —markets; —paints; — points out; —pushes; —tempts.

(See employee, clerk, worker.)

SALIVA

verbs

absorb—; convey—; drivel—; drool—; emit—; excrete—; issue—; ooze—; pour out—; remove—; secrete—; slaver—; slobber—; swallow—; —aids; —defiles; — flows; —mixes; —moistens; —sterilizes.

SALLIES

adjectives

erratic; piquant; impotent; brilliant; massed; liveliest; occasional; sudden; futile; hot; outrageous; bitter.

SALONS

adjectives

glittering; philosophical; illegal; artistic; gaudy; gilded.

SALOON

adjectives

gorgeous; gilded; shadowy; luxurious; spacious; decorous; old-time; mirrored.

verbs

abolish—; assemble in—; crowd—; denounce—; frequent—; furnish—; hie to—; license—; line—; maintain—; permit—; renounce—; tax—; wreck—; —clamors; —reeks of; —resounds.

(See tavern, restaurant, inn, hotel.)

SALT

adjectives

insinuating; resultant; solid; valuable; mineral; specific; complex; relaxing; systematic; desolating; insoluble; deliquescent; shrill; atmospheric; iodized; celery.

verbs

add—; apply—; conserve—; dab in—; dash —; dissolve—; export—; imbue with—; immerse in—; impregnate with—; iodize—;

lack—; powder—; prepare—; preserve in —; refine—; require—; season with—; spice with—; sprinkle—; —destroys; —influences.

(See mustard, sugar, spice.)

SALTY
adverbs
impossibly; extremely; dangerously; satisfactorily; unnecessarily; bitterly; stingingly; sharply; unexpectedly; unsavorily; brackishly; disagreeably; impossibly; unpleasantly; unpalatably; rankly; unappetizingly; inexcusably.

SALUBRIOUS
adverbs
invigoratingly; stimulatingly; measurably; unquestionably; bracingly; usefully; definitely; obviously; manifestly; famously; notably; reputably; undeniably; advantageously.

SALUTATION
adjectives
rude; elaborate; original; friendly; courteous; cordial; mock; boisterous; impressive; noisy; grateful; murmured; expressive; pleasant; grim; crude;. hearty.

verbs
acknowledge—; condense—; discharge—; dispense with—; exchange—s; express—; gain—; greet with—; ignore—; rehearse—; return—; shout—; word—; —befits; —compliments; —favors; —honors.

(See greeting, kiss, embrace.)

SALUTE
adjectives
obedient; reverential; characteristic; rattling; roistering; royal; noisy; parting; graceful; sketched; customary; silent; presidential.

verbs
acknowledge—; bestow—; bow to—; conceive—; fire—; give—; greet with—; master —; perform—; present—; return—; —announces; —compliments; —expresses; —favors; —honors; —troubles.

(See greeting, kiss.)

SALUTE (v)
adverbs
courteously; formally; cordially; thunderously; respectfully; civilly; vehemently; gravely; obediently; fraternally; affectionately; obsequiously.

(See hail, greet.)

SALVATION
adjectives
lovely; eternal; certain; promised; rosy; imaged.

verbs
achieve—; desire—; despair of—; exhort—; find—; gain—; interfere with—; offer—; plead—; preach—; prove—; relish—; secure—; seek—; suffer—; venture—; win—; work out—; —depends on; —opens to.

(See atonement, deliverance.)

SALVE
verbs
apply—; anoint with—; concoct—; daub—; mix—; smear—; spread—; —comforts; —consoles; —cures; —eases; —heals; —mitigates; —palliates; —soothes.

(See lotion, balm, liniment, poultice, ointment.)

SAMENESS
adjectives
deadly; long; illusive; very; dull; boring; repetitious.

SAMPLE
adjectives
original; fair; random; disheartening; odd; pretty; splendid; generous.

verbs
apply for—; collect—s; examine—; furnish —; judge by—; match—; obtain—; present with—; secure—; show—; survey—s; view —; witness—; —confirms; —illustrates; —represents; —serves.

(See merchandise, goods, example, specimen.)

SANATIVE
adverbs
commendably; approvedly; acceptably; reputably; exceptionally; assuredly; securely; conclusively; decisively; demonstrably; conspicuously; successfully; unusually; miraculously; marvelously; unexpectedly; unfailingly.

ally; contemptibly; boorishly; disagreeably; meanly; unpleasantly; gracelessly; grossly; keenly; brilliantly; effectively.

SATIRIZE (v)
adverbs
spitefully; pungently; ruthlessly; delicately; effectively; comically; bitterly; scorchingly; passionately; politically; socially; diabolically; astutely; acrimoniously.
(See ridicule, lash.)

SATISFACTION
adjectives
relaxing; inexpressible; tolerable; aesthetic; obtrusive; obscure; proud; mutual; partial; subjective; excessive; complete; unspeakable; unbounded; suitable; comfortable; outward; disguised; evident; anxious; fine; phonetic; nostalgic; mirthful; immense; mournful; peculiar; compensating, lasting; enduring; all-around; absolute; elegant; unctuous; sweet; unique; lively; ferocious; melancholy; subtle; smug; inward; grim; cold; unhappy; hearty; elevated; mental; mundane; unconcealed; pecuniary; hauling; unfeigned; rash; physical; wholesome; pleasurable; unmarried; meager; indwelling; paltry; complacent; sinister; deep; lasting; inner; fleeting; unnatural; universal; obvious; drunken; full; solemn; secret; ample; heartfelt; vicarious; internal; permanent; extreme; reasonable; ultimate; keenest; lofty; honest.

verbs
achieve—; afford—; beam in—; conceal—; consume with—; crave—; derive—; demand —; desire—; experience—; express—; feign —; gain—; heighten—; indulge in—; lessen —; offer—; procure—; scorn—; yield—; — results; —soothes; seek—.
(See delight, contentment, gratification, happiness, enjoyment.)

SATISFACTORY
adverbs
highly; charmingly; wholly; genuinely; providentially; luckily; gratifyingly; acceptably; reasonably; vastly; unexpectedly; profoundly; particularly; absolutely; unusually; socially; financially; universally; generally; officially; utterly; entirely; seldom; rarely; scarcely; happily.

SATISFIED
adverbs
completely; perfectly; adequately; sufficiently; utterly; wholly; pleasantly; happily; contentedly; luckily; altogether; comfortably; complacently; easily; serenely; cheerfully.

SATISFY (v)
adverbs
temporarily; amply; abundantly; aesthetically; uniquely; pecuniarily; vicariously; sexually; reasonably; ultimately; keenly; rationally; intellectually; philosophically; lustfully; lasciviously; sensually.
(See appease, gratify.)

SATYRIC
adverbs
horribly; leeringly; foully; evilly; frightfully; hideously; monstrously; repulsively; grinningly.

SAUCE
adjectives
luscious; delicate; unstudied; well-seasoned; inimitable; tasty; sizzling.

SAUCY
adverbs
impertinently; incredibly; incurably; impudently; boldly; prettily; insolently; pertly; grossly; unpleasantly; disrespectfully; oddly; singularly; inexplicably; brazenly; smartly; cheaply; audaciously; flippantly; presumptuously; unpardonably; inexcusably; brashly; discourteously; amazingly; singularly; dreadfully; foolishly; dangerously.

SAUNTER (v)
adverbs
lazily; leisurely; unconcernedly; carelessly; brazenly; boldly; nonchalantly.
(See loiter, linger.)

SAVAGE
adverbs
cruelly; bestially; unbelievably; inhumanly; brutally; ferociously; fiercely; furiously; barbarously; pitilessly; ruthlessly; unmercifully; grossly; relentlessly; wildly; singularly; lawlessly.

SAVAGERY
adjectives
asserted; untamed; absolute; idiotic; genial; degraded; outlying; eternal; methodized; abject.

adjectives

incurable; hostile; primitive; squalid; shiftless; sensitive; naked; brown; superstitious; unchristian; innocent; guileless; malicious; carnivorous; dreadful; livid; rudimentary; untutored; howling; sentimental; splendid; malignant.

verbs

appease—; civilize—; condemn—; encourage—; fear—; incite—; quell—; quiet—; soothe—; tame—; —attack; —beset; —charm; —distress; —guide; —inhabit; —murder; —overtake; —rage; —spare; —stampede; —worship.

(See monster, barbarian, Indian, ferocity, native.)

SAVE (*v*)

adverbs

prudently; judiciously; scrupulously; substantially; phenomenally; spectacularly; privately; unprecedentedly; miraculously; penuriously; rashly; courageously; heroically.

(See rescue, deliver.)

SAVING

adjectives

considerable; great; guaranteed; substantial; systematic; conventional; miraculous; phenomenal; bankable; epigrammatic; unbelievable; additional; important; exciting; tremendous; aggregate; definite; private; valuable; unprecedented; supreme; sensational; extraordinary; spectacular.

SAVINGS

verbs

acquire—; afford—; amass—; apply—to; bequeath—; deplete—; deposit—; effect—; entrust with—; exhaust—; heap—; hoard—; preserve—; put by—; rake together—; retire on—; store—; treasure up—; —accrue; —accumulate; —dwindle; —pension.

(See money, profits, income, earnings.)

SAVOR

adjectives

luscious; sharp; immortal; odious; putrid; lovely; appetizing.

verbs

blend—; destroy—; dispel—; lack—; lose —; perfect—; relinquish—; retain—; —al-

lures; —baits; —beguiles; —departs; —differs; —excites; —relishes; —tempts; —varies.

(See flavor, taste, fragrance, perfume, odor.)

SAY (*v*)

adverbs

plaintively; fiercely; cryptically; artlessly; graciously; tremulously; compassionately; complacently; impatiently; brokenly; casually; hoarsely; ruefully; reflectively; insistently; decisively; unsteadily; consolingly; acutely; deprecatingly; reflectively; roisterously; resignedly; emotionally; passionately; soothingly; involuntarily; wistfully; craftily; sententiously; reassuringly; searchingly; tentatively; doggedly; dogmatically; derisively; exultingly; sardonically; impetuously; musingly; coaxingly; wrathfully; authoritatively; emphatically; triumphantly; candidly; blandly; demurely; naively; impetuously; brusquely; magnanimously; philosophically; bluntly; dubiously; tremulously; sensitively; ostentatiously; insinuatingly; decisively.

(See speak, utter.)

SAYING

adjectives

humorous; skin-deep; magnanimous; faithful; blunt; apt; prudent; sententious; bold; quaint; pregnant; mirthful; well-known; pithy; indiscreet; needle-pointed; witty; dim; deft; true; wise.

verbs

accept—; advance—; amend—; attribute—to; compose—; contradict—; heed—; quote —; recall—; refer to—; —amplifies; —angers; —attests; —emphasizes; —epitomizes; —summarizes; —voices.

(See adage, epigram, quotation, motto.)

SCAB
(*industry*)

verbs

disband—s; lynch—; manhandle—; oust—; prohibit—s; protect—; threaten—; —s offend; —s organize; —rebels; —resists; —troubles; —s unite.

(See striker, rioter.)

SCALES

adjectives

grander; chromatic; glistening; diatonic; extensive; colossal; sordid; stupendous; gen-

adverbs
admirably; usefully; satisfactorily; advantageously; fortunately; grittily; disagreeably; unluckily; ordinarily; unpleasantly; unpalatably; terribly; dreadfully.

SANGUINE
adverbs
groundlessly; unreasonably; overly; cheerfully; absurdly; brightly; optimistically; buoyantly; happily; enthusiastically; unwarrantably; foolishly; confidently; ardently; warmly; earnestly; excitedly; characteristically; naturally; inherently.

SANITARY
adverbs
wholly; satisfactorily; surprisingly; completely; safely; meticulously; carefully; inelligently; adequately; extremely; sufficiently; uncommonly; highly; scrupulously.

SANITY
verbs
approach—; attest to—; derange—; display —; doubt—; enjoy—; forsake—; gain—; guard—; jeopardize—; question—; recover —; restore to—; retain—; return to—; test —; —flags; —languishes; —wanes.
(See reason, knowledge, sense.)

SAP
adjectives
torpid; impregnate; sciential; tasty.

SAPIENT
adverbs
acutely; cunningly; discerningly; perceptibly; sensibly; intelligently; profoundly; reasonably; subtly; pompously; proudly; garrulously; chattily; brightly; jocosely; astutely; slyly; cannily; cleverly; piercingly; sharply; shrewdly; soundly; nimbly; wittily.

SAPLINGS
adjectives
flimsy; round; silvered; spiny; sturdy; bent; twisted; hardy.

SARCASM
adjectives
coarse; chilling; taunting; evident; good-natured; needless; irritating; sweeping; quiet; elaborate; cutting; sneering; juster; mocking; withering; hurtling; keener; pre-

meditated; deadly; biting; mild; veiled; obvious; bludgeoning; savage; shivering; painful.

verbs
employ—; flout—; gird in—; indulge in—; pour forth—; vary—; vent—; temper—; —affronts; —bites; —cuts; —detracts; —embitters; —flays; —insults; —piques; —scars; squelches; —strikes; —taunts; —scathes; —smarts.
(See cynicism, invective, mockery, derision, irony.)

SASH
adjectives
tarnished; silken; flaunting; voluminous.

SATCHEL
verbs
check—; clasp—; cram—; dig into—; explore—; guard—; hug—; mislay—; probe —; replenish—; stuff—; tuck in—; —bulges; —contains; —discloses; —swings.
(See bag, baggage, grip, brief-case.)

SATIN
adjectives
lustrous; glossy; shimmering; creamy; gleaming; sheeny; wrinkled; warm.

SATIRE
adjectives
delicate; sharp-pointed; effective; harmless; humorous; scorching; coarse; sober; cosmic; irresistible; shy; genial; deadly; nobler; modest; mild; personal; implied; biting; social; unsparing; scathing; keen; critical; ribald; savage; political.

verbs
aim—at; direct—; employ—; fear—; flash —; interpret—; introduce—; partake in—; resent—; sharpen—; soften—; subject in—; wield—; —amuses; —cuts; —declaims; —denounces; —derides; —exaggerates; —exposes; —jeers; —lashes at; —reproves; —ridicules; —runs riot.
(See irony, jest, joke, mockery.)

SATIRICAL
adverbs
bitterly; cruelly; stingingly; curiously; cleverly; unexpectedly; unnecessarily; scathingly; savagely; derisively; ironically; caustic-

adverbs

sincerely; piously; devoutly; strangely; suddenly; rapturously; contentedly; serenely; recently; naturally; ecclesiastically; ceremonially; actually; reverently; fervently; solemnly; radiantly; zealously.

SANCTIMONIOUS

adverbs

absurdly; ridiculously; affectedly; ostentatiously; laughably; insincerely; disagreeably; pretentiously; smoothly; blandly; suavely; unctuously; prudishly; pharasaically; hollowly; intolerably.

SANCTION

adjectives

philosophical; express; tacit; highest; pragmatic; legislative; rational; theologic; divine; unequivocal; venerable.

verbs

abolish—s; announce—; invoke—s; lend—; offer—; receive—; regard—; require—; seek—; —allows; —assures; —authorizes; —benefits; —confirms; —encourages; —establishes; —permits; —pleases; —supports.

(See approval, indorsement, confirmation, approbation.)

SANCTION (v)

adverbs

unequivocally; solemnly; expressly; philosophically; tacitly; ecclesiastically; legislatively; beneficently; paternally.

(See approve, conform.)

SANCTITY

adjectives

marital; purest; superior; profound; angelic; quiet; magical; supposed; humorless.

verbs

abrogate—; approach—; assume—; cloak in—; conceive in—; defile—; exhibit—; fame for—; hallow—; honor—; intrude upon—; possess—; question—; retain—; simulate—; tamper with—; translate—; vindicate—; violate—; —decays; —invades.

(See holiness, piety, sacredness.)

SANCTUARY

adjectives

startled; heavenly; ancient; tapering; desecrated; vast; veiled; lifelong.

verbs

admit to—; afford—; crowd—; dedicate—; defile—; dwell in—; embrace—; enshrine in—; expel from—; frequent—; gain—; hallow—; inhabit—; raze—; seek—; unveil —; —consoles; —invites; —protects; —shelters.

(See refuge, immunity, cathedral, church, temple, retreat.)

SAND

adjectives

ribbed; spangling; tinted; unending; milky; drooping; sea-deserted; shifting; pathless; torrid; angry; damp; quick; perpetual; swampy; conniving; silver; sounding; slippery; sun-bleached; restless; drifting; slushy; bituminous; dissolving; auriferous; wrinkled; ruby; dreary; worthless; clinging; treeless; sweltering; coralline; wan; volatile; shallower; parched; sinking; sighing; endless; penurious; tropic; stinging; swishing.

verbs

bury in—; crush into—; elevate—; finger—; heap—; intermix with—; lose in—; overlay with—; plod through—; plough through—; polish with—; precipitate—; shovel—; sift —; trace in—; tread—; wade through—; wrinkle—; —hems; —shifts; —smooths.

(See grit, powder, dust.)

SANDALS

adjectives

placid; ambrosial; winged; tropic; worn.

SANDPIPER

verbs

bog—; decoy—; gun for—; —arrays; —bobs; —booms; —bows; —darts; —defies; —flits; —flutes; —glides; —honks; —patters about; —probes; —sails; —settles down; —soars; —squats; —whirs; —zigzags.

(See bird.)

SANDWICH

verbs

broil—; consume—; devour—; fill—; garnish—; gobble—; lunch on—es; munch—; pack—es; relish—; savor—; serve—; spread —; sup on—es; toast—; —appeals; —refreshes.

(See food.)

ally; contemptibly; boorishly; disagreeably; meanly; unpleasantly; gracelessly; grossly; keenly; brilliantly; effectively.

SATIRIZE (v)

adverbs

spitefully; pungently; ruthlessly; delicately; effectively; comically; bitterly; scorchingly; passionately; politically; socially; diabolically; astutely; acrimoniously.

(See ridicule, lash.)

SATISFACTION

adjectives

relaxing; inexpressible; tolerable; aesthetic; obtrusive; obscure; proud; mutual; partial; subjective; excessive; complete; unspeakable; unbounded; suitable; comfortable; outward; disguised; evident; anxious; fine; phonetic; nostalgic; mirthful; immense; mournful; peculiar; compensating; lasting; enduring; all-around; absolute; elegant; unctuous; sweet; unique; lively; ferocious; melancholy; subtle; smug; inward; grim; cold; unhappy; hearty; elevated; mental; mundane; unconcealed; pecuniary; hauling; unfeigned; rash; physical; wholesome; pleasurable; unmarried; meager; indwelling; paltry; complacent; sinister; deep; lasting; inner; fleeting; unnatural; universal; obvious; drunken; full; solemn; secret; ample; heartfelt; vicarious; internal; permanent; extreme; reasonable; ultimate; keenest; lofty; honest.

verbs

achieve—; afford—; beam in—; conceal—; consume with—; crave—; derive—; demand —; desire—; experience—; express—; feign —; gain—; heighten—; indulge in—; lessen —; offer—; procure—; scorn—; yield—; — results; —soothes; seek—.

(See delight, contentment, gratification, happiness, enjoyment.)

SATISFACTORY

adverbs

highly; charmingly; wholly; genuinely; providentially; luckily; gratifyingly; acceptably; reasonably; vastly; unexpectedly; profoundly; particularly; absolutely; unusually; socially; financially; universally; generally; officially; utterly; entirely; seldom; rarely; scarcely; happily.

SATISFIED

adverbs

completely; perfectly; adequately; sufficiently; utterly; wholly; pleasantly; happily; contentedly; luckily; altogether; comfortably; complacently; easily; serenely; cheerfully.

SATISFY (v)

adverbs

temporarily; amply; abundantly; aesthetically; uniquely; pecuniarily; vicariously; sexually; reasonably; ultimately; keenly; rationally; intellectually; philosophically; lustfully; lasciviously; sensually.

(See appease, gratify.)

SATYRIC

adverbs

horribly; leeringly; foully; evilly; frightfully; hideously; monstrously; repulsively; grinningly.

SAUCE

adjectives

luscious; delicate; unstudied; well-seasoned; inimitable; tasty; sizzling.

SAUCY

adverbs

impertinently; incredibly; incurably; impudently; boldly; prettily; insolently; pertly; grossly; unpleasantly; disrespectfully; oddly; singularly; inexplicably; brazenly; smartly; cheaply; audaciously; flippantly; presumptuously; unpardonably; inexcusably; brashly; discourteously; amazingly; singularly; dreadfully; foolishly; dangerously.

SAUNTER (v)

adverbs

lazily; leisurely; unconcernedly; carelessly; brazenly; boldly; nonchalantly.

(See loiter, linger.)

SAVAGE

adverbs

cruelly; bestially; unbelievably; inhumanly; brutally; ferociously; fiercely; furiously; barbarously; pitilessly; ruthlessly; unmercifully; grossly; relentlessly; wildly; singularly; lawlessly.

SAVAGERY

adjectives

asserted; untamed; absolute; idiotic; genial; degraded; outlying; eternal; methodized; abject.

SAVAGES

adjectives

incurable; hostile; primitive; squalid; shiftless; sensitive; naked; brown; superstitious; unchristian; innocent; guileless; malicious; carnivorous; dreadful; livid; rudimentary; untutored; howling; sentimental; splendid; malignant.

verbs

appease—; civilize—; condemn—; encourage—; fear—; incite—; quell—; quiet—; soothe—; tame—; —attack; —beset; —charm; —distress; —guide; —inhabit; —murder; —overtake; —rage; —spare; —stampede; —worship.

(See monster, barbarian, Indian, ferocity, native.)

SAVE (v)

adverbs

prudently; judiciously; scrupulously; substantially; phenomenally; spectacularly; privately; unprecedentedly; miraculously; penuriously; rashly; courageously; heroically.

(See rescue, deliver.)

SAVING

adjectives

considerable; great; guaranteed; substantial; systematic; conventional; miraculous; phenomenal; bankable; epigrammatic; unbelievable; additional; important; exciting; tremendous; aggregate; definite; private; valuable; unprecedented; supreme; sensational; extraordinary; spectacular.

SAVINGS

verbs

acquire—; afford—; amass—; apply—to; bequeath—; deplete—; deposit—; effect—; entrust with—; exhaust—; heap—; hoard—; preserve—; put by—; rake together—; retire on—; store—; treasure up—; —accrue; —accumulate; —dwindle; —pension.

(See money, profits, income, earnings.)

SAVOR

adjectives

luscious; sharp; immortal; odious; putrid; lovely; appetizing.

verbs

blend—; destroy—; dispel—; lack—; lose—; perfect—; relinquish—; retain—; —al-

lures; —baits; —beguiles; —departs; —differs; —excites; —relishes; —tempts; —varies.

(See flavor, taste, fragrance, perfume, odor.)

SAY (v)

adverbs

plaintively; fiercely; cryptically; artlessly; graciously; tremulously; compassionately; complacently; impatiently; brokenly; casually; hoarsely; ruefully; reflectively; insistently; decisively; unsteadily; consolingly; acutely; deprecatingly; reflectively; roisterously; resignedly; emotionally; passionately; soothingly; involuntarily; wistfully; craftily; sententiously; reassuringly; searchingly; tentatively; doggedly; dogmatically; derisively; exultingly; sardonically; impetuously; musingly; coaxingly; wrathfully; authoritatively; emphatically; triumphantly; candidly; blandly; demurely; naively; impetuously; brusquely; magnanimously; philosophically; bluntly; dubiously; tremulously; sensitively; ostentatiously; insinuatingly; decisively.

(See speak, utter.)

SAYING

adjectives

humorous; skin-deep; magnanimous; faithful; blunt; apt; prudent; sententious; bold; quaint; pregnant; mirthful; well-known; pithy; indiscreet; needle-pointed; witty; dim; deft; true; wise.

verbs

accept—; advance—; amend—; attribute—to; compose—; contradict—; heed—; quote—; recall—; refer to—; —amplifies; —angers; —attests; —emphasizes; —epitomizes; —summarizes; —voices.

(See adage, epigram, quotation, motto.)

SCAB
(industry)

verbs

disband—s; lynch—; manhandle—; oust—; prohibit—s; protect—; threaten—; —s offend; —s organize; —rebels; —resists; —troubles; —s unite.

(See striker, rioter.)

SCALES

adjectives

grander; chromatic; glistening; diatonic; extensive; colossal; sordid; stupendous; generous; artistic; lavish; prodigal; elaborate; manifest; glittering; gigantic; diminutive; realistic; defective; adequate; ambitious; industrial; burnished; respectable; miniature.

verbs
collect—; detach—; form—; peel off—; penetrate—; separate—; shed—; strip of—; —armor; —cover; —defend; —enhance; —fall; —overlap; —overlay; —protect; —radiate.
(See flake, film.)

SCALP

adjectives
bare; fearful; transformed; clean; sickly; dry; itching; diseased; scaly.

verbs
adorn—; affect—; apply to—; cover—; crust —; cut—; distend—; heal—; imbed in—; irritate—; lacerate—; massage—; move—; pierce—; rip—; strip—; tear—; wound—; —erodes; —reddens; —tenses; —tingles.
(See head, skin.)

SCAMP

adjectives
slick; premature; pitiful; conscienceless; frolicsome; potential; worthless; wicked; unsocial.

SCAMPER (v)

adverbs
hurriedly; swiftly; playfully; boisterously; friskily; joyously; blithely.
(See run, hasten.)

SCAN (v)

adverbs
earnestly; anxiously; minutely; industriously; wearily; studiously; critically; eagerly; casually; superficially; desultorily; intently; pedantically.
(See look, distinguish.)

SCANDAL

adjectives
darker; latest; typical; inconspicuous; frightful; amazing; frequent (pl); fantastic; judicial; family; appalling; tea-table; foul; vulgar; flagrant; grave.

verbs
air—; bear—; blaze into—; breathe—; curb —; degenerate into—; despise—; dig up—; diffuse—; disclose—; discredit—; dissect—; enjoy—; face—; free from—; garnish with —; involve in—; monger—; shroud in—; spread—; wipe away—; —allures; —arises; —damages; —defaces; —defames; —disgraces; —excommunicates; —harms; —injures; —offends; —persecutes; —shames; —shocks; —trickles in.
(See infamy, aspersion, slander, gossip.)

SCANDALOUS

adverbs
unfortunately; openly; uncommonly; arrantly; terribly; shamefully; undeniably; flagrantly; admittedly; highly; regrettably; sadly; deplorably; grossly; notably.

SCANT

adverbs
dangerously; alarmingly; indecently; pitiably; inexplicably; unmercifully; shamefully; curiously; significantly; fearfully.

SCAR

adjectives
honorable; raised; deep; mental; private; frightful; hideous; dreadful; unsightly; fratricidal.

verbs
bear—; expose—; inflict—; jest at—; plaster —; retain—; reveal—; seam with—s; —attests to; —blemishes; —disfigures; —mars; —marks; —proves; —remains; —results from; —sustains; —traces.
(See blemish, defect, flaw, sore.)

SCARCE

adverbs
alarmingly; seriously; critically; locally; universally; lamentably; fearfully; uncommonly; unusually; curiously; unaccountably; inexplicably; inconveniently; miserably; unexpectedly; evidently; deplorably; remarkably; singularly; suddenly.

SCARCITY

adjectives
restful; increasing; definite; chronic; noticeable; dangerous; fearful.

SCARE

adjectives
baseless; wild; sorry; hopeless.

verbs
exaggerate—; foment—; heed—; manufac-

ture—; occasion—; report—; strike with—; work—; —arouses; —fizzles out (colloq.); —overcomes; —seizes; —stimulates; —terrifies; —unnerves; —excites; —fades.

(See fright, terror, fear, dread, anxiety.)

SCARE (v)
adverbs
instinctively; baselessly; unavoidably; agitatingly; dreadfully; abominably; waggishly.

(See frighten, terrify.)

SCARED
adverbs
terribly; shockingly; awfully; irrecoverably; frightfully; unmercifully; cruelly; brutally; desperately; apparently; somewhat; wildly; foolishly; hideously; ignorantly; miserably; heartlessly; secretly; suddenly; mortally.

SCARF
adjectives
flaunting; downy; fluttering; traditional; square; fringed; flamboyant; daring; flashing.

SCATTER (v)
adverbs
profusely; liberally; generously; promiscuously; philanthropically; confusedly; haphazardly; carelessly.

(See separate, dispel.)

SCATTERED
adverbs
widely; pitifully; wastefully; erratically; lavishly; wantonly; fortunately; luckily; sparsely; extravagantly; thinly; thickly; singularly; intentionally; cleverly; diplomatically; profitably; intentionally.

SCENARIO
verbs
alter—; collaborate on—; complete—; compose—; condense—; detail—; draw up—: elaborate on—; fill in—; outline—; purchase—; reject—; rewrite—; sketch—; submit—; —calls for; —depicts; —dramatizes; —portrays; —thrills; —unfolds.

(See story, play.)

SCENE
adjectives
striking; moving; appropriate; painful; pastoral; mad; magnificent; solemn; shameless; sanguinary; sublime; grotesque; ted-

ious; frightful; idyllic; desolate; lively; licentious; dramatic; affecting; decorous; chaotic; animating; hopeful; delicious; brilliant; semi-tragic; violent; passionate; comical; pitiable; circling; martial; distant; enchanting; lofty; remote; novel; mythological; celestial; garish; foregoing; barren; fine; enveloping; cheerless; troubled; riotous; visionary; sylvan; wondrous; convivial; mountain; sunny; powerful; trial; tropical; odious; immediate; binding; classic; picturesque; exquisite; murky; shifting; droll; torturing; grateful; flattering; varied; melodramatic; death-bed; adventurous: squalid; fateful; historic; astonishing; mournful; pirate; pathetic; turbulent; previous; terse; wild; imposing; conspicuous; animated; human; dreadful; memorable; engrossing; realistic; night; impressive; imprisoned; mimic; shocking; pungent; horrible; distressing; harrowing; preliminary; soul-searching; ennobling; fearful; dismal; stirring; rollicking; vivid; agitating; perilous; heroic; touching; awful; renovated; sequestered; strange; trying; toiling; festive; tragic; quaint; singular; universal; monotonous; precarious; verdant; pacific; tranquil; beauteous.

verbs
alter—; applaud—; behold—; cloud—; conceive—; conjure up—; contemplate—; detail—; dispatch to—; dominate—; dramatize—; eavesdrop upon—; enact—; flee—; hover over—; indulge in—; overshadow—; portray—; reconstruct—; reproduce—; retire from—; smirk at—; storm across—; stumble upon—; visualize—; weigh—; —depicts; —drifts; —motivates; —shifts; —takes momentum.

(See aspect, spectacle, view, place, scenery.)

SCENERY
adjectives
picturesque; distant; rugged; salient; impressive; glorious; noble; savage; diversified; quieting; grandiose; monstrous; fascinating; superlative; mountainous; sumptuous; gaudy; animated; admirable.

verbs
admire—; behold—; contemplate—; design—; devour—; enjoy—; feed on—; light—; present—; view—; —affects; —attracts; —awes; —changes; —delights; —enhances;

1036

—enraptures; —enthralls; —impresses; —inspires; —magnetizes.

(See landscape, scene.)

SCENT

adjectives

foreign; pleasing; floral; alluring; spicy; faint; delicious; keen; remarkable; patriarchal; chosen; dusty; dry; sweet; delicate; exalted; lingering; hot; flower; pungent; cunning; unmemoried; impromptu; dull; peppery; balmy; pretty.

verbs

abhor—; breathe—; convey—; derive—from; detect—; discern—; employ—; eschew —; extract—; follow—; impregnate with—; inhale—; load with—; lose—; pick out—; pursue—; recognize—; recover—; seek—; sniff up—; stimulate—; visualize—; —aids; —disguises; —indicates; —overwhelms; —perceives; —permeates; —pervades; —recalls; —rises; —survives; —wanes; —yields to.

(See essence, fragrance, aroma, odor.)

SCENT (v)

adverbs

instinctively; fragrantly; deliciously; pungently; delicately; brazenly; boldly.

(See perfume.)

SCENTED

adverbs

permanently; odiously; disgustingly; fragrantly; sweetly; exotically; expensively; exquisitely; delicately; opulently; seductively; alluringly; excitingly; pleasantly; nauseatingly; sickeningly; cheaply; mysteriously; evanescently; delightfully; cleverly.

SCEPTRE

adjectives

social; pacific; golden; age-old; jeweled; beauteous; royal; magic.

verbs

bear—; confer—on; entitle to—; govern with—; invest with—; ornament—; rule with—; shake—; sway—; swear by—; touch with—; wield—; —awes; —dignifies; —empowers; —signifies; —symbolizes.

(See baton, power, staff.)

adjectives

preconcerted; rigorous; diverse (pl); fixed; timed; daily; temporary.

verbs

abolish—; adhere to—; alter—; arrange—; consult—; discard—; establish—; expand—; fall behind—; follow—; insert in—; maintain—; map out—; observe—; note—; present—; publish—; refer to—; slash—; threaten—; throw off—; —regulates; —sets forth; —specifies.

(See list, calendar, itinerary.)

SCHEME

adjectives

curious; artistic; nameless; recognized; comprehensive; suitable; subtile; beautiful; selling; ambitious; philanthropic; systematic; ingenious; illusory; unphilosophical; mature; marvelous; impractical; dualistic; seditious; educational; critical; far-reaching; imperial; iconographic; poaching; dubious; hostile; gigantic; cherished; social; multiform (pl); elaborate; improvident; decorative; extensive; despotic; rascally; visionary; promising; constructive; wild; speculative; gardening; unbodied; prearranged; entangled; abominable; interesting; tortuous; iniquitous; rational; ludicrous; extravagant; feasible; generous; well-weighed; detailed; warm; cheery; perfidious; chimerical; digesting; eternal; desolate; providential; prodigal; cowardly; particular; flying; fantastic; vast; homely; harmonious; artless; selfish; colossal; bold; notable; advantageous; flimsy; seductive; wonderful; darling; complicated; shallow; monotonous.

verbs

abandon—; administer—; adopt—; back out of—; blast—; broach—; commit to—; concoct—; contemplate—; dally with—; demonstrate—; devise—; discern—; foist—upon; formulate—; fulfill—; further—; immerse in—; launch—; mature—; mull over—s; organize—; promote—; prosecute—; puzzle out—; resurrect—; scrap—; scrutinize—; seethe with—s; spin—; stymie—; undertake —; view—; —concentrates on; —goes awry; —hatches; —intrigues; —unfolds.

(See idea, project, plan.)

SCHEME (v)

adverbs

covetously; traitorously; diabolically; viciously; abominably; extravagantly; chimerically; artlessly; advantageously; systematically; politically; seditiously; tortuously; perfidiously.

(See plan, plot.)

SCHEMING

adjectives

wily; political; amiable; nefarious; wicked; skillful.

adverbs

innocently; mischievously; childishly; pleasantly; mysteriously; secretly; openly; brazenly; maliciously; meanly; cleverly; politically; astutely; adroitly; madly; viciously; criminally; heartlessly; cattily; brutally; dangerously; lovingly; hatefully; successfully; artfully; ingeniously; cunningly; craftily; sharply; slyly; warily; unscrupulously; insidiously; disloyally; treacherously; thoughtfully; prudently.

SCHOLAR

adjectives

learned; elegant; tolerable; potential; distinguished; convent; renowned; eminent; quiet; reserved; brilliant; famous; studious; ivory-towered; absent-minded; profound; reputed; classical; astonished; feeble; famishing; desperate; crude; credulous; facile; austere; advanced; professional; rude; ripe; amiable; painstaking; imaginative; pedantic; competent; able; grammatical; true; refractory.

verbs

discipline—; enlighten—; guide—; honor—; instruct—; reward—; test—; tutor—; train —; —acknowledges; —acquaints with; — attains; —attends; —comprehends; — crams; —embraces; —follows; —inquires; —investigates; —merits; —professes; — searches.

(See reader, student, pupil, disciple, follower.)

SCHOLARLY

adverbs

extremely; amazingly; brilliantly; deeply; profoundly; singularly; eminently; particularly; reasonably; broadly; assiduously; industriously; forbiddingly; abstrusely; alarmingly; splendidly; consciously.

SCHOLARSHIP

adjectives

theological; eminent; profound; deficient; unusual.

SCHOOL

adjectives

vigorous; trivial; hostile; hungering; monastic; cursory; archaeological; law; creditable; fashionable; eclectic; spasmodic; collegiate; skill-contending; elaborate; up-to-date; hard-boiled; realistic; red-brick; immemorial; illustrious; foremost; decadent; haggard; magazine; formal; parochial; consummate; evolutionary; subordinate; toilful; celebrated.

verbs

approve—; attend—; bar from—; disband —; endow—; enroll in—; enter—; exclude from—; expel from—; father—; foster—; found—; graduate from—; impair—; join —; maintain—; rank—; rate—; revisit—; —attracts; —designates; —examines; — flourishes; —prepares; —suspends; — thrives.

(See college, institution, seminary, library, university.)

SCHOOL-BOY

verbs

chastise—; discipline—; enlighten—; examine—; harass—; impress—; oppress—; rebuke—; reprimand—; reproach—; tutor—; —attends; —cheers; —comprehends; —derides; —detects; —enjoys; —s gather; — pens; —romps; —sports; —taunts; —violates.

(See student, pupil, scholar.)

SCHOOLING

verbs

afford—; confine to—; continue—; ignore—; lack—; neglect—; overlook—; profit by—; refuse—; test—; utilize—; value—; —edifies; —enlightens; —grounds; —imbues; — infuses; —instills; —overcomes; —polishes; —prepares; —trains.

(See training, preparation, education.)

SCHOONER

adjectives

splendid; helpless; respectable; dilapidated; coasting; piratical; trading.

verbs
anchor—; becalm—; con—; convert—; convey by—; design—; fit out—; handle—; launch—; navigate—; rig—; steer—; —bears off; —clears; —cruises; —gleams; —graces; —heels; —plies; —ports; —rushes; —sheers; —shoves off; —signals; —skims; —sounds; —tacks; —tosses.
(See boat, launch, ship.)

SCIENCE

adjectives
substantial; principal; adequate; universal; physical; pseudo; mysterious; experimental; practical; laborious; economic; dominant; non-remunerative; biological; kindred (pl); contiguous; astronomical; industrial; spatial; liberal; specific; miracle; profane; systematic; political; grotesque; falsified; deepest; hypnotic; abstract; speculative; occult; intricate; daring; applied; imaginary; sister; pure; auxiliary; mechanical; visionary; various (pl); direct; bloodless; collateral.

verbs
acclaim—; applaud—; apply—; bolster by —; correlate—s; elucidate—; foster—; further—; grapple with—; live for—; pertain to—; suppress—; —contributes to; —contrives; —demonstrates; —dissects; —explores; —flourishes; —investigates; —proves; —pursues; —reveals; —scoffs at; —scorns —surpasses; —sustains; —teaches; —tests; —trains; —utilizes; —voices; —wages a fight.
(See economics, anatomy, psychology.)

SCIENTIFIC

adverbs
carefully; meticulously; accurately; highly; gravely; extremely; necessarily; scarcely; distinctly; profoundly; undeniably.

SCIENTIST

adjectives
heckling; over-impulsive; distinguished; attuned; pure; dissecting; rejuvenated; equipped; enraptured; objective; skilled; famous.

verbs
enrage—; honor—; perplex—s; puzzle—s; —concludes; —considers; —converts; —cultivates; —deduces; —delves; —devotes; —discerns; —discloses; —disputes; —dissects; —envisions; —examines; —fathoms; —

formulizes; —infers; —reasons; —researches; —seeks; —solves; —stresses; —studies; —verifies.
(See naturalist, philosopher.)

SCION

adjectives
dormant; remaining; fiery; illustrious; gentler; decadent; dissipated; royal.

SCISSORS

verbs
grind—; ply—; resharpen—; wield—; —clips; —crops; —dangles; —nicks; —pares; —pieces; —pierces; —removes; —shears; —smooths; —snips.
(See shears.)

SCOLD (v)

adverbs
harshly; pedantically; maddeningly; monotonously; irritatingly; exasperatingly; malignantly; shrewishly.
(See reprimand, lecture.)

SCOLDING

verbs
addict to—; incur—; inflict—; justify—; merit—; relent—; rue—; vent—; —abuses; —bites; —corrects; —curbs; —cuts; —descends upon; —disciplines; —disturbs; —mortifies; —rebukes; —reproaches; —shames.
(See lashing, rebuke, ridicule.)

COPE

adjectives
ample; determined; economic; confined; unlimited; gracious; intellectual; international; institutional; plentiful; utmost; unrestricted; free; comprehensive; unusual; unsuspected.

verbs
appreciate—; afford—; ascertain—; broaden —; comprehend—; confine—; desire—; dissipate—; dwarf—; enlarge—; exceed—; extend—; gain in—; limit—; measure—; muse over—; narrow—; question—; restrict—; survey—; widen—; —embraces; —extends; —ranges.
(See limit, range, extent.)

SCORCH (v)

adverbs
superficially; ruinously; hopelessly; carelessly; partially; markedly; obviously.
(See burn, shrivel.)

SCORE

adjectives
mortal; creditable; voluminous; operatic; trifling; one-sided; brilliant; breath-taking.

verbs
collate—s; compose—; compress—; copy—; distribute—; familiarize with—; mark—; note—; play—; practice—; recall—; rehearse—; strike off—; tabulate—.

(See music, manuscript, account, reckoning.)

SCORE (v)

adverbs
deftly; precisely; accurately; brilliantly; repeatedly; victoriously; creditably; overwhelmingly.

(See record, enter.)

SCORN

adjectives
sullen; compassionate; rising; indignant; ineffable; casual; virtuous; supercilious; helpless; hopeless; merry; revengeful; unconcealed; quiet; tameless; haughty; curious; intolerable; unaffected; languid; tender; triumphant; indescribable; infidel; shameful; profound; defiant; hard; superficial; superior; writhing; bitter; frank; casual; withering; sensitive; mingled; magnanimous; spitting; fine; chivalric; idle; constant; contemptuous; amused; foul; old-fashioned; supreme; ribald; dazzling; womanly; unutterable; unsavory; incredulous; incalculable; contemptuous.

verbs
bristle in—; cloak in—; convey—; deride in —; expose to—; express—; feign—; heap—; imply—; point in—; quiver in—; regard with—; sneer in—; snort in—; submit to—; treat with—; wither with—; —deepens; —grows; —offends.

(See disdain, derision, contempt.)

SCORN (v)

adverbs
theoretically; unutterably; sullenly; indignantly; superciliously; haughtily; intolerably; triumphantly; indescribably; casually; contemptuously; hatefully.

(See reject, disregard.)

SCORNFUL

adverbs
arrogantly; pompously; insolently; unbear-

---

ably; offensively; youthfully; blithely; ridiculously; ignorantly; significantly; pityingly; unpleasantly; defiantly; learnedly; utterly; thoughtlessly; laughingly; malignantly.

SCOUNDREL

adjectives
unscrupulous; upstanding; infamous; pompous; church-going; blatant; unprincipled; hypocritical; infernal; murderous; remorseless; dissolute; swindling; insolent.

verbs
associate with—; berate—; harbor—; master—; oust—; punish—; regiment—s; rebuke—; reprimand—; shelter—; —degrades; —eludes; —evades; —shocks; —sullies; —tricks.

(See profligate, villian, rogue, criminal.)

SCOURGE

adjectives
national; appointed; dreadful; appalling; inexorable; lifted; controversial; fatal; chastening; penitential; dreaded.

verbs
afflict with—; anticipate—; bemoan—; check—; curb—; cure of—; deplore—; halt —; incur—; lift—; overcome—; prevent—; stamp out—; succumb to—; —befalls; —besets; —destroys; —exterminates; —plagues; —ravishes; —routs; —settles on; —spreads; —wipes out.

(See curse, disease, plague.)

SCOUTING

verbs
discover—; encourage—; engage in—; enjoy—; foster—; found—; instruct in—; perform—; practice—; train in—; venture into —; —conduces to; —drills; —engenders; —offers; —prepares; —teaches; —toughens.

(See athletics, exercise, activity.)

SCOWL

adjectives
envious; unbecoming; slight; swarthy; anxious; sullen; suffering; malignant; fierce; terrific; lowering.

verbs
assume—; cast—; draw into—; exhibit—; gather into—; ignore—; incur—; perpetuate—; receive—; send forth—; —darkens;

—departs; —expresses; —fouls; —glowers;
—relents; —sours; —threatens; —wilts; —
withers.

(See frown, glare, look, sneer.)

SCOWL (v)
adverbs
morosely; vindictively; bitterly; savagely;
threateningly; pugnaciously; belligerently;
enviously; sullenly; malignantly; fiercely;
rudely; uncouthly.

(See frown.)

SCRAMBLE
adjectives
ethical; wild; persistent; rough; unseemly;
exhilarating; nerve-destroying; fearful;
noisy.

verbs
decipher—; define—; degenerate into—: interpret—; protest—; regard—; survey—;
—confuses; —disorders; —disperses; —displeases; —disturbs; —hampers; —impedes;
—perplexes; —upsets; —wanes.

(See rush, struggle.)

SCRAPE
adjectives
unfortunate; typhoid; frequent (pl); tight.

SCRAPS
adjectives
sundry; reminiscent; abject; babbling; infected; disdained; discreditable.

SCRATCH (v)
adverbs
industriously; eagerly; perplexedly; harass-
edly; composedly; complacently; reflectively; meditatively; uncouthly.

(See scribble, scrawl.)

SCRATCHING
verbs
induce—; necessitate—; weary of—; —
annoys; —chafes; —eases; —endangers;
—gratifies; —infects; —inflames; —irks;
—irritates; —mars; —relieves; —vexes.

SCRAWL
adjecives
unhallowed; blotted; rapid; tragic; anguished; hurried; illegible.

SCRAWL (v)
adverbs
illegibly; laboriously; feebly; crudely; rudely; clumsily; hurriedly; unconventionally.

(See scribble, scratch.)

SCRAWNY
adverbs
dingily; haggardly; pitiably; terribly; inexplicably; decrepitly; horridly; scurvily;
sorrily; pitifully; feebly.

SCREAM
adjectives
half-stifled; ear-splitting; feminine; frantic;
faint; long; mocking; unearthly; eloquent;
inarticulate; defiant; hoarse; sharp; piercing; querulous; shrill; piteous; pretty; multitudinous (pl); pulsating; ecstatic; suppressed.

verbs
emit—; issue—; muffle—; pour forth—; resound with—s; restrain—; silence—; stifle
—; suppress—; —alarms; —curdles; —
freezes; —lances; —penetrates; —pierces;
—rends; —rocks; —shakes; —shatters; —
terrorizes.

(See cry, yell, noise, howl, roar.)

SCREAM (v)
adverbs
piercingly; shrilly; madly; frantically; triumphantly; agonizedly; harshly; mockingly;
eloquently; ecstatically; piteously.

(See yell, shriek, screech.)

SCREECH (v)
adverbs
dissonantly; insanely; wildly; bestially;
hideously; irrationally; shamefully; ribaldly.

(See scream, shriek.)

SCREEN
adjectives
featureless; leafy; costly; omnipresent;
mendacious; little; hand; impenetrable;
luminous; stubble; theoretical; shadowy;
fluorescent.

verbs
contrive—; employ—; fold—; frame—;
hinge—; insert—; necessitate—; observe
through—; project on—; remove—; view
on—; —encloses; —envelops; —guards; —

obscures; —prevents; —protects; —shelters; —shields; —shrouds; —wards off.

SCREEN (v)
adverbs
protectively; effectually; leafily; faithfully; modernistically; coveniently.
(See protect, conceal.)

SCRIBBLE (v)
adverbs
carelessly; unbeautifully; furiously; illegibly; unreadably; crabbedly; grotesquely; characteristically.
(See scrawl, scratch.)

SCRIBBLED
adverbs
weakly; dimly; faintly; coarsely; grossly; childishly; illegibly; crookedly; sprawlingly; finely; clearly; feebly; desperately; hurriedly; hastily; hopefully; eagerly; carelessly; untidily; secretly.

SCRIBE
adjectives
romantic; daily; deft; professional; poison-spirited; capable.

SCRIPT
adjectives
legible; spidery; unfinished; tiny; unreadable.

verbs
abolish—; clarify—; comprehend—; decipher—; decode—; direct from—; form—; imitate—; interpret—; practise—; recognize—; reproduce—; revise—; study—; translate—; —attracts; —awes; —confuses; —differs; —puzzles; —resembles.
(See handwriting, writing, manuscript.)

SCRIPTURAL
adverbs
genuinely; authentically; authoritatively; piously; incontrovertibly; convincingly; persuasively; undeniably; provokingly; unanswerably; formidably; comfortingly; prophetically; highly.

SCRIPTURES
verbs
accept—; attack—; bolster with—; cite—; con—; embody in—; embrace—; employ—; enjoy—; limit—; mark—; memorize—;

mouth—; recall—; refer to—; regard—; review—; study—; —enlighten; —guide; —illuminate; —reveal; —sanctify.
(See Bible, Gospel, writing.)

SCROLL
adjectives
scented; bible; brilliant; talismanic; unsullied; graven; awful; gentle; parchment.

SCRUB (v)
adverbs
scrupulously; diligently; spotlessly; industriously; methodically; ambitiously; tirelessly; vigorously; ceaselessly.
(See rub, polish.)

SCRUPLES
adjectives
weak; conscientious; ceremonious; utmost; immovable; commendable; spiritual; tiresome; religious; desperate; formal; wayward; ceremonial; confirmed.

verbs
avoid—; banish—; cling to—; disregard—; dull—; entertain—; express—; lack—; mold —; overcome—; override—; question—; raise—; shape—; sharpen—; shelve—; silence—; stand on—; tamper with—; —plague; —restrain; —trouble; —weigh upon.
(See qualm. doubt, skepticism, suspicion, hesitation.)

SCRUPULOUS
adverbs
habitually; carefully; dependably; unusually; remarkably; admirably; commendably; highly; vigilantly; laudably; reliably; painstakingly; genuinely; meticulously; honestly.

SCRUTINIZE (v)
adverbs
avidly; critically; intently; cannily; quizzically; keenly; minutely; circumspectly; cautiously; persistently; suspiciously; hostilely; irreverently; boldly; shrewdly.
(See examine, inspect.)

SCRUTINY
adjectives
persistent; prolonged; assiduous; suspicious; terrible; distant; calm; curious; intent; searching; accurate; hostile; critical; sullen;

deliberate; attentive; cool; irreverent; silent; keen; overclose; bold; telescopic; appalling; strictest; shrewd; ignorant; earnest; wondering.

verbs
avoid—; cringe under—; defy—; discard on—; invite—; lead to—; meet—; resent—; sharpen—; stretch—; subject to—; threaten with—; undergo—; —detects; —discloses; —disqualifies; —informs; —reveals; —rewards; endure—; expose to—.
(See look, examination, search, inquiry.)

SCUFFLE

adjectives
rough; momentary; noisy; veritable; violent.

verbs
encounter—; join in—; lament—; subdue in—; —bursts forth; —confuses; —cripples; —disturbs; —ensues; —irks; —irritates; —menaces; —rages; —results in; —roars; —threatens; —upsets; —vexes; —wearies.
(See fight, struggle.)

SCULPTOR

verbs
acclaim—; award to—; criticize—; model for—; pose for—; —adorns; —carves; —chisels; —conceives; —engraves; —executes; —expresses; —finishes; —forms; —hews; —immortalizes; —molds; —shapes.
(See artist, painter.)

SCULPTURE

adjectives
monumental; shapeless; classic; antique; symbolic; mortuary; shadowy; matchless; colossal.

SCULPTURE (v)

adverbs
curiously; quaintly; deftly; exquisitely; monumentally; modernistically; bizarrely; intricately.
(See carve, engrave.)

SCUM

adjectives
precocious; muddy; leprous; vulgar; common.

verbs
clear of—; collect—; form—; gather—; purge—; reject—; retain—; sift off—;

strain—; throw off—; work up—; —covers; —films; —floats; —rises; —settles; —thickens; —veils.
(See dross, dirt, debris, filth.)

SCURRILOUS

adverbs
illegally; unpardonably; meanly; maliciously; basely; vulgarly; damagingly; hideously; intentionally; unforgivably; unforgettably; foully; indecently; unnecessarily; vilely; audaciously; boldly; challengingly; tauntingly; opprobriously.

SCURVY

verbs
afflict with—; communicate—; cure of—; ease—; heal of—; remedy—; salve—; suffer from—; —blemishes; —blights; —mars; —scourges; —spreads; —visits; —wipes out.
(See disease.)

SCUTTLED

adverbs
shamefully; ignominiously; secretly; necessarily; finally; desperately; furtively; reluctantly; completely.

SEA

adjectives
fair; boisterous; bland; sterile; sepulchral; savage; motionless; circumfluous; billowy; depraved; turbulent; choppy; coral; shoreless; crystal; glistening; varied; multitudinous (pl); unknown; shimmering; full-toned; homeless; orient; whispering; foaming; rocking; walled; moon-lit; heartless; glassy; sullen; primeval; tideless; wrinkled; insatiate; dense; flowing; undreamed; rough; complaining; unsalted; spacious; calmest; discharged; laughing; tropic; rushing; unfirm; sharp; voracious; wild; abhorred; remorseless; tranquil; treacherous; chainless; illumined; choral; uncanny; dim; leaden; tempestuous; sleeping; raging; troubled; ancient; isolating; throbbing; islanded; arctic; silken; mossy; opaline; empty; whelming; soundless; heaving; slimy; polished; gradual; agitated; murderous; summer; sparkling; plangent; democratic; wondering; lucent; unfathomed; climbing; hoary; intervening; straitened; waveless; arching; corpse-encumbered; misty; unpastured; wan; interlunar; undulating; distant; tossing; molten; full; boiling; unreluctant; peaceful; sandy; terrestrial; neglected; slumbrous; lulled; surging; inward; ugly;

extended; stainless; inviolate; violent; tumbling; careening; hindering; rainy; elongated; moral; winter; spendthrift; changeless; shoaling; rolling; enchanted; azure; delicious; phosphoric; mighty; placid; brilliant; wasting; sunny; pleasant; shivering; windy; abysmal; immemorial; trackless; barren; milky; harmonious; ordinary; narrow; rippling; tinted; incessant; southern; swollen; unresting; stern; limpid; farthest; glad; dancing; haughty; familiar; unstable; invisible; triumphant; rosy; perfumed; incarnadined.

verbs
cast up by—; challenge—; chart—; embark on—; fan—; head out for—; launch on—; plow through—; streak—; traverse—; —allures; —beats against; —bristles; —chastises; —chops; —dashes; —foams; —hems in; —murmurs; —s pile up; —pounds; —pursues; —retreats; —ripples; —rustles; —sighs; —sleeps; —sweeps; —thrashes; —thunders; —whispers; —yields up.
(See lake, ocean, wave, river, surf.)

SEAL

adjectives
dangling; sulphur; violated; experimental; sweet; wax; official; broken.

SEAL (v)

adverbs
hermetically; effectively; mechanically; scientifically; officially; automatically; nominally; legally; bindingly.
(See confirm, attest.)

SEALED

adverbs
hermetically; tightly; completely; successfully; properly; finally; officially; securely; safely; confidently; expertly; sufficiently; satisfactorily; hopelessly; firmly; legally.

SEAMAN

adjectives
distant; broken; disbanded (pl); skillful; proficient; doughty; unimaginative; conscientious; obsequious; groaning.

SEAMED

adverbs
oddly; conspicuously; remarkably; extremely; senilely; frostily; merrily; terribly; deeply.

SEAMS

adjectives
fossiliferous; chintz-welted; innumerable; whitened.

SEAPORT

adjectives
old; drowsy; conspicuous; populous; busy; modern.

SEARCH

adjectives
diligent; preliminary; keen; futile; quiet; breathless; fruitless; unreasonable; evident; deliberate; repeated; systematic; reckless; exhaustive; resolute; protracted; obnoxious; blindfolded; vain; intensive; vague; patient; relentless; superstitious; terrestrial; proposed; personal; narrow; prolonged; studious; frantic; roaming; vigorous; weary; nationwide.

verbs
baffle in—; cease—; conduct—; commence —; devote to—; discontinue—; entail—; enter into—; entrust—to; escape—; instigate —; institute—; justify—; relinquish—; renew—; undertake—; venture on—; weary of—; —ascertains; —consumes; —extends to; —pains; —reveals; —results in; —uncovers; —unearths.
(See examination, exploration, scrutiny, inquiry.)

SEARCH (v)

adverbs
deliberately; diligently; frenziedly; blindly; frantically; intently; rigorously; fruitlessly; cautiously; tirelessly; systematically; recklessly; protractedly; vainly; relentlessly; vaguely; legally; indefatigably.
(See hunt, seek.)

SEARCHING

adjectives
patient; intelligent; laborious; restless.

adverbs
unusually; rigorously; thoroughly; profoundly; uncommonly; rigidly; unpleasantly; heartlessly; inescapably.

SEARCH-LIGHT

verbs
desire—; exhibit—; fit with—; supply—; suspend—; switch on—; —beams; —dazzles; —diffuses; —enables; —exposes; —

facilitates; —flickers; —gleams; —illumines; —pierces; —penetrates; —reflects; —reveals; —signals.
(See light.)

SEASON
adjectives
singing; sickly; glorious; buried; tempestuous; heated; due; ordinary; rainy; favored; sultry; propitious; modish; virtuous; unapparent; festive; winter; holiday; gala; due; faithful; adverse; gentle; true; ominous; pestilential; youthful; beneficent; suitable; advancing; autumnal; convenient; unchanged.

verbs
adapt to—; divide into—s; fill—; inaugurate—; launch—; measure—s; —s alternate; —advances; —clothes; —creeps along; —develops; —drifts by; —fades; —flowers; —lapses; —matures; —s merge; —proceeds; —progresses; —promises; —ripens; —rolls around; —s vary; —waxes.
(See autumn, spring, summer, winter.)

SEASON (v)
adverbs
pungently; deftly; professionally; skillfully; richly; deliciously.
(See flavor.)

SEASONABLE
adverbs
pleasantly; safely; congruously; stylishly; fashionably; reasonably; appropriately; carefully; fastidiously; conveniently; happily; luckily; agreeably; fairly; sensibly.

SEAT
adjectives
proffered; rustic; glorious; battered; pleasant; splayed; favorite; airy; chiefest; princely; storied; regal; supreme; cheap; blissful; dismal; shady; secure; venerable; rural; capacious; luxurious; exalted; imperial; ancestral.

verbs
arrange—s; discover—; emerge from—; fill—s; group—s; mark—; number—s; occupy—; offer—; order—; pad—; proffer—; range—s; relinquish—; reserve—; slump in —; vacate—; wedge into—; —accommodates; —collapses.
(See chair, saddle.)

SEAT (v)
adverbs
musingly; peacefully; airily; cozily; carelessly; abruptly; wearily; drowsily; idly; calmly; rustically; regally; blissfully; exaltedly; imperially; ostentatiously; modestly; demurely; unobtrusively.
(See usher, establish.)

SEATED
adverbs
firmly; gingerly; shakily; nervously; permanently; resolutely; immovably; shyly; timidly; determinedly; finally; primly; demurely; stiffly; gravely; pompously; carefully; respectfully; slouchily; disrespectfully; lazily.

SECESSION
adjectives
successful; timely; foolish; peaceable.

SECLUDED
adverbs
carefully; happily; distantly; completely; pleasantly; comfortably; desirably; terribly; desolately; palatially; unsociably; conveniently; agreeably; inhospitably; delightfully; inexplicably; singularly; curiously; significantly.

SECLUSION
adjectives
obliterating; wearisome; elegant; mummied; dignified; studied; comforting; deep; haughty; bleak; aristocratic; motionless; strict; sweet; utter; tropical; slothful; ascetic; comparative; sullen; torpid; flowery; virtual; sunshiny; blank.

verbs
advise—; advocate—; afford—; attempt—; contemplate in—; emerge from—; enjoy—; gain—; hide in—; interrupt—; meditate in —; offer—; prize—; raise in—; rouse from —; seek—; strive for—; subject to—; bores; —consoles; —dulls; —stagnates; —disciplines.
(See isolation, loneliness, concealment, retirement, retreat.)

SECOND
adjectives
condemned; supercharged; frozen; significant; reckless; precise; fleeting; precious; recaptured; wasted; breathless.

SECRECY

adjectives

mysterious; enjoined; half-pretended; inviolate; romantic; strictest; indispensable; profound; infinite; tremendous; necessary; sworn.

verbs

delve into—; encroach upon—; intrude upon —; obscure with—; pervade—; pierce—; — fosters; —mystifies; —solaces; —veils.

(See seclusion, privacy, retirement, retreat, solitude.)

SECRET

adjectives

unnecessary; enrapturing; golden; tender; yearning; solemn; terrible; guilty; precious; close-locked; fatal; sublime; effective; minute; open; delicious; damaging; dreadful; mysterious; unrevealed; innocent; priceless; efficient; scientific; ultimate; subtle; treasured; serious; sterile; elfish; grim; divine; curious; shameful; conventual; vital; untold; elemental; unsavory.

verbs

betray—; disclose—; discover—; divulge—; entrust—; explore—; expose—; exult in—; ferret into—; ferret out—; glean—s; guard —; harbor—; hug—; impart—; laden with —s; penetrate—; probe—; pry into—; recount—; rediscover—; rejoice in—; relieve of—; relish—; reveal—; secure—; share—; spill—; take into—; unbosom—; unearth—; unfold—; unlock—; utter—; wheedle—; wrest—from; wring—from; yield—; — breaks; —leaks out; —mystifies.

(See confidence, mystery.)

adverbs

apparently; closely; carefully; profoundly; inviolably; necessarily; dangerously; darkly; pleasantly; mysteriously; deeply; furtively; vexatiously; foolishly; wisely; inscrutably; childishly.

SECRETARY

adjectives

indefatigable; confidential; delinquent; honorary; obsequious; legation; subservient; household; flippant; suave; diplomatic.

verbs

acquaint—; confide in—; depend on—; despatch—; dispense with—; entrust—; provide with—; —attends; —records; —transacts.

(See assistant, accessory.)

SECRETION

adjectives

nauseating; acrid; animal; pungent; endocrinous; curdy; life-giving.

verbs

deposit—; discharge—; emit—; extract—; furnish—; influence—; inject—; limit—; pour—; stimulate—; suppress—; throw off —; undergo—; —covers; —flows; —emanates; —exudes; —increases; —issues; — oozes.

(See liquid, saliva, bile.)

SECRETIVE

adverbs

curiously; furtively; mysteriously; unpleasantly; unnecessarily; oddly; importantly; absurdly; ridiculously; laughably; foolishly; craftily; extraordinarily; inordinately; unreasonably; senselessly; habitually; fantastically; crazily; morbidly; comically.

SECT

adjectives

persecuted; denominational; dissenting; unresting; reigning; separated; dogmatical.

verbs

attach to—; distinguish—; divide into—s; extirpate—; honor—; found—; originate—; persecute—; profess—; scatter—; test—; — adheres; —believes; —confounds; —deviates; —distracts; —endures; —observes; — banishes; —springs up; —worships.

(See party, religion.)

SECTION

adjectives

fresh; concluding; pointed; elongated; adjunctive; remote; identical; covered; rugged; rural; insurgent; progressive; benighted; geographical; colored; peaceful; pure; omitted; subsequent; luscious; internal.

verbs

break up into—s; combine—s; curtain off—; desert—; designate—; detach—; divide into —s; enlarge—; present—; rate—; split up into—s; unite—s; —constitutes; —s join.

(See division, compartment, department, segment.)

SECURE

adverbs

entirely; remarkably; financially; reasonably; probably; unusually; extraordinarily; prosperously; fortunately; undeniably; palpably; dependably; reliably; confidently; authentically; happily.

SECURE (v)

adverbs

conditionally; expeditiously; triumphantly; blamelessly; questionably; privately; eventually; legitimately; promptly; fortunately; effectually; financially.

(See gain, obtain.)

SECURITY

adjectives

unfathomable; false; stable; specific; mundane; comparative; fancied; individual; absolute; carnal; imperfect; universal; symbolized; tolerable; proper; reasonable; effectual; foreign; financial; smiling; essential; contented.

verbs

attain—; build up—; dwell in—; enjoy—; evince—; guarantee—; imperil—; insure—; lull into—; maintain—; preserve—; receive —; ruffle—; threaten—; undermine—.

(See impregnability, independence, safety.)

SEDATE

adverbs

gravely; comically; habitually; naturally; pleasantly; priggishly; ridiculously; peculiarly; unusually; properly; modestly; serenely; thoughtfully; calmly; occasionally; forbiddingly; curiously.

SEDATIVE

adjectives

admirable; efficient; bitter; harmful.

verbs

act as—; addict to—s; administer—; employ—; prescribe—; —calms; —eases; —lulls; —mitigates; —palliates: —quells; —quiets; —relieves; —weakens; —soothes.

(See medicine, opiate.)

SEDENTARY

adverbs

disagreeably; unfortunately; monotonously; conveniently; comfortably; harmfully; injuriously; necessarily; providentially; tediously.

SEDGE

adjectives

waving; rustling; bonnet; thick.

SEDIMENT

adjectives

ignoble; dark; useless.

SEDITION

verbs

convict of—; direct—; protest against—; seethe with—; —agitates; —arouses; —disorders; —disparages; —distracts; —disturbs; —incites; —offends; —prejudices; —upsets.

(See treason, disturbance, agitation, commotion.)

SEDITIOUS

adverbs

viciously; desperately; meanly; secretly; vilely; dangerously; alarmingly; powerfully; churlishly; insidiously; furtively; loudly; resentfully; aggressively; actively; openly; audaciously; boldly; influentially.

SEDUCTION

adjectives

vulgar; didactic; deliberate; lulling; invisible.

SEDUCTIVE

adverbs

mysteriously; deliberately; utterly; delightfully; disturbingly; provokingly; intentionally; cleverly; designedly; diabolically; successfully; bewilderingly; amazingly; irresistibly; unquestionably; wondrously; marvelously; unexpectedly; remarkably; surprisingly; coolly; radiantly; joyously; quietly; consciously; tauntingly; tormentingly; overwhelmingly; provocatively; unconsciously.

SEE (v)

adverbs

vividly; graphically: objectively; subjectively; dimly; faintly; distinctly; picturesquely; nakedly; comprehensively; belatedly; previously.

(See view, observe, notice.)

SEED

adjectives

deathless; fruitful; heavenly; worthy; spurting; generous; untainted; true; blind; vigorous; healthy; sanguine; diversified; noxious; alated; degenerate; extensive; foreign; winged; spiritual; germinating; shriveled.

verbs
bear—; bruise—; carry—; implant—; propagate—; scatter—; sow—; —clings; —falls; —flowers; —fructifies; —germinates; — matures; —splits; —springs open; —springs up; —yields.
(See germ, grain.)

SEEDY
adverbs
disagreeably; unpleasantly; decrepitly; sorrily; shabbily; wearily; distressingly; pitiably; miserably; lamentably; deplorably; carelessly; raggedly; wretchedly; unhappily; unusually; unnecessarily; gracelesssly; desolately.

SEEK (*v*)
adverbs
frivolously; sensually; patiently; idly; sedulously; contemptuously; unavailingly; desperately; habitually; persistently; instinctively; contentiously; adventurously; diligently; vainly; aimlessly; scientifically; involuntarily; tirelessly; faithfully; impiously; perseveringly; industriously; obstinately.
(See search, hunt.)

SEEKER
adjectives
frivolous; sincere; tranquil; selfless; inactive; inexperienced; vivacious; sensation.

SEERS
adjectives
profound; pretentious; discomfited; infallible; vegetarian; solitary; statistical; worldly-wise; omniscent.

SEGMENTS
adjectives
decorated; manageable; separated; equal.

verbs
arrange—; compose—; compress—; designate—; divide—; join—; rivet—; unite—; —constitute; —form.
(See section, division, department, part.)

SEGREGATE (*v*)
adverbs
racially; designedly; dictatorially; vicious-

ly; invidiously; seasonally; virtually; diplomatically.
(See isolate, separate.)

SEGREGATED
adverbs
carefully; inhospitably; cruelly; unnecessarily; happily; preferably; mercilessly; significantly; thoughtfully; intolerantly; arrogantly; illegally; undemocratically; uncharitably; perniciously.

SEIZE (*v*)
adverbs
peremptorily; selfishly; impulsively; roughly; rapaciously; greedily; lustfully; diabolically; bestially; unceremoniously; summarily; rudely; uncouthly; desperately; arbitrarily; illegally.
(See snatch, grasp.)

SEIZURE
adjectives
prolonged; epileptic; impending; arbitrary; convulsive; permanent; abrupt; peremptory; illegal; unwarranted.

SELECT (*v*)
adverbs
intelligently; discreetly; painstakingly; arbitrarily; tastefully; variously; fastidiously; ostentatiously; judiciously; exquisitely; infallibly; methodically; legitimately.
(See choose, pick.)

SELECTION
adjectives
marvelous; smartest; extensive; huge; enormous; perverse; customary; dazzling; unusual; noteworthy; careful; judicious; vocational; grand; current; natural; exquisite; unlimited; intelligent; methodical; representative; widest; infallible; artificial; dire; euphuistic; copious; fine; vast; occasional; rapid; conscious; singular; eager; immediate; legitimate; confident; complete; varied.

SELF
adjectives
inmost; past-created; unchanged; progressive; insignificant; whimsical; full-formed; reverend; beautiful; profane; gushing; substantial; piquant; buoyant; perfect; pretended; fancied; malignant; dead; worthless; central; bold; customary; real; gracious; wittiest; sweet; maternal; irregular; tortured; double; forgotten.

SELF-APPRECIATION

verbs

bear—; dissipate—; flush with—; inflate—;
inspire—; promote—; puff up with—; resort
to—; —contents; —provokes; —rewards.
(See egotism, self-esteem.)

SELF-CONFIDENCE

adjectives

sturdy; brave; youthful; sublime; brash;
bright; hard-won; serene.

SELF-CONSCIOUSNESS

adjectives

sharp; perpetual; absurd; puerile; exaggerated; embarrassed; obvious.

verbs

affect—; afflict with—; attain—; blush in—;
conquer—; defeat—; dispel—; divert from
—; free from—; ignite—; nettle by—; overcome—; plague with—; relinquish—; rout
—; simper in—; sweep away—; triumph
over—; —absorbs; —affects; —annoys; —
hinders; —irks; —provokes; —sensitizes.
(See awkwardness, clumsiness, embarrassment.)

SELF-CONTROL

adjectives

persistent; rigid; systematic; supreme; long-
practiced; resolute; wondrous.

SELF-ESTEEM

verbs

alter—; build—; center in—; enlarge—;
favor—; flatter—; impair—; lower—; modify—; pique—; polish—; raise—; smite—;
value—; —assures; —grounds on; —melts;
—overrates; —profits.
(See egotism, conceit, pride, vanity.)

SELFISH

adverbs

incredibly; shamelessly; lazily; incurably;
inherently; habitually; naturally; unbelievably; atrociously; thoughtlessly; abominably; cruelly; unforgivably; shamefully;
blithely; heedlessly; undutifully; ungrate-
ably; remarkably; arrantly; egregiously;
grossly; stingily; arrogantly; sordidly; indolently; uncommonly: unhappily; miserably; grossly; greedily; avariciously; blatantly; openly; curiously; strangely .

SELFISHNESS

adjectives

inconsiderate; blind; intense; enlightened;
rigid; obstinate; sordid; willful; cold; debasing; ghastly; overweening; shallow; individual; solitary; petty; sheer; querulous;
intelligent.

verbs

censure—; coddle—; conquer—; decry—;
foster—; inculcate—; indulge in—; nurse—;
practice—; pursue—; overcome—; oppose
—; restrain—; route—; screen—; transcend
—; —angers; —centers; —concentrates; —
covets; —curses; —embroils; —narrows; —
pains; —pampers.
(See jealousy, ingratitude, materialism,
egotism, cruelty.)

SELF-RELIANCE

verbs

admire—; appreciate—; beget—; breed—;
demand—; destroy—; display—; encourage
—; engender—; esteem—; evince—; foster
—; generate—; implant—; inculcate—; infuse—; instil—; praise—; prize—; smother
—; stifle—; urge—; value—; —fortifies; —
sustains.
(See confidence, faith, assurance.)

SELF-RESPECT

verbs

betray—; brace—; breed—; debase—; degrade—; destroy—; foster—; heighten—;
hoist—; humble—; inculcate—; lower—;
maintain—; nurture—; promote—; sustain
—; reduce—; value—; weaken—; wound—.
(See pride, vanity, egotism, respect.)

SELF-RESTRAINT

verbs

discard—; esteem—; exercise—; impose—;
train in—; value—; —abstains; —binds; —
coerces; —checks; —curbs; —declines; —
desists; —disciplines; —fetters; —forbears;
—governs; —impels; —inures; —moderates; —shackles; —restricts; —tempers.
(See discipline, training, restraint, control.)

SELL (v)

adverbs

systematically; professionally; constructively; rationally; profitably; legitimately; irregularly; intelligently.
(See exchange, transfer.)

adjectives

gross; glorified; restored; corruptible; deserted; petty.

SEMBLANCE

adjectives

tragic; striking; equal; princely; simple; rare; ghostly; sham; grotesque; airy; figurative; bustling; outward.

verbs

admit—; afford—; ascertain—; assume—; bear—; communicate—; discern—; expose—; furnish—; impart—; maintain—; offer—; recognize—; regard—; reveal—; ridicule—; scrutinize—; sustain—; uncover—; wear—of; —approximates; —burlesques; —caricatures; —copies; —deceives; —mirrors; —parallels; —simulates; —smacks of.

(See appearance, aspect, look, similarity.

SEMINARY

verbs

enroll in—; father—; found—; —breeds; —cherishes; —cultivates; —disciplines; —enlightens; —equips; —expands; —expels; —flourishes; —fosters; —inculcates; —informs; —infuses; —instructs; —nurtures; —polishes; —prepares; —propagates; —qualifies; —refines; —trains.

(See college, school, institution, university.)

SENATE

adjectives

venerable; complaisant; servile; reverend; venal; strong; popular.

SENATORS

adjectives

energetic; businesslike; influential; odious; easily-influenced; brilliant; lame-duck; independent.

verbs

convoke—; embroil—; impeach—; muster—; support—; —address; —adjourn; —admit; —assemble; —campaign; —confirm; —convene; —demand; —formulate; —legislate; —orate; —propose; —sit; —stampede; —filibuster.

(See legislator, congressman, judge, lawyer.)

SEND (v)

adverbs

swiftly; despairingly; providentially; equitably; expressly; anonymously; simultaneously; tirelessly; incessantly; vigorously; peremptorily; promptly; precipitately.

(See forward, dispatch.)

SENILE

adverbs

terribly; tragically; pathetically; dingily; ridiculously; desolately; rosily; drunkenly; lamentably; crabbedly; feebly; disgustingly; horribly; weakly; degenerately; gracelessly; depressingly; startlingly; woefully; hopelessly; prematurely; mournfully.

SENILITY

adjectives

sheer; sham; self-indulgent

SENSATION

adjectives

enlightening; disagreeable; wonderful; delicious; sinking; buoyant; literary; tingling; satisfying; pleasing; overpowering; formless; void; spry; variable; sparkling; luxurious; burning; queer; beneficent; strong; tremendous; strange; overnight; immense; peculiar; perverted; unique; smashing; prodigious; profound; tactual; creeping; enormous; bright; funny; crazed; broken; refined; horrible; aristocratic; restful; exuberant; stinging; abrupt; curtain; passive; reigning; advertising; inner; tactile; absorbing; outstanding; atrocious; heavy; nervous; wretched; darting; pricking; extraordinary.

verbs

convey—; create—; excite—; derive—; experience—; fan—; illustrate—; impart—; interpret—; inspire—; lower—; jade with —; overshadow—; parade—; perceive—; produce—; retain—; revive—; stir—; transmit—; —agitates; —animates; —arouses; —enkindles; —enraptures; —fascinates; —flushes; —flusters; —galvanizes; —impresses; —infects; —inflames; —infuriates; —intoxicates; —penetrates; —perishes; —perturbs; —petrifies; —pierces; —piques; —overwhelms; —ravishes; —renders; —ruffles; —rushes; —staggers; —startles; —strikes; —warms; —entrances; rekindle—; report—; reproduce—.

(See perception, consciousness, mood, emotion, feeling, sensationalism.)

SENSATIONAL

adverbs

definitely; curiously; intentionally; shockingly; offensively; singularly; undeniably; garishly; wickedly; extraordinarily; downright; cleverly; tremendously; profitably; deliberately; designedly; purposely; adroitly; ingeniously; attractively; dramatically; spectacularly; surprisingly.

SENSATIONALISM

verbs

abominate—; abhor—; addict to—; avoid —; bear—; condone—; detest—; deplore—; dispose toward—; dodge—; eschew—; frown upon—; incline toward—; recoil from—; refrain from—; reject—; shun—; shy from—; —blazons; —cheapens; —corrupts; —defiles; —disgusts; —publicizes; —sullies.

(See notoriety, publicity, sensation.)

SENSE

adjectives

real; miraculous; pleading; evil; indefatigable; cowering; abounding; moral; accommodated; final; soothing; confused; instinctive; crude; vulgar; intuitive; prophetic; exaggerated; dreary; supplementary; aesthetic; helpless; wakeful; superstitious; false; disparaging; practical; deepening; different; unscientific; distinct; inward; common; crushing; artistic; vigorous; corporeal; elementary; glimmering; intellectual; penetrating; cruel; mystical; colder; sterling; surly; strictest; baffled; extravagant; sickening; normal; suffocating; human; secret; dusty; serene; shrewd; automatic; unwitting; insidious; critical; curious; divers (pl); literal; momentary; accretive; mobile; external; exhilarating; genuine; superior; just; dull; seeming; modest; jubilant; cultivated; mysterious; innate; brute; scriptural; academic; imperturbable; half-conscious; delicate; lingering; practical; devout; sobering; pedagogical; magnetic; noisome; leaping; ethnological; renewed; morbid; anguished; realizing; universal; humble; dimmer; rhetorical; subtile; eminent; sardonic; impaired; hazy; pleasant; constant; tacit; painful; stable; jealous; complimentary; puzzled; narrow; uncanny; absorbed; dewy; rigorous; caviling; kennel; boiling; precocious; jaded; blunted; perceptive; untechnical; warring; palpitating; esoteric; dismal; arithmetical; architectonic; half-dormant; degraded; irresistable; pseudo-pantheistic; nascent; sudden; immanent; plain; wretched; terrible; withering; odious; balancing; apparent; military; dim; symbolic; inborn; reputable; etymological; hypothetical; ineffaceable; eternal; sleepy; inarticulate; pedantic; acquired; implicit; benumbed; solemn; keener; reverted; exterior; lofty; magic; stored; languid; testifying; lively; finer; abstract; social; quibbling; amiable; earnest; material; mobile; offended; sound; exceeding; deficient; due; mechanical; seeing; pathological; receptive; grosser; slumbering; acute; gratified; oppressive.

SENSE (v)

adverbs

intuitively; instinctively; vaguely; uncannily; morbidly; nervously; miraculously; prophetically; secretly; automatically; mysteriously; jealously; precociously; keenly.

(See recognize, perceive.)

SENSE of HUMOR

verbs

cultivate—; derange—; develop—; display —; dull—; exhibit—; foster—; instil—; lack —; necessitate—; pervert—; prize—; require—; treasure—; value—; —eases; —lightens; —responds; —rewards.

(See wisdom, knowledge, ability.)

SENSES

verbs

annihilate—; assail—; awaken—; benumb —; bereave—; blunt—; cultivate—; conquer —; deaden—; deprave—; distort—; doubt —; dull—; educate—; enrapture—; govern —; gratify—; heighten—; inflame—; impair —; injure—; lose—; outrage—; overwhelm —; paralyze—; perceive by—; possess—; purify—; quicken—; refine—; regain—; stimulate—; stir—; titillate—; vex—; —convey; —deceive; —delude; —dictate; —disconcert; —endow; —estrange; —guide; —play; —respond; —stifle; —stray; —swim; —tingle; —conflict.

(See emotion, feeling, sensation, mood.)

SENSIBILITIES

verbs

awaken—; benumb—; blunt—; cloud—; cultivate—; deaden—; discern—; dull—; dwarf—; engender—; lose—; offend—;

paralyze—; perceive—; restore—; revive—; resuscitate—; sharpen—; stupefy—; surrender to—.

(See senses.)

SENSIBILITY
adjectives
quivering; refined; finer; glowing; elegant; profound; natural; tender; delicate; exquisite.

SENSIBLE
adverbs
undoubtedly; scarcely; financially; economically; practicably; solidly; profoundly; usually; stolidly; soundly; substantially; particularly; honestly; thoughtfully; wisely; instinctively; crudely; cruelly; serenely; shrewdly; curiously; dully; imperturbably; pleasantly; painfully; dismally; eminently; remarkably; sincerely; apparently; palpably; evidently; manifestly; highly; altogether; entirely; commendably; laudably; admirably; delightfully; refreshingly; inherently; naturally; innately; discreetly; sagely; gravely; stodgily; odiously; oppressively.

SENSITIVE
adverbs
morbidly; unusually; unreasonably; curiously; oddly; extravagantly; nervously; timidly; shyly; awkwardly; extremely; unfortunately; unnaturally; foolishly; ridiculously; absurdly; deplorably; distressingly; heartbreakingly; preposterously; terribly.

SENSITIVENESS
adjectives
astonishing; pardonable; quivering; morbid; abnormal; fantastic; artistic; overstrained; excessive; infinite; unnatural; emotional; perilous; womanly; feverish.

verbs
dull—; lack—; sharpen—; —pains; —pierces; —prompts; —shocks; —varies; —wrings.

(See feeling, emotion, pain.)

SENSUAL
adverbs
coarsely; basely; grossly; dissolutely; vilely; undeniably; unfortunately; scandalously; broadly; indecently; deplorably; flagrantly; outrageously; utterly.

SENSUOUS
adverbs
keenly; artistically; refreshingly; poetically; enthusiastically; eagerly; appreciatively; responsively; acutely; intensively; quickly; poignantly; avidly; deeply; profoundly; unusually; alertly.

SENSUOUSNESS
adjectives
inert; controlled; rarefied; captivating; rare.

SENTENCE
(general)
adjectives
dispossessed; suspended; extravagant; turgid; involved; hurried; merciful; animated; charming; epigrammatic; vigorous; memorable; concluding; inconerent; suggestive; characteristic; functionary; fragmentary; monotonous; lucid; obscure; final; irritable; drastic; angry; incoherent; weird; vibrant; telegraphic; haunting; jerky; dreadful; dumb; childish; swift; stimulating; discreet; scathing; mangled; whispered; favorite; frigid; oracular; appalling; too-lenient; pithy; hard; immediate; consecutive; fresh; slovenly; declarative.

SENTENCE
(punishment)
verbs
advocate—; annul—; commute—; deal out —; defer—; execute—; faint at—; impose —; justify—; mete out—; pass—; proclaim —; pronounce—; —binds; —expires.

(See judgment, punishment, justice.)

SENTENCES
(words)
verbs
balance—; build—; construct—; declaim—; disclaim—; detach—; embody—; hurl—; mutter—; paraphrase—; quote—; recast—; recollect—; reconstruct—; round—; sum up —; toss—; transcribe—; —pound; —roll; —swing.

(See thought, paragraph, idea, word.)

SENTIMENT
adjectives
affectionate; baseless; filthy; tender; favorable; contradictory; ennobling; growing; mawkish; elevated; incongruous; liberal; enduring; aristocratic; patriotic; frivolous; secret; universal; public; delicate; fresh;

fiery; emotional; poetical; mingled; vague; noble; kindly; recurring; adverse; collective; profane; grateful; delicious; natural; absorbing; vivid; congenial; generous; traditional; buried; maudlin; trivial; warm; creeping; virtuous; humanizing; chivalric; ominous; unaltered; national; pious; exotic; elusive; romantic; artistic; unexpressed; pompous; unexaggerated; altruistic; enduring; detached; silky; potent; heroic; similar; sympathetic; moral; confused; warm; affectionate; false; serious; decisive; contemptuous; fitting; noble; slighting; perpetual; lackadaisical; bombastic; opposite; wintry; endearing; uneasy; stubborn; grandiose; aroused; excessive; muddled; growing; outspoken; pretty; exalted; puerile; minority; masculine; morbid; paltry; reactionary; delectable.

verbs

arouse—; awaken—; check—; communicate —; control—; consummate—; convey—; corrupt—; crystallize—; discard—; echo—; encourage—; express—; gag—; induce—; inscribe—; moderate—; reflect—; sweep—; venerate—; voice—; —blossoms; —blurs; —chills; —defies; —expresses; —falls; —flits; —flowers; —grows; —hangs; —nurtures; —possesses; —reflects; —shifts; —shapes; —solidifies; —swings; —switches; —survives; —veers; —violates; —works.

(See feeling, emotion, tenderness, sentimentality.)

SENTIMENTAL

adverbs

pleasantly; extremely; absurdly; touchingly; incurably; secretly; openly; probably; romantically; feelingly; unusually; somewhat; deeply; profoundly; particularly; ostentatiously; mawkishly; sincerely; genuinely.

SENTIMENTALISM

adjectives

racial; unmanly; romantic; spurious; feigned; western.

SENTIMENTALIST

adjectives

gushing; slobbering; sincere.

SENTIMENTALITY

adjectives

sheer; foolish; posturing; stupid; queer; betraying; unnatural; silly; erotic; sallow.

verbs

affect—; appeal to—; avoid—; burlesque—; confess—; depreciate—; detect—; discard —; dismiss—; disparage—; display—; evince—; exclude—; exhibit—; express—; feign—; profess—; reject—; ridicule—; scoff at—; shun—; —complicates; —creeps; —exaggerates; —oozes; —riles (colloq.); —softens.

(See sentiment.)

SENTINELS

adjectives

watchful; dauntless; delinquent; vigilant; cheerful; motionless; faithful; sleeping.

SENTRIES

adjectives

successive; pacing; red-coated.

SENTRY

verbs

address—; appoint—; circumvent—; discharge—; elude—; escape—; evade—; ignore—; lure—; post—; replace—; salute—; shun—; stand—; —abandons; —accosts; —admits; —advances; —alarms; —arouses; —bars; —challenges; —dozes; —escorts; —guards; —hails; —intrenches; —paces; —patrols; —signals; —warns.

(See patrol, guard.)

SEPARATE (v)

adverbs

cruelly; symmetrically; partially; insuperably; formally; nominally; subsequently; legally; permanently; effectually; physically; fatally; inevitably; deplorably; eternally; conventionally; gradually; austerely.

(See sever, divide.)

SEPARATION

adjectives

physical; unavoidable; laborious; uncertain; prolonged; fatal; inevitable; deplorable; eternal; earthly; conventional; gradual; forcible; austere; subsequent; mysterious; compulsory.

verbs

cement—; effect—; endure—; hazard—; propose—; recommend—; —accomplishes; —bisects; —breaches; —disengages; —disjoins; —dismembers; —enforces; —isolates; —jeopardizes; —reconciles; —rends; —sad-

dens; —segregates; —severs; —splices; —
sunders; —unleashes; —wrings.

(See exile, divorce, excommunication, departure, seclusion.)

SEPULCHER

adjectives
fair; uncovered; enormous; magnificent;
dreamless; august; tenantless; immense.

SEPULCHRAL

adverbs
deeply; coldly; hollowly; darkly; gauntly;
dreadfully; alarmingly; woefully; lugubriously; gloomily; miserably; incongruously;
inexplicably; curiously; preposterously; absurdly; designedly; terrifyingly; inauspiciously; repulsively; needlessly; terribly; unwontedly; mournfully; bafflingly.

SEQUENCE

adjectives
logical; invariable; melancholy; historical;
natural; dramatic; impressive; unusual;
fragmentary; consecutive; chronological;
true; interminable; rapid; intended; inflexible; honorable; chromatic; passionate; coherent; single; listless.

SERAPH

adjectives
burning; unseen; sinless.

SERENADE

verbs
applaud—; compose—; execute—; perform
—; praise—; silence—; sing—; utter—; —
arouses; —awakens; —charms; —enchants;
—enraptures; —entertains; —expresses; —
extols; —moves; —soothes; —stills; —stirs;
—thrills; —unfolds.

(See music, song.)

SERENITY

adjectives
conceited; domestic; undisturbed; cloudless;
calm; symmetrical; ineffable; celestial; wondrous; stern; sweet; unalterable; supreme;
radiant.

verbs
bask in—; bathe in—; bear—; blast—; discompose—; disperse—; disturb—; menace
—; recover—; repose in—; threaten—; —

breaks; —dominates; —charms; —composes; —enchants; —pacifies; —radiates;
—reconciles; —reigns; —ruffles.

(See calm, complacency, composure.)

SERFDOM

verbs
abolish—; deliver from—; denounce—; emancipate from—; eradicate—; liberate
from—; reduce to—; release from—; sink
into—; —binds; —debases; —constrains;
—enchains; —fetters; —harnesses; —oppresses; —represses; —shackles; —subjugates; —suppresses; —tethers; —tramples;
—enslaves.

(See slavery, bondage, servitude.)

SERIES

adjectives
attractive; interesting; stately; well-known;
periodical; distinct; regressive; definite; extensive; painstaking; rhythmic; continuous;
ingenious; graduated; unbroken; deliberate.

verbs
alternate—; arrange in—; blend into—;
break—; chain in—; compile—; construct
—; continue—; deliver—; discontinue—;
edit—; endure—; engage in—; enumerate
—; extend—; file in—; follow in—; grade
in—; interrupt—; issue—; join in—; partition—; pen—; prolong—; protract—; publish—; record—; regulate—; relate—;
sponsor—; sum up—; tabulate in—; wind
in—.

(See row, set, group.)

SERIOUS

adverbs
gravely; critically; extremely; unquestionably; apparently; evidently; manifestly;
curiously; secretly; palpably; ominously;
portentously; mysteriously; admittedly; oddly; resolutely; decidedly; emphatically;
grimly; severely.

SERIOUSNESS

adjectives
conscientious; portentous; unpleasant; nervous; unnecessary; owl-like; touching; especial; melancholy; ironic; sudden; apparent;
pitiful; mock; reverential; surpassing.

verbs
abate—; acknowledge—; aggravate—; alleviate—; assuage—; compensate for—; conjecture—; decry—; detect—; determine—;

1054

diminish—; doubt—; estimate—; exaggerate—; heighten—; intensify—; ignore—; judge—; magnify—; minimize—; mitigate—; modify—; reflect upon—; recognize—; —assures; —invades; —sobers.

(See gravity, earnestness, solemnity.)

SERMON
adjectives
extempore; controversial; funeral; soft; assize; elaborate; erudite; incomparable; splendid; stirring; sincere; brilliant.

verbs
acclaim—; borrow—; deliver—; design—; extol—; feed on—s; misinterpret—; prepare—, polish up—; revise—; —bores; —censures; —declaims; —discourses on; —edifies; —elucidates; —enlightens; —eulogizes; —exhorts; —expatiates on; —expounds; —guides; —harangues; —inspires; —moralizes; —rebukes; —reproves; —thunders; —uplifts; —wearies.

(See oration, address, homily, speech.)

SERMONIZE (v)
adverbs
allegorically; monotonously; paternally; morally; bombastically; mawkishly; conventionally; turgidly; irritably; animatedly; epigrammatically; characteristically; religiously; fanatically.

(See compose, preach.)

SERPENT
adjectives
poisonous; fiery; gilt; immense; treacherous; cursed; troubled; traitorous; writhing; lumbering; belligerent; venomous; monstrous; swollen.

verbs
exhibit—; slay—; —beguiles; —buzzes; —churns; —coils; —entwines; —glides; —hisses; —rustles; —sibilates; —spirals; —stings; —strikes; —struggles; —uncoils; —undulates; —writhes; —envenoms.

(See dragon, snake, reptile.)

SERUM
verbs
administer—; dilute—; derive—; devise—; discover—; drain—; employ—; impregnate with—; infuse—; inoculate—; inject—; introduce—; invent—; prepare—; rush—; —assists; —checks; —combats; —controls; —exempts; —generates; —immunizes; —in-

sures; —moderates; —neutralizes; —overcomes; —remedies; —stagnates; —stems.

(See medicine, fluid, remedy, tonic, antitoxin.)

SERVANT
adjectives
cloistered; shining; numerous (pl); diligent; good natured; gracious; primitive; menial; indentured; authorized; private; confidential; natural; trustworthy; domestic; voluntary; respectful; solitary; stolid; disinterested; faithful; zealous; vile; gentle; assigned; laden; magnanimous; noiseless; unjust; inattentive; corrupt; public; flowered; natty; obedient; docile; superannuated; sorrowful.

verbs
bond—; command—; commend—; curse—; discharge—; dismiss—; employ—; extol—; humble—; rebuke—; reimburse—; reproach—; reprove—; retain—; reward—; sack—; station—; —announces; —attends; —beguiles; —betrays; —devotes; —details; —enlightens; —humbles; —identifies; —obeys; —pilfers; —ushers in; reprimand—.

(See matron, slave, assistant.)

SERVE (v)
adverbs
deftly; graciously; whole-heartedly; elegantly; gratuitously; conspicuously; unwittingly; valiantly; judiciously; indifferently; admirably; exclusively; eminently; generously; simultaneously; gloriously; faithfully; apathetically; tenderly.

(See deal, distribute.)

SERVICE
adjectives
right; courteous; efficient; thoughtful; unmatched; celebrated; gracious; willing; flawless; fine; unusual; alert; deft; helpful; extra; fast; expert; gallant; lip; financial; insurgent; domestic; unedifying; invidious; trustworthy; distinguished; meritorious; inestimable; deferred; memorial; typographic; professional; priestly; peaceful; suitable; religious; imposing; costly; gratuitous; humblest; valuable; haulage; exalted; gruelling; maximum; reluctant; economical; perfunctory; abiding; engineering; impressive; essential; thankless; desperate; dependable; perpetual; honorable; promising; brisk; consecrated; immense; unionized; superior; committal; disastrous; proffered; beneficial; table; scant; eminent; civil; diplomatic;

scientific; gloomy; garrison; reasonable; unselfish; surgical; superlative; industrial; imperative; utility; erection; unique; satisfactory; management; continuous; lasting; hazardous; charitable; meticulous; unmenaced; silver; ceremonious; arduous; glorious; solitary; strenuous; specific; secretarial; mutual; hateful; particular; duteous; advisory; supervisory; auxiliary; filial; golden; dependable; prompt; consular; diffused; manifold (pl); musical; meager.

verbs
abandon—; arise in—; attend—; attribute —; bribe—; call for—; command—; conduct —; correlate—; crave—; culminate—; dedicate—; dislocate—; dispense with—; display—; dispose of—; distinguish—; draw into—; engage in—; enlist—; experience—; force from—; induce into—; introduce into —; lay down—; maintain—; modernize—; obligate to—; paralyze—; participate in—; prepare for—; press into—; provide—; regiment into—; render—; review—; reward—; slash—; sublimate—; supplant—; suspend—; terminate—; toil in—; unify—; volunteer—.
(See work, employment, practice.)

SERVICEABLE
adverbs
extremely; undeniably; valuably; helpfully; practically; infinitely; generously; unusually; highly; conveniently; extraordinarily; obediently.

SERVILE
adverbs
obsequiously; disgustingly; pitiably; cringingly; miserably; innately; sickeningly; pitifully; abjectly; unctuously; blandly; basely; humbly; meekly; ingratiatingly; fawningly; subserviently; remarkably; significantly; oddly; inexplicably; unaccountably; openly.

SERVITOR
adjectives
faithful; swarthy; favored.

SERVITUDE
adjectives
penal; involuntary; loving; political; gilded; marital; prisoned; martial.

verbs
abolish—; bear—; betray into—; debase by —; deliver from—; drag into—; free from

—; lead into—; liberate from—; reduce to —; resign to—; sentence to—; subject to—; —degrades; —chains; —enslaves; —expires; —fetters; —harnesses; —shackles; —weighs upon.
(See bondage, serfdom.)

SESSION
adjectives
executive; prolonged; nominal; secret; winter; all-night; plenary; extraordinary; lengthy; fruitless; extra; special.

verbs
adjourn—; attend—; complicate—; conclude —; convoke—; disband—; dismiss—; disperse—; emphasize—; extend—; open—; prolong—; protract—; resume—; wind up —; —administers; —achieves; —accomplishes; —appropriates; —assembles; —convenes; —deliberates; —effects; —formulates; —frames; —legislates; —recesses.
(See court, meeting, conference, assembly, council.)

SET
adjectives
unreasonable; artistic; brawling; unwelcome; gambling; hard-drinking; military; basic; uncut; prosaic; deplorable; intelligent; fair; poisonous; shiftless; social.

verbs
accumulate—; acquire—; associate in—s; arrange—s; classify in—s; collect—; compile—; complete—; compose—; compound —; conclude—; consort in—s; constitute—; create—; cut—; designate—; dispose of—; dissolve—; divide—; effect—; employ—; form—; fuse—; muster—; pair off in—s; procure—; sever—; sort into—s; supply—; weld—; —comprises; —includes.
(See series, group.)

SET (*v*)
adverbs
cunningly; perceptibly; resolutely; grimly; firmly; stubbornly; sternly; ingeniously; illogically; intuitively; primly; obstinately; deliberately; calmly; relentlessly; coquettishly; daintily; partially; courageously; awkwardly.
(See place, establish.)

SET-BACK
verbs
bear—; brood over—; endure—; fear—;

meet with—; suffer—; —abashes; —confuses; —crushes; —dejects; —discourages; —hinders; —humiliates; —impedes; —mortifies; —rebuffs; —relapses; —retards; —retrogrades; —reverses; —weakens.

(See disaster, calamity, mishap, misfortune.)

SETTING
adjectives
irrational; incongruous; atmospheric; half-comic; contemporary; tragic; insensitive; balanced; pastoral; superb; romantic; brilliant; gorgeous; drab; cumbrous; suggestive.

verbs
—assures; —calls for; —confuses; —depicts; —enhances; —extorts; —hinders; —impedes; —implies; —necessitates; —obstructs; —provides.

(See background, scene, environment.)

SETTLE (*v*)
adverbs
traditionally; cozily; sparsely; voluntarily; colonially; permanently; conclusively; mercilessly; satisfactorily; peacefully; amicably; contentedly; thinly; vaguely; prosperously; pecuniarily; arbitrarily; harmoniously.

(See adjust, fix.)

SETTLEMENT
(*colony*)
verbs
abandon—; attack—; attempt—; defend—; desert—; endanger—; establish—; forsake —; fortify—; garrison—; guide—; imperil —; oppress—; plant—; ravage—; reinforce —; rule—; tyrannize over—; —decays; —colonizes; —dwindles; —governs; —flourishes; —languishes; —perishes; —pioneers; —progresses; —prospers; —thrives.

(See colony.)

SETTLEMENT
(*decision*)
verbs
appeal for—; award—; arrange for—; arrive at—; balk at—; conclude—; confirm —; contract—; delay—; denounce—; dictate —; dispute—; effect—; favor—; gain—; hasten—; negotiate—; pledge—; postpone

—; procure—; question—; ratify—; —determines; —disposes of; —grants; —provides for; —stipulates.

(See litigation, compromise, decision, adjustment.)

SETTLEMENT
(*general*)
adjectives
amicable; prosperous; sparse; rapid; pecuniary; ultimate; defenseless; pretty; lasting; flourishing; equitable; arbitrary; scattered (pl); organized; peaceful; stable; separate; speedy; quiet; numerous (pl); sensible; penal; discordant; harmonious; ecclesiastical; parochial; upper; important.

SETTLER
adjectives
important; befuddled; outlying; early; staunch; brave; hardy; pious; first.

SEVER (*v*)
adverbs
permanently; completely; fatally; partially; hopelessly; voluntarily; legally; financially; economically; socially.

(See divide, separate.)

SEVERE
adverbs
harshly; gravely; puritanically; rigorously; rigidly; uncompromisingly; inflexibly; unsparingly; arbitrarily; domineeringly; imperiously; sternly; unmitigatedly; unrelentingly; relentlessly; odiously; atrociously; detestably; tyrannically; haughtily; brutally; needlessly; intolerably; abominably; barbarously; unwisely; senselessly; unreasonably; warrantably; properly.

SEVERITY
adjectives
unjust; uncompromising; stern; unsmiling; inexorable; unrelaxed; exemplary; unbending; extraordinary; mingled; brutal; presaging; intemperate; amused; burlesque; unnecessary; wholesome; hypocritical; righteous; relentless; formidable; calm; clearcut; merciless; just; unusual; ill-directed.

verbs
abate—; abolish—; accentuate—; acknowledge—; aggravate—; allay—; ameliorate —; apologize for—; assuage—; determine —; ease—; extenuate—; heighten—; ignore —; impose—; increase—; intensify—; judge

with—; magnify—; mitigate—; modify—;
palliate—; relax—; relieve—; scrutinize—;
vary—; —exacts; —tires; —wears down.
(See cruelty, hardness, harshness.)

SEW (v)
adverbs
domestically; exquisitely; delicately; professionally; habitually; fastidiously; artistically.
(See stitch, fasten.)

SEWAGE
verbs
carry off—; convey—; discharge—; dispose
of—; drain—; filter—; wallow in—; —
breeds; —contaminates; —emanates from;
—fouls; —hatches; —infects; —overflows;
—pollutes; —precipitates; —reeks;
spreads; —taints.
(See junk, garbage, filth, waste.)

SEX
adjectives
immured; gentle; fragile; inconstant; variable; bewitching; sterner; respective; dominant; grasping; enigmatical; weaker; dependent; deadlier.

verbs
arouse—; characterize—; cloak—; conceal
—; debauch—; destroy—; determine—; distinguish—; equalize—s; eulogize—; honor
—; pervert—; purify—; respect—; screen
—; segregate—s; shroud—; unite—s; —
boasts; —claims; —emphasizes; —mystifies.
(See males, women, distinction.)

SHACKLES
verbs
fuse—; liberate from—; rend—; sever—;
sunder—; tear—; throw off—; unleash—;
weld—; —bind; —burden; —encumber; —
frustrate; —hamper; —link; —restrict; —
restrain; —torture; —yoke.
(See chain, fetter.)

SHADE
adjectives
thick; cool; melancholy; symbolic; desolate;
chequered; odorous; forlorn; deepest; awful; grim; heavenly; thorny; various (pl);
numberless (pl); noonday; minutest; venerable; fleeting; solemn; unmoving; exact;
consecrated; sullen; tender; tremulous; illustrious; brilliant; translucent; smoky; emphatic; summer; deepening; silent; bashful;
evening; tangled; mottled; somber; sprouting; hideous; harmonious; complementary;
finer; doleful; religious; grateful; waning;
murky; fragrant; mellow; tufted; peaceful;
leafy; veiled; vengeful; popular; floating;
suburban; stunted; dewy; midnight; natu-
ral-looking; beautiful; quivering; reluctant;
delicate; cerise; endless; partial; pulsating;
pointed; blank; balmy; weltering; imperial;
arching; pastel; blending; slender; new;
pleasant; smart; wanted; solid; virile;
lengthened; plain; popular; rich; exclusive;
inviting; welcome; pendent; unexpected;
endless; moonlight; implacable; steadfast; monastic; wandering; audacious;
blessed; heterogeneous; powerful; disfiguring; lucid; wider; wavering.

verbs
abandon—; afford—; bury in—; gain—;
illuminate—; recline in—; repose in—; retire to—; search for—; seek—; welcome—;
—curtains; —deepens; —dims; —eclipses;
—envelops; —obscures; —overcasts; —
screens; —shelters; —shrouds; —veils.
(See darkness, gloom, shadow.)

SHADE (v)
adverbs
dismally; somberly; sullenly; invitingly;
coolly; monastically; partially.
(See screen, cloud.)

SHADOW
adjectives
silvery; wandering; magnified; somber; impervious; stupendous; pale; brooding; luminous; gathering; swift; spectral; gentle;
misty; lengthening; majestic; grotesque;
thoughtful; sudden; protecting; eloquent;
mellow; flocking; thin; transparent; tremulous; clear; portentous; monstrous; dappled;
opaque; vague; lifelong; walking; gigantic; ghostly; heavy; deepest; magic-lantern;
condemning; swimming; grim; gloomy;
cool; noble; fantastic; horrible; mysterious;
moonlight; twilight; dim; baleful; popular;
softest; absurd; skulking; rustling; illuminated; distorted; flickering; haughty; intermittent; dense; violet; shapeless; evening;
rosy; empty; translucent; sinister; weird;
glimmering; defensive; fitful; ghastly;
straight; unnatural; celestial; meager;
ambrosial; apotheosized; vaporous; gusty;
noisome; shining; slatted; illusive; impalpable; slanting; elongated; transparent;
changing; whispering; misty; bold; dread;

veiled; solemn; encroaching; lifeless; thickening; bounding; trembling; houseless; liquid; citron; characteristic; lessening; disturbing; meaner; lank; chiseled; constitutional.

verbs
banish—; cast—; clutch at—; devise—; emerge from—; extend—; grope in—; haunt—; lurk in—; penetrate—; pierce—; repose in—; —blots; —casts; —creeps; —crouches; —dances; —dims; —disintegrates; —eclipses; —encircles; —engulfs; —falls; —flickers; —flits; —hangs; —haunts; —hovers; —hugs; —lengthens; —loiters; —looms; —melts; —plays; —radiates; —retreats; —shifts; —shrouds; —stretches; —trembles; —tosses.

(See shade, ghost, phantom, reflection.)

SHADY
adverbs
refreshingly; gratifyingly; pleasantly; excessively; beautifully; attractively; fortunately; questionably; suspiciously; darkly; invitingly; providentially.

SHAFT
adjectives
serene; granite; spotless; clustering; various (pl); rich; oblique; fluted.

verbs
ascend—; cleave—; descend—; erect—; grasp—; ground—; imbed—; loose—; mount—; sink—; shoulder—; splinter—; straddle—; suspend from—; —bears; —commemorates; —projects; —protrudes; —soars; —supports; —sustains; —towers.

(See column, post, tower, spear, arrow, lance, handle.)

SHAGGY
adverbs
roughly; softly; expensively; pleasantly; naturally; warmly; fashionably; extremely; slightly; beautifully; stylishly; untidily.

SHAKE
adjectives
impressive; impatient; melancholy; solemn; nervous; dubious; significant; respectful; weary.

SHAKE (v)
adverbs
convulsively; nervously; agitatedly; furiously; rudely; violently; negatively; skeptically; energetically; pitilessly; inwardly; pathetically; lustily; viciously; vigorously; sternly; ominously; vehemently; passionately.

(See jar, jolt.)

SHAKESPEARE
verbs
analyze—; commemorate—; criticize—; discuss—; disparage—; glorify—; honor—; idolize—; immortalize—; laud—; perform —; perpetuate—; portray—; revere—; venerate—; worship—; —depicts; —dramatizes; —eternizes; —excels; —lives.

(See literature, artist, poet, creator, dramatist.)

SHAKY
adverbs
tremulously; feebly; weakly; nervously; insecurely; helplessly; hopelessly; desperately; undeniably; obviously; hazardously; perilously; ominously; critically; precariously; forlornly; incurably; infirmly; decrepitly; embarrassingly.

SHALLOW
adverbs
extremely; pleasantly; safely; scandalously; impracticably; desperately; dangerously; obviously; particularly; sufficiently; fortunately; conveniently; unduly; disappointingly.

SHAM
verbs
cloak—; denounce—; discard—; disclose—; divulge—; expose—; fabricate—; uncover —; penetrate—; rebuke—; resort to—; reveal—; suppress—; unveil—; —deceives; —defrauds; —deludes; —disguises; —distorts; —feigns; —imposes upon; —mimics; —perverts; —pretends; —simulates.

(See fake, imitation, deception, counterfeit, hypocrisy.)

SHAME
adjectives
divulged; alluring; sweet; irreparable; maiden; perpetual; conscious; notable; eternal; stinging; sluggish; pure; innocent; passing; burning; penetrative; treble; bashful; sudden; blushing; wounding; virtuous; guilty; tender; murderous; notorious; sec-

ret; ingenious; infernal; deep; passionate; blighting; primal; engendered; earthly; naked; desolate; cherished; disgusting; defiant; tolerated; humble; utter; girlish; villainous; angry; lovely; crying; unvalued; lasting; natural.

verbs
accept—; avenge—; bequeath—; blush in—; bow in—; cloak—; condemn—; cover—; cower in—; cringe in—; deaden to—; disparage—; endure—; evoke—; expel in—; flush with—; hide in—; impute to—; put to —; rid of—; sink with—; slink away in—; suffer—; —blots; —burns; —debases; —defames; —defiles; —degrades; —dishonors; —humiliates; —mixes; —overcomes; —possesses; —scandalizes; —slurs; —stains; —stigmatizes; —sullies; —sweeps; —taints; —tarnishes; —villifies; —disgraces; bring to—.

(See humiliation, disgrace, dishonor, mortification.)

SHAME (v)
adverbs
consciously; viciously; ingeniously; jealously; disgustingly; traitorously; lustfully; vindictively.

(See humiliate, mock.)

SHAME-FACED
adverbs
embarrassingly; sheepishly; guiltily; foolishly; ridiculously; comically; absurdly; unnecessarily; instantly; curiously; significantly; amazingly; modestly; demurely; timidly; fearfully; childishly; awkwardly.

SHAPE
adjectives
vague; graceful; fundamental; sublime; stray; vampire; manifold (pl); imagined; lordly; phantom; ultimate; globular; nobler; streaming; slim; articulate; withered; invisible; various (pl); questionable; uniform; unaccustomed; goodly; delicate; monstrous; expanded; chimerical; clownish; archaic; convenient; cowled; gaudy; false; coarser; uncouth; transitory; prodigious; obscene; execrable; original; orthodox; delusive; lusty; checkered; perfect; glorious; exquisite; stalwart; airy; tangible; dim; minutest; distinctive; oblong; unimagined; quaint; imposing; stately; pillared; elliptic;

gross; human; unique; pigmy; symmetrical; castled; alien; swarthy; habitable; nameless; peculiar; frightful; loathly.

verbs
alter—; caricaturize—; define—; delineate —; depict—; determine—; dim—; discern —; disguise—; distort—; draft—; hack at —; hack into—; hew into—; knead—; lick into—; modify—; mold—; obscure—; outline—; pad—; perceive—; regard—; sketch —; twist into—; —assumes; —suggests.

(See figure, feature, form, outline.)

SHAPE (v)
adverbs
adroitly; divinely; deftly; skillfully; professionally; gracefully; delicately; conveniently; conventionally; exquisitely; distinctively; quaintly; elliptically; symmetrically.

(See form, fashion, mould.)

SHAPELESS
adverbs
lumpishly; cumbrously; heavily; grotesquely; carelessly; awkwardly; fantastically; coarsely; grossly; loutishly; gawkily; consciously; hopelessly; pitiably; miserably; wretchedly; curiously; utterly; pathetically.

SHAPELY
adverbs
beautifully; alluringly; perfectly; divinely; seductively; prettily; unusually; remarkably; strikingly; noticeably; conspicuously; attractively.

SHARE
adjectives
ample; proportionate; individual; sufficient; adequate; full; fertile; fair; due; horrid; considerable; major; requisite; insignificant; proper; scanty; eccentric; usual; corresponding.

verbs
accept—; acquire—; adjust—; allocate—; allot—; apportion—; assign—; assume—; bequeath—; claim—; command—; consume —; deprive of—; disclaim—; distribute—; divert—; draw—; forfeit—; issue—; net—; partake of—; procure—; reap—; refuse—; regulate—; retain—; scorn—; usurp—; waive—; —doubles; —drops; —entitles.

(See part, investment, portion, proportion.)

SHARE (v)

adverbs

vicariously; affectionately; profitably; unsparingly; philanthropically; richly; equitably; gratuitously; faithfully; proportionately; adequately.

(See apportion, divide.)

SHARK

verbs

elude—s; repel—s; —s abound; —attacks; —bolts; —devours; —s endanger; —overturns; —plunges; —preys upon; —pursues; —s ravage; —skims; —skulks; —thrashes; —s victimize.

(See whale, fish.)

SHARP

adverbs

maliciously; unnecessarily; deliberately; bitterly; viciously; purposely; hatefully; spitefully; resentfully; venomously; designedly; cunningly; insinuatingly; incisively; antagonistically; needlessly; unwisely; mercilessly; obnoxiously; churlishly; snarlingly; rancourously; unsparingly; bitingly; adroitly; strategically; unwontedly; naturally; subtly; sensibly; schemingly; extremely; alertly; shrewdly; mysteriously; indubitably; obviously; supremely; unexpectedly; infallibly; infinitely; broadly; precociously; sympathetically; astoundingly; sagaciously; politically; cleverly; profoundly; deeply.

SHATTER (v)

adverbs

utterly; devastatingly; ruinously; spiritually; morally; physically; economically; financially; fundamentally.

(See shiver, demolish.)

SHAVE (v)

adverbs

daily; industriously; fastidiously; neatly; cleanly; closely; meticulously; customarily; habitually.

(See cut, clip.)

SHEARS

adjectives

abhorred; sounding; large; sharp.

verbs

apply—; blunt—; edge—; employ—; clip with—; file—; grind—; manipulate—; sharpen—; whet—; —bristle; —curtail; —level; —lop off; —reduce; —shave.

(See scissors.)

SHEATH

verbs

deposit in—; discard—; divest of—; draw from—; enclose in—; ensconce in—; extract from—; penetrate—; pierce—; pluck from —; repose in—; rest in—; withdraw from —; —encases; —encompasses; —enfolds; —envelops; —girds; —houses; —preserves; —protects; perforate— .

(See envelope, case.)

SHEAVES

adjectives

scattered; nodding; ripened; rusted.

SHED

adjectives

battered; nightly; tumbling; rickety.

SHED (v)

adverbs

periodically; seasonally; annually; naturally; normally; wastefully; luminously.

(See discard, cast.)

SHEEN

adjectives

starlight; spangled; dissolving; changing; original; placid; glistening; glorious; wavy; weird; alternate; superb; tremulous; variegated; metallic; dazzling; lustrous; smoky.

SHEEP

verbs

auction—; breed—; clip—; confine—; cross —; domesticate—; fleece—; herd—; market —; shear—; shelter—; slaughter—; tend —; —bleat; —browse; —climb; —graze; —huddle; —pasture; —produce; —ramble; —roam; —secrete; —straggle; —stray; —taint; —flock.

(See lamb, livestock, animal.)

SHEEPISH

adverbs

somewhat; obviously; naturally; naively; blushingly; absurdly; comically; laughably; ludicrously; awkwardly; guiltily; modestly; bashfully; uncomfortably; adorably.

SHEETS
(general)

adjectives

cotton; stray; smooth; crisp; winding; bedraggled; tattered; torn; dampened; silver; unintermitting; delicious; loneliest; slumbrous; troublesome; standard; stinging; ghostlike; written.

verbs

air—; befoul—; begrime—; bleach—; crease—; deodorize—; disinfect—; dispose of—; flounce—; fumigate—; gather—; hem —; launder—; pin—; plait—; reverse—; roll—; ruck—; ruffle—; rumple—; stain—; smooth—; snuggle in—; sully—; tuck in—; wrinkle—.

(See pillow, cloth, fabric.)

SHELF

adjectives

crowded; empty; pendent; continental; hanging; china.

verbs

adhere to—; bolster—; brace—; deplete—; deposit on—; dislodge from—; disorder on —; elevate—; hoist to—; incline—; lodge on—; prop—; recline on—; replenish—; repose on—; suspend from—; —facilitates; —rocks; —slopes; —sustains; —totters; —supports.

(See ledge, board.)

SHELL
(*cannon*)

verbs

clinch—; crack—; deflect—; rain—s; —annihilates; —blots out; —bursts; —crashes; —cripples; —demolishes; —detonates; —devastates; —discharges; —dismembers; —effaces; —erases; —obliterates; —plasters; —puffs; —rends; —screams; —sighs; —shatters; —smoulders; —uproots; —whines: —whistles; —whizzes.

(See bomb, grenade, shot, projectile.)

SHELL
(*general*)

adjectives

curved; fantastic; skimmed; hissing; rifled; awe-inspiring; orchestra; blazing; almond-shaped; veined; withered; crumbling; bivalve; splitting; knife-edged; screeching; chorded; spherical; tainted; sputtering; outgrown; box-like; misgrown; clinging; microscopic; single; solid; glass; bursting; soundless; woody; reflecting; sea; castaway.

SHELTER

adjectives

offered; sacred; solacing; delightful; generous; despicable; treacherous; grateful; hospitable; insufficient; rude; continual; artificial; noontide; respectable; safe; honorable.

verbs

abandon—; afford—; avail oneself of—; deny—; escort to—; expose—; extend—; gain—; grant—; imperil—; jeopardize—; maintain—; obtain—; procure—; retreat to —; scurry for—; secure—; seek—; utilize —; withdraw from—; —nurtures; —screens; —wards off.

(See haven, sanctuary, security, defense.)

SHELTER (*v*)

adverbs

paternally; faithfully; gratefully; generously; hospitably; artificially; protectively; honorably.

(See defend, protest.)

SHELTERED

adverbs

carefully; extremely; tenderly; unduly; prudishly; protectively; safely; warmly; securely; satisfactorily; duly; grudgingly; hospitably; painfully; comfortably; adequately; affectionately; permanently; insecurely; temporarily; pleasantly; barely.

SHEPHERD

adjectives

faithful; erratic; wandering; boding; homeless.

SHERIFF

adjectives

varlet; burly; brooding; mean.

verbs

authorize—; baffle—; commission—; delegate—; dodge—; elude—; empower—; evade—; frustrate—; perplex—; thwart—; vest in—; —apprehends; —compels; —confines; —deputizes; —enforces; —escorts; —grapples; —implicates; —incriminates; —repossesses; —restrains; —sanctions; —serves; —snares.

(See police, officer, constable.)

SHIELD

adjectives

mirrored; brazen; gilded; caudal; serried; ponderous; bright; protecting; worthless; clanging; dusky; siliceous; heraldic.

verbs

adorn—; batter—; bear—; emblazon—; engrave—; forge—; polish—; split—; —burdens; —protects.

(See badge, emblem, armor, screen.)

SHIFT (v)
adverbs

nervously; obligingly; uneasily; restlessly; momentarily; visibly; impatiently; inoffensively; perceptibly.

(See turn, change.)

SHIFTLESS
adverbs

incurably; habitually; constitutionally; inherently; naturally; oddly; curiously; singularly; unpardonably; crazily; offensively; provokingly; audaciously; openly; negligently; foolishly; loutishly; lazily; indolently; untidily; nonchalantly; indifferently; shamefully; grossly; unwarrantably; improvidently; stupidly; senselessly; stolidly; ineptly.

SHIFTY
adverbs

untrustworthily; shamefully; terribly; inherently; naturally; disgracefully; obviously; manifestly; miserably; wickedly; extremely; cleverly; adroitly; notably; notoriously; insidiously; treacherously; dangerously; despicably; contemptibly; artfully; warily; infamously.

SHIMMER (v)
adverbs

sparklingly; gloriously; metallically; tremulously; gildedly; brightly.

(See shine, flicker.)

SHIN
verbs

abrade—; bandage—; bare—; bark—; batter—; brace—; bruise—; buffet—; expose —; fracture—; gash—; lacerate—; pad—; rend—; scrape—; shield—; skin—; splinter —.

(See leg.)

SHINE (v)
adverbs

serenely; auspiciously; brilliantly; glaringly; perpendicularly; lucidly; radiantly; hazily; luminously; gloriously; goldenly; dazzlingly; feverishly; fitfully; tremulously; majestically; intermittently; fiercely; capriciously.

(See gleam, glitter.)

SHINY
adverbs

attractively; conspicuously; brilliantly; garishly; brightly; gloriously; momentarily; gaudily; unbearably; unpleasantly; gorgeously; proudly; glitteringly; scintillatingly; luminously; phosphorescently; unfashionably; conspicuously; intolerably; admirably; commendably; amazingly; singularly; peculiarly.

SHIP
adjectives

opposing; stratosphere; rolling; advertising; hostile; full-rigged; fearful; turbine-driven; stranded; tempest-winged; ocean-going; expected; blowing; distressed; pursuing; isolated; laboring; embryo; stately; rickety; shapely; specter; cloud; disastrous; myriad (pl); gallant; dismantled; water-logged; butchered; deep-water; whaling; leather-armored; unfortunate.

verbs

abandon—; apportion—; board—; charter —; delay—; drive—; escort—; man—; moor—; navigate—; nose—; propel—; scuttle—; —anchors; —bears; —blows; —bounds; —churns; —crawls; —flounders; —grounds; —lurches; —plies; —plows; —rears; —runs; —sails; —scuds; —shears; —shudders; —sidles; —slithers; —steams; —swings; —tosses; —turns.

(See boat, motorboat, aeroplane, launch.)

SHIP (v)
adverbs

seasonally; internationally; expressly; disastrously; promptly; customarily; faithfully.
(See transport, dismiss, send.)

SHIPMENT
verbs

allow—; admit—; authorize—; bear—; charge with—; check—; consign—; convey —; curtail—; dispose of—; exclude—; guarantee—; imperil—; insure—; limit—; obtain —; pledge—; prohibit—; release—; safeguard—; slate—; tax—; transport—; underwrite—; verify—; —burdens; —includes.

(See goods, merchandise.)

SHIRK (v)
adverbs

timidly; faithlessly; pusillanimously; basely; meanly; cowardly; ingeniously; falsely.
(See neglect, avoid, evade.)

SHIRT

adjectives

fringed; clammy; foul; higher; homespun; woven; unwearable; ruffled; spotless; sleeveless; pleated; wrinkled; irreproachable; fringed; buckskin; hair; dress; work; shrunken.

verbs

attire in—; damage—; divest of—; doff—; don—; expose—; mend—; patch—; pierce —; rend—; shred—; slit—; starch—; strip off—; stuff—; tatter—; tuck—; vend—; —frays; —shields; —swathes.

(See clothing, dress, garment.)

SHIVER

adjectives

cold; electric; simultaneous; protesting; timid; live; nervous.

verbs

allay—s; calm—s; repress—; restrain—; tremble with—; —agitates; —betrays; —convulses; —disquiets; —perturbs; —quavers; —ripples; —runs; —stirs.

(See sob, sigh, thrill, shudder.)

SHIVER (v)

adverbs

involuntarily; coldly; abnormally; timorously; inwardly; ceaselessly; feverishly.

(See shake, tremble.)

SHOALS

adjectives

narrow; dangerous; sable; deadly; treacherous.

verbs

circumvent—; encounter—; escape—; espy —; evade—; extricate from—; discern—; flounder on—; ground on—; risk—; snag on —; sight—; shunt—; —abound; —endanger; —force; —imperil; —jeopardize; —menace; —restrain.

(See reefs, rocks, shore, coast, island.)

SHOCK

adjectives

suggestive; surgical; psychic; paralyzing; overpowering; foaming; immediate; terrific; thundering; surging; unlooked-for; stern; moral; galvanic; dreadful; irresistible; fearful; quivering; rude; feeble; desolating; shivering; shattering; acknowledged; tremendous; harmonious; sudden; jangling; violent; visiting; stunned; physical; sublunar.

verbs

absorb—; attribute—; cushion—; displace —; outweigh—; receive—; subject to—; suffer—; survive—; withstand—; throw off —; —s ensue; —freezes; —galvanizes; —occurs; —persists; —reacts; —recurs.

(See collision, impact, agitation.)

SHOCK (v)

adverbs

morally; profoundly; astoundingly; unspeakably; physically; paralyzingly; terrifically; irresistibly; tremendously; violently; surgically.

(See terrify, astound.)

SHOCKED

adverbs

immeasurably; intensely; duly; indignantly; suddenly; terribly; awfully; incalculably; horribly; desperately; alarmingly; appallingly; fearfully; wildly; miserably; perilously; genuinely; manifestly; shamefully; cruelly; irrecoverably; obviously.

SHOCKING

adverbs

tragically; terribly; scandalously; outlandishly; unexpectedly; grossly; unquestionably; oddly; horribly; undeniably; miserably; wretchedly; shamefully; brutally; needlessly.

SHOD

adverbs

daintily; finely; extravagantly; expensively; stylishly; fashionably; incongruously; inharmoniously; crudely; heavily; warmly; insufficiently; coarsely; cloddishly; carelessly; comfortably; wretchedly; miserably; poorly; ridiculously; inadequately; meanly; raggedly; outlandishly; conspicuously; tastefully; well.

SHOES

adjectives

clumsy; capacious; preposterous; patched; silken; russet; worn; well-cut; abusive; sorry-looking; little; sun-baked; spiked; tin; tattered; irksome; nail-clad; battered; flimsy.

1064

verbs
don—; bear—; fashion—; gloss—; hurl—; manufacture—; mend—; polish—; retrieve —; revamp (colloq.)—; sheathe in—; sole —; —compress; —crunch; —nip; —pinch; —support; —squeeze; —torture.

SHOOT (v)

adverbs
accurately; obliquely; involuntarily; professionally; skillfully; fatally; tragically; maniacally; blindly; wildly.
(See fire, discharge.)

SHOP

adjectives
endless; exclusive; garish; desolate; filth-strewn; multiple (pl); inviting; showy; decent; dull; dingy; discriminating; intrepid; out-of-the-way; glittering; fashionable; specialty; matrimonial; dirty.

verbs
clutter up—; enlarge—; equip—; line—; loot—; man—; patronize—; support—; —accommodates; —adjusts; —caters to; —dispenses; —disposes of; —expands; —furnishes; —offers; —prospers; —purveys; —flourishes; —pledges; —retails; —stocks; —thrives; —undersells; —vends.
(See factory, garage, store.)

SHOP (v)

adverbs
voraciously; meticulously; tirelessly; fashionably; daily; gregariously; industriously; enthusiastically; vigorously; insensately.
(See purchase, visit.)

SHORE

adjectives
fading; pebbled; happy; fertile; beaten; swampy; receding; desolate; concave; exalted; far-off; crescent; rocky; sundered; emerald; inhospitable; waveless; dreadful; solitary; sighing; grateful; gloomy; clifflike; scanty; delicious; shining; smiling; sterile; verdant; lily-lined; melancholy; pastoral; slimy; celestial; treeless; craggy; hoary; lonely; tumbling; accessible; pleasant; crepuscular; laughing; wasting; rival; kindred; upbraiding; sunny; bold; beautiful; chill; distant; furrowed; pitiless; sordid; porous; proximate; cressy; crumbling; friendlier; cheerless; peopled; savage; darksome; teeming; unprotected; changeless; boundless; tranquil; ghostly; mist-

covered; peaceful; rugged; breezy; caressing; lonesome; radiant; spicy; stormless; bloody; imagined; weary; sandy; wintry; arid; perilous; alluvial; heterogeneous; echoic.

verbs
batter—; behold—; blockade—; buffet—; buttress—; coast to—; dash upon—; espy —; explore—; fortify—; frequent—; gain —; hail—; hasten to—; intrench on—; kiss —; maroon on—; pace—; patrol—; plant on—; ramble on—; repel from—; roam—; saunter on—; seek—; skirt—; strive for—; stroll along—; view from—; wash—; win —; —resounds; —tapers.
(See coast, island, beach, shoals, rocks.)

SHORT

adverbs
ridiculously; offensively; delightfully; agreeably; pitifully; disappointingly; relatively; tragically; scandalously; mercifully; wantonly; humanely; unreasonably; dramatically; disgustingly; smartly; inexcusably; characteristically; shamefully; curiously; extremely; remarkably; unconscionably; unpardonably; unexpectedly.

SHORTCOMING

adjectives
intellectual; obvious; spiritual; convenient; pleasant.

verbs
adjust—; atone for—; balance—; betray—; cloak—; compensate for—; condemn—; cope with—; correct—; counteract—; countervail —; denounce—; develop—; discern—; disclose—; divulge—; equalize—; expose—; indicate—; neutralize—; nullify—; overcome—; reconcile to—; redeem—; reproach —; reprove—; reveal—; perceive—.
(See defect, deficiency, failing, failure, imperfection.)

SHORT-HANDED

adverbs
obviously; manifestly; unfortunately; undeniably; lamentably; dreadfully; curiously; admittedly; helplessly; desperately; despairingly; distressingly; painfully; inconveniently; unprofitably; gloomily; sadly.

SHORT-SIGHTED

adverbs
deplorably; unintelligently; formidably; in-

auspiciously; unforgivably; politically; horribly; despicably; improvidently; foolishly; unhappily; disastrously; ruinously; calamitously; unpardonably; ineptly; hopelessly; irretrievably; lamentably; tragically; sorrily; selfishly; unwarrantably.

SHOT

adjectives

quick; succulent; tender; successive (pl); effectual; candid; chance; sprouting; calamitous; stray; deflected; pelting; native; hostile; scattering (pl); desultory; wondrous; hopeful; pendulous; argumentative; deadsure; steady.

verbs

fill with—; hurl—; pour—; pump—; —beats; —belches; —bombards; —cracks; —fusillades; —nicks; —rains; —reverberates; —ricochets; —spatters; —sprays; —sputters; —streams; —thunders; —wails; —whistles; —whizzes.

(See bullet, shell, gun-fire, projectile, missile.)

SHOULDER

verbs

brush—; huddle—; lower—; shrug—; strengthen—; —dislocates; —droops; —flinches; —humps; —hunches; —inclines; —rubs; —sags; —stoops; —twitches; —wriggles.

SHOULDER (v)

adverbs

courageously; staunchly; vigorously; gallantly; bravely; patiently; reluctantly; stalwartly; promptly.

(See assume, bear.)

SHOULDERS

adjectives

naked; drawn; lofty; weary; careless; bowed; patient; shabby; unworthy; averted; decisive; slim; competent; reluctant; indolent; stooped; drooping; slender; quaking; resolute; dislocated; glorious; glimmering; disproportionate; milk-white; misshapen; ponderous; stalwart; heavy; broad; collective; strapping; submissive; hunched; shining; unresponsive; massive; slouching; willing; artful; half-nude; lurching; glossy; immortal; bony; jutting.

SHOUT

adjectives

faint; confused; unrestrained; clamorous; answering; universal; exultant; joyous; defiant; reckless; unreal; melancholy; gratified; uproarious; tumultuous; derisive; enthusiastic; untimely; windy; lusty; painful; distant; muffled; tiny; incessant; rough; cordial; deferential; blithesome; sporadic; deafening; involuntary.

verbs

muffle—; mute—; raise—; restrain—; stifle —; still—; smother—; —alarms; —arises; —breaks; —deafens; —dims; —s drown out; —entreats; —penetrates; —pierces; —rends; —rings; —resounds; —rouses; —splits; —spurs; —stabs; —startles; —terrifies; —thunders; —weaves.

(See call, cry, yell, shriek.)

SHOUT (v)

adverbs

profanely; turbulently; obstreperously; vociferously; jovially; dramatically; hoarsely; ecstatically; derisively; furiously; impatiently; triumphantly; stentoriously; defiantly; clamorously; recklessly; enthusiastically; roughly; cordially; fraternally; deafeningly; blithesomely.

(See yell, call.)

SHOVE (v)

adverbs

rudely; uncouthly; vulgarly; boisterously; playfully; bullyingly; brutally; carelessly; vigorously.

(See crowd, push.)

SHOVEL

verbs

apply—; brandish—; discard—; employ—; muster—s; scoop in—; till with—; —burrows; —clatters; —cuts; —delves; —discloses; —excavates; —exposes; —gouges; —grates against; —lays bare; —unearths.

SHOW
(colloq)

verbs

acclaim—; applaud—; back—; censor—; conclude—; extol—; finance—; flock to—; hail—; offer—; produce—; render—; review—; revise—; stage—; —beguiles; —draws; —traduces.

(See circus, display, exhibition, play, performance.)

SHOW (v)

adverbs

distinctly; conclusively; vaguely; picturesquely; deftly; negatively; devoutly; conspicuously; adroitly; accurately; unequivocally; ingeniously; photographically; subsequently; reluctantly; ostentatiously; delusively; spectacularly; formidably; imperially.

(See display, exhibit.)

SHOWER

adjectives

genial; fiery; russet; intellectual; frizzling; passing; dewy; honeyed; arrowy; icy; myriad; soft; winking; sprinkling; sulphurous; frequent; gracious; fruitful; distilling; ambient; blinding; shimmering; pelting; rainbow-winged; sunlit; continual; whitening; accidental; dropping; scant; summer; spectacular; vernal; falling; heavy.

verbs

long for—; welcome—; —abates; —chills; —continues; —darkens; —deluges; —diminishes; —gushes; —inundates; —issues; —lets up; —plunges; —streams; —surges; —whirls.

(See rain.)

SHOWER (v)

adverbs

generously; genially; unstintedly; fruitfully; ceaselessly; intermittently; vernally.

(See rain, pour.)

SHOWMANSHIP

verbs

applaud—; proclaim—; —acclaims; —advertises; —attracts; —bandies; —dazzles; —embellishes; —emblazons; —features (colloq.); —flames; —flashes; —garnishes; —glitters; —heralds; —parades; —publicizes; —promulgates; —trumpets.

(See display, exhibition.)

SHOWS

adjectives

kingly; unrivaled; temporal; regional; grouped; ostentatious; brilliant; delightful; brave; giddy; miserable; triumphal; frightful; delusive; hideous; spectacular; venerable; outstanding; sorry; harmless; formidable; glittering; pitiful; master; extensive; tumultuous; idle; elaborate; detestable; farcical; mock; brilliant; shallow; rich; gaudy; gallant; brave; imperious; full; phantasmagoric; spangled; marionette.

SHOWY

adverbs

garishly; ornately; cheaply; miserably; unnecessarily; unduly; disgracefully; tawdrily; grossly; foolishly; stupidly; childishly; gracelessly; elaborately; deceptively; gorgeously; pompously; magnificently; inordinately; delusively; expensively; outlandishly; fantastically; excessively.

SHREDS

verbs

bind—; cement—; convert into—; lacerate into—; pare—; reduce to—; rend into—; sever—; snatch—; snip—; tatter into—; tear to—; wear to—.

(See fragment, pieces.)

SHREW

adjectives

chirping; aquatic; occasional; ferret; curst; humorous; noisy; blatant; clamant; raucous.

SHREWD

adverbs

suavely; infinitely; uncannily; adroitly; cleverly; subtly; urbanely; artfully; designingly; slyly; insidiously; dangerously; admirably; practically; commercially; alarmingly; extremely; astoundingly; singularly; thoughtfully; profoundly; precociously; obviously; amazingly; unexpectedly; socially; deliberately; politically; sagaciously; cautiously; wisely; invariably; habitually; customarily; astutely; deftly.

SHREWDNESS

adjectives

infinite; uncanny; apparent; cynical; suave.

verbs

acquire—; ascertain—; commend—; contrive with—; cultivate—; demand—; develop—; discern—; exercise—; gain—; inherit —; intensify—; lack—; mark—; parallel—; penetrate—; recognize—; respect—; reveal —; value—; —dazzles; —discriminates; —endows; —foresees; —impresses; —qualifies.

(See diplomacy, tact, skill, ingenuity.)

SHREWISH

adverbs

disagreeably; scurrilously; scandalously; unpleasantly; intolerably; unbearably; poignantly; sarcastically; unbelievably; notoriously; inexcusably; outlandishly; infamously; inordinately; despicably; contemptibly; abominably; trenchantly; particularly; brutally; scorchingly; cruelly; bitterly; mercilessly.

SHRIEK

adjectives
vehement; myriad; wailing; hilarious; faint; passionate; inquiring; shrill; piercing; loud; unrestrained; great; long; ghastly; sensational; frantic; delirious; discordant; piteous; demoniacal.

verbs
drown out—; emit—; muffle—; restrain—; stifle—; utter—; —alarms; —chills; —curdles; —echoes; —harrows; —penetrates; —petrifies; —pierces; —rends; —resounds; —rings; —rouses; —smothers; —splits; —startles; —unnerves.
(See cry, shout, call, yell.)

SHRIEK (*v*)

adverbs
agonizingly; heartrendingly; imperatively; stridently; shrewishly; vehemently; passionately; unrestrainedly; piteously; discordantly; demoniacally.
(See yell, scream.)

SHRILL

adverbs
piercingly; cuttingly; alarmingly; horribly; murderously; intolerably; fearfully; incredibly; horridly; raucously; suddenly; contemptibly; disagreeably; naturally; incurably; desperately; cruelly; undisguisedly; deliberately; designedly; purposely; meanly; penetratingly; sharply.

SHRINE

adjectives
popular; tourist; despoiled; innumerable (pl); unhallowed; mysterious; desecrated; veritable; haunted; exploited; cherished; celebrated; echoing; secret; competing; wayside; nameless; inmost; fragrant; happy; gloomy; unrivaled; miraculous.

verbs
abandon—; banish from—; bar from—; consecrate—; contaminate—; convert into —; dedicate—; deface—; defile—; desecrate —; dismantle—; enthrone in—; exalt—: hallow—; immortalize—; invade—; isolate —; mutilate—; penetrate—; pervert—;

prostitute—; sanctity—; seclude in—; sequester in—; transgress—; violate—; worship in—; —symbolizes.
(See altar, tomb, sanctuary, temple.)

SHRINK (*v*)

adverbs
perceptibly; timorously; modestly; instinctively; visibly; dumbly; involuntarily; shyly.
(See recoil, wince.)

SHRINKING

adverbs
shyly; painfully; coldly; terribly; desperately; visibly; instinctively; pitiably; guiltily; pathetically; timidly; submissively; servilely; slavishly; basely; tragically; inwardly; noticeably; childishly; perceptibly; pitiably; unaccountably; significantly.

SHRIVEL (*v*)

adverbs
abnormally; prematurely; markedly; partially; ruinously; sadly; tragically.
(See shrink, dwindle.)

SHRIVELED

adverbs
slightly; meagerly; cadaverously; gauntly; emaciatedly; haggardly; scrawnily; skinnily; dreadfully; curiously.

SHROUD

adjectives
vibrant; bloody; flecked; misty; sable; spotted; leafy; clinging; rattling; streamlined; putrid; thin.

verbs
clothe in—; discard—; divest of—; invest in —; —circumscribes; —cloaks; —darkens; —dims; —disguises; —eclipses; —enfolds; —envelops; —obscures; —overcasts; —screens; —shades; —veils.
(See raiment.)

SHROUD (*v*)

adverbs
effectually; permanently; modestly; closely; protectively; partially; darkly; somberly; gloomily.
(See screen, cloak.)

SHRUB

adjectives
blossoming; aromatic; crowding (pl); luxuriant; ornamental; skirting; tranquil; unpruned; widowed; warm-tinted; stunted.

verbs

blast—; blight—; choke—; cultivate—; debilitate—; eradicate—; extirpate—; fertilize—; impoverish—; starve—; strangle—; trim—; uproot—; —beautifies; —declines; —droops; —s enhance; —fades; —flourishes; —graces; —luxuriates; —languishes; —thrives; —trembles; —wanes.

(See bush, honeysuckle, bud, plant.)

SHRUGS

adjectives

expressive; dumb; impertinent; good-natured; impatient; indifferent; significant; contemptuous.

SHUDDER

adjectives

strong; involuntary; passing; ecstatic; visible; slight; repressed; pious; elaborate; intuitive; violent.

verbs

arrest—; elicit—; excite—; feign—; impel —; induce—; inspire—; occasion—; provoke —; repress—; restrain—; —agitates; —betrays; —convulses; —disconcerts; —electrifies; —paralyzes; —perturbs; —ripples through; —ruffles.

(See shiver, sob, sigh.)

SHUDDER (v)

adverbs

spasmodically; physically; instinctively; figuratively; apprehensively; involuntarily; violently; feverishly; abnormally; perceptibly.

(See tremble, shake, shiver.)

SHUFFLE (v)

adverbs

noiselessly; slyly; wearily; uncouthly; sluggishly; clumsily; imperturbably; drearily.

(See drag, walk.)

SHUN (v)

adverbs

timorously; fastidiously; aristocratically; intelligently; cautiously; scrupulously; systematically; studiously.

(See elude, shift, avoid.)

SHUT (v)

adverbs

clamorously; obligingly; stealthily; inexor-

ably; convulsively; sullenly; mysteriously; impatiently; drowsily; abruptly; cautiously.

(See close, exclude.)

SHUTTER

adjectives

awry; heavy-barred; supplementary; iron-cased; closed.

verbs

draw—; elevate—; unfold—; —bars; —blinds; —eclipses; —mantles; —masks; —obscures; —rattles; —restrains; —shades; —veils.

(See screen.)

SHUTTLE

verbs

propel—; swivel—; —alternates; —gyrates; —lurches; —oscillates; —pulsates; —quivers; —revolves; —rotates; —see-saws; —swerves; —swirls; —trembles; —trundles; —wabbles; —whirls; —vibrates.

SHY

adverbs

awkwardly; uneasily; childishly; self-consciously; timidly; uncomfortably; engagingly; embarrassingly; charmingly; painfully; peculiarly; strangely; unwontedly; becomingly; unnaturally; fearfully; clumsily; foolishly; ridiculously; pitiably; touchingly; adorably; comically; absurdly; exquisitely; habitually; deliciously; extremely; incredibly; oddly; curiously; unnecessarily.

SHYNESS

adjectives

delicious; provincial; confused; virgin; rural; exquisite; innate; wonted; girlish; unconquerable; maiden; blushing.

verbs

blush in—; falter in—; feign—; flinch in—; overcome with—; quail in—; —abashes; —afflicts; —arrests; —blenches; —bridles; —confuses; —constrains; —cows; —curbs; —daunts; —deters; —distorts; —distresses; —fetters; —humiliates; —leashes; —overawes; —overwhelms; —perturbs; —represses; —restrains; —smothers.

(See bashfulness, modesty.)

SIBILANT

adverbs

softly; affectedly; ridiculously; laughably; hissingly; toothlessly; lispingly; comically;

warningly; persistently; curiously; derisively; mockingly; disturbingly; pitiably; unpleasantly; strangely; disagreeably.

SICK

verbs

comfort—; heal—; palliate—; prescribe for —; rebuild—; reclaim—; regenerate—; rehabilitate—; relieve—; rescue—; restore—; revive—; soothe—.

(See patient, invalid.)

adverbs

chronically; continually; seriously; habitually; unfortunately; unusually; curiously; oddly; strangely; unaccountably; inexplicably; seriously; critically; recently; definitely; unfortunately; frequently; squeamishly; feverishly; mentally; dangerously; painfully; embarrassingly; inopportunely; inconveniently; awkwardly; desperately; slightly; unendurably.

SICKEN (v)

adverbs

visibly; swooningly; biliously; fatally; tragically; woefully; gradually; speechlessly; mutely; nauseatingly.

(See disgust, languish.)

SICKLY

adverbs

distressingly; unfortunately; bafflingly; always; strangely; inexplicably; wretchedly; unhappily; apparently; curiously.

SICKNESS

adjectives

speechless; desperate; prolonged; swooning; everlasting; pining; violent; bilious; deadly; lasting; soul.

verbs

allay—; alleviate—; banish—; check—; combat—; conquer—; convalesce from—; curse—; eradicate—; feign—; induce—; occasion—; subdue—; —abates; —afflicts; —aggravates; —besets; —cankers; —confines; —cripples; —desolates; —harasses; —heals; —incommodes; —indisposes; —induces; —invalids; —maims; —oppresses; —overcomes; —predisposes; —racks; — ravages; —sears; —seizes; —smites; — sours; —torments; —undermines; —vitiates; —wastes; —withers.

(See ailment, disease, illness, malady.)

SIDE

adjectives

ludicrous; balanced; unbaked; instrumental; paternal; humane; gruesome; seamy; rusty; perilous; luminous; unengaged; massive; verdant; windy; pierced; liberal; stretched-out; obverse; ample; sorrowful; practical; engaging; interminable; nobler; tangled; grassy; ridiculous; bank; valuable; translucent; hairy; wounded; gaping; deep; precipitous; semi-nomadic; perpendicular; distinctive; sloping; lighter; respective; intellectual; outward; emotional; shrinking; spiritual; extravagant; fathomless; pierced; showy; administrative; executive; psychological; spotted; gorgeous; brawny; craggy; neglected; aesthetic; diametrical; opposite; fanciful; starboard; maternal; ventral; exposed; protected; dreamy; winning; objective; superstitious; shuddering; woolly.

SIDE-SPLITTING

adverbs

absurdly; mirthfully; uproariously; boisterously; comically; ridiculously; laughably; farcically; drolly; tumultuously; prankishly; outlandishly; merrily; ludicrously.

SIDEWALK

adjectives

swarming; gravel; moving; unpaved; scented; innocent-looking; broken; wide; cobbled; brick; winding; slippery.

verbs

fence—; gad about—; jog along—; pace—; patrol—; promenade—; ramble along—; saunter along—; straggle along—; traverse —; trudge over—; —crumbles; —deviates; —glistens; —jams.

(See walk.)

SIEGE

adjectives

vigorous; lingering; wanton; severe; bitter; disastrous; moving; protracted; creditable; wreckful; amiable; fatal; famous; fearful; implacable; repeated; hateful; bloody.

verbs

brave—; breast—; endure—; engage in—; extend—; intrench against—; lay—; maintain—; parry—; prolong—; protract—; repel—; resist—; submit to—; survive—; yield to—; weather—; withstand—; —anni-

hilates; —beleaguers; —devastates; —grips; —impoverishes; —lags; —ravages; — starves; —undermines; —blockades.
(See attack, blockade.)

adjectives
meshed; trembling; captious.

verbs
—filters; —purges; —refines; —separates; —sifts; —sorts; —strains; —winnows.

SIFT (*v*)
adverbs
mechanically; academically; curiously; patiently; industriously; painstakingly; suspiciously; legally; automatically.
(See investigate, bolt.)

SIGH
adjectives
gasping; thriftless; gusty; impatient; aimless; fruitless; expiring; deep; burning; sharp; puzzled; plenteous (pl); perpetual; relieved; desponding; perfumed; vain; friendly; delicious; reproachful; sultry; monitorial; lingering; compassionate; mournful; sympathetic; piteous; profound; heavy; quick; slumberous; useless; contrite; false; wistful; feeble; thirsty; pensive; alien; restful; repentant; half-forlorn; audible; inauspicious; inharmonious; short; joyous; passing; impatient; interjectional; watery; philosophic; wasteful; sumptuous; sad; amorous; short; tantalizing; gasping; exasperated; mistaken; miserable; odorous; reckless; infallible; comprehensive; relaxing; desolate; feigned; inaudible; occasional; sorry; yearning; pleased; stifled; disgusted; loud; long; persuasive; gratified; moral; involuntary; relieved; thriftless; convulsive.

verbs
breathe—; burst into—; draw—; elicit—; evoke—; heave—; hush—; muffle—; murmur—; mute—; restrain—; smother—; stifle—; suppress—; utter—; whisper—; — betrays; —bursts from; —deprecates; — flutters; —laments; —racks; —rends; — stirs; —wrings.
(See groan, sob, moan, murmur.)

SIGH (*v*)
adverbs
dismally; profoundly; soulfully; romantically; audibly; pensively; retrospectively; sentimentally; plaintively; appealingly; woefully; tremulously; dejectedly; reminiscently; nostalgically; wistfully; involuntarily; eloquently; compassionately; contritely; forlornly; desolately; inaudibly.
(See grieve, lament.)

SIGHT
adjectives
inward; melting; wondrous; novel; weird; startling; wide; stirring; goodly; uncommon; piteous; enraptured; stimulating; irresistible; aching; holiest; impressive; dilated; refreshing; dismal; touching; remarkable; doleful; spiritual; richer; purer; fairer; heterogeneous; dubious; ravishing; amusing; cheery; instructive; wretched; portentous; clouded; exhilarating; imposing; horrifying; unusual, curtained; solemn; gorgeous; triumphant; precious; fearful; loveliest; continuous; infant; grand; thrilling; unaided; disturbing; curious; quickened; wished; ludicrous; marvelous; appalling; translatable; ghastliest; gallant; truest; bleared; distressing; horrible; swimming; majestic; fine; exceptional; welcome; powerful; sickening; glorious; purblind; joyful; inspiring; all-searching; steadfast; unacquainted; approved; gladdened; straining; extraordinary; splendid; worthless; loathsome; lucent; unveiled; absolute; deadening; glistening; bewildered; unaided; mortal; awful; sorry; genial; saltatory; nocturnal; priceless; secret; whimsical; prettiest; feebler; perfect.

verbs
abhor—; blur—; check—; cloud—; confuse —; conjure—; control—; dim—; distort—; distract—; dull—; focus—; impair—; intensify—; loathe—; lose—; obscure—; obstruct—; recover—; regain—; rely upon—; restore—; sharpen—; shun—; sink from—; stimulate—; tuck out of—; veil—; visualize —; —dazzles; —dissipates; —declines; — enriches; —fails; —invigorates; —outrages; —pollutes; —weakens.
(See vision, view, phenomenon, spectacle, mirage.)

SIGHTLY
adverbs
agreeably; pleasantly; splendidly; magnifi-

cently; unusually; delightfully; extraordinarily; unexpectedly; gloriously; gorgeously; beautifully; entrancingly; remarkably; exceptionally; impressively; thrillingly; dramatically; inexpressibly.

SIGN
adjectives
encouraging; mournful; conspicuous; deep-drawn; premonitory; ideographic; ghastly; indubitable; extreme; hopeful; mute; incomprehensible; regretful; fraternal; important; fluttering; perpetual; visible; ambitious; assured; supplementary; watery; subtle; undoubted; geometric; inauspicious; palpable; bursting; celestial; impressive; depressing; labial; creaking; ominous; frantic; peculiar; optimistic; fragrant; lying; visible; eloquent; translucent; manifold (pl); fearful; natural; symbolic; cabalistic; physical; doubtful; infallible; obscure; elaborate; mysterious; decreased; useless; evident; abject; imperial; characteristic; affecting; faintest; conclusive; sacred; discernible; lamentable; perceptible; talismanic.

verbs
betray—; discern—; drape—; evince—; experience—; interpret—; mistakes—s; question—; trace—s; visit—; watch for—; wipe out—; —appears; —characterizes; —glares; —warns.
(See emblem, indication, signal, notice, mark.)

SIGN (v)
adverbs
legally; formally; perfunctorily; nominally; bindingly; willingly; felicitously.
(See signify, indicate.)

SIGNAL
adjectives
emergency; customary; imperceptible; suggestive; descriptive; preconcerted; true; prompt; cautionary; warning; unheeded.

verbs
await—; beat—; blaze—; breathe—; dispatch—; disperse at—; drum—; exchange —s; flash—; flourish—s; flout—; heed—; gather at—; interpret—; issue—; predetermine—; prescribe—; respond to—; —cautions; —summons; —winks.
(See alarm, beacon, sign.)

SIGNATURE
adjectives
bold; scrawling; sundry; conscious; sprawling; scribbled; unreadable.

verbs
affix—; attest to—; counterfeit—; dash off —; duplicate—; embellish—; enter—; familiarize with—; identify—; pen—; produce —; scratch out—; scrawl—; scribble—; stereotype—; strike out—; submit—; trace —; transcribe—; verify—; vouch for—; witness—; —endorses; —flows; —ripples from; —seals; —s tally.

SIGNIFICANCE
adjectives
drear; mental; emotional; lofty; ghastly; particular; sufficient; supreme; intense; tremendous; spiritual; sad; unsuspected; historic; sound; functional; representative; special; popular; malign; symbolical; mystifying; double; profound; dramatic; ultimate; fine; enormous; vital; tragic; social; immense; contemptuous; intrinsic; lasting; artistic; cruel; prophetic; rude; poignant; gloomy; threatening; highest; arresting; larger; stinging; deep; permanent; transcendent; insolent; convincing; musical; ominous; prime; curious; minor; fatal; moral.

verbs
acquire—; assign—; assume—; attach—; attain—; awaken to—; broaden—; consider —; convey—; dwell upon—; eschew—; fathom—; feel—; forget—; grasp—; heighten—; measure—; narrow—; unfold—; —grows; —overshadows.
(See importance, consequence, import, meaning.)

SIGNIFICANT
adverbs
horribly; menacingly; portentously; pleasantly; happily; immensely; remarkably; distinctly; suddenly; curiously; ominously; deliberately; unmistakably; alarmingly; threateningly; openly; marvelously; tremendously; auspiciously; cruelly.

SIGNIFY (v)
adverbs
clearly; concretely; vividly; undeniably;

affirmatively; comprehensively; plainly; obviously; graphically.

(See show, indicate.)

SILENCE

adjectives

profound; obstinate; mysterious; complete; discomfited; infant; horrid; sullen; majestic; pale; sickening; indignant; melodious; deep; sarcastic; reverent; roaring; morose; heated; honorable; listening; chilling; awkward; demure; musing; stagnant; suitable; unaccountable; voluptuous; resentful; horrified; fearful; astonished; expectant; respectful; oppressive; dignified; deathly; distressful; chagrined; awed; luxurious; bashful; stern; total; snowy; religious; solemn; involuntary; warm; perfumed; defiant; apologetic; lazy; everlasting; moody; attentive; absolute; abstracted; heavy; motionless; stifling; tense; sympathetic; discreet; slumberous, limp, sunlit; momentary; industrious; embarrassed; somber; sulky; dogged; prevailing; hushed; depressing; blank; mute; fruitful; punctuated; painful; broken; ominous; mannerless; grateful; awful; funeral; universal; gathered; uninterrupted; silvery; infinite; tearless; appalling; fragile; eloquent; severe; sepulchral; thoughtful; dismal; empty; thick; sunken; mysterious; guilty; enforced; strange; magical; solvent; freezing; infuriated; bewildered; vibrant; imperative; curious; cold; complete; long; meditative; inhuman; gracious; intense; passive; spellbound; noisy; monumental; museful; brooding; perfect; breathless; lengthened; white; hostile; hideous; dignified; poetic; disciplined; sacred; smiling; forbidding; aggravating; tangible; flushing; unreproved; unsociable; stern; grim; comparative; arid; appealing; maiden; azure; deafening; rapturous; horrible; simple; welcome; bashful; mournful; enamored; despairing; pregnant; shaded; eternal.

verbs

acquiesce in—; appraise—; awaken—; bear—; break—; cajole into—; constrain—; covet—; drop into—; endure—; enjoin—; feel—; impose—; inculcate—; interpret—; lapse into—; lie in—; maintain—; penetrate —; plead for—; preserve—; press into—; put to—; quench—; reduce to—; reflect in —; relapse into—; retreat in—; rip—; sift —; sink into—; slump into—; survey in—; wrap in—; worship—; —cloaks; —descends; —enchants; —encompasses; —en-

sues; —explodes; —falls; —fills; —follows; —grows; —hammers; —hangs; —imposes; —pervades; —pounces; —prevails; — reigns; —rolls; —settles; —sinks; —supervenes; —swallows; —throbs; —troubles.

(See hush, quiet, stillness.)

SILENCE (v)

adverbs

effectually; completely; mysteriously; sarcastically; discreetly; awkwardly; sternly; apologetically; momentarily; grimly.

(See suppress, hush.)

SILENT

adverbs

absolutely; remarkably; unusually; pleasantly; practically; sufficiently; warrantably; reasonably; positively; significantly; usually; reticently; gravely; alarmingly; amusedly; impressively; dangerously; ominously; indulgently; haughtily; angrily; happily; magnanimously; charitably; bewilderingly; strangely; singularly; maddeningly; obstinately; stolidly; sadly; sullenly; mischievously; furtively; stealthily; warily; cautiously; carefully; naturally; guardedly; breathlessly; dreadfully; terrifyingly; gloomily.

SILHOUETTE

adjectives

dark; sliding; streamline; sleek; shadowy; grim; fitted; meager.

SILK

adjectives

watered; seeded; pompadour; domestic; heavy; fresh; delicate; faded; exquisite; glistening; pleated; scarlet; flimsy; newspun; delicate-filmed.

verbs

apparel in—; arrange—; array in—; attire in—; bale—; begrime—; braid—; cast off —; divest of—; drape—; dress in—; entwine—; export—; fabricate—; fringe with —; import—; impregnate—; invest in—; lace—; mat—; net—; plait—; shear—; shred—; skein—; spin—; tangle—; veil in —; warp—; weave—; —fades; —rustles; —tears.

(See handkerchief, cloth, gauze, lining, linen.)

SILLY

adverbs

miserably; incurably; senselessly; stupidly;

loutishly; clownishly; purposely; amusingly; entertainingly; feignedly; absurdly; laughably; imprudently; indiscreetly; hopelessly; disagreeably; intolerably; disgustingly; contemptibly; curiously; pitiably; lamentably; deplorably; wretchedly; disastrously; utterly; hopelessly.

SILVER

adjectives
sheeny; quivering; rippling; transparent; gleaming; wavering; glowing; burnished; shimmering; filigree; massive.

verbs
bedeck with—; burnish—; caparison in—; chase (emboss)—; devaluate—; fabricate—; fashion—; glorify with—; hoard—; mine—; refine—; work in—; —blazons; —coruscates; —enriches; —glints; —glitters; — glows; —tarnishes.
(See metal, steel, jewel.)

SIMILAR

adverbs
indistinguishably; bewilderingly; inconveniently; dangerously; curiously; strangely; naturally; laughably; somewhat; congenially; sufficiently; accidentally; intentionally; deliberately.

SIMILARITY

adjectives
assumed; singular; increasing; psychological.

verbs
attend with—; direct attention to—; discern —; indicate—; observe—; regard—; sense —; —bewilders; —bores; —ceases; —confuses; —echoes; —flusters; —reflects; — mirrors; —parallels; —perplexes; —reproduces; —strikes.
(See identity, resemblance.)

SIMILE

adjectives
absurd; chilling; amiable; expressive; good; swift; felicitous; sickly; oft-repeated; natural; arctic; happy; apt.

verbs
employ—; enlist—; garble—; resort to—; revel in—; —alludes; —colors; —contrasts;

—conveys; —clarifies; —expresses; —implies; —paints; —parallels; —pictures; — strikes.
(See metaphor, comparison.)

SIMPER (*v*)

adverbs
affectedly; coyly; bashfully; embarrassedly; coquettishly; naively; childishly.
(See smile, smirk.)

SIMPERING

adverbs
coyly; demurely; deliberately; foolishly; provokingly; cleverly; designingly; senselessly; hopefully; flirtatiously; ridiculously; archly; cunningly; subtly; wittingly; girlishly; craftily; engagingly.

SIMPLE

adverbs
beautifully; expensively; unnecessarily; utterly; delightfully; artlessly; graciously; refreshingly; intelligibly; pleasantly; fortunately; needlessly; starkly; childishly; severely; chastely; elegantly; gracefully; tastefully; harmoniously; appropriately; ingenuously; naively; bluntly; foolishly; delicately; daintily; charmingly; idiotically; crazily; inanely; fatuously; mindlessly.

SIMPLICITY

adjectives
rich; extreme; precise; subtle; orthographic; sublime; gradual; impressive; chaste; touching; primitive; everlasting; striking; thoroughgoing; scanty; unostentatious; severe; studied; luminous; noble; childlike; solid; medieval; pathetic; laughable; courteous; classic; majestic; low; rude; idyllic; healthful; fundamental; patrician; stolid; limpid; naive; habitual; grave; unique; native; frank; austere; unconscious; sad; patriarchal; serious; absolute; affectionate; stunning; miraculous; antique; pastoral; poignant; inscrutable; rustic; cheerful; exquisite; polite; boyish; striking; vigorous; venerable.

verbs
abandon—; acclaim—; achieve—; advocate —; afford—; applaud—; aspire to—; commend—; desert—; feign—; forsake—; glory in—; inspire—; pretend—; relinquish—; seek—; simulate—; welcome—; —allures;

—attracts; —beguiles; —charms; —deceives; —delights; —disarms; —enchants; —entrances; —fascinates; —inveigles; — refreshes; —renounces.

(See innocence, sincerity, frankness, plainness.)

SIMPLIFY (v)
adverbs
extremely; amazingly; precisely; subtly; orthographically; impressively; fundamentally; uniquely.

(See arrange.)

SIMULATE (v)
adverbs
ingeniously; deftly; artfully; skillfully; professionally; traitorously; slyly; insidiously; venomously.

(See feign, pretend.)

SIMULATED
adverbs
carefully; cleverly; fraudulently; deceptively; adroitly; skillfully; wickedly; deliberately; viciously; artfully; secretly; successfully; mendaciously; smoothly; accurately; exactly; correctly; authentically; theatrically; dramatically; spectacularly; impressively; graphically; wonderfully.

SIN
adjectives
maddening; fundamental; unpardonable; original; dark; deadly; fleshly; grievous; cardinal; damning; regretted; heinous; familiar; unexpiated; shameful; untold; vilest; hidden; foul; mystic; implied; besetting; appalling; bygone; cunning; virtuous; intellectual; grave; venial; detested; imaginary; delightful; conscious; characteristic; precious; penitential; disorderly; superficial.

verbs
abandon—; absolve of—; abstain from—; acknowledge—; ameliorate—; atone for—; banish—; clean from—; commit—; compensate for—; conceive in—; deliver from—; do penance for—; divest of—; excoriate—s; expiate—; extenuate—; forsake—; grapple with—; inherit—; lapse into—; offer for —s; overcome—; pardon—; plunge into—; purge of—; relinquish—; repeat—; reproach—; reveal—; shrive of—; steep in—; stray into—; uncover—; unveil—; wash away—; wallow in—; whip for—; wrestle with—; —corrupts; —damns; —defiles; —

depraves; —flourishes; —hardens; —pollutes; —purges; —surges; —tortures; — traduces; —transgresses; —weighs upon.

(See iniquity, licentiousness, abomination, evil, crime, lust.)

SIN (v)
adverbs
fundamentally; incorrigibly; unwittingly; grievously; egregiously; carnally; intellectually; venially; knowingly; unsuspectingly; lustfully.

(See transgress, trespass.)

SINCERE
adverbs
unaffectedly; charmingly; graciously; affably; cordially; pleasantly; utterly; delightfully ; ardently; honestly; remarkably; plainly; genuinely; dependably; scrupulously; earnestly; fervently; enthusiastically; punctiliously; particularly; reliably.

SINCERITY
adjectives
evident; transparent; artistic; flaming; perfect; despairing; well-feigned; worshiping; obvious; impetuous; unaffected; noble; deep; forlorn; sterling; grave; violent; fierce; youthful; bashful; robust; abominable; sorrowful; patent; grim.

verbs
attest to—; cherish—; declare—; doubt—; express—; feign—; impeach—; impugn—; maintain—; pledge—; pretend—; question —; ring with—; smack of—; stir—; test—; value—; verify—; vow—; —beguiles; — burns; —deludes; —falters; —impresses; — pervades; —vacillates.

(See candor, simplicity, earnestness, honesty, innocence, integrity.)

SINFUL
adverbs
deliberately; wilfully; maliciously; blasphemously; coarsely; consciously; boldly; audaciously; defiantly; impiously; brazenly; openly; flagrantly; incredibly.

SING (v)
adverbs
fervently; quaveringly; nocturnally; effortlessly; audibly; angelically; lustily; bewitchingly; blithely; responsively; derisively; impetuously; exultingly; merrily; conscientiously; extemporaneously; vigorously;

raptly; melodiously; vibrantly; hilariously; magnificently; discordantly; vociferously; throatily; congregationally; professionally; lucretively.

(See hum, croon.)

SINGER

adjectives

notable; malignant; eloquent; inimitable; flattering; pensive; cunning; skillful; splendid; renowned; trained; unseen.

verbs

acclaim—; accompany—; applaud—; belittle—; extol—; prepare—; train—; —carols; —enraptures; —enthralls; —executes; —s harmonize; —impresses; —intones; —matures; —modulates; —pitches; —renders; —stirs; —syncopates; —thrills; —trills; —uplifts.

(See choir, chorus, singing, musician, artist.)

SINGING

adjectives

magical; merry; remote; clear; concerted; congregational; delectable; interlaced; comic; vociferous; fervent; hearty; throaty.

verbs

accompany—; arrange—; coach—; direct—; dominate—; harmonize—; modulate—; rejoice in—; syncopate—; —amuses; —diverts; —echoes; —penetrates; —pervades; —precipitates; —smites; —voices.

(See singer, music.)

SINGSONG

adverbs

intolerably; monotonously; dully; droningly; tediously; unbearably; lullingly; soothingly; drowsily; deliberately; dreamily; sleepily; prosaically; persistently; interminably; endlessly; maddeningly; outlandishly; disagreeably.

SINISTER

adverbs

horribly; ominously; portentously; alarmingly; terrifyingly; deliberately; oppressively; gloomily; unhappily; disturbingly; distressingly; significantly; unmistakably; darkly; hopelessly; fearfully; dismally; deplorably; insidiously; uncommonly; actually; unquestionably; seriously; undoubtedly.

SINK (v)

adverbs

exhaustedly; despondently; swiftly; fatally; gratefully; unfathomably; dejectedly; partially; relaxedly; markedly; continuously.

(See fall, descend.)

SINLESS

adverbs

impossibly; immaculately; chastely; incredibly; sacredly; divinely; beatifically; blessedly; angelically; immortally; eternally; seraphically; innocently.

SINNER

adjectives

tortured; corrigible; wretched; vile; rebellious; ever-living; obdurate; dainty; reckless; hardened.

SINUS

verbs

cauterize—; congest—; drain—; infect—; inflame—; irrigate—; obliterate—; obstruct —; suppurate—; tap—; —clogs; —discharges; —poisons; —secretes; —tortures; —undermines; —racks.

(See sore, cavity, opening.)

SIP (v)

adverbs

demurely; sparingly; fastidiously; aristocratically; delicately; sickeningly; disgustingly; noisily; vulgarly.

(See drink, absorb, suck.)

SIRE

adjectives

sweet; sapient; heathen; illustrious; loving.

SIREN

verbs

resist—; withstand—; yield to—; —allures; —attracts; —beckons; —bewitches; —cajoles; —captivates; —charms; —enamours; —entices; —fascinates; —impels; —inveigles; —intrigues; —lures; —magnetizes; —tempts; —screams; —seduces; —shrieks; —wheedles.

(See lover, woman.)

SISTER

adjectives

impressionable; droll; diverting; desolate; fair; erring; beauteous; barren; unchaste;

weird; hard-boiled; woodland; honored; religious; sterner; younger; incredulous; innocent.

verbs
adore—; caress—; cherish—; claim—; dote on—; embosom—; embrace—; endear to—; esteem—; favor—; glorify—; idolize—; prize—; revere—; worship—.
   (See mother.)

SISTERLY
adverbs
warmly; sympathetically; comfortingly; tenderly; affectionately; assiduously; persistently; adroitly; patiently; indulgently; hopefully; insistently; consistently; cleverly; impulsively; noticeably; carefully; unfailingly; pleasantly; agreeably.

SIT (*v*)
adverbs
decorously; ignominiously; mutely; moodily; calmly; inscrutably; placidly; unobtrusively; picturesquely; impassively; dejectedly; disconsolately; despondently; voicelessly; spiritlessly; dispiritedly; quiescently; majestically.
   (See rest, repose.)

SITE
adjectives
admirable; impregnable; noble; suitable; magnificent; restricted; appropriate; splendid.

SITUATE (*v*)
adverbs
conveniently; centrally; fortunately; geographically; romantically; favorably; picturesquely; alarmingly; dramatically; uniquely; remotely; depressingly; dismally; secludedly; ridiculously; precariously; perilously; anomalously.
   (See place, establish.)

SITUATION
adjectives
sentimental; silly; messiest; equivocal; dramatic; ticklish; cheerful; recurrent; enviable; unpleasant; extreme; alarming; horrifying; tragic; embarrassing; peculiar; speech; tense; detrimental; momentous; dangerous; farcical; desolate; unique; slippery; economic; international; effective; social; urgent; charming; analogous; painful; dependent; aggravating; remote; material; depressing; financial; defiant; unhappy; countless (pl); rational; humorous; precise; secluded; curious; relative; important; insular; hopeless; lonesome; incredible; immoral; dismal; strategical; favorable; arduous; defenseless; conspicuous; parlous; dispersed; pragmatic; dismaying; strained; unfortunate; picturesque; melancholy; appalling; commanding; accessible; ridiculous; subordinate; paradoxical; delicate; difficult; much-coveted; awkward; isolated; distressing; diplomatic; precarious; sequestered; desperate; exposed; forfeited; military; healthy; romantic; comfortable; fearful; perilous; ironic; anomalous.

verbs
alleviate—; alter—; analyze—; barge into (colloq.)—; contemplate—; control—; crash into—; define—; denounce—; dismiss—; dramatize—; clarify—; command—; conceive—; confess—; cope with—; create—; cripple—; deal with—; divulge—; evaluate —; exaggerate—; excogitate—s; gloss over —; grapple with—; grasp—; handle—; master—; plunge into—; ponder over—; relieve—; remedy—; resolve—; save—; sense —; size up—; soften—; sum up—; take stock of—; trace—; unscramble—; utilize—; view—; visualize—; —aggravates; —appeals; —s arise; —baffles; —calculates; —carries; —clears; —confronts; —demonstrates; —develops; —discloses; —disturbs; —dominates; —eases; —grows; —illuminates; —intensifies; —portrays; —recurs; —relaxes; —relinquishes; —revolves; —solves; —suffers; mull over—; neglect—; overdramatize—.
   (See position, condition, predicament.)

SIZE
adjectives
enormous; remarkable; immense; cap; apparent; defined; prodigious; stunted; comparative; generous; respectable; stupendous; imposing; sensational; unusual; unwieldy; minute; inexpensive; substantial; convenient; formidable; monstrous; gargantuan; heroic; graduated; sample; small; serving; requisite; undue; tangible.

verbs
attenuate—; augment—; calibrate—s; compute—; diminish—; distend—; estimate—; exaggerate—; exceed—; expand—; fix—; gauge—; grade—s; graduate—s; inflate—; magnify—; modify—; plumb—; reduce—;

register—; restrict—; standardize—; surpass in—; swell—; tabulate—s; vary—; —dwindles; —s range from; —shrinks.

(See dimension, measurement, extent, magnitude.)

SKELETON

adjectives

decaying; sheeted; fleshless; homogeneous; rickety; moldering; colossal; human; metallic; uncouth; bleached; grinning; moldy.

verbs

build on—; cremate—; disinter—; embalm —; exhume—; expose—; inter—; preserve —; prop—; reduce to—; shrivel to—; uncover—; unearth—; —bears; —crumbles; —grins; —reveals; —supports; —sustains.

SKEPTIC

adjectives

obstinate; staunch; satisfied; complete; confirmed.

verbs

assure—; brook—; overawe—s; overwhelm —s; impress—; persuade—; quiet—; stagger—s; —cavils; —challenges; —demurs; —discredits; —disputes; —dissents; —distrusts; —entertains; —doubts; —hesitates; —queries; —vacillates; —wavers.

(See atheist, critic, heretic.)

SKEPTICAL

adverbs

openly; publicly; scoffingly; jeeringly; derisively; contemptuously; significantly; conspicuously; persistently; obstinately; stubbornly; stolidly; distrustfully; arrogantly; oddly; curiously; extremely; profoundly; secretly.

SKEPTICISM

adjectives

pretended; indulgent; cold; inveterate; painful; native; learned; extreme; happy; definite; flippant; worthwhile; safe; rationalistic.

verbs

assume—; attribute to—; betray—; break down—; collapse into—; confute—; criticize—; deny—; dispose to—; excuse—; fall into—; incline to—; incur—; involve—; justify—; lament—; minimize—; profess—; prompt—; rebuke—; regard—; taint by—;

—amuses; —asserts; —overthrows; —persuades; —prevails; —sweeps; —vanishes.

(See atheism, disbelief, doubt.)

SKETCH

adjectives

pastel; charming; unfinished; occasional; faint; historical; insufficient; vigorous; impressionistic; autobiographical; loose; effective; brief; colossal; concise; panoramic; biographical; hospital; vivid; vignette; critical; characteristic; orchestral; malignant; dramatic; imaginative; good-humored; accompanying; rambling; belated; spirited; despairing; ingenious; lifelike.

verbs

dash off—; design—; disclose—; draft—; execute—; reproduce—; scrutinize—; submit—; trace—; transcribe—; —charts; —delineates; —depicts; —details; —diagrams; —enlightens; —facilitates; —guides; —illustrates; —outlines; —portrays; —prescribes; —represents; —sets forth.

(See drawing, design, illustration, plan, outline.)

SKETCH (*v*)

adverbs

realistically; vaguely; imperfectly; roughly; artistically; vividly; graphically; covertly; ridiculously; satirically; impressionistically; autobiographically; panoramically; biographically; dramatically; imaginatively; ingeniously.

(See draw, portray.)

SKETCHY

adverbs

inadequately; unsatisfactorily; carelessly; unserviceably; hopelessly; disappointingly; singularly; curiously; ineffectively; provokingly; inexcusably; unpardonably.

SKI (*v*)

adverbs

boisterously; dexterously; artfully; professionally; sportively; amateurishly; daringly.
(See slide, skim.)

SKIFF

verbs

batter—; buffet—; convoy—; embark on—; man—; navigate—; punt—; ram—; scull —; swamp—; waft—; —bears; —conveys;

—drifts; —glides; —plies; —puts to sea; —sallies forth; —scuds; —sweeps; —weighs anchor.
(See boat.)

SKILL

adjectives
experimental; inordinate; persevering; diagnostic; dangerous; tactical; moderate; ancient; profound; manual; technical; artistic; trained; superior; exceptional; subtle; acquired; dramatic; linguistic; deft; infinite; descriptive; acknowledged; inventive; competent; matchless; tattered; martial; prodigious; strict; uncanny; untaught; professional; diplomatic; considerable; consummate; daredevil; executive; shallow; exquisite; simple; barren; quaint; detached; methodic; journalistic; masterly; practical; unavailing; athletic; unusual; creative; analytical, potent; monastic; unsurpassed; fearful; unfaltering; comparative; mechanical; rare; quick; sufficient.

verbs
absorb—; acquire—; applaud—; capitalize —; challenge—; confound—; contend with —; develop—; devise—; discern—; display —; evince—; execute with—; exhaust—; exhibit—; extol—; manifest—; overestimate —; surpass—; transfer—.
(See ability, faculty, ingenuity, capability.)

SKILLED

adverbs
moderately; exceptionally; professionally; profoundly; subtly; definitely; admittedly; infinitely; matchlessly; prodigiously; uncannily; diplomatically; consummately; exquisitely; quaintly; rarely; undeniably; incontrovertibly; unusually; creatively; powerfully; fearfully; comparatively; notably; strikingly; diabolically; marvelously; incredibly; dangerously; obviously; constitutionally; naturally; innately; inherently; instinctively; capably; competently; proficiently; deftly; discreetly; conveniently.

SKILLFUL

adverbs
amazingly; remarkably; particularly; miraculously; eminently; conspicuously; unusually; genuinely; admittedly; adequately; presumably; brilliantly; famously; inexpressibly; modestly.

SKIM (v)

adverbs
cursorily; perfunctorily; carelessly; hastily; rapidly; studiously; critically.
(See scan, read.)

SKIMP (v)

adverbs
penuriously; niggardly; meanly; parsimoniously; selfishly; fanatically.
(See save.)

SKIMPY

adverbs
ridiculously; fantastically; comically; absurdly; inexcusably; outrageously; miserably; inadequately; pitifully; pitiably; pathetically; grotesquely; ingenerously; stingily; carelessly; awkwardly; unbecomingly; unfashionably; uncomfortably; unfortunately.

SKIN

adjectives
clear; ruddy; tanned; mortal; dainty; tawny; parchment; tender; dry; scratchy; shaggy; accumulated; tough; defensive; roughened; ivory; olive; ardent; incarnate; wrinkled; transparent; sensitive; sleekest; edible; sunburned; lustrous; untanned; sallow; gay; dead; painted; scaling; waxy; bronzed; superfluous; crinkled; redundant; mottled; narrow.

verbs
affect—; aggravate—; bathe—; chafe—; dust—; enervate—; expose—; harden—; inflame—; ingrain—; injure—; irritate—; macerate—; paint—; pat—; peel—; prick —; pull off—; rejuvenate—; rinse—; rub —; ruffle—; safeguard—; save one's—; scratch—; shed—; smear—; soften—; soothe —; sponge—; ulcerate—; —adapts; — blanches; —erupts; —forms; —furrows; — glows; —jaundices; —parches; —quivers; —scars; —shrinks; —splits; —stains; — thickens; —warts; —wrinkles.
(See epidermis, surface.)

SKIRT

adjectives
sable; close-clinging; silken; short; awful; antiquated; tight; divided; ample; jaunty; flared; voluminous; fleecy; cloudy; smooth; draggled; vaporous; gaudy; wide; hoop; gloomy; umbrella; rustling; gathered; pleated; slit; form-fitting; wrinkled.

verbs
accoutre in—; attire in—; bare—; baste—; cling to—; divest of—; enfold in—; garb in —; gusset—; hem—; pleat—; rig in—; rumple—; ruffle—; soil—; strip off—; swaddle in—; tack—; tuck in—; —cloaks; —s flutter; —mantles; —swathes; —s swirl; —s swish.

(See dress.)

SKITTISH
adverbs
nervously; wildly; fearfully; spiritedly; alarmingly; dangerously; absurdly; ridiculously; laughably; outlandishly; awkwardly; simperingly; fatuously; wantonly; capriciously; captiously; unreliably; unsteadily; undependably; unsteadily; erratically; unpredictably; vexatiously; remarkably.

SKULKING
adverbs
furtively; warily; cautiously; soundlessly; fearfully; constantly; unhappily; miserably; wretchedly; guiltily; frightfully; watchfully; secretly; abjectly; pitiably.

SKULL
adjectives
brainless; eyeless; cast-iron; perfect; grinning; gleaming; empty.

verbs
abrade—; batter—; compress—; contuse—; crack—; crush—; drain—; fracture—; imbed in—; lacerate—; measure—; mummify —; penetrate—; perforate—; pierce—; scrape—; split—; tap—; trepan—; trephine —; —contracts; —deflects; —protects.

(See head, brain, mind.)

SKUNK
verbs
rear—; skin—; trap—; —burrows; —controls; —defiles; —depredates; —digs; — ejects; —exudes; —grunts; —hibernates; — inhabits; —plagues; —preys on; —robs; — secretes; —squirts; —stalks; —stinks.

(See animal.)

SKY
adjectives
flooded; crystal; far; distant; radiant; moon-lit; nether; insufficient; thickening; sweltering; fair; twinkling; viewless; ancient; fantastic; lurid; starry; cloudless; turbulent; glowing; wintry; unruffled; interesting; frightening; dappled; stormy; sullen; balmy; leaden; empty; kindred; utmost; mature; beneficent; natural; elusive; upper; smiling; wonted; sunset; pathless; flaming; glorious; broad; frowning; domestic; copper; velvety; violent; nocturnal; delicious; curdled; humid; bright; narrowing; arched; burning; grinning; showery; granite; haunted; overcast; bitter; palpitating; deep; luminous; roseate; unconscious; lulling; sounding; ethereal; blinding; shrinking; softest; western; boundless; sapphire; barren; serene; enchanting; fragrant; alien; frosty; embroiling; triumphant; lowering; changing; unbarred; tidy; middle; pitiless; flawless; palpitant; fated; envious; star-studded; living; rosy; stainless; candid; gorgeous; peacock; tropic; hueless; sultry; night; summer; windless; resplendent; adverse; spacious; turquoise; sombre; placid; menacing; universal; primrose; angry; wonted; steely; vaulted; winking; saffron; nimbus.

verbs
clothe—; fleck—; flutter from—; freak—; gaze at—; gild—; lighten—; rule—; scan —; streak—; weave across—; —blackens; —blazes; —broods; —casts; —clouds; — darkens; —entrances; —glows; —marbles; —obscures; —patterns; —rifts; —curdles.

(See heaven, cloud.)

SLABS
adjectives
mortuary; thick; steaming; monolithic; shattered; boneless; original; huge; sepulchral.

SLACK
adverbs
weakly; lazily; shiftlessly; indolently; incorrigibly; habitually; naturally; inherently; innately; curiously; dreadfully; unpardonably; inexcusably; intolerably; unprofitably; thriftlessly; negligently; improvidently; uncommonly; utterly; apathetically; dangerously; languidly; carelessly; heedlessly; thoughtlessly; inconsiderately; clumsily; indifferently.

SLACKEN (v)
adverbs
materially; markedly; appreciably; gradually; abruptly; experimentally; comparatively.

(See reduce, loosen.)

SLANDER

adjectives

cursing; malicious; honest; cruel; lame;. covered; cunning; abominable; impossible; libelous.

verbs

acquit of—; babble—; decry—; disprove—; inveigh against—; refute—; spread—; vindicate of—; —bespatters; —blackens; — brands; —calumniates; —defames; —deprecates; —derogates; —detracts; —disparages; —incenses; —infuriates; —libels; — maligns; —stigmatizes; —traduces; —vilifies.

(See aspersion, calumny, libel, malediction.)

SLANDER (v)

adverbs

libelously; scurrilously; foully; viciously; hatefully; vindictively; criminally; illegally; spitefully; maliciously; cunningly; cruelly; covertly; abominably; libelously.

(See defame, traduce.)

SLANDEROUS

adverbs

shamefully; boldly; altogether; openly; actually; admittedly; unexpectedly; shockingly; disgracefully; utterly; infamously; notoriously; uncommonly.

SLANG

adjectives

picturesque; vulgar; descriptive; polyglot; current; sporting; two-fisted; bold; understandable; local; accepted.

verbs

adopt—; ban—; colloquialize—; debar—; evolve—; express in—; frown upon—; interpret—; invent—; popularize—; taboo—; translate—; —amuses; —assumes; —colors; —corrupts; —enlivens; —invigorates; — mutilates; —revises; —spreads; —tends; — vulgarizes.

(See jargon, language.)-

SLANGY

adverbs

disagreeably; unpleasantly; trenchantly; catchily; cheaply; coarsely; unnecessarily; crudely; tawdrily; boorishly; loutishly; ignorantly; gruffly; churlishly; indelicately; remarkably; gracelessly.

SLAP (v)

adverbs

smartly; brutally; cruelly; viciously; impatiently; indignantly.

(See box, strike.)

SLAP-DASH

adverbs

carelessly; blithely; hastily; nonchalantly; excitedly; hurriedly; untidily; thoughtlessly; inconsiderately; boyishly; inexcusably; habitually; incorrigibly; hopelessly; unsatisfactorily; unpleasantly; unluckily.

SLASH (v)

adverbs

ruthlessly; economically; murderously; energetically; conclusively; furiously; vindictively; bestially.

(See cut, gash.)

SLATTERNLY

adverbs

wretchedly; miserably; untidily; intolerably; incorrigibly; unattractively; unpleasantly; unfortunately; actually; carelessly; unconventionally; nonchalantly; desperately; sadly; hopelessly; habitually; unwontedly; displeasingly; offensively.

SLAUGHTER

adjectives

needless; terrific; deep; deadly; dreadful; ignoble; red; fratricidal; ruthless; sheer; persistent; brutal; indiscriminate; terrible; hopeless; unheard-of; causeless; awful; unworthy; fearful; subsequent; treacherous; incidental; wholesale.

verbs

avenge—; check—; condone—; countenance —; curb—; denounce—; exonerate of—; justify—; implicate in—; prosecute for—; regret—; restrain—; subdue—; succumb in —; stem—; —debauches; —decimates; — defiles; —deletes; —depraves; —ravages; —shames.

(See bloodshed, massacre.)

SLAUGHTER (v)

adverbs

professionally; blindly; ruthlessly; carelessly; bellicosely; insensately; needlessly; ignobly; indiscriminately; causelessly; treacherously; fearfully.

(See butcher, kill.)

SLAVE

adjectives

perfidious; veriest; humble; submissive; observant; delegated; fugitive; mercenary; ferocious; cringing; sceptered; myriad (pl); devilish; absconding; tawdry; supernumerary; thin; swarming (pl); pernicious; hollow-chested; runaway; factious; transgressing; crouching; drunken; absolute; faithful; purchased; fingering; past-saving; unmannerly; meanest; refractory; groveling; classified; insulting; monastic; luxurious; sanguine; base; superfluous; liberated; gigantic; loathed.

verbs

awe—; chastise—; emancipate—s; castigate —; fetter—; lash—; leash—s; liberate—s; manacle—; market—s; oversee—s; repress —; return—; shackle—s; spare—; subdue —; subjugate—s; trade in—s; tyrannize over —; yoke—s; —attends; —bows; —s colonize; —drudges; —ministers to; —reveres; —s revolt; —salaams.

(See servant, captive.)

SLAVERY

adjectives

virtual; social; voluntary; blissful; abject; merciful; mechanical.

verbs

abolish—; ban—; deliver from—; denounce —; drudge in—; efface—; enforce—; lead into—; liberate from—; outlaw—; perpetuate—; prohibit—; redeem from—; sell into —; subject to—; submit to—; suppress—; traffic in—; —binds; —crushes; —chains; — demoralizes; —fetters; —flourishes; —manacles; —restrains; —shackles; —subjugates.

(See bondage, enslavement, captivity.)

SLAVISH

adverbs

amazingly; unspeakably; meanly; servilely; pitiably; unbearably; totally; willingly; cheerfully; sullenly; temporarily; rebelliously; patently; mockingly; devotedly; ludicrously; ridiculously; apparently; pathetically; humbly; basely; manifestly; contentedly; contemptibly; openly; markedly; exaggeratedly.

SLAY (v)

adverbs

treacherously; traitorously; vindictively; re-

vengefully; soullessly; nefariously; heartlessly; ruthlessly.

(See kill, slaughter.)

SLEEK

adverbs

smoothly; glossily; extremely; inordinately; unpleasantly; blandly; smugly; consciously; remarkably; excessively; suavely; attractively; unbelievably.

SLEEP

adjectives

flattering; noble; comfortable; common noonday; night; profound; trembling; bankrupt; heavy; eternal; pink-tinged; magnetic; fatal; transient; smiling; bestial; tranquil; scanty; deep; secret; marble; breathing; quiet; restful; sound; unbroken; refreshing; wintry; dreamless; peaceful; fitful; beloved; mystic; metamorphic; downy; lethargic; unstirring; portioned; poppied; sudden; drunken; alcoholic; short; convulsed; uninterrupted; fevered; pleasing; enchanted; mysterious; stealthy; startling; forgetful; hypnotic; frozen; troubled; filmy-eyed; speechless; violated; watchful; solacing.

verbs

arouse from—; beguile in—; call in—; desire—; disturb—; feign—; incline to—; induce—; intensify—; lack—; lull to—; mutter in—; produce—; relieve—; repose in—; require—; rock to—; rouse from—; secure —; sink into—; trail into—; —curtains; — curtails; —engulfs; —insures; —overpowers; —reigns; —renews; —soothes; — steals; —transfers.

(See repose, rest, slumber.)

SLEEP (v)

adverbs

heavily; peacefully; stertorously; profoundly; habitually; fitfully; comfortably; transiently; tranquilly; dreamlessly; alcoholically; hypnotically.

(See doze, slumber.)

SLEEPLESS

adverbs

vigilantly; alertly; nervously; deliriously; feverishly; anxiously; distressingly; painfully; unfortunately; remarkably; puzzlingly; unaccountably; incurably; alarmingly; disturbingly; unhappily; excitedly; curiously; wakefully; restlessly; restively; apprehensively; uneasily; vexatiously; ironically; inconveniently; dangerously; confoundedly; strangely.

SLEEPY

adverbs

uncontrollably; irresistibly; inordinately; strangely; oddly; curiously; particularly; significantly; extremely; alarmingly; dangerously; specially; unusually; wretchedly; miserably; naturally; abnormally; surprisingly; unaccountably; inexplicably; mysteriously; conveniently; perilously; confoundedly; strangely.

SLEET

adjectives

slapping; driving; eddying; arrowy; stimulated; shiny; dangerous.

verbs

brave—; encounter—; melt—; precipitate —; —assails; —bites; —blasts; —blights; —devastates; —endangers; —glazes; —impairs; —imperils; —nips; —pelts; —penetrates; —pierces; —pinches; —rattles on; —ravages; —thaws.

(See ice, snow, hail.)

SLEETY

adverbs

miserably; fearfully; dangerously; suddenly; wretchedly; unmanageably; dreadfully; terribly; freezingly; disagreeably; unpleasantly; frightfully; chillingly; bitterly; perilously; hazardously.

SLEEVE

adjectives

puffed; long; short; flowing; pendent; capacious; tapered; luxurious; charming; slashed; lounging; molded; draw-string.

verbs

adorn—; alter—; append—; baste—; chuckle into—; cuff—; drape—; embellish —; extend—; flounce—; fray—; frill—; fringe—; hem—; knit up—; ruffle—; rumple—; shred—; starch—; tatter—; trim —; —girds.

SLENDER

adverbs

gracefully; unusually; remarkably; delightfully; pleasantly; attractively; exceptionally; marvelously; extremely; beautifully; exquisitely; youthfully; prettily.

SLEUTH

verbs

employ—; engage—; tip off (colloq.)—; — analyzes; —apprehends; —beguiles; — cloaks—; cross-examines—; —deduces; — detects; —discloses; —disguises; —divulges; —dodges; —exposes; —fathoms; —ferrets out; —grills; —interrogates; —investigates; —mystifies; —outwits; —overhauls; — peers; —pries into; —probes; —prowls; — queries; —questions; —ransacks; —reveals; —scents; —scrutinizes; —shadows; — threshes out; —traces; —tracks down; — trails; —uncovers; —unearths; —unmasks; —veils.

(See detective.)

SLIDE (v)

adverbs

imperceptibly; appreciably; terrifyingly; greasily; languidly; violently; deftly; cautiously.

(See glide, slip.)

SLIM

adverbs

boyishly; girlishly; childishly; delightfully; gracefully; unusually; extremely; normally; abnormally; attractively; noticeably; youthfully; unwontedly; distressingly; admirably; pleasantly.

SLIME

adjectives

subsiding; blistering; brute; primeval; bestial.

SLIP

adjectives

artless; warped; native; costly; silken; shapely; sheeny; fitted; necessary.

SLIP (v)

adverbs

stealthily; elusively; artfully; treacherously; evanescently; surreptitiously; insidiously; silently.

(See slide, glide.)

SLIPPER

adjectives

mended; imaginary; high-heeled; fur-lined; flowered; sharp-pointed; comfortable; battered; pinching.

adverbs

unmanageably; always; alarmingly; perilously; dangerously; hazardously; terribly; desperately; wretchedly; miserably; disturbingly; evidently; dreadfully; frightfully; unusually; extremely.

SLOGAN

verbs

adopt—; assail—; chant—; chorus—; dramatize—; coin—; flaunt—; hail—; offer—; rally to—; reject—; shout—; shrill—; thunder—; —elaborates; —rings; —stirs; —symbolizes; —takes hold; —wafts.
(See motto, cry, phrase.)

SLOP (*v*)

adverbs

carelessly; disgustingly; violently; abruptly; clumsily.
(See soil, drink.)

SLOPE

adjectives

fruitful; inaccessible; dappled; parallel; inclined; haunted; sunny; springing; grassy; intervening; declivitous; luminous; gentler; slippery; verdant; scarred; swelling; reverse; trampled; precipitous; rapid; flattish; upland; glimmering; terraced; neglected; westering; desert; wooded; monotonous; savage.

verbs

afford—; avoid—; capsize on—; careen down—; grade—; level—; maintain—; scale—; scamper down—; skirt—; sustain —; —ascends; —banks; —distorts; —endangers; —inclines; —lurches; —recedes; —sags; —streams; —tilts.
(See bank, hill.)

SLOPE (*v*)

adverbs

gradually; markedly; steeply; gently; greenly; inaccessibly; grassily; swellingly; precipitously.
(See incline.)

SLOTH

adjectives

silken; dilatory; cowardly; cushioned; sensual; deliberate; drowsy.

adverbs

notoriously; habitually; naturally; incorrigibly; incurably; lazily; indolently; evidently; openly; admittedly; brazenly; laughingly; unaccountably; drowsily.

SLOUCH (*v*)

adverbs

heavily; carelessly; sullenly; obnoxiously; wearily; visibly; deliberately.
(See droop, hang.)

SLOUGH

adjectives

dreadful; pestiferous; humble; deadly; dreaded.

SLOVENLY

adverbs

inexcusably; unreasonably; shamefully; sadly; embarrassingly; unpardonably; lazily; shamelessly; unpleasantly; repulsively; curiously; negligently; thoughtlessly; insouciantly; casually; nonchalantly; laughingly; unbecomingly; discourteously; crassly; boorishly; outlandishly; outrageously; scandalously; unnecessarily; offensively.

SLUGGISH

adverbs

strangely; stupidly; loutishly; dully; torpidly; indolently; inertly; supinely; negligently; carelessly; indifferently; lethargically; strangely; unwontedly; unusually; exceptionally; intolerably; provokingly; vexatiously; hopelessly; wretchedly; unprofitably.

SLUMBER

adjectives

refreshed; pleasant; profound; heavy; dreamless; weary; unnatural; troubled; breathless; rigid; riveted; shady; careless; charmed; sufficient; famous; alert; eternal; fearful; soft; noontide; tickled; enervating; tranquil; healthful; colossal; unconscious; stagnant; prostrate; silent; lighter; dusty.

verbs

blast—; burst from—; consume in—; curtail —; doze into—; induce—; shatter—; toss in —; —enfolds; —envelops; —grips; —reanimates; —regenerates; —relaxes; —renews; —revitalizes; —revives; —seizes.
(See sleep.)

SLUMBER (v)

adverbs

refreshingly; sweetly; pleasantly; profoundly; dreamlessly; enervatingly; tranquilly; healthfully.

(See doze, sleep.)

SLUMP

verbs

allay—; alleviate—; balance—; check—; counteract—; curb—; descend into—; emerge from—; halt—; mitigate—; moderate —; stem—; suffer—; survive—; —abates; —depresses; —endangers; —fizzles out (colloq.); —jeopardizes; —reduces; —relaxes; —retards; —slackens; —troubles.

(See depression, fall, melancholy.)

SLUMS

verbs

abolish—; comb—; dismantle—; efface—; eradicate—; erase—; explore—; exterminate—; infest—; level—; prowl about—; lurk in—; raze—; rise from—; roam—; root out—; scour—; skulk in—; stamp out —; wallow in—; —breed; —congest; —deface; —defile; —pollute; —reek; —screen; —sully; —teem.

(See district.)

SLUSHY

adverbs

miserably; unhealthfully; disagreeably; wretchedly; messily; unpleasantly; unusually; deucedly.

SLY

adverbs

subtly; surreptitiously; furtively; actually; insidiously; abominably; dangerously; warily; undiscoverably; undoubtedly; extremely; successfully; miserably; hatefully; maliciously; cleverly; adroitly; astutely; politically; commercially; trickily; curiously; marvelously.

SMACK

adjectives

emphatic; hearty; clamorous; affectionate; loud; stunning.

SMALL

adverbs

gracefully; pleasantly; prettily; infinitesimally; minutely; extraordinarily; pitifully; pathetically; miserably; compactly; handily; conveniently; daintily; delicately; miraculously; unbelievably.

SMALLNESS

adjectives

compact; frivolous; suggestive; aristocratic; dainty; handy.

SMALLPOX

verbs

afflict with—; characterize—; contract—; convey—; diagnose as—; expose to—; exterminate—; extirpate—; immunize to—; infect with—; inoculate against—; isolate —; prevent—; quarantine—; succumb to—; transmit—; usher in—; —communicates; —confines; —disfigures; —incubates; —invalids; —marks; —pits; —prostrates; —ravages; —scars; —taints; —vitiates.

(See epidemic, measles, disease.)

SMART

adverbs

comically; facetiously; banteringly; foolishly; jestingly; cleverly; felicitously; uncommonly; brilliantly; unusually; thoroughly; ingeniously; amazingly; admirably; wonderfully; wittily; drolly; sparklingly; acutely; capably; cunningly; craftily; sensibly; reasonably; sagely; prudently; subtly; consciously; impressively; learnedly; notoriously; proverbially; assiduously; alertly; sedulously; earnestly; actively.

SMARTNESS

adjectives

figure; lasting; style; exceptional; distinguished; dramatic; stimulating; superficial; uncouth; fabulous; slovenly; alert; conservative; demure; forced; clumsy

SMASH (v)

adverbs

relentlessly; ruthlessly; vigorously; impulsively; violently; thunderously; terrifically; frightfully.

(See wreck, crush.)

SMELL

adjectives

offensive; pungent; rutting; rank; sharp; foul; conglomerate; musty; villainous; luscious; putrid; faint; concentrated; warning; sickish; sweet; dreadful; grateful; elegant; pervading; spicy; powerful; rebellious; horrid; unholy; evil; heavy; acrid; fishy; damp; moldy; balsam; overpowering; breathless; heavenly; balmy; odious; cold; oppressive; dank.

verbs
abhor—; abominate—; banish—; deodorize —; inhale—; intensify—; loathe—; recognize—; relish—; retain—; waft—; —asphyxiates; —assails; —clings; —corrupts; —edges; —entices; —floats; —gags; —incenses; —irritates; —lures; —mingles; —nauseates; —offends; —permeates; —pervades; —ranks; —repels; —revolts; —sickens; —suggests; —taints; —tempts.

(See fragrance, stench, scent, odor.)

SMELL (v)

adverbs
repulsively; objectionably; heavenly; evilly; repugnantly; offensively; noisomely; pungently; abominably; provokingly; potently; sweetly; odiously; dankly; delectably.

(See scent, perfume.)

SMELLY

adverbs
hideously; odiously; horridly; sickeningly; nauseatingly; startlingly; definitely; disgustingly; unbearably; curiously; overpoweringly; suffocatingly.

SMILE

adjectives
rustic; uneasy; gracious; regretful; winning; surprised; radiant; broad; bitter; reminiscent; whimsical; wreathed; metallic; faint; apologetic; affectionate; sweet; amiable; solitary; pitying; ridiculous; quizzical; spicy; special; contagious; fawning; amused; icy; wistful; courteous; crafty; withering; beaming; ravished; enormous; uncontrolled; sickly; sly; maternal; eager; naked; frank; joyous; complacent; brilliant; answering; forced; angry; sympathetic; wanton; contemptuous; deadly; sad; simulated; audible; illumined; parting; approving; ironical; mocking; sudden; indulgent; welcoming; irradiating; agreeable; restrained; watery; rare; playful; superior; arch; perpetual; innocent; big; somber; polished; responding; irrepressible; religious; peculiar; convenient; everlasting; tolerant; vapid; priceless; vague; racked; complicated; smart; polite; murderous; disdainful; sunny; indomitable; sinister; diabolical;

complaisant; dim; patient; haughty; endless; rapid; passing; benign; lurid; crooked; placid; hot; grave; malicious; incredulous; timid; nervous; kind; involuntary; smothered; ardent; bland; provocative; peerless; vivacious; mellow; wan; new; quiet; calm; abrupt; loving; sagacious; buoyant; greasy; sardonic; conciliatory; sidelong; nasty; dawning; grim; ironical; false; meaning; sustaining; saucy; atoning; cynical; prodigal; charming; natural; indifferent; tolerant; wry; little; visible; mournful; weary; patronizing; languid; deprecating; fitful; humorous; seductive; sarcastic; mutual; idiotic; frigid; enrapt; doleful; hospitable; doubtful; ingratiating; counterfeit; curious; mischievous; childlike; exultant; saturnine; speculative; pensive; immutable; condescending; pert; impish; roguish; ghastly; rueful; hollow; unctuous; inane; joyless; wild; satirical; reassuring; slow; hideous; flattering; listless; parting; fleeting; engaging; severe; immortal; insipid; moonshine; fascinating; facile; beatific; restless; scornful; bosomed; wondering; moony; senile; ambrosial; covert; airy; incisive; faded; shy; social; angelic; envious; debonair; bashful; artificial; waking; antiseptic; paternal; dubious; hungry; pale; ready; clear; thoughtless; gentle; infectious; conscious; timorous; haughty; frequent; backward; enamored; obnoxious; pallid; derisive; beguiling; excited.

verbs
achieve—; answer with—; bestow—; cloud —; conceal—; crinkle into—; extinguish—; extract—; flash—; grant—; illuminate with —; induce—; loosen—; manage—; mock—; permit—; provoke—; quench—; repress—; rouse—; share—; shed—; suppress—; throw—; toss—; wear—; wreathe in—; wrinkle into—; —abashes; —basks; —confronts; —contorts; —creases; —crinkles; —deludes; —departs; —disconcerts; —disparages; —fades; —flashes; —flickers; —hides; —hovers; —lightens; —lingers; —mantles; —plays; —reassures; —renders; —reveals; —twitches.

(See grin, laughter, smirk.)

SMILE (v)

adverbs
delightedly; approvingly; shrewdly; affectionately; cherubically; reluctantly; ecstatically; whimsically; tolerantly; radiantly; indulgently; benevolently; tremulously;

grimly; sympathetically; blandly; beamingly; wanly; auspiciously; impudently; disarmingly; mischievously; magnanimously; unctuously; contemptuously; lewdly; winsomely; wryly; languidly; artificially; automatically; apathetically; benignly; contagiously; ingratiatingly; facetiously; superciliously; superficially; demurely; guilelessly; angelically; affably; ambiguously; coyly; cynically; cunningly; exultantly; exaggeratedly; cryptically; ruefully; benevolently.

(See grin, laugh.)

SMIRK

adjectives

conscious; genteel; empty; confidential; nasty.

verbs

affect—; check—; curb—; force—; raise—; repress—; restrain—; wipe away—; wither with—; —dampens; —depresses, —derides; —disdains; —droops; —flushes; —indicates; —reveals; —ridicules; —scorns; —sinks; —sours.

(See grin, smile.)

SMIRK (v)

adverbs

unpleasantly; slyly; treacherously; cynically; sarcastically; hideously; covertly; artificially; obnoxiously; satirically; saturninely.

(See sneer, simper.)

SMITE (v)

adverbs

ruthlessly; resoundingly; mercilessly; cruelly; bestially; heartlessly; shatteringly.

(See strike, hit.)

SMOKE

adjectives

after-dinner; favorite; stale; filthy; suffocating; thin; ribbon; pallid; curling; sulphur; helpless; inky; lurid; eddying; leaping; bituminous; faint; dense; resinous; blinding; sour; crooked; foul; columned; acrid; venomous.

verbs

enfold with—; spurt—; —asphyxiates; —belches; —billows; —blinds; —blackens; —blights; —carries; —chokes; —clouds; —conceals; —curls; —dissolves; —drifts; —eclipses; —emits; —envelops; —floats; —gags; —grimes; —hangs; —hovers; —

looms; —obscures; —overcomes; —penetrates; —pervades; —pours; —puffs; —reeks; —screens; —seeps in; —shrouds; —shuts out; —smothers; —smudges; —soars; —spirals; —stifles; —suffocates; —swirls; —uncurls; —veils; —vitiates; —whirls; —wraps; —wreathes.

(See fumes, haze, mist, soot, fog.)

SMOKE (v)

adverbs

complacently; jovially; fraternally; leisurely; somnolently; gravely; endlessly; atrociously; deliciously; philosophically; reflectively; meditatively; incessantly.

(See fume, reek.)

SMOKY

adverbs

densely; alarmingly; suffocatingly; terribly; dangerously; dingily; invisibly; perilously; unpleasantly; unbearably; disagreeably; odiously; acridly; blindingly; abominably; hazardously.

SMOOTH

adverbs

politely; mysteriously; significantly; amiably; civilly; genteely; courteously; craftily; obsequiously; good-temperedly; suavely; urbanely; suspiciously; sweetly; graciously; ingratiatingly; fashionably; alluringly; superficially; seductively; hypocritically.

SMOOTH (v)

adverbs

diplomatically; socially; mechanically; skillfully; artfully; benevolently.

(See stroke, calm.)

SMOOTHNESS

adjectives

polished; fashionable; exclusive; alluring; oily; excessive; matronly; surface.

SMOTHER (v)

adverbs

fatally; painfully; incontinently; politely; insidiously; socially; economically; politically; viciously.

(See repress, extinguish.)

SMOULDERING

adverbs

slowly; dangerously; luridly; fantastically; glowingly; alarmingly; actively; dully;

dimly; faintly; perilously; hazardously; hatefully; evidently; persistently; steadily; apparently.

adverbs
unacceptably; carelessly; illegibly; dingily; grimily; grittily; darkly; unpleasantly; offensively; unattractively; amazingly; inexplicably; deliberately; intentionally; impossibly; contemptibly; disagreeably.

SMUG
adverbs
unbearably; disgustingly; disagreeably; irritatingly; unreasonably; ridiculously; pompously; chestily; overly; vexatiously; maddeningly; ostentatiously; complacently; pretentiously; laughably; contentedly; priggishly; imperturbably.

SMUGGLING
verbs
abandon—; abolish—; charge with—; cloak —; confess to—; convict of—; countenance —; cover—; deter—; disclose—; engage in —; expose—; frown upon—; justify—; practice—; screen—; suppress—; traffic in —; uncover—; —defrauds; —mulcts; — profits; —violates.
(See robbery, theft.)

SNAIL
verbs
cultivate—; prey on—; search for—; uncover—; —buries; —crawls; —emerges; — hides.
(See animal.)

SNAKE
adjectives
sinuous; sacred; venomous; gaping; dazzling; strong; quick; watching; hissing; gigantic; poisonous.

verbs
cage—; capture—; charm—; —coils; —constricts; —contorts; —crawls; —deposits eggs; —drapes around; —drops upon; — emerges; —encircles; —engulfs its prey; —entwines; —feigns; —frightens; —glides; —hibernates; —hisses; —lunges; —poisons; —recoils; —retreats; —scurries; —seizes; —slides; —slithers; —squirms; —stalks; —stings; —stirs; —strangles its prey; — strikes; —struggles; —suns itself; —surprises its prey; —swallows its prey; —

sways; —terrorizes; —thrashes about; — threatens; —twines; —twists; —undulates; —vibrates; —whips its tail; —worms its way; —wraps around; —wriggles; — writhes; —zigzags.
(See lizard, reptile.)

SNAKY
adverbs
circuitously; sinuously; insidiously; maliciously; artfully; craftily; subtly; slanderously; insinuatingly; surreptitiously; deceitfully; despicably; treacherously; wilily; subtly; archly; crookedly.

SNAP (v)
adverbs
explosively; exultantly; joyously; irritatingly; nervously; intermittently; repeatedly.
(See snarl, growl.)

SNAPPY
adverbs
disagreeably; bracingly; stimulatingly; coldly; unpleasantly; extremely; bitterly; cruelly; stingingly; harshly; exceedingly; terribly; dreadfully.

SNARE
adjectives
silken; wavering; female; alluring; sensual; treacherous; drowsing; harmless; opal; lying; elfish; marvelous; sentimental; cursed.

verbs
bait—; decoy into—; entangle in—; escape —; lure into—; mend—; plant—; —attracts; —deludes; —entices; —intrigues; —menaces; —tempts; —victimizes.
(See cobweb, net, trap.)

SNARL (v)
adverbs
tigerishly; fiendishly; formidably; fiercely; viciously; portentously; furiously; rapaciously; terrifyingly; bestially; diabolically.
(See growl, snap.)

SNARLS
adjectives
perfect; hoarse; angry; rasping; screaming.

SNATCH (v)
adverbs
instantaneously; swiftly; thievingly; insolently; hurriedly; selfishly; callously; gluttonously.
(See grasp, grab.)

adverbs

notoriously; infamously; reputedly; disagreeably; detestably; abominably; atrociously; shamefully; wickedly; viciously; maliciously; incurably; fearfully; strangely; naturally; habitually; alarmingly; suspiciously; furtively; guiltily.

SNEER

adjectives

dull; veiled; significant; copious (pl); perceptible; subtle; drifting; powdery; haughty; frozen; bitter; infernal; chronic; sinister; twisted; mocking.

verbs

check—; curb—; curl into—; force—; indulge in—; parry—; repress—; restrain—; wither with—; —affronts; —castigates; —chides; —derides; —desecrates; —disparages; —gibes; —jeers; —mocks; —outrages; —rebukes; —scorns; —taunts.

(See jeer, ridicule, contempt.)

SNEER (*v*)

adverbs

derisively; contemptuously; aristocratically; scornfully; hatefully; superciliously; fastidiously; priggishly.

(See jeer, smirk.)

SNEEZE (*v*)

adverbs

violently; explosively; abruptly; repeatedly; significantly; obstreperously; exasperatingly.

(See cough.)

SNICKER

verbs

check—; curb—; disregard—; restrain—; voice—; —admonishes; —chides; —derides; —disparages; —insults; —issues; —mimics; —scoffs; —taunts; —withers; —twits.

(See giggle, laughter, smirk, grin.)

SNICKER (*v*)

adverbs

contemptuously; indecently; irreverently; ribaldly; ludicrously; exasperatingly; slyly; maliciously; irresistibly; insolently.

(See titter, smirk, simper.)

SNIFF

adjectives

tremendous; sarcastic; hearty; prodigious; premonitory.

SNIFF (*v*)

adverbs

greedily; haughtily; warily; instinctively; audibly; suspiciously; ostentatiously.

(See scent, smell.)

SNOB

verbs

crush—; deflate—; humble—; loathe—; pique—; sober—; —affects; —apes; —assumes; —condescends; —cringes; —cuts (colloq.); —disdains; —flushes; —humiliates; —inflates; —overbears; —overweens; —preens; —pretends; —puffs up; —regards; —scoffs at; —scorns; —swaggers; —swells; —worships.

(See hypocrite.)

SNOBBISH

adverbs

unwarrantably; groundlessly; absurdly; curiously; oddly; meanly; grossly; crudely; crazily; pompously; bombastically; cheaply; laughably; arrogantly; haughtily; ridiculously; ludicrously; particularly; uncommonly; unpardonably; unbearably; disagreeably; unpleasantly.

SNORE

adjectives

simultaneous; melodious; feminine; smothered; annoying; regular; buzzing.

SNORE (*v*)

adverbs

intoxicatedly; sonorously; peacefully; stertorously; irritatingly; exasperatingly; melodiously; incessantly; annoyingly; perpetually.

(See sleep, slumber, breathe.)

SNORT

adjectives

impatient; angry; loud; trumpeting; audible; roaring.

SNORT (*v*)

adverbs

impatiently; indignantly; audibly; trumpetingly; roaringly; terrifically; disgustingly; violently; vulgarly.

(See snarl, growl.)

SNOW

adjectives

wintry; flaky; feathery; melting; downy; driven; whirling; benumbing; trackless;

eternal; summer; innocent; chilling; caressing; consecrated; glittering; shrinking; powerful; winged; rugged; drifting; crunching; scattering; untrampled; dazzling; solidified; crisp; sharp; virgin; unfathomable; shrouded; pure; homogeneous; receding; perpetual; wondrous; strange; crusted; dissolving; frozen; sculptured; flying; unsunned; sparkling; untrodden; hard; heavy; wasting; powdery; whipped; crackling; dreaded.

verbs
crunch—; scan—; scrunch (colloq.)—; sculpture in—; stamp—; thaw—; —avalanches; —blankets; —caps; —crowns; —dazzles; —deadens; —diminishes; —drifts; —envelops; —falls; —flashes; —flurries; —glistens; —hides; —hushes; —lies; —mantles; —masks; —muffles; —pelts; —penetrates; —piles; —retreats; —ribs; —sails; —scuds; —sculptures; —settles; —shrouds; —sifts; —tinges; —tints; —veils; —wraps.
(See snowflakes.)

SNOW-BLIND
adverbs
completely; momentarily; temporarily; frantically; terrifyingly; suddenly; perilously; inopportunely; curiously; merely; unluckily; tormentingly.

SNOWFLAKES
verbs
drive—; —accumulate; —adorn; —bite; —blanch; —checker; —chill; —cling; —dazzle; —deluge; —fleck; —frost; —glitter; —nip; —obscure; —shudder; —silver.
(See snow, crystal, flake.)

SNOWY
adverbs
beautifully; exquisitely; fortunately; spectacularly; brilliantly; dazzlingly; dangerously; unbelievably; deeply; persistently; incredibly; unseasonably; unexpectedly; surprisingly; perilously; blindingly; hazardously; dreadfully; fearfully; frightfully; suddenly; windily.

SNUB
adjectives
deliberate; suggestive; cold; shrewd; nasty.

verbs
construe as—; expose to—; resent—; risk—;

rue—; —abashes; —bewilders; —discomposes; —disconcerts; —discredits; —humbles; —humiliates; —overwhelms; —petrifies; —reddens; —reproaches; —slurs; —staggers; —stuns; —takes down a peg.
(See insult, rebuff, rebuke.)

SNUB (v)
adverbs
deliberately; coldly; acrimoniously; invidiously; permanently; contemptuously; hatefully; conceitedly.
(See ignore, disregard.)

SNUG
adverbs
compactly; securely; safely; closely; comfortably; happily; fortunately; pleasantly; warmly; reasonably; agreeably; delightfully; luckily; sufficiently; satisfactorily; deliciously.

SOAP
verbs
adulterate—; enrich—; rinse off—; —agrees with; —deodorizes; —disinfects; —fortifies; —invigorates; —lathers; —launders; —laves; —protects; —purges; —refreshes; —restores; —saturates; —scours; —shampoos; —soothes; —stimulates; —tingles.
(See lather, lotion.)

SOAPY
adverbs
sufficiently; warmly; satisfactorily; pleasantly; reasonably; slightly; strongly; occasionally; unpleasantly; pungently; comfortably; comfortingly.

SOAR (v)
adverbs
magnificently; lazily; serenely; majestically; pretentiously; daringly; gracefully; incessantly; loftily; effortlessly; daringly; transcendingly.
(See fly, mount.)

SOB
adjectives
tearless; dying; convulsive; hysterical; heaving; tremulous; noiseless; desolate; innumerable (pl); loud; indignant; audible; hopeless; diminished; confused; gulping; choked; painful; feeble; commingled (pl); conventional; wild; stifled; gasping; panting; racking; renewed; stormy; deep.

verbs
burst into—s; check—; heave—; repress—; restrain—; smother—; stifle—; strangle—; suppress—; whimper—; —disarms; —engulfs; —gurgles; —lacerates; —laments; —melts; —moves; —overwhelms; —racks; —rends; —shakes; —softens; —touches; — wells up; —wrings.

(See moan, murmur, sigh, shiver, shudder.)

SOB (v)
adverbs
piteously; audibly; miserably; bleakly; passionately; hysterically; violently; convulsively; bitterly; monotonously; tearlessly; tremulously; rackingly; pantingly; gaspingly.

(See weep, cry.)

SOBBING
adjectives
gentle; frightened; unrestrained; monotonous.

adverbs
convulsively; heavily; desolately; lonesomely; heartbreakingly; repentantly; remorsefully; bitterly; cruelly; miserably; loudly; quietly; silently; interminably; continually; unreasonably; absurdly; ridiculously; deliberately; purposefully; profitably; suddenly; violently; unaccountably; hysterically; grievously; angrily; happily; nervously.

SOBER
adverbs
unusually; gravely; unwontedly; uncommonly; extremely; unquestionably; occasionally; usually; seldom; rarely; scarcely; reluctantly; habitually; substantially; moderately; drearily; dismally; pensively; thoughtfully; speculatively; wistfully; wishfully; reasonably; dispassionately; judicially; suddenly; earnestly; judiciously; amazingly; strangely; studiously; alarmingly.

SOBRIETY
verbs
commend—; conduce to—; dispose toward —; dwell in—; lack—; maintain—; moderate—; persist in—; preserve—; pursue—; restore—; suspend—; —represses; —restrains; —spares; —tempers.

(See temperance, moderation, gravity.)

SOCIABLE
adverbs
delightfully; sincerely; charmingly; agreeably; habitually; extremely; usually; rarely; scarcely; affably; genially; highly; cordially; familiarly; quietly; noisily; hilariously; heartily; gracefully; chattily; unusually; exceedingly; extraordinarily; clumsily; suddenly; unexpectedly; excessively; designedly; chummily; warmly; truly; uncommonly; remarkably; significantly; ostentatiously.

SOCIAL
adverbs
pleasantly; agreeably; genially; jovially; happily; festively; sportively; affably; usually; highly; companionably; remarkably; openly.

SOCIALISM
verbs
advocate—; combat—; define—; frown upon—; oppose—; prate of—; promote—; rant against—; reject—; —burrows into; —cankers; —confiscates; —controls; —disposes of; —ebbs; —equals; —flourishes; —frees; —humanizes; —levels; —liberates; —manifests; —paralyzes; —regulates; —relinquishes; —remedies; —shares; —shatters; —undermines; —wages; —wars against.

(See communism, liberalism, modernism, nationalism.)

SOCIALIST
verbs
silence—; —abolishes; —bands; —cements; —clashes; —discards; —distributes; —expatiates on; —hails; —harangues; —heckles; —indoctrinates; —organizes; —prates; —rants; —spreads; —theorizes; —undermines.

(See anarchist, communist.)

SOCIETY
adjectives
plutocratic; polished; vigorous; cultivated; fashionable; cold; open; integrated; agreeable; desolate; exotic; honorable; competitive; provincial; artistic; civilized; charitable; cheerful; distinguished; human; frivolous; shattered; unevolved; distinct; formal; martyrized; decorous; polite; heartless; inorganic; intellectual; fastidious; insensitive; brilliant; literary; aristocratic; primitive; high-toned; perpetual; congenial;

purified; benevolent; exclusive; peripatetic; reputable; sordid; monastic; immoral; notorious; respectable; wild; scientific; contemporary; industrial.

verbs
abandon—; admit to—; debar from—; denounce—; deprive—; destroy—; displease —; elevate—; expel from—; introduce into —; mingle with—; negate—; plunge—; purge—; redeem—; remodel—; shun—; step into—; usher into—; —animates; —arrays; —binds; —brands; —campaigns; —conciliates; —conforms; —controls; —copes; —disintegrates; —establishes; —expands; —expels; —frowns upon; —lauds; —obligates; —organizes; —outlaws; —plagues; —polishes; —recruits; —rends asunder; —revolutionizes; —sanctions; —serves; —shackles; —springs from; —uproots; —wars on; —withdraws.

(See brotherhood, community, companionship, state.)

SOCIETY
(association)
verbs
address—; conciliate—; convoke—; disband —; found—; harangue—; head—; league in—; link in—; mobilize—; muster—; preside over—; sever—; —adjourns; —assembles; —convenes; —defines; —disseminates; —elects; —flocks to; —pledges; —preys; —promulgates; —supports.

(See league, association, club, guild, lodge.)

SOD
adjectives
peace-giving; stubborn; velvet; verdant; spongy; lifeless; moldering.

SODA
verbs
bottle—s; cap—s; carbonate—; charge—; color—; dispense—; dissolve in—; down—; flavor—; manufacture—; mix—; prepare—; purvey—s; siphon—; sweeten—; —effervesces; —exhilarates; —refreshes.

(See beverage, drink, liquor.)

SODDEN
adverbs
dismally; gloomily; heavily; irretrievably; disagreeably; unpleasantly; strangely.

SOFA
adjectives
imposing; embroidered; matted; satin-damask; comfortable; battered.

verbs
bolster—; crouch behind—; curl in—; ensconce in—; loll on—; lounge on—; prop —; perch on—; recline on—; refurbish—; renovate—; repose on—; slump on—; straddle—; upholster—; —accommodates; —bears; —beckons; —graces; —sinks; —supports; —sustains.

(See couch.)

SOFT
adverbs
deliciously; adorably; pleasantly; delightfully; comfortably; admirably; conveniently; invitingly; warmly; comfortingly; curiously; particularly; commendably; pliably; delicately; tenderly; compassionately; sympathetically; gently; adaptably.

SOFT-HEARTED
adverbs
leniently; indulgently; judiciously; understandingly; occasionally; pliably; naturally; usually; unwontedly; graciously; hospitably; admirably; curiously; charitably; generously; magnanimously; notoriously; foolishly; usually.

SOFTNESS
adjectives
passionate; sapping; lovely; liquid; musical; purring; tremulous; feline; infinite; melting; bewitching; displeasing; velvet; shy; unbelievable; sudden; cat-like.

SOFT-SPOKEN
adverbs
blandly; usually; habitually; normally; pleasantly; agreeably; delightfully; deceivingly; indulgently; naturally; invariably; curiously; admirably; deliberately; purposely.

SOGGY
adverbs
unpleasantly; unserviceably; curiously; unwholesomely; heavily; irredeemably; unfortunately; unprofitably; admittedly; irremediably; unexpectedly; remarkably; dreadfully.

adjectives

humid; volcanic; fenny; blood-stained; hallowed; luxuriant; teeming; sterile; sifted; repressed; alluvial; enchanted; thirsty; marshy; unbroken; unproductive; friendly; noxious; ill-smelling; fertile; wholesome; friable; sacred; desolate; accursed; fruitful; parched; arid; sandy; indistinguishable; ancient; smoking; niggardly; poor; rich; radiant; favored; fallow; cultivated; kind; surrounding; ungrateful; neglected; peaty; wretched; congenial; tillable; swampy; burning; mangled; barren; foreign; adjacent; drenched; crusty; virgin; exhausted; devastated; mortal; tropic; native; alien; nitrous; conquered; oozy; crumbling.

verbs

cleave—; conserve—; cultivate—; devitalize—; drain—; enrich—; fertilize—; furrow—; harrow—, irrigate ; impregnate—; preserve—; pry from—; renew—; renounce —; revitalize—; ridge up—; rob—; root in —; scratch—; set foot on—; smell—; sow—; starve—; till—; wring from—; —begrimes; —blesses; —erodes; —procreates; —satisfies; —smudges.

(See land, earth, ground, farm.)

SOIL (v)

adverbs

carelessly; obnoxiously; markedly; hopelessly; disgustingly; annoyingly; exasperatingly.
(See taint, spoil.)

SOJOURN

adjectives

dreary; aimless; endless; short; enforced; protracted; permanent; bloody; previous; brief; accursed; autumnal; obscure; pleasant.

SOLACE

adjectives

individual; airy; idle; melancholy; immeasurable; ecstatic; scant; repenting; little.

verbs

afford—; accord—; bestow—; decline—; derive—; extend—; grant—; offer—; proffer —; reject—; tender—; volunteer—; yield —; —allays; —appeases; —assuages; —beguiles; —cheers, —comforts; —draws; — diverts; —mitigates; —palliates; —salves; —smooths.

(See comfort, consolation.)

adjectives

fanatical; languid; wilted; faceless; gallant; brave; illiterate; true; trusty; rough; career; drunken; godless; volunteer; surviving; harassed; well-tried; distinguished; capable; maddened; struggling; brutal; sausage-legged; valiant; weary; rowdy; unrelenting; mercenary; butchered; disbanded; decorative; deluded; accomplished; improvident; straggling; disorderly; good; hardy; wandering; disaffected; lion-hearted; stout; demoralized; gaunt; intrepid; stern; fearless; hot-tempered; heroic; veteran; lice-ridden; sentimental; indomitable; obdurate; eager; doughty; steady; fortunate; condemned; besotted; chivalrous; vulgar; magnanimous; forlorn; staring; resolute; inebriated; weary; mutilated; sleepy; disillusioned.

verbs

arm—; command—; conciliate—; court-martial—; dispatch—; drill—; harry—; mobilize—; mow down—; quarter—; train—; — advance; —barricade; —beleaguer; —besiege; —brandish; —break step; —bristle; —bluster; —campaign; —charge; —coerce; —crusade; —desert; —enlist; —enroll; — engage; —flock; —garrison; —invade; — intrench; —jostle; —lay siege; —mutiny; — patrol; —parry; —plod—; rake; —repulse; —retaliate; —revive; —slog; —snipe; — squander; —storm; —surrender; —tramp; —trudge; —ward off; —wield.

(See besieger, infantry, army, invader, militia.)

SOLDIERY

adjectives

ruthless; insolent; ferocious; desperate; sanguine; brutal; well-clad; riotous; vagabond; grim-faced; licentious; architectural; fierce.

SOLEMN

adverbs

unduly; curiously; ceremoniously; sacredly; piously; religiously; devoutly; reverentially; fervently; ritualistically; judicially; sternly; austerely; ponderously; gravely; seriously; alarmingly; forbiddingly; unnecessarily; ominously; portentously; depressingly; impressively; magnificently; extraordinarily; gravely; grimly; ridiculously; absurdly; ludicrously; unreasonably; occasionally; unexpectedly; unusually; curiously; strangely; reverently; uncommonly.

adjectives

severe; majestic; religious; rare; mysterious; quaint; guarded; significant; pretentious; accustomed; symmetrical; grievous; unutterable; impressive; formal; professional; inaccessible; profound; dismal; preternatural; sweet; shallow; mournful; livid; royal.

verbs

alleviate—; dedicate in—; ease—; enthrone in—; impress—; maintain—; mar—; perform with—; preserve—; relax—; ruffle—; sustain—; temper—; —abashes; —awes; —chastens; —dampens; —dazzles; —depresses; —deters; —glooms; —inspires; —oppresses; —pervades; —sobers; —subdues.

(See ceremony, gravity, seriousness.)

SOLICIT (v)

adverbs

impudently; courteously; importunately; pertinaciously; timorously; underhandedly; earnestly; pressingly; urgently; insinuatingly.

(See request, ask, seek.)

SOLICITATION

adjectives

hinted; earnest; sickening; pressing; tearful; urgent; insinuating.

verbs

brush aside—s; dismiss—; elicit—; endure —; ignore—; pursue—s; yield to—; —s carry weight; —influences; —irks; —moves; —plagues; —provokes; —riles (colloq.); —ruffles; —sways; —touches; —vexes; —wrings.

(See request, invitation, entreaty.)

SOLICITORS

adjectives

best-moving; fair; government; prominent; insistent.

SOLICITOUS

adverbs

tenderly; anxiously; eagerly; frantically; curiously; strangely; pretentiously; ostentatiously; cursorily; lovingly; affectionately; protectively; absurdly; ridiculously; responsibly; forebodingly; terribly.

adjectives

constant; peculiar; passionate; quiet; liveliest; dismal; tenderest; loving; frozen; selfish; affectionate; profound; glorious; trembling; pitying; sincere; voluntary; paternal; friendly; deep.

verbs

allay—; assuage—; blench in—; cloak—; conceal—; deserve—; display—; distrust—; dwell in—; ease—; exhibit—; expose—; feign—; manifest—; relieve—; relish—; screen—; —besets; —deters; —harrows; —haunts; —obsesses; —perturbs; —preys on; —unnerves; —wracks; —wrings; inspire—.

(See anxiety, misgiving, care, concern, attention.)

SOLID

adverbs

unusually; satisfactorily; fortunately; securely; stably; remarkably; immovably; finally; desirably; sufficiently; safely; financially; structurally; commercially; warrantably; splendidly; undoubtedly; unbreakably.

SOLIDARITY

verbs

cement—; cleave—; compromise—; disrupt —; endanger—; fracture—; gnaw at—; hazard—; impair—; jeopardize—; link in —; maintain—; mar—; menace—; mould —; nurse—; preserve—; rend—; rupture—; sap—; shake—; split—; strain—; sustain —; threaten—; undermine—; weld—; —crumbles; —disintegrates; —prevails; —totters.

(See power, authority, leadership, union.)

SOLIDITY

adjectives

combined; moral; little; primitive; costly; imposing; mellow; false; stable.

SOLIDS

adjectives

atomic; precipitated; flaccid; geometrical; quiescent; elastic.

verbs

compress—; congeal into—; convert into—; dissolve—; excrete—; liquefy—; pierce—; precipitate—; pulverize—; vaporize—; —cohere; —contract; —disintegrate; —displace; —expand.

(See mass.)

SOLILOQUIZE (v)

adverbs

philosophically; morbidly; dejectedly; monotonously; ceaselessly; academically; sepulchrally.

(See utter, talk.)

SOLILOQUY

verbs

breathe—; deliver—; emit—; indulge in—; murmur—; mutter—; reflect in—; unfold —; utter—; voice—; —considers; —contemplates; —discourses; —expatiates on; —mediates; —moves; —ponders; —reasons; —reproaches; —reveals; —revolves; —touches.

(See speech, talk.)

SOLITARY

adverbs

restfully; delightfully; formidably; gloomily; forbiddingly; cheerlessly; pathetically; unhappily; remotely; alarmingly; disagreeably; desperately; desolately; impossibly; tragically; preferably; comfortably; selfishly; unexpectedly; undesirably; uncommonly; curiously; amazingly; insistently.

SOLITUDE

adjectives

mighty; unhallowed; dismal; heaving; tranquil; great; sylvan; proud; expectant; gladsome; splendid; social; musing; crowded; decent; dreary; sealed; oppressive; perfect; wildest; unbroken; mountain; vast; misty; populous; convenient; careless; morose; meditative; patient; arctic; fearful; rural; chilly; mystic; unweeping; delicious; utter; obscure; midnight; grave; dewy; gigantic; twilight; artificial; deep; majestic; moorland; solemn; inaccessible; sullen; serene; pastoral; restored.

verbs

abandon to—; abide in—; afford—; burden —; bear—; crave—; encompass—; endure —; evince—; incline to—; loathe—; long for—; mope in—; muse in—; ponder in—; recall in—; relegate to—; relish—; retire to—; sequester in—; shatter—; shun—; suffer—; welcome—; yearn for—; —cloaks; —deceives; —depresses; —detaches; —isolates; —penetrates; —stagnates.

(See isolation, loneliness, seclusion.)

---

adverbs

scarcely; highly; instantly; chemical ily; obviously; manifestly; conve handily; quickly; adaptably; comm

SO (exp

verbs

approach—; arrive at—; clarify— hend—; demonstrate—; disagree facilitate—; formulate—; furnish— offer—; reach—; seek—; trace— cides; —implies; —points; —rack

(See explanation, interpretation

adjectives

dilute; saline; partial; attenuat commonplace; classic; irritatir colloidal; formless; transpare pacific; ultimate; dirt; deod(vious; antiseptic; adaptive; del sequent; rational; supernatural cessful; supersaturated; pract ing; contemporary; sensible ideal; peaceful; ordinary; lof

verbs

dilute—; dip—; gargle—; inj with—; sponge—; —mixes; seek—.

(See mixture, juice, liquid,

adverbs

definitely; accurately; pro mechanically; scientifically; structively; ingeniously; p(ally; partially.

(See clear, explain.)

adverbs

responsibly; reputedly; r ably; safely; financially; r ably; satisfactorily; fortu

verbs

alleviate—; brighten—; in—; reflect—; relax—; —; sink into—; sulk i abashes; —awes; —dam

deepens; —dejects; —depresses; —envelops; —glooms; —illuminates; —oppresses; —permeates; —pervades; —saddens; —shadows; —weights.

(See darkness, melancholy, gravity, gloom.)

SOMBRE

adverbs

lugubriously; gloomily; dismally; unaccountably; unnecessarily; unpleasantly; richly; sumptuously; harmoniously; fashionably; conventionally; disagreeably; overwhelmingly; mournfully; gravely; gruesomely; terribly; hauntingly; horribly.

SOMERSAULT

verbs

achieve—; avert—; avoid—; culminate in —; execute—; perfect—; perform—; practices; reverse—; —amazes; —astounds; —climaxes; —inverts; —surprises.

(See trick, leap.)

SOMETHING

adjectives

indefinable; coquettish; intangible; infinitesimal; misty; solemn; inestimable; unnatural; ghastly; unnamable; curious.

SOMNOLENT

verbs

overwhelmingly; unaccountably; irresistibly; strangely; dully; overpoweringly; uncontrollably; inexplicably; abnormally; embarrassingly; alarmingly; inexpressibly.

SON

adjectives

... ; mutilated; slow-minded; intended; disgrace; accursed; hardy; illegitimate; ... ess; instinctive; lawful; patriotic; enigmatic; murdered; hapless; prodigal; equi-... ; misunderstood; degenerate; virtuous; ...ished; blooming; surviving; indolent; ...vant; unkempt; gallant; ransomed; ... illustrious; dutiful; purblind; film-... g; admirable; accursed; docile; stal-...; valiant; obedient; accomplished; ...ard; humbled; tortured; first-born; ...nting; ungracious; goodly; brisk; eld-...andsome; patriotic; elegant; amiable; ...earted; insignificant; mercenary; un-...ciated; rude; energetic; exiled.

...te—; bear—; beget—; castigate—;

chastise—; conceive—; crave—; discipline —; disinherit—; disown—; endear to—; expel—; guide—; hunger for—; inculcate in —; ingrain in—; instill in—; pamper—; renounce—; yearn for—; —assumes; —begets; —cherishes; —inherits; —relinquishes; —toddles.

(See child, offspring, daughter.)

SONG

adjectives

emotional; melodious; dramatic; characteristic; throbbing; shanty; voluntary; comic; faultless; boisterous; spiritual; mournful; scurrilous; pealing; solemn; humorous; ineffable; choral; monotonous; rapturous; tranquil; echoing; vapid; immortal; buoyant; deathless; cheerful; weird; antiquated; impassioned; speechless; perpetual; artful; amorous; affectionate; irksome; unconnected; everlasting; protracted; joyous; provoking; unmusical; indolent; savage; drawling; ringing; lifeless; ribald; generous; gusty; rich; blithe; unpremeditated; mystic; shrill; laborious; foolish; magnetic; quivering; syncopated; pastoral; dropping; wondrous; jubilant; plaintive; tragic; parting; chastening; saucy; desperate; ear-breaking; coarse; sunny; eddying; arduous; grandest; wailing; fatal; medicinal; worthless; doleful; visible; yearning; piquant; rollicking; fiery; stifling; hideous; twilight; adventurous; belligerent; noble; nuptial

verbs

accompany—; break out into—; breathe—; carol—; chant—; compose—; dash into —; diffuse—; echo—; execute—; exploit —; flood with—; hum—; improvise—; intone—; lilt—; perform—; pipe—; perpetuate—; render—; stifle—; strike up—; trill —; twitter—; warble—; whistle—; —breaks out; —descends upon; —dwindles; —expresses; —evolves; —laments; —merges; —moderates; —modulates; —pierces; —s pour; —quavers; —recaptures; —ripples; —shatters; —subsides; —swells; —uplifts; —vibrates.

(See melody, jazz, ditty, incantation, music, chant, refrain, carol, hymn.)

SONGSTER

adjectives

exquisite; plumed; lingering; feathered; lifeless; medieval; radio.

SONNET

adjectives

commendatory; true; glowing; halting; wailful; memorable; soaring; conventional; stock; beauteous; insincere.

verbs

compose—; consecrate—; dash off—; dedicate—to; indite—; peruse—s; scan—; transcribe—; weave—; —amuses; —delights; —expresses; —glorifies; —immortalizes; —impresses; —reflects; —rhymes; —sentimentalizes; —treats of; —versifies.

(See poem.)

SONOROUS

adverbs

impressively; unctuously; chantingly; deeply; profoundly; resoundingly; challengingly; richly; magnificently; splendidly; remarkably; strangely; compellingly; majestically; regally; authoritatively.

SOOT

verbs

—begrimes; —besmears; —besmirches; —blackens; —blots; —blurs; —contaminates; —defiles; —eclipses; —flocculates; —jets; —obscures; —reeks; —screens; —settles; —smears; —smirches; —smudges; —soils; —sullies; —tarnishes; —veils.

(See carbon, powder, dust, smoke, fog.)

SOOTHE (v)

adverbs

maternally; infinitely; benevolently; compassionately; harmoniously; effectually; pleasingly.

(See pacify, calm.)

SOOTHING

adverbs

refreshingly; comfortingly; curatively; graciously; serenely; mildly; pleasantly; softly; gratefully; quietly; coolly; gently; blandly; especially; satisfyingly; remarkably; marvelously; tenderly; maternally; mercifully.

SOPHISTICATED

adverbs

consciously; impressively; proudly; vivaciously; absurdly; ridiculously; haughtily; pretentiously; extremely; unexpectedly; bitterly; stylishly; fashionably.

SOPHISTICATION

adjectives

subtle; sly; cool; quaint; hard-boiled; studied; brittle; surface; cruel.

verbs

acquire—; breed—; cultivate—; develop—; discard—; ingrain—; jar—; mould—; pierce—; stamp with—; shock—; —attracts; —beguiles; —bores; —enhances; —glosses; —impresses; —polishes; —reeks; —varnishes; —veneers.

(See manner, style.)

SOPHISTRY

adjectives

subtle; pompous; wild; delinquent; apparent.

SOPRANO

verbs

acclaim—; applaud—; present—; train—; —carols; —cracks; —cultivates; —enthralls; —entrances; —executes; —exercises; —expresses; —flutes; —lilts; —modulates; —moves; —performs; —renders; —strains; —tours; —trills; —twitters.

(See singer, choir, chorus.)

SORCERER

adjectives

miserable; hostile; unfortunate; accused; wicked.

SORDID

adverbs

disagreeably; undoubtedly; atrociously; curiously; basely; uncommonly; unreasonably; unbelievably; incredibly; unthinkably; outrageously; outlandishly; scandalously; terribly; fearfully; detestably; barbarously; unspeakably; stingily; grossly; miserably; churlishly; greedily; foully; unaccountably; unwarrantably; strangely; utterly; undeniably.

SORE

adjectives

swollen; embossed; inward; festering; ever-fretting; raw; horrid.

verbs

aggravate—; cauterize—; diagnose—; disinfect—; dress—; extirpate—; irritate—; lance—; lick—; salve—; treat—; —atrophies; —breaks out; —cankers; —chafes; —defaces; —discharges; —disfigures; —envenoms; —festers; —ferments; —infects; —inflames; —occurs; —persists; —rankles; —responds; —scabs; —suppurates; —taints; —throbs.

(See rash, inflammation, canker, abscess, blister, boil.)

adverbs
painfully; curiously; extremely; miserably; infectiously; dangerously; alarmingly; unaccountably; strangely; fearfully; feverishly; unfortunately; cruelly; exceedingly; naturally.

SORROW

adjectives
dreaming; querulous; sole; profound; despondent; inextinguishable; poignant; sacred; slow; imperious; human; stormy; transient; impetuous; faithless; helpless; unfeigned; sleepless; premature; stifled; domestic; dying; eternal; bitter; silent; deep; hearty; trampling; mortal; uncheered; sentimental; dark; dumb; passionate; crushing; unmitigated; sincere; romantic; imagined; fantastic; foolish; vehement; dried; accumulated; gnarling; noisy; desperate; oppressive; peculiar; grievous; dull; present; aesthetic; inarticulate; strange; concealed.

verbs
afflict with—; appease—; assail with—; assuage—; brim with—; cast—; cloak—; console—; contain—; couch in—; crush—; depict—; derive—; fade out of—; inflict—; intensify—; lament—; multiply—s; relieve—; remedy—; restrain—; share—; swallow—; unfold—; —befalls; —blights; —burdens; —chastens; —consumes; —darkens; —deepens; —embraces; —mars; —overburdens; —overwhelms; —purges.

(See commiseration, sadness, suffering, grief.)

SORRY

adverbs
pitifully; wretchedly; sincerely; genuinely; truly; pitiably; miserably; grievously; profoundly; deeply; abjectly; remorsefully; embarrassingly; humbly; bitterly; regretfully; penitently; admittedly; extremely; immeasurably; reasonably; somewhat.

SORT

adjectives
particular; unsatisfactory; enthusiastic; whimsical; barren; vulgar; prophetical; stimulating; grossest; truest; meanest; desultory; outspoken; odd.

SOUL

adjectives
repentant; harmonic; circling; stormy; witty; genial; learned; troubled; hopeful; flaming; lost; living; amiable; kindred; sinful; erring; frank; reviving; poisonous; ardent; aesthetic; pagan; raptured; maddened; pervading; poetic; wronged; cheated; stagnant; unblemished; zealous; sensitive; loving; neat; gentle; departed; passive; tortured; malignant; impassive; noblest; helpless; starved; susceptible; silly; ravished; withered; luckless; chastened; desolate; lofty; singular; eager; radiant; wondrous; vile; daring; suspended; genial; trusting; polluted; vigorous; willing; separate; fettered; visionary; human; righteous; heroic; grateful; ingenious; deathless; rapt; naked; lifted; ecstatic; flagging; heated; dear; dawning; deluded; vitriolic; artist; full; loyal; groveling; solitary; agitated; gross; fainting; secret; silent; resolute; defeated; common; maddening; divine; brooding; incarnate; harmonious; convivial; morbid; comprehensive; speaking; priceless; wounded; craven; inmost; smitten; offending; spheric; guilty; poisonous; tender; pervading; universal; delicious; haughty; debilitated; passionate; progressive; saturate; feeble; liberal; multitudinous (pl); plastic; unripened; unstained; antique; agitated; festered; regal; truthful; trembling; kingly; emaciated; torpid; nimble; embryonic; redeemed; manly; devastated; reptile; shuddering; unwasting; frivolous; exploring; blotched; dead; scintillating; ransomed; pious; enthralling; delicate; pessimistic; tardy; virile; active; dauntless; altered; crude; eccentric; wakeful; elevated; cavalier; cantankerous; bleeding; clearest; stubborn; yearning; truant; dying; prevailing; introspective; credulous; misguided; exalted; angelic; cautious; charitable; grieved; timid; ardent; merry; spotted; callous; watchful; jealous; departed; intercurrent; countless (pl); rational; hungry; abstracted; wiser; patient; inviolable; obstinate; sordid; guileless; preserved; rich; bewildered; mean; knightly; sober; hideous; distracted; practical; simple; immortal; torn; famished; straying.

deepens; —dejects; —depresses; —envelops; —glooms; —illuminates; —oppresses; —permeates; —pervades; —saddens; —shadows; —weights.

(See darkness, melancholy, gravity, gloom.)

SOMBRE
adverbs
lugubriously; gloomily; dismally; unaccountably; unnecessarily; unpleasantly; richly; sumptuously; harmoniously; fashionably; conventionally; disagreeably; overwhelmingly; mournfully; gravely; gruesomely; terribly; hauntingly; horribly.

SOMERSAULT
verbs
achieve—; avert—; avoid—; culminate in —; execute—; perfect—; perform—; practise—s; reverse—; —amazes; —astounds; —climaxes; —inverts; —surprises.

(See trick, leap.)

SOMETHING
adjectives
undefinable; coquettish; intangible; infinitesimal; misty; solemn; inestimable; unnatural; ghastly; unnamable; curious.

SOMNOLENT
adverbs
overwhelmingly; unaccountably; irresistibly; strangely; dully; overpoweringly; uncontrollably; inexplicably; abnormally; embarrassingly; alarmingly; inexpressibly.

SON
adjectives
giddy; mutilated; slow-minded; intended; scapegrace; accursed; hardy; illegitimate; reckless; instinctive; lawful; patriotic; enigmatic; murdered; hapless; prodigal; equivocal; misunderstood; degenerate; virtuous; astonished; blooming; surviving; indolent; observant; unkempt; gallant; ransomed; poor; illustrious; dutiful; purblind; film-loving; admirable; accursed; docile; stalwart; valiant; obedient; accomplished; wayward; humbled; tortured; first-born; enchanting; ungracious; goodly; brisk; eldest; handsome; patriotic; elegant; amiable; free-hearted; insignificant; mercenary; unappreciated; rude; energetic; exiled.

verbs
alienate—; bear—; beget—; castigate—;

chastise—; conceive—; crave—; discipline —; disinherit—; disown—; endear to—; expel—; guide—; hunger for—; inculcate in —; ingrain in—; instill in—; pamper—; renounce—; yearn for—; —assumes; —begets; —cherishes; —inherits; —relinquishes; —toddles.

(See child, offspring, daughter.)

SONG
adjectives
emotional; melodious; dramatic; characteristic; throbbing; shanty; voluntary; comic; faultless; boisterous; spiritual; mournful; scurrilous; pealing; solemn; humorous; ineffable; choral; monotonous; rapturous; tranquil; echoing; vapid; immortal; buoyant; deathless; cheerful; weird; antiquated; impassioned; speechless; perpetual; artful; amorous; affectionate; irksome; unconnected; everlasting; protracted; joyous; provoking; unmusical; indolent; savage; drawling; ringing; lifeless; ribald; generous; gusty; rich; blithe; unpremeditated; mystic; shrill; laborious; foolish; magnetic; quivering; syncopated; pastoral; dropping; wondrous; jubilant; plaintive; tragic; parting; chastening; saucy; desperate; ear-breaking; coarse; sunny; eddying; arduous; grandest; wailing; fatal; medicinal; worthless; doleful; visible; yearning; piquant; rollicking; fiery; stifling; hideous; twilight; adventurous; belligerent; noble; nuptial

verbs
accompany—; break out into—; breathe—; carol—; chant—; compose—; dash into —; diffuse—; echo—; execute—; exploit —; flood with—; hum—; improvise—; intone—; lilt—; perform—; pipe—; perpetuate—; render—; stifle—; strike up—; trill —; twitter—; warble—; whistle—; —breaks out; —descends upon; —dwindles; —expresses; —evolves; —laments; —merges; —moderates; —modulates; —pierces; —s pour; —quavers; —recaptures; —ripples; —shatters; —subsides; —swells; —uplifts; —vibrates.

(See melody, jazz, ditty, incantation, music, chant, refrain, carol, hymn.)

SONGSTER
adjectives
exquisite; plumed; lingering; feathered; lifeless; medieval; radio.

SOLILOQUIZE (v)

adverbs

philosophically; morbidly; dejectedly; monotonously; ceaselessly; academically; sepulchrally.

(See utter, talk.)

SOLILOQUY

verbs

breathe—; deliver—; emit—; indulge in—; murmur—; mutter—; reflect in—; unfold —; utter—; voice—; —considers; —contemplates; —discourses; —expatiates on; —mediates; —moves; —ponders; —reasons; —reproaches; —reveals; —revolves; —touches.

(See speech, talk.)

SOLITARY

adverbs

restfully; delightfully; formidably; gloomily; forbiddingly; cheerlessly; pathetically; unhappily; remotely; alarmingly; disagreeably; desperately; desolately; impossibly; tragically; preferably; comfortably; selfishly; unexpectedly; undesirably; uncommonly; curiously; amazingly; insistently.

SOLITUDE

adjectives

mighty; unhallowed; dismal; heaving; tranquil; great; sylvan; proud; expectant; gladsome; splendid; social; musing; crowded; decent; dreary; sealed; oppressive; perfect; wildest; unbroken; mountain; vast; misty; populous; convenient; careless; morose; meditative; patient; arctic; fearful; rural; chilly; mystic; unweeping; delicious; utter; obscure; midnight; grave; dewy; gigantic; twilight; artificial; deep; majestic; moorland; solemn; inaccessible; sullen; serene; pastoral; restored.

verbs

abandon to—; abide in—; afford—; burden —; bear—; crave—; encompass—; endure —; evince—; incline to—; loathe—; long for—; mope in—; muse in—; ponder in—; recall in—; relegate to—; relish—; retire to—; sequester in—; shatter—; shun—; suffer—; welcome—; yearn for—; —cloaks; —deceives; —depresses; —detaches; —isolates; —penetrates; —stagnates.

(See isolation, loneliness, seclusion.)

SOLUBLE

adverbs

scarcely; highly; instantly; chemically; easily; obviously; manifestly; conveniently; handily; quickly; adaptably; commendably.

SOLUTION
(explanation)

verbs

approach—; arrive at—; clarify—; comprehend—; demonstrate—; disagree with—; facilitate—; formulate—; furnish—; gain—; offer—; reach—; seek—; trace—; —coincides; —implies; —points; —racks.

(See explanation, interpretation.)

SOLUTION
(general)

adjectives

dilute; saline; partial; attenuated; elusive; commonplace; classic; irritating; logical; colloidal; formless; transparent; decent; pacific; ultimate; dirt; deodorizing; obvious; antiseptic; adaptive; delightful; consequent; rational; supernatural; basic; successful; supersaturated; practical; satisfying; contemporary; sensible; equitable; ideal; peaceful; ordinary; lofty.

SOLUTION
(mixture)

verbs

dilute—; dip—; gargle—; inject—; saturate with—; sponge—; —mixes; —strengthens; seek—.

(See mixture, juice, liquid, medicine.)

SOLVE (v)

adverbs

definitely; accurately; promptly; swiftly; mechanically; scientifically; ultimately; constructively; ingeniously; practically; basically; partially.

(See clear, explain.)

SOLVENT

adverbs

responsibly; reputedly; reputably; admirably; safely; financially; manifestly; acceptably; satisfactorily; fortunately; absolutely

SOMBERNESS

verbs

alleviate—; brighten—; brood in—; **droop** in—; reflect—; relax—; relieve of—; **ruffle** —; sink into—; sulk in—; sustain—; — abashes; —awes; —dampens; —darkens; —

adjectives
commendatory; true; glowing; halting; wailful; memorable; soaring; conventional; stock; beauteous; insincere.

verbs
compose—; consecrate—; dash off—; dedicate—to; indite—; peruse—s; scan—; transcribe—; weave—; —amuses; —delights; —expresses; —glorifies; —immortalizes; —impresses; —reflects; —rhymes; —sentimentalizes; —treats of; —versifies.
 (See poem.)

SONOROUS

adverbs
impressively; unctuously; chantingly; deeply; profoundly; resoundingly; challengingly; richly; magnificently; splendidly; remarkably; strangely; compellingly; majestically; regally; authoritatively.

SOOT

verbs
—begrimes; —besmears; —besmirches; —blackens; —blots; —blurs; —contaminates; —defiles; —eclipses; —flocculates; —jets; —obscures; —reeks; —screens; —settles; —smears; —smirches; —smudges; —soils; —sullies; —tarnishes; —veils.
 (See carbon, powder, dust, smoke, fog.)

SOOTHE (v)

adverbs
maternally; infinitely; benevolently; compassionately; harmoniously; effectually; pleasingly.
 (See pacify, calm.)

SOOTHING

adverbs
refreshingly; comfortingly; curatively; graciously; serenely; mildly; pleasantly; softly; gratefully; quietly; coolly; gently; blandly; especially; satisfyingly; remarkably; marvelously; tenderly; maternally; mercifully.

SOPHISTICATED

adverbs
consciously; impressively; proudly; vivaciously; absurdly; ridiculously; haughtily; pretentiously; extremely; unexpectedly; bitterly; stylishly; fashionably.

adjectives
subtle; sly; cool; quaint; hard-boiled; studied; brittle; surface; cruel.

verbs
acquire—; breed—; cultivate—; develop—; discard—; ingrain—; jar—; mould—; pierce—; stamp with—; shock—; —attracts; —beguiles; —bores; —enhances; —glosses; —impresses; —polishes; —reeks; —varnishes; —veneers.
 (See manner, style.)

SOPHISTRY

adjectives
subtle; pompous; wild; delinquent; apparent.

SOPRANO

verbs
acclaim—; applaud—; present—; train—; —carols; —cracks; —cultivates; —enthralls; —entrances; —executes; —exercises; —expresses; —flutes; —lilts; —modulates; —moves; —performs; —renders; —strains; —tours; —trills; —twitters.
 (See singer, choir, chorus.)

SORCERER

adjectives
miserable; hostile; unfortunate; accused; wicked.

SORDID

adverbs
disagreeably; undoubtedly; atrociously; curiously; basely; uncommonly; unreasonably; unbelievably; incredibly; unthinkably; outrageously; outlandishly; scandalously; terribly; fearfully; detestably; barbarously; unspeakably; stingily; grossly; miserably; churlishly; greedily; foully; unaccountably; unwarrantably; strangely; utterly; undeniably.

SORE

adjectives
swollen; embossed; inward; festering; ever-fretting; raw; horrid.

verbs
aggravate—; cauterize—; diagnose—; disinfect—; dress—; extirpate—; irritate—; lance—; lick—; salve—; treat—; —atrophies; —breaks out; —cankers; —chafes; —defaces; —discharges; —disfigures; —en-

venoms; —festers; —ferments; —infects; —inflames; —occurs; —persists; —rankles; —responds; —scabs; —suppurates; —taints; —throbs.

(See rash, inflammation, canker, abscess, blister, boil.)

adverbs
painfully; curiously; extremely; miserably; infectiously; dangerously; alarmingly; unaccountably; strangely; fearfully; feverishly; unfortunately; cruelly; exceedingly; naturally.

SORROW

adjectives
dreaming; querulous; sole; profound; despondent; inextinguishable; poignant; sacred; slow; imperious; human; stormy; transient; impetuous; faithless; helpless; unfeigned; sleepless; premature; stifled; domestic; dying; eternal; bitter; silent; deep; hearty; trampling; mortal; uncheered; sentimental; dark; dumb; passionate; crushing; unmitigated; sincere; romantic; imagined; fantastic; foolish; vehement; dried; accumulated; gnarling; noisy; desperate; oppressive; peculiar; grievous; dull; present; aesthetic; inarticulate; strange; concealed.

verbs
afflict with—; appease—; assail with—; assuage—; brim with—; cast—; cloak—; console—; contain—; couch in—; crush—; depict—; derive—; fade out of—; inflict—; intensify—; lament—; multiply—s; relieve—; remedy—; restrain—; share—; swallow—; unfold—; —befalls; —blights; —burdens; —chastens; —consumes; —darkens; —deepens; —embraces; —mars; —overburdens; —overwhelms; —purges.

(See commiseration, sadness, suffering, grief.)

SORRY

adverbs
pitifully; wretchedly; sincerely; genuinely; truly; pitiably; miserably; grievously; profoundly; deeply; abjectly; remorsefully; embarrassingly; humbly; bitterly; regretfully; penitently; admittedly; extremely; immeasurably; reasonably; somewhat.

SORT

adjectives
particular; unsatisfactory; enthusiastic;

whimsical; barren; vulgar; prophetical; stimulating; grossest; truest; meanest; desultory; outspoken; odd.

SOUL

adjectives
repentant; harmonic; circling; stormy; witty; genial; learned; troubled; hopeful; flaming; lost; living; amiable; kindred; sinful; erring; frank; reviving; poisonous; ardent; aesthetic; pagan; raptured; maddened; pervading; poetic; wronged; cheated; stagnant; unblemished; zealous; sensitive; loving; neat; gentle; departed; passive; tortured; malignant; impassive; noblest; helpless; starved; susceptible; silly; ravished; withered; luckless; chastened; desolate; lofty; singular; eager; radiant; wondrous; vile; daring; suspended; genial; trusting; polluted; vigorous; willing; separate; fettered; visionary; human; righteous; heroic; grateful; ingenious; deathless; rapt; naked; lifted; ecstatic; flagging; heated; dear; dawning; deluded; vitriolic; artist; full; loyal; groveling; solitary; agitated; gross; fainting; secret; silent; resolute; defeated; common; maddening; divine; brooding; incarnate; harmonious; convivial; morbid; comprehensive; speaking; priceless; wounded; craven; inmost; smitten; offending; spheric; guilty; poisonous; tender; pervading; universal; delicious; haughty; debilitated; passionate; progressive; saturate; feeble; liberal; multitudinous (pl); plastic; unripened; unstained; antique; agitated; festered; regal; truthful; trembling; kingly; emaciated; torpid; nimble; embryonic; redeemed; manly; devastated; reptile; shuddering; unwasting; frivolous; exploring; blotched; dead; scintillating; ransomed; pious; enthralling; delicate; pessimistic; tardy; virile; active; dauntless; altered; crude; eccentric; wakeful; elevated; cavalier; cantankerous; bleeding; clearest; stubborn; yearning; truant; dying; prevailing; introspective; credulous; misguided; exalted; angelic; cautious; charitable; grieved; timid; ardent; merry; spotted; callous; watchful; jealous; departed; intercurrent; countless (pl); rational; hungry; abstracted; wiser; patient; inviolable; obstinate; sordid; guileless; preserved; rich; bewildered; mean; knightly; sober; hideous; distracted; practical; simple; immortal; torn; famished; straying.

verbs

beguile—; beleaguer—; benefit—; bruise—; clothe—; clutter—; commit—; consign—; crush—; deliver—; deplore—; drain—; drown—; empty—; ennoble—; enrapture—; explore—; feast—; feed—; fire—; fortify—; gratify—; harrow—; impel—; incarnate—; incrust—; inflame—; loose—; mask—; mold —; nourish—; perjure—; pour—; purge—; purify—; rack—; raise—; release—; rend —; reveal—; salve—; satisfy—; saturate—; scourge—; sear—; search—; sell—; shadow —; smite—; soothe—; stain—; steep—; stir —; surrender—; tear— touch— transplant —; unburden—; untrim—; unveil—; wrap —; weary—; wrench—; —awakens; —bows; —breathes; —cries; —dares; —exults; —flames; —grieves; —governs; —lives; —palsies; —pants; —perishes; —quails; —quickens; —rebels; —revolts; —sees; —shudders; —struggles; —thirsts for; —wakens; —wavers; —wells up.

(See spirit.)

SOUND

adjectives

incongruous; obdurate; joyful; financial; explosive; ecstatic; numerous (pl); roaring; hissing; peculiar; quavering; plaintive; sprinkled; similar; lamentable; languid; unauthorized; elementary; crisp; muffled; unearthly; affrighting; thundering; lulling; empty; winged; perfidious; tinkling; imposing; ear-splitting; flat; petulant; scratching; powerful; human; horrid; answering; pulsating; puffing; monotonous; cropping; discordant; ominous; multitudinous (pl); articulate; distinct; terrible; mysterious; harmonious; faint; moaning; jarring; agreeable; perfect; blithe; thwacking; sad; romantic; weird; furtive; immortal; obnoxious; maddening; unresting; hideous; menacing; onomatopoeic; agglomerative; endearing; tuneful; stormy; incessant; plain; strange; dentilingual; obstructed; hoarse; chuckling; caressing; murmuring; animated; understanding; munching; increasing; howling; hollow; sullen; meaningless; cruel; heterogeneous; droning; pinging; wandering; delicious; cracking; kindred; spiritual; convulsed; clattering; perpetual; humming; evil; flattering; various (pl); murderous; consecutive; rumbling; gurgling; sensuous; rattling; joyous; dubious; rushing; monosyllabic; muttering; celestial; sweet; stealthy; whizzing; soothing; slight; throaty; suggestive; melodious; eminent;

confused; melancholy; healing; whistling; vague; clashing; raving; siren; repining; soft; recurrent; lambent; portentous; carefree; grunting; mirthful; false; sighing; raspy; idle; vocal; conversational; hammering; chirping; shocking; rhythmic; blissful; scientific; droll; harsh; fundamental; continuous; appalling; ghostly.

verbs

absorb—; alter—; attune to—; carry—; communicate—; deaden—; detect—; dilute —; direct—; disguise—; echo—; elicit—; emit—; give forth—; induce—; lessen—; limit—; mellow—; muffle—; interpret—; sharpen—; smother—; transmit—; waft—; visualize—; smother—; —alarms; —babbles; —ceases; —comforts; —dins; —echoes; —emanates; —s emerge; —falls; —s gibber; —s gurgle; —lulls; —penetrates; —reawakens; —reechoes; —registers; —reverberates; —scatters; —s trouble; —vanishes.

(See noise.)

adverbs

fortunately; wholesomely; securely; luckily; admirably; commendably; satisfactorily; unusually; magnificently; splendidly; impressively; gloriously; perfectly; remarkably; excellently; sufficiently; superbly; miraculously.

SOUND (v)

adverbs

peremptorily; exasperatingly; incessantly; harshly; audibly; incredibly; importunately; celestially; mournfully; incongruously; thunderously; monotonously; discordantly; ominously; mysteriously; jarringly; thwackingly; weirdly; obnoxiously; portentously; appallingly.

(See express, hear.)

SOUNDLESS

adverbs

breathlessly; curiously; strangely; eerily; mysteriously; oddly; extraordinarily; miraculously; admirably; pleasantly; fortunately; furtively; stealthily; carefully; cautiously; warily; perfectly; remarkably; incredibly.

SOUP

adjectives

thick; substantial; hearty; savory; scalding; canned.

verbs

administer—; bolt—; brew—; concoct—; dispatch—; gulp—; guzzle—; imbibe—; ladle—; prepare—; relish—; savor—; season—; sip—; spice—; strain—; swill—; —gelatinizes; —invigorates; —nourishes; —replenishes; —scalds; —tempts; —thickens; —tickles the palate.

(See broth, food, liquid.)

SOUR

adverbs

disagreeably; acridly; yeastily; pleasantly; horribly; startlingly; unexpectedly; oddly; mustily; offensively; inedibly; overly; extremely; curiously; unpalatably; unpleasantly; rancidly.

SOURCE

adjectives

copious (pl); reliable; various (pl); authentic; abundant (pl); external; outside; delightful; usual; proximate; inexhaustible; scanty; respectable; distorted; vital; real; occult; festering; fruitful; paternal; worthwhile; known; classical; valuable; bounteous; recurrent; vulgar; artificial; full-fed; radiant; prolific; frequent; unrelated; continued; grand; editorial; important; shallow; true; inactive; miscellaneous; invisible; authoritative.

verbs

attack—; borrow from—; determine—; dry up—; flow from—; emanate from—; exhaust —; poison—; replenish from—; search for —; spring from—; stamp out—; strike at —; tap—; trace to—; track down—; utilize —; —constitutes; —feeds; —supplies.

(See origin, beginning.)

SOUTH

adjectives

aromatic; fragrant; far; soft; fiery; quiet; feudal; warm.

SOVEREIGN

adjectives

neutral; successive (pl); ruthless; ambitious; legitimate; hapless; territorial; hereditary; joint; youthful; sceptered; vigilant; squatter; spiritual; unchallenged; inscrutable; tribal; feeble; diminished; glorious; gracious; individual.

SOVEREIGNTY

verbs

ascend to—; assume—; endanger—; exercise —; exert—; extend—; gain—; impair—; invest with—; jeopardize—; limit—; maintain—; relinquish—; respect—; retain—; usurp—; weaken—; yield—; —crumbles; —spreads; —sways; —totters; —wields.

(See crown, dominion, power.)

SOW (v)

adverbs

mechanically; scientifically; scatteredly; widely; sparsely; thickly; luxuriantly.

(See scatter, plant.)

SPACE

adjectives

shoreless; encumbered; furlong; ample; plenteous; eternal; coming; boundless; allotted; inconsiderable; porous; astonishing; globular; unnecessary; limitless; tumultuous; immense; adequate; stabling; intervening; trackless; vast; endless; editorial; unoccupied; wide; infinite; successive (pl); watery; projecting; sufficient; weary; choking; unbounded; awful; pervading; shaded; hoary; stellar; vaulted; neutral; storage; restricted; azure; generous; interminable; imaginary; dimensional; intermediate; ethereal; tenantless; breathing; grudging; surface; mightiest; betokened; available; soundless; angry.

verbs

acquire—; augment—; confine to—; cramp for—; dash—; define—; determine—; devote—; diminish—; encamp on—; estimate —; evacuate—; extend—; grant—; insert in —; lack—; limit—; lodge in—; narrow—; nestle in—; penetrate—; permeate—; pervade—; provide—; regulate—; stare in—; tenant—; transmit through—; withdraw from—; —accommodates; —dwindles; —expands; —ranges.

(See capacity, area.)

SPACIOUS

adverbs

adequately; satisfactorily; delightfully; wonderfully; amply; unexpectedly; amazingly; uncommonly; extremely; unnecessarily; admirably; commendably; extraordinarily; magnificently; splendidly; remarkably; conveniently; charmingly; reasonably; vastly.

verbs

disclose—; relax in—; reveal—; revel in—; survey—; —affords; —allows; —dazzles; —emancipates; —enables; —enthralls; —facilitates; —frees; —gives scope; —leaves; —liberates; —overawes; —overwhelms; —permits; —unfolds.

(See luxury, comfort, vastness.)

SPAN

adjectives

incredible; toil-stained; fleeting; artistic; infinitesimal; pitiful; allotted; sapphire; natural; life; useful.

verbs

abbreviate—; bridge—; elongate—; fuse—; interlink—; limit—; prolong—; protract—; reduce—; shorten—; stretch—; survive—; terminate—; unite—; —breaches; —elapses; —extends; —spreads; —stretches.

(See bridge, spread, extent.)

SPANK (v)

adverbs

resoundingly; heartlessly; cruelly; penally; repeatedly; viciously; explosively.

(See whip, paddle.)

SPARE (v)

adverbs

mercifully; generously; benevolently; willingly; voluntarily; magnanimously; nobly; benignantly.

(See save, refrain.)

SPARKLE

adjectives

fiery; exciting; phosphoric; odd; epigrammatic; conversational.

SPARKLE (v)

adverbs

splendidly; radiantly; frostily; keenly; luminously; phosphorically; gaily; spectacularly.

(See glitter, gleam.)

SPARKLING

adverbs

brightly; youthfully; ingenuously; happily; comically; brilliantly; wittily; facetiously; humorously; pleasantly; whimsically; nonsensically; fantastically; drolly; scintillatingly; delightfully; entrancingly; piquantly; thrillingly; stimulatingly.

adjectives

wandering; poor; glimmering; smoldering; enkindling; glowing; broad; bold; angry; starry; numbered; primitive; benignant; luminous; involuntary; immortal; feeble; hot; compensatory; latent; dubious; lively.

verbs

apply—; extinguish—; fan—; kindle—; quench—; smother—; snuff out—; —dazzle; —die; —dwell; —endanger; —enkindle; —flicker; —fly; —glow; —grow; —ignite; —illuminate; —inflame; —radiate; —shoot from; —smoulder; —strike; —tremble.

(See light, fire, flame, flash.)

SPARROW

verbs

—busies; —chases; —cheers; —chirps; —circles; —drifts; —flocks; —flutters; —s haunt; —perks up; —plagues; —robs; —soars; —steals; —thrives on; —tucks away; —twitters; —wanders; —warbles; —wheels; —whistles.

(See bird.)

SPARTAN

adverbs

resolutely; intrepidly; dauntlessly; determinedly; unflinchingly; marvelously; invincibly; fearlessly; heroically; valiantly; doughtily.

SPASM

adjectives

blind; unseemly; terrible; temporary; social; fierce; clonic; tonic; violent; sudden; painful.

verbs

afflict with—s; alleviate—; assuage—; burst into—; characterize by—s; check—; contract in—s; diagnose—; excite—; mitigate —; moderate—; pacify—; prevent—; prolong—; quell—; reduce—; relieve—; subdue —; —affects; —agonizes; —convulses; —denotes; —jerks; —lessens; —overcomes; —passes; —ruffles; —seizes; —strains; —s wrack.

(See convulsion, fit, contraction.)

SPASMODIC

adverbs

convulsively; curiously; strangely; inexplicably; regularly; oddly; terrifyingly; violently; bafflingly; perplexingly; heartbreakingly; unpredictably.

SPEAK (v)
adverbs
epigrammatically; euphemistically; characteristically; impressively; vaguely; pompously; grandiloquently; verbosely; melodiously; euphonically; pointedly; periodically; mournfully; rationally; derogatorily; disparagingly; judiciously; coaxingly; optimistically; respectfully; articulately; conservatively; tremulously; uncompromisingly; reassuringly; energetically; laconically; icily; mellifluously; glibly; contemptuously; indulgently; discursively; tensely; venomously; circuitously; edifyingly; directly; simply; impudently; figuratively; passionately; sublimely; scurrilously; precipitantly; solicitously; warily; emphatically; volubly; ironically; negatively; persuasively; exquisitely.
(See talk, say, express.)

SPEAKER
adjectives
distinguished; influential; conspicuous; adequate; fluent; brilliant; liberal; adroit; inspiring; dependable; impressive; boring; eloquent; timorous; scarred; hardy; flippant; principal; effective; polished; obstreperous; finished; handicapped; unintelligible; scintillating; deft.

verbs
applaud—; badger—; compliment—; confuse—; divert—; eulogize—; heckle—; introduce—; jibe—; laud—; silence—; —addresses; —admonishes; —articulates; —besmirches; —blares; —castigates; —chastises; —condemns; —conveys; —disclaims; —delivers; —digresses; —drawls; —drives home; —enunciates; —expatiates; —expostulates; —fulminates; —gesticulates; —gestures; —harangues; —insinuates; —inveighs against; —laments; —orates; —pounds; —prates; —proclaims; —rants; —raps; —rebuts; —refutes; —shocks; —slanders; —slings; —slurs; —snaps; —stammers; —stutters; —utters; —discourses.
(See debater, orator, politician, minister.)

SPEAR
adjectives
battled; glittering; enormous; broad; well-balanced; serried; splintering; stabbing; bloody; couched; barbed; beaming; shadowy; poisoned; brazen-headed.

verbs
arm with—; barb—; brandish—; cast—; edge—; extract—; fashion—; fling—; hurl —; impale on—; let fly—; level—; taper—; —s bristle; —fells; —flies; —gores; —penetrates; —perforates; —pricks; —punctures; —riddles; —spikes; —stabs; —staves in; —whirs; —whizzes.
(See dart, lance, missile.)

SPECIALIST
adjectives
celebrated; pretended; minute; cold-blooded; qualified; experienced; high-priced.

verbs
baffle—; consult—; employ—; engage—; recommend—; recruit—s; —advocates; —analyzes; —assures; —concludes; —s confer; —counsels; —diagnoses; —discerns; —exhorts; —prescribes; —relieves; —resurrects; —restores.
(See expert, physician, scholar.)

SPECIALTY
verbs
characterize—; designate—; determine—; devote to—; emphasize—; engage in—; excel in—; foster—; indicate—; master—; recognize—; restrict to—; stress—; warrant—.
(See work, science, art, knowledge.)

SPECIES
adjectives
particular; gigantic; important; superior; representative; prehistoric; foreign; tropical; new; dominant; extinct; distinct; collective; terrestrial; principal; mimetic; delightful; incipient; corresponding; subtle; unique; domesticated; nobler; nigh-perfected; rare.

verbs
breed—; classify—; corrupt—; cross—; discover—; elevate—; exalt—; exterminate—; group—; inbreed—; perpetuate—; preserve —; propagate—; refine—; reproduce—; revive—; segregate—; uplift—; vitiate—; —abounds; —congregates; —degenerates; —embraces; —evolves; —includes; —ornaments; —rehabilitates; —relates; —survives.
(See race, group, classification, variety, category.)

1102

adverbs

highly; helpfully; particularly; accurately; singularly; intimately; markedly; appropriately; typically; usually; uncommonly; satisfactorily; duly; conveniently; pertinently; advantageously; especially; minutely; sufficiently; conclusively; ·opportunely.

SPECIFICATIONS

adjectives

factory; provisional; essential; exact; strict; broad; detailed; minute; manufacturing; stated; licensed; general; sweeping; all-inclusive.

verbs

abide by—; adhere to—; cleave to—; deviate from—; diverge from—; draw—; embody in—; follow—; require—; standardize —; —call for; —conform; —define; —demand; —describe; —designate; —detail; —determine; embrace; enumerate, — itemize; —particularize; —regulate.

(See regulations, definition, details, items.)

SPECIFY (v)

adverbs

definitely; distinctly; provisionally; essentially; strictly; broadly; minutely; generally.

(See designate, name.)

SPECIMEN

adjectives

stalwart; active; unique; marvelous; abundant (pl); splendid; favorable; knobby; sundry (pl); hard-looking; precious; complete; admirable; acknowledged; superb; handsome; genuine; huge; lingering; superior; excellent; sickly; occasional; ferocious; prolonged; pleasing; puny; given; enormous; good-looking; unfair.

verbs

attract—; bag—; collect—s; dissect—; exhibit—; guard—; hunt—; mount—; preserve—; prize—; pursue—; search for—; seek—; snare—; stalk—; stuff—; trap—; value—; —evades; —exemplifies; —illustrates.

(See animal, sample.)

SPECK

adjectives

frothy; nebulous; morbid; inconsequential; eccentric; tiniest; swimming; microscopic; isolated; brilliant; shadowy; furthest; pitted.

adverbs

unpleasantly; unfortunately; unluckily; prettily; beautifully; artificially; inconveniently; unsalably; unprofitably; completely; strangely; oddly; perplexingly; unaccountably; inexplicably.

SPECTACLE
(general)

adjectives

ghastly; pleasant; wild; impressive; weird; singular; garish; bewildering; placid; awful; imposing; depressing; appalling; revolting; remarkable; religious; owl-eyed; solemn; lordly; striking; stupendous; damp; theatrical; picturesque; hideous; finer; shameful; elaborate; fairy; odious; inspiring; unhallowed; impassioned; fearful; miserable; gorgeous; sly; beaming; savage; gala; silent; triumphant; pitiful; novel; benevolent; magnificent; direful; daring; wondrous; entrancing; ignoble; attractive; unwonted; unexpected; unique; grandmotherly; extraordinary; splendid; everlasting; mossy; monstrous; menacing; chorographic; unprecedented.

SPECTACLE
(show)

verbs

unfold—; view—; witness—; —affords; —appeals; —caricatures; —fascinates.

(See exhibition, show, display.)

SPECTACLED

adverbs

heavily; forbiddingly; formidably; grimly; primly; unwillingly; unattractively; unbecomingly; horribly; comically; carefully; helpfully; carefully; skilfully; finally; stylishly; protectively; fashionably; demurely; deceptively.

SPECTACLES
(glasses)

verbs

adjust—; blink through—; exhibit—; prescribe—; toy with—.

SPECTACULAR

adverbs

highly; impressively; magnificently; splendidly; brilliantly; regally; royally; colorfully; gorgeously; gloriously; imposingly; majestically; dazzlingly; processionally; dramatically; fantastically; unusually; sensationally; superbly.

SPECTATORS

adjectives
passing; broad; bold; angry; unpracticed; indifferent; festive; singular; curious; distinguished; impartial; patient; unlearned; passive; crowded; astonished; dignified; plebeian; bored; ambitious; attentive; callous.

verbs
accommodate—; affront—; amaze—; amuse—; astound—; attract—; awe—; beguile—; bore—; cheat—; dazzle—; dumbfound—; electrify—; enrage—; entrance—; impress—; petrify—; regale—; scan—; stun—; thrill—; —applaud; —behold; —clamor; —cram; —disperse; —fret; —gasp; —heckle; —irk; —jam; —lure; —marvel; —pour; —rivet; —witness.
(See hearer, crowd, bystander, audience.)

SPECTER

adjectives
ridiculous; gibbering; looming; dancing; ghastly; gloomy; ghostly; confused; grim; grisly; horrid.

verbs
cast—; fight off—; goggle at—; —dissolves; —dreads; —evaporates; —fades; —floats; —glares; —glowers; —haunts; —looms; —melts away; —penetrates; —permeates; —petrifies; —plagues; —terrifies; —vanishes.
(See apparition, phantom, ghost.)

SPECULATE (v)

adverbs
disastrously; rashly; divertingly; chimerically; philosophically; casually; adroitly; financially; contemplatively; ridiculously; abstractly; vaguely; theoretically; ingeniously; shrewdly.
(See meditate, guess.)

SPECULATION

adjectives
grandest; casual; discursive; sympathetic; delighted; daring; philosophic; adroit; colossal; presumptuous; abstruse; financial; humble; enthusiastic; humanitarian; idle; imaginative; contemplative; doubtful; loftier; fantastic; visionary; ridiculous; moody; gambling; delectable; awful; mercenary;

disastrous; abstract; rational; improbable; favorite; empty; vague; sad; wild; unpremeditated; amused; adventurous; original; heedless; affectionate; erring; theoretical; ingenious; prejudicial; deep.

verbs
absorb in—; admonish—; arouse—; denounce—; deter from—; discourage—; dismiss—; dominate—; engage in—; hush—; indulge in—; license—; plunge into—; prohibit—; restrain—; resume—; risk in—; stake on—; torture—; —chances; —endangers; —fascinates; —gropes; —jeopardizes; —lures; —prohibits; —ventures.
(See gambling, meditation, transaction.)

SPECULATOR

adjectives
unscrupulous; dauntless; ingenious; grasping; keen; able; scientific; curbstone; shrewd; plunging; rich.

SPEECH

adjectives
thoughtless; voluble; angry; goodly; copious; long; stirring; maiden; gracious; heartless; chanting; epigrammatic; purest; wholesome; noblest; unrestrained; irrelevant; whispered; ambiguous; occasional; dual; sacred; moderate; impromptu; dedicatory; average; normal; saucy; meaningless; familiar; true; strict; after-luncheon; nebulous; laughing; decent; much-abused; impertinent; strong; vague; well-prepared; oracular; disrespectful; impressive; indignant; devoted; candid; elaborate; derogatory; characteristic; voiceless; extraordinary; eloquent; perfunctory; persuasive; masterly; articulate; demonstrative; rough; facetious; muddled; rasping; plaintive; powerful; whining; fraudulent; graceless; sibilant; complimentary; winged; taciturn; resistance; appropriate; sententious; consonantal; immemorial; intolerant; yearning; pedantic; supposititious; seditious; appreciative; villainous; patriotic; intelligible; expressive; champagne; stump; explosive; inflammatory; treasonable; high; momentous; pursuing; melted; deprecatory; flattering; lazy; composite; private; deliberating; flamboyant; explicit; flirtatious; fluent; luxuriant; royal; ghost-written; effective; reserved; rhetorical; voluble; fastidious; stifled; funeral; artistic; morning; inaudible; incharitable; wandering; dangerous; previous; strict; corrupted; free; manly;

broken; rattling; skillful; triumphant; graceful; higher; untimely; aimless; desolate; florid; fervid; common; impudent; nasal; uncensored; farewell; long-winded; memorized.

verbs
adjust—; ape—; augment—; book—; coach —; color—; compose—; confine—; cultivate —; deliver—; deprecate—; dismiss—; embellish—; endow—; extend—; flood—; incorporate in—; interlard—; intersperse—; polish—; pour forth—; prolong—; recite—; reel off—; respond to—; salt—; spout—; stumble through—; suppress—; time—; — appraises; —betrays; —declaims; —degenerates; —drones; —eulogizes; —flows; —glitters; —humors; —matures; —mingles; —thunders; —transcends; —wearies.
(See lecture, recital, declamation, discourse, oration, address.)

SPEECHLESS
adverbs
suddenly; strangely; utterly; curiously; embarrassingly; pathetically; bashfully; awkwardly; ineptly; shyly; clumsily; timidly; boorishly; loutishly; overwhelmingly; emotionally; miserably; wretchedly; unaccountably.

SPEED
adjectives
violent; dependable; superior; furious; imagined; convenient; breakneck; impressive; wonted; requisite; initial; amazing; thrilling; noiseless; specified; railway; evil; frightful; uninterrupted; incredible; utmost; high; accelerated; skyey; desired; fabulous; surprising; sufficient; diminished; careless; incredible; flashing; electric; lightning; moderate; reasonable; sustained; intoxicating; bidding.

verbs
accelerate—; arrest—; attain—; check—; curb—; diminish—; exceed—; gauge—; goad to—; maintain—; moderate—; propel at—; regale—; slacken—; spur to—; sustain —; throttle—; urge—; —alarms; —endangers; —exhilarates; —facilitates; —intoxicates; —jeopardizes; —menaces; —outstrips; —spurts.
(See momentum, velocity.)

SPEEDY
adverbs
incredibly; increasingly; effortlessly; mercifully; crazily; tragically; awkwardly; uncomfortably; distressingly; painfully; breathlessly; impetuously; perilously; unaccountably; surprisingly; astonishingly; moderately; dangerously; lightly; remarkably; precipitately; incalculably.

SPELL
adjectives
potent; unsolvable; heavenly; fascinating; mesmeric; drowsy; breathing; springtime; subtle; melancholy; hideous; maddened; baleful; appreciable; beguiling; cabalistical; funereal; wondrous; ineffable; savage; mighty; undying; wizard.

verbs
allay—; assuage—; cast—; conjure up—; exercise—; exert—; intensify—; overcome —; struggle under—; weave—; wield—; —bewitches; —charms; —enthralls; —fascinates; —hypnotizes; —lures; —magnetizes; —overwhelms; —permeates; —persists; —prevails; —ruffles; —entrances.
(See charm, enchantment, glamor, incantation.)

SPELL (v)
adverbs
accurately; promptly; involvedly; complicatedly; abbreviatedly; originally.
(See unravel, unfold.)

SPELLBOUND
adverbs
rapturously; raptly; earnestly; intently; magically; fascinatedly; eagerly; completely; utterly; curiously; strangely; marvelously; involuntarily; helplessly.

SPEND (v)
adverbs
tranquilly; recklessly; exclusively; lavishly; rashly; affluently; liberally; fabulously; idly; clandestinely; royally.
(See expend, squander.)

SPHERE
adjectives
glimmering; exalted; higher; bewildering; wheeling; murderous; mortal; youthful; native; diurnal; dusky; starriest; lucid; kingless; sublunary; luscious; ripe; great; mental; unthinking; crystal; softer; danc-

ing; stormy; pure; social; destined; heavenly; singing; unknown; calmer; mundane; alien; blazing; martial; political; far-off; willing; different; enchanted; celestial; humble; reachless; sensuous; untrodden; benighted; legitimate; whirling; poised; interstellar.

verbs
allot—; broaden—; confine to—; deepen—; dominate—; emerge from—; enlarge—; extend—; invade—; limit—; narrow—; penetrate—; permeate—; pierce—; preserve—; reject from—; restrict—; rule—; tread—; widen—; —s narrow; —s overlap; —ranges.
(See jurisdiction, region, position, province, globe.)

SPICE
adjectives
pungent; rich; strange; bartered; powerful; strong; odorous.

verbs
adulterate—; blend with—; impart—; infuse—; inject—; savor—; —bites; —embalms; —flavors; —nauseates; —pervades; —pickles.; —preserves; —scents, —seasons.
(See mustard, flavoring.)

SPICY
adverbs
pleasantly; fragrantly; pungently; redolently; lingeringly; arrestingly; refreshingly; freshly; pleasingly; strongly; delicately; exquisitely; enchantingly; charmingly; delectably; intoxicatingly; richly; attractively; exotically.

SPIDER
adjectives
intrusive; bloated; putrid; weaving; hardy.

verbs
—attacks; —clambers up; —clings; —constructs; —dances; —dangles; —devours; —emerges; —entices; —envenoms; —s infest; —inhabits; —lies in wait; —loops; —paralyzes; —poisons; —s possess; —preys upon; —scrambles; —scurries; —snares; —spins; —stalks; —strikes; —suspends from; —traps; —weaves.
(See insect.)

SPIN (v)
adverbs
scientifically; assiduously; tirelessly; automatically; vigorously; industriously; dizzily; monotonously; sickeningly.
(See twirl, whirl.)

SPINE
verbs
brace—; compress—; curve—; damage—; dislocate—; expose—; fracture—; impair—; inflame—; inject into—; irritate—; lacerate—; protect—; puncture—; sheathe—; strengthen—; support—; tap—; x ray—; —bristles; —controls; —flashes; —quivers; —shudders; —transmits.
(See bone.)

SPINELESS
adverbs
utterly; despicably; contemptibly; cravenly; arrantly; palpably; obviously; notoriously; confessedly; openly; pitiably; shamefully; ingloriously; infamously; terribly; unconscionably; recreantly; distressingly; pitifully; disgustingly.

SPINSTER
adjectives
ardent; unpredictable; resigned; anemic; withered; hopeless; contented; man-shy; miserable.

SPIRE
adjectives
humble; ornate; tapering; slender; friendly; jagged; feathery; tranquil; flaming; graceful; gleaming; soaring; mountain; steadfast; diminishing; rocky; numberless (pl); octagonal; exquisite; far-off.

verbs
ascend—; clamber up—; descend—; discern—; erect—; impale on—; mount—; raze—; scale—; surmount—; suspend from—; —s bristle; —s cluster; —looms; —s shimmer; —soars; —tapers; —topples.
(See tower, stalk.)

SPIRIT
adjectives
abiding; absent; adventurous; aggravated; aggressive; airy; alleged; altruistic; animal; animating; apathetic; ardent; arrogant; artistic; aspiring; audacious; barren; beauteous; becoming; bellicose; belligerent; benevolent; bodiless; benignant; blessed;

boastful; bold; boundless; braced; braver; brazen; bubbling; buoyant; burgeoning; Byronic; burlesquing; calculating; cernuous; combative; charming; chaste; chastened; cherished; chimerical; churlish; commercial; common; compassionate; competitive; complacent; confident; congenial; contagious; contented; contrite; courageous; courtier; craving; creative; critical; damned; dangerous; darksome; dedicated; dejected; demonic; determined; devilish; disconsolate; disembodied; divine; drooping; earnest; ebbing; electric; embittered; emancipated; emulous; encumbered; enlightened; enlivened; enticing; ephemeral; equable; erect; erring; ever-soaring; ethereal; excellent; excited; evil; exclusive; exuberant; facinorous; faint; fallen; familiar; fantastic; fastidious; fervent; festive; feverish; fiery; fighting; flabby; flaming; flashy; flexible; fluttering; foreign; fractious; fraternal; free; fresh; gay; generous; genial; gentle; gloomy; glorious; goaded; grave, gray; grudging; guiding; hackneyed; happy; harassed; hardy; haughty; heedless; helpless; heroic; high; horrible; hospitable; hostile; huge; illustrious; imaged; immaterial; immortal; impatient; imperial; imperishable; impertinent; impetuous; inborn; incongruous; inconstant; indefatigable; independent; indignant; indomitable; inexorable; inexpiable; insurgent; internal; intrepid; introspective; intuitive; invincible; irascible; iron; joyous; judicial; kindly; kindred; kingly; laboring; laggard; lavish; leading; lewd; liberal; lonely; lovable; low; lustrous; magnanimous; majestic; malicious; malignant; managing; martial; masculine; meanest; mercenary; mercurial; migratory; militant; ministering; misguided; mixed; moderate; moving; mutinous; mysterious; nameless; neighboring; neutral; nimble; normal; noble; noxious; obdurate; paradoxical; parting; patronizing; perfect; persecuting; pert; perturbed; pervading; petulant; philanthropic; philosophical; poetic; practical; predominant; presumptuous; profane; prosaic; proscriptive; provincial; public; purest; purged; pythonic; quaint; queer; querulous; rabid; questioning; racial; radical; rallied; rampant; ransomed; rapacious; rare; rational; reasonable; rebellious; regenerate; released; repugnant; resolute; responsive; restless; romantic; roving; ruling; sacerdotal; sacred; scattered; scientific; searching; secret; secular; self-conscious; sensitive; serene; serious;

silent; skipping; skittish; lewd; sleeping; slothful; slow; smoothed; smug; soaring; soldiering; solemn; somber; sound; sparkling; stanch; stern; stout; submissive; supercilious; sympathetic; tempered; tolerable; tolerant; tough; traditional; tragic; troubled; turbulent; tumultuous; unbridled; uncaged; undefiled; unfair; unfettered; unhaggling; unhappy; unmoved; unnatural; unquiet; unresting; valiant; valorous; valuable; vanguard; vanishing; vanquished; vital; vehement; venomous; vivid; volatile; wandering; wanton; warlike; weak; weary; weeping; wicked; wild; worthy; wounded; zealous.

verbs

allude to—; annihilate—; affront—; bolster —; bruise—; burn—; chafe—; commend—; commune with—; comprehend—; drink of —; drench—; exalt—; exorcise—; fetter—; flood—; hamper—; humble—; immortalize —; implant—; inflame—; inject—; oppose —; purge—; raise—; re-animate—; recapture—; reveal—; reverence—; stamp out—; submerge—; sustain—; symbolize—; teach—; typify—; violate—; war against—; wash—; worship—; yield to—; —abides; —actuates; —animates; —appeases; —arises; —awakens; —blights; —bolsters; —breathes; —broods; —buoys; —caters; —cheers; —climbs; —communes with; —communicates; —conjures; —connotes; —conquers; —conveys; —dampens; —daunts; —departs; —displays; —diverts; —embodies; —endows; —engages; —excites; —exhausts; —exhibits; —expands; —expresses; —extracts; —fatigues; —frets; —haunts; —imbibes; —imbues; —impoverishes; —inculcates; —indulges; —infuses; —lags; —lingers; —maintains; —molests; —narrows; —obscures; —overrules; —paralyzes; —partakes; —perceives; —permeates; —pervades; —pierces; —pours out; —preserves; —prevails; —rankles; —reflects; —reigns; —relates; —reveres; —revives; —sinks; —stalks; —stems; —stimulates; —stirs; —strengthens; —strives; —succumbs; —survives; —summons; —swells; —tempers; —tires; —touches; —unfolds; —uplifts; —wails; —wars; —washes. (See soul, life, specter.)

SPIRITED

adverbs

ardently; briskly; unusually; uncommonly; exceedingly; alertly; busily; friskily; vivaciously; unwontedly; delightfully; splendidly; actively; intelligently.

SPIRITUAL
adverbs

naturally; personally; subjectively; devoutly; faithfully; piously; religiously; reverently; instinctively; celestially; gloriously; intuitively; beautifully; immoderately; blessedly; humbly; solemnly; consciously; innately; simply; inherently.

SPIT
verbs

eject—; emit—; excrete—; exude—; moisten with—; regurgitate—; slaver—; slobber—; squirt—; —drivels; —drools; —nauseates; —showers; —slobbers.

(See saliva, liquid, sputum, expectoration.)

SPIT (v)
adverbs

venomously; vulgarly; carelessly; disgustingly; nauseatingly; incessantly; obstreperously; accurately; explosively.

(See sputter.)

SPITEFUL
adverbs

naturally; habitually; always; detestably; dangerously; maliciously; viciously; abominably; incorrigibly; incurably; atrociously; hatefully; enviously; unhappily; unfortunately; strangely; absurdly; deplorably; bitterly; cruelly.

SPLASH
adjectives

gaudy; tremendous; quickening; confounded; tiny; ignominious; audible; weltering; rhythmic.

verbs

avert—; raise—; —begrimes; —besmirches; —deluges; —douses; —drenches; —fouls; —inundates; —moistens; —ruffles; —rumples; —showers; —smears; —smudges; —souses; —spatters; —swashes.

(See wave, water, liquid.)

SPLEEN
adjectives

merry; scornful; weakest; testy; heaving.

verbs

affect—; enlarge—; excise—; excite—; provoke—; remove—; rile (colloq.)—; ruffle

—; vent—; vex—; —depresses; —enlarges; —execrates; —ferments; —functions; —governs; —secretes.

(See bile.)

SPLENDID
adverbs

gorgeously; luminously; brilliantly; vividly; dazzlingly; radiantly; richly; sumptuously; artistically; extraordinarily; amazingly; regally; unexpectedly; barbarically; fantastically; romantically; imposingly; impressively; majestically; imperially; royally; colorfully; imperishably; unforgettably; ornately; dramatically; ceremonially; ritualistically.

SPLENDOR
adjectives

oriental; reflected; intrinsic; glamorous; divine; temporal; lonely; dazzling; scarlet; superficial; infernal; reminiscent; dark; transitory; prodigious; immense; liquid; intellectual; hurrying; vermeil; profuse; passionless; clinging; celestial; sumptuous; lofty; spectral; barbaric; mild; queenly; magnificent; external; meaning; wasteful; crimson; faded; lurid; mellow; dewy; new; starry; chilled; sultry; ancient; modest; baleful; meridian; opulent; prismatic; radiant; scaly; level; unhealthy; monarchical; visionary; chromatic; delusive; arrogant; lustrous; vulgar.

verbs

belittle—; blur—; crown—; envy—; mar—; rejoice in—; —blazes; —blinds; —bursts forth; —crowns; —dazzles; —intoxicates.

(See brilliance, glory, grandeur.)

SPLINT
verbs

apply—; bear—; bind—; discard—; improvise—; pad—; wear—; —affords; —assures; —bolsters; —braces; —maintains; —necessitates; —props; —protects; —serves; —supports; —sustains; —trusses; —underpins.

(See brace, protection.)

SPLINTER
verbs

cleave into—s; draw—; eject—; extract—; impale on—; pluck—; remove—; rend into —s; sever into—; shiver into—s; transfix on

1108

—; withdraw—; —barbs; —gashes; —gauges; —infects; —perforates; —pierces; —punctures.

(See fragment, piece.)

SPLIT

verbs
cement—; fuse—; intervene—; wedge in—; weld—; —bisects; —breaches; —disjoins; —disrupts; —extends; —fractures; —gapes; —halves; —leaves; —mars; —rives; —shatters; —shivers; —splinters; —widens.

(See breach, crack.)

SPLURGE
(*colloq.*)

verbs
create—; cut—; deplore—; indulge in—; lament—; reproach—; rue—; —beguiles; —celebrates; —dazzles; —deludes; —displays; —exhibits; —flaunts; —flourishes; —glitters; —swaggers; —shows off; —splashes.

(See extravagance, waste, demonstration.)

SPOIL (*v*)

adverbs
ultimately; hopelessly; sadly; disastrously; effectively; partially; sickeningly.

(See plunder, damage.)

SPOILS

adjectives
envied; frequent; glittering; private; recking; sluttish; consecrated; trophied.

verbs
appropriate—; cache—; capture—; confiscate—; covet—; display—; dispose of—; exhaust—; exhibit—; filch—; hunger for—; lust for—; pilfer—; pillage for—; pounce upon—; plunder for—; prize—; purloin—; reap—; retain—; sack—; scramble for—; seize—; swoop to—; value—; win—; wrench—; —accrue; —allure; —attract.

(See loot, graft.)

SPONGE

verbs
apply—; dampen—; fish for—s; hook—; infiltrate—; market—; moisten—; mop with —; rinse—; saturate—; scour with—; swab with—; —absorbs; —soaks up; —sucks up.

SPONGY

adverbs
usefully; naturally; profitably; convenient-

ly; adaptably; flexibly; yieldingly; absorbently; pleasantly; comfortably; hopelessly; porously; swampily; quaggily; dangerously; impassably.

SPONSER (*v*)

adverbs
enthusiastically; financially; annually; necessarily; faithfully.

(See indorse, finance.)

SPONSOR

verbs
acquire—; conciliate—s; gain—; inspire—s; obligate to—; redeem—; seek—; —assures; —contracts; —discharges; —encourages; —exhorts; —finances; —furthers; —guarantees; —indorses; —observes; —pioneers; —pledges; —vouches for.

(See contributor, owner, manager.)

SPONTANEOUS

adverbs
eagerly; obviously; enthusiastically; utterly; manifestly; remarkably; absolutely; palpably; unquestionably; warmly; fervently: heartily; undoubtedly; intensely; exceptionally; sympathetically; unusually.

SPOOKY

adverbs
designedly; deliberately; pleasantly; mischievously; unusually; mysteriously; disagreeably; creepily; dismally; desolately; alarmingly; weirdly; uncannily; eerily; fearfully; wretchedly; miserably; uncomfortably; startlingly; horribly; ominously.

SPORT

adjectives
false; rare; willing; noisy; spectator; cruel; merry; sanguinary; biologic; equestrian; rustic; glorious; healthy; solitary; competitive; childish; malicious; domestic.

verbs
coach—; engage in—; enthuse about (colloq.)—; excel in—s; follow—; forsake —; hurl into—; indulge in—; pursue—; revive—; take up—; —attracts; —beguiles; —diverts; —endangers; —enlivens; —fascinates; —invigorates; —strains; —takes hold; —wearies.

(See amusement, diversion, fishing, frolic, game, golf, baseball, etc.)

SPORT (v)

adverbs

ludicrously; boisterously; enthusiastically; animatedly; merrily; competitively; childishly; rustically; noisily; uncouthly.
  (See frolic, play.)

SPOT

adjectives

secluded; sheltered; distinguishable; tuneful; convenient; hovering; dusky; delicious; threadbare; unpromising; chosen; hallowed; shady; retired; dreary; sunlit; selfsame; forsaken; elevated; sleek; wet; treacherous; sore; unknown; dry; beauty; mildewed; curious; desolate; seductive; devoted; perceptible; faulty; unsightly; formidable; sequestered; secure; moist; sacred; swampy; malarial; plague; trysting; vital; lovely; haunted; drearest; barren; memorable; remote; vicious; infinitesimal; secure; insidious; weak; doleful; consecrated; solitary; dreariest; neglected; limited; tender; designated; unfertile; isolated; vulnerable; silent; tranquil; burning; loathsome; ulcer; sanctified; attention-arresting; favorable; veritable; wave-walled.

verbs

bear—s; confine—; designate—; detect—; efface—; eradicate—; lurk near—; incrust —; obliterate—; patch—; scatter—s; scour —; —attracts; —s bespatter; —s besmirch; —betokens; —blemishes; —blurs; —blotches; —s checker; —connotates; —defiles; — mars; —represents; —smudges; —sullies; — transfixes.
  (See freckles, mark, blemish.)

SPOTLIGHT

verbs

concentrate—; eclipse—; elude—; evade—; extinguish—; focus—; obscure—; retire from—; share—; shrink from—; shun—; shy from—; steal—; —dazzles; —diffuses; —disperses; —flickers; —glares; —glimmers; —guides; —illuminates; —penetrates; —pierces; —plays upon; —radiates; —scintillates; —shimmers.
  (See light, limelight.)

SPOUSE

adjectives

indignant; tempestuous; expatriated; faithful; repulsive; pesty; skillful; plighted; exquisite; preternatural; waxen.

SPRAWL (v)

adverbs

grotesquely; drunkenly; violently; lazily; indolently; clumsily; uncouthly.
  (See spread, lie.)

SPRAWLY

adverbs

inconveniently; awkwardly; inexpediently; unnecessarily; terribly; unhandily; unfortunately; undesirably; objectionably.

SPRAY

adjectives

belching; out-wafting; glistening; salt-sea; bloomy; brackish; heavy; vagrant; beechen; sleepless; bent; white-hot; trailing; radiant; dissolving; drooping; yeasty; blinding; delicate; saltless; birchen; seething; writhen; flying; lofty; tumbling; sheeted; misty; deadly.

verbs

diffuse—; distil—; expel—; —beclouds; — befogs; —disinfects; —evaporates; —fizzes; —foams; —fumigates; —gleams; —glitters; —hazes; —mists; —moistens; —obscures; —overcasts; —radiates; —saturates; — sparkles; —spatters; —spumes; —drenches.
  (See fountain, mist, moisture, steam, vapor.)

SPRAY (v)

adverbs

periodically; scientifically; automatically; annually; agriculturally.
  (See scatter, sprinkle.)

SPREAD

adjectives

stunning; mortal; cloudless; dainty; solemn; delicious; immeasurable; tasty; delectable; eye-filling.

verbs

augment—; confine—; diminish—; enhance —; enlarge—; exaggerate—; expand—; extend—; extenuate—; heighten—; intensify —; limit—; magnify—; prevent—; reduce —; swell—; —embraces; —ranges.
  (See cover, extent.)

SPREAD (v)

adverbs

insidiously; contagiously; swiftly; malicious-

ly; spaciously; industriously; generously; parsimoniously; invidiously; internationally.
(See expand, circulate.)

SPREE
adjectives
gigantic; conquering; periodic; prolonged; measured; violent; headlong.

SPRIGHTLY
adverbs
inordinately; exceedingly; unusually; extremely; pleasantly; nimbly; delightfully; gleefully; divertingly; merrily; briskly; vivaciously; alertly; blithely; vigorously; joyously; mercurially.

SPRING
adjectives
trickling; sparkling; hasty; delightful; elegant; plashy; convulsive; fruitless; smiling; wayside; copious; muscular; bubbling; sagging; clear; perpetual; tongue-tied; secret; crystal; bitter; inexhaustible; powerful; quivering; amorous-breathing; bursting; fern-wreathed; purling; covert; young; whispering; tardy; lasting; latent; limpid; filthy; lagging; balmy; exulting; budding; portentous; endless; sinuous; babbling; unfading; living; phantom; fathomless; unsealed; humbler; unusual.

verbs
apostrophize—; bid—to; greet—; hail—; prophesy—; reveal—; salute—; taste—; welcome—; —adorns; —arrives; —boasts; —breathes; —brings; —bursts; —calls forth; —comes; —cries; —departs; —flies; —flourishes; —forsakes; —greets; —laughs; —murmurs; —questions; —returns; —rushes; —says good-bye; —smiles; —spreads; —supplies; —takes leave; —takes wing; —unbosoms; —unlocks; —visits; —wakens; —whips away; —works.
(See autumn, summer, winter.)

SPRING
(*well*)
verbs
contaminate—; drain—; drill—; emanate from—; issue from—; pollute—; seep into —; tap—; trace—; vent—; —advances; —awakens; —babbles; —discharges; —dribbles; —gurgles; —gushes; —jets; —murmurs; —oozes; —opens; —originates in; —

pulsates; —refreshes; —reinforces; —rises; —swashes; —swells; —trickles.
(See fountain, geyser, well, brook.)

SPRING (*v*)
adverbs
agilely; impetuously; hazardously; independently; amazingly; spontaneously; impulsively; joyously; viciously; vindictively; dexterously.
(See leap, bound.)

SPRINKLE (*v*)
adverbs
freshly; thickly; uniformly; liberally; profusely; delicately; sporadically.
(See scatter, spray.)

SPRITE
adjectives
elfin; shadowy; bright-eyed; wretched; dusky; melancholy; airy; elusive; devilish; mischievous; impish.

SPRUCE
adverbs
jauntily; nattily; unusually; habitually; attractively; smugly; carefully; designedly; unwontedly; remarkably; consciously; admirably; proudly; curiously; noticeably; conspicuously.

SPRY
adverbs
ostentatiously; absurdly; foolishly; proudly; pretentiously; resolutely; conspicuously; fatuously; deceptively; jauntily; curiously; showily; remarkably; unusually; ridiculously; crookedly; actively; naturally; habitually; pleasantly; alertly.

SPUNKY
adverbs
delightfully; sufficiently; smartly; inherently; merrily; actually; independently; absurdly; comically; ridiculously; extremely; unreasonably; uncommonly.

SPUR
adjectives
pricking; sluggish; continental; continual; clanking; dizzy; knightly; goading.

SPURIOUS
adverbs
disgracefully; obviously; evidently; manifestly; shamefully; cleverly; deceptively; in-

geniously; unquestionably; transparently; admittedly; unexpectedly; daringly; outrageously; ostensibly; visibly; ridiculously; cheaply.

SPUTTER (v)
adverbs
irately; indignantly; furiously; vindictively; violently; obnoxiously; vulgarly.
(See spit.)

SPUTTERING
adverbs
constantly; fitfully; fretfully; unreasonably; tetchily; shrewishly; irritably; ill-temperedly; futilely; uselessly; vainly; loudly; sullenly; excitedly; eternally.

SPUTUM
verbs
charge—; cough up—; discharge—; emit—; examine—; expectorate—; sterilize—; test —; —accumulates; —characterizes; —congests; —contaminates; —conveys; —dries; —disseminates; —endangers.
(See spit.)

SPY
adjectives
true; prying; universal; omnipresent; unfortunate; jealous; traveling; clumsy; frail; involuntary.

SPY (v)
adverbs
pryingly; jealously; professionally; slyly; involuntarily; insidiously; unscrupulously; traitorously; treacherously; suspiciously; omnisciently; cautiously.
(See watch, search.)

SPYING
verbs
charge with—; cloak—; convict of—; detect—; deter—; disclose—; expose—; goad into—; harry—; mask—; penalize—; perpetrate—; reveal—; uncover—; —acquaints one with; —adorns; —betrays; —brands; —divulges; —enables; —informs; —intrigues; '—jeopardizes; —menaces; —reveals; —stigmatizes; —unveils.
(See curiosity, examination, search, discovery, scrutiny.)

SQUABBLE
adjectives
personal; contemptible; musty; money; petty; grudge; lulling; vulgar; miserable.

verbs
obviate—; arbitrate—; avert—; avoid—; check—; conclude—; curtail—; intervene in —; join in—; judge—; pacify—; precipitate —; preclude—; stage—; subdue—; terminate—; —breaches; —disconcerts; —embroils; —estranges; —expires; —fractures; —ill-becomes; —mars; —rages; —ruptures; —threatens; —vexes.
(See fight, quarrel, dispute.)

SQUAD
adjectives
trained; investigation; motorized; formidable; awkward; mustering; firing; death; narcotic.

verbs
augment—; bar from—; bolster—; captain —; caution—; condition—; disband—; dispatch—; enlarge—; flank—; limit—; maintain—; mobilize—; muster—; quarter—; reanimate—; regiment—; reinforce—; reinstate—; rejuvenate—; revamp (colloq.)—; —assembles; —demolishes; —disperses; —embarks; —huddles; —intrenches; —mobilizes; —patrols; —sallies forth; —s troop.
(See gang, band, group.)

SQUADRON
adjectives
outflanking; feinting; reconnoitering; rushing; prancing; blockading; retreating; magnificent; kindred; lucid; thundering; watchful; well-built: woven-winged; murderous.

SQUALID
adverbs
miserably; wretchedly; incredibly; impossibly; inexpressibly; utterly; pitiably; deplorably; lamentably; shamefully; unnecessarily; needlessly; grossly; terribly; horribly; hopelessly.

SQUALOR
verbs
abolish—; endure—; eradicate—; fester in —; purge—; thrive amidst—; —begrimes; —blots; —contaminates; —corrupts; —de-

bases; —defaces; —defiles; —emphasizes; —offends; —pollutes; —rankles; —reeks; —smothers; —sullies; —tarnishes.
(See dirt, filth, abomination.)

SQUANDER (v)
adverbs
recklessly; rashly; improvidently; liberally; royally; prodigiously; fantastically; wantonly.
(See waste, spend, expend.)

SQUARE
adjectives
quaint; open; desolate; inverse; drawling; fountained; principal; hollow; dusty; silent; diagonal; budding; conspicuous; perfect.

SQUAT (v)
adverbs
vulgarly; cozily; somnolently; pugnaciously; characteristically; habitually; complacently; threateningly.
(See corner, crouch.)

SQUATTERS
verbs
allure—; attract—; dislodge—; encourage —; evict—; invite—; tax—; tempt—; — abound; —claim; —colonize; —deprive; — domesticate; —encamp; —lease; —settle on; —tenant; —usurp.
(See denizen.)

SQUAWK (v)
adverbs
cacophonously; raucously; indignantly; hideously; persistently; plaintively; endurably.
(See squeal, yell.)

SQUEAK
adjectives
shrill; impassioned; high-pitched; serene; tiny; persistent; elusive.

SQUEAKY
adverbs
shrilly; comically; curiously; oddly; unfortunately; annoyingly; embarrassingly; vexatiously; alarmingly; ominously; unfortunately; unluckily; treacherously; dangerously; provokingly.

SQUEAL (v)
adverbs
piteously; shrilly; agonizingly; piercingly;

penetratingly; desolately; wrathfully; impassionedly.
(See cry, yell.)

SQUEAMISH
adverbs
unusually; delicately; extremely; terribly; prudishly; pretentiously; ostentatiously; presumably; notoriously; fastidiously; daintily; absurdly; comically; ridiculously; helplessly; disgustingly; overly; nervously.

SQUEEZE
adjectives
brotherly; mollifying; affectionate; hard; warm; tender.

SQUEEZE (v)
adverbs
imploringly; passionately; mollifyingly; affectionately; fraternally; warmly; tenderly; oppressively, impetuously.
(See compress, crowd.)

SQUINT (v)
adverbs
drolly; sinisterly; suspiciously; knowingly; penetratingly; affectedly; comically; threateningly.
(See wince, peer.)

SQUIRE
adjectives
stupid; rustic; ponderous; parliamentary; proper; blunt.

SQUIRREL
adjectives
flippant; tawny; watchful.

verbs
protect—s; tame—s; —barks; —burrows; —cracks; —curses; —darts; —digs; — dodges; —evades; —flirts its tail; —frolics; —gathers; —harvests; —hides; —jeers; — munches; —nibbles; —quivers; —scampers; —shies; —stores; —trembles; —whisks himself off.
(See animal, chipmunk.)

STAB
adjectives
adroit; bleeding; gashed; hateful; verbal.

verbs
deflect—; inflict—; —agonizes; —convulses; —despatches; —excruciates; —impales; —

inflames; —gushes; —gnaws; —lacerates; —penetrates; —perforates; —pierces; —punctures; —slays; —throbs; —twinges; —twitches.

(See wound.)

STAB (v)

adverbs

adroitly; fatally; dangerously; hideously; vindictively; passionately; treacherously.

(See pierce, thrust.)

STABILITY

adjectives

emotional; social; razor-keen; great; civic.

verbs

afford—; ascertain—; assure of—; attain—; cherish—; commend—; confirm—; destroy —; determine—; detract from—; endanger —; forfeit—; insure—; investigate—; jeopardize—; maintain—; measure—; necessitate—; nurture—; offer—; question—; reinforce—; restore—; retain—; secure—; sustain—; value—; wreck—; —hinges on; —insures; —ruffles; —totters; —wanes.

(See permanence, constancy, firmness, strength, steadiness.)

STABILIZE (v)

adverbs

economically; effectively; politically; democratically; emotionally; governmentally; legislatively; socially.

(See fix.)

STABLE

adverbs

reliably; dependably; fortunately; securely; safely; entirely; financially; emotionally; creditably; eminently; commercially; indestructibly; delightfully; supposedly; presumably; reputably; uncommonly; solidly.

STAFF
(cane)

verbs

arm with—; bear—; brandish—; cudgel with—; discard—; flourish—; flutter on—; relinquish—; shatter—; shoulder—; splinter —; surrender—; wield—; —bludgeons; —braces; —deflects; —sags; —supports; —sustains; —sways.

(See cane, baton, stick.)

STAFF
(general)

adjectives

knotted; managerial; faithful; official; efficient; consultant; inventive; research; energetic; intelligent; glittering.

STAFF
(personal)

verbs

appoint to—; augment—; clutter—; ·discharge—; employ—; evacuate—; inspect—; resign from—; recruit—; suspend from—; —surrenders.

(See personnel.)

STAFF (v)

adverbs

efficiently; faithfully; officially; scientifically; periodically; annually; seasonally.

(See support, provide.)

STAGE

adjectives

verdant; primitive; well-set; mental; commencing; formative; inglorious; momentous; incipient; successive (pl); veiled; obstructed; various (pl); miraculous; analytic; realistic; developmental; trembling; uncertain; restorative; early; domestic; infantile; tentative; rudimentary; middle; well-trod; experimental; indifferent; tragic; legitimate; explosive; worthier; hypothetical; pudding; condensed; baffling; intermediate; infectious; important; imperceptible; dilapidated; milky; maturing; initial; diminutive; perilous; naked; painful; buskined; regressive; embryonic; uncontrollable; usurped.

verbs

abandon—; advance—; cherish—; conceive —; connect—s; dedicate to—s; define—; desert—; destine for—; devote to—; elevate —; exalt—; extol—; forsake—; frisk onto —; glorify—; hoot off—; install—; perform —; prostitute—; quit—; relinquish—; renounce—; retire from—; set—; strut upon —; unsettle—; vindicate—; wed to—; —allures; —attracts; —debases; —entices; —fascinates; —immortalizes; —impassions; —notorizes; —seduces; —succeeds; —s unfold.

(See board, footlights, platform, theatre.)

STAGE (v)

adverbs

stupendously; spectacularly; awesomely; grandiosely; handsomely; dramatically.

(See produce, effect.)

STAGE-FRIGHT

verbs

afflict with—; induce—; intensify—; manifest—; quell—; smite with—; subdue—; suffer—; surmount—; vanquish—; —abates; —barbs; —chills; —consumes; —curdles; —disconcerts; —distresses; —harasses; —hounds; —irks; —nauseates; —overawes; —overcomes; —overwhelms; —plagues; —racks; —ruffles; —sickens; —tenses; —terrifies.

(See fright, fear, terror, nervousness.)

STAGEY

adverbs

absurdly; pretentiously; undisguisedly; outlandishly; transparently; ridiculously; obviously; fantastically; outrageously; flimsily; cheaply; manifestly; disagreeably; unpleasantly; undeniably; bombastically; pompously; laughably; patently.

STAGGER (v)

adverbs

intoxicatedly; weakly; clumsily; stumblingly; helplessly; blindly; faintingly.

(See reel, sway.)

STAGNANT

adverbs

hopelessly; unfortunately; putridly; pestiferously; dangerously; inexplicably; palpably; uselessly; completely; dully; carelessly; indifferently; stolidly; contentedly; lazily.

STAIN

adjectives

primal; perspiration; tender; cloudy; hot; tyrant; haunting; powder; indelible; imputed; crimson; inborn; ineradicable.

STAIRCASE

adjectives

labored; pinched; twisted; steep; monumental; marble; secret; palatial; principal; quaint; little; lofty; filthy; winding; mossy; graceful.

STAIRS

adjectives

broken; skatish; lazar; mountain; wooden; singing; cramped; dingy; ill-kept; cold; cheerless; rocking; interminable; dark; winding; discolored; spacious; polished; dim; tackled; corkscrew.

verbs

ascend—; avoid—; bear up—; blockade—; bolt down—; bounce down—; bound from —; clamber up—; clatter down—; climb—; descend—; design—; grope on—; guide down—; labor up—; limp up—; mount—; pause on—; scale—; scramble up—; scurry up—; skip up—; survey from—; tear up—; thrust down—; thunder down—; topple from —; totter on—; tumble from—; vault—; —creak; —diverge; —spiral; —wind.

(See ladder, step.)

STAKE

adjectives

black; windward; sharp-pointed; metal.

verbs

affix to—; avoid—; drive—; extract—; hitch to—; impale on—; implant—; moor to—; plant—; sink—; shackle to—; suspend from—; transfix to—; withdraw—; —directs; —fences; —guides; —indicates; —marks; —penetrates; —signalizes.

(See post.)

STALACTITES

verbs

—bracket; —dazzle; —derive from; —fashion; —gleam; —glitter; —glimmer; —incrust; —line; —ornament; —radiate; —spur; —stud; —suspend; —taper.

(See icicle.)

STALE

adverbs

uselessly; terribly; obviously; unluckily; alarmingly; indubitably; mustily; unprofitably; tastelessly; inexcusably; unacceptably; disgustingly; wearily; injuriously; unhealthfully; unwholesomely; unwarrantably; objectionably; disagreeably; unpleasantly.

STALENESS

verbs

bar—; estimate—; incur—; loathe—; resent —; resist—; —alters; —flattens; —prevails; —provokes; —offsets; —shames.

(See odor, stench, smell.)

adjectives
green; juicy; martial; tall; withered.

verbs
attach to—; cast away—; crush—; dry—;
gather—; pile—; shake—; sickle—; —
bears; —connects; —curves; —s elevate;
—juts; —protrudes; —rises; —springs; —
supports; —sways; —s tangle; —tapers; —
waves.
(See stem.)

STALK (*v*)
adverbs
dramatically; implacably; grimly; jauntily;
nonchalantly; haughtily; stealthily; martially; vigorously; triumphantly; swaggeringly.
(See stride, strut.)

STALWART
adverbs
sturdily; remarkably; huskily; resolutely;
valorously; intrepidly; trustworthily; amazingly; conspicuously; unusually; remarkably; marvelously; uncommonly; obviously;
vigorously; doggedly; splendidly; dependably; uncommonly; naturally; reliably.

STAMENS
verbs
bear—; examine—; form—; support—; —
burst; —cohere; —contain; —discharge;
—shed; —split open.

STAMINA
verbs
break—; calculate—; deteriorate in—; develop—; evince—; lack—; exhaust—; increase—; lower—; possess—; preserve—;
require—; restore—; supply—; test—; —
ebbs; —endures; —lessens; —mounts; —
resists; —succumbs; —wanes; —withstands.
(See strength, endurance.)

STAMMER (*v*)
adverbs
chokingly; inarticulately; laboriously; confusedly; hesitatingly; incoherently; timidly;
embarrassedly.
(See stumble, falter.)

STAMP
adjectives
broken; legal; indelible; legislative; witching; occasional; intellectual; unmistakable;
rubber.

verbs
affix—; attach—; bear—; collect--; design
—; display—; hammer—; impress—; issue
—; lick—; mark—; moisten—; pound—;
provide—; sponge—; —adheres; —attests;
—authorizes; —certifies; —s cover; —guarantees; —seals; —signifies; —sticks; —validates; —warrants.
(See label, mark, impression.)

STAMP (*v*)
adverbs
petulantly; angrily; indelibly; violently;
vigorously; viciously; ruthlessly; impotently; unmistakably; permanently.
(See imprint, impress.)

STANCH
adverbs
loyally; fearlessly; unwaveringly; steadily;
firmly; reliably; admirably; commendably;
laudably; unusually; marvelously; courageously; gallantly; intrepidly; valiantly; valorously; unexpectedly; enthusiastically; eagerly; earnestly; immovably.

STAND
adjectives
drowsy; desperate; stubborn; unalterable;
dimension; brutal; last; unflinching; lofty;
unequivocal; final; roadside; definite.

verbs
advocate—; appreciate—; criticize—; depend on—; drive from—; hold—; maintain
—; plan—; prepare for—; reiterate—; resist—; retain—; —annoys; —arrests; —
checks; —recoups; —refreshes; —repels.
(See position, opinion.)

STAND (*v*)
adverbs
preeminently; militantly; stalwartly; indubitably; obediently; squarely; habitually; tremulously; haughtily; forlornly; conspicuously; precariously; courageously; picturesquely; valiantly; meekly; irresolutely; ostentatiously; sullenly; boldly; perilously; wistfully; unfalteringly; erectly.
(See endure, bear.)

STANDARD
adjectives
critical; ethical; altered; accepted; zoned;
inherent; abstract; superior; dingy; infallible; artistic; accursed; unrivaled; barbarian; highest; hackneyed; crafty; persistent;

quantitative; capricious; moral; minimum; tentative; legal; well-defined; average; ordinary; tattered; acknowledged; shadowy; unconscious; secular; ponderous; proud; lofty; prospective; artificial; dietary; unhonored; exacting; rigorous; tangible; intellectual; inflexible; journalistic; accessible; rising; rigid; incontestable; single; recognized; unimpeachable; complaisant; conventional.

verbs

accept—; adopt—; advance—; apply—; attain—; conform—; desert—; deviate from —; elevate—; establish—; degrade—; formulate—; frame—; improve—; indoctrinate —; judge—; lift to—; lower—; maintain—; measure up to—; obtain—; prescribe—; preserve—; raise—; rally to—; reconcile—; record—; represent—; require—; serve—; set—; unfurl—; uplift—; violate—; —s collapse; —s conform; —s dictate; —s melt away; —prevails; —reflects.

(See flag, ideal.)

STANDARDIZATION

verbs

adopt—; advocate—; apply—; approve—; assume—; demand—; devise—; encourage —; examine—; formulate—; necessitate—; overcome—; perfect—; promise—; —insures; —progresses; —rears.

(See system.)

STANDING

adjectives

scholastic; better; scientific; legal; worldwide; logical; amateur; requisite; social.

verbs

aspire to—; better—; command—; confine —; create—; declare—; elevate—; esteem —; exceed in—; favor—; grade—; honor —; inquire as to—; judge—; reckon—; regain—; respect—; threaten—.

(See position, reputation, status.)

STANDPOINT

adjectives

elementary; artistic; favorable; psychoanalytic; outside; critical; prejudiced; academic; anagogic; decorative; practical; pagan; unbiased.

verbs

adopt—; alter—; assume—; compare—; contemplate—; criticize—; direct—; insure

—; interpret—; maintain—; measure—; move—; occupy—; regard—; sanction—; select—; shake—; view from—; —affords; —contents.

(See view, position, conception.)

STANZA

adjectives

elegiac; quaint; complicated; pious; long; staccato; unrhyming; experimental; sweeping.

STAR
(*actor*)

verbs

abuse—; admire—; advertise—; celebrate —; credit—; direct—; discover—; distinguish—; glimpse—; glorify—; groom—; hail—; highlight—; interview—; laud—; mob—; present—; publicize—; uncover—; —appears; —attracts; —delights; —interprets; —performs; —portrays; —thrills; —triumphs.

(See hero, actor, artist.)

STAR
(*celestial*)

verbs

discern—; —appears; —beams; —dims; —s flee; —gleams; —glitters; —guides; —hangs; —kindles; —lingers; —s perform; —plumes; —s reign; —s revolve; —s shed radiance; —spangles; —s unfold; —s wander; —s wane.

(See sun.)

STAR
(*general*)

adjectives

celestial; sanguine; mightiest; innumerable (pl); unsetting; evening; air-dissolved; bright; unchanging; ever-burning; polar; gold; glistening; innocent; scattered (pl); literal; happy; glory-beaming; sparkling; luckiest; tenderer; blinking; wide; pink; shy; waking; charitable; blazing; soaring; scintillating; dynastic; solemn; guiding; keen; fixed; remote; fiery; consenting; swart; panting; periodical; tremulous; folding; occulted; azure; guardian; teeming (pl); fragrant; ushering; brooding; meliorating; vagabond; mighty; deathless; wizard; wild; dying; friendly; summer; equidistant; secret; dumb: twinkling; unfinished; vanished; intense; steadfast; burning; patient; watery; pendulous; sentinel; rushing; solitary; dependent; baneful; wheeling; glancing; lurid; bright; downcast; tranquil; solid; winking; sliding; clear; intimate; obscure; gaudy; actual; moist; melancholy; declining; luminous; alien; beamless; prickly; pilot; budding; imperial; favorable; unanchored; cooperative; untroubled; lonely; elderly; newest; white; splendor-winged; utmost; journeying; attending; remorseless; truer; tyrant; palpitating; unstable; fortunate; sinking.

STARCH
verbs
apply—; convert—; dip into—; immerse in —; lose—; object to—; prepare—; remove —; store up—; —finishes; —galls; — hardens; —irritates; —stiffens.
(See food, constituent, carbohydrate.)

STARE
adjectives
studious; dull; stupid; algid; defiant; disfigured; glassy; fascinated; hostile; audible; vacant; grave; angry; meditative; absentminded; sidelong; frigid; concentrated; appraising; unwinking; gloomy; fixed; dreamy; long; admiring; wondering; irreverent; stony; maniac; noncommittal; disgusted; spectral; superior; wild; bemused; questioning; hesitating; incredulous; hungry; sullen; limpid; owlish; insolent; unmitigated; oily; fascinated; solemn; wide-eyed.

verbs
blanket—; comprehend—; cast—; fix—; note —; prolong—; transfer—; —absorbs; —arouses; —astonishes; —excites; —irritates; —provokes; —startles.
(See look.)

STARE (v)
adverbs
impudently; fixedly; sullenly; persistently; solemnly; abstractedly; impassively; hypnotically; perplexedly; obtrusively; moodily; hostilely; arrogantly; apathetically; incredulously; fixedly; truculently; speculatively; insolently; fascinatedly; morbidly; rudely; vacantly.
(See look, gaze.)

STARLIGHT
adjectives
glittering; cool; boundless; glorious; pale; bright; shining; wondrous; magic; romantic.

verbs
be wrought by—; emerge from—; exhibit —; reveal—; shed—; view—; —appears; —awes; —cheers; —comforts; —creeps; — dimples; —embraces; —frames; —glitters; —guides; —scatters; —spangles; —splits; —unfolds; —works.
(See light, star.)

STARLING
verbs
introduce—; naturalize—; rid of—s; —s blot out; —s damage; —dives; —s feast on; —passes over; —quarters; —robs; —thrives.
(See bird.)

STARRY
adverbs
luminously; brilliantly; luckily; fortunately; unusually; brightly; helpfully; romantically; desirably; providentially; auspiciously; remarkably; amazingly.

START
adjectives
theatrical; undisguised; palpable; rheumatic; infinite; hopeful; reluctant; convulsive; guilty; running; involuntary; troubled; vigorous; tremulous; slight; longing; answering; painful; terrified; sudden; fitful.

START (v)
adverbs
violently; precipitately; perceptibly; distractedly; simultaneously; impetuously; reluctantly; jauntily; involuntarily; tremulously; fitfully.
(See embark, launch.)

STARTLE (v)
adverbs
inexpressibly; abruptly; playfully; ludicrously; stupidly; repeatedly.
(See scare, surprise.)

STARTLING
adverbs
unbelievably; unusually; utterly; alarmingly; extremely; unpleasantly; suddenly; strangely; curiously; disconcertingly; painfully; terribly; dreadfully; fearfully; tremendously; remarkably; singularly; oddly; appallingly; disturbingly; unexpectedly; disagreeably; peculiarly.

adjectives
absolute; oxygen; bitter; aesthetic; mental; cruel; slow.

verbs
alleviate—; avoid—; brave—; conceal—; endure—; face with—; hide—; influence—; perish by—; produce—; overcome—; reduce —; reveal—; stave off—; subject to—; — burdens; —devastates; —stalks; —threatens; —victimizes; —weakens.
(See hunger, suffering, need, death.)

STARVE (v)
adverbs
deliberately; cruelly; pennilessly; genteelly; parsimoniously; penuriously; niggardly; mentally; gradually; agonizingly; ceaselessly; miserably.
(See weaken.)

STATE
(condition)
verbs
aggravate—; allay—; alleviate—; arrest—; assuage—; attribute—; breed—; cloak—; comprehend—; conceal—; condemn—; ease —; establish—; excite—; expose—; induce —; intensify—; palliate—; prolong—; relieve—; restore—; resuscitate—; reveal—; revive—; screen—; shroud—.
(See condition, predicament, plight.)

STATE
(general)
adjectives
happy; unpropitious; deplorable; ordered; hopeful; kingly; humble; healthy; wandering; transitional; insipid; distended; totalitarian; bastard; sepulchral; disordered; throned; altered; lamentable; turbulent; dropsical; political; fossil; semi-conscious; feverish; frenzied; blissful; burdened; needful; pathetic; flourishing; honorable; excessive; deplorable; slovenly; anterior; cramped; crude; relaxed; supernal; deluded; spirited; ecstatic; variable (pl); dejected; inarticulate; primitive; impressible; autonomous; surrounding; morbid; feeble; former; dilapidated; democratic; semi-liquid; peaceful; enlightened; industrious; homogeneous; populated; tangled; emotional; authoritative; opulent; neurotic; compound; deliberate; existing; destitute; well-settled; semisavage; impressible; comatose; depressed; corresponding; ordered; indissoluble; dread-

ful; bedraggled; retired; bulwarked; infant; transitional; social; primordial; slow; undetermined; scrambled; unsteadfast; neutral; passionless; dormant; exalted; perpetual; stronger; neutral; anomalous; unravaged; decapitated; unpleasant; knotted; unassailable; embryonic; conflicting; solitary; regal; stoic; vacillating; unique; frail; loose; electrical; quiescent; unwonted; melancholy; miserable; joyless; alarming; wretched; troubled; fair; outcast; forlorn; self-governing; distracted; dissolved; candid; enfeebled; pitiful; rebellious; palmy; coward; rapid; disadvantageous; natural; joyful; stable; budding; unwelcome; savage; apparent; enviable; desirable.

STATE
(political)
verbs
ally with—; annex—; bow to—; carve out —; dominate—; empower—; encroach upon —; enslave—; evacuate—; exalt—; forfeit to—; found—; industrialize—; infringe upon—; invade—; partition—; quell—; reduce—; subdue—; subjugate—; unite—; vanquish—; weld—; yield to—; —administers; —appropriates; —domiciles; —exercises; —s federate; —maintains; —persecutes; —racks with; —requisitions; — tramples; —tyrannizes; —wields.
(See empire, commonwealth, republic, country, nation.)

STATE (v)
adverbs
parenthetically; succinctly; tersely; concisely; impressively; broadly; specifically; metaphorically; authoritatively; emphatically; laconically; explicitly; solemnly; officially; substantially; tranquilly.
(See say, affirm, declare.)

STATELY
adverbs
becomingly; unusually; habitually; naturally; inherently; attractively; beautifully; proudly; regally; royally; majestically; magnificently; splendidly; appropriately; pompously; ceremoniously; gravely; properly; graciously; impressively.

STATEMENT
adjectives
misleading; big; hurtful; irrefutable; preceding; explicit; souring; terse; emphatic; fallacious; sententious; itemized; facetious;

contradictory; lucid; cardinal; unproved; colorless; written; definite; ineradicable; judicious; conflicting; defamatory; comparative; quaint; admirable; humorous; adroit; confident; intelligible; inaccurate; conservative; groundless; naked; specious; plausible; previous; remarkable; uncompromising; hazardous; ridiculous; penetrating; accompanying; publicized; distorted; oracular; attributive; precise; ingenuous; comprehensive; sensible; trifle-sounding; absurd; startling; hyperbolical; vague; foregoing; elucidated; derogatory; fervid; immortal; amazing; reiterated; graphic; detailed; articulate; erroneous; periphrastic; sweeping; dogmatic; positive; direct; superfluous; candid; authoritative; substantial.

verbs
allude to—; alter—; amplify—; base—on; bolster—; buttress—; certify to—; cite—; compile—; contradict—; controvert—; convey—; correlate—; dig up—; discredit—; draft—; edit—; elaborate—; elicit—; evade —; exaggerate—; extract—; fling out—; follow up—; heed—; impugn—; infer from —; issue—; label—; misquote—; modify—; qualify—; quote—; reiterate—; rest upon—; subsidize—; transmit—; unravel—; utter—; verify—; weigh—; —challenges; —depresses; —discloses; —implies; —jars; — justifies.
(See allegation, assertion, declaration, expression, remark.)

STATESMAN
adjectives
influential; sagacious; unhackneyed; darksome; bold; eminent; contending; practised; astute; senile; distinguished; wary; brash; far-seeing; liberal; haughty; dogmatic; brilliant; deft.

verbs
acclaim—; commemorate—; honor—; laud —; —arbitrates; —confers; —contracts; — counsels; —directs; —emancipates; —elevates; —executes; —exhorts; —formulates; —forges; —furthers; —governs; —guides; —helms; —manipulates; —negotiates; — steers; —struggles; —takes over; —transacts; —uplifts.
(See diplomat, legislator, ambassador, statesmanship.)

STATESMANSHIP
adjectives
businesslike; perjured; treacherous; inade-

quate; clear-sighted; far-seeing; conservative; pitiful.

verbs
acclaim—; cloak in—; demonstrate—; discern—; employ—; endow with—; exercise —; —alleviates; —averts; —dodges; — eases tension; —extricates; —flounders; — lightens; —machinates; —maneuvers; — pilots; —smooths; —steers; —unravels.
(See statesman, diplomacy, management.)

STATION
adjectives
enviable; desolate; supernatural; allotted; recruiting; way; unmoving; equivocal; biological; unshrinking; elevated; responsible; dust-driven; distributing; intermediate; fragile; conspicuous; meteorological; dingy; smoky; native; low; service; future; passenger; retreading; control; prostrate; dinky.

verbs
accumulate at—; confine to—; deposit at—; maintain—; remain at—; trundle to—; wait at—; —distributes; —quarters.
(See place, post, location.)

STATION (*v*)
adverbs
ingeniously; elevatedly; conspicuously; intermittently; frequently; advantageously.
(See post, place.)

STATIONARY
adverbs
mysteriously; alarmingly; bewilderingly; apparently; deliberately; helpfully; significantly; curiously; evidently.

STATISTICS
adjectives
complex; staple; stupendous; controversial; appalling; cold; official; available; accurate; scanty; untrustworthy; glowing; devastating; remarkable; pitiless; convincing; definite.

verbs
combine—; compile—; dig into—; eschew —; marshal—; plow through—; quote—; — arm; —bury under; —demonstrate; —dis-

close; —embrace; —hammer; —substantiate; —support; —terrify; —unleash; —verify.

(See list, information, book, knowledge.)

STATUE

adjectives
gigantic; plaster; impulsive; urgent; sepulchral; sylvan; portrait; earthen; colossal; symbolic; charming; strict; grotesque; memorial; emblematic; insignificant; mutilated; grave; multi-farious (pl); magic; marble; rigorous; dominating; painted.

verbs
carve—; cast—; chisel—; disrobe—; erect —; exhibit—; hew—; inscribe on—; model —; mould—; mount—; mutilate—; perch on—; prize—; prop—; shatter—; straddle —; topple—; unveil—; value—; —adorns; —commemorates; —depicts; —embellishes; —honors; —illustrates; —portrays; —symbolizes.

(See figure, masterpiece, monument, plaque.)

STATURE

adjectives
intellectual; veritable; simulated; commanding; mental; physical; moral; unusual; frail; gigantic; diminutive; stately; proud; dilating; slender; apparent; middle; financial; intellectual; political; herculean; unusual; exceptional; colossal; tall.

verbs
achieve—; alter—; attain—; augment—; check—; determine—; exalt—; extend—; heighten—; lack—; limit—; magnify—; measure—; stunt—; surpass in—; —bulks; —dwindles; —looms; —overawes; —towers.

(See height, growth, development.)

STATUS

adjectives
recognized; financial; front-rank; primitive; honorific; present; moral; usual; definite.

verbs
abandon—; acquire—; alter—; approve—; ascertain—; assume—; attack—; attain—; confuse—; corrupt—; defend—; define—; degrade—; designate—; detect—; determine —; dignify—; discredit—; elevate—; ennoble—; exalt—; forfeit—; glorify—; grant —; humble—; improve upon—; impugn—; insure—; investigate—; maintain—; merit

—; recover—; relinquish—; restore—; resurrect—; retain—; revolutionize—; suspend—; sustain—; taint—.

(See position, standing, state, condition.)

STATUTE

adjectives
penal; contravened; dead; oppressive; protective; unfair; age-old; unenforced; heartless; unjustifiable.

verbs
advocate—; abolish—; abrogate—; annul—; codify—; comply with—; countermand—; decry—; denounce—; discard—; doom—; enact—; enforce—; evade—; flout—; formulate—; frame—; ignore—; infringe—; invoke—; nullify—; observe—; ratify—; repeal—; retract—; transgress—; uphold—; veto—; violate—; void—; —annuls; —authorizes; —bans; —bars; —classifies; —decrees; —delegates; —enlightens; —empowers; —establishes; —exists; —legalizes; —limits; —prescribes; —prohibits; —provides.

(See law, legislation.)

STATUTORY

adverbs
impressively; inescapably; recently; unfortunately; luckily; inflexibly; vexatiously; curiously; wisely.

STAY

adjectives
fruitless; protracted; transient; pertinacious; subsequent; laggard; unprofitable; prolonged; tremulous; short; pleasant; amusing; lengthy.

verbs
abandon—; anticipate—; conclude—; discontinue—; enforce—; extend—; grant—; interrupt—; plead for—; press for—; prolong—; protract—; resume—; terminate—; welcome—; —defers; —elapses; —expires; —relaxes; —reprieves; —retards; —wanes.

(See stand, support.)

STAY (v)

adverbs
unobtrusively; adamantly; stubbornly; miraculously; traditionally; customarily; habitually; perpetually; temporarily; fruitlessly; protractedly; transiently; briefly; pertinaciously.

(See remain, lodge.)

STEADFAST

adverbs

loyally; dutifully; affectionately; properly; dependably; reliably; faithfully; eagerly; enthusiastically; zealously; filially; lovingly; fondly; piously; fervently; ardently; unwaveringly; curiously; remarkably; utterly.

STEAL (v)

adverbs

furtively; craftily; slyly; insidiously; basely; covertly; subtly; discreetly; mercilessly; noiselessly; jealously; suspiciously; ominously.

(See rob, plunder.)

STEALING

verbs

charge with—; convict of—; deplore—; disclose—; forsake—; indict for—; penalize—; practise—; rebuke for—; reduce to—; relinquish—; renounce—; reproach for—; resort to—; reveal—; scorn—; —defiles; —degrades; —deprives; —dishonors.

(See theft.)

STEALTHY

adverbs

guiltily; necessarily; warily; unusually; suspiciously; extraordinarily; remarkably; mischievously; furtively; carefully; naturally; uncommonly; craftily; cleverly; adroitly; mysteriously; cautiously; suspiciously; gingerly.

STEAM

adjectives

corrosive; scalding; fainting; sanguine; oppressive; exhaust; unsavory; poisonous; fragrant; spouting; hot; stinking; hissing; rich.

verbs

compress—; gauge—; generate—; harness—; inhale—; meter—; spew—; spout—; spray—; vent—; —befogs; —bursts; —clouds, —condenses; —drenches; —forces; —jets; —mists; —moistens; —obscures; —propels; —scalds; —wilts.

(See mist, spray, smoke.)

STEAMER

adjectives

charter; borrowed; prosaic; boarded; tramp; coastwise; filibustering; delinquent; lazy; dismantled; ocean; sumptuous; elegant; warping.

verbs

convoy—; launch—; —circumnavigates; —ferries; —glides; —hauls; —maneuvers; —plies; —rolls; —rots; —rusts; —speeds; —transports.

(See boat, launch, motor-boat, ship.)

STEAM-SHOVEL

verbs

—batters; —burrows; —s clank; —deepens; —devours; —discloses; —effaces; —erases; —excavates; —facilitates; —gorges; —gnaws at; —gulps; —hollows; —levels; —ravages; —swallows; —trenches; —unearths.

STEED

adjectives

bounding; angular; proud; fiery; flying; dashing; ribbed; unmanageable; mangy; fine-limbed; snowy; mercurial; heavenly; resistless; prancing; border; mottled; fire-breathing; well-proportioned; riderless; reinless; strong; livid; headstrong; frantic; smoking; noble; mighty; shadowy; aerial; stalwart; spirited; wild.

STEEL

adjectives

vengeful; ingot; thrusting; rushing; coarse; thin; nervous; well-tempered; field; jagged; massive; gleaming; shrewd; scorching; mirroring; unpolished; toughened; incomplete; brandished; lateral; carbonized; flashing; molten; crashing; fiery; roweled.

verbs

alloy—; analyze—; cast—; clash against—; compound—; convert into—; deoxidize—; desulphurize—; encase in—; forge—; frame with—; ladle—; lathe—; magnetize—; melt—; mold—; polish—; process—; purify—; roll—; smelt—; tap—; temper—; test—; weld—; —armors; —congeals; —corrodes; —decomposes; —deflects; —oxidizes; —reinforces; —resists; —transmits.

(See iron, lead, metal.)

STEEP

adverbs

precipitously; alarmingly; impossibly; startlingly; unexpectedly; perilously; hazardously; suddenly; starkly; abruptly; unreasonably; excessively; remarkably; incalculably;

inaccessibly; boldly; exorbitantly; extravagantly; unwarrantably; unreasonably; painfully; formidably; forbiddingly; curiously; particularly; immoderately.

STEEPNESS
verbs
bolt—; cap—; culminate—; elevate—; exaggerate—; mount—; surmount—; —declines; —exalts; —impresses; —inspires; —looms; —overwhelms; —soars; —towers.
(See height, altitude.)

STEER (v)
adverbs
erratically; unerringly; dexterously; deftly; skillfully; cautiously; accurately; conscientiously.
(See control, guide.)

STEM
adjectives
enchanted; deathless; gnarled; immovable; tapering; supple; tough; knotted; fibrous; apparent; sacred; insignificant; succulent; climbing; nourishing; straggling; fan-edged; fruitless; slender; bending.

verbs
clasp—; crop—; ground—; heighten—; hinge on—; level—; pivot on—; pluck from —; snip—; spring from—; sway on—; —curves; —extends; —forks; —rises; —supports; —sustains.
(See stalk.)

STENCH
adjectives
noisome; fetid; obscene; horrible; nasty; intolerable; nauseating.

verbs
cast—; diffuse—; emit—; inhale—; —assails; —clings; —contaminates; —corrupts; —defiles; —galls; —lingers; —nauseates; —offends; —overcomes; —overwhelms; —penetrates; —pervades; —pollutes; —reeks; —sickens; —taints; —thickens; —turns.
(See odor, smell, staleness.)

STEP
adjectives
decisive; quickened; radical; important; imperious; weary; restless; tremulous; painful;

pilgrim; homeless; elastic; impudent; lascivious; desperate; fainting; toiling; firm; unfaltering; cautious; single; false; dragging; light; fleet; ungainly; rugged; swinging; uncertain; innumerable; listless; fearless; certain; tottering; rapid; mincing; echoless; zigzag; winding; incomprehensible; successive; witching; assured; gradual; vast; desirable; inadvertent; laggard; graceful; stately; devious; backward; conquering; unpracticed; uneven; timid; reeling; feeble; dictating; trembling; buoyant; practicable; pregnant; irrevocable; gigantic; grassy; drastic; vacillating; sagging; suspended; joyful; dignified; requisite; sedative; long; slow; concluding; still; instinctive; honest; resounding; slackened; furtive; ponderous; social; doubtful; disordered; inevitable; slippery; military; languid; reluctant; ample; rustic; rude; parting; shuffled; hospitable; crunching; boundless; measurable; precautionary; gentle; weak; flagging; rosy; stone; jerky; comely; confident; hasty; gradual; immense; unhurrying; beehived; springy; homeward; irreverent; hushed; decorous; constructive; haughty; threatening; stealthy; undeviating; indispensable; silken; wandering; logical; subsequent; dainty; hazardous; momentous; bold; panting; finite; erratic; deft; noiseless; palsied; tottering; impious; soldierly; intermediate; martial; disspirited; stiff.

verbs
acclaim—; advance—; advocate—; applaud —; appraise—; approve—; ascend—; avert —; comprehend—; contrive—; defend—; design—; devise—; frame—; graduate—; lay out—; loll on—; lumber up—; map out —s; mount—; ooze down—s; plan—; reconsider—; regard—; regret—; retrace—s; rue —; scale—s; slant down—; slip down—s; steal down—s; survey—; systematize—; toil up—; trip down—; urge—; weigh—; —commences; —intrudes; —retreats; —s retrograde.
(See ladder, stairs, footstep, advance.)

STEP (v)
adverbs
discreetly; mincingly; awkwardly; clumsily; boldly; gingerly; defiantly; noiselessly; deliberately; resolutely; reluctantly; majestically; fearlessly; shufflingly; stealthily.
(See stride, pace.)

STERILE

adverbs
safely; securely; absolutely; warrantably; completely; assuredly; protectively; supposedly; presumably; carefully.

STERILITY

adjectives
general; panting; superficial; artistic; painful; shamed.

verbs
advocate—; bewail—; decry—; determine —; induce—; produce—; —annuls; —blasts; —blights; —dashes; —deprives; —devitalizes; —disconcerts; —emasculates; —frustrates; —nullifies; —thwarts.
(See weakness, fatigue.)

STERN

adverbs
gravely; puritanically; rigorously; uncompromisingly; inflexibly; unsparingly; arbitrarily; imperiously; severely; tyrannically; brutally; odiously; atrociously; needlessly; intolerably; senselessly; unreasonably; properly; necessarily.

STERNNESS

adjectives
strange; awful; considerable; unwonted; black; meaningful; frowning.

STEW

adjectives
hot; sickly; peppered; savory-looking; terrible.

verbs
bolt—; brew—; compound—; concoct—; dispatch—; fare on—; gulp—; prepare—; relish—; savor—; season—; sniff—; swill—; —blisters; —quells; —satiates; —seethes; —simmers; —slakes; —whets.
(See meat, food.)

STICK

adjectives
dead-brown; gnarled; knobbed; thick; knotted; sturdy; twisted; pointed.

verbs
arm with—; bear—; belabor with—; brandish—; deflect with—; fling—; flog with—; flourish—; goad with—; hurl—; prop on—; repulse with—; splinter—; thrash with—; thrust—; thwack with—; twirl—; wave—; whack with—; whittle—; —coerces; —intimidates; —supports; —sustains.
(See cane, baton, club.)

STICK (v)

adverbs
tenaciously; manfully; faithfully; firmly; adhesively; sturdily; jealously.
(See jab, stab.)

STICKY

adverbs
unaccountably; perniciously; inconveniently; unpleasantly; disagreeably; terribly; unexpectedly; hatefully; inexcusably; carelessly; messily; unfortunately; handily; usefully; serviceably; properly; suitably; adaptably; amazingly; dependably; insufficiently.

STIGMA

adjectives
infernal; irredeemable; lifelong; viscid; social; scandalous.

verbs
abolish—; bear—; destroy—; efface—; endure—; eradicate—; escape—; extricate—; incur—; inveigh against—; nullify—; purge of—; shun—; suffer—; tolerate—; vindicate of—; wipe out—; —aggravates; —brands; —clings; —defames; —detracts from; —humiliates; —marks; —ostracizes; —reflects upon; —sullies; —taints; —traduces; —defiles.
(See disgrace, dishonor.)

STILETTO

verbs
bury—; edge—; extract—; fling—; hilt—; hurl—; impale on—; plunge—; sheathe—; withdraw--; —s clash; —cleaves; —gashes; —lacerates; —penetrates; —perforates; —pierces; —pricks; —punctures; —rends; —severs; —slashes; —slits; —sunders.
(See knife.)

STILL

adverbs
alarmingly; desolately; lonesomely; absolutely; strangely; peculiarly; curiously; oddly; gruesomely; pleasantly; comfortably; serenely; calmly; refreshingly; appropriately; happily; contentedly; peacefully; suddenly; unaccountably; exceptionally; unusually; remarkably; amazingly; mysteriously; significantly; appallingly.

adjectives

comparative; monastic; prolonged; modest; gloomy; hideous; solemn; earnest; ominous; deathly; profound; appalling; majestic; deepest; utter; glittering; sepulchral; ghostly; unearthly; weird; succeeding; sullen; soft; rural; reverential; curtained; outdoor; sacred; abysmal; intense; fetid; prevailing; suffocating; sabbatical; willful; pensive; deep; black; obstinate; sunny; absolute; audible; dreaming; unwonted; midnight; hushed; awed.

verbs

break—; cherish—; endure—; murmur in—; penetrate—; permeate—; perpetuate—; pervade—; prolong—; rend—; resound in—; ruffle—; shatter—; shroud in—; —calms; —dejects; —depresses; —envelops; —grips; —haunts; —pervades; —reigns; —soothes; —stifles; —sulks; —unnerves.

(See calm, hush, silence.)

STILTED

adverbs

formally; uncomfortably; uneasily; stupidly; ineptly; unfortunately; curiously; crudely; awkwardly; terribly; nervously; gracelessly; pretentiously; absurdly; fantastically; outlandishly; bombastically; bashfully; inexpertly; grossly; unwontedly; unreasonably.

STIMULANT

adjectives

active; overpowering; mental; excellent; strange; intoxicating; favorite; necessary; helpful.

verbs

abstain from—; addict to—; administer—; avoid—; dilute—; impart—; indulge in—; infuse—; inject—; introduce—; prescribe—; require—; —agitates; —buoys; —compresses; —electrifies; —enkindles; —excites; —flushes; —galvanizes; —impassions; —inflames; —intoxicates; —provokes; —quickens; —reanimates; —rejuvenates; —rekindles; —revives; —shocks.

(See coffee, tonic, medicine, alcohol, whiskey.)

STIMULATE (v)

adverbs

lasciviously; artificially; alcoholically; electrically; simultaneously; instantaneously; erotically; refreshingly; injuriously; healthfully; beneficially; perniciously; agreeably; languidly; morbidly; sexually; psychologically.

(See incite, excite.)

STIMULATION

adjectives

sensory; self-satisfying; unnatural; psychological; sexual; useless; painful; gentle.

verbs

acquire—; afford—; convey—; derive—; furnish—; impart—; indulge in—; offer—; provide—; resist—; supply—; yield to—; —accelerates; —overexerts; —quickens; —subsides.

(See excitement, exhilaration.)

STIMULUS

adjectives

temporary; peculiar; reviving; new; sufficient; provocative; external; intellectual; immense; artificial; natural; native; unsound; keen; biting; sharp.

verbs

add—; afford—; apply—; balance—; furnish—; gain—; implant—; lessen—; react to—; reduce—; respond to—; want—; —allures; —assails; —baits; —declines; —diminishes; —incites; —induces; —produces; —recedes; —responds; —survives; —tempts; —wanes.

(See impetus, inducement, incentive.)

STING

adjectives

momentary; jealous; sudden; unworthy; painful; galling; rancorous; brutish; fiery; myriad; careless; venomous.

verbs

allay—; alleviate—; escape—; inflict—; mitigate—; palliate—; relieve—; salve—; treat—; wince at—; —envenoms; —incenses; —inflames; —irritates; —lancinates; —nettles; —perforates; —piques; —poisons; —pricks; —punctures; —rends; —tingles.

(See bite.)

STINK

verbs

(See stench.)

adverbs

parsimoniously; fanatically; meanly; niggardly; selfishly; scandalously; unwontedly.
  (See limit, restrain.)

STIPULATE (v)

adverbs

solemnly; financially; specifically; shrewdly; generally; minutely.
  (See agree, state.)

STIR

adjectives

fluttering; quick; multitudinous; tremulous; nervous; gentle; tremendous; angry; noiseless; pleasant; enormous; ceaseless; restless; subdued; faint; considerable; unnoticed.

verbs

agitate—; brook—; create—; embroil in—; endure—; quash—; quell—; restrain—; subdue—; suppress—; tolerate—; —bustles; —convulses; —disconcerts; —disquiets; —distracts; —diverts; —ebbs; —excites; —intensifies; —persists: —perturbs; —sharpens; —subsides.
  (See commotion, agitation, movement, activity.)

STIR (v)

adverbs

contentiously; frantically; emotionally; spiritually; imperceptibly; profoundly; incessantly; restively; caressingly; tremulously; ceaselessly; agitatedly.
  (See move, arouse, rouse.)

STIRRUPS

verbs

adjust—; discard—; loll on—; maintain—; mount by—; polish—; post on—; reinforce —; rise in—; slip from—; stand up in—; strain—; suspend—; weaken—; —afford; —bear; —brace; —dangle; —enable; —gird; —hang; —receive; —relieve; —support; —sustain.

STITCH (v)

adverbs

patiently; diligently; dexterously; cleverly; ceaselessly; indefatigably; industriously; skillfully.
  (See sew, fasten.)

verbs

alternate—; bias—; dissolve—; interlace—; interlink—; rend—; unravel—; —baste; —bind; —conjoin; —fuse; —hem; —insure; —knit; —reinforce; —restrain; —seal; —save; —tack; —unite.

STOCK
(finance)

verbs

bear—; bull—; burden with—; certify—; counterfeit—; dabble in—; devaluate—; dispose of—; dump—; inflate—; invest in—; issue—; juggle—; liquidate—; market—; recommend—; renew—; retain—; relinquish —; speculate with—; stabilize—; traffic in —; unload—; —ascends; —booms; —crashes; —dwindles; —fluctuates; —impoverishes; —oscillates; —skyrockets (colloq.); —soars; —toboggans; —vacillates.
  (See business, investment, capital, thermometer, barometer, shares.)

STOCK
(general)

adjectives

chitinous; parent; diversified; rejuvenated; calcareous; gilt-edged; inferior; reputable; revolutionary; rolling; suspicious; peaceful; heterogeneous; degenerate; serious; enormous; linguistic; inclusive; parish; tremendous; replaceable; sapling; surplus; extensive; common; fine; venturesome; pioneer; deficient; pathetic; ranging; selected; wild.

STOCKING

adjectives

foul; prosaic; merino; silk; wool; rayon; cotton; webbed; coarse; rough; rubber; wrinkled; rolled.

STOCKY

adverbs

sturdily; huskily; stalwartly; thickly; exceptionally; remarkably; distinctly; peculiarly; unusually; noticeably; unforgettably; chubbily; brawnily.

STOICAL

adverbs

marvellously; naturally; philosophically; courageously; intrepidly; calmly; serenely; valiantly; inflexibly; patiently; coolly; imperturbably; immovably; resolutely; exceptionally.

adverbs

strangely; dully; apathetically; singularly; oddly; curiously; unaccountably; inscrutably; irritatingly; vexatiously; shockingly; callously; abysmally; hopelessly; inexplicably; incurably.

adjectives

tripartite; grateful; excellent; heroic; distended; empty; lean; outraged; unbounded; queasy; nervous; upset; hollow; bulging; protruding.

verbs

abuse—; alkalize—; constrict—; cramp —; derange—; dilate—; displace—; distend—; drain—; empty—; flood—; incise—; irritate—; knead—; lodge in—; offend—; overload—; pump from—; purge —; reduce—; remove from—; scald—; sour —; strangulate—; turn—; upset—; wash out —; —assimilates; —converts; —distresses; —excretes; —falls; —houses; —prolapses; —protests; —reduces; —regurgitates; —retains; —revolts; —shrinks; —turns.

adjectives

mossy; sacrificial; senseless; heavy; ragged; jagged; votive; pallid; timeworn; graven; veritable; ribbed; crumbling; moldering; ancient; crystal; shattered; stumbling; quarried; flying; wrought; misshapen; scarlet; flawless; contumelious; cold; miry; typical; sizzling; destructive; corresponding; hollow; coarse; lithographic; sun-heated; precious; dangerous; showering; blasted; unpolished; barren; silent; greasy; monumental; enameled; uneven; rifted; breathing; bruising; solemn; rigid; massive; splintered; nameless; smoldered; chiseled; perfect; priceless.

verbs

carve in—; cast in—; chisel in—; dislodge —; face—; fashion of—; heave—; hew from—; hurl—; inscribe on—; perpetuate in—; project—; quarry—; rib with—; unveil—; work in—; —bruises; —crushes; — erodes; —facets; —s rattle; —rumbles; — supports; —sustains; —wedges.

(See rock, gem, jewel.)

adverbs

roughly; unpleasantly; ruggedly; disagreeably; impassably; curiously; amazingly; indescribably; terribly; unmanageably; cruelly.

adverbs

cautiously; humbly; dejectedly; wearily; miserably; subserviently; abjectly; obsequiously.

(See bend, descend.)

adjectives

sudden; tender; multiple; occasional; traffic; express; surprising.

adverbs

abruptly; suddenly; instantaneously; instinctively; imperiously; constantly; effectually; timorously; virtually.

(See halt, pause.)

verbs

employ—; fasten—; perforate—; ram in—; stave in—; tamp—; valve—; —checks; — chokes; —corks; —dams; —gags; —insures; —obstructs; —plugs; —restrains; —seals; —stems.

(See plug.)

adjectives

hideous; wholesome; commodious; hidden; heterogeneous; priceless; strange; corner; frugal; department; fragrant; truly-beautiful; tributary; increasing; plundered; rich; chain; vegetable; bounteous; sorrowful; shoe; overflowing; swanky; smart; glistening; plentiful; wondrous; inexhaustible; gorgeous; mystic; unprotected; ordnance; milky; humble; exclusive; abundant; reliable; provident; vast; cooperative; subsistence; gigantic; literary; undiminished; mustering; huge; immense; proud; untried; prodigious; lavish; winnowing; present; colorful; sparkling; absorbing; exciting; action; adventure; entertaining; amazing; amusing; picked; delightful; captivating; thrilling; true.

verbs

canvass—s; departmentalize—; draw from

—s; expand—; patronize—; —adjusts; —
branches out; —caters to; —dispenses; —
disposes of; —flourishes; —guarantees; —
markets; —purveys; —renovates; —retails;
—services; —thrives; —undersells; —unloads; —vends; —wholesales.

(See market, shop, source, supply, provision, food.)

STORE (v)
adverbs

providentially; consequently; secretly; bounteously; inexhaustibly; abundantly; immensely; lavishly; prodigiously; adequately.

(See save, hoard.)

STORK
adjectives

stilted; devouring; brisk; unwelcome; gawk-
y; awkward.

verbs

alarm—; gun for—; stir up—; —claws; —
fishes; —floats; —gyrates; —hovers; —
rakes; —sails over; —skims; —soars; —
strokes; —wades; —wheels.

(See bird.)

STORM
adjectives

teacup; lurid; freezing; irresistible; majestic; blinding; blustering; tumultuous; driving; maddened; harsh; adverse; murky;
wintry; fearful; mocking; wrestling; gathering; factual; insatiate; devastating; cyclonic; purifying; conflicting; rising; surly;
mingling; slanted; revolving; violent; forgotten; howling; bloody; persistent; rushing; clarifying; dissipated; psychologic;
terrific; heavy; raging; confluent; coming;
shipwrecking; vicious; beating; expiring;
pelting; financial; cyclic; unkind; transitory; recurrent; coast; whistling; perfect;
subsiding; blinding; appraising; commingling (pl); rollicking; savage; full-grown;
slanting; driving; momentary; deluging;
long-continued; tremendous; theologic; a-
wakening; wreckful; drenching; political.

verbs

allay—; battle through—; encounter—; fly
before—; foretell—; front—; ride—; scoff
at—; shelter from—; stir up—; survive—;
tarry in—; unleash—; weather—; —abates;
—batters; —brawls; —breaks; —brews; —
bursts; —calms; —develops; —flashes; —
gathers; —grumbles; —lashes; —rages; —

roars; —seethes; —thunders; —wears out;
—whips through; —whistles.

(See blizzard, hurricane, lightning, rain.)

STORM (v)
adverbs

overpoweringly; relentlessly; furiously; irresistibly; thunderously; passionately; devastatingly.

(See fume, rage.)

STORMY
adverbs

wildly; drearily; inordinately; terribly;
perilously; tempestuously; thunderously;
gustily; roughly; furiously; relentlessly;
alarmingly; extraordinarily; violently;
fiercely; intensely; unusually; disastrously;
dreadfully; fearfully; unusually; extremely;
uncommonly; cyclonically; icily.

STORY
adjectives

pathetic; candid; stirring; mouthed; chivalrous; complicated; wonderful; plausible;
ludicrous; priceless; naive; moving; roaring; sublime; unexpurgated; eye-opening;
authentic; detailed; graphic; specious; woeful; improbable; harrowing; idyllic; rambling; poignant; outrageous; self-told; true;
ill-natured; gripping; unpublished; painful;
legendary; rudimentary; mystery; absorbing; stupendous; incredible; cruel; mournful; inimitable; apocryphal; unembellished;
shameful; threadbare; circumstantial;
speaking; typical; thrilling; perishing; revealing; hackneyed; dubious; ribald; conflicting; calumniating; unfinished; veritable;
dismal; squalid; wondrous; well-known;
age-worn; amusing; time-honored; unbelievable; priceless; adventure; self-effacing;
blood-curdling; delectable; inspiring; pungent; fictitious; witty; racy; rapid; complete; amorous; laborious; heroic; commonplace; smooth-flowing; sea; fruitful; innocent; eloquent; darling; appropriate;
absurd; perpetual; horrid; abominable;
unconnected; tragic; curious; edifying;
lustful; copious; spicy; readable; ridiculous; realistic; uppermost; lame; finest;
romantic; monotonous; facetious; sad;
thought-provoking; sordid; slanderous;
eventful; melodramatic; uninterrupted;
homely; accredited; grim; tender; didactic;
unbiased; tribal; mess-worn; disastrous;
well-told; instructive; fascinating; upper;
shallow; garbled; delicious; hall-marked;

unreticent; heinous; elaborate; sensational; exquisite; accepted; harrowing; alive; complete; distinguished; deep; entertaining; horror; full-blooded; intimate; inside; light; swift-moving; top-notch; veracious; well-written; well-paced.

verbs
accumulate—s; belittle—; bolster—; cast—; circulate—; climax—; conceive—; concoct —; construct—; dash off—; criticize—; devour—; discredit—; dominate—; dramatize —; dwarf—; embroider—; enact—; fabricate—; fashion—; forge—; hail—; interpret—; invent—; issue—; load—; manufacture—s; narrate—; overload—; paint—; peg away at—; pour out—; present—; peruse—; question—; recapitulate—; reel off —; reiterate—; relate—; release—; relish —; scoff at—; scotch—; spin—; thread—; transcend—; turn out—; verify—; wade thru—; weave—; worm out—; —centers; —confirms; —consoles; —corroborates; — degenerates; —denounces; —depends; — elicits; —emanates; —embellishes; —engrosses; —enhances; —etches; —fascinates; —flows; —hurtles; —implicates; —inspires; —lacks; —links; —marches; —moves; — originates; —pictures; —pieces; —plunges; —progresses; —recounts; —regales; — reigns; —revolves; —rounds off; —shapes; —skirts; —slanders; —slants; —survives; —throws; —tingles; —touches; —travels; —unfolds.
(See legend, fiction, prose, "movie," history, narrative, myth, narration, manuscript, anecdote, book, episode, novel.)

STOUT
adverbs
brawnily; vigorously; unexpectedly; incredibly; invincibly; dependably; unusually; reliably; intrepidly; unbelievably; fortunately; remarkably; surprisingly; uncommonly.

STOUT-HEARTED
adverbs
intrepidly; fearlessly; ridiculously; uncommonly; admirably; undauntedly; immovably; cheerfully; steadfastly; wonderfully; valiantly; boldly; unfailingly; gaily; heroically; pluckily; resolutely; confidently; indomitably; uncommonly; spunkily.

STOUTNESS
verbs
accentuate—; augment—; deplore—; de-

ride—; exaggerate—; magnify—; mitigate —; predispose to—; reduce—; ridicule—; scoff at—; snigger at—; tend toward—; —aggravates; —deforms; —discommodes; —distorts; —dwarfs; —embarrasses; —endangers; —hampers; —hinders; —inconveniences; —mars; —renders ugly; —restrains; —restricts; —stagnates; —threatens; —towers; —wanes.
(See obesity.)

STOVE
adjectives
solemn; nameless; diminutive; roaring; hot; ancient; fiery; sputtering.

verbs
bask by—; consign to—; dampen—; draft —; extinguish—; feed—; hover over—; kindle—; quench—; replenish—; tend—; —affords; —comforts; —diffuses; —dies; —fumes; —insures; —reeks; —roars; — smoulders; —thaws.
(See fire, flame.)

STRAIGHT
adverbs
invariably; perfectly; unwaveringly; commendably; undeniably; exactly; accurately; correctly; admirably; unquestionably; uncommonly; exceptionally; unerringly; authentically; officially; conveniently; comparatively.

STRAIGHTFORWARD
adverbs
commendably; admirably; eminently; unusually; manifestly; evidently; reliably; unquestionably; delightfully; helpfully; artlessly; candidly; unaffectedly; naturally; inherently; obviously; bluntly; ingenuously; childishly; remarkably; uncommonly; scrupulously.

STRAIN
adjectives
sunny; metaphysical; inspiring; harmonious; terrific; bastard; impure; celestial-ordered; subtle; indomitable; echoing; windy; wild; passionate; parting; true-breeding; jubilant; self-same; soft; andante; majestic; exalted; tidal; lofty; untaught; ceaseless; meditative; strenuous; thrilling; singular; unwonted; sublime; aesthetic; adoring; onward; seraphic; taut; minor; thrilling; virile; homiletic; heated; mystical; musical; haunting; audacious; furious;

melancholy; shrill; intellectual; magic; creeping; nameless; unending; delicious; solemn; ventriloquous; gloomy; exultant; epic; lamentable; humorous; immortal; nervous; ravishing; fluent; intense; melodious; dirgeful; noble; thrilling; severe; pompous; intolerable; arresting; serious; mournful; extraordinary; full-fraught; sententious; chaste; racial; emotional; semi-humorous; muscular; individual; violent; true; profitless; indigenous; tender; steady; existing; successive (pl); mystic; pathetic; half-forgotten; polemic; vicious; curious; iterant; somber; martial; tremendous; terrible; inspired; syncopated; subdued; evoked; local; humble; unpolished; sweet; fierce; divine; crushing; enchanting; inevitable.

verbs
avoid—; develop—; disturb—; endure—; entail—; impose—; lift—; mutate—; relieve of—; overtake—; remove—; risk—; slacken—; stand—; subject to—; withstand —; —swells.
(See tension, exertion, stress.)

STRAIN (v)
adverbs
incompatibly; prodigiously; inordinately; feebly; passionately; furiously; intellectually; lamentably; excessively.
(See force, stretch.)

STRAIT-LACED
adverbs
absurdly; extremely; priggishly; puritanically; ridiculously; immovably; austerely; arbitrarily; unreasonably; unfortunately; rigidly; unwisely; uncompromisingly; forbiddingly; peremptorily; inexorably; tyrannically; foolishly; prudishly.

STRAITS
adjectives
pecuniary; dire; interminable; imaginary; sounding; desperate; narrow; great; bitter.

STRAND
adjectives
braided; remotest; everlasting; rippling; deserted; great; deep; dark; tragic; mysterious; siren-footed; genial; intertwisted (pl); blistering; dreary; uneven; lonely.

STRANGER
adjectives
formidable; mysterious; unutterable; illustrious; witless; unfriended; well-bred; wandering; forlorn; curious; waiting; humble; unsuspecting; audacious; comparative; thorough; inferior; wayfaring; dreadful; distinguished; swarthy; total; casual; ungenial; sympathetic; neat; unsavory; strange; queer; fluttering; passing; houseless; adulated; unnaturalized; insignificant; unheralded; blooming; detested; shrewd; plain-spoken; earth-born; rough-looking; drunken; drawling-voiced.

verbs
acquaint—with; admit—; appraise—; apprehend—; beguile—; bilk—; confide in—; cultivate—; deceive—; defraud—; delude —; discuss—; distrust—; dupe—; enlighten—; entertain—; exclude—s; extend to—; greet—; guide—; hail—; harbor—; implicate—; inform—; interrogate—; investigate—; mislead—; question—; receive—; regard—; salute—; snarl at—; trail—; usher in—; victimize—; welcome—.
(See alien, immigrant, newcomers, foreigners.)

STRANGLE (v)
adverbs
cruelly; excruciatingly; demoniacally; fiendishly; deliberately; maniacally; lustfully; sordidly; horridly; sensationally; horribly; amorously.
(See choke, kill.)

STRAP
verbs
affix—; braid—; buckle—; clasp—; detach —; reinforce—; rend—; sever—; slacken —; tense—; —binds; —couples; —curbs; —fetters; —impedes; —leashes; —links; —restrains; —supports; —sustains.
(See leash, belt, band.)

STRATEGIC
adverbs
cleverly; opportunely; conveniently; expediently; diplomatically; profoundly; secretly; wisely; prudently; discreetly; brilliantly; cunningly; craftily; insidiously; cannily; successfully; splendidly; usefully; profitably; immeasurably; financially; politically; commercially.

adjectives

successful; deadlier; vicious; daring; clumsy; clever; brilliant; military.

verbs

conceive—; concoct—; devise—; employ—; frame—; hatch—; practice—; resort to—; —accomplishes; —baffles; —baits; —befools; —beguiles; —bluffs; —confounds; —decoys; —defrauds; —deludes; —distracts; —diverts; —entices; —frustrates; —hoodwinks; —lures; —rebuffs; —repulses; —routs; —snares; —succeeds; —thwarts.

(See fraud, strategy, deception.)

STRATEGY

adjectives

half-baked; adroit; military; triumphant; ancient; superlative; absurd; sound; naval; aggressive; offensive; thrill-packed.

verbs

achieve—; administer—; adopt—; advise—; approve—; beguile with—; condemn—; counsel—; direct—; effect—; employ—; execute—; fashion—; frame—; guide—; pilot —; plan—; prescribe—; proceed with—; resort to—; steer—; work out—; —defeats; —outwits; —stems from.

(See maneuver, method, stratagem.)

STRAW

adjectives

patient; plaiting; helpful; apparent; damp; frowzy; synthetic; oaten.

verbs

bale—; bed with—; bleach—; discard—; embed in—; glean—; macerate—; plait—; scatter—; shed—; stuff with—; thresh—; weave—; —insures; —litters; —pads; — protects; —thatches.

(See chaff, hair, hay.)

STRAY (v)

adverbs

ostensibly; widely; irrationally; idiotically; adventurously; lustfully; senselessly.

(See roam, wander.)

STREAK

adjectives

ruthless; momentary; rotary; blood-red; uncouth; dingy; shy; cruel; tenderer; glimmering; faithless; vivid; zigzag; dancing; evident; pale; amphibious; glittering; long

adverbs

dingily; unfortunately; carelessly; sorrily; strangely; unaccountably; shabbily; dimly; luminously; curiously; disagreeably; faintly; shamefully; unattractively; unpleasantly.

STREAM

adjectives

swampy; bounding; echoing; whispering; turning; turbid; crystalline; rude; sharp; rippled; torrent; crystal; playful; straining; purling; shoreless; sluggish; eddying; immemorial; rushing; muddy; murmuring; trickling; rock-encumbered; translucent; fiery; feeding; dancing; summer; gliding; eternal; forbidden; steady; reedy; milky; sullen; solitary; gentle; sourceless; augmented; intervening; surcharged; trembling; fervid; plashing; cooling; glacial; salutary; lucid; sylvan; brown; quickening; livelier; fond; silly; wizard; tributary; voiceless; slender; flashing; lurid; cleansing; impetuous; yellow; constant; placid; fertilizing; simpering; bashful; unreluctant; fascinating; chiding; precipitous; intermittent; volcanic; ever-flowing; precious; fleeting; gushing; inert; navigable; pebbly; constant; enormous; comet-like; wayward; muddied; merry; visible; mighty; rapid; irrigating; whispering; living; delicate; substantial; boundless; celestial; Stygian; picturesque; bleeding; branching; feeble; blended; innumerable (pl); accepted; running; hairy; hurrying; hidden; formidable; indolent; reverent; sinister; pale; melancholy; doubled; storied; haunted; equable; formless; continuous; languid; cascading; copious; swollen; flowing; leaping; exuberant; bone-dry; imperial; golden; attractive; rippling; mountain; icy; undulating; petty; epigrammatic; diverging; inland; shallow; joyous; electric; gracious; singing; motionless; childhood; ignoble; lyrical; venomous; traffic; subterranean; returning; limpid; salt; mighty; numerous; brackish; foaming; verbose; dwindling; desolate; flattering; adventurous; brimming.

verbs

bridge—; ford—; head—; purify—; trace —; —boils; —bubbles; —clogs; —complains; —disappears; —drifts; —dwindles; —s harass; —s languish; —s meander; — narrows; —races; —ripples; —shimmers;

—s splash; —trickles; —tumbles; —washes; —s wind.

(See brook, creek, river.)

STREAM (v)

adverbs
tortuously; monotonously; unceasingly; perpetually; giddily; incessantly; boundingly; turbulently; turbidly; torrentially; eddyingly; translucently; copiously; exuberantly; undulatingly; subterraneanly; limpidly.

(See gush, pour, run.)

STREET

adjectives
dingy; medieval; winding; disreputable; squalid; crooked; blazing; quiet; sleepy; narrow; shaded; paved; silent; filthy; attractive; monotonous; littered; still; prominent; startled; unlovely; crowded; embowered; desolate; misty; impassable; moon-lit; forbidden; greasy; populous; unwatered; prominent; darksome; glaring; gutted; deep; darkling; sloppy; racy; straggling; arcaded; dusty; fearful; surging; charted; tortuous; peopled; intersecting; waking; dazzling; slippery; sunny; irregular; frozen; principal; wandering; obscure; deserted; adjacent; respectable; starry; twilight; glittering; little; clean-washed; ill-kept; palaced; corresponding; throngful; unpaved; spacious; rugged; murmuring; roaring; crooked; sultry; marching; residential; adroit; sunburnt; arid; gray; miry; melancholy; thronged.

verbs
amble about—; bedeck—; clutter—; deface —; front—; gain—; lay out—s; litter—; maintain—; patrol—; parade—; ramble thru—; roam—; strew—; stride thru—s; thread—s; throng in—; trudge along—; wander down—; —bakes; —flanks; — joins; —s shine; —swarms; —thunders.

(See sidewalk, lane, avenue, alley, thoroughfare.)

STRENGTH

adjectives
humble; fragile; clumsy; monstrous; raw; hairy; exhaustless; repellant; numerical; vigorous; passionate; sacred; augmented; national; united; central; shining; living; immortal; undivided; superhuman; effective; untiring; elastic; needless; superior; full; remarkable; herculean; barbaric; concentrated; masterful; magnificent; unwasting; natural; alcoholic; unyielding; unimaginative; rockbound; dogged; joyous; remaining; sudden; brute; double; ultimate; lusty; victorious; fear-crazed; desperate; thoughtful; enormous; awkward; voting; unconquerable; immense; immeasurable; silent; lavish; social; impregnable; sturdy; intellectual; unaided; determined; party; sinewy; tensile; massive; artistic; irresistible; renovated; intense; dominating; prodigious; financial; drowsy; superior; revived; aggressive; firm; lasting; muscular; evident; innate; banded; unbroken; conscious; reserved; lofty; excellent; steadfast; divine; ruthless; huge; comparative; placid; relative; pungent; unabated; manlier; solid; sufficient; concentrated; incredible; residing; surprising; unerring; matchless; authorized; spiritual; moral; gigantic; inseverable; skilled; sober; nervous; ambitious; passionless; lyric; honorable; unfolding; mysterious; welded; splendid; fiery; infinite.

verbs
accumulate—; augment—; betray—; confer —upon; conserve—; deny—; derive—; diffuse—; diminish—; drain—; endow with —; equal—; exhaust—; gain—; gather—; husband—; imbibe—; indicate—; maintain —; match—; measure—; muster—; pit—; possess—; pray for—; preserve—; prune—; recover—; regain—; reserve—; restore—; restrain—; sap—; scatter—; signify—; strain—; tax—; undermine—; unite—; — declines; —endures; —falters; —flows; — manifests itself; —spends itself.

(See energy, fortitude, force, power, health, impregnability.)

STRENUOUS

adverbs
disagreeably; dangerously; zealously; eagerly; laboriously; painfully; terribly; extremely; arduously; incredibly; dreadfully; impossibly; energetically; doggedly; vigorously; intensely; indefatigably; wearisomely; formidably; remarkably; unbelievably; unspeakably; unusually; exceptionally; particularly; singularly; peculiarly; unwholesomely.

STRESS

adjectives
unavailing; emotional; special; urgent; adamantine; particular; critical; unobtrusive; unnatural; artificial; plastic; tremendous; intestinal.

verbs

allay—; alleviate—; attach—to; avoid—; demand—; ease—; emphasize—; entail—; lay—upon; mitigate—; occasion—; palliate —; pronounce—; redouble—; relax—; subject to—; —accentuates; —aggravates; — declines; —taxes; —tenses; —wanes; — weighs upon.

(See emphasis, accent, pressure, strain.)

STRESS (v)

adverbs

faintly; markedly; precisely; particularly; exclusively; repeatedly; adamantinely; artificially; obtrusively; vigorously.

(See accent, emphasize.)

STRETCH (v)

adverbs

inordinately; gruesomely; indulgently; beauteously; dismayingly; generously; moderately; tightly; abnormally; piteously; consciously; symmetrically; interminably, indolently; casually.

(See extend, spread.)

STRETCHES

adjectives

sun-scorched; haggard; symmetrical; lilac; mighty; magnificent; interminable; treeless; ample; fragrant; indolent; endless; barren; mysterious; fertile; mossy; casual; wide.

STRICT

adverbs

unreasonably; particularly; singularily; needlessly; narrowly; dogmatically; narrowmindedly; intolerantly; uncharitably; unnecessarily; foolishly; unwisely; cruelly; bitterly; moderately; severely; oddly; illogically; inconsistently; brutally; piously; conventionally; viciously; habitually; dreadfully; wisely; sensibly; moderately; uncommonly; austerely; uncompromisingly; terribly; hideously.

STRICTNESS

verbs

adhere to—; ameliorate—; conform to—; diminish—; ease—; enforce—; infringe—; mitigate—; relax—; violate—; —crushes; —demands; —disciplines; —domineers; — exacts; —hampers; —impresses; —inures; —oppresses; —overrides; —restricts; —revolts; —strains; —taxes; —tramples; — tyrannizes; —yokes.

(See severity, rules, harshness.)

STRIDE

adjectives

heavy; tumultuous; nervous; proud; rhythmical; careless; consuming; self-assuring; enormous; slouching; unprecedented; swinging; prodigious; immense; disordered; free; athletic; short; lofty; majestic; irregular; fearless; formidable; sinking; ravishing; restless; martial; manly; rapid; sober.

verbs

accelerate—; break—; burlesque—; exaggerate—; halt—; hasten—; lengthen—; mimic—; quicken—; regain—; regulate—; relax—; ridicule—; secure—; smooth—; spur to—; —covers; —devours; —outdistances; —overhauls; —shuffles; —spurts; —strains; —taxes.

(See step, walk, pace, gait.)

STRIDE (v)

adverbs

vigorously; austerely; grimly; furiously; swiftly; dramatically; fearlessly; tirelessly; sturdily; rhythmically; prodigiously; athletically; majestically; martially; rapidly; soberly.

(See strut, stalk.)

STRIDENT

adverbs

unpleasantly; raucously; disagreeably; loudly; harshly; quarrelsomely; inelegantly; naturally; insistently; hatefully; offensively; coarsely; cruelly; brutally; pugnaciously; daringly; suddenly; broadly; repulsively; shockingly; disgustingly; ridiculously.

STRIFE

adjectives

unprofitable; elemental; deadly; stern; sexual; frivolous; murderous; fragrant; patient; sacrificial; noble; ambiguous; harmonious; domestic; continued; fruitful; party; barren; unceasing; eternal; vain; inward; harmless; civil; victorious; bloody; dying; absorbing; ignoble; midnight; surging; household; languid; sordid; political; ineffectual; harsh; expiring; constant; idle; inevitable; whirlwind; turbulent; industrial; uncongenial; tortured; feverish; unselfish; victorious; convulsive; theological; varied; bitter; selfish; inhuman; classic; dawning; spiritual; perpetual; unreposing; useless; foolish.

verbs

avert—; maneuver—; perpetuate—; plague with—; renew—; stir up—; —afflicts; —breaks out; —breeds; —brings; —dissolves; —flares; —harasses; —locks; —prolongs; —racks; —seethes; —surges; —tears.

(See discord, dissension, fued, conflict, contention, competition.)

STRIKE

verbs

avert—; ban—; break—; condemn—; crush —; deal with—; direct—; engage in—; foment—; forbid—; forestall—; handle—; interfere in—; precipitate—; prolong—; resort to—; stage—; stave off—; submit without—; support—; terminate—; tolerate—; weigh—; —breaks out; —develops; —s drag on; —embroils; —grips; —intervenes; —paralyzes; —rages; —spreads; —threatens; —wanes; breed—.

(See strife, conflict, feud.)

STRIKE (*v*)

adverbs

firmly; sullenly; pronouncedly; simultaneously; forcibly; spontaneously; instinctively; energetically; significantly; thunderously; heavily; intermittently; aimlessly; accidently; swiftly; mysteriously.

(See hit, slap.)

STRIKERS

verbs

acquit—; bow to—; champion—; conciliate —; disperse—; exonerate—; harangue—; pacify—; placate—; unite—; —arbitrate; —arm; —bar; —charge; —cooperate; —deride; —evict; —heckle; —intimidate; —jeer; —organize; —picket; —pillage; —relent; —repudiate; —riot; —sit down; —taunt; —violate; —demand.

(See rioters, crowd.)

STRIKING

adverbs

conspicuously; impressively; significantly; unusually; ominously; brilliantly; gorgeously; blatantly; garishly; gaudily; unbecomingly; inelegantly; magnificently; gloriously; beautifully; satisfactorily; artistically; luminously; overwhelmingly; delicately; daringly; boldly.

STRING

adjectives

hampering; friendly; sleeping; trembling; sinless; dissonant; silken; melodious; speaking; clanging; stubborn; tinkling; twined; tremulous; consecrated; quivering; veritable; sturdy; dusty; gouty; tightening; dangling; wayward; vibrating; tuneful; slackened.

verbs

braid—; cleave—; draw—; plait—; secure with—; sever—; shred—; slash—; stretch —; sunder—; suspend from—; tense—; —couples; —girds; —sustains; —yokes.

(See cord, leash, chains.)

STRINGENT

adverbs

unwisely; disagreeably; unbearably; intolerably; unintelligently; necessarily; inescapably; terribly; irritatingly; vexatiously; dangerously; ominously; unreasonably; injudiciously; stupidly; inexpediently; ill-advisedly; absurdly.

STRINGY

adverbs

unpleasantly; inconveniently; disagreeably; necessarily; unavoidably; naturally; gummily; uselessly; sufficiently; satisfactorily.

STRIP

adjectives

tenacious; popular; marginal; shadowy; pestilential; tiny; strong.

STRIPES

adjectives

brisk; contrast; vivid; severe; oblique; polychromatic; longitudinal; bright; broad; service; tiny.

STRIVE (*v*)

adverbs

ineffectually; laboriously; ambitiously; earnestly; indomitably; energetically; incessantly; valiantly; patiently; bull-headedly; stubbornly; ineffectively; nobly; dutifully; filially; fiercely; seditiously; diligently; vainly.

(See try, struggle.)

STRIVING

adjectives

human; eternal; earnest; ineradicable; hopeful; wishful; useful; bitter; wistful; vain.

STROKE (v)

adverbs

reflectively; meditatively; caressingly; affectionately; tenderly; absently; moodily; gently.

(See calm, smooth, touch.)

STROKES (boating)

verbs

accelerate—; coach—; develop—; employ—; execute—; invigorate—; pace—; perfect—; polish—; regulate—; scull with—; synchronize—; time—; —cut; —exhaust; —lash; —outdistance; —overhaul; —propel; —strain; —tax; —tell; —tire; —weary.

(See blow.)

STROKES (general)

adjectives

fatal; parliamentary; overhand; crowning; silver; unkind; vulgar; paralytic; heavy; bloodless; careful; cautious; ignorant; vicious; prevailing; impulsive; vigorous; concussive; subtle; blessed; specious; fragrant; lusty; spasmodic; rapid; rhythmic; blind; mortal; apoplectic; disastrous; mortuary; oft-repeated; calumnious; forceful; stinted; fanciful; hostile, curious; brilliant; terrific; coarse; sturdy; despairing; measured; unprecedented.

STROLL

adjectives

aimless; meditative; memorable; undisturbed.

STROLL (v)

adverbs

leisurely; languidly; dejectedly; philosophically; reflectively; nonchalantly; idly; contemplatively; pleasantly; dreamily

(See roam, ramble.)

STRONG

adverbs

brutally; remarkably; physically; powerfully; vigorously; vitally; incontestably; pitilessly; tenaciously; toughly; unquestionably; indubitably; remarkably; exceedingly; undeniably; manifestly; evidently; unexpectedly; determinedly; resolutely; cruelly; unyieldingly; incredibly; obviously; supremely; amazingly; incalculably.

STRONGHOLD

adjectives

impregnable; unconquerable; abandoned; gloomy; ruined.

verbs

abandon—; abdicate—; bar—; barricade—; bolt—; bombard—; escort to—; fortify—; garrison—; imperil—; intrench in—; invade —; jeopardize—; maintain—; menace—; padlock—; patrol—; repel from—; retire to —; retreat to—; screen—; subject—; —preserves; —shields.

(See fortifications, castle, citadel.)

STRUCTURE

adjectives

pyramidal; interesting; domineering; intricate; cosmical; rudimentary; ill-smelling; intended; fanciful; economic; serpentine; naked; mossy; asteriated; elaborate; circular; bonelike; metropolitan; solid; classical; dignified; ephemeral; ambitious; hideous; cellular; imposing; confused; rhythmical; chemical; vernacular; inner; stereotyped; cell; restless; inorganic; sensible; spiritual; streamlined; feathery; phantasmic; substantial; worldly; choral; patchwork; ecumenical; jointed; industrial; commodious; natural; unsightly; hair-growing; administrative; flexible; complicated; institutional; airy; continuous; underlying; ill-conceived; flimsy; internal; laminated; graceful; grave; supporting; artistic; various (pl); unwieldy; rambling; uniform; fragile; stately; urbane; sensible; unambitious; synthetic; magnificent; patriarchal; barn-like.

verbs

bind—; bore into—; complete—; elevate—; erect—; house in—; obliterate—; prop up —; rebuild—; tear down—; threaten—; underlie—.

(See building, edifice, frame, mansion.)

STRUGGLE

adjectives

tragic; intestinal; convulsive; protracted; brutal; obstinate; ineffectual; actual; intense; constant; inner; impending; arduous; continuous; painful; confused; perpetual; unending; imperialist; tremendous; fearful; dying; dire; terrific; heroic; vehement; strenuous; vain; gallant; victorious; stouthearted; prodigious; embittered; wild; unceasing; spiritual; thwarted; savage; sustained; eternal; ancient; deplorable; unequal; herculean; impotent; universal; un-brotherly; awful; bitter; foolish; lifelong; passionate; severe; inevitable; internecine; sanguine; subjective; desperate; slight; despairing; unaided; bloody; sharp; titanic; doubtful; bootless; parochial; fierce; unlettered; unremitting; brilliant; pioneer; apprehended; hidden; obscure; rough; melancholy; muscular; writhing; selfish; ardent; human; evident; moral; expressionable; creative; momentous.

verbs

desert—; engage in—; finance—; indulge in —; intercede in—; localize—; look upon—; participate in—; settle down to—; undergo —; wage—; yield in—; —culminates; —eliminates; —emaciates; —fills; —resolves; —harries; —summons; —swings in.

(See combat, contention, fight, effort, exertion, contest.)

STRUGGLE (v)

adverbs

flounderingly; terrifically; frantically; vainly; heroically; vigorously; savagely; weakly; feebly; manfully; ingeniously; obstinately; gallantly; turbulently; protractedly; vehemently; herculeanly; bootlessly; momentously.

(See labor, grapple.)

STRUT (v)

adverbs

stalwartly; vainly; proudly; conceitedly; arrogantly; pompously; complacently; jauntily; preposterously; magnificently; vulgarly; pugnaciously; valiantly.

(See swell, swagger.)

STUBBORN

adverbs

obstinately; astonishingly; surprisingly; naturally; incorrigibly; wonderfully; unexpectedly; infinitely; implacably; sternly; bull-headedly; doggedly; brutally; inveterately; desperately; inflexibly; habitually; obdurately; viciously; dreadfully.

STUBBORNNESS

adjectives

infinite; impious; implacable; stern; vainglorious; bull-headed.

verbs

allay—; conciliate—; decry—; denounce—; display—; evince—; exhibit—; moderate—;

rebuke—; relax—; reproach—; reprove—; revolt at—; submit to—; —goads; —irks; —resists; —riles (colloq.); —stiffens; —withstands; —yields to.

(See obstinacy, perversity.)

STUDENT

adjectives

diligent; research; discriminating; deep; promising; earnest; fastidious; formal; impartial; docile; special; facetious; ardent; aspiring; insatiable; careless; assiduous; indefatigable; veritable; irresponsible; tireless; thorough; languid; abstract; unprejudiced; historical; noble; able; sober-minded; learned; painstaking; talented; subsequent; tireless; candid; self-helping; laboratory; divinity; apathetic; enthusiastic; agile; negligent; inquisitive; critical; philosophical; scientific; thoughtful; impassioned.

verbs

assign—; bewilder—; baffle—; delude—; discipline—; dismiss—; edify—; enlighten —; enroll—; examine—; expound to—s; grade—; guide—; herd—s; honor—; inculcate in—; indoctrinate—s; ingrain—; initiate—; propound to—s; rear—; recruit—s; reprimand—; reproach—; tutor—; vex—s; —acquires; —advances; —attains; —attunes himself to; —s carouse; —concentrates; —cows; —crams; —cuts; —dips into; —drills; —familiarizes himself with; —flunks (colloq.); —gleams; —interprets; —peruses; —prepares; —qualifies; —translates; —wades through.

(See reader, pupil, graduate, apprentice, classmate.)

STUDIO

adjectives

shabby; wonderful; separate; silk-hung; aggressive; lofty; colossal; comfortable; broadcasting.

STUDIOUS

adverbs

earnestly; curiously; keenly; avidly; eagerly; energetically; tirelessly; actively; naturally; feverishly; gravely; seriously; resolutely; delightfully; overly; alarmingly; profoundly; deeply; uncommonly; happily; ambitiously; obviously; diligently; enthusiastically; oppressively; solemnly; erratically; spasmodically; occasionally.

adjectives

antiquarian; unsympathetic; superficial; graduate; modern; comparative; remarkable; illuminating; long-continued; scientific; painstaking; extraordinary; systematic; unfavorable; preparatory; revealing; proper; comprehensive; extensive; booklined; judicial; concise; forthright; up-to-the-minute; provocative; expert; full-length; fundamental; flippant; exhaustive; philosophical; continuous; assiduous; daring; delightful; watchful; careful; serious; old; desperate; concentrated; patient; theological; authoritative; morbid; analytical; technical; advanced; striking; instructive; candid; crude; suggestive; academic; intensive; satirical; vigorous; compulsory; fossil; obvious; diversified; profitless; linguistic; detailed; actual; thorough; curious; measured; topographical; ornamental; valuable; practical; searching; artistic; cartographic; tempting; clever; immediate; qualitative; perpetual; useless; passionate; lifetime; whimsical; sample; persistent; slight; consecutive; historic; constant; sociological; diligent; rational; economic; indispensable; illusory; rough-hewn; brilliant-hued; convincing; long-interrupted; solitary; utmost; exalted; laborious; statistical; contrapuntal; profound; daily; conscientious; energetic; sublime; penetrating; vivid; incessant; exciting; complicated; mathematical; desultory; previous; ethnographical; probing; intimate; monumental.

verbs

carry on—s; commence—; confine—; delve into—; devote time to—; direct—; distract from—; embrace—of; engage in—; engross in—; enlarge range of—; facilitate—; focus —on; further—; guide—s; impel—; incorporate—; neglect—; plunge into—; proclaim —of; pursue—;. select—; simplify—; specialize in—; stabilize—; standardize—s; thirst for—; toy with—; undertake—; — compensates; —discloses; —edifies; —enlightens; —occupies; —reveals; —rewards; —sharpens; absorb in—; apply—; buckle down to—.

(See curriculum, research, learning, application, history, English, science, etc.)

STUDY (v)

adverbs

desultorily; diligently; extensively; minutely; assiduously; scrupulously; meticulously; persistently; exhaustively; historically; systematically; conscientiously; earnestly; fervently; obstinately; theoretically; monastically; unremittingly; indefatigably; abstractly; philosophically.

(See muse, concentrate.)

STUFF

adjectives

pleasing; fiery; masquing; dismal; immortal; rich; colored; mortifying; stern; garden; embroidered; vitriolic; proud; branded; stinging; warming; luminous.

STUFFY

adverbs

intolerably; overwhelmingly; absurdly; uncommonly; odorously; aristocratically; elegantly; pedantically; snuffily; uncomfortably; distressingly; oppressively; stupidly; unbearably; clamorously; noisily; swarmingly

STUMBLE (v)

adverbs

blindly; stupidly; awkwardly; falteringly; inadvertently; drunkenly; soddenly; vacantly.

(See trip, fall.)

STUN (v)

adverbs

momentarily; physically; emotionally; staggeringly; spiritually; utterly; partially; terrifically.

(See overcome, bewilder.)

STUNTED

adverbs

cruelly; crookedly; distressingly; criminally; pitiably; oddly; wretchedly; miserably; dwarfishly; scrawnily; elfishly; queerly; unfortunately; incredibly; hopelessly; pudgily.

STUPEFIED

adverbs

oddly; suddenly; astonishingly; bewilderingly; grievously; queerly; curiously; dopily; soddenly; utterly; strangely; helplessly; hopelessly; maliciously; hypnotically; sleepily; mysteriously; unaccountably; dazedly.

STUPID

adverbs

abysmally; strangely; unutterably; vacuously; ridiculously; oddly; peculiarly; curiously; unaccountably; irritatingly; vexatiously; shockingly; fatally; callously; carelessly; hopelessly; unpardonably; inexplicably; innately; soddenly; sullenly; grossly; direly; blankly.

STUPIDITY

adjectives

innate; sodden; impenetrable; ineffable; sullen; stultifying; blundering; pompous; designed; gross; useless; current; vacant; insuperable; dire.

verbs

bemoan—; betoken—; bewail—; contemplate —; decry—; deplore—; deride—; disclose —; display—; evince—; feign—; manifest —; marvel at—; observe—; overcome—; realize—; reveal—; ridicule—; shriek at—; stress—; —confounds; —flabbergasts colloq.); —overwhelms; —prejudices.

(See inefficiency, mediocrity, imbecility, inability, dullness, incompetence, ignorance.)

STUPOR

adjectives

dull; partial; obstructing; vacant; empty; silly; blank.

verbs

arouse from—; bring on—; collapse in—; induce—; shock into—; —benumbs; —binds; —blunts; —deadens; —dulls; —envelops; —ensues; —exhausts; —overtakes; —paralyzes; —petrifies; —prostrates; —shatters; —stuns; —suspends; —overcomes.

(See coma, lethargy, languor, unconsciousness.)

STURDY

adverbs

splendidly; admirably; remarkably; surprisingly; stoutly; healthily; vigorously; boyishly; magnificently; stockily; brawnily; enviably; physically.

STYLE

adjectives

slenderizing; tailored; frilly; florid; artificial; dashing; architectural; concise; effective; halting; figurative; extra-colloquial; episodical; anithetical; correct; pleasing; all-pervading; comprehensible; heathenish; slovenly; fantastic; grotesque; balanced; conservative; honorable; latinized; showy; literary; satirical; classic; unsurpassed; impeccable; authentic; complimentary; trim; genuine; sparkling; alert; distinctive; ad-

vance; permanent; commanding; behavioristic; friendly; clear; baronial; polished; brilliant; admirable; rushing; secular; barbaric; lucid; unacademic; dapper; legitimate; single; expensive; established; important; gigantic; swagger; magniloquent; pianoforte; loving; conventional; vigorous; monumental; captivating; pungent; simple; habitual; inherited; arrogant; offensive; flamboyant; browbeating; ceremonious; limited; piquant; epistolary; representative; soft; journalistic; swashbuckling; engaging; dramatic; unambiguous; elegant; ambitious; burial; peculiar; learned; elevated; cataloguing; quiet; incongruous; inoffensive; handsome; fitted; architectural; sleek-fitting; youthful; decent; becoming; pointed; pathetic; superior; interesting; cryptic; ostentatious; stilted; nervous; lucid; epigrammatic; forcible; inimitable; laminated; logical; bald; imperial; reprehensible; thrill-provoking; metrical; dissimilar; typical; sonorous; conceivable; didactic; historic; successive (pl); rebellious; prose; puny; damnatory; native; patriarchal; exclamatory; unequaled; poetic; fine; wrought; singular; dazzling; appropriate; favored.

verbs

acclaim—; adopt—; affect—; approve—; breed—; burlesque—; characterize—; cling to—; cloak—; coarsen—; conceive—; conform to—; couch—; cramp—; cultivate—; design—; develop—; distinguish—; distort —; elaborate—; fabricate—; fashion—; fix —; flag—; formulate—; introduce—; lack —; mar—; mature—; model—; modify—; mold—; polish—; popularize—; purify—; refine—; ridicule—; satirize—; set—; strain —; study—; —bears; —s decree; —discriminates; —embraces; —expresses; —glitters; —indicates; —lends charm; —palls; —takes your fancy; —varies.

(See form, manner, character, fashion.)

STYLE (*v*)

adverbs

smartly; individually; spectacularly; exquisitely; casually; correctly; euphemistically; universally.

(See fashion, create.)

STYLISH

adverbs

conventionally; extremely; elegantly; properly; unusually; curiously; engagingly; enchantingly; inordinately; consciously; noticeably; conspicuously; impressively; imposingly; aristocratically; undeniably; amazingly; astoundingly; skillfully; expensively; naturally; delightfully; charmingly; beautifully; agreeably.

SUAVE

adverbs

unctuously; blandly; resolutely; steadily; deliberately; ominously; politely; ceremoniously; chivalrously; conspicuously; gently; helpfully; craftily; adroitly; disarmingly; charmingly; engagingly; unwontedly; painstakingly; diplomatically; carefully; warily; cleverly.

SUBCONSCIOUSNESS

verbs

arouse from—; control—; fix in—; induce —; influence—; penetrate—; pervade—; reduce to—; —clings to; —dematerializes; —disembodies; —dwells; —ensues; —retains; —reigns; —roams; —spiritualizes; —strays; —wanders.

(See mind, intellect.)

SUBDUE (v)

adverbs

valiantly; unconditionally; absolutely; ignominiously; degradingly; compulsorily.

(See conquer, overpower.)

SUBJECT

adjectives

contemporary; congenial; cognate; bruited; unhappy; abstract; apt; truer; humble; elevated; practical; tragical; touching; imaginable; despairing; dutiful; recurring; distressed; rebellious; incongruous; turbulent; daring; controversial; unruly; absorbing; varied (pl); analogous; fruitful; painful; related; utilitarian; historical; well-determined; idealistic; copious (pl); immediate; hypnotic; impressionable; intoxicating; diversified; rich; miscellaneous (pl); delicate; responsive; base; scriptural; antiquated; facetious; non-technical; allegorical; extraneous; unpleasant; proposed; dominant; precipient; docile; kindred; thinking; suitable; abstruse; dehydrated; unwelcome; invaluable; horrified; corpulent; unwilling; traitorous; ephemeral; foolscap; stern; passive; coherent; striking; ethical; admissable; tributary; somber; decorative; obscure; vexed; isolated; leisure; least; unfortunate; tempted; philosophical; sentient; dehumanized; aggrieved; obtuse.

verbs

abuse—; allude to—; ally to—; approach—; assail—; bedevil—; branch off—; broach—; brood over—; brush upon—; circumvent—; comment on—; comprehend—; converse on —; debate on—; delve into—; depict—; dismiss—; draw upon—; edit—; evade—; exhaust—; exorcise—; expatiate on—; expound—; grasp—; hurry through—; introduce—; investigate—; master—; mention—; nourish—; obscure—; phrase—; ponder over—; pursue—; return to—; scorn—; shake—; summarize—; tackle—; wrap oneself up in—; —associates; —baffles; —s bruit; —deals; —engages; —exalts; —illuminates; —s interweave; —intrigues; —s range; —reacts; —recurs; —stimulates; —takes shape; —throws; —treats; —unfolds; —warms; harp on—.

(See matter, proposition, question, history, English, etc.)

SUBJECT (v)

adverbs

minutely; perpetually; humiliatingly; rigorously; civilly; morally; debasingly; tyrannically; dictatorially.

(See expose, uncover.)

SUBJECTION

adjectives

entire; debasing; discomfited; enforced; civil; total; absolute; moral; humble.

verbs

accomplish—; achieve—; assail—; batter to —; coerce into—; complete—; contrive—; culminate in—; curb—; exempt from—; gain—; halt—; reduce to—; repress—; resist—; restrain—; secure—; terminate—; undermine—; wrestle into—; —binds; —oppresses; control—.

(See discipline, enslavement, exposure, subjugation, subserviency.)

SUBJUGATION

verbs

endure—; escape—; lead into—; liberate from—; reduce to—; resist—; —bridles; —blights; —constrains; —curbs; —enslaves; —fetters; —leashes; —muzzles; —restricts; —shackles; —suppresses; —weighs upon; —yokes.

(See bondage, enslavement, subjection.)

SUBMARINE

verbs

batter—; charter—; command—; communicate with—; engulf—; ground—; navigate —; propel—; ram—; scuttle—; swamp—; —s blockade; —convoys; —descends; —dips; —dives; —ejects; —endangers; —escorts; —explores; —founders; —immerses; —s patrol; —plummets; —plunges; —probes; —scurries; —settles; —slides; —sounds; —squats; —submerges; —tips; —torpedoes.

SUBMERGE (v)

adverbs

forcibly; totally; completely; fatally; instinctively; involuntarily.

(See plunge, sink.)

SUBMISSION

adjectives

unconditional; absolute; calm; vile; dishonorable; willing; unexpected; hopeless; tame; humble; quiet; ignominious; coy; continued; supine; abject; prompt; slavish; degrading; piteous; gentle; formal; proud; patient; pretended; deprecating; compulsory; mute.

verbs

advise—; advocate—; bait into—; bend in —; bow in—; coerce into—; compel—; cuff into—; demand—; endure—; enforce—; enjoin—; exact—; force into—; reduce to—; resign to—; tame into—; tolerate—; yield to—; —chastens; —humbles; —humilitates; batter into—.

(See acquiescence, compliance, obedience.)

SUBMISSIVE

adverbs

obsequiously; compliantly; loyally; passively; obediently; modestly; meekly; humbly; philosophically; necessarily; quietly; apathetically; dully; grimly; apparently; perfectly; shamelessly; appallingly; incredibly; strangely; pathetically; pliantly; weakly; calmly; resolutely; imperturbably; stolidly; stupidly; curiously; mysteriously; evidently; tragically; presumably.

SUBMIT (v)

adverbs

graciously; willingly; passively; uxoriously; spinelessly; coyly; voluntarily; placidly; informally; tamely; ignominiously; uncondi-tionally; docilely; apathetically; supinely; slavishly; mutely; deprecatingly.

(See surrender, yield.)

SUBORDINATE

adverbs

gracefully; cheerfully; respectfully; deferentially; carefully; cautiously; unfailingly; abjectly; slavishly; miserably; wretchedly; pleasantly; courteously; obediently; contentedly; admiringly; willingly; admittedly; apparently.

SUBPOENA

verbs

default—; dispatch—; evade—; issue—; request—; serve—; —apprehends; —arraigns; —bids; —calls upon; —commands; —compels; —constrains; —informs; —instructs; —orders; —requires; —specifies; —summons.

(See order, command.)

SUBSCRIBE (v)

adverbs

heartily; sincerely; earnestly; willingly; immediately; annually; cheerfully; voluntarily.

(See sign, agree.)

SUBSCRIPTION

adjectives

voluntary; annual; huge; cheerful; suggested.

verbs

advance—; afford—; bestow—; cancel—; conclude—; confer—; contribute—; donate —; entrust with—; favor with—; increase —; plead for—; pledge—; raise—; reduce —; renew—; swamp with—s; —aids; —assists; —s pour in; —reinforces; —relieves; —rescues; —succors.

(See contribution.)

SUBSERVIENCY

adverbs

assail—; bow in—; cower in—; cringe in—; decry—; emancipate from—; grovel in—; kneel in—; prostrate in—; reduce to—; stoop in—; submit to—; —abases; —defaces; —degrades; —discountenances; —humiliates; —oppresses; —yokes.

(See subjection.)

SUBSERVIENT

adverbs

willingly; unfortunately; humbly; meekly; slavishly; wretchedly; abjectly; helplessly; sullenly; agreeably; deferentially; respectfully; voluntarily; eagerly; zealously; remarkably; amazingly; oddly; strangely; unaccountably; curiously; unwontedly.

SUBSIDE (v)

adverbs

abruptly; gradually; growlingly; brokenly; ultimately; spontaneously; markedly; intermittently.

(See sink, fall.)

SUBSIDY

verbs

advance—; appropriate—; disburse—; expend—; yield—; —abets; —assists; —bolsters; —enables; —encourages; —fosters; —furthers; —protests; —rejuvenates; —relieves; —rescues; —resuscitates; —succors; —supports; —sustains; —wrests.

(See aid, gift.)

SUBSIST (v)

adverbs

frugally; intellectually; meagerly; precariously; scantily; barely; penuriously.

(See maintain, exist.)

SUBSISTENCE

adjectives

meager; precarious; degraded; scanty; bare; mere.

verbs

animate—; destroy—; ennoble—; justify—; maintain—; preserve—; prolong—; protract —; rely on for—; revive—; support—; vitalize—; vivify—; invest—; wrest—; —furnishes; —wanes; —waxes.

(See livelihood, living, employment.)

SUBSTANCE

adjectives

natural; softening; unsightly; poisonous; combustible; essential; spiritual; tremendous; obstructing; tolerated; sterner; toxic; demulcent; emotional; intellectual; earthly; noble; insulating; viscid; gelatinous; perfumed; innocuous; permeable; authenticating; inert; injurious; scanty; metallic; waste; watery; abrasive; adulterate; pulpy; deleterious; luminous; delicate: innumerable (pl); gummy; artificial; material; life-giving; synthetic; convertible; reorganized; vital; incorruptible; homogeneous; prepared; solid; bituminous; dilated; harsh; caustic; refulgent; rebellious; vitreous; glossy; tenacious; malleable; gaseous; porous; desiccated; durable; mollifying; slovenly; putrid; versatile.

verbs

absorb—; administer—; alter—; compound —; condense—; convert—; dehydrate—; desiccate—; disperse—; dissolve—; embody in—; employ—; express—; fritter away—; lack—; lose—; market—; oxidize—; pulverize—; reach—; reflect—; secrete—; value —; —activates; —congeals; —crumbles; — disintegrates; —endures; —ossifies; —petrifies; —produces; —resists; —yields; produce—.

(See chemical, essence, material, matter.)

SUBSTANTIAL

adverbs

admirably; unusually; remarkably; financially; structurally; commendably; luckily; acceptably; satisfactorily; unexpectedly; agreeably; amazingly; delightfully; providentially.

SUBSTITUTE

adjectives

improvised; sufficient; acceptable; comprehensive; facile; agreeable; ancient; temporary; satisfactory; reasonable; ingenious; occasional; wooden; bloodless; plausible; inadequate; appropriate; selective; human; solid.

verbs

accept—; accredit—; approve—; authorize —; commend—; commission—; concede to —; consent to—; consider—; create—; delegate—; deprecate—; discard—; employ—; frown upon—; grant—; hail—; indorse—; invest—with; offer—; regard—; reimburse —; reject—; sanction—; weigh—; yield to —; —conforms to; —constitutes; —replaces; —supersedes; —supplants; empower—.

(See delegate, agent, representative.)

SUBSTITUTE (v)

adverbs

successfully; definitely; deftly; slyly; insidiously; ingeniously; plausibly; adequately; appropriately; invidiously.

(See exchange.)

SUBTERFUGE

verbs

cloak in—; employ—; resort to—; screen—; veil in—; —beguiles; —conceals; —counterfeits; —deceives; —deludes; —dodges; —eludes; —evades; —falsifies; —feigns; —glosses over; —impostures; —juggles; —misleads; —misrepresents; —obscures.

(See evasion, artifice.)

SUBTLETY

adjectives

ceremonious; absurd; obvious; airy; delicate; hidden; natural; shadowy; time-woven.

verbs

bare—; comprehend—; discern—; enlighten—; interpret—; mask in—; pierce—; see through—; —beguiles; —cloaks; —curtails; —deludes; —disguises; —hints; —misleads; —obscures; —pervades; —prompts; —screens; —shrouds; —suggests; —veils.

(See cunning, deceit, distinction.)

SUBURB

adjectives

smiling; residential; initial; dingy; depressing; thriving; adjoining; flourishing; smug; convenient; fragrant; charming; obscure; foreign; immediate; picturesque; shabby; gardened; mysterious; remote.

SUBVERT (*v*)

adverbs

monstrously; utterly; viciously; completely; insidiously; secretly; debasingly; civilly; politically; governmentally.

(See overthrow, destroy.)

SUBWAY

verbs

construct—; dash into—; flow from—; jam—; —bears; —bores; —conveys; —courses; —extends to; —facilitates; —hums; —replaces; —roars; —screams; —traverses; —tunnels; —unloads; —unites.

(See train, railroad, tunnel.)

SUCCEED (*v*)

adverbs

patently; credibly; notably; inevitably; eminently; legitimately; admirably; scholastically; financially; triumphantly; precociously; superficially; materialistically; phenomenally; significantly; sensationally; ephemerally; commercially; economically.

(See attain, accomplish.)

SUCCESS

adjectives

scholastic; undoubted; international; popular; bad; social; pretentious; booming; enduring; grand; prodigious; mounting; continued; alternate; dawning; instantaneous; pecuniary; inferior; competitive; particular; tremendous; unexampled; imperial; unreached; triumphant; checkered; immense; precocious; transient; superficial; proper; political; indifferent; ill; clumsy; material; brilliant; emphatic; petty; overawed; ultimate; gratifying; enduring; lasting; unbroken; substantial; howling; phenomenal; significant; outstanding; fugitive; considerable; conspicuous; soaring; universal; overnight; amazing; sensational; artistic; .perfect; superb; grandiose; ephemeral; commercial; financial; poor; youthful; extraordinary; definite; prompt; unqualified; dramatic; equal; dubious; established; signal; double; spontaneous; notable; permanent; marvelous; facile; astonishing; monetary; evanescent; sufficient; well-merited; temporary; economic; noticeable; growing; worldly; eventual; reigning.

verbs

achieve—; aspire to—; assure—; attain—; attend with—; beset—; claim—; correlate—; crown with—; earn—; enjoy—; fight to—; flush with—; glean—; hinder—; impede—; jeopardize—; predict—; reckon with—; score—; secure—; smash into—; taste—; train for—; —arises; —attests to; —blasts; —comes; —completes; —crowns; —embitters; —emboldens; —encourages; —hails; —hinges; —insures; —paves; —pays for; —pursues; —signalizes; —springs; —tempts; —wears.

(See fortune, victory, triumph, achievement, supremacy, wealth, fame.)

SUCCESSFUL

adverbs

happily; unusually; consistently; fortunately; triumphantly; extremely; unexpectedly; luckily; felicitously; buoyantly; hilariously; thrillingly; boisterously; excitedly; highly; incomparably; uncommonly; marvelously.

SUCCESSION

adjectives
uninterrupted; dreary; perpetual; observed; lashing; swift; delicious; destined; strange; rapid; continual; sweet; tragic; barbarous; fierce; hereditary; rigid; melodious; medieval; connected; fortuitous; constant.

SUCCOR

verbs
afford—; cherish—; extend—; find—; gain—; furnish—; lend—; plead for—; refuse—; reject—; render—; seek—; withdraw—; withhold—; yield—; —cheers; —nurtures; —relieves; —supports; —sustains.
(See aid, help, relief, assistance.)

SUCCULENT

adverbs
lusciously; deliciously; delightfully; palatably; nutritiously; strangely; unexpectedly; especially; unusually; incomparably; agreeably; pleasantly; delicately; commendably; healthfully.

SUCCUMB (v)

adverbs
fatally; feebly; unconditionally; weakly; gradually; partially; dangerously; ultimately; unresistingly; promptly
(See submit, sink, yield.)

SUCK (v)

adverbs
thirstily; vigorously; greedily; insatiably.
(See absorb, imbibe.)

SUDDEN

adverbs
rudely; unfortunately; startlingly; whimsically; intentionally; astonishingly; mercifully; shockingly; amusingly; disconcertingly; ridiculously; laughably; offensively; inexcusably; unforgivably; dangerously; unreasonably; lamentably; unintentionally; abruptly; breathlessly; unpardonably; precipitately; prematurely.

SUE (v)

adverbs
importunately; legally; litigiously; ruthlessly; vindictively; logically; irrationally.
(See prosecute, arrest.)

SUFFER (v)

adverbs
agonizingly; distressingly; severely; stoically; intensely; dismally; atrociously; grievously; acutely; keenly; proportionately; deservedly; heroically; mentally; extensively; mutely; monetarily; infinitely; miserably; chronically; wretchedly.
(See endure, bear.)

SUFFERER

adjectives
lifelong; innocent; glorious; distinguished; chronic; mighty; indignant; surviving; wretched; immediate.

verbs
agonize—; attend—; cheer—; comfort—; condole with—; console—; convulse—; crucify—; deliver—; depress—; disburden—; ease—; flog—; nurse—; soothe—; treat—; wrack—; wrap up—; wring—; —baffles; —endures; —groans; —laments; —moans; —rallies; —retaliates; —revives; —survives.
(See invalid, victim.)

SUFFERING

adjectives
prolong; imitative; indignant; passive; self-inflicted; awful; needless; subtle; intense; meek; angelic; vicarious; spiritual; supreme; cruel; ignominious; pecuniary; virtuous; fictitious; tempestuous; poignant; unnecessary; protracted; inevitable; patient; unmerited; terrible; acute; untold; petty; decisive; universal; mortal; everlasting.

verbs
antidote—; appease—; assuage—; augment—; avoid—; bear—; doom to—; endure—; exhibit—; experience—; fight—; impose—; indulge—; lessen—; minimize—; palliate—; perfect through—; persevere in—; probe—; prolong—; quench—; reassure—; remedy—; —aggravates; —alleviates; —burdens; —convinces; —defaces; —diminishes; —entails; —expiates; —mitigates; —obviates; —racks; protract—.
(See distress, pain.)

SUFFICIENT

adverbs
sufficient; luckily; gratifyingly; wonderfully; quite; satisfactorily; admirably; luxuriantly; abundantly; amply; copiously; inexhaustibly; amazingly; happily; fortunately.

SUFFOCATION

verbs

avert—; await—; doom to—; escape—; face with—; forestall—; hazard—; rescue from—; result in—; risk—; stave off—; verge on—; —cuts short; —ensues; —follows; —impends; —looms; —menaces; —occurs; —severs; —supervenes; —threatens; —wipes out.

(See drowning, failure.)

SUFFRAGE

adjectives

popular; unsolicited; unrestricted; universal; unappreciated.

verbs

authorize—; campaign for—; claim—; confer—on; curtail—; demand—; deny—; deprive of—; endow with—; enjoy—; entitle to—; extend—; gain—; merit—; relinquish—; restore—; restrict—; revoke—; sanction—; solicit—; throttle—; yield—; —voices.

(See right, vote.)

SUGAR

adjectives

swarthy; permissible; vital; energy-giving; tasty.

verbs

abstain from—; adulterate—; box—; consume—; convert—; crystallize—; cure with—; decompose—; dissolve—; excrete—; grade—; granulate—; market—; prepare—; pulverize—; purify—; refine—; transform into—; utilize—; —candies; —honeys; extract—.

(See nectar, sweetness.)

SUGGEST (v)

adverbs

promptly; slyly; insidiously; respectfully; tactfully; whimsically; sagaciously; facetiously; pacifically; deftly; mildly; casually; subtly; wistfully; significantly; poetically; gloomily; sardonically; rationally; contemptuously; craftily; irrelevantly; hypnotically; specifically.

(See intimate, hint, insinuate.)

SUGGESTION

adjectives

taunting; detailed; sinful; compelling; hypnotic; sound; sensible; inexhaustible; meritless; wild; plausible; pregnant; delicate; obvious; subtle; delusive; least; startling;

perpetual; hopeful; fantastic; imaginative; timorous; sorrowful; rational; implied; ironical; pantomimic; illusory; remotest; reasonable; helpful; adverse; constructive; outside; ashamed; pained; casual; inspiring; terrifying; native; endless; mute; practical; specific; opulent; timely; cheerful; bare; solemn; hopeful.

verbs

acknowledge—; adopt—; afford—; combat—; conceive—; contribute—; convey—; dare—; enforce—; frame—; hazard—; launch—; offer—; propound—; put forth—; reject—; submit—; venture—; waive—; yield to—; —alludes to; —assumes; —counsels; —dies; —expedites; —facilitates; —hints; —misleads; —prescribes; —recommends; —speculates; —stimulates; —surmises; —theorizes.

(See intimation, hint, insinuation, implication, innuendo.)

SUICIDE

adjectives

involuntary; would-be; eventual; political; cold; brave; planned.

verbs

avert—; commit—; conceal—; contemplate—; feign—; flirt with—; goad to—; grieve over—; incite to—; resign to—; resort to—; reveal—; —allures; —betrays; —closes; —dramatizes; —exposes; —frees; —mystifies; —relinquishes.

(See death, murder.)

SUIT

adjectives

elaborate; exclusive; hopeless; washable; riding; luxury; classic; play; tardy; excellent; humble; strong; imported; new; striking; summer; choice; suave; durable; draped; wool; terraced; charming; sumptuous; business; fresh; smart; dressy; distinctive; smooth; conservative; sturdy; worsted; fine; rainy-day; losing; faded; pepper-and-salt; habitual; boldest; sober; customary; gorgeous; libel; honest; superb; neat; repeated; wrong; presumptuous.

verbs

adorn—; alter—; apparel in—; array in—; attire in—; divest of—; doff—; don—; fray—; garb in—; mend—; tatter—; vest in—;

—disguises; —mantles; —protects; — shields.

(See uniform, coat, overcoat, garment.)

SUIT (v)

adverbs
specifically; exactly; definitely; admirably; logically; rationally; precisely; peculiarly; superbly.

(See fit, adapt.)

SUITABLE

adverbs
eminently; wholly; ineffably; conveniently; opportunely; seasonably; comfortably; stylishly; highly; delightfully; unquestionably; fortunately; appropriately; becomingly; providentially; beautifully.

SUITOR

adjectives
unnumbered (pl); bashful; anxious; importunate; eligible; princely; renowned; bold; probable; accepted; slighted; scrupulous; pernicious; woeful.

verbs
attract—s; bind—; cherish—; discourage—; encourage—; gain—; secure—; slight—; — adores; —affiances; —aspires to; —bids for; —bows; —s clamor for; —idolizes; —implores; —importunes; —kneels; —offers; — pleads; —plights; —presses; —professes; — reveres; —solicits; —s throng; —vows; — woos; —troths.

(See lover, sweetheart.)

SULK (v)

adverbs
obstinately; glumly; adamantly; persistently; mutely; unreasonably; miserably; hatefully; woefully.

(See pout, brood.)

SULKY

adverbs
disagreeably; actively; poutingly; glumly; noisily; grimly; dangerously; unpleasantly; vengefully; hatefully; smoulderingly; unaccountably; unreasonably; absurdly; ridiculously; oddly; comically; strangely; gloomily; intolerably.

SULLEN

adverbs
desperately; glumly; dourly; inveterately; habitually; usually; incorrigibly; defiantly; perversely; stolidly; silently; moodily; obstinately; ungraciously; uncivilly; resentfully; angrily; shamefully; disagreeably; unpleasantly; obviously; undisguisedly.

SULTRINESS

verbs
droop in—; swelter in—; —chokes; —dampens; —depresses; —disheartens; —dispirits; —envelops; —flushes; —frets; —glooms; — oppresses; —permeates; —prostrates; — reeks; —seethes; —simmers; —smothers; — sulks; —weighs upon.

(See heat, weather.)

SULTRY

adverbs
unpleasantly; disagreeably; ominously; significantly; distressingly; wretchedly; miserably; strangely; oppressively; smotheringly; curiously; steamily; inauspiciously; intolerably; uncomfortably; alarmingly; extremely; breathlessly.

SUM

adjectives
nominal; fabulous; moderate; untold; successive (pl); meager; pitiful; gross; vast; reasonable; stupendous; trifling; substantial; lawful; formidable; exorbitant; munificent; phonetic; staggering; utmost; unprecedented; round; appalling; pretty; small; enormous; paltry; objective; aggregate; satisfying; tabled; tidy; specified; high; modest.

verbs
accrue—; accumulate—; aggregate—; allot —; amass—; arrive at—; audit—; bestow —; calculate—; check—; compute—; disburse—; discount—; distribute—; embezzle —; entail—; expend—; file—; issue—; necessitate—; realize—; reckon—; register—; represent—; subscribe—; —diminishes; — dwindles; —soars; —staggers.

(See amount, list, number, overhead, profits.)

SUMMARIZE (v)

adverbs
roughly; casually; generally; completely; concisely; statistically; luminously; logically; vividly; convincingly; intelligibly.

(See add, combine.)

adjectives
statistical; running; intimate; authoritative; apt; contradictory; luminous; logical; concise; slumberous; singular; striking; necessary; helpful.

SUMMER

adjectives
parting; bitter; relentless; broiling; costly; gorgeous; slow; humid; troubled; hot; promised; husky; trailing; northern; luxurious; strenuous; exciting; colorful; proud; economic; delicate; heavy; perished; perpetual; epitomized; immediate.

verbs
await—; bask in—; bear the stamp of—; long for—; prolong—; suspend for—; thrive in—; usher in—; welcome—; yearn for—; —begets; —blooms; —breeds; —burgeons; —colors; —conceives; —dresses; —enriches; —fades; —gilds; —kisses; —mellows; —parches; —renews; —unfolds; —vitalizes; —wanes; —waxes; —wilts; —yields.
(See autumn, spring, winter, season.)

SUMMIT

adjectives
peaked; serene; towering; jagged; snow-clad; feathery; ornamental; dreadful; topmost; snowy; wild; pathless; lone; seared; blasted; sacred; sloping; breathless; flowering; hoary; islanded; unique; subordinate; commanding; bleak; sunburned; roofless; unscaled; intangible; toppling.

verbs
achieve—; ascend to—; aspire to—; cap—; clamber to—; crown—; grope for—; link—; mount to—; plunge from—; precipitate from—; scale—; soar to—; strive for—; topple from—; view from—; —allures; —climaxes; —crests; —culminates; —erodes; —tempts.
(See crown, culmination, height, pinnacle.)

SUMMON (v)
adverbs
domineeringly; commandingly; dictatorially; dogmatically; harshly; sternly; peremptorily; courteously; unceremoniously; tersely; arrogantly; emphatically; petulanly; urgently; vociferously.
(See command, call.)

SUMMONS

adjectives
emphatic; collective; peremptory; gracious; petulant; authoritative; coincident; silent; final; hasty; urgent; dread; long-waited; vociferous; strange.

verbs
abrogate—; announce—; answer—; countermand—; dismiss—; dispatch—; enforce—; heed—; ignore—; nullify—; quash—; serve with—; —apprehends; —arraigns; —bids; —cites; —coerces; —commands; —demands; —directs; —informs; —notifies; —orders.
(See call, invitation, mandate, order, command.)

SUMPTUOUS
adverbs
comfortably; surprisingly; actually; luxuriously; delightfully; unexpectedly; miraculously; significantly; invitingly; unnecessarily; extravagantly; pleasantly; designedly; lavishly.

SUN
adjectives
noontide; withdrawing; scarlet; warm; pleasant; never-hurrying; soul-expanding; waning; devouring; traveling; extinguished; external; burning; keen; morning; night; meridian; invisible; declining; rising; dipping; lowering; centrifugal; dazzling; unconquered; pitiless; kindling; blazing; bronze; material; sinking; fierce; retiring; vanished; setting; cruel; earthly; ancient; climbing; ardent; glorious; outdoor; brazen; dying; cloudless; scorching; lurid; rounding; smoldering; tropic; vertical; slanting; circling; majestic; vernal; merciless; killing; radiant; mimic; autumn; descended, glaring; unveiled; temperate; retreating; warmer; conflagrant; sickly; wheeling; early; impassioned; surviving; unruly; gaudy; fair; utmost; worshipped; garish; hateful; insistent; fervent; uncurled; central; bleak; naked; universal; smiting; westering; liberal; vaporous; broiling; blushing; sleepy; fierce; ruddy; sudden; sovereign; treacherous; unshaded; alien; bloody; earth-invisible (pl).

verbs
bask in—; bathe in—; block off—; eclipse —; expose to—; obscure—; protect from—; revel in—; salute—; scorn—; shield from—;

1146

squint at—; worship—; —anneals; —ascends; —bakes; —beats down; —blinds; —blisters; —blushes; —breaks; —burnishes; —climbs; —clouds; —clothes; —creeps; —crowns; —dazzles; —declines; —dims; dips; —dogs; —draws; —drenches; —eclipses; —fades; —filters; —flames; —flays; —floods; —gilds; —gyrates; —haunts; —heralds; —melts; —mirrors; —nourishes; —paints; —parches; —peeps out; —penetrates; —pours; —presses down; —radiates; —renews; —retreats; —salutes; —sears; —shadows; —shines; —sinks; —smiles upon; —smites; —stimulates; —strikes; —tinges; —vanishes; —veils; —wearies; —withdraws; —withers.

(See moon, heat, sunlight.)

SUNLIGHT

adjectives
morning; flowing; bright; thinned; reflected; hazy; marvelous; ardent; roseate; windy; sweet; slanting; choicer; naked; mellow; purging; stealing; unfallen; glancing; blinding; forenoon; laughing; dancing; imprisoned; watery; joyous; quivering; pitiless; mocking; parting; dappled; shaded; healthful; spring-eyed.

verbs
bask in—; emerge into—; flash in—; —arises; —dies; —exposes; —filters; —hallows; —lingers; —penetrates; —quivers; —slides through; —streams; —touches.

(See moonbeam, light, sun.)

SUNNY

adverbs
radiantly; pleasantly; happily; wholesomely; delightfully; cheerily; vivaciously; merrily; brightly; blithely; buoyantly; helpfully; winsomely; exultantly; optimistically; sparklingly; jauntily.

SUNSET

adjectives
forlorn; crimson; sunken; hollow; brilliant; sinking; fiery; dying; silent; pompous; lingering; glorious; peaceful; polychrome; fading; refulgent; wintry; bloody.

verbs
cloud—; loiter till—; linger to—; obscure —; view—; —beams; —colors; —dazzles; —declines; —diffuses; —eclipses; —enchants; —enthralls; —entrances; —gilds;

—gleams; —glimmers; —glows; —glowers; —radiates; —reflects; —scintillates; —shimmers.

(See twilight, daylight, dawn.)

SUNSHINE

adjectives
perpetual; brilliant; sudden; sparkling; searching; westering; tawny; cruel; eternal; clear; radiant; embodied; vital; glancing; dreaming; tingling; satin; sweet; mellow; vivid; open; harsh; broad; pitiless; illimitable; everlasting; imprisoned; peaceful; unclouded; beauteous; precious; continuous; genial; merciless.

verbs
drink in—; flood with—; luxuriate in—; —bleaches; —bursts forth; —caresses; —dances; —energizes; —enlivens; —filters through; —flatters; —gladdens; —glitters; —greets; —illumines; —melts; —parches; —permeates; —pervades; —renews; —shimmers; —showers.

(See light, moonbeam, sunlight, sun.)

SUNSHINY

adverbs
brilliantly; gorgeously; gloriously; delightfully; unusually; fortunately; luckily; wonderfully; marvelously; dazzlingly; faintly; scarcely; hotly; unbearably; intolerably; scorchingly; burningly; mercilessly; glaringly.

SUP (v)

adverbs
sumptuously; regally; bountifully; clandestinely; domestically; fraternally; formally; genially.

(See dine, eat.)

SUPERCILIOUS

adverbs
intolerably; uncivilly; deplorably; haughtily; stupidly; oddly; magnificently; laughably; arrogantly; proudly; offensively; ridiculously; incurably; unpardonably; smugly; irritatingly; insolently; presumptuously; coolly; insufferably; condescendingly; purposely; splendidly; brashly; brazenly; idiotically; ostentatiously; rudely; egotistically; conceitedly; pretentiously; unblushingly; impudently; saucily; swaggeringly; flippantly; shamelessly.

SUPERINTENDENT

adjectives
tutorial; strict; immediate; personal; careful; watchful.

verbs
closet with—; consult—; —admonishes; —arbitrates; —commends; —deliberates; —dickers with; —directs; —exhorts; —goads; —governs; —guides; —manages; —officiates; —pilots; —prescribes; —presides; —pulls strings; —regulates; —sacks; —steers.
(See manager, employer, boss.)

SUPERIOR

adjectives
race; intellectual; immediate.

SUPERIORITY

adjectives
feline; racial; cool; innate; muscular; spurious; numerical; overwhelming; intellectual; essential; absolute; economic; whimsical; scornful; astonishing; obvious; compassionate; ineffable; menaced; lofty; simpering; contemptuous; historical; infinite; fancied; dignified; inherent; masculine; base; adventitious; conscious; immense; extraordinary; assumed.

verbs
acclaim—; achieve—; assert—; assume—; attest to—; belittle—; challenge—; consider —; demonstrate—; disclose—; display—; enhance—; evince—; exaggerate—; exalt—; exhibit—; manifest—; proclaim—; prove—; regard—; reveal—; verify—; vie for—; weigh—; —eclipses; —outshines; establish —.
(See supremacy, eminence.)

SUPERSEDE (v)

adverbs
gradually; temporarily; invidiously; ultimately; logically; expectedly.
(See replace, supplant.)

SUPERSTITION

adjectives
barbarous; colorful; idle; monstrous; exploded; fantastic; capricious; brutal; religious; ethnic; silly; deepest; contemporary; narrow; vain; enormous; popular; conflicting; pure; childish; puerile; vulgar; imaginative; pestilent; singular; degrading; illustrious; bizarre; insatiate; grossest; primitive; unbelievable; fanciful; confused; ancient; haunting; pre-existing.

verbs
abolish—; efface—; encrust with—; eradicate—; explode—; free from—; ignore—; refute—; revive—; rid of—; swallow—; —beguiles; —blinds; —chains; —deludes; —dominates; —dupes; —enslaves; —fetters; —persists; —prejudices; —prevails; —shackles; —shrouds; —subjugates; —warps.
(See fanaticism, ignorance, prejudice, myth.)

SUPERSTITIOUS

adverbs
absurdly; sincerely; ridiculously; unreasonably; foolishly; terribly; fearfully; honestly; gullibly; nervously; incredibly; fanatically; piously; exceedingly; curiously; oddly; strangely; credulously; romantically; fearsomely; inveterately; incurably; anxiously.

SUPERVISE (v)

adverbs
personally; intelligently; successfully; strictly; cautiously; professionally.
(See manage, direct.)

SUPERVISION

adjectives
constant; censorial; direct; rigid; jealous; provincial; voluntary; human; chilling; controlling; governmental; strict; careful.

verbs
assume—; enforce—; maintain—; prescribe —; recommend—; relax—; retain—; subject to—; —administers; —chains; —curbs; —fetters; —guides; —irks; —leashes; —pilots; —restrains; —restricts; —wanes.
(See management, control.)

SUPPER

adjectives
champagne; bountiful; scanty; hearty; solemn; sumptuous; bare; rich.

verbs
bid to—; bolt—; climax—; conclude—; cram in—; deprive of—; devour—; gobble —; gorge—; grace—; gulp—; relish—; savor—; summon to—; —nauseates; —refreshes; —reinvigorates; —renews; —satiates; —tickles the palate.
(See meal, luncheon, breakfast, dinner.)

SUPPLANT (v)

adverbs

inevitably; permanently; ultimately; temporarily; unexpectedly; ruthlessly; dictatorially.

(See supersede, replace.)

SUPPLE

adverbs

youthfully; incredibly; naturally; slenderly; sturdily; amazingly; extremely; uncommonly; admirably; particularly; delightfully; unusually; remarkably; fortunately.

SUPPLEMENT (v)

adverbs

elaborately; fully; completely; authoritatively; definitely; adequately.

(See add, complete.)

SUPPLICATION

adjectives

formal; strong; affecting; frantic; fervent; piteous; reverent; honest.

SUPPLIES

adjectives

stable; continuous; inexhaustible; plentiful; abundant; precarious; visible; regulated; virgin; providential; needed; pecuniary; liberal; considerable; limited; constant; deficient; perennial; adequate; unbounded; scant; table; ample; warlike; extensive; dependable; bountiful; countless; permanent; miserable; muddy; vast; commercial.

SUPPLY

verbs

augment—; avail oneself of—; bolster—; check—; crave—; curb—; curtail—; deplete —; dispense—; entreat—; exceed—; exhaust—; facilitate—; guarantee—; insure —; procure—; replenish—; stabilize—; stock with—; warehouse—; —dwindles; —evaporates; —flows.

(See store, merchandise, stock, surplus, product.)

SUPPLY (v)

adverbs

bounteously; liberally; indifferently; exclusively; infallibly; amply; abundantly; plentifully; faithfully; scantily; continuously; pecuniarily; adequately; permanently; commercially; liberally.

(See furnish, yield.)

SUPPORT

adjectives

substantial; powerful; generous; overwhelming; intermediate; eloquent; wholesale; warm; earnest; mere; thoughtful; zealous; uniform; effective; firm; frail; elusive; principal; hearty; abated; stalwart; urgent; ephemeral; enthusiastic; scarce; vigorous; adequate; superficial.

verbs

angle for—; barter for—; bestow—upon; command—of; consolidate—; derive—; earn —; enlist—; foster—; lend—; lessen—; line up—; maintain—; muster—; pledge—; rally to—; repel—; repudiate—; seek—; share in—; whip up—; —comforts; —consoles; —dissolves; —fails.

(See living, help, livelihood, assistance.)

SUPPORT (v)

adverbs

adequately; steadfastly; appreciatively; respectfully; structurally; plausibly; conscientiously; adamantly; abundantly; substantially; theoretically; warmly; zealously; effectively; heartily; enthusiastically; vigorously.

(See defend, back.)

SUPPORTERS

adjectives

shadowy; ardent; persistent; staunchest; faithful; devoted; fanatical; unconditional; jubilant; regular.

verbs

alienate—; assure of—; estrange—; gather —; lure—; rally—; vex—; —advance; —authenticate; —back; —bear; —bolster; —cheer; —comfort; —expedite; —foster; —found; —further; —maintain; —promote; —sustain.

(See contributor, friend, advocate.)

SUPPOSE (v)

adverbs

rationally; erroneously; falsely; fallaciously; unsuspectingly; hopefully; optimistically.

(See assume, presume.)

SUPPOSITION

adjectives

false; analogous; indolent; staggering; contrary; probable; mitigating.

verbs

argue on—; concede—; confirm—; contradict—; forsake—; grant—; hazard—; maintain—; overthrow—; refute—; speculate on —; support—; unfold—; weigh—; work on —; —alludes; —assumes; —carries weight; —conjectures; —hints; —originates in; — presumes; —presupposes; —surmises; — theorizes; ridicule—.

(See assumption, guess, hypothesis, conjecture.)

SUPPRESS (v)

adverbs

silently; insidiously; traitorously; ruthlessly; undemocratically; viciously; vindictively; overtly; covertly; rigorously; generally; summarily; studiously; tyrannically.

(See repress, restrain.)

SUPREMACY

adjectives

literal; feudal; authorized; universal; maritime; scholarly; secular; naval; ecclesiastical; political; restored; righteous; long-sought; matrimonial; domestic.

verbs

achieve—; acknowledge—; admit—; assert —; battle for—; bolster—; confirm—; demonstrate—; dispute—; insure—; maintain —; preserve—; prove—; renounce—; reveal —; seek—; struggle for—; surrender—; veil —; —crumbles; —sways; —totters.

(See domination, success, achievement, victory.)

SURE-FOOTED

adverbs

amazingly; sufficiently; particularly; unfailingly; fortunately; assuredly; comfortingly; luckily; alertly; gracefully; faithfully; confidently; intrepidly; fearlessly; unquestionably; reliably; trustworthily.

SURF

adjectives

booming; roaring; boiling; raging; damaging; foamy; retreating; relentless; murderous; turmoiling.

verbs

—agitates; —babbles; —batters; —billows; —boils; —booms; —breaks; —buffets; — chops; —deluges; —drenches; —foams; — froths; —hisses; —inundates; —licks; — murmurs; —pounds; —ripples; —roars; —

seethes; —sluices; —sprays; —spumes; — surges; —swashes; —swells; —washes.

(See billow, wave, breaker.)

SURFACE

adjectives

silky; simmering; inferior; temporary; highway; brushed; rough; sparkling; shaggy; heaving; mirror-like; limiting; leaden; inelastic; refracting; troubled; raised; rugged; crawling; vibratory; undulating; reasonable; polished; sensitive; smooth; gleaming; faceted; rolling; agitated; glassy; intellectual; lumpy; metallic; unbroken; radiant; vitreous; sloping; broad; burnished; sprayed; convex; prismatic; sluggish; slotted; plaited; external; tourist; warmer; exposed; muddy; bright; stony; pliant; tenacious; general; plane; driving; suede-like.

verbs

abrade—; becalm—; burnish—; corrugate —; dent—; detect upon—; dip below—; duck below—; engrave on—; explore—; face—; finish—; flash upon—; furrow—; glaze—; inflame—; level—; mar—; penetrate—; plunge beneath—; polish—; probe below—; ruffle—; rumple—; scan—; scour —; scratch—; skim—; smite—; smooth—; veneer—; venture upon—; warp—; weather —; wrinkle—.

SURGE

adjectives

eternal; furious; relentless; toiling; fiery; sulphurous; knelling; rolling; volcanic; boiling; whispering; roaring; restless; broken; imperious.

SURGE (v)

adverbs

confusedly; wildly; thunderously; turbulently; violently; relentlessly; sulphurously; volcanically; boilingly; roaringly; imperiously.

(See swell, heave.)

SURGERY

adjectives

plastic; radical; painful; bold; bloody; magic; life-saving.

verbs

advise—; baffle—; botch—; defy—; employ —; hail—; perform—; practise—; rally from—; resort to—; skill in—; survive—; weather—; —adjusts; —binds; —converts; —delivers; —endangers; —facilitates; —

reanimates; —reconstructs; —rectifies; — rehabilitates; —rejuvenates; —removes; — renovates; —repairs; —restores; —resuscitates; —staunches.

(See operation, remedy, medicine.)

SURLY

adverbs

bluntly; terrifyingly; cruelly; unnecessarily; heedlessly; inexcusably; discourteously; disrespectfully; unpardonably; unwarrantably; boorishly; angrily; roughly; intolerably; churlishly; unaccountably; strangely; curiously; alarmingly; darkly; ominously; unusually.

SURMISE

adjectives

false; intellectual; vague; anxious; wide; wild.

verbs

advance—; concede—; denounce—; form—; grant—; hazard—; offer—; refute—; resort to—; speculate on—; submit—; —alleges; —alludes to; —assumes; —coincides with; —conjectures; —hints; —postulates; —presumes; —presupposes; —suggests; —theorizes.

(See guess, conjecture.)

SURMISE (v)

adverbs

shrewdly; intuitively; rationally; slyly; astutely; vaguely; anxiously; pessimistically; jealously; enviously.

(See suppose, guess.)

SURMOUNT (v)

adverbs

exultantly; victoriously; boisterously; triumphantly; ambitiously; incredibly.

(See conquer, overcome.)

SURPASS (v)

adverbs

amazingly; exultantly; exceedingly; incredibly; astoundingly; spectacularly; sensationally.

(See excel, exceed.)

SURPLUS

adjectives

destructive; labor; unavoidable; re-invested; unsellable; huge; undistributed; profitable.

verbs

accrue—; accumulate—; afford—; amass—; avert—; discard—; disclose—; dispose of —; exaggerate—; invest—; market—; pile up—; reveal—; squander—; swallow—; — assures; —augments; —brims; —burdens; —congests; —deluges; —floods the market; —gorges; —gluts; —insures; —overflows; —strains; —supersaturates; —weighs upon.

(See excess, supply.)

SURPRISE

adjectives

unspeakable; dull; wistful; pleasant; perpetual; quaint; unfortunate; unfeigned; amiable; delightful; unaffected; infinite; contemptuous; calm; charming; effusive; admiring; geological; solemn; shameful; sordid; sweet; bewildered; acceptable; painful; strange; melancholy; glad; excessive; hollow; curt; pompous; horrified; agreeable; blank; puzzled; annoyed; dramatic; drab; swift; exquisite; cordial; inexcusable; continual; quick; speculative; tremendous; mingled; hurt; immense; comic.

verbs

affect—; anticipate—; conceal—; express—; feign—; gape in—; induce—; manifest—; occasion—; prepare—; reveal—; strike with —; —bewilders; —dazzles; —electrifies; — flabbergasts; —overwhelms; —petrifies; — ruffles; —rumples; —shocks; —staggers; — startles; —stuns; —throws one off guard.

(See amazement, miracle, astonishment.)

SURPRISE (v)

adverbs

curiously; agreeably; innocently; utterly; mildly; faintly; mutually; unspeakably; amiably; quaintly; unfeignedly; delightfully; infinitely; painfully; excessively; exquisitely; cordially; tremendously; comically.

(See astonish, amaze.)

SURRENDER

adjectives

easy; traitorous; joyous; pusillanimous; instant; unconditional; forced; forlorn; verbal; resigned; peaceable.

SURRENDER (v)

adverbs

utterly; impatiently; meekly; affectionately; peaceably; unconditionally; voluntarily;

graciously; traitorously; forlornly; pusillanimously.

(See yield, abandon.)

SURROUND (v)

adverbs
opulently; inextricably; enthusiastically; triumphantly; fraternally; apprehensively; artificially; uncongenially; felicitously; luxuriously; tranquilly; picturesquely; grotesquely; nobly; trivially; quaintly; rustically; pastorally; inspiringly.

(See entrench, inclose.)

SURROUNDINGS

adjectives
artificial; uncongenial; iron; appalling; felicitous; tropical; sociable; pleasant; superb; smart; cultural; refined; luxurious; tranquil; picturesque; dignified; affectionate; unique; harsh; primitive; grotesque; grander; indulgent; noble; trivial; quaint; frigid; charming; beautiful; dingy; rustic; pastoral; unwonted; inspiring; modern.

verbs
absorb in—; acclimate to—; acquaint with —; adapt to—; alter—; blind to—; condition by—; contemplate—; darken—; deduce from —; encompass—; engross in—; escape—; explore—; inspect—; orient to—; pervade —; recognize—; reconnoiter—; regard—; rise above—; scan—; scrutinize—; skirt—; survey—; transcend—; —breed; —depress; —enchant; —enthrall; —foster; —impress; —oppress; —suggest; —symbolize.

(See environment, circumstances, conditions.)

SURVEILLANT

adverbs
warily; vigilantly; suspiciously; significantly; carefully; alertly; inquisitively; constantly; watchfully; incessantly; generally; conscientiously; meticulously; punctiliously; dependably; reliably.

SURVEY

adjectives
mournful; calm; ordnance; cursory; interior; official; leisure; compiled; recent; hopeless; impassioned; casual; severe; quick; optimistic; independent; sweeping; chronological; decisive; ·unbiased; preliminary; perspective; impartial; exhaustive.

verbs
authenticate—; check—; cite—; condense—; conduct—; contemplate—; extend—; initiate —; regard—; scan—; —astounds; —calculates; —catalogues; —computes; —confirms; —demonstrates; —discloses; —discovers; — embraces; —enables; —enumerates; —estimates; —evaluates; —gauges; —indicates; —informs; —measures; —probes; —records; —reveals; —scales; —startles; —uncovers; —verifies.

(See study, investigation, examination.)

SURVEY (v)

adverbs
extensively; gloomily; tranquilly; critically; curiously; morbidly; maliciously; suspiciously; officially; leisurely; optimistically; unbiasedly; impartially.

(See view, examine.)

SURVIVAL

adjectives
unique; barbaric; unconscious; fortunate; race; evolutionary; bare.

SURVIVE (v)

adverbs
vigorously; miraculously; heroically; undauntedly; staunchly; courageously.

(See live, exist.)

SURVIVORS

adjectives
terrified; ill-fated; reimbursed; heroic; injured; struggling; belated.

SUSCEPTIBILITY

adjectives
morbid; exquisite; excessive; strong; foolish; obvious; observant; moral; vivid; extreme; patent.

verbs
affect—; allay—; augment—; cancel—; conceal—; compensate for—; counteract—; cultivate—; excite—; exempt from—; increase —; intensify—; neutralize—; promote—; raise—; repress—; sense—; sharpen—; stir —; —endangers; —exposes; —inclines; — jeopardizes; —predisposes; —tends toward.

(See propensity, inclination, tendency.)

SUSCEPTIBLE

adverbs
highly; unusually; easily; emotionally; extremely; quickly; alarmingly; romantically;

strangely; curiously; uncommonly; amazingly; inherently; naturally.

SUSPECT

verbs

absolve—; acquit—; bail—; challenge—; clear—; cross-examine—; defend—; detain —; discharge—; dismiss—; exculpate—; exempt—; exonerate—; free—; grill—; harbor—; hold—; jail—; liberate—; lynch—; question—; release—; retain—; round up —s; shake—; trap—; vindicate—; whitewash—; —denies; —defends; —escapes; —vindicates.

(See prisoner, criminal.)

SUSPECT (*v*)

adverbs

unjustifiably; shrewdly; secretly; previously; gravely; unfairly; generally; justly; insanely; jealously; personally; intrusively.

(See surmise, doubt.)

SUSPENSE

adjectives

absorbed; waiting; agonizing; irresolute; tremulous; sultry; lowering; painful; frighted; unrelaxed; dramatic; clever; intolerable; agitated; prolonged; awful; tedious; awakening.

verbs

allay—; alleviate—; bear—; cower in—; ease—; face—; flinch at—; heighten—; intensify—; lessen—; maintain—; mitigate—; moderate—; palliate—; preserve—; relinquish—; survive—; sustain—; swoon in—; withdraw—; —abates; —agonizes; —embarasses; —relaxes; —rends; —shatters; —strains; —subsides; —taxes; —tenses; —wanes; —weighs upon.

(See perplexity, excitement, tension, anxiety, uncertainty.)

SUSPENSION

adjectives

premature; simultaneous; mature; critical; permanent; definite.

SUSPICION

adjectives

mingled; habitual; mean; mutual; bitter; aggressive; horrible; overawing; harsh; common; inscrutable; special; deep; plentiful; lingering; unworthy; dull; aroused; lively; hard; terrible; prying; jealous; waked; chilly; furtive; infusing; perpetual;

groundless; merest; faint; horrid; diminished; tormented; additional; shrewd; excited; angry; unmanly; personal; general; intrusive; sharp; sly.

verbs

absolve of—; allay—; arouse—; brand with —; breed—; cherish—; confirm—; conquer —; consolidate—s; dispel—; entertain—; evade—; excite—; ground—; heighten—; inspire—; justify—; lull—; occasion—; regard with—; resent—; sweep aside—; veil —; voice—; —crosses the mind; —dawns upon; —deepens; —grows; —pervades; —prevails; —thickens.

(See distrust, jealousy, anxiety, doubt.)

SUSPICIOUS

adverbs

unreasonably; jealously; meanly; cruelly; foolishly; dangerously; terribly; ridiculously; warily; extravagantly; inordinately; curiously; significantly; fearfully; uncertainly; vaguely; definitely; oddly; absurdly; needlessly; wildly; strangely; disagreeably; unpleasantly; odiously; perplexingly; unworthily; craftily.

SUSTAIN (*v*)

adverbs

precisely; spiritually; materially; faithfully; casually; honorably; unanimously; magnificently; heroically; vigorously; faithfully; disastrously; courageously.

(See support, uphold.)

SUSTENANCE

verbs

afford—; arrest—; avail of—; begrudge—; deprive of—; dispatch—; dispense—; exhaust—; furnish—; grant—; grope for—; grovel for—; obtain—; offer—; plead for —; proffer—; provide—; refuse—; strive for—; struggle for—; suspend—; tender—; yield—; extract—.

(See living, livelihood.)

SWAB

verbs

begrime—; besmirch—; brush with—; contaminate—; dab with—; discard—; disinfect with—; dispose of—; foul—; introduce —; precipitate on—; rinse—; saturate—; scour with—; smudge—; taint—; —absorbs; —purges; —soaks up; —sponges.

(See sponge, mop.)

SWAGGER

adjectives

lordly; indolent; imposing; consequential; new; boxy; outstanding; shallow; jaunty; loose; brusque; impudent.

SWAGGER (v)

adverbs

theatrically; boisterously; obstreperously; pretentiously; shamelessly; impudently; dramatically; indolently; jauntily; nonchalantly.
(See swell, strut.)

SWAIN

adjectives

low-spirited; responsive; bashful; rustic; lusty; laboring; ephemeral; despairing; awkward; forlorn; ashy; country; reaping; wary; mistrustful.

verbs

deride—; ground—; impassion—; —attracts; —bewitches; —captivates; —caresses; —cherishes; —courts; —declares; —enamours of; —endears; —pleads; —prates of; —proclaims; —professes; —reveres; —serenades; —woos; —yearns.
(See lover, sweetheart, peasant.)

SWALLOW

adjectives

skimming; twittering; innumerable (pl); blithe; garrulous; chaffering; beauteous.

verbs

—arranges; —banks; —busies; —chirps; —circles; —s colonize; —dares; —s flock; —flutters; —journeys; —migrates; —swims low; —smooths; —snatches; —spreads wings; —sweeps; —twitters.
(See bird, martin.)

SWALLOW (v)

adverbs

avidly; vigorously; hastily; glumly; greedily; thickly; embarrassedly; spasmodically.
(See gulp, eat.)

SWAMP

adjectives

torrid; busy; moss-hung; impassable; fetid; pestilential; tamarack; tangled; unsightly; overtowering; adjacent; brackish; tropical; unhealthy; lonely; salty; inaccessible; social.

verbs

bog in—; brave—; drain—; foul in—; frequent—; hazard—; infest—; inhabit—; meander through—; mire in—; prowl in—; restore—; roam—; skirt—; slog through—; stray into—; traverse—; vanish into—; wallow through—; —breeds; —endangers; —enfolds; —engulfs; —jeopardizes; —mars.
(See marsh, mire, morass, mud.)

SWAMPY

adverbs

muddily; quaggishly; squashily; softly; unwholesomely; malarially; pestilentially; irremediably; hopelessly; unpleasantly; impracticably; disturbingly; distressingly; dangerously; deplorably; undesirably; unfortunately; unhealthfully; unluckily.

SWAN

adjectives

mysterious; drowsy; floating; solitary; ruthless; ruffling; graceful; dying.

verbs

—arches; —chants; —dips; —floats; —idles on water; —immerses; —lies; —mantles; —murmurs; —nibbles; —probes; —sails; —shies away, —steers; —strays; —swims; —trumpets; —wanders; —whoops; —flocks.
(See bird, duck, goose.)

SWANKY

adverbs

absurdly; luxuriously; pompously; arrogantly; superbly; aggressively; ostentatiously; extraordinarily; stylishly; sumptuously; elegantly; manifestly; flauntingly; gorgeously; conspicuously; consciously; quietly; genuinely.

SWARM

adjectives

unsuspected; solar; countless (pl); snow-soft; bony; prodigious; tremendous; ignoble; invading; droning; singing; meteoric; thieving; prolific.

verbs

capture—; disperse—; herd—; restrain—; rout—; smoke—; stir up—; —bristles; —buzzes; —clamors; —clusters; —converges on; —deluges; —emigrates; —filters from;

—focuses on; —hums; —multiplies; —over-whelms; —pours out; —presses; —settles; —surges; —teems; —throngs.
(See hive, horde, crowd.)

SWARM (v)
adverbs
noisomely; prodigiously; prolifically; thunderously; multitudinously; spectacularly; rushingly; engulfingly.
(See flock, cluster.)

SWAY
adjectives
illimitable; righteous; feeble; departed; unquestioned; long-time; potent; ancient; undisputed; mightier; steadfast; insolent; kindred; arbitrary; gracious; territorial; viceregal; double; singular; patriarchal; unconquerable; antique; despotic; sovereign; frigid; intolerable; murmurous; usurped; omnipotent; mischievous.

verbs
administer—; augment—; cripple—; deaden—; diminish—; exercise—; exert—; extend—; invalidate—; paralyze—; scotch—; undermine—; strengthen—; wield—; —controls; —dominates; —dwindles.
(See dominion, influence, power.)

SWAY (v)
adverbs
dizzily; rhythmically; musically; gently; indolently; perilously; alluringly; entrancingly; violently; restlessly; emotionally; psychologically; tremendously; dreamily; religiously.
(See lurch, swing.)

SWEAR (v)
adverbs
vigorously; fiercely; ferociously; solemnly; lustily; audibly; roundly; abominably; traitorously; earnestly.
(See curse, affirm, testify.)

SWEAT
adjectives
bitter; body; profuse; chilly; bloody; cold; tremendous; copious; continual; peasant; goblin.

verbs
check—; glisten with—; induce—; secrete—; —beads; —chills; —develops; —diffuses; —diminishes; —drenches; —drips;

—droops; —glistens; —pours off; —rolls; — stains; —starts; —wilts.
(See perspiration.)

SWEAT (v)
adverbs
copiously; prodigiously; profusely; tremendously; coldly; abnormally.
(See perspire, exude.)

SWEEP
adjectives
outward; wavering; everlasting; soft; long; heaving; exulting; comprehensive; windy; majestic; gentle; irresistible; pitiless; magnificent; wild; enormous; dramatic; dread; liberal; joyous; shining; semi-circular.

verbs
condense—; deflect—; determine—; direct—; enlarge—; extend—; limit—; magnify—; realign—; restrict—; shift—; switch—, —declines; —deviates; —diverges; —embraces; —expands; —ranges; —swerves; —zigzags.
(See speed, range.)

SWEEP (v)
adverbs
capriciously; irresistibly; bitterly; majestically; resistlessly; frightfully; terrifically; silently; mutely; hoarsely; gracefully; surreptitiously; vigorously; tumultuously; relentlessly; heartlessly; confusedly; magnificently; dramatically.
(See carry, move, sway.)

SWEETHEART
verbs
adore—; betroth to—; caress—; cherish—; devote to—; dismiss—; estrange—; forsake—; gain—; idolize—; jilt—; libel—; reject—; revere—; treasure—; woo—; yearn for—; —bewitches; —captivates; —charms; —enchants; —endears; —enraptures; —infatuates.
(See lover, mistress, siren, swain.)

SWEETNESS
adjectives
liquid; mournful; seductive; subtle; womanly; voluptuous; brooding; wild; earnest; penetrating; venerable; palling; ineffable; tender; wanton; balmy; admirable; listless; enduring; deceptive; ravishing; continuous; infantile; exceeding; unbelievable; luscious; drowsy; patient; plaintive; withering;

strained; direful; earthly; penetrative; alarming; awful; saucy; summer; capricious; fragrant; cloying; singular; sacred; wayward; sunny; girlish; prattling; secret; twittering; benign; candied; profuse; simpering.

verbs
adulterate—; affect—; commend—; emit—; enjoy—; feign—; inhale—; inject—; relish —; savor—; —allures; —baits; —cloys; —deceives; —depresses; —nauseates; —permeates; —revolts; —sickens; —smothers; —tempts.
(See nectar, fragrance, sugar, candy.)

SWELL (v)
adverbs
abnormally; hideously; pretentiously; indignantly; gently; powerfully; perceptibly; proudly; enormously; voluptuously; bulbously; incredibly; spectacularly.
(See expand, dilate.)

SWELLING
adjectives
imperceptible; proudest; puffy; slight; harmless; stormy; unfathomed; alternate; hive-like; solemn; gentle; cockney; serious; enormous; voluptuous; bulbous; secret.

verbs
accentuate—; allay—; alleviate—; avert—; characterize by—; compress—; diagnose—; ease—; extend—; overcome—; reduce—; remedy—; restrain—; vent—; —abates; —dilates; —diminishes; —disfigures; —distends; —dwindles; —ebbs; —exaggerates; —indicates; —mars; —presses; —projects; —protrudes; —stiffens; —subsides; —tortures; —wanes.
(See inflammation.)

SWERVE (v)
adverbs
deviously; perilously; dangerously; fatally; erratically; drunkenly.
(See deviate, turn.)

SWIFTNESS
adjectives
incredible; electric; tireless; usual; feline; stunning; menacing; bounding; amazing; wave-like.

SWIM (v)
adverbs
desperately; heroically; vigorously; unflaggingly; lustily; courageously; boldly; staunchly; gallantly.
(See float, move.)

SWINDLE
adjectives
churlish; loving; squealing; enormous; obstinate; snorting; public; huge; monstrous; wide-spread.

verbs
disclose—; execute—; guard against—; participate in—; penalize—; perpetrate—; reveal—; uncover—; unearth—; —bilks; —deprives; —despoils; —diverts; —extorts; —fleeces; —impoverishes; —infuriates; —mulcts; —rooks; —shears; —strips.
(See fake, fraud.)

SWING
adjectives
sensuous; breathless; undulating; rhythmic; unrestricted; smooth; romantic; graceful; saber; glittering; unerring; sweet; fascinating; swaying; crazed.

SWING (v)
adverbs
gracefully; playfully; noiselessly; creakingly; recklessly; gratingly; peremptorily; grotesquely; adroitly; lazily.
(See sway, wave.)

SWIRL
adjectives
eddying; unmistakable; nasty.

SWIRL (v)
adverbs
turbulently; dizzily; incessantly; aimlessly; eddyingly; vertiginously.
(See whirl, twist.)

SWOON
adjectives
profound; interlunar; deathlike; summer; drunken; amorous; sweet; pretended; opportune.

SWORD
adjectives
deputed; drawn; shining; unsheathed; glittering; angry; bold; senseless; naked; virgin; pitiless; reeking; tapered; temporal;

victorious; handsome; self-pointed; ponderous; unsullied; theological; tyrannous; prompted; swift; leaden; two-edged; flaming; boisterous; trusty; noisy; grasping; rusty; knightly; ornamented; sated.

verbs

accoutre with—; affix—; arm with—; bear —; besmirch—; brandish—; draw—; edge —; equip with—; extract—; fall before—; fence with—; flaunt—; flourish—; govern by—; insert—; oppose with—; perish by—; plunge—; purge by—; send home—; sheathe —; slash with—; slay with—; smite with—; stain—; strike with—; swish—; temper—; thrust—; unsheathe—; wave—; wear—; wield—; win by—; woo with—; —clanks; —s clash; —s cut; —drips; —flames; — flashes down; —glitters; —hacks; —pierces; —s slash against; —stuns; —whirs; — wounds.

(See knife, rapier, lance, cutlass, stiletto.)

SYCOPHANCY

adjectives
prodigious; courtly; crude.

verbs

approve—; brand with—; detect—; favor —; forbid—; induce—; lament—; patronize —; ply—; practise—; pursue with—; reject —; resist—; ridicule—; —infests; —irks; —irritates; —nauseates; —pollutes; —wins. (See flattery.)

SYLLABLES

adjectives
ponderous; liquid; redundant; hideous; hissing; stressed; difficult; long; staccato; unaccented.

SYLVAN

adverbs
delightfully; refreshingly; shadily; sweetly; songfully; pleasantly; charmingly; fragrantly; attractively; spaciously.

SYMBOL

adjectives
mystic; prefiguring; appropriated; rigid; graphic; repulsive; shining; magic; national; valiant; barren; companionable; impressive; universal; sacred; accidental; elaborate; mingled (pl); living; everlasting; hallowed; suggestive; dramatic; revolutionary; crude; archaic; sound.

verbs

compose—; comprehend—; conceive—; define—; engrave—; examine—; inquire into —; interpret—; regard—; renounce—; seek —; study—; substitute—; value—; —denotes; —overshadows; —proves; —represents; —signifies; —suggests; —typifies.

(See attribute, device, emblem, mark, sign.)

SYMBOLIC

adverbs
mystically; inscrutably; significantly; faintly; clearly; definitely; intentionally; artistically; mysteriously; curiously; abstrusely; cleverly; consistently; conspicuously; apparently.

SYMMETRY

adjectives
studied; adolescent; absolute; vertical; artificial; admirable; exquisite; broken; structural; rare; matchless; bilateral; sinewy; perfect.

SYMPATHETIC

adverbs
delightfully; warmly; lovingly; companionably; comfortingly; ardently; understandingly; intelligently; cooperatively; actively; zealously; energetically; feelingly; compassionately; indignantly; touchingly; harmoniously; pitifully; altogether; heartily; cordially; effusively; amiably; affectionately; helpfully; humanely; benevolently; generously.

SYMPATHIZE (*v*)

adverbs
gushingly; profoundly; effusively; complacently; keenly; warmly; earnestly; paternally; spontaneously; compassionately; frankly. (See understand.)

SYMPATHY

adjectives
vivacious; fatherly; imperfect; awful; silent; active; understanding; filial; instinctive; unspoken; poetic; trivial; genuine; noble; mock; wholehearted; extensive; delighted; tender; vivid; rebel; secret; loving; intelligent; consoling; utter; spiritual; glorious; passionate; nameless; inexplicable; irrepressible; frightened; reverent; fervent; mysterious; intense; mystic; irresistible; inborn; jeering; natural; impotent; mental; infinite; effusive; unconscious; energetic;

fanciful; fervid; spasmodic; boundless; divided; middle; conditional; placid; ardent; morbid; painful; presumed; healing; patient; cordial; magnetic; imaginative; practical; flaunted; respective; apparent; generous; prudent; subtle; spontaneous; warm; instantaneous; tentative; majestic; sincere; emotional; elaborate; profound; fraternal; unwelcome; synthetic; affectionate; peculiar; sobbing; loving; indissoluble; young; sweet; deferential; intelligent; kindly; passionate; adaptable; demonstrative; impersonal; gentle; radical; frank; solemn; universal; fearful.

verbs

afford—; alienate—s; arouse—; attract—; bestow—; desire—; elicit—; engage—; enlist—; evince—; exercise—; extend—; exude —; feign—; flare up in—; gain—; lack—; limit—; pledge—; reject—; shut off from—; spare—; steel against—; stir—; suppress—; whip up—; win—; woo—; —binds; —consoles; —cools; —eases; —lashes together; —moves; —tempers; —touches; —twinges; —unites.

(See compassion, pity, tenderness, affection.)

SYMPHONIC
adverbs

triumphantly; gloriously; brilliantly; dazzlingly; hamoniously; blaringly; delicately; beautifully; tenderly; merrily; scarcely; thunderously; soothingly; pleasantly; ineffably; impressively; splendidly; magnificently.

SYMPHONY
adjectives

light; airy; pathetic; descriptive; majestic; massive; angelic; universal; seraphic; pert; marvelous; awe-inspiring.

verbs

attend—; compose—; constitute—; develop —; direct—; execute—; introduce—; interpret—; join in—; perform—; present—; produce—; score—; —bursts forth; —charms; —delights; —enchants; —entices; —floats; —provokes; —thrills; —uplifts.

(See music, composition, orchestra.)

SYMPTOMS
adjectives

alarming; positive; terrifying; terminal; prevailing; anomalous; marked; inward; subsequent; dangerous; ominous; warning; dramatic; serious; peculiar; premonitory; unpleasant; distressing; hysterical; troublesome; insidious; bellicose; mitigated; feverish; characteristic; aggravated; decisive; individual; constant; threatening; recurring.

verbs

aggravate—; allay—; alleviate—; attend with—; complicate—; deprecate—; describe —; detail—; develop—; discern—; distrust —; eliminate—; enumerate—; evaluate—; evince—; exhibit—; give rise to—; heed—; ignore—; interpret—; mask—; observe—; regard—; relieve—; subdue—; —abate; —accompany; —advance; —appear; —confound; —continue; —decline; —distress; —indicate; —manifest; —mark; —subside; —vanish; —vary.

(See evidence, sign, indication.)

SYNCHRONIZE (v)
adverbs

delicately; nicely; scientifically; automatically; exactly.

SYNCOPE
verbs

endure—; expire from—; induce—; lapse into—; produce—; suffer—; —contracts; —endangers; —strains; —unnerves.

SYNDICATE
verbs

appoint to—; combine in—; empower—; form—; head—; —adjourns; —contracts for; —controls; —directs; —disposes of; —dupes; —forces; —introduces; —manages; —meets; —promotes; —purchases; —pushes; —raises; —schemes; —transacts; —undertakes.

(See committee, board, group, association, concern.)

SYNTHESIS
verbs

arise from—; comprehend—; construct by—; delve into—; devise—; disclose—; effect—; employ—; exhibit—; facilitate—; form—; hail—; observe—; produce by—; unite in—; —compounds; —restores; —results in; —yields.

(See combination, method.)

SYPHILIS
verbs

afflict with—; campaign against—; contract

—; control—; cure—; diagnose as—; eradicate—; expose—; fear—; indicate—; inflict with—; recognize—; relieve—; reveal—; stamp out—; suspect—; test for—; treat—; —attacks; —cripples; —destroys; —devastates; —menaces; —ravages; —strikes; —yields to.

(See disease.)

SYRINGE
verbs
compress—; employ—; exhaust—; fit—; force from—; inject with—; manipulate—; squeeze—; —cleanses; —discharges; —draws in; —ejects; —emits; —pours; —spouts; —sprinkles into; —squirts.

(See pump.)

SYSTEM
(general)
adjectives
pure; monetary; runaway; star; terrestrial; flexible; rational; corporate; constitutional; delicate; cumbrous; foul; elective; optical; pernicious; maudlin; digestive; mythic; rotting; intricate; dark; prefectorial; monarchical; nervous; overtaxed; routined; innovating; differing; bloc; reducing; judicial; enormous; expensive; utmost; proposed; gymnastic; defective; cumbersome; complicated; correlated; absolute; anatomical; preposterous; stellar; pedantic; beneficent; feudal; ecclesiastical; rigorous; harmonious; sequential; barbarous; infallible; elliptic; native; addled; metrical; prudent; tragic; voluntary; atrocious; equitable; selfish; medieval; debased; feasible; vicious; respected; effective; rapid; voluminous; defensive; conventual; diverse; elevated; closed; expiring; weak; inferior; scientific; harmful; equivalent; merit; subtle; formidable; existing; elastic; extraordinary; philosophic; sympathetic; competitive; imperial; reflective; disastrous; antiquated; subversive; respiratory; vascular; chronological; vigilant; unstable; impersonal; representative; profit; excellent; severe; fruit-

less; vain; infant; patronage; magnificent; distribution; experimental; ethical; full; compact; discordant; regulated; imperial; antiseptic; abstruse; drying.

SYSTEM
(plan, scheme, etc.)
verbs
accept—; adapt to—; adhere to—; adopt—; afford—; apply—; base on—; brace—; buck —; cling to—; consolidate—; contrive—; corrupt—; curb—; demonstrate—; devise—; discard—; disrupt—; dominate—; elucidate —; entrench—; establish—; evolve—; extend—; fashion—; father—; formulate—; forsake—; found—; inaugurate—; incorporate in—; install—; institute—; "knock"—; map out—; master—; modify—; mold—; outmode—; overthrow—; promulgate—; reduce to—; reform—; restore—; shake—; shatter—; subscribe to—; supervise—; vindicate—; wed to—; —bars; —decrees; —disintegrates; —functions; —governs; —hinges on; —insures; —rears; —totters.

(See plan, program, scheme, method, order.)

SYSTEM
(human body)
verbs
absorb into—; alkalize—; animate—; break down—; build up—; deplete—; derange—; drain—; emaciate—; fetter—; gear—; impoverish—; invade—; invigorate—; involve —; nourish—; poison—; purge—; recharge —; regulate—; relieve—; tone up—; traverse—.

(See body.)

SYSTEMATIC
adverbs
habitually; naturally; carefully; cautiously; painfully; pedantically; punctiliously; meticulously; incredibly; painstakingly; satisfactorily; commendably; admirably; tiresomely; needlessly; overly; unnecessarily; occasionally; emphatically.

T

TABERNACLE

adjectives

cloudy; mortal; earthly; quivering; fleshy; incarnate; spiritual.

verbs

abide in—; achieve—; conceive—; construct —; create—; disseminate through—; dwell in—; erect—; establish—; fill—; form—of; frequent—; inhabit—; lay foundation of—; occupy—; organize—; people—; permeate —; put together—; raise—; revere—; shun —; take up one's abode in—; —arises; — breeds; —brings forth; —fosters; —stands; —teems with.

(See church, temple, tent.)

TABLE

adjectives

shrouded; imperial; padded; tottering; wine-smeared; transparent; warped; toler-able; comely; bounteous; clean; zinc-topped; work; modest; rude; separate; abundant (pl); sphered; banqueting; polished; clut-tered; immense; hospitable; gaming; sturdy; extension; reading; well-spread; cheerful; washing; rickety; weather-beaten.

verbs

adorn—with; burrow under—; carve—; compose—of; construct—; clutter—; drape —; drum upon—; emboss—; fashion—; fur-nish—; gild—; grace—; gorge at—; head —; inlay—; litter—; load—with; pile on—; prepare—; spread—; support—; —bears; —groans; —stands; —sustains.

(See desk, bench, furniture.)

TABLOID

verbs

decipher—; interpret—; launch—; —abuses; —**adulterates**; —clamors; —commits; — cries out; —defiles; —disseminates; —holds forth; —horrifies; —inculcates; —nurtures; —pictures; —prostitutes; —seduces; — teems with; —violates; —vulgarizes.

(See press, newspaper.)

TABOO

verbs

countenance—; denounce—; enforce—; ig-nore—; impose—; observe—; remove—; set up—; —bans; —bars; —debars; —excludes; —forbids; —hampers; —hinders; —inhibits; —interdicts; —prohibits; —restrains; —re-stricts; —stands in the way.

(See ban, restriction.)

adverbs

racially; conventionally; inanely; snobbish-ly; socially; piously; ceremonially; strictly; traditionally; ecclesiastically; irrationally; inexplicably; utterly; politically; seriously; curiously; gravely.

TABULATE (*v*)

adverbs

tirelessly; accurately; industriously; statis-tically; neatly; mathematically.

(See record, arrange.)

TACIT

adverbs

implicitly; unobtrusively; inferentially; in-articulately; usually; timorously; validly; legally.

TACITURN

adverbs

provokingly; reticently; shyly; morosely; gloomily; observantly; amazingly; deliber-ately; habitually; naturally; unusually; in-curably; usually; inexplicably; unaccount-ably; interestingly; curtly; laconically; no-toriously; secretively; evasively; incredibly; strangely; usually; oddly; peculiarly; invet-erately; consistently; extraordinarily.

TACT

adjectives

subtle; external; sympathetic; gracious; del-icate; unerring; perfect; cheerful; diplo-matic; exquisite; rare; pecuniary; admir-able; female; genuine; discriminating; re-quisite; faultless; extraordinary; critical; consummate; customary; fine.

apply—; bring—into play; cast—to the winds; discard—; dispense with—; employ —; enlist—; evince—; make away with—; practice—; require—; shelve—; throw aside —; throw—overboard; utilize—; —brings to bear; —conduces; —serves; —subserves.

(See diplomacy, shrewdness, discretion.)

TACTFUL

adverbs

easily; graciously; pleasantly; affably; urbanely; agreeably; ingratiatingly; pleasingly; inoffensively; diplomatically; prudently; discreetly; unusually; notoriously; signally; significantly; gratefully; gracefully; helpfully; serviceably; unwontedly; carefully; cautiously; warily; sympathetically; unctuously; deliberately; wisely; tenderly; acutely; delicately; shrewdly; expertly; reasonably; profoundly; cleverly; thoughtfully; subtly; courteously; chivalrously; politely

TACTICS

adjectives

piscatory; able; skillful; terrorist; astute; medieval; imperfect; preliminary; wily; militant; tough; company; defensive; cautious; amazing; successful; driving; obstructive; ingenious; original; matrimonial; similar; turncoat.

verbs

adopt—; apply—; base—on; condone—; credit—; denounce—; develop—; devise—; dispute—; employ—; engage in—; influence —; introduce—; modify—; predict—; resort to—; revamp (colloq.)—; shift—; vary—; —aim; —assist; —cause; —demand; —effect; —enable; —evolve; —produce; —protect; —result in; —revolt; —shift.

(See maneuver, strategy, plan.)

TACTLESS

adverbs

unfortunately; unwittingly; thoughtlessly; ineptly; blunderingly; awkwardly; gracelessly; cruelly; embarrassingly; unluckily; clumsily; innocently; bluntly; ungraciously; carelessly; brutally; unfeelingly; unsympathetically; coldly; strangely; unexpectedly; lamentably; deplorably; unpardonably; insufferably; unpleasantly; disagreeably; unpredictably; blindly.

TADPOLE

verbs

convert—into; evolve from—; swarm with —s; view—; —adheres to the surface; — approaches; —s attach themselves; — breathes; —breeds; —changes to; —clings; —develops into; —emerges; —glides; — hatches; —is transformed into; —metamor-

phoses; —nibbles; —regenerates; —rushes; —sallies; —undergoes transformation; — wiggles; —wriggles.

(See fish.)

TAIL

adjectives

real; curling; flickering; forked; prehensible; stumpy; monstrous; false; fantastic; lambent; lashing; deadly; stinging; scraggy.

verbs

agitate—; cover—; fasten—; flick—; flourish—; hitch—; infest—; swish—; toss—; wag—; whisk—; —balances; —collides with; —dangles; —dashes; —hangs; — jerks; —lashes; —quivers; —slaps; — smacks; —strikes; —sweeps; —swings; — taps; —twitches; —whacks; —whisks; — wiggles.

(See braid, hair, end, rear.)

TAILOR

adjectives

trained; efficient; master; custom; union; experienced; faultless; loquacious; careful; hand; fine; lusty; soft; skillful; artistic; elaborate; casual; provincial; meticulous.

verbs

—accoutres; —alters; —apparels; —arrays; —attires; —biases; —borders; —designs; — drapes; —fits out; —flounces; —frills; — fringes; —gears; —hems; —outfits; —refurbishes; —renovates; —rigs; —seams; — sheathes; —styles; —tacks.

TAILOR (v)

adverbs

expertly; superbly; smartly; properly; stylishly; luxuriously; expensively; handsomely; faultlessly; exquisitely; flawlessly; scientifically; meticulously; impeccably; artistically.

(See fit, clothe.)

TAINT (v)

adverbs

disgustingly; sickeningly; dangerously; poisonously; partially; subtly; odorously; vilely.

(See corrupt.)

TAINTED

adverbs

unfortunately; ineradicably; indelibly; undisguisedly; fatally; indubitably; vilely; slightly; terribly; lamentably; strangely; unexpectedly; immeasurably; infectiously; noxiously; disgracefully; dangerously; completely; curiously; thoroughly; undeniably; unpleasantly; disagreeably; inexplicably.

TAKE (v)

adverbs

selfishly; invariably; graciously; voluntarily; figuratively; consciously; voraciously; recklessly; unhesitatingly; reluctantly; forcibly; sparingly; literally; ostentatiously; affectionately; seriously; indiscriminately; ostensibly; ceremoniously; roughly.

(See seize, apprehend.)

TAKING

adverbs

marvellously; attractively; charmingly; remarkably; prettily; beautifully; unusually; especially; pleasantly; interestingly; arrestingly; irresistibly; curiously; extraordinarily; enchantingly.

TALE

adjectives

half-told; monotonous; scandalous; sentimental; apocryphal; unbelievable; ecclesiastical; ridiculous; gloomy; foam-like; specious; supernatural; wondrous; pathetic; dismal; legendary; instructive; untold; tedious; mournful; exquisite; beautiful; passionate; flattering; effective; grievous; enchanting; true; riotous; shameful; diverting; evil; extraordinary; soothing; idle; definite; harrowing; melancholy; heavy; romantic; childish; uneventful; successful; crowning; gruesome; desolating; horrible; blissful; sensible; tragic; blood-curdling; artless; ever-young; saddest; magical; incoherent; tempting; merry; wild; transmitted; improbable; family; baseless; unpainted; tavern; taking; piteous; unvarnished; facetious; incomprehensible; intoxicating; sinister; amorous; long-winded; thrilling; melodramatic; mystic; abbreviated; touching; boastful; analogous; trifling; debonair; mingled (pl); seafaring; graphic; metrical; idle; free.

verbs

bear—; beguile with —s; center—; close—; compose—; conceive—; concoct—; construct —; depict—; drink in—; embody in—; follow up—; pervade—; plunge into—; pour out—; relate—; revive—; spin—; testify to —; treat—; unfold—; vary—; weave—; —s abound; —s drift into mind; —enhances

in interest; —entertains; —lengthens; —portrays; —progresses.

(See legend, narrative, narration, novel, story, "yarn," poem.)

TALENT

adjectives

genuine; distinguished; peculiar; superficial; satirical; histrionic; stifled; dramatic; marked; copious; kindred; administrative; brilliant; hidden; intuitive; inherited; native; undisciplined; vivid; social; admirable; innate; conspicuous; rare; precocious; evinced; delicate; original; sturdy; eminent; inconsiderable; gastronomic; choice; undoubted; uncommon; musical; wild; inventive; practical; interior; inborn; extraordinary; rising; latent; constructive; outside; mediocre; undoubted; comic; adoring; culinary; military; exquisite; budding.

verbs

applaud—; bring to light—; call upon—; confine—; cultivate—; demonstrate—; detect—; develop—; discover—; display—; dissipate—; enlist—; esteem—; eulogize—; expand—; exploit—; extol—; glorify—; inherit—; laud—; magnify—; misuse—; nurture—; panegyrize—; pay tribute to—; pervert—; prostitute—; smother—; stifle—; trace—; transcend—; weigh—; worship—; —buds; —decays; —germinates; —issues from; —ministers; —nourishes; —sprouts; —sustains; —transcends.

(See ability, mentality, intelligence, capacity, genius, skill.)

TALENTED

adverbs

eminently; conspicuously; extraordinarily; genuinely; peculiarly; particularly; remarkably; admirably; uncommonly; ingeniously; amazingly; signally; dazzlingly; surprisingly; splendidly; magnificently.

TALK

adjectives

buoyant; hearty; revolutionary; comprehending; fanciful; heartening; ineffable; passionate; furtive; prodigious; vainglorious; blasphemous; sneering; obscene; scandalous; heated; vigorous; unpleasant; willful; casual; yelling; loud; arduous; tedious; fragmentary; elliptical; rambling; everlasting; brilliant; indeterminate; bawdy; unmeaning; customary; spontaneous; vile; unmannerly; imperious; assuming; endless;

racy; confounded; solemn; droning; abundant; convincing; delightful; straight; impersonal; unusual; wanton; desultory; masculine; common; sprightly; buzzing; provincial; vain; loose; boyish; stimulating; inflammatory; inane; frivolous; vague; enjoyable; wicked; malignant; stammering; pious; discursive; alluring; facile; empty; silly; heart-searching; interesting; poetic; half-whispered; tumultuous; eloquent; bantering; wearisome; spasmodic; confidential.

verbs

cease—; compose—; deliver—; distinguish —; hush—; muffle—; mute—; muzzle—; silence—; stifle—; still—; substantiate—; tone down—; —allures; —annoys; —baits; —charms; —convinces; —distracts; —disturbs; —diverts; —edifies; —elucidates; — enlightens; —induces; —interests; —rumors.

(See speech, conversation, discourse, lecture.)

TALK (v)

adverbs

ramblingly; briskly; indefinitely; garrulously; animatedly; fluently; tediously; volubly; amicably; articulately; indiscreetly; blithely; shrewdly; casually; incoherently; pathetically; vivaciously; informally; interminably; mysteriously; unceasingly; eloquently; affectedly.

(See converse, speak.)

TALKATIVE

adverbs

incorrigibly; fluently; garrulously; chattily; informatively; incessantly; pleasantly; graciously; sociably; inveterately; naturally; habitually; incurably; happily; foolishly; loosely; effusively; eloquently; gushingly; prolixly; glibly; flippantly; unwisely; indiscreetly; imprudently; endlessly; tiresomely; strangely; remarkably; marvelously; incredibly; wearisomely; repetitively.

TALL

adverbs

slenderly; extraordinarily; splendidly; handsomely; lankily; absurdly; magnificently; commandingly; cadaverously; gauntly; awkwardly; laughably; gawkily; consciously; proudly; admirably; wonderfully; amazingly; unfortunately; ungainly; immeasurably; unusually; incredibly; attractively; conveniently.

TALLOW

verbs

affect—; boil—; compress—; convert into—; dissolve—; harden—; ignite—; liquefy—; melt—; mold—; purify—; refine—; separate—; solidify—; yield—; —consolidates; —confuses; —lumps; —thaws; —thickens.
(See wax.)

TALONS

verbs

bag with—; bare—; clip—; clutch in—; grasp in—; hook—; lay hold with—; pare —; pinion with—; retain in—; seize in—; sharpen—; —claw; —clench; —clinch; — detain; —gash; —gripe; —lacerate; —rend; —scar; —slash; —tear; —throttle.
(See fang, claw.)

TAME

adverbs

strangely; unexpectedly; finally; curiously; affectionately, tractably; unusually; downright; harmlessly; vexatiously; uninterestingly; dully; insipidly; submissively; lamentably; deplorably; compliantly; dutifully; apparently; obediently; surprisingly; sycophantically; tediously; insufferably.

TAME (v)

adverbs

partially; domestically; thoroughly; sufficiently; subtly; assiduously; rationally.
(See discipline, conquer.)

TAMELESS

adverbs

ardently; vehemently; enthusiastically; irrepressibly; utterly; violently; wildly; absolutely; savagely; ferociously; impatiently; stormily; inordinately; boisterously; crazily; riotously; temperamentally.

TANGIBLE

adverbs

comfortably; solidly; comfortingly; incontrovertibly; actually; finally; scarcely; ultimately; eventually; unexpectedly.

TANGLE

adjectives

dense; hopeless; confused; shining; mossy; feudal; matted; mazy; hereditary; complicated; blossoming; unexpected.

verbs

decipher—; dissolve—; elucidate—; extricate from—; fathom—; key—; liquidate—; resolve—; unravel—; unriddle—; unsnarl —; —confounds; —convulses; —deranges; —disconcerts; —dishevels; —jumbles; —meshes; —muddles; —perplexes; —perturbs; —puzzles; —ruffles; —rumples; —shuffles; —weaves; —webs.

(See intricacy, entanglement, mystery, riddle.)

TANGLE (v)

adverbs

perplexingly; desperately; hopelessly; complicatedly; designedly; confusedly; haphazardly; diplomatically; economically.

(See involve, perplex.)

TANGLED

adverbs

hopelessly; terribly; unfortunately; financially; curiously; embarrassingly; inextricably; strangely; deplorably; lamentably; oddly; darkly; odiously; laughably; ineptly; awkwardly; uncommonly; ridiculously; ludicrously; unskilfully; perplexingly; bewilderingly; guiltily; innocently; unwittingly; gullibly; helplessly; pitifully.

TANK
(general)

adjectives

special; septic; large; spacious; clogged; rusty; useful.

TANK
(military)

verbs

armor—; bullet-proof—; construct—; convert into—; design—; evade—; man—; manoeuvre—; mount—; propel—; surrender —; turret—; —attacks; —bombards; —caterpillars; —climbs; —crushes; —disperses; —lumbers; —negotiates; —repels; —rolls; —rumbles; —wheels.

TANTALIZING

adverbs

idly; absurdly; tormentingly; playfully; unbearably; teasingly; incalculably; terribly; oddly; merrily; continually; comically; outlandishly; uncommonly.

TAP (v)

adverbs

nervously; impatiently; rudely; gracefully;

lightly; significantly; intermittently; irritatingly; incessantly; periodically.

(See rap, knock.)

TAPE

verbs

rend—; shred—; —adheres; —agglutinates; —binds; —cements; —cleaves; —clings; —coheres; —conglutinates; —couples; —glues; —gums; —seals; —shackles; —unites.

(See ligature, band, bandage.)

TAPER

adjectives

glimmering; gleaming; beaming; midnight; waxen; burning; sickly; flickering; tall; graceful; slender.

verbs

glut with—s; obscure—; quench—; snuff out—; —beams; —diffuses; —flames; —flares; —flickers; —flutters; —gleams; —glimmers; —glows; —gutters; —illuminates; —radiates; —scintillates; —shadows; —twinkles.

(See candle, wick, light.)

TAPERING

adverbs

gracefully; symmetrically; slenderly; gradually; suddenly; eventually; unfortunately; beautifully; lamentably; unexpectedly.

TAPESTRY

adjectives

star-inwoven; fluttering; desolate; sun-colored; blossoming; luxuriant; low-toned; smirched; enameled.

verbs

embellish—; exhibit—; hang—; line—; mount—; mutilate—; prize—; rend—; shade —; suspend—; value—; weave—; —adorns; —beautifies; —decorates; —depicts; —landscapes; —portrays.

(See picture, painting.)

TARDY

adverbs

unfortunately; disastrously; unluckily; extremely; unaccountably; deleteriously; unreasonably; needlessly; infamously; unaccountably; indiscreetly; lamentably; deplorably; fatally; unconscionably; habitually; characteristically; exasperatingly; inexcusably; unpardonably; discourteously; impolitely; grossly; indecorously; surprisingly; disappointingly; irreparably.

TARGET

adjectives

uplifted; flaming; sensible; suitable; vulnerable; conspicuous; momentary; superb; helpless; receptive; rapid; moving; human; disappearing.

verbs

align with—; batter—; buffet—; collide with —; deflect from—; deflect—; deviate from —; direct toward—; diverge from—; fall short of—; flay—; level at—; rebound from —; riddle—; smite—; speed toward—; steer toward—; swerve from—; thwack—; — eludes.

(See mark, object.)

TARIFF

verbs

abolish—; absorb in—; adopt—; bandy—; bear—; bruit about—; exact—; legislate—; levy—; modify—; nullify—; parry—; rate —; reciprocate—; reduce—; regale with—; regulate—; revise—; scrap—; set—; silence —; slash—; steer—; yield—; —bamboozles (colloq.); —discourages; —distrains; — fades; —flows; —impedes; —limits; —prohibits; —protects; —ranges; —rates; —restrains; —restricts; —schedules; —subsides; —touches upon; —veers toward.

(See taxes, amount.)

TARNISHED

adverbs

slightly; remediably; temporarily; momentarily; wholly; unfortunately; curiously; ingloriously; morally; deeply; irrecoverably; pitiably; deplorably; unluckily; irretrievably; suddenly; hopelessly; sadly; manifestly.

TART

adverbs

sharply; pleasantly; interestingly; disagreeably; unnecessarily; keenly; discriminatingly; tastefully; laughably; cleverly; piquantly; poignantly; bewilderingly; ungraciously; deliberately; unpleasantly; gracelessly; tactlessly; extremely; suddenly; overly; inexcusably.

TASK

adjectives

barren; acrid; incongruous; diabolical; humble; pensive; considerable; self-imposed; toilsome; glorious; zealous; perilous; imaginative; present-day; uninspired; unpleasing; weary; appalling; tremendous; difficult; strenuous; bleak; ungracious; painful; willing; inevitable; hazardous; dormant; amusing; staggering; cheerless; mental; pedagogical; delightful; knotty; spiritual; irksome; arduous; dreaded; hopeless; delicate; simplified; futile; endless; unfulfilled; impossible; herculean; costly; thankless; onerous; graceful; alloted; anxious; abhorrent; rough; pleasing; laborious; unnatural; noble; primary; astounding; prosaic; formidable; musical; colossal; congenial; recurring; neglected; ungrateful; vulgar; heavy; exacting; suitable; disheartening; menial; priestlike; self-appointed; troublesome; tender; distasteful; useless; easy, discordant; venturesome; intellectual; sales; basic; discouraging; joyous; docile; fatiguing; appalling; dizzy; sublime.

verbs

absorb in—; accept—; achieve—; allot—; appoint—; approach—; assign—; assume —; attempt—; buckle down to—; charge with—; complicate—; confront—; consecrate to—; dedicate to—; develop—; devote to—; discharge—; dispose of—; ease—; engage in—; engross in—; enlist in—; entrust —; essay—; expend on—; facilitate—; fit for—; fulfill—; glorify—; impose—; intrust —; inure to—; lighten—; lump—s; perform —; plunge into—; prescribe—; present—; rally to—; render—; reward—; rob—; set to—; shirk—; shoulder—; shunt—; spur on to—; toil at—; undertake—; view—; whittle down—; —bores; —confronts; —consumes; —exhausts; —fatigues; —involves; —taxes; —wearies.

(See labor, chore, work, job.)

TASTE

adjectives

worst; impeccable; distinctive; congenial; artificial; pictureque; startling; acrid; artistic; luxurious; agreeable; aesthetic; considerable; fanciful; unpleasant; barbarous; educated; nauseous; bizarre; provincial; fastidious; incongruous; desultory; native; refreshing; controlling; exquisite; intellectual; superior; bookkeeping; cultivated; unusual; costly; execrable; elevated; vulgar;

classical; horrible; magic; varying; ludicrous; lustrous; cosmopolitan; barbaric; philanthropic; tangy; good; scientific; admirable; ancestral; erroneous; musical; precious; astringent; literary; uncertain; developed; popular; brazen; massive; instinctive; diminished; enlightened; ephemeral; pronounced; elegant; mortal; clean; honorable; gross; individual; delicious; aromatic; radical; savage; odious; characteristic; surprising; questionable; critical; unperverted; inimitable; plebeian; histrionic; taffy; bitter; schoolmastery; fashionable.

verbs

accumulate—; alter—; betray—; concoct—; criticize—; cultivate—; deprave—; disguise —; dispel—; elevate—; endure—; feign—; gratify—; impair—; indulge in—; manifest —; minister to—; modify—; outgrow—; overrate—; pander to—; pervert—; possess —; polish—; purify—; refine—; reflect—; relish—; simplify—; spice—; —appeais; —bites; —blossoms; —characterizes; —clings; —collapses; —crystallizes; —discriminates; —guides; —gormandizes; —intoxicates; —lingers; —nauseates; —rasps; —reflects; —sickens; —smacks of.

(See desire, craving, impulse, inclination, flavor, appreciation.)

TASTE (v)

adverbs

sparingly; tentatively; fastidiously; perniciously; poisonously; odiously; horribly.

(See relish, eat.)

TASTEFUL

adverbs

delicately; deftly; naturally; richly; chastely; instinctively; inherently; innately; unerringly; exquisitely; fastidiously; quaintly; ingeniously; intrinsically; discriminatingly; expertly; correctly; academically; admirably.

TASTY

adverbs

pleasantly; unusually; gracefully; beautifully; delicately; delightfully; unexpectedly; surprisingly; deliberately; laboriously; invitingly; luxuriously; artistically.

TATTLE (v)

adverbs

childishly; faithlessly; traitorously; pettishly; hatefully; peevishly; vindictively.

(See babble, gossip.)

TATTLING

adverbs

maliciously; garrulously; innocently; cheerily; cheerfully; deliberately; dangerously; purposely; intentionally; childishly; meanly; mischievously; idly; diffusely; endlessly; snidely; dangerously; viciously; vindictively; malignantly; venomously; inanely; mindlessly; senselessly; thoughtlessly; witlessly; contemptibly; despicably; basely.

TAUNT

adjectives

parting; bitter; stinging; unmerited; unfeeling; good; reproachful.

verbs

bristle at—s; disregard—; fling—; hurl—; ignore—; repay—; repress—; restrain—; stifle—; tolerate—; utter—s; —affronts; —brands; —cuts; —disparages; —irks; —irritates; —jeers; —lashes; —outrages; —pervades; —ridicules; —slurs; —stings; —twits.

(See jeer, insult, reproach.)

TAUT

adverbs

curiously; nervously; dangerously; solidly; securely; sufficiently; perilously; finally; completely; lamentably; deplorably; inconveniently; rigidly; strangely; unaccountably.

TAVERN

adjectives

dusky; uninviting; well-restored; popular.

verbs

beguile in—; frequent—; frolic at—; haunt —; patronize—; regale in—; relax in—; reside at—; revel in—; stagger from—; visit —; weary of—; —accommodates; —beckons; —dispenses; —diverts; —lodges; —lures; —resounds; —rings; —welcomes.

(See hotel, inn.)

TAWDRY

adverbs

cheaply; unacceptably; reprehensibly; inexcusably; definitely; positively; inconceivably; incredibly; emphatically; admittedly; inadmissibly; disagreeably; contemptibly; insubstantially; obtrusively; dreadfully; noticeably; conspicuously; undisguisedly; blatantly; inordinately; extremely; sordidly; meanly; cheaply; offensively.

adjectives

confiscatory; direct; excessive; equitable; ingenious; oppressive; unequal; stealthy; extortionate; merciless; enormous; staggering; arbitrary; unpitying; burdensome.

TAXES

adjectives

hidden; local; inspection; prohibitive; punitive; social; fantastic; exclusive; grievous; external; superfluous; onerous; arbitrary; oppressive; exceptionable; inequitable; personal; incredible; odious.

verbs

abscond with—; apply—; appraise for—; appropriate from—; assess—; authorize—; default—; denounce—; derive—; discount—; divert from—; dodge—; eliminate—; enact —; evade—; exempt from—; extort—; grumble about—; impose ; inveigh against —; legislate—; levy—; outlaw—; question —; rate—; reduce—; repeal—; squeeze—; —accrue; —burden; —constitute; —crush; —defray; —design; —enable; —extend; — impoverish; —mount; —prorate; —ruin; — stifle; —support; —total; —yield; expend—.
(See tariff.)

TAXI

verbs

avail oneself of—; commandeer—; employ —; flag—; hail—; hire—; license—; man—; mobilize—s; pursue in—; recruit—s; resort to—; scramble for—; whistle for—; —careens; —conveys; —s file by; —meanders; —pick its way; —rolls away; —rumbles; —scuds; —s scurry; —skids; —swerves; — threads thru traffic; —transports; —traverses; —whizzes.
(See automobile.)

TAXPAYERS

verbs

address—; besiege—; burden—; coerce—; delude—; harass—; impoverish—; irk—; overburden—; promise—; ruffle—; soothe —; stir—; swindle—; tyrannize over—; — array against; —band; —campaign for; — declaim; —decry; —elect; —groan; — clamor; —league; —moan; —petition; — protest; —repudiate; —rise; —unite; — voice.
(See citizen, public, people.)

adjectives

numberless (pl); well-creamed; smuggled; elemental; contraband; rare; licorice; softened; melodious; perfumed; fragrant; aphrodisiac.

verbs

abstain from—; addict to—; brew—; concoct—; dispatch—; dispense—; drain—; entertain at—; flavor—; gulp—; ice—; imbibe—; import—; quaff—; sip—; spice—; strain—; sweeten—; swill down—; —appeases; —moistens; —quenches; —revives; —simmers; —stimulates; —thickens.
(See coffee, drink, beverage.)

TEACH (v)

adverbs

professionally; explicitly; elaborately; exclusively; extensively; laboriously; effectually; systematically; dispassionately; ethically; scrupulously; conscientiously; competently; eminently; zealously; erroneously; inspirationally.
(See instruct.)

TEACHABLE

adverbs

easily; scarcely; hardly; eagerly; responsively; clearly; manifestly; readily; ordinarily; extraordinarily; unusually; alertly; quickly; intelligently; admirably; exceptionally; surprisingly.

TEACHER

adjectives

perspicacious; competent; well-trained; mute; pious; imaginative; established; enthusiastic; delightful; admirable; discontented; notable; eminent; fledged; brilliant; illustrious; foremost; understanding; zealous; distinguished; religious; discouraged; primary; incapable; stimulating.

verbs

commend—; disqualify—; extol—; honor—; prejudice—; revere—; —adjusts; —breeds; —coaches; —cultivates; —disciplines; —discourses; —drills; —edifies; —emancipates; —enlightens; —equips; —expounds; — fledges; —fosters; —guides; —harangues; —hews; —holds forth; —illumines; —impregnates; —inculcates; —indoctrinates; — infiltrates; —infuses; —interprets; —initiates; —inspires; —instils; —instructs; — liberates; —matures; —molds; —nurtures;

—poises; —prepares; —shapes; —sheds light; —sows; —rears; —tutors; —uplifts. (See master, orator, scholar.)

TEACHING

adjectives

assiduous; blind; austere; orthodox; political; time-honored; positive; inspired; inner; basic; rational; erroneous; stern; polytheistic; ethical; false; lofty; skeptical.

verbs

accept—; acquaint with—; adhere to—; advance—; afford—; bias—; blind to—; certify for—; contradict—; convey—; demonstrate—; enlarge—; evolve—; follow—; glean from—; heed—; introduce—; labor at —; memorize—; practise—; prejudice—; propagandize—; reiterate—; reject—; standardize—; suppress—s; treasure—; — affords; —directs; —embraces; —enlightens; —guides; —inculcates; —infuses; — instils; —matures; —qualifies; —prepares; —unveils.

(See doctrine, gospel, precept, instruction, profession.)

TEA-CUP

adjectives

rattling; tiny; dainty; china; fragile.

TEAM

adjectives

well-matched; splendid; phlegmatic; ill-mated; willing; panting; serviceable.

verbs

acclaim—; assemble—; captain—; cleave—; coach—; condition—; discipline—; dominate —; drill—; forsake—; harangue—; harness —; heckle—; inspire—; instil in—; mobilize—; oppose—; rend—; reward—; sever —; subsidize—; transport—; —bows; —concedes; —conquers; —contends; —cooperates; —drubs; —files out; —flounders; — hampers; —manoeuvers; —proselytes; — surmounts; —trains; —triumphs; —upsets; —vanquishes.

(See crew, athlete, contestant.)

TEAR (v)

adverbs

distractedly; viciously; hideously; extensively; impatiently; ravenously; rudely; wolf-ishly; literally; wantonly; ceaselessly; ruthlessly; dreadfully.

(See divide, sever.)

TEARFUL

adverbs

touchingly; maddeningly; vexatiously; deliberately; purposely; profitably; pathetically; sympathetically; pitiably; unfortunately; readily; easily; ridiculously; comically; ludicrously; hysterically; nervously; timidly; shyly; bashfully; tragically; angrily; fearfully; overwhelmingly; embarrassingly; helplessly; anxiously; happily; boisterously; noisily; piteously.

TEARS

adjectives

superabundant; solemn; unshed; melodious; sorrowful; hysterical; timid; passionate; unavailing; heartbroken; fruitless; flowing; glowing; dying; passion-ridden; soul-brought; subduing; glorious; silent; weak; unreclaiming; stealing; idiot; sharp; sweet; bitter; dewy; struggling; treacherous; crystal; impending; grateful; honest; frozen; immortal; happy; salt; undropped; scalding; maudlin; untimely; eternal; joyful; repentant; unremembered; plenteous; tributary; emotional; ungovernable; immense; kindred; continual; gathering; contending; solemn; reminiscent; unavailing; sparkling; briny; unconscious; sympathetic; noiseless; sleepless; merry; crocodile; foolish; supplicating; patriotic; obsequious; excessive; imploring; intermittent; future; celestial; smarting; spiteful; involuntary; resistless; furious; parting; softening; mingled; submissive; saccharine; foreboding; purple; stanchless; contrite; peevish; quenched; humble; feigned; brimming; noble; penitential; dreadful; transparent; vanished; impotent; silver-shedding; mighty; fertile.

verbs

agitate to—; allay—; bathe in—; blind with —; brush away—; burst into—; check—; conceal—; consecrate with—; dab at—; dim with—; dissolve into—; dry—; emit —; feign—; flood with—; give vent to—; ignore—; inspire—; melt down—; move to —; provoke—; relieve—; secrete—; shed —; snivel in—; stem—; sting to—; summon —; swallow—; tinge with—; water with —; wink back—; wipe away—; wring—; —bedew; —blind; —choke; —dissolve; — dry up; —fall; —flow; —glisten; —glitter; —gush forth; —impassion; —melt; —move; —rack; —rain down; —scald; —soften; — start; —sting; —stream down; —sway; —

touch; —tremble; —trickle; —wash away; —well up; —wet; blink back—.

(See lamentation, dew, grief.)

TEASE (v)

adverbs
wilfully; provokingly; irritatingly; exasperatingly; bullyingly; boisterously; slyly; insidiously; viciously; vindictively; subtly; blithely.

(See torment, harass.)

TEASING

adverbs
blithely; playfully; persistently; comically; merrily; wildly; noisily; tormentingly; foolishly; inordinately; pestiferously; ludicrously; nonsensically; absurdly; merrily; airily; immoderately; hilariously.

TECHNICAL

adverbs
clearly; purely; merely; probably; narrowly; strictly; wholly.

TECHNICALITIES

verbs
acquire—; avoid—; bores one with—; botch —; bungle—; denote—; detail—; discard —; dispense with—; dissolve—; enlighten —; exhibit—; explain—; ignore—; insist upon—; master—; necessitate—; plague with —; simplify—; strip—; weigh—; —bewilder; —confuse; —particularize; —perplex.

(See detail, technique.)

TECHNICALITY

adjectives
theological; ecclesiastical; selling; trivial; tiny.

TECHNIQUE

adjectives
comprehensive; scarce; specified; perfected; grooming; inborn; natural; creative; operating; educational; photographic; administrative; first-rate; incredible; piano; impressionistic; remarkable; dramatic; masterly; sterile; histological; surgical; brushing; delicate; facile; amazing; complex.

verbs
acclaim—; achieve—; acquire—; attain—; change—; commend—; contrive—; crown —; dispatch with—; display—; develop—; devise—; employ—; endow with—; evolve —; excel in—; exhibit—; forge—; formu-

late—; improve—; introduce—; laud—; master—; perfect—; practise—; revolutionize—; stamp with—; suggest—; —aids; —enhances; —equips.

(See skill, method, manner.)

TEDIOUS

adverbs
intolerably; monotonously; profoundly; irksomely; tiresomely; uniformly; boringly; terribly; wearisomely; inordinately; feebly; exhaustingly; dully; mortally; prosily; disgustingly; unbearably; wearily; flatly; stupidly.

TEDIUM

verbs
allay—; chafe at—; decry—; disperse—; divert from—; ease—; relieve—; revolt at —; —assails; —beguiles; —bores; —burdens; —disintegrates; —exhausts; —fags; —fatigues; —harasses; —irks; —jades; —overwhelms; —prostrates; —sours; —stagnates; —strains; —taxes; —vexes; —wearies; —weighs upon.

(See monotony, weariness.)

TEETER (v)

adverbs
precariously; dizzily; dangerously; comically; drunkenly; weakly; painfully.

(See sway, balance.)

TEETH

adjectives
feeble; mottled; dazzling; tortuous; milky; ravenous; sharpened; jagged; clenched; hooked; pearly; tartarous; compressed; ferocious; flashing; foam-laced; blunted; glittering; chattering; convulsive; horrid; neglected; decayed; black; lacquered; wolfish; short; ivory; gnashing; snowy; close-shut; dagger-like; grinding.

verbs
abscess—; brace—; clamp—on; clench in—; cut—; dislodge—; drill—; engage with—; extract—; gnash—; grate—; grit—; groove —; imbed—in; lock—; polish—; retain—; —chatter; —crunch; —cut; —disintegrate; —emerge; —erupt; —flash; —gnaw; —lacerate; —pierce; —poison; —project; —reduce.

(See fang, bone.)

TELEGRAM

adjectives
congratulatory; visual; ocular; co-working; worrying; speedy.

verbs
acknowledge by—; convey—; decipher—; decode—; dispatch—; seal—; unfold—; —advises; —alarms; —announces; —authorizes; —s bombard; —confirms; —congratulates; —discloses; —divulges; —directs; —excites; —informs; —orders; —s pour in; —protests; —reveals.
(See letter, dispatch, news, message.)

TELEGRAPH (v)

adverbs
swiftly; instantly; faithfully; peremptorily; authoritatively; fraternally.
(See communicate, dispatch.)

TELEGRAPHIC

adverbs
mysteriously; swiftly; emotionally; marvellously; silently; confidentially; comically; fleetly; unmistakably; mercifully; sympathetically.

TELEPATHIC

adverbs
emotionally; sympathetically; instinctively; unmistakably; mysteriously; naturally; definitely; demonstrably; presumably; distinctly; possibly; imaginably; curiously; strangely; admissibly; credibly.

TELEPHONE

adjectives
limitless; effective; clattering; mute.

verbs
acquire—; communicate by—; confirm by—; disconnect—; drone into—; inform by—; install—; necessitate—; remove—; repair—; scurry to—; sever—; —assists; —awakens; —clamors; —distracts; —diverts; —eases; —enables; —facilitates; —jangles; —lightens; —persists; —shrills.

TELESCOPE

verbs
contemplate through—; design—; direct—at; discern through—; level—at; mount—; peek through—; peer through—; perceive through—; rivet—on; scan with—; squint into—; study through—; survey with—; —aids; —clarifies; —discovers; —distinguish-es; —enlarges; —enlightens; —facilitates; —magnifies; —ranges; —reveals; —sweeps the heavens.
(See microscope.)

TELESCOPIC

adverbs
amazingly; incredibly; marvellously; authentically; credibly; highly; evidently; conveniently; compactly; cleverly; handily; disconcertingly.

TELL (v)

adverbs
succinctly; impassively; hysterically; vehemently; conclusively; frankly; vigorously; jestingly; vividly; reluctantly; impressively; vaguely; musically; candidly; effectively; complacently; fluently; simply; circumstantially; reverently; artfully; reproachfully; accordingly; bluntly; genially; dispassionately; arrogantly; fervently; glibly; poignantly; gravely; inconsistently.
(See communicate, speak.)

TELLING

adverbs
vividly; trenchantly; brilliantly; eloquently; unusually; impressively; uniquely; significantly; graphically; dramatically; vigorously; authoritatively; positively; sensationally; remarkably; extremely; singularly; marvellously.

TELLTALE

adverbs
undisguisably; innocently; embarrassingly; indubitably; convincingly; ineradicably; inescapably; manifestly; ridiculously; undeniably; significantly; remarkably; conspicuously; noticeably; visibly; graphically.

TEMPER

adjectives
generous; reckless; subjective; suspended; creative; critical; gusty; querulous; peevish; suspicious; inflammable; gracious; charitable; terrible; ethereal; youthful; judicial; penurious; violent; dauntless; ruffled; indolent; collective (pl); frayed; bad; easy; convivial; uncertain; predominant; revengeful; skeptical; chivalrous; complacent; malignant; malleable; slumbering; imperious; independent; fixed; haughty; jarring; serene; buoyant; amiable; indifferent; chastened; earthly; ruthless; jovial; unspent; unsunned; fiery; lively; loquac-

ious; self-willed; passionate; columned; delicate; noble; docile; imperturbable; characteristic; mirthful; sweet; queer; philosophic; irritable; lethargic; meek; placid; sunny; equable; changeable; curious; polemical; cold; irreligious; merry; conciliatory; unforgiving; fretful; invincible; pedantic; heroic; unaltered; keen; despondent; ungovernable; inquisitive; impatient; admirable; combative; childish; turbulent; choleric; gunpowder; aspiring; dignified; villainous; boisterous; resentful; coddled; schizoid; benevolent; calm; ferocious; submissive; confident; crusading; eddying; iron-like; tart; feeble.

verbs
allay—; assuage—; blunt—; calm—; chasten—; compose—; curb—; dulcify—; exhibit —; fire—; ignite—; lull—; manifest—; moderate—; mollify—; pacify—; palliate—; quell—; quench—; restrain—; rule—; smooth—; sober—; subdue—; sweeten—; —blazes; —erupts; —explodes; —flames; —flares; —foams; —foments; —fumes; — seethes; —simmers; —snaps.
(See ire, anger, disposition, temperament.)

TEMPERAMENT
adjectives
adventurous; uncertain; artistic; cheerful; nervous; bilious; romantic; brooding; poetical; fierce; ardent; sanguine; morbid; observing; restless; nerveless; classic; highbred; individual; aspiring; unchangeable; philanthropic; sprightly; apathetic; emotional; mercurial; equable; grave; warlike; peculiar; heroic; inborn; fervent; oratorical; impetuous; undisciplined; genial; melancholy; mournful; indolent; pugnacious; fitful; delicate; rare; sunny; passionate; peculiar; physical; overcharged.

verbs
attune—to; bend—; characterize—; curse with—; display—; dispose toward—; exhibit—; fire—; foment—; harmonize—s; imbue with—; incline toward—; inflame—; influence—; inherit—; modulate—; mollify —; mould—; warp—; wrestle with—; —s clash; —flares; —indicates; —piques; — seethes; —simmers.
(See character, disposition.)

TEMPERAMENTAL
adverbs
highly; inconveniently; tempestuously; pro-

vokingly; bewilderingly; naturally; proverbially; characteristically; insufferably; unpredictably; allegedly; unmanageably; uncontrollably; violently; interestingly; perplexingly.

TEMPERANCE
verbs
advocate—; campaign for—; commend—; exhort—; laud—; pledge—; promote—; — abstains; —allays; —alleviates; —chastens; —composes; —denies; —forbears; —mitigates; —moderates; —refrains; —sobers; — softens; —spares; —tranquillizes.
(See moderation, sobriety, restraint.)

TEMPERATE
adverbs
definitely; mildly; judiciously; moderately; calmly; pleasantly; safely; honestly; cautiously; discreetly; prudently; reasonably; certainly; occasionally; habitually; naturally; soberly; consistently; modestly; quietly; inveterately; surprisingly; meticulously; punctiliously; scrupulously; usually.

TEMPERATURE
adjectives
accurate; congenial; equable; unexpected; high; balmy; tepid; terrestrial; physical; low; critical; ruinous; debilitating; varying; aggregate; uniform; intolerable; mean; cheap; consistent; elevated.

verbs
ascertain—; determine—; expose to—of; indicate—; maintain—; measure—; record —; regulate—; swelter in—of; —chars; — chills; —chafes; —climbs; —congeals; — descends; —fluctuates; —flushes; —fuses; —ignites; —mounts; —nips; —parches; — petrifies; —pinches; —refreshes; —sinks; —skyrockets (colloq.); —soars; —thaws; —toboggans.
(See mercury, barometer, meter, weather.)

TEMPEST
adjectives
terrible; howling; winter; renewed; spiritbrewed; shadowy; embattled; hideous; giddy; aerial; social; weltering; thundering; laboring; furious; careening; commanding; ruinous; damaging.

verbs
calm—; still—; sway in—; —abates; —agitates; —batters; —bellows; —blusters; —

buffets; —churns; —clamors; —crackles; —devastates; —drenches; —fumes; —howls; —lashes; —rages; —roars; —seethes; —shrieks; —subdues; —swells; —uproots; —whisks; —whistles; —subsides.

(See gale, hurricane, storm.)

TEMPESTUOUS
adverbs
violently; uncontrollably; passionately; stormily; dangerously; unmanageably; remarkably; unusually; insufferably; notoriously; sensationally; melodramatically; feverishly.

TEMPLE
adjectives
druidical; blushing; foreign; mystical; unworthy; versatile; abolished; graceful; wind-swept; throbbing; soniferous; burning; shattered; hairy; pagan; proud; pillared; wooden; gorgeous; projecting; ancient; holy; arching; magnificent; veined; heated; solemn; sumptuous; shattered; battered; numerous (pl); anointed; airy; glass; monumental.

verbs
attend—; banish from—; beseech in—; blaspheme—; bow in—; commune in—; convert into—; dedicate—; defile—; degrade—; desecrate—; design—; enshrine in—; erect —; expel from—; found—; ordain—; profane—; purge—; quarter in—; refuge in—; rend—; retire to—; sully—; swear by—; taint—; visit—; whip from—; —rises; —sanctifies.

(See church, tabernacle, cathedral.)

TEMPORAL
adverbs
evanescently; merely; transitorily; briefly; fleetingly; fugitively; perishably; transiently; mutably; precariously; impermanently; painfully; unhappily; frailly; ephemerally; utterly; sadly; uncertainly; insecurely.

TEMPORARY
adverbs
fortunately; merely; definitely; presumably; luckily; unfortunately; probably; presumably; definitely; supposedly; allegedly.

TEMPT (*v*)
adverbs
diabolically; fiendishly; insidiously; viciously; lewdly; appetizingly; intolerably; unwit-

tingly; irresistibly; unduly; incestuously; mystically; maddeningly; goadingly.

(See induce, lead.)

TEMPTATION
adjectives
constant; incestuous; sore; stronger; fierce; irresistible; external; various (pl); succulent; inviting; urban; insidious; testy; urgent; mystical; repeated; enticing; usurped.

verbs
accede to—; avoid—; conquer—; deliver from—; fling aside—; grapple with—; heighten—; intensify—; prevail against—; resist—; shun—; steel to—; subdue—; succumb to—; surrender to—; vanquish—; withstand—; wrestle with—; subdue—; —allures; —attracts; —baits; —beckons; —beguiles; —biases; —goads; —lures; —overcomes; —overwhelms; —seduces; —spurs; —sways; —tantalizes.

(See desire, passion, appetite.)

TEMPTING
adverbs
delectably; alluringly; subtly; viciously; cleverly; slily; guilelessly; seductively; irresistibly; curiously; strangely; exotically; perilously; boldly; wickedly; deliciously; charmingly; pleasurably; insidiously.

TENABLE
adverbs
scarcely; soundly; rationally; reasonably; logically; incontrovertibly; obviously; undeniably; easily; manifestly; validly; legally; satisfactorily; basically; effectively; inferentially; sensibly; fundamentally; essentially.

TENACIOUS
adverbs
stubbornly; obstinately; piously; dogmatically; doctrinally; doggedly; toughly; persistently; obdurately; resolutely; grimly; uncompromisingly; indomitably; stiffly; fanatically; inexplicably; disagreeably; ungraciously; tactlessly; surprisingly; churlishly; grossly; vexatiously.

TENACITY
adjectives
unyielding; peculiar; pathetic; amazing; bulldog; breathless; obstinate; desperate;

extraordinary; unmatched; dogged; agonized; marvelous.

verbs
buckle with—; cling with—; display—; exhibit—; inherit—; marvel at—; value—; —droops; —fails; —flags; —flinches; —impresses; —irks; —piques; —rankles; —resists; —riles (colloq.); —stiffens; —wavers; —yields to.
(See impregnability, stubbornness, persistence, strength.)

TENANT
adjectives
delinquent; peripatetic; impoverished; previous; worshipful; shuddering; defaulting; noisome; troublesome.

TEND (v)
adverbs
progressively; auspiciously; affectionately; subversively; obliquely; sedulously; faithfully; maternally; materially; religiously; fervently.
(See contribute, incline.)

TENDENCY
adjectives
pensive; sadistic; moralizing; abnormal; consequent; contrary; general; inevitable; exhibitionistic; decadent; abortive; immoral; dominant; latent; worldly; picturesque; belated; remote; revolutionary; marked; overruling; hereditary; evil; boyish; vicious; rationalistic; opposing; neurotic; abounding; pernicious; ambivalent; diverging; apprehensive; curtailed; philosophical; unconscious; speculative; primitive; morbid; life-abridging; transitory; herding; incestuous; rising; tubercular; undevout; natural; progressive; youthful; extravagant; erratic; notable; irreligious; conflicting; realistic; cancerous; centripetal; social; chronic; growing; powerful; stubborn; pseudo-classic; gravitating; materializing; obnoxious; dispositional; constitutional; pragmatic; aggravating; prevalent; remarkable; dangerous; healthy; observable; incorrigible; curious; devotional; pernicious; dispersive; culinary; commercial; monopolistic.

verbs
augment—; bolster—; check—; combat—; counteract—; counterbalance—; cultivate—; decry—; deplore—; deprecate—; dispose of —; eliminate—; encourage—; exhibit—; foster—; inherit—; neutralize—; nurse—; nurture—; observe—; offset—; outgrow—; overcome—; perceive—; promote—; reflect —; resist—; restrain—; smother—; stifle—; temper—; warp—; —conduces toward; —endangers; —jeopardizes; —predisposes.
(See inclination, proclivity, disposition.)

TENDER
adverbs
affectionately; maternally; infinitely; mercifully; passionately; amorously; impulsively; impetuously; eagerly; amiably; gently; curiously; naturally; oddly; unexpectedly; lovingly; caressingly.

TENDERNESS
adjectives
respectful; wounded; tearful; solemn; passionate; renewed; marked; sexual; dawning; yearning; melting; latent; pardonable; quaint; compassionate; human; spontaneous; newborn; bountiful; boundless; exquisite; conjugal; maternal; growing; unutterable; secondary; paternal; natural; deep; laughing; patriarchal; credulous; brief; immense; profound; elephantine; saddened; masculine; ineffable; touching; increasing; pathetic; grateful; infinite; unaccustomed; majestic; flowery; rugged; zealous; connubial; wishful; infinite; malicious; grave; wild; ineffable; excessive; rough; unvarying; flavorsome; graceful; universal; etherealized; brooding; shy; surpassing; patronizing; ideal; searching; sufficient; eternal; heavenly; uneradicated; peculiar.

verbs
affect—; arouse—; cherish—; display—; evince—; excite—; exhibit—; infuse—; inspire—; move to—; propitiate in—; relent in—; sense—; temper with—; treasure—; —assuages; —captivates; —charms; —disarms; —engages; —floods; —melts; —mitigates; —mollifies; —pervades; —pierces; —stirs.
(See love, kindness, compassion, pity, mercy.)

TENDON
verbs
bind—; cleave—; dissect—; incise—; lacerate—; penetrate—; pull—; rend—; seg-

ment—; sever—; strain—; strip—; —couples; —jams; —knots; —pains; —supports; —unites.

(See muscle, ligament.)

TENEMENTS
adjectives
spacious; frail; tessellated; dreary; newly-painted; fire-trap; dilapidated; unsafe; nauseating; filthy; close-packed; unsightly; disgusting; squalid.

verbs
condemn—; decry—; dwell in—; eject from —; evict from—; inhabit—; inveigh against —; poke about—; raze—; reside in—; roost in—; scurry through—; —breed; —confine; —defile; —dot; —engender; —harden; —overspread; —reek; —sully.

(See building, structure, home, slums.)

TENOR
adjectives
constant; noiseless; general; loud; expressionless; diminutive; same; habitual; operatic; even.

TENSE
adverbs
nervously; utterly; anxiously; rigidly; stiffly; terribly; oddly; uneasily; apprehensively; dreadfully; curiously; visibly; noticeably; manifestly; fearfully; self-consciously; excitedly; eagerly; unusually; remarkably; feverishly; warily; watchfully; quietly.

TENSION
adjectives
diminished; surface; severe; tremendous; increased; relieved; ocular; wonted; nervous; mental; spasmodic; unendurable; vigorous; bitter; emotional; extreme; unnatural; ominous; elastic; awful; high; electric.

verbs
allay—; alleviate—; ameliorate—; blunt—; ease—; erase—; generate—; inure to—; reduce—; relax—; release—; relieve—; soothe—; stir up—; sustain—; —burdens; —exhausts; —flares; —heightens; —jades; —mounts; —prostrates; —snaps; —strains; —taxes; —unnerves; —wearies.

(See misapprehension, anxiety, fear, strain, intensity.)

TENT
adjectives
invading; striped; tall; mat-walled; little; swarthy; stationary; convenient; superfluous; abominable; gauze; solitary; prim; tight.

verbs
assemble in—; avail oneself of—; batter—; buffet—; dwell in—; encamp in—; pelt—; pitch—; stake—; whisk away—; —affords; —comforts; —conceals; —enshrouds; —envelops; —flaps; —flutters; —obscures; —preserves; —shelters.

(See canvas, home, house, pavilion.)

TENTACLES
adjectives
long; trailing; murderous; multitudinous; clutching.

verbs
clutch in—; deliver from—; disengage—; elude—; ensnare in—; escape—; evade—; expand—; extricate from—; hug in—; liberate from—; relax—; release from—; seize in—; sever—; unloose—; —cling to; —contract; —entwine; —grasp; —retain; —smother; —snatch; —suffocate.

(See grasp, grip, talons, claw, clutch.)

TENURE
adjectives
property; fixed; solitary; lifelong; permanent; indefinite.

TEPID
adverbs
sickeningly; nauseously; uninterestingly; pleasantly; harmlessly; agreeably; safely; disagreeably.

TERM
(general)
adjectives
stringent; mechanistic; concrete; triumphant; remunerative; inexorable; appreciative; uncompromising; precise; brilliant; purposed; mysterious; familiar; interchangeable; plain; warm; ambiguous; proffered; unexpired; dubious; unhallowed; disastrous; convincing; abusive; modest; sudden; limited; strong; vile; festival; subsequent; equivalent; respectable; growling; impending; vague; hyperbolical; personal; unqualified; successful; downright; specific; generous; explicit; glowing; wrathful; con-

ciliatory; budget; honorable; obscure; silent; rash; affectionate; convertible; installment; speedy; anagogic; emphatic; disapproving; attractive; original; indefinite; complied; gross; measured; absolute; uncalculating; following; misapplied; extravagant; equal; silken; liberal; uncouth; synonymous; flattering; satisfactory; hyperbolical; chameleon; advantageous; immense; tedious; convenient; endurable; psychoanalytic; unreasonable; generic; relative; intimate; eloquent; terrible; tender; fashionable; amicable; equivocal; favorable; complimentary; penitentiary; recollected; degrading; much-abused; express; comprehensive; antiquated; impressive; feeble; technical; essential; respectful; fundamental; abominable; unmistakable; graphic; energetic; monetary; figurative; opprobrious; unmistakable.

TERM
(words)
verbs

accentuate—; amplify—; analyze—; apply —; clarify—; cloak in—s; clothe in—s; coin—; condense—; confine—; corrupt—; couch in—; define—; derive—; employ—; illustrate—; interpret—; object to—; paraphrase—; stilt—; stress—; voice in—s; — bewilders; —colors; —confuses; —degenerates; —disgraces; —embraces; —emphasizes; —expresses; —implies; —insinuates; —veils.

(See phrase, expression, word.)

TERM (v)
adverbs

vulgarly; improperly; euphemistically; confidentially; appropriately; aptly; irrelevantly; sneeringly; jestingly; satirically; equivocally; degradingly; technically; graphically; figuratively; opprobriously; affectionately; modestly; wrathfully; ambiguously; hyperbolically.

(See call, name.)

TERMAGANT
adverbs

brazenly; uncontrollably; boisterously; savagely; rudely; incredibly; obviously; laughably; ridiculously; unreasoningly; habitually; oddly; crazily; biliously; excitably; pugnaciously; truculently; bewilderingly; cruelly; scurrilously; obscenely.

TERMINATE (v)
adverbs

abruptly; tediously; innocently; happily; disastrously; seedily; inevitably; effectually; fatally; legitimately; swiftly; successfully; amazingly.

(See end, conclude.)

TERMITES
verbs

control—; deter—; exterminate—; infest with—; resist—; seethe with—; shield from —; teem with—; trample—; —abound; — ally with; —attack; —blight; —bore through; —burrow; —colonize; —construct; —deface; —despoil; —destroy; —devastate; —devour; —excavate; —forage; —gnaw; —hollow out; —impair; —incubate; —injure; —invade; —menace; —moult; — mound; —mutilate; —nest; —overrun; — penetrate; —raid; —ravage; —raise; — sap foundations; —store; —swarm; — tunnel through; —undermine.

(See ant, insect.)

TERMS
(conditions)
verbs

accede to—; acknowledge—; acquiesce to —; adopt—; allude to—; approve—; assent to—; challenge—; comply with—; concede to—; confine to—; consent to—; consider —; contract on—; corroborate—; couch in —; dictate—; disclose—; divulge—; enforce—; haggle over—; impose—; indorse —; mince—; propound—; ratify—; regard —; restrict to—; shorten—; sign—; submit —; subscribe to—; translate into—; yield to—; —apply; —conciliate; —imply; —include; —pacify; —placate; —yoke.

(See condition, demand, proposition, provision, limitation.)

TERRACE
adjectives

successive (pl); sloping; spacious; narrow; zigzag; beautiful; rounded; landscaped.

TERRESTRIAL
adverbs

manifestly; disappointingly; materially; comfortably; obviously; ridiculously.

TERRIBLE
adverbs

utterly; consummately; unbearably; appallingly; fascinatingly; luridly; overwhelmingly; indescribably; astoundingly; portentously.

TERRIFIED
adverbs

utterly; basely; brutally; cruelly; mercilessly; irrationally; unusually; highly; dismally; hopelessly; desperately; distressingly; painfully; pathetically; secretly; dreadfully; inwardly; strangely; curiously; wildly; violently; hysterically.

TERRIFY (v)
adverbs

pusillanimously; psychically; unreasoningly; manifestly; irrationally; superstitiously; secretly; frantically; vicariously; immoderately; direly; blindly; overwhelmingly; supernaturally; abjectly.

(See frighten, scare.)

TERRITORY
adjectives

extensive; adjacent; contiguous; debatable; adjoining; valuable; disputed; immense; imperial; worthless; contracted; neutral; condemned; excellent; dangerous; virgin; ideal; productive; paltry; vast; annexed; choice; rich; unassigned; inexhaustible; restricted; best; protected.

verbs

abandon—; absorb—; administer—s; annex —; border—; cede—; claim—; commandeer —; covet—; devastate—; dispose of—; embrace—; endow with—; expropriate—; flank—; forfeit—; fortify—; gain—; impound—; invade—; lay waste—; lease—; mandate—; partition—; patrol—; ravage —; reconquer—; retain—; reward with—; rule—; seek—; skirt—; traverse—; value —; yield—; —confronts; —flourishes; — revolts; —seethes.

(See district, province, locality, jurisdiction, country.)

TERROR
adjectives

mute; avowed; blasphemous; striking; pusillanimous; loving; mutual; bodily; abject; abysmal; mysterious; coquettish; conventional; chastening; conquering; psychic; manifest; rattling; hasty; inconceivable; avenging; haunting; forest; imaginary; instinctive; vague; limitless; unreasoning; sheer; absurd; majestic; dissolving; wild;

grisly; superstitious; shuddering; bouncing; roaring; rigid; secret; breathless; dispelled; vigorous; frantic; natural; undefinable; solemn; rhythmic; deadly; fantastic; vicarious; tinkling; vengeful; faltering; prudential; dreadful; groundless; panicky; moderate; anticipative; veritable; pregnant; scattered; cold; paralyzing; dire; sickly; blind; constant; soul-chilling; overwhelming; unreasonable; supernatural; suppressed; simultaneous; efficient; increasing; unconvinced; ignoble.

verbs

allay—; attest to—; beleaguer by—; bend in—; blanch with—; cower in—; dispel—; entertain—; flinch in—; hesitate in—; incite—; inspire—; live in—; pale in—; palpitate in—; paralyze—; plunge into—; prostrate with—; quake in—; quiver in—; read—; retreat in—; sense—; shrink in—; shudder in—; squirm in—; tremble in—; —aggravates; —catches; —chills; —deters; —harrows; —haunts; —looms; —nauseates; —overwhelms; —petrifies; —racks; —recoils; —reigns; —seizes; —shapes itself; —springs; —stalks; —strikes; —stuns; — weighs upon.

(See dread, dismay, fear, alarm, fright, consternation.)

TERRORISM
verbs

assail—; castigate—; check—; curb—; inflict—; have recourse to—; revolt against —; subject to—; suppress—; tolerate—; —cankers; —coerces; —crushes; —dictates; —domineers; —oppresses; —overrides; — persecutes; —ravages; —reigns; —restrains; —rides roughshod; —snuffs out; —stings; —tyrannizes; —tramples; — wreaks; —yokes.

(See tyranny, intimidation.)

TERRORIST
verbs

quail before—; root out—s; —bridles; — coerces; —desecrates; —devastates; —domineers; —intimidates; —outrages; —pillages; —plunders; —ravages; —restrains; —retaliates; —sheds; —shocks; —suppresses; —tramples; —usurps.

(See anarchist, striker, revolutionist.)

TERROR-STRICKEN
adverbs

disastrously; nervously; awfully; unaccountably; unmercifully; tragically; utterly; hopelessly; curiously; helplessly; pitiably; irrecoverably; direly; sorely; unduly; grievously; naturally; inevitably; appallingly.

TERSE
adverbs
carefully; incisively; bitterly; cuttingly; sarcastically; insolently; indifferently; coldly; officially; wearily; cautiously; discreetly; formidably; rigidly; frigidly; curiously; perplexingly; unreasonably; unnecessarily; brusquely; bluntly; ominously; significantly; oddly.

TEST
adjectives
microscopic; summit; crucial; quick; fiery; acid; practical; universal; elaborate; exhaustive; innumerable (pl); conceiving; grueling; stringent; selective; triumphant; bacteriological; preliminary; careful; rigid; convincing; dangerous; supreme; experimental; actual; great; definite; discriminative; supplementary; instrumental; theological; temporal; complicated; infallible; provocative; prescribed; routine.

verbs
apply—; broaden—; cite—; concoct—; confront with—; conceive—; conduct—; —confirm—; devise—; employ—; essay—; exercise—; fail in—; flunk (colloq.)—; grapple with—; institute—; perform—; question—; rehearse—; repeat—; subject to—; submit to—; survive—; undergo—; utilize—; work out—; wrestle with—; —analyzes; —ascertains; —appraises; —authenticates; —confirms; —determines; —discloses; —dissects; —judges; —overwhelms; —reveals; —springs; —verifies; —vindicates; —weighs.
(See experiment, examination, criterion.)

TEST (v)
adverbs
scientifically; experimentally; practically; thoroughly; periodically; crucially; elaborately; exhaustively; rigidly; definitely; discriminatively; theologically; infallibly; provocatively.
(See quiz, question.)

TESTIFY (v)
adverbs
ethically; essentially; obstreperously; traitorously; flatteringly; falteringly; abundant-

ly; mutely; unflinchingly; solemnly; unequivocally; corroboratively; irrelevantly; negatively; consequently; unanimously; unbiasedly; personally; unimpeachably; conflictingly; sincerely; incontrovertibly; emphatically.
(See assert, tell.)

TESTIMONIAL
adverbs
vividly; reminiscently; suggestively; intimately; pleasantly; flatteringly; deservedly; significantly; unforgettably; indelibly; permanently.

TESTIMONY
adjectives
solitary; jubilant; concurrent; equivocal; miraculous; honeyed; corroborative; irrelevant; remarkable; appreciative; negative; contemporary; inward; consequential; unsupported; indubitable; unanimous; abundant; silent; sufficient; unbiased; uniform; princely; magnificent; personal; willing; ample; unimpeachable; genuine; unique; conflicting; venerable; clear; professional; precious; enthusiastic; damaging; glorious; cheerful; sincere; explicit; oral; unbroken; incontrovertible; emphatic.

verbs
adduce—; analyze—; authenticate—; bear —; blast—; cite—; conform—; contradict—; corroborate—; deduce—; deliver as—; deny —; dispute—; expose—; express—; falsify —; file—; impair—; marshal—; perjure—; punctuate—; question—; record—; refute —; repudiate—; reverse—; review—; substantiate—; sustain—; uncover—; undermine—; uphold—; verify—; —authenticates; —bears; —carries weight; —conflicts; —convinces; —deludes; —differs; —discloses; —disturbs; —divulges; —floods; —reveals; —stuns; —vindicates; —warrants.
(See evidence, proof, declaration.)

TEXT
adjectives
trivial; pregnant; trite; faultless; miraculous; holy; sanguine; adopted; descriptive; infallible; authentic; expanded; obscene; widely-used; brilliant; edited.

verbs
acquaint with—; adhere to—; allude to—; analyze—; bear upon—; contemplate—; con-

tradict—; convey—; copyright—; digress from—; engross in—; explore—; express in —; follow—; heed—; peruse—; ponder—; pore over—; ransack—; regard—; reflect on—; review—; revise—; scan—; scrutinize—; supplement—; tamper with—; transform—; —depicts; —informs; —portrays.

(See matter, composition, book, story, subject, topic, theme.)

TEXTURE
adjectives
mysterious; basic; satiny; exquisite; grainy; permanent; delicate; misty; superb; soft; fine; springy; homely; unstylish; porous; rude; harmonic; historical; slippery; exclusive; crinkled; sheer; delicious; substantial; orthodox; even; fragile; smooth; shimmering; translucent; bubbled; surface; peach-like.

THANK (v)
adverbs
adequately; inarticulately; devoutly; cordially; heartily; formally; humbly; profusely; reverently; sincerely; appreciatively; fulsomely; haughtily; cursorily; dutifully; churlishly.

(See appreciate.)

THANKFUL
adverbs
utterly; delightedly; joyously; gratefully; unusually; particularly; singularly; exceptionally; enthusiastically; devoutly; reverently; deeply; profoundly; appreciatively; inordinately; obviously; earnestly; sincerely; truly; redundantly; unquestionably; remarkably; peculiarly.

THANKLESS
adverbs
dismally; sadly; ungraciously; grimly; heartbreakingly; utterly; bitterly; tragically; distressingly; drearily; cruelly; amazingly.

THANKS
adjectives
distracted; allegiant; humble; shy; fulsome; haughty; savage; impious; cordial; lively; dutiful; public; hearty; beggarly; silent; churlish; mumbled; half-hearted.

verbs
accept—; acknowledge—; declare—; derive —; express—; extend—; feign—; gush—;

inspire—; offer—; overflow with—; proclaim—; proffer—; render—; return—; reward with—; tender—; —beguile; —gratify.

(See gratitude, appreciation.)

THATCHED
adverbs
attractively; recently; picturesquely; admirably; quaintly; satisfactorily; inadequately; thickly; greenly; fragrantly; curiously; intricately; generously; sparsely; thinly; stingily.

THEATRE
adjectives
legitimate; elegant; stupendous; imaginary; sensational; outdoor; woody; vast; gigantic; sublime; air-cooled; immense; comfortable; pleasant; troublesome; costly.

verbs
acclaim—; convert—; flow from—; forsake —; frequent—; install in—; jam—; participate in—; reject—; renounce—; storm—; —affords; —allures; —beckons; —beguiles; —claims; —diverts; —emblazons; —fascinates; —glitters; —immortalizes; —inspires; —presents; —publicizes; —relaxes; —solaces; pack—.

(See opera, footlights, stage, drama.)

THEATRICAL
adverbs
absurdly; ridiculously; professionally; unexpectedly; skilfully; artistically; surprisingly; laughably; imposingly; impressively; pompously; bombastically; extravagantly; crassly; affectedly; crudely; showily; insincerely; gaudily; sensationally; consummately.

THEFT
verbs
accomplish—; acquire by—; apprehend for —; bewail—; charge with—; commit—; denounce—; disclose—; divulge—; forestall —; insure against—; penalize—; plan—; plot—; reveal—; uncover—; —baffles; —distresses; —impoverishes; —violates.

(See plagiarism, robbery.)

THEME
adjectives
lofty; abstract; everlasting; anti-social; pathetic; prolific; gracious; inspiring; majestic; unpleasant; paramount; inviting;

curious; earnest; amusing; unsympathetic; spiritual; characteristic; animating; exotic; weak; idle; imperial; debatable; supermundane; pastoral; poetic; varying; irksome; inexhaustible; realistic; extraneous; fruitful; favorite; rusty; dangerous; conversational; immediate; romantic; human; pregnant; copious (pl); prevailing.

verbs
allot—; alter—; clothe—; color—; comprehend—; criticize—; discard—; dramatize—; elucidate—; embellish—; embody—; evolve —; exhaust—; expatiate on—; expound—; found—; give rise to—; handle—; harp on —; interpret—; intertwine—; launch—; plunge into—; revert—; set forth—; tackle —; unfold—; variate—; vary—; ventilate —; voice—; weave—; —deals; —depicts; —dominates; —portrays; —stands upright; —symolizes.

(See text, subject, topic, idea, essay, composition.)

THEOLOGICAL
adverbs
strictly; narrowly; bigotedly; dogmatically; completely; soundly; devoutly; liberally; restrictively; obstinately; broadly; intolerantly.

THEOREM
verbs
admit—; analyze—; apply—; base on—; comprehend—; contrive—; expound—; fashion—; formulize—; ground on—; ponder —; refer to—; regard—; unfold—; —assumes; —derives from; —postulates; —proves; —solves.

(See problem, principle, law, formula.)

THEORETICAL
adverbs
obstinately; absurdly; impractically; unreasonably; infeasibly; stupidly; impracticably; impossibly; absolutely; merely; vaguely; presumably; fanatically; obscurely; entirely.

THEORIZE (v)
adverbs
philosophically; abstractly; optimistically; plausibly; psychoanalytically; experimentally; atomically; coherently; psychologically; nebulously; poetically; geometrically;

destructively; ingeniously; extravagantly; classically; absurdly; relatively; dynamically; morally; politically; economically; vaguely.

(See philosophize, talk.)

THEORY
adjectives
favorite; plausible; vibratory; psychoanalytic; experimental; undulatory; imaginative; unsound; universal; constructive; atomic; fanciful; antediluvian; coherent; unsatisfactory; elaborate; psychological; rounded; shaky; buttressed; nebulous; physical; artistic; vague; communistic; protectionist; elliptic; geometrical; evolutionary; color; straightforward; antiquated; ethical; mistaken; collision; philosophical; aesthetic; destructive; cherished.; reprehensible; underlying; ingenious; deliberate; extravagant; chemical; classical; absurd; unsupported; oft-expressed; plausible; preconceived; tremendous; fantastic; secular; fossilized; coherential; radical; original; futile; abstract; relative; dynamic; irreconcilable; musical; impracticable; utopian; moral; religious; vague; suicide; economic.

verbs
abandon—; absorb in—; accept—; adopt—; advance—; antiquate—; apply—; arrive at —; authenticate—; base on—; blast—; check—; commit to—; comprehend—; conceive—; confirm—; contradict—; corroborate—; crush—; defend—; demolish—; devise—; discard—; discredit—; dismiss—; disprove—; dispute—; elaborate—; embrace —; entertain—; evolve—; exhaust—; explode—; explain—; hail—; hazard—; illustrate—; incline to—; incorporate in—; investigate—; maintain—; nurse—; outline—; propound—; refute—; reject—; relinquish —; scorn—; set forth—; speculate on—; submit—; subscribe to—; substantiate—; support—; test—; unveil—; upset—; verify —; visualize—; —s clash; —concludes; —deludes; —holds water; —opposes; —proposes; herald—.

(See idea, interpretation, hypothesis, logic.)

THERAPY
adjectives
vaccine; occupational; analytic; radio.

verbs
apply—; baffle—; devise—; expound—

hail—; herald—; practise—; prolong—; protract—; recommend—; revolutionize—; —ameliorates; —mitigates; —palliates; — rectifies; —relieves; —restores; —resuscitates; —revives.

(See cure, treatment.)

THERMOMETER
verbs
consult—; disinfect—; grade—; immerse—in; insert—; impair—; obscure—; shake down—; shatter—; suspend—; —ascends; —deceives; —dives; —indicates; —measures; —ranges from; —records; —registers; —reveals; —rises; —skyrockets (colloq.); —soars; —testifies; —toboggans; —warns; —wavers.

(See meter, price, barometer, mercury.)

THESIS
adjectives
aesthetic; alternative; voluminous; graduate; requisite; dull; pedantic; plagiarized; useless; incompetent; startling; established; brilliant; heavily-footnoted; well-documented.

verbs
acclaim—; analyze—; applaud—; build—; compose—; criticize—; dash off—; elaborate on—; formulate—; illustrate—; peruse—; propound—; submit—; support—; sustain — ;—airs; —brings to light; —comments on; —compiles; —discusses; —dissertates; —embraces; —expatiates; —proposes; —recites; —theorizes; —treats of; —ventilates.

(See manuscript, book, composition, essay.)

THICK
adverbs
substantially; satisfactorily; acceptably; admirably; commendably; impenetrably; sufficiently; tremendously; unimaginably; distressingly; unmanageably; densely; suffocatingly; unreasonably; impassably; curiously; strangely; undesirably.

THICKET
adjectives
bowery; high; spicy; neighboring; branch; straggling; impenetrable; shady; grotesque; dripping; miniature; cool; darksome; fragrant; leafless; impervious; thorny; prickly.

verbs
conceal in—; frequent—; lop off—; nest in —; plunge into—; prune—; spring from—;

stir among—s; trim—; uproot—; —affords; —s choke; —s eclipses; —hinders; —impedes; —obscures; —restrains; —rustles; —shelters.

(See bush, jungle.)

THICK-SET
adverbs
solidly; substantially; sturdily; healthily; stoutly; remarkably; noticeably; staunchly; unusually; particularly; conspicuously; singularly; curiously; uncommonly.

THIEF
adjectives
arrant; filthy; door-waylaying; contented; self-satisfied; insect; child; low; vile; sacreligious; adulterous; practised; slovenly; deformed; unimaginative; hard-headed; raw-boned; snaky-haired; dwarfish; injured; timorous; subtle; merciless; escaped; deft; honorable.

verbs
apprehend—; convict—; grapple with—; handcuff—; incarcerate—; interpret—; parole—; penalize—; pinion—; sentence—; —assaults; —bilks; —defrauds; —eludes; —evades; —extorts; —filches; —fleeces; —loots; —marauds; —mulcts; —palms; —pilfers; —plunders; —poaches; —purloins; —rifles; —rooks; —sacks; —strips.

(See highwayman, gangster, kidnapper, intruder, robber.)

THIEVISH
adverbs
impishly; naturally; habitually; watchfully; incorrigibly; viciously; incurably; wickedly; inveterately; loutishly; dangerously; remarkably; uncommonly; trickily; mischievously; smartly; furtively; stealthily; adroitly; dexterously; cunningly; artfully; ingeniously

THIN
adverbs
astonishingly; extremely; excessively; tenuously; pathetically; insecurely; alarmingly; dangerously; palpably; flimsily; unsatisfactorily; terribly; sufficiently; extraordinarily; expensively; dreadfully; incredibly; conveniently.

THING
adjectives
goodly; extravagant; travailing; heterogen-

eous; existing; fantastic; disproportioned; blind; sharp; single; terrestrial; unutterable; fragile; brute-hooved; insatiable; living; delightful; horrible; atrocious; subtle; elusive; unstable; contemptible; inexplicable; faraway; sublunary; terrene; inanimate; glorious; good; ignoble; treacherous; dreadful; distressful; ill-used; quixotic; ridiculous; painful; groping; plaguy; exasperating; sacred; intangible; desirable; manifold; plaintive; pitiful; semi-accidental; demented; secondary; devastating; rustling; created; willful; grotesque; logical; miserable; haunting; hazardous; interesting; essential; peculiar; prudent; traditional; dark; irrelevant; manly; trivial; infinite; unusual; feathered; kingly; horrid; castaway; venomous; pesky; flimsy; improbable; external; roguish; weird; piquant; odious; powerless; hateful; indispensable; insulting; complete; sinister; heartbreaking; inferior; incongruous; squirming; unheeded; petty; mealy mouthed, ticklish; accepted; unpardonable; incalculable; divine; blamed; mischievous; rightful; immaterial; serious; unprecedented; salutary; omnipotent; creaking; unchained; momentous; detestable; arduous; portentous; unintelligible; interminable; devilish; needful; senseless; hidden; spectral; rotten; native; fresh; priceless; fearful; extraordinary; bohemian; combustible; vast; stupid; terrible; creepy; uncommon; melancholy; valueless; gaudy; dear; vulgar; formed; precious; pinched; subordinate; ruthless; brittle; selfsame; unkind.

THINK (v)
adverbs
abstractly; sensually; despairingly; humorously; frenziedly; contemplatively; habitually; desolately; conscientiously; precisely; instinctively; vaguely; incessantly; idly; poetically; deliberately; remorsefully; constructively; grimly; anxiously; candidly; erratically; scoffingly; divergently; morosely; desultorily; contemptuously; connectedly; hysterically; rapturously; shrewdly; vehemently; dispassionately; diversely; independently; grievously; dismally; creatively; wishfully; incisively; psychoanalytically; subtly; cunningly.
(See meditate, muse.)

THINKING
adjectives
independent; ill; archaic; infantile; infer-

ior; sustained; honest; clear; differentiated; exact; thorough; inventive; original; grievous; dismal; untrammeled; conceptive; creative; wishful; accurate; incisive; psychoanalytic; spacious; subtle; cunning; symmetrical.

verbs
absorb in—; avoid—; bias—; betray—; clarify—; confuse—; discipline—; distract —; divert—; encourage—; engender—; engross in—; exercise—; foster—; give food for—; guide— ;indulge in—; influence—; lose in—; nurture—; occupy in—; pervert —; prejudice—; stimulate—; trust to—; — depresses; —digresses; —focuses on; — penetrates; —revolves about.
(See thought, contemplation, reflection, meditation.)

THIN SKINNED
adverbs
unfortunately; delicately; inordinately; sensitively; terribly; evidently; acutely; abnormally; unusually; exceptionally; strangely; absurdly; unreasonably; noticeably; palpably; foolishly.

THIRST
adjectives
immortal; unqeunchable; insatiable; vulgar; sanctifying; hot; burning; eternal; baffled; fierce; aimless; inextinguishable; human; ardent; opulent; wholesome; reckless; inordinate; universal; pretended; exacting; unhallowed; incessant; savage; slakeless; feverish; parching; urgent; intolerable; perpetual; frantic; distressing; pallid; acquired; marked.

verbs
allay—; arouse—; assuage—; create—; experience—; extinguish—; gratify—; indulge in—; intensify—; kindle—; overcome by—; quell—; quench—; satiate—; satisfy—; sharpen—; slake—; stimulate—; subdue—; suffice—; whet—; —maddens; —plagues; —rages; —torments.
(See appetite, desire, craving, longing.)

THIRSTY
adverbs
continually; painfully; terribly; habitually; strangely; feverishly; inordinately; crazily; constitutionally; curiously; cravingly; des-

perately; alarmingly; inveterately; cruelly; conveniently; avidly; significantly; dreadfully; evidently; suddenly; distressingly.

THORN
adjectives
flowering; barren; fruitful; poisonous; pungent; prickly; mean; insipid; venomed; cruel; blazing; piercing; wind-warped.

verbs
bristle with—s; escape—s; impale on—; snag on—; —barbs; —s crucify; —s fence about; —s harass; —lacerates; —lancinates; —penetrates; —pierces; —plagues; —pricks; —punctures; —rends; —spikes; —s torture.

(See sting, needle, nail.)

THORNY
adverbs
painfully; extremely; dangerously; perilously; strangely; intolerably; undesirably; disagreeably; thickly; unpleasantly; unexpectedly; surprisingly; disadvantageously; inconveniently; slightly; terribly; exceptionally; unusually; unfortunately.

THOROUGHBRED
adverbs
unmistakably; conspicuously; unquestionably; warrantably; decidedly; authentically; highly; obviously; manifestly; palpably; patently; positively; absolutely; notably.

THOROUGHFARE
adjectives
dusty; celebrated; bewildering; glistening; busy; trodden; ambitious; murmurous; tumultuous.

verbs
amble down—; blockade—; clog—; clutter —; cut—; direct to—; enter—; evade—; extend—; file along—; forsake—; frequent —; intersect—; jam—; line—; litter—; obstruct—; pave—; proceed down—; promenade—; strike—; traverse—; —deviates; —swerves; —winds in and out.

(See highway, avenue, street.)

THOUGHT
adjectives
undecided; lingering; leading; angry; systematic; chiming; dream; naked; shining; horrible; flurried; importunate; lofty; numbing; forcible; effective; translucent; marvel-

ous; golden; vagrant; fiery; poetic; habitual; self-torturing; abstract; impassioned; appalling; boundless; high; myriad; accidental; dissonant; unseasonable; restless; ripe; clever; heaven-born; speculative; divine; bitter; darting; darkling; complacent; carking; ill; longing; faithful; soft; unresisting; ennobled; metaphysical; contemplative; virtuous; inscrutable; sober; sinful; impetuous; distracting; knitted; narrow; exhilarating; trustful; teeming; pensive; empirical; moody; innermost; reproachful; contradictory; gentle; dying; odious; adventurous; holy; quiet; eclectic; invisible; wrecked; desponding; roving; hairy; engrossing; brutal; viper; dangerous; discontented; rebellious; selfsame; interesting; economic; studious; suggesting; unutterable; painful; sifted; transcending; endless; fond; thankful; satirical; sorrowful; awakened; disconnected; woundless; haunting; persistent; rash; irreverent; sorry; benighted; uncertain; wistful; morbid; anxious; oftspurned; lifting; frail; tumultuous; incestuous; constant; laborious; treasonable; grand; pleasant; heartwarming; paramount; insupportable; presumptuous; mere; mournful; monopolized; everpresent; halfformed; collateral; associated; winged; pedantic; serene; tangible; unwelcome; soaring; pacific; shattered; clamorous; gastronomic; ungovernable; lawless; rational; misanthropic; unfathomable; licentious; flattering; chaotic; slaughterous; freezing; somber; fleeting; concentrated; morbid; luminous; far-soaring; indistinct; philosophic; intimate; compelling; celebrated; vain; unquiet; intransigent; unschooled; unpractised; swift; passing; dismal; genial; hasty; likely; formless; hateful; thornless; manlike; matchless; aidless; unstained; loving; innocent; deliberate; dreamy; harsh; confused; exhaustive; vigorous; questioning; humiliating.

verbs
absorb in—; analyze—s; appraise—; arrest —; associate with—; awaken—; banish—; bias—s; blend—s; brood over—; center—s upon; check—; cherish—; clarify—s; collect—s; color—; comprehend—; compress—; confirm—; convey—; counterbalance—; cultivate—; dally with—; disclose—; disorder —s; distort—s; divert—s; divine—; dwell upon—; echo—s; efface—; electrify—; embody in—; endure—; engage in—; engross in—; enlarge upon—; enrich—s; entertain

—; erase—; etch—; evoke—; exclude—; execute—; expand—; expel from—s; expose—s; fashion—; formulate—s; furnish food for—; further—; fuse into—s; govern —s; grasp—; groove—s; hamper—; harbor—; immerse in—; impart—; implant—; impregnate with—; induce—; indulge in—; —; interpret—; interrupt—; isolate—; jot down—; kindle the pulse of—; lose in—; impede—; mould—; nurse—; obliterate—; occupy with—; open avenues of—; parallel —; paralyze—s; perpetuate—; preserve—; prompt—; purify—s; react upon—; read—s; recoil from—; reflect—s; reject—; restate —; reveal—; round out—s; saturate—s; scramble—s; scoff at—; shape—s; shrink from—; spit out—; stimulate—; tincture —s; toy with—; transcribe—s; tremble at —; unite—s; utter—; vent—s; vitiate—; voice—; weigh—; wrap in—; —appeals; — corrodes; —creeps into; —crosses the mind; —s crowd; —dominates; —enraptures; — enthralls; —escapes; —filters into; —flashes; —germinates; —haunts, —impresses; — intrudes; —leans toward; —leaps into; — matures; —numbs; —obsesses; —oppresses; —permeates; —perturbs; —petrifies; —possesses; —presents itself; —s ramble; —recalls; —recurs; —relapses into; —s revert to; —s revolve about; —shakes; —shifts to; —sobers; —springs from; —stings; — strikes; —suggests; —swirls up; —symbolizes; —terrifies; —torments; —uplifts; —s waver.

(See idea, concept, conception, consideration, imagination, opinion, meditation.)

THOUGHTFUL
adverbs
graciously; pleasantly; courteously; considerately; agreeably; unusually; quietly; busily; naively; unfailingly; remarkably; marvellously; practically; helpfully; prudently; providently; tactfully; sensibly; thoroughly; completely; charmingly; studiously; earnestly; gravely; seriously; judicially; deliberately; significantly; wonderfully; soberly; profoundly; deeply; dreamily; wistfully.

THOUGHTLESS
adverbs
carelessly; selfishly; dreamily; blindly; innocently; youthfully; boyishly; girlishly; blithely; unwittingly; unconsciously; cruelly; bitterly; meanly; inconsiderately; ungraciously; impolitely; discourteously; terribly;

dangerously; significantly; desperately; hopelessly; unpardonably; inexcusably; remarkably; strangely; incredibly; gaily.

THRASH (v)
adverbs
brutally; soundly; wildly; cruelly; viciously; bestially; penally; fiercely; passionately.
(See beat, whip.)

THREAD
adjectives
imaginary; aimless; scarlet; dramatic; protecting; snagged; sacred; broken; crossed; delicate; ligneous; gossamer; basting; swift-running; darkened; fluffy; wool-like; rhyming; knotted; allotted; frayed.

verbs
baste with—; cleave—; dangle by—; draw —; entwine in—; fray—; loop—; reinforce —; rend—; sever—; shear—; stitch with—; sunder—; suspend from—; tack—; weave —; wear to—.
(See cotton, fibre, string, cord.)

THREAD (v)
adverbs
skillfully; dexterously; delicately; complicatedly; involvedly; intricately; unerringly.
(See wind, weave.)

THREADBARE
adverbs
shabbily; shockingly; dreadfully; dingily; carelessly; pathetically; diaphanously; pitiably; miserably; curiously; inexplicably; mustily; desperately; cruelly; unutterably; sadly; grotesquely; fantastically; unnecessarily; parsimoniously; terribly; distressingly; painfully; humiliatingly; shamefully; nonchalantly; imperturbably.

THREAT
adjectives
invincible; silent; bawling; thundering; terrible; cloudy; stifled; obscure; serious; muttered; ruffian; dark; playful; mysterious; desperate; fearful; insolent; parting; fantastic; bitter; petty; absurd; contemporaneous; drunken; implied; private; tense; whispered; violent; sullen; tyrannous; sibylline.

verbs
aim—at; bandy—s; fling—at; fulminate—; hurl—; mutter—; retract—; resort to—s;

roar—; thunder—; thwart—; unleash—; veil—; yield to—s; —alarms; —bluffs; — browbeats; —coerces; —compromises; — cows; —daunts; —deters; —disconcerts; — distresses; —hangs over; —haunts; —indicts; —intimidates; —jeopardizes; —menaces; —obsesses; —perturbs; —preys upon; —stings; —unnerves; —weighs upon; — awes.

(See menace, oath, curse, imprecation.)

THREATEN (v)
adverbs
illimitably; direfully; darkly; terrifyingly; sinisterly; seriously; adroitly; mutteringly; sullenly; violently; tyrannically; bitterly.

(See menace, portend.)

THREATENING
adverbs
undeniably; plainly; odiously; hatefully; alarmingly; significantly; seriously; gravely; desperately; clearly; definitely; absolutely; positively; graphically; sensationally; dramatically; obviously; terribly; dreadfully; ominously; curiously; darkly; mysteriously; palpably; obscurely; vaguely; dimly; feebly; violently; truculently; absurdly; ridiculously; openly; apparently; frankly; furtively; stealthily.

THRESHOLD
adjectives
unhallowed; shadowed; sacred; glimmering; dread; lucky.

verbs
achieve—; arrive at—; attain—; bar from —; bestride—; block—; cloud—; dwell on —; enter—; file through—; flank—; gain —; huddle at—; reach—; reverence—; screen—; seek—; skirt—; strand at—; stumble over—; veil—.

(See entrance, gate, door.)

THRIFT
adjectives
prudent; extreme; constant; balanced; contented; pecuniary; incomprehensible; reasonable.

verbs
demand—; emphasize—; encourage—; enforce—; extol—; foster—; imbue with—; implant—; inculcate—; ingrain—; necessitate—; practise—; preach--; stress—; — grudges; —infects; —redeems; —saves.

(See economy, frugality.)

THRIFTLESS
adverbs
inexcusably; habitually; naturally; inherently; strangely; picturesquely; presumably; possibly; odiously; hopelessly; incurably; incorrigibly; carelessly; thoughtlessly; improvidently; distressingly; shabbily; deplorably; lamentably; provokingly; intolerably; insufferably; vexatiously; terribly; blithely; gaily; insouciantly.

THRIFTY
adverbs
fortunately; carefully; providently; shrewdly; invariably; unfailingly; wisely; sagely; sensibly; happily; pleasantly; profitably; distinctly; moderately; judiciously; graspingly; overly; uncomfortably; ostentatiously; flourishingly; manifestly; enviably; admirably; commendably; laudably; unusually; habitually; naturally; intensely; inherently; innately; particularly; commercially; happily; luckily; thoughtfully.

THRILL
adjectives
double; distinguished; charmful; warming; renewed; shuddering; delicious; awed; amazed; intoxicating; continuous; restoring; silent; incredulous; horrible; tragic; metallic; original; sympathetic; supernal; biggest; involuntary; vicarious; nascent; poetic; gentle; unpleasant; amusing; exultant; compensating; electric; passionate; comforting; equestrian; eloquent.

verbs
cherish—; crave—; derive—from; excite—; experience—; furnish—; gain—; glow with —; inspire—; itch for—; respond to—; seek —; sense—; —enthuses (colloq.); —fires; —flushes; —impassions; —infects; — pierces; —prickles; —shoots through; — stabs; —tickles; —vibrates through; — warms; —warns; —tingles.

(See shiver, vibration, excitement, tremor.)

THRILL (v)
adverbs
blissfully; tenderly; involuntarily; vicariously; poetically; exultantly; passionately; eloquently.

(See excite, arouse.)

adverbs

enchantingly; interestingly; excitably; tremendously; emotionally; unutterably; remarkably; apparently; evidently; visibly; terribly; utterly; strangely; oddly; marvellously; inexpressibly; utterly; magnificently; splendidly; completely; unwontedly; apparently; immensely; thoroughly; indescribably; positively.

THRILLING

adverbs

utterly; indescribably; unusually; inexpressibly; marvellously; tremendously; superbly; magnificently; immensely; completely; unusually.

THRIVE (*v*)

adverbs

miraculously; bountifully; exceedingly; markedly; amazingly; prodigiously.

(See prosper, succeed.)

THRIVING

adverbs

steadily; gradually; remarkably; amazingly; indubitably; miraculously; incredibly; deservedly; unquestionably; suddenly; curiously; strangely; marvellously; splendidly; stupendously; salubriously; slowly; substantially; pleasantly; happily.

THROAT

adjectives

sinewy; blithest; dreadful; lucid; thundering; soft; impudent; thick; stretching; dazzling; unslaked; slender; infantile; sanded; sore; creamy; harsh; irritated; parched; shaggy; quivering; warbling; swan-like; exquisite; mellow; feminine; supple; scorched; swelling; brown; bursting; corded; careless; listless; myriad (pl); furry; incapable; snowy; slit; gushing; vulture; dividing; careless.

verbs

clear—; clutch—; congest—; disinfect—; dust—; ease—; emerge from—; clog—; infect—; inflame—; introduce into—; irritate —; lacerate—; lodge in—; massage—; medicate—; paint—; ram down—; ravage —; seize by—; sponge—; spray—; strain—; swab—; tickle—; ulcerate—; —contracts; —swells; —tightens.

adjectives

rhythmic; trembling; belated; harmonic; fondest; minutest; romantic; exulting; fleeing; steady; fluttering; heart; ecstatic; blissful.

THROB (*v*)

adverbs

palpitatingly; violently; rapidly; riotously; swiftly; visibly; fitfully; tumultuously; rhythmically; romantically; exultingly; ecstatically; blissfully.

(See pulsate, beat.)

THRONE

adjectives

angelic; heavenly; sanguine; everlasting; jeweled; conspicuous; tear-gemmed; ivory; maiden; towering; empyreal; usurped; sunlike; crystalline; venerable; unenvied; western; lofty; dynastic; sullen; sublime; tarnished; boundless; glorious; cambric; malignant; stately; universal; meridian; ancestral; rocky; peaceful; disputed; constellated; forsaken; tottering; sovereign; blissful; imperial; sapphire; moldy.

verbs

abandon—; abdicate—; accede to—; ascend; aspire to—; attend—; bow before—; burnish—; covet—; defy—; depose from—; desert—; ensconce on—; establish on—; forsake—; gain—; lay claim to—; loll on—; occupy—; overthrow—; plant on—; relinquish—; renounce—; restore to—; retire from—; seek—; usurp—; vacate—; vest in —; win—; —authorizes; —empowers; —tyrannizes; seize—.

(See kingdom, kingship, power, sovereignty, seat, chair.)

THRONG

adjectives

trampling; demoniac; well-dressed; countless (pl); burdened; motley; shadowy; grateful; tumultuous; ragged; threadbare; accusing; ill-bred; billowy; worshipping; sinless; unreposing; innumerable (pl); riotous; fearful; eager; thoughtless; seething; lean; exultant; hungry; starving; ghostly; angelic; excited; expectant; blood-washed; terror-stricken; beauteous; bewinged; adoring; laughing; chattering; moveless; trembling; crushed-down; spectral; listening; sceptered; invisible; festal; armed; emotional; spending; foolish; shining; pros-

trate; immense; base; impish; multitudinous; bestial; pressing; teeming; shoeless;
struggling; shaggy; ravenous; unhealthy;
edifying; toiling; whirling; amorous; moil-
ing.

verbs

disband—; disperse—; muster—; pacify—;
plunge through—; provoke—; rejoin—;
scatter—; silence—; slip through—; —assembles; —concentrates; —clamors; —converges on; —deluges; —eddies 'round; —
flocks; —masses; —mills about; —mobs;
—presses; —swarms; —focuses on.
   (See mob, crowd, multitude.)

THRONG (v)

adverbs

tumultuously; ceaselessly; demoniacally;
countlessly; innumerably; seethingly hungrily; expectantly; multitudinously; incongruously; bestially; moilingly
   (See swarm, congregate.)

THROW (v)

adverbs

violently; recklessly; haughtily; deliberately; dejectedly; bodily; savagely; profligately; passionately; lavishly; systematically;
significantly; defiantly; adroitly.
   (See hurl, heave.)

THRUSH

verbs

—bodes; —cheers; —choruses; —gushes; —
hymns; —moults; —pipes; —pours forth;
—retires; —trills.
   (See bird.)

THRUST

adjectives

vain; repeated (pl); vital; prompt; final;
shrewd-planned; unlikely; sore; tireless; unlucky.

THRUST (v)

adverbs

impudently; impatiently; brutally; determinedly; agilely; obtrusively; conspicuously;
methodically; resolutely; demurely; belligerently; rudely; wrathfully.
   (See stab, stick.)

THUMB

adjectives

black; shuffling; peaked; vigorous; wadded; solitary; broken; waving; fatty.

verbs

bind—; brush with—; crush—; deform—;
dislocate—; extend—; flex—; knead with
—s; lacerate—; manipulate—; sever—;
sprain—; twiddle—s; —gropes; —throbs.
   (See finger.)

THUMP (v)

adverbs

furiously; emphatically; repetitiously; impatiently; indignantly; thunderously; powerfully; dramatically.
   (See beat, hit.)

THUNDER

adjectives

howling; blasting; intermittent; interrupted;
heavy; frightful; thrilling; melodious;
mountain; angry; swarthy; sullen; editorial; muttering; branding; oracular; sus
pended; flameless; ominous; harmless; rumbling; direful; serious; muffled; wrathful;
lounging; artillery; hateful; clothed; incessant; threatening; stage; earthly; sweet;
rattling; brazen; volleying.

verbs

brave—; shoot forth—; —blusters; —
booms; —claps; —crashes; —deafens; —
detonates; —dins; —discords; —disturbs;
—echoes; —fulminates; —menaces; —petrifies; —pierces; —rattles; —rends;; —reverberates; —roars; —rolls; —rumbles; —
shatters; —shocks; —splits; —startles; —
threatens; —volleys.
   (See lightning, detonation, noise, discharge, report, explosion.)

THUNDER (v)

adverbs

appallingly; violently; ominously; tremendously; terrifically; frightfully; rumblingly;
muffledly; wrathfully; threateningly; repeatedly; awesomely.
   (See crash, resound.)

THUNDEROUS

adverbs

ominously; positively; portentously; triumphantly; enthusiastically; acclaimingly;
mutinously; threateningly; significantly;
swellingly; curiously; strangely; deafeningly; splendidly; loyally.

THWART (v)

adverbs

effectually; diligently; successfully; tempo-

rarily; discouragingly; righteously.
(See defeat, baffle.)

THWARTED

adverbs
dangerously; hopelessly; suddenly; painfully; distressingly; unfairly; meanly; odiously; hatefully; cruelly; desperately; curiously; strangely; inscrutably; adroitly; maliciously; cleverly; ingeniously; artfully; craftily; shrewdly; inexplicably; stealthily; quietly; successfully; helplessly; unaccountably; maliciously; dreadfully; discouragingly.

TICKER-TAPE

verbs
festoon with—; insert—; perforate—; read —; shower with—; stabilize—; steady—; —announces; —clutters; —communicates with; —fluctuates; —indicates; —informs; —lists; —litters; —notifies; —oscillates; — quotes; —records; —transmits; —unreels; —vacillates.

TICKET

verbs
arm with—; counterfeit—s; discard—; dispense—s; enumerate—s; grant—; hawk—s; purchase—; register—s; speculate on—s; stamp—s; tag with—s; —admits; —authorizes; —betokens; —checks; —enables; — evidences; —informs; —indicates; —labels; —permits; —testifies to; —vouchsafes.
(See ballot, coupon, label, permit, certificate.)

TICKLE (v)

adverbs
humorously; boisterously; playfully; teasingly; verbally; rudely; roughly; clownishly.
(See tease.)

TICKLED

adverbs
roguishly; mischievously; merrily; enormously; gleefully; ridiculously; obviously; visibly; prankishly; jubilantly; exceedingly; inordinately; wickedly; naughtily; amazingly.

TIDE

adjectives
undulating; brimming; ebbing; insurging; aerial; eventful; boundless (pl); multitudinous (pl); human; restless; falling; arrested; waveless; silent; terrible; mysterious; tossing; joyous; sidereal; ancient; surging; chafing; reactionary; capricious; passionate; forward-flowing; sultry; confused; overwhelming; subsiding; tumultuous; headlong; swollen; rippling; greenblue; conflicting; theologic; over-running; hastening; primal; refluent; glassy; brimful; rising; whelming; billowing; retiring; fickle; pellucid; foaming; interminable; incoming; trackless; latent; lulling; adverse; patriotic; sucking; angry; roving; golden; hurrying; flooding; perennial; contrary; westering; crystal; turbid; dusty-gray; misty; river; silvery; summer; deep-breathing; sliding; treacherous; rhythmic.

verbs
battle with—; breast—; drift with—; harness—; oppose—; stem—; swim with—; yield to—; —crawls out; —deluges; —ebbs; —fluctuates; —inundates; —invades; moans, —overtakes; —recedes; —regresses; —retires; —retreats; —roars; —swamps; —swells; —throbs; —wanes; —washes; — withdraws.
(See flow, flood, current.)

TIDINGS

adjectives
dismal; bad; joyful; unpleasant; frightful; inarticulate; glad; blissful; unimpeded; evil; gracious; accurate; astonishing; startling; heart-stirring; swift; hopeless.

TIDY

adverbs
scrupulously; painfully; terribly; carefully; unwontedly; unusually; dreadfully; spotlessly; remarkably; unexpectedly; suddenly; attractively; invitingly; pleasantly; agreeably; sufficiently; cosily; alluringly; distressingly; starkly; oppressively; miraculously; incredibly.

TIE

adjectives
subtle; weakened; cunning; common; primary; senseless; sordid; lifelong; mysterious; tenderest; singular; indissoluble; deep; domestic; silken; conjugal; sacred; foppish; unsubstantial; frail.

TIE (v)

adverbs
securely; fantastically; heroically; intri-

cately; involvedly; complicatedly; firmly; cunningly; indissolubly.
(See fasten, bind.)

TIER

adjectives
ascending; graceful; proportioned; blazing.

TIES

verbs
acknowledge—; adhere to—; cement—; cherish—; dissolve—; forsake—; knit—; preserve—; rend—; renounce—; saddle with—; sever—; shatter—; strain—; sunder —; treasure—; —affiliate; —bind; — couple; —fetter; —link; —obligate; — pledge; —restrain; —restrict; —shackle; — weaken.
(See bond, band, obligation.)

TIFF

adjectives
domestic; daily; lifelong; hateful; unnerving.

TIGER

adjectives
tawny; brindled; enraged; pouncing; man-eating; mangled; shrinking; clawing; murderous; lightning-fast; muscled; vicious; cunning; lunging; circling; snapping; growling; leaping; skulking; furious; mighty; teeth-baring; ferocious; creeping; catapulting; royal; determined; striped; spotted; fractious; frenzied; deadly; Sumatra; sabre-toothed; swift; slinking; villainous; demoniac; coughing; treacherous; cantering.

verbs
cage—; exterminate—s; infuriate—; lash—; perform with—s; train—; —climb; — crouches; —depredates; —devours; — haunts; —s infest; —lashes out at; — maims; —marauds; —mauls; —mews; — paws; —preys; —purrs; —rages; —ravages; —rends; —roars; —romps; —seizes; —slithers along the path; —snarls; — springs; —tears.
(See animal, lion, leopard.)

TIGERISH

adverbs
vaguely; furtively; fawningly; warily; vigilantly; fearsomely; attractively; slinkingly; alluringly; seductively; alarmingly; dangerously; contemptibly; slinkily; fiercely; per-

ceptibly; indubitably; unmistakably; fatally; indescribably; inexpressibly; inescapably; undeniably.

TIGHT

adverbs
uncomfortably; sufficiently; unfortunately; fatally; terribly; occasionally; dreadfully; happily; blithely; completely; painfully; odiously; distressingly; gloriously; blissfully; permanently; momentarily; disgracefully; shamefully; strangely; unusually; ridiculously; dangerously; injuriously; revealingly; satisfactorily.

TIGHTEN (*v*)

adverbs
gradually; partially; remorselessly; lovingly; passionately; abruptly; insidiously; subtly.
(See grip, squeeze.)

TIGHTS

verbs
accoutre in—; array in—; attire in—; bare —; cavort in—; divest of—; doff—; don—; equip with—; fray—; spangle—; strip of —; tatter—; vest in—; —display; —enable; —expose; —facilitate.
(See costume, uniform, garment.)

TILT (*v*)

adverbs
awkwardly; negligently; jauntily; nonchalantly; precariously.
(See teeter, sway.)

TIMBER

adjectives
shaky; massive; long-used; slashed; marketable; reverberating; rotten; superb; fringing; graceful; useful.

verbs
avail oneself of—; blast—; conserve—; debark—; fell—; knot—; level—; market—; preserve—; process—; provide—; raze—; reinforce—; strip of—; treat—; value—; —decays; —erodes; —jams; —rots.
(See log, beam, wood.)

TIMBERED

adverbs
heavily; profitably; densely; wisely; fortunately; well; luckily; thickly; amazingly; sparsely; thinly; negligibly; valuably; reputedly; allegedly; immensely.

adjectives

valuable; sufficient; troublous; inexpedient; curious; happy; righteous; irresponsible; unconscionable; precious; primitive; arduous; historic; auspicious; predestined; patristic; solemn; evil; official; tolerating; troubled; reasonable; unfit; glorious; fantastic; thoughtless; later; frivolous; rococo; dark; considerable; former; palmy; unsettled; priceless; injurious; appointed; bygone; substantial; fruitful; halycon; impatient; fleeting; ample; boundless; descending; civilized; recorded; intervening; trying; woeful; sorry; appreciable; casting; measurable; degenerate; fittest; unseasonable; stormy; mutual; lessened; uneasy; turbulent; indefinite; despicable; unquiet; factious; immemorial; sacred; fated; apostolic; moral; periodic; unused; record-breaking; virtuous; distracted; tuning; affirmed; chaotic; opportune; fitting; abundant; corroding; pairing; exciting; unemployed; sultry; costly; millennium; propitious; rough-and-tumble; subversive; potential; scented; calamitous; gleaning; leisure; unborn; melodious; charitable; barbarous; anxious; flowering; ridiculous; blissful; squalid; dicing; administrative; invaluable; mournful; pleasant; specified; remote; pointed; abysmal; thin-faced; terrible; discouraging; feudal; stirring; naughty; restless; statutory; perilous; altered; conquering; shadowed; accustomed; unhallowed; limited; envious; significant; awful; intermediate; various (pl); classic; inconvenient; broadening; inevitable; breathing; regenerated; prehistoric; equinoctial; scriptural; scant; dusky; ill-devouring; portentous; assigned; limited; disorderly; revolutionary; unaccustomed; hasty; balmy; prosperous; guilty; growing; distant; profitable; subsequent; enormous; rippling; amphibious; short; swift-footed; regretted; spacious; cloudless; discouraging; stormy; unfavorable; fairy; future; due; consumed; emotional.

verbs

abide—; allot—; begrudge—; beguile—; bide for—; budget—; calculate—; conserve —; consume—; devote—to; devour—; endure—; engross—; exhaust—; fritter away —; indicate—; inform of—; lack—; lavish —on; limit—; mark—; measure—; prolong —; protract—; record—; reveal in—; spare —; squander—; "stall for"—; tarry for—;

terminate—; while away—; —advances; —approaches; —blots out; —discloses; —disintegrates; —dissolves; —dwindles; —elapses; —expires; —fades; —flies; —flits; —glides on; —heals; —marches on; —matures; —mellows; —nears; —outmodes; —presses; —races; —ripens; —recedes; —rolls around; —rolls back; —shadows; —tempers; —unfolds; —vanishes; —vindicates; —wanes; —withers.

(See interval, hour, leisure, month, instant, moment, day.)

TIMED

adverbs

opportunely; wisely; seasonably; wonderfully; fatally; precisely; meticulously; exactly; uncannily; viciously; brutally; heinously; tragically; carefully; scientifically; automatically; cautiously; cleverly; auspiciously; apparently; murderously; punctiliously; promptly; considerately; thoughtfully; graciously; obviously.

TIMELY

adverbs

pleasantly; fortunately; altogether; unusually; particularly; singularly; providentially; remarkably; miraculously; marvellously; curiously; felicitously; wonderfully.

TIMID

adverbs

modestly; constitutionally; shyly; bashfully; groundlessly; anxiously; deliciously; unreasonably; unwontedly; tremulously; childishly; nervously; foolishly; incredibly; naturally; vaguely; momentarily; secretly; excessively; strangely; distressingly; incomprehensibly; temperamentally; helplessly; hopelessly; unaccountably; uneasily; queerly; curiously; genuinely; unaffectedly; significantly.

TIMIDITY

adjectives

modest; early; scrupulous; constitutional; ill-grounded; shy; bashful; refined; anxious; delicious; skulking; irrational; sententious; unwonted; tremulous.

verbs

conceal—; conquer—; cower in—; despise —; feign—; flinch in—; induce—; inspire —; master—; mock—; overcome—; pretend —; prevail over—; quail in—; retire in—; reveal—; simulate—; smite with—; suffer

—; —abashes; —besets; —cows; —daunts; —deters; —dismays; —distresses; —haunts; —overwhelms; —petrifies.

(See cowardice, bashfulness, shyness, modesty, fear.)

TIMOROUS
adverbs
shyly; bashfully; self-consciously; modestly; guiltily; sheepishly; naturally; inherently; merely; habitually; usually; foolishly; sadly; pitiably; miserably; unfortunately; childishly; wretchedly; unreasonably; needlessly; strangely; oddly; curiously; inexplicably; unaccountably; ridiculously; positively; actually.

TINGE
adjectives
sunset; bright; silky-green; confidential; pantheistic; mauve; transient; sanguinary; abundant; slight.

TINGE (v)
adverbs
brilliantly; markedly; slightly; occasionally; deeply; transiently; luridly.

(See imbue, color.)

TINKER
adjectives
itinerant; mean; preaching; strong.

TINKLE
adjectives
inviting; pleasant; cheery; liquid; laughing; lilting.

TINNY
adverbs
unpleasantly; inexcusably; unacceptably; disagreeably; curiously; raucously; intolerably; strangely; unpalatably; tawdrily.

TINT
adjectives
vivid; dismal; acquainted; delicate; pearly; exquisite; unobtrusive; shifting; somber; prophetic; smoky; rainbowed; combative; bloody; delicate; gathering; changing; positive; beauteous; prismatic; prevailing; general; brilliant; mellow; harmonious; tender; original.

TINT (v)
adverbs
delicately; gracefully; richly; vividly; somberly; beauteously; prismatically; brilliantly; harmoniously; mellowly.

(See tinge, color.)

TINY
adverbs
unbelievably; incredibly; infinitesimally; microscopically; minutely; extremely; remarkably; actually; marvelously; positively; dwarfishly; insignificantly; elfishly; fantastically; unimaginably; grotesquely; terribly.

TIP
verbs
cap—; crown—; daub on—; gild—; impale on—; veneer—; whet—; —bristles; —penetrates; —pierces; —projects; —protrudes; —punctures; —stabs.

(See edge, point.)

TIPSY
adverbs
gloriously; shamefully; helplessly; comically; sadly; alarmingly; insecurely; happily; foolishly; comically; ridiculously; laughably; ludicrously; grossly; crassly; offensively; disagreeably; unpleasantly; hopelessly; inordinately; slightly; extremely; terribly; continually; occasionally; definitely; indubitably; suddenly; inexplicably; undeniably; hilariously; noisily; boisterously; uproariously; sullenly.

TIRADE
adjectives
jeering; tedious; patriotic; shrill; positive; cumulative; belated; bitter; lengthy.

verbs
declaim in—; deliver—; fulminate—; halt —; launch—; pour out—; prolong—; rant —; recite—; silence—; spout—; utter—; — anathematizes; —castigates; —censors; — chastises; —declaims; —defames; —denounces; —deprecates; —disparages; —excoriates; —execrates; —harangues; —inveighs against; —lampoons; —lashes; — reprimands; —reproaches; —reproves; — thunders.

(See diatribe, scolding, invective, speech.)

adjectives

spare; pneumatic; first; strong; deflated; retreaded; worn; slippery; useless.

verbs

deflate—; depress—; dilate—; distend—; fray—; gauge—; imbed in—; inflate—; mount on—s; perforate—; pierce—; pump —; puncture—; retread—; scrape—; value —; vulcanize—; —erodes; —grazes; —pads; —preserves; —skids.

TIRE (v)

adverbs

acutely; rapidly; abnormally; sadly; noticably; patently.

(See exhaust, bore.)

TIRESOME

adverbs

pedantically; monotonously; gushingly; garrulously; dully; uninterestingly; prosaically; long-windedly; endlessly, pleachilly; tediously; irksomely; boresomely; intolerably; unpleasantly; harmlessly; disagreeably; undeniably; terribly; needlessly; dreadfully; unfortunately; abominably; disgustingly; desperately; droningly.

TIRING

adverbs

unexpectedly; unwittingly; uncommonly; extraordinarily; dangerously; extremely; unintentionally; terribly; dreadfully; unwontedly; sadly; unfortunately; strangely; curiously; oddly; unnecessarily; needlessly; distressingly; painfully; obviously; palpably; inconsiderately; unaccountably; terrifically; grievously; unwarrantably; pitifully; seriously; oppressively; profoundly; inordinately.

TISSUE

adjectives

superficial; rich; silver; muscular; dermatoid; vegetable; damaged; disposable; cellular; social; desensitized; adipose; glandular; fibrous; abundant; innermost; plaited; excess; transpicuous; siliceous.

verbs

abscess—; canker—; consume—; cramp—; crush—; curette away—; desiccate—; destroy—; distend—; excise—; graft—; harden—; incise—; infect—; inflame—; inject into—; invade—; involve—; knead—; massage—; mould—; nourish—; regenerate

—; support—; suture—; transplant—; —degenerates; —infiltrates; —languishes; —relaxes; —shrivels; —wastes; —withers.

TITANIC

adverbs

monstrously; tremendously; unbelievably; unimaginably; superbly; magnificently; gloriously; majestically; overwhelmingly; gorgeously; stupendously; inconceivably; cumbersomely; incomparably; unsurpassably.

TITLE

adjectives

honorary; precarious; elusive; religious; fabulous; trumped-up; bombastic; imposing; soul-stirring; vague; successive (pl); preliminary; forfeited; neglected; optimistic; seductive; pompous; impressive; shrill; legitimist; grotesque; attractive; hereditary; quaint; numerous (pl); clerical; imperial; distinguishing; illogical; vainglorious; appertinent; fantastic; ingenious; significant; ironic; prescriptive; smoothing; subscriptive; whimsical; homely; honorable; resounding; worse; dubious; newly-obtained; suggestive.

verbs

assume—; award—; bear—; claim—; covet —; decorate with—; defile—; degrade—; disparage—; dub with—; earn—; inherit—; invent—; renounce—; respect—; retain—; revere—; surrender—; underline—; usurp —; —awes; —connotes; —cows; —distinguishes; —epitomizes; —implies; —impresses; —misleads; —symbolizes; —signifies; —veils.

(See name, degree, nickname, rank.)

TITLED

adverbs

nobly; grandly; gloriously; proudly; royally; imperially; austerely; ecclesiastically; divinely; piously; devoutly; legitimately; officially; absurdly; bombastically; ridiculously; ironically; truly; self-; vainly; foolishly; unreasonably; realistically; popularly; ignominously; jeeringly; affectionately; lovingly; derisively; comically; shamefully.

TITTER

adjectives

slight; shamefaced; electric; damaging; explosive.

TITTER (v)

adverbs

affectedly; irrepressibly; involuntarily; girlishly; unsophisticatedly; explosively; naively; rudely; comically; hysterically; affectedly; coyly.

(See laugh, giggle.)

TOAD

adjectives

loathed; soft; sizable; well-fed; blinking; ugly; venomous; bucolic.

verbs

infest with —s; —burrows; —s bury themselves; —creeps; —croaks; —emits a noise; —hibernates; —hops; —jumps; —leaps; —metamorphoses; —plagues; —secretes; —springs; —squats; —vaults.

TOAST

adjectives

complimentary; appropriate; enthusiastic; celebrated; tasty; scorching; crisp; ·burned; crackling; crunching.

verbs

cheer—; drink—; hail—; join in—; propose —; rejoice in—; suggest—; utter—; voice —; acclaims—; —commemorates; —compliments; —eulogizes; —extols; —flatters; —glorifies; —hallows; —honors; —pledges; —solemnizes.

(See tribute, praise, sentiment, bread.)

TOAST (v)

adverbs

convivially; appropriately; crisply; cracklingly; victoriously; fraternally; boisterously.

(See congratulate, celebrate.)

TOBACCO

adjectives

aromatic; heavy; suggestive; coarse.

verbs

abhor—; abstain from—; addict to—; age —; auction—; blend —s; consume—; crave —; cross —s; cultivate—; cure—; denicotinize—; ferment—; filter—; grade—; hunger for—; inhale—; market—; mellow—; mentholize—; moisten—; plug—; powder—; purvey—; ripen—; roast—; scent—; store —; toast—; yearn for—; —braces; —calms; —clouds; —deteriorates; —discolors; —dulls; —impairs; —irritates; —lifts; —ma-

tures; —ravages; —reeks; —repels; —soothes; —steadies; —stunts; —tempts; —tranquillizes; —undermines; —vitiates.

TOE

adjectives

jagged; elfin; pliant; superfluous; contemptuous; shuffling; blunt; nimble; outraged; fantastic; dance-weary; festered; infected.

verbs

amputate—; bare—; brace—; bruise—; cramp—; crush—; dance on—; deform—; dislocate—; distort—; flex—; fracture—; pad—; sever—; skip on —s; splint—; stub —; teeter on—; web—; —pinches; —projects; —protrudes.

TOIL

adjectives

precarious; unhonored; manly; unrequited; exhausting; terrible; profitable; wholesome; philanthropic; unremitting; irksome; contented; hideous; pernicious; happy; filthy; sporadic; wasting; eager; smiling; rugged; blundering; griping; unceasing; earnest; delicious; fragrant; loving; arduous; sickening; desperate; earthly; successful; anxious; double; brave; stormy; noble; honest; meridian; ferocious; sultry; humble; squalid; elaborate; unrepaid; spasmodic; wasting; sullen; drudging; captive; patient; unhallowed; benignant; productive; fatiguing; congenial; ingenious; unusual; incessant; pernicious; sportive.

verbs

abate—; achieve by—; amass by—; cease—; consume in—; delight in—; ease—; hallow —; mitigate—; necessitate—; obviate—; plunge into—; relax—; reward—; shirk—; slacken—; —exhausts; —fags; —fatigues; —jades; —strains; —taxes; —wearies.

(See labor, drudgery, work, effort.)

TOIL (v)

adverbs

patiently; laboriously; ceaselessly; uncomplainingly; manfully; bodily; stealthily; painfully; assiduously; conscientiously; vigorously; sickeningly; precariously; exhaustingly; philanthropically; irksomely; incessantly; arduously; fatiguingly; perniciously.

(See work, labor.)

TOILER

adjectives
self-sufficient; patient; possessionless; laborious.

TOILET

adjectives
elaborate; hasty; unfinished; hurried.

TOILSOME

adverbs
terribly; dreadfully; undesirably; inescapably; unavoidably; brutally; cruelly; bitterly; exhaustingly; horribly; curiously; inordinately; extremely; unexpectedly; shockingly; miserably; wretchedly; shamefully; monotonously; tediously.

TOILWORN

adverbs
terribly; pathetically; significantly; apparently; palpably; extremely; unusually; miserably; obviously; evidently, wretchedly; lamentably; unaccountably; unexpectedly; deplorably; pitiably; inexcusably; remarkably; unmistakably; utterly.

TOKEN

adjectives
unmistakable; especial; tiniest; expressive; personal; unanimous; crushing; unique; singular; mystic; sensible; glorious; visible; palpable; bounteous; beauteous; outward; tremendous; sunny; amorous; leaden; irritating; meaningful.

TOLERABLE

adverbs
scarcely; barely; fairly; apparently; easily; eventually; finally; gradually; evidently; hardly; actually.

TOLERANCE

adjectives
kindly; legal; habitual; courteous; lazy; contemptuous; scientific; moral; apathetic; easygoing; amused; mischievous; indolent; gentle.

verbs
acclaim—; achieve—; advocate—; bear with —; breed—; cherish—; commend—; exemplify—; exhort—; foster—; further—; lack—; nurture—; preach—; preserve—; regard with—; sustain—; temper with—; —ameliorates; —pervades.
(See charity, forbearance, kindness, benevolence.)

TOLERANT

adverbs
sensibly; generously; broadly; wisely; discreetly; diplomatically; tactfully; overly; indulgently; reasonably; moderately; unusually; inordinately; unwisely; charitably; foolishly; rabidly; patiently; calmly; imperturbably; quietly; serenely; easily; mildly; sagely; marvellously; magnanimously; splendidly.

TOLERATE (*v*)

adverbs
eternally; consciously; patiently; magnanimously; generously; legally; courteously; lazily; contemptuously; morally; indolently; gently.
(See endure, permit.)

TOLERATION

adjectives
universal; further; religious; generous; absolute; quiet; superficial; indifferent; continued.

TOLL

adjectives
devilish; patient; terrible; enormous; death; preposterous.

verbs
assess—; augment—; bear—; charge—; deflate—; demand—; enforce—; exact—; fix —; levy—; quote—; rate—; set—; take—; subject to—; —burdens; —enables; —mounts; —taxes; —yields.
(See price, payment, tap.)

TOLL (*v*)

adverbs
solemnly; mournfully; dismally; repetitiously; funereally; fatally; heavily; vibrantly.
(See ring, clang.)

TOMB

adjectives
rock-hewn; sumptuous; brazen; dateless; neglected; wandering; ancestral; vacant; gilded; traditional; crumbling; antenatal; interdicted; indefinable; fin-winged; flowering; melancholy; untimely; fiery; ponderous; lingering; wintry; vast; impregnable; ferocious; watery; murmurous; slender; unlamented; reverend; drear; somber; miry.

verbs
adorn—; bar—; consign to—; deface—; de-

file—; delve in—; desecrate—; disinter from —; erect—; explore—; guard—; haunt—; illuminate—; incarcerate in—; inter in—; mould in—; patrol—; register upon—; rest in—; seal—; shadow—; unearth—; wreath —; —depresses; —envelops; —muffles; —receives; —reeks; —shrouds; —yields up.

(See shrine, grave, monument.)

TOMB-LIKE

adverbs

coldly; horribly; unbearably; supernaturally; terribly; fearfully; wretchedly; intolerably; frighteningly; appallingly; gruesomely; grimly; depressingly; dispiritingly; dismally; woefully; forbiddingly; curiously; grotesquely; fantastically.

TOME

verbs

compose—; concoct—; criticize—; dash off —; deliver—; immortalize—; inscribe—; pen—; polish—; pour forth—; publish—; wade through—; —commemorates; —eulogizes; —honors; —soliloquizes; —treats.

(See book, volume.)

TONE

adjectives

faltering; contemptuous; deprecating; soothing; passive; clear; angelic; deep-strung; provocative; milder; customary; diverse (pl); rueful; answering; solitary; frightened; braggart; ethereal; saddened; dearest; varying (pl); suggestive; victory; vindictive; low; lover-like; gentlest; confidential; sweet; gracious; joyous; regretful; rich; smothered; imperative; sanctimonious; moral; elastic; agitated; startled; careless; romantic; senatorial; breathless; pleading; pitiful; conciliatory; anguished; dictatorial; pastel; dominant; ringing; wailing; dark; bright; intermediate; marine; modified; colorful; didactic; inward; free; callous; hearty; beautiful; unceremonious; unconscious; boisterous; sullen; timid; flippant; blunt; nasal; moral; beseeching; shapeless; mean; menacing; soft; stentorian; confident; savage; faltering; preoccupied; child-like; earnest; imperious; dispassionate; conversational; scorching; intimate; sarcastic; threatening; soul-stirring; exulting; solemn; yearning; vibrating; impatient; luscious; tremulous; philosophic; supercilious; enamored; altered; crimson; distressful; amicable; honeyed; cathedral; ironical; displeasing; monotonous; ordinary; listless; aggressive; ivory; melodious; melting; tranquil; caressing; intriguing; half-pensive; indescribable; transient; well-guarded; promiscuous; martial; subdued; authoritative; maniac; unctuous; contrasting; assured; measured; despairing; archaic; mournful; whining; composite; paternal; drawling; bellicose; officer-like; ruminative; piping; metallic; bantering; incongruous; well-remembered; fretful; exquisite; hollow; vigorous; vexed; animated; witching; clarion; constituent; agonized; eager; healthy; complimentary; brisk; audible; penetrating; subduing; dreamy; piqued; apologetic; fluttering; caustic; proper; courteous; argumentative; nauseated; good-humored; haunting; dulcet; wonted; general; imperious; abominable; doubtful; abrupt; terrified; wheedling; innocent; considerable; tranquil; scoffing; thin; emphatic; sepulchral; liquid; silvery; jocular; harmonious; insolent; condescending; wistful; suppressed; fundamental; reflective; blustering; reproachful; controversial; burnt; unworldly; respectful; precious; lachrymose; unemotional; hungry; revolutionary; convinced; indifferent; untrammeled; strong; expostulating; insinuating; stately; inadequate; feeble; ever-pealing; grown-up; reminiscent; determined; musing; thoughtful; unmusical; exotic; mimic; professional; lugubrious; mordant; suppressed; mollified; frosted.

verbs

accentuate—; adopt—; alter—; amplify—; chasten—; deepen—; elevate—; falsify—; govern—; impart—; inflect—; lack—; lend —; lower—; magnify—; mimic—; modulate—; muffle—; silence—; strengthen—; subdue—; utter—; —betrays; —chastises; —elevates; —expresses; —harmonizes; —indicates; —irritates; —manifests; —mocks; —nettles; —predominates; —reproaches; —reproves; —reveals; —reverberates; —vibrates.

(See note, sound.)

TONGUE

adjectives

serpent; tuneful; partial; piercing; hissing; envious; forked; golden; indignant; wagging; moistened; dead; prattling; cloven; wily; complaining; lambent; gluttonous; foamless; evil; caustic; raise; immortal; furred; feverish; quivering; rapid; dominant; slick; leaping; unbound; classic; calumnious; lolling; earnest; unintelligible; gossiping; faltering; shrewish; gentle; polished; carping; cautious; boyish; halting; biting; coated; hasty; scoffing; silent; slurring; fervent; perfidious; flattering; fine-dividing; ancient; glowing; base; boundless; romancing; casual; heedless; proper; multitudinous (pl); uncivilized; oily; bitter; unbridled; joyous; unwilling; iron; soul-subduing; persuasive; slanderous; malicious; double; nimble; national; candied; pleading; discreet; lamenting; droning; viperish; railing; forbidden; woe-wearied; facile; flexible; foul; censorious; unintelligible; ill; lying; pliant; learned; modern; pioneer; glib; railing; nerveless; boastful; unknowable; brazen; liquid; soothing; slippery; stammering; scorched; teasing; glowing; shallow; whispering; pleasing; immortal; cynical; masterful; captious; gentle; guileless; inestimable; woodland; mother; selfsame.

adjectives
blister—; bridle—; candy—; chafe—; clip cluck—; curb—; discipline—; envenom—; examine—; fur—; furrow—; hold—; hush —; hypnotize—; inflame—; insert—; irritate—; lap with—; loosen—; mute—; paralyze—; provoke—; roll off—; sever—; silence—; smack—; stifle—; still—; suppress —; swab—; tempt—; tickle—; tie—; train —; wag—; —charms; —cleaves to; — falters; —laps; —lashes; —licks; —moistens; —projects; —protrudes; —rasps; — relishes; —savors; —slanders; —slips; — traduces; —voices; —wounds.

TONGUE-TIED
adverbs
deplorably; congenitally; lamentably; unfortunately; pitiably; pathetically; wretchedly; miserably; clumsily; awkwardly; unluckily; embarrassingly; shockingly; uncomfortably; bashfully; shyly; timidly; self-consciously; guiltily; curiously; unwontedly; unusually; peculiarly; strangely; unaccountably; suddenly; apparently.

TONIC
adjectives
valuable; intellectual; antiseptic; exhilarating; bracing; useful; provocative; bitter; healthful; mental; excellent.

verbs
addict to—s; administer—; consume—; dose

with—; prescribe—; recommend—; —bolsters; —builds up; —enriches; —nauseates; —purges; —reanimates; —rejuvenates; — renews; —renovates; —restores; —resuscitates; —revivifies; —stimulates.
(See laxative, medicine, wine.)

TONIC
adverbs
refreshingly; wholesomely; definitely; effectively; really; dependably; reliably; assuredly; strongly; splendidly; invigoratingly; desirably; noticeably; evidently; positively; indubitably; admirably; wonderfully; commendably; marvellously; miraculously; incredibly; unexpectedly; delightfully; satisfactorily; remarkably; particularly .

TONSILS
verbs
apply to—; attack—; coat—; disease—; drain—; enlarge—; envelope ; excite—, extract—; infect—; inflame—; invade—; swab—; swell—; —envenom; —filter; — indicate; —poison; —project; —suppurate; —ulcerate; paint—; scrutinize—; sever—; shrink—.

TOOL
adjectives
unconscious; passive; obedient; legitimate; vital; tempered; shaped; dexterous; edged; brittle; trenchant; unaccustomed; ready; obsolete; congenial; subservient; exquisite; keen.

verbs
apply—; devise—; employ—; enlist—; fashion—; guide—; hew with—; manipulate—; mechanize—; operate—; skill with—; stamp —; strain—; tax—; utilize—; wield—; — bevels; —bores; —eases; —facilitates; — lightens; —smooths.
(See instrument, apparatus, machine.)

TOOLING
adjectives
vigorous; firm; dazzling.

TOOTH
adjectives
rankling; determined; raging; rotten; cavity-eaten; filled; aching; film-covered; sparkling; false; broken; jagged.

verbs
(See teeth.)

TOOTHACHE

adjectives
serious; agonizing; unrelieved; comic; painful.

TOOTHLESS

adverbs
hideously; repulsively; pitifully; incoherently; unintelligibly; powerlessly; infirmly; utterly.

TOOTHSOME

adverbs
especially; particularly; agreeably; surprisingly; definitely; actually; unexpectedly; delectably; deliciously; lusciously; temptingly; extremely; undeniably; unusually; uncommonly; invitingly; pleasantly

TOP

adjectives
slender; inviolate; grisly; hill; sterile; gloomy; sun-bleached; singed; massive; eminent; pryamided; lofty.

TOP-HEAVY

adverbs
dangerously; inartistically; unfortunately; peculiarly; unsatisfactorily; objectionably; oddly; strangely; unluckily; hazardously; clumsily; awkwardly; impractically; unreliably; riskily; obviously; manifestly; unreasonably; crazily; unacceptably; abnormally; precariously; insecurely; uncommonly.

TOPIC

adjectives
dangerous; recondite; related; aforementioned; conversational; wary; religious; hackneyed; various (pl); disagreeable; dreadful; current; absorbing; conservative; tempting; concrete; conceivable; numerous (pl); forbidden; doubtful; political; one-sided; allied; abandoned; important; tiresome; celestial; magazine; commonplace; complicated; wholesome.

verbs
absorb in—; air—; analyze—; argue—; condense—; converse on—; digress from—; disclose—; dismiss—; dissect—; dissertate on—; divert from—; do justice to—; exhaust—; expatiate on—; expound—; grapple with—; limit—; obscure—; probe—; propose—; pursue—; rant about—; resume—;

revive—; seize upon—; shrink from—; unfold—; ventilate—; —fascinates; —treats of.
(See subject, theme, question.)

TOPSY-TURVY

adverbs
unpleasantly; crazily; carelessly; inexcusably; disagreeably; negligently; objectionably; untidily; hastily; irremediably; terribly; oddly; fantastically; unexpectedly; gaily; perplexingly; inextricably; madly; mischievously; deliberately; inconsiderately; thoughtlessly; heedlessly; wildly; wantonly.

TORCH

adjectives
inverted; bridal; fiery; nuptial; smoldering; flaring; feeble; extemporized; broidered; incandescent; blazing; extemporary; processional.

verbs
apply—; bear—; eclipse—; employ—; extend—; extinguish—; flourish—; obscure—; quench—; screen—; smother—; snuff out—; thrust—; —beams; —chars; —dazzles; --enkindles; —flares; —flashes; —flickers; —gleams; —glimmers; —ignites; —radiates; —scintillates; —scorches; —sheds; —shimmers; —singes; —smoulders.
(See lamp, flame, light.)

TORMENT

adjectives
happy; numberless (pl); invented; abiding; exhausted; human; eternal; haunting; protracted; dreadful; perpetual; exquisite; especial; endless; continual; studied.

verbs
allay—; alleviate—; bear—; dull—; ease—; endure—; experience—; induce—; inflict—; mitigate—; occasion—; suffer—; tolerate—; —agonizes; —crushes; —curses; —galls; —gnaws; —rends; —rings; —shatters; —sours; —wracks.
(See punishment, anguish, itching, torture.)

TORMENT (v)

adverbs
constantly; protractedly; exquisitely; endlessly; diabolically; cruelly; heartlessly; unrelentingly; barbarously; devilishly; fiendishly.
(See hurt, pain, torture.)

TORMENTING

adverbs

vaguely; distinctly; mischievously; wantonly; offensively; vexatiously; intolerably; insufferably; unbearably; unwittingly; wilfully; deliberately; intentionally; constantly; unconsciously; purposely; viciously; maliciously; venomously; childishly; youthfully; blithely; continually; consistently; particularly; peculiarly; abominably; detestably; atrociously; facetiously; foolishly.

TORNADO

flounder in—; stagger in—; totter in—; —batters; —blasts; —bowls over; —cripples; —devastates; —ebbs; —effaces; —exterminates; —gyrates; —howls; —levels; — mangles; —plays havoc; —prostrates; — razes; —revolves; —rips over; —roars; — rotates; —scuttles; —smashes; —spends itself; —swamps; —swirls; —topples; — wheezes; —whistles

(See storm, hurricane, wind.)

TORPID

adverbs

safely; securely; wanly; peculiarly; seasonally; naturally; stupidly; dully; merely; apathetically; terribly; unaccountably; unusually; alarmingly; helplessly; hopelessly; particularly; oddly; peculiarly; uncommonly, mercifully; inertly; contentedly; sluggishly; remarkably; inexplicably; habitually.

TORPOR

adjectives

momentary; guilty; heavy; vegetable; dead; frozen; intellectual; delicious; blank; dazed; death-like.

TORRENT

adjectives

wild; rushing; impetuous; irregular; tempestuous; streaming; furious; fiery; thundering; driving; angry; boiling; muddy; seething; dangerous; racing; living; windy; drenching; rapid, turbid; plunging; instantaneous; silver; deep; narrow; swirling; eddying; restless; tremendous; resistless; noisy; mad; fierce; hushed; flashing; swift; foaming; raging; radical; icy; mountain; descending; lava; turbulent; pent-up.

verbs

check—; dam—; immerse in—; pacify—; slacken—; staunch—; stem—; swell into—; tranquillize—; —batters; —buffets; —cascades; —deluges; —devastates; —foams; —gushes; —inundates; —issues from; — roars; —rolls; —surges; —sweeps; — swirls; —washes; —waves.

(See maelstrom, storm, rain, flood, stream.)

TORRENTIAL

adverbs

unusually; unseasonably; unexpectedly; suddenly; alarmingly; destructively; calamitously; disastrously; violently; viciously; swirlingly; inescapably; windily; frigidly; lamentably; mercilessly; furiously; perilously; frightfully; terribly; indescribably; incomparably; tragically; ominously; positively; actually.

TORRID

adverbs

unpleasantly; unfortunately; mercilessly; cruelly; intolerably; unbearably; parchingly; distressingly; injuriously; disastrously; calamitously; unexpectedly; unseasonably; suddenly; terribly; curiously; oddly; particularly; usually; uncommonly; painfully; inescapably.

TORSO

adjectives

slender; youthful; well-proportioned; antique.

TORTUOUS

adverbs

circuitously; painfully; perplexingly; wonderfully; intricately; unusually; arduously; unnecessarily; craftily; sinuously; deceptively; bewilderingly; distressingly; bothersomely; deliberately; objectionably; unpleasantly; disagreeably; maddeningly; discouragingly; vexatiously; curiously; unreasonably; confusingly; needlessly; terribly; dreadfully; tiresomely.

TORTURE

adjectives

excruciating; bitter; mental; lingering; physical; everlasting; exquisite; measured; hideous; endless; unrepressed; horrible; innate; slow; consuming; supreme; secret; utmost; tightening; eternal; memorable; rational; intense; untold; subtle; curdling; cruel; abominable; righteous; fiendish; burning; showy; grating.

verbs
avert—; contrive—; devise—; endure—; enforce—; palliate—; release from—; submit to—; subject to—; —benumbs; —convulses; —crucifies; —harrows; —lingers; —racks.
(See ordeal, torment, punishment, pain.)

TORTURE (v)
adverbs
excruciatingly; bitterly; lingeringly; physically; hideously; horribly; secretly; irrationally; exquisitely; barbarically; grotesquely.
(See torment, hurt, pain.)

TOSS
adjectives
tremendous; pretty; merry; coquettish; disdainful; careless.

TOSS (v)
adverbs
angrily; carelessly; restlessly; arrogantly; indiscriminately; restively; fretfully; impatiently; pettishly; coyly; coquettishly; disdainfully.
(See hurl, heave.)

TOTAL
adjectives
impressive; alarming; tremendous; enormous; attainable; staggering; incorrect; huge; amazing; erroneous.

verbs
amass—; appraise—; ascertain—; assess—; augment—; balance—; calculate—; check—; compile—; compute—; determine—; dispute —; divulge—; estimate—; integrate—; plumb—; rate—; reckon—; reveal—; underestimate—; weigh—; whittle down—; — aggregates; —astounds; —embraces; — mounts; —soars; —staggers; —totters.
(See amount.)

TOTAL
adverbs
finally; undeniably; grossly; substantially; presumably; indivisably; tentatively; staggeringly; roughly; unconditionally.

TOTTERING
adverbs
tremulously; waveringly; uncertainly; odd-

ly; queerly; agedly; helplessly; pitiably; extremely; effetely; dejectedly.

TOUCH
adjectives
starry; soft; pleading; composing; distinctive; fairy; casual; impassioned; featherlike; caustic; felicitous; innumerable (pl); vivifying; continuous; magic; daughterly; hasty; corroding; subtile; exciting; nurselike; unwonted; polluting; passing; consoling; mortal; mysterious; sophisticated; chilling; dramatic; flexible; quivering; aristocratic; truthful; celestial; pardonable; luxurious; masterly; satiric; humorous; soothing; alien; simplifying; lively; mellow; sensitive; couturier; musical; demoralizing; clinging; crowning; icy; dreamy; uncivil; desperate; glowing; unfelt; ethereal; ironical; sweetest; inspiriting; fascinating; facile; convincing; tainting; finishing; summery; immaculate; all-pervading; immediate; caressing; arch; slight; incautious; simple; deathly; discriminative; abominable; skillful; beastly; plastic; innocent; vulgar; sparkling; superficial; faultless; final; classic; rare; grotesque; lyrical; inimitable; passionate; sophisticated; trial-fire.

verbs
avert—; avoid—; evade—; sense—; sensitize—; —benumbs; —brushes; —chills; — comforts; —contaminates; —defiles; —degrades; —electrifies; —excites; —grazes; —impassions; —petrifies; —pollutes; —reveals; —revolts; —tickles.
(See contact.)

TOUCH (v)
adverbs
delicately; affectionately; lingeringly; reverently; piquantly; inadequately; profoundly; confidingly; genuinely; inexpressibly; angelically; timidly; respectfully; fitfully; cautiously.
(See finger, feel.)

TOUCHDOWN
verbs
achieve—; aim at—; annul—; avert—; bid for—; block—; charge for—; clamor for—; culminate in—; pass to—; pile up—s; plunge for—; prevent—; recall—; score—; sneak over—; stem—; sweep for—; void—; yield—; —climaxes; —demoralizes; —determines.

TOUCHING

adverbs

infinitely; poignantly; extremely; unusually; positively; utterly; tenderly; hauntingly; curiously; pathetically; thrillingly; overwhelmingly; incomparably; unexpectedly; undeniably.

TOUCHY

adverbs

absurdly; unreasonably; vexatiously; significantly; arrogantly; indescribably; nervously; cholerically; churlishly; pugnaciously; curiously; strangely; inexplicably; unaccountably; inherently; naturally; unbecomingly; unpleasantly; disagreeably; atrociously; painfully; distressingly; ridiculously.

TOUGH

adverbs

disagreeably; unpleasantly; unpalatably; inedibly, unwarrantably; inadmissibly; curiously; unreasonably; unpardonably; outrageously; scandalously; shamefully; troublesomely; wantonly; dreadfully; inconceivably; uncommonly; extraordinarily; singularly; particularly; viciously; wickedly; ridiculously.

TOUGHNESS

verbs

acquire—; augment—; boast of—; deplore —; glory in—; mitigate—; preserve—; — affords; —breasts; —defies; —endures; — insures; —protects; —rebuffs; —repels; — resists; —supports; —sustains; —withstands; —yields.

(See strength, tenacity.)

TOUR

adjectives

prolonged; extended; creative; systematic; walking; triumphal; protracted; lecture; expensive; reconnoitering; memorable.

verbs

arrange—; cater for—; conclude—; conduct —; direct—; embark on—; extend—; guide —; map out—; organize—; plan—; project —; protract—; recruit for—; sponsor—; standardize—; —attracts; —broadens; — covers; —embraces; —includes; —provides; —skirts; —touches.

(See journey, trip, voyage, excursion.)

TOUR (v)

adverbs

enthusiastically; extendedly; listlessly; hurriedly; drearily; wearily; indefatigably; systematically.

(See travel, visit.)

TOURISTS

adjectives

guileless; romantic; rewarded; listless; hurried; dreary; clever; experienced; wary; weary.

verbs

accommodate—; accompany—; attract—; cater to—; convey—; divert—; entertain—; exploit—; guide—; lecture to—; lure—; shelter—; —consult; —embark; —flock; — marvel at; —mill; —motor; —purchase; — sail; —throng; —view.

(See traveler, passenger.)

TOURNAMENT

adjectives

mock; chivalric; independent; open; national; amateur.

verbs

advance in—; cheer—; color—; compete in —; conduct—; dominate—; emerge from—; engage in—; enter—; judge—; referee—; triumph in—; vie in—; witness—; —excites; —glorifies; —impassions; —publicizes; —rages.

(See contest, game.)

TOWEL

adjectives

ragged; hospitable; cordial; snowy; rough; rubbing; huge; crumpled; soggy.

verbs

begrime—; besmirch—; boil—; defile—; disinfect—; embroider—; employ—; filch—s; launder—; rack—; scour—; spatter—; sully —; swab with—; wrap in—; whip—; — absorbs; —envelops.

(See napkin, handkerchief, cloth.)

TOWER

adjectives

preserved; flying; immortal; quaint; opal; crumbling; meridian; warlike; weird; machicolated; tranquil; nodding; martial-like; impertinent; rent; gigantic; stalagmite; feudal; baroque; temporary; square; leaning; low; tottering; church; strong; topless; irregular; showy; flanking; worn; lurching; gleaming; stone; stunted; upper; shattered; slender; ivy-mantled; precipitous; stately; fortified; moldering; massive; overthrown; marshalled; external; shining; turret; skyey; rustic; ecclesiastical; barbaric; cylindrical; movable; tall; time-twin (pl).

verbs
ascend—; assail—; besiege—; clamber up —; convey to—; dismantle—; encompass—; erect—; flank—with; fortify—; hover over —; imprison in—; incarcerate in—; level—; mount—; raze—; repose in—; scale—; storm—; summon to—; surmount—; surround—; topple from—; view from—; —caps; —commemorates; —dominates; —flanks; —frowns; —honors; —looms; —rears; —soars; —symbolizes.
(See pinnacle, peak, mountain, spire.)

TOWER (v)
adverbs
magnificently; sublimely; martially; gigantically; precipitously; massively; awesomely; prodigiously; impressively.
(See rise.)

TOWN
adjectives
mute; quaint; storm-swept; tumultuous; queer; many-languaged; self-respecting; terror-stricken; combustible; seven-faced; drowsy; murmuring; imaginary; scenic; shapeless; provincial; breeding; sedate; everyday; defenseless; cheerful; industrial; bustling; rebel; high-perched; gray; placid; peaceful; beleaguered; adjacent; toiling; natal; inland; pretentious; ragged; haunted; dark; majestic; resurrecting; glittering; adverse; walled; retreating; famished; prosperous; hapless; picturesque; spiry; forest-girdled; benighted; populous; burning; lesser; native; festival; crude; ambitious; abominable; harbor; massive; cosmopolitan; fortified; insignificant; extraordinary; outlying; veritable; fated; colorful; straggling; wondrous; filthy; fascinating; respective; inexorable; thriving; corrupt; dirty; permanent; petty; snow-thatched; grass-grown; bleak.

verbs
abide in—; allude to—; assault—; besiege —; border—; distinguish—; evacuate—; extend—; father—; flank—; forsake—; found

—; govern—; guide—; inhabit—; invade—; loot—; make the rounds of—; parade—; people—; potter about—; reclaim—; reconnoiter—; scurry around—; set foot in—; skirt—; sojourn in—; throng—; settle in—; trek across—; trudge around—; wall—; —booms; —flourishes; —s snuggle; —springs up; —thrives; —throngs.
(See city, neighborhood, community, village.)

TOXIC
adverbs
indubitably; truly; dangerously; fatally; alarmingly; curiously; evidently; apparently; immediately; instantly; deeply; palpably; cruelly; usually; irremediably; disturbingly; terribly; incontrovertibly.

TOXIN
verbs
dilute—; dispel—; inject—; liberate—; neutralize—; purge of—; secrete—; succumb to —; —circulates; —envenoms; —s fatigue; —invades; —overruns; —poisons; —pollutes; —s propagate; —ravishes; —taints; —vitiates; —weakens.
(See poison, germ.)

TOY
adjectives
tremulous; rude; lamenting; saccharine; adorable; vulgar; battered; inconstant; amorous; expensive; attractive; fond; imaginative; fairy; trifling; garish.

verbs
absorb in—s; caress—; cherish—; deprive of—s; disburse—s; engross in—s; fondle—; model—; regard—; reward with—s; tempt with—s; tinker with—s; weary of—s; wheedle—s away; —amuses; —beguiles; —cheers; —caricatures; —delights; —distracts; —diverts; —excites; —fascinates; —solaces.
(See rattle, doll.)

TOY (v)
adverbs
valiantly; irresistibly; idly; amorously; vulgarly; triflingly; adoringly; quaintly.
(See play, sport.)

TRACE (v)
adverbs
skillfully; accurately; roughly; laboriously;

painfully; unconsciously; ethnologically; unmistakably; perceptibly.

(See investigate, search.)

TRACEABLE
adverbs

easily; dimly; vaguely; distinctly; reasonably; calculably; obviously; discernibly;
hardly; actually; conclusively; manifestly;
clearly; allegedly; presumably; vestigially;
objectively; psychologically; physically.

TRACES
adjectives

ancient; historical; corroding; abundant;
generous; partial; servile; tangled; archaeological; anthropological; ethnological;
slight; marked; effacing; sensible; unmistakable; perceptible; undiscovered; phantom;
visible; surviving.

verbs

bear ; confirm ; convey—, detect—; dim
—; disclose—; discover—; eclipse—; efface
—; eradicate—; erase—; examine—; obscure—; obliterate—; outline—; recognize
—; record—; reveal—; scent—; scrutinize
—; stumble upon—; uncover—; unearth—;
veil—; verify—; —disappear; —vanish.

(See evidence, impression, mark, sign,
multiply.)

TRACK
adjectives

steep; indelible; foamy; beaten; zigzag;
ant; well-chosen; sorrowless; myriad (pl);
luminous; resplendent; untraveled; vengeful; receding; shining; adjacent; unending;
thirsty; glistening; cloud-swept; solar; suitable; grooved.

verbs

blot out—; careen down—; clear—; deduce
from—; efface—; eradicate—; erase—; espy
—; expunge—; follow in—; jump—; obliterate—; steal across—; stumble upon—;
trace—; uncover—; —s afford; —s bear evidence; —s betoken; —s blaze; —s denote;
—enables; —ensnares; —s indicate; —s record; —s reveal.

(See course, groove, trail, trace.)

TRACKLESS
adverbs

bewilderingly; terrifyingly; utterly; hopelessly; completely; incredibly; appallingly;
dismally; overwhelmingly; dishearteningly;
absolutely.

TRACT
adjectives

inflammable; latent; controversial; much-
desired; distributing; uncultivated; wicked;
untrodden; considerable; inviting; stifling;
dry; missionary; irritable; theologic;
marshy; vast; diffusing; humane; alimentary; generous; tender; digestive; adjoining; singular; broad; large; partisan.

verbs

claim—; confine—; cultivate—; enlarge—;
entitle to—; expand—; explore—; fence in
—; grant—; harrow—; limit—; plow—;
reclaim—; sow—; stake out—; till—; work
—; —bears; —flourishes; —fructifies; —
ranges; —thrives.

(See farm, area, district, field, land.)

TRACTABLE
adverbs

easily; pleasantly; agreeably; conveniently;
handily; deceptively; amazingly; unexpectedly; accommodatingly; docilely; surprisingly; dully; quietly; humbly; willingly;
happily; fortunately; suddenly; grudgingly;
momentarily; amenably; apparently; delightfully; silently; wearily; placidly; tearfully.

TRADE
adjectives

considerable; clandestine; immense; peaceable; savory; melancholy; depressed; dreadful; monstrous; profitable; flourishing; military; lucrative; constant; discordant; penitent; languishing; abominable; essential;
harsh; vilest; illicit; wholesale; hereditary;
doubtful; permanent; beastly; external; sedentary; diverted; stagnated; unlawful; intermediary; earthly; reciprocal; thriving;
frivolous; magnificent.

verbs

abandon—; alienate—; augment—; blockade—; bolster—; cement—; conciliate—;
cut into—; decrease—; discontinue—; disrupt—; dominate—; encourage—; endanger
—; engage in—; establish—; expand—; facilitate—; foster—; hamper—; impede—;
increase—; inspire—; make roads upon—;
monopolize—; nurture—; originate—; ply
—; promote—; pursue—; regiment—; relinquish—; restrain—; revive—; spur—;
stimulate—; strangle—; strengthen—; stymie—; swamp with—; swell—; tackle—;

teach—; threaten—; traffic in—; trample down—; —collapses; —dwindles; —freezes; —jumps up; —lures; —slumps.

(See employment, market, exchange, commerce, industry, calling, business.)

TRADEMARK

verbs

acquaint with—; appropriate—; glorify—; patent—; popularize—; recognize—; stamp —; —attests to; —betokens; —distinguishes; —emblazons; —guarantees; —heralds; — indicates; —insures; —labels; —represents; —symbolizes; —vouches.

(See label, copyright, patent.)

TRADESMEN

verbs

bargain with—; barter with—; dicker with —; cater to—; —deal in; —dispense; —dispose of; —engage in; —haggle; —hawk; — market; —peddle; —ply; —purvey; —retail; —trade; —traffic in; —transact; — vend; —vie.

(See hawker, merchant, salesman.)

TRADITION

adjectives

sacred; mysterious; precise; ancient; soberest; superstitious; venerable; cumulative; social; historic; culinary; inherited; patriotic; simple; saner; time-honored; sentimental; exquisite; ghostly; current; moldy; gentlemanly; ritualistic; intellectual; unscientific; sporting; hospitable; family; high; rare; sweet; dim; hoary; liberal; heroic; aesthetic; untrustworthy; living; remote; medieval; decorous; poetic; remarkable; pleasant; tribal; conventional; popular; established; cherished; imperial; renowned; fine; immutable.

verbs

absorb—; acquire—; adhere to—; annihilate —; authenticate—; "ballyhoo"—; bare—; batter—; better—; bound by—; break down —; cast aside—; carry on—; cherish—; conform to—; continue—; create—; cut loose from—; defend—; derive from—; destroy —; disclose—; discrepit—; disregard—; dissolve—; emancipate—; emasculate—; embody in—; endure—; enrich—; establish —; exist in—; express—; force—; fortify—; found—; glory in—; guard—; honor—; ignore—; illustrate—; imbue—; impair—; imperial—; infuse—; ingrain—; inherit—; "junk"—; limit—s; maintain—; mock—;

nourish—; nurture—; observe—; perpetuate —; preserve—; profit by—; rear in—; relate—; relinquish—; repudiate—; revive—; respect—; root in—; saturate with—; shake off—; shatter—; smash—; stand for—; steep in—; stick to—; strangle—; sweep away—; take over—; tinge with—; trace—; undermine—; unfold—; violate—; weld—; —accentuates; —ascribes; —binds; —blinds; — brands; —carries on; —colors; —describes; —determines; —dictates; —enriches; —fetters; —governs; —hands down; —immortalizes; —narrates; —preserves; —persists; —prescribes; —recounts; —regulates; —reports; —rules; —stands; —threatens; —s topple.

(See belief, attitude, culture, habit, custom, usage.)

TRADITIONAL

adverbs

devoutly; deeply; racially; innately; reverently; profoundly; curiously; manifestly; pleasantly; seriously; ineradicably; conventionally; delightfully; apparently; popularly; locally; indestructibly; inflexibly; vaguely; clearly.

TRADUCE (v)

adverbs

viciously; scandalously; libelously; hatefully; savagely; vindictively; revengefully.

(See slander, assail.)

TRAFFIC

adjectives

congested; rushing; metropolitan; aerial; dense; heavy; incessant; petty; abominable; ceaseless; roaring; terminate; din-producing; wearisome.

verbs

avert—; check—; choke—; congest—; control—; converge—; direct—; engage in—; escape—; evade—; facilitate—; guide—; hamper—; impede—; jam—; obstruct—; paralyze—; quell—; regulate—; retard—; shun—; speed—; support—; tangle—; — blares; —clogs; —confuses; —converges; —endangers; —flows; —jangles; —jeopardizes; —roars; —surges; —sweeps by; — thunders.

(See intercourse, exchange, commerce.)

TRAGEDY

adjectives

poetic; vast; shocking; unimaginable; de-

rived; inexcusable; bourgeois; radical; unequalled; dark; bombastic; dream; philosophic; classical; bloody; supreme; fantastic; stark; nocturnal; ancient; national;
countless (pl); tribal; dismal; terrible; impressive; domestic; timeless; climacteric;
successful; terrestrial; world; unavoidable.

verbs
avert—; banish—; bear—; belittle—; bewail—; decry—; deplore—; develop into
—; disclose—; facilitate—; heighten—; intensify—; lament—; mourn—; play—;
plot—; plunge into—; precipitate—; sense
—; shudder at—; skirt the edge of—; stay
—; submerge—; suffer—; surmount—;
verge on—; —afflicts; —appalls; —bereaves; —curdles; —curses; —deals a blow;
—depresses; —descends; —distorts; —excites; —foredooms; —harrows; —haunts;
—mows down; —oppresses; —overtakes; —
purges; —racks; —rends; —sears; —
shakes; —shocks; —sours; —spells; —unfolds; —weighs upon; —wrings.
(See melodrama, atrocity, outrage, calamity, drama, catastrophe.)

TRAGIC
adverbs
overwhelmingly; calamitously; bitterly;
cruelly; incredibly; unexpectedly; dismally;
appallingly; shockingly; devastatingly; unmitigatedly; hopelessly; unrelievedly; utterly; splendidly; superbly; highly; profoundly; consummately; incalculably; immeasurably.

TRAIL
adjectives
hurrying; downward; sidling; lonesome;
traveled; resplendent; recent; dusty; endless; milky; unique; pungent; majestic;
arduous; hour-old; winding; sinuous; well-
worn; twisting; elusive; spiritual; ancestral.

verbs
blaze—; break—; clarify—; clutter—; construct—; deviate from—; diverge from—;
efface—; erase—; explore—; forsake—; illuminate—; jog along—; lay out—; map—;
mark—; obliterate—; obscure—; obstruct
—; plunge along—; pursue—; scan—;
shadow—; skirt—; stir up—; strike into—;
veil—; —bewilders; —recedes; —threads
its course; —twists; —veers; —winds.
(See track, road, lane.)

TRAIL (v)
adverbs
demurely; faithfully; humbly; tediously;
arduously; sinuously; twistingly; elusively;
incessantly.
(See follow, trace.)

TRAIN
adjectives
reaper; starry; unparalleled; funeral; illustrious; imperial; crawling; belated; night;
retreating; prodigious; express; inferior;
gigantic; suburban; shining; grisly; hurtling; fast-flying; virgin; complicated;
pointed; harmless; crack; long-laid; additional; pensive; vagrant; incoming; unfeeling; unpainted; gloom-stricken; wooden;
immediate; melancholy; haughty; celestial;
pompous; sweeping; streamlined.

verbs
assign to—; board—; collide with—; consign to—; convey—; couple—; derail—;
flag—; fuel—; hop aboard (colloq.)—; insert in—; launch—; section—; schedule—s;
scurry for—; shunt—; signal—; switch—s;
transport by—; —bears; —chugs (colloq.);
—conveys; —departs; —facilitates; —
glides; —plunges; —puffs; —pulls into; —
rattles; —rocks; —rolls; —shunts; —
shrieks; —steams; —sways; —sweeps away;
—thunders; —wheels away; —whistles; —
whizzes; —winds its way.
(See automobile, locomotive, trolley-car.)

TRAIN (v)
adverbs
exquisitely; sedulously; scientifically; specially; competently; intellectually; judiciously; technically; adequately; intensively;
monastically; academically; arduously;
systematically; subtly; theoretically.
(See discipline, teach.)

TRAINED
adverbs
successfully; highly; moderately; skilfully;
adequately; recently; well-; badly; inadequately; consummately; carefully; scarcely;
cleverly; marvelously; brilliantly; cruelly;
mercilessly; patiently; persistently; consistently; effectively; sufficiently; specifically;
constantly.

TRAINING
adjectives
continuous; intellectual; judicious; vicious;

elementary; technical; valuable; preparatory; rigid; persistent; watchful; ethical; industrial; disciplinary; adequate; rural; intensive; lifelong; monastic; requisite; vocational; classical; scholarly; precedent; supplementary; arduous; superficial; loving; pious; admirable; secretarial; practical; systematic; rigorous; amatory; leisurely; stabilized; subtle; architectural; theoretical.

verbs

entrust to—; fit for—; imbibe—; persevere with—; prescribe—; relax—; subject to—; undergo—; —accustoms; —breeds; —disciplines; —equips; —forearms; —habituates; —hardens; —impregnates; —inculcates; —infuses; —instils; —inures; —matures; —mellows; —polishes; —prepares; —qualifies; —sharpens; —smooths; —veneers.
(See preparation, education, discipline, exercise.)

TRAIT
adjectives

redeeming; petty; striking; intellectual; boyish; ridiculous; bestial; dominant; overbearing; predominating; advanced; distinguished; outstanding; conspicuous; royal; feminine; multiplex (pl); noble; salient; common; singular; outward; scrupulous; generous; sectional; characteristic; humane; national; essential; desirable; lasting; hereditary; notable; varied (pl); obnoxious; introvert; quantitative; childish; valuable; visible; physiological; ostensible.

verbs

assentuate—; acquire—; breed—s; commend —; cultivate—; discover—s; emphasize—; exhibit—; foster—; illuminate—s; intensify —; manifest—; play a part in—; portray —; relate—; stamp—; value—; —allures; —appears; —attracts; —betokens; —characterizes; —distinguishes; —s etch deeper; —fascinates; —indicates; —individualizes; —s stamp out.
(See characteristic, habit, quality.)

TRAITOR
verbs

accuse—; banish—; denounce—; dub—; exile—; expose—; hiss—; hoot—; ostracize —; outlaw—; proclaim—; pursue—; redeem—; scorn—; sneer at—; spurn—; subdue—; —betrays; —debases; —demeans;

—falsifies; —loses caste; —repudiates; —secedes.
(See betrayer, conspirators, plotters, criminal.)

TRAITOROUS
adverbs

despicably; abominably; stealthily; furtively; unbelievably; unexpectedly; suddenly; curiously; detestably; murderously; meretriciously; insidiously; atrociously; odiously; hatefully; venomously; vilely; grossly; ungratefully; confessedly; traceably; evidently; incalculably; cleverly; invidiously; utterly; presumably; allegedly.

TRAJECTION
adjectives

free; limited; swift; uncanny.

TRAMP
adjectives

collier; measured; penniless; steady; dusty; derisible; plashy; echoing; impecunious; dingy; clattering; sullen; beggarly.

TRAMP (v)
adverbs

ruthlessly; vigorously; sullenly; monotonously; dingily; indefatigably; remorselessly.
(See march, trudge.)

TRAMPLE (v)
adverbs

ruthlessly; heedlessly; speedily; cruelly; viciously; contemptuously; heartlessly.
(See tramp, stamp.)

TRANCE
adjectives

spectral; rigid; magic; mystic; compassionate; blissful; icy; stupid; restless; ecstatic; cataleptic; dizzy; spiritual; stilly; lethargic; doleful; speechless; detested.

TRANQUIL
adverbs

sweetly; amazingly; restfully; contentedly; incredibly; suddenly; surprisingly; refreshingly; delightfully; naturally; habitually; always; seldom; enviably; admirably; happily; contentedly; blissfully; extremely; uncommonly.

TRANQUILITY
adjectives

wishless; misty; dignified; well-regulated;

mist-wrapped; divine; magnanimous; honey-sweet; sumptuous; profound; flustered; long-desired; monotonous; perfect; serene; dry; physical; innocent; boresome; empty; dull.

verbs
break—; disturb—; lull into—; recapture —; recollect in—; shatter—; tolerate—; — alleviates; —assuages; —becalms; —chastens; —composes; —deadens; —depresses; —dulcifies; —pacifies; —settles over; — smooths; —smothers; —stagnates; —subdues.
(See calm, apathy, quiet.)

TRANSACT (v)
adverbs
profitably; industriously; efficiently; ethically; momentously; monetarily; fraudulently; spiritually; nefariously; discreditably; philosophically; ephemerally.
(See conduct, negotiate.)

TRANSACTION
adjectives
momentous; mercantile; monetary; notorious; important; fraudulent; clouded; private; flowery; spiritual; extortionate; nefarious; discreditable; philosophical; ritualistic.

verbs
abandon—; bind to—; carry on—; conceal —; conduct—; consummate—; divulge—; draft—; engage in—; endanger—; execute —; facilitate—; insure—; negotiate—; nullify—; outline—; participate in—; plan—; press—; profit by—; promote—; reject—; release from—; rue—; underwrite—; withdraw from—; —obligates; —stipulates.
(See procedure, deal, bargain, intercourse.)

TRANSCEND (v)
adverbs
boundlessly; gloriously; infinitely; obviously; markedly; amazingly; spectacularly.
(See surpass, excel.)

TRANSCENDENTAL
adverbs
presumably; indubitably; impractically; satisfactorily; altogether; curiously; obviously; incalculably; loosely; strictly.

TRANSCRIBE (v)
adverbs
faithfully; diligently; laboriously; patiently; indefatigably; industriously; ambitiously; accurately.
(See copy, write.)

TRANSCRIBED
adverbs
carefully; accurately; usually; responsibly; legally; necessarily; scrupulously; immediately; intelligibly; perfectly; punctiliously; painstakingly; mechanically; scientifically; carelessly; imperfectly.

TRANSFER (v)
adverbs
temporarily; satisfactorily; forcibly; rapidly; professionally; individually.
(See shift, change.)

TRANSFIGURED
adverbs
radiantly; gloriously; celestially; divinely; brilliantly; glowingly; piously; devoutly; unimaginably; incredibly; beauteously; luminously; curiously; brightly; spiritually; idealistically; marvelously; miraculously; supernaturally; utterly; suddenly.

TRANSFORM (v)
adverbs
miraculously; magically; ingeniously; topographically; uniquely; supernaturally; amazingly; extensively; spectacularly.
(See change.)

TRANSFORMATION
adjectives
magical; striking; bucolic; epic; weird; successive (pl); solemn; tremendous; ingenious; unique; supernatural; topographical.

verbs
achieve—; analyze—; condone—; discern —; facilitate—; undergo—; —accentuates; —alters; —deviates; —innovates; —introduces; —modifies; —modulates; —revamps; —swerves from.
(See fermentation, change, alteration, transition.)

TRANSFORMED
adverbs
marvelously; miraculously; suddenly; gloriously; divinely; utterly; luminously;

strangely; peculiarly; oddly; unaccountably; inexplicably; radiantly; grotesquely; palpably; manifestly; unbelievably; undeniably; incredibly.

TRANSGRESS (v)

adverbs

outrageously; repetitiously; wantonly; venially; notoriously; incestuously; egregiously.
  (See sin, violate.)

TRANSIENT

adverbs

painfully; lamentably; fortunately; fleetingly; merely; pathetically; sadly; tragically; ephemerally; bitterly; meteorically; brilliantly.

TRANSITION

adjectives

ethnological; soft; terrible; quick; hard; sudden; awful; perilous; stormy; violent; delicious; fine; necessary; painful; bitter; swift.

verbs

accomplish—; balk at—; bemoan—; complete—; decry—; denounce—; endure—; necessitate—; smooth—; trace—; undergo —; undertake—; —converts; —involves; —matures; —mellows; —revolutionizes; —ripens.
  (See change, modification, transformation.)

TRANSITIONAL

adverbs

expediently; merely; conveniently; practically; feasibly; quickly; profitably; suitably; advantageously; briefly; serviceably; presumably; probably; adaptably; providentially; helpfully; admirably; aptly.

TRANSITORY

adverbs

briefly; ephemerally; impermanently; perishably; sadly; lamentably; unhappily; mortally; evanescently.

TRANSLATE (v)

adverbs

literally; fluently; extensively; faithfully; flawlessly; exquisitely; freely; exactly; copiously; skillfully; mentally.
  (See interpret, construe.)

TRANSLUCENT

adverbs

mysteriously; strangely; incredibly; scientifically; unbelievably; uncommonly; admirably; commendably; sufficiently; surprisingly; pleasantly; attractively; conveniently; cleverly; agreeably; reasonably; surprisingly; unexpectedly; usefully; practically; satisfactorily.

TRANSPARENT

adverbs

entirely; inconveniently; uncomfortably; delightfully; attractively; unexpectedly; amazingly; conveniently; admirably; commendably; satisfactorily; oddly; comically; absurdly; shamefully; unnecessarily; remarkably; uncommonly; highly; exceptionally; perfectly.

TRANSPLANT (v)

adverbs

unceremoniously; agriculturally; patiently; skillfully; ingeniously; successfully; prudently.
  (See shift, move, change.)

TRANSPLANTED

adverbs

carelessly; unskilfully; unsuccessfully; seldom; easily; safely; skilfully; carefully; successfully; often; usually; unwisely; clumsily; inexpertly; improperly; properly; experimentally.

TRANSPORT (v)

adverbs

swiftly; recklessly; laboriously; dramatically; periodically; annually; regularly; seasonally; continuously; deftly; uniquely.
  (See move, ship.)

TRANSPORTATION

adjectives

water; ruined; laborious; swift; air; faultless; reckless.

verbs

accelerate—; afford—; assign—; assure of —; avail of—; block—; cripple—; direct —; disrupt—; expedite—; facilitate—; grant—; hamper—; impede—; manage—; rate—; retard—; slacken—; —cements; —communicates with; —enables; —links; —unites.
  (See shipment, conveyance.)

adjectives
unyielding; baited; palpable; dramatic; dreaded; ridiculous.

verbs
bait—; circumvent—; elude—; evade—; inveigle into—; lure into—; mask—; spring —; warn of—; —beguiles; —claws; —decoys; —deludes; —dupes; —ensnares; — grasps; —gulls; —hoaxes; —masks; — menaces.
(See pitfall, net, snare, ambush.)

TRAPPED

adverbs
hideously; helplessly; hopelessly; desperately; abominably; maliciously; grimly; unspeakably; utterly; inescapably; fatally; precariously; perilously; permanently; terribly; horribly; frightfuly; appallingly; shockingly; frantically; cleverly; cunningly; finally; ultimately; legally; subtly; adroitly; treacherously.

TRASHY

adverbs
utterly; abominably; terribly; cheaply; worthlessly; horribly; unspeakably; undisguisedly; irretrievably; irredeemably; grossly; crassly; irreclaimably; unacceptably; hopelessly; disagreeably; disgustingly; manifestly; undeniably; arrantly.

TRAVEL

adjectives
earthly; dreary; unknown; riotous; air; irrelevant; tiresome; horseback; prudent; extensive; transient; frequent; equatorial; continental; nomadic; fatiguing.

verbs
afford—; extend—s; facilitate—; forsake —; long for—; modernize—; recall—s; recite—s; recount—s; relinquish—s; widen—s; —acquaints one with; —broadens; — cultivates; —cultures; —edifies; —educates; —endangers; —enlightens; —polishes; — veneers.
(See tour, cruise, adventure, education.)

TRAVEL (*v*)

adverbs
extensively; circuitously; luxuriously; methodically; laboriously; perceptibly; sedately; expensively; advantageously; recklessly.
(See tour, journey.)

adverbs
widely; highly; broadly; brilliantly; unusually; admirably; wonderfully; far; much; frequently; infrequently; seldom; little; marvelously; extensively.

TRAVELER

adjectives
ephemeral; zealous; wayworn; elegant; weary; cheerful; defenseless; mysterious; unprotected; unwary; desperate; expectant; unprofessional; dawdling; dispirited; shrewd; contemporary; present; thoughtful; economical; colonial; veteran; hoary; storm-tossed; late-arriving; rustic; gaping; sleepless; well-assorted (pl); discriminating; unwilling; fastidious; casual; reputable; disconcerting; arctic; wise; sophisticated; refined; seasoned; epicurean.

verbs
accommodate—; cater to—s; comfort—; enchant—s; enthrall—s; exhaust—; fatigue —; guide—; lecture to—; organize—; plunder—s; route—s; waylay—s; welcome —; —journeys; —lingers; —s mill about; —plans; —prolongs; —protracts; —repairs to; —resides at; —roams; —roves; — views; —wearies of; —wends; —witnesses.
(See marcher, tourists.)

TREACHEROUS

adverbs
abominably; dangerously; alarmingly; ominously; portentously; slyly; smoothly; insidiously; hypocritically; flatteringly; furtively; cleverly; disloyally; despicably; boldly; hideously; subtly; maliciously; grossly; deliberately; adroitly; vilely; astutely; inscrutably; undoubtedly; infinitely; deeply; darkly.

TREACHERY

adjectives
cruel; meditated; base; subtle; signal; bitter.

verbs
condemn—; court-martial for—; disclose—; denounce—; expose—; fear—; frame—; plot—; resort to—; screen—; shroud—; stoop to—; suspect—; uncover—; untangle —; veil—; —baits; —beguiles; —betrays; —debases; —deceives; —decoys; —deludes;

—dishonors; —disillusions; —engulfs; —lures; —lurks; —pollutes; —snares; —stains; —sullies.

(See insincerity, ingratitude, infidelity, betrayal.)

TREAD

adjectives

hasty; quick; elastic; viewless; swinging; limping; winter; victorious; slow; measured; firm; fairy; martial; sacred; monotonous; stately; imperious; stealthy; nervous; delicate; resilient; pointed; scandaled; thundering; persistent; springy; self-assured; conquering; undazzled; muffled; backward; unflinching; cat-like; clanging.

TREAD (v)

adverbs

sorrowfully; lightly; boldly; profanely; noiselessly; soundlessly; cautiously; rhythmically; painfully; consciously; gaily; unheedingly; tenderly.

(See walk, proceed.)

TREASON

adjectives

strong; household; detested; pretended; unpardonable; domestic; manifest; ugly; certain; passive; defiant; proud.

verbs

accuse of—; acquit of—; arraign for—; charge with—; cite—; combat—; commit—; condemn for—; confess—; convict of—; deny—; exile for—; indict for—; penalize for—; revenge—; unveil—; uncover—; —betrays; —breaches; —corrupts; —debases; —degrades; —demeans; —dishonors; —stigmatizes.

(See betrayal, crime, treachery.)

TREASONABLE

adverbs

indubitably; utterly; wickedly; admittedly; allegedly; subtly; frankly; assuredly; immeasurably; deliberately; indefeasibly; indefensibly; defiantly; arrantly; unutterably; daringly; boldly; peculiarly; palpably; highly; dangerously; darkly.

TREASURE

adjectives

valued; countless (pl); inexhaustible; sacred; royal; patrimonial; garnered; priceless; celestial; subsequent; vast; portable; precious; costly; heavenly; accursed; life-time; perishing; dear-bought; self-consuming; chaste; autumn; nobler; numbered (pl); eternal; drainless; sterling; superfluous; golden; accumulated; notable; earthly; ruffling; orphaned; long-lost; sleeping; cherished; unsuspected; dewy; longed-for; purloined; buried.

verbs

accumulate—; adorn—; amass—; appraise —; bury—; cache—; cherish—; disclose—; dispose of—; dive for—; exaggerate—; explore for—; extort—; garner—; harbor—; hoard—; impound—; lavish—upon; pilfer —; reclaim—; reveal—; salvage—; secrete —; seek—; stow away—; swallow—; uncover—; unearth—; —astounds; —dazzles; —enriches.

(See wealth, money.)

TREASURED

adverbs

highly; greatly; carefully; piously; affectionately; fondly; lovingly; tenderly; always; truly; especially; deeply; openly; strangely; oddly; unaccountably; sincerely; nationally; decorously; ceremoniously; insistently.

TREASURY

adjectives

exhaustless; infinite; provincial; veritable; depleted; enfeebled; anemic; national; vest-pocket.

verbs

augment—; bankrupt—; deplete—; divert from—; drain—; embarrass—; embezzle from—; raid—; reinforce—; replenish—; replete—; repose in—; stabilize—; tap—; —accrues; —accumulates; —amasses; —appropriates; —authorizes; —declines; —inflates; —issues; —languishes; —lifts; —mounts; —recalls; —swells; —totters.

(See coffer, bank, reserve.)

TREAT

adjectives

popular; delightful; optical; splendid.

verbs

afford—; extend—; indulge in—; luxuriate in—; offer—; procure—; provide—; relish —; rejoice in—; revel in—; welcome—; yield—; —absorbs; —amuses; —delights; —enlivens; —fascinates; —gladdens; —regales; —solaces; —tickles.

(See dainty, entertainment, feast, repast.)

TREAT (v)

adverbs

rationally; barbarously; circumspectly; humanely; systematically; tenderly; adequately; harshly; elaborately; brutally; deferentially; compassionately; reverently; mercilessly; roughly; histrionically; elaborately; objectively; sympathetically; essentially; hospitably; conscientiously; jocosely; capriciously; contemptuously; surgically; medically; courteously.

(See behave, act.)

TREATISE

adjectives

extensive; erudite; laborious; scholarly; distinguished; lucid; philosophical; pedagogical; far-sighted; important; abstruse; pedantic; musical; celebrated; voluminous; masterly; hard-headed; distinct; elaborate; valuable.

verbs

absorb in—; acclaim—; commend—; comprehend—; condense—; consolidate—; denounce—; illustrate—; peruse—; present—; produce—; publish—; revise—; summarize —; write—; —airs; —boxes; —deals with; —digresses; —discourses; —dissertates; — does justice to; —elaborates on; —exhausts; —extends; —sets forth; —recites; —unfolds; —wearies.

(See dissertation, article, book.)

TREATMENT

adjectives

miraculous; infamous; prompt; acoustical; diabetic; proposed; triple-acting; drastic; abominable; scientific; superficial; dietary; persuasive; bold; thematic; heroic; jocose; intelligent; technical; contemptuous; harsh; pessimistic; realistic; cruel; proper; humane; psychoanalytic; symphonic; affectionate; unjust; preferential; successful; osteopathic; unfilial; inhuman; barbarous; severe; well-considered; judicious; summary; sufficient; axial; statistical; ceiling; appropriate; harmonic; architectural; voluntary; hospitable; routine; cathartic; attentive; torturing; ruthless; reliable; competent; delicate; insolent; surgical; standard; sportive; interior; scandalous; harmonious; remote; beautifying; preferential; perfidious; ungenerous; respectful; conscientious; preventive; courteous; hypnotic; capricious; impolite;

antiquated; immediate; mosaic; realistic; playful; disrespectful; frank; artistic; original.

verbs

acquaint with—; administer—; adopt—; advise—; advocate—; alter—; apply—; attribute—; carry on—; check—; commence—; conduct—; confer—on; constitute—; consult for—; co-ordinate—; counsel—; discard—; discontinue—; direct—; employ—; endure —; excel in—; expose—; extend—; facilitate —; indicate—; improve—; institute—; modernize—; modify—; neglect—; outline—; place—; prescribe—; prolong—; protract—; pursue—; question—; recommend—; regulate—; render—; repeat—; require—; respond to—; resume—; skill in—; standardize—; subject to—; tolerate—; undergo—; urge—; yield to—; —accomplishes; —allays; —ameliorates; —antidotes; —assuages; —falls; —incenses; —metes out; — misleads; —mitigates; —perseveres; —palliates; —relieves; —remedies; —represents; —varies.

(See cure, method, act, performance, usage.)

TREATY

adjectives

far-sighted; separate; successive (pl); defensive; definitive; supplementary; ambiguous; secret; advantageous; pleasing; monstrous; equitable; obnoxious; outrageous; violated.

verbs

abrogate—; adopt—; comply with—; condition—; condemn—; confirm—; conform to —; contract—; create—; discharge—; disregard—; dissolve—; draft—; frame—; ignore—; infringe upon—; negotiate—; nullify—; observe—; press—; ratify—; repudiate—; rip—; sanction—; scrap—; sign—; trample—; transgress—; violate—; void—; —affords; —aims; —allies; —binds; —cements; —circumvents; —concludes; —embroils; —guarantees; —insures; —leagues; —pledges; —stipulates; —strengthens; — ties; —unites.

(See lease, covenant, agreement.)

TREE

adjectives

rich; ominous; whispering; brittle; cringing; wide-spreading; ragged; overgrown; tropical; trimmed; stately; fledged; interposing; accursed; tangled; wind-swept; well-branched; kindred; assailed; dusty; feathery; tottering; cleft; stunted; hardy; well-cared-for; thread-like; gloomy; embowering; breathless; slender; white-starred; paradise; low; scrubby; dewy-tasseled; resinous; over-hanging; murdered; stretching; mute; shady; patriarchal; tufted; shining-leaved; enticing; notched; waking; unhewn; draped; rejoicing; water-loving; bare; genealogic; unwaving; darling; immortal; blasted; flowering; somber; unguarded; unlawful; lofty; senseless; yielding; parched; pleached; deserted; spectral; exotic; celestial; drooping; attractive; rifled; hoary; sheltering; forbidden; fantastic; stubby; dooryard; deciduous; prostrate; perfect; tempting; pomegranate; coveted; dripping; new-leafed; gnarled; denuded; sturdy; hollow; wayside; virtuous; twisted; interdicted; sprawling; friendly; lusty; gracious; listening; half-budded; slumberous; massive; blossoming; venerable; indigenous; faded; voluptuous; overarching; magnificent; broad-armed; sapient; naked; centennial; hereditary; tortured; undecaying; celestial; waving; fruit-laden; aromatic; bending; long-lived; eldest; full-branched; girdled; gaunt; unbrageous; glittering; gift-bearing; over-leaning; contorted; quivering; luxuriate; antique; trysting; intolerable; shivering; ornamental; pauper; spicy; shadowy; glistening; blessed; unaccustomed; short; majestic; lowering; misshapen; grafted.

verbs
blight—; clamber up—; conserve —s; cultivate —s; dot with —s; fell—; fertilize —s; graft—; hack at—; hew—; label—; level—; nest in—; prune—; raze—; suspend from—; tap—; thin out—; transplant—; uproot—; —affords; —bears; —bends; —blooms; —blossoms; —bows under; —buds; —s cluster; —creaks; —dips; —falls; —flanks; —flourishes; —flowers; —forms; —forsakes; —fructifies; —garlands; —hints; —lashes; —lifts; —loads; —obscures; —occupies; —overspreads; —plunges; —relinquishes; —rises; —rustles; —scourges; —screens; —shades; —sheds; —shelters; —shimmers; —shivers; —shrouds; —soars; —spreads; —s straggle; —sways; —swishes; —thrives; —throws; —thunders; —topples; —totters; —towers; —whips; —whispers; —writhes; —yields.

(See leaf, branch, oak, elm, etc.)

TREMBLE (v)
adverbs
fearsomely; fearfully; violently; inwardly; abominably; visibly; spasmodically; nervously; morbidly; abnormally; agitatedly.
(See shiver, move.)

TREMBLING
adverbs
helplessly; dreadfully; uncertainly; uncontrollably; awkwardly; perceptibly; pitiably; ineptly; paralytically; weakly; feebly.

TREMOR
adjectives
touching; nervous; sharp; immeasurable; emotional; eager; slight; awful; luminous; fierce; earthquake.

verbs
allay —s; excite to —s; inspire—; record—; respond to—; stir with —s; —agitates; —alarms; —convulses; —creeps; —dislodges; —indicates; —jars; —jolts; —jostles; —jounces; —pulsates; —ripples thru; —shocks; —swells; —terrifies; —trickles; —warms; —quivers.
(See agitation, earthquake, shiver, shudder.)

TRENCH
adjectives
slimy; abhorred; trial; current; political; bold; bloody; artificial; flanking; adjacent; defensive; muddy.

TRENCHANT
adverbs
effectively; unusually; famously; remarkably; wonderfully; cleverly; aptly; uncommonly; powerfully; tellingly; savagely; viciously; unmercifully; sarcastically; drolly; brutally; bluntly; sharply.

TRENCHES
verbs
beseige—; blast—; bolster—; bombard—; burrow—; confine to—; excavate—; fortify —; flow from—; lodge in—; maintain—; map—; patrol—; plan—; raid—; repulse from—; scoop out—; straggle to—; stream to—; swarm from—; tunnel—; —afford; —deface; —furrow; --shelter; —shield.
(See ditch, drain, fortification.)

TREND

adjectives

significant; important; radical; philosophic; noticeable; recent; future; mystical; practical; probable; impressive; unhealthy; gambling; significant.

verbs

affect—; approve—; detect—; discern—; divert—; emphasize—; encourage—; foster—; govern—; hail—; herald—; illustrate—; indicate—; influence—; obscure—; promote —; recognize—; regulate—; retard—; reverse—; scotch—; sense—; sway—; warp —; —departs from; —deviates; —inclines toward; —shifts; —signifies; —swerves.

(See mode, fashion, style, tendency.)

TRESPASS (v)

adverbs

nefariously; boldly; illegally; brazenly; lawlessly; flagrantly.

(See transgress, intrude.)

TRESPASSER

verbs

admonish—; banish—; bar—; caution—; dispel—; eject—; expel—; inveigh against —; oust—; penalize—; prosecute—; —encroaches on; —infringes on; —intrudes; —invades; —obtrudes; —offends; —oversteps; —violates.

(See aggressor, intruder.)

TRESS

adjectives

raven; ebon; flaming; beauteous; unbound.

TRIAL

adjectives

repeated; fiery; ancient; memorable; ludicrous; harassing; speedy; hurried; religious; gracious; mutual; intensified; terrible; weary; still; bitter; countless (pl); impartial; unnecessary; supreme; petty; amicable; mock; grueling.

verbs

appeal—; arraign for—; arrange for—; bear—; behold—; bias—; challenge to—; conclude—; conduct—; determine—; docket —; judge—; prejudice—; preside over—; protract—; scorn—; summon for—; warrant—; —absolves; —acquits; —airs; —

clears; —commences; —discloses; —exculpates; —exonerates; —notorizes; —publicizes; —ventilates; —whitewashes.

(See effort, attempt, endeavor, tribunal, examination.)

TRIBAL

adverbs

ceremonially; strictly; narrowly; originally; characteristically; singularly; peculiarly; exclusively; oddly; actually; apparently; obviously; manifestly; conspicuously.

TRIBE

adjectives

beaten; finny; kindred; rebellious; malignant; predatory; cervine; hostile; crushed; pastoral; illustrious; sylvan; scattered (pl); swarming (pl); cognate; barbarian; unfriendly; neighboring; scaly; contemptible; perishing; indolent; wandering; protected; aboriginal; feline; feathered; unlearned; thriftless; primitive; unnumbered (pl); invisible; swarthy; powerful; fierce; native; carnivorous.

verbs

affiliate with—; ban from—; band in—; cement—; evolve from—; exterminate—; father—; found—; head—; inflame—; mobilize—; muster—; perpetuate—; scatter—; unite—; weld—s; —expands; —multiplies; —ostracizes; —prospers; —survives; —thrives; —vanishes; —wanes.

(See clan, family.)

TRIBULATIONS

verbs

afflict with—; allay—; assuage—; augment —; ease—; encounter—; endure—; experience—; lament—; mitigate—; mourn—; occasion—; palliate—; suffer—; —consume; —distress; —harass; —harrow; —rack; —subdue; —weigh upon.

(See affliction, trouble.)

TRIBUNAL

adjectives

legal; international; judicious; secret; tardy; independent; impartial; peaceful; revolutionary; bustling; arbitral; mock; revolting; supreme; military; just; righteous.

verbs

adjourn—; appeal to—; bias—; convoke—; hamper—; prejudice—; resort to—; —adjudicates; —arbitrates; —awards; —brings in a verdict; —confirms; —decides; —determines; —dooms; —evaluates; —judges; —passes an opinion; —proclaims; —reviews; —sentences; —sets aside; —settles.

(See court, jury.)

TRIBUTE

adjectives
tardy; august; odorous; extravagant; sincere; unconscious; significant; fitting; requisite; eloquent; noble; unwilling; touching; impressive; remarkable; manifold (pl); expressive; everlasting; elaborate; grim; extraordinary; floral; stipulated; joyous; sisterly; generous; anonymous; spontaneous; obtrusive; virgin; poetic; personal; russet; complacent; curious; honorable; intuitive; magnificent; whole-hearted.

verbs
accept—; acknowledge—; award—; bestow —; decline—; decry—; demand—; disdain —; extort—; grant—; indulge—; lavish—; levy—; merit—; offer—; owe—; pour—; scorn—; yield—; —acclaims; —compliments; —flatters; —glorifies; —indemnifies; —lauds; —recompenses; —remunerates; —rewards.

(See graft, tax, bribe.)

TRICK

adjectives
psychological; innocent; hideous; juggling; juvenile; perfidious; foremost; scurvy; forgotten; unwarrantable; commercial; ultramontane; pretty; strategic; singular; sardonic; harsh; perverse; ingenious; admiration; momentary; raw; artistic; speeding; ceremonious; unconsidered; shy; mad; fantastical; innate; nasty; extra; cowardly; abominable; ugly; amusing; political; unbecoming; barbarous; stage; trashy; unworthy; fascinating; mathematical; valorous; favorite; villainous; practical.

verbs
concoct—; contrive—; devise—; discern—; disclose—; hatch—; master—; perform—; perpetrate—; practise—; reveal—; spring —; study—; —ambushes; —baffles; —bewilders; —bores; —confounds; —deceives; —defrauds; —deludes; —mystifies; —amuses.

(See puzzle, manipulation, fraud, deceit, magic, mystery.)

TRICK (v)

adverbs
ridiculously; mystifyingly; deftly; unscrupulously; psychologically; perfidiously; singularly; sardonically; ingeniously; amusingly; mathematically; villainously; practically; politically.

(See deceive, fool.)

TRICKERY

adjectives
obvious; successful; low; transparent; base; foreign; shameless.

verbs
disclose—; employ—; fear—; foil—; hint at—; resort to—; scorn—; sense—; surmise —; suspect—; uncover—; unearth—; —baffles; —baits; —bilks; —deceives; —decoys; —defrauds; —deludes; —ensnares; —gulls; —infuriates; —swindles; —victimizes.

(See cunning, hyprocisy, deception, deceit, fraud.)

TRICKSY

adverbs
cleverly; playfully; whimsically; childishly; wildly; uncontrollably; nonsensically; clownishly; roguishly; mischievously; waggishly; comically; laughably; farcically; ludicrously.

TRICKY

adverbs
subtly; cunningly; insidiously; surreptitiously; artfully; slyly; craftily; deceitfully; delightfully; dangerously; cleverly; adroitly; alarmingly; mischievously; playfully; harmlessly; provokingly; disagreeably; plaguedly; foolishly; maneuveringly; underhandedly.

TRIFLE

adjectives
consequential; unspeakable; useless; glittering; laborious; insignificant; nameless; countless (pl); honest; musical; merest; satirical; inconsiderable; inconsequential; important; enchanted; silliest; logical; careless; petty; pedantic.

TRIFLE (v)

adverbs
leeringly; ridiculously; ludicrously; un-

speakably; insignificantly; illogically; inconsequentially; pettishly; pedantically.

(See toy, play.)

TRIFLES

verbs

belittle—; chatter about—; discount—; disregard—; emphasize—; fret over—; ignore —; minimize—; omit—; scrutinize—; shelve —; skim over—; skip—; stress—; underestimate—; —irk; —irritate; —pique; —rile (colloq.); —plague.

(See insignificance, trivialities.)

TRIFLING

adverbs

absurdly; foolishly; facetiously; flippantly; languidly; senselessly; nonsensically; giddily; airily; ridiculously; farcically; clownishly; intolerably; vainly; uncommonly.

TRIGGER

verbs

caress—; cock—; draw—; ease—; finger—; flick—; fondle—; gear—; jam—; jerk—; jiggle—; oil—; lock—; lubricate—; release—; snap—; wedge—; —clicks; —controls; —discharges; —endangers; —menaces; —recedes; —threatens.

(See knob, lever.)

TRIM

adverbs

naturally; pleasantly; agreeably; usually; habitually; unwontedly; stiffly; jauntily; daintily; smoothly; delicately; neatly; unusually; particularly; noticeably; conspicuously; indescribably; painfully; marvelously; delightfully.

TRIM (v)

adverbs

cautiously; judiciously; exquisitely; gaudily; garrishly; tastefully; symbolically; neatly; fastidiously.

(See arrange, adjust.)

TRIP

adjectives

fairy; perilous; constant; phantasmagoric; periodic; bridal; shopping; foreign; innumerable (pl); mysterious; ghastly; infernal; stimulating; overland; sight-seeing; curious; delightful; strenuous; previous.

verbs

conclude—; contemplate—; depart on—; embark on—; entrain on—; extend—; journey on—; plan—; prolong—; protract—; sally forth on—; —acquaints one with; —embraces; —enchants; —enlightens; —fatigues; —intrigues; —proceeds; —progresses; —relaxes; —spans; —traverses.

(See flight, journey, excursion, quest, tour.)

TRIP (v)

adverbs

rhythmically; gaily; dexterously; lightly; noiselessly; blithely; strenuously; fantastically.

(See dance, move.)

TRIPPING

adverbs

lightly; gaily; merrily; jauntily; blithely; nimbly; tunefully; pleasantly; childishly; girlishly; joyously; happily; beautifully; quickly; buoyantly; ecstatically; melodiously.

TRITE

adverbs

monotonously; tiresomely; vapidly; disagreeably; invariably; trivially; facetiously; fatuously; intolerably; sententiously; uninterestingly; wearily; tediously; flatly; senselessly; vacuously; prosily.

TRIUMPH

adjectives

unworthy; pitiless; crowning; consummate; delusive; melancholy; fiendish; hideous; intoxicating; rare; dawning; gay; paltry; splendid; rhetorical; superficial; turbulent; forensic; ill-concealed; temporary; bitter; assured; absent; unsought; demiurgic; vindictive; final; social; unapproachable; intimate; inimitable; chuckling; strategic; recent; brilliant; nameless; unspeakable; perpetual; wearisome; secure; permanent; malicious; veritable; ultimate; dramatic; awful; debonair; personal; scornful; delirious; ultimate; unmistakable; conscious; passionate; unbroken; remorseless; diplomatic; ceremonial; marvelous; magnificent; peaceful; glorious; melodious; laboring; slight; shameful; contemptible; veritable; bacchanal; temporary.

verbs

acclaim—; attend with—; belittle—; blaze into—; boast—; commemorate—; concede —; congratulate one on—; dilute—; emerge in—; exult in—; foreshadow—; frustrate—; gain—; hail—; mar—; presage—; record —; rejoice in—; return in—; signalize—; sing of—; spur to—; thwart—; witness—; —elates; —emancipates; —flushes; —vanquishes.

(See conquest, ovation.)

TRIUMPH (v)

adverbs

markedly; notably; supremely; gloriously; pitilessly; consummately; intoxicatingly; rhetorically; forensically; politically; strategically; ultimately; diplomatically; veritably.

(See win, succeed.)

TRIUMPHANT

adverbs

proudly; elatedly; justly; naturally; exultingly; wholly; gloriously; splendidly; magnificently; happily; radiantly; delightedly; joyously; jubilantly; merrily; laughingly; heartily; mockingly; jeeringly; scoffingly.

TRIVIAL

adverbs

absurdly; foolishly; altogether; wholly; senselessly; nonsensically; ridiculously; intolerably; uncommonly; insignificantly; inconsequentially; particularly; vexatiously; bothersomely; cheaply; childishly.

TRIVIALITIES

verbs

amplify—; babble—; charge with—; clarify —; cloak in—; content with—; discard—; dismiss—; escape—; evade—; flounder on —; magnify—; prate about—; scoff at—; scorn—; shrink from—; —arise; —bore; —crop up; —harass.

(See trifles.)

TROLLEY-CAR

verbs

collide with—; derail—; jam—; man—; outstrip—; pilot—; schedule—s; stream from—; —accelerates; —clatters; —converges on; —crawls along; —disburdens; —jangles by; —jars; —jolts; —lurches; —rumbles; —screeches; —tears.

(See train.)

TROOPING

adverbs

merrily; noisily; gaily; purposefully; sullenly; angrily; boisterously; truculently; pugnaciously; ominously; threateningly; menacingly; mischievously; derisively; happily; shyly; defiantly; resolutely; encouragingly; triumphantly; laughingly.

TROOPS

adjectives

dispirited; sleepy; ragged; shoeless; ill-equipped; mutinous; light-armed; furious; hated; vulgar; servile; available; predatory; parti-colored; raw; flexible; scattered; exhausted; obtained; infectious; radiant; mercenary; wearied; supplementary; fresh; disembarking; organized; disciplined.

verbs

accoutre—; amass—; arm—; assemble—; ban—; conceal—; concentrate—; dispatch —; disperse—; draft—; enhearten—; enlist —; enforce with—; equip—; garrison—; halt—; harry—; mass—; mobilize—; muster —; quarter—; transport—; yield to—; —advance; —beleaguer; —besiege; —bolster; —charge; —coerce; —disband; —drive; —invade; —mutiny; —occupy; —patrol; —pour into; —reconnoitre; —retaliate; —rout; —storm; —throng.

(See brigade, army, besieger, invader, militia.)

TROPHY

adjectives

glorious; grisly; evil-smelling; ghastly; bloody; shining; melancholy; ostentatious.

verbs

acquire—; annex—; attain—; award—; carry off—; cherish—; clinch—; collect—s; compete for—; contend for—; covet—; display—; engrave—; exhibit—; gain—; gather—s; merit—; procure—; recover—; regain—; relinquish—; retain—; retrieve—; treasure—; value—; —commemorates; —elates; —honors; —signifies; —symbolizes.

(See laurels, monument, memorial, medal.)

adverbs

narrowly; essentially; fundamentally; peculiarly; definitely; scientifically; geographically; preferably; characteristically; distinctly; presumably; unpleasantly; agreeably; intolerably.

TROT (*v*)

adverbs

doggedly; obediently; faithfully; listlessly; monotonously; diligently; jubilantly.

(See gallop, run.)

TROUBLE

adjectives

wretched; associate; endless; unfortunate; personal; perpetual; disciplinary; monetary; annoying; powerful; inflammatory; joyful; intolerable; vague; obscure; major; nocturnal; infinite; lifelong; hesitant; poor; delicious; cruel; constant; garrulous; complex; distressing; pathetic; contagious, invincible, luxurious; measurable.

verbs

afflict with—; anticipate—; arrest—; attend with—; avert—; avoid—; bear—; bewail —; breed—; compensate for—; cure—; diagnose—; endure—; experience—; explore —; foment—; instigate—; lament—; localize—; minimize—; mourn—; pour out—s; probe—; remedy—; repay—; stir up—; undergo—; ward off—; —besets; —blasts; — blights; —crops up; —deranges; —harasses; —haunts; —irks; —irritates; —looms; — lurks; —manifests itself; —originates in; —piques; —preys upon; —rankles; —recurs; —ruffles; —rumples; —seethes; — simmers; —smites; —strikes; —waxes; — weighs upon; —wracks.

(See affliction, hardship, difficulty, adversity, obstacles, tribulation.)

TROUBLE (*v*)

adverbs

impudently; perpetually; vaguely; obscurely; nocturnally; infinitely; distressingly; profoundly.

(See disturb, irritate.)

TROUBLED

adverbs

nervously: frenziedly; unnaturally; laughably; ridiculously; pathetically; lamentably; curiously; abnormally; naturally; touchingly; supremely; unduly; deeply; indescrib-

ably; perceptibly; suspiciously; significantly; pitiably; miserably; terribly; tenderly.

TROUBLESOME

adverbs

persistently; increasingly; sometimes; slightly; devilishly; deucedly; perplexingly; mysteriously; conspicuously; palpably; visibly; manifestly; unusually; naturally; particularly; diplomatically; vexatiously; distressingly; painfully; consistently; remarkably; deliberately; despicably; grossly; boldly; defiantly; intentionally; always.

TROUSERS

adjectives

voluminous; baggy; fluttering; plaid; mustard-colored; creaseless; sport.

verbs

alter—; array in—; bare—; divest of—; doff—; don—; drape—; fray—; garb in —; hitch up—; peg—; pleat—; refurbish—; rend—; retrieve—; strip of—; sunder—; tatter—; vest in—; —clothe; —cover; — protect.

(See clothing.)

TRUANT

adverbs

vexatiously; intolerably; deliberately; heedlessly; carelessly; triflingly; negligently; indifferently; worthlessly; incorrigibly; derisively; brazenly; inexplicably; unaccountably; wantonly; unprofitably; unendurably; bafflingly.

TRUCE

adjectives

reasonable; temporary; faithless; broken; perpetual.

verbs

adopt—; agree to—; arrive at—; beseech —; clamor for—; consent to—; declare—; effect—; hail—; hamper—; impede—; invite—; petition for—; plead for—; press for—; proclaim—; project—; refuse—; reject—; rejoice in—; sign—; welcome—; — arrests; —checks; —curtails; —liberates; — lulls; —pacifies; —reprieves; —rescues; — suspends.

(See halt, peace, respite.)

TRUCK

adjectives
rumbling; passing; clattering.

verbs
assign to—; consign to—; fuel—; guide—; license—; lubricate—; manoeuvre—; overhaul—; recondition—; shift—; —bears; —booms; —chugs (colloq.); —clatters; —conveys; —groans; —jars; —jolts; —pounds along; —roars; —rolls; —rumbles; —swerves; —transports.

(See cart, automobile, bus, vehicle.)

TRUCULENT

adverbs
unbearably; offensively; boldly; daringly; intolerably; boorishly; unmistakably; openly; brutally; challengingly; brazenly; grossly; ominously; inordinately; alarmingly; disagreeably; unreasonably; always; sullenly; singularly; curiously; uncommonly; viciously; vengefully; villainously.

TRUDGE (v)

adverbs
wearily; monotonously; heavily; tirelessly; lazily; solemnly; indefatigably; bravely; buoyantly; patiently; laboriously.

(See walk, proceed.)

TRUE

adverbs
apparently; positively; unquestionably; avowedly; confessedly; admittedly; professedly; palpably; essentially; obviously; evidently; manifestly; officially; reliably; solemnly; disagreeably; accidentally; fundamentally; profoundly; disgracefully; unpleasantly; horribly; intrinsically; gloriously; unanswerably; painfully; heavily; ironically; shockingly; sublimely; universally.

TRUMPET

adjectives
shattering; martial; hideous; silver; snarling; hostile; fierce; discordant; splitting; unblown.

verbs
flourish—s; hearken to—; sound—; toot—; —alarms; —awakens; —blares; —blasts; —blazes; —calls forth; —deafens; —hails; —

heralds; —mobilizes; —musters; —proclaims; —rends; —resounds; —reverberates; —screams; —shatters; —trills.

(See bugle, loudspeaker.)

TRUNK

adjectives
formless; nameless; forest; ungainly; uniform; overhanging; prostrate; silicified; comfortable; quivering; columnar; palpitating; charred; ghostlike; scraggy; knotty; fleshy; decaying; crackling; gnarled; split; ponderous; hoary; fibrous; barky; crashing; moss-grown.

TRUST

adjectives
gentle; boyish; investment; serene; guileless; humble; honorable; unfaltering; blind; changeless; fearless; devoted; stupendous; buoyant; false; unswerving; impious; important; instinctive; delusive; serious; theologic; complete; earnest; human; commercial; implicit; dreadful; sacred; unattainable; ample.

verbs
abuse—; afford—; bestow—; betray—; breach—; breed—; charge with—; cherish—; confide—in; encourage—; entertain—of; fix—; foster—; found—on; inspire—; misplace—; nurse—; nurture—; relinquish—; retain—; root—; rue—; shake—; shatter—; shock out of—; strengthen—; violate—; —crumbles; —falters; —flatters; —reposes in; —wanes; —wavers.

(See hope, assurance, faith, confidence, idealism.)

TRUST (v)

adverbs
implicitly; assuredly; fondly; indolently; tacitly; shrewdly; reverentially; credulously; explicitly; guilelessly; delusively; amply; unfalteringly.

(See rely, depend.)

TRUSTFUL

adverbs
innocently; gullibly; overly; wistfully; childishly; foolishly; unwisely; inordinately; singularly; particularly; incredibly; unbelievably; curiously; remarkably; peculiarly; uncommonly; idiotically; touchingly; unaffectedly; pitifully; confidently; terribly; ingenuously; naively.

TRUSTWORTHY

adverbs

admirably; commendably; unusually; exceptionally; absolutely; utterly; uncommonly; singularly; obviously; apparently; undoubtedly; dependably; truly; supposedly; presumably.

TRUTH

adjectives

disagreeable; dual; unlovely; conceivable; accidental; fundamental; invincible; profound; pursuing; abstract; gloomy; clear; hackneyed; striking; delicious; innocent; disgraceful; unpleasant; intense; solemn; transparent; undoubted; distracted; distorted; outspoken; unconscious; searching; fragmentary; absolute; disguised; horrible; bare; consequent; hateful; perfect; sweet; unfaltering; gracious; useful; innate; unequivocal; practical; rigorous; intrinsic; perennial; granite; austere; unadulterated; glorious; crystal; rudimentary; unsophisticated; dramatic; perverting; palpable; historic; objective; unanswerable; demonstrated; religious; astounding; established; magnificent; slighted; moral; painful; remorseless; hideous; burning; lasting; indelible; priceless; unfathomable; domestic; injured; flattering; apparent; immutable; heavenly; benignant; heavy; consolatory; revered; crushing; valid; constant; barbed; naked; substantial; shocking; unornamented; golden; unvarnished; obvious; stretched; serviceable; scattered; droll; general; solid; unique; humbling; unrecognized; melancholy; informing; appalling; sober; relative; heartrending; comparative; dawning; naturalistic; formidable; imageless; irrefragable; physical; maiden; effectual; royal; sacred; essential; precious; unwelcome; bitter; underlying; stately; steadfast; necessary; good; symmetrical; sublime; indestructible; philosophical; extraordinary; approximate; divine; pure; indwelling; guileless; brilliant; strenuous; sensuous; inviolable; poignant; universal.

verbs

accept—; acknowledge—; adumbrate—; affirm—; annihilate—; apprehend—; approach—; arrive at—; ascertain—; assert —; attest to—; blurt out—; cherish—; cloud —; color—; commit to—; communicate—; compromise—; conceal—; consecrate to—; contradict—; convey—; counterfeit—; credit —; demand—; demonstrate—; deny—; determine—; discern—; disclose—; dispute—; distort—; divulge—; dodge—; dress up—; embroider—; emphasize—; establish—; evade—; expose—; face—; falsify—; flinch before—; forecast—; foster—; foreshadow —; garble—; gloss over—; grace with—; grasp—; herald—; imitate—; impart—; inspire—; intermingle with—; misrepresent —; modify—; obscure—; obstruct—; open —; persuade one of—; pervert—; preach —; probe for—; proclaim—; propagate—; question—; re-echo—; reflect on—; refuge in—; reject—; repudiate—; reveal—; seduce from—; seek—; shadow—; shrink at —; simulate—; sift—; skirt—; smother—; stretch—; stumble over—; support—; sustain—; upholster—; utter—; value—; varnish—; verify—; voice—; vouch for—; warp—; welcome—; —blazes; —burns; — dawns upon; —emerges from; —flatters; — looms; —pierces; prevails; —shines; — triumphs; —vanquishes.

(See gospel, integrity, verity, veracity, sincerity, realism, reality.)

TRUTHFUL

adverbs

dependably; reliably; absolutely; always; altogether; painfully; brutally; fanatically; childishly; completely; dangerously; evidently; reputedly; allegedly; avowedly; inconveniently; usually; notably; fairly; scarcely; faithfully; precisely; literally; glumly; innocently; technically; volubly; statistically; sensationally; frankly; vividly; graphically; impressively; simply; artfully; bluntly; glibly; reluctantly; gravely.

TRY (v)

adverbs

exceedingly; sorely; insistently; surreptitiously; deliberately; variously; perfunctorily; conscientiously; piteously; energetically; manfully; sorely; convulsively; obstinately; blunderingly; elaborately; abominably; faithfully; vainly; nervously; falteringly; guiltily; strenuously.

(See attempt, endeavor.)

TRYST

adjectives

clandestine; childish; bloody; moonlight; amorous; fatal.

1217

verbs

agree upon—; anticipate—; appoint—; cloak—; curtail—; fulfill—; hamper—; impede—; keep—; observe—; plan—; pledge to—; shroud—; suggest—; veil—; —allures; —beguiles; —transgresses; —violates.

(See appointment, place, meeting.)

TUB

adjectives

odious; fermenting; insignificant; daily; refreshing.

verbs

convey in—; dip into—; drain—; emerge from—; ground—; immerse in—; invert—; plug—; plunge into—; propel—; scour—; scuttle—; soak in—; submerge in—; swamp —; swish in—; tap—.

(See kettle, vat, barrel.)

TUBE

adjectives

pneumatic; elegant; ivory; tortuous; magic; hollow; perforated; delicate; slender; golden; railway; twisted.

verbs

coke—; clog—; convolute—; couple—s; dam —; deflate—; dilate—; distend—; drain—; inflate—; insert—; line—; narrow—; obstruct—; penetrate—; perforate—; pierce—; plug—; puncture—; riddle—; seal—; tap—; throttle—; value—; —bursts; —conveys; —expands; —transmits.

(See nozzle, pipe, conduit, tunnel.)

TUBERCULOSIS

verbs

allay—; check—; combat—; contract—; convey—; diagnose as—; predispose to—; succumb to—; tend toward—; wipe out—; —blasts; —blights; —decimates; —devours; —eats; —impairs; —infects; —moulders; —ravages; —saps; —scathes; —taints; —taxes; —undermines; —wastes.

(See consumption, disease.)

TUCK (v)

adverbs

cautiously; mentally; meticulously; picturesquely; snugly; cozily.

(See fold, press.)

TUFT

adjectives

feathery; obligatory; flowery; amber; inky.

TUG (v)

adverbs

hysterically; drowsily; repeatedly; nervously; agitatedly; repetitiously; exasperatingly.

(See pull, draw.)

TUGBOAT

adjectives

vulgar; little; innumerable (pl); straining; squat; sturdy; pug-nosed.

verbs

employ—; guide—; pilot—; ram—; recruit —; —batters; —bestirs; —chugs (colloq.); —draws; —exerts; —s flock about; —hauls; —plies; —puffs; —s retire; —scurries; —snorts; —steams; —strains; —struggles; —s surround; —tows.

(See boat, motor-boat, launch.)

TULIP

adjectives

red; gold; grandiose; lovely; beauteous.

TUMBLE (v)

adverbs

clownishly; comically; clumsily; drunkenly; wretchedly; abruptly; precipitately.

(See fall, heave.)

TUMOR

verbs

confine—; diagnose—; dissolve—; excise—; extirpate—; incise—; reduce—; relieve—; restrict—; treat—; —atrophies; —blocks; —cankers; —compresses; —distends; —enlarges; —expands; —hardens; —invades; —infiltrates; —obstructs; —protrudes; —subsides; —ulcerates.

(See cancer, abscess, growth.)

TUMULT

adjectives

murmuring; fast-gathering; tempestuous; growing; intestinal; formidable; sickening; ensuing; portentous; wild; rolling; surging; internal; inward; passionate; ceaseless; fiery; civic.

verbs

calm—; quell—; restrain—; —bewilders; —breaks loose; —ceases; —dies; —disconcerts; —disorders; —embroils; —ensues; —muddles; —rages; —reigns; —roars; —ruffles; —subsides; —wanes; —waxes.

(See clamor, confusion, disturbance, commotion, noise, turmoil.)

TUMULTUOUS

adverbs

terribly; unmanageably; boisterously; truculently; inordinately; ungovernably; riotously; uproariously; dangerously; dreadfully; fearfully; alarmingly; ominously; significantly; threateningly; lawlessly; defiantly; boldly; grossly; portentously; desperately; derisively; angrily; triumphantly; madly; crazily; deafeningly; hilariously; drunkenly.

TUNE

adjectives

lingering; stirring; plaintive; warbling; fat; fulsome; light; touching; melodious; sentimental; half-remembered; loyal; saucy; enthralling; trivial; tremulous; mysterious; merry; pathetic; greedy; fandango; superfluous; tempting; ecstatic; facile; catchy; pert; lilting; rollicking; romantic.

verbs

accompany—; arrange—; bleat—; carol—; chant—; coax—from; compose—; fake (colloq.)—; fiddle—; harmonize—; hum—; march to—; modulate—; orchestrate—; recall—; render—; score—; strike up—; synchronize—; transpose—; trill—; twitter—; vocalize—; warble—; yodel—; —amuses; —delights; —lilts.

(See ditty, air, incantation, song, music.)

TUNE (v)

adverbs

automatically; professionally; skillfully; accurately; melodiously; delicately; deftly.

(See adjust.)

TUNEFUL

adverbs

pleasantly; merrily; happily; melodiously; musically; rhythmically; childishly; naturally; delightfully; simply; sweetly; smoothly; harmoniously; joyously; joyfully; boyishly.

TUNIC

adjectives

sleeveless; spotless; ungirlish; velvet; adamantine; rich; gauzy; revealing.

TUNNEL

adjectives

deep-level; brilliant; unsupported; signaled; clattering; hot; long; snowy; stuffy.

verbs

blast—; blockade—; bore—; burrow—; drive—through; engineer—; gouge out—; guide through—; patrol—; project—; seal —; —couples; —facilitates; —gapes; —links; —pierces; —penetrates; —unites; —yawns.

(See tube, conduit, pipe.)

TURBID

adverbs

peculiarly; singularly; slightly; unfortunately; significantly; unpleasantly; momentarily; temporarily; definitely; particularly; noticeably; obviously.

TURBULENCE

adjectives

licentious; bloody; infantile; bewildering; riotous; frightening; raucous; nasty.

TURBULENT

adverbs

shamefully; riotously; raucously; ruthlessly; desperately; tumultuously; mutinously; uproariously; unmanageably; ungovernably; violently; recklessly; frightfully; implacably; unappeasably; vengefully; brazenly; murderously; unreasoningly; wildly; furiously; madly; dangerously; ominously; significantly.

TURF

adjectives

trodden; moss-inwoven; firm; flowery; frost-bit; close-cropped; wet; spongy; emerald; springing; fine; mountain; ragged; crisp; compact; unscarred.

verbs

corrugate—; delve in—; furrow—; fertilize—; gambol on—; level—; mar—; plow under—; replace—; smooth—; tamp—; trim—; —beautifies; —blankets; —extends; —greens; —mats; —pads; —mow.

(See meadow, grass, tract, ground.)

verbs
carve—; dine on—; domesticate—; gun for
—; market—s; pluck—; roast—; savor—;
spice—; —dances about; —displays feathers; —s flock; —flutters; —gobbles; —gyrates; —hovers; —preens; —rakes; —
ranges; —stirs up; —strokes; —struts; —
symbolizes; —wheels.
(See bird, fowl, rooster.)

TURMOIL

adjectives
fierce; urban; destructive; strenuous; stern;
bloody; hideous; historic; whizzing; noisy.

verbs
embroil in—; ferment—; foment—; provoke
—; quiet—; throw into—; tranquillize—;
—accompanies; —agitates; —confuses; —
convulses; —deranges; —dishevels; —disquiets; —distracts; —diverts; —follows; —
persists; —perturbs; —prevails; —ruffles;
—seethes; —tangles.
(See commotion, tumult, confusion.)

TURN

adjectives
romantic; radical; light; extravagant; ostentatious; countless (pl); sensational; administrative; thoughtful; comic; sudden;
good; fanciful; melodic; sentimental; epi-
grammatical; satirical; intimate; unquiet;
conversational; unexpected; cynical; artificial; marvelous.

TURN (v)

adverbs
snarlingly; tortuously; petulantly; sinuously; deviously; abruptly; reluctantly; gracefully; deliberately; solemnly; imploringly;
exultingly; doggedly; awkwardly; distractedly; insensibly; instinctively; wearily; amiably; insolently; involuntarily; perversely;
radiantly; wistfully; simultaneously; disdainfully; capriciously; resolutely; grudgingly; noiselessly; miraculously; indifferently; discreetly; energetically; listlessly;
treacherously.
(See spin, revolve.)

TURNING

adjectives
incessant; gentle; fateful; acute; accurate.

TURRET

adjectives
squat; glittering; highest; equal; sequestered; fading; fort.

verbs
armor—; beseige—; command—; festoon—;
fortify—; hover over—; imprison in—;
level—; mount to—; perch on—; plate—;
raze—; surmount—; topple from—; train
—s; view from—; —looms; —revolves; —
rotates.
(See tower, spire, cannon.)

TURTLE

verbs
capture—; crush—; market—s; relish—;
stew—; —s abound; —attains; —breeds;
—burrows; —calls; —creeps; —deposits
eggs; —exudes; —hibernates; —hisses; —
paddles; —perseveres; —protrudes; —snaps
at; —snatches; —submerges; —swims; —
swishes; —withdraws.
(See reptile.)

TUSKS

adjectives
enormous; ingrown; valuable; sharp;
spiral; protective.

TUTOR

adjectives
threadbare; lively; shrewd; deft; skilled;
wise; experienced.

TWANG

adjectives
nasal; familiar; peevish; provincial; annoying.

TWANG (v)

adverbs
exasperatingly; nasally; sharply; tunelessly; harshly; hideously; annoyingly; peevishly.
(See sound.)

TWEEDS

adjectives
imported; sturdy; roughish; rugged; inevitable; exquisite; handsome; hand-loomed.

TWIG

adjectives
tired; overhanging; unsightly; fragile;
hardwood; insignificant; bleak; upreared;

nervous; gleaming; thorny; threatening; ice-coated; crackling.

verbs
bend—; brace—; burden—; clip—; deform —; gather—s; glean—s; ingraft—; prune —s; restrain—; snip off—; support—; thin out—s; —bears; —projects; —protrudes; —shoots out; —spreads.
(See branch, stem.)

TWILIGHT
adjectives
brightening; silvery; sad; deepening; dark; gruesome; obscure; intermediate; shadowy; cool; brilliant; dubious; rainy; darkling; dim; amber; perpetual; magical; unhurried; blank; uncomfortable; slow-dropping; white; disastrous; sulphurous; mystic; thickening; fading; wintry; gathering; winsome; mournful; ancient; departing; hollow; summer; hot; breathless; hesitant; lingering; hushed; mellow; stilly; dense; chilling; luminous; balmy; sympathetic; beautiful, closing.

verbs
approach—; bathe in—; flicker in—; melt into—; reflect—; twinkle in—; —bedims; —creeps upon; —curtails; —curtains; —declines; —deepens; —descends; —diffuses; —dims; —drapes; —fades; —gathers 'round; —glimmers; —hazes; —obscures; —screens; —shades; —shadows; —veils; —wanes; —wraps; —yields to.
(See night, dusk, evening, light, shadow.)

TWILIGHT
adverbs
faintly; delicately; rosily; dully; dimly; windily; fearsomely; beautifully; seductively; romantically; unforgettably; roseately; coldly; darksomely.

TWIN
adjectives
tributary; fraternal; identical.

adverbs
identically; attractively; apparently; interestingly; affectionately; perplexingly; inseparably.

TWINE (*v*)
adverbs
caressingly; nervously; tortuously; affection-

ately; complicatedly; intricately; involvedly; abundantly.
(See cling, fasten.)

TWINGE
adjectives
warning; smart; hereditary; conscience; painful.

TWINKLE
adjectives
humorous; rapid; peculiar; vicious; merry; mischievous; lewd.

TWINKLE (*v*)
adverbs
jovially; frostily; softly; luminously; merrily; humorously; peculiarly; mischievously.
(See shimmer, shine.)

TWINKLING
adverbs
brightly; keenly; sharply; affectionately; fondly; mischievously; laughingly; distinctly; irregularly; unmistakably; wittily; brilliantly; intermittently; regularly; indulgently; actually; significantly.

TWIRL (*v*)
adverbs
nonchalantly; languidly; fiercely; gallantly; sophisticatedly; idly; picturesquely.
(See whirl, revolve.)

TWIST
adjectives
infernal; dexterous; restless; worst; spiral; heroic; antique; unusual; brutal.

TWIST (*v*)
adverbs
deftly; drearily; slyly; dexterously; insidiously; craftily; tortuously; superciliously; infernally; ruthlessly; restlessly; brutally; viciously.
(See contort, coil.)

TWIT (*v*)
adverbs
facetiously; vindictively; maliciously; remorselessly; hatefully; spitefully; humorously; comically; blithely; impudently.
(See chide, reproach.)

adjectives

involuntary; vicious; innocent; agonized; virulent.

TWITCH (v)

adverbs

convulsively; weakly; spasmodically; abnormally; morbidly; pathologically; agitatedly; agonizingly.
(See snatch, jerk.)

TWITCHING

adjectives

uneasy; nervous; spasmodic; convulsive.

TWITTER (v)

adverbs

melodiously; sweetly; blithesomely; merrily; innumerably; irritatingly; maddeningly.
(See chirp, sing.)

TWO-FACED

adverbs

despicably; undoubtedly; contemptibly; deceptively; smoothly; smugly; suavely; grossly; subtly; unexpectedly; shamefully; treacherously; disloyally; naturally; craftily; adroitly; artfully; cunningly; slyly.

TYPE

adjectives

innocent; contemplative; existing; rugged; barren; conspicuous; temperamental; severe; shiftless; civilized; austere; myriad (pl): constitutional; conventional; coadequate; psychologic; dominant; nonpareil; sturdy; various (pl); individual; girlish; attentive; established; militant; conceivable; pompous; delicious; feline; ritualist; unchangeable; spirited; aristocratic; unscrupulous; dignified; tender; vulgar; manufactured; dominant; prevalent; fatalistic; chest-heaving; unrealized; faddist; charming; aesthetic; engrossing; delectable; bachelor; evanescent; heroic; spontaneous; gamin; characteristic; unfamiliar; representative; transcendent; malignant; florid; picturesque; myopic; marrying; original; objectionable; intellectual; innumerable (pl); indigenous; ethnic; conceivable; ingenue;

lax; crackling; beautiful; primitive; preferred; didactic; elaborate; primeval; favorable; man-hunting; superficial; hideous; perverted; uncanny; consummate; sunny; manifold (pl); lofty.

TYPE (v)

verbs

breed—; cast—; characterize—; classify—; conceive—; conform to—; denote—; depict —; designate—; determine—; distinguish—; efface—; enact—; exploit—; fall into—; hew—; idealize—; mold—; portray—; register—; reproduce—; revert to—; specify —; warp—; —embodies; —embraces; —includes; —mystifies; —perplexes.
(See symbol, style, class, model, print.)

TYPE (v)

adverbs

individually; swiftly; accurately; originally; consummately; characteristically.
(See represent.)

TYPEWRITER

verbs

bang—; instruct on—; lubricate—; manipulate—; master—; necessitate—; overhaul —; peck at—; pound on—; service—s; silence—; —clicks; —clatters; —disconcerts; —distracts; —disturbs; —eases; —enables; —facilitates; —lightens; —plagues; —rings; —shifts.

TYPHOON

verbs

—abates; —batters; —devastates; —endangers; —howls; —rages; —ravages; —revolves; —roars; —shrieks; —subsides; —sweeps; —topples; —trammels; —uproots; —whirls.
(See hurricane, blizzard, storm.)

TYPICAL

adverbs

absolutely; entirely; truly; accurately; dependably; reliably; substantially; realistically; symbolically; curiously; incidentally; satisfactorily; approximately; exactly; unerringly; distinctly; indicatively; graphically.

TYRANNICAL

adverbs

quietly; adroitly; unendurably; imperiously;

confidently; socially; selfishly; hopelessly; sweetly; gracefully; wantonly; unscrupulously; insupportably; inexorably; cruelly; vindictively; remorselessly; ruthlessly; intolerably; unreasonably; dangerously; viciously; heartlessly; recklessly; outrageously.

TYRANNY

adjectives

municipal; barefaced; odious; clerical; decided; quiet; adroit; unendurable; imperious; worn-out; watchful; confident; social; selfish; hopeless; legal; grinding; sweet; graceful; wanton; petty; unscrupulous; exacting; insupportable.

verbs

exercise—; impose—upon; inflict with—; germinate—; overthrow—; resist—; revolt against—; savor of ; subject to—; —abuses; —crushes; —distresses; —enslaves; —fetters; —harasses; —oppresses; —restricts; —shackles; —tramples; —treads on; —yokes.

(See despotism, domination, persecution.)

TYRANT

adjectives

unpersuaded; professed; inexorable; implacable; early; despotic; cunning; cruel; sportive; petty; vindictive; remorseless; domestic; power-mad; avaricious; guiltiest; benevolent; invaluable; feminine; pious; sanguinary; ambitious; maniacal; haughty; cloud-piercing; usurping.

verbs

oppose—; play—; prove—; rebel against—; repel—; resist—; serve—; submit to—; —administers; —arrogates; —assumes; —beguiles; —butchers; —coerces; —crushes; —dictates; —domineers; —enslaves; —oppresses; —overrides; —persecutes; —subjugates; —tramples; —usurps; —wields; yokes.

(See dictator, oppressor; monarch; sovereign.)

U

UBIQUITOUS

adverbs

valuably; extraordinarily; comically; importantly; dominantly; aggressively; conspicuously; pompously; curiously; apparently; eagerly; officiously; ostentatiously; undeniably; proudly; quietly; assertively; enterprisingly; busily; actively; patronizingly.

UGLINESS

adjectives

racy; grotesque; ultimate; shapeless; unmitigated; bare; insipid; ferocious; grim; bestial.

verbs

abhor—; accentuate—; aggravate—; deplore—; dispel—; efface—; enhance—; heighten—; lament—; level—; mitigate—; portray—; revolt at—; —blemishes; —defaces; —deforms; —distorts; —embitters; —mars; —pervades; —robs; —sours; —weighs upon.

(See squalor, deformity.)

UGLY

adverbs

awkwardly; fantastically; grotesquely; amusingly; repulsively; pathetically; unbelievably; distressingly; angularly; terribly; horribly; oddly; touchingly; grievously; ludicrously; ridiculously; deplorably; lamentably; singularly; drolly; strangely; queerly; curiously; forbiddingly; frightfully; grossly; clumsily; hideously; grimly; shockingly.

ULCER

verbs

afflict with—s; cauterize—; detect—; expose —; poultice—; probe—; remedy—; salve—; suffer from—; —blemishes; —blights; —cankers; —cicatrizes; —deteriorates; —devours; —disfigures; —erodes; —festers; —infiltrates; —inflames; —rankles; —ravages; —scars; —scathes; —spreads; —taints.

(See abscess, canker, inflammation, blister, sore, cancer.)

ULCEROUS

adverbs

unfortunately; fatally; seriously; slightly; annoyingly; unpleasantly; disagreeably; presumably; obviously; gnawingly; dangerously; alarmingly; chronically; recently; acutely; painfully; disturbingly; distressingly; unaccountably; finally; extremely.

ULTIMATE

verbs

acclaim—; achieve—; afford—; anticipate —; apply—; attain—; dedicate to—; delay —; demand—; determine—; employ—; gain—; necessitate—; proclaim—; seek—; survive—; temporize—; undergo—; waive —; —endures.

(See extreme, goal, aim.)

adverbs

irrevocably; eventually; significantly; tragically; fatally; decisively; unchangeably; hopelessly.

ULTIMATUM

verbs

accede to—; acknowledge—; bow to—; comply with—; contemplate—; contest—; decree—; deliver—; draw up—; enforce—; execute—; file—; ignore—; issue—; reject —; resist—; retract—; slap down—; thunder—; —admonishes; —demands; —impends; —stipulates; —threatens; —warns.

(See warning, demand, challenge, proposition.)

UMBRAGEOUS

adverbs

refreshingly; pleasantly; gloomily; alarmingly; dismally; mysteriously; delightfully; coolly; gratefully; sensitively; curiously; uncommonly; exceptionally; highly; unexpectedly; surprisingly; suddenly; deeply.

UMBRELLA

adjectives

ubiquitous; formidable; protective; leaking.

verbs

arm with—; borrow—; brandish—; discard —; display—; employ—; flourish—; loll under—; mislay—; resort to—; —affords;

—eclipses; —hoods; —insures; —obscures; —obstructs; —screens; —shades; —shelters; —shrouds.

(See pavilion, cane, canopy.)

UMPIRE
verbs
appeal to—; bias—; boo—; bribe—; mob—; prejudice—; protest to—; "razz"—; —admonishes; —arbitrates; —awards; —bars; —confers with; —decides; —determines; —expels; —hands down a decision; —mediates; —penalizes; —referees.

(See judge.)

UNABASHED
adverbs
courageously; frankly; innocently; childishly; boldly; clearly; admirably; surprisingly; entirely; obviously; defiantly; positively; curiously; steadily; strangely; oddly; marvelously; remarkably; fearlessly; calmly; serenely; quietly; composedly; justly, bravonly.

UNACCEPTABLE
adverbs
obviously; cheaply; unfortunately; deplorably; utterly; curiously; vexatiously; embarrassingly; awkwardly; palpably; crudely; shamefully; outrageously; scandalously; seriously; hopelessly.

UNACCOMMODATING
adverbs
gruffly; ungraciously; embarrassingly; grimly; brusquely; crudely; vexatiously; churlishly; sternly; harshly; indifferently; coolly; curiously; strangely; nonchalantly; coldly; cruelly; crisply; bitterly; appraisingly; imperturbably; disturbingly; distressingly; hopelessly; perplexingly; bewilderingly; unconscionably; absurdly; insolently.

UNACCOMPANIED
adverbs
rarely; lonesomely; occasionally; forlornly; courageously; singularly; oddly; preferably; usually; noticeably; obviously; invitingly; manifestly; precariously; embarrassingly; boldly; daringly; challengingly; unfortunately; audaciously; brazenly; oddly; mysteriously; significantly; foolishly; inadvertently.

UNACCOUNTABLE
adverbs
strangely; outlandishly; utterly; perplexingly; bafflingly; apparently; curiously; challengingly.

UNACCUSTOMED
adverbs
apparently; obviously; manifestly; curiously; oddly; significantly; embarrassingly; awkwardly; clearly; appallingly; crudely.

UNADORNED
adverbs
chastely; severely; casually; deliberately; humbly; noticeably; indifferently; carelessly; distinctly; purposely; vexatiously; intentionally; significantly; curiously; remarkably; conspicuously.

UNAIDED
adverbs
surprisingly; obviously; remarkably; utterly; proudly; triumphantly; completely; curiously; manifestly; distinctly; supposedly; presumably; prescriptively; avowedly.

UNALTERABLE
adverbs
deplorably; inconveniently; officially; constitutionally; unfortunately; definitely; presumably; supposedly; luckily; tragically; wretchedly; obviously; regrettably.

UNANIMOUS
adverbs
whole-heartedly; enthusiastically; warmly; practically; absolutely; eagerly; ardently; vociferously; astonishingly; significantly; comfortingly; completely; cheerfully; sensibly; reassuringly; emphatically; impressively; promptly; gladly; miraculously; happily.

UNAPPETIZING
adverbs
dingily; insipidly; colorlessly; miserably; utterly; unfortunately; curiously; unhappily; suddenly; surprisingly; disappointingly; desperately; hopelessly; completely; dismally;

UNAPPROACHABLE
adverbs
sternly; unaccountably; reticently; gloomily;

harshly; cruelly; austerely; pompously; arrogantly; imperially; brutally; coldly; unfortunately; strangely; manifestly; forbiddingly; fearfully; frightfully; gravely; rigorously; unsmilingly; tragically; oddly.

UNASSAILABLE
adverbs
virtuously; pompously; officially; self-righteously; powerfully; imperially; royally; safely; securely; righteously; judicially; constitutionally; happily; arrogantly; presumably; haughtily; hatefully; oddly; monstrously; heartbreakingly; abominably.

UNASSUMING
adverbs
modestly; quietly; demurely; sweetly; shyly; unobtrusively; attractively; charmingly; unaffectedly; delightfully; pleasantly; habitually; naturally; agreeably; artlessly; naively; ingenuously; informally.

UNATTRACTIVE
adverbs
awkwardly; grotesquely; repulsively; unbelievably; pitiably; oddly; angularly; deplorably; strangely; fantastically; pathetically; distressingly; terribly; horridly; touchingly; ridiculously; lamentably; singularly; drolly; queerly: curiously; crudely; painfully.

UNAUTHORIZED
adverbs
blatantly; boldly; brazenly; daringly; unluckily; tragically; foolishly; rashly; recklessly; obviously; palpably; gravely; defiantly; carelessly.

UNAVOIDABLE
adverbs
regrettably; completely; vexatiously; unfortunately; unluckily; awkwardly; embarrassingly; humiliatingly; mortifyingly; incontrovertibly; frankly; fatally; allegedly; manifestly; evidently; obviously; curiously; undoubtedly; legally.

UNAWARE
adverbs
blissfully; innocently; happily; astonishingly; oddly; ironically; curiously; singularly; incredibly; strangely; incongruously; stupid-

ly; carelessly; heedlessly; blithely; nonchalantly; blindly; absurdly.

UNBALANCED
adverbs
dangerously; obviously; palpably; outlandishly; grotesquely; crazily; manifestly; tragically; oddly; singularly; naturally; peculiarly; definitely; presumably; allegedly; unhappily; unfortunately; irresponsibly; curiously; overwhelmingly; incurably; irremediably; deplorably; wretchedly; dangerously; utterly; recently; temporarily.

UNBECOMING
adverbs
utterly; entirely; wholly; frightfully; indecorously; terribly; immodestly; uncommonly; palpably; frankly; awkwardly; exceptionally; discreditably; unworthily; extremely; shamefully; disgracefully.

UNBENDING
adverbs
cruelly; gravely; pompously; austerely; coldly; harshly; severely; bitterly; proudly; taciturnly; implacably; unappeasably; naturally; pridefully; horribly; preposterously; inconceivably; proudly.

UNBIASED
adverbs
delightfully; dependably; truly; actually; sincerely; commendably; admirably; laudably; warrantably; personally; broadly; allegedly; reputedly; avowedly; indisputably; palpably; absolutely; wholly; dispassionately; disinterestedly; fortunately; tolerantly; judiciously; luckily.

UNBURDEN (v)
adverbs
deliberately; remorsefully; articulately; freely; faithfully; tremulously; unconsciously.
(See relieve, empty.)

UNBUSINESSLIKE
adverbs
astonishingly; flippantly; astoundingly; disappointingly; surprisingly; curiously; absurdly; disagreeably; disconcertingly; perplexingly; disturbingly; foolishly; seriously; palpably; strangely; unaccountably; remarkably; amazingly; uncommonly; facet-

iously; annoyingly; impractically; suspiciously; evasively; equivocally; shiftily; indecisively; oddly; impossibly.

UNCANNY
adverbs
alarmingly; peculiarly; weirdly; curiously; strangely; inexplicably; unaccountably; harrowingly; oppressively; mysteriously; viciously; vaguely; unreasonably; hauntingly; gloomily; indefinably; obscurely; inescapably; absurdly; inscrutably; eerily.

UNCEREMONIOUS
adverbs
delightfully; independently; casually; pleasantly; brusquely; facetiously; gruffly; hastily; smilingly; nervously; agreeably; portentously; ominously; naturally; usually; remarkably; singularly; unexpectedly; oddly; peculiarly; characteristically; suddenly; marvellously.

UNCERTAIN
adverbs
timidly; clumsily; shyly; tremulously; blindly; feebly; pathetically; curiously; strangely; vexatiously; indecisively; oddly; miserably; wretchedly; terribly; peculiarly; singularly; significantly; awkwardly; nervously.

UNCERTAINTY
adjectives
unconscious; momentary; prevalent; full; horrible; anxious; tremulous; painful; intolerable; pleasing.

verbs
abolish—; consume—; destroy—; dispel—; efface—; erase—; exhibit—; extinguish—; falter in—; flounder in—; hesitate in—; sweep aside—; vacillate in—; wallow in—; waver in—; —clouds; —dogs; —muddles; —perplexes; —persists; —pervades; —plagues; —prevails; —shrouds; —unnerves; —veils.
(See misapprehension, ambiguity, hesitation, doubt.)

UNCHANGEABLE
adverbs
obstinately; stubbornly; obdurately; egotistically; manifestly; obviously; hopelessly; vexatiously; fatefully; dependably; official-ly; authoritatively; definitely; cruelly; legally; constitutionally; humanly.

UNCHARITABLE
adverbs
selfishly; narrowly; intolerantly; dogmatically; naturally; unfortunately; stubbornly; harshly; thoughtlessly; sternly; abominably; curiously; viciously; disagreeably; coldly; callously; grimly; heartlessly; terribly.

UNCHRISTIAN
adverbs
dreadfully; blatantly; defiantly; definitely; positively; abominably; appallingly; shockingly; boldly; openly; curiously; savagely; barbarously; cruelly; selfishly; flauntingly; gracelessly; indifferently; callously; horribly.

UNCIVIL
adverbs
deliberately; intentionally; significantly; challengingly; rudely; plainly; clearly; inexcusably; unpardonably; contemptibly; arrogantly; crudely; curtly; gruffly; boorishly; churlishly; dangerously; defiantly; boldly; audaciously; curiously; particularly; grossly.

UNCLEAN
adverbs
odiously; squalidly; grossly; obscenely; singularly; indescribably; detestably; abominably; despicably; offensively; disgustingly; impiously; carelessly; arrantly; grievously; scandalously; disastrously; shamefully; infamously; infectiously; horribly; noxiously; deleteriously.

UNCOMFORTABLE
adverbs
definitely; painfully; distressingly; unpleasantly; horribly; dangerously; utterly; coldly; dimly; obscurely; inexcusably; shamefully; uneasily; genuinely; needlessly; extremely; exceedingly; curiously; devilishly; confoundedly; thoroughly; strangely; physically; angrily; embarrassingly; outrageously.

UNCOMMUNICATIVE
adverbs
disagreeably; unsociably; resolutely; doggedly; awkwardly; taciturnly; secretively;

deliberately; stubbornly; loyally; silently; profoundly; determinedly; unpleasantly; desperately; hopelessly; reticently; obstinately; evasively; unflinchingly; exceptionally; immovably; extraordinarily; hopelessly.

UNCOMPLAINING

adverbs

submissively; humbly; curiously; docilely; wisely; fearfully; meekly; singularly; doggedly; resolutely; sullenly; cheerfully; timidly; astutely; craftily; suspiciously; helplessly; shrewdly; patiently; sagaciously; discreetly; cunningly; prudently; knowingly.

UNCOMPLIMENTARY

adverbs

obviously; openly; subtly; maliciously; enviously; terribly; suavely; derisively; cunningly; insidiously; meanly; jealously; smartly; venomously; scandalously; deleteriously; libellously; slightly; highly; unreasonably; curiously; singularly; particularly; smoothly; definitely; contemptibly; deliberately; dreadfully; appallingly; shockingly.

UNCOMPROMISING

adverbs

stiffly; rigidly; unappeasably; obstinately; stubbornly; doctrinally; piously; dogmatically; puritannically; impossibly; terribly; disagreeably; unpleasantly; austerely; severely; sternly; cruelly; brutally; frankly; boldly; truculently; turbulently; gruffly; callously; definitely; indomitably; inexorably; resolutely; fanatically; proudly; arrogantly.

UNCONCERNED

adverbs

indifferently; nonchalantly; blithely; happily; selfishly; thoughtlessly; blindly; ignorantly; pathetically; terribly; deliberately; inconsiderately; curiously; ominously; apparently; singularly; absurdly; strangely; unnaturally; abominably.

UNCONDITIONAL

adverbs

presumably; allegedly; entirely; happily; fortunately; liberally; definitely; constitutionally; practically; generously; broadly; flatly; gloriously; triumphantly; reliably.

UNCONGENIAL

adverbs

unhappily; obviously; bitterly; oddly; surprisingly; helplessly; terribly; dreadfully; intolerably; unfortunately; hopelessly; desperately; singularly; definitely; temperamentally; ominously; fearfully.

UNCONSCIOUS

adverbs

blindly; childishly; selfishly; pathetically; happily; blissfully; momentarily; temporarily; singularly; apparently; obviously; manifestly; presumably; undoubtedly.

UNCONSCIOUSNESS

verbs

approach—; arouse from—; avert—; diagnose—; dope into—; drug into—; fade into —; feign—; hover near—; lapse into—; pretend—; repose in—; shock into—; sink into—; stun into—; —deadens; —endures; —paralyzes; —persists; —seals; —terrifies. (See coma, lethargy.)

UNCONSTITUTIONAL

adverbs

odiously; presumably; flagrantly; supposedly; lamentably; dangerously; daringly; defiantly; trickily; craftily; definitely; manifestly; openly; incontrovertibly; postively; decidedly; flagitiously; unfortunately.

UNCONVENTIONAL

adverbs

absurdly; ridiculously; flauntingly; flagrantly; daringly; slightly; oddly; peculiarly; astonishingly; surprisingly; quaintly; sweetly; singularly; notionally; delightfully; outlandishly; shamefully; purposely; attractively; refreshingly; vexatiously; bewilderingly; unpleasantly; boorishly; crudely.

UNCOUTH

adverbs

rudely; boorishly; naturally; inexcusably; lamentably; awkwardly; fantastically; inordinately; contemptibly; colossally; shockingly; drunkenly; impudently; morosely; unpleasantly; disagreeably; deliberately; boisterously; blatantly; offensively; insufferably; innately; intolerably; unbearably.

UNCOUTHNESS

adjectives
vain; awkward; embarrassing.

UNCOVER (v)

adverbs
mercilessly; ruthlessly; searchingly; diligently; fruitfully; formidably; slyly; grimly; cruelly; despotically; cunningly.
(See reveal, disclose.)

UNCTUOUS

adverbs
disgustingly; professionally; pedantically; smugly; blandly; intolerably; obsequiously; submissively; deceptively; ominously; maddeningly; solemnly; softly; persuasively; carefully; properly; ingratiatingly; suavely; adroitly.

UNDAUNTED

adverbs
resolutely; intrepidly; courageously; blithely; gaily; serenely; calmly; curiously; remarkably; gallantly; laughingly; grimly; absurdly; foolishly; daringly; recklessly; apparently; singularly; confidently; amazingly.

UNDECIPHERABLE

adverbs
sadly; strangely; unfortunately; childishly; dimly; curiously; singularly; vexatiously; awkwardly; disappointingly; heartbreakingly; inexcusably; unpardonably; unreasonably; significantly; deliberately; intentionally; craftily; purposely; cruelly.

UNDEMONSTRATIVE

adverbs
habitually; naturally; inherently; significantly; coolly; surprisingly; perplexingly; churlishly; ungratefully; meanly; disappointingly; shyly; bashfully; modestly; awkwardly; demurely; augustly; sternly; forbiddingly; painfully; curiously; oddly; calmly; chillingly; unluckily; unfortunately; temperamentally.

UNDERGO (v)

adverbs
heroically; gallantly; stoically; generously; willingly; staunchly; courageously; peacefully.
(See endure, experience.)

UNDERHANDED

adverbs
wickedly; curiously; significantly; nefariously; despicably; detestably; craftily; shrewdly; carefully; mysteriously; cunningly; abominably; adroitly; atrociously; cruelly; disgracefully; basely; viciously; grossly.

UNDERNOURISHED

adverbs
pathetically; cruelly; undeniably; positively; definitely; obviously; miserably; wretchedly; pitiably; dangerously; alarmingly; desperately; helplessly; hopelessly; unconsciously; generally; surprisingly; deplorably; unwisely; impecuniously; dreadfully; terribly; inexcusably; recently; emphatically; bitterly.

UNDERPAID

adverbs
contemptibly; inexcusably; cruelly; terribly; needlessly; obviously; absurdly; remarkably; preposterously; presumably; manifestly; definitely; wretchedly; miserably; unwarrantably; emphatically.

UNDERSCORE (v)

adverbs
heavily; blackly; redundantly; indelibly.
(See mark.)

UNDERSELL (v)

adverbs
astutely; ethically; secretively; legitimately; momentously; boldly; financially; desperately.
(See transact, win.)

UNDERSTAND (v)

adverbs
literally; distinctly; cleverly; dimly; sympathetically; expressly; properly; assuredly; intimately; vaguely; keenly; accurately; theoretically; adequately; subtly; exceptionally; shrewdly; sympathetically; tacitly.
(See comprehend, discern.)

UNDERSTANDING

adjectives
friendly; robust; keen; previous; courteous; prospective; analytical; theoretical; adequate; subtle; slow; unconscious; instinctive; definite; speedy; cynical; cordial; synthetic; useful; retrospective; close; general; comprehensive; masculine; profound; dis-

cursive; exceptional; enlarged; vague; chronic; secret; veiled; barren; shrewd; human; distinct; mutual; kind; sympathetic; furtive; mean; emotional; tacit; verbal; momentary; consummate; full-bodied.

verbs

achieve—; acquire—; arrive at—; attain—; awaken—; blossom into—; chill—; convey to —; demonstrate—; destroy—; display—; engrave on—; enlarge—; enlighten—; enrich —; enter into—; escape—; evince—; feign —; foster—; further—; gain—; grasp—; grope for—; illuminate—; impart—; impede—; inhibit—; lack—; lead to—; manifest—; obtain—; promote—; reflect—; require—; school—; seek—; swell—; temper with—; yield to—; —dawns; —discerns; — discriminates; —harmonizes; —pacifies; — tranquillizes; —triumphs.

(See insight, knowledge, commonsense, intellect, learning.)

adverbs

sympathetically; generously; pleasantly; unusually; remarkably; helpfully; patiently; profoundly; momentarily; marvellously; mercifully; completely.

UNDERTAKE (v)

adverbs

sporadically; rashly; reluctantly; successfully; boldly; ill-advisedly; illicitly; scientifically; desperately; hazardously; perilously; grimly; ridiculously; arduously; financially.

(See assume.)

UNDERTAKING

adjectives

scientific; tangible; desperate; unconnected; momentous; remarkable; bold; spurious; aimless; conciliatory; hazardous; chimerical; illicit; solemn; important; tremendous; munificent; unparalleled; perilous; grim; exciting; ridiculous; involved; arduous; herculean; stupendous; desperate; formidable; financial.

verbs

abandon—; analyze—; bind to—; commend —; conceive—; desert—; encourage—; endanger—; essay—; forego—; forestall—; forsake—; insure—; jeopardize—; laud—; outline—; plan—; relinquish—; promote—; renounce—; tackle—; venture on—; withdraw from—; —embraces; —endeavors; —

flourishes; —promises; —thrives.

(See enterprise, plan, deal, program.)

UNDISMAYED

adverbs

gallantly; confidently; optimistically; curiously; admirably; wondrously; apparently; evidently; fortunately; recklessly; pathetically; courageously; singularly; fanatically; zealously; blindly; imperturbably; astonishingly; surprisingly; remarkably; significantly; audaciously; absurdly; arrogantly; brashly.

UNDISTURBED

adverbs

serenely; blindly; stoically; pedantically; witlessly; irresponsibly; calmly; vexatiously; infuriatingly; strangely; amazingly; suspiciously; blandly; unaccountably; surprisingly; philosophically.

UNDULATE (v)

adverbs

restlessly; incessantly; sinuously; gently.

(See wave, curve.)

UNDULATING

adverbs

regularly; smoothly; endlessly; restlessly; dizzily; disturbingly; monotonously; ceaselessly; pleasantly; arably; advantageously; fortunately; crazily; fascinatingly; delightfully; curiously; vastly; extensively; mysteriously; iridescently; colorfully; singularly; marvellously; incessantly; continuously.

UNDUTIFUL

adverbs

curiously; desperately; disagreeably; cruelly; heartbreakingly; incorrigibly; blindly; bitterly; inexcusably; terribly; singularly; coldly; strangely; unquestionably; unbelievably; incredibly; preposterously; shamefully; miserably; unwarrantably; unconcernedly.

UNEASINESS

adjectives

longing; vague; transitory; abrupt; idle; restless; faint; unhappy; growing.

verbs

afflict with—; allay—; assuage—; burden with—; calm—; dispel—; experience—; inspire—; ridicule—; scoff at—; sense—; sweep away—; —accompanies; —distresses;

—dwells in; —envelopes; —gnaws at; —haunts; —oppresses; —persists; —pervades; —prevails; —shrouds; —stabs; —takes hold; —unnerves; —weighs upon; —yields.

(See impatience, discomfort, discontent, anxiety.)

UNEASY
adverbs
naturally; timidly; shyly; unacountably; suddenly; justifiably; unusually; extremely; unnecessarily; needlessly; oddly; ominously; visibly; seriously; obviously; inexplicably; painfully; foolishly; distinctly; inordinately; apparently; profoundly.

UNEDUCATED
adverbs
frankly; unfortunately; academically; supposedly; paradoxically; blessedly; blatantly; strangely; apparently; coarsely; grossly; avowedly; allegedly; manifestly.

UNEMOTIONAL
adverbs
coldly; sternly; gravely; terrifyingly; brutally; harshly; austerely; stoically; unbelievably; unnaturally; abnormally; strangely; singularly; frightfully; ungenerously; stingily; selfishly; terribly; peculiarly; notoriously; reputedly; ostensibly; presumably; conspicuously.

UNEMPLOYED
adverbs
idly; lazily; indolently; unfortunately; miserably; helplessly; inadvertently; unhappily; temporarily; evidently; frequently; manifestly; involuntarily.

UNEMPLOYMENT
adjectives
technological; devastating; partial; continued; nation-wide; artificially-relieved; supposed; appalling; dreaded; frightening.

verbs
absorb—; analyze—; augment—; banish—; bewail—; cancel out—; cause—; check—; decrease—; decry—; deplore—; fear—; increase—; insure against—; legislate against —; lament—; outlaw—; predict—; reduce —; relieve—; remedy—; tackle—; —breeds; —depresses; —deprives; —diminishes; —dwindles; —endangers; —mitigates; —oppresses; —overwhelms; —rav-

ages; —satirizes; —scourges; —shelves; —sweeps; —victimizes.

UNEVEN
adverbs
curiously; perilously; raggedly; roughly; inconveniently; unpleasantly; unjustly; inequitably; unfairly; meanly; disagreeably; absurdly; sadly; crookedly.

UNEVENTFUL
adverbs
tiresomely; dully; flatly; uninterestingly; boresomely; monotonously; curiously; unexpectedly; unpardonably; undeniably; tediously; restfully; fortunately; blessedly; smoothly; conspicuously; placidly; utterly; happily.

UNEXPECTED
adverbs
provokingly; bewilderingly; curiously; utterly; unfeignedly; pitifully; sadly; completely; tragically; suddenly; stunningly; startlingly; terribly; obviously; manifestly; undoubtedly.

UNFAILING
adverbs
blessedly; presumably; generously; usually; reliably; notoriously; reputedly; supposedly; manifestly; miraculously; apparently; conspicuously; notably; dependably; reliably.

UNFAIR
adverbs
manifestly; terribly; openly; flagrantly; abominably; shamefully; cruelly; bitterly; egregiously; despicably; maliciously; unmistakably; daringly; deliberately; dishonorably; uncommonly; secretly; greedily; arrogantly; high-handedly; atrociously.

UNFAIRNESS
verbs
ameliorate—; avenge—; avert—; betray—; condone—; denounce—; deplore—; disclose —; divulge—; mitigate—; rebuke—; remedy—; reveal—; uncover—; —colors; —distorts; —embroiders; —garbles; —glosses over; —taints.

(See injustice, partiality, grievance, wrong.)

UNFAITHFUL

adverbs

notoriously; allegedly; conspicuously; flagrantly; openly; terribly; carelessly; cruelly; irresponsibly; treacherously; curiously; secretly; furtively; actually; presumably; recklessly; undependably; intolerably; abominably; wickedly; viciously; reprehensibly; provokingly; vexatiously; unbearably; unprofitably; deplorably; uselessly; surreptitiously; heinously; wretchedly; miserably; definitely; despicably; detestably; dreadfully; worthlessly; incorrigibly.

UNFAITHFULNESS

verbs

absolve of—; atone for—; avenge—; bear —; breed—; charge—; display—; evince —; expiate—; forgive—; foster—; frown upon—; punish—; regret—; repent—; rue —; —beckons; —disgraces; —dishonors; — tempts.

(See infidelity, insincerity, treachery.)

UNFAMILIAR

adverbs

sadly; embarrassingly; awkwardly; admittedly; evidently; obviously; unconcealably; tragically; helplessly; hopelessly; self-consciously; openly; shamelessly; unsophisticatedly; dreadfully; ineptly; oddly.

UNFASHIONABLE

adverbs

daringly; audaciously; carelessly; slouchily; untidily; dowdily; independently; boldly; recklessly; openly; definitely; admittedly; artistically; strikingly; smartly; ridiculously; bizarrely; ludicrously; intentionally; serenely; indifferently; consciously; naturally; curiously; magnificently; arrogantly; negligently; barbarically; casually; nonchalantly; happily; blithely; thoughtlessly; emphatically; positively; flippantly; notoriously; unashamedly; interestingly; vexatiously; laughingly; foolishly; unwisely.

UNFASTEN (v)

adverbs

readily; automatically; easily; tremblingly; carelessly; artfully; deftly; customarily; strategically.

(See release, relieve.)

UNFATHOMABLE

adverbs

obscurely; mysteriously; darkly; dimly; vaguely; impenetrably; nebulously; perplexingly; eternally; wondrously; abstrusely; muddily; mystically; occultly; inscrutably; puzzlingly; reconditely; unaccountably; unreasonably; irrationally; profoundly; abysmally; infinitely; perpetually; forever.

UNFAVORABLE

adverbs

definitely; unappeasably; uncompromisingly; defiantly; rebelliously; forbiddingly; discouragingly; resolutely; sternly; implacably; emphatically; downright; openly; secretly; surreptitiously; ominously; undeniably; influentially; indifferently; actively; mildly; positively; energetically; dangerously; frankly; expressly; harshly; powerfully; lamentably; fortuitously; stubbornly.

UNFEELING

adverbs

callously; cruelly; coldly; downright; evidently; curiously; strangely; obdurately; implacably; terribly; preposterously; extremely; inexplainably; utterly; harshly; stubbornly; wickedly; brutally; unbelievably; selfishly; incredibly; unimaginably; singularly; viciously; stonily; inhumanly; sternly; austerely; heartlessly.

UNFEIGNED

adverbs

clearly; unquestionably; perceptibly; ingenuously; apparently.

UNFILIAL

adverbs

unnaturally; strangely; horribly; appallingly; incredibly; unreasonably; utterly; unimaginably; astoundingly; justifiably; eventually; sadly; deplorably; wretchedly; miserably; curiously; strangely; remarkably; terribly; inexplicably; ungratefully; inconsiderately; heartbreakingly; surprisingly; stonily; openly.

UNFINISH (v)

adverbs

deservedly; carelessly; sadly; incomprehensibly; unwisely; improvidently.

(See cease, stop.)

UNFIT

adverbs

palpably; altogether; manifestly; allegedly; presumably; ostensibly; utterly; temperamentally; physically; morally; lamentably; deplorably; miserably; wretchedly; curiously; downright.

UNFLINCHING

adverbs

courageously; sturdily; staunchly; boldly; steadily; splendidly; chivalrously; admirably; surprisingly; quietly; imperturbably; firmly; gallantly; heroically; marvellously; magnificently.

UNFOLD (v)

adverbs

beauteously; swiftly; joyously; vividly; prominently; maturely.

(See reveal, uncover.)

UNFORGIVING

adverbs

uncompromisingly; sternly; austerely; seriously; gravely; censoriously; callously; unmercifully; coldly; obdurately; stubbornly; hopelessly; wretchedly; unfortunately; curiously; pharisaically; harshly.

UNFORTUNATE

adverbs

sadly; miserably; tragically; wretchedly; chronically; direly; unexpectedly; suddenly; shamefully; surprisingly; terribly; really; unusually; strangely; oddly; naturally; extremely.

UNFREQUENTED

adverbs

usually; perilously; dangerously; hazardously; notoriously; notably; conspicuously; riskily; unpleasantly; desolately; gloomily; eerily.

UNFRIENDLY

adverbs

cruelly; bitterly; terribly; unreasonably; meanly; hatefully; spitefully; strangely; unwontedly; suddenly; curiously; unwarrantably; disagreeably; snobbishly; inexcusably; churlishly; boorishly; narrow-mindedly; intolerantly; uncharitably; discouragingly; painfully; extremely; uncommonly.

UNFURL (v)

adverbs

automatically; gallantly; awesomely; impressively; picturesquely.

(See release, unfold.)

UNGAINLY

adverbs

miserably; unfortunately; comically; undeniably; terribly; dreadfully; unpleasantly; sadly; curiously; particularly; conspicuously; pathetically; oddly; clumsily; positively; laughably; regrettably; unsuitably; nonchalantly; carelessly; slouchily; indifferently; blandly.

UNGENEROUS

adverbs

surprisingly; suddenly; appallingly; unexpectedly; curiously; unluckily; shockingly; miserably; short-sightedly; foolishly; unwisely; intolerantly; uncharitably; bigotedly; narrowly; terribly; dreadfully; uncommonly.

UNGODLY

adverbs

shamefully; unconscionably; surprisingly; flagrantly; openly; flauntingly; shockingly; appallingly; atrociously; blasphemously; impiously; despicably; offensively; heartbreakingly; viciously; daringly; wickedly; conspicuously; dreadfully; strangely.

UNGOVERNABLE

adverbs

sadly; gracelessly; conspicuously; heinously; highly; inexplicably; atrociously; incomprehensibly; suddenly; sometimes; habitually; boldly; defiantly; mutinously; hopelessly; dreadfully; dangerously; violently; curiously; occasionally; eventually; admittedly; terribly.

UNGRACIOUS

adverbs

curtly; strangely; oddly; significantly; conspicuously; unaccountably; curiously; momentarily; deliberately; intentionally; pointedly; dreadfully; unwontedly; purposely; regrettably; sadly; unfortunately; inadvertently; clumsily; unintentionally; awkwardly; snobbishly.

UNGRATEFUL

adverbs

boorishly; ignorantly; selfishly; indifferently; thoughtlessly; callously; incredibly; unbelievably; oddly; terribly; crassly; grossly; significantly; dreadfully; coldly; stupidly; shamefully; remarkably; unpardonably; astoundingly; cruelly; arrogantly.

UNGUARDED

adverbs

carelessly; inadvertently; momentarily; indifferently; temporarily; insecurely; crassly; strangely; inexplicably; happily; unaccountably; blessedly; advantageously; fortuitously; trustfully; stupidly; incautiously; unexpectedly; seldom; rarely.

UNHANDY

adverbs

deucedly; vexatiously; terribly; foolishly; wastefully; frequently; dreadfully; downright; admittedly; curiously; short-sightedly; extravagantly.

UNHAPPINESS

verbs

bear—; curse with—; dispel—; endure—; evince—; exhibit—; languish in—; lessen—; mitigate—; mollify—; soothe—; suffer—; undergo—; —afflicts; —blasts; —blights; —burdens; —clouds; —crucifies; —dampens; —dejects; —depresses; —desolates; —pervades; —prostrates; —racks; —sprouts; —stabs; —torments; —weighs upon.

(See pathos, distress, misery, sadness.)

UNHAPPY

adverbs

cruelly; bitterly; sadly; desolately; gloomily; moodily; naturally; terribly; dreadfully; unaccountably; inexplicably; curiously; particularly; selfishly; childishly; painfully; admittedly; sullenly; particularly; helplessly; hopelessly; desperately; suddenly; eventually; openly; obviously; frankly; wretchedly; miserably.

UNHEALTHY

adverbs

definitely; terribly; curiously; naturally; apparently; malarially; obviously; manifestly; unfortunately; wickedly; oddly; positively; miserably; wretchedly; congenitally.

UNHOLY

adverbs

frightfully; blasphemously; impiously; terribly; accursedly; profanely; sacrilegiously; wantonly; carelessly; recklessly; appallingly; flippantly; execrably; damnably; dreadfully; horribly.

UNIFORM

adjectives

brilliant; handsome; full; striking; undress; continuous; resplendent; finished; glittering; shabby; outstanding; greasy; practical; gorgeous; dress; gaudy.

verbs

array in—; besmirch—; bestow—s; defile—; discard—; dishonor—; divest of—; don—; espy—; frill—; invest in—; march in—; masquerade in—; recognize—; strip of—; tatter—; —attracts; —denotes; —flatters; —impresses; —symbolizes; —stamps one as; —betokens.

(See tights, clothing, dress.)

adverbs

monotonously; wearisomely; conveniently; adaptably; comfortably; assuredly; pleasantly; tiresomely; flatly; uninterestingly; beautifully; symmetrically; presumably; allegedly; obviously; conspicuously; economically; dependably; reliably; conventionally.

UNIFORM (*v*)

adverbs

gaudily; gaily; impressively; dramatically; vividly; patriotically; brilliantly; somberly; drably.

(See garb, dress.)

UNION

adjectives

splendid; contingent; mystic; eternal; solemn; incestuous; ultimate; conjugal; habitual; unjust; constant; indissoluble; potent; powerful; fertile; conscious; perpetual; existing; legislative; precipitate; unfathomable; moribund; hurried; illicit; fruitful; visible; labor; celestial; consummate; checkoff; complete; substantial; immemorial; perfect; fructifying; loathed; confederated; outstanding.

verbs

band into—; bind into—; consummate—; defend—; destroy—; disrupt—; encourage—; enter into—; foster—; further—; hallow—;

hinder—; impede—; lack—; partition—; preserve—; promote—; protect—; rend—; signify—; solemnize—; sunder—; —affords; —enables; —flourishes; —insures; —strengthens; —suffers.

(See marriage, connection, matrimony, attachment, coalition, combination.)

UNIONS

verbs

affiliate with—; alienate—; ally—; arbitrate—; betray—; cement—; centralize—; combat—; consolidate—; crush—; effect—; enlist in—; enroll in—; dispel—; foster—; head—; install—; league with—; mediate with—; operate—; pacify—; recruit for —; rend—; rule—; scorn—; sympathize with—; —achieve; —band; —call out; —challenge; —clash with; —demand; —embroil; —foment; —link; —merge with; —picket; —preserve; —protect; —strike; —support.

(See strikers, labor.)

UNIT

adjectives

regulatory; myriad (pl); topical; versatile; efficient; functioning; fire-fighting; unmanageable; single; sounding; inseparable; research; harmonious; primary; mechanical; similar; parallactic; potent; political; arbitrary; perfected.

verbs

affiliate with—; amass—; complete—; demolish—; design—; dissolve—; integrate—; isolate—; mould—; partition—; perform as —; rend—; replenish—; shatter—; strengthen—; sunder—; —expands; —swells.

(See cell, property, part.)

UNITE (*v*)

adverbs

stubbornly; strangely; fraternally; substantially; indissolubly; cordially; subsequently; promptly; unanimously; vigorously; ultimately; dramatically; politically; spiritually; harmoniously; enduringly; strategically; logically; morally; fundamentally; practically.

(See join, ally.)

UNITY

adjectives

distinct; unbroken; political; wielded; necessary; rigorous; dramatic; essential; artistic; pervading; territorial; moral; contin-

ental; spiritual; internal; harmonious; enduring; dim; compendious; lasting; brilliant; uncompounded; early; strategic; dramatic; imperial; logical; solid; fundamental; practical; mad.

verbs

accomplish—; achieve—; bind in—; blend in—; clamor for—; commend—; demand—; demolish—; endanger—; foster—; further —; impair—; jeopardize—; lack—; necessitate—; preserve—; promote—; rend—; sunder—; unfold—; verify—; want—; work for—; —enables; —insures; —perpetuates; —persists; —pervades; —prevails; —resists; —rules; —strengthens.

(See harmony, cooperation, agreement.)

UNIVERSAL

adverbs

fundamentally; woefully; universally; significantly; strikingly; curiously; ominously; surprisingly; astonishingly; terribly.

UNIVERSE

adjectives

moral; mad; vast; practical; lampless; useless; illimitable; well-conducted; visible; enduring; conceivable; spiritual; collective; boundless; insubstantial; harmonious; infinite; wise; myriad (pl); expanding; malign; aerial; material; incomprehensible; offensive; effectless; objective; foundering.

verbs

bound—; cloak—; cloud—; comprise—; contemplate—; "debunk"—; dim—; dwell in —; embrace—; encompass—; fathom—; glory in—; govern—; illumine—; impart to —; interpret—; limit—; map—; pervade—; re-create—; regard—; save—; scan—; shroud—; span—; sunder from—; survey—; —acclaims; —evolves from; —links; —mystifies; —mourns; —seethes; —teems; —whirls.

(See creation, life.)

UNIVERSITY

adjectives

studious; sedate; well-rounded; theological; splendid; great; significant; national; state.

verbs

affiliate with—; converge upon—; endow—; enroll in—; enter—; expel from—; found—; guide—; —advances; —breeds; —disciplines; —edifies; —enlightens; —equips; —

facilitates; —fosters; —functions; —furthers; —grounds one in; —honors; —imparts; —instructs; —mothers; —nurtures; —offers; —polishes; —prepares; —primes; —proselytes; —qualifies; —rears; —subsidizes; —verses one in.

(See college, institution, school.)

UNJUST
adverbs

cruelly; bitterly; keenly; unaccountably; unexpectedly; palpably; uncommonly; arrantly; wantonly; intolerably; illogically; vengefully; inexcusably; hatefully; hideously; miserably; wretchedly; incredibly; openly; crassly; stupidly; gravely; seriously; inadvertently; deliberately; intentionally; incredibly; inexplicably; remarkably; incomprehensibly.

UNKEMPT
adverbs

surprisingly; carelessly; deliberately; coolly; nonchalantly; comfortably; provokingly; shamefully; dowdily; embarrassingly; inexcusably; unfortunately; casually; notoriously; conspicuously; unconcealably; horribly; unluckily; deplorably; scandalously; merrily; blowzily; boldly; audaciously; flagrantly.

UNKNOWABLE
adverbs

obscurely; eternally; mysteriously; latently; darkly; dimly; vaguely; impenetratingly; incomprehensibly; perplexingly; wonderfully; mystically; occultly; inscrutably; puzzlingly; elusively; unaccountably; inexplicably; unreasonably; tormentingly; irrationally; profoundly; abysmally; infinitely; perpetually.

UNLAWFUL
adverbs

definitely; implicitly; riskily; perilously; strictly; positively; absurdly; specifically; explicitly; actually; allegedly; presumably; probably; certainly; avowedly; admittedly.

UNLIKELY
adverbs

naturally; utterly; legally; morally; particularly; emphatically; positively.

UNLOCK (v)
adverbs

automatically; readily; rustily; smoothly; easily; temporarily; dexterously.

(See unfasten, release.)

UNMANNERLY
adverbs

strangely; grossly; barbarously; naturally; incredibly; crassly; stupidly; boorishly; cruelly; rustically; provincially; unpleasantly; foolishly; apparently; manifestly; embarrassingly; shamefully; gracelessly; naively; ignorantly; unsophisticatedly; unluckily; wretchedly; unpardonably; oddly; conspicuously; remarkably; highly; uncommonly; unwontedly; disagreeably.

UNMERCIFUL
adverbs

cruelly; coldly; miserably; hatefully; inflexibly; stubbornly; boorishly; brutally; selfishly; unyieldingly; dreadfully; intractably; shamefully; scandalously; wickedly; immovably; sternly; inscrutably; mysteriously; strangely; significantly; remarkably; unwontedly; unaccountably; oddly; surprisingly.

UNMISTAKABLE
adverbs

clearly; explicitly; positively; manifestly; obviously; conspicuously; conveniently; safely; felicitously; fortunately; luckily; happily; definitely; purposely; singularly; designedly.

UNNERVED
adverbs

strangely; naturally; shakily; utterly; oddly; curiously; probably; completely; unreasonably; foolishly; shockingly; palpably; apparently; mysteriously; conspicuously; tremulously; helplessly.

UNOBJECTIONABLE
adverbs

personally; entirely; quite; naturally; pleasantly; harmlessly; manifestly; locally; politically; financially; generally; reasonably; frankly; wholly; fairly; presumably; singularly; altogether.

UNOSTENTATIOUS
adverbs

modestly; quietly; serenely; carefully; calmly; curiously; preferably; always; strangely; shyly; bashfully.

UNPALATABLE

adverbs

strangely; altogether; manifestly; curiously; noxiously; disagreeably; disgustingly; hopelessly; terribly; wretchedly; impossibly; embarrassingly; cruelly; bitterly; disappointingly; outlandishly; dreadfully.

UNPARLIAMENTARY

adverbs

openly; manifestly; wholly; foolishly; ignorantly; boldly; flauntingly; consciously; obstinately; absurdly; entirely; evidently; conspicuously; loosely; casually; carelessly.

UNPERTURBED

adverbs

quietly; strangely; confidently; optimistically; trustfully; curiously; particularly; noticeably; altogether; serenely; certainly; palpably; hopefully.

UNPOPULAR

adverbs

generally; strangely; noticeably; significantly; desperately; currently; terribly; definitely; conspicuously; apparently; manifestly; disturbingly; miserably; mysteriously; curiously; distinctly; emphatically; intensely; seriously; consciously.

UNPREJUDICED

adverbs

admirably; nobly; particularly; admittedly; distinctly; emphatically; curiously; palpably; commendably; dependably; hearteningly; judicially; gravely; honorably; honestly; entirely; wonderfully; happily.

UNPREPARED

adverbs

grossly; carelessly; unpardonably; miserably; palpably; inadvertently; wantonly; financially; socially; wretchedly; undisguisedly; openly; admittedly; unluckily; laughably; comically; tragically; ridiculously; nonchalantly; blithely; merrily.

UNPRESENTABLE

adverbs

horribly; laughably; ridiculously; embarrassingly; muddily; soggily; carelessly; altogether; shamefully; comically; ludicrously; utterly; messily; cruelly; bashfully; obviously; momentarily; always.

UNPROFITABLE

adverbs

disastrously; probably; sadly; extremely; terribly; naturally; seasonally; curiously; suddenly; desperately.

UNQUESTIONABLE

adverbs

utterly; admittedly; luckily; absolutely; momentarily; recognizably; palpably; socially; financially.

UNRAVEL (*v*)

adverbs

persistently; easily; intelligently; patiently; diligently; monotonously.

(See open, reveal.)

UNREAL

adverbs

darkly; abstrusely; obscurely; immaterially; indefinably; chimerically; phantasmally; vaguely; nebulously; evanescently; fantastically; strangely; fabulously; queerly; mystically; insubstantially; virtually; enigmatically; subtly; wildly; spectrally; dimly.

UNREASONABLE

adverbs

foolishly; blunderingly; ridiculously; absurdly; ludicrously; extravagantly; senselessly; egregiously; preposterously; comically; monstrously; fantastically; grotesquely; outlandishly; strangely; manifestly; patently; palpably; perversely; pathetically; grossly; incredibly.

UNREGENERATE

adverbs

obviously; manifestly; evidently; pitiably; stubbornly; obstinately; unfortunately; openly; flagrantly; blasphemously; flippantly; audaciously; impiously; terribly; dreadfully; impenitently.

UNRELENTING

adverbs

wilfully; indomitably; bitterly; sternly; obdurately; pitiably; lamentably; unpardonably; unreasonably; pitilessly; inexorably; obstinately; stubbornly; mulishly; doggedly; perversely; fanatically; pig-headedly; contumaciously; bigotedly; implacably; rancourously; vengefully; ruthlessly; maliciously; cruelly; unmercifully.

UNRELIABLE

adverbs

unfortunately; manifestly; entirely; unluckily; desperately; admittedly; obviously; terribly; actually; furtively; secretly; downright; notoriously; infamously; shamefully; wickedly; palpably; certainly.

UNREST

adjectives

wearisome; secret; political; sickening; unsettled; vain; essential; bitter; ghoulish; eager; sweet.

verbs

allay—; assuage—; calm—; cloak—; cope with—; dispel—; dwell in—; incite—; provoke—; quell—; silence—; still—; stave off—; subdue—; —disconcerts; —gnaws; —irks; —irritates; —racks; —rends; —smoulders; —spreads; —wanes; —weighs upon; —wrings.

(See restlessness, confusion, dissatisfaction, discontent.)

UNRESTRAINED

adverbs

excessively; rakishly; wildly; playfully; wickedly; hilariously; gleefully; joyously; crazily; airily; youthfully; ludicrously; brazenly; monstrously; outlandishly; delightfully; recklessly; wantonly; amazingly; audaciously; impetuously; ardently; heedlessly; indiscreetly.

UNRIGHTEOUS

adverbs

openly; unheedingly; deliberately; heinously; wickedly; impiously; blasphemously; deplorably; wretchedly; miserably; heathenishly.

UNRUFFLED

adverbs

admirably; surprisingly; restrainedly; wonderfully; utterly; calmly; actually; apparently; palpably; evidently; strangely; curiously; fortunately; securely; beautifully.

UNRULY

adverbs

ominously; dreadfully; unmanageably; obstinately; significantly; terribly; oddly; uproariously; boisterously; viciously; politically; truculently; dangerously; violently; unreasonably; ungovernably; obstreperously; jeeringly; designedly; maliciously; viciously; alarmingly; turbulently.

UNSAVORY

adverbs

notoriously; slightly; decidedly; extremely; admittedly; terribly; undisguisedly; dreadfully; manifestly; wickedly.

UNSCATHED

adverbs

mercifully; apparently; blessedly; surprisingly; gloriously; happily; luckily; unexpectedly; blissfully; evidently.

UNSCRUPULOUS

adverbs

notoriously; shamefully; cleverly; astutely; adroitly; infamously; reputedly; allegedly; curiously; terribly; extremely; shamelessly; triumphantly; arrogantly; openly; cruelly; bitterly; desperately; hard-heartedly; greedily; meanly; aggressively; boldly; daringly; criminally; selfishly; hatefully; atrociously.

UNSEASONABLE

adverbs

manifestly; surprisingly; unhealthfully; unprofitably; dangerously; desperately; hazardously; undeniably; highly; uncommonly; curiously; strangely; oddly; significantly; ominously; definitely.

UNSEEMLY

adverbs

desperately; shamefully; unpleasantly; disagreeably; surprisingly; unpardonably; absolutely; inexcusably; indefensibly; daringly; flauntingly; miserably; wantonly; frightfully; horridly; impertinently; blatantly.

UNSELFISH

adverbs

utterly; unnecessarily; ostentatiously; delightfully; remarkably; always; altogether; downright; absurdly; generously; altruistically; charitably; thoughtfully; considerately; graciously; courteously; unexpectedly; usually; naturally; habitually; tenderly; lovingly; extremely; uncommonly; singularly; unexpectedly; unwontedly; sweetly.

UNSETTLED

adverbs

curiously; indecisively; obviously; manifestly; unfortunately; evidently; pitiably; dangerously; temporarily; pathetically; miserably; secretly; confusedly; mentally; financially; sadly; temperamentally; habitually; naturally.

UNSIGHTLY

adverbs

hideously; loathesomely; disgustingly; shabbily; filthily; repulsively; horridly; shockingly; monstrously; gruesomely; dreadfully; positively; terribly; unbearably.

UNSKILFUL

adverbs

naturally; pitiably; awkwardly; clumsily; ineptly; inexpertly; ignorantly; carelessly; heedlessly; pathetically; unacceptably; grossly; undeniably; surprisingly; miserably; terribly; criminally; admittedly; undisguisedly; naively; shyly; self-consciously.

UNSOCIABLE

adverbs

painfully; shyly; disagreeably; terribly; awkwardly; naturally; naively; ungraciously; selfishly; inconsiderately; unwontedly; habitually; unpardonably; miserably; reticently; gravely; surprisingly; unfortunately; pitifully; inexcusably; strangely; offensively.

UNSOPHISTICATED

adverbs

naively; undisguisedly; apparently; palpably; manifestly; ludicrously; ridiculously; embarrassingly; shyly; consciously; painfully; childishly; innocently; awkwardly; clumsily; unhappily; unfortunately; laughably; pathetically.

UNSOUND

adverbs

unfortunately; curiously; inexcusably; untenably; ridiculously; absurdly; dreadfully; wickedly; admittedly; miserably; dangerously; significantly; manifestly; openly; daringly; utterly; unreliably.

UNSPARING

adverbs

sternly; harshly; gravely; unjustly; obstinately; inflexibly; fanatically; narrowly; bigotedly; ridiculously; bitterly; cruelly; unreasoningly; unreasonably; obdurately; gravely; solemnly; frightfully.

UNSTABLE

adverbs

lamentably; deplorably; miserably; ridiculously; obviously; dangerously; alarmingly; ominously; desperately; manifestly; perilously; unpardonably; carelessly; notoriously; flagrantly; unforgivably.

UNSUBSTANTIAL

adverbs

baselessly; fabulously; fantastically; fancifully; suppositiously; virtually; mockingly; illusively; mythically; notionally; romantically; visionarily; quixotically; whimsically; ethereally; tenuously; chimerically.

UNSUITABLE

adverbs

distinctly; positively; altogether; wholly; entirely; incongruously; socially; awkwardly; absurdly; foolishly; extravagantly; unbecomingly; comically; outlandishly; inappropriately; shockingly; crudely; horribly; laughably; singularly.

UNSYSTEMATIC

adverbs

carelessly; bewilderingly; confusingly; chaotically; terribly; unpardonably; inexcusably; criminally; provokingly; irritatingly; inconveniently; vexatiously; ruinously; ignorantly; foolishly; confoundedly; strangely; lazily; negligently; heedlessly; unwarrantably.

UNTENABLE

adverbs

fallibly; unreliably; inaccurately; insubstantially; absolutely; manifestly; carelessly; inconclusively; fallaciously; ultimately; obviously; absurdly; hopelessly; wholly; ridiculously; laughably.

UNTIMELY

adverbs

strangely; obviously; unfortunately; politically; financially; distressingly; terribly.

UNTOUCHED

adverbs

curiously; singularly; momentarily; mercifully; fortunately; blessedly; strangely; absolutely; carefully; providently; luckily; heedfully; apparently; absolutely.

UNTRAMMEL (*v*)

adverbs

entirely; nominally; legally; apparently; obviously.

(See release, free.)

UNTUTORED

adverbs

naively; unbelievably; miraculously; marvelously; curiously; childishly; utterly; obviously; manifestly; miserably; wretchedly; helplessly; distressingly; pathetically; pitiably; fortunately; palpably; blessedly; gloriously; apparently; brilliantly.

UNUSUAL

adverbs

extremely; fortunately; luckily; believably; apparently; obviously; manifestly; gloriously; mercifully; unfortunately; significantly; delightfully; altogether.

UNWARRANTABLE

adverbs

obviously; naturally; altogether; legally; socially; conventionally; decently; judicially; politically; terribly; admittedly; absurdly; ridiculously; ludicrously; wretchedly; miserably; indefensibly; dreadfully; altogether; downright; utterly.

UNWARY

adverbs

youthfully; flippantly; heedlessly; bravely; foolishly; naively; carelessly; ignorantly; wantonly; ridiculously; unbelievably; absurdly; blithely; inconceivably; rashly; witlessly.

UNWEARIED

adverbs

incredibly; fondly; affectionately; helpfully; patriotically; resolutely; intrepidly; unbelievably; miraculously; splendidly; incomprehensibly; lovingly; desperately; marvelously; strangely; oddly; fanatically; amazingly; remarkably.

UNWIELDY

adverbs

awkwardly; clumsily; terribly; unpleasantly; embarrassingly; disagreeably; massively; altogether; manifestly; inconveniently; lumberingly; vexatiously; plaguedly; confoundedly; singularly.

UNWILLINGNESS

adjectives

sheer; dull; deliberate; obstinate; studied.

verbs

acknowledge—; announce—; assert—; aver —; conquer—; contain—; deplore—; dis-

cern—; dispel—; display—; dissolve—; emphasize—; express—; indicate—; justify—; maintain—; overcome—; prevail against—; subdue—; surmount—; sweep away—; swerve from—; voice—; —irks; —persists, —piques; —riles (colloq.).

(See indisposition, reluctance.)

UNWISE

adverbs

incredibly; stubbornly; absurdly; habitually; naturally; obstinately; outrageously; palpably; obviously; cruelly; undeniably; flagrantly; fantastically; politically; terribly; utterly; absolutely; bitterly; disastrously; calamitously.

UNWOMANLY

adverbs

strangely; unbelievably; hoydenishly; terribly; lamentably; deplorably; surprisingly; utterly; dreadfully; ungraciously; curiously.

UNWORLDLY

adverbs

curiously; piously; peculiarly; wholly; indubitably; admirably; blessedly; happily; serenely; blandly; truly.

UNWORTHY

adverbs

entirely; deeply; utterly; undeniably; despicably; contemptibly; sadly; selfishly; lamentably; indisputably; peculiarly; particularly; censoriously; outrageously; bitterly.

UPBRAID (*v*)

adverbs

viciously; vindictively; brutally; obstreperously; laughingly; ferociously; unjustly; volubly; rigorously; paternally; hatefully; jealously.

(See chide, rebuke.)

UPHEAVAL

adjectives

volcanic; economic; religious; devastating; sensuous; business; fatal; passionate; violent; sudden; wild.

verbs

avert—; precipitate—; quash—; quell—; suppress—; —agitates; —arouses; — awakens; —characterizes; —convulses; — dashes; —demolishes; —discloses; —elevates; —jars; —jolts; —jounces; —levels; —prostrates; —razes; —reveals; —revolutionizes; —uncovers.

(See uprising, convulsion, revolution, strike.)

UPHOLD (v)

adverbs

staunchly; faithfully; patiently; patriotically; virtually; solemnly; fiercely; gallantly; extraordinarily; economically; politically; philosophically; metaphysically; nationally.

(See support, defend.)

UPRIGHT

adverbs

splendidly; reputably; admittedly; virtuously; admirably; sincerely; openly; unfailingly; conspicuously; estimably; honorably; boldly; undauntedly; firmly; stably.

UPRISING

adjectives

sudden; armed; courageous; seditious; concerted; marvelous; feared; wide-spread; national; growing .

verbs

annihilate—; blot out—; check—; defeat—; foment—; forestall—; incite—; inspire—; instigate—; provoke—; smash—; squelch —; stem—; subdue—; suppress—; swamp —; —breaks out; —peters out (colloq.); — seethes; —spreads; —violates.

(See upheaval, revolution, strike.)

UPROAR

adjectives

wild; everlasting; positive; stupendous; tremendous; furious; musical; ghastly; stultifying.

verbs

hush—; muffle—; mute—; quash—; quell—; silence—; stifle—; still—; subdue—; suppress—; —abates; —bewilders; —confuses; —deafens; —drowns out; —mounts; — pierces; —rends; —shatters; —splits; — startles; —subsides; —swells; —thunders.

(See clamor, disturbance, din, fracas, roar, rumble.)

UPROARIOUS

adverbs

boisterously; comically; foolishly; hilariously; clownishly; merrily; blithely; gaily; amusingly; divertingly; farcically; fantasti-

cally; inimitably; excitedly; hysterically; enthusiastically; jubilantly; exultantly; triumphantly; rampantly; irrepressibly; laughingly.

UPSET

adverbs

peculiarly; utterly; strangely; significantly; inconsolably; grievously; wearily; nervously; physically; mentally; cruelly; miserably; bitterly; oddly; curiously; amazingly; remarkably; mysteriously; unexpectedly; suddenly; inexplicably; unaccountably.

UPSET (v)

adverbs

ultimately; practically; physically; emotionally; incomprehensibly; cruelly; gravely.

(See otherthrow, overpower.)

URBAN

adverbs

smoothly; distinctly; self-consciously; insistantly; ridiculously; scarcely; absurdly; pseudo-; recently; ridiculously; earnestly.

URBANE

adverbs

pleasantly; courteously; unusually; markedly; conspicuously; agreeably; ingratiatingly; skilfully; smoothly; carefully; diplomatically; serenely; complaisantly; graciously; splendidly; elegantly; unfailingly; resolutely; imperturbably; quietly; tolerantly; indulgently.

URGE

adjectives

biological; evolutionary; irresistible; sudden; strong; deep-seated; universal; self-satisfying; demon-like; glandular; swarthy; creative.

verbs

awaken—; check—; choke back—; conquer —; counteract—; dull—; gratify—; quell—; resist—; restrain—; smother—; squelch—; stem—; stifle—; —impels; —overpowers; —overwhelms; —seizes; —swells; intensify —.

(See importunity, desire, impulse.)

URGE (v)

adverbs

diplomatically; passionately; secretly; blandly; disingenuously; plausibly; insolently; ineffectually; blatantly; eloquently; importunately; explicitly; enthusiastically; continually; persistently; ostentatiously; strenuously; powerfully; insidiously; traitorously; clamorously; mutely; irresistibly.

(See impel, incite.)

URGENT

adverbs

vitally; terribly; essentially; immediately; pressingly; personally; sorely; desperately; dreadfully; ominously; significantly; extremely; supremely; singularly; particularly; peculiarly; presumably; conspicuously; momentously; gravely; seriously.

URINE

verbs

acidify—; analyze—; cloud—; contaminate —; convey—; darken—; dilute—; discharge —; drain—; draw off—; egest—; eliminate —; emit—; evacuate—; excrete—; expel—; extract—; purge of—; retain—; saturate with—; secrete—; store—; tap—; vent—; void—; —accumulates; —colors; —concentrates; —emanates; —indicates; —passes; —pollutes; —reeks; —stinks.

(See liquid, odor, excretion.)

USAGE

adjectives

laudable; hereditary; abnormal; pedantic; traditional; general; effective; cruel; diplomatic; sinister; ill; grammatical; established; symphonic; immemorial; dietetic; rough; traditional; troglodytic; social; common.

verbs

accustom to—; approve—; condemn—; condone—; decry—; determine—; encourage—; foster—; govern—; marvel at—; practise—; prescribe—; promote—; rebuke—; recommend—; reproach—; reprove—; set forth —; subject to—; violate—; —infringes; —offends; —persists; —prevails; —sanctions; —violates.

(See procedure, use, custom, fashion, conventionality.)

USE

adjectives

refined; repeated; unsuspected; unspecified; excessive; experimental; inordinate; lavish; economical; amiable; creative; unsparing; assiduous; infrequent; habitual; vain; ignoble; senseless; consistent; occasional; farreaching; unholy; grave; prolonged; long-

continued; brutal; outspoken; diligent; narrow; respective; increased; decorative; metaphorical; unwonted; temporary; transcendent; domestic; particular; remarkable; infinite; ample; imperfect; growing; barren; congenial; valuable; fruitful; effective; uncaged; exclusive; imaginative; specific; instinctive; unreasoning; judicious; singular; delicate; efficient; dexterous; brilliant; constant; immediate; charitable; plentiful; deliberate; recurrent; varied (pl); concealed; common; accepted; mandatory; precocious; subordinate; unauthorized; industrious; ultimate; indiscriminate; immoderate; unnatural; voluntary; homespun.

verbs

accede to—; addict to—; advance—; advocate—; approve—; assure of—; authorize —; begrudge—; bid for—; concede—; condemn—; confer upon—; confine—to; consider—; counsel—; crave—; cultivate—; curb—; curtail—; debar—; debase—; decline—; decry—; deprecate—; design for—; develop—; disclaim—; discontinue—; discourage—; encourage—; enforce—; enjoin from—; exhort—; facilitate—; foster—; frown upon—; grant—; guide—; impair—; impede—; induce—; inspire—; involve—; master—; obviate—; offer—; outlive—; petition for—; pledge—; ponder—; press to—; prolong—; prompt—; propose—; provoke—; protest—; recommend—; request—; resort to—; restrain—; restrict—; ridicule —; suppress—; tender—; —dishonors; —entails; —facilitates; —habituates; —hardens; —insures.

(See service, need, employment, application.)

USE (v)

adverbs

indiscriminately; similarly; mercifully; promiscuously; universally; exclusively; extensively; lavishly; chiefly; conspicuously; intermittently; ostentatiously; effectively; officially; simultaneously; artfully; deftly; tenderly; ethically; magnanimously; economically; creatively; assiduously; consistently; diligently; domestically; congenially; singularly; judiciously; dexterously; ultimately; voluntarily.

(See employ, utilize.)

USEFUL

adverbs

conveniently; constantly; wholly; unusually;

particularly; specially; peculiarly; amazingly; wonderfully; admirably; curiously; frequently; remarkably; unexpectedly; politically; suddenly; actually; extremely; marvellously; socially; adaptably; invariably; dependably; downright.

USEFULNESS
adjectives
sheer; varied; desultory; partial; increased; high; conspicuous; extraordinary; practical; lively; prodigious; preeminent.

verbs
acclaim—; acquire—; appreciate—; augment—; belittle—; commend—; consider—; contemplate—; discern—; disclose—; hamper—; heighten—; impair—; judge—; lack —; laud—; measure—; minimize—; outlive —; recognize—; regard—; reveal—; weigh —; —ceases; —ebbs; —impresses.
(See value, advantage, benefit.)

USELESS
adverbs
eventually; definitely; utterly; absolutely; probably; finally; ultimately; absurdly; certainly; fantastically; ridiculously; possibly; undoubtedly; completely; pathetically; admittedly; unaccountably; manifestly; obviously.

USELESSNESS
verbs
decry—; deplore—; disclose—; fall into—; inveigh against—; overcome—; rebuke—; scoff at—; set forth—; —burdens; —irks; —irritates; —oppresses; —riles (colloq.); —stigmatizes; —vexes; —weighs upon.
(See futility, waste.)

USHER (*v*)
adverbs
hospitably; gallantly; politely; formally; habitually; professionally.
(See escort, introduce.)

USUAL
adverbs
altogether; scarcely; quite; absolutely; too; rather; admittedly.

USURP (*v*)
adverbs
treacherously; violently; murderously; dictatorially; tyrannically; illegally; sternly; vigorously; politically; arbitrarily.
(See seize, take.)

UTENSIL
adjectives
washing; primitive; cooking; valuable; practical.

verbs
blacken—; cleanse—; discard—; edge—; employ—; encumber—; equip with—s; exhibit—; fashion—; grind—; pilfer—; plate —; polish—; renew—; rinse—; scour—; scrape—; sharpen—; soak—; —enables; — facilitates.
(See instrument, knife, fork, cup, kettle, tool.)

UTILITARIAN
adverbs
handsomely; truly; altogether; sordidly; plainly; entirely; possibly; conveniently; admittedly; warrantably; sensibly; obviously; distinctly.

UTILITY
(*general*)
adjectives
respectable; universal; industrial; misconceived; practical; social; ultimate; heartless; essential; vulgar; definite; wide; obvious.

UTILITY
(*public utility*)
verbs
cater to—; charge—with; dance attendance to—; enrich—; govern—; head—; inveigh against—; investigate—; legislate against —; regulate—; tax—; —s amass; —bribes; —s "crack"; —s crack up (colloq.); —s facilitate; —s function; —s grind; —s lobby; —s perform; —s profit; —s rule; — serves; —s subserve; —tyrannizes.
(See power, company.)

UTILIZE (*v*)
adverbs
economically; effectively; politically; strategically; heartlessly; obviously; essentially; prodigiously; potently.
(See use, employ.)

UTOPIA
adjectives
mechanistic; economic; incorrigible; long-awaited; planned.

verbs
abide in—; cherish—; contrive—; depict—;

desert—; desire—; dream of—; dwell in—; fancy—; forsake—; gain—; hail—; imagine—; inspire—; picture—; portray—; predict—; proclaim—; promise—; quit—; relinquish—; renounce—; reside in—; strive for—; struggle for—.

(See heaven, perfection, ideal.)

UTOPIAN
adverbs
brightly; cheerfully; desirably; airily; illusively; promisingly; elusively; roseately; romantically; fancifully; phantasmally; hopefully; optimistically; whimsically; seriously; boldly; fallaciously; fantastically; notionally; chimerically; ingeniously.

UTTER (*v*)
adverbs
drolly; involuntarily; tremulously; decisively; articulately; prophetically; disparagingly; foolishly; coaxingly; mechanically; inarticulately; impassionately; lyrically; incisively; exquisitely; indiscriminately; voluntarily; specifically; delicately; deliberately.

(See speak, say.)

UTTERANCE
adjectives
bare; mordant; effective; unblushing; rapid; impassioned; mere; audible; rhythmical; graphic; broken; ill-considered; discouraging; homogeneous; full; characteristic; rending; death-defying; articulate; private; prophetic; premature; lyrical; exquisite; lofty; historic; incisive; noble; perfect; calm; lively; spontaneous; loving; imperfect; unheard; monotonous; mastered; public; hearty; numberless (pl); recent; glowing; rapid; fiery; supreme; impressive; simulated; intimate; recorded; luminous; harmonized; caustic; practical; injudicious; brute; spasmodic; simple; indistinct; expansive; vivid; roseate; important; grave; reasonable; powerful; weighty; precise.

verbs
acclaim—; clarify—; clothe—; condense—; deprecate—; magnify—; muffle—; mumble —; mute—; mutter—; rue—; silence—; smother—; stifle—; still—; voice—; weigh —; —astounds; —electrifies; —irks; —perplexes; —rings out; —sears; —shocks; —startles; —stuns.

(See exclamation, drawl, expression, statement.)

UXORIOUS
adverbs
noticeably; absurdly; notoriously; openly; absurdly; ridiculously; conspicuously; foolishly; outlandishly; obviously; ludicrously.

V

adjectives

dull; prospective; stony; rectangular; soundless; blank; utter; absolute; astounding; complete.

VACANT

adverbs

apparently; recently; obviously; coldly; mysteriously; forbiddingly; dismally; unexpectedly; gloriously; opportunely; actually; presumably; allegedly; seldom; happily; fortunately; unfortunately; unprofitably; gloomily; blankly; seasonally; temporarily; frequently.

VACATION

adjectives

memorable; peaceful; unspoiled; thorough; complete; thrilling; never-to-be-forgotten; carefree; summer; inclusive; unique; pictorial; glorious; frequent (pl); restful; giddy; wild; joyous; longed-for; wonderful.

verbs

advise—; conclude—; counsel—; crave—; curtail—; depart on—; extend—; grant—; loll on—; lounge on—; merit—; necessitate —; prolong—; protract—; recommend—; reward with—; terminate—; warrant—; yearn for—; —distracts; —diverts; —reanimates; —refreshes; —relaxes; —renews; —restores; —unbends; —vivifies; —wanes.

(See recess, rest, respite.)

VACATION (v)

adverbs

luxuriously; jovially; sumptuously; fraternally; memorably; peacefully; thrillingly; uniquely; gloriously; giddily; joyously; exquisitely.

(See refresh, travel.)

VACCINATION

verbs

advise—; compel—; employ—; prescribe—; procure—; submit to—; undergo—; —assures; —benefits; —discommodes; —erases; —erupts; —immunizes; —inflames; —insures; —modifies; —safeguards; —scars; —stamps out.

(See operation, serum.)

VACCINE

verbs

assimilate—; diffuse—; dispense; —glycerinate—; inject—; inoculate with—; insert —; introduce—; prepare—; prescribe—; sensitize—; utilize—; —builds up; —exempts; —immunizes; —induces; —inflames; —insures; —irritates; —modifies; —protects; —resists; —safeguards; —stimulates.

VACILLATE (v)

adverbs

irresolutely; weakly; pusillanimously; irrationally; indecisively; desultorily; improvidently.

(See sway, waver.)

VACILLATING

adverbs

vexatiously; hopelessly; indecisively; wantonly; intolerably; foolishly; incorrigibly; habitually; strangely; absurdly; mindlessly; incurably; naturally; inherently; irresolutely; deplorably; unfortunately; sluggishly; helplessly; lamentably; feebly; witlessly; remarkably; inordinately; unreasonably; unbearably; disgustingly.

VACUOUS

adverbs

deplorably; wantonly; sluggishly; lamentably; irremediably; irrecoverably; helplessly; pitiably; strangely; mysteriously; unaccountably; suddenly; unintelligibly; irresponsibly; evidently; manifestly; curiously; grotesquely; miserably; wretchedly.

VACUUM

adjectives

luminous; sterile; dreary; absolute.

verbs

achieve—; create—; employ—; exhaust to —; fill—; induce—; obtain—; reduce to—; require—; seal—; utilize—; valve—; —fails; —retains; —preserves.

VAGABOND

adjectives

incorrigible; royal; nondescript; seedy; precious; wandering; romantic; clever-appearing; lazy; roaming; alluring.

adverbs

delightfully; whimsically; foolishly; notionally; irresponsibly; crazily; elfishly; irrepressibly; merrily; blithely; wholesomely; gaily; happily; uncontrollably; wittily; affably; genially.

adverbs

awkwardly; fantastically; inordinately; offensively; contemptibly; amusingly; artlessly; morbidly; prodigiously; complacently; colossally; tediously.

VAGARIES

adjectives

superstitious; metaphysical; strange; queer; unusual; wild.

VAINGLORIOUS

adverbs

bombastically; egregiously; incredibly; disgustingly; curiously; unreasonably; absurdly; insanely; harmlessly; ridiculously; ludicrously; laughably; sadly; extremely; manifestly; blindly; pompously; fantastically; preposterously; singularly.

VAGINA

verbs

abscess—; dilate—; distend—; drain—; examine—; explore—; incise—; infect—; inflame—; inseminate—; insert into—; invade—; irritate—; lacerate—; line—; obstruct—; occlude—; plug—; probe—; suppurate—; syringe—; —discharges; —emits.

VALE

adjectives

hopeless; melancholy; pleasant; fast-filling; sequestered; horrid; well-watered; hollow; simmering; shadowy; sunny; dimpling; dimmer; grassy; tuneful; gloomy; lonely; wondrous; intervening; dewy; spicy; luxuriant; smooth; sinuous; dreary; long; lit; deep.

VAGRANT

adjectives

scattered (pl); undeveloped; apprehended; arrested.

verbs

(See valley, dale.)

adverbs

blithely; gaily; jauntily; happily; carelessly; irresponsibly; suspiciously; joyously; alertly; profitably; enviably; inconveniently; selfishly; luxuriously; habitually; pleasantly; nervously; furtively; stealthily; merrily; nonchalantly; delightfully; wretchedly; uncertainly; miserably; lonesomely; preferably; hazardously; independently; innocently; harmlessly.

VALEDICTORY

adverbs

sadly; seriously; appraisingly; analytically; admonitory; complimentarily; apparently; manifestly; obviously; warningly; critically; bitterly; affectionately; fondly; touchingly; affectingly; conventionally; comprehensively.

VAGUE

adverbs

intentionally; perplexingly; embarrassingly; obscurely; dimly; stupidly; precariously; ambiguously; unintelligibly; distressingly; mysteriously; unwisely; uncertainly; casually; airily; delusively; evasively; subtly; inconclusively; darkly; abstrusely; impenetrably; remotely; unwarrantably; foolishly; speciously; misleadingly; tenuously; terribly; nonsensically; senselessly; completely; perilously; fearfully; alarmingly; ominously; significantly; fantastically; needlessly; unreliably.

VALET

adjectives

inestimable; obsequious; bowing; quiet; effective; artful; deft; efficient; silk-hosed.

VALIANT

adverbs

resolutely; steadily; unfalteringly; boldly; admirably; wonderfully; marvellously; particularly; amazingly; gloriously; notably; surpassingly; incomparably; immeasurably; indescribably; intrepidly; superhumanly; superbly; splendidly; magnificently; unforgettably; fearlessly; supremely.

VAGUENESS

adjectives

mysterious; comprehensible; voluptuous; studied; calculated; intentional.

VALID

adverbs

reasonably; undoubtedly; assuredly; legally; financially; manifestly; obviously; evidently; reputably; presumably; probably; unquestionably; altogether; substantially; effectively; curiously; definitely.

VALIDITY

adjectives
incontestable; legal; objective; eternal; supreme; scientific; independent; demonstrated; definite.

verbs
analyze—; attack—; avow—; challenge—; defend—; destroy—; discuss—; dispute—; emphasize—; endanger—; exhibit—; honor —; imperil—; impugn—; interfere with—; jeopardize—; maintain—; preserve—; question—; respect—; stamp with—; sustain—; test—; view—; —signifies; —stands.
(See value, position.)

VALLEY

adjectives
fantastic; stretching; fertile; overshadowed; precipitous; placid; solitary; sun-baked; pleasant; delectable; tributary; lofty; rugged; canyon-like; seductive; miserable; heated; copse-clad; picturesque; fabled; serene; blooming; fog-obscured; profound; irregular; branching; beautiful; breathless; solitary; pastoral; fruitful; wooded; flowering; watered; lovely; nest-like; desolate; immense; widening; conspicuous; shallow; redolent; grassy; oblivious; receding; haystack-dotted; verdant; cozy; little; terrible; formless; tiny; untenable; hill-beholden; flat-bottomed; dizzy; lonely; mountain; dusky; southern; imperial; winding; viewless; pathless.

verbs
command—; dash to—; devastate—; discern —; dot—; dwell in—; fill—; haunt—; inhabit—; overrun—; overspread—; penetrate —; people—; permeate—; pervade—; revisit—; ring through—; settle in—; view—; —awakes; —bestirs; —blossoms; —bristles; —dozes; —endures; —glistens; —inspires; —sleeps; —snuggles; —thickens; —waxes; —winds.
(See plain, dale, dell.)

VALOR

adjectives
deliberated; heroic; exceeding; unquestioned; unaffected; loyal; naked; idealized; sheer; free; honorable; bloody; dormouse; personal; distinguished; approved; deliber-

ate; self-respecting; desperate; redoubled; unsurpassed; truculent; mock; reverend; true; frantic; indomitable; patient; pristine; individual; splendid.

verbs
awaken—; call forth—; confirm—; consecrate—; counterfeit—; dedicate to—; discard—; dispense with—; display—; endow with—; gape at—; herald—; impeach—; impugn—; marvel at—; practise—; proclaim—; report—; reward—; tax—; —beggars description; —bewilders; —confounds; —dazzles; —figures; —vanishes.
(See courage, heroism, morale.)

VALOROUS

adverbs
highly; wonderfully; intrepidly; amazingly; commendably; unusually; uncommonly; admirably; tremendously; brilliantly; resolutely; stubbornly; incredibly; invincibly; remarkably.

VALUABLE

adverbs
curiously; exceptionably; exceptionally; extremely; marvellously; seriously; magnificently; incredibly; incalculably; immeasurably; unbelievably; significantly; wonderfully; oddly; unexpectedly; rarely; immensely; enormously; suddenly; immediately; absurdly; fabulously; extraordinarily.

VALUATION

adjectives
false; mental; cordial; fair; common; altered; assessed; improper; reduced.

VALUE

adjectives
historical; rental; thrilling; artistic; independent; priceless; desirable; anticipatory; investment; inestimable; speculative; apologetic; determining; relative; unjust; intrinsic; unescapable; additional; material; positive; restorative; fictitious; sacred; tremendous; incalculable; opposite; symbolic; demonstrated; excellent; amazing; therapeutic; important; outstanding; fundamental; remarkable; heating; exchange; retail; sheer; energy-yielding; sound; uniform; decorative; grand; verified; memorable; prime; essential; food; big; extraordinary; aesthetic; compensating; monetary; unappreciable; local; caloric; asserted; intellectual; independent; prodigious; aggregate; annual;

potential; comparative; vitamin; immeasurable; psychological; paper; survival; practical; marvelous; rare; half-mystical; chief; extra; cultural; reasonable; literary; scientific; full; proper; sensational; nominal; numerical; psychopathic; ultimate; property; fallacious; thrifty; fancy; representative; mere; sentimental; emotional; educational; uncertain; needful; economic; nutritional; permanent; enormous; corresponding; distinct; immense; determinate; splendid; exciting; enduring; customary; specific; beneficial; affective; expressive; unprecedented; conducive; consequent; ethical; critical; diagnostic; refrigerating; social; sacred; unexpected; varying; unrivaled; cherished; additive; face; fluctuating; surprise; moral; extrinsic; compelling; unbelievable; irresistible; exceptional; unbeatable; good; true; unmatchable; surpassed; supreme; entire; lasting; questionable; documentary; exquisite; cash; insulation; top; conspicuous; negotiable; rachitic; fabulous; honest; eye; experimental; brighter; market; dollar; unusual; quality; heart-warming; transcendental; crowning; genuine; scarcity; specified; delusive; peculiar.

verbs

abuse—; advance—; advertise—; analyze —; appraise—; ascertain—; ascribe—to; assess—; attach—to; atribute—to; audit—; authenticate—; belittle—; bolster—; boast —; broadcast—; calculate—; certify—; cite —; comprehend—; compute—; contribute—; debase—; declare—; deflate—; demonstrate —; depreciate—; depress—; determine—; detract from—; dilute—; discount—; dispute—; distort—; dwell upon—; emasculate —; enhance—; establish—; estimate—; exploit—; fathom—; grasp—; impair—; intensify—; judge—; maintain—; misjudge—; negate—; overestimate—; predetermine—; preserve—; proclaim—; rate—; readjust—; reckon—; recognize—; repudiate—; salvage —; sense—; share—; stress—; substantiate —; tender—; testify to—; verify—; vindicate—; weigh—; yield—; —dawns upon; —diminishes; —enriches; —fluctuates; — —hurtles; —inheres; —leaps; —melts away; —mounts; —shrivels; —soars.

(See esteem, usefulness, worth, significance, importance.)

VALUE (v)

adverbs

inordinately; adequately; artistically; his-

torically; pricelessly; sacredly; symbolically; extraordinarily; aesthetically; locally; potentially; immeasurably; psychologically; scientifically; emotionally; economically; politically; ethically; critically; morally; transcendentally; genuinely.

(See estimate, prize.)

VANDAL

adjectives

arrogant; literary; lawless.

VANISH (v)

adverbs

ultimately; mysteriously; utterly; simultaneously; noiselessly; speedily; swiftly; wholly; magically; completely.

(See disappear.)

VANISHING

adverbs

mysteriously; inconsiderately; strangely; inconveniently; magically; outlandishly; deliberately; curiously; strangely; suddenly; unaccountably; mischievously; fantastically; impishly; selfishly.

VANITY

adjectives

flattering; awkward; fantastic; soothed; foolish; petty; violent; generous; roused; racial; inordinate; mundane; unpunctured; courageous; offensive; contemptible; amusing; ingenuous; artless; punctured; insatiable; reawakened; earthly; morbid; literary; innocent; wounded; motherly; restless; complacent; professed; chargeable; prodigious; colossal; selfish; sanguine; ingenious; offended; sheer; masculine; outworn; trampled; tedious; unconscious; ill-bred.

verbs

appease—; betray—; cater to—; conceal—; counteract—; down—; eradicate—; exhibit —; gratify—; humble—; indulge—; irritate —; loathe—; measure—; mollify—; pander to—; prick—; puncture—; ridicule—; ruffle —; satirize—; tickle—; yield to—; —angers; —cloys; —despoils; —diminishes; — functions; —nauseates; —operates; —repulses; —singes; —stirs.

(See egotism, conceit, pedantry, futility.)

VAPID

adverbs

disappointingly; disagreeably; hopelessly; unbelievably; utterly; strangely; unexpectedly; hopelessly; monotonously; uninterestingly; curiously; horribly.

VAPOR

adjectives
oracular; sulphurous; obscuring; aqueous; portentous; black; deathly; foul; gross; swimming; sealike; miasmatic; sunless; steaming; impalpable; misty; sympathetic; poisonous; smoke; soothing; relieving; oracular; radiant; noxious; agitated; rent; gaseous; invisible; stifling; gloomy; midnight; wintry; milky; hideous; imponderable; unctuous; quivering; dim; noontide; suffocating; temperate; corrosive; mercury; ghostly; pale; murky; noxious; alcoholic; quick; evil; diaphanous; motionless.

verbs
diffuse—; distill—; emit—; exhale—; free —; inhale—; liquefy—; —arises; —asphyxiates; bedims, —befogs, —clouds; —condenses; —eddies; —explodes; —floats; — fumes; —hovers over; —infiltrates; —melts; —obscures; —offends; —permeates; — reeks; —rises; —shrouds; —smothers; — vanishes; —veils.
(See haze, fog, fume, mist, moisture.)

VAPOROUS

adverbs
curiously; strangely; terribly; confusingly; alarmingly; insecurely; mysteriously; intensely; foggily; mistily; steamily; bewilderingly; unhealthfully; dankly; hotly; suffocatingly; mustily.

VARIABLE

adverbs
vexatiously; mysteriously; irritatingly; unpredictably; strangely; unreasonably; mischievously; absurdly; inexplicably; unwarrantably; unstably; unreliably; provokingly; remarkably; unaccountably; intensely; inconveniently; uncomfortably; uselessly; unnecessarily.

VARIANCE

adjectives
internal; usual; perpetual; wide; noticeable.

VARIATION

adjectives
graceful; periodic; momentary; secular; diurnal; visible; sure; divers (pl); incessant; discreet; seasonal; occasional; skillful; fantastic; pyro-technical; erratic; verbal; slight; injurious; pleasing; distracting; endless; beneficial; numerous (pl); dignified; appreciable; perpetual; transient; emotional.

verbs
account for—; afford—; ascertain—; augment—; calculate—; check—; condone—; correct—; countenance—; decry—; determine—; discern—; disclose—; discount—; dispel—; evolve—; record—; register—; result in—; welcome—; —arises; —deviates; —modifies; —modulates; —occurs.
(See difference, discrepancy, deviation, change, alteration, modification.)

VARIEGATED

adverbs
beautifully; iridescently; colorfully; opalescently; constantly; unpredictably; remarkably; amazingly; curiously; unusually; mysteriously; handsomely.

VARIETY

adjectives
extraordinary; unmotived; improved; dominant; endless; interesting; considerable; immense; amazing; enchanting; distinct; natural; delicious; continental; boundless; manifold (pl); impressive; multiform (pl); infinite; internal; cultivated; epileptic; sportive; splendid; tubular; crafty; graceful; multifarious (pl); bewildering; coarse; picturesque; aquatic; stout; rich; external; embarrassing; tumultuous; stubborn; inordinate; fresh; dull; conceivable; hideous; gorgeous; agreeable; clinging; remarkable; accurate; distinct; limited; wide; colorful.

verbs
achieve—; afford—; crave—; demand—; display—; distinguish by—; encourage—; foster—; indulge in—; infuse—; inspire—; lack—; offer—; procure—; value—; want —; yield—; —animates; —dazes; —diversifies; —diverts; —enlivens; —entertains; — seasons; —spices.
(See collection, change, violation.)

VARLET

adjectives
wicked; abominable; graceless; crimson; incontinent; naughty.

VARNISH (v)

adverbs
sickly; sleekly; luxuriously; thickly; lustrously; smoothly.
(See polish, shine.)

VARY (v)

adverbs

widely; radically; infinitely; indefinitely; heterogeneously; periodically; incessantly; bewilderingly; distinctly.

(See charge, modify.)

VASE

adjectives

exquisite; ponderous; cloisonne; priceless; broken; patched; inimitable.

VASSAL

adjectives

rebellious; gallant; skillful; tributary; belligerent; dreaded; duteous; humble; obsequious.

VASSALAGE

adjectives

commercial; hereditary; economic; complete; effectual.

VAST

adjectives

populous; current; fathomless; boundless; unimagined.

adverbs

enormously; mysteriously; stupendously; impossibly; overwhelmingly; strangely; colossally; prodigiously; astonishingly; marvellously; extraordinarily; miraculously.

VASTNESS

adjectives

tangled; mysterious; encircling; physical; unending.

verbs

bridge—; comprehend—; explore—; measure—; scale—; scan—; span—; survey—; —affords; —allows; —astounds; —awes; —bewilders; —bulks large; —cows; —embraces; —enraptures; —extends; —fascinates; —impresses; —inspires; —intrigues; —looms; —overawes; —overwhelms; —staggers; —stuns; —transcends.

(See spaciousness, magnitude, size.)

VAT

verbs

age in—; char—; contaminate—; deplete—; drain—; ferment in—; immerse in—; label

—; plunge into—; replenish—; store in—; submerge in—; tap—; —diffuses; —emits; —preserves; —reeks.

(See kettle, tub.)

VAULT

adjectives

choked-up; adjoining; gloomy; intersecting; unribbed; majestic; lurid; heavenly; deep; midnight; opaque; celestial; noxious; sinuous; fathomless; wintry; starry; measurable; lofty; inexhaustible; resounding; dungeon-like; imbowered; azure; ebon; dankish; flaming; funereal.

verbs

amass in—; consign to—; defile—; deposit in—; desecrate—; engrave on—; entomb in —; filch from—; haunt—; inscribe on—; inter in—; invade—; pillage—; plunder—; repose in—; seal—; store in—; stow in—; —depresses; —honors; —insures; —muffles; —receives; —reeks; —resounds; —safeguards.

(See cellar, tomb, box.)

VAULT (v)

adverbs

agilely; skillfully; precipitately; rashly; vigorously; lightly; thrillingly.

(See jump, spring.)

VAULTED

adverbs

ethereally; beautifully; immensely; magnificently; splendidly; brilliantly; safely; closely; tightly; securely.

VAUNT

adjectives

obligatory; vainglorious; ostentatious; nauseating.

VAUNT (v)

adverbs

arrogantly; unduly; obstreperously; vaingloriously; ostentatiously; belligerently; verbally.

(See boast, extol.)

VAUNTING

adjectives

compulsory; idle; boastful.

VEGETABLES

adjectives

frozen; thriving; indigenous; succulent; unpalatable; flabby; shade-living; out-of-season; fresh; raw; green.

verbs
bed out—; broil—; consume—; cultivate—; delve among—; fertilize—; hawk—; husband—; label—; market—; partake of—; pluck—; nurse—; prize—; purvey—; reap —; —relish—; savor—; sow—; sprout—; steam—; transplant—.
(See peanut, plant, fruit, food, peas, etc.)

VEGETATION

adjectives
spontaneous; riotous; luxuriant; decaying; exuberant; tropical; treacherous; aboreal; delicate; objectionable; reeking; thriving; velvet; noxious; spiteful; repulsive; slumbering; coarse; variegated; vigorous.

verbs
tame—; —bourgeons; —buds; —bursts forth; —chokes; —curtains; —eclipses; — flourishes; —flowers; —germinates; — mantles; —obscures; —overruns; —overspreads; —pullulates; —screens; —shades; —shadows; —shoots up; —smothers; — sprouts; —strangles; —thickens; —veils.
(See vegetables.)

VEHEMENCE

adjectives
noisy; unaccountable; petitionary; earnest; suppressed; essential; passionate; excessive; sudden; lively; hasty; wild; corresponding; equal.

VEHEMENT

adverbs
unnecessarily; absurdly; laughably; earnestly; foolishly; wildly; loudly; enthusiastically; zealously; ridiculously; gravely; seriously; passionately; forcibly; energetically; pleadingly; fanatically; oddly; singularly; dogmatically; unwisely; vexatiously.

VEHICLE

adjectives
muddled; passing; appropriate; gleaming; favored; poor; groaning; abused; motor; wind-driven; fluid; mechanical; propelled; nominal; crazy; festive; lumbering; sole; back-country; humble; mimic; commonplace; up-to-date; moldering.

verbs
accelerate—; brake—; draw—; fuel—; guide—; impair—; lubricate—; park—; pilot—; —bears; —conveys; —jars; —jolts; —jounces; —rattles; —roars by; —trundles; —whizzes by.
(See cart, conveyance, carriage, chariot, truck.)

VEIL

adjectives
emerald; snowy; inmost; pitchy; misty; dusky; leafy; gloomy; intervening; star-studded; lucid; ugly; solemnizing; gauzy; impenetrable; twilight; obligatory; tangled; mystic; turbid; close-spun; diaphanous; hieroglyphic; sinuous; overhanging; filmy; trembling; fluttering; raw; golden-tissued; borrowed; adamantine; amethystine; fleecy; fearful; maiden.

verbs
bare—; bedeck with—; cast off—; discard —; dispel—; divest of—; doff—; don—; drape—over; draw—; envelop in—; maintain—; penetrate—; rend—; suspend—over; withdraw—; —beguiles; —billows behind; —conceals; —curtains; —deceives; —deludes; —dims; —disguises; —eclipses; — mantles; —muffles; —obstructs; —obscures; —screens; —shades; —shadows.
(See mask, cloak, disguise, fabric, cloth.)

VEIL (v)

adverbs
curiously; unconsciously; impenetrably; skillfully; gloomily; mystically; diaphanously.
(See conceal, hide.)

VEILED

adverbs
beautifully; closely; mysteriously; heavily; luminously; colorfully; provocatively; secretly; furtively; remarkably; marvellously; splendidly; lightly; thinly; deeply; mystically; symbolically; resolutely; exotically.

VEINS

adjectives
hepatic; freezing; moralizing; throbbing; masterful; aging; scorching; rapid; sap-transmitting; sacred; flushed; sanguine; philosophical; prevalent; cloven; idealistic; empty; azure; agreeable; languid; strenuous; whimsical; merry; swollen; fluent; purple-pulsing; translucent; humorous; dra-

matic; varicose; heroic; melodic; equivocating; contaminated; superstitious; prominent; benignant; enamored; prolific; satirical; sluggish; indurated; furtive; rich; laboring; reminiscent; didactic.

verbs
abscess—; attack—; block—; calcify—; compress—; constrict—; dilate—; disperse through—; distend—; drain—; inflame—; inject into—; issue from—; ligature—; occlude—; puncture—; stir in—; tap—; traverse—; trickle through—; —anastomose; —atrophy; —branch off; —clot; —convey; —degenerate; —harden; —proliferate; —pulsate; —thicken; —ulcerate.
(See blood-vessel, artery.)

VELOCITY
adjectives
high; angular; extraneous; extravagant; accentuated; unrelaxed; inconceivable; ascertained; elliptic; linear; standard; undetermined.

verbs
accelerate—; ascertain—; attain—; check—; determine—; diminish—; gain—; heighten —; measure—; stablize—; —abates; —declines; —dwindles; —ebbs; —endangers; —fluctuates; —subsides; —vacillates; —wanes.
(See momentum, speed.)

VELVET
adjectives
prodigious; slashed; fawn-tinted; transparent; smooth; ruffled; regal; wrinkled; flattering.

verbs
array in—; attire in—; bask on—; crumple —; divest of—; garb in—; lounge in—; ruffle—; rumple—; swathe in—; upholster in—; —adds; —colors; —enhances; —enriches; —signifies; —symbolizes.
(See linen, silk.)

VENDIBLE
adverbs
readily; conveniently; easily; profitably; remarkably; extremely; universally; marvellously; incredibly.

VENERABLE
adverbs
ripely; reputably; extraordinarily; signally; conspicuously; notoriously; estimably; distinctly; nobly; justly; illustriously; virtuously; splendidly; eminently.

VENERATE (v)
adverbs
highly; deeply; religiously; superstitiously; profoundly; obsequiously; humbly; abjectly.
(See respect, esteem.)

VENERATION
adjectives
superstitious; unsympathetic; striking; partial; profound; defective; high; special; deep; remarkable.

VENGEANCE
adjectives
savage; hoarded; gratified; eternal; heroic; bloody; dark; spiteful; cowardly; exemplary; political; vulgar; dastardly; brooding; ample; summary; popular; kindred; pleasing; fiery; worthy; wreakful; satisfied; instant; indiscriminate; gloomy; legal; ripened.

verbs
achieve—; bear—; claim—; clamor for—; conspire—; crave—; demand—; enact—; exact—; forego—; pledge—; press for—; promise—; pursue—; rain—on; seek—; swear—; vow—; wreak—; yield—; —overtakes.
(See revenge, retribution.)

VENGEFUL
adverbs
openly; notoriously; spitefully; murderously; naturally; temperamentally; remarkably; cruelly; bitterly; unrestrainedly; dangerously; secretly; alarmingly; fanatically; wickedly; unforgivingly; reprehensibly; curiously; outrageously; furtively; stealthily; savagely.

VENOM
adjectives
subtle; palsying; spider; lasting; rank.

verbs
anoint with—; antidote—; assimilate—; extract—; immunize to—; infuse—; inject—; neutralize—; resist—; steep in—; succumb to—; suck up—; weaken—; —courses through; —deadens; —overcomes; —paralyzes; —rankles; —seeps through; —stuns.
(See poison, toxin.)

VENOMOUS

adverbs

notoriously; incredibly; hatefully; unfortunately; incurably; fatally; mortally; naturally; terribly; manifestly; horribly; fearfully; conspicuously; outrageously; reprehensibly; uncommonly; highly; intensely.

VENTILATE (v)

adverbs

adequately; thoroughly; defectively; healthfully; beneficially; automatically.

VENTILATION

adjectives

controlled; defective; adequate; automatic; necessary; healthful.

verbs

accomplish—; adjust—; afford—; allow—; facilitate—; furnish—; impair—; lack—; offer—; prescribe—; prevent—; promote ; require—; stabilize—; starve for—; systematize—; want—; —reanimates; —refreshes; —restores; —revivifies.

(See breathing, respiration.)

VENTURE

adjectives

advantageous; revolutionary; maiden; disillusioning; successful; uncertain; amateur; scientific; short-lived; private; matrimonial; speculative; prodigious; fruitful; maritime; succeeding; money-making; biographical; profitable.

verbs

abandon—; acclaim—; back—; contemplate —; decry—; defeat—; denounce—; disclose —; embark on—; encourage—; endanger—; eye—; finance—; forsake—; further—; gamble on—; imperil—; insure—; menace —; promote—; pursue—; relinquish—; threaten—; undertake—; stake on—; withdraw from—; —crashes; —entails; —flourishes; —tempts; —thrives.

(See effort, enterprise, project, undertaking.)

VENTURE (v)

adverbs

buoyantly; soothingly; boldly; timidly; hazardously; trustfully; wistfully; occasionally; cautiously; oracularly; imperiously; openly; solemnly; daringly; rashly; madly; sullenly;

complacently; tactfully; timorously; fruitlessly; profitably.

(See dare, risk.)

VENTURESOME

adverbs

distressingly; boyishly; joyously; fantastically; disturbingly; unaccountably; alarmingly; colossally; terribly; dramatically; crazily; spectacularly; notoriously; strangely; singularly; amazingly; recklessly; incredibly; foolishly; boldly; bravely; audaciously; romantically; vicariously; courageously; unnecessarily; disconcertingly; ostentatiously; showily; daringly.

VERACIOUS

adverbs

naturally; habitually; dependably; utterly; absolutely; reliably; strictly; wholly; courageously; boldly; defiantly.

VERACITY

adjectives

scrupulous; attested; unalloyed; simple; inflexible; proved; innate.

verbs

affirm—; assure of—; authenticate—; confirm—; contravene—; demand—; discipline to—; dispute—; doubt—; gainsay—; impugn —; insure of—; maintain—; profess—; question—; reassert—; rebut—; refute—; regard—; repudiate—; swear to—; trust—; vow to—.

(See honesty, truth, frankness.)

VERANDA

adjectives

spreading; glass-enclosed; canvas-covered; sunken; shady; cool.

VERB

verbs

abuse—; accentuate—; adorn with—; avoid —; bandy—s; bristle with—; classify—; choose—; coin—; condense—; conjugate—; corrupt—; cull—s; decide on—; dedicate —; discard—; dispense with—; elect—; eliminate—; employ—; encounter—; eschew —; espouse—s; examine—s; exclude—s; explore—; fancy—; fix upon—; gasp at—; gather—; go in quest of—; grind out—s; identify—; indulge in—; inspire—; intone—; lavish—; manipulate—; marvel at—; misemploy—; modify—; overwork—; pluck—; prefer—; probe—; reel off—s; reject—; repudiate—s; sanction—; search for—; scrutinize—; seek—; select—; shun—; tabulate —s; thirst for—; —accomplishes; —achieves; —alludes to; —animates; —appeals; —asserts; —bites; —caps; —carries out; —colors; —compels; —complements; —completes; —connotes; —consummates; —controls; —conveys; —crowns; —crystallizes; —declares; —defines; —delineates; —depicts; —derives from; —denotes; —distorts; —drives home; —effects; —energizes; —enlivens; —enriches; —exaggerates; —expresses; —frolics; —fulfills; —gyrates; —impels; —implies; —imports; —improves; —indicates; —informs; —interprets; —invigorates; —kindles; —maintains; —moves; —overshadows; —penetrates; —perfects; —performs; —s plunge into; —portrays; —predicates; —provokes; —renders complete; —responds; —rounds out; —rouses; —seals; —s seethe with; —signifies; —s spring into; —states; —stimulates; —strengthens; —suggests; —supplies action; —swings into action; —urges; —wages; analyzes—; —purports.

VERBOSE

adverbs
incurably; tiresomely; inveterately; monotonously; wearisomely; awkwardly; unexpectedly; grossly; crassly; ineptly; clumsily; childishly; garrulously; fulsomely; terribly; extravagantly; unacceptably; unfortunately.

VERDANT

adverbs
delightfully; luxuriantly; invitingly; alluringly; lushly; properly; unexpectedly; gratifyingly; brilliantly; remarkably; unusually; beautifully.

VERDICT

adjectives
lawful; unanimous; manic-depressive; inevitable; consistent; emphatic; intelligent; differing; favorable; adverse; contrary; just; preposterous; fair; inexplicable.

verbs
affect—; appeal—; arrive at—; bias—; carry—; cast—; clarify—; confirm—; contest—; dally with—; deliver—; denounce—; determine—; disclose—; dispute—; elicit—; enter—; evolve—; influence—; justify—; maintain—; ponder—; prejudice—; present —; pronounce—; propound—; question—; render—; return—; reverse—; secure—;

sustain—; venture—; verify—; voice—; warrant—; —awards; —dooms; —involves; —misjudges; —startles.
(See judgment, award, finding, decision.)

VERDURE

adjectives
lush; perpetual; profuse; deepening; rank; gloomy; restful; living; perennial; vigorous; tropical; virgin; black; complex; endless; vivid; close-cropped; unchanging.

verbs
clothe in—; prune—; reflect—; thin out—; trim—; —blankets; —cloaks; —colors; —curtains; —flourishes; —freshens; —mantles; —obscures; —overspreads; —screens; —shades; —smothers; —veils.
(See grass, vegetation.)

VERGE

adjectives
utmost; inclusive; uppermost; farthest; beetling; extreme; outward.

verbs
achieve—; ascend to—; approach—; attain —; skirt—; steer to—; tread on—; —borders; —bounds; —encloses.
(See boundary, edge.)

VERIFICATION

adjectives
official; decisive; experimental; attempted.

VERIFY (v)

adverbs
unaccountably; accurately; substantially; impartially; officially; experimentally; decisively; specifically.
(See confirm, prove.)

VERITY

adjectives
continual; intense; eternal; conditional; fundamental; bitter; faithful.

verbs
acclaim—; adulterate—; apprehend—; arm with—; demonstrate—; deny—; establish—; evidence—; garble—; ponder—; proclaim —; pronounce—; realize—; reveal—; substantiate—; sustain—; testify to—; unfold —; utter—; voice—.
(See veracity, reality.)

VERMIN

adjectives
creeping; invisible; filthy; parasitic; unpleasant.

verbs
abhor—; breed—; dispel—; eradicate—; exterminate—; swarm with—; —abound; —carry; —contaminate; —defile; —endanger; —infect; —infest; —nauseate; —offend; —overrun; —plague; —pollute; —thrive.
(See insects, cockroach, bug.)

VERMINOUS

adverbs
dangerously; filthily; disgustingly; deplorably; hopelessly; unhealthfully; unsanitarily; unfortunately; damnably; grossly; terribly; dreadfully; unspeakably; indescribably; irremediably; foully; revoltingly; awfully, incredibly.

VERSATILE

adverbs
delightfully; amazingly; charmingly; curiously; admirably; surprisingly; incredibly; marvellously; unbelievably; eminently; illustriously; uncommonly; distinctly; conspicuously; consummately; remarkably; highly.

VERSATILITY

adjectives
vivacious; enormous; characteristic; established; apparent.

verbs
acclaim—; acquire—; appreciate—; attain—; commend—; display—; evince—; exhibit—; marvel at—; value—; —affords; —amazes; —astounds; —embraces; —enables; —excels; —staggers.
(See skill, ability.)

VERSE

adjectives
unpremeditated; mature; evocative; ironic; abominable; flower-sweet; golden; deathless; luxurious; dramatic; magnificent; prosaic; little; magnanimous; well-cadenced; jolly; metaphysical; immortal; marvellous; graceful; introspective; devotional; macaronic; malicious; supererogatory; graceful; slumberous; polished; society; various (pl); measured; heroic; flattering; homely; blank; realistic; faultless; exquisite; sonorous; caustic; singable; sanguinary; halting; rustic; numerous (pl); neglected; faltering;

patriotic; poetic; fascinating; goodly; doggerel; trashy; matchless; piercing; common; undistinguished; musical; balanced; classical; mournful; distinctive; satiric; quillwrit; soothing; galloping; insulting; delicate; melodious; non-dramatic; sorrowful; alliterative; inspired; tolerable; ennobling; clever; octosyllabic; circulated; mechanical; commonplace; comic; unfinished; coarse; outstanding; ridiculous; assonanced; occasional.

verbs
bawl—; carol—; compose—; dash off—; declaim—; divide into—s; enumerate—s; inscribe—on; improvise—; measure—; memorize—; peruse—; polish—; quote—; render —; scan—; scrawl—; sing—; —delights; —effloresces; —eulogizes; —proclaims; —rhymes; —sings of.
(See poetry, poem.)

VERSED

adverbs
well; remarkably; consummately; learnedly; completely; unusually; extraordinarily; supremely; distinctly; effectively.

VERSIFIER

adjectives
ingenious; skillful; mere; melodious.

VERSIFY (*v*)

adverbs
wittily; cleverly; beautifully; exquisitely; scurrilously; ingeniously; melodiously; skillfully.
(See write, compose.)

VERSION

adjectives
corrected; discordant; condensed; spirited; difficult; vamped-up; coarse; dramatic; rhymed; brisk; virulent; defunct; trimmed-down; garbled; thrilling; pedantic; useful; varying (pl); different; radical; scurrilous; casual; faithful; authorized; modified; artistic; classic; exaggerated; improved; authentic; appealing.

verbs
afford—; authenticate—; color—; confirm —; dash off—; distort—; garble—; illustrate—; maintain—; modify—; offer—; pervert—; simplify—; sustain—; unearth—; varnish—; verify—; —s conflict; —contradicts; —differs; —falsifies; —glosses over;

—interprets; —misrepresents; —slanders.
(See comparison, description, meaning.)

VESICAL
verbs
compress—; contract—; dilate—; distend—;
drain—; excise—; incise—; inflame—; irritate—; occlude—; pierce—; puncture—;
strangulate—; tap—; —bursts; —dries up;
—expands; —protrudes; —shrinks; —shrivels.

(See cell, cavity, sac.)

VESSEL
(boat)
verbs
abandon—; batter—; buffet—; captain—;
embark on—; equip—; fit out—; fuel—;
ground—; helm—; man—; moor—; navigate—; pilot—; punt—; rig out—; scull—;
strand—; waft—; —conveys; —departs; —
plies; —plows; —sallies forth; —scuds; —
shoves off; —skims; —straggles in; —tosses;
—weighs anchor.

(See launch, boat, motor-boat, ship.)

VESSEL
(general)
adjectives
primitive; anchored; ship-wrecked; surrendered; tossing; precious; perished; contaminated; rowing; excretory; convenient; rich-
laden; populous; disabled; earthen; effective; weather-beaten; superb; foundering;
communicating; fragile; overcrowded; cap-
illary; half-empty; sacred; lymphatic; puny;
puffing; staggering; seaworthy; gentle; endangered; straggling; suspicious; suitable.

VEST
adjectives
jeweled; warm; bedecked; plain; stylish.

VEST (v)
adverbs
exclusively; specifically; diplomatically; legislatively; religiously; temporarily.
(See invest.)

VESTIBULE
adjectives
crowded; well-designed; monumental.

VESTIGE
adjectives
last; remaining; enormous; lone.

verbs
bear—; discern—; disclose—; display—; exhibit—; mark—; recognize—; reveal—;
stamp out—; uncover—; unearth—; —betokens; —evidences; —fades; —indicates;
—remains; —survives; —tesifies to.
(See sign, mark, trace, remnant, remains.)

VESTIGIAL
adverbs
probably; undoubtedly; apparently; manifestly; unmistakably; possibly; credibly;
curiously; interestingly; traceably; definitely.

VESTMENT
adjectives
gorgeous; coarse; tattered; purchasable; antique; glorious; somber.

VESTURE
adjectives
imperfect; muddy; pretty; mechanic; napless; choral; pompous; linen; fatal.

VETERAN
adjectives
shoeless; surviving; wary; old; experienced; seasoned; war-worn; gallant; right-
minded; decrepit; battered; stalwart; in-
valided; grim-visaged; hardy; callous.

VETO
adjectives
suspensive; exasperating; equivocal; final;
overruled.

verbs
anticipate—; clamp down—; exercise—;
fear—; override—; sustain—; table—; —
annuls; —checks; —curtails; —dashes the
hopes; —debars; —declines; —excludes; —
nullifies; —overrides; —overrules; —quash-
es; —quells; —rejects; —sets aside; —
stems; —voids; —withholds.
(See vote, restriction, prohibition.)

VEX (v)
adverbs
intolerably; shrewdly; exceedingly; maddeningly; bitterly; ceaselessly; mutely; horridly; violently; mentally; fiercely; tryingly.
(See irritate, annoy.)

VEXATION
adjectives
silent; resentful; mutual; insupportable;
horrid; extreme; evident; puzzled; fierce;

tearful; violent; mental; bitter; trying.

verbs
allay—; arouse—; bear—; conceal—; conciliate—; disclose—; display—; evince—; exhibit—; feign—; foment—; fret in—; incite—; induce—; occasion—; overcome—; palliate—; provoke—; restrain—; writhe in—; —cankers; —irks; —gnaws at; —riles (colloq.); —ruffles; —sours.

(See anger, annoyance, displeasure, irritation, ire, chagrin.)

VEXATIOUS

adverbs
especially; unusually; naturally; occasionally; recently; particularly; monotonously; pettily; terribly; inopportunely; plaguedly; deucedly; intolerably; unfortunately; unimaginably; horribly.

VEXED

adverbs
definitely; unreasonably; foolishly; senselessly; unfairly; deeply; unjustly; distinctly; quickly; easily; unhappily; miserably; wretchedly; ill-temperedly; annoyingly; bitterly; plaguedly; pathetically; sorely; grievously; frightfully; intolerably; distressingly; unbearably; furiously; mightily; hotly.

VIAL

adjectives
wrathful; blasting; tiny; bitter; poisonous.

verbs
analyze—; charge—; despatch—; drain—; eject—; filter—; imbibe from—; inhale from —; label—; quaff from—; seal—; snuff up from—; sterilize—; swill—; uncork—; —befuddles; —enlivens; —envenoms; —paralyzes.

(See medicine, glass bottle.)

VIANDS

adjectives
ruder; exotic; mortal; dainty; ready-baked; tasty; savory.

verbs
bolt—; despatch—; devour—; display—; do justice to—; fall to—; gobble—; gulp—; market—; nibble—; preserve—; purvey—; regale with—; relish—; savor—; tuck in—; —nourish; —revive; —tempt.

(See food, victuals, provisions, fare.)

VIBRATE (v)

adverbs
resonantly; discordantly; tunelessly; curiously; rhythmically; mournfully; audibly; sonorously; tremulously; mysteriously.

(See swing, vacillate.)

VIBRATING

adverbs
constantly; thunderously; regularly; tremulously; sympathetically; rapidly; curiously; magically; tunefully; mysteriously; noisily; silently; strangely; secretly; incomprehensibly; dependably; inexplicably; ominously; steadily.

VIBRATION

adjectives
stimulating; rhythmical; deep; touching; braced; nervous; constant; superimposed; mysterious; longitudinal; brave; mournful; audible; sonorous; heart-quaking; rapid; tremulous; ravishing; isochronous; uncomfortable; definite.

verbs
avert—; curb—; record—s; transmit—; —agitates; —ceases; —churns; —disconcerts; —disquiets; —jars; —jiggles; —joggles; —jolts; —jostles; —jounces; —oscillates; —perturbs; —pitches; —pulsates; —rocks; —throbs.

(See pulse, earthquake.)

VICARIOUS

adverbs
altogether; comfortably; perilously; wholly; strangely; generously; curiously; merely.

VICE

adjectives
solemn; enemy; ultimate; incurable; selfish; discordant; encroaching; virtuous; kindred; respective; disgusting; monstrous; gilded; beneficial; hereditary; distinguished; black; ineffable; distorted; plausible; infamous; searing; overshadowing; ruling; alluring; reckless; engendering; unmarred; trivial; heathen; distressing; deliberate; fashionable; supreme; depicting; abstract; notorious; hateful; gross; coarse; bold; reputed; solitary; ingrained; popular; essential; embodied; walking; redeeming; filthy.

verbs
abandon—; addict to—; campaign against check—; clothe in—; combat—; commercial-

ize—; condemn—; condone—; confess—; crusade against—; curb—; cure—; denounce —; expose—; fall into—; forsake—; foster —; indulge in—; renounce—; reveal—; smack of—; sow—; stem—; stray into—; succumb to—; uncover—; weed out—; — corrupts; —debauches; —demoralizes; — depraves; —desecrates; —flourishes; — fouls; —perverts; —stains; —sullies; — taints; lapse into—.

(See knavery, lawlessness, licentiousness, crime.)

VICINITY

adjectives
immediate; apogeal; perilous; proximate.

verbs
abandon—; acquaint one with—; adjoin—; approach—; betake oneself to—; border—; comb—; converge on—; denude—; devastate—; drift to—; encircle—; encompass—; expel from—; flank—; forsake—; frequent —; guard—; patrol—; picket—; prowl about—; ramble about—; roam—; rove—; screen—; shroud—; skirt—; stroll about—.

(See locality, neighborhood.)

VICIOUS

adverbs
notoriously; famously; incomparably; alarmingly; criminally; heinously; nefariously; brutally; incredibly; indescribably; incomparably; wholly; politically; obviously; deplorably; manifestly; terribly; basely; grossly; obscenely; morally; notably; indefensibly; dangerously; intolerably.

VICIOUSNESS

adjectives
inherent; senile; compounded; essential; natural; characteristic.

VICISSITUDES

adjectives
myriad; sublime; sweet; sudden; mortal; sad; strange.

verbs
acquaint one with—; avert—; control—; decry—; denounce—; deplore—; dwell upon —; forecast—; forestall—; foretell—; hazard—; meet—; prepare for—; prophesy—; risk—; suffer—; welcome—; —alter; —imperil; —jeopardize; —revolutionize; — threaten.

(See change, misfortune.)

VICTIM

adjectives
unsuspicious; noble; unfortunate; struggling; hapless; miserable; desirable; ulster-clad; prospective; unspotted; penitent; wretched; choking; immediate; bridal; potential; slaughtered; unresisting; deluded; hunted; illustrious; innumerable (pl); unthinking; contemptible; cowering; countless (pl); unshriven; unnamed; supposed; ingenuous; mutilated; livid; squalid; multifarious (pl).

verbs
avenge—; bait—; beguile—; bilk—; console—; decoy—; defraud—; dupe—; ease —; ensnare—; entice—; exonerate—; goad —; harass—; harrow—; lure—; maim—; martyrize—; sacrifice—; snare—; solicit—s; succor—s; trap—; wrack—; wring—; — bewails; —decries; —despairs; —endures; —grieves; —laments; —languishes; — mourns; —pines; —suffers; —testifies; — tolerates; —succumbs to.

(See prey, quarry, amateur.)

VICTOR

adjectives
laurel-crowned; joyless; loving; upborne; modest.

VICTORIOUS

adverbs
ultimately; finally; eventually; immediately; recently; grandly; brilliantly; magnificently; gloriously; splendidly; royally; modestly; triumphantly; quietly; logically; reasonably; suddenly; unexpectedly; deservedly; happily; luckily; blessedly; utterly.

VICTORY

adjectives
smashing; splendid; subsequent; glorious; brilliant; dialectic; decisive; barren; undeclining; approaching; partisan; ultimate; triumphant; sweeping; marvelous; inevitable; overwhelming; publicized; enormous; fresh; unvarying; superb; prospective; world-famous; ineffective; self-assured; bloody; wholesome; retributive; manifold (pl); signal; endless; speedy; secret; obligatory; gladsome; strategic; Pyrrhic.

verbs
acclaim—; achieve—; advance to—; anticipate—; assure of—; botch—; celebrate—; chalk up—; clinch—; commemorate—;

crown with—; emerge with—; eventuate in —; fall short of—; gain—; glorify—; goad to—; grace—; grind out—; guide to—; hail —; inspire—; insure—; magnify—; pledge to—; proclaim—; promise—; purchase—; radiate—; rob of—; romp to—; result in—; salute—; score—; seal—; sense—; signify —; snatch—; spur to—; sweep to—; temper —; wreathe in—; wrest—from; —demoralizes; —eludes; —evades; —overwhelms; — routs; —vanquishes.

(See conquest, advantage, triumph, success, supremacy.)

VICTUALS
verbs
bolt—; consume—; deluge with—; deplete —; despatch—; devour—; dispense—; furnish with—; gobble—; gorge—; gulp—; laud—; munch—; praise—; preserve—; prepare—; provide—; purvey—; refrigerate—; relish—; replenish—; savor—; stint on—; stock with—; —attract; —lure; —nourish; —refresh; —renew; —restore; —tempt.

(See food, viands.)

VIEW
(general)
adjectives
extensive; provincial; splendid; comprehensive; topographical; modern; regimentalist; historical; respective (pl); foregoing; definite; monarchical; wide; representative; personal; broad; solemn; reiterated; clashing; enlarged; spiritual; systematized; theological; religious; divergent; masculine; gloomy; prehistoric; realistic; bloody; rationalist; stereopticon; philosophic; dismayed; differing; pessimistic; magnificent; distinct; enchanting; optimistic; perspective; dubious; architectural; humanistic; infinite; dynamic; trustworthy; lucid; celebrated; exaggerated; prophetic; benighted; interesting; experimental; anti-democratic; vivid; complete; unmitigated; intensive; spectacular; elaborate; successive (pl); deliberate; panoramic; dissolving; sentimental; esthetic; superb; metaphysical; charitable; illuminated; individualistic; unbounded; intellectual; peculiar; unwashed; liberal; nihilistic; sudden; injurious; aberrant; unobstructed; continuous; partial; stable; mischievous; worldly; unfavorable; glorious; luminous; lofty; idealistic; impressive; practical; prevalent; ample; mechanical; cynic; human; similar; mystical; sharp; clear;

orthodox; believing; angelic; erroneous; nerve-trying; subjective; romantic; beautiful; shuddering; hopeless; dismal; sympathetic; primitive; cheerful; gorgeous; old-fashioned; superficial; many-sided; fascinating; mortal; rosy; undulating; startled; disparaging; dignified; prudent; calm; sanguine; deep; advanced; materialistic; despairing; evolutionary; irresponsible; investigating; charming; disheartened; constitutional; rational; especial; collateral; dissolving; limited; pecuniary; tenable; straining; benevolent; theoretic; matured; retrospective; unfair; uninterrupted; rigid; indescribable; dissolving; sightless; enlightened; melancholy; cross-section; partial; stately; conservative; top-lofty; settled; picturesque; disputed; world-famous; thrilling; splendid; skyline; river; exceptional; overpowering; orthodox.

VIEW
(intellectual)
verbs
advertise—; air—; alter—; analyze—; arrive at—; balance—; bias—; bolster—; broaden—; cancel—; cherish—; clarify—; color—; conceive—; conciliate—; confide—; confirm—; countenance—; credit—; demonstrate—; dispute—; distort—; embrace—; entertain—; establish—; evaluate—; exchange—s; expose—s; expound—; falsify—; fix—; formulate—; grasp—; illustrate—; inculcate—; indoctrinate—; indorse—; influence—; inspire—; integrate—s; interpret —; justify—; lack—; maintain—; narrow —; nurse—; object to—; oppose—; originate —; present—; proclaim—; profess—; reconsider—; repudiate—; retain—; reveal—; set forth—; shape—; share—; shift—; substantiate—; sum up—; support—; sustain—; thwart—; uphold—; voice—; warp—; warrant—; —prevails; —shocks.

(See belief, aim, mission, notion, aspect, perspective, perception, opinion.)

VIEW
(landscape, sight, etc.)
verbs
afford—; bare to—; beautify—; blemish—; cloud—; command—; contemplate—; deface —; distort—; dull—; emblazon—; enjoy—; exalt—; frame—; gaze at—; glimpse—; mar—; obliterate—; obscure—; obstruct—; photograph—; pop into—; portray—; preserve—; rivet upon—; screen—; shade—; sketch—; telescope—; vanish from—; —

blurs; —dazzles; —enchants; —enkindles; —enraptures; —enthralls; —impassions; —impresses; —inspires; —petrifies; —unfolds.

(See sight, scene, prospect, panorama, landscape.)

VIEW (v)

adverbs

regretfully; historically; cynically; sardonically; incessantly; dispassionately; faintly; fitfully; hastily; curiously; extensively; solemnly; philosophically; optimistically; charitably; idealistically; subjectively; sympathetically; objectively; theoretically; panoramically.

(See regard, see.)

VIEWPOINT

adjectives

hard-boiled; short-sighted; national; practical; impersonal; unbiased; fresh; optimistic; evolutionistic; customary; universal; sociological; pessimistic; prejudiced.

VIGIL

adjectives

tearless; lone; late; bitter; dangerous; heart-chilling; weary; solemn; unhallowed; anxious; tongueless.

verbs

allay—; arrest—; curtail—; dread—; ease —; eke out—; endure—; interrupt—; maintain—; necessitate—; prolong—; protract—; relax—; relinquish—; resume—; slacken—; survive—; suspend—; sustain—; terminate —; —fatigues; —tells; —weakens; —wearies; —weighs upon.

(See vigilance, interest, watch, scrutiny.)

VIGILANCE

adjectives

eternal; remarkable; utmost; constant; increasing; unceasing; determined; extraordinary; redoubled; jealous; habitual; stern.

verbs

admonish—; circumvent—; ease—; enforce —; escape—; exhort—; heighten—; intensify—; lighten—; maintain—; mitigate—; necessitate—; reduce—; relax—; sharpen —; slacken—; —declines; —discovers; —insures; —lapses; —safeguards; —subsides; —wanes; —wearies.

(See interest, vigil, caution.)

VIGILANT

adverbs

eternally; constantly; unrelentingly; carefully; intelligently; ordinarily; usually; uncommonly; especially; particularly; unremittingly; cruelly; lovingly; fondly; affectionately; gently; anxiously; fearfully; timidly; nervously; sternly; harshly; curiously; inquisitively; inexcusably; vexatiously; inescapably.

VIGNETTE

verbs

adorn with—s; dash off—; embellish with —s; enamel—; etch—; execute—; frame—; impress—; print—; sketch—; stipple—; varnish—; —delineates; —depicts; —describes; —illustrates; —ornaments; —pictures; —portrays.

(See portrait, picture, sketch.)

VIGOR

adjectives

mortal; ethereal; disciplined; hybrid; prime; uninterrupted; florid; excessive; tireless; sinewy; remarkable; accustomed; terse; quickened; coarse; wild; dramatic; muscular; athletic; wonted; intellectual; pristine; furious; rude; aggressive; manly; plastic; incisive; contrary; bodily; selfish; incredible; extraordinary; original; renewing; increased; peristaltic; conscious; customary; dynamic; remorseless; emulating; recuperative; glorious; determined; rustic; redoubled; lusty; classic; especial; elastic; hardy; graceful; masculine; mighty; purposeful; youthful; mental; terrible; unabated; astonishing; superabundant; full; sudden; original; unimpaired; native; offhand; renovated.

verbs

acquire—; demand—; deplete—; display—; endow with—; enhance—; exert—; exhibit —; infuse—; inject—; instill—; lessen—; maintain—; perform with—; preserve—; radiate—; renew—; retain—; restore—; sap up—; stimulate—; store up—; sustain —; —buttresses; —fades; —fortifies.

(See force, energy, "pep", strength.)

VIGOROUS

adverbs

splendidly; sufficiently; brawnily; healthily; warrantably; actually; fortunately; necessarily; apparently; mysteriously; manifestly; uncommonly; remarkably; luckily.

VILIFY (v)

adverbs

blackly; wrathfully; maliciously; malignantly; cruelly; viciously; jealously; furiously; terribly; coarsely; rudely; hatefully; grossly.
(See slander, traduce.)

VILLA

adjectives

glittering; enchanting; expensive; commodious; peaceful; dainty; restful; gaudy; handsome; spacious; suburban; voluptuous; sumptuous; medieval.

VILLAGE

adjectives

smiling; toy-like; poverty-stricken; cool; shady; damp; worn-out; patriarchal; incurious; straggling; dependent; adjacent; innumerable (pl); obscure; rustic; neighboring; ordinary; provincial; whitewashed; poor; dusky; ghost-like; pathetic; retired; pleasant; well-ordered; preoccupied; miserable; insensible; rural; native; deserted; squalid; insignificant; forsaken; producing; self-supporting; isolated; delightful; stupid-looking; little; stony; picturesque; manufacturing; sprawling; embowered; remote; shabby; lovely; sweet; smiling; red-roofed; helpless; pastoral; benighted.

verbs

abide in—; arouse—; border—; commute from—; desert—; devastate—; dot with—s; ensconce in—; flank—; forsake—; frequent —; inhabit—; lull—; nestle in—; quarter in—; raze—; repair to—; skirt—; storm—; —expands; —flourishes; —hums; —straggles; —thrives.
(See neighborhood, community, town, city.)

VILLAGER

verbs

alarm—; beseech—; bilk—; dominate—; educate—; enslave—; harangue—; plague —; rook—; rouse—; summon—; swindle —; tax—; —bands; —commutes; —cultivates; —descends upon; —flocks to; —markets; —prospers; —rises; —scatters; — thwarts.
(See citizen, individual, inhabitant, taxpayer, public.)

VILLAIN

adjectives

plain-dealing; replenished; ungrateful; dissembling; precise; white; sweet; monstrous; soulless; repulsive; murdering; rich; senseless; false; infernal; cursed; notorious; prodigious; wicked; skulking; accomplished; penurious; scheming; murderous; shag-haired; fine; hoary; inflexible; trusty; honorable; abandoned; atrocious; deliberate; cool.

verbs

apprehend—; banish—; band—; condemn —; curtail—; denounce—; expose—; ferret out—; incarcerate—; inveigh against—; jail—; portray—; prosecute—; reveal—; scourge—; seize—; sniff out—; —s band; —betrays; —confesses; —conspires; —defiles; —desecrates; —eludes; —evades; —plots; —seduces; —slanders; —transgresses.
(See profligate, actor, scoundrel, criminal, monster, character.)

VILLAINOUS

adverbs

unmistakably; utterly; despicably; unhappily; terribly; dreadfully; unspeakably; infamously; conspicuously; incredibly; unimaginably; remarkably; contemptibly; defiantly; openly; secretly; blandly; actually; manifestly.

VILLAINY

adjectives

cold-blooded; multiplying; deliberate; unusual; naked; superfluous; reeking; systematic; stupendous; vocal; sensual; deliberate; demoniacal; subtle.

verbs

accuse of—; charge with—; denounce—; deplore—; detect—; disclose—; expose—; forsake—; involve—; lapse into—; practise—; punish—; renounce—; resort to—; reveal —; rue—; sink into—; turn from—; uncover —; —defames; —degrades.
(See sin, wickedness, crime.)

VINDICATE (v)

adverbs

amply; sufficiently; triumphantly; gallantly; honorably; magnanimously; heroically; creditably; ingeniously; simply.
(See justify, correct.)

VINDICATION

adjectives

alleged; gloomy; culminating; prompt; attempted; triumphant; labored; simple; creditable; vicarious; ingenious; mischievous; pampered.

VINDICTIVE

adverbs

utterly; openly; secretly; defiantly; violently; dangerously; furtively; alarmingly; portentously; ominously; oddly; peculiarly; smoothly; cruelly; bitterly; brutally.

VINDICTIVENESS

adjectives

satanic; detestable; vicious; spiteful; hateful.

verbs

appease—; assert—; assuage—; calm—; dispose toward—; ease—; express—; indulge in—; justify—; harbor—; quell—; relax—; relent—; reveal—; satisfy—; temper—; tranquillize—; warrant—; —grows; —subsides; —wanes; —wakes.

(See hatred, animosity, contempt.)

VINE

adjectives

withering; never-flowering; gadding; tangled; clinging; trellised; scented; delicate; springing; arching; thorny; sovereign; trailing; delicious; intricate; clustering; bordering; ambitious; well-pruned; perfume-breathing; flaming; riotous; luxuriant; creeping; strangling; ambrosial; cloistral; rose-flecked; immense; parasitic; sweet; breathed; interwoven; twisted; choice.

verbs

bunch on—; graft into—; husband—; load —; lop—; prune—; screen with—s; smother in—s; support—; transplant—; —bears; —bows with; —clambers; —clings; —creeps; —embowers; —enriches; —entwines; —flourishes; —overspreads; —scents; —thickens; —thrives; —trails; —yields.

(See honeysuckle, etc.)

VINEYARD

adjectives

sloping; blood-tinctured; terraced; luscious; productive.

VIOLATE (v)

adverbs

flagrantly; expressly; palpably; basely; grossly; flatly; wickedly; persistently; undisguisedly; expressly; criminally; spiritually.

(See transgress, trespass.)

VIOLATION

adjectives

gross; flat; denouncing; wide-spread; wicked; conscious; signal; persistent; undisguised; express.

verbs

condone—; constitute—; disapprove of—; disclose—; dismiss for—; frown on—; ignore—; justify—; penalize—; protest—; wink at—; —desecrates; —encroaches upon; —infringes; —nullifies; —ostracizes; —piques; —repudiates; —riles (colloq.); —tramples; —transgresses; —voids.

(See breach, infringement, infraction.)

VIOLATOR

adjectives

apparent; sacrilegious.

verbs

apprehend—; check—; denounce—; disclose —; exile—; fine—; jail—; "nab"—; pounce upon—; punish—; seize—; trail—; —abuses; —baffles; —breaks; —despoils; —disregards; —eludes; —encroaches; —evades; —infringes; —mulcts; —profanes; —ravishes.

(See criminal.)

VIOLENCE

adjectives

frightful; murderous; unlooked-for; sheer; spontaneous; physical; reckless; passionate; high-handed; unwonted; brutal; unjustifiable; glorious; unscrupulous; theatric; impetuous; irreconcilable; ghostly; gentle; midnight; unreasoning; swift; bloody; needful; uncommon; loud; extreme; odious; meditated; irregular; personal; momentary; aggressive; stunning; sacrilegious; devilish; cowardly; invisible; undiminished; occasional; tragic; threatening; restless; increasing; quiet.

verbs

advocate—; allay—; avert—; balk at—; bar—; burst into—; condone—; cow by—; curb—; denounce—; deplore—; deprecate —; discountenance—; employ—; foment—; frustrate—; incite—; indulge in—; inflame to—; instigate—; lull—; pacify—; precipitate—; provoke—; quell—; resort to—; restrain—; subdue—; —erupts; —rages.

(See malice, impetuosity, indignation, intensify, fury, anger.)

VIOLENT

adverbs

ungovernably; dangerously; lawlessly; youthfully; heedlessly; lamentably; deplorably; openly; actively; defiantly; insurgently; restively; mutinously; rebelliously; tumultuously; treasonably; incorrigibly; persistently; obstinately.

VIOLET

adjectives

glowing; blue-veined; royal; nodding; shrinking; purple; dewy; first; blown; lucid.

VIOLIN

adjectives

alto; beautiful; masterful; priceless.

VIPER

adjectives

universal; jumping; startled.

VIRGIN

adjectives

wily; white-robed; young; budding; vestal; regarded; pale-eyed; poor; learned; powerful; ill-drawn; ultimate; charming; bashful; blushing.

verbs

befit—; bestow upon—; defile—; deflower —; despoil—; esteem—; play the—; respect —; revere—; seduce—; sully—; touch—; —binds; —brags; —captives; —exults; — flaunts; —flouts; —glories; —scolds; — stifles.

(See girl, woman, wife.)

VIRGINITY

adjectives

pretty; irrevocable; indestructible; antiquated; long-preserved.

verbs

acknowledge—; ascribe—; blemish—; dig-

nify—; preserve—; pride oneself on—; profess—; question—; stain—; taint—; take—; tarnish—; threaten—; violate—; worship —; —imparts.

(See chastity, purity, virtue.)

VIRTUE

adjectives

disinterested; hereditary; acquired; slender; manly; unselfish; self-abnegating; conscious; commonplace; attractive; negative; imputed; stellar; domestic; sounding; sterling; vestal; infinite; peculiar; rigid; heroic; admirable; rare; impregnable; barbaric; paltry; distinguished; new-built; abstract; consummate; sober; well-known; surface; unassailable; exemplary; external; unpretending; perfect; unquestionable; diuretic; delightful; dominant; fanciful; honorable; active; ennobling; illustrious; beaming; wondrous; proud; suffering; healing; probable; proverbial; outraged; distressed; aromatic; contradictory; magnetic; outstanding; prime; redeeming; humble; lofty; wearied; beatific; grateful; possible; personal; ever-flourishing; supposed; unique; political; simple; superstitious; thoughtful; godlike; chief; inimitable; boasted; excellent; artificial; manifold (pl); legitimate; proper; nameless; eminent; high; spirited; preserved; knightly; intrinsic; certain; sublime; eclipsed; natural; unbecoming; old-fashioned; healing; ruining; comely; sweet; rude; ruffled; right; strict; sober; solid; public; prosaic; pure; nectarous; disputable; injurious; liberal; politic; cardinal; low; succored; religious; infant; medicinal; flowering; severe; reawakening; moral; middle; untainted; fundamental; marvelous; tangible; loving; aristocratic; definite; traditional; boasted; small; philanthropic; powerful; cheap; incessant; rural; befriending; feminine; bastard; sundry (pl); leading; private; uncertain; amiable; grand; special; soporific; prodigious; ignominious.

verbs

acclaim—s; blot out—; commend—; cultivate—s; defend—; delight in—; embody—s; emphasize—s; esteem—; exemplify—; extol —s; forsake—; foster—; hail—; impart—to; implant—; incarnate—s; inculcate—; instil—; magnify—s; nurture—; observe—s; preserve—; proclaim—s; question—; recognize—s; redeem—; relinquish—; reward—; scoff at—; scorn—; sing—s; stray from—;

sustain—; —distinguishes; —prevails; —triumphs; —uplifts; embrace—.

(See chastity, integrity, morality, courage, prudence, honesty, fortitude, temperance, justice.)

VIRTUOUS
adverbs
pretentiously; unctuously; pharasaically; ostentatiously; actually; notably; entirely; conspicuously; apparently; supposedly; utterly; unquestionably; manifestly; palpably; definitely; remarkably; honestly; sincerely.

VIRULENT
adverbs
disastrously; unfortunately; cruelly; bitterly; admittedly; unusually; terribly; remarkably; insidiously; unbelievably; uncommonly; highly; dreadfully; dangerously.

VIRUS
verbs
allay—; antidote—; check—; combat—; confine—; counteract—; immunize to—; inactivate—; infect with—; inject—; isolate—; neutralize—; weaken—; —attacks; —consumes; —devastates; —inflames; —invades; —paralyzes; —prostrates; —ravages.

(See germ, disease, poison, venom.)

VISAGE
adjectives
grotesque; tawny; shattered; unmutilated; gory; grim; great; bloody; impassive; wrinkled; puckered; swarthy; fierce; monstrous; storied; infernal; importing; bleared; silver; favored; borrowed; illuminated; horrent; ironical; sickly; grotesque; hard-favored; glimmering; revolting; saintly; unrepentant; dark; passionless; weatherbeaten; leathery; pale; choleric; ancient; coppery.

VISIBLE
adverbs
easily; undoubtedly; dimly; clearly; usually; wholly; completely; faintly; brightly; obscurely; distinctly; conspicuously; embarrassingly; inadvertently; unavoidably; purposely; inconveniently; awkwardly.

VISION
(eyesight, etc.)
verbs
astigmatize—; augment—; blur—; cloud—; conserve—; correct—; dazzle—; deprive of —; dim—; distort—; dull—; eclipse—; focus—upon; impair—; infract—; measure —; obscure—; obstruct—; preserve—; quicken—; ravage—; refract—; scathe—; screen—; sharpen—; shield from—; value —; veil—; warp—.

(See sight.)

VISION
(general)
adjectives
sudden; frightful; telescopic; sun-compelling; moral; transitory; tender; ravishing; foregone; delightful; alleged; vivid; specialized; remarkable; appointed; angelic; sweet; light; radiant; rectified; fresh; stunted; mental; early; concentrated; failing; gloomy; spiritual; horrible; calm; relentless; prophetic; useful; disturbing; embodied; unremembered; anxious; uncertain; harassing; artless; dying; frightful; dreadful; singular; ecstatic; tranced; charmed; skyey; world; unforgettable; transcendent; myopic; subjective; halting; transient; dim; fatal; chill; airy; baseless; blissful; narrating; painful; unreal; troubled; mysterious; culminating; morning; earthly; infinite; subtle; alluring; enchanted; unsubstantial; heavenly; saintly; rapturous; entrancing; hawk-like; glorious; cosmic; aesthetic; imaginary; extended; inspiring; subsequent; importunate; cold; confused; delirious; paradisical; impaired; encompassed; tranquil; ominous; pleasing; beautiful; long-promised; discriminating; beatific; downcast; obscure; lucid; hallowed; intellectual; unaided; creative; crystal; cradled; mental; clear; midday; pious; unclouded; overwhelming; singular; bored; sweet; rare; yearning; everlasting; earth-dimmed; defective; philosophical; vague; sun; window; fruitless; far-seeing; apocalyptic.

VISION
(imagination)
verbs
blur—; cherish—; conjure up—; fire by—; flirt with—; fulfill—; resolve—; reveal—; shake off—; train on—; —appears; —arises; —dances; —dawns upon; —dazes; —departs; —fascinates; —flashes before; —flees; —flits; —foretells; —haunts; —materializes; —prophesies.

(See imagination, phantom, dream, phantasy, mirage, nightmare, image.)

adverbs

fantastically; quixotically; chimerically; ephemerally; unsubstantially; imponderably; tenuously; mystically; mythically; fancifully; uncommonly; highly; inanely; vacuously; airily; blankly; dreamily; groundlessly.

VISIT

adjectives

delightful; dramatic; ultimate; surreptitious; unlooked-for; flying; proffered; cordial; doubtful; courteous; unceremonious; yearly; imperial; casual; frequent (pl); distinguished; intended; transient; extraordinary; dreaded; volunteered; ill-timed; agreeable; unavailing; momentous; intemperate; meditated; unwelcome; gentle; prolonged; approaching; parochial; wonted; flying; last-mentioned; hurried; occasional; untimely; perfunctory; domiciliary; impending; stated; cool; comfortable; quiet; happy; pleasant; well-rounded.

verbs

abbreviate—; alternate—; cancel—; close —; conclude—; curtail—; defer—; depart on—; draw out—; extend—; plan—; prolong—; protract—; reciprocate—; resume —; return—; season—; schedule—; terminate—; welcome—; —delights; —wearies.
(See vacation, interview.)

VISIT (v)

adverbs

habitually; customarily; traditionally; periodically; seasonally; surreptitiously; cordially; courteously; ceremoniously; annually; imperially; agreeably; momentously; intemperately.
(See call, journey.)

VISITANT

adjectives

ghostly; weird; undesirable; strange.

VISITATION

adjectives

wide-spread; loving; gentle; transient; providential; heavenly; supernatural; troublesome; undeserved; nightly; sudden.

VISITING

adjectives

compunctious; continual; yearly; routine.

adjectives

transient; assiduous; unseen; anonymous; favored; struggling; nightly; distraught; gaping; pedestrian; enthusiastic; transcendental; dwindling; prominent; casual; uninitiated; wondering; gentle; frequent; haggard; savage; constant; distinguished; celestial; wandering; pauper; ordinary; belated; time-stealing; transitory; accustomed; dreadful; unwelcome.

verbs

amuse—; anticipate—; ban—; bar—; beam at—; confront—; discourage—; elude—; embrace—; entertain—; exclude—; greet—; hail—; ignore—; limit—; receive—; regale —; salute—; shun—; welcome—; —bore; —distract; —divert; —interrupt; —stream in; —surge in; —throng; —weary.
(See guest, listener.)

VISTA

adjectives

economic; pillared; enticing; distant; boundless; backward; frequent; mental; stately; unexpected; spectral.

verbs

cloud—; gaze at—; glory in—; obscure—; pore over—; rivet upon—; scan—; screen —; stare at—; survey—; —dazzles; —enraptures; —enthralls; —extends; —glitters; —opens before; —yawns.
(See view, landscape.)

VITAL

adverbs

obviously; indisputably; clearly; admittedly; curiously; strangely; significantly; particularly; absolutely; fundamentally; palpably; manifestly; remarkably.

VITALITY

adjectives

undreamed-of; intellectual; sportive; hilarious; protracted; restless; aggressive; creative; genuine; lingering; sparkling; continued; departing; brisk; enfeebled; abounding; mental; characteristic; inherent; forgotten; enormous; subterranean; unfailing; immaculate; vigorous; dimensional; glorious; unrivaled; inexhaustible; persistent; overpowering; brutal; miserable; great; low.

verbs

absorb—; acquire—; brim with—; build—; charge with—; concentrate—; conserve—; deprive of—; destroy—; detract from—; dull—; endow with—; exhaust—; glow with —; impair—; instil—; invest with—; lack —; maintain—; preserve—; recruit—; reduce—; reinforce—; renew—; rob of—; retain—; sap—; spare—; sustain—; throb with—; undermine—; —ebbs; —endures; — wanes; —wavers.

(See strength, health.)

VITAMINS

adjectives

toxic; essential; prevailing; helpful; overemphasized.

verbs

classify—; condense—; demand—; despatch —; enrich in—; instil—; lack—; measure —; necessitate—; prate of—; require—; rob of—; —build resistance; —deteriorate; — immunize; —nourish; —sustain.

(See nourishment, food.)

VITUPERATE (v)

adverbs

bitterly; cruelly; insidiously; vitriolically; personally; emotionally; exceedingly; viciously; craftily; savagely; sardonically; snarlingly; horribly; jubilantly; shrilly; stridently; vulgarly; unspeakably.

(See vilify, slander.)

VITUPERATION

adjectives

personal; emotional; nasty; vitriolic.

VITUPERATIVE

adverbs

profanely; obscenely; loudly; blatantly; boisterously; insanely; furiously; justly; unreasonably; terribly; unjustly; coarsely; openly; particularly; shamefully; blisteringly; brutally; unspeakably; incredibly; noisily; shamelessly; publicly; scathingly.

VIVACIOUS

adverbs

delightfully; pleasantly; merrily; nonsensically; comically; entertainingly; divertingly; extremely; uncommonly; highly; amusingly; excitably; enthusiastically; briskly; restlessly; alertly.

VIVACITY

adjectives

violent; nervous; ingenuous; high; unflagging; immense; unsurpassable; unabated; exuberant; sparkling; pert; artificial; unbelievable.

verbs

awaken—; cultivate—; destroy—; display —; lack—; preserve—; recapture—; value —; —animates; —bubbles; —cheers; —declines; —delights; —enlivens; —endears; —exhilarates; —gladdens; —infects; —inspirits; —refreshes; —tires; —vivifies; — wanes.

(See gayety, liveliness, animation.)

VIVID

adverbs

extremely; supernaturally; terribly; frightfully; beautifully; admirably; commendably; unusually; splendidly; wonderfully; miraculously; unbelievably; uncommonly; particularly; peculiarly; curiously; mysteriously; delightfully.

VIVIDNESS

adjectives

shocking; painful; tremendous; transparent; burning; bright; startling; journalistic.

VIXENISH

adverbs

impishly; comically; childishly; significantly; portentously; unbecomingly; ridiculously; unwarrantably; inexplicably; suddenly; hysterically; violently; surprisingly; unwontedly; alarmingly; dreadfully; momentarily.

VOCABULARY

adjectives

lurid; workable; adequate; copious; fundamental; enormous; scientific; picturesque; fashionable; full; varied; working; reading; reserve; valuable; speaking; built-up; stimulated; choice; wide; notable; well-balanced; normal; brilliant; scant; lively; rich; racy; saucy; unusual.

verbs

acquire—; add to—; adopt—; aggrandize —; amass—; analyze—; arrange—; augment—; better—; broaden—; build—; color —; compare—; compile—; contrast—; criticize—; cultivate—; culture—; derive—; develop—; display—; eliminate from—; employ—; enhance—; enlarge—; enrich—; examine—; exhaust—; familiarize oneself with —; furnish with—; gather—; improve—; increase—; limit—; make—active; mature —; narrow—; ransack—; refine—; require —; retain—; select—; simplify—; strengthen—; swell—; vary—; vulgarize—; weaken —; —accrrues; —aids; —amazes; —astounds; —colors; —derives from; —embraces; —equips; —excels; —expresses; —flowers; —fructifies; —grows; —includes; —indicates; —insures; —invigorates; —multiplies; —provides; —ranges; —reveals.

VOCAL CHORDS
verbs
discipline—; distend—; ease—; elongate—; impair—; injure—; irritate—; rasp—; soothe—; strain—; tax—; tighten—; train —; trap—; weaken—; —change; —contract; —emit; —lengthen; —quiver; —utter; —vibrate.

VOCALIST
adjectives
eminent; prominent; wonderful; thrilling.

verbs
acclaim—; accompany—; applaud—; arrange for—; laud—; train—; —carols; —enraptures; —enthralls; —entrances; —executes; —improvises; —intones; —lilts; —quavers; —records; —renders; —scales; —thrills; —trills; —twitters.
(See singer, soprano, choir.)

VOCALIZATION
adjectives
enormous; delicious; picturesque; proper.

VOCATION
adjectives
perilous; sane; sacred; legitimate; peaceful; lifelong.

verbs
desert—; employ in—; enter—; fit for—; forsake—; master—; overcrowd—; prepare for—; pursue—; qualify for—; skill in—; —allures; —attracts; —beckons; —demands; —exacts; —fascinates; —interests; —necessitates; —requires; —treats of.
(See hobby, employment, industry, calling, teaching, law, etc.)

VOCIFERATION
adjectives
harsh; ferocious; raging.

VOCIFEROUS
adverbs
unnecessarily; comically; naturally; carnestly; excitedly; hysterically; enthusiastically; riotously; shrilly; clamorously; inexcusably; disagreeably; unbecomingly; coarsely; surprisingly; grossly; foolishly; unfortunately.

VOGUE
adjectives
instigated; appreciable; tremendous; immense; decorative; fashionable.

verbs
adhere to—; alter—; create—; design—; devise—; dictate—; dignify—; emulate—; establish—; exalt—; fashion—; foster—; glorify—; maintain—; outlive—; popularize —; —dies; —diminishes; —fades; —glitters; —persists; —prevails; —wanes.
(See mode, fashion.)

VOICE
adjectives
able; abrupt; accusing; admirable; admonishing; affectionate; agonized; agitated; airy; alarmed; alien; angelic; angry; antagonistic; anxious; apocalyptic; apologetic; appropriate; arbitrary; assuring; audible; authoritative; awe-struck; babbling; baritone; barren; base; bass; beautiful; beguiling; bellowing; beloved; bemused; bewildered; bitter; blatant; bleating; bluff; blunt; blurred; booming; breathless; brisk; buzzing; broken; calm; caressing; carrying; cavernous; celestial; charming; checked; cheerful; cheering; childish; choked; clamoring; clarion; clashing; clear; clinging; cold; collective; commanding; compelling; complete; concentrated; contentious; controlling; convinced; corrupted; courteous; cracked; crashing; crisp; croaking; darkening; deceptive; decisive; decorous; deep; deferential; deliberate; demoniac; desired; determined; dictatorial; discordant; disembodied; dispassionate; dissentient; dissenting; distant; distinct; divine; doleful; dominant; dragging; dreaded; droning; drunken; dry; dull; eager; ear-deafening; earnest; easy; effective; elegant; eloquent; embarrassed; erect; exasperating; excited; exhilarating; expressionless; exquisite; extinguished; extraordinary; exultant; faint; false; falsetto;

faltering; familiar; far-away; far-off; far-ringing; fascinating; fearful; fear-struck; feeble; feigned; feminine; fiendish; fine; firm; flexible; flowing; flute-like; flutter-ing; foghorn; frequent; fretful; fresh; frightened; full; functioning; gentle; ghost-ly; gibing; gleeful; glorious; godly; good; gorgeous; gracious; great; growling; gruff; guiding; guttural; habitual; half-hesitant; half-whispered; hard; harsh; harmonious; hearty; heathen; heavenly; heavy; helpless; high; high-pitched; hoarse; hollow; horri-ble; hurried; hushed; husky; icy; ignorant; imaginary; impassioned; impressive; im-proved; impelling; imperative; inarticulate; inaudible; incarnate; incessant; incisive; in-dependent; indistinct; ineffectual; inexor-able; infallible; inflexible; inner; insinuat-ing; insolent; inward; iron; irritable; jerky; jubilant; labored; languid; languorous; laughing; lazy; leafy; level; lifeless; lifted; lingering; lisping; living; loathing; loud; loving; low; lowered; low-keyed; low-pitch-ed; lusty; magnificent; magniloquent; ma-jestic; manful; manly; masculine; match-less; maudlin; measured; meek; melancholy; mellifluous; mellow; melodious; melting; merciless; metallic; meteoric; mighty; min-gled (pl); mirthful; modulated; monoton-ous; monstrous; mortal; motherly; mourn-ful; multitudinous (pl); muffled; mumbling; murmuring; musical; mute; myriad (pl); mysterious; nagging; nasal; native; na-tural; odious; offended; oily; omniscient; ominous; painful; palpitant; parrot-like; passionate; patient; patriotic; peaceful; peevish; penetrating; perpetual; pertinent; pettish; petulant; phantom-like; piercing; piping; pitying; placating; plaining; plain-tive; playful; pleading; pleasant; polite; powerful; prodigious; purring; puzzled; quarreling; quavering; querulous; question-ing; quiet; quivering; rapid; raised; rasp-ing; raucous; reckless; recognized; reedy; remarkable; reminiscent; reprehensible; re-proachful; resonant; respectful; responsive; reverential; ringing; rough; rowdy; rusty; sacred; sad; salutary; sardonic; savage; secret; seductive; sepulchral; seraphic; ser-ious; shaken; sharp; short-breathed; shriek-ing; shrill; silky; silvery; singsong; sleep-thick; slender; slow; slurring; smooth; smothered; snapping; snarling; snuffling; sobbing; soft; solemn; sonorous; soothing; sorrowful; soul-piercing; soul-subduing; sprightly; stammering; stately; stationary; steady; stentorian; stern; stifled; still; stir-ring; strained; strange; strangled; stricken; strident; strong; stumbling; stupendous; subdued; subterranean; sudden; suitable; suppressed; surmounting; suspicious; sweet; swelled; synchronized; taunting; tearful; tender; tentative; tenuous; thick; thin; thun-dering; tiny; toneless; tottering; tragic; tranquil; transcendent; transformed; trans-ported; trembling; tremulous; triumphant; troubled; trumpeting; tyrannical; uncertain; unctuous; uneducated; unearthly; unheeded; universal; unmistakable; unmodulated; un-moved; unrestrained; unruffled; unruly; unshaded; unshaken; unsteady; unsyllabic; uttered; vacuous; vague; velvet; venal; venomous; veritable; vigorous; virgin; vociferous; vulgar; wailing; warbled; warning; weary; welcoming; well-attuned; well-bred; well-known; well-modulated; well-tuned; wheedling; whining; whisper-ing; wistful; wondering; woodland; wond-rous; wretched; yawning; yearning; young; impatient; impersonal.

verbs

acclaim—; attune to—; blot out—; candy —; choke—; control—; dampen—; discip-line—; disguise—; drop—; drown out—; dull—; echo—; exercise—; guard—; hark-en to—; heed—; hush—; irritate—; laud —; lift—; mellow—; modulate—; muffle —; mute—; muzzle—; pitch—; place—; re-cognize—; silence—; still—; strain—; study —; sugar—; sweeten—; thrill to—; throttle —; tinge—; train—; —awakens; —bawls; —beguiles; —booms; —breaks; —carols; —carries; —censures; —changes; —charms; —chokes; —cracks; —cuts; —deepens; —drones on; —dwindles; —enraptures; —fascinates; —flags; —flames; —floats up; —lashes; —murmurs; —palpitates; —pene-trates; —pierces; —quavers; —ranges; —rasps; —registers; —resounds; —rings out; —rises; —rolls; —sharpens; —slurs; —squeaks; —stirs; —swells; —thickens; —throbs; —thunders; —tightens; —trails off; —trembles; —twitters; —vibrates; —warms; —wavers; —wheedles; —whines; —whis-pers; —wracks; —wrings.

(See sound, utterance, tone.)

VOICE (*v*)

adverbs

tenderly; harmoniously; accusingly; antag-onistically; anxiously; authoritatively; blunt-ly; exultantly; ominously; sternly; patriot-ically; lustily; audibly; monotonously; petu-

1268

lantly; raucously; reproachfully; sepulchrally; vulgarly; vigorously; vociferously; venomously.

(See express, say.)

VOID

adjectives
trackless; foggy; pale; bare; absolute; mysterious; boundless; populous; fathomless; immeasurable; illimitable; blank.

adverbs
legally; unluckily; apparently; manifestly; unfortunately; blessedly; fortunately; utterly; recently; temporarily; hopelessly; undeniably; definitely; curiously.

VOLCANO

adjectives
extinct; perilous; concealed; slumbering; barren; drowned; spiritual; smoldering.

verbs
fling into—; gaze into—; pacify—; placate —; toss into—; —activates; —awakens; — belches; —buries; —chokes; —destroys; — devastates; —discharges; —ejects; —embroils; —emits; —endangers; —erupts; — flows; —foments; —fulminates; —fumes; — lies dormant; —looms; —quiets; —rampages; —rises; —roars; —rumbles; —seethes; —simmers; —sleeps; —smoulders; — spews forth; —strangles; —streams over; —threatens; —vents.

(See eruption, crater.)

VOLITION

adjectives
distinct; special; true; passionate; conscious; particular.

VOLLEY

adjectives
severe; fine; bombastic; pyrotechnic; instantaneous; incessant; intermitting; useless; deafening.

verbs
blast—; discharge—; flash—; fulminate—; prolong—; renew—; —assaults; —bombards; —crashes; —decimates; —destroys; —detonates; —devastates; —echoes; — flares; —levels; —rattles; —razes; —rends; —resounds; —rings out; —roars; —rolls; —rumbles; —shatters; —splits; —thunders; —wreaks.

(See gun-fire, shots, fussilade.)

VOLUBILITY

adjectives
startling; accustomed; infinite; fierce.

VOLUBLE

adverbs
usually; habitually; comically; chattily; torrentially; ridiculously; unnecessarily; peculiarly; characteristically; momentarily; unusually; hysterically; excitedly; officiously; vexatiously; intolerably; amusingly.

VOLUME

adjectives
separate; immense; added; record; sympathetic; respective; published; comfortable; ambitious; increasing; unprecedented; random; dusky; ragged; penultimate; inexhaustible; thumb-scarred; pale; magnificent; enormous; arid; precious; attractive; ponderous; endless; unlimited; growing; rushing; valuable; library; thundering; remarkable; swelling; respectable; charming; solemn; supplementary; worthless; far-reaching; poetic; tasteful; long-coveted; subsequent; forthcoming; dog-eared; serried (pl); tremendous; substantial; collected; thrilling; proud; pathetic; posthumous; universal; fascinating; masterful; brilliant; momentous; sturdy; vast; venerable; splendid; printed; blinding; mere; bulky; sulphurous; enormous; weighty; instructive; stray; odd; scholarly; sumptuous; inspired; comprehensive.

verbs
author—; autograph—; bind—; browse through—; compile—; con—; confiscate—; consult—; curtail—; delve into—; display —; entitle—; fray—; illustrate—; immerse in—; interpret—; peruse—; ponder—; prepare—; prize—; publish—; review—; revise—; scan—; skim over—; summarize—; tackle—; value—; —airs; —circulates; — condemns; —deals with; —discourses on; — dissertates; —diverts; —exposes; —libels; —narrates; —plagiarizes; —recites; —recounts; —relates; —slanders; —treats of; —unfolds; —ventilates; devote—to.

(See book, manuscript, story, work, tome.)

VOLUMINOUS

adverbs
overwhelmingly; stupendously; inclusively; pedantically; ambitiously; monumentally; sufficiently; immensely; manifestly; absurdly; unnecessarily.

VOLUNTARY

adverbs

freely; generously; impetuously; eagerly; earnestly; energetically; emphatically; unmistakably; undoubtedly; unquestionably; usually; frankly; necessarily; amicably; delightfully; completely.

VOLUNTEERS

adjectives

raw; devoted; zealous; tireless; fanatic; susceptible; doughty; brave.

verbs

acclaim—; arm—; command—; compose of —; discipline—; equip—; furnish—; honor —; laud—; plead for—; quarter—; recruit —; rig out—; train—; transport—; —bid for; —brave; —comprise; —defend; —disband; —enlist; —offer; —proffer; —serve; —storm; —tackle; —tender.

(See soldier, recruit.)

VOLUPTUARY

adjectives

cautious; refined; hedonistic.

VOLUPTUOUS

adverbs

pleasantly; buxomly; luxuriously; delightedly; naturally; habitually; notoriously; conspicuously; openly; utterly; unmistakably.

VOLUPTUOUSNESS

adjectives

inebriating; supposed; gorgeous.

VOMIT (v)

adverbs

nauseatingly; sickeningly; disgustingly; recurringly; drunkenly.

VOMITING

verbs

allay—; ameliorate—; check—; curtail—; diagnose—; encourage—; force—; forestall—; induce—; produce—; stem—; stimulate to—; —cleanses; —dislodges; —eases; —ejects; —eliminates; —endangers; —expels; —indicates; —purges; —sheds; —unburdens; —vents; —weakens.

(See nausea.)

VORACIOUS

adverbs

overweeningly; rabidly; insatiately; incredibly; dreadfully; unspeakably; frightfully; unbelievably; wolfishly; bestially.

VORACITY

adjectives

impotent; insatiable; unscrupulous.

VORTEX

verbs

form—; sweep into—; tumble into—; —agitates; —billows; —boils; —churns; —circumvolutes; —convolutes; —eddies; —engulfs; —expands; —foams; —gyrates; —immerses; —pirouettes; —revolves; —ripples; —rotates; —submerges; —surges; —swells; —swirls; —trundles; —twirls; —whirls.

(See whirlpool, maelstrom.)

VOTARY

adjectives

boyish; dull; firm; mistaken.

VOTE

adjectives

majority; overhanging; overwhelming; disputed; injudicious; unanimous; purchasable; direct; negative; reluctant; decisive; ignorant; appalling; valid; dissenting; simple; plurality; deciding; heavy; loyal; crooked.

VOTE (v)

adverbs

unanimously; progressively; overwhelmingly; democratically; inconsistently; regularly; affirmatively; loyally; intelligently; legally; judiciously; ignorantly; decisively.

(See elect, declare.)

VOTERS

adjectives

independent-minded; submissive; patient; stupid; blinded; purchased; intelligent; thinking.

verbs

address—; appeal to—; assure—; beguile —; coerce—; dictate to—; divide—; harangue—; pledge to—; poll—; promise—; sway—; woo—; —acknowledge; —approve; —ballot; —choose; —determine; —elect; —endorse; —overwhelm; —reign; —rule; —select; —stream to; —subscribe to; —support; —sustain; —vacillate; —voice.

(See constituent, public, citizen.)

VOTES

verbs

aggregate—; alienate—; amass—; angle for —; apportion—; assure of—; bag—; bias —; calculate—; campaign for—; compute —; conciliate—; corral—; gain—; gather —; guarantee—; hazard—; imperil—; influence—; insure—; jeopardize—; line up —; muster—; poll—; procure—; promise—; record—; recount—; register—; risk—; separate—; sew up—; split—; sway—; swing —; void—; win—; —determine; —pile up; —pour in.

(See election, nomination, plurality, ballot.)

VOTIVE

adverbs

sacredly; sacrificially; devoutly; undeniably; apparently; sincerely, truly; completely; contritely.

VOW

adjectives

earthly; capricious; rash; musical; unheedful; violated; truant; passionate; unbroken; moist; bridal; ardent; intermingled; sainted; hollow; frail; noble; slighted; monastic; limber; monkish; solemn; marital; sacred; dread; grateful; self-imposed; idle; generous; heavenly; serviceable.

verbs

annul—; breathe—; commit to—; comply with—; contract—; declare—; desecrate—; discharge from—; divorce from—; embody in—; enforce—; forfeit—; fulfill—; heed—; ignore—; infringe—; liberate from—; maintain—; observe—; pursue—; register—; relax—; respect—; sanctify—; slacken—; solemnize—; swear to—; undertake—; violate—; —binds; —burdens; —chains; — fetters; —pledges; —prohibits; —restrains; —restricts; —weighs upon.

(See pledge, oath, promise, contract.)

VOW (v)

adverbs

patiently; passionately; languidly; capriciously; rashly; ardently; nobly; magnanimously; monastically; sacredly; generously; maritally.

(See promise, swear.)

VOWEL

adjectives

open; various (pl); softening; euphonious;

nasalized; drawled; guttural; mispronounced; throaty.

verbs

ablaut—; accent—; accentuate—; articulate —; discard—; economize on—s; emphasize —; employ—; lengthen—; misuse—; pronounce—; silence—; shorten—; stress—; umlaut—; trip up on—s; —changes; — sharpens.

(See sound.)

VOYAGE

adjectives

prosperous; loving; projected; aimless; tedious; eventful; magnificent; determinate; stormy; tempestuous; ill-fated; frequent (pl); uncertain; romantic; perilous; mysterious; homeward.

verbs

brave—; chart—; conclude—; curtail—; delay—; deviate from—; embark on—; extend —; hazard—; plan—; prolong—; protract —; set forth on—; terminate—; venture upon—; —broadens; —embraces; —fascinates; —lures; —intrigues; —refreshes; — relaxes; —touches upon; —tranquillizes.

(See journey, trip.)

VOYAGER

adjectives

dusty-throated; battered; uninstructed; seasick.

VULGAR

adverbs

incredibly; strangely; habitually; unwontedly; grossly; boorishly; defiantly; crassly; strangely; purposely; arrantly; definitely; openly; conspicuously; shamefully; carelessly; unmistakably; singularly; surprisingly; intentionally; deliberately; flagrantly.

VULGARITY

adjectives

patent; hideous; rude; vigorous; impertinent; unutterable; innumerable (pl); purseproud; finished; pathetic; stupid; private; blatant; odious; intense; superlative; petty; universal; studied.

verbs

abhor—; blush at—; breed—; countenance —; deplore—; descend to—; exhibit—; flaunt—; frown upon—; recoil from—; —

coarsens; —debases; —degrades; —irks; —mortifies; —ostracizes; —repels; —shocks; —surrounds.

(See coarseness.)

VULNERABLE

adverbs

sadly; unfortunately; admittedly; wretchedly; miserably; probably; unluckily; terribly; alarmingly; portentously; ominously; significantly; dangerously; perilously; carelessly; incautiously; criminally; dreadfully; unbelievably; unforgivably; negligently; unhappily.

VULTURE

adjectives

famished; gnawing; carrion; hovering; greedy; swooping; ugly.

verbs

—circles; —clutches; —descends; —devours; —dives; —divests; —flutters; —glides; —gorges; —hisses; —hovers over; —picks clean; —plucks; —pounces upon; —preys upon; —ravishes; —regurgitates; —scales; —scavenges; —seizes; —soars; —shrieks; —subsists; —swoops down; —whirls.

(See bird, eagle, hawk.)

W

WADE (v)

adverbs

laboriously; conscientiously; cautiously; fastidiously; carefully.

(See swim.)

WAFT (v)

adverbs

delicately; pungently; insidiously; gently; capriciously.

(See carry, float.)

WAG (v)

adverbs

humorously; sardonically; slowly; feebly; mutely; wordlessly; sagely; cryptically.

(See nod, move.)

WAGE

adjectives

preposterous; satisfactory; aggregate; hard-earned; comparative; prevailing; monetary; actual; scanty; unsteady; uncertain; exorbitant; inflated; youthful; daily; living.

WAGER

verbs

accept—; agree upon—; cast—; chance—; claim—; contest—; decide—; determine—; force—; frame—; gamble on—; lay—; propose—; record—; release from—; speculate on—; stake—on; transact—; venture—; —challenges; —hazards; —pledges.

(See bet, gambling.)

WAGES

verbs

advance—; boost—; default—; determine—; distribute—; engage for—; expend—; fix—; forfeit—; grudge—; halve—; increase—; invest—; level—; lift—; proportion—; raise—; rate—; realize—; reap—; reduce —; regulate—; scale—; scorn—; serve for —; slash—; squander—; step up—; stimulate—; supplement—; tabulate—; withhold —; —compensate; —conform; —decline; —indemnify; —remunerate; —reward; —soar.

(See income, earnings, fee, pittance, living, livelihood.)

WAGGISH

adverbs

jocosely; facetiously; fatuously; banteringly; boastfully; drolly; clownishly; pleasantly; foolishly; playfully; intolerably; disagreeably; smartly; conceitedly; whimsically; fantastically; vexatiously; disgustingly; merrily; mischievously.

WAGON

adjectives

ancient; lumbering; serviceable; jolting; creaking; wobbling; emigrant; clanking; broken-down; hooded; ramshackle; vengeful.

verbs

brake—; cart on—; convoy—; dispatch—; draw—; harness to—; hitch—; journey by —; —conveys; —creeps along; —draws up; —jolts; —jounces; —rattles; —rolls; —transports.

(See caravan, automobile, cart, vehicle.)

WAIL

adjectives

piteous; faint; infantile; obstreperous; lusty; articulate; windy; inward; melodramatic; thin; fretful; dismal; doleful; dying; hideous; damned; confused; heartbroken; young; passionate; patriotic; pathetic; murmured; tender; moaning; wild; liquid; weird; far-off; mournful; amazed; angry; nightly; flute-like.

verbs

emit—; prolong—; set up—; shrill—; utter —; —complains of; —deplores; —deprecates; —grieves; —laments; —mourns; —pierces; —rends; —rings out; —rises; —wrings.

(See cry, howl, lamentation.)

WAIL (v)

adverbs

distressfully; mournfully; dismally; piteously; inarticulately; fretfully; dolefully; passionately; wildly; weirdly; mournfully; lustily; obstreperously.

(See moan, lament.)

adverbs

mournfully; incessantly; continually; intermittently; hopefully; piously; confoundedly; petulantly; disagreeably; feebly; vociferously; loudly; wistfully; ostentatiously; pitifully; hungrily; sleepily; drowsily; insincerely; tiresomely; monotonously; desperately; vexatiously; pettishly.

WAIST

adjectives

snug; thickening; imperceptible; tapering; enormous; collective; trackless; slender; winsome; wasplike; well-fitting; capacious.

WAIT (*v*)

adverbs

breathlessly; passively; sadly; reverently; anxiously; exultantly; mutely; devotedly; placidly; instinctively; calmly; apprehensively; boldly; hungrily; morbidly; disastrously; indecisively; tensely.

(See pause, delay.)

WAITER

adjectives

smug; oblivious; rowdy; obsequious; swarthy; corpulent; stately; efficient.

verbs

beckon to—; bid—; bow—out; employ—; engage—; rebuke—; reproach—; ring for —; signal—; summon—; tip—; uniform—; —announces; —approaches; —attends; — directs to; —fumbles; —hovers near; —informs; —recommends; —serves; —suggests.

(See matron, nurse, servant.)

WAITING

adverbs

silently; doggedly; resolutely; hopelessly; helplessly; intolerably; restlessly; feverishly; optimistically; trustfully; happily; forlornly; eagerly; boisterously; cruelly; miserably; interminably; insistently.

WAIVE (*v*)

adverbs

magnanimously; willingly; voluntarily; deliberately; nobly; generously; affectionately; informally.

(See dispense, relinquish.)

WAKEFUL

adverbs

nervously; mysteriously; alertly; anxiously;

miserably; wretchedly; vigilantly; habitually; watchfully; unnaturally; peculiarly; strangely; significantly; fortunately; luckily; suddenly; feverishly; comfortably.

WALK
(general)

adjectives

solar; winding; strenuous; long; sunken; gravel; aimless; sanguine; flagged; exhilarating; cheerful; moderate; cloistered; lumbering; obscure; sunny; rough; windy; fatiguing; leisurely; lingering; tangling; cultured; mincing; haphazard; laurel; solitary; hedge-lined; contemplative; rampart; willowy; shady; slow; undulating; rhythmic; moonlight; enrapturing; roaming; royal; humble; swarming; tremendous; silent; visionary; smart; mind-clearing; dark; night; restless; glorious; opposite; spacious; sequestered; imposing; tangling; lazy; murmuring; substantial; oval; umbrageous.

WALK
(path)

verbs

beautify—; border—; block—; bound—; circle—; designate—; elevate—; enclose—; fence in—; flank—; intersect—; occupy—; parallel—; pave—; plank—; promenade—; repair—; run up—; seclude—; shade—; skirt—.

(See lane, alley, path.)

WALK (*v*)

adverbs

cavalierly; gingerly; sprightly; blindly; spirally; deliberately; defiantly; meekly; humbly; unsteadily; characteristically; mutely; monotonously; untiringly; tempestuously; stealthily; strenuously; musingly; restlessly; languidly; foppishly; aimlessly; wantonly; reflectively; defiantly; jauntily; calmly; briskly; warily; abstractedly; sedately; haphazardly; contemplatively; lazily.

(See trudge, stroll.)

WALLET

verbs

adorn—; appropriate—; cram—; emboss—; engrave—; examine—; filch—; guard—; lift—; mulct of—; palm—; pilfer—; prize —; protrude from—; rifle—; stuff—; swell —; thrust into—; —bulges; —wears.

(See bag, purse.)

adverbs

bestially; voluptuously; hoggishly; disgustingly; revoltingly; carnally; lewdly; insatiably; vulgarly.

(See flounder, grovel.)

WALLS

adjectives

naked; massive; rugged; crannied; crumbling; shattered; eloquent; high; espaliered; garden; bartizan; sapphire; gloomy; adamantine; tired; thick; crenelated; staring; tinted; forsaken; weltering; well-built; verdurous; unsurmounted; emblazoned; proscenium; continuous; impregnable; imperial; pretty; impassable; forested; outward; obliterated; impenetrable; celestial; beauteous, ruined; munimental; abdominal; dignified; flaming; expressionless; far-reaching; buttressed; decaying; wicked; dainty; trembling; moldering; ancient; ruinous; humid; courteous; chancel; battlemented; venerable; dungeon; illuminated; exterior; everlasting; dull; damp; fluttering; roofless; low; unplastered; paneled; high-jutting; pictured; dark; grimy; prison; frowning; fortress; tottering; inaccessible; protecting; sheer; remote; unbroken; leafy-bannered; conventual; vertical; steep; jointed; rocky; lengthy; living; soft; evenly-tinted; gleaming; mossy; shiny; sunny; yonder; wailing; rose-bannered; garden; wind-proofed; austered; cerulean; majestic; towering; girdling; unornamented; unfinished; moaning; mountain; lofty; protecting; silver-seamed; somber; melted; unpeopled; projecting; brazen; eternal; intervening; triple; leprous; lateral; beloved; multitudinous; blistered; fragmentary; rustling; weathered; ageless; scarped; confining; mirrored; moss-covered; dingy; distempered.

verbs

barricade behind—; batter down—; bedaub —; clamber over—; decorate—; deface—; drape—; drive to—; emboss—; erect—; flank—; fortify—; fresco—; harbor within —; mount—; paper—; pierce—; rib—; scale—; scan—; smite—; surmount—; vault—; —arise; —confine; —crumble; — defend; —enclose; —envelop; —gird; — impede; —partition; —obscure; —shelter; —shield; —shoulder; —surround.

(See fence, barricade, fortification.)

WALTZ

adjectives

lilting; wheeling; ingratiating; old-fashioned; whirling; graceful; appealing.

verbs

compose—; embrace in—; enjoy—; fling into—; introduce—; popularize—; portray —; sway to—; whirl in—; —calms; —enthralls; —entrances; —graces; —gyrates; —relaxes; —revolves; —rolls; —survives; —thrills.

(See dance, minuet.)

WALTZ (v)

adverbs

gracefully; harmoniously; deftly; energetically; charmingly; seductively; rhythmically; liltingly; ingratiatingly; appealingly.

(See dance, trip.)

WAN

adverbs

pitifully; unfortunately; alarmingly; miserably; feebly; unhealthily; wretchedly; dreadfully; unaccountably; unusually; naturally; strangely; curiously; unnaturally; ghastly.

WAND

adjectives

opiate; streaked; potent; scribbling; snake-encircled; certain; sable.

verbs

bear—; brandish—; cleave—; endow—; fashion—; flex—; flourish—; magnetize—; ply—; smite with—; splinter—; split—; strike with—; stroke—; tip—; whittle—; —charms; —chastises; —enchants; — guides; —mesmerizes; —mystifies; —symbolizes.

(See baton, cane, scepter, twig.)

WANDER (v)

adverbs

desolately; erratically; deviously; dilatorily; errantly; listlessly; aimlessly; disconsolately; blindly; ruefully; stupidly; hopelessly; promiscuously; rashly; wearily.

(See roam, ramble.)

WANDERER

adjectives

bodiless; fantastic; forlorn; night; weary; unwilling; immortal; archetypical; blithe; half-frozen; long-lost; undisciplined.

WANDERING

adjectives

eccentric; devious; difficult; weary; sleepless; restless; vague; unquiet; aimless; accidental; dream-led; enfranchised; much; occasional.

adverbs

inanely; fruitlessly; incessantly; doggedly; hopefully; idly; actually; mentally; confusedly; nervously; nonchalantly; irresponsibly.

WANDERINGS

verbs

cease—; chart—; color—; condemn to—; describe—; embark on—; experience in—; extend—; narrate—; prolong—; protract—; record—; relate—; retire from—; unfold—; weary of—; —aberrate; —age; —amuse; — embrace; —interest; —thrill.

(See travel, voyage.)

WANDERLUST

adjectives

unconquerable; reoccurring; uncontrollable.

verbs

extinguish—; nip—; obey—; quash—; quell —; quench—; resist—; stamp out—; subdue —; succumb to—; surrender to—; yield to —; suppress—; —fires; —grips; —impels; —overwhelms; —perishes; —prods; —pushes; —seizes; —urges.

(See desire, longing, impulse.)

WANT

adjectives

abject; burning; thirsty; fiery; gnawing; acute; actual; spontaneous; unreflected; needful; artificial; common; utter; frank; fearless; passionate; respective; material; immediate; total; unpardonable; unbounded; shameful; endless; wondrous; tender; squalid; divine; present; narrow; curious; presumptive; ripe; absolute; modest; lower; spiritual; conscious; returning; sufficient.

verbs

administer to—s; anticipate—s; come to—; consult—s; correct—; diminish—s; discharge —s; express—; gratify—; impoverish with —; intensify—; mark by—; occasion—; provide for—s; reduce to—; subject to—; suffer—; —blemishes; —goads on; —s multiply.

(See need, lack, necessity, destitution.)

WANT (v)

adverbs

desperately; distressingly; intensely; vaguely; immediately; manifestly; particularly; shamelessly; absolutely; immodestly; spiritually; wistfully; conspicuously; abjectly; passionately.

(See need, desire.)

WANTON

adverbs

recklessly; playfully; immorally; irrepressibly; loosely; unrestrainedly; wickedly; provocatively; delightedly; hilariously; drunkenly; airily; emotionally; insanely; crazily; childishly; ludicrously; pitiably; brazenly; audaciously; heedlessly; imprudently; incorrigibly; eccentrically; monstrously; lawlessly; outlandishly; unwontedly; bafflingly.

WAR

adjectives

suicidal; glorious; brooding; vigorous; impious; exhausting; guerrilla; diabolical; ruthless; expensive; aggressive; ferocious; defensive; internecine; offensive; desolating; mimic; mustering; bitter; grim; impending; universal; increasing; horrible; aboriginal; glorified; inevitable; imminent; classical; barbarous; undeclared; virtuous; fratricidal; open; manful; cormorant; victorious; fearful; intrepid; successive (pl); deadly; successful; tribal; unearthly; meritorious; righteous; unholy; interminable; raging; ensuing; disastrous; banded; brutal; pelting; unvanquished; unjust; incessant; rebellious; devastating; nonsparing; silvan; plangent; elemental; imperialist; contemplated; ghastly; mercenary; renewed; silent; sanguinary; strenuous; social; servile; innocent; irrepressible; intellectual; contumelious; beastly; mad-brained; realistic; fierce; courageous; petty; theologic; religious; witching; tremendous; passive.

verbs

abstain from—; aggravate—; anticipate—; avert—; banish—; cease—; control—; dedicate to—; determine—; dramatize—; dread —; drift into—; embrace—; entangle in—; enter—; envisage—; fend off—; flame into —; foment—; gird for—; halt—; launch—; localize—; muster for—; outlaw—; plunge into—; prolong—; promote—; provoke—; resort to—; romanticize—; stage—; stave off—; stem—; survive—; taboo—; throttle

—; vilify—; wage—; witness—; —arises; —bestializes; —blasts; —bristles; —drags on; —endangers; —entangles; —looms; — overclouds; —overshadows; —progresses; —rages; —ravages; —runs rampant; —sunders; —terminates; —vilifies.

(See fight, combat, battle, warfare.)

WARD

adjectives
unguarded; close; legitimate; hard; slow-turning; airy; intricate; mutinous; surgical; gracious.

WARDROBE

adjectives
sophisticated; natty; all-occasion; personalized; endless; summer; outdoor; holiday.

verbs
attain—; augment—; complete—; delete—; envy—; equip with—; expend on—; fit out with—; luxuriate in—; mend—; mutilate —; perfect—; provide—; purchase—; renew—; repair—; replenish—; restore—; —suffers; —suffices.

(See clothing, apparel.)

WARE

adjectives
varnished; universal; tawdry; gaudy.

WARES

verbs
auction—; bargain for—; bid for—; cheapen —; dispense—; display—; dispose of—; examine—; hawk—; inflate—; inspect—; liquidate—; loot—; market—; peddle—; pilfer—; proclaim—; purvey—; put—under the hammer; retail—; scatter—; test—; undersell—; vend—; —allure; —depreciate.

(See merchandise, product.)

WARFARE

adjectives
manful; curious; dulcet; cruel; chivalrous; incessant; nightly; friendless; deadly; desperate; foreign; unceasing; offensive; tremendous; unrelenting; eternal; aggressive; wanton; devastating; hopeless; internecine; sylvan; perpetual; unsuccessful; bloody; critical; protracted; vigorous; disjointed; impending; predatory; guerrilla; mimic; licentious; partisan; heartrending.

verbs
abolish—; arm for—; array for—; balk at —; carry on—; conclude—; decry—; engage in—; force into—; incite—; inflame to—; initiate into—; instigate—; kindle—; light the torch of—; mobilize for—; precipitate into—; resign to—; revolt at—; threaten—; train for—; —devastates; —exterminates; —menaces; —pillages; —plunders; — seethes; —takes toll; —undermines; — wreaks.

(See hostility, war, struggle, conflict.)

WARLIKE

adverbs
insatiably; recklessly; criminally; bestially; flagrantly; viciously; inherently; foully; systematically; abominably; inhumanly; atrociously; brutally; infamously; iniquitously; nefariously; scandalously; savagely; ferociously; vilely; wickedly; barbarously; incorrigibly; unfeelingly; sinfully; horribly; unspeakably; fiendishly; flagitiously; villainously; needlessly; indecently.

WARM

adverbs
unseasonably; uncomfortably; unreasonably; curiously; terribly; comfortably; securely; gratefully; surprisingly; slightly; dreadfully; suffocatingly; unnecessarily; extremely; sufficiently; pleasantly.

WARM (v)

adverbs
perceptibly; appreciably; uncomfortably; frightfully; dangerously; significantly.

(See heat, arouse.)

WARM-HEARTED

adverbs
delightfully; impulsively; lovingly; generously; philanthropically; naturally; dependably; especially; marvelously; pleasantly; wonderfully; altruistically; cordially; hospitably; unusually; uncommonly; sincerely; conspicuously; genuinely; really; truly; always; frankly; earnestly.

WARMTH

adjectives
genial; comfortable; thrilling; redolent; juvenile; life-giving; personal; soft; native; grateful; bright; added; balmy; considerable; unseemly; vivacious; trustworthy; deceitful; feeble; loathy; refreshing; virile; varying; peculiar; ethereal; brooding; pas-

sionate; heartfelt; tongueless; friendly; dissolving; tingling; true; human; added; eccentric; rugged; confiding; voluptuous; fostering; utmost.

verbs

accustom to—; afford—; bask in—; diffuse —; drowse in—; enjoy—; excite—; exude —; glow with—; impart—; inhale—; provide—; radiate—; regain—; retain—; sense —; swelter in—; temper with—; welcome—; —animates; —chafes; —comforts; —flushes; —fuses; —lingers; —pervades; —renews; —revives; —revivifies; —thaws.

(See glow, geniality, fervor, ardor, heat.)

WARN (*v*)

adverbs

providentially; solemnly; amply; sufficiently; grimly; prophetically; urgently; graciously; forcefully; subtly; soberly; earnestly; faithfully.

(See admonish.)

WARNING

adjectives

grim; prophetic; ecclesiastical; celestial; competent; sundry (pl); gracious; urgent; open; preliminary; startling; eternal; slender; forceful; important; hoarse; subtle; timely; anonymous; displeasing; terrible; anxious; secular; fair; pathetic; sober; earnest; paradoxical.

verbs

accept—; broadcast—; convey—; disregard —; distribute—s; explode—; furnish—; heed—; ignore—; issue—; protest—; regard —; rumble—; signal—; sound—; stress—; tender—; voice—; yield to—; —alarms; — impends; —terrifies.

(See counsel, portent, admonition.)

WARRANT

adjectives

external; lawful; bloody; sufficient; seeming; scriptural; doubtful; valid; avowed; infallible; further.

verbs

arm with—; draw up—; exercise—; flourish —; issue—; procure—; resort to—; retain on—; swear out—; wield—; —accredits; — apprehends; —authorizes; —commissions; —delegates; —deputizes; —empowers; — permits; —pledges; —proclaims; —protects.

(See authority, mandate, summons.)

WARRANTABLE

adverbs

thoroughly; entirely; soundly; altogether; wholly; justly; properly; safely; reasonably; sufficiently; probably; presumably; supposedly; definitely.

WARRIOR

adjectives

sullen; painful; intrepid; inferior; flaming; simple-minded; charging; care-stricken; delighted; naked; redoubtable; savage; struggling; indefatigable; stern-faced; discomfited; long-dead; gloomy-looking; veteran; fierce; illustrious; exhausted; devilish; magnificent; invincible; tiny; dauntless; fell-handed.

verbs

acclaim—; arm—; beribbon—; commemorate—; conciliate—; confer upon—; decorate—; dedicate to—; distinguish—; draft —; elevate—; emulate—; ennoble—; enshrine—; esteem—; exalt—; exhort—; glorify—; hail—; honor—; idealize—; immortalize—; knight—; laud—; lionize—; pacify —; pay homage to—; rank—; revere—; reward—; salute—; worship—; —combats; —engages; —intrenches; —s mobilize; — parries; —perishes; —repels; —sheathes; —wields.

(See soldier, fighter, hero.)

WARSHIP

verbs

anchor—; bomb—; command—; confine on —; engage—; evade—; dodge—; scale—; —blockades; —bombards; —conveys; —convoys; —founders; —hems in; —maneuvers; —s mass; —patrols; —plies; —raids; — rakes; —rams; —retaliates; —rolls; — rushes; —sallies; —shells; —threatens; — transports.

(See boat, ship, army.)

WART

verbs

apply to—; burn—; cauterize—; cut—; daub on—; detach—; dissect—; excise—s; grease—; incise—; patch—s; peel—; remove—; salve—; sever—; subject to—s; treat—; —appears; —blemishes; —bulges; —s develop; —disfigures; —erupts; —flattens; —maligns; —mars; —protrudes; — swells; —thickens; —vanishes.

(See sore, wound.)

adverbs

habitually; constantly; necessarily; alertly; uncommonly; significantly; extraordinarily; noticeably; nervously; wisely; ordinarily; curiously; tiresomely; conspicuously; timidly; sagaciously; deliberately; anxiously; admirably.

WASH (*v*)

adverbs

surreptitiously; scrupulously; listlessly; fastidiously; habitually; laboriously; deliberately.

(See clean, scrub.)

WASHING

verbs

obviate—; require—; subject to—; —ablutes; —cleanses; —deodorizes; —deterges; —disinfects; —elutriates; —expurgates; —eliminates; —laves; —lixiviates; —purges; —purifies; —refreshes; —renews; —vivifies.

(See bath, water.)

WASPS

adjectives

injurious; stinging; buzzing; rowdy.

verbs

avoid—; classify—; —barb; —burrow; —buzz; —dig; —excavate; —hum; —flit; —molest; —nest; —paralyze; —poison; —provision; —pursue; —snare; —sting; —store; —tunnel; —wing.

(See hornet, insect, bee.)

WASTE

adjectives

unbridled; trackless; wandering; sinful; deliberate; dismal; encompassing; watery; woeful; colorless; indeterminate; gloomy; senseless; vast; thriftless; solemn-sounding; stupendous; unnecessary; terrible; inexcusable; wintry; glimmering; unproductive; arctic; barren; widening; sprinkled; spiritual; lonely; putrid; melancholy; simple; premature; colossal; tragic; aching; positive; nitrogenous; inward; desolate; hurried; remote; snowy; frightful; hopeless; burning; pathless; muscular; weltering; garden; flowering; sanctuary; shoreless; lavish; unpardonable; fruitless; boundless; ruinous; digestive; uninhabited; woodland; full; sandy; merciless; monstrous; howling; arid; frozen; turbid; war-worn; useless;

dreary; dangerous; sterile; insidious; desert; wanton; verdant; enormous; tedious; billowy; illimitable; untamed; profligate; dread; moldering.

verbs

abate—; bewail—; check—; countenance—; curb—; curtail—; decry—; detect—; diminish—; discharge—; eliminate—; excrete—; harvest—; imply—; incur—; manufacture —; rebuke for—; reproach for—; restore —; result in—; retrieve—; rid of—; upbraid for—; wipe out—; withdraw—; —abuses; —accumulates; —appals; —declines; —denudes; —desecrates; —diminishes; —dissipates; —endangers; —shrinks; —squanders; —threatens.

(See junk, mess, garbage, extravagance.)

WASTE (*v*)

adverbs

unprofitably; improvidently; rashly; carelessly; heedlessly; deliberately; woefully; senselessly; stupendously; unnecessarily; unproductively; spiritually; ruthlessly; fruitlessly; wantonly; profligately.

(See sqaunder, dissipate.)

WASTE-BASKET

verbs

cast into—; consign to—; cram into—; deluge—; empty—; find in—; mouse around —; relegate to—; stuff—; —provides; —serves; —overflows.

(See basket.)

WASTED
(*emaciated*)

adverbs

pitiably; remarkably; haggardly; gauntly; helplessly; lankly; feebly; desperately; wretchedly; extremely.

WASTEFUL

adverbs

criminally; wickedly; extremely; wantonly; thoughtlessly; inconsiderately; immoderately; terribly; carelessly; negligently; foolishly; enormously; indolently; improvidently; ignorantly; crazily; unconscionably; inordinately; egregiously; atrociously; incredibly; miserably; extremely; imprudently; wretchedly.

WATCH

adjectives

happy; railroad; neglected; solitary; clamorous; fierce; advised; adventuring; vigilant; tireless; celestial; sympathetic; expensive; airy; couchant; brotherly; breathless; unnatural; strict; unceasing; patient; furtive; incessant; faithful; thrilling.

verbs
adjust—; check—; consult—; embellish—; engrave—; fondle—; illuminate—; jewel—; lubricate—; observe—; overwind—; pawn —; refer to—; regulate—; rely upon—; repair—; set—; snatch—; value—; wind—; —fails; —informs; —reminds; —runs down.
  (See dial, clock.)

WATCH (v)

adverbs
vigilantly; anxiously; surreptitiously; sullenly; furtively; narrowly; assiduously; disconsolately; absently; minutely; keenly; vaguely; listlessly; slyly; idly; breathlessly; wistfully; apprehensively; attentively; stealthily; greedily; incessantly; moodily; covertly; defiantly; somberly; pensively; lazily; faithfully.
  (See observe, scrutinize.)

WATCHER

adjectives
indolent; wingless; unsuspected; lone; sleepless.

WATCHFUL

adverbs
carefully; cautiously; responsibly; properly; stingily; greedily; hungrily; coldly; slyly; alertly; wisely; justifiably; sagaciously; inquisitively; curiously; maliciously; fondly; devotedly; jealously; enviously; constantly; anxiously; timidly.

WATCHFULNESS

adjectives
incumbent; calm; heavy; stealthy; constant; suspicious; assiduous; sharp; alert; silent; strenuous.

WATER

adjectives
poisonous; murky; wrinkled; brackish; gentle; golden; pellucid; swishing; impounded; shining; marching; sunny; purplish; winding; honeyed; unshaken; precious; steaming; greasy; saline; putrid; bitter; gliding; hidden; rampant; sky-hued; limpid; rocking; darkening; stagnant; shadowless; hurrying; clear; sparkling; hot; glittering; silvery; seaward; surplus; numberless (pl); glistening; emerald; thundering; sleepy; blessed; ready; burning; blue-bosomed; streaming; muddy; invisible; huddling; climbing; living; wind-swept; lonely; reflecting; cleansing; ornamental; brooding; yielding; insipid; weary; swollen; navigable; transparent; festering; reef-strewn; trackless; starlit; moving; virgin; shoal-impatient; swift; giddy; annihilating; quivering; seething; placid; rose-white; glaring; restless; heaving; meager; dropping; sluggish; bickering; reviving; ebbing; imprisoned; dreamy; land-locked; crystal; flowing; gloomy; turbid; broken; perilous; vivifying; healing; moon-clear; tepid; enchanted; cloistered; sunshiny; fetid; dreary; azure; fastflowing; moon-lit; angry; wasteful; perennial; pliant; unsuspected; hydrant; chanting; loathsome; abundant; fluvial; smooth; idle; silent; booming; still; wide; sweltering; distilled; darkling; inviolable; flashing; scalding; treacherous; devouring; circumfluous; glorious; mysterious; dimpled; surging; life-giving; purling; fleecy; sweet; trickling; blushing; journalistic; tree-fringed; bleak; deep; cold; tributary; bubbling; warm; slow-moving; filthy; odorous; spreading; stormy; nearing; glorious; unclean; distant; glassy; roaring; wild; troubled; retreating; glimmering; western; fleeting; imprisoned; mountainous; jumbled; brilliant; benevolent; green; unknown; unstirring; august; tangy; medicinal; forest; fretting; polished; fatal; sharked; slimy; resistant; rushing; lisping; peaceful; smitten; milky; calm; sliding; tormented; rippling; tideless; running; unruffled; teeming; inundating; mute; destined; faint; black; turbulent; adjacent; fragrant; phosphorescent; unflinching; invisible; frothy.

verbs
administer—; agitate—; cart—; cast upon —; chart—; contaminate—; dabble in—; dam up—; dilute with—; distil—; disturb —; draw—; excrete—; filter—; frisk in—; gaze upon—; harness—; immerse in—; infest—; ingest—; pacify—; partake of—; plod through—; plunge into—; ply with—; pollute—; resort to—; saturate with—; slither into—; slash—; smooth—; steep in—; submerge in—; suck up—; —babbles; —drenches; —dribbles; —drips; —engulfs; —evaporates; —glimmers; —gurgles; —

gushes; —invigorates; —laps; —lashes; —murmurs; —oozes out; —penetrates; —precipitates; —quenches; —recedes; —ripples; —roars; —seeps in; —simmers; —snuffs out; —spurts; —stagnates; —subsides; —surges; —stains; —swells; —swirls; —trickles in.

(See moisture, bath, liquid, pond, juice, lava.)

WATER (v)
adverbs
diligently; literally; faithfully; daily; constantly; superfluously; patiently.
(See refresh, supply.)

WATERFALL
adjectives
ethereal; sheeted; distant; babbling; misty; overhanging; sudden; blazing; dashling; living; roaring; gamboling; rainbowed; graceful.

verbs
approach—; bridge—; erode into—; span —; view—; —cascades; —churns; —deluges; —descends; —endangers; —froths; —gurgles; —s lace; —leaps; —pitches; —roars; —rolls; —rumbles; —scuds over; —sprays; —threatens; —thunders; —tinkles.
(See cataract, spray, mist.)

WAVE
adjectives
sanguine; dark; voiceless; weltering; moon-whitened; tremendous; accompanying; playful; petulant; warring; transcendent; plunging; troubled; unnumbered (pl); sloping; foaming; sordid; successive (pl); tidal; glowing; bounteous; scornful; long; throbbing; turbid; surging; bright; translucent; dignified; furious; lava; fleecy; towering; gliding; rugged; all-powerful; rolling; never-tiring; feathery; lustrous; charming; fluctuating; delicate; glittering; eternal; greedy; burning; whirling; immeasurable; lapsing; flashing; drunken; dividual (pl); yeasty; sparkling; fierce; green; wintry; dull; monstrous; amber; petrified; vivid; haunted; oblivious; rippling; inveterate; hurrying; turbulent; startled; bellowing; rebellious; reckless; inflated; chilly; mounting; softening; impressive; weltering; painted; great; white-crested; pent; impetuous; flinging; whispering; hiding; fiery; yellow; breaking; indented; wobbly; uneven; glossy; frolicsome; audacious; gleam-

ing; lasting; tempestuous; surf; glooming; dissolving; sheltering; dashing; sullen; conquered; starry; blackening; high-rolling; engulfing; melodious; wireless; caressing; calm; ruthless; careless; moon-lit; mirrored; full-flushed; late; rhythmical; curling; ever-deepening; undulating; tossing; wide-wallowing; blind; restless; migratory; lustrous; tractable; bounding; peaceful; dashing; refluent; shattered; wan; slumberous; sparkling; tepid; intermingled (pl); electric; brimming; peaked; mountainous; slimy; salt; wandering; pandemic; infinitesimal; frantic; breaking; foam-figured; whistling; slight; creative; lambent; thin-edged; unfathomable; lonely; mournful; eerie; uncharted; rival; enormous; conflicting; angry; burnished; grassy; conciliatory; crisp; dimpled; quivering; advancing; noble; sympathetic; spent; implacable; ruffled; alarming; loyal, urgent; wildered; jostling; rising; shallow; fretting; mighty; mimic; sonorous; receding; gurgling; siren-haunted; sun-kissed; charmed; frothy; inconstant; unsullied; raging; heaving; peristaltic; stormy; summer; western; blind.

WAVE (v)
adverbs
gaily; gracefully; magically; helplessly; frantically; amicably; cheerfully; energetically; desolately; tremulously; rhythmically; constantly; languidly; erratically; impudently; mournfully; eloquently; gently; contemptuously; surreptitiously.
(See flaunt, brandish.)

WAVER (v)
adverbs
indecisively; irresolutely; weakly; morbidly; vacillatingly; erratically; doubtfully.
(See vacillate.)

WAVERING
adverbs
feebly; decrepitly; indecisively; hesitantly; weakly; finally; seldom; vexatiously; foolishly; irresponsibly; weakly; shyly; timidly; terribly; anxiously; strangely.

WAVES
verbs
breast—; command—; launch upon—; ride —; stem—; walk upon—; —batter; —beat; —break; —buffet; —chant; —dance; —dash; —emanate; —fall; —fizzle; —foam; —lap; —lash; —lift their heads; —lull;

—pound; —rage; —recede; —ripple; —rise; —show their teeth; —sigh; —slap; —slop; —swamp; —toss their manes; —tremble; —tumble; —vibrate.

(See ocean, breaker, billow, maelstrom.)

WAX

adjectives
yielding; incorruptible; plastic; soft; dental.

verbs
accumulate—; bleach—; candle—; collect—; derive—; extract—; fuse—; impress on—; model in—; mould—; plug with—; scrape —; seal with—; secrete—; wick—; yield—; —adheres; —melts; —polishes; —seals; —smooths; —waterproofs.

(See candle, putty.)

WAX (v)

adverbs
mightily; indignantly; boisterously; prodigiously; abnormally; spectacularly.

(See grow, increase.)

WAY

adjectives
abnormal; absolute; admirable; abstract; accommodating; admonitory; adroit; advantageous; agitated; agreeable; aimless; airy; allegorical; ancient; ambitious; amorous; applauded; arched; appointed; artful; assured; astounding; avoidable; bachelor; busy; calculating; caressing; categorical; celestial; challenged; chance; characteristic; charming; cheap; cheerful; childish; comical; circuitous; cold; comfortable; compact; companionable; comparative; complete; composed; comradely; confidential; convenient; cordial; creative; critical; cynical; dank; dark; darkling; dauntless; defiant; deep; delicate; delicious; delightful; deprecating; desolate; desultory; devious; dignified; dim; direct; disagreeable; dishonest; disorderly; distant; distempered; divers (pl); divine; dogged; dolorous; doubtful; doubtless; dreamy; dull; dusty; easy; eccentric; effective; endearing; egoistic; elaborate; enigmatical; enlightened; erring; everlasting; existing; execrable; expeditious; expensive; explicable; expressive; false; fantastic; farthest; fathomable; fiery; flaming; flowered; foul; fumbling; genial; glib; gloomy; good-humored; gracious; gratifying; grave; grim; guileless; happy; half-frightened; hateful; hearty; heavenward;

heavy-hearted; heedful; heterogeneous; hilarious; honorable; humble; idiomatic; idle; illogical; immortal; imperious; impersonal; impetuous; impregnable; incomprehensible; inconsequent; indefinite; indifferent; indirect; inexplicable; infinite; inflexible; ingenious; inscrutable; insolent; insular; inspired; intimate; introverted; irregular; invisible; irresistible; irritating; jerky; jostling; kind; laborious; lampless; labyrinthine; languid; last; laudable; lawful; leafy; learned; legendary; leisure; listless; lofty; loitering; lonely; luxurious; magical; marvelous; melancholy; mild; military; mischievous; modern; monstrous; moon-lit; muddled; murderous; muffled; mysterious; mystical; narrow; nasty; negative; noiseless; objective; night-wandering; nudging; obscure; obedient; offensive; oily; old; organic; original; ostentatious; outmoded; over-darkened; particular; peaceable; passive; paved; pebbly; peculiar; penetrating; peremptory; perfunctory; perilous; perplexing; picturesque; pilgrim; plausible; practical; prefatory; preoccupied; priestly; primrose; privy; promiscuous; promising; prosperous; provincial; provoking; prudent; public; quaint; queer; quick; rakish; random; rational; ready; realistic; reasonable; reassuring; reckless; reflective; respected; restless; restrained; restricted; roundabout; rude; rugged; safe; satisfactory; scaly; scornful; scrupulous; secret; self-chosen; self-made; self-pleasing; servile; shameful; facile; sharp; sheepish; shy; silly; sinuous; slimy; slippery; sodden; soft; solitary; sophisticated; sound; spasmodic; special; spectacular; spiky; spirited; sporadic; spring; squalid; starry; steadfast; stiff-necked; stolid; strange; stylish; sublime; subterranean; successful; sunken; supernatural; suspicious; symmetrical; sympathetic; systematic; temporary; tainted; tentative; theological; thorny; toilsome; tortuous; trackless; tranquil; treacherous; tricky; tumultuous; unaccountable; unceremonious; unchristian; uncompromising; uncouth; undynamic; unemotional; unerring; unexpected; uneven; unfriendly; ungenerous; ungracious; unhandsome; unimpassioned; unique; unkindled; unknown; unmeaning; unmerciful; unmistakable; unmitigated; unobtrusive; unpremeditated; unskilled; unslackened; unsuspected; untrodden; untutored; unwithered; upland; varied; venturous; vigorous; vulgar; wandering; wanton; wary; weary; weedy; whimsical; wildering; willowy; winding; woodland; workable; conscientious; constrained; contrary; half-fascinated.

verbs
adapt to—s; bar—; betray—; block—; bluff —; clutter—; contemplate—; demonstrate —; designate—; devise—; discern—; disclose—; elbow—; emulate—s; err in—; explore—; forge—; forsake—s; grope—; guide—; hew—; illumine—; inaugurate—; initiate in—s; inspire—; interpret—; lurk along—; mark—; mend—s; muddle—; pave —; pick—; plod—; plow—; point out—; pursue—; renounce—s; retrace—; smash—; smooth—; stray from—; strew—; thread—; veer from—; wangle—; welter—; wend—; worm—; yield—.

(See fashion, highway, gate, alley, avenue, manner, course, habit, lane.)

WAYWARD
adverbs
reprehensibly; heartbreakingly; incredibly; miserably; wretchedly; pitiably; curiously; remarkably; unaccountably; unmanageably; incorrigibly; strangely; haplessly; peculiarly; unfortunately; uncommonly; singularly; hopelessly; desperately; childishly.

WAYWORN
adverbs
terribly; weakly; feebly; pitiably; pathetically; undoubtedly; naturally; credibly; extremely; completely; utterly; ominously; momentarily; dreadfully.

WEAK
adverbs
pathetically; terribly; unusually; naturally; extremely; inordinately; significantly; palpably; languidly; remarkably; strangely; curiously; unexpectedly; surprisingly; unaccountably; distressingly; disappointingly; fatally; mortally; alarmingly; unfortunately.

WEAKEN (v)
adverbs
painfully; constitutionally; unsuspectedly; alarmingly; tragically; treacherously; precipitately; materially; basically; ostensibly; insidiously.
(See impair, decline.)

WEAKNESS
adjectives
cold-pale; youthful; normal; mortal; an-

archical; potential; veriest; hereditary; childish; extraordinary; disordered; bodily; relative; physical; endearing; momentary; incurable; inherent; curious; unworthy; progressive; absolute; overmastering; confessed; extreme; deadly; amiable; earthly; intellectual; fatal; permanent; contemptible; prevalent; inborn; hollow.

verbs
arise from—; betray—; bewail—; blame—; confess to—; conquer—; deride—; dress up —; exploit—; increase—; indicate—; lament —; overcome—; pander to—; parade—; produce—; redeem—; reproach for—; speculate upon—; spurn—; —assails; —forfeits; —impairs; —prostrates; —thwarts; induce —.

(See infirmity, inability, disability, impotence, frailty, helplessness.)

WEAL
adjectives
common; public; universal; all-embracing.

WEALTH
adjectives
incipient; personal; incalculable; flowing; estimated; melodic; comparative; boundless; enormous; wanton; ill-gotten; unlimited; diminished; fabulous; proverbial; maiden; undeveloped; mineral; independent; movable; sole; hoarded; substantive; intellectual; growing; concentrated; complacent; monopolistic; lavished; priceless; crystal; progressive; natural; tremendous; material; conspicious; squandering; magic; unwieldy; veritable; many-sided; lacteal; emotional; religious; disregarded; physical; inherited; immense; spiritual; available; gleaned; sparkling.

verbs
accumulate—; affect—; apportion—; attain —; confer—; confiscate—; consume—; destroy—; diffuse—; dissipate—; drain—; efface—; euphemize—; forfeit—; gather—; groan with—; hoard—; labor for—; lavish —; load with—; lust for—; obviate—; plunder—; redistribute—; reject—; roll in—; scatter—; scramble for—; squander—; tap —; tax—; toil for—; winnow—; —destines; —menaces; —multiplies; —surpasses.

(See fortune, affluence, legacy, capital, luxury, money, riches, plenty.)

WEALTHY

adverbs

gorgeously; enormously; comfortably; fortunately; pleasantly; agreeably; serenely; snugly; enviably; complacently; sufficiently; smugly; graciously; fabulously; independently; substantially; tremendously; conspicuously; immensely; crassly; excessively; fairly.

WEAPON

adjectives

slight; spiritual; enticing; ancipital; lethal; unsheathed; respectable; resistless; fierce; habitual; mimic; economic; inadequate; ceremonial; saintly; climatic; pitiless; prohibited; keen; formidable; devastating; ghastly; idle; defensive; fatal; blood-tipped; effective; primitive; death-dealing; trusty; lavish; dripping; heroic; dangerous; imperial; competent.

verbs

brandish—; conceal—; devise—; discredit —; display—; draw—; flourish—; forge—; furnish with—; resort to—; scorn—; sheathe —; stroke—; shield from—; temper—; wield—; wrest—; —s clang; —s clash; — cracks; —s crash; —flashes; —intimidates; —roars; —coerces.

(See arms, cannon, bow, cutlass, dagger, missile, gun, sword.)

WEAR

adjectives

abundant; minimum; worthy; immediate; superfluous; forcible; fashionable; prolonging; satisfactory.

WEAR (v)

adverbs

habitually; absurdly; customarily; religiously; gracefully; conventionally; invariably; jauntily; loosely; haughtily; superfluously; fashionably.

(See use, sport.)

WEARINESS

adjectives

elemental; humble; delicious; despairing; simple; utter; exasperated; satisfied; sheer; mortal; everlasting; blissful; silent; colossal; never-ending; eternal.

verbs

allay—; alleviate—; assuage—; augment—; complain of—; endure—; induce—; mitigate —; relieve—; result in—; succumb to—; — besets; —consumes; —creeps; —deters; — diminishes; —drags; —engulfs; —irks; — irritates; —oppresses; —overtakes; —overwhelms.

(See impotence, fatigue, languor, exhaustion, lassitude, lethargy, ennui.)

WEARISOME

adverbs

intolerably; tediously; monotonously; profoundly; irksomely; terribly; inordinately; exhaustingly; prosily; disgustingly; unbearably; stupidly; vexatiously; annoyingly; excessively; utterly; painfully; dreadfully.

WEARY

adverbs

naturally; inordinately; terribly; utterly; strangely; pitifully; forlornly; physically; nervously; unutterably; immeasurably; profoundly; extremely; mortally; inexpressibly; distressingly; pathetically; sadly.

WEASEL

verbs

—claws; —climbs; —constructs; —defends; —deposits; —inhabits; —pillages; —preys on; —plunders; —slays; —swims.

(See animal.)

WEATHER

adjectives

fair; green; heavy; high; windy; frosty; prized; harsh; inclement; bitter; portentous; overhung; unsullied; thick; warm; sunshiny; damp; foggy; sticky; summer; capricious; foul; whirling; militant; ripening; bright; hard; glad; wintry; unseasonable; darkening; somber; common; extreme; unfavorable; sultry; gypsy; mild; blue; rough; oppressive; humid; starless; unsettled; loud; delicious; glorious; golden; wilting; surface; tough; ripening; gusty; blusterous; unpropitious; cloudless; feverish; detestable; intemperate; singing.

verbs

anticipate—; bare to—; bear—; becloud—; chart—; conjecture on—; converse about—; endure—; expose to—; exult in—; forecast —; predict—; prophesy—; stomach—; unsettle—; —affects; —brightens; —clears; —damages; —dejects; —demoralizes; —depresses; —discourages; —disheartens; —en-

livens; —frowns; —hovers; —invigorates; —limits; —modifies; —permits; —thickens.
(See climate, cold, heat.)

WEATHER-BEATEN

adverbs

curiously; hopelessly; sturdily; dingily; apparently; admittedly; probably; naturally; obviously; palpably; manifestly; laughingly; harmlessly; oddly; shabbily; dingily.

WEATHERED

adverbs

decrepitly; invincibly; sturdily; anciently; admirably; pitifully; languidly; outrageously; definitely; agedly; gauntly; desperately; hopelessly.

WEAVE (v)

adverbs

deceptively, coarsely; subtly; laboriously; ingeniously; inextricably; deftly; skillfully; dexterously; artfully.
(See braid, fabricate.)

WEB

adjectives

singularly-formed; mysterious; bandana; tangled; dark; illuminated; contrapuntal; atrocious; unfinished; intricate; thick-spun; frail; luminous; wondrous; graceful-looking; braided.

verbs

avoid—; elude—; escape—; evade—; spin —; weave—; wreathe—; —ambushes; —attracts; —baits; —beguiles; —convolutes; —curves; —decussates; —enmeshes; —entangles; —entwines; —intersects; —lures; —reticulates; —snares; —traps; —vibrates.
(See cobweb, trap, net.)

WED (v)

adverbs

auspiciously; admirably; happily; gaily; blissfully; genially; perfunctorily; passionately.
(See marry, unite.)

WEDDING

verbs

approve of—; attend—; bar from—; bless —; celebrate—; ceremonialize—; contemplate—; entertain at—; feast at—; officiate at—; perform—; ritualize—; witness—; —binds; —cements; —contracts; —joins; —pledges; —ties; —unites.
(See nuptials, matrimony, marriage.)

WEEDS

adjectives

hardy; pageant; luxuriant; offensive; sea; bladdery; troublesome; unwholesome; mourning; coarse; brittle; silver-budded; fancy; rank; dank; valueless; wretched-looking; little; scented; flowerless; loathed; huddling; clinging; convent; blossoming; amphibious; bending; noisome; fragrant; deleterious; undulating; ineradicable; wasting; encumbering; swaying; thin; choking; noxious; unsightly; berry-spotted.

verbs

clear of—; exterminate—; eradicate—; nip —; pluck—; sever—; suffocate by—; teem with—; —attain; —choke; —crowd; —cumber; —deprive; —destroy; —entwine; —fringe; —hamper; —hinder; —overgrow; —parch; —strangle.
(See grass, plant.)

WEEDY

adverbs

excessively; horribly; hopelessly; inordinately; extraordinarily; naturally; offensively; vexatiously; terribly; unnecessarily; inexcusably; carelessly; hideously; rankly; unwholesomely; disgustingly; discouragingly.

WEEK

adjectives

consecutive (pl); bewildering; tempestuous; momentous; previous; ensuing; successive (pl); eventful; disturbing; dreary; happy; intoxicating; long; tedious; weary.

verbs

abide—; beguile—; celebrate—; commemorate—; endure—; extend—; fix—; forecast —; fritter away—; gain—; outlast—; prolong—; reckon—s; remain—; survive—; terminate—; tolerate for—; while away—; —elapses; —expires; —inaugurates; —lapses; —marks; —s stretch.
(See month, day, hour, time.)

WEEP (v)

adverbs

pitifully; plaintively; piteously; bitterly; wildly; tumultuously; sentimentally; pathetically; intermittently; stormily; hysterically; abundantly; furiously; copiously; ludicrously; sympathetically.
(See lament, moan.)

WEEPING

adjectives

responsive; mysterious; incessant; hysterical; violent; passionate; continual; ludicrous; sore; chronic; wild; focused; untimely.

WEIGH (v)

adverbs

gravely; judiciously; reflectively; empirically; correctly; onerously; heavily; minutely; momentously; ponderously.

(See balance, estimate.)

WEIGHT

adjectives

nightmare; slumberous; undue; soft; dark; mass; excess; increasing; overwhelming; panting; superior; sweet; enormous; withering; unsolicited; panting; patent; caressing; portcullis; co-extensive; lesser; dead; comfortable; unaccustomed; hard; icy; noticeable; prodigal; definite; descending; weary; augmented; emotional; specific; idle; crushing; finite; momentous; ponderous; relative; surplus; massive; cruel; exceptional; light; sufficient; combined.

verbs

adjust—; ascertain—; attain—; bear—; carry—; cast off—; convey—; determine—; exert—; flounder under—; groan under—; manipulate—; match—; modify—; propel —; regulate—; shoulder—; support—; suspend—; unburden—; vary in—; —balances; —bruises; —burdens; —compresses; —constricts; —crumples; —crushes; —descends; —diminishes; —fatigues; —oppresses; — overwhelms; —submerges.

(See load, heaviness, burden.)

WEIRD

adverbs

strangely; gloomily; uncannily; terribly; dismally; fearfully; mysteriously; darkly; curiously; fantastically; grotesquely; incomprehensibly; unpleasantly; disagreeably; peculiarly; eerily.

WELCOME

adjectives

formal; courteous; healthful; comfortless; chill; familiar; tepid; hearty; smiling; preposterous; cordial; awkward; unclouded; pathetic; homely; triumphant; pure; majestic; friendly; noisy; kindred; heart-sped; royal; dismal; generous; intuitive; gracious; unquestioned; premeditated; scant; boisterous; kindly; languid; urbane; immemorial; unostentatious; frank; energetic; extraordinary; joyous; hospitable; genial; cheerful; reverend; warm; lavish; frolic.

verbs

assure—; bark—; bid—; bow—; embrace in—; extend—; greet with—; hail—; insure —; nod—; offer—; overstay—; rejoice in—; roar—; salute—; shout—; smile—; thunder —; win—; —cools; —flatters; —greets; — heartens; —rings.

(See greeting, friendship.)

adverbs

gratefully; refreshingly; cordially; sincerely; hospitably; warmly; truly; unexpectedly; supremely; encouragingly; frankly; acceptably; pleasantly; genially; graciously.

WELCOME (v)

adverbs

smilingly; spaciously; hospitably; enthusiastically; fondly; heartily; affectionately; ecstatically; gleefully; courteously; majestically; generously; languidly; urbanely; ostentatiously; frankly; energetically; joyously; genially; lavishly.

(See greet, hail.)

WELD (v)

adverbs

electrically; sturdily; staunchly; firmly.

WELDING

adjectives

intimate; sturdy; gradual; necessary.

WELFARE

adjectives

immediate; bodily; real; general; human; material; permanent; spiritual; financial; commercial; national; eternal.

verbs

administer—; advance—; aid—; concern—; consider—; consult—; contribute to—; determine—; devote to—; disregard—; encourage —; endanger—; forward—; foster—; further—; ignore—; impair—; improve—; jeopardize—; neglect—; overlook—; plan —; promote—; raise—; regard—; respect —; sacrifice—; safeguard—; seek—; serve —; study—; threaten—; —ascends; —flourishes; —thrives.

(See good, health, happiness, well-being.)

adjectives

deep; calm; handsome; stone; decorated; poisoned; projected; fathomable; crystal; transparent; mossy; extreme; babbling; connected; polluted; harmonious; bubbling.

verbs

bare—; case—; contaminate—; drain—; drill—; emanate from—; excavate—; issue from—; line—; pollute—; probe—; pump from—; sink—; sound—; submerge in—; tap—; test—; —affords; —bubbles; —facilitates; —offers; —overflows; —springs up; —yields.

(See spring, shaft, source, fountain, volcano.)

adverbs

gloriously; splendidly; magnificently; wholly; gaily; entirely; seldom; recently; finally; radiantly; miraculously; happily; fortunately; luckily; naturally; surprisingly; extremely; incomparably; sturdily; rosily.

WELL-BEING

verbs

administer to—; advance—; afford—; bask in—; contribute toward—; desire—; discern —; encourage—; envy—; indicate—; jeopardize—; promote—; sense—; serve—; threaten—; wrap up in—; —flourishes; —permeates; —pervades; —prospers; —thrives.

(See welfare.)

WELL-BRED

adverbs

extremely; satisfactorily; gratifyingly; acceptably; unusually; delightfully; extraordinarily; beautifully; marvelously; surprisingly; unexpectedly; obviously; manifestly; meticulously; charmingly; naturally.

WELL-INFORMED

adverbs

remarkably; eminently; illustriously; exceptionally; consummately; distinctly; particularly; marvelously; wonderfully; profoundly; incredibly; surprisingly; undeniably; intelligently; unusually; certainly; impressively.

WELL-MEANING

adverbs

possibly; probably; apparently; evidently; manifestly; painfully; obviously; hopefully; awkwardly; clumsily; sufficiently.

adjectives

sublimated; faded; bountiful; infinite; flameless; unfooted; shadowy; vagrant; rich; glowing; fiery; crimson; bloody.

verbs

determine—; drift to—; establish in—; filter into—; invade—; migrate to—; penetrate—; pioneer—; settle in—; —absorbs; —attracts; —beckons; —calls; —flourishes; —importunes; —invites; —lures; —offers; —retreats; —thrives.

(See territory, country, region, locality.)

WET

adverbs

terribly; obnoxiously; unwholesomely; soppily, hopelessly; unseasonably; swampily; quaggily; mysteriously; strangely; disgustingly; unpleasantly; unhealthfully; utterly.

WETNESS

adjectives

dripping; sticky; red; annoying; permanent.

WETTING

adjectives

hearty; customary; voluntary; necessary.

WHALE

adjectives

wanton; large-finned; awkward; belching; monstrous; trained.

verbs

conserve—; derive from—s; dissect—; encounter—; exterminate—; glimpse—; harpoon—; haul in—; land—; market—; pursue—; sight—; spot—; strand—; strip—; value—; —s frequent; —gives battle; —s haunt; —inhabits; —looms; —plunges; —preys upon; —spouts; —submerges; —tows; —yields.

(See shark, fish, animal.)

WHEAT

adjectives

fruitless; scythed; yellowing; tender; nodding; ripe; whole; cracked; ground; bleached.

verbs

attack—; consume—; convert—; cultivate—; enrich—; glean—; grind—; harvest—; import—; market—; mill—; pulverize—; sow —; thresh—; trade in—; winnow the chaff from—; —booms; —fails; —flourishes; —fluctuates; —germinates; —matures; —ripens; —ripples; —thrives.

(See crop, harvest, grain, cereal, grass, plant.)

WHEEDLING

adverbs

teasingly; coaxingly; flatteringly; fondly; carefully; foxily; tenderly; persistently; successfully; constantly.

WHEEL

adjectives

ardent; muffled; toothed; sentient; tardy; interior; flaming; buckled; whirling; fervid; humming; formidable; jarring; worm-eaten; gilded; living; westering; broad-tired; massive; shining; wobbling; rolling; restless; ponderous; creaking; glowing; retreating; worn-out; waggly; spinning; whirring; gambling.

verbs

derail—; grip—; lubricate—; maneuver—; pad—; realign—s; shatter—; tread—; trundle—; twirl—; —clicks; —creaks; —deviates; —drones; —encompasses; —encircles; —girdles; —facilitates; —gyrates; —lurches; —jars; —jolts; —jounces; —pivots on; —recoils; —responds; —revolves; —rumbles; —spins; —swerves; —twirls; —whirls.

(See helm, cycle.)

WHEEL (v)

adverbs

automatically; serenely; sharply; swiftly; dizzily; drunkenly; mechanically; ceaselessly; whirringly; smoothly.

(See roll, move.)

WHEREABOUTS

verbs

allude to—; ascertain—; bare—; betray—; bring to light—; conceal—; confirm—; determine—; discern—; disclose—; discover —; divulge—; establish—; expose—; fix—; inform of—; report—; reveal—; screen—; solve—; trace—; unearth—; veil—; verify —; —baffles; —creeps out; —mystifies.

(See existence, position, place.)

WHIFF

adjectives

jealous; subtle; odorous; suggestive; gentle.

WHIM

adjectives

wild; eccentric; epicurean; delightful; illogical; abrupt; mere; ornamental; arbitrary; idle; anti-social; inconvenient; humorous; arrant; curious; mad; silly.

verbs

accede to—; conceive—; deny—; deplore—; discard—; dismiss as—; excite—; grant—; gratify—; humor—; indulge in—; outgrow —; play up to—; provoke—; satisfy—; smother—; yield to—; —intoxicates; —irritates; —piques; —riles (colloq.); —seizes.

(See humor, fad, fancy, caprice.)

WHIMPER (v)

adverbs

fretfully; distractedly; pusillanimously; reproachfully; feebly; pitifully; nervously; weakly; brokenly; hysterically; fruitlessly.

(See weep, cry.)

WHIMPERING

adjectives

nervous; secret; everlasting; continual; frightened; pitiful.

WHIMSICAL

adverbs

ludicrously; fancifully; fantastically; amusingly; pleasantly; cleverly; subtly; agreeably; fascinatingly; charmingly; grotesquely; outlandishly; delightfully; immensely; absurdly; unusually; oddly.

WHINE

adjectives

shrill; pusillanimous; friendly; cracked; peculiar; hungry; begging.

verbs

choke back—; discern—; elicit—; emit—; provoke—; restrain—; smother—; stifle—; subdue—; —distresses; —expresses; —irks; —irritates; —laments; —moves; —riles (colloq.); —s subside; —touches.

(See moan, sob, complaint.)

WHINE (v)

adverbs

piteously; wretchedly; churlishly; shrilly; pusillanimously; beggingly; mournfully; intolerably; hungrily.

(See whimper, cry.)

WHINNY

adjectives

colt-like; shrill; nervous; excited.

WHIP

adjectives

gigantic; remorseless; cutting; keen; deadly; brutal.

verbs

apply—; brandish—; crack—; cut with—; flick—; flog with—; lay on—; prod with—; utilize—; yield to—; —accelerates; —belabors; —bestirs; —coerces; —crackles; —cracks; —flays; —cuts; —impels; —induces; —lashes; —pricks; —reddens; —scourges; —spurs; —stimulates; —stings; —urges; —goads.

WHIP (v)

adverbs

unmercifully; deservedly; savagely; brutally; remorselessly; viciously.
(See beat, thrash.)

WHIPPOORWILL

verbs

—calls; —moans; —reiterates; —vociferates; —wails.
(See bird.)

WHIRL

adjectives

little; powdery; foamy; continuous; social; giddy.

WHIRL (v)

adverbs

crazily; dizzily; madly; gaily; joyously; incessantly; furiously; giddily; continuously.
(See revolve, swirl.)

WHIRLPOOL

adjectives

everlasting; continued; foamy; fatal; heartless.

verbs

avoid—; drift into—; escape—; ferment—; flounder in—; quiver in—; sweep into—; yield to—; —agitates; —batters; —boils; —buffets; —churns; —dashes; —eddies; —endangers; —foams; —froths; —gyrates; —imperils; —jostles; —jounces; —menaces;

—plays; —roars; —seethes; —spouts; —sucks; —swirls; —threatens; —whips.
(See maelstrom, vortex, waves.)

WHIRLWIND

adjectives

drear; cloudy; weltering; dark; awful; rending; eddying; good; undulating; toying; fatal; unexpected.

WHISK (v)

adverbs

deftly; cleverly; eagerly; abruptly; resolutely; noiselessly; cunningly.
(See sweep, whirl.)

WHISKERS

adjectives

solitary; grizzled; sere; miserable; half-starved; shaggy; educated; combed; closely-cropped; bushy; unruly; optimistic; huge; fuzzy; bountiful; unkempt; ingrown.

verbs

affect—; clip—; crop—; cultivate—; discard—; lop off—; pluck—; respect—; ruffle —; rumple—; shag—; shampoo—; shear—; smooth—; stroke—; thin out—; trim—; —adorn; —cloak; —disguise; —fringe; —gray; —quiver; —transform; —tuft.
(See moustache, mane, hair, beard.)

WHISKEY

adjectives

indispensable; hot; commissary; straight; blended; bonded; young; medicinal; cheap; smooth; fiery; burning; synthetic.

verbs

abstain from—; addict to—; age—; assimilate—; bond—; bootleg—; bottle—; consume—; dispatch—; distil—; drain—; inure to—; legalize—; prohibit—; quaff—; refine—; sip—; swill—; tax—; value—; —anaesthetizes; —befogs; —deadens; —dulls; —enlivens; —flows; —flings down; —inebriates; —enslaves; —intoxicates; —narcotizes; —perverts; —revives; swig—.
(See brandy, liquor, alcohol, gin, wine.)

WHISPER

adjectives

delightful; gentle; sullen; friendly; dainty; icy; sibilant; soothing; awe-stricken; stirring; naked; subdued; ragged; little; rapid; hysteric; broken; persuasive; insistent; stage; imperturbable; laughing; silken;

stealthy; confidential; frantic; resolute; ceaseless; indolent; answering; intense; solemn; unnatural; keen; wheezing; busy; blasphemous; significant; low; muttered; hoarse; failing; vibrating; swelling; precautionary; benignant; bearded; husky; multitudinous (pl); fierce; tragic; hollow; ghostly; hideous; bass; audible; hurried; frightened; serene; overt; eloquent; agonized; strained; occasional; caressing; complaining; fanatical; distressed.

verbs
amplify—; conspire in—s; converse in—s; convey in—; drown out—; emit—; harken to—; hush—; inform in—; muffle—; overhear—; raise above—; reduce to—; resort to—; revive—; stifle—; suppress—; —beckons; —buzzes; —dies; —distracts; —diverts; —hints; —prompts; —quavers; —rebukes; —sears; still—.
(See sound, tone, noise, hum.)

WHISPER (v)
adverbs
hoarsely; treasonably; brokenly; passionately; impressively; eagerly; tremulously; urgently; mysteriously; audibly; affectionately; discreetly; petulantly; breathlessly; fiercely; savagely; feebly; defiantly; appealingly; compassionately; insidiously; vehemently; feverishly; stealthily; overtly; eloquently; impressively.
(See gossip, speak.)

WHISTLE
adjectives
noiseless; plaintive; hoarse; careless; expressive; fierce; denouncing; shrill; incessant; congratulatory; occasional.

verbs
blow on—; toot—; —alarms; —announces; —awakens; —beckons; —deafens; —distracts; —drowns out; —pierces; —proclaims; —rends; —screams; —shrieks; —shrills; —signals; —sounds; —splits; —startles; —wails; —warns.
(See warning, flute, note, scream.)

WHISTLE (v)
adverbs
sharply; briskly; piercingly; incisively; warningly; desperately; weirdly; thinly; tunelessly; mockingly; gently; repetitiously; melodiously; plaintively.
(See sound, sing.)

WHITE
adjectives
pure; new; snow; artemisia; frosty; clinging; unendurable; moon-washed; brilliant; beach; billowy; delicate; silvery; translucent; uncanny; popular; smart; plain; wanted; smooth; dazzling; creamy; foaming; shining; whirling; argent; deadly; immaculate; bloodless; slashing; luminous.

adverbs
ghastly; utterly; suddenly; brilliantly; dingily; dustily; dully; nervously; sickly; frightfully; gleamingly; blazingly; chalkily; ghostly; surprisingly; inappropriately; startlingly.

WHITE-LIVERED
adverbs
disgustingly; foolishly; shamefully; terribly; despicably; contemptibly; obviously; manifestly; notoriously; infamously; unusually; spinelessly; abjectly; helplessly; undisguisedly; hideously; terribly.

WHITENESS
adjectives
dazzling; splendid; immaculate; gleaming; downy; pristine; spotless; ghastly; unbroken; chalky; silent; bony; evanescent; dead; odious.

WHITEWASHED
adverbs
neatly; gleamingly; recently; tidily; sanitarily; pleasantly; conveniently; hilariously; quickly; diplomatically; wisely; cheaply; delightfully; cheerfully; ingeniously; thoughtfully; carefully; deceptively; artistically.

WHOLE
adjectives
consistent; magnificent; stupendous; homogeneous; coherent; immeasurable; complete; great; weltering.

WHOLESOME
adverbs
pleasantly; delightfully; palatably; tastily; notably; admittedly; soundly; nutritiously; splendidly; happily; admirably; commendably; attractively; smilingly; rosily; sturdily.

WHOOP (v)
adverbs
hideously; madly; wildly; insanely; barbar-

ously; terrifyingly; viciously; insistently; hysterically.

(See cry, yell.)

WICK

adjectives

flaring; homemade; burned; cotton; low.

verbs

enkindle—; ignite—; immerse—; lower—; raise—; renew—; saturate—; smother—; snuff out—; soak—; —blazes; —diffuses; —flares; —flickers; —flutters; —glimmers; —glows; —illumines; —radiates; —scintillates; —sears; —singes; —sparkles.

(See candle.)

WICKED

adverbs

scarcely; slightly; interestingly; alluringly; terribly; brutally; heinously; undeniably; palpably; manifestly; nefariously; unspeakably; inexpressibly; dreadfully; obscenely; conspicuously; notoriously; infamously.

WICKEDNESS

adjectives

loathsome; idolatrous; flagrant; unforgivable; exceeding.

verbs

acquit of—; atone for—; breed—; condone —; convert from—; denounce—; deplore—; disclose—; do penance for—; expiate—; expose—; extirpate—; forsake—; impute— to; inveigh against—; paint—; purge of—; renounce—; repent—; reproach for—; reveal—; rue—; shrive of—; stamp out—; stew in—; work—; —corrupts; —prevails; —reigns; —taints.

(See lawlessness, abomination, iniquity, licentiousness, immorality, evil.)

WIDE

adverbs

amply; sufficiently; generously; unexpectedly; capaciously; voluminously; exceptionally; particularly; peculiarly; conveniently; commodiously; spaciously; advantageously; tremendously; immensely; adequately; suitably; properly; fortunately; outlandishly; unnecessarily.

WIDEN (v)

adverbs

perceptibly; appreciably; gradually; mark-

edly; proportionately; sufficiently; immeasurably; illimitably.

(See broaden, increase.)

WIDE-SPREAD

adverbs

unfortunately; manifestly; remarkably; amazingly; alarmingly; fearfully; luckily; dangerously; profitably; ineradicably; presumably; allegedly; fantastically; curiously.

WIDOW

adjectives

charming; agreeable; disconsolate; brokenhearted; wanton; childless; perverse; loving; pious; sentimental; virginal; lusty; unpensioned; polygamous; intrepid; austere; superabundant (pl).

WIELD (v)

adverbs

magically; potently; honorably; viciously; dictatorially; tyrannically; cunningly; dangerously; slyly; hatefully; deceitfully; craftily; subtly; ambitiously; ambiguously; virtuously; vigorously; powerfully; ruthlessly.

(See employ, use.)

WIFE

adjectives

shrewish; meek-eyed; worthy; tearful; disrespectful; legitimate; stainless; delicate; profligate; faithless; high-corseted; prideful; sprightly; bejeweled; coquettish; devoted; high-spirited; splendid; querulous; flattered; unsustained; exemplary; playful; dutiful; burdensome; slovenly; frantic; respective (pl); conquering; affectionate; trustful; sainted; temporary; spotless; forward; churchly; begotten; bullied; gracious; beaten; affianced; patient; sweet; virtuous; pale-faced; murdered; undivorced; unalienable; whimpering; smooth-haired; celebrated; amiable; strong-willed; tyrannical; diminutive; mercenary; constant; lewdtongued; chaste; lawful; attractive; innocent; young; execrable; shameless; nervous; simple; common-law; slippery; perjured; aristocratic; pale-cheeked; tender; prudent; pining.

verbs

adore—; alienate—; caress—; choose—; cohabit with—; court—; desert—; embrace—; escort—; estrange from—; extol—; forsake —; intimidate—; seduce—; seek—; slander

—; strike—; take—; win—; —begets; —betrays; —comforts; —conceives; —haggles; —inspires; —mothers; —nags; —presides over; —rails; —shares.
(See mate, husband, mistress.)

WIG

adjectives
glossy; curly; formidable; elastic; frizzled; obvious; tangled; little; flaxen; towering; comical-looking.

WILD

adjectives
vast; impenetrable; sequestered; hidden; unapprehensive; dawning; fretted; luscious; untrodden; dreary.

adverbs
apparently; terribly; unmanageably; rankly; rampantly; fantastically; outrageously; outlandishly; savagely; ungovernably; naturally; inexpressibly; inordinately; boisterously; crazily; frantically; unconscionably; inveterately; hopelessly; manifestly; extraordinarily; pestiferously.

WILDCAT

adjectives
docile; cunning; vicious; sly; dangerous.

verbs
encounter—; skin—; trap—; —carries away; —claws; —depredates; —devours; —glares; —growls; —preys on; —roams; —slinks; —springs; —stalks.
(See animal.)

WILDERNESS

adjectives
vast; sub-arctic; intricate; unwithered; howling; watery; uneasy; rough; trackless; ancient; woody; indiscriminate; equal; untamed; obscure; pristine; remote; reluctant; barren; virgin; leafy; boundless; tangled; lonely; glowing; native; world-wide; unsettled; death-fraught; untrodden; broad; wild; shadowed; frozen; tangled; snowy; intricate; fertile; wasteful; uninhabited; untraveled; savage; measureless; constellated; adoring; interminable; pathless; untamable; marshy; inquiring; parched; arid.

verbs
brave—; circumvent—; clear—; dare—; explore—; fertilize—; flee into—; forsake—; frequent—; infest—; inhabit—; issue from

—; level—; penetrate into—; pioneer into —; plunge into—; range—; retire to—; roam—; skirt—; subdue—; tame—; tangle in—; traverse—; venture into—; —beckons; —broods; —cloaks; —extends; —fascinates; —lures; —screens; —shrouds; invade—.
(See jungle, forest, desert.)

WILDNESS

adjectives
dreaming; wailing; graceful.

WILES

adjectives
intrinsic; instinctive; wanton; insidious; manifold; feminine; endearing; imaginary; winning; subtle; deceitful; crafty.

verbs
discern—; disguise—; fall victim to—; pierce—; resist—; resort to—; succumb to —; yield to—; —allure; —attract; —bait; —deceive; —defraud; —delude; —dupe; —ensnare; —entangle; —gull; —hook; —inveigle; —lure; —seduce; —succeed; —trap.
(See trick, deception, ruse, cunning.)

WILFUL

adverbs
naturally; inveterately; uncontrollably; notoriously; wickedly; stubbornly; foolishly; unreasonably; unmanageably; erratically; fanatically; impudently; inconsiderately; ungraciously; rudely; grossly; brutally; selfishly.

WILL
(*document*)

verbs
abide by—; attest to—; comply with—; contest—; direct in—; discharge—; dispute—; evidence—; execute—; file—; invalidate—; negate—; nullify—; observe—; probate—; seal—; set aside—; stipulate in—; witness —; wrangle over—; —assigns; —bequeaths; —bestows upon; —confers on; —consigns; —contributes to; —declares; —decrees; —discloses; —dispenses; —disposes of; —doles out; —endows; —enriches; —entrusts with; —estranges; —grants; —invests; —metes out; —restores; —settles; —subsidizes; —transfers.
(See contract, legacy, document.)

(general)

adjectives

passionless; individual; vulgar; overmastering; ambitious; cheerful; irresistible; unstable; grumbling; ill; intense; fiery; gracious; incorporated; inexorable; virtuous; devilish; firm-set; indomitable; unconquerable; holy; rational; never-daunted; vigorous; strenuous; inscrutable; powerful; regenerate; hindering; sturdy; unreined; invincible; tyrant; fallible; tormenting; idiotic; uncontrolled; dauntless; overruling; nerveless; natural; arbitrary; potent; genuine; good; lordly; sublime; basic; universal; arch-imperial; opposing; mutual; imperious; cruel; incorruptible; sensory; sovereign; sanguine; self-determined; undivided; sacred; honest; expressive; tremendous; lawless; clearly-expressed; tempered; despotic; tyrannic; benumbed; entangled; tendril-like; royal; imperative; imminent; unrelaxing; gracious.

verbs

accede to—; annihilate—; assert—; bend to —; blind—; blunt—; control—; curb—; effect—; .energize—; enforce—; exercise—; express—; flout—; harden—; impose—; ignore—; liberate—; mold to—; obey—; oppose—; perform—; restore—; subject to—; subjugate—; subordinate—; weaken—; work—; yield to—; —s clash; —moves; —prevails; indulge—.

(See preference, desire, determination, willpower.)

WILLFULNESS

verbs

brook—; curb—; decry—; denounce—; deplore—; dispel—; dispose toward—; dissolve—; endure—; govern by—; incline toward—; put up with—; relax—; relent—; repent—; rue—; tolerate—; —irks; —irritates; —piques; —riles (colloq.); —succumbs to; —yields to.

(See perversity, obstinacy, stubbornness.)

WILLING

adverbs

usually; graciously; politely; considerately; indulgently; generously; agreeably; pleasantly; helpfully; indifferently; enthusiastically; surprisingly; suspiciously; curiously; generously; unexpectedly.

WILLINGNESS

adjectives

gruff; repeated; obvious; ready; surface.

WILLOW

adjectives

idling; silken; sprouting; shivery; weeping; slender.

WILLPOWER

verbs

breed—; cultivate—; discern—; display—; evince—; exhibit—; foster—; inherit—; lack —; lower—; necessitate—; rejuvenate—; require—; stimulate—; test—; want—; weaken—; —banishes; —curbs; —determines; —directs; —dominates; —droops; —flags; —flinches; —perseveres; —rebels; —rejects; —relaxes; —resists; —swerves; —wavers.

(See will, strength, desire, power.)

WIN (*v*)

adverbs

strategically; decisively; effectually; spectacularly; phenomenally; competitively; gallantly; substantially; intrepidly; treacherously.

(See triumph, achieve.)

WINCE (*v*)

adverbs

visibly; perceptibly; markedly; painfully; abruptly; revealingly; guiltily.

(See recoil, shrink.)

WINCING

adverbs

fearfully; constantly; suddenly; significantly; tremulously; painfully; haggardly; arrantly; senselessly; timidly; abjectly; indescribably; secretly; inwardly; openly; miserably; wretchedly; timorously; dreadfully; pathetically; curiously.

WIND

adjectives

crannying; worldly; southerly; good; swift; ill; cruel; biting; wandering; whispering; boisterous; hurtling; rolling; rough; poisonous; shrill; mad; curdling; dew-impearled; wild; chilling; whimsical; ocean; continuous; noiseless; streaming; sharp; rising; wailing; wanton; rude; nimble; special; spleenless; contrary; passing; foul; bleak; whitening; viewless; red-hot; roaring; crackling; fierce; gentle; dirty; sunny; bitter; keen; merry; favoring; shifting; restless; sleepy; sudden; sleety; gusty; cutting; whistling; murderous; dirgeful; pensive; uplifting; soughing; dying; wrinkling; wooing; weighty; unwilling; intricate; doleful; dead; hollow; moaning; mysterious; lulled; light; baffling; fabulous; azure; listening; inanimate; wintry; desert; woven; ferocious; delicate; fresh; panting; ravishing; hurricane; amorous; luscious; weak; tearing; felon; sportive; driving; boisterous; impetuous; mournful; adverse; piercing; tempestuous; contending; baleful; perverse; thirsty; ill-dispersing; tossing; monotonous; soothing; bracing; rustling; throwing; contrary; supple; wrecking; careless; bone-piercing; prevailing; serviceable; sighing; beating; impotent; fitful; quickening; petulant; winged; clinging; weary; lowered; treacherous; awakening; billowy; warring; fickle; life-breathing; unseen; frolic; screaming; dull; illuminated; sole; buffeting; eddying; gathering; marsh-bred; evil; murmuring; swift-winged; merciful; idle; sounding; sweeping; false; rainless; hot; stormy; furious; powerful; withering; warbling; frosty; surly; wave-building; parching; burdened; ungovernable; suffocating; burning; shrieking; repining; stray; drying; unwholesome; inconstant; soothed; mighty; worn-out; unfettered; prophetic; rushing; unbreathed; vagrant; lazy; summer; icy; unleashed; pious; relentless; hungry; odorous; cold; riotous; mounting; intermitting; lapsing; insulting; invisible; laughing; morning; voiceless; howling; translucent; stifling; lifting; visiting; speaking; wicked; tainted; chainless; forgetting; nimble; noble; envious; endless; blustering; mindless; melodious; life-breathing.

verbs

bear on— breast—; expose to—; harness—; ride—; ripple in—; sniff—; soar on—; still —; —abates; —assails; —bites; —blasts; —blusters; —breathes; —buffets; —caresses; —chants; —chills; —s conflict; —cuts; —dallies; —diminishes; —disturbs; —enfolds; —etches; —extinguishes; —grieves; —howls; —hums; —knifes; —lashes; — moans; —mourns; —murmurs; —rages; — rakes; —ranges; —rattles; —roars; — ruffles; —rustles; —scatters; —scourges; — shrieks; —sighs; —sings; —slaps; —slashes; —smites; —snaps; —soughs; —stings; —strips; —sweeps; —swells; —swirls; — threatens; —tugs; —twists; —uproots; —

veers; —wafts; —wails; —wanders; — whines; —whips; —whispers; —whistles; —winnows; shelter from—.
(See gale, blizzard, air, breeze.)

WIND (v)

adverbs

tortuously; sinuously; picturesquely; intricately; monotonously; incessantly.
(See coil, curve.)

WINDMILL

verbs

agitate—; becalm—; drive—; employ—; outmode—; —churns; —circumvolves; — clatters; —s dot; —flaps; —gyrates; — quivers; —revolves; —rotates; —spins; — swirls; —twirls; —whirls.
(See propeller.)

WINDOW

adjectives

embayed; downy; hallowed; eye-like; stained-glass; pictured; foul; shattered; gaping; modern; prominent; bay; oriel; goggle-eyed; mullioned; iron-barred; steamy; irregular; lofty; filmy; diamond-paned; jeweled; dusky; glittering; dark; eastern; grimy; shuttered; thick; curtained; heat-clouded; latticed; emblazoned; delicate; panoramic; countrified; translucent; unglazed; scullery; fading; outjutting; shop; showy; fitted; rusty; iron-grilled; arched; tight; shut; barred; dingy; transparent; panting; regular; memorial; well-glazed; viewless; moon-lit.

verbs

beat on—; besiege—s; besmirch—; besmudge—; confront—; curtain—; drum on —; frame—; glower through—; jimmy—; peep out—; peer through—; pelt—; pour through—; putty—; rap on—; scour—; screen—; scrutinize through—; seal—; shade—; shatter—; spatter—; view from —; weatherstrip—; yank up (colloq.)—; — admits; —affords; —discloses; —glitters; — rattles; —vents; —ventilates.
(See glass, opening.)

WINDOW-PANE

adjectives

shining; grimy; well-fitted; dirt-streaked.

WINDY

adverbs

gustily; terribly; fatally; alarmingly; ominously; frigidly; freezingly; hotly; bitterly;

scorchingly; dreadfully; curiously; increasingly; cruelly; bitterly; bitingly; cuttingly; deucedly; plaguedly; infernally.

WINE

adjectives
diluted; sepulchral; generous; home-brewed; scuppernong; fierce; costly; agitated; raging; nectareous; new; copious; opulent; thick-purpled; straining; windy; heady; wholesome; fermented; medicated; mirthful; remembering; resplendent; inspiring; split; murmuring; heart-warming; splashing; foaming; frothing; forbearing; glimmering; palmy; enchanted; unmingled; fiery.

verbs
age—; brew—; chill—; cure in—; derive —from; distil—; ferment into—; gulp—; guzzle—; heat with—; imbibe—; ply with —; quaff—; reek of—; regale with—; savor —; sip—; sour—; swill—; value—; —animates; —dulls; —enlivens; —exhilarates; —flows; —flushes; —heats; —inflames; — inspires; —inspirits; —putrefies; —relaxes; —revives; —stimulates; —tempts; —warms; —intoxicates.
(See beverage, alcohol, liquor, champagne, beer.)

WING (*v*)
adverbs
gaily; sublimely; tirelessly; gracefully; joyously; unflaggingly; angelically; serenely; powerfully.
(See fly, float.)

WINGS
(*general*)
adjectives
leathern; curbed; trustless; joyous; fiery; hovering; glad; crumpled; snowy; divine; speckled; untiring; budding; light; steady; spacious; gleaming; huge; shadowy; flagging; redoubled; errant; overhanging; vibrating; folded; fateful; peaceful; rushing; silken; scare-crow; glowing; restless; futile; celestial; peerless; feeble; odoriferous; linen; fluttering; expanded; wide-open; invisible; noiseless; slow; laboring; winnowing; swift-rushing; feathered; untried; reverberate; mighty; motionless; fearless; aggressive; plume-plucked; sumptuous; wandering; wavering; dusky; sheltering; grisly; joyful; dawn-white; intended; outspread; rich; ruffled; viewless; hurrying;

trembling; filmy; ebon; languid; nimble; dewy; aerial; twinkling; fanning; aurora; oaring; angelic; cherubic; parental; luminous; airy; unhallowed; immortal; overshadowing; gelid; moving; murmurous; gorgeous; quivering; outstretched; healing; unsustaining; enchanted; gauzy; jealous; unconquerable; multicolored; daedal; drooping; serene; expanded; inconstant; sunny; shower-struck; thunderous; rugged; sounding; unfledged; mealy; gaudy; velvet; fairy; shadowing; glassy; parted; tremulous; glossy; imprisoned; downy; sportive; swift; wheeling; laden; clanking; dye-dusty; unconfined; quickening; mutable; radiant; shrouding; rustling; bruised; agile; dipping; merciful; melancholy; blessed; shivering; glancing; quivering.

verbs
clip—; disable—; flap—; flit on—; fracture —; gather beneath—; hover on—; lend—; pluck—; preen—; prune—; singe—; soar on—; sprout—; strengthen—; take to—; try —; tuck under—; waft on—; —beat; — droop; —enable; —enfold; —flag; —flutter; —liberate; —quiver; —rustle; —wither.

WINGS
(*parts of a building*)
verbs
add—; explore—; extend into—; face—; flank—; gain access to—; haunt—; install —; level—; partition—; raze—; renovate —; restore—; seal—; shout from—; skirt —; skulk in—; view from—; —adjoin; — annex; —append; —project; —supplement.
(See passage, addition.)

WINK
adjectives
single; significant; unfatherly; lasting; cunning; impudent; sly; furtive; suggestive; pitying.

verbs
burlesque—; discern—; exaggerate—; exchange—s; swap—s (colloq.); tip—to; — allures; —amuses; —beckons; —beguiles; — betokens; —conveys; —denotes; —discloses; —distorts; —distracts; —entices; —expresses; —flirts; —indicates; —lures; —passes between; —prompts; —warns.
(See look, grin.)

WINK (v)

adverbs

coyly; triumphantly; significantly; wickedly; broadly; saucily; cunningly; impudently; furtively; suggestively.

(See blink, overlook.)

WINNER

adjectives

outstanding; capable; bread; practical; consistent.

verbs

acclaim—; announce—; applaud—; award to—; crown—; declare—; dispute—; emerge —; entertain—; fete—; glorify—; hail—; herald—; honor—; judge—; proclaim—; publicize—; reward—; —annexes; —profits; —reaps; —surmounts.

(See champion, hero, conqueror.)

WINSOME

adverbs

bonnily; sweetly; consciously; happily; merrily; rosily; graciously; innocently; childishly; youthfully; quietly; laughingly; irresistibly; wholly; alluringly; incomparably; daintily; airily; blithely; wholesomely; truly.

WINTER

adjectives

withered; rough; tedious; semi-arctic; dreadful; belated; rude; terrible; dreary; oblivious; laggard; bitter; brown; collapsing; stern; grand; dumb; dogged; brilliant; fatal; weeping; immortalizing; veritable; polar; trembling; monstrous; cheerless; unearthly; oppressive.

verbs

approach—; evade—; survive—; usher in —; —benumbs; —bites; —blankets; — blasts; —blights; —cloaks; —continues; — declines; —exterminates; —frosts; —glistens; —grips; —impoverishes; —nips; — persists; —presses; —relaxes; —roars; — wanes; —whips across.

(See cold, blizzard, storm, fall.)

WINTRY

adverbs

bracingly; bitterly; invigoratingly; snappily; nippingly; frigidly; delightfully; pleasantly; gloriously; picturesquely; delightfully; freezingly; unpleasantly; bleakly; barely.

WIPE (v)

adverbs

gently; timidly; sedately; quietly; hastily; mechanically; cautiously; medicinally.

(See whisk, obliterate.)

WIRE

adjectives

vertical; braided; flaxen; silver; tattered; telephone; leased; old-fashioned; singing; magnetic; envious; flexible; gilded; cunning.

verbs

base—; coat—; encase—; entwine—; fish with—; insulate—; tape—; —binds; — braces; —communicates with; —conveys; —electrifies; —furnishes; —hums; —reinforces; —transmits; —vibrates.

(See cable.)

WIRY

adverbs

inexhaustibly; sturdily; huskily; indefatigably; untiringly; dependably; wonderfully; amazingly; unbelievably; marvellously.

WISDOM

adjectives

divine; slow; memorable; infinite; wasted; practical; united; quaint; astute; stupendous; assimilable; incomparable; weighty; unseasonable; smiling; ancient; surpassing; calculating; revered; peculiar; limitless; protecting; profound; powerless; worldly; polished; political; moral; heavenly; determined; rich; presumptuous; ripe; deep; aphoristic; sufficient; Magian; supreme; collective; gnomic; honest; dark; musical; parabolical; selfsame; cunning; divine; mature; inner; magisterial; earthly; passionstarved; sifted; ruthless; superhuman; eternal; detestable; conceited; whimsy; sinister; crooked; undefiled; incomprehensible; pointed; prophetic; modest; housewifey; vulgar; fair; just.

verbs

accumulate—; belittle—; bow to—; challenge—; cloak—; conceal—; disclose—; distil—from; doubt—; enthrone in—; garner—; impugn—; inspire with—; invoke—; judge—; lack—; manifest—; partake of—; require—; school in—; seek—; simulate—; steep in—; temper with—; unfold—; yield to—; —decrees; —guides; —ripens; —rules; —warns.

(See information, philosophy, erudition, learning, intelligence, enlightenment, knowledge.)

WISE

adverbs

infinitely; unassailably; astutely; incomparably; surpassingly; particularly; ripely; expertly; sufficiently; supremely; honestly; darkly; cunningly; cleverly; divinely; magisterially; genially; ruthlessly; eternally; detestably; whimsically; significantly; pointedly; prophetically; affectionately; modestly; indubitably; scarcely; financially; discreetly; practically; profoundly; politically; usually; selfishly; surprisingly; undeniably; instinctively; intuitively; sensibly; judicially; capably; sagaciously; acutely; intelligently; sagely; cannily; coolly; equitably; solidly; discerningly.

WISE-CRACKING

adverbs

ridiculously; entertainingly; divertingly; amusingly; cleverly; nonsensically; comically; continually; crazily; smartly; clownishly; drolly; ludicrously; facetiously; waggishly; ridiculously.

WISH

adjectives

ardent; pious; gnawing; lifelong; reasonable; earnest; idle; faint; conscious; homicidal; audible; changing; vague; unrealized; cruel; forbidden; utmost; eager; doleful; docile; distinct; avaricious; fondest; irreconcilable; unaccomplished; slight; irrational; lawless; humble; incestuous; willful; repressed; poor; petty; inordinate; dignified; urgent; ambitious; sensual; venturous; fervent; careless; vehement; added; repressed; ardent; fleeting; anxious; dying; granted; dominant; feeble; foolish; dubious; helpless; passing; pious.

verbs

abandon—; accede to—; achieve—; acquiesce to—; anticipate—; assent to—; betray—; cater to—s; comply with—; conceive—; convey—; defy—s; disclose—; entertain—; express—; favor—; fulfill—; govern—; grant—; gratify—; harbor—; honor—; indicate—; indulge—; inform of —; manifest—; mask—; override—; real-

ize—; repress—; satisfy—; submit to—; subordinate—; uphold—; voice—; yield to —; —consumes; —materializes; —prevails.

(See desire, want, need.)

WISH (v)

adverbs

heartily; devoutly; earnestly; ardently; solemnly; fervently; craftily; seriously; deliberately; viciously; conscientiously; piously; fondly; irrationally; vehemently; foolishly; vainly.

(See desire, want.)

WISP

adjectives

stringy; dewy; lazy.

WISTFULNESS

adjectives

pathetic; queer, tearful.

WIT

adjectives

licentious; shallow; out-of-fashion; undergraduate; blunted; scholarly; fresh; mellow; simple; bitter; obscene; mighty; sarcastic; keen; sprightly; mobile; caustic; courteous; admirable; perplexed; mixed; sparkling; comic; foolish; open; fastidious; paradoxical; sparkling; prodigal; unstrained; inexhaustible; insidious; conversational; vigorous; shrewd; homely; quick; trenchant; various (pl); inimitable; threadbare; human; metaphysic; crack-brained; unseasonable; native; loyal; microscopic; shattered; merciless; strayed; rude; aimless; sharpened; diabolic; assured; fouled; fogged; worthless; acidulous; sluggish; sudden; acute; dextrous; light; confounded; spontaneous; verbal; alert; subtle; delicate; unpremeditated; ebullient; satirical; airy; incomparable; exhilarating; eminent; unmatched; vulgar; ready.

verbs

clothe in—; dampen—; display—; draw—; dull—; exhibit—; grasp—; infuse—; inject —; kindle—; match—; pervert—; refine—; scatter—; sharpen—; tinge with—; — amuses; —beguiles; —bores; —cuts; —delights; —flashes; —flourishes; —flowers; — flows; —penetrates; —rebounds; —scathes; —scintillates; —shines; —sparkles; —totters; —victimizes.

(See understanding, humor, banter, repartee, witticism.)

WITCH

adjectives

soul-killing; potent; wrinkled; foul; reputed.

WITCHCRAFT

verbs

charge with—; condemn—; delve into—; embrace—; employ—; exercise—; explode —; hang for—; practise—; resort to—; suspect of—; —bewitches; —charms; —conjures up; —enchants; —flourishes; —intrigues; —mesmerizes; —presages; employ—; exercise—.

(See enchantment, magic, mysticism.)

WITCHERY

adjectives

dear; languorous; traditional; strange; romantic.

WITHDRAW (v)

adverbs

honorably; modestly; steadily; definitely; hostilely; apologetically; involuntarily; mysteriously; courteously; formally; gracefully; shamefacedly; noiselessly; precipitately; unmolestedly; pusillanimously.

(See retreat, retract.)

WITHDRAWAL

adjectives

timely; unmolested; contemporaneous; early.

verbs

advise—; advocate—; announce—; attend —; begrudge—; contemplate—; consider—; curtail—; promote—; recommend—; regard —; shrink from—; subject to—; —closes; —devoids; —disturbs; —ebbs; —evacuates; —strains; —taxes.

(See removal, departure, evacuation.)

WITHERED

adverbs

pitiably; helplessly; remarkably; surprisingly; gauntly; desperately; paralytically; perceptibly.

WITHHOLD (v)

adverbs

deliberately; purposely; mystically; insidiously; venomously; hatefully; relentlessly; tenaciously; perfidiously.

(See deny, refuse.)

WITHSTAND (v)

adverbs

manfully; gallantly; vigorously; staunchly; stalwartly; admirably; perpetually; economically; boldly.

(See resist, oppose.)

WITLESS

adverbs

provokingly; utterly; absolutely; helplessly; crazily; pitiably; pathetically; miserably; wretchedly; piteously; allegedly; vexatiously.

WITNESS

adjectives

mute; trustworthy; laughing; material; missing; singular; actual; striking; eloquent; perjured; divers (pl); long-lost; perpetual; impartial; terror-stricken; awful; creditable; reluctant; silent; surviving; all-judging; eternal; too-willing; followed; crushing; credible; thorough; steadfast; relentless; petrified; sympathizing.

verbs

bear—; bias—; bribe—; cite—; coach—; confront with—; contradict—; cross-examine —; intimidate—; introduce—; prejudice—; present—; produce—; rake up—s; suborn —; subpoena—; summon—; —acknowledges; —alleges; —attests to; —authenticates; —avers; —bears on; —beholds; —certifies; —confesses; —confirms; —contends; —contradicts; —corroborates; —damns; —endorses; —evidences; —falsifies; —impugns; —perjures; —pictures; —pleads; —records; —reports; —reveals; —seals; —signs; —substantiates; —supports; —testifies; —upholds; —verifies; —views; —vouches for; —vows.

(See observer, bystander, evidence.)

WITTICISM

adjectives

characteristic; pert; neat; coarse; constrained; obscene; painful; withering.

verbs

banter—s; evoke—; exchange—s; flash—; indulge in—s; roar at—; trade—s; —bites; —glitters; —retorts; —salts; —scintillates; —sparkles; —spices; —stings.

(See wit, joke, jest, humor.)

adverbs

profoundly; divertingly; amusingly; delightfully; uncommonly; extremely; mischievously; comically; roguishly; mischievously; scintillatingly; brilliantly; splendidly; unusually; broadly; drolly; facetiously; fatuously; pleasantly; smartly; whimsically; waggishly; cruelly; merrily; fantastically; sparklingly.

WIZARD

adjectives

reputed; doting; egregious; glancing; baffled; bounteous; aged.

WOE

adjectives

silent; unavailing; gloomy; unwieldy; unutterable; comic; lesser; intolerable; outward; imaginative; holy; speechless; bitter; endless; tedious; unreposing; human; immedicable; life-consuming; harboring; guilty; pious; tedious; immortal; irredeemable; wearied; earthly; conscious; unprevailing; nameless; imaginary; discordant; impending; eternal; black; worthless; outward; everlasting; mortal; incommunicable; ending; thankless; stagnant; perplexing; lofty; great; rank; inexpressible; constant; wanton; insuperable.

verbs

afflict with—; allay—; alleviate—; babble —; bewail—; bow in—; burden with—; ease—; exclaim—; hide—; induce—; nurse —; occasion—; overcome with—; palliate —; predict—; recompense for—; remedy—; sink into—; spin out—; suffer—; triumph over—; whimper of—; —curses; —lacerates; —overwhelms; —rends; —saddens; —sours; —wracks; —wrings.

(See grief, sadness, sorrow.)

WOEFUL

adverbs

sadly; dolefully; habitually; utterly; wretchedly; helplessly; terribly; naturally; pathetically; pitiably.

WOLF

verbs

pay a bounty on—s; —s assemble; —s chase; —s devastate; —s infest; —s overpower; — preys on; —prowls; —pursues; —ranges; —runs down; —skulks; —slinks; —snarls; —stalks; —s terrorize; —s troop; —s visit. (See animal.)

WOLVES

adjectives

famished; snapping; snarling; mangled; bloodless; shrewd; rabid; human; ravenous; fearful; genteel; universal.

WOMAN

adjectives

abject; accomplished; admirable; affected; affectionate; aggressive; ambitious; amiable; appealing; aproned; artful; ashy-hued; attractive; beautiful; awe-stricken; baby-faced; bedraggled; bedridden; bent; bewitching; brawny; bread-winning; brilliant; broken-hearted; bustling; careworn; celebrated; charming; chaste; childless; clear-eyed; clear-headed; clever; clinging; comely; compassionate; composed; consonant; corpulent; courageous; crabby; crisp; cruel; curious; cynical; decent; decrepit; defenseless; delicate; desireful; determined; devout; discontented; distinguished; dutiful; dowdyish; dressed; earthly; economical; ecstatic; elaborate; elegant; embroidering; emerging; enduring; energetic; equable; erring; estimable; excellent; exemplary; fair-faced; fanatic; fantastic; fascinating; fashionable; fervent; feverish; flashy; flat; foolish; forsaken; fragile; frantic; frightened; fruitful; frigid; frowsy; full-blossomed; garrulous; gaunt; ghastly; glamorous; glittering; gray; grim; grizzled; handsome; happy; hard-faced; hard-worked; headstrong; haughty; heartless; helpless; heroic; hesitating; high-minded; home-keeping; home-loving; hypersensitive; hysterical; idealistic; illiterate; imperious; impish; implacable; importunate; impressible; incorrigible; indefatigable; independent; indigent; industrious; infidel; informal; insipid; intelligent; intrepid; jealous; jocose; large-souled; lewd; limping; listless; lithe; little; lonely; loitering; long; loose; loquacious; lovely; lumpish; lustful; managing; marble-limbed; mean; middle-aged; mincing; miserable; miserly; modern; modest; morbid; mortal; motherly; much-loved; mulatto; mystic; new; nice; noble; observant; odious; old; over-virtuous; over-worked; over-wrought; pale; perfidious; perjured; pernicious; pinched; pitiless; plain-featured; plainly-dressed; plump; poor; preeminent; presumptuous; pretty; promiscuous; prosaic;

prosperous; proud; prudent; querulous; radiant; rapacious; remarkable; repentant; resolute; respected; reticent; rheumatic; romantic; sad-eyed; scrawny; seductive; self-loving; sensible; sensitive; serene-eyed; serious; shabby; shadowy; shallow; showy; shrewd; shriveled; silken-tressed; silly; slatternly; slender; slim; smooth-limbed; sorrowful; sour-faced; sporting; spotless; square-browed; stalwart; stout; striking; sumptuous; super-annuated; superior; sweet; sweet-voiced; tactful; tattling; tawdry; tenacious; tender; terrified; timid; timorous; tremendous; tremulous; unconstant; uncultivated; uncultured; unenlightened; unescorted; unkempt; unprotected; unworldly; vain; versatile; virtuous; vivacious; warm-hearted; wayside; wayward; weak-willed; wearied; wearisome; weeping; weird; well-dressed; well-favored; white-faced; wilted; witchlike; withered; witty; wooden; worldly; wretched; wrinkled; young.

WOMANLY
adverbs
truly; sweetly; graciously; delightfully; comfortingly; quietly; gracefully; compassionately; serenely; gently; hospitably; pleasantly; naturally; unusually; particularly; remarkably; surprisingly; unexpectedly; attractively; extremely.

WOMB
adjectives
solemn; hollow; tortured; unfathomed; shuddering; fruitful.

verbs
abscess—; develop in—; displace—; empty —; enter—; infect—; incise—; lacerate—; manipulate—; retain in—; support—; ulcerate—; —atrophies; —bends; —contracts; —discharges; —dilates; —dislodges; —distends; —encloses; —engenders; —enlarges; —expels; —falls; —involutes; —manipulates; —pulsates; —quickens; —relaxes; —sags; —yields.

WOMEN
verbs
appeal to—; ban—; bar—; cater to—; charm—; consort with—; defame—; defile —; degrade—; disparage—; emancipate—; enchant—; enfranchise—; enlighten—; liberate—; persecute—; rally—; rape—;

ravish—; spurn—; sway—; typify—; uplift —; —bear; —beget; —beguile; —charm; —conceive; —flock about; —inflame; —labor; —mature; —provide; —nag; —scold.
(See damsel, girl, daughter.)

WONDER
adjectives
natural; varied (pl); small; breathing; envious; utmost; ignorant; lying; listening; breathless; midnight; despairing; sickened; perplexed; sullen; admiring; prodigious; curling; universal; elderly; loving; ornithological; vague; admiring; scornful; peerless; unreasoning; troubled; stupid; reverent; unimaginative; dramatic; lustrous; incredulous; estimable; unearthed; perpetual; isolated; speculative; special; snaky; late; scientific; supernatural; overwhelming; comedy; half-reproachful; silent; effusive.

verbs
acclaim—; bare—s; delve into—s; disclose —s; excite—; explore—s; gain—; gape at —; hail—; inspire—; marvel at—; occasion —; overcome with—; reveal—; stare with —; strike with—; —allures; —amazes; —astounds; —awes; —baffles; —bewilders; —dazzles; —dumbfounds; —mystifies; —petrifies; —startles.
(See curiosity, astonishment, incredulity, admiration, miracle, marvel.)

WONDER (v)
adverbs
confusedly; desperately; wistfully; anxiously; idly; uneasily; vaguely; irrelevantly; distractedly; detachedly; abjectly; capriciously; gloomily; blindly; ironically; uncomfortably; dazedly; sneeringly; miserably; enviously.
(See marvel, amaze.)

WONDERFUL
adverbs
utterly; amazingly; spectacularly; mysteriously; magically; unsurpassably; incredibly; fantastically.

WOO (v)
adverbs
roughly; affectionately; tenderly; timorously; ardently; vigorously; genially; subtly; lackadaisically; abortively; eloquently; earnestly; amusingly.
(See court, love.)

1300

WOOD
(forest)

verbs

comb—; encamp in—; flank—; forsake—; frequent—; infest—; inhabit—; nest in—; prowl—; roam—; rove—; scour—; shelter in—; skirt—; thread through—; —blooms; —extends; —flowers; —obscures; —ranges; —screens; —shades; —shadows; —veils.

(See jungle, forest.)

WOOD
(general)

adjectives

sheltering; bushy; stormy; untrodden; boundless; split; green; tangled; sportive; intricate; wild; solemn; extensive; rippling; swampy; sonorous; violet; echoing; odorous; interminable; scented; ancient; plundered; darkling; dense; vernal; thorny; glowing; gloomy; snow-choked; mistrustful; rooky; soft-textured; crimson; sleeping; unfrequented; pathless; stilly; tuneful; dusky; rare; volumned; native; visionless; round-bosomed; primitive; fragrant; budding; naked; shaded; resinous; haughty; high; beechen; desolate; shining; wet; wide-stretching; sun-bedappled; trackless; dim-seen; distant; unshorn; ragged; aromatic; branching; rank; intervening; thick; ruined; gray-colored; delightsome; changing; hanging; whispering; shaggy; surrounding; dewy; variegated; chestnut; prehistoric; waving; precious; mazy; legendary; oracular; musical; autumnal; pheasant; inaccessible; ruthless; vast; competing; dreadful; deaf; dull; virgin; fatal; magnificent; wild; primeval.

WOOD
(material)

verbs

bevel—; carve in—; char—; chisel—; compress—; debark—; enkindle—; hack—; hew —; gather—; glean—; level—; model in—; plan—; sand—; sear—; shatter—; shave—; splinter—; whittle—; —blazes; —braces; —erodes; —hardens; —petrifies; —rots; —supports.

(See forest, carpenter, board, log, timber.)

WOODCHUCK

verbs

—hole; —burrows; —claws; —damages; —defends; —digs; —holes up; —pops into its hole; —preys on; —pursues; —rips; —tears; —slays; —snatches; —waddles away.

(See animal.)

WOODCOCK

verbs

bag—; decoy—; gun for—; —booms;—defies; —flits; —flocks; —glides; —honks; —inflates; —nips; —probes; —squats; —whirs; —zigzags.

(See bird.)

WOODED

adverbs

densely; thickly; valuably; wonderfully; profitably; beautifully; venerably; gently; sparsely; thinly; carefully; scientifically; intelligently; selectively; variously; impenetrably; gratefully; pleasantly.

WOODPECKER

verbs

—axes; —bores; —chisels; —clings; —digs; —hammers; —laps; —pecks; —prevents; —protects; —taps.

(See bird.)

WOOL

adjectives

soft; unbleached; mineral; ticklish; prickly.

verbs

bear—; brush—; card—; comb—; line with —; market—; oil—; rumple—; shear—; sort—; value—; weave of—; yield—; —affords; —comforts; —frays; —insures; —shelters; —shields.

(See cloth, leather, cotton.)

WORD

adjectives

abhorred; abounding; abrupt; abused; action; agonizing; altered; amazing; ambiguous; amusing; angry; appropriate; archaic; ardent; articulate; astonishing; audible; balanced; barbarous; barbed; bare; barren; bawled; biographical; biting; bitter; blameful; bland; blasphemous; blazing; blessed; bludgeoning; blundering; blunt; boastful; brave; bracketed; brawling; brotherly; brief; broken; burning; cabalistic; careless; caressing; casual; celebrated; certain; ceremonial; chanted; cheering; cherished; choice; choleric; coarse; coaxing; coined; comfortable; comforted; common-sense; comprehensive; conciliatory; conquering; considerate; consoling; constructive; contumelious; conventional; cordial; courteous; cruel; cunning; cutting; dainty; dangerous; daring; deadly; deathful; deathless; debasing; defensive; deliberate; delicate; deprecatory; derisive; descriptive; devastating; devout; dismal; disputatious; distinct; distracted; divided; doubtful; dread; dreadful; dying; eager; earnest; eloquent; elusive; emotional; emphatic; empty; encouraging; endearing; enriched; equivocal; eternal; explanatory; excusing; exotic; evangelical; explicit; extended; exultant; faithful; faltering; famed; fancy; farewell; fatal; favorite; feeble; fervent; fiery; fitting; flaming; flat; flattering; flowery; flying; foul; frequent; frivolous; futile; general; generous; gentle; genial; gigantic; glorious; glowing; golden; good; Gordian; graceful; gracious; grand; grateful; grave; great; half-extinguished; happy; hard; harsh; hasty; healing; heart-easing; heartrending; hesitant; hideous; high; high-born; homely; honest; honeyed; honorable; honored; hopeful; horrible; hot; household; hyphenated; identical (pl); idle; ill; imbedded; impious; imposing; impressive; inappropriate; inarticulate; incarnate; incautious; incoherent; incongruous; indignant; inexcusable; insane; inspiring; insulated; insulting; interchangeable; interrogative; iron; irrevocable; irritable; isolated; jeering; joking; just; keenly-felt; light; lilting; liquid; living; loved; loving; low-pitched; low-spoken; low-toned; luminous; lying; magic; magnanimous; majestic; matchless; meandering; meaningful; measured; meditated; mellifluous; mellow; melting; memorable; merciful; mere; metaphorical; meticulous; mighty; modified; momentary; momentous; monosyllabic; monotonous; moral; mortal; motherly; moving; much-abused; musical; muttered; mystic; naive; naughty; nauseous; nice; necromantic; noble; noisy; noted; obscure; obsolete; odd; odious; offending; oft-repeated; ominous; oppressive; orthodox; overpowering; passing; passionate; pathetic; peerless; perennial; persuasive; petulant; pithy; pitiful; plain; plausible; pleading; plighted; plump; plundered; poetic; poignant; polysyllable; pompous; portentous; potent; precious; precise; pregnant; provocative; quaint; qualified; queer; quenchless; quick; quickening; quiet; rabble-rousing; racy; radical; ragged; rallying; rapturous; rare; rash; ravishing; ready; reasoning; reconciling; recreative; reread; reproachful; repulsive; resonant; restless; revengeful; ringing;

rough; rude; sacred; scientific; scornful; scurrilous; seafaring; sea-going; senseless; serious; serviceable; shy; shameful; sharp; significant; simple; simple-seeming; single; smooth; sneering; sober; soft; soggy; solemn; soothing; soulful; spoken; standardized; stemmed; stifled; stinging; stirring; stormy; strange; strong; stumbling; submissive; successful; sugared; sulphurous; sumptuous; superfluous; sweet; swelling; sympathetic; talismanic; tender; thick; thin; thoughtful; thought-up; threatening; torrential; touching; transparent; tremulous; trite; trenchant; tricky; tumbled; twanging; ugly; unalterable; unchosen; uncomprehended; uncompromising; undecided; understandable; unfamiliar; unfeeling; unflattering; unforgettable; ungrateful; unhappy; unheeded; universal; unkind; unlucky; unmistakable; unmodest; unmodulated; unmoving; unpleasant; unspeakable; unusual; unmuttered; unwinged; unwonted; useless; uttered; vague; veritable; vilified; vituperative; vivid; vulgar; wandering; warning; weak; weird; whirling; whispering; wild; wily; wise; witty; woeful; wondrous; woolly; worthless; woven; written; yearning; superlative; suppliant; suspicious.

WORD (v)

adverbs

courteously; succinctly; cautiously; ingeniously; deftly; insidiously; theoretically; meticulously; religiously; musically; quaintly; modestly; vaguely; vividly; sulphurously.

(See express, speak.)

WORDS

verbs

accept—; amend—; blink at—; boggle over —; breathe—; burble (colloq.)—; clip—; coax—; comprehend—; confirm—; conjure up —; contradict—; convey—; coo—; coin —; cram—; crowd—; cull—; debase—; decipher—; define—; derive—; detect—; digest—; discharge—; dissect—; distort—; dog—; drawl—; drink—; emphasize—; employ—; encounter—; enunciate—; epitomize—; exchange—; exemplify—; fear—; flounder for—; fondle—; forge—; fumble with—; grasp—; grope for—; hang on—; hum—; hurl—; interpose—; interpret—; interrupt—; loose—; measure—; meditate upon—; mince—; misuse—; modify—; mould—; mouth—; muffle—; mumble—; play on—; ponder—; prune down—; quote

—; recall—; record—; reject—; relay—; retract—; rob of—; scrutinize—; search for —; seek—; set forth—; shun—; shy at—; snap at—; snarl—; span—; speak—; spread —; stem—; strain—; string—; stumble through—; swallow—; sweep—; tangle—; tap—; trade—; toss—; toy with—; transcribe—; utter—; verify—; voice—; weave —; weigh—; wrench—; —add; —arrest; —awaken; —boom; —burst; —cluster; —come forth; —crash; —designate; —drift; —drone; —echo; —elude; —embed; —embody; —escape; —expound; —express; —fail; —filter; —flash; —fling; —float; —flow; —gull; —haunt; —imply; —imprison; —inspire; —leak out; —make sense; —overwhelm; —play; —pour; —rebound; —resuscitate; —ring; —rise; —salve; —set forth; —signify; —shower; —slur; —stab; —stare; —sting; —storm; —strangle; —suggest; —surge; —sweep; —symbolize; —toll; —trail; —trickle out; —vibrate; —waft; —wing; —drip.

(See idiom, metaphor, derivative, expression, thought.)

WORDY

adverbs
endlessly; tiresomely; inexpertly; grossly; intolerably; disappointingly; incomprehensibly; monotonously; wearisomely; impossibly; tediously; repetitiously; vilely; confoundedly; unsatisfactorily; crudely.

WORK

adjectives
able; abortive; absurd; accessible; accomplished; admired; aesthetic; aggressive; airy; alleged; ambitious; analogous; anatomical; architectural; arduous; artistic; authentic; authoritative; barbarous; beneficent; biographical; blessed; blundering; brain-directed; celebrated; bread-winning; calamitous; caretaking; catalogue; chamber; changeless; characteristic; charming; cherished; choicest; clean; clerical; colossal; commemorative; compassionate; comprehensive; conscienceless; conscientous; conspicuous; constructive; contemporary; continued; creative; creditable; critical; damp; defective; dental; desolate; destructive; desultory; development; dignified; diplomatic; diversified; domestic; dramatic; dreary; drudgery; durable; easy; ecclesiastical; editorial; egocentric; elaborate; elegant; embroidered; entertaining; epoch-making; exact; executive; exhaustive; experimental;

explicable; expressive; exquisite; extemporaneous; extension; exterior; extravagant; fanciful; fascinating; fatiguing; fiendish; finicky; flourishing; free-lance; frenzied; ghastly; gigantic; graceful; grim; hand; harassing; hard; harmonious; hasty; hazardous; heartbreaking; helpless; home; hospital; humblest; humorous; idealistic; immediate; immoral; immortal; impassioned; imperishable; important; imposing; impressive; incomparable; indifferent; individual; ingenious; inimitable; inner; intellectual; intensive; interesting; irregular; irreligious; irreproachable; journalistic; laboratory; laborious; lacework; lax; licentious; literary; lofty; long-baffled; luminous; lyrical; majestic; makeshift; manifold (pl); masterful; masterly; mature; mechanical; memorable; menial; meretricious; meritorious; merry; monumental; multitudinous (pl); mystical; mythological; nefarious; new; noble; noted; noteworthy; objective; operative; orchestral; ornamental; outer; painful; patriotic; peaceful; permanent; perpendicular; persistent; philanthropic; philosophic; photographic; pianoforte; pioneer; piquant; pleasant; ponderous; popular; practical; profitable; prose; radiant; redeeming; regretful; remarkable; remunerate; reposing; representative; reproductive; risky; rhapsodical; routine; rudimentary; ruinous; rural; scandalous; sensational; sensitive; serious; sham; shielding; short; shriving; significant; sinful; sinless; solid; solitary; spontaneous; startling; statistical; steady; stellar; stern; subsequent; straightforward; stupendous; substantial; subtle; superficial; supplementary; suspended; symbolic; symphonic; systematic; tasteful; tawdry; technical; tedious; theological; theoretical; ticklish; tiring; titanic; toilsome; tolerable; unaccountable; tragic; unfruitful; unhallowed; uniting; unnecessary; unremitting; unsatisfactory; unstinted; unworthy; uplifting; urgent; valorous; variegated; valuable; vigorous; vital; vocal; voluntary; wearisome; well-composed; wholesome; winter; wondrous; worldly; master.

verbs
abandon—; acclaim—; accomplish—; buckle down to—; carry on—; christen—; comprehend—; conceive—; conclude—; delegate—; deprive of—; detail—; differentiate—; digest—; discredit—; distinguish—; dive into—; drug with—; efface—; embark upon

—; enlarge—; execute—; flinch at—; force
—; foster—; fulfill—; hamper—; hinder—;
immerse in—; impair—; improve—; investigate—; issue—; knock off—; mar—; master
—; merge—; minimize—; nurture—; outdo
—; perfect—; perform—; pigeonhole—;
prosecute—; provide—; reconstruct—; recount—; regulate—; remunerate for—;
retard—; shirk—; simplify—; submit—;
supplement—; suspend from—; swamp with
—; terminate—; thrive on—; undo—; wind
up with—; wrestle with—; —blunts; —
ceases; —commences; —confirms; —confounds; —constitutes; —devolves; —eases;
—encumbers; —engrosses; —ennobles; —
entails; —exacts; —extolls; —galls; —
glorifies; —honors; —imbeds; —involves;
—inspires; —overwhelms; —rectifies; —
suspends.

(See drudgery, duty, enterprise, job, labor,
occupation, business, grind.)

WORK (v)
adverbs
diligently; feverishly; passionately; energetically; zealously; automatically; faithfully;
diurnally; persistently; furiously; simultaneously; concertedly; strenuously; indefatigably; minutely; assiduously; prodigiously;
unremittingly; sedulously; spasmodically;
continuously; effectually; exquisitely; harmoniously; independently; conscientiously;
competently; listlessly.

(See labor, toil.)

WORKABLE
adverbs
splendidly; altogether; happily; practically;
conveniently; opportunely; entirely; absolutely; easily; satisfactorily; adequately; actually; readily; luckily.

WORKERS
adjectives
energetic; subservient; mechanical; brisk;
overburdened; copious; deceased; eligible;
subtle; indefatigable; zealous; offending;
routine; faithful; prodigious; bunchy; conservative; inert; chosen; ardent; methodical; swarming; migratory; rotund; rosy;
noble; able-bodied; relief.

verbs
address—; battle—; bind—; discharge—;
engage—; entitle—; exhaust—; exploit—;
fag—; fatigue—; ferret out—; goad—; harangue—; house—; incite—; inveigle—; lock

out—; master—; oust—; oversee—; prod
—; refresh—; regiment—; reimburse—; reinstate—; reward—; ride—; speed—; spur
—; superintend—; —accomplish; —arbitrate; —contribute; —lag; —parade; —pile
into; —plunge into; —relax; —strain; —
strike; —toil; —unionize; —weary.

(See labor, employee, striker.)

WORKMANSHIP
adjectives
exquisite; impeccable; intricate; meticulous;
domestic; experienced; sterling; intrinsic;
reliable; perfect; exacting; gossamer-like;
cumbrous; competent; masterly; expert; cunning; delicate; fine; highest; elaborate; artistic; crude.

WORLD
adjectives
giddy; operatic; expectant; epicurean; outside; drowsy; immense; custom-laden; organic; humming; polite; gloomy; tolerant;
good-tempered; well-breeding; impure; industrial; pagan; demolished; shadowy; unspotted; mighty; unsympathizing; noisy; unending; suffering; romantic; naughty; dim-
eyed; injurious; contemporary; insulted; innumerable (pl); interminable; mundane;
fantastic; unconscious; dissolving; pitiful;
countless (pl); frozen; bustling; spiritual;
intellectual; candid; uncounted (pl); disordered; supernatural; financial; dense; degenerate; commonplace; everyday; sensual;
untraveled; breathing; diagrammed; wondering; invisible; hollow-hearted; crashing;
assembled; unimaginable; fictitious; globular; convex; boisterous; workaday; clamorous; grieved; shaggy; material; flaming;
unseen; busy; turbulent; alien; dingy; congregated; sorrowful; exclusive; neglected;
seething; limited; conscious; benighted; listening; intelligible; contradictory; pulseless;
writhing; famous; teeming; spacious; thinking; unusual; busy; witty; recreant; pendant; frantic; recorded; lazy; working;
manifold; extraordinary; falling; unfamiliar; new-born; atheistic; chilling; arduous;
contemptible; snowy; approving; archetypal; war-convulsed; desert; heaving; unbelieving; quivering; false; monstrous; selfish; despicable; contumelious; fashionable;
angry; inexpressive; rain-wet; fast; moving; distasteful; decomposed; ever-advanc-
ing; godless; hero-worshipping; fighting;
monotonous; corrupted; sin-bound; sympa-

1304

thizing; unremembered; celestial; hoary; altered; heartless; obscure; splendor-winged; divided; fascinating; undiscriminating; literary; careless; censorious; enduring; undisparaged; undespoiled; amphibious; merciless; unfriendly; insipid; infinite; watery; artistic; insecure; imaginative; unfathomable; sphered; warring; carping; commercial; merry; interdependent; well-loved; beautiful; beggared; distraught; sacrilegious; insurgent; shabby; golden; unsteady; dim; mazed; beseiged; offended; ancient; waiting; rough; eugenic; supernatural; external; mechanized; enlightened; white; voiceless; antique; vegetable; unappreciative; practical; ranking; inaccessible; united; boundless; imperfect; mechanistic; resplendent; civilized; panicky; indifferent; simple; violent; unstable; perfumed; ghostly; somber; dream; cautious; feminized, surrounding; spacious; groaning; resplendent; primeval; renovated; too-busy; sublime; thankless; faithless; wide; lampless; apostate; unroofed; war-pliant; hostile; fallen; imperfect; ungoverned.

verbs

bedevil—; befuddle—; benefit—; bestride —; blight—; confront—; consolidate—; contemplate—; convulse—; disease—; dislocate—; doom—; dwarf—; encompass—; enrich—; entangle—; flood—; grace—; heal —; hide from—; ignore—; isolate from—; people—; present to—; proclaim to—; redeem—; reform—; renounce—; revolutionize—; roam—; rock—; shape—; stir—; storm—; struggle with—; survey—; trample on—; transfigure—; triumph over—; withdraw from—; —acclaims; —acknowledges; —collapses; —crumbles; —rejects; —revolves; —slumbers; —teems with; —turns.

(See mankind, humanity, individual, globe, earth, creation, universe.)

WORLDLINESS

verbs

abhor—; achieve—; attain—; declaim—; decry—; denounce—; deplore—; envelop in —; exhibit—; feign—; forsake—; gain—; pretend—; purge of—; quit—; reject—; renounce—; supplant—; wrap in—; —callouses; —centers; —cloaks; —doubts; —hardens; —polishes; —questions; —veneers.

(See erudition, ambition, cynicism, experience.)

WORLDLY

adverbs

godlessly; selfishly; egotistically; covetously; immensely; pitiably; extraordinarily; lazily; contemptibly; deplorably; monstrously; heartlessly; gracelessly; stubbornly; callously; mercenarily; inexplicably; unreasonably; irritatingly; insensately; irreligiously; sacrilegiously; atheistically; irreverently; irrevocably; apostately; horribly; impiously; perversely; fanatically; recklessly; avowedly; blasphemously; profanely; heartbreakingly; grievously; obstinately; obdurately; unhappily; irrationally; unreasonably; openly.

WORM

adjectives

destitute; surfeited; unwholesome; obscene; invisible; lowly; humble; pollution-nourished; sluggish; nameless; voracious; resuscitated; venomous; reluctant; fiery; trodden; dead; crawling; lucky; worthless; velvet; vile.

verbs

angle with—; attract—s; bait with—; crush —; dig for—; excavate for—; hook—; impale—; —s annihilate; —attacks; —bores; —burrows; —creeps; —gnaws; —infects; —pupates; —screws; —slithers; —spirals; —symbolizes; —wriggles.

(See bait, animal.)

WORN

adverbs

shabbily; uselessly; irrecoverably; terribly; naturally; utterly; dingily; undesirably; utterly; pitifully; miserably; dreadfully.

WORRIED

adverbs

unnaturally; nervously; excitedly; terribly; miserably; frantically; pitiably; keenly; significantly; perceptibly; indescribably; deeply; unduly; touchingly; abnormally; naturally; curiously; lamentably; pathetically; ridiculously; ludicrously.

WORRY

adjectives

manifold (pl); mental; faint; territorial; eternal; death-dealing.

verbs

afflict with—; allay—; bear—; beset with —; betray—; dispel—; drown—; experience

—; immerse in—; induce—; occasion—; plunge into—; relieve of—; submerge in—; imburden—; —harasses; —harrows; —haunts; —hounds; —lashes; —oppresses; —plagues; —preys upon; —racks; —rends; —retards; —rings; —shatters; —weighs upon.

(See **anxiety, misgivings, liability, care.**)

WORRY (v)

adverbs

morbidly; miserably; neurotically; perpetually; abnormally; needlessly; desperately.

(See **fret, vex.**)

WORSHIP

adjectives

pagan; outward; astral; mystical; inhuman; spiritual; reverent; sane; idealistic; silent; cynical; imploring; coterie; divine; passionate; reverential; ardent; worthy; unhesitating; continual; interrupted; lifelong.

verbs

bow in—; chant—; congregate for—; defile —; desecrate—; dogmatize—; exalt—; intone—; join in—; kneel in—; lead—; perform—; persecute—; rejoice in—; renounce —; ridicule—; ritualize—; scorn—; sing—; —deifies; —exalts; —glorifies; —idolizes; —invokes; —lauds; —supplicates; —survives.

(See **cult, devotion, adoration, love, prayer, mass.**)

WORSHIP (v)

adverbs

blindly; inconsistently; religiously; solemnly; idolatrously; mystically; reverently; silently; passionately; ardently; continually.

(See **adore, reverence.**)

WORSHIPERS

adjectives

insensate; false; frenzied; vulgar; idol; heathen; devout.

verbs

address—; awe—; convoke—; electrify—; elevate—; hallow—; inspire—; preach to —; —adore; —beseech; —bow; —deify; —enshrine; —give thanks; —glorify; —invoke; —kneel; —pay homage; —pay tribute; —petition; —prostrate; —revere; —sacrifice; —supplicate; —vow.

(See **church-goers, priest, minister.**)

WORSHIPFUL

adverbs

fatuously; foolishly; obviously; conspicuously; devotedly; devoutly; faithfully; fanatically; sincerely; gloriously; admirably; ostentatiously; unctuously; smugly; blandly; truly; laudably; pharasaically; humbly; abjectly; adoringly; meekly.

WORTH

adjectives

transcendent; priceless; individual; passing; inestimable; artistic; imaginary; venerable; intrinsic; known; matchless; martial; nameless; sterling; high; unspeakable; additional; spiritual; reverend; divine; ultimate; genuine.

verbs

appraise—; appreciate—; ascertain—; assert—; assess—; attest to—; challenge—; degrade—; derive—from; determine—; disclose—; display—; endow with—; establish —; estimate—; exhibit—; gauge—; judge —; measure—; probe—; prove—; question —; reflect upon—; signify—; stamp—; weigh—; —ascends; —depreciates; —mounts; —skyrockets.

(See **value, merit, ability.**)

WORTHLESS

adverbs

terribly; undeniably; altogether; absolutely; hopelessly; scandalously; abominably; curiously; peculiarly; outlandishly; trashily; shabbily; miserably; wretchedly; atrociously; completely; contemptibly.

WORTHLESSNESS

verbs

acknowledge—; admit—; balance—; bare —; bemoan—; betray—; bewail—; concede —; consider—; contemplate—; decry—; denounce—; deplore—; divulge—; evidence—; expose—; inveigh against—; lapse into—; mask—; regard—; reveal—; ridicule—; scoff at—; scorn—; stray into—; unveil—.

(See **futility, inferiority, inefficiency, mediocrity, stupidity.**)

WORTHY

adverbs

completely; utterly; laudably; meritoriously; notably; conspicuously; sincerely; truly; incomparably; surpassingly; extraordinarily; amazingly; obviously; recognizably; manifestly; singularly.

WOUND

adjectives

sharp; starched; gaping; unprobed; obstinate; desperate; lifelong; unhealed; sterile; sharp; unadvised; stiffening; self-inflicted; dark; bleeding; ancient; external; immedicable; ghastly; fatal; infected; punctured; lacerated; mortal; grievous; suppurating; cruel; serious; aching; frightful; reeking; recurring; raw; numerous (pl); surface; immediate; hideous; disastrous; severe.

verbs

allay—; alleviate—; assuage—; balm—; caress—; cauterize—; cleanse—; disinfect —; drain—; dress—; inflict—; irrigate—; pack—; probe—; soothe—; staunch—; suck —; swab—; weather—; —bleeds; —punctures; —scars.

(See cut, laceration, injury.)

WOUND (v)

adverbs

indirectly; mortally; spiritually; dangerously; frightfully; cruelly; seriously; severely; critically; sorely; fatally; internally; grievously; hideously; disastrously.

(See hurt, injure.)

WRAITH

adjectives

meek; likely; unusual.

WRANGLE

adjectives

bloody; vestry; conjugal; political; brutal.

verbs

arbitrate—; avert—; curb—; curtail—; engage in—; incite—; instigate—; quell—; subdue—; —annoys; —arises; —bickers; — breaches; —clashes; —disputes; —distracts; —diverts; —ebbs; —embroils; — estranges; —jars; —jolts; —shocks; — wanes.

(See brawl, dispute, argument, quarrel.)

WRANGLE (v)

adverbs

stridently; vociferously; indignantly; furiously; conjugally; politically; brutally; viciously; vindictively; heatedly; incessantly; jealously; pettishly; argumentatively.

(See quarrel, argue.)

WRAP (v)

adverbs

snugly; clumsily; punctiliously; impeccably; festively; meticulously; competently; artistically; crudely.

(See cover, conceal.)

WRAPPER

adjectives

protective; formless; holiday.

verbs

bind—; cast off—; divest of—; enclose in —; husk—; invest in—; package in—s; penetrate—; pierce—; seal—; shed—; strip off—; superimpose—; —affords; —armors; —envelops; —girds; —insures; —preserves; — protects; —safeguards; —shelters; — shields; —swathes.

(See envelope, lining, cover.)

WRATH

adjectives

tiger-like; indignant; dead; volcanic; infinite; jealous; immoderate; swollen; righteous; unconscious; intolerable; glutinous; treacherous; mingled; passionate; desolating; whimsical; vindictive; drunken; popular; fiercest; uncaged; chastening; scornful; patient; ill-suppressed; silent; bitter; naked; envious; stormy; celestial; crazy; awakened; relentless; intense; mysterious; helpless; deathless; senile; destructive; parental; eternal; reproachful; unholy; headlong; foolish; revengeful; celebrated; threatening; righteous.

verbs

appease—; brave—; bring to—; burst into —; dampen—; draw—; encounter—; endure—; escape—; explode in—; fire with —; incur—; mollify—; move to—; pacify —; placate—; provoke—; repent—; rouse —; slake—; uncork—; vent—; —abates; — abuses; —bites; —blazes —clouds; —descends upon; —melts; —oppresses; — smoulders.

(See ire, anger, indignation, rage.)

WRATHFUL

adverbs

desperately; dangerously; inordinately; brutally; ominously; portentously; alarmingly; terribly; frightfully; unusually; unmitigably; unreasoningly; insensately; senselessly.

adjectives
wanton; flavored; branching; rosy; light; variegated; flimsy; summer; noble; festal; odorous; bridal.

adjectives
isolated; passive; sunken; pensile; irredeemable; silent; human; stunted; profitable; dilapidated; emotional; colossal; leafless; pulverized; shattered; crimson; moral; mangled; horrid; centennial; complicated; dreaded; ghastly; pitiable.

verbs
avert—; avoid—; escape—; explore—; glean from—; investigate—; perish in—; probe—; rummage through—; salvage—; survive—; —annihilates; —blights; —defaces; —demolishes; —devastates; —disheartens; —encumbers; —impairs; —impedes; —mars; —obstructs; —scars; —scathes; —strews.

(See ruins, debris, remains, accident.)

adverbs
deliberately; wantonly; revengefully; vindictively; desperately; hideously; disastrously; spiritually; destructively; insanely; treacherously.

(See destroy, ruin.)

verbs
—bubbles along; —busies; —chatters; —cheers; —cuddles; —dances; —hops; —peeps; —runs; —skips; —warms.

(See bird.)

adverbs
violently; abruptly; distressfully; simultaneously; drastically; fiercely; disastrously; diabolically; rudely.

(See seize, grasp.)

adverbs
persuasively; religiously; prodigiously; arduously; ignominiously; industrially; economically; politically; wrathfully; fanatically; fiercely.

(See contend, fight.)

verbs
coach—; manage—; train—; —batters; —buffets; —contends; —crouches; —dives; —engages; —fends; —flattens; —flings; —feints; —grapples; —groans; —grunts; —hugs; —hurls; —locks; —pancakes; —pinions; —rams; —scrambles; —spread-eagles; —strains; —strips; —tackles; —trains; —tussles; —vies for; —wards off.

adjectives
wondrous; mutinous; timorous; base; despairing; stupid; extreme; trembling; pretty; utter; short-sighted; imperturbable; tame; hollow-eyed; miserable; pitied; profligate; loathed; restless; fanatical; scandalous; enormous; self-nurtured; abandoned; nameless; barbarous; famishing; hunted; ephemeral; execrable; caitiff; shattered; delicate; disobedient; cruel; disabled; cowering; intense; fond; tortured; rude; miserable; famished; dishonest; drunken; jealous; deceptive; violent; sodden; smoky; inhuman; stupid; dew-bedabbled; conscious-stricken; odious; needy; houseless; irreparable; filthy.

adverbs
miserably; pitiably; wordlessly; silently; utterly; inexpressibly; unspeakably; helplessly; feebly; hopelessly; cruelly; bitterly; singularly; inconsolably; disconsolately.

adverbs
ecstatically; uncomfortably; uneasily; nervously; oppressively; distressfully; impatiently; impulsively; slickly; deftly; slyly.

(See move, writhe.)

adverbs
fiercely; hysterically; vehemently; imperiously; convulsively; wildly; demoniacally; jubilantly; barbarically; sickeningly; fiendishly; iniquitously.

(See clutch, grasp.)

adverbs
carelessly; furiously; curiously; impatiently; prematurely; superciliously; fastidiously; scornfully.

(See pucker, crease.)

adverbs

oddly; deeply; remarkably; excessively; terribly; merrily; agedly; uncommonly; curiously; noticeably; surprisingly; perceptibly.

WRINKLES

adjectives

upright; facial; weeping; frown-caused.

verbs

acquire—; avoid—; decry—; deplore—; knead—; smooth—; —appear; —blemish; —corrugate; —crease; —deepen; —disfigure; —distress; —furrow; —line; —mar; —ruffle.

WRISTS

adjectives

fettered; limp; blue-veined; gallant; compact; slim; strong.

verbs

adorn—; band—; bare—; benumb—; bind —; brace—; bruise—; dislocate—; distort —; encircle—; extend—; flex—; fracture —; grasp—; handcuff—; lacerate—; manipulate—; misshape—; paralyze—; prick —; seize by—; sprain—.

(See arm, hand, joint.)

WRIT

adjectives

ingenious; hallowed; apostolic; moving; deathless; legal.

verbs

apply for—; draw up—; file—; grant—; honor—; refuse—; respect—; —absolves: —accords; —allows; —authorizes; —confirms; —decrees; —disposes; —empowers; —evicts; —exempts; —exonerates; —immunizes; —informs; —legalizes; —pardons; —privileges; —releases; —sanctions; — summons; —verifies.

(See decree, award, decision, edict, order.)

WRITE (v)

adverbs

diplomatically; admirably; bombastically; trenchantly; graphically; crudely; barbarously; devastatingly; convincingly; pornographically; scintillatingly; profusely; magnanimously; scientifically; laboriously; ironically; irresolutely; irresistibly; pretentious-

ly; tremulously; elegantly; desultorily; anonymously; satirically; hypothetically; harshly; affectionately; expressly; faultlessly; industriously; legibly; prosaically; salaciously; erotically; sensuously; contemporaneously; authoritatively; genially; avidly; solemnly; incoherently; vigorously; urgently; dogmatically; didactically; eclectically; voluminously; inscrutably; realistically; cynically.

(See compose, inscribe.)

WRITER

adjectives

outstanding; foremost; verbose; nature; world-famous; fatigued; controversial; credible; ancient; profane; neo-romantic; prolific; theoretic; travel; authoritative; ecclesiastical; illustrious; distinguished; public; opera; miscellaneous; quaint; sociological; sensational; inspiring; discouraged; unscientific; impressionistic; well-known; promising; juvenile; wretched; designing; seduced; eminent; vivacious; historical; roguish; original; anonymous; polemical; tragic; imaginative; convincing; passionate; discriminating; splendid; creative; influential; monkish; native; fertile; talented; thoughtful; philosophical; early; copious; ghost; practised; vigorous; estimable; nondescript; classic; revolutionary; charming; meritorious; previous; prose; diestical; voluminous; reputed; embryo; entertaining.

verbs

acclaim—; honor—; immortalize—; inspire —; laud—; —climaxes; —clothes in; — colors; —composes; —concocts; —couches in; —dashes off; —decries; —depicts; — elucidates; —eulogizes; —fabricates; —fascinates; —infers; —interprets; —libels; — molds; —narrates; —pens; —plagiarizes; —portrays; —recounts; —relates; —reports; —slanders; —soliloquizes; —styles; —unfolds; —vitalizes; —voices; —weaves.

(See dramatist, novelist, journalist, author, poet.)

WRITHE (v)

adverbs

spiritually; convulsively; sickeningly; agonizingly; pitiably.

(See wriggle, struggle.)

WRITHING

adjectives

mental; gnarled; imaginative; splendid; ignominious.

adjectives

superb; first-class; breezy; contrapuntal; philosophical; epistolary; biographical; voluminous; humorous; undecipherable; wedge-shaped; hieroglyphic; tropical; free-lance; controversial; metaphorical; foremost; impressive; contemporary; descriptive; elaborate; clear; ghost; imaginative; copious; tragic; historical; propagandist; theoretical; inter-twisted; classic; commercial; prophetical; pernicious; dimmed; superb; representative; figurative; straightforward; unfinished; undistinguished; phonetic; miscellaneous; clerkly; distinct; admirable; sacred; cryptic; dramatic; poignant; unacademic; unpublished; excellent; lucid; scholarly; stylistic.

verbs

abridge—; acclaim—; analyze—; ban—; comprehend—; dissect—; disseminate—; engross in—; ferret out—; herald—; immortalize—; interpret—; laud—; permeate—; peruse—; pervade—; pervert—; probe—; prostitute—; publish—; rival—; —air; —dissertate; —embody; —embrace; —enthrall; —impassion; —inspire; —live; —particularize; —treat of; —ventilate.

(See editorial, epistle, epigram, handwriting, literature, prose, poetry.)

WRONG

adjectives

avenged; uncomplaining; revenging; cruel; deadly; great; bitter; ruthless; grievous; deep; hideous; fancied; intrinsic; culminating; enforced; irrevocable; willful; private; petty; perfidious; inevitable; early; fierce; trifling; illegal; foul; heinous; hoarded; irreparable; unredeemed; diabolic; mutual; deplored; inexpiable; accumulated; brazen; abstract; secret; drastic.

verbs

amend—; avenge—; challenge—; combat—; defeat—; denounce—; discern—; efface—; expose—; extenuate—; heal—; implant—; intend—; perpetuate—; redress—; reform —; remedy—; repent—; reproach—; reveal—; sustain—; —blemishes; —blots; —corrupts; —harasses; —injures; —mars; —offends; —oppresses; —weighs upon.

(See guilt, evil, injustice, grievance, crime.)

adverbs

utterly; absolutely; altogether; singularly; curiously; completely; wickedly; mischievously; deliberately; blunderingly; knowingly; outrageously; scandalously; brutally; cruelly; fatally.

WRONG (v)

adverbs

grievously; irreparably; deeply; grossly; iniquitously; ignominiously; insidiously; dishonestly; treacherously; egregiously; ruthlessly; diabolically; secretly.

(See deceive, trick.)

WRONG-DOING

verbs

ameliorate—; atone for—; avert—; campaign against—; check—; condone—; countenance—; decry—; deplore—; expiate—; inveigh against—; penalize—; quell—; reprove—; —despoils; —embitters; —invalidates; —saps; —undermines.

(See wrong, crime, sin.)

WRY

adverbs

fantastically; comically; decrepitly; curiously; cynically; pathetically; congenitally; pitiably; miserably; tragically; hopelessly; irremediably; permanently.

X

X-RAY

verbs

blur—; diagnose by—; dim—; examine under—; employ—; introduce—; observe—; resort to—; scrutinize—; study—; —delin-eates; —depicts; —discloses; —outlines; —photographs; —reveals; —shadows; —traces.

(See picture, microscope, photograph.)

Y

YACHT

adjectives
graceful; magnificent; furtive; converted.

verbs
batter—; board—; buffet—; captain—; christen—; collide with—; dock—; ground —; guide—; lash—; launch—; luxuriate on —; navigate—; pilot—; provision—; quarter on—; ram—; refurbish—; salvage—; scuttle—; swamp—; waft—; —flounders; —reels; —signals.
(See launch, boat, motor-boat, ship.)

YAMMERING

adverbs
hungrily; excitedly; pathetically; pitifully; pitiably; miserably; touchingly; affectingly; heartbreakingly; agonizedly; painfully; distressingly; pleadingly; wretchedly; hopefully; clamorously; feebly; despairingly; madly; dolefully; exhaustedly.

YAPPING

adverbs
spitefully; derisively; threateningly; disagreeably; noisily; clamorously; unpleasantly; grossly; coarsely; excitedly; viciously; eagerly; uncontrollably; unmanageably; alarmingly; snappishly; menacingly; fearfully.

YARD

adjectives
bustling; spacious; industrial; back; snowy; discreet; embowered; obscure; diminutive.

verbs
border—; bound—; circumscribe—; clutter —; confine to—; embrace—; encamp in—; enclose—; fence—; festoon—; flank—; garland—; litter—; provision—; restock—; romp in—; skirt—; span—; survey—; — affords; —extends.
(See area, garden, park.)

YARN
(*colloq.*)
(*tale*)

verbs
blast—; climax—; color—; debunk—; digress from—; embroider—; exaggerate—; explode—; fabricate—; magnify—; narrate

—; recite—; recount—; relate—; retail—; spin—; stretch—; swap—s; terminate—; unfold—; varnish—; weave—; —delights; — distracts; —enthralls; —thrills.
(See story, tale.)

YARN
(*general*)

adjectives
mingled; rollicking; mystical; interminable; periodic; unlikely.

YARN
(*thread*)

verbs
arrange—; baste—; chain with—; entwine in—; fabricate—; interlace—; knit with—; pad with—; rend—; spin—; tack with—; twist—; unravel—; unsnarl—; unwind—; weave—; web—.
(See knitting, thread.)

YAWN

adjectives
smothered; suppressed; slight; prodigious; prolonged; imitative.

verbs
camouflage—; choke back—; conceal—; gag —; interpret—; muzzle—; restrain—; smother—; stifle—; suppress—; veil—; — betrays; —implies; —indicates; —insults; —masks; —silences; —widens.

YAWN (*v*)

adverbs
ferociously; prodigiously; drowsily; audibly; lazily; dreamily; surreptitiously; furtively; secretly; imitatively.

YAWNING

adverbs
embarrassingly; uncontrollably; significantly; undisguisedly; openly; unaccountably; impolitely; discourteously; deliberately; suggestively; unconscionably; wearily; drowsily; sleepily; oddly; continually; prodigiously; nonchalantly; indifferently; audibly; monstrously; loudly; ridiculously; cavernously; frankly; purposely; unconsciously; inadvertently.

adjectives

virgin; elder; young; declining; golden; eternal; blighted; fineless (pl); desolate; vanished; studious; early; tender; childish; dying; successful; important; dangerous; unripe; formative; mature; short; undawned; magnificent; allotted; varied; revolving; troublous; mellowed; plenteous; good; healing; quiet; ominous; countless (pl); reluctant; exasperating; imperial; creeping; cruel; revealing; experimental; enormous; unfulfilling; previous; mighty; mournful; blessed; blooming; arduous; impatient; u-nique; gilded; rolling (pl); adolescent; ensuing; silent; rare; beauteous; endless; far; distant; synodical; sidereal; peaceful; sanguine; weary; infinite; rapid; dreary; advancing; active; green; inverted; vernal; hopeless; innocent; tempestuous; sleeping; gracious; darkling; hallowed; ravaged; subsequent; trembling; iron-footed; fleeting; flying; rolling; slanting; lengthened; lapsing; strong; bitter; impending; heavy-footed; paltry; dreaded; long-vanished; grueling; extinguished; unreluctant; soon-ended; envenomed; recent (pl); peaceful; precious; disastrous; lying; moldering; turbulent; successive (pl); achieving; consecutive (pl); troubled; illimitable; pregnant; alternate (pl); merry; blissful; absent; industrious; memorable; probationary; un-reckoned; columned; bountiful; swelling; long-buried; departed; eventful; canceled; straitened; ill-starred; terrible; innumerable (pl); ragged; blurred; laborious; fabulous; ripened; hoarded; changing; wasted; withering; fiscal; plenteous; execrated.

YEARN (v)

adverbs

vaguely; tenderly; passionately; pensively; compassionately; ineffably; deeply; honestly; restlessly; mutely; inchoately.
(See desire, wish.)

YEARNING

adjectives

rhythmical; passionate; affectionate; anguished; nebulous; poignant; strange; heavenly; pitiful; keen; mortal; tender; intense; silent; precious; innermost; moral; equal; double; inchoate; naive; ineffable; restless; awful; natural; deep; honest; earnest.

verbs

allay—; cherish—; crush—; disclose—; dull—; ease—; gratify—; intensify—; mitigate—; palliate—; quell—; quench—; reveal—; satiate—; satisfy—; slake—; smother—; stifle—; suppress—; —intoxicates; —overwhelms; —seizes.
(See craving, longing.)

adverbs

anxiously; affectionately; fondly; lovingly; amorously; solicitously; hungrily; wearily; eagerly; manifestly; ambitiously; politically; conspicuously; obviously.

YEARS

verbs

advance in—; blank out—; curtail—; devote—to; dream away—; ease—; enliven—; enumerate—; extend—; forsee—; order—; prolong—; record—; rob of—; romp through—; shorten—; span—; survive—; —accumulate; —age; —creep by; —dim; —expire; —file by; —fly; —gnarl; —intervene; —lapse; —mature; —mellow; —parch; —race by; —ripen; —sear; —shrivel; —steal by; —twist.
(See months, time.)

YELL

adjectives

mingled (pl); incessant; long-drawn; simultaneous; fiendish; exultant; doleful; demoniac; jubilant; sickening; frantic; mocking; responsive; excited; deafening; barbaric; fierce; clamorous; triumphant; taunting; distressful; shrill; blood-curdling.

verbs

emit—; muffle—; mute—; muzzle—; restrain—; smother—; stifle—; suppress—; —agonizes; —alarms; —betrays; —discloses; —echoes; —penetrates; —pierces; —rends; —rings out; —shatters; —shrills; —startles.
(See shout, shriek, cry.)

YELL (v)

adverbs

stridently; enthusiastically; violently; furiously; barbarically; viciously; mockingly; demoniacally; fiercely; clamorously; triumphantly; tauntingly; fiendishly; jubilantly; exultantly.
(See cry, bellow.)

adjectives

dazzling; brass; gay; soft; durable; rich; canary; cheerful; bright; eye-taking.

adverbs

dreadfully; deeply; uncommonly; perceptibly; agedly; significantly; ominously; sadly; sorrily; darkly; biliously; mopishly; desperately.

adjectives

throaty; deep; hot; unmistakable; hostile.

adjectives

pyramidal; gigantic.

adjectives

excellent; abundant; desired; glorious; astounding; bloodless; remarkable; reassuring; prosperous; fabulous.

verbs

conserve—; consume—; curtail—; augment —; deplete—; disperse—; enhance—; estimate—; exhaust—; forecast—; garner—; market—; multiply—; squander—; treasure —; value—; —accrues; —ascends; —descends; —exceeds; —floods; —gluts; —mounts; —replenishes; —soars; —swells.
(See harvest, crop.)

adverbs

unequivocally; copiously; ostensibly; dejectedly; reluctantly; submissively; unwillingly; gracefully; blindly; prudently; begrudgingly; heroically; gallantly; abundantly; pusillanimously; gloriously.
(See submit, surrender.)

adverbs

suddenly; warmly; reluctantly; ardently; eagerly; agreeably; politely; courteously; finally; grudgingly; inconsistently; unwillingly; voluntarily; eventually; harmoniously; helpfully; pleasantly; suavely; urbanly.

adjectives

unsought; galling; oppressive; detested; equal; brazen; chafing; heavy; bloody; tyrannical; cruel; servile; insufferable; harnessed.

verbs

bow to—; cast off—; deliver from—; ease —; emancipate from—; endure—; escape—; evade—; harness to—; liberate from—; rend—; sever—; subject to—; throw off—; tolerate—; unburden—; —couples; —curbs; —detains; —enslaves; —fetters; —irritates; —limits; —manacles; —restrains; —restricts; —shackles; —subjugates; —tethers.
(See manacle, chain, authority, band, tyranny.)

verbs

beget—; befriend—; cherish—; conceive—; defend—; devour—; fledge—; guard—; harass—; mother—; nest—; nurse—; prey upon—; protect—; raise—; restrain—; shield—; succor—; suckle—; teach—; wean —; —mature; —take wings; —test.
(See offspring, child.)

adverbs

adorably; sweetly; refreshingly; ridiculously; ecstatically; rapturously; delightfully; unsuitably; unfortunately; charmingly; appealingly; shyly; absurdly; hopelessly; extremely; wretchedly; terribly; childishly; blithely; happily; joyously; hilariously; infinitely; immortally; unbelievably; excitably; ardently; ingenuously; vividly; gloriously; splendidly; exuberantly; radiantly; blessedly.

adjectives

abashed; sturdy; thoughtless; inquisitive; impatient; irresponsible; vigorous; inexperienced; admiring; sensitive; adolescent; nondescript; impertinent.

verbs

adopt—; amuse—; chasten—; discipline—; divert—; entertain—; guide—; nurse—; scold—; sober—; subdue—; —clambers; —clamors; —naps; —plagues; —questions; —romps; —scampers; —scurries; —wearies.
(See child.)

adjectives

courteous; ardent; home-keeping; poetic; ingenuous; unarmed; dashing; immortal;

glorious; vigorous; ambitious; extreme; un-thinking; affected; studious; guarded; sanc-timonious; illiterate; splendid; self-enamor-ed; affluent; dazzling; uncouth; philosophi-cal; smiling; malignant; ill-fed; hopeless; facile; mortal; sensitive; foolhardy; ventur-ous; gracious; fragrant; exuberant; fertile; inexperienced; tenacious; timid; sinless; academic; sportive; heroic; everlasting; pensive; busy; handsome; perpetual; roman-tic; straying; overconfident; thankful; rev-erend; scorbutic; martial; willful; sweet; disdainful; radiant; burning; early; rau-cous; unhardened; restless; blessed; mis-chievous; moonish; unhappy; deflowered; fine; gallant; pretty; saintly; virtuous; be-reaved; eager; personable; fresh; ill-kept; afflicted; tranquil; reckless; wasted; self-willed; haughty; extreme; lonely; expand-ing; refined; obstreperous; thoughtful; con-secrated; protracted; shaggy-headed; rustic; lusty; high-spirited; inexplicable; venture-some; bruised; unregenerate; shrinking; soothing; callow; unsociable; unspent; dire; complaining; hapless; scant; loquacious; insensible; impetuous; fair-haired; illustri-ous; weather-beaten; departed; emulous; lumbering; corrupt; upright; trembling; joyous; tattered; haggard; fadeless; dumb; wooden; dissolute; unfriended; misguided; wretched; passionate; absurd; fantastic; in-flammable; ill-boding; dark; irrepressible; yearning; visioning; smirking; emaciated; personable; curly-headed; fervent; handy; flaming; swart; shambling; dapper; post-war; close-lipped; alert.

verbs

attain—; burden—; cherish—; clutch—; commune with—; conscript—; corrupt—; counsel—; curtail—; depict—; discipline—; distress—; exalt—; extend—; exult in—; govern—; guide—; infuse—; inject—; instil —; lecture to—; maintain—; mar—; person-ify—; prate of—; prepare—; prolong—; quell—; recall—; recapture—; reflect on—; regain—; reminisce of—; reproach—; revel in—; revert to—; ripen into—; rob of—; sacrifice—; stride toward—; struggle to—; survive—; swamp—; symbolize—; — blooms; —emulates; —fades; —fires; — ignites; —impassions; —inspires; —in-spirits; —invigorates; —matures; —mel-lows; —pervades; —reveres; —strays; — surmounts; —sweeps aside; —vaults; — wanes.

(See girl, childhood, maturity.)

YOUTHFUL

adverbs

delightfully; refreshingly; touchingly; wondrously; manifestly; charmingly; sur-prisingly; unbelievably; ingenuously; allur-ingly; adorably; artlessly; innocently; joy-ously; radiantly; blithely; cheerily; raptur-ously; gloriously; splendidly; adventurous-ly; sweetly; restlessly; mischievously; bless-edly; eagerly.

YOUTHFULNESS

adjectives

abounding; joyous; perpetual; mercurial; sparkling.

Z

ZANY

adverbs

amusingly; divertingly; ridiculously; absurdly; nonsensically; utterly; laughably; farcically; clownishly; mischievously; roguishly; playfully; cleverly; ingeniously.

ZEAL

adjectives

untiring; equal; puritan; inconsiderate; unflagging; lofty; cruel; wise; undaunted; peaceful; reformatory; misguided; overtaxed; artistic; benevolent; ancestral; unflinching; high-bred; unselfish; neverwearying; fervent; divine; wavering; accustomed; missionary; indiscreet; plastic; flaming; indomitable; flagging; incredible; hot; ardent; characteristic; solemn; noble; petulant; insensate; unwearied; humble; furious; commendable; religious; pious; upright; immoderate; diminishing.

verbs

attend with—; burn with—; check—; constrain—; cool—; counterfeit—; devote with —; display—; express—; extinguish—; feign—; fire with—; flush with—; heighten —; imbue with—; infuse—; inject—; inspire —; instil—; intensify—; lack—; match—; misguide—; promote—; quench—; regain—; share—; sharpen—; slake—; stimulate—; want—; —blazes; —burns; —consumes; — declines; —ebbs; —goads; —impassions; — melts; —quickens; —spurs; —subsides; — surges; —wanes; —waxes.

(See "pep", ardor, enthusiasm, intensity, fervor, eagerness, energy.)

ZEALOTS

adjectives

religious; wild; fiery; graceless; poetic; crazy-brained; patriotic.

ZEALOUS

adverbs

earnestly; actively; ardently; passionately; energetically; impetuously; eagerly; nervously; excitedly; absurdly; irresistibly; helpfully; extraordinarily; serviceably; delightfully; ridiculously; seriously; devoutly; piously; remarkably; distinctly; efficiently; boldly; willingly; generously.

ZEBRA

verbs

alarm—; cage—; captivate—; cross with—; domesticate—; exterminate—; fetter—; snare—; team with—; thrash—; —abounds in; —balks; —bolts; —bounds; —frequents; —grazes; —herds; —leaps; —pulls; — scurries; —sniffs; —springs.

(See animal, horse.)

ZENITH

verbs

achieve—; ascend to—; attain—; culminate in—; elevate to—; skyrocket to (colloq.)—; toboggan from—; topple from—; whirl to—; —climaxes.

(See height, pinnacle, fame, summit, peak.)

ZEPHYR

adjectives

reckless; delicious; sweet; playful; gracious.

ZERO
(*rating*)

verbs

achieve—; bestow—; concede—; degrade to —; dole out—; fling—; impose—; incur—; merit—; rate—; scorn—; solicit—; tender —; threaten—; withdraw—; —confounds; —contradicts; —destroys; —disorders; — strikes.

(See punishment, reward, grade.)

ZEST

adjectives

special; sporting; prodigious; insatiable; inherent; hearty; adventurous; savage; scalping; rollicking; invidious; soldierly; smiling; inextinguishable; exquisite; glorious; hungry; infinite; keen; unflagging; eager; special; cynical; monotonous.

verbs

afford—; arouse—; augment—; curb—; derive—; devour with—; enhance—; excite—; harness—; impart—; inspire—; repress—; savor with—; stimulate—; subdue—; whet —; —animates; —burns; —charms; —ebbs;

—enlivens; —fortifies; —heartens; —invigorates; —pervades; —promotes; —reassures; —refreshes; —restrains; —suffuses; —sustains; —wanes.

(See zeal, ardor, fervor, flavor.)

ZESTFUL

adverbs

eagerly; alertly; happily; earnestly; avidly; energetically; enthusiastically; unusually; marvelously; unexpectedly; remarkably; inordinately; curiously; miraculously; incalculably; splendidly; superbly; joyously; helpfully; ardently; delightfully; boyishly; youthfully; noticeably; unwontedly.

ZIGZAG

adverbs

interestingly; purposely; profitably; curiously; conveniently; oddly; artistically; peculiarly; miserably; clumsily; adroitly; cleverly; intentionally; characteristically; quaintly; disagreeably; attractively; unexpectedly; deliberately.

ZONE

adjectives

temperate; frozen; arctic; inner; verdant; fringed; bodiced; interminable; fortunate; arable; wide-spread.

verbs

amplify—; apportion—; belt—; bisect—; carve out—; chop up—; circumscribe—; detach—; encircle—; encompass—; enlarge—; flank—; incise—; intersect—; invade—; label—; measure—; outline—; overreach—; pare—; patrol—; penetrate—; permeate—; prescribe—; restrict to—; skirt—; slice up —; subdivide—; swerve from—; widen—; —insulates; —isolates; —partitions; —secludes; —segregates.

(See section, neighborhood, area, locality, whereabouts.)

room of his father: for Hiram was ever a lover of David.

2 And Solomon sent to Hiram, saying,

3 Thou knowest how that David my father could not build a house unto the name of the LORD his God, for the wars which were about him on every side, until the LORD put them under the soles of his feet.

they had anointed him king in place of his father; for Hiram always loved David. **2** And Solomon sent word to Hiram, **3** "You know that David my father could not build a house for the name of the LORD his God because of the warfare with which his enemies surrounded him, until the LORD put

---

Solomon arranges for the stone himself, quarrying it in the hill country of Ephraim, with hired Phoenician stonemasons to do the actual cutting. These experts are from Gebel, i.e., Byblos, twenty miles north of Beyrouth.

The material for this chapter is from the biography, except for vss. 3-6, which are a Deuteronomic interlude.

5:1. The spelling of the name varies, but **Hiram** is correct, being a shortened form of אחירם (ʾaḥirām), "brother of Ram [the lofty one]."

The name **Tyre** means "rock," and the city was originally built on a rocky islet half a mile from the shore. This rock was a mile long by three quarters of a mile broad. Its double harbor, north and south, made it a famous port, since one harbor or the other was generally accessible in any weather. This was important because the whole coast line was most difficult for sailing ships, being a sandy lee shore with few harbors, and the ships were unable to do much more than sail before the wind, since tacking was an unknown art. Alexander the Great built a causeway sixty yards wide and thus captured the city which had successfully resisted many sieges, even that by the Babylonians. Since that time sand has drifted up from the south, and now the site of ancient Tyre is joined to the mainland by an isthmus half a mile broad.

The LXX and Lucian have here a curious variant, according to which Hiram sent his servants to anoint Solomon. This custom is vouched for in the Tell el-Amarna tablets as a ceremony by which the suzerain confirmed the appointment of his vassal. Winckler suggested that the gifts mentioned in vs. 11 were actually a permanent tribute paid annually to the Tyrian king (Eberhard Schrader, *Die Keilinschriften und das Alte Testament*, ed. H. Zimmern and H. Winckler [3rd ed.; Berlin: Reuther & Reichard, 1902-3], I, 237-38).

3-6. The Deuteronomic explanation for David's not having built the temple is that David was too busy establishing the kingdom. The explanation given in II Sam. 7

---

workmen. When he contracted with King Hiram of Tyre for the materials with which to build the temple, he raised a levy of forced labor and dispatched his men into Hiram's country to prepare the timber for shipment. **And he sent them to Lebanon, ten thousand a month in relays; they would be a month in Lebanon and two months at home** (vs. 14). Solomon was wise enough to see that the keeping of home contacts is essential to the morale of men abroad. The nature of man demands some place where he can feel "at home." Home is the spot where our spirits in the presence of love relax from the strain put upon us by the pressure of work. Home is the circle where listening ears allow us to unpack our hearts with words, knowing that understanding sympathy will keep what is worth while and throw away the waste. Home is the environ-

ment where little ones lean on us and look up to us, thereby causing us to stand a bit more firmly and feel a bit taller. Home is the place where we are appraised not in terms of market price but on the basis of what we are, where a Bob Cratchit is a hero to Tiny Tim, however he may be scorned as an underling at the office.

How morale deteriorates when home life is disrupted is shown in time of war. Absentee husbands and fathers, working mothers, uprooted families transplanted by war's emergencies—these are factors which bear fruit in sexual irregularities, multiplied divorces, juvenile delinquency, and many other ills. The prolonged absence of the Hebrew workmen in a foreign land would have tended to weaken both their family ties and their national loyalty. Perhaps we should not read too much into the record here. How much Solomon had his eye on pre-

---

ehum, Baanah.

f the people of

, two thousand

iah, three hun-

seven hundred

Seraiah, Re-el-ai'ah, Mor'decai, Bilshan, Mispar, Big'vai, Rehum, and Ba'anah.

The number of the men of the people of Israel: **3** the sons of Parosh, two thousand one hundred and seventy-two. **4** The sons of Shephati'ah, three hundred and seventy-two. **5** The sons of Arah, seven hundred and

of **Seraiah**, the order of **Nehemiah** and "Azariah" may be Zerubbabel, a Persian **Bigvai** is mentioned as governor of ley, *Aramaic Papyri*, No. 30, l. 1; Josephus, too, mentions a e in Palestine [*Antiquities* XI. 7), and a **Rehum** figures official contemporary with Nehemiah (cf. 4:8-9, 17, 23). able of proof, would explain the preponderance of foreign are non-Jewish and distinctly postexilic in type. **Bigvai** is rubbabel ("Seed of Babylon"), **Mordecai** (an abbreviation nt *Marduk*) and **Bilshan** (probably the popular abbrevia- n names.

THE PRINCIPAL LIST (2:2*b*-67)

ts the number of each clan that returned, followed by a sts, concluding with a listing of donations to the temple by headings into different categories, begins, contrary to with a list of laymen rather than priests and Levites. at the original lay list (vss. 3-20), wherein the clans are ounded them, has been supplemented several times (vss. h identify those returning by geographical names. "book of genealogy" (Neh. 7:5), a stress on number e to regard the list as an official Persian census of the Pfeiffer, *Introduction to the Old Testament* [New York: 836; G. Hölscher, *Die Bücher Esra und Nehemia* [4th ed., Tübingen: J. C. B. Mohr, 1923], II, 503-4). This concept use of geographical rather than personal names, but n a tally of immigrants, and vss. 65-67, inexplainable as te to an account of a return (cf. Rudolph, *op. cit.*, pp.

found they are not all of the same order. In addition ames (e.g., vs. 4, **Shephatiah**, "The Lord Judges") there viation (e.g., vs. 9, **Zaccai** for such a name as Zechariah, animal names (e.g., vs. 3, **Parosh**, "Flea"; vs. 5, **Arah**, 19, **Hashum**, "Broad Nose"). Interesting is **Pahath-moab** name but the title "Governor of Moab." The foreign (vs. 14), and **Ater** (vs. 16) reflect the Exile. er remote ancestors, the words **sons of** should here be

2*b*-35=Neh. 7:7*b*-38; I Esdras 5:7-23)

) BY FAMILY (2:2*b*-20)

in Babylonia and among Arabs, but only the Chronicler re-exilic descendant of Asher, a "chief of princes" who e" (I Chr. 7:39-40). Of widely differing totals in the rs to have been either 652 (as in the M.T. of Neh. 7:10

6 The children of Pahath-moab, of the children of Jeshua *and* Joab, two thousand eight hundred and twelve.

7 The children of Elam, a thousand two hundred fifty and four.

8 The children of Zattu, nine hundred forty and five.

9 The children of Zaccai, seven hundred and threescore.

10 The children of Bani, six hundred forty and two.

11 The children of Bebai, six hundred twenty and three.

12 The children of Azgad, a thousand two hundred twenty and two.

13 The children of Adonikam, six hundred sixty and six.

14 The children of Bigvai, two thousand fifty and six.

seventy-five. 6 The sons of Pa'hath-mo'ab, namely the sons of Jeshua and Jo'ab, two thousand eight hundred and twelve. 7 The sons of Elam, one thousand two hundred and fifty-four. 8 The sons of Zattu, nine hundred and forty-five. 9 The sons of Zac'cai, seven hundred and sixty. 10 The sons of Bani, six hundred and forty-two. 11 The sons of Be'bai, six hundred and twenty-three. 12 The sons of Azgad, one thousand two hundred and twenty-two. 13 The sons of Adoni'kam, six hundred and sixty-six. 14 The sons of Big'vai, two thousand and

and I Esdras 5:10 in the Lucianic recension) or 752 (with the LXX^BA of Neh. 7:10 and the Lucianic Greek text there).

6. Pahath-moab ("Governor of Moab") designates an early Hebrew person who ruled Moab. Under David (II Sam. 8:2) and Solomon, Judeans dominated Moab. The Chronicler suggests that Judeans ruled Moab (Neh. 3:11) and lists a Judean Saraph ("Serpent") as ruler of Moab (I Chr. 4:22). The clan was subdivided into those of **Jeshua and Joab** (cf. 8:9; Neh. 3:19).

7. Elam is used by the Chronicler to designate a Benjaminite (I Chr. 8:24). The name probably has connection with the country east of the Tigris (Gen. 10:22) later ruled by Cyrus, a place to which exiled Israelites were sent (Isa. 11:11).

10. Bani (בני) appears as "Binnui" (בנוי) in Neh. 7:15 and as "Bunni" (בני) in Neh. 10:15. Since two names are found in the list in both Ezra 10:29, 34 and Neh. 10:13-15, 10:15, it is probable that the original list contained two very similar names, representing different clans, and that identical spelling in the C.T. caused the loss of one here. Read for 642 the 648 of Neh. 7:15 and I Esdras 5:13.

12. Azgad ("Gad Is Strong") like Gaddiel ("Gad Is God") in Num. 13:10 contains the name of the god Gad, "Fortune" (cf. Gen. 30:11; Isa. 65:11). For the **one thousand two hundred and twenty-two** of Ezra read 2,222 with the Lucianic recension of Ezra and Nehemiah (cf. Neh. 7:12). The text in Ezra is easily explained by the loss of a letter which makes two thousand (אלפם) read **one thousand** (אלף). The loss was easy before **two hundred** (מאתים), which begins with the same letter that was lost.

13. Adonikam ("My Lord Has Arisen") has the element Adoni- ("My Lord") found in the early names Adoniram (I Kings 4:6) and Adonijah (I Kings 1:8; II Sam. 3:4), where it substitutes for the name of God. Read 667 with Neh. 7:18 and I Esdras 5:14 for the **six hundred and sixty-six** of Ezra.

14. Bigvai (cf. vs. 2), a Persian name, could be a clan name no earlier than the time of the Exile. Greek texts and Josephus (*Antiquities* XI. 7) show that the first

colonies or those who crossed the continent by covered wagon? It was such nameless men who became the first Christian missionaries to the Gentiles (Acts 11:20), and thereby changed the course of Western history. Lists of names like these may be inaccurate or ambiguous, and are certainly tedious reading in public worship or private devotion today; but they remind us of humanity's unpayable debt to nameless men and women who have made posterity their heavy debtors by the courage and persistence that were the historical price of our human heritage.

...he LORD my God hath given ...y side, *so that there is* neither ...evil occurrent.

...old, I purpose to build a ...name of the LORD my God, ...ake unto David my father, ..., whom I will set upon thy ...om, he shall build a house

...re command thou that they ...es out of Lebanon; and my ...with thy servants: and unto ...ire for thy servants accord-...ou shalt appoint: for thou ...*re is* not among us any that ...timber like unto the Sido-

...me to pass, when Hiram ...of Solomon, that he re-...nd said, Blessed *be* the ...ch hath given unto David ...s great people.

them under the soles of his feet. 4 But now the LORD my God has given me rest on every side; there is neither adversary nor misfortune. 5 And so I purpose to build a house for the name of the LORD my God, as the LORD said to David my father, 'Your son, whom I will set upon your throne in your place, shall build the house for my name.' 6 Now therefore command that cedars of Lebanon be cut for me; and my servants will join your servants, and I will pay you for your servants such wages as you set; for you know that there is no one among us who knows how to cut timber like the Sido'nians."

7 When Hiram heard the words of Solomon, he rejoiced greatly, and said, "Blessed be the LORD this day, who has given to David a wise son to be over this great peo-

...ding is contrary to the true and primitive worship of the God of the ...hould involve a tent. The explanation given in I Chr. 22:8 is that ...f blood and therefore not fit to build the temple.

...v sāṭān (**adversary**) is used in its original sense of any human agent. ...e of God's heavenly court. His particular duty is to travel to and fro ...if men are actually as good as they claim to be. If they are not, his ...m before the throne of God. Later the word becomes a proper name, ...r. 21:1 (cf. II Sam. 24:1) Satan is the enemy of God. In the N.T. ...e kingdom of evil.

...of Lebanon were famous from antiquity, their wood being hard ...against dry rot and insects. According to Pliny the cedar roof of ...at Ephesus lasted for four hundred years. The wood is close-grained ...rably suitable for carving. Its fragrance is most marked. Cedars ...the whole of the Lebanon, the Anti-Lebanon, and thence north ...urus Mountains. They were in great demand throughout the Near ...which have always been treeless country. The Assyrian advances ...anean from the twelfth century B.C. onward had in part these ...ve.

...e **Sidonians** (Phoenicians) in crafts of every kind was well known ...cf. the embroidered robes of Andromache and the silver bowl of ...VI. 290; XXIII. 741-44).

...d how much he was ...o his men in the home-...t in the Hebrew tradi-...furnished the tough ...tion together. Totali-...imes have minimized ...development of na-...experiment in weak-...ake of strengthening ...ccessful. The home is

the primary training ground for promoting community and national welfare. And unless the individual learns the squad movements of social action in the family circle, he is ill-fitted to move up to the front line problems of citizenship. Unless we learn to live worthily in our little worlds, we shall not be worth much as workers in the large world.

"The eyes of a fool are in the ends of the earth" (Prov. 17:24). This bit of Hebrew

15 The children of Adin, four hundred fifty and four.

16 The children of Ater of Hezekiah, ninety and eight.

17 The children of Bezai, three hundred twenty and three.

18 The children of Jorah, a hundred and twelve.

19 The children of Hashum, two hundred twenty and three.

20 The children of Gibbar, ninety and five.

21 The children of Beth-lehem, a hundred twenty and three.

fifty-six. 15 The sons of Adin, four hundred and fifty-four. 16 The sons of Ater, namely of Hezeki'ah, ninety-eight. 17 The sons of Be'zai, three hundred and twenty-three. 18 The sons of Jorah, one hundred and twelve. 19 The sons of Hashum, two hundred and twenty-three. 20 The sons of Gibbar, ninety-five. 21 The sons of Bethlehem,

---

syllable is Persian *baga-* ("God"). Aramaic papyri spell **Bigvai** (בגוי‎) as בגוהי‎, the name of a Persian governor of Judea (Cowley, *op. cit.*, No. 30, l. 1; No. 32, l. 1; cf. p. 109).

16. Ater as Hebrew could be either "Cripple" or "Lefty," but is probably the very common abbreviated name Etir, found often in business documents of the Neo-Babylonian and Persian periods. The spelling of the name is the same as that of the element Etir in the names in Aramaic endorsements on cuneiform tablets (Louis Delaporte, *Épigraphes araméens* [Paris: Paul Geuthner, 1912], p. 52, No. 38; p. 57, No. 53). For **of Hezekiah** read "namely of Hezekiah," since the Babylonian name, given in the Exile, had displaced the old clan name **Hezekiah.**

Here I Esdras 5:15 adds four names not in the list in the Hebrew text. The first two are corruptions of Ezra 2:31 (Bewer, *Der Text des Buches Ezra*, pp. 21-22) but from Neh. 10:18-19 it is clear that the other two (υἱοὶ Ἀζούρου, 432, υἱοὶ Ἀννιας [for αυδιας], 101) represent the Azzur of Neh. 10:17, and a corruption of Hodijah of Neh. 10:18 (KJV), now lost from the Hebrew lists. Bewer arbitrarily assumes that the 101 of I Esdras 5:15 was originally 110 in order to obtain a larger grand total.

17-19. I Esdras 5:16 supports the order of verses in Neh. 7:22-24 (cf. Neh. 10:18-19), where the substance of vs. 19 here appears before that of vs. 17. **Bezai** abbreviates Bezalel (10:30; cf. Exod. 31:2; 35:30). **Jorah** ("Autumn Rain"; cf. Deut. 11:14; Jer. 5:24; Hos. 6:3), unique in Ezra, is "Hariph" in Neh. 7:24; 10:19 and originally in I Esdras 5:16. Since Arabic *harîf* means either "freshly gathered fruit" or "autumn rain," it has been argued that **Jorah** and Hariph may be equivalents (Martin Noth, *Die israelitischen Personennamen im Rahmen der Gemeinsemitischen Namengebung* [Stuttgart: W. Kohlhammer, 1928; "Beiträge zur Wissenschaft vom Alten und Neuen Testament"], pp. 228, 244; cf. Rudolph, *op. cit.*, p. 8).

20. Gibbar appears in Neh. 7:25 as the place name "Gibeon," perhaps because of proximity to the names that follow, but Gibeon, northwest of Jerusalem, should not appear before vs. 25 in a list which works northward. The LXXᴬ vocalizes Gaber which is probably the abbreviated Babylonian name Gabria (for Ilu-gabri) found in cuneiform tablets of the Persian period.

(2) By City (2:21-35)

21-28. (Cf. Neh. 7:26-32; I Esdras 5:17-21.) With vss. 21-28 the introductory formula changes from "the sons of" to **the men of,** and the listing is by geographical home rather than by ancestor. The significance of the shift is not clear. It may indicate later supplementation from another source, but some have thought that it indicated a different type of citizen. K. F. Keil suggested that the previous clans were all of Jerusalem, in contrast to those listed geographically (*Chronik, Esra, Nehemia und Esther* [Leipzig: Dorffling & Franke, 1870; "Biblischer Commentar über das Alte Testament"], pp. 415-17), but the figures given are much too large. Others have suggested that those in vss. 3-20

22 The men of Netophah, fifty and six.

23 The men of Anathoth, a hundred twenty and eight.

24 The children of Azmaveth, forty and two.

25 The children of Kirjath-arim, Chephirah, and Beeroth, seven hundred and forty and three.

26 The children of Ramah and Gaba, six hundred twenty and one.

one hundred and twenty-three. 22 The men of Neto'phah, fifty-six. 23 The men of An'athoth, one hundred and twenty-eight. 24 The sons of Az'maveth, forty-two. 25 The sons of Kir'iathar'im, Chephi'rah, and Be-er'oth, seven hundred and forty-three. 26 The sons of Ramah and Geba, six hun-

---

were landed property holders, the freemen, the "people of the land," in contrast to those without property, "the poor of the land" (II Kings 25:12; Jer. 40:7), who were not listed by clan (Eduard Meyer, *Die Entstehung des Judenthums* [Halle: M. Niemeyer, 1896], pp. 152 ff.; Rudolf Kittel, *Geschichte des Volkes Israel* [2nd ed.; Stuttgart: W. Kohlhammer, 1929], III, 359-61; Rudolph, *op. cit.*, p. 20).

It is uncertain whether the places mentioned represent pre-exilic ancestral homes to which the immigrants returned or centers at which returning Jews actually settled. From vss. 1, 70 it is clear that the Chronicler thought that all Jews could return to their pre-exilic homes. It is significant that there is no reference to towns of the Negeb, far in the south, which Jeremiah (13:19) claims were plundered in 598 B.C. and cut off from Judah so that no prisoners were taken from that region in 586 B.C. (Albrecht Alt, "Judas Gaue unter Josia," *Palästinajahrbuch*, XXI [1925], 108). The towns listed begin with the southernmost, in the vicinity of Bethlehem, and proceed northward through familiar sites that appear largely to have escaped the destruction which made the rest of Judea quite a desolate region during the Exile.

21-22. For **The sons of Bethlehem** read "the men of Bethlehem," with vss. 22 ff.; Neh. 7:26. **Bethlehem** is modern Beit Laḥm, about five miles south of Jerusalem. **Netophah** is probably Khirbet Bedd Fālûḥ, about three miles south of Bethlehem, near the road to Tekoa, the home of Amos (Alt, "Das Institut im Jahre 1931," *Palästinajahrbuch*, XXVIII [1932], 9 ff.; Konrad Kob, "Netopha," *ibid.*, pp. 47-54).

23. Anathoth, home of some of David's men (II Sam. 23:27), of Abiathar (I Kings 2:26), and of Jeremiah (1:1; 32:6-15), is Râs el-Kharrûbeh near 'Anâta, about three miles northeast of Jerusalem.

24. Read "men of" as in Neh. 7:28 and I Esdras 5:18 instead of **sons of.** For **Azmaveth** read "Beth-azmaveth," as in Neh. 7:28 and I EsdrasAB 5:18. It is modern Hizmeh, about five miles north-northeast of Jerusalem. The name is Canaanite, preserving the divine name Mot now found in the Ugaritic texts.

25. As in vs. 24, read "men of" with Neh. 7:29 and I Esdras 5:19. **Kiriatharim** ("Village of Cities") is obviously an error for "Kiriath-jearim" ("Village of the Woods") as Neh. 7:29 and the LXX show (cf. Josh. 9:17; 15:9; etc.). It is probably Tell el-Azhar, about nine miles from Jerusalem toward Lydda, nearly six miles southwest of Gibeon. **Chephirah** is Nhirbet el Kefîreh, five miles west of Gibeon, commanding its approaches from the west, about two miles north of Kiriath-jearim. **Be-eroth,** which presumably guarded Gibeon from the north, is not yet exactly identified but Eusebius locates it "under the hill of Gabaon" (Erich Klostermann, *Das Onomasticon der biblische Ortsnamen* [Leipzig: J. C. Hinrichs, 1904]; cf. Peter Thomsen, "Palästina nach dem Onomasticon des Eusebius," *Zeitschrift des deutschen Palästina-vereins*, XXVI [1903], 97-188).

26. Read "men of" with Neh. 7:30 and I EsdrasAB 5:20. **Geba** is modern Jeba', a Benjaminite town commanding the pass at Michmas, east of **Ramah,** which as modern Er-Râm is five miles north of Jerusalem, opposite Bethel. **Ramah** was a frontier outpost of Benjamin, lying between the ancient kingdoms of Israel and Judah (I Kings 15:17, 22).

27 The men of Michmas, a hundred twenty and two.

28 The men of Beth-el and Ai, two hundred twenty and three.

29 The children of Nebo, fifty and two.

30 The children of Magbish, a hundred fifty and six.

31 The children of the other Elam, a thousand two hundred fifty and four.

32 The children of Harim, three hundred and twenty.

33 The children of Lod, Hadid, and Ono, seven hundred twenty and five.

dred and twenty-one. 27 The men of Michmas, one hundred and twenty-two. 28 The men of Bethel and Ai, two hundred and twenty-three. 29 The sons of Nebo, fifty-two. 30 The sons of Magbish, one hundred and fifty-six. 31 The sons of the other Elam, one thousand two hundred and fifty-four. 32 The sons of Harim, three hundred and twenty. 33 The sons of Lod, Hadid, and

27. **Michmas,** modern Mukhmâs (cf. I Sam. 14:5), lies northeast of Geba, on the road from Jericho to Ai.

28. **Bethel** and **Ai** cross the border of Judah-Benjamin into former Ephraimite territory. Alt ("Judas Gaue unter Josia," pp. 108-9) has argued that it was Josiah's policy of expansion that added the marginal district to Judah in pre-exilic times. **Bethel,** modern Beitîn, lies on the road to Shechem (Nablus), about twelve miles north of Jerusalem. **Ai** ("The Ruin") was et-Tell near Dēr Dīwân, on a rocky terraced mound almost two miles east of **Bethel.** Excavation shows the site deserted from about 2200 B.C., except for a few houses about 1000 B.C. Although it is improbable that the place was resettled in any serious fashion during the postexilic period, Rudolph would identify it with Aiath (Isa. 10:28) and Aija (Neh. 11:31).

29-35. (Cf. Neh. 7:33-38; I Esdras 5:21-24.) From "men of" the formula changes to **"sons of,"** as in vss. 3-20, indicating another source. Since the names from vs. 33 are indisputably geographical, it must be true of the whole list that "sons of" must mean "inhabitants of" (cf. Joel 3:6).

29. Most MSS of I Esdras 5:21 support Ezra in reading "sons of" rather than "men of." Nebai (Neh. 10:19) and Nob (Neh. 11:32; cf. Isa. 10:32) suggest a reading Nub or Nob for **Nebo** here (Meyer, *op. cit.,* pp. 145, 149). It has nothing to do with Mount Nebo (Deut. 32:49) or Nebo of Trans-Jordan (Num. 32:3) but is probably Beit Nûbā, north of Aijalon (Yâlō).

30. **Magbish** is omitted in Neh. 7:33-34, but appears as "Magpiash" in Neh. 10:20. Its location is uncertain but the name signifying "made massive" or "heaped up" suggests a place. Etymological difficulty prevents acceptance of C. R. Conder's identification with Khirbet Maḥbiyeh, about four miles northwest of Nebo (Nûbā) (*Map of Western Palestine* [London: Ordnance Survey Office, 1880], Sheet XXI, sec. JV; cf. F. M. Abel, *Géographie de la Palestine* [Paris: J. Gabalda, 1938], II, 398, *s.v. Nébo*).

31. **Other Elam** contrasts with the Elam of vs. 7. Conder (*loc. cit.*) identifies this place with Beit 'Alam, about three and a half miles south of Khirbet Maḥbiyeh and somewhat west-southwest of Nûbā. The total is the same as that in vs. 7, but Rudolph (*op. cit.,* p. 9) rightly insists that such a coincidence does not justify the omission of vs. 31. The larger figure of 2,254 in the LXX of Ezra and Nehemiah, which apparently derives from an alternate Hebrew text, is preferable.

32. Conder (*loc. cit.*) identified **Harim** with Khirbet Hôrân, about one mile northwest of Khirbet Maḥbiyeh (cf. vs. 30).

33. **Lod,** modern Ludd or Lydda, lies in the Plain of Sharon, about eleven miles southeast of Jaffa. **Hadid,** modern el-Hadîtheh, about three and one-quarter miles northeast of **Lod** (Alt, "Das Institut im Jahr 1927," *Palästinajahrbuch, XXIV* [1928], 71-72). **Ono,** modern Kefr 'Anā, lay northwest of **Lod,** almost due east of Jaffa.

These cities, far from Jerusalem, may have been added to Judah under Josiah in pre-exilic times (Alt, "Judas Gaue unter Josia," pp. 110-11), but in postexilic times they

34 The children of Jericho, three hundred forty and five.

35 The children of Senaah, three thousand and six hundred and thirty.

36 ¶ The priests: the children of Jedaiah, of the house of Jeshua, nine hundred seventy and three.

37 The children of Immer, a thousand fifty and two.

38 The children of Pashur, a thousand two hundred forty and seven.

39 The children of Harim, a thousand and seventeen.

Ono, seven hundred and twenty-five. 34 The sons of Jericho, three hundred and forty-five. 35 The sons of Sena'ah, three thousand six hundred and thirty.

36 The priests: the sons of Jedai'ah, of the house of Jeshua, nine hundred and seventy-three. 37 The sons of Immer, one thousand and fifty-two. 38 The sons of Pashhur, one thousand two hundred and forty-seven. 39 The sons of Harim, one thousand and seventeen.

---

appear to have been in a neutral zone between the provinces of Ashdod and Samaria (Neh. 6:2; Alt, "Judas Nachbarn zur Zeit Nehemias," *Palästinajahrbuch*, XXVII [1931], 72, n. 5). Rudolph (*op. cit.*, pp. 20-21) holds that this verse cannot refer to the time of Cyrus or Darius and must be a supplement from a later period.

34. Jericho lies at the ruins of Tell es-Sulṭân, about a mile and a half northwest of modern Jericho, at the eastern foot of the Judean hills. Formerly under control of the Northern Kingdom (cf. I Kings 16:34; II Kings 2:4 ff.), Jericho by late pre-exilic times came under the authority of Judah presumably during the reign of Josiah (Alt, "Judas Gaue unter Josia," p. 109), and it appears to be Judean in the time of Nehemiah (cf. Neh. 3:2).

35. Senaah was probably classical Magdalsenna ("Tower of Sena'a"), controlling the route from the Jordan Valley to Baal Hazor. Abel (*op. cit.*, II, 455) identifies it with the ruin Sheikh Tarûni near Khirbet el 'Auja el Fôqa, about eight miles northeast of Jericho.

b) TEMPLE MINISTRANTS (2:36-58=Neh. 7:39-60; I Esdras 5:24-35)

After the laymen, the list includes those who ministered in the temple, presented by classes and assigned to clans according to ancestors as in vss. 3-20.

(1) PRIESTS (2:36-39)

36-39. Very early the tribe of Levi became official priests; in the Deuteronomic Code the priests are called "the sons of Levi." In David's court his priest Abiathar (I Sam. 22:20; 23:6) served with Zadok (II Sam. 15:27, 36), who was not of the ancient priesthood and possibly not of Levitical lineage. With the banishment of Abiathar (I Kings 1:25, 42 ff.) his post was given to Zadok (I Kings 1:32 ff.), who dominated the Jerusalem temple priesthood. In the Ezekiel Code the priests are called "sons of Zadok." In the Holiness Code (Lev. 17–26) the priests are called "the sons of Aaron" (Lev. 21:1), a restriction perhaps due to the non-Zadokite priests whose legitimacy was denied by the Zadokite group. Thus in Neh. 10:38 the priests are "the sons of Aaron." But later tradition furnished a priestly genealogy for Zadok, appropriate to his eminent position, as a descendant of the eldest son of Aaron (I Chr. 24:3).

Only four clans of priests are listed in Ezra 2 but the number of individuals is proportionately very large (4,289), approximately one tenth of those returning. During the Exile the priests more than others must eagerly have awaited the opportunity to return to rebuild the temple and participate in its cultus. Each of the clans appears related to members of the priestly courses in David's temple, as recognized by the Chronicler. A **Jedaiah** (vs. 36) was the head of the second course of priests in David's temple (I Chr. 24:7). **Jedaiah** is identified as being **of the house of Jeshua,** presumably Jeshua the high priest (vs. 2). Such identification of **the house of Jeshua,** as of the clan of **Jedaiah,** must be a later insertion, made after the return of Jeshua and his

40 ¶ The Levites: the children of Jeshua and Kadmiel, of the children of Hodaviah, seventy and four.

41 ¶ The singers: the children of Asaph, a hundred twenty and eight.

42 ¶ The children of the porters: the children of Shallum, the children of Ater,

40 The Levites: the sons of Jeshua and Kad'mi-el, of the sons of Hodavi'ah, seventy-four. 41 The singers: the sons of Asaph, one hundred and twenty-eight. 42 The sons of the gatekeepers: the sons of Shallum, the sons of Ater, the sons of Talmon, the sons

---

establishment as high priest (Kittel, *Geschichte des Volkes Israel*, III, 396-97). Since **Jeshua,** but not **Jedaiah,** occurs in 10:18 ff., it appears that the Chronicler equated the names.

Immer (vs. 37) was in the sixteenth course of priests in David's temple (I Chr. 24:14). **Harim** (vs. 39) was a priest in the third course (I Chr. 24:8). **Pashhur** (vs. 38), who bears an Egyptian name like some other Levites, should belong to the early period. Since a priest **Pashhur,** the descendant of Malchijah, is mentioned in Neh. 11:12 (cf. I Chr. 9:12), it is possible that he is of the same clan, and that the distinguished remote ancestor Malchijah was the member of the fifth course of priests in David's organization (I Chr. 24:9).

(2) LEVITES (2:40)

40. All Levites were originally regarded as priests, equal to the Zadokites (Deut. 18:6-8), but after the Deuteronomic reform in actual practice they were degraded to become the hereditary servants of the acting priests (Num. 3:9-10), compelled to contribute part of their tithe to the priests (Num. 18:21-29; Neh. 10:38). They acted as butchers of sacrifices, doorkeepers, singers (I Chr. 15:22), scribes, teachers (II Chr. 35:3; Neh. 8:7, 9), and even temple beggars (II Chr. 24:5 ff.). Such secularization greatly depleted the numbers willing to serve in the temple after 586 B.C., for many apparently entered secular employment. Thus very few (seventy-four) Levites are mentioned here, and Ezra found it difficult to get any Levites to return (8:18 ff.). If Neh. 3:17 ff. seems to imply any great number of Levites in Jerusalem, it was perhaps because many could have been recruited from those who had remained in secular service in Judea (Meyer, *op. cit.,* pp. 176 ff.; Kittel, *op. cit.,* III, 394, 404 ff.; Rudolph, *op. cit.,* p. 22).

For **Jeshua and Kadmiel** read "Jeshua, namely of Kadmiel" with Neh. 7:43, for **Jeshua** was the great ancestor and the others named are but subdivisions of the clan. Instead of **sons of** (בני) I Esdras 5:26 has the name "Bannas," but other Greek texts suggest either "Bani" (בני) or "Bunni" (בני), as in vs. 10. Levites with both names occur in Neh. 9:4-5. The word **of** before **the sons of** must be omitted as due to dittography.

(3) SINGERS (2:41)

41. The singers, called "The holy singers" in I Esdras 5:27, were a single clan, the descendants of **Asaph,** one of three Levites whom David set over the song in the temple (I Chr. 15:16; cf. I Chr. 6:31-32, 39). Since only men served in the temple, the singers of vs. 65 were a different and secular group. Under Nehemiah they lived near Jerusalem (Neh. 12:29) and received regular support (Neh. 11:22 ff.) but when neglected, they, like the Levites, turned to secular work in the fields (Neh. 13:10).

(4) PORTERS (2:42)

42. The gatekeepers of the temple are not mentioned in extant pre-exilic literature, although Samuel apparently kept the door of a shrine (I Sam. 3:15). Postexilic gatekeepers did more than tend the door (I Chr. 9:17-32). They are sometimes regarded as Levites (I Chr. 9:26; II Chr. 8:14; 23:4; etc.; Neh. 12:25; 13:22) but sometimes are differentiated as here (II Chr. 35:15).

Shallum, Talmon, and **Akkub** appear in I Chr. 9:17 with **Shallum** as chief. A **Shallum** occurs as ancestor of a gatekeeper in the time of Jeremiah (Jer. 35:4). **Talmon**

the children of Talmon, the children of Akkub, the children of Hatita, the children of Shobai, *in* all a hundred thirty and nine.

43 ¶ The Nethinim: the children of Ziha, the children of Hasupha, the children of Tabbaoth,

44 The children of Keros, the children of Siaha, the children of Padon,

45 The children of Lebanah, the children of Hagabah, the children of Akkub,

46 The children of Hagab, the children of Shalmai, the children of Hanan,

47 The children of Giddel, the children of Gahar, the children of Reaiah,

48 The children of Rezin, the children of Nekoda, the children of Gazzam,

49 The children of Uzza, the children of Paseah, the children of Besai,

50 The children of Asnah, the children of Mehunim, the children of Nephusim,

of Akkub, the sons of Hati'ta, and the sons of Sho'bai, in all one hundred and thirty-nine.

43 The temple servants:[d] the sons of Ziha, the sons of Hasu'pha, the sons of Tabba'-oth, 44 the sons of Keros, the sons of Si'aha, the sons of Padon, 45 the sons of Leba'nah, the sons of Hag'abah, the sons of Akkub, 46 the sons of Hagab, the sons of Shamlai, the sons of Hanan, 47 the sons of Giddel, the sons of Gahar, the sons of Re-ai'ah, 48 the sons of Rezin, the sons of Neko'da, the sons of Gazzam, 49 the sons of Uzza, the sons of Pase'ah, the sons of Besai, 50 the sons of Asnah, the sons of Me-u'nim, the sons of

[d] Heb *nethinim*

---

is a postexilic Aramaic form of Solomon, abbreviated as "Telem" in 10:24. **Akkub** and **Ater** (or Etir; cf. Exeg. on vs. 16) are found as abbreviated Neo-Babylonian names.

(5) TEMPLE SERVANTS (2:43-54)

The **Nethinim** are literally those "given" or "dedicated" as **temple servants**. The Chronicler reports that David and the princes dedicated them for the service of the Levites (8:20). Some were Hebrews (I Sam. 1:11, 24-28) but more frequently they were foreigners, captives of war, who became temple slaves (Num. 31:30, 47) and "hewers of wood and drawers of water" in the cult (Josh. 9:27). Such **temple servants** are strongly parallel to the Babylonian *shirkûtu* (R. P. Dougherty, *The Shirkûtu of Babylonian Deities* [New Haven: Yale University Press, 1923]). They dwelt in the "house of the Nethinim" (Neh. 3:31; cf. Babylonian *Bît Shirki*), supervised by overseers (Neh. 11:21; cf. *Rāb Shirki*). When they married outside of their class, their offspring too were reckoned as temple servants (cf. Mishnah: Kiddushin III. 12; Yebamoth II. 4).

The names of the **temple servants** are significantly largely foreign. Two names are national rather than personal. **Meunim** (vs. 50) were the Arabs at Ma'an (I Chr. 4:39-41; II Chr. 26:7) and the **Nephisim** (vs. 50) are the Naphish Ishmaelites (Gen. 25:15; I Chr. 1:31; 5:19). **Ziha** (vs. 43) and **Asnah** (vs. 50) are Egyptian; **Barkos** (vs. 53) is Edomite; **Rezin** (vs. 48) is probably Aramaean (cf. Isa. 7:1 ff.); and **Sisera** (vs. 53) is non-Semitic (cf. Judg. 4:1–5:31). Many names are such informal nicknames as might be given to servants. **Hasupha** ("Quick," vs. 43), **Gahar** ("Humble," vs. 47), and **Neziah** ("Faithful," vs. 54) express approval, while **Lebanah** ("White," vs. 45); **Giddel** (for "Gadhol," "Big," vs. 47), **Nekoda** ("Spotted" or "Freckled," vs. 48), **Paseah** ("Lame," vs. 49) **Hakupha** ("Stooped," vs. 51), and **Harsha** ("Deaf" or "Dumb," vs. 52) indicate physical condition. **Hatipha** ("Snatched," vs. 54) and **Mehida** (for "Mehira," "Bought," vs. 52) indicate how the servants were acquired.

45-46. After **Akkub** I Esdras 5:30 and the LXX of Neh. 7:48 have additional names "Outa" and "Ketab" (cf. "Ketar" in LXX of Neh. 7:48), which are probably corruptions of names now lost in Hebrew lists. Read "Shalmai" for **Shamlai**, with Neh. 7:48 and Hebrew *Qerê* in 2:46.

47. Vocalization in I Esdras[A] 5:30 (Καθουα) suggests reading for **Giddel** the "Gadhol" (גדול) found often in the Aramaic papyri.

51 The children of Bakbuk, the children of Hakupha, the children of Harhur,

52 The children of Bazluth, the children of Mehida, the children of Harsha,

53 The children of Barkos, the children of Sisera, the children of Thamah,

54 The children of Neziah, the children of Hatipha.

55 ¶ The children of Solomon's servants: the children of Sotai, the children of Sophereth, the children of Peruda,

56 The children of Jaalah, the children of Darkon, the children of Giddel,

57 The children of Shephatiah, the children of Hattil, the children of Pochereth of Zebaim, the children of Ami.

58 All the Nethinim, and the children of Solomon's servants, *were* three hundred ninety and two.

59 And these *were* they which went up from Tel-melah, Tel-harsa, Cherub, Addan, *and* Immer: but they could not show their father's house, and their seed, whether they *were* of Israel:

60 The children of Delaiah, the children of Tobiah, the children of Nekoda, six hundred fifty and two.

Nephi'sim, 51 the sons of Bakbuk, the sons of Haku'pha, the sons of Harhur, 52 the sons of Bazluth, the sons of Mehi'da, the sons of Harsha, 53 the sons of Barkos, the sons of Sis'era, the sons of Temah, 54 the sons of Nezi'ah, and the sons of Hati'pha.

55 The sons of Solomon's servants: the sons of So'tai, the sons of Hasso'phereth, the sons of Peru'da, 56 the sons of Ja'alah, the sons of Darkon, the sons of Giddel, 57 the sons of Shephati'ah, the sons of Hattil, the sons of Po'chereth-hazzeba'im, and the sons of Ami.

58 All the temple servants[d] and the sons of Solomon's servants were three hundred and ninety two.

59 The following were those who came up from Tel-me'lah, Tel-har'sha, Cherub, Addan, and Immer, though they could not prove their fathers' houses or their descent, whether they belonged to Israel: 60 the sons of Del-ai'ah, the sons of Tobi'ah, and the sons of Neko'da, six hundred and fifty-two.

[d] Heb *nethinim*

---

(6) Descendants of Solomon's Servants (2:55-58)

55-58. A subdivision of the **temple servants** are **the sons of Solomon's servants,** who are included among the temple servants in Neh. 10:28 and in the total in vs. 58. Nothing certain is known of their history or function. They may be Canaanite prisoners of war, possibly Gibeonites (Josh. 9:27; I Kings 9:20-21; I Chr. 8:7-9; Rudolph, *op. cit.,* p. 23), who became state slaves (Isaac Mendelsohn, "State Slavery in Ancient Palestine," *Bulletin of the American Schools of Oriental Research,* No. 85 [1942], pp. 16-17). Like the **temple servants,** their names are informal and descriptive: **Peruda** (or "Perida" in Neh. 7:57) is "Lonely" or "Solitary" (vs. 55); **Hattil,** "The Babbler" (vs. 57); and **Darkon,** "Rough" (vs. 56). **Giddel** (vs. 56) should be "Gadhol," as in vs. 47. **Hassophereth** (vs. 55) means "The Teacher" and **Pochereth-hazzebaim** is "The Gazelle Hunter" (vs. 57; cf. Rudolph, *op. cit.,* p. 14). Although a relatively large number of names of the temple servants are given, the group itself was quite small—**three hundred and ninety-two**—averaging about eight per family.

c) Uncertified Clans (2:59-63=Neh. 7:61-65; I Esdras 5:36-40)

The Mishnah declares that Ezra did not rest until Babylonia was "sieved like fine meal" (Kiddushin IV. 1. 69*b*, 71*b*; Yalkut II. 106-7), and that Ezra himself had his own line certified before he left Babylonia (Baba Bathra 15*a*). Pure-blooded Jews were called "fine meal" and the others were designated "mixed dough" (Hugo Graetz, "Illegitime Mischehen in Judäa," *Monatsschrift für Geschichte und Wissenschaft des Judenthums,* XXVIII [1879], 481-508). It is usually assumed that such racial consciousness and striving for purity did not exist until the reforms of Ezra (9:1–10:44) and Nehemiah (13:23-30), but the great list implies the keeping of strict genealogical records during the Exile. There may have been little such concern in Palestine, but there was evidently such interest abroad, especially among such conservative folk, as contributed to the Return.

61 ¶ And of the children of the priests: the children of Habaiah, the children of Koz, the children of Barzillai; which took a wife of the daughters of Barzillai the Gileadite, and was called after their name:

62 These sought their register *among* those that were reckoned by genealogy, but they were not found: therefore were they, as polluted, put from the priesthood.

63 And the Tirshatha said unto them, that they should not eat of the most holy things, till there stood up a priest with Urim and with Thummim.

61 Also, of the sons of the priests: the sons of Habai′ah, the sons of Hakkoz, and the sons of Barzil′lai (who had taken a wife from the daughters of Barzil′lai the Gileadite, and was called by their name). 62 These sought their registration among those enrolled in the genealogies, but they were not found there, and so they were excluded from the priesthood as unclean; 63 the governor told them that they were not to partake of the most holy food, until there should be a priest to consult Urim and Thummim.

The six clans, three lay and three priestly, who remained uncertified were appended to the great list. These may have derived from proselytes or may have lacked proper credentials. **Their seed** (vs. 59) means **their descent.** They came from five Babylonian places not yet identified. Since the element Tel- means a ruined mound of an earlier habitation (Josh. 8:28; Deut. 13:16; Jer. 49:2) at least two places were Jewish resettlements.

61. Omit the introductory **the sons of** with Neh. 7:63 and I Esdras 5:38. **Habaiah** is unique but its variant "Hobiah" may be related to the abbreviation "Hubbah" in I Chr. 7:34 (*Qerê*, Vulg.). **Hakkoz** ("The Thorn") also appears without the article as Koz (I Chr. 4:8; Neh. 3:4, 21). It is argued from Neh. 3:4, 21 that the clan was later reinstated. Possible relationship to the ancient nonpriestly **Barzillai** (II Sam. 17:27; 19:32-37; I Kings 2:7) doubtless brought into question the status of the priestly clan of **Barzillai.**

62. Their registration is, lit., "their writing," which is described as **those that were reckoned by genealogy.** This "writing" is a priestly list like the list of Levites in Neh. 12:22-23 and the much later list of priests mentioned by Josephus (*Against Apion* I. 7). It is preferable to read, "They sought in their writing," as in the Syriac. It is better to read, with Neh. 7:64, "They were not found," since the subject is the clan, not the writing in which the other priests (cf. vss. 39-42) were listed.

Uncertified laymen could doubtless remain in the community, possibly with some restrictions, until lineage could be established. But the priests posed a greater problem because of their prerogatives and the possibility of contaminating the cultus. To avoid defilement of holy things by uncertified priests those challenged were "desecrated from the priesthood." "Desecrated," a term in late Hebrew usage, is preferable to **polluted.**

63. The order restricting the uncertified priests was given by the **Tirshatha,** the Jewish authority in charge. **Tirshatha** is not the title **governor** but an Iranian epithet "The One to Be Feared," which could signify "His Excellency." Its use in Neh. 8:9; 10:1 for Nehemiah as governor is responsible for the intrusion of Nehemiah into I Esdras 5:40 alongside the epithet transliterated as "Attharias." The Syriac text of I Esdras has Nehemiah alone, but the Peshitta declares that "the heads of Israel" gave the order.

According to the M.T., the uncertified priests were forbidden to share in **the most holy food,** special portions reserved for male descendants of Aaron (Lev. 2:3; 7:31-33), but I Esdras 5:40 excluded them from "all holy things," the ordinary priestly food (Lev. 7:3-6; 10:14; 22:10, 13*b*). This is interpreted in the RSV as **they were excluded from the priesthood** (vs. 62). The exclusion was not intended to be permanent, but only until a divine decision could be made through the sacred lot, the **Urim and Thummim** (cf. I Sam. 14:41). Rabbinical tradition lists the sacred lot as among things lacking in the postexilic temple (Tosephta Sota XIII. 2; Yalkut II. 150. 568; Yoma 21*b*), and despite Josephus (*Antiquities* III. 8. 9), there is no evidence for sacred lot in the postexilic temple. The rabbis regarded the statement in vs. 63 as meaning "until the dead

64 ¶ The whole congregation together *was* forty and two thousand three hundred *and* threescore,

65 Besides their servants and their maids, of whom *there were* seven thousand three hundred thirty and seven: and *there were* among them two hundred singing men and singing women.

66 Their horses *were* seven hundred thirty and six; their mules, two hundred forty and five;

67 Their camels, four hundred thirty and five; *their* asses, six thousand seven hundred and twenty.

68 ¶ And *some* of the chief of the fathers,

64 The whole assembly together was forty-two thousand three hundred and sixty, 65 besides their menservants and maidservants, of whom there were seven thousand three hundred and thirty-seven; and they had two hundred male and female singers. 66 Their horses were seven hundred and thirty-six, their mules were two hundred and forty-five, 67 their camels were four hundred and thirty-five, and their asses were six thousand seven hundred and twenty.

68 Some of the heads of families, when

are resurrected" or "until Elijah comes" (Tosephta Sota XIII. 1; Sota 48*b*; Ketuboth 24*b*; Shebuoth 16*a*; Jerusalem Kiddushim IV. 1; Tosaphoth Yoma 21*b*).

A priest would be appropriate in pre-exilic times when any Levite could use the lot (Deut. 33:8), but it was later restricted to the high priest (Exod. 28:30; Lev. 8:8; Num. 27:21; cf. "a priest" in Neh. 7:65). The "high priest" is specified in the Peshitta, Vulg., and I Esdras^ALN. If the high priest is meant, it would indicate that none was yet recognized in the community and the date of the document must be before 520 B.C.

d) SUMMARIES (2:64-67=Neh. 7:66-69; I Esdras 5:41-43)

(1) CONGREGATION (2:64)

64. Together indicates that all of the lists were used in the total. As in 1:9-11, the figures do not agree in all versions and there is a discrepancy between the given grand total and that obtained by addition. By emendation (vss. 12, 16, 31) Bewer (*Der Text des Buches Ezra,* p. 33) derives a sum 32,360, ten thousand less than that in vs. 64. Rudolph (*op. cit.,* p. 25) assumes that the difference is due to the inclusion of women in the given total, as in vs. 65. By adding "from twelve years old," I Esdras 5:41 excludes children, since adulthood was reckoned from that age (cf. Luke 2:42).

(2) PRIVATE PROPERTY (2:65-67)

65-67. It has been argued that the great list ended with the total in vs. 64, and that what follows has been added by the Chronicler (Hölscher, *Esra und Nehemia,* II, 504), but the arguments are not persuasive (cf. Rudolph, *op. cit.,* pp. 7, 9-10). **Besides** indicates that what follows was not counted in the **assembly.** The **servants** or "slaves" were private property, as were the **singers,** whose secular role is seen by the inclusion of women who were not employed in the temple. Such **singers,** to be differentiated from those in vs. 41, entertained the wealthy and served as minstrels (II Sam. 19:35; II Chr. 35:25; Eccl. 2:8).

The animals (vss. 66-67) were needed for the caravan. **Mules** were sometimes used to carry burdens (II Kings 5:17; cf. Judith 2:17; 15:11) but were generally prized for riding (II Sam. 13:29; 18:9), while **asses** were used as pack animals (II Sam. 16:1), and I Esdras 5:43 here calls them "beasts of burden" (ὑποζύγια). Read **their asses** with seven MSS, the LXX, Vulg., and Ethiopic versions and the other nouns in the verses.

3. TEMPLE DONATIONS (2:68-70=Neh. 7:70-73; I Esdras 5:44-46)

68-70. Vss. 68-69 have been regarded as dislocated, originally following either 1:11 (Hölscher, *loc. cit.*) or 8:36 (C. C. Torrey, *The Composition and Historical Value of*

68-70. *Building Campaigns in Every Generation.*—However inaccurate may be the total figures given for the temple building fund in

vs. 69, there is one touch of agelong human nature in vs. 68 which every minister or layman who has ever shared in a church building cam-

when they came to the house of the LORD which *is* at Jerusalem, offered freely for the house of God to set it up in his place:

69 They gave after their ability unto the treasure of the work threescore and one thousand drams of gold, and five thousand pounds of silver, and one hundred priests' garments.

70 So the priests, and the Levites, and *some* of the people, and the singers, and the porters, and the Nethinim, dwelt in their cities, and all Israel in their cities.

3 And when the seventh month was come, and the children of Israel *were* in the cities, the people gathered themselves together as one man to Jerusalem.

they came to the house of the LORD which is in Jerusalem, made freewill offerings for the house of God, to erect it on its site;

69 according to their ability they gave to the treasury of the work sixty-one thousand darics of gold, five thousand minas of silver, and one hundred priests' garments.

70 The priests, the Levites, and some of the people lived in Jerusalem and its vicinity;[e] and the singers, the gatekeepers, and the temple servants lived in their towns, and all Israel in their towns.

3 When the seventh month came, and the sons of Israel were in the towns, the people gathered as one man to Jerusalem.

[e] 1 Esdras 5. 46. Heb lacks *lived in Jerusalem and its vicinity*

Ezra-Nehemiah [Giessen: J. Ricker, 1896; "Beihelte zur Zeitschrift für die alttestamentliche Wissenschaft"], pp. 30-34; *Ezra Studies*, pp. 256, 267). But in the first instance the reason for the disruption of context by the long list is left unexplained, while in the latter one must overlook the fact that Ezra's gifts were already delivered in 8:33 ff. It is better to see the passage as original in the list (cf. Rudolph, *op. cit.*, p. 10).

II. BUILDING THE TEMPLE UNDER DARIUS (3:1–6:22)

A. RECONSTRUCTION OF THE ALTAR AND RE-ESTABLISHMENT OF SACRIFICES (3:1-6)

Throughout this narrative concerned with the cultus the Chronicler's interests and literary habits are observable. What, if any, sources were at his disposal cannot now be determined. It is probable that some sound tradition lay behind the story of the reconstruction of an early altar before the temple was rebuilt. It could exist without the temple and was greatly needed for the rehabilitation of the cult. David had an altar in Jerusalem before the construction of the temple (II Sam. 24:25) and sacrifices continued to be made there even after the temple was destroyed (Jer. 41:5; Hag. 2:14). Less plausible is the Chronicler's inference that the depleted and distressed community at once instituted a sacrificial system on the grand scale that the Chronicler himself knew.

1. ERECTION OF THE ALTAR (3:1-3a=I Esdras 5:47-50a)

3:1. Comparison of vs. 1 with I Esdras 5:47 and Neh. 7:73b shows that the material formed the conclusion of the document incorporated in Ezra 2:2-70. In Nehemiah it introduces the narrative of the reading of the law in the reign of Artaxerxes but here, as in I Esdras, it leads to the erection of an altar prior to the building of the temple in a much earlier period. Such differences in context have compelled some modification in content.

The **seventh month** would fit the context in Nehemiah, where the next previous date is the sixth month, when the walls were completed (Neh. 6:15; 7:1). But since the **seventh month** was a festal period when there would be great need for an altar, the

---

paign will recognize at once. Idealize his history as the Chronicler may well have done, he is nevertheless frank enough to admit that some of the heads of families **made freewill offerings for the house of God . . . according to their ability,** but he also implies that some others gave only sparingly and under pressure, and

that some did not give at all. So has it been with church building funds from that day to this.

3:1-13. *Youth and Age in Changing Times.*— An even more authentic touch of human nature, under the stress of one of the most poignant of human experiences, quickens into life for us

2 Then stood up Jeshua the son of Jozadak, and his brethren the priests, and Zerubbabel the son of Shealtiel, and his brethren, and builded the altar of the God of Israel, to offer burnt offerings thereon, as *it is* written in the law of Moses the man of God.

3 And they set the altar upon his bases; for fear *was* upon them because of the people of those countries: and they offered

2 Then arose Jeshua the son of Jo'zadak, with his fellow priests, and Zerub'babel the son of She-al'ti-el with his kinsmen, and they built the altar of the God of Israel, to offer burnt offerings upon it, as it is written in the law of Moses the man of God. 3 They set the altar in its place, for fear was upon them because of the peoples of the lands,

time would also be appropriate for the Ezra narrative. Nevertheless, the taboos prevailing at the beginning of the **seventh month** (cf. vs. 6) raise some question as to the validity of the date for the Ezra narrative. The numerical reckoning of the **seventh month,** which was Ethanim in the pre-exilic Canaanite calendar (I Kings 8:2) and Tishri in the postexilic Babylonian one, reflects the postexilic change in calendar, when the Babylonian names (cf. 6:15; Neh. 1:1; 2:1; 6:15) had not yet come into general use (cf. Hag. 1:1, 15; etc.).

The year date is difficult to determine since there was none in the original document. The Chronicler apparently considered it to be during the first year of Cyrus (1:1) but Rudolph (*op. cit.*, p. 29) contends that six months would be too short for the return and settlement, and suggests possibly the second or even third year of Cyrus as the actual date. Since Babylon fell in 539 B.C. and the gods were returned during the rest of that year (1:3), the actual interval of preparation and return may have been longer than six months. But it is obvious that the Chronicler identified Sheshbazzar with Zerubbabel and thinks of the days of Darius I as in I Esdras (cf. I Esdras 5:2, 6).

The assembly, according to Ezra, was held in **Jerusalem,** but Nehemiah, which reflects a much later date, located it in the plaza before "the Water Gate" (cf. Neh. 8:1) in restored Jerusalem, while I Esdras 5:47, influenced by I Esdras 9:38, placed it in the plaza before the temple porch. The latter would be appropriate only if it is understood as being before the temple ruins, since in I Esdras, as in Ezra, the temple is not yet rebuilt.

2. Jeshua and **Zerubbabel** (2:2) indicate the time of Darius rather than that of Cyrus (cf. Hag. 1:1–2:23 and Zech. 1:1–8:23). Elsewhere **Zerubbabel,** as secular ruler, is mentioned first (vs. 8; 2:2; 4:3; 5:2; Neh. 12:1) but **Jeshua** precedes him here where matters of cult are involved. Surprisingly, Jeshua's title "high priest" is here omitted (cf. Neh. 12:10 ff.; Hag. 1:1, 14; 2:2). **His brethren** used of **Jeshua** means **his fellow priests;** used of **Zerubbabel,** it signifies not princely brothers but fellow laymen.

The **altar** was hastily constructed in less than a day (vs. 6) of field stones in accordance with the earliest prescriptions for altars in **the law of Moses** (Exod. 20:25; cf. Deut. 27:6). It was described by Hecataeus of Abdera (cf. Josephus *Against Apion* I. 22) and lasted down to Maccabean times (I Macc. 4:47, 54). **Man of God** is applied not only to Moses (cf. Deut. 33:1; Josh. 14:6; I Chr. 23:14; II Chr. 30:16) but also to Samuel (I Sam. 9:6), Elijah (I Kings 17:18), and Elisha (II Kings 4:7) as a prophetic title. It is used also of David (Neh. 12:24, 36) and of Timothy (I Tim. 6:11; II Tim. 3:17).

3a. The **bases** of the altar signify "foundation" rather than "site," since the altar was erected on a platform or pavement (cf. Ezek. 43:13-14, 17). But Josephus, influenced by the Greek text, paraphrases, "He then built the altar on the same place it formerly had been built" (Josephus *Antiquities* XI. 4. 1).

the confused palimpsest of obscure history that has come down as ch. 3. Whatever may have been the chronological and ceremonial confusion that have been so carefully disentangled by the Exeg., every subsequent older generation knows only too well the nostalgia for "the days that are no more"[3] that still throbs with such moving pathos within this brief account. The tears of older folk who could remember the size and splendor of Solomon's former temple were mingled with the shouts of happy young people

[3] Tennyson, *The Princess,* Part IV.

burnt offerings thereon unto the LORD, *even* burnt offerings morning and evening.

4 They kept also the feast of tabernacles, as *it is* written, and *offered* the daily burnt offerings by number, according to the custom, as the duty of every day required;

5 And afterward *offered* the continual burnt offering, both of the new moons, and of all the set feasts of the LORD that were consecrated, and of every one that willingly offered a freewill offering unto the LORD.

and they offered burnt offerings upon it to the LORD, burnt offerings morning and evening. **4** And they kept the feast of booths, as it is written, and offered the daily burnt offerings by number according to the ordinance, as each day required, **5** and after that the continual burnt offerings, the offerings at the new moon and at all the appointed feasts of the LORD, and the offerings of every one who made a freewill offering to the

---

A difficult and confused Hebrew text lies behind the translation **for fear was upon them because of the peoples of the lands.** It is best explained as an intrusive comment which may once have explained some such word as "adversaries" in 4:1. Rudolph (*op. cit.*, p. 28) regards the gloss as relevant, indicating that the motive for restoring the cultus was to assure the help of God against their enemies. The **people of those countries** were the non-Jews sent in to repopulate the land (4:9-10) but the Chronicler would also include those Jews who had remained in the land and married Gentile women (cf. 6:21).

2. INSTITUTION OF PROGRAM OF OFFERINGS (3:3*b*-6=I Esdras 5:50*b*-53)

3*b*-4. Burnt offerings in the earliest postexilic period would probably have followed the simple prescriptions of the Deuteronomic Code (Deut. 12:5-7, 13-14, 27), but the Chronicler doubtless regarded them as following the priestly practices of his own day (Num. 28:1-8; cf. Exod. 29:38-42). The sacrifices were prescribed **as each day required** (cf. Neh. 11:23). This is specified as being either according to **custom** (cf. I Sam. 27:11; Gen. 40:13) or according to the **ordinance** (Lev. 5:10; 9:16; Neh. 8:18), since the Hebrew word used (*mishpāṭ*) can mean either. The latter is perhaps intended (cf. Neh. 8:18) since the complete expression is frequently found in later legislation regarding the **feast of booths** (cf. Num. 29:18, 21, 24, 27, 30, 33).

The **feast of tabernacles** or **booths,** originally a Canaanite agricultural festival (Judg. 9:27), named for the temporary shelters of branches (cf. Neh. 8:15) erected in the fields for the harvest laborers (cf. Isa. 1:8; 4:6; Jonah 4:5) is the oldest festival in the Hebrew cultic calendar. Frequently called simply "the feast" or "the feast of the Lord," it is the only one mentioned in the historical literature (Judg. 9:27; I Sam. 1:1 ff.; I Kings 12:32). Originally a joyous harvest celebration at the close of the year (Exod. 34:22; 23:16; Deut. 16:13-16), in the later Priestly Code it lost its joyful character, and beginning on the fifteenth day of the seventh month (Lev. 23:33-36, 39-43; Num. 29:12-40) it lasted eight days.

5-6. The Chronicler's hand is most apparent here where he assumes that from its completion the altar was as busy with offerings as it was later in his own day. The offerings are listed as in the priestly legislation (Num. 28–29). The **continual burnt offering** was that repeated with regularity **morning and evening** (vs. 3). The pre-exilic burnt offering was made each morning and a meal offering was made each evening (I Kings 18:29-30; II Kings 16:15), but later priestly legislation called for two burnt offerings, morning and evening, each accompanied by a subordinate meal offering (Num. 28:3-8). The latter, which prevailed in the Chronicler's day (cf. I Chr. 16:40; II Chr.

---

who knew nothing beyond or before the comparative drabness and smallness of the new. **The old men who had seen the first house, wept with a loud voice when they saw the foundation of this house being laid, though many shouted aloud for joy; so that the people could**

not distinguish the sound of the joyful shout from the sound of the people's weeping (vss. 12-13).

That same strange mingling of the diverse emotions of age and youth over the same situation can still be heard by sensitive ears at

6 From the first day of the seventh month began they to offer burnt offerings unto the Lord. But the foundation of the temple of the Lord was not *yet* laid. **7** They gave money also unto the masons, and to the carpenters; and meat, and drink,	Lord. **6** From the first day of the seventh month they began to offer burnt offerings to the Lord. But the foundation of the temple of the Lord was not yet laid. **7** So they gave money to the masons and the carpenters, and food, drink, and oil to the

---

13:11; 31:3) is here clumsily transported back to the simple ritual of the early postexilic period. Such a burnt offering is later called simply the "continual" (Dan. 11:31).

With the **new moon** a new month began and it was the sign of a period of danger and taboo, when labor had to cease and sacrifices had to be made. Important sacrifices were held by clans (I Sam. 20:6) and in court (I Sam. 20:5) at that time. Pre-exilic prophets condemned **new moon** celebrations (Isa. 1:14; Hos. 2:11) apparently because of association with Canaanite rites. Although there is abundant evidence for observance of **new moons** in the early cultus, there is no pre-exilic legislation regarding it. Later legislation is found in Num. 28:11-15. The **new moon**, superseded by the sabbath, continued down into late times (Judith 8:6; Col. 2:16). Reference to the sabbath, frequently associated with the continual sacrifices (Num. 28:9 ff.; II Chr. 2:4; 8:13; Neh. 10:33) and **new moons** (Amos 8:5), is missing here in Ezra but is found in I Esdras 5:52, where it may be original.

The **set feasts** were **the appointed feasts** recurring yearly at fixed times (cf. Gen. 1:14). Those meant here are doubtless those of the later priestly calendar (Lev. 23:1-44), the Passover, the feast of Weeks, New Year, the day of Atonement, and the feast of Booths. **A freewill offering** was a sacrifice made usually in thanksgiving and was not mandatory by law or because of a vow (cf. 1:4; Deut. 12:17; Lev. 22:17 ff.; Num. 15:1 ff.). No such offerings are mentioned in I Esdras 5:53 but instead sacrifices due to vows, presumably those made for the safe journey from Babylonia. These are linked to the following verse: "And all they that made any vow to God began to offer sacrifices to God from the new moon of the seventh month." Some have preferred this version (Gustav Jahn, *Die Bücher Esra [A und B] und Nehemja* [Leiden: E. J. Brill, 1909], p. 30), and Batten (*Ezra and Nehemiah*, p. 111) has regarded the Hebrew of Ezra as ungrammatical, since the reference to freewill offerings dangles awkwardly, but as Bewer insists (*Der Text des Buches Ezra*, p. 40), the reference goes back to **they offered burnt offerings** in vs. 3*b*. The M.T., grammatically correct, seems distinctly preferable. The Chronicler may have thought of the offerings brought from Babylonia to the temple (1:4).

The **first day of the seventh month** was a most holy time during which later legislation decreed that no servile work was to be done (Lev. 23:23-25; Num. 29:1). If such prohibition also existed earlier, it would be extremely unlikely that the labor here described took place on that day. **But the foundation of the temple of the Lord was not yet laid** interprets a Hebrew text which is, lit., "But the temple of the Lord was not restored." Thus there need be no direct reference to a **foundation**.

B. Work on the Temple (3:7–6:22)
1. Work Begins (3:7-13)

The conclusion of vs. 6 leads to preparation for the rebuilding of the temple. It is evident that the narrative here has been influenced by the Chronicler's account of the building of Solomon's temple (II Chr. 2; cf. I Kings 5). Such literary dependence need not indicate unhistorical character since the process of building a temple at Jerusalem would necessarily involve the same problems and procedures in every age (cf. Rudolph, *op. cit.*, p. 31).

a) Supplies and Labor (3:7-9=I Esdras 5:54-58)

7. Coined **money** was known in the Persian period but was not common until later. Precious metals were still weighed out. Solomon's "hire" was paid in commodities (I Kings

and oil, unto them of Zidon, and to them of Tyre, to bring cedar trees from Lebanon to the sea of Joppa, according to the grant that they had of Cyrus king of Persia.

8 ¶ Now in the second year of their coming unto the house of God at Jerusalem, in the second month, began Zerubbabel the son of Shealtiel, and Jeshua the son of Jozadak, and the remnant of their brethren

Sido'nians and the Tyrians to bring cedar trees from Lebanon to the sea, to Joppa, according to the grant which they had from Cyrus king of Persia.

8 Now in the second year of their coming to the house of God at Jerusalem, in the second month, Zerub'babel the son of She-al'ti-el and Jeshua the son of Jo'zadak made a beginning, together with the rest of their

---

5:6, 11), and references here to **food, drink, and oil** indicate that such was still the basic medium of payment. The **masons** were miners who quarried the stone (cf. I Kings 5:15; Isa. 5:2; 22:16). **Carpenters** were "engravers" who worked in many mediums. Batten (*op. cit.*, p. 119) plausibly suggests that they dressed and carved the temple stones, but the term also described wood carvers and those who chased metals.

Zidon and **Tyre** were famous in antiquity for their trade (Ezek. 27), especially for **cedar trees from Lebanon** brought from the mountains nearby. Because the cedars furnished the long, massive, tough beams essential for the construction of such large structures as palaces and temples, the forests of Lebanon supplied all the kingdoms of the Near East. As Solomon (I Kings 5:6-10) and Nehemiah (Neh. 2:8) needed cedars for their building, so new cedars would be necessary for rebuilding the burned temple (II Kings 25:8-9). No royal grant of timber is mentioned in the Cyrus edict (Ezra 1:2-4; 6:3-5), and the parallel passage in I Esdras 4:48, which refers to such a grant but assigns the act to Darius, is probably based on Ezra 3:7, with some influence possibly from Neh. 2:8. Josephus here (*Antiquities* XI. 4. 1), influenced by I Esdras, describes a shipment of logs in the days of Darius, which he claims was ordered by Cyrus.

8. From 4:24; 5:16 it would appear that **the second year** refers to the first attempts at reconstruction of the temple in the reign of Cyrus. But in blundering fashion the Chronicler introduces **Zerubbabel** and **Jeshua** of the time of Darius I (521-485 B.C.). For him Zerubbabel was Sheshbazzar. Both I Esdras and Josephus place the events during the reign of Darius I. Work on the temple began on the twenty-fourth day of the sixth month of the second year of Darius (Sept. 21, 520 B.C.) according to Hag. 1:15. Although the Chronicler finds it impossible to do so, historically an abortive attempt at rebuilding by Sheshbazzar in the time of Cyrus must be kept separate from the successful one by Zerubbabel during the reign of Darius. Influence of the Chronicler's narrative of the building of Solomon's temple (II Chr. 3:2) may be seen in the statement that work began in the **second month** (Iyyar, i.e., May). But it is plausible that the work should have started then, when the rainy season had ended and the harvest was gathered (Kittel, *Geschichte des Volkes Israel*, III, 428-29; Rudolph, *loc. cit.*). **Began** dangles incompletely in the Hebrew text, without specifying the action begun. **Made a beginning** does not reflect the awkwardness of the original. The Chronicler's sentence might well be completed, as in I Esdras 5:57, by supplying "And they laid the foundation of the house of God."

The subject of **began** is extremely long and complex. It suggests that in Hag. 1:12, 14, but there Haggai is silent regarding the priests and Levites in whom the Chronicler is much interested. To Haggai, who never mentions Babylonian Jews, the **remnant** means

---

almost any wedding. It is even more evident through periods of rapid and far-reaching change in the life of a community, a nation, or a generation. It recurs likewise in the experience of almost every church, especially in changing city or suburban or rural neighborhoods, when a strategic site has to be given up, or a

beloved building torn down, or a traditional program radically modified. The older members weep nostalgic tears as they look back to the way things were when they were young; but their eventual successors, with no such memories of "the good old days," look forward in hope and faith, and are in a mood to celebrate.

the priests and the Levites, and all they that were come out of the captivity unto Jerusalem; and appointed the Levites, from twenty years old and upward, to set forward the work of the house of the LORD.

9 Then stood Jeshua *with* his sons and his brethren, Kadmiel and his sons, the sons of Judah, together, to set forward the workmen in the house of God: the sons of Henadad, *with* their sons and their brethren the Levites.

10 And when the builders laid the foundation of the temple of the LORD, they set the priests in their apparel with trumpets, and the Levites the sons of Asaph with cymbals, to praise the LORD, after the ordinance of David king of Israel.

11 And they sang together by course in praising and giving thanks unto the LORD; because *he is* good, for his mercy *endureth* for ever toward Israel. And all the people

brethren, the priests and the Levites and all who had come to Jerusalem from the captivity. They appointed the Levites, from twenty years old and upward, to have the oversight of the work of the house of the LORD. 9 And Jeshua with his sons and his kinsmen, and Kad'mi-el and his sons, the sons of Judah, together took the oversight of the workmen in the house of God, along with the sons of Hen'adad and the Levites, their sons and kinsmen.

10 And when the builders laid the foundation of the temple of the LORD, the priests in their vestments came forward with trumpets, and the Levites, the sons of Asaph, with cymbals, to praise the LORD, according to the directions of David king of Israel; 11 and they sang responsively, praising and giving thanks to the LORD,

"For he is good,
   for his steadfast love endures for ever
      toward Israel."

---

those who had not been exiled, while the Chronicler applies the term to the returned exiles alone. The **Levites** (cf. 2:40) were assigned **to have the oversight of the work** (cf. Neh. 11:16). The Hebrew word used means "to be pre-eminent," and used by the Chronicler it has the sense "to oversee" or "to superintend." The **twenty years** minimum age for Levites contrasts with the twenty-five (Num. 8:24) and thirty (Num. 4:3) years of the priestly legislation. Harmonizers have suggested that the difference was due to the scarcity of Levites at the time when many were needed, or that the younger men would be needed for the work of heavy transport. It is questionable whether the Levites were used to any great extent for actual manual labor (cf. vs. 9). More likely the difference in age reflects the practice of the Chronicler's own time (cf. I Chr. 23:24-27; II Chr. 31:17), before changing social and economic conditions compelled a change in age.

9. The names must be emended as in the RSV, in accordance with the Greek texts, to include "Binnui" (בנוי), whose name has been translated as **his sons** (בניו), and "Hodaviah" (הודויה or הודוה, "Hodevah," in Neh. 7:43), which has been corrupted to the graphically similar **Judah** (יהודה). But a **Judah** does appear elsewhere as the head of a family of Levites (Neh. 12:8). **Henadad** does not appear in 2:40, but is mentioned in Neh. 3:18, 24; 10:9, and may have been introduced here secondarily from Nehemiah. It is separated from the other names by text in the M.T. but is joined with them in I Esdras 5:58. Meyer (*Entstehung des Judenthums*, p. 177) believed the name to be missing in 2:40 because the family had not gone into captivity but had remained in Palestine. **Stood . . . together** means were mutually responsible. **To set forward** (cf. vs. 8) is properly rendered in I Esdras by "to serve as taskmasters" (ἐργοδιῶκται). While some MSS read "the doers of the work" instead of **the workmen,** it is better to read with the M.T. "the doing of the work." Here "work" is the task of rebuilding (cf. Hag. 1:14) and must not be restricted simply to "worship" as Meyer inclines to suggest (*ibid.,* p. 195).

b) SUBFOUNDATION LAID AND DEDICATED (3:10-11=I Esdras 5:59-62)

10-11. The celebration occurred before the temple was completed (4:1-3) but there is no specific reference to a **foundation** in the verse (cf. vs. 6). For **they set** read with thirteen MSS, the LXX, and I Esdras, "they stood," which the RSV interprets

shouted with a great shout, when they praised the Lord, because the foundation of the house of the Lord was laid.

12 But many of the priests and Levites and chief of the fathers, *who were* ancient men, that had seen the first house, when the foundation of this house was laid before their eyes, wept with a loud voice; and many shouted aloud for joy:

13 So that the people could not discern the noise of the shout of joy from the noise of the weeping of the people: for the people shouted with a loud shout, and the noise was heard afar off.

And all the people shouted with a great shout, when they praised the Lord, because the foundation of the house of the Lord was laid. **12** But many of the priests and Levites and heads of fathers' houses, old men who had seen the first house, wept with a loud voice when they saw the foundation of this house being laid, though many shouted aloud for joy; **13** so that the people could not distinguish the sound of the joyful shout from the sound of the people's weeping, for the people shouted with a great shout, and the sound was heard afar.

---

came forward. The Hebrew "dressed" is interpreted as **in their apparel** and in I Esdras "clad in vestments" (ἐστολισμένοι). Josephus expands this to "adorned with their customary garments." It is possible that a word, perhaps "in fine linen" (בוץ), has dropped from the text. The **trumpets** were the long tubelike clarions with flaring bell such as are portrayed among the plunder of the temple on the Arch of Titus at Rome. They were the priests' instruments (cf. Num. 10:8), used on ceremonial occasions (cf. I Chr. 16:6). The Levites played **cymbals** (cf. II Sam. 6:5; I Chr. 15:19). The Levitical musicians were the **sons of Asaph** (2:41). David was the one who ordered the Levites to be musicians, according to the Chronicler (II Chr. 29:25-26). The Hebrew "they answered" is properly interpreted as **they sang responsively.** Josephus and I Esdras 5:61 indicate that hymns were sung; the line of song quoted here (found also in Pss. 106:1; 136:1; cf. Jer. 33:10 ff.), was a favorite of the Chronicler (cf. I Chr. 16:34; II Chr. 5:13; 7:3). **Toward Israel** was added early by someone who did not recognize the quotation.

c) POPULAR REACTION TO THE BUILDING (3:12-13=I Esdras 5:63-65)

12-13. Popular reaction to the temple must be understood in the light of Hag. 2:1-4, in which the prophet encourages the people who were disappointed with the appearance of the structure. Any **old men** who had seen the first temple would have been greatly in the minority in the crowd in 520 B.C., since that temple had been destroyed sixty-six years before.

Part of vs. 12 is in Hebrew quite rough and grammatically impossible, reading, lit., ". . . the old man who had seen the first house in its establishment, this the house, with their eyes. . . ." The expression "this the house" may be a correct gloss to the pronoun "its" (Rudolph, *op. cit.*, p. 30); or the pronoun זה, "this," may be a fragment of an original verb נבזה, "despised," in a parenthetical comment explaining the weeping on such an occasion: ". . . at the time of its rebuilding the house was despised in their eyes" (Arnold B. Ehrlich, *Randglossen zur hebräischen Bibel* [Leipzig: J. C. Hinrichs, 1914], VII, 163; Bewer, *op. cit.*, pp. 45-46). This conforms to the sense of Hag. 2:3. According to I Esdras 5:65, "The people did not hear the trumpets because of the weeping of the people," a view reflected by the Peshitta. But the Chronicler believed that the complaints of the weepers were concealed by the loud shouts of the others who outnumbered them. Josephus explains: "But the people in general were content with their present condition, and because they were allowed to build themselves a temple they desired no more, and neither considered nor remembered nor tormented themselves at all with the comparison of that one and the former temple, as though this were below their expectations" (*Antiquities* XI. 4. 2).

The intrusion of several words in vs. 13 obscures the meaning. Of three occurrences of **the people** only the last seems original. The first instance is lacking in the Vulg. and the second, which may be a dittograph, is missing in the LXX. Ehrlich's emendations

4 Now when the adversaries of Judah and Benjamin heard that the children of the captivity builded the temple unto the LORD God of Israel;

4 Now when the adversaries of Judah and Benjamin heard that the returned exiles were building a temple to the LORD, the

---

further improve the text, reading **discern** as singular and inserting the preposition "of" before the first occurrence of **sound**. As emended, vs. 13 should read: "And there was not a discerning of the sound of the shout of joy from the sound of weeping, for the people were shouting a great shout."

2. THE SAMARITAN CONFLICT (4:1–6:22)

In ch. 4 the Chronicler explains why the temple, begun during Cyrus' reign (539 530 B.C.), was not finished until the time of Darius I (521-486 B.C.). Ignoring economic reasons (Hag. 1:9) and Jewish reluctance to undertake the task (Hag. 1:2), he suggests that the delay was due to persecution by the neighbors of the Jews, whose offer of co-operation was rejected (4:1-5). He illustrates such persecution by offering excerpts from an Aramaic source (cf. Intro., p. 557) which showed that in all periods, through correspondence with the Persian court, the enemies of the Jews tried to stop the reconstruction of Jerusalem and succeeded temporarily (4:6-24).

Through his usual confusion of Zerubbabel with Sheshbazzar, the Chronicler transports events of the time of Darius I back to that of Cyrus. Thus he is enabled to expound his views that the returned exiles began work on the temple at once, and that from the beginning the Jews rejected the contamination of associating with foreigners, no matter what religion they professed. While the actual date of the first open break between the returned Jews and their neighbors cannot yet be determined, tension between them must have increased from the very start on economic and political as well as religious grounds. As J. W. Rothstein's correct interpretation of Hag. 2:14*b* shows, already by the time of Haggai "the people of the land" were regarded as "unclean" (*Juden und Samaritaner* [Leipzig: J. C. Hinrichs, 1908; "Beiträge zur Wissenschaft vom Alten Testament"], pp. 31-41).

a) OFFER OF ASSISTANCE (4:1-2=I Esdras 5:66-69)

4:1. The **adversaries,** now identified in vss. 2, 9-10, may once have been explained here rightly by the migrant gloss "the peoples of the lands," now in 3:3. They appear to be the folk of mixed blood inhabiting the province of Samaria, where the Hebrews of the Northern Kingdom had dwelt. Although tradition associates **Benjamin** with the northern tribes at their secession (I Kings 11:32, 36; 12:17, 20; Hos. 5:8), ultimately it was linked with Judah (cf. Jer. 33:12-13), where it is regularly associated in postexilic sources (cf. 2:20-34; I Chr. 7–8; 9:7-9; 12:2-7; Neh. 11:7 ff.). **The LORD** represents the proper name of the Jewish God which was probably pronounced "Yahweh."

4:1-24. *Sectarianism and Racialism.*—Whatever the chronological confusions, and the variety of sources both Hebrew and Aramaic that have been interwoven into this puzzling chapter, as these have been so strangely mingled by the Chronicler and so patiently disentangled by present-day scholarship, there is one aspect of this chapter which modern eyes, in the light of subsequent history, must note with sadness of heart. The offer of co-operation by the Samaritans, with its reminder of a common heritage in faith and worship—**Let us build with you; for we worship your God as you do** (vs. 2*b*)—is curtly rebuffed by the exclusiveness characteristic of sectarianism in every age, and of racialism in every land: **You have nothing to do with us in building a house to our God** (vs. 3). This refusal of the returned exiles in Jerusalem to allow their Samaritan coreligionists any share in the worship of the rebuilt temple, a refusal which according to Josephus actually dated from the end of the Persian period, is here projected back by the Chronicler to this first attempt to rebuild the temple—in the face of his own admission in II Chr. 34:9 that money had earlier been sent from Samaria for the repair of the temple under Josiah. The Chronicler is of course in entire sympathy with the stress of

2 Then they came to Zerubbabel, and to the chief of the fathers, and said unto them, Let us build with you: for we seek your God, as ye *do;* and we do sacrifice unto him since the days of Esar-haddon king of Assur, which brought us up hither.

3 But Zerubbabel, and Jeshua, and the rest of the chief of the fathers of Israel, said unto them, Ye have nothing to do with us

God of Israel, 2 they approached Zerub'babel and the heads of fathers' houses and said to them, "Let us build with you; for we worship your God as you do, and we have been sacrificing to him ever since the days of E'sar-had'don king of Assyria who brought us here." 3 But Zerub'babel, Jeshua, and the rest of the heads of fathers' houses in Israel said to them, "You have

---

2. As I Esdras 5:68 shows (cf. Ezra 4:3), "and to Jeshua," now lost from the M.T., should be added after **Zerubbabel. We seek your God** (cf. 6:21) reflects the tradition in II Kings 17:25-28, 32 (cf. Josephus *Antiquities* IX. 9. 3). According to II Chr. 34:9, money was sent from Samaria for the temple in the time of King Josiah. Later the sons of the governor of Samaria (cf. Neh. 2:9-10) bore the good Jewish names Delaiah and Shelemiah; the Jews in Egypt, when their temple was destroyed, appealed to the Samaritans for aid in 408 B.C. (Cowley, *Aramaic Papyri,* pp. 108-24); and the relative of a Jewish high priest married the daughter of the governor of Samaria (Neh. 13:28). They accepted the Jewish Pentateuch as their sacred scripture. Thus, essentially Jewish in religion, the Samaritans felt they had a common interest with the Jews in their cult and made an apparently sincere offer of co-operation. Josephus claims that they were permitted to worship at the temple after its completion (*Antiquities* XI. 4. 3; XVIII. 2. 2).

Some have seen a political motive in the Samaritan offer. The Samaritans under the Assyrians and Neo-Babylonians had prestige as the ruling group in the province until the Persian rule began. Jewish newcomers from the East, who had the consent and support of the Persian court and could thus form a new and powerful upper class in the region, were menacing the established position of the Samaritans. By joining the new Jewish group in their venture the Samaritans may have sought identification with them and thus a salvaging of something of their political position (Rudolph, *op. cit.,* pp. 33-34).

Reference to Assyrian King **Esar-haddon** (680-669 B.C.) shows that the adversaries were not those settled in Samaria after its conquest by Sargon in 721 B.C. (II Kings 17:24 ff.) but a group exiled there later. Esar-haddon's annals indicate that the Syrian coast was subdued and organized as an Assyrian province from which Syrians were exiled and to which Eastern folk were sent for settlement in 677-676 B.C. (D. D. Luckenbill, *Ancient Records of Assyria and Babylonia* [Chicago: University of Chicago Press, 1926-27], II, 211-12, sec. 527; A. T. Olmstead, *History of Assyria* [New York: Charles Scribner's Sons, 1923], pp. 374-75). The neighboring province of Samaria may then have received the Easterners mentioned in vs. 2. It has also been suggested that the settlement was made in connection with the fall of Tyre and Esar-haddon's Egyptian campaign of 671 B.C. (Rudolph, *op. cit.,* p. 33).

b) REJECTION OF ASSISTANCE (4:3=I Esdras 5:70-71)

3. The Jewish rejection was, lit., "It is not for you and for us," which is properly interpreted as **You have nothing to do with us** or, in the Amer. Trans., "You have nothing in common with us." **We ourselves together** signifies the Jews banded together against

---

both Ezra and Nehemiah on racial purity as a prerequisite for any sharing in the worship of the God of their fathers. But as Julius A. Bewer [4] points out in his discussion of the book of Ruth, the "broader sympathies" and "larger-hearted

[4] *The Literature of the Old Testament and Its Historical Development* (rev. ed.; New York: Columbia University Press, 1933), pp. 282, 284.

view" so memorably set forth in that exquisite little idyl did not prevail against the "nativists, led by Nehemiah and Ezra."

In the light of the tragic story of anti-Semitism down the centuries, of its cruel climax in mid-twentieth century Germany, and of its ominous echoes in other countries, one can only speculate as to how different the course of history

to build a house unto our God; but we ourselves together will build unto the LORD God of Israel, as king Cyrus the king of Persia hath commanded us.

4 Then the people of the land weakened the hands of the people of Judah, and troubled them in building,

5 And hired counselors against them, to frustrate their purpose, all the days of Cyrus king of Persia, even until the reign of Darius king of Persia.

nothing to do with us in building a house to our God; but we alone will build to the LORD, the God of Israel, as King Cyrus the king of Persia has commanded us."

4 Then the people of the land discouraged the people of Judah, and made them afraid to build, 5 and hired counselors against them to frustrate their purpose, all the days of Cyrus king of Persia, even until the reign of Darius king of Persia.

---

the Samaritans. **We alone** follows the Vulg. and I Esdras, but such a meaning for the M.T. is not otherwise supported in Hebrew.

Cyrus . . . commanded us appeals to the royal edict (1:2-3; 5:13, 15; 6:1-4) to exclude Samaritans, taking advantage of a technicality to exclude undesirables. The Chronicler believed that none but returned Jewish exiles built the temple. Jewish reluctance to co-operate may have been due historically to the fact that the Samaritans were not pure monotheists but had merely added the Jewish God, as the god of the land, to their regular pantheon (II Kings 17:29-34a; cf. *ibid.*).

c) PLOTS AND FRUSTRATIONS (4:4-5 = I Esdras 7:72-73)

From an Aramaic document at his disposal (cf. Intro., pp. 557-58) the Chronicler presented evidence of the scheming antipathy of the adversaries who sought royal support in preventing Jewish reconstruction. Only part of the material refers to the temple, and that from the time of Darius (5:1–6:15). None was available from the periods of Cyrus and Cambyses to explain the stoppage to which the Chronicler's verse (4:24) would intend the opposition to refer. Apparently because the Chronicler desired to lead directly from the completion of the temple (5:15) to reinstitution of cultic services as a preliminary to the story of Ezra (7:1–10:44), he shifted the later material of 4:6-23, which would have interrupted his narrative, from after 5:1–6:18 to its present location. He was more concerned with the religious history than with accurate chronology. Evidently for him the data from the reigns of Xerxes and Artaxerxes amply illustrated the type of opposition which he believed also marked the period prior to Darius. With the shift the statement in 4:6 was translated from Aramaic to Hebrew and the reference to the letter in vs. 7 was but partially so translated.

4. Weakened the hands (cf. Neh. 6:9), lit., "relaxing the hands," an old Hebrew idiom (cf. II Sam. 4:1; Isa. 13:7; Jer. 6:24; 50:43; etc.), means to cause someone to lose heart and be discouraged to the point of inefficiency and even of inability to work. It is now found in a Hebrew ostracon from Lachish, referring to a prophet accused of lowering the morale of the country in a critical moment (Harry Torczyner, *et al., The Lachish Letters* [London: Oxford University Press, 1938], pp. 104-5, 117, No. VI, l. 6).

The **hired counselors** could have been Jewish traitors (cf. Neh. 6:12-13) or, since the term is used of royal advisers (7:28), bribed Persian officials. The accusations are general, presumably because specific data were lacking for the early Persian period. The Chronicler records a persistent tradition of the beginning of the temple by Sheshbazzar during the reign of Cyrus, but he could supply no details. It was common knowl-

---

might have been had the wider horizons and sympathies of the books of Ruth and Jonah prevailed instead of the relentless racialism of Ezra, had these proffered seeds of co-operation in work and worship instead of the dragon's teeth of racial prejudice and arrogance been

sown in Palestine 2,400 years ago. The Chronicler is at least explicit in his summary of the bitter harvest: **Then the people of the land discouraged the people of Judah, and made them afraid to build, and hired counselors against them to frustrate their purpose.** . . .

6 And in the reign of Ahasuerus, in the beginning of his reign, wrote they *unto him* an accusation against the inhabitants of Judah and Jerusalem.

7 ¶ And in the days of Artaxerxes wrote Bishlam, Mithredath, Tabeel, and the rest of their companions, unto Artaxerxes king of Persia; and the writing of the letter *was* written in the Syrian tongue, and interpreted in the Syrian tongue.

6 And in the reign of Ahasu-e′rus, in the beginning of his reign, they wrote an accusation against the inhabitants of Judah and Jerusalem.

7 And in the days of Ar-ta-xerx′es, Bishlam and Mith′redath and Tab′e-el and the rest of their associates wrote to Ar-ta-xerx′es king of Persia; the letter was written in

edge, from the work of Haggai and Zechariah, that the temple was actually constructed by Zerubbabel and Jeshua in the time of Darius. The Chronicler harmonizes his traditions in part by identifying the leaders of the two periods and in part by the contradictory hypothesis of a compulsory work stoppage between the reigns.

d) Reigns of Xerxes and Artaxerxes (4:6-24)

(1) Complaints Made to Xerxes and Artaxerxes (4:6-16=I Esdras 2:16-24)

6. As indicated above, **Ahasuerus** here is anachronistic if it refers to Xerxes. Both I Esdras and Josephus omit this verse. **Ahasuerus** (cf. Esth. 10:1; Dan. 9:1) is a corrupt form of a Persian name. It has been called a corruption of Cyaxares, confused with the name Xerxes. This has been taken as evidence that the Chronicler shared the later Jewish concept of Persian chronology which, faulty and unhistorical, recognized Cyaxares (II), a fictitious Median king reputed to be the son of "Darius the Mede" (Dan. 5:31) and the successor of Cyrus (C. C. Torrey, "Medes and Persians," *Journal of the American Oriental Society,* LXVI [1946], 3, 6-9). This ingenious interpretation would explain the unusual order of kings in vss. 6 ff. but it is not persuasive. More likely is the usual identification with Xerxes (486-465 B.C.). In explaining the unhistorical sequence of kings, Xerxes and Artaxerxes have been regarded as being used as typical Persian names (Alfred Bertholet, *Die Bücher Esra und Nehemia* [Tübingen: J. C. B. Mohr, 1902; "Kurzer Hand-Commentar zum Alten Testament"], p. 13). We probably have here a genuine reference to King Xerxes which has been drawn from its proper chronological position in the original Aramaic document (see *ibid.* and Rudolph, *op. cit.,* pp. 35, 37, 41).

The **accusation** is not explicit. Presumably the Chronicler (or the author of the Aramaic source) did not regard it as being as important or as relevant as those letters given in full. Lack of detailed knowledge of events in Palestine during the time of Xerxes makes it impossible to recover the substance of the letter or its occasion. **The beginning of his reign** means Xerxes' accession year, when he ascended the throne (December, 486 B.C.) to fill out the last year of his predecessor before beginning his own first year on April 6, 485 B.C. A papyrus describes such a year as "the beginning of the reign, when . . . the king sat upon his throne" (Cowley, *op. cit.,* p. 16, No. 6, ll. 1-2).

7. Like vs. 6, the letters to **Artaxerxes** I (464-423 B.C.) are out of chronological order. The two Artaxerxes letters are combined in I Esdras 2:16 by listing together all the senders. Josephus (*Antiquities* XI. 2. 1) corrects the chronology of both the M.T. and I Esdras by making Cambyses (530-522 B.C.) the recipient of the letter. He prefaces the document with a statement that during the reign of Cyrus the satraps were bribed to oppose Jewish reconstruction without the knowledge of Cyrus, who was preoccupied with

Then the work on the house of God which is in Jerusalem stopped. (Vss. 4-5a, 24.) In these sensitive matters, not least, the children on both sides reap what their fathers have sown; and the history not only of the Jewish people, but of our Western civilization as well, might have

been different had the outlook of the books of Ruth and Jonah prevailed over that of Ezra.

And yet, just as we are on the point of such speculation about what the course of history might have been and was not, a realistic question arises to give us pause. In the pathetically

8 Rehum the chancellor and Shimshai the scribe wrote a letter against Jerusalem to Artaxerxes the king in this sort:

Aramaic and translated./ 8 Rehum the commander and Shim'shai the scribe wrote a letter against Jerusalem to Ar-ta-xerx'es the

f Heb adds *in Aramaic,* indicating that 4. 8-6. 18 is in Aramaic. Another interpretation is *The letter was written in the Aramaic script and set forth in the Aramaic language*

---

war elsewhere. Thus he does what the Chronicler leads one to expect by his vs. 24. But he does so only by mentioning the reconstruction of the temple which he already found in I Esdras 2:18, 20, although it is not in any of the Artaxerxes correspondence in the M.T. which should postdate the completion of the temple (but cf. 6:14).

The senders of the first letter (vs. 7) were the Persian **Mithredath** (Old Persian *Mithradata;* cf. 1:8) and the Aramaean **Tabe-el** (like Hebrew Tobiah), about whom nothing more definite is known. It has been conjectured that **Tabe-el** was a Jew, sympathetic toward rebuilding Jerusalem, who wrote the Aramaic document (cf. Intro., pp. 557-58) to **Mithredath** (cf. LXX^B) for transmission to the king (H. H. Schaeder, *Iranische Beiträge I* [Halle: M. Niemeyer, 1930], pp. 16-17). The M.T., however, only permits both men to share in sending the letter. Despite I Esdras 2:16, **Bishlam** is not a proper name but the Aramaic for "in peace." It could be part of a salutation in a letter (cf. vs. 17; 5:7), but the verse is not an introduction in form, and the word order would be unusual for a salutation. Rudolph (*op. cit.,* p. 34) therefore suggests reading בירושלם, "against Jerusalem," for בשלם, **Bishlam.**

Although vs. 7 is in Hebrew, its original Aramaic is still evident in the spelling of **unto** and in the use of loan words for **companions** (vss. 9, 17, 23; 5:3, 6; 6:6, 13) and **letter** (vss. 18, 23; 5:5). **Writing,** too, is an Aramaic word, a gloss to explain the Persian loan word for **letter. Written** could refer to the use of square **script** or to the use of **the Aramaic language. In the Syrian tongue** is, lit., **in Aramaic** the language which was the lingua franca of the Persian Empire (R. A. Bowman, "Aramaeans, Aramaic, and the Bible," *Journal of Near Eastern Studies,* VII [1948], 65-90). The last occurrence of **in the Syrian tongue,** not found in the LXX, is probably an addition, inserted as in Dan. 2:4 to indicate transition to the Aramaic language which follows (4:8–6:18).

8-16. The second Artaxerxes letter is given in full. Within vss. 8-11*a* are several introductions to the letter, each differing in the identification of the senders. Vss. 9-10, which interrupt the narrative, are an interpolated explanatory comment identifying the **companions** of the senders (cf. Torrey, *Ezra Studies,* p. 178). Schaeder (*Iranische Beiträge* I, p. 22) assumes that the long list of vss. 9-10 originally followed vs. 11*b*, but that the Chronicler first omitted them and later put them back in the margin whence they migrated to the present position after vs. 8, where they are relevant. As the letter actually begins in vs. 11*b*, the senders are now grouped anonymously under a general title. Josephus makes Cambyses the recipient of the letter (cf. vs. 7) instead of Artaxerxes.

Each section of the complex (vss. 8-11*a*) concludes with a peculiar expression, lit., **and thus** (vs. 8) or **and now** (vss. 10, 11), usually incorrectly translated **in this sort, as follows,** or "at such a time" (vs. 11). Such an expression regularly in the Aramaic papyri marks the division between the salutation and the body of the letter (Cowley, *op. cit.,* No. 17, l. 2; No. 21, l. 3; No. 26, l. 1; No. 37, l. 2; etc.).

8. Rehum ("Merciful") abbreviates such an Akkadian name as *^mRahim-ili* or *^mRahim-sharri.* His title was "Holder of a (royal) decree," the Aramaic equivalent of

---

weak and difficult situation of these returning exiles, amid the racial, cultural, and spiritual mixtures and dilutions that surrounded them, would their great heritage of prophetic and ethical religion have been preserved for posterity without the hard protective shell of the

rigid racialism that speaks out so positively, not only in vs. 3*b*, **We alone will build to the LORD, the God of Israel,** but likewise throughout both Ezra and Nehemiah? Would Judaism, the law and the prophets alike, have survived amid the rising flood of Hellenistic syncretism through

9 Then *wrote* Rehum the chancellor, and Shimshai the scribe, and the rest of their companions; the Dinaites, the Apharsathchites, the Tarpelites, the Apharsites, the Archevites, the Babylonians, the Susanchites, the Dehavites, *and* the Elamites,

10 And the rest of the nations whom the great and noble Asnapper brought over, and set in the cities of Samaria, and the rest *that are* on this side the river, and at such a time.

king as follows — 9 then wrote Rehum the commander, Shim'shai the scribe, and the rest of their associates, the judges, the governors, the officials, the Persians, the men of Erech, the Babylonians, the men of Susa, that is, the Elamites, 10 and the rest of the nations whom the great and noble Osnap'par deported and settled in the cities of Samar'ia and in the rest of the province

---

Persian *farmānkara*. He was not a military leader but a bureaucrat representing the king (Herzfeld, *Zoroaster and His World*, I, 171; the Persian equivalent, *prmnkr*, is found in Cowley, *op. cit.*, No. 26, ll. 4, 8). The title was borrowed from Assyria, where it was held by officials of high rank, sometimes even by the chief priest (E. G. Klauber, *Politisch-Religiöse Texte aus der Sargonidenzeit* [Leipzig: E. Pfeiffer, 1913], pp. xxiv-xxv; cf. No. 137, reverse, l. 2; No. 103, reverse ll. 9-10; No. 111, reverse l. 4; No. 116, reverse l. 3). Klauber calls the official the "reporter," the meaning found also in I Esdras 2:17, 25 and in Josephus, who interprets the title "the recorder of all things that happen" (*Antiquities* XI. 2. 1). Such royal investigators were sent out yearly to the Persian satrapies to investigate and report conditions (Xenophon *Cyropaedia* VIII. 6. 16). Neither **chancellor** nor **commander** adequately renders the title or function.

Shimshai is found frequently in Akkadian records as *mShamshai*, an abbreviation of a name including the name of the Babylonian sun-god Shamash. Since a common **scribe** would not be mentioned in the salutation, **Shimshai** must be an official. Rudolph (*op. cit.*, p. 42) identifies him as Rehum's secretary. He probably was such a royal appointee as the scribe attached to officials during the Persian period to spy upon them and report directly to the king (Herodotus *History* III. 128; cf. George Rawlinson, *The History of Herodotus* [New York: D. Appleton & Co., 1859], II, 426, n. 9). Thus both men were required to investigate suspicious acts such as the fortification of Jerusalem. **Letter** here represents an Akkadian word (*egirtu*) borrowed by both the Aramaic and the Hebrew languages.

9-10. The list of names is a commentary on the "adversaries" (vs. 1), "the people of the land" (vs. 4). Although the M.T. treats all the names as gentilics, and some are definitely geographic, many are official titles.

The **Dinaites** are **the judges** (Persian *dâtabhar*), found often in the Aramaic papyri (Cowley, *op. cit.*, No. 6, l. 6; No. 8, l. 24; No. 27, l. 9; No. 80, l. 8; No. 82, l. 1). The Lucianic recensions of the LXX and of I Esdras 2:17 translate as **judges**, and Josephus calls them "the judges of the council" (*Antiquities* XI. 2. 1). Herodotus (*History* III. 31) claims that their authority derived from the king, and a papyrus links them with "observers" and "police" as part of the spy network of the province (Cowley, *op. cit.*, No. 27, ll. 8-9).

The **Apharsathchites** were not **governors** but "envoys" (Persian *frēstaka* or *fraistaka*; Rudolph, *op. cit.*, p. 36, cites Wilhelm Eilers, *Iranische Beamtennamen in der keilschriftliche Überlieferung* [Leipzig: F. A. Brockhaus, 1940], pp. 39, n. 1, 100; cf. Herzfeld,

---

the centuries between the O.T. and the N.T., except within that shell of legalism and exclusivism which Ezra himself did so much to create and to harden? The same kind of question, in terms not so much racial as cultural and theological, has faced the younger Christian

churches in India and China. And if Judaism had not survived as a distinctive culture and faith, would there have arisen any Jesus of Nazareth four hundred years after Ezra, or any Christian church universal under Paul? Who of us is wise enough to answer these highly

11 ¶ This *is* the copy of the letter that they sent unto him, *even* unto Artaxerxes the king; Thy servants the men on this side the river, and at such a time.

12 Be it known unto the king, that the Jews which came up from thee to us are

Beyond the River, 11 and now this is a copy of the letter that they sent — "To Ar-ta-xerx'es the king: Your servants, the men of the province Beyond the River, send greeting. 12 And now be it known to the king that the Jews who came up from you to us

---

Zoroaster and His World, I, 171) . I Esdras 6:7, translating the "Apharsachites" of Ezra 5:6; 6:6, has "governors." None of the many explanations of the **Tarpelites** is convincing but its position suggests some kind of **officials.** The **Apharsites** are usually rendered as **Persians** (so also Rudolph, *loc. cit.*) but Herzfeld relates them to a possible Neo-Babylonian official, the *amiprasakanu*, whose identity is yet undetermined (Herzfeld, *Zoroaster and His World,* I, 171) . Since the -*ka* sign is damaged in the text, the name is probable but not certain. Harry Torczyner ("Aryans and non-Aryan Persians in the Bible," *Bulletin of the Jewish Palestine Exploration Society,* XIV [1947-48], pp. 1, 6) regards the **Archevites** (ארכויא) as representing the Aryans, the "free-born" Persians (αριακοι) and the **Tarpelites** (reading טפליא and comparing שרביט for שביט) as "affiliated" or "dependent" Persians, the Babylonians and Shushanites that follow in the list. But this hypothesis depends on reading "Persians" for titles otherwise identifiable (**Apharsites** and **Apharsathchites**) and if the affiliated Persians are those listed, **Tarpelites** should appear just before the ethnic names.

Archevites are doubtless the **men of Erech** (Gen. 10:10) , of the ancient city Uruk (modern Warka) in southern Babylonia. Since the other names are those of cities, the **Babylonians** apparently are those of the city of Babylon. **Susanchites** were men of the city of Shushan or **Susa** (Neh. 1:1; Dan. 8:2; Esth. 1:2, 5; 3:15) , the capital of ancient Elam. **Dehavites** must be revocalized with two MSS and LXX[B] and translated **that is** linking the **Susanchites** with the **Elamites,** which was doubtless originally an explanatory gloss to the less familiar **Susanchites.** The **Elamites** were a non-Semitic folk who dwelt in the great plain of the lower Tigris, along the northern shore of the Persian Gulf, and in the mountains enclosing the plain to the north and east. They frequently joined the Babylonians against the Assyrians (George G. Cameron, *History of Early Iran* [Chicago: University of Chicago Press, 1936], pp. 4-5) .

Asnapper is certainly a corruption of Ashurbanipal, the last Assyrian king (669-633 B.C.) , since only he captured Shushan (Susa) from which the captives (vs. 9) were brought (H. Gelzer, "Die Colonie des Osnappar," *Zeitschrift für aegyptische Sprache,* XIII [1875], 81-82; Cameron, *History of Early Iran,* pp. 198-207) . **Deported and settled** indicates that the Hebrew exile was not unique but a regular political technique used by the Assyrians with rebels. In exile people would be too busy adjusting to a new environment to be a threat to Assyria. Read the plural, **cities of Samaria,** with the LXX and Vulg. (cf. II Kings 17:24-26) .

11. After the long list, a brief reference to the letter is needed to resume the subject. The salutation here greatly resembles that in the Aramaic papyri when a superior is addressed (Cowley, *op. cit.,* No. 30, l. 1; cf. No. 17, l. 1) .

12. **Be it known to the king** is appropriate for the report of royal informants and may have been a standard formula for introducing such reports (cf. vs. 13; 5:8) . Such

---

speculative questions, much less to presume to correct the actual course of history? All that we can fairly say is that Ezra and Nehemiah did then prevail over the authors of Ruth and Jonah, but that Jesus and Paul were later, "in God's own good time," raised up out of that very heritage. This also "is the LORD's doing;

it is marvelous in our eyes" (Ps. 118:23) . And in this reminder from the actual course of history there is agelong encouragement for all who to this day have to live and work in a world where sectarianism and racialism are still powerful, sowing their dragon's teeth as of old.

come unto Jerusalem, building the rebellious and the bad city, and have set up the walls *thereof,* and joined the foundations.

have gone to Jerusalem. They are rebuilding that rebellious and wicked city; they are finishing the walls and repairing the foun-

---

a report would normally reach the king indirectly through a scribe who would read it to him. Some Assyrian reports addressed to the king contain personal notes to the scribal intermediaries. One begins: "To king Sargon himself, my lord, may this come . . . . Speak as follows to the king, my lord . . ." (Leroy Waterman, *Royal Correspondence of the Assyrian Empire* [Ann Arbor: University of Michigan Press, 1930], Part II, p. 217, No. 1027). Another appends the note: "Whoever you are O scribe who reads this, do not conceal it from the king your lord. Speak kindness before the king. May Bel (and) Nabû command kindness for you before the king" (*ibid.,* Part II, p. 371, No. 1250). The very formula may be reflected in the appended note: "Now I have written to the king my lord. May the king my lord know" (*ibid.,* Part I, pp. 120-21, No. 177; Part II, p. 29, No. 753).

Came up from you, lit., "came up from with you," need not imply a return from Ezra's group, for the expression may be merely geographical, meaning "from the East," where the king was. Since Nehemiah arrived at Jerusalem and built the walls before Ezra came (cf. Intro., pp. 561-62), the reference could not be to Ezra and his group. Rudolph (*op. cit.,* pp. 44-45) dates this incident shortly before 445 B.C., possibly in 448 B.C., while the satrap Megabyzos was in revolt against Artaxerxes. **Rebellious and wicked** describe Jerusalem from the standpoint of overlords who had to send expeditions to crush rebels in the western provinces (II Kings 18:7-11, 13-20; 24:1-2; 25:1-6, 25-26).

The correspondence here is not concerned with the temple, as in I Esdras 2:18, 20, but with the city walls. The temple was finished by the time of Artaxerxes (but cf. 6:14). The Chronicler in placing the letter here merely illustrates the hostility of the adversaries. Torrey ("Medes and Persians," p. 2) contends that the Chronicler understood that the adversaries were playing a trick; by a lying accusation regarding the city wall the enemies succeeded in stopping all construction, including the temple, which was their real goal. But there is no temple mentioned in Ezra and its presence in I Esdras is easily explained as due to a misunderstanding of "palace" in Ezra 4:14 as "temple" since the same Hebrew word is used for both (Rudolph, *op. cit.,* p. 43, n. 1).

Since the walls are still incomplete in vs. 13, "have finished the walls" (ASV) or **have set up the walls** is surely wrong. One can read **are finishing,** but it is preferable to follow Rudolph's emendation (*ibid.,* p. 38), which suggests that the verb "they have begun" (ושריו) has been lost by haplography after the very similar "the walls" (שוריא), and that the verb following should be read "to finish," thus, "they have begun to finish the walls."

The long debated **foundations,** which represents a hitherto enigmatic Aramaic word ('*ushshayyā*'), is now explained plausibly as a distinctly Mesopotamian architectural term (Sumerian *USH;* Akkadian *ushshu*) referring to a subfoundation double the thickness of the planned walls into which the walls were laid (Sidney Smith, "Foundations: Ezra iv, 12; v, 16; vi, 3," in I. Epstein, E. Levine, and C. Roth, eds., *Essays in Honor of the Very Reverend Dr. J. H. Hertz* [London: E. Goldston, 1944], pp. 385-96). The *ushshu* is mentioned in an Akkadian building inscription by Artaxerxes (Ernst Herzfeld, *Altpersische Inschriften* [Berlin: Dietrich Reimer, 1938], p. 45, No. 22, 1. 5; R. G. Kent, "Old Persian Texts," *Journal of Near Eastern Studies,* IV [1945], 228). Perhaps such a structure is what Darius describes in his record of the building of his palace at Susa when he says, "Downward the earth was dug, until I reached rock in the earth. When the excavation had been made, rubble was packed down, some 40 cubits in depth, another (part) 20 cubits in depth. On that rubble the palace was constructed." (R. G. Kent, *Old Persian* [New Haven: American Oriental Society, 1950], pp. 142-44, Darius Susa F., ll. 22-27, sec. 3e; cf. George G. Cameron, *Persepolis Treasury Tablets* [Chicago: University

13 Be it known now unto the king, that, if this city be builded, and the walls set up *again, then* will they not pay toll, tribute, and custom, and *so* thou shalt endamage the revenue of the kings.

14 Now because we have maintenance from *the king's* palace, and it was not meet for us to see the king's dishonor, therefore have we sent and certified the king;

15 That search may be made in the book of the records of thy fathers: so shalt thou find in the book of the records, and know that this city *is* a rebellious city, and hurt-

dations. 13 Now be it known to the king that, if this city is rebuilt and the walls finished, they will not pay tribute, custom, or toll, and the royal revenue will be impaired. 14 Now because we eat the salt of the palace and it is not fitting for us to witness the king's dishonor, therefore we send and inform the king, 15 in order that search may be made in the book of the records of your fathers. You will find in the book of the

---

of Chicago Press, 1945], p. 17, n. 112.) Since architectural problems differed in stony Jerusalem from those in muddy Mesopotamian plains, the easterners who wrote the letter apparently applied the term they knew to some similar process employed by the Jews. With such a meaning for **foundations** the verb is best translated "being dug out" with the American Jewish Translation, supported by the Peshitta. Obviously the work was not very far along and the officials believed that prompt action would prevent the fortification of Jerusalem.

13. Tribute is an Akkadian loan word (*mandatu*) meaning a more or less voluntary gift made to an overlord (cf. Neh. 5:4 KJV). Usually closely linked with it is the *biltu*, the assessed tribute imposed by the overlord. That is apparently related to the second term in the series (Aramaic בלו) which is attested as "his tax" (בלוה) in an Aramaic ostracon from Egypt (Mark Lidzbarski, *Ephemeris für semitische Epigraphik* [Giessen: A. Töpelmann, 1908], II, 238-39). The third term, usually translated **custom** or **toll** because of its similarity to the Hebrew verb "go" (הלך), is still another Akkadian word (*ilku*) meaning *corvée*, taskwork, or feudal service owed the overlord, or its cash equivalent. It occurs (as הלך) in the Aramaic notes in the margins of cuneiform tablets concerned with the *ilku* (Delaporte, *Épigraphes araméens*, p. 67, No. 73; p. 70, No. 78; pp. 70-71, No. 79).

Revenue is but an incorrect guess based on context. The difficult word is probably a Persian adverb meaning "in the end" (as in the ASV) or "finally" (Persian *apatam-am*; Schaeder, *Iranische Beiträge* I, p. 74). The warning **thou shalt endamage** would hardly be addressed to a king by his subjects. Better sense is given by a simple emendation (reading מלכי מהנזק for מלכים תהנזק), "My king will be damaged" (Kittel, *Geschichte des Volkes Israel*, III, 601, n. 1; Rudolph, *op. cit.*, p. 39).

14. Since **we eat** incorrectly translates the verb "we have salted" (*melaḥnā'*), it is preferable to revocalize the word as the noun "our salt" (*milḥanā'*), reading, "Our salt is the salt of the palace" (Eberhard Nestle, *Marginalien und Materialien* [Tübingen: J. J. Heckenhauer, 1893], pp. 30 ff.; cf. Rudolph, *op. cit.*, p. 40). The reference is to a salt covenant (cf. Lev. 2:13; Num. 18:19; II Chr. 13:5) whereby contracting parties pledge to help and defend one another. Modern Arabs say "There is salt between us" and modern Persians describe a disloyal person as "untrue to salt" (H. C. Trumbull, *The Covenant of Salt* [New York: Charles Scribner's Sons, 1899]; W. R. Smith, *Lectures on the Religion of the Semites* [3rd ed.; New York: The Macmillan Co., 1927], p. 270; Adela M. Goodrich-Freer, *Arabs in Tent and Town* [London: Seeley, Service & Co., 1924], pp. 115-18). **Not fitting** represents the Persian *ariyaka*, "worthy of an Aryan" (Isidor Scheftelowitz, *Arisches im Alten Testament* [Berlin: S. Calvary & Co., 1901], I, 79). **Dishonor** is, lit., "nakedness" (cf. Gen. 9:22-23).

15. The book of the records is actually, as in I Esdras, the LXX^L, and Vulg., "books of memoranda," records kept by the Persian bureaucrats and their predecessors (cf.

ful unto kings and provinces, and that they have moved sedition within the same of old time: for which cause was this city destroyed.

16 We certify the king that, if this city be builded *again,* and the walls thereof set up, by this means thou shalt have no portion on this side the river.

17 ¶ *Then* sent the king an answer unto Rehum the chancellor, and *to* Shimshai the scribe, and *to* the rest of their companions that dwell in Samaria, and *unto* the rest beyond the river, Peace, and at such a time.

18 The letter which ye sent unto us hath been plainly read before me.

19 And I commanded, and search hath been made, and it is found that this city of old time hath made insurrection against kings, and *that* rebellion and sedition have been made therein.

20 There have been mighty kings also over Jerusalem, which have ruled over all *countries* beyond the river; and toll, tribute, and custom, was paid unto them.

records and learn that this city is a rebellious city, hurtful to kings and provinces, and that sedition was stirred up in it from of old. That was why this city was laid waste. 16 We make known to the king that, if this city is rebuilt and its walls finished, you will then have no possession in the province Beyond the River."

17 The king sent an answer: "To Rehum the commander and Shim'shai the scribe and the rest of their associates who live in Samar'ia and in the rest of the province Beyond the River, greeting. And now 18 the letter which you sent to us has been plainly read before me. 19 And I made a decree, and search has been made, and it has been found that this city from of old has risen against kings, and that rebellion and sedition have been made in it. 20 And mighty kings have been over Jerusalem, who ruled over the whole province Beyond the River, to whom tribute, custom, and toll were paid.

N. Schneider, "Die Urkundenbehälter von Ur III und ihre archivalische Systematik," *Orientalia,* N.S.IX [1940], 7; Cameron, *Persepolis Treasury Tablets,* pp. 9 ff., 20-23). **Your fathers** is not "your ancestors" but "your predecessors," the Babylonian kings. The Persians regarded themselves as the legitimate successors of the Neo-Babylonians, for the writers here have in mind the earlier revolts leading to the destruction of Jerusalem. Nothing certain is known of Palestinian revolts under the early Persian kings. But the incidents of Zech. 6:9-15 and the sudden disappearance of Zerubbabel suggest that the Jews may have proved rebellious during the reign of Darius (A. T. Olmstead, *History of the Persian Empire* [Chicago: University of Chicago Press, 1948], pp. 138-39).

(2) LETTER OF ARTAXERXES TO REHUM AND SHIMSHAI (4:17-22=I Esdras
2:25-29)

17. Instead of Artaxerxes I (cf. vs. 8), Josephus has Cambyses, whom he describes as "naturally bad." **Answer** represents a Persian word (*paitigāma*) which in modern Persian (*paigam*) means "message" (Scheftelowitz, *op. cit.,* I, 51). The abrupt **To Rehum** is characteristic of address to an inferior also in the Aramaic papyri (Cowley, *op. cit.,* No. 26, l. 1). **Peace** or "well-being" suggests the χαίρειν of Greek letters (cf. Acts 15:23; 23:26; Jas. 1:1) but it is also found alone in the papyri (*ibid.,* Nos. 39, 42, etc.), where it may be an abbreviation of the lengthy salutation, "The welfare of . . . may the god seek abundantly at all times" (*ibid.,* No. 30, ll. 1-2; No. 17, ll. 1-2; No. 21, l. 2, etc.).

18. Plainly read is rather "translated," since it is a technical term referring to extempore translation by a scribe, in the presence of the king, of material written in a foreign language into Persian, which the king could understand. Its Hebrew equivalent is in vs. 7. In Neh. 8:8 the term is used for translation from Hebrew to Aramaic (cf. Schaeder, *Iranische Beiträge I,* pp. 1-14). Since all versions, including the LXX, are confused by the term, its use here argues against fabrication of the letter in the late period and for the originality of the document containing it.

19-20. Search has been made implies search in the Babylonian files. Like the Assyrians, they must have kept full reports on political events in all areas of their

21 Give ye now commandment to cause these men to cease, and that this city be not builded, until *another* commandment shall be given from me.

22 Take heed now that ye fail not to do this: why should damage grow to the hurt of the kings?

23 ¶ Now when the copy of king Artaxerxes' letter *was* read before Rehum, and Shimshai the scribe, and their companions, they went up in haste to Jerusalem unto the Jews, and made them to cease by force and power.

24 Then ceased the work of the house of God which *is* at Jerusalem. So it ceased unto the second year of the reign of Darius king of Persia.

21 Therefore make a decree that these men be made to cease, and that this city be not rebuilt, until a decree is made by me.

22 And take care not to be slack in this matter; why should damage grow to the hurt of the king?"

23 Then, when the copy of King Artaxerx'es' letter was read before Rehum and Shim'shai the scribe and their associates, they went in haste to the Jews at Jerusalem and by force and power made them cease.

24 Then the work on the house of God which is in Jerusalem stopped; and it ceased until the second year of the reign of Darius king of Persia.

---

empire (cf. vs. 15; Waterman, *Royal Correspondence,* Part IV, pp. 23-24). **Ruled over all . . . beyond the river** is an unhistorical exaggeration since **Jerusalem** never approximated rule over all Palestine and Syria. The verse looks like an expression of Jewish nationalistic pride and as such may be a Jewish expansion of a more moderate statement. But Batten (*Ezra and Nehemiah,* pp. 178-79) suggests that the threat of a strong Judean king, such as is found in the cuneiform record of Hezekiah's strong resistance to Sennacherib (Luckenbill, *Ancient Records of Assyria and Babylonia,* II, 119-21, sec. 240) may have been sufficient to move a suspicious Persian ruler to such action.

21-22. Since only the king had the prerogative to do so (cf. 6:12), **make a decree** shows the men to be his representatives. **Until a decree is made by me,** lacking in I Esdras, may be a later addition, anticipating the granting of permission in Neh. 2:4-6. "The throne" would properly interpret **the kings** of the M.T.

(3) Work Stopped at Jerusalem (4:23-24=I Esdras 2:30)

23-24. Rehum's title (vss. 8, 9, 17) has been lost here as one MS, the LXX[L], and the Peshitta show. **By force and power** is, lit., "by arm and force." "Arm" is often a symbol of strength (Ezek. 31:17; Prov. 31:17; Dan. 11:15, 31). **Power** or "force" (חיל) is used for "army" in the Aramaic papyri. In I Esdras the text is interpreted, "with horsemen and a multitude in battle array," and Josephus does likewise. Rudolph (*op. cit.,* p. 44) plausibly suggests that whatever had been built in Jerusalem was then destroyed, leaving the desolation which caused Nehemiah's grief (Neh. 1:3). Vs. 24 is probably due to the Chronicler, who disturbed the original order of the Aramaic document (cf. Intro., p. 559) and then had to revert to the situation in vs. 5 in order to resume his narrative in ch. 5. The expression **king of Persia**, which he uses elsewhere (vss. 5, 7; 1:1-2, 8; 3:7; 7:1) supports this view. The word **then** which introduces the verse and relates it to the chronological sequence that precedes (Darius, vss. 2-3; Xerxes, vs. 6; and Artaxerxes, vss. 7-22), suggests that the Chronicler may have confused Darius I (522-486 B.C.) with Darius II (423-404 B.C.), which would be too late for the completion of the temple. Schaeder regards **then** as a reference to events in the days of Cyrus which he believes were originally in the Aramaic document but were omitted because the Chronicler had already dealt with them (1:1–4:4). Schaeder (*Iranische Beiträge* I, p. 23) suggests that **then** was copied unthinkingly, thus making a false chronology. This hypothesis cannot be proved. Rudolph (*op. cit.,* pp. 39-40) believes that the Chronicler who wrote the verse in Hebrew wrote "Thus" (כזאת) in Hebrew, which was corrupted to **then** when it was translated into Aramaic (אדין > באדין > בדין > כדן < כזאת).

5 Then the prophets, Haggai the prophet, and Zechariah the son of Iddo, prophesied unto the Jews that *were* in Judah and Jerusalem in the name of the God of Israel, *even* unto them.

2 Then rose up Zerubbabel the son of Shealtiel, and Jeshua the son of Jozadak, and began to build the house of God which *is* at Jerusalem: and with them *were* the prophets of God helping them.

5 Now the prophets, Hag′gai and Zecha-ri′ah the son of Iddo, prophesied to the Jews who were in Judah and Jerusalem, in the name of the God of Israel who was over them. 2 Then Zerub′babel the son of She-al′ti-el and Jeshua the son of Jo′zadak arose and began to rebuild the house of God which is in Jerusalem; and with them were the prophets of God, helping them.

---

e) Reign of Darius (5:1–6:22)

The story of the temple, interrupted at 4:5, is resumed in 5:1–6:18, part of the Aramaic document already encountered in 4:6-23. As the sequence of kings shows, 5:1–6:18 must have preceded 4:6-23 originally.

After brief reference to resumption of work on the temple under the stimulus of Haggai and Zechariah (5:1-2) the writer describes an official investigation of the Jewish activity in Jerusalem (5:3-5) and incorporates verbatim the official report to the king (5:6-17), which explains the situation the officials found (5:8) and gives a statement of the Jewish defense (5:11-16). The officials called for a check of Jewish claims and requested further instructions (5:17).

(1) The Temple Building Is Begun (5:1-2=I Esdras 6:1-2)

5:1-2. In Darius' second year (520 B.C.), after Haggai's first prophecy (Aug. 29, 520 B.C.; cf. Hag. 1:1), the work on the temple was resumed (Sept. 21, 520 B.C.; cf. Hag. 1:15). The date in Hag. 1:1 was doubtless the source of both that in Ezra 4:24*b* and I Esdras 6:1. The name **Haggai** is found frequently in the postexilic periods in the cuneiform records of Babylonia as well as in the Aramaic papyri. The paternity of **Haggai** is never given, but he is always called "the prophet" (Hag. 1:1, 12; 2:1, 10; cf. Ezra 6:14). The RSV wrongly follows I Esdras here in omitting the title. **Zechariah** ("God Has Remembered"), on the basis of Zech. 1:1, should be the "descendant" of **Iddo** the prophet rather than his **son** or "grandson." In cuneiform records of the period the third name in a paternal record usually refers to a distinguished ancestor whose name is proudly perpetuated. According to the Chronicler (II Chr. 13:22) "Iddo the prophet" was a person of distinction in the time of King Abijah (913-911/910 B.C.). Such abbreviation of genealogy is found elsewhere in the cases of Ezra (7:1; cf. I Chr. 6:14-15), Laban (Gen. 29:5; cf. Gen. 24:24), and Jehu (I Kings 19:16; II Kings 9:20; cf. II Kings 9:2, 14).

The God of Israel is found elsewhere several times, particularly in the Aramaic material (6:14; 7:15; I Chr. 5:26), but the Chronicler usually has "The LORD, the God of Israel" (cf. I Chr. 15:12, 14; 16:4, 36; etc.), which I Esdras and the LXX^A have here. **Even unto them:** The last word in vs. 1 dangles awkwardly, disconnected and meaningless. Its alternate translation, **who was over them,** makes good sense, although the ambiguous pronoun could mean either the Jews or the prophets.

For **Zerubbabel** and **Jeshua** see Exeg. on 2:2; 3:2. **Began to build** need not mean ignorance of the work of Sheshbazzar since he is mentioned in vs. 16. The Aramaic word here translated **began,** like later Greek ἤρξατο (ἤρξαντο), is often redundantly prefixed to a verb in narration without temporal significance (Gustaf Dalman, *The*

5:1–6:22. Prophetic Persistence Through Obstructions.—Resuming his story of the rebuilding of the temple that had been interrupted in 4:6, the Chronicler avails himself of further Aramaic source material bearing on the political legitimacy of the undertaking, as having the written sanction of a Persian king and his officials. In so doing he gives incidental recognition (5:1-2) to the actual movers in the whole enterprise, the prophets **Haggai and Zechariah.** The respective roles of the prophet and the layman in every constructive achievement, then

3 ¶ At the same time came to them Tatnai, governor on this side the river, and Shethar-boznai, and their companions, and said thus unto them, Who hath commanded you to build this house, and to make up this wall?	3 At the same time Tat′tenai the governor of the province Beyond the River and She′thar-boz′enai and their associates came to them and spoke to them thus, "Who gave you a decree to build this house and to

Words of Jesus, tr. D. M. Kay [Edinburgh: T. & T. Clark, 1909], pp. 26-28; Torrey, *Ezra Studies,* p. 51, note d, p. 189). But since apparently little evidence remained of the former work, which seems limited to substructure (vs. 16), Zerubbabel actually began again with a new substructure (3:10-11). **Rebuild** is more accurate. While **helping** could mean manual labor, it is probable that the prophetic "help" means moral support and encouragement (cf. 6:14). The same verb is used in the Aramaic version of the Behistun inscription in the sense of "support" in Darius' claim " (the God) Ahuramazda helped me" in battle (Cowley, *op. cit.,* pp. 251-59, ll. 2, 5, 13, 19, 28). Josephus, too, interpreted it as moral support, claiming that the prophets "urged them to take courage and not to be apprehensive of any untoward action by the Persians" (*Antiquities* XI. 4. 5).

(2) OFFICIAL INVESTIGATION OF THE BUILDING OF THE TEMPLE (5:3-5 = I Esdras 6:3-6)

The narrative of the investigation by officials of the Persian court was begun and the line of questioning was indicated, but when the writer realized that the story would be duplicated in the letter to follow (vss. 3-4; cf. vss. 9-10), he stopped abruptly and appended the letter itself (Rudolph, *op. cit.,* p. 51).

3. The date intended by **at the same time** cannot be determined closely, but the narrative suggests that it was soon after building was begun, when enough had been done to attract attention to the project. External walls had been raised (vs. 8) and work was progressing rapidly. Since the beginning of Darius' reign was marked by revolts throughout the empire, alert officials reported the seeds of sedition wherever they began to sprout. The tone of the letter suggests a routine visit by unbiased officials (vs. 17), but the Chronicler (4:5) and Josephus regard it as part of a deliberate campaign of harassment of the Jews, perpetrated by the Samaritans through persuasion or bribery of local officials. Josephus (*Antiquities* XI. 4. 4) departs from biblical tradition to reflect the natural concern of the official who inquired "who it was that had given them permission to build the temple in such a way that it was more like a fortress than a sanctuary."

Since Zerubbabel is not mentioned specifically in vss. 5, 9, and **the elders** are mentioned, some have dated the visit after the sudden disappearance of Zerubbabel. While it is true that he may have been included in the list of elders, silence regarding him in this situation is surprising, and may possibly be evidence for the date of this episode. A. T. Olmstead linked Zerubbabel's disappearance with a Jewish revolt timed to coincide with that of Nebuchadrezzar III and with Darius' Egyptian campaign ("Darius and His Behistun Inscription," *American Journal of Semitic Languages and Literatures,* LV [1938], 410-12; cf. the same author's *History of the Persian Empire,* pp. 138-40). But it has been shown that the revolts were past, and for Zerubbabel's disappearance one must "presuppose a comparatively peaceful situation in the Persian Empire," perhaps "immediately after the Jews resumed work on the temple, i.e., somewhere in the latter part of Darius' second year of reign" (519 B.C.; Arno Poebel, "The Duration of the Reign

and now, are shrewdly suggested in 5:2: the laymen **rose up**—and there was no enduring accomplishment until they did; but **with them were the prophets of God helping them.** There is likewise specific mention (vss. 14, 16) of the apparently abortive early attempt at rebuilding	under Cyrus, made by Sheshbazzar (1:8, 11), whom later tradition, as the Exeg. points out, either slurred over, or confused with Zerubbabel, or sought to erase altogether. Into most of the major accomplishments of history go such premature attempts and failures. Their final

4 Then said we unto them after this manner, What are the names of the men that make this building?

finish this structure?" 4 They^g also asked them this, "What are the names of the men

g Gk Syr: Aramaic *We*

---

of Smerdis, the Magian, and the Reigns of Nebuchadnezzar III and Nebuchadnezzar IV," *American Journal of Semitic Languages and Literatures,* LVI [1939], 145). Rudolph (*loc. cit.*), because he believes that the inner walls were erected and the temple almost completed, dates the incident to 517 B.C., closer to 515 B.C. when the temple was finished (6:15) than to its beginning in 520 B.C. But this hypothesis rests heavily upon a faulty interpretation of a word (אשרנא in vs. 3 below) which he translates as "paneled."

Tattenai, formerly identified with **Ushtannu** (Hystanes), the satrap over Babylonia and Trans-Euphratia (Bruno Meissner, "תתני," *Zeitschrift für die alttestamentliche Wissenschaft,* XVII [1897], 191-92), was apparently his subordinate. He is almost certainly mentioned in a business document of the time of Darius I as "the governor [NAM=*pakhat*] of Trans-Euphratia" (A. T. Olmstead, "Tattenai, Governor of 'Across the River,'" *Journal of Near Eastern Studies,* III [1944], 46). The title **governor** is thus quite elastic, sometimes indicating the great satrap, sometimes, as here, his subordinate, ruling but part of the satrapy, and at times even a more limited subordinate (Hag. 1:1) whose authority was confined to Judea, a part of Trans-Euphratia (cf. Abel, *Géographie de la Palestine,* II, 115, n. 3). Albrecht Alt would interpret the latter as simply "commissioner," insisting that the official had but temporary authority to complete a limited and specific task to which he was appointed ("Die Rolle Samarias bei der Entstehung des Judentums," *Festschrift Otto Procksch* [Leipzig: J. C. Hinrichs, 1934], pp. 23-24).

Shethar-bozenai need not be emended to Shatibarzana (cf. Rudolph, *op. cit.,* p. 46; cf. Cowley, *op. cit.,* pp. 11-12, No. 5, l. 16) since it would form a good Persian name (Shathrabujyāna; "Delivering the Kingdom"), which may also be found in the papyri (Raymond A. Bowman, "An Aramaic Journal Page," *The American Journal of Semitic Languages and Literatures,* LVIII [1941], 305, 312; col. C, l. 4). The second element of the name is found alone as an epithet in the Aramaic incantations (J. A. Montgomery, *Aramaic Incantation Texts from Nippur* [Philadelphia: University Museum, 1913], No. 40, ll. 17-18, cf. pp. 252-54). Like Shimshai (4:8), this official was probably a royal scribe. **Their companions** are identified as "the investigators" (vs. 6).

This wall is proved an incorrect translation by the several occurrences of the Aramaic word it represents (*'ushsharnâ*) in the papyri (Cowley, *op. cit.,* No. 26, ll. 5, 9, 21; No. 27, l. 18; No. 30, l. 11). There the term refers to materials required to repair a boat, to objects stolen from a temple, and to some material from a temple which could be burned. It has been recognized that the word "must be taken in a wide sense" (*ibid.,* p. 102). It has been well translated as "material" or "equipment" by Harry Torczyner who, however, finally wrongly identifies the word here in Ezra with the building itself ("Anmerkungen zu den Papyrusurkunden von Elephantine," *Orientalische Literaturzeitung,* XV [1912], 399). The Greek χορηγία, used by the LXX here and in vs. 9, seems appropriate for it can mean "supplies" (for war) or "apparatus" (for a banquet or for the stage). In Ezra it could refer either to prepared stones, beams, or other materials awaiting the builders, or to equipment or furnishings for the completed temple.

4. "We told them" of the ASV, appropriate in the letter that follows (vss. 7-17), is out of place in a narrative in the third person. **They also asked** is better but inexact, since the verb of the M.T. is **said.** Render with the LXX, Ethiopic, Peshitta versions and one

---

achievement is made possible by a creative combination of the initiative of men with the ripeness of the times and the conditions, under what 5:5 calls **the eye of their God**—a symbol of "providential watchfulness" (Exeg.). Such co-operation between different callings, and

between different generations, is energized by the religious faith that can continue to say alike of unfinished tasks from the past and of new beginnings for the future, **We are the servants of the God of heaven and earth** (5:11).

In chs. 5–6 the Chronicler is plainly concerned

5 But the eye of their God was upon the elders of the Jews, that they could not cause them to cease, till the matter came to Darius: and then they returned answer by letter concerning this *matter*.

6 ¶ The copy of the letter that Tatnai, governor on this side the river, and Shethar-boznai, and his companions the Apharsachites, which *were* on this side the river, sent unto Darius the king:

7 They sent a letter unto him, wherein was written thus; Unto Darius the king, all peace.

who are building this building?" 5 But the eye of their God was upon the elders of the Jews, and they did not stop them till a report should reach Darius and then answer be returned by letter concerning it.

6 The copy of the letter which Tat'tenai the governor of the province Beyond the River and She'thar-boz'enai and his associates the governors who were in the province Beyond the River sent to Darius the king;

7 they sent him a report, in which was written as follows: "To Darius the king, all

MS, "they said to them as follows." It is lacking in I Esdras and may be an addition from vs. 9 (so Meyer, *Entstehung des Judenthums*, p. 26; Hermann Guthe and L. W. Batten, *The Books of Ezra and Nehemiah* [Leipzig: J. C. Hinrichs, 1901; "The Sacred Books of the Old Testament"], p. 34; Rudolph, *op. cit.*, pp. 46-47). **What are the names?** Lit., "Who are they, the names?" an idiom found also in Judg. 13:17. The names, which may have included Zerubbabel and Jeshua, are nowhere preserved. After answering the first question (vs. 3), the names may have been forgotten as unimportant. More likely they were sent in a separate list. In I Esdras 6:12 it is said that the Jews were required to furnish such a list "in writing."

5. The eye of their God symbolized providential watchfulness (Pss. 33:18-19; 34:15-16). **The matter**, elsewhere translated "the decree" (6:14) is here **a report**, in the sense customary in Akkadian (cf. 4:8; Dan. 6:2). **The report** is the letter that follows (vss. 7-17). **The answer** (cf. 4:18, 23) is found in 6:6-12. **By letter** is implied by the narrative but has no counterpart in Aramaic.

(3) REPORT OF TATTENAI TO DARIUS (5:6-17=I Esdras 6:7-22)

6. Copy (cf. 4:11, 23) and **letter** (cf. 4:8, 11) are loan words from the Persian and Akkadian respectively. **Apharsachites** are not the governors (RSV); the latter renders "the rulers" (οἱ ἡγεμόνες) of I Esdras 6:7. Nor is the term a transcription of Greek ἔπαρχος, **governor** (Torrey, *Ezra Studies*, p. 174; contra W. F. Albright, "The Date and Personality of the Chronicler," *Journal of Biblical Literature*, XL [1921], 114). The LXX and Vulg. treat it incorrectly as a proper name. Herzfeld (*Zoroaster and His World*, I, 171) identified the **Apharsachites** with the "Apharsites" of 4:9. Eilers most plausibly identifies them with the Persian *frasaka*, "investigator," which is also implied by the "watcher" (*nawaṭir*) of the Ethiopic version (cf. Rudolph, *op. cit.*, p. 50).

7. A letter (cf. 4:17) is preferable to **a report** since it represents the Persian word used in 4:17. The **all** of **all peace** is unique in Aramaic epistolary salutation, but the word is attested by I Esdras 6:8 where, however, as "all things" it is transferred to the next sentence. The word translated **all** is really an adverb (J. A. Montgomery, "Adverbial *kúlla* in Biblical Aramaic and Hebrew," *Journal of the American Oriental Society*, XLIII [1923], 391-95). The expression resembles superficially the "Heartiest greetings" (πλειστα χαιρειν) or "Many greetings" (πολλα χαιρειν) sometimes found in Greek letters of Hellenistic Egypt. But it is probably a token abbreviation of a longer Aramaic greeting

to make full use of all Aramaic sources at his disposal, showing the political approval given by various Persian kings to the rebuilding of the temple. In ch. 6 he cites a memorandum of Cyrus to his officials, and another of instruction by Darius I (under whom the temple was

completed in 515 B.C.), promising both official sanction and financial support in the great task, in accordance with Persian policy in these matters. Either because he found the name of Artaxerxes interpolated in his texts, or because he himself was confused as to the Persian king

8 Be it known unto the king, that we went into the province of Judea, to the house of the great God, which is builded with great stones, and timber is laid in the walls, and this work goeth fast on, and prospereth in their hands.

9 Then asked we those elders, *and* said unto them thus, Who commanded you to build this house, and to make up these walls?

peace. 8 Be it known to the king that we went to the province of Judah, to the house of the great God. It is being built with huge stones, and timber is laid in the walls; this work goes on diligently and prospers in their hands. 9 Then we asked those elders and spoke to them thus, 'Who gave you a decree to build this house and to finish this

---

(cf. 4:17; 7:12) such as "The welfare (שלם) of ——— may the Gods altogether (כלא) seek abundantly at all times" (Cowley, *op. cit.*, p. 140, No. 41, l. 1). Since "and now," which usually marks the end of the salutation (cf. 4:12, 13, 17), is missing here, Bewer (*Der Text des Buches Ezra*, p. 58) regards the **all** as an early corruption of that expression.

8. For **be it known** see Exeg. on 4:12. **The province of Judea,** a subdivision of the satrapy of "Babylon and Trans-Euphratia," may represent such an administrative division as that over which Assyria formerly had appointed a "district ruler" (*ambêl-pakhati;* cf. Abel, *op. cit.*, II, 115).

I Esdras 6:8 has additional material, at least part of which apparently has been lost from the M.T. since some of the data is presupposed later (e.g., "those elders" in vs. 9). Therefore, after **the province of Judea,** read, "We found in the city of Jerusalem the elders of the Jews building . . . ," which must be genuine (cf. Guthe and Batten, *op. cit.,* p. 35; Bewer, *loc. cit.;* Rudolph, *loc. cit.*). The object of "building" is **the house.** Thus what is translated **to** is actually an Aramaic indicator of the object. **The great God** has long been regarded as strange for a Persian official and therefore evidence of Jewish composition. But as I Esdras 6:9 shows, **great** here modifies not **God** but **the house of . . . God.** Thus we read, "We went to the province of Judea [and we found, in the city of Jerusalem, the elders of the Jews building] the great house of God."

As the Greek versions show, **great stones** is certainly wrong. The LXX has "choice" for **great,** while I Esdras 6:9 has the double translation "polished and costly" (cf. I Kings 7:9-11) with no indication of size. The usual explanation, deriving **great** from "round," is forced and impossible (Batten, *Ezra and Nehemiah,* p. 140). The word (גלל) is now found in Aramaic also on a series of mortars and pestles of gray-green chert from Persepolis (E. F. Schmidt, *The Treasury of Persepolis* [Chicago: University of Chicago Press, 1939], pp. 61-62 and Fig. 41) which bear in part the inscription "[So and so] made this mortar of *gll*" (עבד הון זנה זי גלל). It is encountered also in a Mandaic incantation text, where Cyrus H. Gordon translates it as "unsplit stone" (גלאלא) ("Aramaic and Mandaic Magical Bowls," *Archiv Orientalni,* IX [1937], pp. 96-97 and Pl. XII, Bowl M, l. 20). Although its etymology remains uncertain, the context suggests some kind of stone or "stone" in general. The Semitic **stones** here and in 6:4 may then be an explanatory gloss to the foreign word.

Timber is laid in the walls (cf. 6:4) is too ambiguous for identifying the type of construction. Timber with brick is found even in early times in Egypt, Babylonia, and Greece, but stone and timber, a weak combination, is more rare. Cretan houses of

---

under whom the task was finished, he ascribes the latter document to Artaxerxes. Complicated as are these textual and chronological problems, they suggest the difficulties against which the returning exiles labored, and the importance to them of official support against the opposition of their neighbors and the paucity of their own resources, thus confirming the picture of poverty

and apathy given in the books of Haggai and Zechariah. More important than official support in overcoming these obstacles was the indomitable Hebrew faith reflected in 6:12, 22. The God whom they served would **overthrow** their enemies, provide new allies, and give them strength of hand and joy of heart for **the work of the house of God, the God of Israel.**

10 We asked their names also, to certify thee, that we might write the names of the men that *were* the chief of them.

11 And thus they returned us answer, saying, We are the servants of the God of heaven and earth, and build the house that was builded these many years ago, which a great king of Israel builded and set up.

12 But after that our fathers had provoked the God of heaven unto wrath, he gave them into the hand of Nebuchadnezzar the king of Babylon, the Chaldean, who destroyed this house, and carried the people away into Babylon.

13 But in the first year of Cyrus the king of Babylon, *the same* king Cyrus made a decree to build this house of God.

structure?' 10 We also asked them their names, for your information, that we might write down the names of the men at their head. 11 And this was their reply to us: 'We are the servants of the God of heaven and earth, and we are rebuilding the house that was built many years ago, which a great king of Israel built and finished. 12 But because our fathers had angered the God of heaven, he gave them into the hand of Nebuchadnez'zar king of Babylon, the Chalde'an, who destroyed this house and carried away the people to Babylonia. 13 However in the first year of Cyrus king of Babylon, Cyrus the king made a decree that this

masonry had great wooden beams tying in the stone both horizontally and vertically (J. D. S. Pendlebury, *The Archaeology of Crete* [London: Methuen & Co., 1939], pp. 98, 132, 188; and Pls. XXI, 1; XXIX; XXX, 1). But this is not the usual conception of the Jewish temple and is improbable. Stone and wood were used together in the walls of the temple court (cf. I Kings 6:36; 7:12) but scarcely in the walls of the temple itself. Rudolph, thinking of his interpretation in vs. 3, regards the wood as paneling for the inner walls (cf. I Kings 6:15), but this, too, is improbable. The reference is probably to the fixing of cedar beams into and across the walls to support the roof (cf. I Kings 6:9). **Goeth fast on** or **goes on diligently** interprets a Persian word (Old Persian *usprna*) which Schaeder identifies (in a personal communication to Rudolph, *loc. cit.*) as "completely." Read here, "And that work is being done thoroughly" (cf. 6:8, 12-13; 7:17, 21, 26).

11-17. This long Jewish answer to the first question of the officials (vss. 3, 9), a long-range historical review, was a favorite device of Jewish writers (cf. Neh. 9:6-37). A more direct answer could have been given, but this type of answer is certainly more effective. Because of its apologetic tone and because its course of history is that stressed by the Chronicler, many conclude that the Chronicler has worked it over or may have even written it himself. But since the explanation is a Jewish defense, such as might be expected under the circumstances, there seems no good reason to challenge its validity as an actual scribal record of the Jewish answer.

11. Answer, here used of oral response, is the same Persian word elsewhere used of a "letter" (4:17; 5:7). The **great king,** of course, was Solomon (I Kings 5:1–7:51).

12. Angered or **provoked . . . unto wrath** implies very violent anger, for the verb, meaning "to tremble violently," is also used of the movement of earthquake. When the people ignored or rejected an agreement made between their fathers and God (cf. Jer. 7:17-20; 11:1-12), it was believed that God need no longer defend Israel but could become their vengeful enemy (II Chr. 36:14-16). **Gave them** expresses the belief that God could and did use foreign people as instruments for the punishment of Israel (cf. 1:2; Judg. 2:13-15; 4:1-2; 6:1; etc.). Nebuchadrezzar II (604-562 B.C.) besieged and destroyed Jerusalem in 586 B.C. and carried off many Jews to Babylon (Jer. 39:1-18; II Kings 24:1–25:30). **Chaldean** indicates the tribal groups from which Nebuchadrezzar descended; not of the line of old Babylonian kings but of a nomadic tribe that settled at the headwaters of the Persian Gulf about the tenth century B.C. and became the Neo-Babylonian rulers after the decline and fall of Assyria.

13. With this verse the narrative reaches the point at which 1:1 begins. If the Chronicler were author, we should expect a reference to the return from Babylon, one

14 And the vessels also of gold and silver of the house of God, which Nebuchadnezzar took out of the temple that *was* in Jerusalem, and brought them into the temple of Babylon, those did Cyrus the king take out of the temple of Babylon, and they were delivered unto *one*, whose name *was* Sheshbazzar, whom he had made governor;

15 And said unto him, take these vessels, go, carry them into the temple that *is* in Jerusalem, and let the house of God be builded in his place.

16 Then came the same Sheshbazzar, *and* laid the foundation of the house of God

house of God should be rebuilt. 14 And the gold and silver vessels of the house of God, which Nebuchadnez'zar had taken out of the temple that was in Jerusalem and brought into the temple of Babylon, these Cyrus the king took out of the temple of Babylon, and they were delivered to one whose name was Shesh-baz'zar, whom he had made governor; 15 and he said to him, "Take these vessels, go and put them in the temple which is in Jerusalem, and let the house of God be rebuilt on its site." 16 Then this Shesh-baz'zar came and laid the founda-

---

of his favorite themes. **King of Babylon** (cf. 1:1) is corrected to "king of Persia" in the Peshitta, but it is justified in I Esdras by the explanation "the first year that Cyrus reigned over the country of Babylon." For the **decree** cf. 1:2-4; 6:3-5.

14. For **vessels** see 1:7-11; 6:5; II Kings 25:13-17. The **temple of Babylon**, "his own temple" in I Esdras 6:18, was Esagila, of which Nebuchadrezzar calls himself "patron." Herodotus (*History* I, 181-83) describes some of the glories of that temple (cf. G. R. Tabouis, *Nebuchadnezzar* [New York: McGraw Hill Book Co., 1931], pp. 29 ff.; Vincent Scheil and M. Dieulafoy, *Esagil ou le Temple de Bêl-Marduk à Babylone* [Paris: Imprimerie Nationale, 1913]. **Whose name was Sheshbazzar** (cf. 1:8) is, lit., Sheshbazzar, his name." The expression "his name" is good Persian and must not be omitted with the Greek versions, H. L. Strack (*Grammatik des biblisch Aramäischen* [4th ed.; Leipzig: J. C. Hinrichs, 1905], p. 3*, note s), and Bewer (*op. cit.,* p. 60) as an accidental anticipation of the **whom he had made,** which has the same consonantal structure (שמה). "His name" also occurs in the Aramaic copy of the Behistun Inscription after proper names where the Old Persian text has *nāma,* and also in several other papyri (Cowley, *op. cit.,* Nos. 28, 33, 66:1, and the Ahiqar Papyrus; cf. Dan. 2:26; 4:8, 19; Antoine Meillet, *Grammaire du Vieux-Perse,* ed. E. Benveniste [Paris: É. Champion, 1931], p. 179; E. L. Johnson, *Historical Grammar of the Ancient Persian Language* [New York: American Book Co., 1917], p. 234, sec. 596). In 1:8 **Sheshbazzar** was simply "prince of Judah." His title, here translated **governor,** is an ambiguous one (cf. Exeg. on vs. 3). Like Zerubbabel (Hag. 1:1) and Nehemiah (Neh. 5:14), he would be ranked below Tattenai (Ezra 5:3). Possibly the title here was equivalent to the later Greek ethnarch. Others posit for him more limited authority, temporary assignment to a specific task (cf. vs. 3) and some render "deputy" (cf. Kurt Galling, *Syrien in der Politik der Achaemeniden* [Leipzig: J. C. Hinrichs, 1937; "Der Alte Orient"], p. 32; Rudolph, *op cit.,* pp. 62, 64).

15. The usual interpretation has a contradiction between the two parts of the verse, the first half presumes a standing temple while the second permits the building of one. Batten (*op. cit.,* pp. 137-38) omits reference to **the temple,** and implies storage in Jerusalem in some temporary place. The word translated **temple** here and in vs. 14 may also be translated "palace" (cf. 4:3; Dan. 4:29; 5:5; 6:18). Bewer (*loc. cit.*) therefore avoids the contradiction by translating "palace," implying the governor's palace. Rudolph (*op. cit.,* p. 52) objects, but his solution through an explicatory conjunction ("it, namely the House of God, shall be built") is implausible and unsatisfactory. It is probable that **the temple** here anticipates the building of such a structure. The same word, **place** or **site,** is used in an Aramaic papyrus for the site of the former Jewish temple in Egypt on which a new one was to be built (Cowley, *op. cit.,* No. 32, l. 8).

16. Laid the foundation involves Sheshbazzar in an act elsewhere assigned to Zerubbabel (4:12). Here men of the time of Zerubbabel refer to Sheshbazzar as someone who lived some time before. Tradition of the return and attempt at reconstruction under

which *is* in Jerusalem: and since that time even until now hath it been in building, and *yet* it is not finished.

17 Now therefore, if *it seem* good to the king, let there be search made in the king's treasure house, which *is* there at Babylon, whether it be *so*, that a decree was made of Cyrus the king to build this house of God at Jerusalem, and let the king send his pleasure to us concerning this matter.

6 Then Darius the king made a decree, and search was made in the house of the rolls, where the treasures were laid up in Babylon.

tions of the house of God which is in Jerusalem; and from that time until now it has been in building, and it is not yet finished.'

17 Therefore, if it seem good to the king, let search be made in the royal archives there in Babylon, to see whether a decree was issued by Cyrus the king for the rebuilding of this house of God in Jerusalem. And let the king send us his pleasure in this matter."

6 Then Darius the king made a decree, and search was made in Babylonia, in the house of the archives where the docu-

Sheshbazzar persisted and could not be ignored, even though, for sentimental as well as historical reasons, Zerubbabel was associated with the building of the second temple. The persistent memory of an earlier attempt at building embarrassed later generations who could not explain the failure of so holy a mission, and it confused historians of later times who tried to record the history of the temple. Sheshbazzar's acts were first slurred over, then deliberately identified with those of Zerubbabel. Deliberate attempts were made in ancient times to erase Sheshbazzar from Jewish history, and such efforts have continued down to our own day. But it is likely that a relatively small but enthusiastic group returned in the time of Cyrus and also that an attempt at building the temple was made. Conditions were even more unfavorable then than in the time of Haggai, and the crude beginning was abortive. About eighteen years later traces of the effort were no longer discernible and a new beginning had to be made.

For **foundation** see Exeg. on 4:12. Not **laid** but "gave" is the verb used here (cf. 4:12). Guthe and Batten (*op. cit.*, p. 63) see Persian influence here, since Old Persian *dâ* means both "give" and "make," and in trilingual inscriptions Babylonian "give" (*nadânu*) has the same significance, presumably under Persian influence. Such use of "give" is also found in the Aramaic papyri (Cowley, *op. cit.*, No. 81, l. 111; Ahiqar, l. 170).

17. With vs. 16 the Jewish account is finished. The transition to the officials' own request is marked by **Now, therefore** or **Therefore**—literally the same "and now" which elsewhere separated the salutation from the body of the letter (4:8, 10, 11). **If it seem good** is a characteristic deferential statement used in correspondence of the Persian period when subordinates ventured to make suggestions or petitions to their superiors. Similar usage is found in the papyri (Cowley, *op. cit.*, No. 27, ll. 19, 21, 22; No. 30, l. 23a; No. 31, l. 22. The **treasure house** is, lit., "the house of the treasures." **The royal archives** reflects the translation of I Esdras 6:21. No archival rooms have yet been found at Babylon, but they must have been similar to those excavated at the treasury at Persepolis. There documents were deposited in several rooms adjacent to the Court of Reception. Nearly eight hundred clay tablets were found in a tablet room, while in the papyrus and parchment room nearby only a few bits of charred cloth and some clay labels (*bullae*) bearing the seals of Darius and Xerxes bore witness to the very hot fire that had destroyed the flammable contents of the room at the burning of Persepolis (Schmidt, *Treasury of Persepolis*, pp. 33-37, Fig. 11). **Babylon** would be a natural place to look for early records of Cyrus. It was there that Hormuzd Rassam found the famous and valuable Cyrus Cylinder now in the British Museum (cf. O. E. Hagen, "Keilschrifturkunden zur Geschichte des Königs Cyrus," *Beiträge zur Assyriologie*, II [1891-93], 205).

(4) ANSWER OF DARIUS (6:1-12=I Esdras 6:23-34)

The requested search for Cyrus' edict (5:17) is first described (vss. 1-2) and its substance is quoted (vss. 3-5) before Darius' own instructions to his officers are given.

2 And there was found at Achmetha, in the palace that *is* in the province of the Medes, a roll, and therein *was* a record thus written:

3 In the first year of Cyrus the king, *the same* Cyrus the king made a decree *concerning* the house of God at Jerusalem, Let

ments were stored. 2 And in Ecbat'ana, the capital which is in the province of Media, a scroll was found on which this was written: "A record. 3 In the first year of Cyrus the

His orders grant the Jews permission to build the temple without molestation and provide for its support when it is finally completed (vss. 6-12). As a result of the king's assistance the temple was finished (vss. 14-15) and dedicated (vss. 16-18). The Chronicler then appended a description of the Passover and the feast of Unleavened Bread, which fell due shortly after the dedication of the building (vss. 19-22).

6:1-2. Then means when the report (5:7-17) was received at the Persian court. Instead of **made a decree** one expects an informal "gave an order" here, but the Persian king used only the decree in his administration. **House of the rolls** is, lit., "house of letters" or "house of documents." Josephus and I Esdras interpret it as **archives.** Since such rooms for documents were found in association with the treasury at Persepolis (cf. 5:17) it is not necessary to transpose the text to read "the storeroom where the documents were stored" (Julius Wellhausen, "Die Rückkehr der Juden aus dem babylonischen Exil," *Nachrichten von der königliche Gesellschaft der Wissenschaft zu Göttingen* [1895], p. 176; Torrey, *Ezra Studies,* p. 192; Rudolph, *op. cit.,* p. 54), and we can retain with the M.T., **where the treasures were laid up.** Although search may have been made **in Babylon,** as had been suggested (5:17), the edict was actually found at **Ecbatana** (modern Hamadân), the former capital of Media which, because of its elevation and pleasant climate, became the summer resort of the Persian kings. Cyrus spent two summer months in **Ecbatana,** three spring months in Susa, and the rest of the year at Babylon (Xenophon *Cyropaedia* VIII. 6. 22; Strabo *Geography* XI. 13. 1). Shortly after his accession Cyrus retired to Ecbatana (539-538 B.C.), leaving the government at Babylon first to his general Gobryas and later to Crown Prince Cambyses (cf. Nabonidus Chronicle, col. III, ll. 24 ff. in Sidney Smith, *Babylonian Historical Texts,* p. 118; Olmstead, *History of the Persian Empire,* p. 57). Read neither **palace** nor **capital** to designate **Ecbatana** but translate "fortress" (Akkadian *birtu*) as descriptive of a fortified city. Such usage is regular in the Aramaic papyri of the Persian period; in the Behistun Inscription the word is used to translate Old Persian "stronghold" (*didā;* Cowley, *op. cit.,* Behistun Inscription, ll. 77-78). Ecbatana was a great fortress, as classical and other writers testify (Herodotus *History* I. 98; Judith 1:2-4; cf. Zend-Avesta, the second fargard of the Vendidad Jemshid). Since the record was probably a single sheet of parchment or papyrus (Bowman, "Aramaeans, Aramaic, and the Bible," p. 77), **a roll** is preferable to **a scroll,** which suggests something more formal and elaborate.

3-5. (Cf. 5:13-15.) Both 5:13-15 and 6:3-5 deal with the same situation; the former as narrative, the latter as prescription. Strong resemblances have led some to regard 6:3-5 as a corruption of 5:13-15, so that 6:3-5 might be emended on the basis of 5:13-15. Thus 6:4 has been excised because it was not in the other passage, and the text of 5:15*b* has been substituted for 6:5*b* by some (cf. Batten, *op. cit.,* pp. 143-44). But 5:15*b* seems to be superfluous, and 6:5*b* is quite appropriate in its present context (cf. Bewer, *op. cit.,* p. 62, n. 1). Since Aramaic tends toward stereotyped forms of expression, in the same situation some identical vocabulary and word order might be expected. Furthermore, **the first year of Cyrus** (cf. 1:1) and **Cyrus the king . . . made a decree** quote Tattenai's letter (5:13), just as an Aramaic memorandum later reflects passages in the official letter to which it responds (Cowley, *op. cit.,* cf. No. 32 with No. 30). Bickerman contends that 6:3-5 represents a written document in contrast to the oral heraldic proclamation in 1:1-4 (cf. 1:1). Plausible is the suggestion that 6:3-5 is not a formal decree but the abstraction of relevant portions of a more extensive document which may have been

the house be builded, the place where they offered sacrifices, and let the foundations thereof be strongly laid; the height thereof threescore cubits, *and* the breadth thereof threescore cubits;	king, Cyrus the king issued a decree: Concerning the house of God at Jerusalem, let the house be rebuilt, the place where sacrifices are offered and burnt offerings are brought; its height shall be sixty cubits and its breadth sixty cubits, 4 with three courses of great stones and one course of timber; let the cost be paid from the royal treasury.
4 *With* three rows of great stones, and a row of new timber: and let the expenses be given out of the king's house:	

concerned with permission for rebuilding the temples of other gods also (Galling, *op. cit.*, p. 31; Cyrus Cylinder, ll. 30-36; Sidney Smith, *op. cit.*, p. 91, col. 6, l. 18). It has been supposed that the builders in the time of Darius had either the edict or an abstract of it, apparently as part of the temple archives (Rudolph, *op. cit.*, p. 53). **Record** (vs. 2), lit., "memorandum," favors the idea of abstraction of data from a more extensive document. A similar memorandum in the Aramaic papyri deals with official permission to rebuild the Jewish temple in Egypt (Cowley, *op. cit.*, pp. 122-24, No. 32), and the same word "memorandum" is found frequently on the reverse of the papyri bearing the Behistun Inscription (*ibid.*, No. 61, ll. 1, 10; No. 63, ll. 10, 12, 14; No. 68, l. 2).

3. Several MSS and the versions show the translation "the house of God which is in Jerusalem" (cf. vs. 12; 4:24; 5:2, 16); cf. the statement in the papyri, "the temple of Yahu the God which is in the fortress Yeb" (*ibid.*, No. 30, l. 6). Such a reference to the temple here appears to be a superscription, possibly to distinguish the Jerusalem grant from others which may have been in the same document. The designation **the place where sacrifices are offered** suggests the official Persian description of the Jewish temple in Egypt as "the house of the sacrificial altar" (*ibid.*, No. 32, ll. 3-4).

Because the verb means not **laid** but **brought,** there have been many attempts to emend the word translated **foundations** (*ushshu* as in 4:12). It has been altered to "his fire offerings" (Paul Haupt in Guthe and Batten, *op. cit.*, p. 36) or **burnt offerings** (Torrey, *Ezra Studies,* p. 192). In the present context, however, not **offerings** but some transition to the following building instructions is expected. The architectural term **foundations,** as "substructure," suits the present context and needs no emendation. As "let them carry," the verb might refer to carrying the fill for the substructure. If "carry" could have the sense of "bear" or "support," as in English, **foundations** could be the subject, connected with the dimensions of the building: "And its substructures shall support its height," etc. Unfortunately since such use is not attested, the problem remains unsolved.

A dimension is lacking in the specifications. Data about Solomon's temple, the pattern here, shows that due to the many references to **cubits,** a scribe has omitted some Hebrew text, including the height of the building, which is thirty cubits in I Kings 6:2. The **sixty** now attached to **its height** is the missing measure of length (cf. I Kings 6:2; II Chr. 3:3; see Rudolph, *op. cit.*, pp. 54-55). The **breadth** measure has been assimilated to the previous **sixty** and should be "twenty" as the Peshitta shows (cf. I Kings 6:2; II Chr. 3:3; Ezek. 41:2). Since the **cubit** varied in length, the size of the building cannot be determined. The Jewish **cubit** was about 17.6 inches but Ezek. 41:8 mentions a "great cubit," apparently the royal cubit, described as "a cubit and a handbreadth" (about 20.57 inches at Jerusalem), which must have been used for such a building.

4. **Courses** is now attested as an Akkadian word (*nadbak*) in a tablet of the time of Nebuchadrezzar, in which a foreman of bricklayers specifies the number of bricks in each **course** in the construction of a palace wall (H. F. Lutz, *Neo-Babylonian Administration Documents from Erech* [Berkeley: University of California Press, 1927], p. 74, No. 82, ll. 3, 11). As in 5:8, **great stones** is incorrect. Instead of **new timber,** read with the LXX^AB and two MSS **one course of timber** (cf. I Kings 6:36; 7:12). The specifications are for the walls of the temple court and must not refer to the temple walls, which apparently had no binding timbers (cf. 5:8).

5 And also let the golden and silver vessels of the house of God, which Nebuchadnezzar took forth out of the temple which *is* at Jerusalem, and brought unto Babylon, be restored, and brought again unto the temple which *is* at Jerusalem, *every one* to his place, and place *them* in the house of God.

6 Now *therefore,* Tatnai, governor beyond the river, Shethar-boznai, and your companions the Apharsachites, which *are* beyond the river, be ye far from thence:

7 Let the work of this house of God alone; let the governor of the Jews and the elders of the Jews build this house of God in his place.

---

5 And also let the gold and silver vessels of the house of God, which Nebuchadnez′zar took out of the temple that is in Jerusalem and brought to Babylon, be restored and brought back to the temple which is in Jerusalem, each to its place; you shall put them in the house of God."

6 "Now therefore, Tat′tenai, governor of the province Beyond the River, She′thar-boz′enai, and your associates the governors who are in the province Beyond the River, keep away; 7 let the work on this house of God alone; let the governor of the Jews and the elders of the Jews rebuild this house

---

5. It was expected that the temple vessels taken by the Babylonians would be restored to Jerusalem (cf. Jer. 27:21-22), and postexilic Jews believed that one of the first acts of Cyrus after his capture of Babylonia was their return (cf. 1:7-11; 5:14-15). Since the subject is the **vessels,** the words **and also let . . . be . . . brought,** lit., "and let it go," are awkward. But it is unnecessary to make the verb plural to agree with the subject from which it is so far separated (Ehrlich, *Randglossen zur hebräischen Bibel,* VII, 168; contra Eduard König, *Historisch-comparative Syntax der hebräischen Sprache* [Leipzig: J. C. Hinrichs, 1897], sec. 348*t*; cf. Rudolph, *op. cit.,* p. 56). It may be translated according to its sense as "and let it [all] come . . ." (Torrey, *Ezra Studies,* p. 193). **Every one to his place,** impossible here, is perhaps an intrusion under the influence of "upon its place" in 5:15. **And place them** includes an object not in the M.T. which has "you shall lay down." The best sense is obtained by emending the text to read, "And let it all be caused to be deposited . . ." (*ibid.*). Such emendation is favored by the fact that the verb is translated passively in the versions and the result (וינחת) has some graphic similarity to the present text (ותחת).

6-12. With **now** in vs. 6 attention shifts abruptly to Darius' answer to the officials (cf. 5:6) who had asked for instructions (5:17). Such a sharp transition, without formal epistolary introduction, suggests that a portion of the text is missing between vs. 5 and vs. 6. **Now,** here as elsewhere (cf. 4:8, 10; 5:17), seems to mark a transition, a shift from reference to Cyrus' edict to Darius' own order based on the edict. But the connection between vs. 2 and vs. 3 is too close and smooth to conjecture that the salutation and part of the letter ever stood there. Josephus, too, felt the need for some introduction here, and he supplied a covering letter for the Cyrus edict, but there is nothing in the M.T. or in I Esdras to support his informal, rather Hellenistic note (*Antiquities* XI. 4. 7). It is proposed to introduce something like "Thereupon Darius wrote to Tattenai . . ." (cf. Rudolph, *op. cit.,* p. 48), but there is no present means for recovering the text which was lost so early that none of the versions preserve a trace of it.

6. With **now** Darius begins to explain "his pleasure" (5:17) about the Jewish temple. Since his throne was still somewhat uncertain at the beginning of his reign, he found it expedient to confirm Cyrus' edict and thereby to gain the good will of the Jews who could form for him a buffer against Egypt (Olmstead, *History of the Persian Empire,* pp. 140-41). In the Gadatas inscription, too, in his "policy towards the gods" Darius is motivated by the concern of his "forefathers towards the god . . ." (Botsford and Sihler, *Hellenic Civilization,* p. 162).

7. This verse is better translated, "Let the governor of the Jews and the elders of the Jews alone for the work of that house of God; and let them build that house of God upon its site" (cf. Vulg.; Torrey, *Ezra Studies,* p. 193, note n). **The governor,** a gloss

8 Moreover I make a decree what ye shall do to the elders of these Jews for the building of this house of God: that of the king's goods, *even* of the tribute beyond the river, forthwith expenses be given unto these men, that they be not hindered.

9 And that which they have need of, both young bullocks, and rams, and lambs, for the burnt offerings of the God of heaven, wheat, salt, wine, and oil, according to the

of God on its site. **8** Moreover I make a decree regarding what you shall do for these elders of the Jews for the rebuilding of this house of God; the cost is to be paid to these men in full and without delay from the royal revenue, the tribute of the province from Beyond the River. **9** And whatever is needed — young bulls, rams, or sheep for

---

for agreement with 5:3, is responsible for the further expansion to "Zerubbabel, the servant of the Lord" in I Esdras 6:27. As might be expected of a distant king, the Aramaic text has "that house of God" instead of **this.**

8. In the ambiguous text here, **do to the elders** could mean, as in I Esdras 6:27-28, "work along with the elders," but such help would have been refused (cf. 4:2-3). **Do for these elders** is less likely than "do about those elders." As in vs. 7 the pronouns indicate remote objects, "those elders," "that house," and "those men." Vs. 8*b* is introduced by an explicative conjunction, "namely."

Reaffirming Cyrus' edict (6:4), Darius orders the **expenses** of building withheld from **the royal revenue**—lit., from **the king's goods**—collected by his agents in Trans-Euphratia. Since it represents a Persian word for "thoroughly" (cf. 5:8), **in full** is better than **forthwith. That they be not hindered,** presumably referring to the workmen, reflects the LXX and Peshitta, but the M.T. has "that it may not be made to stop," which refers to payments for the work. "Without stopping" is therefore more accurate than **without delay.**

The verse has been ridiculed as unauthentic because Hag. 2:3; Zech. 4:7-10 reflect no use of such funds (Jahn, *Esra [A und B] und Nehemja,* p. 54; Hölscher, *Esra und Nehemia,* II, 514), but it would be difficult to collect the grant from hostile officials far from the court even if it were made (cf. Batten, *Ezra and Nehemiah,* p. 146; Rudolph, *op. cit.,* pp. 56-57). Furthermore, since the work was not stopped by the officers (cf. 5:8), it is probable that before any grant could be collected the plans and construction would be too far advanced to admit any major changes.

9-10. Part of the expenses of the cult, too, were to be paid by the king. On the assumption that a Persian king would not be likely to make such concessions and would be uninterested in such details of Jewish cult, these verses have been regarded as unhistorical forgeries. But the Persepolis treasury texts show just such royal concern for detail (cf. Cameron, *Persepolis Treasury Tablets,* pp. 12-13). Such interest is known to have extended to the cult of subject peoples. Cyrus was concerned with Babylonian gods and temples (cf. 1:2-3). Cambyses was personally concerned about Egyptian temples and the distribution of supplies for their sacrifices (cf. Olmstead, *History of the Persian Empire,* p. 91; Wilhelm Spiegelberg, ed., *Die sogennante demotische Chronik* [Leipzig: J. C. Hinrichs, 1914], pp. 32-33). He showed special concern for the Jewish temple in Egypt (Cowley, *Aramaic Papyri,* p. 113, No. 30, ll. 13-14). Darius I also supported a foreign god favored by his predecessors and reproved an official for taxing a religious community and for making them cultivate unhallowed ground (cf. Botsford and Sihler, *op. cit.,* p. 162). Darius II later sent to Egypt detailed orders for the keeping of the Jewish festival of Unleavened Bread (and Passover?) and, in granting permission to rebuild the Jewish temple in Egypt, the types of sacrifice permitted were specified (Cowley, *op. cit.,* No. 21 and No. 32).

It may be deduced from vs. 10 that not all sacrifices but only the daily burnt offerings and their supplements which were connected with prayers for the royal house were supplied (Bertholet, *Esra und Nehemia,* p. 27; Rudolph, *op. cit.,* pp. 58-59). Cyrus, too, expected daily intercession with the Babylonian gods he had re-established (Cyrus

appointment of the priests which *are* at Jerusalem, let it be given them day by day without fail:

10 That they may offer sacrifices of sweet savors unto the God of heaven, and pray for the life of the king, and of his sons.

11 Also I have made a decree, that whosoever shall alter this word, let timber be pulled down from his house, and being set up, let him be hanged thereon; and let his house be made a dunghill for this.

burnt offerings to the God of heaven, wheat, salt, wine, or oil, as the priests at Jerusalem require — let that be given to them day by day without fail, 10 that they may offer pleasing sacrifices to the God of heaven, and pray for the life of the king and his sons. 11 Also I make a decree that if anyone alters this edict, a beam shall be pulled out of his house, and he shall be impaled upon it, and his house shall be made a

---

Cylinder, ll. 34-36). Later Jews in Egypt similarly offered to pray and sacrifice on behalf of a Persian official who might help with the restoration of their temple (Cowley, *op. cit.,* p. 114, No. 30, ll. 25-28).

Thus the substance of vss. 9-10 is historically probable, but they can also be challenged on other grounds. The accuracy of terminology and the knowledge of Jewish practices there demonstrated may be explained as due to the influence of a Jewish secretary, like the later Ezra, as advisor to the royal court (Rudolph, *op. cit.,* pp. 57-58). But the verses are just such an expansion as the Chronicler might make in the interest of the cultus and there are definite indications of the Chronicler's literary style. The sacrifices are listed in an order favored by the Chronicler (I Chr. 29:21; II Chr. 29:21, 32; Ezra 6:17; 7:22; 8:35) and the expression **day by day** is such as he favors (I Chr. 12:22; 16:23; II Chr. 8:13; 24:11; 30:21). The verses are best explained as an expansion by the Chronicler (cf. Torrey, *Composition,* p. 10; *Ezra Studies,* p. 158).

Wheat was offered as fine flour, either alone (Lev. 5:11-13), mixed as dough (Lev. 2:1-3), or as cakes (Lev. 2:4 ff.). Josephus here specifies "fine flour." **Salt** (cf. 7:22) was offered with all oblations (Lev. 2:13; Mark 9:49), and meal offerings are particularly specified as needing **salt** seasoning (Lev. 2:13). **Wine** was presented as a libation with every public burnt offering (Exod. 29:40-41; Lev. 23:13, 18, 37; Num. 15:24; etc.). It was poured from a chalice to the base of the altar (Ecclus. 50:15; cf. Josephus *Antiquities* III. 9. 4). Olive **oil** figured prominently in the meal offering. **Sweet savors,** as the odor of sacrifice, here means the regular **pleasing sacrifices** (cf. Exod. 29:18, 25; Lev. 1:9, 13, 17; etc.).

11-12. Severe penalties were prescribed for those who violated the royal decree. Neither **hanged** nor "fastened" (ASV) reflects the violence of the act. The M.T. has, lit., "let a timber be pulled away from his house and, when erected, let him be struck upon it." The victim was **impaled** on the sharpened timber. It was thrust into the body either just below the ribs or between the legs (cf. W. D. Birch and T. G. Pinches, *The Bronze Ornaments of the Palace Gates of Balawat* [London: Society of Biblical Archaeology, 1902], pp. 2*b*, 4*b*, 10*a*; Pls. B2, D4, J3). The Assyrians used impalement to punish only the most abhorrent crimes (Olmstead, *History of Assyria,* pp. 87, 112, 308, 551; Bruno Meissner, *Babylonien und Assyrien* [Heidelberg: C. Winter, 1920], I, 112), and Herodotus (*History* III. 159) calls it a Persian practice also. The **house** of the offender was pulled down (cf. Dan. 2:5; 3:29) and the ruin was made into a **dunghill** or public privy (II Kings 10:27; J. A. Montgomery, *A Critical and Exegetical Commentary on the Book of Daniel* [New York: Charles Scribner's Sons, 1927; "International Critical Commentary"], pp. 148-49).

Warnings of punishment for violation of royal decree are not unusual. Unlike the Daniel passages, vs. 12 promises additional punishment for future kings or people who would change the decree favoring the temple. The KJV wrongly makes **alter** (vs. 12) refer to the temple, but the implied object of the verb, as vs. 11*a* shows, is the **edict.** As usual in such threats, God is expected to defend the decree and the temple, since he would be vitally concerned and would survive the king himself.

12 And the God that hath caused his name to dwell there destroy all kings and people, that shall put to their hand to alter *and* to destroy this house of God which *is* at Jerusalem. I Darius have made a decree; let it be done with speed.

13 ¶ Then Tatnai, governor on this side the river, Shethar-boznai, and their companions, according to that which Darius the king had sent, so they did speedily.

14 And the elders of the Jews builded, and they prospered through the prophesying of Haggai the prophet and Zechariah the son of Iddo. And they builded, and finished *it*, according to the commandment of the God of Israel, and according to the commandment of Cyrus, and Darius, and Artaxerxes king of Persia.

15 And this house was finished on the third day of the month Adar, which was in the sixth year of the reign of Darius the king.

dunghill. 12 May the God who has caused his name to dwell there overthrow any king or people that shall put forth a hand to alter this, or to destroy this house of God which is in Jerusalem. I Darius make a decree; let it be done with all diligence."

13 Then, according to the word sent by Darius the king, Tat'tenai, the governor of the province Beyond the River, She'thar-boz'enai, and their associates did with all diligence what Darius the king had ordered. 14 And the elders of the Jews built and prospered, through the prophesying of Haggai the prophet and Zechari'ah the son of Iddo. They finished their building by command of the God of Israel and by decree of Cyrus and Darius and Ar-ta-xerx'es king of Persia; 15 and this house was finished on the third day of the month of Adar, in the sixth year of the reign of Darius the king.

The God who has caused his name to dwell there is a distinctly Hebraic expression, common in Deuteronomic literature (cf. Deut. 12:11; 14:23; 16:2, 6, 11; 26:2; etc.). Its Jewishness has been explained as due to Jewish advice in the drafting of the document in the Persian chancellory (Bertholet, *op. cit.*, pp. 27-28; Rudolph, *op. cit.*, p. 58). The **name** of God, representing his revealed character and attributes, is sometimes equivalent to the person of God (Pss. 5:11; 7:17; 20:1), and in the late Jewish period it becomes a substitute for "God" (Lev. 24:11-16). The Persian word translated **done with speed** or **done with all diligence** is better rendered as "done thoroughly" (cf. 5:8; 6:8).

(5) COMPLETION OF THE TEMPLE (6:13-18=I Esdras 7:1-9)

Darius' officials (5:3) promptly followed his orders. With "they decided to act accordingly," Josephus implies reluctance, in keeping with his idea of bribed officials (cf. 4:7), but it does not represent the M.T. In vs. 13 as in vs. 12, read "thoroughly" instead of **speedily.**

14. The narrative in vs. 14 reflects the situation in 5:1-2. The same Aramaic word is used for both the **command** of God and the **decree** of the Persian kings. The **commandment** of God may rest ultimately on II Sam. 7:12-13; I Kings 5:4-5, but more directly upon Ezra 1:2. The **decree of Cyrus** is in 1:2-3; 6:3-5; that of **Darius** is in 6:7-8. Since the temple was finished under Darius I (vs. 15), the reference to **Artaxerxes** (464-423 B.C.) must be an addition made by someone who thought of the king's aid to Ezra (7:12-27) and Nehemiah (Neh. 2:5-8), and especially of the king's intention (Ezra 7:27). But a tradition persisted that there was some rebuilding of the temple in the time of **Artaxerxes** (cf. S. A. Cook, "I Esdras" in R. H. Charles, ed., *The Apocrypha and Pseudepigrapha of the Old Testament* [Oxford: Clarendon Press, 1913], p. 13).

15. About four and a half years after it was started (Sept. 21, 520 B.C.; cf. Hag. 1:14-15) the temple was finished. **Adar** (February-March) was the last Babylonian month. The **third day** (Mar. 12, 515 B.C.) of the M.T. is less likely than the "twenty-third day" of I Esdras 7:5 (Apr. 1, 515 B.C.), since the "twenty" is easier lost than gained in the text. Furthermore, the **third day** was a sabbath, when no work could be done, while the "twenty-third day" was a Friday (F. X. Kugler, *Von Moses bis Paulus* [Münster in Westfalen: Aschendorff, 1922], p. 215). It is unnecessary to substitute "they continued"

16 ¶ And the children of Israel, the priests, and the Levites, and the rest of the children of the captivity, kept the dedication of this house of God with joy,

17 And offered at the dedication of this house of God a hundred bullocks, two hundred rams, four hundred lambs; and for a sin offering for all Israel, twelve he goats, according to the number of the tribes of Israel.

18 And they set the priests in their divisions, and the Levites in their courses, for the service of God, which *is* at Jerusalem; as it is written in the book of Moses.

19 And the children of the captivity kept the passover upon the fourteenth *day* of the first month.

16 And the people of Israel, the priests and the Levites, and the rest of the returned exiles, celebrated the dedication of this house of God with joy. 17 They offered at the dedication of this house of God one hundred bulls, two hundred rams, four hundred lambs, and as a sin offering for all Israel twelve he-goats, according to the number of the tribes of Israel. 18 And they set the priests in their divisions and the Levites in their courses, for the service of God at Jerusalem, as it is written in the book of Moses.

19 On the fourteenth day of the first month the returned exiles kept the passover.

---

for **was finished** (so Batten, *op. cit.*, p. 149) since the verb is Akkadian and usage in that language permits a translation "completed" when used of finishing a temple (Carl Bezold, *Babylonisch-Assyrisches Glossar* [Heidelberg: C. Winter, 1926], p. 59, col. 2, *s.v. așû*, III₁), as also in later Targumic Aramaic (Marcus Jastrow, *A Dictionary of the Targumim* [New York: G. P. Putnam's Sons, 1903], II, 1567, *s.v.* שֵׁיצִי). Because of its precise date and because he feels that vs. 14 closes an episode, Torrey (*Ezra Studies*, p. 158) regards vs. 15 as a new section (6:15-18) by the Chronicler, but that would leave unexplained the transition from Aramaic to Hebrew at vss. 18-19.

16-18. The ceremony of dedication at the completion of the temple is reminiscent of that of the time of Solomon (I Kings 8). Such celebration is historically probable and the report may rest on the temple archives. Such stress on priestly activity is widely regarded as evidence of the Chronicler's authorship, but in several instances the evidence points away from him. The tripartite concept of the restored community (vs. 16) suggests the Chronicler's view but **all Israel** and the sacrifice of **twelve he-goats** (cf. 8:35), representing **the tribes of Israel** (vs. 17), indicate that there is a more inclusive view operative in the narrative. The sacrifices, too, are relatively modest when compared with those at the earlier dedication (I Kings 8:5), especially according to the Chronicler's account (II Chr. 7:5). In Lev. 4:13-21 the **sin offering** calls for a bullock rather than a he-goat.

With renewal of sacrifices the temple staff was inducted (vs. 18), and I Esdras 7:9 adds that doorkeepers were stationed at every gate (cf. I Esdras 1:16). Organization of the clergy into **divisions** and **courses** is traced to **the book of Moses** (cf. 3:2), but Pentateuchal law contains no such provisions. The reference, however, may be simply to priestly dedication (Exod. 29:1-46; Lev. 8:1-36) and the appointment of Levites (Num. 3:5-9; 8:5-22). It has been recognized that if the Chronicler were the author, one should expect reference to Davidic authority for clerical organization, since that was his understanding of its origin (cf. 3:10; 8:20; I Chr. 23:1–26:32; Neh. 12:24, 45; cf. Rudolph, *op. cit.*, p. 61). For **the service of God** read with the Peshitta and the LXXᴸ "the service of the house of God," since "house" has been lost from the M.T.

(6) The Feasts of Passover and Unleavened Bread (6:19-22=I Esdras 7:10-15)

The Aramaic section is concluded with vs. 18, and the Hebrew language, dropped at 4:6, is resumed. As most authorities agree, the author is the Chronicler. But it has been suggested that he has only adapted one of his sources, fitting it to its present context and modifying it to suit his own ideas (Batten, *Ezra and Nehemiah*, pp. 151-52).

19. The **passover**, originally a pastoral festival, finally was regarded as celebrating

20 For the priests and the Levites were purified together, all of them *were* pure, and killed the passover for all the children of the captivity, and for their brethren the priests, and for themselves.

21 And the children of Israel, which were come again out of captivity, and all such as had separated themselves unto them from the filthiness of the heathen of the land, to seek the LORD God of Israel, did eat,

22 And kept the feast of unleavened bread seven days with joy: for the LORD had

20 For the priests and the Levites had purified themselves together; all of them were clean. So they killed the passover lamb for all the returned exiles, for their fellow priests, and for themselves; 21 it was eaten by the people of Israel who had returned from exile, and also by every one who had joined them and separated himself from the pollutions of the peoples of the land to worship the LORD, the God of Israel. 22 And they kept the feast of unleavened bread seven days with joy; for the LORD had made

---

Israel's deliverance from Egyptian bondage (Exod. 12:1-30). It is not mentioned in the earliest Hebrew legislation but is prominent in the later codes and is described at length by the Chronicler (II Chr. 35:1-19). The **fourteenth day of the first month,** i.e., Nisan (cf. Exod. 12:2-3, 6), in 515 B.C. was April 21, shortly after the completion of the temple. Torrey (*Composition,* p. 10) holds the Chronicler responsible for the chronology which neatly makes the Passover occur right after the dedication. The expression **the children of the captivity,** excluding non-exiled Jews, presents the Chronicler's conception of the restored community, but it is slightly expanded in vs. 21. The "children of Israel" found here in I Esdras 7:10, however, is not original but is derived from I Esdras 7:6 (=Ezra 6:16).

20. The pro-Levite bias of the Chronicler (II Chr. 29:34) is seen in his insistence that **the Levites** killed the sacrifice for the priests (II Chr. 35:3-6, 10-11, 14). Vs. 20*b* shows that only the Levites **were purified.** A later writer who missed them added **the priests. Purified themselves together,** lit., "purified themselves as one," is properly translated as "purified themselves to a man" by the Amer. Trans. **Pure** or **clean** is a technical term meaning "ceremonially clean." This signifies freedom from such contamination as would prevent the ritual act from being efficacious. Such purification was done with water (cf. Exod. 29:4; Num. 8:7), just as Babylonian priests purified themselves with river water before entering the sanctuary (Johannes Pedersen, *Israel, Its Life and Culture, II-III* [London: Oxford University Press, 1940], pp. 747-48).

21. The community of vs. 19 was augmented by **every one who had joined them,** by proselytes drawn from Gentiles and half-caste Jews who had intermarried with the Gentiles (cf. 9:1-2, 12, 14; Neh. 13:23-24). According to Jewish legislation, all "clean" Jews were expected to share the Passover under penalty of ostracism (Num. 9:13); circumcised foreigners could participate on the same basis as the Jews (Num. 9:14); but all uncircumcised were forbidden to partake (Exod. 12:43-45, 48-49).

Filthiness or **pollutions** means "ceremonial uncleanness," just the opposite of the ceremonial purity of vs. 20. In I Esdras 7:13 it is interpreted as "the abominations" or "the detestable things" (βδέλυγμα; cf. Luke 16:15; Matt. 24:15; etc.), the influences of foreign culture, particularly in religion (cf. 9:1, 11; Neh. 13:23-24, 26). The tragedy of Babylonian captivity was attributed to such foreign contamination (9:13-14), and later Jewish exclusiveness and the strong aversion to mixtures are deeply rooted in this antipathy to non-Jewish influence. **To seek** (cf. 4:2) is distinctly the Chronicler's own term. Although it has been interpreted as **to worship,** the word may have been weakened to merely "revere" (S. R. Driver, *Introduction to the Literature of the Old Testament* [9th ed.; New York: Charles Scribner's Sons, 1913], p. 536, No. 7). The implied object of **did eat** is the Passover, which is made explicit in the LXX.

22. The **feast of unleavened bread,** originally a Canaanite harvest festival (Exod. 34:18-26 [J]; 23:14-16 [E], followed on the day after the Passover, the fifteenth day (cf. Lev. 23:6), and continued for **seven days. Turned the heart** means "changed the mind" (or "the will" or "the purpose"). **King of Assyria** is anachronistic in the Persian period.

made them joyful, and turned the heart of the king of Assyria unto them, to strengthen their hands in the work of the house of God, the God of Israel.

7 Now after these things, in the reign of Artaxerxes king of Persia, Ezra the son of Seraiah, the son of Azariah, the son of Hilkiah,

2 The son of Shallum, the son of Zadok, the son of Ahitub,

them joyful, and had turned the heart of the king of Assyria to them, so that he aided them in the work of the house of God, the God of Israel.

7 Now after this, in the reign of Ar-ta-xerx'es king of Persia, Ezra the son of Serai'ah, son of Azari'ah, son of Hilki'ah, 2 son of Shallum, son of Zadok, son of Ahi'-

Jewish scholars assume a Persian king and Josephus so translates it (*Antiquities* XI. 4. 8). **Assyria** may be loose usage or even a scribal error for "Syria" (cf. Hölscher, *Esra und Nehemia,* II, 516). The unidentified **king** is most probably Artaxerxes, whose harshly unfavorable decision (4:21-22) is about to be changed in the following narrative (7:1-28), which the Chronicler here anticipates. Artaxerxes is recalled as a supporter of the work of both Ezra and Nehemiah and as beautifier of the house of the Lord (7:27). As the versions show, **the work of the house of God, the God of Israel** is awkward in the M.T. Expected is either "the house of the God of Israel" (as in the LXX) or "the house of the Lord, the God of Israel" (as in the Vulg., I Esdras, and Peshitta).

III. Ezra's Return (7:1–8:36)
A. Introduction of Ezra (7:1-10=I Esdras 8:1-8)
1. Genealogy of Ezra (7:1-5)

7:1-5. The general chronological note, **after these things** (cf. II Chr. 32:1; Esth. 2:1; 3:1), covers an interval of 117 years, between the completion of the temple (6:15) and the journey of Ezra to Judah (7:7).

Ezra ("Help") abbreviates such a full name as Azariah (cf. 2:2). The genealogy supplied (vss. 1:5) is an unhistorical reflection of the conviction of the Chronicler's age that so important a person as Ezra must have had a significant ancestry. As priest (cf. vss. 11-12, 21), he was not only a descendant of Aaron (vs. 5), like all Jewish priests returned from Babylonia (8:2), but he was also related to the house of the high priest. Such relationship was suggested perhaps by the name of Ezra's father, **Seraiah** (vs. 1), which was the same as that of the high priest slain at the fall of Jerusalem, about 188 years before Ezra's arrival in Palestine (cf. II Kings 25:18-21). Since about five generations separated Ezra from the high priest **Seraiah**, Ezra could not have been his son. If the link with the family of the house of the high priest is intended, the genealogy should have been carried down to a high priest closer to Ezra. The missing generations have been explained by supposing that from the time of **Seraiah** onward the family of Ezra was not directly in the line of the high priest but collateral to it (Ernst Bertheau, *Die Bücher Esra, Nechemia und Ester,* ed. Victor Ryssel [2nd ed.; Leipzig: S. Hirzel, 1887; "Kurzgefasstes exegetisches Handbuch zum Alten Testament"], p. 88; Keil, *Chronik, Esra, Nehemia und Esther,* p. 457).

7:1-26. *Ezra: The "Ready Scribe."*—At last we meet the hero whose name the whole book bears; but at first only through an introduction in the third person, evidently written long afterward by some author (either the Chronicler or some intermediate redactor), whose major interests are at any rate those of the Chronicler. His emphasis is still, as in chs. 5–6, on the political approval and financial support given by different Persian kings to the rebuilding of the temple; but even more now (cf. vss. 6-10 with vss. 25-26) on the special qualifications of Ezra to teach and enforce the law of Moses in the full authoritative sense which it had acquired in the Jerusalem community by the time of the Chronicler—as **statutes and ordinances** laid down by God himself, under penalties that included not only **imprisonment** and **banishment,** but even **death** (vs. 26).

3 The son of Amariah, the son of Azariah, the son of Meraioth,

4 The son of Zerahiah, the son of Uzzi, the son of Bukki,

5 The son of Abishua, the son of Phinehas, the son of Eleazar, the son of Aaron the chief priest:

6 This Ezra went up from Babylon; and he *was* a ready scribe in the law of Moses, which the LORD God of Israel had given: and the king granted him all his request, according to the hand of the LORD his God upon him.

tub, 3 son of Amari'ah, son of Azari'ah, son of Merai'oth, 4 son of Zerahi'ah, son of Uzzi, son of Bukki, 5 son of Abi'shu-a, son of Phin'ehas, son of Elea'zar, son of Aaron the chief priest — 6 this Ezra went up from Babylonia. He was a scribe skilled in the law of Moses which the LORD the God of Israel had given; and the king granted him all that he asked, for the hand of the LORD his God was upon him.

The genealogy is based on data in I Chr. 6:3-15, 50-53 (cf. Neh. 11:11), but comparison shows the list in Ezra to be textually defective (cf. Rudolf Kittel, *Die Bücher der Chronik* [Göttingen, Vandenhoeck & Ruprecht, 1902; "Handkommentar zum Alten Testament"], pp. 39-42). Assuming three generations to a century, the present list would reach back only about 567 years, not to Aaron but to about the time of Saul (*ca.* 1150 B.C.). In addition to the generations missing between the fall of Jerusalem and Ezra, the present list lacks the generations named in I Chr. 6:8b-12a, which were lost apparently accidentally, due to the similarity of names. A scribe's eyes passed from one **Amariah** (cf. I Chr. 6:7) to another (cf. I Chr. 6:11), omitting the seven intervening names. The genealogy does, however, share the glaring error of I Chr. 6:12 in identifying **Zadok** as the son of **Ahitub** (cf. 7:2). If I Sam. 2:22-36 has any real value, **Zadok** cannot be identified as the son of **Ahitub**, Abiathar's grandfather (cf. William R. Arnold, *Ephod and Ark* [Cambridge: Harvard University Press, 1917], pp. 14-15). This faulty genealogy is secondary to the Ezra narrative and does not represent Ezra's true ancestry, which must have been originally simply "Ezra the son of Seraiah."

2. SUMMARY OF EZRA'S CAREER (7:6-10)

6. This Ezra, repeating the subject of vs. 1 after the long genealogical insertion, identifies the person of the genealogy with the principal character in the narrative that follows. The M.T. permits **from Babylon,** but **from Babylonia** is more likely since, in late Jewish use the term but rarely refers to the city. **Scribe** (cf. 4:8) can mean an official secretary of the court (cf. II Sam. 8:17; II Kings 18:18, 37; 19:2; Esth. 3:12; 8:9). It is argued that Ezra, like the later Jewish exilarch (*rēsh gālūthā'*), was a high court official who advised the king in all matters concerning the Jewish people (cf. Neh. 11:24; H. H. Schaeder, *Esra der Schreiber* [Tübingen: J. C. B. Mohr, 1930; "Beiträge zur historischen Theologie"], pp. 46-49; cf. Rudolph, *op. cit.,* p. 73). The word translated **ready** (*māhir*) is used of scribes in Egypt in the sense of "experienced" or "skillful" (W. M. Müller, *Asien und Europa* [Leipzig: W. Engelmann, 1893], p. 173) and elsewhere during the Persian period and before. An Aramaic papyrus calls Ahiqar, an Assyrian scribe, "a wise and skillful [מהר] scribe" (Cowley, *Aramaic Papyri,* p. 212, l. 1; cf. pp. 220, 226). It is the Chronicler who transformed Ezra the royal official to the later distinctly Jewish Bible scribe, the specialist in scripture, more familiar in his own day (cf. I Chr. 2:55; Neh. 12:26; Ecclus. 38:24–39:11; Matt. 2:4).

It is said of Ezra that the king **granted him all his request,** but the Ezra story begins abruptly and there is preserved no account of Ezra's session with the king, such as is found in the story of Nehemiah (cf. 2:1-8). The nature of **his request** can be learned only from the edict of the king (vss. 13-26). It would appear that as an official in the Persian court Ezra persuaded the king that it would be to the advantage of the empire to establish Jewish law as normative in Palestine. Apparently convinced that peace and

7 And there went up *some* of the children of Israel, and of the priests, and the Levites, and the singers, and the porters, and the Nethinim, unto Jerusalem, in the seventh year of Artaxerxes the king.

8 And he came to Jerusalem in the fifth month, which *was* in the seventh year of the king.

7 And there went up also to Jerusalem, in the seventh year of Ar-ta-xerx'es the king, some of the people of Israel, and some of the priests and Levites, the singers and gate-keepers, and the temple servants. 8 And he came to Jerusalem in the fifth month, which

---

security would be fostered by such a measure, and that the re-establishment of the Jewish cult at Jerusalem would result in greater loyalty of his subjects and the support of the powerful Jewish God for the royal house, Artaxerxes **granted him all that he asked.** The **hand of the LORD** (vs. 28; 8:22, 31; cf. 7:9; 8:18; Neh. 2:8, 18) indicates the favor of God. **According to the hand** implies success in proportion to God's support, but the sense is improved by following the LXX in reading, **for the hand of the LORD . . . was upon him.**

7-8. Because in vs. 7 attention is turned suddenly but briefly from Ezra to returning exiles, the verse has been regarded as an addition to the text (Josef Markwart, *Fundamente israelitische und jüdische Geschichte* [Göttingen: Dieterich, 1896], p. 34; Sigmund Mowinckel, *Ezra den Skriftlaerde* [Kristiania: 1916], p. 2; Hölscher, *op. cit.*, II, 518). But a simple emendation from **and there went up** (ויעלו) to "he sent up" (ויעל) would refocus the attention on Ezra and eliminate the chief motive for omitting the verse (Rudolph, *op. cit.*, p. 67). The classes of people mentioned are those found in Ezra 2:1-70, but Hölscher argues that the treatment of **the singers and gate-keepers** as distinct from **the Levites** (2:41; 3:10) is contrary to the Chronicler's point of view, and is thus evidence for the secondary character of the verse. It is true that the **singers and gate-keepers** are not named among the returning Jews in 8:15 ff., but they are here a later addition derived from the Levites in 8:18-19, probably under the influence of 7:24, and possibly also with 2:41-42 in mind (*ibid.*, p. 72). Vs. 8, which almost duplicates vs. 7b, has also been regarded as an addition (Martin Noth, *Überlieferungsgeschichtliche Studien I* [Halle: M. Niemeyer, 1943], p. 125), but the verse does advance the thought, reverting to Ezra from his companions and specifying **the fifth month** (July-August) as part of the date.

One of the most perplexing and controversial problems of Ezra-Nehemiah is that of the date of Ezra's arrival in Jerusalem. Traditionally **Artaxerxes** is identified with Artaxerxes I (464-424 B.C.), whose **seventh year** was 458 B.C. Since Ezra followed Nehemiah to Palestine (cf. Intro., pp. 561-62) and was not his contemporary, the **Artaxerxes** must have been Artaxerxes II (404-359 B.C.), whose **seventh year** was 398 B.C. (H. H. Rowley, *The Servant of the Lord and Other Essays on the Old Testament* [London: Lutterworth Press, 1952], pp. 131-59). It is always possible that Ezra may have come to Jerusalem some time during the reign of Artaxerxes I, after the end of the first administration of Nehemiah in 432 B.C. (Neh. 5:14), but any satisfactory date in this period is highly conjectural, without textual support. Some have arbitrarily assigned Ezra's arrival to the thirty-second year of Artaxerxes I (433/432 B.C.), when Nehemiah left (W. H. Kosters, *Die Wiederherstellung Israels in der persischen Periode* [tr. A. Basedow; Heidelberg: J. Hörning, 1895], pp. 95 ff., 116; Bertholet, *Esra und Nehemia*, pp. 30-31; R. H. Kennett, *Old Testament Essays* [Cambridge: Cambridge University Press, 1928], p. 85; formerly also W. F. Albright, *The Archaeology of Palestine and the Bible* [New York: Fleming H. Revell Co., 1932], p. 219). Others have sought textual support for a date in the "thirty-seventh year" of Artaxerxes I (428 B.C.) by assuming the loss of "thirty" (שלשים) from the text due to similarity to the beginning of the spelling of seven (שבע) in vss. 7-8 (Markwart, *op. cit.*, p. 36; Bewer, *Der Text des Buches Ezra*, p. 68; W. F. Albright, *From the Stone Age to Christianity* (2nd ed.; Baltimore: Johns Hopkins Press,

9 For upon the first *day* of the first month began he to go up from Babylon, and on the first *day* of the fifth month came he to Jerusalem, according to the good hand of his God upon him.

10 For Ezra had prepared his heart to seek the law of the LORD, and to do *it,* and to teach in Israel statutes and judgments.

11 ¶ Now this *is* the copy of the letter that the king Artaxerxes gave unto Ezra the

was in the seventh year of the king; 9 for on the first day of the first month he began[h] to go up from Babylonia, and on the first day of the fifth month he came to Jerusalem, for the good hand of his God was upon him. 10 For Ezra had set his heart to study the law of the LORD, and to do it, and to teach his statutes and ordinances in Israel.

11 This is a copy of the letter which King

[h] Vg See Syr: Heb *that was the foundation of the going up*

1946), p. 366; Rudolph, *op. cit.,* pp. 71, 168). The date cannot be determined accurately but it must have been at least after the first administration of Nehemiah.

9. Chronological data already given in vss. 7-8 is recapitulated here. Such information, lacking in the present Ezra narrative, must have been drawn by the Chronicler from the now missing beginning of Ezra's own report. **He began to go up** attempts to make sense of a corrupt Hebrew text, **that was the foundation of the going up.** For **the foundation** (*yeṣudh*) read the verb "was decided upon" (*yiṣṣadh;* cf. Esth. 1:8). Earlier, perhaps, **the first month** was followed by an explanatory gloss "that is [the month] Nisan," of which נסן, "Nisan," was lost because of some similarity to the verb יסד, "was decided upon" (cf. Ehrlich, *Randglossen zur hebräischen Bibel,* VII, 171; Rudolph, *op. cit.,* p. 67). Thus we translate, "For upon the first of the month (that is Nisan) the going up was decided upon." Such emendation avoids a conflict with 8:31, according to which the departure occurred on the twelfth day (Apr. 16, 398 B.C.) instead of the **first day** (Apr. 5, 398 B.C.). There need be no contradiction in any case since there was some delay (8:15-30) before the actual departure.

10. This verse comments on vs. 6, explaining the reason for Ezra's success through divine support and portraying him as the ideal Jewish scribe dedicated to the threefold task of seeking the law, obeying it, and propagating it. **Set his heart** means "set his mind" (cf. 1:1). The **law of the LORD** is "the law of Moses" (vs. 6). **To seek the law** means **to study** it, to determine its implications for daily life. Such study ultimately produced the oral law and the Talmud. But study was not enough, for it was obedience to the law that led to a virtuous life. Thus Judaism stresses activity rather than belief as the avenue to salvation. Such emphasis is found insistently in the older Hebrew legislation. Scribal legalism was not merely individual but also social. The learned had a missionary task to perform. **Statutes and ordinances** are terms found in earlier legislation (cf. Exod. 15:25; Josh. 24:25; I Sam. 30:25), especially in Deuteronomy where they are synonyms (Deut. 4:1, 5, 8, 14; 5:1; 11:32; 12:1; 26:16). **Statutes** originally meant something "inscribed" and a related word in Arabic means "to be right" or "to be obligatory." **Ordinances,** lit., **judgments,** signify legal decisions based on an earlier inscribed code.

B. EZRA'S COMMISSION (7:11-26=I Esdras 8:8-24)
1. INTRODUCTION (7:11-12)

An editorial verse in Hebrew (vs. 11) introduces a long document (vss. 12-26) which, like all official correspondence in the book, is written in the Aramaic language (cf. 4:8-22; 5:6–6:12). Purportedly a royal decree, it contains Ezra's commission, a statement of his authority, and a list of powers at his disposal to assure the success of his mission. The phraseology of the decree is very surprising for a Persian ruler, since it shows intimate acquaintance with Jewish terminology (cf. vss. 13, 15) and with cultic distinctions and practices prevailing in the later Jewish temple (cf. vs. 24). Such Jewishness has led to a charge that the document was forged (cf. Torrey, *Ezra Studies,* pp. 157-58; Pfeiffer, *Intro. to O.T.,* p. 826), or at least that an original document has been edited, supplemented, or even rewritten by a Jew (Driver, *Intro. to Literature*

priest, the scribe, *even* a scribe of the words of the commandments of the Lord, and of his statutes to Israel.

12 Artaxerxes, king of kings, unto Ezra the priest, a scribe of the law of the God of heaven, perfect *peace,* and at such a time.

Ar-ta-xerx'es gave to Ezra the priest, the scribe, learned in matters of the commandments of the Lord and his statutes for Israel: 12 "Ar-ta-xerx'es, king of kings, to Ezra the priest, the scribe of the law of the

---

of O.T., p. 550). A plausible explanation is presented by those who regard Ezra as an official in the Persian court, the adviser to the king for Jewish affairs (cf. vs. 6). As such, Ezra himself could have written the document or dictated its terms to be endorsed by the king and issued as an official decree (Meyer, *Entstehung des Judenthums,* pp. 64 ff.; Kittel, *Geschichte des Volkes Israel,* III, 583; Schaeder, *Esra der Schreiber,* pp. 9, 42, 55; Rudolph, *op. cit.,* pp. 73, 76).

11. Copy (cf. 4:11; 5:6) implies a written source behind the Aramaic text. **Artaxerxes** (cf. vss. 7-8) is the king according to the M.T. and I Esdras, but Josephus, aware of chronological difficulty in conflict with dates in Nehemiah, and believing that Ezra has preceded Nehemiah, has substituted "Xerxes" (485-465 B.C.), the predecessor of Artaxerxes I, as the one who gave Ezra his commission. Vs. 11*b* obviously is a later gloss on **the scribe,** based on the substance of vs. 10.

12. The title **king of kings,** used here in the superscription, was frequently employed by the Persian rulers (cf. Dan. 2:37), as by the Babylonians before them (Ezek. 26:7). Ezra is identified as **priest,** but, as in the Aramaic papyri (Cowley, *op. cit.,* No. 30, ll. 1, 18; No. 38, ll. 1, 12), the word used is Hebrew (*kōhēn*) rather than Aramaic (*kumrā*). Thus it would appear that the Hebrew term had been adopted in official use (cf. Schaeder, *Esra der Schreiber,* p. 43). Apparently on the basis of the genealogy of vss. 1-5, Ezra is identified as the "chief priest" in I Esdras 9:40 and Josephus (*Antiquities* XI. 5. 1), but that is incorrect. Schaeder (*Esra der Schreiber,* pp. 46-48) has also insisted that the second title of Ezra, **scribe of the law,** was in the Persian period an official one, a trace of which is found in the later name of the secretariat for law (*dādh dawirih*). Here the term used for **law** is Persian (*dāt*) rather than Hebrew (*tôrāh;* cf. 3:2). The concept was always important in Persian thought. Nor did the Persians distinguish sharply between sacred and secular law. In the Avesta, the Persian holy book, as also in later Pahlavi literature, there is no distinction between moral and legal crimes, between ecclesiastical and civil jurisprudence, for the priestly code of the Avesta, the Vendidad, is a medley of all sorts of ritual, moral, civil, and even hygienic laws (James Darmesteter, *The Zend-Avesta;* Part I, "The Vendidad" [Oxford: Clarendon Press, 1880; "The Sacred Books of the East"], pp. lxx-lxxi, lxxxii, lxxxiv).

Under such circumstances Ezra might be expected to be successful in gaining royal support in his attempt to introduce sacred **law** into the Judean province. He was directed to set up authorities in a secular manner (vs. 25), and his law was to be regarded as equivalent to the law of the king (vs. 26). Royal support was doubtless forthcoming on the assumption that the land could be made secure and peaceful for Persia through the instrumentality of Jewish law (cf. Rudolph, *op. cit.,* p. 76). Identification of the **law** as that of the **God of heaven** (cf. 5:11; 6:9) has led Schaeder (*Esra der Schreiber,* pp. 48-49) to insist that Ezra was secretary for Jewish affairs in the Persian court.

The verse literally concludes "finished, and now." The words **and now** are the normal conclusion of the salutation of a letter (cf. 4:10), but "finished" (cf. 5:16) is a corruption which has no counterpart in the versions and is therefore omitted entirely in the RSV. Part of the corrupt word (גמר) is probably a distorted fragment of the word "peace" (שלם) and its remainder (יר) is a likely distorted duplication of the letters which follow (רב; Bewer, *op. cit.,* p. 69). The presence of "peace" in the Peshitta and I Esdras 8:9 seems to support the addition of the word "peace" in emending the text.

13 I make a decree, that all they of the people of Israel, and *of* his priests and Levites, in my realm, which are minded of their own free will to go up to Jerusalem, go with thee.

14 Forasmuch as thou art sent of the king, and of his seven counselors, to inquire concerning Judah and Jerusalem, according to the law of thy God which *is* in thine hand;

15 And to carry the silver and gold, which the king and his counselors have freely offered unto the God of Israel, whose habitation *is* in Jerusalem,

16 And all the silver and gold that thou canst find in all the province of Babylon,

God of heaven. And now 13 I make a decree that any one of the people of Israel or their priests or Levites in my kingdom, who freely offers to go to Jerusalem, may go with you. 14 For you are sent by the king and his seven counselors to make inquiries about Judah and Jerusalem according to the law of your God, which is in your hand, 15 and also to convey the silver and gold which the king and his counselors have freely offered to the God of Israel, whose dwelling is in Jerusalem, 16 with all the silver and gold which you shall find in the whole province of

2. Permission to Return (7:13-14)

13. This verse is strongly Jewish in terminology. **Any one . . . who freely offers** represents an expression unusual in Aramaic but common in later Hebrew, especially in the work of the Chronicler (I Chr. 29:5, 6, 9, 14, 17; II Chr. 17:16; cf. Ezra 1:6; 2:68; Neh. 11:2). Such usage, the distinction between **priests** and **Levites** (cf. 2:36, 40), and the use of **people of Israel** to designate secular persons in contrast to the clergy, where the Persians would say "Jews" (cf. 4:12, 23; 5:1, 5; 6:7-8, 14), all suggest Jewish rather than Persian composition. Since those wanting to go to Judah were to go **with** Ezra, his commission included leading a caravan to Jerusalem.

14. The Persian king ruled absolutely, without a regularly established council. But he occasionally called in judges, political or military experts, or even just the "noblest Persians" as advisers (Herodotus *History* III. 31; VII. 8; VIII. 67). In Esth. 1:14 the counselors are described as "the seven princes of Persia and Media, who saw the king's face, and sat first in the kingdom." The basis for the number **seven** cannot yet be determined, but as late as the revolt of Cyrus the Younger (403-401 B.C.) the council consisted of seven of the most distinguished Persians of his staff (Xenophon *Anabasis* I. 6. 4-5). **To make inquiries** means "to investigate," as in 4:15, 19; 5:17; 6:1. Thus Ezra was to investigate the degree to which Jewish law was being effectively obeyed in Judah.

Your God indicates that there was no ambiguity regarding the nature of the **law.** It was distinctly Jewish and not confused with Persian legislation. **In your hand** identifies the law as that favored and promoted by Ezra. The nature of this **law,** much debated, is not yet certainly identified. It was a code already known to the people (vs. 25; Neh. 8:1), but the law brought by Ezra from Babylonia cannot be identified with any special code of the Bible. It was probably a form of the Deuteronomic Code, with which there had been considerable concern during the Exile, but it was a form of that code that had been somewhat modified in the direction of the Priestly Code developed during the Exile (cf. Neh. 8:1-2).

3. Gifts for the Temple (7:15-19)

15-16. With (vs. 16) indicates that two distinct groups of donors are mentioned in vs. 16, since vs. 16a is not qualified by vs. 16b, which certainly refers to Jews. The phrases **all the silver and gold** and **in the whole province** suggest a large group of donors. Some have seen here the influence of 1:4, and possibly the story of the Exodus (Exod. 10:25; 12:35-36; cf. Torrey, *Ezra Studies,* p. 158). As an alternative it has been proposed that Ezra was privileged to levy a tax on Jewish property in Babylonia for

with the freewill offering of the people, and of the priests, offering willingly for the house of their God which *is* in Jerusalem:

17 That thou mayest buy speedily with this money bullocks, rams, lambs, with their meat offerings and their drink offerings, and offer them upon the altar of the house of your God which *is* in Jerusalem.

18 And whatsoever shall seem good to thee, and to thy brethren, to do with the rest of the silver and the gold, that do after the will of your God.

19 The vessels also that are given thee for the service of the house of thy God, *those* deliver thou before the God of Jerusalem.

20 And whatsoever more shall be needful for the house of thy God, which thou shalt have occasion to bestow, bestow *it* out of the king's treasure house.

Babylonia, and with the freewill offerings of the people and the priests, vowed willingly for the house of their God which is in Jerusalem. **17** With this money, then, you shall with all diligence buy bulls, rams, and lambs, with their cereal offerings and their drink offerings, and you shall offer them upon the altar of the house of your God which is in Jerusalem. **18** Whatever seems good to you and your brethren to do with the rest of the silver and gold, you may do, according to the will of your God. **19** The vessels that have been given you for the service of the house of your God, you shall deliver before the God of Jerusalem. **20** And whatever else is required for the house of your God, which you have occasion to provide, you may provide it out of the king's treasury.

---

the funds, but there is no evidence for such action (Carl Siegfried, *Esra, Nehemia und Esther* [Göttingen: Vandenhoeck & Ruprecht, 1901; "Handkommentar zum Alten Testament"], p. 52). The non-Jewish donors were probably "his lords'" (cf. 8:25). Delivery of the gifts is mentioned in 8:24-26, 33-34.

17-18. Knowledge of Hebrew terminology and custom is evident in these verses. Not only the proper sacrifices are mentioned, but also the **cereal offerings** and **drink offerings** that regularly accompanied them (cf. Num. 15:1-10). But the usage is not that preferred by the Chronicler for designating the sacrificial animals. **Speedily** should be rendered "faithfully" (cf. 5:8; 6:8, 12, 13). Since it is assumed (vs. 18) that the collected funds will be more than enough for the sacrifices, the surplus is to be disposed of under Ezra's direction, but only for such cult purposes as will please the Jewish God. **Will of . . . God** represents a word meaning "pleasure" or "desire," found only here and in late Hebrew. **Your brethren** means Ezra's fellow priests.

19. Vessels should be "utensils" in a wider sense than pots and jars, as the LXX (σκεύη) shows (cf. 1:10-11). Although I Esdras 8:17 seems to interpret them as temple vessels that had been plundered (1:7-11; 5:14; 6:5), this is but an assumption. They may have been dedicated by their donors to the **service** of the temple. The abrupt **God of Jerusalem** would be unique in the Aramaic documents. Since the LXX and Vulg. have "in Jerusalem," it is probable that the Peshitta is right in reading "the God who is in Jerusalem" (cf. 1:3). But it is possible also that the original text was "the God of Israel, who is in Jerusalem" (cf. vs. 15).

4. Additional Funds (7:20-24)

20-24. If additional funds are needed for the temple beyond the donations, such requirements are to be met by a grant of funds from **the king's treasury** (cf. 5:17; 6:1). **You may provide it** seems addressed to Ezra, who was not in position to draw on royal funds. Therefore there is incorporated in Ezra's orders a special section (vss. 21-24) which is addressed to **the treasurers** who are to pay the funds (cf. 1:8). These officials are to take orders from **Ezra** (cf. vs. 12), but in a businesslike way practical limits are put on his possible demands (vs. 22). Again **speedily** is "faithfully" or "exactly" (cf. 5:8).

The Chronicler's tendency to exaggerate statistics concerning the temple (cf. I Chr. 29:7) has led those who regard him as the author here to be suspicious of the royal grants (Jahn, *Esra [A und B] und Nehemja*, p. 63). The list of gifts and prerogatives

21 And I, *even* I Artaxerxes the king, do make a decree to all the treasurers which *are* beyond the river, that whatsoever Ezra the priest, the scribe of the law of the God of heaven, shall require of you, it be done speedily,

22 Unto a hundred talents of silver, and to a hundred measures of wheat, and to a hundred baths of wine, and to a hundred baths of oil, and salt without prescribing *how much.*

23 Whatsoever is commanded by the God of heaven, let it be diligently done for the house of the God of heaven: for why should there be wrath against the realm of the king and his sons?

24 Also we certify you, that, touching any of the priests and Levites, singers, porters, Nethinim, or ministers of this house of God, it shall not be lawful to impose toll, tribute, or custom, upon them.

21 "And I, Ar-ta-xerx′es the king, make a decree to all the treasurers in the province Beyond the River: Whatever Ezra the priest, the scribe of the law of the God of heaven, requires of you, be it done with all diligence, 22 up to a hundred talents of silver, a hundred measures of wheat, a hundred baths of wine, a hundred baths of oil, and salt without prescribing how much. 23 Whatever is commanded by the God of heaven, let it be done in full for the house of the God of heaven, lest his wrath be against the realm of the king and his sons. 24 We also notify you that it shall not be lawful to impose tribute, custom, or toll upon any one of the priests, the Levites, the singers, the doorkeepers, the temple servants, or other servants of this house of God.

---

has been called "not quite incredible" (Torrey, *Ezra Studies*, p. 206, note u) , but Meyer did not think the sums mentioned excessive (*Entstehung des Judenthums*, pp. 68-69) . Egyptian records reveal both Persian interest in the sacrificial cultus of their subjects and Persian generosity in supporting it (Speigelberg, *Die sogennante demotische Chronik,* pp. 32-33; cf. Olmstead, *History of the Persian Empire,* p. 91) .

Since no uniform standard of weight was recognized in the ancient Near East, even for weights bearing the same name, the actual measure of Persian generosity cannot be determined. **Talents** weighed about sixty-five pounds each. **Measures** represents the *kôr,* which held about eleven and two-thirds bushels of grain (however, see Vol. I, p. 155) . **Baths** held about nine gallons apiece. **Oil** translates a word meaning "anointing," apparently an abbreviation of the Hebrew expression "the oil of anointing" (cf. Exod. 25:6; 29:7; etc.) . The same word is used in 6:9 and in the Aramaic papyri, but one would not expect a Persian official to use it without Jewish prompting or instruction. There would not be a very heavy demand for **salt** (cf. 6:9) , and no limit was set for its expenditure.

23. The motive for royal support of the temple was to win the favor of the Jews and their God and to prevent their antipathy against the royal family and the Persian Empire. Practical considerations doubtless prevailed. Artaxerxes II long hoped to emulate his predecessors as conquerors of Egypt. The weak Egyptian kings of the Twenty-eighth and Twenty-ninth Dynasties (525-332 B.C.) seemed to hold promise of Persian victory, and a friendly Palestine on the flank and rear would be a military necessity for success.

24. All temple attendants (cf. 2:36, 40-43) were to be exempt from **tribute, custom, or toll,** by which is meant taxes and forced labor (cf. 4:13) . The clergy were often granted special privileges and exemptions (J. A. Wilson in Pritchard, *Ancient Near Eastern Texts,* p. 212) . The Gadatas inscription reflects just such favors by Darius and his predecessors (Botsford and Sihler, *Hellenic Civilization,* p. 162) , and Josephus (*Antiquities* XII. 3. 3) claims that Antiochus the Great later granted such exemption from taxation. The list of attendants certainly shows Jewish influence in its compilation. Since **singers** represents a word (*zammar*) signifying either "singer" or "player," the term "musicians" presents the same ambiguity as the Aramaic word. **Ministers** or **servants**

25 And thou, Ezra, after the wisdom of thy God, that *is* in thine hand, set magistrates and judges, which may judge all the people that *are* beyond the river, all such as know the laws of thy God; and teach ye them that know *them* not.

26 And whosoever will not do the law of thy God, and the law of the king, let judgment be executed speedily upon him, whether *it be* unto death, or to banishment, or to confiscation of goods, or to imprisonment.

25 "And you, Ezra, according to the wisdom of your God which is in your hand, appoint magistrates and judges who may judge all the people in the province Beyond the River, all such as know the laws of your God; and those who do not know them, you shall teach. 26 Whoever will not obey the law of your God and the law of the king, let judgment be strictly executed upon him, whether for death or for banishment or for confiscation of his goods or for imprisonment."

is related to the term "service" in vs. 19. It is properly rendered as "menials," since it presumably refers to "the sons of Solomon's servants" of 2:55.

5. Ezra and the Law (7:25-26)

25-26. With **you, Ezra** the letter again turns to Ezra himself. **The wisdom of your God** means "the law of your God" (cf. vs. 14). The equation of **wisdom** and **law,** found frequently in late Hebrew, anticipates the usage in Ben Sirach (Ecclus. 15:1; 19:20; 21:11; 24:23-29; 34:8). This too is evidence for Jewish composition. A secular organization was to be set up for judging in accordance with the law of Ezra. **Magistrates** and **judges** are synonymous terms. Only the latter (*dayyān*) is used in the Aramaic papyri of the Persian period (cf. 4:9). The former is Hebrew (cf. 10:14) and is not used elsewhere in Aramaic. Instead, the LXX^ABL have "scribes and judges," which presupposes an original "secretaries and judges." Such "scribes" were secular officers, like the "notaries of the provinces" mentioned in the Aramaic papyri (Cowley, *Aramaic Papyri,* p. 53, No. 17, ll. 1, 6).

All the people seems to mean all Jews and Gentiles of Syria and Palestine (Torrey, *Ezra Studies,* p. 206, notes u, v), but **such as know the laws of your God** limits the authority to Jews alone, wherever they were found in **the province Beyond the River** (cf. Batten, *Ezra and Nehemiah,* pp. 313-14; Meyer, *op. cit.,* p. 67). The injunction to **teach** the law to those ignorant of it doubtless refers to those Jews who had abandoned Judaism and to the more remote Jewish groups who had not kept abreast of the development of Jewish law. Official control over all Jews in the West, even outside of Palestine, is well illustrated by the instructions sent to Egypt about the observance of the feast of Unleavened Bread in 419 B.C. (Cowley, *op. cit.,* pp. 60-62).

26. Royal approval made Jewish law **the law of the king,** and willful disobedience to it was to be punished with the same severity used against other law breakers. **Speedily** is better rendered **strictly** here (cf. 5:8). The punishments, arranged with decreasing severity, gave Ezra power which he appears to have been reluctant to use. Ezra's friends threaten **confiscation** and **banishment** (cf. 10:8), but there is no evidence of the execution of that threat. The rendering **banishment** assumes that the problematical word שרשׁו represents a Semitic root (שׁרשׁ), which can mean "uproot" (Ps. 52:5 [Hebrew 52:7]); from this an abstract noun **banishment** can be produced. Such etymology is rejected by Batten (*op. cit.,* p. 316), who nevertheless regards the conjectured meaning as most probable. But somewhere in a truly Persian list should be found "beating," the most common Persian form of punishment. The LXX^AB, indeed, renders the M.T. as "chastisement" (παιδείαν; cf. Heb. 12:5, 7-11; Prov. 15:5; and often in the LXX). If this is the correct interpretation of the word, it may be non-Semitic, possibly an abbreviation of "the scourge," "whip," or "thong" (*sraoshô-careman*), one of the two implements for beating mentioned in the later Persian law book (Vendidad IV, 17-21; V, 43-44; etc.; cf. Darmesteter, *The Zend-Avesta,* p. xcvi, n. 3).

27 ¶ Blessed *be* the LORD God of our fathers, which hath put *such a thing* as this in the king's heart, to beautify the house of the LORD which *is* in Jerusalem:

28 And hath extended mercy unto me before the king, and his counselors, and before all the king's mighty princes. And I was strengthened as the hand of the LORD my God *was* upon me, and I gathered together out of Israel chief men to go up with me.

27 Blessed be the LORD, the God of our fathers, who put such a thing as this into the heart of the king, to beautify the house of the LORD which is in Jerusalem, 28 and who extended to me his steadfast love before the king and his counselors, and before all the king's mighty officers. I took courage, for the hand of the LORD my God was upon me, and I gathered leading men from Israel to go up with me.

6. EZRA'S POEM OF PRAISE (7:27-28)

27-28. The Aramaic edict is followed by a doxology in Hebrew (vss. 27-28). With these verses begins the Ezra document (cf. Intro., pp. 556-57) which, with some exceptions, is written in the first person. Ezra supposedly is the speaker throughout. The beginning of the Ezra document, now lost (Batten, *op. cit.*, p. 316), must have given some account of Ezra's audience before the king and his counselors (vss. 14, 28), which resulted in his winning the right to go to Judea to establish Jewish law there. Some of the data of the original document must have been used by the Chronicler for his editorial introduction (vss. 1-26), but the beginning of the Ezra document was omitted, apparently because its substance was greatly duplicated in the Artaxerxes letter (vss. 12-26).

In I Esdras 8:25 (LXXᴬ) vs. 27 is introduced by the note, "Then said Esdras the scribe . . . ," but this is obviously a late editorial note identifying the speaker of the "I" section, for it is missing in I Esdrasᴮᴸ. **Such a thing as this,** lit., "like this," refers not to the preceding document but to the whole idea of Ezra's return and all it implied. Thus I Esdras has "these things." Those things most in the writer's mind are then specified. **In the king's heart** means "in the king's mind" (cf. 6:22). A similar view is found in I Sam. 21:12; Job 22:22, as well as in the Ahiqar papyri (Cowley, *op. cit.*, p. 225, l. 163). **Beautify** represents a word much used under the influence of the book of Isaiah (cf. 10:15; 44:23; 49:3; 55:5; 60:7, 9, 13, 21; 61:3; cf. Exod. 8:9 [Hebrew 8:5]; Judg. 7:2; Ps. 149:4; Arvid S. Kapelrud, *The Question of Authorship in the Ezra-Narrative* [Oslo: J. Dybwad, 1944], p. 43). Although much support of the temple is attributed to Artaxerxes, there is no evidence that he was responsible for such building or decoration of the temple as is implied in 6:14.

Extended means "offered," as in I Chr. 21:10. The idiom means "to let one find mercy" (cf. Gen. 39:21). **Steadfast love** (*hésedh*) is often used by the Chronicler and by the later psalmists, but it is not found in the Jewish papyri. There, however, in a similar context, the word "mercy" (*raḥmin*), as also used in Neh. 1:11 (cf. Neh. 9:19, 27-28, 31), is found. For **counselors** see vs. 14. **I was strengthened** means "I strengthened myself," in the sense of **I took courage** (cf. II Chr. 15:8). For **hand of the LORD** see 7:6. **Gathered** implies a process of selection. Later Jewish tradition insisted that Ezra himself selected those who were to return, that, as Rabbi Eleazar said, "Ezra did not go up from Babylon until he made it like pure sifted flour . . . " by sifting those of pure lineage ("fine

27-28. Ezra's Doxology.—Not only "Ezra's memoirs" in the first person, but an authentic note of firsthand religion appears at last in this hymn of praise. It is **the God of our fathers** who has moved the Persian king's heart and strengthened Ezra's hand for this great undertaking; it is his guiding **hand** that has called forth and led this little company across the desert. The Chronicler in his later time looks back on that journey as Leonard Bacon in 1833 looked back on the

founding of New Haven, two hundred years earlier, and on the landing of the Pilgrims at Plymouth in 1620:

> O God, beneath thy guiding hand
> Our exiled fathers crossed the sea.

In that American hymn, as in this Jewish doxology, patriotism and religion meet and blend in a paean of praise and thanksgiving.

8 These *are* now the chief of their fathers, and *this is* the genealogy of them that went up with me from Babylon, in the reign of Artaxerxes the king.

2 Of the sons of Phinehas; Gershom: of the sons of Ithamar; Daniel: of the sons of David; Hattush.

3 Of the sons of Shechaniah, of the sons of Pharosh; Zechariah: and with him were reckoned by genealogy of the males a hundred and fifty.

8 These are the heads of their fathers' houses, and this is the genealogy of those who went up with me from Babylonia, in the reign of Ar-ta-xerx'es the king: 2 Of the sons of Phin'ehas, Gershom. Of the sons of Ith'amar, Daniel. Of the sons of David, Hattush, 3 of the sons of Shecani'ah. Of the sons of Parosh, Zechari'ah, with whom were

unmixed meal") from the intermarried peoples ("mixed dough"; Babylonian Talmud, Kiddushin 69*b*, 71*b*, cf. Jerusalem Talmud, Kiddushin IV, 1; cf. Haggada, Yalkut II, 1067).

C. Those Returning with Ezra (8:1-14=I Esdras 8:28-40)

8:1-14. In accordance with the royal edict (7:13), Ezra planned to lead back those Jews who desired to go to Judea. Josephus (*Antiquities* XI. 5. 2) adds a comment that a copy of the royal correspondence was sent by Ezra to his kinsmen in Media (cf. II Kings 17:6) and that "many of them, taking along their possessions also, came to Babylon out of longing to return to Jerusalem. But the Israelite nation as a whole remained in the country." As usual, he omits the extended lists of returnees given in the Bible, lest it interrupt the flow of his narrative.

The authenticity of the list has been challenged by those who regard it as an invention, based on 2:1-70 and interrupting the connection between 7:28 and 8:15 (cf. Hölscher, *Esra und Nehemia*, II, 493, 519-20). But the originality of the list has been vigorously defended (cf. Rudolph, *Esra und Nehemia*, p. 79). The expression "chief men" of 7:28 is related to the **chief of their fathers** in vs. 1, and vs. 15 fits well as the resumption of narrative when the author has interpolated a relevant list (cf. Noth, *Überlieferungsgeschichtliche Studien* I, p. 125).

It is incorrect to regard the genealogy as "an extract of those in Ezr 2 and Neh 7" (Kapelrud, *op. cit.*, p. 45), for there are important differences. Unlike that in 2:1-70, this genealogy first lists the priests (vs. 2), with no heading to identify them. Only the ancestral names indicate the priestly connection. Those listed are not Zadokites (cf. 2:36) but descendants of Aaron who became prominent in Babylonia between the time of Zerubbabel and Ezra and were not yet recognized as dominant in Palestine as late as the time of Ezra (10:18 ff.; cf. Kittel, *Geschichte des Volkes Israel*, III, 402-7). The descendants of the two Aaronitic families are later most important, according to the Priestly Code (cf. Num. 3:1 ff.; 25:6-15). It has been conjectured that the priests are here listed first in deference to Ezra the priest (7:11-12), and that the family of **Phinehas** precedes because that was the one to which Ezra belonged (7:5; cf. Rudolph, *op. cit.*, p. 79). But **Ithamar** was the youngest son of Aaron (Exod. 6:23) and might therefore be listed second. In Neh. 10:6 **Daniel** appears among the priests sealing the covenant. Since Ezra later selected a dozen priests who came up with him (vs. 24), the two men mentioned must have been family heads, as among the laymen.

Hattush was an individual, a prince of the line of David through Solomon and Zerubbabel. The words **of the sons of Shecaniah** (vs. 3) refer to **Hattush** and indicate

8:1-20. The Caravan on Its Way.—Again the narrative in the first person is interrupted by the insertion of another of the genealogical lists of which the Chronicler was so fond; but at last in vs. 15 the caravan begins to "get organized" for its long journey. Then Ezra discovers (vss. 15-20) that he has with him for the proper service of the temple neither Levites nor their helpers the Nethinim, an interesting hint that there were plenty of plausible reasons why the ma-

4 Of the sons of Pahath-moab; Elihoenai the son of Zerahiah, and with him two hundred males.

5 Of the sons of Shechaniah; the son of Jahaziel, and with him three hundred males.

6 Of the sons also of Adin; Ebed the son of Jonathan, and with him fifty males.

7 And of the sons of Elam; Jeshaiah the son of Athaliah, and with him seventy males.

8 And of the sons of Shephatiah; Zebadiah the son of Michael, and with him fourscore males.

registered one hundred and fifty men. 4 Of the sons of Pa'hath-mo'ab, Eli-e-ho-e'nai the son of Zerahi'ah, and with him two hundred men. 5 Of the sons of Zattu,ⁱ Shecani'ah the son of Jahazi'el, and with him three hundred men. 6 Of the sons of Adin, Ebed the son of Jonathan, and with him fifty men. 7 Of the sons of Elam, Jeshai'ah the son of Athali'ah, and with him seventy men. 8 Of the sons of Shephati'ah, Zebadi'ah the son of Michael, and with him eighty men.

ⁱ Gk 1 Esdras 8. 32. Heb lacks of Zattu

that he was the grandson (cf. 5:1) of Shecaniah (I Chr. 3:22). According to J. W. Rothstein and Johannes Hänel (*Kommentar zum ersten Buch der Chronik* [Leipzig: A. Deichert, 1927; "Kommentar zum Alten Testament"], p. 43), "and the sons of Shemaiah" is to be omitted in I Chr. 3:22, which would make **Hattush** the son of Shecaniah as here and I Esdras 8:29.

It is largely the list of lay families (vss. 3-14) that causes the genealogy to be regarded with suspicion, since many of the family names found in 2:3 ff. (=Neh. 7:8 ff.) are encountered here. Although the names of remote ancestors are identical, there is some difference in order. All the names found in vss. 3-14 are encountered among the first thirteen names in ch. 2, but only a dozen families are found here in ch. 8. "Arah" and "Zaccai" are surprisingly missing, and no names beyond 2:15 are found. Although it is not mentioned specifically, the number twelve is presumably selected to represent the twelve Hebrew tribes, for the symbolism occurs elsewhere in the Ezra narrative (cf. vss. 24, 35). Although **Jeshaiah** and **Athaliah** (vs. 7) are Benjaminite (cf. Neh. 11:7; I Chr. 8:26), it is impossible to assign the families mentioned to the twelve original Hebrew tribes.

The formula here calls for listing the ancestral name, the family leader who returned with Ezra, identified by his father's name, together with the sum of the males of that family who returned at that time. Where the formula is incomplete (vss. 5, 10) the need for restoration of text is apparent, and in the one instance of departure from the formula (vs. 13) the change is significant. Thus the name of the father of **Zechariah** (vs. 3) no longer survives. In vs. 4 **Pahath-moab** (2:6) apparently has come to indicate the family of Jeshua alone (2:6) since "Joab" appears independently later in the list (vs. 9). Missing in vs. 5 is the name of the remote ancestor, but it can be restored as "Zattu" (2:8) on the basis of the "Zathoes" of the LXX. Similarly, in vs. 10 the LXX ("Boani") and I Esdras^AB ("Banias") indicate that the missing ancestral name was "Bani" (cf. 2:10). **Ebed** ("Servant of . . .") in vs. 6 (cf. Judg. 9:26) could be an abbreviation of such a name as "Abdiel," but the Greek texts suggest an original "Obed" (Ruth 4:17, 21; I Chr. 2:12; Matt. 1:5), which abbreviates **Obadiah** (cf. vs. 9). The name **Jeshaiah** (vs. 7) is identical with the name "Isaiah." The feminine name **Shelomith** (vs. 10; cf. Lev. 24:11) should be vocalized "Shelomoth" (cf. I Chr. 23:9; 24:22; 26:25-28), as the Greek versions show. **Hakkatan** ("The Little One") in vs. 12 may be an epithet meaning either "small" or "young" (cf. Judg. 3:9 and "James the less" in Mark 15:40).

jority of the exiles preferred to remain in the relative comfort and security of Babylon, rather than to risk so long and dangerous a journey to what proved to be so precarious a livelihood. But with the help of **a man of discretion** and

by **the good hand of our God upon us** (vs. 18), this ceremonial lack was supplied. As so often in the undertakings that make history, both human wisdom and divine guidance and blessing "had a hand" in the outcome.

9 Of the sons of Joab; Obadiah the son of Jehiel, and with him two hundred and eighteen males.

10 And of the sons of Shelomith; the son of Josiphiah, and with him a hundred and threescore males.

11 And of the sons of Bebai; Zechariah the son of Bebai, and with him twenty and eight males.

12 And of the sons of Azgad; Johanan the son of Hakkatan, and with him a hundred and ten males.

13 And of the last sons of Adonikam, whose names *are these*, Eliphelet, Jeiel, and Shemaiah, and with them threescore males.

14 Of the sons also of Bigvai; Uthai, and Zabbud, and with them seventy males.

15 ¶ And I gathered them together to the river that runneth to Ahava; and there

9 Of the sons of Jo'ab, Obadi'ah the son of Jehi'el, and with him two hundred and eighteen men. 10 Of the sons of Bani,ʲ Shelo'mith the son of Josiphi'ah, and with him a hundred and sixty men. 11 Of the sons of Be'bai, Zechari'ah, the son of Be'bai, and with him twenty-eight men. 12 Of the sons of Azgad, Joha'nan the son of Hak'katan, and with him a hundred and ten men. 13 Of the sons of Adoni'kam, those who came later, their names being Eliph'elet, Jeu'el, and Shemai'ah, and with them sixty men. 14 Of the sons of Big'vai, Uthai and Zakkur, and with them seventy men.

15 I gathered them to the river that runs

ʲ Gk 1 Esdras 8. 36. Heb lacks *Bani*

In vs. 13 the formula is broken and three names are given without reference to paternity. The word translated **last** is obscure in the context. It is unnecessary to omit the word as a dittograph (cf. Ehrlich, *Randglossen zur herbräischen Bibel*, VII, 174; Bewer, *Der Text des Buches Ezra*, p. 74; Hölscher, *op. cit.*, II, 520). **Who came later** is nonsense in the light of the **went up with me** in vs. 1. The LXXᴬᴮ and I Esdras, which have "the last ones," show the way to the proper interpretation. The three individuals comprise the last of the family of **Adonikam** (2:13) that remained in Babylonia. The three men were apparently of equal rank.

Of the family of **Bigvai** (2:14), **Uthai** appears to have been the son of **Zabbud** (or **Zakkur**), as the reading in I Esdras shows (cf. Bewer, *loc. cit.*). The Greek versions show that in agreement with the single name the correct reading of the M.T. is "with him" rather than **with them**. After the corruption of the text to read two names, the text was altered to **with them** in agreement, and that "correction" is found in the Vulg., Peshitta, and about ninety MSS. **Zabbud** represents the written tradition of the M.T., but Hebrew oral tradition, supported by the Vulg. and the LXXᴸ has **Zakkur**. The names are easily confused in writing and it is impossible to determine which was original.

D. Acquisition of Temple Servants (8:15-20=I Esdras 8:41-49)

15. As with every large caravan about to get under way, an open space away from the big city was used as an assembly point where the people could be organized and the equipment prepared for the expedition (cf. Jer. 41:17). Here the emigrees **abode . . . in tents** during the necessary period. Ezra's camp was located on a stream flowing toward **Ahava,** a place not yet certainly identified. Instead of **river,** translate "stream" or "canal" (cf. Ezek. 1:1; 3:15). Identification which would place **Ahava** on the Euphrates must be wrong since that river would not be described as in vs. 15. Many attempts at identification have been made, but the most probable links it with modern Mečin, the classical Maschana or Scenae, on the canal now called Ad-Duǧejl (Alois Musil, *The Middle Euphrates* [New York: Czech Academy of Sciences and Arts, 1927], Appendix XX, pp. 360-63). The classical name, which means "tented settlement," suits well the description of **Ahava.** The place is located on the transport route along the right bank of the Tigris River at the point where it branches into two caravan routes, one leading northwest, the other going westward across central Mesopotamia.

Some have seen the prototype of the **three days** in the Nehemiah memoirs (Neh.

abode we in tents three days: and I viewed the people, and the priests, and found there none of the sons of Levi.

16 Then sent I for Eliezer, for Ariel, for Shemaiah, and for Elnathan, and for Jarib, and for Elnathan, and for Nathan, and for Zechariah, and for Meshullam, chief men; also for Joiarib, and for Elnathan, men of understanding.

to Aha'va, and there we encamped three days. As I reviewed the people and the priests, I found there none of the sons of Levi. 16 Then I sent for Elie'zer, Ar'i-el, Shemai'ah, Elna'than, Jarib, Elna'than, Nathan, Zechari'ah, and Meshul'lam, leading men, and for Joi'arib and Elna'than, who

---

2:11; Kapelrud, *op. cit.,* p. 46), but three days is only a reasonable time to delay for organization (cf. vs. 32 for disbanding the caravan). It was apparently on the third day that the absence of the Levites was discovered, but it was not until the twelfth day that the lack was remedied and the caravan was ready to depart (vs. 31).

Perhaps in ancient times, as today in mass migrations, the chieftains rode together in advance of the caravan, followed by the various households together with their stock. At each encampment the families erected tents in a place selected by the family leader so that a halted caravan was actually a series of family camps (Charles M. Doughty, *Travels in Arabia Deserta* [New York: Random House, 1946], pp. 257, 161-62; cf. C. P. Grant, *The Syrian Desert* [New York: The Macmillan Co., 1938], p. 226). Stress on family groups explains the family structure of the genealogy. Thus, too, the absence of Levites was detected when Ezra **reviewed the people and the priests.**

The Levites apparently refused to leave their security and position in Babylonia for the insecurity of menial duties in the Jerusalem temple (cf. Neh. 13:10). Later Jews, embarrassed by such reluctance, rationalized the Levites' behavior by explaining that since Abraham had once dwelt in Babylonia, and the Babylonian language was similar to Hebrew, the Levites and other Jews felt at home there (Tosephta Baba Kama VII, 3; Pesaḥim 87b). Some insisted that Levites were in the caravan (cf. 7:7), but that they were old men who had made themselves unfit for temple service by biting off their fingers (cf. Lev. 21:16-24) rather than play their instruments at Nebuchadrezzar's orders (Yalkut II, 884; Midrash Tehillim, 137). But Ezra found no Levites and had to recruit some.

16. A group of men were appointed to represent Ezra in the gathering of the Levites. They are called **leading men,** but aside from **Zechariah** (vss. 3, 11) and **Shemaiah** (vs. 13), who bear very common names, none is listed among the family leaders in the genealogy (vss. 3-14). Nor can it be determined just how many members the delegation had. The M.T., LXX, and Vulg. list eleven; I Esdras^AB has ten; while I Esdras^L has only seven. Several names seem to be duplicated. **Elnathan** appears thrice and the abbreviation **Nathan** once, while **Jarib** and **Joiarib** are variants of the same name. One **Elnathan** may be a corruption of another name for which six MSS have "Jonathan." **Joiarib** and **Elnathan,** now separated from the others at the end of the verse, obviously duplicate the earlier **Jarib** and **Elnathan,** as I Esdras^L shows. Their omission restores to the noun "chieftains" (lit., "heads") its adjectival modifier "intelligent," so that all men listed, not just the last two, are characterized as "intelligent leaders," as in I Esdras 8:44.

Grammatical ambiguity makes possible the translations "I sent to Eliezer" as well as **I sent for Eliezer,** as though the men were located somewhere apart from Ezra in Babylonia. But Ezra sent them to Iddo (vs. 17). No preposition is given in the Vulg. and the Lucianic Greek texts, apparently because it was recognized as the sign of the object, as in Aramaic (E. F. Kautzsch, *Gesenius' Hebrew Grammar,* tr. A. E. Cowley [2nd English ed.; Oxford: Clarendon Press, 1910], sec. 143e; cf. Driver, *Intro. to Literature of O.T.,* p. 538, No. 39; Torrey, *Ezra Studies,* p. 265; Bewer, *op. cit.,* p. 75), and the translation should be "I sent Eliezer."

17 And I sent them with commandment unto Iddo the chief at the place Casiphia, and I told them what they should say unto Iddo, *and* to his brethren the Nethinim, at the place Casiphia, that they should bring unto us ministers for the house of our God.

18 And by the good hand of our God upon us they brought us a man of understanding, of the sons of Mahli, the son of Levi, the son of Israel; and Sherebiah, with his sons and his brethren, eighteen;

were men of insight, 17 and sent them to Iddo, the leading man at the place Casiphi'a, telling them what to say to Iddo and his brethren the temple servants[k] at the place Casiphi'a, namely, to send us ministers for the house of our God. 18 And by the good hand of our God upon us, they brought us a man of discretion, of the sons of Mahli the son of Levi, son of Israel, namely Sherebi'ah with his sons and kins-

[k] Heb *nethinim*

---

17. **I sent them with commandment** reflects the conflate reading of the M.T., but only one of the ideas, either "send" or "command," should be translated. Hebrew oral tradition and the Peshitta call for "I commanded them," as in the American Jewish Translation. This is understood as meaning "directing them [to]" or "I dispatched them" (cf. Exod. 6:13; Jer. 27:4). Hebrew written tradition, the LXX[AB], and Arabic versions call for a translation **I sent them.** The **Iddo** (אדו) to whom the delegation was sent must not be confused with the Iddo (עדו) of I Kings 4:14; Zech. 1:7; II Chr. 12:15, which is spelled differently. The name abbreviates one containing the element "Lord" (*'ādhôn*), such as Adonijah. It may be found in Neo-Babylonian texts as *mid-du-u-a* (Oluf Krückmann, *Neubabylonische Rechts- und Verwaltungs-texte* [Leipzig: J. C. Hinrichs, 1933], No. 9, l. 38). Like the leaders who accompanied Ezra (8:1, 16), **Iddo** is a "head" or **leading man** of the Jews.

Iddo was found at **the place Casiphia** which also is not yet identified but must have been near **Ahava.** Because 9:8 uses **place** for the holy place in Jerusalem, it has been suggested that **Casiphia** was a sanctuary, a Babylonian Jewish "temple" parallel to the Jewish temples in Egypt (Laurence E. Browne, "A Jewish Sanctuary in Babylonia," *Journal of Theological Studies,* XVII [1916], 400-401; cf. the same author's *Early Judaism* [Cambridge: Cambridge University Press, 1920], p. 53). It has also been conjectured that **Casiphia** was a training school for Levites (Bertheau, *Esra, Nechemia und Ester,* p. 104). But it is more probable that **Casiphia** was a city or village with a large Jewish colony. **Place** is used of a city in Hebrew when its name is already known (cf. II Kings 18:25), but the word may be used here as a determinative, an aid in reading as in Akkadian (cf. Gen. 12:6; Jer. 19:13; cf. W. E. Staples, "The Reading of Hebrew," *American Journal of Semitic Languages and Literatures,* LVIII [1941], 139-45). It has been suggested that the name **Casiphia** has been distorted to Ctesiphon, the city lying just across the river from Seleucia (Hugo Winckler, "Kasiphja-Ktesiphon," *Altorientalische Forschungen* [Leipzig: E. Pfeiffer, 1901], Reihe 2, Bd. III, pp. 509-30). Such identification cannot be regarded as certain, but the site would be suitable if the antiquity of Ctesiphon could be demonstrated archaeologically.

The senseless combination "his brother the Nethinim" in the M.T. has been corrected to **his brethren the Nethinim.** It is better to read with the versions, "Iddo and his brethren." But **Iddo** was probably a Levite rather than one of the Nethinim and **brethren** here merely indicates mutual interest and professional relationship, as elsewhere (cf. 3:2). As I Esdras shows, originally the text had "and the Nethinim," but the conjunction was lost accidentally since it was identical with the last letter of **his brethren.** Thus we should read, "Iddo and his brethren and the Nethinim." **Ministers** is, lit., "servants," but as a cultic title it could be applied even to priests (cf. Exod. 28:35; 30:20); here it indicates menial servants, the lowly assistants of the priests.

18-20. Josephus summarizes these verses but, as usual, in the interest of the narrative he supplies no names. **The good hand** is as in 7:6. As I Esdras[AB] shows, the **man of discretion** was **Sherebiah,** who plays an important role in the Ezra story (8:18, 24; Neh. 8:7; 9:4-5; 10:12; 12:8, 24). Thus **and** before his name should be regarded as explicative

19 And Hashabiah, and with him Jeshaiah of the sons of Merari, his brethren and their sons, twenty;

20 Also of the Nethinim, whom David and the princes had appointed for the service of the Levites, two hundred and twenty Nethinim: all of them were expressed by name.

21 ¶ Then I proclaimed a fast there, at the river of Ahava, that we might afflict our-

men, eighteen; 19 also Hashabi'ah and with him Jeshai'ah of the sons of Merar'i, with his kinsmen and their sons, twenty; 20 besides two hundred and twenty of the temple servants, whom David and his officials had set apart to attend the Levites. These were all mentioned by name.

21 Then I proclaimed a fast there, at the

(cf. 6:8), translated **namely. Sherebiah** is traced to Jacob **(Israel)** through **Levi** (cf. Exod. 6:19; Num. 3:20). All of the Levites mentioned were of the line of **Merari** the son of **Levi** (cf. I Chr. 6:47), the family which traditionally served the tent of meeting (Num. 4:29-33, 42-45) and helped to bear the tabernacle (Num. 10:17). **Hashabiah** is listed with **Jeshaiah** (vs. 7) as being of the sons of **Merari** (I Chr. 6:44-45). The antecedent of **his brethren** is Sherebiah of vs. 18, but **their sons** refers to the families of **Hashabiah** and **Jesaiah.**

Only thirty-eight Levites were assembled, but the number of servants was swelled by the relatively large number of **Nethinim** (cf. 2:43) who were induced to go to Jerusalem. Because the **Nethinim** are not mentioned in vs. 15, the reference to them has been regarded as an addition to the text. But 7:7 lists them as among those who returned with Ezra, and it is probable that with so few Levites returning, some special inducements may have been offered to bring servants of any order to the temple. The unusual form of the relative pronoun in vs. 20 suggests that the clause, **whom David and the princes,** etc., may have been added to the text. Since the Chronicler uses the relative particle several times (I Chr. 5:20; 27:27), this may be the work of his hand. There was no need to comment on the origin of the Nethinim here, and it is only here that there is preserved the tradition that **David and the princes** were responsible for instituting the **Nethinim.** The Chronicler elsewhere declares that the temple cultus derived from the time of David, but the **Nethinim** do not come into prominence until the postexilic period.

Mentioned by name is associated with lists of names elsewhere in the work of the Chronicler (I Chr. 12:31; 16:41; II Chr. 28:15; 31:19) and in Num. 1:17. It indicates that a full list was available and could have been given but was omitted because too many names were involved.

E. FINAL PREPARATION BEFORE DEPARTURE (8:21-23=I Esdras 8:50-53)

Ezra assumed leadership at once, and as leader combined his secular and religious functions in seeking the protection of God for his caravan. He had assured the king that God would protect his own and therefore did not request a bodyguard (vs. 22), but he was aware of the robbers who would try to loot his caravan (vs. 31) to get the rich and valuable treasure he carried (vss. 25-28). Through fasting and prayer he sought divine protection (vss. 21-23), and the temple treasure was placed in the charge of God's holy priests (vss. 24-30). The move was successful, for although the caravan was attacked they finished the journey safely (cf. vss. 23, 31).

21-23. The self-inflicted hunger pains of a **fast** were calculated to influence God to pity the fasting petitioner (cf. II Sam. 12:16 ff.; Isa. 58:3) and thus gain a favorable

---

21-36. *Prayer and Fasting.*—Here some sense of historical reality and religious urgency breaks through the genealogical and ceremonial framework within which the Chronicler is so concerned to set his story; and we begin to feel something of the firsthand authenticity that is

so marked in Nehemiah's memoirs. Ezra proclaims a period of fasting and prayer, because he is ashamed to ask the king for a military guard after he has so explicitly put his reliance on **the hand of our God** (vs. 22) for guidance and protection.

selves before our God, to seek of him a right way for us, and for our little ones, and for all our substance.

22 For I was ashamed to require of the king a band of soldiers and horsemen to help us against the enemy in the way: because we had spoken unto the king, saying, The hand of our God *is* upon all them for good that seek him; but his power and his wrath *is* against all them that forsake him.

23 So we fasted and besought our God for this: and he was entreated of us.

24 ¶ Then I separated twelve of the chief of the priests, Sherebiah, Hashabiah, and ten of their brethren with them,

river Aha'va, that we might humble ourselves before our God, to seek from him a straight way for ourselves, our children, and all our goods. 22 For I was ashamed to ask the king for a band of soldiers and horsemen to protect us against the enemy on our way; since we had told the king, "The hand of our God is for good upon all that seek him, and the power of his wrath is against all that forsake him." 23 So we fasted and besought our God for this, and he listened to our entreaty.

24 Then I set apart twelve of the leading priests: Sherebi'ah, Hashabi'ah, and ten of

---

answer to prayer. The **right way** means a **straight** or "even" way (cf. Isa. 26:7; Jer. 31:9). In I Esdras^{AB} 8:50 it is interpreted as a "favorable journey" (εὐοδίαν). The Amer. Trans. renders it "a safe journey." Because of danger of ambush by local raiders who would plunder the caravan while passing through lonely desert wastes en route to the west, during the Persian period the government in control sometimes on request furnished a military escort (cf. Neh. 2:9), just as the Turks supplied janizaries during the early part of the Ottoman period (cf. Grant, *op. cit.*, pp. 128, 137-39) and the French did in Syria in modern times. The rendering **band of soldiers**, lit., "a force" (cf. 4:23), represents a word used in the Jewish papyri for the detachment of soldiers posted at Assuan, and also in the Behistun papyri for the Assyrian and Persian armies. **To help us,** like the M.T., implies a readiness of the Jews themselves to fight, but **to protect us,** which is based on the Greek versions, stresses absolute dependence upon the armed escort. The great concern was felt for the children and possessions. The word translated **little ones** (vs. 21) is found frequently in early Hebrew but is relatively rare in the late period (cf. Isa. 9:6; Esth. 3:13; 8:11; II Chr. 20:13; 31:18). The Greek versions translate it as **our children. Substance** (Hebrew *rekhûsh;* cf. 1:4, 6) can mean "livestock," as in I Esdras 8:50, but here the broader interpretation of the term, accumulated **goods,** is preferable since Ezra sought safe arrival not only of his beasts but of the treasure (vss. 25-28) being delivered.

In Ezra's refusal to ask for a bodyguard some have seen a rebuke to Nehemiah for lack of faith and a lauding of Ezra as superior (cf. Kapelrud, *Question of Authorship in the Ezra-Narrative,* pp. 52-53). It is thus supposed that the Ezra narrative here is dependent upon Nehemiah and is thus historically improbable. It may, however, be merely the expected contrast between the realistic and practical administrator Nehemiah and the religious idealist Ezra.

F. DELEGATION TO TRANSPORT TREASURE (8:24-30=I Esdras 8:54-60)

Lacking an armed bodyguard, Ezra sought some way to protect the treasure entrusted by the Persian court for delivery to the temple in Jerusalem. As material set apart for divine use, the vessels and the metals were **holy unto the LORD** (vs. 28). Both men, as priests and Levites (cf. Lev. 21:6; II Chr. 23:6), and temple paraphernalia (cf.

To Americans, vss. 21-23 may well seem the most momentous in the entire book in their far-reaching historical consequences. William Bradford's *History of Plymouth Plantation* tells us that this was the text of John Robinson's last sermon at Leyden, before he sent his little

band of Pilgrims forth in 1620 to face the perils of the North Atlantic in autumn, and the rigors of "a stern and rock-bound coast" [5] through that first terrible winter at Plymouth,

[5] Felicia Dorothea Hemans, "The Landing of the Pilgrim Fathers."

25 And weighed unto them the silver, and the gold, and the vessels, *even* the offering of the house of our God, which the king, and his counselors, and his lords, and all Israel *there* present, had offered:

26 I even weighed unto their hand six hundred and fifty talents of silver, and silver vessels a hundred talents, *and* of gold a hundred talents;

their kinsmen with them. 25 And I weighed out to them the silver and the gold and the vessels, the offering for the house of our God which the king and his counselors and his lords and all Israel there present had offered; 26 I weighed out into their hand six hundred and fifty talents of silver, and silver vessels worth a hundred talents, and

---

Josh. 6:19; Zech. 14:20-21) were consecrated and were then no longer subject to common use but were henceforth surrounded by taboos and restrictions placed on all of God's property. Only holy men should handle holy things. The knowledge that the valuables belonged neither to Ezra nor the people but to their God would serve to make the holy men guarding the wealth unquestionably honest and especially vigilant until their responsibilities should be discharged in Jerusalem. Implied also is the fact that God would in a special way protect what was his own.

24. Set apart means selected for the special task. **Twelve** was a popular number among the Hebrews, but it is here not a symbol for the twelve tribes since all of the clerics were of the same tribe. No laymen were permitted to handle holy things. In addition to the dozen priests there were as many Levites selected (cf. vs. 30). Since **Sherebiah** and **Hashabiah** were not priests (cf. 8:2) but leaders of Ezra's newly acquired Levites (cf. vss. 18-19), it is necessary to read with I Esdras the conjunction "and" before each name. It has been suggested that something like "and the Levites" has been omitted after **priests** (Torrey, *Ezra Studies*, p. 266). Josephus (*Antiquities* XI. 5. 2) identifies the group as "treasurers who were of priestly descent." **Their brethren** means the Levites.

25. Of the treasure the **silver** and **gold** constituted the **freewill offering** (vs. 28) collected in Babylonia for the temple (cf. 7:15 ff.). In addition to the **king** and **counselors** (vs. 25) mentioned in 7:15, the M.T. adds a third group, **his lords,** which appear as "leaders" in the LXX and "grandees" or "noblemen" in I Esdras. Josephus here omits the third group as in 7:15. Unworked precious metal, presumably in bars or ingots, is listed by weight alone, but the manufactured articles are listed by number and appraised value. As elsewhere, **vessels** may better be translated "implements" (cf. 1:7). In listing the treasure the most common and abundant metal is listed first, then gold, and finally the rare and valuable objects.

26. The figures here given, much too large to be historically probable, are doubtless the Chronicler's contribution, for he becomes overly enthusiastic in his statistics where the temple is concerned (cf. II Chr. 7:5), even where his figures can be checked against an earlier source (II Sam. 24:24; I Chr. 21:25).

The **hundred talents** assigned to the silver vessels does not represent the M.T., which has, lit., "a hundred silver vessels worth talents." It has been proposed to read the **talents** as dual, "two talents," rather than as plural (Bewer, *Der Text des Buches Ezra,* p. 77; cf. Rudolph, *Esra und Nehemia,* p. 82). But such a modest sum seems inappropriate in the light of the other figures. It is more probable that the actual figure, which should follow **talents,** has been lost from the text (cf. Meyer, *Entstehung des Judenthums,* p. 69; Torrey, *Ezra Studies,* p. 266). Since a **talent** weighed about sixty-five

---

during which half the company of the "Mayflower" perished. Thus the "idealized history" of the Chronicler kindled some at least of the spiritual dynamic that sustained a longer and riskier journey than Ezra's, and through the "Mayflower Compact" signed in Provincetown Harbor became a creative part of the social

and religious heritage of American democracy. The congregation at Leyden, like the caravan at the river Ahava, proclaimed a "day of solleme humiliation . . . powering out prairs to ye Lord with great fervencie, mixed with abundance of tears." Robinson's sermon on this text took most of the day "very profitably," and his

27 Also twenty basins of gold, of a thousand drams; and two vessels of fine copper, precious as gold.

28 And I said unto them, Ye *are* holy unto the LORD; the vessels *are* holy also; and the silver and the gold *are* a freewill offering unto the LORD God of your fathers.

29 Watch ye, and keep *them,* until ye weigh *them* before the chief of the priests and the Levites, and chief of the fathers of Israel, at Jerusalem, in the chambers of the house of the LORD.

30 So took the priests and the Levites the weight of the silver, and the gold, and the vessels, to bring *them* to Jerusalem unto the house of our God.

a hundred talents of gold, 27 twenty bowls of gold worth a thousand darics, and two vessels of fine bright bronze as precious as gold. 28 And I said to them, "You are holy to the LORD, and the vessels are holy; and the silver and the gold are a freewill offering to the LORD, the God of your fathers. 29 Guard them and keep them until you weigh them before the chief priests and the Levites and the heads of fathers' houses in Israel at Jerusalem, within the chambers of the house of the LORD." 30 So the priests and the Levites took over the weight of the silver and the gold and the vessels, to bring them to Jerusalem, to the house of our God.

pounds (cf. 7:22), the silver gift would come to more than twenty-one tons, while the **hundred talents** of gold would come to about three and a quarter tons, worth considerably more than the silver. The ratio of silver to gold in the Persian period is as yet unknown, but in the Chaldean age, just before the Persian conquest, the ratio of silver to gold varied between ten and thirteen to one (W. H. Dubberstein, "Comparative Prices in Later Babylonia," *American Journal of Semitic Languages and Literatures,* LVI [1939], 23).

27. The **bowls** are of the same type as those in 1:10. The term rendered **drams** or **darics** is spelled as in I Chr. 29:7 (*'adharkōnîm*) rather than as in Ezra 2:69 (cf. Neh. 7:70-72). However, the confusion in the LXX^{ABL} suggests that the spelling of the M.T. was once that in 2:69, for the error there, "the road" (τὴν ὁδόν), points to a confusion of the Hebrew "road" (דרך) with the beginning letters of **darics** (דרכ [מנים]).

The list of treasure concludes with the unique vessels of special type and great value. They are described as being as **precious as gold,** but Josephus calls them "more precious than gold," which would account for their being last in a list that is apparently in an ascending scale. Since the same word is used in Hebrew for both **copper** and **bronze,** the nature of the material is uncertain and it has even been suggested that it was "a rare amalgam" (George Rawlinson, *Ezra and Nehemiah* [New York: Anson D. F. Randolph & Co., 1891], p. 23). The description given here seems to favor copper as a metal of beauty that could be highly polished. The KJV omits the modifier found in the M.T., which in the RSV is translated **bright,** apparently because the LXX has

departing flock never forgot what he said to them:

I charge you before God and his blessed Angels to follow me no further than I follow Christ, . . . and if God shall reveal anything to you by any other Instrument of his, be as ready to receive it as ever you were to receive any truth by my ministry. [Two days later they left Leyden], that goodly and pleasant citie, which had been their resting place near 12 years; but they knew they were pilgrimes, and looked not much on those things, but lift[ed] up their eyes to ye heavens, their dearest cuntrie, and quieted their spirits.[6]

[6] George F. Willison, *Saints and Strangers* (New York: Reynal and Hitchcock, 1945), pp. 119-20.

So Ezra's faith and courage for his journey across the Arabian Desert quickened the Pilgrims' faith and courage that dared both the Atlantic and the winter wilderness two thousand years later, passing over thus into the spiritual heritage of the western continent to mold the history of the New World. In view of the historical results of the journeys of both these little companies, the religiously minded among their children's children have had reason aplenty to join in the grateful acknowledgment of their "founding fathers": **The hand of our God was upon us, and he delivered us from the hand of the enemy and from ambushes by the way** (vs. 31*b*).

31 ¶ Then we departed from the river of Ahava on the twelfth *day* of the first month, to go unto Jerusalem: and the hand of our God was upon us, and he delivered us from the hand of the enemy, and of such as lay in wait by the way.

32 And we came to Jerusalem, and abode there three days.

31 Then we departed from the river Aha'va on the twelfth day of the first month, to go to Jerusalem; the hand of our God was upon us, and he delivered us from the hand of the enemy and from ambushes by the way. 32 We came to Jerusalem, and

---

"glittering" and I Esdras has "glittering like gold." In the Amer. Trans. it is interpreted as "burnished." But the M.T. has "reddened" (cf. Arabic *ṣahiba*, "be red") and the term appears to be a translation of the Akkadian "red-gleaming copper" (*sipparu russu*).

G. Departure and Arrival (8:31-36 = I Esdras 8:61-64)

The first stage of the journey to Jerusalem began on the first of the first month (7:9) in the seventh year of Artaxerxes (7:7-8). But Josephus, basing his narrative on I Esdras 8:6 (=Ezra 7:8), wrongly places the movement during the seventh year of Xerxes (479 b.c.), which is too early. The delay at Ahava (cf. 8:15 ff.) took some time, but after the temple servants were gotten and the caravan organized, the departure was made on the twelfth day of the first month (Apr. 16, 398 b.c.).

31. We departed translates a word used among nomads meaning "pull up stakes" and then "depart," a word rare in late Hebrew (Job 4:21; 19:10) as might be expected, but it is appropriate here for the departure of a tented community (cf. 8:15). Josephus declares that the group "set out from the Euphrates" but that is much less likely than from the Tigris. The route along the Euphrates would be difficult and dangerous during early spring (Rawlinson, *Ezra and Nehemiah*, pp. 32-35). Musil (*Middle Euphrates*, p. 361) says: "There was no corn ripe as yet in early April on the Euphrates, and the Jews would therefore have found neither food for themselves nor pasture for their animals. Moreover, the chiefs of the different settlements along the Euphrates, always more or less independent, would undoubtedly have troubled them with their demands. The chiefs from the surrounding country would not have hesitated to fall upon a body of strangers not protected by Persian soldiery and who, as they knew or at least imagined, had plenty of money and supplies." The alternate route, longer but safer, through more inhabited territory "led first along the right bank of the Tigris northward nearly as far as Mosul of today; then it turned west along the foot of the northern mountain range and went through the region between the desert and the settled country as far as the Euphrates, which it reached at the ford of Thapsacus in the neighborhood of the present Bâlis ruins" (*ibid.*).

Ezra's journey took four months, culminating at Jerusalem on the first day of the fifth month (7:9), July 31, 398 b.c., including necessary delays and the journey from Syria southward to Jerusalem. Strabo (*Geography* XVI. 1. 8, 26-27) describes the same route as traveled by merchants of his day, and indicates that it took twenty-five days from the ford of the Euphrates (at Anthemusia) to Scenae (=Ahava) on camel back (Musil, *op. cit.*, pp. 361-62). Ezra's large group with its livestock could scarcely match the speed of small merchant caravans.

32. Upon arrival at **Jerusalem** there were **three days** of encampment, apparently for rest and orderly demobilization of the caravan. Immigrants would have to be settled and the inevitable conflicts between the newcomers and the people in the land would have to be adjusted. Because in Neh. 2:11 a similar interval followed Nehemiah's arrival, vs. 32 here has been regarded as a borrowing from that passage by the Chronicler (cf. Siegfried, *Esra, Nehemia und Esther*, p. 60; Kapelrud, *op. cit.*, p. 57), but there is nothing implausible in the narrative here. In fact, such a period would be even more necessary with Ezra's caravan than with Nehemiah's smaller company.

33 ¶ Now on the fourth day was the silver and the gold and the vessels weighed in the house of our God by the hand of Meremoth the son of Uriah the priest; and with him *was* Eleazar the son of Phinehas; and with them *was* Jozabad the son of Jeshua, and Noadiah the son of Binnui, Levites;

34 By number *and* by weight of every one: and all the weight was written at that time.

35 *Also* the children of those that had been carried away, which were come out of the captivity, offered burnt offerings unto the God of Israel, twelve bullocks for all Israel, ninety and six rams, seventy and seven lambs, twelve he goats *for* a sin offering: all *this was* a burnt offering unto the LORD.

there we remained three days. 33 On the fourth day, within the house of our God, the silver and the gold and the vessels were weighed into the hands of Mer'emoth the priest, son of Uri'ah, and with him was Elea'zar the son of Phin'ehas, and with them were the Levites, Jo'zabad the son of Jeshua and No-adi'ah the son of Bin'nui. 34 The whole was counted and weighed, and the weight of everything was recorded.

35 At that time those who had come from captivity, the returned exiles, offered burnt offerings to the God of Israel, twelve bulls for all Israel, ninety-six rams, seventy-seven lambs, and as a sin offering twelve he-goats; all this was a burnt offering to

---

33-34. On the **fourth day,** after the caravan had disbanded, Ezra turned to the less pressing but important duty of delivering the temple treasure. It was presumably turned in at "the chambers," the storerooms or treasuries of the temple (cf. vs. 29; Neh. 10:37-39). Since the M.T. says that the things were "weighed out upon the hands" of the treasurers, it is better to read **weighed into the hands of . . .** rather than "under the direction of . . ." (Torrey, *Ezra Studies*, p. 267). **By the hand of** is certainly too ambiguous, since it is clear from the M.T. that **Meremoth** was the recipient of the treasure, not the one bringing it. In businesslike fashion the goods were checked **by number and by weight** against the inventory at Jerusalem. Such concern about accounting has led to the conclusion that the Ezra document is no mere memoir or edifying treatise but an actual report back to the king and court regarding the progress of the tasks to which Ezra was entrusted (cf. Rudolph, *op. cit.,* pp. 83-84). Because "the same peculiar construction and the same words" are used in I Chr. 28:14-18, it has been suggested that the Chronicler has written this passage (Torrey, *loc. cit.*), but both passages are concerned with tabulation, and the agreement is not as verbally exact as the theory implies. The **priest, Meremoth,** is mentioned as having come up from Babylonia at an earlier day (cf. 2:61). Since he was of the family of Koz, who could not authenticate their right to priestly office (2:61-62), and since he is mentioned without priestly title as a builder of the wall in the days of Nehemiah (Neh. 3:4, 21), the presence of the title **priest** here is significant. It has been conjectured that Meremoth's double share of work on the wall (Neh. 3:4, 21) gained his priestly investiture (cf. Aage Bentzen, "Priesterschaft und Laien in der jüdischen Gemeinde des fünften Jahrhunderts," *Archiv für Orientforschung,* VI [1931], 285). Such evidence would indicate the priority of Nehemiah's arrival and activity in Jerusalem (cf. Rowley, *Servant of the Lord,* pp. 158-59). **Eleazar** may be the priest accused of marrying a foreign wife in 10:18. **Jozabad** and **Noadiah** were Levitical assistants to the priests. A **Jozabad** was one of the chief Levites who had oversight of the outside business of the temple in the days of Nehemiah (Neh. 11:16), a role in which he appears to be functioning here. A Levite of the same name married a foreign woman (10:23). **Noadiah** appears only here, but he is of the important family of **Binnui** which, like that of **Jeshua,** is listed as having come up from Babylonia with Zerubbabel (Neh. 12:8).

35-36. Appended to the Ezra narrative are these verses in which the Chronicler's hand is apparent both in interest and style. But the content need not be regarded as unhistorical, at least in its broad outlines, although the Chronicler may have heightened

36 ¶ And they delivered the king's commissions unto the king's lieutenants, and to the governors on this side the river: and they furthered the people, and the house of God.

the Lord. 36 They also delivered the king's commissions to the king's satraps and to the governors of the province Beyond the River; and they aided the people and the house of God.

some of the details. The verses complete the episode by disposing of elements presumably neglected in the Ezra document: the presenting of the sacrifices at the temple (7:17) and the delivery of royal instructions (cf. 7:21) to the secular officials of the western provinces. Both matters lie within the peculiar interests of the Chronicler, for they concern the history and fortunes of the temple.

At that time (vs. 34 KJV) is an example of faulty verse division, since it should introduce vs. 35, as in the RSV, which here follows the LXX^AB. Josephus (*Antiquities* XI. 5. 2) indicates that the sacrifices were made "when he [Ezra] had given these [treasures] over to the priests." The nature of the **offerings** is not clear. He explains them not as special gifts but as regular "whole burnt offerings customarily made." But the verse here stresses that it was the returning Jews, not those already in the land, who made the sacrifices. This would suggest that they may have been, like the thanksgiving (*tôdhāh*) sacrifices (Lev. 7:11-12; 22:29-30) or "joyous sacrifices" (*šalmê simḥāh*) of the later period, thanksgiving for a safe journey. In I Esdras 8:66 the sacrifice is called a "peace offering" (σωτηρίον), the word regularly used in the LXX to translate the Hebrew *shélem*. But only a portion of the peace offerings and thank offerings was burned; the rest was eaten by the worshiper and his friends. The only public peace offerings were the two lambs at Pentecost (cf. Lev. 23:19). Public sacrifices, as a rule, were either **burnt offerings** (*'ōlāh*) or the **sin offering** (*ḥaṭṭā'th*). Therefore Josephus declares the sacrifices were "as an atonement for sins," and thus agrees with the M.T., which mentions a **sin offering**. The term **sin offering** may apply only to the **twelve he-goats** (cf. 6:17; Lev. 7:1-38).

The figures in this verse indicate the author's belief that the restored community represented all the twelve tribes of Israel (cf. vss. 1-14, 24), since all sacrifices are twelve or multiples of it. Obviously the **seventy-seven** lambs is corrupt and should be "seventy-two," as is rendered in I Esdras^AL and Josephus. The figures here presented suggest those of the tribal sacrifices at the dedication of the early altar according to Num. 7:12-88, but the number of **rams** is extraordinarily large, for in Num. 7:87-88 the number of rams and lambs is identical.

36. For **commissions** the M.T. has, lit., "the laws" (Persian *data*; cf. 7:12), but the meaning is clearly weakened to mean "instructions" or "orders." The **commissions** here mentioned are usually identified as those incorporated in the king's letter (7:21-24), but the latter are addressed to the "treasurers" whereas the officers here mentioned as the **king's lieutenants** are his **satraps** (Persian *khshathrapāvan*) and **governors** (Babylonian *paḥatu*; cf. 5:3, 6, 14; 6:6, 7, 13). The **satraps** were the vice-regents of satrapies, and as such, among the highest officials in the kingdom. **Governors** was a Semitic title which in the Persian period was ambiguous and could be applied to any official, including the satrap himself (cf. 5:3). Here, as in Daniel (3:2-3, 27; 6:7) and Esther (3:12; 8:9), the Persian and Babylonian titles are found side by side. It is sometimes assumed that **governors** is an explanatory gloss to **satraps** (Batten, *Ezra and Nehemiah*, p. 330) or vice versa (Bertholet, *Esra und Nehemia*, p. 38), and Guthe has suggested that the conjunction might be explicative, "namely" (cf. 6:8; 8:18).

They furthered or **they aided** reflects a verb meaning "to lift" or "to carry," which is extended to mean "they gave support to," as in the Amer. Trans. (cf. 1:4; I Kings 9:11; Esth. 9:3). In the M.T. the subject could be Ezra and his companions, the **they** of vs. 36a, but Josephus (*Antiquities* XI. 5. 2) clarifies the subject as the officials who received the royal orders, for he says: "Being compelled to carry out his [Artaxerxes'] commands they [the officials] honored the Jewish nation and assisted it in all necessary ways."

643

9 Now when these things were done, the princes came to me, saying, The people of Israel, and the priests, and the Levites, have not separated themselves from the people of the lands, *doing* according to their abominations, *even* of the Canaanites, the Hittites, the Perizzites, the Jebusites, the Ammonites, the Moabites, the Egyptians, and the Amorites.	9 After these things had been done, the officials approached me and said, "The people of Israel and the priests and the Levites have not separated themselves from the peoples of the lands with their abominations, from the Canaanites, the Hittites, the Per'izzites, the Jeb'usites, the Ammonites, the Moabites, the Egyptians, and the Amo-

The transition from 8:36 to 9:1 is decidedly too abrupt to be original. The necessary sequel to ch. 8 is Neh. 7:70-73, which is quite out of place in the story of Nehemiah. The entire passage Neh. 7:70–8:18 belongs between Ezra 8 and Ezra 9 (Torrey, *Ezra Studies,* p. 256). Rudolph (*op. cit.,* p. 85; cf. pp. 14-15) would move from 8:36 to Neh. 7:72*b*.

IV. MIXED MARRIAGES (9:1–10:44)
A. REPORT OF MIXED MARRIAGES (9:1-2=I Esdras 8:68-70)

9:1. After these things had been done suggests that the crisis of chs. 9–10 occurred during the fifth month, shortly after Ezra's arrival at Jerusalem (cf. 7:8-9), but Josephus claims it was "some time afterwards," and 10:6-9 indicates a date in the ninth month (Dec. 14, 398 B.C.), almost five months after Ezra's arrival. The events of the seventh month (Neh. 7:70–8:18) had thus intervened, and **these things** must refer to the acceptance of the law and the celebration of the feast of Tabernacles (Neh. 8:1-18), a part of the Ezra story that has been transported to the book of Nehemiah. The proper order of the Ezra narrative would have Neh. 7:70–8:18 between Ezra 8 and 9 (cf. Torrey, *Ezra Studies,* pp. 255-60).

Since it is unlikely that Ezra would have remained so long ignorant of the situation concerning mixed marriages, or would have made no attempt to combat that trend, the account of earlier, futile attempts by Ezra to solve the problem may have been editorially suppressed by the Chronicler as being unworthy behavior by the community he recognized as ideal (cf. 4:1; 5:1). But it is possible also that Ezra himself had omitted from his official report the previous failures in favor of the detailed account of the more successful measures which is preserved (cf. Rudolph, *op. cit.,* pp. 85, 87).

The term **princes** (*sārîm,* vs. 2) is used by Nehemiah for district leaders (Neh. 3:9; 12:31-32). **Peoples of the lands** (cf. 3:3) are those found in Judea by those who returned from the Exile. The long list of people which follows is intended as a commentary on **peoples of the lands.** But the list is a worthless and unhistorical addition to the text, since it includes people who had long since disappeared from the scene, exterminated or assimilated by the Canaanites and Hebrews. **Canaanites, Hittites, Perizzites, Jebusites, Egyptians,** and **Amorites** were no threat to the Jews in the time of Ezra. For **Amorites** I Esdras 8:69 has "Edomites," which would be historically suitable since the Edomites pushed into southern Judea during the Exile and formed part of the population when Ezra arrived (cf. Neh. 2:19). **Ammonites,** too, were still active in Palestine (cf. Neh. 4:3, 7; 13:7-8), as were the **Moabites** (cf. Isa. 25:10-11; Ps. 83:6; Neh. 13:1). **Ammonites** and **Moabites** may appear because of Deut. 23:3-4 (cf. Neh. 13:1), and the list may well have been derived by the Chronicler from the injunction against foreign contacts in Deut. 7 (especially vss. 1, 3-4).

9:1-15. Family Complications.—Hard as some of us find it to sympathize with Ezra's acute concern and ruthless attitude toward mixed marriages, as that attitude appears in chs. 9–10, there is one aspect of his prayer of public confession that has touched our own consciences to the quick. Under the influence of the greater Hebrew prophets and of the Christian "social gospel," we have felt it a part of our responsibility as Christian ministers to declare and

2 For they have taken of their daughters for themselves, and for their sons: so that the holy seed have mingled themselves with the people of *those* lands: yea, the hand of the princes and rulers hath been chief in this trespass.

3 And when I heard this thing, I rent my garment and my mantle, and plucked off the hair of my head and of my beard, and sat down astonished.

rites. 2 For they have taken some of their daughters to be wives for themselves and for their sons; so that the holy race has mixed itself with the peoples of the lands. And in this faithlessness the hand of the officials and chief men has been foremost."

3 When I heard this, I rent my garments and my mantle, and pulled hair from my

2. The negative statement of vs. 1 becomes positive accusation here. **They** refers to the Jewish men. **Holy race** is, lit., **holy seed** (cf. Isa. 6:13), the "seed of Abraham" (II Chr. 20:7), the "holy people" (Deut. 7:6). Believing that God abhorred mixtures (cf. Lev. 19:19), the Jews were rebuked for mingling with their non-Jewish neighbors. Jewish leaders rather than the average Jews were guilty of the practice of foreign marriages. **Rulers** represents a Babylonian title for a variety of appointed **officials**, from governors to simple deputies, and in the Persian period even for superintendents or foremen (cf. Ezek. 23:6, 12, 23; Jer. 51:23, 57; Isa. 41:25). Its degradation in the post-exilic period is apparent in its listing between the nobles and the people (Neh. 4:14). Here they are probably only local deputies or minor leaders. The **princes** or **officials** (cf. vs. 1) should probably be identified with the "nobles," for in Neh. 4:14, in a listing similar to that found here, the officials linked with the "deputies" are called "nobles" (*ḥôrîm*) instead of **princes** (*sārîm*), as here. The two titles are usually regarded as identical (Meyer, *Entstehung des Judenthums*, p. 132) and it has been proposed to omit the former title since the **princes** in vs. 1 are the informers (cf. Hölscher, *Esra und Nehemia*, II, 522) and the LXX^AB has but one title. But the two groups need not be identical, for the **princes** of vs. 1 may be those who returned with Ezra, while those in vs. 2 may represent those long resident in Judah (Rudolph, *op. cit.*, p. 86).

The Hebrew word translated **trespass** suggests perfidy and is best rendered **faithlessness**. The LXX has "breach of covenant" (ἀσυνθεσία). The word, characteristic of late Hebrew, is often used by the Chronicler (cf. I Chr. 9:1; 10:13; II Chr. 28:19; 29:19; 33:19; 36:14).

B. Ezra's Reaction to the Mixed Marriages (9:3-15)

1. Ezra's Mourning (9:3-5=I Esdras 8:71-73; cf. Neh. 13:23-28)

Sensitive Ezra was severely shaken by the news that there were Jews who were married to foreigners, since he knew that the entire community was endangered by their misbehavior. Unlike Nehemiah (13:25), Ezra's action was turned against himself. So different are the reactions in the same situation that it has been regarded as evidence of a basic difference in personality, which makes it highly improbable that Nehemiah can be "simply Ezra (i.e., the Chronicler) under another name," as Torrey (*Ezra Studies*, p. 248) has declared (cf. Batten, *op. cit.*, p. 46).

3. **Rent my garment** expresses very violent action, originally the tearing off of all clothing to the point of nakedness (cf. Mic. 1:8; Isa. 20:2-4), although the practice was severely modified later (Morris Jastrow, tr., "The Tearing of Garments as a Symbol of Mourning," *Journal of the American Oriental Society*, XXI [1900] 23-39; "Baring of

confess the sins of our own day and generation; but we have not always been equally ready to recognize our individual and group responsibility as sharers in these social sins. We do well to note that Ezra himself had no slightest share in the sins of his people which he so movingly

confesses in vss. 3-15; and yet, like a true shepherd of souls, he identifies himself with his wandering and wayward flock before the judgment seat of God. From beginning to end, the words **we**, **us**, and **our** appear in his prayer of confession: **O my God, I am ashamed and**

4 Then were assembled unto me every one that trembled at the words of the God of Israel, because of the transgression of those that had been carried away; and I sat astonished until the evening sacrifice.

head and beard, and sat appalled. 4 Then all who trembled at the words of the God of Israel, because of the faithlessness of the returned exiles, gathered round me while I sat appalled until the evening sacrifice.

the Arm and Shoulder as a Sign of Mourning," *Zeitschrift für die alttestamentliche Wissenschaft*, XXII [1902], 117-20). The attention that Ezra attracted indicates that he did more than minor damage to his clothing. The M.T. has simply **my garment**, using a general word for clothing, which the LXX and Syriac wrongly understood as the plural, **my garments**. Undergarment must be meant here, since an outer garment, a **mantle**, was also worn. The description of the **mantle** (Exod. 28:31-35) suggests that it was fashioned like a Greek chiton with a neck-hole in the midst of the cloth and highly embroidered or otherwise decorated. Mantles were worn by kings and men of high station (Immanuel Benzinger, *Hebräische Archäologie* [Freiburg i. B.: J. C. B. Mohr, 1894], p. 100). In I Esdras 8:71 the word is rendered as "holy garment," presumably influenced by the use of the term mantle as part of the high priest's vestments (Exod. 28:31-32).

Pulled hair is preferable to **plucked off the hair,** since the M.T. indicates that but part of the hair was pulled. Such plucking was the counterpart of the more formal cutting or shaving of hair as a sign of mourning (Amos 8:10; Jer. 16:6; Ezek. 7:18; Job 1:20), a practice forbidden by Hebrew law (Lev. 19:27; 21:5; Deut. 14:1; Ezek. 44:20).

Overcome by emotion, Ezra fell to the ground. **Appalled** merely suggests the emotion of terror and awe involved in the Hebrew word. "Horror-stricken" is preferable, since the word is used in Hebrew to describe objects that cause horror and abhorrence (cf. Dan. 9:27). The expression of sorrow was genuine, but Ezra seems to have made use of the occasion deliberately to gather a crowd and set the stage emotionally for his message. Josephus (*Antiquities* XI. 5. 3) interprets Ezra's experience by saying: "He reasoned that if he commanded them to put away their wives and children born to them he would not be listened to [so] he remained lying on the ground." Ezra has been called a "master of psychology" (Kittel, *Geschichte des Volkes Israel*, III, 595), and such seems to be the case since he renounced the use of force, despite his great authority (cf. 7:25-26), and used such subtle means to influence men to do what he desired of their own volition (cf. Rudolph, *op. cit.*, p. 170).

4. The plight of Ezra, lying torn and disheveled in the street before the temple (cf. 10:1), stunned by the shock of the terrible news, would naturally attract a crowd of pious Jews, particularly if he was recognized as the prominent religious leader who but recently had led the community to an acceptance of the law (cf. Neh. 9–10). Doubtless it was the spectacle of silent Ezra himself rather than a full knowledge of the situation behind his shock and grief that gathered and held the people. Hence **because of the faithlessness,** etc., in vs. 4 is awkward in its present place. Its inappropriateness is sensed by I Esdras, where it is freely translated as "while I mourned for the iniquity," while Josephus (*loc. cit.*) states that Ezra acted thus "because the chief men among the people were guilty of the charge." The difficult words fit better at the conclusion of vs. 3 (Ehrlich, *Randglossen zur hebräischen Bibel*, VII, 177; Bewer, *Der Text des Buches Ezra,* pp. 80-81). **The words of the God of Israel** need not refer to an exact passage of scripture

blush to lift my face to thee, my God, for our iniquities have risen higher than our heads, and our guilt has mounted up to the heavens. From the days of our fathers to this day we have been in great guilt. . . . Behold, we are before thee in our guilt, for none can stand before thee be-

cause of this. (Vss. 6-7, 15.) The first person plural in his prayers was possibly part of the secret of the radical reforms Ezra was apparently able to bring about during his own lifetime, and of the far-reaching influence which he certainly exerted over successive generations.